THE
1900
FREE PUBLIC LIBRARY
OF THE CITY OF TRENTON,
NEW JERSEY.
SEAL OF THE CITY OF TRENTON
1792.

Chambers World Gazetteer

Chambers World Gazetteer

An A-Z of Geographical Information

Edited by
Dr David Munro

CHAMBERS
CAMBRIDGE

CAMBRIDGE EDINBURGH
NEW YORK NEW ROCHELLE MELBOURNE SYDNEY

Published jointly by W & R Chambers Limited
43-45 Annandale Street, Edinburgh EH7 4AZ, and
The Press Syndicate of the University of Cambridge
The Pitt Building, Trumpington Street, Cambridge CB2 1RP
32 East 57th Street, New York, N.Y. 10022, USA
10 Stamford Road, Oakleigh, Melbourne 3166, Australia

First published 1895
Fifth Edition 1988

British Library Cataloguing in Publication Data
Munro, David
Chambers world gazetteer : an A-Z of
geographical information – 5th ed.
1. Gazetteers
I. Title
910′.3′21
G103.5

ISBN 1-85296-200-3

Typeset by H. Charlesworth, Ltd., Huddersfield

Printed and bound in Great Britain
at The Bath Press, Avon

Contents

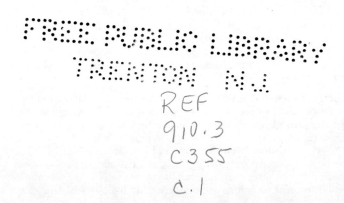

Preface

So Geographers, in Afric maps,
With Savage pictures fill their gaps,
And o'er unhabitable downs
Place elephants for want of towns.
Jonathan Swift

Chambers World Gazetteer is a geographical dictionary of world places listed alphabetically from the city of Aachen in West Germany to the city of Zwolle in the Netherlands. The Gazetteer includes information not only on cities, regions, countries and physical features but also on national parks and international economic and cultural regions such as the Alpe Adria and Regio Basiliensis in Europe and the Mano River Union and Senegambia in West Africa.

The Gazetteer is worldwide in scope but there is obviously a limit to the number of places and the extent of information included in this volume. The decision to include or not to include a particular location has been based on a number of criteria. Initially, an attempt has been made to include information on all first order administrative divisions and their capitals, either as individual entries or in tabular form under the Administrative division section of country entries. Wherever it is thought reasonable to do so, second-order administrative divisions are also included. For the USA each of the 50 states has an individual entry but counties (of which there are over 3,000) are listed in tabular form under each state. For France, on the other hand, there are individual entries for each of the 22 regions and each of the 95 departments.

Cities and towns have generally been selected firstly for their administrative function. Capitals or chief towns of administrative divisions have individual entries except on occasions where the name of the town is the same as the name of the region or district and little additional information is available relating to that place. Cities and towns have secondly been selected on the basis of population, the population threshold being different for each country. Clearly an arbitrary decision to include all towns with a population, say, greater than 50,000 would exclude nearly all towns from small countries such as Belize where the capital has a population of less than 3,000 inhabitants and the only major city and port, Belize City, has a population of nearly 40,000. Each country therefore has a different threshold which relates to the size and demographic patterns of that country. For Japan the threshold population is 200,000, giving a total of 94 entries in the Gazetteer, while for Hungary the cut-off point is 20,000, to give a total of 61 entries. The actual number of town and city entries for a particular country may often be greater than the total number over a particular threshold since capitals of regions, as described above, will also be included even if their population is less than the threshold figure. For example, a town such as Bar-le-Duc in France, with a population of just over 20,000, will be included because it is the capital of the Meuse department of Lorraine, even though the cut-off figure for France is 30,000.

If the Gazetteer only included towns and cities on the basis of administrative function and population many interesting and important locations would be missed. Many places have therefore been included because they are of special interest as locations of historic, religious, industrial or touristic significance or simply because they have been the scene of some event that has had worldwide cover in the news. These entries have been selected purely subjectively as locations that stand out in the wide range of contemporary source material that has been used in the compilation of this volume. Special interest locations include great archaeological sites such as

Machu Picchu in Peru, Tadmur (Palmyra) in Syria and Angkor in Cambodia; famous religious sites such as Fatima in Portugal, Lumbini in Nepal and Adam's Peak in Sri Lanka; fast-developing tourist centres such as the Costa del Sol on the Mediterranean coast of Spain, the island resort of Phuket in south Thailand and Albena on the Black Sea coast of Bulgaria; significant industrial sites such as the Itaipu hydroelectric scheme on the river Paraná in Brazil and the oil terminal of St Fergus in north-east Scotland; sites featured in the news of recent years such as the Palestinian refugee camps of Bourj Barajneh and Chatila, the South African squatter camps at Crossroads and KTC, and Chernobyl, site of the 1986 nuclear accident in the Soviet Union.

There are additional places that have been included purely for curiosity value. These include the town of Okinawa in Bolivia which is largely populated by Japanese inhabitants, Truth or Consequences in New Mexico, USA, which was renamed after a radio programme and Cooee in Queensland, Australia where a 'cooee'-calling contest takes place every August.

Since the publication of the last edition of *Chambers World Gazetteer*, in 1965, the world has seen many changes. To keep up with these changes is a difficult task, but one that is made easier with the assistance of modern technology. This edition has been compiled with the aid of the computing facilities in the Department of Geography at the University of Edinburgh where attention has been focused on geographical information systems and an easily updatable world geographical database has been developed.

The information included in the Gazetteer has been culled from a wide range of up-to-date sources. Statistical data on the populations and areas of regions and towns has been extracted from statistical yearbooks and from material supplied directly from statistical departments of individual countries. Economic information has been obtained from chambers of commerce worldwide and tourist information has been selectively drawn from the literature produced by government tourist departments. Additional information has been supplied by university departments from as far afield as Oulu and Kabul, and help with pronunciation has been obtained from a broad spectrum of staff, students and visitors who have either been resident in or have passed through the University of Edinburgh. The editor is grateful to all who have supplied information and to those government representatives who have viewed the entries for their country. Every effort has been made to ensure the accuracy of information quoted in *Chambers World Gazetteer* but any comments and corrections for future editions are welcomed.

For want of accurate information the classical cartographers drew 'elephants for want of towns'. By contrast, the modern geographer is overwhelmed with facts and figures that change from day to day. Errors of omission and subjectivity are inevitable in a work of this kind, but it is hoped that the places of the world have not been represented, in the words of Alexander Pope, 'chaos-like together crush'd and bruis'd'. At worst, they may appear 'as the world, harmoniously confus'd'.

Guidance notes

We have set out a typical entry from *Chambers World Gazetteer* on pp. x and xi.

Order

We have arranged the entries in alphabetical order. Where places that share the same name are concerned, we have applied the following conventions:

where the same name applies to places in different countries, the entries are arranged in alphabetical order of country; e.g. **Córdoba** in Argentina is listed before **Córdoba** in Colombia;

where the same name applies to places in different administrative regions within particular countries, the entries are arranged in alphabetical order of region; e.g. **Bloomington** in the USA is listed in order of the states Illinois, Indiana and Minnesota;

where the same name applies to different places or features in the same country, the entries are generally listed in order of region/provinces, then town, then physical features; e.g. the province of **Orense** in Spain comes before the town of the same name, and the province of **Ontario** in Canada comes before Lake **Ontario**.

Place-names

In our choice of headwords, we have adopted the following place-name conventions:

for country entries, the headword is in the English form, e.g. **Finland**, not Suomi, and **Brazil**, not Brasil;

for all other entries, the headword is in the local form, e.g. **Beograd**, not Belgrade;

where physical features extend over international boundaries and different names or spellings apply, the headword is in the English form, e.g. **Tagus**, not Tajo or Tejo;

where a name incorporates a definite article or a generic term, the specific part usually comes first in the headword, e.g. **Alamos, Los; Everest, Mount; Europa, Picos de;**

where the addition of a generic term to a specific form results in a compound word, that form is generally used, e.g. **Ounasjoki** (Ounas River) in Finland;

the Pin-yin system of Romanization is used in the spelling of Chinese names;

Albanian names are spelt in the indefinite form e.g. **Tiranë**, not Tirana.

Cross-references

Our cross-referencing system is clear and comprehensive so that, if places are known by alternative names, readers are easily referred from one name to the other; e.g.

Cologne, city in West Germany. See Köln.
Salisbury, capital of Zimbabwe. See Harare.

Maps

Most country entries are accompanied by an up-to-date map, showing the administrative divisions within the country concerned. The capital of the country is indicated by ■.

Pronunciation

We give help with the pronunciation of names that we feel will be especially difficult for readers. Often, a stress mark is sufficient; e.g. **Ham'eln**. In other cases we have used a simple respelling scheme (see p.xiii). Where places have the same names and the same pronunciation, we give help with the first entry only; e.g. **Granada**, *gra-na'THa*.

Every pronunciation given refers to all following places of the same name, until a change is indicated.

Measurements

We give all distances, heights and extents in metric units, and temperatures in degrees Celsius. See p.xviii for a useful conversion guide.

Specimen entry

Liechtenstein *lᴋʜ'ten-shtīn*, official name Principality of Liechtenstein, FÜRSTENTUM LIECHTENSTEIN (Ger), an independent Alpine principality in central Europe, situated between the Austrian prov of Vorarlberg (E) and the Swiss cantons of St Gallen and Graubünden (W); timezone GMT +1; area 160 sq km; fourth smallest country in the world; land boundary 76 km; capital Vaduz; pop(1985) 27,076; the average population density in 1985 was 169 inhabitants per sq km; the Liechtensteiners are of Alemannic origin; the official language is German but the populace speaks it in the form of an Alemannic dialect; the predominant faith is Roman Catholic (86.9%); the currency is the Swiss franc; membership Council of Europe, CEPT, EFTA, EPO, EUTELSAT, International Court of Justice, IAEA, INTELSAT, ITU, UNCTAD, UNIDO, UNICEF, UPU, WIPO.

Physical description. Liechtenstein is bounded on the W by the R Rhine, whose valley occupies about 40% of the country. This broad flood plain, where much of the agriculture is concentrated, lies at a mean alt of 450 m. Much of the rest of the country is mountainous, rising to 2,599 m in the Grauspitz. The mountains are extensively forested with meadows at higher levels. The plains, once marshy, are now drained and cultivated.

Climate. The climate is mild, in spite of the mountain situation. In winter, temperatures rarely fall below −15° C, while in summer the average high temperature varies between 20° C and 28° C. Mean annual rainfall varies between 1,050 mm and 1,200 mm, rising to 1,800 mm in the Alpine regions. The warm south wind (Föhn) greatly influences the climate and enables grapes and maize to flourish.

Government and constitution. Liechtenstein is a constitutional monarchy ruled by the hereditary princes of the House of Liechtenstein. The present constitution of 5 Oct 1921 provides for a unicameral parliament (*Diet*) of 15 members elected for 4 years. The country is governed jointly by the Prince, who is Head of State, and the parliament. On parliamentary recommendation the Prince appoints a government of 5, a prime minister and 4 councillors, for a 4-year term.

Industry. Despite its small size and limited natural resources, Liechtenstein has, since the 1950s, developed from a poor hill-farming area to a highly-industrialized nation with a per capita income higher than that of its rich neighbour, Switzerland. This transition has led to the immigration of foreign workers (Swiss, Austrians,

Pronunciation
Official name
Timezone
Population
Language
Religion
Currency
International organization membership
Physical description
Climate
Rainfall
Government and constitution

Germans, Italians, Spaniards). In 1985, 44.1% of the labour force was employed in industry and commerce. The industrial sector is export-based and centred on specialized and high-tech production. The most important industries include metalworking, engineering and instrument making, and also more traditional industries such as chemicals, pharmaceuticals, textiles, ceramics, and foodstuffs. There has been a rapid growth in the export of high-technology goods, metals, ceramics and chemicals, mainly to Switzerland (under customs union) and re-exports to West Germany and the USA. Imports, mainly from EEC and EFTA countries, consist largely of raw materials and foodstuffs. International banking and finance (attracted by the favourable tax structure and legal system), the sale of postage stamps, and a flourishing tourist industry, bring in important revenue. Tourism has become increasingly important to the economy, the number of visitors reaching 85,851 in 1985.

Industry

Economy

Agriculture. In 1986 less than 3% of the workforce was employed in agriculture. The rearing of cattle, for which the Alpine pastures are well suited, is highly developed. Livestock, vegetables, corn, wheat, potatoes, and grapes are the main agricultural products. Nearly 35% of the total land area of the country is covered by forest, 41% of which is regularly used for timber extraction and 91% of which is public property belonging to the 11 communes and the 8 Alpine cooperatives.

Agriculture

Administrative divisions. The Principality is divided into two districts, Oberland (Upper Country) and Unterland (Lower Country), which are divided into 11 communes. The Oberland contains the communes of Vaduz, Balzers, Triesen, Triesenberg, Schaan, and Planken, while the communes of Eschen, Mauren, Gamprin, Ruggell, and Schellenberg lie in the Unterland.

Administrative divisions

Commune	*area (sq km)*	*pop (1985)*
Balzers	19.6	3,460
Eschen	10.3	2,785
Gamprin	6.1	927
Mauren	7.5	2,703
Planken	5.3	293
Ruggell	7.4	1,326
Schaan	26.8	4,697
Schellenberg	3.5	674
Triesen	26.4	3,043
Triesenberg	29.8	2,241
Vaduz	17.3	4,927

Abbreviations and contractions

AD	anno Domini
admin	administrative, administration
Afrik	Afrikaans
agric	agriculture
Alb	Albanian
alt	altitude
anc	ancient
approx	approximately
Arab	Arabic
arrond	arrondissement
ASSR	Autonomous Soviet Socialist Republic
Aug	August
b.	born
BC	before Christ
Belg	Belgian
Bhut	Bhutanese
Bret	Breton
Bulg	Bulgarian
c	century
c.	circa
°C	Celsius
C	Cape
CAR	Central African Republic
Chin	Chinese
Co	county
cu	cubic
Czech	Czechoslovakian
d.	died
Dec	December
Dan	Danish
dept	department
dist	district
div	division
Du	Dutch
e	estimated
E	east, eastern
Eng	English
Esk	Eskimo
Feb	February
Fin	Finland, Finnish
Flem	Flemish
Fr	French
Gael	Gaelic
Ger	German
GMT	Greenwich Mean Time
govt	government
Gr	Greek
ha	hectares
Heb	Hebrew
Hind	Hindi
Hung	Hungarian
I	island
Indon	Indonesian
Is	islands
Ital	Italian
Jan	January
Jap	Japanese
km	kilometre
kw	kilowatt
Kor	Korean
L	Lake
Lat	Latin
m	metres
mm	millimetres
Malay	Malaysian
max	maximum
min	minimum
mn	million
Mt	Mountain/Mount
Mts	Mountains
N	north, northern
Nor	Norwegian
Nov	November
Oct	October
orig	originally
Pol	Polish
pop	population
Port	Portuguese
prov	province
pt	point
R	River
rep	republic
Rom	Romanian
Rus	Russian
S	south, southern
Sansk	Sanskrit
Sept	September
Serb	Serbian
Sing	Singalese
Slov	Slovenian
Sp	Spanish
sq	square
St	Saint
stat	statistical
SSR	Soviet Socialist Republic
Swed	Swedish
Turk	Turkish
UAR	United Arab Republic
UK	United Kingdom
USA	United States of America
USSR	Union of Soviet Socialist Republics
Viet	Vietnamese
W	west, western
Yug	Yugoslavian

Key to pronunciation

Vowel sounds

ay	= a in fate	*oo*	= oo in moon
a	= a in lad	*u*	= u in but
ah	= a in father	*ü*	= *Ger* ü, *Fr* u, etc. (nearly *ee*)
e	= e in led	*œ*	= *Ger* ö, *Fr* œu, etc. (nearly as *u* in fur)
ee	= e in we		
ė	= e in other		Diphthongs
i	= i in lid	*yoo*	= u in tube
ī	= i in mine	*aw*	= aw in saw
o	= o in lot	*ow*	= ow in cow
ō	= o in vote	*oy*	= oy in boy

The *tilde* sign (˜) over a vowel denotes that it is nasalized, i.e. pronounced partly through the nose. The nasalized -ai-, -ei-, and e after i is represented by *ĩ*, e.g. **Ain, Reims, Amiens** (*ĩ, rĩs, am-yĩ*). In Portuguese the sounds *ee* and *oo* are sometimes nasalized, appearing as *ẽẽ*, e.g. **Coimbra**, and *õõ*. The Arabic guttural *'ain* is represented by the conventional inverted comma ('), e.g. **'Adan**.

Consonant sounds

The consonants b, d, f, h, j, k, l, m, n, p, r, t, v, w, y (not used as vowel), z, have in English unambiguous values, and are used for these values.

g	= g in get	*y'*	= final y sound as in *Fr* **Dordogne**, (*dor-don´y'*), or y sound after palatalized consonants, as in *Russ* **Tyumen'** (*tyoo-myayn´y'*)
s	= s in set		
ch	= ch in church		
sh	= sh in shore		
th	= th in thin	*l'*	= unvoiced final consonant as in *Fr* **Grenoble** (*gre-nob´l'*)
zh	= z in azure, s in pleasure		
TH, DH	= th in this		
KH	= ch in Scots loch		

Accentuation

The sign ´, denoting that the preceding syllable is stressed, has been used in headwords and/or alternative titles where phonetic respelling has been deemed unnecessary. Stress is not shown in Chinese names, which are evenly accented; nor is it generally indicated in French names, where the correct effect is better obtained by slightly raising the pitch of the voice on the final syllable.

Abbreviations of international organizations

AAPSO	Afro-Asian People's Solidarity Organization
ACP	States of Africa, the Caribbean and the Pacific (Associated with the EEC)
ADB	Asian Development Bank
AfDB	African Development Bank
AFESD	Arab Fund for Social and Economic Development
AID	US Agency for International Development
AIOEC	Association of Iron Ore Exporting Countries
AMAL	Afwaj al-Muqawama al-Lubnaniyya (Shi'ite Muslim group in Lebanon)
ANC	African National Congress
ANRPC	Association of Natural Rubber Producing Countries
ANZUS	ANZUS Council: treaty signed by Australia, New Zealand and the United States
APACL	Asian People's Anti-Communist League
APC	African Peanut (Groundnut) Council
ARTDO	Asian Regional Trade Development Organization
ASEAN	Association of Southeast Asian Nations
ASPAC	Asian and Pacific Council
ASSIMER	International Mercury Producers Association
BADEA, BDECA	Arab Bank for Economic Development in Africa
Benelux	Belgium, Netherlands, Luxembourg Economic Union
BIS	Bank for International Settlements
BLEU	Belgium-Luxembourg Economic Union
CACM	Central American Common Market
CARICOM	Caribbean Common Market
CARIFTA	Caribbean Free Trade Association
CCC	Customs Cooperation Council
CDB	Caribbean Development Bank
CEAO	West African Economic Community
CEMA, CMEA	Council for Mutual Economic Assistance
CENTO	Central Treaty Organization
CEPT	Conférence Européene des Administrations des Postes et des Télécommunications
CERI	Centre for Educational Research and Innovation
CIPEC	Intergovernmental Council of Copper Exporting Countries
COMECON	Council for Mutual Economic Aid
CPU	Commonwealth Press Union
DAC	Development Assistance Committee (OECD)
EAMA	African States associated with the EEC
EC	European Communities
ECA	Economic Commission for Africa (UN)
ECE	Economic Commission for Europe (UN)
ECGD	Export Credits Guarantee Department, UK
ECLA	Economic Commission for Latin America (UN)
ECOSOC	Economic and Social Council
ECOWAS	Economic Community of West African States (French abbreviation CEDEAO)
ECU	European Currency Unit
ECWA	Economic Commission for Western Asia (UN)
EDF	European Development Fund
EEC	European Economic Community
EFTA	European Free Trade Association
EIB	European Investment Bank
ELDO	European Space Vehicle Launcher Development Organization
EMA	European Monetary Agreement
EMS	European Monetary System
ENTENTE	Political-Economic Association of Ivory Coast, Dahomey, Niger, Upper Volta and Togo

EPO	European Patent Organization
EPTA	Expanded Programme of Technical Assistance (UN)
ESCAP	Economic and Social Commission for Asia and the Pacific (UN)
ESRO	European Space Research Organization
Euratom	European Atomic Energy Community
EUTELSAT	European Telecommunications Satellite
FAO	Food and Agriculture Organization (UN)
FLNC	Congolese National Liberation Front (Zaire)
FLS	Front Line States (Angola, Botswana, Mozambique, Tanzania, Zambia)
FRELIMO	Mozambique Liberation Front
GATT	General Agreements on Tariffs and Trade (UN)
G-77	Group of 77
GCC	Gulf Cooperation Council
IAEA	International Atomic Energy Agency (UN)
IADB	Inter-American Defense Board
IATA	International Air Transport Association
IATP	International Association of Tungsten Producers
IBA	International Bauxite Association
IBEC	International Bank for Economic Cooperation
IBRD	International Bank for Reconstruction and Development (World Bank) (UN)
ICA	International Cooperative Alliance
ICAC	International Cotton Advisory Committee
ICAO	International Civil Aviation Organization (UN)
ICCAT	International Commission for the Conservation of Atlantic Tunas
ICCO	International Cocoa Organization
ICEM	Intergovernmental Committee for European Migration
ICES	International Cooperation in Ocean Exploration
ICFTU	International Confederation of Free Trade Unions
ICJ	International Court of Justice
ICO	International Coffee Organization
ICRC	International Committee of the Red Cross
ICSU	International Council of Scientific Unions
IDA	International Development Association (IBRD Affiliate) (UN)
IDB	Inter-American Development Bank
IDB	Islamic Development Bank
IEA	International Energy Agency (associated with OECD)
IFAD	International Fund for Agricultural Development (UN)
IFC	International Finance Corporation (IBRD Affiliate) (UN)
IHO	International Hydrographic Organization
IIB	International Investment Bank
ILO	International Labour Organization (UN)
ILZSG	International Lead and Zinc Study Group
IMCO	Inter-government Maritime Consultative Organization
IMF	International Monetary Fund (UN)
IMO	International Maritime Organization (UN)
INCB	International Narcotics Control Board
INOC	International Olympic Committee
INRO	International Natural Rubber Organization
INTELSAT	International Telecommunications Satellite Organization
INTERPOL	International Criminal Police Commission
IOC	International Olympic Committee
IOOC	International Olive Oil Council

IPC	Integrated Programme for Commodities (Common Fund)
IPDC	International Programme for the Development of Communication
IPI	International Press Institute
IPU	Inter-Parliamentary Union
IRC	International Rice Council
ISO	International Sugar Organization
ITC	International Tin Council
ITU	International Telecommunications Union (UN)
IUCN	International Union for the Conservation of Nature and Natural Resources
IUS	International Union of Students
IUSY	International Union of Socialist Youth
IWC	International Whaling Council
IWC	International Wheat Council
LAIA	Latin American Integration Association (Spanish form: Aladi)
LDC	Less Developed Country
LME	London Metal Exchange
MFA	Multi-Fibres Arrangement
MPLA	Angolan People's Liberation Movement
NAM	Nonaligned Movement
NAMUCAR	Naviera Multinacional Caribe
NATO	North Atlantic Treaty Organization
OANA	Organization of Asian and Pacific News Agencies
OAPEC	Organization of Arab Petroleum Exporting Countries
OAS	Organization of American States
OAU	Organization of African Unity
OCAM	Afro-Malagasy and Mauritian Common Organization
OCLAE	Latin American Continental Students Organization
ODA	Official Development Assistance
ODECA	Organization of Central American States
OECD	Organization for Economic Cooperation and Development
OIC	Organization of the Islamic Conference
OMVS	Organization for the Development of the Senegal River Valley
OPEC	Organization of Petroleum Exporting Countries
OSF	OPEC Special Fund
PAHO	Pan American Health Organization
PAIGC	African Party for the Independence of Guinea-Bissau and Cape Verde
PANA	Pan-African News Agency
PLO	Palestine Liberation Organization
PLF	Palestine Liberation Front
SADCC	South African Development Coordination Committee
SCAR	Committee of the International Council of Scientific Unions for promoting Antarctic Research
SCOR	Committee of the International Council of Scientific Unions for promoting Oceanographic Research
SELA	Latin American Economic System
SITC	Standard International Trade Classification
SPC	South Pacific Commission
TAZARA	Tanzania-Zambia Railway
TBD	Trade and Development Board (UN)
UDEAC	Economic and Customs Union of Central Africa
UDEAO	West African Customs Union
UDI	Unilateral Declaration of Independence
UEAC	Union of Central African States
UN	United Nations
UNCDF	United Nations Capital Development Fund
UNCTAD	UN Conference on Trade and Development
UNDP	UN Development Programme

UNEP	UN Environment Programme
UNESCO	UN Educational, Scientific, and Cultural Organization
UNHCR	UN High Commission for Refugees
UNICEF	UN Children's Fund
UNIDO	UN Industrial Development Organization
UNIFIL	UN Interim Force in Lebanon
UNRRA	UN Relief and Rehabilitation Administration
UNRWA	UN Relief and Works Agency
UPEB	Union of Banana Exporting Countries
UPU	Universal Postal Union (UN)
USDA	United States Department of Agriculture
WACL	World Anti-Communist League
WCL	World Confederation of Labour
WEU	Western European Union
WFC	World Food Council (UN)
WFDY	World Federation of Democratic Youth
WFP	World Food Programme (UN/FAO)
WFTU	World Federation of Trade Unions
WHO	World Health Organization (UN)
WIPO	World Intellectual Property Organization (UN)
WMO	World Meteorological Organization (UN)
WPC	World Peace Council
WPFC	World Press Freedom Committee
WSG	International Wool Study Group
WTO	World Tourism Organization
WTO	Warsaw Treaty Organization (Warsaw Pact)

Conversion guide

All measurements in *Chambers World Gazetteer* are given in metric units. We suggest multiplying as shown below for *approximate* imperial equivalents. *Exact* equivalents can be calculated by using the figures in parentheses.

Length		**Multiply by**
millimetres	→ inches	0.04 (0.394)
centimetres	→ inches	0.4 (0.3937)
metres	→ yards	1.1 (1.0936)
kilometres	→ miles	0.6 (0.6214)

Area		
square metres	→ square yards	1.2 (1.196)
hectares	→ acres	2.5 (2.471)
square kilometres	→ square miles	0.4 (0.386)

Temperatures are given in degrees Celsius. The scale below shows equivalent Fahrenheit temperatures.

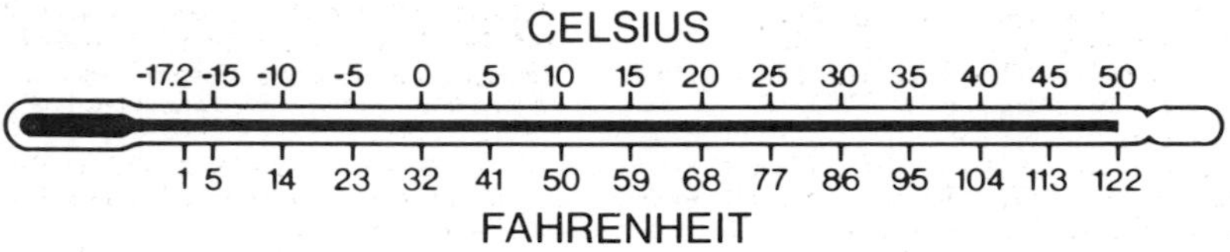

Acknowledgements

The editor is indebted to the following individuals who assisted with editorial research and the compilation of the text: Diane Brown, Chris Burns, Rosalind Cummins, Sir John Fayrer, Lorna Fraser, Janet Gibson, Judith Gillespie, David Gray, Kenneth Mitchell, Ian Smith, Jane White and Bob Woods. For technical advice and assistance the editor is grateful to Alan Alexander, Steve Dowers, Vicky Eachus, Richard Healey, Margaret Leeman and Tom Waugh. Maps of the administrative divisions of the world were prepared by Morag Gillespie and Anona Lyons of the Drummond Street Reprographics Unit, Edinburgh.

To the many organizations, institutions, government agencies and individuals who supplied information used in this publication the editor extends his grateful thanks.

A

Aachen *ah'KHen*, AIX-LA-CHAPELLE *eks-la-sha-pel* (Fr), 50 47N 6 04E, pop(1983) 243,700, manufacturing city in Köln (Cologne) dist, Nordrhein-Westfalen (North Rhine-Westphalia) prov, W Germany; 64 km WSW of Köln, Germany's most westerly city, lying near the Dutch and Belgian borders in a forest-ringed basin in the foothills of the Eifel and the Ardennes; the Bad Aachen hot springs are noted in the treatment of gout, rheumatism and sciatica; the city has associations with Charlemagne; 32 German kings were crowned here; technical college; railway; economy: textiles, glass, machinery, chemicals, light engineering, foodstuffs, rubber products; monuments: 15th-c cathedral, town hall (1350); event: international riding, jumping and driving tournament.

Aaiun, El, Western Sahara. See La'youn.

Aalborg, town in Denmark. See Ålborg-Nørresundby.

Aa'len, 48 49N 10 06E, pop(1983) 62,800, industrial and commercial city in Stuttgart dist, Baden-Württemberg prov, W Germany; 70 km E of Stuttgart, on the R Kocher; former Free Imperial City (1360-1802); railway; economy: machine and hand tools, iron and steel, motor vehicles and components, railway vehicles and equipment, textiles, ironworking, leather goods.

A'ali en Nil, area of S Sudan. See Upper Nile.

Aalst *ahlst*, dist of Oost-Vlaanderen (East Flanders) prov, Belgium; area 469 sq km; pop(1982) 262,368.

Aalst, A'LOST (Fr), 50 57N 4 03E, pop(1982) 78,707, capital town of Aalst dist, Oost-Vlaanderen (East Flanders) prov, Belgium; 28 km NW of Bruxelles, on the R Dender, here canalized; part of the Greater Bruxelles commuter belt; hops cultivated in neighbouring villages are marketed here; railway; economy: cotton, textiles, engineering, motor vehicle assembly, maize and wheat starch, derivatives (glucose, dextrose, etc); monuments: 13th-c town hall, church of St Martin (1480); events: carnival procession (Shrove Sunday); St Martin's Fair (Shrove Tuesday).

Aanekoski *a'ne-kō'ski*, 62 36N 25 44E, pop(1982) 11,284, town in Keski-Suomi prov, E central Finland; at the S end of L Keitele, 38 km N of Jyväskylä; established in 1932; railway; economy: paper, chemicals, timber products, hydroelectric power.

Aarau *ar'ow*, 47 24N 8 04E, pop(1980) 15,788, capital town of Aargau canton, N Switzerland; on the R Aare, 37 km W of Zürich, below the vine-clad Jura Mts; railway; economy: textile machinery, shoes, iron and steel, optical instruments; preserves the old tradition of bell-founding.

Aare *ah're*, AAR *ar* (Fr), largest river entirely in Switzerland; emerges from Grimselsee (L Grimsel), Berner Alpen (Bernese Alps) and flows N then W through Brienzer See (Lake of Brienz), past Interlaken, through Thuner See (Lake of Thun), and then NW past Thun and Bern; it enters Bieler See (L Biel) as Hagneck Canal and leaves it as Aare Canal at Nidau, then flows generally NE, past Solothurn, Olten and Aarau to the Rhine; length 295 km; catchment area 17,779 sq km; navigable from the Rhine to Thun.

Aargau *ar'gow*, ARGOVIE *ar-go-vee'* (Fr), canton in N Switzerland; pop(1980) 453,442; area 1,404 sq km; capital Aarau; chief towns Brugg, Reinach, Zofingen and Baden; drained by the R Aare, a tributary of the Rhine; joined the Confederation in 1803; the German language is spoken by the majority of inhabitants.

Aba *a'ba*, 5 06N 7 21E, pop(1981e) 241,900, town in Imo state, S Nigeria, W Africa; 56 km NE of Port Harcourt; railway; economy: food products, brewing, animal feed, chemicals, textiles and glass.

Abaco *a'ba-kō*, island group in the N Bahamas, E of Grand Bahama I; extends in an arc from Great Abaco I (SW) to Little Abaco I (NW), and includes numerous cays; pop(1980) 7,324; area 1,680 sq km.

Ābādān', 30 20N 48 16E, pop(1985e) 294,068, oil port in Khuzestān prov, W central Iran; close to the Iraq border; on Ābādān I, in the delta of the Shatt al'Arab, at the head of the Arabian Gulf; terminus of Iran's major oil pipelines; airport; severely damaged in the Gulf War.

Ābay Wenz, river in E Africa. See Blue Nile.

Abbé *a-bay'*, lake on the Ethiopia-Djibouti frontier, NE Africa; located 145 km WSW of Djibouti, noted for its populations of pink flamingoes, ibises and pelicans; additional interesting features include limestone spires and sulphur-laden vapour streams; receives the R Awsah.

Abbottabad *ab'ut-a-bad*, 34 12N 73 15E, pop(1981) 66,000, city in North-West Frontier prov, Pakistan; 116 km N of Rawalpindi and 217 km E of Peshawar; at an alt of 1,255 m in the Himalayas, on the newly constructed Karakoram highway; market town for the surrounding area and a popular hill station health resort; named after Major Abbott, a British officer who 'pacified' the area between 1849 and 1853; Kakul military college.

ABC Islands, an abbreviated name often applied to the 3 main islands of Aruba, Bonaire and Curaçao in the S Netherlands Antilles which are situated off the N coast of South America in the Caribbean.

Abéché *a-bay-shay'*, 13 49N 20 49E, pop(1979e) 54,000, capital of Oauddaï prefecture, E central Chad, N central Africa; E of N'Djamena; airport.

Abengourou *a-ben-goo'roo*, dept in SE Ivory Coast, W Africa; pop(1975) 177,692; area 6,900 sq km; the W border is formed by the R Comoé; capital Abengourou.

Åbenrå *o'bun-ro'*, AABENRAA, 55 03N 9 25E, pop(1981) 15,341, fishing town and capital of Sønderjylland county, on the Åbenrå Fjord, an inlet of the Lille Bælt (Little Belt), SE Jylland (Jutland), Denmark; rail terminus; economy: engineering; the town has largest harbour in S Jylland.

Abeokuta *a bay'ō-koo-ta*, 7 10N 3 26E, pop(1981e) 345,000, capital of Ogun state, SW Nigeria, W Africa; on the Ogun river, 80 km N of Lagos; founded in mid 1820s as a refuge against slave raiders; airfield; railway; economy: textiles, brewing and metals; events: the Akogun, Giriwo and Gelede festivals are held in May, Nov and Dec.

Abercarn', formerly NEWBRIDGE, 51 39N 3 08W, pop(1981) 16,866, town in Blaenau Gwent dist, Gwent, SE Wales; 20 km N of Cardiff, in Islwyn urban area; economy: coal, iron, tinplate.

Abercorn, town in Zambia. See Mbala.

Aberdare *a-ber-dayr'*, 51 43N 3 27W, pop(1981) 31,684, town in Cynon Valley dist, Mid Glamorgan, S Wales; 32 km NNW of Cardiff; economy: engineering, printing.

Aberdare Mountains *a-ber-dayr'*, mountain range in W central Kenya, E Africa; NNW of Nairobi and SW of Mount Kenya; lying N-S between the Equator and 1°S, the highest peaks are Lesitama (3,994 m), Kinangop (3,906 m) and Kipipiri (3,349 m).

Aberdeen', DEVANA (anc), 57 10N 2 04W, pop(1981) 190,465, seaport capital of Grampian region, NE Scotland; on the North Sea, between the rivers Dee (S) and Don (N), 92 km NE of Dundee; a royal burgh since 1179; the city has won the 'Britain in Bloom' competition several times; university (1494); airport (at Dyce, 9 km NW); railway; ferries to Orkney and Shetland; helicopter port; economy: port trade and fishing, finance, oil supply service, tourism; monuments: Aberdeen is known as 'The

Granite City' owing to this local stone having been used in many of the buildings; Art Gallery; Gordon Highlanders Regimental Museum; maritime museum; 16th-c house of Sir George Skene, Provost of Aberdeen from 1676 to 1685; St Machar's cathedral (1131); Bridge of Dee (1500) with 7 arches which span 122 m; the Brig o' Balgownie, which spans the river Don in a 19 m-wide arch, was completed c.1320 and repaired in 1607; event: Aberdeen festival (July-Aug).

Aberdeen, 45 28N 98 29W, pop(1980) 25,956, county seat of Brown county, NE South Dakota, United States; 250 km NNW of Sioux Falls; railway; economy: distribution centre in an agricultural region, trading in grain and livestock.

Abergavenny *a-ber-ga-ven'i*, GOBANNIUM (anc), 51 50N 3 00W, pop(1981) 14,398, town in Monmouth dist, Gwent, SE Wales; N of Pontypool, at the junction of the Usk and Gavenny rivers; railway; economy: agricultural trade, iron.

Abergele *-gel'i*, 53 17N 3 34W, pop(1981) 12,596, town in Colwyn dist, Clwyd, NE Wales; also in Abergele-Rhyl-Prestatyn urban area; railway; economy: quarrying.

Abertillery-Brynmawr *-til-ayr'i-brin-mahr*, 51 45N 3 09W, pop(1981) 28,351, coal-mining town in Blaenau Gwent dist, Gwent, SE Wales; 48 km NW of Bristol.

Aberystwyth *a-ber-ist'with*, 52 25N 4 05W, pop(1981) 11,170, university and resort town in Ceredigion dist, Dyfed, W Wales; at the mouth of the Ystwyth and Rheidol rivers, on Cardigan Bay; the city was built around a castle of Edward I in 1227; college of University of Wales (1872); National Library of Wales (1955); railway; economy: boatbuilding, brewing, agricultural trade; event: university theatre summer season.

Abhā *ab'ha*, 18 00N 42 34E, pop(1974) 30,150, town in Asīr prov, SW Saudi Arabia; 192 km SE of Al Qunfudhah; on a plateau in the upper reaches of the Wadi Bisha; administrative capital of the Asīr prov; alt 2,438 m; airfield.

Abidjan *a-bee-jan'*, coastal dept in S Ivory Coast, W Africa; pop(1975) 1,389,141; area 14,200 sq km; bounded in the W by the R Bandama; lagoons stretch along much of the coast; capital Abidjan; chief towns Grand Bassam, Bingerville and Anyama; economy: cement and petroleum processing, petroleum reserves offshore.

Abidjan, 5 19N 4 01W, pop(1980) 1,690,000, industrial seaport capital of Ivory Coast, W Africa; on the N shore of Ebrié lagoon, 240 km W of Sekondi-Takoradi (Ghana) and 320 km S of Bobo-Dioulasso (Burkina); became capital of the French Ivory Coast colony in 1935; the city has expanded since the 1920s with the addition of port facilities in the early 1950s; university (1958); Abidjan-Port-Buet airport; railway N to Burkina; economy: farm machinery, metallurgy, motor car assembly, electrical appliances, plastics, soap, coffee and cocoa trade, timber products, tobacco, food processing, beer, chemicals; monument: Ifan museum.

Abilene *ab'e-leen*, 32 28N 99 43W, pop(1980) 98,315, county seat of Taylor county, NW central Texas, United States; 225 km W of Fort Worth; university (1891); railway; economy: aircraft, electronic equipment, missile components, agricultural and oil-field equipment, food products, clothing; nearby is Dyess Air Force Base.

Ab'ingdon, 52 07N 0 15E, pop(1981) 29,558, town in Vale of White Horse dist, Oxfordshire, S central England; on the R Thames, 10 km S of Oxford; economy: leather, brewing.

Ablad, Bahr el, river in NE Africa. See White Nile.

Åbo, town in Finland. See Turku.

Aboisso *a-boy'sō*, coastal dept in SE Ivory Coast, W Africa; pop(1975) 148,823; area 6,250 sq km; dominated by Lagune Aby and the lake created by the Ayamé dam; capital Aboisso; chief towns Ayamé, Adiaké and Assinia.

Abomey *a-bo'may*, 7 14N 2 00E, pop(1979) 41,000, town in Zou prov, S Benin, W Africa; 105 km NNW of Porto Novo; former capital of the Kingdom of Dahomey; the Portuguese burned the city and abandoned it to the French in 1892; connected to the coastal railway in 1905; monuments: Royal Palace of Djema including the tomb of King Gbehanzin (still guarded by women) and a historical museum.

Abrak Kheitan, 29 20N 48 00E, pop(1980) 105,095, S suburb of Al Kuwayt (Kuwait City), State of Kuwait, at the head of the Arabian Gulf.

Abruzzi *ah-broo'tsee*, ABRUZZESE, ABRUZZO, region of E central Italy, comprising the provs of Chieti, L'Aquila, Pescara, and Teramo; pop(1981) 1,217,791; area 10,795 sq km; poor agricultural area, with arable farming possible only in valleys running down from the Appennino (Apennines) to the Adriatic Sea; centre for developments in tourism and winter sports; in the valley 'Val Vibrata', which runs for 15 km along the coast of the region, there are numerous small businesses (leather, knitwear, furniture, etc) set up with aid from Cassa per il Mezzogiorno, the S Italy Development Agency.

Abruzzi, national park in the southernmost part of Abruzzi region, E central Italy, in the valley of the upper Sangro; area 400 sq km; established in 1922; there are beautiful beech forests; the resort village of Pescasseroli is in the centre of the park.

Abu Dhabi, one of the seven member states of the United Arab Emirates. See Abū Ẓabī.

Abu Simbel *ah-boo sim'bel*, 22 22N 31 38E, site of ancient temples of Rameses II (c.1250 BC) by L Nasser, S Egypt; 280 km S of Aswân; discovered in 1812; relocated above the water level of L Nasser when the area was flooded in 1966; the site is 5 hours by hydrofoil and 30 mins by plane from Aswân.

Abū Ẓabī, ABU DHABI *a'boo dah'bee*, largest of the seven member states of the United Arab Emirates; bounded NW by Qatar, S and W by Saudi Arabia, and N by the Arabian Gulf; it stretches from the base of the Qatar Peninsula in the W to Dubayy (Dubai) in the NE; the terrain is barren with vast areas of desert and *sabkhah* (salt flats); area 67,600 sq km; coastline 400 km; pop(1980) 449,000; capital Abū Ẓabī; main oasis settlement Al 'Ayn; economy: Abū Ẓabī is the principal centre of offshore oil production; the main onshore fields are Bū Haşā, Al' Asab, and Murban-Bab; the main offshore fields are Umm Shaif, Mubarraz, and Zakum; a fourth field, Al-Bandaq, lies partly in Qatar waters; Abū Ẓabī produces about 750,000 of OPEC's production quota for the UAE of 950,000 barrels per day (1986); it is also the main exporter of liquefied natural gas in the lower Gulf area; Dās I, collection point for the surrounding oil and gas fields, is the centre of an expanding petrochemical and gas liquefaction industry; at the Ar Ru'ays industrial city complex, 250 km W of Abū Ẓabī city, areas are set aside for the production of iron and steel, petrochemicals, and light industries; there is a power and desalination complex at Taweelah.

Abū Ẓabī, ABU DHABI, 24 28N 54 25E, pop(1980) 242,985, capital town of Abū Ẓabī emirate and the United Arab Emirates, SE Arabian Peninsula; situated on an island in the Arabian Gulf; the town is laid out in a geometric grid pattern; Mina Zayed is its port; airport; economy: oil-related industries.

Abuja *a-boo'ja*, 9 05N 7 30E, proposed new capital of Nigeria in Federal Capital Territory, central Nigeria, W Africa; in 1976 it was decided to build a new capital for Nigeria in order to relieve the increasing pressure on the infrastructure of Lagos; the city is under construction at the geographical centre of the country, S of Kaduna to which it will be linked by a new road; the development is under the supervision of the Federal Capital Development Authority; since the celebration of National Day in Abuja in 1982 some government offices have already moved to the new capital.

Ābuye Mēda, 10 30N 39 49E, mountain in NE Shewa region, E central Ethiopia; height 4,200 m.

Abyān, governorate of SW South Yemen; formerly the Third Governorate; chief town Zinjibār.

Abyssinia, NE Africa. See Ethiopia.

Acadia, LAFAYETTE, national park on the coast of Maine, United States; SE of Bangor; protects granite peaks on

Mount Desert Island and a promontory on the mainland; established in 1929.

Acapulco or **Acapulco de Juárez** *a-ka-pool'kō dhay whah'-reth*, 16 51N 99 56W, pop(1980) 409,335, port and resort town in Guerrero state, S Mexico; on the Pacific Ocean, 310 km SSW of Ciudad de México (Mexico City); airfield; most popular tourist resort in Mexico, with approx 20 beaches and 250 hotels; monument: in the centre of the city is Fort San Diego, scene of the last battle for Mexican independence.

Acaraí, Serra *a-ka-ra-ee'*, AKARAI MOUNTAINS, mountain range of N South America on the Brazil-Guyana border; length 129 km; forms N watershed of Amazon basin (continued by the Serra de Tumucumaque); rises to 396 m.

Accra' or **Greater Accra**, coastal region in S Ghana, W Africa; pop(1984) 1,420,066; area 2,030 sq km; capital Accra; chief towns Tema, Legon, Dawhenya; economy: petroleum and salt mining, cement, aluminium and salt processing.

Accra, 5 33N 0 15W, pop(1970) 636,067, seaport capital of Ghana, W Africa; on the coast of the Gulf of Guinea, 415 km WSW of Lagos; the city has grown from 3 forts and trading posts, James (British), Crèvecœur (French) and Christianborg (Danish), the last mentioned being the seat of government now called Osu Castle; Accra became capital of Ghana in 1957; the area around the harbour called Jamestown is the seat of the Queen Mother of the Ga people; to the E is the Markola market; university (1948) at Legon 13 km W; airport at Kotoka (10 km from Accra); railway; economy: food processing, fishing, brewing, engineering, scrap metal trade, export of zoo animals, cacao, gold, timber, fruit.

Ac'crington, 53 46N 2 21W, pop(1981) 36,657, town in Hyndburn dist, Lancashire, NW England; 8 km E of Blackburn; railway; economy: coal, textiles, engineering, bricks.

Aceh or **Daerah Istemewa Aceh** *ahch'ay*, ATJEH, ACHEEN, ATCHIN, special territory of Indonesia in N Sumatera; ethnic groups include the Gayo, Batak and Alas people; pop(1980) 2,611,271; area 55,392 sq km; capital Banda Aceh; economy: copra, tobacco, timber, coffee, rubber, palm oil, tea, rice, sisal, pepper, natural gas; the 9,464 sq km Gunung Leuser National Park surrounds Mt Leuser (3,381 m) in the Bukit Barisan range and the Alas Valley on the border of Sumatera Utara prov; orang-utan, rhinoceros, elephant, tapir, sun bear, macaque, mouse deer are amongst the animals to be found here.

Achaea, nome (dept) of Pelopónnisos region, Greece. See Akhaia.

Ack'lins Island, island in the Bahamas, SE of Crooked I, bounded E by Mayaguana Passage; pop(1980) 616; area 497 sq km; chief settlements Snug Corner and Spring Point; economy: agriculture and fishing.

Aconcagua, region in central Chile. See Valparaíso.

Aconcagua, Cerro *a-kon-kag'wa*, 32 39S 70 01W, mountain rising to 6,960 m in Mendoza prov, Andina, W Argentina; in the Andes, E of the Chilean border; 112 km WNW of Mendoza; the highest peak in the Western hemisphere; Uspallata Pass is at its S foot; first ascended in 1897 by the Fitzgerald expedition.

Acor, Serra de *a-kor'*, mountain range, Coimbra dist, central Portugal; a SW extension of the Serra da Estrêla lying E of Coimbra and rising to 1,340 m.

Açores, Ilhas dos *a-zōr'esh*, AZORES *a-zorz'* (Eng) ('islands of the hawks'), pop(1981) 243,410; island archipelago of volcanic origin lying 1,400-1,800 km W of the Cabo da Roca on the mainland of Portugal between lat 39 43N and 36 55N and long 24 46W and 31 16W; a Portuguese autonomous region divided into 3 dists: Angra do Heroísmo, Ponta Delgada and Horta; represented by five members in the Portuguese Parliament; the nine largest islands lie in three widely separated groups, to the NW Flores and Corvo, in the centre Terceira, Graciosa, São Jorge, Faial and Pico, and to the E Santa Maria with the Formigas Islands and São Miguel, the principal island; settled by Portuguese since 1439; in 1466 the islands were made over to Isabella of Burgundy, thereafter there was a considerable influx of Flemish settlers; the chief town is Ponta Delgada; economy: agriculture with exports of grain, fruit, tea and tobacco; exposed throughout the year to strong winds, in summer blowing from the NE and in winter from the SW; Pico (2,351 m) is the highest peak in the Azores and also in Portugal.

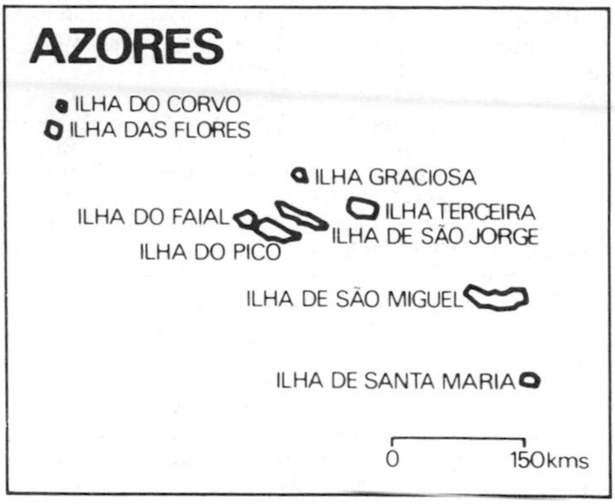

Acquaviva *ahk-wah-vee'vah*, castle (dist) in the Republic of San Marino, central Italy; area 4.86 sq km; pop(1980) 1,087; population density in 1980 was 223 inhabitants per sq km; economy: cement production.

Acre *ak'ray*, state in Norte region, NW Brazil; bounded S by Bolivia and Peru along the Acre and Abuna rivers and W by Peru; lies within the tropical rainforest basin of the Amazon; crossed by the upper Jurua and Purús rivers; pop(1980) 301,303; area 152,589 sq km; capital Rio Branco; economy: rubber, chestnuts.

Acre, town and dist in Israel. See 'Akko.

Ada *ay'da*, 5 47N 0 42E, town in Volta region, SE Ghana, W Africa.

Adam, Mount, 51 34S 60 05W, mountain on the island of West Falkland, Falkland Is, situated S of Hill Cove Settlement, rising to 700 m.

Adamaoua *ad-am-ah'wah*, prov in N central Cameroon, W Africa; comprising the central Massif d'Adamaoua; chief town Ngaoundéré; pop(1984e) 400,000; a former native kingdom settled by Fulah tribes in the 15th century; economy: livestock, cereals, coffee, groundnuts, vegetables, bauxite.

Adam's Peak, SRI PADA (Sing), 6 49N 80 30E, sacred mountain in Sri Lanka rising to 2,243 m NE of Ratnapura; in Dec-April pilgrimages are made to the foot-shaped hollow found on the mountain's summit, believed to be the footprint of Buddha by Buddhists, of Adam by Muslims, of God Siva by Hindus and of St Thomas, the Apostle, by some Christians.

'Adan, governorate of SW South Aden; formerly the First Governorate; chief town Aden ('Adan).

Adana *a'da-na*, SEYHAN *say-han'*, prov in S Turkey, bounded S by the Mediterranean Sea; pop(1980) 1,485,743; area 17,253 sq km; capital Adana; chief towns Ceyhan, Kozan and Ozmaniye; drained by the R Seyhan.

Adana, 37 00N 35 19E, pop(1980) 574,515, commercial capital of Adana prov, S Turkey; on the R Seyhan; 4th largest city in Turkey; railway; airfield.

Adapazarı *a-da-pa-za-ru'*, SAKARYA, 40 46N 30 23E, pop(1980) 130,977, capital of Sakarya prov, NW Turkey; on the W bank of the R Sakarya; trade centre for the surrounding agricultural region which produces tobacco, sugar-beet, grains; railway.

Addis Ababa *a'dis a'bu-bu*, ADIS ABEBA, 9 02N 38 42E, pop(1984e) 1,412,575, capital of Ethiopia, NE Africa; alt 2,400 m; founded by Menelik II in 1887, replacing Intotto as capital in 1889; occupied by Italy between 1936 and 1941 when it was declared capital of Italian East Africa; headquarters of UN Economic Commission for Africa; also headquarters of the Organization of African Unity (OAU); university (1950); railway connection with

Djibouti completed in 1917 (782 km); airport (Bole, 8 km); monuments: national museum, St George cathedral, emperor Menelik II's tomb.

Addison, 41 56N 87 59W, pop(1980) 29,759, residential town in Du Page county, NE Illinois, United States; 30 km W of Chicago.

Addo Elephant, national park in Cape prov, South Africa; 6 km N of Port Elizabeth; area 68.52 sq km; established in 1931; over 100 Addo elephants are preserved here.

Adelaide *ad'el-ayd*, 34 56S 138 36E, pop(1986) 993,100, port capital of South Australia and urban centre of Adelaide stat div, S South Australia; on the Torrens river where it meets the St Vincent Gulf, at the foot of the Mount Lofty Range; founded in 1837, it was the first municipality in Australia to be incorporated (1840); Adelaide Festival Centre, situated on the banks of the Torrens river, comprises a concert theatre, a drama theatre, an experimental theatre, an amphitheatre, galleries and restaurants; to the W of the city are fine beaches, including Maslin Beach, the first nude bathing beach in Australia; some of Australia's best wines are to be found in McLaren Vale, to the S of the city; 2 universities (1874, 1966); railway; airfield; economy: oil refining, motor vehicles, electrical goods, shipbuilding, trade in wool, grain, fruit and wine; monuments: the South Australian Museum contains a vast collection of aboriginal art; the Art Gallery of South Australia; the Constitutional Museum traces political history; Ayers House, dating from 1846, is the headquarters of the South Australian National Trust; Maritime museum in Port Adelaide; events: Adelaide arts festival, held every 2 years; Adelaide Cup Day (May); the Adelaide statistical division is an area with close economic and social contact with Adelaide urban centre and with a boundary that circumscribes anticipated urban development during the last 2 decades of the 20th century; it comprises 5 subdivisions and 35 local government areas with a total pop of 954,080:

Statistical subdivision / *Local govt area*	*pop(1981)*
Eastern	
Adelaide	11,190
Burnside	38,690
Campbelltown	44,300
East Torrens	5,220
Kensington and Norwood	8,990
Onkaparinga	100
Payneham	17,100
Prospect	19,160
St Peters	8,710
Stirling	13,550
Unley	36,730
Walkerville	7,020
North Eastern	
Enfield	50,900
Gumeracha	950
Salisbury	33,670
Tea Tree Gully	69,080
Para	
Elizabeth	33,310
Gawler	6,300
Light	900
Munno Para	27,620
Salisbury	54,560
Southern	
Brighton	20,320
Glenelg	13,550
Happy Valley	20,490
Marion	68,780
Mitcham	61,690
Noarlunga	62,630
Willunga	6,340
Western	
Enfield	17,120

contd

Statistical subdivision / *Local govt area*	*pop(1981)*
Henley and Grange	15,870
Hindmarsh	7,810
Port Adelaide	36,480
Thebarton	9,500
West Torrens	46,220
Woodville	79,230

Adélie, Terre *a-day'lee*, ADÉLIE COAST or ADELIE LAND (Eng), part of French Southern and Antarctic Territories in Antarctica between 66° and 67° S, 136° and 142° E; area of about 432,000 sq km; first seen by Captain Dumont d'Urville of the French navy in 1840; explored by Mawson 1911-14 and 1929-31; French territory since 1938; the French Polar Expedition maintains a research station at Base Dumont d'Urville.

Aden *ay'den*, 'ADAN, 12 50N 45 00E, pop(1981e) 264,326, seaport capital in 'Adan governorate, South Yemen; on the Gulf of Aden, approx 160 km E of the Bāb al Mandab strait at the entrance to the Red Sea; situated on the volcanic Aden peninsula; capital of former Aden protectorate; in medieval times it was a busy port on the Arab trade route between the Red Sea, the Arabian Gulf and India; after the opening of the Suez Canal in 1869 it became an important coaling station and transshipment point; made a British crown colony in 1937; became capital of the independent republic in 1968; airport; economy: oil refining, shipping.

Aden, Gulf of, W arm of the Red Sea, lying between South Yemen (N) and Somalia (S); connected to the Red Sea by the Strait of Bāb al Mandab; linked to the Indian Ocean by that area between the island of Socotra and the S coast of Oman; geologically an extension of the Great Rift Valley; length 885 km.

Adige *a'dee-jay*, ETSCH (Ger), ATH'ESIS (anc), river in N Italy, rising S of Passo di Resia in 3 small Alpine lakes; flows E into the Trentino as far as Merano, then generally S past Bolzano, Trento, and Rovereto, then SE across the Po plain, past Verona and Legnago, and E to the Adriatic Sea, 8 km SE of Chioggia; length 408 km; after the Po it is the chief river of Italy; tributaries include the Noce, Isarco and Avisio rivers.

Adirondack Mountains *ad-e-ron'dak*, mountain range lying largely in NE New York state, United States; stretches from Utica in the SW to L Champlain in the NE; rises to 1,629 m at Mt Marcy; named after an Indian tribe; source of the Hudson and Ausable rivers; locations such as Lake Placid are noted winter resorts.

Adis Abeba, capital of Ethiopia. See Addis Ababa.

Adıyaman *a-du'ya-man*, prov in S Turkey, bounded S and E by the R Euphrates (Firat); pop(1980) 367,595; area 7,614 sq km; capital Adıyaman; economy: grain, tobacco, cotton.

Admiralty Islands, island group in Manus prov, N Papua New Guinea; Manus is the main island; other islands include Momote, Rambulyo, Lou, Baluan, Tong, Bipi; chief town Lorengau; the islands became a German protectorate in 1884 and an Australian mandate in 1920; economy: fishing, copra.

Ado-Ekit'i, 7 40N 5 16E, pop(1981e) 291,200, town in Ondo state, SW Nigeria, W Africa, 40 km N of Akure.

Adour *a-door'*, river in SW France rising in the central Pyrénées near Pic du Midi de Bigorre; flows N and then W to enter the Bay of Biscay near Bayonne; length 335 km; navigable to Dax; tributaries Midouze, Luy, and Nive rivers.

Adrar', department of central Algeria, N Africa; area 422,498 sq km; pop(1982) 151,309; chief town Adrar.

Adrar, region in central Mauritania, NW Africa; pop(1982e) 60,000; area 215,300 sq km; mainly desert with occasional oases; capital Atar; chief towns Chrerick, Chinguetti, Ouadane and Ain Safra.

Adrar des Iforhas *a-drar' dayz ee-fo'ras*, massif in NE Mali,

W Africa; at the SW end of the Hoggar (Ahaggar) massif; rising to over 1,000 m.

Adriatic Sea *ay-dree-a'tik*, arm of the Mediterranean Sea, lying between the E coast of Italy and the Balkan Peninsula (Yugoslavia and Albania); the Gulf of Venice lies at its head in the NW and in the S it is separated from the Ionian Sea by the Strait of Otranto; length 805 km; width 93-225 km; max depth 1,250 m; highly saline owing to excessive evaporation and the small input of fresh water; the Po and Adige rivers continually deposit sediment along the coast; sandspits are common along the NW coast; the coast of Yugoslavia, which is developing into a major tourist resort, is rugged and irregular, with many offshore islands and sheltered bays; lobster, sardines and tuna are the chief catches of the rich fisheries; Venice, Rijeka, Ancona, Bari and Brindisi are the main ports.

Adula Gruppe, mountain range in Lepontine Alps, Ticino and Graubünden cantons, SE Switzerland; highest peak is the Rheinwaldhorn (3,403 m); Hinterrhein river, a headstream of the Rhine rises here and flows E through the Rheinwald valley.

Adzopé *ad-zō'pay*, dept in SE Ivory Coast, W Africa; pop(1975) 162,837; area 5,230 sq km; bounded E by the R Komé; capital Adzopé; chief towns Bouape and Bettie.

Aegean Islands *ee-jee'an*, island group and region of Greece; pop(1981) 428,533; area 9,122 sq km; name generally applied to the islands of the Aegean Sea, including Lésvos, Khíos, Sámos, Límnos, and Thásos; the region comprises the nomoi (depts) of Khíos, Kikládhes, Lésvos, Sámos, and Sporádhes.

Aegean Sea, E arm of the Mediterranean Sea; bounded by Greece to the W and N, Turkey to the NE and E, and the islands of Crete and Rhodes forming the S limit; the sea is thickly dotted with islands on which the Aegean civilization of 3,000-1,000 BC flourished, particularly the Kikládhes (Cyclades) and the Sporádhes (Dodecanese) groups; length (N-S) 645 km; width 320 km; linked to the Black Sea by the Dardanelles Strait, the Sea of Marmara and the Bosporus; greatest depth of 2,013 m is found off N Crete; named after the legendary Aegeus, who drowned himself in the belief that his son Theseus had been killed; fishing for sardine and sponge is an important industry; natural gas has been found off the NE coast of Greece.

Aegina, Greek island. See Aíyna.

Aetolia and Acarnania, nome (dept) of Sterea Ellás-Évvoia region, Greece. See Aitolía and Akarnanía.

Afghanistan *af-gan'i-stan*, official name Republic of Afghanistan, DE AFGHANISTAN JAMHURIAT, republic in S Asia; bounded N by Turkestan SSR (Soviet Union), E and S by Pakistan and W by Iran, while a narrow tongue in the extreme NE extends to touch the Xinjiang Uygur autonomous region of China and Kashmir, India; timezone GMT $+4\frac{1}{2}$; area 647,497 sq km; capital Kābul; chief towns include Mazār-e Sharīf, Herāt, Kandahār; pop(1984e) 14,366,434 plus an estimated $2\frac{1}{2}$ mn nomadic tribesmen and 3 mn who are living in Pakistan and Iran as refugees; Pathans are the main ethnic group, but also present are Tajik, Hazara, Turkoman and Uzbek minorities; official languages are Pushtu, Dari (Persian) and Russian, with some English, French and German spoken; Islam is the main religion, mostly of the Sunni sect, although there is a minority of around 1 mn Shi'a Moslems; the unit of currency is the Afghani, which is subdivded into 100 puls; national holidays 21 March (Nowroz or New Year's Day), 27 April (Saur Revolution Day), 4 June (Id-ul-Fitr), 17-18 July (Republic Day), 27 August (Id-ul-Adha), 31 Aug (Pushtoonistan Day), 9 Sept (Parliament Day), 25 Sept (Ashura), 15 Oct (Day of Deliverance), 24 Oct (United Nations Day), 5 Dec (Prophet's birthday); membership of Islamic Development Bank, ILO, IMF, UN, WHO, World Bank.

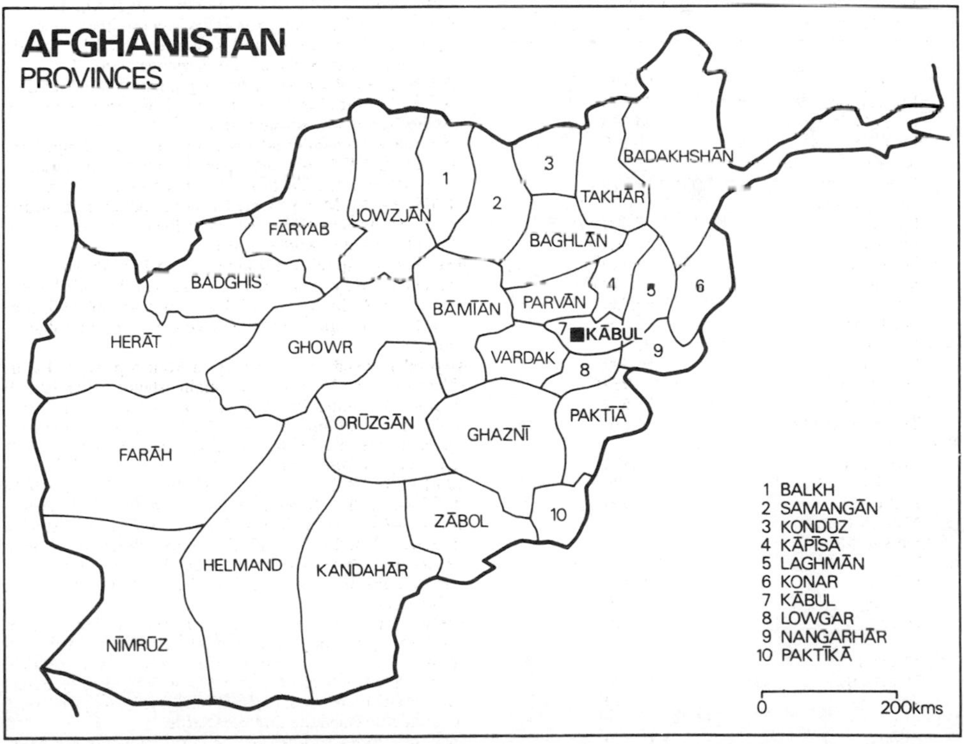

Physical description. Afghanistan is a mountainous country centred on the Hindu Kush system, which reaches heights of over 7,320 m and is the 2nd highest range in the world. Peaks are highest in the centre and the NE of the country. Many secondary ranges spread out from the Hindu Kush, which are vegetated with mountain forest and topped with alpine tundra. NW of the Hindu Kush, heights decrease rapidly to 200 m towards the Afghanistan border with the USSR. S of the Hindu Kush lie arid uplands descending into desert in the SW, which are vegetated mostly by scrub. Heights of 200-500 m are found along the boundary with Iran. NW of the Hindu Kush system is the fertile valley of Herāt, lying on the R Hari Rud. Afghanistan is landlocked and is over 500 km distant from the nearest ocean.

Climate. Afghanistan has a continental type climate, winter severity being increased by the effects of altitude. Summers are warm everywhere except on the highest peaks. The mountainous S protects Afghanistan from the summer monsoonal rains, such that hardly any rain falls during June to Oct. Rain mostly occurs during spring and autumn. Annual rainfall averages 338 mm. Winters can be cold with considerable snowfall at higher altitudes, but the lower elevations of Afghanistan, particularly in the S, have a desert or semi-arid climate, where winters are milder.

History, government and constitution. Afghans (ancestors of the Pathans) first formed a nation in 1747 under Ahmed Shah Durrani, although the modern-day state now extends beyond the original boundaries. Britain saw Afghanistan as a bridge between India and the Middle East but failed to gain control during a series of Afghan Wars, the last of which was in 1919. The feudal monarchy survived until after World War II, when the constitution became more liberal under a series of Soviet-influenced 5-year economic plans. In 1973 the king was deposed, the 1964 constitution abolished and a republic formed. A new constitution was adopted in 1977 but a coup in the following year installed a new government under the communist leader, Noor Mohammed Taraki. A further coup in Sept 1979 brought to power Hafizullah Amim. Under the pretext of a 1978 Treaty of Friendship, this event precipitated the invasion of Afghanistan by USSR forces and the establishment of Babrak Karmel as head of state. A 36-member Central Committee elects a 9-member Politburo, while the 65-member Revolutionary Council elects a 7-member Presidium. Head of state is the General Secretary of the Politburo and President of the Revolutionary Council and the Presidium. The regime has met heavy guerrilla resistance from the Mujahideen (Islamic fighters) and its influence extends effectively over only 20% of the population.

Economy. Since the late 1970s most sectors of the economy have been affected by civil war, in particular the sugar and textile industries. Agriculture has traditionally been the basis of the economy, the main crops being wheat, fruit and vegetables, maize, barley, cotton, sugar-beet and sugar cane. Sheep, cattle and goats are also important and 80% of the forest cut annually is used as fuel wood. Industrial activity concentrates on food processing, textiles, leather goods, plastics, furniture, footwear and mechanical spares. Natural gas production in the N is largely for export to the USSR. The major trade partners are the USSR and other COMECON countries.

Administrative divisions. Afghanistan is divided into the following 29 provinces:

Province	*area (sq km)*	*pop(1984e)*
Badakhshān	540,280	47,403
Bādghīs	227,437	21,858
Baghlān	536,783	17,109
Balkh	635,332	12,593
Bāmīān	291,476	17,414
Farah	254,820	47,788
Fāryab	588,452	22,279
Ghaznī	702,054	23,378
Ghowr	366,823	38,666
Helmand	562,043	61,828
Herāt	868,564	61,315
Jōwzjān	683,870	25,553
Kābul	1,659,377	4,585
Kandahār	625,101	47,676
Kāpisā	271,915	1,871
Konar	271,470	10,479
Kondūz	606,211	7,827
Laghmān	337,274	7,210
Lowgar	234,789	4,652
Nangarhār	812,466	7,616
Nīmrūz	112,536	41,356
Orūzgān	482,091	29,295
Paktīā	525,389	9,581
Paktīkā	266,139	19,336
Parvān	548,001	9,399
Samangān	284,351	15,465
Takhār	564,545	12,376
Vardak	312,135	9,023
Zābol	194,710	17,293

Af'rica, after Asia, the 2nd largest continent, extending S from the Mediterranean Sea; bounded W by the Atlantic Ocean and E by the Indian Ocean and the Red Sea; bisected by the Equator which passes through the states of Gabon, Congo, Zaire, Uganda, Kenya and Somalia; measures 8,000 km in length by 7,200 km in breadth; area c.29.8 mn sq km; rises to the volcanic peak of Mt Kilimanjaro (5,895 m); major rivers include the Congo, Niger, Nile and Zambezi; major cities with a pop in excess of one million persons include Cairo, Alexandria, Kinshasa, Casablanca, Johannesburg, Algiers, Lagos, El Giza, Addis Ababa and Cape Town.

Afyonkarahısar *af-yon'ka-rah-i-sar*, mountainous prov in W Turkey; pop(1980) 597,516; area 14,230 sq km; capital Afyon; Mt Emir in the N and L Akeshir in E; drained by R Akar; chief opium-producing area of Turkey.

Agadez *ag-a-des'*, dept in central Niger, W Africa; generally a low-lying, hot desert region with virtually no rainfall; in the N is the high Hamada Maguene plateau and in the W central area the Aïr massif rising to 1,944 m at Mount Greboun; between these is the Ténéré du Tafassasset desert; area 634,209 sq km; pop(1977e) 95,000; comprises 2 arrond; capital Agadez; chief towns Bilma, Djado; economy: salt, coal and uranium mining, tin and uranium processing.

Agadez, 17 00N 7 56E, pop(1977) 20,475, capital of Agadez dept, central Niger, W Africa; 700 km ENE of Niamey at the foot of the Aïr mountains; an ancient caravan trading city with a 16th-c mosque; the former capital of a Tuareg kingdom; there are fine examples of Sudanic mud architecture and the city is renowned for its traditional silversmiths and leatherworkers; airfield; economy: tourism, trading and salt.

Agadir *a-ga-deer'*, 30 30N 9 40W, pop(1982) 110,479, seaport in Agadir prefecture, Sud prov, W Morocco, N Africa; on the Atlantic coast, 120 km S of Essaouira, 303 km SW of Marrakech and 8 km N of the mouth of the R Sous; occupied by Portuguese who named it Santa Cruz 1505-41; taken by the French in 1913; extensive rebuilding after the 1960 earthquake which killed 12,600 people; airport; economy: fishing, tourism; monument: 16th-c kasbah fortress; event: African People's Arts Festival in July.

Agaña *a-gah'nya*, 13 28N 144 45E, port and capital town of Guam, Mariana Is, W Pacific Ocean, on the W coast of the island on Agaña Bay; anchorage at Apra Harbour; a US naval base covers much of the harbour; taken by the Japanese in 1941 and destroyed during its recapture by the Americans in 1944; monument: cathedral (1669).

Agboville *ag-bō-veel'*, dept in SE Ivory Coast, W Africa;

pop(1975) 141,970; area 3,850 sq km; capital Agboville; chief towns Yepo and Azaguié; the railway from Abidjan runs SE-NW across the dept.

Agen *a-zhã*, 44 12N 0 38E, pop(1982) 32,893, agric centre and capital of Lot-et-Garonne dept, Aquitaine region, SW France; between the R Garonne and a steep hill; road and rail junction; the centre of a fertile fruit-growing dist watered by the Garonne Canal and especially famous for its plums and prunes; Joseph Scaliger and the barber-poet Jasmin were natives; monuments: 11th-c St Carpais cathedral and 4 Renaissance mansions joined to form a museum containing a fine ceramic collection as well as paintings by Goya and Boudin.

Agincourt *a-zhin-coor*, AZINCOURT, village in Pas-de-Calais dept, Nord-Pas-de-Calais, NW France; NW of Arras, celebrated for the bloody battle in which the English forces of Henry V defeated a larger French army on 25 Oct 1415.

Agra *ah'gru*, 27 17N 77 58E, pop(1981) 770,000, city in Uttar Pradesh, NE India; S of the R Yamuna, 190 km SSE of Delhi; founded in 1566 by Akbar; former Mogul capital until 1659 when Aurungzebe removed to Delhi; seat of the government of North-West Provinces (1835-62); beseiged during the Indian Mutiny (1857); university (1927); airfield; linked to Delhi, Gwalior, Jaipur and Kanpur by rail; economy: glass and leather handicrafts, carpets; monuments: the Taj Mahal (1630-48), built in pure white marble by Shah Jahan as a memorial to his favourite wife Arjmand Banu; fort containing the Pearl Mosque of Shah Jahan (Moti Masjid); the Mirror Palace (Shish Mahul); the Great Mosque; to the N at Sikandra is the tomb of Akbar.

Ağri *a-ru'*, mountainous prov in E Turkey, bounded E by Iran; pop(1980) 368,009; area 11,376 sq km; capital Karaköse (Ağri); drained by R Murat; the prov has a large Kurdish pop.

Ağrı Dağı or **Büyük Ağrı Dağı** *bü-yük u-ru' da-u*, GREAT MT ARARAT *a'ru-rat*, 39 44N 44 15E, highest peak in Turkey; situated on the border between Kars and Ağri provs, E Turkey, close to the frontier with Iran and the USSR; height 5,165 m; it is the alleged landing place of Noah's Ark; Küçük Ağrı Dağı (Little Ararat) lies to the SE and rises to 3,907 m.

Agrigento *ah-gree-jen'to*, prov of Sicilia region, Italy; pop(1981) 466,495; area 3,041 sq km; capital Agrigento.

Agrigento, formerly GIRGENTI *jeer-jen'tee*, AKRAGAS (Gr), 37 19N 13 35E, pop(1981) 51,325, capital town of Agrigento prov, Sicilia, Italy; on the S coast 99km SSE of Palermo; sulphur mines; railway; monuments: several ruined temples, in particular the Temple of Concord (5th c BC, converted into a church in the Middle Ages) and the Temple of Juno Lacinia (5th-c BC).

Agrínion *ah-gree'nee-on*, formerly VRAKHORI, 38 38N 21 25E, pop(1981) 45,087, main town of Aitolía and Akarnanía nome (dept), Sterea Ellás-Évvoia region, Greece; NW of L Trikhonís, on the main highway between Árta and Návpaktos; airfield; economy: centre for local tobacco trade; event: Papastratia festival of cultural and sporting events (June).

Aguadulce *ag-wa-dool'see*, 8 06N 80 31W, pop(1980) 10,665, town in Coclé prov, central Panama, Central America; on the Inter-American Highway, SW of Panamá City; its port is 5 km from the town; large salt-beds nearby.

Aguán *a-gwan'*, river in N Honduras, Central America; rises S of Yoro and flows approx 240 km ENE across the N lowlands to meet the Caribbean Sea at Santa Rosa Aguán, E of Trujillo.

Aguascalientes *ag'was-kal-yen'tays* ('warm waters'), state in central Mexico; bounded E, N and W by Zacatecas and S by Jalisco; situated on the central plateau with broken ranges of the Sierra Madre Occidental in the W and SW; the land is lower in the E; in the centre of the state lies the Aguas Calientes river valley; drained by the Río de Aguas Calientes; the state contains several sulphuric thermal springs; pop(1980) 503,410; area 5,471 sq km; capital Aguascalientes; economy: mining (gold, silver, copper, lead, zinc), brewing, alcohol, food processing, textiles, agriculture (vines, maize, garlic, sorghum, onions, peppers, alfalfa, wheat).

Aguascalientes, 21 51N 102 18W, pop(1980) 359,454, capital of Aguascalientes state, central Mexico; alt 1,888 m; founded in 1575, the town is named after its numerous hot mineral springs; the town is built over an ancient network of tunnels; state capital since 1835; university; railway; economy: viticulture; monument: the government palace, once the castle of the Marqués de Guadalupe, contains colourful murals around the inner courtyard.

Agulhas, Cape *a-gool'yas* (Port, 'needles'), 34 50S 20 00E, the most southerly point of the African continent, 160 km ESE of the Cape of Good Hope, South Africa; running past it, round the whole S coast, is a reef, the Agulhas Bank, an important fishing ground; in 1852 the troopship *Birkenhead* was wrecked off the cape with the loss of over 400 men.

Ahaggar *ah-he-gahr'*, HOGGAR, mountain range in S Algeria, N Africa; rises to 2,918 m at Mt Tahat which is the highest point in Algeria; peaks rise from a plateau with a mean elevation of about 2,000 m; isolated rock peaks include Iharen (1,732 m), Ilamane (2,758 m), and the 'mountain of goblins', Garet el Djenoun (2,327 m), which is according to legend, a holy mountain.

Ah'len, 51 46N 7 53E, pop(1983) 53,200, manufacturing city in Münster dist, Nordrhein-Westfalen (North Rhine-Westphalia) prov, W Germany; 27 km SE of Münster; railway; economy: footwear, enamel, coal mining nearby.

Ahmadabad *ah'ma-da-bad*, AHMEDABAD, 23 00N 72 40E, pop(1981) 2,515,000, commercial centre and industrial city in Gujarat, W India; lies on the R Sabarmati, 440 km N of Bombay; founded in 1411 by Ahmad Shah I, Sultan of Gujarat; fell to the Moguls in 1572 and thereafter enjoyed a period of prosperity; a British trading post opened here in 1619 and by the early 19th century the British controlled the city; centre of Gandhi's activities during the 1920s and 30s; airfield; railway; economy: cotton industry (established in the early 19th century); monuments: temples, mosques, forts and Gandhi's Sabarmati Ashram.

Aḩmadī, Al *al a-ma-dee'*, 29 05N 48 10E, pop(1980) 23,875, town in E Kuwait, 30 km S of Al Kuwayt (Kuwait City); linked by pipeline to its port and loading terminal, Mīnā' al Aḩmadī, 8 km ESE on the Arabian Gulf; residential community for the surrounding oil fields, developed after 1946; economy: oil, natural gas, chemicals.

Ahmadpur East *ah'mud-poor*, 29 06N 71 14E, pop(1981) 57,000, city in Punjab prov, Pakistan; SW of Bahawalpur; former capital of Bahawalpur state; railway; wheat, cotton and millet are the main local products.

Ahr, river in Nordrhein-Westfalen (North Rhine-Westphalia), W Germany; rises near Blankenheim and flows 90 km E to meet the Rhine near Sinzig; the valley has been noted for its wine since Roman times and is the most northerly wine-growing area in Germany.

Ahuachapán *a-wa-cha-pan'*, dept in W El Salvador, Central America; bordered W by Guatemala and S by the Pacific Ocean; pop(1971) 183,682; area 1,281 sq km; capital Ahuachapán; chief towns Tacuba and Atiquizaya; the Río de Paz forms its W boundary.

Ahuachapán, 13 57N 89 49W, pop(1980) 69,852, capital town of Ahuachapán dept, W El Salvador, Central America; near the Guatemala border, 35 km WSW of Santa Ana; alt 753 m; railway; an important distribution centre; economy: coffee trade, geothermal power plant (1975).

Ahvāz *ah-waz'*, 31 19N 48 42E, pop(1983) 470,927, industrial capital of Ahvāz dist, Khuzestān, SW Iran; 544 km SW of Tehrān, on the R Kārūn; oil was discovered nearby in the early 20th century; airfield; railway.

Ahvenanmaa *ah'ven-an-ma*, ÅLAND *aw'land* (Swed), ('land of waters'), an island group forming an autonomous admin dist (*mahkunta*) of Finland at the S end of the Gulf of Bothnia between Sweden and Finland; area 1,552 sq km; pop(1982) 23,196; the resort town of Maarianhamina, situated on the S coast of the island of Ahvenanmaa, is the dist capital; 80 out of a total of 6,554 islands are inhabited; other islands include Eckero, Lemland, Lumparland and Vardo; the islands are governed by an elected *landstig*; Swedish is the first language.

Aiea *ī-ay'a*, 21 23N 157 56W, pop(1980) 32,879, town in Honolulu county, Hawaii, United States; residential suburb 12 km W of Honolulu, on Pearl Harbor, Oahu I.

Aigües-Tortes *ayg'wes tor'tes*, ('winding waters'), national park in Lérida prov, Cataluña, NE Spain; established in 1955; area 105 sq km; in a valley at an alt of 1,500 m rising to 3,000 m; between the Noguera de Tort and Noguera Pallaresa valleys; glacially eroded landscape with lakes (St Maurice), woods and snow-covered peaks (Colomés); chamois, wild goat, ibex, wild boar and capercaillie are protected here.

Ain *ī*, dept in Rhône-Alpes region of E France lying between the rivers Rhône and Saône and comprising 4 arrond, 41 cantons and 419 communes; pop(1982) 418,516; area 5,762 sq km; capital Bourg-en-Bresse; fertile plains in the N, pasturage by the R Saône, swampy in the S and mountainous in the E which is furrowed N-S by spurs of the Jura Mts; the Dombes area, dotted with lakes and lying to the S of Bourg-en-Bresse, is a high plateau formed from Ice Age detritus; interesting caves near Nantua (Grotte du Cerdon); vineyards, pasture and timber clothe the valleys; spa at Divonne-les-Bains; economy: poultry, meat, cereals, wine and Roquefort and Gruyère cheese.

Ain, river in E France rising in the central Jura Occidentale near Nozeroy; flows SSW through the Jura and Ain to the R Rhône 29 km above Lyons; length 200 km; tributary R Bienne.

Aïn Diab *īn dyab'*, 33 20N 71 25W, pop(1982) 329,006, municipality in Centre prov, W Morocco, N Africa; a W suburb of Casablanca; a seaside resort town.

Aïn-Chock *īn-chok'*, 33 19N 71 24W, pop(1982) 422,095, a municipality in Centre prov, W Morocco, N Africa; a SE suburb of Casablanca.

Aïn-es-Sebaâ *īn-es-se-bah'*, 33 20N 71 25W, pop(1982) 468,123, municipality of Centre prov, W Morocco, N Africa; a NE suburb of Casablanca.

Aïoun el Atrous *a-yoon el at-roos'*, 16 43N 9 30W, capital of Hodh el Gharbi region, S Mauritania, NW Africa; 725 km E of Saint Louis (Senegal); airfield.

Aïr *ayr*, AZBINE *az-bee'na*, mountain massif in N Niger, W Africa; a S extension of the Hoggar (Ahaggar) massif; the highest peak is Mount Greboun (1,944 m); uranium deposits are located at Arlit and Akouta.

Airdrie *ayr'dree*, 55 52N 3 59W, pop(1981) 45,747, town in Monklands dist, Strathclyde, W central Scotland; in Clydeside urban area, 17 km E of Glasgow; railway; economy: pharmaceuticals, glass.

Aire, river rising in the Pennines, North Yorkshire, N England; flows 112 km S and SE to meet the R Ouse above Goole; above Leeds it passes through Airedale, which gives its name to a breed of dogs; the Aire Gap is an important route through the Pennines.

Aisén or **Aysen** *ī-sen'*, AISÉN DEL GENERAL CARLOS IBAÑEZ DEL CAMPO, region in S Chile; bordered E by Argentina; comprises the provs of Coihaique, Aisén, General Carrera and Capitan Prat; pop(1984) 70,600; area 108,997 sq km; capital Coihaique; economy: sheep raising, mining; L General Carrera lies on the Argentina border (E); in the W is Laguna San Rafael National Park whose main feature is the San Rafael glacier.

Aisne *ayn*, dept in Picardie region of N France, comprising 5 arrond, 42 cantons and 817 communes; pop(1982) 533,970; area 7,369 sq km; capital Laon; main industrial centre located at St Quentin; level and fertile in the N and hilly in the S; watered by the R Aisne, R Oise and canals such as the St Quentin Canal, which links the city of that name to the industrial cities of Belgium and N Germany; there are many World War I battlefields and war memorials.

Aisne, river in NE France rising near Vaubecourt in the Ardennes Occidentales; flows NNW then W to the R Oise near Compiègne; length 280 km; tributary R Aire.

Aitolía and Akarnanía *eet-ōl'yu and a-kur-nay'nee-u*, AETOLIA AND ACARNANIA (Eng), nome (dept) of Sterea Ellás-Évvoia region, Greece; pop(1981) 219,764; area 5,461 sq km; capital Mesolóngion.

Aitutaki *ī-too-ta'kee*, 18 52S 159 46W, coral atoll of the Cook Is, S Pacific, 224 km N of Rarotonga; area 17.9 sq km; pop(1981) 2,335; the low lying hills rise to 120 m and are flanked by banana plantations and coconut groves.

Aiud *a-yood'*, 46 19N 23 43E, pop(1983) 28,334, town in Alba county, W central Romania; on the R Mureş, 25 km NNE of Alba Iulia; established in the 12th century; railway; economy: wine and agricultural trade, textiles, paper.

Aix-en-Provence *eks-ã-pro-vãs*, 43 31N 5 27E, pop(1982) 124,550, ancient city in Bouches-du-Rhône dept, Provence-Alpes-Côte d'Azur region, SW France; 30 km N of Marseille in a fertile plain surrounded by mountains; archbishopric; thermal springs; university (1409); casino and nightclubs; the town was founded as Aquae Sextiae in 123 BC by the Roman consul Caius Sextius; the artist Paul Cézanne (1839-1906) was born and died here; important centre for Provençal literature since the 15th century; airport; railway; economy: olive oil, fruit, almond processing; monuments: many fountains, especially along the Cours Mirabeau; 11-16th-c St Saver cathedral; a baroque hôtel de ville (1658); several art galleries including the Musée Granet which houses a fine collection of French, Flemish, Dutch and Italian paintings; events: International Music Festival in July-Aug; Saison d'Aix with open-air performances from June to Sept.

Aíyion *ay'yee-on*, 38 15N 22 05E, pop(1981) 25,723, town in Akhaïa nome (dept), Pelopónnisos region, Greece; on the S coast of the Korinthiakós Kólpos (Gulf of Corinth), 35 km E of Pátrai; railway.

Aíyna *ī'yee-na*, AEGINA *ee-jī-na* (Eng), island in the Saronikós Kólpos (Saronic Gulf), Greece, SW of Athínai (Athens); area 83 sq km; pop(1981) 11,127; chief town Aíyna; the island is a popular resort; monument: Temple of Aphaia.

Ajaccio *a-zhak'si-o*, *a-yat'chō* (Ital), 41 55N 8 40E, pop(1982) 55,279, seaport and capital of Corse-du-Sud dept, Island of Corsica, France; lying on the W coast of the island in a sheltered bay at the head of the Golfe de Ajaccio; Corsica's 2nd largest port; airport 7 km from the city; railway (to Bastia and Calvi); car ferries to Marseille, Toulon and Nice; casino; founded by the Genoese in 1492; made capital of Corsica in 1811 by Napoleon; economy: fishing and timber trade; monuments: Maison Bonaparte, the birthplace of Napoleon.

Ajka *o-i'ko*, 47 4N 17 31E, pop(1984e) 31,000, town in Veszprém county, W Hungary; on R Torna, W of Veszprém; railway; economy: agricultural trade, mining, aluminium products, electric power.

'Ajmān *aj-man'*, smallest of the seven member states of the United Arab Emirates, entirely surrounded by the territory of Shāriqah except on the coast; 'Ajmān has 2 separate enclaves in the Hajar Mts; area 250 sq km; pop(1980) 36,100; capital 'Ajmān; the emirate is relatively undeveloped with no significant oil or gas reserves yet discovered.

'Ajmān, 25 25N 55 30E, capital town of 'Ajmān emirate, United Arab Emirates, SE Arabian Peninsula; on the Arabian Gulf; economy: shipping.

Ajmer *uj-meer'*, 26 28N 74 37E, pop(1981) 374,000, city in Rajasthan, NW India; 345 km SW of New Delhi; believed to have been founded in 145 AD, but largely developed in the 12th century; former military base of the Moguls against the Rajputs; linked by rail to Ahmadabad, Jaipur, Bikaner and Bhilwara; economy: cotton, marble; monuments: the dargah, tomb of St Moinuddin Chisti, a centre of Muslim pilgrimage; the palace of the emperor Akbar.

Akashi *a-ka'shee*, 34 39N 135 00E, pop(1980) 254,869, town in Hyōgo prefecture, Kinki region, S Honshū island, Japan; W of Ōsaka on the coast between Harima-nada Sea and Ōsaka-wan Bay; railway.

Akas'sa, 4 19N 6 02E, seaport in Cross River state, Nigeria; on the R Niger delta at the centre of onshore and offshore oil and gas fields.

Akershus *ak'ers-hoos*, AGGERSHUS, a county of E Norway lying between Oslofjorden (Oslo Fjord) and L Mjösa, drained chiefly by the R Glåma; area 4,916 sq km; pop(1983) 376,202; capital Oslo; in 1948 part of it was incorporated in Oslo.

Akhaïa *a-kī'ya*, ACHAEA *a-kee'a* (Eng), nome (dept) of N Pelopónnisos region, SW Greece, bounded N by the Korinthiakós Kólpos (Gulf of Corinth); pop(1981) 275,193; area 3,271 sq km; capital Pátrai; produces wine, olives, fruit, sheep and goats.

Akharnái *ah-KHur-nay'*, ACHARNAE (Lat), 38 05N 23 44E, pop(1981) 40,185, town in Attikí nome (dept), Sterea Ellás-Évvoia region, Greece; 10 km N of Athínai (Athens); the setting for Aristophanes' *Acharnians*; an ancient Mycenean site; railway.

Akhelóös *ahk-hel-o'os*, ACHELOUS *a-kil-ō'us* (Eng), 2nd longest river of Greece; rises in the Píndhos Mts S of the Métsovon gap; flows S through mountain gorges to the fertile Agrínion plain and discharges into the Ionian Sea opposite Kefallinía I, 29 km W of Mesolóngion; length 220 km.

Akita *ah-kee'ta*, 39 44N 140 05E, pop(1980) 284,863, port capital of Akita prefecture, Tōhoku region, N Honshū island, Japan; on the W coast, on the Sea of Japan, at the mouth of the Omono river; university (1949); railway; event: 5-7 Aug, Kanto Festival, a parade where men try to balance 'Kanto', long bamboo poles hung with many lighted lanterns, on their foreheads, shoulders, hips or chins.

Akjoujt *ak-zhoo'zhut*, 19 44N 14 20E, capital of Inchiri region, W Mauritania, NW Africa; on the Route du Mauritanie, 290 km ESE of Nouadhibou.

'Akko, ACRE *ay'kur*, sub-district of North dist, NW Israel; bounded N by Lebanon and W by the Mediterranean Sea; pop(1983) 276,334; area 936 sq km.

'Akko, PTOLEMAIS (anc), 32 55N 35 04E, pop(1982e) 39,100, ancient town in North dist, NW Israel; a resort centre on the Mediterranean Sea; 'Akko became capital of the Crusader kingdom after Jerusalem was captured by the Saracens in 1187; railway; ancient and modern harbour; monuments: huge crypt of the Knights Hospitaller of St John, 18th-c city walls and several mosques.

Akosombo *a-ko-sōm'bo*, 6 17N 0 03E, town in Volta region, SE Ghana, W Africa; at the S end of L Volta; site of the Volta Dam which generates electricity both for S Ghana and for export; there is a ferry link on L Volta to Yapei.

Akranes *ah-kra-nes'*, 64 19N 22 05W, fishing port in Vesturland region, W Iceland; on Faxaflói (Faxa Bay), N of Reykjavík; pop(1983) 5,349; there is a ferry link with Reykjavík; a town since 1941; economy: fishing, cement.

Akron (Greek, 'summit'), 41 05N 81 31W, pop(1980) 237,177, county seat of Summit county, NE Ohio, United States; on the Little Cuyahoga river, 56 km SSE of Cleveland; a city since 1865; university (1913); railway; airfield; economy: metal products, rubber, machinery; polymer research centre; monuments: Goodyear World of Rubber Museum, E.J. Thomas Performing Arts Hall, Blossom Music Centre.

Akrotiri *ahk-re-tee'ree*, a bay on the S coast of the Mediterranean island of Cyprus; Limassol is the main port town; there is a British base at Akrotiri on the peninsula that separates Akrotiri Bay (E) from Episkopi Bay (W).

Aktyubinsk *ak-tyoo'byinsk*, 50 16N 57 13E, pop(1983) 218,000, capital city of Aktyubinskaya oblast, NW Kazakhskaya (Kazakhstan) SSR, Soviet Union; in the S foothills of the Ural'skiy Khrebet (Ural Mts) range, on the left bank of the R Ilek, a tributary of the R Ural; established in 1869; railway; airport; economy: ferroalloy and chromium plants, engineering, manufacture of agricultural machinery, chemicals, building materials, knitwear, clothing, furniture, and foodstuffs.

Akure *a-koo'ray*, 7 14N 5 08E, pop(1969e) 82,461, capital of Ondo state, SW Nigeria, W Africa; 225 km ENE of Lagos; economy: palm oil, wood products, brewing.

Akureyri *ah-koo-ray'ree*, 65 41N 18 04W, 3rd largest town and capital of Nordurland, N Iceland; 436 km NE of Reykjavík; pop(1983) 13,745, the most important centre of trade, industry and education in N Iceland; attained municipal status in 1862; skiing at Hlíðarfjall 3 km from the town; economy: food processing; monuments: Lystigarðurinn park contains over 400 species of Icelandic plants; 3 memorial museums in honour of Icelandic poets.

Akuse *a-koo'sa*, 6 04N 0 12E, town in Volta region, SE Ghana, W Africa; on the R Volta.

Akyab', capital of Arakan state, W Burma. See Sittwe.

Alabam'a, state in SE United States; bounded W by Mississippi, N by Tennessee, E by Georgia, and S by Florida and the Gulf of Mexico; the R Alabama, which is formed by the confluence of the Tallapoosa and Coosa rivers at the centre of the state, flows SW to join the R Tombigbee, forming the R Mobile; the R Tombigbee enters from Mississippi and flows S to join the R Alabama near the Gulf coast; the R Mobile flows a short distance S to empty into Mobile Bay, an arm of the Gulf of Mexico; the R Tennessee flows in a loop W through the N part of the state before re-entering Tennessee; the R Chattahoochee follows the lower part of Georgia state border; the highest point is Mt Cheaha (734 m); Alabama includes 3 distinct regions: (1) a mountainous NE, (2) a coastal plain in the S, and, in between, (3) the rolling plain of the Appalachian Piedmont; the chief farm products are cattle, poultry, cotton, soybeans and peanuts; manufacturing industry, which accounts for more than half of the state's income, produces chemicals, textiles, paper products and processed food; the iron and steel industry is centred on Birmingham; electrical power is supplied by the hydroelectric schemes of the Tennessee Valley Authority in the N; other minerals contributing to the state's income are coal, oil and stone; lumbering and fishing are also important; the first permanent settlement was established by the French on the site of Mobile in 1711; N Alabama became part of the USA in 1783, the remainder being acquired by the Louisiana Purchase in 1803; the 22nd state to be admitted to the Union in 1819; seceded from the Union in 1861; slavery was abolished in 1865, but Alabama refused to ratify the 14th Amendment to the US Constitution and was placed under military rule in 1867; the state was finally re-admitted to the Union in 1868 but Federal troops remained in the state until 1876; also known as the 'Heart of Dixie' or the 'Camellia State'; pop(1980) 3,893,888; area 131,994 sq km; capital Montgomery; other major cities are Birmingham, Mobile and Huntsville; the state is divided into 67 counties:

County	*area (sq km)*	*pop(1980)*
Autauga	1,552	32,259
Baldwin	4,131	78,556
Barbour	2,298	24,756
Bibb	1,625	15,723
Blount	1,672	36,459
Bullock	1,625	10,596
Butler	2,025	21,680
Calhoun	1,589	119,761
Chambers	1,550	39,191
Cherokee	1,438	18,760
Chilton	1,807	30,612
Choctaw	2,363	16,839
Clarke	3,198	27,702
Clay	1,573	13,703
Cleburne	1,459	12,595
Coffee	1,768	38,533
Colbert	1,531	54,519
Conecuh	2,220	15,884
Coosa	1,708	11,377
Covington	2,699	36,850
Crenshaw	1,589	14,110

contd

County	*area (sq km)*	*pop(1980)*
Cullman	1,919	61,642
Dale	1,459	47,821
Dallas	2,535	53,981
De Kalb	2,023	53,658
Elmore	1,617	43,390
Escambia	2,473	38,440
Etowah	1,409	103,057
Fayette	1,638	18,809
Franklin	1,672	28,350
Geneva	1,503	24,253
Greene	1,641	11,021
Hale	1,719	15,604
Henry	1,448	15,302
Houston	1,500	74,632
Jackson	2,782	51,407
Jefferson	2,909	671,324
Lamar	1,573	16,453
Lauderdale	1,719	80,546
Lawrence	1,802	30,170
Lee	1,583	76,283
Limestone	1,453	46,005
Lowndes	1,856	13,253
Macon	1,596	26,829
Madison	2,096	196,966
Marengo	2,553	25,047
Marion	1,932	30,041
Marshall	1,474	65,622
Mobile	3,219	364,980
Monroe	2,649	22,651
Montgomery	2,062	197,038
Morgan	1,495	90,231
Perry	1,869	15,012
Pickens	2,314	21,481
Pike	1,747	28,050
Randolph	1,518	20,075
Russell	1,648	47,356
Shelby	2,080	66,298
St Clair	1,680	41,205
Sumter	2,358	16,908
Talladega	1,958	73,826
Tallapoosa	1,823	38,676
Tuscaloosa	3,474	137,541
Walker	2,090	68,660
Washington	2,811	16,821
Wilcox	2,296	14,755
Winston	1,594	21,953

Alagoas *a-la-gō'as*, state in Nordeste region, NE Brazil; bordered E by the Atlantic, S by the Río São Francisco; its coastal plain rises to the W; pop(1980) 1,982,591; area 27,731 sq km; capital Maceió; economy: textiles, agriculture, cattle raising, fishing, offshore oil; to the W is part of the Paulo Alfonso National Park, containing the Paulo Alfonso Falls, once one of the great falls of the world; they are now used for hydroelectric power; little water passes over them now except in the rainy season.

Alagón *a-la-gōn'*, river in W Spain, rising to the E of the Sierra de Peña de Francia, Castilla-León, Spain, flowing generally SW to the R Tagus near Alcantara; length 201 km; tributaries Perales, Jerte, Hurdano, Angeles, Rivera Bronce, Arroyo Grande and Arrago rivers.

Alajuela *a-la-way'la*, prov of N Costa Rica, Central America; bounded N by Nicaragua; located largely in tropical lowlands drained by the Río Frío and the Río San Carlos; the Cordillera del Guanacaste and the Cordillera de Tilarán extend along the W boundary; the SE corner is occupied by the Cordillera Central; contains the volcanoes of Arenal (1,633 m), Viejo (2,060 m), and Poás (2,704 m); pop(1983e) 413,765; area 9,753 sq km; capital Alajuela; chief towns San Ramón, Grecia, and Quesada; traversed in the S by the Inter-American Highway.

Alajuela, 10 00N 84 12W, pop(1983e) 42,579, capital town of Alajuela prov, central Costa Rica, on the Inter-American Highway, 19 km NW of San José; centre of an important sugar-growing and cattle-raising district; it is now a mid-summer resort for the people of San José; alt 952 m; railway; economy: agricultural trade, fish processing.

Alameda *a-le-mee'da*, 37 46N 122 15W, pop(1980) 63,852, city and port in Alameda county, W California, United States; on an island in E San Francisco Bay, S of Oakland.

Al'amos, Los, 35 52N 106 19W, pop(1980) 11,039, community in Los Alamos county, N New Mexico; 56 km NW of Santa Fe in the Jemez Mts; a nuclear research centre since 1943; the first nuclear weapons were developed here during World War II.

Alamo'sa, 37 28N 105 54W, pop(1980) 6,830, county seat of Alamosa county, S Colorado, United States; settled in 1878; to the NE is the Great Sand Dunes National Monument.

Al-Anbār, governorate in W Iraq, bounded NW by Syria, SW by Jordan, and S by Saudi Arabia; pop(1977) 466,059; area 89,540 sq km; capital Ar Ramādī; chief towns Hīt and Al Hadīthah; drained by the R Euphrates (Al-Furāt) in the E; largely desert in the W.

Åland, island group in Finland. See Ahvenanmaa.

Alaska *a-las'kah*, state in United States; bounded N by the Beaufort Sea and Arctic Ocean, W by the Chukchi Sea, Bering Strait and Bering Sea, S by the Gulf of Alaska and the Pacific Ocean and E by Canada (Yukon territory and British Columbia); drained by the Yukon river which crosses the state E-W and its tributaries (the Porcupine, Tanana and Koyukuk rivers); also drained by the Colville, Kuskokwim, Susitna and Copper rivers; in the N of Alaska is the low North Slope which rises southwards to the Brooks Range, the northernmost part of the Rocky Mts; the Kuskokwim Mts rise in the SW; Alaska continues SW with the Aleutian Islands and the Aleutian mountain range; the Chugach Mts lie along the S coast of Alaska; the Wrangell Mts in the SE extend as far as the Yukon border to meet the St Elias Mts; Alaska rises to 6,194 m in Mt McKinley, situated in Denali National Park in S central Alaska; in the S are Lake Clark and Katmai national parks, in the SE is Wrangell-St Elias National Park; economy: oil and natural gas (on the North Slope), tourism, food processing, paper and lumber, seafood, dairy products; discovered by Russians, the first permanent settlement was made on Kodiak Island in 1792; Alaska was managed under the trade monopoly of the Russian-American Fur Company from 1799 to 1861; in 1824 negotiations with Britain and the USA set the Russian border at 54 40N; the Russians began to withdraw from the American coast and Alaska went into a period of decline; in 1867 the USA bought Alaska for $7,200,000; the purchase was negotiated by Secretary of State Seward and for many years afterwards the land was known as 'Seward's Folly'; gold was discovered in 1889 (at Nome) and in 1902 (at Fairbanks); the disputed boundary with British Columbia was settled in favour of the USA in 1903; the region was finally given a representative in Congress in 1906 and received territorial status in 1912; during World War II the Aleutian islands of Attu and Kiska were occupied by the Japanese from June 1942 to Aug 1943; the present constitution was adopted in 1956 and Alaska was granted statehood in 1959 (49th state); the discovery in 1968 of large oil reserves led to the building of a crude-oil pipeline from the North Slope S to Valdez (begun in 1975); pop(1980) 401,851; area 1,484,165 sq km; capital Juneau; major city: Anchorage; the state is divided into 23 boroughs:

Borough	*area (sq km)*	*pop(1980)*
Aleutian Islands	28,314	7,768
Anchorage	4,503	174,431
Bethel	93,870	10,999
Bristol Bay	1,381	1,094

contd

Borough	area (sq km)	pop(1980)
Dillingham	119,709	4,616
Fairbanks North Star	19,250	53,983
Haines	6,172	1,680
Juneau	6,828	19,528
Kenai Peninsula	41,746	25,282
Ketchikan Gateway	3,229	11,316
Kobuk	82,142	4,831
Kodiak Island	12,470	9,939
Matanuska-Susitna	63,705	17,816
Nome	62,065	6,537
North Slope	236,483	4,199
Prince of Wales-Outer Ketchikan	19,916	3,822
Sitka	7,639	7,803
Skagway-Yakutat-Angoon	34,421	3,478
Southeast Fairbanks	62,839	5,676
Valdez-Cordova	101,995	8,348
Wade Hampton	46,322	4,665
Wrangell-Petersburg	15,509	6,167
Yukon-Koyukuk	413,657	7,873

Alaska, Gulf of, N part of the Pacific Ocean, lying between the Alaskan Peninsula in the W and the mainland Alaskan Panhandle in the E; main arms are the Shelikof Strait, Cook Inlet, Prince William Sound, Yakutat Bay and Cross Sound; the warm Alaskan Current, entering from the SE, keeps the ports ice-free; Valdez is the most important port, being the terminus of the Trans-Alaskan Pipeline from North Slope.

Álava *a'la-va*, southern and largest of the three Basque provs in N Spain; bounded on the SW by the R Ebro; part of a plain that includes outlying ranges of the eastern Cordillera Cantabrica; pop(1981) 260,580; area 3,047 sq km; capital Vitoria; economy: mining, iron and steel products, table wines produced at Areta and Llodio.

Alavus *ah'la-voos*, 62 35N 23 35E, pop(1982) 10,601, town in Vaasa prov, W central Finland; situated midway between Vaasa and Jyväskylä; established in 1974.

Alayskiy Khrebet, one of the W ranges of the Tien Shan mountain system, SW Kirgizskaya SSR, S Soviet Union; extends c.320 km E from the R Sokh to the upper reaches of the R Karadar'ya on the Chinese frontier; rises to a max height of 5,880 m in the W; traversed by the Osh-Khorog highway; bounded S by the R Kyzylsu.

Alba *al'ba*, county in W Central Romania, situated to the N of the Transylvanian Alps and watered by the R Mureş; pop(1983) 419,807; area 6,231 sq km; capital Alba Iulia; a wine-producing region also noted for fruit and poultry.

Alba Iulia *al'ba yoo'lya*, APULUM (Lat), 46 04N 23 33E, pop(1983) 59,369, capital of Alba county, W central Romania; on the R Mureş; founded by the Romans in the 2nd century AD; former seat of the princes of Transylvania and from 1599-1601 the capital of the united principalities of Transylvania, Walachia and Moldavia; railway; economy: wine trade and manufacture of footwear, soap, furniture; monuments: 12th-c Romanesque church; Bathyaneum building.

Albacete *al-ba-thay'tay*, hilly prov in Castilla-La Mancha, SE central Spain; pop(1981) 334,468; area 14,862 sq km; capital Albacete; the Júcar and Segura rivers form a number of reservoirs that supply power and irrigation; economy: mining, livestock, rice, olive oil; footwear and clothing are widely produced in towns like Almansa, Caudete and Hellin.

Albacete, 39 00N 1 50W, pop(1981) 117,126, capital of Albacete prov, Castilla-La Mancha, SE Spain; 251 km SE of Madrid; bishopric; centre of the fertile La Mancha wine producing region; the surrounding swamps were drained in the 19th century when an irrigation canal was built; railway; formerly had an extensive trade in cutlery, and still famous for its souvenir knives (navajas) and daggers (puñales); economy: footwear, clothing, tools, wine, flour; monument: 16th-c cathedral; events: fairs and fiestas of Albacete with bullfights, folk music and sporting events in Sept.

Al-Bahra Al-Ah'mar, governorate in Egypt; pop(1976) 56,191; area 203,685 sq km; capital Al-Ghurdaqah.

Albania *al-bay'ni-a*, SHQIPNI, SHQIPRI or SHQIPËRI (Alb), official name People's Republic of Albania, REPUBLICA POPULLORE SOCIALISTE E SHQIPËRISË (Alb), a socialist republic in the W part of the Balkan Peninsula, bounded on the W by the Adriatic Sea, NE by Yugoslavia and SE by Greece; coastline 418 km in length; area 28,748 sq km; timezone GMT + 1; capital Tiranë; chief towns Shkodër, Durrës, Vlorë, Korçë and Elbasan; currency the lek (100 qintars); pop(1980) 2,671,700; Albanians form the majority of the population (96%), there are also Greeks (over 2%), Vlachs, Gypsies and Bulgarians; the language is Albanian, with two dialects, Gheg (N of R Shkumbin) and Tosk in the S; although Albania is constitutionally an atheist state, the population is mainly Muslim in

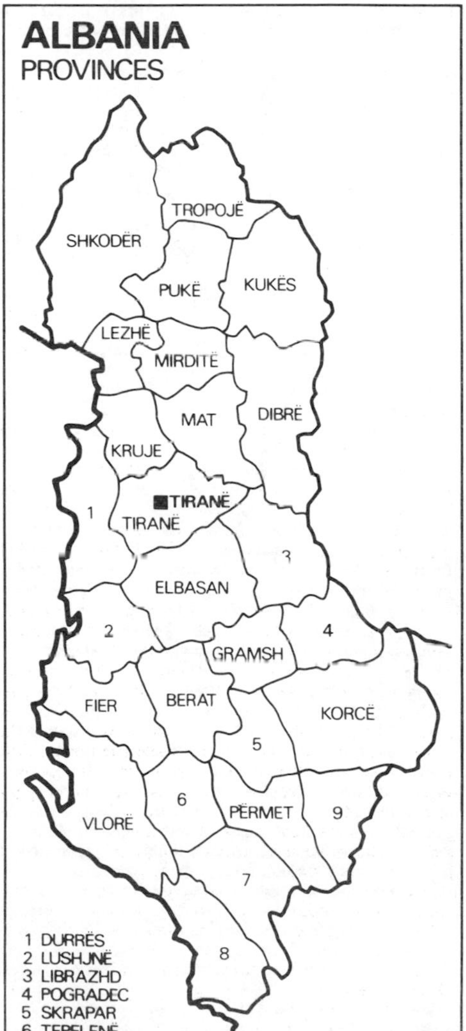

origin, with some Christians, Orthodox and Catholic; the rate of natural population increase is high (20.1 per 1,000); half of the population is concentrated in the W low-lying area, which occupies only one quarter of the country's territory; national holiday 29 Nov (Liberation Day); membership of CEMA, FAO, IAEA, IPU, ITU, UN, UNESCO, UPU, WFTU, WHO, WMO; Albania has not participated in CEMA since the 1961 dispute with the Soviet Union and withdrew from the Warsaw Pact in Sept 1968.
Physical description. Albania is a mountainous country, still one of the most inaccessible and untravelled in Europe; the North Albanian Alps in the N rise to 2,692 m; rivers include the Drin in the N, Shkumbin and Seman in the centre, and Vijosë in the S; the SE part of L Scutari lies on the N border; the large tectonic lakes of Ohrid and Prespa, in the SE, are partly in Albania; there are many lagoon-lakes in the lowlands and small karst and glacial lakes in the uplands.
Climate. The climate is Mediterranean-type; on the plains in the summer the weather is hot and dry (average July temperature 24°-25°C) and thunderstorms are frequent and severe; in the winter it is mild, damp and cyclonic (average January temperature 8°-9°C); winters in the mountains can be severe, with snow cover lasting several months; annual precipitation in the mountains exceeds 1,000 mm.
Government and constitution. The present political structure is derived from the Constitution of 14 March 1946 as amended in 1950, 1955, 1960 and 1963; in Dec 1976 a new Constitution was adopted by which Albania became a Socialist People's Republic; the supreme legislative body is the single-chamber People's Assembly of 250 deputies which meets twice a year; election to the People's Assembly is by universal suffrage (at 18 years) every 4 years; the People's Assembly adopts laws, confirms the state budgets and national economic plans, elects the Presidium of the People's Assembly and forms the government of Albania (the Council of Ministers); effective rule is exercised by the Albanian Labour Party (founded in Nov 1941) whose governing body is the Politburo.
Economy. The seventh 5-year plan, covering 1981-85, was particularly concerned with industrial expansion, especially in the oil, mining and chemical industries. It is now stated that economic policy is founded on the 'revolutionary principle of self-reliance'.
Industry and trade. All industry is nationalized down to the smallest workshops. Much of the country's manufacturing industry is concentrated in the cities of Tiranë, Durrës, Shkodër, Vlorë, Korçë and Elbasan. The principal industries are agricultural product processing, textiles, oil products and cement. There are 1981-85 trade agreements with Bulgaria, Czechoslovakia, North Korea, Poland, Vietnam and Yugoslavia; and Albania also trades with Italy, France and India. Exports include crude oil, bitumen, chrome, nickel, copper, tobacco, fruit and vegetables.
Energy. There are hydroelectric power plants on the Mat, Bistritsa, Drin, and other rivers. The Lenin Hydroelectric Power Plant was built near Tiranë with Soviet assistance. The oil industry is being rapidly expanded; it is produced chiefly at Qytet Stalin where a pipeline connects with the port of Vlorë. Natural gas is also extracted.
Agriculture and forestry. In 1970 there were 5,990 sq km of arable land, the main crops being wheat, sugar-beet, maize, potatoes, fruit, grapes and oats. As much as 56% of cultivated land is now irrigated. Albania is committed to eliminating all private farming through the progressive transformation of farm co-operatives into state farms. Forty seven per cent of the territory of Albania is forest land.
Communications. The Albanian portion of the new rail link from Shkodër to Titograd in Yugoslavia was completed in early 1985. Total length of railways in 1983 was 253 km. A ferry service from Trieste to Durrës opened in Nov 1983. There are regular scheduled flights from Tiranë (Rinas Airport) to Beograd (Belgrade), Bucureşti (Bucharest), Budapest and East Berlin.
Administrative divisions. The country is divided into 26 provinces (*rrethet*):

Province	*area (sq km)*	*pop(1980)*
Berat	1,026	147,200
Dibrë	1,569	128,300
Durrës	859	209,500
Elbasan	1,466	197,600
Fier	1,191	203,400
Gjirokastër	1,137	58,500
Gramsh	695	36,300
Kolonjë	805	21,600
Korçë	2,181	193,000
Krujë	607	88,200
Kukës	1,564	81,900
Lezhë	479	50,500
Librazhd	1,013	59,300
Lushnjë	712	110,900
Mat	1,028	64,300
Mirditë	698	42,400
Përmet	930	35,200
Pogradec	725	59,000
Pukë	969	42,400
Sarandë	1,097	74,400
Shkodër	2,528	198,600
Skrapar	775	39,800
Tepelenë	817	43,300
Tiranë	1,222	297,700
Tropojë	1,043	38,800
Vlorë	1,609	149,600

Albany *ol'ba-ni*, 34 57S 117 54E, pop(1981) 15,222, resort and seaport in Lower Great Southern stat div, Western Australia, on the S coast of Australia, SE of Perth; founded in 1826, Albany is one of the oldest towns in Australia; it was used as a stopover point for vessels on their way to India; in 1985 the entrance to the Princess Royal Harbour was renamed the Atatürk Entrance in remembrance of the Anzac troops who left from here for Gallipoli in 1915; railway; airfield.

Albany, 31 35N 84 10W, pop(1980) 74,059, county seat of Dougherty county, SW Georgia, United States; on the R Flint, 124 km SE of Columbus; railway; economy: peanut and pecan processing; aircraft assembly; manufactures fertilizers, pharmaceuticals, and wood and cotton products.

Albany, 42 39N 73 45W, pop(1980) 101,727, capital of state in Albany county, E New York, United States; on the R Hudson, 232 km N of New York City; the 2nd oldest continuously inhabited settlement in the 13 original colonies, being settled by the Dutch in 1614; surrendered to the English in 1664; capital of state since 1797; 2 universities (1844, 1848); railway; monuments: State Capitol, Schuyler Mansion (British General Burgoyne was a prisoner-guest here after the Battle of Saratoga in 1777); event: annual Tulip Festival.

Albany, 44 38N 123 06W, pop(1980) 26,546, city in Linn county, W Oregon, United States; on the Willamette river, 32 km S of Salem; founded in 1848; railway.

Albarracin, Sierra de, *al-va-ra-theen'*, mountain range in Aragón and Castilla-La Mancha regions of E central Spain, rising to 1,855 m; the old walled town of Albarracin at 1,182 m is a national monument and centre of timber production; S of the town are the caves of El Callejon de Plou and Cueva del Navazo with prehistoric paintings of hunting scenes.

Albe'na, 43 20N 28 05E, resort town in Varna okrug (prov), E Bulgaria; situated in a bay of the Black Sea, 30 km N of Varna; 7 km of sandy beaches.

Albert, Lake, LAKE MOBUTO SESE SEKO (Zaire), lake in E central Africa; situated in the W Rift Valley on the frontier between Zaire and Uganda, Lake Albert is the northernmost of the central African lakes; approx 160 km long and 40 km wide; alt 619 m; receives the Victoria Nile (NE) and Semliki (SW) rivers; the Albert Nile flows

N from it; European discovery by Samuel Baker (1864); named after Queen Victoria's consort; forts were established between 1885 and 1890 by both Stanley and Emin Pasha; the main lakeside settlements are Kesenye and Mahagi-Port (Zaire) and Butiabi (Uganda).

Albert Nile, upper reach of the R Nile in NW Uganda, E Africa; issues from the NE corner of L Albert, close to the Victoria Nile Delta; flows NE past Pakwach, Obongi and Loropi before crossing into Sudan at Nimule; once in Sudan the river is known as the Bahr el Jebel until its meeting point with the Bahr el Ghazal to form the White Nile.

Alberta *al-ber'ta*, province in W Canada; bordered W by British Columbia, S by the United States, E by Saskatchewan and N by Northwest Territories (Mackenzie district); the majority of the prov is a rolling plain except for the fringe of the Rocky Mts in the W and for the NE corner of Alberta, which lies in the Canadian Shield; the N half of the prov has great rivers, lakes and forests with large areas of open prairie; the S consists largely of rolling treeless prairie with irrigated land in the far S and E; drained by the Peace, Slave and Athabasca rivers in the N and the North Saskatchewan, Red Deer and Bow in the S; the largest of Alberta's lakes are L Athabasca, L Claire and Lesser Slave Lake; the Rocky Mts in SW Alberta contain Jasper, Banff and Kootenay national parks; in the far S of the prov is Waterton Lakes National Park, while in the N, extending into Mackenzie dist of Northwest Territories, is Wood Buffalo National Park; pop(1981) 2,237,724; area 638,233 sq km; the prov is divided into 15 census divisions; capital Edmonton; major towns: Calgary and Medicine Hat; economy: oil, natural gas, grain, cattle, timber products, coal, food processing, chemicals, fabricated metals; Alberta was originally part of Rupert's Land, the territory granted to the Hudson's Bay Company in 1670; sovereignty was acquired by the Dominion in 1870; law and order was effectively established in 1874 by the North West Mounted Police from Winnipeg who made their base at Fort Macleod, approx 160 km S of Calgary; Alberta became a prov on 1 Sept 1905; the prov is governed by a Lieutenant-Governor and an elected 79-member Legislative Assembly.

Alberto M. de Agostini *al-ber'tō em'ay dhay a-gos-tee'nee*, national park in Magallanes region, S Chile; area 7,900 sq km; established in 1965; the park includes part of Tierra del Fuego and some small islands to the S.

Alberton, 26 16S 28 08E, pop(1980) 230,667, city in Transvaal prov, South Africa; a SE suburb of Johannesburg; railway.

Albi *al-bee*, 43 56N 2 09E, pop(1982) 48,341, artistic centre and capital of Tarn dept, Midi-Pyrénées region, S France, on a height near the R Tarn in the foothills of the Massif Central 80 km NE of Toulouse; scene of the suppression of the 13th-c Albigensian heretics or Cathares, who believed that the earth was created by the devil and that salvation could only be achieved by concentrating on the heavenly life to come; birthplace of the artist Toulouse-Lautrec (1864-1901); archbishopric; railway; economy: textiles, steel, aniseed, wine; monuments: brick-built Gothic St Cécile cathedral and Palais de la Berbie, formerly the archbishop's palace with a collection of paintings by Toulouse-Lautrec and other French artists; noted for its foie gras truffe; events: theatre festival (July), musical festival (Aug), international amateur film festival (Aug) and son et lumière recalling the Albigensian crusade (during the summer months).

Ålborg-Nørresundby *ol'bor nu'ru-sonn'boo*, AALBORG, 57 02N 9 54E, pop(1983) 154,755, commercial town and capital of Nordjylland county, N Jylland (Jutland), Denmark; situated on both sides of the Limfjorden (Lim Fjord); university (1973); a road and railway bridge and the Limfjorden Tunnel, opened in 1969, lead to Nørresundby on the N side of the fjord; economy: foodstuffs, engineering, shipbuilding, cement manufacturing; monuments: Ålborghus Castle (1539).

Albufeira *al-boo-fay'ra*, 37 05N 8 15W, pop(1981) 14,196, fishing village and resort, Faro dist, S Portugal; 43 km W of Faro, in a bay on the S coast in the centre of a fig and almond growing area, the picturesque Moorish-style Albufeira is Portugal's busiest seaside resort with beaches, golf and watersports.

Albula Alpen *al'boo-la*, ALBULA ALPS (Eng), mountain group in the Rhaetian Alps, Graubünden canton, SE Switzerland, N of St Moritz; crossed by Albula Pass which leads from Upper Engadine to Albula valley; length 25 km; height 2,312 m; railroad passes through Albula Tunnel, just S of the Pass; R Albula rises in the Rhaetian Alps, 8 km N of St Moritz, flows NW to the Hinterrhein N of Thusis; length 36 km.

Albuquerque *al-be-kir'ki*, 35 05N 106 39W, pop(1980) 331,767, county seat of Bernalillo county, central New Mexico, United States; largest city in the state, situated on the Rio Grande; settled in 1706; later a military post during the Mexican War of 1846-70; a city since 1890; 2 universities (1889, 1940); railway; airport; economy: agricultural trade, timber, electronics, processed foods, railway engineering; nearby is the Atomic Energy Commission installation; monuments: church of San Felipe de Neri (1706), the Old Town Plaza, National Atomic Museum; events: Feria Artesana (Aug), International Balloon Fiesta (Oct).

Albury-Wodon'ga, 36 03S 146 53E, pop(1981) 53,214, urban centre in Murray stat div, SE New South Wales, Australia; an amalgamation of 2 towns, on the border between Victoria and New South Wales; the pop includes 18,142 residents in that part of Wodonga situated in Victoria; water sports at L Hume; economy: trade in wool, grain, fruit and wine.

Alcalá de Guadaira *al-ka-la' dhay gwa-dhee'ra*, 37 20N 5 50W, pop(1981) 45,352, city in Sevilla prov, Andalucia, SW Spain; 12 km SE of Sevilla; railway; economy: metal products, foodstuffs, flour, olive oil.

Alcalá de Henares *al-ka-la' dhay ayn-a'rays*, COMPLUTIM (anc), ALKAL'A (Arab), 40 28N 3 22W, pop(1981) 142,862, town in Madrid prov, central Spain, on the left bank of the R Henares, 25 km ENE of Madrid; birthplace of Cervantes (1547), the architect Bustamente and Catherine of Aragón; it had a famous university, founded in 1498 but moved to Madrid in 1836; the first polyglot Bible was published here in 1517; the town was rebuilt after the Civil War; economy: plastics, chemicals, electrical appliances and pharmaceuticals; monuments: 16th-c College of San Ildefonso (former univ), its chapel with a monument to Cardinal Cisnero, founder of the university; church of St Mary where Cervantes was baptized in 1547.

Alcalde Díaz *al-kal'day dee'as*, pop(1980) 10,298, town in Panamá prov, Panama, Central America.

Alcazar de San Juan *al-ka'thar dhay san hwan*, 39 24N 3 12W, pop(1981) 25,185, town in Ciudad Real prov, Castilla-La Mancha, S central Spain; 90 km NE of Ciudad Real; railway; the surrounding La Mancha plain is associated with the novel *Don Quixote*; economy: woollens, wine, olives.

Alcira *al-thee'ra*, SUERO or SAETABICULA (anc), 39 09N 0 30W, pop(1981) 37,446, city in Valencia prov, E Spain; on R Júcar, 35 km S of Valencia; economy: rice, oranges, textiles, cattle.

Alcobendas *al-koo-ben'das*, 40 32N 3 38W, pop(1981) 63,507, town in Madrid prov, central Spain; 17 km NE of Madrid; economy: cosmetics, thermal and acoustic insulators.

Alcoy', 38 43N 0 30W, pop(1981) 65,908, industrial town in Alicante prov, Valencia, E Spain; at the foot of the Sierra de Montcabrer and the confluence of the Serpis, Molinar and Barchell rivers; railway; to the S is the Carrasqueta Pass (1,024 m); economy: paper, textiles, agric machinery and olives; monuments: the churches of St Mary (1767) and Santo Sepulcro; event: Moors and Christians Fiesta in April with mock battles, fireworks and bellringing to commemorate the fighting between Moors and Christians.

Alda'bra, 9 25S 46 20E, coral atoll nature reserve in SW Indian Ocean, NW of Madagascar; 1,200 km SW of the island of Mahé; an outlying dependency of the Seychelles; area 154 sq km; the group also includes the smaller atolls of Assomption, Astove and Cosmoledo Is; occupied by scientific staff; habitat of the giant land tortoise; nature reserve established in 1976.

Aldan *awl-dan'*, river in S Yakutskaya ASSR, Rossiyskaya, E Soviet Union; rising in the W Stanovoy Khrebet range, close to the border with Amurskaya oblast; flows N then E past Tommot (head of navigation) and Chagda, continues N and NW to join the R Lena 160 km N of Yakutsk; length 2,240 km; drainage basin area 702,000 sq km; navigable for 1,610 km; coal deposits in the S Yakutian basin in the upper Aldan river provide fuel for the power station at Chul'man; chief tributaries include the Uchur, Maya, and Amga rivers.

Alderney *awl'dur-nee*, AURIGNY (Fr), RIDUNA (anc), one of the Channel Is, off the coast of French Normandie, W of Cherbourg; situated NE of Guernsey and separated from the Cotentin peninsula by the Race of Alderney; in the Bailiwick of Guernsey; the island has its own legislative assembly; pop(1981e) 2,086; area 8 sq km; chief town Saint Anne.

Aldershot *awl'der-shot*, 51 15N 0 47W, pop(1981) 54,358, town in Rushmoor dist, Hampshire, S England; 13 km W of Guildford; military depot; railway; economy: engineering, electrical goods.

Ald'ridge, 52 36N 1 55W, pop(1981) 17,589, town in Walsall borough, West Midlands, central England; 5 km NE of Walsall; economy: engineering, plastics.

Aleg', 17 02N 13 58W, capital of Brakna region, W Mauritania, NW Africa; SE of Nouakchott; the Lac d'Aleg lies to the NW.

Aleksinac *a-lek'see-nats*, 43 31N 21 42E, pop(1981) 67,286, town in E central Srbija (Serbia) republic, Yugoslavia; on R Morava; railway; economy: coal mining, fruit, vegetables, tobacco.

Alençon *a-lâ-sô*, 48 27N 0 04E, pop(1982) 32,526, capital of Orne dept, Basse-Normandie region, NE France; at the junction of the rivers Sarthe and Briante in an agric region; railway; associated with lace-making; monuments: Notre Dame cathedral (1444) and exhibition at the Pont Neuf School of Lace.

Alentejo, Portugal. See Alto Alentejo and Baixo Alentejo.

Aleppo, city in NW Syria. See Ḥalab.

Alerces, Los *a-ler'says*, Andean national park in W Chubut prov, Patagonia, Argentina; area 1,875 sq km; established in 1937; SW of the Cordillera Esquel; borders W with Chile; contains several small lakes.

Alessandria *ah-les-sahn'dree-ah*, prov of Piemonte region, NW Italy; pop(1981) 466,102; area 3,561 sq km; capital Alessandria.

Alessandria, 44 55N 8 37E, pop(1981) 100,523, capital town of Alessandria prov, Piemonte region, NW Italy; on R Tanaro, NW of Genova; railway; economy: wine, engineering.

Ålesund *awl'e-soond*, AALESUND, 62 28N 6 11E, pop(1983) 34,895, seaport city in Møre og Romsdal county, W Norway; N of Bergen, on several islands off the W coast; a great fire in 1904 destroyed almost all of the town's old timber houses which were later rebuilt in stone; an important centre for Arctic fishing grounds; economy: fish processing, shipyards, clothing.

A'letsch, glacier in Valais and Bern cantons, S central Switzerland, W and S of the Aletschhorn; composed of the Great Aletsch Glacier, Upper Aletsch Glacier and Middle Aletsch Glacier; area 117.6 sq km; length 23.6 km; the largest glacier in Europe.

A'letschhorn, 46 28N 8 00E, mountain in the Berner Alpen (Bernese Alps), Valais canton, Switzerland, 8 km SSE of the Jungfrau; height 4,195 m.

Alexandria *al-ig-zan'dree-a*, EL ISKANDARÎYA *is-kan-de-ree'e*, 31 13N 29 55E, pop(1976) 2,317,700, seaport capital of Alexandria governorate, N Egypt; on the Mediterranean coast, 180 km NW of Cairo; 2nd largest city of Egypt and the country's main port; founded in 332 BC by Alexander the Great; capital of the Ptolemies between 304 and 30 BC when it was the largest known city; a former centre of Hellenistic and Jewish culture; noted for its famous royal libraries; Aristarchus and Euclid studied at its ancient university; occupied by Julius Caesar (47 BC); after the death of Antony and Cleopatra, Octavian (subsequently Augustus) entered the city (30 BC) claiming it as part of the Roman Empire; at that time its 'free' pop was in the order of 300,000 people plus a larger number of slaves; captured in 642 AD by the Arabs who moved the capital to Cairo; Alexandria was an insignificant town when taken by Napoleon in 1798 and retaken by the British 3 years later; its importance was re-established in 1819 when Mohammed Ali ordered the construction of a canal from the R Nile to the city; the canal carried trade but was also a source of irrigation water for surrounding land; university (1942); railway; airport (at 8 km); economy: car assembly, oil refining, natural gas processing, food processing, trade in cotton, vegetables and grain; monuments: Catacombs of Kom El Shugafa dating from the 1st and 2nd centuries AD consist of three tiers of burial shafts; Graeco-Roman museum with exhibits dating from the 3rd century BC; Pompey's Pillar, raised in 297 AD in memory of Emperor Diocletian; Serapium temple ruins; the mosque of Abu'l Abbas; Al Montaza, summer residence of the ex-king Farouk.

Alexandria, 40 38N 22 28E, pop(1981) 10,543, town in Imathía nome (dept), Makedhonia region, Greece.

Alexandria, 43 59N 25 19E, pop(1983) 47,730, capital of Teleorman county, S Romania; N of the R Danube; railway; economy: wood products, light engineering, grain.

Alexandria, 55 59N 4 36W, pop(1981) 26,329, town in Dumbarton dist, Strathclyde, W central Scotland; on the R Leven, 5 km N of Dumbarton; railway; economy: photographic equipment, distilling.

Alexandria, 31 18N 92 27W, pop(1980) 51,565, resort and parish seat of Rapides parish, central Louisiana, United States; on the Red river, 155 km NW of Baton Rouge; the city was burned to the ground by Federal troops during the Civil War in 1864; university; railway; airfield; economy: agricultural trade, valves, lumber, paper, soaps and cleansers; monument: Plantation Homes.

Alexandria, 38 48N 77 03W, pop(1980) 103,217, port and residential city, NE Virginia, United States; on the R Potomac, 10 km S of Washington, DC; railway; airport (Washington National); monument: Mount Vernon; home of George Washington, 1st president of the United States.

Alexandroúpolis *ah-lek-sahn-droo'pol-ees*, DEDÉAGACH *da'-da-ah-ahch* (Turk), ALEXANDROPLE (Eng), 40 51N 25 53E, pop(1981) 34,535, capital town of Évros nome (dept), Thraki region, Greece; near the frontier with Turkey, on R Évros; airfield; railway; local ferries; economy: centre for local tobacco trade; event: Navy Week (June-July).

Alfiós *ahl-fee-os'*, ALPHEEUS *al-fee'us* (Eng), river in W Pelopónnisos region, S Greece; rises in the Taïyetos Mts, flows NW through Arkadhía and Ilia nomoi (depts) to discharge into the Ionian Sea near Pírgos; Olympia is on its N bank; length 110 km.

Alföld *awl'fuld*, Great Plain region of S Hungary and extending into N Yugoslavia and W Romania; lying E of the R Danube between the N central mountains of Hungary and the S foothills of the Carpathian Mts; this flat, monotonous geographical region covers about half of Hungary and is crossed by a system of canals that water a fertile region that produces large quantities of grain and fruit; livestock graze the arid grasslands which are known as *pusztas*; national parks at Hortobágy, Bükk and Kiskunság.

Alfreton *awl'fre-ton*, 53 06N 1 23W, pop(1981) 21,338, town in Amber Valley dist, Derbyshire, central England; 15 km S of Chesterfield; railway; economy: textiles.

Algarve *al-gar'vay* (Arab 'al gharb', the west), a region and prov of S Portugal co-extensive with Faro dist; bounded to W and S by the Atlantic, to the N by the Alentejo region and to the E by the R Guadiana which follows the Spanish frontier; the Algarve is separated from the rest of Portugal by hills extending to the SW point of the country at Cabo de São Vincente; capital Faro; main resort area of Portugal; area 5,072 sq km.

Algeciras *al-heth-ee'ras, al-je-see'ras* (Eng), 36 09N 5 28W, pop(1981) 86,042, seaport and resort in Cádiz prov, Andalucia, SW Spain; at the southern tip of the Iberian peninsula on the W side of the Algeciras bay, opposite Gibraltar; car ferries to Canary Is, Melilla, Tangier and Gibraltar; railway; watersports; beaches at El Rinconcillo and La Línea; economy: exports including oranges and cork and the manufacture of paper; monument: remains of Old Algeciras founded by the Moors in 713 under the name of 'Al-Gezira al-Khadra' (green island); events: fair and fiestas with bullfights in June; patronal fiestas in Aug with underwater fishing competitions and bullfights; Festival of Spain in Aug with a regatta.

Alger *al-zhay'*, ALGIERS *al-jeerz'*, 36 50N 3 00E, pop(1984) 2,442,303, seaport capital of Algeria, N Africa; in Sidi M'Hamed daira, Alger dept, N Algeria, N Africa; 805 km SSW of Marseilles (France); founded by the Berbers on the site of Roman Icosium during the 10th century; Turkish rule was established in 1518 by Barbarossa and the city was later used as a base for Barbary pirates; the French took Alger in 1830; during World War II the city became Allied headquarters and seat of De Gaulle's provisional government; University of Algeria (1879); university of sciences and technology (1974); railway; airport; economy: trade, commerce and administration, wine; monuments: Sidi Abderrahman mosque, dedicated to the town's protector who died in 1471; Sidi Mohammed Sherif mosque with unusual octagonal minaret; Djama Djehid mosque (16th-c); cathedral; national library; the Bardo museum housed in an 18th-c Moorish villa; museum of antiquities, founded by Stephane Gsell, with mosaics, religious treasures and Roman precious metal workings; national museum of fine arts houses important examples of African paintings and sculptures.

Algeria *al-jee'ri-a*, L'ALGÉRIE (Fr), official name The Democratic and Popular Republic of Algeria, AL-JUMHURIYA AL-JAZAIRIYA (Arab), a N African republic bounded W by Morocco, SW by Western Sahara, Mauritania and Mali, SE by Mali, E by Libya, NE by Tunisia and N by the Mediterranean Sea; area 2,460,500 sq km; timezone GMT +1; capital Alger (Algiers); chief towns include Constantine, Oran, Skikda, 'Annaba, Mostaganem, Blida and Tlemcen; pop(1984e) 21,351,000; 99% of the pop are of Arab-Berber origin with less than 1% of European origin; 99% of the pop is Sunni Muslim; the unit of currency is the dinar; national holidays 5 July (Independence Day), 1 Nov (Revolution Day), 19 June (Overthrow of Ben Bella) and numerous Islamic festivals; membership of AfDB, AIOEC, Arab League, ASSIMER, FAO, G-77, GATT (de facto), IAEA, IBRD, ICAO, IDA, Islamic Development Bank, IFAD, ILO, ILZSG, IMF, IMO, INTELSAT, INTERPOL, IOOC, ITU, NAM, OAPEC, OAU, OIC, OPEC, UN, UNESCO, UPU, WHO, WIPO, WMO.

Physical description. From the Mediterranean coast, mountains rise in a series of ridges and plateaux to the Atlas Saharien, part of the Atlas Mts which extend NE from Morocco. The majority (91%) of the population is located on the narrow coastal plain where mountain valleys drop down to meet the sea. To the S of the Atlas Saharien is the vast Algerian sector of the Sahara desert, a dry sandstone plain dissected by valleys. In the NE of this region is a major depression, the Chott Melrhir, which extends E into Tunisia. In the far south the Ahaggar (Hoggar) Mts rise to 2,918 m at Mt Tahat.

Climate. The northern coastal region which accounts for about one-sixth of the country's total area experiences a typical Mediterranean climate. Rainfall which is higher along the coast ranges between an annual average of 400 and 800 mm mostly falling in Nov-March. Above about 900 m rain turns to snow and can lie for a number of weeks. Alger (Algiers), situated on the coast, is representative of this region with an annual rainfall of 760 mm and average max daily temperatures ranging between 15°C and 29°C. The remaining five-sixths of the country experiences an essentially rainless Saharan climate. In Salah is representative of this region with an average annual rainfall of less than 20 mm and average max daily temperatures ranging between 21°C and 45°C.

History, government and constitution. The indigenous peoples of N Africa, known to the Romans as 'Berbers', have been driven back from the coast by a succession of invaders including Phoenicians, Romans, Vandals, Arabs, Turks and French. It was the Arabs who had the most significant impact between the 8th and 11th centuries with the introduction of both Islam and the Arabic language. The French began a colonial campaign in 1830 eventually establishing control over the whole of Algeria by 1902. A revolutionary independence movement, the National Liberation Front (FLN), engaged in a guerrilla war with French forces from 1954 until the signing of the Evian Accord in March 1962. After a ceasefire, elections were held and Algeria gained full independence from France. A new constitution was adopted in 1963. The first president of independent Algeria, Ahmed Ben Bella, was subsequently replaced after a bloodless coup in 1965 which led to the dissolution of the National Assembly and the suspension of the constitution. The country was governed by decree until 1976 when an election was followed by the adoption of a new constitution. A legislative National People's Assembly with 261 members is elected every 5 years. An executive president, also elected for a 5-year term, appoints a cabinet of about 26 ministers. State security is in the hands of a High Security Council. The socialist FLN is the only political party.

Economy. Following independence in 1962 the Algerian government nationalized all major foreign business interests, many private Algerian companies and about one-third of arable land. Although employing 35% of the workforce agriculture accounts for less than 10% of national income. Crops grown principally along the N coast include wheat, barley, oats, grapes, citrus fruits and vegetables. Algeria is far from self-sufficient in terms of food production and still requires to import approx one-third of its needs. Industrial activities include food processing, textiles and clothing. Petroleum products account for about 30% of national income. Algerian crude oil extraction represented less than 5% of OPEC countries' total production for 1984, but natural gas reserves are estimated to be the 4th largest in the world after the USSR, Iran and the USA. Algeria's development in the 1980s is centred on the production of natural gas and gas derivatives. Pioneer in the development of liquid natural gas, Algeria in association with Italy has constructed the first trans-Mediterranean gas pipeline. Main trading partners include France, West Germany, Japan, the US and Italy.

Administrative divisions. Algeria is divided into 31 departments (*wilaya*) which are sub-divided into *daira*:

Department	*area (sq km)*	*pop(1982)*
Adrar	422,498	151,309
Al Asnam	8,676	973,469
Alger	785	2,165,691
'Annaba	3,489	604,898
Batna	14,881	646,330
Béchar	306,000	174,568
Bejaïa	3,442	624,452
Biskra	109,729	615,015
El Blida	3,703	1,041,487
Bouira	4,517	421,225
Constantine	3,561	757,687
El Djelfa	22,903	389,440
Guelma	8,624	616,229
Jijel	3,704	572,644
Laghouat	112,052	371,863

contd

Department	*area (sq km)*	*pop(1982)*
Lamdjya	6,704	535,414
Mascara	5,845	502,022
Mostaganem	7,023	848,900
M'Sila	19,824	500,364
Oran	1,820	833,507
Ouargla	559,234	237,527
Oum-el-Bouaghi	8,123	441,114
Saida	106,777	436,031
Sétif	10,350	1,088,663
Sidi bel Abbès	11,648	591,787
Skikda	4,748	562,340
Tamanrasset	556,000	63,592
Tébessa	16,574	423,202
Tiaret	23,455	695,665
Tizi-Ouzou	2,756	959,640
Tlemcen	9,283	648,327

Alham'bra, 34 08N 118 06W, pop(1980) 64,615, city in Los Angeles county, SW California, United States; a residential area, c.8 km ENE of Los Angeles; founded in 1881; railway.

Aliákmon *ah-lee-ahk'mon*, HALIACMON *hay-lee-ak'mun* (anc), river in W Makedhonia region, N Greece; rises near the Albanian border, 40 km WSW of Kastoría; flows SE past Nestórion and Neápolis, then turns NE to discharge into the Thermaïkós Kólpos (Gulf of Salonika) between Kateríni and Thessaloníki; length 297 km; the longest river in Greece.

Alicante *al-ee-kan'tay*, prov in Valencia region, E Spain; bounded E by the Mediterranean, N by Valencia and W by Albacete and Murcia; although mountainous in the N fertile valleys give way to a coastal plain which widens in the S; rocky coastline to the N and salt lagoons to the S; pop(1981) 1,148,597; area, 5,863 sq km; capital Alicante; economy: metal products, timber, fishing; footwear in towns like Elche, Elda, Monovar and Petrel, carpets in Crevillente; citrus fruit and olives around Alicante, Elche, Alcoy and Orihuela.

Alicante, LUCENTUM (Lat), 38 23N 0 30W, pop(1981) 251,387, seaport and capital of Alicante prov, SE Spain; 422 km SE of Madrid; airport; railway; car ferries to Marseilles, Oran, Ibiza and Palma de Mallorca; its climate makes it a popular winter resort; economy: metal products, textiles, paper, tobacco, fertilizer, exports fruit and wine; monuments: the palm-lined Alicante promenade with its marble pavement; castle of St Barbara originally built by the Carthaginians; church of St Mary, a former mosque rebuilt in the 14th century; event: bonfires in June in honour of St John with parades, fireworks, riding contests and the burning of figures made of wood and cardboard.

Alice Springs, 23 42S 133 52E, pop(1981) 18,395, urban centre in Northern Territory, central Australia; railway terminus; airfield; administrative and supply centre for the settlements and cattle stations of the Outback; monuments: aviation museum; 11 km from Alice Springs is the Château Hornsby Winery, central Australia's first winery; 100 km W of Alice Springs, on the way to Ayers Rock, is a camel farm; 119 km to the W is Hermannsburg Mission, established by Lutheran missionaries in 1877, and now home to approx 400 Aborigines; 111 km E of Alice Springs in the East MacDonnell ranges is the Arltunga goldfield reserve with ruins dating from central Australia's gold-mining era; events: Camel Cup camel races in May; Bangtail Muster with rodeos, parades and cattle round ups (May); Alice Springs Show Day (5 July); Henley-on-Todd Regatta, with mock yacht races on the dry bed of the Todd river (Aug).

Aligarh *a-lee-gur'*, KOIL, 27 54N 78 04E, pop(1981) 320,000, city in Uttar Pradesh, N central India; E of the R Yamuna, N of Agra; formerly an important stronghold of the Jats, Afghans and Mahattras; university (1921) replaced the former Anglo-Oriental College founded in 1875; linked by rail to Delhi and Moradabad; monument: fort (1524).

Alimniá *ahl-eem-nee-ah'*, island of the Sporádhes, Greece, in the SE Aegean Sea, W of Ródhos (Rhodes); area 7 sq km.

Alk'maar, 52 38N 4 44E, pop(1984e) 83,892, city and municipality in Noord Holland prov, W Netherlands; on the Noord Holland Canal, 8 km from the North Sea coast and 32 km NNW of Amsterdam, surrounded by a ring of tree-shaded canals; founded in the 10th century and received its charter in 1254; railway; economy: engineering, paper, textiles, foodstuffs (canneries and chocolates), organ building; monuments: town hall (16-17th-c); church of St Laurens (15th-c); many architectural monuments and old beautiful guild and burgher houses of the 16th and 18th centuries; event: cheese market every Friday morning (end of April until mid-Sept).

Allahabad *ah'lu-hu-bahd* ('city of God'), 25 25N 81 58E, pop(1981) 642,000, city in Uttar Pradesh, NE India; on the N bank of the R Yamuna, N of its junction with the Ganga (Ganges) river, 560 km SE of New Delhi; built on the site of Prayag, an ancient Indo-Aryan city; the mythical Saraswati R meets the Yamuna and the Ganga rivers at sacred Sangam where a large Hindu religious festival (Kumbh Mela) is held every 12 years; centre of Hindi literature; founded by Akbar in 1583; Treaty of Allahabad (1765) granted the administration of Bengal, Bihar and Orissa to the East India Company; ceded to the British in 1801; airfield; rail link to Kanpur; economy: cotton, sugar; monuments: Great Mosque; Sultan Khossor's caravanserai; fort containing the carved Asoka pillar (240 BC).

Allegheny Mountains *al'e-gen-ee, -gay'nee*, ALLEGHENIES, mountain range in the E USA; W part of the Appalachian Mts; extends over 805 km from N Pennsylvania, SSW through W Maryland, E West Virginia and SW Virginia; forms the watershed between the Atlantic and the Mississippi river; the mountains include several fairly parallel ridges, which run NE to SW (including Laurel Hill, Negro Mt and Shavers Mts); the range contains the highest point in Pennsylvania (Mt Davis, 979 m) and in West Virginia is Spruce Knob, 1,481 m, highest peak in the Alleghenies; the mountains are rich in timber, coal, iron and limestone.

Allen Park, 42 16N 83 13W, pop(1980) 34,196, town in Wayne county, SE Michigan, United States; 16 km SW of Detroit.

Allentown, 40 37N 75 29W, pop(1980) 103,758, county seat of Lehigh county, E Pennsylvania, United States; on the R Lehigh, 77 km N of Philadelphia; railway.

Allep'pey, 9 30N 76 22E, pop(1981) 373,512, port in Kerala, S India; on an inlet on the Malabar coast, S of Cochin; known as the 'Venice of India'; terminus of inland waterways from N and S; economy: trade in coffee and pepper; event: Onam snake boat races (Aug-Sept).

Allgäuer Alpen *ahl'goy-*, ALLGÄU ALPS (Eng), mountain range between Bayern (Bavaria) prov, W Germany, and Tirol, Austria; extending E from the Bodensee (L Constance) along the Austro-German border to the Lech river valley, forming W division of Bavarian pre-Alps; highest peak is the Madelegabel (2,645 m); Lech and Iller rivers rise here; noted for its intensive cattle-rearing (the Allgäu breed being famous) and its highly developed dairying industry; also many spas and medicinal springs locally.

Allier *al-yay*, dept in Auvergne region of central France, comprising 3 arrond, 34 cantons and 320 communes; in the upper basins of the Loire, Allier and Cher rivers where they cut the Massif Central; low spurs of the Mts d'Auvergne run in from the S, wooded and vine-clad; pop(1982) 369,580; area 7,340 sq km; capital Moulins; main industrial centre at Montluçon on the R Cher (chemicals, rubber and foundries); rich in minerals which include coal, iron, antimony and kaolin; spas at Vichy,

Neris-les-Bains, Châteauneuf-les-Bains and Bourbon-l'Archambault; Beauvoir (at Échassières) and La Palice (at Lapalisse) are châteaux worth visiting; near St Gervais are the 68 m-high hydro-electric Barrage de Besserve and the Viaduc des Fades, which is claimed to be the highest railway viaduct in Europe.

Allier, river in central France rising in the Cévennes; flows NNW to the R Loire below Nevers; navigable to Issoire; length 410 km; famous gorges S of Brioude; tributaries Alagnon, Sioule and Dore rivers.

Alloa *al'ō-a*, 56 07N 3 49W, pop(1981) 26,428, capital of Clackmannan dist, Central region, central Scotland; on the R Forth, 10 km E of Stirling; economy: textiles, brewing, engineering.

Alma-Ata *al'mu-a'ta*, formerly VERNYI (-1921), 43 15N 76 57E, pop(1983) 1,023,000, capital city of Alma-Atinskaya oblast and Kazakhskaya SSR, Soviet Union; in the N foothills of the snow-capped Zailiyskiy Alatau range, c.300 km from the Chinese frontier; established in 1854 as a military fortress and trading centre; after the 1887 earthquake, when all but one of the town's 1788 houses were destroyed, it was decreed that only single-storey houses of wood should be built, with a few exceptions in the town centre; famous for its Aport apples which can weigh up to 500 gm each; a noted tourist and athletic centre; university (1934); Academy of Sciences (1968); railway; airport; economy: coal-fired power plant, machine building, engineering, printing, film-making, foodstuffs, tobacco, textiles, and leather; monument: Ascension cathedral, erected in 1904, is the 2nd tallest wooden building in the world.

Almanzora *al-man-tho'ra*, river in Almeria prov, S Spain; rising on NW slopes of the Sierra de los Filabres it flows E and SE to meet the Mediterranean E of Vera; length 130 km.

Almelo *ahl'mul-ō*, 52 22N 6 42E, pop(1984e) 62,941, city and municipality in Overijssel prov, E Netherlands; 14 km NW of Hengelo; railway; economy: fashion fabrics and household textiles, technical textile products, recreational products.

Almería *al may-ree'a*, mountainous prov in Andalucia region, SE Spain; situated by the Mediterranean; drained by the R Almanzora; pop(1981) 405,313; area, 8,774 sq km; capital Almería; economy: in the Sierras there are rich mines of copper, iron, mercury, silver and lead; a major cement plant with quarry and port facilities is located at Carboneras; fruit and vegetable cultivation are important.

Almería, UNCI (anc), PORTUS MAGNUS (Lat), (Arab 'Al-Mariyya', mirror of the sea), 36 52N 2 27W, pop(1981) 140,946, Andalucian seaport and capital of Almería prov, S Spain; 563 km SSE of Madrid; railway; airport; car ferries to Melilla; occupied by Carthaginians, Romans and Moors as an important trade centre; economy: metal work, textiles, chemical products, horticulture; monuments: Alcazaba fortress, castle of San Cristóbal, 16th-c Gothic cathedral; events: 10-day fiestas in Aug; winter fiestas (Dec-Jan); Costa del Sol Car Rally in Dec.

Almirante *al-me-ran'tee*, 9 20N 82 22W, pop(1980) 10,561, port town in Bocas del Toro prov, NW Panama, Central America; on the Caribbean coast, 16 km WSW of Bocas del Toro; a major banana-shipping port until the plantations were abandoned in 1929; railway.

Al-Muthanna, governorate in S central Iraq, bounded S by Saudi Arabia, and E by Kuwait; pop(1977) 215,637; area 49,206 sq km; capital As Samawah; the R Euphrates (Al-Furāt) crosses W-E in the N.

Alness, 57 42N 4 15W, pop(1981) 6,289, town in Ross and Cromarty dist, Highland region, N Scotland; on the R Alness, on the N side of the Cromarty Firth, 5 km W of Invergordon; railway; the town expanded in the 1970s in connection with North Sea oil developments.

Alnwick *an'ik*, 55 25N 1 42W, pop(1981) 7,500, market town in Alnwick dist, Northumberland, NE England; on the R Aln, 48 km N of Newcastle upon Tyne; monument: castle, seat of the Dukes of Northumberland.

Alor Setar or **Alur Setar** *ah'lor stahr*, 6 06N 100 23E, pop(1980) 69,435, capital of Kedah state, NW Peninsular Malaysia, SE Asia; 475 km NNW of Kuala Lumpur at the junction of the Kedah and Padang Terap rivers; airfield N of Anak Bukit; monuments: Zahir mosque; Balai Besar (Great Hall), built in 1898 and used as an audience hall by the sultans of Kedah; sultan's palace at Anak Bukit; state museum; well preserved Malay fort at Kuala Kedah fishing village.

Alost, town in Belgium. See Aalst.

Alpe Adria *alp ay'dree-a*, a working association of 11 neighbouring regions in Austria, W Germany, Italy and Yugoslavia, linked by cultural and economic interests; established in 1978 on the initiative of the Italian prov of Veneto; comprises Oberösterreich, Salzburg and Steiermark federal states in Austria, Veneto, Lombardy, Trentino-Alto Adige, Friuli-Venezia Giulia regions in Italy, Bayern in W Germany and Hrvatska (Croatia) and Slovenija republics in Yugoslavia; pop(1981) 35,600,000.

Alpes Cottiennes *alp kot-ee-yen*, COTTIAN ALPS (Eng), a division of the W Alps in SE France along the French-Italian frontier, extending from the Alpes Maritimes at Maddalena Pass to the Alpes Graian at Mont Cenis; the highest peak is Monte Viso (3,851 m).

Alpes-de-Haute-Provence *alp-de-ōt-pro-vãs*, largely mountainous dept in Provence-Alpes-Côtes d'Azur region of SE France at the S end of the Alps, comprising 4 arrond, 32 cantons and 200 communes; pop(1982) 119,068; area 6,925 sq km; capital Digne; the highest point is Mt Pelat (3,052 m); the Durance and Verdon rivers are dammed to provide hydroelectric power; 16 km SW of Castellane is the spectacular Grand Canyon du Verdon, a natural fault in the limestone with wild gorges and dramatic cliffs that vary in height from 250 m to 700 m; there is an observatory at Forcalquier, a location chosen for its pure atmosphere.

Alpes-Maritimes *alp-ma-ree-teem*, dept in Provence-Alpes-Côte d'Azur region of SE France bordering Italy and lying at the S end of the French Maritime Alps whose spurs run S to the Mediterranean Sea; comprises 2 arrond, 46 cantons and 163 communes; pop(1982) 881,198; area 4,299 sq km; capital Nice; the Côte d'Azur forms the most westerly part of the French Riviera and here are the famous coastal resorts of Nice, Cannes, Antibes and Menton; the R Var and its tributary the R Tinée flow N-S to meet the sea W of Nice; NW of Nice is the artists' resort of Vence where D.H. Lawrence died in 1930; interesting caves and prehistoric sites near St Cézaire; spa at Berthemont-les-Bains; Parc National du Mercantour is located N of St Martin-Vesubie, which is one of the finest summer resorts and mountaineering centres in Europe; ski stations and resorts at Auron, Beuil, Isola, Gréolières and Valberg; the château at Gourdon (9-17th-c) is worth visiting; the Alpes Maritimes or Maritime Alps which stretch across the Italian frontier, present 80 km of rocky summits, the highest being Cima Sud Argentera (3,297 m) in Italy; the Col de Restefond (2,802 m) is the highest of the Alpine road passes; economy: winter and summer tourism, glass-works at Biot, sheep-rearing and the manufacture of cheese in upland areas, roses and jasmin cultivated in the area of Châteauneuf and Opio, perfume manufactured at Grasse.

Alphen aan den Rijn *ahl'fun an den rīn*, 52 08N 4 40E, pop(1984e) 54,560, industrial city and municipality in Zuid Holland prov, W Netherlands; on the R Rhine, 30 km NE of Rotterdam; its Avifauna bird sanctuary (open Mar-Oct) has over 10,000 birds of 400 different species.

Alps, the principal mountain range of Europe, covering 259,000 sq km between lat 43-48N and long 5-17E, in Switzerland, France, Germany, Austria, Liechtenstein, Italy and Yugoslavia; they stretch in parallel chains over 1,000 km in a SW to NE direction from the Colle d'Altare, close to the Mediterranean coast in the Golfo di

Genova, to the Hochschwab in E Austria; the source of many great European rivers - drained by the R Rhine to the North Sea, by the R Po (and the Tagliamento, Piave and Adige) to the Adriatic, and by the R Rhône to the Mediterranean; there are 5 watersheds - Mediterranean-Adriatic, Adriatic-North Sea, North Sea-Mediterranean, Adriatic-Black Sea and Black Sea-North Sea, with hydrographic centres at the minor peaks of Wyttenwasserstock and Pizzo Lunghino; the highest range is Mont Blanc (4,807 m); I. Western Alps: (1) Alpes-Maritimes (Cima Sud Argentera 3,297 m) (2) Alpes Cottiennes or Cottian Alps (Monte Viso 3,851 m) (3) Alpes Dauphine (Barre des Écrins 4,101 m) (4) Alpes Graian (Gran Paradiso 4,061 m); II. Middle Alps: (1) Alpi Pennine (Mont Blanc 4,807 m; Monte Rosa 4,634 m; Matterhorn 4,477 m) (2) Alpi Lepontine (3,553 m) (3) Alpi Retiche or Rhaetian Alps (Piz Bernina 4,049 m) (4) Berner Alpen or Bernese Alps (Finsteraarhorn 4,274 m; Aletschhorn 4,195 m; Jungfrau 4,158 m) (5) Alpi Orobie (6) Ötztaler Alpen (Wildspitze 3,774 m) (7) Dolomiti or the Dolomites (Marmolada 3,342 m) (8) Lechtaler Alpen (3,038 m) III. Eastern Alps: (1) Zillertaler Alpen or Alpi Aurine (3,510 m) (2) Kitzbühler Alpen (2,559 m) (3) Karnische Alpen or Carnic Alps (2,781 m) (4) Julijske Alpe or Julian Alps (Triglav 2,863 m) (5) Hohe Tauern or Noric Alps (Groß Glockner 3,797 m) (6) Niedere Tauern (2,863 m); notable passes include the Mont Cenis, St Bernard (Little and Greater), Gemmi, Simplon, St Gotthard, Splugen, Stilfserjoch (Stelvio), Brenner; there are railway tunnels at the Col de Fréjus, Lotschberg, Simplon and St Gotthard; the range was originally formed by a collision between the African and European tectonic plates; frost and rain, rivers and glaciers have removed large masses and carved the mountains into their present form; Alpine towns have manufactures concerned with native and imported products such as textiles, clocks, chocolate and wooden goods, but since the 19th century mountaineering and downhill skiing have been important; the tourist facilities are highly developed with hotels, mountain huts, rack-and-cable railways and cableways; in 1911 Karl Blodig was the first man to climb all the peaks over 4,000 m in height.

Al-Qādisiyah, governorate in S central Iraq; pop(1977) 423,006; area 8,569 sq km; capital Ad Dīwānīyah; drained by the R Euphrates and its numerous channels.

Als, ALSEN *ol'sun* (Ger), Danish island in the Lille Bælt (Little Belt), off E coast of S Jylland (Jutland), separated from mainland by the Alsensund, SW of Fyn I; area 321 sq km; chief towns Sønderborg, Nordborg and Augustenborg; administered by Sønderjylland county; beautiful beaches make it a popular tourist resort; belonged to Germany until 1920.

Alsace *al-sas'*, ELSASS (Ger), ALSATIA (Lat), ('those who live beyond the Rhine'), region of NE France comprising the depts of Bas-Rhin and Haut-Rhin, part of the Upper Rhine Plain on the frontier with Germany, 13 arrond, 75 cantons and 896 communes, on the W side of the Rhine valley and the E slopes of the Vosges; pop(1982) 1,566,048; area 8,280 sq km; at one time part of Lorraine before becoming part of the German Empire; the Treaty of Westphalia in 1648 returned most of Alsace to France but in 1871 after the Franco-Prussian War it was once more ceded to Germany and made part of the imperial territory of Alsace-Lorraine; in 1919 it was again returned to France; it is one of the most agriculturally fertile and industrially productive regions of France; the Alemanic dialect 'Elsasserdeutsch' is still spoken; the region is traversed S-N by the rivers Rhine and Ill; the chief towns are Strasbourg, Mulhouse and Colmar; Mulhouse is the main industrial centre while Strasbourg, the capital, is the seat of the Council of Europe and the European Parliament; there are spas at Niederbronn-les-Bains, Pechelbronne and Morsbronn; Albert Schweitzer (1875-1965), the doctor, organist and missionary, was born in Kayserberg; the wine towns and vineyards of Alsace can be explored by following the well sign-posted 180 km 'Route du Vin d'Alsace', along the E slopes of the Vosges; part of the Vosges Regional Nature Park (Parc des Vosges du Nord) is located in Bas-Rhin dept; economy: wine, beer, pottery, chemicals, paper, printed fabrics, textile dyeing and spinning, machinery and car manufacture.

Al'ta, 69 57N 23 10E, pop(1980) 13,378, town on the N coast of Finnmark county, N Norway; 146 km S of Hammerfest, at the mouth of the R Altaelv; economy: salmon-fishing, slate-working.

Alta Verapaz *al'ta vay-ra-pas'*, mountainous dept in N central Guatemala, Central America; pop(1982e) 383,178; area 8,686 sq km; capital Cobán; drained by the Cahabón and Polochic rivers; slopes N into the Petén lowlands; bounded W by the Río Chixoy and SE by the Sierra de las Minás; economy: a pipeline carries oil from a field in the extreme NW to the refinery near Puerto Barrios; apart from an area in the N of the dept devoted to coffee growing much of the land is given over to subsistence agriculture, forestry, or is agriculturally undeveloped.

Al'taelv, ALTA RIVER, river in N Norway, rises on Finnish border S of Kautokeino; flows N through Finnmark county to discharge into Altafjorden (Alta Fjord), an inlet of the Arctic Ocean, at Alta; length 200 km; the upper course is called the R Kautokeino.

Altai Shan *al-tī shan*, ALTAI MOUNTAINS, major mountain system of central Asia; extends from the USSR in the NW, SE along the border between Xinjiang aut region, NW China and Mongolia, into Mongolia itself; source of the Irtysh and Ob rivers; the highest point of the Russian Altai is Mt Bolukha (4,506 m); in Mongolia the Youyi Feng peak rises to 4,374 m; the average height of the range is 2,000 to 3,000 m above sea-level.

Altamira, Cuevas de *kway'vas dhay al-ta-mee'ra*, caves with Paleolithic paintings of animals, 24 km W of Santander, Santander prov, N Spain; restored in 1974.

Altar', 1 40S 78 25W, extinct Andean volcano in central Ecuador, rising to 5,270 m on the border of Chimborazo and Morona-Santiago provs, 15 km E of Riobamba; its two snow-capped peaks resemble an altar.

Altay *al'tī*, ALTAI, AERHATAI SHAN, 46 40N 92 45E, capital of Govĭaltay county, SW Mongolia; on the N edge of the Gobi Desert, WSW of Ulaanbaatar; a centre of livestock breeding.

Alt'dorf or **Altorf**, 46 52N 8 36E, pop(1980) 8,200, capital town of Uri canton, central Switzerland; at SE tip of Urner See (L Urner), 32 km SE of Luzern; starting point of the road over Klausen Pass (1,948 m); railway; monuments: Wilhelm Tell monument (1895); Capuchin monastery (1581), the earliest in Switzerland; event: Schiller's *Wilhelm Tell* is played annually.

Altenburg *ahl'tun-boork*, 50 59N 12 27E, pop(1981) 55,827, manufacturing town in Altenburg dist, Leipzig, S central East Germany; in R Pleisse valley, 64 km E of Weimar; former capital of the Duchy of Saxe-Altenburg (1826-1918); railway; economy: tourism, clothes.

Alto Alentejo *al-to a-lā-tay'zhoo*, (Arab 'alem Tejo', beyond the Tagus), an agricultural prov of SE central Portugal formed in 1936 from the former Alentejo region, lying to the SE of the R Tagus and including most of Portalegre and Évora dists; an often barren, low lying plain with cork tree forests, heaths and maquis; there are many prehistoric standing stones and chambered cairns (antas); the chief town is Évora.

Alto Paraguay *pa-ra-gwī'*, dept in Occidental region, NE Paraguay; bordered E by Brazil along the Río Paraguay, NE and N by Bolivia; pop(1982) 4,535; area 37,000 sq km; capital Fuerte Olimpo; part of the low lying and often flooded Chaco plain.

Alto Paraná *pa-ra-na'*, dept in Oriental region, SE Paraguay; bordered E by Brazil and Argentina along the Río Paraná; a high thickly-forested region, drained by many rivers with waterfalls and rapids; pop(1982) 188,351; area 13,498 sq km; capital Puerto Presidente Stroessner; because of its fertile soil, rich vegetation and hydroelectric potential it is one of Paraguay's most productive depts; Itaipú hydroelectric plant is one of the world's largest with an output of 12·6 GW; several dams have been built along the Río Paraná.

Alton, 51 09N 0 59W, pop(1981) 14,366, town in East Hampshire dist, Hampshire, S England; 16 km SE of Basingstoke; railway; economy: engineering, electrical goods; monuments: 13-15th-c church of St Lawrence; Chawton, home of Jane Austen, who lived here from 1809 to 1817; Curtis Museum.

Alton, 38 53N 90 11W, pop(1980) 34,171, town in Madison county, SW Illinois, United States; on R Mississippi, 35 km N of St Louis; railway.

Altoo'na, 40 31N 78 24W, pop(1980) 57,078, town in Blair county, central Pennsylvania, United States; 144 km E of Pittsburgh; railway; economy: manufacturing and repair shops for state railway; 8 km W is the scenic Horseshoe Curve of the railway.

Altos, Los, 37 23N 122 07W, pop(1980) 25,769, city in Santa Clara county, W California, United States; a residential area, 10 km S of Palo Alto, in the foothills of the Santa Cruz Mts.

Altrincham *awl'tring-am*, 53 24N 2 21W, pop(1981) 39,693, town in Trafford borough, Greater Manchester, NW England; 13 km SW of Manchester; railway; economy: engineering, market gardening.

Altun Shan, ALTYN TAGH, ASTIN TAGH, ALTUN MOUNTAINS, mountain range in SE Xinjiang aut region, NW China; central offshoot of the Kunlun Shan range; extends ENE along the Xinjiang-Qinghai border between Tarim Pendi and Qaidam Pendi basins; average height is between 3,500 and 4,000 m; the highest peak, Mt Altun, rises to 5,798 m.

Alturas, Serra das *al-too'ras*, mountain range, Braga dist, N Portugal, rising to 1,279 m in the NE and 1,256 m at Cabreira in the SW.

Alvão, Serra de *al-vown'*, mountain range, Vila Real dist, N Portugal; NW of Vila Real, rising to 1,283 m.

Alvelos, Serra de *al-ve'los*, mountain range, Castelo Branco dist, E central Portugal; W of Castelo Branco, rising to 1,084 m.

Älvsborg or **Elfsborg** *elfs'bor*, a county of SW Sweden, W of L Vänern, borders with Norway in the NW; land area 11,394 sq km; pop(1983) 425,178; capital Vänersborg; chief towns Borås, Trollhattan and Alingsås.

Al-Wadi Al-Jadid', governorate in S central Egypt; pop(1976) 84,645; area 376,505 sq km; capital El Khârga.

Alzette *ahl-zet'*, river in Luxembourg, rising WNW of Esch; flows E and N to meet the R Sûre at Ettelbruck; length 65 km.

Amagasaki *a-ma-ga-sa'kee*, 34 42N 135 23E, pop(1980) 523,650, town in Hyōgo prefecture, Kinki region, S Honshū island, Japan; W of Ōsaka; railway.

Amaliás *ah-mah-lee'ahs*, 37 48N 21 21E, pop(1981) 14,698, town in Ilía nome (dept), Pelopónnisos region, Greece, near the W coast, on the main highway between Pírgos and Pátrai.

Amambay *am-am-bī'*, dept in Oriental region, E central Paraguay; bordered E (along the Sierra Amambaí) and N (along the Río Apa) by Brazil; has a humid, subtropical climate; in the N of the dept is the Cerro Cora National Park; pop(1982) 68,422; area 12,933 sq km; capital Pedro Juan Caballero.

Amapá *a-ma-pa'*, territory in Norte region, N Brazil; bordered N by Guiana, E by the Atlantic, S by the Amazon delta and W by the Jari river; lies in tropical rainforest area; pop(1980) 175,257; area 140,276 sq km; capital Macapá; economy: mining (manganese), rubber, chestnuts, timber; in the N is the Cabo Orange National Park; Amapá also boasts Brazil's only standard-gauge railway which carries manganese from the mining town of Icomiland to the new pellet plant at Pôrto Santana, S of Macapá; in 1967 US billionaire, Daniel K. Ludwig, launched forestry and rice growing projects on a 150,000 sq km piece of land in W Amapá terr and E Pará state along the banks of the Jari river; the company town of Monte Dourado grew rapidly in association with this project.

Amarante *a-ma-ran'ti*, 41 16N 8 05W, pop(1981) 6,987, small, picturesque, wine-producing town in Porto dist, N Portugal; on R Tâmega, 63 km E of Porto; renowned for its phallic cakes baked on the first Saturday in June for the festival of São Gonçalo, patron saint of married couples and lovers; monuments: 16th-c Renaissance 'Philippine' style convent of São Gonçalo and the tiled church of São Pedro.

Amarela, Serra de *a-ma-re'la*, mountain range, Braga dist, N Portugal; part of the Peneda-Gerês National Park lying between the R Lima and R Cávado near the Spanish frontier and rising to 1,361 m.

Amaril'lo, 35 13N 101 50W, pop(1980) 149,230, county seat of Potter county, NW Texas, United States; 180 km N of Lubbock; railway; airport; economy: commercial, banking, and industrial centre for the Texas panhandle; oil refining, meat packing, flour milling, zinc smelting, helicopters and synthetic rubber.

Amasya *a-ma'syah*, prov in N Turkey; bounded N by Canik Mts; pop(1980) 341,387; area 5,520 sq km; capital Amasya; economy: opium, wool, fruit, tobacco, lead, gold and silver.

Amazon, major river in South America. See Amazonas.

Amazonas *a-ma-zō'nas*, state in Norte region, NW Brazil; bordered by Venezuela (N), Colombia (NW), Colombia and Peru (W); crossed W-E by the middle Amazon (called the Solimões above the influx of the Río Negro); situated within the tropical rainforest basin of the Amazon; crossed by numerous tributaries of the Amazon, including the rivers Negro, Branco, Jurua and Purus (the world's most crooked river); pop(1980) 1,430,089; area 1,564,445 sq km; capital Manaus; economy: forestry, fishing; rivers are the principal form of transport to the interior of the state; environmentalists are concerned at the widespread burning of the Amazonian forest (the world's largest forest, which is estimated to contain a third of the planet's trees and to supply half of its oxygen); it is reckoned that 4% of the forest is destroyed annually to make way for new settlements, ranches and industries; in the NW is the Río Negro Nature Reserve.

Amazonas, AMAZON (Eng), RÍO DE LAS AMAZONAS (Sp), river in N South America, considered to be the largest river in the world by volume and the 2nd longest; its two major headstreams, the Marañón and the Ucayali, rise in the Andes of Peru, approx 150 km from the Pacific; they cross the lowlands of N Peru, meet and form the Amazon to the S of Iquitos, Peru; the river then flows E into Acre state, N Brazil at a point just S of the Equator; in Brazil it is called the Solimões until the influx of the Río Negro; it flows E across Amazonas and Pará states, then forms the border between Pará and Amapá states before entering the Atlantic in a wide delta; the Amazon drains a basin of approx 7,000,000 sq km and has more than 1,100 tributaries, of which 17 are over 1,600 km long; the rivers of the Amazon basin carry one-fifth of the world's running water; despite difficulty in navigation, ocean steamers sail up river as far as Iquitos, 3,680 km from the Atlantic; the deepest point of the Amazon (37 m) is at the influx of the Trombetas river; at the delta the Pará and Amazon rivers form a large island, the Ilha de Marajó; the length measured from L Lauricocha, at the headwaters of the Marañón, is 6,280 km; the length measured from L Vilafro following the Ucayali and Apurímac headwaters to the mouth of the Amazon via the Canal do Norte is 6,449 km; most shipping uses the Breves Straits and the Río Pará to reach the ocean, a total distance of 6,751 km (88 km longer than the Nile); principal tributaries include the Napo, Putamayo, Caqueta, Trombetas, Jurua, Purus, Madeira, Tapajos, and Xingu rivers; northern tributaries flood in June, southern in March or April; river levels at Manaus fluctuate by more than 15 m; fresh water from the Amazon is estimated to extend up to 300 km from the coast; the northern channels of the Amazon delta are made dangerous by a frequent tidal bore (*Pororoca*) which sweeps up river at a speed of up to 65 km per hour, generating waves sometimes 5 m in height; cargo launches use the Amazon to link with the interior, carrying fish, cedarwood, flour, rubber, and jute;

the Amazon was discovered by Vicente Yáñez Pinzón in 1500; it was first descended in 1541 by Orellana, and first ascended in 1637 by Pedro Texeira; steam ships first sailed the river in 1853; in 1866 the Amazon was opened to world shipping and in 1929 free navigation of the river was guaranteed by treaty between Colombia and Brazil.

Amazonas, administrative territory in SE Colombia, South America; a densely forested lowland region lying just S of the Equator; bounded S by Peru along the Putumayo and Amazon rivers, and E by Brazil; crossed by the Río Caquetá; the Río Apaporis forms the territory's NE boundary; pop(1985) 13,210; area 109,665 sq km; capital Leticia.

Amazonas, dept in N Peru, situated at the W edge of the Amazon basin; bordered N by Ecuador; crossed by the Río Marañón; pop(1981) 254,560; area 41,297 sq km; capital Chachapoyas.

Amazonas, federal territory in SW Venezuela; bounded S by Brazil along the Serra Imeri and the Serra Tapirapecó, SE along the Serra Parima, and W Colombia along the rivers Orinoco, Atabapo and Negro; includes W outliers of the Guiana Highlands in E; watered by the Orinoco river; pop(1980) 45,600; area 170,503 sq km; capital Puerto Ayacucho.

Amazonia *a-ma-zon'ya*, national park in NW Pará state, Nordeste region, NE Brazil; area 10,000 sq km; established in 1974.

Ambato *am-ba'tō*, 1 18S 78 39W, pop(1982) 100,454, capital of Tungurahua prov, in the Andean Sierra of central Ecuador; on the Río Ambato, S of Quito; to the SE lies Tungurahua volcano and to the SW Chimborazo; the town was almost completely destroyed by an earthquake in 1949; known as the 'garden city of Ecuador', Ambato has a notable weekly market; railway; economy: textiles, rugs, drinks, tobacco, food processing, chemicals, motor vehicles; events: fruit and flower festival in Feb.

Ambergris Cay *am'ber-grees*, low lying peninsula of the W Caribbean Sea; Corozal dist, N Belize, Central America; southernmost tip of the Yucatan peninsula, separated by a channel from the mainland of Belize; chief resort town San Pedro.

Ambleside, 54 26N 2 58W, pop(1981) 3,188, town in South Lakeland dist, Cumbria, NW England; N of L Windermere; monuments: 19th-c church of St Mary; 18th-c tollhouse on a bridge over the R Rothay.

Ambon *ahm'bōn*, AMBOINA, 3 41S 128 12E, pop(1980) 79,636, seaport capital of Maluku prov (Moluccas), Indonesia; on Ambon Bay on the island of Ambon, off the SW coast of the island of Seram; university (1962); airfield.

Ameland *ah'mul-ahnt*, one of the West Frisian Is, in Friesland prov, N Netherlands, between the North Sea (N) and the Waddenzee (S); area 57 sq km; length 22 km; width 6.5 km; chief villages Hollum, Nes and Ballum; ferry from Nes to Holwerd on the mainland; the N shore is protected by dunes; there is a lighthouse (NW).

American Samoa *sa-mō'ah*, territory of the United States, in the central S Pacific Ocean, some 3,500 km NNE of New Zealand, comprising 5 principal islands, all of volcanic origin, and 2 coral atolls; timezone GMT −11; area 197 sq km; pop(1980) 32,297; capital Fagatogo; the bulk of the population is located on the 2 main islands of Tutuila and Ta'u; the people of American Samoa are largely of Polynesian origin and are United States nationals; in recent years there has been a large out-migration to the United States; Christianity is the dominant religion; the official language is English.

Physical description and climate. American Samoa consists of the main island of Tutuila (109 sq km) and the islands E and N of it which include Aunu'u, the Manu'a Group (Ta'u, Olosega, Ofu), and the atolls of Swain's I and the uninhabited Rose I. The 5 main islands are volcanic and hilly with large areas still covered by thick bush and forest. Tutuila, the westernmost island, rises to 653 m, while Ta'u rises to 970 m. Swain's and Rose islands are low-lying atolls. The climate is tropical maritime with a small annual range of temperature and plentiful rainfall. The average annual rainfall is 5,000 mm. In Pago Pago, on Tutuila I, annual rainfall is 4,850 mm, average Jan temperature is 28.3°C, and average July temperature 26.7°C.

History, government and constitution. The United States acquired rights to American Samoa following a Commission set up in 1899 to resolve the dispute over rights to the Samoan islands between the UK, Germany, and the United States. Germany acquired rights to Western Samoa while the USA acquired rights to the islands now known as American Samoa. The islands of Tutuila and Aunu'u were ceded by their chiefs to the USA in 1900, the islands of the Manu'a group in 1904 and Swain's I in 1925. The islands were under the administration of the United States Department of the Navy until 1951. Today, American Samoa is an unincorporated and unorganized territory of the United States, administered by the Department of the Interior. In 1948 a bicameral legislature was established, allowing the Samoans to have advisory legislative functions. The constitution of 1960 which was revised in 1967 provides for a limited law-making authority. The governor is the administrative head of the executive branch. The legislature, known as the *Fono*, comprises the senate and the house of representatives. The senate consists of 18 members, chosen by county councils according to Samoan custom, while the 21 representatives are chosen by popular vote.

Economy. Many of the islanders are smallholding farmers, growing bananas, breadfruit, cassava, yams, pineapples, and vegetables. Most commercial farms are in the Tafuna plains and W Tutuila, the principal crops being taro, breadfruit, yams, bananas, and coconuts. Fish canning is important, employing the 2nd largest number of people (after the government). The canneries at Pago Pago date from 1954. Tuna fishing and local inshore fishing are both expanding. Chief exports are canned tuna, watches, pet foods, and handicrafts.

Administrative divisions. American Samoa is divided into 15 counties which are grouped into Eastern, Western, and Manu'a districts.

Americana *a-may-ree-ka'na*, 22 44S 47 19W, pop(1980) 121,743, town in São Paulo state, Sudeste region, SE Brazil; NW of São Paulo; the area was settled by Confederate refugees from the S of the USA after the Civil War, although most of the original settlers soon returned to the United States; railway; economy: textiles, mechanics, tyre-manufacturing.

Amerrique, Sierra de *a-mer-ee'kay*, mountain range in Chontales and Río San Juan depts, S central Nicaragua, Central America; forming a section of the main continental divide; bounded W by Lago de Nicaragua; extends approx 48 km SE from Camoapa; forms the watershed between rivers flowing E into the Caribbean Sea (Río Escondido, Río Punta Gorda) and that flowing W into Lago de Nicaragua (Río Oyate).

Am'ersfoort, 52 09N 5 23E, pop(1984e) 86,896, commercial city and municipality in NE Utrecht prov, W Netherlands; 19 km NE of Utrecht, at the confluence of several small rivers, which, further downstream, form the R Eem; surrounded by a vast area of forest and heathland; many of its inhabitants commute to the nearby provincial capital of Utrecht and to Amsterdam, 50 km away; received its charter in 1259 and developed around the cloth-manufacturing and brewing industries; birthplace of Oldenbarneveldt; railway; economy: electrical engineering, motor vehicles, machines, chemicals, foodstuffs; monuments: Onze Lieve Vrouwe church (with a 15th-c carillon tower), Gothic church of St George (begun in 1243 and completed in 1534).

Am'ersham, 51 40N 0 38W, pop(1981) 21,492, residential town in Chiltern dist, Buckinghamshire, S central England; 21 km SE of Aylesbury; railway; economy: furniture, radio-isotopes.

Ames *aymz*, 42 02N 93 37W, pop(1980) 45,775, town in Story county, central Iowa, United States; on the R Skunk, 45 km N of Des Moines; university (1858); railway.

Amiens *am-yĩ*, SAMAROBRIVA (anc), 49 54N 2 16E, pop(1982) 136,358, agric market town and capital of Somme dept, Picardie region, N France; 130 km N of Paris on the left bank of the R Somme; university (1964); railway; bishopric; economy: textiles and food processing, market-gardens irrigated by canals sell fruit and vegetables; war-time cemeteries at Arras to the E; monuments: 13th-c Gothic cathedral of Notre-Dame, the largest in area in France, known for its statuary, carvings and art galleries.

Amindivi Islands, island group of India. See Lakshadweep.

Amirantes *a'mir-ants*, a group of coral islands in the SW Indian Ocean, 800 km N of Madagascar and 240 km WSW of the island of Mahé; administered by Seychelles, the group includes the islands of St Joseph, Poivre, Daros, Desneuf and Marie Louise Is; noted for deep sea diving and fishing; copra is the main product.

Amman', governorate (*muhafaza*) of the East Bank, central Jordan; bounded E by Saudi Arabia and SW by the Dead Sea; capital Amman; chief towns Mādabā and Zarqa.

Amman, 31 57N 35 52E, pop(1980e) 1,232,600, industrial and commercial capital city of the Hashemite Kingdom of Jordan; in Amman governorate, East Bank, 80 km ENE of Jerusalem, on the R Zarqa; became the capital of Transjordan in 1923; by the 13th century BC Amman was an established city controlling the Desert Highway, a historic trade route linking Egypt and the Red Sea with the Levant and Tigris-Euphrates basin; noted for its locally-quarried coloured marble; airport; railway; monuments: Roman amphitheatre (1st-c BC) and remains of a temple.

Am'manford, 51 48N 3 59W, pop(1981) 10,757, coal mining town in Dinefwr dist, Dyfed, SW Wales; 27 km ESE of Carmarthen; railway.

Ammersee *ah'mur-zay*, LAKE AMMER (Eng), lake in S Bayern (Bavaria) prov, W Germany, 35 km SW of München (Munich), on the Bavarian plateau; area 47.5 sq km; max depth 83 m; average depth 38 m; length 16 km; width 3-6 km; inlet R Ammer, outlet R Amper; surrounded by forest-covered morainic hills; many attractive resorts around its shores.

Amorgós, easternmost island of the Kikládhes, Greece, in the Aegean Sea, SE of Náxos; area 121 sq km; Amorgós is the main settlement; the island rises to a height of 822 m.

Amoy, town in Fujian prov, SE China. See Xiamen.

Amparai, AMPARA, 7 17E 81 41E, pop(1981) 16,213, capital of Amparai dist, Eastern prov, Sri Lanka; on the E edge of Gal Oya national park; airfield.

Ampato, Nevado de *nay-va'dō dhay am-pa'tō*, Andean massif rising to 6,310 m in Arequipa dept, S Peru; situated in the Cordillera Occidental, 64 km NW of Arequipa; nearby is the Cañon del Colca, thought to be the world's deepest canyon.

Ampos'ta, oilfield in the W Mediterranean off the Costa Dorada, E Spain; discovered in 1971 and on stream in autumn 1972.

Amraoti, city in India. See Amravati.

Amravati *um-row'tee*, AMRAOTI, 20 58N 77 50E, pop(1981) 261,000, city in Maharashtra, W central India; site of the Great Stupa (AD 200) of the Andhra Dynasty; the largest cotton market in India is located here; railway link to Nagpur in the NE.

Amritsar *um-rit'sur* ('pool of immortality'), 31 35N 74 57E, pop(1981) 589,000, city in Punjab, NW India; centre of the Sikh religion; founded in 1577 by Ram Das around a sacred tank, known as the pool of immortality; the Golden Temple, found at the centre of the tank, is particularly sacred to Sikhs; under the gold and copper dome the sacred book of the Sikhs, Granth Sahib, is kept; the centre of the Sikh empire in the 19th century and of modern Sikh nationalism; the Amritsar massacre of Indian nationalists took place in April 1919; a battle between the Indian Army and Sikh militants inside the Golden Temple, led to the death of a Sikh leader in June 1984; university (1969); airport.

Amstelveen *ahm'stul-vayn*, 52 18N 4 50E, pop(1984e) 68,518, city and municipality in Noord Holland prov, W Netherlands; economy: civil and electrical engineering, shipbuilding, machine construction, concrete products, foodstuffs, packages and packaging materials.

Amsterdam *ahm'stur-dahm'*, *am'stur-dam* (Eng), 52 23N 4 54E, pop(1984e) 994,062, major European port and capital city of the Netherlands, in Noord Holland prov, W Netherlands; at the junction of the R Amstel and the Ij inlet which is an arm of the Ijsselmeer; railway; airport at Schiphol (one of the largest and most modern in Europe); municipal university (1632), free university (1880); together with its 10 outer suburbs, Amsterdam represents the largest urban concentration in the *Randstad*, an enormous industrial belt which stretches between Ijmuiden, at the opening of the North Sea Canal into the sea, and Hilversum to the SE; Amsterdam's growth from a small fishing village in the 13th century was rapid, especially after the foundation of the Dutch East India Company in 1602 and as a result of the Treaty of Westphalia (1648), which closed the R Schelde to navigation and temporarily destroyed the commerce of Antwerpen; the whole of the centre of the city was destroyed by bombing in 1940; it was later rebuilt to adapt to the demands of modern traffic, with clear zoning of administrative, commercial, residential and cultural activities; the important harbour industry which developed after World War II was stimulated by the construction of a giant petro-chemical and chemical complex linked by pipeline to the oil port of Rotterdam; the port, 2nd largest in the Netherlands after Rotterdam, is an important transshipping point for goods such as mineral oils, ores, coal, grain, oil-seed and animal feed; important cultural centre with the world-famous Concertgebouw Orchestra; one of the world's greatest banking centres; economy: shipbuilding, steel, engineering, motor and aircraft manufacturing, textiles, brewing, foodstuffs, publishing and printing, chemicals and pharmaceuticals, data processing and office equipment, cigarettes, electricity production; diamond-cutting was introduced after the sacking of Antwerpen in 1576 and developed into a specialized industry; monuments: House of Anne Frank; Rembrandt House (1606), since 1911 a museum with drawings and etchings; Oude Kerk (consecrated in 1306), the city's oldest church with 16th-c stained glass; 15th-c Nieuwe Kerk; 17th-c royal palace; event: international Windjammer Regatta 'Sail Amsterdam' (Aug).

Amsterdam, Île de, 37 52S 77 32E, volcanic island in S Indian Ocean; part of the French Southern and Antarctic Territories; area 54 sq km; discovered in 1633 by the Dutch explorer, Van Diemen; annexed by France in 1843.

Amstetten *am'shtet-en*, 48 08N 14 52E, pop(1981) 21,989, capital of Amstetten dist, W Niederösterreich, NE Austria, 130 km W of Wien (Vienna).

Am-Timan *am-tee-man'*, 10 59N 20 18E, capital of Salamat prefecture, SE Chad, N central Africa; 560 km ENE of N'Djamena.

Amudar'ya, OXUS (anc), river predominantly in S Soviet Union; formed by the junction of the Vakhsh and Pyandzh rivers, 29 km SW of Nizhni Pyandzh, on the Soviet-Afghanistan frontier; flows W past Termez, forming the border between Afghanistan (S) and the USSR (N) for c.320 km; at Bosaga the river turns NW and continues through Turkmenskaya and Uzbekskaya republics, past Chardzhou and Turtkul', to discharge into the Aral'skoye More (Aral Sea) where it forms a wide delta; length 1,415 km; drainage basin area 309,000 sq km; the largest river of central Asia, it is an important source of irrigation water; the river flows swiftly until it reaches the Peski Karakumy (Kara-Kum Desert) where its course braids into several channels.

Amuku, Lake *a-moo-koo'*, 3 43N 59 25W, small lake in Rupununi dist, SW Guyana, South America; on W bank of the R Rupununi in an extensive savannah; supposed site in colonial days of the fabled golden city, Manoa, and of Raleigh's El Dorado.

Amundsen Sea *ah'men-sen*, S arm of the Pacific Ocean off the Walgreen Coast of Marie Byrd Land, Antarctica; between Thurston I (E) and Siple I (W).

Anadolu *a-nu-dō-loo'*, ANATOLIA *a-nu-tō'lee-u*, Asiatic region of Turkey, usually synonymous with Asia Minor; it is a mountainous peninsula between the Black Sea (N), Aegean Sea (W), and the Mediterranean Sea (S).

Anadyr Gulf, inlet of the NW Bering Sea, Soviet Union. See Anadyrskiy Zaliv.

Anadyrskiy Zaliv, ANADYR GULF, inlet of the NW Bering Sea, NE Siberian Rossiyskaya, Soviet Union; S of the Chukotskiy Poluostrov peninsula, extending from Mys Chaplino (Cape Chaplin) in the N to Mys Navarin (Cape Navarin) in the S; the rivers Velikaya and Anadyr' drain into the gulf.

Anáfi *ah-nah'fee*, 36 23N 25 44E, island of the Kikládhes, Greece, in the Aegean Sea, between Thíra and Astipálaia; area 38 sq km; Anáfi is the main settlement.

Anaheim *a'na-hīm*, 33 50N 117 55W, pop(1980) 219,311, city in Orange county, SW California, United States; 37 km SE of Los Angeles, on the coastal plain; founded by Germans in 1857 as a cooperative community; railway; Disneyland (opened 1955).

Anam'bra, state in S Nigeria, W Africa; pop(1982e) 5,735,400; area 17,675 sq km; the R Niger follows the W border; capital Enugu; chief towns Abakaliki, Onitsha, Nsukka and Awgu; named after the R Anambra, a tributary of the R Niger; the main ethnic group are the Igbos; natural resources include iron ore, ceramic clay, silica sand, limestone, salt, coal, lead, zinc, oil and natural gas; economy: mining, car manufacture, cement processing, brewing, rice, vegetable oil refining and food processing.

Anantang, Pakistan. See Islamabad.

Anápolis *a-na'po-lees*, 16 19S 48 58W, pop(1980) 160,571, town in Goiás state, Centro-Oeste region, W central Brazil; SW of Brasília; railway; economy: important trading centre for rice, maize, coffee, soya beans, cattle.

Anatolia, Asiatic region of Turkey. See Anadolu.

Ancash *ang'kash*, dept in N Peru; bordered by the Pacific (W) and bounded by the Río Marañón (E); crossed N-S by the Cordillera Blanca, part of the Cordillera Occidental and now a national park; pop(1981) 818,289; area 36,308 sq km; capital Huaráz; in the E of the dept are the extensive 2,500-year-old ruins of Chavín, set in 7 underground levels; the ruins are noted for their unusually carved stone heads and relief work; original Chavín culture spread from the coast to encompass a large part of Peru, with Chavín de Huantar acting as a crossroads for trade between coast, sierra and jungle from 800 to 200 BC.

Anchorage, 61 13N 149 54W, pop(1980) 174,431, city and seaport in S central Alaska, United States; at the head of Cook Inlet; largest city in the state; founded in 1918 as a railway construction camp; the city was severely damaged by an earthquake in 1964; important transportation hub and a major administrative and commercial centre in the state; a vital defence centre, with Fort Richardson military base and Elmendorf Air Force Base nearby; university (1957); airport; railway; monuments: Earthquake Park, National Bank Heritage Library; events: Iditarod Sled Race (March), Great Alaska Shootout (Nov), Fur Rendezvous (Nov).

Ancona *ahng-kō'nah*, prov of Marche region, E central Italy; pop(1981) 433,417; area 1,937 sq km; capital Ancona.

Ancona, 43 37N 13 31E, pop(1981) 106,498, seaport and capital town of Ancona prov, Marche region, E central Italy; on the Adriatic coast; a naval and commercial port; bishopric; airfield; rail junction; ferries to Greece and Yugoslavia; economy: shipbuilding, trade in grain and pharmaceuticals; monuments: Arch of Trajan (AD 115), cathedral of San Ciriaco (12th-c); events: International Angling and Water Sports Fair (June-July).

Andalucia or **Andalusia** *an-da-loo-thee'a*, a large and fertile autonomous region of S Spain comprising the provs of Almería, Cádiz, Córdoba, Granada, Huelva, Jaén, Málaga and Sevilla; pop(1981) 6,440,987; area 87,268 sq km; Andalucia is dominated by the great basin of the R Guadalquivir and to the S by the Betic Cordillera which rise to 3,481 m at Cerro de Mulhacén in the Sierra Nevada, Spain's highest peak; the higher altitudes are covered with steppe vegetation and maquis scrub which is grazed by goats while on lower ground the mountain slopes are covered with forests of cork-oak and chestnut; the region is more densely populated on the S coastal strip which is known internationally for its tourist resorts on the Costa del Sol and the Costa de la Luz; agriculture is largely based on sugar-cane, fruit, bananas, wine and cotton; Málaga, Cádiz and Algeciras are the main industrial cities and ports in the region; from the 8th century it was under Moorish rule - Lower Andalucia until the 13th century, Upper Andalucia until the late 15th century.

Andaman and Nicobar Islands *an'da-man and nik-ō-bahr'*, a union territory of India comprising 2 island groups in the Bay of Bengal; separated from Burma, Thailand and Sumatra by the Andaman Sea; pop(1981) 188,254; area 8,293 sq km; over 300 islands, stretching 725 km N to S, are the summits of a submarine ridge which is connected to the Arkan Yoma in W Burma; both groups became a state of the republic of India in 1950; the Andaman Is were the site of a British penal colony (1858-1945); Cellular Jail in the penal town of Port Blair has since been made a national shrine; Port Blair is the administrative centre and only town of the Andaman Is; Port Blair is connected to Calcutta and Madras by boat; the inhabitants of the Andaman Is are the Negritos, who are related to SE Asian ethnic groups; the mountainous Nicobar Is, whose inhabitants are of Mongoloid stock, lie S of the Andamans; this group of 19 islands was occupied by Denmark (1756-1848), but annexed to the UK in 1869; the chief town of Nicobar is Nankauri; both island groups are covered in tropical forest; monsoon storms are frequent during May-Oct; economy: fishing, rubber, fruit, rice, hardwood timber; most foodstuffs are imported; event: Durga Puja (Sept-Oct).

Andaman Sea, NE arm of the Indian Ocean; bounded E by Burma and Thailand, N by the Gulf of Martaban and the delta of the Irrawaddy river, S by Sumatra and W by the Andaman and Nicobar Islands; linked to the Pacific Ocean by the Strait of Malacca and to the Bay of Bengal by the Ten Degree Channel and numerous other passages through the Andaman and Nicobar Islands.

Anderlecht *ahn'dur-leKTt*, 50 50N 4 18E, pop(1982) 94,715, town in Brussel dist, Brabant prov, Belgium; a W suburb of Bruxelles.

Anderson, 40 10N 85 41W, pop(1980) 64,695, county seat of Madison county, central Indiana, United States; 52 km NE of Indianapolis; railway.

Anderson, 34 31N 82 39W, pop(1980) 27,313, county seat of Anderson county, NE South Carolina, United States; 44 km SSW of Greenville; railway; economy: commercial centre in farming area; manufactures include textiles, fibreglass and sewing machines.

Andes, Los *lōs an'days*, 32 50S 70 36W, pop(1982) 34,648, capital of Los Andes prov, Valparaíso, central Chile; alt 820 m; railway; set in a wealthy agricultural, fruit-farming and wine-producing area; monuments: in the Plaza de Armas there are monuments to José de San Martín and Bernardo O'Higgins; there is also a monument to the Clark brothers who built the Trans-Andean railway.

Andes, Los, major mountain range in South America, running parallel to the Pacific coast from Tierra del Fuego (S) to the Caribbean (N); passes through the countries of Argentina, Chile, Bolivia, Peru, Ecuador, Colombia and Venezuela; extends over 6,437 km; rises to 6,960 m in the Cerro Aconcagua (Argentina), the highest point in South America and in the western hemisphere; the source of the Cauca, Magdalena, Orinoco, Amazon (Marañón and Ucayali) and Pilcomayo rivers, and all large rivers of Argentina except the Paraná; in places, especially N Argentina, Bolivia, Peru and Colombia, the

Andes spread out over high plateaux in several parallel ranges (cordilleras); in the S the Andes are broken up into blocks separated by channels; a range in Tierra del Fuego runs along the S coast; from S Chile the Cordillera Agostini range runs N between the Chile frontier and Patagonia (Argentina), with many lakes and peaks between 1,800 and 3,600 m; the range, which runs from approx 42°S northwards along the Chile-Argentina border to Bolivia, contains the highest peaks of the system, including Pular (6,225 m) in Chile; Aconcagua (6,960 m), Mercedario (6,770 m), Bonete (6,872 m) and Pissis (6,858 m) in Argentina; and Ojos del Salado (6,908 m), Tupungato (6,800 m), Llullaillaco (6,723 m), Incahuasi (6,709 m) and Tres Cruces (6,330 m) on the border between Chile and Argentina; there are many lakes and tourist resorts in Chile and Argentina between 39° and 42°S (Nahuel Huapí, Llanquihue, Ranco, Todos los Santos); at approx 23° to 28°S lies the Puna de Atacama, a desolate plateau region with an average height of 3,350 to 3,900 m, bordered on the W in Chile by the Cordillera Domeyko; the central part of the Andes in Bolivia covers approx two-fifths of the country in an elevated plateau, or *altiplano*, of 3,000 to 3,600 m and encloses L Poopó and L Titicaca (part of which is in Peru); the main range in Bolivia is the Cordillera Real, with peaks at Ancohuma (6,388 m), Illimani (6,402 m) and Illampu (6,485 m); the Andes in Bolivia also split into E and W mountain ranges, the Cordillera Oriental and Occidental (the latter being a continuation of the western volcanoes of Peru, and containing Bolivia's highest peak, the Nevado Sajama, 6,542 m); from Bolivia the Andes extend NW to travel the length of Peru in many separate ranges; these include the Cordillera Oriental in the SE; the Cordillera Occidental along the coast; the Cordillera de Carabaya (SE Peru, an extension of Bolivia's Cordillera Real) and Cordillera Huayhuash (in central Peru, N of Lima, forming a watershed between the Marañón and the Pacific streams); the highest peaks in Peru include Huascarán (6,768 m), Coropuna (6,425 m), Auzangate (6,394 m), Ampato (6,310 m) and Salcantay (6,271 m); in Ecuador, under the name of Cordillera Real, the Andes system narrows and runs nearly due N to the Colombian border; the highest peaks of Ecuador, many of which are active, include Chimborazo (6,310 m), Cotopaxi (5,896 m), Cayambe (5,790 m), Antisana (5,704 m); in Colombia the Andes spread out into 3 great ranges, the Cordillera Occidental near the coast; the Cordillera Central, between the Cauca and Magdalena river valleys, and the Cordillera Oriental in the interior (this range extends into Venezuela as the Cordillera de Mérida); highest points in Colombia include Tolima (5,215 m), Huila (5,750 m) and Ruiz (5,399 m); the Andes continue NE into Venezuela as the Sierra Nevada (or Cordillera) de Mérida, rising to 5,007 m in the Pico Bolívar; in E Panama and NW Colombia is the connecting range of the Serraní del Darién, which is said to link the Andes with the Central American ranges and thus with the Sierra Madre and the Rocky Mountains of North America.

Andhra Pradesh *an-dra pru-daysh'*, state in S India; bounded E by the Bay of Bengal; pop(1981) 53,403,619; area 276,814 sq km; divided into 23 administrative dists; capital Hyderabad; Andhra was constituted a separate state on 1 Oct 1853, on its partition from Madras; in Nov 1956 the Telanganga area of the former Hyderabad state was added to the region; in Apr 1960 parts of the Chingleput and Salem dists of Madras were transferred to Andhra Pradesh in exchange for a section of Chittoor dist; the state has a unicameral Legislative Assembly with 295 seats; the main agricultural crops are sugar cane, groundnuts, cotton, rice and tobacco; chief industries include textile manufacturing, sugar-milling, chemicals, cement, fertilizer, paper, carpets, woodcrafts, natural gas (Reyzole), oil refining and shipbuilding (Vishakhapatnam); events: Sankrant (Jan), Ugadi (April) and Chaturthi (Aug-Sept).

Andikíthira *un-dik-ee'thee-ru*, 35 52N 25 18E, Greek island in the Mediterranean Sea, between Pelopónnisos and Kríti (Crete); area 20 sq km; Potamós is the main settlement.

Andina *an-dee'na*, mountainous region of W Argentina comprising the provs of Catamarca, La Rioja, Mendoza, San Juan and Neuquén; bordering Chile these provs are traversed N-S by the Andes which rise to 6,960 m at Aconcagua; area 523,203 sq km; pop(1980) 2,277,988.

Andizhan *an-dyi-zhahn'*, ANDIJAN, 40 48N 72 23E, pop(1983) 247,000, capital city of Andizhanskaya oblast, E Uzbekskaya SSR, Soviet Union; in the fertile Fergana plain, surrounded on all sides by mountain ranges; the city was destroyed by an earthquake in 1902 but was soon rebuilt; railway; economy: electrotechnical industries, cotton-ginning, vegetable oil, machinery, footwear, knitwear, and clothing; there are deposits of oil and gas in the city.

Andorra or in full **the Valleys of Andorra** *an-do'ra*, VALLS D'ANDORRA (Cat), VALLÉE D'ANDORRE (Fr), official name Principality of Andorra, PRINCIPAT D'ANDORRA, a small, semi-independent, neutral state on the S slopes of the central Pyrenees between France and Spain; the border with Spain is 36.6 km long and with France 63.7 km; timezone GMT +1; area 468 sq km; pop(1982) 39,940; capital Andorra la Vella which is 613 km from Madrid, 208 km from Barcelona, 882 km from Paris and 757 km from Marseille; the language of the country is Catalan but French and Spanish are also spoken; French francs and Spanish pesetas are the accepted currency and the national budget is expressed in pesetas; membership of UNESCO.

Physical description. Andorra is a mountainous country with altitudes ranging from 2,946 m at Coma Pedrosa to 840 m at the confluence of the Valira and Runer rivers; it occupies two valleys (del Norte and del Orient) of the R Valira which flows S to join the R Segre at Seo de Urgel in Spain.

Climate. Winters are cold but dry and sunny, with the lowest average monthly rainfall (34 mm) in Jan and the average daily temperatures between Dec and Feb lying between a max of 6°C and a min of −1°C. The midsummer months are slightly drier than spring and autumn.

Government and constitution. Claiming to be one of the oldest states in Europe, Andorra has been under the joint protection of France and Spain since 1278; the Co-Princes of the Principality are the President of France and the Bishop of Urgel who hold legislative and juridical powers and represent the state internationally; the Co-Princes are represented by their respective *Veguers* and by Episcopal and French *Batlles* (civil magistrates) with responsibility for law and order and for overall administration policy. By decree of these representatives, one government was established in Andorra on 15 Jan 1981. The Consell General de Les Valls (General Council) appoints the Head of the Government, and he in turn designates the members of his government of four councillors; these four councillors are elected from each of the seven parishes (*parròquies*) to the General Council. Each parish is administered by a *Comú*.

Natural resources. Since 1929 hydroelectric power has been developed on the two arms of the R Valira (30,000 kW capacity in 1983); over half of the country's electricity production is exported; potatoes are produced in the highlands and tobacco in the valleys. Forest land (pine, fir, oak, birch, box-tree) covers 41% of Andorra, pasture 44% and agricultural land 6.5%.

Economy. There is no restriction on currency exchange and there are neither direct taxes nor value-added taxes; these factors favour imports and low prices. The economy is largely based on tourism, commerce, tobacco, construction and forestry; in recent years there have also been considerable developments in the textile, publishing, leather, mineral water and furniture industries alongside traditional cigar and cigarette production. The mountain slopes have been developed for skiing at 5 resorts which have among them 37 km of ski runs; an estimated 8 million tourists visit Andorra each year.

Transport. There are airports at La Seu-Andorra and at La Seo de Urgel in Spain; the road into the valleys from Spain is open all year round, and that from France is closed occasionally in winter; there are 186 km of road in Andorra; there are coach connections to railway termini at L'Hospitalet, La Tour de Carol, Puigcerda and Lleida.
Administrative divisions. Andorra is divided into 7 parishes (*parròquies*) as follows:

Parish	*pop(1982)*
Andorra la Vella	15,698
Canillo	794
Encamp	4,558
Escaldes	10,758
La Massana	2,705
Ordino	780
Sant Julià	4,647

Andorra la Vella *-vel'ya*, ANDORRA LA VIEJA (Sp), ANDORRE LA VIELLE (Fr), pop(1982) 15,698, one of the seven parishes of the Principality of Andorra with a capital town of the same name located on the E side of the Pic d'Enclar (2,317 m), 613 km NE of Madrid; alt 1,029 m; airports at La Seu-Andorra and at Seo de Urgel in Spain.

Andover *an'dō-vėr*, 51 13N 1 28W, pop(1981) 30,932, town in Test Valley dist, Hampshire, S England; 21 km NW of Winchester; railway; economy: printing, engineering.

Andropov, formerly RYBINSK (-1984), 58 03N 38 50E, pop(1983) 247,000, river port and manufacturing town in Yaroslavskaya oblast, European Rossiyskaya, Soviet Union; extends 22 km along both banks of the R Volga, just below the Rybinsk dam and reservoir; one of the oldest trading and industrial settlements on the R Volga; named after president Andropov; railway; economy: manufacture of printing presses, road-building machines, snow-ploughs, aircraft engines, and river vessels.

An'dros, island in the W Bahamas, W of New Providence I, on the Great Bahama Bank; largest island in the Bahamas; pop(1980) 8,397; area 5,955 sq km; chief towns are on the E coast and include Mars Bay, Moxey Town, Andros Town and Morgan's Bluff; the W shore is a long, low, barren bank.

Án'dros, northernmost island of the Kikládhes, Greece, in the Aegean Sea, between Évvoia and Tínos; area 380 sq km; length 40 km; length of coastline 177 km; chief town is Ándros on the E coast; there are bathing beaches at Batsí and Gávrion; rises to 994 m in the centre of the island.

Andujar *an-doo'har*, 38 03N 4 05W, pop(1981) 34,946, city in Jaén prov, Andalucia, S Spain; on the R Guadalquivir, 75 km E of Córdoba; railway; airfield; economy: timber, furniture, pottery, mineral springs.

Anécho *a-nay'chō*, 6 17N 1 40E, pop(1977) 13,300, town in Maritime region, S Togo, W Africa; 44 km E of Lomé; former slave trading town and capital of Togo under the Germans and French; noted for its German colonial houses; railway.

Anega'da, pop(1980) 169, island of the British Virgin Islands in the Lesser Antilles chain of the E Caribbean; 40 km NE of Tortola Island; a flat island surrounded by reefs; area 34 sq km.

Aneto, Pico de *pee'kō thay an-ay'tō*, 42 37N 0 40E, highest peak of the Pyrenees mts, rising to 3,404 m in Huesca prov, NE Spain.

Angara *un-gu-ra'*, river in Irkutskaya oblast and Krasnoyarskiy kray, SE Siberian Rossiyskaya, Soviet Union; a SW outlet of the Ozero Baykal (L Baikal); flows NNW past Irkutsk and Bratsk, then turns W at Kata to join the R Yenisey 56 km SSE of Yeniseysk; length 1,779 km; drainage basin area 1,039,000 sq km; a constant discharge of large volumes of water and constricted, steep-sided valley slopes cut into resistant rocks render the river particularly suitable for hydroelectric power generation; there are dams and power stations at Irkutsk (1958), Bratsk (1961), and Ust'ilimsk; the river is navigable between Irkutsk and Bratsk; there are iron, coal, and gold deposits in the Angara basin; chief tributaries include the Irkut, Belaya, Iya, Kova, Mura, and Chuna rivers.

Angarsk *un-garsk'*, 52 31N 103 55E, pop(1983) 251,000, town in Irkutskaya oblast, Rossiyskaya, Soviet Union; at the junction of the Kitoi and Angara rivers, 50 km NW of Irkutsk; one of Siberia's youngest towns, established in 1949; it has one of the highest birthrates in the country; a station on the Trans-Siberian railway; economy: woodworking, clothing, oil refining, chemicals, plastics, construction materials, electromechanical plant; monuments: Palace of Culture (1955), House of Communications.

Angel Falls, 5 57N 62 33W, waterfall in Bolívar state, SE Venezuela, South America; on an affluent of the Río Caroní; drops from a plateau in the Guiana Highlands; the highest waterfall in the world with a total drop of 979 m; named after the US aviator, Jimmy Angel, who crashed nearby in 1937.

Angeles, Los *lōs an-KHe'lays*, 37 28S 72 21W, pop(1982) 74,899, capital of Bío-Bío prov, Bío-Bío, central Chile; railway; economy: set in a wine, fruit and timber district.

Angeles, Los *los an'jé-leez*, 34 04N 118 15W, pop(1980) 2,966,850, seaport capital of Los Angeles county, California, United States; founded in 1781 on a Spanish grant; originally called Nuestra Señora Reina de Los Angeles; captured by Commodore Stockton of the US Navy in 1846; incorporated as a town in 1850; Los Angeles grew after the arrival of the Southern Pacific Railroad and the discovery of oil nearby in 1894; the city has expanded, absorbing towns, villages and independent cities such as Santa Monica, Beverly Hills, Culver City and Redondo Beach; 5 universities; railway; 3 airports (Los Angeles, Long Beach, Santa Clara); the city has a harbour on San Pedro Bay, 40 km S of the city centre; economy: military and civil aircraft, machinery, petroleum products, electronic equipment, glass, chemicals, oil refining, fish canning and distributing; Los Angeles harbour ships oranges, grain and dairy products; Hollywood, a district of Los Angeles, is a major centre of the American film and television industry; monuments: Los Angeles County Museum of Art; the 28-storey City Hall; Old Mission Church (c.1818), now a museum; La Brea tar pits; the Hollywood Bowl; Hollywood Wax Museum; Universal Film Studios; Disneyland.

Ångermanälven *ong'-er-man-el-fen*, ANGERMAN (Eng), river in central Sweden, rising in the Kjölen Mts; flows SE and S through Västerbotten and Västernorrland counties past Vilhelmina, Sollefteå and Kramfors; discharges into Gulf of Bothnia 16 km NE of Härnösand; length 450 km, navigable length 50 km; course marked by cataracts and waterfalls, source of hydroelectric power.

Angers *ã-zhay*, JULIOMAGNUS (anc), 47 30N 0 35W, pop(1982) 141,143, capital of Maine-et-Loire dept, Pays de la Loire region, S France; on the R Mayenne above its junction with the R Loire; bishopric; railway; formerly capital of Anjou prov; economy: centre of Anjou wine trade and the production of the celebrated Cointreau liqueur, electrical machinery; monuments: St Maurice cathedral, 13th-c château and museums with interesting art treasures, especially tapestries; event: Festival of Dramatic Art (June) in the castle.

Angkor *ahng-kor'*, 13 26N 103 50E, Khmer ruins 6 km N of Siem Reap, to the N of Tonlé Sap (lake), NW Cambodia; extends over an area of 107 sq km which was designated a national park in 1925; includes the ruins of the ancient capital, Angkor Thom; it is moated and surrounded by a square wall, with broad avenues leading to the Bayon or temple; the Royal palace and other temples are decorated with stone carvings which depict Khmer and Hindu life; Angkor Wat (temple) is the best preserved monument of Khmer art and is dedicated to the god Vishnu; Angkor complex was completed in the 12th century after the building of Angkor Wat; abandoned in 1443 as the capital in favour of Phnom Penh; the complex was discovered in 1860 amidst thick jungle.

Anglesey *ang'gl-see*, Wales. See Ynys Môn.

Angmagssalik *ahng-mahg'sa-lik*, 65 35N 38 00W, settlement and trading post on the E coast of Greenland, just below the Arctic Circle; used as an air base during World War II; Mt Forel (3,360 m) rises to the N.

Angol', 37 48S 72 43W, pop(1982) 32,029, capital of Malleco prov, La Araucanía, Chile; SSE of Concepción; railway; founded by Valdivia in 1552; destroyed by Indians 7 times and rebuilt; monuments: the Dillman Bullock regional museum contains stone-age Indian artefacts; the Vergel experimental fruit-growing station is worth seeing; 35 km W is the Parque Nacional Nahuelbuta.

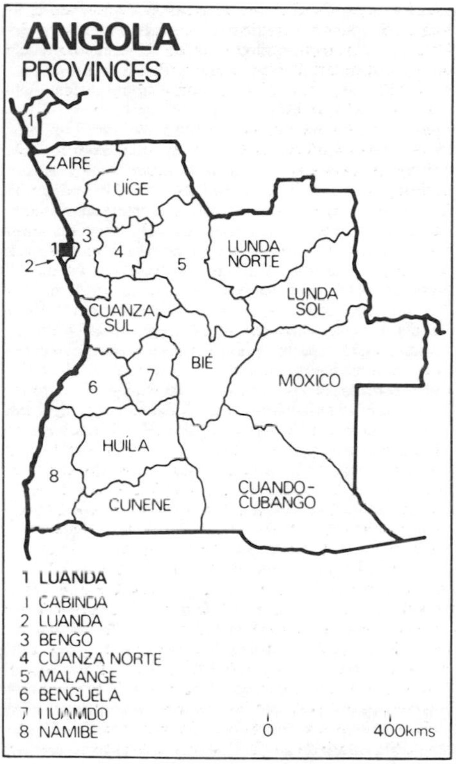

Angola *ang-gō'la*, official name People's Republic of Angola, REPÚBLICA POPULAR DE ANGOLA (Port), a republic of SW Africa bounded S by Namibia, E by Zambia and N by Zaire, with the separate prov of Cabinda enclosed by the Congo; timezone GMT +1; area 1,245,790 sq km; pop(1984e) 7,770,000; capital Luanda; chief towns Huambo, Benguela, Lobito, Namibe (Moçâmedes), Cabinda, Malanje and Lubango; major ethnic groups include the Bakongo, the Mbundu, the Ovimbundu, the Lunda-Tchokwe, the Nganguela, the Nyaneka-Humbe, the Herero and the Ambo; there are about 100 sub-groups; despite a major exodus of Europeans during 1974-75 following independence there remain approximately 30,000 Europeans (mainly Portuguese); 68% are Roman Catholic and 20% Protestant; the official language is Portuguese; Bantu dialects also spoken include Umbundu (38%), Kimbundu (27%), Lunda (13%) and Kikongo (11%); the unit of currency is the kwanza of 100 lewi; national holiday 11 Nov (Independence Day); membership of AfDB, FAO, G-77, GATT (de facto), ICAO, IFAD, ILO, IMO, INTELSAT, ITU, NAM, OAU, SADCC, UN, UNESCO, UNICEF, UPU, WFTU, WHO and WMO.

Physical description. Angola has a narrow coastal plain which widens in the N towards the delta of the R Congo. Inland lies a high plateau with a mean elevation of 1,200 m and with peaks rising to 1,500 m in the S. Within the central massif of the Bié Plateau is the highest point in Angola, Serro Môco (2,619 m). To the N and E of the high plateau the land slopes gradually towards the basins of the Congo and Zambezi rivers. Numerous rivers rise in the plateau, the most important of which are the Cubango, Cuito, Cuando, Cuilo, and Cuango. Few of these rivers are navigable for any great length in Angola.

Climate. Much of Angola experiences a tropical plateau climate with a single wet season between Oct and March and a long dry season. Above 1,500 m temperatures are more temperate, frost can occur and the dry season is shorter. Huambo (alt 1,700 m) is representative of this upland region with an average annual rainfall of 1,450 mm and average max daily temperatures ranging between 24°C and 29°C. On the coast both temperature and rainfall are much reduced by the cold Benguela current which flows S-N along the shore. This region is semi-desert as far N as Luanda, with a gradual increase in rainfall northward. The extreme dryness of the S is well represented by Namibe (Moçâmedes) with an average annual rainfall of 55 mm and average max daily temperatures ranging between 22°C and 29°C, but in the far N average annual rainfall reaches 600 mm.

History, government and constitution. The Portuguese explorer, Diogo Cão, was the first European to explore Angola when he landed at the mouth of the R Congo in 1483. The area became a Portuguese colony and remained so until its independence 5 centuries later. For a brief period between 1641 and 1648 the Dutch seized Luanda and Benguela. Prior to the abolition of slavery an estimated 3,000,000 Angolan slaves were sent to Brazil in the space of 3 centuries. It was during the Berlin West Africa Congress of 1884-85 that Angola's boundaries were formally defined. In 1951 Angola became an Overseas Province of Portugal but prolonged internal revolt led to a military coup in Portugal in 1974 and the granting of full independence in 1975. Since the collapse of the first government of independent Angola three internal factions have engaged the country in civil war - the Marxist MPLA (Popular Movement for the Liberation of Angola), UNITA (the National Union for the Total Independence of Angola) and the FNLA (National Front for the Liberation of Angola). Between Aug 1975 and Dec 1976 the USA supplied arms to the FNLA and UNITA and at the request of the MPLA Cuban combat troops began arriving in substantial numbers in 1976. In Aug 1975 South African forces occupied an area along the Angola-Namibia frontier in order to protect a hydroelectric station. They withdrew from combat in 1976, but were again active in S Angola between Aug 1981 and Jan 1984. Angola has also given refuge to members of the Namibian independence movement SWAPO (South West African Peoples' Organization) who have launched attacks on Namibia from Angolan territory. Similarly, in 1977-78 the Front for the Liberation of the Congo (FLNC) launched 2 raids into Zaire from Angolan territory. Though civil war has continued for over a decade Angola officially remains a one-party state, governed by a president (also head of state) who exercises power via an executive council of appointed ministers (about 20) and a National People's Assembly of 203 elected and 20 appointed members.

Economy. Despite years of civil war Angola is largely self-sufficient in food crops such as cassava, corn, vegetables, plantains and bananas. In addition coffee, cotton, sisal, timber, tobacco, palm oil and maize are exported. Angola has reserves of diamonds, manganese, iron ore, gypsum, asphalt, limestone, salt and phosphates, but the extraction and refining of oil (215,000 barrels per day in 1984), has accounted for over 75% of the country's recent export earnings. Most of the oil reserves are located off the coast of Cabinda prov in the Kambala and Livuite fields. The principal industrial activities are oil refining, food processing, and the manufacture of textiles, cement, paper and pulp. Angola's main trading partners are Portugal, Cuba, West Germany, the USA, the UK, Canada and Japan.

Communications. There is a total road network of 73,828 km in Angola of which 8,577 km is surfaced. The railway system extends to 3,189 km with main lines from Lobito S to Benguela and then E via Huambo to Zaire; from Namibe (Moçâmedes) E past Lubango, Quipungo, Kuvango terminating at Menongue, with a branchline between Lubango and Chiange (S); from Luanda NE to Caxito and E to Malanje, with a branchline to Dondo (S). There is a short line between Gunza (Porto Amboium) on the coast and Gabela. There is an airport at Luanda and airfields at Cabinda, M'Banza Congo, Damba, Ambriz, Malanje, Saurimo, Chitato, Luau, Luena, Lobito, Benguela, Huambo, Kuito, Namibe and Ondjiva.

Administrative divisions. Angola is divided into the 18 provs of Cabinda, Cuanza Norte, Cuanza Sul, Cuando-Cubango, Cunene, Benguela, Bié, Bengo, Huambo, Huíla, Luanda, Lunda Norte, Lunda Sul, Malanje, Moxico, Namibe, Uige and Zaïre.

Angoulême *ã-gool-em,* ICULISMA (anc), 45 39N 0 10E, pop(1982) 50,151, industrial town and capital of Charente dept, Poitou-Charentes region, W France; on R Charente within ancient ramparts; bishopric; railway; economy: brandy, paper and felt slippers, motors, alternators, gears, engineering; monument: 12th-c St Pierre cathedral.

Angoumois *a-goo-mwa,* former prov of W France, now occupying most of Charente and part of Dordogne depts; the former capital was Angoulême.

Angra do Heroísmo *an'gra do ay-ro-ees'mo* ('bay of heroism'), dist in the Portuguese autonomous region of the Azores; situated in the central Azores archipelago, E Atlantic; includes the volcanic islands of Terceira, São Jorge and Graciosa Is; divided into 5 councils and 43 parishes; area, 703 sq km; the chief town is Angra do Heroísmo; pop(1981) 75,010; its name commemorates the resistance to the Miguelists (1828-32); the most severe earthquakes took place in 1614, 1800, 1801, 1841 and 1980; the islands are famous for their therapeutic hot sulphur springs and the fertile land produces cereals, vegetables, broad beans, kidney beans, potatoes, chestnuts, grapes and oranges.

Angra do Heroísmo, 38 40N 27 14W, pop(1981) 18,294, fortified chief town and seaport of Angra do Heroísmo dist, Portuguese autonomous region of the Azores; at the head of a deep bay on the S coast of Terceira I; bishopric of the Azores, founded in 1464, it was until 1832 the capital of the Azores; exports wine, fruit, flax and grain, manufactures tobacco and soap and distils alcohol; airport at Lajes; events: festival of Espírito Santo after Easter; Cidade festival in June and festival of Our Lady of Serreta in Sept.

Anguilla *an-gwil'a,* most northerly of the Leeward Is, E Caribbean, 112 km NW of St Kitts and 8 km N of St Martin; a British dependent territory; timezone GMT −4; the unit of currency is the East Caribbean dollar; area 155 sq km; capital The Valley; other main settlements South Hill, The Quarter Stony Ground; main seaports Road Bay and Blowing Point; pop(1974) 6,500; the dominant faith is Christianity; English is the official and spoken language; airport (Wallblake).

Physical description and climate. The territory of Anguilla also includes Sombrero I (where there is a lighthouse station) and several other offshore islets and cays. Anguilla I is a low lying, coral island covered in scrub. The climate is tropical with a low and erratic rainfall ranging from 550 mm to 1,250 mm per annum. The hurricane season is from July to October.

History, government and constitution. English settlers from St Kitts colonized the island in 1650. From 1825, Anguilla became more closely associated with St Kitts and was ultimately incorporated in the colony of St Kitts-Nevis-Anguilla. On 19 Dec 1980 Anguilla was formally separated from the colony though a *de facto* separation had been in force since 1971. Anguilla is now a separately administered dependency of the UK. According to the 1982 constitution, executive power is vested in the governor who is appointed by the British sovereign. The Legislative Assembly consists of 7 elected members, 2 nominated members, and 2 official members.

Economy. The tourist industry has developed rapidly in recent years with plans to construct international standard hotels. Fishing is also important to the economy with lobster-farming receiving considerable investment. The lobsters are exported mainly to Puerto Rico. Agriculture is limited by the low rainfall but some crops are grown, notably pigeon peas, corn, and sweet potatoes. Salt, produced by natural evaporation in 2 salt ponds, is exported mainly to Trinidad.

Angus, district in Tayside region, E Scotland; pop(1981) 93,038; area 2,023 sq km; a former Scottish county; chief town Forfar.

Anhui *an-whay,* ANHWEI, prov in E China; bordered W by Henan and Hubei provs, N by Shandong and Jiangsu provs, E by Jiangsu and Zhejiang provs and S by Jiangxi prov (along the Chang Jiang river); crossed in the S half of the prov by the Chang Jiang river valley and lakes leading onto the river and in the N by the Huai He river valley; Huaibei Plain, part of the North China Plain, is situated in the N of Anhui; the prov contains several large lakes including Chengdong Hu and Wabu Hu which lie to the NW of Hefei; to the SE of Hefei in the centre of the prov is Chao Hu lake (area 782 sq km); Anhui consists mostly of plains and hills which rise SW into the Dabie Shan mountains; pop(1982) 49,665,724; area 139,900 sq km; capital Hefei; principal town Huainan; economy: agriculture, mining.

Anhwei, province in E China. See Anhui.

Anjalankoski *ahn'yal-an-ko'ski,* 60 52N 26 50E, pop(1982) 20,079, town in Kymi prov, SE Finland; established in 1975; railway.

Anjou *an'joo, ã-zhoo,* 45 36N 73 36W, pop(1981) 37,346, town in S Québec, SE Canada; a N suburb of Montréal; situated between the Rivière des Prairies and the St Lawrence river.

Anjou *ã-zhoo,* former prov in the Paris Basin of NW France, now occupying the dept of Maine-et-Loire and small parts of Indre-et-Loire, Mayenne and Sarthe; former capital was Angers; Henry II of England, first of the Plantagenets or Angevins, was son of Geoffrey Plantagenet, Count of Anjou; Anjou gave a line of kings to Sicily and Naples.

Anjouan *ãzh-wã',* JOHANNA, NZWAMI, 12 15S 44 25E, pop(1980) 148,000, island of the Comoros group in the Mozambique Channel; situated between Grande Comore and Mayotte; area 424 sq km; chief town and port Mutsamudu; the highest peak is Mt Nyingui.

Ankara *ang'ka-ra,* mountainous prov in Turkey; pop(1980) 2,854,689; area 30,715 sq km; capital Ankara; the R Sakarya forms part of its W boundary.

Ankara, ANCYRA, ANGORA (anc), 39 55N 32 50E, pop(1980) 1,901,282, capital city of Ankara prov and the Republic of Turkey, W central Turkey; on a tributary of the R Ova, at the centre of the Anatolian plateau; administrative, commercial, and cultural centre; 2nd largest city in Turkey; formerly an important location on the caravan route from Istanbul to the E; government was transferred here from Istanbul in 1923; university (1946); Hacettepe University (1967); technical university (1956); railway; airport; economy: textiles, mohair, leather, cement.

Ann Arbor, 42 17N 83 45W, pop(1980) 107,966, county seat of Washtenaw county, SE Michigan, United States; 57 km W of Detroit; founded in 1824; university (1841); railway; economy: cameras, computers, scientific equipment and car parts.

'Annaba *an'a-ba,* formerly BÔNE (Fr), 36 55N 7 47E, pop(1982) 340,517, seaport in 'Annaba dept, N Algeria, N Africa; on the Mediterranean coast, W of Tunis; nearby are the remains of Hippo Regius, an ancient Phoenician and Roman port; airport; economy: iron ore, steel.

Annan, 54 59N 3 16W, pop(1981) 8,314, capital of Annandale and Eskdale dist, Dumfries and Galloway, S

Scotland; on the R Annan, 25 km SE of Dumfries; railway.

Annap'olis, 38 59N 76 30W, pop(1980) 31,740, capital of state in Anne Arundel county, central Maryland, United States; port on the S bank of the R Severn; named after Princess (later Queen) Anne in 1695; railway; economy: business and shipping centre; US Naval Academy (1845); site of the statehouse where the treaty that ended the American War of Independence was ratified in 1784.

Annapurna-Himal *an-na-poor'na-hi-mahl'*, mountain massif of the central Himalayas, Nepal, central Asia; Annapurna I was first climbed in 1950 by Maurice Herzog's French expedition and was at that date the highest mountain climbed by man; approx 56 km long, the range includes Annapurna I (8,091 m), Annapurna II (7,937 m), Annapurna III (7,556 m), Annapurna IV (7,525 m), Gangapurna (7,455 m), Annapurna South (7,219 m), Glacier Dome (7,193 m), Nilgiri East (7,134 m), Nilgiri West (7,055 m), Machhapuchhre (7,993 m), Lamjung Himal (6,931 m), Hiunchuli (6,441 m) and Mardi Himal (5,127 m); the range encloses a high mountain valley; Annapurna region is part of the Pokhara trekking region and is recommended for trekking in all but the coldest months, giving the trekker splendid views of snow peaks and glaciers.

Annecy *an-see*, 45 55N 6 08E, pop(1982) 51,993, industrial town and capital of Haute-Savoie dept, Rhône-Alpes region, E France; in the foothills of the French Alps on the N shore of the Lac d'Annecy; bishopric; railway; economy: textiles, watches, paper, bearings; the old quarter close to the lake has narrow streets with arcades and is dissected by canals; its aspect and climate have made the town a popular resort; it is on the route to the Little St Bernard and Mt Cenis passes.

Annecy, Lac d', lake in Haute-Savoie dept, Rhône-Alpes region, E France; area 27 sq km; located in the French Alps with the town of Annecy at the N end and the resort of Talloires on the E shore.

Annil el Azraq, CENTRAL, region of central Sudan, NE Africa; area 53,716 sq km; pop(1983) 4,012,543; chief town Wadi Medani; crossed by the Blue Nile (Bahr el Azraq).

Anniston, 33 39N 85 50W, pop(1980) 29,523, county seat of Calhoun county, NE Alabama, United States; 90 km ENE of Birmingham; railway; economy: manufacturing, including textiles, microwave ovens, factory-built homes, and vaccines; event: Shakespeare Festival (summer).

Áno Liósia, 38 05N 23 42E, pop(1981) 16,862, town in Attikí nomo (dept), Sterea Ellás-Évvoia region, Greece; an outer suburb of Athínai (Athens).

Anshan, AN-SHAN, 41 05N 122 58E, pop(1984e) 1,258,600, town in Liaoning prov, NE China; organized mining and smelting began here c.100 BC; iron ore deposits were rediscovered by the Japanese in the early 1900s; railway; economy: site of China's largest iron and steel complex (producing 25% of the country's annual output of steel), agricultural machinery, construction materials, chemicals, textiles, porcelain, electrical appliances; monuments: Qianlian Shan (Thousand Lotuses Hill), a 10th-c Buddhist hermitage, named after the lotus-like cloud formations which surround the hill-top; Eryijiu (19 Feb) park in the E of the city, named after the date in 1948 when the People's Liberation Army finally gained control of Anshan; approx 10 km SE of Anshan is the Tanggangzi hot springs park, once a fashionable resort for the wealthy, the park now contains a sanatorium for steelworkers.

Antaibao *an-tī-bow*, 35 00N 111 20E, pop(1986e) 20,000, a new industrial town and major opencast coal mining development on the open loess plateau of S Shanxi prov, NE central China; near the border with Henan prov, NE of Xi'an; the town has developed from a small village noted for its cave dwellings since the opening of the mine in 1985; the mine is administered jointly by Chinese and US companies; airfield.

Antakya *an-ta-kyah'*, HATAY, ANTIOCH *an'ti-ok*, ANTIOCHIA (anc), 36 12N 36 10E, pop(1980) 94,942, capital of Hatay prov, S Turkey; near the Mediterranean, 90 km W of Ḥalab (Aleppo) in Syria; founded in 300 BC, the city rivalled Alexandria; capital of Syria until 64 BC; centre of early Christianity; destroyed by earthquake in 526 AD; economy: tobacco, olives, cotton, grain.

Antalya *an-tal'ya*, maritime prov in SW Turkey, bounded S by the Mediterranean Sea; pop(1980) 748,706; area 20,591 sq km; capital Antalya.

Antalya, ADALIA, ATTALEIA (anc), 36 54N 30 42E, pop(1980) 173,501, seaport capital of Antalya prov, SW Turkey; on a narrow coastal plain of the Mediterranean Sea; founded in the 2nd century BC; nearby are deposits of chrome and manganese; airport; economy: food processing and trade in agriculture and forest produce; event: film and art festival in Oct.

Antananarivo *an-ta-nan-a-ree'vō*, TANANARIVE, TANANARIVO ('city of the thousand'), 18 52S 47 30E, pop(1985e) 662,585, capital of Madagascar; situated on a basalt ridge overlooking the Betsimitatra and Laniera plains in the E central part of the island in a prov of the same name; alt 1,245-1,469 m; known as Antananarivo since 1975, the city is divided into the upper and lower towns; university (1955); casinos; Mohamasina sports stadium and racecourses; Ivato airport (12 km from city); rail connections with Toamasina and Antsirabe; economy: textiles, tobacco, food processing; monuments: Queen's palace, Ambohitsorahitra palace, prime ministers' tombs, museum of art and archaeology, Zoma market.

Antarctic Circle, imaginary line on the surface of the Earth at 66 30S, marking the southernmost point at which the sun can be seen during the summer solstice and the northernmost point at which the midnight sun can be seen in S polar regions.

Antarctica *ant-ark'tik-a*, S Polar continent nearly 15.5 mn sq km in extent, surrounded by an ice-filled ring of ocean waters in which are scattered island groups partly of polar and partly of sub-polar character. Apart from the Graham Land peninsula and the islands to the N the continent lies S of 65° S, almost entirely within the Antarctic Circle. In most places along the 22,400 km coastline, the shore reaches the sea in high ice cliffs which rise steeply at a very short distance inland. The most southerly shores are near the 78th parallel in the Ross and Weddell Sea. The continent is divided into Greater and Lesser Antarctica which are separated by the Transantarctic Mts which rise to 5,140 at Vinson Massif, 4,528 m at Mt Kirkpatrick and 4,351 m at Mt Markham. The continent is uninhabited. There are no flowering plants, grasses or large mammals, but species of algae, moss, lichen and sea plankton provide food for fish, birds, whales and seals. Baleen whales, which spend part of the summer in the zone 480 km N of the pack ice, have been extensively exploited and have declined in numbers since the peak fishing seasons of the early 1930s; the shrimp-like krill are also fished by Russian and Japanese fishermen in Antarctic waters. Significant scientific exploration of the continent has taken place since the 1890s following the expedition of Borchgevrink (1899) which was the first to establish a winter base in Antarctica. The S Pole was first reached by Amundsen in Dec 1911 a month before the fateful expedition of Capt Robert Scott who died with 3 other members of his team on the return trip from the pole.

Glaciation. The surface of the Antarctic continent consists almost entirely of an ice sheet with an average depth of 1,500 m overlying rock. The form of glaciation is that of continental inland ice which moves slowly towards its periphery, pushing long tongues into the sea and creating shelf ice over large areas. Drift ice develops along the whole coastline.

Icebergs. Icebergs are found in large numbers in waters contiguous to the Antarctic continent. The size of bergs varies in the oceans bordering the continent and with the season. The largest bergs in Antarctic waters are of the tabular type, ranging in height from 10 to 60 m, and in length from a few hundred metres to 12 m.

Pack ice. The Antarctic pack ice is composed of (a) sea

ice frozen in the open sea, (b) detached fragments of fast ice formed along the coastline, and (c) disintegrated particles of land ice. The N limit of the pack ice is variable and the location of the extreme edge varies seasonally. During late winter and spring the edge extends to its most northerly limit. There is a wide difference in the range of movement of the pack in different longitudes. Except on the Pacific coast and the W portion of the Weddell Sea, it is probable that nearly all parts of the continental coast and the fixed shelf ice are free of pack ice at times in the late summer.

Climate. The wind system on the continent is caused by the vast high pressure area which overlies the Antarctic. Outward blowing winds prevail; and since the coast trends generally E-W, these winds, deviated to the left by the Earth's rotation, blow from the SE; on the W of the Ross Sea, where the coast trends N-S, for the same reason they blow from the SW. They are often of hurricane force, characterized by an absence of humidity and a rising temperature due to adiabatic conditions. Blizzards are very common in the Antarctic, but usually do not extend far out over the sea. They are rare during Nov, Dec and Jan, but are frequent during the autumn and winter months. Rain occurs frequently along the W coast of Graham Land and in N regions. The lowest temperature ever recorded on Earth was −88.3°C at the USSR Vostok Station.

Ownership. During International Geophysical Year (1957-58) 12 countries maintained 65 bases in Antarctica. An Antarctic Treaty was signed by these nations in 1959 in Washington. The treaty referred to the area S of 60° S, exclusive of the high seas, providing for international co-operation in scientific research, but prohibiting military operations, nuclear explosions and the disposal of radioactive waste. Territorial claims have been made by the UK (British Antarctic Territory), Norway (Dronning Maud Land), France (Terre Adélie), Australia (Enderby Land, Wilkes Land, George V Coast and part of Oates Coast), New Zealand (160° E to 150° W), Chile (90° W to 53° W) and Argentina (74° W to 25° W).

Antequera *an-tay-kay'ra*, ANTICARIA (anc), pop(1981) 35,171, city in Málaga prov, Andalucia, S Spain; near the R Guadalhorce, 62 km N of Málaga; railway; economy: textiles, sugar, grain; monuments: the castle was the first stronghold in the Kingdom of Granada to be recaptured from the Moors (1410); nearby are prehistoric dolmens or funerary chambers.

Antibes *ã-teeb*, ANTIPOLIS (anc), 43 35N 7 07E, pop(1982) 63,248, fishing port and fashionable resort on the Riviera, in Alpes-Maritimes dept, Provence-Alpes-Côte d'Azur region, SE France; facing Nice across a long bay; the town is best known for its luxurious villas and hotels sheltered by the pines of the Cap d'Antibes; a well-known flower-growing centre; at Golf-Juan, 3 km W of Antibes, Napoleon landed with 1,000 men on his return from Elba in March 1815; railway; economy: perfumes, flowers, olives, fruit, chocolates; monuments: a number of Roman remains and several museums, including the Musée Picasso which contains ceramics, drawings and paintings presented by Picasso after World War II.

Anti'gonish, 45 39N 62 00W, pop(1981) 18,110, town in Antigonish county, Nova Scotia; on George Bay; founded in 1784 by disbanded men of the Nova Scotia Regiment; St Francis Xavier University (1853).

Antigua *an-tee'ga*, island in the Leeward group of the Lesser Antilles, E Caribbean, 40 km S of Barbuda; area 280 sq km; rises to 470 m in the W; capital St John's.

Antigua *an-tee'gwa*, ANTIGUA GUATEMALA, 14 33N 90 42W, pop(1983e) 26,631, capital city of Sacatepéquez dept, S Guatemala, Central America; SW of Guatemala City; founded in 1543 by the Spanish after the earlier capital, Ciudad Vieja, was destroyed by flood; capital of the republic until it was largely destroyed by earthquake in 1773; the ancient city flourished in the 18th century with many churches, a university (1680), a printing press (founded 1660), and a reputed population of about 60,000; monument: cathedral (1534); events: Holy Week processions.

Antigua and Barbuda *bar-byoo'da*, group of 3 islands in the Leeward group of the Lesser Antilles, E Caribbean; timezone GMT −4; area 442 sq km; capital St John's; other main town Codrington; pop(1984e) 79,000; the people are almost entirely of African Negro descent; English is the official language; Christianity is the dominant religion; the unit of currency is the Eastern Caribbean dollar; membership of CARICOM, Commonwealth, G-77, ICAO, ILO, IMF, ISO, OAS, UN, UNESCO.

Physical description and climate. The 2 main islands in the group are Antigua (280 sq km) and Barbuda (161 sq km). Redonda (1 sq km) is an uninhabited rocky island

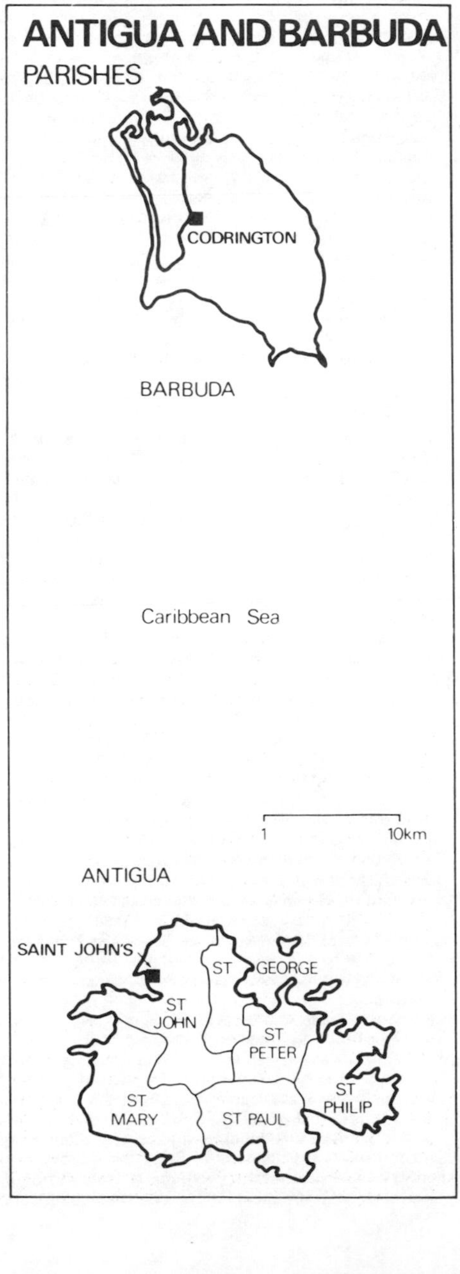

situated 40 km to the SW of Antigua. The W part of Antigua is composed of volcanic rock and rises to 470 m at Boggy Peak. Low lying limestone platforms occupy the E and N areas rising to no more than 153 m. Barbuda lies some 40 km N of Antigua. It is a flat coral island reaching only 44 m at its highest point with a large lagoon on its W side. The climate is tropical with temperatures ranging from 24°C in Jan to 27°C in Aug and Sept, and a mean annual rainfall of 1,000 mm. There is a hot season from May to Nov.

History, government and constitution. When Columbus landed on Antigua in 1493 he named it after the church of Santa Maria de la Antigua in Seville, Spain. English settlers colonized the island in 1632 and in 1667 it was formally ceded to Britain by the Treaty of Breda. Barbuda was colonized from Antigua in 1661. The 2 islands were administered as part of the Leeward Is Federation from 1871 until 1956. In 1967 Antigua became an associated state of the UK and independence was achieved on 1 Nov 1981. The 1981 Constitution provides for a governor and a bicameral legislature consisting of a 17-member senate and a 17-member house of representatives.

Economy. In 1981 tourism accounted for 40% of national income. It is the principal source of foreign exchange for the country with the USA its major market. Sugar was the major export earner until 1960 when prices fell dramatically. By 1972 production had virtually ceased. Attempts were made to revive the industry in 1980 to meet local demand.

Anti-Lebanon, mountain range on the Lebanon-Syria frontier. See Sharqi, Jebel esh.

Antilles *an-til'eez*, the whole of the West Indies except the Bahamas. A hypothetical island, Antilia, had figured in old sea charts as early at least as 1424; that name was applied in 1493 by Peter Martyr d'Anghiera to the West Indies. The Greater Antilles include Cuba, Jamaica, Hispaniola (Haiti and the Dominican Republic) and Puerto Rico; the Lesser Antilles are divided into the Windward Is to the S, the Leeward Islands to the N, and the Netherlands Antilles off the coast of Venezuela.

Antioch, city in Turkey. See Antakya.

Antioch *an'tee-ok*, 38 01N 121 48W, pop(1980) 42,683, city in Contra Costa county, W California, United States; on the San Joaquin river, 48 km ENE of Oakland; railway; economy: site of a power plant of the Central Valley Project.

Antioquia *an-tyō'kya*, mountainous dept in NW central Colombia, South America; extends along the Cauca valley; flanked by the Cordillera Central and the Cordillera Occidental; bounded W by the Río Atraro and E by the Río Magdalena; pop(1985) 3,720,025; area 63,612 sq km; capital Medellín.

Antisana *an-tee-sa'na*, 0 30S 78 13W, Andean volcano in Napo prov, N Ecuador, 48 km SE of Quito; height 5,704 m; the crater, which is still active, emits sulphurous gases; there is a village of the same name on its NW slopes.

Antofagasta *an-tō-fa-gas'ta*, region in N Chile; situated between the Andes and the Pacific Ocean, bordering with Argentina (E) and Bolivia (NE); comprises the provs of Tocopilla, El Loa and Antofagasta; largely an arid region including part of the Desierto de Atacama in the W and the Andean peaks of Cerro Pular, Volcán Llullaillaco and Volcán Azufre; watered by the Loa river; pop(1984) 333,900; area 125,253 sq km; capital Antofagasta; chief towns Tocopilla and Calama; economy: shipping and mining (the world's largest underground copper mine is situated at Chuquicamata, N of Calama).

Antofagasta, 23 38S 70 24W, pop(1982) 166,964, port and capital of Antofagasta prov, Antofagasta, Chile; largest city in northern Chile; developed as a result of mineral and agricultural trade with Europe in the 19th century; modern sports stadium at S end of the city; many fine public gardens and beaches; university (1956); railway; airport; economy: exports nitrates and copper; monuments: a Bolivian silver refinery dating from 1868; a huge anchor is set high in the mountains and was used as a navigational aid by shipping; geographical and archaeological museums; local holiday 19 June (Day of San Pedro, patron saint of the fishermen).

An'trim, AONTROIM (Gael), county in NE Northern Ireland; bounded W by Co Derry (Londonderry) along the R Bann, SW by Lough Neagh, S by Co Down along the R Lagan, N by the Atlantic Ocean and the North Channel and E by the Irish Sea; consists mainly of a basalt plateau rising in the N and E with the Antrim Mts; slopes gradually inland to Lough Neagh; major rivers include the Bann, Main, Bush and Lagan; the county includes the islands of Rathlin, the Skerries and the Maidens; the basalt rock formation, the Giant's Causeway, is situated on the N coast; pop(1981) 642,267; area 2,831 sq km; county town Belfast; principal towns Lisburn, Ballymena and Carrickfergus; economy: Irish linen, textiles, cattle and sheep raising, agriculture (potatoes, flax, oats); shipbuilding; Antrim is divided into 9 districts:

District	*area (sq km)*	*pop(1981)*
Antrim	563	44,384
Ballymena	638	54,426
Ballymoney	419	22,873
Belfast	140	295,223
Carrickfergus	87	28,458
Larne	338	28,929
Lisburn	444	82,091
Moyle	495	14,252
Newtownabbey	152	71,631

Antrim, 54 43N 6 13W, pop(1981) 22,342, town in Antrim dist, Antrim, NE Northern Ireland; on the NE shore of Lough Neagh, 22.5 km NW of Belfast; railway; economy: textiles (linen); monuments: Antrim's round tower, which is 27 m high and dates from c.900 AD, is one of the finest in Ireland; the ruins of Antrim Castle (built in 1662, extended in 1816 and seriously damaged by fire in 1922).

Antsirana'na, ANTSERANA ('the port'), formerly DIEGO-SUAREZ (Port), 12 19S 49 17E, pop(1978e) 48,000, port at the N end of the island of Madagascar beyond the Massif du Tsaratanana; chief town of a prov of the same name; originally named after 2 Portuguese admirals who discovered the harbour in the 16th century; formerly an important military base; the town has Arab, Indian and Pakistani quarters; the Ambre mountain nature reserve is nearby, and 75 km S is the sacred L Anivorano where offerings are made to crocodiles during Fijoroana ceremonies; airfield; difficult road access; economy: naval shipyard.

Antwerp, city in Belgium. See Antwerpen.

Antwerpen *ant'ver-pen* (Fr), ANT'WERP (Eng), prov of N Belgium, bordering the Netherlands; area 2,867 sq km; pop(1982) 1,571,092; drained by the R Schelde (Scheldt); comprises the 3 dists of Antwerpen, Mechelen and Turnhout; capital Antwerpen; chief towns Lier, Mechelen and Turnhout.

Antwerpen, dist of Antwerpen prov, Belgium; area 1,001 sq km; pop(1982) 916,780.

Antwerpen, ANVERS *ã-vayr*, 51 13N 4 25E, pop(1982) 183,025, capital city of Antwerpen dist, Antwerpen prov, N Belgium; on the right bank of the R Schelde (Scheldt), 88 km from its estuary with the North Sea; chief port of Belgium and 4th largest port of the world; world-famous centre of the diamond industry; chartered in 1291; centre of the medieval cloth trade with England; home of Rubens; its zoo is one of the most famous in the world; colonial university (1920); railway; economy: shipbuilding and repairing, oil refining, synthetic fibres, plastics, petrochemicals, agrochemicals, oils and fats, motor vehicles, automobile components, animal feedstuffs, foodstuffs, household machines, diamonds; monuments: cathedral of Our Lady (1352), largest Gothic church in Belgium; town hall (16th-c); church of St Jacob (15-16th-c).

Anuradhapura *an-a-rahd-e-poor'a*, 8 20N 80 25E,

pop(1981) 35,981, capital of Anuradhapura dist, North-Central prov, Sri Lanka; 205 km N of Colombo; Sri Lanka's first capital; founded in 4th century BC; according to the Mahavansa, the ancient Sinhala chronicle, the city was a model of town planning and was divided into precincts according to caste; monuments: Sri Mahabodhi Tree is allegedly the oldest tree in the world (2,200 years) and is all that remains of the Bo tree beneath which Buddha found Enlightenment (in 1966 enclosed in a golden railing); the Thuparama Dagaba is the oldest of Sri Lanka's shrines (*dagabas*), built to enshrine Buddha's collarbone, and owes its present bell shape to 1840s reconstruction.

Anvers, city in Belgium. See Antwerpen.

Anya'ma, 5 29N 4 04W, town in Abidjan dept, SE Ivory Coast, W Africa; NNW of Abidjan; railway.

Anyang *an-yang*, 37 23N 126 55E, pop(1983e) 291,919, town in Kyŏnggi prov, NW Korea; railway.

Anzoátegui *an-swa'tay-gee*, state in NE Venezuela; bounded N by the Caribbean and S by the Orinoco river; largely comprises *llanos* plain in the S and low lying coastal hills in the NE; pop(1980) 689,555; area 43,283 sq km; capital Barcelona.

Aomori *ow'mo-ree*, 40 50N 140 43E, pop(1980) 287,594, port capital of Aomori prefecture, Tōhoku region, N Honshū island, Japan; on the N coast, in Taradate-kaikyō Bay; railway; event: 2-7 Aug, Nebuta Festival, a parade with floats and dancers.

Aosta *ah-o'stah*, prov of Valle d'Aosta region, NW Italy; pop(1981) 112,353; area 3,263 sq km; capital Aosta.

Aosta, AOSTE (Fr), 45 43N 7 19E, pop(1981) 37,194, capital town of Aosta prov, Valle d'Aosta region, NW Italy; in the fertile valley of the R Dora Baltea, ringed by mountains; largely French-speaking; railway; important traffic junction for routes across the Alps; economy: ironworking industry, tourism; monuments: the old town is surrounded by well-preserved Roman walls, with 20 towers.

Aozou Strip *ow'zoo*, 100 km-wide strip of mountainous desert in Borkou-Ennedi-Tibesti prefecture, N Chad, N central Africa; disputed territory on the frontier with Libya who occupied the area in 1973; Libya's claim to Aozou is based on an unratified 1935 agreement between France and Italy; the area is rich in uranium and mineral deposits.

Apeldoorn *a'pel-dōrn*, 52 13N 5 57E, pop(1984e) 144,108, commercial city and municipality in Gelderland prov, E Netherlands; 27 km N of Arnhem, on the E edge of the Veluwe (a region of sandy woods and heathland, which rises to 110 m), between the Rhine, Ijssel and Eem rivers; a fashionable residential town with fine parks; railway; economy: metalworking, paper, textiles, chemicals, fishing nets, veal and veal products, computers; monument: Het Loo (1685), the royal country residence since the time of William of Orange, is 2 km N of the town.

Apennines, mountain range in Italy. See Appennino.

Aphrodisias, ancient city of Turkey. See Geyre.

Apia *a'pee-u*, 13 48S 171 45W, capital town of Western Samoa, on the N coast of Upolu I, in the SW Pacific Ocean; pop(1981) 33,000, a fast expanding cluster of villages; churches and trading companies line its waterfront.

Apo, Mount *ah'pō*, an active volcano and highest mountain in the Philippines, SW of Davao, near SE coast of Mindanao I; rises to 2,954 m; part of a national park.

Appalachian Mountains *a-pa-lay'shun*, *a-pa-lay'chee-an*, APPALACHIANS, mountain system in E North America extending from the Gulf of St Lawrence SSW to central Alabama; lies nearly parallel with the Atlantic coast and consists of various parallel ranges separated by wide valleys; lies mainly between the Coastal Plains and Interior Plains; the Appalachian Mts include the major mountain ranges E of the Mississippi, except for the Adirondack Mts; the highest peak is Mt Mitchell (2,037 m, 35 46N 82 16W) in the Black Mts in Yancey county, North Carolina; the Appalachian Mts may be subdivided into 3 major longitudinal bands on the basis of structure and topography: the Older Appalachians in the E (which contain the highest peaks in the system), the Folded, or Newer, Appalachians in the centre (which include the Great Appalachian Valley), and the Appalachian Plateau in the W (which includes the Catskill, Allegheny and Cumberland Mts); the Older Appalachians are composed of strongly-folded and metamorphosed Palaeozoic rocks, with granite and other igneous intrusions; this range includes from N to S, the Shichshock Mts and Notre Dame Mts (Québec), the White Mts (New Hampshire), Green Mts (Vermont), Berkshire Hills (Massachusetts); from here 2 prongs swing S through New York and New Jersey to meet the Blue Ridge Mts in Pennsylvania; the Blue Ridge Mts continue S through Virginia and North Carolina and into Georgia; the Blue Ridge Mts include the highest peaks of E USA; the central band of Folded or Newer Appalachians includes the Great Appalachian Valley, which is formed N-S by the St Lawrence lowland, the L Champlain lowland and the Hudson river valley; from the Hudson, a chain of longitudinal valleys (the best known is Shenandoah valley in Virginia) continues SW to end in Alabama; the Newer Appalachians lie, on the whole, to the W of this valley; they are composed of folded Palaeozoic strata which have undergone little metamorphosis; the mountains extend over S New York, NW New Jersey, E Pennsylvania, W Maryland, E West Virginia, W and SW Virginia, E Tennessee, NW Georgia and NE Alabama; the westernmost part of the Appalachian Mts, the Appalachian Plateau, stretches from the Mohawk river valley, New York, to near the town of Birmingham, Alabama; it occupies parts of New York, Pennsylvania, Ohio, West Virginia, Kentucky, Tennessee and Alabama; there are glaciers in the parts of the Appalachians which are situated in Canada and in New England; the area is rich in minerals; the area's national parks include the Great Smoky Mountains National Park (Tennessee) and Shenandoah National Park (Virginia).

Appennino *ah-pen-ee'nō*, APENNINES *a'pu-nīnz* (Eng), mountain range extending in a long arc down the whole length of the Italian peninsula, from the Appno Ligure, to the SW corner of Calabria and continuing into Sicilia; length 1,400 km; width 30-150 km; there are 3 divisions: (1) the N division, including the Appno Ligure, Appno Tosco-Emilliano, and the Appno Umbro-Marchigiano, reaching its highest point in Monte Cimone (2,165 m); (2) the central division, including the Appno Abruzzese and the Appno Napoletano, reaching its highest point in the Gran Sasso d'Italia (2,914 m); (3) the S division extends to the Golfo di Taranto and curves round the 'toe' of Italy, including the Appno Lucano and La Sila, reaching its highest point in Monte Pollino (2,248 m); the Taro, Reno, and Panaro rivers rise on the N slopes and flow to the Po and the Adriatic Sea; the Tevere (Tiber), Arno, Magra, and Serchio rivers flow W towards the Ligurian and Tyrrhenian Seas; from the E slope of the mountain range, which falls abruptly to the Adriatic, flow the Biferno, Tronto, Ofanto, Pescara, and Chienti rivers; the S division, particularly the 'toe', has suffered many earthquakes, the worst occurring in 1783 and 1908; there are numerous mineral springs in the foothills; at the foot of the mountains vegetation is typically Mediterranean, with olive groves, vineyards, nut trees and orchards; above this is a zone of open forest, with beeches predominating at lower levels and conifers higher up; above 1,800 m the slopes are covered with stones and scree; the main occupations within the mountainous areas are stock-farming (goats and sheep), some arable farming, and forestry.

Appenzell *ap'pen-tsel*, 47 20N 9 20E, pop(1980) 4,900, capital town of Appenzell Inner Rhoden demicanton, NE Switzerland; 11 km S of St Gallen, in the fertile valley of the R Sitter; railway; event: Landsgemeinde (last Sunday in April), when all the citizens of the Catholic demicanton of Appenzell Inner Rhoden gather to vote on the cantonal laws and taxes.

Appenzell Ausser Rhoden, APPENZELL OUTER RHODES (Eng),

APPENZELL RHODES EXTÉRIEURES (Fr), demicanton in NE Switzerland; pop(1980) 47,611; area 243 sq km; capital Herisau; mountainous in the SE; joined the Confederation in 1513.

Appenzell Inner Rhoden, APPENZELL INNER RHODES (Eng), APPENZELL RHODES INTÉRIEURES (Fr), demicanton in NE Switzerland; pop(1980) 12,844; area 172 sq km; capital Appenzell; drained by the R Sitter; consists mainly of the Alpstein and Säntis massifs; joined the Confederation in 1513.

Appenzell Outer Rhodes, demicanton in Switzerland. See Appenzell Ausser Rhoden.

Appleton, 44 16N 88 25W, pop(1980) 59,032, county seat of Outagamie county, E Wisconsin, United States; on the R Fox, 27 km N of Oshkosh; Lawrence University (1847); railway; economy: food processing, paper, agricultural implements.

Apure *a-poo'ray*, state in W central Venezuela; bordered S along the Río Meta and SW along the Río Arauca by Colombia, N by the Río Apure and E by the Orinoco river; consists of vast *llanos* plains in the Orinoco basin; crossed W-E by numerous rivers linking with the Orinoco; pop(1980) 196,808; area 76,471 sq km; capital San Fernando.

Apure, navigable river in W central Venezuela; formed by the union of the Uribante and Sarare rivers (which rise in Colombia's Cordillera Oriental) in Apure state, 6 km NNE of Guadalito; flows approx 560 km NE and E through the *llanos* to join the Orinoco 120 km ESE of San Fernando; length (with the Río Uribante) 960 km; its major tributaries are the Portuguesa and Santo Domingo rivers.

Apurímac *a-poo-ree'mak*, dept in S central Peru; a mountainous region in the Cordillera Occidental of the Andes; watered by the Río Apurímac and its affluents; pop(1981) 323,346; area 20,654 sq km; capital Abancay.

Apuseni *a-poo-shayn'*, ('west peak'), mountain range in W Romania; N of the Transylvanian Alps and SW of Cluj-Napoca; the highest point is Bihor Peak (1,849 m).

'Aqaba *a'ka-bu*, AELANA *ee-lay'nu* (anc), 29 31N 35 00E, pop(1983e) 40,000, seaport in Ma'ān governorate, East Bank, SW Jordan; 96 km SW of Ma'ān, at the N end of the Gulf of 'Aqaba, on the border with Israel; Jordan's only outlet to the sea; the town commanded the ancient caravan routes from Egypt to Arabia; popular winter seaside resort; airport; railway; on the King's Highway, an ancient trade route through the Red Sea-Jordan rift valley; the port has modern container terminal facilities; a special phosphate exporting terminal links 'Aqaba to the nearby mining area by rail; economy: port trade, thermal power, fertilizer, timber processing, tourism.

Aquila, L' *ah'kwee-lah*, prov of Abruzzi region, E central Italy; pop(1981) 291,742; area 5,035 sq km; capital Aquila.

Aquila, L', AQUILA DEGLI ABRUZZI *-del'yee a-broot'see*, 42 22N 13 24E, pop(1981) 63,678, capital town of L'Aquila prov, Abruzzi region, E central Italy; NE of Rome, surrounded by the limestone heights of the Appno Abruzzese; archbishopric; railway; monuments: church of Santa Maria di Collemaggio (1280), Castello (1534).

Aquitaine *a-kee-ten, a-kwi-tayn* (Eng), AQUITANIA (anc), region of SW France comprising the depts of Dordogne, Gironde, Landes, Lot-et-Garonne, Pyrénées-Atlantiques, 18 arrond, 234 cantons and 2,281 communes; pop(1982) 2,656,544; area 41,308 sq km; united with Gascony under the French crown in the 11th century but acquired by England in 1152 on the marriage of Henry II to Eleanor of Aquitaine; remained in English hands until 1452; the chief town is Bordeaux; the region is drained by the rivers Garonne, Dordogne and Gironde and their tributaries which flow W and NW to the Bay of Biscay; interesting caves with paintings and rock concretions near Les Eyzies, Le Bugue, Montignac (Lascaux) and Rouffignac; the Bergerac and Bordeaux areas are noted for their wines; the Parc des Landes de Gascogne regional nature park caters for riding and canoeing; there are spas at Biarritz, Préchacq-les-Bains, Dax, Tercis-les-Bains, Saubusse-les-Bains and Eugénie-les-Bains; economy: wine, fruit, resin (Mont-de-Marsin), tobacco, shipbuilding, chemicals and oil refining (Bordeaux).

'Araba, Wadi *a'ra-bah*, dry river valley on the Israel-Jordan border, occupying part of the Red Sea-Jordan rift system; extends approx 160 km from the Dead Sea (N) to the Gulf of 'Aqaba (S); N of the Dead Sea it extends into the El Ghor depression.

Arabia *a-ray'bi-a*, Arabia proper, the home of the Arabs, occupies a peninsula of SW Asia bounded N by the Syrian Desert, E by the Gulf (Arabian Gulf), W by the Red Sea and S by the Arabian Sea; area 2,590,000 sq km; divided politically into the states of Saudi Arabia, Yemen, South Yemen, Oman, United Arab Emirates, Bahrain, Qatar and Kuwait; the area is an important world source of petroleum.

Arabian Gulf or **The Gulf** *a-ray'bee-an*, PERSIAN GULF, SINUS PERSICUS (anc), arm of the Arabian Sea with which it is connected via the Gulf of Oman and the Strait of Hormuz; bounded N by Iran, NW by Iraq and Kuwait, W by Saudi Arabia and Qatar, and S by the United Arab Emirates (Trucial Coast); Bahrain and Qeshm (Iran) are the two largest islands; length 885 km; max width 322 km; average depth 100 m; an important source of oil; in the N an oil pipeline links offshore oilfields with Iran and Saudi Arabia via a terminal on Khârg I.

Arabian Sea, NW section of the Indian Ocean; principal arms include (1) the Gulf of Oman (NW), which is linked to the Arabian Gulf by the Strait of Hormuz and (2) the Gulf of Aden (W), which is linked to the Red Sea by the Strait of Bāb al Mandab; bounded N by Pakistan and Iran, E by India, W by Oman and South Yemen and S by the submarine Carlsberg Ridge; Socotra (S Yemen) is the principal island, lying at the entrance to the Gulf of Aden; depths of 2,895 m in the N to 4,392 m in the SW reflect the presence of an alluvial cone at the mouth of the R Indus extending from the continental terrace off the coast of Pakistan into the Arabian Basin; the Arabian Sea is a trade route between the Indian subcontinent and the Arabian Gulf states.

Aracaju *a-ra-ka-zhoo'*, 10 54S 37 07W, pop(1980) 287,934, port capital of Sergipe state, Nordeste region, NE Brazil; on the right bank of the Río Sergipe, 10 km from its mouth; university (1967), railway; airfield; economy: trade in sugar cane, coconuts, oil, rice, coffee, potassium, salt, cattle, textiles.

Araçatuba *a-ra-sa-too'bu*, 21 12S 50 24W, pop(1980) 113,925, town in São Paulo state, Sudeste region, SE Brazil; NW of São Paulo; railway; economy: citrus fruits, cotton, sunflowers, rice, peanuts.

Arad *a'rad*, county in W Romania, on the border with Hungary; crossed by the R Mureş; pop(1983) 505,303; area 7,652 sq km; capital Arad.

Arad, 46 10N 21 19E, pop(1983) 183,774, commercial and industrial capital of Arad county, W Romania; on the R Mureş near the Hungarian frontier; established in the 11th century; transferred from Hungary to Romania in 1920; airfield; railway junction; economy: textiles, lathes, rolling stock, timber, electrical goods, metal goods, wine; monument: 18th-c citadel, built by Empress Maria Theresa.

Arafura Sea *ah-ray-foo'ra*, section of the Pacific Ocean bounded to the N and NE by Indonesia and New Guinea and to the S by Australia; linked to the Coral Sea (E) by the Torres Strait and bounded W by the Timor Sea; the Gulf of Carpentaria lies to the SE; shallow depths of 27 m off New Guinea to 55 m off the N tip of Australia are due to the underlying continental shelf.

Aragón *a-ra-gōn'*, autonomous region and former kingdom of NE Spain comprising the provs of Huesca, Teruel and Zaragoza; pop(1981) 1,196,952; area 47,669 sq km; a featureless upland region which, with Navarre, largely occupies the basin of the R Ebro enclosed by the Pyrenees in the N and the scarp slopes of the Meseta in the SW; the population is sparse and settlement is located close to rivers where there are oases of almonds, figs, vines and olives irrigated for a distance of 90 km by the Canal Imperial which follows the course of the R Ebro.

Aragua *a-ra'gwa*, state in N Venezuela; mountainous near the coast in the N, with fertile valleys in the basin of L Valencia; pop(1980) 854,121; area 5,380 sq km; capital Maracay.

Araguaia *a-ra-gwī'a*, national park in W Goiás state, Centro-Oeste region, W central Brazil; area 5,623 sq km; established in 1959; situated in the N of the world's largest river island (area 20,000 sq km); formed by 2 branches of the Río Araguaia (the Araguaia and the Formoso).

Araguaia, main tributary of the Tocantins river, NE Brazil; rises at 18 00S 53 00W in central Brazil and flows NNE to the Tocantins; forms W boundary of Goiás state with the states of Mato Grosso and Pará; its length is estimated at between 1,770 and 2,410 km; in its mid course it separates into 2 branches and encloses Bananal Island, the world's largest river island (area 20,000 sq km), now containing a national park; its chief tributary, the Garças river, is noted for its mosquitos.

Arāk *ah-rak'*, 34 00N 49 40E, pop(1983) 209,932, capital city of Arāk dist, Markazī, W central Iran; 240 km SW of Tehrān, surrounded by mountains; noted for its rugs and carpets; railway.

Arakan *ar-u-kan'*, RAKHINE *ra-kīn'*, state in W Burma; bordered by Bangladesh (NW) and the Bay of Bengal (W); a narrow coastal strip is separated from inland states by the Arakan Yoma mountain range; there are several offshore islands, the largest of which are Ramree and Cheduba; drained by the Kaladan, Mayu, Lemro and Dalet rivers; pop(1983) 2,045,891; capital Sittwe.

Arakan Yoma *yō'ma*, mountain range in SW Burma; situated between the Arakan coast on the Bay of Bengal and the Irrawaddy river valley; extends from Chin state (N) to the Irrawaddy delta; rises to over 1,980 m; forms a climatic barrier, cutting off central Burma from the effects of the SW monsoon, thus creating a dry zone.

Aral Sea, USSR. See Aral'skoye More.

Aral'skoye More *a-ral'ske-ye mor'ye*, ARAL SEA (Eng), an inland sea and the world's 4th largest lake, covering 67,340 sq km; located E of the Caspian Sea in Central Asian USSR; bounded to the NW, N and E by SW Kazakhstan (Kazakhskaya SSR) and to the SE, S and W by NW Uzbekistan (Uzbekskaya SSR); several small islands are found within the sea; the slightly saline water is a result of geologically recent separation from the Caspian Sea coupled with freshwater input from the Syrdar'ya and Amu Darya rivers without an available outlet; approx 420 km long and 280 km wide with a max depth of 70 m; the lake is generally shallow with navigation restricted to a small area; fishing (carp, perch and pike) is important, while sodium and magnesium sulphate are mined along the shores.

Aran Islands, group of 3 islands off the SW coast of Galway county, Connacht, W Irish Republic; Inishmor, Inishmaan and Inisheer are located at the mouth of Galway Bay; each has an airstrip with flights from Carnmore (6 km E of Galway); boat service from Rossaveel; monuments: several monastic ruins and Dun Aengus fort.

Aranjuez *a-ran-hweth'*, ARAJOVIS (anc), 40 02N 3 37W, pop(1981) 35,936, market town and resort in Madrid prov, central Spain; on the R Tagus, 50 km S of Madrid; economy: trade in fruit and vegetables; monuments: Royal Palace, rebuilt in 1727 by Philip V as a summer residence; Prince's Garden including the Labourer's Cottage and Sailor's House; event: Fiesta of San Fernando in May, with a bullfight and festivities.

Ar'arat, 37 20S 143 00E, pop(1983e) 8,740, city in Central Highlands stat div, Victoria, SE Australia; formerly a gold-mining town; railway; airfield; economy: sheep breeding, wine; monuments: regional art gallery; Langi Morgala folk museum.

Ararat, Mt, mountain in NE Turkey. See Ağrı Dağı.

Arauca *a-row'ka*, intendency in E Colombia, South America; bounded N and E by Venezuela; the N border is formed by the Río Arauca, the S border by the Río Casanare; consists mainly of low grasslands; pop(1985) 16,464; area 23,818 sq km; capital Arauca.

Araucanía, La *la a-row-ka-nee'a*, region of central Chile; S of Río Bío-Bío; comprises the provs of Malleco and Cautin; pop(1984) 675,700; area 31,946 sq km; capital Temuco; chief towns Angol and Villarica; economy: agriculture, forestry; the region includes Los Paraguas, Villarrica and Lanín national parks; inhabited by the Araucanian Indians, whose territory once included almost all of Chile; a warlike people, they resisted Spanish and Chilean rule until 1870; their final revolt ended with the treaty of Temuco (1881).

Arber, Great, mountain in W Germany. See Großer Arber.

Arbīl *ar-beel'*, governorate in the Kurdish Autonomous Region, N Iraq, bounded N by Turkey, and NE by Iran; pop(1977) 541,456; area 14,428 sq km; capital Arbīl.

Arbīl or **Irbil**, ARBELA (anc), 36 12N 44 01E, pop(1970) 107,355, capital town of Arbīl governorate, Kurdish Autonomous Region, N Iraq, 80 km E of Mosul; agricultural trade centre at terminus of railway from Kirkūk.

Arbroath *ar-brōth'*, ABERBROTHOCK (anc), 56 34N 2 35W, pop(1981) 24,119, port in Angus dist, Tayside, E Scotland; on the North Sea, 27 km NE of Dundee; railway; economy: textiles, clothing, engineering, fishing; monument: remains of Arbroath abbey (1178) where the Declaration of Arbroath was signed in 1320 by King Robert the Bruce asserting independence from England.

Arcadia, nome (dept) of Pelopónnisos region, Greece. See Arkadhía.

Arcadia, 34 08N 118 02W, pop(1980) 45,994, city in Los Angeles county, SW California, United States; at the base of the San Gabriel Mts, 21 km ENE of Los Angeles; railway.

Archangel, capital city of Arkhangel'skaya oblast, NW European Rossiyskaya, Soviet Union. See Arkhangel'sk.

Arches, national park in Grand county, E Utah, United States; features wind-eroded natural arch formations; established in 1929; area 332 sq km.

Arctic, that area in the N hemisphere which lies N of the tree-line or, more loosely, to the N of the Arctic Circle; Arctic conditions of climate, vegetation and life forms obtain in Greenland, Svalbard and the N parts of Canada, Soviet Union, Alaska and Iceland.

Arctic Circle, an arbitrary boundary marking the southernmost extremity of the northernmost area of the Earth; the area to the N of the tree-line; placed at 66° 17′ N, but often defined as the area N of 70°.

Arctic Ocean, a body of water lying within the Arctic Circle and centred on the North Pole; the world's smallest ocean, covering 13,986,000 sq km; this area is frozen all year except in its marginal areas; connects with the Pacific Ocean via the Bering Strait, while the Davis Strait and that area between the Greenland and the Norwegian Sea connects it to the Atlantic Ocean; main exchange of water is between the Arctic and the Atlantic due to the narrowness of the Bering Strait restricting flow; outflow forms the cold East Greenland Current, flowing down the E coast of Greenland and the Labrador Current, flowing through Smith Sound and Baffin Bay; nearly landlocked and bounded by USSR, Norway, Greenland, Canada and Alaska; water currents in the Arctic Ocean do not flow out into the Greenland Sea, owing to the rotation of the Earth and to deflection off the coast of North Greenland; this results in heavy-pressure ice off Greenland and Ellesmere Island, which in winter forms hummocky icefields; these icefields break up to form pack-ice during summer and are carried S by surface currents, generally melting before reaching the major shipping lanes; the Arctic Ocean has the widest continental shelves of all oceans, averaging 643 km off the coast of Arctic Siberia and forming a ring enclosing an oval-shaped basin which is only broken by the Greenland Sea; the basin stretches between Svalbard Island and the Bering Strait and is crossed by the Alpha Ridge, the Lomonsov Ridge and the Arctic Mid-Oceanic

Ridge, separating the Canada, Fletcher, Pole and Barents abyssal plains; unexplored until Amundsen's flight over it in 1926; shortest air flights between the continents of the northern hemisphere are across the Arctic; floating ice islands such as Ice-Island T-3 (known since 1952) are used to track the direction and rate of surface circulation; research, involving the study of temperatures, ice regressions and sea species, shows that the Arctic Ocean is experiencing a period of warming.

Ardabīl *ar-du-beel'*, 38 15N 48 18E, pop(1983) 221,970, town in Ardabīl dist, Āzarbāyān-e Sharqī, NW Iran; approx 50 km W of the Caspian Sea, surrounded by mountains.

Ardèche *ar-desh*, mountainous dept in Rhône-Alpes region of E France rising from the R Rhône in the E to the E-facing slopes of the Cévennes (Mt Mezenc 1,754 m); comprising 3 arrond, 33 cantons and 338 communes; pop(1982) 267,970; area 5,529 sq km; capital Privas; cut by the R Ardèche in the SE; there are spas at St Laurent-les-Bains, Vals-les-Bains and Neyrac-les-Bains; there are interesting caves near Orgnac-l'Aven and Bourg-St-Andéol; economy: grain, wine, fruit (in the W and S), coal, iron-ore.

Ardèche, river in E France rising in the Cévennes; flows SE to the R Rhône above Pont-St-Esprit; below the fall of Ray-Pic are the Pont d'Arc, a natural bridge worn in the limestone by the river, and the Ardèche gorge, a favourite canoeing route over rapids; length 120 km; tributary Chassezac.

Ardennes *ar-den'*, dept in Champagne-Ardenne region of NE France on the Belgian border, comprising 4 arrond, 37 cantons and 460 communes; pop(1982) 302,338; area 5,229 sq km; capital Charleville-Mézières; hilly except in SE and NW; watered by the R Meuse, R Aisne and tributaries; economy: the fertile valley of the Aisne and the centre of the dept produce cereals and wine, while in the N cider and beer are made; there are several slate and iron mines.

Ardnamurchan Point *ard na mær'KHan*, 56 44N 6 14W, cape in SW Highland region, W Scotland; at the W end of Ardnamurchan peninsula, on the W coast; N of Mull island and S of Eigg island; westernmost point on the British mainland; the lighthouse (1849) has a fixed light which is visible for 29 km.

Ardros'san, 55 39N 4 49W, pop(1981) 11,421, seaport in Cunninghame dist, Strathclyde, SW Scotland; on Ayr Bay, near the Firth of Clyde, 51 km SW of Glasgow; railway; ferry service to Arran; economy: engineering, transport equipment; monument: ruins of 12th-c Ardrossan castle, destroyed by Cromwell.

Arecibo *a-ray-see'bō*, 18 29N 66 42W, pop(1980) 86,766, port on N coast of Puerto Rico, E Caribbean; 65 km W of San Juan; an old colonial city with fine beaches; airfield (F)

Arendal *a'run-dal*, 58 27N 8 56E, pop(1980) 11,501, seaport and administrative capital of Aust-Agder county, S Norway; on the Skagerrak, 72 km NE of Kristiansand; economy: industry and shipping.

Arequipa *a-ray-kee'pa*, dept in S Peru; bordered W by the Pacific; the E half of the dept is occupied by the Andean Cordillera Occidental; pop(1981) 706,580; area 63,527 sq km; capital Arequipa; in the N of the dept is the Nevado Coropuna (6,425 m), the Nevado de Ampato (6,310 m) and the Cañon del Colca, a gorge cut by the Río Colca near the town of Cabanaconde; at 60 km long and 3,000 m deep, it is considered to be the deepest canyon in the world.

Arequipa, 16 25S 71 32W, pop(1981) 447,431, capital of Arequipa dept, S Peru; situated in a valley at the foot of El Misti volcano (5,843 m); alt 2,380 m; built on the site of an ancient Inca city, it is now the main commercial centre for southern Peru; the city was rebuilt in 1540; because of the danger of earthquakes, many of the old buildings are low, with flat roofs and small windows; 2 universities (1828, 1964); railway; airfield (Rodríguez Ballón) at 5 km; economy: textiles, soap; monuments: the Plaza de Armas is faced on 3 sides by colonial arcaded buildings and on the 4th by the twin-towered cathedral (1612), largely rebuilt in the 19th-c; one of the city's oldest districts is San Lázaro; La Companía church has striking examples of the florid Andean mestizo style of architecture; Puente Bolívar, designed by Eiffel; the walled Santa Catalina convent.

Arezzo *a-ret'so*, ARRETIUM (anc), hilly prov of E Toscana region, NW central Italy; pop(1981) 313,157; area 3,232 sq km; capital Arezzo.

Arezzo, 43 28N 11 53E, pop(1981) 92,105, capital town of Arezzo prov, Toscana region, NW central Italy; near the confluence of the Chiana and Arno rivers, 80 km SE of Firenze (Florence); built on the site of an Etruscan settlement; economy: textiles, furniture, pottery, leather; centre of the antiques trade and trade in olive oil and wine; monuments: church of Santa Maria della Pieve (11-13th-c); Gothic cathedral (begun 1277), with a splendid marble altar by Pisano; events: medieval jousting (June and Sept); Giostra del Saracino (1st Sunday in Sept).

Argentina *ar-jen-tee'na, ar-KHayn-tee'na* (Sp), official name The Argentine Republic, REPÚBLICA ARGENTINA, a republic of SE South America bounded E by the S Atlantic, W by Chile, NE by Uruguay and Brazil and N by Bolivia and Paraguay; timezone GMT −3; total area claimed 3,761,274 sq km; area (American continent) 2,780,092 sq km (excluding the Falkland Is claimed by Argentina); area (Antarctic continent) 964,250 sq km (excluding S Georgia, Orkney Is and S Sandwich Is claimed by Argentina); an Atlantic coastline of 4,725 km; capital Buenos Aires; chief towns Córdoba, Rosario, Mendoza, La Plata, San Miguel de Tucumán; pop(1980) 27,949,480; about 85% are of European origin and 15% of mestizo or S American Indian origin; 90% are nominally Roman Catholic; the official language is Spanish but English, French, German and Italian are widely spoken; the currency is the austral of 100 centavos (formerly the peso); national holiday 25 May (Independence Day); membership of FAO, G-77, GATT, IADB, IAEA, IBRD, ICAC, ICAO, IDA, IFAD, IFC, IHO, ILO, IMF, IMO, INTELSAT, IOOC, ISO, ITU, LAIA, NAM, OAS, PAHO, SELA, UN, UNESCO, UPU, WFTU, WHO, WMO, WSG, WTO.

Physical description. The Andes, which stretch the entire length of Argentina (N-S), form the watershed between the Atlantic and the Pacific as well as the boundary with Chile. The mountains extend far to the E in N Argentina, but their width decreases toward the S. High ranges, plateaux and rocky spurs comprise the NW quarter of Argentina. The high plateaux along the border with N Chile are semi-desert. Aconcagua (6,960 m), Bonete (6,872 m) and Tupungato (6,800 m), the highest peaks, lie along the Argentine-Chilean border. To the E a grassy, treeless plain, the *pampa*, rises gradually from the Atlantic coast to the Andean foothills. S Argentina is made up of a series of uneven, arid steppes, sloping from W to E. The island of Tierra del Fuego, off the S tip, is similar to S Argentina in character. The Paraguay, Paraná and Uruguay rivers drain N Argentina, and join to form the La Plata estuary. To the S many rivers, such as the Colorado and Negro, rise in the Andes and flow to the Atlantic. There are many lakes in the *pampa* and Patagonia regions, the largest being Lago Argentino (1,415 sq km) and Lago Viedma (1,088 sq km) in Santa Cruz prov.

Climate. Most of Argentina lies in the rainshadow of the Andes. The prevailing W winds lose their moisture against the W slopes, and descend into Argentina with increasing temperature and decreasing humidity. The NW corner is dry steppe or elevated desert. NE Argentina has predominantly E and NE winds and a moderately humid sub-tropical climate with temperatures and rainfall averaging 16°C and 500-1000 mm in Buenos Aires. The central *pampa* region and a strip along the foot of the mountains are semi-arid, with temperatures ranging from tropical to moderately cool. Between these two semi-arid areas lies the rainshadow desert, a plateau extending to the coast between 40°S and 50°S;

some rainfall prevents absolute barrenness. The S part is directly influenced by the strong prevailing westerlies.

History, government and constitution. Argentina was settled in the 16th century by the Spanish who approached from the N across the Andes and by sea via the Río de la Plata. A viceroyalty was established with Buenos Aires as its capital and in 1816 independence from Spain was declared with the setting up of the United Provinces of the Río de la Plata. Present-day Uruguay, Paraguay and Bolivia broke away from the Union and in 1853 a federal constitution modelled on that of the USA was established. A war with Paraguay in 1865-70 resulted in the acquisition of territory in the Gran Chaco, but an attempt to gain hold of the Falkland Is (Islas Malvinas) in 1982 failed when occupying Argentine forces were removed by a British Expeditionary Force. The country is governed by a bicameral National Congress consisting of a 192-member House of Deputies elected for 4 years and a 46-member Senate elected for 9 years. A president, who is elected for a 6-year term, appoints governors of the 22 provs.

Economy. Since the opening up of the pampas in the latter half of the 19th century European settlement has brought capital to Argentina, making it one of the leading industrial and agricultural nations of S America. Agricultural produce, chiefly cereals and meat, accounts for about 70% of export earnings. Other farm produce includes potatoes, cotton, sugar cane, sugar beet, tobacco, linseed oil, rice, soya, grapes, olives, and peanuts. Manufacturing industry is largely based on the production of cement, fertilizer, steel, plastics, paper and pulp, textiles, motor vehicles. Oil and gas are exploited, chiefly off the coast of Patagonia and coal, gold, silver, copper, iron ore, beryllium, mica, tungsten, manganese, limestone and uranium are also produced in significant quantities. Argentina's main trading partners are the USSR, Brazil, the Netherlands, the USA, Italy, W Germany, Spain, Japan and Chile.

Administrative divisions. Argentina is divided into a Federal District, 22 provs and a territory as follows:

Division	*area (sq km)*	*pop(1980)*
Federal District		
Buenos Aires	200	2,922,829
National Territory		
Tierra del Fuego	21,263	29,392
Provinces		
Buenos Aires	307,804	10,865,408
Catamarca	99,818	207,717
Chaco	99,633	701,392
Chubut	224,686	263,116
Córdoba	168,766	2,407,754
Corrientes	88,199	661,454
Entre Ríos	76,216	908,313
Formosa	72,066	295,887
Jujuy	53,219	410,008
La Pampa	143,440	208,260
La Rioja	92,331	164,217
Mendoza	150,839	1,196,228
Misiones	29,801	588,977
Neuquén	94,078	243,850
Río Negro	203,013	383,354
Salta	154,775	662,870
San Juan	86,137	465,976
San Luis	76,748	214,416
Santa Cruz	243,943	114,941
Santa Fe	133,007	2,465,546
Santiago del Estero	135,254	594,920
Tucumán	22,524	972,655

Argentino, Lago *ar-KHen-tee'nō*, lake in the S Patagonian Andes in W Santa Cruz prov, Patagonia, S Argentina; area 1,415 sq km; set in a national park, its outlet is into the Santa Cruz river.

Argeş *ar'jesh*, county in S central Romania, situated to the S of the Transylvanian Alps and crossed N-S by the R Argeş; pop(1983) 660,055; area 6,801 sq km; capital Piteşti.

Argeş, river in S Romania, formed by two headstreams rising in the Transylvanian Alps; flows S to meet the R Danube W of Oltenita; linked with Bucureşti by a canal; length 288 km.

Ar'golís, agricultural nome (dept) of Pelopónnisos region, S Greece; pop(1981) 93,020; area 2,154 sq km; capital Návplion; 96 km WSW of Athínai (Athens); produces fruit.

Árgos *ahr'gōs* or *ahr'gus*, 37 38N 22 43E, pop(1981) 20,702, ancient town in Argolís nome (dept), Pelopónnisos region, S Greece; in a fertile plain near the Argolikós Kólpos (Gulf of Argolikós), on the main highway between Trípolis and Kórinthos; railway.

Argovie, canton in Switzerland. See Aargau.

Arguin, Banc d', national park in Dakhlet-Nouadhibou region, W Mauritania, NW Africa; area 11,730 sq km; situated around a bay of same name; established in 1976.

Argyll and Bute, district of Strathclyde region, W Scotland; pop(1981) 68,834; area 6,497 sq km; chief town Lochgilphead; the district includes the island of Bute whose chief town is Rothesay.

Arhangay *ar'KHan-gī*, ARAKHANGAI, county in central Mongolia; pop(1981e) 80,000; area 55,200 sq km; capital Tsetserleg; nearly 16% of the area is under forest; the county is the most productive livestock region of Mongolia, with over 20 farms producing beef cattle and horses; a 180 sq km state farm specializes in meat and milk production.

Århus *or'hoos*, AARHUS, county in E Jylland (Jutland), Denmark; area 4,561 sq km; pop(1983) 578,149; bounded on the E by the Kattegat; capital Århus, chief towns Randers, Grenå, Silkeborg.

Århus, 56 08N 10 11E, pop(1983) 248,509, capital of Århus county, E Jylland (Jutland), Denmark; lies in a wide bay of the Kattegat, S of Ålborg; cultural and educational hub of central Jylland with a university founded in 1928; railway; economy: engineering, foodstuffs, machinery, textiles; monument: cathedral of St Clement (1201).

Arica *a-ree'ka*, 18 28S 70 18W, pop(1982) 120,846, port and capital of Arica prov, Tarapacá, Chile; 19 km S of the Peruvian frontier, on the Pacific coast, SW of La Paz, Bolivia; the most northerly city in Chile; acquired from Peru in 1929; airport (Chaculluta); Arica is connected by rail with La Paz, Bolivia, the steam train (made in Germany in 1924) once used on this line can be seen outside the station; over half the imports and exports of Bolivia flow over Arica's railway; an oil pipeline also links Arica with Bolivia; economy: port trade, fishmeal, tourism; monuments: Pacific War museum on the Morro headland, the scene of a great victory by Chile over Peru on 7 June 1880; in the Plaza de Armas is the San Martín cathedral, built in iron by Eiffel; Eiffel also designed the customs house.

Ariège *ar-yezh*, dept in Midi-Pyrénées region of S France on the Spanish border and the N slopes of the Pyrénées; comprises 3 arrond, 20 cantons and 332 communes; pop(1982) 135,725; area 4,890 sq km; capital Foix; cut N-S by the R Ariège and divided between mountain and valley (Pic de Montcalm 3,080 m); the road from Aix to Puigcerda in Spain crosses the Col de Puy-Morent and a westward route leads into the small state of Andorra; spas at Ussat-les-Bains and Ax-les-Thermes; there are several caves with prehistoric rock paintings near Foix; economy: fertile in the N producing grain, fruit and vegetables, iron and coal.

Ariège, river in S France rising in the E Pyrénées on the border with Andorra; flows NNW to join the R Garonne above Toulouse; length 170 km; tributary Hers.

Arima *u-ree'mu*, 10 38N 61 17W, pop(1980) 24,100, town in N Trinidad, SE Caribbean, 26 km E of Port of Spain, bounded N by the Northern Range; once a flourishing cacao centre; road junction; event: Festival of Santa Rosa (30 Aug).

Aripo, El Cerro del *a-ree'pō*, MT ARIPO *u-ri'pō*, 10 43N 61 15W, mountain peak in the Northern Range, N Trinidad, SE Caribbean; height 940 m; highest point in the Republic of Trinidad and Tobago.

'Arîsh, El *el a-reesh'*, RHINOCOLURA (anc), 31 08N 33 48E, capital of Sinai governorate, NE Egypt; on Mediterranean coast, 145 km E of Port Said; held by Israel (1967-79); railway.

Arizo'na, state in SW United States, bounded W by California and Nevada, N by Utah, E by New Mexico, and S by Mexico; the Colorado river flows generally SW across the NW corner of the state then turns S to form most of the W state border; the R Gila flows W across the S of the state to empty into the Colorado; the Salt river rises in E and flows W to empty into the Gila in S central Arizona; the Hoover Dam causes the Colorado river to swell into L Mead on the Nevada border; the state has several mountain ranges, the highest of which are the San Francisco Mts; the highest point is Humphreys Peak (3,862 m); the Colorado Plateaux (N) are high, dry plains incised by deep canyons, the most famous of which is the Grand Canyon which has been carved out by the Colorado river; the NE corner of the state includes Navajo and Hopi Indian reservations; the S edge of the Colorado Plateaux is marked by an escarpment called the Mogollon Rim; S of this are desert basins interspersed with bare mountain peaks; these give way to relatively low, desert plains in the S; the centre of the state is dominated by a huge area of national and state forest; the climate of the entire state is characterized by scant rainfall and aridity; on irrigated land cattle are grazed and the chief crops are dairy products, cotton, lettuce and hay; tourism is the state's most important industry, with visitors being attracted by famous scenic and cultural sites such as the Grand Canyon, the Petrified Forest, meteor craters, and Indian reservations; manufacturing industries produce computer equipment, aerospace components, timber products and machinery; Arizona produces two-thirds of the nation's copper supply; Spanish exploration began in 1539; the region became part of New Spain (1598-1821) after which it was included in the newly-independent Mexico; the region was acquired by the United States in the Treaty of Guadalupe Hidalgo (1848) and the Gadsden Purchase of 1853; Arizona was organized as a separate territory in 1863, but until 1886 suffered from frequent attacks from Apache Indians, led by Cochise and later by Geronimo; it became a state (48th) in 1912; also known as the 'Grand Canyon State'; pop(1980) 2,718,215; area 295,121 sq km; capital Phoenix; other major cities include Tucson, Mesa and Tempe; the state is divided into 14 counties:

County	*area (sq km)*	*pop(1980)*
Apache	29,149	52,108
Cochise	16,167	85,686
Coconino	48,381	75,008
Gila	12,355	37,080
Graham	12,038	22,862
Greenlee	4,776	11,406
Maricopa	23,730	1,509,052
Mohave	34,541	55,865
Navajo	25,883	67,629
Pima	23,886	531,443
Pinal	13,892	90,918
Santa Cruz	3,219	20,459
Yavapai	21,120	68,145
Yuma	25,984	90,554

Arkadhia, ARCADIA *ar-kay'di-a* (Eng), nome (dept) of Pelopónnisos region, Greece; pop(1981) 107,932; area 4,419 sq km; capital Trípolis; a mountainous area, rising in the N to Killíni (2,376 m); lower areas of plain are situated around Trípolis and Megalópolis, drained by the R Alfiós and its tributaries.

Arkansas *ar'kan-saw, ar-kan'sas*, river in S central USA; rises in the Sawatch Range of the Rocky Mountains in central Colorado; flows generally ESE across the Great Plains of SE Colorado, through S Kansas past Wichita, through NE Oklahoma past Tulsa and into Arkansas where it flows between the Boston Mts (N) and the Ouachita Mts (S); the Arkansas then flows past Fort Smith and Little Rock and joins the Mississippi river S of Memphis; length 2,333 km; major tributaries: the Cimmaron, Canadian, Neosho and Verdigris rivers; navigable for its length in Arkansas.

Arkansas *ar'kan-saw*, state in S central United States; bounded W by Texas and Oklahoma, N by Missouri, E by Tennessee and Mississippi, and S by Louisiana; the Mississippi river follows the E border; the R Arkansas flows SE, bisecting the state on its way to meet the Mississippi; the Red river flows through the extreme SW corner of the state, forming part of the Texas border; the Boston Mts, part of the Ozark Plateau, rise in the NW, and the Ouachita Mts in the W; the highest point is Mt Magazine (860 m); the mountainous region of the N and W is bisected by the Arkansas river valley; in the S and E are extensive plains; over half of the state is covered by commercial forest; chief agricultural products are poultry, soybeans, rice (Arkansas is the nation's leading producer), cattle, dairy, and cotton; manufacturing industries, which are located along the banks of the R Arkansas, produce processed foods, electrical equipment, paper, timber products and chemicals; Arkansas leads the nation in bauxite production and also produces petroleum and natural gas; the attraction of the state's forests, lakes and streams makes tourism a major state industry; the first white settlement in the area was established by the French in 1686 when the region became part of French Louisiana; Arkansas was ceded to the US as part of the Louisiana Purchase in 1803; in 1812 the state became part of the Territory of Missouri; it became a separate territory in 1819, and entered the Union as a state (25th) in 1836; seceded from the Union in 1861; although occupied by Union troops in 1863, Arkansas was not re-admitted to the Union until 1868; also known as the 'Land of Opportunity'; pop(1980) 2,286,435; area 135,403 sq km; capital Little Rock; other chief cities include Fort Smith, North Little Rock and Pine Bluff; the state is divided into 75 counties:

County	*area (sq km)*	*pop(1980)*
Arkansas	2,616	24,175
Ashley	2,428	26,538
Baxter	1,420	27,409
Benton	2,192	78,115
Boone	1,518	26,067
Bradley	1,700	13,803
Calhoun	1,633	6,079
Carroll	1,648	16,203
Chicot	1,687	17,793
Clark	2,254	23,326
Clay	1,667	20,616
Cleburne	1,433	16,909
Cleveland	1,557	7,868
Columbia	1,994	26,644
Conway	1,451	19,505
Craighead	1,854	63,239
Crawford	1,544	36,892
Crittenden	1,557	49,499
Cross	1,617	20,434
Dallas	1,737	10,515
Desha	1,940	19,760
Drew	2,161	17,910
Faulkner	1,677	46,192
Franklin	1,583	14,705
Fulton	1,602	9,975
Garland	1,708	70,531
Grant	1,646	13,008
Greene	1,505	30,744
Hempstead	1,885	23,635
Hot Spring	1,599	26,819
Howard	1,492	13,459
Independence	1,984	30,147
Izard	1,511	10,768
Jackson	1,646	21,646
Jefferson	2,293	90,718
Johnson	1,758	17,423
Lafayette	1,347	10,213
Lawrence	1,531	18,447
Lee	1,565	15,539
Lincoln	1,461	13,369
Little River	1,342	13,952
Logan	1,864	20,144
Lonoke	2,036	34,518
Madison	2,176	11,373
Marion	1,526	11,334
Miller	1,609	37,766
Mississippi	2,330	59,517
Monroe	1,583	14,052
Montgomery	2,012	7,771
Nevada	1,612	11,097
Newton	2,140	7,756
Oauchita	1,916	30,541
Perry	1,430	7,266
Phillips	1,781	34,772
Pike	1,555	10,373

contd

County	*area (sq km)*	*pop(1980)*
Poinsett	1,981	27,032
Polk	2,236	17,007
Pope	2,132	39,021
Prairie	1,706	10,140
Pulaski	1,994	340,613
Randolph	1,706	16,834
Saline	1,885	53,161
Scott	2,330	9,685
Searcy	1,737	8,847
Sebastian	1,391	95,172
Sevier	1,456	14,060
Sharp	1,576	14,607
St Francis	1,659	30,858
Stone	1,576	9,022
Union	2,738	48,573
Van Buren	1,843	13,357
Washington	2,473	100,494
White	2,704	50,835
Woodruff	1,539	11,222
Yell	2,418	17,026

Arkhangel'sk *urk-han'gilsk*, ARCHANGEL (Eng), 64 32N 40 40E, pop(1983) 399,000, port and capital city of Arkhangel'skaya oblast, NW European Rossiyskaya, Soviet Union; on the R Severnaya Dvina, on an inlet of the Beloye More (White Sea); one of the largest sea and river ports in the USSR; the harbour is often icebound during the winter; established in the 16th century by the Muscovy Company, it was the first Russian seaport before the building of St Petersburg (Leningrad) in 1703; railway; airfield; economy: fishing, clothing, knitwear, footwear, seaweed processing, shipbuilding and repairing, transport equipment, timber industries; monument: monastery dedicated to the Archangel Michael, after whom the city is named.

Arklow *ark'lō*, INBHEAR MOR (Gael), 52 48N 6 09W, pop(1981) 8,646, seaport and resort in Wicklow county, Leinster, E Irish Republic; on Irish Sea at mouth of R Avoca, S of Dublin; railway; economy: fishing, tourism, pottery.

Arlberg *arl'berk*, 47 09N 10 12E, mountain massif in the Lechtal Alps on the border between the Tirol and Vorarlberg states, W Austria; forms the watershed between the Rhine and Danube rivers; a favourite area for winter sports with resorts at St Anton, Lech, Zürs, Stuben and Klösterle; hang-gliding school at Lech; there are two road passes (Arlberg Road and Flexen Road).

Arles, ARLES-SUR-RHÔNE *arl-sür-rōn*, 43 41N 4 38E, pop(1982) 50,772, old town in Bouches-du-Rhône dept, Provence-Alpes-Côte d'Azur region, SE France; 72 km NE of Marseille, lying to the S of the point where the R Rhône divides into the Grand Rhône and the Petit Rhône to form the silted-up Camargue delta; formerly an important crossroads and capital of Provence; Van Gogh lived and painted here in 1888-89 before being admitted to a mental home near St Rémy; railway; economy: boatbuilding, metal work, foodstuffs, hats; monuments: Roman remains including the huge arena and theatre and several art museums.

Ar'lington, 32 44N 97 07W, pop(1980) 160,113, town in Tarrant county, N Texas, United States; 20 km E of Fort Worth; university (1895); railway; economy: iron and steel, auto and aircraft parts, electronic and oil-field equipment, rubber products, and mobile homes.

Arlington, county of Virginia state, United States; a suburb of Washington, DC; area 68 sq km; pop(1980) 152,599; site of the Arlington National Cemetery (1920) with a memorial amphitheatre and Tomb of the Unknown Soldier; the US Dept of Defense headquarters are located in the Pentagon Building.

Arlington Heights, 42 05N 87 59W, pop(1980) 66,116, town in Cook county, NE Illinois, United States; 40 km

NW of Chicago; railway; event: Budweiser Million (Aug).

Arlington, Upper, 40 00N 83 04W, pop(1980) 35,648, town in Franklin county, central Ohio, United States; on the R Scioto, 13 km NNW of Columbus.

Arlon *ar-lõ'*, dist of Luxembourg prov, SE Belgium; area 317 sq km; pop(1982) 47,334.

Arlon, AARLEN *ahr'lun*, OROLAUNUM (Lat), 49 41N 5 49E, pop(1982) 22,364, capital town of Arlon dist, Luxembourg prov, SE Belgium; on a high plateau in the Ardennes, near the Luxembourg border; railway; monument: St Donat's church (1626).

Armadale, 55 54N 3 42W, pop(1981) 9,527, town in West Lothian dist, Lothian, central Scotland; 4 km W of Bathgate and 11 km SW of Linlithgow.

Armagh *ar-mah'*, ARD MHACHA (Gael), county in SE Northern Ireland; bounded E by Co Down along the Newry river, N by Lough Neagh, NW by Co Tyrone along the R Blackwater and S and SW by the Republic of Ireland; major rivers include the Blackwater, Newry, Callan and Bann; rises to 577 m in Slieve Gullion in the S of the county; pop(1981) 118,820; area 1,254 sq km; county town Armagh; major towns include Lurgan and Portadown; economy: agriculture (potatoes, flax, apples), linen; Armagh is divided into 2 districts:

District	*area (sq km)*	*pop(1981)*
Armagh	672	47,618
Craigavon	382	71,202

Armagh, 54 21N 6 39W, pop(1981) 12,700, county town of Armagh in Armagh dist, SE Northern Ireland; an ancient and historic city, Armagh was the seat of the kings of Ulster from 400 BC to 333 AD; in the 5th c Armagh became the religious centre of Ireland when St Patrick was made archbishop in 445 and a church and monastery were established here; the town became an important centre for education; it was subjected to several raids by Danes; Brian Boru (the Celtic king) and his son were buried here after the Battle of Clontarf (1014); the town was destroyed in 1566 by Shane O'Neill and was burned in 1642; economy: textiles (linen), engineering, shoes, food processing; monuments: St Patrick's cathedral (Protestant, built in 1834) stands on the site of the original church founded in 445; St Patrick's cathedral (Roman Catholic, built between 1840 and 1873 in neo-Gothic style); Armagh is the seat of both the Protestant and the Catholic archbishops; observatory (1791); Royal School (1627), founded by Charles I; 3 km SW of Armagh is Navan Fort, palace of the kings of Ulster, known then as Emania.

Armagnac *ar-man-yak*, dist in SW France, now mostly in Gers dept, Aquitaine; known for its brandy; the chief town is Auch.

Armenia *ar-may'nya*, 4 32N 75 40W, pop(1985) 186,604, capital of Quindío dept, W central Colombia, South America; founded in 1889; university (1962); railway; airfield (El Edén) at 13 km; economy: coffee processing, foodstuffs, drinks.

Armenia, Soviet republic. See Armyanskaya.

Armenia *ar-mee'nee-a*, MIN'NI (anc), ancient kingdom largely occupying the present-day Van region of E Turkey and parts of NW Iran and SW USSR; located SE of the Black Sea and SW of the Caspian Sea; today Turkish Armenia comprises the NE provs of Turkey; chief towns Kars, Erzurum, Erzincan; the area was ruled by the Ottoman Turks from 1514, with E territory ceded to Persia in 1620 and further districts lost to Russia in 1828-29; Armenian nationalism arose in the 19th century with claims that E Anatolia was the original homeland of the Armenians, that the territory had been occupied by force by Seldjukis, Ottomans and finally Turks and that a series of massacres had taken place in the 1890s and again in 1915; since 1973 Armenian claims have been backed by terrorist activities.

Ar'midale, 30 32S 151 40E, pop(1981) 18,922, urban centre in Northern stat div, NE New South Wales, Australia; university (1954); agricultural centre of the sheep-rearing New England area; railway; airfield.

Armoricain, Massif *mas-eef ar-mor-ee-kayn*, low lying hills in Bretagne and Normandie regions of W France, rising to 417 m at Monts des Avaloirs in the Alpes Mancelles.

Armyanskaya, ARMENIYA SSR, ARMENIA *ar-mee'nee-a* (Eng), constituent republic of the Soviet Union, in S Transcaucasia, bounded N by Gruzinskaya (Georgia) SSR, E by Azerbaydzhanskaya SSR, SE by Iran, SW by Nakhichevanskaya ASSR (of the Azerbaydzhanskaya SSR), and NW by Turkey; the republic is mountainous with an average elevation of 1,800 m, rising to 4,090 m at Mt Aragats in the W; the Ozero Sevan in the E is the largest lake; the Araks is the chief river; pop(1983) 3,219,000; area 29,800 sq km; capital Yerevan; economy: extraction and processing of building materials, chemicals (chiefly synthetic rubber and fertilizers), carpet weaving, electrical engineering, foodstuffs, machine tools, and textiles; the chief industrial centres are Yerevan, Leninakan, Alaverdi, Kafan, Kirovakan, Daval, Megri, and Oktemberyan; 8 hydroelectric power stations on the R Razdan have recently been completed; agriculture is concentrated in the Araks valley and in the vicinity of Yerevan; chief crops include grains, cotton, tropical fruits, grapes, olives, and some industrial crops; livestock raising is the chief occupation in mountainous areas; Armenia was proclaimed a Soviet Socialist Republic on 29 Nov 1920 and a constituent republic of the USSR in 1936; Soviet Armenia lays claim to Turkish Armenia, including the holy mountain of Ararat.

Arn'hem, 52 00N 5 53E, pop(1984e) 291,399, capital city of Gelderland prov, E Netherlands; on the right bank of the lower Rhine, near its junction with the R Ijssel, 53 km ESE of Utrecht; part of the city lies in the hills at the edge of the Veluwe, a vast area of woods and moorland; seat of the law courts, of several government agencies and of the provincial government; founded on the site of a Roman settlement; received its charter in 1233; flourished throughout the Middle Ages as a river trading port; heavily damaged in World War II; railway; economy: tin-smelting, man-made fibres, salt, pharmaceuticals, chemicals, consumer products, electricity generation, engineering; monuments: 15th-c Grote Kerk; town hall (1540); St Walburgisbasiliek (1422), oldest church in the town; Dutch open air museum (N); safari park; Burgers Zoo.

Arnhem Land, the peninsular N projection of N Australia E of Darwin, named after the Dutch ship which arrived here in 1618; the principal town is Nhulunbuy; now a reserve for Aborigines.

Arnold, 53 01N 1 07W, pop(1981) 37,765, town in Newark dist, Nottinghamshire, central England; 6 km NE of the centre of Nottingham; economy: public utilities.

Arns'berg, dist in Nordrhein-Westfalen (North Rhine-Westphalia) prov, W Germany; pop(1983) 3,613,900; area 7,999 sq km; capital Arnsberg.

Arnsberg, 51 25N 8 02E, pop(1983) 76,100, manufacturing city in Arnsberg dist, Nordrhein-Westfalen (North Rhine-Westphalia), W Germany; on R Ruhr, 67 km SSE of Münster; railway.

Ar'ran, island in Strathclyde region, W Scotland; separated from the W coast mainland by the Firth of Clyde and from the Kintyre peninsula by the Kilbrannan Sound; area 430 sq km; rises to 874 m at Goat Fell; chief towns are Brodick, Lamlash, Lochranza; ferry links between Brodick and Ardrossan and Lochranza and Claonaig; monuments: Brodick castle, garden and country park, ancient seat of the Dukes of Hamilton; Bronze Age Moss Farm Road stone circle; 13-14th-c Lochranza castle.

Arras', 50 17N 2 46E, pop(1982) 45,364, old frontier town and capital of Pas-de-Calais dept, Nord-Pas-de-Calais region, N France; between Lille and Amiens; bishopric; formerly famous for its tapestries; many war cemeteries nearby; 10 km N is the Vimy Ridge memorial, a tribute to the 75,000 Canadians who died there in 1917; birthplace of Robespierre; Flemish-style houses overlook the two great market (Saturday) squares; railway; economy:

agricultural equipment, engineering, sugar-beet, vegetable oil, hosiery.

Arrecife de Lanzarote *a-ray-thee'fay dhay lan-tha-ro'tay*, PUERTO ARRECIFE, 28 57N 13 37W, pop(1981) 29,502, seaport and capital of Lanzarote I, Las Palmas prov, Canary Is; on the S coast of the island; airport; monuments: castles of San Gabriel and San José; the town has picturesque old streets with an arcaded market square.

Ārsī, ARUSI, ARUSSI, mountainous region in central Ethiopia, NE Africa; pop(1984e) 1,662,233; area 23,500 sq km; mountain peaks include Bada (4,133 m) and K'ech'a Mt (4,190 m); L Ziway is situated on the NW border; capital Āsela.

Ár'ta, nome (dept) of Ipiros region, W Greece; pop(1981) 80,044; area 1,662 sq km; capital Árta; produces grain, cotton and fruit; Tzouměrka rises to 2,429 m in the Pindhos range.

Árta, AMBRACIA (anc), 39 09N 20 59E, pop(1981) 18,283, agric market town and capital of Árta nome (dept), Ipiros region, W Greece, on the left bank of R Árakhthos; Greek Orthodox bishopric; economy: leather, textiles, tobacco, fruit, cotton and grain; monuments: church of Ayía Theodóra (13th-c), church of Panayía Parigorítissa (13th-c).

Arthur's Pass, main mountain pass through the Southern Alps, N central South Island, New Zealand; alt 924 m; discovered by the surveyor and explorer, Sir Arthur Dobson in 1864 while searching for a short route from the Canterbury Plains to Westland; set in a 944 sq km national park of the same name established in 1929.

Artigas *ar-tee'gas*, dept in NW Uruguay; bordered N and E along the Río Quarai by Brazil and W along the Río Uruguay by Argentina; drained by the Arroyo Tres Cruces Grande and the Arroyo Cuaró Grande; SE are the Cerros de Catalán; pop(1985) 68,994; area 11,738 sq km; capital Artigas; the dept was formed in 1884.

Artigas, 30 25S 56 28W, pop(1985) 34,156, capital of Artigas dept, NW Uruguay; on the Río Quarai where it follows the frontier with Brazil; railway; airfield; economy: agriculture, cattle-raising.

Artois *ar-twa*, ARTESIUM (Lat), former prov of NE France now occupying the dept of Pas-de-Calais; its former capital was Arras; during the 11th, 12th and 14th centuries as part of Flanders the region was part of the Austrian and Spanish Netherlands; ceded to France in 1659; at Lillers the first European artesian well was sunk in 1126.

Artvin *art-vun'*, CORUH *cho-roo'*, mountainous prov in NE Turkey, bounded NW by the Black Sea and N by the USSR; pop(1980) 228,997; area 7,436 sq km; capital Artvin; economy: grain, tobacco.

Arua *a'roo-a*, 3 02N 30 56E, pop(1980) 9,633, town in Nile prov, Uganda, E Africa; close to Uganda's frontier with Zaire, 160 km WNW of Gulu; railway.

Aruba *ar-oo'ba*, island of the S Netherlands Antilles, Windward Is, E Caribbean, 30 km N of the Paraguana Peninsula, Venezuela; formally separated from the Netherlands Antilles Federation in 1986, the island is now a self-governing member of the Kingdom of the Netherlands; composed of coralline limestone fringing an igneous core; rises to 189 m at Jamanota in the hilly SE; the Hooiberg (167.5 m) is a cone-shaped hill which rises sharply in the NW; area 193 sq km; pop(1981) 60,312; capital Oranjestad; airport; economy: tourism, oil refining, rum distilling, cigarettes, beverages.

Arucas *ar-oo'kas*, 28 08N 18 32W, pop(1981) 25,770, town at the N end of Gran Canaria I in the Canary Is, Canarias autonomous region of Spain; 18 km W of Las Palmas; economy: sugar-cane, brandy, tourism.

Arun, river rising in West Sussex, S England; flows 58 km W and S to meet the English Channel at Littlehampton.

Arunachal Pradesh *ahr-u-nah'chal pru-daysh'*, formerly NW FRONTIER AGENCY OF ASSAM, union territory in NE India; bounded N by Tibet, E by Burma and W by Bhutan; pop(1981) 628,050; area 83,578 sq km; created in Jan 1972; there are 9 administrative dists, including Dibang Valley, West Kameng, East Kameng, West Siang, East Siang, Lohit, Tirap, Upper Subansiri, Lower Subansiri; capital Itanagar; the territory is governed by a Council of Ministers and a 30-member Legislative Assembly; 60% of the land is covered by forest; economy: rubber, coffee, coconut, fruits, spices, wood products; ruins of ancient Mayapur lie N of Itanagar.

Arusha *a-roo'sha*, 3 21S 36 40E, pop(1978) 55,281, capital of Arusha region, NE Tanzania, E Africa; at the S foot of Mount Meru, 322 km W of Tanga; in 1929 the railway reached the town which was used as a base for trips to Mount Kilimanjaro, the Ngorongoro Crater and the national parks of N Tanzania; economy: tourism, clocks and watches, leatherworking, cutlery, textiles, meerschaum pipes, tyres, radios, coffee, cotton, timber, electrical goods.

Arusi, region of Ethiopia. See Ārsī.

Arva'da, 39 48N 105 05W, pop(1980) 84,576, city in Jefferson county, N central Colorado, United States; a largely residential suburb 10 km NW of Denver; economy: processed foods, beer and chemicals.

Arvayheer *ar-vay-KHeer*, ARVAYKHEER, ARRAY HEER, 46 15N 102 46E, capital of Övör-Hangay county, central Mongolia; linked NW by road to Ulaanbaatar; economy based on stock breeding.

Ås *os*, 59 56N 10 45E, pop(1980) 11,013, suburb of Oslo in Akershus county, SE Norway.

Asadābād, 34 52N 71 09E, pop(1984e) 2,290, capital of Konar prov, E Afghanistan; on R Kunar, S of the Hindu Kush Mts, near the Pakistan frontier and ENE of Kābul; airfield.

Asahikawa *a-sa-hee-ka'wa*, ASAHIGAWA, 43 46N 142 23E, pop(1980) 352,619, town in Hokkaidō prefecture, W central Hokkaidō island, Japan; NE of Sapporo; railway; economy: wood products, saké, textiles.

Asamankese *a-sa-man-ke'say*, 5 51N 0 40W, pop(1970) 101,144, town in Eastern region, SE Ghana, W Africa; economy: civil engineering.

Asansol *us-un-sōl'*, 23 40N 86 59E, pop(1981) 365,000, industrial city in West Bengal, E India; NW of Calcutta; linked by rail to Dhanbad and Durgapur; the Burnpur industrial centre lies 4 km from the city; economy: coal, aluminium.

Ascension, 7 56S 14 25W, a small, arid, volcanic island in the S Atlantic, 1,125 km NW of St Helena; British territory; area 88 sq km; pop(1983e) 1,400, in 1922 administration passed from the Admiralty to the Colonial Office and the island was annexed to St Helena; there is a British Forces contingent (mainly RAF) on the island; an airfield (Miracle Mile) near Georgetown; a cable station links the island with St Helena, Sierra Leone, St Vincent, Rio de Janeiro and Buenos Aires; the highest point is Green Mountain (859 m); a mountain farm produces fruit and vegetables and supports 70-100 pigs and some cattle; a breeding ground for sea turtles, the sooty tern and partridges; rabbits and goats also common; discovered by the Portuguese on Ascension Day 1501, but uninhabited until the exile of Napoleon to St Helena in 1815, when a small British naval garrison was placed here; in 1942 the US Government established an air base which was subsequently reoccupied in connection with the extension of the Long Range Proving Ground for guided missiles centred in Florida; US National Aeronautic and Space Administration opened a Tracking Station at the Devil's Ashpit in 1966; Atlantic Relay Station for BBC opened at English Bay and Butt Crater in 1966; British forces were sent to the island in April 1982 in support of the Falkland Islands Task Force.

Aschaffenburg *a-shaf'en-boork*, 49 58N 9 08E, pop(1983) 59,600, river port in Unterfranken dist, NW Bayern (Bavaria), W Germany, on the right bank of the R Main, 34 km ESE of Frankfurt; ceded to Bayern by Austria in 1814; railway; economy: an important centre of the West German clothing industry and transshipment point for water-borne traffic on the R Main; monuments: Schloss Johannisburg Palace (1605-14), former residence of the archbishops of Mainz.

Ascoli Piceno *as'kō-lee pee-chay'nō*, prov of Marche region, E central Italy; pop(1981) 352,567; area 2,088 sq km; capital Ascoli Piceno.

Ascoli Piceno, 42 52N 13 35E, pop(1981) 54,928, capital town of Ascoli Piceno prov, Marche region, E central Italy; 25 km from the Adriatic coast at the confluence of the Castellano and Tronto rivers, surrounded on 3 sides by mountains of the Appno Umbro-Marchigiano; the painter and architect Cola Filotesio dell'Amatrice worked here between 1519 and 1542; railway; monuments: Gothic hall-church of San Francesco (1262-1371); event: Quintana medieval jousting (1st Sunday in Aug).

Āsela *a-se'lay*, ASELLE, 7 58N 39 04E, pop(1984e) 36,720, capital of Ārsī region, Ethiopia, NE Africa; 140 km SSE of Addis Ababa.

Aselle, city in Ethiopia. See Āsela.

Ashanti *a-shan'tee*, hilly region in S central Ghana, W Africa; the R Afram flows SE from its source W of Mampong; the Oda and Ofin rivers flow SW from their sources near Kumasi; L Bosumtwi, SE of Kumasi, is Ghana's only natural lake; pop(1984) 2,089,683; area 25,123 sq km; capital Kumasi; chief towns Obuasi, Mampong, Juaso and Bekwai; formerly an African kingdom, then British protectorate; at war with Britain 1807-26, 1873-74 and 1895-96; part of Digya National Park located in NE; economy: gold mining, diamond processing.

Ashby-de-la-Zouch *ash-bi-de-la-zoosh'*, 52 46N 1 28W, pop(1981) 11,900, market town in North West Leicestershire dist, Leicestershire, central England; 26 km WNW of Leicester; economy: coal, soap, foodstuffs, agricultural trade; monument: 15th-c castle where Mary Queen of Scots was imprisoned in 1569.

Ashdod *ash-dōd'*, 31 48N 34 38E, pop(1982e) 62,000, seaport in South dist, W Israel; on the Mediterranean Sea, 40 km S of Tel Aviv-Yafo; the present city was founded in 1956 as the major port of S Israel; railway; ancient and modern harbour; important port of call for cruise ships.

Asheville, 35 36N 82 33W, pop(1980) 53,583, county seat of Buncombe county, W North Carolina, United States; on the R French Broad, on a plateau in the Blue Ridge Mts; settled in 1794, achieving city status in 1835; university; railway; popular mountain resort; economy: tourism; manufactures electrical equipment, textiles, clothing, timber and tobacco; monument: Colburn Mineral Museum; home of the writer, Thomas Wolfe.

Ashford, 51 09N 0 53E, pop(1981) 45,962, town in Ashford dist, Kent, SE England; on the Great Stour river, 21 km SW of Canterbury; railway junction; economy: engineering, perfume.

Ash'ington, 55 11N 1 34W, pop(1981) 28,116, town in Wansbeck dist, Northumberland, NE England; 8 km E of Morpeth; economy: coal, engineering.

Ashkhabad *as-KHe-bat'*, formerly POLTORATSK (1919-27), 37 58N 58 24E, pop(1983) 338,000, capital city of Ashkhabadskaya oblast and S Turkmenskaya SSR, Soviet Union; situated close to the Iranian border, the city stands at the centre of an oasis, bounded N by the Peski Karakumy (Kara-Kum Desert) and S by the Khrebet Kopet-Dag range; established in 1881 as a military fortification; university (1950); on the Trans-Caspian railway; a canal brings water from the R Amudar'ya to the city; airport; economy: solar research and development, foodstuffs, manufacture of carpets, glass, and machinery.

Ashland, 38 28N 82 38W, pop(1980) 27,064, town in Boyd county, NE Kentucky, United States; on the R Ohio, 170 km ENE of Lexington; railway; economy: river and railway shipping point for coal, clay and timber; iron and steel, coke, refined oil, chemicals, clothing and mining equipment.

Ashmore and Cartier Islands, uninhabited Australian external territory in the Indian Ocean 320 km off the NW coast of Australia; timezone GMT +8; area about 3 sq km; the Ashmore Islands (Middle, East and West islands) and Cartier Island came under the authority of the Commonwealth of Australia in 1931; formerly administered by the Northern Territory, it became a separate Commonwealth Territory in 1978; responsibility for administration rests with the Minister for Territories and Local Government; in 1983 Ashmore reef was declared a national nature reserve.

Ashqelon *ash'ke-lon*, sub-district of South dist, central Israel; bounded W by the Mediterranean Sea; pop(1983) 203,743; area 1,272 sq km.

Ashqelon, 31 40N 34 35E, resort and ancient Philistine city in South dist, W Israel; on the Mediterranean Sea, 56 km S of Tel Aviv-Yafo; the ancient quarter lies 2 km S in a national park; railway; Mediterranean terminal of an oil pipeline from Elat on the Gulf of 'Aqaba.

Ashton-in-Makerfield *-mayk'-*, 53 29N 2 39W, pop(1981) 28,411, town in Tameside borough, Greater Manchester, NW England; 8 km S of Wigan; economy: engineering.

Ashton-under-Lyne *-līn'*, 53 29N 2 06W, pop(1981) 44,196, town in Tameside borough, Greater Manchester, NW England; 10 km E of Manchester; railway; economy: engineering, machinery, leather, plastics, textiles, cigarettes, cotton, chemicals.

'Āsi *a'see*, ORONTES *ō-ron'tees*, ('the rebel river'), river in SW Asia; rises in the El Beqa'a valley near Baalbek in Lebanon; flows N between the Jebel esh Sharqi (Anti-Lebanon) and Jebel Liban (Lebanon) ranges then flows through W Syria passing Ḥimş and Ḥamāh; in N Syria it forms part of the Turkish border then turns abruptly W then SW past Antakya to discharge into the Mediterranean Sea S of Samandag; length 384 km; used for irrigation, particularly in Syria where a dam at Ḥimş (said to date from the time of the Pharaohs) impounds the Bahrat Ḥimş.

Asia *ay'zha*, the largest continent; bounded N by the Arctic Ocean, E by the Pacific Ocean, S by the Indian Ocean and W by Europe; measures 8,560 km in length by 9,600 km in breadth; area including Asian USSR c.44 mn sq km; the principal mountain system is the Himalayas, rising to 8,840 m at Mt Everest; the people of Asia form over half the pop of the world, with a density of over 75 persons per sq km; major ethnic groups include Caucasian, Mongolian, Malayan, Dravidian and Negroid; major rivers include the Chiang Jiang (Yangtze), Huang He (Yellow River), Brahmaputra, Irrawaddy, Indus and Ganga (Ganges); major cities with a pop in excess of 5 million persons include Tōkyō, Shanghai, Calcutta, Beijing, Bombay, Seŏul, Manila, Jakarta, Delhi and Bangkok.

Asīr *a-seer'*, tribal prov of SW Saudi Arabia, bounded N by Hejāz, E by Najd, S by Yemen, and W by the Red Sea; consists of the arid Tihama coastal plain backed by a mountain range which rises to 3,133 m at Jebel Abhā, the highest peak in Saudi Arabia; one of the chief agricultural areas of the country; chief towns Abhā, Şabyā, and Jīzān; acknowledged the rule of Ibn Sa'ud in 1926; made a division of Saudi Arabia in 1930.

As'ker, 59 52N 10 26E, pop(1980) 35,941, town in Akershus county, SE Norway; railway.

Askim *as'keem*, 59 15N 11 10E, pop(1980) 12,069, town in N of Østfold county, SE Norway; near E bank of R Glåma, 53 km SE of Oslo; railway.

Askøy *ask'u-u*, 60 24N 5 10E, pop(1980) 17,080, town in Hordaland county, SW Norway.

Asmera *as-me'ra*, ASMARA, 15 20N 38 58E, pop(1984e) 275,385, capital of Ērtra region, Ethiopia, NE Africa; situated at 2,350 m above sea-level, 65 km SW of Mits'iwa (Massawa), its port on the Red Sea coast; occupied by Italians in 1889, replacing Mits'iwa as regional capital in 1897; occupied by British forces in 1941; university (1958); airport (Yohannes IV, 9.5 km); monuments: cathedral (1922), archaeological museum.

Asnam, Al *al as-nahm'*, CHELIFF, ECH *shay-leef'*, 36 11N 1 21E, pop(1982) 179,123, town in Algeria, N Africa; WSW of Alger; railway.

Aspen, 39 12N 106 49W, pop(1980) 3,678, resort town in Pitkin county, W central Colorado, United States; an old silver-mining town now converted into a year-round resort and cultural centre with ski slopes nearby; events: music and film festivals.

Asprópirgos *ah-spro'pir-gos*, 38 03N 23 35E, pop(1981) 11,816, town in Attikí nome (dept), Sterea Ellás-Évvoia region, Greece; W of Athínai (Athens).

Assaba *as-sah'ba*, AÇBA, region in S Mauritania, NW Africa; pop(1982e) 152,000; area 36,500 sq km; capital Kiffa; chief towns Kankossa and Zrafiét.

Assam', state in E India; bounded NW by Bhutan and SE by Bangladesh; pop(1981) 19,902,826; area 78,523 sq km; divided into the 9 administrative dists of Chachar, Darrang, Goalpara, Kamrup, Karbi Anglong, Lakhimpur-Dibrugarh, North Chachar Hills, Nowgong, Sibsagar; almost completely separated from India by Bangladesh; Assam has a unicameral legislature of 126 members; crossed by the R Brahmaputra (Jamuna); the world's largest river island of Majuli is a pilgrim centre; became a British protectorate in 1826 at the close of the Burmese War; annexed to Bengal in 1839; detached from Bengal in 1874; joined the Eastern Districts of Bengal in 1905 on the partition of Bengal; separated again in 1912; with the partition of India in 1947, almost all of the Muslim district of Sylhet was given to Pakistan, while Dewangiri was ceded to Bhutan; Meghalaya state, previously within Assam, was created in 1972; capital Dispur; economy: oilfields producing almost half of India's crude oil, oil refining, timber, tea, rice, jute, cotton and oilseeds; event: Bohang Bihu (April).

As'sen, 53 00N 6 34E, pop(1984e) 46,745, capital city of Drenthe prov, N Netherlands, 26 km S of Groningen, at the confluence of 2 inland waterways, Drentse Hoofdvaart and Noord-Willemskanal, in attractive wooded surroundings; important junction for inland shipping; railway; economy: oil and gas; became an independent community in 1807 and received its charter in 1809 from King Louis Bonaparte.

Assiniboine *a-si'nu-boyn*, river in S Canada; rises in E Saskatchewan prov, to the N of Yorkton; flows SE to the mouth of the Qu'Appelle river, then E through S Manitoba past Brandon and Portage la Prairie to join the Red river at Winnipeg; length 1,070 km; its principal tributary is the Souris river.

Assiout, town in Egypt. See Asyût.

Asti *as'tee*, prov of Piemonte region, NW Italy; pop(1981) 215,382; area 1,510 sq km; capital Asti.

Asti, 44 54N 8 13E, pop(1981) 77,681, capital town of Asti prov, Piemonte region, NW Italy; at the centre of a fertile wine-producing area (Asti Spumante), at the junction of the Tanaro and Borbore rivers; bishopric; railway; economy: textiles, chemicals, glass, food products, tourism; event: Palio race (mid-Sept).

Astipálaia *ahs-tip-ah'lu-yu*, 36 32N 26 23E, island of the Sporádhes, Greece, in the S Aegean Sea, WSW of Kós; area 97 sq km; pop(1981) 1,030; Astipálaia is the main settlement.

Astrakhan', formerly KHADZHI-TARKHAN, 46 22N 48 04E, pop(1983) 481,000, capital city of Astrakhanskaya oblast, SE European Rossiyskaya, Soviet Union; on a huge island in the Volga delta; 75 km of dykes protect the city from the Volga's floodwaters; alt 22 m below sea-level; founded in the 13th century; university (1919); the most important river and seaport in the Volga-Caspian basin; railway; airport; economy: fishing and fish processing, woodwork, metalwork, ship repair, chemicals, textiles, cotton, foodstuffs, transport equipment, and river vessels; a major transshipment centre for oil, fish, grain, and wood; monument: 16th-c white-walled Kremlin fortress.

Asturias *as-too'ree-as*, autonomous region and former principality of N Spain co-extensive with the prov of Oviedo; pop(1981) 1,129,556; area 10,565 sq km; a mountainous region extending along the Bay of Biscay to the W of Santander prov; the Cordillera Cantabrica which occupy most of the region rise to 2,646 m in the Picos de Europa which are famous for rock-climbing, hunting and fishing; the agriculture of the fertile Oviedo basin is largely based on maize, fruit and livestock; nearly half of Spain's coal is supplied from the mines of Asturias where the mining of fluorspar, zinc and iron have also helped to promote industry in Oviedo and Gijón.

Asunción *a-soon-syōn'*, 25 15S 57 40W, pop(1982) 455,517, federal and dept capital in Central dept, Oriental, SW Paraguay; an important transport and commercial centre on the shores of a bay on the E bank of the Río Paraguay; established in 1537, this was the first permanent Spanish settlement in the La Plata region of which it was capital until replaced by Buenos Aires in 1580; 2 universities (1890, 1960); railway; airport (Presidente General Stroessner) at 15 km; economy: food processing, footwear, textiles; monuments: the city is laid out in the colonial rectangular style and is built on a low hill topped by the large modern church, La Encarnación; none of the public buildings in Asunción date earlier than the last half of the 19th century; the government palace was built during the Triple Alliance War in the style of the Louvre; the congressional palace and the cathedral are in the Plaza Constitución; to the SW of this square is the Plaza de los Héroes, with the Pantheon of Heroes: begun during the Triple Alliance War and finished in 1937, it is based on Les Invalides in Paris; it now contains the tombs of 2 unknown Paraguayan soldiers and of Marshal Estigarribia, the victor of the Chaco War in the 1930s; across the river is the reservation of the Maca Indians, brought from the Chaco.

Asuncion, La, 11 06N 63 53W, pop(1980) 9,000, capital of Nueva Esparta state, NE Venezuela; on Isla de Margarita; economy: cotton, sugar, distilling.

Aswân *a-swahn'*, SYENE (anc), 24 05N 32 56E, pop(1976) 144,377, capital of Aswân governorate, S Egypt; on the E bank of the R Nile, 900 km S of Cairo; Elephantine I on the R Nile is the oldest inhabited area of Aswân; Aswân Dam at First Cataract and limit of river navigation S of Aswân was built in 1898-1902; Aswân High Dam further S at the head of L Nasser was completed in 1971; railway; airfield (8 km); economy: steel, textiles, winter tourism; monuments: Aswân museum; the Roman Nilometer; temples of Ptolemy VII (2nd-c BC), Seti I and Rameses II; Tombs of the Ancient Nobles carved out of the hillside on the W bank of the Nile; Aga Khan Mausoleum on the W bank; Coptic monastery of St Simeon (6th-c); temples of Philae; temple of Kalabsha, dating from the reign of the Roman Emperor Augustus, transported 55 km from its original site and re-erected near the Aswân High Dam.

Asyût, ASSIOUT *as-ee-oot'*, LYCOPOLIS (anc), 27 14N 31 07E, pop(1976) 213,983, capital of a governorate of the same name, central Egypt; on the W bank of the R Nile, 380 km S of Cairo; nearby are the ruins of Tel el Amarna; university (1957); railway; economy: pottery, wood and ivory crafts.

Atacama *a-ta-ka'ma*, region of N Chile; bordered by the Andes and Argentina (W); comprises the provs of Chañaral, Copiapó and Huasco; watered by the Copiapó and Huasco rivers; includes the Andean peaks of Volcán Copiapó, Nevado Tres Cruces and Cerro Dos Hermanos, the last two lie on the Argentinian border; pop(1984) 212,900; area 74,705 sq km; capital Copiapó; chief towns Vallenar and Chañaral; an Inca smelting complex was discovered in the Copiapó valley in 1981; economy: fishing; mining (copper, iron); agriculture; the Huasco valley is noted for its wine production; at Huasco there is a mechanical pier for loading the iron ore mined at Algorrobo.

Atacama, Desierto de, arid desert area in N Chile; extends 960 km S from the Peru border to the Río Copiapó; the desert is included in parts of Tarapacá, Antofagasta and Atacama regions; at 600 m, the desert is a series of dry salt basins bounded W by the Pacific coastal range and E by the Cordillera de Domeyko, a flanking range of the Andes which separates the desert from the Puna de Atacama, the high Andean tableland on the Argentina-Chile border; there is almost no vegetation and the desert is claimed to be the world's driest area; the town of Calama recorded a 400-year drought up to 1971; of the streams descending from the Andes, only the Río Loa reaches the Pacific; water is piped to the towns and nitrate fields from the Cordillera; the desert was ceded to Chile by Peru and Bolivia in 1883-84; included in the salt basins are the Pampa del Tamarugal (a desert plateau, 290 km long and 32 km wide) in Tarapacá and Antofagasta regions (NW); the pampa is rich in nitrates, iodine and borax; the salt desert of Salar de Punta Negra in Antofagasta region contains borax deposits.

Atacazo *a-ta-ka'sō*, 0 22S 78 35W, extinct Andean volcano in Pichincha prov, N central Ecuador; 19 km SW of Quito; height 4,410 m.

Atafu *a-ta-foo'*, formerly DUKE OF YORK ISLAND, 8 40S 172 40W, low lying atoll of Tokelau, S Pacific Ocean, 496 km N of Western Samoa; area 2.03 sq km; pop(1981) 554.

Atakora *a-ta-kō'ra*, prov in NW Benin, W Africa; dominated by the Atakora Mts; the R Pendjara flows NE and then SE forming part of Benin's N border; the R Mekrou flows NE across the prov from its source in the Atakora Mts; chief towns Djougou, Natitingou, Bassila; Boucle de la Pendjari National Park lies to the N; economy: gold mining.

Atakora, CHAINE DE L'ATAKORA (Fr), low mountain range mainly in NW Benin, W Africa; c.210 km long and rising to about 750 m.

Atakpamé *a-tak-pa'ma*, 7 34N 1 14E, pop(1977) 21,800, chief town of Des Plateaux region, S Togo, W Africa; on the railway between Lomé and Blitta; at the centre of Togo's cotton growing belt; famous for the Tchebe 'stilt dance'; economy: textiles, trade in coffee.

Atar *a'tar*, 20 32N 13 08W, pop(1976) 16,326, capital of Adrar region, W Mauritania, NW Africa; located on Route du Mauritanie, NE of Nouakchott, 420 km E of Nouadhibou; airfield.

Atbara *at'ba-ra*, 17 42N 34 00E, pop(1983) 73,009, town in Northern region, Sudan, NE Africa; on the R Atbara at its junction with the R Nile, 16 km N of Ed Damer; Lord Kitchener's army defeated the Khalifa's troops here in 1898; railway junction; airfield.

Atebubu *at-e-bu'bu*, 7 47N 1 00W, town in Brong-Ahafo region, central Ghana, W Africa.

Ath *aht*, AAT *aht* (Flem), dist of Hainaut prov, S Belgium; area 487 sq km; pop(1982) 77,264.

Athabasca *a-tha-bas'ka*, lake in central Canada; situated in NE Alberta and NW Saskatchewan; area 8,080 sq km; length 335 km; receives the Athabasca and Peace rivers in the SW, drained in the NW by the Slave river which links it to the Great Slave Lake and from there by the Mackenzie river to the Arctic Ocean; large deposits of oil sand are mined in this area.

Athabasca, river in W central Canada; southernmost tributary of the Mackenzie river; rises in the Rocky Mts on the border between Alberta and British Columbia, to the N of Mt Columbia; flows through Jasper national park and then NE to enter L Athabasca in a delta at the SW opposite Fort Chipewyan; length 1,231 km; major tributaries include the Pembina, Lesser Slave, La Biche and Clearwater rivers.

Athens, capital city of Greece. See Athínai.

Ath'ens, 33 57N 83 23W, pop(1980) 42,549, county seat of Clarke county, N Georgia, United States; on the R Oconee, 95 km ENE of Atlanta; settled in 1785; university (1801); railway; economy: poultry processing; manufactures clocks and watches, and textiles.

Ath'erton, 53 31N 2 31W, pop(1981) 22,032, town in Salford borough, Greater Manchester, NW England; 18 km WNW of Manchester; railway; economy: engineering, textiles, drinks.

Athínai *ah-thee'ne*, ATHENS *ath'énz* (Eng), ATHENAE (anc), 38 00N 23 44E, pop(1981) 862,133, Greater Athens 3,027,331, capital city of Greece; in a wide coastal plain between the Ilissus and Cephissus rivers, surrounded by hills rising to 1,413 m at Párnis and 1,026 m at Imittós; political, economic, and cultural centre of Greece; an ancient Greek city-state extending over Attiki by the 7th century BC; reached a height of economic and cultural prosperity under Pericles (460-431 BC); taken by the Romans in 146 BC; visited by St Paul in 54 AD; part of the Ottoman Empire in 1456; capital of modern Greece since 1835; university (1837); railway; 2 airports at Ellinikó; its shipping lines are based at Piraiévs (Piraeus), one of the principal ports of the Mediterranean; economy: textiles, machine tools, shipbuilding, chemicals, food processing; monuments: a number of hills rise out of the plain of Attikí, among them the Acropolis (156 m), which was built on as early as Mycenaean times, the Hill of the Nymphs (105 m), and the Pnyx (110 m), meeting place of the Assembly in ancient Athínai; there are numerous museums, including the National Archaeological Museum which houses the finest collection of Greek art in the world; monuments of ancient Athínai located on the Acropolis include the Parthenon (5th-c BC), temple of the city's guardian goddess Athena, wrecked by an explosion in 1682; the Propylaea (437-432 BC); the temple of Athena Niki (432-421 BC); the Ionic Erechtheion (421-406 BC); the Acropolis museum, situated at the SE corner of the Acropolis, containing a fine collection of Greek sculpture; S of the Acropolis are the Odeon of Herod Atticus (2nd-c BC), the portico of Eumenes, remains of the Asklepieion, the rock-cut theatre of Dionysus (4th-c BC), and the site of the Odeum of Pericles; to the N of the Acropolis lies the excavated area of the Ancient Agora (market-place), and further E there are more Roman remains (market, Hadrian's Library, Tower of the Winds); other monuments include the Olympieion, which dominates the area E of the Acropolis; the Arch of Hadrian (AD 131-132), which marks the boundary between the ancient city and the Roman extension; the Stadion, a large marble structure with seating for 70,000 spectators which occupies the same site as its ancient predecessor; monuments of the modern city, which dates from the reign of King Otto I (1834-62), include the former royal palace (1834-38), now the Parliament Building; to the S and E of the palace is the National Garden, one of the city's relatively few open spaces; events: Carnival (Feb); Athínai Festival of Music and Drama (July-Sept); folk dancing in open-air theatre (May-Sept); son et lumière (April-Oct).

Athlone *ath-lōn'*, ÁTH LUAIN (Gael), 53 25N 7 56W, pop(1981) 14,426, town in Westmeath county, Leinster, central Irish Republic; on R Shannon, W of Dublin; technical college; barracks; radio transmitter; river boating centre; railway; economy: textiles, industrial and electrical cable; monuments: remains of town wall, 13th-c Franciscan abbey, 13th-c castle; event: all-Ireland amateur drama contest in July.

Athy *uth-ī'*, BAILE ÁTHA H-Í (Gael), 52 59N 6 59W, pop(1981) 5,565, market town in Kildare county, Leinster, E Irish Republic; on R Barrow on a branch of the Grand Canal SW of Dublin; railway; economy: agricultural trade, peat moss factory; monument: Woodstock Castle (12th-c).

Ati *ah-tee'*, 13 11N 18 20E, capital of Batha prefecture, central Chad, N central Africa; between N'Djamena and Abéché.

Atitlán, Lago de *a-teet-lan'*, lake in Sololá dept, SW central Guatemala, Central America; 64 km W of Guatemala City; area 388 sq km; length 38 km; occupies the crater of an extinct volcano; it is over 300 m deep with no visible outlet and is surrounded by high cliffs; on its shores are the inactive volcanoes of Atitlán and Tolimán (S), and San Pedro and Santa Clara (SW); fishermen supply the markets of the region with fish and freshwater crabs from the lake.

Atiu *a-tee-oo'*, formerly ENUAMANU, 20 00S 158 07W, coral island of the Cook Is, S Pacific, 184 km NE of Rarotonga; area 27 sq km; pop(1981) 1,225; rises to 90 m; fertile volcanic soils cover the slopes of the hills; pineapples, oranges, taro, and coffee are grown; Takitaki cave, inhabited by birds, is a popular tourist attraction.

Atjeh, territory of Indonesia. See Aceh.

Atlan'ta, 33 45N 84 23W, pop(1980) 425,022, capital of state in Fulton county, NW Georgia, United States;

largest city in the state, situated close to the R Chattahoochee, near the foothills of the Appalachian Mts; the region was ceded by Creek Indians in 1821 and the city founded at the end of the railway in 1837 when it was called Terminus; re-named Atlanta in 1845; a Confederate supply depot in the Civil War, and burned by General Sherman in 1864; capital of Georgia since 1887; 4 universities (1835, 1836, 1865, 1913); railway; airport; economy: industrial, transportation, commercial and financial centre of the state; manufactures include aircraft, automobiles, textiles, food products, steel, furniture and chemicals; monuments: High Museum of Art, Alliance Theatre, Oakland Cemetery, Martin Luther King historic site, Grant Park; the home and grave of Martin Luther King Jr.

Atlantic City, 39 21N 74 27W, pop(1980) 40,199, town in Atlantic county, SE New Jersey, United States; on the Atlantic coast, 96 km SE of Philadelphia; railway; popular seaside resort with famed boardwalk (over 6 km long); also known for its casinos.

Atlantic Ocean, body of water extending in an 'S' shape from the Arctic to the Antarctic, separating the continents of North and South America (W) from Europe and Africa (E); area c.82,217,000 sq km; connected to the Arctic Ocean by (1) the Greenland Sea, via the Denmark Strait, (2) the Norwegian Sea and (3) Baffin Bay, via Nares Strait and Davis Strait; connected to the Pacific Ocean by the Drake Passage, the Straits of Magellan and the Panama Canal, via the Caribbean Sea; connected to the Indian Ocean by the Suez Canal, via the Mediterranean Sea and by that area between Antarctica and Africa. Principal arms in the W are the Labrador Sea, the Gulf of Mexico and the Caribbean Sea; in the E the North Sea, Baltic Sea, Mediterranean Sea and Black Sea, the Bay of Biscay and the Gulf of Guinea; in the S the Weddell Sea. The continental shelf is narrow off the coast of Africa and Spain but broader in NW Europe with depths of 90 m off the S coast of Ireland and 550 m off the S coast of Norway; the continental shelf is wider off the E coast of N and S America with depths of 3.6 m near Boston and 120 m at the mouth of the Río de la Plata; the continental shelves fall away to deep abyssal plains reaching depths of 5,725 m in the Argentine abyssal plain and 4,875 m in the Demerara abyssal plain beyond the continental shelf and alluvial cone at the mouth of the R Amazon; average ocean depth 3,660 m; the ocean floor is separated from that of the Arctic by a submarine ridge system running between SE Greenland and Scotland; the 'S' shaped, submarine Mid-Atlantic Ridge runs between Iceland and the Antarctic Circle dividing the ocean floor into eastern and western sections; the ridge is the centre of earthquake and volcanic activity, being offset by numerous faults across its entire length; as new igneous rock is formed at the axis of the ridge in a spinal rift valley, the older crust moves away on each side to cause sea-floor spreading such that North and South America are moving away from Africa and Europe; divergent plate motion is estimated to occur at a rate of 2.0 cm per year in the North Atlantic S of Iceland, 3.0 cm per year at the Equator and 4.1 cm per year in the South Atlantic; the Rio Grande and Walvis ridges are lateral ridges which may have formed as a result of drifting; main plates are the North American, Eurasian, African and South American; subduction as a result of contact with the Caribbean plate has formed the Puerto Rico Trench, where the Atlantic's deepest point of 8,648 m is found; a shallow submarine ridge lies across the Straits of Gibraltar separating the Atlantic from the more saline Mediterranean water; oceanographic information dates from the Challenger Expedition (1872-76); surface circulation patterns in the Atlantic are the result of the rotation of the Earth, wind systems, topography and water density; major movement is clockwise in the North Atlantic and counter-clockwise in the South Atlantic; main currents include the Gulf Stream or North Atlantic Drift, the North Equatorial Current, Canary Current, Equatorial Counter Current, South Equatorial Current, Brazil Current and the Benguela Current; the Sargasso Sea is a sluggish region which exists at the centre of movement in the North Atlantic; main islands include Iceland, Færøerne (Faeroe Is), the British Isles, the Island of Newfoundland, the Azores, Bermuda, Madeira and the Canary Islands, the Cape Verde Islands, Trinidad and Tobago, Ascension, St Helena, the Martin Vaz Islands, Trinidad, Tristan da Cunha group, Gough, the Falkland Islands, and South Georgia; mineral resources of the Atlantic include manganese nodules, found off the coasts of Brazil and Argentina in the deep South Atlantic and in the North American Basin; offshore oil and gas, found off the coast of SW Africa, the tip of Argentina, in the Brazil Basin, in the Angolan Basin and the Caribbean; metal-rich sediments are found in association with the Mid-Atlantic Ridge; diamonds are mined off SW Africa and gold off Nova Scotia; best fishing areas correspond to those areas of greatest phytoplankton abundance, where nutrients are washed down from the land or where coastal or equatorial upwelling occurs. The Atlantic is an important international communications highway, particularly for oil tanker traffic from the Middle East to Europe, as the Suez Canal is limited to ships with a loaded draught of 11 m.

Atlántico *at-lan'tee-kō*, dept in N Colombia, South America; bounded N by Caribbean sea, E by the upper Río Magdalena and S by the Canal del Dique; pop(1985) 1,406,545; area 3,382 sq km; capital Barranquilla.

Atlántida *at-lan'tee-da*, maritime dept in N Honduras, Central America; pop(1983e) 242,235; area 4,248 sq km; capital La Ceiba.

Atlantique *at-lã-teek'*, coastal prov in S Benin, W Africa; chief towns Ouidah, Allada; economy: petroleum, cement processing.

Atlas Mountains, a system of folded mountain chains in Morocco, Algeria and Tunisia, NW Africa; associated geologically with the similar folded chains of the W Mediterranean basin; includes (1) the volcanic Anti-Atlas range in SW Morocco which runs SW-NE for 250 km and rises to heights over 2,500 m and is connected to the main Atlas range by a ridge which peaks at Jbel Siroua (3,304 m); (2) the Haut Atlas range which is the largest range in the group, running SW-NE for 650 km from Morocco's Atlantic coast near Agadir and rising to Jbel Toubkal (4,165 m), the highest point in Morocco; (3) to the N, the Moyen Atlas rising to 3,343 m at Caberral; (4) E-W along Morocco's Mediterranean coast the Er Rif mountains which rise to over 2,000 m at Jbel Tidighine (2,496 m) and Jbel Taghzout (2,459 m); (5) the Atlas Saharien which extends NE of the Haut Atlas across N Algeria rising to its highest point at Djebel Aissa (2,236 m); (6) the Tell Atlas, a smaller coastal range running along Algeria's Mediterranean seaboard.

At-Ta'mīm, governorate in N Iraq; pop(1977) 495,425; area 9,426 sq km; capital Kirkūk; bounded N by the R Az-Zāb al-Kabir.

Attapu, ATTOPEU *a-tō'pu*, prov (*khowèng*) of S Laos, SE Asia; capital Attapu.

Attersee or **Kammersee** *at'er-zay* or *kam'er-zay*, LAKE ATTER or KAMMER (Eng), 47 55N 13 32E, lake in Vöcklabruck dist, Oberösterreich, N Austria, E of Salzburg; extends from the limestone walls of the Höllengebirge in the SE to the low hills of the Alpine foreland; area 45.9 sq km; length 20 km; width 2-3 km; max depth 171 m; largest Alpine lake in Austria; lakeside summer resorts at Seewalchen, Kammer, Weyregg, Steinbach and Weissenbach.

Attica, nome (dept) of Sterea Ellás-Évvoia region, E Greece. See Attikí.

Attikí, ATT'ICA (Eng), nome (dept) of Sterea Ellás-Évvoia region, E Greece, bounded S and E by the Aegean Sea; pop(1981) 342,093; area 3,381 sq km; capital Athínai (Athens); between Athínai and Soúnion there are numerous holiday resorts on the coast, which is known as the 'Attic Riviera' or 'Coast of Apollo'; the E coast to the S of Marathón has also become a popular holiday area.

Attleboro, 41 57N 71 17W, pop(1980) 34,196, town in

Bristol county, SE Massachusetts, United States; near the Rhode Island border, 19 km NE of Providence, Rhode Island; railway.

Atuntaqui *a-toon-ta'kee*, 0 21N 78 10W, pop(1982) 12,247, town in Imbabura prov, in the Andean Sierra of N central Ecuador; W of Ibarra and NE of Quito; railway; economy: clothes, textiles.

Aube *ōb*, dept in Champagne-Ardenne region of NE France, comprising 3 arrond, 32 cantons and 430 communes; pop(1982) 289,300; area 6,004 sq km; capital Troyes; centre of the sparkling Champagne wine area; the dry chalk of the Champagne-Pouilleuse is arid except for the fertile ribbon of the R Aube which flows NW-SE; the R Seine flows in a similar direction further S; extensive woodland; the Parc de la Forêt de l'Orient regional nature park caters for riding, water sports and fishing; economy: hosiery, wine, forest products, grain and vegetables.

Aube, river in NE France rising in the plateau of Langres; flows NW by Bar and Arcis to the R Seine N of Romilly-sur-Seine; length 248 km.

Au'burn *aw'burn*, 32 36N 85 29W, pop(1980) 28,471, town in Lee county, E Alabama, United States; 80 km ENE of Montgomery; university (1856); railway; economy: textiles.

Auburn, 42 56N 76 34W, pop(1980) 32,548, county seat of Cayuga county, central New York, United States; at the N end of L Owasco, 40 km WSW of Syracuse; founded in 1793; railway; monuments: Cayuga museum of history and art, Owasco Stockaded Indian Village.

Auburn, 47 18N 122 14W, pop(1980) 26,417, city in King county, W central Washington, United States; situated 16 km ENE of Tacoma; railway.

Auch *ōsh*, ELIMBERRUM or AUGUSTA AUSCORUM (Lat), 43 39N 0 36E, pop(1982) 25,543, ancient town and capital of Gers dept, Midi-Pyrénées region, S France on R Gers; archbishopric; known for its Armagnac eau-de-vie and pâté de foie gras; an important city in Roman Gaul and former capital of Gascony and Armagnac; a long stairway of 200 steps leads down from the Place Salinis to the river; railway; economy: furniture, hosiery; monuments: folk museum; St Pierre cathedral; statue of d'Artagnan who was immortalised by Dumas in *The Three Musketeers*.

Auckland *awk'-*, 36 55S 174 43E, pop(1981) 144,963 (city), 769,558 (urban area), seaport city in Central Auckland, North Island, New Zealand; on a narrow isthmus between Waitemata and Manukau harbours; principal port of New Zealand; founded in 1840; capital of New Zealand (1840-65); Waitemata Harbour is spanned by the Auckland Harbour Bridge; to the NE of Auckland is Rangitoto, a volcanic island; in the suburb of Mount Wellington is the New Zealand Heritage Park, with displays featuring the nature, culture and agriculture of New Zealand; university (1958); railway; airport; economy: textiles, footwear, clothing, chemicals, steel, electronics, carpets, plastics, food processing, vehicle assembly; monuments: Howick colonial village; Auckland War Memorial museum contains New Zealand's largest collection of Maori artifacts; the Museum of Transport and Technology has an early flying machine invented by the New Zealander, Richard Pearse.

Aude *ōd*, dept in Languedoc-Roussillon region of S France on the Golfe du Lion, comprising 3 arrond, 34 cantons and 437 communes; pop(1982) 280,686; area 6,139 sq km; capital Carcassonne; mountainous in the S; on the N slopes of the Pyrénées and furrowed W-E by a large depression in which flows the R Aude; watered by the Canal du Midi which links the R Garonne with the Rhône; Les Corbières, a spur of the French Pyrénées rising to 1,231 m at Bugarach and stretching towards the Cévennes, are heavily wooded with extensive vineyards producing rich, fruity VDQS appellation wine; sparkling white wine is produced around Limoux; more fertile in the N where cereals, olives and almonds are grown; Quillan and Limoux are small manufacturing towns; Narbonne is noted for its white honey; along the coast are lagoons rich in fish; minerals: iron, lead, cobalt, etc; there are spas at Ginoles-les-Bains, Escouloubre-les-Bains and Rennes-les-Bains.

Aude, river in S France rising in the Pyrénées-Orientales near Pic de Carlitte; flows N to Carcassonne then E to the Golfe du Lion E of Narbonne; length 220 km; tributary Fresquel.

Augrabies Falls *o-grab'eez* ('place of great noise'), national park in NW Cape prov, South Africa; S of the Kalahari Gemsbok park; area 54.03 sq km; the falls, which drop 191 m through a series of rapids, were discovered in 1824; includes the Klipspringer Trail into the longest granite canyon in the world.

Augsburg *owgs'boork*, AUGUSTA VINDELICORUM (anc), 48 22N 10 54E, pop(1983) 246,700, industrial and commercial city in Schwaben dist, S Bayern (Bavaria) prov, W Germany; at the confluence of the Lech and Wertach rivers, 48 km WNW of München (Munich); founded by the Romans, it is the oldest city on the popular tourist route, the 'Romantic Road', which runs from the Main valley via Augsburg to Füssen; the world's first social settlement, the Fuggerei, is here; university (1970); railway; economy: textiles, threads, cotton fabrics, fabric printing and finishing, jet aircraft, machine building, heavy engineering and steel fabrication, construction; monuments: Renaissance town hall (1615-20), St Ulrich's Minster (1500), Rococo Schaezler Palais; event: Mozart Summer Festival.

Augus'ta, 33 28N 81 58W, pop(1980) 47,532, county seat of Richmond county, E Georgia, United States; on the R Savannah, 166 km ENE of Macon; founded c.1717 as a river trading post; changed hands many times during the War of Independence; capital of Georgia 1786-95; housed Confederate powder works during the Civil War; a popular resort with a notable golf club; railway; airfield; economy: trade and industrial centre; manufactures include textiles, fertilizers, chemicals and bricks.

Augusta, 44 17N 69 50W, pop(1980) 21,819, state capital of Maine, United States; on the R Kennebec 72 km from its mouth, and 40 km NE of Lewiston; in Kennebec county, S Maine; airfield.

Aunis *ō-nees*, former prov of W France now occupying with part of Saintonge the dept of Charente-Maritime; it was formerly under the control of Poitou and the capital was La Rochelle.

Aurangābād *ow'rung-gah-bahd*, 24 46N 84 23E, pop(1981) 316,000, historic city in Bihar, E India; lies to the E of the R Son, 64 km W of Gaya; economy: silk; monuments: many notable Mogul monuments and cave temples.

Aurillac *ō-ree-yak*, 44 55N 2 26E, pop(1982) 33,197, market town, tourist centre and capital of Cantal dept, Auvergne region, S central France; on the R Jordanne; to the NE is the volcanic Plomb du Cantal; the town is associated with Gerbert, the shepherd-boy who became the first French Pope, Sylvester II, in the year 999; he is credited with having made an astrolabe and a weight-driven clock, and with having introduced arabic numerals to W Europe after a visit to Arab-occupied Spain; railway; economy: umbrellas, leather goods.

Aurora *aw-rō'ra*, 39 44N 104 52W, pop(1980) 158,588, town in Arapahoe county, N central Colorado, United States; a residential suburb 10 km E of Denver; railway; economy: agricultural trade, electrical products, aircraft parts and oil-field equipment.

Aurora, 41 45N 88 19W, pop(1980) 81,293, town in Kane county, NE Illinois, United States; 59 km W of Chicago; railway.

Auroville *ow'rō-vil*, city in Tamil Nadu, SE India; international utopian city under construction NW of Pondicherry.

Aurskog-Holand *owr'skōg-hōlant*, 59 55N 11 27E, pop (1980) 12,344, town in Akershus county, SE Norway.

Aust-Agder *owst-ahg'der*, formerly NEDENES *nay'de-nays*, a county of S Norway bounded on the S by the Skagerrak, drained chiefly by the Otra, Nidelva and Tovdalselva rivers; area 9,212 sq km; pop(1983) 92,738; capital Arendal.

Austin *aw'stin*, 30 17N 97 45W, pop(1980) 345,496, capital of state in Travis county, S central Texas, United States; on the Colorado river, 236 km WNW of Houston; first settled in 1835 and made capital of the independent Republic of Texas in 1839; in 1842 the Texas government moved to Houston for fear of marauding Mexicans and Indians, but returned to Austin in 1845 when Texas joined the Union as a state; 2 universities (1876, 1881); railway; airfield; economy: commercial centre for an extensive agricultural region; electronic and scientific research; event: Aqua Festival (Aug).

Austral Islands, French Polynesia. See Tubuai, Îles.

Australasia *o-stral-ay'zha*, a term etymologically equal to *Southern Asia*, used to indicate Australia, Tasmania, New Zealand, New Guinea (including New Britain), New Caledonia and Vanuatu; often described as equivalent to all of Oceania below the Equator and N of 47°S; the term is not commonly used in these areas.

Australia *o-strayl'ya*, official name Commonwealth of Australia, an independent country forming the smallest continent in the world; situated entirely in the S hemisphere; lies between 113 09E and 153 39E and 10 41S and 43 39S with almost 40% of its land mass lying N of the Tropic of Capricorn; bounded N by the Timor and Arafura seas, NE by the Coral Sea, E by the South Pacific Ocean, and S and W by the Indian Ocean; timezones: Western Australia GMT +8, Northern Territory and South Australia GMT +9½, New South Wales, Queensland, Tasmania, Victoria and Australian Capital Territory GMT +10; area 7,692,300 sq km; capital Canberra; principal towns Melbourne, Brisbane, Perth, Adelaide and Sydney; pop(1986) 16,248,836; pop comprises 1% Aborigine and Asian and 99% Caucasian, largely of British, Maltese, Italian, Greek, Dutch and Polish descent; English is the official language; under 30% of the pop are Anglican, over 25% are Roman Catholic; the currency is the Australian dollar of 100 cents; national holidays 26 Jan (Australia Day), 25 April (Anzac Day), the Queen's Birthday; membership of ADB, AIOEC, ANZUS, CIPEC, Colombo Plan, Commonwealth, DAC, ELDO, ESCAP, FAO, GATT, IAEA, IATP, IBA, IBRD, ICAC, ICAO, ICO, IDA, IEA, IFAD, IFC, IHO, ILO, ILZSG, IMF, IMO, INTELSAT, INTERPOL, IOOC, IPU, IRC, ISO, ITC, ITU, IWC (International Whaling Commission), IWC (International Wheat Council), OECD, UN, UNESCO, UPU, WHO, WIPO, WMO, WSG.

Physical description. The Australian continent consists largely of plains and plateaux, three-quarters of which lie at an average alt of 600 m above sea-level. The West Australian Plateau, which occupies nearly half the whole area, is composed of ancient rocks similar to those of Africa. In the centre of the plateau, around the town of Alice Springs, are the MacDonnell Ranges, which rise to 1,524 m at Mt Liebig and 1,510 m at Mt Zeil. NW is the Kimberley Plateau rising to 936 m at Mt Ord and W are the Hamersley Ranges rising to 1,226 m at Mt Bruce. Most of the plateau is dry and barren, comprising flat desert including the Gibson Desert (W), the Great Sandy Desert (NW), the Great Victoria Desert (S) and the Simpson Desert (central). S of the Great Victoria Desert is the Nullarbor Plain which is traversed by the Trans-Australian Railway. The Eastern Highlands or Great Dividing Range extends in a zone 150-400 km wide parallel to the E seaboard from Cape York Peninsula, N Queensland to S Victoria. In SE New South Wales it rises to 2,228 m in Mount Kosciusko, Australia's highest mountain, in the section known as the Australian Alps. The range consists of a series of blocks uplifted during the Tertiary period, separating the fertile plains of the E coast from the vast West Australian Plateau. Between the W Plateau and the E Highlands lies a broad synclinal lowland belt extending from the Gulf of Carpentaria S through Queensland, where there is a vast artesian basin, into the Murray-Darling plains, which have been filled up since tertiary times with waste materials derived mainly from the E Highlands. Unlike the Gulf of Carpentaria, which is a N unfilled section of the syncline, the V-shaped Spencer's and St Vincent's gulfs W of Adelaide are rift valleys formed by downthrows on the margin of the upthrust blocks of the Flinders and Barrier ranges. Off the NE coast of Australia, stretching for over 1,931 km, is the Great Barrier Reef. The island of Tasmania, a S extension of the E Highlands, rises to 1,617 m at Mt Ossa and is separated from the mainland by the Bass Strait. In the W and S of the continent are numerous dry salt lakes, which rarely fill with water. The country's longest river is the Murray, its chief tributaries are the Darling, Murrumbidgee and Lachlan.

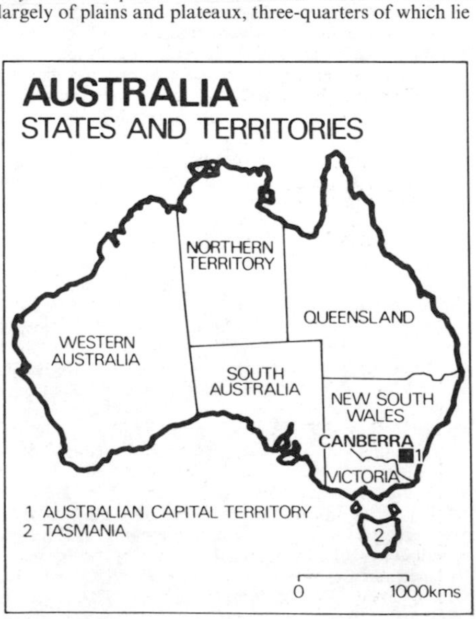

Climate. The disposition of the highlands close to the E coast is unfortunate for Australia which lies mainly in the belt of the SE Trades, its longer E-W axis being in near alignment with those winds. Only the two S corners reach far enough S to catch rainfall from the westerlies in winter, and only the two N peninsulas extend far enough N to receive any considerable rains from the summer NW monsoon. Darwin in Northern Territory has an average daily temperature of 26°-34°C in Nov and 19°-31°C in July, with a max rainfall of 386 mm in Jan during the period of the 'Willy Willie' tropical storms, falling to 0 mm in July. More than a third of the country receives under 260 mm mean annual rainfall and less than a third receives over 500 mm. Half of Australia has a rainfall variability of more than 30%, with many areas experiencing prolonged drought. Alice Springs, situated at the heart of desert and semi-arid central Australia, has average daily temperatures of 4°-19°C in July and 21°-36°C in Jan, with min and max monthly average rainfall figures of 8 mm (July-Sept) and 43 mm (Jan). Fertile land with a temperate climate and reliable rainfall is limited to the lowlands and valleys and highland slopes in the E and SE within 400 km of the coast, and a small triangular region in the SW corner. The population of Australia is concentrated in these two regions. Melbourne has average daily temperatures of 6°-13°C in July, the coldest month, and 14°-26°C in Jan-Feb, with monthly rainfall averaging between 48 and 66 mm. In Tasmania climatic conditions vary between mountain and coast. The W is exposed to the stormy W winds which bring heavy rainfall (over 2,500 mm per annum in places). The E lowlands have a much lower rainfall (500-700 mm per annum). Owing to the relative warmth of the Southern Ocean, winters are mild at sea-level and summers are not excessively hot. Hobart, representative of the lowland area, has an average daily temperature of 4°-11°C in July and 12°-22°C in Jan.

History, government and constitution. The first European

visitors to Australia were the Dutch who explored the Gulf of Carpentaria in 1606 and landed in 1642. Over a century later Captain James Cook finally took British possession of Australia in 1770. No longer able to deport petty criminals to America, Britain decided in 1786 to establish a penal colony to be called New South Wales. The first group of convicts arrived on 26 Jan 1788. In 1829, all the territory now known as Australia was constituted a dependency of Britain. Increasing numbers of settlers were attracted to Australia. Spanish Merino sheep were imported at the end of the 18th century, the first shipment of wool being exported to London in 1807. Gold was discovered at Bathurst, New South Wales, in 1851, and later at Ballarat and Bendigo, Victoria. Transportation of convicts to E Australia ended in 1840, but continued until 1853 in Tasmania and until 1868 in Western Australia. A second gold rush took place in 1892-93 with the discovery of gold at Coolgardie and Kalgoorlie. In 1850 a British Act of Parliament set up Legislative Councils, with freedom to amend Colonial constitutions. The colonies drafted their own constitutions and set up their own governments, New South Wales in 1855, Tasmania and Victoria in 1856, South Australia in 1857, Queensland in 1860 and Western Australia in 1890. In 1901 the Commonwealth of Australia was established with Canberra chosen as the site for its capital. The legislature comprises a bicameral Federal Parliament with a 64-member Senate elected for 6 years and a 125-member House of Representatives elected every 3 years. The Prime Minister and the cabinet ministers are responsible to the House. The head of state is the Governor-General representing the Queen as Queen of Australia, who presides over an Executive Council. Five states have bicameral parliaments comprising a Legislative Council and a House of Assembly. Queensland has a unicameral Legislative Assembly. Northern Territory with a unicameral Legislative Assembly has been self-governing since 1978. The Australian Capital Territory has a legislative body responsible to a federal minister.

Economy. Australia's economy has traditionally been based on agriculture and mining. Australia is the world's largest wool producer, and a top exporter of veal and beef. The country's most important crop is wheat, most of which is exported to China, Japan, Egypt, Indonesia and the Soviet Union. Other important cereals include barley, oats, maize and sorghum. Discoveries of petroleum reserves, bauxite, rutile, ilmenite, nickel, lead, zinc, copper, tin, uranium, iron ore and other minerals in the early 1960s have turned Australia into one of the world's major mineral producers. Commercial oil production began in 1964 when the Moonie oilfield in Queensland came on stream. The Gippsland basin produces two-thirds of Australia's oil and most of its natural gas, but major discoveries have been made off the NW coast. Manufacturing industry has expanded rapidly since 1945, the fastest-growing industries being those connected with engineering, car manufacture, metals, textiles, clothing, chemicals and food processing. Australia is now an important exporter of steel-mill products. Also important is shipbuilding with yards at Whyalla, Adelaide, Brisbane, Maryborough, Newcastle, Sydney and Melbourne.

Administrative divisions. Australia is divided into 6 states and 2 territories:

Division	*area (sq km)*	*pop(1986e)*
States		
New South Wales	801,428	5,605,269
Queensland	1,727,200	2,675,313
South Australia	984,000	1,393,813
Tasmania	67,800	449,135
Victoria	227,600	4,207,689
Western Australia	2,525,500	1,496,059
Territories		
Australian Capital Territory	2,400	263,156
Northern Territory	1,346,200	158,402

Australian Alps, chain of mountains in SE Australia forming the S part of the Great Dividing Range; extends approx 300 km SW from Australian Capital Territory to the Goulburn river, Victoria; includes the Snowy Mts, Bowen Mts and Barry Mts, Victoria; the Australian Alps rise to 2,228 m at Mount Kosciusko, the highest peak in Australia.

Australian Antarctic Territory, Antarctic territory situated S of 60° S and lying between 142° and 136° E (excluding Terre Adélie); claimed by Australia in 1936; area 6,043,852 sq km of land and 84,798 sq km of ice shelf; a scientific station was established in MacRobertson Land at Mawson in 1954; Davis base in the Vestfold Hills was established in 1957; Australia assumed custody of the US Wilkes Station on the Budd Coast in 1959 and subsequently replaced it by the Casey Station in 1961; Australia is a party to the 1959 Antarctic Treaty.

Australian Capital Territory, territory in SE Australia; bordered on all sides by New South Wales; mountainous in the S, the territory drops N through low hills to the urbanized floodplains of the Murrumbidgee and Molonglo rivers; pop(1986) 263,156; area 2,400 sq km; up to 60% of the workforce is employed by the government; the manufacturing sector is largely associated with government contract work in electronics and computing; the Australian Capital Territory was created in 1911 to provide a location for the national capital, Canberra; state holidays Canberra Day (March), Bank Holiday (August), Labour Day (Oct).

Austria *os'tree-ah*, ÖSTERREICH *u'ster-rīKH* (Ger), official name Republic of Austria, REPUBLIK ÖSTERREICH, a federal republic in central Europe bordered to the N by W Germany and Czechoslovakia, to the S by Italy and Yugoslavia, to the W by Switzerland and Liechtenstein and to the E by Hungary; timezone GMT +1; area 83,854 sq km; pop(1981) 7,555,338; capital Wien (Vienna); major cities include Graz, Linz, Salzburg, Innsbruck and Klagenfurt; the language is German; 98.1% of the population is German, 0.7% is Croatian and 0.3% is Slovene; the religion of 85% of the population is Roman Catholic; the unit of currency is the schilling of 100 groschen; national holiday 26 Oct; membership of EFTA, free trade agreement with EEC, GATT, ADB, DAC, ECE, EMA, FAO, IBRD, ICAC, ICAO, IDA, IDB, IEA, IFAD, IFC, ILO, IMF, IMO, INTELSAT, INTERPOL, ITU, IWC, UN, UNESCO, UPU, WFTU, WHO, WIPO, WMO, WTO, WSG.

Physical description. Situated at the E end of the Alps, Austria is almost entirely mountainous. The ranges of the Ötztal, Zillertal, Hohe Tauern and Niedere Tauern stretch eastwards from the main Alpine massif and after attaining heights of more than 3,750 m at Grossglockner (3,797 m) and Wildspitze (3,774 m) slope away into the

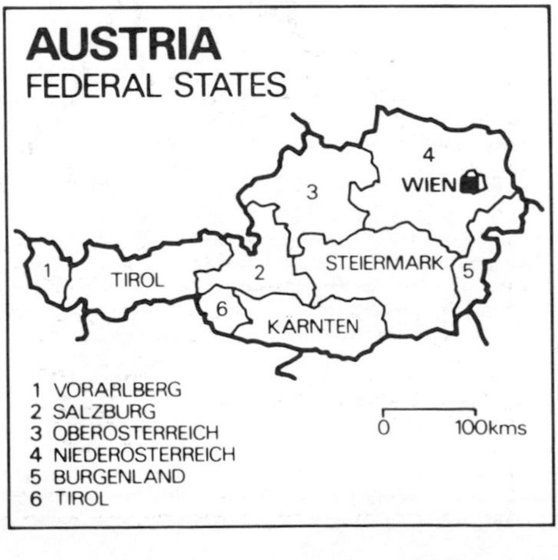

Hungarian plain. The chief passes into Italy are the Brenner and Plöcken. The country lies, with the exception of Vorarlberg state, in the drainage basin of the R Danube and its tributaries, the Lech, Inn, Traun, Raab and Drau rivers. Neusiedler See on the E frontier with Hungary is the largest lake.

Climate. Austria can be divided into 3 climatic regions: (1) the Alps - often sunny in winter but cloudy in summer; (2) the Danube valley and Wien basin - the driest region where winter snow is rarely deep; (3) the SE including Steiermark and Kärnten - a region of heavy thunderstorms, where winters can be severe but summers are warmer and sunnier than N of the Alps. In general the summer months are wettest although rainfall is often heavy and of short duration. Winters are cold throughout the country and are coldest when E to NE winds bring low temperatures from E Europe and Russia. Some N-S running Alpine valleys experience a warm, dry wind known as the Föhn which is most frequent in autumn and spring and can be responsible for fires and snow-melt leading to avalanches.

History, government and constitution. The state of Austria grew out of the Eastern Mark ('March' or frontier land), which was founded as an outpost of the empire of Charlemagne. In time the mark became a duchy and passed to the Hapsburg family in 1282. After 1438 the heads of this house held almost uninterruptedly the position of Holy Roman Emperor, and Austria became the leading state in Germany. On the extinction of the Holy Roman Empire in 1806, the Hapsburgs declared themselves Emperors of Austria, ruling over territory in present-day Hungary, Czechoslovakia, Yugoslavia, and Poland. The Austrian Federal Republic was established in 1919 on the break-up of the Austro-Hungarian Empire. Political disagreements in the early 1930s resulted in the establishment of an authoritarian state under Chancellor Dollfuss and in March 1938, as a result of the *Anschluss*, Austria was incorporated into the German Reich under the name Ostmark. In April 1945 a provisional government restored the Republic of Austria which was jointly occupied by British, American, French and Russian troops until 1955 when the country was finally recognized as an independent democratic state. In Oct 1955 the National Assembly passed the Federal Constitutional Law on the Neutrality of Austria. Since then Austria has been a haven for refugees from many states in E Europe and Asia. The Parliament or Federal Assembly includes a National Assembly (*Nationalrat*) and an Upper House (*Bundesrat*); 183 deputies are elected to the National Assembly and 63 members to the Upper House. The President as Head of State holds office for 6 years and appoints the Federal Chancellor. The Nationalrat, which is elected for 4 years, approves federal legislation and also any newly appointed government. Each province is administered by its own government headed by a Governor elected by the provincial parliament.

Agriculture and forestry. Although only 20% of the total area of Austria is arable land and 28.8% is pasture, over 300,000 farms (1980) produce 99% of the country's food needs. Between 1970 and 1980 the agricultural workforce was reduced by about 25% as a result of mechanization. Austria's principal agricultural areas are the regions to the N of the Alps and along both sides of the R Danube to the plains of the E frontier with Hungary. Here there is crop-farming and cattle-farming as well as orchards and vineyards. On lower and middle mountain slopes there is more forestry and cattle breeding; 44.2% of Austria is under forest; 58.8% of farm and forest production is accounted for by small, privately owned holdings of 0.02-0.1 sq km, 39.3% by medium-sized holdings of 0.1-1 sq km.

Industry. Since prehistoric times ore-yielding rock strata have provided a wide range of metal and mineral resources. In Eisenerz, Steiermark, iron ore is obtained by opencast mining in the Erzberg Mts. Foundries are located nearby at Donawitz and the raw steel is processed into high-grade steel at Donawitz, Judenburg, Kapfenberg, Kindberg, Kreiglach (Steiermark) and Ternitz (Tirol). The second major iron and steel centre is Linz which is linked to the steel towns of Krems and Liezen by the R Danube. The LD method of oxygen-blown steel which was developed in Austria is now used worldwide to produce high-grade steel. In addition to iron, Austrian mines also produce lignite, lead ore, zinc ore, antimony ore, graphite, talc, anhydrous gypsum, kaolin, clay and salt. Also important is the processing of raw aluminium, refined lead, antimonial lead, electrolytic tin and sintered magnesite. Oil and natural gas are extracted from fields NE of Wien (Vienna) and from the region between the Enns and Inn rivers. Oil refining and associated petrochemical industries are located at Schwechat. There are 4 pipelines transporting natural gas to industrial centres throughout Austria and two transit pipelines crossing from COMECON countries to Italy and W Germany. Since the end of World War II Austria has tried to expand its finished goods sector using traditional commerce and small industries to produce textiles, paper, ceramics, wood products, clothing, chemicals, foodstuffs, glassware, metal goods, electrical goods and vehicles. Austria's major trading partner is W Germany.

Communications. There are 355 km of navigable inland waterways with two river ports at Linz and Wien. There are international airports at Wien, Graz, Linz, Klagenfurt, Salzburg and Innsbruck.

Administrative divisions. Austria is divided into 9 federal states (*länder*) as follows:

Federal State	*area (sq km)*	*pop(1981)*
Burgenland	3,966	272,274
Kärnten	9,533	536,727
Niederösterreich	19,171	1,439,137
Oberösterreich	11,979	1,270,426
Salzburg	7,154	441,842
Steiermark	16,387	1,187,512
Tirol	12,647	586,139
Vorarlberg	2,601	305,615
Wien	415	1,531,346

The federal states are divided into 98 districts (*Bezirke*).

Austvågöy *owst-vo-gu'ü*, ØSTVÅGØY or ØSTVAAGØY, Norwegian island in the Norwegian Sea, largest of the Lofoten group, 88 km W of Narvik, separated from Hinnöy (E) by a narrow strait; rises to 1,055 m; area 526 sq km; length 53 km; width 18 km; administered by Nordland county; Svolvær, on the E coast, is the chief town.

Auvergne *o-vern'y'*, region and former prov of central France comprising the depts of Allier, Cantal, Haute-Loire and Puy-de-Dôme, 14 arrond, 154 cantons and 1,308 communes; pop(1982) 1,332,678; area 26,013 sq km; the region is named after the Arverni whose chieftain, Vercingetorix, was the most famous opponent of Caesar in the Gallic Wars; from a Roman prov it became a duchy, a county, and (10th century) a principality which was united to France in 1527; Haute-Auvergne is the mountainous part to the W and Basse-Auvergne the valley of the R Allier; some of the great rivers of France start their journeys here - the Loire, Cher, Allier, Dordogne and the Lot; there are numerous hydroelectric barrages (at Sarrans and Bort-les-Orgues); the capital, Clermont-Ferrand, marks the division between the 'Limagne', the low-lying fertile valley of the Allier, and the high volcanic plateaux to the SW; the high ground begins dramatically, immediately W of Clermont-Ferrand, with the solitary peak of Puy-de-Dôme rising to 1,463 m; the highest peaks in the Auvergne are found in the Monts Dore, with the Puy de Sancy at 1,886 m.

Auxerre *ō-ser'*, AUTISSIODORUM (Lat), 47 48N 3 32E, pop(1982) 41,164, market town and capital of Yonne dept, Bourgogne, central France; on the R Yonne and surrounded by orchards and vineyards; one of the oldest towns in France; bishopric; railway; economy: wine, paints, metal goods; monuments: the St Étienne cathedral; abbey church of St Germain with 9th-c frescoes which are the oldest of their kind in France.

Auyu'ittuq, national park in Franklin dist, Northwest Territories, N Canada; on SE Baffin island, at the N end of the Cumberland Peninsula; dominated by the Penny Highlands which rise to over 2,100 m and are capped by the Penny Ice Cap, c.5,700 sq km of solid ice; Auyuittuq National Park also contains glaciers in the valleys surrounding the Penny Highlands; area 21,471 sq km; the park was established in 1972.

Auzangate *ow-sang-ga'tay*, 13 47S 71 15W, Andean peak rising to 6,394 m in a spur of the Cordillera de Carabaya which is part of the Cordillera Occidental, Cuzco dept, SE Peru.

Avarua, 21 12S 159 46W, port and capital town of the Cook Is, S Pacific, on the island of Rarotonga; Rarotonga International Airport opened in 1973 is W of the town; economy: fruit canning.

Ave *a'vay*, river in Porto dist, N Portugal, rising in the Serra da Cabreira and flowing into the Atlantic at Sul de Vila do Conde; length 85 km; navigable 2 km as far as Vila do Conde; area of basin, 1,395 sq km; principal tributaries Este and Vizela.

Avebury *ayv'bėr-i*, 51 27N 1 51W, village in North Wiltshire dist, Wiltshire, S England; on the R Kennet, 15 km SW of Swindon; monuments: the village is located within a Neolithic earthwork with a stone circle, the largest megalithic monument in England; nearby Silbury Hill is the largest prehistoric construction in Europe; the West Kennet long barrow, containing 30 burials in 5 chambers, is the largest chambered tomb in England; Windmill Hill is one of the oldest known Neolithic sites, with remains dating back to about 3,100 BC.

Aveiro *a-vay'ro*, dist of NW Portugal bordering the Atlantic, part of prov of Beira Litoral; area, 2,708 sq km; drained by R Vouga which forms a lagoon 47 km long by 7 km wide at its mouth; divided into 19 councils and 198 parishes; pop(1981) 622,988; economy: cereals, wool, vegetables, meat, dairy produce, cork, resin, timber, fruit, wine, brandy, fishing, salt, seaweed and the manufacture of fertilizer, paper, motor engines, chemicals and ceramics; minerals: antimony, arsenic, wolfram, manganese, copper, coal, lead; airfields at São Jacinto, Espinho, Esmoriz and Maceda; the dist includes the important demarcated wine area of Bairrada.

Aveiro, TALABRIGA (anc), 40 37N 8 35W, pop(1981) 29,200, capital of Aveiro dist, Portugal; ancient port and fishing town lying on E side of R de Aveiro, 67 km S of Porto; associated with 16th-c Newfoundland cod-bank fishing; bishopric; traversed by canals; railway; economy: ship repair, salt from the salt-pans on the shores of the Aveiro estuary, seaweed for use as fertilizer, porcelain and ceramics; monuments: cathedral (1464) and many fine burghers' houses; events: industrial and trade fair at the end of March; municipal holiday on 12 May; Ria festival, regatta of seaweed-fishers in second half of July; pilgrimage of São Paio da Torreira, the blessing of the boats in September.

Avellino *a-vel-lee'nõ*, ABELLI'NUM (anc), prov of Campania region, S Italy; pop(1981) 434,021; area 2,802 sq km; capital Avellino.

Avellino, 40 49N 14 47E, pop(1981) 56,892, capital town of Avellino prov, Campania region, S Italy; in the Appennino, 45 km E of Napoli (Naples); centre of an agricultural and wine-growing area; monument: restored 10th-c cathedral.

Aveyron *a-vay-rõ*, mountainous dept in Midi-Pyrénées region of S France lying close to the S edge of the Massif Central; comprises 3 arrond, 46 cantons and 304 communes; pop(1982) 278,654; area 8,735 sq km; capital Rodez; the dept is crossed by the Lot, Aveyron, Viaur and Tarn rivers which are separated by hills; the R Truyère, a tributary of the R Lot in the NE is dammed for hydroelectric power; in the N are wild basaltic spurs of the Mts du Cantal and in the S are limestone spurs of the Cévennes (Causse du Larzac); spa at Cransac; economy: stock-rearing, Roquefort cheese, coal, iron, gloves (Millau).

Aveyron, river in S France rising in the Causse de Sauveterre limestone plateau of the Massif Central; flows W to meet the R Tarn below Montauban; length 250 km; tributary Viaur.

Aviemore, 57 12N 3 50W, pop (1981) 2426; town in Badenoch and Strathspey dist., Highland region, N central Scotland; on the R Spey, 19 km SW of Grantown, 18 km NE of Kingussie; skiing and winter sports centre, all-year tourist resort; situated between the Cairngorms to E and Monadhliath Mountains to W; economy: tourism.

Avignon *a-veen-yõ*, former prov of SE France largely in Vaucluse dept; its capital was the city of Avignon.

Avignon, AVENIO (Lat), 43 57N 4 50E, pop(1982) 91,474, walled capital of Vaucluse dept, Provence-Alpes-Côte d'Azur region, SE France, at the foot of a chalk hill on the left bank of the R Rhône; a popular tourist centre; archbishopric; a papal residence between 1309 and 1376; the centre of an important school of painting; John Stuart Mill the philosopher died and was buried here in 1873; railway; economy: chemicals, soap, paper, man-made fibres; monuments: the vast Gothic Palais des Papes; ruins of the 12th-c Pont St Benezet, subject of the folk-song 'Sur le Pont d'Avignon'; many fine churches and museums.

Ávila *a'vee-la*, prov in Castilla-León region, N Spain; separated from Madrid prov by the Sierra de Guadarrama; mountainous to the S and flat to the N where it forms part of the central plateau (Meseta); pop(1981) 178,997; area 8,048 sq km; capital Ávila; economy: tourism, wine, livestock (chiefly Merino sheep), timber products.

Ávila or **Ávila de los Caballeros**, AVELA, ABULA or ABYLA (anc), 40 39N 4 43W, pop(1981) 41,735, ancient walled city, capital of Ávila prov, Castilla-León, central Spain; at the foot of the Sierra de Guadarrama; 115 km W of Madrid; alt 1,130 m; bishopric; railway; birthplace of Queen Isabella, St Teresa; economy: wine, livestock; monuments: cathedral (11th-c); town walls; churches of St Peter and St Vincent; monastery of St Thomas; events: Holy Week; Fiesta of St John in June; summer fiesta with a battle of flowers in July and Fiesta of St Theresa in Oct with a parade of giant figures and masks and dancing.

Ávila, El *el a'vee-la*, national park in N Venezuela; on the Caribbean, directly E of Caracas; area 851 sq km; established in 1958.

Avilés *a'vee-les*, 43 35N 5 57W, pop(1981) 86,584, seaport in Oviedo prov, Asturias, N Spain; on the R de Avilés estuary, 6 km from the coast; railway; airport; economy: shipbuilding, steel, metal products, fishing, textiles; monuments: churches of St Francis and St Nicholas of Bari (14th-c), with the tomb of Pedro Menendez, the conqueror of Florida; events: Bullo fiesta at Easter with folk music, parades, regatta and cattle show; fair in Aug.

Avon *ay'von*, county in SW England; bounded W by the R Severn estuary; includes parts of the Cotswolds and Mendip Hills; pop(1981) 915,176; area 1,347 sq km; county town Bristol; chief towns include Bath and Weston-super-Mare; economy: food processing, high technology; the county is divided into 6 districts:

District	*area (sq km)*	*pop(1981)*
Bath	29	80,771
Bristol	110	390,697
Kingswood	48	84,495
Northavon	462	119,297
Wansdyke	323	76,733
Woodspring	375	163,183

Avon (Celtic, 'river' or 'stream'), river rising at Naseby in Northamptonshire, central England; flows 75 km SW through Warwickshire and Hereford and Worcester to meet the R Severn at Tewkesbury in N Gloucestershire.

Avon, river rising in NW Wiltshire, S England; flows 112 km S, W and NE through Bath and Bristol to meet the Bristol Channel at Avonmouth.

Awaso *a-wa'sō*, 6 20N 2 22W, town in Western region, W Ghana, W Africa; on the railway between Dunkwa and Goaso.

Awe, picturesque loch in Strathclyde region, W Scotland; length 37 km; SE of Oban; drained by the R Awe; many early lake dwelling sites (crannogs) have been discovered; Ben Cruachan rises to 1,124 m to the N; hydroelectric power station; Inverliever Forest lies W; monuments: 15th-c Kilchurn castle, Inishail chapel.

Axim *ash-eem'* or *ak'sim*, 4 53N 2 14W, town in Western region, W Ghana, W Africa; originally a fort built by the Portuguese.

Ayacucho *a-ya-koo'chō*, dept in S Peru; mountainous dept crossed by the Cordilleras Occidental and Central; bordered by the Río Mantaro (N) and the Río Apurímac (NE); pop(1981) 430,289; area 45,503 sq km; capital Ayacucho; the last great battle in the war of independence was fought near Ayacucho (on 9 Dec 1824); Bolívar's forces decisively defeated those of the Viceroy, thus gaining political independence from Spain for most of South America.

Āybak *ī'bak*, AIBAK, SAMANGĀN, 36 16N 68 01E, pop(1984e) 5,413, capital of Samangān prov, N Afghanistan; on R Khulm, NNW of Kābul.

Aydın *ī-dun'*, maritime prov in W Turkey, bounded W by the Aegean Sea; pop(1980) 652,488; area 8,007 sq km; capital Aydın; drained E-W by the R Menderes; has deposits of iron, copper, lignite, emery, arsenic, magnesite, mercury; economy: cotton, tobacco, fruit and grain.

Ayer Itam or **Ayer Hitam** *ī'er ee'tam*, 5 25N 100 14E, pop(1980) 35,550, town on the island of Pulau Pinang (Penang), Pulau Pinang state, NW Malaysia, SE Asia; W of George Town; monument: Kek Lok Si (temple of paradise), the largest Buddhist temple in Malaysia, built 1890-1904.

Ayers Rock *ayrz*, ULURU (Abor), 25 18S 131 18E, inselberg in SW Northern Territory, N Australia; 32 km E of Mt Olga (546 m), in the 1,325 sq km Uluru National Park, 450 km SW of Alice Springs; rises from the desert to a height of 348 m; 3.6 km long, 2.4 km wide and 8.8 km in circumference; 20 km NW of Ayers Rock is the resort town of Yulara.

Ayia Napa *ay'ya na-pa*, 34 59N 34 00E, pop(1981e) 850, old fishing village in Famagusta dist, SE Cyprus; Ayia Napa and nearby Paralimni have become the second most important tourist areas on the island, with numerous hotels and self-catering complexes; monument: monastery of Ayia Napa, completed by the Venetians just prior to the Turkish occupation of 1570.

Aylesbury *aylz'ber-i*, 51 50N 0 50W, pop(1981) 52,914, county town in Aylesbury Vale dist, Buckinghamshire, S central England; N of the Chiltern Hills, 60 km NW of London; railway; economy: furniture, chemicals, food processing, engineering; monuments: 13th-c St Mary's church.

Aylesford *aylz'ford*, 51 18N 0 27E, pop(1981) 21,204, town linked with East Malling in Tonbridge and Malling dist, Kent, SE England; on the R Medway, 5 km NE of Maidstone; railway.

'Ayn, Al, 24 11N 55 45E, pop(1980) 101,663, rapidly developing new city in Abū Ẓabī emirate, United Arab Emirates, SE Arabian Peninsula; 150 km E of the coastal city of Abū Ẓabī; situated close to the Oman frontier in the W foothills of the Hajar Mts; surrounded by sand dunes, some in excess of 30 m high; there are date and palm plantations adjacent to the commercial centre; the city has developed on the site of an oasis village; one of the fastest-growing cities in the Middle East; university (1977); E terminus of the highway from Abū Ẓabī; 16 km S is the Al 'Ayn National Park; economy: small industrial areas to the S of the city (cement manufacturing); monuments: fort, several ancient archaeological sites in the vicinity; events: Islamic festivals.

Ayr, 55 28N 4 38W, pop(1981) 49,522, capital of Kyle and Carrick dist, Strathclyde, SW Scotland; on the Firth of Clyde, at the mouth of the R Ayr, 19 km SW of Kilmarnock and 48 km SW of Glasgow; railway; economy: metal products, machinery, carpets, tourism; monuments: Loudoun Hall (built in the late 15th, early 16th-c for a rich merchant) is one of Scotland's oldest examples of Burgh Architecture; the Tam o' Shanter Museum, a museum to the poet Robert Burns and once a brewhouse which Douglas Graham of Shanter (whom Burns wrote of as Tam o' Shanter) supplied with malted grain; 3 km S of Ayr is the town of Alloway, where Robert Burns was born in 1759; 19 km SSW of Ayr is Culzean castle (1777), designed by Robert Adam; between the castle and Ayr itself is a hill known as the 'electric brae' where an optical illusion makes vehicles appear to go downhill when they are actually going up.

Āzarbāyān-e Gharbī *ah'zur-bī-yan-e gar-vee*, mountainous province in NW Iran, bounded N and W by Turkey, and NE by the USSR; pop(1982) 1,407,604; area 38,850 sq km; capital Orūmīyeh.

Āzarbāyān-e Sharqī, mountainous prov in NW Iran, bounded N and NE by the USSR; pop(1982) 3,197,685; area 67,102 sq km; capital Tabrīz.

Azerbaydzhanskaya, AZERBAYDZHAN SSR, AZERBAIJAN *a-zer-bī-jahn'ski-a*, constituent republic of the Soviet Union, in the E part of Transcaucasia, bounded E by the Caspian Sea and S by Iran; the Nakhichevanskaya ASSR and the Nagorno-Karabakhskaya Autonomous Oblast are part of the republic; the main axis of the Bol'shoy Kavkaz (Greater Caucasus) range crosses the N part of the republic and runs into the Apsheronskiy Poluostrov (Apsheron Peninsula); the Malyy Kavkaz (Lesser Caucasus) range occupies the SW, separated from the mountains to the N by the plain of the R Kura; the highest peak is Mt Bazar-Dyuzi (4,480 m) in the NE; forests cover 10.5% of the total area; pop(1983) 6,399,000; area 86,600 sq km; capital Baku; chief towns Kirovabad and Sumgait; economy: oil extraction and refining; iron, steel, aluminium, copper, chemicals, cement, building materials, foodstuffs, textiles, fishing, timber industries, salt extraction; oil is extracted on the Apsheronskiy Poluostrov, in the Kura-Araks lowland, and in offshore areas (Neftyanyye Kamni); the most important industrial cities are Baku, Kirovabad, Nukha, Stepanakert, Nakhichevan', and Lenkoran'; chief agricultural products are grain, cotton, rice, grapes, fruit, vegetables, tobacco, and silk; c.70% of the cultivated land is irrigated; Azerbaydzhanskaya was proclaimed a Soviet Socialist Republic on 28 April 1920 and a constituent republic of the USSR in 1936; it comprises 2 divisions:

Division	*area (sq km)*	*pop(1983)*
Nagorno-Karabakhskaya (autonomous region)	4,400	168,000
Nakhichevanskaya (ASSR)	5,500	257,000

Azogues *a-sō'gays*, 2 46S 78 56W, pop(1982) 14,548, capital of Cañar prov, in the Andean Sierra of S central Ecuador; NE of Cuenca; railway; economy: pesticides, mineral products; a centre of the Panama hat industry.

Azores, Portuguese autonomous region. See Açores, Ilhas dos.

Azov, Sea of *a'zof*, AZOVSKOYE MORE (Rus), NE gulf of the Black Sea, in S European USSR, in the SE Ukraine; separated from the main body of the Black Sea by the Kerch Strait (Kerchenskiy Proliv); its main arms are the Gulf of Taganrog (Taganrogskiy Zaliv) to the NE and the Sivash Sea to the W; the Sivash or Putrid Sea is mostly swamp, being almost completely cut off from the Sea of Azov by the sandpit called the Tongue of Arabat (Arabat'skaya Strel'ka); fed by the Don and Kuban rivers; the water of the Black Sea is shallow and almost fresh, tending to freeze over during Nov-March; the max depth is 15.3 m; river deposits cause further shallowing and silting of harbours; an important source of freshwater fish for Soviet Russia.

Azraq, Bahr el, river in NE Africa. See Blue Nile.

Azuay *a-sway'*, mountainous prov in the Andean Sierra of S central Ecuador; intersected by fertile valleys with a semi-tropical, humid climate; pop(1982) 442,019; area 8,098 sq km; capital Cuenca; economy: drinks, tobacco, dairying, fruit canning, textiles, motor vehicles.

Azuero *a-sway'rō*, peninsula in W central Panama, Central America; on the Pacific Ocean coast; forms the W side of the Golfo de Panamá; length 80 km; includes the provs of Los Santos, Herrera, and part of Veraguas; rises to 829 m at Cerro Canajagua; terminates in Punta Mala (Mala Point) in the SE.

Azusa *a-zhoo'sa*, 34 08N 117 52W, pop(1980) 29,380, city in Los Angeles county, SW California, United States; at the foot of the San Gabriel Mts, 21 km E of Pasadena.

B

Baalbek *bahl'bek*, HELIOPOLIS (anc), 34 00N 36 12E, town in the El Beqa'a governorate of E Lebanon; at the W foot of the Jebel esh Sharqi mts; the Phoenicians built a temple to the sun-god, Baal, here; later associations with the Roman god, Jupiter; an important centre of Muslim Shi'ite activity and base for the Iranian Revolutionary Guard.

Babahoyo *ba-ba-ho'yō*, 1 53S 79 31W, pop(1982) 42,266, capital of Los Ríos prov, W central Ecuador; on the Río Babahoyo NE of Guayaquil; university (1971); economy: flour milling.

Babeldoab *beb-el-dō'ap*, BABELTHUAP, PALAU, rugged and densely wooded island, largest of the Belau group in the W Caroline Is, W Pacific Ocean; area 367 sq km; Micronesia's 2nd largest island (next to Guam); the highest point is Mt Ngerchelechuus; airport; there are prehistoric terraces with monoliths between Ollei and Mengellang villages.

Ba'bil, BABYLON *ba'bi-lun*, governorate in S central Iraq; pop(1977) 592,016; area 5,503 sq km; capital Al Ḩillah; traversed in the W by the R Euphrates (Al-Furāt).

Babylon *ba'bi-lun*, 32 33N 44 25E, ancient ruined city in Babil governorate, S central Iraq, N of Al Ḩillah, close to the R Euphrates; it was the chief city of Mesopotamia, rising to importance when Hammurabi made it the capital of his kingdom of Babylonia (c1760-1600 BC); the Hanging Gardens of Babylon were one of the Seven Wonders of the World.

Babylonia *ba-bi-lō'ni-a*, ancient empire of Mesopotamia, limited historically to the first dynasty of Babylon established by Hammurabi (c.1760 BC) and to the Neo-Babylonian period after the fall of the Assyrian Empire; coincides with the plain between Baghdād, Iraq, and the Persian Gulf.

Bacău *bak-a'oo*, county in E central Romania, with the E Carpathian Mts to the W; watered by the Bistriţa and Siret rivers; pop(1983) 700,303; area 6,606 sq km; capital Bacău; an important oil producing region.

Bacău, 46 32N 26 59E, pop(1983) 165,655, capital of Bacău county, E central Romania; on the R Bistriţa, and to the E of the E Carpathian Mts; airfield; railway junction; economy: chemicals, wood products, textiles, food processing, leather, light engineering, petroleum, paper, pulp.

Bačka Palanka or **Palanka** *bach'ka pa'lan-ka*, 45 14N 19 24E, pop(1981) 58,155, town in autonomous province of Vojvodina, NW Srbija (Serbia) republic, Yugoslavia; on R Danube, 32 km W of Novi Sad; railway.

Bacolod *bah-kō'lod*, 10 38N 122 58E, pop(1980) 262,415, seaport in Negros Occidental prov, Western Visayas, Philippines; 480 km SSE of Manila, on NW coast of Negros I; university (1941); railway; airfield; economy: sugar refining, fishing, rice.

Bács-Kiskun *bach-keesh'koon*, county in S Hungary; situated on the Great Plain (Alföld) between the R Danube and R Tisza and bounded to the S by Yugoslavia; pop(1984e) 564,000; area 8,363 sq km; capital Kecskemét; chief towns include Kiskunfélegyháza, Nagykörös and Kiskunhalas; 42% of the population lives in 6 towns, the rest in 105 villages and small settlements; the country's largest orchard can be found at Kecskemét; a quarter of the hydrocarbons produced in Hungary come from this county; national park at Kiskunság; economy: grain, fruit, vegetables, wine, paprika, food processing, poultry, livestock breeding, hydrocarbons, engineering, enamel, knitwear, lace.

Bad Godesberg, spa in W Germany. See Bonn.

Bad Homburg, VOR DER HÖHE BAD HOMBERG *baht hom'burg, for der hœ'e*, 50 17N 8 33E, pop(1983) 50,600, city in Darmstadt dist, Hessen (Hesse) prov, W Germany; at the foot of the Taunus Mts, 28 km ENE of Wiesbaden; mineral baths, health and tourist resort; economy: pharmaceuticals, health foods, paints, electrical insulation materials, industrial products, foodstuffs.

Bad' Lands, arid region of SW South Dakota and NW Nebraska, United States; an area of barren, eroded landscapes and fossil deposits E of the Black Hills.

Bad Salzuflen *baht zahlts-oof'lun*, 52 08N 8 44E, pop(1983) 51,000, spa city in Detmold dist, NE Nordrhein-Westfalen (North Rhine-Westphalia) prov, W Germany, 72 km SW of Hannover; railway.

Badajoz *ba-THa-hoth'* or *bad'a-joz* (Eng), prov in Extremadura region, W Spain; bounded on the W by Portugal; a prov of low hills and plains traversed by the R Guadiana; pop(1981) 635,375; area 21,657 sq km; capital Badajoz; largest prov in Spain; economy: olive oil, wine, tanning, foodstuffs, canning, textiles; hydroelectric power at Talarrubias.

Badajoz, PAX AUGUSTA (anc), 38 50N 6 59W, pop(1981) 114,361, capital of Badajoz prov, SW Spain, on R Guadiana, near Portuguese frontier; 401 km SW of Madrid; bishopric; former Moorish capital; birthplace of Louis Morales; airport; railway; economy: tinned vegetables, textiles.

Badakhshān *bad-ak-shan'*, prov in the Hindu Kush Mts of NE Afghanistan; bounded E by Pakistan and N by the USSR, with a narrow corridor stretching E to meet China; pop(1984e) 540,280; area 47,403 sq km; capital Feyzābād.

Badalona *ba-THa-lō'na*, BAETULO (anc), 41 26N 2 15E, pop(1981) 227,744, industrial seaport and outer suburb 10 km NE of Barcelona city in Barcelona prov, Cataluña, NW Spain; economy: shipbuilding, glass, textiles and exports; monument: on a nearby hill is the 15th-c monastery of San Jeronimo de la Murtra.

Baden *bah'den*, THERMAE PANNONICAE (anc), ('baths'), 48 01N 16 14E, pop(1981) 23,140, capital of Baden dist, Niederösterreich, NE Austria; 30 km S of Wien (Vienna), on the R Schwechat; connected to Wien by tram; the principal Austrian spa with sulphurous waters; casino.

Badenoch and Strathspey, district in Highland region, N Scotland; pop(1981) 12,402; area 2,319 sq km; chief town Kingussie; includes the resort towns of Aviemore and Grantown on Spey and the Cairngorm skiing developments.

Baden-Württemberg *bah'den vür'tem-berk*, prov in SW corner of W Germany, bounded on the W by France and on the S by Switzerland; comprises the administrative dists of Stuttgart, Karlsruhe, Freiburg and Tübingen; area 35,751 sq km; pop(1983) 9,243,300; capital Stuttgart; chief towns Karlsruhe, Freiburg and Ulm; chief rivers are the Danube, Rhine and Neckar; mountain ranges include the Schwarzwald (Black Forest) (SW), Schwäbische Alb (Swabian Jura) (SE) and Odenwald (N); SE includes N part of the Bodensee (L Constance); economy: precision engineering and the optical industry, electrical engineering, machine construction, textiles, motor vehicles; the 2nd largest tourist area in W Germany; the Schwarzwald is as famous for its health resorts and mineral springs as it is for its wooden clocks.

Bādghīs *bad'gis*, BADGHISAT, prov in NW Afghanistan; bounded N by the USSR; pop(1984e) 227,437; area 21,858 sq km; capital; Qal'eh-ye Now.

Badulla *ba-dul'a*, 6 59N 81 03E, pop(1981) 33,068, capital of Badulla dist, Uva, S Sri Lanka; at the centre of the

Uva Basin, within a tea-growing region; terminus of the mountain railway from Colombo.

Baerum *ba'rum*, LYSAKER *loo'sa-ker*, 59 56N 10 45E, pop(1980) 80,253, port and suburb of Oslo in Akershus county, SE Norway; at the head of Oslofjorden; the explorer Fridtjof Nansen died on his estate near here; economy: chemicals.

Bafatá *bu-fu-ta'*, region in central Guinea-Bissau, W Africa; pop(1979) 116,032.

Bafatá, 12 09N 14 38W, pop(1979) 13,429, town in Guinea-Bissau, W Africa; on the R Geba, 105 km ENE of Bissau.

Baffin Bay *baf'in*, an ice-blocked Arctic gulf, lying between Greenland (E) and Baffin, Bylot, Devon and Ellesmere islands (W); connected to the Arctic Ocean in the N by way of Smith Sound and Nares Strait and to the Atlantic Ocean in the S by the Davis Strait; length c.1,125 km; width ranges from 113 km to 644 km; although depths exceed 2,470 m, ice cover and the presence of numerous icebergs, brought by the Labrador Current from the Arctic, limit navigation to the summer; the bay was first entered in 1585 by John Davis and later explored by William Baffin in 1616; an important whaling area in the 1800s; seafowl and fur-bearing animals are found along the coastline.

Baf'fin Island, largest and easternmost island in the Canadian Arctic Archipelago; in SE Franklin dist, Northwest Territories, in the Arctic Ocean between 61°52′ and 73°51′N and 61°19′ and 90°11′W; separated from Labrador by the Hudson Strait; separated from Greenland to the E by the Davis Strait and Baffin Bay; area 318,186 sq km; length approx 1,600 km; width 209-725 km; the irregular coastline contains several deep bays including Frobisher Bay and Cumberland Sound (SE), Eclipse Sound (NE) and Admiralty Inlet (NW); mostly a plateau rising to approx 915 m; to the E there are mountain ranges with glaciers and snow fields; in the S are Nettiling and Amadjuak lakes; the island has several peninsulas including Hall, Cumberland and Foxe (S), Borden and Brodeur (N); the chief settlements are Frobisher Bay and Lake Harbour in the S and Pond Inlet in the NE; most of the inhabitants are Eskimos; first visited by Martin Frobisher in 1576-78; in 1614 William Baffin studied the island and bay during his search for the Northwest Passage.

Bafoussam *ba-foo'sam*, 5 31N 10 25E, pop(1984e) 88,000, capital of Ouest prov, Cameroon, W Africa; 270 km N of Douala; headquarters of Union of Arabica Coffee Cooperatives (UCCAO), which organizes the collection, processing, packaging and export of coffee; airfield; economy: coffee growing and trading centre, agricultural services, animal fodder, wood carving.

Bafu'ru Plateau, province of central Congo, W Africa; area 38,400 sq km; pop(1980) 102,670; capital Djambala.

Baghdād *bag'dad, bag-dad'* (Eng), governorate in central Iraq; pop(1977) 3,189,700; area 5,023 sq km; capital Baghdād; comprises the Euphrates-Tigris lowland.

Baghdād, 33 20N 44 26E, pop(1970) 2,183,760, capital city of Baghdād governorate and the Republic of Iraq; on R Tigris; commercial and transportation centre; founded in 762 on the W bank of the river; under the caliph Harun ar-Rashid Baghdād rose to become one of the greatest cities of Islam; the city is still enclosed on 3 sides by the ancient walls; university (1922); railway; airport; economy: oil refining, distilling, tanning, tobacco, textiles and cement.

Baghlān *bag-lan'*, prov in NE central Afghanistan; N of Kābul; pop(1984e) 536,783; area 17,109 sq km; capital Baghlān Jadid; connected by road to Kābul in the S; Salang Pass and tunnel, lying on the main Soviet supply route from the USSR border to Kābul, has been the focus of resistance activity by the Mujahideen guerrillas since the Russian invasion of Afghanistan in 1979.

Baghlān or **Baghlān Jadid**, 36 11N 68 44E, pop(1984e) 43,000, capital of Baghlān prov, NE central Afghanistan; on the major road between Kābul and Kondūz.

Baguio *bag'ee-ō*, 16 25N 120 37E, pop(1980) 119,009, summer capital of the Philippines, in Benguet prov, NW Luzon I; mountain resort town and official summer residence of the Philippines president; a city since 1909; 2 universities (1911, 1948); event: summer festival.

Bahamas *ba-hah'maz*, official name Commonwealth of the Bahamas, archipelago consisting of some 700 low lying islands and over 2,000 cays, forming a chain which extends approx 800 km SE from the coast of Florida; timezone GMT −5; area 13,934 sq km; capital Nassau; major town Freeport; pop(1980) 209,505; more than 75% of the population live on either New Providence or Grand Bahama; the pop comprises 85% black and 15% white (mostly English, American, and Canadian descent); English is the official language; the dominant religion is Christianity; the unit of currency is the Bahamian dollar; membership of CARICOM, CDB, Commonwealth, FAO, G-77, GATT (de facto), IBRD, ICAO, IDB, ILO, IMF, IMO, INTERPOL, ITU, NAM, OAS, PAHO, UN, UNESCO, UPU, WHO, WIPO, WMO, WTO.

Physical description and climate. The coralline limestone islands of the Bahamas comprise the two oceanic banks of Little Bahama and Great Bahama. They tend to be long, narrow, and low, the highest point being only 120 m above sea-level. The climate is subtropical with an average winter temperature of 21°C and an average summer temperature of 27°C. Mean annual rainfall varies from 750 mm to 1,500 mm, largely concentrated in May-June and September-October. Hurricanes are frequent between June and November.

History, government and constitution. The Bahamas were visited by Christopher Columbus in 1492 but it was not until 1647 that the first permanent European settlement was established by a group of English and Bermudan religious refugees. The islands became a British Crown Colony in 1717 and in the earlier period of British occupation they became notorious as the rendezvous of buccaneers and pirates. During the American Civil War they were used as a base for blockade-runners. Independence was achieved on 10 July 1973. The Commonwealth of the Bahamas has a bicameral House of Assembly with 43 elected members and a senate with 16 nominated members. Head of state is the British monarch, represented in the Bahamas by a governor-general.

Economy. Tourism is the mainstay of the economy employing 66% of the labour force and accounting for 25% of national income. The main tourism centres are New Providence (Nassau and Paradise I) and Grand Bahama. The 2nd most important sector of the economy is finance. The Bahamas' status as a tax haven has contributed significantly to its growth as an international banking centre. Other important industries include oil refining, fishing, rum and liqueur distilling, and the manufacture of cement, pharmaceuticals, and steel pipes. There is an oil transshipment point at South Riding Point on Grand Bahama I. Chief exports include petroleum and petroleum products, rum, salt, fish, and pulp-wood. The USA is the chief trading partner supplying 74% of imports and receiving 41% of total exports (1984). Other trading partners include Canada, UK, and other EEC countries. Agriculture employs around 7% of the total labour force and approx 142 sq km of land is cultivated, the chief agricultural products being fruit and vegetables.

Island groups. The Bahamas comprise the following 17 islands and island groups:

Islands	*area (sq km)*	*pop(1980)*
Abaco	1,680	7,324
Acklins I	497	616
Andros	5,955	8,397
Berry Is	31	509
Biminis, Cay Lobos, Cay Sal	28	1,432
Cat I	388	2,143
Eleuthera, Harbour I,		

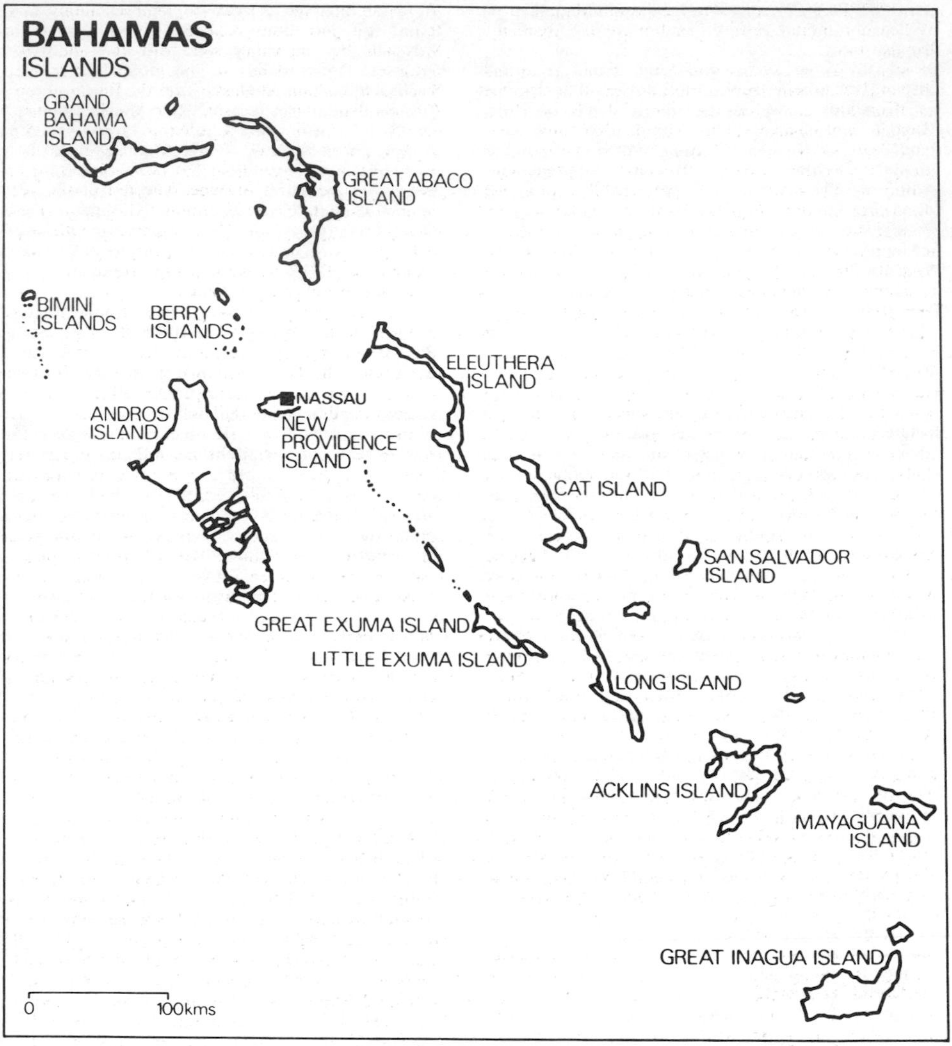

contd

Islands	*area (sq km)*	*pop(1980)*
Spanish Wells	518	10,600
Crooked I	217	517
Exuma & Cays	290	3,672
Grand Bahama	1,372	33,102
Inagua	1,545	939
Long Cay	23	33
Long I	595	3,358
Mayaguana	285	476
New Providence	207	135,437
Ragged Is	36	146
San Salvador & Rum Cay	233	804

Bahawalnagar *bu-hah'vul-nu-gur*, 29 24N 71 47E, pop(1981) 74,000, town in Punjab prov, Pakistan; 169 km NE of Bahawalpur; economy: pottery, trade in wheat, millet.

Bahawalpur *bu-hah'vul-poor*, 29 57N 73 23E, pop(1981) 178,000, town in Punjab prov, Pakistan; on the edge of the Thar desert, to the SSE of Multan near the R Sutlej; connected by railway to Sukkur; founded in 18th century; former capital of the princely state of Bahawalpur; ceded to Pakistan in 1947; university (1975); economy: textiles, soap, machinery.

Bahia *ba-ee'a*, state in Nordeste region, NE Brazil; bounded E by the Atlantic, N by the Río São Francisco; in the NW is the Barragem do Sobradinho Dam; pop(1980) 9,454,346; area 561,026 sq km; capital Salvador; chief towns include Vitória da Conquista, Feira de Santana, Itabuna; economy: agriculture; chemical and petrochemical industries; oil; in the far N is part of the Paulo Alfonso National Park; on the SE coast is the 140-sq km Monte Pascoal National Park (1961), rising to 536 m in Monte Pascoal; Brazil was first claimed for Portugal by Pedro Álvares Cabral on 22 April 1500, when he stepped ashore at Pôrto Seguro in SE Bahia state.

Bahía Blanca *ba-hee'a blan'ka*, 38 45S 62 15W, pop(1980) 220,765, city in Buenos Aires prov, Litoral, E Argentina; at the head of the Bahía Blanca Bay, SW of Buenos Aires; comprises the city proper and 5 ports on Río Naposta including the naval base of Puerto Belgrano; founded in 1828; university (1956); railway; airport (Comandante Espora); economy: oil refining, wool and food processing, timber trade, fishing.

Bahía de Caráquez *ba-ee'a dhay ka-ra'kes*, 0 38S 80 24W, pop(1982) 12,360, Pacific Ocean seaport in Manabí prov, W Ecuador; on the seaward S end of an inlet; economy: banana trade.

Bahía, Islas de la, BAY ISLANDS (Eng), island group and dept of Honduras in the W Caribbean Sea off the N coast of Honduras; comprises the resort islands of Utila, Roatán and Guanaja and several islets and cays; pop(1983e) 18,744; area 259 sq km; visited by Columbus in 1502; chief town Roatán; Roatán I is mountainous with tropical vegetation and is protected by a coral reef; the people are descended from British immigrants and from 5,000 Negroes and Caribs brought here at the end of the 18th century by the British from the West Indies; held by Britain 1850-58, then ceded to Honduras; economy: boat-building, bananas and coconuts.

Bahir Dar, 11 33N 37 25E, pop(1984e) 54,800, town in Gojam region, Ethiopia, NE Africa; N of the Choke range, close to the outflow of the Blue Nile from T'ana Hāyk' (L Tana).

Bahr el Ghazal', area of S Sudan, NE Africa; (province prior to 1983); area 77,625 sq km; pop(1983) 2,265,510.

Bahrain', official name State of Bahrain, group of 35 islands comprising an independent state in the Arabian Gulf midway between the tip of the Qatar Peninsula and mainland Saudi Arabia; at 25 km the Saudi-Bahrain causeway is the longest in the world; timezone GMT +3; area 678 sq km; capital Al Manāmah; other city Al Muharraq; pop(1983e) 400,000; the pop is 73% Arabic and 9% Iranian, with Pakistani and Indian minorities; two-thirds are Shi'a Muslim and about 30% are Sunni Muslim; Arabic is the official language but English, Farsi and Urdu are also spoken; the currency is the Bahrain dinar; national holiday 16 Dec (National Day); membership of Arab League, FAO, G-77, GATT, GCC, IBRD, ICAO, Islamic Development Bank, ILO, IMF, IMO, ITU, NAM, OAPEC, OIC, UN, UNESCO, UPU, WHO, WMO.

Physical description. The island of Bahrain is approx 48 km in length and 13-16 km in width, with a total area of 562 sq km. Largely composed of sand-covered limestone, it rises to a central plateau 30-60 m in elevation, its highest point being Jabal Dukhan (135 m). The island is largely bare and infertile except for a narrow strip of land in the N. In general the soils are poor and saline, supporting little vegetation. In 1973 work commenced on 31 major drainage schemes to remove salinity and a fertile belt has been created between Jidhafs and Wasmiah by importing soil with the addition of fertilizers. Other islands in the group include Nabih Saleh, Jidda, Umm Al-Nassan and the Hawār group.

Climate. Bahrain has 3 seasons. Dec-March is typified by cool N or NE winds with a little rain (average of 35 mm in Dec). From the end of March temperatures rise to reach a peak in Aug, although a cool N *Bara* sometimes reduces temperatures in June. The rest of the year is dominated by the *Shamal*, a moist NE wind, or the hot, sand-bearing *Qaws* from the S. Summer months are hot and humid with an average temperature of 36°C and a humidity of 97% in Sept, but temperatures fall from Oct to an average of 19°C in January.

History, government and constitution. During the period of the Dilman civilization (2000-1800 BC) Bahrain was a flourishing centre of trade. Since the late 18th century, the country has been governed by the Khalifa family, originally part of the Anaiza tribal confederation of the Arabian Peninsula. In 1861 Bahrain concluded a treaty of protection with the UK which precluded the shaikh from entering into relationships with any other foreign power. This treaty, which had been entered into with other Arabian Gulf shaikdoms, was terminated by the UK in 1971 and after failing to enter into a union with Qatar and the 7 Trucial shaikdoms Bahrain became independent as the State of Bahrain. In May 1973, an experimental parliamentary system was established under a new constitution. This lasted for two years before the National Assembly was disbanded in 1975. Bahrain is a constitutional monarchy governed by the Amir who appoints a Council of Ministers headed by a prime minister. The 6 towns and cities of Bahrain are administered by one central municipal council.

Economy. Bahrain was one of the first of the Arab states to discover oil (1931) and was the first to establish an oil refinery. Apart from lime and gypsum, petroleum and natural gas are the only significant natural resources, but oil is refined not only from Bahrain's own oil fields but also from the Abu Safaa offshore field which is operated by Saudi Arabia. Industrial zones have been developed at Mina Sulman, Ma'meer and Abu Gazal. Using bauxite from Australia, smelters produce aluminium for export to the Far East. Because of its position at the centre of the Gulf, Bahrain is used by many marine companies as a main port for shipments to be re-exported to other Gulf states and as a centre for ship repair. Bahrain has also become an important regional centre for banking and commerce. Pearl fishing during June-Oct was formerly an important source of income but trade depression and competition from Japanese cultured pearls has virtually eliminated this source of income.

Baia Mare *ba'ya ma'ray*, 47 39N 23 36E, pop(1983) 129,719, capital of Maramureş county, N Romania; situated to the W of the Rodnei Mts; part of Hungary during World War II; airfield; railway; economy: metallurgy, chemicals, fruit, wine, livestock; monuments: St Stephen Tower (14th-c); mint museum.

Baikal, Lake, lake in S Siberia, Soviet Union. See Baykal, Ozero.

Băileşti *ba-eel-esht'*, 44 01N 23 20E, pop(1983) 22,029, town in Dolj county, S Romania; 48 km SW of Craiova; railway; economy: agricultural centre for grain and livestock; tanning and food processing.

Bairnsdale *bayrnz'dayl*, 37 51S 147 38E, pop(1983e) 10,040, town in East Gippsland stat div, SE Victoria, Australia; on the Mitchell river near the entrance to L King; railway; economy: centre of a wine-producing area; near the town is the 4 sq km MacLeod's Morass game reserve, established to conserve waterfowl.

Baixo Alentejo *bīsh'yoo a-lā-tay'zhoo*, agricultural prov of S Portugal formed in 1936 from the former Alentejo (Arab 'alem Tejo', beyond the Tagus) region, includes most of Beja dist, bounded to the S by the Algarve, to the N by the Alto Alentejo, to the W by the Atlantic and to the east by the Spanish frontier; the prov has a fifth of Portugal's total coastline but less than 1% of the country's total fish catch; area, 13,614 sq km; the chief town of lower Alentejo is Beja; cork-oak is widely distributed and makes an important contribution to the economy which, despite the aridity of much of the soil, is also largely based on corn-growing, cattle-rearing, pig-farming and charcoal-burning; the province is also famous for the Alter Real breed of horse which has been reared here since the 18th century and is particularly prized for dressage; the population is sparse, with concentrations of people living in a few small towns and villages and the majority widely dispersed occupying large isolated farms.

Baja *bo'yo*, 46 12N 18 59E, pop(1984e) 40,000, town in Bács-Kiskun county, S Hungary; on R Danube S of Budapest; college of engineering; railway; economy: corn and cattle trade, textiles.

Baja California Norte *ba'ha ka-lee-for'nya nor'tay*, state in NW Mexico; bounded N by California (USA), NE by Sonora, W by the Pacific Ocean, E by the Golfo de California and S by Baja California Sur; N half of a peninsula; apart from a narrow coastal strip on the Pacific, the state is largely mountainous, with (N-S) the Sierra de Juárez, Sierra San Pedro Mártir and Sierra de San Borja; also within the state are Isla Angel de la Guarda in the Golfo de California and Isla Cedros and Isla Guadalupe in the Pacific; pop(1980) 1,225,436; area 69,921 sq km; capital Mexicali; major towns: Tijuana and Ensenada; economy: agriculture (cotton, wheat, olives, vines, barley, fruit), fishing and fish processing, cotton cleaning, dairy products, wine and beer, textiles, tanning, chemicals.

Baja California Sur *soor*, state in NW Mexico; bounded N by Baja California Norte, W and S by the Pacific Ocean and E by the Golfo de California; the state is low in the W and high in the E, with (N-S) the Sierra de Santa Lucía, Sierra de la Giganta and Sierra de San Lázaro; also included are several small offshore islands in the Golfo de California; pop(1980) 215,139; area 73,475 sq km; capital La Paz; economy: agriculture (cotton, wheat, alfalfa, maize, citrus fruit, dates, olives, figs, vines, onions), cattle and goat raising, mining (salt, gypsum, copper), fishing and fish processing, oil (edible), tourism.

Baja Verapaz *ba'ha vay-ra-pas'*, mountainous dept in central Guatemala, Central America; pop(1982e) 152,374; area 3,124 sq km; capital Salamá; traversed W-E by the Sierra de Chuacús in the S; the Río Grande forms its S boundary with Guatemala dept; economy: nickel mining W of Salamá.

Bajram Curri *bee'ram ku'ri*, 42 20N 20 04E, town and capital of Tropojë prov, N Albania; N of the R Drin, close to the border with Yugoslavia.

Bakau *ba-kow'*, 13 29N 16 41W, pop(1980) 11,300, town in The Gambia, W Africa; on the left bank of the R Gambia estuary, 11.3 km WNW of Banjul.

Bakersfield, 35 26N 119 01W, pop(1980) 105,611, capital of Kern county, S central California, United States; on the Kern river, at the S end of the San Joaquin Valley, c.160 km NNW of Los Angeles; the city developed after oil was discovered here in 1889; railway; economy: commercial and industrial centre.

Bākhtarān *baKH-ta-ran'*, formerly KERMĀNSHĀHĀN, mountainous prov in NW Iran, bounded W by Iraq; pop(1982) 1,030,714; area 23,667 sq km; capital Bākhtarān.

Bākhtarān, formerly KERMĀNSHĀH *ker-man-sha'*, 34 19N 47 04E, pop(1983) 531,350, capital of Bākhtarān dist, Bākhtarān, NW Iran; 416 km WSW of Tehrān; trade centre for surrounding agricultural region; airfield.

Bakony *bo'kony'*, wooded mountain range N of L Balaton in the Transdanubian Highlands of W Hungary; rises to 702 m at Mt Köris; bauxite is mined.

Baku *ba-koo'*, 40 22N 49 53E, pop(1983) 1,638,000, seaport capital of Azerbaydzhanskaya SSR, Soviet Union; on the Apsheronskiy Poluostrov (Apsheron Peninsula), on the W coast of the Caspian Sea; industrial, scientific, and cultural centre; university (1919); railway; airport; economy: oil refining, gas-processing, metalworking, machine building, petrochemicals, manufacture of tyres, solar research and development; connected by a double oil pipeline with Batum on the Black Sea; monuments: Kiz-Kalasyi (Virgin's Tower), dating from the 1st half of the 12th century; Shirvan Shah's Palace, surrounded by the citadel wall and now housing the Baku Museum.

Bakwanga, town in Zaire. See Mbuji-Mayi.

Balaton *bo'lo-ton*, lake in W central Hungary; W of the Danube and S of the Bakony Mts of Transdanubia; area 598 sq km; length 77 km; width 8-14 km; largest and shallowest lake in Central Europe; Hungary's largest recreation area with resorts at Siófok, Keszthely and Balatonfüred (spa with carbonic waters).

Balbriggan *bal-bri'gun*, BAILE BRIG IN (Gael), 53 37N 6 11W, pop(1981) 6,708, fishing port and resort in Dublin county, Leinster, E Irish Republic; N of Dublin; railway; economy: tourism, hosiery.

Baldwin Park, 34 04N 117 58W, pop(1980) 50,554, city in Los Angeles county, SW California, United States; 26 km E of Los Angeles.

Balē, mountainous region in S Ethiopia, NE Africa; pop(1984e) 1,006,491; area 124,600 sq km; the highest peak is Batu (4,307 m); the land dips towards the SE and the Somali frontier; rivers include the Genale Wenz (SW border) and Wabe Shebele Wenz (E border); chief town Goba; includes a national park of same name (area 1,675 sq km).

Baleares, Islas *ees'las bal-ay-ah'rays*, BALEARIC ISLANDS *bal-e-ar'ik* (Eng), island archipelago of 5 major islands and 11 islets in the W Mediterranean near the E coast of Spain that forms the Baleares autonomous region of Spain; capital Palma de Mallorca; pop(1981) 655,909; area 5,014 sq km; the region consists of two groups of islands, the E and larger group comprising the two chief islands of Mallorca or Majorca, Menorca or Minorca, and the smaller island of Cabrera with several islets and the W group comprising Ibiza, Formentera (known as the Pitiusas or Pine Islands), and several islets; the islands have picturesque scenery and a mild climate making them popular as tourist resorts; airports at Palma de Mallorca, Ibiza and Mahon; car ferries to Barcelona, Alicante and Valencia in Spain, Genoa in Italy and Marseilles in France; economy: fruit, wine, grain, cattle, fishing, textiles, chemicals, cork, timber.

Balearic Islands, Spanish autonomous region. See Baleares.

Bali *bah'li*, island province of Indonesia; lying between the island of Jawa (W) and Lombok (E); a mountainous island with peaks rising to 3,142 m at Gunung Agung in the E; pop(1980) 2,469,920; area 5,561 sq km; capital Denpasar; a chiefly Hindu population with a language derived from the Palava script of S India; the Dutch gained full control of the island by 1908; the island now has a highly developed tourist industry with resorts at Legian and Kuta beaches; economy: rice, cattle, coffee, copra, salt, onions.

Balıkesir *ba-lu'ke-sir*, prov in NW Turkey, bounded N by the Sea of Marmara and W by an inlet of the Aegean Sea; pop(1980) 853,177; area 14,292 sq km; capital Balıkesir; economy: grain and opium.

Balıkesir, 39 38N 27 52E, pop(1980) 124,051, capital town of Balıkesir prov, NW Turkey; centre of a rich agricultural region; road and rail junction; airfield; food processing, rugs, textiles.

Balkh *balk*, prov in N Afghanistan; bounded N by the USSR; pop(1984e) 635,332; area 12,593 sq km; capital Mazār-e-Sharīf.

Balkhash, Ozero, crescent-shaped lake in SE Kazakhstan SSR, Soviet Union; 160 km W of the Chinese border; area 18,300 sq km; length 605 km; max width 74 km; max depth 26 m; it has a low, sandy S shore and a high, rocky N shore; its chief inlet is the R Ili and it has no outlet; the salt content increases towards the E; salt extraction and fishing are important activities; there are extensive copper deposits on the N shore (Kounradskiy); principal harbours are Burylbaytal and Burlyu-Tobe; there are deserts to the S (Peski Sary-Ishikotrau, Peski Muyunkum); the lake is thought to have formed part of a much more extensive sheet of water of which the Ozero Sasykkol' and Ozero Alakol' lakes to the E are also remaining portions.

Bal'larat, BALLAARAT, 37 36S 143 58E, pop(1983e) 36,550, city in Central Highlands stat div, SW central Victoria, Australia; NW of Melbourne; railway; centre of a wool-producing dist; in 1851 the largest gold reserves in the country were discovered here; the famous Eureka Stockade, the gold-diggers' rebellion against state authority, took place here in 1854; economy: textiles, brewing, metal products; monuments: a reconstruction of the Eureka Stockade; Sovereign Hill historic park, a reconstruction of the gold-digging village; gold museum; Adam Lindsay Gordon's cottage, home of the Australian poet; vintage trams run on a short track beside L Wendouree in the NW of the town.

Ballater *bal'a-tur*, 57 03N 3 03W, pop(1981) 1238, village on R Dee in SW Grampian region, Scotland, 13 km E of Balmoral castle; tourism.

Ballina *ba'li-nu*, BÉAL ÁTHA AN FHEADHA (Gael), 52 49N 8 26W, pop(1981) 7,858, market town in Mayo county, Connacht, W Irish Republic; on R Mayo; angling centre; railway; event: Moy Festival in July to celebrate the famous salmon of the R Moy.

Ballinasloe *ba-lin-us-lō'*, BÉAL ÁTHA NA SLUAGH (Gael), 53 20N 8 13W, pop(1981) 6,481, market town in Galway county, Connacht, W Irish Republic; on R Suck; railway; economy: agricultural market town for E Galway; event: Oct fair is the largest livestock fair in Ireland.

Ballincollig *ba-lin-ko'lig*, BAILE AN CHULLAIGH (Gael), 51 54N 8 35W, pop(1981) 7,231, agricultural market town in Cork county, Munster, S Irish Republic; near R Lee, W of Cork.

Balln'gry, 56 11N 3 19W, pop(1981) 7,021, town in Dunfermline dist, Fife, E Scotland; 5 km NW of Lochgelly.

Ballyclare *ba-li-clayr'*, BEALACH CLAIR (Gael), 54 45N 6 00W, pop(1981) 6,159, town in Newtownabbey dist, Antrim, NE Northern Ireland; 16 km SW of Larne; economy: textiles, engineering.

Ballymena *ba-li-mee'na*, AN BAILE MEANACH (Gael), 54 52N 6 17W, pop(1981) 28,166, town in Ballymena dist, Antrim, NE Northern Ireland; on the Braid river, railway; economy: textiles, engineering, footwear, food processing, tobacco, tyres.

Ballymoney, BAILE MONAIDH (Gael), 55 10N 6 30W, pop(1981) 5,679, town in Ballymoney dist, Antrim, NE Northern Ireland; 11 km SE of Coleraine; railway; economy: textiles, food processing, medical supplies, mineral waters.

Balmor'al, 57 02N 3 15W, castle in SW Grampian region, Scotland, on the R Dee; royal summer residence in Scotland since mid-19th-c.

Balqā', Al, governorate (*muhafaza*) of the East Bank, Jordan, bounded W by the R Jordan; capital Salt.

Balsas, Río *bahl'sahs*, RÍO DE LAS BALSAS, river in S central Mexico; rises in N Puebla and Tlaxcala; as the Atoyac it flows S and SW through Puebla, curving W into Guerrero where it is called the Mezcala; continues W and S, through Guerrero then along the Guerrero-Michoacán border where it forms the El Infiernillo Dam; enters the Pacific Ocean at 17 55N 102 10W; the Balsas is unnavigable due to rapids; the river valley is partly irrigated and produces various crops including coffee, maize, cotton, sugar cane and tropical fruit.

Baltic Sea *bawl'tik*, OSTSEE (Ger), MARE SUEVICUM (anc), an arm of the Atlantic Ocean enclosed by Denmark, Sweden, W Germany, E Germany, Poland, USSR, Finland and Sweden; covers an area of 422,170 sq km; connected to the North Sea by the Kattegat, Skagerrak and Danish Straits (Öresund, Great Belt and Little Belt) and by the Kiel Canal, across the Jutland Peninsula; chief arms of the Baltic are the Gulf of Bothnia, Gulf of Finland, the Gulf of Riga, the small Gulf of Gdańsk and Meckenburg Bay; main islands include Hiiumma, Saaremaa, Åland, Gotland, Öland, Bornholm, Rügen, Fehmarn and the insular part of Denmark; major rivers flowing into the Baltic include the Dal, Ljusan, Storsjon, Angerman Älv, Ume Älv, Lule Älv, Torne Älv, Kemi, Neva, Daugava, Nemar, Wista and Oder; mean depth 55 m; the deepest point is the Gotland Deep (approx 463 m); the low salinity of the Baltic, which is the result of the influx of fresh water, coupled with its general shallowness, causes large areas, particularly in the NE, to freeze over in winter, making navigation impossible for 3 to 5 months yearly; the main ports include Rostock, Lübeck, Kiel (E and W Germany); Gdańsk, Gdynia (Poland); Leningrad, Tallinn, Paldiski, Riga, Liepaja, Kaliningrad (USSR); and Copenhagen, Stockholm and Helsinki (Scandinavia); navigated since ancient times, particularly in connection with the amber found along the coast in former E Prussia; the Hanseatic League dominated commerce during the Middle Ages.

Baltimore *bol'-*, 39 17N 76 37W, pop(1980) 786,775, port in N Maryland, United States; on the R Patapsco, at the upper end of Chesapeake Bay; purchased in 1729 by the Maryland legislature who developed the settlement as a seaport and shipbuilding centre; achieved city status in 1797; the British attack on Fort McHenry in 1814 inspired Francis Scott Key to write the *Star Spangled Banner*; 6 universities; railway; airport; largest city in the state; economy: trade in coal, grain and metal products; major industries include shipbuilding, food processing, copper and oil refining, and the manufacture of chemicals, steel and aerospace equipment; monuments: Inner Harbour, museum of art, Walters art gallery, Morris A. Mechanic Theatre; event: Preakness Festival (May).

Balúchistán *ba-loo-chi-stan'*, prov in W and SW Pakistan; pop(1981) 4,305,000; area 347,190 sq km; bounded W by Iran, N by Afghanistan and S by the Arabian Sea; capital Quetta; mountainous terrain, covered for the most part by desert; economy: cotton, natural gas, fishing, salt trade; British influence dates from the Afghan Wars; treaties of 1879 and 1891 brought the N section of the prov under direct British control; incorporated into Pakistan in 1947-48.

Balzar *bal-sar'*, 1 25S 79 54W, pop(1982) 17,627, town in Guayas prov, W Ecuador; on the Río Picon, N of Guayaquil.

Balzers *bal'zers*, 47 04N 9 32E, pop(1985) 3,460, commune in Oberland dist, Principality of Liechtenstein, central Europe; area 19.6 sq km; economy: optical engineering, semiconductors, heating accessories, synthetic fibres, precision instruments.

Bamako *ba-ma-kō'*, region in W central Mali, W Africa; pop(1971) 958,767; area 90,100 sq km; low lying with higher ground SW of Bamako; the R Niger flows SW-NE across the region, receiving the R Sankarani near the capital, Bamako; chief towns Banamba, Dioïla, Kangaba, Kolokani, Koulikoro, Kati and Nara; Koulikoro, NE of Bamako, is the terminus of the railway which runs from Dakar in Senegal; economy: textiles, food processing, metals.

Bamako, 12 40N 7 59E, pop(1976) 404,022, river-port capital of Mali, W Africa; on the R Niger; botanical gardens; zoo; airport; railway; economy: power plant, ceramics, food processing, pharmaceuticals, metals, textiles, cycles, chemicals, tobacco.

Bambari *bam-ba'ree*, 5 40N 20 37E, chief town of Ouaka prefecture, Central African Republic; on the R Ouaka, 260 km NE of Bangui.

Bam'berg, 49 54N 10 54E, pop(1983) 70,600, river port and manufacturing city in Oberfranken dist, N Bayern (Bavaria) prov, W Germany; on the R Regnitz near its confluence with the Main, 48 km W of Bayreuth; on the Main-Danube Canal; railway; alt 262 m; university; economy: engineering, textiles, floor coverings, carpets, electrical goods; monuments: early 13th-c Romanesque cathedral, former Benedictine Abbey of Michaelsberg (1009-1803); events: Calderon Festival (July); the Bamberg Symphony Orchestra has an international reputation.

Bam'ble, ØDEGÅRDENS VERK *u'da-gor-duns vark*, 58 59N 9 38E, pop(1980) 12,434, town on E coast of Telemark county, SE Norway; economy: timber, mining.

Bamburgh *bam'bur-u*, BERBANBURH (anc), coastal village in Berwick-upon-Tweed dist, Northumberland, NE England; capital of the kingdoms of Bernicia and Northumbria during the 6-8th centuries; monuments: museum commemorating Grace Darling who was born and buried here; Bamburgh Castle was allegedly built by Ida, first king of Bernicia, in the 6th century.

Bamen'da, 5 55N 10 09E, pop(1984e) 64,000, capital of Nord-Ouest prov, Cameroon, W Africa; 350 km N of Douala and 435 km NW of Yaoundé; alt 1,520 m; an English-speaking area, the town comprises the Mantontown (lower town) and the Bafreng-town (upper town), the former being densely populated and characterized by craft workers; tea plantations at Ndu were introduced by the British in 1957; airfield (Bali, 20 km); economy: coffee trading centre, agricultural services.

Bāmīān *bam-ee-an'*, BAMIYAN, prov in N central Afghanistan; pop(1984e) 291,476; area 17,414 sq km; capital Bāmīān.

Bāmīān, 34 50N 67 50E, pop(1984e) 8,062, capital of Bāmīān prov, N central Afghanistan; was a major caravan centre between India and central Asia; prominent centre of Buddhism in the 7th century and a Muslim fortress town in the 9-12th centuries; airfield.

Bamingui-Bangoran *ba-meen'gee-ban'go-ran'*, prefecture in N Central African Republic; bordered N by the frontier with Chad where it follows the Aouk river; the land rises to the Massif des Bongos in the S and SE; the Saint Floris and Bamingui-Bangoran national parks are located in the NE and W of the prefecture respectively; pop(1968) 27,700; area 58,200 sq km; chief town Ndélé; other towns include Bangoran, M'Bala, Bagara and Yangéné.

Bamingui-Bangoran, national park in W Bamingui-Bangoran prefecture, N Central African Republic; area 10,700 sq km; established 1933.

Ban Hat Yai *bahn haht yī*, HAT YAI, 7 00N 100 28E, pop(1982) 108,389, city in S Thailand, near the Malaysian frontier; railway; airfield.

Banbridge, DROICHEAD NA BANNA (Gael), 54 21N 6 16W, pop(1981) 9,650, town in Banbridge dist, Down, SE Northern Ireland; on the R Bann, 35 km SW of Belfast; economy: textiles (linen), engineering, footwear, rope and fishing nets.

Banbury *ban'ber-i*, 52 04N 1 20W, pop(1981) 38,191, town in Cherwell dist, Oxfordshire, S central England; on the R Cherwell and Oxford Canal, 35 km N of Oxford; in the 17th century the cross famous in nursery rhyme was destroyed (replaced 1858) by the Puritans, for whom the place was noted in contemporary satire; railway; economy: aluminium, car parts, printing, electrical goods, foodstuffs.

Banda Aceh *ban'da ahch'ay*, formerly KOETARADJA or KUTARAJA, 5 30N 95 20E, pop(1980) 53,668, capital of Aceh special territory, N Sumatera, Indonesia; at the N tip of the island of Sumatera; over several centuries strong trade links with the Arab world developed; a predominantly Muslim city; university (1961); railway; airfield.

Banda Sea, sea in the Malay Archipelago, Indonesia; lies E of the Sulawesi (Celebes) Islands, W of the Kei Islands, S of the Maluku (Moluccas) and N of Timor; includes the 10 volcanic Banda Islands; reaches a depth of 4,511 m.

Bandai Asahi *ban'dī ah-sah-hee*, national park in N central Honshū island, Japan; in SW Tōhoku and NE Chūbu regions; contains several volcanic peaks, rising to 2,024 m; last great eruption in 1888; area 1,896 sq km; established in 1950.

Bandar Abbās *ban-dar' a-baz'*, 27 11N 56 17E, pop(1983) 174,950, seaport capital of Bandar' Abbās dist, Hormozgān, SE Iran; 35 km SSW of Kermān, on the N shore of the Strait of Hormuz; airfield; economy: tourism, fishing, maritime trade.

Bandar Seri Begawan *bahn'dahr ser-ee be-gah-wan*, formerly BRUNEI TOWN, 4 56N 114 58E, pop(1971) 72,481, capital of Brunei, SE Asia; located in Brunei-Muara dist, 20 km from the mouth of the Brunei river; airport; the town wharf has been used mainly for local vessels since the opening of a deep-water port at Muara in 1972; monuments: Mesjid Sultan Omar Ali Saifuddin mosque (1958), Churchill Museum, Sultan Hassanal Bolkiah Aquarium.

Bandarban *bahn'dur-bun*, region in SE Bangladesh; bounded W by Chittagong region, S and E by Burma; pop(1981) 171,000; area 4,501 sq km; chief town Bandarban.

Bandeira, Pico da *pee'kō da ban-day'ra*, 20 25S 41 40W, mountain in SE Brazil; rising to 2,890 m on the border between Minas Gerais and Espírito Santo states, 320 km NNE of Rio de Janeiro; situated in the Serra do Caparaó, part of the coastal escarpment; just to the S is the Caparaó National Park; until comparatively recently it was thought to be the highest mountain in Brazil (the Pico da Neblina and Pico 21 de Março on the frontier with Venezuela are higher).

Bandundu *ban-doon'doo*, region in W Zaire, central Africa; pop(1981e) 4,119,524; area 295,658 sq km; capital Bandundu; chief towns include Bolobo, Inongo and Kikwit; L Mai-Ndombe is in the N and the R Kasai, a major tributary of the R Zaire (Congo) flows WNW across the region; the 2 major tributaries of the R Kasai, the R Kwango and the R Kwilu, both flow N.

Bandun'du, BANNINGVILLE (-1966), 3 20S 17 24E, pop(1970) 74,467, capital of Bandundu region, W Zaire, central Africa; 195 km SW of Inongo, on the R Kasai near its junction with the R Kwango; railway; airfield.

Bandung *bahn-doong'*, 0 32N 103 16E, pop(1980) 1,201,000, capital of Jawa Barat prov, W Jawa, Indonesia; 180 km SE of Jakarta, surrounded by mountains; Sundanese cultural centre; founded in 1810; site of the first Indonesian rock festival in 1975; Catholic university (1955); institute of technology (1959); nuclear research centre; railway.

Banff, 57 40N 2 31W, pop(1981) 3,938, capital of Banff and Buchan dist, Grampian region, NE Scotland; on the N coast, on the left bank of the R Deveron; joined to the town of Macduff on the right bank; economy: fishing; monuments: museum, Duff House, designed by William Adam.

Banfora *ban-fō'ra*, 10 36N 4 45W, pop(1985e) 17,589, town in SW Burkina, W Africa; 72 km SW of Bobo Dioulasso; formerly part of the Ivory Coast (1919-32); economy: agricultural trade.

Bangalore *bang-gal-or'* ('city of beans'), 12 59N 77 40E, pop(1981) 2,914,000, capital of Karnataka, S central India; 290 km W of Madras and 830 km SE of Bombay; founded in 1537; former military headquarters of the British administered dist of Mysore (1831-1947); linked by rail to Mysore, Madras and Hyderabad; airfield; economy: aircraft, machine tools, light engineering, electronics, trade in coffee.

Bangassou *bā-ga'soo*, 4 41N 22 48E, chief town in M'bomou prefecture, SE Central African Republic; on the R Bomou, 470 km ENE of Bangui.

Banghāzī *ben-gah'zi*, BENGHAZI (Eng), 32 07N 20 05E, pop(1982) 650,000, seaport in Banghāzī prov, N Libya, N Africa; on the Gulf of Sirte, 645 km E of Tarābulus (Tripoli); first settled by Greeks who remained until the end of the 3rd century BC; the modern town is partly situated on the Hellenistic and Roman towns of Berenice; the Turks controlled the town from the 16th century until 1911 and the Italians from 1911 until 1942; used as a military and naval supply base during World War II; the ruler of the Sensui Muslim brotherhood resides here; university (1955); airport (29 km).

Bangkok *bang-kok*, 13 44N 100 30E, pop(1982) 5,018,327, capital city of Thailand; on Chao Praya R, 25 km from its mouth on the Bight of Thailand; developed as a major city after the Burmese invasions of the late 18th century; capital of Thailand since 1782; the old city is noted for its many canals; since 1955 the headquarters of the SE Asia Treaty Organization; 8 universities; accessible to small ocean-going vessels; rail links with Cambodia and Malaysia; airport; economy: commerce, paper, ceramics, textiles, timber, aircraft, matches, food processing, cement; monuments: the Grand Palace; temples of the Golden Buddha and Reclining Buddha; 60 km W of Bangkok is the Phra Pathom Chedi, the world's tallest Buddhist monument, which marks the spot where Buddhism was introduced; Ayutthaya, 70 km N of Bangkok was capital of Thailand (1350-1767).

Bangladesh *bahng-lah-desh'*, formerly EAST PAKISTAN, official name People's Republic of Bangladesh, GANA PRAJATANTRI BANGLADESH, Asian republic lying between the foothills of the Himalayas and the Indian Ocean; bounded W and NW by West Bengal (India), E by Assam Tripuria (India), SE by Burma and S by the Bay of Bengal; timezone GMT +6; area 143,998 sq km; capital Dhākā; Chittagong in the SE is the 2nd largest town and Bangladesh's chief port; Khulna, with its seaport at Chalna, is the 3rd largest town and an important industrial region; pop(1984) 99,585,000; one of the world's most densely populated areas, the highest densities being along the lower Ganges (Padma) and Meghna rivers; ethnic groups include 98% Bengali, 300,000-400,000 Biharis and less than 1 million tribals; Bengali (called Bangla in Bangladesh) is the official language, English is used for official, legal and commercial purposes and is spoken and understood by most educated people, while dialects are retained by tribal people; 83% of the pop is Muslim, mostly of the Sunni sect, 16% Hindu, less than 1% Buddhist, Christian or other; Bangladesh is a secular state; the taka, a new currency, was floated in 1976; national holidays 26 March (National Day), 1 May, 21 Feb (Martyrs' Day), 14, 15 or 16 April (Pahela Baishak, the Bengali New Year); membership of ADB, Afro-Asian People's Solidarity Organization, Colombo Plan, Commonwealth, ESCAP, FAO, G-77, GATT, IAEA, IBRD, ICAO, IDA, Islamic Development Bank, IFAD, IFC, ILO, IMF, IMO, INTELSAT, INTERPOL, IOC, IRC, ITU, NAM, OIC, UN, UNCTAD, UNESCO, UPU, WHO, WFTU, WMO, WTO.

Physical description. Bangladesh is for the most part a vast, low lying alluvial plain, cut by a network of rivers, canals, swamps and marsh. The 3 main rivers are the Ganges (Padma), the Brahmaputra (Jamuna) and the Meghna and these meet in the S to form the largest delta in the world. The plain is nowhere above 30 m and is therefore subject to frequent flooding, which although depositing silt and so maintaining soil fertility, does cause severe damage. In 1984 severe flooding killed 600 people and made 30 mn homeless. The clay and sand coastline of Chittagong in the E is much more stable and is backed by the fertile valleys and peaks of Chittagong Hill Tracts, which rise to 1,200 m. Hill areas are found in the E regions of Comilla, Mymensingh and Sylhet, reaching some 240 m, which are actually foothills of the Assam mountains. The country is covered by lush vegetation, with bamboo and palm forests in the E, mixed monsoon forest in the Madhuper jungle, central Bangladesh and vast areas of the S delta region covered in mangroves and hardwood forest, called Sundarbans. Royal Bengal Tiger, crocodiles, pythons, cheetahs and monkeys are found in the Sundarbans, while panthers and wild-boar are found in the Sylhet forest.

Climate. Bangladesh has a tropical monsoon climate, with a hot season lasting from March to June when rain occurs in heavy thunderstorms. The heat is made uncomfortable by the humid conditions and temperatures are generally higher inland than on the coast. The main rainy season of the SW monsoon lasts from June to Sept and rain is heavy and frequent during this time, being brought by depressions in the Bay of Bengal. Sept to Nov is a period of less reliable rainfall, but is generally associated with cyclones which develop in the Bay of Bengal and cause sea surges such as to cause widespread inundation of the low lying coastal areas. The cool season lasts from Sept to Nov.

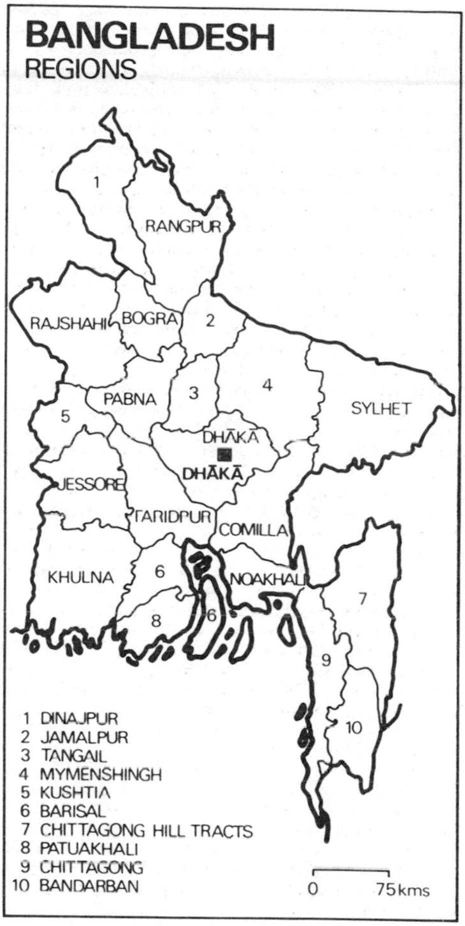

History, government and constitution. Bangladesh was part of the State of Bengal, until under British influence a Muslim East Bengal was created in 1905, separate from Hindu West Bengal. The split was unsuccessful and Bengal was reunited in 1911. When India became independent in 1947 and the state of Pakistan was formed Bengal was again partitioned, with West Bengal remaining in India and East Bengal forming East Pakistan. Disparity in investment and development between East and West Pakistan, which were separated by over 1,610 km, coupled with language differences, forced East Pakistan to seek autonomy, Sheikh Mujib, leader of the Awami League, started the rebellion in 1971 which led to East Pakistan's independence after India had allied itself with Bangladesh and defeated the Pakistani troops. Bangladesh formed its first government in 1972. Sheikh Mujib, who was the first president, suspended the constitution in 1975 and was assassinated shortly afterwards during an army coup. Two further coups followed in 1975 and 1977. A fourth military coup occurred on 23 March 1982, deposing President Sattar who was replaced by Lieut-General Hossain Mohammad Ershad. The constitution was suspended in 1982 but restored again in 1986. Parliament has one 300-member chamber, where 30 seats are reserved for women. Members are elected every 5 years by all citizens over 18 years.

Economy. Agriculture accounted for 57% of the national income in the mid 1980s, employing 85% of the working population. Sixty four per cent of the total area is under cultivation and 80% of this is sown to rice, while 9% supports jute. Bangladesh is required to import foodgrains to feed its growing population. Bangladesh supplies 80% of the world's jute which constitutes 56% of Bangladesh's total exports. Although jute is facing competition from polypropylene, this synthetic fibre's petroleum origin means that its present competitive price cannot be assumed to hold in the future, therefore the government of Bangladesh is concentrating on the development of jute and the exploitation of new markets, especially in the developing world. Bangladesh is the world's 5th largest producer-exporter of tea and a massive tea industry and plantation rehabilitation project is under way. Tobacco and sugar are also important export crops. Manufacturing industry is based on production from jute mills, paper mills, aluminium works, textile mills, match factories, glass works and shipyards. Huge reserves of natural gas, coal, peat, limestone and some heavy minerals are known. Main trade partners include the USA, Mozambique, Iran, Pakistan, Sudan, Japan and W Europe.

Administrative divisions. Bangladesh is divided into 21 regions and 64 districts as follows:

Region/District	*area (sq km)*	*pop(1981)*
Bandarban	4,501	171,000
Barisal	7,298	4,667,000
Barisal	2,416	1,837,000
Bhola	2,755	1,171,000
Jhalakati	751	587,000
Perojpur	1,375	1,072,000
Bogra	3,888	2,728,000
Bogra	2,922	2,109,000
Joypurhat	966	619,000
Chittagong	7,456	5,491,000
Chittagong	5,213	4,465,000
Cox's Bazar	2,243	1,026,000
Chittagong Hill Tracts	8,680	580,000
Chittagong Hill Tracts	6,090	302,000
Khagrachari	2,590	278,000
Comilla	6,599	6,881,000
Brahmanbaria	1,876	1,728,000
Chandpur	1,656	1,796,000
Comilla	3,067	3,357,000
Dhākā	7,469	10,014,000
Dhākā	1,468	4,023,000
Gazipur	1,820	1,177,000
Manikganj	1,370	1,063,000
Munshiganj	988	1,066,000
Narayanganj	708	1,357,000
Narsingdi	1,116	1,328,000
Dinajpur	6,565	3,200,000
Dinajpur	3,447	1,804,000
Panchaghar	1,300	578,000
Thakurgaon	1,818	818,000
Faridpur	6,880	4,764,000
Faridpur Sadar	2,082	1,315,000
Goalanda	1,103	678,000
Gopalganj	1,484	981,000
Madaripur	1,113	942,000
Sariatpur	1,098	848,000
Jamalpur	3,349	2,451,000
Jamalpur	2,033	1,531,000
Sherpur	1,316	920,000
Jessore	6,572	4,020,000
Jessore	2,593	1,706,000
Jhenaidah	1,960	1,114,000
Magura	1,035	611,000
Narail	984	589,000
Khulna	12,167	4,329,000
Bagerhat	3,939	1,226,000
Khulna	4,470	1,748,000
Satkhira	3,758	1,355,000
Kushtia	3,439	2,292,000
Chuadanga	1,160	654,000
Kushtia	1,567	1,236,000
Meherpur	712	402,000
Mymenshingh	9,668	6,568,000
Kishoreganj	2,551	1,894,000
Mymenshingh	3,999	3,087,000
Netrokona	3,118	1,587,000
Noakhali	5,459	3,816,000
Feni	984	899,000
Lakshmipur	1,423	1,121,000
Noakhali	3,053	1,796,000
Pabna	4,730	3,424,000
Pabna	2,330	1,547,000
Sirajganj	2,400	1,877,000
Patuakhali	4,095	1,843,000
Barguna	1,442	712,000
Patuakhali	2,652	1,131,000
Rajshahi	9,455	5,270,000
Naogaon	3,460	1,730,000
Natore	1,862	1,068,000
Nowabganj	1,673	933,000
Rajshahi	2,460	1,539,000
Rangpur	9,595	6,510,000
Gaibandha	2,157	1,576,000
Kurigram	2,272	1,326,000
Lalmonirhat	1,212	749,000
Nilphamari	1,631	1,151,000
Rangpur	2,323	1,708,000
Sylhet	12,715	5,656,000
Hobiganj	2,515	1,278,000
Moulvi Bazar	3,165	1,171,000
Sunamganj	3,535	1,429,000
Sylhet	3,500	1,778,000
Tangail	3,403	2,444,000

Bangor, BEANNCHAR (Gael), 54 40N 5 40W, pop(1981) 46,585, resort town in North Down dist, Down, SE Northern Ireland; on the S shore of Belfast Lough; site of a missionary abbey (founded c.555 by St Comgall); the abbey was destroyed by Danes in the 9th c, rebuilt in 1120, taken over by Franciscans in 1469 and dissolved in 1542; railway; economy: tourism, engineering; monument: ruins of the abbey church.

Bangor, 53 13N 4 08W, pop(1981) 13,002, town in Arfon dist, Gwynedd, NW Wales; SW of Conwy, opposite the island of Anglesey; university (1884); railway; economy: chemicals; engineering; electrical goods; tourism.

Bangor, 44 48N 68 46W, pop(1980) 31,643, county seat of Penobscot county, E central Maine, United States; on the R Penobscot; Husson College (1898); Business College (1891); Northern Conservatory of Music (1929); railway; airfield; economy: electronics, turbines, footwear, paper, timber.

Bangui *bahn'gwee*, 4 23N 18 37E, pop(1981) 387,100, capital of Central African Republic; on the R Ubangi, 1,030 km NNE of Brazzaville; founded in the late 19th century; airport; economy: timber products, cigarettes, metal products, office machinery, beer; monument: Boganda Museum.

Bangweulu, Lake *ban-gway-oo'loo*, lake in N Zambia, S central Africa; on the border between Luapula and Northern provs, E of Mansa; drained S by the Luapula river which flows on to form Zambia's NW border; Chisi island lies at the centre of the lake; European discovery by David Livingstone in 1868; lakeside settlements include Lubwe, Chilubi and Samfya.

Banhine, national park in Gaza prov, Mozambique, SE Africa; area 7,000 sq km; established in 1972.

Baní *ba-nee'*, 18 19N 70 21W, pop(1982e) 97,990, town in Peravia prov, Dominican Republic; on the S coast of the island of Hispaniola, 4.8 km from the Caribbean Sea; on the Sanchez highway between Santo Domingo and Azua; surrounded by fertile agricultural land.

Bani *ba'nee*, river in central Mali, W Africa; formed by the confluence of the Baoulé and Bagoé rivers in Sikasso region, 160 km E of Bamako; flows NE through Ségou and Mopti regions to join the R Niger at Mopti; length 370 km.

Banja Luka *ba'nya loo'ka* ('St Luke's bath'), 44 47N 17 11E, pop(1981) 183,618, spa town in Bosna-Hercegovina republic, W central Yugoslavia; on R Vrbas; badly damaged by an earthquake in Oct 1969; university (1975); railway; economy: tourism, coal mining, textiles; monument: Ferhad Pasha mosque.

Banjarmasin *bahn'jar-mah-sin*, BANDJARMASIN, 3 22S 114 33E, pop(1980) 281,673, capital of Kalimantan Selatan prov, S Borneo, Indonesia; on R Martapura near its junction with the R Barito; predominantly Islamic; noted for its precious and semi-precious stones; university (1961); airfield; economy: rubber, timber and pepper export.

Ban'jul, local government area in The Gambia, W Africa; pop(1983) 44,186; area 12.7 sq km; the chief cities are Banjul, capital of The Gambia, and the surrounding urban area of Kombo St Mary.

Banjul, BATHURST (-1973), 13 28N 16 35W, pop(1983) 44,186, seaport capital of The Gambia, W Africa; situated on the Island of St Mary in the R Gambia estuary 195 km SE of Dakar; established in 1816 as a settlement for freed slaves; on the N side of the R Gambia is Fort Bullen which was built in 1826 to protect Banjul; airport at Yundum (27 km from the city).

Bann, major river in Northern Ireland; rises in the Mourne Mts; flows 40 km NW to enter the S end of Lough Neagh; flows out of the N end of Lough Neagh for 53 km, through Lough Beg and past Coleraine to enter the Atlantic; sometimes referred to as the Upper and Lower Bann river.

Banningville, town in Zaire. See Bandundu.

Bann'ockburn, 56 06N 3 55W, village in Stirling dist, Central region, Scotland; SSE of Stirling; to the W took place the battle (24 June 1314) in which Robert Bruce, by defeating Edward II of England, won Scotland's independence.

Banská Bystrica *bahn'skah bis-tri-tsa*, 48 44N 18 50E, pop(1984) 73,258, capital of Stredoslovenský region, Slovak Socialist Republic, E central Czechoslovakia; in the foothills of the Low Tatra Mts, at the junction of the Hron and Bystrica rivers; founded in 13th century; railway; economy: veneer, pulp and plywood; formerly an important gold-mining town.

Banstead, 51 19N 0 12W, pop(1981) 35,679, residential town linked with Tadworth in Reigate and Banstead dist, Surrey, SE England; part of Greater London urban area; 5 km E of Epsom; railway; economy: pharmaceuticals.

Baotou *bow-to*, PAO-T'OU, 40 38N 109 59E, pop(1984e) 1,063,600, town in Nei Mongol aut region, N China; situated on the Huang He (Yellow river); largest industrial city in Inner Mongolia; railway; airfield; economy: steel, iron, aluminium reduction, chemicals, fertilizers, cement, food processing, textiles; monument: Wudang Zhao (Wudang pagoda), a small Buddhist pagoda.

Ba'qūbah *ba-koo'ba*, 33 45N 44 40E, pop(1970) 39,186, capital town of Diyāla governorate, E central Iraq; on R Diyāla, 60 km NNE of Baghdād.

Bar *bahr*, ANTIBARIUM (anc), 42 05N 19 06E, pop(1981) 32,535, industrial port in Crna Gora (Montenegro) republic, Yugoslavia; on the Adriatic coast, SE of Titograd; centre of a fruit-growing region and also a summer resort with water-skiing at Sutomare by L Scutari; former seat of the Primate of Serbia; formerly held by Venice, Turkey and Albania until annexed to Montenegro in 1878; the town comprises Novi Bar (New Bar) with its port facilities, and Stari Bar old town, which is now mostly in ruins; railway terminus; car ferries to Bari in Italy and to Kérkira (Corfu) and Igoumenitsa in Greece; economy: tourism, fruit trade, bauxite.

Baracaldo *bar-a-cal'do*, 43 17N 2 59W, pop(1981) 117,422, industrial town in Vizcaya prov, Pais Vasco (Basque Country), N Spain; on the left bank of the R Nervion, just W of Bilbao; railway; economy: a leading iron and steel centre; electrical equipment.

Barahona *ba-re-hō'na*, 18 13N 71 07W, pop(1982e) 74,632, port and chief town of Barahona prov, Dominican Republic; on S coast, W of Santo Domingo; tourist beaches nearby; airfield; the centre of a sugar and coffee growing area.

Barakī Barak, BARAKI RAJAN, 33 54N 68 58E, pop(1984e) 1,245, prov capital of Lowgar, E Afghanistan; lies to the SW of Kābul and to the S of the R Logar.

Barani *ba-ra'ni*, 13 09N 3 51W, town in NW Burkina, W Africa.

Baranya *bor'on-yo*, county in S Hungary; dissected by Mecsek Mts in the NW and bounded to the S by Yugoslavia; the R Danube passes through the E part of the county; pop(1984e) 434,000; area 4,487 sq km; capital Pécs; chief towns include Mohács; 56% of the population lives in 5 towns and two-thirds of the 291 villages have less than 500 inhabitants; one in six settlements has a largely German population and in 119 communes Southern Slavs account for a share of the residents; 58,000 small privately-owned farms produce one-third of the county's agricultural output; spa at Harkany; economy: mining, leather, porcelain, food processing, grain, wine, pig and cattle breeding; minerals: coal, iron ore and uranium.

Barbados *bar-bay'dos*, most easterly of the Caribbean Is, in the Atlantic Ocean between 13° and 14°N and 59° and 60°W, 160 km E of St Vincent and 320 km NW of Trinidad; timezone GMT −4; area 430 sq km; capital Bridgetown; other main town Speightstown; pop(1980) 248,983; most people are concentrated in the S Bridgetown, St Michael, and Christ Church areas; 80% of the population are of African descent, 16% are of mixed race, and 4% are European; English is the official language; Protestant Christianity is the dominant religion; the unit of currency is the Barbados dollar; membership: CARICOM, Commonwealth, FAO, GATT, G-77, IADB, IBRD, ICAO, IDB, IFAD, IFC, ILO, IMF, IMO, INTELSAT, INTERPOL, ISO, ITU,

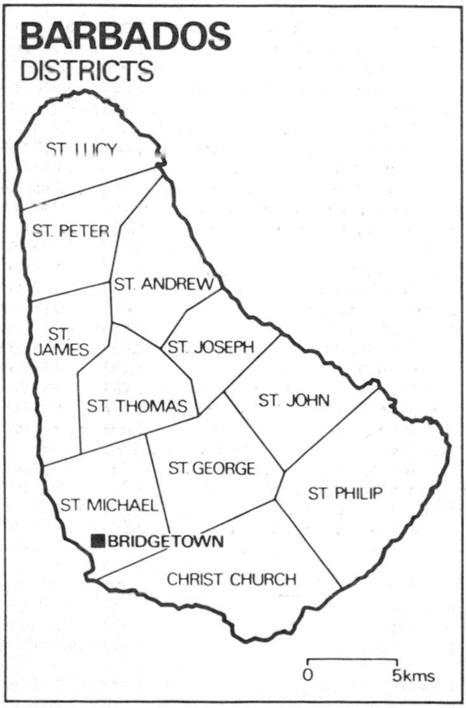

IWC, NAM, OAS, PAHO, SELA, UN, UNESCO, UPU, WHO, WMO.

Physical description and climate. Barbados is a small triangular shaped island extending 32 km from NW to SE and ringed by a coral reef. Scotland District in the NE is an area of rugged terrain rising to 340 m at Mt Hillaby. The rest of the island consists of a series of tablelands of coral limestone formation. Although there are no rivers, deep gullies fill with water during periods of heavy rainfall. The climate is tropical with an average annual temperature of 26.5°C and a mean annual rainfall of 1,420 mm. There is a hot and rainy season from June to Dec when temperatures range from 23°C to 30°C and humidity is high. NE trade winds blow steadily during the dry season from Dec to May. Annual rainfall varies from 1,250 mm on the coast to 1,875 mm in the interior.

History, government and constitution. Barbados was colonized by the British in 1627 and remained under the direct rule of the British Crown until self-government was attained in 1961. The island became an independent sovereign state within the Commonwealth on 30 November 1966. Executive power rests with the prime minister who is appointed by the governor-general. The legislature comprises a governor-general, a 21-member senate, and a house of assembly with 27 elected members.

Economy. Services (including tourism) account for over 70% of national income. Tourism is the major industry and most important foreign-exchange earner. The agricultural sector accounts for about 7% of national income, the main crop being sugar cane. Sugar has traditionally been the mainstay of the economy, with rum and molasses being produced as by-products, but there has recently been a tendency to diversify into other crops. In 1983, sugar cane covered a total area of 141 sq km (approximately 80% of total arable land) and over 85% of production was exported. A project to revive the cotton industry is under way with 0.8 sq km initially planted. Other crops include bananas, onions, and vegetables. Industry accounted for 20% of GDP in 1981 and manufactured exports have now supplemented sugar as the second most important foreign exchange earner. Natural gas reserves are being exploited in the St Andrew dist. The major sectors of growth include the manufacture of garments, electronic and electrical equipment, and medical supplies. In 1981, the principal imports were machinery and transport equipment, manufactured goods, mineral fuels, foodstuffs, and chemicals, mainly from the USA, the UK, CARICOM countries and Canada. The principal exports were sugar, molasses, syrup, electronic assembly goods, clothing, foodstuffs, and rum. The USA receives approximately 30-35% of the total value of exports and the CARICOM countries 20-30%.

Administrative divisions. Barbados is divided into 11 districts as follows:

District	*area (sq km)*	*pop(1980)*
St Michael	38.9	99,953
Christ Church	57.1	40,790
St George	44.0	17,361
St Philip	59.5	18,662
St John	33.7	10,330
St James	31.1	17,255
St Thomas	33.7	10,709
St Joseph	25.9	7,211
St Andrew	36.2	6,731
St Peter	33.7	10,717
St Lucy	36.2	9,264

Communications. Grantley Adams International Airport is located 18 km from Bridgetown.

Barberton, 41 00N 81 39W, pop(1980) 29,751, town in Summit county, NE Ohio, United States; on the R Tuscarawas, 11 km SSW of Akron; railway.

Barbuda *bar-byoo'da*, island in the Leeward group of the Lesser Antilles, E Caribbean, 40 km N of Antigua of which it is a dependency; area 161 sq km; it is a flat coral island reaching only 44 m at its highest point; there is a large lagoon on the W side; main settlement Codrington.

Barcelona *bar-thay-lō'na*, prov in Cataluña, NE Spain, situated on the Mediterranean coast; includes the S facing slopes and spurs of the E Pyrenees and fertile lowland coastal plain drained by the R Llobregat; pop(1981) 4,618,734; area 7,733 sq km; capital Barcelona; resort towns such as Sitges on the Costa Dorada; the most densely populated and highly industrialized part of Spain; economy: agric products include olives, almonds, fruit, vegetables and some cereals; industrial products include cement, cork, textiles, chemicals, paper, glass and pharmaceuticals.

Barcelona, BARCINO or BARCINONA (anc), 41 21N 2 10E, pop(1981) 1,754,900, major seaport and capital of Barcelona prov, NE Spain; also capital of Cataluña region; 621 km NE of Madrid; 2nd largest city in Spain; divided into the old town and the newer Barceloneta on a tongue of land at the port; universities (1440 and 1968); airport; railway; car ferries to Mahon, Palma de Mallorca, Ibiza, Canary Is; centre of Catalan art and literature; economy: textiles, petrochemicals (Martorell), oil refining, engineering; monuments: Gothic Quarter including the 13th-c cathedral, the Ramblas, palace of the kings of Aragón, Church of the Holy Family where Gaudi first started to work in 1884, Museum of Catalan Art, Maritime Museum, Bishop's Palace, Palace of la Virreina art gallery including works of Antonio Gaudi; events: Fiesta of St Anthony in Jan with blessing of animals and parades; Palm Market; Holy Week; Corpus Christi; Fiesta Mayor in Sept with street bonfires.

Barcelona *bar-say-lō'na*, 10 08N 64 41W, pop(1981) 156,461, capital of Anzoátegui state, Venezuela; on the SW bank of the Río Neveri, 5 km from the Caribbean; railway; airport; monument: in the town are the ruins of the Casa Fuerte, a relic of the War of Independence.

Barcelos *bar-sel'os*, 41 32N 8 37W, pop(1981) 10,800, picturesque old town on N bank of R Cávado, Braga dist, N Portugal; 18 km W of Braga; produces characteristic regional pottery cockerels which have become an emblem of Portugal; railway; events: Das Cruzes festival at the beginning of May with processions and the fishermen's festival in Sept.

Bardejov *bard'ye-yof*, BARTFELD (Ger), 49 18N 21 14E, pop(1984) 26,502, town in Východoslovenský region, Slovak Socialist Republic, E Czechoslovakia; on R Topla, N of Prešov, in the N Carpathian Mts near the frontier with Poland; hot springs nearby; railway.

Bareilly *bu-ray'lee*, BARELI, 28 22N 79 27E, pop(1981) 438,000, industrial city in Uttar Pradesh, N India; 190 km NE of Agra, E of the R Ramganga; linked to Rampur by rail; founded in 1537; a Mogul capital in 1657; ceded to the British in 1801; played a leading role in the Indian Munity of 1857.

Barents Sea, BARENTSOVO MORE (Rus), BARENTS HAVET (Nor), a shallow arm of the Arctic Ocean, lying N of Norway and European USSR; bounded by Svalbard (Spitsbergen) and Zemlya Frantsa Josifa (Franz-Josefland) in the N and Novaya Zemlya in the W; connects with the Kara Sea, through the straits of Matochkin Shar, Karskiye Vorotaa and Yugorski Shar and with the Norwegian Sea between North Cape and Svalbard; the warm North Cape Current, which is a continuation of the North Atlantic Drift, disperses pack ice in the S; Murmansk and Vardö ports are ice-free throughout the year.

Bargoed *bahr-goyd'*, 51 43N 3 15W, pop(1981) 15,374, town in Rhymney Valley dist, Mid Glamorgan, S Wales; N of Cardiff in Islwyn urban area; railway.

Bari *ba'ree*, prov of Puglia region, SE Italy; pop(1981) 1,464,627; area 5,128 sq km; capital Bari.

Bari, 41 07N 16 52E, pop(1981) 371,022, seaport and capital town of Bari prov, Puglia region, SE Italy; on a peninsula in the Adriatic Sea, WNW of Brindisi; an important industrial and commercial centre; archbishopric; university (1924); naval college; airport (9 km W of the town at Palese); car ferries; economy: petrochemicals, shipbuilding; site of Italy's first atomic power station; monument: in the centre of the old town is the cathedral of San Nicola (begun 1087); events: festival of St Nicholas - procession of fishing boats (8 May); Fiera del Levante (Levante Fair), annually in Sept.

Barinas *ba-ree'nas*, state in W Venezuela; bounded S by the Río Apure and W by outliers of the Cordillera de Mérida, and situated in a region of *llanos* plains, the state is drained by numerous secondary tributaries of the Orinoco, including the Apure, Santo Domingo and Guanare rivers; pop(1980) 318,401; area 35,187 sq km; capital Barinas; oil is piped from Barinas to Puerto Cabello.

Barinas, 8 37N 70 12W, pop(1981) 110,462, capital of Barinas state, W Venezuela; SE of Maracaibo, in the E foothills of the Cordillera de Mérida; university (1975); airfield.

Barisal *bur'i-sal*, region in S Bangladesh; on the Ganges river delta; includes Barisal, Bhola, Jhalakati and Perojpur districts; pop(1981) 4,667,000; area 7,298 sq km.

Barisal, 22 41N 90 20E, pop(1981) 172,905, river port capital of Barisal region, S Bangladesh; on a tributary at the mouth of the R Ganga (Ganges); Barisal Guns are natural phenomena which sound like distant cannon fire or thunder and are thought to be of seismic origin; economy: trade in jute, rice, betel nuts, oilseed and fish.

Baritu *ba-ree'too*, national park in NE Salta prov, Argentina; area 724 sq km; established in 1974; borders E with Bolivia.

Bar'king and Dagenham *-dag'en-em*, 51 33N 0 08E, pop(1981) 149,930, industrial borough in Greater London, England; on the R Roding, 15 km ENE of central London, N of the R Thames; railway; economy: electrical equipment, chemicals; monuments: 7th-c Barking Abbey and Valence Manor House (1600).

Barlavento *bar-la-ven'to*, group of windward islands and a district, Cape Verde Is, comprising the islands of Santo Antão, São Vicente, Santa Luzia, São Nicolau, Sal and Boa Vista; area 2,230 sq km; pop(1980) 107,968, the district of Barlavento is divided into 7 local government *concelhos* or councils.

Bar-le-Duc *bar-le-dük* or **Bar-sur-Ornain** *or-nĩ* ('duke's fortress'), 48 47N 5 10E, pop(1982) 20,029, capital of Meuse dept, Lorraine region, NE France; on the R Ornain and the Marne-Rhine Canal; economy: textiles, brewing, metal goods, hosiery.

Barnaul *bar-na-ool'*, 53 20N 83 40E, pop(1983) 561,000, capital city of Altayskiy kray, SW Siberian Rossiyskaya, Soviet Union; on the left bank of the R Ob' where it meets the R Barnaulka; established in 1730 as a silver-smelting centre; mining school; meteorological observatory (1841); railway; airfield; steamship dock; economy: heavy engineering and the manufacture of clothing, textiles, motor-vehicle engines, building materials, and foodstuffs.

Bar'net, 51 40N 0 13W, pop(1981) 292,441, largely residential borough of N Greater London, England; includes the suburbs of Barnet, East Barnet, Friern Barnet, Hendon and Finchley; railway; economy: finance, leather, scientific instruments; monument: 13th-c Chipping Barnet church.

Barns'ley, 53 34N 1 28W, pop(1981) 77,616, urban area pop(1981) 128,157, coal-mining town in Barnsley borough, South Yorkshire, N England; on the R Dearne, 18 km N of Sheffield; noted for its glass-blowing in the 17th century; railway; economy: coal, glass, carpets, clothing, foodstuffs, engineering; monuments: 15th-c church of St Mary, Monk Bretton priory (3 km NE).

Barn'staple, 51 05N 4 04W, pop(1981) 24,878, port town in North Devon dist, Devonshire, SW England; on the R Tow, 55 km NW of Exeter; birthplace of John Gay who wrote *The Beggars' Opera*; railway; economy: engineering, trade in wool and cattle.

Baros'sa, pop(1981) 28,750, a NE suburb of Outer Adelaide stat div, South Australia; the Barossa valley is a noted wine-producing area; event: wine festival every 2 years to celebrate the grape harvest (alternates with Adelaide Festival of Arts).

Barquisimeto *bar-kee-see-may'tō*, 10 03N 69 18W, pop(1981) 497,635, capital of Lara state, N Venezuela; university (1968); railway; airfield; monuments: the cathedral is a modern structure of free-form concrete and glass; in front of the modern Palacio Municipal is a large square with a bronze equestrian statue of Bolívar.

Barra Mansa *ba'ra man'sa*, 22 35S 44 12W, pop(1980) 123,335, town in Rio de Janeiro state, Sudeste region, SE Brazil; NW of Rio de Janeiro; railway; economy: cattle raising.

Barracoot'a, gas field in the Bass Strait, off the S coast of Victoria, Australia.

Barranquilla *ba-ran-keel'ya*, 11 00N 74 50W, pop(1985) 1,120,975, modern industrial capital of Atlántico dept, N Colombia, South America; on the Río Magdalena, 18 km from its mouth; Colombia's principal Caribbean port; the river has been deepened to enable river-port facilities to be extended to ocean-going vessels; founded in 1721; the first free industrial and trade zone in Colombia; headquarters of the Corporación Financiera del Norte, a regional private development corporation; 3 universities (1941, 1966, 1967); bull ring; in 1919 Barranquilla opened the first air terminal in Latin America; airport (Ernesto Cortissoz) at 10 km; economy: commerce, foodstuffs, footwear, drinks, tobacco, furniture, textiles, petrochemicals and Latin America's first caprolactam plant producing the basic material used to make nylon.

Barrhead, 55 48N 4 24W, pop(1981) 18,418, town in Renfrew dist, Strathclyde, W Scotland; in Clydeside urban area, on the R Levern, 11 km SW of Glasgow; railway.

Barrie, 44 22N 79 42W, pop(1981) 38,423, town in SE Ontario, SE Canada; on the SW shore of L Simcoe, 80 km N of Toronto; railway; racetrack; site of a Winter Carnival which attracts ice motorcyclists and dog sledders.

Barroso, Serra de *bar-ro'so*, mountain range, Vila Real dist, N Portugal; lying to the NW of the Barragem do Alto Rabagão and rising to 1,208 m.

Barrow, river in S Irish Republic, rising in Slieve Bloom Mts of Kildare; flows 190 km E and S to meet the Atlantic Ocean at Waterford Harbour; tributaries R Nore; navigable to Athy.

Barrow-in-Furness, 54 07N 3 14W, pop(1981) 50,625, port town in Barrow-in-Furness dist, Cumbria, NW England; on Furness peninsula, 19 km NW of Lancaster; railway; economy: shipbuilding, engineering, paper, chemicals, offshore gas services.

Barry, 51 24N 3 18W, pop(1981) 46,520, resort town in Vale of Glamorgan dist, South Glamorgan, S Wales; on the Bristol Channel, SW of Cardiff; railway; economy: engineering.

Bartlesville, 36 45N 95 59W, pop(1980) 34,568, county seat of Washington county, NE Oklahoma, United States; on the R Caney, 66 km N of Tulsa; railway; economy: distribution centre for a rich oil-producing region; monuments: Price Tower, Nellie Johnstone oil well (replica of the first commercial well in the state).

Baruun Urt *ba'roon oort*, 46 80N 113 80E, capital of Sühbaatar county, SE Mongolia; mining centre and market for agricultural produce.

Basauri *bas-ow'ree*, 43 13N 2 54W, pop(1981) 51,996, S suburb of Bilbao in Vizcaya prov, Pais Vasco (Basque Country), N Spain.

Bascilicata *bah-zeel-ee-kah'tah*, LUCANIA (anc), mountainous region of S Italy, comprising the provs of Potenza and Matera; pop(1981) 610,186; area 9,990 sq km; agricultural area producing wheat, maize, wine, olives, and chestnuts; 30% of the working population are employed in agriculture; the discovery of methane deposits at Ferrandina helped the chemicals industry to develop in the prov of Matera; drained by the Agri and Basento rivers which rise in the Appno Lucano.

Ba'sel, BASLE *bahl* (Eng), BÂLE *bahl* (Fr), 47 35N 7 35E, pop(1980) 182,143, capital of Basel-Stadt demicanton and of Basel canton, NE Switzerland; on the R Rhine, 69 km N of Bern; centre of the transnational Regio Basiliensis 'natural region' which has been promoted since 1963; the oldest Swiss university (1460); Basel is a major European communications crossroads and Switzerland's leading transshipment centre; the city is a river port (opened 1924) at the terminus of Rhine navigation; railway junction; international airport, Basel-Mulhouse, on French territory and shared with France; Basel is on the direct N-S route from Hamburg to Italy, either via the St Gotthard Tunnel or the Great St Bernard Tunnel; the city is a major centre of international commerce, the home of many headquarters of banking, finance, forwarding agencies and insurance companies; headquarters of the Bank for International Settlements; the Swiss Industries Fair, the largest convention and fair organization in Switzerland, is held every year in the newly opened European World Trade and Convention Centre; the city is divided by the R Rhine into Grossbasel (Greater Basel), on the steep left bank, and Kleinbasel (Lesser Basel) on the right bank; there are notable zoological and botanical gardens; early development of the city was related to the silk and dye industries; the printing machine and book trade began in Basel in the 15th century; the city left the German empire for the Swiss Confederacy in 1501 and became an influential centre during the Reformation, with Erasmus, Oecolampadius, Euler and Johann Bernoulli among its teachers; today Basel is a major cultural centre with 26 museums and 13 theatres; the space-age pylon at the 'Three Countries Corner' or 'Dreilaendereck', on a promontory jutting out into the R Rhine, symbolizes Basel's location at the junction of France, Germany and Switzerland; the first Zionist conference was held here in 1897; in 1969 it voted against union with Basel-Land, and since then many emigrants have left to enjoy the relatively cheaper standard of living outside; Basel has the highest proportion of old people in Switzerland (20% of the population); headquarters and laboratories of the major Swiss pharmaceutical companies (Roche, Ciba-Geigy and Sandoz); salt works further up the Rhine exploit one of Switzerland's few natural resources, and guarantee self-sufficiency in salt; economy: pharmaceuticals, synthetics, agrochemicals, chemicals, textiles, metallurgy, engineering, foodstuffs; monuments: the red-sandstone Gothic minster (until 1528 a cathedral), consecrated in 1019 but largely rebuilt in 1356 after an earthquake and fire, has fine towers and cloisters, and an apse and Romanesque gate of 1185; town hall (1504-1514); town mansions and corporate houses (15th and 16th centuries); Spalentor (1400); events: 3-day Basel Carnival (Fasnacht).

Basel-Country, demicanton in Switzerland. See Basel-Land.

Basel-Land *bas'el-land*, BASEL-COUNTRY (Eng), BÂLE-CAMPAGNE *bahl-kā-pah'nyu* (Fr), demicanton in NE Switzerland; pop(1980) 219,822; area 428 sq km; capital Liestal; lies on the N slopes of the Jura Mts; joined the Confederation in 1501; the German language is spoken by the majority of inhabitants.

Basel-Stadt *bas'el-shtaht*, BASEL-TOWN (Eng), BÂLE-VILLE *bahl-veel'* (Fr), demicanton in NE Switzerland; pop(1980) 203,915; area 37 sq km; capital Basel; the demicanton comprises two suburbs and the city of Basel.

Basel-Town, demicanton in Switzerland. See Basel-Stadt.

Basento *ba-zen'to*, river in Basilicata region, S Italy; rises in the Appno Lucano, 18 km SSW of Potenza; flows N and ESE to the Golfo di Taranto, 24 km ESE of Pisticci; length 149 km.

Basildon *baz'il-don*, 51 34N 0 25E, pop(1981) 95,338, residential town in Basildon dist, Essex, SE England; NE of London and 16 km SSW of Chelmsford; a 'new town' development (1949) designed to accommodate overspill from London; railway; economy: motor vehicles.

Basiliensis, Regio *rej'i-ō ba-sil-yen'sis*, transnational 'natural region' encompassing the frontier districts of France, Switzerland and W Germany, in the Upper Rhine Valley, between the Jura Mts and the Black Forest; administrative centre Basel; regional centres at Mulhouse and Freiburg; pop(1984e) 2,077,797; area 234 sq km; international cooperation between local governments, industries and universities promoted since 1963.

Basingstoke *bay'zing-stōk*, 51 16N 1 05W, pop(1981) 73,492, town in Basingstoke and Deane dist, Hampshire, S England; 27 km NE of Winchester; headquarters of the UK Civil Service Commission; railway; economy: engineering, printing, publishing, electronics, light engineering; monuments: Willis Museum; Silchester Roman site (17 km N).

Basle, city in Switzerland. See Basel.

Basque Provinces, autonomous region in N Spain. See Pais Vasco.

Basrah, Al *baz'ru*, governorate in SE Iraq, at the head of the Arabian Gulf; pop(1977) 1,008,626; area 19,702 sq km; capital Al Basrah; traversed NW-SE by the Shatt al'Arab.

Basrah, Al, 30 30N 47 50E, pop(1970) 333,684, port capital of Al Basrah governorate, SE Iraq, at the head of the Shatt al'Arab R, c.120 km from the Arabian Gulf; administrative and commercial centre; known in *Arabian Knights* as Bassorah; university (1967); railway; airport; economy: oil refining, manufacture of fertilizers; the port was closed in Sept 1980 as a result of the conflict with Iran.

Bas-Rhin *ba-rī*, dept in N half of the Alsace region of E France on the German frontier, comprising 7 arrond, 44 cantons and 514 communes; pop(1982) 915,676; area 4,787 sq km; capital Strasbourg; the R Rhine dissects the dept N-S; the Rhône-Rhine and Marne-Rhine Canals converge on Strasbourg; in the W the Vosges Mts rise to 1,098 m; extensive vineyards and orchards; there are spas at Niederbronn, Pechelbronne and Morsbronn; part of the Parc des Vosges du Nord regional nature park is within the dept; economy: beer, wine, paper, machinery, coal, iron.

Bassar *ba'sar*, 9 18N 0 53E, pop(1977) 17,500, town in Centrale region, Togo, W Africa; N terminus of the Togolese railway.

Basse, local government area in The Gambia, W Africa; pop(1983) 111,335; area 2,008 sq km.

Bassein *ba-sayn'*, 16 46N 94 45E, pop(1983) 355,588, port and capital of Irrawaddy division, SW Burma; W of Rangoon; railway; airfield.

Basse-Koto *bas-kō'tō*, prefecture in S Central African Republic; pop(1968) 183,223; area 17,550 sq km; the R Bangui flows through the prefecture to join the R Ubangi on the S border of the country as does R Kotto which also forms the prefecture's E border; chief town Mobaye; other towns include Alindao, Bangoro, Mokassa, Harga, Fouroumbala and Kembe.

Basse-Normandie *bas-nor-mâ-dee*, region of NW France comprising the depts of Calvados, Manche and Orne, 11 arrond, 140 cantons and 1,808 communes; pop(1982) 1,350,979; area 17,589 sq km; lies on the coast of the English Channel between Brittany and Haute-Normandie; its main towns are Caen and the port of Cherbourg; from the Collines de Normandie (417 m) and the NW extremity of the Collines du Perche (314 m) in the Armorican Massif, the region is drained by the rivers Touques, Dives, Orne and Vire which flow N to the Baie de la Seine; the Cotentin peninsula extending N into the English Channel culminates in the granite cliff of the Nez de Jobourg; close to the bay of Mont-St-Michel, the warm air of the Gulf Stream produces semi-tropical vegetation; extensive woodlands (Bocage Normand) S of Caen; noted for the production of Calvados from the distilled spirit of cider; the epic World War II cross-Channel invasion by the Allied Forces to free Europe in June 1944 centred on the beaches of the Calvados coastline.

Bass'enthwaite, lake in the Lake District of Cumbria, NW England; 5 km NW of Keswick; Skiddaw Forest lies E and Thornthwaite Forest lies W.

Basse-Terre *bas-ter'*, one of the 2 main islands of the Overseas Department of Guadeloupe, Lesser Antilles, E

Caribbean; separated from Grande-Terre I by the narrow Rivière Salée; area 848 sq km; pop(1982) 141,313; capital Basse-Terre; the terrain is mountainous with Grande Soufrière, an active volcano, rising to 1,484 m; the Natural Park of Guadeloupe covers 300 sq km of forest land in the centre of the island.

Basse-Terre, 16 00N 61 42W, pop(1982) 13,656, port and capital town of the Overseas Department of Guadeloupe, Lesser Antilles, E Caribbean; on the SW coast of Basse-Terre I, 168 km NNW of Fort-de-France, Martinique; monuments: cathedral and nearby ruins of Fort St-Charles.

Basseterre *bas-ter'*, 17 17N 62 43W, pop(1980) 14,725, capital and chief port of St Kitts-Nevis, N Leeward Is, E Caribbean, on the SW coast of St Kitts I; distribution centre for exports to neighbouring islands; Golden Rock International Airport is 3 km to the N; economy: electrical components, garments, data processing, beverages, rum products; monument: cathedral.

Bassila *ba-see'la*, 9 01N 1 46E, town in Atakora prov, W central Benin, W Africa; 130 km NNW of Savalou close to the Benin-Togo border.

Bastia *bas-tee'a* (Ital 'bastiglia', fortress), 42 40N 9 30E, pop(1982) 45,081, port and capital of Haute-Corse dept, NW Corsica, France; in the NE corner of the island on the narrow Cap Corse between the mountains and the sea; railway; airport 21 km S of the town; founded by the Genoese in 1380; the capital of Corsica until 1811; the largest port and chief town of the island; the town comprises the Terra Vecchia of the old fishing village, the Terra Nuova round the Citadel overlooking the harbour, the original Bastia settlement and the modern housing area of St Joseph; the Old Port to the S is used by yachts and fishing boats while the New Port to the N handles shipping from Marseille, Nice, Toulon, Livorno and Elba.

Bastogne *bahst-o'ny'*, BASTENAKEN *bahs'tun-ahk-un* (Flem), dist of Luxembourg prov, SE Belgium; area 1,043 sq km; pop(1982) 36,322.

Bat Yam *bat' yam'*, 32 01N 34 45E, pop(1982) 134,500, seaside resort town in Tel Aviv dist, W Israel; on the Mediterranean Sea, SW of Tel Aviv-Yafo; established in 1926.

Ba'ta, 1 57N 9 50E, pop(1983) 24,100, chief town and seaport on the coast of mainland Río Muni, Equatorial Guinea, W central Africa; 240 km SSE of the capital Malabo, on Bioko island and 160 km N of Libreville (Gabon); airfield; economy: timber export.

Bath, AQUAE CALIDAE (Lat), AKERMANCEASTER (Anglo Saxon), 51 23N 2 22W, pop(1981) 79,965, spa town in Bath dist, Avon, SW England; on R Avon, 19 km ESE of Bristol; noted since Roman times for its hot springs; chartered in 1189; railway; technical university (1966); economy: tourism, printing, plastics, engineering, monuments: Roman baths, 15th-c Roman bath museum, abbey church, notable Georgian crescents; events: Mid-Somerset festival (March), festival of the arts (May).

Batha *ba'tha*, prefecture in Chad, N central Africa; pop(1979) 354,000; area 88,800 sq km; a low lying desert region; L Fittri lies in the SW, there are a number of rivers in the S which flow into L Fittri the largest being the R Batha; capital Ati; chief towns Yao, Mangalme and Am Djémena.

Bathgate, 55 54N 3 38W, pop(1981) 14,477, chief town of West Lothian dist, Lothian, central Scotland; 9 km S of Linlithgow, 29 km SW of Edinburgh; railway; economy: steel, electronics, machinery.

Bath'urst, 33 27S 149 35E, pop(1981) 19,640, urban centre in Central West stat div, New South Wales, Australia; on the Macquarie river, W of Sydney; railway; airfield; one of the country's oldest towns, with many 19th-c buildings; economy: plastics, food processing, tanning.

Bathurst and Melville Islands, islands off the NW coast of Northern Territory, N Australia; approx 80 km N of Darwin; pop(1981) 1,586; area 7,487 sq km; these islands are Aboriginal communities; the Tiwis lived here for thousands of years with little or no contact with the mainland Aboriginal tribes; the town of Nguiu on Bathurst I was founded as a Catholic mission in 1911; today the town has a pop of 1,000; economy: wood-carving and pottery.

Bat'ley, 53 44N 1 37W, pop(1981) 45,591, town in Leeds borough, West Yorkshire, N England; part of West Yorkshire urban area; 10 km SSW of Leeds; woollen shoddy was first manufactured here; railway; economy: coal, textiles, foodstuffs, engineering, chemicals, plastics, textile machinery.

Batman', ILUH, 37 52N 41 02E, pop(1980) 86,172, city in Siirt prov, E Turkey; E of Diyarbakır.

Batna *bat-na'*, 35 34N 6 10E, pop(1982) 179,775, chief town of Batna dept, N Algeria, N Africa; 97 km SSW of Constantine; founded by the French in 1748 as a military outpost; numerous Roman ruins in the area include Lambèse and Timgrad; railway.

Baton Rouge *bat-en roozh'*, 30 27N 91 11W, pop(1980) 219,419, capital of state in East Baton Rouge parish, SE Louisiana, United States; a deep-water port on the Mississippi river, 116 km WNW of New Orleans; ceded by France to Britain in 1763, but later taken by Spain; the town was ceded to France and then in 1803 ceded to the USA as part of the Louisiana Purchase; in 1810 the town declared its independence under the name Feliciana but after Louisiana joined the Union in 1812 Baton Rouge was incorporated (1817) as a town within that state; state capital 1849-61 and since 1882; university (1860); railway; airfield; economy: oil refining, petrochemical industries, food processing, machinery, foundries, and ironworks; monuments: State Museum, Riverside Museum, the old capitol, Huey Long grave and memorial.

Battambang *bat-tam-bang*, province in W Cambodia, pop(1981) 551,860; bounded W and NW by Thailand, S by Pursat prov, N and E by Siem Reap-Oddar Meanchey prov and E by Tonlé Sap (lake); crossed by the Sangker river; major rice-growing region; Battambang-Phnom Penh road was a major target during the civil war in an effort to stop the supply of rice to Phnom Penh; chief city and Cambodia's 2nd largest city is Battambang, a market town, with several rice mills and a textile industry.

Batticaloa *bat-i-ke-lō'a*, 7 43N 81 42E, pop(1981) 42,934, capital of Batticaloa dist, Eastern prov, Sri Lanka; on a lagoon, known as Batticaloa Lake, an inlet of the Bay of Bengal; during colonial times it was second in importance to Trincomalee; 72% of the pop of the dist are Tamil; the 'singing fish' phenomenon is associated with Batticaloa, with unexplained humming of the surf at full moon; monument: remains of Dutch fort, built in 1602.

Battle Creek, 42 19N 85 11W, pop(1980) 35,724, town in Calhoun county, S Michigan, United States; 35 km E of Kalamazoo; railway; economy: breakfast foods.

Batu, 6 55N 39 49E, mountain in NW Balē region, S Ethiopia, NE Africa; height 4,307 m.

Batu Pahat *bah'too pah'hat*, BANDAR PENGGARAM *ban-dar' peng-ga'ram*, 1 50N 102 48E, pop(1980) 64,727, port town in Johor state, S Peninsular Malaysia, SE Asia; near the mouth of the R Batu Pahat, 96 km NW of Johor Baharu; conference centre.

Bauchi *bow'chee*, state in NE central Nigeria, W Africa; pop(1982e) 3,877,100; area 64,605 sq km; drained by the Gongola river; capital Bauchi; chief towns Gombe, Azare, Misau and Ningi; a 19th century kingdom ruled by the Fulah tribe until the British gained control in 1902; the pop comprises a number of ethnic groups including the Tangale, the Waja, the Fulani and the Hausa; about 90% of pop engaged in farming; main cash crops are cattle, cereals and cotton; Yankara game reserve, established in 1972 (area 2,078 sq km); economy: reserves of gold, colombite, cassiterite, coal, limestone, iron ore, antimony and marble; meat canning, groundnut processing, oil mills, cotton ginning, wire and cable production, brick production, cement processing and tourism.

Bauchi, 10 16N 9 50E, pop(1981e) 186,000, capital of Bauchi state, NE central Nigeria, W Africa; 460 km SW of Maiduguri, 105 km NE of Jos and 234 km SE of Kano; founded in 1809; formerly called Yakoba; railway; economy: motor vehicles.

Bauru *bow-roo'*, 22 19S 49 07W, pop(1980) 180,093, town in São Paulo state, Sudeste region, SE Brazil; NW of São Paulo; railway; economy: rice, maize, cattle; founded at the end of the 19th century; near the town is the Horto Florestal, an experimental forestry station which opened in 1928.

Bavaria, prov in W Germany. See Bayern.

Bavaria, Upper, dist of W Germany. See Oberbayern.

Bavarian Alps, mountain range between southern W Germany and Austria. See Bayerische Alpen.

Bavarian Forest, mountain range in W Germany. See Bayerische Wald.

Bawku *bo'koo*, 11 05N 0 11W, town in Upper region, N Ghana, W Africa.

Bay City, 43 36N 83 54W, pop(1980) 41,593, county seat of Bay county, E Michigan, United States; at the head of Saginaw Bay, 21 km N of Saginaw; railway; economy: shipbuilding, machinery.

Bay Islands, Honduras. See Bahía, Islas de la.

Bayamo *bī-a'mō*, 20 23N 76 39W, pop(1983e) 103,366, capital of Granma prov, SE Cuba; surrounded by pasture land 96 km WNW of Santiago de Cuba; road and rail junction; airfield; founded in 1513, it was one of Cuba's leading towns during the colonial era; Céspedes initiated the revolt against Spain here in 1868; former gold mines nearby.

Bayamón *bī-a-mōn'*, 18 24N 66 10W, pop(1980) 196,207, city in Puerto Rico, E Caribbean; on R Bayamón, SW of San Juan; railway; economy: food processing, sugar.

Bayan Har Shan, BAYAN HAR MOUNTAINS, mountain range in central Qinghai prov, W central China; southern offshoot of the Kunlun Shan range; source of the Huang He (Yellow river); elevation ranges from 5,000 to 6,000 m; rises to 5,442 m at Mt Yagradaze.

Bayan-Hongor *ba'yan-KHon'gōr*, BAYAN KHONGOR, county in SW Mongolia; pop(1981e) 61,000; area 116,000 sq km; bounded S by the People's Republic of China; crossed by many rivers including the Baydrag Gol and the Dzag Gol; capital Bayanhongor; more than 10 hot and cold mineral springs are found in the county; lynx, ibex, antelope, wild camel (khavtgai) and the Gobi bear (masalai) are found; economy: cattle and goat farming (Bayan Hongor county supports the greatest numbers of goats in Mongolia); gold, copper and coal mining; marble and granite quarrying; printing, wood processing, food processing.

Bayan Hongor, BAYAN KHONGOR, 46 42N 100 9E, capital of Bayan-Hongor county, SW Mongolia; on Urd Tamir river, WSW of Ulaanbaatar; economy: stock breeding, timber, mining and food processing.

Bayan-Ölgiy *ba'yan ul'gi*, BAYAN OELGI, county in NW Mongolia; pop(1981e) 72,000; area 45,800 sq km; capital Ölgiy; bounded N by USSR and W by the People's Republic of China; lies in the mountainous Mongolian Altai; larches, pine, poplars and willows cover the county; wolves, bears, foxes and lynxes are common; mineral resources include coal, fluorspar, sulphur, marble and lime; stock rearing, particularly cattle, is the main occupation; wood-processing, printing and wool laundry are the chief industries.

Bayerische Alpen *bī'rish al'pen*, BAVARIAN ALPS *buv-ay'ree-un* (Eng), mountain range between S Bayern (Bavaria) prov, W Germany and Tirol, Austria; extending E and W from the Bodensee (L Constance) to Salzburg; highest peak is the Zugspitze (2,962 m); part of the northern calcareous alps; subsidiary ranges are the Wettersteingebirge, Karwendelgebirge and Nordkette; chief resort is Garmisch-Partenkirchen; the Allgäuer Alpen (Allgäu Alps) form its W section; in Austria it is also called the Tirol Alps.

Bayerische Wald *-vahlt*, BAVARIAN FOREST (Eng), mountain range bounded on the NW by the rivers Chamb and Regen and on the SW by the Danube valley, extending SE to the Linz basin in Austria and merging on the N into the Böhmerwald (Bohemian Forest) in Czechoslovakia; the 2 principal ranges include the Vorderer Wald and the Hinterer Wald; highest peak is the Einodriegel (1,126 m); largest continuous forest in Europe; contains Germany's first national park.

Bayern *bī'ern*, BAVARIA *buv-ay'ree-u* (Eng), prov in SE W Germany, bounded on the E by Czechoslovakia and on the S by Austria; comprises the administrative dists of Oberbayern, Niederbayern, Oberpfalz, Oberfranken, Mittelfranken, Unterfranken and Schwaben; area 70,553 sq km; pop(1983) 10,969,500; capital München (Munich); chief towns Augsburg, Passau, Nürnberg, Würzburg and Regensburg; chief rivers are the Danube, Isar, Lech and Main; surrounded by mountain ranges, Bayerische Wald (Bavarian Forest) (E), Fichtelgebirge (NE) and Bayerische Alpen (Bavarian Alps) (S); economy: electrical and mechanical engineering, clothing; the largest prov in W Germany, also Europe's oldest existing political entity; many spas and climatic health resorts S of München (Bad Tolz, Bad Wiessee, Bad Reichenhall); in the W is the 'Romantic Road'.

Baykal, Ozero *bī-kal'*, LAKE BAIKAL (Eng), crescent-shaped lake in S Siberia, on the border between Irkutskaya oblast and Buryatskaya ASSR, Rossiyskaya, Soviet Union; the largest freshwater lake in Eurasia and deepest in the world; area 31,500 sq km; length (SW-NE) 636 km; width 24-80 km; max depth 1,620 m; lies in a deep tectonic basin bordered W by the Baykal'skiy Khrebet range, NE by the Barguzinskiy Khrebet range, and S by the Khrebet Khamar Daban range; the lake is fed by 336 rivers and streams but its only outlet is the Angara, a chief tributary of the Yenisey; there are 22 islands in the lake, the largest of which is Ostrov Ol'khon (length 51 km); there are many hot springs on its shores and earthquakes are frequent; the lake freezes over Jan-April; the Trans-Siberian railway passes round the rocky S shore; Genghis Khan, the Mongol leader, is said to have been born to the SE of the lake.

Baykal-Amur Magistral (BAM), railway in SE Siberian Rossiyskaya, Soviet Union, on a line some 150-300 km N of the Trans-Siberian railway; links the town of Lena, near Ust Kut on the R Lena, with Komsomol'sk-na-Amure in Khabarovskiy kray; length 3,200 km; extensive swamps, taiga forest, permafrost, river seismic problems (R Olekma), and severe continental weather conditions greatly hampered construction of the line; there are railheads at Ust Kut, Tynda, Urgal, and Komsomol'sk-na-Amure; several industrial enterprises are planned in the zone served by the railway which includes rich copper deposits at Udokan, coking coal and high-grade iron ore in the area of Chulman and Aldan to the N, timber resources, and valuable deposits of asbestos and lead-zinc ores; the area is also rich in hydroelectric resources.

Bayonne *ba-yōn'*, 40 40N 74 01W, pop(1980) 65,047, town in Hudson county, NE New Jersey, United States; on the peninsula between Upper New York Bay and Newark Bay, 8 km SW of Jersey City; railway; economy: petroleum refining and exporting, chemicals; the city is linked to Staten Island by the Bayonne Bridge.

Bayreuth *bī-royt'*, 49 56N 11 35E, pop(1983) 71,100, industrial and marketing town, capital of Oberfranken dist, NE Bayern (Bavaria) prov, W Germany; on a tributary of the R Main, 66 km NE of Nürnberg; world famous as a festival city committed to the operas of Wagner; university (1975); railway; economy: electricity supply; monuments: 16th-c old palace, new palace (1753), Wagner theatre (1872-76); events: Richard Wagner Festival (July-Aug).

Baytown, 29 43N 94 59W, pop(1980) 56,923, town in Harris county, SE Texas, United States; on Galveston Bay, 36 km E of Houston; railway; economy: oil refining, chemicals, synthetic rubber and steel.

Beaconsfield *bek'unz-feeld*, 51 37N 0 39W, pop(1981) 13,317, town in South Bucks dist, Buckinghamshire, S central England; 8 km SE of High Wycombe; railway; economy: scientific instruments.

Bearsden, 55 56N 4 20W, pop(1981) 27,183, capital of

Bearsden and Milngavie dist, Strathclyde, W central Scotland; in Clydeside urban area, on the line of the Antonine Wall, 8 km NW of Glasgow; railway; largely a residential town.

Beatrice *bee'a-tris*, oil field in the Moray Firth, off the NE coast of Scotland, United Kingdom; linked by pipeline to Nigg in Ross and Cromarty.

Beau Bassin-Rose Hill *bō bas-sã-*, 20 14S 57 27E, pop(1981e) 86,549, residential township in Plaines Wilhems dist, W Mauritius; S of Port Louis; economy: clothes, handcrafts, copper products.

Beauce *bōs*, flat, fertile pays of the Paris Basin, N central France between Étampes, Pithiviers, Orléans, Châteaudun and Chârtres (its chief town); near Orléans the farmland gives way to forest because of the change from loess to sand deposits.

Beaufort Sea *bō'fort*, pack ice-covered region of the Arctic Ocean, N of Alaska and W of the Arctic archipelago of Canada; part of the deep Arctic basin, which becomes shallow over the continental shelf of Canada; in 1968 a vast deposit of oil was discovered at Prudhoe Bay which was linked by pipeline to Valdez on the Gulf of Alaska; first ice crossing by Stefánsson in 1915 and by Storkenson in 1918.

Beaujolais *bō-zho-lay*, a sub-division of the old prov of Lyonnais in E central France, now forming the N part of Rhône and a small part of Loire dept; it is a granite upland on the edge of the Massif Central; the slopes above the river valleys yield a good Burgundy wine of the name, the centre of the trade being at Villefranche; the N part of the dist is known as Beaujolais Villages; there is a clearly signposted 'Route du Beaujolais.'

Beaumont *bō'mont*, 30 05N 94 06W, pop(1980) 118,102, county seat of Jefferson county, SE Texas, United States; a modern deep-water port on the R Neches, 125 km ENE of Houston; founded in 1835; university; railway; airfield; economy: shipbuilding, oil refining, petrochemicals.

Beauport *bō-por'*, 46 52N 71 12W, pop(1981) 60,447, town in S Québec, SE Canada, 8 km NE of Québec on the St Lawrence river, opposite the S end of the Ile d'Orléans; settled in 1634; it was here that the French encountered General Wolfe's forces in 1759; railway.

Beauvais *bō-vay*, CAESAROMAGUS or BELLOVACUM (Lat), 49 25N 2 08E, pop(1982) 54,147, market town and capital of Oise dept, Picardie region, N France; on the R Thérain, 76 km N of Paris; bishopric; railway; economy: agric equipment, rayon, tiles, fruit, dairy produce; monument: tallest cathedral in France (68 m).

Beavercreek, 40 43N 80 37W, pop(1980) 31,589, town in Greene county, W Ohio, United States; 11 km SE of Dayton.

Beaverton, 45 29N 122 48W, pop(1980) 30,582, city in Washington county, NW Oregon, United States; 11 km W of Portland; founded in 1868; railway.

Beb'ington, 53 22N 3 01W, pop(1981) 62,236, town in Wirral borough, Merseyside, NW England; on Wirral peninsula, 5 km S of Birkenhead; includes Port Sunlight on the R Mersey, a model town built in 1888 for the employees of a local soap and margarine factory; the terminus of the Manchester Ship Canal lies to the SE; railway; economy: chemicals, soap and detergent, edible oils.

Béchar *bay-shar'*, department of W Algeria, N Africa; area 306,000 sq km; pop(1982) 174,568; chief town Béchar.

Bed'ford, 52 08N 0 29W, pop(1981) 77,014, county town in North Bedfordshire dist, Bedfordshire, S central England; a residential town 32 km SE of Northampton and 75 km N of London; John Bunyan (1628-88) was imprisoned here for 12 years, during which time he wrote *The Pilgrim's Progress*; railway; economy: foodstuffs, engineering.

Bedfordshire, county in S central England; bounded NW by Northamptonshire, NE by Cambridgeshire, SE by Hertfordshire and W by Buckinghamshire; drained W-E by the R Ouse; pop(1981) 507,054; area 1,235 sq km; county town Bedford; chief towns include: Luton, Dunstable and Biggleswade; economy: distribution centre, motor vehicles, bricks, wheat, barley; the county is divided into 4 districts:

District	*area (sq km)*	*pop(1981)*
Luton	43	164,743
Mid Bedfordshire	504	102,533
North Bedfordshire	476	133,116
South Bedfordshire	212	106,662

Bed'lington, 55 08N 1 35W, pop(1981) 15,072, town in Wansbeck dist, Northumberland, NE England; on the R Blyth, 7 km SE of Morpeth; economy: coal, electronics.

Bedwas *bed'wahs*, 51 35N 3 10W, pop(1981) 8,923, town in Rhymney Valley dist, Mid Glamorgan, S Wales; N of Cardiff in Caerphilly-Bedwas urban area.

Bed'worth, 52 29N 1 28W, pop(1981) 29,277, town in Nuneaton and Bedworth dist, Warwickshire, central England; part of Coventry-Bedworth urban area; 5 km S of Nuneaton; economy: engineering, textiles.

Będzin *be'-jeen*, 50 19N 19 07E, pop(1983) 77,000, city in Katowice voivodship, S Poland; on R Czarna Przemsza, NE of Kraków; railway; economy: coal mining, non-ferrous metals foundry; monument: castle (1364) with regional museum.

Beersheba *beer-shee'bu*, BE'ER SHEVA, sub-district of South dist, S Israel; bounded W by Egypt and E by Jordan; pop(1983) 275,018; area 12,835 sq km.

Beersheba, 31 15N 34 47E, pop(1982) 112,600, industrial town in South dist, S Israel; on the N edge of the Negev desert; southernmost Israelite city in ancient times with ruins lying E of the modern town; desert farming research centre; university (1965); railway; airfield; oil pipeline.

Beeston, 52 56N 1 12W, pop(1981) 65,198, town linked with Stapleford in Broxtowe dist, Nottinghamshire, central England; 5 km SW of Nottingham; railway; economy: engineering, pharmaceuticals, textiles.

Begumgonj *bay'gum-gunj*, 22 59N 91 04E, pop(1981) 69,623, town in Noakhali dist, Noakhali region, S Bangladesh; E of Noakhali; railway.

Behar'a, governorate in N Egypt; pop(1976) 2,517,292; area 4,589 sq km; located within the Nile delta; capital Damanhûr.

Beihai *bay-hī*, PEIHAI, 21 28N 109 06E, pop(1984e) 171,600, city and port in Guangxi aut region, S China; on the Gulf of Tongking; special economic zone; economy: centre for fishing and for local communications; monument: Mount Guantou, in the SW of the city, contains a natural cave with a forest of peculiarly-shaped rocks at its entrance which echo the sound of the sea.

Beijing *bay-zhing*, PEIPING, PEKING, 39 55N 116 25E, municipality pop(1982) 9,230,687, urban centre pop(1984e) 5,754,600, capital city and municipality of NE China; the Jundu Shan mountains rise to the W; part of the NE border is formed by the Great Wall of China; municipality area 17,800 sq km; from the early 10th century Beijing was the secondary capital of the Liao dynasty and then the capital city of succeeding dynasties, namely: the Jin, Yuan, Ming and Qing; it was made the capital of China in 1949; university (1898); Qinghua University (1950); railway; airport; economy: rapid development since 1949 in textiles, petrochemicals, light and heavy engineering and electricity production; monuments: the Imperial Palace, former home of the Chinese emperors, is situated in the centre of Beijing; it was built during the Yuan dynasty (1279-1368), then rebuilt by the 3rd Ming emperor, Yong Le (1403-24), using hundreds of thousands of workers; surrounded by a moat and a 10.7 m-high wall, the Imperial Palace consists of 6 main palaces and numerous smaller buildings with a total of over 9,000 rooms; formerly known as the 'Forbidden City', no commoner or foreigner was allowed to enter the Imperial Palace without special permission; an imperial decree also ordained that no building in Beijing could be higher than the palace, most of which is 2 storeys high; art treasures from the palace were looted during the Japanese occupation of Beijing in the 1930s and by the

Guomindang (Nationalists) in 1949 before their retreat to Taiwan; Tian'anmen square is the largest public square in the world, covering 0.4 sq km; on one side of the square is Tian'anmen (the Gate of Heavenly Peace), a huge stone gate with a wooden roof, built in 1417 and restored in 1651; the rostrum on top is used by China's leaders on special occasions; the 36 m-high obelisk in the centre of the square was erected as a tribute to the heroes of the Chinese Revolution; the Mao Zedong Memorial Hall which faces the Tian'anmen gate was begun in 1976 and inaugurated on 9 Sept 1977, the anniversary of Chairman Mao's death; Niu Jie, built in 996, is Beijing's oldest Muslim temple; nearby is the Fayuan Si temple, completed in 696, which contains a rare religious collection of Buddhist antiques; in the SE of Beijing, Tiantan (the Temple of Heaven), built in the 15th century, contains the Hall of Prayer for Good Harvests, the Imperial Vault of Heaven and the Circular Mound Altar of Heaven; Yiheyuan (the Summer Palace) is situated approx 11 km NW of Tian'anmen square; the original palace, built in the 12th century, was destroyed by the British and French in 1860; the present palace was built in 1888; in the N of the grounds is Longevity Hill, which overlooks Kunming lake in the S: a favourite spot for Sunday picnics; in the SW of the city is Lugouqiao bridge, also known as the Marco Polo bridge; the bridge, 235 m long and supported by 11 archways, contains 485 carved stone lions on its 280 balustrades, which were retained when the bridge was widened in 1969; 75 km NW of Beijing at Badaling is part of the Great Wall; in a valley to the N of Beijing are the tombs of 13 Ming emperors; the sacred road leading to the Ming tombs is lined with statues of legendary animals and humans.

Beira *bay'ra*, 19 46S 34 52E, pop(1980) 214,613, seaport capital of Sofala prov, Mozambique, SE Africa; 190 km SW of the mouth of the R Zambezi at the mouth of the Buzi and Pungué rivers 725 km NNE of Maputo and 450 km SE of Harare (Zimbabwe); with its well developed harbour facilities it is Mozambique's main port, one of 3 major outlets for mineral production; occupied by the Portuguese in 1506; founded in 1891 as the seat of the Mozambique Company; administration was transferred to the Mozambique government in 1942; linked by rail to Zaire, Malawi, Zambia and Zimbabwe; airport.

Beira Alta *bay'eer-a al-ta* ('upper edge or shore'), mountainous prov of N Portugal formed in 1936 from the former region of Beira, includes parts of Guarda and Viseu districts from the wooded highlands and high peaks of the Serra da Estrêla to the valleys of the Douro and Mondego; geologically a continuation of the cordilleras of central Spain; the chief town is Guarda but the largest is Viseu; area 9,426 sq km.

Beira Baixa *bay'eer-a bīsh'ya*, ('lower edge or shore') agricultural prov of N central Portugal formed in 1936 from the former Beira region, includes most of Castelo Branco dist extending over an infertile plain between the southern foothills of the Serra da Estrêla and the R Tagus; the chief towns are its capital, Castelo Branco, and Covilhã; area 7,416 sq km; in the river valleys the farming is mixed, with the production of grain, vegetables and fruit; elsewhere the predominant type of farming on large estates is single-crop grain production.

Beira Litoral, *bay'eer-a lee-toor-ahl'* ('coastal edge or shore'), prov of N central Portugal formed in 1936 from the former Beira region, includes parts of Aveiro, Coimbra and Leiria dists covering coastal dunes, pinewoods, marshy river estuaries and salt-pans; area, 7,444 sq km; the chief town is Coimbra; noted for the production of full-bodied red and sparkling demarcated wines at Bairrada.

Beirut, governorate and capital city of Lebanon. See Beyrouth.

Beja *bay'zha*, dist in S Portugal, part of the former Baixo Alentejo prov, lying between the Atlantic and the Spanish border; area, 10,240 sq km; pop(1981) 188,420; divided into 14 councils and 90 parishes; economy: textiles, ceramics, grain, rice, potatoes, onions, tomatoes, wine, fruit, cork, wood, acorns, meat, skins, dairy produce, sheep, pigs; minerals: lead, copper, iron, manganese, zinc, sulphur; airfields at Beja and Amaraleja.

Beja, PAX JULIA (anc), 38 01N 7 52W, pop(1981) 19,700, agricultural market town and capital of Beja dist, Portugal; 136 km SE of Lisbon, on gently rolling uplands between the basins of R Sado and R Guadiana; railway; airfield; NATO airbase; monuments: the castle (1300), Rainha Dona Leonor museum, with a fine collection of azulejos tiles; events: municipal holiday in the first week of May; São Lourenço and Santa Maria fairs in Aug with bullfights.

Béja *bay-zha'*, 36 52N 9 13E, pop(1984) 46,708, capital of Béja governorate, N Tunisia, N Africa; 90 km W of Tunis; railway.

Bejaïa *bi-jah'ee-ya*, 36 49N 5 03E, pop(1982) 145,052, chief town of Bejaïa dept, N Algeria, N Africa; on the Mediterranean coast, E of Alger; railway.

Békés *bay'kaysh*, county in SE Hungary; bounded to the S by Romania; watered by the Körös and Berettyo rivers; pop(1984e) 429,000; area 5,632 sq km; capital Békéscsaba; chief towns include Orosháza, Gyula, Békés and Szarvas; the Gyoma printing house is noted for facsimile editions of old codices and bibles; Békés county was the rural base of the labour movement during the early 20th century; thermal baths at Gyula, Gyoma; economy: grain, fruit, vegetables, sausages, bus chassis, plate-glass and heat-insulating glass, corn harvesters, knitwear.

Békés, 46 47N 21 09E, pop(1984e) 22,000, town in Békés county, SE Hungary; on R Körös, 9 km NE of Békéscsaba; railway; economy: trade centre in agricultural region; textiles.

Békéscsaba *bay'kaysh-cho'bo*, 46 40N 21 05E, pop(1984e) 69,000, capital of Békés county, SE Hungary; NE of Szeged; railway; economy: Persian-style rugs and carpets, textiles, food processing.

Bekka, The, governorate of Lebanon. See Beqa'a, El.

Bekwai *bek-wi'*, 6 28N 1 29W, town in Ashanti region, S central Ghana, W Africa; S of Kumasi and SW of L Bosumtwi.

Belait *bal-īt'*, dist of Brunei, SE Asia; bounded N by the South China Sea, E by Tutong dist and on all other sides by the East Malaysian state of Sarawak; pop(1981) 49,590; Kuala Belait, Seria and Badas are the major towns; Belait river is the main waterway; economy: oil and gas.

Belau or **Palau** *pe-la'oo*, official name Republic of Belau, a group of small islands and islets, the smallest of the 4 political units to emerge out of the US Trust Territory of the Pacific Islands, W Pacific Ocean; lying about 7° 30′ N of the equator, and c.960 km E of the Philippines; the westernmost cluster of the 6 major island groups that make up the Caroline Is; timezone GMT +10; area 494 sq km; pop(1980) 12,177; 65% of Belau's resident population live in the capital Koror; Palauan is the major language but English is generally used as the language of business and government on Koror I.

Physical description. The Belau archipelago consists of some 350 islands, islets and atolls strewn along a line from Angaur to the atoll of Kayangel, 200 km NE. The islands vary in size from small uninhabited islets to 367 sq km Babeldoab, the main island and the 2nd largest in Micronesia (after Guam). Formerly the Rock Is, the Floating Garden Is are undercut mounds of limestone in a wide lagoon on the W side of Belau. Formed as ancient reefs, this uninhabited 200-island complex is now thickly covered with dark vegetation. The largest islands of Belau were formed by Eocene volcanic activity and are composed of basalt and andesite. Babeldoab rises to 200 m and is fringed by mangrove swamps. Angaur and Peleliu are low platform and reef islands. At the northernmost tip of the archipelago is the coastal atoll of Kayangel.

Climate. The climate of Belau is sunny and warm all year round. Humidity is high, the annual mean being 82%; mean annual temperature being 27°C. Average annual rainfall is 3,810 mm, falling most heavily between May and Sept. Typhoons can be expected at any time throughout the year.

History, government and constitution. The islands were held by Germany between 1899 and 1914. Belau came under Japanese administration from 1920, when Japan's rule in Micronesia was recognized by a League of Nations Mandate. In September 1944, US Marines invaded Peleliu and Anguar, which were used as bases from which to launch their attack on the Philippines. In 1946, the US took control of the Caroline, Marshall, and Marianas Is (except Guam) as a trusteeship of the US. Belau was one of the 6 districts of this Trust Territory of the Pacific Islands. In 1979, the Constitution of the Republic of Belau was defined, and in 1980 was ratified by the people of Belau. The Constitution sets up a democratic, representative form of government with elements of 2 governmental systems, the modern democratic system, and the system of hereditary chiefs. The Constitution stipulates that the chiefs are an advisory body, but in reality they wield considerable influence, especially in the state government.

Economy. Agriculture, fisheries and tourism are considered to be Belau's most favoured areas of development. There is considerable agricultural land capable of growing taro, pineapple, breadfruit, bananas, yams, citrus fruit trees, coconuts, pepper and pandanus, melons and some vegetables, but most agriculture is of basic subsistence type. There are a few commercial farms on Babeldoab I growing cash crops. Belau grants fishing rights to companies and associations from Japan, Taiwan, the Philippines, and the US, who fish mainly for tuna. Although there is considerable potential for tourism, the industry's growth is slowed by limited infrastructure.

Belawan *be-la'wan*, 3 46N 98 44E, seaport in Sumatera Utara prov, Indonesia; on the NE coast of the island of Sumatera, at the mouth of the R Deli, N of the commercial city of Medan; economy: the outlet for 65% of Indonesia's exports, chiefly of rubber, tobacco, palm oil, sisal and coffee.

Belém *be-lem'*, 1 27S 48 29W, pop(1980) 755,984, port capital of Pará state, Norte region, N Brazil; at the mouth of the Tocantins river; founded in 1616; university (1957); railway; airport; monuments: cathedral (1748); the Paz Theatre is one of the largest in the country; Santo Aleixandre, an 18th-c church, is now the Museum of Religious Art; the Goeldi Museum comprises a museum, a zoological garden and a botanical exhibit; the 17th-c Mercês Church is the oldest church in Belém; the Basilica of Nossa Senhora de Nazaré (built in 1909) has beautiful marble-work and stained glass windows; events: accession of Pará to independent Brazil (15 Aug); Our Lady of Nazaré, known as Cirio, the festival of candles (2nd Sunday and 4th Monday in Oct).

Bélep, Îles *bay'lep*, island group 50 km NW of the French overseas territory of New Caledonia in S Pacific Ocean; area 70 sq km; pop(1976) 686.

Belfast, BEAL FEIRSTE (Gael), 54 35N 5 55W, pop(1981) 358,991, capital of Northern Ireland in Belfast dist, Antrim, NE Northern Ireland; at the mouth of the Lagan river, on Belfast Lough; Belfast's original settlement and castle were destroyed in 1177; the 17th-c Plantation of Ulster brought English and Scottish settlers to Belfast which became a centre of Irish Protestantism; after 1685 and the Revocation of the Edict of Nantes, the Irish linen industry attracted large numbers of Huguenots; the city grew rapidly in the 19th century with the expansion of industry; Belfast became the capital of Northern Ireland in 1920; the city has well-defined Nationalist (Catholic) and Unionist (Protestant) areas and has been disrupted by civil unrest since 1968; Queen's University of Belfast (1908); railway; airfield; airport (Aldergrove International, W of Belfast); economy: shipyards, aircraft, linen, engineering, footwear, food processing; monuments: neo-Renaissance style city hall (1900); to the E of city hall is a memorial to the *Titanic* which was built in a Belfast shipyard in 1912; St Anne's cathedral (begun in 1898) contains the tomb of Lord Carson, Unionist leader, who died in 1935; the Ulster Museum contains early Celtic finds and the treasure recovered in 1968 from a Spanish galleon which sank off the Giant's Causeway in 1588; Parliament House, former seat of the Northern Ireland parliament, is situated in the suburb of Stormont.

Belfast Lough *loKH*, inlet on the E coast of Northern Ireland; extending inland between Co Antrim (N) and Co Down (S); provides a natural harbour 19 km long by 5-11 km wide; the city of Belfast is situated at the head of the lough, on the Lagan river; other towns on its shore are Newtownabbey and Carrickfergus (N), Bangor and Holywood (S).

Belfort *bel-for*, 47 38N 6 50E, pop(1982) 52,739, old fortified town and capital of the Territoire de Belfort dept, Franche-Comté region, NE France; on the R Savoureuse between the Vosges and the Jura; part of the dept of Haut-Rhin that was left to France on the cession of Alsace to Germany in 1871; railway; economy: chemicals, engineering, electrical machinery, textiles, plastics and locomotives; monument: the Lion of Belfort carved in 1880 by the sculptor Bartholdi to commemorate the heroism of the townsfolk during the 100-day seige of 1870; events: Trade Fair in May-June; 'Summer Nights' in the Citadel in June-July.

Belfort, Territoire de *bel-for*, dept in Franche-Comté region of E France, bounded on the S by Switzerland; comprises 1 arrond, 14 cantons and 100 communes; pop(1982) 131,999; area 610 sq km; capital Belfort.

Belgaum *bayl'gowm*, 15 54N 74 36E, pop(1981) 300,000, city in Karnataka, S India; 402 km SSE of Bombay, E of the dividing ridge of the W Ghats; connected to Pune by rail; economy: cotton cloth; monument: fort, captured in 1818 by the British; Jain temples.

Belgium *bel'jum*, official name Kingdom of Belgium, ROYAUME DE BELGIQUE *bel-zheek'* (Fr), KONINKRIJK BELGIË *bel'KHee-u* (Flem), a kingdom of NW Europe, bounded N by the Netherlands, S by France, E by West Germany and Luxembourg, and W by the North Sea; coastline 64 km; area 30,540 sq km; timezone GMT +1; capital Bruxelles (Brussels); chief towns Antwerpen, Gent, Charleroi, Liège, Brugge, Namur and Mons; pop(1983) 9,858,017; a line drawn E-W a little S of Bruxelles divides the population, by race and language, into two approximately equal parts; N of the line the inhabitants are

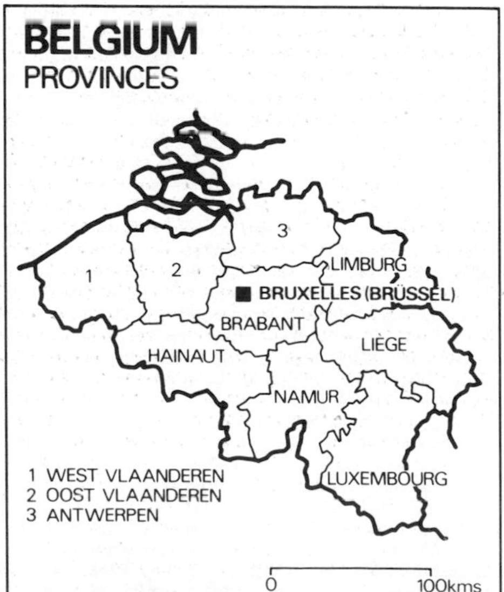

Flemings of Teutonic stock who speak Flemish, while S of the line they are French-speaking Latins known as Walloons; ethnic divisions 55% Fleming, 33% Walloon, 12% mixed or other; 56% of the population speak Flemish (Dutch), 32% speak French, and 1%, mainly along the E border, speak German; a linguistic frontier has now been fixed between the Dutch-speaking, French-speaking and German-speaking parts of Belgium; the city of Bruxelles and dist of Brussel are bilingual; 75% of the population are Roman Catholic; the Belgian currency is the franc of 100 centimes; national holiday 21 July (National Day); membership of Benelux Economic Union, Council of Europe, NATO, OECD, ADB, DAC, ECOSOC, EEC, EIB, ELDO, EMS, ESRO, FAO, GATT, IAEA, IBRD, ICAC, ICAO, ICES, ICO, IDA, IEA, IFAD, IFC, ILO, IMF, IMO, INTELSAT, IOOC, IPU, ITC, ITU, OECD, UN, UNESCO, UPU, WEU, WHO, WIPO, WMO, WSG.

Physical description. The total area of 30,540 sq km comprises 28% cultivated land, 24% meadow and pasture, 20% forest and 28% urban. The country is mostly low-lying, but there are some hilly dists, notably in the SE where a spur of the Ardennes separates the valleys of the Meuse and Moselle. The Ardennes region consists of forested hills with an average elevation of 300-500 m. Most of the area is covered by fertile soils which have been intensively cultivated for hundreds of years, but along the Dutch border the Kempen is composed of marshes and coal-bearing heaths, with considerable reclaimed and irrigated patches. The main river systems, the Sambre-Meuse and Schelde, drain towards the mouths of the Rhine across the Dutch border. Belgium has a low-lying, dune-fringed coastline of 64 km along the North Sea, between the mouth of the R Schelde and the French border.

Climate. The climate is cool and temperate with strong maritime influences. In the higher SE dists, hot summers alternate with cold winters. Average daily sunshine amounts range from approx 2 hours a day in Jan to between 7 and 8 hours in June.

History, government and constitution. The territory of the modern kingdom of Belgium has been subject to many different political régimes. It formed part of the Roman Empire, and then passed under the dominion of the Franks. As the feudal system arose, the country was distributed under a number of quasi-independent dukes and counts. These provs were absorbed from 1385 onwards by the House of Burgundy, and they continued under that rule till the downfall of Charles the Bold in 1477. With his daughter Mary, they then passed to the House of Hapsburg and remained with the Spanish branch of that line till the Peace of Utrecht in 1713, being known as the Spanish Netherlands to distinguish them from the N provs, which in the reign of Philip II had revolted from Spain and formed a Protestant republic, while the S provs continued subject to the Roman Catholic Church. In 1713 the Spanish provs were transferred to Austria as the Austrian Netherlands. The country was conquered by the French in 1794 and formed part of the French Republic and Empire until 1815. Thereafter it was united with the Netherlands. But this union of two countries differing essentially in language, religion and historic feeling did not prove successful. In 1830 the Belgians rebelled; the European powers intervened, and Belgium was recognized as an independent kingdom under Leopold of Saxe-Coburg. According to the Constitution of 1931, Belgium is a hereditary and constitutional monarchy. Legislative power is vested in the King, the Senate and the Chamber of Representatives. For both Senate and Chamber all elections are held on the basis of universal suffrage. As of 1 Oct 1980, Wallonia and Flanders have regional 'subgovernments' with elected regional councils and executive officials. Wallonia has a separate Walloon Cultural Council. The Belgian enclave of Baarle-Hertog in the Netherlands has an area of 7 sq km.

Industry and trade. Belgium was one of the earliest countries in Europe to industrialize, its initial development being based on the rich coalfields along the foothills and valleys of the Ardennes, and on the long-established textile industry of Flanders. An important iron and steel industry, dependent upon imported raw materials from Luxembourg and Germany, has given rise to a wide range of related metallurgical and engineering industries. Major industries include engineering and metal products, processed food and beverages, chemicals, basic metals, textiles, glass, and petroleum. Six trusts control the greater part of Belgian industry. A full economic union (Benelux Economic Union) between Belgium, Netherlands and Luxembourg, came into force on 1 Jan 1948. Major exports include iron and steel products, finished or semi-finished precious stones (diamonds), refined petroleum products and textile products. Major trade partners include Luxembourg, West Germany, France, the Netherlands, the UK, Italy and the USA.

Agriculture. Belgian farming is prosperous with many intensively cultivated smallholdings owned by industrial workers, as well as larger, highly-mechanized farms. Agriculture in the early 1980s constituted less than 4% of national income. Livestock production predominates. On arable land wheat, potatoes, sugar-beet, flax, other vegetables and hay are the main crops. Only 3% of the workforce is employed full-time in agriculture.

Administrative divisions. Belgium is divided into 9 provinces as follows:

Province	*area (sq km)*	*pop(1982)*
Antwerpen	2,867	1,571,092
Brabant	3,358	2,222,974
Hainaut	3,788	1,296,719
Liège	3,863	998,007
Limburg	2,422	720,766
Luxembourg	4,441	222,437
Namur	3,666	408,134
Oost-Vlaanderen	2,982	1,332,547
West-Vlaanderen	3,134	1,081,913

Belgorod *byel'go-rot*, 50 38N 36 36E, pop(1983) 268,000, capital city of Belgorodskaya oblast, European Rossiyskaya, Soviet Union; on the R Severskiy Donets; a centre of scientific research and planning for exploitation of the Kursk magnetic anomaly, an extensive area of iron ore deposits; railway; economy: building materials, machinery, foodstuffs.

Belgrade, capital of Yugoslavia. See Beograd.

Beli Manastir *be'lee ma'nas-tir*, 45 45N 18 36E, pop(1981) 53,409, town in NE Hrvatska (Croatia) republic, Yugoslavia; 24 km N of Osijek, near the Hungarian frontier; railway; economy: foodstuffs.

Belize *be-leez'*, formerly BRITISH HONDURAS (-1973), independent state in Central America; bounded N by Mexico, W and S by Guatemala and E by the Caribbean Sea; area 22,963 sq km; max length 280 km; max width 109 km; capital Belmopan; chief towns Belize City, Dangriga, Punta Gorda, San Ignacio; timezone GMT −6; pop(1980) 145,353; one-third of the population lives in Belize City; the main racial groups are Creoles, Spanish-Mayan Mestizos, Caribs, E Indians, Spanish and European and Canadian Mennonites; about 60% of the pop are Roman Catholic; English is the official language, but Spanish and local Mayan dialects are also spoken; the currency is the Belize dollar of 100 cents; national holidays 9 March (Baron Bliss Day), 10 Sept (National Day), 21 Sept (Independence Day), 12 Oct (Pan American Day), 19 Nov (Garifuna); membership of Commonwealth, CARICOM, CDB, IDA, IFC, IMF, UN.

Physical description. Lying on the Caribbean coast of Central America between the Río Hondo (N) and the Sarstoon river (S), Belize has an extensive coastal plain that is swampy in the N but gradually gives way to more fertile land further S. From the SW the Maya Mts extend almost to the E coast, rising to 1,120 m at Victoria Peak in the Cockscombs. Flanking this area are pine ridges, tropical forests, savannas and farm land growing fruit, rice and sugar. The Belize river dissects the country W-E. The inner coastal waters are protected by the world's 2nd longest barrier reef, a line of coral reefs dotted with palm and mangrove islets called *cayes*.

Climate. The climate is generally subtropical but is tempered by trade winds. On the coast temperatures range from 10°C to 35.6°C, but in the mountains the range is greater. Rainfall which varies from year to year ranges from an average of 1,295 mm in the N to 4,445 mm in the S. There is a dry season from Feb to May and a brief dry spell in Aug. Hurricanes in 1961 (Hattie) and 1978 (Greta) have caused severe damage.

History, government and constitution. Belize was colonized in the 17th century by shipwrecked British sailors and disbanded soldiers from Jamaica who acquired rights to engage in the logwood industry following the Treaty of Paris in 1763. Spanish attacks on British settlers continued until the 'baymen', with British naval support, won a victory at the Battle of St George's Cay in 1798. In 1862 British Honduras was formally created a British colony under the administration of Jamaica. The link with Jamaica was severed in 1884 and in 1954 the constitution was changed to allow universal adult suffrage. In 1961 a ministerial system of government was created and in 1964 internal self-government was granted. Changing its name to Belize in 1973 full independence was eventually achieved in 1981. Guatemalan claims over Belize territory have ensured that a British military presence is still maintained to defend the country.

Economy. Traditionally based on timber and forest products the economy has recently relied more on agriculture, producing sugar (Corozal and Orange Walk dists), citrus fruit (Stann Creek dist), cocoa (Stann Creek dist), rice (Toledo dist), tobacco, bananas and beef. Sugar and citrus account for 70% of exports by value. There is also a significant fishing industry (shrimp, lobster, conch). A small industrial sector is based on boatbuilding, the processing of food products and the manufacture of textiles, furniture, batteries and cigarettes. Most consumer goods and capital equipment are imported. Major trade partners include the USA, Canada, the UK and other Caribbean countries.

Administrative divisions. Belize is divided into 6 districts as follows:

District	*area (sq km)*	*pop(1980)*
Belize	4,202	50,801
Cayo	5,336	22,837
Corozal	1,859	22,902
Orange Walk	4,735	22,870
Stann Creek	2,175	14,181
Toledo	4,647	11,762

Belize, dist in Belize, Central America, pop(1980) 50,801; area 4,202 sq km; chief town Belize City; watered by the Belize and Sibun rivers; Maya ruins at Altun Ha.

Belize City, 17 29N 88 10W, pop(1980) 39,771, seaport capital of Belize dist, Belize, Central America; at the mouth of the Belize river where it meets the Caribbean Sea; former capital of Belize until 1970; occasionally badly damaged by hurricanes; airport; economy: commerce, tourism, fishing.

Belize River, chief river of Belize, Central America; rises in NE Guatemala E of Doleres and flows NE 290 km to meet the Caribbean Sea N of Belize City.

Bell, 33 59N 118 11W, pop(1980) 25,450, city in Los Angeles county, SW California, United States; a residential city 10 km SSE of Los Angeles.

Bell Gardens, 33 58N 118 10W, pop(1980) 34,117, city in Los Angeles county, SW California, United States; a residential suburb SE of Los Angeles, near Bell.

Belle-Ile *bel-eel*, island in N Bay of Biscay off the coast of Morbihan dept, W France; S of the Presqu'île de Quiberon; area 90 sq km; 17 km long by 5-10 km wide; main town is Le Palais; boat service to Port Maria on the mainland; associated with poets, painters and actresses such as Sarah Bernhardt.

Belleville, 38 31N 89 59W, pop(1980) 41,580, county seat of St Clair county, SW Illinois, United States; 22 km SE of East St Louis; railway.

Belleville, 40 47N 74 09W, pop(1980) 35,367, town in Essex county, NE New Jersey, United States; on the R Passaic, 6 km N of Newark, railway.

Belle'vue, 47 37N 122 12W, pop(1980) 73,903, city in King county, W central Washington, United States; E of Seattle.

Bellflower, 33 53N 118 09W, pop(1980) 53,441, city in Los Angeles county, SW California, United States; 23 km SE of Los Angeles.

Bellingham, 48 46N 122 29W, pop(1980) 45,794, port and capital of Whatcom county, NW Washington, United States; on Bellingham Bay in the S of the Strait of Georgia, 128 km N of Seattle; railway; economy: shipping, processing and industrial centre.

Bellingshausen Sea *bel'ingz-how-zen*, arm of the South Pacific Ocean bordering Antarctica; lies between Alexander Island and Thurston Island; named after Fabian Gottlieb von Bellingshausen (1778-1852), who commanded the Russian expedition of 1819-21 which discovered Alexander Island.

Bellinzona *bel-in-tsō'na*, BELLENZ *bel'ents* (Ger), 46 12N 9 02E, pop(1980) 16,743, capital city of Ticino canton, S Switzerland; near the R Ticino 147 km SE of Bern; railway.

Bellshill, 55 49N 4 02W, pop(1981) 39,676, town in Motherwell dist, Strathclyde, central Scotland; in Clydeside urban area, 4 km NW of Motherwell; railway; economy: engineering, distributive trades.

Belluno *bel-loo'nō*, prov of Veneto region, N Italy; pop(1981) 220,335; area 3,678 sq km; capital Belluno.

Belluno, 46 08N 12 13E, pop(1981) 36,634, capital town of Belluno prov, Veneto region, N Italy; on R Piave; nearby there is a winter sports area; railway; economy: wax, electrical goods, silk; monument: cathedral (begun in 1517).

Belmopan *bel-mō-pan'*, 17 18N 88 30W, pop(1980) 2,935, capital of Belize, Central America and chief town of Cayo dist; between the Belize and Sibun rivers, 80 km W of Belize City, near the junction of the Western and Hummingbird Highways; capital of Belize since 1970 when the town was established as the new administrative centre of the country; a new settlement at the Valley of Peace for the resettlement of refugees from El Salvador and Guatemala was made permanent in 1985; economy: administration, matches.

Belo Horizonte *be'lō o-ree-zon'tay*, 19 54S 43 54W, pop(1980) 1,441,567, commercial and industrial capital of Minas Gerais state, Sudeste region, SE Brazil; N of Rio de Janeiro at an alt of 800 m above sea-level; designed and built in the 1890s, it was Brazil's first planned modern city; 3 universities (1927, 1954, 1958); railway; airfield; an airport at Lagoa Santa, 39 km from Belo Horizonte, was opened in Jan 1984; the Minascentro, a Convention Centre for exhibitions and congresses, was opened in the city centre in 1984; 8 km from the centre is the suburb of Pampulha with notable modern architecture largely designed by the Brazilian architect, Oscar Niemeyer, who later designed Brasília; the Mineirão sports stadium is the 2nd largest in Brazil; Belo Horizonte's industrial area is approx 10 km from the city centre, and has become the 3rd largest industrial centre in Brazil; economy: commerce, mining, steel, car industry; monuments: around the main square, the Praça da Assembléia, are the modern legislative Assembly, Banco do Brasil and Museum of Modern Art; a monument in the Parque de Mangabeiras commemorates the visit of the Pope in 1982.

Beloit', 42 31N 89 02W, pop(1980) 35,207, city in Rock county, S Wisconsin, United States; on the R Rock where it follows the Illinois state border; railway.

Belorussia, constituent republic of the Soviet Union. See Belorusskaya.

Belorusskaya, BELORUSSIYA SSR, BELORUSSIA, WHITE RUSSIA, constituent republic of the Soviet Union, in the W part of European USSR, bounded W by Poland; the terrain is predominantly flat with a zone of hills and moraines in the NW rising to a max elevation of 345 m; in the S is the marshy Poles'ye Nizmennost; chief rivers are the Dnepr, its tributaries the Pripyat' and Sozh, Zapadnaya Dvina, and the Neman; there are c.11,000 lakes; forests, primarily coniferous, cover one-third of the area; pop(1983) 9,807,000; area 207,600 sq km; capital Minsk; chief towns Gomel', Vitebsk, Mogilev, Bobruysk, Grodno, and Brest; economy: machine tools, motor vehicles, agricultural machinery, glass, foodstuffs, chemicals (mineral fertilizers), textiles, artificial silk, flax, and leather, peat extraction, petroleum extraction and refining (Novopolotsk and Mozyr'), electrical engineering, electronics, salt extraction (salt beds in the S cover an area of some 20,000 sq km); power plants have been built in Baranovichi, Grodno, Molodechno, and Lida; farmland covers 46% of the total land area; meat and dairy production are the main agricultural activities but Belorusskaya is the most important flax-growing area in the Soviet Union; proclaimed a Soviet Socialist Republic in Jan 1919; the republic is divided into 6 oblasts:

Oblast	*area (sq km)*	*pop(1979)*
Brestskaya	32,300	1,363,000
Gomel'skaya	15,798	1,599,000
Grodnenskaya	25,000	1,131,000
Minskaya	22,014	1,556,000
Mogilevskaya	20,719	1,249,000
Vitebskaya	19,683	1,385,000

Bel'per, 53 01N 1 29W, pop(1981) 17,426, town in Amber Valley dist, Derbyshire, central England; on the R Derwent, 11 km N of Derby; railway; economy: textiles, engineering.

Belukha, Gora *byil-oo'KHu*, 49 46N 86 40E, highest peak in the Altay range, on the border between Rossiyskaya and Kazakhskaya SSR, Soviet Union; height 4,506 m; situated at the E end of the Katunskiy Khrebet range; gives rise to 16 glaciers.

Ben M'Sick *ben mus-eek'*, 33 21N 71 24W, pop(1982) 637,445, municipality in Centre prov, W Morocco, N Africa; an E suburb of Casablanca.

Benal'la, 36 35S 145 58E, pop(1983e) 8,750, city in Goulburn stat div, NE Victoria, Australia; NNE of Melbourne, SW of L Mokoan; railway; monuments: regional art gallery, Pioneers Museum.

Benares, city in N India. See Varanasi.

Ben'del, state in SW Nigeria, W Africa; pop(1982e) 3,924,400; area 35,500 sq km; formerly the Mid-West region; bounded S by the Bight of Benin and E by the R Niger; generally low lying except in the N where land rises to about 570 m; capital Benin City; ports at Warri, Koko, Burutu and Forcados; tanker terminals at Escravos and Forcados; ethnic groups include Edo, Urhobo, Itsekiri, Ishan and Ijaw; economy: oil, iron ore, natural gas, limestone, lignite, rubber, crêpe, timber, cement, glassware, carpets, boat building, brewing and flour milling.

Ben'digo, 36 48S 144 21E, pop(1983e) 32,880, city in Loddon-Campaspe stat div, N central Victoria, Australia; NNW of Melbourne; the centre of a wine-producing area; gold was panned here until the 1950s; railway; economy: agricultural trade, textiles, rubber, railway engineering; monuments: the Central Deborah gold mine; wax museum; reconstructed Sandhurst Town; the Bendigo Pottery, Australia's oldest pottery, founded in 1858; Chinese Joss House, the only surviving Chinese Joss House of the 1860s; event: Chinese Dragon Festival at Easter.

Benevento *bay-nay-ven'to*, prov of Campania region, S Italy; pop(1981) 289,143; capital Benevento.

Benevento, 41 08N 14 46E, pop(1981) 62,636, capital town of Benevento prov, Campania region, S Italy; 57 km NE of Napoli (Naples), on a flat-topped hill between the rivers Sábato and Calore; economic and communications centre of the fertile Benevento basin; railway; economy: leather, matches, Strega liqueur, confectionery; monuments: cathedral (1200); Porta Aurea, a magnificent arch erected in 114 AD to honour the emperor Trajan.

Ben'fleet, 51 33N 0 35E, pop(1981) 50,926, town in Castle Point dist, Essex, SE England; part of Southend urban area; railway; economy: engineering.

Bengal, Bay of, arm of the Indian Ocean, on S coast of Asia; bounded by India and Sri Lanka in the W, by Bangladesh in the N and in the E by Burma, the Andaman Islands and the Nicobar Islands; 2,090 km long by 1,610 km wide, with depths ranging from 2,390 m in the N to 4,145 m off the continental terrace of Sri Lanka; Andaman and Nicobar Islands separate it from the Andaman Sea; receives many large rivers including the Krishna, Godavari, Mahanadi, Ganges, Brahmaputra, Irrawaddy, Salween; main ports: Madras, Vishākhapatnam, Calcutta, Chittagong and Akayab; subject to heavy monsoon rains and cyclones.

Benghazi, city in Libya. See Banghāzī.

Bengkulu *beng-koo'loo*, province of Indonesia; in the SW corner of Sumatera I; traversed by the Barisan Mts which are separated from the Indonesian Sea by a narrow coastal strip; pop(1983) 768,004; area 21,168 sq km; capital Bengkulu; economy: coal, gold, silver.

Bengkulu, 3 46S 102 16E, pop(1980) 31,866, capital of Bengkulu prov, Indonesia; on the SW coast of Sumatera I; once a centre of the pepper trade; held by the British from 1685 until 1824 when it was ceded to the Dutch; airfield.

Benguela *beng-ge'lu*, 12 34S 13 24E, pop(1970) 40,996;

capital of prov of same name, W Angola, SW Africa; on railway and main road 31 km S of Lobito; founded in 1617; a railway was built in the 1920s to extract minerals (copper) from central Angola and Zaire; airfield.

Benguela Current, a cold ocean current which moves in a northerly direction along the SW coast of Africa.

Ben'ha, 30 28N 31 11E, capital of Qalyûbîya governorate, Egypt, NE Africa; E of the Dumyât branch of the Nile, 45 km NNW of Cairo; railway; economy: cotton, grapes.

Beni *be'nee*, department in N Bolivia; bordered by Brazil (NE, along the Guaporé and lower Mamoré rivers) and by the Beni river (W and NW); extensive tropical lowlands (*llanos*) in the S, change to dense forests, mainly along the rivers, in its N and NE sections; drained by the Río Mamoré and its affluents which comprise Bolivia's chief river transportation network; pop(1982) 217,700; area 213,564 sq km; capital Trinidad; chief towns Riberalta, Guayaramerín; economy: the region flourished during the late 19th century owing to the rubber boom, this has now been replaced in part by the cattle industry.

Beni Mellal *ben-ee me-lahl'*, 32 22N 6 29W, pop(1982) 95,000, capital of Beni Mellal prefecture, Centre prov, Morocco, N Africa; 289 km S of Fès, between the Moyen Atlas and the Tadla plain; centre of olive and mulberry-growing region; an artificial lake nearby is formed by the Bin el Oudane Dam.

Beni Suef *ben-ee su-ayf'*, BANI SUWAYF, 29 05N 31 05E, pop(1976) 118,148, capital of Beni Suef governorate, N central Egypt; on the W bank of the R Nile, 110 km SSW of Cairo; railway; economy: cotton processing.

Benidorm *bay-nee-dorm'* or *ben'i-dorm* (Eng), 38 33N 0 09W, pop(1981) 24,983, resort town in Alicante prov, E Spain on the Mediterranean Costa Blanca; there are two beaches on either side of a rocky promontory.

Benin *ben-een'*, formerly DAHOMEY (-1975), official name The People's Republic of Benin, RÉPUBLIQUE POPULAIRE DU BENIN (Fr), a republic in W Africa, bounded N by Niger, E by Nigeria, NW by Burkina and W by Togo; pop(1985e) 3,932,000, area 112,622 sq km; timezone GMT +1; capital Porto Novo (nominal), political and economic capital Cotonou; chief towns include Oiudah, Abomey, Kandi, Parakou and Natitingou; 99% of the Beninese are black Africans of 42 ethnic groups, the most important being the Fon, Adja, Yoruba and Bariba; there is a small European community; French is the official language but local languages such as Fon (47%) and Yoruba (9%) (mainly in S) and Adja (12%), Bariba (10%), Somba (5%) and Aizo (5%) are important; the majority of the pop follows local beliefs (70%) the remainder being either Christian (15%) or Muslim (15%); the unit of currency is the franc CFA; membership of AfDB, CEAO, EAMA, ECA, ECOWAS, Entente, FAO, G-77, GATT, IBRD, ICAO, ICO, IDA, IFAD, ILO, IMF, IMO, INTERPOL, ITU, NAM, Niger River Commission, OAU, OCAM, UN, UNESCO, UPU, WFTU, WHO, WIPO, WMO, WTO.

Physical description. Benin rises from a 100 km-long sandy coast with lagoons to low lying plains. Thereafter the land rises steeply to a savannah plateau at around 400 m. The Atakora Mts rising to heights over 500 m lie to the NW. Towards the NE the land falls towards the Alibori river valley which, along with the R Sota, joins the much larger valley of the R Niger which forms part of the NE border between Benin and Niger. Other important rivers include the Pendjari and Mékou which flow N from the Atakora Mts; the R Ouémé, with its tributaries, the Okpara and the Zou, and the R Kouffo flow S to the Gulf of Guinea.

Climate. Benin has a tropical climate which can be divided into 3 zones: (1) in the S there is rain throughout the year, especially during the 'Guinea Monsoon' (May to Oct); (2) in the central area there are 2 rainy seasons with maxima in May-June and Oct; (3) in the N these rainy seasons merge into one (July to Sept). The N dry season (Oct to April) is hot, has very low humidity and is subject to the dry and often dust-laden *harmattan* wind

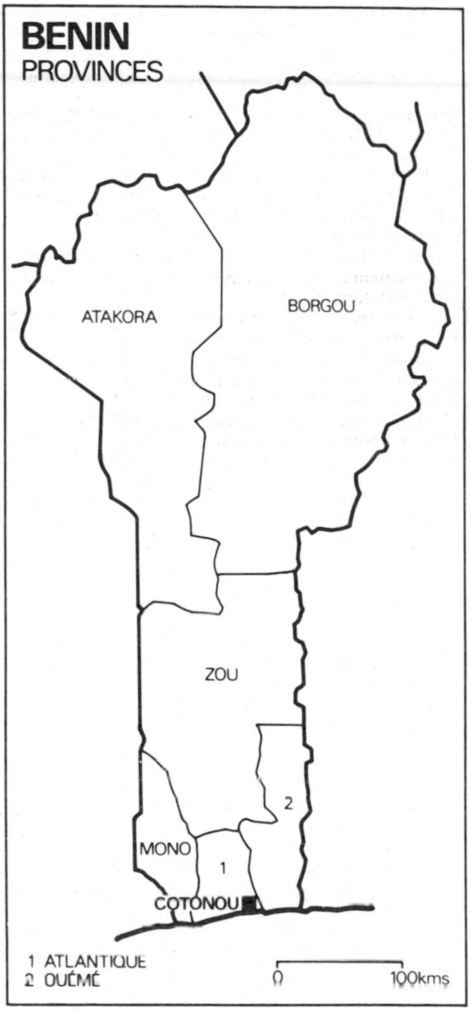

which blows from the NE. The average annual rainfall in Cotonou is 1,300 mm.

History, government and constitution. In pre-colonial times Benin was a collection of small, frequently warring principalities. The most powerful of these was the Fon Kingdom of Dahomey, founded in the 17th century, which had its base in Abomey. The Portuguese engaged in colonial activities centred around the slave trade, but finally, in 1892, the King of Dahomey was subjugated by the French and the country became the French Protectorate of Dahomey. The protectorate became a territory within French West Africa in 1904, became an independent republic within the French community in 1957 and finally achieved full independence in 1960. Its name was changed from Dahomey to Benin in 1975 and a new constitution was adopted in 1977 establishing a unicameral legislature with a 336-member National People's Assembly, a national executive council and a president, all elected from the sole political party. The civilian government is Soviet-modelled. The first elections under the new constitution were held in 1979.

Economy. Benin has no known natural resources in commercial quantity except for a small oilfield discovered 16 km offshore in the Gulf of Guinea. Agriculture plays an important role (45% of national income) and is based on the export of palm oil products, cashew nuts and sea products. The service sector accounts for 45% of national income and industrial activity based on food processing, textiles, beverages and cement accounts for a further 10%. Benin's main trading partners are France, other EEC countries, Nigeria, China, Japan and the USA.

Administrative divisions. Benin is divided into the 6 provinces of Atakora, Atlantique, Borgou, Mono, Ouémé and Zou. These provinces are further subdivided into 84 districts.

Benin, Bight of, arm of the Atlantic Ocean N of the Gulf of Guinea; forms a wide bay on the S coast of Togo, Benin and the SW coast of Nigeria; Lagos is the chief port.

Benin City *be-neen'*, 6 19N 5 41E, pop(1981e) 183,000, capital of Bendel state, SW Nigeria, W Africa; W of the R Niger, 240 km E of Lagos; taken by the British in 1897; university (1970); airport; economy: wood, brewing, textiles, chemicals and animal feed; monuments: museum, royal palace.

Benoni *bu-nō'nee*, 26 12S 28 18E, pop(1980) 206,810, city in Transvaal prov, South Africa; 27 km E of Johannesburg; railway; economy: engineering, gold mining.

Bénoué *bay'noo-ay*, national park in Cameroon, W Africa; area 1,800 sq km; established in 1968; bounded S and E by the river after which it is named; wildlife includes buffalo, waterbuck, lion, giraffe, rhinoceros, Derby eland and hippopotamus.

Bent'ley, 53 34N 1 08W, pop(1981) 34,453, town in Doncaster borough, South Yorkshire, N England; just N of Doncaster; railway; economy: coal mining.

Bentong *ben-toong'*, 3 35N 101 45E, pop(1980) 22,921, town in W Pahang state, central Peninsular Malaysia, SE Asia; NE of Kuala Lumpur; tin-mining town.

Benue *bay'noo-ay*, state in S central Nigeria, W Africa; pop(1982e) 3,870,300; area 45,174 sq km; the Benue and Niger rivers form the N and W borders of the state; capital Makurdi; chief towns Katsina-Ala, Gboko, Oturkpo and Idah; about 70% of the pop is engaged in farming; ethnic groups include the Idoma, the Igala and the Tiv; economy: coal, limestone, marble, oil, cement, timber, bricks, cotton, brewing and sanitary ware.

Benue, BEBOUÉ (Fr), major tributary of the R Niger in Nigeria, W Africa; rises in Cameroon N of N'gaoundéré; flows N to Garoua and then generally WSW across E and S central Nigeria; navigable below Garoua; passes Yola, Numan, Ibi and Makurdi to join the R Niger at Lokoja; the main tributaries are the Gongola, Donga, Taraba, Katsina, Okwa and Wase rivers; length 1,295 km.

Benxi *ben-chee*, PEN-CH'I, 41 21N 123 45E, pop(1984e) 810,500, town in Liaoning prov, NE China; railway; economy: steel, cement, coal mining.

Beograd *bay-o'graht*, BELGRADE (Eng) ('white mountain'), SINGIDUNUM (anc), 44 50N 20 30E, pop(1981) 1,407,073, modern capital city of Yugoslavia and of the republic of Srbija (Serbia); situated at the junction of the Danube and Sava rivers; since World War II the new district of Novi Beograd has been developed on the left bank of the R Sava; university (1863); arts university (1957); airport; railway; an important centre of communication; seat of an Orthodox patriarch and a Roman Catholic archbishop; economy: machine tools, electrical equipment, light engineering, motor vehicles, pharmaceuticals, textiles, foodstuffs; monuments: Kalemegdan fortress; Prince Eugene's Gate (1719), built to commemorate victory over the Turks; Orthodox cathedral; palace of Princess Ljubica; museum of the Serbian Orthodox Church; St Mark's church; tomb of Sheikh Mustapha; Jewish historical museum; national museum; museum of contemporary art; events: international film festival in Feb; 'Belgrade Spring', light music and folk music in May; International Festival of Modern Dramatic Art in Sept; Belgrade Music Festival in Oct.

Beqa'a, El *el be-kah'*, THE BEKKA, governorate (*moafazat*) of E Lebanon; bounded NE and E by Syria; subdivided into the 5 divisions (*cazas*) of Hermel, Baalbek, Zahlé, Beqa'a al Gharbi and Rachaïya; capital Zahlé; chief towns Hermel and Baalbek; comprises a high plateau varying in altitude from 800 m to 1,150 m; the Jebel esh Sharqi (Anti-Lebanon) range extends along the E frontier with Syria, rising to peaks above 2,000 m; drained N-S by the R Līṭāni; the Beqa'a valley has been of strategic importance to both Israel and Syria and has been the centre of Muslim Shi'ite activity; the R Līṭāni was the limit of the 1978 Israeli invasion of S Lebanon; economy: poultry production, sheep rearing, wheat, vineyards.

Berat *bay-rat'*, prov of S central Albania; area 1,026 sq km; pop(1980) 147,200; capital Berat.

Berat, formerly BELIORAD, ANTIPATREIA or PULCHERIOPOLOIS (anc), 40 42N 19 56E, pop(1975) 30,000, town and capital of Berat prov, S central Albania; on the R Osumi, 48 km NE of Vlorë, at the foot of the Tomorrit Mts (2,480 m); became bishopric in the 10th century; consists of an upper town or citadel (rebuilt by Byzantines in the 13th century) which contains many old churches, a lower left-bank town with a 15th-c mosque, and the modern right-bank town; the autocephalic Albanian Orthodox Church was proclaimed here in 1922; economy: trade centre for the surrounding tobacco-growing, horticulture and viticulture region; manufacture of cotton textiles, processing of olive oil and tobacco; monuments: remains of a 13th-c fortress, residential blocks from the Middle Ages, 13th-c church of Ste Mary of Vlakhern, 18th-c cathedral.

Berbera *bur'bu-ru*, 10 28N 45 02E, pop(1982) 55,000, port in Woqooyi Galbeed prov, Somalia, NE Africa; on the Gulf of Aden coast, 225 km SE of Djibouti and 240 km S of Aden (South Yemen); winter capital of British Somaliland until 1941 when Hargeysa became capital; airfield.

Berbérati *ber-bay-rah-tee'*, 4 19N 15 51E, pop(1981) 95,000, chief town in Haute-Sangha prefecture, SW Central African Republic; 314 km W of Bangui; airfield.

Berchem *ber'KHum*, 50 47N 3 31E, pop(1982) 45,128, town in Antwerpen dist, Antwerpen prov, Belgium; a SE industrial suburb of Antwerpen.

Berekum *be-re-kum'*, 7 30N 2 40W, town in Brong-Ahafo region, W Ghana, W Africa; W of Sunyani.

Bergama *bergah'ma*, PERGAMON, PERGAMUM (anc), 39 08N 27 10E, pop(1980) 38,000, town in İzmir prov, W Turkey; N of İzmir; once capital of the ancient kingdom of Pergamum and of the Roman prov of Asia; parchment is supposed to have been invented here; the library of Bergama with over 200,000 volumes was given by Mark Antony to Cleopatra; monuments: Asclepieion and Acropolis with ruins of the temples of Trajan and Dionysos, sanctuary of Athena and altar of Zeus.

Ber'gamo, prov of Lombardia region, N Italy; pop(1981) 896,117; area 2,758 sq km; capital Bergamo.

Bergamo, 45 42N 9 40E, pop(1981) 122,142, capital town of Bergamo prov, Lombardia region, N Italy; between the rivers Brembo and Serio, NE of Milano (Milan); Bergamo was the first seat of the Republican Fascist government set up in N Italy by Mussolini after his fall from power (1943); the new (lower) town extends out over the plain; railway; economy: textiles, cement, printing, electrical switches; monuments: the old town, on a hill strongly fortified by the Venetians, has a fine Romanesque basilica (1137-1355) and a 15th-c cathedral.

Bergen, city in Belgium. See Mons.

Ber'gen, 60 23N 5 20E, pop(1983) 207,292, seaport and administrative capital of Hordaland county, SW Norway; standing on a promontory at the head of a deep bay; an old shipping and trading town and an important tourist and cultural centre; founded 1070 by King Olaf Kyrre; damaged by fire in 1702, 1855 and 1916; occupied by Germans in April 1940 and held until the end of World War II; birthplace of the composer Grieg (1843-1907); see of the Lutheran bishop of Bergen; university (1948); rail terminus; airport; economy: shipyards, engineering, paper, fishing, fish products, pottery, offshore oil services; monuments: restored 13th-c cathedral, Hanseatic museum.

Bergenfield, 40 56N 74 00W, pop(1980) 25,568, town in

Bergen county, NE New Jersey, United States; 14 km E of Paterson; railway.

Bergheim *berk'hīm*, 50 57N 6 38E, pop(1983) 54,200, city in Köln (Cologne) dist, Nordrhein-Westfalen (North Rhine-Westphalia) prov, W Germany, W of Köln.

Bergisch-Gladbach *ber'gish glaht'bahkh*, 50 59N 7 09E, pop(1983) 100,900, industrial city in Köln (Cologne) dist, Nordrhein-Westfalen (North Rhine-Westphalia) prov, W Germany, E of Köln; chief town of the Rhineland-Berg area; noted for its paper-making industry.

Bering Sea *bay'ring*, part of the Pacific Ocean, lying between Siberia on the W and Alaska on the E and bounded to the S by the Aleutian Islands and the Aleutian Trench; the Bering Strait (90 km wide at its narrowest point) connects it to the Chukchi Sea and the Arctic Ocean; the Diomede Islands lie in the centre of the strait; area 2,274,020 sq km; ice-bound from Nov to May; the warm Japan Current has little influence so far N; St Lawrence, St Matthew and the Pribilof islands lie within the USA section of the sea; boundary between USSR and USA divides the Bering Sea; depths reach 3,960 m in the SW over the Bering abyssal plain, but in the NE there is a mean depth of 27-73 m over the continental shelf; its largest arms are the Gulf of Anadyr (Anadyrskiy Zaliv), Norton Sound and Bristol Bay; discovered and explored first in the 17th century, but the potential of seal-fur wealth was not realized until the voyages of Vitus Bering in 1728 and 1741; the seal herd was threatened with extinction as a result of over-exploitation, but herds were built up after the 1911 agreement by the UK, the USA, the USSR and Japan to regulate sealing; sea otters, although protected by the 1911 agreement, are almost extinct today.

Berkeley *bur'kli*, 37 52N 122 16W, pop(1980) 103,328, city in Alameda county, W California, United States; residential suburb N of Oakland, on the E shore of San Francisco Bay; university (1868); monument: university art museum.

Berkhamsted *berk'am-sted*, formerly GREAT BERKHAMSTED, 51 46N 0 35W, pop(1981) 16,878, town in Dacorum dist, Hertfordshire, SE England; in the Chiltern Hills, 40 km NW of London; railway; economy: engineering, electrics.

Berkshire or **Royal Berkshire** *bark'shir*, county of S England; bounded W by Wiltshire, N by Oxfordshire, NE by Buckinghamshire, S by Hampshire and SE by Surrey; drained by the Kennet and Thames rivers; pop(1981) 681,226; area 1,259 sq km; county town Reading; chief towns include Newbury, Windsor, Maidenhead, Bracknell; economy: engineering, high technology, pharmaceuticals, plastics; the county is divided into 6 districts:

District	*area (sq km)*	*pop(1981)*
Bracknell	109	82,512
Newbury	705	121,398
Reading	40	133,540
Slough	28	97,389
Windsor and Maidenhead	198	133,300
Wokingham	179	115,103

Berlin *ber-leen'*, 52 32N 13 25E, former capital of Germany, partitioned in 1945 into East Berlin and West Berlin; founded in 13th century; former residence of the Hohenzollerns and capital of Brandenburg; later capital of Prussia, becoming an industrial and commercial centre in the 18th century; in 1949 West Berlin became a province of the Federal Republic of Germany and East Berlin a county of the German Democratic Republic; the two halves of the city are separated by a wall built in 1961 to prevent the movement of citizens from E to W.

Berlin, East, pop(1981) 1,145,743, county and capital of the German Democratic Republic (E Germany); political, economic and cultural centre of the country; linked to the Oder and Elbe rivers by canals; area 403 sq km; seat of the Council of State, the Council of Ministers and govt ministries; the largest industrial centre in the country; German Academies of Sciences (1700); Humboldt University (1810); 5 colleges and 18 technical schools; recreation centres developed in lake area to the SE; railway; 2 airports; economy: mechanical and electrical engineering, electronics, motor vehicles, chemicals, food processing; monuments: Pergamum museum, national gallery, Rotes Rathaus (red town hall); events: annual festival of dramatic art and music and annual political song festival.

Berlin, West *ber-leen*, 52 32N 13 25E, pop(1983) 1,854,500, a West German enclave lying entirely within E Germany; area 480 sq km; railway; according to the constitution of 1 Sept, 1950, Berlin is simultaneously a prov (*Land*) of the Federal Republic (though not yet formally incorporated) and a city; university (1946); economy: non-ferrous metals, machine tools, office equipment, stationery, pharmaceuticals, chemicals, brewing, soft-drinks, fibre-cement products, toys, electrical cables and wires, clothing, steel construction.

Bermejo *ber-me'KHō*, 22 10S 64 40W, pop(1976) 11,462, town in Acre prov, Tarija, S Bolivia; lies on the Río Bermejo, on the border with Argentina; railway; economy: oil refining.

Bermuda *ber-myoo'da*, formerly SOMERS IS, a British self-governing dependency in the Western Atlantic about 900 km E of Cape Hatteras, North Carolina at 32° N 65° W, comprising about 138 low lying coral islands and islets of which 20 are inhabited and 7 are linked by causeways and bridges; the whole group is shaped like a fishhook, measuring 35 km in maximum extent from E to W and 22 km from N to S with an average width of less than 1.6 km; to the W of the Main Island and linked by bridges are Somerset, Boaz and Ireland Is; to the E of the Main Island are St George's and St David's Is; area 53 sq km; pop(1980) 54,670, the highest point is Gibb's Hill (78 m); capital Hamilton on Great Bermuda; deepwater ports at Hamilton, St George (St George's I) and Freeport (Ireland I); timezone GMT −4; about two-thirds of the pop are black, the remainder being mainly of British or Portuguese stock; the official language is English; the main religions are Anglican (37%), Roman Catholic (14%); the main airport is at Kindley Field (US Naval Air Station and civil airport); motor cars have been allowed on the islands since 1947; the currency is the Bermuda dollar of 100 cents; public holidays: Jan, New Year's Day; Good Friday; 24 May, Bermuda Day; June, Queen's Birthday; August, Cup Match; 2 August, Somer's Day; 1st Monday in Sept, Labour Day; November, Remembrance Day; December, Christmas and Boxing Day.

Climate. The climate of Bermuda is sub-tropical and is much influenced by the warmth of N Atlantic waters; the islands are generally humid, with rain well distributed throughout the year; summers are warm to hot and the winters mild with occasional warm, sunny days.

History. The islands obtain their name from a Spanish mariner, Juan Bermudez, who discovered the group in the early 16th century; following the wrecking of Sir George Somers's ship *Sea Venture* here in 1609, the islands were colonized in 1612 under an extended Virginia Company charter; a charter of 1615 by the islanders was annulled in 1684 when the British Crown took over the government of Bermuda. During the 17th century the economy was based on whaling, ship-building and tobacco-growing. Because it is a natural fortress, defended by an extensive barrier reef and entered through two narrow channels, it has been of great value as a naval station. Until 1862 the colony was also an important penal settlement. With the inauguration of steamship services during the 19th century, the islands enjoyed a prosperous trade in agricultural products, particularly with the E coast of the USA, and from 1901 there has been a steady growth in tourism. A new constitution providing internal self-government came into force in June 1968 when the first general elections were held. Kindley Field air base has been leased to the US government for 99 years.

Government. The British Government is represented by a Governor who is responsible for external affairs, defence, internal security and the police; the Legislature consists of the Queen, the Senate and the House of Assembly, the latter comprising 40 members elected from 20 constituencies for a period of 5 years; 5 members of the Senate are appointed by the Governor on the advice of the Premier and 3 on the advice of the Opposition Leader; the Cabinet is headed by the Premier and at least 6 members of the Legislature.

Economy. The main exports are petroleum products, pharmaceuticals and aircraft supplies; boat building and ship repair are also important industries; year-round tourism is the main foreign exchange earner, and in recent years international company business in the fields of insurance and investment has become important (5,938 international companies in 1984).

Agriculture and fisheries. As a result of building development, the area of arable land is decreasing. Vegetable production, which is still important, is supplemented by citrus and banana plantations. Since 1976 a Fisheries Development Programme has promoted the utilization of less common species and has provided a Fish Landing and Processing Centre marketing a variety of products.

Administrative divisions. Bermuda is divided into 9 parishes:

Parish	*pop(1980)*
St George's	4,587
Hamilton	3,784
Smith's	4,463
Devonshire	6,843
Pembroke	12,060
Paget	4,497
Warwick	6,948
Southampton	4,613
Sandy's	6,255

Bern, BERNE (Fr), canton in W Switzerland; pop(1980) 912,022; area 6,887 sq km; capital Bern; chief towns Biel, Moutier, Thun, Burgdorf and Interlaken; drained by the Aare and Emme rivers; mountainous in the NW and S; lakes include Thuner See, Brienzer See and Bieler See; joined the Swiss Confederacy in 1353.

Bern, 46 57N 7 28E, pop(1980) 145,254, federal capital of Switzerland and of Bern canton, W Switzerland; on R Aare 94 km SW of Zürich; the home of international organizations such as the Telegraph and Postal Unions; Bern allegedly takes its name from the bear which was the first animal caught by Duke Berchtold after founding the city in 1191; university (1834); railway junction; airport at Belpmoos; economy: textiles, machinery, chocolate, pharmaceuticals, foodstuffs, graphic trades, electrical equipment, engineering; monuments: Gothic cathedral (1421-1573), late-medieval town hall, clock tower; has many broad arcade-lined streets and a baroque old quarter; many museums, including the Kunstmuseum, which houses the world's largest collection of the works of Paul Klee; event: 'Zibelemärit', centuries-old market held on the 4th Monday of Nov each year.

Bernardo O'Higgins, region in S Chile. See Libertador General Bernardo O'Higgins.

Bernardo O'Higgins, national park in Magallanes-La Antártica Chilena region, S Chile; borders E with Argentina's Los Glaciares National Park; rises to 3,600 m; area 17,610 sq km; established in 1970.

Berne, city and canton in Switzerland. See Bern.

Berner Alpen, BERNESE ALPS (Eng), BERNESE OBERLAND, ALPES BERNOISES (Fr), mountain range in Bern and Valais cantons, Switzerland; a N division of the Central Alps, extending from Lac Léman (Lake of Geneva) to Grimsel Pass; highest peak is the Finsteraarhorn (4,274 m); also includes the Aletschhorn and Jungfrau (4,158); drained on the N by the Saane, Simme, Kander and other streams, and on the S by the Rhône, which is fed by the Aletsch and Rhône glaciers; there are numerous tourist resorts including Interlaken (principal gateway to the Berner Alpen), Grindelwald, Kandersteg and Leukerbad.

Bernese Alps, mountain range in Switzerland. See Berner Alpen.

Bernese Oberland, mountain range in Switzerland. See Berner Alpen.

Bernina, Piz *peets ber-nee'na*, peak in the central Alps, SE Switzerland, 14 km SSE of St Moritz, on the Italian border; highest of the Bernina Alps, part of Rhaetian Alps; Bernina Pass is 16 km SE of St Moritz, near Bernina Hospice; height 4,049 m; length 39 km.

Beroun *ber'own*, 49 58N 14 05E, pop(1984) 23,595, town in Středočeský region, Czech Socialist Republic, W Czechoslovakia; on R Berounka, 25 km WSW of Praha (Prague); railway; economy: iron, textiles.

Berounka *ber'own-ka*, river in W Czechoslovakia formed by the meeting of the Mze and Radbuza rivers near Plzeň; flows about 110 km N and NE to R Vltava near Praha (Prague).

Berry *ber-ree*, former prov of central France, now occupying the depts of Indre and Cher; its capital was Bourges; the greater part is constituted by the fertile Champagne Berrichonne dist around Châteauroux, Issoudun and Bourges.

Berry Islands, archipelago in the NW Bahamas, on the NE edge of the Great Bahama Bank, NE of Andros I; pop(1980) 509; area 31 sq km; comprises a number of cays (Sandy Cay, Whale Cay, Hoffmans Cay, etc) in an arc which extends NE then NW from the N tip of Andros I; airports on Great Harbour Cay and Chub Cay.

Bertoua *ber-too'a*, 4 34N 13 42E, pop (1984e) 22,000, capital of Est prov, Cameroon, W Africa; 350 km NE of Yaoundé; primarily an administrative and commercial town; railway; airfield.

Berwickshire, district in Borders region, SE Scotland; pop(1981) 18,270; area 876 sq km; chief town Duns.

Berwick-upon-Tweed *ber'ik-*, 55 46N 2 00W, pop(1981) 12,989, town in Berwick-upon-Tweed dist, Northumberland, NE England; on the North Sea at the mouth of the R Tweed, on the Scottish-English border; Spittal and Tweedmouth districts lie to the S of the R Tweed; disputed by England and Scotland, it changed ownership 14 times; part of England since 1482; railway; economy: foodstuffs, salmon fishing, engineering; monuments: 16th-c ramparts; parish church of the Holy Trinity (1652); 16 km SW is Flodden Field where a memorial commemorates the battle of 1513 in which King James IV of Scotland was killed in battle by the English; 12 km SW is 15th-c Norham Castle, formerly a border fortress of the Bishop of Durham.

Ber'wyn, 41 51N 87 47W, pop(1980) 46,849, residential town in Cook county, NE Illinois, United States; 16 km W of Chicago.

Besançon *bė-zã-sõ*, VESONTIO OR BESONTIUM (anc), 47 15N 6 00E, pop(1982) 119,687, industrial town and capital of Doubs dept, Franche Comté region, NE France; on the R Doubs, on the NW edge of the Jura; former capital of Franche-Comté; university (1485); archbishopric; a strategic site between the Vosges and the Jura since Gallo-Roman times; birthplace of Victor Hugo and of the Lumière brothers who invented cinematography; the first factory in the world to produce artificial fibres was established here in 1890; clock-making brought here from Switzerland in 18th century; railway; economy: watches, clocks and artificial silk; monuments: the citadel on a high rock overlooking the river, Roman remains and several museums.

Beskids or **Beskidy**, mountain group in the Carpathian range on the Polish-Czechoslovak frontier; rises to 1,725 m at Babia Gora.

Bes'sacarr, 53 31N 1 06W, pop(1981) 19,062, town SE of Doncaster in Doncaster borough, South Yorkshire, N England; 4 km SE of Doncaster.

Bess'emer, 33 24N 86 58W, pop(1980) 31,729, town in Jefferson county, N central Alabama, United States; 18 km SW of Birmingham; named after Henry Bessemer, inventor of the Bessemer Process; railway; economy: iron and steel.

Bethel Park, 40 20N 80 01W, pop(1980) 34,755, town in Allegheny county, W Pennsylvania, United States; 12 km SSW of Pittsburgh.

Bethlehem *beth'li-hem*, sub-district of Judea-Samaria dist, Israel, in the Israeli-occupied West Bank.

Bethlehem, BEIT LAHM (Arab), 31 42N 35 12E, pop(1980) 14,000, Biblical town in Jerusalem governorate, Israeli-occupied West Bank, W Jordan; 8 km SSW of Jerusalem; the birthplace of Jesus and the home of David; in 386 AD St Jerome came to Bethlehem and here prepared the Vulgate, his Latin version of the Bible; trade centre for the surrounding agricultural area; university (1973); monuments: Church of the Nativity, built by Constantine 330 AD above the chamber in which Jesus is said to have been born; to the N of the town is the grave of Rachel, who died giving birth to Benjamin (a place of pilgrimage for pious Jews); Monastery of Elijah (6th-c, later restored).

Bethlehem, 40 37N 75 23W, pop(1980) 70,419, town in Northampton county, E Pennsylvania, United States; on the R Lehigh, 8 km E of Allentown; university; railway; economy: the traditional steel industry is being gradually replaced by a wider range of high-technology industries.

Bettembourg *bet-ā-boor'*, 49 31N 6 06E, pop(1981) 5,813, town in Esch-sur-Alzette canton, Luxembourg dist, S Luxembourg; on the S side of the R Alzette, 10 km S of Luxembourg; its Parc Merveilleux (entertainment park) attracts thousands of visitors annually; economy: metal products and car accessories.

Bet'tendorf, 41 32N 90 30W, pop(1980) 27,381, town in Scott county, E Iowa, United States; on the Mississippi river, E of, and adjacent to, Davenport; event: international folk festival (May).

Beveren *bay'vur-en*, 51 13N 4 15E, pop(1982) 40,892, town in Sint-Niklaas dist, Oost-Vlaanderen (East Flanders) prov, Belgium.

Beverley, 53 51N 0 26W, pop(1981) 19,687, county town and market town in Beverley dist, Humberside, NE England; 12 km NW of Kingston-upon-Hull; administrative centre of Humberside, railway; economy: engineering.

Beverly, 42 33N 70 53W, pop(1980) 37,655, town in Essex county, NE Massachusetts, United States; on the Atlantic coast, on Massachusetts Bay, 26 km NE of Boston; railway; event: Shakespeare programme at North Shore Music Theatre in May.

Beverly Hills, 34 04N 118 25W, pop(1980) 32,367, residential city in Los Angeles county, SW California, United States; surrounded by Los Angeles; extends (N) to the slopes of the Santa Monica Mts; the home of many television and film celebrities.

Bex'hill or **Bexhill-on-Sea**, 50 50N 0 29E, pop(1981) 35,402, residential and resort town in Eastbourne dist, East Sussex, SE England; part of Hastings-Bexhill urban area; on the English Channel, 7 km W of Hastings; railway; economy: engineering; monuments: De la Warr Pavilion (1936); 15th-c Herstmonceux castle (9 km NW), which has housed a royal observatory since 1949.

Bex'ley, 51 27N 0 10E, pop(1981) 214,078, residential and industrial borough of SE Greater London, England; includes the suburbs of Bexley, Crayford, Erith and part of Chislehurst and Sidcup; railway; economy: engineering, chemicals, petroleum products, food processing; monuments: 12th-c Lessness abbey and 13th-c St Mary's church.

Beyla *bay'la*, 8 42N 8 39W, town in SE Guinea, W Africa; 220 km SSE of Kankan.

Beyrouth *bay-root'*, BEIRUT, governorate (*moafazat*) of W central Lebanon; bounded W by the Mediterranean Sea; no administrative subdivisions; capital Beyrouth.

Beyrouth, BEIRUT, BERYTUS (anc), 33 52N 35 30E, pop(1980e) 702,000, seaport capital of Beyrouth governorate and the state of Lebanon, W central Lebanon, SW Asia; capital city of the republic since 1920; situated on a promontory which juts into the Mediterranean Sea; financial, educational and commercial centre; the city is divided between rival political and religious factions; the 'Green Line' refers to the division of the city during the 1975-76 civil war into the Muslim (W) and Christian (E); an Israeli attack on Palestinian and Syrian forces in June 1982 led the following Sept to the evacuation from the city of Palestinians to camps such as Sabra, Chatila and Bourj Barajneh; American University (1866, new charter 1920); Lebanese University (1953); Arab University (1960); railway; airport; monuments: Grand Seraglio (formerly a Turkish barracks and at one time seat of the government); cathedrals of St Elie and St George; national museum with a notable collection of Phoenician, Roman, Greek and Byzantine antiquities.

Béziers *bayz-yay*, BAETERRAE SEPTIMANORUM or JULIA BETERRAE (Lat), 43 21N 3 13E, pop(1982) 78,477, town in Hérault dept, Languedoc-Roussillon region, S France; on a height overlooking the R Orb; the Canal du Midi, linking the Atlantic to the Mediterranean, meets the R Orb at Béziers, descending 30 m through the 9 locks of Fonserranes; railway; economy: centre of S French wine trade, chemicals and fertilizers; event: the Festival of St Aphrodise with the Procession du Camel in March-April.

Bhadgaon *bad'gown*, BHAKTAPUR' ('city of the devotees'), 27 41N 85 26E, pop(1971) 40,112, city and religious centre in central Nepal, central Asia; 14 km E of Kathmandu, in the Kathmandu Valley; alt 1,400 m; probably founded by King Ananda Malla in 889 AD; shaped like a conch-shell, the urban area occupies 10 sq km; economy: processing of grain and vegetables grown in the surrounding area; pottery and weaving are traditional crafts; monuments: Durbar Square is the focal point of the city, with many temples and architectural showpieces including the Lion Gate, the Golden Gate, the Palace of 55 Windows, the Bell of Barking Dogs, Batsala Temple and a replica of the Pashupatinath Temple.

Bhairab *bī'rub*, BHAIRAB BAZAR, 24 04N 91 00E, pop(1981) 635,663, town in Mymenshingh dist, Mymenshingh region, N central Bangladesh.

Bhavnagar or **Bhaunagar** *baw'nu-gur*, 21 46N 72 14E, pop(1981) 308,000, port city in Gujarat, W India; on the Gulf of Khambhāt, an inlet of the Arabian Sea; founded in the mid-13th century; economy: bricks, tiles, metal products, cotton.

Bhopal *bō-pahl'*, 23 20N 77 53E, pop(1981) 672,000, capital of Madhya Pradesh, central India; 170 km ENE of Indore, in the Vindhya range; former capital of a principality; founded in 1723 by Dost Mohammed Khan; ruled by the begums of Bhopal (1844-1926); fort established in 1728; concluded a treaty of dependence with Britain in 1818 and acceded to India in 1947; scene of a major industrial disaster which killed c.2,500 people and left 100,000 homeless in Dec 1984; university (1970); airfield; linked to Jhansi by rail; economy: cotton, electrical goods and jewellery; monument: Taj-ul s-Masajid mosque.

Bhután *boo-tahn'*, DRUK-YUL *drook-yool* (Bhut), official name Kingdom of Bhután, state in the E Himalayas, lying between 26° 45′ and 28° 00′ N and between 89° and 92° E; bounded N by the Tibet region of China and S, E and W by India; timezone GMT +5½; capital Thimphu; area 46,600 sq km; 305 km from E to W; pop(1986e) 1,484,000; most of the people live in the Himalayan foothill region; ethnic groups include Bhote (60%), Nepalese (25%) and indigenous or migrant tribes (15%); official languages are Dzongkha (a Tibetan dialect mostly spoken by Bhotes), Nepali and various dialects of Nepalese and English; Lamaistic Buddhism (75%) and Buddhist-influenced Hinduism (25%) are the main religions; paper currency is the ngultrum, while tilchung is the silver currency, Indian currency is also legal tender; use of both Indian and Bhutánese currency has caused the decline of barter as the main method of exchange; national holidays 17 Dec (King's birthday), 11, 12, 13 Nov; membership of ADB, Colombo Plan, FAO, G-77, IBRD, IDA, IFAD, IMF, NAM, UNESCO, UPU, UN, WHO.

Physical description and climate. From the high peaks of the Eastern Himalayas which reach heights of 7,315 m in the N, the land runs down through forested mountain ridges with fertile valleys to low foothills which meet the Duars Plain in the S. Many rivers including the R Manas flow down to meet the R Brahmaputra. Climatic conditions range from permanent snowfields and glaciers in the high Himalayas to subtropical forest in the S. The more densely populated valleys of central Bhután are temperate. Violent thunderstorms and torrential rain are common, with an average of 1,000 mm of rain in the central valleys and 5,000 mm in the S.

History, government and constitution. British involvement in Bhután dates from a treaty of 1774 between the East India Company and the ruler of Bhután. In 1865 the government was granted a subsidy and in 1910 Britain agreed to minimal interference in internal affairs but offered advice on external affairs. A special treaty arrangement with India, signed in 1949, allows Bhután control over its internal affairs but requires a similar consultation with India in foreign relations. From 1907 the country was governed by a Maharajah, now addressed as the King of Bhután. In Oct 1969 the absolute monarchy was replaced by a form of democratic monarchy, although the King remains head of government and head of state. The King is advised by a 9-member Royal Advisory Council and a 6-member Council of Ministers. The 150-member unicameral legislative National Assembly or *Tsongdu*, which meets twice a year, comprises village elders, monastic representatives and administrative officials who are elected every 3 years. There are no legal political parties.

Economy. The economy of Bhután is largely based on agriculture which accounts for about 50% of national income. The main crops are rice, wheat, maize, mountain barley, potatoes, vegetables and fruit, especially oranges. The country is nearly self-sufficient in food and exports cereals and fruit. There is a forested area of 2,840 sq km of which 2,738 ha is productive plantation forest. Industry accounts for 10% of national income and is mostly centred on the production of local handicrafts, food processing, cement processing and plywood manufacture. Handicrafts and timber are the chief exports, while textiles and cereals are the main imports. India is the chief trading partner.

Administrative divisions. The 4 regions (east, central, west and south) are divided into 17 districts each under a governor (*dzongda*). The majority of Butánese live close to a castle-monastery (*dzong*) around which a village has developed. The most powerful of these have given their name to geographical divisions of the country.

Bia *bee'a*, national park in SW Ghana, W Africa; area 78 sq km, established in 1974.

Biafra, Bight of *bee-a'fra*, part of the Atlantic Ocean, lying in the E bay of the Gulf of Guinea; extends from the mouth of the R Niger in the N to the coast of N Gabon in the E; Bioko (Equatorial Guinea) is the chief island.

Biała Podlaska *byow'a pod-la'ska*, voivodship in E Poland, on the frontier with the USSR; traversed W-E by R Krzna; pop(1983) 294,000; area 5,348 sq km; capital Biała Podlaska; chief towns include Międzyrzec Podlaski, Łosice and Radzyń Podlaski; famous horse stud farm at Janów Podlaski.

Biała Podlaska, 52 03N 23 05E, pop(1983) 44,400, capital town of Biała Podlaska voivodship, E Poland; on R Krzna, near the USSR frontier; railway; economy: wool, furniture; monument: 17th-c Radziwiłł mansion.

Białowieża *bya-wov-ye'zha*, 52 41N 23 50E, resort village in Białystok voivodship, E Poland; at the centre of the Białowieża Forest; seat of several scientific institutes.

Białowieża, oak, pine and spruce forest on the Polish-USSR frontier; total area 1,290 sq km; area in Poland 580 sq km; 50.7 sq km constitute the Białowieża National Park in Poland (formed in 1921); extensive swamps; formerly a hunting reserve of the Polish monarchy; contains reserves of European bison and Biłgoraj pony.

Białystok *byow-o-shtok'*, voivodship in E Poland; on the frontier with the USSR; traversed E-W by R Narew; includes part of the Białowieża Forest of which 580 sq km is in Polish territory and 50.7 sq km constitute the Białowieża National Park; pop(1983) 660,000; area 10,055 sq km; capital Białystok; chief towns include Bielsk Podlaski and Hajnówka.

Białystok, 53 09N 23 10E, pop(1983) 240,300, industrial capital of Białystok voivodship, E Poland; on the Polasie plain near the Knyszyńska Forest; largest city in NE Poland; developed as a textile centre during the 19th century; first Council of Workers' Delegates with first workers' and peasants government and Provisional Revolutionary Committee formed here in 1918; the city was rebuilt after 1945; medical academy; railway; economy: cotton, wool, tools, food processing, power; monuments: Revolutionary Movement Museum; residence of the Branicki family, designed by Tilman van Gameren; church of St Roch (1924); Baroque town hall; event: national festival of music and poetry in April.

Biankou'ma, dept in W Ivory Coast, W Africa; pop(1975) 75,711; area 4,950 sq km; capital Biankouma.

Biarritz *bee-ar-eets*, 43 29N 1 33W, pop(1982) 28,000, fashionable resort town in Pyrénées-Atlantiques dept, Aquitaine, SW France; on the Bay of Biscay; noted for its mild climate and beaches.

Bibiani *bee-bya'nee*, 6 30N 2 08W, town in Western region, W Ghana, W Africa; on the railway between Awaso and Goaso.

Bicester *bis'ter*, 51 54N 1 00W, pop(1981) 16,021, town in Cherwell dist, Oxfordshire, S central England; 18 km NE of Oxford; railway; economy: engineering, livestock and agricultural trade.

Biddulph *bi'dëlf*, 53 08N 2 10W, pop(1981) 16,798, town in Staffordshire Moorlands dist, Staffordshire, central England; 12 km N of Stoke-on-Trent; economy: coal, textiles, engineering.

Bideford *bid'e-ford*, 51 01N 4 13W, pop(1981) 18,874, town linked with Northam in Torridge dist, Devonshire, SW England; on the R Torridge, 58 km NW of Exeter; economy: transport equipment.

Biel *beel*, BIENNE *byen* (Fr), 47 09N 7 16E, pop(1980) 53,793, industrial and commercial town in Bern canton, Switzerland; near Bieler See (L Biel), at the foot of the Jura Mts, 27 km NNW of Bern; the people of Biel are bilingual, speaking both French and German; railway junction; economy: scientific instruments, engineering; monuments: 17th-c town hall, 15th-c church; has a charming old town centre on a hill above the new market place.

Bielefeld *bee'le-felt*, 52 02N 8 31E, pop(1983) 307,900, industrial city in Detmold dist, NE Nordrhein-Westfalen (North Rhine-Westphalia) prov, W Germany; 61 km E of Münster, at an important pass through the Teutoburger Wald (Teutoburg Forest); university (1969); railway; economy: linen, clothing, textiles, foodstuffs, fisheries, beer and soft drinks, sewing machines, motor-cycles, shipping, building and furniture fittings, pharmaceuticals, chemicals, business machinery, machine tools, printing and packaging materials; event: Linen Weavers' Festival (May).

Bielsko-Biała *byel-shko-byow'a*, voivodship in S Poland; on the frontier with Czechoslovakia; N of the Beskid Mts and traversed S-N by R Soła; pop(1983) 857,000; area 3,704 sq km; capital Bielsko-Biała; chief towns include Oświęcim, Cieszyn and Żywiec.

Bielsko-Biała, BIELITZ *bee'lits* (Ger), 49 50N 19 00E, pop(1983) 172,000, industrial capital of Bielsko-Biała voivodship, S Poland; in the valley of the R Biała near the Beskid Mts; noted as a major producer of textiles; film studios; railway; economy: textiles, textile machinery, motor vehicles, gliders, electrical engineering, power.

Bienne, town in Switzerland. See Biel.

Biferno *bee-fer'no*, TIFERNUS (anc), river in S central Italy, rising in the Appno Napoletano; flows 83 km NE to the Adriatic Sea, 3 km SE of Termoli.

Big Bend, national Park in W Texas, United States; an area of mountain and desert on a big bend of the Rio Grande, on the Mexican frontier; established in 1944; area 2,833 sq km.

Big'gin Hill, 51 18N 0 02E, pop(1981) 13,925, town in Bromley borough, Greater London, England; 6 km E of Warlingham; airfield.

Biggleswade *big'lz-wayd*, 52 05N 0 17W, pop(1981) 10,954, town in Mid Bedfordshire dist, Bedfordshire, S central England; on R Ivel, 15 km SE of Bedford; airfield; railway; economy: engineering.

Bihać *bee'hach*, 44 49N 15 53E, pop(1981) 65,544, town in NW Bosna-Hercegovina republic, Yugoslavia; on R Una, 100 km W of Banja Luka; railway; economy: hydroelectric power, agricultural trade.

Bihar or **Behar** *bee-har'*, state in E India; bounded N by Nepal, E by West Bengal, S by Orissa, SW by Madhya Pradesh and W by Uttar Pradesh; pop(1981) 69,823,154; area 173,876 sq km; capital Patna; the state is divided into 10 divisions and 38 dists; Bihar is governed by a 325-member Legislative Assembly; the state is crossed by the R Ganga (Ganges) and many of its tributaries including the Son, Gardak and Ghaghara rivers; to the S of the R Ganga the Rajmahal Hills stretch NE-SW; the Hazaribagh Range and the Ranchi plateau are located in the extreme S; Bihar has the greatest mineral deposits of any Indian state; coal is the principal mineral; Bihar is the only Indian state producing copper; over 25% of the cultivable area is irrigated; chief agricultural crops include rice, jute, sugar cane, oilseed, wheat and maize; industries include iron and steel, machine tools, fertilizers, electrical engineering, paper milling and cement.

Bihor *bee'KHor*, county in NW Romania, on the Hungarian frontier; pop(1983) 650,707; area 7,535 sq km; capital Oradea.

Bijagos *bee-zhu-gosh'*, ARQUIPÉLAGO DOS BIJAGŌS (Port), an archipelago off the coast of Guinea-Bissau, W Africa; consists of numerous small islets and 15 larger islands including Orango, Formosa, Caravela and Roxa; the town of Bolama is located on an island of the same name.

Bijeljina *bee-ye'lyin-a*, 44 46N 19 14E, pop(1981) 92,808, town in NE Bosna-Hercegovina republic, Yugoslavia; near the frontier with Srbija (Serbia), 48 km NE of Tuzla; railway; economy: grain and cattle trade.

Bijelo Polje *bee-ye'lo pol'ye*, formerly AKYALE (Turk), 43 03N 19 42E, pop(1981) 55,634, town in E Crna Gora (Montenegro) republic, Yugoslavia; on R Lim, 72 km NE of Titograd.

Bikaner *bi-ku-neer'*, 28 01N 73 22E, pop(1981) 280,000, city in Rajasthan, NW India; in the Thar Desert; linked by rail to Ajmer and Delhi; founded in 1488, capital of the former state of Bikaner; joined with Rajasthan in 1949; economy: woollen goods, leather work, carpets, camels; monuments: 16th-c Rajput palaces.

Bikini *bee-kee'nee*, atoll in the Marshall Is, W Pacific, 3,200 km SW of Hawaii; from 1946-58 the Americans carried out 23 nuclear tests on Bikini; the first H-bomb was tested here; the inhabitants were evacuated from the island in Feb 1946 but many returned in 1972, only to be evacuated again when it was discovered that they had ingested the largest dose of plutonium ever monitored in any population.

Bilbao *bil-ba'o*, 43 16N 2 56W, pop(1981) 433,030, major seaport and industrial capital of Vizcaya prov, N Spain; 395 km N of Madrid; founded in 1300; university (1886); airport; railway; bishopric; monuments: 14th-c cathedral; art museum; churches of St Anton and St Nicholas de Bari; economy: iron, steel, chemicals, shipbuilding, fishing; events: machine tool fair in March; Semana Grande in Aug, with bullfights, concerts, folk events and a pilgrimage to San Roque followed by a trade fair.

Bilecik *bi-le-jik'*, hilly prov in NW Turkey; pop(1980) 147,001; area 4,307 sq km; capital Bilecik; drained by the R Sakarya.

Billericay *bil-er-ik'i*, 51 38N 0 25E, pop(1981) 30,609, town in Basildon dist, Essex, SE England; 8 km E of Brentwood; railway.

Billingham, 54 36N 1 17W, pop(1981) 36,712, industrial town in Stockton-on-Tees dist, Cleveland, NE England; 4 km NE of Stockton-on-Tees; railway; economy: chemicals.

Billings, 45 47N 108 30W, pop(1980) 66,798, county seat of Yellowstone county, S Montana, United States; largest city in the state, situated on the R Yellowstone, near the Crow Indian Reservation; railway; airfield; economy: sugar, livestock, wheat and wool trade, oil refining, sugar refining, meat packing, and flour milling; event: International Livestock Exposition (Oct).

Bil'ma, 18 46N 12 50E, town in Agadez dept, NE Niger, W Africa; on a caravan route from Tripoli to L Chad; economy: salt, agricultural trade.

Biloxi *be-lok'see*, 30 24N 88 53W, pop(1980) 49,311, town in Harrison county, SE Mississippi, United States; on the Gulf of Mexico at the mouth of the R Biloxi; named after an Indian tribe; the first permanent white settlement in the Mississippi valley; railway; economy: tourism, boatbuilding, shrimp and oyster fisheries; Keesler Air Force Base.

Biltine *beel-teen'*, prefecture in E Chad, N central Africa; pop(1979) 175,000; area 46,850 sq km; there are extensive seasonal floodplains; the Massif du Kapka rises in the centre of the prefecture; capital Biltine; chief towns Guéréda, Iriba and Arada.

Biltine, 14 30N 20 53E, capital of Biltine prefecture, E central Chad, N central Africa; 80 km N of Abéché.

Bimini Islands *bi'mi-nee*, island group in the NW Bahamas, on the Straits of Florida, 176 km W of Nassau; comprises a string of cays extending 72 km N-S; pop(1980) 1,432; area 28 sq km; chief town Alice Town; airport on S Bimini.

Bing Bong, 15 37S 136 21E, town in NW Northern Territory, Australia; on the Gulf of Carpentaria on the NE coast; E of Bing Bong Creek and N of Borroloola; the Sir Edward Pellew group of islands lies offshore.

Binga, Mount *bing'ga*, 19 47S 33 03E, mountain in Manica prov, W central Mozambique, SE Africa; rising to 2,436 m near the border with Zimbabwe, it is the highest peak in Mozambique.

Bingerville *bing'ger-veel*, 5 20N 3 53W, town in Abidjan dept, S Ivory Coast, W Africa; 11 km E of Abidjan; the French capital of Ivory Coast 1900-35.

Binghamton, 42 06N 75 55W, pop(1980) 55,860, county seat of Broome county, S New York, United States; on the R Susquehanna, 105 km S of Syracuse; university (1946); railway; airfield; Robertson Centre for the arts and sciences.

Bingöl *bing-ul'*, mountainous prov in E Turkey; pop(1980) 228,702; area 8,125 sq km; capital Bingöl.

Bío-Bío *bee'ō bee'ō*, region of S central Chile; an inland region following the Bío-Bío valley; bordered E by Argentina and the Andes; comprises the provs of Ñble, Bío-Bío, Concepción and Arauco; in the E is L Laja, at the foot of Antuco volcano; Copahue volcano is on the Argentinian border; pop(1984) 1,558,700; area 36,939 sq km; capital Concepción; chief towns Los Angeles, Chillán (birthplace of Bernardo O'Higgins) and Lebu; economy: agriculture, petrochemicals, steel, carbon; the region contains Laguna del Lajo, Tolhuaca, Nahual Buta and Cerro Ñielol national parks.

Bio'ko, formerly FERNANDO PO, FERNANDO POO (-1973), MACIAS NGUEMA BIJOGO (-1979), island in the Bight of Biafra, off the coast of Cameroon, W Africa; area 2,017 sq km; island prov of Equatorial Guinea of volcanic origin rising to 3,007 m at Pico de Basilé; the chief town and capital of Equatorial Guinea is Malabo (formerly Santa Isabel), other towns include Luba (formerly San Carlos) and Riaba (formerly Conception); visited by the Portuguese in 1471, the island was originally named after the navigator Fernão do Po; variously occupied by British, Portuguese and Spanish; between 1973 and 1979 the island was named after a president of Equatorial Guinea who was ousted in a coup in 1979; economy: coffee, cocoa and copra.

Biom'bo, region in Guinea-Bissau, W Africa; pop(1979) 56,463.

Birao *beer-ow'*, 10 11N 22 49E, chief town in Vakaga

prefecture, NE Central African Republic; in a swampy area near the Sudan frontier, 805 km NE of Bangui; on the caravan route to Dafur.

Birhan, 10 45N 37 55E, mountain in the Choke range, Gojam region, central Ethiopia, NE Africa; 48 km NNE of Debra Markos; height 4,154 m.

Birkenhead, 36 49S 174 43E, pop(1981) 21,324, city in Central Auckland, North Island, New Zealand; on N shore of Waitemata Harbour.

Birkenhead, 53 24N 3 02W, pop(1981) 99,529, urban area pop(1981) 280,521, town in Wirral borough, Merseyside, NW England; on the Wirral peninsula opposite Liverpool, to which it is linked under the R Mersey by rail and road tunnels; railway; economy: shipbuilding, clothing, engineering, food processing, the export of flour and machinery, the import of grain and livestock.

Birkirka'ra, 35 53N 14 30E, pop(1983e) 17,861, town in N central Malta; 5 km SW of Valletta.

Bîrlad *beer'lad*, 46 14N 27 40E, pop(1983) 66,476, town in Vaslui county, E Romania; railway.

Bir'mingham, 52 30N 1 50W, pop(1981) 1,006,527, city and county town in West Midlands, central England; part of West Midlands urban area and Britain's 2nd largest city; 175 km NW of London; the name is derived from the dwelling place (*ham*) of the Beoroma family (*ing*); a noted centre for metalwork since the 16th century; developed rapidly in the Industrial Revolution in an area with a large supply of iron ore and coal; University of Birmingham (1900); University of Aston at Birmingham (1966); National Exhibition Centre (1976); Aston Science Park; regional media centre for television and radio; railway; economy: engineering, vehicles, plastics, chemicals, electrical goods, machine tools, glass; monuments: 18th-c church of St Philip, cathedral of St Chad (1839), Aston Hall (1618-35); event: international showjumping championships (April).

Birmingham, 33 31N 86 48W, pop(1980) 284,413, county seat of Jefferson county, N central Alabama, United States; 135 km NNW of Montgomery; largest city in the state; Samford University (1842); railway; airfield; economy: leading iron and steel centre in the south; iron, coal and limestone are mined in the area; other manufactures include metal products, transportation equipment, chemicals, and food products; centre for commerce, banking and insurance; monuments: Alabama Symphony, Sloss Furnaces, iron statue of Vulcan (mythical god of the forge); event: festival of the arts (April).

Birni n'Konni *birn'ing kō'nee*, 13 49N 5 19E, town in Tahoua dept, SW central Niger, W Africa; S of Tahoua, close to Nigerian border; economy: trade, agriculture, power plant.

Birżebbuġa *beerd-ze-boo'jah*, 35 49N 14 32E, pop(1983e) 5,470, town in SE Malta; lying between St George's Bay and Pretty Bay which are inlets of the larger Marsaxlokk Bay; noted for lace manufacture.

Biscay, Spanish prov. See Vizcaya.

Biscay, Bay of *bis'kay*, GOLFE DE VIZCAYA (Sp), GOLFE DE GASCOGNE (Fr), arm of the Atlantic Ocean, bounded to the E by the W coast of France and to the S by the N coast of Spain; lies between the Isle d'Ouessant (Ushant Island) and Ortigueira (Cape Ortegal); irregular coasts with many fine harbours; known for its strong currents and sudden storms; resorts such as Biarritz are located along the straight, sandy shores of the SE French coast; major ports include St Nazaire, La Rochelle, San Sebastian and Santander.

Bishop Auckland, 54 40N 1 40W, pop(1981) 23,898, town in Wear Valley dist, Durham, NE England; on the R Wear, 15 km SW of Durham; railway; economy: electrical goods, engineering.

Bishopbriggs *bish-op-rigs'*, 55 54N 4 14W, pop(1981) 23,501, town in Glasgow City dist, Strathclyde, W central Scotland; in Clydeside urban area, 5 km N of Glasgow; railway.

Bishop's Stortford *stor'ford*, 51 53N 0 09E, pop(1981) 22,791, town in East Hertfordshire dist, Hertfordshire, SE England; on the R Stort, 13 km N of Harlow; birthplace of Cecil Rhodes; railway; airport (Stansted); economy: petroleum products, engineering, scientific instruments.

Bis'kra, department of NE Algeria, N Africa; area 109,729 sq km; pop(1982) 615,015; chief town Biskra.

Bismarck, 46 48N 100 47W, pop(1980) 44,485, capital of state in Burleigh county, central North Dakota, United States; on the R Missouri; established in 1873; territorial capital in 1883 and state capital in 1889; railway; airfield; economy: trade and distribution centre for agricultural region; oil refining (nearby oil reserves in Williston Basin); manufactures food products and machinery; monuments: Camp Hancock Museum, Heritage Centre; event: Folkfest (Sept).

Bismarck Archipelago, island group NE of New Guinea, SW Pacific, comprising New Britain, New Ireland, Admiralty Is, and Lavongai; area 49,709 sq km; all are mountainous with several active volcanoes; Rabaul, on the Gazelle Peninsula of New Britain, was the former capital of the Territory of New Guinea; site of Japanese naval and air bases in World War II.

Bismarck Sea, SW arm of the Pacific Ocean; to the NE of New Guinea and the NW of New Britain; 805 km E-W; Battle of the Bismarck Sea on 2-3 March 1943 saw the destruction of a Japanese naval force by US aircraft and naval units.

Bissau *bee-sow'*, region in Guinea-Bissau, W Africa; pop(1979) 109,214.

Bissau, BISSÂO, 11 52N 15 39W, pop 105,273, seaport capital of Guinea-Bissau, W Africa; on Bissau Island in the R Geba estuary; established in 1687 as a fortified slave trading centre, it became a free port in 1869; in 1941 the capital was moved here from Bolama; airfield; monuments: national museum, cathedral.

Bistriţa *bee'street-sa*, 47 8N 24 30E, pop(1983) 67,311, capital of Bistriţa-Năsăud county, N Romania, established with another 6 Transylvanian towns by German colonists in the 12-13th centuries; part of Hungary during World War II; railway; economy: wine, timber and agricultural trade, footwear, food processing, brewing; monuments: Gothic Evangelical church and Greek-Catholic church with interesting frescoes.

Bistriţa-Năsăud *bee'street-sa-na-sa-ood'*, county in N Romania, in the W foothills of the E Carpathian Mts; crossed by the R Someş; pop(1983) 309,758; area 5,305 sq km; capital Bistriţa; a notable wine-producing area.

Bitlis *bit-lis'*, prov in SE Turkey; pop(1980) 257,908; area 6,707 sq km; capital Bitlis; includes W part of L Van Gölü; economy: grain, vegetables, tobacco; noted former centre of the order of Whirling Dervishes.

Bitola or **Bitolj** *bee'to-lah*, MONASTIR (Turk), 41 01N 21 21E, pop(1981) 137,835, town in Makedonija (Macedonia) republic, Yugoslavia; 112 km S of Skopje; formerly a strategic nodal point at the intersection of the main E-W and N-S roads of the S Balkans; 2nd largest town in Makedonija; railway; skiing in the nearby Pelister range where there is a national park (120 sq km) established in 1949; monuments: the excavations at Heraclea; Ajdar Kadi mosque; event: 'Ilinden Days' festival of folk music in July-Aug.

Biumba *be-yoom'ba*, 1 36S 30 02E, pop(1978) 519,968, city and prefecture in Rwanda, central Africa; 39 km N of Kigali; alt 2,300 m.

Biwa-ko *bee'wa-kō*, LAKE BIWA, LAKE OMI *ō'mee*, the largest lake in Japan; in Shiga prefecture, Kinki region, central Honshū, Japan; 8 km NE of Kyōto; area 676 sq km; 64 km long; 3-19 km wide; 96 m deep; the only outlet is the R Seta at the S end of the lake; a 12 km-long canal connects the lake with Kyōto.

Biysk *byee'eesk*, 52 40N 85 00E, pop(1983) 221,000, town in Altayskiy kray, Rossiyskaya, Soviet Union; on the R Biya, in the N foothills of the Altay range; established in 1709 as a military fortress and became a city in 1782; rail terminus; economy: chemicals, cotton textiles, clothing, power station equipment.

Bizerte *bi-zur'te*, HIPPO DIARRHYTUS (Lat), 37 18N 9 52E, pop(1984) 94,509, capital of Bizerte governorate, N

Tunisia, N Africa; 60 km NNW of Tunis; strategically important owing to its prominent position on the Mediterranean coastline; the town has been occupied by the Romans, the Vandals, the Arabs, the Moors, the Spaniards (1534-72) and the French who occupied the town in 1881 and rebuilt the disused port (1895); Bizerte was heavily bombed by the Allies during World War II when it was a German base, but was rapidly rebuilt in the post-war era; a French naval base until 1963; there is a kasbah in the old city; railway; event: Bizerte Festival (July-Aug).

Bjorneborg, town in Finland. See Pori.

Black Forest, mountain range in W Germany. See Schwarzwald.

Black River, district in W Mauritius; area 259 sq km; pop(1983) 37,470; the Black River bisects the Tamarin lagoon, a popular bathing resort.

Black Sea, EUXINE SEA, PONTIUS EUXINUS (anc), CHERNO MORE (Bulg), MAREA NEAGRA (Rom), CHERNOYE MORE (Rus), KARADENIZ (Turk), inland sea of 413,365 sq km between Europe and Asia; connected to the Mediterranean in the SW by the Bosporus, the Sea of Marmara and the Dardanelles; 1,210 km long by 120-560 km wide, with a maximum depth of 2,246 m; bounded to the N and NE by the Ukrainian SSR, Russian SFSR and Georgia SSR, with Turkey to the S and Bulgaria and Romania to the W; together with the Caspian and Aral seas, the Black Sea was once part of a large body of water, but during the Tertiary period the Black Sea separated from the Caspian Sea to join the Mediterranean; the Sea of Azov is the largest arm, joined via the Kerch Strait; steep, rocky coasts in the S and NE, sandy shores to the N and NW; receives fresh water from the Danube, Dneister, the Southern Bug, Dnieper, Rion, Kizil, Irmak and the Sakarya rivers; the denser stagnant lower layer is devoid of marine life; an outward low-salinity surface current from the Bosporus exists, while denser, saline water enters the Black Sea by way of a submarine inward current; fishing is important especially in the N, where herring, mackerel, pike and bream are caught; navigated since ancient times, its shores were colonized by the Greeks in the 8th-6th centuries BC and by the Romans in the 3rd-1st centuries BC; the Genoese established colonies in the 13th century along its shores, and from the 15th to the 18th centuries the Black Sea was within the Turkish empire; Russian ambition to gain control of the Bosporus and the Dardanelles led to a dispute with the Ottoman Empire; in 1774 the Russians gained the right to trade in the Black Sea following the Treaty of Kainarji; 10 years later Austria gained the right to trade in its waters, and following the treaty of Amiens in 1802 French and British ships were admitted; the Treaty of Paris in 1856 opened it up to the commerce of all nations and closed it to ships of war; the USSR unsuccessfully proposed control of the Black Sea and revision of the status of the Turkish Straits after World War II.

Blackburn, 53 45N 2 29W, pop(1981) 110,254, town in Blackburn dist, Lancashire, NW England; 13 km E of Preston, on the Leeds-Liverpool Canal; railway; economy: engineering, textiles, paper, electronics.

Blackburn, Mount, 61 44N 143 26W, dormant volcano in SE Alaska, United States; situated in the Wrangell Mts, 160 km ENE of Valdez; in the Wrangell-St Elias National Park and Preserve; height 5,160 m; highest peak in the Wrangell Mts.

Blackpool, 53 50N 3 03W, pop(1981) 148,482, town in Blackpool dist, Lancashire, NW England; on the Irish Sea coast, 25 km W of Preston; the largest holiday resort in N England, with an estimated 8.5 mn visitors annually; railway; economy: tourism, electronics, engineering, transport equipment; monuments: observation tower, Grundy art gallery; events: ballroom dancing championships (summer); musical festival (summer); agricultural show (summer); illuminations (autumn).

Blacksburg, 37 14N 80 25W, pop(1980) 30,638, town in Montgomery county, W Virginia, United States; 45 km W of Roanoke; university.

Blackwood, 51 41N 3 13W, pop(1981) 13,278, town in Islwyn dist, Gwent, SE Wales; N of Abercarn; railway.

Blaenau Ffestiniog *blī'now fest-in'yog*, 52 59N 3 56W, locality in Merionnyd county, Gwynedd, NW Wales; N of Ffestiniog; power station; private railway line; centre for slate and granite quarrying.

Blagoevgrad *blag-o'yev-grat*, an okrug (prov) in SW Bulgaria, on the NW edge of the Pirin Planina (Pirin Mts) and on the frontier with Yugoslavia and Greece; traversed N-S by the R Struma; area 6,464 sq km; pop(1981) 338,000.

Blagoevgrad, formerly GORNA DZHUMAYA (-1950), 42 01N 23 05E, health resort and capital of Blagoevgrad okrug (prov), SW Bulgaria; situated near the R Struma; railway; economy: tobacco processing; monument: ruins of Roman settlement are situated nearby.

Blaine, 45 10N 93 13W, pop(1980) 28,558, town in Anoka county, SE Minnesota, United States; suburb 21 km N of Minneapolis.

Blairgowrie *blayr-gow'ree*, 56 36N 3 21W, pop(1981) 7,184, town in Perth and Kinross dist, Tayside, E Scotland; on the R Ericht, 27 km NW of Dundee; the centre of a soft fruit growing area; monument: to the W of Blairgowrie is Ardblair Castle, built in the 16th century on the foundations of a 12th-c castle.

Blaj *blazh*, 46 10N 23 57E, pop(1983) 22,812, town and cultural centre in Alba county, W central Romania; established in the 13th century; railway junction; theological seminary; economy: alcohol, tiles; monuments: 18th-c cathedral and archiepiscopal palace.

Blanca, Laguna *la-goo'na blan'ka*, national park in S Neuquén prov, Andina, Argentina; SW of Zapala; area 82.5 sq km; L Blanca situated in the N of the park.

Blantyre *blan-tīr'*, 14 46N 35 00E, pop(1984e) 333,800, town in Southern region, S Malawi, SE Africa; situated in a hilly region 60 km SW of Zomba; alt 1,040 m; Church of Scotland mission founded here in 1876; named after David Livingstone's birthplace in Scotland; became a British consular post in 1883 and a township in 1895; Malawi's main commercial and industrial centre; has expanded from a 1966 pop of 109,000; nearby are the Kapachira Falls; railway; Chileka airport 11 km N; economy: tea, coffee and rubber trade, brewing, distilling, hides and skins, crafts; monuments: museum, Roman Catholic and Anglican cathedrals.

Blantyre, 55 47N 4 06W, pop(1981) 19,948, town in Clydeside urban area, Hamilton dist, Strathclyde, W central Scotland; just NW of Hamilton; railway: monuments: Livingstone National Memorial, in a block of 18th-c mill tenements where the missionary and explorer, David Livingstone, was born in 1813.

Blarney *blar'nay*, 51 56N 8 34W, pop(1981) 1,500, small village in Cork county, Munster, S Irish Republic; 8 km NW of Cork; visitors to Blarney Castle are supposed to gain the power of eloquent speech from the rush of blood to the head as they hang upside down to kiss the Blarney Stone - a legend dating from the 16th century when Lord Blarney, by pure loquaciousness, avoided acknowledging to Queen Elizabeth's deputy that the lands of Blarney were held as a grant from the Queen and not as a chiefship.

Blejsko Jezero *blet'sko ye-ze'ro*, LAKE BLED (Eng), lake in NW Slovenija republic, Yugoslavia; 48 km NW of Ljubljana; a popular all-year-round tourist region with many hotels and a spa in the village of Bled noted for its solar treatment; a favourite summer resort for Beograd diplomats; Tito had a villa on the S side of the lake; skiing complex nearby at Zatrnik.

Blekinge *blay'king-e*, a county of S Sweden on the Baltic coast; land area 2,909 sq km; pop(1983) 152,118; capital Karlskrona; chief towns Ronneby and Karlshamn.

Bletch'ley, 52 00N 0 46W, pop(1981) 38,273, town in Milton Keynes dist, Buckinghamshire, S central England; 20 km E of Buckingham; railway; economy: light engineering.

Blida *blee'da*, EL BOULAIDA, 36 30N 2 50E, pop(1982) 197,261, chief town of El Blida dept, N Algeria, N Africa;

40 km SW of Alger; dating from the 16th century Blida was occupied by the French in 1839; earthquakes in 1825 and 1867; railway.

Bloemfontein *bloom-fon-tayn'*, 29 07S 26 14E, pop(1980) 230,688, capital of Orange Free State prov, E central South Africa; 160 km ESE of Kimberley and 370 km SW of Johannesburg; judicial capital of South Africa; originally a Boer farmstead sited near a spring called the 'fountain of flowers' or Bloemfontein; developed into a fort in 1846 under Major H.D. Warden; seat of government of Orange River Sovereignty and of Orange Free State Republic 1849-57; the failure of a conference here in 1899 between Sir Alfred Milner and President Kruger led to the outbreak of the Boer War on 11 Oct 1899; Lord Roberts took the city in March of the following year; university (1855); airfield; railway; economy: trade centre for Orange Free State prov and Lesotho; railway engineering, food processing, glassware, furniture, plastics, fruit canning; monuments: Anglican cathedral, national museum (1877), war museum (1931).

Blois *blwa*, BLESAE (anc), 47 35N 1 20E, pop(1982) 49,422, market town and capital of Loir-et-Cher dept, Centre region, central France; on the R Loire, 53 km SW of Orléans; Denis Papin, inventor of an early form of pressure cooker, was born here in 1648; railway; economy: wood, grain, wine, shoes, chocolate and porcelain; monuments: magnificent 13th-c château with royal associations, originally built to defend the bridge over the R Loire; 9 km NE is the Château de Menars, the home of Madame de Pompadour, favourite of Louis XV.

Bloomfield, 40 48N 74 12W, pop(1980) 47,792, town in Essex county, NE New Jersey, United States; 6 km N of Newark.

Bloomington, 40 29N 89 00W, pop(1980) 44,189, county seat of McLean county, central Illinois, United States; 56 km ESE of Peioria; university (1850); railway.

Bloomington, 39 10N 86 32W, pop(1980) 52,044, county seat of Monroe county, S Indiana, United States; 72 km SSW of Indianapolis; university (1820); railway; economy: limestone, coal mining, agricultural trade.

Bloomington, 44 50N 93 17W, pop(1980) 81,831, town in Hennepin county, SE Minnesota, United States; suburb 18 km S of Minneapolis; railway.

Blue Mountain, mountain peak rising to 2,256 m in Portland parish, Surrey county, on the Caribbean I of Jamaica.

Blue Mountains, national park in E New South Wales, Australia; the Blue Mountain Range is part of the Great Dividing Range; area 2,159 sq km; established in 1959.

Blue Nile, ĀBAY WENZ (Ethiopia), BAHR EL AZRAQ (Sudan), upper reach of the R Nile, NE Africa; length within Ethiopia 800 km; total length 1,450 km; issues from the SE corner of T'ana Hāyk' (L Tana), which is located in the Gojam region of Ethiopia; flows SE along the NE edge of the Choke Mts then turns S and W along the border between the Gojam and Welega regions of Ethiopia towards the Sudanese frontier; crosses into Sudan at Bumbadī and flows into a lake created by the Roseires Dam; on reaching Khartoum it joins the White Nile to form the R Nile proper; during its period of high flood the Blue Nile accounts for almost 70% of the R Nile's flow but during low water this figure falls to less than 20%.

Blue Ridge Mountains, mountain range, SE USA; E portion of the Appalachian Mts; extends NE-SW for approx 1,050 km from S Pennsylvania, through Maryland, Virginia and North Carolina to N Georgia; generally a narrow linear ridge in form, 16-24 km wide; it widens in North Carolina and includes the Black Mts and Great Smoky Mts (both in W North Carolina); at this point the ridge includes the E part of Tennessee and a small portion of NW South Carolina; the Blue Ridge Mts rise to 2,037 m in Mt Mitchell in the Black Mts at 35 46N 82 16W, this is the highest point in North Carolina; the Blue Ridge Mts also contain the highest peaks in Georgia: Brasstown Bald (1,458 m at 34 53N 83 49W), in Virginia: Mt Rogers (1,746 m at 36 40N 81 33W) and in South Carolina: Sassafras Mt (1,083 m at 35 04N 82 47W); the range also includes the Great Smoky Mountains National Park (area 2,092 sq km, established in 1934); further N in Virginia is the Shenandoah National Park (area 849 sq km, established in 1935); the region is famous for its wooded scenery and timber is the major resource here; some of the remote Blue Ridge valleys, especially in the S, shelter mountain people who have kept many old ways of life and speech.

Blue Springs, 39 01N 94 17W, pop(1980) 25,927, town in Jackson county, W Missouri, United States; 16 km SE of Independence.

Blue'fields, 12 00N 83 49W, pop(1978) 18,252, port and capital town of Zelaya dept, E Nicaragua, Central America; S of the point where the Río Escondido enters the Caribbean Sea; most important of Nicaragua's 3 Caribbean ports; its outer port is El Bluff; airfield; main exports: bananas, cabinet woods, frozen fish, shrimps, and lobsters.

Blumenau *bloo-men-ow'*, 26 55S 49 07W, pop(1980) 144,785, commercial and industrial town in Santa Catarina state, Sul region, S Brazil; on the Río Itajaí; university; railway; situated in a district settled mostly by Germans; monument: German immigrant museum.

Blyde River Canyon, national nature reserve, Transvaal prov, South Africa; a deep canyon incised into the edge of the escarpment round the perimeter of the S African plateau.

Blyth *blīTH*, 55 07N 1 30W, pop(1981) 35,056, port town in Blyth Valley dist, Northumberland, NE England; on the R Blyth, 18 km N of Newcastle upon Tyne; economy: light engineering, fishing, coal and timber trade.

Bo *bō*, dist in Southern prov, Sierra Leone, W Africa; pop(1974) 217,711; area 5,219 sq km; capital Bo.

Bo, 7 58N 11 45W, pop(1974) 39,000, capital of dist of same name in Southern prov, Sierra Leone, W Africa; 177 km ESE of Freetown; airfield.

Boa Vista *bō'a veesh'ta*, 16 11N 22 57W, flat, sandy island in the Barlavento or windward group of Cape Verde, popular with tourists; area 620 sq km; pop(1980) 3,397, there are 12 beaches, the longest being Santa Monica (35 km); fishing, particularly for shellfish, is also important; the chief town is Sal-Rei; salt is mined for export.

Boaco *bwah'kō*, dept in central Nicaragua, Central America; bounded SW by Lago de Nicaragua; the Río Grande de Matagalpa forms part of its N boundary with Matagalpa dept; E part occupied by the Montañas de Huapi; pop(1981) 88,862; area 5,398 sq km; capital Boaco; chief towns Camoapa and San Francisco.

Boaco, 12 28N 85 41W, pop(1978) 8,684, capital town and agricultural centre of Boaco dept, S central Nicaragua, Central America; 72 km NE of Managua; railway; economy: livestock trade, timber.

Bobigny *bō-been-yee*, 48 55N 2 27E, pop(1982) 42,727, industrial suburb of Paris and capital of Seine-Saint-Denis dept, Ile-de-France region, lying N of Paris; once known for its market-gardens.

Bobo Dioulasso *bo'bo dyoo-las'ō*, 11 11N 4 18W, pop(1985) 231,162, city in SW Burkina, W Africa; 322 km WSW of Ouagadougou; railway; airfield.

Bobruysk *be-broo'yisk*, 53 08N 29 10E, pop(1983) 214,000, town in Mogilevskaya oblast, Belorusskaya SSR, Soviet Union; on the R Berezina; founded in the 16th century and fortified by Alexander I; railway; harbour; economy: woodworking, machine building, chemicals, tyres, leatherwork.

Boca Raton *bō-ka ra'tōn*, 26 21N 80 05W, pop(1980) 49,505, town in Palm Beach county, SE Florida, United States; on the Atlantic Ocean, 25 km N of Fort Lauderdale; university (1964); railway; economy: tourism, computers, plastics.

Bocas del Toro *bō'kas del to'rō*, prov in NW Panama, Central America; bounded N by the Golfo de los Mosquitos, an inlet of the Caribbean Sea, and W by Costa Rica; drained by the Río Changuinola; includes the archipelago of Bocas del Toro; pop(1980) 53,487; area 8,917 sq km; capital Bocas del Toro; other chief town Almirante; economy: agriculture (bananas, cacao, abacá); the banana railways provide links between Guabito on the Costa Rican frontier, Changuinola, and Almirante; formed in 1903 out of Colón prov; includes the Laguna de Chiriquí.

Bocas del Toro, 9 20N 82 15W, pop(1980) 2,520, Caribbean port and capital of Bocas del Toro prov, NW Panama, Central America; at S tip of Isla Colón; founded by Negro immigrants in the early 19th century; destroyed by fire in 1904 and 1907; terminus of a pipeline carrying Alaskan oil from the Pacific port of Puerto Armuelles.

Bocholt *boKH'olt*, 51 50N 6 35E, pop(1983) 65,300, manufacturing city in Münster dist, NW Nordrhein-Westfalen (North Rhine-Westphalia) prov, W Germany, near the Netherlands frontier; railway; economy: textiles.

Bochum *boKH'oom*, 51 28N 7 12E, pop(1983) 391,300, industrial and commercial city in the Ruhr valley, Düsseldorf dist, Nordrhein-Westfalen (North Rhine-Westphalia) prov, W Germany; 59 km SSW of Münster, between the rivers Emscher and Ruhr; originally developed around the coal and steel industries; university (1965); home of the German Shakespeare Society; railway; economy: steel, motor vehicles, radio and television sets.

Bocşa *bōk'sha*, 45 23N 21 47E, pop(1983) 21,783, health resort town in Caraş-Severin county, W Romania; railway; economy: mining, tanning.

Bodensee *bō'den-zay*, LAKE CONSTANCE (Eng), LACUS BRIGANTINUS (anc), lake on the N side of the Swiss Alps forming a meeting point of Switzerland, Austria and W Germany; area 541.2 sq km; length 64 km; part of the course of the R Rhine which enters at the SE end; the island of Mainau is N of Konstanz; island of Reichenau is W of Konstanz; the NW arm is known as the *Überlingersee*; the chief towns on the shore are Konstanz, Friedrichshafen, Lindau and Bregenz.

Bod'min, 50 29N 4 43W, pop(1981) 12,269, town in North Cornwall dist, Cornwall, SW England; 42 km W of Plymouth and S of Bodmin Moor; economy: electrical goods, engineering.

Bodø *bo'dœ*, 67 18N 14 26E, pop(1983) 33,642, seaport and administrative capital of Nordland county, N Norway; 160 km SW of Narvik, opposite the Lofoten Is; received its municipal charter in 1816; developed with the expanding herring fisheries in 2nd half of the 19th century; rebuilt in modern style after fire damage during May 1940; technical colleges; rail terminus, airfield links town with Scandinavian network of air services; economy: fisheries, shipyards.

Boeotia, prov of Greece. See Voiotía.

Boghotu, Pacific island. See Santa Isabel.

Bognor Regis *bog'nor ree'jis*, 50 47N 0 41W, pop(1981) 53,175, coastal resort town in Arun dist, West Sussex, S England; on the English Channel, 20 km W of Worthing; the suffix 'Regis' dates from 1929 when King George V came to recuperate here; railway; economy: tourism, electrical engineering.

Bo'gong, Mount, 36 45S 147 21E, highest peak in Victoria state, Australia; rises to 1,986 m in the Australian Alps.

Bogotá *bō-gō-ta'*, formerly SANTA FE DE BOGOTÁ, 4 38N 74 05W, pop(1985) 3,967,988, federal capital of Colombia, in Cundinamarca dept, central Colombia, South America; the city stands on a plateau at 2,650 m and covers over 210 sq km; the administrative, commercial and financial centre of Colombia; once the centre of the Chibcha culture, the city was founded in 1538 by the Spanish; formerly capital of Greater Colombia and of New Granada; 15 universities; railway; airport (El Dorado) at 9.5 km; monuments: around the central Plaza Bolívar old colonial buildings include the cathedral, the Museum of Colonial Art, the Palace of San Carlos, the house of the Marqués de San Jorge (now an archaeological museum), the Municipal Palace, the National Capitol, and the churches of San Ignacio, Santa Clara, and San Agustín; at the Parque Santander is the Gold Museum, housing a priceless collection of pre-Colombian art and jewellery including Colombia's largest and most valuable collection of emeralds; a funicular railway and cable car link the city with the Monserrate peak national park, which offers fine views; at the foot of Monserrate, to the E of the city, is the Quinta de Bolívar colonial mansion, formerly the home of Simón Bolívar.

Bogra *bō'gru*, region in N central Bangladesh; includes Bogra and Joypurhat districts; pop(1981) 2,728,000; area 3,888 sq km; chief town Bogra.

Bogra, 24 52N 89 29E, pop(1981) 68,749, market town in Bogra dist, Bogra, N central Bangladesh; 112 km S of Rangpur and NE of Rajshahi; railway.

Bohemia *bō-hee'mee-a*, ČECHY *che'KHi* (Czech), BÖHMEN *bu'men* (Ger), historic prov of W Czechoslovakia, bounded E by the historic prov of Moravia, W and S by W Germany and Austria and N by E Germany and Poland; natural boundaries include the Erzgebirge (N), Bohemian Forest (SW) and the Sudetes Mts (NE); chief rivers include the Elbe (Labe), Vltava (Moldau), Ohre (Eger), Jihlava and Jizera; major towns include Praha (Prague), Ceské Budějovice, Plzeň and Ústí nad Labem; under Hapsburg rule from the early 16th century until 1918; after World War II it became a prov of Czechoslovakia, but in 1949 it was divided into a number of administrative units which later (1968) became part of the Czech Socialist Republic of W Czechoslovakia.

Bohemian Forest, mountain range in W Germany and Czechoslovakia. See Böhmerwald.

Bohinjsko Jezero *bo'hint-sko*, BOHINJ *bo'hin-ya* (Eng), lake and resort area in NW Slovenija republic, Yugoslavia; situated 56 km NW of Ljubljana, surrounded by mountains of the Julian Alps; winter sports on Mt Vogel which has snow until April.

Böhmerwald *bœ'mer-valt*, BOHEMIAN FOREST (Eng), ČESKÝ LES (Czech), forested mountain range along the boundary between Bayern (Bavaria) prov, W Germany and Bohemia, W Czechoslovakia; the main range is split into a low NW section, a higher SE massif, and a parallel S subsidiary range, the Bayerische Wald (Bavarian Forest); the highest peak on the German side of the frontier is Grosser Arber (Great Arber) (1,457 m); Bayern, Vltava, Regen and Ilz rivers rise here.

Bohol *bō-hol'*, island in Visayas group, S central Philippines; separated from Mindanao (S) by Bohol Strait; Cebu I lies W and Leyte I NE; area 4,116 sq km; chief town Tagbilaran.

Bohol Sea *bō-hol*, sea of the Philippine Is; bounded S by Mindanao I, N by Bohol I, NW by Negros and Cebu islands, NE by Leyte and W by the Sulu Sea; linked to the Philippine Sea by the Surigao Straits; main islands: Camiguin and Siquijor.

Bohumin *bo'hoo-meen*, NOVY BOHUMIN, 49 55N 18 20E, pop(1984) 25,268, town in Severomoravský region, Czech Socialist Republic, central Czechoslovakia; on R Odra, NNE of Ostrava, near the Polish frontier; railway; economy: oil, iron, chemicals.

Boise *boy'zee*, 43 37N 116 13W, pop(1980) 102,451, capital of state in Ada county, SW Idaho, United States; on the R Boise; railway; airfield; largest city in the state; economy: trade and transportation centre; food processing and light manufacturing; monuments: Old Idaho Penitentiary, Idaho State museum.

Bokaro Steel City *bō-kah'rō*, 23 46N 85 55E, pop(1981) 261,000, city in Bihar, E India; linked E to Dhanbad by rail; Bokaro reservoir lies to the W; surrounded by coalfields; the city's economy is based on steel production.

Boké *bō-kay'*, 10 56N 14 17W, town in W Guinea, W Africa; 60 km NNW of Conakry; railway; economy: bauxite mining.

Boksburg, 26 13S 28 15E, pop(1980) 150,287, city in Transvaal prov, South Africa; 21 km SE of Johannesburg; centre of the E Rand gold mining area; coal was discovered here in 1887; railway; economy: electrical equipment, freight cars, soap, fruit canning, gold mining.

Bol, 13 27N 14 40E, capital of Lac prefecture, W Chad, N central Africa; on the E shore of L Chad.

Bola'ma, 11 35N 15 30W, seaport in Bolama-Bijagos

region, Guinea-Bissau, W Africa; on Bolama Island in the Bijagos archipelago 32 km SSE of Bissau; temporarily occupied by the British in the 18th century; capital of the former Portuguese Guinea until 1941 when Bissau became capital.

Bolama-Bijagos *bō-la'ma-bee-zhu-gosh'*, region in SW Guinea-Bissau, W Africa; pop(1979) 25,473.

Bolan Pass, Pakistan. See Quetta.

Bole *bō'lay*, 9 03N 2 23W, town in Northern region, NW central Ghana, W Africa; situated between Sunyani and Wa, close to the Ivory Coast border.

Bolgatanga *bōl-ga-tang'ga*, 10 44N 0 53W, pop(1982) 47,858, capital of Upper region, N Ghana, W Africa; 150 km N of Tamale, between Tamale and Ouagadougou (Burkina); economy: civil engineering.

Bol'ingbrook, 41 02N 88 01W, pop(1980) 37,261, town in Will county, NE Illinois, United States; 40 km SW of Chicago.

Bolívar *bo-lee'var*, dept in NW Colombia, South America; bounded N by the Caribbean sea and E by the Río Magdalena whose affluents, the San Jorge, Cauca and Sinú rivers, water the alluvial forested lowlands and savannahs; pop(1985) 1,199,437; area 25,978 sq km; capital Cartagena.

Bolívar, mountainous prov in the Andean Sierra of central Ecuador; bordered by Chimborazo prov (E) and by the Cordillera de Guaranda (W); watered by the Río Chimbo; pop(1982) 152,101; area 4,105 sq km; capital Guaranda; economy: sheep and cattle raising, timber.

Bolívar, state in SE Venezuela; bordered E by Guyana, S along the Sierra Pacaraima by Brazil and N by the Orinoco river; watered by Caroni, Paragua and Caura rivers, tributaries of the Orinoco; largely covered by the Guiana Highlands; in the N of the state is the Guri dam and hydroelectric plant; in the centre of the state is the Angel Falls, the world's highest waterfall; pop(1980) 666,362; area 237,908 sq km; capital Ciudad Bolívar.

Bolívar, Ciudad, 8 08N 63 23W, pop(1981) 182,941, capital of Bolívar state, SE Venezuela; on Orinoco river; the river's narrows gave the town its former name of Angostura; it was here that a physician invented Angostura bitters in 1824, the factory moved to Port of Spain in 1875; Bolívar came here after defeat to reorganize his forces and was joined by British legionnaires; it was in this town that he was declared President of Gran Colombia (Colombia, Ecuador and Venezuela); in return for British aid in the battle of Carabobo, Bolívar granted British forces the right to march through any city in Gran Colombia; university; airfield; economy: trading in beans, skins, gold and diamonds; monument: on a hill in the centre of the town is the Zanuro hill fort (1902).

Bolívar, Pico, Andean peak in Mérida state, W Venezuela; 13 km ESE of Mérida; at 5,007 m it is the highest peak of the Cordillera de Mérida and of Venezuela; crowned with a bust of Bolívar.

Bolivia *bo-liv'ee-a*, official name Republic of Bolivia, REPÚBLICA DE BOLIVIA, a republic of W central S America; bounded N and E by Brazil, W by Peru, SW by Chile, S by Argentina and SE by Paraguay; timezone GMT −4; area 1,098,580 sq km; capital (govt) La Paz; legal and judicial capital Sucre; pop(1983e) 6,081,722; the pop comprises 30% Quechua Indian, 25% Ayamará Indian, 25-30% mixed and 5-15% European; in 1940 a Jewish settlement was established E of La Paz and recently Japanese families have settled in Santa Cruz; Quechua, Ayamará and Spanish are official languages; 95% are Roman Catholic; national holiday 6 Aug (Independence Day); the currency is the peso boliviano of 100 centavos; membership of FAO, G-77, IADB, IAEA, IATP, IBRD, ICAO, ICO, IDA, IDB, IFAD, IFC, ILO, IMF, INTELSAT, INTERPOL, ISO, ITC, ITU, LAIA, NAM, OAS, PAHO, SELA, UN, UNESCO, UPU, WHO, WMO, WTO.

Physical description. The land-locked republic of Bolivia is bounded to the W by the Cordillera Occidental of the Andes which rises to 6,542 m at Sajama, the country's highest volcanic peak. This range is separated from the Cordillera Real to the E by the flat, 400 km long Altiplano plateau which lies 3,600 m above sea-level. The two major lakes in this region are L Titicaca and L Poopó. The Altiplano, which was the centre of early Indian culture, is the most densely populated part of the country. E of the Cordillera Real the Oriente foothills descend SE into the dry, scrub-covered Chaco and NE into dense tropical forest. Several rivers including the Beni, Itonomas and Paraguá flow down from the Andes to meet the Río Guaporé where it follows the frontier with Brazil.

History, government and constitution. From the early 16th century Spanish imperial interests centred around the mineral wealth of the Altiplano and in particular the silver mines of Potosí. The independence movement resulted in the liberation of Bolivia by General Sucre in 1825 and in the following year a constitution was established. As a result of war with her neighbours territory was lost to Chile (1879-84), Brazil (1903) and Paraguay (1935). Bolivia has a bicameral legislature or Congress comprising a Senate of 27 members (3 from each dept) and a Chamber of Deputies with 117 members elected for 4 years. The president appoints a cabinet of 15 ministers. Since 1966 there have been over a dozen changes of government in Bolivia.

Economy. Bolivia is still largely dependent on minerals for its foreign exchange. Although silver is largely exhausted it has been replaced by tin, tungsten, antimony, lead and gold. One-fifth of the world's tin has been supplied by Bolivia. The country is self-sufficient in petroleum and gas with pipelines to Argentina and Chile. Bolivia's main trading partners are Argentina, Brazil, the USA, the UK, and Japan.

Agriculture. Although Bolivia imports large quantities of grain the country is self-sufficient in sugar, rice and cotton which have recently been grown in the less developed Oriente (E) regions. Since 1952 land reform has divided most of the larger estates, chiefly in the Altiplano where potatoes, cereals, cotton, and livestock are the main products. Resettlement programmes have located many Altiplano families in the tropical Oriente.

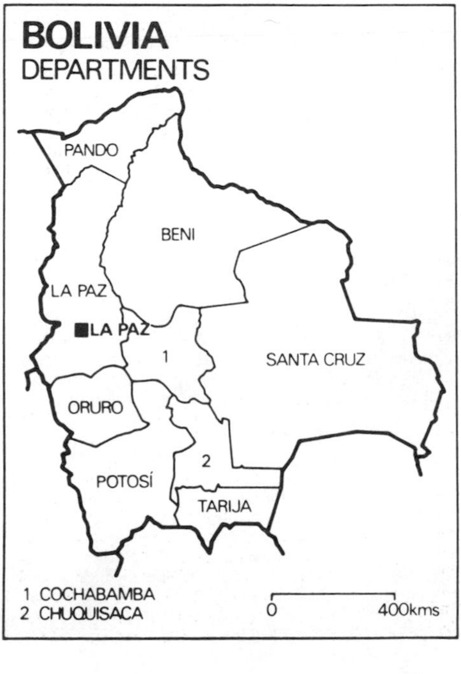

Illegally-produced cocaine is also a major source of income from agricultural land.
Administrative divisions. Bolivia is divided into 9 departments as follows:

Department	*area (sq km)*	*pop(1982)*
Beni	213,564	217,700
Chuquisaca	51,524	435,406
Cochabamba	55,631	908,674
La Paz	133,985	1,913,184
Oruro	53,588	385,121
Pando	63,827	42,594
Potosí	118,218	823,485
Santa Cruz	370,621	942,986
Tarija	37,623	246,691

Bolligen *bo'lig-un*, 46 59N 7 30E, pop(1980) 32,312, town in Bern canton, Switzerland.

Bologna *bo-lōn'ya*, agricultural prov of Emilia-Romagna region, N Italy; pop(1981) 930,284; area 3,701 sq km; capital Bologna.

Bologna, 44 30N 11 20E, pop(1981) 459,080, capital city of Bologna prov, Emilia-Romagna region, N Italy; 83 km N of Firenze (Florence), on a fertile plain at the foot of the Apennines; one of the most ancient cities of Italy, enclosed by the remains of its 8 km circuit of 13-14th-c walls; archbishopric; late 12th-c university, one of the 2 prototypal universities of Europe, founded from the early law school; airport (7 km NE at Borgo Panigale); rail junction; economy: manufacture of pasta and sausages (mortadella), shoes, chemicals, engineering, precision instruments, and publishing; monuments: church of San Petronio (begun 1390); church of San Domenico (begun 1235) containing the tomb of the saint for whom it is named; 2 leaning towers, originally built for defensive purposes in the 12th century - the Asinelli has a height of 97.6 m and leans 1.23 m from the vertical, and the Garisenda is 48 m high and is 3.22 m aslant; the Pinacoteca Nazionale has some of the best works of Bolognese painters of the 15-19th centuries.

Bol'shoy Kavkaz, GREATER CAUCASUS, mountain range in SW European Rossiyskaya, and Gruziya and Azerbaydzhan republics, Soviet Union. See Kavkaz.

Bolsover *bol'zo-ver*, 53 14N 1 18W, pop(1981) 11,540, town in Bolsover dist, Derbyshire, central England; 9 km SE of Chesterfield.

Bolton *bōl'ton*, formerly BOLTON-LE-MOORS, 53 35N 2 26W, pop(1981) 143,921, town in Bolton borough, Greater Manchester, NW England; 18 km NW of Manchester; centre of the wool industry until the 18th century when it became an important cotton centre; railway; economy: engineering, textiles, paper, chemicals; monuments: textile machinery museum containing inventions that revolutionized the cotton industry, including Crompton's mule, Hargreaves's jenny and Arkwright's water-frame; Hall i' th' Wood local history museum.

Bolu *bo-loo'*, maritime prov in N Turkey, bounded N by the Black Sea; pop(1980) 471,751; area 11,051 sq km; capital Bolu; economy: opium, flax, cereals, tobacco.

Bolzano *bol-tsa'no*, BOZEN *bō'tsen* (Ger), prov of Trentino-Alto Adige region, N Italy; pop(1981) 430,568; area 7,400 sq km; capital Bolzano.

Bolzano, 46 30N 11 20E, pop(1981) 105,180, capital town of Bolzano prov, Trentino-Alto Adige region, N Italy; on R Isarco, SSW of the Brenner Pass; chief commercial, industrial, and tourist centre of the region; the people are mainly German-speaking; winter sports; economy: steel production, textiles, distilling, wine, canning, pianos, tourism.

Bomaderry, Australia. See Nowra-Bomaderry.

Bomba'li, dist in Northern prov, Sierra Leone, W Africa; pop(1974) 233,626; area 7,985 sq km; capital Makeni.

Bombay', 18 55N 72 50E, pop(1981) 8,227,000, port capital of Maharashtra, W India; largest city of India; has W India's only natural deep-water harbour; geologically a part of peninsular India, which is thought to be the oldest part of the sub-continent; Bombay was originally a cluster of 7 islands called Heptanasia by Ptolemy (150 AD); ceded to Portugal as a mission centre and trading post in 1534 by the Sultan of Gujarat; ceded to Britain in 1661 in a marriage treaty between Charles II and Infanta Catherine of Portugal; headquarters of the East India Company (1685-1708); the name Bombay is derived from Mumbadevi, patron goddess of the Koli fisherfolk; the city expanded with the development of the cotton industry and the railway system during the 1860s; 2 universities (1916, 1957); airport; linked by rail to Ahmadabad and Pune; economy: textiles, carpets, machinery, chemicals, petroleum refining; a nuclear reactor is located at Trombay; monuments: the Afghan church (1847) is dedicated to those British soldiers killed during the Sind and Afghan campaigns; the Gateway of India, a stone archway designed in the Gujarat style of the 16th-c and built to commemorate the visit to India in 1911 of King George V and Queen Mary; Mani Bhavan (Gandhi Memorial); Raudat Tahera, a marble mosque and mausoleum with 4 silver doors; Victoria and Albert Museum.

Bonaire *bon-ayr'*, island of the S Netherlands Antilles, Windward Is, E Caribbean, 60 km N of Venezuela; composed of coralline limestone fringing an igneous core; rises to 241 m in the hilly NW; there is a low lying coastal plain in the S; area 288 sq km; length 35 km; pop(1981) 8,753; capital Kralendijk; airport; economy: tourism, salt mining, textiles; the Washington-Slagbaai National Park, established in 1969, covers an area of 59 sq km; there is also an underwater park (60 sq km).

Bondi *bon'dī*, a well-known resort beach in the Sydney suburb of Waverley, New South Wales, SE Australia.

Bondoukou *bon-doo'koo*, dept in E Ivory Coast, W Africa; pop(1975) 296,551; area 16,530 sq km; bounded W by the R Komoé and SE by the R Ba; capital Bondoukou; chief towns Bandoli, Saleye and Tanda; economy: cocoa.

Bo'ness *bō-ness'*, BORROWSTOUNNESS (anc), 56 01N 3 37W, pop(1981) 14,641, town in Falkirk dist, Central region, central Scotland; on the S shore of the Firth of Forth, 26 km WNW of Edinburgh; economy: timber, engineering; monuments: Bo'ness museum; Kinneil Roman Fortlet; Kinneil House, to the W of Bo'ness, was the seat of the Dukes of Hamilton in the 16-17th centuries and was also where James Watt developed his invention of the steam engine; Bo'ness and Kinneil Railway is a working steam railway system.

Bongor *bon-gor'*, 10 18N 15 20E, capital of Mayo-Kebbi prefecture, SW Chad, N central Africa; on the R Logone where it follows the Cameroon frontier, 210 km S of N'Djamena; founded in 1910 by Germans; airfield.

Bongos, Massif des *bong'gō*, mountainous massif in Central African Republic; the main peaks are Mt Tousoro (1,330 m) and Mt Koudo (1,310 m).

Bonin Islands, group of volcanic islands in the W Pacific Ocean. See Ogasawara-shotō.

Bonn, 50 43N 7 06E, pop(1983) 292,900, capital city of W Germany, in Köln dist, S Nordrhein-Westfalen (North Rhine-Westphalia) prov; on the R Rhine, 25 km SSE of Köln (Cologne); founded as one of the earliest Roman forts on the Rhine; since the incorporation of Bad Godesberg into the city, it has possessed a renowned spa resort within its boundaries; capital of W Germany since 1945; birthplace of Beethoven; university (1818); railway; economy: plastics, packaging materials, aluminium; monument: 11-13th-c Minster; event: International Beethoven Festival every 3 years in Sept.

Bonny, 4 25N 7 10E, town with tanker terminal facilities, Rivers state, S Nigeria, W Africa; on the Gulf of Guinea, S of Port Harcourt.

Bonnyrigg, 55 52N 3 07W, pop(1981) 14,399, town in Midlothian dist, Lothian, E central Scotland; 9.5 km SE of Edinburgh and 3 km SW of Dalkeith; economy: food, engineering.

Bonthe *bon'tee*, island dist in Southern prov, Sierra Leone, W Africa; pop(1974) 80,606; area 3,458 sq km; capital Bonthe.

Bonthe, 7 32N 12 30S, capital of dist of same name, Southern prov, Sierra Leone, W Africa; on E coast of Sherbro Island, 137 km SE of Freetown; airfield.

Bootle, 53 28N 3 00W, pop(1981) 70,610, seaport in Liverpool borough, Merseyside, NW England; N of the R Mersey; extensive docks; railway; economy: tin, tanning, engineering and the export of timber.

Bophuthatswana *bo-poo-tats-wah'na*, locally BOP, independent black homeland in South Africa; pop(1984e) 1,667,478; area 44,000 sq km; comprises 7 separate units of land in Cape, Orange Free State and Transvaal provs, close to the frontier with Botswana; granted self-government in 1971 and independence in 1977 by South Africa; independent status not recognized internationally; main languages are English, Afrikaans and Setswana; over 368,000 people are commuters or migrant workers in South Africa; economy: brewing, tanning, furniture, maize, beef; major platinum mines at Rustenberg, Western and Impala mines account for about a third of world production of platinum group metals; other important metals include copper, nickel, gold, chromium (Rustenberg and Marico), vanadium (Brits), asbestos, iron ore, diamonds, limestone, manganese and fluorspar; generates the largest national income of the 4 'independent' homelands.

Boquerón *bo-kay-rōn'*, dept in Occidental region, W Paraguay; bordered W by Bolivia, SW and S by Argentina along the Río Pilcomayo; in the NW half of the dept is part of the Gran Chaco plain; low grasslands are in the SE; pop(1982) 14,685; area 44,000 sq km; capital Pedro P. Peña.

Boquerón Abad *bō-kay-rōn' a-badh'*, narrow gorge on Huánuco-Loreto dept border, N central Peru; situated in the Cordillera Azul, the gateway to the Amazon river basin; the trans-Andean highway passes through it; sometimes called Boquerón Padre Abad.

Bor, 44 05N 22 06E, pop(1981) 56,486, town in E Srbija (Serbia) republic, Yugoslavia; 25 km NNW of Zajecar; railway; economy: major copper-mining centre.

Bora-Bora, small island in Îles sous le Vent (Leeward Is) group of the Archipel de la Société (Society Is), French Polynesia, S Pacific Ocean; pop(1977) 2,572; area 36 sq km.

Borås *boo-raws'*, 57 44N 12 55E, pop(1982) 100,759, industrial town in Älvsborg county, SW Sweden; 56 km E of Göteborg (Gothenburg); founded in 1632 by Gustavus Adolphus; railway; economy: textile mills, several large mail-order businesses.

Bordeaux *bor-dō*, BURDIGALA (Lat), 44 50N 0 36W, pop(1982) 211,197, inland port and capital of Gironde dept, Aquitaine, SW France; on the R Garonne; one of the chief ports of France as well as being the cultural and commercial centre for the whole SW region; 480 km SW of Paris and 100 km from the Atlantic; held by the English for 300 years; temporary seat of government in 1870, 1914 and 1940; the city is notably well laid out, its spaciousness dating from the extensive building in the 18th century, when prosperity followed the establishment of the colonial empire; industrial site with deep water quays on the right bank of the Garonne; the famous Bordeaux wines are produced in the region of the town; to the N is the Médoc (Châteaux Lafite, Latour, Margaux); to the S the Graves and Sauternes; between Garonne and Dordogne rivers is the Entre-deux-Mers; archbishopric; university (1441); railway; Mérignac international airport; economy: shipbuilding, chemicals, wine trade, oil-refining, fishing; monuments: in the centre of town, the church of St Seurin (12-15th-c); Grand Theatre (1773-80); 486 m long Pont de Pierre (1813-21).

Borders, region in SE Scotland; bounded N by Lothian region, NE by the North Sea, W by Strathclyde region, SW by Dumfries and Galloway and SE by England, partly along the Cheviot Hills and the R Tweed; crossed E-W by the Southern Uplands; drained by the Tweed, Teviot, Jed Water, Yarrow Water, Whiteadder Water and Ettrick Water; pop(1981) 99,784; area 4,672 sq km; capital Newtown St Boswells; major towns include Hawick, Peebles and Galashiels; economy: livestock, forestry, textiles; the Borders region is divided into 4 districts:

District	*area (sq km)*	*pop(1981)*
Berwickshire	876	18,270
Ettrick-Lauderdale	1,356	31,725
Roxburgh	1,540	35,277
Tweeddale	899	14,512

Borehamwood *bōr'am-wood*, 51 40N 0 15W, pop(1981) 28,397, town just outside Greater London urban area, in Hertsmere dist, Hertfordshire, SE England; 4 km N of Edgware; centre of the film industry; railway.

Borge *borg*, 68 15N 13 50E, pop(1980) 10,873, town in Østfold county, SE Norway; on R Glåma, SE of Oslo; railway junction; former meeting place of the law-making Borgarthing; the explorer Amundsen was born in the village of Vedsten near here; economy: timber, paper, electrical equipment, chemicals, hydroelectricity.

Børgefjell *bur'yu-fyel*, mountain range in S Nordland county, N central Norway, S of the Vefsna river valley, near the Swedish border; rises to 1,703 m at Kvigtind peak, 72 km SSE of Mosjøen; contains the Børgefjell National Park which covers 1,000 sq km.

Borgerhout *bor'gur-howt*, 51 13N 4 27E, pop(1982) 43,556, town in Antwerpen dist, Antwerpen prov, Belgium; an E suburb of Antwerpen.

Borgo Maggiore *bor'go mag-yor'e*, castle (dist) in the Republic of San Marino, central Italy; pop(1980) 3,939; economy: pottery.

Borgou *bor'goo*, prov in NE Benin, W Africa; the R Alibori flows NE across the prov to join the R Niger on the NE border; chief towns Parakou, Kandi, Nikki; the Benin sector of the W National Park is located in the N; a railway linking Niamey (Niger) to the coast runs N-S through the prov; economy: iron ore mining.

Borkou-Ennedi-Tibesti *bor-koo-ee-ne-di-tee-bes'tee*, prefecture in N Chad, N central Africa; pop(1979) 88,000; area 600,350 sq km; the Tibesti mountains rise in the N to the highest peak in Chad -- Emi Koussi 3,415 m; there are extensive seasonal floodplains in SW and N; the Plateau de Basso lies in the SE; capital Faya; chief towns Zouar, Oum Chaloumba, Nédédlèy, Aozou, Faya Largeau, Fada and Bardai; remained under French military administration until 1965; the territory known as the Aozou Strip in the N has been claimed by Libya since 1969 and was occupied in 1973; economy: livestock, uranium.

Borkum *bor'koom*, 53 35N 6 40E, westernmost German North Sea island of Ostfriesische Inseln (East Frisian Is), at the mouth of the R Ems, 42 km NW of Emden; Nordseebad Borkum is a popular tourist resort; area 30.7 sq km.

Borlänge *boor'leng-u*, 60 29N 15 25E, pop(1982) 46,763, town in Kopparberg county, central Sweden; 192 km NW of Stockholm; railway; economy: steel and iron.

Borneo *bor'nee-ō*, island in SE Asia, E of Sumatera, N of Jawa and W of Sulawesi; 3rd largest island in the world; comprises the Malaysian states of Sarawak and Sabah and the former British protectorate of Brunei in the N; the remainder of the island comprises the 4 provs of Kalimantan which form part of Indonesia; formerly divided between the British and the Dutch; area 484,330 sq km; mountainous in the N rising to 4,094 m at Mt Kinabalu in Sabah; the interior is densely forested; economy: rice, pepper, copra, tobacco, oil, bauxite, iron.

Bornes, Serra de *bor'nish*, mountain range E of Mirandela, NE Portugal, between R Tua and R Sabor, rising to 1,202 m.

Born'holm, Danish island in Baltic Sea, 40 km S of Sweden, 168 km ESE of København (Copenhagen); pop(1983) 47,313; area 588 sq km; length 37 km; rises to 162 m; constitutes a county of Denmark; economy: fishing, fish-processing, farming, tourism; taken by Sweden in 1645 and returned to Denmark in 1660; administrative capital and chief port is Rønne, situated on W coast; N and central area are of granite.

Bor'no, state in NE Nigeria, W Africa; pop(1982e) 4,780,000; area 116,400 sq km; the W edge of L Chad lies in the NE corner of the state; capital Maiduguri; chief towns Biu, Dikwa, Gwoza, Nguru, Geidam, Gashua, Monguno, Potiskum and Bama; about 75% of the pop is engaged in agriculture, chiefly cattle raising in the W and N and rice growing in the E where there are irrigation schemes at Gjibo and Yedseram; there are polder drainage projects on the shore of L Chad at Kirenowa and Baga; economy: fisheries, gum arabic, groundnut processing, leather tanning, confectionery and soap.

Boromo *bo-rō'mō*, 11 47N 2 54W, town in NW Burkina, W Africa; between Ouagadougou and Bobo Dioulasso.

Bo'rovets, 42 18N 23 34E, ski resort in the Rila Planina (Rila Mts), Sofiya okrug (prov), W Bulgaria; at the foot of Mt Moussala, 70 km SE of Sofiya; alt 1,300 m.

Borsa *bor'sha*, 47 39N 24 40E, pop(1983) 27,539, resort town in Maramureş county, N Romania; on W slopes of the Carpathian Mts; railway; economy: tourism, timber.

Borsod-Abaúj-Zemplén *bor'shod-o'bo-we-zem'playn*, county in NE Hungary; pop(1984e) 801,000; area 7,248 sq km; three separate counties until 1950; capital Miskolc; chief towns include Sátoraljaujhely; 45% of the population reside in Miskolc and 6 other towns; 33% of arable land is state owned, 65% cooperative and 1% private; national park at Bükk Mt; new towns built at Kazincarcika and Leninváros; spas at Mezokovesd, Sarospatak, Miskolctapolca and Lillafüred; economy: mining, steel, nitrogen fertilizer, PVC powder, ethylene, chemicals, petrochemicals, refining, wine (Tokay); minerals: coal, iron ore.

Borūjerd *bō-roo-jerd'*, 33 55N 48 50E, pop(1983) 177,524, town in Borūjerd dist, Lorestān, W Iran, surrounded by mountains.

Bosanska Gradiška or **Gradiška** *bo'san-ska gra'dish-ka*, formerly BERBIR, 45 09N 17 15E, pop(1981) 58,095, town in N Bosna-Hercegovina republic, Yugoslavia; on R Sava, 40 km N of Banja Luka.

Bosanska Krupa or **Krupa** *kroo'pa*, 44 53N 16 10E, pop(1981) 55,229, town in NW Bosna-Hercegovina republic, Yugoslavia; on R Una; railway; economy: timber, bauxite.

Bosna-Hercegovina *bos'na-her-tse-go-vee'na*, BOSNIA AND HERZEGOVINA (Eng), a constituent republic of central Yugoslavia; pop(1981) 4,124,256; area 51,129 sq km; capital Sarajevo; chief towns include Banja Luka, Zenica, Tuzla and Mostar; the region became an Austrian protectorate in 1878 and was eventually annexed by Austria in 1908; in 1918 the two provs were allotted to Yugoslavia; a mountainous region including part of the Dinaric Alps, it is noted for its limestone gorges.

Bosnia and Herzegovina, republic of Yugoslavia. See Bosna-Hercegovina.

Bosporus, strait in NW Turkey. See Karadeniz Boğazi.

Bosques Petrificados *bos'kays pet-ree-fee-ka'THōs*, PETRIFIED FORESTS (Eng), natural monument in E Santa Cruz prov, Patagonia, Argentina; area 100 sq km; established in 1954; contains 70,000 year-old araucaria trees, averaging 3 m in circumference and 15-20 m in height.

Bossangoa *bo-san-gō-a'*, 6 27N 17 21E, chief town in Ouham prefecture, N Central African Republic; on the R Ouham, 274 km NW of Bangui.

Bossier City *bō'zher*, 32 31N 93 44W, pop(1980) 50,817, town in Bossier parish, NW Louisiana, United States; on the Red river, opposite Shreveport; railway; Barksdale Air Force Base.

Boston, 52 59N 0 01W, pop(1981) 34,453, port town in Boston dist, Lincolnshire, E central England; on the R Witham, 45 km SE of Lincoln, in fertile wheat-growing fens; railway; economy: light engineering.

Boston, 42 22N 71 04W, pop(1980) 562,994, capital of state in Suffolk county, E Massachusetts, United States; on Massachusetts Bay, at the mouth of the Charles river; settled in 1630 and made capital of the Massachusetts Bay Colony in 1632; achieved city status in 1822; a centre of opposition to British trade restrictions and scene of the Boston Tea Party (Dec 1773); centre of the Unitarian church movement; noted for its colleges and universities (1869, 1898, 1906); Conservatory of Music; railway; airport; economy: commerce, finance, electronics, printing and publishing; historic sites: Boston Tea Party ship and museum, Christ Church (1723), Paul Revere's house, Faneuil Hall (1742); museum of fine art; event: Boston Marathon run on Patriot's Day, April.

Bosumtwi *bō-soom'twee*, 6 32N 1 20W, lake in S Ashanti region, S central Ghana, W Africa; the only natural lake in Ghana; situated in an 8 km-wide basin with no surface outlet; area 48 sq km; average depth 70 m.

Botany Bay, a shallow inlet 8 km S of Sydney, New South Wales, Australia; ringed by residential suburbs of Sydney; Captain Cook made his first landing here in 1770, naming the bay after the number of new plants discovered by Sir Joseph Banks, his botanist; the site was chosen as a penal settlement in 1787, but on arrival it was found to be unsuitable and a location at Sydney Cove (on which arose Sydney) was chosen; the name Botany Bay, however, was for many years synonymous with Australian convict settlements.

Botev *bot'ef*, formerly YUMRUKCHAL (-1950), 42 43N 24 55E, highest peak of the Stara Planina (Balkan Mts) of N central Bulgaria, SW Romania and E Yugoslavia; height 2,376 m.

Botevgrad *bo'tef-grat*, formerly ORKHANIYE (-1934), 42 55N 23 47E, pop(1981e) 20,000, city in Sofiya okrug (prov), W central Bulgaria; in the Botevgrad valley NE of Sofiya; economy: agriculture and woodwork.

Bothnia, Gulf of *both'nee-ah*, N arm of the Baltic, between Sweden and Finland; bounded to the S by the Åland Is; length 644 km; width 80-241 km; max depth 100 m; islets and sandbars impede navigation; surface waters of low salinity; generally freezes over in winter.

Botoşani *bō-tō shan'*, county in NE Romania, to the E of the E Carpathian Mts, on the Ukrainian frontier; pop(1983) 459,268; area 4,965 sq km; capital Botoşani.

Botoşani, 47 44N 26 41E, pop(1983) 94,536, capital of Botoşani county, NE Romania; established in the 14th century; railway; economy: grain and livestock trade; clothes, paper, brewing; 15th-c monastery with frescoes.

Botrange *bōt rãzh'*, 50 30N 6 05E, mountain in the Hohe Venn (N section of the Ardennes), E Liège prov, Belgium; 8 km NNE of Malmédy; the highest mountain in Belgium; height 694 m.

Botswa'na, official name Republic of Botswana, S African republic bounded S by South Africa, W and N by Namibia and E by Zimbabwe; timezone GMT +2; area 582,096 sq km; pop(1981) 941,027; capital Gaborone; chief towns Francistown, Lobatse, Selebi-Phikwe, Orapa and Jwaneng; the majority of the pop is Tswana (94%) with a few Bushman (5%) and Europeans (1%); 20% are Christian, the remainder following local beliefs; the official language is English but the national language is Setswana; the unit of currency (since 1976) is the pula of 100 thebes; national holiday 30 Sept (Independence Day); membership of AfDB, the Commonwealth, FAO, G-77, GATT (de facto), IBRD, ICAO, IDA, IFAD, IFC, ILO, IMF, INTERPOL, ITU, NAM, OAU, SADCC, UN, UNESCO, UPU, WHO, WMO.

Physical description. Botswana is a landlocked, undulating sand-filled plateau with a mean elevation of about 1,000 m. The majority of the people live in the fertile E area which is bordered E by the R Limpopo. To the W of this area the environment changes progressively through dry scrubland and savannah to the sand-covered Kalahari Desert which only receives water during the wet season. What little water there is drains into natural hollows or pans where swamps develop during the rainy season, drying out to salt pans in the heat of the dry season. In the Ngamiland and Chobe dists (NW) conditions are in complete contrast, with a varied fauna and flora associated with the rich Okavango river delta. To the E of the delta are the Makgadikgadi salt pans which are occasionally flooded by the Okavango delta.

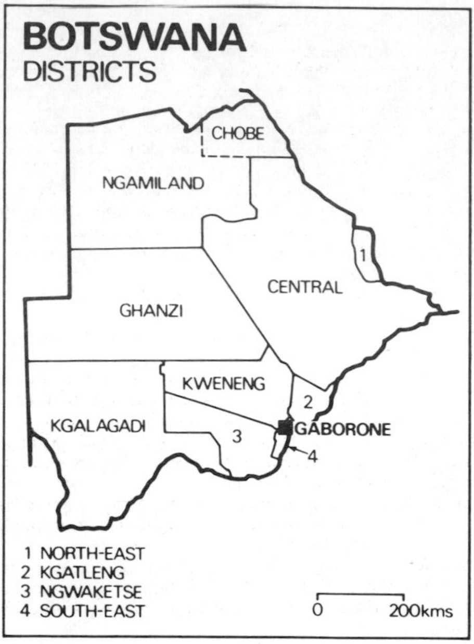

Deciduous forest is found in the extreme N and NW where momgongo, baobab, mophane and morula are the most notable tree species.

Climate. Botswana has a largely sub-tropical climate but in the S and W conditions become more arid. In the N and E rainfall is higher and falls almost totally during the summer months (Oct-April). Francistown (alt 1,004 m) is representative of this region with an annual average rainfall of 450 mm and average max daily temperatures ranging between 23°C and 32°C. The remainder of the country is mainly desert or scrubland and is, in large part, comprised of the Kalahari Desert. Annual rainfall is erratic, decreasing S and W to below 200 mm. In winter, nights can be cold with occasional frost.

History, government and constitution. During the 19th century the area now known as Botswana was visited by Robert Moffat and later by his son-in-law, David Livingstone, who established a mission amongst the nomadic herdsmen and the Bechuana farmers, remaining there until the 1850s. Under threat of settlement by South African Boers from the Transvaal prov, the territory came under British protection in 1885. The S part of this territory became a Crown Colony and subsequently part of the Cape Colony (now part of Cape prov, South Africa). The remaining N section continued under British administration as the Bechuanaland Protectorate. While the constitution of the Union of South Africa (1909) was being drafted the local inhabitants of Bechuanaland, Basutoland (now Lesotho) and Swaziland all declared their wish not to be part of the Union. In 1920 the British created 2 advisory councils, one for Africans and the other for Europeans and in 1938 tribal treasuries were established for local chiefs. Following the Constitution of 1961 self-government was achieved in 1964 and in the following year the seat of government was moved from Mafeking to Gabarone. In 1966, after a general election, the Bechuanaland Protectorate became the independent Republic of Botswana and a sovereign member of the Commonwealth. The country is governed by a legislative National Assembly comprising 32 elected, 4 nominated and 2 ex-officio members. A president appoints a cabinet of about 15 members.

Economy. More than 80% of the pop is dependent on subsistence farming which is largely based on the rearing of livestock. Annual production is varied, being highly susceptible to drought and disease (1977-78 outbreak of foot-and-mouth disease). In addition unfenced land makes breeding control and pasture improvement difficult. Much of the meat produced is sold to the Botswana Meat Commission in Lobatse which has the country's only abattoir. Crop-growing is relatively unimportant, but the main subsistence crop is drought-resistant sorghum which is grown in addition to maize, millet, beans and cowbeans. The main cash crops include cotton, groundnuts and sunflower seeds. The Botswana Agricultural Marketing Board, established in 1974, has done much to improve the arable situation by setting annual guaranteed fixed prices. Mineral extraction has been of major importance to the economy since the 1970s, Botswana being the 2nd largest producer of nickel in Africa, 3rd largest producer of diamond and 4th largest producer of cobalt. By 1981 the country's diamond production represented 13% of the world total. It was in 1967 that the Orapa was located (the world's second largest diamond pipe). There are also mines at Lethlakane and Jwaneng. Copper-nickel matte which is mined at Selebi-Phikwe is also important, the USA buying the entire 1981 production for refining in Louisiana. Coal is mined at Morupule and substantial reserves of brine exist in the Sua Pan (part of the Makgadikgadi Pans in Central district). Other mineral reserves include asbestos, talc, manganese, gypsum, gold, chromium, silver and platinum-group metals. Manufacturing industry, which has only developed significantly in recent years, is dominated by livestock processing with products including hides, dairy produce, soap and bonemeal. Botswana's profuse wildlife in areas such as the Gemsbok national park attracts large numbers of tourists. Major trade countries include the EEC, the USA and other African countries.

Administrative divisions. Botswana is divided into 9 districts and 6 independent townships as follows:

District	*area (sq km)*	*pop(1981)*
Central	147,730	323,328
Chobe	5,120	36,636
Ghanzi	117,910	19,096
Kgalagadi	106,940	24,059
Kgatleng	7,960	44,461
Kweneng	35,890	117,127
Ngamiland	129,930	75,997
Ngwaketze	28,470	119,653
South-East	1,780	30,649
Independent township	*area (sq km)*	*pop(1981)*
Gaborone	97	59,657
Francistown	79	31,065
Lobatse	30	19,034
Selebi-Phikwe	50	29,469
Orapa	10	5,229
Jwaneng	100	5,567

Bottom, The, 17 42N 63 26W, capital town of Saba I, N Netherlands Antilles, E Caribbean, 48 km NW of St Kitts; built within an extinct crater.

Bott'rop, 51 31N 6 55E, pop(1983) 113,400, coal-mining and industrial city in Düsseldorf dist, Nordrhein-Westfalen (North Rhine-Westphalia) prov, W Germany, 8 km NNW of Essen; railway.

Bouaflé *bwa'flay*, dept in central Ivory Coast, W Africa; pop(1975) 263,609; area 8,500 sq km; part of Bandama Blanc lake is located in the NE; capital Bouaflé; chief town Sinfra.

Bouaké *bwa'kay*, dept in central Ivory Coast, W Africa; pop(1975) 808,048; area 23,670 sq km; the railway from Abidjan runs N across the dept; capital Bouaké; chief towns Beoumi, Marabadiassa, Fetekro, Sakassou, Tiekissou, Toumodi and Yamoussoukro (capital designate of the Ivory Coast).

Bouaké, 7 42N 5 00W, pop(1975) 173,248, capital of dept

of same name, Ivory Coast, W Africa; 290 km NNW of Abidjan; an old Muslim trading town; railway; airfield; economy: agricultural trade, textiles, clothing.

Bouar *boo-ar'*, 5 58N 15 35E, pop(1981) 51,000; chief town in Nana-Mambéré prefecture, W Central African Republic; 113 km WSW of Bozoum.

Bouba Ndjidah *boo'ba un-jee'da*, national park in Nord prov, N Cameroon, W Africa; area 2,200 sq km; established in 1968; situated on the frontier with Chad; wildlife includes buffalo, elephant, monkey, warthog, rhinoceros, hippopotamus, various antelope and panther; created originally as a forest and hunting reserve in 1947 in order to protect Derby elands and rhinoceros.

Bouches-du-Rhône *boosh-du-rōn*, ('mouths of the Rhône'), maritime dept in Provence-Alpes-Côte d'Azur region of SE France on the Rhône delta and in the angle between the R Rhône (on the W) and the R Durance (on the N), comprising 4 arrond, 47 cantons and 119 communes; pop(1982) 1,724,199; area 5,087 sq km; capital Marseille; several low spurs of the Alpes-Maritimes (eg St Victoire, which was much painted by Cézanne, and Les Alpilles) run E-W; the plain between them and the sea is the stony and arid La Crau which is watered by canals and occasionally planted with fruit trees; the watery plain in the delta is La Camargue, pastureland long associated with wild horses, bulls and the celebrated French 'cowboy', but increasingly being given over to rice fields and vineyards; the Parc de la Camargue regional nature park and reserve caters for naturalists and pony trekking; many coastal lagoons (eg Étang de Berre and Étang de Vaccares) and inland ponds; near Marseille are some islands, on one of which is the famous 16th-c Chateau d'If made famous in Dumas' *Count of Monte Cristo*; the village of Les Baux-de-Provence, on a high spur of Les Alpilles, gave its name to the mineral bauxite which was first discovered nearby in 1822; white coastal limestone used in the construction of the Suez Canal is quarried at Calenque de Port Miou; petrol refineries at Martigues; towns include Arles, Aix-en-Provence and Tarascon.

Boucle de Baoulé *boo'kl dė bow-lay'*, national park in E Kayes region, W Mali, W Africa; area 3,500 sq km; as the name implies it is partly bounded by the R Baoulé; established in 1953.

Boucle de la Pendjari *boo-kl' de la pen-dja'ree*, national park in N Benin, W Africa; as the name implies it is partly bounded by a bend in the R Pendjari which forms part of the N Benin border; area 2,755 sq km; established in 1961.

Bouenza *boo-en'za*, province of S Congo, W Africa; area 12,265 sq km; pop(1980) 161,320; capital N'Kayi.

Bougainville *boo'gan-vil*, 6 12S 155 15E, mountainous volcanic island in N Solomons prov, Papua New Guinea, SW Pacific, 480 km NW of Guadalcanal, length 190 km; width 50 km; rises to 2,743 m at Mt Balbi in the interior of the island; chief port Kieta; economy: copper-mining at Panguna.

Bougouni *boo-goo'nee*, 11 25N 7 28W, pop(1971) 9,300, town in Sikasso region, S Mali, W Africa; 145 km SSE of Bamako; economy: power plant.

Bou-Hed'ma, national park in Tunisia, N Africa; area 162 sq km; established in 1936.

Bouira *bwee'-ra*, department of N Algeria, N Africa; area 4,517 sq km; pop(1982) 421,225.

Boujdour *boozh-door'*, prov in Western Sahara, NW Africa; pop(1982) 8,481; area 100,120 sq km; claimed by Morocco.

Boujdour, 26 08N 14 33W, pop(1982) 3,597, capital of Boujdour prov, Western Sahara, NW Africa.

Boulder, 40 01N 105 17W, pop(1980) 76,685, resort county seat of Boulder county, N central Colorado, United States; in the Rocky Mts, 40 km NW of Denver; founded in 1858; university (1876); mineral springs; railway; economy: aircraft, computers, electronic equipment, chemicals and sporting goods; event: Kinetic Conveyance (May).

Boulogne or **Boulogne-sur-Mer** *boo-lon'y'-sür-mer*, 50 43N 1 37E, pop(1982) 50,000, seaport in Pas-de-Calais dept, Nord-Pas-de-Calais, NW France; on the coast of the English Channel, S of Calais; the principal commercial harbour and fishing port of France; ferry and hovercraft links with Dover and Folkestone.

Boulogne-Billancourt *boo-lon'y'-bee-yâ-koor*, 48 50N 2 14E, pop(1982) 102,595, industrial and residential suburb of Paris in Hauts-de-Seine dept, Ile-de-France region, central France; on the R Seine; formed in 1925 by amalgamating Boulogne-sur-Seine and Billancourt; the former next to the Bois de Boulogne is residential while the latter is industrial; economy: lamps and lighting equipment, PVC compounds, automobiles, agric and forestry machinery, machine tools.

Boulsa *bool-sa'*, 12 41N 0 29W, town in Burkina, W Africa; SE of Kaya.

Bouna *boo'na*, dept in NE Ivory Coast, W Africa; pop(1975) 84,290; area 21,470 sq km; the Black Volta river follows the E frontier with Ghana; Comoé National Park occupies a large area of the dept; capital Bouna; chief towns Sapoutan, Kakpin, Nassian and Bania.

Boundary Peak, 37 51N 119 23W, mountain in W Esmeralda county, SW Nevada, United States; highest peak in Nevada state; height 4,006 m.

Boundia'li, dept in N Ivory Coast, W Africa; pop(1975) 132,278; area 10,095 sq km; the R Bagoé flows N through the dept; capital Boundiali.

Bountiful, 40 53N 111 53W, pop(1980) 32,877, town in Davis county, N Utah, United States; a residential suburb 13 km N of Salt Lake City; railway; settled by Mormons.

Bourbonnais *boor-bon-ay*, former prov of central France, now occupying the dept of Allier and parts of Cher, Puy-de-Dôme and Creuse; the capital was Moulins; formerly a duchy (1327-1523).

Bourge-en-Bresse *boor-kã-bres* or **Bourg** *boor*, 46 13N 5 12E, pop(1982) 43,675, market town and capital of Ain dept, Rhône-Alpes region, E France on the R Reyssouze; united with Savoy in 1272 then with France in 1601; well known to gourmets, especially for its fish and game (from La Dombes), frogs' legs in cream, and local wines (Seyssel-Montagnieu-Cerdon); railway; economy: trades in grain, chickens, wine and livestock; monuments: in the old quarter are the Bishop's Palace and Notre Dame church; in the SE suburb of Brou is the Flamboyant Gothic monastery of Brou built by Margaret of Austria in 1505-36, now housing the municipal library and museum; events: an international motorcycle race every year (1st Sunday of May); there is a weekly market and a big cattle fair every month; Bréssan enamel jewellery is a local art.

Bourges *boorzh*, AVARICUM (anc), 47 09N 2 25E, pop(1982) 79,408, ancient ducal town and capital of Cher dept, Centre region, central France; at the confluence of the rivers Auron and Yèvre, on the Canal du Berry; bishopric; railway; economy: hardware, linoleum, textiles; agric equipment; monuments: the 13th-c cathedral of St-Étienne; Palais Jacques Cœur built in 1443 by the king's silversmith; many fine Renaissance houses.

Bourget, LAC DU BOURGET *lak du boor-zhay*, lake in the Savoie dept, Rhône-Alpes region, E France; area 45 sq km; 18 km long by 2-3 km wide and 60-100 m deep; largest lake in France; boat trips on the lake; overlooked by the resort of Aix-les-Bains to the E; on the W bank is the richly decorated Benedictine abbey of Hautecombe, burial place of the princes of Savoie.

Bourgogne *boor-gon'y'*, BURGUNDY (Eng), region and former prov of E central France comprising the depts of Côte-d'Or, Nièvre, Saône-et-Loire and Yonne, 15 arrond, 169 cantons and 2,040 communes; pop(1982) 1,596,054; area 31,582 sq km; formerly the kingdom of Burgundia or Burgundy (in the 5-10th centuries); a famous wine-producing area with notable wines from Beaujolais, Beaune, Chablis, Côte de Beaune, Gevrey Chambertin, Mâcon and Meursault; from the wooded Monts du Morvan (902 m) in the centre of the region flow the Yonne, Cure and Armançon rivers which converge en route to the R Seine near Paris; the chief town is Dijon; the French poet and novelist Lamartine was born in Mâcon in 1790; industry is centred on Le Creusot which straddles the Canal du Centre; there are interesting caves at Arcy-sur-Cure; the Parc de Morvan regional nature park caters for riding, canoeing, shooting and fishing; there are spas at Pouques-les-Eaux, St Honoré-les-Bains, Bourbon-Lancy and Maizières.

Bourj Barajneh *boorzh bar-azh'ne*, Palestinian refugee camp on the outskirts of Beyrouth (Beirut), Lebanon; created following the evacuation of Palestinians from the city after Israeli attacks on Palestinians and Syrians in June 1982; scene of a prolonged seige in 1987.

Bournemouth *born'-muth*, 50 43N 1 54W, pop(1981) 145,704, resort town in Bournemouth dist, Dorset, S England; on Poole Bay, 40 km SW of Southampton; railway; economy: tourism, printing, engineering.

Bouvetøya, BOUVET ISLAND *boo'vay*, 54 26S 3 24E, uninhabited island in the S Atlantic about 2,400 km SW of the Cape of Good Hope and about 1,600 km N of Antarctica; a Norwegian dependency claimed by Norway in 1927, under Norwegian sovereignty in 1928 and declared a dependency in 1930; area 57 sq km; discovered in 1739 by the French navigator, Pierre Bouvet; Britain raised a flag on the island in 1825 but waived its claim in favour of Norway in 1930.

Bovec *bo'vets*, PLEZZO (Ital), FLITSCH (Ger), 46 20N 13 33E, village and winter sports resort in Slovenija republic, NW Yugoslavia; in the Soča valley, on the road to Treviso in Italy; cableway from Bovec to winter sports area in the Kanin range (2,585 m); chair-lift and ski-tow facilities.

Bowie, 39 00N 76 47W, pop(1980) 33,695, residential town in Prince George's county, central Maryland, United States; 25 km W of Annapolis; railway.

Bowling Green, 36 59N 86 27W, pop(1980) 40,450, county seat of Warren county, S Kentucky, United States; on the R Barren, 105 km SE of Owensboro; university (1906); railway; economy: trade in tobacco, corn, livestock and dairy products; manufactures include textiles, clothing and automobiles.

Bowling Green, 41 23N 83 39W, pop(1980) 25,728, county seat of Wood county, N Ohio, United States; 29 km S of Toledo; university (1910); railway.

Boyacá *bō-ya-ka'*, dept in E central Colombia, South America; the Cordillera Oriental rises in the E; pop(1985) 1,089,387; area 23,189 sq km; capital Tunja; economy: agriculture, steel (Paz del Rio); the historic bridge at Boyacá was the scene of Simón Bolívar's decisive victory over the Spanish in 1819 that ensured Colombia's independence.

Boyali *bō-yah'lee* or **Boali**, 4 47N 19 09E, chief town of Ombella-Mpoko prefecture, Central African Republic; NW of Bangui.

Boyne, river in E Irish Republic, rising in the Bog of Allen, Kildare county, Leinster; flows 110 km NE to meet Irish Sea near Drogheda; Battle of the Boyne was fought at Oldbridge near Drogheda in 1690.

Boynton Beach, 26 32N 80 04W, pop(1980) 35,624, beach resort in Palm Beach county, SE Florida, United States; on the Atlantic Ocean, 20 km S of West Palm Beach; railway.

Bozoum *bo-zoom'*, 6 16N 16 22E, chief town in Ouham-Pendé prefecture, NW Central African Republic; on the R Ouham, 322 km NW of Bangui.

Braband, North, prov in the Netherlands. See Noord Brabant.

Brabant *bra'bunt*, BRABAND *brah'bahnt* (Flem), prov of central Belgium; area 3,358 sq km; pop(1982) 2,222,974; comprises the 4 dists of Brussel, Halle-Vilvoorde, Leuven and Nivelles; capital Bruxelles; chief towns Vilvoorde, Leuven, Halle and Nivelles; drained by the Demer and Senne rivers.

Brač *bratch*, 3rd largest of the Adriatic islands of Yugoslavia, situated on the Dalmatian coast in Hrvatska (Croatia) republic, SW of Split; mostly bare rock or maquis grazed by sheep; resorts at Supetar and Postira on the N coast, Bol on the S coast, Milna to the W and Sumartin to the E. Postira was the birthplace of the Croatian writer Vladimir Nazor.

Brack'nell, 51 26N 0 46W, pop(1981) 52,836, industrial town in Bracknell dist, Berkshire, S England; 6 km E of Wokingham; meteorological centre; railway; economy: engineering, electronics, finance.

Bradenton *bray'den-ton*, 27 30N 82 34W, pop(1980) 30,170, county seat of Manatee county, SW Florida, United States; on Tampa Bay, at the mouths of the Braden and Manatee rivers; railway; economy: a winter resort and shipping centre for citrus fruit; travertine quarries nearby.

Brad'ford, 53 48N 1 45W, pop(1981) 295,048, town in West Yorkshire, N England; part of West Yorkshire urban area; 15 km W of Leeds and 310 km NNW of London; 19th-c development was based on the textile industry; university (1966); railway; economy: textiles, textile machinery, coal, engineering, micro-electronics; monuments: city hall (1873), wool exchange (1867), art gallery (1904), 15th-c cathedral.

Braemar *bray-mar'*, 57 01N 3 24W, village in SW Grampian region, Scotland, 10 km W of Balmoral castle; tourism; Highland games (Aug).

Bra'ga, mountainous dist in NW Portugal, part of Minho prov; area 2,730 sq km; pop(1981) 708,924; drained by R Cávado and R Ave; rises to almost 2,000 m in the Serra do Gerês; divided into 13 councils and 511 parishes; economy: meat, honey, dairy produce, cork, wood, resin, vegetables, grain, fruit, wine and small industries such as papermaking, linen, textiles, leather, cutting instruments and crafts; produces the famous light vinhos verdes, wines from grapes that are often grown on high 'cruzelas' or trellises.

Braga, BRACARA AUGUSTA (anc), 41 32N 8 26W, pop(1981) 63,800, industrial capital of Braga dist and fourth largest city in Portugal; 371 km N of Lisboa and 53 km NNE of Porto; former capital of the old region of Entre Minho and Douro; seat of the Primate of Portugal; economy: motor vehicles, electrical appliances, leather and textiles; monuments: 11th-c cathedral, university; events: Holy Week with processions; Midsummer celebrations with folk events and processions; São Miguel fair and agricultural show at the end of Sept.

Bragança *bra-gã'sa*, mountainous dist of NE Portugal, part of Trás-os-Montes prov, bounded by Spain and R Douro; drained by R Tua and R Sabor; area 6,545 sq km; pop(1981) 184,252; chief town Bragança; divided into 12 councils and 298 parishes; airfield; railway; economy: cork, wood, resin, meat, dairy produce, skins, grain, vegetables, fruit, wine, leather goods, textiles; minerals: antimony, arsenic, lead, chromium, iron, manganese, gold, silver, quartz, talc and wolfram.

Bragança, BRAGANZA (Eng), JULIOBRIGA (anc), 41 48N 6 50W, pop(1981) 13,900, capital of Bragança dist, NE Portugal; on N Douro plateau, 10 km from the Spanish border; bishopric; original seat of the House of Bragança which ruled Portugal from 1640 to 1910; monuments: castle built by Sancho I in 1187, cathedral, 12th-c town hall and Baçal Abbey; agricultural centre, silk-weaving still flourishes; events: Cantarinhas fair in May; municipal holiday at the end of Aug; São Mateus fair in Sept.

Brahestad, town in Finland. See Raahe.

Brahmanbaria *bra-mun-bar'yu*, 23 58N 91 04E, pop(1981) 87,570, town in Brahmanbaria dist, Comilla, SE Bangladesh; ENE of Dākā.

Brahmaputra *bra-me-poot-ra*, YARLUNG ZANGBO (Chinese), JAMUNA (Bang), river in SW China and India; rises in the Gangdisê Shan (Kalias Range) of the Himalayas in Xizang aut region as the Maquan He river; flows E to be joined by the Raka Zangbo river, then E to the S of Lhasa, where it is joined by the Lhasa He river and becomes the Yarlung Zangbo Jiang; the river continues E then turns to flow S into NE Assam, India; near the town of Sadiya it is joined by the Dibang and Lohit rivers and becomes the Brahmaputra; the river then flows WSW through Assam then S into Bangladesh where the bulk of the water continues S as the Jamuna river while the Brahmaputra follows the old river bed in a curve to the E of the Jamuna; the Brahmaputra continues S to join the Padma in forming a vast delta before flowing into the Bay of Bengal; length approx 2,895 km; length in Chinese territory approx 1,800 km.

Brăila *bra-ee'la,* county in E Romania, pop(1983) 393,291; area 4,724 sq km; capital Brăila.

Brăila, 45 17N 27 58E, pop(1983) 224,998, river port and capital town of Brăila county, E Romania; on the R Danube; includes the suburbs of Brăilita, Nedelcu P. Chercea and Radu Negru; established in the 14th century; ceded to Romania in 1829; railway; economy: grain trade, shipyards, pulp, paper, food processing, steel, textiles.

Braintree, 51 53N 0 32E, pop(1981) 31,139, town in Brain'tree dist, Essex, SE England; 17 km NE of Chelmsford; railway; economy: printing, engineering.

Brak'na, region in SW Mauritania, NW Africa; pop(1982e) 171,000; area 33,000 sq km; capital Aleg; chief towns Bogué, Mal, Aslat, Regba and Néré; the R Sénégal follows the S border where a rich alluvial soil supports agriculture.

Brak'pan, 26 15S 28 22E, pop(1980) 79,732, town in Transvaal prov, South Africa; 32 km E of Johannesburg; railway; a gold mining centre.

Brampton, 43 42N 79 46W, pop(1981) 149,030, town in SE Ontario, SE Canada; 25 km W of Toronto; railway; economy: textiles, footwear, dairy products, flowers.

Brand'berg, KÖNIGSTEIN, 21 10S 14 33E, mountain in W Namibia, SW Africa; height 2,606 m; located N of Wulvis Bay; highest point in Namibia.

Brandenburg, BRANDENBURG AN DER HAVEL *brahn'dun-boork an der haf'el,* 52 25N 12 34E, pop(1981) 94,680, industrial city in Brandenburg dist, Potsdam, central East Germany; on R Havel, W of Berlin; former centre of the Prussian prov of Brandenburg, part of which is now in Poland; railway; economy: steel, textiles.

Brandon, 49 50N 99 57W, pop(1981) 36,242, town in SW Manitoba, S Canada; on the Assiniboine river, 208 km W of Winnipeg; founded in 1778; railway link established in 1881, grew rapidly as a wheat market for the expanding agricultural economy of the surrounding countryside; university (1899); railway; airfield; economy: meat packing, light engineering; situated at the centre of a rich mixed-farming area, the major areas of interest are wheat, barley, oats, flax, dairying, livestock and market gardening; N of the town is the Dominion Experimental Farm; event: Manitoba Provincial Exhibition (July).

Brantford, 43 09N 80 17W, pop(1981) 74,315, town in SE Ontario, SE Canada; on the Grand river, 80 km W of L Ontario; in 1784 the British Crown granted the Indians of the Six Nations a reserve extending along the Grand river; these tribes had fought with the British in the American War of Independence; they were led by the Mohawk chief Joseph Brant; the reservation gradually shrank and in 1830 the Indians ceded Brant's Ford to European settlers; it was incorporated as a city in 1877; railway; economy: precision tools, chemicals, transportation equipment, paper products, electrical goods; monuments: Her Majesty's Chapel of the Mohawks (1785) is the oldest Protestant church in Ontario; the Brant county museum contains a collection of Six Nations artifacts; in the centre of the city is the Bell Memorial to Alexander Graham Bell, inventor of the telephone; on the opposite side of the Grand river is the Bell Homestead, former home of the inventor who came to Canada from Scotland.

Brasília *bra-seel'ya,* fed dist in Centro-Oeste region, W central Brazil; pop(1980) 1,176,935; area 5,814 sq km; capital Brasília; economy: commerce, administration, agriculture, cement, construction; over half the pop is contained in 7 satellite cities of Brasília; 280 sq km were designated a national park in 1961.

Brasília, 15 45S 47 57W, pop(1980) 410,999, capital of Brazil in Brasília fed dist, Centro-Oeste region, W central Brazil; construction began in 1956 and the capital was moved from Rio de Janeiro in 1960; the city was laid out in the shape of a bent bow and arrow; residential areas lie along the curve of the bow; at right angles to these residential areas is the arrow; at the tip of the arrow is the Praça do Tres Poderes, containing the Congress buildings, the Palácio do Planalto (President's office) and the Supreme Court building; W of this square lie the cathedral and the Ministry buildings; the cultural and recreational zones and commercial and financial areas lie on either side of the intersection of the bow and arrow; near the lake is the Palácio da Alvorada, the president's residence; university of Brasília (1962); airport; economy: centre of government and administration; light industry; monuments: Brasília is famous for its wealth of modern sculpture; events: on the first Sunday in each month, the states of Brazil take it in turn to raise the flag in the Praça dos Tres Poderes, accompanied by a cultural presentation.

Braşov *bra-shov',* county in central Romania, in the E Transylvanian Alps; pop(1983) 665,097; area 5,351 sq km; capital Braşov.

Braşov, KRONSTADT (-1918), STALIN (1950-1960), 45 39N 25 35E, pop(1983) 331,240, industrial capital of Braşov county, central Romania; founded in the 13th century by the Teutonic Knights; an important medieval trade centre; ceded by Hungary after World War I; also a summer resort and winter sports centre; university (1971); railway junction; economy: textiles, lorries, tractors, metallurgy, ball bearings, chemicals, machinery.

Brass, 4 20N 6 15E, town with tanker terminal facilities, Rivers state, S Nigeria, W Africa; on the R Niger delta, SW of Port Harcourt; linked by pipeline to offshore oil fields.

Bratislava *brat'yis-la-wa,* POSONIUM (Lat), 48 10N 17 08E, pop(1984) 401,383, river port and capital of Západoslovenský region and Slovak Socialist Republic, S central Czechoslovakia; on R Danube; 2nd largest city in Czechoslovakia; university (1919); technical university (1938); satellite settlements include Štrkovec, Trávniky, Ostredky, Pošeň, Záluhy, Podvornice, Rovnice, Dúbravka and Lamač; the new town of Petržalka (Petzwald) is under construction on the right bank of the R Danube; a stronghold of the Great Moravian Empire in the 9th century it later became capital of Hungary (1541-1784); Hungarian monarchs were crowned here until 1835 and the Hungarian Diet met here until 1848; centre of emergent Slovak national revival, it was incorporated into Czechoslovakia in 1918; airport (Vajnory); railway; economy: food processing, petrochemicals, agrochemicals, oil refining, textiles, paper, electrical equipment, mechanical engineering, trade in agricultural products; monuments: Mirbach palace, Lenin's museum, pharmaceutical museum; events: musical festivals.

Bratsk, 56 10N 101 30E, pop(1983) 231,000, youngest Siberian city in Irkutskaya oblast, Rossiyskaya, Soviet Union; on the R Angara, 600 km downstream from Irkutsk; on the S edge of the Sredne Sibirskoye Ploskogor'ye (Central Siberian Plateau); established in 1955 in association with the construction of the Bratsk hydroelectric power plant, the largest in the world (completed in 1964); port on the shore of Bratsk reservoir which was formed from the confluence of the Oka, Iya, and Angara rivers and was completed in 1965; railway; airfield; economy: aluminium plant, timber industries.

Braulio Carrillo *brow-lee-ō kar-ee'yō,* national park in central Costa Rica, Central America; N of San José; established in 1978; area 320 sq km; rising to 2,906 m at Barba volcano which is largely covered by rainforest.

Braunschweig *brown'shvīk,* BRUNSWICK (Eng), dist of E Niedersachsen (Lower Saxony) prov, W Germany; pop(1983) 1,619,500; area 8,093 sq km; c pital Braunschweig.

Braunschweig, 52 17N 10 28E, pop(1983) 257,100, capital of Braunschweig dist, E Niedersachsen (Lower Saxony) prov, W Germany; manufacturing and commercial city on the R Oker; capital of free state of Braunschweig until its incorporation into Niedersachsen in 1946; the Mittelland Canal runs N of the town; technical university (1745); railway; economy: chemical engineering, foodstuffs, sugar, food processing machinery, construction, packaging, lorries, precision engineering; monument: Romanesque cathedral (1173-95).

Brava *brah'va*, 14 52N 24 42W, island in the Sotavento or leeward group of Cape Verde; area 67 sq km; pop(1980) 6,984, 1 hour by ferry from Fogo I; rises to 961 m at Fontaínhas peak; the chief town is Nova Sintra; Furna is the only port.

Bray, BRI CHUALLAN (Gael), 53 12N 6 06W, pop(1981) 23,358, town in Wicklow county, Leinster, E Irish Republic; on Irish Sea, S of Dublin; railway; economy: film-making studios.

Brazil *bra-zil'*, BRASIL (Port), official name The Federative Republic of Brazil, REPÚBLICA FEDERATIVA DO BRASIL (Port), a republic situated in E and central South America, extending from 5°N to 34°S, and broadest at 7°S; bounded N by Colombia, Venezuela, Guyana, Surinam and Guiana, E by the Atlantic, W by Colombia, Peru, Bolivia and Paraguay and S by Argentina and Uruguay; its land frontiers extend for 15,719 km, and its coastline for 7,408 km; Brazil has 4 timezones ranging from GMT −2 in the Atlantic islands off the E coast to GMT −3 in the E (including the cities of São Paulo, Rio de Janeiro and Brasília), GMT −4 in the mid-W, and GMT −5 in the state of Acre in the extreme W; area 8,511,965 sq km; capital Brasília; principal cities São Paulo, Rio de Janeiro, Belo Horizonte, Recife and Salvador; pop(1980) 119,002,706; ethnic groups include Portuguese, Italian, German, Japanese, black, and Amerindian, comprising 55% white, 38% mixed, and 6% black; the official language is Portuguese; 89% of the pop is Roman Catholic, the rest are Protestant or Spiritualist; the currency is the cruzado of 100 centimos; on 1 March 1986 the Brazilian currency, the cruzeiro, was devalued; 1 cruzado = 1,000 cruzeiros; national holidays: 21 April (Tiradentes), 1 May (Labour Day), 7 Sept (Independence Day), 12 Oct (Nossa Senhora Aparecida), 2 Nov (All Souls' Day), 15 Nov (Day of the Republic); membership of FAO, G-77, GATT, IADB, IAEA, IBRD, ICAC, ICAO, ICO, IDA, IDB, IFAD, IFC, IHO, ILO, IMF, IMO, INTELSAT, IPU, IRC, ISO, ITU, IWC, OAS, PAHO, SELA, UN, UNESCO, UPU, WHO, WIPO, WMO, WTO.

Physical description. Brazil is divided into two structural regions. In the N lies the Amazon basin and in the centre and S lies the Brazilian plateau. Three-eighths of Brazil is made up of plains and lowlands including the Amazon basin in the N, part of the Río de la Plata basin in the S and SW and a thin coastal plain along the Atlantic coast. The remaining five-eighths of Brazil is divided into two plateaux, the vast, rolling central plateau of the Brazilian Highlands, rising to 2,890 m at Pico da Bandeira, and the Guiana Highlands, which lie only partly in Brazil and contain Brazil's highest peak, Pico da Neblina (3,014 m). The low lying Amazon basin, once an inland sea, is now drained by rivers that carry one-fifth of the earth's running water. Beyond the alluvial floodplain of the Amazon which covers less than 2% of the river valley the soils are heavily leached and infertile. Where the forest canopy is cleared soils are susceptible to erosion after tropical rainstorms. The Brazilian plateau lies to the S and E of the Amazon basin and is highest near the Atlantic coast; it lies between the Amazon and Río de la Plata river basins and has an average height of 600-900 m. Brazil has no mountains as high as the Andes, the average alt of Brazil is 500 m. The vegetation of the upland plateau country changes from a thorny scrub forest in the N to a wooded savannah (*campo cerrado*) that covers over 2 million sq km of the interior. The country is divided by 8 river systems, the most important being the Amazon (N), the São Francisco (central) and the Paraguay, Paraná and Uruguay (S). On the Atlantic is a thin coastal strip 100 km wide. Although this area comprises only 7.7% of Brazil's total land area it contains 30% of the country's population.

Climate. Brazil lies almost entirely within the tropics, with the Equator passing through the N part of the country near Macapá and the Tropic of Capricorn through the SE, near São Paulo. The physical geography divides the country into 4 climatic regions - the Amazon basin, the Brazilian plateau, the tropical coastlands and the southern states of Paraná, Rio Grande do Sul and Santa Catarina. In the Amazon basin annual rainfall is between 1,500 and 2,000 mm; there is no dry season, the climate is typically tropical with average midday temperatures between 27° and 32°C; frost is rare, and night temperatures seldom fall below 10°C. Belém, at the mouth of the Amazon, is the wettest location, the heaviest rains falling between Jan and May, with temperatures ranging between 22° and 32°C. At Manaus, in the central part of the region, the period from June to Sept is drier than at Belém with temperatures between 24° and 33°C. Sena Madureira in the extreme SW of the region is in the shadow of the Andes and is therefore wetter, with heaviest rainfall between Dec and March, and average daily temperatures between 17° and 34°C. There is little variation in average monthly temperatures, but there is less midday humidity during the dry season and in the wet season there is more cloud, higher humidity and higher night temperatures. At Brasília, which is representative of this area, temperatures range between 13° and 32°C in the dry season and 17° to 31°C in the wet season. In the Brazilian plateau there is a more distinct wet and dry season. With the exception of the NE, this region has an annual rainfall of 1,250-1,500 mm, most rain falling between Oct and April. The dry region in the NE has less than 750 mm of rain per year, and is susceptible to prolonged droughts. The town of Iguatú, for example, has daily temperatures of 21° to 36°C, and monthly rainfall of as little as 3 mm in Aug rising to 185 mm in March. The narrow coastal strip has a hot, tropical climate, but the months during which the greatest amount of rain falls vary greatly from N to S. Near the mouth of the Amazon all months are wet, but rainfall is greatest from Dec to May. From approx 3°S to Bahia at 14°S the wettest months are from May to Aug. Temperatures at Recife, situated on this part of the coast, range from 22° to 30°C, with as little as 25 mm rainfall in Oct compared with 277 mm in June. S of Bahia the rainy period changes again, with most rain falling between Nov and April. Rio de Janeiro in this area has a daily temperature range from 17° to 29°C, with up to 137 mm of rain in Dec and as little as 41 mm in Aug. Brazil's southern states lie outside the tropics, and have a seasonal, temperate climate similar to that of Uruguay or N Argentina. Temperatures at Pôrto Alegre range from 9° to 31°C. On the coast rainfall is well distributed throughout the year, although the cooler months of April-Sept can be slightly wetter. Inland, frosts are quite common during the winter (April-Sept), but the wettest months are during the summer, unlike the coastal district.

History, government and constitution. Brazil was discovered for the Portuguese by Pedro Alvares Cabral in 1500. The first settlement was established at Salvador da Bahia, with a second at São Vicente, near Santos, in 1507 and a third at Olinda, near Recife, in 1537. Settlement was concentrated on the N and E coasts, with settlers bringing cattle, sugar cane and slaves with them. During the 16th and 17th centuries the provinces of Bahia, Pernambuco and Paraíba were the world's prime source of sugar. The original 13 feudal principalities of Brazil were replaced in 1572 by a Viceroyalty, and the division of the country into north and south with capitals at Salvador and Rio de Janeiro. The Portuguese court was driven to Brazil by Napoleon in 1808 and on 7 Sept 1822 the Regent, Pedro (son of King João VI of Portugal) declared Brazilian independence and was crowned king of Brazil on 1 Dec. Dom Pedro abdicated in 1831 following a military revolt. Nine years later his son, Dom Pedro II, became the second emperor. Political power remained in the hands of wealthy landowners whose huge estates produced most of the country's income. The abolition of slavery and a war with Uruguay culminated in a coup by the army and plantation owners who declared a republic in 1889. The period from 1889 to 1930 was one of expansion and increasing prosperity, Brazil attracting large numbers of European immigrants. In 1930 a revolution headed by Getúlio Vargas, Governor of Rio Grande do Sul, deposed President Wáshington Luís. Vargas assumed power, first as provisional president, then as dictator. He was forced to resign in October 1945. A liberal republic was restored in 1946, but government instability, high inflation and a fear of radical political philosophies led to a military coup in March 1964. The constitution of 1967 declared Brazil a federative republic with broad powers granted to the federal government. The form of government has been a military-backed presidential regime since 1964, with compulsory universal suffrage for those over the age of 18, except illiterates. Since 1979 a process of liberalization (*abertura*) has allowed the return of political exiles to stand for state and federal offices. The bicameral National Congress consists of 69 senators (3 from each state) elected for 8 years and 479 deputies elected for 4 years by proportional representation weighted in favour of less populous states. State governors with limited powers are elected every 4 years.

Economy. The early economy of Brazil was based on sugar cane, cattle and the discovery of precious metals. Between 1698 and 1725 gold was found in Minas Gerais, Mato Grosso and Goiás and in 1729 diamonds were discovered in Minas Gerais. The gold rush lasted 100 years, then petered out. In more recent times important mineral resources have included iron ore, manganese, bauxite, nickel, uranium and gemstones. Principal agricultural products, which along with mineral ores account for almost half of Brazil's export earnings, include coffee, soya beans, sugar cane, cocoa, rice, beef and maize. Brazil's industry, which is mostly located in the SE states, accounts for almost 35% of the national income and 60% of exports. Principal industries are steel, chemicals, petrochemicals, machinery, motor vehicles, consumer goods, cement, lumber and shipping. Although offshore oil production has increased since the 1960s, 48% of Brazil's imports in 1985 were accounted for by crude oil. To supply a rapidly growing demand for energy there have been large investments in hydroelectricity, cane alcohol, coal and nuclear power. Hydroelectricity is the

second most important source of energy in Brazil, accounting for 90% of all electricity consumed in 1985. The most important hydroelectric scheme is that of the Itaipu dam on the Río Paraná. Set up in conjunction with Paraguay, it is said to be the world's largest hydroelectric complex. A second scheme on the Río Pará (Tucurui Dam) in NE Brazil has also been completed. In 1974 the Proálcool programme was set up to substitute cane alcohol for oil products; Brazil has now become a world leader in the development of alcohol fuel. A coal plan, Procarvão, is being carried out to increase the output of saleable coal from reserves in the S of Brazil. A nuclear plant was established at Angra dos Reis in 1982. Major trade partners include the USA, W Germany, Japan, the Netherlands, Argentina, the USSR, and Italy.

Agriculture. Brazil is one of the world's largest farming countries, being largely self-sufficient in food production except for wheat. Seventeen per cent of the country is cultivable or suitable for grazing, with agriculture employing 35% of Brazil's population, accounting for approx 12% of its national income and almost 40% of exports. Brazil is the world's largest exporter of coffee, supplying approx one-third of the world's coffee output, although coffee's proportion of total exports fell to 10% in 1983. Brazil is the second largest exporter of cocoa and soya beans, and a major exporter of meat, sugar cane and cotton. Other important agricultural products include butter, maize and oranges. In Dec 1981 the total number of cattle in Brazil was 93 million. Brazil's timber reserves are the third largest in the world, but continuing destruction of the Amazon rainforest is causing much concern among scientists and ecologists. In recent times Brazil has been extending cultivation in order to increase its agricultural exports. The most important of these developments is soya bean production in the states of Mato Grosso do Sul, Rio Grande do Sul, São Paulo and Paraná. Brazil has also expanded cultivation of sugar cane, necessary for the production of fuel.

Communications. In recent years the road network has been extended into the NW through the Amazon rainforest. The southernmost of 2 major roads, the Rodovia Transamazônica, runs through the N of Pará state, then swings SW to cross the S of Mato Grosso state. In the N the Rodovia Perimetral Norte, or Perimetral North Highway, runs from Macapá on the coast parallel with the Venezuelan border through Amapá, Pará, Roraima and N Amazonas states until it nears the Colombian border, where quicksand has forced the virtual abandonment of this trunk road. Linking these 2 roads is the Rodovia Panamericana, which passes down through Roraima and Amazonas to join the Rodovica Transamazônica W of the Madeira river. The Perimetral North Highway is being constructed to assist in the extraction of bauxite deposits in NW Brazil. These new roads which cut through the Amazon basin are little more than dirt tracks, occasionally topped with gravel. The trunk road from Pôrto Velho to Manaus was sealed in 1975. New highways have superseded many of the 19th-c railways which pushed inland from ports and were designed to remove primary produce for markets in SE Brazil and the N Atlantic seaboard. Most of these railways were built by private foreign capital and few were linked until the 1950s. In the NE 2 railway lines were built by the government, from Forteleza to Baturité and Camocim to Sobral, in response to the 1877-79 drought.

Administrative divisions. Brazil is divided into 5 geographical regions which are subdivided into 23 states, 3 territories (Amapá, Fernando de Noronha and Roraima) and 1 federal territory (Brasília) as follows:

Region/state	*area (sq km)*	*pop(1980)*
Centro-Oeste		
Brasília	5,814	1,176,935
Goiás	642,092	3,859,602
Mato Grosso	881,001	1,138,691
Mato Grosso do Sul	350,548	1,369,567
Nordeste		
Alagoas	27,731	1,982,591
Bahia	561,026	9,454,346
Ceará	150,630	5,288,253
Fernando de Noronha	26	1,279
Maranhão	328,663	3,996,404
Paraíba	56,372	2,770,176
Pernambuco	98,281	6,141,993
Piauí	250,934	2,139,021
Rio Grande do Norte	53,015	1,898,172
Sergipe	21,994	1,140,121
Norte		
Acre	152,589	301,303
Amapá	140,276	175,257
Amazonas	1,564,445	1,430,089
Pará	1,250,722	3,403,391
Rondônia	243,044	491,069
Roraima	230,104	79,159
Sudeste		
Espírito Santo	45,597	2,023,340
Minas Gerais	587,172	13,378,553
Rio de Janeiro	44,268	11,291,520
São Paulo	247,898	25,040,712
Sul		
Paraná	199,554	7,629,392
Rio Grande do Sul	282,184	7,773,837
Santa Catarina	95,985	3,627,933

Area figures for Pará state include 2,680 sq km in dispute with Amazonas and figures for Ceará state include 2,614 sq km in dispute with Piauí state.

Brazos *bra'zos*, river in S USA; formed in W Texas by the Double Mountain Fork and Salt Fork rivers; flows generally SE through Texas, past the towns of Mineral Wells and Waco to enter the Gulf of Mexico at Freeport; length 1,947 km; major tributaries: the Clear Fork, Little and Navasota rivers; used for irrigation, hydroelectricity and flood-control.

Brazzaville *braz'a-vil*, 4 14S 15 14E, pop(1980) 422,402, river-port capital of the Congo, W Africa; on the right bank of the R Zaire in Pool prov, 385 km ENE of Pointe-Noire; the Zairian capital of Kinshasa (Leopoldville) is situated on the opposite bank; terminus of a railway which begins at Pointe-Noire on the Atlantic coast; founded in 1880 by Savorgnan de Brazza and was used as a base for French territorial claims in the area; largely undeveloped until its strategic position and radio station were utilized during World War II when it was the headquarters of the Free French forces; university (1961); airport; economy: banking, chemicals, metallurgy, food processing, textiles, timber.

Brčko *burch'ko*, 44 52N 8 49E, pop(1981) 82,768, town in NE Bosna-Hercegovina republic, Yugoslavia; on R Sava, N of Tuzla; railway; economy: fruit, coal mining, foodstuffs.

Brea *bree'a*, 33 55N 117 54W, pop(1980) 27,913, city in Orange county, SW California, United States; 16 km N of Anaheim.

Brechin *bree'KHin*, 56 44N 2 40W, pop(1981) 7,692, town in Angus dist, Tayside, E Scotland; on the South Esk river, 12 km W of Montrose; monument: 11th-c round tower is one of 2 remaining round towers of the Irish type in Scotland.

Břeclav *bret'slaw*, LUNDENBURG (Ger), 48 65N 16 51E, pop(1984) 24,896, town in Jihomoravský region, Czech Socialist Republic, W central Czechoslovakia; on R Dyje, near the border with Austria, SE of Brno; railway.

Brecon Beacons, national park in Wales; area 1,434 sq km; established in 1957; parts in Gwent, Dyfed, Powys and Mid Glamorgan; the 3 main peaks of 'The Beacons' being Pen-y-Fan, Corn Du and Cribyn rise to c.900 m; the park area includes the historic sites of Brecon cathedral, Llanthony Priory and Llangorse Lake; information centres are located at Brecon, Craig-y-nos, Abergavenny and Llandovery.

Breda *bray'da*, 51 35N 4 45E, pop(1984e) 153,517, industrial city in Noord Brabant prov, S Netherlands; at the confluence of the Mark and Aa rivers, 22 km W of Tilburg, near the Belgian border; seat of a Catholic bishop; important cultural centre, headquarters of numerous research and educational institutes; Breda, protected by a castle, developed in the 12th century and obtained its charter in the middle of the 13th century; well-known for 'the Compromise of Breda', a protest against Spanish tyranny (1566), and Charles II's manifesto or 'Declaration of Breda', made before his restoration to the British throne in 1660; railway; economy: engineering, synthetic fibres, foodstuffs, matches, brewing, power tools, tourism; monuments: Breda castle (built in 1350, enlarged in 1538 and now Holland's Military Academy); 18th-c town hall; Gothic cathedral (1510).

Bred'bury, 53 25N 2 05W, pop(1981) 28,558, town linked with Romiley in Stockport borough, Greater Manchester, NW England; 4 km ENE of Stockport, railway.

Bregenz *bray'gents*, BRIGANTIUM (anc), 47 31N 9 46E, pop(1981) 24,561, capital of Vorarlberg, W Austria, on the shores of the Bodensee (L Constance) at the foot of the Pfänder (1,064 m); cableway to the summit of Pfänder; railway station; monument: St Martin's tower, a relic of the medieval fortifications.

Breithorn *brīt'horn*, 46 29N 7 52E, peak in the Pennine Alps, on the Italian-Swiss border, S of Zermatt, between the Matterhorn and Monte Rosa; height 4,165 m.

Bremen *bray'men*, prov in N of W Germany, completely surrounded by the prov of Niedersachsen (Lower Saxony); includes the ports of Bremen and Bremerhaven; area 404 sq km; pop(1983) 676,900; economy: merchant, fishing and naval vessels (built and serviced), aircraft, oil refining, machine construction, electrical engineering, coffee and tea processing.

Bremen, 53 05N 8 48E, pop(1983) 545,100, commercial city and capital of Bremen prov, W Germany; on both banks of the lower R Weser, 94 km SW of Hamburg; 2nd largest seaport and maritime trading city in West Germany, carrying on a considerable trade in grain, cotton and tobacco; university (1970); during the 1970s the population declined by about 10% as shipyards began to merge; railway; economy: shipbuilding and repairing, machine building, steel, oil refining, chemicals, electrical equipment, gas compressors, electronic control systems, aerospace, motor vehicles, textiles, cigarettes and tobacco, coffee-roasting and brewing; monuments: 11th-c cathedral, Gothic town hall (1405-10).

Bremerhaven *bray'mer-hav-en*, 53 34N 8 35E, pop(1983) 137,300, seaport in Bremen prov, W Germany; on the E bank of the Weser estuary, 56 km N of Bremen; railway; became a city in 1851 and united with Wesermunde in 1938; for many years it was Europe's largest fishing port, but in the early 1980s it suffered from a decline in deep sea fishing; economy: trawling, shipbuilding and repairing, machinery construction.

Bremersdorp, town in Swaziland. See Manzini.

Bremerton, 47 34N 122 38W, pop(1980) 36,208, port in Kitsap county, W central Washington, United States; on an arm of the Puget Sound, 24 km W of Seattle; founded in 1891; the population trebled during World War II in association with the development of Puget Sound Navy Yard; railway.

Brenner Pass *bren'ner*, BRENNERO *bray'nay-ro* (Ital), 47 02N 11 32E, mountain pass in the central Tirol Alps on the border between Italy and Austria; alt 1,371 m; on the main route between Bolzano and Innsbruck; open at all seasons of the year, the lowest pass over the main chain of the Alps.

Brent, 51 34N 0 17W, pop(1981) 253,275, borough of NW Greater London, England; includes the suburbs of Wembley and Willesden; site of Wembley Football Stadium; railway; economy: foodstuffs, engineering, electrical equipment; events: Rugby League Cup final (May); Football Association Cup final (May); Royal International Horse Show (July); Horse of the Year Show (Oct).

Brent, gas field in the North Sea, E of the Shetland Is; linked by 447 km of pipeline to St Fergus in Grampian Region, Scotland, and from there a further 222 km to the fractionation and ethylene plants of Mossmorran, Fife.

Brent'wood, 51 38N 0 18E, pop(1981) 51,643, town in Brentwood dist, Essex, SE England; 17 km SW of Chelmsford; railway; economy: transport equipment, engineering.

Brescia *bray'shah*, BRIXIA (anc), prov of Lombardia region, N Italy; pop(1981) 1,017,093; area 4,758 sq km; capital Brescia.

Brescia, 45 33N 10 13E, pop(1981) 206,661, industrial town and capital of Brescia prov, Lombardia region, N Italy; on the highway between Milano and Verona; rail junction; economy: textiles, clothing, shoes, iron and steel (approximately 100 private steel companies producing rods, bars, special steel, wire, etc), metallurgical products, transport equipment, machine tools, precision engineering, hardware; centre of Italy's firearms industry, having one-third of Europe's small arms market, and a substantial proportion of the rifle market; market centre for local agricultural produce; monuments: Tempio Capitolino, a Corinthian temple built in AD 72, and other Roman remains; Renaissance town hall (1492-1508).

Brest, 48 23N 4 30W, pop(1982) 160,355, fortified port and naval station in Finistère dept, Bretagne region, NW France; on the Atlantic coast; a fine natural harbour on the Penfeld estuary, which is fed by the rivers Aulne and Elorn, it was used as a German submarine base in World War II; railway; the town was rebuilt after being totally destroyed during the War; extensive dockyards, dry-docks, naval stores and arsenals.

Brest *bryest*, BREST LITOVSK, BRZESCNAD BUGIEM (Pol), 52 08N 23 40E, pop(1983) 208,000, river port capital city of Brestskaya oblast, Belorusskaya SSR, Soviet Union; on the R Mukhavets at its junction with the R Bug, on the Polish border; founded by Slavs in 1017; a major transportation centre; railway; economy: foodstuffs, instrument-making, electrical engineering, electronics.

Bretagne *bre-tan'y'*, BRITTANY (Eng), region and former prov of NW France comprising the depts of Côtes-du-Nord, Finistère, Ille-et-Vilaine and Morbihan, 15 arrond, 194 cantons and 1,265 communes; pop(1982) 2,707,886; area 27,208 sq km; the prominent NW peninsula is bounded on the N by the English Channel and in the S by the Bay of Biscay and inland by the regions of Pays de la Loire and Basse-Normandie; the chief towns are Nantes, Rennes and the ports of Lorient, Quimper and Brest; while the coastline (Armor) is rugged and striking, the interior (Arcoet) is generally bleak, except for the Lanvaux dist, with large tracts of heathland rising to 391 m at Monts d'Arrée and 326 m at Montagne Noire; incorporated into France as a prov in 1532; the region is noted for its concentration of megalithic monuments (Carnac); there is a tidal power station at Rance at the mouth of the R Vilaine; the majority of France's naval and fishing fleets are manned by Breton sailors; among gourmets, the area is noted for its seafood, onions, artichokes, strawberries and Breton Muscadet wine.

Brezh'nev, NABEREZHNYYE CHELNY (-1985), 55 42N 52 19E, pop(1983) 394,000, town in NE Tatarskaya ASSR, Soviet Union; on the S shore of Nizhnekamsk reservoir; named after President Brezhnev.

Bria *bree-ah'*, 6 32N 22 00E, chief town in Haute-Kotto prefecture, E Central African Republic; on the R Kotto, 177 km NE of Bambari.

Bridgend, 51 31N 3 35W, pop(1981) 31,579, town in Ogwr dist, Mid Glamorgan, S Wales; on R Ogwr, 25 km W of Cardiff; railway; economy: engineering, machinery, sewing machines, hardware, electrical equipment.

Bridgeport, 41 11N 73 12W, pop(1980) 142,546, port town in Fairfield county, SW Connecticut, United States; on

Long Island Sound at the mouth of the R Pequonnock, 27 km SW of New Haven; university (1927); railway; economy: electrical goods, machinery.

Bridgetown, 13 06N 59 36W, pop(1980) 7,552, seaport and capital city of Barbados, West Indies, on Carlisle Bay in the SW of the island; a new deep-water harbour has been built to the NW of the city by joining Pelican I to the mainland; the resort of Paradise Beach is N of Bridgetown; economy: sugar manufacturing; monuments: cathedral; one of the earliest monuments commemorating Admiral Lord Nelson.

Bridg'water, 51 08N 3 00W, pop(1981) 31,011, town in Sedgemoor dist, Somerset, SW England; on the R Parrett, 15 km NNE of Taunton; birthplace of Robert Blake (1598-1657), Oliver Cromwell's admiral; railway; economy: textiles, footwear, electrical goods, plastics; monuments: 14th-c church of St Mary, Admiral Blake museum; 6 km ESE is the site of the Battle of Sedgemoor at which James VII defeated the Duke of Monmouth (1685).

Bridlington, 54 05N 0 12W, pop(1981) 28,970, port and resort town in East Yorkshire dist, Humberside, NE England; on the North Sea, 40 km N of Kingston-upon-Hull; railway; economy: transport equipment.

Brid'port, 50 44N 2 46W, pop(1981) 10,791, market town in West Dorset dist, Dorset, S England; 23 km W of Dorchester; railway.

Brienz, Lake of, lake in Switzerland. See Brienzer See.

Brienzer See *bree-ents'ar zay*, LAKE OF BRIENZ (Eng), lake in Bern canton, central Switzerland, in the Berner Alpen; R Aare enters the lake at NE, leaves at SW, connecting it with Thuner See; Brienz is the main lakeside town; area 29.8 sq km; 14 km long and between 2 and 2.5 km wide; max depth 259 m; lies between the limestone ridge of the Brienzer Grat and the Jurassic Faulhorn group; it was originally connected with Thuner See, but now lies 7 m higher.

Brig'house, 53 42N 1 47W, pop(1981) 32,558, town in Calderdale borough, West Yorkshire, N England; part of West Yorkshire urban area; on the R Calder, 7 km N of Huddersfield; economy: engineering, textiles, textile machinery.

Bright'on, 50 50N 0 10W, pop(1981) 137,985, resort town in Brighton dist, East Sussex, SE England; part of Brighton-Worthing-Littlehampton urban area; on the English Channel, 77 km S of London; in 1782 the Prince of Wales, later George IV, took up residence here; University of Sussex (1961), 5 km NE; railway; economy: food processing, furniture; monuments: Royal Pavilion (1811), designed by John Nash; events: Brighton Festival (May); London-Brighton veteran car run (Nov).

Brikama *bree-ka'ma*, local govt area in The Gambia, W Africa; pop(1983) 137,194; area 1,759.3 sq km.

Brikama, 13 16N 16 39W, pop(1980) 11,500, town in The Gambia, W Africa; 21 km S of Banjul.

Brindisi *breen'dee-see*, BRUNDI'SIUM (anc), prov of Puglia region, S Italy; pop(1981) 391,064; area 1,836 sq km; capital Brindisi.

Brindisi, 40 37N 17 57E, pop(1981) 89,786, seaport and capital of Brindisi prov, Puglia region, S Italy; 104 km SE of Bari, on the Adriatic; has an inner and an outer harbour; since ancient times Brindisi has been an important centre of trade with the E Mediterranean; used by the Crusaders as a naval base; the poet Virgil died here in 19 BC on his return from Greece; archbishopric; airport (6 km NE); railway; monuments: 18th-c cathedral, Castello Svevo (1233).

Brisbane *briz'ben*, 27 30S 153 00E, pop(1986) 1,171,300, state capital of Queensland, Australia; urban centre in Brisbane stat div, Queensland, Australia; on the Brisbane river; founded in 1824 as a penal colony; capital of Queensland since 1859; University of Queensland (1909) in St Lucia suburb, Griffith University (1971) in Nathan suburb; railway; airport; economy: commerce, oil refining, chemicals, engineering, shipbuilding, cement, clothing, food processing and trade in agricultural produce; monuments: the City Hall, built of Queensland sandstone in 1930, houses an art gallery, museum, library and concert hall; Lone Pine Koala Sanctuary; botanical gardens at Mount Coot-tha; Government House, the Governor's residence since the 1920s; Queensland maritime museum includes the city's dry dock which dates from 1881; event: Brisbane Royal Show (Aug); the city of Brisbane is divided into 176 suburbs, the largest of which include Inala, Coorparoo, The Gap, Kedron and Wynnum; Brisbane statistical division with a total pop of 1,096,200 comprises 10 suburbs:

Suburb	*area (sq km)*	*pop(1981e)*
City of Brisbane	1,220	736,660
Albert	71	11,640
Beaudesert	95	2,910
Caboolture	201	19,400
Ipswich	122	73,020
Logan	241	87,370
Moreton	200	16,070
Pine Rivers	357	61,210
Redcliffe	35	44,030
Redland	537	43,890

Bristol, BRICGSTOW (anc), 51 27N 2 35W, pop(1981) 420,234, city in Avon county, SW England; 187 km W of London; county town and administrative centre of Avon county: an important shipping centre with ports at Avonmouth, Royal Portbury and Portishead; gained county status in 1373 from Edward III; university (1909); 2 airports; railway; economy: shipbuilding, aircraft construction, engineering, tobacco processing, trade in food, petroleum products, metals; monuments: 12th-c cathedral, Roman Catholic cathedral (1973), 14th-c St Mary Redcliffe, Clifton suspension bridge (1864); Brunel's SS *Great Britain*, the world's first ocean-going propellor-driven ship, rests restored where she was launched in 1843.

Bristol, 41 40N 72 57W, pop(1980) 57,370, town in Hartford county, central Connecticut, United States; 24 km SW of Hartford.

Bristol Channel, an inlet of the Atlantic Ocean and an extension of the R Severn estuary, between Wales and England; extends 128 km E-W, with a width varying from 5 km to 80 km at its mouth; chief towns on the Welsh (N) coast include Cardiff, Swansea and on the English (S) coast Ilfracombe and Weston-super-Mare; tributaries include the Taff, Towy, Parrett, Taw and Torridge rivers.

British Antarctic Territory, British colonial territory lying between 20° and 80° W and S of 60° S, including the South Orkney Islands, the South Shetland Islands, the Antarctic Graham Land Peninsula and all adjacent lands, and the land mass extending to the South Pole; formerly part of the Falkland Islands Dependencies until this territory was formed in 1962; area 5.7 mn sq km of which 388,500 is land; most of the islands are rugged with glaciers, while the peninsula is mountainous, rising to about 3,600 m at Mt Jackson; the main continental area is covered by ice and fringed by floating ice shelves; there are no permanent inhabitants, the population solely consisting of scientists of the British Antarctic Survey; the territory is administered by a High Commissioner resident in the Falkland Is; there are scientific bases at Rothera on Adelaide I, Halley on the Caird coast, Signy on Signy I, Faraday on the Graham Peninsula and Fossil Bluff in George IV Sound (summer only); scientific bases were established in 1943-44, mostly on sites previously used as whaling or sealing stations.

British Columbia, mountainous province in SW Canada; bordered N by Yukon and Northwest Territories (Mackenzie district), E by Alberta, S by the United States, NW by Alaska and W by the Pacific Ocean; the Rocky Mts lie to the E; the Coast Mts along the W coast are deeply indented; the largest islands off the coast are Queen Charlotte Island (comprising Graham Island and Moresby Island) and Vancouver Island; the ranges are cut by fertile valleys of the Fraser, Thompson and Columbia rivers and their tributaries; NE British Columbia forms part of the Great Plain; the largest of the prov's numerous lakes are Williston, Okanagan, Kootenay, Kinbasket and the Arrow Lakes; in the Selkirk Mts (SE) is the 1,349 sq km Glacier National Park, established in 1886; pop(1981) 2,744,467; area 892,677 sq km; capital Victoria; major towns: Vancouver, Kamloops, Prince George, New Westminster and Burnaby; economy: timber products, hydroelectric power, mining (coal, copper, silver, gold, molybdenum), tourism, oil and natural gas, fishing, dairy products, cattle; Captain Cook landed on the W coast of Vancouver I in 1778; by 1786 a flourishing fur trade had developed between the British and the coastal Indians; the Hudson Bay Company controlled the fur trade as far S as Oregon; Fort Victoria was established in 1843 to secure the British claim which the American settlers refused to recognize; the border between British Columbia and the United States was settled by the Oregon Treaty of 1846; Vancouver I became a colony in 1846; with the discovery of gold in the Fraser river in 1858 large numbers of people came to settle in this area; the British government subsequently formed the colony of British Columbia which was merged with Vancouver I in 1866; British Columbia entered the Federation of Canada in 1871, with the promise that a railway would be constructed to the Pacific; in 1885 the Canadian Pacific Railroad was completed; the completion of the Panama Canal in 1915 opened European markets to British Columbian products, enhancing the development of Vancouver as a major Canadian port; British Columbia is governed by a Lieutenant-Governor and an elected 57-member Legislative Assembly.

British Indian Ocean Territory, British territory in the Indian Ocean 1,899 km NW of Mauritius and 3,380 km E of Mombasa, comprising the Chagos Archipelago; the islands (including Diego Garcia, Peros Banhos and Salomon) cover some 54,400 sq km of ocean and include 6 main island groups situated on the Great Chagos Bank; land area 60 sq km; acquired by France in the 18th century because of their importance astride the trade route to the E, the islands were annexed by Britain in 1814 and were administered as a dependency of Mauritius until the British Indian Ocean Territory was established in 1965; the territory at that time also included the islands of Aldabra, Desroches and Farquhar, which were transferred to the Seychelles in 1976; there is no permanent population; the territory was established to meet UK and US defence requirements in the Indian Ocean; there is a UK-US naval support facility on the island of Diego Garcia; the former population of 1,200 Ilois, descended from slaves introduced to work on copra plantations, was resettled on Mauritius before the establishment of the naval base; the islands have a tropical maritime climate with rainfall between 2,290 and 2,540 mm per year; the average temperature on Diego Garcia is 27°C.

Brittany, region in France. See Bretagne.

Brive-la-Gaillarde *breev-la-ga-yard*, 45 09N 1 32E, pop(1982) 54,032, town in Corrèze dept, Limousin region, S central France; 83 km SSE of Limoges, on the R Corrèze; on the road and rail route between Paris and Toulouse and from Bordeaux to Clermont-Ferrand; economy: textiles, fruit-growing and market-gardening; event: Saturday market.

Brixham *brik'sem*, 50 23N 3 30W, pop(1981) 15,500, resort town in Torbay dist, Devonshire, SW England; 8 km S of Torquay; William of Orange landed here in 1688; economy: tourism, fishing.

Brno *bœr'no*, BRÜNN (Ger), 49 11N 16 39E, pop(1984) 380,871, industrial capital of Jihomoravský region, Czech Socialist Republic, central Czechoslovakia; at the junction of the Svratka and Svitava rivers; 3rd largest city in Czechoslovakia; university (1919); technical university (1899); university of agriculture (1919); music conservatory; the Bren gun, later made in the UK, was developed in Brno; founded in 10th century; became part of Bohemia in 1229; King Wenceslaus made it a free city in 1243; formerly capital of Austrian crownland of Moravia; Napoleon made his headquarters here during the Battle of Austerlitz in 1805; airport (Cernovice); railway; economy: machinery, textiles, armaments, chemicals, trade in vegetables.

Broadmeadows, 37 45S 144 58E, pop(1983e) 108,100, NW suburb of Melbourne, Melbourne stat div, S Victoria, Australia.

Broad'stairs, 51 22N 1 27E, pop(1981) 22,186, resort town in Thanet dist, Kent, SE England; SE of Margate, on the English Channel; railway; economy: electrical goods; monument: Bleak House, where Charles Dickens wrote *David Copperfield*.

Brockton, 42 05N 71 01W, pop(1980) 95,172, town in Plymouth county, SE Massachusetts, United States; 35 km S of Boston; settled in 1700, achieving town status in 1821; railway; economy: electronics, leather, footwear.

Broken Arrow, 36 03N 95 48W, pop(1980) 35,761, city in Tulsa county, NE Oklahoma, United States; a suburb 20 km SE of Tulsa; railway.

Broken Hill, 31 57S 141 30E, pop(1981) 26,913, mining town in Far West stat div, New South Wales, Australia; centre of silver, lead and zinc mining; the town is administered by the Barrier Industrial Council; the School of the Air was founded here in 1956 and the Royal Flying Doctor Service took the town as its base in 1938; monuments: the 19th-c Afghan Mosque was built by Pakistanis and Afghans who handled camel trains based at Broken Hill.

Brokopon'do, dist in central Surinam, NE South America; the country's largest inland waterbody, W. J. Van Blommestein Meer reservoir, is in the N; further N still is the Brownsberg Nature Park; area 21,440 sq km; pop(1980) 20,249; capital Brokopondo.

Brom'ley, 51 32N 0 00, pop(1981) 282,394, residential borough of SE Greater London, England; includes the suburbs of Bromley, Orpington, Beckenham and Penge; railway.

Bromley Cross, 53 36N 2 24W, pop(1981) 21,728, town linked with Bradshaw in Bury borough, Greater Manchester, NW England; 5 km N of Bolton; railway.

Bromo, Gunung *goo'nung brō'mō*, 7 55S 112 55E, active volcano in E Jawa, Indonesia; rises to 2,614 m in the Tengger range; last erupted in 1930; scene of the Kasada festival when offerings to the god of fire are thrown into the crater.

Broms'grove, 52 20N 2 03W, pop(1981) 25,177, town in Bromsgrove dist, Hereford and Worcester, W central England; 20 km SW of Birmingham; railway; economy: engineering, transport equipment.

Brønderslev *bru'nur-slev*, 57 16N 9 58E, pop(1981) 10,748, town in N Nordjyllands county, N Jylland (Jutland), Denmark; railway; economy: engineering.

Brong-Ahafo *brong-ah'fō*, region in central Ghana, W Africa; pop(1984) 1,179,409; area 39,709 sq km; higher ground in the SW and centre falls towards the NE and the shores of L Volta; the R Tain flows SE then NE to join the Black Volta river; the R Tano flows S from source near Wenchi; capital Sunyani; chief towns Kintampo, Goaso; the NE half of Digya National Park is located in the SE; economy: gold mining.

Bronx or **The Bronx**, borough of New York City and county of New York state, United States; a mainland borough of N New York City; area 109 sq km; pop(1980) 1,168,972; bisected by the R Bronx; Fordham University (1841); named after Jonas Bronck, an early Dutch settler.

Brook Park, 41 24N 81 51W, pop(1980) 26,195, town in Cuyahoga county, NE Ohio, United States; 15 km SW of Cleveland.

Brookfield, 43 04N 88 09W, pop(1980) 34,035, city in Waukesha county, SE Wisconsin, United States; 20 km W of Milwaukee.

Brooklyn, borough of New York City, co-extensive with Kings county, New York state, United States; area 182 sq km; pop(1980) 2,230,936; at the SW corner of Long

Island; linked to Staten I over the Narrows by the Verrazano Bridge (1964); Long Island University (1926); economy: shipbuilding, engineering, food processing, footwear, trade in grain.

Brooklyn Center, 45 05N 93 20W, pop(1980) 31,230, town in Hennepin county, SE Minnesota, United States; residential suburb 13 km NNW of Minneapolis.

Brooklyn Park, 45 06N 93 23W, pop(1980) 43,332, town in Hennepin county, SE Minnesota, United States; suburb 15 km NW of Minneapolis; railway.

Brossard, 45 28N 73 32W, pop(1981) 52,232, town in S Québec, SE Canada; on the W shore of the St Lawrence river, opposite Montréal; railway.

Brown'hills, 52 39N 1 55W, pop(1981) 18,200, town in Walsall borough, West Midlands, central England; 8 km NE of Walsall; economy: coal mining.

Brownsville, 25 54N 97 30W, pop(1980) 84,997, county seat of Cameron county, S Texas, United States; port on the Rio Grande river near its mouth, opposite Matamoros, Mexico; the establishment of Fort Texas here (1846) resulted in the Mexican War; renamed Fort Brown after Major Jacob Brown who died commanding its defence; the town grew up around the fort and served as an important Confederate port during the Civil War; railway; airfield; economy: trade, processing, and distributing centre for the irrigated lower Rio Grande valley; oil-related industries; event: Charro Days (Feb).

Brownwood, 31 42N 98 58W, pop(1980) 44,337, county seat of Brown county, central Texas, United States; 108 km SE of Abilene; university; railway; economy: processing and shipping centre for an agricultural area.

Broxburn, 55 52N 3 33W, pop(1981) 12,032, town in West Lothian dist, Lothian, E central Scotland; 18 km W of Edinburgh; economy: food, textiles, machinery.

Bruges, town in Belgium. See Brugge.

Brugge *broog'ge*, dist of West-Vlaanderen (West Flanders) prov, Belgium; area 651 sq km; pop(1982) 255,166.

Brugge, BRUGES *brüzh*, 51 13N 3 14E, pop(1982) 118,048, port and capital town of Brugge dist, West-Vlaanderen (West Flanders) prov, NW Belgium; 12 km S of the seaport of Zeebrugge, with which it is connected by the Boudewijn Canal; known as the 'Venice of the north', it is one of the best preserved medieval cities in Europe; the city was the chief market town of the medieval Hanseatic League and a major centre of the woollen and cloth trade; trade declined from the 15th century as a result of competition with Antwerpen and the silting-up of the R Zwyn which connected it to the North Sea; other canals connect Brugge with Oostende, Nieuwpoort, Veurne, Gent and Sluis; railway; economy: the port handles crude oil, coal, iron ore, general cargo and fish; manufactures: steel, cotton, furniture, brewing, precast concrete, paints, outboard motors, lawn mowers, lace; monuments: Gothic town hall (1376-1420); chapel of the Holy Blood (the name commemorates the gift to the city in 1150 of a few drops of Christ's blood); church of Our Lady (12-13th-c); halle (13-14th-c, with a belfry of the 13-15th-c); events: Procession of the Holy Blood (every year on Ascension Day), Pageant of the Golden Tree (every 5th year).

Brunei *broo'nī*, official name State of Brunei Darussalam, THE ISLAMIC SULTANATE OF BRUNEI; state on the NW coast of Borneo, SE Asia; bounded to the NW by the South China Sea, and on all other sides by the E Malaysian state of Sarawak; divided into two sections by the Limbang river valley of Sarawak; timezone GMT +8; area 5,765 sq km; capital Bandar Seri Begawan (formerly Brunei Town); other towns include Kuala Belait, Seria and Tutonga; pop(1983) 214,000, ethnic groups include (65%) Malay and (20%) Chinese; the official language is Malay, but English is widely spoken; dialects of the non-Malay indigenous peoples are spoken in the interior; Islam is the official religion of Brunei; the Malay people are Muslim, while the Chinese are either Buddhist, Confucianist, Taoist or Christian; some of the indigenous people follow traditional animist religions; the currency is the Brunei dollar of 100 sen, interchangeable at par with the Singapore dollar (until 1972 interchangeable with the Malaysian dollar); national holidays 23 Feb (National Day), 31 May (founding of the Royal Brunei Regiment), 15 July (the Sultan's birthday), 29 Sept (Constitution Day); all Islamic holidays are also observed; membership of ASEAN, INTERPOL, OIC; rejected membership of the Federation of Malaysia in 1963.

Physical description. Brunei consists of a swampy coastal plain, which rises through foothills to a mountainous region on the border with Sarawak. Agriculture is located mainly on the cleared areas of the alluvial, swampy coastal plains. Equatorial rain forest covers 75% of the land area. The valleys of the Belait and Tutong rivers are in the W and consist mostly of a series of swamps.

Climate. A tropical climate is found throughout Brunei, with high temperatures and humidity and no marked seasons. The average daily temperature ranges from 24°C to 30°C, while annual rainfall averages 2,540 mm on the coast, reaching 5,080 mm in the interior. Annual humidity averages between 67% and 91%.

History, government and constitution. Formerly a powerful Muslim sultanate, its name in the form of Borneo was given by Europeans to the whole island. Reduced to its present size by the mid-19th century, Brunei came under British protection in 1888. In 1983 Brunei became a fully independent state. The constitution dates from 1959 with amendments in 1965. The country is a constitutional monarchy with the Sultan as head of state. He is advised by a Privy Council, a Legislative Council, a Religious Council and a Council of Succession. The 20-member Legislative Council is appointed by the Sultan and presided over by a Speaker. Brunei's legal system is based on Islamic law. The last elections held in Brunei were in March 1965, since then elections have been postponed indefinitely. The only political party is the exiled, anti-government Brunei People's Party.

Economy. With no industrial sector, the economy of Brunei is largely dependent on oil and gas resources, principally based on the Seria oilfield which was discovered in 1929 and the Lumut gas liquefaction plant. The main agricultural subsistence crops are rice, bananas and peppers, but Brunei imports some 80% of its food. 110 sq km of rubber plantation have been abandoned since World War II owing to falling prices for natural rubber. Timber exports are limited although forest-processing industries are being developed. The main trading partners are the UK and Japan.

Administrative divisions. Brunei is divided into the 4 dists of Belait, Tutong, and Brunei-Muara in the W and Temburong in the E, each of which are administered by a District Officer. Municipal authorities are found in Bandar Seri Begawan, Kuala Belait, Seria and Tutong.

Brunei Town, former name of the capital of Brunei, SE Asia. See Bandar Seri Begawan.

Brunei-Muara, dist of Brunei, SE Asia; bounded N by the South China Sea, W by the dist of Tutong, E by Brunei Bay and S by the E Malaysian state of Sarawak; pop(1981) 114,310; Bandar Seri Begawan (capital of Brunei) and Muara are the main towns.

Brunswick, dist and city in W Germany. See Braunschweig.

Brunswick, 41 14N 81 51W, pop(1980) 28,104, county seat of Medina county, NE Ohio, United States; 32 km SSW of Cleveland.

Brussel *bru'sul*, dist of Brabant prov, Belgium; area 162 sq km; pop(1982) 994,774.

Brussels, capital city of Belgium. See Bruxelles.

Bruxelles *brük-sel*, BRÜSSEL (Flemish), BRUSSELS *bru'sulz* (Eng), BROUCSELLA (anc), 50 50N 4 21E, pop(1982) 138,893 (excluding the suburbs), commercial and cultural city in Brussel dist, Brabant prov, Belgium; capital of Belgium and Brabant prov, lying at the geographical mid-point of the country where the hills of the valley of the Senne (tributary of the R Schelde) merge into the Flemish plain; divided into the Lower Town, intersected by several branches of the R Senne, and the Upper Town, set on the crest of the hills to the E, as well as the several dists adjacent in the E and N; around the inner city are 18 suburbs which are connected to it but have independent administration; headquarters of the country's most important financial institutions, also of the European Economic Community, NATO and numerous international organizations; linked to the North Sea by the Willebroek Canal and to the coal-mining area of S Belgium by the Charleroi Canal; the linguistic frontier between the Flemish and the Walloons runs only a few kilometres S of the city; officially Bruxelles is bilingual, but in the central section French predominates, whereas most of the suburbs are Flemish-speaking; archbishopric; Bruxelles National Airport (Zaventem); railway; underground system; Free University of Bruxelles; St Louis and St Aloysius private universities; Protestant Faculty of Theology; Royal Military School; 5 royal academies of fine arts and 5 royal conservatories; industry has largely moved out of the city to adjacent locations with greater financial incentives; the economic base of central Bruxelles is now almost entirely related to the service sector; economy: textiles, clothing, synthetic fibres, lace, carpets, porcelain, glass, cement, oil refining, fertilizers, chemicals, detergents, tyres, mechanical and chemical engineering, electromechanical equipment, electronics, office equipment, lead and zinc smelting, aluminium, household electrical goods, construction, motor vehicles, robotics, publishing, nuclear industry, brewing, cigarettes and tobacco, frozen food products, confectionery; monuments: town hall (15-18th-c), royal palace (1827-29, completely rebuilt 1905); Palais de la Nation (1779-83); cathedral (13-15th-c), church of Notre-Dame de la Chapelle (begun in 1210); event: Ommegang (processions, first Thursday in July).

Bryan, 30 40N 96 22W, pop(1980) 44,337, county seat of Brazos county, E central Texas, United States; 140 km NW of Houston; railway; economy: aluminium products, furniture, building materials, chemicals, electronic components.

Bryansk *bree-ansk'*, formerly BRYN', later DEBRIANSK, 53 15N 34 09E, pop(1983) 418,000, capital city of Bryanskaya oblast, central European Rossiyskaya, Soviet Union; on the R Desna; an independent principality until 1356; in 1956 the neighbouring industrial city of Bezhitsa became part of Bryansk; railway; economy: steam power plant, woodworking, the manufacture of wool, textiles, fertilizers, and refrigerator vehicles.

Bryce Canyon, national park in S Utah, United States; features curiously eroded rock formations; established in 1928; area 144 sq km.

Brymbo-Gwersyllt *brim'bō-gwer'silt*, 53 04N 3 01W, pop(1981) 13,382, town outside Wrexham in Wrexham Maelor dist, Clwyd, NE Wales; railway; economy: steel.

Bubanza *boo-ban'za*, 3 05S 29 22E, capital of prov of the same name, Burundi, central Africa; N of Bujumbura.

Bu'ca, 38 22N 27 10E, pop(1980) 103,105, town in İzmir prov, W Turkey; E of İzmir.

Buçaco *boo-sa'koo*, BUSACO (Eng), forest in Aveiro dist, Portugal; 27 km NE of Coimbra; designated a national park; contains 400 native and 300 exotic tree species; scene of battle (1810) in which British and Portuguese forces under Wellington defeated Napoleon's third attempt to conquer Portugal; monuments: palace, Carmelite convent, Cruz Alta and an arboretum; area 1.5 sq km.

Bucaramanga *boo-ka-ra-mang'ga*, 7 08N 73 10W, pop(1985) 493,929, capital of Santander dept, N central Colombia, South America; NNE of Bogotá, in the Cordillera Oriental at 1,018 m; university (1947); known as the 'garden city of Colombia'; founded in 1622, the city expanded in the second half of the 19th century; the Parque Santander lies at the heart of the modern city, while the Parque García Romero is at the heart of the colonial area; to the SW of Bucaramanga is an amusement park; nearby Barrancabermeja is the petroleum centre of Colombia; railway; economy: coffee, cacao, tobacco, cotton.

Buchanan *bu-ka'nun*, GRAND BASSA, 5 57N 10 02W, seaport in Liberia, W Africa; 97 km ESE of Monrovia; coastal terminus of railway which runs NE across the country to Yekapa; airfield.

Bucharest, capital of Romania. See Bucureşti.

Buckhaven *buk-hay'vĕn*, 56 11N 3 03W, pop(1981) 18,265, port town in Kirkcaldy dist, Fife, E Scotland; on the N shore of the Firth of Forth, 11 km NE of Kirkcaldy; monument: Buckhaven Fishing Museum.

Buckie, 57 40N 2 58W, pop(1981) 7,839, port town in Moray dist, Grampian region, NE Scotland; on Spey Bay, on the North Sea, 21 km E of Elgin; economy: fishing, tourism; monument: Buckie Maritime museum.

Buckinghamshire, county in S central England; bounded N by Northamptonshire, E by Bedfordshire and Hertfordshire, SE by Greater London, S by Berkshire and W by Oxfordshire; drained by the Ouse and Thames rivers; crossed in the S by the Chiltern Hills; pop(1981) 567,979; area 1,883 sq km; county town Aylesbury; chief towns include Bletchley, High Wycombe and Buckingham; economy: agriculture, furniture, bricks, printing, high technology; the county is divided into 5 districts:

District	*area (sq km)*	*pop(1981)*
Aylesbury Vale	904	133,109
Chiltern	201	92,320
Milton Keynes	310	124,343
South Bucks	144	62,488
Wycombe	324	155,719

Buckley, 53 11N 3 04W, pop(1981) 16,663, town in Wrexham Maelor dist, Clwyd, NE Wales; railway; economy: engineering.

Bucureşti, *boo-koo-resht'*, municipality with suburban communes in S Romania, including the city of Bucureşti; pop(1983) 2,227,568; area 1,521 sq km.

Bucureşti BUCHAREST (Eng), CETATEA DAMBOVIŢEI (anc), 44 25N 26 07E, pop(1983) 1,995,156, capital and largest city of Romania; on the R Damboviţa (a tributary of the R Danube); founded in the 14th century, the fortified city established itself as an important commercial centre on the trade route to Constantinople, becoming capital of the principality of Walachia in 1698 and of Romania in 1861; between 1948 and 1956 Bucureşti served as the headquarters of the Cominform (formerly located in Beograd); university (1864), technical university (1819); an oil pipeline links Bucureşti with Ploeşti; airport (Baneasa); railway; economy: engineering, metallurgy, machinery, oil refining, textiles, chemicals, food processing, motor vehicles; monuments: 18th-c Domnita Baleasa church, Palace of the Republic (former Royal Palace),

Palace of St Synod, 17th-c St George church, the Athenaeum arts and music centre.

Budapest *boo'do-pesht*, 47 29N 19 05E, pop(1984e) 2,064,000, capital of Hungary; a city with county status on the R Danube where it enters the Great Plain (Alföld); largest city in Hungary and the country's most important industrial centre; area 525 sq km; Budapest is divided into 22 metropolitan districts, but the city consists of two distinct halves, the old-world Buda on the hilly ground on the W bank and the modern regularly laid out Pest on the E bank; the unification of the two parts took place in 1873; the old part of Pest which is the centre of business and commerce is contained within the 'Innere Ring-Strausse' of boulevards, while two outer rings extend through the newer parts of the town; Buda stands on the site of the Roman colony of Aquincum, its geographical position ensuring its importance as a trade centre; the city reached its height as a cultural and trading centre during the 15th century; Eötvöos Loránd University (1635); University of Medicine (1769); University of Economic Science (1948); University of Horticulture (1853); Hungarian Academy of Sciences; National Theatre and State Opera House; railway; airport (Ferihegy, 16 km from city centre); economy: iron, steel, chemicals, pharmaceuticals, textiles.

Budva *bood'va*, 42 17N 18 50E, seaport and resort town in Crna Gora (Montenegro) republic, Yugoslavia; on the Adriatic, 40 km WSW of Titograd; consists of the old town and a resort area to the S; large naturist beach at Jaz.

Buéa *boo-ay'a*, 4 09N 9 13E, pop(1984e) 34,000, capital of Sud-Ouest prov, Cameroon, W Africa; 16 km NNE of Limbe and 70 km W of Douala, at the foot of Mount Cameroon; alt 1,000 m; noted for its pleasant climate, the former German colonial governor (General von Puttkamer) transferred his headquarters here from Douala for the benefit of his officers' health; capital of a German colony between 1901 and 1909; now located in an English-speaking area; railway; airfield (Tiko, 15 km).

Buena Park *bway'na*, 33 52N 118 00W, pop(1980) 64,165, city in Orange county, SW California, United States; W of Fullerton.

Buenaventura *bwen-a-ven-too'ra*, 3 51N 77 06W, pop(1984e) 122,500, Pacific seaport in Cauca dept, SW Colombia, South America; on the Bahia de Buenaventura, 128 km NW of Cali; Colombia's most important Pacific trading port; founded in 1540; railway; economy: fishing, fish canning, trade in coffee, hides, gold, platinum, sugar.

Buenos Aires *bway'nōs ī'rays*, prov in Litoral region, E Argentina; flat *pampa* land situated between Paraná and Plata rivers (N) and Río Negro (S); pop(1980) 10,865,408; area 307,804 sq km; capital La Plata; chief towns include Mar del Plata and Bahía Blanca; major agricultural prov of Argentina; economy: maize, wheat, sorghum, flax; cattle and sheep raising; timber; granite, gypsum, sand, limestone and quartzite mining.

Buenos Aires, 34 40S 58 30W, pop(1980) 2,908,001, federal capital of Argentina in Gran Buenos Aires federal dist, Litoral, E Argentina; on S bank of Río de la Plata; founded in 1536 by Pedro de Mendoza as the city of the 'Puerto de Santa Maria del Buen Aire'; destroyed by Indians but re-settled in 1580; formerly capital of the Spanish viceroyalty of La Plata which encompassed Uruguay, Paraguay, S Bolivia and Argentina; suburbs include Avellaneda (industrial), Olivos (residential), San Isidro (sporting and leisure resort), Quilmes (industrial), Tigre and the old port dist of La Boca; horse racing course; 9 universities; metro; railway; airport (Ezeiza) 35 km from the city; 2 airfields; economy: brewing, textiles, ironware and glass (Quilmes); monuments: national gallery, opera house; the Plaza de Mayo at the city centre is surrounded by interesting buildings including the town hall (Cabildo); presidential palace (Casa Rosada); cathedral containing the tomb of the liberator General San José de San Martín.

Buenos Aires, Lago, LAGO GENERAL CARRERA (Chile), lake in the Patagonian Andes of Argentina and Chile; situated in NW Santa Cruz prov, Patagonia, S Argentina and E General Carrera prov, Aisen del General Carlos Ibañez del Campo, S Chile; area 2,240 sq km; length 128 km; up to 20 km wide; it is divided N-S by the international line; the outlet is the Baker river in the SW arm of the lake.

Buffalo, 42 53N 78 53W, pop(1980) 357,870, county seat of Erie county, W New York, United States; port on the R Niagara at the NE end of L Erie; 2nd largest city in the state; 2 universities (1846, 1867); railway; economy: motor vehicles and vehicle parts, machinery, steel; monuments: Albright-Knox art gallery, science museum; 27 km N are the Niagara Falls.

Bug, river in E central Poland and E USSR; rises near USSR-Polish frontier and flows 772 km NW and W to meet R Wisła (Vistula) NW of Warszawa (Warsaw); length in Poland 587 km; navigable for 587 km; tributaries include Krzna and Liwiec rivers.

Buhuşi *boo-hoosh'*, 46 41N 26 45E, pop(1983) 20,669, town in Bacău county, NE central Romania; on R Bistriţa; railway; economy: textiles, distilling, oil refining.

Bui *bwee*, 8 11N 2 10W, dam on the Black Volta river, in Brong-Ahafo region, W Ghana, W Africa.

Bui, national park in W Brong-Ahafo region, W central Ghana, W Africa; area 3,074 sq km; established in 1971.

Buin *bween*, 33 45S 70 48W, pop(1982) 23,419, town in Maipo dist, Santiago, central Chile; railway.

Bujumbura *bow-jum-bow'ra*, 3 22S 29 21E, pop(1979) 172,201, port and capital of Burundi, central Africa, also capital of prov of same name; at the NE extremity of L Tanganyika; alt 805 m; formerly named Usumbura; founded in 1899 by German colonists; university (1960); airport; economy: coffee and cotton processing, brewing, cement, textiles, soap, shoes and metal working.

Bukavu *boo-ka'voo*, COSTERMANSVILLE (-1966), 2 30S 28 49E, pop(1976e) 209,051, capital of Kivu region, E Zaire, central Africa; on the shore of L Kivu, about 1,600 km ENE of Kinshasa; centre of a major mining and processing region (tungsten, columbium, tin and tantalum).

Bukhara *boo-ka'ra*, 39 47N 64 26E, pop(1983) 200,000, capital city of Bukharskaya oblast, Uzbekskaya SSR, Soviet Union; on the lower course of the R Zeravshan and the Shkhrud irrigation canal system; famed for its ancient artistic trades (gold embroidery, silk weaving); railway; economy: foodstuffs, cotton ginning, manufacture of fur and silk textiles, solar research and development; it has the largest karakul-skin processing plant in the USSR; monuments: mausoleum of Ismail Samani (late 9th or early 10th century); Ark Fortress, housing the museum of local history; Mir-i-Arab Medresseh (1534), now a Muslim theological training college; Kalyan Mosque, with the highest minaret in the city (46.5 m).

Bukit Mertajam *boo'kit mer-tah'jam*, 5 21N 100 27E, pop(1980) 28,675, town in Pulau Pinang state, NW Malaysia, SE Asia; SE of Butterworth; railway.

Bukittinggi *boo-ke-ting'gee*, formerly FORT DE KOCK, 0 18S 100 20E, town in Sumatera Barat prov, Indonesia; in the highlands of W Sumatera I, N of Padang; the cultural centre of the Minangkabau people.

Bükk *buk*, forested mountain range and national park in NE Hungary; a S spur of the Carpathians; national park (area 387.7 sq km) established in 1976.

Bulawayo *boo-la-way'yō*, 20 10S 28 43E, pop(1982) 414,000, capital of Matabeleland North prov, Zimbabwe, S Africa; 370 km SW of Harare and 880 km from Johannesburg (South Africa) by road; founded in 1893; railway junction; airport; economy: commercial, industrial and tourist centre; asphalt contractors, agricultural equipment, confectionery, electrical equipment.

Bulgan *bool'gan*, county in N Mongolia; pop(1981e) 40,000; area 50,000 sq km; capital Bulgan; bounded N by the USSR; crossed by the rivers Selenge Mörön, Egiyn Gol, Ideriyn Gol and the Ohrhon Gol; noted for an abundance of medicinal herbs; mixed forest covers 30% of the county, supporting the wood-processing and printing industries; stock breeding is important, with

85% of cattle held by agricultural associations; mineral resources include coal, lime, rock crystal, copper, turquoise emerald and molybdenum.

Bulgaria *bul-gay'ree-a*, BULGARIYA, BLGARIYA *bul-gah'ree-ya*, official name People's Republic of Bulgaria, NARODNA REPUBLIKA BULGARIYA (Bulg), republic and socialist state in the E part of the Balkan Peninsula, SE Europe; bounded to the N by Romania, the W by Yugoslavia, the SE by Turkey, the S by Greece and the E by the Black Sea; timezone GMT +2; area 110,912 sq km; pop(1982) 8,905,581; capital Sofiya; chief towns include Plovdiv, Varna, Ruse, Bourgas, Stara Zagora and Pleven; the pop is 85.3% Bulgarian, 8.5% Turk, 2.6% Gypsy and 2.5% Macedonian; the government promotes atheism but the religious background of the pop is 85% Bulgarian Orthodox and 13% Muslim; national holidays 24 May (Day of Slav and Bulgarian Letters and Culture), 9 and 10 Sept (Liberation from Fascism Day); the unit of currency, which is linked to the Russian rouble, is the lev of 100 stotinki; membership of Warsaw Pact, CEMA, FAO, IAEA, ICAO, ILO, IMO, IPU, ITC, IWC, UNESCO, UPU, WFTU, WHO, WIPO, WMO, WTO.

Physical description. Central Bulgaria is traversed W-E by the Stara Planina (Balkan Mts) rising to heights in excess of 2,000 m; the Rhodopi Planina (Rhodope Mts) of SW Bulgaria, which separate Bulgaria from Greece, rise to nearly 3,000 m just S of Sofiya; the Bulgarian lowlands stretch S from the R Danube with an average width of 100 km; the Bulgarian rivers either flow N from the watershed of the Stara Planina to the Danube or S to the Aegean; the major rivers of Bulgaria include the Maritsa, Iskur, Yantra and Struma.

Climate. The climate is largely continental with hot summers and cold winters, but to the S the climate is transitional towards that of the Mediterranean with winters that are milder and moister; the exposed uplands experience extremes of temperature; on the Black Sea coast winters are slightly warmer but NE winds blowing cold air from Russia can cause very cold spells.

History, government and constitution. The Bulgars, a Finno-Ugrian people, crossed the Danube in the 7th century and gradually merged in the Slavonic pop. The Bulgarian empire, which at one time achieved great power, waged perpetual war on the Byzantines until it was destroyed by the Turks in the 14th century. Bulgaria remained under Turkish rule until 1878, although full independence was not achieved until 1908. Between 1908 and 1946, when a socialist People's Republic was proclaimed, Bulgaria was a kingdom; in 1947 the 'Dimitrov' constitution replaced the existing 'Turnovo' constitution of 1879; this constitution was in turn replaced in May 1971 when a single-chamber National Assembly was established consisting of 400 members elected for 5 years; the National Assembly elects a State Council which unites the legislative and executive powers; the Council of Ministers is a supreme, executive and administrative organ accountable to the State Council and the National Assembly; there is no constitutional single Head of State but some of the functions of a Head of State are carried out by the Chairman of the State Council; the largest socio-political organization in Bulgaria is the Fatherland Front which was founded in 1942; the two main political forces in the country directing the development of a socialist society are the Bulgarian Communist Party and the Bulgarian Agrarian Party; local administration is in the hands of People's Councils elected for a term of two and a half years.

Trade and industry. The major industries that have developed since the war are food processing, machine building, chemicals, metal products, electronics, textiles

and clothing, with machinery and equipment accounting for nearly 50% of all exports (1983); fuel and minerals make up about 50% of the country's imports; nearly 80% of Bulgaria's trade is with the Soviet Union and other Eastern bloc countries.

Agriculture. Bulgaria is self-sufficient in agricultural produce which is still the mainstay of the economy despite recent industrialization; agriculture employs about 20% of the workforce producing some 25% of national income and exports; the main crops are grain, fruits, vegetables, rice, tobacco, sheep, hogs, poultry, cheese, sunflower seeds, unginned cotton and attar of roses; since the 1970s, 75% of farmland is held by agro-industrial complexes which are amalgamations of collective and state farms with food-processing plants and farm machinery stations.

Administrative divisions. The country is divided into 28 provinces or *okruzi* (sing. *okrug*) as follows:

Province	*area (sq km)*	*pop(1981)*
Blagoevgrad	6,464	338,000
Burgas	7,605	435,000
Gabrovo	2,068	178,000
Khaskovo	4,008	296,000
Kŭrdzhali	4,020	286,000
Kyustendil	3,002	199,000
Lovech	4,129	211,000
Mikhailovgrad	3,628	236,000
Pazardzhik	4,379	322,000
Pernik	2,355	175,000
Pleven	4,364	373,000
Plovdiv	5,612	753,000
Razgrad	2,646	193,000
Ruse	2,595	297,000
Shumen	3,374	252,000
Silistra	2,859	174,000
Sliven	3,618	236,000
Smolyan	3,518	174,000
Sofiya	7,310	309,000
Sofiya(city)	1,113	1,070,358
Stara Zagora	5,013	411,000
Tolbukhin	4,716	252,000
Tŭrgovishte	2,754	172,000
Varna	3,810	467,000
Veliko Tŭrnovo	4,719	347,000
Vidin	3,066	169,000
Vratsa	4,006	291,000
Yambol	4,162	205,000

Bum Bum, 4 27N 118 04E, island off the SE coast of Sabah state, E Malaysia; SE Asia; situated opposite Semporna; the chief village is Bum Bum.

Bunbury *bun'ber-ee*, 33 20S 115 34E, pop(1981) 21,749, resort and port in South-West stat div, Western Australia, Australia; on Koombana Bay, 180 km S of Perth; first settled by Lieut Bunbury in 1836; declared a city in 1979; railway; airfield; economy: crab fishing, superphosphates, computing software, timber, grain, mineral sands.

Bun'daberg, 24 50S 152 21E, pop(1981) 32,560, seaport in Wide Bay-Burnett stat div, Queensland, Australia; on the Burnett river, 380 km NNW of Brisbane; railway; airfield; economy: sugar, rum distilling, brewing, engineering, tomatoes; monuments: Bundaberg historical museum; monument to Bert Hinkler who made the first solo flight from London to Australia in 1928.

Bungoma *boong-gō'ma*, 0 34N 34 34E, pop(1979) 25,000, town in central Western prov, Kenya, E Africa; 35 km NNE of Kakamega, near the Ugandan border; railway.

Buraydah *boor-ī'du*, BURAIDAH, 26 20N 44 08E, pop(1974) 69,940, oasis town in Qassim prov, N central Saudi Arabia, 336 km NW of Ar Riyāḑ (Riyadh); airfield; noted for its camel and cattle markets.

Bur'bank, 34 11N 118 19W, pop(1980) 84,625, city in Santa Clara county, SW California, United States; 16 km NNW of Los Angeles, in the San Fernando Valley; settled in 1887; a noted centre of the film industry.

Burbank, 41 46N 87 48W, pop(1980) 28,462, town in Cook county, NE Illinois, United States; 20 km SW of Chicago.

Burdur *boor-door'*, mountainous prov in SW Turkey; bounded SE by Elmali Mts; pop(1980) 235,009; area 6,887 sq km; capital Burdur; economy: opium, hemp, grain, vegetables, attar of roses.

Burewala or **Mandi Burewala** *boor-ay'vahl-u*, 30 05N 72 47E, pop(1981) 86,000, agricultural market town in S Punjab prov, Pakistan; 102 km E of Multan.

Burgas or **Bourgas** *boor-gas'*, okrug (prov) of E Bulgaria bordering the Black Sea; area 7,605 sq km; pop(1981) 435,000; the area includes a number of seaside resorts including Nesebur and Sozopol; along the Gulf of Burgas lie the salt lakes of Pomorie, Atanasovo, Burgas and Mandra.

Burgas, 42 30N 27 29E, pop(1981) 173,078, commercial seaport, health resort and industrial capital of Burgas okrug (prov), E Bulgaria; on the Gulf of Burgas (Burgaski Zaliv) in the Black Sea; founded in the 18th century on the site of 14th-c Pirgos; airport; railway; economy: machinery, textiles, food processing; monuments: Department of Bulgarian Iconography in the district art gallery; Otmanli People's Parkland; event: international folklore festival.

Burgenland *boor'gen-lant*, federal state in E Austria on the Hungarian frontier, comprising 9 dists and 138 communities; pop(1981) 272,274; area 3,966 sq km; capital Eisenstadt; the Neusiedler See is central Europe's only steppe lake; it is a predominantly agricultural state, the main products being wheat, maize, vegetables, fruit, and a large variety of renowned wines; economy: canning of agricultural produce, sugar-processing; home of the Croat ethnic group which settled here in the 16th century after fleeing from their S Slav homes before advancing Turkish armies; formed in 1921 from German-speaking border areas of what had previously been Hungary.

Burgess Hill, 50 57N 0 08W, pop(1981) 23,631, town in Mid Sussex dist, West Sussex, S England; 15 km N of Brighton; railway.

Burgos or **Burgo** *boor'gos*, mountainous prov in Castilla-León region, N Spain; traversed by the Douro (Duero) and Ebro rivers with the Cordillera Cantabrica to the N and outliers of the central plateau (Meseta) in the S; pop(1981) 363,474; area 14,309 sq km; capital, Burgos; economy: forestry, livestock, food processing.

Burgos, 42 21N 3 41W, pop(1981) 156,449, capital of Burgos prov, N Spain; on R Arlanzón, 243 km N of Madrid; former capital of Old Castile; archbishopric; railway; monuments: cathedral (1221); castle of counts of Castile; home and burial site of El Cid; economy: textiles, motor accessories, silk, chemical products, nails, clothes; Santa Maria de Gerona nuclear power station (460 MW) opened in 1971; events: Corpus Christi with a great procession to the monastery of Las Huelgas and fair and fiestas of St Peter in June with bullfights, parades and concerts.

Burgundy, region in France. See Bourgogne.

Burkina *boor-kee'na*, official name People's Republic of Burkina, BURKINA FASO, formerly UPPER VOLTA (-1984), then officially RÉPUBLIQUE DE HAUTE-VOLTA (Fr), a landlocked republic in W Africa, bounded N by Mali, E by Niger, SE by Benin, S by Togo and Ghana and SW by Ivory Coast; area 274,540 sq km; timezone GMT; pop(1985e) 6,773,931; capital Ouagadougou; chief towns include Bobo Dioulasso, Koudougou, Ouahigouya, Kaya, Banfora, Tougan, Dédougou, Dori, Diébougou, Tenkodogo and Fada N'Gourma; there are over 50 tribes including the Mossi (48%), Gourma (5%) and Fulani nomads (10%) in the N, Lobi-Dagari (7%), Mandé (7%) in the SE, Bobo (7%) in the SW, Sénoufo (6%), and Gourounsi (5%); the official language is French, but 50% of the pop speak local languages of the Sudanic group (Moré, Dioula and Gourmantche); most (65%) of the pop follow local beliefs; the remainder are either Muslim (about 25%) or Christian (10%, mainly Roman Catholic); the unit of currency is the franc CFA; national holidays 3 Jan (Anniversary of the Revolution), 11 Dec (Republic Day); membership of AfDB, CEAO, EAMA, ECA, EIB (associate), Entente, FAO, G-77, GATT, IBRD, ICAO, IDA, IDB (Islamic Development Bank), IFAD, IFC, ILO, IMF, INTELSAT, INTERPOL, IPU, IRC, ITU, NAM, Niger River Commission, OAU, OCAM, OIC, UN, UNESCO, UPU, WCL, WFTU, WHO, WIPO, WMO and WTO.

Physical description. Burkina lies on a platform of ancient crystalline rock which is covered with sandstone in the S. The land is generally tilted southward so that most rivers flow S to the R Volta (the Volta Noire, Volta Rouge and Volta Blanche rivers), or to the R Niger. Many of the rivers are reduced during the dry season making navigation impossible. In the S there are wooded savannahs, while in the N the plains dry out into semi-desert.

Climate. Burkina has a tropical climate which is hot all year round, with a mean temp of 27°C during the dry season from Dec to May. There is a rainy season between June and Oct with violent storms in Aug. From Nov to March the dry, dusty *harmattan* wind blows from the NE. Generally, rainfall decreases from S to N. At Ouagadougou the average rainfall is 894 mm.

History, government and constitution. In the 18th and 19th centuries the Mossi, a Voltaic tribe, became the dominant African group with a large empire controlled from Ouagadougou. French colonial interests culminated in the creation of Upper Volta which was constituted in 1919 out of parts of Upper Senegal and Niger (created 1904). Abolished in 1932, most of the territory was joined to the Ivory Coast. In 1947 the original borders were reconstituted and autonomy within the French community followed in 1958. Upper Volta became fully independent in 1960. Restored in 1970, the constitution was suspended between 1974 and 1978. A new constitution of 1977 which allowed for the election of a 57-member National Assembly was further suspended in 1980. The Republic of Upper Volta was renamed Burkina Faso in 1984. Burkina is governed by a 12-member People's Salvation Council (CSP).

Economy. Burkina is an agricultural country with 90% of the pop involved in producing 50% of the national income during the early 1980s. Agriculture is largely at the subsistence level and is subject to drought conditions (eg 1973-74). The main subsistence crops are sorghum, millet, maize, and rice. Important cash crops include cotton, groundnuts, sesame, sugar cane and livestock. Though there are no known reserves of coal or petroleum there are reserves of titanium, limestone, iron ore, vanadium, manganese, zinc, nickel copper, phosphate and gold. The main manufactured products are processed foods, cigarettes, shoes and bicycles. Burkina's main trading partners are France, Ivory Coast, the USA, W Germany, Japan and the Netherlands.

Administrative divisions. Burkina is divided into 25 provinces:

Province	*pop(1985e)*
Bam	175,130
Bougouriba	213,019
Boulgou	358,617
Burkina	582,012
Comoé	210,758
Ganzourgou	149,744
Gnagna	147,570
Gourma	231,073
Houet	370,847
Kénédougou	118,603
Kossi	244,320
Nahouri	88,287
Namentenga	329,751
Nouhoun	240,318
Oubritenga	787,011
Passoré	262,548
Poni	216,604
Sahel	265,428
Sanmatenga	340,938
Sissli	144,642
Soum	159,975
Sourou	279,186
Tapoa	110,599
Yatenga	636,991
Zoundwéogo	109,960

contd

The depts are divided into 44 *cercles* or subdepts.

Burlingame *bur'ling-gaym*, 37 35N 122 21W, pop(1980) 26,173, city in San Mateo county, W California, United States; a residential suburb on the W shore of San Francisco Bay, 24 km S of San Francisco.

Burlington, 43 19N 79 48W, pop(1981) 114,853, town in SE Ontario, SE Canada; on L Ontario, 8 km N of Hamilton; railway.

Burlington, 40 49N 91 14W, pop(1980) 29,529, county seat of Des Moines county, SE Iowa, United States; on the Mississippi river, 94 km SSW of Davenport; railway; economy: a shipping and manufacturing centre.

Burlington, 36 06N 79 26W, pop(1980) 37,266, city in Alamance county, N central North Carolina, United States; 32 km E of Greensboro; railway; economy: industrial centre in an agricultural region; manufactures textiles.

Burlington, 44 29N 73 12W, pop(1980) 37,712, county seat of Chittenden county, NW Vermont, United States; port on E side of Lake Champlain, 54 km WNW of Montpelier; settled in 1773, achieving city status in 1865; university (1791); airport; railway; economy: food processing, timber, printing, electronics; event: Champlain Discovery (June).

Burma *bur'ma*, official name The Socialist Republic of the Union of Burma, PYIDAUNGSU SOCIALIST THAMMADA MYANMA NAINGNGANDAW *pyī-tah-win-zoo' sō-shal-ist ta'ma-da myan-ma' ning-ung-gan-da'* (Burm), republic in SE Asia; bordered by China (N and NE), Laos and Thailand (E), India (NW), Bangladesh (W), and by the Bay of Bengal and the Andaman Sea (W); timezone GMT +6½; area 678,576 sq km; capital Rangoon; chief cities include Mandalay, Henzada, Pegu, Myingyan; pop(1981) 36,196,000; ethnic groups include Burman (72%), Karen (7%), Shan (6%), Indian (6%), Chinese (3%), Kachin (2%), Chin (2%); the official language is Burmese, but minority ethnic groups also have their own languages; 85% of the pop practise Theravada Buddhism, an older form of Buddhism; the currency is the kyat (of 100 pyas); national holidays 4 Jan (Independence Day), 12 Feb (Union Day), 2 March (Peasants' Day), 11 March (Full Moon of Tabaung), 27 March (Resistance Day), 17 April (Burmese New Year), 24-26 April (Thingyan); 9 May (Full Moon of Ksonn), 7 July (Full Moon of Waso), 19 July (Martyrs' Day), 4 Oct (Thadingyut); 2 Nov (Dewali Tazaundaing), 12 Nov (National Day), 17 Dec (Karen New Year); membership of ADB, Colombo Plan, FAO, G-77, GATT, IAEA, IBRD, ICAO, IDA, IFC, IHO, ILO, IMF, IMO, INTERPOL, IRC, ITU, UN, UNESCO, UPU, WHO, and WMO.

Physical description. The largest country on the SE Asian mainland, Burma is rimmed in the N, E and W by mountain ranges rising in the N to over 5,500 m. Burma's highest peak, Hkakabo Razi (5,881 m), is situated on the N border with China. The mountains are a continuation of the high plateaux of S China, stretching down into Burma in a series of ridges and valleys. In the centre of the country lies the valley of the Irrawaddy and Chindwin rivers which rise in the high mountains to the N. Burma's principal rivers, the Irrawaddy, the Salween and the

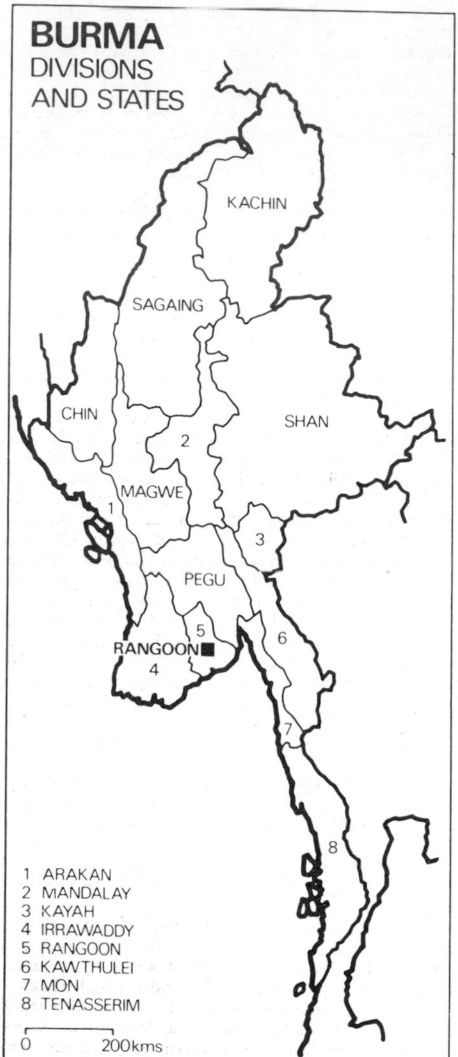

Sittang, all run from N to S, separating the Burmese mountain ranges in a series of river valleys. To the S of Rangoon is the Irrawaddy river delta, which extends over 240 km of tidal forest. The majority of the population is situated in the central low lying part of Burma, in the valleys of the Irrawaddy, Chindwin, Salween and Sittang rivers.

Climate. Burma has a tropical monsoon type of climate with a marked change between the cooler, dry season of Nov-April and the hotter, wet season of May-Sept. This seasonal contrast is caused by the great reversal of winds which affects south Asia. The dry season is dominated by the NE monsoon and the wet season by the SW monsoon, which blows off the Indian Ocean. Locally the main climatic differences depend on altitude and the degree of exposure to the rainy SW monsoon. The coastal and higher mountains of the E and N have heavy rainfall ranging from 2,500 to 5,000 mm a year. Since the interior lowlands are sheltered from the direct effect of the SW monsoon, they may receive as little as 1,000 mm of rain or even less. Mandalay lying inland receives only 3 mm in Jan and Feb, and a max of 160 mm in July. Over most of Burma, at least three-quarters of the annual rainfall occurs during the season of the SW monsoon. In the lowlands, and especially on the coast, temperatures are high all year round, the highest occurring during March-May, before the heaviest rains. Although temperatures are lower in the hills, the climate below 1,200 m is hot and tropical for most of the year. High humidity renders the high temperatures on the coast even more unpleasant. Even inland the heat of the rainy season is oppressive. The dry season is distinctly cooler and more pleasant in the interior, especially in the N uplands.

History, government and constitution. First unified during the 11th century by King Anawrahta, Burma remained independent until 1287 when Kubla Khan's Mongol hordes invaded the country. A second dynasty was established in 1486 but was plagued by internal disunity and, from the 16th century onwards, by intermittent wars with Siam (now Thailand). A new dynasty was established in 1752 and Burma was reunited under King Alaungpaya. Under his and his successor's rule Burma repelled the Chinese but came into conflict with the British, who were vying with the French for dominance in the area. Burma was eventually annexed to British India during the 3 Anglo-Burmese wars between 1824 and 1886. Burma's last king, Thibaw, was exiled by the British and the monarchical system abolished. Burma was separated from India in 1937 and was granted a constitution which provided a limited measure of self-government. Under the leadership of the People's Freedom League (AFPFL) the various groups and regions within Burma joined to form the Union of Burma which formally came into existence on 4 Jan 1948 as a fully independent nation outside the Commonwealth of Nations. The Burmese government, headed by Prime Minister U Nu, was controlled by the AFPFL and followed a policy of parliamentary democracy, dedicated to the creation of a socialist welfare state. In 1958 a split in the AFPFL led to a political crisis and an army takeover. Elections held in 1960 led to U Nu regaining power with his faction of the AFPFL renamed the Union Party. A second coup in March 1962 established a new revolutionary government. Twelve years later, in March 1974, a new constitutionally elected single-party system of government was installed and the country became the Socialist Republic of the Union of Burma. This followed the approval by referendum in 1973 of a new constitution designed to establish a one-party socialist republic. The 464-member People's Assembly (*Pithu Hluttaw*) elects a 29-member State Council, a prime minister and a council of ministers. The president is elected by the State Council. Each state is governed by a number of locally elected People's Councils.

Economy. The economy of Burma is largely dependent on agriculture and forestry which account for nearly 50% of national income and employ over 70% of the workforce. The main agricultural products are rice, beans, maize, sugar cane, pulses and oilseed. The forest industry is a major supplier of teak and other hardwoods for fuel and export. Major industries include agricultural processing, textiles and footwear, pharmaceuticals, fertilizers, wood and wood products and petroleum refining. Mineral resources include zinc and lead from Shan state, tin from Tenasserim, copper, gypsum, limestone, chromium, asbestos, oil and coal. The country's main exports are rice, teak and minerals. Major trade partners include Singapore, Western Europe, China, the UK and Japan.

Administrative divisions. Burma is divided into 14 administrative divisions 7 of which are states as follows:

Division	*pop(1983)*
Arakan State	2,045,891
Chin State	368,985
Irrawaddy	4,991,057
Kachin State	903,982
Kawthulei State	1,057,505
Kayah State	168,355

contd

Division	*pop(1983)*
Magwe	3,241,103
Mandalay	4,580,923
Mon State	1,682,041
Pegu	3,800,240
Rangoon	3,973,782
Sagaing	3,855,991
Shan State	3,718,706
Tenasserim	917,628

Burnaby, 49 16N 122 58W, pop(1981) 136,494, town in S British Columbia, SW Canada; an E suburb of Vancouver; Simon Fraser University (1963), railway.

Burnham-on-Sea *ber'nĕm-*, 51 15N 3 00W, pop(1981) 17,341, resort town linked with Highbridge in Sedgemoor dist, Somerset, SW England; on Bridgewater Bay on the Bristol Channel, 12 km N of Bridgewater; railway.

Burn'ley, 53 48N 2 14W, pop(1981) 77,127, town in Burnley dist, Lancashire, NW England; at the junction of the Brun and Calder rivers, 35 km N of Manchester; railway; economy: engineering, textiles, chemicals, aerospace equipment, vehicle parts.

Burnsville, 44 47N 93 17W, pop(1980) 35,674, town in Dakota county, SE Minnesota, United States; 26 km S of Minneapolis.

Burntwood, 52 42N 1 55W, pop(1981) 29,085, town in Lichfield dist, Staffordshire, central England; 12 km N of Walsall.

Burrel *boo'rel*, 41 37N 19 59E, town and capital of Mat prov, N central Albania; 37 km NNE of Tiranë, on the R Mat; police training school.

Bursa *boor-sah'*, maritime prov in NW Turkey, bounded NW by the Sea of Marmara; pop(1980) 1,148,492; area 11,043 sq km; capital Bursa; economy: tobacco, fruit and grain.

Bursa, BRUSA, PRUSA (anc), 40 12N 29 04E, pop(1980) 445,113, capital city of Bursa prov, NW Turkey; 5th largest city in Turkey; commercial and industrial centre; noted for its silk textiles; founded at the end of the 3rd century BC; railway; airfield; economy: motor car assembly, soft drinks; monument: Green mosque (1421).

Burton, 42 59N 84 17W, pop(1980) 29,976, town in Genesee county, E Michigan, United States; SE of, and adjoining, Flint.

Burton-upon-Trent, BURTON-ON-TRENT, 52 49N 1 36W, pop(1981) 59,595, town in East Staffordshire dist, Staffordshire, central England; on the R Trent, 15 km SW of Derby; railway; economy: brewing, foodstuffs, rubber products, tyres.

Buru *bur'oo*, mountainous, forested island in Maluku prov, Indonesia; island of the Moluccas group W of Seram and E of Sulawesi (Celebes); area 8,803 sq km; rises to 2,429 m at Mt Tomahu; taken by the Dutch in 1683.

Burundi *bu-roon'dee*, official name Republic of Burundi, a republic in central Africa, bounded N by Rwanda, E and S by Tanzania, SW by L Tanganyika and W by Zaire; timezone GMT +2; area 27,834 sq km; pop(1984) 4,691,000; in 1984 the UNHCR recorded 256,300 refugees mainly from Zaire and Rwanda; capital Bujumbura; chief towns Bubanza, Ngozi, Muyinga, Muramvya, Gitega, Bururi and Rutana; the pop comprises Hutu (85%), with Tutsi (14%), Pygmy (1%) and a few Europeans and S Asians; the chief religions are Roman Catholic (62%), Protestant (5%), local religious beliefs (32%) and Muslim (1%); official languages are French and Kirundi with Swahili being spoken along L Tanganyika and in the Bujumbura area; the unit of currency is the Burundi franc; national holiday 1 July (Independence Day); membership of AfDB, EAMA, ECA, FAO, G-77, GATT, IBRD, ICAO, ICO, IDA, IFAD, IFC, ILO, IMF, INTERPOL, ITU, NAM, OAU, UN, UNESCO, UPU, WHO, WIPO, WMO and WTO.

Physical description. Burundi lies across the Nile-Congo watershed and is bounded W by the narrow plain of the R Ruzizi (NW) and L Tanganyika (W). The R Malagarasi forms the S border with Tanzania, and the R Akanyaru follows the N border with Rwanda. Lakes Rugwero and Tshohoha are located on the N frontier with Rwanda. The interior is a plateau at an average height of about 1,500 m sloping E toward Tanzania and the R Maragarazi valley. The highest point in Burundi is Mount Karonje (2,685 m). The R Nile's most southerly tributary, the R Luvironza, rises in the S.

Climate. Burundi has an equatorial climate that varies with altitude and by season. A dry season occurs from June to Sept, the rest of the year being moderately wet. The average annual rainfall in Bujumbura (alt 805 m) is 850 mm per year.

History, government and constitution. Since the 16th century the country was ruled by the Tutsi kingdom under a number of *mwamis* ('kings'). Following German military occupation in 1890 the area was included in German East Africa. During World War I the Belgians took control and in 1919 Burundi became a League of Nations mandated territory administered by the Belgians. After World War II it was joined with Rwanda and became the UN Trust Territory of Ruanda-Urundi (1946). UN elections in 1961 led to internal self-government in 1962 and full independence later the same year. The suspension of the constitution in 1966 was accompanied by the appointment of a new prime minister and king, the latter being deposed in the same year with Burundi being declared a republic in the process. In 1972 the Council of Ministers was dissolved and civil war escalated. Later in the same year the government was recalled only to be deposed in a military coup in 1976. This event produced a revolutionary council and a military president. Civilian government was restored in 1982 with a National Assembly, an executive president, a Council of Ministers and military governors for the provinces.

Economy. Agriculturally the country is marginally self-sufficient in food, the main subsistence crops including manioc, yams, corn and haricot beans. Cash crops include coffee, cotton and tea. Industry centres around light consumer goods such as shoes, soap, beverages and blankets. Tin and basserite ceased to be mined in 1979 and 1980 respectively. There are reserves of rare earth metals, peat, nickel, tungsten, columbium, tantalum and phosphate at various locations. Main trading partners are Belgium, Luxembourg, West Germany, France, Kenya, Japan, the UK, the USA and the Netherlands.

Administrative divisions. Burundi is divided into the 8 provinces of Bujumbura, Bubanza, Muramvya, Ngozi, Gitega, Ruyigi, Bururi and Muyinga, which are subdivided into 18 arrondissements and 78 communes.

Bururi *boo-roo'ree*, 3 57S 29 35E, capital of prov of same name, Burundi, central Africa; 66 km SW of Gitega.

Bury *ber'i*, 53 36N 2 17W, pop(1981) 62,181, town in Bury borough, Greater Manchester, NW England; 8 km E of Bolton; home town of Robert Peel (founder of the British police force) and John Kay (inventor of the 'flying shuttle' weaving loom); railway; monuments: Lancashire Fusiliers museum with memorabilia of the division which guarded Napoleon while in exile on St Helena; city museum with the Wrigley collection of 19th-c English paintings.

Bury St Edmunds *ber'i-*, BEODERICSWORTH (Anglo-Saxon), 52 15N 0 43E, pop(1981) 31,178, market town in St Edmundsbury dist, Suffolk, E England; on the R Lark, 37 km NW of Ipswich and 45 km E of Cambridge; burial place of King Edmund who was later canonized; the 7th-c monastery, converted to an abbey in 1032, was a major centre for the production of illustrated manuscripts including the *Bury Bible*; railway; economy: brewing, agricultural machinery, precision engineering, electronics, cameras; monuments: 11th-c abbey, 15th-c cathedral of St James, 14-15th-c church of St Mary, Suffolk Regiment museum, Moyes Hall museum.

Busembatia *bus cm-baht'ee-a*, 0 46N 33 37E, town in Busoga prov, Uganda, E Africa; NW of Jinja; railway.

Būshehr *boo-sheer'*, prov in SW Iran, bounded W by the Arabian Gulf; pop(1982) 356,216; area 27,699 sq km; capital Būshehr.

Būshehr, BUSHIRE, 28 59N 50 50E, pop(1983) 120,948, seaport capital of Būshehr dist, Būshehr, SW Iran; on a peninsula which juts into the Arabian Gulf; one of the chief ports of Iran; founded in 1736; the British used it as a base for their Persian Gulf fleet in the 18th century; airfield.

Busia *boo'si-ya*, 0 28N 34 07E, pop(1979) 25,000, town in W Western prov, Kenya, E Africa; on the frontier with Uganda, 27 km SSW of Tororo.

Buskerud *boos-ke-rood'*, a county of S Norway, drained chiefly by the Lågen and Hemsil rivers; area 14,933 sq km; pop(1983) 217,348; capital Drammen; chief towns include Hønefoss and Kongsberg.

Busoga *boo-sō'ga*, prov of SE Uganda, E Africa; bounded S by L Victoria; chief town Jinja.

Bus'selton, 33 43S 115 15E, pop(1981) 6,463, resort town in South-West stat div, Western Australia, Australia; on S shore of Geographe Bay, S of Bunbury and 190 km SSW of Perth; founded by John Busselton in 1832; railway; economy: wine, vegetables, grain, dairy products, fishing.

Butare *boo-ta'ra*, 2 34S 29 43E, pop(1978) 21,691, capital of prefecture of same name, Rwanda, central Africa; 71 km SSW of Kigali; alt 1,748 m; originally called Astrida after the Belgian queen; university (1963); founded in 1927.

Butte *byoot*, 46 00N 112 32W, pop(1980) 37,205, county seat of Silver Bow county, SW Montana, United States; on a plateau in the Rocky Mts; railway; airfield; economy: mining of copper, zinc, silver, manganese, gold, lead and arsenic; monument: World Museum of Mining.

But'termere, lake, village and fell in the Lake District of Cumbria, NW England; SW of Keswick; joined to the Crummock Water (NW) by a short stream.

Butterworth, 5 25N 100 22E, pop(1980) 77,982, city in Pulau Pinang state, NW Peninsular Malaysia, SE Asia; on the Strait of Malacca, 382 km NW of Kuala Lumpur; airfield; railway; ferry to George Town on Pinang island (*pulau*).

Bux'ton, AQUAE ARNEMETIAE (Lat), 53 15N 1 55W, pop(1981) 20,282, spa town in High Peak dist, Derbyshire, central England; 34 km SE of Manchester; radioactive springs; railway; economy: scientific instruments, limestone; event: well-dressing on Ascension Day.

Buzău *book-za'oo*, county in SE central Romania, in the SE foothills of the Transylvanian Alps; crossed by the R Buzău; pop(1983) 518,030; area 6,072 sq km; capital Buzău; oil, timber, wine-producing and agriculture are important.

Buzău, 45 09N 26 49E, pop(1983) 126,780, commercial and industrial capital of Buzău county, SE central Romania; on the R Buzău; railway junction; economy: timber, grain and wine trade, chemical equipment, glass, metal, oil refining, textiles; monument: 17th-c cathedral.

Bydgoszcz *bid-goshtch'*, voivodship in N central Poland; bounded on the E by R Wisła (Vistula) and watered by Brda, Wda and Noteć rivers; the city of Bydgoszcz is bypassed by the Noteć Canal and the Bydgoszcz Canal links the Wisła and Oder (Odra) river basins with other central European waterways; Bydgoszcz Canal planned in 1766 by the Polish geographer F. Czaki; region includes the Tuchola Forest; pop(1983) 1,064,000; area 10,349 sq km; capital Bydgoszcz; chief towns include Inowrocław, Chojnice and Świecie.

Bydgoszcz, BROMBERG *brom'berk* (Ger), 53 10N 18 00E, pop(1983) 357,700, river port capital of Bydgoszcz voivodship, N central Poland; on R Brda near its confluence with the Wisła (Vistula); an important river communications centre; granted urban status in 1346; sports stadium and centre; railway; airport; economy: radios, telephones, bicycles, footwear, light engineering; monuments: 16th-c Poor Clare's church, Leon Wyczołkowski museum of art, philharmonic hall, 18-19th-c half-timbered granaries; events: festival of ancient music; Polish piano competitions.

Bytom *bit'om*, BEUTHEN *boy'ten* (Ger), 50 21N 18 51E, pop(1983) 238,000, mining city in Katowice voivodship, S Poland; NW of Katowice; lead and silver mines important in 12th century when the city was founded; now an important Silesian coal and ore mining centre; centre of Polish independence organizations during the plebiscite of 1921; incorporated into Germany until 1945; railway; economy: coal, zinc, lead mining, metallurgy, clothing; monuments: medieval city walls, 13-14th-c Gothic church of St Mary, Upper Silesian museum.

C

Caaguazú *ka-a-gwa-soo'*, dept in Oriental region, SE central Paraguay; E of Asunción; pop(1982) 299,227; area 14,409 sq km; capital Coronel Oviedo.

Caazapá *ka-a-sa-pa'*, dept in Oriental region, SE Paraguay; bounded S and SW by the Río Tebicuary; pop(1982) 109,510; area 9,496 sq km; capital Caazapá.

Cabañas *ka-van'yas*, dept in N El Salvador, Central America; bounded NE by Honduras; pop(1971) 139,312; area 1,075 sq km; capital Sensuntepeque; chief towns Victoria and Ilobasco; the Río Lempa forms its N boundary.

Cabeço Rainha *kab-ay'soo rin'ya*, 39 51N 7 48W, mountain, W of Castelo Branco, E central Portugal, rising to 1,080 m.

Cabimas *ka-bee'mas*, 10 26N 71 27W, pop(1981) 140,435, town in Zulia state, W Venezuela; on the E shore of L de Maracaibo.

Cabinda *ku-been'du*, prov of Angola on the SW coast of Africa, N of the R Congo; bounded W by the Atlantic and surrounded by the Congo, it is separated from the rest of Angola; area 7,270 sq km; chief town Cabinda; attached to Angola in 1886 by agreement with Belgium; oil is extracted from the offshore Kambala and Livuite fields.

Cabinda, 5 35S 12 12E, seaport capital of prov of same name, NW Angola, SW Africa; 55 km N of the R Congo estuary and 105 km WNW of Boma (Zaire); economy: oil refining.

Cabo Delga'do, prov in NE Mozambique, SE Africa; pop(1980) 940,000; area 82,625 sq km, R Rovuma forms N border with Tanzania and R Lúrio forms S border with Nampula prov; capital Pemba; chief towns include Mocímboa da Praia, Montepeuz, Palma and Ibo.

Cabo Orange *ō-ran'zhay*, national park in N Amapá terr, Norte region, N Brazil; area 6,190 sq km; established in 1980.

Cabreira *kab ray'ra*, 41 38N 8 03W, highest point of Serra de Cabreira mountain range, Braga dist, N Portugal, rising to 1,261 m.

Cabrera *kab-ray'ra*, 39 15N 2 58E, small island in the Mediterranean Balearic Is, Baleares autonomous region, Spain; 15 km S of Mallorca.

Cabriel *kab-ree-el'*, river rising in the Sierra de Cuenca, Castilla-La Mancha, Spain; flowing SSE then SE to meet the R Júcar at Cofrentes; the river is dammed at Contreras to form a reservoir; the river forms part of the W boundary with Valencia region; length 263 km.

Čačak or **Chachak** *chah'chahk*, 43 54N 20 22E, pop(1981) 110,676, town in W central Srbija (Serbia) republic, E Yugoslavia; 96 km S of Beograd; railway; economy: fruit trade.

Cáceres *ka'the-res*, prov in the upper part of Extremadura region, W Spain; in the R Tagus basin; bounded to the W by Portugal; mountainous in the N and flat in the S below the R Tagus; nuclear power station at Almarez; pop(1981) 414,744; area 19,945 sq km; capital Cáceres; economy: cotton, clothes, chemicals, pharmaceuticals, ceramics, metal products, canning, olives, fruit, vegetables, livestock.

Cáceres, QAZRIS (Arab), 39 26N 6 23W, pop(1981) 71,852, walled town and capital of Cáceres prov, W Spain; on the R Cáceres; 297 km WSW of Madrid; a Roman settlement was founded here in the 1st century BC; railway; economy: pharmaceuticals, chemicals, textiles, leather; monuments: the centre of the old walled town is the Plaza Santa Maria; Lower Golfines Palace; church of San Mateo; Maltravieso cave paintings.

Cacheu *ku-shay'oo*, region in Guinea-Bissau, W Africa; pop(1979) 130,227.

Čadca *chat'sa*, 49 26N 18 45E, pop(1984) 21,480, town in Středoslovenský region, Slovak Socialist Republic, central Czechoslovakia; near the Polish frontier, N of Žilina; railway; economy: textiles.

Cad'er Id'ris ('chair of Idris'), 52 42N 3 54W, mountain ridge in Gwynedd, NW Wales; SW of Dolgellau; rises to 892 m at Pen-y-Gader.

Cádiz *ka'deeth* or *ke-diz'* (Eng), prov in Andalucia region, SW Spain; facing the Atlantic (Gulf of Cádiz), the Mediterranean and the Strait of Gibraltar; crossed in the NW by the R Guadalquivir; Punta Tarifa is the southernmost point of Europe, pop(1981) 1,001,716; area 7,385 sq km; capital Cádiz; economy: famous for its Jerez sherry; steelworks at Campo de Gibraltar; shipyard at Puerto Real; natural gas offshore.

Cádiz, GADIER or GADES (anc), (Arab 'gaddir', fortress), 36 30N 6 20W, pop(1981) 157,766, seaport and capital of Cádiz prov, Andalucia, SW Spain; on a promontory in the Bay of Cádiz, projecting NW from the Isla de León; 663 km SSW of Madrid; bishopric; university; airport; railway; car ferries to Casablanca and Canary Is; naval harbour of La Carraca; economy: shipbuilding and export of sherry, fish, salt and olives; Spanish treasure ships from the Americas made Cádiz one of the wealthiest ports in Europe during the 16-18th centuries; Sir Francis Drake burned the ships of Philip II at anchor here in 1587; monuments: 18th-c cathedral; chapel of Santa Catalina containing Murillo's last work; events: Holy Week; Fiestas Típicas Gaditanas in May, Festival of Spain in Aug with a regatta and Trofeo Internacional Ramon, an international football competition, in August.

Caen *kã*, 49 10N 0 22W, pop(1982) 117,119, port and capital of Calvados dept, Basse-Normandie region, NW France; on the R Orne, 15 km S of the R Seine; university (1432, refounded in 1809); airport; railway; the town is linked to Ouistreham by a canal; the local limestone was used to build many of the cathedrals and churches of S England; principal seat of William the Conqueror; Beau Brummel died in the lunatic asylum here; economy: tourism, commerce and steel; monuments: abbey church of St-Étienne with the tomb of William the Conqueror; church of St-Pierre with its famous clock tower.

Caernarfon or **Caernarvon** *kahr nahr'von*, 53 08N 4 16W, pop(1981) 9,431, historic county town in Arfon dist, Gwynedd, NW Wales; yachting centre; economy: agricultural trade, plastics, metal products; monument: 13th-c castle, birthplace of Edward II.

Caerphilly *kar-fil'i*, 51 35N 3 14W, pop(1981) 28,971, town in Rhymney Valley dist, Mid Glamorgan, S Wales; N of Cardiff in Caerphilly-Bedwas urban area; the town gives its name to a fine white cheese; railway; economy: cheese, textiles, engineering; monument: castle (c.1270), built by Edward I.

Cagayan de Oro *ka-gī'an day ō'rō*, 8 29N 124 40E, pop(1980) 227,312, city in Misamis Oriental prov, Northern Mindanao, Philippines; on NW coast of Mindanao I, near the mouth of the R Cagayan; university (1933); airfield.

Cagliari *kal'ya-ree*, CAR'ALES (anc), prov of S Sardegna (Sardinia) Italy; pop(1981) 730,473; area 6,895 sq km; capital Cagliari.

Cagliari, 39 13N 9 08E, pop(1981) 233,848, seaport and capital of Cagliari prov, S Sardegna (Sardinia), Italy; on the S coast of the island in the wide Golfo de Cagliari (Gulf of Cagliari), with salt lagoons on either side; the oldest part of the town is situated on the slopes of a precipitous hill, around the foot of which are the newer districts and suburbs; archbishopric; university (1606); airport; railway; ferries to Napoli (Naples), Civitavecchio and Palermo; economy: oil terminal, petrochemicals; monuments: cathedral (1312), Roman amphitheatre, museum of archaeology; events: Santa Maria di Bonaria - patronal festival (24 April); Sagra di San Efisio costume festival (beginning of May).

Caguas *kag'was*, 18 14N 66 04W, pop(1980) 117,959, inland city of Puerto Rico, E Caribbean; at the centre of a fertile valley 25 km S of San Juan.

Cahors *ka-or*, 44 27N 1 27E, pop(1982) 20,774, ancient town and capital of Lot dept, Midi-Pyrénées region, S central France; on a bend of the R Lot; birthplace of the statesman Gambetta; known for its full-bodied, dry red wine and its truffles; bishopric; railway; monuments: 3-towered Pont de Valentre (1308); 11th-c cathedral of St-Étienne.

Caicos Islands *kay'kos*, island group in the W Atlantic, SE of the Bahamas, forming a British dependent territory with the Turks Is; includes the islands of S Caicos, E Caicos, Middle (or Grand) Caicos, Providenciales and W Caicos; settled by Loyalist planters from the S States of America after the War of Independence; after the abolition of slavery in 1838 the planters left the islands to their former slaves.

Cairngorms, The, CAIRNGORM MTS, mountain range in NE central Scotland, part of the Grampian Mts; a granite mountain mass in SE Highland and SW Grampian regions; rises to 1,309 m in Ben Macdhui; between the rivers Dee (S) and Spey (N); winter sports area.

Cairns *kayrnz*, 16 51S 145 43E, pop(1981) 48,557, resort and seaport in Far North stat div, on the NE coast of Queensland, Australia; starting point for tours to the Great Barrier Reef, the Atherton Tableland and the Cape York Peninsula; offshore are Green Island, Fitzroy Island and Arlington Reef; railway; airfield; economy: agricultural trade, timber, mining, sugar, deep-sea fishing for black marlin (Sept-Dec).

Cairo *kī'rō*, EL QÂHIRA (Arab), 30 03N 31 15E, pop(1984e) 9,500,000 (Greater Cairo), capital of Egypt and Cairo governorate; at the head of the R Nile delta on the W bank, 180 km SE of Alexandria and 130 km W of Suez; largest African city; originally founded as El Fustat in 642 AD by the Arabs; a new capital city was founded beside El Fustat in 969 AD by Jauhar (a Fatimite general); occupied by the British 1882-1946; Cairo University (1908); Ain Shams University (1950); American University (1919); railway; airport; economy: tourism, cement, chemicals, leather, textiles, brewing, food processing; monuments: mosque of Amur (7th-c); mosque of Kait Bey (15th-c); the Muslim university (972 AD) is housed in the mosque of El Azhar, the world's leading centre of Islamic learning; mosque of Ibn Touloun (878 AD); mosque of Sultan Hassan (14th-c); Roda island in the R Nile is where the biblical figure Moses is reputed to have been found in the bulrushes; major archaeological sites nearby including Heliopolis, the pyramids at El Gîza and the ruins of Memphis; Egyptian museum of antiquities with exhibits that include treasures from Tut Ankh Amun's tomb; Coptic museum; museum of Islamic art; royal library.

Caithness, district in Highland region, N Scotland; pop(1981) 27,380; area 1,776 sq km; chief town Wick.

Cajamarca *ka-KHa-mar'ka*, mountainous dept in N Peru; crossed by Cordillera Oriental; bordered N by Ecuador, E by the Río Marañón; pop(1981) 1,045,569; area 35,417 sq km; capital Cajamarca.

Cajon, El *el ku-hōn'*, 32 48N 116 58W, pop(1980) 73,892, city in San Diego county, S California, United States; 19 km E of San Diego.

Čakovec *chah'ko-vets*, CSAKATHURN *cha'ka-toorn* (Ger), CSÁKTORNYA *chak'tor-nya* (Hung), 46 24N 16 26E, pop(1981) 116,825, town in N Hrvatska (Croatia) republic, Yugoslavia; railway; economy: wine trade, petroleum.

Calabar *ka'lu-bar*, 4 56N 8 22E, pop(1981e) 256,000, seaport capital of Cross River state, Nigeria, W Africa; near the mouth of the R Calabar, 560 km ESE of Lagos; known as Old Calabar until 1904; university (1975); airfield; tanker terminal; economy: cement, palm oil, rubber and wood.

Calabria *ka-lab'ree-a*, *ka-lay'bri-a* (Eng), region of S Italy, occupying the 'toe' of the country, between the Ionian and Tyrrhenian seas; comprises the provs of Cosenza, Catanzaro, and Reggio di Calabria; pop(1981) 2,061,182; area 15,079 sq km; capital Catanzaro; chief towns Cosenza, Crotone, Reggio di Calabria, and Locri; in the N is La Sila (Botte Donato, 1,929 m) and in the S the Aspromonte range (Montallo, 1,956 m) separated by an expanse of low-lying land, once marshy and malaria-ridden, which is located between the Golfo di Santa Eufemia in the W and the Golfo di Squillace in the E; the coast is much indented with bays and coves; underdeveloped area with mixed Mediterranean agriculture, producing wheat, olives, figs, wine, and citrus fruit; there is a newly developed industrial area at Crotone, supplied by electric power from a number of dams in the Sila range; mineral resources include rock salt from Lungro and sulphur from Strongoli; the region is much subject to earthquakes, floods, and erosion.

Calabria, national park in Calabria region, S Italy; area 170 sq km; established in 1968.

Calais *kal-ay'*, *kal'ay* (Eng), 50 57N 1 52E, pop(1982) 76,935, seaport in Pas-de-Calais dept, Nord region, NW France; on the Pas de Calais (Straits of Dover) at the shortest crossing to England; 34 km ESE of Dover and 238 km N of Paris; railway; airport; ferry services to Dover and Folkestone; economy: tulle and machine-made lace, passenger and commercial port; monuments: Rodin's famous sculpture of the 6 burghers commemorating the surrender of the town to Edward III after an 8-month siege.

Calama *ka-la'ma*, 22 27S 68 56W, pop(1982) 61,727, modern capital of Elloa prov, Valparaíso, N Chile; NE of Antofagasta; alt 2,250 m; railway; airfield; economy: explosives manufacturing.

Călăraşi *ka-la-rash'*, county in SE Romania, bounded to the S by the R Danube which follows the frontier with Bulgaria; pop(1983) 310,388; area 4,959 sq km; capital Călăraşi; the area is noted for fruit-growing and wine production.

Călăraşi, KALARASH, 44 12N 27 22E, pop(1983) 63,005, capital of Călăraşi county, SE Romania; on R Byk; railway; economy: fruit, wine trade, pulp, clothing, foodstuffs.

Calcutta *kal-ku'ta*, 22 36N 88 24E, pop(1981) 9,166,000, port capital of West Bengal, E India; on the R Hugli in the delta of the R Ganga (Ganges), 128 km from the Bay of Bengal; 2nd largest city in India; chief port of E India; founded in 1690 by the British East India Company; in 1756 the Nawab of Bengal captured Calcutta, imprisoning the garrison overnight in a confined guardroom of Fort William known as 'the black hole of Calcutta'; capital of British India (1773-1912); Maidan, 3 sq km of parkland in the city centre, was originally cleared from jungle to prevent surprise attacks on Fort William; Chowringhee (Jawaharlal Nehru Road), once an old pilgrim route to Kalighat, is now Calcutta's main thoroughfare; 2 universities (1857, 1962); airport (Dum Dum); railway; economy: textiles, chemicals, paper, metal, jute; monuments: Ochterlony Monument, erected in honour of Gen David Ochterlony who brought the Nepal War to a successful conclusion; N of the Maidan is the Raj Bhaven, built as the palace residence of the governor of Bengal; St John's cathedral (1787); Nakhoda mosque (1926) is the chief mosque of the Muslim population of Calcutta; Marble Palace (1835) is built with 90 varieties of marble; mirror-encrusted Jain temples (1867) are surrounded by ornamental gardens and figures, the chief image having a necklace of gold and a diamond in his head; the Hindu Bengali Temple of Kali

(1809) is built on a sacred site associated with the small toe of a goddess who fell there.

Caldas *kal'das*, mountainous dept in central Colombia, South America; follows the Cauca valley between the Cordillera Central (E) and the Cordillera Occidental (W); includes the Nevado del Ruiz on Tolima dept border; pop(1985) 789,730; area 7,888 sq km; capital Manizales.

Caldas da Rainha *kal'das da rin'ya* ('the queen's hot springs'), 39 24N 9 08W, pop(1981) 16,900, spa town in Leiria dist, central Portugal, with warm sulphur springs; railway; economy: ceramics; events: Midsummer 'holy bath' celebrations, 23-25 June.

Calder *kol'der*, river rising S of Burnley in Lancashire, NW England; flows 56 km E through W Yorkshire to meet the R Aire at Castleford; it is joined by the R Colne NE of Huddersfield.

Calder, river rising N of Colne, central Lancashire, NW England; flows 25 km NW to meet the R Ribble near Whalley.

Caldera *kal-day'ra*, 9 55N 84 51W, port in Puntarenas prov, W Costa Rica, Central America; S of Puntarenas on the Golfo de Nicoya.

Caldicot, 51 36N 2 45W, pop(1981) 12,296, town in Monmouth dist, Gwent, SE Wales; E of Newport; railway.

Caledon *kal'e-don*, river in Lesotho and South Africa; length about 480 km; a major tributary of the Orange river which it joins by flowing into the lake created by the Hendrik Verwoerd dam near Bethulie, on the border between Orange Free State prov and Cape prov; for much of its upper reaches it forms Lesotho's N frontier with South Africa before flowing through the Orange Free State prov.

Caledonian Canal, a line of inland navigation following the Great Glen (Glen Mor) in Highland region, Scotland; extends from Inverness in the NE to Loch Eil near Fort William in the SW, passing through Lochs Ness, Oich and Lochy and 35 km of man-made channels which were excavated between 1803 and 1847; there are 29 locks; total length 96 km.

Calera, La *la ka-lay'ra*, 32 47S 71 16W, pop(1982) 33,738, town in Quillota dist, Valparaíso, central Chile; railway.

Calgary, 51 05N 114 05W, pop(1984) 619,814, town in S Alberta, SW Canada; on the Bow river where it meets the Elbow river, near the foothills of the Rocky Mts; centre of a rich grain and livestock area; from the mid-1800s the site of Calgary was visited by fur trappers, hunters and gold prospectors; in 1875 the North West Mounted Police began the building of a fort, the forerunner of modern Calgary; the settlement grew after the arrival of the Canadian Pacific Railroad (CPR) in 1883, and Calgary was chosen by the CPR as the headquarters of their land settlement and irrigation schemes; in 1886 after a large part of Calgary was destroyed by fire a city edict made it mandatory to construct new buildings of sandstone; in 1914 oil was found to the S of Calgary; university (1945); airport; economy: communications and transport centre, meat packing, oil refining; monuments: the Glenbow Alberta art gallery and museum contains mementoes from pioneering days; Heritage Park open-air museum; on St George's Island in the Elbow river are Dinosaur Park and Calgary Zoo; Calgary Tower (1967) at 190 m is the 2nd tallest structure of its kind on the American continent; the Centennial Planetarium was built to mark Canada's 1967 Centennial Year; event: the Calgary Stampede in July, with rodeo competitions, chuckwagon races, stage shows, trade and livestock exhibitions and a cattle stampede.

Cali *ka'lee*, 3 24N 76 30W, pop(1985) 1,398,276, capital of Valle de Cauca dept, W Colombia, South America; the 3rd largest city in Colombia at the centre of a rich sugar-producing region; founded in 1536; 2 universities (1945, 1958); railway; airport (Palmaseca) at 17.5 km; monuments: many of the possessions of Cali's last Royal Sheriff have been preserved in the colonial ranch-house of Cañas Gordas; the church and 18th-c monastery of San Francisco houses a collection of paintings by former monks and abbots; Cali's oldest church, La Merced, with its adjoining convent, houses the museum of colonial art and the archaeological museum; at the centre of Cali, in the Plaza de Caicedo, are the cathedral, national palace and a statue of one of the independence leaders, Joaquín Caicedo y Cuero; modern art museum; events: national art festival in June; annual fair in Dec with bullfights, masquerade balls and sporting contests.

Calicut *kal'i-kut*, KOZHIKODE *kō'zhe-kōd*, 11 15N 75 43E, pop(1981) 546,000, port city in Kerala, SW India; university (1968); on the Malabar Coast of the Arabian Sea, 530 km WSW of Madras; linked by rail to Mangalore, Coimbatore and Ernakulam; a trade centre since the 14th century; Vasco da Gama's first Indian port of call in 1498; the city gave its name to calico cotton; economy: textiles and trade in timber, spices, tea, coffee and cashew nuts.

Califor'nia, state in SW United States; bounded N by Oregon, E by Nevada, SE by Arizona (following the Colorado river), S by Mexico and W by the Pacific Ocean; California is mountainous in the N, W and E, with dry, arid depressions in the S (Mojave and Colorado deserts) and SE (Death Valley); the Klamath Mts rise in the N; in the W the Coast Ranges extend the length of California running parallel to the Pacific; in the E the Sierra Nevada follows the Nevada state frontier, rising to 4,418 m at Mt Whitney (highest point in the state); in the W foothills of the Sierra Nevada is the area known as the Mother Lode, a belt of gold-bearing quartz; Yosemite National Park, Kings Canyon National Park and Sequoia National Park are situated in the Sierra Nevada; the Sierra Nevada and Coast Ranges are separated by the Central Valley which is drained by the San Joaquin and Sacramento rivers; irrigation wells and a state water distribution system have turned the Central Valley into one of the USA's major producers of fruit, vegetables, grain and livestock; Redwood National Park, with its giant redwood trees, is NW of San Francisco near the Pacific Ocean; a zone of faults, known as the San Andreas Fault, extends S from N California along the coast, through the San Francisco peninsula, and SE towards the head of the Golfo de California; movement along part of this zone caused the San Francisco earthquake of 1906; economy: just S of San Francisco is Silicon Valley, the centre of the US microelectronics industry; other industries include food processing, machinery, transportation equipment, fabricated metals, cotton, wine (vineyards are to be found in over 40 Californian counties); first colonized by Spaniards in the mid-18th century, settlers from the E began to arrive during the mid-19th century particularly after the discovery of gold in the Mother Lode country (1848); Californians drove out the last Mexican governor in 1845 and the territory was formally ceded to the USA in 1848 by the treaty of Guadalupe-Hidalgo; California became the 31st state of the Union in 1850; large numbers of settlers moved into California with the development of new industries, and immigrants from the central 'Dust Bowl' states arrived (1936-38); between 1940 and 1950 the state had the USA's highest rate of population increase (53%) as a result of the expansion of military services and Pacific trade; also known as the 'Golden State'; pop(1980) 23,667,902; area 406,377 sq km; capital Sacramento; major towns: San Francisco, Los Angeles, Oakland and San Diego; the state is divided into 58 counties:

County	*area (sq km)*	*pop(1980)*
Alameda	1,914	1,105,379
Alpine	1,919	1,097
Amador	1,531	19,314
Butte	4,280	143,851
Calaveras	2,655	20,710
Colusa	2,995	12,791
Contra Costa	1,898	656,380
Del Norte	2,618	18,217

contd

County	*area (sq km)*	*pop(1980)*
El Dorado	4,459	85,812
Fresno	15,543	514,621
Glenn	3,429	21,350
Humboldt	9,305	108,514
Imperial	10,850	92,110
Inyo	26,580	17,895
Kern	21,138	403,089
Kings	3,619	73,738
Lake	3,281	36,366
Lassen	11,838	21,661
Los Angeles	10,582	7,477,503
Madera	5,577	63,116
Marin	1,360	222,568
Mariposa	3,786	11,108
Mendocino	9,131	66,738
Merced	5,054	134,560
Modoc	10,566	8,610
Mono	7,847	8,577
Monterey	8,588	290,444
Napa	1,934	99,199
Nevada	2,496	51,645
Orange	2,075	1,932,709
Placer	3,682	117,247
Plumas	6,690	17,340
Riverside	18,756	663,166
Sacramento	2,525	783,381
San Benito	3,609	25,005
San Bernardino	52,166	895,016
San Diego	10,951	1,861,846
San Francisco	120	678,974
San Joaquin	3,679	347,342
San Luis Obispo	8,601	155,435
San Mateo	1,162	587,329
Santa Barbara	7,145	298,694
Santa Clara	3,362	1,295,071
Santa Cruz	1,160	188,141
Shasta	9,844	115,715
Sierra	2,493	3,073
Siskiyou	16,331	39,732
Solano	2,168	235,203
Sonoma	4,170	299,681
Stanislaus	3,916	265,900
Sutter	1,565	52,246
Tehama	7,678	38,888
Trinity	8,294	11,858
Tulare	12,501	245,738
Tuolumne	5,808	33,928
Ventura	4,841	529,174
Yolo	2,636	113,374
Yuba	1,664	49,733

California, Golfo de, GULF OF CALIFORNIA (Eng), arm of the Pacific Ocean, located between the Mexican mainland and Baja California to the W; to the N is the Colorado river delta, which separates the gulf from the Salton Sea and Imperial Valley; the gulf broadens and deepens towards the S, reaching a max depth of 2,595 m; 1,130 km long by 80-130 km wide; tourism, fishing and the harvesting of sponge, pearl and oyster are important.

Callao *kal-yah'ō*, maritime dept and constitutional prov in W Peru; on the arid Pacific littoral between Lima and the sea; comprises the territory around the port and a few islands, forming an enclave in Lima dept; pop(1981) 443,413; area 73 sq km; capital Callao.

Callao, 12 05S 77 08W, pop(1972) 296,220, port and capital of Callao dept and constitutional prov, W Peru; the town's port handles 75% of Peru's imports and approx 25% of its exports; the inner harbour covers 1 sq km; Drake and others raided Callao in the 16th century; occupied by Chile (1879-84); the present town was built after the earthquake of 1746; the port is linked by rail with Lima; airport; monument: the Real Felipe fortress (1774), last stronghold of the Royalists in S America, withstood a year-long siege in 1826.

Calne, 51 27N 2 00W, pop(1981) 10,289, town in North Wiltshire dist, Wiltshire, S England; 8 km E of Chippenham; economy: electronics, engineering.

Caloocan *ka-lō-ō'kan*, 14 38N 120 58E, pop(1980) 467,816, city on Luzon I, Philippines; just N of Manila.

Caltanissetta *kal-ta-nee-set'ta*, NISSA (anc), prov of Sicilia region, S Italy; pop(1981) 285,829; area 2,106 sq km; capital Caltanissetta.

Caltanissetta, 37 29N 14 04E, pop(1981) 61,146, capital town of Caltanissetta prov, Sicilia region, S Italy; 34 km SW of Enna; railway; economy: sulphur mines.

Calumet City, 41 37N 87 32W, pop(1980) 39,697, town in Cook county, NE Illinois, United States; on Indiana border, 32 km S of Chicago; economy: steel.

Calvados *kal-va-dos*, maritime dept in Basse-Normandie region of NW France, comprising 4 arrond, 48 cantons and 704 communes; pop(1982) 589,559; area 5,548 sq km; capital Caen; dissected by the R Orne with the wooded Bocage Normand to the SW and traversed N-S by several lines of low hills, mostly rich pasture, in Auge and the plain of Caen; the dangerous reef extending for 25 km along the coast between the Orne and Vire rivers is called Les Calvados after a vessel of the Spanish Armada wrecked on it; the well-known eau-de-vie, calvados, is made here; sea-water treatment establishment at Trouville; son-et-lumière at Balleroy.

Cam, GRANTA (anc), river in Cambridgeshire, E central England; rises W of Thaxted and flows 64 km N through Cambridge to meet the R Ouse S of Ely.

Camagüey *ka-ma-gway'*, formerly PUERTO PRÍNCIPE *pwer'to preen'si-pay*, largest prov of Cuba, bounded N by the archipelago de Camagüey; in a tropical zone, the prov is generally low and level; there are swamps along the Caribbean coast; drained by the San Pedro, Najasa, and Caunao rivers; area 14,134 sq km; pop(1981) 664,566; capital Camagüey; other main town Nuevitas; there are deposits of iron, copper, chromium, and marble.

Camagüey, 21 25N 77 55W, pop(1983e) 253,836, capital city of Camagüey prov, E central Cuba; 570 km SE of La Habana (Havana); founded in 1515 when it was known as Puerto Príncipe; became capital of the Spanish W Indies in the 19th century; railway; on the Central Highway; its port is Nuevitas, 72 km ENE; formerly important as a cattle and sugar centre; notable ballet company; monuments: cathedral (rebuilt 1617); notable Jesuit church; the Casa Jesús Suárez Gayol was the home of a revolutionary who was killed with Che Guevara in Bolivia.

Camargue *cam-arg*, dist in R Rhône delta, Bouches-du-Rhône dept, SE France; an alluvial island largely consisting of saltmarsh and lagoon; the area around the salt water lake, Étang de Vaccares, is a nature reserve for migratory birds including the flamingo; there is an information centre at Ginès; in recent years much of the land to the N has been drained, desalinated, irrigated and planted with rice and vines, but the bulls and horses for which the Camargue is famous still exist on a number of ranches; the chief locality is Saintes-Maries-de-la-Mer; there are facilities for boating and riding.

Camaril'lo, 34 13N 119 02W, pop(1980) 37,797, city in Ventura county, SW California, United States; 13 km E of Oxnard; railway.

Camas *ka'mas*, 37 24N 6 01W, pop(1981) 25,327, town in Sevilla prov, Andalucia, S Spain; just W of Sevilla; economy: soap, olives.

Cam'berley, 51 19N 0 44W, pop(1981) 45,716, residential town linked with Frimley in Surrey Heath dist, Surrey, SE England; part of Aldershot urban area; 10 km N of Aldershot; Royal Staff College; railway; economy: electrical goods, engineering.

Cambodia *kam-bō'dee-a*, KAMPUCHEA *kam-pu-chee'a*, official name Democratic Kampuchea, PEOPLE'S DEMOCRATIC REPUBLIC OF KAMPUCHEA, formerly KHMER REPUBLIC (1970-75), republic of S Indo-China, SE Asia; bounded N by Thailand and Laos, E and SE by Vietnam, W by Thailand and SW and S by the Gulf of Thailand; timezone GMT +7; area 181,035 sq km; capital Phnom Penh; the 2nd largest town is Battambang; pop (1981) 5,756,141; 93% of the pop is Khmer (Kampuchean), 4% Vietnamese and 3% Chinese; before 1975 95% of the pop practised Theravada Buddhism; in 1976 Buddhism was abolished as the state religion; there are Roman Catholic and Muslim minorities; Khmer is the official language but French is also widely spoken; national holiday 17 April; membership of ADB, Colombo Plan, ESCAP, FAO, G-77, GATT, IAEA, IBRD, ICAO, IDA, ILO, IMF, IMO, INTERPOL, IRC, ITU, Mekong Committee, NAM, UN, UNESCO, UPU, WFTU, WHO, WMO.

Physical description. Cambodia occupies an area that surrounds the Tonlé Sap (lake), a freshwater depression on the Cambodian Plain which is crossed by the floodplain of the Mekong river in the E. The highest land in the country is found in the SW, where the Chaîne des Cardamomes range runs for 160 km across the Thailand border and rises to 1,813 m at Phnom Aural. Standing between the Tonlé Sap and the sea, this mountain range acts as a watershed and is subject to the heaviest monsoon rainfall. Monsoon floods during the wet season (May-Oct) cause the R Mekong to reverse the flow of the Tonlé Sap river and so seasonally inundate the Tonlé Sap and its surrounding forest area.

Climate. The Cambodian climate is of the tropical monsoon type, dominated by S and SE winds during May-Sept, the season of greatest rainfall, and N to NE winds from Oct to April, the dry season. The mountain region in the SW has heavy rainfall on those slopes which face the Gulf of Thailand, sheltering other areas of the country from the effects of the monsoon. Temperatures are high in the lowland region throughout the year, with humidity being at its greatest during the period of the monsoon. At Phnom Penh average monthly precipitation is highest in Oct (257 mm), and lowest in Jan (7 mm).

History, government and constitution. Cambodia was originally part of the Kingdom of Fou-Nan, which was taken over by the Khmers during the 6th century and ruled by their monarchs from Angkor during the 9-13th centuries. Cambodia was in dispute with the Vietnamese and the Thais from the 15th century onwards. In 1863 Cambodia was established as a French Protectorate which was recognized by Thailand in exchange for the provinces of Battambang and Siem Reap. These provinces came back to Cambodia after the Franco-Thai Convention of 1904 and the Franco-Thai Treaty of 1937. In 1904 the province of Stung Treng, previously under the administration of the Laos government, became part of Cambodia. Cambodia gained independence from France in 1953, when Prince Sihanouk, the son of the reigning monarch, became Prime Minister. Prince Sihanouk was deposed in 1970 after a long period of economic difficulty, and on 9 Oct 1970 the Kingdom of Cambodia became the Khmer Republic. Fighting broke out throughout the country, involving troops from N and S Vietnam, the USA, Republican and anti-Republican troops. The situation degenerated into civil war in 1973 when direct involvement by the USA and Vietnam ceased. The surrender of Phnom Penh to the Khmer

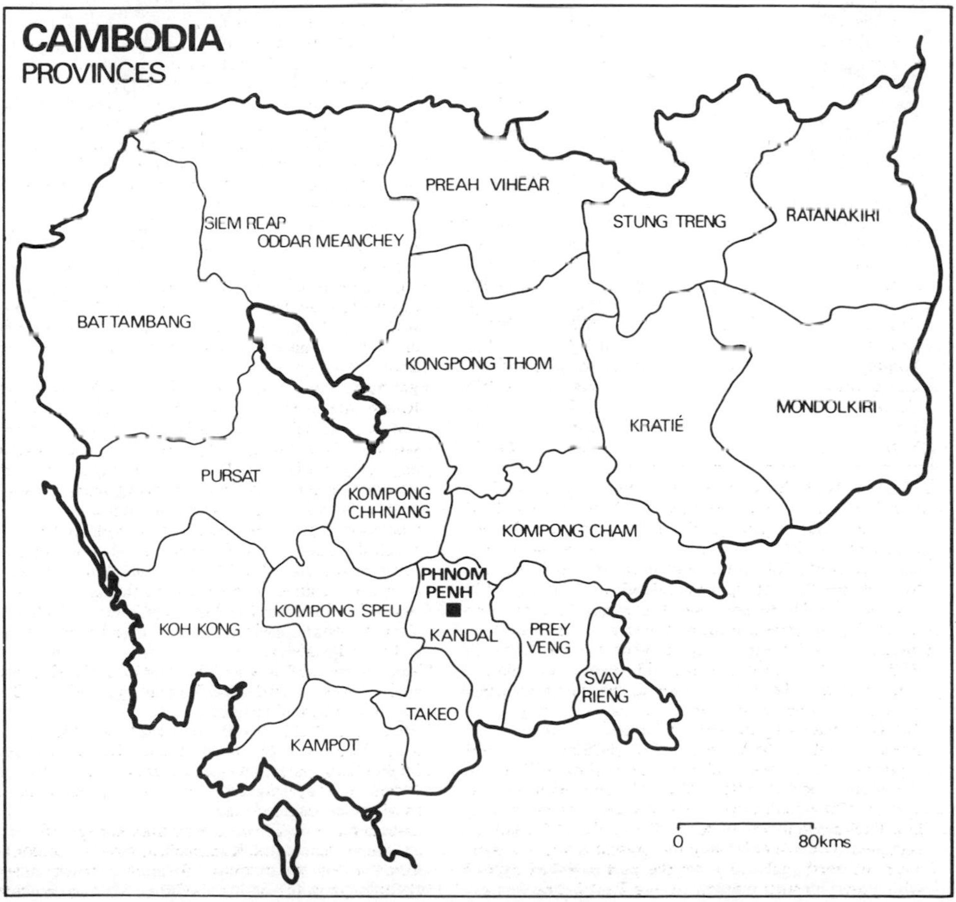

Rouge in 1975 ended the 5-year war, but established a government which cut Cambodia off from the rest of the world, expelling all foreigners and forcing out the city populations to work in the fields. Fighting occurred during 1977-78 and on 7 Jan 1979 Phnom Penh was captured by the Vietnamese, causing the Prime Minister Pol Pot to flee. On 8 Jan 1979 the Vietnamese-backed Kampuchean United Front for National Salvation established a People's Revolutionary Council, with a 117-member National Assembly being elected in May 1981 for a 5-year term. A new constitution in June 1981 replaced the Revolutionary Council by appointing a 7-member Council of State and a 16-member Council of Ministers. In 1982 the Khmer Rouge, the Son Sann's Kampuchean People's National Liberation Front and Prince Sihanouk's group formed a coalition government which was officially recognized by the USA.

Economy. The majority of the Cambodian population are employed in subsistence agriculture, chiefly growing rice and corn. The forests of Cambodia provide raw material for local timber industries. Other traditional manufacturing industries include rice milling and fish processing. Industrial development was disrupted by civil war, but since 1970 motor-assembly and cigarette manufacturing have been established. In April 1975 a programme for repairing war-damaged factories started. Cambodia has the greatest freshwater fisheries in SE Asia at Tonlé Sap, but since 1966 production has declined by one-third. Shortage of fossil fuels slows industrial development. The oil refinery at Kompong Som, which came into production in 1969, was closed due to war damage in 1971. Chief exports are natural rubber, pepper, rice and wood. Imports arrive mostly in the form of international food aid and economic aid from the Soviet bloc. Vietnam and the USSR are the chief trading partners. In 1978 money was abolished and no wages were paid, but the use of money was restored in 1980.

Administrative divisions. Cambodia is divided into the 18 provinces (*khet*) of Battambang, Kampot, Kandal, Koh Kong, Kompong Cham, Kompong Chhnang, Kompong Speu, Kompong Thom, Kratié, Mondolkiri, Preah Vihear, Prey Veng, Pursat, Ratanakiri, Siem Reap-Oddar Meanchey, Stung Treng, Svay Rieng, Takeo.

Cam'borne, 50 12N 5 19W, pop(1981) 34,774, industrial town linked with Redruth in Kerrier dist, Cornwall, SW England; 18 km W of Truro; a former tin-mining centre; railway; economy: mining, engineering.

Cambridge *kaym-*, 43 22N 80 20W, pop(1981) 77,183, town in SE Ontario, SE Canada; SW of Toronto; railway.

Cambridge, CANTABRIGIA (Lat), 52 12N 0 07E, pop(1981) 91,167, county town in Cambridge dist, Cambridgeshire, E central England; on the R Cam, 82 km N of London; university (12th-c); railway; economy: electronics, printing, cement, flour, scientific instruments; monuments: churches of St Benedict and the Holy Sepulchre; events: May Week, college boat races (June), festival of Ceilidhs (Sept).

Cambridge, formerly NEW TOWNE (-1638), 42 22N 71 06W, pop(1980) 95,322, county seat of Middlesex county, E Massachusetts, United States; on the Charles river, 5 km W of Boston; founded in 1630, achieving city status in 1846; the first printing press in the USA was set up here in 1640; Harvard University (1636) is the oldest US college; Massachusetts Institute of Technology (1859) moved from Boston in 1915; railway; economy: electronics, glass, scientific instruments, photographic equipment, printing and publishing.

Cambridgeshire, county of E central England; bounded N by Lincolnshire, NE by Norfolk, E by Suffolk, S by Essex and Hertfordshire, W by Bedfordshire and Northamptonshire; drained by the Nene, Ouse and Cam rivers; flat fenland lies to the N; pop(1981) 578,734; area 3,409 sq km; county town Cambridge; chief towns include Peterborough, Ely and Huntingdon; economy: grain, vegetables, food processing, electronics, engineering; the county is divided into 6 districts:

District	*area (sq km)*	*pop(1981)*
Cambridge	41	91,167
East Cambridgeshire	655	53,864
Fenland	552	67,701
Huntingdon	924	124,253
Peterborough	334	133,140
South Cambridgeshire	903	108,609

Cam'den, 51 33N 0 09W, pop(1981) 172,014, borough of N Greater London, England; N of the City of Westminster; includes the suburbs of Hampstead, St Pancras and Holborn; named after an 18th-c Lord Chancellor; university (1826); railway stations at Euston (1849), King's Cross (1852) and St Pancras (1874); monuments: British Museum, John Keats House, Gray's Inn, Lincoln's Inn, Telecom (orig. Post Office) Tower (1964).

Camden, 39 56N 75 07W, pop(1980) 84,910, county seat of Camden county, W New Jersey, United States; a port on the E bank of the R Delaware, opposite Philadelphia; a city since 1828; home of the poet Walt Whitman 1873-92; university (1934); railway; economy: oil refining, shipbuilding, textiles, food processing, radio and television equipment.

Cameron Highlands, district in Pahang state, central Peninsular Malaysia, SE Asia; an upland area on the Perak frontier, E of Ipoh, developed as a hill resort district in the 1940s; the chief stations include Ringlets, Tanah Rata and Berinchang.

Cameroon *kam-u-roon'*, official name the Republic of Cameroon, RÉPUBLIQUE DU CAMEROON (Fr), a W African republic bounded SW by Equatorial Guinea, S by Gabon, SW by the Congo, E by the Central African Republic, NE by Chad and NW by Nigeria; timezone GMT +1; area 475,439 sq km; pop(1984e) 9,576,000; capital Yaoundé; chief towns Ngaoundéré, Bertoua, Maroua, Douala, Garoua, Bamenda, Bafoussam, Ebolowa and Buéa; main ethnic groups include Cameroon Highlanders (31%), Equatorial Bantu (19%), Kirdi (11%), Fulani (10%), Northwestern Bantu (8%), Eastern Nigritic (7%); approx half the pop hold local beliefs, the remainder being Christian (one-third) or Muslim (one-sixth, mainly in the N); official languages are French and English with 24 major African language groups also represented; the unit of currency is the franc CFA; national holiday 20 May (National Day); membership of AfDB, EAMA, ECA, EIB (associate), FAO, G-77, GATT, IAEA, IBRD, ICAC, ICAO, ICO, IDA, IDB (Islamic Development Bank), IFAD, IFC, ILO, IMF, IMO, INTELSAT, INTERPOL, IPU, ISO, ITU, Lake Chad Basin Commission, NAM, Niger River Commission, OAU, OIC, UDEAC, UN, UNESCO, UPU, WHO, WIPO, WMO and WTO.

Physical description. Cameroon can be divided into four geographical regions. The low coastal plain is characterized by equatorial forest rising to a central plateau region reaching elevations of over 1,300 m. The W region along the frontier with Nigeria is forested and mountainous rising to 4,070 m at Mount Cameroon, an active volcano, which is the highest peak in W Africa. Further E in N central Cameroon, the land rises towards the Massif d'Adamaoua. Towards L Chad the terrain changes to low savannah and semi-desert with national parks and reserves at Bénoué, Waza, Faro, Bouba Ndjidah and Kala-Malque. Major rivers flowing from the central plateau to the Gulf of Guinea include the Sanaga (length 525 km). The M'Bakou reservoir and the S tip of L Chad are the only major areas of water within the country.

Climate. The N of the country has a wet season between April and Sept, the remainder of the year being dry, with an annual rainfall between 1,000 and 1,750 mm. The N plains are semi-arid. The equatorial S has rain throughout the year with 2 wet seasons and 2 dry seasons. Yaoundé is representative of the south with an average annual rainfall of 4,030 mm and max daily temperatures ranging between 27°C and 30°C. A small area of Mount

Cameroon is one of three places in the world to receive more than 10,000 mm of rain per annum, the others being the Hawaiian Islands and Assam (India).

History, government and constitution. First explored by the Portuguese navigator Fernando Po, and later by traders from Spain, the Netherlands and Britain, there was an attempt in 1884 by France, Germany and Britain to annexe the area. The German consul from Tunisia gained control after a treaty agreed with the Douala people and subsequently Germany was able to expand its colonial territory through treaties with the French and British. In 1914 the country was invaded by France and Britain and in 1919 a declaration divided Cameroon between these two countries. This declaration was confirmed by a mandate of the League of Nations in 1922. After the fall of France in 1940 General de Gaulle's troops took the territory by force for the Free French. The United Nations turned the British and French mandates into trusteeships in 1946. The UN voted in 1958 to end the French trusteeship and in 1960 French Cameroon acquired independence as the Republic of Cameroon. A year later, in 1961, the population of British Cameroon voted on their future. The northern sector voted to become part of Nigeria and the southern sector voted to become part of the Republic of Cameroon. The same year the latter area was reunified with French Cameroon and the Federal Republic of Cameroon came into being. From that date till 1972 the republic was governed as a federation with E and W Cameroon having separate parliaments. A referendum in 1972 supported the abolition of the federal system and the country's name was changed to the United Republic of Cameroon. The 'United' was dropped from the name after a constitutional amendment in 1984. The 1972 constitution provided for a president (also head of state), an executive prime minister, a cabinet of ministers and a National Assembly (120 members), which is elected for 5-year terms. Local government of the 10 provs is by appointed governors. Tribal laws and customs are honoured as long as they do not contradict the formal court system.

Economy. Agriculture has traditionally been central to the Cameroon economy, employing about 80% of the workforce and accounting for a significant proportion of export earnings. The country is the world's 5th largest cocoa producer and is also an important supplier of coffee. Other export crops include cotton, rubber, bananas and timber. Industry is limited to light manufacturing, assembly and domestic processing with the exception of the aluminium plant at Edé which produces between 40,000 and 50,000 tonnes per annum (1985). Crude oil extraction has expanded significantly since 1977 providing an important source of export income during the early 1980s. Cameroon is nearly self-sufficient in the production of fertilizer materials, cement and crude oil. Gold, bauxite, natural gas and tin are also extracted. Tourism is an important source of income, one of the principal attractions being the wildlife which is protected in a number of national parks and reserves. The main trading partners are France, the USA, West Germany, Japan, Italy, the Netherlands and the USSR.

Administrative divisions. Cameroon is divided into 10 provinces:

Province	*pop(1984e)*	*chief town*
Centre	1,598,000	Yaoundé
Est	460,000	Bertoua
Littoral	1,398,000	Douala
Nord	571,000	Garoua
Nord-Ouest	1,119,000	Bamenda
Ouest	1,274,000	Bafoussam
Sud-Ouest	743,000	Buéa
Sud	394,000	Ebolowa
Extrème-Nord	1,619,000	Maroua
Adamaoua	400,000	Ngaoundéré

Cameroon, Mount, MONGO-MA-LOBA, 4 14N 9 10E, volcanic massif in S Cameroon, W Africa; runs inland for 23 miles from the Gulf of Guinea; with its main peak at 4,070 m, the massif is the highest mountain group in W Africa; erupted in 1922, last eruption in 1959; first ascended by Richard F. Burton and G. Mann in 1861.

Cami, Lago, lake in Chile and Argentina. See Lago Fagnano.

Camiri *ka-mee'ree*, 20 08S 63 33W, pop(1976) 19,499, town in Cordillera prov, SW Santa Cruz, S Bolivia; airfield; economy: oil refining.

Campana *kam-pa'na*, 34 10S 59 55W, pop(1980) 51,498, town in Buenos Aires prov, Litoral, E Argentina; on R Paraná, 72 km NW of Buenos Aires; railway; economy: meat, grain, oil.

Campania *kam-pa'nee-a*, *kam-pay'ni-a* (Eng), region of S Italy, extending from the Appno Napoletano (Neapolitan Apennines) in the E to the coast of the Tyrrhenian Sea, here much indented; comprises the provs of Caserta, Benevento, Napoli, Avellino, and Salerno; pop(1981) 5,463,134; area 13,598 sq km; chief towns Napoli (Naples), Salerno, Benevento, and Caserta; it is a fertile low-lying agricultural area, well watered by the rivers Garigliano, Volturno, and Sele; intensively cultivated, producing wheat, citrus fruits, wine, vegetables, fruit and tobacco; there are ancient sites at Pompeii, Herculaneum, Paestum, and Velia.

Campbell, 37 17N 121 57W, pop(1980) 27,067, city in Santa Clara county, W California, United States; 8 km SW of San José.

Campbell Island, 52 33S 169 09E, volcanic island of New Zealand; situated 590 km S of Stewart island and 720 km S of Invercargill in the SW Pacific; area 114 sq km; discovered in 1810; economy: seal fur trade.

Campeche *kam-pay'chay*, state in SE Mexico; in the W of the Yucatán peninsula; bounded N by the Gulf of Mexico; SW by Tabasco, S by Guatemala, E by Quintana Roo and NE by Yucatán; comprises vast, tree-covered lowlands made up of porous limestone; in the W the Isla del Carmen, a long bar, separates the Gulf of Mexico from the Laguna de Términos, which is fed by subterranean streams and by the Río Candelaria; major rivers: Río Candelaria, Río Champotón; the land is marshy in the W and along part of the coastline; pop(1980) 372,277; area 50,812 sq km; capital Campeche; economy: agriculture (maize, cocoa, sugar cane, citrus fruit, rice, bananas, pineapples), cattle and pig raising, fishing and fish processing.

Campeche, 19 50N 90 30W, pop(1980) 151,805, seaport capital of Campeche state, SE Mexico; on the Bahía de Campeche in the Gulf of Mexico, on the W coast of the Yucatán peninsula; university (1756); Spaniards first arrived here in 1517; in the 17th century the town was fortified against pirates; railway; monuments: Campeche contains several 16th and 17th-c churches, an ancient fort and parts of the old walls built to protect the town.

Campina Grande *kam-pee'na gran'day*, 7 15S 35 53W, pop(1980) 222,102, town in Paraíba state, Nordeste region, NE Brazil; NW of Recife; university (1966); railway; economy: vegetable oils, light industry; monument: museum of modern art.

Campinas *kam-pee'nas*, 22 54S 47 60W, pop(1980) 566,627, town in São Paulo state, Sudeste region, SE Brazil; NW of São Paulo; 2 universities (1941, 1962); agricultural institute; railway; airport; economy: cotton, maize, sugar cane, coffee; monuments: fine cathedral, old market and colonial buildings.

Campo Grande *kam'pō gran'day*, 20 24S 54 35W, pop(1980) 282,857, capital of Mato Grosso do Sul state, Centro-Oeste region, W central Brazil; SE of Corumbá; university (1970); railway; airport; economy: rice, soya beans, wheat; monument: the Regional Indian Museum has exhibits and handicrafts of the local Pantanal and Mato Grosso Indians.

Campobasso *kam-po-bas'so*, prov of Molise region, Italy; pop(1981) 235,847; area 2,909 sq km; capital Campobasso.

Campobasso, 41 33N 14 39E, pop(1981) 48,291, market town and capital of Campobasso prov, Molise region, Italy; 88 km NNE of Napoli (Naples); bishopric; railway; economy: soap, cutlery; monuments: Romanesque church, 16th-c Castello di Monforte.

Campos *kam'pos*, 21 46S 41 21W, pop(1980) 178,457, town in Rio de Janeiro state, Sudeste region, SE Brazil; 56 km from the mouth of the Río Paraíba, in one of the largest sugar-producing zones in Brazil; railway; airfield; economy: sugar cane, alcohol production, mining of limestone and marble, oil.

Canada *kan'e-da*, formerly BRITISH NORTH AMERICA (-1867), independent country in N North America; bordered S by the United States, W by the Pacific Ocean, NW by Alaska, N by the Arctic Ocean and Baffin Bay, NE by the Davis Strait and E by the Labrador Sea and the Atlantic Ocean; area 9,971,500 sq km; capital Ottawa; pop(1983) 24,907,100; ethnic groups are 45% of British origin, 29% of French origin, 23% of other European origin and 1.5% indigenous Indian and Eskimo; the official languages are English and French; religion is predominantly Roman Catholic (49%), with 18% United Church and 12% Anglican; the currency is the Canadian dollar of 100 cents; national holidays 1 July (Canada Day), Labour Day (Sept), Thanksgiving (Oct), 11 Nov (Remembrance Day); membership of ADB, Colombo Plan, the Commonwealth, DAC, FAO, GATT, IAEA, IBRD, ICAO, ICES, ICO, ICRC, IDA, IDB (Inter-American Development Bank), IEA, IFAD, IFC, IHO, ILO, ILZSG, IMF, IMO, INTELSAT, INTERPOL, IPU, ISO, ITC, ITU, IWC (International Whaling Commission), IWC (International Wheat Council), NATO, OAS (observer), OECD, PAHO, UN, UNCTAD, UNESCO, UPU, WHO, WIPO, WMO and WSG.

Timezones. Canada is divided into the following timezones:

Region	±GMT
W Yukon	−9
Yukon and Pacific	−8
Mountain	−7
Central	−6
Eastern	−5
Atlantic	−4
Newfoundland	−3

Physical description. The landscape of Canada is dominated in the NE by the pre-Cambrian Canadian Shield, an area of relatively undisturbed ancient rock which extends from Ellesmere and Baffin islands, the coast of Labrador and the highlands of E Québec to the flat plains of N Ontario in the SW and the tundra of the Northwest Territories, Manitoba and Saskatchewan. Its lowest point is located in Hudson Bay. In the E the mountains of Nova Scotia and New Brunswick are an extension of the Appalachian system. In S Québec and Ontario lie the fertile St Lawrence lowlands, bordering the Great Lakes and the deeply faulted valley of the St Lawrence river. S and W of the Canadian Shield flat prairie country stretches W to the Western Cordillera which includes the Rocky Mts, the Cassiar Mts and the Mackenzie Mts, Columbia, the Yukon and part of W Alberta. The Coast Mts which flank a rugged, heavily indented coastline rise

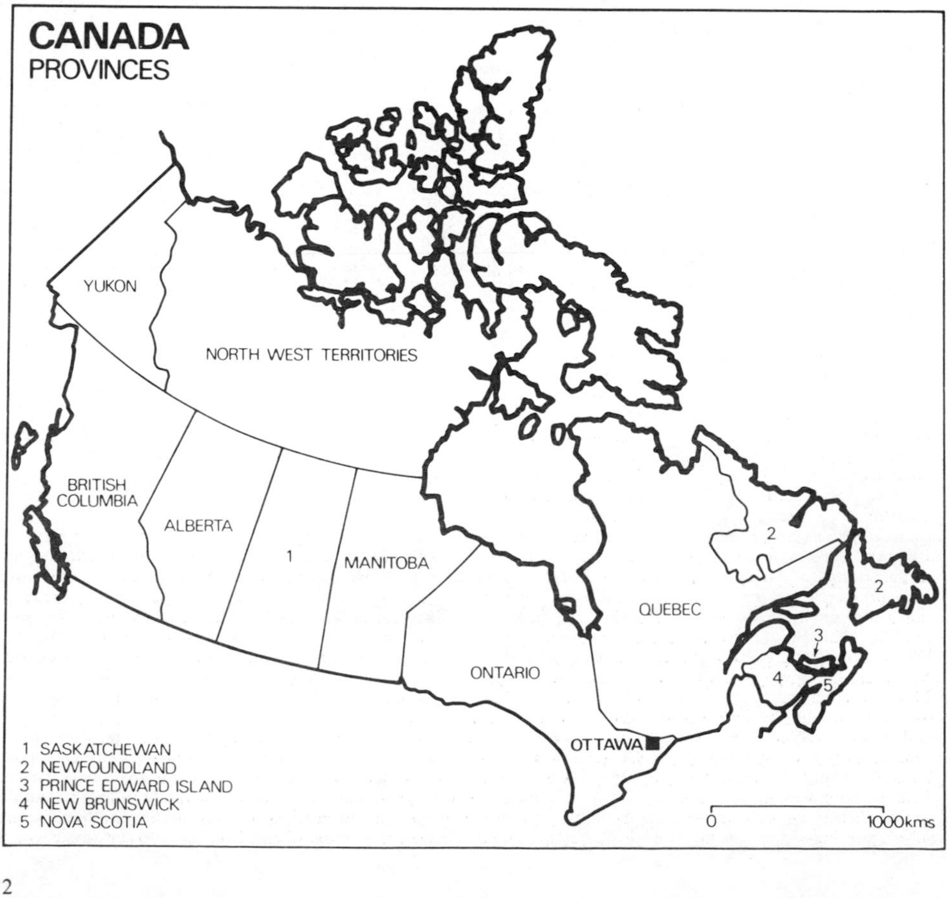

to 5,950 m at Mt Logan, the highest peak in Canada. Canada's major rivers include the Yukon and Mackenzie rivers in the W, the North Saskatchewan, South Saskatchewan, Saskatchewan and Athabasca rivers in central Canada and the Ottawa and St Lawrence rivers in the E.

Climate. Only a narrow strip of Canada close to the United States border has a temperate climate with cold winters. Apart from Hudson Bay which is frozen over for approx 9 months of the year, the N coast of Canada is permanently ice-bound or severely obstructed by ice floes. Only the Pacific coast of British Columbia, the Atlantic coast of Newfoundland and the provinces S of the Gulf of St Lawrence have harbours which do not regularly freeze in winter. The low lying land to the E of the Rocky Mts presents no barrier to cold air from the Canadian Arctic which sweeps S and E in winter and spring. Warmer maritime air from the Pacific Ocean only reaches the area of Canada to the W of the Rocky Mts in British Columbia. The W coast and some inland valleys of British Columbia have mild winters and warm summers, with rain falling throughout the year. On the Atlantic shores winter temperatures are warmer than those of the interior, but the summer temperatures are lower as a result of the cold Labrador current. Much of the S interior of Canada has high summer temperatures and long, cold winters.

History, government and constitution. In 1497 John Cabot landed on the E coast of Canada, thinking he had found the route to China. The country was visited by the Portuguese a few years later and in 1504 St John's, Newfoundland, was established as the shore base for the English fisheries. In 1534 Jacques Cartier landed at Gaspé and claimed land for France. He explored part of the country in 1535 and in 1541 made his 3rd voyage there in the first French colonizing expedition to North America. Sir Humphrey Gilbert visited Newfoundland in 1583 and claimed it for England, making it England's first overseas colony. In 1608 Samuel de Champlain founded the city of Québec, the first permanent settlement in Canada. Explorers and missionaries penetrated W to the Great Lakes and beyond in search of the NW passage to Asia. In 1670 the fur trading Hudson's Bay Company was founded. By 1696 the British were in open conflict with the colonists of New France. By the treaty of Utrecht (1713) France surrendered the Hudson's Bay and Acadia (Nova Scotia), Newfoundland to the British, while after the Seven Years' War, during which Wolfe captured Québec (1759), the Treaty of Paris gave to Britain all of France's possessions in North America except the islands of St Pierre and Miquelon. New France then covered little more than the St Lawrence valley, but the Québec Act (1774), besides attempting to conciliate French colonists who remained in possession under British rule, created the prov of Québec, which extended to the Ohio and Mississippi rivers. After an unsuccessful invasion of Canada the boundary was settled around the Great Lakes in 1783. Migration of loyalists to Canada from the USA after the Wars of Independence resulted in the prov of Québec being divided into Upper and Lower Canada. These provs were reunited in 1841 as Canada. In 1867 the Dominion of Canada was created by the confederation of Québec, Ontario, Nova Scotia, and New Brunswick. Rupert's Land and Northwest Territories were bought from the Hudson's Bay Company in 1869-70. Manitoba became a prov in 1870 and in 1871 British Columbia agreed to join the confederation after the promise of a transcontinental railroad. Prince Edward Island entered the confederation in 1873. The discovery of gold in the Klondike in 1896 began a wild gold rush and Yukon terr came under the control of Canada in 1898. Agriculture in the central prairies boomed in the late 19th century and Alberta and Saskatchewan were made provs in 1905. Newfoundland was the last to enter the confederation in 1949. In 1982 full responsibility for Canada's constitution was granted by the British monarch to the Canadian parliament in an amendment to the North America Act of 1867. The enactment of the Canada Act in 1982 was the last act of the UK parliament in relation to Canadian constitutional affairs. In the same year the Canadian government passed the Constitution Act which added a charter of rights to the existing Canadian constitution. Canada is governed by a bicameral federal parliament which includes a Senate of 104 nominated members and a House of Commons of 282 elected members. The provinces have the authority to administer and legislate on education, property laws, health and local affairs. The British monarch is head of state and is represented by a Governor-General, appointed on the advice of the Canadian prime minister, usually for a 5-year term of office.

Economy. From an economy traditionally based on the export of natural resources and agricultural products Canada has developed into a modern industrial nation. However, Canada remains the world's 2nd largest exporter of wheat, accounting for over 20% of the global wheat trade. Forest covers 44% of Canada's total land area, with the export of forest products accounting for approx 15% of the country's total export trade. Altogether, farm, forest and fish products provide approx 25% of Canada's exports. Mineral deposits are widespread, with Canada the world's largest producer of asbestos, zinc, silver and nickel; the 2nd largest producer of potash, gypsum, molybdenum and sulphur; and a leading producer of uranium, titanium, aluminium, cobalt, gold, lead, copper, iron and platinum. Canada is a major producer of hydroelectricity, oil and gas and is a net exporter of energy (mainly gas and electricity). The country's major exports are in motor vehicles and parts, lumber, woodpulp and newsprint, crude and fabricated metals, natural gas, crude petroleum and wheat. The major export partners are the USA, the EEC and Japan. Manufacturing industries are largely based in the cities of SE Canada where one-quarter of the workforce generate about 50% of Canada's wealth. Major industries include food processing, timber products, motor vehicles, chemicals, petroleum products, machinery and metal products.

Administrative divisions. Canada is divided into 10 provinces and 2 territories (Northwest Territories and Yukon):

Province/territory	*area (sq km)*	*pop(1981)*
Alberta	638,233	2,237,724
British Columbia	892,677	2,744,467
Manitoba	547,704	1,026,241
New Brunswick	71,569	696,403
Newfoundland	371,635	567,681
Northwest Territories	3,246,389	45,471
Nova Scotia	52,841	847,442
Ontario	916,734	8,625,107
Prince Edward Island	5,660	122,506
Québec	1,357,655	6,438,403
Saskatchewan	570,113	968,313
Yukon	531,844	22,135

Canadian, river in S central USA; rises in the Sangre de Cristo Mts in NE New Mexico, near the Colorado border; flows S and E through New Mexico then generally E through N Texas and Oklahoma to join the Arkansas river in E Oklahoma, 42 km SE of Muskogee; length 1,458 km; major tributary: the North Canadian river; dammed by the Conchas Dam in NE New Mexico, to the NW of Tucamari, used for flood-control and irrigation.

Canadian Shield, LAURENTIAN PLATEAU, vast area of ancient pre-Cambrian rocks which covers over half of Canada; in the shape of a horseshoe its S boundary runs approx from the coast of Labrador, around Hudson Bay, through Québec and Ontario and through the Winnipeg, Great Slave and Great Bear lakes to the Arctic near the mouth of the Mackenzie river; the Shield extends into the USA to include the Adirondack Mts of New York state, Upper Michigan Peninsula, N Wisconsin and NE Minnesota; this stable area of granites, gneisses and sedimentary rocks has been subjected to minimal mountain-building activity since pre-Cambrian times; it is well watered with lakes and swamps, remnants of Pleistocene glaciation; the region is generally infertile, but is a rich source of minerals, forest products and hydroelectricity.

Çanakkale *cha-nak'ka-le*, maritime prov in NW Turkey, bounded N by the Sea of Marmara and W by the Aegean Sea; pop(1980) 391,568; area 9,737 sq km; capital Çanakkale (Dardanelli).

Çanakkale Boğazi, DARDANELLES *dar-du-nelz'*, HELLESPONT *he'lus-pont* (Eng), HELLESPONTUS (anc), narrow strait in NW Turkey, connecting the Aegean Sea (W) and the Sea of Marmara (E), and separating the Gelibolu (Gallipoli) peninsula of European Turkey from Anadolu (Anatolia); length 65 km; width varies from 1.6 to 6.4 km; in Greek mythology the Hellespont was the scene of the legend of Hero and Leander.

Cañar *kan-yar'*, prov in the Andean Sierra of S central Ecuador; watered by Naranjal or Cañar river; pop(1982) 174,510; area 3,184 sq km; capital Azogues; economy: tobacco and mineral products.

Cañar, 2 38S 78 57W, pop(1982) 10,534, town in Cañar prov, S central Ecuador; N of Cuenca; famous for its double weaving.

Canarias, Islas *ees'las kan-ar'i-as*, CANARY ISLANDS (Eng), island archipelago in the Atlantic Ocean 100 km off the NW coast of Africa, W of Morocco and S of Madeira; forms the Spanish autonomous region of Canarias which is divided into the provs of Las Palmas de Gran Canaria and Santa Cruz de Tenerife; the island group comprises Tenerife, Gomera, La Palma and Hierro in Santa Cruz de Tenerife prov and Lanzarote, Fuerteventura and Gran Canaria (Grand Canary) as well as the barren and uninhabited islands of Alegranza, Graciosa and Isla de Lobos, all in Las Palmas prov; pop(1981) 1,367,646; area 7,273 sq km; Las Palmas is the largest town in the Canary Is; all the islands are volcanic and mountainous, the Pico de Teide rises to 3,718 m at the centre of a national park on the Island of Tenerife; three other national parks are also notable for their interesting volcanic formations and unusual Mediterranean and African flora; the mild, subtropical climate attracts tourists but the islands can be subject to tornadoes and drought; as a result there is a striking difference in value between irrigable and non-irrigable land; where irrigation is possible the volcanic soil produces very rich crops of fruit and vegetables (bananas, tomatoes, potatoes are the characteristic exports); the islands are a port of call on the South African liner service; Spain established sovereignty in 1479, completing the conquest of the remaining islands in 1495; the Canary Is were described by the elder Pliny (who explained the name as referring to the many dogs found on Gran Canaria (Lat 'canis', a dog) in connection with an expedition of the king of Mauretania; economy: agriculture, fishing, tourism, canning, textiles, leatherwork, footwear, cork, timber, chemical products and metal products at Telde.

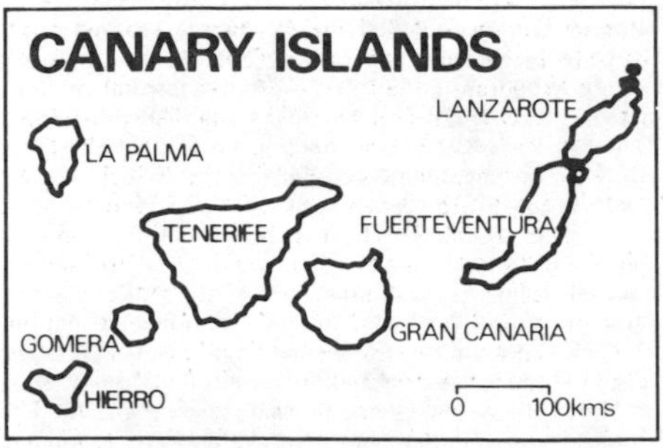

Canary Islands, Spanish autonomous region. See Canarias.

Canaveral, Cape, CAPE KENNEDY (1963-73), 28 28N 80 28W, cape in Brevard county, E Florida, United States; on the E coast of the Canaveral peninsula; site of John F. Kennedy Space Center; US manned space flights have been launched from here since 1961.

Can'berra, 35 18S 149 08E, pop(1986) 285,800, national and regional capital in Australian Capital Territory, SE Australia; on the Molonglo river, SW of Sydney; building started in 1913 and the Commonwealth Parliament was moved from Melbourne in 1927; Australian National University (1946); railway; airport; pop includes 19,056 residents of Queanbeyan on the border with New South Wales; monuments: Australian war memorial; Australian national gallery; Telecom tower on Black Mountain; high court of Australia; Parliament House.

Cancún *kan-koon'*, 21 08N 86 45W, pop(1980) 27,500, city and resort island on the NE coast of Quintana Roo, Mexico; developed during the late 1970s as a major beach resort.

Canea, nome (dept) of Kríti I (Crete), Greece. See Khaniá.

Canelones *ka-nay-lō'nays*, dept in S Uruguay; at the mouth of the Río de la Plata, just N of Montevideo; bordered W and N by Río Santa Lucía; mostly lowland, with fine beaches along its coast; pop(1985) 359,349; area 4,752 sq km; capital Canelones; chief towns Pando, La Paz, Las Piedras and Santa Lucía; economy: agriculture, fruit, wine, olives, cattle; in the centre of the dept is the F.D. Roosevelt National Park; the dept was formed in 1816.

Canelones, 34 32S 56 17W, pop(1985) 17,316, capital of Canelones dept, S Uruguay; N of Montevideo, in a grain-growing area; railway.

Canendiyú *ka-nen-dee-yoo'*, dept in Oriental region, E central Paraguay; bordered N and E by Brazil (E along the Río Paraná, N along the Cordillera Mbaracayú); pop(1982) 65,807; area 13,953 sq km; capital Salto del Guairá.

Canillo *ka-neel'yo*, pop(1982) 794, one of the seven parishes of the Principality of Andorra with a village seat of the same name situated 8 km NE of Andorra la Vella in the Valira del Orient valley; alt 1,560 m.

Çankırı *chan-ku-ru'*, mountainous prov in N Turkey; pop(1980) 258,436; area 8,454 sq km; capital Çankırı.

Canna (Norse *kanne*, island like 'a pot'), island in Highland region, W Scotland; separated from the island of Rhum (SE) by the Sound of Canna and from the island of Skye (N) by the Cuillin Sound; length 8 km; width 0.8 km; ferry link with Mallaig via Eigg and Rhum; pop(1981) 24; economy: sheep, lobster fishing.

Cannanore Islands, island group of India. See Lakshadweep.

Cannes *kan*, 43 33N 7 00E, pop(1982) 72,787, fashionable resort town on the French Riviera in Alpes-Maritimes dept, Provence-Alpes-Côte d'Azur region, SE France; situated on the Golfe de la Napoule, a bay of the Mediterranean; the town extends crescent-shaped for about 6 km along the Rade de Cannes with its beaches and yachting harbours; low, wooded hills protect Cannes on the N from the Mistral wind; the mildness of the winter and temperate climate of summer attract many visitors; first made popular as a resort by Henry Lord Brougham who built a villa here in 1834; originally a winter resort often frequented by royalty, but in more recent times it has become a summer resort with a large number of N American visitors; the main tourist centre is the Boulevard de la Croisette with magnificent views across the waterfront; about 1.5 km offshore lie the wooded Iles de Lerins; railway; airport; 3 casinos; events: International Film Festival in April-May and International Fireworks Festival in August.

Can'nock, 52 42N 2 01W, pop(1981) 54,583, town in Cannock-Great Wyrley urban area, Cannock Chase dist, Staffordshire, central England; 13 km NE of Wolverhampton; economy: engineering.

Cano *ka'noo*, active volcano on Fogo I, Cape Verde, rising to 2,829 m; the last major eruption was in 1847; the highest mt in the Cape Verde archipelago.

Canoas *ka-nō'as*, 28 55S 51 10W, pop(1980) 213,999, town in Rio Grande do Sul state, Sul region, S Brazil; just N of Pôrto Alegre; railway; airport; economy: oil refining, plastics, glass.

Cantabria *kahn-tab'ree-ah*, autonomous region of N Spain co-extensive with the prov of Santander; stretches across the Cordillera Cantabrica (1,382 m) to the headwaters of the R Ebro; pop(1981) 510,816; area 5,289 sq km; its capital, the city of Santander, is one of the leading ports of N Spain.

Cantabrica, Cordillera *kahn-tab'ree-kah*, CANTABRIAN MTS (Eng), mountain range in N Spain, extending 500 km W-E from Galicia along the Bay of Biscay to the Pyrenees and forming a barrier between the sea and the central plateau (Meseta) of Spain; in the Picos de Europa massif the highest point is 2,648 m; the mts are rich in minerals as well as being a source of hydroelectric power.

Cantal *kã-tal*, dept in the Auvergne region of central France, comprising 3 arrond, 26 cantons and 258 communes; pop(1982) 162,838; area 5,726 sq km; capital Aurillac; one of the most mountainous areas of France, traversed from the NE by the Mts d'Auvergne, terminating in the Plomb du Cantal; the Mts de la Margeride (outliers of the Cévennes) run up from the SE to meet them in the middle, and other ranges converge at their S end in the centre of the dept; stock-rearing is the main occupation; hydroelectric Barrage de l'Aigle 11 km W of Mauriac; spa at Chaudes-Aigues; the 15-18th-c château at Tournemire is worth visiting; the Parc des Volcans regional nature park lies partly within the dept.

Can'terbury, DUROVERNUM (Lat), CANTWARABURH (Anglo-Saxon), 51 17N 1 05E, pop(1981) 39,742, market town linked with Blean in Canterbury dist, Kent, SE England; St Augustine began the conversion of England to Christianity here in 597 AD when he baptized King Ethelbert, King of Kent; archbishop Thomas Becket was murdered (1170) by Henry II's knights in Canterbury cathedral; important literary associations with Chaucer, Marlowe, Defoe, Dickens and Maugham; granted a Mayor in 1158; university (1965); railway; economy: engineering, glass; monuments: 11-15th-c cathedral; churches of St Dunstan, St George, St Martin, St Mildred and St Peter; St Augustine's College; the Weavers, half-timbered Tudor houses; city walls; event: cricket festival (Aug).

Canton, capital of Guangdong prov, S China. See Guangzhou.

Canton 40 48N 81 23W, pop(1980) 94,730, county seat of Stark county, E Ohio, United States; 32 km SSE of Akron; railway; home and burial place of President McKinley, 25th president of the United States.

Can'vey Island, 51 32N 0 35E, pop(1981) 35,338, town in Castle Point dist, Essex, SE England; on R Thames estuary E of London; economy: electronics, printing.

Canyon de Chelly *shay*, national monument in NE Arizona, United States; established in 1931 to protect notable cliff dwellings; area 339 sq km.

Cap Vert or **Cape Ver'de**, Dakar region, W Senegal, W Africa; the most westerly point of the African continent; 2,400 km SW of Casablanca (Morocco) and 2,980 km ENE of Natal (Brazil).

Cape Breton Island, island in Nova Scotia prov, E Canada; separated from the mainland in the S by the Strait of Canso and almost bisected by Bras d'Or Lake, an arm of the sea which enters from the E, and is connected by a short canal with St Peter's Bay to the S; chief towns are Sydney, Glace Bay and Louisburg; much of the NW is set aside as Cape Breton Highlands National Park, established in 1936 as a tourist area; comprises the counties of Inverness, Victoria, Cape Breton and Richmond; area 10,295 sq km; pop(1981) 169,985; there are many of Scottish descent who speak Gaelic; there are ferry links from North Sydney to Argentia and to Port aux Basques (Newfoundland); economy: dairy farming, fishing, timber, coal mining, gypsum; Cabot made his first landing here; as a colony it was originally French (Ile Royale), and was not taken by the British until 1758; it was joined to Nova Scotia in 1820.

Cape Coast, 5 10N 1 13W, pop(1982) 72,959, seaport capital of Central region, S Ghana, W Africa; on the Gulf of Guinea, between Sekondi-Takoradi and Accra; the name is corrupted from Cabo Corso (Port); occupied in succession by Portuguese, Dutch, Swedes and Danes from the 15th century; in 1662 it became a British possession; the British fort changed hands a number of times and is now partly used as a prison; university (1962); economy: civil engineering.

Cape Cod, a sandy peninsula of SE Massachusetts state, United States; length 105 km; width up to 32 km; bounded E by the Atlantic and W by Cape Cod Bay; crossed by the 13 km Cape Cod Canal; on 15 May 1602 Bartholomew Gosnold recorded, 'Near this cape...we took great store of codfish...and called it Cape Cod'; pilgrims from the *Mayflower* landed near Provincetown in Nov 1620; airfield at Provincetown.

Cape Coral, 26 29N 81 58W, pop(1980) 32,103, town in Lee county, SW Florida, United States; at the mouth of the Caloosahatchee river, 14 km SW of Fort Myers.

Cape Girardeau *je-rar'dō*, 37 19N 89 32W, pop(1980) 34,361, town in Cape Girardeau county, SE Missouri, United States; on the Mississippi river, 48 km NNW of its junction with the R Ohio; university; railway; economy: timber, furniture, electrical goods.

Cape Province, KAAP'PROVINSIE (Afrik), prov in W South Africa; pop(1985) 5,041,137; area 641,379 sq km; bounded W by the Atlantic Ocean and S by the Indian Ocean; NW frontier with Namibia formed by the Orange river which is joined by the Vaal river at Douglas and the Caledon river near Bethulie; mountain ranges along the Great Escarpment include the Stormberg (Drakensberg), the Winterberg, the Sneeuberge, continuing W to the Nuweveldberge, Konnsberg and Roggeveldberge mts; the Kougaberg, Swartberge, Langeberg and Oilifantsrivierberg are part of the Cape fold mountains; the Cape of Good Hope (Kaap die Goeie Hoop) lies S of Cape Town; the most S point of the African continent is Cape Agulhas, where the Atlantic Ocean meets the Indian Ocean; the prov is noted for its profusion and variety of flora (noted by both Carl von Linné and Charles Darwin) with at least 18 genera with 20 or more interrelated varieties; flora best observed at the Cape Floral Kingdom reserve on Table Mountain; capital Cape Town (Kapstad); chief towns include Port Elizabeth, East London, Victoria West, Beaufort West, Upington, Vryburg and Mosselbaai, first settlement founded by Jan van Riebeeck of the Dutch East India Company in 1652; a British possession between 1795 and 1803 and again in 1806; as a result of the Convention of London the colony was formally passed over to the British in 1814; in 1850 the colony was given its own parliament and in 1910 it became part of the Union of South Africa; economy: grape growing and wine production (all of South Africa's vineyards being located within 160 km of Cape Town), diamonds (Kimberley), vehicles, grain, fruit, pottery, timber, engineering, distilling, textiles, furniture.

Cape Town, KAPSTAD, KAAPSTAD (Afrik), 33 56S 18 28E, pop(1985) 776,617, Greater Cape Town 1,911,521 (including Goodwood, Bellville, Wynberg), seaport capital of Cape prov, South Africa; on Table Bay at the foot of Table Mountain (1,080 m); legislative capital of South Africa; the original settlement was established in 1652 by Jan van Riebeeck as a victualling station for the Dutch East India Company; occupied by the British in 1795; Cape Malays are descendants of the E Indian slaves brought in by the Dutch in early colonial days; nuclear power station at Koeberg; university (1829); railway; airport; economy: commerce, textiles, trade in wool, mohair, grain, fruit, wine and oil; monuments: national gallery, statue to Jan van Riebeeck and his wife; Castle of Good Hope (1666), the oldest colonial building in South Africa, with a military and marine museum and the Fehr collection of antique furniture and glassware; Koopmans de Wet House (1777); Groote Kerk, the oldest church in the city; Union Houses of Parliament.

Cape Verde, most westerly point of the African continent. See Cap Vert.

Cape Verde *kayp vurd*, official name Republic of Cape Verde, REPUBLICA DE CABO VERDE (Port), island group in the Atlantic Ocean off the West Coast of Africa about 500 km W of Dakar, Senegal, lying between 17 12N and 14 48N and between 22 44W and 25 22W; the archipelago, consisting of 10 islands and 8 islets, is divided into 2 main groups which define their position in relation to the prevailing NE wind: the Barlavento, or Windward group in the N and the Sotavento, or leeward group in the S; the windward group includes the islands of Santo Antão, São Vicente, Santa Luzia, São Nicolau, Sal and Boa Vista; the leeward group includes the islands of São Tiago, Maio, Fogo and Brava; capital Praia on São Tiago I; the main ports are at Mindelo and Praia; area 4,033 sq km; pop(1980) 296,093, timezone GMT −1; about 50% of the population lives on São Tiago I; about 60% of the population is of mixed black African and European descent and most of the rest are black African; the dominant religion is Roman Catholic; the official language is Portuguese but a form of creole is commonly spoken; the currency is the escudo Caboverdianos; there are airports on all major islands except for Brava I, and an international airport (Amilcar Cabral) is located on Sal I; there are ferry connections between the islands of São Vicente and Santo Antão and the islands of Fogo and Brava; membership of UN, OAU and an ACP state of the EEC.

Physical description. The island group is of volcanic origin, all the islands being mountainous except for Boa Vista, Maio and Sal; the highest peak is Cano (2,829 m), an active volcano on Fogo I; coastal plains are semi-desert and the mountains are either covered with savanna or thin forest; except for Santo Antão all the islands are noted for their fine sandy beaches.

Climate. The islands are at the N limit of the tropical rain belt and have a low and unreliable rainfall, most of which occurs during Aug and Sept; the climate is cooler and damper in the uplands where most cultivation is to be found; there have been periods of severe and prolonged drought; there is only a small range of temperature throughout the year and the tropical heat and high humidity can be uncomfortable except when the islands are fanned by NE sea breezes.

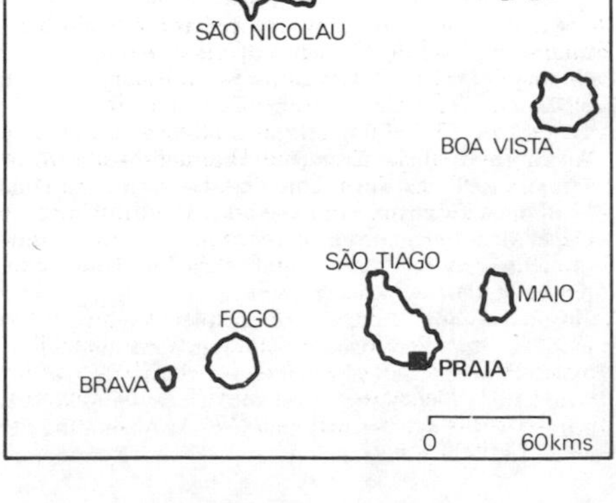

History, government and constitution. The islands were discovered by Portuguese navigators in the mid-15th-c and were quickly colonized by Portuguese settlers as well as being used as a penal colony. Cape Verde became an overseas province of Portugal in 1951 and eventually gained full independence in July 1975 when a unicameral People's National Assembly consisting of 56 members was elected. The sole legal party is the Partido Africano da Independencia de Cabo Verde. The islands were administered with Portuguese Guinea (now Guinea-Bissau) until 1879, but the Constitution of 1981 discounted a possible future union with Guinea-Bissau. Members of the Assembly who are elected for a 5 year term elect a President who appoints and leads a Council of Ministers.

Economy. As a colony of Portugal Cape Verde was an important victualling point for transatlantic shipping but more recently the economy of the islands has suffered from a need for substantial food imports required to support a large population that has been faced with the effects of a decade-long drought. More than 300,000 people left the islands in the late 1960s and early 1970s and unemployment reached a total of 80% by 1976. About 70% of the workforce are farmers who occupy irrigated inland valleys where they raise livestock and subsistence crops of maize, beans, potatoes, cane sugar, bananas, yams and coffee, but since 1975 fishing has gained in importance; the main exports are fish, cane sugar, coffee, bananas, meat and hides. Salt, limestone and volcanic silica ash (pozzolana) are also mined and exported.

Administrative divisions. Cape Verde is divided into 2 *distritos* (districts), each of which is divided into 7 *concelhos* (councils). Santo Antão I comprises 3 councils and São Tiago comprises 4 councils. The area and population of the 10 islands are as follows:

Island	*area (sq km)*	*pop(1980)*
Barlavento		
Santo Antão	779	43,198
São Vicente	227	41,792
Santa Luzia	36	0
São Nicolau	388	13,575
Sal	216	6,006
Boa Vista	620	3,397
Sotavento		
Maio	269	4,103
São Tiago	991	145,923
Fogo	476	31,115
Brava	67	6,984

Capelle aan den Ijssel *kah-pel'e an den ī'sel*, 51 56N 4 22E, pop(1984e) 53,444, municipality in Zuid Holland prov, W Netherlands; on the R Ijssel, 8 km E of Rotterdam in the *Randstad* conurbation.

Capellen *kah-pe'lan*, canton in W part of Luxembourg dist, W Luxembourg; area 199 sq km; pop(1981) 27,159; bounded to the W by Belgium; traversed by the Mamer and Eisch rivers; capital Capellen.

Cap-Haïtien *kap-a-ee-syĩ*, CAP HAITIEN *kap hay'shen* (Eng), locally LE CAP *le kap'*, 19 47N 72 17W, pop(1975) 54,691, port and chief town of Nord dept, N Haiti, E Caribbean; 136 km N of Port-au-Prince; trade centre for the fertile Plaine du Nord; founded 1670 by the French; devastated by an earthquake in 1842.

Cappadocia, geographical region of Turkey. See Kapadokya.

Capri *ka'pree*, CAP'REAE (anc), island in Napoli prov, Campania region, Italy; lying off the tip of Sorrento peninsula, in the Tyrrhenian Sea; area 10.5 sq km; length 6 km; maximum width 2.5 km; its rugged limestone crags rise to a height of 589 m; capital Capri; the Grotta Azzurra (Blue Grotto) on the N coast of the island is a great tourist attraction.

Caquetá *ka-kay-ta'*, dept in S Colombia, South America; tropical forest region on the Equator; bounded W by

Cordillera Oriental, S by the Río Caquetá; drained by the Caguán and Yarí rivers, affluents of the Caquetá; pop(1985) 177,259; area 88,965 sq km; capital Florencia.

Carabobo *ka-ra-bō'bō*, state in N Venezuela; bordered N by the Caribbean; mountainous region with narrow coastal lowlands; crossed by a coastal hill range; includes large section of L Valencia (E); pop(1980) 1,019,042; area 4,647 sq km; capital Valencia; the most developed agricultural and industrial region of Venezuela.

Caracal *ka-ra-kal'*, 44 07N 24 18E, pop(1983) 34,337, town in Olt county, S Romania; 136 km SW of Bucureşti; railway; economy: textiles, furniture.

Caracas *ka-ra'kas*, federal dist in N Venezuela; bordered N by the Caribbean; pop(1980) 2,074,203; area 119 sq km; capital Caracas.

Caracas, 10 30N 66 55W, pop(1981) 1,162,952, federal capital of Venezuela, in Caracas fed dist, N Venezuela; alt 120-960 m; founded in 1567; 3 universities (1725, 1953, 1970), metro (opened Jan 1983); railway; airfield (Maiquetía) and airport (Simón Bolívar), both 28 km from Caracas; a comparatively low pass in the mountains (1,040 m) gives access to Caracas's port, La Guaira, and to its international and domestic airports; in the W of the city, near the government offices in the Palacio Miraflores and Palacio Blanco, is the industrial suburb of Catia; most of the city's factories are situated in the suburb of Antímano; Altamira and El Paraíso (SW) are residential suburbs; Caracas is the business, cultural and industrial centre of Venezuela; the proportionate growth of Caracas since the war has been greater than that of any other Latin American capital; monuments: the Plaza Bolívar, flanked by the cathedral and several government buildings, has an equestrian statue of Bolívar; the Panteón Nacional has Bolívar's tomb and was built as a tribute to all of Venezuela's national heroes; the Casa Natal del Libertador is a reconstruction of Bolívar's birthplace and a museum; the Capitolio Nacional, with its painted ceilings, houses a bronze urn containing the 1811 Declaration of Independence.

Caramulo, Serra do *ka-ra-moo'loo*, mountain range, N central Portugal, W of Viseu, rising to 1,071 m; vintage motor museum in the village of Caramulo.

Caransebeş *kar-an-say'besh*, 45 23N 22 13E, pop(1983) 31,198, town in Caraş-Severin county, W Romania; on R Timiş; established in the 12th century; theological academy; Teius recreation centre is SW; airfield; railway junction; economy: wood products and fruit trade.

Caraş-Severin *ka'ras she've-rin*, county in W Romania; in the W foothills of the Transylvanian Alps, on the frontier with Yugoslavia; pop(1983) 402,939; area 8,503 sq km; capital Reşiţa; economy: mining and chemicals.

Carazo *ka-ra'so*, maritime dept in Nicaragua, Central America; bounded W by the Pacific Ocean; pop(1981) 109,450; area 950 sq km; capital Jinotepe, economy: coffee growing.

Car'bondale, 37 44N 89 13W, pop(1980) 26,287, town in Jackson county, S Illinois, United States; 27 km W of Marion; university (1874); railway.

Carcassonne *kar-ka-son*, CARCASO (anc), 43 13N 2 20E, pop(1982) 42,450, ancient city and capital of Aude dept, Languedoc-Roussillon region, S France; on the R Aude and the Canal du Midi, lies in the fertile foothills of the Pyrénées; the town is divided into 2 parts: the Ville Basse (Lower Town), laid out in a regular grid plan and ringed by boulevards, and the Cité, a heavily fortified area which lies above the right bank of the R Aude; the Cité is the most complete example of a medieval fortified town to have been preserved intact in France; in ancient times it was the junction of E-W and N-S trading-routes; origin of a recipe for cassoulet; bishopric; railway; economy: hosiery, tanning, wine; monuments: the Cité (alt 200 m), elliptical in plan, is surrounded by a double circuit of walls and towers, there are 54 towers (11-13th-c), 2 gates and the basilica of St-Nazaire (5th-c, rebuilt 11-13th-c), in the Ville Basse there is the cathedral of St Michel (late 13th-c, restored after a fire in 1840) and the Gothic church of St Vincent (late 13th-c); event: Feast of the Patron St Gimer (May).

Carchi *kar'chee*, prov in the Andean Sierra of N Ecuador; bordered N by Colombia; pop(1982) 127,779; area 3,750 sq km; capital Tulcán; chief towns El Angel, San Gabriel; economy: tobacco, dairying, food processing, textiles, flour milling.

Cardamomes, Chaîne des *kar'da-moms*, CARDAMOM MOUNTAINS (Eng), mountain range following the SE Thailand and Cambodian frontier, lying to the E of Chanthaburi; the highest peak is Phnom Aural (1,813 m); length 160 km; subject to heavy monsoon rains; densely vegetated.

Cardiel, Lago *kar-dyel'*, lake in W central Santa Cruz prov, Patagonia, S Argentina; area 458 sq km; width 22 km.

Car'diff, CAERDYDD (Welsh), 51 30N 3 13W, pop(1981) 266,267, capital of Wales, in Cardiff dist, South Glamorgan, S Wales; at the mouth of the Taff, Rhymney and Ely rivers, on the Bristol Channel; a Roman fort was founded here during the 1st century AD; a Norman castle was built on the same site c.1090 and a city charter was granted in 1147; the construction of a canal leading to the Merthyr Tydfil coal mining area in 1794 and the later development of a harbour in the 1830s resulted in a dramatic expansion of the population; official capital of Wales since 1955; university (1893); college of music and drama; cultural and economic centre of Wales; railway; economy: administration, steel, car components, cigars; monuments: national museum, city hall, Llandaff cathedral, Welsh National Folk Museum, Cardiff castle.

Carei *ka-ray'*, 47 40N 22 28E, pop(1983) 26,933, town in Satu Mare county, N Romania; near the Hungarian border; ceded to Romania in 1919; railway; economy: agricultural equipment, paper, machinery, chemicals; monuments: interesting buildings around the central market place; 15th-c castle.

Careysburg *kā'riz-*, 6 30N 10 32W, town in Liberia, W Africa; 29 km ENE of Monrovia.

Cargados Carajos Islands *kahr-gah'dōs ka-rah'zhōs*, ST BRANDON (Eng), small island group NE of Mauritius in the Indian Ocean; a dependency of Mauritius with Agalega Is.

Caribbean Sea, *kar-i-bee'an* or *kah-rib'e-an*, arm of the Atlantic Ocean, lying between the West Indies and Central and South America; separated from the Gulf of Mexico by the Yucatán Channel; linked to the Pacific by the Panama Canal; inter-island passages linking with the Atlantic include Windward Passage, the Mona Passage and the Anegada Passage; the Caribbean is composed of the Yucatan, Colombian and Venezuelan basins, with depths ranging from 6 m on the continental shelf off Nicaragua to 5,058 m on the floor of the Venezuelan Basin; the Cayman Trench between Cuba and Jamaica falls to 6,950 m below sea-level, the Caribbean's deepest point; area 1,942,500 sq km; surface water enters through the straits of the Lesser Antilles, is warmed as it moves anti-clockwise entering the Gulf of Mexico via the Yucatán Passage; lower salinity than the Atlantic; Christopher Columbus first visited the Caribbean in 1493; the Caribbean is named after the Carib Indians; the islands of the Caribbean stretching in an arc from Puerto Rico to Trinidad were known as the Caribee Is; the main island groups are the Greater and Lesser Antilles.

Carinthia, federal state of Austria. See Kärnten.

Carlisle *kar-līl'*, LUGUVALIUM (Lat), 54 54N 2 55W, pop(1981) 73,233, county town in Carlisle dist, Cumbria, NW England; at the W end of Hadrian's Wall, at the confluence of the Eden and Caldew rivers; airfield (Crosby); railway junction; economy: foodstuffs, metal goods, textiles, engineering; monuments: 11-12th-c cathedral, 11th-c castle, 18th-c church of St Cuthbert; event: Great Fair (last Saturday in Aug).

Carlow *kar'lō*, CHEATHARLACH (Gael), county in Leinster prov, SE Irish Republic; situated between the Slieve Ardagh Hills (W) and the Wicklow Mts (E) where the Barrow and Slaney rivers water rich farm land; the Blackstairs Mts rise in the S; pop(1981) 39,820; area 896 sq km; capital Carlow.

Carlow, 52 50N 6 55W, pop(1981) 13,164, capital of Carlow county, Leinster, SE Irish Republic; technical college; railway; economy: barley malting, sugar-beet, footwear; monuments: Carlow Castle (12th-c), cathedral (19th-c), Browne's Hill tumuli (3 km E).

Carls'bad, 33 10N 117 21W, pop(1980) 35,490, health resort in San Diego county, SW California, United States; on the Gulf of Catalina on the Pacific Ocean, 6 km S of Oceanside; mineral springs and beaches; railway.

Carlsbad, 32 25N 104 14W, pop(1980) 25,496, county seat of Eddy county, SE New Mexico, United States; on the R Pecos, 110 km S of Roswell; railway; economy: potash mining and refining; tourism; the Carlsbad Caverns national park is nearby.

Carl'ton, 53 22N 1 06W, pop(1981) 46,119, town in Newark dist, Nottinghamshire, central England; E of Nottingham; railway; bricks, mining, hosiery, furniture.

Carluke *car-look'*, 55 45N 3 51W, pop(1981) 11,674, town in Clydesdale dist, Strathclyde, central Scotland; 8 km NW of Lanark; railway; economy: food and pharmaceuticals.

Carmarthen, 51 52N 4 19W, pop(1981) 14,491, county town of Dyfed in Carmarthen dist, Dyfed, SW Wales; on the R Towy 13 km N of the Bristol Channel; chartered in 1227; railway; economy: dairy products, pharmaceuticals, flour milling, agricultural trade.

Carmelo *kar-may'lō*, 34 00S 58 20W, pop(1985) 14,127, river port in Colonia dept, S Uruguay; on the Río Uruguay; a free port; a launch service runs between Carmelo and Tigre in Argentina.

Car'nac, 47 35N 3 05W, location in Morbihan dept, Bretagne (Brittany), NW France; near the Quiberon peninsula; site of over 3,000 megalithic dolmens and menhirs (standing stones or stones set up in aligned rows), dating from the 3rd and 4th millennia BC.

Carnar'von, 24 51S 113 45E, pop(1981) 5,053, fishing port in Central stat div, Western Australia, Australia; on the Gascoyne river, N of Shark Bay; the 40 m-wide main street dates from the era of the camel caravans; named after Lord Carnarvon in the 1880s; satellite communications station; railway; airfield; economy: fishing, fruit.

Car'nic Alps, KARNISCHE ALPEN (Ger), ALPI CARNICHE (Ital), S Alpine mountain range on the border between Italy and Austria; highest peak is Hohe Warte (2,780 m); the range is crossed by the Plöcken Pass.

Carnoustie *kahr-noo'stee*, 56 30N 2 44W, pop(1981) 9,225, resort town in Angus dist, Tayside, E Scotland; on the E coast, 17 km ENE of Dundee; railway; the town's golf courses include one of championship status.

Carolina *ka-rō-lee'na*, 18 23N 65 05W, pop(1980) 165,954, 3rd largest city in Puerto Rico, E Caribbean; ESE of San Juan; economy: textiles, sugar.

Carpathian Mountains *kar-pay'THi-an*, a mountain system of E central Europe forming the E wing of the great Alpine uplift. It extends 1,400 km in a semi-circle from Bratislava on the R Danube to Drobeta-Turnu Severin on the same river, traversing at its ends Czechoslovakia and Romania and in the middle portion forming the boundary between Czechoslovakia and Poland, and crossing SW Ukrainian SSR. It constitutes the watershed between the Baltic and the Black Sea, and from W to E the main divisions are the Malé Karpaty (Little Carpathians); Bilé Karpaty (White Carpathians); Beskydy (Beskids); Nizké Tatry (Low Tatra); Vysoké Tatry (High Tatra); Carpatii Orientali (E or Romanian Carpathians); and Carpatii Meridionali (Transylvanian Alps). The highest point is Negoiul (2,548 m). The range is rich in minerals and coal deposits and is generally forested to a height of 1,200 m.

Carpathians, mountains in Czechoslovakia. See Karpaty.

Carpatii Meridionali *kar-pat'see mer-id-ee-on-a'lee*, TRANSYLVANIAN ALPS (Eng), mountain range in central Romania; a S branch of the E European Carpathian Mts; the highest peak is Negoiul (2,548 m), the highest point in Romania; there are 3 longitudinal zones with newer rocks to the E, older rocks at the centre and volcanic peaks with craters in the W; includes the national park of Retezat (130 sq km) established in 1935.

Carpatii Orientali, ROMANIAN CARPATHIANS (Eng), mountain range running N-S in E Romania; part of the E European Carpathian Mts; rises to 2,305 m at Pietrosu.

Carpentaria, Gulf of *kahr-pen-tay'ree-a*, sea forming a great inlet on the N coast of Australia between Cape Arnhem and Cape York; bounded N by the Arafura Sea and linked to the Coral Sea by the Torres Strait; 595 km long by 491 km wide; shallow depths of 24-55 m, since the gulf is located over a continental shelf; named by Tasman in 1642 in honour of the Governor-General of the Dutch East Indies; bauxite deposits are found on its E shore.

Carrantuohill *kar-an-too'ul*, mountain in SW Irish Republic in the Macgillycuddy's Reeks range, rising to 1,041 m; the highest peak in the Irish Republic.

Carrickfergus, CARRAIG FHEARGHAIS (Gael), 54 43N 5 49W, pop(1981) 17,633, seaport and resort town in Carrickfergus dist, Antrim, NE Northern Ireland; on the N side of Belfast Lough, 19 km NE of Belfast; William III landed here before the battle of the Boyne, as did a French force in 1760; railway; economy: textiles, precision engineering, tobacco processing; monuments: the remains of Carrickfergus castle (built in 1180 by John de Courcy, the Norman conqueror of Ulster); it was captured by King John in 1210 and remained an English garrison until 1928; part of the castle contains a local history museum; the 4-storey keep (27 m high) contains a regimental museum; the 17th-c North Gate (now restored) was part of the town's fortifications.

Carrick-on-Suir *ka-rik-on-shoor'*, CARRAIG NA SIÚRE (Gael), 52 21N 7 25W, pop(1981) 5,566, market town in Tipperary county, South Riding, Munster, S Irish Republic; on R Suir, E of Clonmel; railway; monuments: 14th-c castle and abbey.

Carrollton, 32 57N 96 55W, pop(1980) 40,595, town in Dallas county, NE Texas, United States; a suburb 21 km NNW of Dallas; railway; economy: metal products, aircraft parts, and electronic equipment.

Carson, 33 48N 118 17W, pop(1980) 81,221, city in Los Angeles county, SW California, United States; NW of Long Beach.

Carson City, 39 10N 119 46W, pop(1980) 32,022, capital of state and an independent city, W Nevada, United States; near L Tahoe, 41 km S of Reno; economy: trade centre for a mining and agricultural area; monument: Nevada State Museum; event: Nevada Day (Oct).

Cartagena or **Cartagena de los Indes** *kar-ta-KHay'na*, 10 24N 75 33W, pop(1985) 529,622, port capital of Bolívar dept, NW Colombia, South America; on the Caribbean coast SW of Barranquilla; founded in 1533 by Pedro de Heredia as a storehouse for Peruvian treasure bound for Spain; the fortified city was sacked by Sir Francis Drake in 1586; access for ships from the up-river ports is via the Canal del Dique, built by Spain in 1650; university (1824); airfield (Crespo) at 1.5 km; economy: oil-refining, chemicals, plastics; events: festival of the Virgin of La Candelaria (2 Feb) and independence of Cartagena (11-14 Nov).

Cartagena, CARTHAGO NOVA (Lat), 37 38N 0 59W, pop(1981) 172,751, fortified seaport and naval base in Murcia prov, SE Spain; on a bay of the Mediterranean, 48 km S of Murcia; Spain's leading commercial port and principal naval base; the hill-protected harbour is one of the best in the Mediterranean; formerly the largest naval arsenal in Europe; founded by the Carthaginian leader Hasdrubal in 221 BC; railway; airports at Murcia and San Javier; watersports; economy: food processing, clothes, metallurgy and glass works, exports and oil refining at nearby Escombreras; 15 km canal to supplement drinking water built from San Javier; monuments: the castle of la Concepción and the 13th-c church of Santa Maria la Vieja; events: famous procession in Holy Week and Virgen del Monte Carmel patronal festival in July.

Cartago *kar-tah'gō*, prov in central Costa Rica, Central America; located on the E slopes of the Cordillera de

Talamanca; drained by the Río Reventazón and its tributaries; contains the volcanoes of Turrialba (3,339 m) and Irazú (3,432 m); pop(1983e) 259,916; area 3,125 sq km; capital Cartago; chief towns Turrialba, Paraíso and Tejar; served by the Inter-American Highway.

Cartago, 9 50N 83 52W, pop(1983e) 27,929, capital town of Cartago prov, central Costa Rica; at the foot of the Irazú volcanic peak, on the Inter-American Highway, 22 km ESE of San José; founded in 1563 and was the capital of Costa Rica until 1823; destroyed frequently by Irazú volcano and by earthquakes in 1841 and 1910; alt 1,439 m; monument: cathedral with noted stone figures.

Car'thage, 36 54N 10 16E, ancient town in Tunisia, N Africa; now a suburb of Tunis; founded in 815 BC as the Punic capital; the name means 'new city' (the old city being Utica); from 6th century BC the Carthaginians developed their seapower and trade links here, but the Punic Wars between Carthage and Rome (264-241 BC, 218-201 BC and 149-146 BC) resulted in the eventual destruction of the city; the city was restored as a capital by the Vandals between 439 AD and 533 AD, but was destroyed again by the Arabs in 698 AD; presently there are few remains - the Roman baths of Antonius, remains of the old harbour and an aqueduct of Hadrian; St Louis (Louis IX of France) died here in 1270 whilst on crusade and a chapel was built in his honour (1841); the cathedral was built by Cardinal Lavigerie in 1866; event: International Festival of Carthage (July-Aug).

Caruarú *ka-roo-a-roo'*, 8 15S 35 55W, pop(1980) 137,502, market town in Pernambuco state, Nordeste region, NE Brazil; W of Recife; railway.

Carvoeiro, Cabo *kar-vway'roo*, 39 21N 9 24W, W tip of rocky Peniche Peninsula, on Atlantic coast of Leiria dist, central Portugal.

Casablanca *ka-su-blang'ku*, DAR EL BEIDA (Arab), 33 20N 71 25W, pop(1982) 1,856,669, seaport in Casablanca-Anfa prefecture, Centre prov, W Morocco, N Africa; on the Atlantic coast 90 km SW of Rabat and 290 km SW of Tanger (Tangiers); includes the suburbs of Ben M'Sick, Aïn Diab, Aïn-es-Sebaâ and Aïn Chock; the original port of Anfa was destroyed in 1498 by the Portuguese who rebuilt the city in 1515 and named it Casa Branca ('white house'); the city was seriously damaged by an earthquake in 1755 and subsequently rebuilt; French occupation began in 1907; there was rapid development during 20th century as a result of the development of port facilities and the shipment of mineral resources; the port handles over 75% of Moroccan trade; Churchill and Roosevelt met here in Jan 1943 after the Allied landings in N Africa during World War II; university; railway; airport; economy: tourism, banking, fishing, glass, soap, phosphates and manganese.

Casanare *ka-sa-na'ray*, intendency in E central Colombia, South America; bounded N by Arauca intendency along the Río Casanare, SE by Vichada admin terr and Meta dept along the Río Meta, W by Boyacá dept; pop(1985) 24,443; area 44,640 sq km; capital Yopal; the region was formed in 1950 out of the lowland section of Boyacá.

Cascade Range *kas-kayd'*, mountain range in W North America; extends over 1,120 km from Lassen Peak in N California, where it meets the Sierra Nevada, N through Oregon and Washington to the Fraser river in British Columbia; named after the cascades of the Columbia river where it passes through the mountain range in a canyon 1,219 m deep; the Cascade Range lies nearly parallel with the Pacific Ocean and approx 177-257 km distant from it; it is continued S by the Sierra Nevada of California and N by the Coast Range of British Columbia and Alaska; rises to 4,392 m in Mount Rainier (46 52N 121 45W, in Washington state); the principal peaks in Washington are Mts Rainier, Adams (3,742 m) and Baker (3,285 m); in Oregon, Mts Hood (3,424 m) and Jefferson (3,200 m); in California, Mt Shasta (4,317 m); many of the peaks, including Mts Rainier, Shasta, Adams, Hood, Jefferson and St Helens, are snow-covered volcanic cones; extensive glaciation has left many lakes, of which L Chelan is the largest; glaciers are to be found on the higher peaks, notably those of Mt Rainier; Crater Lake National Park is in the S of the range; the Klamath and Columbia rivers cut through the range from E to W; a 13 km-long railway tunnel goes through the Cascade Range 160 km E of Seattle; the area's chief resources are timber and hydroelectricity.

Cascais *kash-kīsh'*, 38 41N 9 25W, pop(1981) 12,500, fishing port and popular resort on the Costa do Sol in Lisboa dist, central Portugal; 24 km W of Lisbon, on the W side of a rocky bay sheltered from the N winds by the Serra de Sintra; Cascais with its elegant parks and gardens has rapidly become a fashionable tourist resort like its near neighbour Estoril, with watersports and beaches nearby; railway; airfield (Tires); economy: fishing, tourism, electronics and telecommunications; monument: the 17th-c citadel, now the President's summer residence; event: Cascais fair from mid to end of July.

Cascavel *kas-ka-vel'*, 24 59S 53 29W, pop(1980) 100,329, town in Paraná state, Sul region, S Brazil; E of the Río Paraná; economy: maize, soya beans, wheat, timber, cattle raising.

Caserta *ka-zer'ta*, prov of Campania region, S Italy; pop(1981) 755,628; area 2,639 sq km; capital Caserta.

Caserta, 41 04N 14 20E, pop(1981) 66,318, capital town of Caserta prov, Campania region, S Italy; 32 km NNE of Napoli (Naples), at the foot of Monti Tifatini in the N part of the Campanian plain; here, on 29 April 1945, the German forces in Italy signed their surrender; railway; economy: chemicals, soap, trade in olive oil, wine, grain; monument: former royal palace (begun 1752).

Casino *kas-ee'nō*, 28 50S 153 02E, pop(1981) 9,743, town in Richmond-Tweed stat div, NE New South Wales, Australia; S of Brisbane; railway.

Casiquiare, *ka-see-kya'ray*, natural waterway in SW Amazonas federal territory, SW Venezuela; links the Orinoco and the Amazon river basins; branches off from the Orinoco at a point 32 km W of Esmeralda, at 3 10N 65 50W; flows approx 225 km SW and W to join the Río Negro 11 km NNW of San Carlos; the direction of flow is determined by the relevant levels of the two rivers; well-known to early missionaries, the river was made famous by the journey of Humboldt and Bonpland in 1801.

Casper, 42 51N 106 19W, pop(1980) 51,016, county seat of Natrona county, E central Wyoming, United States; largest city in the state, situated on North Platte river, 228 km NW of Cheyenne; the town expanded rapidly after the discovery of oil in the 1890s at Salt Creek, Teapot Dome, and Big Muddy; railway; airfield; economy: distributing, processing and trade centre in a farming, ranching and mineral-rich area, oil refineries, oil-related industries; coal and open-pit uranium mining nearby; monument: Old Fort Casper Museum.

Caspian Sea *kas'pee-an*, or MARE CASPIUM, MARE HYRCANIUM (anc), an inland sea, surrounded on 3 sides by territory of the USSR, and in the S by Iran, the largest inland body of water on Earth, covering 371,000 sq km, with a max depth of 980 m in the S; the shallow N half averages only 5.2 m in depth; intersected by a submarine ridge S of the centre; its low salinity is due to fresh water input, largely from the Volga, Kura, Emba and Terek rivers; the sea is frozen in the N for several months during severe winters; the Caspian has no outlet and has no tides; interregional freight trade is considerable, particularly oil from Baku; Beluga caviar is an important product of the shallow waters in the N; its level varies subject to evaporation and river input; construction of large dams on the Volga has affected the level in recent years; the sea is possibly named after the Caspii tribe which once occupied its S shores.

Castellón de la Plana *kas-tel-yon' day la plah'na*, prov in Valencia region, E Spain; mts in the N and W slope down to a fertile densely populated coastal plain; pop(1981) 431,755; area 6,679 sq km; capital Castellón de la Plana; economy: forestry and livestock in the mts, nuclear power station at Peniscola (500 MW); azulejos tiles, ceramics, linen, chemicals, footwear, canning, clothes, citrus fruit.

Castellón de la Plana, 39 58N 0 03W, pop(1981) 126,464, seaport and manufacturing city, capital of Castellón de la Plana prov, E Spain; 417 km E of Madrid; beaches and a port at El Grao 5 km from Castellón; economy: azulejos tiles, ceramics, footwear, furniture, linen, exports oranges; event: fiesta of St Magdalene in Holy Week with bullfights, regatta, procession and folk events.

Castelo Branco *kash-tay'loo bra'koo*, dist in E central Portugal; area, 6,704 sq km; pop(1981) 234,230; bounded by Spain (E and NE), the R Tagus (S) and the Serra da Estrêla (NW); divided into 11 councils and 156 parishes; extensive forests producing cork, resin and timber; economy: vegetables, horticulture, fruit, wine, meat, skins, dairy produce, textiles, ceramics; minerals: antimony, lead, copper, feldspar, manganese, quartz, titanium, uranium, wolfram, zinc; largest town, Covilhã; airfields at Covilhã and Idanha-a-Nova.

Castelo Branco, 39 50N 7 31W, pop(1981) 21,300, capital of Castelo Branco dist and former capital of the prov of Beira Baixa, E central Portugal; 275 km NE of Lisboa; founded 1209 by Templars; former frontier town of strategic importance; since 17th century celebrated for the colourful embroidered bedspreads known as *colchas*; economy: agriculture especially goat's milk cheese and olive oil, cork and wool; monuments: town wall; bishop's palace with its Baroque garden; churches of São Isabel, Misericordia (1519) and Our Lady of the Piedade with beautiful azulejo tiles; event: a municipal holiday 2 weeks after Easter.

Castilla-La Mancha *kas-teel'ya lah man'cha*, autonomous region of central Spain in the historical region of New Castile, comprising the provs of Albacete, Ciudad Real, Cuenca, Guadalajara and Toledo; pop(1981) 1,648,584; area, 79,230 sq km; there are 913 municipalities; part of the dry treeless and sparsely populated Meseta heartland of Spain rising to 700 m in altitude; the recent construction of reservoirs such as the Embalse de Alarcón 12 km S of Cuenca for irrigation has served to increase grain and chick pea production and has enabled the planting of eucalyptus to take place; rain in the spring and autumn produces grazing for the merino sheep which are brought there from the Extremadura to pasture during the summer.

Castilla-León *kas-teel'ya lay-on*, autonomous region of N Spain in the historical regions of León and Old Castile, comprising the provs of Ávila, Burgos, León, Palencia, Salamanca, Segovia, Soria, Valladolid and Zamora; pop(1981) 2,583,137; area, 94,147 sq km; the northern part of the central plateau (Meseta) bounded in the N by the Cordillera Cantabrica and in the S by the Sierra de Gredos and the Sierra de Guadarrama; the central part of the region is watered by the R Douro (Duero); cattle, fighting bulls and sheep are reared in the uplands which are often planted with cork-oaks; in the lowland valleys the recent construction of reservoirs for hydroelectric power and irrigation has helped improve the cultivation of wheat in Zamora and rye in León.

Castlebar *ka-sul-bahr'*, CAISLEÁN AN BHARRAIGH (Gael), 53 52N 9 17W, pop(1981) 7,423, capital of Mayo county, Connacht, W Irish Republic; on R Castlebar; residential and agricultural market town; Irish Land League founded here in 1879; airfield; railway; economy: linen, hats, bacon; event: international song contest in Oct.

Cas'tleford, 53 44N 1 21W, pop(1981) 39,401, town in Wakefield borough, West Yorkshire, N England; at the junction of the Aire and Calder rivers, 15 km SE of Leeds; railway; economy: coal mining.

Castlemaine *kah'sl-mayn*, 37 05S 144 19E, pop(1983e) 6,810, town in Loddon-Campaspe stat div, central Victoria, Australia; NNW of Melbourne; a former gold-mining settlement; railway; monuments: the centre of town contains well-preserved 19th-c buildings; Castlemaine Market, built in 1862, was restored in 1974.

Castries *kas'trees*, 14 01N 60 59W, pop(1982e) 130,000, port and capital town of St Lucia, Windward Is, E Caribbean; on the NW coast of the island; the town was rebuilt after being destroyed by fire in 1948; Vigie Airport is 3 km to the N; economy: foodstuffs, beverages, tobacco, textiles, wood and wood products, printing and publishing, industrial chemicals, rubber products, metal products.

Castrop-Rauxel *kas'trop-rowks'el*, 51 33N 11 36E, pop(1983) 77,400, industrial city in Arnsberg dist, Nordrhein-Westfalen (North Rhine-Westphalia) prov, W Germany; 51 km SSW of Münster.

Cat Island, elongated island in the central Bahamas, 160 km ESE of Nassau, bounded W by Exuma Sound; pop(1980) 2,143; area 388 sq km; length 80 km; width 5 km; chief settlements Arthur's Town and Port Howe; rises in the N to the highest point in the Bahamas; airfields at Arthur's Town, Hawk's Nest and New Bight.

Catalonia, Spanish autonomous region. See Cataluña.

Cataluña *kah-tuh-loo'nya*, CATALUNYA (Catalan), CATALONIA (Eng), autonomous region of NE Spain, comprising the provs of Barcelona, Gerona, Lérida and Tarragona and formerly including Roussillon and Cerdana; formerly a principality; there are 937 municipalities in the region; pop(1981) 5,956,414; area, 23,305 sq km; the Catalan Mts run parallel to the coast, linking the Pyrenees with the central plateau (Meseta); the region is more densely populated in the fertile river valleys where cereals, olives, almonds, hazelnuts and grapes are grown; industry is centred around Barcelona and there are many tourist resorts along the internationally known Costa Brava; to the N of Lérida many of the rivers that flow down from the Pyrenees have been dammed to provide hydroelectric power; the Catalan language, which is an independent Romance language related to Provençal, has undergone a revival since the death of General Franco in 1975.

Catamarca *ka-ta-mar'ka*, prov in Andina region, NW Argentina; mountainous region in the Andes, bordering with Chile on W; rises in W to 6,908 m at Ojos del Salado on Chile-Argentina border; pop(1980) 207,717; area 99,818 sq km; capital Catamarca; chief towns Londres and Tinogasta; economy: cattle raising, gold, silver, copper, tin and manganese mining, timber.

Catamarca, 28 28S 65 46W, pop(1980) 88,432, capital of Catamarca prov, Andina, NW Argentina; NNW of Córdoba and SSW of San Miguel de Tucumán, in foothills of E Andes; curative thermal springs; railway; economy: agricultural and mining centre, famous for hand-woven ponchos.

Catanduanes *kaht-an-dwahn'es*, island off the SE coast of Luzon I, NE Philippines; area 1,512 sq km; chief town Virac.

Catania *ka-tah'nee-a*, CAT'ANA (anc), prov of Sicilia region, S Italy; pop(1981) 1,005,577; area 3,553 sq km; capital Catania.

Catania, 37 31N 15 06E, pop(1981) 380,328, port and capital of Catania prov, Sicilia region, S Italy; 160 km SE of Palermo, at the foot of Mt Etna (3,332 m), on the E coast of the island; its port ships the produce of the wide and fertile Piana di Catania, the principal grain-growing region of Sicilia; archbishopric; university (1434); airport; railway; economy: shipbuilding, textiles, paper, sulphur processing, tourism.

Catanzaro *ka-tan-dzah'rō*, prov in Calabria region, S Italy; pop(1981) 744,834; area 5,247 sq km; capital Catanzaro.

Catanzaro, 38 54N 16 36E, pop(1981) 100,832, residential town, resort and capital of Catanzaro prov, Calabria region, S Italy; on a rocky hill, 9 km from the Golfo di Squillace; archbishopric; the centre of a citrus-growing area.

Caterham and Warlingham *kay'ter-êm, wor'ling-êm*, 51 17N 0 04W, pop(1981) 30,344, town in Tandridge dist, Surrey, SE England; part of Greater London urban area; on N Downs, 12 km S of Croydon; railway; economy: cosmetics, engineering.

Catió *ka-tyō'*, 11 13N 15 10W, pop(1979) 5,170, town in S Guinea-Bissau, W Africa; SE of Bissau, on the Atlantic coast.

Cat'skill Mountains, mountain group in SE New York state, United States; part of the Appalachian system, situated W of the Hudson river and SW of Albany; rises to 1,282 m at Slide Mt.

Cauca *kow'ka*, dept in SW Colombia, South America; bounded W by the Pacific Ocean; drained by Cauca, Patía and Caquetá rivers, which rise in the region; crossed by the Cordillera Occidental and Cordillera Central; includes the volcanoes of Sotará and Puracé; pop(1985) 674,824; area 29,308 sq km; capital Popayán.

Cauca, river in Colombia, South America; rises in the Cordillera Central, 51 km S of Popayán; main tributary of the Río Magdalena; flows 970 km N through the fertile Cauca valley between the Cordilleras Occidental and Central; receives the Río Nechí in Caribbean lowlands; enters left arm of the Río Magdalena (Brazo de Loba) 48 km SE of Magangué; partly navigable for small craft on its lower and mid course; flows through rainforests and swamps in its lower course near its junction with the Río Magdalena.

Caucasus, major mountain system in SW European USSR. See Kavkaz.

Cauquenes *kow-ke'nays*, 35 58S 72 19W, pop(1981) 25,756, capital of Cauquenes prov, Maule, central Chile; SW of Santiago; railway.

Cávado *ka'va-doo*, river of N Portugal; rises in Serra do Larouco, flows WSW to the Atlantic at Esposende W of Braga; length 118 km; navigable 6 km to Barca do Lago; area of basin 1,648 sq km; principal tributaries include the Homem and Rabagão rivers.

Ca'van, AN CHABHÁIN (Gael), county in Ulster prov, N central Irish Republic; bounded N by N Ireland; drained by Analee, Boyne and Erne rivers; pop(1981) 53,855; area 1,891 sq km; capital Cavan.

Cavan, CABHÁIN (Gael), 54 00N 7 21W, pop(1981) 5,035, agricultural market town and capital of Cavan county, Ulster, Irish Republic; NW of Dublin; bishopric; economy: crystal; event: international song contest in April.

Caxias do Sul *ka-shee'as dō sool'*, 29 14S 51 10W, pop(1980) 198,683, town in Rio Grande do Sul state, Sul region, S Brazil; N of Pôrto Alegre; university (1967); railway; economy: commerce, wine, motor vehicles.

Cayambe *ka-yam'bay*, 0 02N 78 08W, pop(1982) 14,249, town in Pichincha prov, in the Andean Sierra of N central Ecuador; NW of Cayambe volcano; railway; economy: dairy farming and cheese production.

Cayambe, 0 02N 77 58W, extinct Andean volcano on the border between Imbabura, Pichincha and Napo provs, N central Ecuador, just N of the Equator; 64 km ENE of Quito; height 5,790 m; the town of Cayambe lies at its NW foot; the volcano is craterless with a square, snow-capped top.

Cayenne *ka-yen'*, 4 55N 52 18W, pop(1982) 38,135; federal and district capital of French Guiana, NE South America; major port on the island of Cayenne at the mouth of the R Cayenne, on the Atlantic coast; airport (Cayenne-Rochambeau) at 16 km; monuments: the Canal Laussant built by Malouet in 1777; in the Place de Grenoble is the Jesuit-built residence (1890) of the Prefect.

Cayes, Les *lay kay'*, 18 15N 73 46W, pop(1975) 27,222, port and chief town of Sud dept, S Haiti, E Caribbean; 152 km WSW of Port-au-Prince.

Cayman Brac *kay-man' brak*, 19 45N 79 50W, easternmost of the Cayman Is, W Caribbean, 120 km ENE of Grand Cayman I; area 36 sq km; length 19 km; rises to 42 m at the E end of its limestone plateau; noted for its turtles.

Cayman Islands *kay-man'*, *kay'man* (Eng), British dependency in the W Caribbean, comprising the islands of Grand Cayman, Cayman Brac, and Little Cayman, c.240 km S of Cuba; timezone GMT −5; area 259 sq km; capital George Town; other main town West Bay; pop(1979) 16,677; about 60% of the pop is of mixed descent; 35% of the pop is under 18 years of age; English is the official language with Spanish frequently spoken as the 2nd language; Christianity is the dominant religion; the unit of currency is the Cayman Is dollar of 100 cents.

Physical description and climate. Geographically the Cayman Is are part of the Cayman Ridge which extends W from Cuba. Grand Cayman and Little Cayman are flat, little more than 18 m above sea level. Cayman Brac has a central limestone plateau which rises to 42 m at its E end. All the islands are ringed by coral reefs and have minimal surface drainage. The climate is tropical with an average annual rainfall of 1,420 mm. There is a hurricane season from July to Nov. Temperatures average 24°C to 32°C from May to Oct and 16°C to 24°C during the rest of the year.

History, government and constitution. The Cayman Islands were visited by Columbus in 1503 but never settled by the Spanish. In 1670 they were ceded (with Jamaica) by Spain to Britain under the Treaty of Madrid. Later, the islands were colonized by British settlers from the island of Jamaica from where the islands were administered. When Jamaica became independent in 1962 the islands became a separate British Crown Colony. A governor, appointed by and representing the British sovereign, presides over a 15-member legislative assembly and is chairman of an executive council.

Economy. Tourism, international finance, real estate transactions and property development are the most important economic activities. During the period 1976 to 1983 tourism in the Cayman Is grew from 76,596 visitors to more than 300,000 annually. More than 80% of the visitors come from the USA. Cruise ship traffic has increased substantially, exceeding 130,000 per annum. In 1982 there were well over 450 banks and trust companies established on the Cayman Is with George Town having more banks per capita than any other city in the world. There is an oil transshipment terminal off Little Cayman. The only manufacturing industries serve domestic and tourist demand (handicrafts and jewellery). Large-scale agricultural development is limited to a few enterprises based on cattle and poultry production and the growing of vegetables. The government-owned turtle farm on Grand Cayman has been adversely affected by an import ban by the USA. The chief exports in 1982 were tropical fish and primary turtle products, mainly to Jamaica, the UK, the USA, and Costa Rica. Main imports include foodstuffs, textiles, building materials, petroleum products, and automobiles.

Communications. There are airports on Grand Cayman (Owen Roberts) and Cayman Brac (Gerrard Smith) and an airfield on Little Cayman. The main seaport is George Town.

Cayo *ki'o*, dist in Belize, Central America; bounded W by Guatemala and dissected E-W by R Belize; Maya Mountains rise in the S; pop(1980) 22,837; area 5,336 sq km; chief towns Belmopan, San Ignacio, Santa Elena and Benque Viejo del Carmen; Maya ruins at Xunantunich and Caracol; agricultural research station at Central Farm.

Cazin *tsa'zin*, 44 59N 15 57E, pop(1981) 57,110, town in NW Bosna-Hercegovina republic, Yugoslavia; NNE of Bihać.

Ceará *say-a-ra'*, state in Nordeste region, NE Brazil; bounded NE by the Atlantic, W by the state of Piauí, S by Pernambuco state and E by Rio Grande do Norte and Paraíba states; pop(1980) 5,288,253; area 150,630 sq km; capital Fortaleza; chief town Juazeiro do Norte; economy: textiles, food processing, chemicals, timber, metallurgy; in the NW of the state is the Ubajara National Park; the state's area includes 2,614 sq km to be demarcated between Piauí and Ceará.

Cebu *say'boo*, island in Visayas group, S central Philippines; a narrow island lying between Negros I (W) and Bohol I (E); area 4,419 sq km; chief towns Cebu, Lapu-Lapu and Danao.

Cebu, CITY OF CEBU, 10 17N 123 56E, pop(1980) 490,281, seaport in Cebu prov, Central Visayas, Philippines; on E coast of Cebu I; formerly capital of Spanish Philippines; 4 universities (1595, 1919, 1946, 1949); airfield; economy: tobacco and copra trade; monuments: Spanish fort; Santo Niño church, with the cross Magellan set up at the first mass on the island; events: Santo Niño de Cebu, a week-long festival with processions, fireworks and cultural shows in Jan; parade to celebrate the landing of Magellan in 1521.

Cedar Falls, 42 32N 92 27W, pop(1980) 36,322, town in Black Hawk county, E Iowa, United States; on the R Cedar, 10 km W of Waterloo; university (1876); railway.

Cedar Rapids, 41 59N 91 40W, pop(1980) 110,243, county seat of Linn county, E Iowa, United States; on R Cedar, 80 km SE of Waterloo; railway; airfield; economy: cereals, communications equipment and machinery; named after the surging rapids on the river.

Cegléd *se'glayd*, 47 11N 19 47E, pop(1984e) 40,000, town in Pest county, N Hungary; 64 km SE of Budapest; railway; economy: fruit and agricultural trades.

Ceiba, La *la say'ba*, 15 45N 86 45W, pop(1983e) 61,248, port and capital town of Atlántida dept, N Honduras, 64 km E of Tela, on the Caribbean Sea; in a valley at the foot of Pico Bonito (2,580 m); airport (Golosón); railway; boat connections to the Islas de la Bahía (Bay Is), Tela and Trujillo; economy: exports bananas, pineapples, and other fruits; event: carnival (May).

Celaya *say-lah'ya*, 20 31N 100 49W, pop(1980) 219,010, town in Guanajuato state, S central Mexico; alt 1,754 m; railway; monuments: the town is famous for its churches built by Mexico's baroque architect, Tresguerras (1765-1833), a native of the town, and for its sweetmeats, especially a caramel spread called 'cajeta'.

Celebes Sea *se'le-beez*, sea of SE Asia, bounded by islands of Indonesia (W and S), Malaysia (NW) and the Philippines (NE); linked to the Java and Flores seas by the Makassar Strait; max depth 5,090 m.

Celje *tse'lye*, CILLI *chee'lee* (Ger), CLAUDIA CELEIA (anc), 46 15N 15 16E, pop(1981) 63,877, town in Slovenija republic, Yugoslavia; on R Savinja; founded in 1st century by the Roman emperor Claudius; part of Austria until 1918; railway; economy: mining, metallurgy, coal mining, wine trade.

Celle *tsel'le*, 52 37N 10 04E, pop(1983) 71,900, manufacturing city in Lüneburg dist, Niedersachsen (Lower Saxony) prov, W Germany; on R Aller, 35 km NE of Hannover; has one of largest orchid nurseries in Europe; famous for its Provincial Stud Farm; still functions as a garrison town with both German and British troops; railway; economy: televisions, biscuits, paint, machinery and textiles; monuments: medieval castle (formerly the residence of the Dukes of Brunswick-Lüneburg); Renaissance town hall (1530-81).

Celtic Sea *kel'tik*, part of the Atlantic Ocean S of Ireland; separated from the Irish Sea by St George's Channel; linked to the North Sea by the English Channel; the Bristol Channel is the main inlet; average depths of 100-200 m, with depths of 50-100 m over the Nymphe and Labadie Banks.

Central, a low-lying coastal region in S Ghana, W Africa, pop(1984) 1,145,520; area 9,469 sq km; capital Cape Coast; chief towns Winneba, Saltpond; economy: salt and beryllium mining, diamond and salt processing.

Central, region in central Scotland; bounded N and NE by Tayside, E by Fife, SE by Lothian and S and W by Strathclyde; part of the W border lies along Loch Lomond, and part of the NE border lies along Loch Tay; the N part of the region is in the Highlands, and includes the Trossachs, a picturesque range of hills, in the W; the S part of Central region encloses the Forth river valley; drained by the Forth, Carron and Devon rivers; contains several lochs including Lochs Katrine, Lubnaig and Venachar (W) and part of Loch Earn (NE); pop(1981) 273,391; area 2,631 sq km; capital Stirling; major towns include Falkirk, Alloa and Grangemouth (all in the SE, the region's industrial area); Central region is divided into 3 districts:

District	*area (sq km)*	*pop(1981)*
Clackmannan	161	47,855
Falkirk	301	144,361
Stirling	2,170	81,175

Central African Republic, official name The Central African Republic, RÉPUBLIQUE CENTRAFRICAINE (Fr), a republic in central Africa, bounded N by Chad, NE by Sudan, S by Zaire and Congo and W by Cameroon; area 626,780 sq km; timezone GMT +1; there are no railways; there are 453 km of bituminous roads and 10,196 km of improved earth roads and 7,080 km of inland waterways; capital Bangui; chief towns Berbérati, Bouar and Bossangoa; pop(1985e) 2,630,000; there are about 80 ethnic groups most of which have common cultural and linguistic characteristics; major ethnic groups include the Baya (34%), Banda (28%), Sara (10%), Mandjia (9%), Mboum (9%), M'Baka (7%) and a small European community; the majority of the pop is Christian (Protestant 25%, Roman Catholic 25%), the remainder following either local (24%) or Muslim (10%) beliefs; the official language is French but Sangho is widely spoken; the unit of currency is the franc CFA; national holiday 13 Aug; membership of AfDB, Conference of East and Central African States; EAMA, ECA, FAO, G-77, GATT, IBRD, ICAO, ICO, IDA, IFAD, ILO, IMF, INTELSAT, INTERPOL, ITU, NAM, OAU, OCAM, UDEAC, UEAC, UN, UNESCO, UPU, WHO, WIPO and WMO.

Physical description. The Central African Republic is set on a plateau which forms the watershed between the Chad and Congo river basins with a mean elevation of 600 m. Most of the northern rivers drain toward L Chad and southbound rivers flow toward the R Ubangi which forms the country's S border and eventually joins the R Congo. The highest ground is found in the NE (Massif des Bongos) and NW.

Climate. The N half of the country has a single rainy season between May and Sept and although rain falls throughout the year it is minimal during Dec-Feb. The average annual rainfall in the N is between 875 and 1,000 mm and in the S, which has a more equatorial climate, between 1,500 and 2,000 mm.

History, government and constitution. The Central African Republic was, until 1958, one of 4 territories within French Equatorial Africa, then known as Ubangi Shari. In that year it became an autonomous republic within the French community and in 1959 it joined with the other republics to form an economic, technical and customs union. In 1960 the country achieved full independence from France and in 1976 a new constitution was drawn up to provide for a parliamentary democracy and for the country's name to be changed to the Central African Empire. A coup in 1979 deposed the president and abolished the Empire of Emperor Bokassa I. The name of the country was changed to the Central African Republic. A second military coup in 1981 established a 23-member committee for National Recovery (CMRN). The Central African Republic is a one-party state.

Economy. The country's economy is based on agriculture with about 85% of the working pop engaged in subsistence agriculture growing cassava, groundnuts, cotton, maize, coffee, millet, sorghum, tobacco, rice, sesame seed, plantain, bananas and yams. Cash crops include cotton, coffee, peanuts and sesame. Hardwood forests provide mahogany, obeche and limba for export. Diamond mining and reserves of uranium are important to the economy. The main industries, which are largely based in Bangui, include sawmilling, brewing, diamond splitting and leather and tobacco processing. The main trade partners are France, West Germany, the USA, the UK, Israel, Spain, Belgium, Luxembourg and the Netherlands.

Administrative divisions. The Central African Republic is divided into 15 prefectures:

Prefecture	*area (sq km)*	*pop(1968)*
Bamingui-Bangoran	58,200	27,700
Bangui	67	301,793
Basse-Koto	17,550	183,223

contd

Prefecture	*area (sq km)*	*pop(1968)*
Haut-M'Bomou	55,530	53,564
Haute-Kotto	86,650	44,392
Haute-Sangha	44,350	235,306
Kemo Gribingui	37,200	134,031
Lobaye	24,500	150,510
M'bomou	61,150	127,240
Nana-Mambéré	26,600	198,720
Ombella-Mpoko	32,430	94,064
Ouaka	49,900	190,972
Ouham	52,250	262,998
Ouham-Pendé	32,100	232,283
Vakaga	46,500	178,602

These prefectures are subdivided into 47 subprefectures.

Central America, a geographical region that encompasses the independent states to the S of Mexico and to the N of S America; includes Guatemala, El Salvador, Belize, Honduras, Nicaragua, Costa Rica and Panama; the area gained independence from Spain in 1821, the independent states evolving from the former captain generalcies of Guatemala and New Granada.

Central Greece and Euboea, region of Greece. See Sterea Ellás-Évvoia.

Central, Massif *mas-eef sô-tral*, an area of ancient rocks in SE central France, mainly in the depts of Cantal, Haute-Loire and Aveyron, occupying about one-sixth of the country; the highest peak is Puy de Sancy in the Monts Dore (1,885 m) which is the highest point in France outside the Alps and the Pyrenees; there are massive limestone beds with impressive gorges, crags and caves as well as volcanic rocks such as the Monts Dômes which were active about 8,000 years ago; source of the Loire, Allier, Cher and Creuse rivers; there are facilities for winter sports at Le Mont-Dore, Super-Besse and Super-Lioran.

Central Siberian Plateau, upland region in E Siberian Rossiyskaya, Soviet Union. See Sredne Sibirskoye Ploskogor'ye.

Central Valley, GREAT CENTRAL VALLEY, valley in California, United States; situated between the Sierra Nevada (E) and the Coast Range (W); the part to the N of San Francisco is formed by the Sacramento river, the part to the S by the San Joaquin river; together they are used for the Central Valley Project, involving dams and reservoirs used for flood-control, irrigation and hydroelectricity.

Centre, region of central France comprising the depts of Cher, Eure-et-Loire, Indre, Indre-et-Loire, Loir-et-Cher and Loiret, 19 arrond, 192 cantons and 1,841 communes; pop(1982) 2,264,164; area 39,151 sq km; includes the former provs of Orléanais and Touraine and the pays of Beauce, Sologne and Gâtinais, the chief towns are Tours, Orléans, Bourges, Chartres, Vierzon and Châteauroux; the region is traversed by the Loire, Cher and Indre rivers which meet W of Tours; although generally flat the land rises to 434 m in the Collines du Sancerrois, N Cher dept.

Centro-Oeste *sent'trō-wes'tay*, region in W central Brazil; comprises Mato Grosso, Mato Grosso do Sul and Goiás states and Brasília federal territory; most of the region lies within the Brazilian plateau; in the W is part of the Pantanal; principal rivers include the Tocantins, Araguaia, Juruena and Paraguay; pop(1980) 7,544,795; area 1,879,455 sq km; economy: cattle raising, agriculture (especially in Goiás and Mato Grosso do Sul states) rice, soya beans, kidney beans, maize, cotton, babaçu nuts; rubber, mining of iron, manganese, rock crystals.

Cephalonia, Greek island. See Kefallinía.

Ceram, island of Indonesia. See Seram.

Cerritos *se-ree'tos*, 33 52N 118 02W, pop(1980) 53,020, city in Los Angeles county, SW California, United States; NE of Long Beach.

Cerro Largo *ser'rō lar'gō*, dept in NE Uruguay; bordered by the the Río Negro (N and NW), by Brazil along the Río Yaguarão (NE) and by L Mirim (SE); the Cuchilla Grande is in the S; pop(1985) 77,985; area 14,929 sq km; capital Melo; the dept was formed in 1837.

César, El *say'sar*, dept in N Colombia, South America; bordered E by Venezuela; the Río Magdalena forms part of its W boundary; the W is occupied by extensive marshland and part of the lake, Ciénaga de Zapatosa; pop(1985) 584,152; area 22,905 sq km; capital Valledupar.

Česká Lípa *ches'kah leep'a*, BÖHMISCH-LEIPA *boo-mish-lī'pa* (Ger), 50 43N 14 35E, pop(1984) 31,752, town in Severočeský dist, Czech Socialist Republic, W Czechoslovakia; 64 km N of Praha (Prague); railway; economy: fruit trade, textiles, leather; monuments: Augustine monastery, castle.

České Budějovice *ches-keh boo'dye-yow-it-seh*, BUDWEIS *boot'vīs* (Ger), 49 00N 14 30E, pop(1984) 92,826, river port and capital of Jihočeský region, Czech Socialist Republic, W Czechoslovakia; on R Vltava, 120 km S of Praha (Prague); founded in 13th century; railway; economy: brewing, food processing, machinery, timber and metal products; monument: Dominican abbey.

České Zemé, CZECH SOCIALIST REPUBLIC, republic in W Czechoslovakia; pop(1984) 10,328,221; area 78,864 sq km; united with Slovensko (Slovak Socialist Republic) in 1918 to form Czechoslovakia; comprises the former provinces of Bohemia, Silesia and Moravia; bounded N by E Germany (Erzgebirge Mts) and Poland, W by W Germany (Bohemian Forest) and S by Austria; capital Praha (Prague); chief towns include Brno, Plzeň, Ostrava, Ústí nad Labem, České Budějovice; divided into the 7 regions of Severočeský, Západočeský, Středočeský, Jihočeský, Východočeský, Jihomoravský and Severomoravský.

Československo. See Czechoslovakia.

Český Těšín *che'skee tye'sheen*, 49 44N 18 13E, pop(1984) 24,826, town in Severomoravský region, Czech Socialist Republic, central Czechoslovakia; 24 km ESE of Ostrava, near the Polish frontier; formerly part of Poland (1938-39) and Germany (1939-45); railway; economy: textiles, machinery, furniture, food processing.

Cessnock-Bellbird *ses'nok-bel'bird*, 32 51S 151 21E, pop(1981) 16,916, town in Hunter stat div, E New South Wales, Australia; an amalgamation of 2 towns W of Newcastle and N of Sydney.

Ceuta *thay'oot-a*, 35 52N 5 18W, pop(1981) 65,264, free-port and military station, with Melilla a region of Spain; at the E end of the Strait of Gibraltar, on the N African coast of Morocco; a 'plaza de soberania' administered by Cádiz prov, Spain; car ferries to Algeciras; became Spanish in 1580; economy: trade in tobacco, petrol derivatives, lubricants and combustibles, petrol storage and transport; monuments: old fortress at Monte Hacho, cathedral and 18th-c church of Our Lady of Africa.

Cévennes *say ven*, CEBENNA (anc), the chief mountain range in the S of France, on the SE edge of the Massif Central above the Mediterranean coastal plain; its general direction is NE-SW, forming a watershed between the river systems of the Loire, Rhône and Garonne; the central mass lies in Ardèche and Lozère depts, the highest peaks are Mt Mézenc (1,754 m), Mt Lozère (1,699 m) and Mt Aigoual (1,565 m); much of the area is barren limestone waste, interrupted by volcanic rocks; the landscape is varied, ranging from forest to barren grassland, bare moorland and deep gorges such as the impressive Gorges du Tarn between Ste-Énimie and Les Vignes.

Chachani, Nevado de *nay-va'dō thay cha-cha'nee*, Andean volcano in Arequipa dept, S Peru; 24 km N of Arequipa in the Cordillera Occidental, to NW of El Misti volcano; height 6,096 m; there is a meteorological station.

Chaco *cha'kō*, prov in Litoral region, N Argentina; bordered by the Bermejo river (NE) and by the Paraná and Paraguay rivers (E); largely humid, subtropical wooded plain with desert in the NW; the prov forms the S part of the Gran Chaco plain; pop(1980) 710,392; area 99,633 sq km; capital Resistencia; chief town Presidente Roque Sáenz Peña; economy: sorghum, cotton, sugar cane, cattle raising, timber; tannin extraction.

Chaco, national park in SE Chaco prov, Litoral, Argentina; area 150 sq km; established in 1954.

Chaco, dept in Occidental region, N Paraguay; bordered N and W by Bolivia; the majority of the dept is taken up by scrub forest, grassland and desert of the Gran Chaco; pop(1982) 286; area 36,000 sq km; capital Mayor Pablo Lagerenza.

Chad, TCHAD *chad* (Fr), official name Republic of Chad, RÉPUBLIQUE DU TCHAD (Fr), a republic in N central Africa, bounded N by Libya, E by Sudan, S by Central African Republic and W by Cameroon, Niger and Nigeria; area 1,284,640 sq km; pop(1979) 4,405,000; timezone GMT+1; capital N'Djamena (formerly Fort Lamy); chief towns include Moundou, Sarh and Abéché; although N Chad is occupied by Arab desert nomads and S Chad by Negro farmers and herdsmen there are some 200 distinct ethnic groups; French is the official language but Chadian Arabic is widely spoken in the N; there are over 100 languages and dialects spoken; over 50% of the pop is Muslim, the remainder following local religions and Christianity (5%); the unit of currency is the franc CFA; national holiday 13 April; membership of AfDB, CEAO, Conference of E African States, EAMA, ECA, EEC (associate), FAO, G-77, GATT, IBRD, ICAC, ICAO, IDA, Islamic Development Bank, INTELSAT, ITU, IFAD, ILO, IMF, L Chad Basin Commission, NAM, OAU, OCAM, OIC, UN, UNESCO, UPU, WHO, WIPO, WMO.

Physical description. Chad occupies a landlocked and mostly arid, semi-desert plateau on the edge of the Sahara desert with an average alt of 200-500 m above sea-level; the Logone and Chari rivers drain into L Chad in the SW; most other rivers are seasonal, flowing only after rainfall; isolated massifs along the Sudan frontier rise to 1,500 m and in the N the volcanic Tibesti Mts reach a height of 3,415 m at Emi Koussi; the vegetation is generally desert scrub or steppe, with the majority of the population living in the tropical S.

Climate. Between May and Oct the S is moderately wet but dry for most of the rest of the year. At N'Djamena the average annual rainfall is 744 mm. The hot and arid N half of the country is almost rainless. The central plain is hot and dry with a brief rainy season during June-Sept.

History, government and constitution. During the late 19th century the area came under French influence and as part of French Equatorial Africa gained colonial status in 1920. The country was granted autonomy in 1959 and independence in 1960. A constitution was adopted in 1962, but suspended in 1975 when the National Assembly was dissolved. In 1982 a quasi-constitution, the Fundamental Act, provided a juridical framework to enable the promulgation of decrees by the president of the 20-member Council of Ministers. A 30-member National Consultative Assembly was also formed in 1982. The judicial review of legislation is theoretically the responsibility of the Supreme Court.

Economy. The economy of Chad, which has been severely damaged in recent years by drought, plagues of locusts and civil war, has been largely dependent on the export of cotton, kaolin and animal products. Local agriculture in the S is based on the production of cassava, groundnuts, millet, sorghum, rice, yams, sweet potatoes and dates. There is oil exploration in Kanem prefecture with refining facilities in Laï with which it is linked by a pipeline. Deposits of uranium, gold and bauxite exist in the N and salt has been extracted from the area around L Chad. Nigeria, Cameroon and France are major trading partners.

Administrative divisions. Chad is divided into 14 prefectures:

Prefecture	*area (sq km)*	*pop(1979)*
Batha	88,800	354,000
Biltine	46,850	175,000
Borkou-Ennedi-Tibesti	600,350	88,000
Chari-Baguirmi	82,910	676,000
Guéra	58,950	207,000
Kanem	114,520	200,000
Lac	22,320	139,000
Logone-Occidental	8,965	295,000
Logone-Oriental	28,035	307,000
Mayo-Kebbi	30,105	684,000
Moyen-Chari	45,180	524,000
Ouaddaï	76,240	347,000
Salamat	63,000	107,000
Tandjilé	18,045	302,000

In addition there are 54 subprefectures, 27 administrative posts and 9 municipalities.

Chad, TCHAD (Fr), shallow freshwater lake in N central Africa at the meeting point of Chad, Nigeria, Cameroon and Niger; area 10,400 sq km at low water and 20,700 sq km at high water; fed by the Chari-Logone river system from the S and the R Komadugu Yobe from the W, it has no visible outlets, water seeps underground; occasionally, in high water season, it connects with the R Benue system through the Logone and Mayo-Kebbi rivers; the lake is a remnant of a former inland sea, its shoreline expanding and contracting according to the seasons; there is a continuous chain of inhabited islands along the E coast; fishing and natron extraction are important; first reached by Europeans in 1823 (Oudney, Chepperton and Denham); the Frenchman Jean Tilho conducted a thorough hydrographic survey between 1912 and 1917; nearby is Douguia Wildlife Reserve; oil was discovered nearby in Niger.

Chad'derton, 53 27N 2 08W, pop(1981) 33,518, town in Oldham borough, Greater Manchester, NW England; 10 km NE of Manchester and W of Oldham.

Chagang *ja-gang*, JAGANG, prov in N North Korea; bordered N by China along the R Yalu; capital Kanggye.

Chaghcharān *chag-cha-ran'*, CHEGHCHERAN, CHAKHCHARAN, 34 28N 65 21E, pop(1984e) 3,260, capital of Ghowr prov, central Afghanistan; lies to the W of Kābul and E of Herāt on the R Hari-Rūd; airfield.

Cha'gos Archipelago, island group in Indian Ocean. See British Indian Ocean Territory.

Chahar Mahāll va Bakhtīāri *ch-har ma-hal va bak-tee-a'ri*, mountainous prov in W central Iran; pop(1982) 394,357; area 14,820 sq km; capital Shahr-e Kord.

Chalatenango *cha-le-te-nan'gō*, dept in N El Salvador, Central America; bounded NE by Honduras; pop(1971) 186,003; area 2,507 sq km; capital Chalatenango; chief towns Tejutla and La Palma; the Río Lempa forms much of its W and S border.

Chalchuapa *chal-chwa'pa*, 14 00N 89 41W, pop(1980) 56,136, town in Santa Ana dept, W El Salvador, Central America; on the main highway between Santa Ana and Ahuachapán; railway; monument: Tazumal ruin, built in 980 AD by the Pipil Indians.

Chalcidice, nome (dept) of Makedhonia region, Greece. See Khalkidhíki.

Chalfont St Peter, 51 35N 0 34W, pop(1981) 19,609, town linked with Gerrard's Cross in Chiltern dist, Buckinghamshire, S central England; 9 km NW of Uxbridge; railway.

Châlons-sur-Marne *sha-lō-sür-marn*, 48 58N 4 20E, pop(1982) 54,359, important agric market and capital of Marne dept, Champagne-Ardenne region, NE France; on the right bank of the R Marne, in the centre of the great plain of Champagne; railway; crossed by several canals; economy: champagne, beer; monuments: St-Étienne cathedral with a wealth of stained-glass from the 12-13th centuries; 12th-c church of Notre-Dame-en-Vaux with a famous carillon of 56 bells.

Chalon-sur-Saône *sha-lō-sür-sōn*, 46 47N 4 51E, pop(1982) 57,967, industrial and commercial town in Saône-et-Loire dept, Bourgogne region, E central France; on the W bank of the R Saône where it is linked to the R Loire by the Canal du Centre; river port, railway; it is the distribution centre for the wine dist that lies W of the town; birthplace of Nicéphore Niepce (1765-1833), the celebrated pioneer of photography; events: renowned for its twice yearly commercial fairs.

Chambéry *shā-bay-ree*, 45 34N 5 55E, pop(1982) 54,896, capital of Savoie dept, Rhône-Alpes region, SE France; in the gorge linking L Bourget to the R Isère, 14 km S of Aix-les-Bains; produces, and gives its name to, one of the best of the French vermouths; ancient capital of the dukes of Savoy, who ruled from the château which dominates the town with its massive round tower and Italianate chapel; monuments: church of St Pierre with a 9th-c crypt and baptistry; cathedral (originally the chapel of a 13th-c Franciscan monastery, greatly enlarged in the 15th century).

Champagne *shā-pan'y'*, *sham-payn'* (Eng), dist and former prov of NE France, now occupying the depts of Marne, Haute-Marne, Aube and Ardennes with parts of Yonne, Aisne, Seine-et-Marne and Meuse; named 'country of plains' from the great plains near Reims, Châlons-sur-Marne and Troyes; divided into upper and lower Champagne; Brie Champenoise lies in the W; the centre is dry chalkland while to the E there is richer dairying country; the famous wines are produced along the slopes from Reims to Épernay and westwards along the N bank of the R Marne; the name Champagne was also given to flat dists in Normandie, Saintonge and around Le Mans.

Champagne Castle, 29 06S 29 20E, 2nd highest mountain of the Drakensberg range, S Africa; rises to 3,375 m on the Lesotho-Natal frontier; first recorded ascent by A.H. Stocker and F.R. Stocker in 1888.

Champagne-Ardenne *shā-pan'y'-ar-den*, region of NE France comprising the depts of Ardennes, Aube, Marne and Haute-Marne, 15 arrond, 143 cantons and 1,903 communes; pop(1982) 1,345,935; area 25,606 sq km; includes part of the forest-clad Ardennes hill land to the N, the flat, dry chalk Plaine de Champagne near Reims and the area to the S drained by the Seine, Aube and Marne rivers; noted for the production of champagne wine, made from pinot grapes grown on shallow chalky soil; the 120 km long 'Route du Champagne' runs through the vine-growing areas, starting at Reims, dividing into 3 sections; like the adjoining region of Lorraine, there was heavy fighting in Champagne during the last 3 wars between France and Germany, notably the battles for Sedan and Metz; chief towns include Reims, Épernay, Troyes, Chaumont and Charleville-Mézières; between Reims and Épernay is the 'Mountain of Reims' which is largely forest and where the wild boar is still hunted.

Champaign *sham-payn'*, 40 07N 88 15W, pop(1980) 58,133, town in Champaign county, E Illinois, United States; adjacent to Urbana, 72 km ENE of Decatur; railway.

Champasak, prov (*khowèng*) of S Laos, SE Asia; capital Champasak.

Champigny-sur-Marne, *shā-peen-yee-sur-marn*, 48 49N 2 31E, pop(1982) 76,260, residential suburb of Paris in Val-de-Marne dept, Ile-de-France region, central France; on the N bank of a loop of the R Marne.

Chandigarh *chun'di-gahr*, city and union territory in NW India, pop(1981) 450,061; area 114 sq km; the city and surrounding area became a Union Territory in Nov 1966, serving as the joint state capital of the Punjab and Haryana; ultimately to become capital of the Punjab state only, once a capital for Haryana has been built; 27% of the territory is under forest; the city was designed by the French architect Le Corbusier, using the layout of self-contained neighbourhood units for a max pop of 150,000; the town plan includes an 8 km green belt; university (1947); has Asia's largest rose garden; airfield; linked by rail to Delhi.

Chandler, 33 18N 111 50W, pop(1980) 29,673, town in Maricopa county, S central Arizona, United States; 28 km SE of Phoenix; railway; economy: sugar, mobile homes, computer components, and containers; nearby is Williams Air Force Base.

Chandpur *chand'poor*, 23 15N 90 40E, pop(1981) 85,656, town in Chandpur dist, Comilla, SE Bangladesh; lies close to the R Megnha; railway.

Chang or **Ko Chang** *kō chang*, 2nd largest island (*ko*) of Thailand; off the coast of Trat prov, near the NE shore of the Gulf of Thailand; a resort island.

Chang Jiang *chang jahng*, YANGTSE-KIANG, YANGTZE RIVER *yank-si*, longest river in China and 3rd longest in the world; length 6,300 km; its source is the Tuotuo He which flows from the Jianggendiru glacier on the SW slopes of Geladandong peak, the highest peak in the Tanggula Shan range in SW Qinghai prov; it then flows E and is known as the Tongtian He until it nears the Xizang-Sichuan border in SE Qinghai, where it becomes the Jinsha Jiang; the Jinsha Jiang flows S, forming part of the Sichuan-Xizang border then part of Sichuan's border with Yunnan; it flows through the N of Yunnan and along its N border with Sichuan into Sichuan itself where, after passing the town of Yibin in S Sichuan it becomes the Chang Jiang; the Chang Jiang flows NE through the Sichuan basin where it is joined by the Min Jiang, Tuo Jiang, Jialing Jiang and Wu Jiang rivers; at the border with Hubei it forms a series of gorges known as the Yangtze gorges; the Qutang Xia gorge, Wu Xia gorge and Xiling Xia gorge pass through the Wu Shan range; from here the Chang Jiang flows SE and S to enter the Hubei plain where it forms part of the border with Hunan to the S; it is joined by the Qing Jiang and Han Shui rivers and by the rivers of the Dongting Hu lake system; it then flows in a curve NE past Wuhan then SE to the border with Jiangxi where it is joined by the rivers of the Poyang Hu lake system; from here the Chang Jiang flows NE along part of the Jiangxi-Anhui border, through Anhui past Anqing, Tongling and Wuhu and into Jiangsu where it passes Nanjing and Zhenjiang (where it is crossed by the Grand Canal) before curving

SE past Nantong to enter the East China Sea at Shanghai; the Chang Jiang has a drainage area of over 1,800,000 sq km (19% of China's total area); the river provides approx 40% of China's electricity through hydroelectric power stations which are concentrated in the section of the river known as the Jinsha Jiang; this section contains the Hutiao (Tiger Leaping) canyon, one of the world's largest canyons, with a length of 16 km and a drop of 170 m; at its narrowest point, the canyon is only 30 m wide; at the mouth of the Chiang Jiang (Yangtze) gorges, on the border of Sichuan prov, is the Gezhouba water control project; the Gezhouba Dam near Yichang is one of the largest in the world; the Chang Jiang is a major transportation artery between E and W China, being navigable for over 940 km; bridges at Chongqing, Wuhan and Nanjing have now partly solved the problem of N-S communication; the entire length of the river was first navigated in 1986; the Chang Jiang river basin is densely populated and comprises approx one-quarter of China's cultivated land: it contains fertile soil, highly developed agriculture and numerous mineral deposits; there have been plans to channel part of the Chang Jiang 1,000 km to the N where water is scarce.

Changan, capital of Shaanxi prov, central China. See Xi'an.

Changchun *chang-choon*, CH'ANGCH'UN, 43 50N 125 20E, pop(1984e) 1,809,200, capital of Jilin prov, NE China; on the Yitong river in the central part of China's NE plain; Changchun was developed in the period of Japanese military occupation (1933-45) when it was the capital of the puppet state of Manchukuo; university (1958); railway; airfield; economy: electric furnaces, automobiles, light engineering, textiles, food processing, chemicals; Changchun film studio.

Chang-hua *chang-hwa*, county of W Taiwan; area 1,061.7 sq km; pop(1982e) 1,203,970.

Changsha *chang-sha*, CH'ANGSHA, 28 10N 113 0E, pop(1984e) 1,123,900, river port and capital of Hunan prov, SE China; on the lower Xiang river, in intensively cultivated alluvial lowlands; the town was established before 1000 BC and was an early craft and industrial centre; known as an important education centre from 976 AD; Changsha was established as a foreign trade port in 1904; Mao Tse-tung began his conversion to communism here as a student from 1912 to 1918; university (1959); railway; airfield; economy: textiles, food-processing, chemicals, light engineering, electronics; monuments: the Hunan provincial museum contains documents relating to revolutionary history and exhibits from the Han Tomb (dating from 206 BC to 24 AD), discovered at Mawangdui in 1972; Yuelushan Park contains one of China's oldest extant Buddhist temples (Lushan temple, founded in 268 AD); Tianxin Ge, situated on the highest point within the city, is the only remaining part of Changsha's city wall; the Buddhist Kaifu Temple (896 AD) was occupied by a factory during the Cultural Revolution.

Channel Islands, ILES NORMANDES (Fr), island group of the British Isles in the English Channel, W of the Cotentin Peninsula of French Normandie; the principal islands are Guernsey, Jersey, Alderney and Sark; other islands include Herm, Jethou, Brechou, the Caskets, the Minquiers and the Chauseys; the English language predominates in the towns, elsewhere a Norman-French patois is spoken; area 194 sq km; the islands have 6th-c associations with St Helier and St Sampson; granted to the Dukes of Normandy in the 10th century, they were the only part of Normandy remaining with England after 1204; economy: fruit, vegetables, flowers, dairy produce; the islands are a dependent territory of the British Crown with their own legislative assemblies and legal system; the islands are divided into the Bailiwick of Guernsey and the Bailiwick of Jersey; in Guernsey and Jersey, the Bailiff, who is appointed by the Crown, presides over the Royal Court and the representative assembly (the States) and is the head of the island administration.

Chao Phraya *chow prī'a*, river in central Thailand; flows into the Bight of Bangkok, an inlet of the Gulf of Thailand, just S of Bangkok; length 365 km; the river port of Muang Nakhon Sawan has been developed to provide a waterway access to the N and NE regions.

Chaoan, China. See Chaozhou.

Chaouén, town in Morocco. See Chefchaouen.

Chaozhou *chow-jō*, CHAOAN, formerly CHAOCHOW (-1914), 23 22N 116 36E, pop(1984e) 1,202,800, city in Guangdong prov, S China; at the head of the Han river delta, N of Shantou; economy: textiles, porcelain, mining.

Chapala, Lago de *lah'gō day chah-pah'lah*, lake in E Jalisco and NW Michoacán states, SW Mexico; 77 km long E-W; approx 16 km wide; area 3,366 sq km; largest lake in Mexico; situated on the central plateau, 48 km S of Guadalajara; fed by the Río Lerma entering at the E end; drained by the Río Grande de Santiago at Ocotlán at the NE corner; the resort town of Chapala is on the N shore.

Chapel Hill, 35 55N 79 04W, pop(1980) 32,421, residential town in Orange county, N central North Carolina, United States; 18 km WSW of Durham; university (1789); railway.

Chapelcross, nuclear power station, Annandale and Eskdale dist, Dumfries and Galloway, S Scotland; 4 km NE of Annan; Scotland's first gas-cooled reactors came into commercial operation here in 1959-60.

Chapeltown, 53 28N 1 27W, pop(1981) 22,647, town in Sheffield borough, South Yorkshire, N England; N of Sheffield; railway.

Chappaquid'dick (Algonquian, 'separated-island-at'), island to the E of Martha's Vineyard I, United States; in the Nantucket Sound, off the SE coast of Massachusetts.

Chard, 50 53N 2 58W, pop(1981) 9,402, market town in Yeovil dist, Somerset, SW England; 19 km SE of Taunton; economy: lace, clothing.

Charente *sha-rãt*, dept in Poitou-Charentes region of W France, comprising 3 arrond, 35 cantons and 405 communes; pop(1982) 340,770; area 5,956 sq km; crossed by the low spurs of the Mts of Limousin, Poitou and Périgord and watered by the Charente and Vienne rivers; there are considerable heaths and woods; brandy is made here from grapes grown in the Charente basin (eg at Cognac); capital Angoulême, chief towns include Confolens and Cognac; all traffic routes converge at Angoulême; there are interesting châteaux at Cognac (13-16th-c) and Étagnac (11-12th-c).

Charente, river in W France rising SW of Rochechouart in Haute-Vienne dept; flows W through Charente-Maritime dept to the Bay of Biscay opposite Ile d'Oléron; length 360 km; navigable to Angoulême; tributaries Tardoire, Touvre, Seugne and Boutonne rivers.

Charente-Maritime, dept in Poitou-Charentes region of W France, bounded W by the Bay of Biscay and SW by the Gironde estuary; comprises 5 arrond, 45 cantons and 472 communes; pop(1982) 513,220; area 6,864 sq km; mainly flat and in places swampy, watered by the Charente and Gironde rivers; the slopes of the low hills to the N and NE of the Charente R are covered with grapes (for Cognac brandy and wine); capital La Rochelle, chief harbours are Rochefort and Tonnay-Charente, other towns include Saintes and Marennes (celebrated for its oysters); spas at Rochefort and Saujon; the Parc du Marais Poitevin regional nature park lies partly within the dept.

Chargui, Hodh ech *shar-gee'*, desert region in SE Mauritania, NW Africa; pop(1982e) 235,000; area 182,700 sq km; capital Néma; chief towns Oualata, Niout, Néré, Timbédra (airfield), Bassikounou and various waterholes.

Chari *shah-ree'*, river in SW Chad, N central Africa; formed by the junction of the Bamingui and Gribingui rivers 170 km W of N'Délé it is the main tributary of L Chad; flows 800 km NW past Sarh and Bousso to join the R Logone at N'Djamena where it forms the border between Chad and Cameroon before entering L Chad; length including R Bamingui 1,060 km; explored by Heinrich Barth (1852) and Gustav Nachtigal (1872-73).

Chari-Baguirmi *cha-ree-ba-geer'mee*, prefecture in W central Chad, N central Africa; pop(1979) 676,000; area

82,910 sq km; a low lying prefecture drained in the S and W by the Logone (which follows part of the W border), Chari and Erguig rivers; capital N'Djamena; chief towns Bokoro, Massénya and Bousso.

Chārikār *char'i-kar*, 35 02N 69 13E, pop(1984e) 24,580, capital of Parvan prov, E Afghanistan; lies on the main road S to Kābul and close to the S bank of the R Ghorband.

Charleroi *shar-le-rwa*, dist of Hainaut prov, SW Belgium; area 555 sq km; pop(1982) 441,040.

Charleroi, 50 25N 4 27E, pop(1982) 219,579, town in Charleroi dist, Hainaut prov, SW Belgium; on the R Sambre; formerly a fortress, finally dismantled after the mid-19th century; from here in World War I the French were driven back by the Germans (Aug 1914); economy: insulated electric wire and cables.

Charlesbourg *sharl'boorg*, 46 51N 71 16W, pop(1981) 68,326, town in S Québec, SE Canada; 8 km NNW of Québec; first settled in 1659.

Charleston, 32 46N 79 56W, pop(1980) 69,510, county seat of Charleston county, SE South Carolina, United States; a port on the Atlantic Ocean, at the mouths of Ashley and Cooper rivers; the oldest city in the state, founded in 1670; survived attacks by a British Fleet in 1776 and 1779, but was finally captured by Sir Henry Clinton and held by the British 1780-82; site of a convention in Dec 1860 which proclaimed the secession of South Carolina from the Union; the Confederate attack on nearby Fort Sumter on 12-13 April 1861 began the Civil War; the town was finally evacuated by Confederate forces in 1865 after a 2-year siege; devastated by an earthquake in 1886; railway; airfield; economy: fertilizers, chemicals, steel, asbestos, cigars, paper products, textiles and clothing; site of a US naval and air force base; monuments: Charleston Museum, Old Slave Mart Museum and Gallery, Gibbes Art Gallery, and several old colonial buildings.

Charleston, 38 21N 81 38W, pop(1980) 63,968, capital of state in Kanawha county, W West Virginia, United States; at the confluence of Elk and Kanawha rivers; a settlement developed around Fort Lee in the 1780s; a city since 1870; capital of West Virginia 1870-75 and from 1885; railway; airfield; economy: an important transportation and trading centre in the highly industrialized Kanawha valley; manufactures chemicals, glass, primary metals, and various other products based on the salt, coal, natural gas, clay, sand, timber and oil found in the region; event: Sternwheel Regatta (Aug).

Charlestown, 17 08N 62 37W, pop(1980) 1,771, capital and port of Nevis I, St Kitts-Nevis, N Leeward Is, E Caribbean, on the W coast of the island, at the foot of Nevis Peak (985 m); once famous for its thermal springs; economy: garments.

Charleville-Mézières *sharl-veel-may-zyer*, CAROLOPOLIS, ARCAE REMORUM (Lat), 49 44N 4 40E, pop(1982) 61,588, capital of Ardennes dept, Champagne-Ardenne region, NE France; lies within 2 loops of the R Meuse; it was originally 2 independent towns: Charleville, the N half, is laid out on a regular grid plan centred on the spacious Place Ducale, the S part, Mézières, is older, with remains of medieval ramparts; throughout World War I it was in the hands of the Germans; a few hours before the Armistice the German troops opened fire on the town, causing much damage; there was also considerable damage in World War II during the German advance of 1940.

Charlotte, 35 13N 80 51W, pop(1980) 314,447, county seat of Mecklenburg county, S North Carolina, United States; 110 km SSW of Winston-Salem; the Mecklenburg Declaration of Independence was signed here in May 1775; birthplace of James K. Polk, 11th president of the United States; 2 universities (1867, 1946); railway; airfield; largest city in the state; economy: textiles, chemicals, machinery, food and printed materials.

Charlotte Amalie *shar'lut u-mal'yu*, 18 22N 64 56W, pop(1980) 11,756, port and capital city of the US Virgin Is, Lesser Antilles, Caribbean, on the S coast of St Thomas I, on St Thomas Harbour; one of the most popular cruise ship ports in the Caribbean; economy: tourism.

Charlottesville, 38 02N 78 30W, pop(1980) 39,916, independent city and county seat of Albemarle county, central Virginia, United States; on the R Rivanna, 112 km WNW of Richmond; settled in the 1730s; named after the wife of King George III; university (1819); railway; economy: electronics, navigational systems, communications equipment; monuments: Monticello, home of Thomas Jefferson, and Ash Lawn, the home of James Monroe, respectively the 3rd and 5th presidents of the United States.

Charlottetown, 46 14N 63 09W, pop(1981) 15,282, capital of prov in Queen's county, Prince Edward Island, NE Canada; on Hillsborough Bay; founded by the French in the 1720s; prov capital since 1765; university (1969); economy: fishing, trades in textiles, potatoes, dairy products, timber.

Charsadda *char'sud-du*, 34 12N 71 46E, pop(1981) 62,000, city in North-West Frontier prov, Pakistan; site of ancient city taken by Alexander the Great in 326 BC; the headquarters in 1930 of the 'Red Shirt' movement.

Charters Towers, 20 02S 146 20E, pop(1981) 6,823, town in Northern stat div, Queensland, Australia; on Flinders Highway, SW of Townsville; railway; airfield; at the beginning of the 19th century it was the most important gold town in Queensland; a gold mine and houses typical of the period still remain.

Chartres *shahr'tr*, AUTRICUM, CIVITAS CARNUTUM (anc), 48 29N 1 30E, pop(1982) 39,243, capital city of Eure-et-Loire dept, Centre region, N central France; on the left bank of the R Eure, 100 km SW of Paris; bishopric; it is an important agricultural centre and wheat market lying in the fertile Plaine de la Beauce; railway; monuments: abbey church of St Pierre-en-Vallée (11-13th-c); cathedral of Notre-Dame, one of the best preserved Gothic architectural monuments of France, after devastating fires (743, 858, 1020 and 1194) the old Romanesque cathedral, believed to have stood on the site of a Gallo-Roman sanctuary, was replaced by the present day building dating chiefly from 1195 to 1220 and consecrated in 1260; at the W end of the cathedral stand two great towers surmounted by spires, the Clocher Vieux on the right (saved intact from the earlier cathedral, considered a masterpiece of the Romanesque style) and the Clocher Neuf on the left; the Royal Doorway (Portail Royal), decorated with statues which became models for the further development of sculpture (mid 12th-c); the area immediately surrounding the cathedral has been declared a conservation area and much has been done to clean and preserve the buildings; event: students' pilgrimage (April-May).

Châteauguay *shah tō gay'*, 45 22N 73 44W, pop(1981) 36,928, town in S Québec, SE Canada; on the Châteauguay river near its mouth on Lac St Louis, 23 km SW of Montréal; railway.

Châteauroux *shah-tō-roo*, 46 50N 1 40E, pop(1982) 53,967, capital of Indre dept, Centre region, central France; on the R Indre; named from a château built in the 10th century by Raoul le Large; home-town of General Bertrand, one of Napoleon's most loyal soldiers; railway; economy: brewing, woollens, tobacco, agric trade; monument: 10 km E, in the bombed-out castle of Diors, is a museum devoted to the 3 wars, 1870, 1914 and 1939.

Châtelet *shat-lay*, 50 24N 4 32E, pop(1982) 38,272, town in Charleroi dist, Hainaut prov, Belgium.

Chatham *chat'am*, 42 24N 82 11W, pop(1981) 40,952, town in S Ontario, SE Canada; on the R Thames; railway; economy: tobacco, sugar refining, flour milling, canning.

Chatham, 51 23N 0 32E, pop(1981) 66,063, industrial and naval town in the Medway Towns urban area and Rochester upon Medway dist, Kent, SE England; on the R Medway, 45 km E of London; naval base; railway; economy: electrical goods.

Chatham Islands, islands of New Zealand in the SW Pacific Ocean; 850 km E of Lyttelton, South Island; area 963 sq km; comprises the 2 islands of Chatham (Whairikauri) and Pitt (Rangihaute) and some rocky islets; discovered in 1791 by Lt Broughton, of the brig *Chatham*; in 1831, 800 Maoris landed, and in 9 years reduced the aboriginal Morioris from 1,200 to 90; a large brackish lake occupies the interior of Chatham I; economy: sheep-rearing, sealing, fishing.

Chatila *sha-tee'la*, pop(1986) 3,200, Palestinian refugee camp on the outskirts of Beyrouth (Beirut), Lebanon; created following the evacuation of Palestinians from the city after Israeli attacks on Palestinians and Syrians in June 1982; in Sept 1983 Christian Phalangists carried out a massacre here.

Chattanoo'ga (Creek, 'rock-rising-to-a-point'), 35 03N 85 19W, pop(1980) 169,565, county seat of Hamilton county, S Tennessee, United States; a port on the R Tennessee, just N of the Georgia border; almost entirely surrounded by scenic mountains which include Lookout Mt, Signal Mt and Missionary Ridge; settled c.1835 after which it developed as a salt-trading centre; achieved city status in 1851; scene of battles of Chickamauga and Chattanooga (1863) during the Civil War; university (1886); railway; airfield; economy: textiles, chemicals, metal products.

Chaumont *shō-mõ*, 48 07N 5 08E, pop(1982) 29,552, capital town of Haute-Marne dept, Champagne-Ardenne region, NE France; on a height between the rivers Marne and Suize, which join just N of the town; railway; economy: glove-making; monuments: basilica of St Jean (twin-spired church of different periods from Gothic to Renaissance); 27 km NW is the village of Colombey-les-Deux-Églises, home of General de Gaulle, former president of France.

Chaux-de-Fonds, La *shōd-fõ'*, 47 07N 6 51E, pop(1980) 37,234, town in Neuchâtel canton, NW Switzerland; in a bleak valley in the Jura Mts, high above Lac de Neuchâtel, close to the French frontier; the largest watch-making town in Switzerland; built to a grid pattern in the early 19th century after a fire; the Saut-du-Doubs waterfall and gorges are nearby on the French frontier; birthplace of the famous architect Charles-Edouard Jeanneret, better known as Le Corbusier (1887-1965); railway junction; economy: watches, technical instruments; monument: International Watch and Clock museum.

Chaves *sha'vish*, AQUAE FLAVIAE (Lat), 41 45N 7 32W, pop(1981) 12,000, spa town with medicinal hot springs on R Tâmega, Vila Real dist, N Portugal; 66 km NNE of Vila Real; railway; airfield; monuments: twelve-arched Roman bridge; castle on the site of a Roman fortress, once the residence of the first Duke of Bragança; 17th-c Baroque church of the Misericordia with azulejo tile biblical pictures and ceiling paintings; event: Santos fair at the end of Oct.

Cheadle, 53 24N 2 13W, pop(1981) 59,828, town linked with Gatley in Stockport borough, Greater Manchester, NW England; S of Manchester and 4 km W of Stockport; railway; economy: engineering, printing.

Cheb *KHep*, 50 04N 12 20E, pop(1984) 31,333, industrial town in Západočeský region, Slovak Socialist Republic, W Czechoslovakia; in the R Ohre valley, 80 km NW of Plzeň, near the border with W Germany; Wallenstein was assassinated here in 1634; railway; economy: machinery, motorcycles, textiles.

Cheboksary *che-buk-sa'ree*, SHUPASHKAR (Chuvash), 56 08N 47 12E, pop(1983) 364,000, capital city of Chuvashskaya ASSR, NW European Rossiyskaya, Soviet Union; on the R Volga; university (1967); railway; airfield; economy: machine building, textiles, building materials, foodstuffs; monument: Vedenskii cathedral (1657).

Ched'dar, 5 17N 2 46W, pop(1981) 3,900, market town in Sedgemoor dist, Somerset, SW England; 16 km ESE of Weston-super-Mare; famous for the limestone features of the Cheddar Gorge and for the Cheddar cheese originally made here.

Cheefoo, special economic zone in Shandong prov, E China. See Yantai.

Chefchaouen *shef-show-en'*, XAUEN (Sp), CHAOUÉN, CHECHAOUEN, 35 10N 4 16W, pop(1982) 23,563, town in Chefchaouen prefecture, Nord-Ouest prov, N Morocco, N Africa; in the Er Rif Mts, 55 km S of Tétouan; a holy city, founded in the 15th century; known as the 'town of fountains' because of its many gushing springs; monuments: Great mosque, kasbah fortress.

Chegutu *che-goo'too*, formerly HARTLEY, 18 10S 30 14E, pop(1982) 20,000, town in Mashonaland West prov, Zimbabwe, S Africa; 105 km WSW of Harare; railway; economy: farming, mining.

Cheju *che-joo*, prov of Korea, comprising a large volcanic island (Cheju do) 70 km off the SW tip of the Korean Peninsula; rises to 1,950 m in Halla san peak, the highest point in Korea; pop(1984) 482,031; area 1,824 sq km; capital Cheju; connected to the mainland by air and ferry; in the early 1960s Catholic farmers brought 500 sheep from New Zealand and Japan and taught the villagers of Hallim, a small town in the NW of the island, to shear sheep, process the wool and weave; the *tolharubang* (stone grandfathers), black lava statues of a benign old man, once considered fertility gods, are major symbols of Cheju island: reproductions are now sold as souvenirs.

Chekiang, province in E China. See Zhejiang.

Cheliff, Ech, town in Algeria. See Asnam, Al.

Chełm *KHe'oom*, voivodship in E Poland; bounded on the E by R Bug which follows the USSR frontier; pop(1983) 237,000; area 3,866 sq km; capital Chełm; chief towns include Krasnystaw and Włodawa.

Chełm, KHOLM (Rus), 51 08N 23 29E, pop(1983) 57,900, capital of Chełm voivodship, E Poland; near the USSR frontier; manifesto of the Polish Committee of National Liberation proclaimed here in 1944; railway; economy: cement; monuments: 18th-c cathedral, Baroque parish church with interesting polychromes.

Chelms'ford, 51 44N 0 28E, pop(1981) 92,479, county town in Chelmsford dist, Essex, SE England; on the R Chelmer, 48 km NE of London; railway; economy: electronics, furniture; monument: 15th-c cathedral.

Chelsea, central London, England. See Kensington and Chelsea.

Chelsea, 42 23N 71 02W, pop(1980) 25,431, town in Suffolk county, E Massachusetts, United States; on the Mystic river, 5 km NE of Boston; economy: chemicals, paints, footwear.

Cheltenham *chel'ten-em*, 51 54N 2 04W, pop(1981) 84,373, residential town in Cheltenham dist, Gloucestershire, SW central England; on the W edge of the Cotswold Hills, 12 km NE of Gloucester; former spa; railway; events: Cheltenham Gold Cup horse-race (March); National Hunt steeplechases in Prestbury Park; festival of contemporary music (July).

Chelyabinsk *chil-ya'binsk*, TCHELYABINSK, 55 12N 61 25E, pop(1983) 1,077,000, industrial capital city of Chelyabinskaya oblast, W Siberian Rossiyskaya, Soviet Union; on the E slopes of the S Ural'skiy Khrebet (Ural Mts) range; established in 1736 as a Russian frontier outpost; airport; road and rail junction; economy: ferrous metallurgy, machine building, foodstuffs, chemicals.

Chenab *chay'nab*, river in Kashmir and Pakistan; one of the 5 rivers of the Punjab; rises in the Himalayas and flows NW through the Himāchal Pradesh and into Kashmir, cutting into the Pī Pānjāl range, then S past the town of Riāsi and into Punjab prov, Pakistan; joined by the R Jhelum near Jhang Maghiana, the R Ravi NNE of Multan and the R Sutlej to the E of Bahawalpur forming the R Panjnad which joins the R Indus to the NE of Chachran; extensive irrigation canal system links with the R Chenab.

Chengchow, capital of Henan prov, N central China. See Zhengzhou.

Chengde *cheng-de*, JEHOL, 40 59N 117 52E, pop(1984e) 325,800, town in NE Hebei prov, N China; railway; economy: distribution centre for forestry and agricultural products; monuments: Chengde was once the summer home of the Qing emperor, Kang Xi; his summer palace and gardens to the S of the city are now a public park; built between 1703 and 1780, the remaining buildings include 9 temples, some in Chinese style, others influenced by Tibetan temples; the largest of these, the Lamaist-inspired Temple of General Peace (built in 1775), has an area of 199,904 sq m.

Chengdu *cheng-doo*, CHENGTU, 30 37N 104 06E, pop(1984e) 2,539,600, capital of Sichuan prov, SW central China; Chengdu was first built in 200 BC as the Zhou dynastic capital; it was known as the 'city of hibiscus' during the Five Dynasties Period (907-60) when hibiscus was planted all over the town; the apricot tree is the symbol of Chengdu; the town developed after 1949 when the new government decided to make it into a regional industrial base; home of the Sichuan opera; university (1931); railway; airfield; economy: rice, wheat, sweet potatoes, tea, medicinal herbs, tobacco, silk, handicrafts, coal, metallurgy, electronics; monuments: Du Fu Cottage was the home of the Tang poet, Du Fu (712-70), who lived here for 3 years; c.40 km NW of the town on the Min river is the Dujiang Yan Dam, which dates from 250 BC when a trunk canal was cut through Green City Peak mountain and a water distribution network set up to irrigate 13,000 sq km of land; it has been expanded since 1949 and now irrigates over 165,000 sq km; Ching Yang Gong, the oldest and largest Daoist temple in Chengdu, was established during the late Han Dynasty; event: an annual 2-month flower festival, featuring operatic and theatrical performances as well as flowers, is held in Ching Yang Gong, commencing on the 15th day of the 2nd lunar month (Feb-March).

Chenghsien, capital of Henan prov, N central China. See Zhengzhou.

Chengtu, capital of Sichuan prov, SW central China. See Chengdu.

Chepstow, 51 39N 2 41W, pop(1981) 12,457, urban area incorporating Tutshill-Sedbury in Monmouth dist, Gwent, SE Wales; on the R Wye, 22 km ENE of Newport, N of the Severn Road Bridge; railway; economy: light industry, agricultural trade, tourism; monument: 11-13th-c castle; 11th-c St Mary's church, remains of 13th-c town wall and 14th-c town gate; 5 km N are the ruins of Tintern Abbey (1131).

Cher *sher*, dept in Centre region of central France, bounded on the NE by the Loire R; comprises 2 arrond, 35 cantons and 290 communes, pop(1982) 320,174; area 7,235 sq km; consists of plain and well-wooded hills rising to 434 m in the NE; drained by the Cher and Arnon rivers; capital Bourges; there are interesting châteaux at Blancafort (15th-c), Culan (12-15th c) and Ainay le Vieil (Renaissance).

Cher, river in central France rising in the Massif Central E of Aubusson; flows N and NNW to the R Loire near Tours; length 350 km; navigable to Noyers; tributaries Tardes, Arnon, Yeuvre and Sauldre rivers.

Cherbourg *sher-boor*, CARUSBUR (anc), 49 38N 1 37W, pop(1982) 40,500, fortified seaport and naval base in Manche dept, Basse-Normandie, NW France; at the head of the Cotentin peninsula; begun by Vauban in 1687, the harbour was extended by Napoleon; the harbour is protected by a long *digue* or breakwater built in 1853; France's 3rd largest naval base; used by transatlantic shipping; ferry services to Southampton, Weymouth and Rosslare.

Cherepovets *chi-ryi-pe-vyets'*, 59 05N 37 55E, pop(1983) 290,000, port town in Vologodskaya oblast, NE European Rossiyskaya, Soviet Union; on the Volga-Baltic waterway; originated as a tax-exempt settlement near the Voskresenskii monastery; railway; airfield; economy: ferrous metallurgy, chemicals, furniture, shipbuilding.

Cherkassy *chir-ka'see*, 49 27N 32 04E, pop(1983) 259,000, capital city of Cherkasskaya oblast, Ukrainskaya SSR, SW Soviet Union; a port on the NW bank of the Kremenchug reservoir and a fast-growing industrial and cultural centre; founded at the end of the 13th century; it was here that the Cossack leader, Bogdan Khmelnitsky, sent his first letter in June 1648 proclaiming the Ukrainians' wish to unite with Russia; railway; economy: foodstuffs, machine building, chemicals, fertilizers, silk, clothing, knitwear.

Cherni Vruh or **Cherni Vrukh**, also **Cerni Vrah** *cher'nee-vraKH* ('black peak'), 42 34N 23 16E, highest peak of the Vitosha Mts, W Bulgaria, 15 km from Sofiya; height 2,290 m; the upper slopes are a national park and nature reserve but the area is best known as a skiing resort; there is a road to the summit.

Chernigov *cher-nyee'gof*, 51 30N 31 18E, pop(1983) 263,000, river port and capital city of Chernigovskaya oblast, Ukrainskaya SSR, SW Soviet Union; on the right bank of the R Desna; one of the oldest cities in Russia; railway; economy: manufacture of pianos and synthetic fibres, ship repair, wood-work, and foodstuffs; monuments: 11th-c Spaso-Preobrazhenskii cathedral, one of the country's oldest stone buildings; 12th-c cathedral of St Boris and St Gleb (rebuilt after fire damage in 1511); Ukrainian Baroque architecture of the 17-18th centuries, including Lizogub's House (1690s), cathedral (1679-89), and St Catherine's church (1715).

Chernobyl' *cher-no'bil*, 51 16N 30 15E, city in Ukrainskaya SSR, SW Soviet Union; near the junction of the Pripyat and Ushk rivers, N of Kiyev (Kiev); scene of the world's largest known nuclear disaster in 1986.

Chernovtsy *cher-nof'tsee*, formerly CHERNOVITSY, CZERNOWITZ (Ger), 48 19N 25 52E, pop(1983) 232,000, capital city of Chernovitskaya oblast, Ukrainskaya SSR, SW Soviet Union; stretching for 12 km along the banks of the R Prut, in the E foothills of the Carpathians; founded at the beginning of the 15th century; university (1875); railway, airfield; economy: foodstuffs, machine building, manufacture of cotton textiles, clothing, knitwear, and power station equipment; monument: wooden church of St Nicholas (1607).

Cherskogo, Khrebet *cher'sko-ve*, CHERSKI RANGE *cher'skee*, mountain range predominantly in Yakutskaya ASSR, but extending also into W Magadanskaya oblast, Rossiyskaya, NE Soviet Union; extends c.1,000 km SE from the Yana-Indigirka river divide to the R Kolyma; bounded W by the Verkhoyanskiy Khrebet range; consists of a series of short, broken ranges, the summits of which rise to heights of 2,000-2,500 m; rises to 3,147 m at Gora Pobeda in the S section; traversed by the R Indigirka and the Magadan-Yakutsk highway; rich in lead, zinc, molybdenum, and coal.

Chesapeake *ches'a-peek*, 36 50N 76 17W, pop(1980) 114,486, independent city, SE Virginia, United States; 6 km S of Norfolk; formed in 1963 by the merger of the former city of South Norfolk with part of Norfolk county; farmland and part of the Great Dismal Swamp lie within its boundaries; railway; economy: fertilizer, cement and wood products.

Chesapeake Bay, an inlet of the Atlantic Ocean in Virginia (S) and Maryland (N) states, United States; at the mouth of the Susquehanna, Patuxent, Potomac, Chester, Choptank, Nanticoke, Rappahannock and James rivers; part of the Intracoastal Waterway.

Chesh'am, 51 43N 0 38W, pop(1981) 20,935, town in Chiltern dist, Buckinghamshire, S central England, United Kingdom; 40 km NW of London; railway; economy: chemicals, engineering.

Chesh'ire, county of NW central England; bounded W by Wales and N by Merseyside and Greater Manchester; drained by the Mersey, Weaver, Dee, Gowy and Wheelock rivers; the Delamere Forest lies between Chester and Northwich; pop(1981) 929,981; area 2,328 sq km; county town Chester; chief towns include Crewe, Warrington, Widnes, Runcorn, Macclesfield; economy: dairy farming, petrochemicals, motor vehicles; the county is divided into 8 districts:

District	*area (sq km)*	*pop(1981)*
Chester	448	115,600
Congleton	211	79,161
Crewe and Nantwich	431	98,555

contd

District	*area (sq km)*	*pop(1981)*
Ellesmere Port and Neston	82	82,309
Halton	74	122,094
Macclesfield	523	150,086
Vale Royal	384	111,812
Warrington	176	169,372

Cheshunt *ches'unt*, 51 43N 0 02W, pop(1981) 49,718, residential town linked with Waltham Cross in Greater London urban area and Broxbourne dist, Hertfordshire, SE England; 22 km N of London; railway; economy: electronics, horticulture.

Ches'ter, DEVA, DEVANA CASTRA (Lat), CAERLEON (Welsh), LEGACEASTER (Anglo-Saxon), 53 12N 2 54W, pop(1981) 82,363, county town of Cheshire, NW central England; on the R Dee, 305 km NW of London; important Roman port and military centre; railway; economy: light engineering, tourism, car components; monument: 13-15th-c cathedral, city walls, 11th-c St John's church; town hall (1869).

Chester, 39 51N 75 22W, pop(1980) 45,794, town in Delaware county, SE Pennsylvania, United States; port on R Delaware, 22 km SW of Philadelphia; railway.

Ches'terfield, 53 15N 1 25W, pop(1981) 74,180, town in Chesterfield dist, Derbyshire, central England; on the R Rother, 16 km S of Sheffield; railway; economy: engineering, glass, pottery, surgical dressings; monuments: 14th-c church of St Mary and All Saints, Chatsworth House (11 km W).

Chesterfield, Îles, island group comprising 11 uninhabited coral islets NW of the French overseas territory of New Caledonia in the S Pacific Ocean; 550 km W of Bélep Is; area 10 sq km.

Ches'ter-le-Street', 54 52N 1 34W, pop(1981) 34,975, town in Chester-le-Street dist, Durham, NE England; on the R Wear, 9 km N of Durham; on site of Roman station of Concangium; railway; economy: coal mining, chemicals, electrical goods; monuments: 14th-c Lumley castle, church of St Mary and St Cuthbert.

Chetumal *che-too-mahl'*, PAYO OBISPO (-1935), 18 30N 88 17W, capital of Quintana Roo state, SE Mexico; a resort town on the border with Belize, on the Bahía de Chetumal at the mouth of the Río Hondo; airport; economy: trade in livestock, chicle, timber, fruit and henequen.

Cheviot Hills *chee'vi-ot*, hill range on the border between Scotland and England; extends 56 km SW along the frontier between Borders region and Northumberland; rises to 816 m at The Cheviot; gives its name to a famous breed of sheep.

Cheyenne *shī-an'*, 41 08N 104 49W, pop(1980) 47,283, capital of state in Laramie county, SE Wyoming, United States; near the Colorado border, 157 km N of Denver, Colorado; named after an Indian tribe; the city was founded at a railway junction in 1867; territorial capital since 1869; the city prospered with the opening up of the Black Hills gold fields in the 1870s; railway; economy: livestock market and shipping centre; monument: Frontier Days Museum; event: Frontier Days (July).

Chia-i or **Chia-yi** *cha-yee*, 23 38N 120 59E, pop(1982e) 252,906, independent municipality in W central Taiwan; N of T'ai-nan; area 60 sq km.

Chia-i, county in E Taiwan; area 1,891.4 sq km; pop(1982e) 574,712.

Chiang Mai *jee'-eng mī*, 18 48N 98 59E, pop(1982) 104,910, city in NW Thailand; 700 km N of Bangkok, at the foot of Doi Inthanon, Thailand's highest mountain; N Thailand's principal city since 1296 when it was founded by king Meng Rai as the capital of Lan Na Thai kingdom; university; railway; airfield; events: flower festival in Feb; Songkran water-throwing festival in April at the Thai New Year; Loy Krathong in late Nov.

Chianning, former name for capital of Jiangsu prov, SE China. See Nanjing.

Chiapas *chee-ah'pas*, state in S Mexico; situated on the Pacific Ocean between the Istmo de Tehuantepec and Guatemala; bounded W by Veracruz and Oaxaca states, N by Tabasco, E by Guatemala and S by the Golfo de Tehuantepec and the Pacific; the main branch of the Sierra Madre runs parallel and close to the coast; this section includes the peak Volcán de Tacaná (4,092 m), which is situated on the border with Guatemala; drained by the Lacantum, Mezcalapa and Usumacinta rivers; Chiapas contains 2 large reservoirs, the Presa de la Angostura in the S and the Presa Netzahualcóyotl in the W; in the forest of the NE are the ancient Mayan temples of Palenque; pop(1980) 2,096,812; area 74,211 sq km; capital Tuxtla Gutiérrez; economy: agriculture (coffee, cocoa, maize, cotton, sugar cane, rice, tobacco, bananas, oranges), cattle raising, timber, fishing, chalk, sugar refining, cotton processing, textiles, alcohol.

Chiba *chee'ba*, 35 38N 140 07E, pop(1980) 746,430, capital of Chiba prefecture, Kanto region, E Honshū island, Japan; a commuter town 40 km E of Tōkyo, on Tōkyo Bay; university (1949); railway; economy: steel, textiles, paper.

Chicago *shi-kah'gō*, 41 53N 87 38W, pop(1980) 3,005,072, county seat of Cook county, NE Illinois, United States; on L Michigan; 2nd largest city in the USA; built on the site of Fort Dearborn, Chicago was settled in the 1830s; it developed as a result of its strategic position linking the Great Lakes with the Mississippi river after completion of the Illinois and Michigan Canal in 1848 and following the opening of a railway linking it with the E in 1853; acquired city status in 1837; much of the city was destroyed by a fire in 1871; 7 universities; railway; airport; economy: electrical machinery, metal products, steel (one-quarter of the nation's steel is produced in and around the city), food products; printing and publishing; commerce and finance is centred upon 'The Loop' area; transport centre of the USA, with one of the busiest airports in the world and a major inland port; monuments: Lyric Opera, Art Institute, Museum of Science and Industry, Shedd Aquarium, Planetarium; event: Chicago Film Festival (Nov).

Chicago Heights, 41 30N 87 38W, pop(1980) 37,026, town in Cook county, NE Illinois, United States; 43 km S of Chicago; railway.

Chīchāwatni *chee-cha'vat-nee*, 30 32N 72 42E, pop(1981) 50,000, market town in SE Punjab prov, Pakistan; economy: cotton, sugar, grain, timber.

Chichén Itzá *chee-chen' eet-sah'*, 20 40N 88 32W, ruined Maya city in E Yucatán, SE Mexico; 113 km ESE of Mérida in dense tropical jungle; believed to have been founded in the 6th century by the Itzá from Guatemala; in the 10th century the Toltecs from their capital at Tula in the N overran the Yucatán and established their capital at Chichén Itzá; the city then became the focus of Yucatán's religious and political power between the 10th and 13th centuries; the city had almost disappeared by the time Cortés arrived in 1521; in the centre of the city is the Castillo, or Great Pyramid, built in approx 1000 AD and dedicated to the feathered serpent, Quetzalcóatl, whose Maya name was Kukulcan; on top of the Castillo is a hidden sanctuary with a sacrificial *Chac-Mool* altar and throne in the shape of a jaguar, painted in red and inlaid with spots of jade; the Temple of Warriors has columns in the form of serpents and vast pillared chambers; S of this is the Court of the Thousand Columns, with Toltec-style colonnades and square columns which have figures of warriors carved on each side; to the N is the Sacred Cenote, a natural well about 30 m deep which was the centre for pilgrimages and sacrifices to the rain god; excavations of the well have recovered pottery, incense, gold, jade, wood and rubber objects; the largest of the 7 Ball Courts at Chichén Itzá is the largest in Middle America; a sacred game was played here in which the winner was put to death; the S portion of Chichén Itzá is known as Old Chichén.

Chich'ester, 50 50N 0 48W, pop(1981) 27,241, county town of West Sussex, S England; 26 km E of Portsmouth;

founded by the Romans, its 4 main streets meet in a main square; railway; later taken by the Saxons and named after their leader, Cissa; economy: engineering, furniture, agricultural trade; monuments: 11-12th-c cathedral, 12th-c bishop's palace, 13th-c St Mary's hospital, 15th-c market cross, theatre (1962), remains of a Roman villa at Fishbourne (3 km W); event: Chichester Festival Theatre season (Aug-Sept).

Chichibu-Tama *chee'chee-boo-ta-ma*, national park in E Chūbu, W Kanto regions, central Honshū island, Japan; a mountainous area 70 km NW of Tōkyo; area 1,216 m; established in 1950.

Chiclana de la Frontera *cheek-la'na dhay la fron-tay'ra*, 36 26N 6 09W, pop(1981) 36,203, resort town in Cádiz prov, Andalucia, S Spain; 25 km SE of Cádiz; economy: noted for its thermal springs and the manufacture of dolls; fruit and vegetables, timber, wine, dairy products.

Chiclayo *chee-klī'yō*, 6 47S 79 47W, pop(1981) 280,244, capital of Lambayeque dept, NW Peru; situated on a plain near the coast; railway; airfield (Coronel Ruiz) at 2 km; monuments: set around the Plaza de Armas are the new cathedral, the principal club and the Palacio Municipal.

Chico *chee'kō*, 39 44N 121 50W, pop(1980) 26,603, city in Butte county, N central California, United States; in the Sacramento Valley, c.130 km N of Sacramento; university founded in 1860; economy: food processing, timber.

Chico'pee (Algonquian, 'swift water'), 42 09N 72 37W, pop(1980) 55,112, town in Hampden county, SW Massachusetts, United States; on R Connecticut, 5 km N of Springfield and 128 km WSW of Boston, on the R Chicopee at its junction with the R Connecticut; railway; economy: textiles, firearms.

Chicoutimi *shi-koo'ti-mee*, 48 26N 71 06W, pop(1981) 60,064, port and cultural centre in S central Québec, SE Canada; on the Saguenay river at its junction with the Chicoutimi river; situated at the head of navigation of the Saguenay river; university (1969); railway; airfield.

Chiem, lake in southern W Germany. See Chiemsee.

Chiemsee *keem'zay*, LAKE CHIEM (Eng), lake in SE Bayern (Bavaria) prov, W Germany, in the foothills of the Bayerische Alpen (Bavarian Alps); largest lake in Bayern, 64 km ESE of München (Munich); area 82 sq km; max depth 74 m; average depth 29 m; width 5-15 km; inlet is the R Ache, outlet the R Alz; it fills the middle of a basin carved out by an Ice Age glacier; there are 3 islands in the lake; round the shores there are many holiday resorts, largest of these Prien (a health resort).

Chiesanuova *kyay-za-nwō'va*, castle (dist) in the Republic of San Marino, central Italy; area 5.46 sq km; pop(1980) 702; population density in 1980 was 128 inhabitants per sq km.

Chieti *kyay'tee*, TEA'TTE (anc), prov of Abruzzi region, central Italy; pop(1981) 370,534; area 2,587 sq km; capital Chieti.

Chieti, 42 21N 14 10E, pop(1981) 54,927, capital town of Chieti prov, Abruzzi region, E central Italy; 13 km SSW of Pescara; archbishopric; economy: textiles, pasta, bricks; monuments: Gothic cathedral; remains of a Roman theatre, aqueduct, and temples.

Chiguayante *chee-gwa-yan'tay*, 36 55S 73 00W, pop(1982) 34,251, town in Concepción prov, Bío-Bío, central Chile; railway.

Chi-hsi, town in Heilongjiang prov, NE China. See Jixi.

Chihuahua *chee-wah'wa*, mountainous state in N Mexico; bounded N by the USA (New Mexico and Texas), partly along the Río Grande, W by Sonora, SW by Sinaloa, S by Durango and E by Coahuila; the Sierra Madre Occidental rises to 3,000 m; in the N and E are large plains (Llano de los Caballos Mesteños and Bolsón de Mapimí) interrupted by isolated subranges; the plains are drained by the Conchos and Casas Grandes rivers; pop(1980) 1,933,856; area 244,938 sq km; capital Chihuahua; economy: agriculture (wheat, cotton, oats, maize, alfalfa, sorghum, peanuts, vines, apples, walnuts, quinces, plums, pears, figs), cattle, sheep, goat, horse, pig and mule raising, mining (lead, zinc, silver, gold, iron, copper, manganese, fluorite), meat, fruit and vegetable packing, iron and steel, petrochemicals, chemicals, electrical goods, textiles, wine, brewing; Chihuahua is famous for its hairless small dog, which has a constant body temperature of 40°C.

Chihuahua, 28 40N 106 06W, pop(1980) 406,830, capital of Chihuahua state, N Mexico; alt 1,428 m; university (1954); Pancho Villa based his revolutionary activities in the surrounding area, and once captured the city by disguising his men as peasants on their way to the market; railway; economy: mining, cattle raising; 8 km from Chihuahua is one of the largest smelting plants in the world; monument: the cathedral in Plaza Constitución was begun in 1717 and finished in 1789.

Chikwa'wa, dist in Southern region, Malawi, SE Africa; area 4,755; pop(1977) 194,425.

Chile *chi'lee*, official name the Republic of Chile, REPÚBLICA DE CHILE, a republic of SW South America; bounded W by the Pacific Ocean, E by Argentina, NE by Bolivia and NW by Peru; timezone GMT −4; area 756,626 sq km (excluding territory claimed in Antarctica); pop(1984) 11,878,400; capital Santiago; chief towns Valparaíso, Concepción, Talcahuano, Antofagasta, Viña del Mar; Antofagasta, Valparaíso and San Antonio are the main ports; the official language is Spanish; the currency is the peso of 100 centavos; national holidays 21 May (Navy Day), 19 Sept (Independence Day), 12 Oct (Discovery of America); membership of CIPEC, ECOSOC, FAO, G-77, GATT, IADB, IAEA, IBRD, ICAO, IDA, IDB, IFAD, IFC, IHO, ILO, IMF, IMO, INTELSAT, INTERPOL, IPU, ITU, LAIA, OAS, PAHO, SELA, UN, UNESCO, UPU, WHO, WIPO, WMO, WSG, WTO.

Physical description. A narrow coastal belt is backed by a series of Andean mountain ridges which in the N rise to 6,723 m at Llullaillaco on the Argentine frontier. In the centre and S the mountains are lower and in the far S they are ice-capped and separated by sea channels. A central Andean valley, 40-60 km wide at 1,200 m, separates the coastal range from the main inland cordilleras. With its deep alluvial soils and extensive natural irrigation this area is one of the most fertile parts of Chile. In the far NW, between the Andes and the Pacific lies the arid Atacama desert.

Climate. As a result of the country's length, spanning 37° of latitude, and of altitudes that range from Andean peaks to coastal plain, the climate of Chile is varied. Conditions range from extreme aridity in the N Atacama desert to cold, wet and windy in the far S at Tierra del Fuego. In central Chile, where the majority of people live, there is a Mediterranean climate with warm, wet winters and dry summers. At Valparaíso on the coast of central Chile the average temperature in July is less than 12°C and in Jan nearly 18°C, with an average annual rainfall of 505 mm. Further inland, and at a higher elevation, the annual rainfall at Santiago is lower at 375 mm. In the N at Antofagasta annual rainfall drops to just over 12 mm.

History, government and constitution. Originally occupied by South American Indians, the arrival of the Spanish in the 16th century brought Chile into the Viceroyalty of Peru. Independence from Spain was declared in 1810, but the struggle for liberation did not come to an end until Royalist forces were defeated in 1818. The country's first president was General Bernardo O'Higgins. Border disputes with Bolivia, Peru and Argentina resulted in the War of the Pacific (1879-84) and the annexation of nitrate-rich territory around Antofagasta. A dispute with Peru over Tacna (dept in SW Peru) and Arica was not resolved until 1929 when Arica was allotted to Chile and Tacna to Peru. Economic instability and unrest in the late 1920s led to the military dictatorship of Col Ibañez until 1931. In 1938 the Popular Front under Aguirre Cerda came to power and in 1946 Gabriel González Videla, a left-wing radical supported by the communists, was elected to office. In 1973, the 3-year-old Marxist coalition government of Salvador Allende was ousted and a military junta under General Augusto Pinochet took

control, banning all political activity. A new constitution providing for the eventual return to democracy came into effect in 1981.

Economy. The economy of Chile has for over a century been based on agriculture and mining. Wheat, corn, potatoes, sugar beet, fruit and livestock are the major agricultural products for internal consumption and for export through the ports of central Chile. In the N fishing is important, while in the S timber products are of increasing value. Copper from N Chile is a major export earner in addition to the mining of iron ore, nitrates, silver, gold, coal and molybdenum. In the far S the discovery of oil and gas in 1945 has provided a vital source of energy. Manufacturing industry is largely based on steel, wood pulp, cellulose and mineral processing. Major trade partners include the USA, the UK, Venezuela, Japan, Brazil, W Germany, Spain, France and Argentina.

Administrative divisions. Chile is divided into 12 regions which are further subdivided into 51 provinces.

Region	*area (sq km)*	*pop(1984)*
Tarapacá	58,785	263,400
Antofagasta	125,253	333,900
Atacama	74,705	212,900
Coquimbo	40,656	437,200
Valparaíso	16,396	1,316,200
O'Higgins	16,456	586,000
Maulé	30,661	735,400
Bío-Bío	36,939	1,558,700
La Araucanía	31,946	675,700
Los Lagos	68,247	899,300
Aisén	108,997	70,600
Magallanes-Antártica	132,033	116,400

Chiles, Nevado de *chee'lays*, 0 49N 77 45W, extinct Andean volcano on the border between Ecuador and Colombia; rises to 4,768 m, 24 km W of Tulcán.

Chilpancingo *cheel-pahn-seeng'gō*, CHILPANCINGO DE LOS BRAVOS, 17 33N 99 30W, capital of Guerrero state, SW Mexico; university (1867); event: fiesta in the second half of Dec.

Chil'tern Hills, a low chalk hill range in SE England; extends 88 km NE from S Oxfordshire, through Buckinghamshire, Hertfordshire and Bedfordshire; in the SW it is continued as the Berkshire Downs and in the NE as the East Anglian Ridge; rises to 260 m at Coombe Hill SW of Wendover; protection against robbers was afforded by the stewardship of the *Chiltern Hundreds* (Burnham, Desborough and Stoke), still given to a member of the House of Commons to enable him to resign.

Chimaltenango *chee-mal-tay-nang'gō*, mountainous dept in S central Guatemala, Central America; pop(1982e) 267,182; area 1,979 sq km; capital Chimaltenango; chief towns Santa Rosa, Patzicía, and Yepocapo; bounded N by the Río Grande and W by the Río Coyolate; includes the Acatenango volcano.

Chimaltenango, 14 40N 90 48W, capital town of Chimaltenango dept, S central Guatemala, Central America; 32 km W of Guatemala City, on the Inter-American Highway; founded in 1526 just S of an old Indian fortress.

Chimborazo *cheem-bō-ra'sō*, mountainous prov in the Andean Sierra of central Ecuador; Volcán Chimborazo, the highest peak in Ecuador, rises to 6,310 m; pop(1982) 334,100; area 6,522 sq km; capital Riobamba; economy: mining, tobacco.

Chimborazo, 1 28S 78 48W, inactive Andean volcano in Chimborazo prov, central Ecuador; 29 km NW of Riobamba; at 6,310 m it is the highest peak in the Ecuadorean Andes; its cone is partly covered by glaciers.

Chimbote *cheem-bō'tay*, 8 59S 78 38W, pop(1981) 216,406, port in Ancash dept, N Peru; one of the few natural harbours on the W coast and Peru's largest fishing port;

exports fishmeal; a new port has been built to serve the national steel industry.

Chim'bu, province in central Papua New Guinea; bounded to the N by the Bismarck range which rises to 4,508 m at Mt Wilhelm; area 6,100 sq km; pop(1980) 178,013; capital Kundiawa; drained by the Tua and Wahgi rivers.

Chimkent *chim-kyent'*, 42 16N 69 05E, pop(1983) 352,000, capital city of Chimkentskaya oblast, S Kazakhskaya SSR, Soviet Union; between the Badam and Sairam rivers of the Syr-Dar'ya basin; founded in the 12th century; railway; airfield; economy: oil refining, lead processing, and the manufacture of chemicals, pharmaceuticals, furniture, cotton, and building materials.

Chimoio *chi-mō'yō*, 9 04S 33 30E, pop(1980) 68,125, capital of dist of same name and of Manica prov, central Mozambique, SE Africa; situated NW of Beira; railway.

Chin, mountainous state in W Burma; bounded W by Bangladesh and India; includes Rongklang and Letha ranges, rising to 3,053 m at Mt Victoria in the SE; drained by the Manipur, Kaladan, Mi and Pen rivers; pop(1983) 368,985; capital Haka.

Chin Hills, mountain range in Chin state, W Burma. See Rongklang.

China *chī'na*, official name The People's Republic of China, ZHONGHUA RENMIN GONGHE GUO *chung-hwa ren-min kung-hō kwo* (Chinese), a socialist state in central and E Asia, extending from 53°N to 18°N and from 73°E to 134°E; bordered N by the USSR and Mongolia, E by North Korea, the Bo Hai Gulf, Huang Hai (Yellow Sea) and the East China Sea, with Hong Kong and Macao as enclaves on the SE coast, S by the South China Sea, the Gulf of Tongking, Vietnam, Laos, Burma, India, Bhutan and Nepal, and W by India, Pakistan, Afghanistan and the USSR; timezone GMT +8; area 9,597,000 sq km; capital Beijing (Peking); pop(1982) 1,008,175,228; the pop is 93% Han Chinese, the remainder being Zhuang, Uygur, Hui, Yi, Tibetan, Miao, Manchu, Mongol, Buyi, Korean and numerous lesser nationalities of which there are 55 groups with a pop of 67 mn; languages spoken are standard Chinese (Putonghua) or Mandarin (based on the dialect of Beijing), also Yue (Cantonese), Wu (Shanghainese), Minbei (Fuzhou), Minnan (Hokkien-Taiwanese), Xiang, Gan, Hakka dialects and minority languages; pinyin is the official romanized form of writing; China is officially atheist, but the most important religious elements are Confucianism, Taoism, Buddhism and ancestor-worship; 2-3% of the pop is Muslim and 1% Christian; the official currency (*renminbi*) is the yuan or kuai of 100 fen (10 fen = 1 jiao); overseas visitors use foreign exchange certificates; national holiday 1 Oct (National Day); membership of FAO, IAEA, IBRD, ICAO, IDA, IFAD, IFC, IHO, ILO, IMF, IMO, INTELSAT, ITU, Multifiber Arrangement, UN, UNESCO, UPU, WFTU, WHO, WIPO, WMO.

Physical description. Over two-thirds of China is upland hill, mountain and plateau occupied by one-third of the population. The highest mountains of China are to be found in the W, largely in Xizang aut region (Tibet) and Qinghai prov where the Xizang Gaoyuan (Tibetan plateau) rises to an average alt of 4,000 m. Known as 'the roof of the world', its peaks on the border with Nepal include Mount Everest (8,848 m). To the N and E of the Xizang Gaoyuan the land eventually drops down to the desert or semi-desert of Sinkiang and Nei Mongol (Inner Mongolia) at an average alt of 1,000-2,000 m. In the NE the broad and fertile plains of Manchuria are separated from North Korea by the densely forested Changpai Shan uplands. East of the Tibetan plateau and S of Nei Mongol the prosperous Sichuan basin is drained by the Chang Jiang (Yangtze river) which flows E across the S

plains to the East China Sea at Shanghai. The heavily populated S plains and E coast of China have rich, fertile soils and are protected from the N winds.

Climate. The climate of China is varied and can be divided into the following 7 zones: (1) NE China, including the Huang He (Yellow river) valley, part of Nei Mongol and the region known as Manchuria, has cold winters, with strong winds blowing from the N. Summers are warm and humid, but rainfall is unreliable. Both winter and summer temperatures decrease further N, so that in Manchuria rivers are frozen for 4 to 6 months of the year and snow lies for 100 to 150 days. Shenyang, representative of this region, has an average daily temperature of −6° to −18°C in Jan, the coldest month, and 21° to 31°C in July, with rainfall averaging a min of 8 mm in the winter months and a max of 183 mm in July. Beijing, which lies further S and W, has warmer winters, with Jan temperatures ranging between −10° and 1°C. Rainfall is at a min of 4 mm in Jan and a maximum of 243 mm in July. (2) Central China, including the area from Shanghai (E) inland as far as Chongqing in Sichuan prov, in the upper Chang Jiang (Yangtze river) valley. Summers are warm and humid as damp air moves inland off the Pacific. The coastal regions are sometimes subjected to typhoons or tropical cyclones. In the extreme W summer rainfall is lower than on the coast. Temperatures at Shanghai on the E coast of China range between 1° and 8°C in the winter months of Jan and Feb and 23° to 32°C in July and Aug. Rainfall, with a min of 36 mm in Dec, is much higher in the summer months with, on average, 180 mm in the month of June and almost 150 mm in July-Aug. Chongqing in the W averages 5° to 9°C in its coldest winter month of Jan and 25° to 35°C in Aug. Rainfall ranges between a min of 15 mm in the month of Jan and 180 mm in the month of July. The town of Wuhan, situated c.650 km inland from Shanghai in the middle Chang Jiang (Yangtze river) valley, records temperatures of 1° to 8°C in Jan and 26° to 34°C in July-Aug. Rainfall here ranges between 28 mm in Dec and 244 mm in July. (3) S China, including the provinces of Guangdong, Fujian and Jiangxi, lies partly within the tropics and is the wettest part of China in the summer. Typhoons are more frequent here, especially during July-Oct. Coastal conditions are represented by those of Hong Kong, with temperatures ranging between 13° and 17°C in Feb and 26° to 31°C in July-Aug. Summers are hot and humid. Coastal rainfall ranges between 31 mm in Dec and 394 mm in July. Rainfall is heavy from April to Sept both along the coast and inland at Wuzhou, where it ranges between 33 mm in Jan and 206 mm in May. Temperatures here range from 8° to 16°C in Jan and 26° to 32°C in July and August. (4) SW China, including the inland region of China which lies along the border with Vietnam, Laos and Burma, is mountainous with summer temperatures moderated by altitude. Winters are mild with little rain. Summers are wet on the mountains, but sheltered valleys receive little rain. The town of Mengzi in Yunnan prov has a temperature range of 8°-20°C in Dec-Jan and 19°-29°C in July. Rainfall ranges from an average of 8 mm in Jan to 198 mm in Aug, July-Aug being the wettest months. (5) Xizang autonomous region, a high plateau surrounded by mountains, lies above 3,700 m, with extensive areas rising above 4,900 m. Winters are severe with frequent light snow and hard frost. Summers are warm during the daytime, but there is a sharp drop in temperature at night. Lhasa, representative of conditions in the valleys and the SE part of Xizang, has temperatures ranging from −10° to 7°C in Jan and 9° to 24° in July. Rainfall is heaviest in the summer months when moist air is drawn into Xizang by the Asian monsoon winds. Average monthly rainfall figures recorded at Lhasa range from 0 mm in Dec-Jan to 122 mm in July. (6) Xinjiang and the W interior has an arid desert climate. Winters are cold and rainfall is well distributed throughout the year. The town of Kashi is representative of conditions in W Xinjiang at about 1,300 m. Here temperatures range from −11° to 1°C in the coldest month of Jan and 20° to 33°C in July. Rainfall ranges from a min average of 3 mm in Feb and Sept-Oct to a max of 15 mm in Jan. (7) Nei Mongol, comprising mountain ranges and semi-desert lowlands, has an extreme continental-type climate with cold winters and warm summers. Winter temperatures are similar to those of Manchuria and NE China. Ürümqi in N Xinjiang is representative of this region, with Jan temperatures ranging between −11° and −22°C. Strong winds in winter and spring make the weather even colder. Summer temperatures range between 14° and 28°C during July. Rainfall, although scarce, is spread throughout the year, with a min of 8 mm falling in Feb and a max of 43 mm in Oct.

History, government and constitution. Chinese civilization is believed to date from the Xia dynasty (2200-1700 BC) which formed the first Chinese state in the area that is now part of Shaanxi and Henan provs. The Western Zhou dynasty ruled over a prosperous feudal agricultural society from 1066 to 771 BC after which the capital was moved from Xi'an to Luoyang which became the centre of the Eastern Zhou dynasty (770-256 BC), an era that produced the great Chinese philosophers, Confucius and Lao Zi (Lao-tzu). The first emperor of the Qin dynasty, Qin Shi Huangdi (221-10 BC), unified the warring states of China, organizing the country into a hierarchy of prefectures and counties under centralized control. During the Western and Eastern Han dynasties (206 BC-220 AD) China expanded westwards, repelling the Huns in the Mongolian plateau and making contacts with central and W Asia. Buddhism was introduced from India during the second half of this dynasty. After the Han dynasties China was split into the Three Kingdoms (the Wei, Shu and Wu, 220-65 AD), while nomadic tribes from the N and W raided N China. From the 4th century onwards a series of northern dynasties was set up by the invaders while several southern dynasties succeeded one another in the Chang Jiang (Yangtze) valley, with their capital at Nanjing (Jiangsi prov). Buddhism spread during this period and the arts and sciences flourished. China was gradually reunited and work began on the Grand Canal during the Sui (581-618) and Tang (618-907) dynasties. After a period of partition into the Five Dynasties (907-60) there emerged the Song dynasty (960-1279), remembered for literature, philosophy, and the invention of movable type, gunpowder and the magnetic compass. Mongol and Tartar tribes forced the Song to abandon their capital at Kaifeng in 1126 and move to Hangzhou. Eventually in the 13th century, Genghis Khan took control of China and established the Mongol Yuan dynasty (1279-1368). The Grand Canal was completed in the early part of this period, and China was visited by European missionaries and merchants including Marco Polo. During the succeeding Ming dynasty (1368-1644) contacts with the West grew with the arrival of the Portuguese in 1516, the Spanish in 1557, the Dutch in 1606 and the English in 1637. The Manchus, non-Chinese invaders from the north-east, overthrew the Ming dynasty in 1644 and ruled until 1911, enlarging the Chinese empire to include Manchuria, Mongolia, Tibet, Taiwan and the central Asian regions of Turkestan. Despite contact with Europe, only the port of Canton (Guangzhou) was open to foreign merchants. Chinese opposition to foreign imports, in particular opium, led to the Opium War of 1839-42. The Treaty of Nanjing in 1842 effectively opened the ports of Guangzhou, Xiamen, Fuzhou, Ningbo and Shanghai to foreign trade, and Hong Kong was ceded to Britain. A second war with Britain and France (1858-60) resulted in the opening of Tianjin to foreign trade. At the same time, Russia acquired part of China in 1858-60 and later leased Port Arthur (Lüshun) in Liaoning prov SW of Dalian on the Liaodong Bandao peninsula. The Sino-Japanese War of 1895 resulted in the control of Taiwan and Korea passing to Japan. In 1898 Weihai was leased by Britain, Guangzhou (Canton) by France and Jiao Xian (in Shandong prov) by Germany. The last unsuccessful attempt to oppose foreign influence resulted in the Boxer Rebellion of 1900. A mutiny among Chinese troops at Wuchang, Hebei prov, on 10 Oct 1911, finally led to the downfall of Manchu rule. In Feb 1912 the Republic of China was founded by Sun Yatsen. After his death in 1925 the country was unified under Chiang Kaishek who made Nanjing the capital in 1928. Conflict between the nationalists and the communists led to the famous Long March of 1934-35 when the communists made their way to Shaanxi prov in NW China, setting up headquarters at Yan'an under the leadership of Mao Zedong. Eventually defeated by the communists, the nationalists fled to Taiwan in 1950. By then (Oct 1949) the Chinese Communist Party had proclaimed the People's Republic of China with its capital at Beijing. During the first Five-Year Plan (1953-57) industry and commerce, including banking, were nationalized and agriculture collectivized on Soviet lines. The first formal constitution of the People's Republic of China was drawn up in 1954 after the election of deputies to the National People's Congress. In 1958-59 the Great Leap Forward placed emphasis on local rather than central authority, on sex-equality and the establishment of rural communes. Soviet aid and technicians, supplied to China after the revolution, were withdrawn after a dispute between China and the USSR. In 1966 Mao Zedong initiated a period of reform known as the Cultural Revolution. This period was marked by violence and unrest often initiated by militants known as Red Guards. After the death of Chairman Mao in 1976, many policies were reversed in the drive towards rapid industrialization and the opening of wider trade relations with the western world. Under the 1978 constitution China is governed by an elected National People's Congress of 3,000 deputies. The Congress in effect ratifies the programme of the Chinese Communist Party. Responsible to the Standing Committee of Congress, which takes the role of head of state, is a State Council of over 50 ministers led by the prime minister.

Economy. Since 1949 China's economy has been largely based on heavy industry, producing iron and steel, coal, machinery, armaments, textiles and petroleum. In more recent years emphasis has been placed on light industries producing a wide range of household goods and consumables. Special economic zones at locations such as Shenzen have been set up to attract foreign investment. China is rich in mineral deposits. The largest coal mining centres are in Hebei, Shanxi, Shandong, Jilin and Anhui provs. China is a major world producer of wolfram (tungsten ore); other important minerals include iron and tin ores, phosphate rock, aluminium, copper, lead, zinc, antimony, manganese, sulphur, bauxite, salt and asbestos. China is the largest oil-producing country in the Far East with approx 100 oil fields, the largest being those in the E and NE at Daqing, Shengli, Dagang and Karamai. The country also has offshore resources in the Bo Hai gulf (Nanhuanghai basin) and the South China Sea around Hainan (Zhujiangkou and Yinggehai basins). From about 10% of its land area China produces a large percentage of its food requirements, although large quantities of wheat are imported annually. Major subsistence crops include rice, grain, beans, potatoes, tea, sugar, cotton, and oil-seed. China's major trade partners include Japan, Hong Kong, the USA, West Germany, Canada, Australia and Singapore.

Administrative divisions. China comprises 21 provinces, 3 municipalities (Shanghai, Beijing and Tianjin) and 5 autonomous regions (Ningxia, Xinjiang, Guangxi, Xizang and Nei Mongol) as follows:

Division	*area (sq km)*	*pop(1982)*
Anhui	139,900	49,665,724
Beijing	17,800	9,230,687
Fujian	123,100	25,931,106
Gansu	530,000	19,569,261
Guangdong	231,400	59,299,220
Guangxi	220,400	36,420,960
Guizhou	174,000	28,552,997
Hebei	202,700	53,005,875
Heilongjiang	463,600	32,665,546
Henan	167,000	74,422,739
Hubei	187,500	47,804,150
Hunan	210,500	54,008,851
Jiangsu	102,200	60,521,114
Jiangxi	164,800	33,184,827
Jilin	187,000	22,560,053
Liaoning	151,000	35,721,693
Nei Mongol	450,000	19,274,279
Ningxia	170,000	3,895,578
Qinghai	721,000	3,895,706
Shaanxi	195,800	28,904,423
Shandong	153,300	74,419,054
Shanghai	5,800	115,859,748
Shanxi	157,100	252,891,389
Sichuan	569,000	99,713,310
Tianjin	4,000	7,764,141
Xinjiang	1,646,800	13,081,681
Xizang	1,221,600	1,892,393
Yunnan	436,200	32,533,817
Zhejiang	101,800	38,884,603

China also claims the island of Taiwan off its SE coast: pop(1982) 18,270,749; area 36,000 sq km.

Chi-nan, capital of Shandong prov, E China. See Jinan.

Chinandega *chin-an-day'ga*, maritime dept in NW Nicaragua, Central America; bounded NW by the Golfo de Fonseca, NE by Choluteca dept, Honduras, and W by the Pacific Ocean; rises to peaks above 1,000 m in the SE; pop(1981) 228,573; area 4,598 sq km; capital Chinandega; chief towns El Viejo, Corinto, and Chichigalpa; economy: growing of cotton, sugar cane, and bananas.

Chinandega, 12 35N 87 10W, pop(1978) 44,435, capital town of Chinandega dept, NW Nicaragua, Central America; 35 km NW of León; in an agricultural district growing bananas, cotton, and sugar cane; airfield; railway.

Chin-chou, town in Liaoning prov, NE China. See Jinzhou.

Chingo'la, 12 31S 27 53E, pop(1980) 145,869, town in Western prov, W Zambia, S Central Africa; 96 km NW of Ndola; railway; economy: copper mining.

Ching-tao, town in Shandong prov, E China. See Qingdao.

Chinho'yi, SINOIA, 17 21S 30 13E, pop(1982) 24,000, town in Mashonaland West prov, Zimbabwe, S Africa; 105 km WNW of Harare; the nearby Chinhoyi Caves formed out of limestone have been a place of refuge for thousands of years and are now a major tourist attraction; railway.

Chiniot *chin-yōt'*, 31 40N 73 05E, pop(1981) 106,000, agricultural market town in Punjab prov, Pakistan; W of Lahore; near R Chenab; railway.

Chinju *cheen-joo*, 35 10N 128 06E, pop(1983e) 219,496, town in Kyŏngsangnam prov, S Korea; railway.

Chinkiang, town in Jiangsu prov, E China. See Zhenjiang.

Chino *chee'nō*, 34 01N 117 41W, pop(1980) 40,165, city in San Bernardino county, SW California, United States; 48 km E of Los Angeles.

Chios, nome (dept) and island of Greece. See Khíos.

Chipata *che-pah'te*, formerly FORT JAMESON (-1965), 13 40S 32 42E, pop(1980) 32,291, capital of Eastern region, Zambia, S central Africa; 515 km ENE of Lusaka; originally established as a military post in 1898, the town was notorious for its slave-trading activities; became the British South Africa Company's administrative headquarters of NE Rhodesia; airfield at 11.5 km.

Chip'penham, 51 28N 2 07W, pop(1981) 21,532, market town in North Wiltshire dist, Wiltshire, S England; on the R Avon 20 km ENE of Bath; railway; economy: engineering, plastics, electronics, dairy products.

Chipping Sodbury, 51 33N 2 24W, pop(1981) 26,981,

market town in Northavon dist, Avon, SW England; 18 km NE of Bristol; railway.

Chiquimula *chee-kee-moo'la*, mountainous dept in E Guatemala, Central America; bounded E by Honduras; pop(1982e) 215,409; area 2,376 sq km; capital Chiquimula; chief towns Quezaltepeque and Esquipulas.

Chiquimula, 14 48N 89 32W, capital town of Chiquimula dept, E Guatemala, Central America; 104 km ENE of Guatemala City; railway; event: fiesta (12-18 Aug).

Chiradzu'lu, dist in Southern region, Malawi, SE Africa; area 767 sq km; pop(1977) 176,184.

Chired'zi, 21 00S 31 38E, pop(1982) 10,300, town in Victoria prov, Zimbabwe, S Africa; SE of Masvingo; railway.

Chiriquí *chee-ree-kee'*, prov in SW Panama, Central America; bounded W by Costa Rica and S by the Pacific Ocean; drained by the David, Chiriquí, and Fonseca rivers, all flowing into the Golfo de Chiriquí which is an inlet of the Pacific Ocean; pop(1980) 287,350; area 8,758 sq km; capital David; chief towns Pedregal, Puerto Armuelles, and La Concepción; traversed by the Inter-American Highway; there are copper deposits at Cerro Colorado.

Chirisan, national park in S Korea; situated at the junction of the Chŏllapuk, Chŏllanam and Kyŏngsangnam provincial frontiers; Chirisan peak rises to 1,915 m; area 479 sq km; established in 1967.

Chirripó Grande *chee-ree-pō' gran'day*, 9 50N 83 25W, highest peak of Costa Rica and S Central America; situated in the Cordillera de Talamanca, 32 km NNW of Buenos Aires, on the border between the provs of Cartago and Limón; height 3,819 m; the Chirripó National Park, which covers an area of 437 sq km, is the N limit of the shrub-grass vegetation, the *paramo*, which is characteristic of the Andes.

Chishtian Mandi *chisht'yun mahn'di*, 29 44N 72 54E, pop(1981) 62,000, city in Punjab prov, Pakistan; 120 km ENE of Bahawalpur; railway.

Chita *chee-ta'*, formerly INGODINSKOE ZIMOV'E, also CHITINSKAIA, 52 00N 113 35E, pop(1983) 326,000, capital city of Chitinskaya oblast, SE Siberian Rossiyskaya, Soviet Union; at the confluence of the Chita and Ingoda rivers; established by the Cossacks in 1653; became a tax-exempt settlement in 1690; on the Trans-Siberian railway; airport; economy: power plant, manufacture of machine tools and instruments, equipment for the chemical industry, furniture and wood products, foodstuffs, and leather footwear.

Chitip'a, dist in Northern region, Malawi, SE Africa; area 3,504 sq km; pop(1977) 72,316.

Chitré *chee-tray'*, 7 59N 80 25W, pop(1980) 17,080, capital town of Herrera prov, central Panama, Central America; on the peninsula of Azuero, 136 km SW of Panamá City; founded by Indians in 1821; served by a branch of the Inter-American Highway.

Chittagong *chit'u-gong*, region in SE Bangladesh; includes Chittagong and Cox's Bazar districts; pop(1981) 5,491,000; area 7,456 sq km; bounded W by the Bay of Bengal and SE by Burma; capital Chittagong; crossed by the Karnafuli and Sangau rivers; the Karnafuli reservoir is located in the NE.

Chittagong, 22 20N 91 48E, pop(1981) 1,391,877, seaport capital of Chittagong dist, Chittagong, SE Bangladesh; principal port of Bangladesh on the R Karnafuli which flows into the Bay of Bengal; known to Arkan, Arab, Persian, Portuguese and Mogul mariners; conquered by Nawab of Bengal in 1666; ceded to the British East India Company in 1760; the port was damaged during the 1971 Indo-Pakistani war; noted for its many Hindu and Buddhist temples; lies in one of the wettest regions of the world; university (1966); economy: trade in tea, jute, skins and hides; cotton, iron, steel, fruit canning, matches, shipbuilding and oil refining; offshore oil installations established in the 1960s.

Chittagong Hill Tracts, region in SE Bangladesh; includes Khagrachari and Chittagong Hill Tracts districts; bounded E by Burma and W by Chittagong region; pop(1981) 580,000; area 8,680 sq km; hilly area enclosed by the Feni, Karnafuli, Sangu and Matamuhuri rivers; reaches heights of 500-1,000 m in the SE; divided into 4 fertile valleys, separated by ridges; the valleys are covered with thick planted forest, dominated by tall teak trees; Kaptia Lake, covering 686 sq km, was formed when the Karnafuli hydroelectric dam was built at Kaptia; capital Rangamati.

Chitungwi'za, 18 00S 31 08E, pop(1982) 172,600, town in Mashonaland East prov, Zimbabwe, S Africa; SSE of Harare; planned as a new independent suburb of Harare.

Chit'win or **Royal Chitwin**, national Park in S central Nepal, central Asia; between the Sumesar Range (E) and the R Gandak (W); area 932 sq km; established in 1973.

Chobe *chō'bay*, dist in N Botswana, S Africa; NE of Ngamiland dist; pop(1981) 36,636; area 5,120 sq km; chief towns Chobe, Kachikau, Kasane, Ngoma and Pandamatenga; noted for its wildlife, the Chobe National Park was established in 1968.

Chocó *cho-kō'*, dept in W Colombia, South America; bounded W by the Pacific, N by the Caribbean, NW by Panama and E by the Cordillera Occidental; the Atrato and San Juan river valleys run N-S through the length of the dept; both rivers are navigable; pop(1985) 68,506; area 46,530 sq km; capital Quibdó; economy: platinum.

Choiseul *choy'sl*, LAURU (Polynesian), volcanic island of the Solomon Islands group, 48 km SE of Bougainville on the Bougainville Strait, SW Pacific; area 2,589 sq km; length 144 km; width 32 km; occupied by the Japanese during World War II.

Cholet *sho-lay*, 47 04N 0 53E, pop(1982) 56,528, industrial town in Maine-et-Loire dept, Pays de la Loire region, NW France; on the R Moine, 50 km SW of Angers; economy: clothing, especially shoes and handkerchiefs; largely destroyed at the time of the Vendéen counter-revolution (1793) when, after much fighting, it was burned by the Republican Army; the Musée des Guerres de Vendée records these events; event: scene of a Saturday cattle market.

Chŏllanam *chul-lah-nam*, SOUTH CHOLLA, prov in SW Korea; bounded W by the Huang Hai Sea and S by the Korea Strait; includes numerous small islands off the coast of South Korea; drained by the Yŏngsan-gang and the Sŏmjin-gang rivers; rises to 1,187 m in Mudŭng san peak, situated SE of Kwangju; pop(1984) 3,824,322; area 12,189 sq km; capital Kwangju; many of the province's islands are now part of Tadohae national park.

Chŏllapuk *chul-lah-puk*, NORTH CHOLLA, CHŎLLABUK, prov in W Korea; bounded W by the Huang Hai Sea; bordered in the N by the Kŭmgang river; rises to 1,279 m at Paegun san peak on the border with Kyŏngsangnam prov; pop(1984) 2,288,707; area 8,052 sq km; capital Chŏnju.

Choluteca *cho-loo-tay'ka*, dept in S Honduras, Central America, bounded E by Nicaragua and SW by the Golfo de Fonseca; pop(1983e) 289,637; area 4,207 sq km; capital Choluteca.

Choluteca, 13 16N 87 11W, pop(1983e) 53,033, capital town of Choluteca dept, S Honduras, in the plain of Choluteca, 34 km SE of San Lorenzo; economy: timber, coffee growing, cattle raising.

Chomutov *KHom'oot-of*, KOMOTAU (Ger), 50 28N 13 25E, pop(1984) 57,398, industrial town in Severočeský region, Czech Socialist Republic, W Czechoslovakia; 80 km NW of Praha (Prague); railway; economy: coal mining, iron, steel.

Chone *chō'nay*, 0 41S 80 06W, pop(1982) 33,839, town in Manabí prov, W Ecuador; on the Río Chone, NE of Portoviejo.

Ch'ŏngjin *chung-jeen*, 41 50N 129 55E, pop(1972) 265,000, capital of Hamgyŏngnam (North Hamgyong) prov, NE North Korea; situated on the NE coast, on the Sea of Japan; railway.

Ch'ŏngju *chung-joo*, 36 39N 127 27E, pop(1983e) 305,175, capital of Ch'ungch'ŏngpuk prov, Korea; railway.

Chongqing *chung-king*, CHUNGKING, PAHSIEN, 31 08N 104 23E, pop(1984e) 2,733,700, town in Sichuan prov,

SW central China; at the confluence of the Jialing Jiang and Chang Jiang (Yellow) rivers; the old part of the city is situated on a mountainous peninsula between the 2 rivers; established in the 12th century, Chongqing became a treaty port in 1891, but modern development did not begin until 1928; the most important industrial city in SW China; there are hot springs to the N and S of the city; railway; airfield; river transport; economy: steel, machinery, chemicals, textiles, light industry; monuments: the US-Chiang Kaishek Criminal Acts Exhibition Hall was used as a prison in World War II, torture instruments used on communists are displayed here; Sichuan Fine Arts Academy; Chongqing museum.

Chŏnju *chon-joo*, 35 50N 127 04E, pop(1984) 421,751, capital of Chŏllapuk prov, SW Korea; railway; economy: tourism, rice; monuments: c.32 km SW of Chŏnju is Kŭmsan-sa ('Gold Mountain') Temple, one of Chŏllapuk's largest and most important Buddhist shrines, built in 766 AD and enlarged in 1079, it was burned in the Japanese invasion of 1597; the present main hall was rebuilt in the 17th century.

Chontales *chōn-ta'lays*, dept in S central Nicaragua, Central America; bounded W by Lago de Nicaragua and N by the Montañas de Huapi; traversed NNW-SSE by the Sierra de Amerrique which is the watershed between rivers flowing W to Lago de Nicaragua (Río Oyate, Río Mayales) and those flowing E to the Caribbean Sea (tributaries of the Río Escondido); pop(1981) 98,562; area 5,310 sq km; capital Juigalpa; chief towns La Libertad, Acoyapa, and Santo Domingo.

Chor'ley, 53 40N 2 38W, pop(1981) 33,708, town in Preston urban area and Chorley dist, Lancashire, NW England; 16 km NW of Bolton; railway; economy: engineering, textiles, plastics.

Chorrera, La *la chō-re'ra*, 8 51N 79 46W, pop(1980) 37,566, town in Panamá prov, central Panama, Central America; on the Inter-American Highway; its port on the Golfo de Panamá is Puerto Caimito.

Chorzów *KHo-zhoof'*, formerly KRÓLEWSKA HUTA, 50 19N 18 56E, pop(1983) 145,100, industrial city in Katowice voivodship, S Poland; separated from Katowice (SE) by the Voivodship Park of Rest and Culture, the largest urban park in Poland (600 ha); suburbs of Chorzów and Hajduki Wielkie joined with Królewska Huta to form the modern city of Chorzów in the 1930s; sports stadium; railway; economy: steel, coking coal, chemicals, nitrogen, transport equipment; monument: ethnographic museum.

Choybalsan *choy'bal-san*, TCHOIBALSAN, 48 02N 110 10E, capital of Dornod county, NE Mongolia; lies on the R Kerulen; railway; economy: mining, agricultural trade, foodstuffs.

Christ'church, 43 33S 172 40E, pop(1981) 164,680, city in Canterbury, South Island, New Zealand; on the R Avon, on the E coast, NW of its port, Lyttelton Harbour; founded in 1850 by English Anglican colonists; dependent for its prosperity on the rich cornlands and sheep stations of the Canterbury Plains; the 1974 Commonwealth Games were held here in the Queen Elizabeth II Park; University of Canterbury (1873); railway; airport; economy: food processing, wool, chemicals, fertilizers, furniture; monuments: Canterbury museum; Ferrymead Historic Park has examples of early transport; McDougall art gallery.

Christchurch, 50 44N 1 45W, pop(1981) 33,529, residential town in Christchurch dist, Dorset, S England; 8 km E of Bournemouth; centre for recreational sailing; railway; economy: plastics, electronics.

Christmas Island *kris'mas*, 10 25S 105 39E, pop(1983e) 3,000, island in the Indian Ocean 360 km S of Java Head and 1,310 km from Singapore; administered by Australia as an external territory; area 155.4 sq km; annexed by the UK in 1888, placed under the administration of the Straits Settlements in 1889 and incorporated with the Settlement of Singapore in 1900; sovereignty was passed to Australia in 1958; the population includes about 350 Europeans, 1,820 Chinese and 750 Malays; there is a wet season from Nov to April and an annual rainfall of about 2,040 mm; the island's main source of income is derived from the export of rock phosphate and phosphate dust, chiefly to Australia and New Zealand; technical school; airport.

Christmas Island, atoll in Line Is, Pacific Ocean. See Kiritimati.

Chrudim *KHrud'yim*, 49 58N 15 49E, pop(1984) 20,890, town in Východočeský region, Czech Socialist Republic, W central Czechoslovakia; on R Chrudimka, E of Praha (Prague); railway; economy: textiles, footwear.

Chuacús, Sierra de *dhay chwa-koos'*, mountain range in Quiché and Baja Verapaz depts, central Guatemala, Central America; extends some 128 km W-E between Santa Cruz del Quiché and Salamá; continues E as the Sierra de las Minás; forms the divide between the Río Chixoy (N) and the Río Motagua (S).

Chuadanga *chwa-dang'gu*, 23 38N 88 52E, pop(1981) 76,000, town in Chuadanga dist, Kushtia, W Bangladesh; W of Dhākā, near the Indian frontier.

Chūbu *choo'boo*, region in central Honshū island, Japan; bordered by the Sea of Japan (W), Kinki region (S), the Pacific Ocean and Kanto region (E) and Tōhoku region (E and N); a mountainous region with low lying coastal land; in the centre of the region is Chūbu-Sangaku National Park; pop(1980) 19,984,000; area 66,743 sq km; Chūbu region is divided into 9 prefectures as follows:

Prefecture	*area (sq km)*	*pop(1980)*
Aichi	5,114	6,222,000
Fukui	4,188	794,000
Gifu	10,596	1,960,000
Ishikawa	4,196	1,119,000
Nagano	13,585	2,084,000
Niigata	12,577	2,451,000
Shizuoka	7,772	3,447,000
Toyama	4,252	1,103,000
Yamanashi	4,463	804,000

Chūbu Sangaku *sahn'ga-koo*, JAPAN ALPS, national park in Chūbu region, central Honshū island, Japan; area 1,698 sq km; established in 1934; situated in N Chūbu region, in the highest section of the Japan Alps; rises to 3,180 m in Yariga-take peak.

Chubut *choo-boot'*, prov in Patagonia region, S Argentina; crossed by Chubut and Chico rivers; noted lake region includes L Musters, L Colhué Huapí and L Fontana; contains the hydroelectric dam of Futaleufú in W, and the Florentino Ameghino dam in E, used for irrigation, hydroelectricity and flood control; in E, Valdés Peninsula (a haven for wildlife) juts out into the Atlantic; contains several sites of petrified forests (*bosques petrificados*); towns such as Trelew and Madryn were established by Welsh settlers (*Galianos*) who landed at New Bay in 1865; pop(1980) 263,116; area 224,686 sq km; capital Rawson (named after an Argentine Minister of the Interior in the 1860s); chief towns Trelew and Comodoro Rivadavia; economy: sheep and some cattle raising; timber; zinc, clay and gypsum mining; oil; manufacturing.

Chūgoku *choo-gō'koo*, region in S Honshū island, Japan; bounded N and NW by the Sea of Japan, SW by the Kammon Tunnels and the Suō-nada Sea, SE by the Seto Naikai Strait and NE by Kinki region; extending the full length of the region is the Chūgoku-san chi mountain range; pop(1980) 7,586,000; area 31,847 sq km; Chūgoku region is divided into 5 prefectures as follows:

Prefecture	*area (sq km)*	*pop(1980)*
Hiroshima	8,455	2,739,000
Okayama	7,079	1,871,000
Shimane	6,627	785,000
Tottori	3,492	604,000
Yamaguchi	6,095	1,587,000

Chukchi Peninsula, NE extremity of Asia, in Magadanskaya oblast, Rossiyskaya, Soviet Union. See Chukotskiy Poluostrov.

Chukchi Sea *chook'chee*, part of the Arctic Ocean, lying N of Chukotskiy Poluostrov, USSR and the Seward Peninsula, Alaska and to the W of Point Hope, Alaska; separated from the Bering Sea by the Bering Strait; the International Dateline cuts the Chukchi Sea, as does the boundary between the USSR and the USA; depths range between 13-150 m over the wide continental shelf.

Chukotskiy Poluostrov, CHUKCHI PENINSULA, NE extremity of Asia, in Magadanskaya oblast, Rossiyskaya, Soviet Union; bounded N by the Chukchi Sea, E by the Bering Strait, and S by the Anadyrskiy Zaliv gulf of the Bering Sea; at the E end of the Chukotskiy (Anadyrskiy) Khrebet range; rises to heights above 1,000 m; its E point is Mys Dezhneva (Cape Dezhnev).

Chula Vista *choo'la vis'ta*, 32 39N 117 05W, pop(1980) 83,927, city in San Diego county, SW California, United States; S of San Diego, on San Diego Bay.

Ch'unch'ŏn *choon-chun*, 37 56N 127 40E, pop(1983e) 165,275, agricultural market town and capital of Kangwon prov, NE Korea; on R Pukhan, 70 km NE of Sŏul.

Ch'ungch'ŏngnam *choong-chong-nam*, SOUTH CHUNGCHONG, prov in W Korea; bordered W by the Huang Hai Sea; drained by the Kŭmgang river, which also forms part of its S border with Chŏllapuk prov; rises to 878 m at Taedun san peak, also on the border with Chŏllapuk prov; pop(1983e) 3,056,198; area 8,807 sq km; capital Taejŏn.

Ch'ungch'ŏngpuk *choong-chong-puk*, NORTH CHUNGCHONG, CH'UNGCH'ŎNGBUK, prov in central Korea; drained by the Hangang river; rises to 1,242 m at Minjuji san peak on the border with Chôlapuk prov; pop(1984) 1,419,921; area 7,430 sq km; capital Ch'ŏngju; in the SE part of the prov in Songnisan national park is Pŏpchusa temple, once the largest temple in Korea, known to have hosted c.30,000 priests at one gathering; Korea's largest standing image of Buddha (17 m high) is also located here.

Chungking, town in Sichuan prov, SW central China. See Chongqing.

Chuquisaca *choo-kee-sa'ka*, department in S central Bolivia; includes part of the Chaco (E); drained by the upper course of the Pilcomayo and Pilaya rivers; the W part includes outliers of the Cordillera Real with fertile valleys and the E comprises tropical lowland bordering Santa Cruz dept and Paraguay; pop(1982) 435,406; area 51,524 sq km; capital Sucre; economy: oil, agriculture.

Chur *koor*, COIRE *kwar* (Fr), CUERA or QUERA *kway'ra* (Romansch), COIRA (Ital), 46 52N 9 32E, pop(1980) 32,037, capital town of Graubünden canton, SE Switzerland; on the R Plessur, which here flows into the R Rhine, 69 km E of Altdorf; railway; has been a bishopric at least since 452 AD; starting point of the Rhätische Bahn (narrow gauge railway) to St Moritz, the Chur-Arosa line and the Furka-Oberalp line to Brig; monument: 11-12th-c cathedral.

Churchill, river in N Saskatchewan and N Manitoba, Canada; issues from Methy Lake, NW Saskatchewan, flowing SE through Peter Pond Lake and Churchill Lake to L Ile-à-la-Crosse; from there the river flows E through several small lakes, including Knee, Black Bear Island and Otter lakes, then NE through Granville Lake, Southern Indian Lake and on to enter Hudson Bay at the town of Churchill.

Churchill, formerly HAMILTON, river rising in L Ashuanipi, Newfoundland, E Canada; flows 896 km N and SE to meet L Melville at Goose Bay; Churchill Falls, below Lobstick Lake, is a major source of hydroelectric power.

Cicero *si'ser-ō*, 41 51N 87 45W, pop(1980) 61,232, town in Cook county, NE Illinois, United States; industrial suburb 10 km W of Chicago.

Ciechanów *cheKH-an-ov'*, voivodship in NE central Poland; watered by R Wkra; pop(1983) 413,000; area 6,362 sq km; capital Ciechanów; chief towns include Mława, Płonsk and Pułtusk.

Ciechanów, TSEKHANOV (Rus), formerly ZICHENAU (Ger), 52 52N 20 38E, pop(1983) 37,600, capital town of Ciechanów voivodship, NE central Poland; 80 km NNW of Warszawa (Warsaw); railway; monument: 15th-c castle of the Dukes of Mazovia.

Ciego de Avila *syay'gō day a'vee-la*, prov in central Cuba; area 6,485 sq km; pop(1981) 320,961; capital Ciego de Avila; chief towns Morón and Júcaro.

Ciego de Avila, 21 51N 78 47W, pop(1983e) 78,115, capital town of Ciego de Avila prov, central Cuba; commercial centre for rich agricultural region; founded in 1849; railway; economy: centre of dairy farming, cattle and citrus.

Cienfuegos *syayn-fway'gōs*, prov in W central Cuba; land rises in the SE; area 4,149 sq km; pop(1981) 326,412; capital Cienfuegos.

Cienfuegos, 22 10N 80 27W, pop(1983e) 106,478, port and capital of Cienfuegos prov, W central Cuba; on a peninsula on the S coast of the island, 337 km SE of La Habana (Havana); founded in 1819 for French settlers, the original site was destroyed by a storm in 1825; the city has become an important industrial centre with an economy based on tobacco and citrus; has a botanical garden maintained by Harvard University; monuments: Castillo de Jagua (1738-45), museum of decorative arts.

Cieza *thyay'tha*, 38 17N 1 23W, pop(1981) 29,932, city in Murcia prov, SE Spain; on the R Segura, 41 km NE of Murcia; railway; economy: plastics, timber, paper, flour, cereals, fruit and vegetables.

Cimone, Monte *mon'te chee-mo'ne*, highest peak in the Appno Tosco-Emilliano, N Italy, 34 km NW of Pistoia; height 2,165 m.

Cìmpia Turzii *kum'pya toor'zee*, 46 33N 23 53E, pop(1983) 26,592, town in Cluj county, NW central Romania; on R Aries; burial place of Michael the Brave (1601); railway junction; economy: light engineering.

Cìmpina *kam'pee-na*, 45 08N 25 44E, pop(1983) 37,089, summer resort and industrial town in Prahova county, SE central Romania; on R Prahova, in the foothills of the Transylvanian Alps; railway; economy: petrol production and refining, chemicals, engineering, furniture, power plant.

Cìmpulung *kam'poo-loong*, 45 16N 25 03E, pop(1983) 39,777, resort in Argeş county, S central Romania; in S foothills of the Transylvanian Alps; established in the 12th century by German colonists, the town became the first capital of Walachia; railway; economy: lignite mining, pickup trucks, wine, textiles, timber, paper, power.

Cìmpulung Moldovenesc *kam'poo-loong mol-do-vayn-esk'*, 47 32N 25 34E, pop(1983) 21,128, resort town in Suceava county, NE Romania; railway; economy: food processing, cement, furniture, machinery; monument: 18th-c wooden church.

Cincinnati *sin-si-na'ti*, 39 06N 84 01W, pop(1980) 385,457, county seat of Hamilton county, SW Ohio, United States; on R Ohio; Fort Washington built here in 1789; achieved city status in 1819; there were large numbers of German immigrants in the 1840s; birthplace of William Howard Taft; 2 universities (1819, 1831); a noted centre of wine production; railway; economy: aircraft engines, vehicles, chemicals, machinery, food, metal products; monuments: Taft Museum, Contemporary Arts Centre, Kings Island Park; event: Oktoberfest (Sept).

Cinqueterre *cheeng-kwe-te'ru*, Mediterranean coastal region between La Spezia and Levanto on the Riviera di Levante, Liguria, NW Italy; comprises the 5 villages ('cinque terre') of Monterosso al Mare, Vernazza, Corniglia, Manarola, and Riomaggiore; tall, precipitous cliffs fringe the coastline.

Cintra, Portugal. See Sintra.

Cirencester *sī'ren-ses-ter* or *sis'is-ter*, CORINIUM DOBUNORUM (anc), 51 44N 1 59W, pop(1981) 13,783, market town in Cotswold dist, Gloucestershire, SW central England; in the Cotswolds, on the R Churn, 22 km NW of Swindon; 2nd largest town in Roman Britain during 2nd century AD; agricultural college; economy: electrical goods, engineering; monuments: 14th-c church of St John the Baptist, Corinium museum.

Ciskei *sis'kī*, independent black homeland in NE Cape prov, South Africa; pop(1984e) 903,681; area 7,700 sq km; bounded SW by the Indian Ocean; the 4th black homeland to gain independence (1981); its independent status is not recognized internationally; the majority of the pop are Xhosa who are dependent on subsistence agriculture; about 50,000 workers commute daily to East London or King William's Town; over 105,000 people in total are commuters or migrant workers in South Africa; capital Bisho; chief towns include Mdantsane (158,864), Zwelitsha (30,773), Sada (28,966) and Dimbaza (18,715); economy: farming, wood, leather, textiles.

Cisnădie *chees'na-dyay*, 45 42N 24 09E, pop(1983) 21,632, town in Sibiu county, central Romania; 8 km S of Sibiu, in the Transylvanian Alps; railway; economy: fruit, textiles.

Citlaltépetl *seet-lal-tay'pe-tul*, PICO DE ORIZABA, 19 02N 97 02W, highest peak in Mexico, rising to 5,699 m on the border of Veracruz and Puebla states, E Mexico; an extinct volcano, it has been inactive since 1687; first ascended in 1848; situated in the 197.5 sq km Pico de Orizaba National Park which was established in 1936.

Ciudad de México, capital of Mexico. See México, Ciudad de.

Ciudad Real *thyoo-thath' ray-al'*, prov in Castilla-La Mancha region, central Spain; mountainous in the S, SW and NW but largely a flat plain that stretches into Cuenca and Albacete provs; traversed by the R Guadiana; pop(1981) 468,327; area 19,749 sq km; capital Ciudad Real; economy: mining, wine, food processing, clothes, textiles, leather, iron, steel, distilling, motor vehicle battery plant at Manzanares to the E.

Ciudad Real, 38 59N 3 55W, pop(1981) 51,118, capital of Ciudad Real prov, S central Spain, on the fertile La Mancha plain between R Guadiana and R Jabalón, 190 km S of Madrid; bishopric; established in 1255; home of Don Quixote; railway; economy: livestock trade, textiles, pharmaceuticals; monuments: cathedral (1531); church of St Peter; events: Fiestas of the Virgen del Prado in August.

Ciudadela *thyoo-tha-thay'la*, CIUTADELLA DE MENORCA, 40 00N 3 50E, pop(1981) 14,573, small fishing port at the W end of the island of Menorca in the Balearic Is, Baleares autonomous region, Spain; former capital of Menorca; beaches nearby at Santandria Cove, Alganares, Cala Blanca and Cala Banes; economy: fishing, footwear; monuments: 14th-c Gothic cathedral and Naveta de Tudons prehistoric remains.

Clackmannan, district in Central region, central Scotland; pop(1981) 47,855; area 161 sq km; chief town Alloa.

Clac'ton-on-Sea', 51 48N 1 09E, pop(1981) 40,313, resort town in Tendring dist, Essex, SE England; on the North Sea coast, 21 km SE of Colchester; railway; economy: engineering.

Clare, AN CHLÁIR (Gael), county in Munster prov, W Irish Republic; bounded W by Atlantic Ocean and E by Slieve Aughty Mts; dramatic Cliffs of Moher on Atlantic coast; impressive limestone outcrops at Burren; pop(1981) 87,567; area 3,188 sq km; capital Ennis; famous 3-day folk festival at the spa town of Lisdoonvarna in July.

Claremont, 34 06N 117 43W, pop(1980) 30,950, city in Los Angeles county, SW California, United States; at the base of the San Gabriel Mts, 48 km E of Los Angeles; railway.

Clarence *klar'ens*, river in E South Island, New Zealand; rises in the Spenser Mts; flows S and NE between the Kaikoura mountain ranges; enters the Pacific 32 km N of Kaikoura; length 209 km.

Clarksville, 36 32N 87 21W, pop(1980) 54,777, county seat of Montgomery county, N Tennessee, United States; at the confluence of the Cumberland and Red rivers, 65 km NW of Nashville; founded in 1784; university; railway; economy: important processing and market centre for livestock and tobacco.

Clay Cross, 53 10N 1 24W, pop(1981) 22,726, town linked with North Wingfield in North East Derbyshire dist, Derbyshire, central England; 8 km SE of Chesterfield.

Clayton, 37 05S 145 05E, suburb of Melbourne, Victoria, SE Australia; SE of Melbourne city centre; Monash University (1958).

Clearwater, 27 58N 82 48W, pop(1980) 85,528, county seat of Pinellas county, W Florida, United States; a resort on the Gulf of Mexico, 24 km NW of St Petersburg; railway.

Cleckheat'on and Liv'ersedge, 53 43N 1 41W, pop(1981) 26,281, town in Kirklees borough, West Yorkshire, N England; part of West Yorkshire urban area; NW of Dewsbury.

Cleethorpes, 53 34N 0 02W, pop(1981) 33,347, resort town in Cleethorpes dist, Humberside, NE England; SE of Grimsby on the R Humber estuary; railway; economy: fishing.

Clerf *klerf* or **Clerve** *klerv*, river in SE Belgium and Luxembourg, rising NE of Bastogne in Belgium; flows 50 km ENE and S to meet the R Wiltz at Kautenbach in Luxembourg.

Clermont-Ferrand *kler-mõ-fer-rã*, 45 46N 3 04E, pop(1982) 151,092, capital of Puy-de-Dôme dept, Auvergne region, central France; at the foot of the volcanic region of Monts Dômes (W), to the NE it overlooks the fertile Limagne plain; bishopric; university (1896); railway; Clermont-Ferrand has over 20 mineral springs and supplies a good deal of France's bottled mineral water (it comes to the surface just N of the town centre); in the 8th century Clermont was a small town built within ramparts on a small hill, itself an extinct volcano; it became Clermont-Ferrand in 1630 when it merged with its rival neighbour Montferrand; birthplace of the 17th-c philosopher and writer Blaise Pascal; it is the geographical and economic centre of the Massif Central and the centre of the Michelin rubber tyre industry; railway; monuments: cathedral of Notre-Dame, with 12-15th-c stained-glass, begun in 1248 and unique in being built of the local black lava rock; Romanesque basilica of Notre-Dame-du-Port (11-12th-c), in the crypt is a 17th-c Black Madonna.

Clervaux *kler-võ'*, canton in N part of Diekirch dist, N Luxembourg; area 302 sq km; pop(1981) 9,580; traversed N-S by the R Clerf, the R Our follows its E frontier with W Germany; bounded to the W by Belgium; part of the German-Luxembourg Nature Park is located in Clervaux.

Clervaux, 50 03N 6 00E, pop(1981) 1,000, health resort and capital of Clervaux canton, Diekirch dist, N Luxembourg; situated in a deep valley by the R Clerf in the Ardennes; 66 km N of Luxembourg; 85 km of well-marked walks nearby; economy: lifting and handling equipment.

Clevedon *kleev'don*, 51 27N 2 51W, pop(1981) 18,094, summer resort town in Woodspring dist, Avon, SW England; on the R Severn estuary, SW of Bristol; the town has associations with the writers Thackeray and Coleridge; economy: foodstuffs, engineering.

Cleveland *kleev'land*, county of NE England; bounded E by the North Sea, S by North Yorkshire and W by Durham; includes Teesside urban area with port facilities on the R Tees estuary; pop(1981) 567,958; area 583 sq km; county town Middlesbrough; chief towns include Stockton-on-Tees, Hartlepool; economy: iron, steel, chemicals, fertilizers, oil and petrochemicals; the county is divided into 4 districts:

District	*area (sq km)*	*pop(1981)*
Hartlepool	94	94,870
Langbaurgh	240	150,215
Middlesbrough	54	150,430
Stockton-on-Tees	195	172,443

Cleveland, 41 30N 81 42W, pop(1980) 573,822, county seat of Cuyahoga county, NE Ohio, United States; port on L

Erie at the mouth of the R Cuyahoga; developed with the opening of the Ohio and Erie Canal (1827) and became a city since 1836; 3 universities (1826, 1886, 1923); railway; airfield; economy: machinery, metals and metal products, electronics, transportation equipment; medical research centre; monuments: Play House, Holden Arboretum, art museum.

Cleveland, 35 10N 84 53W, pop(1980) 26,415, county seat of Bradley county, S Tennessee, United States; 40 km ENE of Chattanooga; railway.

Cleveland Heights, 41 30N 81 34W, pop(1980) 56,438, town in Cuyahoga county, NE Ohio, United States; 11 km E of Cleveland.

Cleveland Way, long-distance footpath in North Yorkshire, N England; length 150 km; stretches from Helmsley to near Filey.

Clifton, 40 53N 74 09W, pop(1980) 74,388, town in Passaic county, NE New Jersey, United States; NNW of, and adjacent to, Passaic; formerly part of Passaic; railway.

Clinton, 41 51N 90 12W, pop(1980) 32,828, county seat of Clinton county, E Iowa, United States; on the Mississippi river, 48 km NE of Davenport; railway.

Clipperton Island, 10 20N 109 13W, uninhabited island in the Pacific Ocean, 1,000 km SW of Mexico; used as a base by the English pirate, John Clipperton; claimed by France but occupied by Mexico in 1897; administered from French Polynesia.

Clitheroe *kliTH'er-ō*, 53 53N 2 23W, pop(1981) 13,729, town in Ribble Valley dist, Lancashire, NW England; 15 km NE of Blackburn; economy: clothing, textiles, engineering.

Clonmel', CLUAIN MEALA (Gael), 52 21N 7 42W, pop(1981) 14,808, capital of Tipperary county, South Riding, Munster, S Irish Republic; on R Suir; centre of Irish greyhound racing and salmon fishing; railway; economy: agricultural trade, food processing, tourism, footwear, cider, prams.

Clovis *klō'vis*, 36 49N 119 42W, pop(1980) 33,021, city in Fresno county, central California, United States; in the San Joaquin Valley, 13 km NE of Fresno.

Clovis, 34 24N 103 12W, pop(1980) 31,194, county seat of Curry county, E New Mexico, United States; 15 km W of the Texas border; railway; economy: trade centre for a cattle-ranching and farming area; rail junction; nearby is Cannon Air Force Base.

Cluj *kloozh*, county in NE central Romania; N of the Transylvanian Alps; traversed by the R Someş; pop(1983) 740,580; area 6,650 sq km; capital Cluj-Napoca; an agricultural and mining region.

Cluj-Napoca or **Cluj** *kloozh-na'po-ka*, KLAUSENBERG (Ger), 46 47N 23 37E, pop(1983) 304,244, capital of Cluj county, NE central Romania; on the R Someş, in the foothills of the Apuseni Mts; founded in the 12th century by German colonists on the site of a former Roman colony; ceded from Hungary in 1920; the chief cultural and religious centre of Transylvania since the 16th century; university (1872), technical university (1948); botanical gardens; winter sports facilities nearby; airfield; railway; economy: electrical equipment, metallurgy, chemicals, machinery, textiles, footwear; monuments: central square with 16-18th-c houses; Gothic St Michael church; Austrian fort; Franciscan monastery.

Clutha *kloo'tha*, longest river of South Island, New Zealand; rises in L Wanaka, W South Island; flows SE past the towns of Alexandra, Roxburgh and Balclutha to enter the Pacific near Kaitangata; length from its source, the Makarora river, 322 km; there are massive hydroelectric schemes on the Clutha river near Alexandra.

Clwyd *kloo'id*, county in NE Wales; pop(1981) 391,081; area 2,426 sq km; chief town Mold; created in 1974; economy: coal, steel (Shotton, Brymbo), engineering, aircraft, chemicals, plastics, clothing, paper, microprocessors; industry is largely located in the E around Wrexham and Deeside; there are coastal resorts at Colwyn Bay and Rhyl; Clwyd is divided into 6 districts:

District	*area (sq km)*	*pop(1981)*
Alyn and Deeside	154	72,088
Colwyn	553	48,936
Delyn	278	65,030
Glyndŵr	966	40,728
Rhuddlan	109	52,100
Wrexham Maelor	366	113,300

Clwyd, river rising in Gwynedd, NE Wales; flows N 48 km through Clywd to meet the Irish Sea W of Rhyl.

Clyde *klīd*, river in S Scotland; the main headstream, the Daer Water, rises in S Strathclyde, near the Dumfries and Galloway border, 13 km ENE of Thornhill (Dumfries and Galloway) and flows generally N and NW; near Lanark it falls over 98 m via 4 waterfalls in less than 6 km (at the Falls of Clyde, near New Lanark); below Lanark the Clyde flows NW through a fertile area known for its orchards of apples, pears and plums; from here it continues through Scotland's most important industrial area S of Glasgow, then through Glasgow City; at Dumbarton the river expands into the Firth of Clyde, an estuary which extends 103 km W then S to the island of Ailsa Craig (W of Girvan) where it joins the North Channel; the Firth of Clyde is generally 2-30 km wide, widening to approx 60 km at its mouth; length 170 km; catchment area c.3,836 sq km; Glasgow is the head of navigation for ocean-going vessels; used for hydroelectricity; it is linked to the R Forth via a canal; the Clyde valley, or Clydesdale, was noted for its breeding of Clydesdales (draft horses).

Clydebank, 55 54N 4 24W, pop(1981) 51,854, capital of Clydebank dist, Strathclyde, W Scotland; in Clydeside urban area, on the N bank of the R Clyde, 10 km NW of Glasgow; railway; economy: heavy engineering, shipbuilding.

Clydeside, pop(1981) 1,718,423, urban area in W Strathclyde, W central Scotland; comprises the 11 districts of Bearsden and Milngavie, Clydebank, Cumbernauld and Kilsyth, East Kilbride, Eastwood, Glasgow City, Hamilton, Monklands, Motherwell, Renfrew and Strathkelvin; airport; railway; economy: major industrial area of Scotland.

Côa *kō'a*, river in N central Portugal, rises near Sabugal (Guarda dist), flows N to the R Douro near Vila Nova de Fozcôa; length 112 km.

Coahuila *kō-ah-wee'la*, COAHUILA DE ZARAGOZA, state in N Mexico; bounded N by Texas (USA) along the Río Grande, W by Chihuahua and Durango states, S by Zacatecas and E by Nuevo León; crossed N-S by broken ranges of the Sierra Madre Oriental; the NW is arid tableland with depressions; the land is lower in the E; drained by the Río Sabinas and the Río Salado de los Nadadores; the Laguna region in the S, irrigated by the Nazas and Aguanaval rivers, is one of Mexico's major cotton-producing regions; pop(1980) 1,558,401; area 149,982 sq km; capital Saltillo; economy: agriculture (cotton, wheat, grapes, alfalfa, sorghum, maize, walnuts, figs, apples, pomegranates), cattle raising, mining (coal, fluorite, phosphorus and, on a smaller scale, silver, lead, zinc, copper, gold, iron and salt), iron and steel, motor cars, chemicals, textiles.

Coal'ville, 52 44N 1 20W, pop(1981) 28,899, town in North-west Leicestershire dist, Leicestershire, central England; 20 km NW of Leicester, on the edge of Charnwood Forest; economy: engineering, coal.

Coast Mountains, mountain range in W British Columbia and Alaska, extending approx 1,600 km NW-SE between Yukon terr border and the Fraser river, where it meets the N end of the Cascade Range; runs parallel with the Pacific and forms the NW border between British Columbia and Alaska; rises to 4,042 m in Mt Waddington in British Columbia (at 51 22N 125 14W).

Coast Range, mountain belt in W North America, extending along the coast of the Pacific Ocean from Alaska S through British Columbia, Washington, Oregon, California and Baja California (Mexico); beginning in Alaska with the uplands of Kodiak Island, the range continues E and SE with the Kenai Mts, Chugach Mts and St Elias Mts (which rise to 5,950 m in Mt Logan, the 2nd highest peak in North America); the range then continues S along the coast of S Alaska and British Columbia, where it continues on the Alexander Archipelago, Queen Charlotte and Vancouver Islands and is separated from the Coast Mts to the E by several straits along the British Columbia coast; the range reappears on the mainland again in the Olympic Mts of Washington; the system continues S as generally low mts (rising to 600-1,200 m) along the Washington and Oregon coasts to the Klamath Mts on the Oregon-California border; in California to the E of the Coast Range lie the Sacramento and San Joaquin river valleys (known generally as the Central Valley); the range continues S through the Mexican state of Baja California to its southernmost tip.

Coatbridge, 55 52N 4 01W, pop(1981) 50,957, capital of Monklands dist, Strathclyde, W central Scotland; in Clydeside urban area, 14 km E of Glasgow; railway; economy: engineering.

Coatepeque, Lago de *kō-a-te-pay'kee*, lake in Santa Ana and Sonsonate depts, W El Salvador, Central America.

Coatzacoalcos *kwat-sa-kwal'kōs*, PUERTO MÉXICO, 18 09N 94 25W, pop(1980) 186,129, port in Veracruz state, SE Mexico; S of Veracruz; railway; economy: oil and sulphur.

Cobán *kō-ban'*, 15 28N 90 20W, pop(1983e) 43,538, capital town of Alta Verapaz dept, N central Guatemala, Central America; 96 km N of Guatemala City; many coffee, tea and vanilla plantations flourish here; alt 1,320 m; monuments: church of El Calvario (1559); Mayan remains nearby; events: Holy Week; procession of saints (3 Aug); folklore festival (28-29 Aug).

Cóbh *kōv*, formerly COVE OF CORK (-1849), QUEENSTOWN (-1922), 51 51N 8 17W, pop(1981) 8,439, seaport town in Cork county, Munster, S Irish Republic; on S shore of Great Island in Cork Harbour, ESE of Cork; yachting centre; formerly important as a port of call for transatlantic steamers; in 1838 the *Sirius* made one of the first transatlantic steamship crossings from here; a German freighter carrying arms for the 1916 rising was scuttled here; railway; economy: steel (Haulbowline).

Cob'ham, 51 20N 0 24W, pop(1981) 13,936, town linked with Oxshott in Elmbridge dist, Surrey, SE England; on the R Mole, 7 km NW of Leatherhead; railway.

Cobija *kō-bee'ha*, 11 01S 68 45W, pop(1976) 3,650, capital of Pando dept, NW Bolivia; on the Río Acre in N Suarez prov.

Coblenz, dist and town in W Germany. See Koblenz.

Cochabamba *ko-cha-bam'ba*, dept in central Bolivia; includes the Cordillera de Cochabamba, an E branch of the Cordillera Real, which crosses the dept in an arc W-SE, separating the mountainous part (W) from tropical valleys and tropical lowlands (N and E); drained by the Santa Elena and Cotacajes rivers (W), Caine river (S), Chaparé and Ichilo rivers (E); the dept has fertile valleys and mild climate; Cochabamba basin is the greatest grain and fruit producing area in Bolivia; pop(1982) 908,674; area 55,631 sq km; capital Cochabamba; chief towns Quillacollo and Punata; economy: wheat, maize, barley, vegetables, cattle, oil.

Cochabamba, 17 26S 66 10W, pop(1982) 281,962, capital of Cercado prov, Cochabamba, central Bolivia; Bolivia's 3rd largest city, founded in 1542; alt 2,500 m; set in a bowl of rolling hills, it is an important agricultural centre; to the N is Cerro Tunari (5,180 m); there are thermal baths near the city; there is a golf club at L Alalay outside the town; university (1832); railway; airfield (Jorge Wilstermann) at 4 km from the city; economy: oil refining, furniture, footwear, agricultural trade; monuments: the Palacio de Cultura houses a group of local museums under one roof; the main tourist attraction, Los Portales, is on the outskirts of the city, this mansion, once belonging to the tin magnate, Simon Patiño, is now a museum; a monument on La Coronilla hill commemorates the defence of the town by its womenfolk during the War of Independence; events: municipal and retail markets take place on Wednesdays and Saturdays; a local carnival takes place 15 days before Lent.

Cochin *ko'chin*, 9 55N 76 22E, pop(1983) 686,000, naval base and seaport in Kerala, SW India; on the Malabar coast of the Arabian Sea, 1,080 km SSE of Bombay; a Portuguese trading station was established here by Vasco da Gama in 1502; Fort Cochin was the first European settlement in India; the tomb of Vasco da Gama lies in the churchyard; economy: shipbuilding and trade in fruit and cattle.

Cochrane, Lago, lake in Chile and Argentina. See Lago Pueyrredón.

Cockermouth, 54 40N 3 21W, pop(1981) 7,000, town in Allerdale dist, Cumbria, NW England; at the junction of the Cocker and Derwent rivers, 40 km SW of Carlisle; home town of William Wordsworth (1770-1850); economy: footwear.

Cockscomb Basin, region of the Maya mountains, Belize; a forest reserve, part of which was designated the world's first jaguar reserve in 1986; reserve area 14.56 sq km; access via Maya Centre, SW of Dangriga.

Coclé *kō-klay'*, prov in central Panama, Central America; on the Golfo de Panamá, an inlet of the Pacific Ocean; pop(1980) 140,903; area 5,035 sq km; capital Penonomé; chief towns El Valle and Aguadulce; traversed by the Inter-American Highway.

Coco *kō'kō*, formerly SEGOVIA, river in SW Honduras and N Nicaragua, Central America; rises near San Marcos de Colón in Choluteca dept, SW Honduras; flows ENE through Madriz dept, then forms the boundary between Nueva Segovia (N) and Jinotega (S); on reaching Poteca it flows alongside the frontier between Honduras (N) and Nicaragua (S) until it discharges into the Caribbean Sea at Cabo Gracias a Dios; the delta has several islands and 3 main channels; chief tributaries include the Río Bocay, Río Estelí, and Río Huaspuc; length 720 km.

Coco, Isla del *dhel kō'kō*, 5 30N 87 00W, thickly-wooded island and national park in the Pacific Ocean, situated approximately 500 km SW of Osa peninsula, Costa Rica; area 25 sq km; it is the only ocean island belonging to Costa Rica; the national park was established in 1978 and covers a total area of 32 sq km.

Cocos Islands *kō'kōs*, KEELING ISLANDS *kee'ling*, 12 05S 96 53E, pop(1983) 579, 2 separate groups of atolls in the Indian Ocean, 3,685 km W of Darwin, Australia; an Australian external territory comprising 27 small, flat, palm-covered coral islands with a total land area of 14.2 sq km, the main islands are West island (pop 216), which is 10 km in length, has an airport and is mostly occupied by Europeans; Home island (pop 363) is occupied by the Cocos Malay community; Direction, Horsburgh and South Islands and North Keeling Island all lie 24 km N of the group; discovered in 1609 by Captain William Keeling of the East India Company, the islands were settled first in 1826 by Alexander Hare and again in 1827 by John Clunies-Ross, who landed with Malay seamen to exploit the coconut palms; in 1857 the islands were annexed to the British Crown; in 1886 Queen Victoria granted the lands to George Clunies-Ross, retaining certain rights to the Crown, and in 1903 the Cocos group was incorporated with the Settlement of Singapore, having previously been under the control of the government of Ceylon; in 1955 the Cocos islands were placed under Australian administration as the Territory of Cocos (Keeling) Islands; an islands council, established by the Malay community, advises the administrator on all issues; in 1978 the Australian government purchased the Clunies-Ross interests in the islands and a Cocos Malay co-operative was established to manage the islands' copra plantation.

Codlea *kod'lee-a*, 45 43N 25 27E, pop(1983) 23,416, town in Braşov county, Romania; 13 km NW of Braşov; railway; economy: textiles, food processing, wood products, horticulture.

Cody *kō'di*, 44 31N 109 04W, pop(1980) 6,790, resort city in Park county, NW Wyoming; on the Shoshone river, E of Yellowstone National Park; monument: Buffalo Bill Historic Center, a replica of the ranch of this famous frontiersman.

Coeur d'Alene *kord-layn'*, 47 40N 116 46W, pop(1980) 20,054, town in Kootenai county, N Idaho, United States; in the Idaho panhandle, 50 km E of Spokane; a military post was established here, but the site developed following the discovery of silver and lead in 1882; the Coeur d'Alene Lake is a major resort area.

Coffs Harbour, 30 18S 153 08E, pop(1981) 16,020, port in Mid-North Coast stat div, NE New South Wales, Australia; on E coast, S of Brisbane; railway; airfield; economy: bananas, timber.

Coihaique or **Coyhaique** *koy-hī'kay*, 45 34S 72 04W, pop(1982) 22,961, commercial capital of Coihaique prov, and Aisén region, Chile; located in a large valley surrounded by mountains; a base for hiking and skiing excursions in the area.

Coimbatore *kō-im'ba-tōr*, 11 00N 76 57E, pop(1981) 917,000, city in Tamil Nadu, S India; 425 km SW of Madras, N of the R Noyil; commanding the Palghat Gap through the Western Ghats, the city was the stronghold of successive Tamil kingdoms from the 9-17th centuries; ceded to Britain in 1799; linked to Calicut and Tiruppur by rail; university (1971); airfield; economy: market centre for tea, cotton and teak; industries include glass making, electrical goods and fertilizer.

Coimbra *kwēē'bra*, dist in W central Portugal, largely in Beira Litoral prov, bounded by the Atlantic (W) and the Serra de Lousa (E); area 3,956 sq km; pop(1981) 436,324; drained by R Mondego entering the Atlantic at Figueira da Foz; divided into 17 councils and 193 parishes; economy: livestock, horticulture, wine, dairy produce, fruit, rice, olives; minerals: lead, gold, silver, quartz, titanium, wolfram, zinc, coal, tin; airfields at Coimbra, Figueira da Foz and Lousa.

Coimbra, CONIMBRIGA (anc), 40 15N 8 27W, pop(1981) 71,800, capital of Coimbra dist, central Portugal; on R Mondego, 173 km NNE of Lisbon; former capital of Portugal (1139-c.1260); seat of oldest university in Portugal (founded at Lisboa in 1290 and transferred to Coimbra in 1537); episcopal see; economy: paper, tanning, pottery, biscuits, food processing and fabrics; monuments: São Sebastiano aqueduct; monastery of the Holy Cross; the Manueline 16th-c Claustro do Silencio; old cathedral; bishop's palace containing the Machado de Castro national museum; Conimbriga Roman site and the Children's Portugal village nearby; events: Queima das Fitas student festival during the second half of May; Rainha Santa festival, in honour of Santa Isabel at the beginning of June in even-numbered years.

Coire, town in Switzerland. See Chur.

Cojedes *kō-KHay'des*, state in N Venezuela; principally an area of *llanos* plain, watered by secondary tributaries of the Orinoco river; pop(1980) 135,579; area 14,793 sq km; capital San Carlos.

Cojutepeque *kō-hyoo-te-pay'kee*, 13 42N 88 58W, pop(1980) 35,011, capital of Cuscatlán dept, central El Salvador, Central America; 32 km E of San Salvador; railway.

Colac *kō-lak'*, 38 22S 143 38E, pop(1983e) 10,190, town in Barwon stat div, S Victoria, Australia; S of L Colac, SW of Melbourne; in an area containing nearly 30 volcanic lakes, ranging in size from small basins to huge craters such as L Corangamite, the largest lake in Victoria; railway.

Colchester *kōl'ches-ter*, CAMULODUNUM (Lat), COLNECEASTER (Anglo-Saxon), 51 54N 0 54E, pop(1981) 88,847, town in Colchester dist, Essex, SE England; S of the R Colne, 82 km NE of London; University of Essex (1961); claimed to be the oldest town in England; railway; economy: oysters, rose growing; monuments: city walls, 12th-c castle; event: oyster festival (Oct).

Coleraine *kōl-rayn'*, CUIL RAITHIN (Gael), 55 8N 6 40W, pop(1981) 15,967, town in Coleraine dist, Co Derry (Londonderry), N Northern Ireland; on the Bann river, near the N coast; one of the oldest English settlements, the site was given to corporations of the City of London by James I in 1613; New University of Ulster (1965); railway; economy: salmon fishing, whisky distilling, linen, food processing; monument: Mountsandel Fort, a Stone Age circular fort, is situated in the S of the town on the R Bann.

Colhué Huapí, Lago *la'gō kol-hway' hwa-pee'*, lake in S Chubut prov, Patagonia, S Argentina; area 593 sq km; length 96 km; 8-24 km wide; situated 9 km E of L Musters, to which it is linked by a short stream; its outlet is the Río Chico, an affluent of the Chubut river.

Colima *kō-lee'ma*, state in SW Mexico; bounded SW by the Pacific Ocean, N and E by Jalisco and SE by Michoacán; consists of foothills of the Sierra Madre Occidental in the N and E and coastal lowlands in the SW; drained by the Armería and Salado rivers; the Naranjo and Coahuayana rivers form the E border with Jalisco and Michoacán; along the coastline is the Laguna de Cuyutlán, separated from the Pacific by a narrow peninsula; Colima includes the Islas Revillagigedo, 800 km off the coast; pop(1980) 339,202; area 5,191 sq km; capital Colima; economy: agriculture (copra, lemons, bananas, maize, sugar cane, rice, papayas, peppers), fishing, mining (iron, salt), sugar refining, soap.

Colima, 19 14N 103 41W, pop(1984e) 58,000, capital of Colima state, SW Mexico; in the Valle de Colima, SSW of Colima Volcano which last erupted in 1941; university (1867); railway; economy: sugar refining, cigars, shoes and trade in maize, rice.

Coll (Gael, 'hazel'), flat, rocky island in Strathclyde region, W Scotland; 30 km NW of Tobermory, Mull; length 20 km; rises to 103 m at Ben Hogh; ferry links with Tiree and Oban; the chief village is Arinagour; the island is associated with the history of the Clan Maclean.

College Station, 30 37N 96 21W, pop(1980) 37,272, city in Brazos county, E central Texas, United States; 134 km NW of Houston; Mechanical University (1876).

Collie, 33 20S 116 06E, pop(1981) 7,667, town in South-West stat div, Western Australia, Australia; 176 km S of Perth; railway; economy: open-cast coal mining, electricity (Muja power station).

Colmar *kol'mar*, KOLMAR (Ger), 48 05N 7 20E, pop(1982) 63,764, capital of Haut-Rhin dept, Alsace region, E France; on a plain near the vine-covered foothills of the S Vosges Mts, on the R Lauch; birthplace of Bartholdi, the 19th-c sculptor of New York's Statue of Liberty and the Lion of Belfort, and Baron Haussmann, who transformed the face of Paris with his grand boulevards; railway; economy: tourism (an excellent point from which to explore the High Vosges), textiles, foodstuffs, metalworking, market-gardening, wine production; monuments: the old quarter, with its narrow and winding streets, has many burghers' houses of the 16-17th centuries; Maison Pfister (1537, wooden galleries); Gothic Dominican church (13th-c); town hall (18th-c); events: wine fair (mid-August), sauerkraut festival (Sept); well-known for its summer folklore events.

Colne *kōn* or *kōln*, 53 52N 2 09W, pop(1981) 19,173, town in Pendle dist, Lancashire, NW England; 9 km NE of Burnley; railway; economy: textiles, clothing.

Colôane *koo-lō'a-ne*, 22 08N 113 33E, island of the Portuguese overseas prov of Macau, E Asia; W of Hong Kong; linked to the island of Taipa to the N by a causeway (Istmo Taipa-Colôane); pop(1982) with Taipa 7,224; area 7 sq km; the relics of St Francis Xavier are kept here; there are several fine beaches; monument: temple of Tam Kung.

Cologne, city in West Germany. See Köln.

Colombes *ko-lōb*, 48 55N 2 14E, pop(1982) 78,783, industrial and residential suburb of Paris in Hauts-de-Seine dept, Ile-de-France, N central France; international sports stadium.

Colombia *ko-lom'bi-a*, official name The Republic of Colombia, REPÚBLICA DE COLOMBIA, a republic of NW South America, bounded N by Panama and the Caribbean, W by the Pacific Ocean, E by Venezuela, SE by Brazil and S by Ecuador and Peru; timezone GMT −5; area 1,140,105 sq km; pop(1980) 26,823,000; capital Bogotá; chief cities Medellín, Cali and Barranquilla; there are 23 cities with a pop exceeding 100,000; 90% of the pop lives in the temperate valleys of the Andes; ethnic groups include mixtures of Spanish, Indian and Negro origin; the official language is Spanish; 95% of the pop is Roman Catholic; the currency is the peso of 100 centavos; national holiday 30 July (Independence Day); membership of FAO, G-77, GATT, IADB, IAEA, IBRD, ICAC, ICAO, ICO, IDA, IDB, IFAD, IFC, IHO, ILO, IMF, IMO, INTELSAT, INTERPOL, IRC, ISO, ITU, LAIA, NAM, OAS, PAHO, SELA, UN, UNESCO, UPEB, UPU, WFTU, WHO, WIPO, WMO, WSG, WTO.

Physical description. Colombia is the only South American country with a coastline on both the Caribbean and Pacific, with island possessions at San Andrés, Providencia, San Bernardo, Islas del Rosario and Isla Fuerte in the Caribbean and Gorgona, Gorgonilla and Malpelo in the Pacific. On the mainland the central spine of the Andes running N-S branches into 3 distinct ranges which divide the narrow coastal plains from the forested lowlands of the Amazon basin. The Cordillera Central, separated from the Cordillera Occidental by the Río Cauca, rises to heights in excess of 5,000 m, the highest peak in this region being Huila at 5,750 m. To the E beyond the Río Magdalena the Cordillera Oriental surrounds large areas of plateau. The country is drained in 3 directions by rivers that flow into the Pacific, those

which find an outlet to the Caribbean and those which become tributaries of the Amazon and reach the Atlantic. *Climate.* The coastal plains in the NW and W are hot and humid throughout the year with an annual rainfall over 2,500 mm. Heaviest rainfall occurs during the night. On the Caribbean coast there is a drier period from Dec to April. In the Andes an annual rainfall of 1,000-2,500 mm falls evenly throughout the year, the W ranges being wetter than those in the E. The hot, humid tropical lowlands to the E experience an annual rainfall of between 2,000 and 2,500 mm with two relatively wetter periods during Dec-Jan and April-May.
History, government and constitution. Spanish occupation from the early 16th century largely displaced the former Amerindian population which survived to supply peasant labour for large ranches. For nearly 300 years Colombia was governed by Spain within the Viceroyalty of Peru and later the Viceroyalty of New Granada. In 1819, following the campaigns of Simón Bolívar, Colombia gained its independence and formed a union with Ecuador, Venezuela and Panama linked under the banner of Gran Colombia. The secession of Venezuela (1829), Ecuador (1830) and Panama (1903) brought this union to an end. The present constitution dates from 1886, with legislative power exercised by a bicameral Congress composed of a 114-member Senate and a Chamber of Representatives with 199 members elected for 4 years. The president, who is elected for a 4-year term, appoints cabinet ministers and chiefs of administrative departments and is advised by a Council of State whose members are elected by Congress.
Economy. Virtually self-sufficient in food, Colombia employs about one-third of its workforce on the land. Major export crops include coffee, bananas, cotton, sugar, maize, rice, beans, wheat, potatoes and cut flowers. With a manufacturing industry limited to textiles, leather and other local consumer goods there is a heavy dependence on mineral wealth. Gold, silver, platinum and nickel are mined, coal is extracted in the N at El Cerrejón and oil is pumped from the E *llanos* (plains) at Caño Limón, Trinidad and Guayuriba. The Río Magdalena, navigable for 1,400 km, is an important waterway, but the development of the interior has largely been hampered by the lack of good communications. Major trade partners include the USA, W Germany, Venezuela, Japan, France, Ecuador and the UK.
Administrative divisions. Colombia is divided into 23 departments, 4 intendencies and 5 administrative territories as follows:

Division	*area (sq km)*	*pop(1985)*
Departments		
Antioquia	63,612	3,720,025
Atlántico	3,382	1,406,545
Bolívar	25,978	1,199,437
Boyacá	23,189	1,089,387
Caldas	7,888	789,730
Caquetá	88,965	177,259
Cauca	29,308	674,824
César	22,905	584,152
Chocó	46,530	68,506
Córdoba	25,020	878,738
Cundinamarca	22,623	1,358,978
Guajira	20,848	245,284
Huila	19,890	636,642
Magdalena	23,188	760,611
Meta	85,635	321,563
Nariño	33,268	848,618
Norte de Santander	21,658	871,966
Quindío	1,845	375,762
Risaralda	4,140	623,756
Santander	30,537	1,427,110
Sucre	10,917	523,525
Tolima	23,512	1,028,239
Valle de Cauca	22,140	2,833,940
Intendencies		
Arauca	23,818	16,464
Casanare	44,640	24,443
Putumayo	24,885	30,000
San Andrés-Providencia	44	36,515
Administrative territories		
Amazonas	109,665	13,210
Guainía	72,238	3,311
Guaviare	42,327	12,235
Vaupés	65,268	3,414
Vichada	100,242	3,377

Colombo *ke-lom'bō*, originally KALAN-TOTTA, 6 55N 79 52E, pop(1981) 587,647; seaport capital of Colombo dist, Western prov and chief city of Sri Lanka; on the W coast, S of the R Kelani; the outer suburb of Sri-Jayawardenapura has been the official capital of Sri Lanka since 1983; the city has many architectural legacies of the Moors, Portuguese, Dutch and British mixed with modern styles; settled by the Portuguese in 1517 and the Dutch in 1656, the British took control in 1796; the city became Sri Lanka's major port in 1875, with the building of a breakwater and the enlargement of the artificial harbour; used as a British defence base 1942-45; location of the 1950 Commonwealth Conference which established the *Colombo Plan*, a series of recommendations for the economic assistance of S and SE Asia; most of Sri Lanka's road and rail networks converge on Colombo; University of Sri Lanka (1972); University of Sri Lanka, Colombo Campus (1972); economy: oil refining, iron and steel, tea, rubber and cocoa trade; monuments: national museum, Independence Hall, many Hindu shrines (*kovils*) and Moorish mosques.

Colón *ko-lōn'*, dept in N Honduras, Central America; pop(1983e) 128,370; area 8,870 sq km; hilly in the W, flat and fertile in the E; capital Trujillo.

Colón, prov of central Panama, Central America; on the Caribbean coast; divided into W and E sections by the Panama Canal Area; drained by the Coclé del Norte and Indio rivers; pop(1980) 137,997; area 4,961 sq km; capital Colón; chief towns Portobelo and Cristobal; includes the territory of San Blas.

Colón, formerly ASPINWALL, 9 21N 79 54W, pop(1980) 59,840, port and capital city of Colón prov, N Panama, Central America; at the Caribbean end of the Panama Canal; second largest city in Panama; founded in 1850 and named after William Aspinwall, railway builder; railway.

Colonia *kō-lō'nya*, dept in SW Uruguay; on the Río de la Plata at the mouth of the Río Uruguay, opposite Buenos Aires; pop(1985) 112,348; area 5,682 sq km; capital Colonia del Sacramento; chief towns: the ports of Carmelo and Juan Lacaze; there are many colonial towns or *colonias*, settled by European immigrants, eg Colonia Valdense in the SW of the dept is a Waldesian settlement where some of the customs of the Piedmontese Alps still exist; the dept was formed in 1816.

Colonia del Sacramento *del sak-ra-men'tō*, COLONIA, 34 29S 57 48W, pop(1985) 19,077, capital of Colonia dept, SW Uruguay; free zone which juts out into the Río de la Plata; railway; airport; ferry service to Buenos Aires (Argentina); founded by Portuguese settlers from Brazil in 1680; at Real San Carlos, just outside town, are a racecourse and a bullring; monuments: town walls and old colonial buildings; municipal museum in the house of Almirante Brown; mansion of the Viceroy; the house of General Mitre; the Farola.

Colonsay, ST COLUMBA'S ISLE, island in Strathclyde region, W Scotland; N of Islay and W of Jura; separated from Oronsay by a low channel which is dry at low water; rises to 134 m at Carn Mor; the islet of Eilean nan Ron (SW) is a nature reserve with a breeding colony of grey seals; monument: Augustinian priory.

Colora'do, state in W central United States; bounded W by Utah, N by Wyoming and Nebraska, E by Nebraska and Kansas, and S by Oklahoma and New Mexico; the Colorado river rises in the N and flows SW into Utah; the R Arkansas rises in central Colorado and flows S then E into Kansas; the Rio Grande rises in the SW and flows SE into New Mexico; the South Platte river rises in N central Colorado and flows NE into Nebraska; the Rocky Mts run N-S through the centre of the state and are divided into several ranges: Front Range, Sangre de Cristo Mts, Park Range, Sawatch Mts, and San Juan Mts; the highest point is Mt Elbert (4,399 m); E Colorado is part of the High Plains section of the fertile Great Plains and is the centre of cattle and sheep ranching in the state; the Colorado Plateau (W) has many canyons (eg the Black Canyon of the Gunnison National Monument) cut by the Colorado and Gunnison rivers; notable national parks and monuments include Rocky Mountain National Park, Dinosaur National Monument, and Great Sand Dunes National Monument; the chief agricultural products are wheat, hay, corn, sugar-beets and livestock; major industries include food processing, printing and publishing, and the manufacture of electrical and transportation equipment, fabricated metals, chemicals, and lumber, stone, clay and glass products; mineral reserves include oil, coal, and uranium; Colorado has the world's largest deposits of molybdenum; the E part of the state was included in the Louisiana Purchase of 1803 and the W part was gained from Mexico by the Treaty of Guadalupe Hidalgo in 1848; settlement expanded after the gold strike of 1858; Colorado became a territory in 1861 and a state (38th) in 1876; the Ute Indian reservation is located in the SW corner of the state; Colorado is also known as the 'Centennial State'; pop(1980) 2,889,964; area 269,347 sq km; capital Denver; chief cities include Colorado Springs, Aurora, Lakewood and Pueblo; the state is divided into 63 counties:

County	*area (sq km)*	*pop(1980)*
Adams	3,211	245,944
Alamosa	1,869	11,799
Arapahoe	2,080	293,621
Archuleta	3,518	3,664
Baca	6,640	5,419
Bent	3,944	5,945
Boulder	1,929	189,625
Chaffee	2,621	13,227
Cheyenne	4,636	2,153
Clear Creek	1,030	7,308
Conejos	3,338	7,794
Costilla	3,190	3,071
Crowley	2,054	2,988
Custer	1,924	1,528
Delta	2,967	21,225
Denver	288	492,365
Dolores	2,766	1,658
Douglas	2,187	25,153
Eagle	4,394	13,320
El Paso	5,535	309,424
Elbert	4,813	6,850
Fremont	3,999	28,676
Garfield	7,675	22,514
Gilpin	387	2,441
Grand	4,820	7,475
Gunnison	8,419	10,689
Hinsdale	2,899	408
Huerfano	4,118	6,440
Jackson	4,196	1,863
Jefferson	1,997	371,753
Kiowa	4,571	1,936
Kit Carson	5,616	7,599
La Plata	4,399	27,424
Lake	985	8,830
Larimer	6,770	149,184

contd

County	*area (sq km)*	*pop(1980)*
Las Animas	12,405	14,897
Lincoln	6,724	4,663
Logan	4,727	19,800
Mesa	8,603	81,530
Mineral	2,280	804
Moffat	12,303	13,133
Montezuma	5,299	16,510
Montrose	5,824	24,352
Morgan	3,318	22,513
Otero	3,242	22,567
Ouray	1,409	1,925
Park	5,699	5,333
Phillips	1,789	4,542
Pitkin	2,517	10,338
Prowers	4,235	13,070
Pueblo	6,180	125,972
Rio Blanco	8,377	6,255
Rio Grande	2,374	10,511
Routt	6,154	13,404
Saguache	8,234	3,935
San Juan	1,009	833
San Miguel	3,346	3,192
Sedgwick	1,404	3,266
Summit	1,578	8,848
Teller	1,453	8,034
Washington	6,552	5,304
Weld	10,374	123,438
Yuma	6,149	9,682

Colorado, river in SW USA; rises in the Continental Divide in the NW corner of Rocky Mountain National Park, N Colorado; flows generally SW through W Colorado and SE Utah, enters N Arizona through Marble Canyon and turns to flow W through the Grand Canyon; the river turns S at the Hoover Dam and forms part of the Nevada-Arizona border; the Colorado then continues S as the California-Arizona border, then the Arizona border with Mexico and finally forms part of the boundary between Baja California and Sonora before entering the Golfo de California; length 2,333 km; major tributaries: the Gunnison river (Colorado); the Green and San Juan rivers (Utah); the Little Colorado and Gila rivers (Arizona); the Virgin river (Nevada); the Colorado is used extensively for irrigation, flood-control and hydroelectric power as at the Hoover, Davis, Parker and Imperial dams.

Colorado, river in S USA; rises in the Llano Estacado in NW Texas; flows generally SE through Texas, past Austin to enter Matagorda Bay and the Gulf of Mexico; length 1,438 km, major tributaries: the Concho, San Saba and Llano rivers; used for flood-control, hydroelectricity and irrigation.

Colorado Desert, depressed arid region in SE California and N Baja California, United States; area estimated at between 5,180 and 7,770 sq km; situated W of the Colorado river, NW of the Gulf of California and S of the Mojave Desert; crossed by scattered mountain ranges; contains the Salton Sea, a shallow saline lake, situated 71 m below sea-level; the desert is part of the Great Basin.

Colorado, Río, *ree'ō ko-lo-ra'dō*, river, S central Argentina, formed by union of the Río Barrancas and the Río Grande (which rise in the Andes on the Chile border) on Mendoza-Neuquén prov border; flows 860 km SE across N Patagonia along the borders of Mendoza-Neuquén and La Pampa-Río Negro provs to the Atlantic where it forms a delta 130 km S of Bahía Blanca; with the Río Grande it is 1,140 km long.

Colorado Springs, 38 50N 104 49W, pop(1980) 215,150, county seat of El Paso county, central Colorado, United States; a residential and resort city at the foot of Pikes Peak, 102 km S of Denver; university; railway; the nearby mineral springs make it a popular health resort; also nearby is the US Air Force Academy; event: Easter Sunrise Service.

Colquiri *kol-kee'ree*, CENTRO MINERO COLQUIRI, 17 22S 67 08W, pop(1976) 15,350, town in Inquisivi prov, La Paz, Bolivia; economy: this mining centre, once famous for silver and tin, now produces zinc.

Columbia, river in W North America, in NW United States and SW Canada; rises in the Rocky Mts in E British Columbia; flows NW through McNaughton Lake then S through Upper Arrow Lake and Arrow Lake and into Washington state, USA; the Columbia then flows S past Coulee Dam, then W and SE past Richland and Pasco; it is joined by the Snake river near the Washington-Oregon border where it turns W to form the boundary between these 2 states; passes through Portland, Oregon to enter the Pacific Ocean at Cape Disappointment, SW of Tacoma; length 1,953 km; major tributaries include the Kootenai, Clark Fork, Spokane, Okanogan, Yakima, Snake, Umatilla, John Day, Deschutes and Williamette rivers; the river has many rapids and falls along its length, and has cut a gorge through the Cascade range to the E of Portland; the river is a source of irrigation water and hydroelectric power.

Columbia, 38 57N 92 20W, pop(1980) 62,061, county seat of Boone county, central Missouri, United States; 43 km N of Jefferson City; university (1839); railway.

Columbia, 34 00N 81 03W, pop(1980) 101,208, capital of state in Richland county, central South Carolina, United States; at the confluence of the Broad and Saluda rivers which join to form the R Congaree; settled in the early 1700s, it became state capital in 1786 and achieved city status in 1854; 2 universities (1801, 1870); railway; airfield; economy: commercial and trading centre in a rich farming area; printing; manufactures include textiles, plastics, electrical equipment and machinery.

Columbia, 35 37N 87 02W, pop(1980) 26,372, county seat of Maury county, central Tennessee, United States; on the R Duck, 65 km SSW of Nashville; railway; economy: trade and processing centre for beef cattle and tobacco; shipping point for the region's limestone and phosphate deposits; monument: James K. Polk House (1816).

Columbus, 32 28N 84 59W, pop(1980) 169,441, county seat of Muscogee county, W Georgia, United States; port on the R Chattahoochee, 128 km WSW of Macon; important Confederate centre during the Civil War; captured by Federal troops a week after General Lee's surrender at Appomattox; railway; airfield; economy: textiles, iron, processed food, chemicals, and concrete and wood products.

Columbus, 39 13N 85 55W, pop(1980) 30,614, county seat of Bartholomew county, S Indiana, United States; on the E Fork of the R White, 54 km E of Bloomington; railway.

Columbus, 33 30N 88 25W, pop(1980) 27,383, county seat of Lowndes county, E Mississippi, United States; on the R Tombigbee, 130 km N of Meridian; university; railway; airfield; economy: trade, processing and shipping centre for cotton, livestock, dairy and timber region; marble quarrying nearby.

Columbus, 39 58N 83 00W, pop(1980) 564,871, capital of state in Franklin county, central Ohio, United States; at the confluence of the Olentangy and Scioto rivers; laid out in 1812 opposite the earlier settlement of Franklinton; capital of the state since 1824 and a city since 1834; 3 universities (1850, 1870, 1902); railway; airforce base; economy: electronics, machinery, fabricated metals, food products, stone, clay and glass products; major aircraft and automobile parts supplier; important centre for research in science and information technology; monuments: Centre of Science and Industry, Ohio Historical Centre, Ohio Railway Museum, Ballet Metropolitan.

Colwyn Bay, 53 18N 3 43W, pop(1981) 27,683, resort town in Colwyn dist, Clwyd, NE Wales; railway; economy: light engineering; event: annual fishing festival.

Coma Pedrosa *kō'ma pay-dro'sa*, mountain peak in the E central Pyrenees on the N border of the Principality of Andorra with France; height 2,946 m; highest peak in Andorra.

Comayagua *ko-ma-yah'gwa*, dept in central Honduras, Central America; pop(1983e) 211,465; area 5,193 sq km; capital Comayagua.

Comayagua, 14 30N 87 39W, pop(1983e) 28,121, capital town of Comayagua dept, Honduras, 120 km NW of Tegucigalpa; former capital of Honduras until 1870; the first university in Central America was founded here in 1632 but later closed in 1842; monument: cathedral (1685-1715).

Comber, AN COMAR (Gael), 54 33N 5 45W, pop(1981) 7,600, town in Ards dist, Down, SE Northern Ireland; near the head of Strangford Lough, 13 km ESE of Belfast; economy: whisky distilling, engineering.

Combin, Grand, 45 57N 7 18E, peak in Pennine Alps, SW Switzerland; 1 km N of Italian border, 16 km SE of Orsières; height 4,314 m.

Comilla *koo-mil'lu*, KUMILLA, region in SE Bangladesh; includes Brahmanbaria, Chandpur and Comilla districts; pop(1981) 6,881,000; area 6,599 sq km; bounded E by the Tripuria district of Assam, India; capital Comilla.

Comilla, 23 28N 91 10E, pop(1981) 184,132, capital of Comilla dist, Comilla, E Bangladesh; lies E of Dhākā and close to the border with the Tripuria district of Assam, India in the E; linked by rail to Chittagong in the SE; airfield; trade in tobacco, rice, jute, oilseed, sugar cane; manufacture of metal products and soap.

Comino *ko-mee'no*, 36 00N 14 20E, the smallest of the three main islands of the Maltese group, Comino lies midway between Malta and Gozo and is separated from the main island of Malta by the South Comino Channel; area 2.7 sq km; the island, which is a 20-minute boat trip from the main island, has one hotel and no cars; the highest point is 247 m; the chief attraction is the Blue Lagoon; until the 1700s the island was noted as a harbour for pirates.

Commewijne *ko-ma-vī'na*, coastal dist in NE Surinam, NE South America; bounded N by the Atlantic; area 4,110 sq km; pop(1980) 14,351; capital Nieuw Amsterdam.

Como *kō'mō*, prov of Lombardia region, N Italy; pop(1981) 775,979; area 2,067 sq km; capital Como.

Como, 45 49N 9 06E, pop(1981) 95,571, capital town of Como prov, Lombardia region, NW Italy; at the SW end of L Como, surrounded by rocky heights, partly forest-covered; railway; the old town is still mostly encircled by its medieval wall, and there are some Roman remains; economy: silk, motor cycles, glass, furniture, tourism; monuments: town walls; marble cathedral (1396), remodelled in Renaissance style (1487-1596); 11th-c twin-towered church of Sant'Abbondio, modernized in 1587.

Como, Lago di or **Lario**, LAKE COMO (Eng), LARIUS LACUS (anc), narrow fjord-like lake in Como prov, Lombardia region, N Italy; 50 km N of Milan, at the foot of the Bernese Alps; area 146 sq km; length 50 km; at its half-way point, between Menaggio and Varenna, it is 4 km wide; max depth 410 m, deepest of the N Italian lakes; formed by the expansion of the R Adda, which enters at its N and issues at its SE extremity; the promontory of Bellagio divides it into 2 branches, the SW arm, with the town of Como at its S end, and the SE arm, the Lago di Lecco, with the outflow of the R Adda; surrounded by mountains, rising to 2,610 m in Monte Legnone, on whose slopes are plantations of chestnuts and walnuts; lake resorts include Tremezzo and Menaggio; on the SW arm there are numerous villas surrounded by beautiful gardens and vineyards.

Comodoro Rivadavia *kō-mō-dō'rō ree-va-dav'ya*, 45 50S 67 30W, pop(1980) 96,865, seaport and largest city in Chubut prov, Patagonia, S Argentina; 396 km S of Trelew, on the Golfo San Jorge, on the Atlantic coast; university (1961); railway; airfield; natural gas pipeline is linked to Buenos Aires; economy: oil (discovered 1907), petrochemicals; local holidays: 28 July (Founding of Chubut in 1901), 13 Dec (Petroleum Day).

Comoé *ko-mō'ay*, national park, largely in Bouna dept, NE

Ivory Coast; crossed by a river of the same name; area 11,500 sq km; established in 1968.

Comoros *ke-mor'ōs*, official name Federal Islamic Republic of the Comoros, REPUBLIQUE FÉDÉRALE ISLAMIQUE DES COMORES, group of 3 volcanic islands at the N end of the Mozambique Channel between Mozambique and Madagascar; area 1,862 sq km; timezone GMT +3; pop(1980) 356,000; capital and largest city Moroni; Antalote, Cafre, Makoa, Oimatsaha and Sakalava are the main ethnic groups derived from separate waves of immigration from Africa, Arabia, Indonesia and Madagascar; the majority of the population speak Kiswahili, but French and Arabic are also spoken; over 85% of the pop are Shirazi Muslims, the remainder are Roman Catholic; the currency is the franc CFA of 100 cents; membership of AfDB, FAO, G-77, IBRD, IDA, IDB, IFAD, ILO, IMF, ITU, NAM, OAU, OIC, UN, UNESCO, UPU, WHO, WMO.

History, government and constitution. Between 1843 and 1912 France gained control of Grande Comore, Anjouan, Mohéli and Mayotte islands which were placed under the authority of the governor of Madagascar. French companies and Arab merchants established a plantation-based economy producing export crops. In 1947 the islands became a French overseas territory and internal political autonomy was granted in 1961. Agreement was reached with France in 1973 for the eventual independence of Comoros by 1979, but in 1975 the Comoran parliament declared unilateral independence. The island of Mayotte decided to remain under French administration. A constitution was approved by referendum in 1978 establishing the Comoros as a Federal Islamic Republic. As Head of State, the president is elected for a 6-year term. He appoints a prime minister and up to 9 other ministers who collectively form the Council of Government. There is a 39-member unicameral Federal Assembly directly elected every 5 years. Each of the 3 islands is administered by a governor who is nominated by the president and is assisted by 4 commissioners and an elected legislative council.

Economy. Vanilla, copra, cacao, sisal, coffee, cloves, vegetable oils and perfume are the most important products traded chiefly with France, Madagascar, Kenya, Italy, W Germany, Tanzania and the USA.

Administrative divisions. The Comoros group comprises 3 islands:

Island	*area (sq km)*	*pop(1980)*
Grande Comore (Njazidja)	1,148	189,000
Mohéli (Mwali)	290	19,000
Anjouan (Nzwami)	424	148,000

Compton, 33 54N 118 13W, pop(1980) 81,286, city in Los Angeles county, SW California, United States; 19 km S of Los Angeles.

Conakry *ko'nu-kree*, 9 30N 13 43W, pop(1980) 763,000, seaport capital of Guinea, W Africa; on Tumbo island, 710 km SE of Dakar (Senegal) and 130 km NNW of Freetown (Sierra Leone); linked to the mainland by a causeway; established in 1889; technical college (1963); railway terminus; airport; economy: textiles, trade in fruit, iron ore, alumina.

Concepción *kon-sep-syōn'*, 36 49S 73 03W, pop(1982) 206,107, industrial capital of Concepción prov, and Bío-Bío region, central Chile; situated 15 km up the Río Bío-Bío; 3rd largest city in Chile; founded in 1550, it has had to move site more than once because of earthquakes; university (1919); railway; airfield (Carriel Sur) just outside the town centre; economy: coal, steel (Huachipato), textiles, paper, oil refining, ship repairing; SE of the city is the Cerro Caracol with two good viewing points at the Mirador Chileno and the Mirador Alemán; event: craft fair in the Parque Ecuador (Feb).

Concepción *kon-sep-syōn'*, dept in Oriental region, E central Paraguay; bordered E by Brazil along the Río Apa; bounded W by the Río Paraguay, S by the Río Ypané; consists mainly of marshy lowland; pop(1982) 135,068; area 18,051 sq km; capital Concepción.

Concepción, 23 22S 57 26W, pop(1982) 22,866, capital of Concepción dept, Oriental, N central Paraguay; on E bank of the Río Paraguay; railway; economy: free port for Brazil and trade centre of N Paraguay.

Concepción, La, pop(1980) 10,823, town in Chiriquí prov, W Panama, Central America; close to the Costa Rican border, 21 km NW of David; on the Inter-American Highway.

Concord, 37 59N 122 02W, pop(1980) 103,255, city in Contra Costa county, W California, United States; 27 km NE of Oakland, just S of Suisun Bay; railway.

Concord, 42 28N 71 21W, pop(1980) 16,293, town in Middlesex county, E Massachusetts, United States; on the R Concord, 28 km WNW of Boston; railway; in April 1775 British soldiers attempted to seize military stores in Concord but were resisted by minutemen, resulting in battles at Concord and Lexington, which marked the start of the American War of Independence.

Concord, 43 12N 71 32W, pop(1980) 30,400, capital of state in Merrimack county, S New Hampshire, United States; on the R Merrimack, 24 km N of Manchester; established in 1727, achieving town status in 1784 and city status in 1853; state capital since 1808; New Hampshire Technical Institute (1964); railway; economy: electrical goods.

Concordia *kon-kor'dya*, 31 25S 58 00W, pop(1980) 93,618, port in Entre Rios prov, Litoral, E Argentina; on R Uruguay; racecourse; railway; economy: agriculture, fishing, trade in grain and citrus.

Coney Island *kō'nay* (Dutch, 'rabbit'), resort on the S coast of Long Island in Brooklyn borough, New York state, United States; situated S of New York City, near the mouth of the Hudson river; part of Long Island since the silting up of Coney Island Creek; developed as a pleasure resort since the 1840s.

Congleton *kong'gl-ton*, 53 10N 2 13W, pop(1981) 23,590, town in Congleton dist, Cheshire, NW central England; on the R Dane, 18 km NE of Crewe; railway; economy: textiles, clothing, plastics, electrical goods, engineering.

Congo *kong'gō*, official name People's Republic of the Congo, RÉPUBLIQUE POPULAIRE DU CONGO (Fr), a W central African republic bounded W by Gabon, NW by Cameroon, N by the Central African Republic, E and S by Zaire and SW by the Atlantic Ocean; the country encloses, bar its Atlantic Ocean coast, the Angolan prov of Cabinda; timezone GMT +1; area 341,945 sq km; pop(1984e) 1,745,000; capital Brazzaville; chief towns Pointe-Noire (major port), Loubomo and N'Kayi; the pop comprises about 75 tribes, almost all of Bantu origin, and about 15 main ethnic groups, the most important being the Kongo (48%) in the S, Sangha (20%) and M'Bochi (12%) in the N, and Téké (17%) in the central area; there are a number of Europeans, mainly French; half the pop are Christian (40.5% Roman Catholic and 9.5% Protestant), most of the remainder follow local beliefs (47%) or are Muslims (3%); the official language is French; the unit of currency is the franc CFA; national holiday 15 Aug; membership of AfDB, Conference of East and Central African States, EAMA, ECA, EIB (associate), FAO, G-77, GATT, IBRD, ICAO, ICO, IDA, IFAD, IFC, ILO, IMF, IMO, INTELSAT, INTERPOL, ITU, NAM, OAU, UDEAC, UN, UNESCO, UPU, WFTU, WHO, WIPO and WMO.

Physical description. The Congo has a short Atlantic coastline fringing a broad mangrove plain that rises inland to a ridge of mountains reaching 900 m. Lakes Tchibende and Tchimba are located on this coastal plain and the Kouilou R runs SW across it, to enter the Atlantic Ocean near Madingo-Kayes. The R Ogooué (Gabon's main river) rises in this area and flows N. The inland mountain ridge is deeply cut by the R Congo which flows SW to the coast. Beyond the ridge the Niari valley rises up through terraced hills to reach a height of 1,040 m at Mont de la Lékéti on the Gabon frontier. The N is a tilted basin drained by rivers such as the Alima and

the Sangha flowing E and S to meet the Oubangui and Congo rivers which form the country's E and S borders. Dense grassland, mangrove and forest cover most of the country.
Climate. The Congo experiences a hot, humid equatorial climate with an annual rainfall totalling 1,250-1,750 mm. Rainfall decreases near the Atlantic coast and in the S. Temperatures vary little, with average max daily temperatures at Brazzaville ranging between 28°C and 33°C. There is a distinct dry season between June and Sept and a less marked one in Jan.
History, government and constitution. Although the Portuguese visited the coast of the Congo in the 14th century it was the French who eventually penetrated further inland establishing trading posts and a colonial presence in the 19th century. As part of French Equatorial Africa from 1908 to 1958, it was known as the 'Middle Congo'. In 1959 the Congo became a member of the French community and in the following year it became an independent republic. The country's first president was removed after a coup in 1963 and in 1968 a second coup introduced a military leadership which created a one-party Marxist-Leninist state, renaming the country the People's Republic of the Congo. This was the first Marxist state to be established in Africa. The constitution of 1979 restored democracy and provided for an executive president elected for a 5-year term. He is assisted by a Council of Ministers. In addition there is a Central Committee of 60 members and a National Assembly of 153 members.
Economy. Agriculture and forestry have been the traditional basis of the economy. Cash crops include sugar cane, coffee, cocoa, palm oil, tobacco and groundnuts, while the main subsistence crops include manioc, rice, yams, potatoes, maize and bananas. Until 1973 timber was the main source of export income but since then 90% of income has been derived from oil exports. Diamonds, potash and cement are also extracted and produced in significant quantities. Industry is centred around oil refining, timber processing, brewing, sugar refining and soap manufacture. The main trading partners include France, Brazil, West Germany, the USA, Italy, Spain and Japan.
Administrative divisions. The Congo is divided into 9 provinces:

Province	*area (sq km)*	*pop(1980)*
Kouilou	13,694	261,370
Niari	25,942	137,210
Bouenza	12,265	161,320
Lékoumou	20,950	62,730
Pool	34,000	208,420
Bafuru Plateau	38,400	102,670
Cuvette	74,850	121,470
Sangha	55,800	41,360
Likouala	66,044	31,930

Congo, river in central and W Africa; one of the world's major rivers and, at about 4,670 km in length, the 2nd longest in Africa after the Nile; area of basin 3,755,000 sq km (second only to the Amazon, S America); rises as the R Lualaba, which drains L Deleommune (S Zaire), and flows N passing Bukama, Kongolo, Kindu, Ubundu

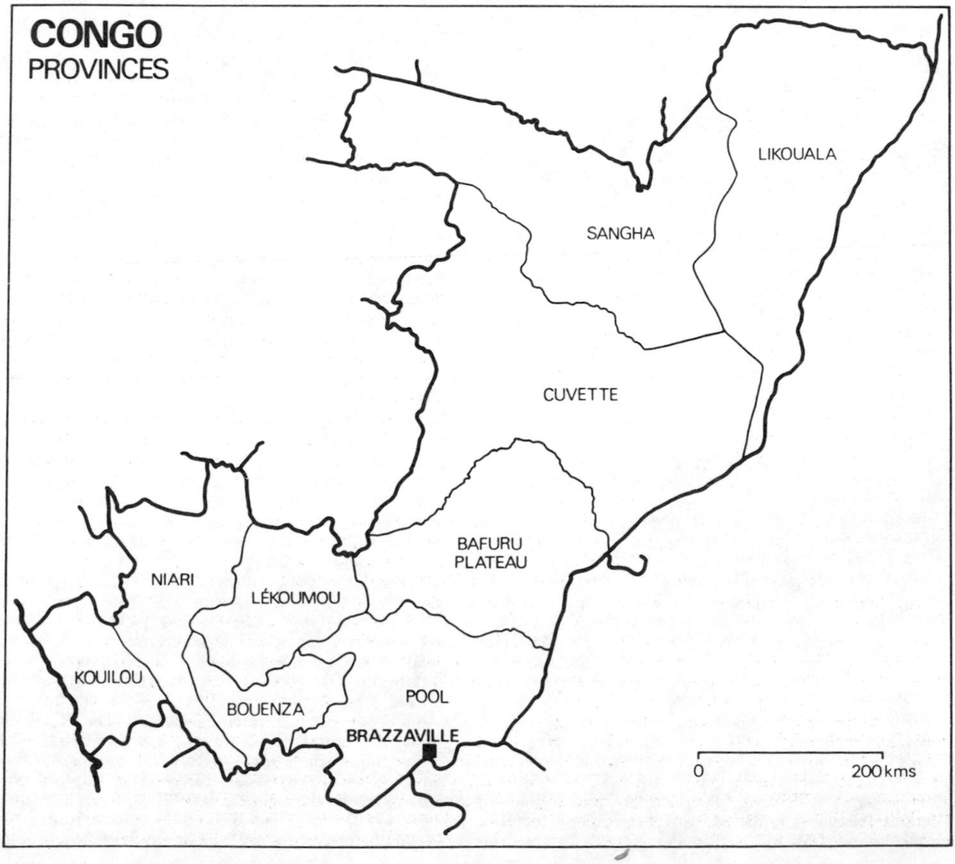

(Pontierville); SE of Kisangani (Stanleyville) it crosses the equator; known from here as the R Zaire it proceeds NW past Basoko and flows in an arc across central Africa past Lisala and Mbandaka; SW of Mbandaka it is known as the R Congo as it re-crosses the equator and is joined from the N by one of its two major tributaries, the Oubangui (which, for the latter part of its course, forms the frontier between NE Congo and Zaire), and forms the frontier between SE Congo and Zaire; flowing SW it passes Bolobo and then receives its other major tributary, the R Kasai, from the E; continues SW with the Congolese and Zairian capitals of Brazzaville and Kinshasa on opposite banks; as the river leaves the edge of the central African plateau it flows through a narrow trench in the Crystal Mountains into the extreme W of Zaire, passes Matadi and Bomi before entering the Atlantic Ocean SSE of Pointe-Noire and W of Bomi; below Matadi it forms the frontier between Zaire and Angola; the ocean tide affects the river for 100 km upstream; the Congo is unusual amongst equatorial rivers in its perennial flow which results from its receiving tributaries from both the N and S hemispheres; the first European discovery of the mouth of the river was made by the Portuguese explorer, Diogo Cão, in 1482 who named it Zaire (corruption of local *zadi* or *great water*); a British explorer, Captain J.K. Tuckey, whilst searching for the source of the Nile in 1816 reached Isangila; between 1866 and 1877 David Livingstone explored the Mweru (Zaire-Zambia frontier) and Bangweulu (Zambia) lakes and reached the Lualaba; Henry M. Stanley associated the Lualaba with the Congo during a major exploration which began at Nyangwe (Zaire) in 1874 and finished at Boma in 1877.

Con'isbrough, 53 29N 1 13W, pop(1981) 16,111, coal-mining town in Doncaster borough, South Yorkshire, N England; 8 km SW of Doncaster; railway; monument: 12th-c Norman castle, the site of Sir Walter Scott's novel *Ivanhoe*.

Con'iston Water, lake in the Lake District of Cumbria, NW England; W of L Windermere and the Grizedale Forest; length 9 km; the village of Coniston lies on the NW shore; on the E shore is Brantwood, the former home of John Ruskin who is buried at Coniston; the Old Man of Coniston rises to 802 m in the W; Sir Malcolm Campbell set up a world water speed record of 141.7 mph on the lake in 1939; Donald Campbell lost his life here in 1967 trying to break the water speed record.

Conn, Lough, *loKH kon*, lake in Mayo county, Connacht, Irish Republic; situated W of the Ox Mountains (Ox Mts); connected to L Cullin.

Connacht *ko'not*, CONNAUGHT, prov in W Irish Republic; comprises the counties of Sligo, Leitrim, Mayo, Roscommon, Galway; bounded NE by Ulster, E by Leinster and S by Clare provs; pop(1981) 424,410, area 17,121 sq km; chief towns include Sligo, Galway and Castlebar.

Connah's Quay, 53 13N 3 03W, pop(1981) 14,756, town in Alyn and Deeside dist, Clwyd, NE Wales; in Connah's Quay-Shotton urban area; airfield; railway; economy: light engineering.

Connaught, prov in Irish Republic. See Connacht.

Connecticut *kon-e'ti-kut*, a New England state in NE United States, bounded W by New York, N by Massachusetts, E by Rhode Island and S by Long Island Sound; the 'Constitution State' or the 'Nutmeg State'; pop(1980) 3,107,576; area 12,667 sq km; one of the original states of the Union, 5th to ratify the Federal Constitution; capital Hartford; other major cities include Bridgeport, New Haven, Waterbury and Stamford; the R Connecticut in the centre, R Housatonic to the W and R Thames in the E flow S through the state to empty into Long Island Sound; the highest point is Mt Frissell (725 m); the coast is predominantly urbanized but the interior is mainly woodland and forest with some cropland producing dairy produce, poultry and tobacco; explored by Adriaen Block in 1614; the state is divided into 8 counties as follows:

County	*area (sq km)*	*pop(1980)*
Fairfield	1,643	807,143
Hartford	1,921	807,766
Litchfield	2,395	156,769
Middlesex	970	129,017
New Haven	1,586	761,337
New London	1,739	238,409
Tolland	1,071	114,823
Windham	1,339	92,312

Connemara *kon-i-ma'ra*, mountainous region in W Galway county, Irish Republic; W of L Corrib; rocky coastline with mountains rising to 765 m at Croagh Patrick in the Twelve Bens.

Con'sett, 54 51N 1 49W, pop(1981) 22,904, town in Derwentside dist, Durham, NE England; 20 km SW of Newcastle upon Tyne; economy: engineering.

Constance, lake in southern W Germany, NE Switzerland and NW Austria. See Bodensee.

Constance, town in W Germany. See Konstanz.

Constance, Lake. See Bodensee.

Constanţa *kon-stan'tsa*, county in SE Romania; bordered by the R Danube (W), the Black Sea (E) and Bulgaria (S); pop(1983) 693,207; area 7,055 sq km; capital Constanţa.

Constanţa, CONSTAN'ZA (Eng), TOMIS, CONSTANTINIANA (anc), 44 10N 28 40E, pop(1983) 315,662, major port and capital of Constanţa county, SE Romania; situated on the W shores of the Black Sea; 3rd largest city in Romania; established in the 7th century BC as a Greek colony; under Roman rule from 72 BC; Ovid lived in exile here; the city was named after Constantine I (4th-c AD); ceded to Romania in 1878; airport; railway; economy: naval shipyards, tourism, textiles, foodstuffs, metal products, soap.

Constantine *kon'stun-teen*, CIRTA (anc), QACENTINA, 36 22N 6 40E, pop(1979e) 350,000, chief town of Constantine dept, NE Algeria, N Africa; 320 km ESE of Alger; the oldest city in Algeria, Constantine has been an important centre since the 3rd and 4th centuries BC; Roman provincial capital of Numidia; destroyed in 311 AD during civil war and rebuilt by Constantine I; seat of successive Muslim dynasties during the Middle Ages and prospered under Turkish rule during the 18th century; French occupation began in 1837; university (1969); railway; airport.

Contadora, Isla *kon-ta-dō'ra*, 8 40N 79 02W, island of Panama; in the Archipieago de las Perlas (Pearl Is), S of Panamá City in the Golfo de Panamá; meeting place of the foreign ministers of Colombia, Mexico, Panama and Venezuela (the Contadora Group) in January 1983 to discuss the economic and socio-political problems of Central America; the resulting solutions became known as the Contadora process.

Continental Divide, GREAT DIVIDE, a line of mountain peaks in North America extending SSE from NW Canada down the W United States into Mexico, Central America and South America where it meets the N end of the Andes; the line marks a watershed which separates west-flowing rivers from those which flow E or N; includes the Rocky Mts in Canada and the USA and the Sierra Madre ranges in Mexico.

Conwy, CONWAY, 53 17N 3 50W, pop(1981) 3,926, historic market town and resort in Aberconwy dist, Gwynedd, NW Wales; at head of Conwy river; economy: engineering, tourism.

Conwy, river in Gwynedd, NW Wales; rises in SW Aberconwy and flows 48 km N through the Vale of Conwy to meet the Irish Sea between Conwy and Llandudno.

Cooee, bay in Queensland state, E Australia; on the coast N of Rockhampton; named after the 'coo-ee', or call of the bushmen; event: annual cooeeing competition (Aug).

Cook Islands, widely scattered group of 15 volcanic and coral islands, centred some 3,200 km NE of New Zealand, S Pacific Ocean, between 8° and 23° S and 156°

and 167° W; the 15 islands of the Cook group include Rarotonga, Mangaia, Atiu, Mauke, Mitiaro, Aitutaki, Palmerston Atoll (Avaru), Penrhyn (Tongareva), Suwarrow (Suvorov), Manihiki (Humphrey I), Rakahanga (Rierson I), Pukapuka (Danger I), Nassau, Manuae, Te Au o tu (Hervey Is) and Takutea; a self-governing country in free association with New Zealand; area 238 sq km; the unit of currency is the New Zealand dollar; timezone GMT −10; capital Avarua; pop(1981) 17,754; 42% of the pop is 14 years of age and under, 52.9% is aged between 15 and 64 (inclusive), and 4.4% is 65 years and over; the population comprises 81.3% Polynesian, 7.7% Polynesian and European, 7.7% Polynesian and other, 2.4% European; Christianity is the dominant religion; English is the official language, with local languages widely spoken; membership of ADB, IDA, IFC, IMF.

Physical description and climate. The Cook Is comprise the Northern Group and the Southern Group. The islands of the Northern Group, except Nassau, are low lying coral atolls with central lagoons. Of the 9 islands of the Southern Group, Palmerston and Manuae are typical atolls, while tiny Takutea, like Nassau, is a low coral island without a central lagoon. The others are mainly volcanic with fringing coral reefs. The highest island, Rarotonga, rises to 650 m. The climate is damp and tropical, with rainfall heavy on the forested volcanic slopes of the S islands. The low lying outer islands are drier, and can even have severe water shortages. The hurricane season is from Nov to April.

History, government and constitution. The islands were placed under British protection between 1888 and 1901, becoming a New Zealand dependency in 1901. They became internally self-governing in 1965, although their association with New Zealand continues. There is an elected 22-member Legislative Assembly with a premier as head of state. An appointed High Commissioner represents the British sovereign and New Zealand interests.

Economy. Many of the islanders are subsistence farmers and fishermen. Export crops include copra, citrus fruits, pineapples, tomatoes, and bananas. Nearly 30% of the pop is engaged in agriculture and fishing industries, 27% engaged in community, social, and personal services, and 43% in other industries. Fruit processing is the main industry. Imports, which far outweigh exports, include foodstuffs, textiles, and fuels. The major trade partner is New Zealand. Tourism is the most rapidly growing industry, especially in the islands of Rarotonga and Aitutaki.

Cook, Mount, 43 37S 170 08E, mountain in W South Island, New Zealand; the highest peak in New Zealand, it rises to 3,764 m in the Southern Alps; the 944 sq km Mount Cook National Park was established in 1953; first ascent on 25 Dec 1894; the national park contains 22 of the 27 peaks in New Zealand which are over 3,050 m; the Tasman Glacier is 29 km long and 2 km wide.

Cook Strait, channel of the Pacific Ocean separating North Island from South Island, New Zealand; 32-130 km wide; discovered by Captain Cook in 1770.

Cookstown, AN CHORR CHRIOCHACH (Gael), 54 39N 6 45W, pop(1981) 7,649, town in Cookstown dist, Tyrone, central Northern Ireland; on the Ballinderry river, 73 km W of Belfast; founded in 1609; economy: textiles, engineering, food processing; monuments: to the S of Cookstown are the remains of Tullaghoge Fort, an early, ring-shaped Celtic fort with a rampart and a ditch; it was the centre for the O'Neill clan in the early Middle Ages.

Coon Rapids, 45 09N 93 19W, pop(1980) 35,826, town in Anoka county, SE Minnesota, United States; suburb on the Mississippi river, 20 km N of Minneapolis; railway.

Copán *kō-pan'*, dept in W Honduras, Central America, bounded W by Guatemala; pop(1983e) 217,258; area 3,200 sq km; capital Copán.

Copán, or **Santa Rosa de Copán**, 14 52N 89 10W, pop(1983e) 19,055, town in Copán dept, W Honduras; the ruins of a great Maya city dating from 800 AD are located W near Santa Rita, close to the Guatemalan frontier.

Copenhagen, capital city of Denmark. See København.

Copiapó *kō-pya-pō'*, 27 22S 70 20W, pop(1982) 65,001, mining centre and capital of Copiapó prov, and Atacama region, N Chile; on the Río Copiapó, set in an area of farms and orchards; railway; airfield; monuments: mineralogical museum containing many of the ores only found in the Atacama desert; there is a monument to Juan Godoy, a pioneer of the mining industry.

Copperbelt, prov in central Zambia, S central Africa; pop(1980) 1,248,888; area 31,328 sq km; watered by the Katwe and Lushwishi rivers; economic centre of Zambia because of vast copper and cobalt reserves; chief mines at Mufulira, Nkana and Chibuluma; capital Ndola; chief towns include Chilonga, Kitwe and Luanshya; a railway from Lusaka runs N and NW through the prov and into Shaba prov, Zaire.

Coquet *ko'ket*, river in Northumberland, NE England; rises on Carter Fell in the Cheviot Hills and flows 64 km NE to meet the North Sea near Amble.

Coquilhatville, town in Zaire. See Mbandaka.

Coquimbo *kō-keem'bō*, region of central Chile; borders with Argentina and the Andes (E); comprises the provs of Elquí, Limarí and Choapa; watered by Elquí, Limarí and Choapa rivers; to the W of the prov are irrigated river valleys; pop(1984) 437,200; area 40,656 sq km; capital La Serena; chief towns Ovalle and Coquimbo; economy: iron-ore mining, agriculture, fishing, tourism; Cerro Tololo, ESE of La Serena, is the largest astronomical observatory in the southern hemisphere; it contains five telescopes, the largest of which is 400 cm; W of Ovalle are the Fray Jorge and Valle del Encantado national parks; there is a pilgrimage on 25-26 Dec each year to Andacollo, SSE of Coquimbo, to the Shrine of the Virgín del Rosario de Andacollo where pre-Conquest dancing still takes place.

Coquimbo, 29 54S 71 25W, pop(1982) 71,079, port capital of Elquí prov, Coquimbo, central Chile; railway; economy: port trade, fishmeal; in 1981 heavy rain uncovered 39 ancient burials of humans and llamas which had been sacrificed, a small museum has been built to exhibit these.

Corabia *ko-ra'bya*, 43 46N 24 31E, pop(1983) 20,765, river port town in Olt county, S Romania; on R Danube, close to the Bulgarian frontier; railway terminus; economy: ceramics, textiles.

Coral Gables, 25 45N 80 16W, pop(1980) 43,241, residential town in Dade county, SE Florida, United States; on Biscayne Bay, 8 km SW of Miami; university (1925); railway.

Coral Sea, SOLOMON SEA, an arm of the Pacific Ocean bounded W by NE Australia, N by Papua New Guinea and the Solomon Is and E by the islands of Vanuatu and New Caledonia; the Tasman Sea lies to the S; there are many coral islands, small island groups of volcanic origin and submarine seamounts; the Lord Howe Seamounts form a central chain; island groups include the Willis Group, Coringa Is, Îles Chesterfield and the Marion Reef; reaches a max depth of 9,175 m in the New Hebrides Trench, between Vanuatu and New Caledonia; the Great Barrier Reef lies along its W edge.

Coral Sea Islands, Territory of the, uninhabited territory in the Coral Sea off the NE coast of Australia, administered by the Australian government since 1969, comprising scattered reefs and islands over a sea area of about 1 million sq km; timezone GMT +10; there is a manned meteorological station on Willis I; islands and reefs include the Great Barrier Reef, Lihou Reef and Cays, Mellish Reef, Marion Reef, Kenn Reef, Frederick Reef, Saumarez Reef, Wreck Reef, Bird I and Cato I.

Coral Springs, 26 14N 80 16W, pop(1980) 37,349, town in Broward county, SE Florida, United States; 24 km NNW of Fort Lauderdale.

Corazón *ko-ra-sōn'*, 0 35S 78 40W, Andean volcano in Pichincha prov, N central Ecuador; 40 km SSW of Quito; snow-capped twin peaks rise to 4,788 m; its crater lake contains sulphurous water.

Corbières *kor-byer*, sparsely populated upland dist in Aude dept, S France, lying between the Massif Central and the Pyrénées with its highest point at Pic de Bugarach (1,231 m); the lower-lying area is known for its full-bodied red wine; the chief locality is Quillan.

Cor'by, 52 29N 0 40W, pop(1981) 48,797, town in Corby dist, Northamptonshire, central England; 10 km N of Kettering; an enterprise zone, formerly based on steelworks which closed in 1980; railway; economy: engineering.

Corcovado *kor-kō-va'dō*, national park in SW Puntarenas prov, Costa Rica, Central America; located at the W end of Osa peninsula and includes also the Isla del Caño; the park was established in 1976 and covers an area of 418 sq km; it consists largely of tropical rainforest.

Cordillera, La *la kor-deel-yay'ra*, dept in Oriental region, W central Paraguay; bounded W and N by the Paraguay and Mandivurá rivers; in SW is L Ypacaraí; pop(1982) 194,826; area 4,948 sq km; capital Caacupé.

Córdoba *kor'dō-va*, prov in Centro region, central Argentina; a humid fertile pampa region with the Sierra de Córdoba in the W and salt marshes in the E and S; NE is the Mar Chiquita salt lake; NW is part of the Salinas Grandes salt desert; crossed by Primero, Segundo, Tercero, Cuarto and Cuinto rivers, some of which are used for irrigation and hydroelectric power; pop(1980) 2,407,754; area 168,766 sq km; capital Córdoba; chief towns Río Cuarto and Villa María; economy: maize, wheat, sheep and cattle raising, manganese, sand, basalt, limestone, marble and granite mining, motor vehicles, tourism.

Córdoba, 31 25S 64 11W, pop(1980) 968,664, capital of Córdoba prov, Centro, central Argentina; on the Río Primero, near the foothills of the Sierra de Córdoba; founded by Cabrera in 1573, Córdoba was renowned as a centre of the Jesuit missions; 3 universities, including Argentina's first university (founded in 1613); railway; airport (Pajas Blancas) 15 km from the city centre; economy: vehicles, textiles, cement, glass; local holidays: 6 July (Foundation of the City), 30 September (St Jerome).

Córdoba, dept in NW Colombia, South America; bounded N by the Caribbean; contains the lakes Ciénaga de los Zambos (E) and Ciénaga Grande (N); pop(1985) 878,738; area 25,020 sq km; capital Montería; economy: agriculture, cattle, tobacco, cacao, cotton, sugar.

Córdoba, 18 55N 96 55W, pop(1980) 126,179, city in Veracruz state, S Mexico; 95 km WSW of Veracruz, in the Sierra Madre Oriental; General Iturbe signed the Treaty of Córdoba here in 1821, freeing Mexico from Spanish colonial rule; railway; economy: coffee, sugar.

Córdoba or **Córdova**, prov in Andalucia region, S Spain; on the R Guadalquivir, crossed E-W by the Sierra Morena in the N; an undulating plain to the S; pop(1981) 717,213; area 13,718 sq km; capital Córdoba; economy: mining, forestry and pasture in the N and agric, olive-growing, vineyards, fruit and vegetables in the S; olive oil, pharmaceuticals, glass, paper, textiles.

Córdoba, 37 50N 4 50W, pop(1981) 284,737, capital of Córdoba prov, Andalucia, S Spain; on R Guadalquivir, 400 km SSW of Madrid; bishopric; airport; railway; economy: tourism, brewing and distilling, wine, olives, textiles, paper, tools, copper; monuments: Mezquita-Cathedral, old Jewish quarter, Moorish Alcazar; events: festival of los Patios Cordobeses in May with decoration of patios, flamenco, a pilgrimage in honour of the Virgen Conquistadora accompanied by highly decorated horse-drawn carriages; fair of Our Lady of la Salud in May and autumn fiestas in Sept with folk dancing.

Córdoba, Sierra de, mountain range of Argentina, largely in W Córdoba prov with outliers in San Luis, Tucumán and Santiago del Estero provs; extends 480 km N-S, covering c.29,800 sq km; comprises three parallel ridges running N-S: Sierra Chica (E), 88.5 km long and rising to 1,829 m; Sierra Grande (centre), 64 km long and rising to 2,330 m, continuing S as the Sierra de Comechingones, 80 km long and rising to 2,205 m; Sierra de Guasapampa (W), 72 km long and rising to 1,370 m, continuing S as the Sierra de Pocho, 64 km long and rising to 1,463 m; generally older than the Andes, the average height is 1,981 m and the highest peak Cerro Champaquí (2,880 m); drained by the rivers Primero, Segundo, Tercero and Cuarto.

Corfu, nome (dept), island, and town in Greece. See Kérkira.

Corinth, nome (dept) of Pelopónnisos region, Greece. See Kórinthos.

Corinto *kō-reen'tō*, formerly PUNTA ICACOS, 12 29N 87 14W, pop(1980e) 12,000, port in Chinandega dept, Nicaragua, Central America; S of Chinandega; chief Pacific port of Nicaragua; founded in 1840; railway; economy: trade in sugar, coffee, hides, timber.

Cork, CHORCAIGH (Gael), county and county borough, Munster, S Irish Republic; prosperous agricultural and industrial county bounded S by Atlantic Ocean and watered by the Lee, Bandon and Blackwater rivers; the Boggeragh and Nagles Mts rise to the NW and N of Cork; pop(1981) 402,465; area 7,459 sq km; capital Cork; supplies of natural gas and oil from fields off Kinsale Head with terminal facilities at Whiddy Island.

Cork CHORCAIGH (Gael), 51 54N 8 28W, pop(1981) 149,792, commercial seaport, county borough and capital of Cork county, Munster, S Irish Republic; on R Lee near its mouth on Lough Mahon; 3rd largest city in Ireland; docks and ferry terminal 4 km downstream; University College Cork (1845); airport; railway, ferries; economy: shipbuilding, brewing, tanning, food processing; monuments: St Finbar's cathedral (built on the site of the original church built by Cork's patron saint), Shandon church, St Mary's cathedral; events: cattle shows in Feb; international folk dance and choral festival.

Corner Brook, 48 58N 57 58W, pop(1981) 24,339, city in Newfoundland, E Canada; on the W coast of the island of Newfoundland at the head of the Bay of Islands and near the mouth of the R Humber; railway; economy: paper, iron, gypsum, cement.

Cornwall, 45 02N 74 45W, pop(1981) 46,144, town in SE Ontario, SE Canada; on the St Lawrence river, at the SW end of L St Francis; on the Canada-USA border; in the 1870s Thomas A. Edison set up the first plant for lighting a factory by electricity in one of Cornwall's cotton mills; railway; canal; connected by bridge with the USA; headquarters of the St Lawrence Seaway; economy: hydroelectric power, furniture, textiles, chemicals, paper; the pop is one-half French-speaking, one-half English-speaking.

Cornwall, county on the Caribbean I of Jamaica; W of Middlesex county to the W of the island; comprises the parishes of Hanover, Westmorland, St Elizabeth, St James, and Trelawny; area 3,912 sq km; pop(1982) 528,781; chief town Montego Bay.

Cornwall or **Cornwall and Isles of Scilly**, county in SW England; includes the Scilly Isles; bounded S by the English Channel, N by Devon and W by the Atlantic Ocean; pop(1981) 432,240; area 3,564 sq km; county town Truro; economy: tin mining, livestock, fishing, tourism; the county is divided into 6 districts and the Isles of Scilly:

District	*area (sq km)*	*pop(1981)*
Caradon	664	68,169
Carrick	461	76,629
Isles of Scilly	16	1,850
Kerrier	473	83,195
North Cornwall	1,195	64,464
Penwith	303	55,691
Restormel	452	79,439

Coro *kō'rō*, 11 25N 69 42W, pop(1980) 1,000, capital of Falcón state, NW Venezuela; on the Gulf of Coro, an inlet of the Caribbean; founded in 1527; railway; airfield; economy: timber, salt, coal, distilling.

Coroa *ko-rō'a*, 41 55N 6 52W, mountain, NW of Bragança near Spanish border, NE Portugal, rising to 1,273 m.

Corona, 33 53N 117 34W, pop(1980) 37,791, city in Riverside county, SW California, United States; 21 km SW of Riverside; railway.

Coronel *ko-ro-nel'*, 36 59S 73 10W, pop(1982) 49,257, port in Concepción prov, Bío-Bío, central Chile; just S of Concepción, in the heart of a coal-mining dist; railway; scene of British naval engagement with a German squadron under von Spee in 1914.

Coronel Oviedo *ko-ro-nel' ō-vyay'dō*, 25 24S 56 30W, pop(1982) 21,782, capital of Caaguazú dept, Oriental, E Paraguay.

Coronie *ko-rō'nee-a*, dist in NW Surinam, NE South America; bounded N by the Atlantic; area 1,620 sq km; pop(1980) 2,777; capital Totness.

Coropuna, Nevado *nay-va'dō kō-rō-poo'na*, snow-capped Andean massif, Arequipa dept, S Peru; in the Cordillera Occidental, 29 km N of Chuquibamba; has several peaks, the highest rising to 6,425 m.

Çorovodë *cho-ro-vo'de*, 40 30N 20 12E, town and capital of Skrapar prov, S central Albania; 32 km SE of Berat, on the R Osum; economy: lignite mining.

Corozal *cor-ō-zahl'*, dist in N Belize, Central America; bounded N and NW by Mexico; pop(1980) 22,902; area 1,859 sq km; capital Corozal; economy: sugar, fruit-growing.

Corozal, 18 23N 88 23W, pop(1980) 6,899, chief town of Corozal dist, Belize, Central America; SW of Chetumal; on Corozal Bay, an inlet of the Bahía Chetumal; airfield; economy: light industry.

Corpus Christi, 27 47N 97 24W, pop(1980) 231,999, county seat of Nueces county, S Texas, United States; a port at the mouth of the R Nueces where it meets Corpus Christi Bay; founded in 1839; university (1947); railway; airfield; economy: petroleum and natural gas centre; oil refining, chemicals, smelting, food processing, fishing (the port is the base for a large shrimp fleet).

Corrèze *kor-ez*, dept in Limousin region of central France, comprising 3 arrond, 36 cantons and 286 communes; pop(1982) 241,448; area 5,857 sq km; on the N boundary rise the Mts du Limousin, and from them 3 chains run S; watered by the Vézère and Corrèze rivers, and in the E by the Dordogne, which forms a section of the boundary between Corrèze and Cantal depts; capital Tulle, chief towns include Brive-la-Gaillarde and Ussel.

Corrib, Lough, *loKH ko'rib*, lake in Galway county, Connacht, W Irish Republic; drains into Galway Bay linked to L Mask (N); area 176 sq km; length 40 km; width 15 km.

Corrientes *kor-yen'tays*, prov in Litoral region, NE Argentina; bordered E by the Río Uruguay where it follows the Brazil and Uruguay border, N by the Río Alto Paraná along the Paraguay border and W by the Río Paraná and the provs of Chaco and Santa Fe; the prov includes the swampland of Esteros del Iberá; pop(1980) 661,454; area 88,199 sq km; capital Corrientes; chief towns Goya and Paso de los Libres; economy: tea, cotton, flax; cattle and sheep raising; basalt mining.

Corrientes, 27 30S 58 48W, pop(1980) 179,590, capital of Corrientes prov, Litoral, NE Argentina; port on Río Paraná opposite Barranqueras (Chaco prov); 40 km below the mouth of the Río Paraguay; founded in 1588 by Alonzo de Vera; site of Graham Greene's novel *The Honorary Consul*; 2 universities (1957, 1961); railway; airfield (Camba Punta) at 10 km; economy: tanning, sawmilling, textiles, vegetable oils.

Corriv'erton, SPRINGLANDS, 5 53N 57 10W, pop(1979e) 17,000, small port in E Berbice dist, NE Guyana, South America; near the mouth of the R Courantyne; daily ferry to and from Nieuw Nickerie (Surinam); although formerly called Springlands, the town is officially referred to as Corriverton as it has been joined with Skeldon to form the Courantyne (Correntyne) river town.

Corse *kors*, CORSICA (Eng) ('the scented isle'), mountainous island and region of France in the Mediterranean Sea, comprising the depts of Corse-du-Sud and Haute-Corse, 5 arrond, 52 cantons and 360 communes; pop(1982) 240,178; area 8,680 sq km; 183 km long by up to 84 km wide; separated from Sardinia to the S by the Strait of Bonifacio; France's largest island and 4th largest in the Mediterranean; the interior is mountainous, rising to 2,710 m at Mont Cinto; although in the W the mountains reach to the coast, in the E there are fertile alluvial plains, edged seawards with lagoons and swamps; it has 1,000 km of superb coastal scenery, with fine beaches, coves, gulfs and mountains rising sheer from the sea; there are numerous short streams, none navigable; the luxuriant growth of vegetation - forest, scrub (maquis), olive trees, orange-groves, vineyards and an abundance of flowers - led Napoleon, a native of the island, to say 'I would recognise Corsica with my eyes closed from its perfume alone'; tourism is important, with holiday activities including sailing, fishing, climbing, skin-diving in the waters around Cap Corse, canoeing in mountain rivers, and skiing at Vergio and Haut-Asco; there are car ferries from Nice, Toulon and Marseille and air services from Paris, Marseille and Nice; capital Ajaccio, chief towns Bastia, Calvi, Corte and Bonifacio; resorts include Propriano (bathing and health resort), Zicavo, Porto, Calvi and Ile-Rousse; an Italian dialect is spoken; economy: corks (Porto-Vecchio), asbestos workings at Canari, vines, olives and fruits, tourism; above the Gulf of Porto, between Porto and Piana, are to be found the curious rock formations known as the 'Calanches', which are granite pinnacles worn into bizarre forms resembling fabulous animals; near the village of Brando there is a stalactitic cave from which there is a fine view; includes the Parc de la Corse regional nature park, covering an area of 1,483 sq km.

Corse-du-Sud, dept in Corse region on the the Island of Corsica, France, comprising 2 arrond, 22 cantons and 124 communes; pop(1982) 108,604; area 4,014 sq km; a high mountain range (2,357 m) extends along the E boundary; many westward flowing rivers including the Gravone and Taravo have their source in these mountains; the W coastline is irregular with many capes and bays; capital Ajaccio.

Cor'sham, 51 26N 2 11W, pop(1981) 11,407, town in North Wiltshire dist, Wiltshire, S England; 6 km SW of Chippenham.

Corsica, France. See Corse.

Cortés *kor-tes'*, dept in NW Honduras, Central America; pop(1983e) 624,090; area 3,951 sq km; capital San Pedro Sula.

Cortez', 37 22N 108 36W, pop(1980) 7,095, town in Montezuma county, SW Colorado; on the R Mancos, S of Grand Junction; adjacent is the Mesa Verde National Park which features ancient cliff dwellings; nearby is the Ute Indian reservation.

Cortina d'Ampezzo, 46 33N 12 08E, tourist centre and winter sports resort in Belluno prov, Veneto region, N Italy, at the E end of the Strada delle Dolomiti, in a wide valley enclosed by the high peaks of the Alpi Dolomitiche (Dolomites); the Winter Olympics were held here in 1956; alt 1,224 m; event: International Sports Film Competition (beginning of March).

Çorum *cho-room'*, prov in N Turkey; pop(1980) 571,831; area 12,820 sq km; capital Çorum; economy: carpet manufacture and fruit-growing.

Coruña, La *la kor-oon'ya*, CORUNNA (Eng), prov in Galicia region, NW Spain; on the rocky indented Atlantic coast, containing the westernmost point in Spain (Cape Finisterre); pop(1981) 1,083,415; area 7,876 sq km; capital La Coruña; economy: mining, timber, food processing, clothes, electrical equipment, metal boxes, tinned fish, textiles.

Coruña, La, CARONIUM (anc), 43 20N 8 25W, pop(1981) 232,356, seaport and capital of La Coruña prov, Galicia, NW Spain; on a promontory on the Atlantic coast, 609 km NW of Madrid; divided into the old town (ciudad vieja) and the new town (ciudad nueva) or fishing quarter (pescaderia); railway, airport; car ferries to the Canary Is; watersports; burial place in San Carlos Gardens of Sir

John Moore (d.1809); economy: oil, iron and steel, shipbuilding, clothes, food canning, fish products, pharmaceuticals; monuments: Hercules Tower, church of Santiago; events: Holy Week; Fiesta of the Virgen del Carmen with procession of boats in July; Fiesta of Maria Pita in Aug and Galician Pilgrimage in Sept.

Corunna, Spanish prov. See Coruña.

Corval'lis, 44 34N 123 16W, pop(1980) 40,960, capital of Benton county, W Oregon, United States; on the Willamette river, 45 km SSW of Salem; founded in 1845; university (1858); railway.

Corvo or **Ilha do Corvo** *kor'voo*, CORVI MARINI (anc) ('crow island'), 39 35N 31 08W, pop(1981) 374, most northerly and smallest island of the Azores, Horta dist, Portuguese autonomous region of the Azores; 25 km from Santa Cruz das Flores, with an area of 17.5 sq km; 7 km long and up to 4.5 km wide; island is made up of the single extinct volcano, Monte Gordo (777 m); Vila Nova de Corvo is the only settlement; economy: stock-farming, fishing, woollens and the gathering of seaweed for the production of agar-agar (gelatine).

Cos, Greek island. See Kós.

Cosenza *ko-sent'sa*, prov of Calabria region, S Italy; pop(1981) 743,255; area 6,649 sq km; capital Cosenza.

Cosenza, 39 17N 16 16E, pop(1981) 106,801, agricultural market town and capital of Cosenza prov, NW Calabria region, S Italy; in the fertile Crati valley, W of La Sila range; archbishopric; railway; economy: textiles, agricultural trade.

Cospicua *ko-spee'kwa*, 35 53N 14 32E, pop(1983e) 9,855, community situated at the E end of the main island of Malta, facing Valletta on the opposite side of the Grand Harbour; with its neighbours, Vittoriosa and Senglea, often known as the 'Three Cities'.

Costa Blanca *blan'ka*, ('white coast'), the coastal resort regions of Murcia, Alicante and part of Almería provs, E Spain; on the Mediterranean coast extending S from Cabo San Antonio to the Punto Almerimar; situated between the Costa del Azahar in the N and the Costa de Almería; a good climate all year round attracts visitors in summer and winter.

Costa Brava *bra'va*, ('wild coast'), the Mediterranean coastal resort region of Cataluña, E Spain, lying to the N of the Costa Dorada.

Costa de Almería, coastal resort region on the Mediterranean coastline of Almería prov, S Spain, between the Costa Blanca to the N and the Costa del Sol to the W.

Costa de la Luz *dhay la loos*, ('coast of light'), resort region on the Atlantic coastline of Huelva and Cádiz provs, S Spain; extending from the mouth of the R Guadiana on the Portuguese border to the most southerly tip of Spain at Tarifa on the Strait of Gibraltar.

Costa de Lisboa or **Costa do Sol**, Atlantic coastline of Portugal between estuaries of R Tagus in the N and R Sado S of Lisboa; the chief resorts are at Cascais and Estoril.

Costa de Prata *pra'ta*, ('silver coast'), stretch of Atlantic coastline in Portugal between Cabo de Roca in the S and R Douro in the N; the chief resorts are at Espinho, Figueira da Foz and Vimeiro.

Costa del Azahar *dhayl az-a-KHar'*, ('orange-blossom coast'), Mediterranean coastal resort region of Castellón de la Plana and Valencia provs, E Spain; lying between the Costa Dorada in the N and the Costa Blanca in the S; the longest stretch of coast in Spain.

Costa del Sol *dhayl sol*, ('coast of the sun'), Mediterranean coastal resort region, Andalucia, S Spain, extending from the end of the Costa de Almería at Punto Almerimar to the most southerly point in Spain at Tarifa.

Costa do Algarve *do al-gar'vay*, S Atlantic coast of Portugal from Cabo de São Vincente in the W to R Guadiana on the Spanish border; the most popular tourist resort area in Portugal, with resorts at Luz de Lagos, Praia da Rocha, Praia do Carvoeiro, Armação de Pêra, Vilamoura.

Costa Dorada *do-ra'da*, ('golden coast'), Mediterranean coastal resort region S of the Costa Brava, Barcelona and Tarragona provs, E Spain, extending about 260 km.

Costa Dourada *do'oo-ra-da* ('golden coast'), Atlantic coastline of W Portugal between the Ponta da Arrifana and mouth of R Sado; the main resorts are Aljezur, Vila Nova de Milfontes and Porto Covo.

Costa Mesa *kos'ta may'sa*, 33 38N 117 55W, pop(1980) 82,562, city in Orange county, SW California, United States; near Newport Bay, 13 km S of Santa Ana.

Costa Rica *kos'ta ree'ka*, official name Republic of Costa Rica, REPÚBLICA DE COSTA RICA, 2nd smallest republic in Central America, bounded W by the Pacific Ocean, N by Nicaragua, E by the Caribbean, and SE by Panama; timezone GMT −6; area 51,022 sq km; capital San José; chief towns Cartago, Heredia, Liberia, Puntarenas, and Limón; pop(1983e) 2,403,781; pop growth rate 3.1% (1960-78); the pop is mainly of Spanish descent; West Indians predominate along the Caribbean coast; the majority of the people live in the Meseta Central around San José; Roman Catholicism is the dominant religion; Spanish is the official language, with a Jamaican dialect of English spoken around Limón; the unit of currency is the colón of 100 centavos; membership of CACM, Central American Democratic Community, FAO, G-77, IADB, IAEA, IBRD, ICAO, ICO, IDA, IDB, IFAD, IFC, ILO, IMF, IMO, INTELSAT, INTERPOL, IPU, ITU, IWC, NAMUCAR, OAS, ODECA, PAHO, SELA, UN, UNESCO, UPEB, UPU, WHO, WMO, WTO.

Physical description. A series of volcanic ridges form the backbone of Costa Rica, stretching from the Cordillera del Guanacaste in the NW through the Cordillera de Tilarán and the Cordillera Central to the Cordillera de Talamanca in the SE. Chirripó Grande (3,819 m) in the Cordillera de Talamanca is the highest peak in Costa Rica and S Central America. The most important structural depression within these highlands is the Meseta Central which covers an area of 5,200 sq km at an altitude of 800-1,400 m and is the economic heart of the country. The W part of this basin is drained by the Río Grande into the Pacific while the NE part is drained by the Río Reventazón through deep gorges into the Caribbean Sea. The lowlands of the Río San Juan on the Nicaraguan border continue S as far as Limón. Near the coast much of this land is swampy, but as the land rises humid tropical forest predominates. In NW Costa Rica,

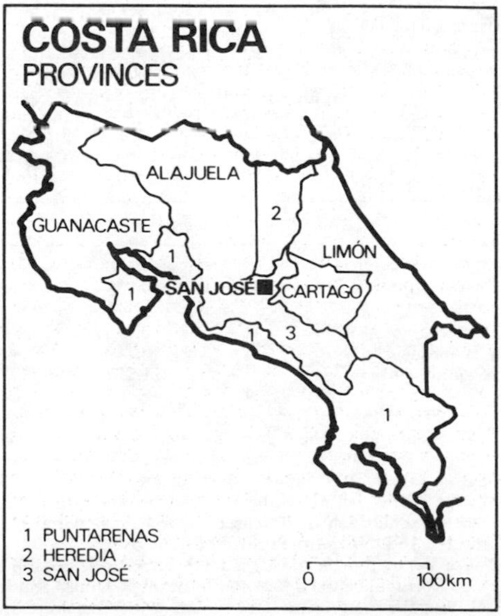

the waters of the Golfo de Nicoya separate the mountains of the mainland from those of the narrow Nicoya peninsula. A lowland savannah extends from just S of the mouth of the Río Grande de Tárcoles along the NE shore of the Golfo de Nicoya towards Nicaragua. The Río General flows through another structural depression in SW Costa Rica.

Climate. The climate is tropical, with a small range in temperature and abundant rainfall. More temperate conditions exist in the central upland areas. There is a dry season from Dec to May. Annual precipitation varies from 1,400 mm in the region of the Río Tempisque in NW Costa Rica to approx 8,000 mm in the Cordillera de Talamanca, with a country average of 3,300 mm. Average annual temperature varies between 26°C on the Atlantic coast and 27.8°C on the Pacific coast.

History, government and constitution. Columbus discovered Costa Rica on his 4th and final voyage to the Americas in 1502. It was named Costa Rica ('rich coast') in the belief that vast gold treasures existed. During the 16th century Spaniards settled in the Meseta Central which was already populated by sedentary Indian farmers. Independence from Spain was declared in 1821 and Costa Rica became a member of the Federation of Central America from 1824 until 1839. The armed forces were abolished in 1948. Costa Rica is a democratic republic governed by a legislative assembly of 57 deputies, elected for 4 years. Executive authority is vested in a president, also elected for 4 years, and a cabinet of 13 members.

Agriculture. Agriculture is the mainstay of the economy, employing almost one-third of the workforce and contributing just over 20% to the national income. The principal agricultural products are coffee, bananas, sugar, and cattle. The Meseta Central, with its rich volcanic soil, is the principal coffee-growing area. Costa Rica was at one time the world's second largest banana exporter but world surplus, high production costs, and increased export duties have led to bananas being replaced by oil palms. Intensive dairying and cattle raising are also important activities. A scheme is under way to divert water from the Laguna de Arenal in E Guanacaste prov to the relatively dry area at the head of the Golfo de Nicoya. It is intended that this shall be a major rice growing region. Timber and fishing also make an important contribution to the economy. Gold and silver deposits are worked in the Cordillera de Tilarán and the Osa peninsula. Bauxite deposits in the Boruca area are yet to be fully exploited. Petroleum exploration is concentrated in the Talamanca valley S of Limón in collaboration with the Mexican government. Manufacturing industry is based on food processing, textiles, fertilizers, plastics, pharmaceuticals and electrical equipment. Major trade partners include CACM countries, the UK, W Germany and the USA.

Administrative divisions. Costa Rica is divided into 7 provinces as follows:

Province	*area (sq km)*	*pop(1983e)*
San José	4,960	890,443
Alajuela	9,753	413,765
Cartago	3,125	259,916
Heredia	2,656	171,688
Guanacaste	10,141	228,249
Puntarenas	11,277	286,082
Limón	9,189	153,638

Communications. The Inter-American Highway crosses Costa Rica from the Nicaraguan border and progresses SE via Liberia, Las Cañas and Alajuela to San José and S to the border with Panama via Cartago and San Isidro del General. Juan Santamaría International Airport is located 16 km from the centre of San José.

Cos'ta Ver'de ('green coast'), stretch of Atlantic coastline in N Portugal between the mouths of the R Douro and R Minho; the main resorts are at Viana do Castelo, Ofir, Póvoa de Varzim, Moledo do Minho and Vila Praia de Ancora.

Costermansville, town in Zaire. See Bukavu.

Cotacachi *kō-ta-ka'chee*, 0 22N 78 22W, extinct Andean volcano in Imbabura prov, N Ecuador; rises to 4,939 m, 24 km W of Ibarra; it has several craters and crater lakes; L Cuicocha is to the S.

Côte d'Or, dept in Bourgogne region of central France, almost entirely on the W bank of the upper Saône R; comprises 3 arrond, 43 cantons and 705 communes; pop(1982) 473,548; area 8,763 sq km; the steep E escarpment of the Massif Central, below which lie Dijon and Beaune, runs NE across the E half of the dept; the Côte d'Or range runs into the hills of Beaujolais, to the Cévennes in the S and into the Ardennes and Vosges in the N; the Mts du Morvan run W towards their S end; W of the escarpment the land drops to the fertile river valley, yielding grain, hemp and market-garden produce; E of the escarpment is higher, well-wooded land, rich in iron and coal; there is some industry, chiefly around Dijon and Chatillon; notable burgundy wines from Beaune, Nuits St Georges and Gevrey Chambertin; capital Dijon, other towns include Beaune, Châtillon-sur-Seine and Montbard; the Parc de Morvan regional nature park lies partly within the dept; spa at Maizières; there are numerous châteaux including Thoisy (Renaissance), Commarin (15-18th-c) and Fontenay Abbey (12th-c).

Cotentin *kot-ã-tẽ*, dist forming a peninsula in the N part of Manche dept, NW France, jutting into the English Channel; an old Norman county, it is named after its former capital Coutances; chief locality is Cherbourg.

Côtes-du-Nord, dept in Bretagne region of W France, bounded on the N by the English Channel; comprises 4 arrond, 52 cantons and 369 communes; a range of hills, rising to 340 m, extends W-E across the S half of the dept; drained by the northward flowing Trieux and Rance rivers; pop(1982) 538,869; area 6,877 sq km; capital Saint-Brieuc.

Cotonou *kō-ton-oo'*, 6 24N 2 31E, pop(1982e) 487,020, port in Ouémé prov, S Benin, W Africa; on a sandspit between the Bight of Benin and L Nokoué; the largest city in Benin; though not the official capital of Benin, the majority of the country's political and economic business is conducted here; seat of the Presidency, most ministries, the National Assembly and all embassies; centre for most commercial activities; university (1970); airport 6 km from the city centre; railway; economy: vegetable oils, soap, power plant.

Cotopaxi *kō-tō-pak'see*, mountainous prov in the Andean Sierra of N central Ecuador; Cotopaxi volcano rises to 5,896 m in the NE; watered by the Río Patate; pop(1982) 277,678; area 6,248 sq km; capital Latacunga; economy: cereal, fruit, vegetables, dairying, iron, steel.

Cotopaxi, 0 40S 78 26W, active Andean volcano in N central Ecuador; on the border of Cotopaxi, Napo and Pichincha provs; 48 km S of Quito; at 5,896 m it is the highest active volcano in the world; contained within a 340-sq km national park established in 1975; a llama breeding station and NASA satellite tracking station are located nearby.

Cotswold Hills or **Cotswolds** *kotz'wōldz*, hill range mainly in Gloucestershire, SE England; extends 80 km NE from Bath to Chipping Camden, separating the lower R Severn from the source of the R Thames; rises to 333 m at Cleeve Cloud, near Cheltenham; gives its name to a breed of sheep; the district is noted for a characteristic mellow-coloured type of stone, of which its picturesque villages are built.

Cottbus *kot'boos*, county in SE East Germany; pop(1981) 884,655; area 8,262 sq km; part of the Lusatia region, it is inhabited by the bilingual Slavic Sorb minority group occupying the districts of Cottbus, Hoyerswerda, Weisswasser, Spremberg, Guven, Forst, Calau and Lübben; 40% of land is farmed, with market-gardening important in the Spreewald; extensive reclamation of former open-cast mine sites; economy: open-cast coal mining, power generation (Boxberg power station, Jänschwalde power station and Schwarze Pumpe gas complex), market-gardening, fish-farming and chemical, textile and glass industries.

Cottbus, KOTTBUS, 51 44N 14 20E, pop(1982) 117,217, capital of Cottbus county, SE East Germany; on R Spree, SE of Berlin, close to the Polish frontier; railway; economy: textiles, metallurgy, electrical machinery.

Cottian Alps, SE France. See Alpes Cottiennes.

Cotuí *kō-twee'*, 19 04N 70 10W, pop(1982e) 95,575, town in Sánchez Ramírez prov, Dominican Republic, 43 km ESE of La Vega; airfield; road junction; silver, gold, and copper were mined nearby in early colonial times.

Council Bluffs, 41 16N 95 52W, pop(1980) 56,449, county seat of Pottawattamie county, SW Iowa, United States; on the Missouri river, opposite Omaha, Nebraska; railway; economy: processed foods, machinery, electrical equipment and fabricated metals; monument: General Dodge House.

Courbevoie *koor-be-vwa*, 48 54N 2 15E, pop(1982) 59,931, industrial and residential NW suburb of Paris in Hauts-de-Seine dept, Ile-de-France region, N central France; economy: petrol products and derivatives, ceramic fibres, food and dietary products.

Courtrai, town in Belgium. See Kortrijk.

Covasna *ko-vas'na*, county in E central Romania, between the Transylvanian Alps and the W Carpathian Mts; pop(1983) 224,280; area 3,705 sq km; capital Sfintu Gheorghe.

Coveñas *ko-ven'yas*, 9 24N 75 33W, seaport and oil terminal in Sucre dept, NW Colombia, South America; linked to E Colombia by a transmontane pipeline.

Coventry *kov'en-tri*, COUENTREY (anc), 52 25N 1 30W, pop(1981) 313,815, modern industrial city in West Midlands, central England; part of Coventry-Bedworth urban area; 150 km NW of London; in 1043 Leofric, Earl of Mercia, founded a Benedictine priory around which the town grew; his wife was the famous 'Lady Godiva'; an important centre of clothing manufacture from the 17th century; University of Warwick (1965); railway; economy: vehicles, machine tools, agricultural machinery, telecommunications equipment, man-made fibres; monuments: old cathedral (1433), destroyed during World War II; new cathedral, designed by Sir Basil Spence and consecrated in 1962; 15-16th-c church of Holy Trinity; St Mary's Hall (1343), built for the merchants' guild; museum of British road transport.

Covilhã *koo-veel-ya'*, 40 17N 7 31W, pop(1981) 22,200, picturesque hill town in Castelo Branco dist, central Portugal, on SE slopes of the Serra da Estrêla; important textile centre and winter sports resort; railway; airfield; monuments: 15th-c church of Santa Maria; chapels of São Martinho and Santa Cruz (16th-c) and town hall.

Covina *ko-vee'na*, 34 05N 117 52W, pop(1980) 33,751, city in Los Angeles county, SW California, United States; at the base of the San Gabriel Mts, 32 km E of Los Angeles.

Covington, 39 05N 84 31W, pop(1980) 49,563, town in Kenton county, N Kentucky, United States; at the junction of the Ohio and Licking rivers; connected to Cincinnati by a suspension bridge; railway; economy: tobacco, meat-packing, paper, sheet metal, machinery and electrical equipment; monuments: cathedral Basilica of the Assumption, Devou Park, Garden of Hope.

Cowdenbeath, 56 07N 3 21W, pop(1981) 12,272, town in Dunfermline dist, Fife, E central Scotland; 8 km NE of Dunfermline; railway; economy: open-cast coal mining.

Cowes *kowz*, 50 45N 1 18W, pop(1981) 16,278, town in Medina dist, Isle of Wight, S England; on R Medina estuary where it meets the N coast of the island; a notable yachting centre; ferries and hydrofoil to Southampton; economy: boat and hydrofoil building, radar, tourism; monuments: Osborne House (East Cowes), summer residence of Queen Victoria and Prince Albert; Cowes castle, built by Henry VIII in 1543, is home of the Royal Yacht Squadron; event: Cowes Week (Aug).

Cozumel, Isla *ko-zoo-mel'*, resort island in the Caribbean, 19 km off the NE coast of Quintana Roo, Mexico; chief town San Miguel; 47 km long by 14.5 km wide; ferry links to Puerto Morelos on the mainland.

Cracow, city and voivodship, Poland. See Kraków.

Craigavon, 54 28N 6 25W, pop(1981) 10,195, town in Craigavon dist, Armagh, S Northern Ireland; a 'new town', just NE of Portadown.

Craiova *kra-yo'va*, 44 18N 23 47E, pop(1983) 260,422, cultural and commercial capital of Dolj county, S Romania; on R Jiu; university (1966); airfield; railway junction; economy: grain trade, electrical engineering, farm machinery, rolling stock, fertilizers, textiles, food processing; monuments: 17th-c Demetrius church; palace of justice museum.

Cram'lington, 55 05N 1 35W, pop(1981) 25,225, an industrial 'new town' under development in Blyth Valley dist, Northumberland, NE England; 12 km N of Newcastle upon Tyne; the town has a projected population of 62,000; railway; economy: engineering, razor blades, tractors.

Cranston, 41 47N 71 26W, pop(1980) 71,992, town in Providence county, E Rhode Island, United States; on R Pawtuxet, 8 km S of Providence; railway.

Crater Lake, circular crater lake in SW Oregon, United States, in the Cascade Range; 9.5 km across; area 52 sq km; 604 m deep; alt 1,879 m; the lake is situated in an enormous pit formed by the destruction of the summit of a prehistoric volcano (now called Mt Mazama); 150-600 m-high cliffs line the shores of the lake; the lake has neither an inlet nor an outlet, but remains at a near-constant level from rainfall and melting snow; Small Wizard Island near the W shore rises 237 m above the surface of the lake and has a crater at the top; the lake is situated in Crater Lake National Park (area 641 sq km, established in 1902); Mt Scott (2,721 m) is the highest of the volcanic peaks in the park.

Crawley, 51 07N 0 12W, pop(1981) 73,376, town in Crawley dist, West Sussex, S England; 43 km S of London; designated a 'new town' in 1947; London (Gatwick) airport lies N; railway; economy: pharmaceuticals, engineering, electronics, furniture.

Cremo'na, prov of Lombardia region, Italy; pop(1981) 332,236; area 1,772 sq km; capital Cremona.

Cremona, 45 08N 10 01E, pop(1981) 80,929, capital town of Cremona prov, Lombardia region, Italy; on the N bank of the R Po; noted for the violin-makers who worked here during the 16-18th centuries (eg Stradivari), railway; an inland port on the Milan-Po Canal; economy: textiles, pasta, dairy products, confectionery; monuments: cathedral in Lombard Gothic style (1107-90); Gothic Palazzo Comunale (town hall, 1206-45), 13th-c Torrazzo, an octagonal tower 111 m high.

Cres *tsress*, 2nd largest of the Adriatic islands of Yugoslavia, in Hrvatska (Croatia) republic; situated S of Rijeka; area 404 sq km; includes the resort and port town of Cres and the picturesque villages of Punta Križa, Osor and Martinšćica; the highest point is Mt Sis (650 m); Lake Vrana is an important water supply for the island and its neighbour, Lošinj.

Crete, region and island of Greece. See Kríti.

Creteil *krê-tay*, 48 47N 2 28E, pop(1982) 71,705, capital of Val-de-Marne dept, Ile-de-France region, France; economy: motors, electrical equipment for automobiles, optical and ophthalmic products, distilling.

Creus, Cabo *kray-oos'*, APHRODISIUM (Gr), 42 19N 3 19E, the most easterly point on the Iberian peninsula; the picturesque fishing village of Cadaques nearby is preserved by local artists and not far away is a house belonging to the artist Salvador Dali.

Creuse *krœz* ('deep'), dept in Limousin region of central France, comprising 2 arrond, 27 cantons and 260 communes; drained by the Creuse R; hilly in the S, where the Plateau de Millevaches links the Mts d'Auvergne with those of Limousin, and along the sides of the Creuse valley; pop(1982) 139,968; area 5,565 sq km; capital Gueret; spa at Évaux-les-Bains.

Creuse, river in central France rising in the plateau of

Millevaches NW of La Courtine; flows NNW in a deep valley to the R Vienne near La Haye-Descartes; length 255 km; tributaries Petite Creuse, Claise and Gartempe rivers.

Crewe *kroo*, 53 05N 2 27W, pop(1981) 59,352, town in Crewe and Nantwich dist, Cheshire, NW central England; NW of Stoke-on-Trent; a major railway junction; economy: chemicals, railway engineering, clothing, vehicles.

Crimea, peninsula in SW Soviet Union. See Krym.

Cristóbal Colón, Pico *pee'kō krees-tō'bal kō-lōn'*, snow-capped Andean peak in Magdalena dept, N Colombia, South America; rises to 5,800 m, 113 km E of Barranquilla; the highest peak in the Sierra Nevada de Santa Marta and in Colombia.

Crna Gora *tsur'na go'ra*, MONTENEGRO *mon-te-nee'grō* (Eng) ('black mountain'), a constituent republic in W Yugoslavia; a mountainous region bounded SW by the Adriatic Sea, SE by Albania and E and N by Srbija (Serbia) and Bosna-Hercegovina; pop(1981) 584,310; area 13,812 sq km; capital Titograd; the mountain town of Cetinje (alt 670 m) was a former capital; until 1918 an independent monarchy; the population is mostly of Serbo-Croat stock; economy: livestock, grain and tobacco.

Croatia, republic of Yugoslavia. See Hrvatska.

Crooked Island, island in the SE Bahamas, separated from Long I (NW) by the Crooked I Passage; pop(1980) 517; area 217 sq km; chief town Colonel Hill; economy: agriculture and fishing.

Crooked Tree, 17 46N 88 33W, village and wildlife sanctuary in N Belize; the sanctuary comprises 3 areas around the Northern and Western lagoons and is an important bird migration site; the village is located on the W shore of Northern Lagoon; area 18.1 sq km; designated in 1981.

Cros'by, GREAT CROSBY, 53 30N 3 02W, pop(1981) 53,853, town in Sefton borough, Merseyside, NW England; at the mouth of the R Mersey, opposite the Crosby Channel, 10 km N of Liverpool; railway.

Cross Fell, highest peak of the Pennine Chain in Cumbria, NW England; rises to 893 m, 32 km SE of Carlisle.

Cross River, state in S Nigeria, W Africa; pop(1982e) 5,546,400; area 27,237 sq km; bounded S by the Gulf of Guinea; the Cross river runs N-S through state; other rivers include the Calabar, the Qua Iboe and the Great and Little Kwa; capital Calabar; chief towns Ogoja, Ikom, Akamkpa, Ikot Ekpene and Eket; there are tanker terminals at Calabar and Kwa Ibo; Cross River is an agricultural state with a variety of food and cash crops including rice, cereals and palms; economy: cement processing (Calabar, Oron), oil extraction and processing in the S, mining of limestone, calcium, salt, zinc, tin ore and lead.

Crosse, La, 43 48N 91 15W, pop(1980) 48,347, county seat of La Crosse county, W Wisconsin, United States; at the junction of the Black and Mississippi rivers, on the Minnesota state border; a trade centre for agricultural produce.

Crossroads, 34 00S 18 36E, pop(1985) 29,262, squatter settlement, Cape prov, South Africa; SE of Cape Town and S of D.F. Malan airport.

Crow'borough, 51 03N 0 09E, pop(1981) 17,078, dormitory town in Wealden dist, East Sussex, SE England; 11 km SW of Tunbridge Wells; railway.

Crow'thorne *crō'-*, 51 23N 0 49W, pop(1981) 19,339, town in Wokingham dist, Berkshire, S England; 6 km SW of Bracknell.

Croy'don, 51 23N 0 06W, pop(1981) 300,508, borough of S Greater London, England; S of Lambeth; includes the suburbs of Croydon and Coulsdon and Purley; railway; airport at Heathrow; economy: commerce, foodstuffs, engineering, electronics, pharmaceuticals; monument: Whitgift's Hospital (1596).

Crozet, Îles de *krō-zay'*, 46 30S 51 00E, group of 5 islands in S Indian Ocean; the 3 main islands are named Île aux Cochons, Île de la Possession and Île de l'Est; part of the French Southern and Antarctic Territories; discovered in 1772 by Marion-Dufresne; annexed by Crozet for Louis XV; area 300 sq km; a meteorological and scientific station has been based at Alfred-Faure on Île de la Possession since 1964.

Cruces, Las *las kroo'sez*, 32 19N 106 47W, pop(1980) 45,086, county seat of Dona Ana county, S New Mexico, United States; on the Rio Grande, 66 km NNW of El Paso, Texas; university (1888); nearby is the White Sands Missile Range, a major military and NASA testing site where the first atomic bomb was tested; the town's name, Spanish for 'the crosses', commemorates the massacre of 40 travellers by Apache Indians in 1830; railway; event: Enchilada Fiesta (Oct).

Cruden Bay, 57 24N 1 51W, village and port in Banff and Buchan dist, Grampian, NE Scotland, United Kingdom; 11 km S of Peterhead near the mouth of the Water of Cruden at the N end of the Bay of Cruden; linked by pipeline to the Forties oil field.

Crystal, 45 03N 93 22W, pop(1980) 25,543, town in Hennepin county, SE Minnesota, United States; suburb 11 km NW of Minneapolis; railway.

Csongrád *chon'grad*, county in S Hungary; part of the Great Plain (Alföld) of SE Hungary, crossed by the Tisza, Maros and Körös rivers; pop(1984e) 453,000; area 4,263 sq km; capital Szeged; chief towns include Makó, Szentes and Hódmezövásárhely; there are 54 villages; 65,000 employed in industry; half of Hungary's oil and natural gas supplied from Csongrád; 3 universities; economy: grain, fruit, oil, natural gas, chemicals, rubber and cable manufacture, agricultural machinery, pottery, furniture, electrical goods, porcelain, hemp, salami, red pepper.

Csongrád, 46 43N 20 12E, pop(1984e) 22,000, market town in Csongrád county, S Hungary; at the junction of the Tisza and Körös rivers; railway; economy: cattle, dairy produce, grain and wine trade.

Cuba *kyoo'ba* (Eng), official name Republic of Cuba, REPÚBLICA DE CUBA, island republic in the Caribbean Sea, W of Haiti, N of Jamaica, and S of Florida; timezone GMT −5; area 110,860 sq km; capital La Habana (Havana); chief towns Santiago de Cuba, Camagüey, Holguín, and Santa Clara; pop(1981) 9,723,605; the people are mainly of Spanish and African origin; Spanish is the official language; before Castro assumed power in 1959, 85% of the population were Roman Catholic; the Castro regime now discourages religious practices and has circumscribed the activities of religious groups; the unit of currency is the peso of 100 centavos; membership: CEMA, ECLA, FAO, G-77, GATT, IADB, IAEA, ICAO, IFAD, IHO, ILO, IMO, IRC, ISO, ITU, IWC, NAM, NAMUCAR, OAS, PAHO, Permanent Court of Arbitration, Postal Union of the Americas and Spain, SELA, UN, UNESCO, UNIDO, UPU, WFTU, WHO, WIPO, WMO, WSG, WTO.

Physical description. The Republic of Cuba is an archipelago comprising the island of Cuba, Isla de la Juventud ('isle of youth'), and c.1,600 islets and cays. The main island of Cuba is 1,250 km long and varies in width from 191 km in the E to 31 km in the W. The coastline is indented by numerous bays and inlets. Much of the S coast (except for the mountainous E part) is low and marshy. The N coast is generally steep and rocky with some of the best harbours in the world. Approx a quarter of Cuba is mountainous. The main ranges include the Sierra del Escambray in the centre, the Sierra de los Organos to the W of La Habana, and the rugged Sierra Maestra in the E. The highest peak in Cuba is Pico Turquino in the Sierra Maestra which reaches a height of 2,005 m. The rest of the island is flat or gently rolling with many wide, fertile valleys and plains.

Climate. The climate is subtropical, warm and humid. The average annual temperature is 25°C, varying from 23°C in winter to 27°C in summer. There is a dry season from Nov to April and a wet season from May to Oct. Mean annual rainfall is 1,375 mm, approx 75% of this

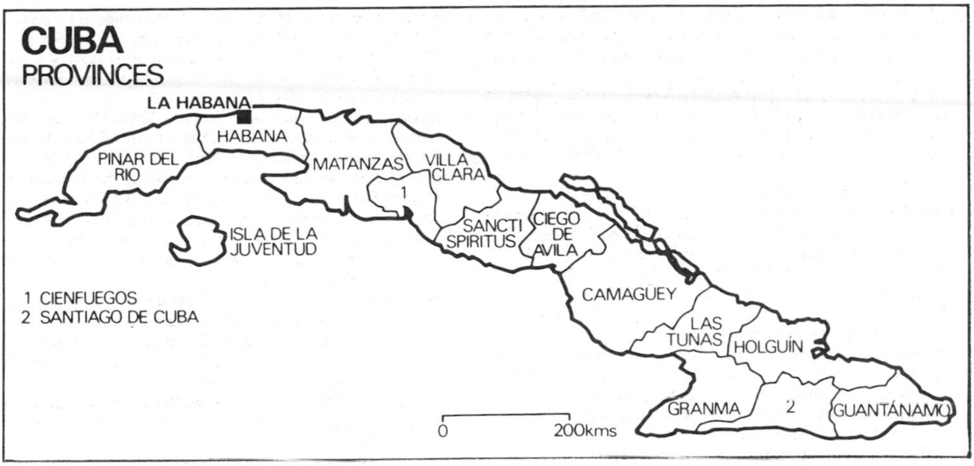

occurring as short, heavy showers during the wet season. Hurricanes are liable to occur between June and Nov.

History, government and constitution. Cuba was visited by Christopher Columbus in Oct 1492 and settled by Spanish sugar cane planters and tobacco farmers from the early 1500s. The native Carib and Arawak Indian population was quickly wiped out and African slaves were brought in to work on the plantations. Antagonism between Spaniards and criollos (native-born descendants of the colonizers) eventually led to the Ten Years' War which broke out on 10 Oct 1868. From 1895 to 1898 rebellion flared up again under José Martí, Cuba's greatest national hero. The USA entered the conflict on the side of the revolutionaries when one of their battleships was blown up in La Habana harbour on 15 Feb 1898. Later that same year, Spain relinquished its rights over Cuba in the Treaty of Paris and independence was proclaimed on 20 May 1902. The USA retained its naval bases on the island and also reserved the right of intervention in Cuban domestic affairs. From 1933 the increasingly corrupt dictatorship of General Batista eventually led to yet another struggle for freedom, this time led by Fidel Castro. On 26 July 1953, an armed opposition group led by Castro failed to capture the Moncada army barracks at Santiago de Cuba. Two years later, after forming a revolutionary group (the '26th of July Movement') in Mexico, Fidel Castro returned to Cuba and began a guerrilla struggle in the Sierra Maestra. Victory came on 1 Jan 1959 and within months Castro set about establishing a communist state. The first socialist constitution came into force on 24 Feb 1976. Executive power is vested in the Council of Ministers, which heads the government. It is appointed by the National Assembly of People's Power on the proposal of the head of state.

Economy. After the 1959 revolution, the large plantation estates were nationalized and land plots of up to 0.66 sq km were distributed to the peasants. In Sept 1982 the total area under cultivation included 33,982 sq km state-owned and 4,754 sq km in the private sector. Cuba is the world's second largest sugar producer. In 1983 sugar accounted for 75% of export earnings. Since 1971, however, attempts have been made to diversify the economy by broadening the industrial base and developing non-sugar agriculture, nickel processing, fishing, and tourism. Other important crops include tobacco, rice, maize, coffee, and citrus fruits. The Vuelta-Abajo district near Pinar del Río is the main tobacco-growing region on the island. Meat production is becoming increasingly important and dairy cattle are being introduced on a large scale. There are also attempts to rehabilitate coffee plantations, mostly located in the mountainous E provinces. Major industries include sugar milling, petroleum refining, food and tobacco processing, and the manufacture of textiles, paper and wood products, metals, and cement. Cuba is the world's fifth largest producer of nickel, accounting for 6% of exports in 1981. Chief exports in 1982 included sugar, nickel, shellfish, and tobacco. Chief imports were capital goods, industrial raw materials, foodstuffs, and petroleum which are imported at subsidized prices, chiefly from the USSR. Subsidized trade accounts for about 88% of the balance of payments. Before Fidel Castro came to power, more than half of Cuba's trade was with the USA. In 1983 the USSR accounted for 86.5% of Cuba's foreign trade. Canadian grain is a major import from non-communist countries. The major non-Comecon trading partners are Canada, Japan, France, Spain, the Netherlands, the UK, and West Germany.

Communications. The Central Highway traverses the island for 1,216 km from Pinar del Río to Santiago de Cuba. José Martí International Airport is located 18 km from La Habana. Chief ports include Antilla, Cienfuegos, Guayabal, La Habana, Mariel, Matanzas, Nuevitas, and Santiago de Cuba.

Administrative divisions. Cuba is divided into 14 provinces and the city of La Habana as follows:

Province	*area (sq km)*	*pop(1981)*
Pinar del Río	10,860	640,740
La Habana	5,671	586,029
Isla de la Juventud	2,199	57,879
Matanzas	11,669	557,628
Cienfuegos	4,149	326,412
Villa Clara	8,069	764,743
Sancti Spíritus	6,737	399,700
Ciego de Avila	6,485	320,961
Camagüey	14,134	664,566
Las Tunas	6,373	436,341
Holguín	9,105	911,034
Granma	8,452	739,335
Santiago de Cuba	6,343	909,506
Guantánamo	6,366	466,609
Ciudad de La Habana	740	1,924,886

Cucamonga *koo-ka-mong'ga*, RANCHO CUCAMONGA, 34 06N 117 35W, pop(1980) 55,250, city in San Bernardino county, SW California, United States; in the foothills of the San Gabriel Mts, just E of Upland.

Cuchumatanes, Sierra los *koo-choo-ma-ta'nes*, mountain range in Huehuetenango and Quiché depts, NW Guatemala, Central America; extends c.160 km NW-SE from the border with Mexico to the Río Chixoy; rises to over 3,500 m; source of the rivers Selegua and Ixcán.

Cúcuta *koo'koo-ta*, 7 55N 72 31W, pop(1985) 440,823,

capital of Norte de Santander dept, NE Colombia, South America; 16 km from the frontier with Venezuela; within a Tax Free Zone; university (1962); founded in 1733, destroyed by an earthquake in 1875 and then rebuilt; because of the town's geographical position as a gateway to Venezuela, Cúcuta was a focal point in the history of Colombia's fight for independence; birthplace of General Francisco de Paula Santander and seat of the Constituent Congress of 1821; railway; airfield; economy: coffee, tobacco, cattle trade.

Cuenca *kwen'ka*, 2 54S 79 00W, pop(1982) 152,406, capital of Azuay prov, in the Andean Sierra of S central Ecuador; a colonial city surrounded by the Tarqui, Yanuncay, Tomebamba and Machángara rivers; 3rd largest city in Ecuador; founded by the Spanish in 1557; 2 universities (1868, 1970); airfield; railway; economy: tobacco, dairy products, meat packing, fruit canning, textiles, leatherworks, motor vehicles, agricultural machinery, chemicals; monuments: on the central Parque Calderón stand both the old cathedral and the new cathedral (finished in 1967); La Concepción, a convent founded in 1599, is now a religious art museum; modern art museum; folk museum; at nearby Baños are sulphur baths; Cuenca, with its water plant, is said to have the best drinking water in Ecuador; the main market takes place on Thursdays.

Cuenca, prov in Castilla-La Mancha region, central Spain; the mountainous N merges into the La Mancha plain in the S; the Tagus and Júcar rivers cross the prov; pop(1981) 210,280; area 17,061 sq km; capital Cuenca; economy: forestry, livestock, electrical equipment, wooden boxes, radio parts; Zorita II nuclear power station (450 MW).

Cuenca, CONCA (anc), 40 05N 2 10W, pop(1981) 41,791, capital of Cuenca prov, E central Spain; overlooking the R Júcar, 167 km ESE of Madrid; bishopric; railway; monuments: the Hanging Houses (Casas Colgadas); Museum of Abstract Art; 13th-c cathedral; events: Holy Week with procession and concerts; Fiesta of Our Lady of la Luz in May-June with a singing competition and Fiesta of San Julian in Sept with bullfights and sporting competitions.

Cuernavaca *kwer-na-vah'ka*, 18 57N 99 15W, pop(1980) 232,355, capital and resort town of Morelos state, S central Mexico; 77 km S of Ciudad de México (Mexico City); alt 1,542 m; university (1939); captured by the Spanish in 1521; railway; monuments: Iglesia de la Asunción cathedral, completed in 1552; nearby is the church of the Tercera Orden (1529), containing a small figure thought to be one of the only 2 statues of Cortés in Mexico; the Regional Cuauhnahuac museum (the Aztec name for Cuernavaca) in the centre of the city contains prehistoric to modern exhibits; the museum is housed in the palace Cortés built for his 2nd wife in 1531; on the rear balcony is a Diego Rivera mural of the conquest of Mexico; the building was the seat of State Legislature until 1967 when the new legislative building was completed; near the railway station is the Teopanzolco pyramid; the Cacahuamilpa caverns are amongst the largest in N America; there are many spas in the surrounding area.

Cugir *koo'jeer*, 45 48N 23 25E, pop(1983) 29,781, town in Alba county, W central Romania; railway terminus; economy: metal, munitions.

Cuiabá *koo-ya-ba'*, 15 32S 56 05W, pop(1980) 167,880, capital of Mato Grosso state, Centro-Oeste region, W central Brazil; situated at the geographical centre of South America; on an upper tributary of the Río Paraguaí; airfield; economy: commercial centre for much of the Mato Grosso, manufacturing (rubber, drinks), cattle raising, tourism; gold was discovered here in 1719; a modern city with an imposing government palace and other buildings grouped around its main square.

Cuilapa *kwee-la'pa*, 14 16N 90 18W, capital town of Santa Rosa dept, SE Guatemala, Central America; 43 km SE of Guatemala City, on the Inter-American Highway between Jutiapa and Guatemala; the capital moved here in 1871 from Santa Rosa; destroyed by earthquake in 1913 after which Barbarena became temporary capital for 7 years.

Culiacán *kool-ya-kahn'*, CULIACÁN ROSALES, 24 50N 107 23W, pop(1980) 560,011, capital of Sinaloa state, NW Mexico; on the Río Culiacán, 208 km NNW of Mazatlán; founded in 1599; university (1873); railway; economy: vegetables, textiles.

Cullod'en, a ridge forming part of Drummossie Muir in Nairn dist, Highland region, Scotland; E of Inverness; here the Duke of Cumberland routed the clans under Prince Charles Edward Stuart (16 April 1746), extinguishing the Jacobite cause; there is a National Trust for Scotland information centre.

Culver City, 34 01N 118 25W, pop(1980) 38,139, city in Los Angeles county, SW California, United States; film studio centre 13 km WSW of Los Angeles.

Cumaná *koo-ma-na'*, 10 27N 64 10W, pop(1981) 179,814, capital of Sucre state, NE Venezuela; founded in 1520, Cumaná was the first Hispanic city to be founded in South America; university (1958); economy: sardine canning; monuments: a new museum (1974) commemorates the 150th anniversary of the battle of Ayacucho; Margarita island nearby is famous for its carnival.

Cum'berland, former county of NW England; part of Cumbria since 1974.

Cumberland, 39 39N 78 46W, pop(1980) 25,933, county seat of Allegany county, NW Maryland, United States; on a N branch of the R Potomac; originally Fort Cumberland; the site of George Washington's first military headquarters; economy: a railway and shipping centre for a coal mining area.

Cumbernauld *kum-bėr-nawld'*, 55 58N 3 59W, pop(1981) 47,901, capital of Cumbernauld and Kilsyth dist, Strathclyde, central Scotland; 20 km NE of Glasgow; designated a 'new town' in 1955; railway; economy: engineering, service industries.

Cum'bria, county in NW England; bounded W by the Irish Sea, NW by the Solway Firth, N by Scotland, S by Lancashire and E by Northumberland, from which it is separated by the Pennines; 40% of the county lies within the Lake District and Yorkshire Dales national parks; created in 1974 from the former counties of Westmorland and Cumberland; pop(1981) 487,038; area 6,810 sq km; county town Carlisle; chief towns include Penrith, Kendal, Lancaster, Barrow-in-Furness; economy: agriculture, tourism, shipbuilding, marine engineering, chemicals; the county is divided into 6 districts:

District	*area (sq km)*	*pop(1981)*
Allerdale	1,257	97,121
Barrow-in-Furness	77	73,189
Carlisle	1,030	101,092
Copeland	737	73,140
Eden	2,158	44,191
South Lakeland	1,551	98,305

Cumnock, 55 27N 4 16W, pop(1981) 9,650, capital of Cumnock and Doon Valley dist, Strathclyde, SE Scotland; 23 km E of Ayr.

Cundinamarca *koon-dee-na-mar'ka*, mountainous dept in the Sabana de Bogotá plateau of the Cordillera Oriental, central Colombia, South America; bounded W by the Río Magdalena; pop(1985) 1,358,978 (excluding Bogotá); area 22,623 sq km; capital Bogotá; on the Río Bogotá is the Salto de Tequendama (Tequendama Falls) which have a drop of 147 m; N of Bogotá is the town of Zipaquirá, famous for its vast rock-salt mine with its underground cathedral, carved out of the salt rock, which took 10 years to complete.

Cuneo *koo'nay-ō*, CONI *kō-nee* (Fr), prov of Piemonte region, NW Italy; pop(1981) 548,452; area 6,902 sq km; capital Cuneo.

Cuneo, 44 24N 7 33E, pop(1981) 55,875, capital town of Cuneo prov, Piemonte region, NW Italy; on a plateau above the junction of the rivers Gesso and the Stura di

Demonte; railway; economy: textiles, silk, food processing, metal products.

Cupar *koo'per*, 56 19N 3 01W, pop(1981) 6,637, market town and capital of North-east Fife dist, Fife, E Scotland; on the R Eden, 16 km NE of Glenrothes, 16 km SSW of Dundee; railway.

Cupertino *kyoo-per-tee'nō*, 37 19N 122 02W, pop(1980) 34,015, city in Santa Clara county, W California, United States; in the Santa Clara Valley, 13 km W of San José.

Curaçao *koo-ra-sah'ō*, largest and most populous island of the Netherlands Antilles, E Caribbean, in the Windward group, 60 km N of Venezuela; composed of coralline limestone fringing an igneous core; the island is generally flat but rises to 373 m in the NW; area 444 sq km; length 58 km; width 13 km; pop(1981) 147,388; capital Willemstad; airport; economy: tourism, oil refining, phosphate mining, ship repairing.

Curepipe *kyoor-peep'*, 20 19S 57 31E, pop(1981e) 56,681, township in Plaines Wilhems dist, W central Mauritius; alt 550 m; Curepipe grew from a small village during the 19th century when cholera and malaria epidemics forced people to leave Port Louis for the cooler, healthier plateau country; economy: woollen yarn, sweaters, dyeing and painting of silk fabrics and sarees.

Curicó *koo-ree-kō'*, 34 59S 71 14W, pop(1982) 51,743, capital of Curicó prov, Maule, central Chile; alt 200 m; railway; a centre of wine production; Curicó's main Plaza de Armas is one of the finest in Chile.

Curitiba *koo-ree-chee'ba*, 25 24S 49 16W, pop(1980) 842,818, commercial and industrial capital of Paraná state, Sul region, S Brazil; SW of São Paulo, on the plateau of the Serra do Mar at an alt of 900 m; university (1959); railway; airfield; monuments: in the city centre is a group of buildings dominated by the Palácio Iguaçu, headquarters of the state and municipal governments; the old municipal government building now houses the Museu Paranaense in Praça Generoso Marques; on Praça Tiradentes is the cathedral built in 1894; the Passeio Público park in the heart of the city has a zoo, a network of canals with boats and a small aquarium; to the N of the city on the shores of L Bacacheri is an Egyptian temple; event: Our Lady of Light (8 Sept).

Curtea de Argeş *koor'tya day ar'jesh*, 45 06N 24 40E, pop(1983) 28,016, resort town in Argeş county, S central Romania; on R Argeş; on S slopes of the Transylvanian Alps; founded in the 14th century; railway; economy: pottery, wood products; monument: 16th-c Byzantine cathedral, burial place of the kings of Romania.

Cuscatlán *koos-ket-lan'*, dept in central El Salvador, Central America; pop(1971) 158,458; area 766 sq km, capital Cojutepeque; chief towns Suchitoto and Tenancingo; drained by the Río Quezalapa, a tributary of the Río Lempa; part of the Lago de Ilopango occupies its SW corner.

Cuttack *kut'ak* ('the fort'), 20 25N 85 57E, pop(1981) 326,000, river port in Orissa, E India; 350 km SW of Calcutta, at the head of the Mahanadi river delta; founded in the 10th century; headquarters of the Mogul and Mahratta conquerors of Orissa; railway; economy: noted for filigree work in both silver and gold; monument: Muslim shrine.

Cuvette *koo-vet'*, province of central Congo, W Africa; area 74,850 sq km; pop(1980) 121,470; capital Owando.

Cuxhaven *kooks-hah'fen*, 53 51N 8 41E, pop(1983) 57,800, seaport in Lüneburg dist, NE Niedersachsen (Lower Saxony) prov, W Germany; on R Elbe estuary, N of Bremerhaven; railway; until 1938 an outlying part of Hamburg prov.

Cuyahoga Falls *koo-ya-hō'ga* (Iroquoian, 'important river'), 41 08N 81 29W, pop(1980) 43,890, town in Summit county, NE Ohio, United States; on the R Cuyahoga, 8 km N of Akron; railway.

Cuzco *koos'kō*, dept in S central Peru; mountainous region set in the Cordillera Oriental which here splits into the Cordillera de Vilcanota and the Cordillera de Carabaya in the S and the Cordillera Vilcabamba in the N; drained by the Apurímac and Urubamba rivers; pop(1981) 832,504; area 84,140 sq km; capital Cuzco; to the NE of Cuzco city is the famous Inca city of Machu Picchu, rediscovered in 1911 by Hiram Bingham; further NE is the Inca city of Vilcabamba, last stronghold of the Incas under Manco II and Tupuc Amaru until it was destroyed by the Spanish in 1572; Vilcabamba was rediscovered by Savoy in 1964.

Cuzco, 13 32S 71 57W, pop(1981) 181,604, capital of Cuzco dept, S Peru; alt 3,500 m; ancient capital of the Inca empire; the city is remarkable for its colonial churches, monasteries and convents and for its extensive Inca ruins; university (1969); railway; airfield; monuments: on the N side of the Plaza de Armas, the heart of the city, is the cathedral (early 17th-c) containing the crucifix of El Señor de las Temblores, object of many pilgrimages and thought to prevent earthquakes; on the E side is the church of La Compania de Jesús, built in the late 17th-c on the site of the Palace of Serpents; to the SE of this square is the church of Santo Domingo, built in the 17th-c on the walls of the Temple of the Sun and from its stones; Inca stonework can be seen in the area to the E of the Plaza de Armas, especially in the street, Callejón Loreto, where the walls of the House of the Women of the Sun are on one side and those of the Palace of the Serpents on the other.

Cwmbran *koom-brahn'*, 51 39N 3 00W, pop(1980) 44,797, county town of Gwent, in Torfaen dist, Gwent, SE Wales, United Kingdom; 24 km NNE of Cardiff; economy: engineering, scientific instruments.

Cyangu'gu, prefecture in Rwanda, central Africa; SW of Kigali at the S end of L Kivu; area 2,226 sq km; pop(1978) 331,380.

Cyclades, nome (dept) and island group of Greece. See Kikládhes.

Cypress, 33 50N 118 02W, pop(1980) 40,391, city in Orange county, SW California, United States; 16 km ENE of Long Beach.

Cyprus *sī'prus*, KYPROS (Gr), KIBRIS (Turk), official name Republic of Cyprus, KYPRIAKI DIMOKRATIA (Gr), KIBRIS CUMHURIYETI (Turk), island republic in the NE Mediterranean Sea, approx 80 km S of Turkey; timezone GMT +3; area 9,251 sq km; capital Nicosia, chief towns Famagusta, Larnaca, Limassol, and Kyrenia; pop(1983e) 659,000; about 77% of the population is Greek-speaking Orthodox Christian and 18% are Turkish-speaking Muslim; virtually all Turks now live in the occupied N sector which comprises 37% of the island; the remaining 5% comprise Armenians, Latins, Maronites, and other minorities; Greek and Turkish are both official languages and English is widely spoken; the unit of currency is the Cyprus pound of 100 cents; membership of the Commonwealth, Council of Europe, FAO, G-77, GATT, IAEA, IBRD, ICAO, ICO, IDA, IFAD, IFC, ILO, IMF, IMO, INTELSAT, INTERPOL, ITU, NAM, UN, UNESCO, UPU, WFTU, WHO, WMO, WTO

Physical description. Cyprus is the third largest island in the Mediterranean after Sicily and Sardinia. The Kyrenia

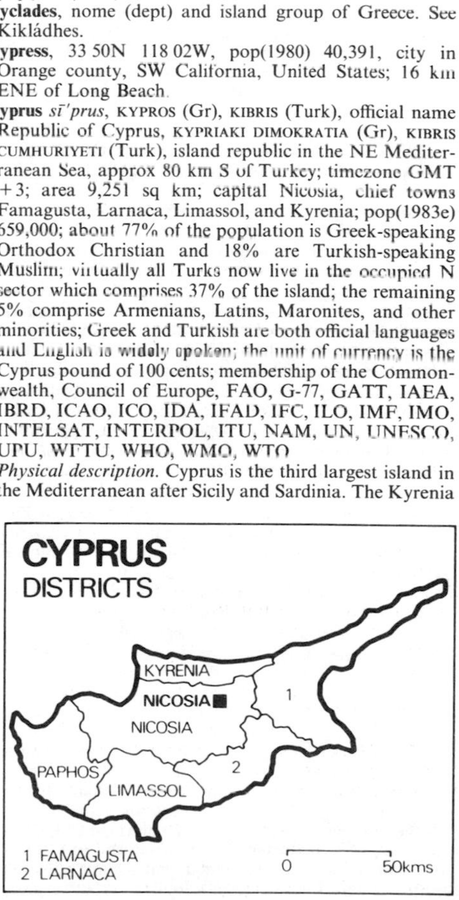

mountain range extends 150 km along the N coast and rises to 1,024 m at Mt Kyparissovouno. The forest-covered Troödos Mts occupy the SW part of the island and rise to 1,951 m at Mt Olympus. These ranges are separated by the fertile Mesaoria plain which extends the length of the island from Morphou Bay (W) to Famagusta Bay (E). The coastline is indented and mostly rocky, but there are several long, sandy beaches. There are no perennial freshwater lakes or rivers, but the numerous watercourses, dry during summer and autumn, often become torrents in winter.

Climate. Cyprus has a typical Mediterranean climate with hot, dry summers and warm, wet winters. The mean annual rainfall for the island as a whole is 500 mm although this varies from 300-400 mm in the central plain to nearly 1,200 mm at the top of the Troödos massif. The mean daily temperature in July and Aug ranges from 22°C on the Troödos Mts to 29°C on the central plain. Winters are mild with a mean Jan temperature of 10°C on the central plain and 4°C on the higher parts of the Troödos Mts. During the winter snow falls frequently on land above 1,000 m.

History, government and constitution. Through the ages Cyprus has been ruled by Romans, Greeks, Egyptians, French, Venetians, Turks, and British. The island was conquered by the Turks in 1571 and Ottoman rule lasted until 1878 when administration was passed to the British. The island was formally annexed by Britain at the outbreak of World War I and it eventually became a Crown Colony in 1925. Greek Cypriot demands for union between Cyprus and Greece led to guerrilla warfare against the British administration and a 4-year state of emergency was declared from 1955 to 1959. Cyprus became an independent republic on 16 Aug 1960. Treaties prohibited partition of the island between Greece and Turkey, and under the terms of the Treaty of Establishment, Britain retained sovereignty over 2 base areas on the island at Akrotiri and Dhekelia. Intercommunal fighting between the 2 groups continued throughout the 1960s. A coup launched by the Greek military junta on 15 July 1974 was followed by a Turkish invasion of the island and subsequent occupation of 37% of the island's territory. More than 160,000 Greek Cypriots were displaced during this Turkish advance. As a result, the island was divided into 2 parts by the Green Line, stretching from the NW coast above Pomos to Famagusta in the E and cutting through the capital, Nicosia. On 15 November 1983, the Turkish Cypriot community occupying the N third of the island declared itself the independent 'Turkish Republic of Northern Cyprus'. This unilateral declaration of independence was recognized only by Turkey. Cyprus is an independent and sovereign republic with a presidential system of government. The president, who is head of state, is elected for a term of 5 years by the Greek community. Legislative power is vested in a 50-member house of representatives, of whom 35 are elected by the Greek community and 15 by the Turkish community. As from December 1983 the Turkish members have ceased to attend.

Economy. The economy of the Greek Cypriot south has largely recovered from the impact of the 1974 Turkish invasion, with light manufacturing industries now constituting the main growth sector of the economy. Chief manufactures include paper, paperboard products, chemicals, food and wine, clothing, footwear, cigarettes, and various other consumer goods. The only heavy industries in Cyprus are petroleum refining, cement production, and electricity generating. During 1980 mineral exports, notably asbestos, clay, chrome, and umber, represented c.4.1% of total exports. Chief exports include clothing, wine and alcoholic beverages, chemicals, machinery and transport equipment, and minerals. Chief trading partners include the EEC, E Europe and the Arab countries. Although the tourist trade suffered considerably as a result of the 1974 hostilities, tourism and services now account for about 15% of national income. Long-stay visitors to Cyprus rose from a total of 47,000 in 1975 to 621,000 in 1983. The Turkish Cypriot economy of the N sector remains heavily dependent on agriculture. The major sources of income are provided by Turkish tourists from the mainland and the export of citrus fruit and vegetables. Chief crops include citrus fruits, potatoes, grapes, cereals, carobs, vegetables, olives, and almonds. Potatoes have replaced table grapes and oranges as the single most important crop and in 1984 they accounted for 46.2% of total agricultural products, the main market being Britain. Various irrigation schemes are designed to increase the area under cultivation.

Communications. There are 10,943 km of roadway in Cyprus, of which 5,277 km are paved and 5,666 km are earth or gravel. There are now no railways on the island. There are international airports at Larnaca and at Paphos. The chief commercial ports presently in operation are those of Limassol and Larnaca on the S coast of the country. Famagusta, the island's chief port prior to the 1974 coup and invasion, is now under Turkish occupation and has been declared by the government of Cyprus closed to shipping and an illegal port of entry.

Administrative divisions. Cyprus is divided into 6 districts as follows:

District	*area (sq km)*	*pop(1973)*
Famagusta	1,970	123,856
Kyrenia	639	32,586
Larnaca	1,126	60,714
Limassol	1,388	124,855
Nicosia	2,726	232,702
Paphos	1,395	57,065

Cyrenaica *sī-ren-ay'i-ka*, region of N Africa between Tripolitania (W) and Egypt (E); takes its name from the Greek colony of Cyrene; a former prov of Libya; a major theatre of operations during World War II.

Czech Socialist Republic, Czechoslovakia. See České Zemé.

Czechoslovakia *chek-os-lo-vah'ki-a*, ČESKOSLOVENSKO (Czech), official name Czechoslovak Socialist Republic, CESKOSLOVENSKÁ SOCIALISTICKÁ REPUBLIKA (Czech), a land-locked federal state consisting of the Czech Socialist Republic (České Zemé) in the W and the Slovak Socialist Republic (Slovensko) in the E; bounded N by Poland, E by USSR, S by Hungary and Austria, SW by W Germany and NW by E Germany; 3,540 km land boundary; area 127,899 sq km; timezone GMT +1; pop(1984) 15,437,038; capital Praha (Prague); chief towns include Bratislava, Brno, Ostrava, Košice, Plzeň and Olomouc; Czech and Slovak are official languages although Hungarian is also widely spoken; 65% of the pop is Czech, 30% Slovak, the remainder comprising Hungarian, German, Polish and Ukrainian groups; the currency is the koruna (Kčs) or crown of 100 haler; national holiday 9 May (Liberation Day); membership of Warsaw Pact, COMECON, CEMA, FAO, GATT, IAEA, ICAO, ICO, ILO, IMO, IPU, ISO, ITC, ITU, UN, UNESCO, UPU, WFTU, WHO, WIPO, WMO, WSG, WTO.

Physical description. The country is divided into two main geographical regions separated by the valley of the R Morava; the first comprises Bohemia and W Moravia, the second E Moravia and Slovakia. The first region is roughly the basin of the Upper Elbe (Labe) and its tributary the Moldau (Vltava) - both navigationally important - and slopes northward to the Erzgebirge; to the E the Moravian plateau gives easy access to the second geographical region of the country which contains the W range of the Carpathians and slopes southwards from the Beskids and (Tatry) Tatra Mts to the R Danube and the Hungarian plains, and whose rivers the Morava, Váh, Nitra, Hron and Ipel join the Danube. The most important waterways are the Elbe, the Oder and the Danube connecting the country with the major seaports of E Germany and Poland. Large dams and reservoirs have been built mainly on the Vltava and the Váh rivers to assist water conservation and to provide energy.

Czechoslovakia has over 22,000 lakes which contain about 60 species of fish. There are over 1,500 mineral springs whose mineral properties have led to the foundation of many spas. The country is richly wooded (35%), chiefly with mixed and coniferous forests, although there are fine beech and oak forests in Slovakia. In remote mountain forests there are still bears and wild boar to be found.

Climate. The climate is typically continental with warm, humid summers and cold, dry winters. In winter snow lies 40-100 days and in low-lying areas fog can persist. There is little variation from E to W, the greatest variations occurring in mountain areas.

History, government and constitution. Formerly ruled by the Austrian Hapsburgs, Czechoslovakia became a separate state in 1918 when Czech lands were united with Slovakia. Mazaryk was elected first president of a parliamentary democracy. Claims of ill-treatment of the German-speaking minority in the Sudetenland during the 1930s gave Hitler an excuse to occupy the region in 1938. After World War II Czechoslovakia again became independent with the loss of some territory to the USSR. The parliamentary democracy was replaced by communist rule following a coup in 1948. An attempt to liberalize the political regime in 1968 was terminated after the intervention of Warsaw Pact troops. Since the constitution of 1960 was amended in 1968, each of the two republics has been governed by a National Council (200 deputies in Czech and 150 in Slovak Socialist Republic) with overall executive and legislative power vested in the Federal Assembly which elects a president. The Federal Assembly comprises the Chamber of Nations, with 75 Czech and 75 Slovak delegates, and the Chamber of the People which has 200 deputies elected by national suffrage. The dominant political party is the Communist Party of Czechoslovakia (KSC).

Economy. The economy of Czechoslovakia is based on the socialist concept of central planning with 5-year economic plans. Major industrial products include iron, steel, chemicals, equipment and machinery, glass, motor vehicles, cement, armaments, wood and paper. Steel production is largely based around the coal fields of Ostrava but attempts have been made to industrialize rural E Slovakia by introducing metal and engineering industries to cities such as Košice. Oil and gas refineries near Bratislava are supplied by pipeline from the USSR. Plzeň is noted for its beer and for the production of motor vehicles. The main agricultural products from state farms, collective farms and private plots (max size 1 ha) are sugar beet, potatoes, wheat, barley and maize. Major trading partners include the E bloc countries, Austria and W Germany.

Administrative divisions. The two Socialist Republics of Czechoslovakia are divided into the following ten *kraj* or regions which are subdivided into 112 districts:

Region	*area (sq km)*	*pop(1984)*
Czech Socialist Republic		
Severočeský	7,810	1,177,391
Západočeský	10,876	876,525
Středočeský	11,003	1,144,360
Jihočcský	11,345	694,112
Východočeský	11,240	1,247,086
Jihomoravský	15,028	2,053,497
Severomoravský	11,067	1,948,997
Slovak Socialist Republic		
Západoslovenský	14,491	1,707,507
Středoslovenský	17,985	1,559,391
Východoslovenský	16,191	1,440,536

Częstochowa *chē-sto-KHov'a*, voivodship in S central Poland, pop(1983) 759,000; area 6,182 sq km; capital Częstochowa; chief towns include Myszków and Lubliniec.

Częstochowa, TSCHENSTOCHAU (Ger), CHENSTOKHOV (Rus), 50 49N 19 00E, pop(1983) 244,100, industrial capital of Częstochowa voivodship, S central Poland; on R Warta; includes the industrial suburb of Nowa Częstochowa and the old Stara Częstochowa based around the market place; technical university (1949); railway; airfield; economy: steel, iron ore mining, chemicals, textiles; monuments: Paulite monastery (1382) on the Jasna Góra hill, with fine Baroque interior and art treasures; museum of iron ore mining; 7th-c burial ground; event: annual national violin festival.

D

Da Hinggan Ling *da hing-an ling*, GREATER KHINGAN RANGE, mountain range in NE Nei Mongol (Inner Mongolia) aut region and N Heilongjiang prov, NE China; runs 1,200 km from NE to SW, from the Heilong Jiang river in the N southwards almost to the border with Hebei prov; average elevation ranges from 1,100 to 1,400 m; rises to 2,029 m in Huanggangliang; the Da Hinggan Ling is one of China's most important natural forested areas; to the E, in NW Heilongjiang prov, is the Xiao Hinggan Ling, the Lesser or Eastern Khingan range.

Da Nang *da nang*, formerly TOURANE, 16 04N 108 13E, pop(1972e) 500,000, seaport in Quang Nam-Danang prov, central Vietnam, Indo-China; on the South China Sea; site of US military base during the Vietnam War.

Da Yunhe *da yoon-ho*, GRAND CANAL, canal in E China; measuring 1,794 km, it is the longest man-made waterway in the world; the canal stretches S from Beijing municipality, through Tianjin municipality and Shandong and Jiangsu provs terminating at Hangzhou in Zhejiang prov; it flows past the towns of Tianjin, Dezhou, Jining, Yangzhou, Wuxi, Suzhou and Hangzhou; building commenced in the 5th-c BC to aid the carriage of tribute rice from the Chang Jiang (Yangtze) Plain to the imperial government in Beijing (Peking); extensions to the original section near Yangzhou were made during the 7th century, when a canal connecting the Huang He (Yellow river) and Chang Jiang (Yangtze river) was built, the entire canal being opened in 610 AD; the N part of the Da Yunhe canal was redredged in the 14th century; the Grand Canal was the major transport artery between N and S China from the 13th century to the early 19th century, its use declined after the construction of railways; the canal connects 5 main rivers, the Hai He, Huang He, Huai He, Chang Jiang and Qiantang; the section from Jiangsu to Zhejiang is open all the year round for shipping; the canal's embankments have masonry towpaths which are still in use; the average width is 30.5 m, although it can become as narrow as 9 m when crossed by stone bridges.

Dabaka'la, dept in NE central Ivory Coast, W Africa; pop(1975) 56,230; area 9,670 sq km; capital Dabakala.

Dabola *da-bō-la'*, 10 50N 11 05W, town in central Guinea, W Africa; on the R Tinkisso, 314 km ENE of Conakry; railway.

Dąbrowa Górnicza *da'bro-va goor-nee-cha*, DOMBROVA (Rus), 53 40N 23 20E, pop(1983) 141,600, city in Katowice voivodship, S Poland; NE of Katowice; nearby coal deposits are amongst the thickest in the world (20 m); recreation centre on artificial L Pogoria; railway; economy: mining, steel.

Dacca, capital of Bangladesh. See Dhākā.

Dachstein *daKH'stīn*, 47 29N 13 36E, highest peak in the Salzkammergut and the name of a region in Salzburg, Oberösterreich and Steiermark states, central Austria; glaciers, ice caves and mountain lakes (Hallstätter See and Gosausee).

Dadra and Nagar Haveli *da-drah'* and *nu-gur ah-vel'i*, union territory in W India; bounded W by the Gulf of Khambhat, an arm of the Arabian Sea; lies between Gujarat and Maharashtra states; crossed by the R Damanganga; pop(1981) 103,677; area 491 sq km; formerly Portuguese territory; occupied in July 1954 by nationalists requesting that the area be incorporated into the Union; in Aug 1961 it became a union territory of India, despite an International Court of Justice ruling at The Hague, which upheld Portugal's claim to the areas; a tribal territory of 72 villages, with administrative headquarters at Silvassa; the territory is under the jurisdiction of Bombay, Maharashtra; agricultural crops include rice, ragi, wheat and millet; forest products are also important; there are no heavy industries; the administrative centre at Silvassa is linked with Bombay and Ahmadabad by rail.

Dagenham, London, England. See Barking and Dagenham.

Dah'lak Islands, archipelago in the SE Red Sea off the coast of Ērtra region, N Ethiopia, NE Africa; separated from the mainland by the Mits'iwa (Massawa) Channel; comprises two large islands and 124 small ones which are mostly uninhabited; stone quarried from Nokra Island was used to rebuild Mits'iwa after it suffered an earthquake in 1921.

Dahomey, W Africa. See Benin.

Dairen, town in Liaoning prov, NE China. See Dalian.

Dakar *du-kar'*, region in W Senegal, W Africa; pop(1976) 984,660; area 550 sq km; known as Cap Vert until 1984; capital Dakar; mostly desert or palm and casuarina plain; L Retba is separated from the Atlantic Ocean by 10 km of sand dunes; an international convention centre is located near Yoff airport; an artists' village and pilot ranch are located at Bambylor; the new town of Pikine has been established near Dakar.

Dakar, 14 38N 17 27W, pop(1979) 978,553, seaport capital of Senegal, W Africa; at the S extremity of the Cape Verde peninsula, the most W point of the African continent; W Africa's 2nd largest port serving Senegal and Mauritania; founded in 1857 by Faidherbe, it subsequently became the capital of French West Africa in 1902 and the capital of Senegal in 1958; between 1924 and 1946 it was part of a separate area known as Dakar and Dependencies; the port was held by Vichy forces during World War II after the fall of France; university (1499); railway terminus; Yoff airport (15 km from city); economy: commerce, soap, leather products, pharmaceuticals, textiles, metal products, plastics, fishing tackle, food processing; monuments: ethnographical museum, Great Mosque (67 m high); notable markets at the Kermel, the Sandaga and the Medina; a Roman Catholic cathedral, consecrated in 1936.

Dakhla *daKH'la*, VILLA CISNEROS (Sp), 23 43N 15 57W, pop(1982) 17,822, capital of Oued Eddahab prov, Western Sahara, NW Africa; airport.

Dakhlet-Nouadhibou *daKH'let-nwad-i-boo'*, region in W Mauritania, NW Africa; pop(1982e) 30,000; area 22,300 sq km; capital Nouadhibou; Mauritania's only railway links Nouadhibou to Zouîrât in Tiris Zemmour region, running E and N parallel to the border with the Western Sahara.

Dakovica *dyak-o'vit-sa*, 42 22N 20 26E, pop(1981) 92,203, town in autonomous province of Kosovo, SW Srbija (Serbia) republic, Yugoslavia; 64 km WSW of Priština, near the Albanian frontier; formerly held by Turkey (-1913), Montenegro (1913-29) and Albania (1941-44); economy: chrome and pyrites mining.

Dakovo *dyak'ko-vo*, 45 19N 18 24E, pop(1981) 52,349, town in N Hrvatska (Croatia) republic, Yugoslavia; SSW of Osijek.

Dalälven *dal-el'vun*, DAL (Eng), river in S central Sweden; formed by two forks, the Österdalälven and the Västerdalälven which join together S of L Siljan; flows SE through Kopparberg and S Gävleborg counties to discharge into the Gulf of Bothnia at Skutskär, SE of Gävle; length 520 km; 2nd longest river in Sweden.

Dalandzadgad *da'lan-dza'da-gad*, 43 34N 104 20E, capital of Ömnögovĭ county, S Mongolia; lies on the NE edge of Gurvan Sayhan Uul; economy: camel breeding, agriculture and salt production.

Dalian *da-lee-en*, LUDA, LU-TA, DAIREN, DALIEN, 38 53N 121 37E, pop(1984e) 1,587,800, port city in Liaoning prov, NE China; at the S end of the Liaodong Bandao peninsula in the Bo Hai gulf; a special economic zone; the port was built between 1899 and 1930 by the Japanese; control of the city passed from Japan to the Soviet Union in 1945; although Soviet occupation ended in 1954, bilingual street signs still remain; Dalian's deep natural harbour is silt-free and ice-free; resort beaches nearby; railway; airfield; economy: diesel engines, shipbuilding, machine tools, chemicals, textiles, glass; the centre of a fruit growing area (well-known for a variety of apples), fishing (especially shellfish).

Dalias *dal-ee'as*, 36 49N 2 52W, pop(1981) 32,929, town in Almería prov, Andalucia, S Spain; 35 km W of Almería; economy: mining, mineral baths nearby.

Dalien, town in Liaoning prov, NE China. See Dalian.

Dalkeith, 55 54N 3 04W, pop(1981) 11,255, capital of Midlothian dist, Lothian, E central Scotland; on the North Esk and South Esk rivers, 10 km SE of Edinburgh; economy: engineering.

Dal'las, 32 47N 96 49W, pop(1980) 904,078, county seat of Dallas county, NE Texas, United States; on the R Trinity; the 7th largest city by pop in the USA, Dallas is the commercial and financial centre of the southwest; named after George Mifflin Dallas, vice-president of the USA (1845-49); the city was founded in 1841 and achieved city status in 1871; President J.F. Kennedy was assassinated here in Nov 1963; 2 universities (1910, 1956); railway; airport; economy: electronic and transportation equipment, machinery, textiles, clothing, leather goods, oil refining.

Dalmatia *dal-may'shya*, a name applied since early times to the strip of territory bordering the Adriatic Sea in Bosna-Hercegovina and Crna Gora (Montenegro) republics, W Yugoslavia; extends from the S end of the island of Pag to Cavtat, S of Dubrovnik; for the most part mountainous and barren with few lines of communication to the interior; excellent harbours at Zadar, Split and Dubrovnik; once part of the Greek province of Illyria settled in the 6th century BC and later occupied by the Slavs in the 7th century AD.

Daloa *dal'wa*, dept in SW central Ivory Coast, W Africa; pop(1975) 369,610; area 15,200 sq km; capital Daloa; chief towns Febiaso and Varoua.

Daly City, 37 42N 122 28W, pop(1980) 78,519, city in San Mateo county, W California, United States; S suburb of San Francisco.

Damanhûr *da man hoor'*, HERMOPOLIS PARVA (anc), 31 03N 30 28E, pop(1976) 188,927, capital of Behara governorate, N Egypt; in the R Nile delta, 60 km ESE of Alexandria; economy: cotton.

Damascus, governorate and capital city of Syria. See Dimashq.

Damāvand, Qolleh-ye *da-ma-vand'*, 35 56N 52 08E, volcanic cone in the Elburz Mts, Māzandarān prov, N Iran, 72 km NE of Tehrān; height 5,670 m; highest peak in Iran; it has a permanent snowcap; Damāvand resort is at its S foot.

Damietta, town and governorate in Egypt. See Dumyât.

Dammām, Ad *ad dam'mam*, 26 20N 50 05E, pop(1974) 127,845, seaport in Eastern prov, E Saudi Arabia; on the W shore of the Arabian Gulf, opposite Bahrain; residential town for the surrounding oilfields; the Ad Dammām oilfield, discovered in 1936, has its centre at Aẓ Ẓahrān (Dhahran), 13 km to the S; modern development began in the late 1940s; centre of commerce and industry; university (1975); railway; economy: chemicals, metallurgy, fertilizers.

Damongo *da-mon'gō*, 9 05N 1 50W, town in Northern region, central Ghana, W Africa; W of Tamale.

Danakil Depression *dan'e-kil*, desert area in NE Ethiopia, NE Africa; occupies parts of Ērtra (SE), Tigray (E), Welo (NE), Hārergē (N) regions; a low-lying region bounded N and E by the Red Sea and by the Rift Valley in the S and W; mountainous in parts, rising to 1,000 m; the land also dips to 116 m below sea-level; an extremely hot area with temperatures soaring close to 60°C; naturally occurring salt reserves have been the centre of the regional economy for centuries; the salt is extracted and then transported by pack animal; the area is inhabited by the Afar people; the region is crossed by the Djibouti-Addis Ababa railway.

Danané *da-na'nay*, dept in W Ivory Coast, W Africa; pop(1975) 170,249; area 4,600 sq km; the R Cess forms the W frontier with Liberia; capital Danané.

Danbury, 41 24N 73 28W, pop(1980) 60,470, town in Fairfield county, SW Connecticut, United States; 32 km NW of Bridgeport; founded in 1685; railway; burned by the British in 1777 during the War of Independence.

Dangriga *dan-gree'ga*, formerly STANN - CREEK, 16 59N 88 13W, pop(1980) 6,661, capital of Stann Creek dist, Belize, Central America; on the Stann Creek river; linked to Belmopan and Belize city by Hummingbird and Western Highways; airfield; port facilities S at Commerce Bight.

Danlí *dan-lee'*, 14 02N 86 30W, pop(1983e) 17,986, town in Paraíso dept, S Honduras, Central America; economy: sugar, aguardiente, tobacco; event: Fiesta del Maíz (last weekend of August).

Danmark. See Denmark.

Danube, *dan'yoob*, DONAU *dōn'ow* (Ger), DUNAV *doo'nav* (Bulg), DUNAI *doo'nī* (Rus), DUNAREA *doo'ner-ya* (Rom), river in central and SE Europe, rising at Donaueschingen in the Black Forest, SW W Germany; flows NE through Bayern (Bavaria), SE across Austria, continuing E and S through Czechoslovakia, Hungary and then forming the main length of the Romania-Bulgaria border; its large swampy delta discharges into the Black Sea in Romania; length 2850 km; second longest river in Europe (the longest is the Volga); of great commercial importance, linked by canals to the Main, Oder and Rhine, and with the Rhine-Main-Danube and Danube-Black sea canals it forms the Trans-Europe Waterway (3500 km); major cities on its banks are Wien (Vienna), Budapest and Beograd (Belgrade); Romanian-Yugoslavian Iron Gate hydro and navigation project on its lower course; over 300 tributaries incl. Lech, Isar, Inn, Morava, Drau, Jiu, Olt, Dambovita.

Danville, 40 08N 87 37W, pop(1980) 38,985, county seat of Vermilion county, E Illinois, United States; on the R Vermilion, 53 km E of Champaign; railway.

Danville, 36 36N 79 23W, pop(1980) 45,642, independent city, S Virginia, United States; on R Dan, 5 km N of North Carolina border; railway; economy: shipping and trading centre; tobacco market.

Danzig, city in Poland. See Gdansk.

Dão *down*, river in Viseu dist, N central Portugal; rises in Serra de Lapa and flows 80 km SW to meet the R Mondego NE of Coimbra; the mountain-bound river valley and surrounding area are noted for the production of most of Portugal's 'vinho maduro' or matured table wine.

Dapaong', 10 58N 0 07E, chief town of Des Savanes region, N Togo, W Africa.

Daqahlîya *da-ka-lee'yu*, governorate in N Egypt; pop(1976) 2,732,756; area 3,471 sq km; capital El Mansûra.

Daqing *da-king*, ANDA, 46 37N 124 59E, pop(1984e) 802,100, city in Heilongjiang prov, NE China; NW of Harbin; the nearby Daqing oil field produces more than half of China's petroleum; a petrochemical complex, initiated in 1982, is now the focus for the expansion of the city with industries producing ethylene products; railway.

Dar es Salaam *dar' es su-lam'* (Arab, 'haven of peace'), 6 51S 39 18E, pop(1978) 757,346, seaport capital of Dar es Salaam region, E Tanzania, E Africa; on the Indian Ocean, 45 km S of Zanzibar and 645 km SE of Nairobi (Kenya); founded in 1882 by Sultan of Zanzibar; occupied by German East Africa Company in 1887; the capital of German East Africa was transferred here from Bagamoyo in 1891; occupied by the British during World War I; capital of Tanzania until 1974 when the more central location of Dodoma was chosen; the city remains the country's main port and industrial, commercial and financial centre; university (1961); airport (12 km W); economy: food processing, cement, glass, craftwork, mosquito coils, car parts, printing, linen, petroleum products, chemicals, pharmaceuticals, pesticides, aluminium and steel, polystyrene products, textiles, clothing, timber, mining machinery, seafoods, brewing, molasses; monuments: national museum, one of Africa's most important archaeological museums containing Dr Louis Leakey's famous Olduvai Gorge finds, amongst which is the skull of *Zinjanthropus boisei* or 'nutcracker man'; Tanzanian State House; monument to Tanganyikan troops who fought with the British in World War II; event: Saba Saba festival during the first week of July to celebrate the foundation of the TANU political party.

Dar'ā, DERRÁ *der'a*, governorate (*mohofazat*) in SW Syria; bounded S by Jordan; pop(1981) 362,969; capital Dar'ā; other chief town Izra.

Dardanelles, strait in NW Turkey. See Çanakkale Boğazi.

Darfur', region (former province in W Sudan, NE Africa; bordered W by Chad, Central African Republic and Libya; area 196,555 sq km; pop(1983) 3,093,699; chief towns El Fasher, Geneina and Nyala (rail terminus); the Jebel Marra rises in the W; there is scrub forest in the S and grassland in the N; there are reserves of zinc, lead and salt; economy: livestock, gum arabic.

Darhan *dar'KHan*, DARKHAN, 48 40N 100 10E, pop(1981e) 52,000; town in Selenge county, N Mongolia; lies E of the R Haraa and NW of Ulaanbaatar; a new city, constructed since 1961; railway; economy: mining, building and foodstuffs.

Darién *dar-yen'*, prov of E Panama, Central America; bounded SE by Colombia and W by the Golfo de Panamá; indented by the Golfo de San Miguel on the W coast; drained by the Chucunaque, Tuira, and Balsas rivers; bounded N by the Cordillera de San Blas; pop(1980) 26,524; least densely populated prov in Panama; area 16,803 sq km; capital La Palma; chief towns Yaviza and El Real; attempted settlement by the Scots in the 1690s (the Darien Scheme) is still remembered in local place names such as Punta de Escoces, Caledonia Bay and Caledonia Mountain; it is proposed that the Inter-American Highway will cross the prov.

Dārjiling or **Darjee'ling**, 27 02N 88 20E, pop(1981) 57,603, hill station in West Bengal, NE India; in the foothills of the Himalayas near the Sikkim state frontier; the inhabitants are mostly Bhutanese and Nepalese; at the centre of a tea-growing region; former summer residence of the Bengal government.

Darling, river in SE Australia; longest tributary of the Murray river; its headstreams, the Dumaresq and Macintyre rivers, join at the New South Wales-Queensland border 280 km SW of Brisbane; the river then flows W and SW along the border, past the town of Mungindi (at this point it is known as the Macintyre or the Barwon); it continues SW through New South Wales, past Bourke and on to join the Murray river; between Mungindi and Bourke it is known as the Barwon or the Darling, after Bourke it is known as the Darling river; length 3,070 km; major tributaries include the Gwydir, Namoi, Castlereagh, Macquarie, Bogan and Warrego rivers; the waters of the Darling are used for irrigation in New South Wales.

Darling Range, mountain range in Western Australia, near Perth; extends 320 km S along the SW coast and rises to 582 m at Mt Cooke.

Dar'lington, 54 31N 1 34W, pop(1981) 86,358, town in Darlington dist, Durham, NE England; on the R Tees, W of Stockton-on-Tees; railway; economy: engineering, textiles.

Darmstadt *darm'shtat*, a S dist of Hessen (Hesse) prov, W Germany; pop(1983) 3,415,000; area 7,446 sq km; capital Darmstadt.

Darmstadt, 49 51N 8 40E, pop(1983) 137,800, capital of Darmstadt dist, S Hessen (Hesse) prov, W Germany; 27 km S of Frankfurt; lies on the edge of the Upper Rhine plain amid the N foothills of the Odenwald; city status in 1330; former capital of Hessen state; the economic and communications centre of S Hessen; aerospace centre; technical university (1895); railway; economy: plastics, cosmetics, chemicals, electronics.

Darsalami *dar-sa-la'mi*, 11 04N 4 19W, town in SW Burkina, W Africa; S of Bobo Dioulasso; railway.

Dart, river in Devon, SW England; rises on Dartmoor and flows 60 km SE past Totnes to meet the English Channel at Dartmouth.

Dart'ford, 51 27N 0 14E, pop(1981) 63,064, market town in Greater London urban area and Dartford dist, Kent, SE England, United Kingdom; 24 km WNW of Chatham, on the R Darent; linked to Essex by the Dartford Tunnel; railway; economy: paper, engineering, pharmaceuticals, cement.

Dartmoor, national park in Devon, S England; area 913 sq km; established in 1951; noted for granite *tors*, many of which have been eroded into odd shapes, and for hanging oak woods; a popular area for walking and riding.

Dartmouth, 44 40N 63 35W, pop(1981) 62,277, port in S Nova Scotia, SE Canada; NE of Halifax; settled in 1751, it became a whaling port in the late 18th century; railway; joined to Halifax by 2 suspension bridges, opened in 1955 and 1970 respectively; event: on the first Wednesday in Aug the Natal Day regatta is held on L Banook.

Dar'wen, 53 42N 2 28W, pop(1981) 31,094, town in South Ribble dist, Lancashire, NW England; 6 km S of Blackburn; railway; economy: chemicals, paint, textiles.

Dar'win, formerly PALMERSTON, PORT DARWIN, 12 23S 130 44E, pop(1981) 56,482, seaport capital of Northern Territory, Australia; on the Beagle Gulf, an inlet of the Clarence Strait; an important communications centre serving Arnhem Land (E) and the surrounding mining districts; the first European settlement of 1869 was destroyed by a hurricane in 1879; in 1942 the city was attacked by the Japanese; rebuilt after the war, Darwin was destroyed by cyclone Tracy in Dec 1974; reconstruction began in 1976; airport; monuments: Government House, built in 1869, is the home of the Administrator of the Northern Territory; Overland Telegraph Memorial, erected in memory of the men who built the overland telegraph line from Adelaide to Darwin, completed on 22 Aug 1872; Stuart Memorial, in memory of John McDouall Stuart who crossed Australia from Adelaide to Darwin between Oct 1861 and July 1862, following a route later chosen for the overland telegraph line and Stuart Highway; Ross and Keith Smith memorial, commemorating the first flight from England by brothers Ross and Keith Smith in Dec 1919; cathedral (1902); Fannie Bay Gaol Museum, in use for nearly 100 years before the last prisoners were transferred to new buildings at Berrimah in 1979; S of Darwin is Australia's first commercial crocodile farm; events: Darwin Beer Can Regatta for craft made almost entirely of beer cans (June); Darwin Royal Show Day in July.

Dar'win, 51 48S 58 59W, settlement on East Falkland, Falkland Is, in the S Atlantic, at the head of Choiseul Sound, on the narrow isthmus that joins the N half of East Falkland to Lafonia in the S; about 70 km from Stanley.

Dasht-e-Kavīr *dasht'e-ka-veer'*, salt desert basin of the central Iranian plateau, SE of the Elburz Mts, N central Iran; length 805 km; width 320 km; strong surface evaporation has created a salt crust covering salt marsh or mud; settlement is confined to the surrounding mountains; extending SE from it is the Dasht-e-Lut, a sand and stone desert.

Dasht-e-Lut *dasht'e-loot'*, sand and stone desert of E Iran; extending SE from the Dasht-e-Kavīr salt desert; length 480 km; width 320 km; mostly dried-out *kavirs* (salt marshes).

Daska *dus'ku*, 32 15N 74 23E, pop(1981) 56,000, city in Punjab prov, Pakistan; SW of R Chenab.

Date Line, an imaginary line, based by international agreement on the meridian of 180° (with deviations to keep certain islands in the same zone as their respective mainlands), at which the date is altered to compensate for the gain or loss of time (1 hour per 15°) which occurs when circumnavigating the globe.

Datong *dah-toong*, TA-T'UNG, 40 12N 113 12E, pop(1984e) 981,000, city in Shanxi prov, NE central China; just S of the Great Wall, W of Beijing (Peking); established in the 4th century as capital of the Northern Wei dynasty; railway; economy: livestock, fur, coal mining, cement, locomotives, soda; monuments: the Jiulong Bi (Nine Dragon Screen), a Ming dynasty screen of multicoloured glazed tiles; 16 km W of Datong are the Yungang Caves, the 53 cave temples contain the earliest examples of Buddhist stone-carving in China, numbering 51,000 bas-reliefs and statues mostly carved between 460 and 494 AD.

Daule *dow'lay*, 1 56S 79 56W, pop(1982) 18,923, town in Guayas prov, W Ecuador; on the Río Daule, N of Guayaquil.

Dauphiné *dō-fee-nay*, former prov in SE France, now occupying the depts of Drôme, Isère and Hautes-Alpes; on passing to Philip V in 1349, both lands and title became the property of the king's eldest son.

Davao *da'vow*, CITY OF DAVAO, 7 05N 125 38E, pop(1980) 610,275, seaport in Davao Del Sur prov, Southern Mindanao, Philippines; at the head of Davao Gulf, SE Mindanao I; founded 1849; formerly held by Japanese; university (1965); airfield; economy: rice, copra, corn trade, pearls; events: tribal festival in Oct; feast of San Pedro in June.

Dav'enport, 41 32N 90 35W, pop(1980) 103,264, county seat of Scott county, E Iowa, United States; on the Mississippi river, opposite Rock Island, Illinois; developed after the building, in 1856, of the first railway bridge across the Mississippi; railway; economy: heavy industrial and agricultural equipment.

Dav'entry, 52 16N 1 09W, pop(1981) 16,193, town in Daventry dist, Northamptonshire, central England; 20 km W of Northampton; radio transmitting station nearby; monument: Iron Age fort.

David *da-veed'*, 8 26N 82 26W, pop(1980) 49,472, capital town of Chiriquí prov, SW Panama, Central America; on the Río David; founded in 1738 as a gold-prospecting camp; its port, Pedregal, is 8 km to the S; railway; on the Inter-American Highway; events: international fair and fiesta (19 March).

Davis, 38 33N 121 48W, pop(1980) 36,640, city in Yolo county, central California, United States; 21 km W of Sacramento; university (1908); railway.

Davis Strait, sea passage between Greenland and Baffin Island, separating Baffin Bay from the Labrador Sea and connecting the Atlantic with the Arctic Ocean; 645 km long by 290 km wide at its narrowest point; route by which the Labrador current brings icebergs from the Arctic into the Atlantic Ocean; named after the British navigator John Davis who first sailed through the strait in 1587; depths of 1,700 m are reached in the middle of the channel.

Davos *da-vōs'*, TAVAU (Romansch), 46 54N 9 52E, pop(1980) 10,468, fashionable summer and winter resort town in Graubünden canton, E Switzerland; in a high valley traversed by the R Landwasser, surrounded by forest-covered mountains, SE of Chur; Davos's fame as a health resort dates from 1860 when Dr Alexander Spengler prescribed the clear mountain air for his tuberculosis patients; also a popular winter sports centre, with the largest skating rink in Europe; a few km S of Davos is the magnificent walking and winter sports area of Rinerhorn; the chief snow fields, shared with Klosters, are reached by the Parsenn funicular, and the Parsenn run is claimed to be the world's finest; alt 1,560 m; railway; bathing beach on the Davoser See (N end of the valley); event: International Ice Hockey Tournament for the Spengler Cup.

Dawḥah, Ad, DOHA *dō'ha*, 25 25N 51 32E, pop(1985e) 150,000, seaport capital of the State of Qatar, on the Arabian Gulf; on the E coast of the Qatar Peninsula; reclamation of the West Bay has created New Dawḥah (area 7.4 sq km) for the location of new housing, foreign embassies, and government offices; chief commercial and communications centre; E terminus of the dual carriageway which links Qatar with the Saudi Arabian road network; university; economy: oil refining, shipping, engineering, foodstuffs, refrigeration and processing plants for preparing prawns for export, and the manufacture of construction materials; there is a pipeline from Musay'īd oil refinery; the Ras Abu Fantas power and distillation plant is situated to the SE; airport; monument: old Turkish fort (1850).

Dawson, 64 04N 139 24W, pop(1981) 1,530, city in W Yukon terr, NW Canada; on the Yukon river, near the Alaskan frontier; established as a mining town during the gold rush of 1896 when its pop reached a total of 25,000.

Daya Bay, site of China's largest nuclear power project in Guangdong prov, S China; 50 km from Hong Kong; designed to supply Hong Kong and Guangdong prov with power in 1993.

Dayr az Zawr *dayr' ez zōr'*, governorate (*mohofazat*) in E Syria; bounded SE by Iraq; pop(1981) 409,130; capital Dayr az Zawr; chief towns Al Mayādīn and Abū Kamāl; traversed NW-SE by the R Euphrates.

Dayr az Zawr, DEIR-EZ-ZOR ('the convent of the groves'), 35 20N 40 05E, pop(1970) 66,143, capital town of Dayr az Zawr governorate, E central Syria; 320 km SE of Ḥalab (Aleppo); situated on the right bank of the R Euphrates which is here bridged 5 times; university; railway; road junction; economy: agricultural production in the Euphrates river valley has increased considerably as a result of land reclamation and irrigation.

Dayton, 39 45N 84 12W, pop(1980) 203,371, county seat of Montgomery county, W Ohio, United States; at the confluence of the Stillwater and Miami rivers, 75 km N of Cincinnati; founded in 1796; 2 universities (1850, 1964); railway; airfield; aviation and aeronautical research centre, home of Wilbur and Orville Wright, the first aviators; event: Dayton Airshow (July).

Daytona Beach, 29 13N 81 01W, pop(1980) 54,176, town in Volusia county, NE Florida, United States; on the Atlantic Ocean, 140 km SSE of Jacksonville; railway; year-round resort, noted for its hard, white beach; event: Summer Speed Week (July).

Dazu *da-zoo*, 29 47N 106 30E, town in Sichuan prov, SW central China; 160 km NW of Chongqing; one of the most important Buddhist archaeological sites in China, containing over 50,000 stone carvings from the 9th to 13th centuries AD; the Buddhist figures at Dazu are depicted as normal human beings in scenes of everyday life, departing from traditional Buddhist art with its images of fear and of the supernatural; 2 km from Dazu is Bei Shan (North Hill), where the first Buddhist shrine was established in 892; Bei Shan contains over 10,000 figures which were sculpted in 290 niches over a period of 250 years from the late Tang to the late Song dynasty; Grotto 136, 'The Wheel of the Universe', contains an intricately carved stone wheel symbolizing the cycle of man's life and the limitless power of Buddhism; this grotto depicts women who subdued wild animals: the female bodhisattvas, Manjusri and Samatabhadra, astride a lion and an elephant; Grotto 245 contains over 1,000 minute figures, including pagodas, temples, dancing sparrows, musicians and dragons; 15 km NE of Dazu is Baoding Shan, containing 10,000 figures sculpted between 1179 and 1249; included in these sculptures is the Sleeping Buddha, a reclining Buddha which measures over 31 m; also at Baoding Shan is the Yuan Jue (Total Awakening) Grotto, famous for its carving of a kneeling god surrounded by Buddhist followers.

De Kalb, 41 56N 88 46W, pop(1980) 33,099, city in De Kalb county, N Illinois, United States; on S branch of the R Kishwaukee, 45 km SE of Rockford; university (1895); railway.

Dead Sea, LACUS ASPHALTITES (anc), (Heb, 'BAHRAT LUT' SEA OF LOT), THE SALT SEA, SEA OF THE PLAIN, EAST SEA (Old Test), inland lake in the Jordan Trough of the Great Rift Valley on the Jordan-Israel border; connected to the Gulf of 'Aqaba by the Wadi Araba; the sea is the lowest point on Earth, lying 394 m below sea-level; fed by the Jordan river to the N, but has no outlet other than by evaporation; one of the most saline lakes in the world, the water is characterized by magnesium, sodium, potassium and calcium salts; large masses of asphalt occasionally appear on the surface; potash and magnesium bromide have been exploited since 1921; sea levels have been falling as the result of water from the R Jordan being used for irrigation and for domestic and industrial supply; there have been plans to link the Dead Sea directly to the Mediterranean in order to stabilize sea levels.

Deal, 51 14N 1 24E, pop(1981) 26,548, resort town in Dover dist, Kent, SE England; 13 km NNE of Dover on the English Channel; a Cinque port; railway; economy: shipyards, fishing, tourism; monument: 16th-c Deal castle, built by Henry VIII.

Dear'born, 42 19N 83 11W, pop(1980) 90,660, town in Wayne county, SE Michigan, United States; on the R Rouge, 16 km W of Detroit; railway; economy: iron and steel, motor vehicles; monuments: Greenfield Village, Henry Ford Museum.

Dearborn Heights, 42 20N 83 18W, pop(1980) 67,706, town in Wayne county, SE Michigan, United States; NW of Dearborn and 20 km W of Detroit.

Dearne Valley *dern*, pop(1981) 89,055, urban area in South Yorkshire, N England; 12 km SE of Barnsley; its centre is at Bolton-upon-Dearne; crossed by the R Dearne which rises E of Huddersfield in W Yorkshire and flows SE into the R Don N of Conisbrough; railway.

Death Valley, SE California, United States; ancient rift valley lake bed beside the Nevada border; a deep and arid desert basin, it is one of the hottest places in the world and contains the lowest point in North America (the Badwater river, alt −86 m); 225 km long; 6-26 km wide; stretches NW from the Mojave desert between the Amargosa Range (E) and the Panamint Range (W); set in a National Monument, area 8,399 sq km, established in 1933; Telescope Peak (height 3,367 m) is the highest peak in the monument; the area receives almost no rainfall (less than 5 cm per year) and has high summer temperatures reaching 74°C (ground) and 57°C (air); the monument contains numerous salt and alkali flats, colourful rock formations, desert plants, small animal life and footprints of prehistoric animals; the valley was named in 1849 by a party of gold prospectors, some of whom died while trying to cross it; in the 1880s large deposits of borax were discovered; Scott's Castle was built by the American adventurer Walter Scott.

Debra Markos *de'bre mar'kōs*, 10 19N 37 41E, pop(1984e) 39,808, capital of Gojam region, W Ethiopia, NE Africa; 240 km NW of Addis Ababa; airfield.

Debra Zeyit *de'bre zayt*, DEBRE ZEIT, 8 50N 39 00E, pop(1984e) 51,143, town in Shewa region, central Ethiopia, NE Africa; SE of Addis Ababa; railway.

Debrecen *deb'ret-sen*, 47 33N 21 42E, pop(1984e) 205,000, capital of Hajdú-Bihar county, E Hungary; city of county rank and economic and cultural centre of the Great Plain (Alföld) region; third largest city in Hungary; in 1849 Louis Kossuth proclaimed the independence of Hungary in the great church in Debrecen; university (1912); University of Agrarian Science (1868); University of Medicine (1951); railway; economy: commercial centre for agricultural region; tobacco trade; pharmaceuticals; agricultural machinery.

Decatur *di-kay'tur*, 34 36N 86 59W, pop(1980) 42,002, county seat of Morgan county, N Alabama, United States; on the R Tennessee, 120 km N of Birmingham; railway; economy: shipyards; manufactures include textiles, plastics, chemicals, bricks, tyres and trailers.

Decatur, 39 51N 88 57W, pop(1980) 94,081, county seat of Macon county, central Illinois, United States; on L Decatur, 56 km E of Springfield; Millikin University (1901); railway; economy: corn, coal; Abraham Lincoln received his first endorsement for the presidential nomination here, in May 1860.

Deccan *de'kun*, DAKSHIN (Sanskrit), eastward sloping plateau occupying most of central S India, S of the Vindhya Mts; bounded by the Eastern Ghats and the Western Ghats; includes most of Karnataka, S Andhra Pradesh, SE Maharashtra and NW Tamil Nadu states; major towns include Hyderabad and Bangalore; average alt 600 m; the area is noted for its cotton production, the rich volcanic soils in the NW being known as 'the black cotton soils'; historically Deccan is the area of India to the S of the R Narbada; during the 17th century most of the Deccan area was united under the Mogul Empire; Hindus began to regain political power here during the early 18th century; the Carnatic plains area of the Deccan plateau became the arena for the British struggle against the French for control of India during the 18th century.

Děčín *dyet'cheen*, TETSCHEN (Ger), 50 48N 14 15E, pop(1984) 54,987, industrial river port town in Severočeský region, Czech Socialist Republic, W Czechoslovakia; on R Labe (Elbe); includes Podmokly on the left bank of the R Elbe; railway; economy: coal mining.

Dédougou *day-doo'goo*, 12 29N 3 25W, town in W Burkina, W Africa; W of Koudougou and the Black Volta river.

Ded'za, dist in Central region, Malawi, SE Africa; area 3,624 sq km; pop(1977) 298,190.

Deerfield Beach, 26 19N 80 06W, pop(1980) 39,193, town in Broward county, SE Florida, United States; on the Atlantic Ocean, 20 km N of Fort Lauderdale; railway.

Dehiwala *day-hee-wah'le*, DEHIWELA, 6 52N 79 52E; pop(1981) 174,385; town in Colombo dist, Western prov, Sri Lanka; S of Colombo on the Indian Ocean; health resort with fine beaches.

Dehra Dun *day'ru doon*, 30 20N 78 03E, pop(1981) 294,000, city in Uttar Pradesh, N India; 60 km NE of Sahranpur; founded in the 17th century by the Sikh guru Ram Rai; market town and administrative centre for surrounding dist; has a noted forest research institute, military training academy and archaeological survey laboratory; railway.

Dej *dezh*, 47 08N 23 55E, pop(1983) 38,229, town in Cluj county, NE central Romania; on R Somes, NNE of Cluj-Napoca; railway junction; economy: grain, fruit, hide trade, oil refining, paper, saltworks.

Del City, 35 26N 97 26W, pop(1980) 28,424, city in Oklahoma county, central Oklahoma, United States; a residential suburb 8 km SE of Oklahoma City.

Del Rio, 29 22N 100 54W, pop(1980) 30,034, county seat of Val Verde county, SW Texas, United States; a port on the Rio Grande river, opposite Ciudad Acuña, Mexico; railway; economy: marketing and distributing centre in a sheep-farming region; nearby is Laughlin Air Force Base.

Del'aware, state in E United States; bounded S and W by Maryland, N by Pennsylvania, and E by New Jersey, Delaware Bay and the Atlantic Ocean; the R Delaware forms the upper part of the E state border, separating Delaware from New Jersey, before emptying into Delaware Bay; the highest point is Ebright Road (135 m); predominantly an industrial state but agricultural products include poultry, soybeans, corn and dairy products; the state's industries are centred around Wilmington, the chief manufactures being chemicals and transportation equipment, processed food, plastics and primary and fabricated metals; several large corporations are based in Wilmington, taking advantage of the state's taxation laws; the original Swedish settlers were supplanted in 1655 by the Dutch who were in turn supplanted by the British in 1664; part of Pennsylvania until 1776; one of the original states and first to ratify the Federal Constitution in Dec 1787; the 'First State' or 'Diamond State'; pop(1980) 594,338; area 5,023 sq km; capital Dover; other chief cities are Wilmington and Newark; the state is divided into 3 counties:

County	*area (sq km)*	*pop(1980)*
Kent	1,547	98,219
New Castle	1,030	398,115
Sussex	2,449	98,004

Delaware, river in Pennsylvania, New York and Delaware states, United States; formed by the meeting of 2 branches in S New York; flows 450 km SE following the state frontiers of Pennsylvania, New York and New Jersey to meet Delaware Bay; navigable to Trenton.

Delémont *del-ay-mõ'*, DELSBERG *dels'berk* (Ger), 47 22N 7 21E, pop(1980) 11,682, capital town of Jura canton, W Switzerland; on the R Sorne, SW of Basel; former residence of the prince-bishops of Basel; railway junction; economy: watch-making; monuments: church of St Marcel (1762-66); there are also many classical 18th-c buildings in the old town above the river; the road between Delémont and Porrentruy is an established scenic route.

Delft, 52 01N 4 22E, pop(1984e) 86,733, ancient city and municipality in W Zuid Holland prov, W Netherlands; on the R Schie, between Rotterdam and 's-Gravenhage; technical university (1863); birthplace of the scholar and statesman Hugo de Groot (1583-1645), of the painter Jan Vermeer, and of the natural scientist Anthoni van Leeuwenhoek (1632-1723), inventor of the microscope; in the 14th century Delft was famous for linen-weaving, and in the 16th century arose the pottery and porcelain industries which brought the town a world-wide reputation; railway; economy: vehicle and machine construction, industrial pharmaceutical products, yeast and alcohol, consumer products, electrical engineering, building materials, paper, cardboard, porcelain; monuments: Nieuwe Kerk (1396-1496), in the choir is the impressive mausoleum of William the Silent, erected at the expense of the United Provinces after his assassination in Delft in 1584; Italian Renaissance town hall; Prisenhof (originally the monastery of St Agatha), residence of the Princes of Orange and scene in 1584 of the assassination of Prince William of Orange, the founder of Dutch independence.

Delgado or **Villa Delgado** *vee'ya del-ga'dō*, 13 40N 89 18W, pop(1980) 84,335, town in San Salvador dept, El Salvador, Central America; a NE suburb of San Salvador.

Delhi *de'li*, union territory in N central India, on the boundary between the states of Haryana and Uttar Pradesh, to the E of the R Yamuna, pop(1981) 6,196,414; area 1,485 sq km; separated from Punjab prov in 1912 and extended in 1915 by the addition of a small part of the United Provinces; became a union territory in Nov 1956; administered by a metropolitan council of 61 members; there are 241 villages; capital Delhi.

Delhi, DILLI (Hind), formerly SHAHJAHANABAD, 28 38N 77 17E, pop(1981) 5,714,000, capital of India and administrative centre of Delhi union territory, N central India; 1,190 km NNE of Bombay and 1,280 km NW of Calcutta; Old Delhi, enclosed within the walls built by Shah Jahan in 1638, lies on the banks of the R Yamuna; historically of strategic importance at the head of navigation on the R Yamuna and guarding the approaches to the fertile Ganges plain from the NW, the direction from which India has been invaded many times; the Mogul architecture and thronged bazaars of Old Delhi sharply contrast with the formal architecture and wide boulevards of New Delhi to the S; largely designed by Sir Edwin Lutyens, New Delhi has been the administrative centre of India since 1912 and is the largest commercial centre in India; with the decline in water transport Delhi became a great railway centre; university (1922); airport (Palam); economy: chemicals, machine tools, clothing, footwear, drinks, food processing, plastics, bicycles, radios and televisions; traditional crafts of Delhi include jewellery, papier mâché, textiles and ivory carving; monuments: Red Fort, with its red sandstone walls and gateways, contains the Mogul palace built by Shah Jahan in the mid-17th century; to the S of the Red Fort, on the banks of the Yamuna is the site called Rajghat, where Mahatma Gandhi was cremated (31 Jan 1948); to the SW of the fort is the great domed Jama Masijid, which is the largest mosque in India (1644-58), built in red sandstone and inlaid with white marble.

Del'menhorst, 53 03N 8 37E, pop(1983) 71,700, commercial and manufacturing city in Weser-Ems dist, Niedersachsen (Lower Saxony) prov, W Germany; 14 km WSW of Bremen; railway; economy: hydraulic excavators and loaders.

Delphi, ancient site in Greece. See Dhelfoí.

Delray Beach, 26 28N 80 04W, pop(1980) 34,325, resort and residential town in Palm Beach county, SE Florida, United States; on the Atlantic Ocean, 28 km S of West Palm Beach; railway; economy: trade centre for flowers, fruit and vegetables.

Delsberg, town in Switzerland. See Delémont.

Delta Amacuro *del'ta a-ma-koo'rō*, federal territory in NE Venezuela; bordered by the Atlantic (E) and Guyana (SE); Trinidad lies in the Caribbean to the N; consists mainly of the large triangle formed by the swampy Orinoco delta; pop(1980) 69,257; area 40,184 sq km; capital Tucupita.

Deman'da, Sierra de la, mountain range of the Cordillera Iberica in Castilla-León and La Rioja regions of N Spain; extends along the Logroño-Burgos prov border, rising to 2,262 m.

Demer, river in NE and central Belgium; rises near Bilzen in Limburg prov; flows W through N Brabant prov, past Diest and Aarschot to the R Dijle at Werchter; navigable below Diest; length 96 km.

Den Haag, city in the Netherlands. See 's-Gravenhage.

Den Helder, 52 57N 4 45E, pop(1984e) 63,826, municipality in N Noord Holland prov, W Netherlands; on the N tip of W Friesland, between the Waddenzee and the open North Sea, opposite Texel I; rail terminus; largest naval port of the Netherlands; ferry services to Texel; economy: fishing, textiles; connected to Amsterdam by the Noord Holland Canal; at the centre of one of the country's prime bulb growing areas.

Dender *den'dur*, DENDRE *dã'dru* (Fr), river in W central Belgium; rises 10 km SW of Soignies, Hainaut prov; flows N past Ath, Lessines, Ninove and Aalst to the R Schelde at Dendermonde; lower course navigable; length 88 km.

Dendermonde *den'dur mōn du*, dist of Oost-Vlaanderen (East Flanders) prov, N Belgium; area 343 sq km; pop(1982) 181,306.

Dendermonde, TERMONDE *ter-möd'* (Fr), 51 02N 4 06E, pop(1982) 42,295, town in Dendermonde dist, Oost-Vlaanderen (East Flanders) prov, Belgium; 19 km W of Mechelen, on the right bank of the R Schelde where the R Dender joins it; monuments: town hall (formerly the 14th-c cloth hall), Gothic church of Our Lady (14-15th-c), former Butchers' Guildhall (1416).

Denizli *de-neez'lee'*, mountainous prov in SW Turkey; pop(1980) 603,338; area 11,868 sq km; capital Denizli.

Denizli, 37 46N 29 05E, pop(1980) 135,373, capital town of Denizli prov, SW Turkey; on a tributary of the R Menderes, 176 km ESE of İzmir; agricultural market centre; badly damaged by earthquakes in 1710 and 1899; nearby are the ruins of ancient Laodicea, including a stadium and 2 large theatres; event: Pamukkale festival (3-5 June).

Denmark, DANMARK *dan'mark* (Dan), official name Kingdom of Denmark, KONGERIGET DANMARK (DAN), a kingdom of N Europe, consisting of (1) the greater part of the peninsula of Jylland (Jutland), (2) a number of islands in the Baltic Sea close to the coast of Jylland, of which the largest are Sjælland (Zealand), Fyn, Lolland, Falster, and much further E, Bornholm, and (3) some of the N Frisian Islands in the North Sea; bounded on the N by the Skagerrak, on the E by the Kattegat, Øresund and the Baltic Sea, on the S by West Germany, and on the W by the North Sea; the southernmost and smallest of the Scandinavian countries; coastline 3,379 km; area (excluding Greenland and the Færøerne Islands) 43,076 sq km; timezone GMT +1; capital København (Copenhagen); chief towns Århus, Odense, Ålborg, Esbjerg, Randers and Kolding; total pop(1983) 5,116,464; population density is 117 inhabitants per sq km; the Danes are a branch of the Scandinavian race and their language is, like Swedish, a derivative of Old Scandinavian, but has been modified by its contact with German; 97% of the population are of the Lutheran Church; there are 5 universities in Denmark (København, Århus, Odense, Roskilde and Ålborg); the Danish currency is the krone of 100 øre; national holiday 16 April (Queen's Birthday); membership of Council of Europe, EEC, ADB, DAC, EMS, ESRO, FAO, GATT, IAEA, IBRD, ICAC, ICAO, ICES, ICO, IDA, IDB, IFAD, IFC, IHO, ILO, IMF, IMO, INTELSAT, IPU, ISO, ITC, ITU, IWC, NATO, OECD, UN, UNESCO, UPU, WHO, WIPO, WMO, WSG.

Physical description. The country is uniformly low-lying, the highest point (Ejer Bavnehöj in E Jylland) being less than 200 m above sea level. There are no large rivers and few lakes, but its shoreline is indented by many lagoons and fjords. The fjords penetrate deeply into the country, the largest being Limfjorden (Lim Fjord) which intersects Jylland and has cut off its N extremity since 1825, when it broke through the isthmus which had till then separated it from the North Sea.

Climate. The climate is much modified by marine influences, and the effect of the Gulf Stream, to give winters that are cold and cloudy but summers that are warm and sunny. Few places have an annual rainfall exceeding 675 mm.

History, government and constitution. First united as a single state over one thousand years ago, Denmark joined with Sweden and Norway under one ruler in 1389. In the 16th century Sweden separated from the union and in 1814, following Danish support of Napoleon, Norway also gained its independence. In 1864 Schleswig Holstein, which had been under Danish control since 1460, was lost to Germany. Denmark has been a constitutional monarchy since 1849, with the present constitution being founded upon the 'Grundlov' (charter) of 5 June, 1953. Prior to that date the country had a bi-cameral legislature, the *Landsting* or Senate elected indirectly for 8 years and the *Folketing* elected directly for 4 years. In 1953 the Senate was abolished and a unicameral system adopted. Legislative power lies with the Queen and the 179-member Diet (*Folketing*) jointly. Iceland gained its independence from Denmark in 1944, but Greenland and Færøerne (Faroe) Is remain dependencies each returning 2 elected members to the Diet.

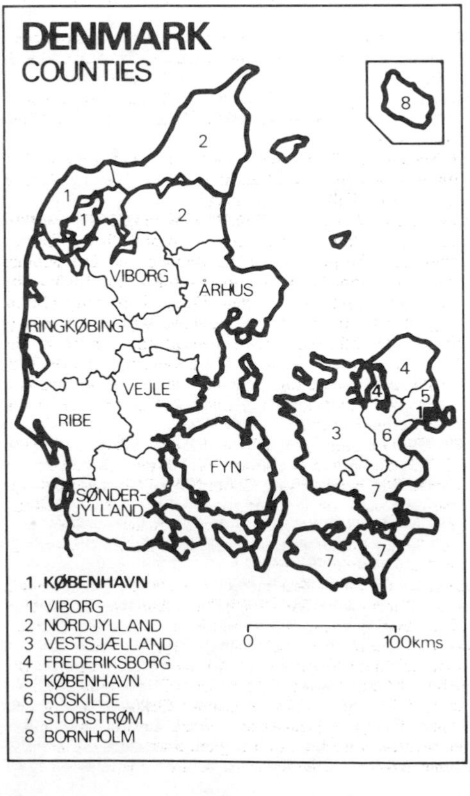

Industry. Denmark's lack of raw materials has limited the country's industrial base to the processing industries (machinery, hardware, shipping, furniture, glass, porcelain, chemicals, pharmaceuticals, etc). The country's main industrial concentrations are located around København, Odense, Århus and Ålborg-Nørresundby. Its principal trading partners are W Germany, Sweden, the UK, the USA, the Benelux countries, Norway, Italy, France and Switzerland. In recent years, windmill production has become one of Denmark's fastest growing industries with exports chiefly to California. Denmark has been a member of the EEC since Jan 1973.

Agriculture and forestry. Denmark's fine marly soil, formed by ground moraines, is largely devoted to intensive agriculture, with 64% of the total land area under arable cropping and 8% under pasture. Eleven per cent of the land area is under forest. The area of cultivated land is 29,000 sq km, most of this (17,000 sq km) being under corn. The average farm size is 0.3 sq km. In recent years, pig breeding has declined significantly in favour of cattle and poultry production, while horticulture and vegetable-growing have increased. Foodstuffs including canned meat, powdered milk and sugar, account for 26% of total exports. The main markets are the EEC, Japan, the USA and Iran.

Administrative divisions. Denmark is divided into 14 counties (*amt*) as follows:

County	*area (sq km)*	*pop(1983)*
København	522	619,687
Frederiksborg	1,347	331,349
Roskilde	891	205,414
Vestsjælland	2,984	277,914
Storstrøm	3,398	258,670
Bornholm	588	47,313
Fyn	3,486	453,773
Sønderjylland	3,930	249,970
Ribe	3,131	214,700
Vejle	2,997	327,102
Ringkøbing	4,853	264,103
Århus	4,561	578,149
Viborg	4,122	230,909
Nordjylland	6,173	482,409

Denmark Strait, an arm of the N Atlantic Ocean between the E coast of Greenland and the NW coast of Iceland, linking the Atlantic Ocean to the Greenland Sea; the cold East Greenland Current flows SW through the channel bringing icebergs and fog, while a section of the warmer Irminger Current flows NE through the Strait around the coast of Iceland; wide continental shelves extend from the coasts of both Greenland and Iceland.

Denny, 56 02N 3 55W, pop(1981) 23,158, town in Falkirk dist, Central region, central Scotland; 8 km W of Falkirk; economy: iron.

Denpasar *den-pah'sahr*, 8 40S 115 14E, pop(1980) 88,142, capital and largest city of the island prov of Bali, Indonesia; university (1962); airport; seaport at Benoa Harbour to the S; monument: the temple and palace of Bali combine to form a museum of Balinese art.

Den'ton, 53 27N 2 07W, pop(1981) 37,764, town in Tameside borough, Greater Manchester, NW England; N of the R Tame and 6 km NE of Stockport; railway; economy: plastics, textiles, scientific instruments.

Denton, 33 13N 97 08W, pop(1980) 48,063, county seat of

Denton county, NE Texas, United States; 58 km NNW of Dallas; 2 universities (1890, 1901); railway; economy: trade, processing, and distributing centre for a large agricultural area; food-processing plants, flour mills, and factories manufacturing building materials, machinery, and clothing.

Denver, 39 44N 104 59W, pop(1980) 492,365, capital of state in Denver county, N central Colorado, United States; largest city in the state and a port on the South Platte river; the gold-mining settlement of Auraria was united with 2 other villages to form Denver in 1860; university (1864); railway; airport; economy: processing, shipping, and distributing centre for a large agricultural area, with stockyards and meat packing plants; manufactures include electronic and aerospace equipment, rubber goods and luggage; monuments: Fornery Transport Museum, US Mint; event: National Stock Show (Jan).

Dera Ghazi Khan *day'ru gah'zee KHan*, 30 05N 70 44E, pop(1981) 103,000, city in Punjab prov, Pakistan; on the Indus Canal; trade and administrative centre for the surrounding wheat and millet growing area; founded in the 15th century; moved to its present site in 20th century as a result of frequent flooding; uranium has been found here.

Dera Ismail Khan *day'ru is-mīl KHan*, 31 51N 70 56E, pop(1981) 68,000, town in North-West Frontier prov, Pakistan; agricultural market and local trade centre 241 km SSW of Peshawar; founded in 1469, the old town was swept away by the R Indus; new town built in 1823; oil discovered in the surrounding region; university (1974); economy: laquered wood, glass and ivory crafts.

Derby *dar'bi*, 52 55N 1 30W, pop(1981) 220,681, city in Derbyshire, central England; on the R Derwent, 56 km NE of Birmingham; in 880 AD the Danes changed the Saxon name of Northworthy to Deoraby; chartered in 1637; railway; economy: aero engines, lawnmowers, sugar refining, textiles, chemicals, plastics, china; monuments: cathedral of All Saints (1525), old silk mill industrial museum.

Derbyshire *dar'bi-shir*, county of central England; bounded NW by Greater Manchester, N by West Yorkshire, NE by South Yorkshire, E by Nottinghamshire, SE by Leicestershire and W by Cheshire and Staffordshire; rises to The Peak at 636 m; drained by Derwent, Dove, Wye and Trent rivers; pop(1981) 910,173; area 2,631 sq km; county town Matlock; chief towns include Derby, Chesterfield, Glossop; economy: textiles, iron smelting, engineering; the county is divided into 9 districts:

District	*area (sq km)*	*pop(1981)*
Amber Valley	265	109,587
Bolsover	160	70,634
Chesterfield	66	96,941
Derby	78	216,897
Erewash	109	102,112
High Peak	541	82,546
North-east Derbyshire	277	96,765
South Derbyshire	339	67,908
West Derbyshire	795	66,783

Derg, Lough, *loch durg*, lake in Galway, Clare and Tipperary counties, Irish Republic; formed by a widening of the R Shannon; Slieve Aughty Mts rise to the W; length 32 km; max width 8 km.

Derry, LONDONDERRY, DOIRE (Gael), county in N Northern Ireland; bounded N by Lough Foyle and the Atlantic Ocean, E by Co Antrim (mostly along the R Bann), SE by Lough Neagh, S and SW by Co Tyrone and NW by the Republic of Ireland; a hilly county with part of the Sperrin Mts rising in the S; drained by the Bann, Roe and Foyle rivers; pop(1981) 186,751; area 2,067 sq km; county town Derry (Londonderry); major towns include Coleraine and Portstewart; economy: mainly agriculture, producing seed potatoes and dairy produce; Derry is divided into 4 districts:

District	*area (sq km)*	*pop(1981)*
Coleraine	485	46,272
Limavady	587	26,270
Londonderry	382	83,384
Magherafelt	573	30,825

Derry, LONDONDERRY (-1984), 55 00N 7 19W, pop(1981) 62,697, county town in Londonderry dist, Derry (Londonderry), NW Northern Ireland; situated on a hill above the R Foyle, 8 km above its mouth into Lough Foyle sea lough, 122 km NW of Belfast; St Columba founded a monastery here c.546 AD and the Celtic settlement of Derry was built around it; the Vikings often raided the area in the 9-10th centuries; in 1613 James I proclaimed the city of Derry to be part of the Corporation of London; it was renamed London-Derry and a Protestant colony was settled here; in 1689 the city was beseiged by James II; under the Rev George Walker the city held out for 105 days until help arrived; 7,000 inhabitants died in the process; the town's name was changed to Derry in 1984; railway; economy: port; textiles (linen shirts), chemicals, engineering, man-made fibres, ceramics; monuments: the centre of the old town is surrounded by walls (built in 1619) which extend for approx 1.5 km and are over 5 m thick; 4 of the original gates are still in good condition: Butcher's Gate, Ferryquay Gate, Shipquay Gate and Bishop's Gate; St Columba's cathedral (Protestant) built 1628-33, restored and added to 1885-87; St Columba's church (Catholic) was built in 1873 in neo-Gothic style, nearby is St Columba's stone; the Guildhall (1912) contains a council chamber and the city museum; monument to George Walker.

Der'venta, 44 59N 17 56E, pop(1981) 57,010, town in N Bosna-Hercegovina republic, Yugoslavia; on R Ukrina, ENE of Banja Luka; railway; economy: timber and fruit trade.

Der'went, river in Derbyshire, central England; rises on the High Peak and flows 96 km S past Derby to meet the R Trent SW of Long Eaton.

Derwent, river in North Yorkshire, NE England; rises S of Whitby and flows 96 km S and W to meet the R Ouse near Goole.

Derwent Water, lake in the Lake District of Cumbria, NW England; extends 5 km S from Keswick; Borrowdale and the Lodore Falls are at its head.

Des Moines *di moyn'*, 41 35N 93 37W, pop(1980) 191,003, capital of state in Polk county, central Iowa, United States; at the junction of the Racoon and Des Moines rivers; developed around a fort established in 1843; a city and state capital since 1900; Drake University (1881); largest city in the state; railway; airport; economy: important industrial and transportation centre in the heart of Iowa's Corn Belt; agricultural processing, machinery manufacture, printing and publishing; monuments: the Capitol, Des Moines Art Centre, Centre of Science and Industry.

Des Plaines *days playnz'*, 42 03N 87 52W, pop(1980) 53,568, city in Cook county, NE Illinois, United States; on the Des Plaines river, 32 km NW of Chicago; railway.

Desē *des'yay*, DESSYE, DESSIE (Ital), 11 05N 39 40E, pop(1984e) 68,848, capital of Welo region, E Ethiopia, NE Africa; on the W edge of the Rift Valley, 250 km NE of Addis Ababa; airfield.

Desertas or **Ilhas Desertas** *di-zer'tash*, 32 32N 16 30W, three Portuguese islets (Ilhéu Chão, Deserta Grande and Ilhéu Bugio) 18 km SW of Madeira, E Atlantic Ocean.

Désirade, La *day-zee-rad'*, island of the Overseas Department of Guadeloupe, Lesser Antilles, E Caribbean; 8 km ENE of Grande-Terre I; area 22 sq km; length 11.2 km; pop(1982) 1,602; chief settlement Grande Anse; economy: fishing, sheep-rearing, sisal, cotton and maize cultivation; there is a cactus plantation on the E coast.

Desna *dyis-na'*, tributary river of the Dnepr, rising S of

Yel'nya, in Smolenskaya oblast, W European Rossiyskaya, W Soviet Union; flows generally S then SW past Bryansk and Chernigov to discharge into the R Dnepr just N of Kiyev; length 1,179 km; chief tributaries Oster, Seym, and Naviya rivers; used mainly for lumber transport.

Dessau *de'sow*, 51 51N 12 15E, pop(1982) 103,380, industrial city in Dessau dist, SW central Halle, East Germany; on R Mulde just S of where it meets the R Elbe, N of Leipzig and SW of Berlin; railway; economy: rolling stock, machinery, electrical equipment, chemicals; monuments: 16th-c palace.

Det'mold, dist of NE Nordrhein-Westfalen (North Rhine-Westphalia) prov, W Germany; pop(1983) 1,796,800; area 6,515 sq km; capital Detmold.

Detmold, 51 55N 8 50E, pop(1983) 67,000, ancient town and capital of Detmold dist, Nordrhein-Westfalen (North Rhine-Westphalia) prov, W Germany; 86 km E of Münster, in the valley of the Werre on the N slopes of the Teutoburger Wald (Teutoburg Forest); alt 134 m; railway; economy: coffee roasting, soft drinks; monuments: Schloss (palace, built 1548-57); the picturesque old town still preserves many 16-17th-c half-timbered houses; Bandel's colossal statue (1875) of Arminius stands on the Grotenburg in the Teutoburger Wald.

Detroit *de-troyt'*, 42 20N 83 03W, pop(1980) 1,203,339, county seat of Wayne county, SE Michigan, United States; port on the R Detroit, W of L St Clair; 6th largest city in the USA; founded by the French as a fur-trading outpost in 1701, it became the trading and political centre for the Great Lakes region; surrendered to the British in 1760 during the Seven Years War, and in turn handed over to the USA in 1796; briefly re-occupied by the British in 1812; capital of state 1837-47; 2 universities (1877, 1933); railway; airport; economy: the nation's leading manufacturer of cars and trucks (one-third of the country's cars are assembled in and around the city); also manufactures aeroplanes, machinery, metal products and food products; printing and publishing; in the early 1980s recession caused high unemployment and a fall in population; monuments: Science Centre, Historical Museum, Institute of Arts, Motown Museum, Belle Isle; event: Freedom Festival (July).

Deurne *dur'nu*, 51 13N 4 28E, pop(1982) 76,744, town in Antwerpen dist, Antwerpen prov, N Belgium; E suburb of Antwerpen.

Deux-Sèvres *de sevr*, dept in Poitou-Charentes region of W France, comprising 3 arrond, 33 cantons and 303 communes; pop(1982) 342,812; area 6,004 sq km; cut by the Sèvre-Niortaise R (flowing W to the Bay of Biscay) and the Sèvre-Nantaise (flowing N to the Loire); drained also by the Thouaret and Boutonne rivers; the N is woody and high, the rest fertile, growing wheat, oats and barley; capital Niort; the Parc du Marais Poitevin regional nature park lies partly within the dept.

Deva *day'va*, 45 53N 22 55E, pop(1983) 75,161, capital of Hunedoara county, W central Romania; on R Mureş; airfield; railway; economy: livestock, timber, fruit trade, tourism, food processing; monuments: 13th-c fortress; castle with archaeological museum.

Deventer *dayf'en-ter*, 52 15N 6 10E, pop(1984e) 64,823, industrial city in S Overijssel prov, E Netherlands, on the right bank of the R Ijssel; well-known for its special gingerbread (Deventer 'koek'); birthplace of the theologian Geert Groote (1340-84), who founded c.1376 the clerical and lay fraternity known as the 'Brotherhood of Common Life'; Deventer was one of Holland's most important trade and cultural centres in the 17th century; railway; economy: carpets, publishing, packaging products, packaging machinery and equipment, precision systems for quality control, bicycles; monument: 14-16th-c Grote Kerk (St Lebuinus, Dutch Reformed).

Devil's Island, French penal colony off the coast of French Guiana. See Iles du Salut.

Deviz'es, 51 22N 1 59W, pop(1981) 12,707, market town in Kennet dist, Wiltshire, S England; on Kennet and Avon Canal, 26 km ESE of Bath; economy: brewing, engineering; monuments: Museum of the Wiltshire Archaeological and Natural History Society, Wiltshire Regimental museum.

Devoll *de'vol*, river in S central Albania; rises at Grámmos on the Greek border and flows 150 km N and W through L Maliq land reclamation area to meet the R Osum NW of Berat where it forms the R Seman.

Dev'on Island, Arctic island in E Franklin dist, Northwest Territories, Canada; situated NW of Baffin Bay; separated from the mainland by the Lancaster Sound; area 55,247 sq km.

Devonport, 41 09S 146 16E, pop(1981) 21,424, port in Mersey-Lyell stat div, Tasmania, Australia; on the N coast of Tasmania, at the mouth of the R Mersey, 72 km WNW of Launceston; ferry to Melbourne; railway; airfield; economy: textiles, carpets, furniture, food processing, trade in paper, timber, agricultural products; monuments: bicycle museum; ship's museum; Aboriginal cultural centre; nearby are the King Solomon Caves.

Devonshire, parish in the Bermuda Islands; pop(1980) 6,843.

Devonshire, county of SW England; bounded SW by Cornwall, E by Dorset and Somerset, NW by the Bristol Channel and Atlantic and S by the English Channel; drained by the Exe, Dart, Torridge and Tow rivers; pop(1981) 958,745; area 6,711 sq km; county town Exeter; chief towns include Plymouth, Torbay, Torquay, Barnstaple; economy: livestock, dairy products, cider; the county is divided into 10 districts:

District	*area (sq km)*	*pop(1981)*
East Devon	817	106,885
Exeter	44	96,516
Mid Devon	916	58,439
North Devon	1,086	79,564
Plymouth	79	245,520
South Hams	887	68,371
Teignbridge	675	96,287
Torbay	63	116,200
Torridge	985	47,568
West Devon	1,160	43,395

Dews'bury, 53 42N 1 37W, pop(1981) 50,046, town in Calderdale borough, West Yorkshire, N England; part of West Yorkshire urban area; on the R Calder 12 km SW of Leeds; railway; economy: coal, textiles, carpets, leather.

Dezfūl *diz-fool'*, 32 20N 48 30E, pop(1983) 140,920, town in Dezfūl dist, Khuzestān, W central Iran; 120 km N of Ahvāz, on the R Dez; near the site of ancient Susa; the town flourished in the 19th century as an administrative centre and as an exporter of indigo; it is now a trade centre for the surrounding irrigated agricultural region; railway; airfield.

Dezhnev, Cape, northeasternmost point of Asia, NE Siberian Rossiyskaya, Soviet Union. See Dezhneva, Mys.

Dezhneva, Mys, CAPE DEZHNEV *dyezh'nyif*, formerly EAST CAPE (-1898), 66 08N 169 40W, northeasternmost point of Asia, NE Siberian Rossiyskaya, Soviet Union; situated at the E end of the Chukotskiy Poluostrov (Chukchi Peninsula), projecting into the Bering Sea; named after the Russian navigator who discovered it in 1648.

Dhah'ran, AẒ ẒAHRĀN, 26 18N 50 05E, town in Eastern province, E Saudi Arabia, 13 km S of Ad Dammān.

Dhākā or **Dacca** *da'ka*, region in central Bangladesh; includes Dhākā, Gazipur, Manikganj, Munshiganj, Narayanganj and Narsingdi districts; pop(1981) 10,014,000; area 7,469 sq km; capital of region and Bangladesh is Dhākā; the world's greatest jute growing region; Madhupur forest lies in the W.

Dhākā, 23 42N 90 22E, pop(1981) 2,365,695, capital city of Bangladesh, in Dhākā region, W of the R Meghna, on a channel of the R Dhaleswari; prior to partition in 1947 it was a small university town, with an estimated population of 250,000; since then large-scale immigration and the growth of industry has caused the population to expand; administrative, commercial and industrial heart of Bangladesh; lies in the centre of the world's greatest jute growing region; former French, Dutch and English trading post; 1608-1704 capital of Mogul province of East Bengal; during 1905-12 it was capital of the British province of East Bengal and Assam; became capital of East Pakistan in 1947; surrendered by the Pakistani army in Dec 1971 to Indian troops to become the capital of Bangladesh; university of Dhākā (1921); Bangladesh University of Engineering and Technology (1961); airport; railway; economy: trade in jute, rice, oilseed, sugar and tea; manufacture of textiles, chemicals, matches, soap, glass and shoes; printing, engineering and boatbuilding are also important; monuments: Suhrawardy Uddyan, formerly the racecourse, is a popular city park, where the oath for independence was taken on 7 March 1971; Central Shahid Minar is a monument to commemorate the martyrs of the Historic Language Movement 1952 and is a symbol of Bangladeshi nationalism; Dhākā has over 1,000 mosques and is known as the 'city of mosques'; Sadarghat market is one of the oldest traditional shopping centres in the city selling books, cloth, garments and shoes; 12 km SE is Langalband, a sacred Hindu site.

Dhanbad *dahn'bahd*, 23 50N 86 30E, pop(1981) 677,000, city in Bihar, E India; in the Damodar Valley, NE of Ranchi; linked by rail to Asansol; centre for the nearby coal-mining industry.

Dhelfoí *del'fi*, DELPHI (Eng), formerly PY'THO, 38 29N 22 30E, village and ancient site in Fokís nome (dept), Sterea Ellás-Évvoia region, Greece, on the slopes of Mt Parnassós, high above the Korinthiakós Kólpos (Gulf of Corinth), 176 km from Athínai (Athens); renowned throughout the ancient Greek world and beyond as the sanctuary of Apollo and the seat of his oracle; considerable remains of the temple and precincts were excavated in the 19th century; alt 520-620 m.

Dhi Qār, governorate in S central Iraq; pop(1977) 622,979; area 13,668 sq km; capital An Naşiriyah; comprises part of the Euphrates-Tigris lowland.

Dhofar *dhō-far'*, prov of S Oman, SE Arabian peninsula; mostly a coastal plain backed by Jabal Samhan hills; chief town Şalālah.

Dibrë *dee'bre*, DIBRA *dee'bra* (Turk), prov of E Albania; area 1,569 sq km; pop(1980) 128,300; capital Peshkopi.

Did'cot, 51 37N 1 15W, pop(1981) 15,204, town in South Oxfordshire dist, Oxfordshire, S central England; 16 km S of Oxford; railway.

Diébougou *dye-boo'goo*, 11 00N 3 12W, town in W Burkina, W Africa; 105 km E of Bobo Dioulasso.

Diefoula *dye-foo'la*, 10 13N 4 43W, town in SW Burkina, W Africa.

Diego Garcia *dee-ay'gō gar-see'a*, 6 34S 72 24E, island in the Chagos Archipelago, Indian Ocean; part of the British Indian Ocean Territory which was established in 1965; an important strategic location in the Indian Ocean with a UK-US naval support base established in 1973; there is no permanent population.

Diekirch *dee'kirKH*, N dist of the Grand Duchy of Luxembourg, comprising the cantons of Diekirch, Redange, Wiltz, Vianden and Clervaux; watered by the Our, Clerf, Wiltz, Alzette and Sûre rivers; pop(1981) 53,363; area 1,157 sq km; capital Diekirch.

Diekirch, canton in SE part of Diekirch dist, E Luxembourg; area 239 sq km; pop(1981) 21,873; traversed W-E by the R Sûre and N-S by the R Alzette.

Diekirch, 49 52N 6 10E, pop(1981) 5,585, resort and capital of the canton and dist of Diekirch, E Luxembourg; on the R Sûre on the border between the Gutland and Ösling regions of the Ardennes; 35 km N of Luxembourg; alt 200 m; economy: tourism, brewing and iron foundry; events: beer festival, 3rd Sunday in July; carnival parade, pilgrimage and procession of the Octave of Our Lady on 5th Sunday after Easter.

Dieppe *dee-ep*, 49 55N 1 05E, pop(1982) 26,000, seaport in Seine-Maritime dept, Haute-Normandie, NW France; below high chalk cliffs on the R Arques where it meets the English Channel, N of Rouen; scene of an ill-fated wartime reconnaissance Allied landing in 1942; ferry links with Newhaven.

Diest *deest*, 50 58N 5 03E, pop(1982) 20,695, market town in Leuven dist, NE Brabant prov, Belgium; on the R Demer, between the fertile Haveland and the wooded Kempen; since the 2nd half of the 13th century, when Diest received its charter, it ranked among the most important towns in Brabant because of its cloth-making, but this has long since disappeared; best known in the country as the 'city of beer'; an ancient fortified town with original ramparts; railway; economy: brewing, footwear, hosiery, foodstuffs; monument: 12th-c Premonstratensian Abbey Averbode (6 km to the W).

Dietikon *dye'tee-kon*, 47 29N 8 25E, pop(1980) 21,765, town in Zürich canton, N Switzerland; on the R Limmat, NW of Zürich; railway; economy: engineering, transport equipment.

Diffa *dee-fa'*, dept in SE Niger, W Africa; a low-lying region with a SE border formed by L Chad; there is an extensive area of sand dunes in the N; area 140,216 sq km; pop(1977e) 150,000; comprises 3 arrond; capital Diffa; chief towns Bosso, Koufey, Mainé-Soroa.

Diffa, 13 28N 12 35E, capital of Diffa dept, SE Niger, W Africa; close to the Nigerian border.

Differdange *dif-er-dãzh'*, 49 32N 5 53E, pop(1981) 8,588, town in Esch-sur-Alzette canton, Luxembourg dist, S Luxembourg; important industrial centre and point of departure for excursions to the French frontier; economy: steel, iron.

Digne *deen'y'*, 44 05N 6 12E, pop(1982) 16,391, capital of Alpes-de-Haute-Provence dept, Provence-Alpes-Côte d'Azur region, SE France; among hills in the Bleone R valley, equidistant from Marseille, Avignon, Nice and Grenoble; railway; a thermal station noted for the treatment of rheumatism.

Digue, La *la deeg*, 4 20S 55 51E, pop(1985e) 2,000, granite island in the Seychelles, Indian Ocean; NE and 3 hours by boat from the main island of Mahé; area 10 sq km; there are tourist facilities.

Digya *dig-ya'*, national park in Brong-Ahafo and Volta regions, central Ghana, W Africa; area 3,126 sq km; established in 1971.

Dihōk, governorate in the Kurdish Autonomous Region, NW Iraq; bounded N by Turkey; the R Tigris forms part of its W border; pop(1977) 250,575; area 6,374 sq km; capital Dihōk; the land rises towards the N border with Turkey

Dihōk, DOHUK, 36 52N 43 01E, pop(1970) 19,736, capital town of Dihōk governorate, Kurdish Autonomous Region, NW Iraq.

Dijon *dee-zhõ*, DIBIO (anc), 47 20N 5 00E, pop(1982) 145,569, industrial and commercial city and capital of Côte d'Or dept, Bourgogne region, E France; at the confluence of the rivers Ouche and Ruzon, on a fertile plain below the steep E edge of the Central Plateau; bishopric; university (1722); railway; it is the historic capital of Burgundy; famous for its restaurants and its mustard, also an important centre of the wine trade; monuments: Palais des Ducs de Bourgogne (Baroque); Gothic church of Notre-Dame; church of St Michel (mixture of Gothic and Renaissance); Palais de Justice (16-17th-c, now the Law Courts), cathedral of St-Benigne (twin-towered Gothic, originally an abbey church); on the W outskirts of the town there are remains of the late 14th-c Chartreuse de Champmol, built by Duke Philippe le Hardi as a ducal mausoleum, but virtually destroyed in the Revolution, now a psychiatric hospital.

Diksmuide *diks-mœy'de*, DIXMUDE *deeks-müd* (Fr), dist of West-Vlaanderen (West Flanders) prov, Belgium; area 362 sq km; pop(1982) 47,565.

Dilbeek *dil'bayk*, 50 51N 4 16E, pop(1982) 35,258, town in Halle-Vilvoorde dist, Brabant prov, Belgium; a W suburb of Bruxelles.

Dili or **Dilly** *di'lee*, 8 35S 125 35E, pop(1980) 65,451, seaport capital of Timor Timur (Loro Sae) prov, Indonesia; on N coast of the island of Timor; former capital of Portuguese Timor until 1975; airfield.

Dimashq *di-mashk'*, DAMASCUS *da-ma'skus*, ESH SHAM *esh-sham'* (Arab), governorate (*mohofazat*) in SW Syria; bounded SE by Jordan and NW by Lebanon; pop(1981) 917,364; the Jebel esh Sharqi (Anti-Lebanon) range in the W is bounded E by a fertile agricultural area (part of the ancient 'Fertile Crescent') which is drained by the R Barada.

Dimashq, DAMASCUS, 33 30N 36 19E, pop(1981) 1,112,214, capital city of Syria, Middle East; 80 km ESE of Beyrouth (Beirut); situated in the E foothills of the Jebel esh Sharqi (Anti-Lebanon) range, on the R Barada; claimed to be the world's oldest continuously inhabited city; mentioned first in Genesis, the city has been conquered by the Assyrians (732 BC), Alexander the Great (333 BC), the Romans (64 BC) under whom it prospered, the Muslim Omayyads (635), the Mongols (1260), Tamerlane (1399), the Turks (1516), and the Allies (1918 and again in 1941 to oust Vichy France); in ancient times it was a great trade and commercial centre on the caravan route to Baghdad; the city is still famous for its crystallized fruits, brass and copper ware, silks, and woodwork; Dimashq was capital of Syria during the 2 years of independence, 1918-20, when the Turkish empire was overthrown by the Arab Revolt; satellite city Dimashq ad-Jadideh; university (1923); airport; railway; monuments: medieval citadel (1219); Great Mosque (8th-c, burned 1893 then restored); the ancient Via Recta, the 'street called Straight', runs E-W for 1,500 m with Roman gateways at either end; event: international fair during the last 2 weeks of Aug.

Dimbokro *deem-bō'krō*, dept in SE central Ivory Coast, W Africa; pop(1975) 475,023; area 14,100 sq km; the R Comoé follows part of the border; capital Dimbokro; chief towns Ouéllé, Daoukro, Boiànda, Bongouanou and Anoumaba.

Dimboviţa *dam'bo-vee-tsa*, county in S central Romania; in the S foothills of the Transylvanian Alps; pop(1983) 549,405; area 4,035 sq km; capital Tìrgovişte.

Dinajpur *din-aj'poor*, region in NW Bangladesh; includes Dinajpur, Panchaghar and Thakurgaon districts; pop(1981) 3,200,000; area 6,565 sq km; formerly a British province of India, but partitioned between India and E Pakistan in 1947; economy based on rice and sugar cane; capital Dinajpur.

Dinajpur, 25 38N 88 44E, pop(1981) 96,718, capital of Dinajpur dist, Dinajpur, NW Bangladesh; on R Punarbhaba, SW of Rangpur, near the Indian frontier; railway; economy: trade in jute, rice, sugar cane, barley, rape and mustard; rice and oilseed milling, soap.

Dinant *dee-nã*, dist of Namur prov, Belgium; area 1,592 sq km; pop(1982) 89,152.

Dinant, 50 16N 4 55E, pop(1982) 12,008, tourist resort in Dinant dist, Namur prov, Belgium; in the upper valley of the R Meuse, under precipitous limestone rocks; famous throughout the Middle Ages for its brass and copperware, the manufacture of which has been recently revived; the town was conquered and destroyed in 1466 by Philip the Good, when 800 of its inhabitants are said to have drowned in the R Meuse; the Furfooz Nature Park is located SE of here; monuments: church of Notre Dame (13th-c); citadel (built by the Dutch government in 1821 on the site of the former fortress which had belonged to the bishops of Liège).

Dina'ric Alps, DINARA PLANINA (Serb), ALPI DINARICHE (Ital), mountain range following the Adriatic coast of Yugoslavia and NW Albania; linked to the main Alpine system via the Julian Alps; rises to 2,522 m at Durmitor; limestone ranges in the Karst region (NW).

Din'der, national park in central Sudan, NE Africa; area 6,397 sq km; established in 1935.

Dingwall, 57 35N 4 26W, pop(1981) 4,842, capital of Ross and Cromarty dist, Highland, N Scotland; at the head of the Cromarty Firth, 18 km NW of Inverness; road and rail junction; railway; monuments: Dingwall Town Hall (built c.1730) with a museum of local history and an exhibition on General Sir Hector MacDonald (1853-1903) who was born near Dingwall.

Dinosaur, national monument in NE Utah and NW Nevada, United States; established in 1915 to protect notable prehistoric animal deposits; area 824 sq km.

Dinslaken *dinz'lah-ken*, 51 34N 6 43E, pop(1983) 60,400, industrial city in Düsseldorf dist, Nordrhein-Westfalen (North Rhine-Westphalia) prov, W Germany; near the R Rhine, 16 km N of Duisburg; economy: steel and plastic strapping.

Diourbel *dyoor-bel'*, arid region in W Senegal, W Africa; pop(1976) 425,113; capital Diourbel; the area of Diourbel and Louga regions combined is 33,547 sq km.

Diourbel, 14 39N 16 12W, pop(1979) 55,307, capital of Diourbel region, W Senegal, W Africa; 130 km E of Dakar on the Dakar-Niger railway; economy: market gardening, peanuts, crafts, textiles.

Dirē Dawa *dir-i de-wah'*, 9 35N 41 50E, pop(1980e) 82,024, town in N Hārergē region, SE Ethiopia, NE Africa; NW of Hārer and NE of Addis Ababa; railway junction; airfield.

Disko, island off the W coast of Greenland, at the head of the Davis Strait; area 8,285 sq km; chief settlement Godhavn; coal deposits.

District of Columbia, federal district in E United States, co-extensive with the city of Washington; bounded W by Virginia and N, E and S by Maryland; pop(1980) 638,333; area 164 sq km.

Divinópolis *jee-vee-no'po-lees*, 20 08S 44 55W, pop(1980) 108,279, town in Minas Gerais state, Sudeste region, SE Brazil; W of Belo Horizonte; railway; economy: light industry, cattle raising.

Divo *dee'vō*, dept in S Ivory Coast, W Africa; pop(1975) 278,526; area 10,650 sq km; capital Divo; chief towns Lakota and Guittri.

Dīwānīyah, Ad *di-wan-ee'yu*, 32 00N 44 57E, pop(1965) 60,553, capital town of Al-Qādisiyah governorate, S central Iraq; 64 km SE of Al Ḩillah, on a channel of the R Euphrates (Al-Furāt); railway.

Diyāla *di-ya'la*, governorate in E central Iraq, bounded E by Iran; pop(1977) 587,754; area 19,047 sq km; capital Ba'qūbah; the land rises towards the E and N; drained by numerous tributaries of the R Tigris.

Diyarbakır *di-yar'ba-kur*, prov in SE Turkey; pop(1980) 778,150; area 15,355 sq km; capital Diyarbakır.

Diyarbakır, AMIDA (anc), 37 55N 40 14E, pop(1980) 235,617, capital town of Diyarbakır prov, SE Turkey; on the R Tigris; agricultural market centre; railway; airfield; economy: textiles, leather and trade in grain, mohair, wool; monument: black basalt fortification walls built during the 4th century.

Djado *jah'dō*, 21 00N 12 20E, an oasis town in Agadez dept, NE Niger, W Africa; on the edge of the Djado plateau.

Djel'fa, El, department of N Algeria, N Africa; in the Atlas Saharien; area 22,903 sq km; pop(1982) 389,440; chief town Djelfa.

Djénné *jay-nay'*, 13 55N 4 31W, pop(1971) 10,900, town in Mopti region, central Mali, W Africa; in the Macina depression, on the R Bani 355 km SSW of Tombouctou; known as the 'Jewel of the Niger', it was probably founded in the 8th century; a mosque built this century replicates the original destroyed in 1830; in past centuries the town rivalled Tombouctou as a centre of Muslim culture; economy: leatherwork, trade.

Djerba, island off Tunisia. See Jerba.

Djibouti *ji-boo'ti*, official name the Republic of Djibouti, JUMHOURIYA DJIBOUTI (Arab), a NE African republic bounded NW, W and S by Ethiopia, SE by Somalia and N by the Gulf of Aden; timezone GMT +3; area 23,310 sq km; pop(1984e) 350,000; capital Djibouti; chief towns Tadjoura, Dikhil, Obock and Ali-Sabieh; ethnic groups include Somali (60%), Afar (5%), French Arab (5%) plus some French, Ethiopians, Italians, Arabs, Greeks, Sudanese and Indians; a large majority of the pop (94%) are Muslim, the remainder being Christian; the official language is Arabic, but French, Somali and Afar are widely used; the unit of currency is the Djibouti franc; national holidays 27 June (Independence Day) and 1 May (Labour Day); membership of AfDB, Arab League, FAO, G-77, IBRD, ICAO, IDA, IDB (Islamic Development Bank), IFAD, IFC, ILO, IMF, IMO, INTERPOL, ITU, NAM, OAU, OIC, UN, UPU, WFTU, WHO and WMO.

Physical description. Situated at the S end of the Red Sea where it meets the Gulf of Aden, Djibouti is separated from the Arabian peninsula by the Strait of Bab al Mandeb. The Gulf of Tadjoura, with the cities of Djibouti and Tadjoura on either side of its mouth, juts deep into the country. Mountains of volcanic origin consist of a series of plateaux dropping down to flat, low lying, rocky desert (an extension of Ethiopia's Danakil desert) which backs a 350 km fertile coastal strip around the Gulf of Tadjoura. Both irrigated agriculture and the highest population density are to be found in this coastal area. The highest point is the Moussa Ali which rises to 2,020 m in the N.

Climate. Djibouti has a semi-arid climate with a hot season from May to Sept. The coastal plain experiences very high temperatures all year round with the max average daily temperature only dropping below 30°C during the months of the low sun (Dec-Feb). The interior highlands (over 600 m) experience slightly lower humidity and temperatures. Rainfall is sparse with an annual average of 130 mm at Djibouti. The rainfall on the coast generally falls between Nov and March whereas in the interior the rain falls between April and Oct (period of the high sun).

History, government and constitution. French interest in this part of NE Africa dates from 1862 when friendship treaties were signed with local chiefs. Two decades later effective occupation of what was called French Somaliland took place. In 1884 the French governor, Lagarde, succeeded in bringing together the 2 protectorates of Obock and Tadjoura and in 1896 Djibouti became the capital of this territory. After World War II the area became a French Overseas Territory with a territorial assembly. In 1967 French Somaliland became the French Territory of the Afars and the Issas (FTAI). In May 1977, following several referenda, Djibouti became the last African country to gain independence from France. The government has a legislative chamber of 65 deputies, an executive prime minister and a council of approx 15 ministers. An elected president is head of state.

Economy. As a result of inadequate rainfall and effectively no rivers, crop-based agriculture is only possible with the aid of irrigation. On the coast date palms, fruit and vegetables are cultivated. The main agricultural activity of the nomadic population is the raising of livestock and on the coast a small fishing industry operates. The economy of the country is not based on agriculture but on the modern port of Djibouti which is well situated to handle ships using the Suez Canal and the Red Sea. The benefits of this port have been undermined in recent years by the adoption of container ships and supertankers which can take the Cape route from America and Europe to the Indian Ocean. Up to 60% of Ethiopia's imports and 40% of its exports came through Djibouti by rail but these figures slumped dramatically and the railway line was closed for a year (1977-78). The industrial sector is small, concentrating on construction materials and the bottling of mineral water. Tourism represents a small but important contribution to the economy. The main trading partners include France, Ethiopia, Japan, Belgium, Luxembourg, the UK, Italy, South Yemen and West Germany.

Administration. Djibouti is divided into the 5 districts of Djibouti, Ali-Sabieh, Tadjourah, Dikhil and Obock.

Djibouti, 11 36N 43 08E, pop(1984e) 180,000, free port capital of Djibouti, NE Africa; on a coral peninsula 565 km NE of Addis Ababa (Ethiopia) and 240 km SW of Aden (South Yemen); a NE terminus of the railway from Addis Ababa which was completed in 1917; the city was built between 1886 and 1900 in the Arab style and in 1896 succeeded Obock as the capital of French Somaliland; became the official port of Ethiopia in 1897 and though its modern port facilities used to deal with a large proportion of Ethiopia's imports and exports this trade has declined dramatically; airport at 6 km; economy: commercial port trade, fishing, tourism.

Djoudj *jooj*, national park in NW Senegal, W Africa; between Senegal and Gorom rivers, NE of Saint-Louis, near the Mauritanian frontier; area 1,600 sq km; established in 1971; 7th largest reserve of ducks and wild pigs in the world; important for migratory birds.

Djougou *joo'goo*, 9 40N 1 46E, town in Atakora prov, NW Benin, W Africa, 113 km WNW of Parakou.

Dnepr *dun-ye'pre*, DNIEPER *nee'pur*, BORYSTHENES (anc), river in European Rossiyskaya, Belorusskaya, and Ukrainskaya republics, W Soviet Union; rises in the S Valdayskaya Vozvyshennost' range, W of Sychevka, N Smolenskaya oblast, Rossiyskaya; flows S and W past Smolensk, turns S at Orsha, flows through Belorusskaya SSR, then makes a wide bend (SE then SW) through Ukrainskaya SSR, past Kiyev (Kiev), Dneprodzerzhinsk, Dnepropetrovsk, and Zaporozh'ye to discharge into the Black Sea at Kherson; length 2,201 km; drainage basin area 504,000 sq km; chief tributaries Ingulets, Orel, Vorskla, Desna, and Sozh rivers; water from the Kakhovka reservoir irrigates large areas of the lower Dnepr basin and also the plain of N Krym (Crimea); it is planned that further development will eventually extract 61% of the river's average discharge and irrigate an area of 30,000 sq km.

Dneprodzerzhinsk *dun-ye'pre-dyer-zhinsk'*, formerly KAMENSKOYE, 48 30N 34 37E, pop(1983) 265,000, industrial river port in Dnepropetrovskaya oblast, Ukrainskaya SSR, Soviet Union, on the R Dnepr; industrial development began in the late 19th century; railway; economy: hydroelectric power plant, manufacture of railway wagons.

Dnepropetrovsk *dun-ye'pre-pye-trofsk'*, EKATERINOSLAV (-1926), 48 29N 35 00E, pop(1983) 1,128,000, port capital of Dnepropetrovskaya oblast, Ukrainskaya SSR, Soviet Union; on the R Dnepr; established in 1783 on the site of a Cossack village; university (1918); railway; airport; economy: ferrous metallurgy, machine building, chemicals, foodstuffs; monument: cathedral (1830-35).

Dnestr *dun-ye'stur*, DNIESTER *nee'stur*, DNIESTR (Pol), river in Ukrainskaya and Moldavskaya republics, W Soviet Union; rising NW of Turka in the Carpathian Mts; flows generally SE through SW Ukrainskaya SSR and E Moldavskaya SSR, discharges into the Dnestrovskiy Liman, a N inlet of the Black Sea, SW of Odessa; length 1,402 km; chief tributaries Bystritsa, Seret, and Zbruch rivers; freezes over from Dec to March; formed the border between Romania and the USSR between 1918 and 1940.

Dnieper, river in W Soviet Union. See Dnepr.

Dniester, river in W Soviet Union. See Dnestr.

Doba *dō-ba'*, 8 40N 16 50E, capital of Logone-Oriental prefecture, SW Chad, N central Africa; 80 km E of Moundou.

Doboj *do'boy*, 44 44N 18 05E, pop(1981) 99,548, town in N Bosna-Hercegovina republic, Yugoslavia; on R Bosna, E of Banja Luka; railway; economy: foodstuffs.

Döbraberg *dœ'brah-berk*, 50 16N 11 37E, mountain in Bayern (Bavaria) prov, W Germany; highest peak (795 m) of the Frankenwald (Franconian Forest), 8 km SW of Selbitz.

Dodecanese ('twelve islands'), nome (dept) and island group of Greece. See Sporádhes.

Dodoma *dō-dō'ma*, 6 10S 35 40E, pop(1984e) 180,000, capital of Tanzania, E Africa; also capital of a region of same name in central Tanzania; at an alt of 1,120 m, 160 km WNW of Kilosa; became capital in 1974 after a 10-year transfer plan; economy: administration and trade in live and stuffed birds.

Doha, capital of the State of Qatar. See Dawḩah, Ad.

Doi Inthanon *doy in'te-nen*, the highest mountain in

Thailand; rises to 2,594 m WSW of Chiang Mai in NW Thailand.

Doldrums, a marine region near the Equator noted for its sultry air, its calms, its light, baffling winds, its local gusts and thunderstorms; lying between the NE and SE trade winds, it varies in width in different longitudes and at different seasons; towards the solstices, these regions move about 5° from their mean positions, towards the N in June and towards the S in Dec.

Dolj *dolzh*, county in S Romania; bounded to the S by the R Danube which follows the Bulgarian frontier; pop(1983) 767,624; area 7,413 sq km; capital Craiova.

Dollard des Ormeaux *do-lar' days or-mō'*, 45 29N 73 48W, pop(1981) 39,940, town in S Québec, SE Canada; at the mouth of the Ottawa river, W of Montréal; railway.

Dolomites, mountain range in NE Italy. See Dolomitiche, Alpi.

Dolomitiche, Alpi *dō-le-mee'ti-ke*, DOLOMITES *dol'ō-mīts* (Eng), Alpine mountain range in Trentino-Alto Adige and Veneto regions, NE Italy; bounded by the Isarco, Adige, Brenta, Piave and Rienza rivers; a dolomitic limestone formation of jagged outlines and isolated peaks, rising to 3,342 m in Marmolada; attracts many tourists, walkers, climbers, and winter sports enthusiasts; winter sports and health resorts include Cortina d'Ampezzo and San Martino di Castrozza; the military roads of World War I, many of them still in good condition, make it possible for non-climbers to reach high altitudes.

Dolores *dō-lō'rays*, 33 34S 58 15W, pop(1985) 12,914, river port in Soriano dept, SW Uruguay; on the Río Salvador.

Dom, 46 06N 7 52E, the highest mountain entirely in Switzerland, rising to 4,545 m NE of Zermatt in the Pennine Alps.

Domagnano *do-man-yah'no*, castle (dist) in the Republic of San Marino, central Italy; area 6.62 sq km; pop(1980) 1,867; population density in 1980 was 282 inhabitants per sq km.

Dombóvár *dom'bō-var*, 46 21N 18 09E, pop(1984e) 21,000, town in Tolna county, S central Hungary; on R Kapos, E of Kaposvár; railway; economy: fruit and vegetable trade.

Dominica *do-min-ee'ka*, DOMINIQUE *do-mee-neek'* (Fr), official name Commonwealth of Dominica, island in the Windward group of the West Indies, E Caribbean Sea, situated between the French island groups of Guadeloupe to the N and Martinique to the S; timezone GMT −4; area 751 sq km; pop(1981) 74,859; capital Roseau; chief towns Portsmouth and Grand Bay; the population is mainly of African, or mixed African and European origin; there is a Carib Indian settlement of about 500; Christianity, largely Roman Catholicism, is the dominant faith; English is the official language with French widely spoken; the E Caribbean dollar, pound sterling, and French franc are all legal tender; airport at Melville Hall, W of Marigot on NE coast; membership of UN, CARICOM, Commonwealth, FAO, GATT (de facto), G-77, IBRD, IDA, IFAD, IFC, ILO, IMF, IMO, INTERPOL, OAS, UNESCO, UPU, WHO, WMO.

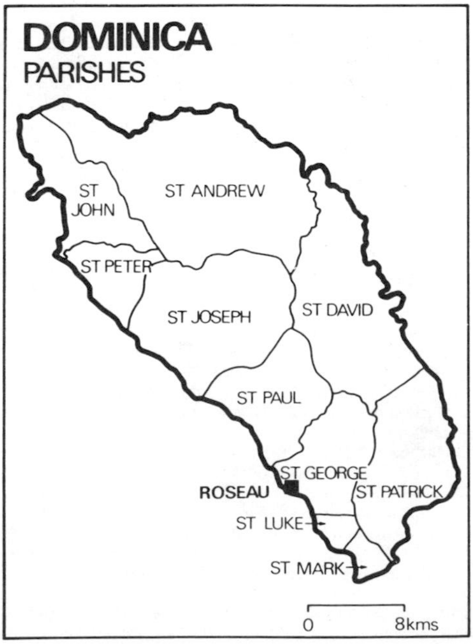

Physical description and climate. The island is roughly rectangular in shape with a deeply-indented coastline. It is c.50 km long and 26 km wide, rising to 1,447 m at Morne Diablotin in the N. Dominica is of volcanic origin, with many fumaroles and sulphur springs. In 1880 there was a great eruption of volcanic ash from the 'Boiling Lake' at the S extremity of the island. A central ridge, with lateral spurs and deeply-incised valleys, occupies the interior of the island. The Clyde, Pagua, Rosalie, Roseau and Layou rivers flow down to the coast from the central mt ridge. Of the total land area 67% is forested. The climate is warm and humid with mean monthly temperatures ranging from 25.6°C to 32.2°C. There is a marked dry season only on the W side of the island. Annual rainfall figures range from 1,750 mm on the coast to 6,250 mm in the mountainous areas where there is a luxuriant tropical vegetation.

History, government and constitution. Dominica was first visited by Europeans when Columbus landed here in 1493. The island was allegedly first seen on a Sunday, hence the origin of its name. The French attempted to colonize the island but in 1748 it was returned to its Carib population on being declared a neutral island. British planters settled in 1763, introducing Negro slaves and Dominica eventually became a British Crown Colony in 1805. From 1958 to 1962 it formed part of the Federation of the West Indies, gaining full independence in 1978. It is an independent republic within the Commonwealth, governed by a house of assembly of 30 members (21 elected). The cabinet is presided over by a prime minister, and an elected president is head of state.

Economy. The main industries are agricultural processing, tourism, the manufacture of soap and other coconut-based products, and cigars. At least 40% of the workforce is engaged in agriculture, largely on plantations producing citrus fruits (notably limes), bananas, coconuts and cocoa. The main agricultural products are raw and sweetened lime juice, lime oil, bay oil, copra, and rum. Pumice is quarried for export and the bottling of water has recently developed. The major trading partners are UK (traditionally taking about 75% of banana exports), the USA, other EEC countries, and other CARICOM countries.

Administrative divisions. Dominica is divided into the 10 parishes of St John, St Andrew, St David, St Peter, St Joseph, St Paul, St George, St Patrick, St Mark, and St Luke.

Dominican Republic, REPÚBLICA DOMINICANA (Sp), republic of the West Indies, comprising the E two-thirds of the island of Hispaniola, bordering W on Haiti; timezone GMT −4; area 48,442 sq km; pop(1981) 5,647,977; capital Santo Domingo; chief towns Santiago, La Vega, San Juan, and San Francisco de Macorís; the people are mostly of Spanish or mixed Spanish and Indian origin; the state religion is Roman Catholicism; Spanish is the official language; the unit of currency is the peso oro of 100 centavos; membership of FAO, G-77, GATT, IADB, IAEA, IBA, IBRD, ICAO, ICO, IDA, IDB, IFAD, IFC, IHO, ILO, IMF, IMO, INTELSAT, INTERPOL, IOOC, IRC, ISO, ITU, OAS, PAHO, SELA, UN, UNESCO, UPU, WFTU, WHO, WMO, WTO.

Physical description and climate. The country is traversed NW-SE by the Cordillera Central, a heavily-wooded

mountain range with many peaks over 3,000 m. The Pico Duarte (3,175 m) is the highest peak in the Caribbean. In the SW, L Enriquillo lies in a broad valley which cuts E-W through the mountains. The Isla Cabritos on the lake is a national park. There is a wide coastal plain in the E with a national park (Este) at the SE tip of the island. Where the Cordillera Oriental falls down to the Bahia de Samana in the E there is the Los Haitises National Park. The climate is tropical maritime with a rainy season from May to Nov. The N flanks of the mountains receive most rainfall. Santo Domingo, on the S coast, has a mean Jan temperature of 23.9°C and a mean July temperature of 27.2°C, and an average annual rainfall of 1,400 mm. Hurricanes may occur between June and Nov.

History, government and constitution. The island of Hispaniola was visited by Columbus in 1492 and became a prominent Spanish colony in the 16th and 17th centuries. The island was partitioned in 1697, the E province of Santo Domingo remaining Spanish and the W third, now the Republic of Haiti, passing into French possession. After being taken over by Haiti on several occasions, Santo Domingo became independent in 1844 under its new name of Dominican Republic. Spain reoccupied it in 1861, to be driven out 4 years later. A new constitution was adopted on 28 November 1966. Executive power is vested in the national congress, comprising a 27-member senate and a 120-member chamber of deputies. All members are elected for 4-year terms, as is the president. The president governs with the assistance of a cabinet, which includes about 17 secretaries of state and the chiefs of the armed forces.

Economy. Approximately 274 sq km of the total land area is cultivable. Sugar cultivation is the principal industry, the largest sugar estates being in the SE of the republic. Two companies produce over 80% of the total, but in all there are 16 sugar 'centrals'. Cocoa, accounting for about 15% of the cultivated land area, is the second principal crop. Other crops grown include coffee (exported mainly to USA), rice, cotton, tobacco, bananas, mangoes, tomatoes, and oranges. In 1980, 45-50% of the workforce was employed in agriculture, mainly on subsistence farms and smallholdings. The major industries are tourism, sugar processing, bauxite, iron, nickel and gold mining, textiles, and cement production. Chief exports include sugar, gold, silver, ferronickel and coffee. The main destinations for exports are the USA (typically 50-55% of the total value), Switzerland, Venezuela, the Netherlands, Puerto Rico, Spain, Japan, and Belgium. Chief imports include foodstuffs, petroleum, industrial raw materials, and capital equipment, the main trading partner being the USA (around 40-45% of the total value). The tourism sector is now an expanding component of the economy, with new resort complexes being developed along a 125 km stretch of coastline between Luperón and Cabrera on the N coast.

Communications. The main ports are Santo Domingo, La Romana, San Pedro de Macorís, Puerto Plata, Barahona, Haina, and Las Calderas. There are 3 international airports: Las Americas, Puerto Plata, and La Romana. 588 km of railway tracks carry sugar from the estates.

Administrative divisions. The republic is divided into 27 provinces.

Province	*pop(1981)*
La Altagracia	100,112
Azua	65,384
Bahoruco	78,636
Barahona	137,160
Dajabón	57,709
Distrito Nacional	1,550,739
Duarte	235,544
Elias Piña	65,384
Espaillat	164,017
Independencia	38,768
María Trinidad Sánchez	112,629

contd

Province	*pop(1981)*
Monte Cristi	83,407
Pedernales	17,006
Peravia	168,123
Puerto Plata	206,757
La Romana	109,769
Salcedo	99,191
Samaná	65,699
San Cristóbal	446,132
San Juan	239,957
San Pedro de Macorís	152,890
Sánchez Ramírez	126,567
Santiago	550,372
Santiago Rodríguez	55,411
El Seibo	157,866
Valverde	100,319
La Vega	385,043

Don, river in SW European Rossiyskaya, Soviet Union; rising in Tul'skaya oblast, SE of Tula; flows generally S past Dankov and Zadonsk, then sweeps round in a wide bend (SE then SW) past Kalach-na-Donu and Rostov-na-Donu, to discharge into the Azovskoye More (Sea of Azov) at its NE end; length 1,958 km; chief tributaries Severskiy Donets, Chir, Ilovlya, Khoper, Sosna, and Voronezh rivers; the lower Don valley between Rostov-na-Donu and Volgograd is largely irrigated; the Tsimlyansk reservoir is linked to the R Volga (E) by the Volga-Don Canal; accessible to seagoing vessels as far as Rostov-na-Donu; there are valuable fisheries, especially on the lower course of the river.

Donau, European river. See Danube.

Don'caster, DANUM (anc), 53 32N 1 07W, pop(1981) 76,042, urban area pop(1981) 133,178, town in Doncaster borough, South Yorkshire, N England; on R Don, 27 km NE of Sheffield; founded as a castle in the 1st century AD and later an important Roman station on the road from Lincoln to York; railway; economy: coal, nylon, rope, machinery and railway engineering; monument: South Yorkshire industrial museum; event: St Leger Stakes, the oldest horse-race in England (Sept).

Donegal *don-i-gol'* or *don'-i-gol*, DÚN NA NGALL (Gael), scenic county in Ulster prov, N Irish Republic; bounded W and N by Atlantic Ocean and E by N Ireland; watered by R Finn and R Foyle; Blue Stack Mts W of Donegal, Derry Eagh in NW and Slieve Snaght in N rising to 752 m at Errigal; pop(1981) 125,112; area 4,830 sq km; capital Donegal; famous for tweed manufacture; deposits of uranium; associated with St Patrick, Station I on L Derg has been an important shrine of pilgrimage for over 1,500 years.

Donets, Northern, river in SW Soviet Union. See Severskiy Donets.

Donetsk, formerly STALINO, STALIN, YUZOVKA, 48 00N 37 50E, pop(1983) 1,055,000, industrial capital city of Donetskaya oblast, Ukrainskaya SSR, Soviet Union; on the R Kal'mius, in the Donbas coal basin where mining dates from 1798; established in 1870; university (1965); railway; airport; road junction; economy: coal mining, metallurgy, mechanical and chemical engineering, machine building, chemicals, light industry, foodstuffs; since 1959 local industry has run on natural gas piped from Stavropol'.

Dongting Hu, lake in N Hunan prov, E central China; area 3,915 sq km; China's 2nd largest freshwater lake (the largest being Poyang Hu lake in Jiangxi prov); fed by the Zi Shui, Li Shui, Yuan Jiang and Xiang Jiang rivers; enters the Chang Jiang (Yangtze river) by a channel situated to the W of Yueyang, on the border with Hubei prov; the area is now reduced to about 2,820 sq km owing to silt deposits from the rivers.

Doornik, town in Belgium. See Tournai.

Dorado, El, 33 12N 92 40W, pop(1980) 25,270, county seat of Union county, S Arkansas, United States; 128 km ESE of Texarkana; oil was discovered here in 1921; economy: oil centre of the state, with several oil refineries and chemical plants.

Dor'chester, DURNOVARIA (anc), 50 43N 2 26W, pop(1981) 14,225, county town in West Dorset dist, Dorset, S England; on the R Frome, 12 km N of Weymouth; the Roman ramparts became known as 'The Walks' in the 18th century; King Athelstan (925-39) established a mint here; Judge Jeffrey's Bloody Assizes were held here in 1685; railway; economy: brewing; event: Thomas Hardy festival (Aug); monuments: Dorset county museum, Dorset military museum, Maiden castle prehistoric fort (3 km S).

Dordogne *dor-don'y'*, dept in Aquitaine region of SW France, comprising 4 arrond, 50 cantons and 555 communes; pop(1982) 377,356; area 9,060 sq km; drained by the westward flowing R Dordogne and its tributaries (Isle, Vézère, and Dronne rivers); formed mainly of the old Guiennese dist of Périgord, whose name is perpetuated in the truffle industry and in its pâtés; there are Celtic and Roman remains; capital Périgueux, chief towns Bergerac, Nontron and Sarlat; there are numerous châteaux including Richemont (16th-c), Beynac (13th-c) and Hautefort (14-17th-c); there are interesting caves near Les Eyzies, Montignac, Rouffignac and Le Bugue.

Dordogne, DURANIUS (anc), river in SW France rising in the Auvergne hills S of Le Mont-Dore; formed by the confluence of the Dor and Dogne rivers in Puy-de-Dôme dept; flows SW and W past Bergerac and Libourne to meet the R Garonne at the Bec d'Ambes where it forms the Gironde estuary; length 472 km; tributaries Maronne, Cère, Diège, Vézère and Isle rivers; the vineyards along the valley slopes include those of St Émilion and Pomerol.

Dordrecht *dor'dreKHt*, DORDT or DORT, 51 48N 4 39E, pop(1984e) 199,156, river port and industrial city in S Zuid Holland prov, W Netherlands; between the rivers Oude, Maas, Merwede and the 2 branches of the Maas, the Noord and the Dordtse Kil, 19 km ESE of Rotterdam; founded in 1008; by 1220 it had become the wealthiest commercial town of the Netherlands, but in the 18th century it was surpassed by Rotterdam; cargo vessels have partly made way for pleasure yachts in the old inner basin and new basins have been dug S of the town to accommodate larger ships; the Synod of Dort, the greatest meeting of the Reformed churches, took place in 1618-19; birthplace of the de Witt brothers (prominent 17th-c politicians) and the painters Bols, Cuyp and van Hoogstratten; railway; economy: shipbuilding, engineering, chemicals; monuments: Grote Kerk (begun c.1300 and rebuilt in the 15th and 16th centuries).

Dori *dō'ree*, 14 03N 0 02W, town in NE Burkina, W Africa; 240 km NE of Ouagadougou.

Dor'king, 51 14N 0 20W, pop(1981) 14,830, market town in Mole Valley dist, Surrey, SE England; on the R Mole, 40 km SW of London; railway; economy: engineering.

Dormagen *dor'mah-gun*, 51 06N 6 50E, pop(1983) 57,300, industrial city in Düsseldorf dist, Nordrhein-Westfalen (North Rhine-Westphalia) prov, W Germany, 16 km S of Düsseldorf.

Dornbirn *dorn'birn*, 47 25N 9 46E, pop(1981) 38,641, capital and largest town of Dornbirn dist, Vorarlberg state, W Austria; at the foot of the Bregenzerwald on the edge of the Rhine valley, 12 km from Bregenz; airfield; economy: textiles and engineering; event: Dornbirn Fair in July-Aug.

Dornod *dor'nōt*, EAST COUNTY (Eng), county in E Mongolia; pop(1981e) 50,000; area 122,000 sq km; bounded N by USSR and E and S by the People's Republic of China; capital Choybalsan; 22% of Mongolia's cultivated land, 54% of its hay-plots and 10% of its pasture lie within this county; economy: beef cattle, coal, copper, iron ore, tungsten, salt, food processing, textiles, vehicle repair.

Dornogovĭ *dor-no-gō'bee*, DORNOGOV, EAST GOBI COUNTY (Eng), county in SE Mongolia; pop(1981e) 40,000; area

111,000 sq km; capital Saynshand; bounded S and E by the People's Republic of China; covered in part by the Gobi Desert; steppe soils are found in the N of the county, while sandy soils are found in the S.

Dorohoi *do-ro-hoy'*, 47 57N 26 31E, pop(1983) 27,495, town in Botoşani county, NE Romania; 120 km NW of Iaşi; established in the 14th century; railway terminus; economy: grain, livestock, timber trade.

Dorset, county of S England; bounded S by the English Channel and from W to E by Devonshire, Somerset, Wiltshire and Hampshire; extensive heathlands and chalk down are drained by the Frome and Stour rivers; pop(1981) 595,415; area 2,654 sq km; county town Dorchester; chief towns include Bournemouth, Weymouth and Poole; economy: tourism, livestock, quarrying: the county is divided into 8 districts:

District	*area (sq km)*	*pop(1981)*
Bournemouth	46	145,704
Christchurch	50	37,986
North Dorset	609	46,774
Poole	64	119,316
Purbeck	405	40,778
West Dorset	1,083	78,849
Weymouth and Portland	42	57,547
Wimborne	355	68,461

Dorsten *dor'stun*, 51 40N 6 55E, pop(1983) 71,700, industrial city in Münster dist, Nordrhein-Westfalen (North Rhine-Westphalia) prov, W Germany; 22 km N of Essen; railway.

Dortmund *dort'moont*, 51 32N 7 28E, pop(1983) 595,200, industrial, mining and commercial city in Arnsberg dist, Nordrhein-Westfalen (North Rhine-Westphalia) prov, W Germany; river port in the Ruhr valley, 50 km S of Münster; connected to the North Sea by the Dortmund-Ems Canal (272 km long); has one of Germany's largest inland harbours; a great sporting centre, with almost 100 sports installations; university (1966); railway; economy: iron and steel, mechanical engineering, construction machinery, non-alcoholic drinks, brewing.

Dos Hermanas *dos her-man'as*, 37 16N 5 55W, pop(1982) 57,357, town in Sevilla prov, Andalucia, S Spain; 11 km S of Sevilla; the scene of a famous pilgrimage on the third Sunday in Oct; economy: plastics, porcelain, iron, animal food, olives.

Dosso *dō'sō*, dept in SW Niger, W Africa; a low-lying region with the R Niger flowing along its SW border; there are seasonal floodplains in the W and E; area 31,002 sq km; pop(1977e) 640,000; comprises 5 arrond; capital Dosso; chief towns Gaya, Birni Ngaouré, Dogondoutchi; economy: phosphate mining.

Dosso, 13 03N 3 10E, capital of Dosso dept, SW Niger, W Africa; 130 km ESE of Niamey; economy: power plant and agriculture.

Dothan, 31 13N 85 24W, pop(1980) 48,750, county seat of Houston county, SE Alabama, United States; 26 km N of the Florida border and 28 km W of Georgia border; railway; economy: manufactures include lumber products, furniture, farm tools, and textiles; nuclear power plant; event: Peanut Festival (Oct).

Douala *doo-a'la*, DUALA, 4 04N 9 43E, pop(1984) 784,000, seaport capital of Littoral prov, Cameroon, W Africa; on the R Wouri estuary, 270 km W of Yaoundé and 25 km from the Gulf of Guinea coast; Mount Cameroon (4,070 m) is nearby; the city has a relatively high non-African population (mainly French and Greek); the English missionary Alfred Saker settled here in 1845; Nachtigal raised the German flag here in 1884 when the town was called Kamerunstadt; capital of German Cameroon between 1885 and 1901 and of French Cameroon between 1940 and 1946; the city acquired its present name in 1907; a bridge over the R Wouri (1,800 m long) to Bonabéri was built in 1955; the city is divided into the three districts of Bell, Akwa (commercial) and Diedo; railway; airport (4 km); economy: economic capital of Cameroon with many import-export companies; one of W Africa's busiest ports trading in bananas, minerals, agricultural services, coffee, cocoa and tobacco trading, timber, plywood, palm oil, brewing and soft drinks, natural rubber, soap, detergent, vegetable oil, cocoa butter and cement; centre for petroleum exploration; industries: aluminium smelting, paper, pulp, textiles, flour milling, metal work, chemicals and food processing; monument: Pagoda of King Manga Bell (royal palace of Asian style).

Doubs *doo*, dept in Franche-Comté region of E France, bounded on the W by the Ognon R and separated from Switzerland on the E by the Jura Mts; comprises 3 arrond, 35 cantons and 592 communes; drained by the Doubs R; pop(1982) 477,163; area 5,234 sq km; capital Besançon; spa at Besançon; interesting caves near Roset-Fluans (Grotte d'Osselle).

Doubs, DUBIS (anc), river in E France rising in the E Jura Mts near the Swiss frontier; flows NE, following the Swiss-French border, into Switzerland then W into France, N and finally SW past Besançon and Dôle to meet the R Saône near Chalon-sur-Saône; length 430 km; tributary R Loué; once a tributary of the Rhine; the deep limestone gorge of Cluse de Doubs at Pontarlier is an important railway route into Switzerland.

Douglas, 54 09N 4 29W, pop(1981) 19,944, seaport capital of the Isle of Man; on the E coast of the Isle of Man, 80 km W of Barrow-in-Furness; railway; economy: tourism; monuments: Manx National Museum; in the S part of the bay, on Conister Rock, is the Tower of Refuge, built in 1832 by Sir William Hilary, founder of the Royal National Lifeboat Institution; just SE of Douglas is Douglas Head promontory, site of a lighthouse.

Dounreay *doon-ray'*, nuclear research station, Caithness, Highland region, N Scotland; on the coast of the Pentland Firth, 13 km W of Thurso.

Douro *do'oo-roo*, *doo'ro* (Eng), DUERO *dway'ro* (Sp), DURIUS (anc), river rising in the Sierra de Urbion in Soria prov, N central Spain, flows 609 km W to Portuguese border which it follows for 107 km in SW direction before turning W across N Portugal, emptying into the Atlantic at São Jõao da Foz near Porto; 322 km in Portugal; used extensively for irrigation and hydroelectric power, five dams built and operated jointly by Spain and Portugal: Barragem de Miranda do Douro, Barragem do Picote, Barragem da Bemposta, Barragem de Aldeladavila and Barragem de Sauceine; length 895 km; navigable 200 km to Barca de Alva; vineyards on terraced slopes of slaty soil in the upper Douro valley or País do Vinho produce port and Mateus Rosé, principal tributaries include the Sabor, Tua, Sousa, Corgo, Tâmega, Águeda, Côa, Távora and Paiva.

Douro Litoral *do'oo-roo lee-toor-ahl'*, prov of NW Portugal formed in 1936 from the former region of Minho or Entre Minho and Douro, includes most of Porto dist; cities: Porto and Penafiel; area 3,248 sq km.

Dover *dō'vėr*, DOUVRES (Fr), DUBRIS PORTUS (Lat), 51 08N 1 19E, pop(1981) 34,304, seaport in Dover dist, Kent, SE England; principal cross-Channel port, the shortest link with France (35 km); the largest of the Cinque ports; railway; monuments: 13-14th-c Dover castle; 13th-c St Edmund's chapel, the smallest chapel in England; Roman painted house (2nd-c AD).

Dover, 39 10N 75 32W, pop(1980) 23,512, capital of state in Kent county, central Delaware, United States; 64 km S of Wilmington; planned in 1717 and made state capital in 1777; city status in 1929; university; railway; economy: trade in fruit and vegetables; event: Old Dover Days (May).

Dovrefjell *dov're-fyel*, DOVREFJELD, mountain plateau in S central Norway, divided from the Jotunheimen range to the N by the Gudbrandsdalen valley, extends 160 km between Romsdalsfjord (Romsdal Fjord) (W) and the Østerdalen valley (E); rises to 2,286 m at Snøhetta; source of the R Driva.

Dowa *dō'wah*, dist in Central region, Malawi, SE Africa; area 3,041 sq km; pop(1977) 247,603.

Down, AN DUN (Gael), county in SE Northern Ireland; bounded W by Armagh along the Newry river, NE by Antrim along the Lagan river, N by Belfast Lough, S by Carlingford Lough and E by the Irish Sea; a hilly county with a coastline indented (N-S) by Strangford Lough, Dundrum Bay and Carlingford Lough; major rivers include the Newry, Lagan, Bann; in the S are the Mourne Mts; rises to 852 m with Slieve Donard in the SE; the Newry Canal connects the Newry river, via the Bann river, with Lough Neagh; pop(1981) 339,229; area 2,448 sq km; county town Downpatrick; major towns Newry, Bangor and Newtownards; economy: agriculture (oats, potatoes, vegetables, stock-rearing), linen; Down is divided into 6 districts:

District	*area (sq km)*	*pop(1981)*
Ards	369	57,626
Banbridge	444	29,885
Castlereagh	85	60,757
Down	646	52,869
Newry and Mourne	895	72,243
North Down	73	65,849

Downers Grove, 41 49N 88 01W, pop(1980) 42,572, town in Du Page county, NE Illinois, United States; 32 km W of Chicago; railway.

Downey, 33 56N 118 25W, pop(1980) 82,602, city in Los Angeles county, SW California, United States; 16 km SE of Los Angeles.

Downpatrick, DUN PADRAIG (Gael), 54 20N 5 43W, pop(1981) 8,245, county town in Down dist, Down, SE Northern Ireland; near the S end of Strangford Lough; one of the chief centres of pilgrimage in Ireland; St Patrick is said to have landed here in 432 and to have founded a church c.440; St Patrick, St Columbus and Bridget of Kildare are buried here; economy: textiles, agricultural trade; monuments: St Patrick's cathedral (1798-1812), containing parts of the earlier cathedral built in the 13th c and also the tomb of St Patrick; 3 km NW of Downpatrick are the remains of Inch abbey, founded c.1187 by John de Courcy; 2 km NE of the town are the remains of the Monastery of Saul, said to be founded by St Patrick in 440.

Downs, low lying chalk hill ranges rising in Dorset and Hampshire and extending into Surrey, Kent and East and West Sussex, S England; the North Downs extend from the chalk cliffs of Dover in the E, through Kent and into Surrey; they are separated from the South Downs by the Weald; the South Downs stretch W to Beachy Head, running parallel to the S coast of England; the North Downs rise to 294 m at Leith Hill and the South Downs to 264 m at Butser Hill.

Drak'ensberg ('dragon's mountain'), KWATHLAMBA, KAHLAMBA, mountain range in South Africa forming the E escarpment of the S African plateau; extending NE-SW through Transvaal, Natal and Cape provs; forms the E frontier of Lesotho with Natal and the W frontier of Swaziland with Transvaal; main peaks, located near the Natal-Lesotho frontier, include Thaban Ntlenyana (3,482 m), Champagne Castle (3,375 m), Mt aux Sources (3,299 m).

Drá'ma, agricultural nome (dept) of Makedhonia region, N Greece; pop(1981) 94,772; area 3,468 sq km; capital Dráma; drained by the R Néstos (Mesta).

Drá'ma, DRABES'CUS (anc), 41 10N 24 11E, pop(1981) 36,109, capital town of Dráma nome (dept), Makedhonia region, N Greece; 36 km NW of Kaválla, at the foot of Mt Falakrón (2,194 m), on a tributary of the R Strimón, which is harnessed to drive oilmills; railway; economy: processes locally produced cotton, rice, and tobacco.

Dram'men, 59 45N 10 15E, pop(1983) 50,581, seaport and administrative capital of Buskerud county, SE Norway; at the mouth of the R Dramselv on a branch of the Oslofjorden (Oslo Fjord), railway; economy: engineering, paper; important port shipping Norwegian timber, cellulose and paper.

Drammen or **Drams'vassdraget**, river in S Norway, rising as R Hallingdalselv on the S slopes of the Hallingskarvet range; flows ENE through Buskerud county to Gol then SSE through L Krøderen to Drammen; discharges into the Drammensfjord, an arm of the Oslofjorden (Oslo Fjord); length 309 km; an important communication line for the timber trade, with saw-mills, pulp manufactures and other ancillary industries on its banks.

Drancy *drã-see*, 48 55N 2 26E, pop(1982) 60,224, town in Seine-Saint-Denis dept, Ile-de-France region, N central France.

Drôme *drōm*, dept in Rhône-Alpes region of SE France, on the E side of the lower Rhône-Saône valley; comprises 3 arrond, 35 cantons and 371 communes; pop(1982) 389,781; area 6,530 sq km; in the E are outliers of the Alpes Cottiennes, covered with woods and pasturage; drained by the westward flowing Isère, Drôme, Aigues and Ouvèze rivers; near the Rhône R the sandy soil is made fertile by irrigation; capital Valence, other towns include Romans, Nyons and Montelimar; there are interesting caves near La Chapelle-en-Vercors (Grotte de la Luire); the Parc du Vercors regional nature park lies partly within the dept.

Drenthe *dren'te*, DRENTE, pop(1984e) 427,300, prov in N Netherlands, bounded on the E by West Germany; land area 2,653 sq km; mostly flat, lying some 10-20 m above sea level; situated in the extreme NE of the wide Geest plains; rises to 32 m in the moraines of Hondsrug, a range of hills some 50 km long stretching from Emmen in the SE to Groningen in the NW; capital Assen; chief towns Emmen and Hoogeveen; economy: arable farming predominates in the 'peat colonies' of E Drenthe, further W it is predominantly livestock or mixed farming on less well-drained clay and peat soils, interrupted by patches of heath and woodland; industry plays only a subordinate role in the economy with petroleum extraction in the SE; the fen colonies are primarily in the S of the prov, around Beilen and Hoogeveen; it is the most thinly populated prov in the Netherlands (density in 1983 was 160 inhabitants per sq km).

Dresden *drays'dun*, 3rd largest county in SE East Germany; pop(1981) 1,804,556; area 6,738 sq km; crossed by important transit roads, railway lines and the R Elbe, the country's largest river; part of the Lusatia region, it is inhabited by the bilingual Slavic Sorb minority group occupying the districts of Bautzen, Kamenz and Niesky; 60% of land is farmed and 25% is under forest; Dresden is the capital and chief industrial centre; steel is important at Riesa, Görlitz and Freital and textile manufacture is mostly located to the E; nuclear research centre at Ressendorf; popular holiday areas are the Elbsandsteingebirge (Saxon Switzerland), the Lusatian Mts and the Zittauer Gebirge.

Dresden, 51 2N 13 45E, pop(1982) 521,011, capital of Dresden county, SE East Germany; on R Elbe, ESE of Berlin, close to the Czechoslovak frontier; heavily bombed during World War II; technical university (1828); Dresden china is manufactured in Meissen; airport; railway; economy: motor vehicles, electronics, pharmaceuticals, food processing, optical instruments.

Drin *dreen*, DRILO (anc), river in Albania; flows N out of L Ohrid into E Albania; turns W in N Albania and flows tortuously to the Adriatic Sea; in its lower course it is partly deflected to the R Bojana (Buenë); length 280 km; copper-ore is mined in the river basin.

Drina *dree'na*, river in Yugoslavia; formed by the junction of the Tara and Piva rivers on the Crna Gora (Montenegro) border; flows 456 km N to meet the R Sava SW of Ruma; used for hydroelectric power; navigable for 330 km.

Drobeta-Turnu Severin or **Turnu Severin** *dro-bet'a-toor'noo se-ve-reen'*, DROBETA (anc), 44 36N 22 39E, pop(1983) 92,235, river port and capital town of Mehedinţi county, SW Romania; on left bank of R Danube where it follows the frontier with Yugoslavia; railway; economy: livestock, timber, grain, fruit trade; aircraft, shipyards, railway wagons, pulp, paper, alcohol, furniture; monuments: remains of Roman city and of Trajan's Bridge.

Drogheda *dro'u-du*, DROICHEAD ÁTHA (Gael), 53 43N 6 21W, pop(1981) 23,615, industrial seaport town in Louth county, NE Leinster, E Irish Republic; on R Boyne, N of Dublin; Irish parliaments met here until 1494; railway; economy: brewing, textiles, chemicals; monuments: Neolithic passage graves at Dowth, Knowth and Newgrange 7 km W; remains of 5th-c monastery at Monasterboice 8 km N; battleground of the Battle of the Boyne (1690) 6 km SW.

Droichead Nua *dro'u noo'a*, formerly NEWBRIDGE, 53 11N 6 48W, pop(1981) 10,716, market town in Kildare county, Leinster, E Irish Republic; on R Liffey ENE of Kildare; the town developed around a barracks built in 1816; railway.

Droitwich *droyt'wich*, 52 16N 2 09W, pop(1981) 18,140, town in Wychavon dist, Hereford and Worcester, W central England; 10 km NE of Worcester; railway; economy: engineering, electrics.

Drôme, river in SE France rising in the Dauphiné pre-Alps, E of Col de Cobre, in Hautes-Alpes dept; flows WNW across Drôme dept to meet the R Rhône below Livron; length 110 km.

Dron'field, 53 19N 1 27W, pop(1981) 22,673, town in North-east Derbyshire dist, Derbyshire, central England; 8 km N of Chesterfield; railway; economy: iron, steel, engineering.

Dronning Maud Land, QUEEN MAUD LAND (Eng), Norwegian Antarctic territory E of British Antarctic Territory and W of Enderby Land, extending to the S Pole; claimed by Norway in 1939; there are scientific bases at Sanae (S Africa) and Novo Lazarevskaya (USSR).

Dronten, pop(1984e) 22,200, municipality in Flevoland, W Netherlands; land area 333 sq km.

Drouzhaba or **Druzba** *droozh'ba*, 43 15N 28 00E, resort town in Varna okrug (prov), E Bulgaria; on the Black Sea, 6 km N of Varna.

Droylsden *droylz'den*, 53 29N 2 09W, pop(1981) 22,624, town in Greater Manchester, NW England; E of Manchester; economy: textiles, engineering, foodstuffs, plastics.

Drysdale River, national park in Western Australia, NW Australia; includes the Drysdale river and the Ashton Mt range; area 4,355 sq km; established in 1974.

Duars *dwarz*, region at the foot of the Himalayas in Bhután and the Indian state of Assam; part of the plain of the Brahmaputra river valley; crossed N-S by the R Manas.

Duarte, Pico *dwar'tee*, formerly MONTE TRUJILLO, mountain in the Cordillera Central of the Dominican Republic, Hispaniola I, West Indies; height 3,175 m; highest peak in the Caribbean.

Dubai, one of the seven member states of the United Arab Emirates. See Dubayy.

Dubayy *doo-bī'*, DUBAI, second largest of the United Arab Emirates, NE of Abū Ẓabī; area 3,900 sq km; pop(1980) 278,000; capital Dubayy; chief town Mina Jebel Ali; Dubayy has separate enclaves in the Hajar Mts; economy: oil was discovered in 1966 while production and export of crude oil commenced in 1969; the main offshore fields are Fath, SW Fath, Falah, and Rashid; Margham is a major onshore oil and gas field which also has a gas gathering system with facilities to transport 8.5 million cubic metres of gas per day to the industrial port complex of Mina Jebel Ali, 35 km SW of Dubayy; Mina Jebel Ali, declared a free trade zone in May 1980, is based on the supply of natural gas to provide electricity and desalinated water and to service petrochemical industries; industries at Mina Jebel Ali include a desalination plant, a copper and aluminium cables factory, an aluminium smelter, and a steel fabrication facility; the older industrial zone of Rashidiya accounts for 40% of Dubayy's processing industries.

Dubayy, DUBAI, 24 10N 55 20E, pop(1980) 265,702, major port and capital of Dubayy emirate, United Arab Emirates, SE Arabian Peninsula; on both sides of Dubayy Creek which discharges into the Arabian Gulf; airport; Port Rashid is its port; economy: building, shipping.

Dub'bo, 32 16S 148 41E, pop(1981) 23,986, town in North-Western stat div, E central New South Wales, Australia; on the Macquarie river, 296 km NW of Sydney; railway; airfield; economy: clothing, flour, sheep and cattle; monuments: Western Plains Zoo, Australia's only open-range zoo.

Dü'bendorf, 47 28N 8 37E, pop(1980) 20,683, town in Zürich canton, N Switzerland, NE of Zürich; economy: engineering, electrics, plastics.

Dub'lin, BAILE ÁTHA CLIATH *bah'lee ah klee* (Gael), county in Leinster prov, E Irish Republic; bisected W-E by R Liffey and the Grand Canal; Wicklow Mts to the S and Irish Sea to the W; pop(1981) 1,003,164; area 922 sq km; capital Dublin.

Dublin, EBLANA (anc), 53 20N 6 15W, pop(1981) 860,619, county borough and capital of Irish Republic; at mouth of R Liffey where it meets the Irish Sea, built on the site of a Viking settlement; the port is connected to the interior by the Grand and Royal Canals; in 1919 1st Sinn Feinn parliament met here; famous former residents have included Oscar Wilde, W.B. Yeats, George Bernard Shaw, Thomas More, Jonathan Swift, R.B. Sheridan, Edmund Burke and James Joyce; natural gas pipeline from Kinsale; airport (10 km from city); railway; ferries to Liverpool and Holyhead; economy: trading port, brewing, distilling, textiles, chemicals, food processing; two universities Trinity College (1591) and University College of the National University of Ireland (1908); monuments: King's Inns, national museum, national gallery, Leinster House, Dublin Castle.

Dubrovnik *doo'brov-nik, doo-brov'nik* (Eng), RAGUSA *ra-goo'sa* (Ital), 42 40N 18 07E, pop(1981) 66,131, port on the Dalmatia coast of Hrvatska (Croatia) republic, W Yugoslavia; capital of Dalmatia; airport (Čilipi, 30 km S); car ferries to Italy and Greece; on the W side of the new harbour is Lapad peninsula with hotels and villas; nearby naturist beach to the S at Mlini; economy: silk, leather, dairy products, liqueurs, tourism; monuments: town wall surrounding the old town; cathedral; Rector's palace; event: Dubrovnik Summer Festival in July-Aug.

Dubuque *de-byook'*, 42 30N 90 41W, pop(1980) 62,321, county seat of Dubuque county, E Iowa, United States; a port on the Mississippi river, 100 km NE of Cedar Rapids; university (1852); railway; economy: shipbuilding, food processing, machinery; monument: Mississippi Stern-wheelers; event: Dubuque Festival (May).

Dudelange or **Forge du Sud** *dü-de-lãzh'*, DÜDELINGEN (Ger), 49 28N 6 05E, pop(1981) 14,074, industrial town in Esch-sur-Alzette canton, Luxembourg dist, S Luxembourg; at the foot of Mt St Jean; 3rd largest town in Luxembourg; economy: steel; monument: Neogothic parish church with Dom. Lang's 'Way of the Cross'; event: popular festival on 2nd Sunday of Sept.

Dud'ley, 52 30N 2 05W, pop(1981) 187,367, town in West Midlands, central England; 12 km W of Birmingham; railway; economy: metal products, clothing, glass, leather; monuments: church of St Thomas the Apostle (1817-19), 13th-c Dudley castle.

Dufourspitze *doof-oor'shpi-tsu*, PUNTA DUFOUR (Ital), 45 57N 7 53E, mountain peak in Valais canton, Switzerland; highest peak of the Monte Rosa group of the Pennine Alps, on the Italian-Swiss border; 2nd highest alpine peak; height 4,634 m.

Duisburg *düs'boorKH*, 51 27N 6 42E, pop(1983) 541,800, industrial and commercial city in Düsseldorf dist, Nordrhein-Westfalen (North Rhine-Westphalia) prov, W Germany; river port on W edge of the R Ruhr, at the confluence of the Ruhr with the Rhine, 19 km NNW of Düsseldorf; largest inland port in Europe; a university town in the Middle Ages; the excellent regatta course in the Wedau sports park has made Duisburg a favoured choice for international rowing regattas; the famous cartographer Gerhard Mercator (1512-94) lived and taught here; railway; economy: Germany's largest producer of steel, copper and zinc works, heavy equipment, plastics, oil refining, brewing, river craft.

Dukeries, The, area of NW Nottinghamshire, central England; includes Sherwood Forest and the parks of former ducal seats at Clumber, Thoresby, Welbeck and Worksop.

Dukhān *dook-han'*, 25 25N 50 50E, pop(1975) 2,000, oil town on the W coast of Qatar Peninsula, State of Qatar; oil was first discovered here in 1939 but was not commercially exploited until after World War II; economy: liquefied natural gas plant; the oilfield is linked by pipeline to the terminal at Musay'īd (Umm Said).

Duluth *de-looth'*, 46 47N 92 07W, pop(1980) 92,811, county seat of St Louis county, NE Minnesota, United States; at the W end of L Superior, opposite Superior; railway; airfield; economy: major lake port handling grain and iron ore; manufactures steel, cement, metal products and electrical equipment; monuments: Aerial Lift Bridge and Leif Erikson Park; event: Grandma's Marathon (June).

Dum Dum, 22 37N 88 25E, pop(1981) 360,288, city in West Bengal, NE India; just NE of Calcutta; airport; former British military station; dumdum bullets were first made here in an ammunition factory; economy: engineering.

Dumai *doo-mī*, 1 39N 101 28E, port in Riau prov, Indonesia; on E coast of the island of Sumatera, opposite Rupat I; its oil refinery is linked to the oilfields at Rumbai near Pekanbaru by a pipeline.

Dumbarton, 55 57N 4 35W, pop(1981) 23,430, capital of Dumbarton dist, Strathclyde, W Scotland; at the confluence of the Leven and Clyde rivers, 22 km NW of Glasgow; Mary Queen of Scots left for France from Dumbarton in 1548, at the age of 5; railway; economy: distilling, electronics; monument: Dumbarton castle, a modern barracks with a 12th-c gateway, a dungeon and a sundial dating from the time of Mary Queen of Scots.

Dumfries *dum-frees'*, 55 04N 3 37W, pop(1981) 32,100, market town and capital of Nithsdale dist, and of Dumfries and Galloway region, SW Scotland; on the R Nith, 97 km SE of Glasgow and 47 km NW of Carlisle; Robert Burns lived here from 1791 until his death in 1796; railway; economy: light engineering, textiles; monuments: Burns's House and Mausoleum; the Old Bridge House (1662); Devorgilla's Bridge, which was originally built in the 13th-c by Devorgilla Balliol who endowed Balliol College, Oxford; local event: Dumfries and Galloway arts festival (May).

Dumfries and Galloway, region in SW Scotland; bounded N by Strathclyde, E by Borders, SE by England (along the R Sark), S by the Solway Firth, Wigtown Bay and Luce Bay and W by Beaufort's Dyke; in the W is a peninsula which is known as the Rinns of Galloway; the region is drained by the Cree, Dee, Nith and Annan rivers; pop(1981) 145,139; area 6,370 sq km; capital Dumfries; major towns include Kirkcudbright and Stranraer; Stranraer is linked by ferry to Larne in Northern Ireland; Dumfries and Galloway is divided into 4 districts:

District	*area (sq km)*	*pop(1981)*
Annandale and Eskdale	1,553	35,467
Nithsdale	1,433	56,217
Stewartry	1,671	23,214
Wigtown	1,713	30,241

Dummersee, 52 30N 8 21E, lake in S Niedersachsen (Lower Saxony) prov, W Germany, on the border between Weser-Ems and Hannover dists; area 16 sq km; max depth 3 m; average depth 2 m; the R Hunte flows through the lake.

Dumyât *dum-yat'*, DAMIETTA *dam-ee-et'a*, PHATNITIC (anc), 31 26N 31 48E, pop(1976) 93,488, port capital of Dumyât governorate, NE Egypt; 13 km from mouth of Dumyât branch of the Nile, NNE of Cairo and 50 km WNW of Port Said; economy: cotton.

Dún Laoghaire *doon-la'ree*, formerly KINGSTOWN, DUNLEARY *dun-lee'ree* (Eng), 53 17N 6 08W, pop(1981) 54,496, borough in Dublin county, Leinster, E Irish Republic; on Irish Sea S of Dublin; fishing port, resort town, yachting centre and dormitory town for Dublin; harbour built by Rennie between 1817 and 1859; named Kingstown when George IV landed here in 1821; railway; ferries to Holyhead.

Duna, European river. See Danube.

Dunajská Streda *doon'ay-skah stre'da*, 48 00N 17 32E, pop(1984) 20,384, town in Západoslovenský region, Slovak Socialist Republic, S central Czechoslovakia; SE of Bratislava, near the Hungarian frontier; railway.

Dunakeszi *doon'o-kes-ee*, 47 31N 19 03E, pop(1984e) 27,000, town in Pest county, N Hungary; N of Budapest; railway; economy: food processing.

Dunántúl *doo'nan-tool*, TRANSDANUBIA *trans-dan-yoo'bee-a* (Eng), geographical region in Hungary, lying W of the R Danube and extending to the Hungarian Alps and S to the R Drava; occupies one-third of Hungary; a hilly and fertile region, noted for livestock and wine production.

Dunarea, European river. See Danube.

Dunaújváros *doon-o-wee-va'rosh*, 47 00N 21 57E, pop(1984e) 62,000, town in Fejér county, central Hungary; on the R Danube; economy: iron and steel, textiles.

Dunav, European river. See Danube.

Dunbar, 56 00N 2 31W, pop(1981) 6,035, resort town in East Lothian dist, Lothian, E Scotland; on the North Sea, 43 km E of Edinburgh; Torness nuclear power station is 7 km to the SE; railway.

Dunblane, 56 12N 3 59W, pop(1981) 6,855, town in Stirling dist, Central region, central Scotland; on the Allan Water, 8 km N of Stirling; monument: 13th-c Dunblane cathedral, restored in 1829-95.

Duncanville, 32 39N 96 55W, pop(1980) 27,781, town in Dallas county, NE Texas, United States; a residential suburb 17 km SSW of Dallas; railway.

Dundalk *dun-dolk'*, DUN DEALGAN (Gael), 54 01N 6 25W, pop(1981) 29,135, capital of Louth county, Leinster, NE Irish Republic; on R Castletown near its mouth on Dundalk Bay; railway; economy: brewing, cigarettes, food processing, textiles, chemicals; monument: Dun Dealgan mound 3 km W, the birthplace of Cuchulain, the legendary leader of the Red Branch Knights, who defended the Cooley Peninsula against the cattle raiders from the W; event: Maytime theatre festival.

Dundee, 56 28N 3 00W, pop(1981) 174,345, port capital of Dundee City dist and Tayside region, E Scotland; on the N side of the Firth of Tay, 29 km E of Perth; a royal burgh since the 12th century; the city developed with the jute manufacturing industry; university (1881); airfield; railway; economy: textiles, paper, confectionery, oil-related industries, electronics; the Firth of Tay is crossed here by rail and road bridges; monuments: Barrack Street natural history museum; Caird Hall (1914-23); Broughty Castle Museum, housed in a former estuary fort, 6 km E of the city centre, contains an exhibition on local history, including exhibits of Dundee's former involvement in the whaling industry; Claypotts Castle, a tower house built between 1569 and 1588.

Dundgovĭ *dund-gō'bee*, DUND GOBI, MIDDLE GOBI (Eng), county in central Mongolia; pop(1981e) 40,000; area 78,000 sq km; part of the Gobi Desert zone; capital Mandalgovĭ; copper, fluorspar, coal, iron ore, turquoise and other semi-precious stones are mined; cattle and camel herding are important.

Dunedin *dun-ee'din*, 45 52S 170 30E, pop(1981) 77,176, city in Otago, SE South Island, New Zealand; on the E coast at the S end of the Otago peninsula; seaport located at Port Chalmers, 13 km NE; its name is derived from the Gaelic form of Edinburgh; founded by Scottish settlers in 1848, Dunedin became an important centre after the discovery of gold in the region; Otago University (1869); railway; airfield; economy: wool, footwear, clothing, agricultural machinery, trade in wool, meat, fruit and dairy produce; monuments: the city's buildings, parks and statues reflect the influence of early Scottish settlers; at the centre of the city is the Octagon and a statue of the

Scots poet, Robert Burns; Dunedin's colonial buildings include the municipal chambers (1878-80), railway station (1904), Fortune Theatre (1869), Bank of New Zealand (1883) and Knox Church (1876); the Early Settlers' Museum contains a collection of items from Dunedin's pioneering era; Hocken Library is a major resource centre for New Zealand history.

Dunedin, 28 01N 82 47W, pop(1980) 30,203, town in Pinellas county, W Florida, United States; on the Gulf of Mexico, 32 km W of Tampa; railway; economy: fruit-processing centre; connected to Dunedin Beach I by a causeway.

Dunfermline *dun-ferm'lin*, 56 04N 3 29W, pop(1981) 52,227, capital of Dunfermline dist, Fife, E Scotland; 27 km NW of Edinburgh; a royal burgh since 1588; ancient residence of Scottish kings and the burial place of several, including Robert the Bruce; birthplace of Charles I and of Andrew Carnegie (1835); railway; economy: textiles, clothing, metal products, electronics; monuments: Dunfermline abbey and palace, on the foundations of a church built by Queen Margaret (11th-c).

Dungan'non, DUN GEANAINN (Gael), 54 31N 6 46W, pop(1981) 8,295, market town in Dungannon dist, Tyrone, S central Northern Ireland; 56 km WSW of Belfast; until the 17th century the town was the major stronghold of the O'Neills, Earls of Tyrone; economy: textiles (linen), engineering, food processing; monuments: 19 km NE of Dungannon, on the W shore of Lough Neagh, is the High Cross of Arboe, a 9th-c restored cross, almost 5 m high; at Beaghmore, 26 km NW of Dungannon, are prehistoric stone circles with grave mounds, built c.1800 BC.

Dungarvan *dun-gar'vun*, DUN GARBHAIN (Gael), 52 05N 7 37W, pop(1981) 6,631, market town in Waterford county, Munster, SE Irish Republic; on Dungarvan Bay SW of Waterford; economy: fishing, leather.

Dungeness Head, 5 55N 0 58E, point on the S coast of Kent, S England; projects into the English Channel SE of Lydd; nearby is Dungeness nuclear power station, with gas-cooled, graphite-moderated reactors which came into commercial operation in 1965 and an advanced gas-cooled reactor in operation in 1983.

Dunhuang *tun-whang*, TUNHUANG, 40 05N 94 45E, town in Gansu prov, NW China; Dunhuang was established in 200 BC; 25 km SE of the town are the Mogao Grottoes, the oldest Buddhist shrines in China; carving began in 366 AD and over the following 1,000 years hundreds of caves were carved out of the steep sandstone cliffs in a layered honeycomb pattern connected by a series of wooden walkways and ladders; the Grottoes were abandoned after the 14th century and accidentally rediscovered in 1900; the scrolls, embroideries, paintings and sutras which they contained were sold or plundered; 62 km SW of Dunhuang are the Yangguan and Hongshan mountain passes, which served as China's gateway into the western world until blocked by Mongols in the 14th century.

Dunkerque *dœ̃-kerk*, DUNKIRK (Eng), DUINEKERKE *dœ'een-kerk* (Flem), 51 02N 2 23E, pop(1982) 73,618, seaport in Nord dept, Nord-Pas-de-Calais region, NW France, at the entrance to the Pas de Calais (Straits of Dover); it is the 3rd largest port of France with extensive docks, deep-water quays and cross-Channel ferry connections to Dover and Harwich; began in the 9th century as a tiny fishing harbour close to the church (or kirk) on the dunes; during World War II the retreating British Expeditionary Force was rescued from the beaches near the town; railway; economy: shipbuilding, oil refining, fishing equipment, cotton spinning.

Dunkirk, France. See Dunkerque.

Dunkwa *doong'kwa*, 5 59N 1 45W, town in Central region, S Ghana, W Africa; between Sekondi-Takoradi and Kumasi; railway junction.

Dunmore Town, town on Harbour I, Eleuthera, Bahamas; former capital of the Bahamas.

Dunmur'ry, 54 33N 6 00W, pop(1981) 14,655, town in Lisburn dist, Antrim, NE Northern Ireland; 6 km SSW of Belfast; economy: engineering.

Dunnet Head, 58 41N 3 22W, cape in NE Highland region, NE Scotland; at the W end of the Pentland Firth, 13 km NE of Thurso; northernmost point of the British mainland.

Dunoon, 55 57N 4 56W, pop(1981) 9,369, town in Argyll and Bute dist, Strathclyde, W Scotland; on the W shore of the Firth of Clyde, 7 km W of Gourock; ferry service to Gourock and Wemyss Bay; event: Dunoon and Cowal Highland Gathering (Aug).

Duns *dunz*, 55 47N 2 20W, pop(1981) 2,253, capital of Berwickshire dist, Borders, E Scotland; 21 km W of Berwick-upon-Tweed; the birthplace of John Duns Scotus (1266-1308), a Franciscan and medieval philosopher; monuments: to the N of the town is Duns Law, a hill (217 m) topped by earthworks of an ancient fort and by the Covenanters' Stone, which commemorates the encampment of the Covenanters' army here in 1639; Manderston, an Edwardian country house, is 3 km E of Duns.

Dunstable, DUROCOBRIVAE (Lat), 51 53N 0 32W, pop(1981) 48,629, town in South Bedfordshire dist, Bedfordshire, S central England; at N end of the Chiltern Hills, 7 km W of Luton; at the junction of the Roman Watling Street and the earlier Icknield Way; Whipsnade Zoo lies nearby; gliding nearby; economy: engineering, paper.

Durance *du-rãs*, river in SE France rising in Hautes-Alpes dept near the Italian border; flows SSW through a series of gorges in the Provence Alps and then W, entering the R Rhône SW of Avignon; length 305 km; tributaries Guisane, Buech, Ubaye, Bleone, Asse and Verdon rivers; provides water for numerous irrigation canals.

Durango *doo-rang'gō*, state in NW central Mexico; bounded N by Chihuahua, W by Sinaloa, SW by Nayarit, SE by Zacatecas and E by Coahuila; crossed NW-SE by the Sierra Madre Occidental; in the E are vast semi-arid plains; drained by the Nazas, Mezquital, de la Sauceda and Aguanaval rivers; the Río Aguanaval forms part of the border with Coahuila; pop(1980) 1,160,196; area 123,181 sq km; capital Durango; economy: agriculture (maize, cotton, wheat, oats, barley, sunflowers, fruit), stock raising, timber, mining (iron, gold, silver, lead, mercury, fluorite), food processing, textiles, chemicals, wine and beer.

Durango *doo-rang'go*, VICTORIA DE DURANGO, 24 01N 104 40W, pop(1980) 321,148, capital of Durango state, NW central Mexico; 903 km NW of Ciudad de México (Mexico City); alt 1,889 m; founded in 1563; university (1957), railway; economy: timber, mining, farming; monument: cathedral (1695); the town is famous for its iron-water spring.

Durango, 43 13N 2 40W, pop(1981) 26,101, city in Vizcaya prov, País Vasco (Basque Country), N Spain; 25 km SE of Bilbao; railway; economy: mining, paper, agricultural trade.

Durazno *doo-ras'nō*, dept in central Uruguay; bordered by the Rincón del Bonete dam (N and NW); the Palmar dam (W) and the Río Yí (S and SW); pop(1985) 53,864; area 14,315 sq km; capital Durazno.

Durazno, 33 22S 56 31W, pop(1985) 27,602, capital of Durazno dept, central Uruguay; N of Montevideo; railway; airfield.

Durban *dur'bun*, PORT NATAL, 29 53S 31 00E, pop(1985) 634,301, seaport in Natal prov, South Africa; on Indian Ocean coast, 485 km SE of Johannesburg; South Africa's busiest port handling annually over 20 mn tons of cargo in the early 1980s; a large proportion of the pop is comprised of Indians who were brought to South Africa in the 1860s to work on the sugar plantations; South Africa's 3rd largest city; the original mission settlement of Berea was established here in 1834; the town was laid out in 1835 and named after Sir Benjamin D'Urban, governor of the Cape Colony; university (1960); railway; airport; economy: shipbuilding, oil refining, chemicals, fertilizers, food processing, textiles; monuments: museum and art gallery; the oldest Hindu temple in South Africa.

Dür'en, MARCODURUM (anc), 50 48N 6 30E, pop(1983) 85,600, industrial city in Köln dist, SW Nordrhein-Westfalen (North Rhine-Westphalia) prov, W Germany; on the R Ruhr, 29 km E of Aachen; railway; economy: chemicals.

Durg *doorg*, DURG-BHILAINAGAR, 21 12N 81 20E, pop(1981) 490,000, city in Madhya Pradesh, central India; SE of the Maikala Range, W of Raipur; railway.

Durgapur *door'gah-poor*, 23 30N 87 20E, pop(1981) 306,000, city in West Bengal, E India; on the R Damodar, NW of the Durgapur Barrage; linked NW to Asansol and SE to Barddhamān by rail; economy: coal mining, iron and steel.

Durham *dur'am*, county in NE England; bounded E by the North Sea, N by Tyne and Wear and Northumberland, W by Cumbria and S by North Yorkshire and Cleveland; rises to the Pennines in the W; drained by the Tees, Derwent and Wear rivers; pop(1981) 607,198; area 2,436 sq km; county town Durham; chief towns include Darlington, Chester-le-Street and Bishop Auckland; economy: coal, engineering, chemicals, agriculture; the county is divided into 8 districts:

District	*area (sq km)*	*pop(1981)*
Chester-le-Street	66	51,956
Darlington	198	98,195
Derwentside	271	88,517
Durham	190	85,639
Easington	143	101,075
Sedgefield	220	93,171
Teesdale	843	24,461
Wear Valley	505	64,184

Durham, 54 47N 1 34W, pop(1981) 41,178, county town of Durham, NE England; on the R Wear; founded in the 10th century by monks who had fled from Lindisfarne; university (1832); railway; economy: administration; textiles, clothing, coal mining, engineering, carpets; monuments: Norman cathedral (1093), castle, Gulbenkian Museum, Durham Light Infantry Museum; event: Durham Rowing Regatta (June); miners' gala (July).

Durham, 36 00N 78 54W, pop(1980) 100,831, county seat of Durham county, N central North Carolina, United States; 32 km NW of Raleigh; settled in 1750; 2 universities (1828, 1909); railway; economy: tobacco, cigarettes, timber, insurance and textiles.

Durmitor *door'mee-tor*, highest mountain in Crna Gora (Montenegro) republic, Yugoslavia; in the Dinaric Alps between the Piva and Tara rivers, rising to 2,522 m.

Durrës *doo'res*, formerly DURAZZO *doo-rat'so* (Ital), DRAJ (Turk), prov of W Albania; area 859 sq km; pop(1980) 209,500; capital Durrës; the dist has a reputation for malaria.

Durrës, 41 18N 19 28E, pop(1980) 65,900, seaport and capital of Durrës prov, W Albania; on the Adriatic Sea, 30 km W of Tiranë; a highway junction and the principal port of the country; railway; founded as Epidamnos in 627 BC, and in 229 BC it was renamed Dyrrhachium; a seaside health resort; the Italians and the Austrians occupied it during World War I when it was capital of Albania (1912-21); the population is largely of Muslim origin; economy: shipbuilding, metalworking, foodstuffs, tobacco, leatherwork, rubber, fishing and fish-packing, tourism; monuments: former royal villa and the remains of Byzantine-Venetian fortifications.

Dursley *durz'li*, 51 42N 2 21W, pop(1981) 12,626, town in Stroud dist, Gloucestershire, SW central England; in the Cotswold Hills, 12 km W of Stroud.

Dushanbe, until 1929 DIUSHAMBE, STALINABAD (1929-61), 38 38N 68 51E, pop(1983) 530,000, capital city of Tadzhikskaya SSR, S Soviet Union; on the R Dushabe, a tributary of the R Vakhsh; alt 750-930 m; university (1948); railway; airfield; economy: electrical engineering, metalworking, machine building, and the manufacture of building materials, textiles, silk, and foodstuffs.

Düss'eldorf, a W dist of Nordrhein-Westfalen (North Rhine-Westphalia) prov, W Germany; pop(1983) 5,113,000; area 5,288 sq km; capital Düsseldorf.

Düsseldorf, 51 13N 6 47E, pop(1983) 579,800, industrial capital of Düsseldorf dist and Nordrhein-Westfalen (North Rhine-Westphalia) prov, W Germany; on the Lower Rhine river, 34 km NNW of Köln (Cologne); university (1965); city status in 1288; birthplace of Heinrich Heine; called the 'office desk of the Ruhr', the city is the administrative centre of the province's heavy industry; the opera house and theatre are among Germany's leading houses; Düsseldorf is also a fashion centre and a city of congresses and trade fairs; railway; economy: iron and steel, aluminium, metalworking, heavy equipment, car components, machine building, machine tools, oil refining, chemicals, fertilizers, petrochemicals, textile fibres, glassware, plastics, electronic materials, paper and packaging, reinforced concrete, photographic products; monument: Schloss Benrath (10 km SE in the dist of Benrath), a Rococo palace built 1755-73.

Dvina, Northern, river in N European Rossiyskaya, Soviet Union. See Severnaya Dvina.

Dvina, Western, river in NW Soviet Union. See Zapadnaya Dvina.

Dyce *dīs*, 57 12N 2 11W, pop(1981) 7,039, town in Aberdeen City dist, Grampian region, NE Scotland; 9 km NW of Aberdeen; railway; Aberdeen airport is on the W side of the town; monuments: at Dyce Old Church are 2 Pictish symbol stones.

Dyfed *duv'id*, county in SW Wales; bounded W by Cardigan Bay and St George's Channel, S by the Bristol Channel, N and E by Powys and SE by W Glamorgan; drained by the Ystwyth, Towy and Teifi rivers; capital Carmarthen; economy: oil refining, dairy products, fishing, coal, tinplate; pop(1981) 330,178; area 5,768 sq km; created in 1974, the county is divided into 6 districts:

District	*area (sq km)*	*pop(1981)*
Carmarthen	1,182	51,798
Ceredigion	1,793	57,459
Dinefwr	971	36,747
Llanelli	234	75,406
Preseli	1,151	69,354
South Pembrokeshire	438	39,414

Dzaoudzi, 12 47S 45 12E, pop(1978) 4,147, capital and 2nd largest commune of Mayotte in W Indian Ocean; area 6.7 sq km; administered by France; located on La Petite Terre island; airport.

Dzavhan *dzav'KHan*, DZA'VAKHAN, county in NW Mongolia; pop(1981e) 80,000; area 82,000 sq km; bounded N by USSR; covers steppe and desert areas; capital Uliastay; stock breeding is the economic base of the county, particularly cattle and sheep; iron, copper, lead, gold and silver are found.

Dzerzhinsk *jer-zhinsk'*, formerly CHERNORECH (-1919) and RASTIAPINO (-1929), 56 15N 43 30E, pop(1983) 269,000, city in Gor'kovskaya oblast, W European Rossiyskaya, Soviet Union; on the R Oka, 32 km W of Gor'kiy (Gorky); became a city in 1930; railway; economy: manufacture of chemicals, construction materials, furniture, and foodstuffs.

Dzhugdzhur, Khrebet *joog-joor'*, mountain range predominantly in Khabarovskiy kray, Rossiyskaya, E Soviet Union; extends c.800 km NNE from the headstreams of the R Uchur (tributary of the R Aldan) along the coast of the Sea of Okhotsk to the R Okhota; rises to 1,906 m at Gora Topko in the central section of the range; continued SW by the Stanovoy Khrebet range; source of the Uchur, Maya, and Ulya rivers.

Dzungarian Basin, basin in N Xinjiang aut region, NW China. See Junggar Pendi.

Dzunnmod *dzoon'möd*, DSUNMOD, 47 50N 106 52E, capital of Töv county, central Mongolia; lies to the S of Ulaanbaatar.

E

Eaglescliffe, 54 30N 1 21W, pop(1981) 16,545, town in Stockton-on-Tees dist, Cleveland, NE England; 5 km SW of Stockton-on-Tees; railway.

Ealing *ee'ling*, 51 31N 0 20W, pop(1981) 279,846, borough of W Greater London, England; 13 km from the centre of London; includes the suburbs of Southall, Ealing and Acton, with industry based at Hanwell and Greenford; railway; airfield at Northolt; economy: engineering, chemicals.

Earl Shil'ton, 52 34N 1 19W, pop(1981) 16,530, town in Hinckley and Bosworth dist, Leicestershire, central England; 6 km NE of Hinckley; economy: footwear, hosiery.

Earn *ern*, loch in Perth and Kinross dist, Tayside, Scotland; 18 km W of Crieff; length (E-W) 10.5 km; a centre for watersports; drained by the R Earn which flows E to meet the R Tay estuary SE of Perth.

East Bank, region in Jordan, E of the R Jordan; comprises the governorates (*muhafazas*) of Amman, Al Balqā', Irbid, Al Karak, and Ma'ān; corresponds roughly with the former Amirate of Transjordan.

East Chicago, 41 38N 87 29W, pop(1980) 39,786, town in Lake county, NW Indiana, United States; on L Michigan, 29 km SE of Chicago; railway; economy: steel and chemicals.

East China Sea, an arm of the Pacific Ocean, bounded E by Japanese islands from Kyūshū to Okinawa, S by Taiwan and W by mainland China; the Yellow Sea lies to the N; linked to the Sea of Japan by the Korean Strait and to the South China Sea by the Formosa Straits; vast oil deposits were discovered in 1980.

East Cleveland, 41 33N 81 33W, pop(1980) 36,957, town in Cuyahoga county, NE Ohio, United States; residential suburb 8 km ENE of Cleveland.

East Coast Bays, 36 42S 174 48E, pop(1981) 28,303, town in Central Auckland, North Island, New Zealand; N of the town of Takapuna.

East Dereham *deer'am*, 52 41N 0 56E, pop(1981) 11,910, town in Breckland dist, Norfolk, E England; 25 km NW of Norwich; economy: agricultural machinery, iron; monument: church of St Nicholas with 16th-c bell tower and tomb of the poet, William Cowper.

East Detroit, 42 28N 82 57W, pop(1980) 38,280, residential town in Macomb county, SE Michigan, United States, 16 km NE of Detroit.

East Flanders, prov of Belgium. See Oost-Vlaanderen.

East Grinstead *grin'sted*, 51 08N 0 01W, pop(1981) 24,183, town in Mid Sussex dist, West Sussex, S England; 18 km SE of Reigate; railway; economy: chemicals, plastics.

East Kilbride, 55 46N 4 10W, pop(1981) 70,676, capital of East Kilbride dist, Strathclyde, W central Scotland; 11 km S of Glasgow in Clydesdale urban area; designated a 'new town' in 1947; railway; economy: engineering, electrical goods, electronics, clothing; just outside the town is Calderglen Country Park.

East Lansing, 42 44N 84 29W, pop(1980) 51,392, town in Ingham county, S central Michigan, United States; E of, and adjoining, Lansing; university.

East London, OOS-LONDEN (Afrik), 33 00S 27 54E, pop(1980) 160,582, seaport in Cape prov, South Africa; at the mouth of the Buffalo river where it meets the Indian Ocean coast, 240 km ENE of Port Elizabeth and 480 km SW of Durban; founded in 1846 as Port Rex; used as a base during the Kaffir War of 1847; its name was changed to East London in 1848; railway terminus; airfield; economy: wool, furniture, glass, fishing, fruit canning.

East Lothian, district of Lothian region, E central Scotland; pop(1981) 80,666; area 713 sq km; chief town Haddington.

East Orange, 40 46N 74 13W, pop(1980) 77,690, town in Essex county, NE New Jersey, United States; residential suburb 6 km WNW of Newark; railway.

East Point, 33 41N 84 27W, pop(1980) 37,486, town in Fulton county, NW Georgia, United States; suburb 9 km SSW of Atlanta; railway; economy: textiles, machinery, chemicals, fertilizer and paper.

East Ret'ford, 53 19N 0 56W, pop(1981) 19,380, town in Bassetlaw dist, Nottinghamshire, central England; on the R Idle, 43 km NE of Nottingham; railway; economy: engineering, dyeing.

East Siberian Sea, part of the Arctic Ocean, stretching from Ostrov Vrangelya (Wrangel Island) in the E to the Novosibirskye Ostrova (New Siberian Islands) in the W; bounded S by the N coast of NE Siberia and N by the edge of the continental shelf; receives water from the Indigirka, Kolyma and Alazeya rivers; ice free and navigable Aug-Sept; its major port is Ambarrchik; the Earth's widest continental shelf lies in the East Siberian Sea, with an average width of 644 km; surface water circulation is from W to E; linked to the Laptev Sea by Proliv Dimitriya Lapteva and Ostrova Anzhu and to the Chukchi Sea by the Proliv Longa.

East St Louis, 38 37N 90 09W, pop(1980) 55,200, town in St Clair county, W Illinois, United States; on the R Mississippi, opposite St Louis; railway; economy: iron and steel products.

East Sussex, county of SE England; bounded S by the English Channel, N by Kent and W by West Sussex; the South Downs lie parallel to the coast and part of the Weald lies to the N; drained by the R Ouse; pop(1981) 657,248; area 1,795 sq km; county town Lewes; chief towns include Brighton, Eastbourne, Bexhill and Hastings; economy: electronics, furniture, service industries; the county is divided into 7 districts:

District	*area (sq km)*	*pop(1981)*
Brighton	58	147,336
Eastbourne	44	77,963
Hastings	30	75,284
Hove	24	85,092
Lewes	292	78,233
Rother	511	75,936
Wealden	837	117,404

Eastbourne, 50 46N 0 17E, pop(1981) 77,963, resort town in Eastbourne dist, East Sussex, SE England; on the English Channel, 30 km E of Brighton; E of the South Downs; the residential suburb of St Leonards lies E; a Crown possession in Saxon times, it was later bought by 3 Sussex families and eventually developed into a fashionable coastal resort in the 18th century; railway; economy: distributive trades; building; monuments: 13th-c Lamb Inn, 14th-c Pilgrims Inn, Towner Art Gallery, Saxon parish church of St Mary; event: international tennis tournament (June).

Easter Island, Pacific Ocean island of Chile. See Pascua, Isla de.

Eastern, region in W Ghana, W Africa; pop(1984) 1,679,483; area 19,833 sq km; includes SW portion of L Volta; the R Birin flows SW from its source near Kibi and the R Volta follows the E border; capital Koforidua; chief towns Oda, Mpraeso and Kibi; economy: aluminium, gold mining, diamond processing.

Eastern Scheldt, estuary in the Netherlands. See Oosterschelde.

Eastleigh *eest'lee*, 50 58N 1 22W, pop(1981) 58,914, town in Eastleigh dist, Hampshire, S England; just N of Southampton; railway; economy: engineering, electrical goods, timber.

Easton, 40 41N 75 13W, pop(1980) 26,027, county seat of Northampton county, E Pennsylvania, United States; at the confluence of R Lehigh and R Delaware, 24 km ENE of Allentown; railway.

Eastwood, 53 01N 1 18W, pop(1981) 18,112, town in Broxtowe dist, Nottinghamshire, central England; 12 km NW of Nottingham; birthplace of D.H. Lawrence in 1885; economy: engineering, coal products.

Eastwood, district in Strathclyde region, W Scotland; pop(1981) 53,572; area 116 sq km; chief town Giffnock.

Eaton Socon, town in Cambridgeshire, England. See St Neots.

Eau Claire *ō klār*, 44 49N 91 30W, pop(1980) 51,509, county seat of Eau Claire county, W Wisconsin, United States; on the Chippewa river, 114 km N of La Crosse; developed with the timber trade in the 1840s; university (1916); railway.

Ebbw Vale *eb'oo*, 51 47N 3 12W, pop(1981) 21,145, mining town in Monmouth dist, Gwent, SE Wales; on the R Ebbw, 56 km NW of Bristol; railway; economy: printing, tinplate, engineering; formerly a major centre of coal mining, iron and steel.

Eberswalde *ay-burs-vahl'du*, 52 50N 13 50E, pop(1981) 53,183, town in Eberswalde dist, Frankfurt, E East Germany; NE of Berlin near the Polish frontier; railway; economy: crane manufacture.

Ebolowa *e-bō-lō'wa*, 2 56N 11 11E, pop(1984e) 30,000, capital of Sud prov, Cameroon, W Africa; 170 km S of Yaoundé; a German fortress is all that remains of old city; a centre for the collection and export of cocoa.

Ebro *e'brō*, IBERIUS (anc), longest river flowing entirely in Spain; rises in the Cordillera Cantabrica and flows SE through Álava, Navarra, La Rioja, Zaragoza and Tarragona provs before entering the Mediterranean at Cape Tortosa; at its mouth the chief port is San Carlos de la Rapita; there are 3 major reservoirs, the Embalse de Sobron in its upper reaches and the Embalses de Mequinenza and de Flix in Zaragoza and Tarragona provs; length 910 km.

Eccles *ek'lz*, 53 29N 2 21W, pop(1981) 37,792, town in Salford borough, Greater Manchester, NW England; 6 km W of Manchester; railway; economy: textiles, engineering.

Echternach *eKH'ter-naKH*, canton in N part of Grevenmacher dist, E Luxembourg; area 186 sq km; pop(1981) 10,653; on the E frontier with W Germany; bounded to the N and E by the R Our and traversed NE-SW by the R Ernz Noire; the 36 ha Echternach Lake is in the centre of a recreation area covering 557 ha.

Echternach, 49 49N 6 25E, pop(1981) 4,000, capital of Echternach canton, Grevenmacher dist, E Luxembourg; on the R Sûre, 34 km NE of Luxembourg; good walking area at the nearby Moellerdall and in the Germany-Luxembourg Nature Park; monuments: basilica with tomb of St Willibrord; 15th-c town hall; parish church of St Peter and St Paul, reputedly the oldest Christian sanctuary in Luxembourg; events: unique dancing procession on Whit Tuesday; International Festival of Classical Music (June-July).

Écija *ay'thee-ha*, ASTIGI (anc), 37 30N 5 10W, pop(1981) 34,619, town in Sevilla prov, Andalucia, S Spain; on the R Genil, 80 km E of Sevilla; noted for horse breeding; railway; economy: metal works, textiles, ceramics, fruit.

Ecuador *ek'wa-dor*, official name The Republic of Ecuador, REPÚBLICA DEL ECUADOR, republic in NW South America straddling the Equator; bounded N by Colombia, S and E by Peru and W by the Pacific Ocean; includes the Galápagos Is 970 km W; timezone GMT −5; area 270,699 sq km; pop(1982) 8,138,974; capital Quito; chief towns Guayaquil, Cuenca, Riobamba, Esmeraldas; the pop is 25% Indian, 55% Mestizo, 10% Spanish and 10% African; 49% of the pop live in the lowland *Costa* between the Andes and the Pacific Ocean, 47% live in the Andean Sierra and 3% in the tropical Oriente to the E; the official language is Spanish and the chief Indian tongue is Quechua; the predominant religion is Roman Catholic; the currency is the sucre of 100 centavos; national holidays 24 July, 10 Aug (National Day), 9 Oct, 12 Oct, 2-3 Nov; membership of Andean Pact, ECOSOC, FAO, G-77, IADB, IAEA, IBRD, ICAO, ICO, IDA, IDB, IFAD, IFC, IHO, ILO, IMF, IMO, INTELSAT, INTERPOL, IRC, ITU, LAIA, NAM, OAS, OPEC, PAHO, SELA, UN, UNESCO, UPEB, UPU, WFTU, WHO, WMO, WTO.

Physical description. Mainland Ecuador is divided into 3 distinct regions - the coastal plain (*Costa*) in the W, which descends from rolling hills in the N to a broad lowland basin averaging 100 km in width before opening out into the Golfo de Guayaquil; the Andean uplands (*Sierra*) in the centre, a series of irregular chains forming 3 main ranges of the Andes and rising to snow-capped peaks which include Cotopaxi (5,896 m), the world's highest active volcano; the forested alluvial plains of the *Oriente* in the E, dissected by rivers flowing down from the Andes towards the Amazon. The Galápagos Is lying in the Pacific nearly 1,000 km W of the coast of Ecuador comprise 6 major islands and many smaller ones with a total land area of about 7,812 sq km. The islands are of volcanic origin and are chiefly basaltic lava flows with shallow, cratered cones, some of which are still active.

Climate. Hot and humid, the *Costa* has a rainy season from Dec to April although rain falls throughout the year. Annual rainfall on the coast varies from 2,000 mm in the N to 200 mm in the S as the dry coastal belt of Peru is approached. In the central Andes temperatures are much reduced by altitude with a climate in Quito characterized by spring-like warm days and chilly nights with frequent heavy rain in the afternoon. The *Oriente* has a typically hot and wet equatorial climate with rainfall evenly distributed throughout the year.

History, government and constitution. Formerly a N part of the great Inca Empire, Ecuador was taken by the

Spanish in 1527 and ruled by them for nearly 300 years within the Viceroyalty of New Granada. In 1822, following the campaigns of Simón Bolívar and Antonio José de Sucre, Ecuador gained independence and was joined with Panama, Colombia and Venezuela to form the Republic of Greater Colombia. Ecuador left the union in 1830 to become an independent republic. Between 1830 and 1947 there were no less than 14 constitutions and between 1925 and 1948 there were 22 presidents, none of whom completed a term in office. The legislative power is in the hands of a unicameral National Congress consisting of a 71-member House of Deputies and 4 permanent committees of 28 members elected every 2 years. The executive includes 12 ministries and several cabinet-level secretariats under the president who is elected for a term of 2 years.

Economy. Agriculture employs nearly 50% of Ecuador's workforce and generates about one-fifth of the national income. Beans, cereals, potatoes and livestock are produced in the *Sierra* to supply staple foods while export crops such as bananas, coffee, cocoa, cane sugar, rice, cotton and vegetable oil are produced in the *Costa*. In recent years the fishing industry has provided significant quantities of shrimp for export. Since 1972 oil has been piped from the *Oriente* to refineries at Esmeraldas, providing a revenue that has helped reduce the country's dependence on fuel imports and on agriculture as a major source of income. New petrochemical and steel industries have added to the manufacturing sector which had largely been based on food processing and textiles. Major trade partners include the USA, Japan, Latin America and the Caribbean, and W Germany.

Administrative divisions. Ecuador is divided into the following 20 provinces:

Province	*area (sq km)*	*pop(1982)*
Costa		
Esmeraldas	15,031	249,008
Manabí	18,853	906,676
Los Rios	6,825	455,869
Guayas	20,246	2,038,454
El Oro	5,810	334,872
Insular		
Galápagos	7,812	6,119
Oriental		
Napo	53,835	115,110
Pastaza	18,238	31,779
Morona Santiago	24,261	70,217
Zamora Chinchipe	23,107	46,691
Sierra		
Carchi	3,750	127,779
Imbabura	4,459	247,287
Pichincha	12,872	1,382,125
Cotopaxi	6,248	277,678
Tungurahua	3,128	326,777
Bolívar	4,105	152,101
Chimborazo	6,522	334,100
Cañar	3,184	174,510
Azuay	8,098	442,019
Loja	11,214	360,767

Edam *ay'dahm* or *ee'dam* (Eng), 52 30N 5 02E, pop(1984e) 24,019, town in E Noord Holland prov, W Netherlands; situated on reclaimed land on the Ijsselmeer, to which it is connected by a canal, 21 km NE of Amsterdam; founded in the 13th century as a customs post; the cheese trade was the source of its prosperity in the 16th and 17th centuries; economy: tourism, textiles, ceramics, dairy products; monument: 15th-c Grote Kerk (has a 17th-c classroom with its original desks).

Ede *ay'de*, 52 04N 5 40E, pop(1984e) 86,816, industrial city in Gelderland prov, East Netherlands, 21 km NW of Arnhem; important for its rayon production.

Ede *ay'day*, 7 44N 4 31E, pop(1975e) 182,000, town in Oyo state, Nigeria, W Africa; 72 km NNE of Ibadan; railway; gold mining nearby.

Eden, river in Cumbria, NW England; rises 16 km SE of Appleby and flows 104 km NW to meet the Solway Firth NW of Carlisle.

Edhessa *ay'thay-sah*, EDES'SA, formerly VODENÁ, 40 48N 22 03E, pop(1981) 16,054, capital town of Pélla nome (dept), Makedhonia region, N Greece; 68 km W of Thessaloníki (Salonica), on a terrace in the foothills of Mt Vérmion.

Edina *e-dī'na*, 44 53N 93 21W, pop(1980) 46,073, town in Hennepin county, SE Minnesota, United States; residential suburb 10 km SW of Minneapolis; railway.

Edinburgh *ed'in-bur-u*, 55 57N 3 13W, pop(1981) 420,169, capital of Lothian region and of Scotland; in E central Scotland, between the Pentland Hills and the S shore of the Firth of Forth, 66 km E of Glasgow; there are port facilities at Leith, which was united with Edinburgh in the 1920s; also incorporates the burghs of Canongate (1856), Portobello (1896) and Granton (1900); Malcolm Canmore (1057-93) built a castle on the castle rock and his wife (St Margaret) added a chapel which is the oldest building in the city; in 1392 Robert the Bruce granted Edinburgh its first charter; Edinburgh became the capital of Scotland after the loss of Berwick in 1482; after the Union of the Parliaments in 1707 Edinburgh's political importance declined, but it remained a centre of intellectual and cultural importance; in the 1760s the New Town designed by James Craig provided new housing for the merchants of Edinburgh, although the business centre remained in the Old Town; at this time the Nor' Loch separating the old and new towns was drained and laid out as gardens (Princes Street Gardens); Edinburgh University (1583); Heriot-Watt University (1966); railway; airport; economy: brewing, distilling, finance, tourism, printing, publishing, trade in grain; monuments: Edinburgh Castle contains a military museum and the Scottish National War Memorial; the oldest section of the castle is St Margaret's Chapel (12th-c), other parts were built by James IV; the Palace of Holyroodhouse is the official residence of the Queen in Scotland; most of the palace was rebuilt for Charles II; Mary Queen of Scots lived here for 6 years; the picture gallery contains portraits of over 70 Scottish kings; beside the palace is Holyrood Park which contains the hill, Arthur's Seat, an extinct volcano with 2 main craters; in the centre of Edinburgh is the Scott Monument (completed in 1844), consisting of a statue of Sir Walter Scott and his dog under a canopy and spire 61 m high, with 64 statuettes of Scott characters; on the top of Calton Hill (alt 107 m), in the centre of the city, is an observatory plus a partly completed reproduction of the Parthenon; this was begun in 1824 to commemorate the Scots who died in the Napoleonic wars, but was never completed due to lack of money; Gladstone's Land, a 6-storey tenement completed in 1620; near Greyfriars Churchyard is a statue of Greyfriars Bobby, the Skye terrier who watched over his master's grave for 14 years after his death in 1858; the house of John Knox, the Scottish reformer, is said to be the only 15th-c house in Scotland; St Giles cathedral dates from the 15th century; outside the cathedral is the Heart of Midlothian, a heart-shaped design in the cobblestones marking the site of the Old Tolbooth which was built in 1466, stormed in 1736 in the Porteous Riots, and demolished in 1817; National Gallery of Scotland; Scottish National Gallery of Modern Art; Scottish National Portrait Gallery; National Museum of Scotland; Museum of Childhood; Wax Museum; Royal Botanic Garden; Edinburgh Zoo (one of Britain's leading zoos, famous for its large breeding colony of Antarctic Penguins); Royal Observatory, on Blackford Hill in the S of the city; Meadowbank Stadium sports complex (opened in 1970 for the Commonwealth Games and host also to the 1986 Commonwealth Games); there is an artificial ski slope to the S of the city; events: folk festival (March); Royal Highland Agricultural Show (June); Military Tattoo (Aug); International Festival, Fringe Festival, Jazz Festival, Film Festival and Highland Games (Aug-Sept).

Edirne *e-dir'ne*, ADRIANOPEL *ay-dree-a-nō'pel*, prov in NW Turkey, bounded N by Bulgaria, W by Greece, and S by an inlet of the Aegean Sea; pop(1980) 363,286; area 6,276 sq km; capital Edirne.

Edirne, ADRIANOPOLIS, HADRIANOPOLIS (anc), 41 40N 26 34E, pop(1980) 71,914, capital of Edirne prov, NW Turkey; near the Bulgarian frontier WNW of İstanbul at the junction of the Maritsa and Tundzha rivers; ancient Thracian town rebuilt and named after the Roman emperor Hadrian in 2nd century AD; railway; economy: textiles, soap, leather, carpets, cheese; event: grease wrestling in May-June.

Edmond, 35 39N 97 29W, pop(1980) 34,637, city in Oklahoma county, central Oklahoma, United States; 20 km N of Oklahoma City; Central State College (1981); railway; economy: trade centre in an oil-producing area.

Edmonds, 47 49N 122 23W, pop(1980) 27,679, city in Snohomish county, NW Washington, United States; on Puget Sound, 24 km N of Seattle; railway.

Edmonton, 53 34N 113 25W, pop(1984) 560,085, capital of Alberta prov, W Canada; situated in the central part of the prov on both banks of the North Saskatchewan river; Edmonton is the most northerly large town in N America; first settled by the rival fur trading companies, Hudson's Bay Co and North West Co; Fort Edmonton was built by Hudson's Bay Co on the North Saskatchewan river, 40 km below the city's present site, in 1795; destroyed by Indians in 1807, it was rebuilt on its present site in 1819 and became an important trading post; the first building outside the fort was erected in 1871 by the Rev George McDougall; reached by the Canadian Pacific Railroad in 1891 and in 1905 was chosen as Alberta's capital; the city grew rapidly after the discovery of oil nearby in 1947; University of Alberta (1906) and Athabasca University (1972); railway; airport (near the town of Devon to the S); airfield (near St Albert to the NW); economy: petrochemicals, retail and trade centre; monuments: the Legislative Building, begun in 1907, is built in the shape of a cruciform of British Columbia granite and sandstone from Alberta; the George McDougall Memorial Shrine and Museum is the oldest building in Edmonton (built in 1871), it is now a museum; events: Klondike Days, an agricultural, livestock and industrial display, with c.200,000 participants dressed in costumes from the Klondike period; included in the celebrations is the 'Sourdough Raft Race' (July).

Edward, Lake, LAKE RUTANZIGE, lake in E central Africa; situated in the W Rift Valley on the frontier between Zaire and Uganda; approx 80 km long and 50 km wide; alt 912 m; receives the Rutshuru river; the Semliki river flows from the N end into L Albert; European discovery by Henry Stanley in 1889.

Edwards Plateau, plateau in SW Texas, United States; max alt approx 762 m; SE extension of the Great Plains; situated to the S and SE of the Llano Estacado; bordered to the S by the Río Grande river valley; drained by the Colorado, Concho, Nueces, San Saba, Llano and Guadalupe rivers; much of the plateau is semi-arid; used for stock raising.

Eeklo *ayk'lō*, dist of Oost-Vlaanderen (East Flanders) prov, NW Belgium; area 334 sq km; pop(1982) 80,082.

Efate *e-fa'tee*, VATÉ *va-tay'* (Fr), SANDWICH ISLAND (Eng), 17 40S 168 23E, volcanic island, Vanuatu, 248 km SE of Espiritu Santo I, SW Pacific; area 985 sq km; length 42 km; width 23 km; capital of Efate and of Vanuatu is at Vila; pop(1979) 18,000.

Ef'es, EPHESUS *ef'e-sus*, 37 55N 27 19E, ancient city of Lydia and chief of the 12 Ionian cities of Asia Minor; at mouth of R Bayindir, near the Aegean coast, S of İzmir; centre of the cult of Cybele (an Anatolian fertility goddess), and later notorious for the licentious worship of Artemis whose temple, the largest classical Greek temple ever built, was one of the Seven Wonders of the ancient world; visited by St Paul; a principal port of the Mediterranean in 2nd century AD; the ruins were excavated during the 19th and 20th centuries; the resort village of Kuşadasi (New Ephesus) lies 12 km SSW on the Aegean coast; a museum at Selçuk houses works of art recovered from Ephesus; Selçuk is also the venue of a camel wrestling festival in Jan; 7 km from Selçuk is the Mereymana chapel where the Virgin Mary is believed to have spent the last days of her life.

Egedesminde *ay'gedh-es-min-de*, 68 50N 53 00W, settlement on the W coast of Greenland; on Disko Bugt, N of the Arctic Circle; named after Hans Egede, the Norwegian missionary who came to Greenland in 1721.

Eger *e'ger*, 47 53N 20 27E, pop(1984e) 64,000, commercial capital of Heves county, N Hungary; on R Eger, SW of Miskolc; archbishopric; thermal springs; noted for its red wine; railway; economy: tobacco and wine trade, machinery; monuments: cathedral, fort, Turkish minaret.

Eg'ham, 51 26N 0 34W, pop(1981) 21,810, residential town in Spelthorne dist, Surrey, SE England; part of Greater London urban area; on R Thames, 30 km WSW of London; railway; economy: distributive trades.

Egmont, Mount, TARANAKI (Maori), 39 18S 174 05E, symmetrical volcanic peak, W North Island, New Zealand; rises to 2,518 m S of the town of New Plymouth; the 335 sq km Mount Egmont national park was established in 1900.

Egypt *ee'jipt*, official name Arab Republic of Egypt, JUMHURIYAT MISR AL-ARABIYA (Arab), formerly UNITED ARAB REPUBLIC; a NE African republic bounded W by Libya, S by Sudan, E by the Red Sea, NE by Israel and N by the Mediterranean Sea; timezone GMT +2; area 1,001,449 sq km; capital Cairo; chief towns include Alexandria, Port Said and Aswân; pop(1984e) 47,049,000; 90% of the pop is of Eastern Hamitic origin, the remainder is largely of Greek, Italian and Syro-Lebanese stock; 94% of the pop is Sunni Muslim, the remainder being largely Coptic Christian; the official language is Arabic with English and French widely spoken; the unit of currency is the gold Egyptian pound; national holiday 23 July (National Day); membership of AAPSO, AfDB, FAO, G-77, GATT, IAEA, IBRD, ICAC, ICAO, IDA, Islamic Development Bank, IFAD, IFC, IHO, ILO, IMF, IMO, INTELSAT, INTERPOL, IOOC, IPU, IRC, ITU, IWC (International Wheat Council), NAM, OAU, OIC, UN, UNESCO, UPU, WHO, WIPO, WMO, WPC, WSG, WTO. Egypt was suspended from the Arab League and OAPEC in 1979.

Physical description. Although Egypt extends to 1,001,449 sq km, 90% of the pop lives on the floodplain of the R Nile on about 40,000 sq km or 3% of the country's area. The R Nile flows N into Egypt from Sudan. It is dammed just S of Aswân where L Nasser was created in the 1960s. N of Cairo the river spreads into a huge delta 250 km across and 160 km from N to S, as it empties into the Mediterranean Sea. Between the Nile and the Red Sea the narrow Eastern Desert rises through a sandy plateau to rocky peaks such as the Shayib el Banat (2,187 m). This region is sparsely inhabited as is the Western Desert which accounts for over two-thirds of the country W of the Nile. Within it are 7 major depressions of which the largest and lowest is the Qattâra Depression which dips 120 m below sea-level. The Faiyûm Depression was connected to the R Nile during the 16th-c BC by canals and presently is a major area for irrigated cultivation. The Sinai Peninsula, separated from the bulk of Egypt by the Red Sea and the Suez Canal, is a desert region with mountains in the S rising to 2,637 m at Gebel Katherîna, Egypt's highest point.

Climate. The greater part of Egypt experiences a desert climate except for an 80 km-wide Mediterranean coastal fringe which has an annual rainfall of 100-200 mm. The coastal winters (Nov-March) are generally warm with occasional cold days when a N wind blows. Summers are hot and sunny though temperatures are often modified by strong onshore breezes. The period between March and early June can be uncomfortably hot on the coast when the dust-laden *khamsin* wind blows N from the

Sahara. Alexandria, situated on the coast at the W edge of the Nile delta, is representative of the coastal region with an annual average rainfall of 180 mm and average max daily temperatures between 18°C and 30°C. Throughout the rest of the country annual rainfall is less than 50 mm. Aswân, which is situated in the S of Egypt on the Nile, is representative of this region with minimal recorded rainfall and average max daily temperatures between 23°C and 42°C.

History, constitution and government. Egypt has existed as a unified state for more than 50 centuries. Neolithic cultures appeared on the Nile around 6,000 BC and agricultural activity began about 3,500 BC. It was about 3,100 BC that central authority became established under the first of the 30 Pharaonic dynasties. The pyramids at El Gîza (including the largest pyramid ever built) were constructed during the 4th dynasty. It was during the New Empire period (1567 to 1085 BC) that ancient Egypt's power, wealth and territorial extent reached its zenith. Cambyses, the son of Persia's Cyrus the Great, launched a military attack in the 6th century BC, removing the last pharaoh of the 26th dynasty and establishing Egypt as a Persian province. Persian influence continued until the conquest of Alexander the Great in the 4th century BC. After Alexander's death (323 BC) the line of Ptolemaic Pharaohs ruled Egypt until the suicide of Cleopatra in 30 BC. Seven centuries of Roman and Byzantine rule came to an end in 672 AD when the Arabs conquered Egypt. In 1798 Napoleon launched a 3-year occupation of Egypt by France, establishing the region's strategic and economic importance midway between Europe and India. The construction of the Suez Canal in 1869 emphasized the importance of Egypt. A revolt in 1879 was eventually put down by British forces in 1882, bringing Egypt into the British sphere of influence. The country became a British protectorate in 1914, but was declared independent in 1922. British influence remained strong and the country was used as a base for Allied forces during World War II. In 1952 King Farouk was deposed by Gamel Abdul Nasser who declared Egypt a republic the following year. Nasser rapidly became an Egyptian and Arab hero as a result of obtaining finance for the building of the Aswân High Dam and his handling of the French, Israeli and British invasion of 1956. The Israeli invasion of 1967 resulted in the loss of the Sinai Peninsula and control over part of the Suez Canal. During the 1970s Nasser's successor, Anwar el-Sadat, regained control through negotiation of the Suez Canal and parts of the Sinai Peninsula. President Sadat was assassinated in 1981. Egypt has a legislative People's Assembly with 392 members (plus up to 10 presidential appointments) which elects a president every 6 years. The president appoints a vice-president, a prime minister and a council of about 28 ministers. In addition, there is a Consultative Council of 210 members (two-thirds elected, one-third nominated).

Economy. Agriculture, restricted to the floodplain of the R Nile, accounts for about one-third of Egypt's national income and employs about 40% of the workforce. The building of the Aswân High Dam extended the area of irrigated cultivation. Main food crops grown include millet, maize, beans, rice, barley, wheat and sugar cane. Cotton is the main export crop in addition to rice, fruit and vegetables. Since wheat is a major import landowners are required to plant cotton on only one-third of their land and use at least another third to grow wheat. Manufacturing industry is based on food processing, textiles, construction, light manufacturing and military equipment. In 1981 Egypt supplied 1% of world oil production. Mineral resources include iron ore which is processed at Helwan near Cairo, aluminium which is processed at Nag Hammadi near Qena, cement which is processed at Helwan and Tourah, gypsum, phosphates, manganese, tin and nitrates (which support the fertilizer industry with plants at Talkha and Abu Qir). The main trading partners for imports are the USA, West Germany, France, Italy and Japan; and for exports Italy, the USSR, the UK, Czechoslovakia, West Germany and Greece.

Administrative divisions. Egypt is divided into 25 governorates:

Governorate	*area (sq km)*	*pop(1976)*
Al-Bahra Al-Ahmar	203,685	56,191
Alexandria	2,679	2,318,655
Al-Wadi Al-Jadid	376,505	84,645
Aswân	1,530	619,932
Asyût	1,530	1,695,378
Behara	4,589	2,517,292
Beni Suef	1,332	1,108,615
Cairo	214	5,084,463
Dumyât	589	557,115
Daqahlîya	3,471	2,732,756
El Faiyûm	1,827	1,140,245
Gharbîya	1,942	2,294,303
El Gîza	1,010	2,419,247
Ismâ'ilîya	1,442	351,889
Kafr el Sheik	3,437	1,403,468
Menûfiya	1,612	1,710,982
Mersa Matrûh	298,735	112,772
El Minya	2,262	2,055,739
Port Said	72	262,620
Qalyûbîya	971	1,647,006
Qena	1,851	1,705,594
Sharqîya	4,180	2,621,208
Sinai	60,174	10,104
Sohâg	1,547	1,924,960
Suez	17,840	194,001

Eibar *ay-bar'*, 43 11N 2 28W, pop(1981) 36,494, town in Guipúzcoa prov, Pais Vasco (Basque Country), N Spain; 45 km E of Bilbao; railway; economy: armaments, iron and steel, compressors, sewing machinery.

Eider *ī'der*, river in Schleswig-Holstein prov, W Germany; rises SW of Kiel, flows W to discharge into the North Sea at Tonning; length 188 km; navigable length 112 km; drainage basin area 1,891 sq km; historic boundary between Schleswig (N) and Holstein (S).

Eidsvoll *ayts'vol*, 60 19N 11 14E, pop(1980) 15,196, town in Akershus county, SE Norway; 48 km NE of Oslo; railway; new constitution drawn up here May 17, 1814 providing for a unicameral national assembly and denying the king an absolute veto.

Eifel *ī'fel*, mountain range of volcanic origin predominantly in W Rheinland-Pfalz (Rhineland-Palatinate) prov, W Germany; bounded on the E by the R Rhine and on the S by the R Mosel; highest point is the Hohe Acht (747 m), average height 600 m.

Eiger *ī'gur*, 46 34N 8 01E, mountain peak with three ridges in the Berner Alpen (Bernese Alps), Bern canton, S central Switzerland; its N face is one of the most formidable climbs in the Alps; height 3,970 m; the Mönch ridge in combination with the W face was the route of the first ascent by Barrington in 1858; the NE Mittellegi ridge was first climbed in 1921; the Nordwand face was first climbed in 1938.

Eigersund or **Egersund** *ay'gur-soon*, 58 33N 6 02E, pop(1980) 11,835, fishing port on the SW coast of Rogaland county, SW Norway; S of Stavanger on the North Sea; railway; monument: folk museum.

Eigg *eg* (Gael, 'eag' notched), island in Highland region, W Scotland; S of Skye and SE of Rhum and 11 km from the mainland (E); area 67 sq km; the whole island is a reserve managed by the Scottish Wildlife Trust; rises to 397 m at the Sgurr of Eigg; historically associated with the Clan Macdonald; ferry connections to Mallaig; economy: cattle, crofting, fishing.

Eindhoven *īnt'hō-ven*, 51 26N 5 30E, pop(1984e) 374,109, modern industrial city in SE Noord Brabant prov, S Netherlands; on the R Dommel, 88 km SE of Rotterdam; airport; railway; technical university (1956); the city developed in the 2nd half of the 19th century around the textile and electric light industries and became, for a while, the largest city in S Netherlands; the modern town is now an important shopping and cultural centre; the Philips Evoluon, a flying saucer-shaped museum of modern technology, draws more than 400,000 visitors annually; the Centre of Micro-Electronics advises companies on the application of electronics technology; 75% of the population is Roman Catholic; economy: engineering, consumer hardware, electric and electronic products, trucks, bus chassis, tractors, engines, aircraft landing gear, military vehicles, glassware, man-made fibres, paper, textiles, tobacco.

Einödriegel *īn'ut-ree-gul*, 48 55N 13 02E, mountain in E Bayern (Bavaria) prov, W Germany; highest peak of the Bayerische Wald (Bavarian Forest) range of the Böhmerwald (Bohemian Forest); height 1,126 m.

Eire, the Republic of Ireland. See Irish Republic.

Eisenach *ī'zun-ahKH*, 50 59N 10 19E, pop(1981) 50,674, town in Eisenach dist, Erfurt, SW East Germany; 50 km W of Erfurt, near the border with W Germany; founded in 12th century; birthplace of Johann Sebastian Bach; railway; economy: motor cars, electrical equipment.

Eisenstadt *ī'zen-shtat*, 47 51N 16 31E, pop(1981) 10,102, capital of Eisenstadt dist and Burgenland state, E Austria; 46 km S of Wien (Vienna); principal seat of the great Esterházy family in the 17th and 18th centuries; Josef Haydn (1732-1809) was Kapellmeister here; economy: wine trade; monuments: Schloss Esterházy, Bergkirche (the mausoleum of Josef Haydn), cathedral; events: Burgenland Wine Week in Aug-Sept and Haydn Memorial Concerts in May-June.

Ekanga'la, new African town in KwaNdebele homeland and in Transvaal prov, South Africa; N of Pretoria, near Bronkhorstspruit.

Ekenas, town in Finland. See Tammisaari.

Ekofisk, oil field in the North Sea linked by pipeline to Teesport, Cleveland, NE England.

El Salvador, country in Central America. See Salvador, El.

Elat *ay-lat'*, 29 33N 34 57E, seaport in South dist, S Israel; on the N shore of the Gulf of 'Aqaba; founded in 1949; there is a nature reserve with an underwater observatory just S of the port on Coral Beach; airfield; terminus of oil pipeline from Ashqelon on the Mediterranean Sea.

Elâziğ *e-la-zu'*, mountainous prov in E Turkey, bounded W by the R Euphrates and SE by the Taurus Mts; pop(1980) 440,808; area 9,153 sq km; capital Elâziğ; economy: fruit, grain and vegetable farming; mining of chromite and lignite.

Elâziğ, 38 41N 39 14E, pop(1980) 142,983, capital of Elâziğ prov, E Turkey; railway; airfield.

El'ba, AITHA'LIA (Gr), IL'VA (Lat), island in the Tyrrhenian Sea, lying between the N Italian coast and the French island of Corse (Corsica), separated from the mainland by the 10 km-wide Strait of Piombino; area 223 sq km; length 27 km; width 18.5 km; chief town and port Portoferraio; the coast is deeply indented; the island consists mainly of granite and porphyry, and has considerable quantities of high-quality iron ore, particularly in the E; Napoleon lived here after his abdication (1814-1815); economy: iron working, tuna and anchovy fisheries, agriculture (fruit and wine), tourism.

Elbasan', prov of central Albania; area 1,466 sq km; pop(1980) 197,600; capital Elbasan; drained by the R Shkumbin; fertile in its flat portions, growing grain, tobacco, olives and fruit.

Elbasan, 41 06N 20 04E, pop(1980) 56,500, industrial town and capital of Elbasan prov, central Albania; 32 km SE of Tiranë; transportation and agric centre in the fertile valley of the R Shkumbin; on the railway from Durrës; became bishopric in the 5th century; economy: cigarettes, olive oil, canned fruit, wood products, ferrous metallurgy; monument: 15th-c Turkish fortress; the fortified part is the old Christian quarter, the outskirts being Muslim.

Elbe *el'be*, LABE *lah'be* (Czech), ALBIS (anc), river in Czechoslovakia, E Germany and W Germany; rises on S slopes of the Riesengebirge, Czechoslovakia; flows S, W and NW in Czechoslovakia, then N across E Germany, turning NW to flow into the North Sea at Cuxhaven, W Germany; length 1,158 km; length in W Germany 227 km (all navigable); chief tributaries Vltava and Ohre in Czechoslovakia, and Mulde, Saale, Schwarze Elster, Havel, and Elde in East Germany; connected by canals with R Oder and Baltic Sea; navigable to beyond Czechoslovakian border.

Elbert, Mount, 39 05N 106 27W, mountain in Lake county, central Colorado, United States; the highest peak in Colorado state, rising to 4,399 m in the Rocky Mts.

Elbląg *el-blã'*, voivodship in N Poland; bounded N by the Baltic Sea, W by R Wisła (Vistula) and at its NE corner the USSR; includes the Żuławy plain; pop(1983) 458,000; area 6,103 sq km; capital Elbląg; chief towns include Malbork and Kwidzyn.

Elbląg, ELBING, 54 10N 19 25E, pop(1983) 115,900, river port capital of Elbląg voivodship, N Poland; on R Elbląg, close to the Baltic Sea; joined the Hanseatic League in 13th century and flourished as an important centre of Polish maritime trade; branch of Gdańsk technical university; railway; boat service across Wisła (Vistula) bay to Krynica Morska and across L Drużno and on Elbląski Canal to Ostróda; economy: marine engineering, clothing; monuments: contemporary art gallery, 13th and early 16th-c Dominican church houses, Gothic church of St Nicholas.

El'brus *el'broos*, 43 21N 42 29E, highest peak of the Kavkaz (Caucasus) range, S European Rossiyskaya, Soviet Union; 64 km SSW of Kislovodsk; height 5,642 m; highest peak in Europe; formed by 2 extinct volcanic cones; situated in the W section of the Bol'shoy Kavkaz (Greater Caucasus) range; its glaciers give rise to the Kuban', Malka, and Baksan rivers.

Elburz *el-boorz'*, mountain range in N Iran, between the Caspian Sea (N) and the Dasht-e-Kavīr salt desert (S); rises to 5,670 m at Qolleh-ye Damāvand (Mt Damāvand), highest peak in Iran; comprises a series of steep, narrow, parallel ridges; the N slopes are deeply dissected by swiftly flowing Caspian coastal streams; the S slopes receive scanty rainfall; traversed by the R Safīd Rūd.

Elche *el'chay*, ILLICIS (Lat), 38 15N 0 42W, pop(1981) 162,873, town in Alicante prov, Valencia, E Spain; on the R Vinalapó, 23 km SW of Alicante; noted for its unique palm forest, the largest in Europe; economy: footwear, cocoa and chocolate, dates, leather goods; monuments: 15th-c Altimira Palace which has been declared a national monument; the Huerto del Cura garden and the Palm Grove; event: Misterio de Elche, a mystery play performed in the church of St Mary in Aug, a privilege granted by Pope Urban VIII.

Elda *el'da*, 38 29N 0 47W, pop(1981) 52,185, town in Alicante prov, Valencia, E Spain; on a fertile plain, 32 km NW of Alicante; economy: important shoe-manufacturing industry; monuments: Moorish castle and 17th-c Franciscan convent.

El'doret, 0 31N 35 17E, pop(1984e) 71,000, town in W central Rift Valley prov, Kenya, E Africa; 129 km NW of Nakuru; founded by Boer settlers from South Africa, it was, until 1912, known simply as 'Sixty-Four'; alt 2,095 m; education centre; economy: farming and grain milling.

Eleuthera *ee-loo'the-ra*, elongated island in the central Bahamas, between Great Abaco I (NW) and Cat I (SE); pop(1980) 10,600; area 518 sq km; named after the Greek word for freedom; chief settlements Governor's Harbour and Hatchet Bay; airports at N Eleuthera, Rock Sound and Governor's Harbour.

Elevsís *ay-layf-sees'*, ELEUSIS *el-yoo'sis* (Eng), 38 04N 23 26E, pop(1981) 20,320, industrial town in Attikí nome (dept), Sterea Ellás-Évvoia region, Greece, on the coast 22 km W of Athínai (Athens); site of ancient Eleusis, home of Eleusinian mysteries; railway.

Elgin, 57 39N 3 20W, pop(1981) 18,908, capital of Moray dist, Grampian region, NE Scotland; on the R Lossie, 8 km S of Lossiemouth and 59 km E of Inverness; railway; economy: food, distilling; monument: ruins of Elgin cathedral, founded in 1224 and burned in 1390.

Elgin, 42 02N 88 17W, pop(1980) 63,798, city in Kane

county, NE Illinois, United States; on the R Fox, 59 km WNW of Chicago; railway.

El'gon, Mount, 1 07N 34 35E, extinct volcano on the frontier between Kenya and Uganda; located NE of Kampala and NW of Nairobi; height 4,321 m; crater 600 m deep and 6.5 km across; first ascent in 1890 by Jackson, Gedge and Martin; a national park of 169 sq km was established in 1968.

Elisabethville, town in Zaire. See Lubumbashi.

Elizabeth, 40 40N 74 13W, pop(1980) 106,201, county seat of Union county, NE New Jersey, United States; on Newark Bay, 8 km S of Newark; railway; a residential suburb of New York City, linked to Staten Island by Goethals Bridge; capital of state 1664-86; economy: oil refining.

Elk Grove Village, 42 01N 87 59W, pop(1980) 28,907, town in Cook county, NE Illinois, United States; suburb 35 km NW of Chicago.

Elkhart, 41 41N 85 58W, pop(1980) 41,305, town in Elkhart county, N Indiana, United States; at the confluence of the St Joseph and Elkhart rivers, 24 km E of South Bend; railway.

Ellesmere Island *el'es-meer*, Arctic island in N Franklin dist, Northwest Territories, Canada; W of NW Greenland, from which it is separated by the Nares Strait; area 196,236 sq km; barren and mountainous island with a large ice-cap in the SE and a fjord coastline; its N point, Cape Columbia, is the northernmost point in Canada.

Ellesmere Port *elz'meer*, 53 17N 2 54W, pop(1981) 65,803, port town in Ellesmere Port and Neston dist, Cheshire, NW central England; 14 km SE of Liverpool, on the R Mersey estuary and the Manchester Ship Canal; railway; economy: oil and petroleum, engineering, paper, chemicals, motor vehicles.

Ellice Islands, SW Pacific island group. See Tuvalu.

Ellon, 57 22N 2 05W, pop(1981) 6,319, town in Gordon dist, Grampian, NE Scotland; on the R Ythan, 24 km N of Aberdeen.

Elmhurst, 41 53N 87 56W, pop(1980) 44,276, city in Du Page county, NE Illinois, United States; residential suburb 26 km W of Chicago; railway.

Elmira *el-mī'ra*, 42 06N 76 48W, pop(1980) 35,327, county seat of Chemung county, S New York, United States; on R Chemung, 75 km W of Binghamton and 9 km N of the Pennsylvania border; railway; monuments: Arnot art museum, Mark Twain's Study (where he wrote *The Adventures of Tom Sawyer* and other stories); Elmira College was one of the first to give degrees to women.

Elsinore, seaport of Denmark. See Helsingør.

Eltepe, mountain in Bulgaria. See Vikhren.

Elvas *ayl'vash*, 38 50N 7 10W, pop(1981) 12,700, market town and former frontier fortress town in Portalegre dist, E Portugal; situated amid orchards of fruit and olives, 18 km W of Badajoz in Spain; built to counter the equally strong Spanish frontier town of Badajoz, the fortifications were reinforced on many occasions from the late medieval period until the late 18th century; noted for olive oil, plums and textiles; monuments: medieval walls, the 13th-c Moorish castle built on the site of a Roman fortress and enlarged in the 15th century; 17th-c Santa Luzia fort; 'Manueline' style cathedral and Amoreira aqueduct; events: Senhor Jesús da Piedade festival and São Mateus fair at the end of Sept.

Elverum *el'vu-room*, 60 54N 11 33E, pop(1980) 16,596, town in Hedmark county, E Norway; SE of Lillehammer, close to the R Glåma; temporary meeting place of Norwegian government Apr 1940; railway; monument: Norwegian Forestry Museum.

Ely *ee'li*, 52 24N 0 16E, pop(1981) 9,122, small city in East Cambridgeshire dist, Cambridgeshire, E central England; in fertile wheat-growing fens, on the R Ouse, 23 km NNE of Cambridge; railway; economy: paper, engineering; monuments: cathedral with an octagonal tower; King's School (1543).

Elyria *i-lir'ee-a*, 41 22N 82 07W, pop(1980) 57,538, county seat of Lorain county, N Ohio, United States; 37 km WSW of Cleveland; railway.

Emathia, nome (dept) of Makedhonia region, Greece. See Imathía.

Em'den, 53 22N 7 12E, pop(1983) 50,900, seaport on the estuary of the R Ems, in Weser-Ems dist, NW Niedersachsen (Lower Saxony) prov, W Germany; 74 km WNW of Oldenburg; has the most westerly German North Sea harbour and the largest after Hamburg and Bremen; situated at the end of the Dortmund-Ems Canal, the port mainly serves the Ruhr (coal, ore and grain); the Ems-Jade Canal also provides a connection with Wilhelmshaven; railway; ferry service to the island of Borkum; economy: fishing, merchant and naval vessels (built and serviced), machine building, motor vehicles, herring fishing.

Emi Koussi *ay-mee koo-see'*, 19 52N 18 31E, mountain in Borkou-Ennedi-Tibesti prefecture, N Chad, N central Africa; 210 km NNW of Faya; height 3,415 m; an extinct volcano with a crater 19 km in diameter and 1,200 m deep; the highest point in the Tibesti mountains and in Chad.

Emilia-Romagna *ay-meel'ya ro-ma'nya*, region of N Italy, comprising the provs of Piacenza, Parma, Reggio nell'Emilia, Modena, Bologna, Ferrara, Ravenna, and Forli; pop(1981) 3,957,513; area 22,126 sq km; extends from the Po valley to the Appno Tosco-Emilliano, and E to the Adriatic coast; economy: agriculture (meat and dairy farming, tomatoes, fruit, wine, sugar-beet, maize, rice); industry: petrochemicals (based on the recently developed resources of oil and natural gas in the Po plain), car manufacture, textiles, shoes, boots; fishing and tourism are important along the Adriatic coast; the ancient Via Emilia, running from Rimini to Piacenza, is an attractive route.

Em'men, 52 48N 6 57E, pop(1984e) 91,010, city in E Drenthe prov, N Netherlands; near the West German border, 45 km SE of Groningen; rail terminus.

Emmen, 47 05N 8 18E, pop(1980) 22,392, town in Luzern canton, Switzerland, N of R Reuss; railway; economy: engineering.

Empalme, El, town in Ecuador. See Velasco Ibarra.

Emporia *em-pō'ree-a*, 38 25N 96 11W, pop(1980) 25,287, county seat of Lyon county, E Kansas, United States; 83 km SW of Topeka; settled in 1856; university (1863); railway; economy: flour mills.

Ems, EEMS (Du), AMISIA (anc), river in Nordrhein-Westfalen (North Rhine-Westphalia) and Niedersachsen (Lower Saxony) provs, W Germany; rises 16 km N of Paderborn; meanders 400 km W and N past the Rhine to the North Sea, forming a 32 km long estuary of which the Dollart is a part; length 328 km, navigable length 238 km; it communicates with the Ruhr through the Dortmund-Ems Canal.

Emsworth, 50 51N 0 56W, pop(1981) 17,713, town linked with Southbourne in Havant dist, Hampshire, S England; 3 km E of Havant; railway.

Enare, lake in Finland. See Inarijärvi.

Encamp *ã-kã'*, pop(1982) 4,558, one of the seven parishes of the Principality of Andorra with a village seat of the same name situated 5 km NE of Andorra la Vella in the Valira del Orient valley; alt 1,315 m; cableway to Engolasters; monument: Notre-Dame de Meritxell, a national shrine on a hill to the N of the village.

Encarnación *en-kar-na-syōn'*, 27 20S 55 50W, pop(1982) 27,632, port capital of Itapúa dept, Oriental, SE Paraguay; on the Río Paraná; railway; connected by a bridge to the Argentinian town of Posadas; economy: export centre for the region's products; the town is now the centre for the construction of the Yaciterá-Apipé dam, which is shared by Paraguay and Argentina; the older, lower part of the colonial town will be flooded when the Yaciterá dam is completed.

Enchi *en'chee*, 5 53N 2 48W, town in Western region, W Ghana, W Africa; W of Dunkwa.

En'field, 51 40N 0 05W, pop(1981) 258,770, borough of N Greater London, England; includes the suburbs of Enfield, Southgate and Edmonton; Enfield Chase, formerly annexed to the Duchy of Lancaster, was split up in

1777, the portion retained by the Crown being purchased by London County Council in 1938 for inclusion in the Green Belt scheme; railway; economy: small arms, electronics, metal and plastic products.

En'ga, province in central Papua New Guinea; rises to 3,902 at the Sugarloaf in the Central range; area 12,800 sq km; pop(1980) 164,870; chief town Wabang.

England *ing'gland*, ANGLIA (Lat), kingdom forming the S part of the island of Great Britain; bounded N by Scotland, S by the English Channel, E by the North Sea and W by Wales, the Atlantic Ocean and the Irish Sea; includes the Isles of Scilly, Lundy and the Isle of Wight; largely undulating lowland rising in the S in the Mendip Hills, Cotswold Hills, Chiltern Hills and North Downs; rises to the N-S ridge of the Pennines in the N and the Cumbria Mts in the NW; drained E by the Tyne, Tees, Humber, Ouse and Thames rivers and W by the Eden, Ribble, Mersey and Severn rivers; the Severn is the

longest river in Great Britain; the Lake District (NW) includes Derwent Water, Ullswater, Windermere and Bassenthwaite; area 130,357 sq km; pop(1981) 46,229,955; capital London; chief cities include Birmingham, Liverpool, Manchester, Newcastle upon Tyne, Bristol, Plymouth, Sheffield, Leeds; the Midlands conurbation, centred on Birmingham, is the main industrial area; chief ports at Grimsby, Immingham, Tilbury, Southampton, Portsmouth; linked to the Channel Is and to Europe by ferry and hovercraft from Folkestone, Dover, Newhaven, Ramsgate, Portsmouth, Southampton, Weymouth, Plymouth, Harwich and Kingston-upon-Hull; since 1974 England has been divided into 46 counties:

County	*area (sq km)*	*pop(1981)*
Avon	1,346	915,176
Bedfordshire	1,235	507,054
Berkshire	1,259	681,226
Buckinghamshire	1,883	567,979
Cambridgeshire	3,409	578,734
Cheshire	2,328	929,981
Cleveland	583	567,958
Cornwall and Isles of Scilly	3,564	432,240
Cumbria	6,810	487,038
Derbyshire	2,631	910,173
Devonshire	6,711	958,745
Dorset	2,654	595,415
Durham	2,436	607,198
East Sussex	1,795	657,248
Essex	3,672	1,474,300
Gloucestershire	2,643	501,673
Greater London	1,579	6,713,165
Greater Manchester	1,287	2,595,753
Hampshire	3,777	1,466,385
Hereford and Worcester	3,926	631,756
Hertfordshire	1,634	956,517
Humberside	3,512	852,420
Isle of Wight	381	118,594
Kent	3,731	1,467,619
Lancashire	3,063	1,376,519
Leicestershire	2,553	844,525
Lincolnshire	5,915	550,758
Merseyside	652	1,511,915
Norfolk	5,368	694,566
North Yorkshire	8,309	666,951
Northamptonshire	2,367	528,448
Northumberland	5,032	299,484
Nottinghamshire	2,164	985,283
Oxfordshire	2,608	519,490
Shropshire	3,490	375,715
Somerset	3,451	427,114
South Yorkshire	1,560	1,303,948
Staffordshire	2,716	1,015,620
Suffolk	3,797	598,335
Surrey	1,679	1,004,332
Tyne and Wear	540	1,142,675
Warwickshire	1,981	476,315
West Midlands	899	2,648,939
West Sussex	1,989	661,847
West Yorkshire	2,039	2,037,165
Wiltshire	3,481	518,545

Englewood *eng'el-wood*, 39 39N 104 59W, pop(1980) 30,021, town in Arapahoe county, N central Colorado, United States; a suburb 10 km S of Denver; railway; economy: precision instruments and metal products.

English Channel, LA MANCHE (Fr), MARE BRITTANNICUM (Lat), arm of the Atlantic Ocean, bounded N by the S coast of England and S by the N coast of France; the Channel has separated England from the continent of Europe since the rise in sea level following the last glacial period; connected to the North Sea by the Straits of Dover in the E where it is only 34 km wide; 565 km long by 240 km wide at its widest point between Lyme Bay, England, and Golfe de St-Malo; Channel crossings by ferry and hovercraft, linking Dover to Dunkerque and Boulogne, Folkestone to Calais and Boulogne, Plymouth to Roscoff, and Portsmouth to Le Havre, Cherbourg and St-Malo via the Channel Is; a Channel tunnel is planned; in 1909 the first aeroplane crossing of the Channel was made by Bleriot; Matthew Webb in 1875 was the first to swim the Channel; the main islands are the Isle of Wight and the Channel Islands of Guernsey, Jersey, Alderney and Sark.

Enid, 36 24N 97 53W, pop(1980) 50,363, county seat of Garfield county, N central Oklahoma, United States; 106 km N of Oklahoma City; Phillips University (1907); railway; economy: trade and processing centre for wheat, dairy cattle, and poultry; oil fields nearby.

En'na, formerly CASTROGIOVANNI, prov of Sicilia region, S Italy; pop(1981) 190,939; area 2,562 sq km; capital Enna.

Enna, 37 34N 14 17E, pop(1981) 27,838, capital town of Enna prov, Sicilia region, S Italy; 99 km SE of Palermo, on a plateau in the centre of the island; railway; economy: sulphur and rocksalt; monument: cathedral (begun in 1307).

Ennis *e'nis*, INIS (Gael), 52 50N 8 59W, pop(1981) 14,640, market town and capital of Clare county, Munster, W Irish Republic; on R Fergus; railway; monuments: 13th-c Franciscan abbey, remains of 12th-c Clare and Killone abbeys nearby.

Enniscorthy *e-nis-kor'thee*, INIS CÓRTHAIDH (Gael), 52 30N 6 34W, pop(1981) 7,261, market town in Wexford county, Leinster, SE Irish Republic; on R Slaney, E of Blackstairs Mts; railway; economy: dairy produce, timber; monuments: St Aidan's cathedral, 12th-c castle.

Enniskillen *e'nis-kil'in*, INIS CEITHLEANN (Gael), 54 21N 7 38W, pop(1981) 10,429, county town in Fermanagh dist, Fermanagh, SW Northern Ireland; on an island in the R Erne, between Lower Lough Erne and Upper Lough Erne; former stronghold of the Maguires; English families were settled here after Tyrone's rebellion; in 1689 William III's forces defeated those of James II here; Enniskillen became a noted Protestant stronghold; airfield (St Angelo); economy: tourism, watersports, engineering, food processing; monuments: all that remains of the castle of the Maguires is a 15th-c keep and 16th-c water gate, with a museum; the Protestant cathedral (dating from the 17-18th centuries) contains the colours of the royal regiments of Enniskillen.

Enns *ens*, river in N Austria; rises in the Niedere Tauern, flowing E through Steiermark then N through Oberösterreich to meet the R Danube SE of Linz; length 254 km; navigable below Steyr.

Enschede *ens'kHay-de*, 52 13N 6 53E, pop(1984e) 248,200, cultural city in E Overijssel prov, E Netherlands; on the Twente Canal, near the West German border; technical university (1961); received its charter in 1325; industrialization began in the 1830s when it became a focal point of the Dutch cotton industry, the city has a textile school; railway; economy: traditional cotton and wool industries, artificial silk, ready-made clothing, textile machinery, chemicals, foodstuffs (milk products), electrical engineering.

Ensenada *en-se-nah'dah*, 31 53N 116 37W, pop(1980) 175,425, port in Baja California Norte state, NW Mexico; 104 km SSE of San Diego (USA); economy: fishing, canning, wineries, olives; the port serves deep-sea vessels, principally trading in cotton; monument: 16 km S of Ensenada is La Bufadora, the largest blowhole on the Pacific coast.

Entebbe *en-te'be*, 0 05N 32 29E, pop(1983e) 20,472, town in S Uganda, E Africa; 25 km SW of Kampala on N shore of L Victoria; founded in 1893; former capital of Uganda (1894-1962); railway; airport.

Entrance, The, 33 24S 151 28E, pop(1981) 37,891, town in Sydney stat div, E New South Wales, Australia; on the E coast; amalgamated with Terrigal, it includes the former urban centre of Terrigal-Wamberal.

Entre Ríos *en'tray ree'ōs*, prov in Litoral region, NE Argentina; established in 1814; bordered by the Río Paraná (W) and the Río Uruguay where it follows the

Uruguay frontier; low, fertile, alluvial area with humid subtropical climate; near Concordia is the Salto Grande dam providing water for hydroelectricity, irrigation, navigation and recreation; pop(1980) 908,313; area 76,216 sq km; capital Paraná; chief towns Concordia and Concepción del Uruguay; economy: maize, wheat, sorghum, flax, maté, sheep and cattle raising, fishing, timber, gypsum and sand mining, meat packing; tourism.

Entrecasteaux Islands, D' *dã-tru-ka-stō'*, volcanic island group in Milne Bay prov, Papua New Guinea, SW Pacific, separated from New Guinea by the Ward Hunt Strait; comprises the islands of Fergusson, Normanby, and Goodenough; area 3,107 sq km.

Enugu *en-oo'goo*, 6 20N 7 29E, pop(1981e) 256,000, capital of Anambra state, Nigeria, W Africa; 195 km NNE of Port Harcourt; established as a result of a silver prospecting expedition discovering coal in the region in 1909; television studio; railway; airfield; economy: metals, food processing, coal, glass, bricks and motor vehicles.

Ephesus, ancient city in Turkey. See Efes.

Épinal *ay-pee-nal*, 48 10N 6 27E, pop(1982) 40,954, fortified capital town of Vosges dept, Lorraine region, E France; on the upper Moselle R; well-known from the 18th century onward for the production of prints; railway; economy: cotton-weaving, light industries; monuments: basilica of St Maurice (13th-c).

Épinay-sur-Seine *ay-pee-nay-sür-sen*, 48 57N 2 18E, pop(1982) 50,314, town in Seine-Saint-Denis dept, Ile-de-France region, N central France.

Epirus, region of Greece. See Ipiros.

Ep'som and Ewell *yoo'ĕl*, 51 20N 0 16W, pop(1981) 66,872, amalgamated towns in Epsom and Ewell dist, Surrey, SE England; part of Greater London urban area; 22 km SW of London; Epsom Downs noted as a horse-racing centre; railway; economy: chemicals, pharmaceuticals; events: the 'Derby' and 'Oaks' horse-races.

Equator *ee-kway'tor*, the terrestrial Equator is the great circle on the Earth's surface, half-way between the poles, dividing the Earth into the northern and southern hemispheres; its own latitude is 0°, and from it latitude is measured in degrees N and degrees S; the celestial Equator is the great circle in the sky in the same plane as the Earth's Equator; when the sun is on it day and night are everywhere equal (hence it is also called the *equinoctial line* or *circle*).

Equatoria, EL ISTIWA'IYA, area of SE Sudan, NE Africa; (province prior to 1983); area 76,495 sq km; pop(1983) 1,406,181; capital Juba; dissected by the Blue Nile.

Equatorial Guinea, official name Republic of Equatorial Guinea, REPÙBLICA DE GUINEA ECUATORIAL, a republic in W central Africa comprising (1) the mainland area (Río Muni) bounded N by Cameroon and E and S by Gabon and (2) the islands of Bioko and Annabón (Pagalu) and the smaller islands of Corisco, Elobey Grande and Elobey Chico (total area 17 sq km) in the Gulf of Guinea; timezone GMT +1; mainland area 26,016 sq km; total area 28,051 sq km; pop(1984e) 275,000, a large number of the population emigrated during the late 1960s and 1970s; of 2,460 km of roads in Río Muni, approx 185 km are paved, the remainder being gravel and earth; of 300 km of roads on Bioko, 146 km are paved; there are no railways in Equatorial Guinea; capital Malabo; chief towns are Bata and Evinayoung on the mainland, and Luba and Riaba on Bioko; on the mainland (Río Muni) the pop is primarily of the Fang ethnic group of Bantu origin; 80% are Roman Catholic, the remainder follow local beliefs; the official language is Spanish; pidgin English and Fang also spoken; the unit of currency is the ekuele; national holiday 12 Oct; membership of AfDB, Conference of East and Central African States, ECA, FAO, G-77, GATT (de facto), IBRD, ICAO, IDA, IFAD, ILO, IMF, IMO, INTERPOL, ITU, NAM, OAU, UN, UNESCO, UPU and WHO.

Physical description. Mainland Río Muni rises sharply from a narrow coast of mangrove swamps towards the heavily-forested African plateau. Here the land is deeply cut by a number of rivers including the Río Mbini (Benito) which rises as the Woleu in Gabon and flows generally W for about 320 km to enter the Gulf of Guinea near Senye. The island of Bioko lying about 160 km NW of the mainland prov is of volcanic origin rising to 3,007 m at Pico de Basilé.

Climate. Both mainland and islands have a hot and humid equatorial climate. The island of Bioko has relatively high rainfall owing to the height of its main peak. Average annual rainfall is almost uniformly around 2,000 mm, with average max daily temperature ranging between 29°C and 32°C.

History, government and constitution. First visited by Europeans in the 15th century, the island of Fernando Póo was claimed by Portugal between 1494 and 1788 but occupied by Britain between 1781 and 1843. Spain acquired the rights to Fernando Póo and Río Muni in 1844 in order to develop coffee and cocoa plantations. In 1904 the Spanish introduced the *patronata* system preventing the local people from indulging in anything but petty trade and forcing most to work on plantations for low wages. A move towards independence began in the 1950s and the colony was granted a form of self-government in 1963. Full independence came in 1968 and following 10 years of harsh dictatorship a coup in 1979 established a military government. The country is governed by a military council of about 19 ministers presided over by a president who is head of state. In 1982 provision was made for a new constitution to establish an elected house of representatives and a smaller state council.

Economy. Equatorial Guinea's economy is largely based on agriculture, the principal cash crop being cocoa which is grown chiefly on Bioko. Coffee and timber are also major exports but bananas, cassava, palm oil and sweet potatoes are also grown. Spain is the country's most important trade partner.

Administrative divisions. Equatorial Guinea is divided into the 7 provs of Annobón (Pagalu), Bioko Norte, Bioko Sur, Centro Sur, Kié-Ntem, Litoral, Wele-Nzas.

Erawan, oil and gas field in the Gulf of Thailand; natural gas first brought to generating stations at Bangkok in 1981; the world's longest pipeline links the field with Bangkok.

Erbeskopf *er'bus-kopf*, 49 42N 7 07E, mountain in S Hessen (Hesse) prov, W Germany; highest peak of the Hunsrück, 11 km NW of Birkenfeld; height 816 m.

Ěrd *ayrd*, 47 19N 19 00E, pop(1984e) 45,000, river port town in Pest county, N Hungary; on R Danube, SW of Budapest; economy: fruit and dairy trade.

Erdenet, 45 10N 97 40E, pop(1978) 35,000, town in Bulgan county, N Mongolia; on a tributary of the Orhon Gol; a new city founded in 1971 with Soviet help; linked by rail to Ulaanbaatar; linked to Darhan by road; economy based on mining and engineering, with future plans to build a carpet factory, a wool laundry and a wood-processing enterprise; State farms provide the town with fresh milk and vegetables.

Erfurt *er'foort*, county in SW East Germany; pop(1981) 1,236,681; area 7,349 sq km; economy: electronics, electrical engineering, telecommunications equipment, farm machinery, motor vehicles (Eisenach), potash and knitwear; 64% of its area is farmed and 22% is wooded; the Thuringian Forest is a popular holiday region; the county has associations with Martin Luther, Goethe, Schiller and Bach; former Buchenwald Nazi concentration camp on the R Ettersberg near Weimar.

Erfurt, 50 58N 11 2E, pop(1982) 212,449, industrial capital of Erfurt county, SW East Germany; colleges of medicine and education; meeting place of the governments of E and W Germany for the first time in 1970; airport; railway; economy: market-gardening, precision tools; monuments: 12th-c cathedral; event: international horticultural show.

Erie *ee'ree*, 42 08N 80 05W, pop(1980) 119,123, county seat of Erie county, NW Pennsylvania, United States; port on L Erie; railway; airfield; a large harbour handles a variety of raw materials; headquarters of Commodore Perry in the 1812 war with Britain.

Erie, Lake, lake in North America, on the frontier between Canada and the USA; 4th largest of the Great Lakes; bounded N by Ontario prov (Canada) and W, S and E by the states of Michigan, Ohio, Pennsylvania and New York (USA); 388 km long by 48-92 km wide; area 25,667 sq km of which 12,769 sq km are in Ontario, Canada; the Detroit river is its inlet from L Huron in the W, via L St Clair; the Niagara river in the E is its outlet to L Ontario; navigation from L Huron to L Erie follows the natural channel of the St Clair river and the Detroit river, but the Welland Ship Canal between lakes Erie and Ontario bypasses Niagara Falls; ice generally closes the lake to navigation from mid-Dec until the end of March; principal US ports are Buffalo and Dunkirk (New York), Erie (Pennsylvania), Conneaut, Ashtabula, Cleveland, Lorain, Sandusky and Toledo (Ohio) and Detroit (Michigan); major Canadian ports are Leamington and Port Colborne; industry is centred on the E and S shores from Detroit to Cleveland and around Buffalo; a fruit-growing area lies along the lake in W New York and NE Ohio; islands include Bass and Kelleys islands (Ohio) and Pelee island (Ontario); forts and trading posts sprang up along the shores of L Erie in the early 17th century; the French and Indian wars gave Britain control of the lake; in Sept 1813, near the end of the War of 1812, the British were defeated at Put-in-Bay in the Battle of Lake Erie; after the war the US-Canadian boundary was established to run approx through the centre of the lake.

Eritrea, region in N Ethiopia. See Ērtra.

Er'langen, 49 35N 11 00E, pop(1983) 102,400, city in Mittelfranken dist, Bayern (Bavaria) prov, W Germany; on the R Regnitz, 19 km NNW of Nürnberg; railway; university (1743); economy: electronics, natural and synthetic fibres and yarns.

Ermoúpolis *er-moo'po-lis*, HERMOUPOLIS (Eng), SÍROS *see'ros* (anc), 37 25N 24 56E, pop(1981) 16,595, capital town of Kikládhes nome (dept), Aegean Islands, Greece; on the E coast of Síros I; local boat service; harbour; economy: boatyards, tourism; event: Navy Week (June-July).

Erne, Lower Lough *ern*, lake in NW Co Fermanagh, SW Northern Ireland; 29 km long; 8 km wide; area 137 sq km; fed by the river Erne, which enters the lake from the SE and flows out from the NW; contains several islands; a 16 km stretch of the river Erne connects Lower Lough Erne with Upper Lough Erne to the SE.

Erne, Upper Lough, lake in SE Co Fermanagh, SW Northern Ireland; 16 km long; 11 km wide; fed from the SE by the R Erne which connects the lake with Lower Lough Erne to the NW.

Erode *e-rōd'*, 11 21N 77 43E, pop(1981) 276,000, city in Tamil Nadu, S India; on the SW bank of the R Cauvery, within a major cotton-growing region; linked NE to Salem and SW to Coimbatore.

Erse'ke, 40 22N 20 40E, town and capital of Kolonjë prov, SE Albania; at the foot of the Grámmos, 32 km S of Korçë.

Ērtra, ERITREA *er-e-tree'a*, region in N Ethiopia, NE Africa; pop(1984e) 2,614,700; area 117,600 sq km; coastal region adjacent to the Red Sea; includes the Dahlak Is; capital Asmera; chief towns Mits'iwa (Massawa), Keren, Adīgrat, Adi Ugrī, Āksum, Ādwa and Āseb; taken by the Italians in 1882 and declared a colony in 1890; used as a base for the Italian invasion of Abyssinia in 1935; made part of Italian East Africa in 1936; taken by the British in 1941; federated to Abyssinia in 1952, finally becoming a province in 1962; a railway originating near Kassala (Sudan) crosses into Ērtra near Teseney and runs E to Mits'iwa (Massawa) on the Red Sea coast.

Erzgebirge *erts'ge-bir-ge*, ORE MTS (Eng), mountain range on the frontier between E Germany and Czechoslovakia rising to 1,244 m at Klínovec in Czechoslovakia and to 1,214 m at Fichtelberg in E Germany.

Erzincan *er-zin-jan'*, mountainous prov in E central Turkey; pop(1980) 282,022; area 11,903 sq km; capital Erzincan; economy: copper mining, leather, textiles.

Erzurum *er-zoo-room'*, mountainous prov in NE Turkey; pop(1980) 801,809; area 25,066 sq km; capital Erzurum.

Erzurum, 39 57N 41 17E, pop(1980) 190,241, capital of Erzurum prov, NE Turkey; on Armenian plateau; agricultural trade centre; university (1958); railway; airfield; economy: iron, copper, sugar, tanning and trade in cattle, grain and vegetables.

Esbjerg *ays'byer*, 55 28N 8 28E, pop(1983) 80,317, seaport on W coast of Ribe county, SW Jylland (Jutland), Denmark; railway; passenger and vehicle ferry connections with Britain and the Færøerne Is; economy: fishing, base for Danish exploration of oil and gas in North Sea, exports agricultural produce; the most important Danish North Sea port.

Esbo, town in Finland. See Espoo.

Escaldes *es-kal'des*, pop(1982) 10,758, one of the seven parishes of the Principality of Andorra with a village seat of the same name situated 2 km NE of Andorra la Vella in the Valira del Orient valley; alt 1,105 m; a popular spa.

Escaut, river in W Europe. See Schelde.

Eschen *e'shen*, 47 13N 9 32E, pop(1985) 2,785, commune in Unterland dist, Principality of Liechtenstein, central Europe; area 10.3 sq km.

Esch-sur-Alzette *esh-sür-al-zet'* or **Esch**, canton in SW part of Luxembourg dist, S Luxembourg; area 243 sq km; pop(1981) 114,474; important wine-producing area; on the S frontier with France; bisected by the R Alzette and its tributary, the R Mess; in the last quarter of the 19th century Brown Jura iron ore deposits were extensively mined; the ore was relatively poor 'minette' or small ore, but heavy industries tended to develop near the mines; the large Arbed steelworks is located at Belval.

Esch-sur-Alzette, 49 30N 5 59E, pop(1981) 25,142, industrial capital of the canton of the same name in S Luxembourg; on the French frontier, 18 km SW of Luxembourg; 2nd largest town in Luxembourg; developed since the coming of the blast furnaces in 1871; Galgebeirg Nature Park is nearby; economy: steel, cement, printing.

Eschweiler *esh'vī-ler*, 50 49N 6 14E, pop(1983) 53,200, manufacturing city in Köln (Cologne) dist, SW Nordrhein-Westfalen (North Rhine-Westphalia) prov, W Germany; 18 km NE of Aachen; railway.

Escondido *es-con-dee'dō*, 33 07N 117 05W, pop(1980) 64,355, city in San Diego county, SW California, United States; 43 km NNE of San Diego.

Escuintla *ays-kweent'la*, maritime dept in S Guatemala, Central America; bounded S by the Pacific Ocean; pop(1982e) 496,522; area 4,384 sq km; capital Escuintla; chief towns San José and Tiquisate; drained by the Coyolate and Guacalate rivers; the coastal plain is devoted largely to cotton growing; it is the richest agricultural dept in the country, producing 80% of the sugar, 20% of the coffee, 85% of the cotton, and 70% of the cattle of the whole country.

Escuintla, 14 18N 90 47W, market town and capital of Escuintla dept, S Guatemala, Central America; 18 km SSW of Palín; Agua volcano is to the N; flourished as a political and indigo-trading centre in the 17th and 18th centuries; railway; famous for its medicinal baths and fruits; economy: meat packing; an industrial park is being developed here; event: fiesta (8-12 Dec).

Eşfahān *es-fa-han'*, mountainous prov in W central Iran; pop(1982) 2,175,150; area 104,550 sq km; capital Eşfahān.

Eşfahān, ISFAHAN, ASPADANA *as-pud-ay'nu* (anc), 32 40N 51 38E, pop(1983) 926,601, capital city of Eşfahān dist, Eşfahān, W central Iran; 336 km S of Tehrān, on the R Zaindeh; 3rd largest city in Iran; airport; railway; economy: steel complex (30 km S of city), noted for its fine carpets, hand-printed textiles, and metalwork; monuments: Lutfullah mosque with blue-tiled dome; 17th-c royal mosque, an outstanding example of Persian architecture; Ali Kapu gate, leading to the former royal gardens; Chihil Satun with 40 pillars is noted as the former throne hall; Jolfa cathedral.

Esher *eesh'er*, formerly ESHER AND THE DITTONS, 51 23N

0 22W, pop(1981) 46,847, residential town linked with Molesey in Epsom and Ewell dist, Surrey, SE England; part of Greater London urban area; 24 km SW of central London; railway; economy: light engineering.

Eskilstuna *esk'il-stoo-na*, 59 22N 16 31E, pop(1982) 89,459, industrial town in Södermanland county, SE Sweden; S of L Mälaren, 72 km W of Stockholm, at NE corner of L Hjälmaren; railway; economy: iron and steel; famous since the 17th century for swords and cutlery; monuments: 12th-c church, town hall (1897).

Eskişehir *es-ki'she-hir*, mountainous prov in NW Turkey, bounded in part by the R Sakarya; pop(1980) 543,802; area 13,652 sq km; capital Eskişehir.

Eskişehir, 39 47N 30 30E, pop(1980) 309,431, industrial capital of Eskişehir prov, NW Turkey, on the R Porsuk; nearby is the ancient Phrygian city of Dorylaeum; noted for its hot mineral springs; road and rail junction; airfield; economy: sugar refining, agricultural implements, textiles, cement.

Esmeraldas *es-may-ral'das*, prov in NW Ecuador; rises from the Pacific coast towards the Andes in the E; bordered NE by Colombia; the indented coastal lowlands are watered by the Esmeraldas and Santiago rivers; humid tropical climate with little seasonal variation; more arid along the coast as a result of the cool Humboldt Current; pop(1982) 249,008; area 15,031 sq km; capital Esmeraldas; economy: tobacco, cacao, cattle ranching, timber, gold mining, oil, gas, food processing.

Esmeraldas, 0 56N 79 40W, pop(1982) 90,360, capital of Esmeraldas prov, NW Ecuador; on the Río Esmeraldas; linked by pipeline with the oilfields of the *Oriente*; university (1970); railway; economy: gold, oil-refining, food processing; nearby are a new power station, a new fishing port and a liquid-gas loading terminal.

España, country of SW Europe. See Spain.

Esperance, 33 49S 121 52E, pop(1981) 6,375, resort and port in South-Eastern stat div, Western Australia, Australia; on Esperance Bay, 344 km S of Kalgoorlie; N Americans established farms here; cruises to the Recherche archipelago; railway; airfield; economy: wheat, oats, barley, cattle, lamb, wool.

Esperanza, La *lah es-pay-ran'sah*, 14 18N 88 19W, capital of Intibucá dept, S Honduras, Central America; in the Sierra de Opalaca at the centre of a fruit-growing area.

Espichel, Cabo de *eesh-pay-shel'*, 38 24N 9 13W, steep headland on Atlantic coast of Setúbal dist, central Portugal, at N end of Baia de Setúbal.

Espierres-Helchin *es-pyer-helKH'in*, 50 43N 3 22E, pop(1982) 75,731, town in Kortrijk dist, West-Vlaanderen (West Flanders) prov, W Belgium.

Espírito Santo *es-pee'ree-tō san'tō*, state in Sudeste region, E Brazil; bordered E by the Atlantic; rises in the W towards the Serra do Caparaó and the Serra dos Aimorés; drained by short coastal streams and by the Doce river; has a low, marshy coastline; pop(1980) 2,023,340; area 45,597 sq km; capital Vitória; economy: coffee, timber in the N, food processing, non-metallic minerals, metallurgy, chemicals; near the coast is the 240-sq km Sooretama Biological Reserve (established in 1943); farther S, to the NW of Vitória, is the 43.5-sq km Nova Lombardia Biological Reserve (established in 1955) in which there is a unique hummingbird sanctuary; in the SW is part of the 162-sq km Caparaó National Park (established in 1961).

Espiritu Santo, 15 15S 166 55E, volcanic island, Vanuatu, 248 km NW of Efate, SW Pacific; area 3,947 sq km; pop(1979) 16,200; main town Santo.

Espoo *es-po'*, ESBO (Swed), 60 08N 25 00E, pop(1982) 145,317, town in Uudenmaa prov, S Finland; c.8 km W of Helsinki; formerly an outer suburb of the capital city; railway; Dipoli conference centre at Otaniemi; established in 1963.

Esquipulas *es-kee-poo'las*, 14 36N 89 22W, town in Chiquimula dept, SE Guatemala; 117 km E of Guatemala City, near the Honduras frontier; meeting place of the 5 Central American presidents in May 1986 to sign a declaration that the Contadora Process was the best political forum for achieving peace and democracy (Esquipulas Summit); monument: church containing the 'Black Christ'.

Essaouira *es-a-wir'a*, 31 30N 9 47W, pop(1982) 42,035, resort and seaport capital of Essaouira prefecture, Tensift prov, W Morocco, N Africa; on the Atlantic Ocean, 172 km N of Agadir; developed by European merchants in the 18th century; landing place of US forces in 1942; economy: fishing, food processing, leather, wool, olive oil.

Es-Semara *ez-say-ma'ra*, prov in Western Sahara, NW Africa; pop(1982) 20,480; area 61,760 sq km; claimed by Morocco.

Es-Semara, 26 44N 11 41W, pop(1982) 17,753, capital of Es-Semara prov, Western Sahara, NW Africa.

Es'sen, 51 28N 6 59E, pop(1983) 635,200, industrial city in Düsseldorf dist, Nordrhein-Westfalen (North Rhine-Westphalia) prov, W Germany; 29 km NNE of Düsseldorf, between the rivers Emscher and Ruhr; owes its importance as a metropolis of the Ruhr and headquarters of many large industrial corporations (including the largest German mining company) to its situation in the middle of the Rhineland-Westphalia coalfield; an important centre of retail trade; bishopric; railway; economy: mining, iron and steel, heavy industry, rolling stock and locomotives, electronics, glass, chemicals, plastics, brewing, soft drinks, building materials, machine tools, building and civil engineering, shipbuilding and repairing, engineering, textiles; monuments: Minster (9-14th-c), one of the oldest churches in Germany; Werden Abbey church; event: Baldeney Festival (climax of the summer season).

Essequibo *e-sė-kee'bō*, largest river in Guyana, South America; draining more than half the total area of the country; rises in the Guiana Highlands on the Brazilian border at 1 12N 58 47W; flows approx 970 km N past Bartica to meet the Atlantic at a 32 km-wide delta, 21 km WNW of Georgetown; its lower course is navigable for large vessels up to Bartica (approx 80 km); its course is interrupted by numerous rapids and falls; major tributaries include the Rupununi, Potaro and Mazaruni-Cuyuni rivers.

Es'sex, county of SE England; NE of London; bounded E by the North Sea and S by the Thames estuary; pop(1981) 1,474,300; area 3,672 sq km; county town Chelmsford; economy: grain, oysters, electronics, motor vehicles, tourism; the county is divided into 14 districts:

District	*area (sq km)*	*pop(1981)*
Basildon	111	152,815
Braintree	612	112,219
Brentwood	149	72,360
Castle Point	44	85,560
Chelmsford	342	138,925
Colchester	334	134,385
Epping Forest	345	116,550
Harlow	26	79,521
Maldon	358	47,867
Rochford	169	73,783
Southend-on-Sea	42	157,083
Tendring	337	114,361
Thurrock	163	127,105
Uttlesford	642	61,766

Ess'lingen, 48 43N 9 19E, pop(1983) 88,400, industrial city in Stuttgart dist, Baden-Württemberg prov, W Germany; in the middle Neckar valley, 10 km ESE of Stuttgart; railway; economy: metal constructions, car bodies and components, machine tools, air conditioning plants; monuments: 8th-c town church, old town hall (half-timbered building of 1430); preserves a number of important historic buildings dating from the time it was a Free Imperial City.

Essonne, dept in Ile-de-France region of N France, comprising 3 arrond, 35 cantons and 196 communes; drained by the R Seine and its tributaries; pop(1982)

988,000; area 1,804 sq km; capital Évry; there is an 18th-c château at Morigny.

Estelí *es-tay-lee'*, dept in NW Nicaragua, Central America; close to the border with Honduras, bounded W by the Cordillera Horno Grande; drained by the Río Estelí and its tributaries; pop(1981) 110,076; area 1,999 sq km; capital Estelí; chief towns La Trinidad and San Juán de Limay; the Inter-American Highway crosses the dept N-S.

Estelí, 13 04N 86 20W, pop(1978) 26,892, capital town of Estelí dept, NW Nicaragua, Central America; in the E foothills of the Cordillera Horno Grande, on the Río Estelí; alt 839 m; on the Inter-American Highway; heavily damaged during the civil wars of 1978-79; site of prehistoric carved stone figures; economy: timber, tanning.

Eston, 54 34N 1 07W, pop(1981) 37,633, town linked with South Bank in Langbaurgh dist, Cleveland, NE England; 6 km E of Middlesbrough; railway.

Estonia, constituent republic of the Soviet Union. See Estonskaya.

Estonskaya, ESTONIA (Eng), constituent republic of the Soviet Union; in NW European USSR, bounded W and N by the Baltic Sea; the terrain is plainlike with traces of ancient glaciation; the largest of the republic's numerous islands are Saaremaa, Hiiumaa, and Muhu; rivers, such as the Narva, tend to be short and carry small volumes of water; there are 1,512 lakes; forests, mainly coniferous, cover 36% of the area; pop(1983) 1,507,000; area 45,100 sq km; capital Tallinn; chief towns Tartu, Narva and Kohtla-Järve; economy: extraction and processing of shale oil, machine building, metalworking, chemical and petrochemical industries (mineral fertilizers), food processing, light industry (cotton fabrics), phosphorite mining, timber-related industries; farmland covers 32% of the total land area; animal husbandry, which specializes in the production of milk and bacon, is the leading branch of agriculture; proclaimed a Soviet Socialist Republic on 21 July 1940.

Estoril *eesh-too-reel'*, 38 42N 9 23W, pop(1981) 16,000, fashionable resort town in Lisboa dist, central Portugal; 21 km W of Lisboa; with radioactive hot springs, fine villas and beaches on the Atlantic coast this location has been frequented for many years by wealthy tourists, convalescing Englishmen and unemployed royalty; railway; Grand Prix motor racing circuit reopened in 1984.

Estrada, La *la es-trah'da*, 42 43N 8 27W, pop(1981) 25,719, agric town in Pontevedra prov, Galicia, NW Spain; 40 km NE of Pontevedra; mineral springs; economy: livestock, cereals, wine, timber.

Estrêla, Serra da *eesh-tray'la*, mountain range, a granite ridge extending 100 km SW from Guarda to S of Coimbra in NE central Portugal; rises to 1,991 m at Malhão de Estrêla or Torre; main watershed and highest mountain range on mainland Portugal, the first area in the country to be designated (1958) a tourist region, winter sports on the central massif are the main attraction with ski-lifts at Piornos (380 m long) and Covões de Loriga (782 m long); peaks at Cabeça Alta (1,283 m) and São Pedro do Acor (1,349 m).

Estremadura *eesh-tre-ma-doo'ra* (Lat 'Extrema Durii', farthest land on the Douro), prov and former region of W central Portugal, comprising the area from the mouth of the R Tagus as far inland as the Ribatejo basin, N to the SW outliers of the Serra da Estrêla and S to the R Sado; the prov includes parts of Lisboa, Setúbal and Leiria dists; area 3,249 sq km; the chief town is Lisboa; the agricultural heart of the province lies to the W around Alcobaça where mixed farming of Mediterranean type predominates with the cultivation of vines, fruit, olives, wheat, maize and vegetables; to the N an upland area of Mesozoic limestone is largely grazed by sheep and goats; on marshy low-lying land in valley basins rice is commonly grown and to the S the mild oceanic climate produces a softer landscape; with the additional attraction of thermal springs at Caldas da Rainha, Estoril, etc this part of the prov has become a popular tourist region as well as being the political and cultural centre of Portugal.

Esztergom *es-ter-gom'*, GRAN (Ger), STRIGONIUM (anc), 47 47N 18 44E, pop(1984e) 31,000, river port town in Komárom county, N Hungary; on R Danube NW of Budapest; a fortress in Roman times, the city became capital of Hungary in the 10th century; birthplace of St Stephen, Hungary's first king; became seat of primate in 1198; school of forestry; thermal springs nearby; railway; economy: coal and lignite mining nearby, wine trade, machinery; monument: 19th-c Basilica, the largest church in Hungary.

Etah, 78 15N 72 00W, Eskimo settlement in NW Greenland; N of Thule on the Nares Strait, opposite Ellesmere I; point of departure for several polar expeditions.

Ethiopia *ee-thee-ō'pee-a*, formerly ABYSSINIA, official name People's Democratic Republic of Ethiopia, HEBRETESEBAWIT ITYOPIA, a state of NE Africa, bounded W and SW by Sudan, S by Kenya, E and NE by Somalia, N by Djibouti and the Red Sea; area 1,221,918 sq km; timezone GMT +3; capital Addis Ababa (Adis Abeba); chief towns Asmera, Jimma, Dire Dawa; pop(1984e) 41,930,118; ethnic groups include Galla (40%), Amhara and Tigray (32%), Sidamo (9%), Shankella (6%), Somali (6%), Gurage (2%); 40-45% are Muslim, and 35-40% are Ethiopian Orthodox; the official language is Amharic but Tigrinya, Orominga, Arabic and English are also spoken; the unit of currency is the Ethiopian birr of 100 cents; national holiday 12 Sept (Popular Revolution Commemoration Day); membership of AfDB, ECA, FAO, G-77, IAEA, IBRD, ICAO, ICO, IDA, IFAD, IFC, ILO, IMF, IMO, INTELSAT, INTERPOL, IPU, ITU, NAM, OAU, UN, UNESCO, UPU, WFTU, WHO, WMO and WTO.

Physical description. Ethiopia is dominated by a mountainous central plateau which is split diagonally by the Great Rift valley. The highest point in Ethiopia is Ras Dashan Mt (4,620 m) in N Gonder region. High peaks in the central plateau also include Birhan (4,154 m), Abuye Mēda (4,200 m), Batu (4,307 m), K'ech'a Mt (4,190 m), Gugē (4,200 m). The plateau is crossed E-W by the Blue Nile which has its source in T'ana Hāyk' (L Tana). Other major lakes in Ethiopia are located on the frontier with Djibouti (L Abbe and Tehīyo Hāyk'), on the border between Shewa and Arsī regions (K'ok'a Hāyk', Ziway Hāyk', Ābiyata Hāyk' and Shala Hāyk') and on the border between Gamo Gofa and Sīdamo regions (Ābaya Hāyk' and Ch'amo Hāyk'). The N extremity of L Turkana crosses Ethiopia's S frontier in Gamo Gofa region. The N and E section of the country which includes parts of Ērtra, Tigray, Welo and Hārergē regions is relatively low lying. The Danakil Depression in the NE dips to 116 m below sea-level.

Climate. A large part of the Ethiopia plateau has a mean elevation of between 1,800 and 2,400 m and experiences a tropical climate which is moderated by higher altitudes and has a distinct wet season (April-Sept). Temperatures are warm but rarely hot all year round. In the E there is frequently a short wet period during April-May before heavier rains arrive during July-Aug. Annual rainfall is in excess of 1,000 mm throughout most of the country but can peak between 1,500 and 2,000 mm in the W. Snow falls on the higher ground but there are no permanent snow fields. Addis Ababa is representative of the upland central plateau region with an average annual rainfall of 1,236 mm and average max daily temperatures ranging between 21°C and 25°C. The hot, semi-arid NE lowlands (Danakil Depression) and SE lowlands (Ogaden area) receive less than 500 mm of rain annually and are highly susceptible to drought.

History, government and constitution. Ethiopia is the oldest independent country on the African continent and was known as Abyssinia until after World War II. It was during the 19th century under Theodore II (1855-68) and Emperor Menelik II (1889-1913) that Abyssinia began its modern development. The Italians occupied Eritrea in

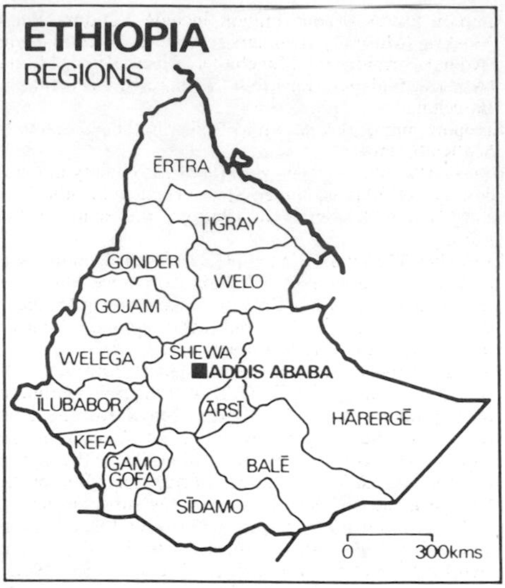

1882 and declared it a colony in 1890. Abyssinia's independence was recognized by the League of Nations in 1923 and a constitution was established in 1931 a year after the Emperor Haile Selassie came to the throne. Disagreement with Italy resulted in the Italian invasion of 1935 and its annexation as Italian East Africa from 1936 until 1941. Haile Selassie returned from exile in 1941 and remained emperor until 1974 when unrest within the country culminated in his removal by the military. A Provisional Military Administrative Council (PMAC) was formed and a programme of nationalization and land reform was initiated. The PMAC were opposed by left-wing civilian groups who had assisted in Selassie's removal but were insistent on a democratic civilian government. This opposition passed through a phase of relatively peaceful protest to assassination of PMAC leaders. This was countered by mass arrests and executions - a period labelled the 'Red Terror' (Nov 1977 to March 1978). The Ethiopians have an ongoing conflict with Somalia based on ethnic and border disagreements and within the country there remains a conflict with regional Eritrean and Tigrean forces. After Selassie's overthrow the 1955 constitution was suspended and parliament dissolved. A large civilian bureaucracy governs the country on a day-to-day basis. The PMAC and the Workers Party of Ethiopia (established in 1984 as the sole political party) hold overall power. The PMAC consists of about 80 appointed members plus an inner central committee and a standing committee. All three are chaired by the head of state who is also chairman of a council of about 27 appointed ministers.

Economy. Agriculture plays a major role in the Ethiopian economy employing over 80% of the pop and generating more than half of the country's income. Approx 66% of agricultural activity is subsistence farming with production of teff, barley, wheat, maize and sorghum. The export market is dominated by coffee which generates between 65% and 75% of foreign exchange earnings. Sugar, cotton, pulses and oil seeds are also exported. Agricultural production was severely reduced during the drought of the early 1980s which affected 11 out of the 15 regions of Ethiopia. Oil and petroleum products, gold, cement and salt are the main minerals to be extracted in small quantities. There is a state-owned oil refinery at Aseb (Ērtra region) on the Red Sea coast. There are reserves of iron ore, copper, gypsum, gems, tin, mercury, coal, sulphur, limestone and mica. Manufacturing industry, which is largely based on supplying local markets, centres on food processing, tobacco and textiles. Main trading partners are Saudi Arabia, Japan, the USA, Italy, Djibouti, Egypt, West Germany and the UK.

Administrative divisions. Ethiopia is divided into 15 regions:

Region	*area (sq km)*	*pop(1984e)*
Addis Ababa	218	1,412,575
Ārsī	23,500	1,662,233
Balē	124,600	1,006,491
Ērtra	117,600	2,614,700
Gamo Gofa	39,500	1,248,034
Gojam	61,600	3,244,882
Gonder	74,200	2,905,362
Hārergē	259,700	4,151,706
Īlubabor	47,400	963,327
Kefa	54,600	2,450,369
Shewa	85,200	8,090,565
Sīdamo	117,300	3,790,579
Tigray	65,900	2,409,700
Welega	71,200	2,369,677
Welo	79,400	3,609,918

Etna, Monte *et'nu*, MOUNT ETNA (Eng), MONGIBELLO *mon-jee-bel'lo* (Sicilian), 37 45N 15 00E, isolated volcanic mountain in Catania prov, E Sicilia, Italy, 29 km NNW of Catania; height 3,323 m; Europe's largest active volcano; it has the form of a truncated cone with an almost circular base 40 km in diameter and 145 km in circumference; there are over 200 subsidiary cones on the flanks of the mountain, the principal being the Monti Rossi (948 m), twin peaks which were cast up in 1669 in the most violent of recorded eruptions; on the SE slope is a large, precipitous cleft, the Valle del Bove, which is 5 km wide and surrounded on 3 sides by rock walls 600-1,200 m high; oranges and lemons grow up to 500 m above sea level, olives and vines to 1,300 m; these fertile lower slopes have one of the most concentrated non-urban populations of the world; from 1,300 m to 2,100 m the vegetation consists of forest trees and maquis; above this there is a desert zone of lava and ashes, snow-covered 9 months of the year; the solar power station *Eurhelios* is on the S slope of Etna, where the sun shines for 3,000 hours each year on average.

Eton, town in Berkshire, England. See Windsor.

Etosha *i-tō'sha*, national park in N Namibia, SW Africa; area 22,270 sq km; established in 1958; encloses the Etosha Pan, a salt-water-filled depression with no outlets.

Ettelbruck *e'tel-brook*, 49 51N 6 06E, pop(1981) 6,044, commercial and tourist town in Diekirch canton, Diekirch, central Luxembourg; 30 km N of Luxembourg; an important rail and road junction at the meeting of three valleys located at the entry to the Ardennes.

Etterbeek *e'tur-bayk*, 50 50N 4 23E, pop(1982) 44,040, town in Brussel dist, Brabant prov, Belgium; an E suburb of Bruxelles.

Eua *ay-oo'ah*, 21 23S 174 55W, island of the Tongatapu group, S Tonga, S Pacific, 40 km SE of Tongatapu; area 87.4 sq km; pop(1984) 4,017; main town 'Ohonua.

Euboea, nome (dept) and island of Greece. See Évvoia.

Euclid *yoo'klid*, 41 34N 81 32W, pop(1980) 59,999, town in Cuyahoga county, NE Ohio, United States; a NE suburb of Cleveland on L Erie.

Eugene *yoo-jeen'*, 44 05N 123 04W, pop(1980) 105,624, capital of Lane county, W Oregon, United States; on the Willamette river, 97 km S of Salem; founded in 1851; university (1872); railway; airfield.

Eungella *yoon-gel'a*, national park in E Queensland, NE Australia; W of Mackay; area 508 sq km; established in 1950; includes a unique tropical rainforest on top of the Clarke Mt range.

Eupen *u'pun*, 50 38N 6 02E, pop(1982) 16,788, town in Verviers dist, E Liège prov, Belgium, S of Aachen and close to the W German frontier; principal town in the German-speaking part of Belgium; a popular health resort (Kneipp water-cure) and holiday centre; Dam of Eupen provides the largest artificial lake in Belgium;

many of the people are descended from French refugees after the Peace of Luneville; railway; economy: textiles, man-made fibres, tourism, cables and wires; monument: St Nicholas church (1727); event: annual carnival (begins first Sunday after 11 Nov).

Euphrates *yoo-fray'teez*, AL FURĀT *el foo-rat'* (Arab), FIRAT *fi'rat* (Turk), largest river in W Asia; length 2,735 km; formed by the confluence of the Kara and Murat rivers, E central Turkey; the Kara or W Euphrates rises in the Kargapazarıı Dağiı, 22 km N of Erzurum, then flows 456 km SW to its junction with the Murat, 8 km NE of Keban; the Murat rises in the mountains of E Turkey, 64 km SW of Büyük Ağrıı Dağiı (Mt Ararat); the combined streams flow generally S to the Syrian border, then SE through the Syrian desert past Ar Raqqah and Dayr az Zawr, crossing into Iraq near Abū Kamāl; it then flows SE through Iraq past Al Fullūjah, Karbalā' and As Samawah; at Al Qurnah, 64 km NW of Al Basrah, it unites with the Tigris to form the Shatt al'Arab, a 192-km stretch of the joint stream which flows into the Arabian Gulf; it has few tributaries and is navigable for shallow-draft vessels as far as Hīt; in its upper course the Euphrates flows swiftly through deep canyons and narrow gorges; it is used extensively for irrigation in Syria; the river's lower course supplies water to Iraq's date plantations through a system of canals (some connecting the Euphrates with the Tigris) and barrages; between Hindīya and As Samawah in central Iraq the Euphrates splits into 2 channels, Shatt al Hindīya and the Shatt al Ḥillah; the lower Tigris and Euphrates drainage basins water Mesopotamia, birthplace of ancient civilizations; the remains of ancient cities such as Babylon, Erech, Larsa, and Borsippa can be found along the present or former banks.

Eure *œrr*, dept in Haute-Normandie region of NW France, comprising 3 arrond, 40 cantons and 676 communes; pop(1982) 462,323; area 6,040 sq km; crossed in the NE by the R Seine; it is flat, fertile and well-wooded; capital Évreux, chief towns Les Andelys and Louviers; the Parc de Brotonne regional nature park lies partly within the dept.

Eure, river in NW France rising in the Collines du Perches (Perche Hills) SW of La Ferté-Vidame in Orne dept; flows ESE through Eure-et-Loire dept to Chartres and then N to meet the R Seine above Pont-de l'Arche; length 225 km; tributaries Avre and Iton rivers.

Eure-et-Loir, dept in Centre region of central France, in the fertile dist of Beauce; comprises 4 arrond, 29 cantons and 402 communes, pop(1982) 362,813; area 5,880 sq km; watered by the Eure and Loir rivers; generally open and flat, except for the low Collines de Beauce and the Collines du Perche, running E-W across it from the hills of Orléans; capital Chartres, other towns include Châteaudun and Dreux, all traffic routes converge on Chartres; there is a 12-17th-c château at Maintenon.

Europa, Picos de *pee'kos THay yoo-ro'pa*, highest range of the Cordillera Cantabrica, in the provs of Santander, León and Asturias, N Spain, rising to 2,570 m at Pico Tesorero; divided into 3 massifs by the rivers Sella, Cares, Duje and Deva; the western mountain mass is known as the Massif of Cornion (2,596 m), the central one as the Massif of the Urrieles and the eastern one as the Massif of Andara (2,441 m); noted for mountaineering, game hunting and fishing.

Europe *yoo'rop*, after Australia, the 2nd smallest continent, forming an extensive peninsula of the eurasian landmass, occupying c.8% of the earth's surface; area including European USSR c.10.5 mn sq km; bounded N and NE by the Arctic Ocean, NW and W by the Atlantic Ocean, S by the Mediterranean Sea and E by Asia beyond the Uralsk'iy Khrebet (Ural Mts); supports over 25% of the pop of the world; politically divided into 32 states (including the Vatican City, Andorra, Monaco and San Marino); major rivers include the Danube, Rhine, Rhône, Loire and Tagus; major mountain systems include the Alps rising to 4,807 m at Mont Blanc and the Pyrénées rising to 3,404 m at Pico de Aneto; cities with a pop in excess of one million include London, Paris, Moskva (Moscow), Leningrad, Madrid, Berlin, Roma (Rome), Birmingham, Manchester, Kiyev (Kiev), Athinai (Athens), Budapest, Bucureşti (Bucharest), Tashkent and Barcelona.

Europort, major European port facility in the Netherlands. See Rotterdam.

Evanston, 42 03N 87 41W, pop(1980) 73,706, city in Cook county, NE Illinois, United States; residential suburb on L Michigan, 24 km N of Chicago; university (1851); railway.

Evansville, 37 58N 87 35W, pop(1980) 130,496, county seat of Vanderburgh county, SW Indiana, United States; on the Ohio river, 46 km ENE of its junction with the R Wabash; university (1965); railway; economy: chemicals, plastics, furniture, refrigerators.

Ev'erest, Mount, SAGARMATHA (Nepali), QOMOLANGMA FENG *chō-me-lung'ma* (Chin), 27 59N 95 26W, mountain peak lying on the border between Nepal and the Tibet region of the People's Republic of China, in the Himalayas of central Asia; at 8,848 m, this is the highest point above sea-level in the world; named after Sir George Everest (1790-1866), who was surveyor-general of India; following attempts in 1921 and 1922, Mallory and Irvine, 2 members of the 1924 British Expedition, climbed beyond 8,534 m but failed to return; in 1952 a Swiss expedition reached 8,599 m; the peak was first reached on 28 May 1953, when Sir Edmund Hillary and Sherpa Tenzing Norkay of Nepal reached the summit in a British expedition under Col John Hunt; claimed by China; in 1952 the Chinese banned the name Everest in favour of Qomolangma Feng ('sacred mother of waters').

Everett, 42 24N 71 04W, pop(1980) 37,195, town in Middlesex county, E Massachusetts, United States; 5 km N of Boston; economy: steel, electrical goods, chemicals, printing.

Everett, 47 59N 122 12W, pop(1980) 54,413, port capital of Snohomish county, NW Washington, United States; on Puget Sound, 40 km N of Seattle, at the mouth of the Snohomish river; railway.

Everglades, S Florida, United States; swampy, subtropical region, length c.160 km, width 80-120 km, area approx 12,950 sq km; covers most of the Florida peninsula S of L Okeechobee; consists of saw grass savannahs and water dotted by clumps of trees; in an area of heavy rainfall only a few metres above sea-level; drainage and reclamation schemes, including thousands of km of canals and ditches, have made a large amount of land productive, mostly in citrus fruits and sugar; parts are heavily wooded with cypress and mangrove; part of the S Everglades judged unfit for cultivation is now in the Everglades National Park (area 5,668 sq km, established in 1947); the park is situated in the S of the Florida peninsula and includes much of Florida Bay, with its many keys.

Evesham *eev'shem*, 52 06N 1 56W, pop(1981) 15,280, town in Wychavon dist, Hereford and Worcester, W central England; in the Vale of Evesham in a fruit and vegetable-growing area; railway; economy: foodstuffs, engineering.

Évora *ay'voo-ra*, fertile lowland dist in SE central Portugal, part of Alto Alentejo prov; area 7,393 sq km; pop(1981) 180,277; bounded on E by Spain; divided into 14 councils and 77 parishes; economy: textiles and carpets, timber, cork, olives, rice, fruit, wine and wheat; minerals: antimony, arsenic, copper, iron, feldspar, quartz; airfield at Évora; main towns at Évora, Estremoz and Vila Vicosa.

Évora, EBORA OR LIBERALITAS JULIA (Lat), 38 33N 7 57W, pop(1981) 34,100, ancient walled market town and capital of Évora dist, S Portugal; 112 km ESE of Lisboa; agricultural centre; railway; airfield; economy: carpets, wool, cork; monuments: early Gothic cathedral (1186); archbishop's palace; Roman temple of Diana where the 1974 revolution was planned; 15th-c church of the Loios; 16th-c Moorish and 'Manueline' Casa Cordovil and the old university (1551); events include: São João fair at the end of June, the largest fair in S Portugal with folk events.

Évreux *ay-vrœ*, CIVITAS EBUROVICUM (anc), 49 00N 1 08E, pop(1982) 48,653, capital of Eure dept, Haute-Normandie region, NW France; in the fertile Iton valley; railway; economy: textiles, rubber goods, chemicals; monuments: cathedral of Notre-Dame, old Bishop's Palace (15th-c), former Benedictine abbey church of St-Taurin with a Romanesque arcade.

Evritanía *ayv-ri-ta-nee'a*, mountainous nome (dept) of Sterea Ellás-Évvoia region, Greece; pop(1981) 26,182; area 1,869 sq km; capital Karpenísion.

Évros *ayv'ros*, E nome (dept) of Thraki region, NE Greece, on the Turkish and Bulgarian borders; pop(1981) 148,486; area 4,242 sq km; capital Alexandroúpolis; produces wheat, tobacco and cotton.

Évry *ay-vree*, 48 34N 2 36E, pop(1982) 29,578, capital of Essonne dept, Ile-de-France region, N central France; 34 km S of Paris.

Évvoia *ay'vi-a*, EUBOEA *yoo-bee'a* (ENG), NEGROPON' (Ital), nome (dept) of Sterea Ellás-Évvoia region, Greece; pop(1981) 188,410; area 4,167 sq km; capital Khalkís.

Évvoia, 2nd largest Greek island, in the Aegean Sea, separated from the mainland of Greece by a narrow channel only 60 m wide at its narrowest point; area 3,655 sq km; length 144 km; length of coastline 678 km; rises to 1,744 m; with the N Sporádhes it forms a nome (dept) of Sterea Ellás-Évvoia region; pop(1981) 185,626; capital Khalkís; chief towns Istiáia, Kími, and Káristos; in recent years the coastal towns and villages have developed into tourist resorts; produces olives, grapes, cereals, sheep and goats.

Exe *eks*, river in Somerset and Devon, SW England; rises on Exmoor and flows 88 km SE and S past Exeter to meet the English Channel at Exmouth.

Exeter *ek'set-er*, ISCA DAMNONIORUM (anc), 50 43N 3 31W, pop(1981) 91,938, county town in Exeter dist, Devonshire, SW England; on the R Exe, 70 km NE of Plymouth; founded by the Romans in the 1st century AD; stone wall erected in 3rd century against Saxon intrusion and subsequent Danish invasions; port status partially restored by the construction of England's first ship canal in 1560; W headquarters of Royalist forces during civil war; university (1955); railway; airfield; economy: agricultural trade, textiles, leather goods, metal products, pharmaceuticals, wood products; monuments: 12th-c cathedral, 12th-c guildhall, maritime museum.

Exmoor, national park in Somerset and Devon, England; area 686 sq km; established in 1954; occupies the coastline between Minehead and Combe Martin Bay; Brendon Hills (E); information centres are located at Lynmouth, County Gate and Dulverton.

Exmouth *eks'muth*, 50 37N 3 25W, pop(1981) 28,661, resort town in Teignbridge dist, Devonshire, SW England; on the R Exe, 15 km SE of Exeter; centre for recreational sailing; railway; economy: engineering.

Extremadura or **Estremadura** *ays-* or *eks-tray-mah-doo'rah*, autonomous region of W Spain on the Portuguese frontier, comprising the provs of Badajoz and Cáceres; pop(1981) 1,064,968; area, 41,602 sq km; a western continuation of the central plateau (Meseta) deeply cut by the R Tagus and R Guadiana, bounded to the N by the Sierra de Gata (1,735 m) and Sierra de Gredos (2,592 m); the region is largely dry and covered with stony moorland grazed by merino sheep; pig-farming is common in the oak forests and, in the valleys, vines, figs, olives and almonds are grown; with the help of irrigation wheat-growing has been extended in the Lower (Baja) Extremadura; in recent years the building of many dams to produce hydroelectric power and the construction of over 350 km of irrigation channels has resulted in the development of industrial plants and some 380 municipalities.

Exuma and Cays *ek-soo'mu*, island group in the central Bahamas, SE of Andros I; the group extends approx 224 km NW-SE and includes Great Exuma I, Little Exuma I, and numerous cays; pop(1980) 3,672; area 290 sq km; chief town George Town (Great Exuma I); airfields at George Town and Staniel Cay.

Eyasi, Lake *e-yah'see*, lake in N Tanzania, E Africa; 153 km W of Arusha; 70 km long and 15 km wide; the fossil bones of *Africanthropus njarasensis* were discovered here in 1935.

Eyre Lakes *ayr*, dry salt lakes in NE South Australia; includes Lake Eyre North (145 km long and 64 km wide, with an area of 7,692 sq km) and Lake Eyre South (61 km long and 26 km wide with an area of 1,191 sq km); Lake Eyre North is normally a shallow pan of glistening white salt; it has filled with water only 3 times since European discovery and stands at 15 m below mean sea-level; it is fed by a series of intermittently flowing rivers, including the Finke, the Diamantina and Cooper Creek; the site of Donald Campbell's world land speed record in 1964 in the *Bluebird Proteus*.

F

Fada N'Gourma *fa'dang goor'ma*, 12 10N 0 30E, town in Burkina, W Africa; 200 km E of Ouagadougou; to the SE on the border with Ghana is the Arly Wildlife Sanctuary (area 760 sq km, established in 1954); to the E is the Burkina section of the W National Park.

Færøerne *faru'*, FAEROE ISLANDS or FAROE ISLANDS *fa'rō*, 62 00N 7 00W, a group of 22 sparsely vegetated volcanic islands in the N Atlantic between Iceland and the Shetland Is; a self-governing region of Denmark since 1948; area 1,399 sq km; pop(1981) 44,070, capital Tórshavn; settled by Norse in the 8th century, it become part of the kingdom of Norway in the 11th century; passed to Denmark in 1380; parliament (*Lagting*), restored in 1852, consists of 32 members; Stromo and Ostero are the largest islands; the Germanic language is similar to Icelandic; economy: export of frozen filleted and salted fish; craft manufactures.

Faetano *fah-ye-tah'no*, castle (dist) in the Republic of San Marino, central Italy; area 7.75 sq km; pop(1980) 778; population density in 1980 was 100 inhabitants per sq km.

Făgăraș *fa-ga-rash'*, 45 50N 24 59E, pop(1983) 39,666, town in Brașov county, central Romania; on R Olt, between Sibiu (W) and Brașov (E); established in the 12th century; railway; economy: fertilizers, plastics.

Fagatogo *fang'a-tōng ō*, 14 17S 140 41W, capital of American Samoa, on the E coast of Tutuila I, in the S Pacific Ocean.

Fagnano, Lago *fag-na'nō*, LAGO CAMI or LAGO YEHUIN (Chile), lake in S part of main island of Tierra del Fuego; width 8 km; mostly in SW of Argentina's Tierra del Fuego national territory, with a small W part in SE Tierra del Fuego prov, Magallanes y la Antarctica Chilena region, Chile; area 593 sq km; length 96 km.

Fahaheel, 29 10N 48 10E, pop(1980) 42,170, town on the Arabian Gulf, E Kuwait; 5 km E of Al Aḩmadī; economy: oil, natural gas.

Faial or **Ilha do Faial** *fi-ahl'* ('beech island'), 38 35N 28 42W, the most westerly island in the central group of the Azores, Horta dist, named after the scrub tree *Myrica faya* which resembles the local beech; the island measures 172 sq km in area and is 22 km long by up to 15 km wide; the highest point is Pico Gordo, a volcano that has been quiescent since 1672; the W tip of the island is formed by the Volcão dos Capelinhos, a submarine volcano which erupted in 1957, burying the village of Comprido; frequent earthquakes, the worst being in 1759-60, 1862, 1926, 1958 and 1980; economy: crafts, farming, a whaling industry now in decline; the fortified main town of Horta is the meeting place of the Parliament of the Azores; the home (1486-1490) of the Nuremburg cosmographer Martin Behaim; airport.

Failsworth *faylz'werth*, 53 31N 2 09W, pop(1981) 20,951, town in Greater Manchester, NW England; 7 km NE of Manchester; railway; economy: electrical goods, engineering, textiles, chemicals, aircraft parts.

Fair' Lawn, 40 56N 74 08W, pop(1980) 32,229, town in Bergen county, NE New Jersey, United States; 5 km ENE of Paterson.

Fair'banks, 64 50N 147 50W, pop(1980) 22,645, city in North Star borough, central Alaska; terminus of the Alaska railway and highway; founded in 1902 after the discovery of gold; university (1922); economy: mining, oilfield services.

Fairborn, 39 49N 84 02W, pop(1980) 29,702, town in Greene county, W Ohio, United States; 16 km NE of Dayton; railway.

Fairfield, 38 15N 122 03W, pop(1980) 58,099, city in Solano county, W California, United States; 24 km NE of Vallejo; adjoins the town of Suisun to the S; railway.

Fairfield, 41 09N 73 15W, pop(1980) 54,849, summer resort town in Fairfield county, SW Connecticut, United States; port on Long Island Sound, 7 km SW of Bridgeport; university (1942); railway; economy: chemicals, engineering; event: Dogwood festival (May).

Fairfield, 39 21N 84 34W, pop(1980) 30,777, town in Butler county, SW Ohio, United States; on R Great Miami, 29 km N of Cincinnati.

Faisalabad *fī-sal-a-bad'*, LYALLPUR, 31 25N 73 09E, pop(1981) 1,092,000, city in Punjab prov, Pakistan; W of Lahore, in an important cotton and wheat growing region; railway; economy: grain, ghee (clarified butter), textiles, flour, soap, chemicals and textile machinery.

Faiyûm, El *fī-yoom'*, AL-FAYUM, 29 19N 30 50E, pop(1976) 167,081, capital of El Faiyûm governorate, Egypt; 90 km SW of Cairo; railway; El Faiyûm was a royal seat in the 12th Pharaonic dynasty (1991-1785 BC); monuments: pyramids of Amenmhet III and Senusertt II.

Fakaofo *fa-kow'fō*, 9 30S 171 15W, low lying atoll of Tokelau, S Pacific Ocean, 432 km N of Western Samoa; area 2.63 sq km; pop(1981) 650.

Falcón *fal-kōn'*, state in NW Venezuela; on the Gulf of Venezuela (NW); consists of N outliers of Andean spurs and coastal lowlands; in the extreme N the Paraguaná Peninsula juts into the Caribbean, pop(1980) 507,899; area 24,790 sq km; capital Coro.

Falkirk, 56 00N 3 48W, pop(1981) 36,880, town in Falkirk dist, Central region, central Scotland; 37 km W of Edinburgh; railway; economy: concrete, casting, printing, coach building; monuments: Falkirk museum, with a display of the region's archaeological history; near Falkirk is a castle of the Roman Antonine Wall.

Falkland Islands *fawk'land*, ISLAS MALVINAS *ee'las mal-vee'nas* (Sp), British Crown Colony in the S Atlantic about 650 km E by N of the Strait of Magellan, situated between 51° and 53° S and between 57° and 62° W. The colony consists of East Falkland and West Falkland, with over 200 small islands covering an area of approx 12,170 sq km; timezone GMT −4; pop(1980) 1,813, of whom 1,000 live in the capital town of Stanley on East Falkland; most of the islanders are of British descent; in the Camp (the countryside other than Stanley) the largest settlement is at Goose Green where there are about 100 residents; the Beauchene Is to the S of the Falkland Is have been designated a bird sanctuary and wildlife and seal reserve; the 3 main religious denominations represented are Anglican, Roman Catholic and United Free Church; there is an airport at Mt Pleasant near Stanley with air links to the UK and to local grass or beach airstrips.

Physical description. The coastline is deeply indented with many good anchorages; the relief is hilly except in Lafonia (the S half of East Falkland), rising to 705 m at Mt Usborne on East Falkland and 700 m at Mt Adam on West Falkland; small streams and lakes are numerous throughout the treeless, peat-covered moorland landscape. West Falkland is separated from East Falkland by the Falkland Sound.

Climate. The islands are characterized by strong winds (a mean annual windspeed of 17 knots), a narrow temperature range (from 19°C in Jan to 2°C in July) and a comparatively low annual rainfall (635 mm) that is fairly evenly distributed throughout the year.

History, government and constitution. The Falkland Is appear on Spanish maps of the early 16th century as the Islas do Sanson. They were seen by several early navigators including, in 1689-90, Capt John Strong, who named the Falkland Sound after Viscount Falkland. De Bougainville established a French settlement from St Malo here in 1764, giving the islands the name Îles Malouines after the fishermen of St Malo who frequently visited the S Atlantic. The French yielded their settlement to the Spanish in 1767 but Britain had already established a base here in 1765. Spain relaxed its hold over the Falkland Is in 1806. In 1820 the islands were occupied in the name of the Rep of Buenos Aires but Britain asserted her possession in 1833. Formal annexation of the Falkland Is and its Dependencies took place in 1908 and 1917. The whole area has been claimed since independence by Argentina. The Falkland Is and its Dependencies were invaded by Argentine military forces in April 1982. A British Task Force was immediately dispatched and, following a fierce conflict in which over 1,000 British and Argentine lives were lost, 12,000 Argentine troops surrendered and the islands were returned to British rule. External affairs and defence are the responsibility of the British Government which appoints Civil and Military Commissioners. Internal affairs are governed by executive and legislative councils, the latter having a majority of elected members. Elected councillors represent 6 constituencies, 3 in Camp and 3 in Stanley. The Civil Commissioner is the Chairman of Executive Council and the President at Legislative Council meetings. The present Constitution came into force in Nov 1977. In Jan 1983 the Falkland Is Government Office was established in London to provide a two-way information service and to assist with development.

Economy. Agriculture is limited to a small area of oats grown for hay and to sheep farming for wool. There are no minerals or manufacturing industries. The chief imports are provisions, alcoholic beverages, timber, clothing and hardware. The Falklands Islands Trading Company, formed in 1851, is the largest single landowner and trading company.

Falkland Sound, an arm of the S Atlantic that separates the islands of West and East Falkland, Falkland Is, extending NE for about 80 km; up to 30 km wide.

Fall River, 41 43N 71 10W, pop(1980) 92,574, town in Bristol county, SE Massachusetts, United States; seaport at the mouth of the Taunton river, 19 km NW of New Bedford; established in 1656; railway; economy: cotton, rubber, paper, clothing; event: arts festival in June.

Falmouth *fal'muth*, 50 08N 5 04W, pop(1981) 18,548, port town linked with Penryn in Carrick dist, Cornwall, SW England; centre for recreational sailing 12 km S of Truro on Falmouth Bay; railway; economy: transport equipment, engineering.

Falster *fahl'stur*, Danish island in Baltic Sea, S of Sjælland (Zealand) and SW of Møn I, separated from S Sjælland by Storstrøm Strait; area 512 sq km; length 45 km; rises to 44 m; 24 km wide in the N, narrowing to 5 km wide in the S; chief towns Nykøbing, Stubbekøbing; S tip (Gedser Odde) is the most southerly point in Denmark; administered by Storstrøm county; beautiful sandy beaches on the E coast.

Fălticeni *fal-tee-chayn'*, 47 27N 26 20E, pop(1983) 25,829, town in Suceava county, N Romania; 104 km WNW of Iaşi; founded in the 18th century; former residence of the first ruler of Moldavia; railway terminus; economy: wood work, tanning.

Falun', 60 37N 15 40E, pop(1982) 51,082, manufacturing town and capital of Kopparberg county, central Sweden; 208 km NW of Stockholm; railway; former copper-mining centre; received municipal charter 1641.

Famagusta *fa-ma-goos'ta*, dist in E Cyprus; area 1,970 sq km; pop(1973) 123,856; capital Famagusta; at present this area is largely under Turkish occupation.

Famagusta, 35 07N 33 57E, pop(1973) 38,960, capital town of Famagusta dist, E Cyprus, on Famagusta Bay; occupies the site of ancient Arsinoë, built in the 3rd century BC by Ptolemy II; strongly fortified by the Venetians in the 15th and 16th centuries; Famagusta was the island's chief port prior to the 1974 coup and Turkish invasion; it is now under Turkish occupation and has been declared by the government of Cyprus closed to shipping and an illegal port of entry; monuments: old town wall (defended by 15 bastions); 14th-c citadel; ruins of the church of St George of the Latins (late 13th-c); cathedral of St Nicholas (early 14th-c French Gothic).

Fan si Pan *fan see pan*, 22 19N 103 46E, the highest mountain in Vietnam, rising to 3,143 m SW of Lao Cai, N Vietnam.

Farāh *fu'ra*, prov in W Afghanistan; bounded to the W by Iran; pop(1984e) 254,820; area 47,788 sq km; capital Farāh; crossed from NE to SW by the R Farāh; S section of prov is desert.

Farāh, FARARUD, 32 23N 62 08E, pop(1984e) 20,605, capital of Farāh prov, W Afghanistan; located S of Herāt and NW of Kandahār; lies in the N tongue of the Khash Desert, on the R Farāh; airfield; market for products of the surrounding agricultural region.

Faranah *fa-ra-na'*, 10 03N 10 45W, town in central Guinea, W Africa; 90 km SSE of Dabola.

Fareham, 50 51N 1 10W, pop(1981) 56,820, town linked with Porchester in Fareham dist, Hampshire, S England; 9 km NW of Portsmouth; railway; economy: engineering, transport equipment, scientific instruments.

Farewell, Cape, Greenland. See Farvel, Kap.

Fargo, 46 53N 96 48W, pop(1980) 61,383, county seat of Cass county, SE North Dakota, United States; a port on the Red river, 300 km E of Bismarck; largest city in North Dakota; established in 1871; university (1890); railway; economy: trade and distribution centre in wheat and livestock region; monument: Bonanzaville, USA; event: Pioneer Days (Aug).

Faridpur *fu-reed'poor*, region in S central Bangladesh; includes Faridpur Sadar, Goalanda, Gopalganj, Madaripur and Sariatpur districts; crossed by the Ganges river; pop(1981) 4,764,000; area 6,880 sq km; capital Faridpur.

Faridpur, 23 29N 89 31E, pop(1981) 66,579, capital of Faridpur Sadar dist and Faridpur region, S central Bangladesh; close to the S bank of the Ganges, 50 km SW of Dhākā; has a noted Muslim shrine; railway; economy: rice, jute, oilseed.

Farim', 12 30N 15 09W, pop(1979) 4,468, town in N Guinea-Bissau, W Africa; on the R Cacheu, NE of Bissau.

Farmington, 36 44N 108 12W, pop(1980) 31,222, town in San Juan county, NW New Mexico, United States; at the confluence of the San Juan, Animas and La Plata rivers; railway; economy: trade centre in oil and farming region; monuments: Aztec Ruins national monument, Chaco Canyon national monument.

Farmington Hills or **Farmington**, 42 28N 83 23W, pop(1980) 58,056, residential town in Oakland county, SE Michigan, United States; 22 km SSW of Pontiac.

Farn'borough, 51 17N 0 46W, pop(1981) 48,294, town in Rushmoor dist, Hampshire, S England; N of Aldershot; air force base and aeronautical research centre; railway; economy: chemicals, electrical goods, scientific instruments; event: biennial air displays.

Farne Islands, THE STAPLES, a group of basaltic islets in the North Sea, 3 km NE of the mainland, Northumberland, NE England; a sanctuary for birds and Atlantic seals.

Farnham *fahr'nėm*, 51 13N 0 49W, pop(1981) 34,852, town in Waverley dist, Surrey, SE England; part of Aldershot urban area; on the R Wey, 15 km WSW of Guildford; railway; economy: engineering, timber.

Farnworth, 53 33N 2 24W, pop(1981) 26,148, town in Salford borough, Greater Manchester, NW England; 4 km SE of Bolton; railway; economy: textiles, engineering, coal.

Faro, national park in Nord prov, Cameroon, W Africa; area 3,300 sq km; established in 1980.

Faro *fa'roo*, dist in S Portugal, co-extensive with the prov of Algarve; area 5,072 sq km; pop(1981) 323,534; divided into 16 councils and 71 parishes; economy: meat, milk, eggs, almonds, olives, figs, horticulture, wine, vegetables, cork, timber; minerals: antimony, barium, copper, manganese, titanium; airport at Faro and airfields at Azeda-Castro Marim, Lagos and Portimão.

Faro, 37 02N 7 55W, pop(1981) 28,200, industrial seaport and capital of Faro dist, S Portugal; on the S coast, 219 km SSE of Lisboa; the port handles wine, cork, fish and fruit; focal point of Algarve tourism; railway; airport; monuments: Renaissance cathedral; churches of the Carmo (Baroque) and of Santo Antonio do Alto (1754); events: Senhora do Carmo fair at the end of July with a display of folk arts and crafts and Santa Iria fair at the end of Aug.

Fårö *fō'ru*, 57 56N 19 10E, Swedish island in Baltic Sea, off SE coast of Sweden, NE of Gotland I, separated from Gotland I by 3 km wide Fårösund, 56 km NE of Visby; area 114 sq km; length 16 km; width 3-13 km; has an indented coastline; administered by Gotland county.

Fārs *fars*, mountainous prov in SW Iran; pop(1982) 2,035,582; area 133,298 sq km; capital Shīrāz.

Farvel, Kap *kap fahr-vel'*, UUMMANNARSUAQ (Esk), CAPE FAREWELL (Eng), 59 45N 44 00W, southernmost tip of Greenland.

Farwaniya, 29 20N 48 00E, pop(1980) 57,715, S suburb of Al Kuwayt (Kuwait City), State of Kuwait, Arabian peninsula; situated just N of Kuwait International Airport.

Fāryab *far'yab*, FARIAB, prov in N Afghanistan; bounded to the N and NW by the USSR; pop(1984e) 588,452; area 22,279 sq km; bisected by the N-flowing Qausar Andkhua river; capital is Meymaneh, which lies on the main road linking Herāt in the SW with Mazār-e Sharif in the NE.

Fatick *fa'teek*, region in W Senegal, W Africa; part of Sine Saloum region until 1984; capital Fatick.

Fátima *fa'ti-ma*, 39 37N 8 38W, pop(1981) 6,500, pilgrimage town, Santarém dist, central Portugal, where three peasant children claimed to have seen the 'Virgin of the Rosary' in 1917, 22 km SE of Leiria; pilgrimages take place from May to Oct on 12th-13th of each month; monuments: the chapel built on the spot where the Virgin appeared and the huge neo-classical Basilica begun in 1928.

Fatshan, town in Guangdong prov, SE China. See Foshan.

Faversham, 51 20N 0 53E, pop(1981) 15,985, port and market town in Swale dist, Kent, SE England; NW of Canterbury, on the R Swale; railway; economy: engineering; monument: church of St Mary of Charity.

Fāw, Al *fa'ō*, FAO, 29 55N 48 26E, oil port in Al Basrah governorate, SE Iraq; 80 km SE of Al Basrah, on the Shatt al'Arab just above its mouth on the Arabian Gulf.

Faw'ley, 50 49N 1 20W, pop(1981) 12,585, town in New Forest dist, Hampshire, S England; on Southampton Water, 16 km S of Southampton.

Faya', LARGEAU *lar-zhō'*, 17 58N 19 06E, capital of Borkou-Ennedi Tibesti prefecture, N Chad, N central Africa; 770 km NE of N'Djamena; a military outpost and oasis in SE Sahara; airfield.

Fayetteville *fa-yet'vil*, 36 04N 94 10W, pop(1980) 36,608, county seat of Washington county, NW Arkansas, United States; 80 km N of Fort Smith; university (1871); railway; economy: farm trade centre and summer mountain resort.

Fayetteville, 35 03N 78 53W, pop(1980) 59,507, county seat of Cumberland county, S central North Carolina, United States; on the Cape Fear river, 80 km S of Raleigh; founded by Scottish settlers in 1739; university (1867); Fort Bragg military reservation lies to the W; railway; economy: textiles, timber, machinery.

Fder'ik, FORT GOURAUD (Fr), 22 40N 12 41W, capital of Tiris Zemmour region, N Mauritania, NW Africa; 240 km N of Atar, on the Route du Mauritanie; railway terminus; airfield.

Feathertop, Mount, 36 53S 147 10E, mountain in E central Victoria, Australia; rising to 1,922 m in the Australian Alps.

Fécamp *fay-kãp*, 49 45N 0 23E, pop(1982) 23,000, port in Seine-Maritime dept, Haute-Normandie, NW France; on the coast of the English Channel between Dieppe and Le Havre; the principal cod-fishing port of France; the first Bénédictine liqueur made from local herbs was produced here in 1510; Guy de Maupassant lived in the town.

Federally Administered Tribal Areas, an area in NW Pakistan; pop(1981) 2,199,000; area 27,220 sq km; bounded N and W by Afghanistan.

Fehmarn *fay'marn*, island in Schleswig-Holstein prov, W Germany; in W Baltic Sea, separated from the mainland by Fehmarnsund (Fehmarn Sound), on NW side of entrance to Mecklenburger Bucht (Bay of Mecklenburg); area 185.3 sq km.

Feira de Santana *fay'ra day san-ta'na*, 12 17S 38 53W, pop(1980) 227,004, town in Bahia state, Nordeste region, NE Brazil; NW of Salvador; railway; economy: beans, maize, cattle; the centre of a cattle breeding and trading area, its Monday market, the Feira do Couro, is said to be the largest in Brazil.

Fejér *fe-yeer*, county in W central Hungary; pop(1984e) 423,000; area 4,374 sq km; bounded E by R Danube with L Velence at its centre; R Sárviz formed by the confluence of Sed and Gaja rivers W of the county capital is paralleled by a canal, both of which drain S to the Danube; capital Székesfehérvár; economy: fruit, grain, wine, livestock, bauxite mining.

Feldberg *felt'berk*, 47 51N 8 02E, mountain in SW Baden-Württemberg prov, W Germany; highest peak in the Schwarzwald (Black Forest), SE of Freiburg; height 1,493 m; noted winter sports resort; Todtnau is at its SW foot.

Feldberg, Great, mountain in W Germany. See Großer Feldberg.

Feldkirch *felt'keerKH*, 47 15N 9 38E, pop(1981) 23,745, capital of Feldkirch dist, Vorarlberg, W Austria, on the R Ill; bishopric; road and rail junction; monument: 12th-c Schattenburg on a rocky hill to the E of the town; event: wine festival in June.

Felixstowe *fee'lik-stō*, 51 58N 1 20E, pop(1981) 24,461, port town and resort in Suffolk Coastal dist, Suffolk, E England; on the North Sea coast, 17 km SE of Ipswich; railway; ferries to Gothenburg, Rotterdam and Zeebrugge; container terminals.

Fel'ling, 54 57N 1 33W, pop(1981) 36,319, town in Gateshead borough, Tyne and Wear, NE England; in Tyneside urban area; S of R Tyne and E of Gateshead.

Femunden *fay'moon-den*, FEMUNDSJÖ, L FEMUND *fay'moon* (Eng), lake in NE Hedmark county, S central Norway, near Swedish border, 32 km SE of Røros; area 201 sq km; length 67 km; drained S by the R Trysilelva, upper course of R Klarålven.

Fens, The or **Fen Country**, flat marshy land surrounding the Wash, in Lincolnshire, Norfolk, Suffolk and Cambridgeshire, E England; extends 112 km N-S and 6 km E-W; watered by the Witham, Welland, Nene and Ouse rivers; the Wash is a remnant of a larger bay of the North Sea that has become silted up by these rivers; the area has been artificially drained since Roman times, but after 1621 major reclamation was carried out under the guidance of the Dutch engineer, Cornelius Vermuyden; drainage was also carried out by the 5th Earl of Bedford after whom the parallel cuts of the Old and New Bedford rivers and the Bedford Level are named; in medieval times there were many important monasteries on 'islands' of dry land amidst the marshy Fens, ie at Medeshamstede (Peterborough), Ely, Crowland, Ramsey, etc; economy: market gardening, fruit, vegetables, grazing.

Ferkéssédougou *fer-kay-say-doo'goo*, dept in N Ivory Coast, W Africa; pop(1975) 90,423; area 17,728 sq km; the railway from Abidjan runs N through the dept; capital Ferkéssédougou; chief towns Kong, Niellé and Wangolodougou.

Fermanagh *fer-man'a*, FEAR MANACH (Gael), county in SW Northern Ireland; bounded NW, W, S and SE by the Republic of Ireland and NE by Co Tyrone; mainly hilly in the NE and SW, rising to 667 m in the very S with Cuilcagh; drained by the R Erne; Upper and Lower Lough Erne run SE-NW through the centre of the county; pop(1981) 51,008; area 1,676 sq km; county town

Enniskillen; economy: agriculture (potatoes); Fermanagh consists only of the district of Fermanagh: area 1,876 sq km; pop(198), 51,008.

Fernando de Magallanes *fayr-nan'dhō dhay ma-gayl-ya'nays*, national park in Magallanes region, S Chile; area 8,000 sq km; comprises a large number of islands; the park was established in 1969.

Fernando de Noronha *fer-nan'dō day no-ro'nya*, terr in Nordeste region, NE Brazil; pop(1980) 1,279; area 26 sq km; a small archipelago 500 km off the NE coast of Brazil; of volcanic origin, the island Fernando de Noronha rises to 321 m and has interesting wildlife; created in 1942, the terr is under military control and only one island (Fernando de Noronha) is inhabited; pop consists mainly of fishermen or civilians working for the military; the islands were discovered in 1503, and were used by pirates for a time; in 1738 the Portuguese built the Fort dos Remédios; remains of the fort still exist, as well as a deserted town nearby; the island was also used as a penal colony.

Fernando Póo, Equatorial Guinea. See Bioko.

Ferndale, 42 28N 83 08W, pop(1980) 26,227, residential town in Oakland county, SE Michigan, United States; 16 km N of Detroit.

Ferndown, 50 48N 1 55W, pop(1981) 24,160, town in Wimborne dist, Dorset, S England; 9 km N of Bournemouth.

Ferrara *fayr-rah'ra*, prov of Emilia-Romagna region, N Italy; pop(1981) 381,118; area 2,631 sq km; capital Ferrara.

Ferrara, 44 50N 11 38E, pop(1981) 149,453, ancient town and capital of Ferrara prov, Emilia-Romagna region, N Italy; 5 km S of the R Po; seat of the Council of Ferrara (1438) and of the Renaissance court of the 15th century; ceded to France (1797-1815); part of the kingdom of Sardinia in 1859; archbishopric; university (1391); railway; monuments: Castello Estense, the 4-towered moated castle of the Este family, begun in 1385 and partly rebuilt after 1554; cathedral of San Giorgio (1135); numerous fine palaces.

Ferrol, El or fully **El Ferrol de Caudillo** *cow-deel'yo*, 43 29N 8 15W, pop(1981) 91,764, old town in La Coruña prov, Galicia, NW Spain; sheltered in a bay, NE of La Coruña; the birthplace of General Franco; Spain's principal naval base on the Atlantic, with shipyards, docks and a Naval Academy; textile manufacture is also important.

Fertö, lake in Austria and Hungary. See Neusiedler See.

Fès or **Fez** *fez*, 34 05N 5 00W, pop(1982) 448,823, city in Fès prefecture, Centre-Nord prov, N central Morocco, N Africa; 240 km ENE of Casablanca; oldest of Morocco's 4 imperial cities; Old Fès (Fès Medina) founded in 808 by Moulay Idriss II whose shrine is still one of the holiest places in Morocco; the Karaouine mosque, which was first built during the 9th century, became famous as a Muslim university; New Fès (Fès Djedid) was founded in 1276 by the Merinade dynasty and includes the Sultan's palace (Dar el Makhzen); modern Fès (the Ville Nouvelle) is situated S of the railway; the city gave its name to a type of red felt hat worn by many Islamic followers; railway; economy: textiles, carpets, leather, soap.

Feteşti *fay-tesht'*, 44 22N 27 51E, pop(1983) 29,874, town in Ialomiţa county, SE Romania; situated E of Bucureşti on R Danube; railway junction; economy: fruit, agricultural trade.

Feyzābād *fi'ze-bad*, FAIZABAD, 37 05N 70 40E, pop(1984e) 9,973, capital of Badakhshān prov, N Afghanistan; lies on R Kokcha and is linked by road to Kānābād; airfield.

Fianarantsoa *fyan-ar-ant-soo'a* ('the town where good is learnt'), 21 27S 47 05E, pop(1978) 55,500, town in SE central Madagascar; 408 km S of Antananarivo in the uplands of the Massif de l'Isalo; chief town of a prov of the same name; founded in 1830 around a village called Ivoneha; formerly an important centre for French Catholic missionaries; there is a rail link to Mankara; economy: rice, tobacco, wine and brandy trade; monuments: Alakamisy-Ambohimaha rock carvings.

Fichtelberg *fik'tel-berk*, mountain in the Erzgebirge range, S of Karl-Marx-Stadt, on the frontier between E Germany and Czechoslovakia; height 1,214 m; the highest mountain in E Germany.

Fichtelgebirge *fiKH'tel-ge-beer-ge*, SMRČINY (Czech), horseshoe-shaped mountain range in NE Bayern (Bavaria) prov, W Germany; the rivers Main, Saale, Eger and Naab rise here; forms the watershed between the Elbe, Rhine and Danube rivers; highest peak Schneeberg (1,051 m); largely covered with fir forests, forming a link between the Erzgebirge and the Böhmerwald (Bohemian Forest).

Fier *fee-er'*, prov of SW Albania; area 1,191 sq km; pop(1980) 203,400; capital Fier.

Fier, 40 43N 19 34E, pop(1975) 28,000, agric centre and capital of Fier prov, S central Albania; 32 km W of Berat, between the Seman and Vijosë rivers, at the S edge of Myzeqe plain; railway; founded in 1877 as a Turkish state; economy: thermoelectric power plant, oil refinery; monument: there are ruins of ancient Apollonia (8 km W).

Fife, or KINGDOM OF FIFE, region in E Scotland; bounded by the Firth of Tay (N), the North Sea (E), the Firth of Forth (S), Central region (SW) and Tayside (W); a low lying region, drained by the Eden and Leven rivers; bounded W by the Lomond Hills; the coast has many small fishing ports such as Anstruther, St Monance, Pittenweem; there are oil, gas and chemical developments in the W at Mossmoran near Kirkcaldy; open-cast coal mining near Lochgelly and Cowdenbeath; much of the interior is farmland; pop(1981) 327,362; area 1,307 sq km; capital Glenrothes; major towns include Dunfermline, Cowdenbeath, Cupar and St Andrews; Fife is divided into 3 districts:

District	*area (sq km)*	*pop(1981)*
Dunfermline	301	122,898
Kirkcaldy	248	142,361
North-east Fife	758	62,103

Figueira da Foz *fee-gay'ee-ra da fozh*, 40 07N 8 54W, pop (1981) 12,800, fishing port and resort in Coimbra dist, central Portugal; at the mouth of the R Mondego, 45 km W of Coimbra; principal base of cod fisheries; manufacture of paper paste; railway; airfield; monuments: 17th-c tiled Paço da Figueira and the Santa Catarina observatory; events: São João festival at the end of June, with bullfights, folk events and midnight procession.

Figueras *fee-gay'ras*, 42 18N 2 58E, pop(1981) 30,532, town in Gerona prov, Cataluña, NE Spain; on the Ampurdan plain, 38 km N of Gerona; railway; economy: metal products, cereals, textiles.

Figura *feeg-yoo'ra*, 35 53N 14 32E, pop(1983e) 5,617, community on the main island of Malta, situated to the SE of Grand Harbour between Paola and Żabbar.

Fiji *fee'jee*, Melanesian island group in the SW Pacific Ocean, lying 4,450 km SW of Honolulu, 2,730 km NE of Sydney, Australia, and 1,770 km N of Auckland, New Zealand; area 18,333 sq km; coastline 1,129 km; timezone GMT +11; capital Suva; chief towns Lautoka, Ba, Labasa, Nadi, Nausori; pop(1981) 646,561; about 90% of the population lives on the 2 main islands of Viti Levu and Vanua Levu; about 90% of the pop is urban; indigenous Fijians, a mixture of Polynesian and Melanesian, comprise 44% of the population, 51% are Indian, 1% European, 1% Chinese, and the rest are mainly other Pacific islanders; native Fijians live throughout the country while the Indo-Fijians concentrate primarily near the urban centres and in the cane-producing centres of the 2 main islands; virtually all native Fijians are Christian (about 85% Methodist and 12% Roman Catholic); about 70% of the Indo-Fijians are Hindu, 25% Muslim, the remainder include Christians; English is the official language; most Fijians speak Bauan, a dialect of the indigenous Fijian language; Hindustani, a locally developed form of Hindi, is spoken by most Indians; the currency is the Fijian dollar; membership of

ADB, Colombo Plan, FAO, G-77, GATT, IBRD, ICAO, IDA, IFAD, IFC, ILO, IMF, INTELSAT, ISO, ITU, South Pacific Forum, UN, UPU, WFTU, WHO, WIPO, WMO, South Pacific Commission, South Pacific Bureau for Economic Cooperation, associate member of EEC, associate member of the Economic and Social Commission for Asia and the Pacific.

Physical description. The Fiji group of 844 islands and islets, about 100 of which are permanently inhabited, covers a land area of 18,333 sq km within a 320 km economic zone of 1,290,000 sq km. The main archipelago lies between 15° and 22° S and 177° E and 174° E. The island of Rotuma and its dependencies were added to the territory in 1881 and are geographically separate. They lie between 12° and 15° S and 175° and 180° E. The territory comprises the large islands of Viti Levu (10,429 sq km) and Vanua Levu (5,556 sq km), and numerous small islands situated mainly in the Lau and Yasawa groups and in the Koro Sea. Most of the larger islands are situated on one of the major earthquake belts of the world and are mainly composed of ancient volcanic and andesitic rock. They are generally mountainous and rugged with sharp peaks and crags, but extensive areas of flat land can be found where the rivers have formed deltas, and there are fertile plains around the coastline. The highest peak is Tomaniivi (Mt Victoria) (1,324 m) on Viti Levu. Chief rivers are the Rewa (navigable for 112 km), Sigatoka, and the Ba, all on Viti Levu. There are no active volcanoes but hot springs occur in isolated places. Most of the smaller islands consist wholly or partly of limestone and there is little vegetation. They generally rise steeply from the shore and have flat-topped profiles. The Great Sea Reef is an extensive coral reef stretching for 483 km along the W fringe of the archipelago. Coral reefs also surround most of the other islands. There is a marked contrast between the wet, windward side (SE) of the islands, covered with dense tropical forests, and the dry, mainly treeless, leeward side.

Climate. The prevailing trade winds blow from the E or SE throughout the greater part of the year. In the wet season, between Nov and April, winds are more variable and it is during these months that tropical cyclonic storms or hurricanes are more likely to develop. Temperatures average 23.2°C to 27.2°C, with extremes ranging from 17.2°C to 33.3°C, and diurnal range of temperature is about 6°C. Average temperature is generally 5° C lower in the mountainous interiors. Annual rainfall varies from 1,905 mm to 3,048 mm, the higher rainfall falling in the E and SE. The windward areas enjoy abundant rainfall, well distributed throughout the year. The leeward (NW) sides, however, have well defined wet and dry seasons. Here most of the rain falls during the hurricane season when the variable winds blow. Humidity on the wet windward slopes averages 74% and may reach saturation point.

History, government and constitution. Discovered by Tasman in 1643 and visited by Captain Cook in 1774, the islands were mainly occupied by sandalwood loggers, mutineers and shipwrecked men. Fiji became an independent state within the Commonwealth on 10 Oct 1970, after 96 years of British colonial rule. An independent republic was proclaimed in October 1987 following a military coup in May 1987. It has a parliamentary system of government. The bicameral parliament consists of a nominated senate and an elected house of representatives. There are 52 members in the house of representatives, 22 elected by the native Fijian community, 22 by the Fiji Indian community, and 8 by other voters. The senate has 22 members appointed for 6-year terms.

Economy. Fiji's economy is primarily agrarian. Some 2,430 sq km of land are in agricultural use. Sugar cane is the principal cash crop, grown mainly on small holdings by tenant farmers. It accounts for more than two-thirds of Fiji's export earnings and about one-quarter of the population depend on it directly for their livelihood. Other cash crops include copra and ginger. Copra provides coconut oil and other products for export and employs nearly as many workers as the sugar industry. Rice, cocoa, maize, tobacco, passionfruit, root crops, and a variety of vegetables and fruits are also grown. There is a small but developing livestock industry. Although there is no large-scale fishing industry, there are government-supervised small unit fishing projects. There is also growing exploitation of the substantial skipjack tuna resources for the local fresh market and for canning. Forests cover 45% of Fiji's land area. A comprehensive pine afforestation programme has been implemented as a basis for a woodpulp/chip and timber export industry. Gold is at present the most important mineral being produced: mining is now confined to the Vatakoula area in N Viti Levu. The expanding industrial sector accounts for 15% of national income and is the 2nd largest employer. Major industries include sugar-milling, the processing of coconut-oil, and gold-mining. There is also a great variety of light industries. Chief exports are sugar, gold, coconut oil, fish products, forestry products and molasses. The major export markets are the UK, Australia, the USA, other EEC countries, New Zealand and Singapore. Tourism plays an important part in the economy, with the total number of visitors rising to 203,600 in 1982. The Pacific Harbour residential resort development, covering 30 sq km at Deuba, 48 km from Suva on Viti Levu, is currently being constructed.

Administrative divisions. Fiji is divided into 4 divisions for administrative purposes. The Western Division is the largest, covering the W side of Viti Levu and the islands to the N and W. The 3 others are Central, Northern, and Eastern.

Filingué *fee-ling'gay*, 14 21N 3 22E, town in Niamey dept, SW Niger, W Africa; NE of Niamey; economy: stock raising and power plant.

Fin'dlay, 41 02N 83 39W, pop(1980) 35,594, county seat of Hancock county, NW Ohio, United States; on the R Blanchard, 64 km S of Toledo; railway; economy: petroleum, gas.

Finger Lakes, a group of long, narrow, finger-like lakes in W New York state, United States; S of L Ontario; includes (W-E) Canandaigua, Keuka, Seneca, Cayuga, Owasco and Skaneateles lakes.

Finistère *fin-e-ster*, dept in Bretagne region of NW France, between the English Channel and the Bay of Biscay; comprises 4 arrond, 49 cantons and 283 communes; pop(1982) 828,364; area 6,733 sq km; the westernmost dept of France; the coast is rugged with large bays and several islands; drained by the Aulne R (forming part of the Brest-Nantes Canal); the climate is damp and gales are frequent; the small sturdy horses of Finistère are widely raised; capital Quimper, chief towns Brest and Douarnenez; includes the Parc d'Armorique regional nature park (642 sq km) which caters for riding, shooting and fishing; there are sea-water treatment establishments at Douarnenez-Tréboul and Roscoff

Finisterre, Cabo, *fin-is-ter'ay* or *fin-is-tayr'*, 42 50N 9 16W, La Coruña, NW Spain; the westernmost point on the Spanish mainland, off which a British fleet under Anson defeated the French in 1747.

Finke Gorge, PALM VALLEY, national park in SW Northern Territory, central Australia; SW of Alice Springs and 19 km S of the missionary town of Hermannsburg; includes the Finke river and Palm Valley with its relict forms of flora.

Finland, SUOMI *soo-o'mi* (Finn), official name Republic of Finland, SUOMEN TASAVALTA (Finn), REPUBLIKEN FINLAND (Swed), a republic of N Europe bounded E by Russia (1,269 km), S by the Gulf of Finland, W by the Gulf of Bothnia and Sweden (586 km) and N by Norway (716 km); coastline 1,100 km; area 338,145 sq km; timezone GMT +2; capital Helsinki; chief towns Tampere, Turku, Espoo and Vantaa; pop(1980) 4,787,800; after Iceland and Norway, Finland is the most sparsely inhabited country in Europe; over half of the pop lives S of a line from Pori to Lappeenranta; since 1950 pop growth has been slow with large numbers emigrating to Sweden; the concentration of the population in the S and SW is the result of considerable rural emigration and urbanization that has accompanied economic growth since the mid-1950s; 48 of the 84 cities of Finland acquired municipal status after 1960; in 1982 94% of the population spoke Finnish as their first language and 6% spoke Swedish; in the Åland islands and in some W and SW towns such as Parainen (Pargas) Swedish is the first language; Russian and Lappish are also spoken; Finnish, with Estonian and Hungarian, belongs to the Finno-Ugric group of languages; 90% of Finnish Lapps live in the Lapland districts of Enontekiö, Inari, Utsjoki and Sodankylä; there is a small gypsy population of about 5,500 concentrated in the S; 90% of the population are of the Lutheran Church; the Finnish currency is the markka (mark, mk) of 100 penni (pennies, p); national holiday 6 Dec (Independence Day); membership of Nordic Council, OECD, Associate member of EFTA, ADB, CEMA, DC, FAO, GATT, IAEA, IBRD, ICAC, ICAO, ICES, ICO, IDA, IDB, IFAD, IFC, IHO, ILO, IMF, IMO, IPU, ITI, IWC, UN, UNESCO, UPU, WHO, WIPO, WMO, WSG.

Physical description. Finland is a low-lying glaciated plateau with an average height of 152 m above sea level. The highest peak is Haltiatunturi (1,328 m) on the NW border with Norway. In the SE there are over 60,000 shallow lakes connected either naturally or artificially to provide a system of inland navigation. Glacial deposits cover the W and S coastlands and the NW-SE alignment of the SE lakes indicates the direction of ice movement during the last period of glaciation. Finland is still emerging from the sea, its area increasing by 7 sq km every year as the land in Ostrobothnia rises 90 cm per year and in the Helsinki area 30 cm. Over one third of the country lies N of the Arctic Circle. The principal rivers are the Tornio and the Kemi (Finland's longest river) which flow S into the head of the Gulf of Bothnia and the Oulu which flows through central Finland to meet the same gulf. The remainder of Finnish rivers are short since their watersheds are close to the coast. The most important watershed is Maanselka, which divides the waters flowing to the Baltic from those draining to the Arctic Ocean and White Sea. Off the broken SW coastline lies Finland's largest archipelago, Saaristomeri, with over 17,000 islands and skerries. To the W are the Åland islands. Most of the country is in the northern coniferous forest zone which is characterized by pine, spruce and birch trees. The Lapland fells are in the Arctic-Alpine zone while the SW coast and archipelago are in the continental European oak zone. There is a higher proportion of swampland than in any other country. Forest land covers 65% of the country, water 10%, and cultivated land 8%.

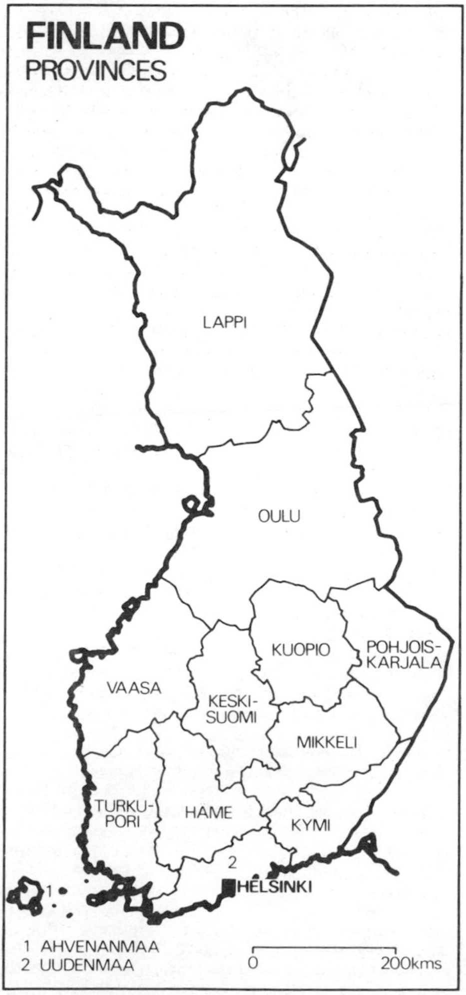

Climate. Despite Finland's northerly location the Finnish climate is ameliorated by the Baltic Sea, the inland waters and the W winds that bring warm air currents from the Atlantic in summer. By contrast, winds from the Eurasian continent bring cold spells in winter and heatwaves in summer. In the S the annual precipitation is 600-700 mm and in the N, where half falls as snow, 500-600 mm. The short dark days of winter are compensated for by summer nights when the sun does not go down beyond the horizon for more than 70 days.

History, government and constitution. From the invasion of Eric IX in 1157 until the cession of Finland to Russia in 1809 the country was ruled by Sweden. During the 19th century the country remained an autonomous Grand Duchy of the Russian Czar with its own constitution and civil service, but at the turn of the century the Czar tried to abolish its autonomous status and the Pan-Slav movement tried to impose orthodoxy and autocracy on the Lutheran and liberal-minded Finns. After the Russian revolution in 1917 Finland became an independent republic. A constitution was established in 1919 and a parliamentary system was created in 1928. Two hundred members are elected by proportional representation to a single-chamber House of Representatives (Eduskunta) for a period of 4 years. Members are elected from 14 electoral districts with an additional representative from the self-governing Åland Islands. The highest executive power is held by the President who is elected for 6 years. A Council of State or Cabinet divided into 13 ministries is responsible for major executive decisions. In each province administrative authority is vested in a provincial board with a governor who is appointed by the President. Under the provincial boards are the local authorities administered by sheriffs in 225 districts and by magistrates in the 'old' cities. For local government the country is also divided into 461 municipalities (*kunta*), 84 of which are cities.

Economy. Since the early 1950s, when Finland was a semi-industrialized country with a large proportion of the population engaged in forestry and farming, rapid economic growth has changed the structure of production and foreign trade. The diversification of exports in the 1960s and 1970s has allowed the metal, engineering, clothing and chemical industries to contribute a greater share to the export market, although the forest industry continues to contribute a high percentage (about 40%). A dependence on raw material and fuel imports has helped strengthen trade links with the Soviet Union since the early 1970s, but over 60% of Finnish trade is with other OECD countries.

Agriculture and forestry. Since the early 1950s the number of people employed in agriculture and forestry has fallen from 46% (1950) to 13% (1980). This is the result of mechanization and emigration to the cities where industrial growth has absorbed many smallholders who used to work in the fields during the summer and in the forests during the winter. The export of surplus farm products has been difficult, and with the volume of agricultural production remaining static there has been a reduction in arable land and a decrease in the number of farms. The chief crops are hay, barley, oats, spring and autumn wheat, rye, sugar beet, potatoes and spring oil-yielding plants. Pine, spruce and birch are the main forest species used in the production of roundwood for the sawn goods, plywood, pulp and paper industries. The volume of the growing stock is estimated at over 1,500 million solid cu m, and the annual growth at over 57 million solid cu m. About 20% of Finnish forests are owned by the state.

Administrative divisions. The country is divided into the following 12 provinces (*lahni*):

Province	*area (sq km)*	*pop(1982)*
Uudenmaa	10,404	1,150,930
Turku-Pori	23,166	707,401
Ahvenanmaa	1,552	23,196
Häme	19,802	668,839
Kymi	12,828	343,055
Mikkeli	21,660	208,523
Pohjois-Karjala	21,585	177,242
Kuopio	19,956	254,056
Keski-Suomi	19,356	244,991
Vaasa	27,319	439,082
Oulu	61,579	426,155
Lappi	98,938	198,011

Finland, Gulf of, an E arm of the Baltic Sea, bounded N by Finland, S by Estonskaya SSR and E by Rossiyskaya SFSR; 4,600 km long and 16-120 km wide; its shallowness and low salinity result in ice cover from Dec to March; Helsinki, Kotka, Vyborg, Leningrad and Tallinn are its main ports.

Fin'nart, 56 07N 4 50W, town in Dumbarton dist, Strathclyde, W Scotland; on the E side of Loch Long, 4 km N of Garelochhead; economy: oil terminal, connected by pipeline to oil refineries at Grangemouth.

Finnmark *fin'mahrk*, FINMARKEN, county of N Norway, lying within the Arctic Circle, drained by the Altaelv and Tana rivers; the N coastline is heavily indented by many fjords including Varangerfjorden (Varanger Fjord) and Porsangen; area 48,649 sq km; pop(1983) 77,383; capital Vadsø; chief towns Hammerfest and Kirkenes.

Fiordland, national park, SW South Island, New Zealand; the largest of New Zealand's national parks, with mountains, lakes and a coastline indented by fiords; area 10,232 sq km; established in 1904.

Fiorentino *fyo-ren-tee'no*, castle (dist) in the Republic of San Marino, central Italy; area 6.57 sq km; pop(1980) 1,392; population density in 1980 was 212 inhabitants per sq km; economy: cement production.

Firenze *fee-ren'tsay*, FLORENCE (Eng), FLORENTIA (anc), prov of Toscana region, Italy; pop(1981) 1,202,013; area 3,880 sq km; capital Firenze.

Firenze, 43 47N 11 15E, pop(1981) 448,331, ancient city and capital of Firenze prov, Toscana region, Italy; on the R Arno, surrounded by foothills of the Appno Tosco-Emilliano; archbishopric; university (1321); European University Institute, founded in 1972 by the EEC; seat of the Accademia della Crusca; founded at the foot of the hill on top of which was the Etruscan town of Faesulae; governed by members of wealthy guilds, the town became an important trading centre by the 12th century and the cultural and intellectual centre of Italy from the Middle Ages; airport; railway; economy: iron and steel, copper products, perfumes and cosmetics, medicinal products, tourism; monuments: the town is famed for its many churches, of which the finest are: (1) Battistero di San Giovanni, an octagonal structure with a dome, founded probably in the early Christian period on the remains of a Roman building and famous for the 3 gilded bronze doors with relief decoration; (2) the Duomo, a vast Gothic cathedral (1296), built by Arnolfo di Cambio, with octagonal dome by Brunelleschi (1420-34), and facade dating from 1875-1887; (3) Franciscan church of Santa Croce (begun in 1295), containing the tombs of Michelangelo, Aliferi, Machiavelli, Rossini, and others; (4) Dominican church of Santa Maria Novella, a Gothic building (1278-1350), with frescoes by Ghirlandaio; (5) church of Santa Maria del Carmine (almost completely rebuilt in 1782 after a fire), with the famous Brancacci chapel, containing frescoes on the lives of the Apostles (1424-27); (6) church of San Lorenzo, originally consecrated by St Ambrose in 393 as Firenze's first cathedral, rebuilt in 1425 by Brunelleschi, containing the Old Sacristy (by Brunelleschi, 1421-28) and the New Sacristy (built by Michelangelo, 1520-24); (7) 13th-c church of San Marco, rebuilt several times; (8) church of the Santissima Annunziata (1250), with forecourt containing frescoes by Andrea del Sarto (1505-14); (8) church of Or San Michele, built in 1284-91 as a corn exchange and rebuilt in 1337-1404. Additional buildings of interest include the Palazzo Vecchio (town hall), built for the Signoria between 1298 and 1314; Palazzo degli Uffizi, built in 1560-74 as government offices and now occupied by the Galleria degli Uffizi, one of the world's great art collections, including major works by North Italian, particularly Venetian, painters, as well as outstanding pictures by Dutch and German masters; Palazzo Medici-Riccardi (1444-52), with its famed chapel (Gozzoli), Palazzo Pitti (15th-c and later), the largest Florentine palace, now housing an art gallery; Ponte Vecchio, Firenze's oldest bridge (rebuilt in 1345 after repeated destruction), spans the R Arno and is famous for its goldsmiths' booths; events: religious festivals throughout the year, particularly at Easter; Gioco del Calcio - historical ball-game (1 May); music festival (May).

Fishguard, 51 59N 4 59W, pop(1981) 4,798, port town in Preseli dist, Dyfed, SW Wales; 20 km N of Haverfordwest, on Fishguard Bay; a passanger ferry links with Rosslare in Ireland.

Fitchburg, 42 35N 71 48W, pop(1980) 39,580, city in Worcester county, N Massachusetts, United States; on the R Nashua, 35 km N of Worcester; railway; founded in 1740, achieving city status in 1872; economy: electrical goods, textiles, paper, footwear, machinery.

Fittri *feet-ree'*, 12 50N 17 30E; shallow freshwater lake 40 km SW of Ati in Batha prefecture, E central Chad, N central Africa; the area varies between 26 and 52 sq km; receives the R Batha; largely overgrown with reeds.

Five Holy Mountains, The, five mountains in China thought in ancient times to be inhabited by the gods. See Wu Yue.

Flacq *flak*, district of E Mauritius; area 297.9 sq km; pop(1983) 109,290; bounded S by the Bambous Mts; tourist resort at Belle Marie Plage.

Flagstaff, 35 12N 111 39W, pop(1980) 34,743, county seat of Coconino county, central Arizona, United States; near San Francisco Peaks; settled in 1876, achieving city status in 1928; university (1899); Lowell Observatory; railway; economy: livestock, timber, tourism; monument: Sunset Crater National Monument.

Flamingo Gorge, a national recreation area surrounding Flamingo Gorge reservoir in SW Wyoming and NE Utah, United States.

Flanders, region in Belgium. See Vlaanderen.

Fleet, 51 16N 0 50W, pop(1981) 27,595, town in Hart dist, Hampshire, S England; 6 km W of Farnborough; railway; economy: electronics.

Fleetwood, 53 56N 3 01W, pop(1981) 28,136, port town in Wyre dist, Lancashire, NW England; on Morecambe Bay, at the mouth of the R Wyre, 13 km N of Blackpool; ferries to Belfast and the Isle of Man; economy: chemicals, plastics, computers, fishing.

Flens'burg, 54 46N 9 28E, pop(1983) 86,400, seaport and

manufacturing city in N Schleswig-Holstein prov, W Germany; at the head of an inlet of the Baltic Sea (Flensburger Forde), near Danish border, 32 km N of Schleswig; Germany's most northerly port and most important town in Schleswig; railway; economy: shipbuilding, engineering, local specialities of Flensburg are rum and smoked eels; monument: St Nicholas church (14-16th-c).

Fleuve, region of Senegal, W Africa. See Saint-Louis.

Flevoland, province of W Netherlands; almost entirely an area of land reclaimed from the Ijsselmeer, comprising an E polder (area 540 sq km) reclaimed in the period 1950-57 and a S polder (area 430 sq km) reclaimed in the period 1959-68; the prov was created in 1986; the chief settlements are Lelystad and Dronten.

Flin Flon, 54 47N 101 51W, pop(1981) 7,894, town in W Manitoba prov, central Canada; 888 km NNW of Winnipeg, on the frontier with Saskatchewan prov; airfield; economy: mining and smelting of gold, silver, copper and zinc.

Flinders Ranges, mountain ranges in SE Australia. See Lofty-Flinders Ranges.

Flint, 53 15N 3 07W, pop(1981) 11,398, town in Delyn dist, Clwyd, NE Wales; near the heavily industrialized area around Chester; railway; economy: paper.

Flint, 43 01N 83 41W, pop(1980) 159,611, county seat of Genesee county, E Michigan, United States; on the R Flint, 93 km NNW of Detroit; established in 1819, achieving city status in 1855; university; railway; economy: vehicles and aeroplane engines.

Florence, prov and city in N central Italy. See Firenze.

Florence, 34 48N 87 41W, pop(1980) 37,029, county seat of Lauderdale county, NW Alabama, United States; on the R Tennessee, next to Wilson Dam; settled in 1818, achieving city status in 1889; university (1872); railway; economy: cotton, aluminium, tiles, textiles, chemicals, boats, tourism; event: W.C. Handy Music Festival (Aug).

Florence, 34 12N 79 46W, pop(1980) 30,062, county seat of Florence county, E South Carolina, United States; 120 km ENE of Columbia; railway; economy: industrial and trade centre; railway engineering.

Florencia *flo-ren'sya*, 1 37N 75 37W, pop(1985) 77,598, capital of Caquetá dept, S Colombia, South America; SE of Popayán; established in 1908, the town has a modern square with sculptures and fountains; airfield; the San Agustín archaeological park is located NW.

Flores *flō'res*, 16 58N 89 50W, capital town of Petén dept, N Guatemala, Central America; on an island in the S part of Lago Petén Itzá; linked by causeway with Santa Elena airfield; nearby are the ruins of Tikal and other Mayan cities.

Flores *flō'res*, island of the Lesser Sunda group, Indonesia; part of the prov of Nusa Tenggara Timur; area 17,144 sq km; chief town Ende; other towns include Ruteng, Maumere and Reo; traversed by a mountain range with active volcanoes rising to heights over 2,500 m and covered by dense tropical forest; formerly held by the Portuguese but came under Dutch rule in 1907; economy: fishing, copra, maize, rice.

Flores or **Ilha das Flores** *flo'reesh* ('island of flowers'), 39 25N 31 15W, the most westerly of the Azores Is, Horta dist, Portuguese autonomous region; 17 km long by up to 14 km wide, with an area of 142 sq km; highest point is the Morro Grande (942 m); here in 1591 Sir Richard Grenville set out in the little *Revenge* which held at bay 15 Spanish warships - the subject of Tennyson's poem; airfield; economy: farming and stock-rearing; Santa Cruz das Flores on the E coast is the main town and port.

Flores *flō'rays*, dept in SW Uruguay; bordered by the Río Yí (N and NW) and the Arroyo Grande (W); pop(1985) 24,381; area 4,519 sq km; capital Trinidad; in the N of the dept is the Gruta del Palacio.

Flores Sea, sea of SE Asia, bounded N by the Indonesian island of Sulawesi and S by the Lesser Sunda Islands; the Java Sea lies W and the Banda Sea lies E; linked to the Timor Sea in the S by way of the Savu Sea and to the Indian Ocean in the S by Selat Lombok strait.

Florianópolis *flō-ree-a-no'po-lees*, 27 35S 48 31W, pop(1980) 153,652, capital of Santa Catarina state, Sul region, S Brazil; on the Atlantic coast between the bays of Baía Norte and Baía Sul on Santa Catarina island; joined to the mainland by 2 bridges, one of these is the Ponte Hercílio Luz, the longest steel suspension bridge in Brazil, closed to traffic in 1983; to the W of the island is the lake, Lagoa da Conceição, a popular leisure resort; there are 42 beaches around the island; 2 universities (1960, 1965); airfield; economy: commerce, fishing, tourism; monument: the Santana Fort now houses a museum of military arms.

Flo'rida, state in SE United States; a long peninsula bounded W by the Gulf of Mexico, N by Alabama and Georgia, E by the Atlantic Ocean, and S by the Straits of Florida and the Gulf of Mexico; the St Johns river rises in E central Florida and flows N to empty into the Atlantic Ocean; the R Caloosahatchee flows W from L Okeechobee into the Gulf of Mexico; the R Apalachicola flows S through the NW of the state to empty into the Gulf of Mexico; the R Perdido follows the W border with Alabama and the St Marys river follows part of the Georgia state border; L Okeechobee in S central Florida is the 4th largest lake wholly within the United States (area: 815 sq km; max depth: 4.6 m); the highest point is located in Walton county (105 m); the Florida Keys Islands stretch in a line SW from the S tip of the state, all linked by a series of causeways; the NW is a gently rolling panhandle area, cut by deep swamps along the coast; central Florida abounds in lakes, around which citrus fruits and other crops are grown; the S is almost entirely covered by the Everglades, a marshy, low lying tropical area unsuitable for cultivation but with a diverse flora and fauna; the E coast in the S of the peninsula is protected from the Atlantic Ocean by sandbars and islands which create shallow lagoons and bays; the sandy beaches and warm, sunny climate attract tourists, making this narrow coastal strip one of the fastest-growing metropolitan areas in the country; attractions include the Everglades National Park, Walt Disney World entertainment park, and the John F. Kennedy Space Center at Cape Canaveral; Florida is the greatest producer of citrus fruits in the USA and the country's 2nd largest producer of vegetables; other agricultural products include sugar cane, tobacco, cattle and dairy products; the chief manufacturing industries include processed foods, chemicals, electrical equipment, transportation equipment and wood products, and phosphate mining; Florida was discovered and settled by the Spanish in the 16th century, ceded to Britain in 1763 and divided into East and West Florida; it was given back to Spain after the War of Independence in 1783; West Florida was gained by the United States in the Louisiana Purchase of 1803 and occupied in 1813; East Florida was purchased for $5,000,000 by the United States in 1819; Florida was admitted as the 27th state to join the Union in 1845, but seceded in 1861; slavery was abolished in 1865 and Florida was re-admitted to the Union in 1868; also known as the 'Sunshine State'; pop(1980) 9,746,324; area 140,798 sq km; capital Tallahassee; other major cities include Jacksonville, Miami, Tampa, St Petersburg and Fort Lauderdale; the state is divided into 67 counties:

County	*area (sq km)*	*pop(1980)*
Alachua	2,343	151,348
Baker	1,521	15,289
Bay	1,971	97,740
Bradford	762	20,023
Brevard	2,587	272,959
Broward	3,149	1,018,200
Calhoun	1,477	9,294
Charlotte	1,794	58,460
Citrus	1,635	54,703
Clay	1,539	67,052
Collier	5,184	85,971
Columbia	2,070	35,399

contd

County	area (sq km)	pop(1980)
Dade	5,083	1,625,781
De Soto	1,654	19,039
Dixie	1,823	7,751
Duval	2,018	571,003
Escambia	1,716	233,794
Flagler	1,278	10,913
Franklin	1,417	7,661
Gadsden	1,347	41,565
Gilchrist	920	5,767
Glades	1,984	5,992
Gulf	1,453	10,658
Hamilton	1,344	8,761
Hardee	1,656	19,379
Hendry	3,024	18,599
Hernando	1,240	44,469
Highlands	2,675	47,526
Hillsborough	2,738	646,960
Holmes	1,269	14,723
Indian River	1,292	59,896
Jackson	2,449	39,154
Jefferson	1,583	10,703
Lafayette	1,417	4,035
Lake	2,480	104,870
Lee	2,088	205,266
Leon	1,758	148,655
Levy	2,860	19,870
Liberty	2,176	4,260
Madison	1,846	14,894
Manatee	1,942	148,442
Marion	4,186	122,488
Martin	1,443	64,014
Monroe	2,688	63,188
Nassau	1,687	32,894
Okaloosa	2,434	109,920
Okeechobee	2,002	20,264
Orange	2,366	471,016
Osceola	3,510	49,287
Palm Beach	5,182	576,863
Pasco	1,919	193,643
Pinellas	728	728,531
Polk	4,740	321,652
Putnam	1,906	50,549
Santa Rosa	2,662	55,988
Sarasota	1,490	202,251
Seminole	775	179,752
St Johns	1,604	51,303
St Lucie	1,511	87,182
Sumter	1,459	24,272
Suwannee	1,794	22,287
Taylor	2,751	16,532
Union	640	10,166
Volusia	2,894	258,762
Wakulla	1,563	10,887
Walton	2,772	21,300
Washington	1,534	14,509

Florida *flō-ree'da*, dept in S central Uruguay; bordered by the Río Yí (N), the Cuchilla Grande Principal and the Arroyo Casupá (E) and the Río Santa Lucía (S); the S end of the Cuchilla Grande range lies in the E; pop(1985) 65,873; area 12,107 sq km; capital Florida; the dept was formed in 1856.

Florida, 34 04S 56 14W, pop(1985) 28,406, capital of Florida dept, S central Uruguay; N of Montevideo; railway; airfield; the town is famous for a folklore festival held here each year on Independence Day.

Flo'rida Keys, S Florida, United States; series of small islands curving approx 240 km SW around the tip of the Florida peninsula, from just S of Miami Beach to Key West, approx 160 km NNE of Havana; the islands include, from NE to SW, Key Largo, Long Key, Key Vaca, Big Pine Key, Sugarloaf Key and Key West; the N islands are part of a coral reef and the S ones part of a former limestone island; tropical products (limes, pineapples, etc) are grown in the S and tarpon fishing attracts sportsmen; in 1935 the islands were struck by a great hurricane which destroyed the half-constructed railway; the Overseas Highway runs from the mainland to Key West, 198 km long, it was built in 1938 to replace the destroyed railway.

Flórina *flō'ree-na*, mountainous nome (dept) in Makedhonia region, N Greece, on the Albanian and Yugoslav borders; pop(1981) 52,430; area 1,924 sq km; capital Flórina.

Flórina, LERIN (Serb), 40 48N 21 26E, pop(1981) 12,562, capital town of Flórina nome (dept), Makedhonia region, N Greece; on a plateau 16 km from the Yugoslav border; agricultural college; economy: trade in fruit, cereals, livestock.

Flo'rissant, 38 48N 90 20W, pop(1980) 55,372, town in St Louis county, E Missouri, United States; suburb 22 km NW of St Louis.

Flotta, 58 49N 3 07W, island in the Orkney group of islands, N Scotland; S of Scapa Flow, to the E of Hoy island; an oil terminal, linked by pipeline to the Piper oil field.

Flushing, seaport in the Netherlands. See Vlissingen.

Focşani *fok-shan'*, 45 41N 27 12E, pop(1983) 77,391, capital of Vrancea county, E Romania; established in the 15th century; seat of the commission for Romanian unification (1859-62); Romanian-German truce signed here in 1917; railway; economy: wine, timber, grain trade, manufacture of textiles, metal products and pharmaceuticals.

Foggia *fod'ja*, maritime prov of Puglia region, SE Italy; pop(1981) 681,595; area 7,185 sq km; capital Foggia.

Foggia, 41 28N 15 33E, pop(1981) 156,467, capital town of Foggia prov, Puglia region, SE Italy; economic centre of the extensive Apulian plain, the Tavoliere di Puglia; almost all the town's medieval buildings were destroyed in an earthquake in 1731; airfield; rail junction; economy: engineering, paper, pasta, olive oil, cheese; monument: cathedral (1179), rebuilt in Baroque style after the 1731 earthquake.

Fogo *fo'go*, 14 53N 24 31W, island in the Sotovento or leeward group of Cape Verde, dominated by the volcanic Cano Peak (2,829 m), the highest mt in the archipelago (last major eruption in 1847); area 476 sq km; pop(1980) 31,115, the chief town is São Filipe on the W shore; coffee, oranges and tobacco are grown.

Fogo, Lagoa do *fo'goo*, ('lake of fire') 37 31N 25 29W, crater lake on Ilha de São Miguel, Azores; 2 km long by 1 km wide, formed during an eruption in 1563.

Föhr *foœr*, 2nd largest island of the Nordfriesische Inseln (North Frisian Is), W Germany; in the North Sea off W coast of Schleswig-Holstein prov; area 82.8 sq km; chief town Wyk.

Foix *fwa*, former prov of S France, now occupying the mountainous Ariège dept; joined to the crown by Henry IV.

Foix, 42 58N 1 38E, pop(1982) 10,044, old agricultural market town and capital of Ariège dept, Midi-Pyrénées region, S France; at the foot of the Pyrénées, on the R Ariège, 75 km S of Toulouse; railway; monuments: triple-towered château (1012); 6 km NW is the subterranean river of Labouiche, with a 2 km boat journey through an illuminated limestone cave.

Fokís *fo-kees'*, PHOCIS *fō'sis* (Eng), nome (dept) of Sterea Ellás-Évvoia region, Greece, bounded S by the Korinthiakós Kólpos (Gulf of Corinth); pop(1981) 44,222; area 2,120 sq km; capital Amfissa.

Folgefonn *fol'gafon*, FOLGEFONNI or FOLGEFONNA, ice field on a plateau in the Hardanger region, S of Hardangerfjorden (Hardanger Fjord), Hordaland county, SW Norway; area 212 sq km; length 35 km; height 1,654 m; extends S from near Sorfjord (Sor Fjord); 3rd largest ice field in Norway; several arms descend from it including the Buarbrae.

Folkestone *fōk'stun*, 51 05N 1 11E, pop(1981) 43,998, seaport and resort in Shepway dist, Kent, SE England;

22 km E of Ashford; a notable bathing resort in the 19th century; birthplace of the physician, William Harvey (1578-1657) who discovered the circulation of the blood; railway; cross-Channel ferries to France; monument: 13th-c church of St Mary and St Eanswythe.

Fond du Lac, 43 47N 88 27W, pop(1980) 35,863, county seat of Fond du Lac county, E Wisconsin, United States; a resort at the S end of L Winnebago; railway.

Fontana, 34 06N 117 26W, pop(1980) 37,111, city in San Bernardino county, SW California, United States; 14 km W of San Bernardino.

Fontenay-sous-Bois *fõt-nay-soo-bwa*, 48 51N 2 28E, pop(1982) 53,019, town in Val-de-Marne dept, Ile-de-France region, N central France; a SE suburb of Paris.

Foraker, Mount, 62 59N 151 29W, mountain in S central Alaska, United States; height 5,304 m; situated 209 km NNW of Anchorage, in Denali National Park and Preserve.

Forest *foray'*, 50 49N 4 19E, pop (1982) 50,477, town in Brussel dist, Brabant prov, Belgium; a suburb of Bruxelles.

Forez *fo-rayz*, former county in central France; a flat region between the Loire and Allier rivers.

Forfar *for'fĕr*, 56 38N 2 54W, pop(1981) 12,770, capital of Angus dist, Tayside, E Scotland; 20 km N of Dundee; economy: textiles, iron works.

Forlì *for-lee'*, FORUM LIV'II (anc), prov of Emilia-Romagna region, N Italy, on the Adriatic Sea; pop(1981) 599,420; area 2,911 sq km; capital Forlì.

Forlì, 44 13N 12 02E, pop(1981) 110,806, industrial town and capital of Forlì prov, Emilia-Romagna region, NE Italy; in the E foothills of the Appno Tosco-Emilliano, on the right bank of the R Montone; on the Via Emilia between Bologna and Rimini; airfield; railway; economy: footwear, felt, textiles, furniture; monument: Romanesque church of San Mercuriale (12th-c).

Form'by, 53 34N 3 05W, pop(1981) 26,711, residential town in Sefton borough, Merseyside, NW England; 17 km N of Liverpool; Ainsdale Nature Reserve is nearby; railway.

Formentera *for-men-tay'ra*, (Lat 'frumentum', wheat), 38 43N 1 26E, island in the Balearic Is, Baleares autonomous region, Spain, south of Ibiza from which it is separated by the Es Freus passage; area, 100 sq km; pop(1981) 3,500; the capital San Francisco Javier is 18 km away from the port of La Sabina; the island is largely formed by two high pine-clad capes (La Mola and Berberia) with a depression in the centre edged by white-sand beaches; event: patronal festival in July.

Formigas or **Ilheu das Formigas** *foor-mee'gash*, ('isles of the ants'), 37 10N 24 55W, uninhabited islets 35 km NE of Ilha de Santa Maria in the Azores archipelago, a subterranean ridge emerging from the water to a height of 11 m in a series of cliffs including the Rocas Formigas and Recife do Dollabarat.

Formosa, See Taiwan.

Formosa *for-mō'sa*, prov in Litoral region, N Argentina; hot, humid region bordered by the Río Pilcomayo where it follows the Paraguayan border, by the Río Bermejo which forms the border with Chaco prov and by the Río Paraguay on the Paraguayan border; pop(1980) 295,887; area 72,066 sq km; capital Formosa; economy: sorghum, cotton, cattle raising, tannin extraction, timber, processing industries.

Formosa, 26 07S 58 14W, pop(1980) 95,067, river-port capital of Formosa prov, Litoral, N Argentina; on the Río Paraguay, in flat, swampy tropical area; railway.

Forres *fo'riz*, 57 37N 3 38W, pop(1981) 8,354, town in Moray dist, Grampian region, NE Scotland; 6 km S of Findhorn Bay and 19 km W of Elgin; railway; monument: NE is Sueno's Stone, an early sculpted monument, 6 m high with elaborate carving.

Forssa *fors'sa*, 60 49N 23 40E, pop(1982) 19,688, town in Turku-Pori prov, SW Finland; situated between Turku and Hämeenlinna; established in 1923; railway.

Fort Collins, 40 35N 105 05W, pop(1980) 65,092, county seat of Larimer county, N Colorado, United States; at the foot of the Rocky Mts, 95 km N of Denver; settled in 1864; university (1870); railway; economy: trade, shipping and processing centre for grain, sugar-beets and livestock.

Fort Dodge, 42 30N 94 11W, pop(1980) 29,423, county seat of Webster county, central Iowa, United States; on the R Des Moines, 109 km NNW of Des Moines; railway; gypsum deposits nearby.

Fort Jameson, town in Zambia. See Chipata.

Fort Lauderdale, 26 07N 80 08W, pop(1980) 153,279, county seat of Broward county, SE Florida, United States; on the Atlantic Ocean, 40 km N of Miami; railway; airport; the city is interwoven with over 400 km of natural and artificial waterways, and is connected by a navigable canal to L Okeechobee; economy: fishing and yachting resort, with one of the largest marinas in the world; manufactures include yachts and electronic products; event: Christmas Boat Parade.

Fort Lee, 40 51N 73 58W, pop(1980) 32,449, town in Bergen county, NE New Jersey, United States; on the Hudson river, 16 km NNE of Jersey City; the site of a fort built, along with Fort Washington, to defend West Point during the War of Independence; it was abandoned when Fort Washington fell to the British in 1776; economy: motion picture film processing; an early centre of the motion picture industry; monument: George Washington Bridge.

Fort McMurray, 56 40N 111 07W, pop(1984) 35,352, town in NE Alberta, W central Canada; on the Athabasca river where it meets the Clearwater river; erected in 1790 by the North West Co and called the Fort of the Forks; it was taken over by Hudson's Bay Co in 1821 and rebuilt and renamed in 1875; situated in the middle of the Great Canadian Oil Sands, deposits of oil-bearing sands estimated to contain enough oil to supply the whole of North America for 60 years; airfield.

Fort Myers, 26 39N 81 52W, pop(1980) 36,638, county seat of Lee county, SW Florida, United States; on the estuary of the R Caloosahatchee; railway; economy: tourism; shipping point for citrus fruits, winter vegetables, and other products.

Fort Pierce, 27 27N 80 20W, pop(1980) 33,802, county seat of St Lucie county, E Florida, United States; on the R Indian (a lagoon), 86 km NNW of West Palm Beach; originally built in 1838 for protection from Seminole Indians; railway; economy: distributing centre for cattle, citrus fruits and vegetables; fishing; tourism.

Fort Portal, 0 40N 30 17E, town in Western prov, Uganda, E Africa; 145 km NNW of Mbarara.

Fort Rosebery, town in Zambia. See Mansa.

Fort Smith, 35 23N 94 25W, pop(1980) 71,626, county seat of Sebastian county, W Arkansas, United States; at the junction of the Arkansas and Poteau rivers, on the Oklahoma border; railway; economy: farm trade centre and major industrial hub; important supply point during the 1848 gold rush.

Fort Victoria, town in Zimbabwe. See Masvingo.

Fort Wayne, 41 04N 85 09W, pop(1980) 172,196, county seat of Allen county, NE Indiana, United States; at the junction of the St Joseph and St Mary rivers where they form the R Maumee; university (1917); railway; monument: Old Fort Wayne.

Fort William, 56 49N 5 07W, pop(1981) 11,061, capital of Lochaber dist, Highland region, W Scotland; on the E side of Loch Linnhe, near the head of the loch; railway; airfield; economy: aluminium, distilling; monuments: Inverlochy castle; N of Fort William is Neptune's Staircase, a series of 8 locks (built 1805-22) which raise the Caledonian Canal by 19.5 m; ESE of Fort William is Ben Nevis, the highest mountain in Britain (height 1,344 m).

Fort Worth, 32 45N 97 18W, pop(1980) 385,164, county seat of Tarrant county, NE Texas, United States; on the W fork of the R Trinity, 50 km W of Dallas; formerly an old cow town, the city is still an important livestock market centre; university (1873); railway; airfield; economy: aircraft and aerospace industries, oil refining and oil-related industries, pharmaceuticals, textiles, and leather goods; monuments: Fort Worth Art Centre, Amon Carter Museum of Western Art, Greer Island Nature Centre; event: Southwestern Exposition (Jan).

Fortaleza *for-ta-lay'za*, 3 45S 38 35W, pop(1980) 647,917, port capital of Ceará state, Nordeste region, NE Brazil; on the Atlantic coast; developed as an important centre for coastal and overseas trade; 2 universities (1955, 1973); railway; airfield; economy: commercial and industrial centre; monuments: a new tourist centre in the old prison on the waterfront includes the Museu de Arte e Cultura Popular; next to the state government building is the mausoleum of President Castello Branco (1964-67); opposite the Mercado Central is a new cathedral, built in a Classical style out of concrete; event: local festival on the last Sunday of July, with raft (*jangada*) races.

Fort-de-France *for-de-frãs'*, formerly FORT ROYAL (Eng), 14 36N 61 05W, pop(1982) 99,844, capital town of the French Overseas Department of Martinique, Lesser Antilles, E Caribbean; since the destruction of St Pierre in 1902 it has been the main commercial and shipping centre of the island; its landlocked harbour covers an area of 40 sq km; Lamentin International Airport is 14 km from the centre of the town; monument: cathedral (1895).

Forth, river in SE central Scotland; formed at Aberfoyle, W Central region, by the confluence of the Duchray Water and the Avondhu which rise on the NE slope of Ben Lomond; the Forth then flows generally E, past Stirling and Alloa, where it begins to widen out into the Firth of Forth estuary; the Firth of Forth extends 82 km from Alloa to the North Sea, where its mouth is bounded by Dunbar (S) and Fife Ness (N); it varies in width from 2.5 km to 28 km; crossed by a road bridge at Kincardine, below Alloa, and by the Forth road and rail bridges at Queensferry, to the W of Edinburgh; length 186 km; major tributaries of the river Forth: Allan Water, Teith and Devon rivers; major tributaries of the Firth of Forth include the Leven, Esk, Avon and Almond rivers; connected with the Clyde via the Forth and Clyde Canal.

Forties, oil field in the North Sea off the NE coast of Grampian region, NE Scotland; linked by pipeline to Cruden Bay, S of Peterhead.

Foshan *fō shan*, NAMHOI, FATSHAN, 23 03N 113 08E, town in Guangdong prov, SE China; settled as early as 2600 BC, Foshan became a well-known religious centre from the 10th century; railway; economy: folk-craft centre, pottery, metal casting, silk, papercutting; monument: the Zhu Miao (Temple of the Ancestors) was built during the Song dynasty (960-1279) and is made of interlocking wooden beams, using no metal or nails.

Fou-hsin, town in Liaoning prov, NE China. See Fuxin.

Foumban *foom-ban'*, 5 43N 10 50E, pop(1984e) 88,000, town in Ouest prov, Cameroon, W Africa; 225 km NNW of Yaoundé; in a strongly Muslim area; seat of the Bamoun Sultanate, a dynasty which began in 1394 under Nchare Yen; airfield; monuments: Sultan's palace built by King Njoya who was inspired by the German governor's residence at Buéa (completed in 1917); King Njoya was deposed by French colonials in 1923 and died in Yaoundé in 1934; Museum of Arts and Traditions (founded in 1930 by Mose Yepap); mosque.

Fountain Valley, 33 42N 117 58W, pop(1980) 55,080, city in Orange county, SW California, United States; SW of Santa Ana.

Four Corners, the point in SW United States, 37N 109W, where Colorado, New Mexico, Arizona and Utah meet.

Fou-shan, town in Liaoning prov, NE China. See Fushun.

Fouta Djallon *foo'ta ja-lon'*, mountainous massif in W central Guinea, W Africa; 22 W African rivers including the Niger, the Sénégal and the Gambia rise in this area.

Foxe Basin *foks*, a shallow basin in Northwest Territories, Canada; N of Hudson Bay; connected to the Atlantic Ocean via Foxe Channel and Hudson Strait; linked to Baffin Bay by the Gulf of Boothia, via the Fury and Hecla Strait; bounded to the N and E by Baffin Island, to the W by Melville Peninsula and to the SW by Southampton I; 550 km long by 360 km wide; ice-clogged for most of the year; named after Luke Foxe, an English navigator who explored Hudson Bay in 1631.

Foyle, Lough, inlet of the Atlantic; on the N coast, bounded W by Donegal, Republic of Ireland and E by Co Derry (Londonderry), Northern Ireland; the mouth itself is only 1.5 km wide; the lake is 24 km long and 16 km wide; fed by the R Foyle.

Franca *fran'ka*, 20 33S 47 27W, pop(1980) 144,117, town in São Paulo state, Sudeste region, SE Brazil; W of Belo Horizonte and N of São Paulo; railway; economy: cotton, coffee, soya beans, cereals, cattle.

France *frans*, GALLIA (anc), official name Republic of France, RÉPUBLIQUE FRANÇAIS *frãn-sez*, republic of W Europe, bounded N and NE by Belgium, Luxembourg and W Germany, E by Switzerland, Italy and Monaco and S by Spain and Andorra; includes the island of Corse (Corsica) in the Mediterranean and the overseas departments of Guadeloupe, Martinique, Guiana, Réunion, St Pierre et Miquelon, Mayotte; France also administers the overseas territories of New Caledonia, French Polynesia, Wallis and Futuna, and the Southern and Antarctic Territories; timezone GMT +1; capital Paris; chief towns Marseille, Lyon, Toulouse, Nice, Strasbourg; area 551,000 sq km; overseas depts area 97,014 sq km; pop(1982) 54,334,871; overseas depts pop(1982) 1,251,843; the pop is largely of Celtic and Latin origin with Teutonic, Slavic, N African, Indochinese and Basque minorities; 90% of the pop are Roman Catholic; the official language is French with Provençal, Breton, Flemish, Catalan, Corsican, Basque and Germanic regional patois; the currency is the French franc of 100 centimes; national holiday 14 July (Bastille Day); membership of ADB, Council of Europe, DAC, EEC, EIB, ELDO, EMA, EMS, ESRO, FAO, GATT, IAEA, IATP, IBRD, ICAC, ICAO, ICES, ICO, IDA, IFAD, IFC, IHO, ILO, IMF, IMO, INTELSAT, IOOC, IPU, IRC, ISO, ITC, ITU, OECD, UN, UNESCO, UPU, WEU, WFTU, WHO, WIPO, WMO, WSG, WTO.

Physical description. Situated between the Atlantic and the Mediterranean, France is a country of low and medium-sized hills and plateaux deeply cut by rivers and bounded to the S and E by large mountain ranges. The open topography of the country has facilitated the movement of peoples and the development of communications which include over 8,600 km of waterways. The principal hill ranges in the interior are the Armorican massif, the Massif Central, the Cévennes, the Vosges and the Ardennes, separated by the Paris and Garonne basins. The country is bounded to the E by the Alps (rising to 4,810 m at Mont Blanc, Europe's highest peak) and the Jura Mts and to the S by the Pyrénées. The principal rivers of France, radiating from the centre of the country, include the Loire (the longest river in France at 1,020 km), Rhône, Seine and Garonne which open out into large estuaries.

Climate. The climate of France ranges from a Mediterranean type in the S with warm, moist winters and hot dry summers to a maritime type in the NW where annual rainfall averages 573 mm and average temperatures range from 3°C in winter to 18°C in summer. The E has a continental type climate with an annual average rainfall of 786 mm reaching a peak in summer, often accompanied by thunderstorms.

History, government and constitution. Prehistoric settlement is indicated by remains of primitive flints from the Lower Palaeolithic, the magnificent carvings and rock-paintings of the Upper Palaeolithic (eg at Lascaux), and later the immense megaliths of the Mediterranean settlers in the Neolithic and Bronze Ages (eg at Carnac). By the 5th century BC Celtic-speaking Gauls were dominant. Between 125 BC and the 5th century AD Gaul was part of the Roman Empire. The Gallo-Roman empire was broken up by the Teutonic Burgundians who settled in the Rhône valley, by Visigoths on either side of the Pyrénées and by Franks in the N. The Frankish Clovis inaugurated the Merovingian epoch in the 5th century as the Franks spread their influence over most of modern

France and SE Germany. In 987, following years of disorder, Hugh Capet founded a feudal monarchy which eventually restored a centralized government. In the 12th century the Plantagenets of England acquired Brittany, Maine, Touraine, Poitou, Guienne and Gascony and were more powerful in France than the French. These territories were gradually recovered by France until in 1453 only Calais remained in English hands. This, too, fell in 1558. The 16th century saw the long struggle between Francis I and the Emperor Charles V, the French Renaissance, and the horrors of the Wars of Religion (1562-95), in which the massacre of St Bartholomew (1572) and the assassination of Henry III (1589) were notable incidents. In the 17th century the kings of France with their ministers, Sully, Richelieu, and Mazarin, restored the power of the monarchy, but under Louis XIV despotism reigned unchecked. In 1789 the bankruptcy of the government after years of economic decay led to the summons of the Estates-General for the first time since 1614. Revolution quickly followed and The First Republic of France was declared in 1792 on the fall of the Bourbon monarchy. For 10 years between 1804 and 1814 the country was ruled by Napoleon I during the period known as the First Empire. The monarchy was restored in 1814 but came to an end in 1848 with the abdication of Louis Philippe and the establishment of the Second Republic. During the period of the Second Empire between 1852 and the Franco-Prussian War of 1870-71, France was ruled by Louis Napoleon. The Third Republic, which was declared in 1870, lasted until the German invasion of France in 1940. The Fourth Republic, established in 1946, was succeeded by the Fifth Republic in 1958. The president, who is elected every 7 years, appoints a prime minister and government and presides over the Council of Ministers which is responsible to the bicameral legislature. There is a National Assembly of 491 deputies and a 304-member Senate elected every 5 years. A 9-member Constitutional Council oversees elections and safeguards the constitution, and an Economic and Social Council advises on Government and Private Members' Bills.

Economy. France is W Europe's foremost producer of agricultural products, chiefly cereals, beef, sugar beet, potatoes, wine, grapes and dairy products, with 35% of land under cultivation. Since 1950 the numbers employed in agriculture have fallen from 25% of the work force to 10% as agricultural technology has been modernized and as industry has attracted people to the cities. The industry of France is powered by coal from the coalfields of N France, Lorraine and the Massif Central, by hydroelec-

tric power from the Alps and by nuclear power generated at some two dozen sites. The metal and chemical industries are based on reserves of iron ore, bauxite, potash, salt and sulphur. Traditionally, heavy industry (steel, machinery, textiles, clothing and chemicals) has been based around the coalfields of the N, but more recently the development of electronics has taken place elsewhere. Tourism and fishing also play an important role in the economy of France. Major trade partners include other EEC countries, the USA, Japan and the USSR.
Administrative divisions. France is divided into 22 regions and 95 departments as follows:

No.	*Region/Department*	*area (sq km)*	*pop(1982)*
	Alsace		
67	Bas-Rhin	4,787	915,676
68	Haut-Rhin	3,523	650,372
	Aquitaine		
24	Dordogne	9,184	377,356
33	Gironde	10,000	1,127,546
40	Landes	9,237	297,424
47	Lot-et-Garonne	5,358	298,522
64	Pyrénées-Atlantique	7,633	555,696
	Auvergne		
03	Allier	7,382	369,580
15	Cantal	5,741	162,838
43	Haute-Loire	4,965	205,895
63	Puy-de-Dôme	7,955	594,365
	Basse-Normandie		
14	Calvados	5,536	589,559
50	Manche	5,938	465,948
61	Orne	6,100	295,472
	Bourgogne		
21	Côte-d'Or	8,765	473,548
58	Nièvre	6,837	239,635
71	Saône-et-Loire	8,565	571,852
89	Yonne	7,425	311,019
	Bretagne		
22	Côtes-du-Nord	6,878	538,869
29	Finistère	6,785	828,364
35	Ille-et-Vilaine	6,758	749,764
56	Morbihan	6,763	590,889
	Centre		
18	Cher	7,228	320,174
28	Eure-et-Loir	5,876	362,813
36	Indre	6,778	243,191
37	Indre-et-Loire	6,124	506,097
41	Loir-et-Cher	6,314	296,220
45	Loiret	6,742	535,669
	Champagne-Ardenne		
08	Ardennes	5,218	303,338
10	Aube	6,002	289,300
51	Marne	8,163	543,627
52	Haute-Marne	6,216	210,670
	Corse		
20a	Corse-du-Sud	4,013	108,604
20b	Haute-Corse	4,555	131,574
	Franche-Comté		
25	Doubs	5,228	477,163
39	Jura	5,008	242,925
70	Haute-Saône	5,343	231,962
90	Terr. de Belfort	610	131,999
	Haute-Normandie		
27	Eure	6,004	462,323
76	Seine-Maritime	6,254	1,193,039
	Ile-de-France		
75	Ville de Paris	105	2,176,243
77	Seine-et-Marne	5,917	887,112
78	Yvelines	2,271	1,196,111
91	Essonne	1,804	988,000
92	Hauts-de-Seine	175	1,387,039
93	Seine-Saint-Denis	236	1,324,301
94	Val-de-Marne	244	1,193,655
95	Val-d'Oise	1,249	920,598
	Languedoc-Roussillon		
11	Aude	6,232	280,686

contd

No.	*Region/Department*	*area (sq km)*	*pop(1982)*
30	Gard	5,848	530,478
34	Hérault	6,113	706,499
48	Lozère	5,168	74,294
66	Pyrénées-Orientales	4,087	334,557
	Limousin		
19	Corrèze	5,860	241,448
23	Creuse	5,560	139,968
87	Haute-Vienne	5,512	355,737
	Lorraine		
54	Meurthe-et-Moselle	5,235	716,846
55	Meuse	6,220	200,101
57	Moselle	6,214	1,007,189
88	Vosges	5,903	395,769
	Midi-Pyrénées		
09	Ariège	4,890	135,725
12	Aveyron	8,735	278,654
31	Haute-Garonne	6,301	824,501
32	Gers	6,254	174,154
46	Lot	5,228	154,533
65	Hautes-Pyrénées	4,507	227,922
81	Tarn	5,751	339,345
82	Tarn-et-Garonne	3,716	190,485
	Nord-Pas-de-Calais		
59	Nord	5,738	2,520,526
62	Pas-de-Calais	6,672	1,412,413
	Pays de la Loire		
44	Loire-Atlantique	6,894	99,498
49	Maine-et-Loire	7,145	675,321
53	Mayenne	5,171	271,784
72	Sarthe	6,245	504,768
85	Vendée	6,721	483,027
	Picardie		
02	Aisne	7378	533,970
60	Oise	5,857	661,781
80	Somme	6,175	544,780
	Poitou-Charentes		
16	Charente	5,953	340,770
17	Charente-Maritime	6,848	513,220
79	Deux-Sèvres	6,004	342,812
86	Vienne	6,084	371,428
	Provence-Alpes-Côte d'Azur		
04	Alpes-de-Haute-Provence	6,944	119,068
05	Hautes-Alpes	5,520	105,070
06	Alpes-Maritimes	4,294	881,198
13	Bouches-du-Rhône	5,112	1,724,199
83	Var	5,993	708,331
84	Vaucluse	3,566	427,343
	Rhône-Alpes		
01	Ain	5,756	418,516
07	Ardèche	5,523	267,970
26	Drôme	6,525	389,781
38	Isère	7,474	936,771
42	Loire	4,774	739,521
69	Rhône	3,215	1,445,208
73	Savoie	6,036	323,675
74	Haute-Savoie	4,391	494,505

Franceville *frãs-veel'*, 1 40S 13 31E, capital of Haut-Ogooué prov, SE Gabon, W central Africa; on the R Ogooué, 512 km ESE of Libreville; founded in 1880 by de Brazza; until 1946 the town was in the Middle-Congo colony; development of the Upper Ogooué has been facilitated by the completion of road links with Ndjolé, Lastrousville and Libreville; National Advanced Police Training Centre; regional television centre; sports stadium; railway; airfield (Albert-Bernard Bongo, 20 km from the city); economy: banking, mining (at Moanda), manufacture of metal alloys and the production of molasses.

Franche-Comté *frãsh-kõ-tay*, region and former prov of E France comprising the depts of Doubs, Jura, Haute-Saône and Territoire de Belfort, 9 arrond, 112 cantons and 1,780 communes; pop(1982) 1,081,049; area 16,202 sq km; it stretches S from Lorraine almost to Geneva, its E boundary following the crests and W slopes of the Jura Mts; the land rises to the Monts Faucilles in the N and to the Vosges in the NE; watered by the Saône, Ognon, Doubs and Ain rivers; the Plaine de Bresse extends into the W Jura dept; the vineyards N of Lons-le-Saunier produce the dry, fragrant, nutty 'vin jaune' of Château-Chalon, rarely met with outside the region; the capital was Dôle, then Besançon; chief towns include Belfort (an important tourist centre for skiing, climbing and walking), Vesoul, Montbéliard and Pontarlier.

Francisco Morazán *mō-ra-zan'*, dept in Honduras, Central America; pop(1983e) 736,272; area 7,943 sq km; capital Tegucigalpa.

Francistown, 21 11S 27 32E, pop(1981) 31,065, independent township in Central dist, Botswana, S Africa; 160 km SW of Bulawayo (Zimbabwe); alt 990 m; area 79 sq km; industrial and commercial centre of Botswana; originally a gold mining settlement; railway; airfield; economy: textiles, light industry, trade, services.

Franconia, Lower, dist of W Germany. See Unterfranken.

Franconia, Upper, dist of W Germany. See Oberfranken.

Franconian Forest, mountain range in W Germany. See Frankenwald.

Frankenwald *frahng'-kun-vahlt*, FRANCONIAN FOREST (Eng), mountain range in NE Bayern (Bavaria) prov, W Germany; S outlier of the Thüringer Wald, W Germany; extends 36 km between R Rodach (NW) and the Fichtelgebirge (SE); highest peak is the Döbraberg (795 m).

Frankfort, 38 12N 84 52W, pop(1980) 25,973, capital of state in Franklin county, N central Kentucky, United States; on the R Kentucky, 83 km E of Louisville; Daniel Boone founded the settlement in 1770; state capital since 1792; site of the graves of Daniel and Rebecca Boone; university; railway; economy: trade and shipping centre for tobacco, livestock and limestone; products include whisky, automobile parts, shoes and metal items; event: Capital Expo (June).

Frankfurt, FRANKFURT AN DER ODER, 52 50N 14 31E, pop(1981) 81,009, capital of region in Frankfurt dist, Frankfurt, E East Germany; 80 km E of Berlin on R Oder, where it follows the frontier with Poland; railway; economy: textiles, machinery, semiconductors.

Frankfurt *frank-foort*, FRANKFURT AM MAIN *am mīn*, 50 07N 8 40E, pop(1983) 614,700, manufacturing and commercial city in Darmstadt dist, Hessen (Hesse) prov, W Germany; river port on the R Main, 27 km N of Darmstadt; the headquarters of the Bundesbank, the leading German stock exchange and numerous banks found here; many international trade fairs; some of Germany's finest health resorts (Bad Hohburg, Bad Nauheim, Bad Soden, Königstein) are practically suburbs of this city; most of the German Emperors were crowned in Frankfurt, Goethe was born in the town and the first German National Assembly met here; university (1914); international junction for rail, road and air traffic; economy: river craft, precision engineering and optical instruments, chemicals, pharmaceuticals, brewing, non-alcoholic drinks, aluminium products, metals, transport equipment, agricultural machinery, packaging, publishing, oil products, building products, domestic appliances, office machines, telecommunications; monuments: Goethe House (rebuilt in 1949); Gothic cathedral (13-15th-c); the Romer (city's ancient town hall); event: International Frankfurt Fair (Aug).

Frankfurt-Oder, county in E East Germany; pop(1981) 704,808; area 7,186 sq km; bounded on the E by the R Oder which plays an important role in international goods transport; 50% of the land is farmed, with vegetables and glasshouse crops as the main products; 36% of the county is under forest largely used for recreational purposes; economy: iron and steel (Ost), cold reduction mill (Eisenhüttenstadt), petrochemicals (Schwedt), paper and pulp (Schwedt), crane works (Eberswalde), semiconductors (Frankfurt), chemical engineering and tyres (Fürstenwalde), cement (Rüdersdorf).

Franklin, district in NE Northwest Territories, Canada; comprises the Canadian Arctic peninsulas of Melville and Boothia and Arctic islands, the largest of which are Baffin, Victoria and the Queen Elizabeth islands; area 1,422,565 sq km; economy: fur trapping.

Franz-Josef Land, archipelago in the Arctic Ocean, NW Soviet Union. See Zemlya Frantsa-Iosifa.

Fraser, river in SW Canada; rises in the Rocky Mts on the Alberta-British Columbia border; flows NW through the Rocky Mountain Trench to Prince George at the NW end of the Cariboo Mts; turns sharply S to flow past Quesnel, Lillooet, Yale and Hope, where it turns W past Chilliwack, Maple Ridge and New Westminster and through a small delta to enter the Strait of Georgia and the Pacific Ocean 16 km S of Vancouver; length 1,368 km; major tributaries include the Nechako, Quesnel, Chilcotin, Thompson and Lillooet rivers; navigable below Yale; above Yale it flows through the canyon of the Fraser river, between mountains rising to over 915 m; the gold rush of 1858 took place along the upper reaches of the river and in 1859 gold was discovered in the Cariboo area further N along the river valley; the river is followed by the Canadian Pacific and Canadian National Railroads.

Fraserburgh *fray'zẽr-bur-u*, 57 42N 2 00W, pop(1981) 12,512, port town in Banff and Buchan dist, Grampian, NE Scotland; on the North Sea, 24 km NW of Peterhead; economy: engineering; fishing (Fraserburgh is the main herring port of ther NE).

Frauenfeld *frow'en-felt*, 47 34N 8 59E, pop(1980) 18,607, capital town of Thurgau canton, NE Switzerland; 34 km NE of Zürich; railway junction; monument: 11th-c castle with a massive 12th-c tower.

Fray Bentos *frī ben'tōs*, 33 10S 58 20W, pop(1985) 20,091, river-port capital of Río Negro dept, W Uruguay; on the Río Uruguay; railway; airfield; ferry; economy: meat packing and canning; an international toll bridge has been built across the R Uruguay to the Argentinian town of Puerto Unzué.

Fredericia *frid-ree'tsi-a*, 55 34N 9 47E, pop(1981) 29,350, port on the Lille Bælt (Little Belt) in Vejle county, E Jylland (Jutland), Denmark; railway; economy: engineering, textiles; founded in the mid 17th century to protect communications with the islands; laid out in a regular pattern.

Frederick, 39 25N 77 25W, pop(1980) 28,086, county seat of Frederick county, W Maryland, United States; 38 km SE of Hagerstown.

Fredericton, 45 57N 66 40W, pop(1981) 43,723, capital of New Brunswick prov, E Canada; in S central New Brunswick, on the St John river; originally settled by Acadians in 1731 and called St Anne's Point; little of this town remained when Fredericton was established in 1785 and renamed in honour of Prince Frederick, 2nd son of George III; in 1787 it took over from St John as capital of New Brunswick; university (1783); railway; airfield; monuments: the York-Sunbury Historical Museum, situated in the former officers' quarters of the British garrison, contains, among other items, replicas of 19th-c Fredericton homes; the Beaverbrook Art Gallery houses a large collection of paintings by Canadian and European artists; opposite the gallery is the Provincial Legislature, built in 1880; Christ Church cathedral, completed in 1853, is one of the best examples of decorated Gothic architecture in N America; Old Government House was built in 1828 as a residence for the prov's lieutenant-governors; the Prince of Wales (later Edward VII) stayed here in 1860; the building is now the headquarters of the Royal Canadian Mounted Police.

Frederiksberg *frid'riks-berk*, 55 42N 12 29E, pop(1981) 88,167, a W suburb of København (Copenhagen), Frederiksborg county, E Sjælland (Zealand), Denmark; area 9 sq km; economy: engineering.

Frederiksborg *frid'riks-bor*, a county of N Sjælland (Zealand), Denmark; bounded on the E by the Øresund, on the N by the Kattegat and on the W by the Isefjord;

area 1,347 sq km; pop(1983) 331,349; capital Hillerød; chief towns Helsingør, Frederiksværk and Frederikssund.

Frederikshavn *-hown*, formerly FLADSTRAND, 57 28N 10 33E, pop(1981) 24,938, seaport on the Kattegat, Nordjylland county, NE Jylland (Jutland), Denmark; railway, ferry services; economy: shipyards, engineering, foodstuffs; received municipal charter 1818.

Frederikssund *frid'rik-soon*, 55 51N 12 05E, pop(1981) 13,584, town in Frederiksborg county, N Sjælland (Zealand), Denmark; economy: engineering.

Frederiksværk og Hanehoved *frid'rik-sverk*, 55 58N 12 02E, pop(1981) 11,559, town in Frederiksborg county, N Sjælland (Zealand), Denmark; railway; economy: engineering, foodstuffs.

Fredrikshamn, port in Finland. See Hamina.

Fredrikstad *fred'rik-stah*, 59 13N 10 57E, pop(1983) 27,578, seaport on W coast of Østfold county, SE Norway; on E shore of Oslofjorden (Oslo Fjord) at mouth of R Glåma; railway; monument: Gamlebyen (Old Town), the only intact 17th-c fortress town in the N.

Free'port, 10 27N 61 25W, pop(1980) 22,301, chief town of Grand Bahama Island in the Bahamas; airport; International Bazaar in the Lucaya area.

Freeport, seaport on Ireland I, Bermuda; modern port facilities include a commercial berth 240 m in length, an oil bunkering station and reception facilities for bulk cement.

Freeport, 42 17N 89 36W, pop(1980) 26,266, county seat of Stephenson county, N Illinois, United States; on the R Pecatonica, 45 km W of Rockford; railway.

Freeport, 40 39N 73 35W, pop(1980) 38,272, town in Nassau county, SE New York, United States; on South Shore, Long Island; summer resort and centre for sailing and fishing; monument: historical museum.

Free'town, dist in Western prov, Sierra Leone, W Africa; pop(1985) 469,776; area 13 sq km; capital Freetown.

Freetown, 8 30N 13 17W, pop(1985) 469,000, seaport capital of Sierra Leone, W Africa, also capital of a dist of the same name; 805 km SE of Dakar; Sierra Leone's best natural harbour; the first European landing by the Portuguese in the 15th century was followed in 1562 by the arrival of Sir John Hawkins; with its origins in the creation of a settlement for freed slaves Freetown was founded in the late 1790s; W Africa's oldest university, Fourah Bay, was founded as a college in 1827; old fort and trading factories at Bunce Island; in colonial times Freetown was an important British naval base and bunkering station on the R Sierra Leone estuary; airport; economy: oil refining, plastics, sugar, cement, footwear, soap, fish processing, trade in platinum, diamonds, gold, chromite, palm kernels, ginger and kola nuts.

Freiberg *frī'berk*, 50 55N 13 21E, pop(1981) 51,377, town in Freiberg dist, Karl-Marx-Stadt, S East Germany; NE of Karl-Marx-Stadt, near R Mulde; founded in 12th century around silver mines; college of technology; railway; economy: electronics, non-ferrous metal works, electrical engineering.

Freiburg *frī'boork*, dist in SW Baden-Württemberg prov, W Germany; pop(1983) 1,869,300; area 9,357 sq km.

Freiburg, canton and town in Switzerland. See Fribourg.

Freiburg im Breisgau *im brīz'gow*, 48 00N 7 52E, pop(1983) 178,400, manufacturing and commercial city in Freiburg dist, Baden-Württemberg prov, W Germany; between the Kaiserstuhl and the Schwarzwald (Black Forest) at the point where the R Dreisam enters the Upper Rhine plain, 128 km SW of Stuttgart; a conference centre and sporting town; university (17th-c); railway; economy: yarns and threads, chemical fibres; monuments: Minster (13-16th-c); the 1,284 m high Schauinsland lies within the city boundaries.

Fremantle *free'man-tl*, 32 07S 115 44E, pop(1981) 22,484, seaport city in Western Australia state, Australia; on the W coast of Australia at the mouth of the Swan river, 10 km SW of Perth, part of Perth metropolitan area; known locally as 'Freo'; founded in 1829 as a penal colony; the city has a notable sailing club; centre for the 1986-87 America's Cup yacht race; railway terminus; economy: shipbuilding, paint, carpets, furniture, trade in petroleum products, iron and steel products, grain, wool, fruit; monuments: the Round House (1830), a former jail; maritime museum.

Fremont *free'mont*, 37 32N 121 57W, pop(1980) 131,945, city in Alameda county, W California, United States; 56 km S of San Francisco, near the S end of San Francisco Bay; economy: micro-electronics, data systems.

French Guiana *gee-ah'na*, LA GUYANE FRANÇAISE, overseas dept of France in South America bordering the Atlantic; situated between 2° and 6°N; bounded W by Surinam along the R Marowijne, E by Brazil, partly along the R Oiapoque (Oyapok) and S by Brazil along the Serra de Tumucumaque; timezone GMT $-3\frac{1}{2}$; area 90,909 sq km; capital Cayenne; pop(1982) 73,022; the pop is comprised of Creoles, Europeans, Amerindians and Negroes; the official language is French, though Creole patois and Indian languages are spoken outside the towns; the majority of the pop is Roman Catholic; the currency is the franc; national holiday 14 July (Bastille Day); membership of WFTU.

Physical description. A low lying country near the coast, French Guiana rises to 396 m in the central Chaîne Granitique and in the S rises towards the Serra de Tumucumaque which reaches 635 m at Mont Saint Marcel. Rivers flowing from the centre and S of the country to meet the Atlantic and E and W border rivers include the Camopi (tributary of the Oiapoque), the Inini, Ouaqui, Tampoc and Marowiny (tributaries of the Marowijne) and the Mana, Sinnamary, Comte and Approuague. French Guiana has many rocky islets along its coast. Of these the most famous is Devil's Island, one of the Iles du Salut.

Climate. French Guiana has a hot and humid tropical climate with a rainy season from Dec-June and a dry period during Aug-Oct. Average daily temperatures at Cayenne on the coast range between 23°C and 33°C and monthly rainfall ranges from 551 mm in May to 31 mm in Sept.

History, government and constitution. French Guiana became a territory of France in 1817. Political prisoners had been sent there in 1798, and an official penal colony

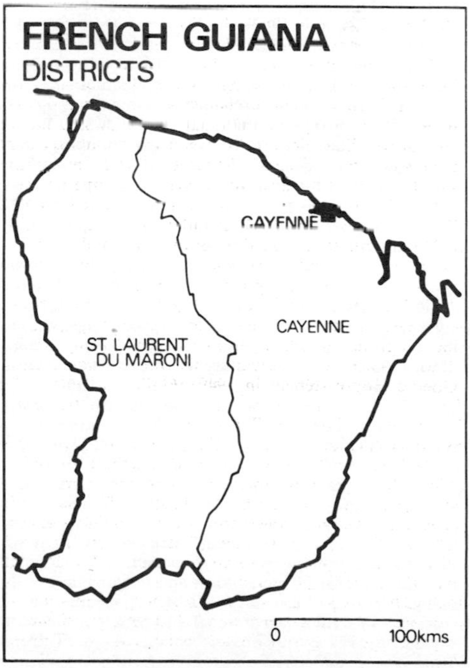

was established in 1852. Convicts were shipped to French Guiana until 1935, using Saint Laurent du Maroni as the port of entry. Most of the penal colonies had closed by 1946. On 19 March 1946 the status of Guiana was changed to that of an overseas department, with the same laws, regulations and administration as a dept in metropolitan France. The seat of the Prefect and of the principal courts is at Cayenne.

Economy. French Guiana's most important natural resource has been its timber, extracted from forests which cover c.80,000 sq km. Mineral resources have been little exploited although bauxite has been located in the Kaw mountains to the E of Cayenne and kaolin has been found at Saint Laurent du Maroni; French Guiana imports most foodstuffs and manufactured goods. Its chief exports include shrimps, rum, essence of rosewood, hardwood timber and gold.

Agriculture. Only 104 sq km of French Guiana is under cultivation, the principal crops being rice, maize, manioc, bananas and sugar cane as well as a variety of fruits, vegetables and spices. Cattle, pigs and poultry are also reared.

Administrative divisions. French Guiana is divided into the 2 dists of Cayenne and Saint Laurent du Maroni.

French Polynesia, official name Territory of French Polynesia, island territory comprising 5 scattered island groups in the SE Pacific Ocean, between the Cook Is to the W and the Pitcairn Is to the E; area 3,941 sq km; coastline 2,525 km; timezone GMT −6; capital Papeete; pop(1977) 137,382; the people are mostly Polynesian, with European and Chinese admixtures; expatriate Frenchmen make up about 15% of the total population, their numbers having increased since the former colonies of France in Africa gained independence; the dominant religion is Christianity (55% Protestant, 32% Catholic); the official language is French but local languages are widely spoken.

Physical description. French Polynesia consists of 5 archipelagoes: the Archipel de la Société (Society Is), 1,535 sq km in area, including Tahiti and Bora-Bora; Tuamotu Archipelago (826 sq km); Archipel des Gambier (11 sq km); Îles Marquises (Marquesas Is), 1,189 sq km in area; and Îles Tubuai (Austral Is), 137 sq km in area. The uninhabited Clipperton I, 1,000 km off the coast of Mexico, is administered by the High Commissioner for French Polynesia but does not form part of the Territory. Most of the islands are volcanic, mountainous, and ringed with coral reefs, standing on submarine reefs aligned NE-SW. The Tuamotu and Gambier groups are mainly low lying coral atolls. Tahiti, largest of the Society Is, rises to 2,237 m.

Climate. The climate is hot and humid from Nov to April, but cooler and drier the rest of the year. Temperatures are moderated by brisk SE trade winds. Tropical storms are less frequent than in the W Pacific but periods of prolonged heavy rain are not unusual.

History, government and constitution. From the mid-19th century French missions began operating in Tahiti and other islands. France declared protectorates progressively from 1842. In Nov 1958, 'French Oceania' became an Overseas Territory within the French community. Under the 1977 Constitution, the islands are administered by an appointed High Commissioner and Council of Government. The 5-member Government Council is elected by a Territorial Assembly of 30 members. 2 deputies and a senator represent French Polynesia in Paris.

Economy. The economy is based on agricultural smallholdings growing vegetables and fruit, and plantations providing coconut oil and copra for export. Coconut trees cover the coastal plains of the mountainous islands and the greater part of the low lying islands. The main industries are tourism and maintenance of the French nuclear test base. Chief imports include metalwork, textiles, petrol, sugar and flour. Chief exports are coconut oil, cultured pearls, vanilla, and citrus fruits. France receives 86% of all exports.

French Southern and Antarctic Territories, TERRES AUSTRALES ET ANTARCTIQUES FRANÇAISES (Fr), French overseas territory, comprising Terre Adélie in Antarctica and the islands of Kerguélen, Crozet, Amsterdam and St Paul in the S Indian Ocean; established in 1935; governed by an administrator and 7-member consultative council which meets twice-yearly in Paris; the 12 members of the Scientific Council are appointed by the senior administrator with approval of the French Minister in charge of scientific research; a 15-member consultative committee on the environment was created in 1982.

Fresno, 36 44N 119 47W, pop(1980) 218,202, capital of Fresno county, central California, United States; c.257 km SE of San Francisco; a city since 1889; university; railway; airfield; situated at the centre of a wine-producing region; Kings Canyon and Sequioa national parks are c.80 km E of here; economy: grapes, grain, cotton, cattle, agricultural machinery, food processing.

Fribourg *free-boor'*, FREIBURG *frī'boork* (Ger), a predominantly rural canton in W Switzerland; pop(1980) 185,246; area 1,670 sq km; capital Fribourg; chief towns Bulle, Gruyères; drained by the R Saane and its tributaries; mountainous in the SE; joined the Swiss Confederacy in 1481; one-third of the canton is German-speaking.

Fribourg, 46 49N 7 09E, pop(1980) 37,400, medieval town and capital of Fribourg canton, W Switzerland; on a peninsula in the R Saane, which flows in a deep valley through the Mittelland, 27 km SW of Bern; founded in 1178 at a ford in the river; persisted as a Catholic stronghold in the Reformation when its neighbours turned Protestant; bishopric; university (1889); railway junction; economy: foodstuffs, engineering; monuments: a noteworthy polychrome tomb in the cathedral of St Nicholas, church of the Woodcutters (13th-c); 16th-c town hall.

Fridley, 45 05N 93 16W, pop(1980) 30,228, town in Anoka county, SE Minnesota, United States; on R Mississippi; railway; in 1965 three tornadoes destroyed large parts of the town.

Friedrichshafen *free'driKHs-hah-fen*, 47 39N 9 29E, pop(1983) 51,800, harbour town in Tübingen dist, S Baden-Württemberg prov, W Germany; on N shore of the Bodensee (L Constance); alt 402 m; railway; economy: metal constructions, vehicles and bulldozers, engineering; birthplace of the Zeppelin.

Friesche Eilanden *free'she ee-lant'en*, FRISIAN ISLANDS *fri'zhun* (Eng), island chain in the North Sea, extending along coasts of the Netherlands, Germany and Denmark; includes: (1) Nordfriesische Inseln (North Frisian Is) off NW coast of Schleswig-Holstein prov, W Germany, and SW coast of Denmark; chief islands (German) Sylt, Föhr, Nordstrand, Pellworm and Amrum; (Danish) Rømø, Fanø and Mandø, plus several uninhabited islands, and Die Halligen (Hallig Is); (2) Ostfriesische Inseln (East Frisian Is) off Niedersachsen (Lower Saxony) prov, W Germany; chief islands Borkum, Juist, Norderney, Langeoog, Spiekeroog and Wangerooge, and 4 uninhabited islands, including Neuwerk and Scharhorn; (3) West Frisian islands off Waddenzee and N Netherlands coast; chief islands Texel, Vlieland, Terschelling, Ameland and Schiermonnikoog, and 4 uninhabited islands.

Friesland *frees'lant*, FRISIA (anc), pop(1984e) 597,200, prov in N Netherlands; includes most of the West Frisian Is; land area 3,352 sq km; in the SW and N it borders on the Ijsselmeer and the Waddenzee; in the S and SE its boundary is the Wouden, an area of sandy ridges with a transition to the morainic plateau of Drenthe; in the E it merges into marshland of Groningen prov; capital Leeuwarden; chief towns Harlingen and Sneek; economy: some arable farming on the coast of the Waddenzee, NW of Leeuwarden, elsewhere livestock farming predominates, specializing in the production of butter and the breeding of Frisian cattle; there are small shipyards building small canal boats of less than 50 tonnes; there are extensive marshlands along the North Sea coast which have been partly reclaimed from the sea and partly developed from the inland freshwater lakes.

Frin'ton-on-Sea, 51 50N 1 14E, pop(1981) 12,689, residential resort town linked with Walton-on-the-Naze in Tendring dist, Essex, SE England; 8 km NE of Clacton-on-Sea; railway.

Frisian Is, North Sea. See Friesche Eilanden.

Friuli-Venezia Giulia *free-oo'lee vay-nayt'sya jool'ya*, region of NE Italy, comprising the provs of Gorizia, Pordenone, Trieste, and Udine; pop(1981) 1,233,984; area 7,843 sq km; economy: agriculture (particularly viticulture), tourism (winter sports in the mountains are being developed); Friulian, a Rhaeto-Romanic dialect, is spoken.

Frome *froom*, 51 14N 2 20W, pop(1981) 19,817, town in Mendip dist, Somerset, SW England; on the R Frome, 17 km S of Bath; a town of Anglo-Saxon origin with narrow alleys and old stone houses; railway; economy: textiles, plastics, printing, engineering, perry making; monument: Longleat House (1568), 8 km NE.

Frosinone *fro-zee-nō'nay*, prov of Lazio region, central Italy; pop(1981) 460,395; area 3,240 sq km; capital Frosinone.

Frosinone, FRUSINO (anc), 41 38N 13 22E, pop(1981) 44,644, agricultural market town and capital of Frosinone prov, Lazio region, central Italy; 80 km ESE of Rome, on a hillside above the Cosa valley, in the foothills of the Appno Abruzzese.

Frunze *froon'zye*, formerly PISHPEK, 42 54N 74 46E, pop(1983) 577,000, capital city of Kirgizkaya SSR, S Soviet Union; in the Chu valley, at the foot of the Kirgizskiy Khrebet range; it is irrigated by 2 small rivers, the Ala-arch and the Ala-medin; major transportation, industrial, and cultural centre; established in 1825; alt 750-900 m; university (1951); railway; airport; economy: manufacture of agricultural machinery, textiles, food, and tobacco products.

Frýdek-Místek *free'dek-mee-stek*, 49 40N 18 30E, pop(1984) 62,398, town in Severomoravský region, Czech Socialist Republic, central Czechoslovakia; on R Ostravice, SE of Ostrava; Frýdek and Místek, on opposite sides of the river, are one commune; railway; economy: timber, textiles.

Fthiótis, *thī-ō'tis*, PHTHIOTIS (Eng) nome (dept) of Sterea Ellás-Évvoia region, Greece, bounded E by Évvoia nome (dept); pop(1981) 161,995; area 4,441 sq km; capital Lamia.

Fuchskauten *fooks'kow-tun*, 50 40N 8 05E, mountain in NE Rheinland-Pfalz (Rhineland-Palatinate) prov, W Germany; highest peak of the Westerwald range, 16 km SW of Dillenburg; height 656 m.

Fuengirola *fweng-hee-ro'la*, 36 32N 4 41W, pop(1981) 30,606, port in Málaga prov, Andalucia, S Spain; 30 km SW of Málaga; beaches nearby; economy: fishing, fish processing, tourism, textiles.

Fuenlabrada *fweng-lah-vra'dha*, 40 16N 3 49W, pop(1981) 77,626, town in Madrid prov, central Spain; 16 km SSW of Madrid; railway; economy: textiles and grain.

Fuerteventura *fwer-tay-ven-too'rah*, 28 25N 14 00W, volcanic Atlantic island in the Canary Is, Las Palmas prov, Canarias region of Spain; situated to the E of Gran Canaria and 105 km W of the coast of Morocco; Betancuria (pop 534) is the main town; area 1,722 sq km.

Fujayrah, Al *al foo-jī'ru*, one of the seven member states of the United Arab Emirates, on the Batinah coast, bounded E by the Gulf of Oman; its territories alternate with the Shāriqah enclaves; the terrain is partly mountainous with a fertile coastal plain and no desert; area 1,150 sq km; pop(1980) 32,200; capital Al Fujayrah; the people live mostly in scattered villages and depend on agriculture for their livelihood.

Fujayrah, Al, 25 10N 56 20E, capital town of Al Fujayrah emirate, United Arab Emirates, SE Arabian Peninsula; on the Gulf of Oman in the E foothills of the Hajar Mts; economy: shipping.

Fuji *foo'jee*, 35 10N 138 37E, pop(1980) 205,751, town in Shizuoka prefecture, Chūbu region, SE Honshū island, Japan; on R Fuji, 32 km NE of Shizuoka; to the N and E lies the Fuji Hakone Izu National Park; railway.

Fuji Hakone Izu *foo'jee hah-kō'nay ee'zoo*, national park in central Honshū island, central Japan; area 1,232 sq km; established in 1936; the park lies to the SW of Tōkyo, extending from Fuji-san volcano S and SE to include the peninsula to the E of Surugawan Bay; in the N of the park is Fuji-san volcano, Japan's highest peak; the centre of the park consists of Hakone, an area formed by the action of a triple volcano; Hakone is a mountain resort and spa town with hot springs; nearby is L Ashi, a crater lake formed c.4,000 years ago (area 7 sq km) and now a popular fishing resort; along the E shore of the lake is the Cryptomeria Avenue, an avenue of c.420 cryptomeria trees which were planted in 1618 along the old Tokaido Highway to provide travellers with shade; the S of the park consists of the Izu peninsula and its offshore islands.

Fujian *foo-kyen*, FUKIEN, mountainous province in SE China; situated on China's SE coast; bordered E by the Taiwan Strait, W by Jiangxi prov along the Wuyi mountains; SE of Nanping is the Daiyun Shan range; drained by the Min Jiang and Jinlong Jiang rivers; the coastline is indented with many harbours and offshore islands; pop(1982) 25,931,106; area 123,100 sq km; capital Fuzhou; chief towns include Xiamen (special economic zone); economy: fruit (lichee, banana, pineapple), flowers, shellfish.

Fuji-san *foo-jee-sahn'*, FUJIYAMA, MOUNT FUJI (Eng), 35 23N 138 42E, highest peak in Japan; in Shizuoka prefecture, Chūbu region, central Honshū, Japan; 88 km WSW of Tōkyo; an extinct volcano which rises to 3,776 m; an isolated peak with an almost perfect cone, its crater has a diameter of c.600 m; the last eruption was in 1707; the mountain is barren and snow-capped; since ancient times it has been sacred; until the Meiji restoration of 1868 no woman was allowed to climb it; there are 5 lakes at the N base of the mountain, the largest, L Kawaguchi, is c.5 km long and 1.5 km wide; Fuji-san volcano is situated in Fuji Hakone Izu National Park.

Fujisawa *foo-jee-sa'wa*, 35 22N 139 29E, pop(1980) 300,248, town in Kanagawa prefecture, Kanto region, E Honshū island, Japan; situated SSW of Tōkyō, on the N shore of Sagami-wan Bay; railway; economy: trade in grain and vegetables.

Fujiyama, mountain in Japan. See Fuji-san.

Fukien, province in SE China. See Fujian.

Fukui *whoo-koo-ee*, 36 04N 136 12E, pop(1980) 240,962, capital of Fukui prefecture, Chūbu region, central Honshū island, Japan; 125 km NNE of Kyōto; railway; economy: silk, rayon, leather, paper, food processing.

Fukuoka *foo-ke-wō'ka*, formerly NAJIME, 33 39N 130 21E, pop(1980) 1,088,588, port capital of Fukuoka prefecture, NE Kyūshū island, Japan; 145 km NNE of Nagasaki, on the S shore of Genkai-nada Sea; Kyūshū University (1911); institute of technology (1909); opened to foreign trade in 1899; rail terminus; airport (Itazuke) at 7 km; economy: chemicals, textiles, paper, metal goods, shipbu ilding; monuments: 16 km from Fukuoka is the Dazaifu Temman gu, one of the most famous shrines in Japan; built in the 10th century in memory of Sugawara Michizane, a patron of the arts and of calligraphy, it was rebuilt during the 16th century and restored in 1950.

Fukushima *foo-ke-shee'ma*, 37 44N 140 28E, pop(1980) 262,837, capital of Fukushima prefecture, Tōhoku region, N Honshū island, Japan; 240 km NNE of Tōkyo; railway; economy: silk.

Fukuyama *foo-ke-ya'ma*, 34 29N 133 21E, pop(1980) 346,030, port town in Hiroshima prefecture, Chūgoku region, SW Honshū island, Japan; at the mouth of the R Ashida on the Huichi-nada Sea, 85 km ENE of Hiroshima; railway; economy: cotton, rubber products, dyes, fertilizer, sugar.

Fulda *fool'du*, 50 32N 9 41E, pop(1983) 56,400, manufacturing city on the R Fulda in Kassel dist, E Hessen (Hesse) prov, W Germany; 86 km NE of Frankfurt am Main; railway; economy: carpets, clothing, industrial textiles; monuments: cathedral (1704-12); the Prince-Bishops of the 18th century endowed it with its Baroque architecture.

Fulda, river in Hessen (Hesse) prov, W Germany; rises on the Wasserkuppe, flows N past Fulda, Hersfeld and Kassel to Munden where it joins the R Werra to form the R Weser; length 218 km; navigable length 109 m; drainage basin area 6,947 sq km; receives the R Eder.

Fulham, London, England. See Hammersmith and Fulham.

Fullerton, 33 53N 117 56W, pop(1980) 102,034, city in Orange county, SW California, United States; 35 km SE of Los Angeles, just N of Anaheim; university; railway; economy: fruit processing and packing, petroleum.

Funafuti *foo-na-foo'tee*, 8 30S 179 12E, port and capital town of Tuvalu, SW Pacific, on the E side of Funafuti atoll; airfield.

Funchal *foo-shal* (Port 'funcho', fennel), dist of Portugal, co-extensive with Madeira Is; area 796 sq km; divided into 11 councils and 53 parishes; pop(1981) 253,891; economy: sugar, fruit, horticulture, grain, wine, meat, wool, dairy products, embroidery.

Funchal, 32 40N 16 55W, pop(1981) 119,481, capital of Portuguese autonomous region of Madeira and Funchal dist, on S coast of Ilha da Madeira; third largest Portuguese city; divided into 5 parishes; episcopal see; exports Madeira wine, embroidery, fruit, fish, dairy produce and wickerwork; there is a colourful market; industries: sugar milling, distilling, tobacco products, soap, canning; important port and resort on transatlantic route; monuments: 'Manuleine' cathedral (1485); 15th-c chapel of Santa Catarina; forts of Our Lady of Conceição, Pico (1632) and São Tiago (1614); 16th-c São Lourenço palace, now the governor's palace, and nearby Jardim de São Francisco; events: municipal holiday in first week of May; Senhora do Monte festival in mid-Aug, with procession, religious and folk events and the São Silvestre festival on New Year's Eve.

Fundy, Bay of, a bay separating the provs of New Brunswick and Nova Scotia, E Canada. The world's greatest tidal height (16.2 m) is used to generate electricity.

Fünen, Danish island. See Fyn.

Furnas, Lagoa das *foor'nash*, 37 30N 25 20W, a crater lake at the W end of Ilha de São Miguel, Azores; 2 km long; after a volcanic eruption in 1630 there emerged a series of hot springs, mud springs, and sulphur and mineral springs, some of which are used for medicinal purposes.

Fürth *fürt*, 49 29N 11 00E, pop(1983) 99,000, manufacturing city in Mittelfranken dist, Bayern (Bavaria) prov, W Germany; at confluence of Regnitz and Pegnitz rivers, 8 km NW of Nürnberg; railway; economy: radios, audio equipment, electronics.

Fushun *foo-shahn*, FOU-SHAN, 41 50N 123 53E, pop(1983e) 1,210,000, city in Liaoning prov, NE China; railway; economy: important base for the coal and oil refining industries; power, steel, machinery, chemicals, pharmaceuticals, electronics, textiles, grain and timber processing, trade in soya beans, rice, wheat, maize, sorghum, peanuts, tobacco, hemp.

Fuxin *foo-shin*, FOU-HSIN, 42 08N 121 39E, pop(1984e) 653,200, city in Liaoning prov, NE China; railway.

Fuzhou *foo-jō*, 26 09N 119 17E, pop(1984e) 1,164,800, provincial capital of Fujian prov, SE China; on the N bank of the Min Jiang river, near the Taiwan Strait and the East China Sea; established in 202 BC, Fuzhou grew in the 6th century and in the 10th century was made capital of an autonomous state; in the early 19th century a Fuzhou official led the first serious military campaign against foreigners attempting to import opium, precipitating the First Opium War; in 1842 it was established as an open port; China's first modern ship was constructed here at the Mawei shipyard; re-opened to the outside world in 1979; Mawei economic and technical development zone specializes in steel; railway; airfield; connected by coastal passenger shipping to Shanghai; economy: fishing, food processing and trade in rice, sugar cane, tea, oranges, fruit; monuments: West Lake Park was first laid out as an imperial garden more than 1,000 years ago; the Twin Pagodas serve as symbols of Fuzhou; the White Pagoda at the foot of Yushan Hill (built in 904, destroyed by fire in 1534 and rebuilt in 1548) is 41 m high, has 8 corners and 7 levels; the Ebony Pagoda at the foot of Wushan Hill (built in 941 and later renovated) is 33.9 m high and similar to the White Pagoda; Yushan and Wushan hills were both established as Daoist mountain retreats with several temples; approx 10 km outside Fuzhou on Drum Hill is the Yongquan Si (Bubbling Spring Temple), containing a tooth of Buddha.

Fyn *foon*, FÜNEN *foon'en* (Ger), Danish island between S Jylland (Jutland) and Sjælland (Zealand), bounded by the Lille Bælt (Little Belt) on W and the Store Bælt (Great Belt) on E; area 3,486 sq km; the largest lake, Arreskov, is drained by the R Odense; the administrative and cultural capital of the island is Hans Andersen's town of Odense; other towns include Svendborg and Nyborg; with small adjacent islands constitutes a county of Denmark; 2nd largest island in Denmark; there is a train ferry from Nyborg to Korsør.

Fyn, a county of Denmark, between Jylland (Jutland) and Sjælland (Zealand); includes Fyn I, Langeland I and several other small islands; area 3,486 sq km; pop(1983) 453,773; capital Odense; chief towns Middelfart, Nyborg and Svendborg.

G

Gabès *ga'bes*, 33 52N 10 06E, pop(1984) 92,259, port and resort capital of Gabès governorate, E Tunisia, N Africa; on the Golfe de Gabès coast, 320 km S of Tunis; located on the site of an ancient Phoenician settlement; an important trade outlet for the Saharan nomads, marking the junction between coastal road and desert tracks; airfield; railway terminus; economy: cement, bricks, potassium processing, petrochemicals, oil refinery and tanker port to the N at Skhira; monuments: mosque of Sidi Bouloubaba, who was appointed to shave the Prophet's face; carpet museum; event: Festival of Sidi Bouloubaba, a festival of music and arts in July.

Gabon *ga-bõn'*, official name the Gabonese Republic, RÉPUBLIQUE GABONAISE (Fr), a republic of W equatorial Africa, bounded S, E and NE by the Congo, N by Cameroon, NW by Equatorial Guinea and W by the Atlantic Ocean; timezone GMT +1; area 267,667 sq km; pop (1984e) 958,000; capital Libreville; chief towns Oyem, Makokou, Lambaréné, Port Gentil, Tchibanga, Mouila, Koulamoutou and Franceville; the indigenous pop comprises approx 40 Bantu tribes which are divided into 4 main groups, the Fang, the Eshira, the Bapounou and the Bateke; about 10% of the people are expatriate Africans and Europeans (mainly French); the majority of the pop are Christian, the remainder following local beliefs; there are a few (less than 1%) Muslims; the official language is French, with Fang, Myene and Bateke dialects also spoken; the unit of currency is the franc CFA; national holidays 12 March (Renovation Day), 17 Aug (Independence Day), also major Christian and Islamic holidays; membership of AfDB, African Wood Organization, Conference of East and Central African States, BDECA (Central African Development Bank), EAMA, EIB (associate), FAO, G-77, GATT, IAEA, IBRD, ICAO, ICCO, ICO, IDA, IDB (Islamic Development Bank), IFAD, IFC, ILO, IMF, IMO, INTELSAT, INTERPOL, IPU, ITU, NAM, OAU, OIC, OPEC, UDEAC, UN, UNESCO, UPU, WHO, WIPO, WMO and WTO.

Physical description. Gabon sits astride the Equator for 880 km from W to E. Its coast is typified by lagoons and estuaries which include Lagune Nkomi, Lagune M'Banio and Lagune Ndogo, and the Gabon and Ogooué estuaries. The land rises in a series of steps toward the African central plateau and is cut by a number of rivers including the Ogooué (the country's main river), the Ivindo (NE), the Komo (NW), the Nyanga (SW) and the Ngounié (W central). Much of the country is within the basin of the R Ogooué which flows from the SE of the country generally NW and W to meet the Atlantic S of Libreville. There are few large waterbodies within Gabon except the Lac Onangué, SW of Lambaréné. The general elevation of the plateau is between 1,000 m and 1,200 m.

Climate. Gabon has a typical equatorial climate with hot, wet, cloudy and humid conditions. Annual average rainfall ranges between 1,250 mm and 2,000 mm inland, with June to Aug being marginally drier than other months. Average rainfall can be greater in coastal areas. The capital, Libreville, has an average annual rainfall of 2,510 mm with an average max daily temperature range between 33°C and 37°C.

History, government and constitution. The first Europeans to visit the area were the Portuguese in the 15th century. The country is named after the Portuguese word 'gabão', a coat with sleeve and hood bearing a resemblance to the shape of the R Komo estuary. During the following century Dutch, British and French traders arrived, France eventually gaining control after signing treaties with coastal chiefs in 1839 and 1841. In 1849 a slave ship was captured by the French and the liberated slaves formed a settlement on a site which was called Libreville (the current capital of Gabon). A number of explorers investigated the interior between 1862 and 1887, the most famous of these being Savorgnan de Brazza who attempted to locate the headwaters of the R Congo. The French occupied Gabon in 1885 but it was not administered by them until 1903. It was in 1910 that Gabon became one of four territories of French West Africa, a federation which remained intact until 1959. The following year Gabon, along with the Central African Republic, Chad and the Congo, became independent. A single-party political system was adopted in 1961. The current constitution provides for an executive president elected for a 7-year term, an appointed council of ministers (about 28 members), and a legislative National Assembly of 84 elected and 9 appointed members serving for a 5-year term.

Economy. Although 65% of the pop is employed in farming, only a small area of land is under cultivation growing corn, coffee, cocoa, bananas, rice, yams and cassava. Low production necessitates a high import (90%) of foodstuffs. Until the discovery of oil, timber extraction formed the basis of the economy. The most valuable timber tree is the okoumé of which Gabon is the world's largest producer. Other timbers extracted include mahogany, izogo, iroko and tchikola mostly converted to plywood, pulp and paper manufacture although an increasing amount is being processed to produce veneers and furniture within the country. Since independence, Gabon has enjoyed rapid economic growth largely owing to the discovery and exploitation of oil, natural gas, and minerals which account for 80% of exports. Crude oil production is mainly derived from offshore fields near Port Gentil. Gabon has reserves of iron ore, gold, lead, zinc, columbium, uranium, tantalum, marble and alabaster, manganese and limestone. Manganese, gold and uranium are extracted in significant amounts. The main industrial activities include timber and mineral processing, food processing and oil refining. The completion of an International Monetary Fund (IMF) programme in 1982 significantly contributed to the development of the economy and an end to debt service difficulties which emerged in the late 1970s. The completion of major roads and the Trans-Gabon railway system has also provided a stimulus to the economy. The main trading partners are France, West Germany, the USA, the UK, the Netherlands, Belgium and Luxembourg.

Administrative divisions. Gabon is divided into 9 provinces:

Province	*area (sq km)*	*pop(1970)*
Estuaire	20,740	195,000
Haut-Ogooué	36,547	127,000
Moyen-Ogooué	18,535	52,000
Ngounié	37,750	130,000
Nyanga	21,285	67,000
Ogooué-Ivindo	46,075	60,000
Ogooué-Lolo	25,380	52,000
Ogooué-Maritime	22,890	120,000
Woleu-Ntem	38,465	148,000

These provinces are sub-divided into 37 départements.

Gaboro'ne, 24 45S 25 55E, pop(1981) 59,657, independent township and capital of Botswana, S Africa; alt 1,006 m; area 97 sq km; located in South East dist, WNW of Pretoria (South Africa); most of the city has developed since it became the capital of Botswana in 1965; Botswana campus of the University of Botswana and Swaziland; airport (2 km); economy: light industry, textiles, trade, services.

Ga'brovo, okrug (prov) of central Bulgaria on the N slopes of the Stara Planina (Balkan Mts), traversed by the R Yantra; area 2,068 sq km; pop(1981) 178,000; an open-air museum was set up in Etur 8 km S of Gabrovo in 1963; fruit-growing area.

Gabrovo, 42 52N 25 19E, pop(1981) 79,523, capital of Gabrovo okrug (prov), central Bulgaria; on the R Yantra; railway; developed as an important industrial town following its liberation in 1877; economy: textiles, metal products, wood, leather.

Gabù *ga-boo'*, region in Guinea-Bissau, W Africa; pop(1979) 104,227.

Gadsden, 34 01N 86 01W, pop(1980) 47,565, county seat of Etowah county, NE Alabama, United States; on the R Coosa, 95 km NE of Birmingham; railway; economy: iron, coal, limestone, sand and clay mining, rubber, metal and textile industries.

Gafsa *gaf'su*, CAPSA (Lat), 34 28N 8 43E, pop(1984) 60,870, capital of Gafsa governorate, central Tunisia, N Africa; 290 km SSW of Tunis; inhabited in palaeolithic times and an important settlement since the Numidian era; the city has developed from a well-watered oasis; airfield; economy: phosphate mining region, tourism, handicrafts, fruit trade; monuments: mosque, ruins of Roman pools.

Gagnoa *gag-nō'a*, dept in S central Ivory Coast, W Africa; pop(1975) 259,504; area 6,900 sq km; capital Gagnoa.

Gaiba, Lago *gī'ba*, lake in E Santa Cruz dept, Bolivia; on the border with Brazil, 129 km N of Puerto Suárez; length 13 km; width 6 km; receives the Río Pando and is connected with Río Paraguay by a NE outlet; also connected by a short stream to L Uberaba (NNW); to NE in Mato Grosso prov, Brazil, is the Cara Cara Biological Reserve.

Gail *gayl*, river in Tirol and Kärnten states, Austria; rises in the Carnic Alps and flows E to meet the R Drau at Villach; length 122 km.

Gainesville, 29 40N 82 20W, pop(1980) 81,371, county seat of Alachua county, N central Florida, United States; 100 km SW of Jacksonville; university (1853); railway; economy: electronic equipment and wood products; monuments: Paynes Prairie State Park, Warrens Cave.

Gainsborough *gaynz'bur-u*, 53 24N 0 46W, pop(1981) 20,593, river port in West Lindsey dist, Lincolnshire, E central England; on the R Trent, 25 km NW of Lincoln; railway; economy: transport equipment, engineering, food processing, timber.

Gairdner, Lake *gard'ner*, shallow salt lake in S central South Australia, Australia; 257 km N of Port Lincoln; 154 km long and 48 km wide, with an area of 4,766 sq km.

Gaithersburg *gay'therz-berg*, 39 08N 77 12W, pop(1980) 26,424, town in Montgomery county, W Maryland, United States; 32 km NW of Washington; railway.

Galán, Cerro *ga-lan'*, Andean peak rising to 6,600 m on the border between Catamarca prov, Andina, and Salta prov, Norte, N Argentina; 40 km SW of Rinconada.

Galápagos *ga-la'pa-gōs*, ARCHIPIÉLAGO DE COLÓN *kol-ōn'*, Ecuadorian island group situated on the Equator, 970 km west of the South American mainland; the Galápagos group includes the 6 main islands of San Cristóbal, Santa Cruz, Isabela, Floreana, Santiago and Fernandina, the last 2 of which are uninhabited; there is also the smaller island of Baltra (with an airport), and the 11 uninhabited islands of Santa Fe, Pinzón, Española, Rábida, Daphne, Seymour, Genovesa, Marchena, Pinta, Darwin and Wolf, and over 40 small islets; the highest peak is Volcán Wolf (1,707 m) on Isabela Island; pop(1982) 6,119; area 7,812 sq km; discovered in 1535 by the Spanish who laid no claim to them; for the next 3 centuries they were frequented only by pirates and political refugees; later used as a whaling supply depot; English names given to the islands by US and British navigators are now mainly used only in scientific literature; with British consent Ecuador took possession in 1832; Darwin visited the islands in 1835; the largest island, Isabela (formerly Albemarle), is 120 km long and forms half the total land area of the archipelago; its notorious convict colony was closed in 1958; the Galápagos Is are divided administratively into the 3 cantons of San Cristóbal, Isabela and Santa Cruz; the administrative centre is Baquerizo Moreno on San Cristóbal, but the largest town is Puerto Ayora on Santa Cruz; of volcanic origin, the islands are almost entirely composed of basaltic lava flows with shallow, cratered cones, some of which are active; the cold Humboldt Current meeting the warmth of the Equator, in addition to constant volcanic activity, has produced an archipelago of diverse vegetation and landforms, from lava deserts to tropical forests; many unique species of flora and fauna evolved independent of

the mainland (and sub-species on different islands); on Isla Fernandina is the largest concentration of marine iguanas, the world's only marine lizards; the largest concentrations of tortoises are to be found on Isabela (6,000 in 1975) and Santa Cruz (3,000 in 1975), with smaller numbers on San Cristóbal (500), Santiago (500) and Pinzón (500) islands; at Academy Bay on Isla Santa Cruz is the Charles Darwin Biological Research Station, established in 1959; in April 1985 a serious fire on Isabela Island destroyed much of the island's unique wildlife; the 6,912-sq km Galápagos National Park was established in 1934.

Galashiels *ga-la-sheelz'*, 55 37N 2 49W, pop(1981) 12,244, town in Ettrick and Lauderdale dist, Borders, SE Scotland; on the Gala Water, 22 km N of Hawick; Scottish College of Textiles; economy: textiles; monument: Abbotsford House, home (1817-22) of the novelist Sir Walter Scott, is 4 km from Galashiels.

Galaţi *ga-lats'*, county in E Romania; bounded to the E by the USSR; pop(1983) 623,450; area 4,425 sq km; capital Galaţi.

Galaţi, GALATZ, 45 27N 28 02E, pop(1983) 285,077, river port and capital town of Galaţi county, E Romania; on the R Danube; an important trading centre since the 16th century and a free port between 1834 and 1883; university (1948); airfield; railway junction; economy: fishing, shipyards, iron, steel, textiles, hardware, petroleum refining, food processing; monument: St George Church (16th-c).

Galdhøpiggen *gal-hup'pig-un*, 61 38N 8 19E, peak in the Jotunheimen range, W Oppland county, S central Norway, 128 km NW of Lillehammer, W of the Glittertind; height 2,469 m; 2nd highest peak in Norway.

Galesburg, 40 57N 90 22W, pop(1980) 35,305, county seat of Knox county, W Illinois, United States; 72 km WNW of Peoria; railway; birthplace of Carl Sandburg.

Galicia *gal-i'sha*, autonomous region of Spain in the NW corner of the Iberian peninsula extending S to the Portuguese border, comprising the provs of La Coruña, Lugo, Orense and Pontevedra; pop(1981) 2,811,912; area, 29,434 sq km; watered by a number of rivers including the R Minho (Miño) all of which are enclosed by ridges of hills; the deep fjord-like inlets (rias) at the river mouths provide the ports of Vigo and La Coruña with protection from the storms that sweep in from the Atlantic; smallholder farms produce maize and wine, but sardine fishing and the mining of wolfram and tin play a more important part in the economy; many Galician smallholders have emigrated to South America; there is a separatist political movement.

Galilee *ga'li-lee*, GALIL (Hebrew), N region of former Palestine and now of Israel, bounded W by the Mediterranean Sea, N by Lebanon, E by Syria, L Tiberias, and the Jordan valley, and S by the Yizre'el (Jezreel) plain; chiefly associated in Biblical times with the ministry of Jesus; after the destruction of Jerusalem (AD 70), Galilee became the main centre of Judaism in Palestine; in 1948 border areas were the scene of fierce fighting during the Arab invasion of Israel.

Galle *gahl*, formerly POINT DE GALLE, 6 01N 80 13E, pop(1981) 76,873, capital of Galle dist, Southern prov, Sri Lanka; on W coast, 116 km SE of Colombo; a major seaport in colonial times until Colombo became the country's main port in 1875; the Portuguese took Galle from the Sinhala kings in 1587; Dutch laid siege to Galle in 1640; noted for its handicrafts of tortoiseshell, ivory, ebony and woven lace, which have been subject to strong Arab influence.

Gallipoli, peninsula of Turkey. See Gelibolu.

Galloway, SW Scotland. See Dumfries and Galloway.

Gal'veston, 29 18N 94 48W, pop(1980) 61,902, summer resort and county seat of Galveston county, SE Texas, United States; a port on Galveston I, at the mouth of Galveston Bay; named after Count Bernardo de Gálvez, viceroy of New Spain; in 1817 the privateer Jean Lafitte established a base here; the city was laid out in a grid pattern in 1839 by Michael B. Menard; in 1900 a hurricane swept water across the low lying island, killing thousands and destroying the city; a 16 km-high sea wall was later erected but the city was again badly damaged by a hurricane in 1961; university; railway; airfield; economy: oil refining, shipbuilding, grain, machinery, chemicals, fishing (especially for shrimp); monuments: antique dollhouse museum, the sailing ship *Elissa*; event: Dickens on the Strand (Dec).

Galway *gol'way*, NA GAILLIMHE (Gael), county in Connacht prov, W Irish Republic; bounded W by Atlantic Ocean; the Twelve Bens rise to the W and the county is drained by the R Clare which joins Lough Corrib at its S end; pop(1981) 172,018; area 5,939 sq km; capital Galway; agriculturally poor mountainous land in W and sheep and cattle farming in the E; tourism and associated craft industries are important.

Galway, GAILLIMH (Gael), 53 16N 9 04W, pop(1981) 41,861, seaport capital of Galway county, Connacht, W Irish Republic; at the head of Galway Bay and S end of L Corrib; includes the resort suburb of Salthill (W) with modern Leisureland complex; university (1849); technical college; airfield at Carnmore (6 km E of city); railway; economy: textiles, chemicals; monuments: the Spanish Arch is a reminder of former trade links with Spain in the Middle Ages; plaque opposite church of St Nicholas commemorates Mayor Lynch who sentenced his own son to death and then, when the official executioner refused to carry out the sentence, hanged him himself; events: annual horse show in July; Galway plate-horse racing in Aug; Irish theatre festival (Jul-Aug); international sea angling festival in Sept; Claddagh summer festival; Sept oyster festival.

Gambaga *gam-ba'ga*, 10 31N 0 22W, town SE of Bolgatanga in Northern region, N Ghana, W Africa.

Gambia, GAMBIE (Fr), river in W Africa; rises in the Fouta Djallon massif in Guinea near the town of Labé and flows for about 800 km W to the Atlantic Ocean; for the last 470 km of its course it runs along the length of The Gambia; passes the towns of Basse, Georgetown, Kuntaur and Kaur; navigable by ocean-going ships for 200 km and by shallower draft craft for its entire length in The Gambia; the river is tidal for 160 km and 60 km during the rainy and dry seasons respectively.

Gam'bia, The, official name The Republic of the Gambia; a W African republic bounded on all sides by Senegal with the exception of its Atlantic Ocean coastline; timezone GMT; area 10,402 sq km; pop(1984) 725,000; there are no railways, 432 km of paved roads, 501 km of improved roads and 400 km of inland waterways; capital Banjul (formerly Bathurst); chief towns Serrekunda, Brikama and Bakau; ethnic groups include Madinka (37.7%), Fula (16.2%), Wolof (14%) and Jola (8.5%), others (13.1%) and non-Gambians (10.5%); 85% of the pop is Muslim, 14% is Christian and 1% follows local beliefs; the official language is English with local tongues such as Madinka, Wolof and Fula also spoken; Arabic is taught in Koranic schools; the unit of currency is the dalasi of 100 butut; national holiday 18 Feb (Independence Day); membership of AfDB, APC, Commonwealth, ECA, ECOWAS, FAO, G-77, GATT, IBRD, ICAO, IDA, Inter-American Development Bank, IFAD, IMF, IMO, IRC, ITU, NAM, OAU, OIC, UN, UNESCO, UPU, WFTU, WHO, WMO and WTO.

Physical description. The Gambia is a strip of land 322 km long from E-W lying along the R Gambia which is navigable by ocean-going ships for 200 km upstream from its estuary. A flat country, especially near the coast, The Gambia does not rise above 90 m.

Climate. The Gambia has a tropical climate with a rainy season extending from June to Sept. Rainfall decreases further inland. The prevailing winds during this period are warm and humid and blow from the SW-W off the S Atlantic. During the dry season the dry and often dust-laden Saharan *harmattan* wind blows from the NE. The climate is most oppressive, especially on the coast, during the wet season owing to high humidity levels and high night-time temperatures. The average annual rainfall at

Banjul is 1,295 mm with average temperatures ranging from 22.8°C (Jan) to 26.7°C (July). Inland temperatures can rise to over 40°C.

History, government and constitution. The Gambia was first visited by Europeans in 1455 when Portuguese explorers sailed up the R Gambia, but the area was not settled until the 17th century. In 1807 the country was administered from Sierra Leone and in 1843 The Gambia became an independent British Crown Colony. In 1866 it was included in the West African Settlements but in 1888 it reverted to separate colonial status. It was not until 1904, after the French had renounced trading rights, that its boundaries were finally defined. The Gambia achieved full internal government from Britain in 1963 and became an independent member of the Commonwealth in 1965. In 1970 it was declared a republic within the Commonwealth. In 1982 The Gambia and Senegal joined to form the Confederation of Senegambia which was designed to integrate their military, economic, communications and foreign policies whilst preserving independence and sovereignty. The government consists of a 43-member House of Representatives (35 elected by popular vote, 4 representing tribal chiefs and 4 nominated), a president (head of state) and a cabinet of about 12 members.

Economy. Agriculture is the most important sector of the economy with groundnuts being the most important cash crop and occupying about half of all cultivated land. Cotton is the other main cash crop. In terms of food crops The Gambia relies heavily on rice but is not yet self-sufficient. Other agriculture includes millet, sorghum, fruit and vegetables and livestock. Industries include groundnut processing, brewing, soft drinks, agricultural machinery assembly, small wood and metal working and clothing. The main exports are groundnuts and groundnut products, fish and palm kernels. Tourism has become an important sector of the economy in recent years with a total of 41,950 visitors to beach resorts in 1983-84. The main trading partners for imports are the UK, China, the Netherlands, Japan, France, Burma, West Germany, and for exports the UK, the Netherlands, France, Italy, Switzerland, Portugal and West Germany.

Administrative divisions. The Gambia is divided into 8 local government areas:

Local govt area	*area (sq km)*	*pop(1983)*
Banjul	12.7	44,186
Kombo St Mary	75.6	101,431
Brikama	1,759.3	137,194
Mansakonko	1,547.5	55,266
Kerewan	2,151.5	112,047
Kuntaur	1,466.5	57,608
Georgetown	1,381.5	68,418
Basse	2,008.0	111,335

Gambier, Archipel des, GAMBIER ISLANDS (Eng), coral island group of French Polynesia, S Pacific Ocean; area 11 sq km; pop(1977) 515; comprises 4 islands and many uninhabited islets, enclosed within a semi-circular outer barrier reef; rises to 482 m at Mt Duff; part of the Tuamotu Archipelago; Mangaréva, the main island and largest of the group, is 8 km long and has Rikitéa as its chief port.

Gamo Gofa, GEMU-GOFA, region in SW Ethiopia, NE Africa; pop(1984e) 1,248,034; area 39,500 sq km; mountainous region rising to 4,200 m at Gugē; the R Omo Wenz flows along the W and N border; chief towns Gīdole and Bako.

Gampaha *gam'pa-ha*, 7 06N 80 00E, pop(1981) 10,456, capital of Gampaha dist, Western prov, Sri Lanka; NE of Colombo.

Gamprin *gam-preen'*, 47 14N 9 31E, pop(1985) 927, commune in Unterland dist, Principality of Liechtenstein, central Europe; area 6.1 sq km.

Gand, city in Belgium. See Gent.

Gandak *gun'duk*, river formed W of Kathmandu, Nepal, by the junction of the Kali Gandaki and Trisuli rivers; flows SW from the foothills of the Himalayas into India then SE to meet the R Ganga (Ganges) opposite Patna; length (including R Kali Gandaki) 675 km.

Gander, 48 58N 54 34W, pop(1981) 10,404, town in E Newfoundland, E Canada; on the island of Newfoundland, NW of St John's; airport; economy: fish processing, oil.

Gandhinagar *gahn'di-nah-gur*, 23 15N 72 45E, pop(1981) 62,443, capital of Gujarat state, W India; 25 km N of Ahmadabad.

Gandia *gan-dee'a*, 38 58N 0 09E, pop(1981) 48,494, town in Valencia prov, E Spain; 68 km SSE of Valencia; port at Grao de Gandia; economy: fruit, brandy, olive oil, cement, velvet, silk, leather, food canning.

Ganga *gung'gah*, GANGES *gan'jeez* (Eng), river in N India; formed in the E Himalayas from the headwaters of the Alaknanda and Pindar streams at Karnapravag; flows W through the Silwalik Range to Hardwar and onto the Ganga Plain; continues SE to Allahabad, where it receives the waters of the Yamuna river and then E to Varanasi; turns NE to Patna and E through the state of Bihar, turning SE into the state of West Bengal where it follows the frontier with Bangladesh; receives water from the R Brahmaputra (Jamuna), 32 km NNW of Faridpur; as the R Padma it continues SE through Bangladesh, joining the R Meghna to the NW of Chandpur; branches into many tributaries and forms the vast Ganga-Brahmaputra delta in the Bay of Bengal, which stretches from the Meghna in the E to the R Hugli in the W; total length 2,510 km; the Ganga is an important trade artery in addition to providing irrigation water to the fertile Ganga Plain where crops of rice, oilseed, sugar cane and cotton are produced in one of the world's most densely populated areas; considered one of the most sacred Hindu rivers.

Gangdisê Shan *gung-di-se*, KAILAS RANGE, mountain range in SW Xizang aut region (Tibet), SW China; situated N of the Himalayas; rises to 6,714 m in Kangrinboqê Feng peak; bounded in the E by the Nyainqêntanglha Shan range; acts as a watershed between the inland drainage system and the Indian ocean drainage system.

Ganges, river in India. See Ganga.

Gannett Peak, 43 10N 109 38W, mountain in Fremont county, central Wyoming, United States; rises to 4,201 m in the Rocky Mts; the highest peak in Wyoming state.

Gansu *kan-soo*, KANSU, prov in N central China; situated in the upper Huang He (Yellow river) valley; bordered N by Mongolia and Nei Mongol aut region (Inner Mongolia), E by Shaanxi prov and Ningxia aut region, S by Qinghai, Sichuan and Shaanxi provs and W by Xinjiang aut region; adjoins the Loess, Inner Mongolia and Tibetan plateaux, with an average alt of 1,000-3,000 m; drained by the Huang He river and its tributaries; its central S border with Qinghai prov lies along the Qilian Shan range; to the N on the Nei Mongol border are the Heli Shan and Longshou Shan ranges; the corridor between these ranges is largely desert or semi-desert; it was a natural route from central China to Xinjiang aut region and central Asia in ancient times and was used for the trading of silk; pop(1982) 19,569,261; area 530,000 sq km; capital Lanzhou.

Ganta *gan'ta*, 7 15N 8 59W, town in Liberia, W Africa; 225 km NE of Monrovia.

Gao *gow*, region in N Mali, W Africa; pop(1971) 630,632; area 808,920 sq km; a flat desert landscape, the only major elevation being the Adrar des Iforhas in the NE; between Gao and Tombouctou, S of the R Niger, are the Mts du Takamadasset and W of Gao is Mount Sounfal; Tombouctou is at the NE end of the Macina depression and lakes in this area include L Faguibine (W), L Haribonga and L Dô (SE); the R Niger flows in an arc across the S of the region past Tombouctou, Gao and Ansongo; capital Gao; chief towns Tombouctou, Goundam, Gourma-Rharous, Kidal, Diré, Bamba, Bourem, Ansongo and Ménaka; economy: salt, uranium, phosphate, manganese and aluminium mining; oil refining; phosphate processing.

Gao, 16 19N 0 09W, pop(1976) 30,714, river-port capital of Gao region, E Mali, W Africa; on the R Niger; once capital of the Songhai empire, Gao houses the mosque of Kankan Moussa and tomb of the Askia dynasty; airfield; from July to Dec there are river connections to Koulikoro; economy: power plant, trade centre, agriculture.

Gaoua *ga'wa*, 10 18N 3 12W, town in SW Burkina, W Africa; 145 km SE of Bobo Dioulasso.

Gap, VAPINCUM (anc), 44 33N 6 05E, pop(1982) 32,097, ancient mountain town and capital of Hautes-Alpes dept, Provence-Alpes-Côte d'Azur region, SE France; on the R Laye, 154 km NNE of Marseille; episcopal see; railway; winter skiing at nearby Ceuse (1,520 m); in this town is the house in which Napoleon spent a night in March 1815 on his way N after escaping from Elba.

Garbsen, 52 25N 9 36E, pop(1983) 57,700, city in Hannover dist, Niedersachsen (Lower Saxony) prov, W Germany, 13 km W of Hannover.

Gard, dept in Languedoc-Roussillon region of S France, on the Mediterranean and the lower Rhône; named after one of its tributaries which cuts it from W to E; comprises 3 arrond, 45 cantons and 353 communes; pop(1982) 530,478; area 5,853 sq km; the NW rises to 1,567 m at Mt Aigoual in the Cévennes, but the S is flat and swampy, with salt marshes and pools; quantities of olives, mulberries (for the important silkworms), grapes (for the abundant local red wines and Montpellier brandy), cherries, apricots, peaches, figs and pears are grown; the famous Pont du Gard aqueduct, one of the most imposing Roman remains in France, was built here by Agrippa in 19 BC to bring water from near Uzès to Nîmes; capital Nîmes, other towns include Alès and Uzès; there are interesting caves near Camprieu (Abîme de Bramabiau); spa at Les-Fumades-les-Bains; Le Duche (Ducal Castle) at Uzès; part of the Parc National des Cévennes lies within the dept (walking, skiing, watersports, caving).

Garda, Lago di *la'go dee gahr'dah*, LAKE GARDA (Eng), LACUS BENACUS (anc), largest Italian lake (named after the village on its E shore), lying between the regions of Lombardia and Veneto, in the provs of Trento, Verona, and Brescia, N Italy; area 370 sq km; length 52 km; width 5-16.5 km; max depth 346 m; separated from the Adige river valley to the E by the 80 km long limestone ridge of the Monte Baldo (2,218 m); receives R Sarca (N), leaving it (SE) as R Mincio, a tributary of the Po; N part of the lake is narrow and fjord-like; the Riviera Bresciana is a fertile strip between Gargnano and Salò on the W side of the lake; olives are grown up to a height of 300 m around the shoreline; resort towns include Riva del Garda, Desenzano, San Zeno di Montagna, Garda, and Sirmione.

Garđar, GARDHAR, 64 05N 21 55W, town in Suđurland, W Iceland; S of Reykjavik; pop(1983) 5,764, economy: shipbuilding, metallurgy, chemicals.

Garden City, 42 20N 83 21W, pop(1980) 35,640, town in Wayne county, SE Michigan, United States; 24 km W of Detroit.

Garden Grove, 33 47N 117 55W, pop(1980) 123,307, residential city in Orange county, SW California, United States; NW of Santa Ana.

Gardena *gar-dee'ne*, 33 53N 118 18W, pop(1980) 45,165, city in Los Angeles county, SW California, United States; suburb 16 km S of Los Angeles.

Gardēz *gar-dez'*, GORDIAZ, 33 37N 69 09E, pop(1984e) 10,469, capital of Paktīā prov, E Afghanistan; lying to the S of Kābul.

Gardunha, Serra da *gar-doon'ya*, mountain range, NE central Portugal, NNW of Castelo Branco, rising to 1,225 m.

Garfield, 40 52N 74 06W, pop(1980) 26,803, town in Bergen county, NE New Jersey, United States; on R Passaic, 8 km SE of Paterson; railway.

Garfield Heights, 41 26N 81 37W, pop(1980) 34,938, town in Cuyahoga county, NE Ohio, United States; 10 km SSE of Cleveland; railway.

Gar'forth, 53 48N 1 24W, pop(1981) 15,992, town in Leeds borough, West Yorkshire, N England; 11 km E of Leeds; railway; economy: coal, transport equipment, timber.

Garland, 32 55N 96 38W, pop(1980) 138,857, town in Dallas county, NE Texas, United States; a suburb 21 km NNE of Dallas; railway; economy: important centre for the research and manufacture of electronic components for aircraft and missiles.

Garonne *gar-on*, GARUMNA (anc), the principal river of SW France, rising in the Val d'Aran, 42 km inside the Spanish border; flows from the central Pyrénées NE and NW through Haute-Garonne, Tarn-et-Garonne, Lot-et-Garonne and Gironde depts past Toulouse, Agen and Bègles to the Bec d'Ambes, 32 km below Bordeaux, where it meets the R Dordogne to form the Gironde estuary; length 575 km; tributaries Neste, Save, Gers, Baise, Salat, Ariège, Tarn and Lot rivers; at Toulouse the Canal du Midi links it with the Mediterranean Sea; it is an important part of the inland waterways of France, serving Toulouse and Bordeaux.

Garoua *ga-roo'a*, GARUA, 9 17N 13 22E, pop(1984e) 93,000, river-port capital of Nord prov, Cameroon, W Africa; on the right bank of the R Bénoué, 645 km NNE of Yaoundé; at the centre of a cotton growing area, commercially established in 1951; the Bénoué-Niger waterway represents a seasonally (July-Sept) navigable 1,600 km route from Garoua to the open sea; the port trades in cotton, cement, salt, groundnuts and petrol products; railway; airport.

Garrigues, Monts *mõ gar-eeg*, low-lying limestone foothills of the Cévennes, S France, extending NE across the depts of Hérault and Gard; the highest point is Pic Saint Loup (658 m).

Gary, 41 36N 87 20W, pop(1980) 151,953, industrial city in Lake county, NW Indiana, United States; on L Michigan, 39 km SE of Chicago; railway; economy: major producer of raw steel.

Gascogne *gas-kony'*, GASCONY (Eng), VASCONIA (Lat), former prov in Aquitaine region, SW France, now occupying the depts of Landes, Gers, Hautes-Pyrénées and parts of Haute-Garonne, Tarn-et-Garonne and Lot-et-Garonne; bounded on the S by the Pyrénées and on the W by the Bay of Biscay; it was separated under first the Basques, then the Franks, who made it a duchy; in 1052 it was again joined to Guienne, remaining in English hands between 1154 and 1453.

Gasto'nia, 35 16N 81 11W, pop(1980) 47,333, county seat of Gaston county, SW North Carolina, United States; 30 km W of Charlotte; railway; economy: textile centre (major producer of fine-combed cotton yarn); also produces textile machinery.

Gateshead, 54 58N 1 35W, pop(1981) 91,893, town in Gateshead borough, Tyne and Wear, NE England; part of Tyneside urban area; S of R Tyne, opposite Newcastle upon Tyne; railway; economy: textiles, engineering, printing, rubber, electrical engineering, glass, plastics, paints, chemicals.

Gâtinais *ga-tee-nay*, pays of the Paris basin, SE of Paris, central France; the chalk is overlain with flinty clay which creates a watery surface to the land.

Gatineau *ga'ti-nõ*, 45 29N 75 40W, pop(1981) 74,988, town in S Québec, SE Canada; on the Ottawa river on the border with Ottawa prov; situated directly N of Ottawa; railway; economy: lumber, paper milling.

Gatos, Los, 37 14N 121 59W, pop(1980) 26,906, city in Santa Clara county, W California, United States; a residential suburb in the foothills of the Santa Clara Mts, 13 km SW of San José.

Gatún *gat-oon'*, lake in Colón prov, N Panama, Central America; it is part of the Panama Canal route which crosses it NW-SE between Juan Gallegos and Barro Colorado islands; area 422 sq km; a high-level reservoir, Madden Dam, feeds the lake and maintains its level at 26 m above sea-level; Barro Colorado I in the lake is a biological reserve for scientific research.

Gävle *yev'lu*, formerly GEFLE *yev'le*, 60 41N 17 10E, pop(1982) 87,621, seaport city and capital of Gävleborg county, E Sweden; 160 km NNW of Stockholm, on the W shore of the Gulf of Bothnia; received city charter in 1446; railway; economy: exports timber and metal ore from its modern port installations; monuments: 18th-c town hall, castle (1583-93); railway museum.

Gävleborg *yev'le-bor*, GAFLEBORG, GEFLEBORG, a county of E Sweden, bounded on the E by the Gulf of Bothnia; drained chiefly by the R Ljusnan; land area 18,191 sq km; pop(1983) 292,739; capital Gävle; chief towns Sandviken, Hofors, Söderhamn and Bollnas.

Gawler *go'ler*, 34 38S 138 44E, pop(1981) 9,433, town in Adelaide stat div, SE South Australia, Australia; on the Gawler river, N of Adelaide; railway; event: the Gawler 3-day equestrian event.

Gaya *ga'ya*, 11 52N 3 28E, town in Dosso dept, SW Niger, W Africa; on the R Niger; railway; economy: textiles.

Ga'za, prov in SW Mozambique, SE Africa; pop(1980) 990,900; area 75,709 sq km; situated on Tropic of Capricorn and bordered E by the R Changane; the R Limpopo flows NW-SE before entering the Mozambique Channel just SW of Xai-Xai; capital Xai-Xai; chief towns include Chibuto and Massingir; railway (from Maputo) runs SE-NW through prov before crossing into Zimbabwe at Chicualacuala; Banhine National Park is located within the prov.

Ga'za Strip, Israeli-occupied district under military administration since 1967; bounded NW by the Mediterranean Sea; area 202 sq km; chief town Gaza; formerly part of Egyptian Sinai; divided into the sub-districts of Gaza, Rafah and Khan Yunis; the ancient Philistine city of Gaza was excavated by Petrie.

Gazanku'lu, national state or non-independent black homeland in Transvaal prov, NE South Africa; S of Venda independent homeland; includes the districts of Giyani, Malamulele, Mhala and Ritavi; pop(1985) 497,213; achieved self-governing status in 1973.

Gaziantep *ga-zee-an'tep*, prov in S Turkey, bounded S by Syria and E by the R Euphrates; pop(1980) 808,697; area 7,642 sq km; capital Gaziantep.

Gaziantep, formerly ANTEP, AINTAB, 37 04N 37 21E, pop(1980) 374,290, capital city of Gaziantep prov, S Turkey, on a tributary of the R Euphrates; 6th largest city in Turkey; important trading and manufacturing centre; noted for its textiles and pistachio nuts; an important strategic centre during the Crusades; it was the centre of Turkish resistance (1920-21) to the French occupation of the region; railway; airfield.

Gdańsk *gda'insk*, voivodship in N Poland; bounded N by the Baltic Sea and E by R Wisła (Vistula); pop(1983) 1,373,000; area 7,394 sq km; capital Gdańsk; chief towns include Gdynia, Tczew, Sopot, Wejherowo and Starogard Gdański.

Gdańsk, formerly DANZIG (Ger), 54 22N 18 38E, pop(1983) 464,600, industrial port and capital of Gdańsk voivodship, N Poland; at the mouth of the Martwa Wisła (a branch of the Vistula); a stronghold of the Dukes of Gdańsk-Pomerania in the 10th century, it gained importance as a major European seaport and for its gold, furniture and clockmaking trades; the Lenin shipyard producing general cargo vessels is the largest in Poland; held by Prussia between 1793 and 1919 when it became a Free City within the Polish tariff area; with Sopot and Gdynia it forms part of the *Tri-city*; university (1970); technical university (1945); maritime research institutes; railway; airport; economy: shipbuilding, textiles, televisions, phosphorus fertilizer, oil refinery, food processing and cold storage; monuments: in the main town - High Gate, Golden Gate, St George Fraternity mansion (1487-94), Artus court; in the old port - Bakers' Gate, archaeological museum, Swan tower, churches of the Virgin Mary and St John and post office where 51 postal employees resisted German attacks for 14 hours on 1 Sept, 1939; in the old town - churches of St Elizabeth and St Catherine, 14th-c Great Mill, mansion of the abbots of Pelplin; in 14th-c old suburb S of main town - national museum, church of the Holy Trinity, small armoury; in the lower town - Royal Granary (1620); events: Gdańsk Festival in Aug, Polish feature film festival in Sept.

Gdynia *gdin'ya*, GDINGEN (Ger), 54 31N 18 30E, pop(1983) 240,200, seaport city in Gdańsk voivodship, N Poland; 20 km NW of Gdańsk on the Bay of Gdańsk (Załoka Gdańska); developed between 1924 and 1929 as a major Baltic port and naval base; included with Sopot and Gdańsk as part of the *Tri-city*; railway; economy: shipbuilding, deep sea fishing; monuments: oceanographic museum, the destroyer *Błyskawica* at the Southern Pier; monument of gratitude to Polish and Soviet soldiers killed during the liberation of the Gdańsk coast during 1945.

Gedaref *ge-da-ref'*, EL QADĀRIF, 14 01N 35 24E, pop(1973) 66,465, town in Eastern region, Sudan, NE Africa; 190 km SSW of Kassala; railway; economy: trade in livestock, grain, cotton and fruit.

Geelong *jee-long'*, 38 10S 144 26E, pop(1986) 148,300, port in Barwon stat div, S Victoria, Australia; on the W side of Corio Bay, part of Port Phillip Bay, SW of Melbourne; Deakin University (1974); railway; economy: aluminium refining, oil refining, motor vehicles, trade in wheat; monuments: many 19th-c villas with beautiful gardens; Geelong's customs house is the oldest wooden building in Victoria and was the town's first telegraph station.

Gejiu *ge-jyō*, KOCHIU, 23 28N 103 05E, pop(1984e) 337,700, mining city in Yunnan prov, SW China; major centre for the exploitation of half the tin reserves of China; on the railway from Kunming to Vietnam, just south of the Tropic of Cancer; tin was used in the minting of bronze coins during the reign of Emperor Qian Long (1731-96).

Gelderland *KHel'der-lant*, GUELDERLAND or GUELDERS (Eng), pop(1984e) 1,735,800, prov in E Netherlands, bounded on the E by W Germany and on the S by the R Maas, the rivers Lek and Ijssel also form part of the boundary; large parts of the landscape have been reclaimed during the past century; land area 5,008 sq km; capital Arnhem; chief towns Apeldoorn and Nijmegen; economy: predominantly mixed farming, some livestock farming (mostly cattle) in the NW; land consolidation and farming co-operative schemes are common; Gelderland is the largest prov in the Netherlands.

Geleen *KHu-layn'*, 50 58N 5 45E, pop(1984e) 177,410, city in Limburg prov, S Netherlands, NE of Maastricht.

Gelibolu *gel-e-be-loo'*, GALLIPOLI *ge-lip'e-lee*, narrow peninsula extending SW from the coast of İstanbul prov, NW Turkey; between the Çanakkale Boğazi (Dardanelles) in the SE and the Aegean Sea in the W; length c.100 km; scene of fierce fighting in 1915-16, during World War I.

Gelligaer *ge-hli-gar'*, 51 40N 3 18W, pop(1981) 16,905, mining town in Rhymney Valley dist, Mid Glamorgan, S Wales; 8 km NNW of Cardiff railway.

Gelsenkirchen *gel'zen-keer-KHen*, 51 30N 7 05E, pop(1983) 295,400, river port and industrial city in Düsseldorf dist, Nordrhein-Westfalen (North Rhine-Westphalia) prov, W Germany; 24 km W of Dortmund; railway; economy: oil refining, chemicals, petrochemicals, glass, plastics, household equipment, milling products including dietary foods.

Gemsbok *gemz'bok*, national park in W Kgalagadi dist, SW Botswana, S Africa; area 24,800 sq km; established in 1971; has a common and open border with South Africa's Kalahari Gemsbok National Park (N Cape Prov).

General Carrera, Lago, lake in Chile and Argentina. See Lago Buenos Aires.

Geneva, city and canton in Switzerland. See Genève.

Geneva, Lake of, Switzerland. See Léman, Lac.

Genève *zhė-nev'*, GENEVA *je-nee'va* (Eng), GENF (Ger), GINEVRA *ji-nayv'ra* (Ital), canton in W Switzerland; pop(1980) 349,040; area 282 sq km; capital Genève; it was an independent, Protestant republic until it joined the Swiss Confederacy in 1815.

Genève, 46 13N 6 09E, pop(1980) 156,505, capital city of Genève canton, W Switzerland; on the R Rhône at the W end of Lac Léman (Lake of Geneva); located at the heart of the European motorway network; known as the 'smallest of big capitals'; former seat of the League of Nations (1920-46), capital of 'la Suisse romande' (French-speaking Switzerland), and a long celebrated intellectual, theological and scientific centre associated with Rousseau, de Saussure, de Candolle; has been almost entirely rebuilt since 1847 in modern style, with widened streets; the Old Town is on the left bank of the R Rhône, where the cultural and artistic life is concentrated, while the railway station and the numerous international organizations are to be found on the right bank; c.200 organizations have their headquarters in Genève, most of them situated around the Place des Nations; Genève was a free city until the end of the 13th century, then an independent Republic until it chose to become a Swiss canton in 1814; Jean Calvin (1509-1564), the Reformer, made the city the 'Protestant Rome'; renowned for its numerous quays and its fountain, Jet d'Eau, which throws jets of water as high as 745 m; the university was developed out of the Academy founded by Calvin in 1559 for the training of Reformed theologians; railway; airport (Coitrin); economy: world capital of high-class watchmaking and jewellery; monument: St Peter's cathedral (12th-c); events: Escalade Day (12 Dec); International Automobile Show (annual).

Genf, city and canton in Switzerland. See Genève.

Genil *hay-neel'*, river rising from a glacier on Valeta Peak in the Sierra Nevada, Andalucia, S Spain; flows WNW to meet the R Guadalquivir near Palma del Río; length 337 km; reservoir at Embalse de Iznajar.

Genk *gengk*, 50 58N 5 30E, pop(1982) 61,643, town in Hasselt dist, Limburg prov, NE Belgium; economy: laminated sheet iron.

Genoa, prov and seaport in NW Italy. See Genova.

Genova *jay'nō-va*, GENOA *jen'ō-a* (Eng), GENUA (anc), GÊNES (Fr), prov of Liguria region, NW Italy; pop(1981) 1,045,109; area 1,831 sq km; capital Genova.

Genova, 44 24N 8 56E, pop(1981) 762,895, seaport and capital of Genova prov, Liguria region, NW Italy; on a semi-circular bay of the Golfo di Genova, in the foothills of the Appno Ligure; the conurbation of Greater Genova extends from Nervi to Voltri for a distance of 35 km along the coast; founded as a Roman trading centre on the Ligurian coast; by the 13th century it had become the leading Mediterranean port; because of its opposition to Venice it was granted special trading rights with Constantinople and the surrounding area; in the 14th century it lost its position to Venice for control of the Levant and declined commercially; included in the Ligurian Republic established by Napoleon in 1797 and given to the king of Sardinia in 1815; birthplace of Christopher Columbus; rebuilt after World War II, it became the largest and busiest port in the Mediterranean; in 1969 Genova was the first Mediterranean port to build container facilities; the modernization of smaller Italian ports such as Livorno and Spezia has taken some trade away from Genoa, which has been superseded by Marseille as the largest Mediterranean port; archbishopric; Academy of Fine Arts (1751); university (1471); Verdi Institute of Music; airport; railway; ferries; economy: oil refining, chemicals, papermaking, textiles, animal feedstuffs, synthetic detergents, toiletries, motor scooters and motorbikes, nuclear and geothermal power plant equipment, sugar refining; monuments: Doge's Palace (13th-c), Gothic church of San Matteo (1278), cathedral of San Lorenzo (consecrated 1118, remodelled in Gothic style in 1307-12), Palazzo Reale (begun 1650), Palazzo Rosso (17th-c, contains a picture gallery), and many other palaces; event: international ballet festival in the park of Villa Gropallo (July).

Gent *KHent*, dist of Oost-Vlaanderen (East Flanders) prov, NW Belgium; area 943 sq km; pop(1982) 485,696.

Gent, GAND *gã'* (Fr), GHENT *gent* (Eng), 51 02N 3 42E, pop(1982) 237,687, river port and capital city of Gent dist, Oost-Vlaanderen (East Flanders) prov, NW Belgium; at the confluence of the Schelde and Leie rivers, the many branches of which intersect the city; with its 5 suburbs it is the 3rd largest urban region in Belgium; 2nd largest port after Antwerpen, the harbour is connected by several canals to the Westerschelde (Gent-Terneuzen Canal) and the North Sea (Brugge-Gent Canal as well as the Brugge-Oostende Canal and the Brugge-Zeebrugge Canal), on the Gent-Terneuzen Canal is a steel mill and many other industrial plants; the main industrial area is N of the old medieval city; Gent is the focus of Flemish nationality; university (1816, since 1930 a Flemish institution); railway; economy: spinning and weaving (employing more than 10,000 people and producing the world-famous Flemish linen), chemicals, integrated steel works, car manufacturing, electrical and electronic engineering, publishing; monuments: cathedral of St Bavo (begun in the 10th century); town hall (15-17th-c); House of Free Boatmen (1531), the most beautiful Gothic guildhall in Belgium; abbey of St Bavo (642), restored several times since the 10th century; castle of Gravensteen (1180-1200).

Gentofte *gen'tof-tu*, 55 46N 12 32E, pop(1981) 66,782, city in København (Copenhagen) county, E Sjælland (Zealand), Denmark; part of Greater København; economy: timber, furniture, engineering, electrics.

George Town, 19 20N 81 23W, pop(1979) 7,617, seaport and capital of the Cayman Is, W Caribbean, on Grand Cayman I; financial and administrative centre; Owen Roberts International Airport is nearby.

George Town, PINANG, PENANG *pen-ang'*, 5 26N 100 16E, pop(1980) 248,241, capital of Pulau Pinang state, W Peninsular Malaysia, SE Asia; on the NE coast of the island of Pulau Pinang (Penang) on a headland known to local Malays as Tanjong; named after King George III of Great Britain; railway; ferry to Butterworth on the mainland; the city has a large Chinese population; economy: electronics, textiles, silk and toy trade; monuments: Fort Cornwallis; St George's church, the oldest Anglican church in SE Asia.

George'town, local government area in The Gambia, W Africa; pop(1983) 68,418; area 1,381.5 sq km; chief town Georgetown.

Georgetown, 6 46N 58 10W, pop(1983e) 188,000, federal and dist capital and major port, E Demerara dist, N Guyana, South America; on right bank at the mouth of R Demerara; the town is a tidal port, protected by a sea wall and a system of dykes; university (1963); railway; airfield (Ogle) at 9.5 km; airport (Timehri) at 40 km; economy: food processing, shrimp fishing; monuments: Georgetown's 19th-c wooden houses supported on stilts and its green boulevards laid along the lines of the old Dutch canals make it a very picturesque city; most of the older buildings are of wood, but a fire in 1945 has resulted in the erection of many concrete buildings in the commercial centre; colonial buildings include the Gothic-style wooden city hall, built in 1887; St George's cathedral (dating from 1892, height 43.5 m) is one of the tallest wooden buildings in the world; the President's Residence is at Guyana House on Main Street (1852); the Law Courts (finished in 1878) are on High Street, the Parliament Building on Avenue of the Republic; at the head of Brickdam (a main street) is an aluminium arch which commemorates independence; opposite this is a monument to the 1763 slave rebellion; the Botanic Gardens, which also include a small zoo, cover over 260 sq km and contain an exotic collection of orchids and palms; there are many sports grounds and clubs on the outskirts of the city.

Georgi Dimitrov *gyor'gi di-meet'rof*, lake in Stara Zagora okrug (prov) of Central Bulgaria, NW of Stara Zagora; takes its name from one of the socialist founders of the modern republic.

Georgia, constituent republic of the Soviet Union. See Gruzinskaya.

Georgia, state in SE United States; bounded W by Florida and Alabama, N by Tennessee and North Carolina, E by South Carolina and the Atlantic Ocean, and S by Florida; the R Savannah flows SE following the South Carolina state frontier to the Atlantic Ocean; the R Chattahoochee flows S, forming part of the W border;

the R Flint flows SSW and joins the R Chattahoochee at the SW corner of the state, forming the R Apalachicola; the Oconee and Ocmulgee rivers join in the SE to form the R Altamaha which flows SE to the Atlantic Ocean; the S end of the Blue Ridge Mts rises in the N; the highest point is Mt Brasstown Bald (1,457 m); the S part of the state is a low coastal plain which is heavily forested; the N includes the fertile Piedmont plateau, the Appalachian plateau and Blue Ridge Mts; the forested S region supplies many local paper mills, and the state leads the nation in the production of pulp; the state's leading industrial products include textiles, transportation equipment, food products and chemicals; nearly half the US crop of peanuts is grown in Georgia; other agricultural crops include cotton, tobacco, corn, poultry, livestock and soybeans; popular tourist resorts include the Golden Isles just off the Atlantic coast and the vast wilderness area of Okefenokee Swamp in the S; discovered by the Spanish, but settled in 1733 as a British colony, the last of the original 13 colonies to be founded; the 4th of the original 13 states (first southern state) to ratify the Constitution (1788); seceded from the Union in 1861; slavery was abolished in 1865, and Georgia became the last state to be re-admitted to the Union, on 15 July 1870; also known as the 'Empire State of the South' or the 'Peach State'; pop(1980) 5,463,105; area 150,946 sq km; capital Atlanta; other major cities are Columbus, Savannah and Macon; the state is divided into 159 counties:

County	*area (sq km)*	*pop(1980)*
Appling	1,326	15,565
Atkinson	894	6,141
Bacon	744	9,379
Baker	902	3,808
Baldwin	668	34,686
Banks	608	8,702
Barrow	424	21,354
Bartow	1,186	40,760
Ben Hill	660	16,000
Berrien	1,186	13,525
Bibb	658	150,256
Bleckley	569	10,767
Brantley	1,157	8,701
Brooks	1,278	15,255
Bryan	1,147	10,175
Bulloch	1,763	35,785
Burke	2,166	19,349
Butts	486	13,665
Calhoun	738	5,717
Camden	1,687	13,371
Candler	645	7,518
Carroll	1,303	56,346
Catoosa	421	36,991
Charlton	2,028	7,343
Chatham	1,152	202,226
Chattahoochee	650	21,732
Chattooga	814	21,856
Cherokee	1,102	51,699
Clarke	317	74,498
Clay	510	3,553
Clayton	385	150,357
Clinch	2,135	6,660
Cobb	892	297,718
Coffee	1,565	26,894
Colquitt	1,448	35,376
Columbia	754	40,118
Cook	606	13,490
Coweta	1,154	39,268
Crawford	853	7,684
Crisp	715	19,489
Dade	458	12,318
Dawson	546	4,774
De Kalb	702	483,024
Decatur	1,524	25,495
Dodge	1,310	16,955

contd

County	*area (sq km)*	*pop(1980)*
Dooly	1,032	10,826
Dougherty	858	100,718
Douglas	528	54,573
Early	1,342	13,158
Echols	1,095	2,297
Effingham	1,253	18,327
Elbert	954	18,758
Emanuel	1,789	20,795
Evans	484	8,428
Fannin	998	14,748
Fayette	517	29,043
Floyd	1,349	79,800
Forsyth	588	27,958
Franklin	686	15,185
Fulton	1,388	589,904
Gilmer	1,110	11,110
Glascock	374	2,382
Glynn	1,071	54,981
Gordon	923	30,070
Grady	1,193	19,845
Greene	1,011	11,391
Gwinnett	1,131	166,903
Habersham	723	25,020
Hall	985	75,649
Hancock	1,222	9,466
Haralson	736	18,422
Harris	1,206	15,464
Hart	598	18,585
Heard	759	6,520
Henry	835	36,309
Houston	988	77,605
Irwin	941	8,988
Jackson	889	25,343
Jasper	965	7,553
Jeff Davis	871	11,473
Jefferson	1,375	18,403
Jenkins	918	8,841
Johnson	796	8,660
Jones	1,024	16,579
Lamar	484	12,215
Lanier	504	5,654
Lauren	2,122	36,990
Lee	931	11,684
Liberty	1,344	37,583
Lincoln	510	6,716
Long	1,045	4,524
Lowndes	1,318	67,972
Lumpkin	746	10,762
Macon	1,050	14,003
Madison	741	17,747
Marion	952	5,297
McDuffie	666	18,546
McIntosh	1,105	8,046
Meriwether	1,316	21,229
Miller	738	7,038
Mitchell	1,331	21,114
Monroe	1,032	14,610
Montgomery	634	7,011
Morgan	907	11,572
Murray	897	19,685
Muscogee	567	170,108
Newton	720	34,489
Oconee	484	12,427
Oglethorpe	1,149	8,929
Paulding	811	26,110
Peach	395	19,151
Pickens	603	11,652
Pierce	894	11,897
Pike	569	8,937
Polk	809	32,386
Pulaski	647	8,950
Putnam	894	10,295
Quitman	380	2,357

contd

County	*area (sq km)*	*pop(1980)*
Rabun	962	10,466
Randolph	1,121	9,599
Richmond	848	181,629
Rockdale	343	36,747
Schley	439	3,433
Screven	1,703	14,043
Seminole	585	9,057
Spalding	517	47,899
Stephens	460	21,763
Stewart	1,175	5,896
Sumter	1,271	29,360
Talbot	1,027	6,536
Taliaferro	510	2,032
Tattnall	1,258	18,134
Taylor	993	7,902
Telfair	1,154	11,445
Terrell	876	12,017
Thomas	1,433	38,098
Tift	697	32,862
Toombs	965	22,592
Towns	429	5,638
Treutlen	525	6,087
Troup	1,076	50,003
Turner	751	9,510
Twiggs	941	9,354
Union	832	9,390
Upson	848	25,998
Walker	1,160	56,470
Walton	858	31,211
Ware	2,358	37,180
Warren	744	6,583
Washington	1,778	18,842
Wayne	1,682	20,750
Webster	546	2,341
Wheeler	777	5,155
White	629	10,120
Whitfield	757	65,789
Wilcox	993	7,682
Wilkes	1,222	10,951
Wilkinson	1,173	10,368
Worth	1,495	18,064

Gera *gay'rah*, county in S East Germany; pop(1981) 740,831; area 4,004 sq km; economy: electronic equipment, precision tools (Jena), high quality consumer goods, steel (Gera), machine tools (Gera, Saalfeld, Zeulenroda), man-made fibres (Rudolstadt-Schwarza), fabrics (Gera, Greiz), china (Kahla) and industrial appliances (Hermsdorf); 50% of the county is farmed and 37% is under forest; flood control, hydroelectric power and water supply are provided by the damming of the R Saale to form the Rohenewarte-Stausee and the Bleil-Sperre near the W German frontier SE of Saalfeld.

Gera, 50 53N 12 11E, pop(1982) 127,347, capital of Gera county, S East Germany; on R Weisse Elster, SW of Leipzig; former capital of the principality of Reuss-Schleiz-Gera; railway; economy: machine tools, food processing, textiles.

Geraldton, 28 49S 114 36E, pop(1981) 20,895, resort and port in Central stat div, Western Australia, Australia; on Indian Ocean, N of Perth; railway; airfield; 2nd largest harbour in Western Australia; economy: superphosphates, boatbuilding, lobster fishing; monuments: Shell museum; the maritime museum contains numerous finds from wrecks which ran aground on the offshore Abrolhos Islands.

Gerês, Serra do *zher-ayz'*, mountain range, Braga dist, N Portugal; on the Spanish border, rising to 1,561 m, forms part of Peneda-Gerês National Park.

Gerlachovsky *ger'le-kof-ske* or **Gerlachovsky Štit** formerly FRANZ JOSEF-SPITZE, STALIN PEAK, highest peak of the Carpathian range and of Czechoslovakia in the Vysoké Tatry (High Tatra), rising to 2,655 m.

Germany, East, official name German Democratic Republic, DEUTSCHE DEMOKRATISCHE REPUBLIK (Ger), socialist republic of N central Europe bounded N by the Baltic Sea, E by Poland W and SW by W Germany and S by Czechoslovakia; in the centre of the country is West Berlin (480 sq km), a W German city the political status of which was defined by the Quadripartite Agreement signed by the UK, France, the USA and the USSR after World War II; timezone GMT +1; area 108,333 sq km; pop(1980) 16,737,000; the pop includes 100,000 Sorbs (Wends), a Slavic national minority group occupying 12 districts in Cottbus and Dresden counties; 64% of the pop are of working age; nearly 55% of the pop are either Roman Catholic or Protestant, the remainder being unattached to any religion; capital East Berlin; chief towns include Leipzig, Dresden, Karl Marx Stadt, Magdeburg, Halle, Rostock and Erfurt; Rostock, Wismar, Stralsund and Sassnitz are major seaports; E Berlin, Riesa and Magdeburg are major river ports; the currency is the Mark der DDR of 100 pfennigs; national holidays May Day, 7 Oct (Founding of GDR); membership of CEMA, COMECON, IAEA, ICES, ILO, IMO, IPU, ITU, UN, UNESCO, UPU, WFTU, WHO, WIPO, WMO, WTO, Warsaw Pact.

Physical description. The N and central parts of the country comprise a 250 km Baltic coastline with dunes and lagoons, backed by a fertile low-lying plain intersected by pine-clad low morainic hills and dotted with many lakes of glacial origin, the largest of which is the Muřritz-See (117 sq km). Further south the land rises into the Lausitzer Bergland, the Elbsandsteingebirge, the Erzgebirge and the spruce and pine-clad Harz Mts of the Thüringer Wald (Thuringian Forest). Only the Fichtelberg and the Auersberg in the Erzgebirge and Brocken in the Harz rise over 1,000 m. Major rivers include the Elbe, with its tributaries the Spree, Havel and Saale and to the E, the Oder, which flows into the Baltic Sea. The rivers of E and W Germany are interconnected by canals, the

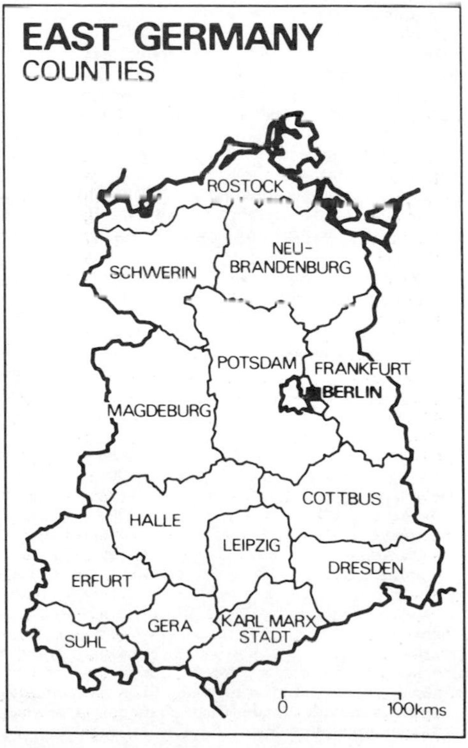

Hohenzollern linking the Oder and Elbe and the Mittelland linking the Elbe and the Ruhr.

Climate. The climate is temperate, with an Atlantic influence giving rise to relatively mild winters and cool summers. The mean annual temperature is 10°C. The weather can be variable, but long spells of cold weather in winter are not uncommon, with the freezing of canals. On the Baltic coast winters are milder and cloudier than further inland, but with the freezing of the Baltic the region can be colder than the North Sea districts of W Germany. In central E Germany rainfall is low in the summer, with an average monthly max of 73 mm in July, and there is more daily sunshine than on the Baltic coast. The S is generally wetter and colder at higher altitude, with snow lying in the mountains for some time. Here the alpine influence is stronger than the oceanic influence of the Atlantic.

Constitution and government. Following the partition of Germany in 1945 E Germany was administered by the USSR, which established the soviet model of government in 1949. In that year the People's Chamber enacted a Constitution of the new German Democratic Republic. After anti-Soviet demonstrations were put down in 1953, the country was recognized by the USSR as an independent republic in 1955, with the E border following the Oder-Neisse rivers. The N part of the former prov of E Prussia, including its capital at Königsberg (Kaliningrad), was transferred to the USSR. In 1968 a new socialist constitution was approved. The People's Chamber, a single-chamber parliament (*Volkskammer*) of 500 deputies, elects the 26-member Council of State (*Stahtsrat*), the Council of Ministers (*Ministerrat*) and the National Defence Council. In 1960 the office of president was abolished and a Council of State was formed comprising a chairman, 6 deputy chairmen and 18 members. The Council is authorized to make decisions and to interpret the law. Effective political control is exercised by the Politburo of the Socialist Unity Party.

Economy. Since World War II the country has had a centrally-planned socialist economy. This has given rise to the creation of state and co-operative farms and to the movement of industry from its traditional centres in Berlin and to the S to the formerly rural N and E. Apart from potash and coal, E Germany has few mineral resources and is heavily dependent on imported oil. Industry is based on the production of specialized industrial equipment, including precision tools, optical instruments and semiconductors. In addition, shipbuilding and the production of chemicals, textiles, motor vehicles and food processing are important. E Germany's main trading partners are its neighbours in the eastern bloc.

Administrative divisions. Since 1952 East Germany has been divided into 15 counties as follows:

County	*area (sq km)*	*pop(1981)*
Berlin	403	1,162,305
Cottbus	8,262	884,655
Dresden	6,738	1,804,556
Erfurt	7,349	1,236,681
Frankfurt-Oder	7,186	704,808
Gera	4,004	740,831
Halle	8,771	1,821,690
Karl Marx Stadt	6,009	1,918,184
Leipzig	4,966	1,402,130
Magdeburg	11,526	1,262,291
Neubrandenburg	10,948	620,760
Potsdam	12,568	1,118,413
Rostock	7,074	889,121
Schwerin	8,672	590,135
Suhl	3,856	549,075

These counties are further divided into 28 urban and 191 rural districts with a total of 7,554 communities, of which 1,028 are towns and cities.

Germany, West, DEUTSCHLAND *doych'lant* or DEUTSCHES REICH *doych-es rīKH'*, official name Federal Republic of Germany, BUNDESREPUBLIK DEUTSCHLAND (Ger), a central European state, bounded E by East Germany (German Democratic Republic) and Czechoslovakia, SE by Austria, SW by Switzerland, W by France, Luxembourg, Belgium and the Netherlands, and N by Denmark, the North Sea and the Baltic Sea; it includes the Nordfriesische Inseln (North Frisian Is), Ostfriesische Inseln (East Frisian Is), Helgoland and Sanddüne Is in the North Sea, and Fehmarn Is in the Baltic Sea; area 249,535 sq km, including West Berlin; timezone GMT +1; federal capital Bonn; largest city West Berlin; chief towns Hamburg, München (Munich), Köln (Cologne), Essen, Frankfurt am Main and Dortmund; total pop(1983) 61,306,700; the population is almost entirely Germanic, both racially and linguistically, speaking either the High German (Hochdeutsch) of cultivated society or the Low German (Platt Deutsch) dialect of the N and NW; an ethnic Danish minority lives in the north; about 44% of the population are Protestant, predominantly Lutherans, and 45% are Roman Catholic, most of whom live in the south; there are 64 universities, with 780,722 students in 1981; the currency is the Deutschmark of 100 pfennig; membership of Council of Europe, EEC, ADB, DAC, EIB, ELDO, EMS, ESRO, FAO, GATT, IAEA, IBRD, ICAC, ICAO, ICES, ICO, IDA, IFAD, IEA, IFC, IHO, ILO, IMF, IMO, INTELSAT, IPU, ITC, ITU, NATO, OECD, UN, UNESCO, UPU, WEU, WHO, WIPO, WMO, WSG, WTO.

Physical description. The terrain of W Germany varies from the plains of the N lowlands through the central uplands and Alpine foothills to the Bayerische Alpen (Bavarian Alps) in the S. The N part of the country lies within the North German Plain where traces of continental glaciation are clearly visible, particularly in the NE where there are extensive moraine-covered uplands and many lakes. The central uplands include the Rheinisches Schiefergebirge (Rhenish Slate Mts) rising to 879 m, the rolling upland and low mountains of Hessen (Hesse) prov, the horst massifs of the Schwarzwald (Black Forest), part of the Harz Mts, and the Odenwald and Spessart. The entire central part of the country has a diversified and fragmented topography, the flat crests of mountains contrasting sharply with steep slopes. The extreme S is occupied by the Bayerische Alpen, whose highest peak, the Zugspitze, rises to 2,962 m. Glacial and karst limestone landforms can be found here. The predominantly low and flat coasts of the North Sea and the Baltic Sea are broken by bays and estuaries. Most of the rivers drain into the North Sea, including the Ems, Weser and Elbe. The Rhine is the main river, crossing the entire country from S to N. The Alpine rivers, including the upper reaches of the Rhine and the right tributaries of the Danube, are fed mainly by snow and glaciers so that their flow is at its maximum in summer. The utility of Germany's natural waterways has been largely increased by an intricate canal organization which connects the principal rivers and facilitates the transport of German goods to all parts of Europe.

Climate. Oceanic influences are most strong in the NW where winters are mild but stormy. Elsewhere a continental climate is general. To the E and S, winter temperatures are lower, with bright frosty weather and considerable snowfall. On occasions, however, the winters can be cold in N Germany, particularly when spells of persistent easterly winds bring cold air from Russia. The average winter temperature in the north is 1.6°C and in the south −2.7°C. Summer temperatures average 16°C in the north and are slightly higher in the south. The average annual precipitation, 600-700 mm in the plains and less than 500 mm in some intermontane basins, increases to 1,400-1,800 mm in the Harz Mts and the Schwarzwald, and exceeds 2,000 mm in some parts of the Bayerische Alpen.

History, government and constitution. The ancient Germans were of Teutonic blood, divided into tribes that were eventually united in the 8th century within the Frankish Empire of Charlemagne. After 918 the monarchy became elective, the third elected King, Otho I, assuming the title of Emperor of the Holy Roman Empire. The elective nature of the monarchy prevented Germany from becoming a united kingdom, and until the 19th century, it remained divided into several hundred states. The conquest of Germany by Napoleon resulted in a considerable reduction in the number of states and in 1814-15, with the Congress of Vienna, the country became a confederation of 39 states under the presidency of Austria. Under the leadership of Bismarck, Prussia succeeded to Austria as the leading German power. By 1871 Bismarck had achieved the complete union of Germany and the foundation of the 2nd Reich, with the King of Prussia as the hereditary German Emperor. The new Empire's aggressive foreign policy endangered the peace of Europe and eventually led to World War I (1914-18). The defeat of Germany brought about the fall of the 2nd Reich and the founding of the democratic

Weimar Republic. Political power passed to the extreme right wing Nazi party and Adolf Hitler became dictator of the totalitarian 3rd Reich in 1933. Acts of aggression led to World War II and a second defeat for Germany resulted in the collapse of the German political régime. The area of Germany was reduced and the country occupied by the UK, USA, France and Russia. Berlin was similarly sectored into 4 occupation zones. The Soviet Union subsequently suggested the establishment of a demilitarized, independent, united Germany, but the other occupying countries responded by declaring the Western occupation at an end with the creation of the Federal Republic of Germany in 1948. Modern West Germany is a democratic and social federal state. The Constituent Assembly (known as the Parliamentary Council) established a Basic Law which was approved by a two-thirds majority of the parliaments of the participating Länder and came into force on 23 May 1949. The head of state is the president, elected for a five-year term by a federal convention composed of the Federal Diet and an equal number of members elected by the Länder parliaments. The highest legislative body is a bicameral parliament comprising the Federal Diet (*Bundestag*) and the federal Council (*Bundesrat*). The Federal Diet, elected for a term of 4 years, enacts legislation, elects the head of the federal government, and participates in the election of the president of the republic. The Federal Council consists of members of the governments of the Länder. Each Land has from 3 to 5 seats in the Federal Council depending on the size of its population. The Federal Government consists of the Federal Chancellor, elected by the Federal Diet on the proposal of the Federal President, and the Federal Ministers, who are appointed and dismissed by the Federal President upon the proposal of the Federal Chancellor.

Economy. West Germany ranks among the world's leading industrial nations. The economy is heavily export orientated, with 25%-30% of West Germany's national income derived from overseas trade. In 1985 industry accounted for 48% of national income, mainly based on iron and steel production, coal mining, cement, the manufacture of steel and metal products, chemicals and textiles, machine construction, the electrical industry and the processing of foodstuffs. Iron, steel, and non-ferrous metals are now mainly processed from imported ores, with West Germany also depending heavily on imported oil and gas. There are, however, considerable reserves of deep-mined coal and open-pit brown coal. Economic strength also depends on technically-advanced manufacturing industries. Chief imports include finished manufactures, agricultural products (world's largest importer), ores and metals, petroleum, rubber, sulphur, cotton, wool, and oils and fats. Exports include chemicals, motor vehicles and iron and steel products. Major trading partners include EEC member countries, Austria, Switzerland and the USA. Since World War II there has been a tendency for manufacturing to move away from the traditional heavy industry locations towards Bayern and Baden-Württemberg which are now important centres of high technology.

Agriculture and forestry. In 1980 nearly 48,000 sq km of the 122,000 sq km of agricultural land were under permanent pasture and grassland, while arable land accounted for 73,000 sq km (29%) of the total area. Agriculture accounted for 3% of national income in 1980, the chief products being grains (wheat, barley), potatoes and sugarbeets. Six per cent of the 27 million workforce are employed in agriculture. Raising livestock, largely for milk and meat products, is more important than cropping. The uplands of central West Germany are mostly devoted to mixed arable and livestock farming with fruit and wine specialization along the valleys of the Rhine and its tributaries.

Administrative divisions. West Germany is divided into 10 provinces (*Länder*). The western sectors of Berlin are governed by the USA, the UK, and France, which together with the USSR have special rights and responsibilities in Berlin. The provinces are further divided into 26 districts.

Province/District	*area (sq km)*	*pop(1983)*
Baden-Württemberg	35,751	9,243,300
Stuttgart	10,558	3,459,700
Karlsruhe	6,919	2,398,000
Freiburg	9,357	1,869,300
Tübingen	8,917	1,516,200
Bayern	70,553	10,969,500
Oberbayern	17,528	3,687,500
Niederbayern	10,332	1,007,500
Oberpfalz	9,691	966,200
Oberfranken	7,231	1,044,800
Mittelfranken	7,245	1,520,700
Unterfranken	8,531	1,199,900
Schwaben	9,994	1,542,900
Berlin(West)	480	1,854,500
Bremen	404	676,900
Hamburg	755	1,609,500
Hessen	21,114	5,565,000
Darmstadt	7,445	3,415,000
Gießen	5,381	968,700
Kassel	8,288	1,181,200
Niedersachsen	47,447	7,248,500
Braunschweig	8,093	1,619,500
Hannover	9,043	2,038,000
Lüneburg	15,346	1,468,700
Weser-Ems	14,965	2,122,300
Nordrhein-Westfalen	34,062	16,836,500
Düsseldorf	5,288	5,113,000
Köln	7,363	3,900,900
Münster	6,897	2,412,000
Detmold	6,515	1,796,800
Arnsberg	7,998	3,613,900
Rheinland-Pfalz	19,848	3,633,500
Koblenz	8,092	1,357,500
Trier	4,925	472,000
Rheinhessen-Pfalz	6,830	1,804,000
Saarland	2,571	1,052,800
Schleswig-Holstein	15,721	2,616,600

Germiston *jer'-*, 26 15S 28 10E, pop(1980) 155,435, city in Transvaal prov, South Africa; W of Johannesburg; railway; economy: textiles, chemicals, steel, engineering and the largest gold refinery in the world.

Gerona *KHay-ro'na*, prov in Cataluña, NE Spain; it includes the E end of the Pyrenees, the plain of Ampurdan (with remains of ancient Greek colonies, Emporion and Rhode), the rocky Costa Brava coast and the easternmost point of continental Spain (Cape Creus); pop(1981) 467,945; area, 5,886 sq km; capital Gerona; formerly a principality of the kingdom of Aragón; economy: synthetic fibres, plastics, textiles, chemicals, tools, rubber tyres.

Gerona, GERUNDA (anc), 41 58N 2 46W, pop(1981) 87,648, fortified town and capital of Gerona prov, Cataluña, NE Spain; near junction of R Onar and R Ter, 721 km NE of Madrid; bishopric; university; airport; railway; car ferries to Ibiza, Barcelona, Málaga; economy: textiles, chemicals, electronics, soap; monuments: 14th-c Baroque and Gothic cathedral, churches of St Felix and Pedro de Galligans; events: Fiestas de San Narciso in Oct-Nov.

Gerrard's Cross, Buckinghamshire, England. See Chalfont St Peter.

Gers *zher*, dept in Midi-Pyrénées region of S France, named from the river which flows S-N through it; comprises 3 arrond, 31 cantons and 462 communes; pop(1982) 174,154; area 6,257 sq km; drained also by the Adour (liable to flood), Arrats, Gimone and Baise rivers; furrowed N-S by the wooded foothills of the Pyrénées; capital Auch, other towns include Condom, Lectoure and Mirande; spa at Barbotan.

Getafe *hay-tah'fay*, 40 18N 3 44W, pop(1981) 127,060, industrial town in Madrid prov, central Spain; 12 km S of Madrid, at the centre of a wide plain; to the E is the Los

Angeles hill with the Heart of Jesus monument; considered the geographical centre of Spain; airport; economy: dairy produce, agric equipment, vehicle parts; monuments: church of St Mary Magdalene, Piarist seminary.

Gett'ysburg, 39 83N 79 27W, pop(1980) 7,194, small town and county seat, Adams county, Pennsylvania, USA. Site of the battle (July 1863), considered to be the turning-point of the Civil War, in which the Union forces under Meade defeated the Confederates under Lee.

Geyre, APHRODISIAS, 37 45N 29 03E, ancient city, SW of Denizli, W Turkey; among the remains is one of the best-preserved stadiums of the Roman world with a seating capacity of 30,000; remains of the temple of Aphrodite; home of Alexander of Aphrodisias, a Greek philosopher (c.200 AD).

Geysir *gee'ser*, 64 19N 20 19W, location in Suðurland, W Iceland which gave its name to the word 'geyser'; used to send up water columns 40-60 metres; 30 km NE of Laugarvatn, E of Reykjavík.

Gezhouba *ge-zhoo-ba*, man-made dam on the Chang Jiang (Yangtze river), Hubei prov, central China; near Yichang; at the mouth of the Chang Jiang (Yangtze) gorges; the largest water control project in the world.

Ghaghara *gug'gur-a*, GOGRA, river in W China, Nepal and N India; rises in the Himalayas in SW Xizang aut region, China; flows SE through Nepal as the R Karnali, where it is joined by the R Seti; continues SE, cutting through the Siwalik range of mountains it enters the Bihar state of India and joins the R Ganga (Ganges) below Chhapra; length 1,030 km.

Ghana *gah'na*, official name Republic of Ghana, a republic of W Africa, bounded W by the Ivory Coast, N by Burkina and E by Togo; area 238,686 sq km; timezone GMT; pop(1984) 12,205,576; capital Accra; chief towns Koforidua, Sekondi-Takoradi, Cape Coast, Kumasi, Sunyani, Tamale, Ho and Bolgatanga; there are 75 distinct tribal groups including the Akan (44%) who predominate in the S and W, the Mole-Dagbani (16%) in the N, the Ewe (13%) in the S, the Ga (8%) in the Accra region and the Fanti in the coastal area; the official language is French but African languages including Akan (44%), Mole-Dagbani (16%) and Ewe (13%) are also important; of religious groups 29% of the pop is Protestant, 14% Roman Catholic, 38% holds local beliefs and 12% is Muslim; the unit of currency is the cedi of 100 pesewas; national holiday 6 March; membership of AfDB, Commonwealth, ECA, ECOWAS, FAO, G-77, GATT, IAEA, IBA, IBRD, ICAO, ICO, IDA, IFAD, IFC, ILO, IMF, IMO, INTELSAT, INTERPOL, IRC, ISO, ITU, NAM, OAU, UN, UNESCO, UPU, WHO, WIPO, WMO, WTO.

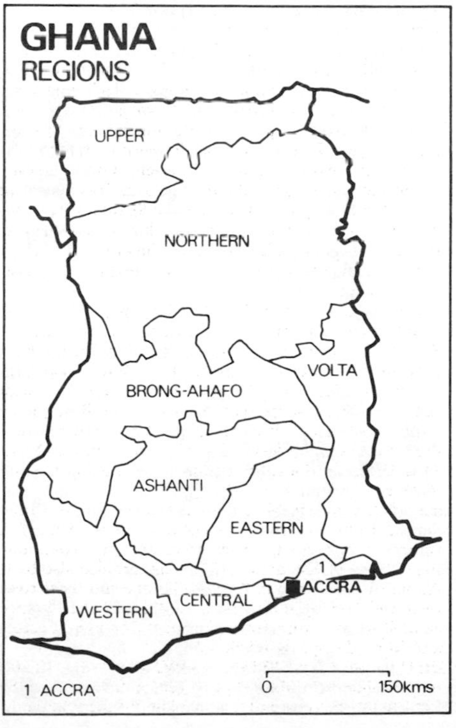

Physical description. Ghana has a coastline typified by sand bars and lagoons. Inland there are low lying plains which lead on to the Ashanti plateau in the W and in the E the R Volta basin which has been dammed to form L Volta. To the E of L Volta there are mountains rising to 885 m at Mount Afadjado. W and NW of L Volta the Black Volta river flows through rising grasslands to meet the Ivory coast frontier which it follows N into Burkina.

Climate. Ghana has a tropical climate which ranges from a warm, dry coastal belt in the SE and a hot humid SW corner to a hot, dry N savannah. The central zone has 2 rainy seasons with maxima in May-June and Oct but in the N these merge into one season (July to Sept). The N dry season is subject to the dry and often dust-laden *harmattan* wind which blows from the NE. At Kumasi the average annual rainfall is 1,400 mm.

History, government and constitution. The state of Ghana was created by the union of 2 former British territories, British Gold Coast, which became a Crown Colony in 1874, and British Togoland. The latter was administered as part of British Gold Coast and in 1957 its people voted to join it to form the state of Ghana which subsequently was declared a fully independent republic within the Commonwealth in 1960. Ghana was the first British colony in Africa to achieve independence and the first African country to join the Commonwealth. The constitution provides for a 140-member parliament elected every 5 years and an executive president elected every 4 years. The president appoints a 20-member cabinet and a Council of State. A coup in 1982 resulted in the suspension of the constitution and the creation of a Provisional National Defence Council.

Economy. Although Ghana is mainly agricultural the country has a diverse resource base which includes commercial reserves of oil, diamonds, gold, manganese, bauxite and wood, all of which are exported. Cocoa, supplying two-thirds of export revenue, is the most important cash crop, but tobacco, cotton, peppers pineapples, avocados and ginger are also exported. Major industries include mining, lumbering, light manufacturing, fishing and aluminium. The main trading partners are the UK, other EEC countries and the USA.

Administrative divisions. Ghana is divided into 9 regions:

Region	*area (sq km)*	*pop(1984)*
Eastern	19,833	1,679,483
Western	24,214	1,116,930
Central	9,469	1,145,520
Ashanti	25,123	2,089,683
Brong-Ahafo	39,709	1,179,409
Northern	70,338	1,162,645
Volta	20,651	1,201,095
Upper	27,319	1,210,745
Accra	2,030	1,420,066

These regions are subdivided into 58 districts which are further divided into 267 administrative districts.

Ghanzi *kan'zee*, dist in W Botswana, S Africa; pop(1981) 19,096; area 117,910 sq km; economy: agricultural trade; capital Ghanzi; other main town Mamuno.

Gharbi, Hodh el *gar-bee'*, desert region in S Mauritania, NW Africa; pop(1982e) 154,000; area 53,400 sq km; capital Aïoun el Atrous.

Gharbîya *gar-bee'yu*, AL-GHARBIYAH, governorate in N

Egypt, pop(1976) 2,294,303; area 1,942 sq km; capital Tanta.

Ghats, Eastern *gahts*, mountain system of the E peninsular region of India, running parallel to the Bay of Bengal and forming the E edge of the Deccan Plateau; extends generally SW from the R Mahanadi in the state of Orissa to the Nilgiri Hills which lie in the states of Kerala and Tamil Nadu and are the junction of the Western and Eastern Ghats; consists of a series of disconnected hill ranges, which include the Velikonda, Nallamala, Seshachalam, Palkonda, Melagiri and Nilgiri hills; heights range from 1,000 to 2,000 m in the N to over 2,000 m in the SW; Doda Betta in the Nilgiri Hills reaches 2,636 m; crossed by numerous rivers including the Krishna, Godavari, Papagini, Sagileru, Gundlakamma and the Nagavali; goldfields are found near the town of Kolar, to the NE of Bangalore.

Ghats, Western, mountain system of W peninsular India, lying parallel to the Arabian Sea and running in a general direction of NW-SE; length c.1,600 km; extends from the R Tapti in the NW to the Cape Comorin, on the S tip of India and joined to the Eastern Ghats in the Nilgiri Hills; forms the W boundary of the Deccan Plateau; Palghat Gap interrupts the chain just to the S of the Nilgiri Hills; acts as the chief watershed of peninsular India and is the source of rivers such as the Krishna, Godavari and the Kaveri; subject to heavy rainfall during the SW monsoon; slopes are generally covered in dense tropical forest vegetation, with bamboo, teak, blackwood and sandalwood being commercially exploited; heights are greatest in the Nilgiri and Cardamon Hills of the S, reaching their highest point at Anai Mudi Peak (2,695 m) in the Cardamon Hills.

Ghaziabad *gah-zee-ah-bahd'*, 28 39N 77 26E, pop(1981) 292,000, city in Uttar Pradesh, NE India; 19 km E of Delhi, on a tributary of the R Yamuna; linked to Delhi in the W and to Moradabad in the E by rail; market town for the surrounding agricultural region; founded in 1740.

Ghaznī *gaz-nee*, prov in E central Afghanistan; pop(1984e) 702,054; area 23,378 sq km; crossed by the main road running from Kābul in the NE to Kandahār in the SW; capital Ghaznī.

Ghaznī, 33 33N 68 28E, pop(1984e) 33,351, capital of Ghaznī prov, E central Afghanistan; SW of Kābul and W of Gardēz; lies on the R Ghaznī; market town for sheep, wool, camel hair, corn and fruit; famed Afghan coats are made in this town; one of Asia's most important cities between 962 and 115 AD; fortress was taken by the British during the Afghan Wars.

Ghent, city in Belgium. See Gent.

Gheorghe Gheorghiu-Dej *gyor'ge gyor'gee-oo-desh*, 46 17N 26 45E, pop(1983) 49,330, town in Bacău county, NE central Romania; S of Bacău; railway; economy: petrochemicals, synthetic rubber.

Gheorgheni *gyor-gayn'*, 46 43N 25 36E, pop(1983) 22,478, town in Harghita county, N Romania; situated W of Piatra-Neamţ in the E Carpathian Mts; Lacul Roşu resort is nearby; railway; economy: timber, distilling.

Gherla *ger'la*, 47 02N 23 55E, pop(1983) 21,964, town in Cluj, NW central Romania; on R Someş, S of Dej; established in 17th century by Armenians; railway; economy: livestock trade, textiles.

Ghor, El *gōr*, depression in Jordan and NE Israel, forming the lower part of the Jordan river valley; extends approx 104 km from L Tiberias (N) to the Dead Sea (S); width varies from 1.6 km to 19 km; S of the Dead Sea it extends into the depression of Wadi 'Araba.

Ghowr *gor*, GHOR, prov in W central Afghanistan; pop(1984e) 366,823; area 38,666 sq km; capital Chaghcharān.

Giant's Causeway, volcanic basalt formation on the N coast of Co Antrim, Northern Ireland; 11 km NE of Portrush; a natural 'pavement' of columnar basalt projecting into the North Channel; formed by the tops of thousands of small basaltic columns (usually hexagonal and 38 to 50 cm in diameter) which resulted from the cooling of a volcanic flow; the columns vary in height, forming 3 natural platforms (the Little, Middle and Grand Causeway) and have several large caves and rock formations; according to legend, the causeway was built by or for giants to travel across to Scotland; a ship from the Spanish Armada was wrecked in Spanish Bay here in 1588.

Gibraltar *jib-rawl'ter*, *KHee-vrahl-tahr'* (Sp), (Arab 'Jebel Tariq', the mountain of Tariq), 36 09N 5 21W, a narrow rocky peninsula rising steeply from the low lying coast of SW Spain at the E end of the Strait of Gibraltar, the gateway between the Atlantic Ocean and the Mediterranean Sea; an important strategic point of control for the W Mediterranean, especially with the extension of British interests in the E and the opening of the Suez Canal; a British Crown Colony; Gibraltar played a key role in Allied naval operations during the two world wars, and has remained a military base for Britain with certain naval, air and communications facilities available to NATO; the coast of Morocco is 32 km across the Strait to the S; 8 km from Algeciras; area 5.86 sq km; length 4.8 km; width 1.2 km, narrowing to the S; pop(1983) 29,073 of whom 20,021 are Gibraltarians and 5,808 are British; English is the official language although Spanish is widely spoken; British currency is used but the Gibraltar government also issues its own banknotes; timezone GMT + 1; airport at North Front, 1.7 km from the town; the town and commercial harbour are situated on the W coast; the harbour has a water area of 2 sq km; car ferries to Tangier; monument: Moorish castle.

Physical description. 'The Rock', as it is frequently called, is 426 m high; the top is a sharp ridge, the N escarpment being completely inaccessible, as is the whole upper length of the E face; the S half of the Rock slopes down to cliffs 30 m high at Europa Point; the Rock is connected to the Spanish mainland by a low lying sandy plain about 1.6 km long and half as wide; there are extensive limestone caves, notably Upper and Lower St Michael's Cave and the Cathedral Cave. The rock is the only place in Europe where monkeys (Barbary apes) run wild.

Climate. Gibraltar has a typical Mediterranean climate with dry summers; winters are wetter than the rest of S Spain due to exposure to Atlantic storms; winds around the Rock are often gusty.

History and government. Occupied since the 8th century, Gibraltar was ceded to Britain by Spain in 1713; it became a Crown Colony in 1830; a Legislative Council was established in 1950, but after a referendum in 1969 it was replaced by a House of Assembly consisting of a Speaker and 15 elected and two ex-officio members; the Governor, who is the Queen's personal representative, is directly responsible for all matters not specifically allocated to ministers such as defence, external affairs and internal security; elections to the House of Assembly take place every 4 years; the main political parties are the Gibraltar Labour Party and Association of Human Rights and the Gibraltar Socialist Labour Party; since 1973 Gibraltar has been part of the EEC by virtue of Article 227(4) of the Treaty of Rome, but at Gibraltar's request, the Community's common tariff arrangements, its Common Agricultural Policy and its value-added taxation system do not apply to Gibraltar.

Economy. There is no agriculture, little livestock and no mineral resources; imports of manufactured goods and food are largely from Portugal, Morocco, Netherlands, Japan, Britain and other Commonwealth countries; few local exports but there is a flourishing entrepôt trade including fuel supplies to shipping; the economy is largely dependent on the presence of British naval and military forces; in 1982 about 60% of GNP was generated by British government expenditure; because of reduced need for naval fleet support services the Royal Naval Dockyard was converted to a commercial yard in 1985.

Gibraltar, Strait of, FRETUM HERCULEUM (Lat), BAB AL ZAKAK (Arab), channel connecting the Mediterranean to the Atlantic; length 60 km; width between the Rock of Gibraltar and Cape Ceuta (the Pillars of Hercules) is 24 km, at the W extremity 40 km and at the narrowest

15 km; the constant E-flowing current balances evaporation from the Mediterranean, which would otherwise become a gradually shrinking salt lake.

Gibson Desert, central belt of the Western Australian Desert; situated between the Great Sandy Desert (N) and the Great Victoria Desert (S); consists of sand dunes, scrub and salt marshes; includes the salt lakes L Disappointment and L Auld; situated in the Gibson Desert is the Rudall River national park.

Gießen or **Giessen** *gee'sen*, dist of Hessen (Hesse) prov, W Germany; pop(1983) 968,700; area 5,381; capital Gießen.

Gießen, 50 34N 8 40E, pop(1983) 73,200, old university town and capital of Gießen dist, Hessen (Hesse) prov, W Germany; on the R Lahn, 56 km N of Frankfurt; university (1607); railway; the chemist Justus von Liebig, the originator of modern nitrogenous fertilizers and inventor of meat extract, lived and taught here from 1834 to 1852.

Giffnock, 55 48N 4 14W, pop(1981) 33,634, chief town of Eastwood dist, Strathclyde, Scotland; in Clydeside urban area, 8 km S of Glasgow; railway.

Gifu *gee'foo*, 35 27N 136 46E, pop(1980) 410,357, capital of Gifu prefecture, Chūbu, central Honshū island, Japan; 32 km NNW of Nagoya; rebuilt after 1891 earthquake and after World War II; cormorant fishing attracts tourists from May to Sept; university (1949); railway; economy: umbrellas, lanterns, fishing; event: naked pilgrim festival on 10 Dec.

Gijón *hee-hōn'*, 43 32N 5 42W, pop(1981) 255,969, seaport and industrial town in Oviedo prov, Asturias, NE Spain; lying between two sheltered bays on the N coast, 29 km N of Oviedo; linked to the former island of Santa Catalina by deposits of alluvial soil; the main outlet for the Asturian coal mines; College of Industry and Nautical Science (1794); birthplace of the 18th-c writer, Jovellanus; economy: shipyards (El Musel), fishing, steel (Verina), motor vehicles, tools, electrical equipment; oilfields 48 km offshore; events: blessing of the sea at the patronal fiesta in June in honour of St John the Baptist and fiestas of solitude in Sept.

Gikongo'ro, prefecture in Rwanda, central Africa; SW of Kigali; area 2,192 sq km; pop(1978) 369,591.

Gīlān *gee-lan'*, prov in NW Iran, bounded NE by the Caspian Sea, pop(1982) 1,581,872; area 14,709 sq km; capital Rasht.

Gilbert Islands, island group of Kiribati, central Pacific Ocean, 1,300 km NW of the Phoenix Is, comprising a chain of 17 coral atolls spread over a length of about 680 km; area 264 sq km; pop(1985) 61,014; most of the atolls are no more than from 200 to 300 m wide, but they may be anywhere from 15 to 100 km long; all have central lagoons except Makin, Kuria, Nukunau, Tamana, and Arorae; capital Tarawa; until 1977 part of the British colony of Gilbert and Ellice.

Gillingham *jil'ing-am*, 51 24N 0 33E, pop(1981) 93,734, industrial and naval town in the Medway Towns urban area, Kent, SE England; on the R Medway, 48 km E of London, adjoining Chatham; railway; economy: engineering, foodstuffs.

Gimie, Mount *zhee-mee'*, mountain on the Windward I of St Lucia in the Caribbean; rising to 950 m E of Soufrière.

Gióna *gee-o'nu*, mountain peak in the Píndhos Mts, Sterea Ellás-Évvoia region, Greece, 18 km NW of Amfissa; height 2,510 m.

Gippsland, district of SE Victoria, Australia; E of Melbourne; mountains in the N drop down to fertile plains in the S; economy: lignite, dairy products, cereals, hops.

Giresun *gee-ru-soon'*, mountainous prov in N Turkey, bounded N by the Black Sea; pop(1980) 480,083; area 6,934 sq km; capital Giresun; economy: copper and zinc mining, grain, forest products.

Giresun, 40 55N 38 25E, pop(1980) 45,690, seaport capital of Giresun prov, N Turkey; on the Black Sea, E of Samsun.

Gironde *zhee-rōd*, dept in Aquitaine region of SW France, bounded on the W by the Bay of Biscay and occupied in the NW by the Gironde estuary; comprises 5 arrond, 63 cantons and 543 communes; pop(1982) 1,127,546; area 10,000 sq km; there are several lakes along the W coastline; drained chiefly by the Dordogne and Garonne rivers; capital Bordeaux, chief towns Libourne and Bègles; notable wines from the Entre-deux-Mers and Médoc areas; the Parc des Landes de Gascogne regional nature park lies partly within the dept.

Gisborne *giz'bern*, 38 41S 178 02E, pop(1981) 29,986, port and resort town in East Coast, North Island, New Zealand; SE of Auckland and NW of Napier, at the head of Poverty Bay; the site of Captain Cook's landing in 1769; railway; airfield; economy: trade in wine and in market garden, farm and forest produce.

Gisenye *gee-sen'yee*, 1 42S 29 15E, pop(1978) 12,436, capital of prefecture of same name, Rwanda, central Africa; on L Kivu close to Rwanda-Zaire frontier.

Gitarama *gee-ta'ra-ma*, prefecture in Rwanda, central Africa; area 2,241 sq km; pop(1978) 602,752.

Gitega *ge-tay'ga*, 5 48S 24 18E, pop(1979) 15,943, capital of prov of same name, Burundi, central Africa; 61 km E of Bujumbura; a former royal residence.

Giurgiu *joor'joo*, county in S Romania; bounded to the S by the R Danube which follows the frontier with Bulgaria; pop(1983) 373,526; area 3,810 sq km; capital Giurgiu.

Giurgiu, 43 53N 25 58E, pop(1983) 62,740, river port and capital town of Giurgiu county, S Romania; on the R Danube; established in the 10th century by Genoese merchants; linked to Ruse in Bulgaria by a bridge; railway; economy: shipyards, oil, building materials, chemicals, food processing, timber trade, textiles; monuments: medieval fortress; clock tower.

Gîza, El *gee'za*, GIZEH, AL-JIZAH, 30 36N 32 15E, pop(1976) 1,246,713, capital of El Gîza governorate, N Egypt; on the W bank of the R Nile, 5 km SW of Cairo; railway; economy: cotton, footwear, brewing, cinema industry; monuments: the pyramids of Cheops, Khafra and Mankara and the Sphinx are located 8 km SW of the city; the Cheops pyramid was one of the Seven Wonders of the World and the largest pyramid ever built; it was originally 235 m square and 147 m high.

Gjirokastër *gyee ro-kah'ster*, ARGYROKASTRON *ar-ye-rok'a-stron* (Gr), prov of S Albania; area 1,137 sq km; pop(1980) 58,500; capital Gjirokastër.

Gjirokastër, 40 05N 20 10E, pop(1975) 22,000, commercial town and capital of Gjirokastër prov, S Albania; 72 km SE of Vlorë, on a left-bank tributary of the R Vijosë; former centre of the Bektashi (Muslim sect); monuments: 18th-c mosques, Orthodox cathedral (1774), citadel (rebuilt in the 19th century on Venetian foundations); in Turkish hands until 1913.

Gjøvik *yu'vik*, 60 47N 10 41E, pop(1983) 26,070, town in Oppland county, S central Norway; on W shore of L Mjösa; railway; economy: glass-making.

Glaciares, Los *lōs gla-sya'rays*, Andean national park in SW Santa Cruz prov, Patagonia, Argentina; area 4,459 sq km; established in 1937; includes the E parts of L Viedma and L Argentino; on W borders Chile and the Chilean National Park, Bernardo O'Higgins.

Glacier, national park in NW Montana, United States; a region of mountains, lakes and small glaciers; part of the Waterton-Glacier Intenational Peace Park; area 4,052 sq km; established in 1910.

Gladbeck *glat'bek*, 51 34N 6 59E, pop(1983) 78,400, industrial city in Münster dist, Nordrhein-Westfalen (North Rhine-Westphalia) prov, W Germany, 35 km WNW of Dortmund.

Gladstone, 23 52S 151 16E, pop(1981) 22,083, port in Fitzroy stat div, Queensland, Australia; situated on the E coast, 96 km SE of Rockhampton, on Port Curtis Inlet; railway; airfield; an outlet for central Queensland's mineral and agricultural resources; has the largest aluminium refinery in the world.

Glåma *glo'ma*, or GLOMMEN, GLOMMA *glom'ma*, river in E Norway, rising in Dovrefjell plateau in Sør-Trøndelag county, issues from L Rien, 32 km NE of Røros; flows S through Øyeren L to Oslofjorden (Oslo Fjord) at Fredrikstad; length 598 km; brings logs to the sawmills and paper-mills further downstream; tributaries Folla, Atna, Rena and Lågen rivers; longest river in Norway.

Glaris, town and canton in Switzerland. See Glarus.

Glarus *gla'roos*, GLARIS *glah-rees'* (Fr), alpine canton in NE Switzerland; pop(1980) 36,718; area 684 sq km; capital Glarus; other towns Näfels, Linthal and Braunwald; occupies the basin of the R Linth and surrounded on 3 sides by mountains; it is linked with the neighbouring canton of Uri by the Klausen Pass; the cotton industry established itself here at an early stage, using hydroelectric power from the R Linth; local culinary specialities are Schabzieger, a herb cheese, and Glarner Pasteten (fruit tarts); joined the Swiss Confederacy in 1352.

Glarus, 47 03N 9 04E, pop(1980) 5,800, capital of Glarus canton, NE Switzerland; at the foot of Glärnisch, 58 km E of Luzern; rebuilt after a fire in 1861; railway; monument: twin-towered Neo-Romanesque church; event: open-air 'parliament' on the first Sunday in May.

Glasgow *glahz'gō* (Celtic 'glas ghu', 'beloved green place'), 55 53N 4 15W, pop(1981) 765,030, capital of Strathclyde region, W Scotland; on the R Clyde, 66 km W of Edinburgh; the largest city in Scotland; the rise of Glasgow as a commercial city dates from the 17th century, expanding with the trade in tobacco, rum and sugar from the Americas; later shipbuilding and associated metal and engineering industries were dependent on Lanarkshire coal and iron; pop(1740) c.17,000, pop(1801) 84,000, pop(1931) 1,093,337; Loch Katrine is the main source of water; University of Glasgow (1451); Strathclyde University (1964); railway; metro; airport (at Abbotsinch, 11 km W); economy: shipyards, commerce, whisky blending and bottling, carpet manufacturing; monuments: Kelvin art gallery and museum; Hunterian art gallery and museum; the Burrell Collection, gifted to Glasgow by Sir William and Lady Burrell; Royal Scottish Academy of Music (1847); Museum of Transport; ruins of 15th-c Cathcart castle; 12th-c cathedral dedicated to St Mungo; Provand's Lordship, the only other surviving medieval building in Glasgow (1471); 15th-c Crookston castle where Darnley and Mary Queen of Scots stayed after their marriage in 1565; Haggs castle (1585) has been turned into a museum of history for children; the Mitchell Library (1874) is the largest public reference library in Scotland; the People's Palace (1898) contains exhibits relating to the history of Glasgow; Regimental Headquarters of the Royal Highland Fusiliers, a museum covering the history of the Royal Scots Fusiliers, the Highland Light Infantry and the Royal Highland Fusiliers; the Victorian tenement museum contains household exhibits from the 19th century; event: Mayfest.

Glas'tonbury, 51 09N 2 43W, pop(1981) 6,700, market town in Mendip dist, Somerset, SW England, on the R Brue, 35 km SW of Bath; a lake village in prehistoric times; according to legend it was here that Joseph of Arimathea brought the Holy Grail, the chalice that was used at the Last Supper; monument: Benedictine abbey.

Glendale, 33 32N 112 11W, pop(1980) 97,172, town in Maricopa county, S central Arizona, United States; 12 km NW of Phoenix; economy: food processing and trade in fruit and vegetables; nearby is Luke Air Force Base.

Glendale, 34 09N 118 15W, pop(1980) 139,060, city in Los Angeles county, SW California, United States; residential and industrial suburb N of Los Angeles; in the SE San Fernando Valley; economy: vehicles.

Glendora, 34 08N 117 52W, pop(1980) 38,654, city in Los Angeles county, SW California, United States; residential city, 35 km ENE of Los Angeles; railway.

Glenrothes *glen-roth'is*, 56 12N 3 11W, pop(1981) 32,971, town in Kirkcaldy dist; capital of Fife region, E Scotland; designated a new town in 1948; a centre for electronic research; airfield; economy: timber, plastics, electronics, machinery, paper.

Glenview, 42 04N 87 48W, pop(1980) 32,060, town in Cook county, NE Illinois, United States; 29 km NNW of Chicago; railway; US naval air station.

Glittertind *glit'ur-tin*, GLITTERTINDEN, 61 40N 8 32E, highest mountain in Norway, a peak in the Jotunheimen range, W Oppland county, S central Norway; height 2,470 m.

Gliwice *glee-veet'sa*, GLEIWITZ (Ger), 50 20N 18 40E, pop(1983) 211,200, city in Katowice voivodship, S Poland; W of Katowice on the Gliwice Canal which connects with the R Oder (Odra) to form a 700 km long waterway to Szczecin; surrounded by parkland and coal fields; Silesian technical university (1945); the first coke-burning smelting furnace in Europe was opened here in 1796; railway; economy: coal mining, steel, iron; monuments: museum of folk sculpture, statue of Chopin, Holy Cross monastery.

Głogów *glog-oof'*, 51 40N 16 06E, pop(1983) 60,100, town in Legnica voivodship, SW Poland; former capital of the Piast kingdom; railway; monuments: 12-15th-c collegiate church, Piast castle and museum.

Glossop, 53 27N 1 57W, pop(1981) 30,040, town linked with Hollingworth in High Peak dist, Derbyshire, central England; 22 km E of Manchester; railway; economy: clothing, engineering.

Gloucester *glos'ter*, GLEVUM (Lat), CAER GLOU (Anglo-Saxon), 51 53N 2 14W, pop(1981) 92,385, county town of Gloucestershire, SW central England; NE of Bristol; connected to R Severn by canal; railway; airfield; economy: boatbuilding, trade in timber and grain; monuments: 13th-c cathedral, Bishop Hooper's Lodging; event: Three Choirs Festival in rotation with Hereford and Worcester (Sept).

Gloucester, 42 37N 70 40W, pop(1980) 27,768, town in Essex county, NE Massachusetts, United States; port on the coast of Cape Ann, 43 km NE of Boston; railway; economy: fishing, fish processing, boat building; tourism; event: St Peter's fiesta (June).

Gloucestershire *glos'ter-shir*, county in the Midlands of SW central England; bounded N by Hereford and Worcester, NE by Warwickshire, E by Oxfordshire, S by Wiltshire and Avon and W by Gwent in Wales; drained by the R Severn; pop(1981) 501,673; area 2,643 sq km; county town Gloucester; chief towns include Cheltenham, Cirencester; economy: fruit growing, arable farming in the Cotswolds; the county is divided into 6 districts:

District	*area (sq km)*	*pop(1981)*
Cheltenham	35	84,373
Cotswold	1,142	68,712
Forest of Dean	528	72,847
Gloucester	33	92,385
Stroud	454	102,021
Tewkesbury	450	81,335

Gniezno *gnyez'no*, GNESEN (Ger), 52 32N 17 32E, pop(1983) 66,100, town in Poznań voivodship, W central Poland; claimed as the first capital of Poland according to a legend which describes how the chieftain of the Polanie tribe saw a nesting white eagle and decided to build a stronghold here; railway; economy: machinery, leather; monuments: cathedral (14-15th-c), archaeological museum, 14th-c Gothic church of St John.

Gnjilane *gan-yee'la-ne*, 42 26N 21 26E, pop(1981) 84,085, town in autonomous province of Kosovo, S Srbija (Serbia) republic, Yugoslavia; 32 km SE of Priština.

Goa, Daman and Diu *gō'a da-mahn and dee'oo*, union territory in W India; bounded by the Arabian Sea in the W, and landward by Gujarat state; pop(1981) 1,082,117; area 3,813 sq km; crossed by railway, running between Dhārwād, Karnataka and Madgaon on the coast; the capital and largest town is Panaji (Panajim); there is a Legislative Assembly of 30 members; Goa was conquered by Muslims in 1312, but became part of the Hindu kingdom of Vijayanagar in 1370; recaptured by Muslims 100 years later; in 1510 Alfonso of Albuquerque captured the coastal region for Portugal; in 1531 the Portuguese captured the Daman area to the N of Bombay, which was ceded to them in 1539 by the Shah of Gujarat; the island of Diu, which lies off the S coast of Gujarat state in the Arabian Sea, was taken by Portugal in 1534; Old Goa was a prosperous port city in the 16th century; in Dec 1961 India occupied the territories and incorporated them into the Indian Union; economy: manganese and iron ore, coastal fishing, rice, wheat, ragi, pulses and fruit; Marmagoa is the main port; there is a daily boat service between Panaji and Bombay; dependent for electric power on neighbouring states.

Goaso *gō-a'sō*, 6 49N 2 27W, town SW of Sunyani in Brong-Ahafo region, SW Ghana, W Africa; railway terminus, with a proposed rail link to Sunyani.

Gobi *gō-bee*, desert in central Asia; area approx 1,295,000 sq km; extends c.1,610 km E-W across SE Mongolia and N China; bounded E by the Da Hinggan Ling range and W by the Tien Shan range; situated on a plateau ranging in height from 915 to 1,525 m; consists of a series of shallow, alkaline basins; the W part of the desert is completely sandy; nearly all the Gobi desert's soil has been removed by strong winds from the NW and deposited in N central China as loess; the narrow grass-covered area which surrounds the Gobi desert supports a small number of nomadic Mongolian tribes, who live by herding sheep and goats; numerous palaeontological finds, including dinosaur eggs, have been made in the desert; prehistoric implements, some approx 100,000 years old, have also been found; inhabited by Mongol nomads, the desert is crossed by many old trade routes.

Godalming, 51 11N 0 37W, pop(1981) 18,882, town in Guildford dist, Surrey, SE England; home of the writer Aldous Huxley (1894-1963); railway; economy: engineering, textiles.

Godavari *go-dah'vu-ree*, GODAVERI, river in central India; rises to the WSW of Maharashtra state in the Western Ghats; flows generally ESE past Nānded and across Andhra Pradesh; forms part of the boundary between Andhra Pradesh and Madhya Pradesh; flows SE through a steep gorge cut in the Eastern Ghats to Rajahmundry to enter the Bay of Bengal by way of 2 mouths at Cape Godavari and Point Narasapatnam; sacred river of the Hindus; has an extensive navigable irrigation canal system; delta of the Godavari was one of the earliest sites of European settlement in India.

Godhavn *gōdh'hown*, QEQRTARSUAQ (Esk), 69 15N 53 33W, fishing settlement on the W coast of Greenland; on Disko I, at the head of the Davis Strait, N of the Arctic Circle; founded in 1733; former whaling station; radio and scientific installations.

Godmanchester, town in Cambridgeshire, England. See Huntingdon.

Gödöllö *gü'dü-lü*, 47 38N 19 25E, pop(1984e) 29,000, town in Pest county, N Hungary; NE of Budapest; university of agricultural science (1945); railway; economy: electrical machinery.

Godthåb or **Godthaab** *got'hop*, NÛK, NUUK (Esk), 64 11N 51 44W, pop(1983e) 9,848, capital and largest town of Greenland; on SW coast, on Davis Strait; founded in 1721 by Hans Egede; ruins of a 10th-c Norse settlement are nearby; economy: fish processing, scientific installations, oil and liquid gas storage.

Gogra, river in India, Nepal, China. See Ghaghara.

Goiânia *gō-yan'ya*, 16 43S 49 18W, pop(1980) 702,858, capital of Goiás state, Centro-Oeste region, W central Brazil; SW of Brasília; founded in 1933, it succeeded Goiás Velho as state capital in 1937; university (1960); railway; economy: rice, cattle raising; in the W of the city is the Parque Mutirama, with a zoo and an 'Educational Park'; the city also has a racecourse and motor racetrack.

Goiás *go-yas'*, state in Centro-Oeste region, W central Brazil; bounded W by the Río Araguaia, N by the Río Tocantins, E by the Serra Geral de Goiás; crossed by several short mountain ranges; pop(1980) 3,859,602; area 642,092 sq km; capital Goiânia; chief town Anápolis; economy: coffee, rice, cattle, minerals (manganese, nickel, gold, quartzite, tin).

Gojam *gō'jam*, region in W Ethiopia, NE Africa; pop(1984e) 3,244,882; area 61,600 sq km; a mountainous region with peaks including Birhan (4,154 m) and Amedamit (3,619 m) both of which are located within the Choke range which runs NW-SE; part of T'ana Hāyk' (L Tana) is located in the NE; capital Debra Markos; chief towns include Dunkur and Mot'a.

Gojra *gōj'ru*, 31 10N 72 43E, pop(1981) 68,000, city in SE central Punjab prov, Pakistan; 47 km SW of Faisalabad; railway; economy: trade in wheat and cotton.

Golan' or **Golan Heights**, AL JAWLĀN (Arab), Israeli-occupied area of Syria administered as a sub-district of North dist, N Israel; situated E of the Sea of Galilee; pop(1983) 19,727; area 1,176 sq km; in 1948 the Israel-Syria border followed the R Jordan; Golan was occupied by Israel in 1967 and later annexed in 1981; several Jewish settlements founded; rises to 1,204 m at Mt Avital.

Golborne *gō'bern*, 53 29N 2 36W, pop(1981) 20,652, town in Wigan borough, Greater Manchester, England; 9 km N of Warrington; economy: textiles, coal, engineering.

Gold Coast, 27 59S 153 22E, pop(1986) 219,300, urban area in Moreton stat div, Queensland, E Australia; pop includes 19,269 residents in the part of Gold Coast within New South Wales; on the E coast, S of Brisbane; railway; airfield; the largest resort region in Australia with restaurants and beaches stretching for 32 km; includes Southport, Surfers' Paradise, Broadbeach and Burleigh Heads; monuments: tourist attractions such as the Dreamworld, Sea World and a bird paradise.

Golden Gate Highlands, national park in the high veld of NE Orange Free State prov, South Africa; wildlife includes wildebeest, blesbok, eland, buffalo, springbok and the rare lammergeyer; area 48 sq km; established in 1963; facilities include 2 rest camps and a youth camp.

Golden Sands, beach resort in Bulgaria. See Zlatni Pyasăci.

Goldsboro, 35 23N 77 59W, pop(1980) 31,871, county seat of Wayne county, E North Carolina, United States; on the R Neuse, 72 km SE of Raleigh; railway; economy: tobacco, textiles.

Golfito *gol-fee'tō*, 8 42N 83 10W, port in the prov of Puntarenas, S Costa Rica, Central America; on an inlet of the Golfo Dulce; airfield.

Golspie *gol'spi*, 57 58N 3 58W, pop(1981) 1,491, capital of Sutherland dist, Highland region, NE Scotland; on the E coast, just N of the Dornoch Firth and 24 km SW of Helmsdale; railway.

Gomel' *go'myi-ly'*, HOMEL, 52 25N 31 00E, pop(1983) 432,000, river port and capital city of Gomel'skaya oblast, Belorusskaya SSR, Soviet Union; on the R Sozh; university (1969); railway; economy: manufacture of machine tools and motor vehicles, instrument-making, electrical engineering, electronics.

Gonaïves *gon-a-eev'*, 19 29N 72 42W, pop(1975) 36,736, port and chief town of Artibonite dept, W Haiti, E Caribbean; on the Golfe de la Gonâve, 112 km NNW of Port-au-Prince; exports agricultural produce from the fertile Artibonite Plain; scene of the proclamation of Haitian independence on 1 Jan 1804.

Gonarezhou *-re'zhoo*, national park in Zimbabwe; area 5,053 km; established in 1975.

Gonâve, Île de la *eel de la go-nav'*, elongated island in the Golfe de la Gonâve, Haiti, E Caribbean; situated between the Canal de la Gonâve (S) and the Canal de Saint Marc (N); area 658 sq km; length 56 km; largely covered by forests.

Gonder *gon'dur*, GONDAR, 12 39N 37 29E, pop(1984e) 68,958, capital of Gonder region, NW Ethiopia, NE Africa; N of T'ana Hāyk' (L Tana), 400 km NNW of Addis Ababa; capital of Ethiopia between 1732 and 1855; a former centre for religion, art, culture, music and learning; occupied by the Italians in 1936 and was the last place in Italian East Africa to fall to British forces during World War II; airfield; monuments: palaces and churches dating from 17th and 18th centuries including Fasilides Castle where Louis XIV's emissary was received in 1699.

Gongola *gong-gō'la*, state in E Nigeria, W Africa, pop(1982e) 4,154,500; area 91,390 sq km; mountainous in the SE (Sheshibi mountains) and NE (Mandara mountains); capital Yola; chief towns Suntai, Wukari, Numan, Jalingo, Gembu, Mubi and Gombi; there are numerous ethnic groups with their own dialects but Hausa and Fulfulde are common to all; one of Nigeria's most important states in terms of livestock; there are game reserves at Sarauna and Kshimbilla; economy: iron ore, lead, limestone, salt, zinc, sugar refining, cotton ginning, livestock trade.

Goodwood, 33 54S 18 32E, pop(1980) 238,102, municipality in Cape prov, South Africa; a SE suburb of Cape Town.

Goole, 53 42N 0 52W, pop(1981) 19,508, port town in Boothferry dist, Humberside, NE England; at junction of Don and Ouse rivers, 37 km W of Kingston-upon-Hull; railway; economy: chemicals.

Goose Green, 51 52S 59 00W, settlement on East Falkland, Falkland Is, in the S Atlantic, at the head of Choiseul Sound, on the narrow isthmus that joins the N half of East Falkland to Lafonia in the S; pop(1980) 100, the second largest settlement in the Falkland Is.

Gopalganj *gō'pal-gunj*, 23 00N 89 48E, pop(1981) 182,338, town in Gopalganj dist, Faridpur, S central Bangladesh; on the W bank of the R Haringhat.

Göppingen *gœp'ing-en*, 48 42N 9 40E, pop(1983) 52,400, town in Stuttgart dist, Baden-Württemberg prov, W Germany, 38 km ESE of Stuttgart; railway.

Gorakhpur *gō'ruk-poor*, 26 45N 83 23E, pop(1981) 306,000, city in Uttar Pradesh, NE India; on the R Rapti, a tributary of the Ghaghara R; founded in 1400 and named after a Hindu saint; a conglomeration of farm villages in a densely populated agricultural region, where the chief crops are rice, cotton and cereals; damaged by earthquake in 1934; airfield; linked E to Lucknow by rail.

Gordon, district in Grampian region, NE Scotland; pop(1981) 62,309; area 2,214 sq km; chief town Inverurie.

Goreme *gor'em-e*, valley in Cappadocia, central Turkey; noted for its cave dwellings.

Gorgān *gor-gahn'*, 36 55N 54 30E, pop(1983) 114,321, town in Gorgān dist, Māzandarān, NE Iran, 296 km ENE of Tehrān, at the edge of the Caspian Sea; railway; airfield.

Gorgol *gor'gol*, region in S Mauritania, NW Africa; pop(1982e) 169,000; area 13,600 sq km; capital Kaédi; chief towns Mbout, Nguiguilore and Maghama; the R Sénégal follows the S frontier with Senegal; there are extensive phosphate reserves.

Gorizia *gō-reet'syah*, GÖRZ *gœrts* (Ger), prov of Friuli-Venezia Giulia region, NE Italy; pop(1981) 144,726; area 466 sq km; capital Gorizia.

Gorizia, 45 57N 13 37E, pop(1981) 41,557, capital town of Gorizia prov, Friuli-Venezia Giulia region, NE Italy; near the Yugoslav frontier, where the fertile valley of the R Isonzo emerges into the plain of Friuli, 35 km NNW of Trieste; archbishopric; railway; economy: cotton, silk, paper, furniture, trade in wine and fruit; monuments: 14th-c cathedral; old castle of the counts of Gorizia.

Gorj *gorzh*, county in SW Romania, in the SW foothills of the Transylvanian Alps; pop(1983) 370,956; area 5,641 sq km; capital Tîrgu Jiu; economy: agriculture and timber trades are important.

Gor'kiy *gor'y'-ki*, GORKY (Eng), formerly NIZHNY NOVGOROD, 56 20N 44 00E, pop(1983) 1,382,000, river port and industrial capital of Gor'kovskaya oblast, E European Rossiyskaya, Soviet Union; at the confluence of the Volga and Oka rivers; established in 1221 as a frontier post; Gor'kiy was famous for its annual trade fairs held from 1817 to 1930 except during the Bolshevik Revolution and the civil war; university (1918); railway; airport; economy: machine building, chemicals, woodworking, foodstuffs.

Görlitz *ger'lits*, 51 9N 15 0E, pop(1981) 80,831, town in Görlitz dist, Dresden, SE East Germany; on the Nysa Łużycka, E of Dresden, where it follows the Polish frontier; railway; economy: manufacture of rolling stock.

Gorlovka *gor'luf-ku*, 48 17N 38 05E, pop(1983) 339,000, town in Donetskaya oblast, Ukrainskaya SSR, Soviet Union; 45 km NE of Donetsk, in the Donets basin; the town developed in 1867 in connection with the coal industry; railway; canal; economy: coal mining, machine building, chemicals, foodstuffs, clothing.

Gornji Milanovac or **Milanovac** *gor'nyee mee-la'no-vats*, 44 01N 20 29E, pop(1981) 50,651, town in central Srbija (Serbia) republic, Yugoslavia; W of Krugujevac; railway.

Gorom Gor'om, 14 26N 0 14W, town in NE Burkina, W Africa; NNW of Dori.

Gorongo'sa, national park in Sofala prov, SE central Mozambique, SE Africa; area 3,770 sq km; established in 1940.

Gorseinon, 51 41N 4 02W, pop(1981) 18,039, town in Lliw Valley dist, West Glamorgan, S Wales; W of Swansea.

Gorzów *gor-zoof'*, voivodship in W Poland; bounded W by R Oder (Odra) which follows the frontier with E Germany; traversed E-W by R Warta, which meets the R Noteć E of Gorzów Wielkopolski; pop(1983) 474,000; area 8,484 sq km; capital Gorzów Wielkopolski; chief towns include Kostrzyn and Choszczno.

Gorzów Wielkopolski *gor-zoof' vyel'ko-pol-ski*, LANDSBERG (Ger), 52 42N 15 12E, pop(1983) 113,000, river port capital of Gorzów voivodship, W Poland; on R Warta; railway; economy: synthetic fibres, silk, timber; monuments: 13-14th-c Gothic cathedral, remains of 14th-c town walls.

Gos'forth, 55 01N 1 36W, pop(1981) 25,384, town in Newcastle upon Tyne borough, Tyne and Wear, NE England; part of Tyneside urban area; a NW suburb of Newcastle upon Tyne.

Goslar *gos'lahr*, 51 55N 10 23E, pop(1983) 52,000, manufacturing town in Hannover dist, SE Niedersachsen (Lower Saxony) prov, W Germany; 37 km S of Braunschweig, on N fringe of the Harz Mts; includes the well-known climatic and winter sports resort of Hahnenklee-Bockswiese at the foot of the 726 m high Bocksberg; railway; monuments: 15th-c town hall; Kaiserpfalz, an imperial palace built 1039-56; Brusttuch burgher house (1526).

Gos'port, 50 48N 1 08W, pop(1981) 70,705, town in Gosport dist, Hampshire, S England; part of Portsmouth urban area; at the entrance to Portsmouth harbour; ferry; economy: chemicals, engineering, distributive trades.

Gostivar *go'stee-var*, 41 47N 20 55E, pop(1981) 101,188, town in NW Makedonija (Macedonia) republic, S Yugoslavia; railway.

Göteborg *yœ'te-bor*, GOTHENBURG (Eng), 57 45N 12 00E, pop(1982) 425,696, seaport and capital city of Göteborg och Bohus county, SW Sweden; at the mouth of the R Göta älv on the Kattegat; 2nd largest city in Sweden; leading port and commercial town; founded in 1619 by Gustavus Adolphus; originated in 1865 what is known as the Gothenburg system for the regulation of the sale of intoxicating liquors; became a free port in 1921; university (1891), technical university (1829); railway; ferry services to England, Denmark and Germany; the Göta Canal links it with the Baltic; economy: shipbuilding, motor vehicles, chemicals, ball-bearings; monument: cathedral (1633), restored 1956-57.

Göteborg och Bohus *-o-bō'hus*, a county of SW Sweden, bounded on the W by the Skagerrak; chief river is the Göta älv; land area 5,110 sq km; pop(1983) 709,447; capital Göteborg (Gothenburg); chief towns Uddevalla and Mölndal; the county includes the islands of Tjörn and Orust.

Gotha *gō'tah*, 50 57N 10 43E, pop(1981) 57,573, town in Gotha dist, Erfurt, SW East Germany; W of Erfurt; founded in 12th century; former residence of the dukes of Saxony-Gotha (1640-1825) and Saxecoburg-Gotha (1826-1918); railway; economy: precision instruments, chemicals, publishing, textiles.

Got'land, GOTTLAND, GOTHLAND, an island county of Sweden, in the Baltic Sea off the SE coast of Sweden; includes the islands of Gotland, Fårö and Karlsö; there are spectacular rock formations at Raukar; land area 3,140 sq km; pop(1983) 55,895; capital Visby; colonized by Germans in 12th century; taken by Sweden in 1280, by Denmark in 1361 and again by Sweden in 1645.

Gottenburg, capital city of Sweden. See Göteborg.

Göttingen *gœt'ing-en*, 51 31N 9 55E, pop(1983) 132,700, university town in Hannover dist, S Niedersachsen (Lower Saxony) prov, W Germany; in the Leine valley at the foot of the Hainberg, 88 km SSW of Braunschweig; university (1737); railway; economy: precision engineering, optical equipment, metalworking; event: Handel Festival (June); many Nobel Prize winners have studied or taught here; also noted as a city of congresses.

Gottwaldov *got-wal'dof*, ZLIN (Ger), 49 14N 17 40E, pop(1984) 84,731, town in Jihomoravský region, Czech Socialist Republic, central Czechoslovakia; on the R Dřevnice, E of Brno in the White Carpathian Mts; railway; economy: footwear, rubber goods, timber, machinery.

Gouda *KHow'da, gow'da* (Eng), 52 01N 4 43E, pop(1984e) 60,026, city in Zuid Holland prov, W Netherlands; 23 km NE of Rotterdam, in a fertile polder area between Utrecht, Rotterdam and 's-Gravenhage, at the confluence of the Gouwe and the Ijssel rivers; railway; economy: stoneware, candles, clay pipes, dairy products; monuments: town hall (1449-59); Janskerk, Holland's longest church, rebuilt in the 16th century with windows containing portraits of 16th-c celebrities including William the Silent, Philip II of Spain and Mary Tudor); noted for its cheese market.

Goulburn *gool'burn*, 34 47S 149 43E, pop(1981) 21,755, agricultural centre in SE New South Wales, Australia; SW of Sydney and NE of Canberra; railway; airfield; to the E is Morton National Park.

Gourock *goo'rok*, 55 58N 4 49W, pop(1981) 11,203, town in Inverclyde dist, Strathclyde, W Scotland; on the S shore of the Firth of Clyde, 4 km W of Greenock; railway; ferry services to Dunoon; monument: on the cliff side is the prehistoric Kempock Stone, once used in rites by fishermen to ensure good weather and by couples about to wed.

Goverla *gu-vyer'lu*, HOVERLA (Pol), 48 09N 24 30E, highest peak in the Ukrainian Carpathian Mts, SW European Soviet Union; 19 km W of Zhabye; height 2,058 m; the R Prut rises at its E foot.

Governador Valadares *go-ver-na-dor' va-la-da'rays*, 18 51S 41 57W, pop(1980) 173,624, town in Minas Gerais state, Sudeste region, SE Brazil; NE of Belo Horizonte; railway; economy: commerce, light industry, mining of semi precious stones, cattle raising.

Govĭaltay *go-al'tī*, GOV'ALTAI, county in SW Mongolia, pop(1981e) 40,000; area 142,000 sq km; in the Altai mountain region; bounded W by the People's Republic of China; capital Altay; desert covers much of the area; crossed by Gichgeniyn Nuru, Aj Bogd Uul and Edrengiyn Nuruu; noted for the abundance of medicinal herbs, such as liquorice, fool's parsley and gentian; Gobi bears (masalai) and wild boars are common in the desert areas; stock farming is important, with 70% of the cattle being kept by agricultural associations.

Gozo *got'zo*, GHAUDEX *gow'desh* (Maltese), GAULUS (anc), 36 00N 14 13E, island in the Maltese group, often called the 'Isle of Calypso'; situated 6 km NW of the main island of Malta and separated from the small island of Comino by the North Comino Channel; area 67 sq km; length of shoreline 43 km; pop(1983e) 23,644 (with Comino); the main towns are Victoria, Xagħra, Nadur and Xewkija; the main seaport is Mġarr Harbour; there is a holiday resort at the fishing village of Marsalforn on the N coast; the island is largely given over to agriculture which is watered by a comprehensive irrigation network; near Xagħra there are two prehistoric temples and two alabaster caves; on the road to Għarb, the Ta' Pinu church is a centre of pilgrimage in an area where local legend claims that the Virgin Mary appeared on several occasions.

Gračanica *gra'chan-it-sa*, 44 43N 18 18E, pop(1981) 54,311, town in NE Bosna-Hercegovina republic, Yugoslavia; on R Spreca, 32 km NW of Tuzla; railway; economy: fruit and sugar-beet trade.

Gracias a Dios *gras-ee-as a dee'os*, easternmost dept in Honduras, Central America; pop(1983e) 35,471; area 16,621 sq km; drained by the Río Patuca; the Río Coco forms its S boundary with Nicaragua; capital Puerto Lempira.

Graciosa or **Ilha Graciosa** *gras-yo'sa*, 39 03N 28 00W, most northerly island in the central Azores, Angra do Heroísmo dist, Portuguese autonomous region of the Azores; measuring 13 km long by up to 7 km wide, with an area of 62 sq km; highest point is the rim of the Caldeira do Enxofre (411 m) at the foot of which lies the spa of Termas do Carapacho, with subterranean mineral springs; main town and port is Santa Cruz; economy: crop-farming, fruit-growing and stock-rearing.

Gradačac *gra'da-chats*, 44 52N 18 26E, pop(1981) 54,281, town in NE Bosna-Hercegovina republic, Yugoslavia; 40 km NNW of Tuzla.

Graf'ton, 29 40S 152 56E, pop(1981) 17,005, town in Mid-North Coast stat div, NE New South Wales, Australia; on the R Clarence, S of Brisbane; railway; airfield; economy: dairy cattle breeding, brewing, timber; event: Jacaranda festival in Sept.

Graham Land, mountainous Antarctic peninsula forming part of the British Antarctic Territory; rises to about 3,600 m at Mt Jackson; the Weddell Sea lies to the E.

Graian Alps *gray'yun*, ALPES GRAIAN (Fr), ALPI GRAIE (Ital), mountain range on the French-Italian frontier, S of the Mont Blanc group; rises to 4,061 m in Gran Paradiso; comprises many glaciers.

Grám'mos, 40 23N 20 45E, mountain in Kolonjë dist, S Albania; on the border with Greece; height 2,503 m.

Grampian, region in NE Scotland; bounded N and E by the North Sea, W by Highland region and S by Tayside; part of the Cairngorms and part of the Grampian Mts lie in the SW; drained by the Spey, Dee, Don, Ythan and Deveron rivers; pop(1981) 471,942; area 8,704 sq km; capital Aberdeen; major towns include Peterhead, Stonehaven, Fraserburgh and Elgin; economy: fishing, farming, oil-related industries, whisky; Grampian is divided into 5 districts:

District	*area (sq km)*	*pop(1981)*
Aberdeen City	184	203,927
Banff and Buchan	1,526	81,699
Gordon	2,214	62,309
Kincardine and Deeside	2,548	42,482
Moray	2,231	81,525

Grampian Mts, mountain system extending SW-NE across Scotland; the S edge forms the natural boundary between the Highlands and the Lowlands; consists of gentle slopes to the S, steep ones to the N; rises to 1,344 m in Ben Nevis, the highest peak in Britain; includes several smaller chains of mountains, among them the Cairngorms, which contain some of the highest peaks (Ben Macdhui, 1,309 m; Cairn Toul, 1,293 m; Cairngorm, 1,245 m); source of the headwaters of the Dee, Don, Spey, Findhorn, Esk, Tay and Forth rivers.

Grampians, mountain range in SW central Victoria, Australia; SW spur of the Great Dividing Range; extends approx 64 km NW from Ararat; rises to 1,167 m at Mt William.

Gramsh, prov of central Albania; area 695 sq km; pop(1980) 36,300; capital Gramsh.

Gramsh, town and capital of Gramsh prov, central Albania; on the R Devoll, 29 km SSE of Elbasan.

Gran, 60 23N 10 32E, pop(1980) 12,347, town in SE corner of Oppland county, S central Norway.

Gran Buenos Aires *gran bway'nōs ī'rays*, federal dist in Litoral region, E Argentina; bordered (E) by the Río de la Plata; pop(1980) 2,922,829; area 200 sq km; federal capital Buenos Aires.

Gran Canaria *gran ca-na'rya*, 28 00N 15 35W, volcanic

Atlantic island in the Canary Is, Las Palmas prov, Canarias autonomous region of Spain; situated between Tenerife I (W) and Fuerteventura I (E); area 1,532 sq km; the highest point is Pozo de las Nieves (1,980 m); the N and W coasts are edged by steep cliffs while the S has wide beaches with tourist facilities; the main town is Las Palmas de Gran Canaria; Telde and Arucas are important industrial centres for sugar cane, distilling, tobacco, chemicals and light engineering; airport on the E coast.

Gran Chaco, El *gran cha'kō* (Spanish, 'the great hunting ground' or 'riches'), an inland plain of South America in Bolivia, Paraguay and Argentina; an area of scrub forest and grassland, almost desert in places, with swamps and in the rainy season great lagoons; it has a tropical savannah climate; slopes SE to the rivers Paraguay and Paraná which, with their tributaries, the Bermejo and the Pilcomayo and other streams, cover vast tracts with their flood-waters and fertilizing clay; comprises (1) the Chaco Boreal (area 259,000 sq km) which lies to the N of the Río Pilcomayo, partly in Bolivia but mostly in Paraguay; (2) the Chaco Central (area 129,500 sq km) which lies between the Pilcomayo and the Bermejo rivers and belongs to Argentina; and (3) the Chaco Austral (area 259,000 sq km) which lies in Argentina S of the Río Bermejo; the region has a sparse population, but is noted for cattle-raising and the extraction of tannin from the quebracho tree (*Schinopsis lorentzii*); disagreement between Bolivia and Paraguay concerning the interstate boundary in the Chaco led to open warfare in 1932-35.

Gran Paradiso *gran pa-ra-dee'sō*, GRAND PARADIS *grã pa-ra-dee* (Fr), highest peak in the Graian Alps, NW Italy, 26 km S of Aosta; height 4,061 m; the whole massif forms with the adjacent territory a national park (700 sq km), established in 1922, in which are the sole surviving wild steinboks.

Granada *gra-na'THa*, dept in W Nicaragua, Central America; bounded E by Lago de Nicaragua; contains Lago de Apoyo and Lago de Tisma; pop(1981) 113,102; area 1,401 sq km; capital Granada; other main town Nandaime.

Granada, 11 58N 85 59W, pop(1978) 56,232, capital town of Granada dept, W Nicaragua, Central America; on the NW shore of Lago de Nicaragua; founded 1524 at the foot of Mombacho volcano; terminus of the railway from the port of Corinto, 190 km to the NW; lake beach; monuments: cathedral, church of La Merced (1781-83); events: Holy Week, Assumption of the Virgin (14-30 Aug).

Granada, prov in Andalucia region, S Spain; bounded to the S by the Mediterranean; drained by the R Genil and its tributaries; includes the Sierra Nevada with its skiing facilities on the slopes of Mulhacén and Veleta; formerly part of a Moorish kingdom which included Almería and Málaga; pop(1981) 761,734; area 12,531 sq km; capital Granada; economy: beer, chemical products, mining, food processing, furniture, mineral water (Lanjarón), electrical appliances, cement, textiles, clothes, paper, carpets (Zubia).

Granada, 37 10N 3 35W, pop(1981) 262,182, capital of Granada prov, Andalucia, S Spain; on R Genil at the foot of Sierra Nevada mountains, 434 km S of Madrid; alt 662-780 m; founded by the Moors in the 8th century; became capital of the Moorish kingdom of Granada in 1238 and remained the last Moorish stronghold in Spain until captured in 1492; archbishopric; university (1531); airport; railway; Fuentevaqueros, 20 km from Granada, was the birthplace of the poet and dramatist, Federico Garcia Lorca; economy: textiles, paper, soap; monuments: 16th-c Gothic and Renaissance cathedral including the Chapel Royal with the tombs of Ferdinand (d.1516) and Isabella (d.1504), Generalife Palace and the Alhambra; events: Conquest Day in January; Holy Week with processions; fiesta of Las Cruces de Mayo in May; international festival of music and dance (June-July); international sports week in winter and Costa del Sol Rally in Dec.

Granby, 45 23N 72 44W, pop(1981) 38,069, town in S Québec, SE Canada; railway; economy: textiles, rubber, chemicals, tobacco, meat processing.

Grand Bahama, island in the NW Bahamas, just W of Great Abaco I; fourth largest island in the Bahamas; pop(1980) 33,102; area 1,372 sq km; length 120 km; chief town Freeport-Lucaya; popular tourist resort; home of the Underwater Explorers' Club; International Bazaar; oil transshipment at South Riding Point.

Grand Bassam, 5 14N 3 45W, town in Abidjan dept, S Ivory Coast, W Africa; 30 km E of Abidjan, at the mouth of the R Comoé; capital of the Ivory Coast until 1900; railway terminus; airport.

Grand Canal, canal in E China. See Da Yunhe.

Grand Canyon, enormous gorge in NW Arizona, United States; 349 km long; 8-25 km wide from rim to rim; maximum depth 1,900 m; the result of large-scale erosion by the Colorado river, which has exposed 1,500 million years of geological formations; the river extends through a high plateau region of 1,524-2,740 m; the portions of the side walls which have formed isolated towers due to erosion by side streams are often referred to as temples; the best known of these are Vishnu Temple, Shiva Temple and Wotan's Throne; the Grand Canyon National Park (4,931 sq km) was established in 1919.

Grand Cayman *kay-man'*, largest of the Cayman Is, W Caribbean; a flat island surrounded by coral reefs; area 197 sq km; length 45 km; max width 13 km; pop(1979) 15,000; capital George Town; has the only commercial turtle farm in the world; Owen Roberts International Airport is located 2.5 km from the capital; tourist development is concentrated along the Seven Mile Beach peninsula.

Grand Comore *ke-mor'*, NJAZIDJA, 11 45S 43 15E, pop(1980) 189,000, largest island of the Comoros group in the Mozambique Channel; area 1,148 sq km; chief town Moroni; steep mountains rise to the peak of Kartala, an active volcano; the island forests produce building timber.

Grand Coulee *koo'lee*, valley in Douglas county, NE central Washington, United States; the 168 m Grand Coulee Dam on the Columbia river was completed in 1942.

Grand Forks, 47 55N 97 03W, pop(1980) 43,765, county seat of Grand Forks county, E North Dakota, United States; at the confluence of the Red Lake and Red rivers, 118 km N of Fargo; university (1883); railway; airfield; economy: dairy products, beet sugar, meat processing, flour mills, grain.

Grand Island, 40 55N 98 21W, pop(1980) 33,180, county seat of Hall county, S Nebraska, United States; on the R Wood near its confluence with the R Platte, 144 km W of Lincoln; railway; economy: horse, mule and cattle market; monument: Stuhr Museum of the Prairie Pioneer; event: Husker Harvest Days (Sept).

Grand Junction, 39 04N 108 33W, pop(1980) 28,144, county seat of Mesa county, W Colorado, United States; at the confluence of the Colorado and Gunnison rivers; railway; economy: agricultural trade, food processing, uranium, oil and coal mining, electronic equipment, tourism (skiing and hunting); event: Coors Bicycle Classic (Aug).

Grand Port, district of SE Mauritius; area 260.3 sq km; pop(1983) 94,490.

Grand Prairie, 32 45N 97 00W, pop(1980) 71,462, town in Dallas county, NE Texas, United States; 18 km W of Dallas; railway; economy: aerospace products, mobile homes, metal goods, plastics, and medical supplies; monument: Six Flags over Texas amusement park.

Grand Rapids, 42 58N 85 40W, pop(1980) 181,843, county seat of Kent county, W Michigan, United States; on the R Grand, 98 km WNW of Lansing; railway; airfield; economy: furniture, machinery, fabricated metals; monuments: art gallery, planetarium and museum.

Grand St Bernard, 45 53N 7 11E, alpine mountain pass between Martigny, Valais canton, Switzerland, and Aosta, Italy, on the Italian-Swiss border, in the SW Pennine Alps, E of the Mont Blanc group; connects the Rhône valley with the Val d'Aosta in Italy; the road is the highest in the Swiss Alps after the Umbrail road, and is usually open only from June until Oct; the construction of the St Bernard Tunnel (5,828 m long) in 1959-63 made the route passable throughout the year; height 2,469 m; nearby there is a hospice run by monks.

Grand Teton *tee'tan*, national park in NW Wyoming, United States; includes the most dramatic area of the Teton range including Grand Teton (4,197 m); established in 1929; area 1,241 sq km.

Grande, Bahía *ba-ee'a gran'THay*, broad inlet of the S Atlantic in SE Santa Cruz prov, Argentina; between the Río Chico estuary (N) and Punta Dungeness (S); 225 km N-S, c.72 km W-E; receives the estuaries of the Coyle, Santa Cruz and Chico rivers; the main town on the bay is Río Gallegos, capital of Santa Cruz prov, where North American bandits Butch Cassidy and the Sundance Kid (Robert Leroy Parker and Harry Longabaugh) robbed the Banco de Londres y Tarapacá in January 1905 and escaped with 20,000 pesos and 280 pounds sterling.

Grande de Matagalpa *gran-day day ma-ta-gal'pa*, GRANDE, river in central Nicaragua, Central America; rising 40 km SW of Matagalpa; flows E through W Matagalpa dept then forms the boundary between Matagalpa (N) and Boaco (S); finally it flows through central Zelaya dept to meet the Caribbean Sea at Río Grande; tributaries include the Río Tuma and Río Murra; length 320 km.

Grande Prairie, 55 10N 118 52W, pop(1981) 25,056, city in W Alberta, W Canada; 455 km NW of Edmonton, near the prov frontier with British Columbia; railway; airfield; economy: livestock and timber trade.

Grande, Río *ree'ō grand'*, *ree'ō gran'day*, (Mexico) RÍO BRAVO, RÍO BRAVO DEL NORTE, river in SW USA and N Mexico; rises in the San Juan Mts of the Rocky Mts in SW Colorado; flows SE through Colorado then generally S through New Mexico, past Albuquerque to the meeting of the New Mexico, Texas and Mexico borders at El Paso (Texas) and Ciudad Juárez (Mexico); the river then flows generally SE to form the border between Texas and the Mexican states of Chihuahua, Coahuila, Nuevo Leon and Tamaulipas; it passes the twin towns of Del Rio (Texas) and Ciudad Acuña (Mexico), Laredo (Texas) and Nuevo Laredo (Mexico) and Brownsville (Texas) and Matamoros (Mexico) to enter the Gulf of Mexico approx 35 km E of Brownsville; length 3,033 km; major tributaries: the Pecos river (Texas) and Conchos river (Mexico); used for irrigation and flood-control in New Mexico, Texas and Mexico; navigation is forbidden by international agreement, vessels can sail only as far as the port of Brownsville.

Grande-Terre *grân-ter'*, one of the 2 main islands of the Overseas Department of Guadeloupe, Lesser Antilles, E Caribbean; separated from Basse-Terre I by the narrow Rivière Salée; area 585 sq km; pop(1982) 157,696; chief town Pointe-à-Pitre; the island is of coral formation and rises to only 150 m; Gosier is the holiday centre of Guadeloupe.

Grand-Lieu, Lac de *lak de grã-lyœ*, lake in Loire-Atlantique dept, Pays de la Loire region, W France; area 37 sq km; 2nd largest lake in France; on the S side of the R Loire, S of Nantes.

Grand-Popo *grã-pō'pō*, 6 19N 1 57E, town in Mono prov, S Benin, W Africa; at the mouth of the R Mono, 88 km W of Porto Novo; railway.

Grangemouth, 56 01N 3 44W, pop(1981) 21,599, port in Falkirk dist, Central region, central Scotland; on the S shore of the Firth of Forth, 5 km E of Falkirk; container port facilities; railway; economy: timber and oil trade, distilling, petrochemicals, oil refining; monument: Grangemouth museum with exhibitions on central Scotland's canals and on James 'Paraffin' Young and the development of the shale oil industry.

Granite City, 38 42N 90 09W, pop(1980) 36,815, town in Madison county, W Illinois, United States; on the R Mississippi, 11 km N of East St Louis; railway.

Gran'ma, prov in SE Cuba, bounded W by the Golfo de Guacanayabo; land rises in the S to peaks over 1,500 m in the Sierra Maestra; drained by the Cauto and Salado rivers, and numerous short streams draining into the Golfo de Guacanayabo from the Sierra Maestra; area 8,452 sq km; pop(1981) 739,335; capital Bayamo; chief towns Manzanillo and Yara.

Grantham *grant'am* or *gran'tham*, 52 54N 0 38W, pop(1981) 31,095, town in South Kesteven dist, Lincolnshire, E central England; on R Witham, 35 km E of Nottingham; market town for rich agricultural region; railway; economy: sausages, engineering, plastics; monuments: 14th-c Grantham House and 14th-c church of St Wulfram.

Grasmere *grahs'meer*, 54 28N 3 02W, pop(1981) 1,100, scenic resort village in Cumbria, NW England; by L Grasmere, 23 km N of Kendal; monument: Dove Cottage, the home of William Wordsworth from 1799 to 1808; church of St Oswald, burial place of William Wordsworth.

Graubünden *grow'bün-den*, GRISONS *gree-zõ'* (Fr), GRIGIONI (Ital), mountainous canton in SE Switzerland; pop(1980) 164,641; area 7,109 sq km; capital Chur; St Moritz, Davos and Arosa are major ski resorts of world fame; largest of the Swiss cantons, covering one sixth of the area of the country; the canton is a high wooded plateau (average height 1,500 m) from which project the snow-covered peaks usually called 'Piz'; drained by the R Inn, here called the En; the Swiss National Park, near Zernez, preserves the traditional flora and fauna of the Alps; 10% of the roads are within tunnels, and the highest pass in Switzerland, Umbrail Pass (2,501 m), is here; one half of the people speak German, one sixth speak Italian, and the remainder speak Romansch, of which there are 2 main dialects; joined the Swiss Confederacy in 1803; the chief local handicrafts are embroidery and handwoven linens.

Grauspitz *grow'spitz*, 47 05N 9 35E, highest peak in the Principality of Liechtenstein, central Europe; in the Rhätikon Alps, on the S frontier with Switzerland.

Gravesend, 51 27N 0 24E, pop(1981) 53,638, industrial town in Gravesham dist, Kent, SE England; on the R Thames, E of London; railway; economy: electrical goods, engineering, printing.

Grays, 51 29N 0 20E, pop(1981) 45,963, town in Thurrock dist, Essex, SE England; on the R Thames, 3 km W of Tilbury; railway.

Graz *grahts*, 47 05N 15 22E, pop(1981) 243,166, capital of Steiermark state, SE Austria; on the R Mur, at the foot of the Schlossberg (473 m); the 2nd largest city in Austria; it is the economic and commercial focus of the whole region; the outskirts of the town are heavily industrialized, and associated with the Graz 'Southeast Fair', an engineering and production display held in May and at the end of Sept; 3.5 km NE of the town is the Piber Stud Farm, where the famous Lippizaner horses are bred for the Spanish Riding School in Wien (Vienna); 2 universities (1585 and 1811); opera house; railway; airport; economy: iron, steel, coal and paper; monuments: Renaissance Landhaus (1557-65), former seat of the Styrian parliament; Landeszeughaus (Provincial Arsenal), with a unique store of 17th-c arms and armour; late Gothic cathedral; 28 m-high clock tower; at Stübing, 15 km N of Graz, is the Austrian open air museum; event: Steirischer Herbst ('Styrian Autumn') in Oct-Nov.

Greasby *greez'bi*, 53 23N 3 06W, pop(1981) 56,225, town linked with Moreton in Wirral borough, Merseyside, NW England; 7 km W of Birkenhead; railway.

Great Australian Bight, area of the Southern Ocean off the S coast of Australia between Cape Pasley (W) and Port Lincoln (E), a distance of 1,448 km; separated from the Spencer Gulf by the Eyre Peninsula; depths range from 70 m over the continental shelf to 5,578 m over the Great Bight abyssal plain.

Great Barrier Reef, coral reef in the Coral Sea off the NE coast of Australia; part of the Coral Sea Islands Territory administered by Australia; 50-150 km offshore and 2,000 km in length, it is the largest accumulation of coral known, yielding trepang, pearl-shell, and sponges to divers; the surf is violent and dangerous, but the intervening channel, clustered with atolls, forms a safe, shallow passage connected by several navigable channels with the deeps of the Coral Sea.

Great Basin, vast interior region in W USA, situated between the Sierra Nevada and the Cascade Range (W) and the Wasatch Range (Rocky Mts) and W face of the Colorado Plateau (E and SE); covers parts of Oregon and Idaho, most of Nevada, W Utah and part of SE California; characterized by rugged N-S mountain ranges; the region has a semi-arid climate and its few streams (the largest are the Humboldt and Carson rivers) drain into saline lakes or sinks; the largest lakes are the Great Salt, Utah, Sevier, Pyramid, and Walker lakes, remnants of the enormous prehistoric lakes, Bonneville and Lahontan, which covered much of the present area of the basin; the basin also includes several deserts: Great Salt Lake Desert, Mojave Desert, Death Valley, Colorado Desert, Black Rock Desert, Smoke Creek Desert and Carson Sink; agriculture is only possible with irrigation; the region has very little timber and the major resources are in minerals and grazing land.

Great Bear Lake, lake in W Mackenzie dist, Northwest Territories, NW Canada; on the Arctic Circle to the E of the Franklin Mts; irregular in shape, the lake is 320 km long and 40-177 km wide; area 31,153 sq km; drained in the SW by the Great Bear river which flows into the Mackenzie river; the lake is navigable for only 4 months of the year because of ice; Fort Franklin on the SW shore near the Great Bear river was Sir John Franklin's winter quarters from 1825 to 1827; in the NE of the lake is the site of Fort Confidence, Franklin's winter quarters in 1837.

Great Belt, Denmark. See Store Bælt.

Great Bitter Lake, The, BUHEIRET MURRAT EL KUBRA (Arab), lake on the Suez Canal between Ismâ'ilîya (N) and Suez (S); the Little Bitter Lake lies SE.

Great Britain *grayt bri'ten*, kingdom of W Europe, comprising the kingdoms of England and Scotland and the principality of Wales, which with Northern Ireland constitutes the United Kingdom of Great Britain and Northern Ireland; timezone GMT; area 244,755 sq km; pop(1981) 55,780,000; the pop is 81.5% English, 9.6% Scottish, 2.4% Irish, 1.9% Welsh and 2% West Indian, Asian and African; English is the official language although Welsh and Gaelic are also spoken by minorities in Wales and Scotland; Wales joined the United Kingdom in 1535, Scotland in 1603 and Ireland in 1801; Great Britain is a kingdom with a monarch as head of state; the country is governed by a bicameral parliament which comprises a 650-member House of Commons and a House of Lords with hereditary peers, life peers, Anglican bishops and law lords; an executive cabinet is appointed by the prime minister; the currency is the pound sterling of 100 pence; membership of ADB, CENTO, Colombo Plan, Council of Europe, DAC, EEC, ELDO, ESRO, FAO, GATT, IAEA, IBRD, ICAC, ICAO, ICES, ICO, IDA, IDB, IEA, IFAD, IFC, IHO, ILO, IMF, IMO, INTELSAT, INTERPOL, IOOC, IPU, IRC, ISO, ITC, ITU, NATO, OECD, UN, UPU, WEU, WHO, WIPO, WMO, WSG.

Administrative divisions. The United Kindom of Great Britain and Northern Ireland comprises the following major constituent countries:

Country	*area (sq km)*	*pop(1981)*
England	130,357	46,229,955
Wales	20,761	2,791,851
Scotland	78,762	5,130,735
Northern Ireland	14,120	1,481,959

Great Divide, United States. See Continental Divide.

Great Dividing Range, mountain range in Queensland, New South Wales and Victoria states, E Australia; extends 3,600 km from Innisfail, NE Queensland S to Melbourne then W to the Victoria border with South Australia; sub-ranges include the McPherson Range, the New England Range, the Australian Alps, the Blue Mts and the Grampians; rises to 2,228 m at Mt Kosciusko.

Great Falls, 47 30N 111 17W, pop(1980) 56,725, county seat of Cascade county, N central Montana, United States; at the junction of the Missouri and Sun rivers; railway; airfield; economy: oil and copper refining, zinc reduction and flour mills; the centre of a large hydro-electric power development; monument: Russell Studio and Museum; event: Russell Art Auction (March).

Great Indian Desert, desert region in NW India and E Pakistan. See Thar.

Great Lakes, in central North America; the largest group of freshwater lakes in the world; connected chain of lakes situated on the Canada-USA border and drained by the St Lawrence river; bordered N by Ontario (Canada), W and S by Minnesota, Wisconsin, Illinois, Indiana, Michigan, Ohio, Pennsylvania and New York; they consist of L Superior, L Michigan (the only one entirely in the USA), L Huron, L Erie and L Ontario; their water surface is approx 245,300 sq km, of which approx 87,270 sq km are in Canada; the USA-Canadian border passes through the approx centre of Lakes Superior, Huron, Erie and Ontario; all are connected by navigable straits and canals: St Mary's river and the Soo canals, Strait of Mackinac, St Clair river and lake, Detroit river, Niagara river, Welland canal and the St Lawrence river and Seaway; from May to December an enormous volume of coal, ore, grain, etc passes through them and the various ship canals to the St Lawrence; the Great Lakes are sometimes taken to include L St Clair.

Great Malvern, 52 07N 2 19W, pop(1981) 30,470, town in Malvern Hills dist, Hereford and Worcester, W central England; popular health resort in the Malvern Hills, 12 km SW of Worcester; railway; economy: engineering, plastics; event: Malvern Festival (May).

Great Plains, region of central North America; a sloping plateau, generally 644 km wide, bordering the E base of the Rocky Mts from Alberta (Canada) in the N, S to the Llano Estacado in E New Mexico and W Texas; includes parts of Alberta and Saskatchewan, the E parts of Montana, Wyoming, Colorado and New Mexico, and the W parts of North Dakota, South Dakota, Nebraska, Kansas, Oklahoma and Texas; the region is generally one of limited rainfall, short grass and large level tracts, although there are areas of highlands (the Black Hills, South Dakota), badlands (South Dakota), sand hills (Nebraska) and lowlands; drained by the headwaters of the Missouri and by the Platte, Republican, Arkansas, Kansas and Canadian rivers; used chiefly for stock grazing and grain growing; contains mineral resources of oil, natural gas, coal and lignite; dry farming on unsuitable land and overpasturing led to the dust storms of the drought years 1934, 1936 and 1937, creating the Dust Bowl, semi-arid regions where wind storms may carry off enormous quantities of topsoil.

Great Salt Lake, large inland salt lake in NW Utah, United States, just NW of Salt Lake City; situated between the Wasatch Range of the Rocky Mts (E) and the Great Salt Lake Desert (W); length 121 km; width 80 km; maximum depth 11 m; average depth 4 m; fed by the Jordan, Weber and Bear rivers; has no outlet and fluctuates greatly in size; major islands: Antelope Island and Fremont Island; its water is 20-27% saline, making it several times more saline than ocean water; sodium chloride (common salt) is extracted for commercial use; crossed by a railway which was completed in 1903; the Great Salt Lake is a remnant of the enormous prehistoric L Bonneville.

Great Salt Lake Desert, arid region in NW Utah, United States; situated to the W of the Great Salt L; extends

177 km S from the Goose Creek Mts; the level part near the Nevada border is known as the Bonneville Salt Flats, where world speed car records were established by Sir Malcolm Campbell (1935), Captain George E T Eyston (1938) and John Cobb (1939).

Great Sandy Desert, N belt of the Western Australian Desert; situated to the N of the Gibson Desert; consists mostly of sand dune, scrub and salt marsh; extends as far as the Indian Ocean in the W.

Great Sandy Desert, arid region in S Oregon, United States; 241 km long; 48-80 km wide; extending roughly NW-SE, the area is largely volcanic and situated on porous mantle rock into which surface waters disappear.

Great Slave Lake, lake in S Mackenzie dist, W Northwest Territories, central Canada; situated near the Alberta border, N of the Caribou Mts; 483 km long; 48-225 km wide; area 28,570 sq km; the North Arm extends approx 129 km NW from the body of the lake; the lake contains numerous islands, including the Simpson Islands; drained in the W by the Mackenzie river; receives the Yellowknife river (N), Slave river (S) and Hay river (SW); the town of Yellowknife on the N shore of the lake is the capital of Northwest Territories.

Great Smoky Mountains, national park on the Tennessee-North Carolina state frontier, United States; protects the largest tract of red spruce and the largest area of hardwood in the USA; rises to 2,025 m at Clingmans Dome.

Great Victoria Desert, VICTORIA DESERT, S belt of the Western Australian Desert; situated to the S of the Gibson Desert and N of the Nullarbor Plain in South Australia and Western Australia.

Great Wall, CHANG CHÊNG, large, man-made, defensive wall in NE China; stretches from Shanhaiguan in NE Hebei prov W in a broken line through Beijing (Peking) municipality, Shanxi prov, Nei Mongol aut region, Shaanxi prov, Ningxia aut region and Gansu prov to the Jiayuguan pass, N Gansu, in the Gobi desert; 6,000 km in length, its continuous length is estimated to have been 50,000 km; built during the Warring States Period (403-221 BC) as strategically placed separate sections, it was connected into one long wall during the period of the first Qin emperor (221 06 BC) by 300,000 men, the majority of whom were political prisoners whose bodies are buried under the wall itself; attempts were made to strengthen the wall with cement and stones during the Ming dynasty (1368-1644); the massive fortification at Jiayuguan pass where the wall ends was built during this period, after the decline in the Silk Road which passed here, to keep out the defeated Mongols who had fled to the NW; a commission was set up in 1979 to preserve the Great Wall as a national monument; the Great Wall of China is the only man-made object visible from satellites in space.

Great Yar'mouth, YARMOUTH, 52 37N 1 44E, pop(1981) 55,398, resort and port town in Great Yarmouth dist, Norfolk, E England; on a peninsula between the North Sea and the confluent mouths of the Bure, Yare and Waveney rivers; once an important herring port; railway; economy: tourism, engineering, oil and gas supply services, paper pulp products, food processing, fishing; monuments: 13-14th-c town walls, 12th-c church of St Nicholas and Elizabethan museum.

Great Zimbabwe *zim-ba'bway*, 20 16S 30 54E, archaeological site in Victoria prov, SE Zimbabwe; 28 km SE of Masvingo and SW of L Kyle; European discovery made by Carl Mauch in 1868; archaeological evidence indicates that the settlement prospered between the 13th and 15th centuries and was the work of a Shona-Karanga society; evolved from humble beginnings into a powerful state ruled by a succession of kings with the Arab gold trade playing an important role in this rise to prominence; its decline during the 15th century is believed to have been due to population pressure; the site includes the Hill Complex (the oldest section), the Great Enclosure or Great House (Imba Huru) and the Valley Complex; the Great Enclosure is an irregular ellipsoid measuring up to 106 m across; the outer walls are over 11 m high and 243 m in circumference; the whole structure contains approx 18,000 cubic metres of stonework which makes it the largest single ancient dwelling structure S of the Sahara; there is a site museum which houses the Great Zimbabwe Birds which were carved in soapstone; one of the more stylized birds is depicted on the Zimbabwe flag, currency and national coat of arms.

Greater Khingan Range, mountain range in Nei Mongol aut region (Inner Mongolia), N and NE China. See Da Hinggan Ling.

Greater Manchester, metropolitan county of NW England; pop(1981) 2,595,753; area 1,287 sq km; bounded N by Lancashire, W by Merseyside, S by Cheshire and E by Derbyshire and West Yorkshire; the metropolitan council was abolished in 1986; county town Manchester; includes 10 boroughs:

Borough	*area (sq km)*	*pop(1981)*
Bolton	140	260,654
Bury	99	176,112
Manchester	116	448,674
Oldham	141	220,017
Rochdale	160	207,430
Salford	97	243,865
Stockport	126	290,422
Tameside	103	217,708
Trafford	106	221,788
Wigan	199	309,083

Greboun, Mount *gre-boon'*, 20 00N 8 38E, mountain in N Niger, W Africa; height 1,944 m; highest peak in Aïr massif and in Niger.

Gredos, Sierra de *gray'THos*, forest-clad mountain range dividing the Castilla-La Mancha, Castilla-León and Extremadura regions of central Spain; rises to 2,592 m at Pico de Almanzor which is the highest peak in the central plateau; a SW continuation of the Sierra de Guadarrama and 40 km W of Madrid.

Greece *grees*, HELLAS (anc), ELLÁS *ay-las'* (Gr), official name The Hellenic Republic, ELLINIKI DIMOKRATIA (Gr), a republic of SE Europe, occupying the S part of the Balkan peninsula and numerous islands in the Aegean and the Ionian seas of the Mediterranean, bounded N by Albania, Yugoslavia, and Bulgaria, E by Turkey and the Aegean Sea, S by the Mediterranean, and W by the Ionian Sea; area 131,957 sq km; length of coastline 15,021 km; timezone GMT +2; capital Athínai (Athens); chief towns Thessaloníki, Pátrai, Iráklion, Vólos, and Lárisa; pop(1981) 9,740,417; 97.7% of the pop are Greek, 1.3% are Turkish, and 1.0% are Vlach, Slav, or Albanian; the predominant faith is Greek Orthodox (98%), with a small number of Muslims (1.3%) concentrated in W Thraki; Greek is the official language, although English and French are widely understood; the Greek currency is the drachma of 100 lepta; national holiday 25 March (Independence Day); membership of EEC, the Council of Europe, EMA, FAO, GATT, IAEA, IBRD, ICAO, IDA, IFAD, IFC, IHO, ILO, IMF, IMO, INTELSAT, IOOC, ITU, NATO, OECD, UN, UNESCO, UPU, WHO, WIPO, WMO, WSG, WTO.

Physical description. The total area of Greece includes 40% meadow and pasture, 29% arable and permanent crop, 20% forest, 11% urban land. The country consists of a large area of mainland which includes the Pelopónnisos, connected to the mainland by the narrow Isthmus of Corinth, and more than 1,400 islands, the largest of which include Kríti (Crete), Évvoia (Euboea), Lésvos (Lesbos), Ródhos (Rhodes), Khíos, Kefallinía, Kérkira (Corfu), Límnos, Sámos, and Náxos. About one fifth of the area of Greece is accounted for by islands. The intricate and rugged coastline has been strongly eroded by weather and water. Nearly 80% of Greece is mountainous or hilly. Makedhonia and Thessalía regions in the NE are separated from Ipiros in the NW by the

Píndhos Mts, a continuation of the Dinaric Alps. An E branch, Óthris, bounds Thessalía on the S. The mountain range along the E coast includes Ólimbos (2,917 m), the highest point in Greece, and continues in the islands of Évvoia, Ándros, Tínos, Míkonos, Náxos, and Armagós. The Píndhos Mts are continued SE in Gióna (2,510 m), form the nome (dept) of Attikí, and re-appear as the islands of Kéa, Kíthnos, Sérifos, and Sífnos. The peninsula of Pelopónnisos consists of the Taïyetos range in the S and the Párnon range in the E, which sweeps round in the islands of Kíthira, Kríti, Kárpathos, and Ródhos, to Anatolia. In the extreme NE of Greece, Thraki is cut off from Bulgaria by the Rodopi Planina (Rhodope Mts). Chief rivers in Greece include the Néstos (Mesta), which rises in Bulgaria, Strimón, Árakhthos, Akhelóös, Aliákmon (longest river lying wholly in Greece), Piniós, and Alfiós. There are numerous small lakes, many of which dry out to mere marshes in summer.

Climate. The climate of the coastal lands and islands is Mediterranean, with mild, rainy winters and hot, dry summers. Rainfall occurs almost entirely in the winter months. E Greece is the driest. The average annual rainfall at Athínai (Athens) is 414 mm. During the summer a persistent northerly wind, known as the *Etesian*, blows across the Aegean. In mountain areas the climate is generally cooler, with severe winters and heavy winter precipitation.

History, government and constitution. In prehistoric times Greece was inhabited by a Mediterranean race whose civilization culminated in the Minoan-Mycenean culture of Kríti (Crete). The Dorians invaded from the N at the beginning of the 12th century BC, capturing the

Pelopónnisos. Subsequently the islands and coastline of Asia Minor were occupied by Æolians, Ionians and later by Dorians. Greek colonies, noted as centres of art, literature and philosophy, were established along the N and S coasts of the Mediterranean and on the shores of the Black Sea. Sicily was in Greek hands and S Italy became Magna Graecia. On mainland Greece there were many city states, the most powerful being the Dorian state of Sparta and the state of Athens. Encroachment of Greek colonies by the Persians culminated in the invasion of Greece by Darius (490 BC) and later by Xerxes (480-79 BC), invasions repelled by the Greeks at Marathon, Salamis, Plataea and Mycale. The Confederation of Delos was formed in 477 BC to resist further Persian aggression. It was at this time that Greek literature and art flourished. The conflict between Sparta and Athens (Peloponnesian War) eventually weakened the country, which was taken by the Thebans (379-71 BC) and later by the Macedonians (338 BC). Under Alexander the Great military expeditions penetrated Asia and Africa, but eventually Macedonian power was broken by the Romans in 197 BC. Subsequently Greece formed part of the Eastern or Byzantine Empire of Rome. In 1453 the Byzantine Empire fell to the Turks who ruled Greece for nearly 4 centuries. A national reawakening began in 1821; and by 1828 with the support of Britain, France and Russia, Greece became a free but weak state. In 1864 Britain ceded the Ionian islands. The Russo-Turkish war of 1877-78 added Thessalía (Thessaly) and part of Ipiros (Epirus). The Greek claim to the S of Makedhonia (Macedonia), Kríti (Crete) and many islands in the Aegean was made good, but acquisitions in Ipiros fell short of national aspirations with the establishment of the new kingdom of Albania. W Thraki (Thrace) was acquired after World War I when over 1.5 mn Greek refugees from Turkey entered the country. A republic was established in 1924, was momentarily interrupted by dictatorship in 1926, and gave place to a restored monarchy in 1935. In 1944 the liberation of Athínai and Pelopónnisos from the Germans was followed by 5 years of civil war, exacerbated by communist support of the rebels. On 21 April 1967, a coup d'état took place and the first of a series of military governments was formed. The monarchy was abolished along with the Constitution of 1952. On the collapse of the government of Lieut-Gen Phaedon Ghizikis in July 1974, the 1952 Constitution was re-introduced in a modified form. A new Constitution was introduced in June 1975, establishing a presidential parliamentary republic which provides for a president as chief of state, and a prime minister as head of government. Government is vested in a unicameral parliament of 300 deputies, elected for 4 years. The executive consists of a president elected by the parliament for 5 years, a prime minister, and a cabinet of about 22 ministers.

Industry. Greece produces a variety of ores and minerals, including iron, magnesite, bauxite, and lignite. There is little coal, and although oil was discovered in 1963 in W central Greece, considerable quantities of fuel have to be imported to meet the country's energy requirements. The Greek economy is characterized by a strong service sector accounting for about 55% of national income, and a relatively large agricultural sector accounting for about 14% of national income. Agriculture, employing 28% of the labour force and occupying just under 30% of the total land area, is based on the production of cereals, cotton, tobacco, fruit, figs, raisins, wine, olive oil and vegetables. The manufacturing industries of Greece are based on the production of processed foods, textiles, metals, chemicals, electrical equipment, cement, glass, transport equipment, and petroleum products. About half of the labour force is self-employed, with 90% of Greek firms employing under 10 workers. The manufacturing-mining sector accounts for just over 30% of national income and about 45% of Greece's exports which include textiles, metal products, cement, chemicals, and pharmaceuticals. Major trade partners include other EEC countries, the USA and Saudi Arabia.

Administrative divisions. Greece is divided into 10 geographical regions, including Greater Athens, which are subdivided into departments (*nomoi*, sing. *nome*):

Region/Nome	*area (sq km)*	*pop(1981)*
Aegean Islands		
Khíos	904	49,865
Kikládhes	2,572	88,458
Lésvos	2,154	104,620
Sámos	778	40,519
Sporádhes	2,714	145,071
Greater Athens	433	3,027,331
Ionioi Nísoi		
Kefallinía	904	31,297
Kérkira	641	99,477
Levkás	356	21,863
Zákinthos	406	30,014
Ipiros		
Árta	1,662	80,044
Ioánnina	4,990	147,304
Préveza	1,036	55,915
Thesprotía	1,515	41,278
Kríti		
Iráklion	2,641	243,622
Khaniá	2,376	125,856
Lasíthi	1,823	70,053
Réthimnon	1,496	62,634
Makedhonia		
Dráma	3,468	94,772
Flórina	1,924	52,430
Grevená	2,291	36,421
Imathía	1,701	133,750
Kastoría	1,720	53,169
Kaválla	2,111	135,218
Khalkidhíki	2,918	79,036
Kilkís	2,519	81,562
Kozáni	3,516	147,051
Pélla	2,506	132,386
Piería	1,516	106,859
Sérrai	3,968	196,247
Thessaloníki	3,683	871,580
Pangaíon Óros	336	1,472
Pelopónnisos		
Akhaïa	3,271	275,193
Argolís	2,154	93,020
Arkadhía	4,419	107,932
Ilía	2,618	160,305
Kórinthos	2,290	123,042
Lakonía	3,636	93,218
Messinía	2,991	159,818
Sterea Ellás-Évvoia		
Aitolía and Akarnanía	5,461	219,764
Attikí	3,381	342,093
Évvoia	4,167	188,410
Evritanía	1,869	26,182
Fokís	2,120	44,222
Fthiótis	4,441	161,995
Voiótia	2,952	117,175
Thessalía		
Kardhítsa	2,636	124,930
Lárisa	5,381	254,295
Magnisía	2,636	182,222
Tríkkala	3,384	134,207
Thráki		
Évros	4,242	148,486
Rodhópi	2,543	107,957
Xánthi	1,793	88,777

Pangaíon Óros (Mount Athos) in Makedhonia is a self-governing theocratic community composed of 20 monasteries.

Greeley, 40 25N 104 42W, pop(1980) 53,006, county seat of Weld county, N Colorado, United States; 80 km N of

Denver; a city since 1885; university; railway; economy: trade and processing centre for an irrigated farming area; event: Independence Stampede (June).

Green Bay, 44 31N 88 00W, pop(1980) 87,899, county seat of Brown county, E Wisconsin, United States; port at the S end of Green Bay, at the mouth of the R Fox; settled in 1745, it is the oldest settlement in Wisconsin; university; railway; airfield; economy: paper and board, fishing.

Green Line, The, dividing line between Muslim W Beyrouth (Beirut) and Christian E Beyrouth, Lebanon, during the 1975-76 civil war.

Greenfield, 42 58N 88 00W, pop(1980) 31,467, residential city in Milwaukee county, SE Wisconsin, United States; 12 km SW of Milwaukee.

Greenland, GRØNLAND *grō'een-lahn* (Dan), KALÂTDLIT-NUNÂT *ke-laht-lit-nu-nat'* (Eskimo), the second largest island in the world (after Australia), situated NE of North America in the N Atlantic and Arctic Oceans; bounded N by the Lincoln Sea, SE by the Denmark Strait, NE by the Greenland Sea, W by Baffin Bay and the Davis Strait; separated from Ellesmere I by the Nares Strait in the NW; timezone GMT 0, −1, −4; area 2,175,600 sq km of which c.16% is ice-free; pop(1984e) 52,347; capital Godthåb; the pop is largely Inuit (Eskimo) with Danish admixtures; both Eskimo dialects and Danish are spoken; the main religions are Lutheran Christianity and Shamanism.

Physical description. Largely covered by an ice-cap that reaches 4,300 m in thickness, the island forms part of the Canadian Shield with Pre-Cambrian granites and gneisses predominating in ice-free areas. The coastline is deeply indented by fjords and the entire island is ringed by coastal mountains that rise to 3,702 m at Gunnbjørn Fjeld in the SE. In the far north, Peary Land has no ice-cap. The largest offshore island is Disko, on which the settlement of Godhavn is located. The natural vegetation includes mosses, lichens, grasses, sedges; on the SW coast, which is influenced by the warmer, wetter N Atlantic Drift, dwarf trees such as birch and dwarf willow are able to grow. Major animal species include polar bear, musk ox, polar wolf, Arctic hare, lemming and reindeer. Less than 5% of Greenland is habitable by man. Greenland was explored by Martin Frobisher and John Davis in the 16th century.

History and government. Settled by seal-hunting Eskimos from N America as early as 2,500 BC, Norse settlers occupied and farmed ice-free areas in the SW during the 12-15th centuries. Resettlement by the Danes in the 1720s resulted in the colonizing of the whole of Greenland by Denmark, the economy of the island largely remaining in the hands of the monopolistic Danish Royal Greenland Trading Company. A Danish-American agreement for the defence of Greenland was signed in 1951, allowing World War II bases to be retained. In 1979 Greenland was granted home rule as a self-governing province of Denmark. Greenland has an elected Provincial Council which sends 2 members to the Danish Parliament. Local government is vested in 19 settlement councils.

Economy. The economy of Greenland is largely dependent on inshore and deep-water fishing based in the SW ports which are ice-free throughout the year. One-sixth of the pop is involved in fishing and processing of cod, capelin, salmon and shrimp. There is some sheep farming in the SW, and traditional hunting for seal and fox furs continues in N and E Greenland. Cryolite is mined at Iviglut. There are also reserves of lead, zinc, molybdenum, uranium and coal.

Greenland Sea, gulf connecting the Atlantic and Arctic Oceans; bounded W by Greenland, E by Svalbard; to the S lies the Norwegian Sea; a cold surface current from the Arctic brings icebergs and fog; depths range from 180 m on the continental shelf to 3,535 m in the abyssal plain; crossed by the Greenland Fracture Zone and separated from the Dumshaf abyssal plain and the Norwegian Sea by the Mid-Atlantic Ridge.

Greenock, 55 57N 4 45W, pop(1981) 59,016, port and chief town of Inverclyde dist, Strathclyde, W central Scotland; on the S shore of the Firth of Clyde, 3 km W of Glasgow; birthplace of James Watt (1736-1819); railway; container port facilities; economy: engineering, electronics, sugar refining; monument: McLean museum with exhibits relating to James Watt.

Greensboro, 36 04N 79 48W, pop(1980) 155,642, county seat of Guilford county, N central North Carolina, United States; 40 km E of Winston-Salem; 2 universities (1891); railway; economy: textiles, tobacco products and electrical machinery.

Greenville, SINOE *sī'nō*, 5 01N 9 03W, town in Liberia, W Africa; at the mouth of the R Sinoe, 250 km SE of Monrovia; airfield.

Greenville, 33 24N 91 04W, pop(1980) 40,613, county seat of Washington county, W Mississippi, United States; a deep-water harbour on L Ferguson, adjoining the Mississippi river, 145 km NNW of Jackson; railway; economy: processing and shipping centre for agricultural products, especially cotton; manufactures include metal products, concrete and automobile parts; event: Delta Blues Festival (Sept).

Greenville, 35 37N 77 23W, pop(1980) 35,740, county seat of Pitt county, E North Carolina, United States; on the R Tar, 52 km SE of Rocky Mount; university (1907); railway; economy: trade in grain, cotton and tobacco products.

Greenville, 34 51N 82 24W, pop(1980) 58,242, county seat of Greenville county, NW South Carolina, United States; 160 km NW of Columbia; 2 universities (1825, 1927); railway; airfield; economy: textiles, clothing, processed foods, pharmaceuticals and fabricated metals.

Greenwich *gren'ij* (Old English, 'Grenawic', green habitation on the bank of a river), 51 28N 0 00, pop(1981) 212,987, borough of E central Greater London, England; S of R Thames; includes the suburbs of Greenwich and part of Woolwich; site of the original Royal Greenwich Observatory now at Herstmonceux; the meridian of longitude is reckoned from this point which is also the source of the world time standard known as Greenwich Mean Time (GMT); birthplace of Henry VIII, Elizabeth I and Mary; railway; monuments: Royal Naval College, National Maritime museum; Greenwich Hospital (1694).

Greifswald *grīfs'vahlt*, 54 6N 13 24E, pop(1981) 61,388, town in Greifswald dist, Rostock, N East Germany; founded in 1250; part of Sweden (1648-1815); university (1456); railway; economy: coal, nuclear power.

Grenå *gray'no*, 56 25N 10 53E, pop(1981) 13,638, town in Århus county, E Jylland (Jutland), Denmark; railway; economy: engineering.

Grenada *gru-nay'da*, most southerly of the Windward Is, E Caribbean, approx 241 km SW of Barbados and 145 km NW of Trinidad; timezone GMT −4; area 344 sq km; capital St George's; chief towns Gouyave, Victoria, and Grenville; pop(1981) 98,000; the majority of the pop is of black African descent; the dominant religion is Roman Catholicism; English is the official language with a French patois widely spoken; the unit of currency is the Eastern Caribbean dollar of 100 cents; membership: CARICOM, FAO, G-77, GATT (de facto), IBRD, ICAO, IDA, IFAD, IFC, ILO, IMF, NAM, OAS, PAHO, SELA, UN, UNESCO, UPU, WHO.

Physical description and climate. The independent state of Grenada includes the main island of Grenada and the S Grenadines, an arc of small islands extending from Grenada N to St Vincent. Grenada itself is 34 km long and 19 km wide and has an area of 311 sq km. It is volcanic in origin with a ridge of mountains which extends the entire length of the island. The highest point is Mt St Catherine which rises to 843 m NE of St George's. The land falls steeply to the sea in the W but more gently in the E and SE. The Grand Etang (530 m) is one of 3 lakes which have formed in the craters of extinct volcanoes. The climate is subtropical with a mean annual temperature of 23°C and rainfall varying from 1,270 mm per annum on the coast to 5,000 mm in the mountainous

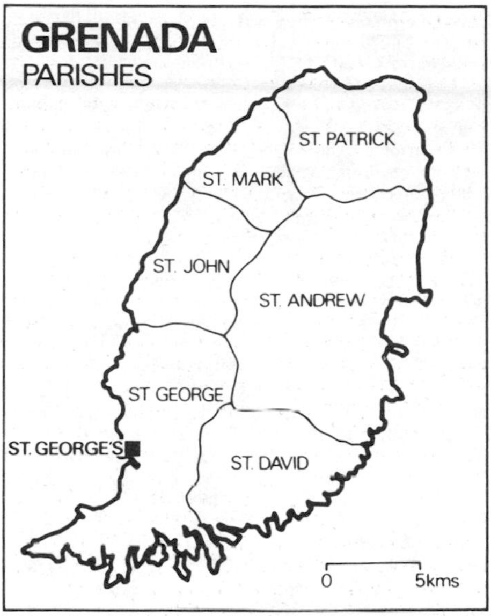

interior. There is a dry, mild season from Jan to May. The rest of the year is wet and humid with temperatures rising to 32°C. The Grenadines tend to be slightly drier than the island of Grenada.

History, government and constitution. Columbus visited Grenada in 1498, naming the island Concepción, but the island remained virtually uncolonized until the mid-17th century when French settlers from Martinique ousted the original Carib inhabitants. Grenada was ceded to Great Britain in 1763, retaken by the French in 1779, then finally ceded to Britain under the Treaty of Versailles in 1783. In 1833 it was included in the general government of the Windward Is and became a British Crown Colony in 1877. In 1962 Grenada became an associated state of Great Britain and in 1974 gained full independence. The 1973 Constitution of Grenada recognizes the British monarch as head of state. There is a bicameral legislature comprising an appointed 13-member Senate and a 15-seat, directly elected House of Representatives. An executive cabinet of 15 ministers is headed by a prime minister. In March 1979 a popular people's revolution was successfully mounted by the opposition, but in 1983 a power struggle led to the killing of the prime minister, Maurice Bishop. A group of Caribbean countries requested the involvement of US troops who invaded the island in Oct 1983 in order to restore stable government.

Economy. The economy is largely based on agriculture which accounts for just over 20% of national income. During the 18th century it was discovered that the island's soil proved ideal for growing spices. The principal crops are fruit and vegetables, cocoa, nutmegs, bananas, and mace. Hurricane Allen destroyed an estimated 40% of the banana crop in Aug 1980. A policy of economic diversification now attempts to introduce crops such as guavas, citrus fruits, avocados, plums, mangoes, and cashew nuts. The most important industry is the processing of agricultural products and their derivatives (sugar, rum, coconut oil, lime juice, honey). The major trade partners are the West Indies, the UK, the USA, the Netherlands and W Germany. Chief exports include clothing, fruit, vegetables, cocoa, nutmeg and mace.

Administrative divisions. Grenada is divided into the 6 parishes of St Patrick, St Mark, St John, St Andrew, St George, St David and the dependency of Carriacou and Petit Martinique in the Grenadines.

Grenadines, The *gren'a-deenz*, group of 600 small islands and islets in the Windward Is, E Caribbean; between St Vincent and Grenada; administered by St Vincent (N Grenadines) and Grenada (S Grenadines); includes the islands of Carriacou, Union, Mustique, Bequia, Canouan and Mayreau.

Grenoble *gre-nob'l'*, CULARO, GRATIANOPOLIS (anc), 45 12N 5 42E, pop(1982) 159,503, ancient fortified city and capital of Isère dept, Rhône-Alpes region, E France; at the confluence of the rivers Isère and Drac, at the S end of the Grande-Chartreuse, in a striking Alpine setting; Mont Blanc is to the NE; the old quarter, towards the R Isère, contains many historic buildings, while beyond this, the new Grenoble spreads out in all directions with broad avenues and high-rise blocks; in the 19th century Grenoble was a pioneer in the generation of hydroelectric power; it prospered during the French colonial period on its trade with the French African colonies, the opening of the Suez Canal, and its local soap industry and oil mills; its industrial progress has continued ever since; the population has risen rapidly from 102,000 since the early 1950s; an important sports and tourist centre; the 1964 Olympic skating championships and the Winter Olympics of 1968 stimulated new building and an increase in tourist traffic; there are facilities for skiing to the E at L'Alpe-d'Huez, Les Deux Alpes and La Grave and to the SW in the neighbourhood of Villard-de-Lans; the recently opened World Trade Centre was designed to help revitalize this ancient city and promote trade relations with French-speaking N Africa, Middle East and other Mediterranean neighbours; the Industrial Science Park (the Zirst), set up at Meylan, 5 km from the city, provides a home for 95 different companies (electrical engineering, telecommunications) providing employment for 3,000 people; bishopric; university (1339); railway; economy: electro-metallurgy, chemicals, plastic products, electrical engineering, nuclear research, glove manufacturing, walnuts (grown in the lower Isère valley between Tullins and St Marcellin); monuments: 12-13th-c cathedral of Notre-Dame with an impressive 15th-c sculptured canopied shrine; 13th-c brick church of St Andre (once the chapel of the ruling Dauphins); Palais de Justice (Law Courts), dating partly from the 15th century with an early Renaissance facade.

Gren'ville, 12 07N 61 37W, town on the island of Grenada, Windward Is, E Caribbean; situated on the E coast.

Gresham, 45 30N 122 26W, pop(1980) 33,005, city in Multnomah county, NW Oregon, United States; 16 km E of Portland, near the Columbia river; railway; economy: in the centre of a fruit-growing region.

Grevená, nome (dept) of SW Makedhonia region, N Greece; pop(1981) 36,421; area 2,291 sq km; capital Grevená; produces wheat, tobacco, dairy products and timber.

Grevenbroich *gray'ven-broiKH*, 51 06N 6 32E, pop(1983) 56,700, city in Düsseldorf dist, W Nordrhein-Westfalen (North Rhine-Westphalia) prov, W Germany; SSW of Düsseldorf; railway; economy: aluminium.

Grevenmacher *gray'ven-maKH'er*, E dist of the Grand Duchy of Luxembourg, comprising the cantons of Grevenmacher, Remich and Echternach; pop(1981) 38,836; area 525 sq km.

Grevenmacher, canton in central part of Grevenmacher dist, E Luxembourg; area 211 sq km; pop(1981) 16,393; important vine-growing area along the R Moselle, producing sparkling wine; on the E frontier with W Germany; traversed by the R Syre which meets the Moselle NE of Grevenmacher.

Grevenmacher, 49 41N 6 27E, pop(1981) 3,000, river port and capital of Grevenmacher canton, Grevenmacher dist, E Luxembourg; 37 km ENE of Luxembourg; dam and lock of the Moselle canal here; economy: foundry; events: wine fair (Thursday after Easter); Easter exhibition of agriculture, viticulture and handicrafts; wine and grape festival during 2nd weekend in Sept.

Greylock, Mount, highest peak in Massachusetts state, NE United States; rises to 1,049 m N of Pittsfield.

Greystones, CLOCH LIATH (Gael), 53 9N 6 04W, pop(1981) 7,442, resort town and fishing port in Wicklow county, Leinster, E Irish Republic; now linked with Delgany; railway.

Griffith, 34 18S 146 04E, pop(1981) 13,187, town in Murrumbidgee stat div, S central New South Wales, Australia; NW of Canberra, at the centre of the fertile Riverina dist, an artificially irrigated area in the S of the state; railway; airfield; economy: rice, wine.

Grims'by, formerly GREAT GRIMSBY, 53 35N 0 05W, pop(1981) 92,596, port town in Great Grimsby dist, Humberside, NE England; on the S side of the R Humber estuary; railway; economy: fishing, fertilizers, chemicals, engineering, trade in fish, coal, grain and timber.

Grimstad *grim'stah*, 58 20N 8 35E, pop(1980) 13,825, town in Aust-Agder county, S Norway; 20 km SW of Arendal in a fertile agricultural region.

Griqualand *gree'kwe-*, region of Cape prov, South Africa; mostly in the 'independent' homeland of Transkei; bounded N by Lesotho; in 1862 settled by Griquas, bushmen of Hottentot descent; West Griqualand, including the diamond fields of Kimberley, became part of the Cape Colony in 1880; East Griqualand was joined to Cape Colony in 1879; chief towns include Kokstad, Kimberley.

Grisons, canton in Switzerland. See Graubünden.

Grodno *grod'nu*, GARDINAS (Lith), 53 40N 23 50E, pop(1983) 230,000, river port and capital city of Grodnenskaya oblast, SE Belorusskaya SSR, Soviet Union; on the R Sozh; railway; economy: manufacture of chemical fibres and mineral fertilizers, power plant, sugar refining.

Groningen *KHrō'ning-en*, pop(1984e) 561,500, prov in N Netherlands, bounded on the E by W Germany and on the N by the North Sea, includes the easternmost West Frisian Is and the W shoreline of the Ems river estuary; the coast is protected by dykes; land area 2,334 sq km; capital Groningen; chief towns Delfzijl and Onstwedde; economy: arable farming predominates in the 'peat colonies' of SE Groningen, elsewhere there is livestock farming on the less well-drained clay and peat soils; after discovery of a large quantity of gas in 1959, an extensive distribution network was constructed, to which almost all the homes and industrial enterprises in the Netherlands are connected.

Groningen, 53 13N 6 35E, pop(1984e) 206,611, capital of Groningen prov, N Netherlands; at the confluence of the Drentse Aa, here called Hoornse Diep, and the Winschoter Diep; see of a Catholic bishop; the most important city in North Netherlands, its market is one of the largest in the country, dealing in cattle, vegetables, fruit and flowers from the surrounding countryside; headquarters of the Dutch Grain Exchange; connected to its outer port, Delfzijl, by the Eems Canal; university (1614); airport; railway; economy: shipbuilding, chemicals, electrical equipment, paper, pipe tobacco, cigarettes, furniture; monuments: 13th-c Martinkerk and town hall (1777-1810).

Großer Arber or **Grosser Arber** *grō'sur*, GREAT ARBER (Eng), JAVOR (Czech), 49 07N 13 09E, mountain in E Bayern (Bavaria) prov, W Germany; highest peak (1,456 m) of the Böhmerwald (Bohemian Forest), near German-Czech border, 14 km N of Regen; R Weisser Regen (White Regen) rises on NW slopes.

Großer Feldberg or **Grosser Feldberg** *felt'berk*, GREAT FELDBERG (Eng), 50 13N 8 28E, mountain in SW Hessen (Hesse) prov, W Germany; highest peak (879 m) of the Taunus range, 10 km WNW of Oberursel.

Großer Plöner See or **Grosser Plöner See** *plœ'nur zay*, PLÖN LAKE *plun* (Eng), 54 10N 10 22E, largest lake of Schleswig-Holstein prov, W Germany, SE of Kiel; area 29 sq km; max depth 60 m; average depth 14 m.

Grosseto *gros-say'tō*, prov of Toscana region, central Italy; pop(1981) 220,905; area 4,496 sq km; capital Grosseto.

Grosseto, 42 46N 11 07E, pop(1981) 69,523, capital town of Grosseto prov, Toscana region, W central Italy; 178 km NW of Roma (Rome), W of the main highway between Genova (Genoa) and Roma; economic centre of the strip of coastal territory known as the Maremma; railway; economy: agricultural engineering and trade in olive oil, cereals; monuments: bastioned fortifications and a 13th-c cathedral.

Großglockner or **Grossglockner** *grōs'glok-nar*, 47 05N 12 44E, mountain in the Hohe Tauern range, Tirol and Kärnten states, S central Austria; height 3,797 m; the highest peak in Austria; first climbed in 1800; feeds the Pasterze glacier; at 2,505 m the Grossglocknerstrasse is Austria's highest pass.

Groznyy *groz'nee*, 43 21N 45 42E, pop(1983) 387,000, capital city of Checheno-Ingushskaya ASSR, SE European Rossiyskaya, Soviet Union; on a tributary of the R Terek, in the N foothills of the Bol'shoy Kavkaz (Greater Caucasus) range; established in 1818 as a fortress; university (1972); railway; airfield; economy: oil refining, manufacture of chemicals and foodstuffs.

Grudziądz *groo'jonz*, GRAUDENZ (Ger), 53 29N 18 45E, pop(1983) 92,800, industrial port in Toruń voivodship, N central Poland; Tuchola Forest nearby; railway; boat service to Gdańsk, Malbork and Warszawa (Warsaw); economy: rubber, agricultural machinery, marine engineering; monuments: 17-18th-c granaries by the river; Baroque buildings of former Jesuit college.

Gruzinskaya, GRUZIYA SSR, GEORGIA (Eng), constituent republic of the Soviet Union, occupying the central and W parts of Transcaucasia, bounded SW by Turkey and W by the Black Sea; the Bol'shoy Kavkaz (Greater Caucasus) range in the N is separated from the Malyy Kavkaz (Lesser Caucasus) in the S by intermontane lowlands; the highest point in the republic is Mt Shkhara (5,203 m) on the N border; chief rivers are the Kura and Rioni; forests cover c.39% of the total territory; pop(1983) 5,134,000; area 69,700 sq km; capital Tbilisi; chief towns Kutaisi, Rustavi, Batumi, Sukhumi, and Poti; economy: mining of manganese, coal, non-ferrous metal ores, and barite; ferrous metallurgy; oil refining; chemicals and petrochemicals; machine building; textile and silk industries; hydroelectric power generation; food processing (especially the production of tea, wines, and preserved foods); the chief branches of agriculture are tea cultivation and fruit growing, especially citrus fruits and viticulture; the Kakhetia region, along the R Alazani, is famed for its orchards and wines; proclaimed a Soviet Socialist Republic on 25 Feb 1921 and became a constituent republic of the USSR in 1936; the republic is divided into 3 autonomous soviet republics and one autonomous region:

Division	*area (sq km)*	*pop(1983)*
Abkhazskaya (aut soviet socialist republic)	8,600	517,000
Adzharskaya (aut soviet socialist republic)	3,000	371,000
Severo-Osetinskaya (aut region)	3,900	98,000

Guadalajara *gwa-THa-la-KHah'ra*, 20 30N 103 20W, pop(1980) 2,244,715, capital of Jalisco state, W central Mexico; 535 km WNW of Ciudad de México (Mexico City); alt 1,567 m; founded in 1530; 2 universities (1792, 1935); railway; airport (Miguel Hidalgo) at 20 km; economy: textiles, clothing, tanning, soap, glass, pottery, food processing; monuments: still contains many colonial buildings including the cathedral (begun in 1561 and finished in 1618); the government palace (1643), where in 1810 Hidalgo gave his first proclamation abolishing slavery; in an old monastery is the Jalisco state museum; Santa Mónica church (1718), with its carved facade; San

Francisco church (1550) and El Carmen church, with its 18th-c rococo pulpit; several colonial buildings including the government palace and the University of Guadalajara contain works of art by the artist Orozco; the contents of the former Orozco museum in Ciudad de México (Mexico City) have been transferred to Guadalajara to the Museo Taller José Clemente Orozco; events: 21 March, a public holiday, commemorates Benito Juárez's birthday; fiesta with concerts, bullfights, sports and exhibitions of Mexican handicrafts (Oct); fiesta in honour of the Virgin of Guadalupe, with music and a fair (28 Oct-20 Dec).

Guadalajara, prov in Castilla-La Mancha region, central Spain, on the dry plateau E of Madrid; watered by the R Tagus and its tributaries; in the N are spurs of the Sierra Guadarrama and the Cordillera Iberica; pop(1981) 143,124; area 12,190 sq km; capital Guadalajara; economy: mining, linen, woollens, electrical equipment, leather, soap, wooden products, machinery, azulejos tiles.

Guadalajara, ARRIACA (anc), (Arab 'Wad Al-Hajarah', river of stones), 40 37N 3 12W, pop(1981) 56,922, capital of Guadalajara prov, central Spain, close to the left bank of the R Henares; 58 km NE of Madrid; railway; economy: leather, soap, linen, woollens, electrical equipment, aviculture; monuments: ducal palace of the Mendozas; chapel of Don Luis de Lucena; church of San Gines; event: Autumn fiesta in Sept with bullfights, sporting contests and an agricultural show.

Guadalcanal *gwa-dul-ku-nal'*, largest of the Solomon Islands, SW Pacific; area 5,302 sq km; length 144 km; width 56 km; capital Honiara; rises to 2,477 m at Mt Makarakomburu; there are extensive plains on the NW coast on which rice and oil palms are cultivated; Henderson Airport is situated 13 km E of Honiara; there is small-scale alluvial gold working centred on the Gold Ridge area; scene of the first World War II Allied Pacific invasion northward (7 August 1942).

Guadalquivir *gwad-al-kee-veer'*, BAETIS (anc), (Arab 'Vad-el-kebir', large river), river rising in the Sierra de Cazorla, Andalucia, S Spain, flowing W to Cordoba then SW to the Atlantic at Sanlúcar de Barrameda; length 657 km; navigable to Sevilla; reservoirs for irrigation and hydroelectric power, the largest being the Pantano de el Tranco de Beas.

Guadarrama, Sierra de *gwad-a-rah'mah*, mountain range lying between Madrid and Segovia in Castilla-León and Madrid regions of central Spain; rises to 2,430 m at the Pico de Penalara.

Guadeloupe *gwad-loop'*, overseas department of France, comprising a group of islands in the central Lesser Antilles, E Caribbean; timezone GMT −4; area 1,779 sq km; capital Basse-Terre; largest town Pointe-à-Pitre; pop(1982) 328,400; 90% of the pop is black or mulatto, 5% Caucasian, less than 5% East Indian, and the remainder Chinese and Lebanese; the dominant religion is Roman Catholicism; French is the official language, spoken mainly in creole dialect; the unit of currency is the French franc; membership of WFTU.

Physical description and climate. Guadeloupe comprises the 7 islands of Grande-Terre, Basse-Terre, Marie-Galante, La Désirade, Îles des Saintes, St-Barthélemy, and the N part of St Martin, plus many small islets. The 2 main islands of Grand-Terre and Basse-Terre, separated by the narrow bridged strait of the Rivière Salée, make up 80% of the total land area and accommodate over 90% of the population. Basse-Terre is mountainous with Grande Soufrière, an active volcano, rising to 1,484 m. Grande-Terre is lower, rising to only 150 m, and is of coral formation. Although most of the islands lie in the Windward group, St Martin and St Barthélemy lie 250 km to the NW in the Leeward Is. The climate is warm and humid with an average annual temperature of 28°C. Rainfall is heaviest between May and Nov.

History, government and constitution. Visited by Columbus in 1493, the islands were occupied by the French in 1635 and later held by the British until 1813 when they were transferred to Sweden. In 1816 the islands were

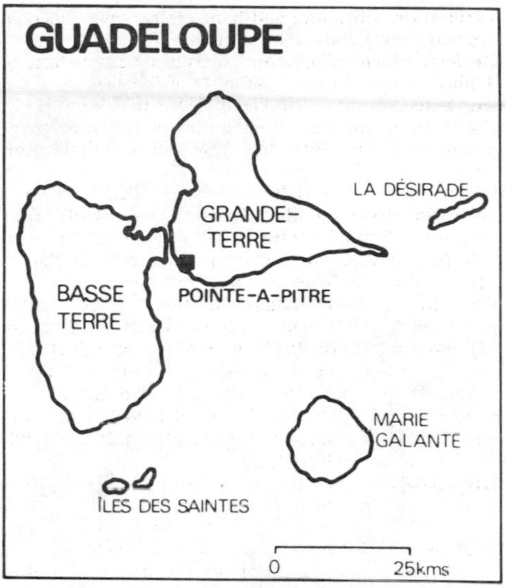

returned to France and in 1946 received departmental status. Guadeloupe became an administrative region in 1973. The department sends 2 senators and 3 deputies to the national assembly in Paris. A commissioner is advised by a 36-member general council and an elected regional council of 41 members.

Economy. Agricultural processing, particularly sugar refining and rum distilling, is the principal industry. Approx 25% of the total area is cultivated, the main crops being sugar cane, bananas, aubergines, and sweet potatoes. Chief imports include foodstuffs, consumer goods, machinery and transport equipment, and fuel. Over 60% of imports are from France. Chief exports include bananas (approximately 55% of total export value), sugar (25% of total export value), and rum. The main destination for exports is France, which takes nearly 70% of all exported products.

Administrative divisions. Guadeloupe is divided into 3 arrondissements which in turn are sub-divided into 34 communes.

Communications. Le Raizet International Airport is located 3 km from Pointe-à-Pitre. The main port is Pointe-à-Pitre.

Guadelupe Mountains, national park in Texas, United States; 160 km E of El Paso; features a major Permian limestone fossil reef; established in 1929; area 2,066 sq km.

Guadiana *gwa-dya'na, gwah-THyah'nah* (Sp), ANAS (anc), river of Spain and Portugal, flowing out of Ojos del Guadiana, a swampy lake region NE of Ciudad Real in S central Spain, flows 338 km W to Portugal then S through Beja dist to the Gulf of Cadiz at Vila Real de Santo Antonio (Faro dist); navigable 72 km to Mertola; length 578 km; principal tributaries include the Caia, Degebe, Cobres, Oeiras, Odeleite and Vascão.

Guainía *gwī-nee'a*, administrative territory in tropical E Colombia, South America; bounded E by Venezuela along the Río Negro, S by Brazil and N by the Río Guaviare; pop(1985) 3,311; area 72,238 sq km; capital Obando.

Guairá *gwī-ra'*, dept in Oriental region, S central Paraguay; pop(1982) 143,374; area 3,202 sq km; capital Villarrica; economy: tobacco, cotton, sugar, yerba maté, hides, meat and wine (produced by the German settlers); mysterious hieroglyphics have been found in the NE of the dept and are claimed by some to be of Viking origin.

Guajira, La *gwa-KHee'ra*, dept in N Colombia, South America; a peninsula on the Caribbean sea; the northernmost part of Colombia and of the South

American continent, it is an arid, sparsely inhabited area; pop(1985) 245,284; area 20,848 sq km; capital Riohacha; economy: coal-mining (El Cerrejón).

Gualeguaychú *gwa-lay-gwī-choo'*, 33 03S 59 31W, pop(1980) 51,057, town in Entre Ríos prov, Litoral, NE Argentina; near the mouth of the Río Gualeguaychú, opposite Fray Bentos (Uruguay); event: carnival at the beginning of March; railway.

Guam *gwahm*, largest and southernmost island of the Mariana Is, W Pacific Ocean, approximately 5,920 km W of Hawaii and 2,400 km E of Manila, situated at 13° N and 144° E; area 541 sq km; capital Agaña; timezone GMT +10; pop(1980) 105,979, including c.20,000 military personnel and their dependants; the population comprises Chamorros (42%), Caucasians (24%), Filipinos (21%), and also small numbers of Japanese, Chinese, Koreans, and other Micronesians; the official languages are Chamorro and English; Catholicism is the dominant religion; the majority of inhabitants live in the N and central part of the island.

Physical description. The island was formed by an uplift of undersea volcanoes and is fringed by a coral reef. It is slightly more than 48 km long and 6.4-16 km wide. S Guam is made up of low volcanic mountains rising to 406 m at Mt Lamlam. The central and N part of the island consists mainly of a high coralline limestone plateau with cliffs that drop precipitously down to a narrow coastal shelf.

Climate. The climate is tropical maritime. Temperatures range between 24°C and 30°C, with a mean annual temperature of 27°C. May and June are the hottest months. Most of the island's annual average of 2,125 mm of rain falls during the wet season, the period from July to December. Guam's tropical humidity is tempered by the prevailing NE trade winds. Tropical storms and typhoons are periodically experienced.

History, government and constitution. Guam is an unincorporated territory of the US. In 1950, administration of the island was transferred from the navy (who held it from 1899) to the Department of the Interior, and the inhabitants became citizens of the US. Guam has an elected governor, a unicameral legislature of 21 members, a non-voting representative in the US Congress, a Superior Court, having jurisdiction over local legal matters, and a US District Court with jurisdiction over federal matters and constitutional issues.

Economy. Guam's economy is highly dependent on government activities. Over 30% of total civilian employment is accounted for by the territorial government. Military installations cover 35% of the surface area of the island. Attempts have been made, however, to shift emphasis of the island's development from economic dependence on the military to diversified industrial and commercial projects. Guam has developed into a significant financial centre with offices of major mainland and Asian banks located on the island. Manufacturing activities include petroleum refining, dairy products, garments, printing, furniture, watches, and a wide range of other products for local markets. Copra, palm oil, and processed fish are also exported. Most of the exports are in the form of cargo in transshipment to the US and the islands of Micronesia. The US provides about 75% of the island's imported goods and receives more than 60% of its exports. Tourism was the most rapidly growing private sector activity in the decade 1973-83. In 1981, 312,000 persons visited Guam, of which 81% were from Japan. Guam's deep water port, Apra, continues to be a significant contributor to the economic growth of the island. There has been an increase in tuna transshipping activities, enhanced by technological advances in the tuna industry. Several inter-island, regional, and international carriers serve Guam's recently constructed air terminal. Guam serves as a transshipment centre for general cargo moving by air and sea. A total of 13 ocean shipping lines call at the island.

Guanacaste *gwa-na-kas'tay*, prov in NW Costa Rica, Central America; bounded N by Nicaragua and W by the Pacific Ocean; includes the peninsula of Nicoya and the lowlands at the head of the Golfo de Nicoya; the Cordillera del Guanacaste and the Cordillera de Tilarán extend along the E border; pop(1983e) 228,249; area 10,141 sq km; capital Liberia; chief towns Nicoya and Tilarán; economy: cattle, maize, rice, cotton, beans, and fruit; manganese is mined at Playa Real; traversed by the Inter-American Highway.

Guanacaste, Cordillera del, mountain range forming the boundary between the provs of Guanacaste (W) and Alajuela (E), NW Costa Rica, Central America; extends 112 km NW-SE from near the frontier with Nicaragua to the Laguna de Arenal; rises to 2,028 m at the volcano of Miravalles.

Guanajuato *gwa-na-hwah'tō*, mountainous state in central Mexico; bounded N by San Luis Potosí, W by Jalisco, S by Michoacán and E by Querétaro; crossed by ranges of the Sierra Madre Occidental; drained by the Río Lerma and its affluents; the Lerma forms part of the border with Michoacán; pop(1980) 3,044,402; area 30,491 sq km; capital Guanajuato; economy: agriculture (wheat, sorghum, maize, barley, chick-peas, alfalfa, carrots), cattle and pig raising, mining (gold, silver, mercury and fluorite), fruit and vegetable packing, petrochemicals, textiles, tourism.

Guanajuato, 21 00N 101 16W, pop(1983e) 45,000, capital of Guanajuato state, central Mexico; in the Sierra Madre Occidental, 355 km NW of Ciudad de México (Mexico City); university (1732); railway; economy: textiles, pottery.

Guangdong *kwang-toong*, KWANGTUNG, prov in S China; bordered S by the South China Sea and Hong Kong, W by Guangxi aut region, N by Hunan and Jiangxi provs and NE by Fujian prov; mountainous in the N; in the SW opposite Hainan island is the Leizhou Bandao peninsula; pop(1982) 59,299,220; area 231,400 sq km; capital Guangzhou; economy: rich agricultural region along the Zhu Jiang (Pearl river) delta, growing rice, wheat, fruit, vegetables, sugar cane and oil-bearing plants; the prov includes numerous islands and reefs of the South China Sea including Hainan island; China's first large nuclear power station is located in Daya Wan bay in S Guangdong, NE of Hong Kong.

Guangxi *kwang-see*, KWANGSI CHUANG, aut region in S China; bordered N by Guizhou and Hunan provs, S by Vietnam and the Gulf of Tongking, W by Yunnan prov and E by Guangdong prov; mountainous region with a low central river basin; drained by the You Jiang, Zuo Jiang, Yu Jiang and Hongshui He; pop(1982) 36,420,960; area 220,400 sq km; capital Nanning; chief towns Beihai, Guilin; economy: agriculture, fishing and mining; the Hongshui He river is the site for new hydroelectric power stations capable of supplying Yunnan, Guizhou and the rest of S China with electricity.

Guangzhou *kwang-jō*, CANTON, KWANGCHOW, 23 08N 113 20E, pop(1984e) 3,221,600, capital of Guangdong prov, S China; on the Zhu Jiang (Pearl river) delta; Guangzhou was founded in 200 BC and developed as a port; considerable urban renewal after 1949; one of 5 Chinese ports opened to foreign trade following the Opium War of 1839-42; university (1958); medical college (1953); special economic zone; railway; airport; economy: important industrial and foreign trade centre in S China, engineering, textiles, shipbuilding, chemicals, clothes; monuments: Yuexiu public park, created in the 1950s, contains an exhibition hall, stadiums, swimming pools, lakes and the Guangdong historical museum; also in Yuexiu Park is the Five Goats Statue: Guangzhou was said to be founded by 5 celestial beings who came down from heaven riding on 5 goats; the Huaisheng mosque (built in 627 AD) is thought to be the oldest mosque in China; the National Peasant Movement Institute, founded in 1924 on the site of a 16th-c Confucian temple, was used to train young communists, with Mao Zedong as its director in 1926; mausoleum of the 72 martyrs; Sun Yatsen memorial hall; event: bi-annual Chinese Export Commodities Fair.

Guantánamo *gwan-ta'na-mō*, easternmost prov in Cuba, bounded E by the Windward Passage separating Cuba from Haiti; drained by the Toa river; area 6,366 sq km; pop(1981) 466,609; capital Guantánamo; other chief town Baracoa; there are copper, manganese, chromium and iron mines on the rocky headland; there is a US naval base on the S coast.

Guantánamo, 20 09N 75 14W, pop(1983e) 171,065, capital of Guantánamo prov, SE Cuba; on a bay of the same name, 81 km ENE of Santiago de Cuba; important trading and processing centre for rich agricultural region; founded in 1797; the sugar industry began here in 1819; railway.

Guaranda *gwa-ran'da*, 1 36S 78 59W, pop(1982) 13,685, capital of Bolívar prov, in the Andean Sierra of central Ecuador; built on 7 hills, it is known as 'the Rome of Ecuador'; the town is the main centre for the wheat and maize-growing Chimbo valley.

Guarda *gwar'da*, dist in NE Portugal, bounded by Spain (E) and R Douro (N), part of Beira Alto prov, area 5,496 sq km; pop(1981) 205,631; divided into 14 councils and 332 parishes; economy: dairy produce, wheat, maize, olives, vegetables, wine, clogs, rope; minerals: arsenic, lead, feldspar, silver, quartz, titanium, uranium, wolfram, tin.

Guarda, 40 32N 7 20W, pop(1981) 13,100, capital of Guarda dist, NE Portugal; situated on a ridge overlooking the entrance to the upper Mondego valley (W) and the Zêzere (SW), 219 km SE of Porto; alt 1,057 m, the highest town in Portugal; founded in 1197 as a frontier guard against the Moors; episcopal see; agricultural centre with leatherwork and distilling; monuments: 12-13th-c Torre de Menagem fortifications; cathedral (begun in 1390 and completed in 16th century); 18th-c churches of the Misericordia and São Vicente.

Guarenas *gwa-ray'nas*, 10 28N 66 38W, pop(1981) 101,742, town in Miranda state, N Venezuela; E of Caracas.

Guárico *gwa'ree-kō*, state in N central Venezuela; bordered N by outliers of the coastal hill range and S by the Orinoco river and its tributaries, the Apure and Portuguesa; a region of *llanos* plain with a tropical climate; pop(1980) 371,423; area 64,961 sq km; capital San Juan de los Morros; 30% of Venezuelan oil is extracted from the S of this state.

Guarulhos *gwa-rool'yōs*, 23 33S 46 39W, pop(1980) 426,693, industrial town in São Paulo state, Sudeste region, SE Brazil.

Guatemala *gwa-tay-mah'la*, official name Republic of Guatemala, REPÚBLICA DE GUATEMALA , northernmost of the Central American republics, bounded N and W by Mexico, SW by the Pacific Ocean, E by Belize and the Caribbean Sea, and SE by Honduras and El Salvador;

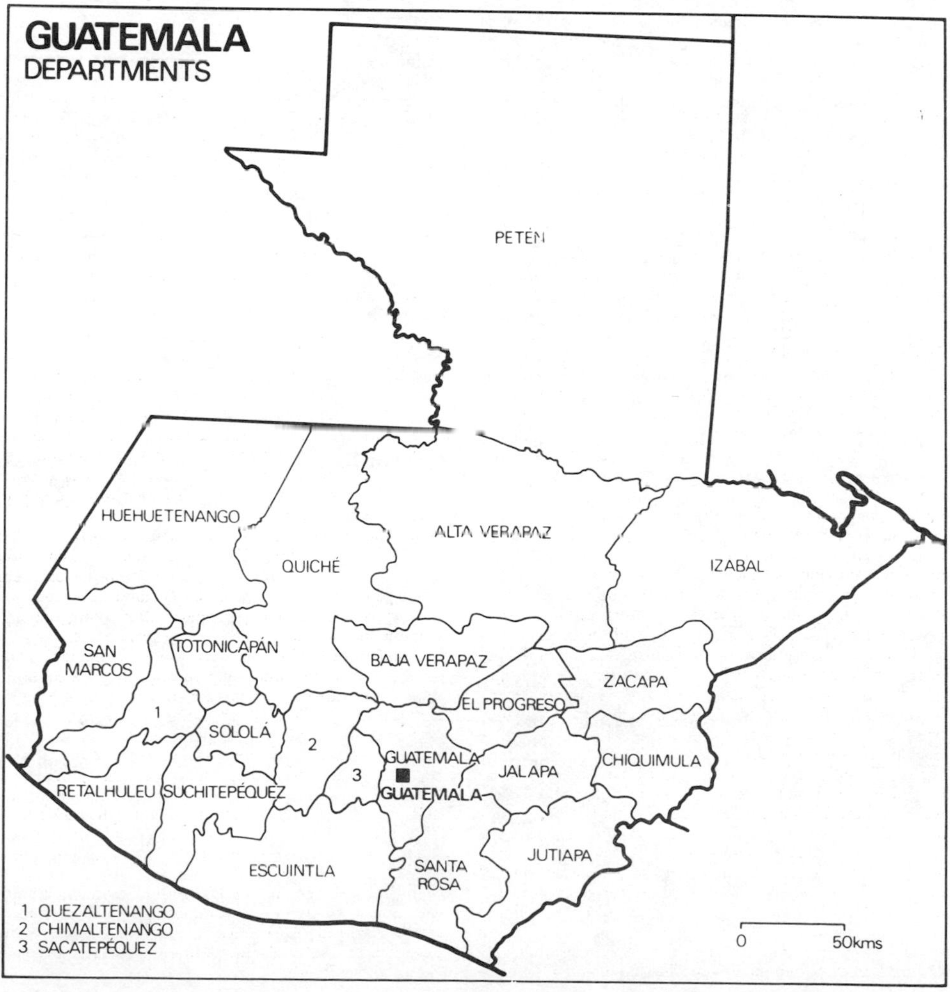

timezone GMT −6; area 108,889 sq km; capital Guatemala City; chief towns Quezaltenango, Escuintla, Antigua, and Mazatenango; pop(1983e) 6,043,559; 41.4% of the population are pure Indian, the remainder are chiefly mestizo and westernized Indian; although Spanish is the official language over 40% of the population speaks an Indian dialect as a primary tongue; Roman Catholicism is the dominant religion; the unit of currency is the quetzal of 100 centavos; national holiday 15 Sept (Independence Day); membership of CACM, FAO, G-77, IADB, IAEA, IBRD, ICAC, ICAO, ICO, IDA, IDB, IFAD, IFC, IHO, ILO, IMF, INTELSAT, INTERPOL, IRC, ISO, ITU, IWC, OAS, ODECA, PAHO, SELA, UN, UNESCO, UPEB, UPU, WFTU, WHO, WMO.

Physical description. More than two-thirds of Guatemala is mountainous and 62% forested. From the narrow Pacific coastal plain, nowhere more than 50 km wide, the highlands rise steeply to heights of between 2,500 m and 3,000 m. These mountains include the Sierra Madre, Sierra los Cuchumatanes, Sierra de Chuacús, and the Sierra de las Minás. The majority of the 33 known volcanoes in the country are concentrated along the S edge of the highlands. Intermontane basins in this volcanic region lie at a height of between 1,500 m and 2,500 m and are drained either by short rivers into the Pacific (Río Coyolate, Río Michatoya) or by longer rivers into the Caribbean (Río Motagua). Lago de Atitlán, ringed by volcanoes, occupies one of these basins W of Guatemala City. Two large valleys extend towards the Caribbean Sea from the highlands: the valley of the Motagua (400 km long) and, further N, the valley of the Río Polochic (298 km long) which drains into the Bahía de Amatique via the Lago de Izabal. To the N, bordering on Mexico and Belize, lies the low undulating tableland of El Petén, geographically a part of the Yucatán peninsula. It covers an area of 36,000 sq km and is covered with dense hardwood forest.

Climate. The Petén lowlands and the Caribbean coast have a humid tropical climate. Altitude modifies the climate further inland. There is a well-marked rainy season from May to Oct, although on the coastal plains the rainfall regime is more variable. In Guatemala City temperatures range from 17.2°C in Jan to 20.6°C in July and the mean annual rainfall is 1,316 mm. Rainfall is heaviest along the slopes exposed to the Caribbean winds and those exposed to the Pacific winds. Annual rainfall in these areas ranges from 1,800 mm to more than 5,000 mm.

History, government and constitution. The Mayan civilization flourished in Guatemala until the Spanish conquest of 1523-24, thereafter the country came under Spanish colonial rule. Independence from Spain was achieved on 15 Sept 1821 when Guatemala became part of the Federation of Central America. When the Federation was dissolved in 1840 Guatemala passed through a series of dictatorships broken only by short periods of representative government. On 23 March 1982 a junta took control of the country in a bloodless coup. The constitution and all political activity was suspended until a further coup on 8 August 1983 eventually led to a return to civilian rule. Guatemala is constitutionally governed by a National Congress of 61 deputies elected for 4-year terms. Executive power is vested in a president and an appointed cabinet of about 10 ministers. Guatemala still maintains a claim over the territory of Belize to the E.

Agriculture and forestry. Agriculture accounts for over 25% of national income, employing 50% of the workforce. Agricultural products account for some 65% of total exports, chiefly coffee, bananas, cotton and sugar. The lower slopes of the highlands, between 600 m and 1,500 m, are planted with coffee which is well suited to the upland soil and climate. Above 1,500 m the land is given over to wheat and the main subsistence crops of maize and beans. Cotton, sugar cane, rice, and beans are grown on the Pacific coastal plain. Cattle raising and beef production in the lowlands is also of importance. Bananas are grown chiefly in the Motagua valley and in the Lago de Izabal district. Land ownership is concentrated in the hands of a small minority of the population. Approx 76% of the population owns only 10% of cultivable land. Forestry accounts for 62% of the total land area, chiefly in Petén dept which is rich in mahogany and other woods.

Industry. Manufacturing industry accounts for 17% of national income, the chief products being foodstuffs, chemicals, textiles, construction materials, tyres, and pharmaceuticals. Newly developing industries include the manufacture of electrical goods, plastic sheet, and metal furniture. There are reserves of nickel in the Lago de Izabal district of E Guatemala. Other minerals such as lead and silver are mined in small quantities. A pipeline carries oil from fields near Rubelsanto in NW Alta Verapaz dept to the port of Santo Tomás de Castilla on the Caribbean Sea. Exploration is continuing in the Rubelsanto area and in the nearby dept of Petén. Guatemala's main trading partners are the USA, CACM countries, Japan, West Germany, and Venezuela.

Administrative divisions. Guatemala is divided into 22 departments as follows:

Department	*area (sq km)*	*pop(1982e)*
Alta Verapaz	8,686	383,178
Baja Verapaz	3,124	152,374
Chimaltenango	1,979	267,182
Chiquimula	2,376	215,409
Escuintla	4,384	496,522
Guatemala	2,126	1,785,665
Huehuetenango	7,403	524,829
Izabal	9,038	290,203
Jalapa	2,063	162,907
Jutiapa	3,219	329,185
Petén	35,854	102,803
El Progreso	1,922	101,203
Quezaltenango	1,951	447,428
Quiché	8,378	430,003
Retalhuleu	1,858	206,543
Sacatepéquez	465	137,815
San Marcos	3,791	552,094
Santa Rosa	2,955	249,930
Sololá	1,061	173,401
Suchitepéquez	2,510	304,826
Totonicapán	1,061	236,033
Zacapa	2,690	149,267

Guatemala, mountainous dept in Guatemala, Central America; pop(1982e) 1,785,665; area 2,126 sq km; capital Guatemala City; chief towns San Pedro Sacatepéquez and Los Dolores.

Guatemala, GUATEMALA CITY, 14 38N 90 22W, pop(1983e) 1,300,000, capital city of Guatemala, Guatemala dept, Central America; on a plateau in the Sierra Madre mountain range; at the summit of the railway from Puerto Barrios to San José; founded in 1776 to serve as capital after the earlier capital, Antigua, was destroyed by earthquake in 1773; rebuilt since its almost total destruction by earthquakes in 1917-18; alt 1,500 m; University of San Carlos (1680) and 4 other universities; airport (La Aurora); economy: foodstuffs, textiles, footwear, tyres, cement; monuments: cathedral (1782-1815, damaged by the 1976 earthquake); churches of Santo Domingo (1782-1807) and San Francisco; on the W outskirts of the city are the Mayan ruins of Kaminal Juyú, a celebrated archaeological site.

Guatopo *gwa-tō'pō*, national park in Miranda and Guárico states, N Venezuela; SE of Caracas; area 926 sq km; established in 1958.

Guaviare *gwa-vya'ray*, administrative territory in S central Colombia, South America; bounded N by Meta dept along the Río Guaviare, S by Caquetá dept along the Río Ajaju; area 42,327 sq km; pop(1985) 12,235; capital San José.

Guayana, Ciudad *gwa-ya'na*, SAN FÉLIX DE GUAYANA, 8 22N 62 37W, pop(1981) 314,497, a new city in Bolívar state, E Venezuela; on Orinoco and Caroní rivers; railway; airfield at Puerto Ordaz; Ciudad Guayana was built to link the 4 separate towns of San Félix, Puerto Ordaz, Palúa and Matanzas; a pop of 1 million is planned; San Félix is a commercial port; Puerto Ordaz is an iron-ore loading port, connected by rail with the open-cast iron mine, Cerro Bolívar; Palúa is an iron-ore terminal; nearby on the R Caroní is the Macagua hydroelectric plant; higher up the river is the Guri dam and hydroelectric plant.

Guayape *gwī-a'pay*, river in E central Honduras, Central America; rises NW of Guayape; flows SE past Guayape, ENE through the Olancho valley, then S to join the Río Guayambre, 37 km SE of Juticalpa, where it forms the Río Patuca; length 240 km.

Guayaquil *gwī-a-keel'*, 2 13S 79 54W, pop(1982) 1,199,344, capital of Guayas prov, W Ecuador; major seaport and commercial city, on the west bank of the Río Guayas; founded by Francisco de Orellana in 1537, the city is named after the legendary Indian prince, Guayas and the princess Quil who allegedly committed suicide rather than surrender to the Spanish; developed as an international sea and river port, serving inland tropical villages and plantations; the first steam boat in Latin America was constructed in shipyards here, and the world's first submarine trial was carried out here; 4 universities (1867, 1958, 1962, 1966); the city has a racecourse, golf, tennis and yachting clubs; railway; airport (Simón Bolívar); ferries and a bridge link the city with Durán, the rail terminal on the east bank of the river; economy: banana trade (the greatest exporter of bananas in the world); mining (sand, clay), drinks, tobacco, meat packing, dairy products, fruit, vegetable and fish packing, vegetable oil production, flour milling, coffee, food processing, sugar refining, animal foodstuffs, textiles, leather, wine, plastics, electrical equipment, motor vehicles, explosives, pharmaceutical products, iron and steel, oil refining, rubber, chemicals, pesticides; monuments: municipal palace and government palace on the river front; liberation monument in the Plaza Centenario (1920); House of Culture, with a notable gold collection; in the city museum there is a collection of Jívaro Indian shrunken heads; Los Libertadores Monument commemorates the meeting in 1822 between Simón Bolívar and José de San Martín; San Francisco church (1603), rebuilt in 1968; Santo Domingo church (1548), the city's oldest church; events: 24 July (Bolívar's birthday) and 25 July (Foundation of the City).

Guayaramerín *gwī-a-ram-ay-reen'*, PUERTO SUCRE, 10 51S 65 23W, pop(1976) 12,520, small town in Vaca Diez prov, Beni, Bolivia; on the Río Mamoré, on the border with Brazil (E), opposite the Brazilian town of Guajará Mirim; a ferry operates between the two towns; airfield.

Guayas *gwī'as*, prov in W Ecuador; bounded W by the Pacific Ocean, S by the Golfo de Guayaquil and E by the Andes; watered by the Río Guayas; pop(1982) 2,038,454; area 20,246 sq km; capital Guayaquil; economy: coffee, cacao, pineapples, wine, dairying, sugar refining, food processing, oil, natural gas, mining, motor vehicles.

Guayas, river in Guayas prov, W central Ecuador; formed by the meeting of several navigable rivers which rise on the W slopes of the Andes; tributaries include the Daule, Vinces, Chimbo (or Yaguachi) and Babahoyo rivers; enters the Gulf of Guayaquil in a wide estuary; length (including the Río Babahoyo headstreams) 160 km; the Guayas is one of the largest river systems on the W coast of South America and waters one of the most fertile regions of Ecuador.

Guaymas *gwī'mas*, 27 55N 110 54W, pop(1970) 103,500, resort and port in Sonora state, NW Mexico; on the Golfo de California, 136 km S of Hermosillo; railway; economy: fishing; monument: 18th-c church of San Fernando.

Gudenå *goo'du-no*, river in N central Jylland (Jutland), Denmark; rises in Viborg county, flows NE through Århus county, discharges into Randers Fjord at Randers; length 157 km; longest river in Denmark.

Guecho *gay'chō*, 43 21N 2 59W, pop(1981) 67,321, outer suburban town NW of Bilbao, in Vizcaya prov, Pais Vasco (Basque Country), N Spain; on Bilbao Bay, 10 km N of Bilbao.

Guékédou *gay-kay'dow*, 8 35N 10 11W, town in S Guinea, W Africa; 220 km SSW of Kankan.

Guelma *gwel'ma*, department in N Algeria, N Africa; area 8,624 sq km; pop(1982) 616,229; chief town Guelma.

Guelph *gwelf*, 43 34N 80 16W, pop(1981) 71,207, town in SE Ontario, S Canada; on the Speed river; 43 km NW of Hamilton; founded in 1827 by John Galt, the Scottish novelist; university (1964); railway; economy: iron, steel, textiles, rubber, chemicals; monuments: the Church of Our Lady cathedral was modelled on the cathedral of Cologne; waterfowl park; electric railway museum; museum for the poet John McCrae.

Guéra *gay'ra*, prefecture in S central Chad, N central Africa; pop(1979) 207,000; area 58,950 sq km; capital Mongo; chief towns Melfi, Bitkine and Chediba; part of Zakouma National Park lies in the SE.

Gueret *gwer-ay*, 46 11N 1 51E, pop(1982) 16,621, capital city of Creuse dept, Limousin region, central France; on a high plateau, 198 km S of Orléans; once the capital of the old prov of Marche; railway; monument: the municipal museum, housed in a large 18th-c house in the centre of a large garden on the S edge of the town contains a collection of 12-15th-c enamelwork from Limoges and elsewhere, including notable ecclesiastical crosses and shrines.

Guernica *ger-nee'ka*, 43 19N 2 40W, pop(1981) 17,836, town in Vizcaya prov, Pais Vasco (Basque Country), NE Spain; 25 km ENE of Bilbao, on an inlet of the Bay of Biscay; German planes bombed the town during the Spanish Civil War; economy: armaments, metal products, furniture, foodstuffs.

Guernsey *gœrn'zay*, 2nd largest of the Channel Is; lies NW of Jersey and W of the Cotentin Peninsula of French Normandie; pop(1981) 53,313; area 63 sq km; chief town St Peter Port; the island gave its name to a sailor's knitted garment and a breed of dairy cattle.

Guerrero *ge-ray'rō*, mountainous state in SW Mexico; bounded by the Pacific Ocean (S), Michoacán (NW and N), México, Morelos and Puebla (N) and Oaxaca (E); crossed W-E by the Sierra Madre del Sur; drained by the Río Balsas; pop(1980) 2,174,162; area 64,281 sq km, capital Chilpancingo; major town: Acapulco; economy: agriculture (maize, copra, coffee), stock raising, fishing, mining (gold, silver, copper, lead, zinc, mercury, barite, bentonite), food processing, ice-making, sugar refining, cotton processing, tourism.

Gugu *goo'goo*, 6 16N 37 25E, mountain in N Gamo Gofa region, SW Ethiopia, NE Africa; height 4,200 m.

Gugule'tu, pop(1985) 76,312, African township SE of central Cape Town, Cape prov, South Africa; W of KTC squatter settlement and Nyanga township.

Guiana Highlands *gee-ah'na*, mountainous tableland mainly in S and SE Venezuela, and extending into Brazil and Guyana, South America; the tableland, a forested plateau, covers half the area of Venezuela; the Highlands extend from the right bank of the R Orinoco to the Brazilian border ranges of Parima and Pacaraima, rising to 2,875 m in Monte Roraima; consists of crystalline rocks with sandstone and lava caps; the vast plateaux are separated by deep valleys and have magnificent waterfalls, including Angel Falls, considered to be the highest waterfall in the world.

Guidimaka *gee-dee-ma-kah'*, region in S Mauritania, NW Africa; pop(1982e) 102,000; area 10,300 sq km; capital Sélibaby; chief towns Harr, Artémou, Samba Kandji and Bouly; the R Sénégal follows the S frontier in an area where rich alluvial soils support agriculture.

Guiglo *gwee'glō*, dept in SW Ivory Coast, W Africa; pop(1975) 137,672; area 14,150 sq km; capital Guiglo; chief towns Péon, Duékoué, Tai and Toulépleu; part of Tai National Park is located in the SE.

Güija, Laguna de *gee'ha*, lake in Jutiapa dept, S Guatemala and Santa Ana dept, NW El Salvador, Central America; SW of Metapán.

Guildford *gil'ford*, 51 14N 0 35W, pop(1981) 63,086, county town in Guildford dist, Surrey, SE England; on the R Wey, 45 km SW of London; originally a ford over the R Wey; University of Surrey (1966); burial place of the Rev Charles Dodgson (Lewis Carroll), author of *Alice in Wonderland*; railway; economy: vehicles, engineering, plastics, pharmaceuticals; monuments: Royal King Edward VI Grammar School (1557), cathedral (completed in 1964), Archbishop Abbot's Hospital, Women's Royal Army Corps museum.

Guilin *gway-lin*, KWEILIN, 25 21N 110 11E, pop(1984e) 446,900, town in Guangxi aut region, S China; on the W bank of the Li river; river boat trips on the Li river through dramatic limestone hills are a major tourist attraction; Guilin contains 90% of China's Muslim population; severely damaged during World War II when it was the site of a US air base; the greater part of the town has been rebuilt since 1960; railway; airfield; economy: grain, fishing, cotton, spun silk, rubber, medicines, machinery; monuments: Reed Flute Cave, formerly used as a refuge from bandits and invading armies, features the enormous Shuiqinggong (Crystal Palace) Grotto with its legendary stone pillar, said to be the Dragon King's magic needle used as a weapon by the Monkey King in the Chinese fable 'Journey to the West'; Zengpiyan Cave was the site of a Stone Age village, remains of humans and animals have been found since excavations began in 1973; in Seven Star Park is the Forest of Tablets, a cave containing many stelae from the Tang and Ming dynasties.

Guimarães *geem-ar-a'ish*, 41 26N 8 19W, pop(1981) 22,100, fortified city in Braga dist, N Portugal; at the foot of the Serra de Catarina, 21 km SE of Braga; first capital of Portugal; economy: textiles; monuments: 10th-c castle which was the birthplace in 1110 of Alfonso Henriques, the first king of Portugal; Ducal palace built by the first Duke of Bragança and chapel of São Miguel (1105) where King Alfonso was baptized; events: Cruzes festival at beginning of May; International Folk Festival at the end of July; pilgrimage to Senhora da Penha at the beginning of Sept.

Guinea *gin'i*, GUINÉE *gee-nay'* (Fr), formerly FRENCH GUINEA, official name The Republic of Guinea, RÉPUBLIQUE DE GUINÉE (Fr), a W African republic bounded NW by Guinea-Bissau, N by Senegal and Mali, E by the Ivory Coast, S by Sierra Leone and Liberia and SW by the Atlantic Ocean; timezone GMT; area 246,048 sq km; pop(1984) 5,579,000; capital Conakry; chief towns Kankan, Kindia, N'Zérékoré and Labé; there are 662 km of railway (Conakry-Kankan), a 134 km line from bauxite deposits at Boké to Port Kamsar and a 144 km line from Conakry to Fria, 4,780 km of paved roads and 1,295 km of inland waterways navigable by shallow draft vessels; ethnic groups include Fulani (40%), Malinké (25%), Susu (11%), Kissi (6%), Kpelle (5%) and others including Dialonka and Loma; 75% of the pop is Muslim, 24% follows local beliefs and 1% is Christian; the official language is French; Fulani, Malinké, Susu, Kissi, Kpelle, Loma, Basari and Koniagi are also officially taught in schools; the unit of currency is the syli of 100 couris; national holiday 2 Oct (Independence Day); membership of AfDB, ECA, ECOWAS, FAO, G-77, GATT, IBA, IBRD, ICAO, ICO, IDA, IDB (Islamic Development Bank), IFAD, ILO, IMF, IMO, INTELSAT, INTERPOL, ITU, Mano River Union, NAM, Niger River Commission, OAU, OIC, UN, UNESCO, UPU, WFTU, WHO, WMO.

Physical description. A coast characterized by mangrove forests rises to a coastal plain between 50 and 60 km wide which is forested and widely cultivated. Beyond this lies the Fouta Djallon massif, about 900 m above the coastal plain. Near the Senegal frontier rise some of the higher peaks including Mt Loura (1,515 m) and Mt Tangue (1,537 m). The E is typified by savannah plains cut by river valleys which flow toward the upper basin of the R Niger. The Guinea Highlands of the S are forested and generally rise above 1,000 m. On the frontier with Liberia is Mt Nimba (1,752 m).

Climate. Guinea has a tropical climate with a wet season extending from early May through to late Oct. During the dry season the average temperature on the coast is 32°C dropping to 23°C in the wet season and becoming cooler further inland. The average annual rainfall at Conakry is 4,923 mm.

History, government and constitution. The French began their incursions into present-day Guinea during the early 19th century claiming the area as a protectorate in 1849. Under the name of Rivières du Sud it was governed with Senegal until its establishment as a separate colony in 1893. The country's current boundaries were defined in the late 19th and early 20th centuries with the division of the coastal Guinea region between France, Britain (Sierra Leone) and Portugal (Guinea-Bissau, formerly Portuguese Guinea). It became a constituent territory within French West Africa in 1904 but reverted to separate colonial status in 1946 as an overseas territory. The post World War II era saw a rise in nationalism which led to the rejection of membership of the proposed French community. Guinea was alone in this stance and became an independent republic in 1958. A military coup in 1984 established a military government headed by a president and a 10-member Council of Ministers.

Economy. Guinea is a largely agricultural country, the majority of the people being subsistence farmers growing rice, maize, yams and cassava. The main cash crops are sugar cane, groundnuts, coffee, bananas, palm kernels and pineapples. Timber is also extracted from areas of rich tropical forest. Guinea is rich in minerals with approx one-third of the world's bauxite reserves, large iron ore reserves and significant diamond, gold and uranium deposits. In NW Guinea, bauxite and alumina operations involving foreign mining companies generate 96% of the country's foreign exchange. Independence brought a fall in production and a deterioration in infrastructure as a result of the withdrawal of French expertise and investment. The main trading partners for imports are France, West Germany, the USA, the USSR, Belgium, Luxembourg and the UK, and for exports the USA, West Germany, the USSR, Spain, Canada and France.

Administrative divisions. Guinea is divided into the 4 regions of Guinée-Maritime, Moyenne-Guinée, Haute-Guinée and Guinée-Forestière. These regions are further subdivided into 33 local government regions.

Guinea, Gulf of, arm of the Atlantic Ocean, lying in the great bend of the West African coast; bounded to the N by the Ivory Coast, Ghana, Tongo, Benin and to the E by Nigeria, Cameroon, Equatorial Guinea and Gabon; the Equator lies to the S; the Bight of Benin and the Bight of Biafra are the major inlets.

Guinea-Bissau *gi-nee-bi-sow'*, official name Republic of Guinea-Bissau, REPUBLICA DA GUINÉ-BISSAU, a republic of W Africa bounded SE by Guinea, N by Senegal and SW by the Atlantic Ocean; timezone GMT; area 36,260 sq km; pop(1984) 842,000; capital Bissau; chief towns Bafatá, Bolama, Gabù, Mansôa, Catió, and Farim; there are no railways, 418 km of bituminous roads and scattered stretches of waterways which are important to coastal commerce; the majority of the pop is of African origin and includes Balanta (30%), Fula (20%), Manjaca (14%), Mandingo (13%) and Papel (7%); there are also some Europeans and Mulatta (less than 1%); most of the pop follows local religious beliefs (60%), the remainder being either Muslims (35%) or Christians (5%); Portuguese is the official language with Criolo and numerous African languages also spoken; the unit of currency is the peso of 100 centavos; national holiday 24 Sept (Independence Day); membership of AfDB, FAO, G-77, GATT (de facto), IBRD, ICAO, IDA, IDB (Islamic Development Bank), IFAD, IFC, ILO, IMF, IMO, ISCON, ITU, NAM, OAU, OIC, UN, UNESCO, UPU, WFTU, WHO, WMO.

Physical description. An indented coast typified by islands and mangrove-lined estuaries is backed by forested coastal plains. Chief rivers flowing from the interior to the Atlantic are the Cacheu, the Geba and the Corubal. A low lying country with savannah-covered plateaux in the S and E, rising to 310 m on the Guinea border. The Bijagos Archipelago, which lies off the coast, includes many heavily-forested islands.

Climate. Guinea-Bissau has a tropical climate with a wet season (June to Oct) followed by a dry season when the dust-laden *harmattan* wind blows in from the Sahara. The average annual rainfall at Bissau is 1,950 mm and temperatures range from 24.4°C to 26.7°C.

History, government and constitution. Guinea-Bissau (formerly Portuguese Guinea) was discovered by Nuno Tristão in 1446, but did not become a separate Portuguese Colony until 1879. Its borders were defined by a convention with France in 1886 but the Portuguese did not gain full control until 1936. In 1952 it became an overseas territory of Portugal and an armed rebellion against colonial rule began in 1961. Independence was declared in 1973 and formally recognized by Portugal in the following year. The constitution provides for a National Assembly but following a coup in 1980 a military government with a president and council of ministers was installed. A new constitution was promulgated by the Revolutionary Council in 1984 and members were elected to a new 150-seat National People's Assembly. There is only one political party in the country, the Partido Africano da Independencia da Guiné e Cabo Verde (PAIGC).

Economy. The country's economy is centred on agriculture with about 90% of the workforce engaged on smallholdings. Food crops include rice on the lowland plains and maize, sorghum, cassava, beans, yams, and cattle and sheep on the higher ground. Peanuts, coconuts, palm oil and groundnuts as cash crops represent substantial export earnings as do shrimps and fish trawled from the waters off the Bijagos Archipelago. Timber is also exported occasionally. Industry is limited to construction, food processing, brewing and soft drinks. There are petroleum resources, bauxite and phosphate reserves. Main trading partners for imports are Portugal, USSR, Sweden, France, West Germany, Belgium, Luxembourg, Italy, the Netherlands, Pakistan, the USA, and the UK, and for exports Portugal, Egypt, Senegal, France, Spain, Cape Verde, West Germany and Algeria.

Administrative divisions. Guinea-Bissau is divided into 8 regions and the capital Bissau:

Region	*pop(1979)*
Bafatá	116,032
Biombo	56,463
Bissau	109,214
Bolama	25,473
Cacheu	130,227
Gabù	104,227
Oio	135,114
Quinara	35,532
Tombali	55,099

Guipúzcoa *gee-pooth'ko-wa*, smallest of the three Basque provs in N Spain, on the Bay of Biscay and the French border; the W spurs of the Pyrenees slope down to a high rocky coastline; pop(1981) 692,986; area 1,997 sq km; smallest Spanish prov; capital San Sebastian; economy: steel, machine tools, electronics, perfume (Zaldibia), precision tools, furniture, livestock, food processing.

Güira de Melena *gwee'ra day may-lay'na*, 22 47N 82 33W, pop(1981) 429,090, capital town of La Habana prov, W Cuba, 40 km SSW of La Habana (Havana); railway.

Guisborough *giz'bur-u*, 54 32N 1 04W, pop(1981) 19,219, town in Langbaurgh dist, Cleveland, NE England; 9 km S of Redcar; economy: light engineering; monuments: 12th-c Augustinian monastery, 15th-c church of St Nicholas.

Guiseley *gīz'li*, 53 53N 1 42W, pop(1981) 30,963, town linked with Yeadon in Leeds borough, West Yorkshire, N England; part of West Yorkshire urban area; 13 km NW of Leeds; railway; economy: engineering, textiles.

Guiyang *kway-yang*, KUEI-YANG, 26 35N 106 40E, pop(1984e) 1,352,700, capital of Guizhou prov, S China; railway; airfield.

Guizhou *gway-jō*, KWEICHOW, prov in S China; bordered S by Guangxi aut region, W by Yunnan prov, N by Sichuan prov and E by Hunan prov; situated in E section of Yunnan-Guizhou plateau; part of the S border with Guangxi is formed by the Nanpan Jiang river; rises in the E with the Miao Ling range, in the N with the Dalou Shan range and in the W with the Wumeng Shan range; drained by the Wu Jiang and Beipan Jiang rivers; in the NW in the Wumeng Shan range is Cao Hai lake (area 46.6 sq km); in SW Guizhou on a headstream of the Dabang river, a tributary of the Beipan Jiang, is Huangguoshu waterfall, one of the largest waterfalls in China; Guizhou contains numerous limestone caverns; pop(1982) 28,552,997; area 174,000 sq km; capital Guiyang; economy: agriculture, timber, minerals, wine.

Gujarat *goo-ja-raht'*, state in W India; bounded N by Pakistan, SW, S and SE by the Arabian Sea and indented in the SW by the Gulf of Kachch (Kutch) and in the SE by the Gulf of Khambhat (Cambay); pop(1981) 33,960,905; area 195,984 sq km; formed in May 1960 from the N and W Gujarati-speaking areas of Bombay state; capital Gandhinagar; the state has 19 districts; Gujarat is governed by a 182-member Legislative Assembly; Gujarat is one of the most industrialized states in India; the chief industries include textiles, electrical engineering, petrochemicals, machine tools, cement, oil refining, fertilizers; the state is the heart of the cotton-growing industry in India; there are about 2 dozen fields with reserves of crude oil and gas; agricultural crops include rice, groundnuts and cotton; airfield at Ahmadabad; 6 universities; in June 1983 a flood caused by the bursting of the Fodana Dam in Saurashtra region caused the deaths of over 600 people and widespread damage to property and crops; archaeological evidence links Gujarat with the Indus civilization of c.3000-1500 BC; Gujarat became an independent sultanate in 1401, but became part of the Mongol Empire in 1572; it retained its own princely rulers under British control; in 1947 the region was organized as part of the state of Bombay.

Gujranwala *gooj-rahn'vahl-a*, 32 06N 74 11E, pop(1981) 654,000, city in NE Punjab prov, Pakistan; 67 km NW of Lahore; Sikh ruler Ranjit Singh born here in 1780; former Sikh capital; railway; economy: copper and brass handicrafts, grain trade.

Gujrat *gooj-raht'*, 32 35N 74 06E, pop(1981) 154,000, city in Punjab prov, E Pakistan; 109 km N of Lahore, between the Jhelum and Chenab rivers; founded in 16th century; railway; economy: gold and silver crafts, trade in wheat, millet, cotton and rice.

Gulf Stream, an ocean current named after the Gulf of Mexico, out of which it flows past Florida, along the E coast of the USA, till it is deflected near the banks of Newfoundland NE across the Atlantic Ocean; part of the N Atlantic anticyclonic circulation; it has an important moderating effect on the climate of NW Europe.

Gulf, The, arm of the Arabian Sea. See Arabian Gulf.

Gulfport, 30 22N 89 06W, pop(1980) 39,676, county seat of Harrison county, SE Mississippi, United States; a port on the Gulf of Mexico, 20 km W of Biloxi; railway; economy: seafood packaging, the manufacture of chemicals, pharmaceuticals, metal products, and clothing.

Gulu *goo'loo*, 2 46N 32 21E, town in Northern prov, Uganda, E Africa; 260 km N of Kampala; railway.

Gümüşhane *gu-mu'sha-ne*, mountainous prov in NE Turkey; bounded N by Rize Mts and S by Erzincan Mts; pop(1980) 275,191; area 10,227 sq km; capital Gümüşhane; economy: forest products, grain and copper mining.

Gümüşhane, 40 26N 39 26E, pop(1980) 12,735, capital of Gümüşhane prov, NE Turkey; NW of Erzurum.

Gunnbjørn Fjeld *goon'byorn*, 68 50N 29 45W, highest mountain in Greenland, rising to 3,702 m.

Guntur *goon-toor'*, 16 23N 80 30E, pop(1981) 368,000, city in Andhra Pradesh, S India; linked NE to Vijayawada by rail; market for the surrounding cotton and tobacco-growing region; founded in the 18th century by the French, but ceded to Great Britain in 1823.

Gurbantunggut Shamo, desert in N Xinjiang aut region, NW China. See Junggar Pendi.

Gurk *goork*, river in Kärnten state, S Austria; rises in the Gurktal Alps at Kuhnsdorf, flowing E then S to meet the R Drau; length 158 km.

Gütersloh *gü'tur-slō*, 51 54N 8 25E, pop(1983) 78,200, city in Detmold dist, N Nordrhein-Westfalen (North Rhine-Westphalia) prov, W Germany; 50 km E of Münster; railway; economy: mineral water, soft drinks, household appliances, mechanical engineering.

Gutland *goot'lant* or **Pays Gaumais** ('good land'), geographical region of S Luxembourg; part of the fertile uplands of Lorraine, extending over sandstone and shell-limestone; an important wine-producing area is to be found on the slopes along the R Moselle between Schengen and Wasserbillig; on the less fertile, Jurassic sandstone table in the centre of the region stands the capital city, Luxembourg; occupies 1,758 sq km (68%) of Luxembourg.

Guyana *gee-ah'na*, official name Cooperative Republic of Guyana, country on the N coast of South America on the Atlantic; situated between 1° and 8°N; bordered E by Surinam, W by Venezuela and S by Brazil; timezone GMT $-3\frac{1}{2}$; area 214,969 sq km; capital Georgetown; pop(1984e) 775,000; pop comprised of East Indian (51%), mixed Afro-Indian (43%), Amerindian (4%), Chinese and European (2%); the official language is English, although Hindi, Urdu and local dialects are also spoken; the main religion is Christianity (57%), followed by Hindu (33%) and Muslim (9%); the currency is the Guyana dollar of 100 cents; national holiday 23 Feb (Republic Day); membership of Commonwealth, CARICOM, ACP/EEC, CDB, FAO, G-77, GATT, IADB, IBA, IBRD, ICAO, IDA, IDB, IFAD, IFC, ILO, IMF, IMO, INTERPOL, IRC, ISO, ITU, NAM, OAS (observer), PAHO, SELA, UN, UNESCO, UPU, WFTU, WHO, WMO.

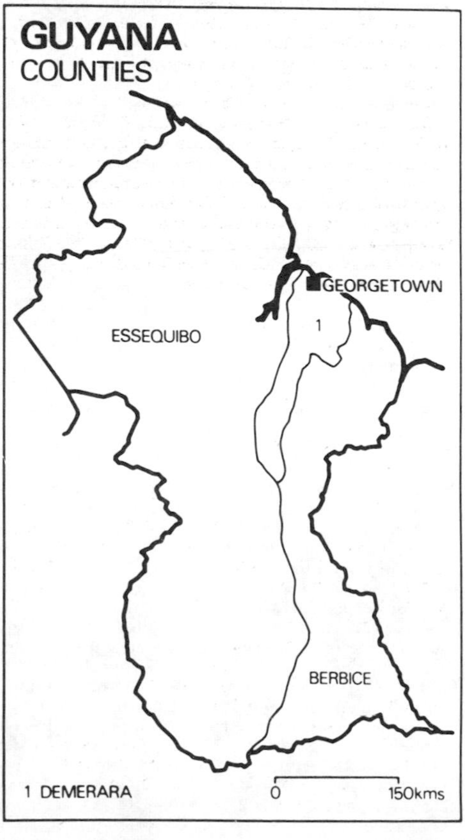

Physical description. Guyana is divided into 3 geographical areas: (1) an inland forest covering approx 85% of the total land area; (2) a grass-covered savannah in the hinterland (covering approx 20,700 sq km); and (3) a coastal plain, 16-65 km wide and 320 km long. Much of the coastal plain lies 1-1.5 m below sea-level at high tide, and is protected and drained by a complex system of sea defences, dams and canals. This is the most populated part of the country, containing about 94% of the pop. Guyana is watered by 3 main rivers which flow N from the Guiana Highlands to reach the Atlantic: the Essequibo, Demerara and Berbice; the upper courses of the rivers have numerous rapids and waterfalls (including the Kaieteur Falls on the R Potaro). In the W of Guyana is the country's highest peak, Monte Roraima, which rises to 2,875 m in the Pakaraima Mountains.

Climate. The Guyana lowlands have a hot, wet, equatorial type climate with constant high humidity and two rainy seasons. On the coast the temperatures are influenced by the cooling NE trade-winds. Georgetown's temperature and rainfall are representative of the coastal lowland area, with min and max temperatures of 23°C and 34°C and highest rainfall during May-July and Nov-Jan. Inland, on the high plateau there is less rainfall and usually one rainy season from April to Sept. Temperatures are much lower here than on the coast, giving rise to a climate that is less oppressive. Temperatures recorded on the plateau range from 16°C to 31°C and rainfall ranges from 252 mm to 51 mm.

History, government and constitution. Guyana was sighted by Columbus in 1498 and settled by the Dutch in the late 16th century. In 1815 the colonies of Essequibo, Demerara and Berbice were officially ceded to the British and were consolidated as British Guiana in 1831. Racial disturbances between East Indians and Blacks erupted in 1962 and independence was eventually granted in 1966. Guyana became a republic on 23 Feb 1970. In 1980 a new constitution was adopted. Guyana has a modified parliamentary government. Legislative power rests with a unicameral 75-member National Assembly, elected by proportional representation every 5 years. Of these seats 12 represent local and regional governments.

Economy. Unemployment, which is high in Guyana, has been strongly affected by labour unrest, low productivity and a high foreign debt. The situation worsened in 1985 when the IMF made Guyana ineligible for further credits due to lack of repayment. The economy of Guyana is largely based on the agricultural production of sugar and rice which accounts for over half of export earnings, and on the mining of bauxite. Principal exports are bauxite, sugar, rice, shrimps, molasses, timber and rum. Major trade partners include the USA, the UK, Trinidad and Tobago, Japan, Canada and Jamaica.

Administrative divisions. Guyana is divided into the 9 districts of North West, Mazaruni-Potaro, Rupununi, Essequibo, Essequibo Islands, W Demerara, E Demerara, W Berbice and E Berbice.

Guyane, overseas dept of France. See French Guiana.

Guyenne or **Guienne** *goo-yen*, ACQUITANIA (Lat), former prov of Aquitaine region, SW France, now occupying the depts of Gironde, Dordogne, Lot, Aveyron, Tarn-et-Garonne and Lot-et-Garonne and including Périgord, Rouergue, Brazidas, Entre-deux-Mers, Médoc and Bourges; bounded on the W by the Bay of Biscay; its former capital was Bordeaux.

Gwalior *gwahl'i-or*, 26 12N 78 09E, pop(1981) 556,000, city and former princely state in Madhya Pradesh, central India; lies between the rivers Sind and Chambal; linked to Agra and Jhansi by rail; dates from the 8th century; within the walls of the fort on Gwalior Rock are ornamental palaces, temples and shrines, with 15th-c sculptures; famed as a cultural centre during the 15th century, the city was held by the Moguls during the 15th and 16th centuries; captured by the British in 1780; in 1947 Gwalior joined with other princely states to become the state of Madhya Bharat; in 1956 Madhya Bharat merged with the state of Madhya Pradesh.

Gwent, county in SE Wales; bounded W by W Glamorgan, NW by Powys, NE by Hereford and Worcester, E by Gloucester and S by the Bristol Channel; capital Cwmbran; drained by the Usk and Wye rivers; economy: coal mining, chemicals, aluminium, tinplate, market gardening, food processing, dairy farming; pop(1981) 439,875; area 1,376 sq km; created in 1974, the county is divided into 5 districts:

District	*area (sq km)*	*pop(1981)*
Blaenau Gwent	127	79,478
Islwyn	99	64,759
Monmouth	824	71,616
Newport	201	133,808
Torfaen	126	90,214

Gweru *gway'roo*, formerly GWELO *gway'lō*, 19 25S 29 50E, pop(1982) 79,000, capital of Midlands prov, Zimbabwe, S Africa; 155 km NE of Bulawayo; by virtue of its central location Gweru is an important communications centre; railway; airfield; economy: administration, shoes, glassware, metal alloys, dairy products, batteries.

Gwynedd *gwin'eTH*, county in NW Wales; bounded N by the Irish Sea, E by Clwyd and S by Powys; includes the island of Anglesey; rises to 1,085 m at Snowdon in Snowdonia national park; drained by the R Conwy; pop(1981) 230,048; area 3,869 sq km; capital Caernarfon; economy: livestock, slate quarrying, textiles, electronics, light engineering, tourism; Holyhead is linked to Dun Laoghaire in Ireland; created in 1974, the county is divided into 5 districts:

District	*area (sq km)*	*pop(1981)*
Aberconwy	606	52,414
Arfon	410	52,072
Dwyfor	620	26,315
Isle of Anglesey	715	66,496
Meirionnydd	1,518	32,027

Gydan, mountain range in NE Soviet Union. See Kolymskiy Khrebet.

Gydanskiy Poluostrov, GYDA PENINSULA (Eng), peninsula in NE Tyumenskaya oblast and NW Krasnoyarskiy kray, Rossiyskaya, Soviet Union; lying between the mouths of the Taz (W) and Yenisey (E) rivers; bounded N by the Karskoye More (Kara Sea), W by Obskaya Guba (Ob' Bay), and NE by Yeniseyskiy Zaliv (Yenisey Gulf); in the N the Gydanskaya Guba (Gyda Bay) divides the main peninsula into 2 smaller ones: Poluostrov Yavay in the W and Poluostrov Mamonta on the E; the land is generally low lying, poorly drained, and tundra-covered.

Gympie *gim'pee*, 26 10S 152 35E, pop(1981) 10,768, market town in Wide Bay-Burnett stat div, SE Queensland, Australia; on the Mary river, N of Brisbane; a former gold-mining town; railway; economy: dairy farming, bananas, pineapples.

Gyöngyös *dyun'dyush*, 47 48N 20 00E, pop(1984e) 38,000, town in Heves county, N Hungary; in the foothills of the Matra Mts NE of Budapest; thermal springs nearby; railway; economy: grain, livestock and fruit trade, textiles, copper, coal mining.

Györ *dyür*, RAAB (Ger), ARRABONA (Lat), 47 41N 17 40E, pop(1981) 125,000, industrial city and capital of Györ-Sopron county, NW Hungary; at the junction of the Rába and Repce rivers with an arm of the R Danube, near the frontier with Czechoslovakia; linked to Neusiedler See (L Fertö) by a canal; bishopric; noted for its modern ballet company; railway; economy: motor vehicles, trucks, steel, machinery; foodstuffs, textiles, distilling; monuments: 18th-c Carmelite convent, cathedral, 18th-c Baroque city hall.

Györ-Sopron *dyür-shop'ron*, county in NW Hungary; bounded N by Czechoslovakia and W by Austria, comprising the N part of the Kisalföld (Little Alföld) region; bisected N-S by the R Rába with part of Neusiedler See (L Fertö); pop(1984e) 430,000; area 4,012 sq km; capital Györ; chief towns include Mosonmagyaróvár and Sopron.

Gyula *dyoo'lo*, 46 38N 21 17E, pop(1984e) 35,000, town in Békés county, S Hungary; on the R Körös, SE of Békéscsaba; the town has medicinal baths containing alkali, iodine and bromine; economy: grain, tobacco and dairy trade, meat processing, chemicals, foodstuffs; monuments: Europe's only surviving brick castle which was built in the 14th century; event: open air summer festival.

Gżira *gzee'rah*, 35 54N 14 30E, pop(1983e) 10,392, community in N central Malta, W of Valletta and overlooking Sliema and Lazzaretto creeks.

H

Ha'apai *ha'pī*, island group of central Tonga, S Pacific, c.160 km N of Tongatapu; area 109.3 sq km; pop(1984) 8,561; main town Pangai (on Lifuka); with the exception of the live volcano Tofua, and the extinct volcano Kao, the islands of this group are flat and coralline; the famous mutiny on *HMS Bounty* took place in Ha'apai waters.

Haar'lem, HARLEM (Eng), 52 23N 4 38E, pop(1984e) 217,191, capital city of Noord Holland prov, W Netherlands; c.7 km from the North Sea coast, on the little R Spaarne, 19 km W of Amsterdam; part of the great conurbation or *Randstad* area; noted centre for tulip, hyacinth, crocus bulbs which are exported all over the world; founded in the 10th century and received its charter in 1245; Haarlem was sacked by the Spaniards (1573); the architect Lieven de Key (1560-1627) founded a school of building here; railway; economy: industrial chemicals and pharmaceuticals, publishing and printing, shipyards, railway works, machine and car-body works, food processing; monuments: 13-17th-c town hall, once the residence of the Counts of Holland; Grote Kerk (1472), one of the largest churches in the Netherlands.

Haarlemmermeer *har'lem-er-mayr*, 52 22N 4 39E, pop(1984e) 83,428, city in Noord Holland prov, W Netherlands; on a fertile polder, 10 km SE of Haarlem; this area of fenland was drained in 1839-52 and the city grew around the village of Hoofddorp.

Habana, La *a-vah'na*, HAVANA (Eng) ('the haven'), 23 07N 82 25W, pop(1983e) 1,972,363, capital city and prov (Ciudad de La Habana) of the Republic of Cuba, on the N coast of the island; San Cristóbal de La Habana, founded on the S coast by Diego Velásquez in 1515, was 4 years later transferred to its present site; the Plaza Revolucionaria is the focal point of modern La Habana with a monument to the national hero, José Martí, in the centre of the square; the main suburb is Marianao, 16 km W of the capital; Ernest Hemingway, a frequent visitor to La Habana, owned an estate on the outskirts of the city; area 740 sq km; university (1721); chief port of the republic; railway; airport; monuments: cathedral, built in Spanish style in 1704; presidential palace (1920); several old fortresses including La Fuerza (1538), the oldest building in Cuba; castles of El Morro (1589-1630) and La Punta (late 16th-c); International Conference Centre; event: carnival in July.

Habana, La, prov in W Cuba, encircling the city prov of Ciudad de La Habana on 3 sides, and bounded S by the Golfo de Batabaná, an inlet of the Caribbean Sea; area 5,671 sq km; pop(1981) 586,029; capital Güira de Melena.

Hab'ra, La, 33 56N 117 57W, pop(1980) 45,232, city in Orange county, SW California, United States; N of Fullerton.

Hachinohe *ha-chee-nō'hay*, 40 30N 141 30E, pop(1980) 238,179, town in Aomori prefecture, Tōhoku region, N Honshū island, Japan; on the E coast, on the Pacific Ocean; 72 km SE of Aomori; railway; economy: steel, iron, chemicals, paper, cement.

Hachiōji *ha-chee-ō'jee*, 35 40N 139 20E, pop(1980) 387,178, town in Tōkyo prefecture, Kanto region, central Honshū island, Japan; 40 km W of Tōkyo; a noted centre of silk weaving for 200 years; railway; economy: textiles, chemicals.

Hackensack, 40 53N 74 03W, pop(1980) 36,039, county seat of Bergen county, NE New Jersey, United States; on the Hackensack river, 11 km ESE of Paterson; named after an Indian tribe; settled by the Dutch in 1647 and later by the British in 1668; used as a camping ground by both sides during the War of Independence; a city since 1929; railway; economy: chemicals, engineering, glass, paper, furniture.

Hackney, 51 33N 0 03W, pop(1981) 180,434, borough of NE central Greater London, England; includes the suburbs of Hackney, Stoke Newington and Shoreditch; said to have been the first place near London provided with coaches let out for hire, hence the expression *hakney coach*, meaning 'a coach that can be hired'; Hackney Marsh is the biggest playing-field in London; railway.

Ḩaḑramawt *ha-dra-mowt'*, governorate of central South Yemen; formerly the Fifth Governorate; chief town Al Mukallā; an intermittent river valley region in South Yemen; extending approx 240 km W-E then SE to the Arabian Sea near Sayḩut; chief tributary Wadi Duan; it is a major agricultural region producing dates, honey, and tobacco.

Haddington, 55 58N 2 47W, pop(1981) 8,139, chief town of East Lothian dist, Lothian, E Scotland; on the R Tyne, 26 km E of Edinburgh; birthplace of John Knox (1505); one of the best-preserved towns in Scotland, Haddington has an almost complete medieval street plan; monuments: buildings include the town house (1748), designed by William Adam; 17th-c Nungate Bridge; St Mary's parish church (built in the late 14th and early 15th-c).

Hadera *hu-day'ru*, sub-district of Haifa dist, N Israel; bounded W by the Mediterranean Sea; pop(1983) 165,743; area 571 sq km.

Haderslev *ha'thers-lev*, HADERSLEBEN *ha-thers-lay'ben* (Ger), 55 15N 9 30E, pop(1981) 19,374, seaport on Haderslev Fjord, Sønderjylland county, SE Jylland (Jutland), Denmark; economy: engineering; monument: 13th-c cathedral.

Hadīthah, Al *ha-dee'thu*, town in Al-Anbār governorate, N central Iraq; on the W bank of the R Euphrates; airfield; railway; economy: power generation, oil refining.

Haeju or **Haiju** *ha-joo*, 38 04N 125 40E, capital of Hwanghainam prov, SW North Korea; a fishing port on an inlet of the Huang Hai (Yellow Sea).

Hafizabad *hah-fiz-ah-bad'*, 32 03N 73 42E, pop(1981) 83,000, city in Punjab prov, Pakistan; 48 km WSW of Gujranwala; railway; economy: trade in wheat, rice, millet and oilseed.

Hafnarfjörður, HAFNARFJÖRDHUR *hap-nur-fyur'door*, 64 04N 21 58W, fishing port in Suðurland, W Iceland; S of Reykjavík; pop(1983) 12,683, economy: fishing, aluminium, electrical appliances.

Hagen *hah'gen*, 51 22N 7 27E, pop(1983) 212,500, industrial city in Freiburg dist, Nordrhein-Westfalen (North Rhine-Westphalia) prov, W Germany; on N fringes of the Sauerland, extending into the valleys of the Ruhr, Ennepe, Lenne and Volme rivers, 48 km ENE of Düsseldorf; railway, situated at the junction of important traffic routes; economy: household goods, ironworking, manufacture of accumulators, foodstuffs, textiles, paper; the Westphalian Open-Air Museum of Technology is situated in the S of the city.

Hagerstown *hay'gerz-*, 39 39N 77 43W, pop(1980) 34,132, county seat of Washington county, NW Maryland, United States; 109 km WNW of Baltimore; railway.

Hague, The, city in the Netherlands. See 's-Gravenhage.

Haifa *hī'fa*, district in N Israel, bounded W by the Mediterranean Sea; divided into the sub-districts of Hadera and Haifa; pop(1983) 576,400; area 854 sq km; capital Haifa.

Haifa, HEFA, 32 49N 34 59E, pop(1982) 226,100, industrial centre and seaport in Haifa dist, NW Israel; on a peninsula which juts into the Mediterranean Sea; 3rd largest city in Israel; university (1963); airfield; railway;

economy: oil and the export of agricultural produce; monument: Bahai Shrine.

Hā'il *ha'il*, 27 28N 42 02E, pop(1974) 40,500, oasis town in Central prov, N Saudi Arabia; 592 km NW of Ar Riyāḍ (Riyadh); on caravan route between Al Madīnah (Medina) and Iraq; airfield.

Hail'sham, 50 52N 0 16E, pop(1981) 16,508, town N of Eastbourne in Wealden dist, East Sussex, SE England; 11 km N of Eastbourne.

Hainan *hī-nan*, island off the S coast of China; separated from the Leizhou Bandao (Luichow Peninsula) by the Qiongzhou Haixia (strait); a prefecture of Guangdong prov; includes the Li and Miao nationality aut areas; rises to 1,879 m at Wuzhi Shan; area 34,000 sq km; opened to tourism and foreign trade in 1982; economy: rubber, coconut, sugar, coffee, cocoa, betel nut, pineapple, fishing; reserves of over 50 minerals including limestone, marble, quartz, china clay and iron ore; principal cities Haikou, Dongfang and the resort port of Yulin; airport at Haikou; 18 ports on its 1,580 km coastline.

Hainaut *en-ō'*, formerly HAINAULT, HENEGOUW *hay'nug-ow* (Flem), HENNEGAU (Ger), prov of S Belgium; area 3,788 sq km; pop(1982) 1,296,719; comprises 7 dists of Ath, Charleroi, Mons, Mouscron, Soignies, Thuin and Tournai; capital Mons; chief towns Tournai, Charleroi and La Louvière; drained by the Schelde, Dender and Sambre rivers; flat and fertile in the N and W, occupied in the S by the spurs of the Ardennes; for long periods between the 11th and the 13th centuries it was united with Flanders; French Hainaut (now part of the dept of Nord) was separated in 1659.

Haiphong *hī-fong*, 20 50N 106 41E, pop(1979e) 1,279,667, seaport in N Vietnam, Indo-China; in the delta of the Red river, 88 km SE of Hanoi and 36 km from the Gulf of Tonkin; established in 1874; 3rd largest city in Vietnam; rail link to Kunming in Yunnan prov, China; economy: plastics, textiles, phosphates, rice.

Haiti *hay'tee, a-ee-tee'* (Fr), official name Republic of Haiti, RÉPUBLIQUE D'HAITI (Fr), republic in the West Indies, occupying the W third of the island of Hispaniola, 80 km E of Cuba; timezone GMT −5; area 27,750 sq km; capital Port-au-Prince; chief towns Port-de-Paix, Cap-Haïtien, Gonaïves, and Les Cayes; pop(1986e) 6,758,000; the majority of the pop is pure Negro (95%), the remainder chiefly mulatto and European; Roman Catholicism and voodoo are the main religions; French, the official language, is spoken by only 10% of the population; Creole French is widely spoken; the unit of currency is the gourde of 100 centimes; membership: UN, FAO, G-77, GATT, IADB, IAEA, IBA, IBRD, ICAO, ICO, IDA, IDB, IFAD, IFC, ILO, IMF, IMO, INTELSAT, INTERPOL, IRC, ITU, OAS, PAHO, SELA, UNESCO, UPU, WHO, WMO, WTO.

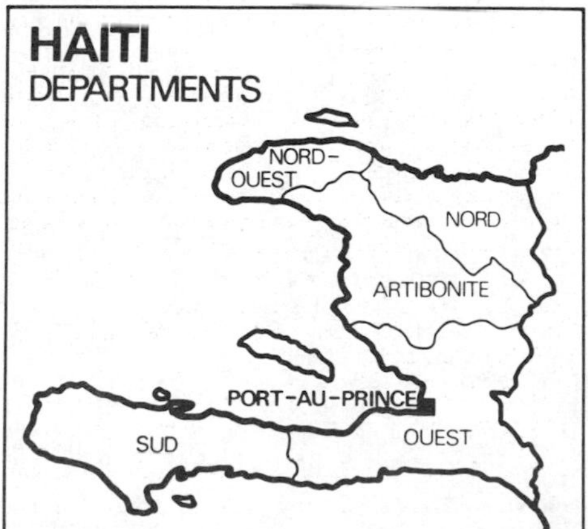

Physical description. Haiti consists of 2 mountainous peninsulas separated by the Golfe de la Gonâve, a deep bay. Mountain and valley topography in general trends WNW to ESE. The Massif du Nord in the N peninsula extends across the border into the Dominican Republic. Several of its ridges rise above 1,500 m. The S peninsula consists of the Massif de la Hotte and, further E, Massif de la Selle. Haiti's highest peak is La Selle (2,280 m). Between these 2 main masses is a deep structural depression called Plaine du Cul-de-Sac, extending from Port-au-Prince to the E side of the country. The plain of the R Artibonite and the Plateau Central are other areas of lowland. The islands of Gonâve, off the W coast, and Tortue, off the N coast, are geologically associated with the surface features of Haiti.

Climate. The climate is tropical maritime with mean monthly temperatures ranging from 24°C to 29°C. Rainfall varies quite considerably over short distances. The annual average over much of the N coast and the mountainous areas of the interior is 1,475 mm to 1,950 mm, but only 500 mm over the leeward or W side of the country. The wet season extends from May to Sept.

History, government and constitution. The island of Hispaniola was discovered by Columbus in 1492. Haiti was created when, under the Treaty of Ryswick (1697), the W third of the island was ceded to France. The country declared its independence in 1804, and from 1822 to 1844, Haiti and Santo Domingo (Dominican Republic), the E part of Hispaniola, were united. From 1915 to 1934 Haiti was under US occupation. The 1957 constitution, as subsequently amended, provides for an executive president who is elected for life. The president is assisted by an appointed council of about 15 secretaries of state. There is also a unicameral National Assembly of 58 deputies elected for 6-year terms by universal suffrage.

Economy. Haiti's economy is based on agriculture which employs 70% of the workforce. Typical holding size is no more than 0.015 sq km. Large plantations, growing coffee, sugar, and sisal, occupy 10% of the arable land area. Other crops include rice, corn, sorghum, and cocoa. New varieties of rice should significantly boost future production, especially in the Artibonite valley. Major industries include sugar refining, textiles, flour milling, cement manufacturing, bauxite mining, tourism, and light assembly industries. Chief exports are coffee, light industrial products, bauxite, essential oils, and sisal. The USA is the main trading partner.

Administrative divisions. Despite constitutional provision for 9 administrative divisions, Haiti is currently divided into 5 departments as follows:

Department	*area (sq km)*	*pop(1977)*
Nord-Ouest	2,750	247,326
Nord	4,100	747,360
Artibonite	6,800	748,357
Ouest	7,900	1,983,826
Sud	6,200	1,041,232

Ha'jar, coastal mountain range in N Oman, SE Arabian peninsula; extends approx 480 km NW-SE parallel to coast of the Gulf of Oman; comprises a series of limestone ridges and tablelands; divided by the Wadi Samā'il into W (Al Hajar al Gharbī) and E (Al Hajar ash Sharqī) sections; the W Hajar is separated from the Gulf of Oman by the fertile Bāṭinah coastal plain; the highest part of the range is the Jabal Akhdar which rises to 3,018 m.

Hajdú-Bihar *hoy'doo-bee'hor*, county in E Hungary; in NE Great Plains (Alföld); drained by the Hortobagy, Berretyo and Kösely rivers; pop(1984e) 552,000; area 6,212 sq km; capital Debrecen; chief towns include Hajdúszoboszló and Hajdúböszörmény; local breeds of cattle are preserved at Hortobágy national park; economy: a flat agricultural region producing grain, vegetables, wine and livestock.

Hajdúböszörmény *hoy'doo-bü'sür-mayny'*, 47 40N 21 30E, pop(1984e) 32,000, town in Hajdú-Bihar county, E Hungary; NNW of Debrecen; livestock trade.

Hajdúszoboszló *hoy'doo-so'bos-lō*, 47 27N 21 22E, pop(1984e) 24,000, resort town in Hajdú-Bihar county, E Hungary; SW of Debrecen; medicinal springs containing iodine, bromine, natrium chloride and bitumen were discovered here in the 1920s when drilling for oil near Hortobágy.

Haka', 22 42N 93 41E, capital of Chin state, NW Burma; W of R Chindwin, near the Indian frontier.

Hakkâri *hak-ya-ree'*, mountainous prov in SE Turkey; bounded E by Iran and S by Iraq; pop(1980) 155,463; area 9,521 sq km; capital Hakkâri; economy: cereals, naphtha.

Hakodate *ha-kō-da'tay*, 41 46N 140 44E, pop(1980) 320,154, port in Hokkaidō prefecture, SW Hokkaidō island, Japan; on a small peninsula in the Tsugaru-kaikyō Strait; one of the first towns to be opened to foreigners after the Treaty of Kanagawa in 1854; former capital of Hokkaidō I; railway; airport at 7 km; economy: fishing, shipbuilding, food processing, cement, timber products; monuments: regional museum containing local archaeological finds and relics of the Ainu civilization; near Hakodate is a Trappist convent founded by French nuns in the 19th century; 6 km from the convent is the Yunokawa onsen hot spring; its waters have a temperature of 30°-60°C and are known for their curative properties; event: snow and ice festival at the end of Jan.

Ḥalab *ha-leb'*, ALEPPO *u-le'pō*, governorate (*mohofazat*) in N Syria; bounded N by Turkey; pop(1981) 1,878,701; capital Ḥalab; chief towns Al Bāb and Manbij; the Buḥayrat al Asad lake forms part of the E border.

Ḥalab, 36 12N 37 10E, pop(1981) 976,727, capital city of Ḥalab governorate, NW Syria; 350 km N of Dimashq (Damascus); chief commercial and industrial centre of N Syria; university (1960); airport; road and rail junction; monuments: citadel, numerous mosques; economy: industrial refrigeration plant; event: Cotton Festival (Sept).

Halden *hal'dun*, formerly FREDRIKSHALD, 59 08N 11 13E, pop(1983) 26,219, seaport and frontier town in SE Østfold county, SE Norway; near the Swedish border, on the Skagerrak; railway; Halden Canal; economy: woodworking, boot and shoe manufacturing; principal area for the timber trade in E Norway; monument: nearby is the 17th-c castle of Fredriksten.

Haleakala Crater *ha-lay-a-ka-la'*, KOLEKOLE, 20 42N 156 16W, dormant volcano in E Maui island, Hawaii, United States; rises to 3,055 m; contains the largest inactive crater in the world: area 49 sq km; 610 m deep, 12 km long, 3.8 km wide and 32 km in circumference; situated in Haleakala National Park.

Halesowen *haylz-ō'wn*, 52 26N 2 05W, pop(1981) 57,532, town in Birmingham borough, West Midlands, central England; 11 km W of Birmingham; economy: engineering, machinery, machine tools, iron founding.

Half Moon Cay, 17 12N 88 33W, small island in W Caribbean Sea, at the S end of Lighthouse Reef, Belize dist; E of Belize City, noted for its breeding colony of red-footed boobies and man-o'-war birds; declared a Crown reserve in 1928 and a natural monument of Belize in 1982; area 0.15 sq km.

Halibut, oil field in the Bass Strait, off the S coast of Victoria, Australia.

Halifax, 44 38N 63 35W, pop(1981) 114,594, seaport capital of Nova Scotia prov, SE Canada; on the E coast of Nova Scotia on a small peninsula; a major transatlantic port and rail terminus; Halifax is joined to the city of Dartmouth to the NE by 2 suspension bridges; the city was founded in 1749 as a military and naval base for the British forces; used in the 1758 expedition against Louisburg, and for British operations in the American Revolution and the War of 1812; a British garrison was stationed here until 1906; Halifax was used as a naval base, convoy terminal and port of embarkation in both world wars; in 1917 a vessel carrying explosives was rammed in the harbour, causing 2,000 fatalities, 10,000 casualties and major damage; this is said to have been the largest single man-made explosion prior to the atomic bomb; in 1945 the naval arsenal exploded; the *Halifax Gazette*, established in 1752, was the first Canadian newspaper; in 1912 victims of the *Titanic* disaster were buried in the suburb of Fairview; University of King's College (1789); St Mary's University (1802); Dalhousie University (1818); Mount St Vincent University (1925); Nova Scotia Technical College (1907); railway; airport; economy: clothing, furniture, food processing, trade in fish and timber; monuments: the Historic Properties area was originally built in the 1800s and was the business centre for the town, among the buildings here are Collins Bank and the Privateers' Warehouse, a stone building which housed cargoes captured by Nova Scotia schooners acting as privateers until the captured ships and cargoes could be auctioned off by the Admiralty; in the centre of Halifax is Citadel Hill (height 82 m) which was formed by glacial deposits; it is now a National Historic Park with museums on the pioneer and military life of early Halifax; a cannon is fired from here every day at noon; the main exhibit of the Maritime Museum of the Atlantic is the 900-ton hydrographic ship, the *Acadia*, which charted the Labrador and Arctic coasts in the early 20th century.

Halifax, 53 44N 1 52W, pop(1981) 77,354, town in Calderdale borough, West Yorkshire, N England; part of Halifax-Sowerby Bridge urban area; on the R Calder, 11 km SW of Bradford; a noted medieval cloth-manufacturing town; railway; economy: textiles, carpets, clothing, engineering.

Halla san, 33 25N 126 30E, highest peak in Korea at 1,950 m; situated on Cheju island off the SW coast of South Korea in Halla san National Park (area 19 sq km; established in 1973).

Halland *ha'land*, a county of SW Sweden, bounded on the W by the Kattegat where there are excellent beaches; the Nissan and Lagan rivers flow across S part of the county; land area 5,448 sq km; pop(1983) 234,388; capital Halmstad; chief towns Varberg and Falkenberg.

Hallandale, 25 59N 80 08W, pop(1980) 36,517, town in Broward county, SE Florida, United States; on the Atlantic Ocean, 24 km N of Miami.

Halle *ha'le*, HAL (Fr), 50 44N 4 14E, pop(1982) 32,249, industrial town in Halle-Vilvoorde dist, W Brabant prov, Belgium; 15 km SW of Bruxelles, on the R Senne and on the canal linking Bruxelles with Charleroi; a well-known place of pilgrimage; close to the linguistic border between Flanders and Wallonia; railway; economy: textiles, leather, foodstuffs, blast furnaces; monument: basilica of Our Lady (14-15th-c).

Halle, county in SW central East Germany; watered by Saale and Elbe rivers; pop(1981) 1,821,690; area 8,771 sq km; major industrial region with chemicals produced at Wittenburg, Wolfen, Halle and Bitterfeld; the new town of Halle Neustadt was specially built for chemical workers; mechanical engineering, rolling stock and footwear are other important industries; there are 83 nature reserves.

Halle, HALLE AN DER SAALE, 51 29N 12 0E, pop(1982) 233,437, capital of Halle county, SW central East Germany; NW of Leipzig, on R Saale; university; Academy of Agricultural Science; birthplace of Georg Friedrich Handel; railway; economy: mechanical engineering, rolling stock, chemicals stock.

Halle Neustadt *ha'lu noy'shtaht*, 51 28N 11 58E, pop(1981) 91,809, city in Halle dist, Halle, SW central East Germany; on the R Saale, on the NW outskirts of Halle; a new town developed for the chemical workers of Halle; railway.

Halle-Vilvoorde *hal'le-veel-vord*, HAL-VILVORDE (Fr), dist of Brabant prov, Belgium; area 943 sq km; pop(1982) 518,962.

Hallig Islands, island group in the North Sea, off NW Germany. See Halligen, Die.

Halligen, Die *dee ha'li-gun*, HALLIG IS *hah'lig* (Eng), island group of the Nordfriesische Inseln (North Frisian Is), NW Germany, in the North Sea, off Schleswig-Holstein coast; eleven islands in total, including Nordstrand, Pellworm, Nordmarsch-Langeness and Hooge.

Hallingskarvet *hal'lin-skar-vet*, HALLINGSKARV, mountain range in S Norway, forming NE section of the Hardangervidda plateau; rises to 1,934 m, 16 km E of Finse; extends 96 km E to W.

Hallstatt *hal'shtat*, 47 34N 13 39E, pop(1981) 1,500, small market town in the Salzkammergut of Oberösterreich state, N Austria; on the SW shore of Hallstätter See, 50 km SE of Salzburg; the first phase of the European Iron Age (8-4th century BC) is known as the Hallstatt period and is characterized by goods from the prehistoric burial tombs found in this area; salt has been mined here for many centuries; event: lake procession at Corpus Christi.

Hallyŏsudo, HALLYŎ WATERWAY, marine national park, Kyŏngsangnam prov, SE Korea; follows SE coastline, from the town of Yŏsu eastwards to near Pusan; the park is the site of an oyster raising industry and encompasses over 400 islands and islets; it was here that Admiral Yi Sun-shin defeated the Japanese in several sea battles during the Japanese invasions of the late 16th century; in 1592 Admiral Yi Sun-shin invented iron-clad warships with as many as 26 cannon on either side; also in the park is Kŏjedo island, Korea's 2nd largest island, situated SW of Pusan and site of a prisoner-of-war camp during the Korean War; the 479-sq km national park was established in 1968.

Halmahera *hal-ma-her'a*, formerly DJAILOLO, island in Maluku prov (Moluccas), Indonesia; largest island of the Moluccas group, situated on the Equator SW of the Philippines; area 17,936 sq km; taken by the Dutch in 1683.

Halm'stad, 56 41N 12 55E, pop(1982) 76,392, seaport and capital city of Halland county, SW Sweden, on the Kattegat; received municipal charter in 1307; the town was rebuilt after a fire in 1619; the old town still preserves the style of that period; railway; economy: tourism, textiles, pulp, paper, dairy produce; monuments: 14th-c church, early 17th-c castle.

Hälsingborg *hel'sing-bor-ye*, HELSINGBORG (Eng), 56 03N 12 43E, pop(1982) 102,951, seaport and commercial town on W coast of Malmöhus county, SW Sweden; on the Øresund (The Sound) opposite Helsingør, Denmark; part of Denmark before 1658; railway; ferry services to Denmark; economy: textiles, machinery, copper-refining, fertilizers and trade in chemicals, timber and paper; monuments: neo-Gothic town hall (1897), 13th-c St Mary's church.

Haltiatunturi *hal'tee-ah-toon'too-ree*, HADEFJALL *hard'a-fyel* (Swed), MT HALTI OR HALTIA *hal'tee-ah* (Eng), 69 17N 21 15E, a mountain in Lappi prov, NW Finland, on the Norwegian frontier; height 1,328 m.

Haltom City, 32 48N 97 16W, pop(1980) 29,014, town in Tarrant county, NE Texas, United States; a suburb 8 km NE of Fort Worth.

Hamadān *ha'ma-dan*, mountainous prov in W Iran; pop(1982) 1,046,628; area 20,172 sq km; capital Hamadān.

Hamadān, 34 48N 48 30E, pop(1983) 234,473, capital city of Hamadān dist, Hamadān, W Iran, 280 km WSW of Tehrān; trade centre for surrounding agricultural region (fruit and grain); alt 1,830 m; economy: noted for its rugs, leather, wood and metal products; monument: tomb of Avicenna (died here in 1037).

Ḩamāh *ha'ma*, governorate (*mohofazat*) in W central Syria; pop(1981) 736,412; capital Ḩamāh; mainly desert except for the area in the vicinity of Ḩamāh which is irrigated by the R 'Āsi (Orontes).

Ḩamāh, EPIPHANIA, 35 09N 36 44E, pop(1981) 176,640, capital town of Ḩamāh governorate W central Syria; 140 km S of Ḩalab (Aleppo); situated on the R 'Āsi (Orontes) where ancient *norias* (waterwheels) are still in operation; university (1960); railway; road junction; monuments: citadel, Azem Palace (now a museum of Islamic art), Great Mosque; economy: agricultural trade, tourism, iron and steel production.

Hamamatsu *ha-ma-mat'tsoo*, 34 42N 137 42E, pop(1980) 490,824, town in Shizuoka prefecture, Chūbu region, central Honshū island, Japan; on the S coast, on the Pacific Ocean, 68 km WSW of Shizuoka; railway; economy: textiles, chemicals, tea, motorcycles, musical instruments.

Hamar *hah'mahr*, formerly STORHAMMER, 60 57N 10 55E, pop(1980) 15,904, agric market town on L Mjøsa, N of Oslo, capital of Hedmark county, E Norway; founded 1152 by the English pope, Adrian IV, the original town was destroyed by the Swedes in 1567; railway; monument: to the W of the town there are ruins of a 12th-c cathedral.

Hambantota *ham-bun-tō'ta*, 6 00N 81 00E, pop(1981) 8,577, town in Hambantota dist, Southern prov, Sri Lanka; on S coast.

Hamburg, 53 33N 10 00E, pop(1983) 1,617,800, industrial port and cultural city on the R Elbe, 109 km from its mouth at Cuxhaven; constitutes a prov of W Germany; area 755 sq km (including the islands of Neuwerk and Scharhörn); university (1919); founded by Charlemagne in the 9th century, Hamburg formed an alliance with Lübeck in the 12th century which eventually led to the formation of the Hanseatic League; largest German port and major European port, and Germany's largest city after Berlin; railway; economy: merchant, fishing and naval vessels (built and serviced), oil, aluminium, copper, zinc, metalworking, electronics, engineering, aircraft, motor vehicles, electrical equipment, packaging, rubber, cosmetics, chemicals, petrochemicals, foodstuffs, brewing, cigarettes; monuments: Renaissance-style town hall (1886-97), St Michael's church (1750-62); events: Hamburger Dom (Nov-Dec); international boat show.

Häme *ha'me*, TAVASTEHUS (Swed), a prov of S Finland; area 19,802 sq km; pop(1982) 668,839; Hämeenlinna is the prov capital although Tampere, near the W border with Turku-Pori prov, is the largest town; the prov is studded with many lakes with L Paijanne forming the E border.

Hämeenlinna *ham'en-leen-a*, TAVASTEHUS *ta-vas'te-hoos* (Swed), 61 00N 24 25E, pop(1982) 42,042, capital town of Häme prov, S Finland; on L Vanajavesi with the Hattelmala hills bounding it to the S; established in 1639; birthplace of the composer Jean Sibelius (1865-1957) and the poet Paavo Cajander (1846-1913); Aulanko National Park is 4.5 km to the N; economy: wood and metal industries.

Hamelin, town in W Germany. See Hameln.

Ham'eln, formerly HAMELIN, 52 07N 9 24E, pop(1983) 57,000, manufacturing town in Hannover dist, S Niedersachsen (Lower Saxony) prov, W Germany; on the R Weser, 40 km SW of Hannover; former medieval market town; famous as the city of the Pied Piper; railway; economy: milling, carpets; monuments: Minster of St Boniface (11-14th-c); events: 'Pied Piper' play (July-Oct).

Hamersley Range *hay'merz-li*, mountain range in NW Western Australia; runs parallel to and S of the Fortescue river; extends 257 km ESE from the Robe river as far as Newman; rises to 1,244 m at Mt Meharry; the great iron-bearing area of Western Australia; the 6,176 sq km Hamersley Range national park was established in 1969.

Hamgyŏngnam, SOUTH HAMGYONG, prov in NE North Korea; bordered SE by the Sea of Japan and the Choson-Man bay; capital Hamhŭng.

Hamgyŏngpuk *ham-gyung-puk*, NORTH HAMGYONG, prov in NE North Korea; bordered N by Jilin prov, China along the R Tumen, E by the Sea of Japan and by the USSR in the extreme NE; capital Ch'ŏngjin.

Hamhŭng *ham-hoong*, 39 54N 127 35E, pop(1972) 420,000, capital of Hamgyŏngnam (South Hamgyong) prov, E North Korea; railway.

Ham'ilton, 37 45S 142 04E, pop(1983e) 10,090, town in South Western stat div, W Victoria, Australia; 280 km W of Melbourne; centre of a sheep-farming area; railway;

airfield; Hamilton community parklands includes a major sporting complex.

Hamilton, parish on the Main Island of Bermuda; pop(1980) 3,784.

Hamilton, 32 18N 64 48W, port, resort and capital of Bermuda, situated in the parish of Hamilton on Great Bermuda or Main I; pop(1980) 1,617, it has a deep harbour approached by a long intricate channel through Two Rock Passage; the port has modern berthing and container facilities for both passenger and cargo ships; founded in 1612; capital of Bermuda since 1815; Bermuda College is based at the Stonington Campus.

Hamilton, 43 15N 79 50W, pop(1981) 306,434, town in SE Ontario, SE Canada; on Hamilton harbour at head (W) of L Ontario; 58 km SW of Toronto; founded in 1813 by George Hamilton; the battle of Stoney Creek took place here in the same year, the battlefield is now a public park; McMaster University (1887); railway; economy: textiles, steel, agricultural machinery, electrical equipment.

Hamilton, 37 46S 175 18E, pop(1981) 91,109, city on North Island, New Zealand; on the R Waikato; New Zealand's largest inland city; noted for horse breeding and agricultural research; N of Hamilton is the town of Ngaruawahia and the Turangawaewae Marae, home of the Maori Queen, where a regatta is held each March; Waikato University (1964); railway; airfield; economy: trade in dairy farm, market garden and forest products; monuments: Waikato art museum contains a collection of Maori artifacts.

Hamilton, 55 47N 4 03W, pop(1981) 51,718, capital of Hamilton dist, Strathclyde, W central Scotland; in Clydeside urban area, 17 km SE of Glasgow; railway; economy: electronics; monuments: the Cameronians Regimental Museum contains a display on the regiment and on the Covenanters; Hamilton district museum; the Old Parish Church (1734) is Hamilton's oldest church and the only church designed by William Adam; just outside Hamilton is Strathclyde country park, which contains Hamilton mausoleum, built in the 1840s by the 10th Duke of Hamilton.

Hamilton, 39 24N 84 34W, pop(1980) 63,189, county seat of Butler county, SW Ohio, United States; on the Great Miami river, 32 km N of Cincinnati; railway.

Hamina *ha'meen-a*, FREDRIKSHAMN *fray'dreeks-ha'man* (Swed), 60 33N 27 15E, pop(1982) 10,369, major port in Kymi prov, SE Finland; situated on a peninsula in the bay of Vehkalahti in the Gulf of Finland, 43 km from the Soviet border, the only crossing open to foreign vehicles; established in 1653; in 1753 the town was named after King Fredrik I of Sweden; in 1809 the Treaty of Hamina ceded the whole of Finland to Russia; economy: timber exports.

Ham'mamet, SIAGU (Lat), 36 25N 10 40E, resort town in NE Tunisia, N Africa; 70 km SE of Tunis on the Mediterranean coast, 85 km N of Sousse; event: International Festival of Hammamet in July-Aug.

Ham'mersmith and Fulham *fool'am*, 51 30N 0 14W, pop(1981) 148,447, borough of W central Greater London, England; N of R Thames; Fulham is the residence of the Bishop of London; location of Wormwood Scrubs prison, Olympia exhibition centre and White City athletics stadium; railway; events: photo world exhibition (May); fine art and antiques fair (June).

Hammond, 41 38N 87 30W, pop(1980) 93,714, town in Lake county, NW Indiana, United States; on the Illinois state border, 32 km SSE of Chicago; railway; economy: steel.

Hampshire, county of S England; bounded S by the English Channel, E by West Sussex and Surrey, N by Berkshire and W by Wiltshire and Dorset; crossed by the North Downs in the NW and W; W of Southampton is the New Forest; pop(1981) 1,466,385; area 3,777 sq km; county town Winchester; chief towns Portsmouth, Southampton; economy: livestock, oil refining, chemicals, pharmaceuticals, electronics, tourism; the county is divided into 13 districts:

District	*area (sq km)*	*pop(1981)*
Basingstoke and Deane	637	130,526
East Hampshire	515	90,613
Eastleigh	80	92,954
Fareham	74	88,609
Gosport	25	78,083
Hart	218	76,158
Havant	56	117,428
New Forest	753	146,134
Portsmouth	37	180,066
Rushmoor	36	78,243
Southampton	49	205,337
Test Valley	637	91,407
Winchester	659	90,827

Hampton, 37 02N 76 21W, pop(1980) 122,617, independent city, SE Virginia, United States; on the Hampton Roads channel, 7 km NE of Newport News; railway; economy: fisheries; monument: nearby is Fort Monroe where Jefferson Davis was imprisoned for 2 years after the Civil War.

Hampton Roads, a channel at the mouth of the James river where it meets Chesapeake Bay, Virginia, United States.

Hamrun *hahm-roon'*, 35 53N 14 30E, pop(1983e) 14,033, industrial town in N central Malta; 3 km SW of Valletta.

Hanau *han'ow*, 50 08N 8 56E, pop(1983) 86,000, industrial city in Darmstadt dist, SE Hessen (Hesse) prov, W Germany; on the R Main, 18 km E of Frankfurt; birthplace of the brothers Jacob and Wilhelm Grimm, authors of the famous fairy tales; railway; economy: precious metals, chemicals, dyestuffs, industrial equipment, galvanizing materials.

Handa, island and nature reserve 5 km NW of Scourie, Sutherland dist, Highland region, NW Scotland; a seabird sanctuary noted for its vast numbers of fulmars, gulls, kittiwakes, shags and skuas.

Handan *hahn-tahn*, HAN-TAN, 36 37N 114 25E, pop(1984e) 954,300, city in S Hebei prov, N China; railway.

Hangang *han-gang*, HAN, 2nd longest river in Korea; rises in the mountains of central Korea; flows 514 km NW past Sŏul to enter the Huang Hai Sea near the border with North Korea.

Hangchow, capital of Zhejiang prov, E China. See Hangzhou.

Hangzhou *hang-jō*, HANGCHOW, 30 18N 120 07E, pop(1984e) 1,222,900, capital of Zhejiang prov, E China; on the Qiantang river at the S end of the Grand Canal which links it to Beijing (Peking); founded in 2200 BC; after the 6th century AD, owing to the extension of the Grand Canal, it grew rapidly as a trade and administration centre; capital of several kingdoms and dynasties between the 8th and 12th centuries; technical university (1927); university (1959); railway; airfield; economy: iron and steel, refining, engineering, hydroelectric power, silk, trade in bamboo, wheat, barley, rice, cotton, sweet potatoes, tea; monument: on the W shore of the West Lake is the monastery of the Spirits' Retreat, a Buddhist temple founded in 326 AD.

Haninge *hah'ning-e*, 59 06N 18 11E, pop(1982) 59,670, town in Stockholm county, SE Sweden, a S suburb of Stockholm.

Hanko *hang'ko*, HANGO *hang'u* (Swed), 59 50N 23 00E, pop(1982) 12,224, industrial town, resort and free port in Uudenmaa prov, S Finland; situated on a peninsula, it is Finland's southernmost town; established in 1874; rail ferry terminal; events: tennis tournament and international sailing regatta in July.

Han-kou, Han-kow, capital of Hubei prov, E central China. See Wuhan.

Hann'over, HANOVER (Eng), dist of Niedersachsen (Lower Saxony) prov, W Germany; pop(1983) 2,038,000; area 9,043 sq km; capital Hannover; formerly a state of NW Germany and an electorate of the Holy Roman Empire (1692-1806), it later became a kingdom (1814-66) and then a province of Prussia (1866-1945).

Hannover, 52 23N 9 44E, pop(1983) 524,300, commercial and industrial capital city of Niedersachsen (Lower Saxony) prov, W Germany, in Hannover dist; on the right bank of the R Leine, 56 km WNW of Braunschweig (Brunswick); chartered in 1241, it became the home of the dukes of Brunswick-Lüneburg (later electors of Hannover) in the early 17th century; technical university (1831); university of medicine (1961); university of veterinary medicine (1913); railway; on the Mittelland Canal; economy: electronics, motor vehicles, tyres, non-ferrous metals, cement, pharmaceuticals, brewing, civil engineering, construction equipment, chemicals (rubber), foodstuffs; monuments: neo-classical Opera House (1845-52), Leine Palace; Gothic Old Town Hall (15th-c); events: Hannover Trade Fair (end April), International Aviation Trade Fair (every 2 years).

Hanoi *ha-noy'*, 21 01N 105 52E, pop(1979e) 2,570,905, capital of Vietnam, Indo-China; situated on Red R, N Vietnam, 88 km W of Haiphong; capital of French Indo-China (1887-1946); university (1956); centre of industry and transport; economy: textiles, tanning, brewing, engineering, rice milling, coal, food processing, tapioca, sesame, millet, wood products, resins and gums, footwear.

Hanover, dist and city in W Germany. See Hannover.

Hanover Park, 41 59N 88 09W, pop(1980) 28,850, town in Cook county, NE Illinois, United States; 43 km WNW of Chicago.

Han-tan, town in Hebei prov, N China. See Handan.

Har Us Nuur, salt lake in W Mongolia; W of Hovd; length 64.4 km.

Ḩaraḑ *har-adh'*, 24 15N 49 00E, pop(1974) 100,000, oil town in Eastern prov, E central Saudi Arabia; 256 km SSW of Az̧ Z̧ahran (Dhahran); railway; airfield; economy: oil (discovered 1949), irrigation.

Harare *ha-rah'ray*, formerly SALISBURY, 17 43S 31 05E, pop(1982) 656,000, capital and largest city of Zimbabwe, S Africa; in Mashonaland East prov at an alt of 1,473 m, 370 km NE of Bulawayo; founded in 1890 and named after Lord Salisbury; railway from Beira on the Indian Ocean coast of Mozambique reached here in 1899; known as the 'sunshine city'; international conference centre; horse-racing and trotting tracks; motor-racing circuit; railway; airport; economy: administration, banking, commerce, asphalt, refrigeration services, plastic packaging, polythene products, agricultural equipment, graphic supplies, paints, adhesives, construction materials, timber, electrical equipment; monuments: Queen Victoria museum; national gallery; national archives; national botanical garden.

Har'bel, 6 19N 10 20W, pop(1981) 60,000, town in Liberia, W Africa; 52 km E of Monrovia on the R Farmington.

Harbin *har'bin*, HAERHPIN, formerly PINKIANG, 45 54N 126 41E, pop(1983e) 2,560,000, capital of Heilongjiang prov, NE China; industrial centre on the Manchurian plain on the Songhua (Sungari) river; founded in the 12th century, Harbin developed as a fishing village; after the construction of the Chinese Eastern Railroad it became a major rail junction; c.500,000 'white' Russians fled to the town after the Russian Revolution of 1917, successfully dominating the city and giving it its Russian flavour; railway; airfield; economy: power-generating equipment, food processing, machinery, linen, sugar refining, paper; monuments: in the public square there is a monument to the Russians who died in World War II; the principal area for recreation, with swimming and boating, is Stalin Park; Harbin Zoo (1954) has successfully bred the rare north-east China tiger; event: the Harbin Summer Music Festival in July.

Hardang'erfjorden, HARDANGER FJORD, *hahr'dang-er* (Eng), inlet of the North Sea, Hordaland county, on SW coast of Norway; extends 179 km inland NE and E; max depth 830 m.

Hardangervidda, *hahr-dang'er-vid-dah*, HARDANGER PLATEAU OF THE VIDDA (Eng), extensive mountain plateau in SW Norway, extending 160 km between the head of Hardangerfjorden (Hardanger Fjord) and the Hallingdal valley; barren bedrock area with an average elevation of 1,067 m, rising to 1,862 m at Hardangerjøkulen; other peaks include Sandfloeggji, Hårteigen and Solfonn; winter sports and tourist area.

Hārer, HARAR, 9 20N 42 10E, pop(1984e) 62,160, capital of Hārergē region, SE Ethiopia, NE Africa; on the edge of the Rift Valley, 360 km E of Addis Ababa; a favourable location on fertile land between the Danakil and Ogaden areas and a temperate climate led to Hārer becoming an important centre for food supply and trade after the 7th century; it reached its peak of eminence during the 16th century; sacked in 1542 and although gradually rebuilt it was never to recover its former status; cave paintings indicate early habitation of this part of NE Africa; visited by the explorer Richard Burton and the French poet Rimbaud; the latter's house still stands; occupied by Egypt between 1875 and 1885; damaged during Italian-Abyssinian War (1936); taken by British forces during 1941; nearby is the village of Kolubi (45 km) where the annual renewal of the miracle of St Gabriel is celebrated each Dec.

Hārergē *ha'rur-ge*, semi-arid region in SE Ethiopia, NE Africa; pop(1984e) 4,151,706; area 259,700 sq km; a generally low lying region with a mountainous spur separating the Ogaden area (SE) from the Ādal-Esa area NW; a few small lakes in the extreme NW include L Kaddabasa and Beda Hāyk'; capital Hārer; chief towns Jijiga, Dirē Dawa.

Hargeysa *har-gay'sa*, 9 31N 44 02E, pop(1982) 70,000, town in Woqooyi Galbeed prov, Somalia, NE Africa; 145 km SW of Berbera; was summer capital (the winter capital being Berbera) of British Somaliland until 1941 when it became the permanent capital; airport.

Harghita *har-gyeet'a*, county in NE Romania, in the W Carpathians; pop(1983) 351,609; area 6,610 sq km; capital Miercurea-Ciuc.

Haringey *har'ing-gay*, 51 35N 0 07W, pop(1981) 203,553, residential borough of N central Greater London, England; includes the suburbs of Wood Green, Hornsey and Tottenham; railway.

Har'lingen, 26 12N 97 42W, pop(1980) 43,543, town in Cameron county, S Texas, United States; 38 km NW of Brownsville; railway; economy: shipping and processing centre in a farming area producing fruit, vegetables and cotton; manufactures include clothing, aircraft, and metal and concrete products.

Harlow *har'lō*, 51 47N 0 08E, pop(1981) 79,521, town co-extensive with Harlow dist, Essex, SE England; 33 km NE of London; designated a 'new town' in 1947; railway; economy: electronics.

Harmanli, town in Bulgaria. See Kharmanly.

Härnösand *her'nœ-sand*, HERNOSAND, 62 37N 17 55E, pop(1982) 27,760, seaport and capital town of Västernorrland county, E Sweden; its centre is on an island at the mouth of the Ångermanälven R in the Gulf of Bothnia; see of a bishop since 1772; railway; formerly an important trading and market town; chartered in 1585; plundered and burnt by the Russians 1721.

Har'penden, 51 49N 0 22W, pop(1981) 28,797, residential town in St Albans dist, Hertfordshire, SE England; 7 km N of St Albans; Rothamsted agricultural experimental station is nearby; railway; economy: electrical goods.

Harper, CAPE PALMAS, 4 25N 7 43W, seaport in Liberia, W Africa; 410 km SE of Monrovia; airfield.

Harris, S part of the Lewis-with-Harris island district in the Western Isles of Scotland; area c. 500 sq km; ferry links between Tarbert and Uig (Skye) and Lochmaddy (N Uist).

Harrisburg, 40 16N 76 53W, pop(1980) 53,264, capital of state in Dauphin county, S Pennsylvania, United States; on the R Susquehanna, 157 km WNW of Philadelphia; scene of many important conventions, in particular the Harrisburg Convention of 1788; site of Camp Curtin, the first Union camp in the Civil War; scene of nuclear power station accident on Three Mile Island; railway; economy:

former steel industry giving way to a more diversified economy based on textiles, paper, machinery, food processing, bricks.

Harrogate *har'u-gayt*, 54 00N 1 33W, pop(1981) 64,915, spa town and conference centre in Harrogate dist, North Yorkshire, N England; 20 km N of Leeds; 88 sulphur, saline and chalybeate springs; railway; monument: Royal Pump Room; events: International Youth Music (April); International Festival of Cycling (June); International Festival (July-Aug).

Harrow *ha'rō*, 51 35N 0 21W, pop(1981) 195,478, residential borough of NW Greater London, England; railway; economy: finance, quarrying; monuments: 11th-c St Mary's church and Harrow school (1571).

Harstad *hahr'stah*, 68 48N 16 30E, pop(1983) 21,773, town in Troms county, N Norway; economy: fish-processing; events: annual festival at end of June, angling contest in summer.

Hartford, 41 46N 72 41W, pop(1980) 136,392, capital of state in Hartford county, central Connecticut, United States; on the R Connecticut; founded by Dutch settlers in 1633; city status in 1784; university; railway; economy: aeroplane parts, motor vehicles, electrical equipment, machinery, metal products; has the world's largest concentration of insurance companies; monuments: the Old State House, Wadsworth Atheneum, Museum of Connecticut History.

Hartlepool *hart'li-pool*, 54 42N 1 11W, pop(1981) 92,133, port town in Hartlepool dist, Cleveland, NE England; 11 km N of Middlesbrough; an advanced gas-cooled nuclear reactor started commercial operation in 1984; railway; economy: engineering, glass and trade in iron, steel and petrochemicals; monument: 12-13th-c St Hilda's church.

Hartley, town in Zimbabwe. See Chegutu.

Harut, river, rising in the Herāt prov of W Afghanistan; flows generally S to the salt marsh and lake of Hamu-e Sāberi in the Nīmūz prov of Afghanistan.

Harvey, 41 36N 87 50W, pop(1980) 35,810, town in Cook county, NE Illinois, United States; 29 km S of Chicago; railway.

Harwich *har'ich*, 51 57N 1 17E, pop(1981) 17,329, port in Tendring dist, Essex, SE England; on the North Sea coast, 26 km E of Colchester; railway; container freight terminal; ferries to Denmark, West Germany and Holland; economy: engineering.

Haryana *hahr-ee-ahn'u*, state in N India; bounded S by Rajasthan, N by Punjab and Himachal Pradesh; the union territory of Delhi indents the E boundary of the state; pop(1981) 12,850,902; area 44,222 sq km; created in Nov 1966 from the Hindi-speaking parts of the state of the Punjab; the capital is Chandigarh, shared with the state of Punjab; the state is governed by a 90-member Legislative Assembly; a university, High Court and other public services are shared with Punjab state; over 82% of the state's labour force is employed in agriculture, growing sugar, cotton and oilseed; water from the Sutlej-Beas scheme irrigates sandy soil in an area where rainfall is erratic; terrain is largely dry and flat; there are deposits of iron ore; major industries include cotton and woollen textiles, agricultural machinery, glass, cement, paper and sugar milling; nearby Delhi provides a large market for the sale of consumer goods manufactured in the state; there is no airport within the state; rail routes cross the state to converge on Delhi.

Hasa, Al *al a-sa'*, former tribal prov of Saudi Arabia; on W coast of Arabian Gulf, bordered W by the sandy Dahnā desert; chief towns Al Hufūf and Al Mubarraz; rich oil-producing area; dates, wheat, and rice are the chief agricultural products; the region was seized from the Turks in 1914 by Ibn Sa'ud and attached to Najd.

Hasakah, Āl *el ha'se-ku*, HASSAKEH, governorate (*mohofazat*) in NE Syria; bounded N by Turkey and E by Iraq; pop(1981) 669,887; capital Āl Hasakah; other chief town Al Qāmishlī; rises to 920 m in the Jabul 'Abd al 'Azīz; drained by the R Khabur, chief tributary of the Euphrates; a new dam on this river is designed to enable the reclamation of 10,000 sq km of land for the production of cotton, rice, cereals, and fruit; the Qaratshūk oilfield is in the extreme NE.

Haskovo, okrug (prov) of Bulgaria. See Khaskovo.

Haslemere *hayz'l-meer*, 51 06N 0 43W, pop(1981) 10,617, town in Waverley dist, Surrey, SE England; 20 km SSW of Guildford; railway; economy: chemicals; event: Dolmetsch Festival of early English music (July).

Haslingden, 53 43N 2 18W, pop(1981) 14,374, town in Rossendale dist, Lancashire, NW England; 6 km SE of Accrington; economy: textiles, engineering, footwear.

Hass'elt, dist of Limburg prov, NE Belgium; area 907 sq km; pop(1982) 354,615.

Hasselt, 50 56N 5 20E, pop(1982) 65,100, industrial town and capital of Hasselt dist, Limburg prov, NE Belgium; between Liège and Antwerpen, on the R Demer; S of the town extend fertile fields and orchards, to the N is the coalfield of Limburg; received town status in the 12th century; here the Dutch defeated the Belgians in 1830; railway; economy: foodstuffs, chemical and electrical engineering; monuments: Gothic cathedral of St Quintin (15th-c), town hall (1675), church of Our Lady.

Hässleholm *hes'lu-holm*, 56 09N 13 45E, pop(1982) 48,827, town in Kristianstad county, S Sweden; NW of Kristianstad; a city since 1914; railway; economy: food processing, textiles, pharmaceuticals.

Hastings *hay'-*, 39 39S 176 52E, pop(1981) 36,083, town in Hawke's Bay, North Island, New Zealand; SW of Napier; at Cape Kidnappers to the E of Hastings is the world's only mainland gannet sanctuary; railway; economy: centre of an important fruit and wine producing area; manufacture of cycles and motor mowers; event: highland games at Easter.

Hastings, 50 51N 0 36E, pop(1981) 75,284, resort town in Hastings dist, East Sussex, SE England; part of Hastings-Bexhill urban area; on the English Channel, 52 km E of Brighton; the Battle of Hastings was fought 9 km NW in 1066; a Cinque port and former base of the Royal Fleet; the town declined as the harbour silted up; railway; economy: tourism, scientific instruments, plastics, engineering, electronics, clothing; monuments: castle (1066), built by William the Conqueror; 14th-c St Clement's and All Saints church; Fisherman's Museum; St Clement's sandstone caves; White Rock Pavilion with a tapestry depicting the Battle of Hastings; Bateman's (17 km NW), 17th-c home of Rudyard Kipling 1902-36.

Hatay *ha-tī'*, maritime prov in S Turkey, bounded W by the Mediterranean Sea, E and S by Syria; Amanos Mts in the W; pop(1980) 856,271; area 5,403 sq km; capital Antakya.

Hat'field, 51 46N 0 13W, pop(1981) 33,296, town in Welwyn Hatfield dist, Hertfordshire, SE England; 30 km N of London; designated a 'new town' in 1948; railway; economy: aircraft, engineering.

Hatfield, 53 36N 0 59W, pop(1981) 20,265, town linked with Stainforth in Doncaster borough, South Yorkshire, N England; 11 km NE of Doncaster; railway; monument: 11th-c village church.

Hattiesburg, 31 20N 89 17W, pop(1980) 40,829, county seat of Forrest county, SE Mississippi, United States; on the R Leaf, 137 km SE of Jackson; university; railway; economy: trade in timber and agricultural produce.

Hattingen *hah'ting-un*, HATTINGEN AN DER RUHR, 51 24N 7 10E, pop(1983) 56,200, industrial town in Arnsberg dist, Nordrhein-Westfalen (North Rhine-Westphalia) prov, W Germany; SE suburb of Essen on the R Ruhr; economy: engineering, machinery.

Hatvan *hot'von*, 47 40N 19 45E, pop(1984e) 25,000, town in Heves county, N Hungary; NE of Budapest; railway junction; economy: textiles, wine, foodstuffs.

Haugesund *how'ge-soon*, 59 25N 5 16E, pop(1983) 27,030, seaport on W coast of Rogaland county, SW Norway; 104 km S of Bergen, on the mainland and 2 islands, on a fjord opposite Stavanger; airport; a monument nearby commemorates the unification of Norway by Harald Haarfagr who is supposedly buried here.

Haute-Corse *ōt-kors*, dept in Corse region, France, at the N end of the Island of Corsica, comprising 3 arrond, 30 cantons and 236 communes; pop(1982) 131,574; area 4,666 sq km; drained by the R Golo; rises to 2,710 m at Monte Cinto; capital Bastia.

Haute-Garonne *ōt-ga-ron*, dept in Midi-Pyrénées region of S France, on the upper Garonne at the Spanish frontier; comprises 3 arrond, 50 cantons and 587 communes; pop(1982) 824,501; area 6,309 sq km; mountainous in the S where the Pyrénées rise to over 3,000 m, and furrowed throughout with the vine-clad Pyrenean foothills which run mainly NE and NW to the valley of the Garonne R; the Canal du Midi and the Canal lateral à la Garonne cut across the NE of the dept; capital Toulouse; all traffic routes converge at Toulouse; spas at Luchon, Barbazan, Encausse-les-Thermes and Salies-du-Salat.

Haute-Kotto *ōt-kō'tō*, prefecture in E Central African Republic; the Massif des Bongos rises in the N; the rivers M'Bari, Kotto and Chinko flow SW; pop(1968) 44,392; area 86,650 sq km; chief town Bria; other towns include Ouadda, Mouka, Yalinga, Mereke, Voulou and Birini.

Haute-Loire *ōt-lwahr*, mountainous dept in Auvergne region of central France, on the upper Loire and the Massif Central; comprises 3 arrond, 33 cantons and 260 communes; pop(1982) 205,895; area 4,977 sq km; the Monts du Velay separate the valleys of the Allier and the Loire, and in the SW rise part of the Monts de la Margeride; capital Le Puy.

Haute-Marne, dept in Champagne-Ardenne region of NE France, on the upper R Marne; comprises 3 arrond, 32 cantons and 395 communes; pop(1982) 210,670; area 6,211 sq km; watered in the E by the R Meuse and in the W by the R Aube; elevated in the S (Plateau de Langres); capital Chaumont, other towns include Langres and Wassy, scene of the massacre which started the Wars of Religion (1562); spa at Bourbonne-les-Bains.

Haute-Normandie, UPPER NORMANDY (Eng), region of W France comprising the depts of Eure and Seine-Maritime, 6 arrond, 110 cantons and 1,421 communes; pop(1982) 1,655,362; area 12,317 sq km; bounded on the N by the English Channel and cut in half by the meandering course of the Lower Seine; the main industrial towns are Rouen and Le Havre; Dieppe is one of the most important ports in France; there are several notable forests including the Foret d'Eawy (beech forest, recently famed for its boar-hunt), Foret d'Eu (one of the 3 ancient forests of Upper Normandy) and the Forest of Brotonne, in which the Brotonne Nature Park (492 sq km) is centred; châteaux include Beaumesnil (12 km SE of Bernay), Champ de Bataille (4 km NW of Le Neubourg) and Vascoeuil (9 km NW of Lyons-la-Forêt); resorts on the Alabaster Coast include Fécamp (also the principal French cod-fishing port), Le Tréport, Ste-Adresse and Étretat; there is a spa at Forges-les-Eaux; the 'Route des Abbeyes' from Rouen to Le Havre along the right bank of the Seine is particularly attractive.

Hautes-Alpes, mountainous dept in Provence-Alpes-Côte d'Azur region of SE France, bounded on the E by Italy; comprises 2 arrond, 30 cantons and 175 communes; pop(1982) 105,070; area 5,549 sq km; watered by the R Durance and its tributaries, also by the Drac and Romanche rivers; rises to 4,103 m in the Massif du Pelvoux (N); capital Gap; includes the Parc du Queyras (593 sq km) regional nature park and part of the Parc National des Écrins, a national park catering for climbing, walking and cycling.

Haute-Sangha *ōt-sā-ga'*, prefecture in SW Central African Republic; a flat region with river valleys running NNW-SSW; rivers include the Boumbé (on the W border with Cameroon), Mambēe and Lobaye (on the SE border with Lobaye prefecture); pop(1968) 235,306; area 44,350 sq km; chief town Berbérati; other towns include Carnot, Bania, Zaorosongou, Babadza, Sosso and Gamboula; economy: diamond mining.

Haute-Saône, dept in Franche Comté region of E France, comprising 2 arrond, 29 cantons and 545 communes; pop(1982) 231,962; area 5,343 sq km; the Ognon R forms part of its S boundary; watered by the upper Saône R and its tributaries, the ground rising on each side of their NE-SW basin; capital Vesoul.

Haute-Savoie, dept in Rhône-Alpes region of E France, on the Swiss border and the S shore of Lac Léman (L Geneva); comprises 4 arrond, 33 cantons and 290 communes; pop(1982) 494,505; area 4,391 sq km; watered by the R Arve; the mountainous terrain at the N end of the French Alps makes it a popular tourist area with resorts at Annecy, Chamonix, Évian-les-Bains; the Alpes de Savoie meet the Alpes du Valais in the culminating peak of Mt Blanc (4,807 m), on the international border; capital Annecy; spas at Luxeuil-les-Bains, Évian-les-Bains and St-Gervais-les-Bains; interesting caves near Thorens-Glières (Grotte de la Diau).

Hautes-Pyrénées, dept in Midi-Pyrénées region of S France, on the Spanish border; comprises 3 arrond, 34 cantons and 475 communes; pop(1982) 227,922; area 4,507 sq km; the Pyrénées rise in the S (over 3,000 m) and the foothills run out in tongues, separated by northward flowing mountain rivers, the chief of which is the Adour; capital Tarbes, chief towns Lourdes and Bagnères-de-Bigorre; interesting caves near Aventignan, Bagnères-de-Bigorre and St-Pé-de-Bigorre; the Parc National des Pyrénées Orientales (474 sq km), situated SW of Tarbes near the Spanish frontier, at an altitude between 1,000 m and 3,300 m, caters for walking, pony trekking, climbing and fishing; spas at Cauterets, Barèges, Capvern and Bagnères-de-Bigorre.

Haute-Vienne, dept in Limousin region of central France, on the upper Vienne R; comprises 3 arrond, 40 cantons and 201 communes; pop(1982) 355,737; area 5,512 sq km; elevated in the centre (Mts de la Marche) and in the S (Mts du Limousin), with the Vienne valley running E-W between; watered also by the Gartempeo, Isle and Tardoire rivers; capital Limoges; chief towns St-Junien and St-Yrieix.

Haut-M'Bomou *ōt-um-bō'moo*, prefecture in SE Central African Republic; several rivers flow SW to join the R Bomu; Mt Koungou rises S of Djéma; pop(1968) 53,564; area 55,530 sq km; chief town Obo; other towns include Zémio, Djéma, Goubére, Kadjéma, Dakoma, Ouando and Bembé Oudaka.

Haut-Rhin, dept in Alsace region of E France, on the German and Swiss borders; comprises 6 arrond, 31 cantons and 377 communes; pop(1982) 650,372; area 3,523 sq km; watered by the Ill R and its tributaries; rises from the Rhine valley in the NE to the heights of the Vosges in the W; some cereals and considerable vines and hops are grown in the W, and there are numerous spas and resorts; capital Colmar, chief towns Guebwiller and Mulhouse; Belfort is administratively separate.

Hauts-de-Seine, dept in Ile-de-France region of N France lying to the W of the city of Paris, comprising 3 arrond, 40 cantons and 36 communes; pop(1982) 1,387,039; area 175 sq km; capital Nanterre.

Havana, capital city of Cuba. See Habana, La.

Hav'ant, 50 51N 0 59W, pop(1981) 50,220, town in Havant dist, Hampshire, S England; part of Portsmouth urban area; 10 km NE of Portsmouth; railway; economy: engineering, scientific instruments.

Haverfordwest, 51 49N 4 58W, pop(1981) 13,871, town in Preseli dist, Dyfed, SW Wales; NNE of Milford Haven, on the W Cleddau river; railway; monuments: 12th-c castle and Augustinian priory.

Haverhill *hay'vě-ril*, 52 05N 0 26E, pop(1981) 16,992, industrial town in St Edmundsbury dist, Suffolk, E England; 26 km SE of Cambridge; economy: electrics, plastics.

Haverhill, 42 47N 71 05W, pop(1980) 46,865, town in Essex county, NE Massachusetts, United States; on the R Merrimack, 24 km NE of Lowell and 3 km S of the New Hampshire border; birthplace of John Greenleaf Whittier; railway; economy: footwear, electrical goods.

Havering *hay'-*, 51 37N 0 11E, pop(1981) 239,344, borough of NE Greater London, England; includes the suburbs of Romford and Hornchurch; railway.

Havířov *ha'veer-of*, 49 46N 18 25E, pop(1984) 90,473,

manufacturing and mining town in Severomoravský region, Czech Socialist Republic, central Czechoslovakia; SE of Ostrava; founded in the 1950s; railway.

Havlíčkův Brod *hayv'leetch koof brot*, formerly NĚMECKÝ BROD, 49 38N 15 46E, pop(1984) 25,122, town in Východočeský region, Czech Socialist Republic, NW central Czechoslovakia; on R Sazava; railway.

Havre, Le *le avr*, formerly LE HAVRE-DE-GRACE, 49 30N 0 06E, pop(1982) 200,411, commercial seaport in Seine-Maritime dept, Haute-Normandie region, NW France; on the English Channel, on the N side of the R Seine estuary, backed by hills and cliffs, 176 km WNW of Paris; it is the principal French port for transatlantic passenger liners and the 2nd port of France after Marseille; the Place de l'Hôtel-de-Ville is one of the largest city squares in Europe; founded by François I in 1517 to replace the silted-up medieval port of Harfleur; later it developed into an important commercial port and after the American War of Independence, it became the main centre for the import of colonial products such as coffee, tobacco, cotton and sugar; it was a naval base under Napoleon I and a major Allied base in World War I; during World War II it suffered heavy destruction and had to be almost completely rebuilt; since the establishment of the pipeline to Paris, oil forms 80% of all commodities handled by the port; to the E of the town is the seaside suburb of Ste-Adresse (fashionable in the 19th century) and the outer suburb of Nice Havrais (the 'Nice' of Le Havre); at the E edge of Le Havre lies the medieval town of Harfleur (its 15th-c steeple, rising 83 m, is an important landmark); monument: church of St Joseph, with an octagonal tower 106 m high.

Hawaii *ha-wah'ee*, Pacific state of the US, a group of 8 major islands and numerous islets in the central Pacific Ocean; the islands are of volcanic origin, with coral reefs; the highest point is Mauna Kea, on Hawaii I (4,201 m); the islands are generally fertile and highly vegetated, although Kahoolawe is arid; over 90% of its flora and fauna are unique to the islands; food processing is the state's leading industry, with pineapples and sugar cane the chief agricultural products; other important products include coffee, cattle, dairy produce, and macadamia nuts; commercial fishing, particularly for tuna, is a major industry; there are defence installations at Pearl Harbor; the first people to reach the islands were the Polynesians over 1,000 years ago; discovered by Captain James Cook in 1778, and named the Sandwich Islands; in 1810 King Kamehameha I united all the islands under his rule, and encouraged trade with the USA; Christian missionaries first visited the islands in 1820; in 1893 the monarchy was overthrown and a request for annexation to the USA was made but was rejected by President Cleveland; his successor, President McKinley, favoured annexation which finally took place in 1898; the islands were made a territory in 1900; on 7 Dec 1941, Japanese planes made a surprise attack on the US naval base at Pearl Harbor on Oahu I, an action which brought the United States into World War II; the Hawaiian Islands were the chief US Pacific base throughout the war, and were under martial law from the day of the Japanese attack until March 1943; Hawaii was finally admitted to the Union as the 50th state in 1959; also known as the 'Aloha State'; pop(1980) 964,691; area 16,705 sq km; capital Honolulu; the 8 principal islands are Hawaii, Kahoolawe, Kauai, Lanai, Maui, Molokai, Niihau and Oahu; the state is divided into 5 counties:

County	*area (sq km)*	*pop(1980)*
Hawaii	10,488	92,053
Honolulu	1,550	762,565
Kalawao	34	144
Kauai	1,612	39,082
Maui	3,021	70,847

Hawaii, largest island and county of the Pacific state of Hawaii, United States; situated SE of Maui; area 10,488 sq km; pop(1980) 92,053; chief town Hilo; includes the Volcanoes National Park which rises to 4,169 m at Mauna Loa; this and the neighbouring Mauna Kea (4,201 m) are 2 of the tallest mountains in the world which rise over 9,000 m from the ocean floor; Hawaii is known as the 'orchid isle' for its fields of orchids and anthurium; it is also the premier astronomical site in the world.

Hawalli, 29 20N 48 10E, pop(1980) 152,270, E suburb of Al Kuwayt (Kuwait City), State of Kuwait.

Hawār', DUKHAN *doo-KHan'*, island off the W coast of the Qatar peninsula, on the Gulf of Bahrain; ownership is disputed between Bahrain and Qatar; a major source of oil was discovered here in 1939.

Hawick *haw'ik*, 55 25N 2 47W, pop(1981) 16,364, capital of Roxburgh dist, Borders, SE Scotland; on the R Teviot, 63 km SSE of Edinburgh and 59 km N of Carlisle; economy: textiles; monument: museum in the ancestral home of the Langlands family.

Hawthorne, 33 55N 118 21W, pop(1980) 56,447, city in Los Angeles county, SW California, United States; 19 km SSW of Los Angeles.

Hay'ling Island, 50 48N 0 59W, pop(1981) 12,737, town E of Portsmouth in Havant dist, Hampshire, S England; S of Havant between Chichester and Langstone harbours; connected to the mainland by Langstone Bridge; max length (N-S) 6 km and max width (E-W) 7 km; ferry to Portsea I.

Hayward, 37 40N 122 07W, pop(1980) 94,167, city in Alameda county, W California, United States; 24 km SE of Oakland; founded in 1854; university; railway; E terminus of the San Mateo Toll Bridge across San Francisco Bay.

Haywards Heath, 51 00N 0 06W, pop(1981) 28,190, residential town in Mid Sussex dist, West Sussex, S England; 20 km N of Brighton; railway.

Hazel Grove *hayz'l*, 53 23N 2 08W, pop(1981) 40,680 town linked with Bramhall in Stockport borough, Greater Manchester, NW England; 4 km SE of Stockport; railway.

Hazleton, 40 57N 75 59W, pop(1980) 27,318, town in Luzerne county, E Pennsylvania, United States; 59 km NW of Allentown; railway; economy: coal.

Heanor *hee'ner*, 53 01N 1 22W, pop(1981) 21,928, town in Amber Valley dist, Derbyshire, central England; part of Nottingham urban area; 5 km NW of Ilkeston; economy: textiles.

Heard and McDonald Islands, island group situated in S Indian Ocean, about 4,000 km SW of Freemantle, Australia; an Australian external territory comprising Heard Island, Shag Island (8 km N of Heard I) and the McDonald Islands (42 km W of Heard I); area 412 sq km; transferred from UK to Australian control in 1947; Heard I is actively volcanic and has a weather station; Heard I rises to over 2,000 m.

Heb'burn, 54 59N 1 30W, pop(1981) 20,021, industrial town in South Tyneside borough, Tyne and Wear, NE England; part of Tyneside urban area; on S bank of the R Tyne, 6 km E of Gateshead; economy: shipbuilding, coal, lead smelting, electronics, chemicals, engineering.

Hebei *he-bay*, HOPEH, prov in N China; bordered N by Nei Mongol aut region (Inner Mongolia), W by Shanxi prov, S by Henan and Shandong provs and E by Liaoning prov and the Bohai Gulf; encloses Beijing (Peking) and Tianjin municipalities in the NE; mountainous in the W and N with low lying land in the E; includes the Damaqun Shan range in the N and the Taihang Shan and part of the Wutai Shan in the W; to the W of Beijing municipality, Xiaowutai Shan (Lesser Wutai mountain) rises to 2,780 m; the Great Wall of China, which starts at Shanhaiguan in the extreme E of the prov, crosses Hebei prov to the E, N and SW of Beijing municipality; the Grand Canal runs SW through Hebei and along part of its border with Shandong; watered by the Hai He and Luan He rivers; pop(1982) 53,005,875; area 202,700 sq km; capital

Shijiazhuang; principal towns Qinhuangdao, Handan, Chengde and Tangshan; economy: trade in grain, cotton, timber, mining products; oil, iron and steel.

Hebrides *heb'ri-deez*, islands lying off the W coast of Scotland; thought to have derived their name from the Greek *Eboudai* which was Latinized by Pliny to *Hebudes*; until the 13th century the Hebrides also included the Kintyre peninsula, the Isle of Man, Rathlin I and islands in the Firth of Clyde; the Western Isles were ceded to Alexander III of Scotland in 1266 by Magnus of Norway; the Norwegian name *Sudreyar* (Southern Islands) was Latinized as *Sodorenses*, a term that survives in the Anglican Bishopric of Sodor and Man; over 500 islands are divided into the Inner and Outer Hebrides.

Hebrides, Inner, group of islands off the W coast of Scotland; the major islands are Skye, Eigg, Coll, Tiree, Mull, Iona, Staffa, Jura and Islay; these are incorporated into Highland and Strathclyde regions.

Hebrides, Outer, group of islands off the W coast of Scotland. See Western Isles.

Hebron *hee'bron*, administered as a sub-district of Judea-Samaria dist, Israel, in the Israeli-occupied West Bank of Jordan.

Hebron, governorate (*muhafaza*) of Jordan in the Israeli-occupied West Bank, W Jordan, bounded E by the Dead Sea; capital Hebron.

Hebron, EL KHALIL (Arab), HEVRON (Hebrew), 31 32N 35 06E, capital city of Hebron governorate (Jordan), Israeli-occupied West Bank, W Jordan; 29 km SSW of Jerusalem; reputedly one of the oldest cities in the world, built 1730 BC; religious centre of Islam; it was the home of Abraham and for a time of David, who ruled the Hebrews from here for 7 years before moving his capital to Jerusalem; monument: shrine of Haram El-Khalil over the Cave of Machpelah.

Hedge End, 50 55N 1 17W, pop(1981) 12,911, town just outside Southampton in Eastleigh dist, Hampshire, S England; a SE suburb of Southampton.

Hed'mark, formerly HEDEMARKEN, a county of SE Norway, bounded on the E by Sweden; area 27,388 sq km; pop(1983) 187,779; capital Hamar; drained chiefly by the R Glåa; the N part of the county is mountainous with peaks including Elgepiggen (1,604 m) and Store Sølnkletten (1,827 m); includes much of L Mjøsa in the W; county of extensive forests, biggest area of farmland in Norway.

Heerlen *hayr'len*, 50 55N 6 00E, pop(1984e) 266,095, industrial city in Limburg prov, S Netherlands; NE of Maastricht, 8 km from the West German border; railway; centre of the Limburg coal basin; economy: fertilizers, yarn and fibre feedstocks, chemicals, plastics, building materials, gas and oil exploration.

Hefei *he-fay*, HOFEI, formerly LUCHOW, 31 55N 117 18E, pop(1984e) 853,100, rapidly growing industrial capital of Anhui prov, E China; railway; airfield; economy: mining, steel, chemicals, textiles; monuments: Hefei museum contains c.100,000 artifacts dating back 7,000 years, these include a 2,000-year-old jade burial suit, stitched with silver thread.

Heidelberg *hī'dul-berk*, 49 23N 8 41E, pop(1983) 133,600, industrial city in Karlsruhe dist, Baden-Württemberg prov, W Germany; lies at the point where the R Neckar emerges from the hills of the Odenwald into the Rhine plain, 18 km ESE of Mannheim; centre of German Calvinism during the 16th century; old university (1711); new university (1928-31); railway; economy: manufacture of printing presses, fountain pens, agric machinery, adhesives and sealing materials, and chemical and physical apparatus, pipelines, cement, plaster; several publishing houses are based in the town; monument: castle (1583-1610).

Heilbronn *hīl'bron*, 49 08N 9 13E, pop(1983) 111,000, industrial river port in Stuttgart dist, Baden-Württemberg prov, W Germany; on R Neckar (here canalised), 43 km N of Stuttgart; railway, harbour; centre of an important wine-producing region; economy: chemicals, metallurgy, paper.

Heilong Jiang, AMUR RIVER, river in NE China and USSR; boundary river between the two countries; the main source is the Ergun He, whose headstream, the Hailar He, rises on the W slopes of the Da Hinggan Ling range in NE Nei Mongol aut region (Inner Mongolia); the N source is the Shilka river which rises in the E foothills of the Hentiyn Nuruu (Kentei mountains); the Ergun He flows NE to form the border between Nei Mongol and the USSR; it joins the Shilka river near the border between Nei Mongol and Heilongjiang prov where it becomes the Heilong Jiang river; it flows E then S forming the border with Amur region (USSR) and is joined by the Zeya river; it continues SE and E along the complete N border of Heilongjiang prov and that of Yevreysk region (USSR); the Heilong Jiang, or Amur, then flows NE through Soviet Khabarovsk Kray to enter the Okhotskoye More (Sea of Okhotsk) via the Amurskiy Liman at the town of Nikolayevsk-na-Amure; major tributaries: the Songhua Jiang, Wusuli Jiang, Zeya, Bureya and In Urmi; the total length is 4,350 km, with 2,965 km within China.

Heilongjiang *hay-loong-ji-ahng*, HEILUNGKIANG, prov in NE China; bordered N by the USSR (along the Heilong Jiang, or Amur, river), E by the USSR (partly along the Wusuli Jiang river), W by Nei Mongol (along the Yilehuli Shan range and Nen Jiang river) and S by Jilin prov; mountainous in the W and N; crossed in the NW by the Xiao Hinggan Ling (Lesser Khingan) range; in the SE are the Zhangguangcai Ling and Laoye Ling ranges and in the E the Wanda Shan range; rises in the NW to 1,398 m in Fengshui Shan; drained by the Heilong Jiang, Wusuli, Songhua Jiang (or Sungari), Nen Jiang and Mudan Jiang rivers; in the E on the border with the USSR is part of Xingkai Hu lake; pop(1982) 32,665,546; area 463,600 sq km; capital Harbin; principal towns Qiqihar and Jixi; economy: grain, timber, oil and mining of coal, gold, copper, aluminium, lead, zinc, silver, cobalt; in the W of the prov is the city of Daqing, built to provide facilities for workers and their families at China's biggest oil field (it supplies half of the country's total production); Daqing also has a large petrochemical plant.

Heilungkiang, prov in NE China. See Heilongjiang.

Heimaey *hī'me-ay*, largest offshore volcanic island of the Vestmannaeyjar group (Westman Is) off the S coast of Iceland; erupted on 2 Jan 1973, causing the evacuation of the entire pop of 5,300; airfield; ferry; important fish processing centre.

Heinola *hay'no-la*, 61 13N 26 05E, pop(1982) 15,733, industrial town and resort in Mikkeli prov, SE central Finland; situated on the R Kymijoki NE of Lahti; established in 1839; economy: power production equipment.

Hejāz *he-jaz'*, former tribal prov of Saudi Arabia; extends along the Red Sea coast and the Gulf of 'Aqaba, bounded N by Jordan, E by Najd, S by Asīr, and W by the Red Sea; comprises the barren Tihama coastal plain and an inland highland region, fertile agricultural land in the S in the vicinity of Makkah (Mecca) and Al Madīnah (Medina); Ibn Sa'ud was declared King of Hejāz in 1926; the formal union of Najd and Hejāz into Saudi Arabia was proclaimed in 1932.

Hekla, 64 01N 19 39W, volcano in SW Iceland, rising to 1,491 m; over 20 recorded eruptions since the 12th century.

Hel'ena, 46 36N 112 02W, pop(1980) 23,938, capital of state in Lewis and Clark county, W central Montana, United States; on the E bank of the Continental Divide, 74 km NNE of Butte; railway; economy: commercial and shipping centre in ranching and mining area; manufactures include machinery, concrete, and paints; the city was founded after the discovery of gold in 1864 at Last Chance Gulch which is now Helena's main street.

Helensburgh *-bur-u*, 56 01N 4 44W, pop(1981) 16,621, town in Dumbarton dist, Strathclyde, W Scotland; on the N shore of the Firth of Clyde, 12 km NW of Dumbarton; railway; popular coastal resort for Glasgow area; economy: coachbuilding; monument: the Hill House (1902-03), designed for W. W. Blackie by Charles Rennie Macintosh.

Hel'goland, HELIGOLAND (Eng), 54 09N 7 52E, rocky North Sea island of the Nordfriesische Inseln (North Frisian Is), in Helgoländer Bucht (Helgoland Bay), Schleswig-Holstein, W Germany, 64 km NW of Cuxhaven, W Germany; area 2.1 sq km; captured from Denmark by the UK in 1807, it was ceded to Germany in 1890 in exchange for Zanzibar.

Heligoland, North Sea island, W Germany. See Helgoland.

Hell, 63 25N 10 54E, village in Nord-Trøndelag, central Norway; on a bay of the Trondheimsfjord, 32 km E of Trondheim; railway junction.

Hellespont, strait of NW Turkey. See Çanakkale Boğazi.

Hellín *el-yeen'*, 38 31N 1 40W, pop(1981) 22,651, industrial city in Albacete prov, Castilla-La Mancha, SE central Spain; near the confluence of the R Segura and R Mundo, 59 km S of Albacete; railway; reservoirs nearby; economy: mining, clothes, silk.

Hell's Canyon, GRAND CANYON OF THE SNAKE, gorge on the Snake river where it follows the Oregon-Idaho state frontier, United States; with a depth of 2,448 m it is one of the deepest gorges in the world; length 64 km.

Helmand *hel'mund*, prov in Afghanistan, stretching from the centre to the S; bounded in the S by the Baluchistan region of Pakistan, the Chagai Hills forming a natural barrier; pop(1984e) 562,043; area 61,828 sq km; crossed by the main road running SE from Herāt to Kandahār; crossed by the SW flowing R Helmand, which rises in the Hindu Kush Mts of NE Afghanistan.

Helmand, longest river in Afghanistan; rises in the Hindu Kush mountains and flows SW to Nīmrūz prov, Afghanistan; flows into the marshy lake of Hamu-e Sāberi; Ghengis Khan (13th century) and Tamerlane (14th century) destroyed the ancient irrigation and river control system; length 1,125 km.

Hel'mond, 51 28N 5 40E, pop(1984e) 60,582, city and municipality in Noord Brabant prov, S Netherlands; 14 km ENE of Eindhoven; railway; economy: motor cars.

Helsingborg, port of Sweden. See Hälsingborg.

Helsingfors, capital city of Finland. See Helsinki.

Helsingør *hel'sing-ur*, ELSINORE (Eng), 56 03N 12 38E, pop(1983) 56,246, seaport on the Øresund, in Frederiksborg county, NE Sjælland (Zealand), Denmark; only 4.5 km from the Swedish town of Helsingborg on the other side of the Øresund; railway; economy: shipbuilding, engineering; monuments: site of Kronborg Castle, dating from the 16th century and famous as the scene of Shakespeare's *Hamlet*; town hall (1855).

Helsinki *hel'seen-kee*, HELSINGFORS *hel'sing-forz* (Swed), 60 08N 25 00E, pop(1982) 483,400, seaport, capital of Finland and Uudenmaa prov, S Finland; on the Gulf of Finland on a peninsula surrounded by islands and protected by fortifications of Suomenlinna; founded by Gustavus Vasa in 1550, N of present site; the heart of the city is based around the harbour where the dominant style of architecture is 19th century neo-classical, designed by the German architect Carl Ludwig Engel; 6 km from the city centre the residential garden city of Tapiola, built in the 1950s, is a model of modern town planning; University of Helsinki (transferred from Turku 1828); technical university (1908); railway; international airport; Olympic Stadium; economy: shipbuilding, textiles, engineering, porcelain, export trade; monuments: cathedral (completed in 1852); Rock Church (Tempeliaukio); Ateneum museum of art and National Museum; open-air museum of country life on the nearby island of Seurasaari.

Helvellyn *hel-vel'in*, 54 32N 3 02W, mountain in the Lake District of Cumbria, NW England; rises to 950 m between Ullswater and Thirlmere.

Hemel Hempstead *hem'sted*, 51 46N 0 28W, pop(1981) 80,340, town in Greater London urban area and Dacorum dist, Hertfordshire, SE England; on R Gade and Grand Union Canal, 11 km NNW of Watford; railway.

Hemingford Grey, town in Cambridgeshire, England. See St Ives.

Hempstead, 40 43N 73 38W, pop(1980) 40,404, residential town in Nassau county, SE New York, United States; on Long Island, 32 km E of New York; Hofstra University (1935).

Henan *he-nan*, HONAN, prov in N central China; bordered S by Hubei prov, E by Anhui and Shandong provs, N by Hebei and Shanxi provs and W by Shaanxi prov; rises S in the Tongbai Shan range, and W in the Funiu Shan, Xionger Shan and Xiao Shan ranges (eastern extensions of the Qinling Shan range); the centre of Henan is crossed by the lower Huang He (Yellow river) valley which then forms part of the border with Shandong prov; drained by the Huai He, Wei He, Zhentou He, Hong He and Ying He rivers; Song Shan peak (1,512 m) is one of China's Five Holy Mountains; pop(1982) 74,422,739; area 167,000 sq km; capital Zhengzhou; principal towns Kaifeng, Luoyang and Puyang; economy: agriculture, mining; as a political and cultural centre of ancient China, Henan was one of the earliest developed regions.

Hendersonville, 36 18N 86 37W, pop(1980) 26,561, town in Sumner county, N central Tennessee, United States; 20 km NE of Nashville; railway.

Hengduan Shan, mountain range in SE Xizang aut region, NW Yunnan prov and W Sichuan prov, SW China; consists of a series of parallel ranges running N to S, including the Nu Shan range in the W and the Daxue Shan and Qionglai Shan ranges in the E, with, among others, the Nu Jiang, Langcang Jiang and Jinsha Jiang rivers running through the parallel intermontane valleys; averages 3,000 to 4,000 m above sea-level; rises to 7,556 m with Gongga Shan peak in the Daxue Shan range.

Hengelo *heng'e-lō*, 52 03N 6 19E, pop(1984e) 76,855, industrial city in E Overijssel prov, E Netherlands, near the German border; railway; salt from water is processed here.

Hen'ley-on-Thames', 51 32N 0 56W, pop(1981) 11,180, town in South Oxfordshire dist, Oxfordshire, S central England; on the R Thames, 10 km NE of Reading; railway; economy: engineering; events: Royal Regatta (July); swan-upping (July).

Hentiy *KHen'tay*, KHENTI, county in N Mongolia; pop(1981e) 50,000; area 85,000 sq km; capital Öndörhaan; bounded N by the USSR; covered by forest-steppe and steppe vegetation; crossed by more than 70 rivers; over 30 mineral springs known; extensive deposits of tin, tungsten, coal, iron ore, gold and copper; stock farming is important; industry: food, power, wood processing and ore mining.

Henzada *hen-za-da'*, 17 63N 95 26E, pop(1983) 283,658, town in Irrawaddy division, S central Burma; on R Irrawaddy; railway.

Herāt *hu-rat'*, HARAT, HEROIVA (anc), prov in W Afghanistan; bounded W by Iran and N by USSR; pop(1984e) 868,564; area 61,315 sq km; crossed by the Paropamisus mountain range and the Hari Rud; linked to Mazār-e Sharīf in the NE and Kandahār in the SW by main roads; a fertile river valley which is noted for its fruit, especially grapes.

Herāt, 34 20N 62 10E, pop(1984e) 159,804, capital of Herāt prov, W Afghanistan; lies close to the Hari Rud; airfield; economy: textile, carpet and weaving industries and market for dried fruits, nuts and wool; lies on the old trade route from Persia to India and on the caravan route from China to central Asia and Europe; became part of a united Afghanistan in 1881; major landmark is the 12th-c Great Mosque.

Hérault *ay-rō*, dept in Languedoc-Roussillon region of S France, bounded S by the Mediterranean (Golfe du Lion), which makes 3 long lagoons in the coastline (Étangs de Thau, de Vic and de Mauguio); comprises 3 arrond, 45 cantons and 343 communes; pop(1982) 706,499; area 6,101 sq km; it rises inland to the SW end of the Cévennes; watered by the Hérault and Orb rivers; capital Montpellier, chief towns Béziers and Sète; spas at Lamalou-les-Bains, Avené-les-Bains and Balaruc-les-Bains; the Parc du Haut-Languedoc regional nature park lies partly within the dept (riding, canoeing); caves near Gignac (Grotte de Clamouse) and Ganges (Grotte des Demoiselles).

Hérault, river in S France rising in the S Cévennes Mts; flows S across Hérault dept to the Golfe du Lion near Agde; length 160 km.

Heredia *ay-ray'dee-a*, prov in NE Costa Rica, Central America; bounded N by Nicaragua; the S part of the prov is traversed by the Cordillera Central with peaks rising to over 2,000 m; tropical lowland occupies the N and central areas; drained chiefly by tributaries of the Río San Juan; pop(1983e) 171,688; area 2,656 sq km; capital Heredia; chief towns Santa Bárbara and Santo Domingo.

Heredia, 10 00N 84 08W, pop(1983e) 29,544, capital town of Heredia prov, Costa Rica, Central America; 10 km NNW of San José; alt 1,137 m; university (1973); railway; airfield; economy: food processing, coffee, cattle.

Hereford, 52 04N 2 43W, pop(1981) 47,804, town in Hereford dist, Hereford and Worcester, W central England; on the R Wye at the centre of a rich farming region; railway; economy: foodstuffs, engineering, cattle, hops, cider; monument: 11th-c cathedral of St Mary and St Ethelbert, with the largest chained library in the world and the famous *Mappa Mundi*, a medieval map of the world; event: Three Choirs Festival in rotation with Gloucester and Worcester (Sept).

Hereford and Worcester *woos'ter*, county of W central England; bounded W by Powys (Wales), SW by Gwent (Wales), S by Gloucestershire, E by Warwickshire, NE by West Midlands, and N by Staffordshire and Shropshire; drained by the Wye and Teme rivers; the Malvern Hills rise SW of Worcester; pop(1981) 631,756; area 3,926 sq km; county town Worcester; chief towns include Hereford, Kidderminster, Great Malvern, Evesham; economy: cattle, horticulture, high technology; the county is divided into 9 districts:

District	*area (sq km)*	*pop(1981)*
Bromsgrove	220	88,070
Hereford	20	47,804
Leominster	932	37,399
Malvern Hills	902	82,213
Redditch	54	66,609
South Herefordshire	905	47,587
Worcester	32	74,790
Wychavon	666	95,381
Wyre Forest	196	91,703

Herford *her'fort*, 52 07N 8 40E, pop(1983) 61,300, manufacturing city in Detmold dist, NE Nordrhein-Westfalen (North Rhine-Westphalia) prov, W Germany; 69 km ENE of Münster, between the Wiehengebirge and the Teutoburger Wald (Teutoburg Forest), at the point where the R Aa flows into the Werre; railway; economy: furniture, textiles, dairy produce.

Herisau *hay'ri-zow*, 47 23N 9 17E, pop(1980) 14,160, capital town of Appenzell Ausser Rhoden demicanton, NE Switzerland; 8 km SW of St Gallen; railway junction.

Hermosillo *er-mō-see'lyō*, 29 15N 110 59W, pop(1980) 340,779, capital of Sonora state, NW Mexico; near the junction of the Zanjón and Sonora rivers, 1,958 km NW of Ciudad de México (Mexico City); a winter tourist resort; university (1938); railway; airfield; economy: fruit, mining of gold, silver and copper.

Hernani *er-na'nee*, 43 16N 1 59W, pop(1981) 30,272, industrial town in Guipúzcoa prov, Pais Vasco (Basque Country), N Spain; on the R Urumea, S of San Sebastian; railway; economy: paper, electronics, elevators, machine tools.

Herne *her'ne*, 51 33N 7 12E, pop(1983) 177,700, industrial city in Münster dist, Nordrhein-Westfalen (North Rhine-Westphalia) prov, W Germany; in the Ruhr valley, 53 km SSW of Münster; established in 1897; railway; economy: civil engineering, construction, chemicals, coal mining.

Herne Bay, 51 23N 1 08E, pop(1981) 26,451, resort town in Canterbury dist, Kent, SE England; 11 km N of Canterbury; railway; economy: engineering.

Her'ning, 56 08N 8 59E, pop(1983) 55,927, commercial city in Ringkøbing county, central Jylland (Jutland), Denmark; railway; economy: clothing.

Herrera *her-ay'ra*, smallest prov of Panama, Central America; occupying the NE part of the peninsula of Azuero; bounded NE by the Golfo de Panamá and N by the Río Santa Maria; pop(1980) 81,963; area 2,427 sq km; capital Chitré; chief towns Parita and Ocú; traversed by a branch of the Inter-American Highway.

Herstal *hers'tahl*, 50 40N 5 38E, pop(1982) 38,189, industrial town in Liège dist, Liège prov, E Belgium, on the R Meuse, NE of Liège; birthplace of Pepin and residence of Charlemagne; railway; economy: engineering, precision casting and forging, military weapons and ammunition, industrial equipment, sporting goods.

Herten *her'tun*, HERTEN IN WESTFALEN, 51 36N 7 08E, pop(1983) 69,000, industrial city in Düsseldorf dist, Nordrhein-Westfalen (North Rhine-Westphalia) prov, W Germany; 16 km N of Essen; economy: coal mining, machinery, foodstuffs.

Hertford *hart'ford*, 51 48N 0 05W, pop(1981) 21,606, county town in East Hertfordshire dist, Hertfordshire, SE England; on R Lee, 32 km N of London; railway; economy: plastics, engineering; monuments: 12th-c Hertford castle; Waltham abbey (20 km SE).

Hertfordshire *hart'ford-shir*, county of SE England; N of Greater London; drained by the Colne and Lee rivers and the Grand Union Canal; pop(1981) 956,517; area 1,634 sq km; county town Hertford; chief towns include St Albans, Harpenden, Welwyn Garden City; economy: wheat, cattle, horticulture, brewing, paper, electronics, pharmaceuticals, aerospace; the county has 10 districts:

District	*area (sq km)*	*pop(1981)*
Broxbourne	52	79,596
Dacorum	210	129,151
East Hertfordshire	477	107,386
Hertsmere	98	87,753
North Hertfordshire	374	107,262
St Albans	161	125,124
Stevenage	25	74,523
Three Rivers	88	77,938
Watford	21	74,462
Welwyn Hatfield	128	93,322

Herzliyya *herts-lee'u*, 32 10N 34 51E, seaside resort town in Tel Aviv dist, W Israel; on the Mediterranean Sea, 15 km N of Tel Aviv-Yafo; founded in 1924 and named after Theodor Herzl, the founder of modern Zionism; railway.

Hessen *he'sun*, HESSE *hes* (Eng), prov in E central W Germany; comprises the three dists of Darmstadt, Gießen and Kassel; drained by the Lahn, Nidd, Fulda and Main rivers; mountain ranges include the Hohe Rhön (E), Westerwald (W), Taunus (SW) and Odenwald (SE); area 21,114 sq km; pop(1983) 5,565,000; capital Wiesbaden; chief towns Kassel, Fulda and Frankfurt am Main; economy: chemicals, precision engineering and optical instruments, motor vehicles, machine construction, foodstuffs; rich in timber, especially the N part of the prov which has 40% of its area covered in mixed forest; the prov has some of Europe's best-known spas (Wiesbaden, Homberg, Ems).

Heswall, 53 20N 3 06W, pop(1981) 31,031, town in Wirral borough, Merseyside, NW England; on the Wirral peninsula, 7 km SE of West Kirby; railway.

Heves *he'vesh*, county in N Hungary; bisected by the R Tarna, with the Matra Mts to the N; pop(1984e) 346,000; area 3,637 sq km; capital Eger; other chief towns include Hatvan and Gyöngyös; famous wine-producing area around Eger; economy: timber, lignite, wine.

Hevros, river in Bulgaria, Greece and Turkey. See Maritsa.

Hexi Corridor *he-shee*, GANSU CORRIDOR, natural corridor from central China through Gansu prov to Xinjiang aut region; situated between the Qilian Shan and Langlong Ling ranges to the S and the Heli Shan and Longshou Shan ranges to the N; length approx 1,200 km; it is the major part of the ancient Silk Road, one of the longest trade routes in the ancient world; from the 3rd century BC onwards, when the Huns seized the route, numerous battles were fought to keep the Hexi Corridor open; during the Han dynasty an extension of the Great Wall went W from Dunhuang almost to Lop Nur lake in E Xinjiang aut region.

Heywood *hay'-*, 53 36N 2 13W, pop(1981) 29,686, town in Rochdale borough, Greater Manchester, NW England; 5 km E of Bury; economy: textiles, leather, transport equipment.

Hhohho *hō'hō*, dist in the Highveld of N Swaziland, SE Africa; chief town Mbabane; asbestos mining at Havelock.

Hialeah *hī-e-lee'a* (Seminole, 'beautiful-prairie'), 25 50N 80 17W, pop(1980) 145,254, town in Dade county, SE Florida, United States; 8 km NW of Miami; railway; economy: printing, clothing, furniture, transportation equipment and building supplies; monument: Hialeah Park Race Track.

Hidalgo *ee-THal'gō*, mountainous state in central Mexico; bounded N by San Luis Potosí, NW by Querétaro along the Moctezuma river, SW by México, SE by Tlaxcala and E by Puebla and Veracruz; crossed NW-SE by the Sierra Madre Oriental; lower in the NE; drained by the Tula, Tulancingo and Amajac rivers; pop(1980) 1,516,511; area 20,813 sq km; capital Pachuca; economy: agriculture (maize, alfalfa, barley, wheat), cattle, sheep, pig and goat raising, iron and steel, machinery, textiles; formerly one of the most important silver-mining areas in the world, Hidalgo is now a centre for the mining of gold, silver, copper, lead, zinc, fluorite, manganese.

Higashi-Ōsaka *hee-ga'shee-ō-sa'ka*, 34 40N 135 35E, pop(1980) 521,558, town in Ōsaka prefecture, Kinki region, S Honshū island, Japan; an E suburb of Ōsaka; university; railway; economy: textiles, leather products, chemicals, machinery.

High Point, 35 57N 80 00W, pop(1980) 63,380, city in Guilford county, N central North Carolina, United States; 22 km WSW of Greensboro; railway; economy: furniture and hosiery.

High Wycombe *wik'em*, formerly CHEPPING WYCOMBE, 51 38N 0 46W, pop(1981) 70,219, town in Wycombe dist, Buckinghamshire, S central England; on R Wye 45 km NW of London; railway; economy: furniture, paper, precision instruments; monument: local history museum.

Highland, region in N Scotland; bounded N and E by the North Sea, SE by Grampian region, S by Tayside, SW by Strathclyde and W by the Minch and the Little Minch; includes the island of Skye and the Inner Hebrides, but not the Outer Hebrides; sparsely inhabited region of great scenic beauty; includes the Grampian, Monadhliath and Cairngorm Mts; crossed by numerous rivers, mountain ranges and lochs; crossed diagonally SW-NE by the lochs of the Great Glen: Loch Linnhe, Loch Lochy, Loch Oich and Loch Ness; this is also the route taken by the Caledonian Canal, which was completed in 1822 to provide a short-cut between Inverness and the W of Scotland; the region rises to 1,344 m in Ben Nevis in the SW, the highest peak in Britain; in the NW of Highland region, at the head of Loch Glencoul, is Eas Coul Aulin waterfall, the highest waterfall in Britain, with a drop of 200 m; in the extreme NE of Highland region is John o' Groats, which lies close to the northernmost point of the British mainland at Dunnet Head; in S Highland region, SE of Fort William is Glencoe, where the Massacre of Glencoe took place in 1692; pop(1981) 200,150; area 25,391 sq km; capital Inverness; major towns include Wick, Dingwall, Thurso, Nairn; economy: forestry, livestock, oil, winter skiing; Highland region is divided into 8 districts:

District	*area (sq km)*	*pop(1981)*
Badenoch and Strathspey	2,319	12,402
Caithness	1,776	27,380
Inverness	2,800	56,770
Lochaber	4,507	20,422
Nairn	422	10,119
Ross and Cromarty	5,000	47,518
Skye and Lochalsh	2,701	11,298
Sutherland	5,865	14,241

Highland, 41 33N 87 28W, pop(1980) 25,935, town in Lake county, NW Indiana, United States; 6 km SE of Hammond; railway.

Highland Park, 42 11N 87 48W, pop(1980) 30,611, residential town in Lake county, NE Illinois, United States; on L Michigan, 40 km N of Chicago; railway.

Highland Park, 42 24N 83 06W, pop(1980) 27,909, town in Wayne county, SE Michigan, United States; surrounded by the city of Detroit.

Higüey *ee-gway'*, 18 40N 68 43W, pop(1982e) 86,383, town in La Altagracia prov, E Dominican Republic, in a fertile agricultural region, 37 km ESE of El Seibo; airfield; established in 1502; monument: basilica of Our Lady of La Altagracia.

Hilden *hil'dun*, 51 10N 6 56E, pop(1983) 54,000, manufacturing city in Düsseldorf dist, Nordrhein-Westfalen (North Rhine-Westphalia) prov, W Germany; near the R Rhine, 11 km SE of Düsseldorf; economy: textiles.

Hildesheim *hil'des-hīm*, 52 09N 9 55E, pop(1983) 101,900, port in Hannover dist, SE Niedersachsen (Lower Saxony) prov, W Germany; 29 km SSE of Hannover, in the fertile valley of the R Innerste; founded in 1300; railway, its port is linked with the Mittelland Canal by a branch canal 13 km long; economy: iron, machinery, hardware, electronics; monuments: St Michael's church (11th-c), Romanesque cathedral (1054-79).

Hillaby, Mount *hil'a-bi*, 13 12N 59 35W, mountain at the centre of the island of Barbados, West Indies, rising to 340 m N of Bridgetown.

Ḥillah, Al *hi'lu*, 32 28N 44 29E, pop(1970) 128,811, capital town of Babil governorate, S central Iraq; 93 km S of Baghdād, on a channel of the R Euphrates; almost wholly built of bricks from the ruins of ancient Babylon; railway.

Hillerød *hi'lur-udh*, 55 56N 12 19E, pop(1981) 25,441, capital of Frederiksborg county, N Sjælland (Zealand), Denmark; railway; economy: engineering; monument: Frederiksborg Castle (1602-1620), built on three islands in a small lake.

Hil'lingdon, 51 32N 0 27W, pop(1981) 230,159, borough of W Greater London, England; bounded W by Buckinghamshire; includes the suburbs of Uxbridge, Ruislip-Northwood, Hayes and Harlington and Yiewsley and West Drayton; Brunel University (1966); Heathrow airport; railway; monument: 14th-c St Dunstan's church.

Hillsboro, 45 31N 122 59W, pop(1980) 27,664, capital of Washington county, NW Oregon, United States; on the Tualatin river, 22 km W of Portland; settled c.1845; railway.

Hilo *hee'lō*, 19 44N 155 05W, pop(1980) 35,269, county seat of Hawaii county, Hawaii, United States; on Hilo Bay, Hawaii I; towering above the city are the volcanic peaks of Mauna Kea and Mauna Loa; Hilo was badly damaged by tsunamis in 1946 and 1960; university; airfield; economy: food processing, sugar, flowers and tourism; events: Merrie Monarch Festival (April), Festival of the Pacific (July).

Hil'versum, 52 14N 5 10E, pop(1984e) 105,570, city in SE Noord Holland prov, W Netherlands; became famous for its radio and television stations; one of the fashionable residential and commuter districts of Amsterdam; the town developed from a small village after the Amsterdam-Amersfoort railway line was built in 1874; economy: textiles, leatherwork, printing, electrical engineering, pharmaceuticals.

Himachal Pradesh *hi-mah'chal pra-daysh'*, state in N India; bounded E by the Xizang auto region (Tibet) of the People's Republic of China, N by Jammu and Kashmir, W by Punjab and S by Haryana and Uttar Pradesh; pop(1981) 4,237,569; area 55,673 sq km; created from 30 former hill states in 1948; in 1954 Bilaspur state merged with Himachal Pradesh, and in Nov 1966 parts of the Punjab were transferred to Himachal Pradesh; achieved full statehood in Jan 1971; the principal language of the state is Pahari; includes 12 districts; capital Simla; the state is governed by a unicameral legislature; 76% of the population are employed in agriculture, growing seed potatoes, wheat, maize, rice and fruit; nearly 40% of the state is under forest, the largest supply of coniferous timber in N India; industry: timber products, salt, handicrafts; crossed by the railways between Simla and Chandigarh and Delhi and Jammu, which pass through Pathankot; crossed by the Siwalik range of mountains, which is a section of the Great Himalayan Range.

Himalayas *hi-mahl'ya* or *him-a-lay'a* (Sansk 'abode of snow'), central Asia; a gigantic wall of mountains lying N of the Indus and Brahmaputra rivers; the Himalayas are not a single range but a series of parallel ranges, generally rising towards the N; beyond lies the Tibetan plateau at over 3,000 m above sea-level; the Himalayas rise as a great curve from the Pamirs in the NW, stretching over 2,400 km to the borders of Assam and China in the E, where the R Brahmaputra cuts through in a succession of gorges; the land rises up to the foothills of the Himalayas from the swampy grassland of the Ganges Basin, known as *terai* in Nepal and *duars* in Bengal; beyond boulder-strewn, forest-clad talus slopes (*bhabar*) the land rises through the Siwaliks foothills to the 3 main ranges of the Himalayas, the Outer, Middle and Inner Himalayas; this three-fold arrangement is lost in the E and becomes 5 ranges in Kashmir - the Lesser and the Great Himalayas, the Zāskār Range, Ladākh Range and the Karakorams; Mt Everest, the highest peak in the world, rises to 8,848 m on the Nepal-Tibet border; other major peaks include K2 in the Karakorams (8,611 m), Kangchenjunga on the India-Nepal border (8,586 m), Makalu in Nepal (8,475 m), Dhaulagiri in Nepal (8,167 m), Nanga Parbat in Kashmir (8,126 m), and Annapurna in Nepal (8,091 m). Geologically the Himalayas are comparatively young mountains and belong to the great Tertiary mountain-building period when the Alps and the Andes also arose; the range is the approximate boundary between the Mongoloid and the Indo-Afghan races, the Tibeto-Chinese and the Indo-Germanic languages; in Hindu mythology the mountains are highly revered.

Himeji *hee-may'jee*, 34 50N 134 40E, pop(1980) 446,256, town in Hyōgo prefecture, Kinki region, S Honshū island, Japan; 51 km WNW of Kōbe; railway; economy: textiles, chemicals, metal goods, electrical appliances, precision instruments; monument: the Himeji-jō (Castle of the White Heron), completed in 1617; event: castle festival on 22 June.

Ḥimş *homs*, governorate (*mohofazat*) in Syria; bounded NW by Lebanon and SE by Jordan and Iraq; pop(1981) 812,517; capital Ḥimş; other chief town Tadmur (Palmyra); mostly desert; comprises the N part of the Jebel esh Sharqi (Anti-Lebanon) range (NW); drained by the R 'Āsi (Orontes); traversed W-E by an oil pipeline which passes through Tadmur.

Ḥimş, EMESA *e'me-sa* (anc), 34 44N 36 43E, pop(1981) 354,548, industrial capital city of Ḥimş governorate W central Syria; on the R 'Āsi (Orontes), 160 km N of Dimashq (Damascus); commercial centre in well-irrigated area; road and rail junction; economy: oil refining, sugar refining, manufacture of textiles, cement, metals, silk, rayon and fertilizers, and production of industrial refrigeration plant; monuments: mausoleum containing the tomb of Khaled Ibn Al-Walid, the great commander of the Muslim armies who brought Islam to Syria in 636.

Hinck'ley, 52 33N 1 21W, pop(1981) 35,611, town in Hinckley and Bosworth dist, Leicestershire, central England; 20 km SW of Leicester; railway; economy: footwear, hosiery, textiles.

Hindley, 53 32N 2 35W, pop(1981) 21,493, town in Wigan borough, Greater Manchester, NW England; 4 km SE of Wigan; railway; economy: coal, textiles, rubber, paint.

Hindu Kush *hin'doo koosh*, PAROPAMISUS (anc), mountain range in central Asia, an extension of the Himalayan system and the 2nd highest mountain range in the world, covering some 805 km; runs WSW from the SW corner of the Pamir Plateau, NW Frontier prov of Pakistan, to the Bāmīān prov of NE Afghanistan; rises to 7,690 m in Tirich Mir on the Chittral border; 4 subsidiary ridges fan out from the main range; from Bāmīān it is continued SW by the Kūh-e Bābā; crossed by several passes; the Salang Tunnel on the border of the Baghlān and Parvān provs of Afghanistan, is the main break in the system, which allows Kābul to be linked to the area N of the Hindu Kush and the USSR; peaks of the Hindu Kush are permanently snow-covered and have little vegetation; Alexander the Great and Tamerlane followed the passes of the Hindu Kush in their invasions of India.

Hink'ley Point, nuclear power station, Somerset, SW England, on the coast of Bridgwater Bay, W of Stolford; gas-cooled, graphite-moderated reactors came into commercial operation in 1965 and advanced gas-cooled reactors in 1976, 1978.

Hinnøy *hin'u-oo*, HINDOY, island in the Norwegian Sea off the NW coast of Norway, belonging to the Vesterålen group; largest island in Norway; rises to 1,267 m in the SW (Moysalen peak); area 2,198 sq km; length 88 km; the N of island is administered by Troms county while the S is administered by Nordland county.

Hiratsuka *hee-ra'tse-ka*, 35 20N 139 19E, pop(1980) 214,293, town in Kanagawa prefecture, Kanto region, central Honshū island, Japan; on N shore of Sagami-wan Bay, 30 km WSW of Yokohama; railway; economy: textiles.

Hiroshima *hi-re-shee'ma*, *hee-ro'shi-ma*, 34 23N 132 27E, pop(1980) 899,399, capital of Hiroshima prefecture, Chugōku region, S Honshū island, Japan; on the S coast, in Hiroshima-wan Bay; on the delta of the R Ota; founded in 1594 as a castle on the Isle of Hiroshima; the city served as a military headquarters in the Sino-Japanese War (1894-95) and the Russo-Japanese War (1904-05); an atomic bomb was dropped here on 6 Aug 1945: c.150,000 people were killed or wounded and 75% of the buildings were destroyed or severely damaged; the town was rebuilt in 1958; university (1949); railway; airport at 7 km; shipping services; economy: naval shipyards, car manufacturing, chemicals, textiles, food processing; monuments: in Peace Memorial park are the Cenotaph (which contains the names of the bomb victims of 1945), the Eternal Flame, the Fountain of Prayer and the Peace Memorial museum; the Peace Memorial museum contains a display and short film on the aftermath of the atomic bomb; also in Peace Memorial park is the shell of the Industrial Exhibition Hall, the only building to survive the holocaust, now known as the Atom Dome; Ri jô Castle, built on the Isle of Hiroshima and destroyed by the atom bomb, was rebuilt in 1958 and now contains a museum with displays of ancient pottery, maps, manuscripts and weapons; events: 15 July, celebrations at Miyajima (Itsukushima shrine); Peace Festival in the Peace Memorial Park on 6 Aug.

Hispanio'la, formerly SANTO DOMINGO, 2nd largest island of the Greater Antilles, E Caribbean; between Cuba (W) and Puerto Rico (E), separated from the former by the 88 km-wide Windward Passage, and from the latter by the 120 km-wide Mona Passage; the W third of the island is occupied by Haiti, the rest by the Dominican Republic; the island is predominantly mountainous, traversed NW-SE by several forested ranges, in particular the Cordillera Central where the highest peak in the West Indies rises to 3,175 m (Pico Duarte); largest river is the Artibonite, flowing mostly through Haitian territory; the island was named by Columbus La Isla Española when he made his first landing here in 1492.

Hitachi *hee-ta'chee*, 36 35N 140 40E, pop(1980) 204,596, industrial city in Ibaraki prefecture, Kanto region, E Honshū island, Japan; on the E coast, on the Pacific Ocean, 30 km NE of Mito; railway.

Hitch'in, 51 57N 0 17W, pop(1981) 33,744, town in North Hertfordshire dist, Hertfordshire, SE England; 13 km NE of Luton; railway; economy: engineering, flour, parchment.

Hitra, *hit'rah*, formerly HITTEREN, Norwegian island in the Norwegian Sea off W coast of Norway, WSW of the entrance to Trondheimsfjord (Trondheim Fjord), 59 km W of Trondheim; area 571 sq km; length 46 km; width 19 km; administered by Møre og Romsdal county.

Hjälmaren *yel'mar-en*, HJÄLMAR (Eng), lake in Västmanland, Södermanland and Örebro counties, SE Sweden; extends from Örebro in W to Eskilstuna in E; E of L Vänern and N of L Vättern; area 484 sq km; max depth 28 m; linked with L Mälaren to NE by Hjälmare Canal.

Hjørring *yœr'ring*, 57 28N 9 59E, pop(1981) 23,697, city in Nordjylland county, NE Jylland (Jutland), Denmark; railway; economy: shipbuilding.

Hkakabo Razi *ka-ka'bō rah'zee*, 28 17N 97 46E, mountain in Kachin state, N Burma; the highest peak in Burma, it rises to 5,881 m on the border with China.

Hlohovec *lo'ho-wets*, 48 26N 17 49E, pop(1984) 22,633, town in Západoslovenský region, Slovak Socialist Republic, S central Czechoslovakia; on R Váh, NW of Nitra; railway; economy: agricultural centre.

Hlučín *loot'cheen*, 49 54N 18 11E, pop(1984) 23,124, town in Severomoravský region, Czech Socialist Republic, central Czechoslovakia; NW of Ostrava, near the Polish frontier; railway.

Ho *hō*, 6 38N 0 38W, pop(1982) 39,958, capital town of Volta region, SE Ghana, W Africa; NE of Akosombo, near the Togo border; economy: civil engineering.

Ho Chi Minh *hō chee min*, THANH PHO HO CHI MINH, SAIGON *sī-gon*, 10 46N 106 43E, pop(1979e) 3,419,978, largest city in Vietnam, Indo-China; on R Saigon, S Vietnam, 54 km from its mouth on the South China Sea; jointly administered with Cholon city to the SW; the chief industrial centre of Vietnam; named after the leader of the communist Viet-Minh League which declared Vietnam an independent republic in 1946; airport; economy: textiles, rubber products, soap, rice milling, brewing, distilling, seafood exports, food processing, bamboo and rattan exports, fruit and vegetables.

Hobart *hō'bart*, 42 54S 147 18E, pop(1986) 180,300, seaport and state capital in Hobart stat div, SE Tasmania, Australia; on the Derwent river at the foot of Mt Wellington; founded in 1804 as a penal colony; capital of Tasmania since 1812 and a city since 1842; University of Tasmania (1890); railway; airport; economy: textiles, clothes, zinc, paper, food processing.

Hobbs, 32 42N 103 08W, pop(1980) 29,153, city in Lea county, SE New Mexico, United States; 105 km ENE of Carlsbad and 6 km W of the Texas border; economy: developed after the discovery of oil and natural gas in 1927; chemical industries; thoroughbred horses are raised in the area.

Hoboken *hō-bō'ken*, 40 44N 74 02W, pop(1980) 42,460, city in Hudson county, NE New Jersey, United States; port on the Hudson river, on the N edge of Jersey City; a former resort for New Yorkers; achieved city status in 1855; a railway terminus, it is linked to Manhattan by tunnels and ferries; economy: electronics, electrical equipment, chemicals.

Hochvogel *hōKH'fō-gul*, 47 23N 10 27E, peak in the Allgäuer Alpen (Allgäu Alps), S Bayern (Bavaria) prov, on Austro-German border, 13 km E of Obersdorf; height 2,593 m.

Hoddesdon *hodz'den*, 51 46N 0 01W, pop(1981) 38,111, town in Broxbourne dist, Hertfordshire, SE England; part of Greater London urban area; 5 km S of Ware; economy: foodstuffs, engineering, chemicals.

Hódmezövásárhely *hōd'mez-ü-va'shar-hay*, 46 28N 20 22E, pop(1984e) 54,000, town in Csongrád county, S Hungary; near R Tisza, NE of Szeged; railway; agriculture school; economy: grain and cattle trade, electronics, agricultural machinery, pottery, timber, textiles.

Hodonin *hod'on-yeen*, 48 51N 17 09E, pop(1984) 26,160, town in Jihomoravský region, Czech Socialist Republic, central Czechoslovakia; on R Morava, SE of Brno; Thomas G. Masaryk born here; railway; economy: petroleum, food processing.

Hoek van Holland *hook van hol'ant*, HOOK OF HOLLAND (Eng), cape on the SW coast of Zuid Holland prov, S SW Netherlands; N of the mouth of the Nieuwe Mass river; also the name of a port situated 27 km WNW of Rotterdam; ferry links with the UK.

Hof *hōf*, 50 18N 11 55E, pop(1983) 52,500, manufacturing town in Oberfranken dist, NE Bayern (Bavaria) prov, W Germany; on the R Saale, 50 km NNE of Bayreuth; railway; economy: textiles, brewing, machinery.

Hofei, capital of Anhui prov, E China. See Hefei.

Hoffman Estates, 42 03N 88 10W, pop(1980) 37,272, town in Cook county, NE Illinois, United States; 40 km NW of Chicago.

Hofsjökull *hofs'ye-kootl*, glacier of central Iceland; 3rd largest glacier in Iceland; area 994 sq km.

Hoh Xil Shan, mountain range in NE Xizang aut region (Tibet) and SW Qinghai prov, SW China; S offshoot of the Kunlun Shan range; extends E to adjoin the Bayan Har Shan range.

Hohe Acht *hō'u ahKHt'*, 50 22N 7 00E, highest peak of the Eifel range, W Rheinland-Pfalz (Rhineland-Palatinate) prov, W Germany, 3 km E of Adenau; height 747 m.

Hohe Rhön *hō'u run*, mountain range in E Hessen (Hesse) and NW Bayern (Bavaria) provs, W Germany; main range of the Rhön Mts; highest peak is the Wasserkuppe (950 m); a notable gliding centre.

Hohe Tauern *hō'e tow'arn*, mountain range of the Eastern Alps in Tirol and Kärnten states of W Austria, rising to 3,797 m at Grossglockner, the highest peak in Austria; the Venediger group, the most westerly part of the Hohe Tauern, has numerous glaciers; 10,000 sq km have national park status.

Hohhot *hoo-hay-hot*, HUHOHAOT'E, HUHEHOT, formerly KWESUI ('green city'), 40 49N 111 37E, pop(1984e) 778,000, capital of Nei Mongol aut region (Inner Mongolia), N China; area 65 sq km; founded in 1581 and extended in 1735, its name was changed to Hohhot in 1954; owing to the threat of invasion by the Soviet Union a 7,000 metre-long tunnel system has been built to allow evacuation to the Daqing mountains; railway; airfield; economy: textiles, clothing, sugar refining, cigarettes, food products, dairy products, machinery, electronics, televisions, building materials, musical instruments; monuments: White Pagoda; Dayao Stone-Age village, discovered in 1973; tomb of Wang Zhaojun.

Hoima *hō-ee'ma*, 1 25N 31 22E, town in Western prov, Uganda, E Africa; 50 km SW of Masindi.

Hokkaidō *hah-kī'dō*, YEZO, EZO, northernmost and 2nd largest island of the Japanese archipelago; bounded by the Sea of Japan (W), the Pacific Ocean (E) and the Sea of Okhotsk (NE); separated from Honshū I to the S by the Tsugaru-kaikyō Strait, from Sakhalin I to the N by the La Pérouse (or Sōya-kaikyō) Strait and from the Kuril'skiye Ostrova Is to the NE by the Nemuro-kaikyō Strait; the island measures 418 km N-S, 450 km E-W, with an irregularly shaped peninsula in the SW; Hokkaidō is largely mountainous with active and inactive volcanic cones in the central area; there are numerous hot springs in the SW; rises in the centre to 2,290 m at Mt Asahi-dake in Taisetsuzan national park; pop(1980) 5,576,000; area 83,513 sq km; economy: rice, rye, sugarbeet, grazing, forestry, fishing, and mining of iron, gold, chrome; oil and natural gas; originally populated by the Ainu, Hokkaidō served as an island of exiles; fear of Russian invasion led to the building of fortifications on the island in 1812 and to colonization schemes after 1868; Hokkaidō is now popular as a winter sports resort.

Holbæk *hol'bek*, 56 33N 10 19E, pop(1981) 20,634, town on the Isefjord, Vestsjælland county, NW Sjælland (Zealand), Denmark; railway; economy: engineering.

Holguín *ol-geen'*, prov in E Cuba, bounded NE by the Atlantic Ocean; hilly in the SE; area 9,105 sq km; pop(1981) 911,034; capital Holguín; chief towns Banes and Antilla; economy: farming and sugar cane.

Holguín, 20 54N 76 15W, pop(1983e) 192,182, capital town of Holguín prov, E Cuba; 104 km NNW of Santiago de Cuba; communication and trading centre for agricultural region; founded in 1523; the new Lenin district is built on former flat wasteland; college of technology; railway.

Holland. See Netherlands, The.

Holland, 42 47N 86 07W, pop(1980) 26,281, town in Ottawa county, W Michigan, United States; on L Michigan, 40 km WSW of Grand Rapids; railway; summer resort; event: Tulip Time Festival (May).

Holland, North, prov in the Netherlands. See Noord Holland.

Holland, South, prov in the Netherlands. See Zuid Holland.

Hollingworth, town in Derbyshire, England. See Glossop.

Hollywood, dist of Los Angeles city, California, United States; centre of the American film and television industries.

Hollywood, 26 01N 80 09W, pop(1980) 121,323, resort town in Broward county, SE Florida, United States; on the Atlantic Ocean, 12 km S of Fort Lauderdale; railway; particularly favoured as a place for retirement.

Holmfirth-Honley *hōm-*, 53 35N 1 46W, pop(1981) 21,148, town in Kirklees borough, West Yorkshire, N England; part of West Yorkshire urban area; on the R Holm, 7 km S of Huddersfield; railway.

Holon *hō-lōn'*, 32 01N 34 46E, pop(1982) 134,600, town in Tel Aviv dist, W Israel; SE of Tel Aviv-Yafo.

Holstebro *hŏl'ste-brō*, 56 22N 8 38E, pop(1981) 28,270, town in Ringkøbing county, W Jylland (Jutland), Denmark; railway; economy: engineering, foodstuffs.

Holy Island, LIN'DISFARNE, island in the North Sea off the E coast of Northumberland, NE England; 15 km SE of Berwick-upon-Tweed; accessible at low water from the mainland by a causeway built in 1954; area 10 sq km; monument: Lindisfarne priory (1093), built on the site of an earlier 7th-c cathedral founded by St Aidan; the colony of Columban monks reached its greatest glory under St Cuthbert, and the famous illuminated manuscripts known as the *Lindisfarne Gospels* were written here.

Holyhead, CAER GYBI (Welsh), 53 19N 4 38W, pop(1981) 12,652, chief town and port on the island of Yns Môn (Anglesey) in Isle of Anglesey dist, Gwynedd, NW Wales; on the N coast of Holyhead island; airport; railway, ferry to Dun Laoghaire in Ireland; economy: engineering, transport equipment, tourism.

Holyoke *hō'li-ōk*, 42 12N 72 37W, pop(1980) 44,678, city in Hampden county, SW Massachusetts, United States; on the R Connecticut, 13 km N of Springfield; city status in 1873; railway; economy: leading US manufacturer of fine writing and envelope paper; Holyoke power dam on the R Connecticut just N of Holyoke at the Hadley Falls.

Holywell, 53 17N 3 13W, pop(1981) 11,160, town in Delyn dist, Clwyd, NE Wales; 6 km NW of Flint; the 'Welsh Lourdes', a place of pilgrimage since the 7th century; St Winefride (Gwenfrewi), who was beheaded in the 7th century, is honoured in the 15th-c St Winefride's chapel which stands above the healing spring; events: pilgrimages in June and Nov.

Holywood, ARD MHIC NASCA (Gael), 54 38N 5 50W, pop(1981) 9,462, town in North Down dist, Down, E Northern Ireland; a suburb of Belfast on the S shore of Belfast Lough, 9.5 km NE of Belfast; economy: engineering; monument: ruins of a monastery, founded originally in the 7th century, replaced in the 13th century by Franciscans and later burned in 1572.

Honan, province in E central China. See Henan.

Honan, town in Henan prov, E central China. See Luoyang.

Honduras *hon-doo'ras*, *hon-dyoo'ras* (Eng), official name Republic of Honduras, REPÚBLICA DE HONDURAS (Sp), a Central American republic, bounded SW by El Salvador, W by Guatemala, E and SE by Nicaragua, N by the Caribbean Sea, and S by the Pacific Ocean; timezone GMT −6; area 112,088 sq km; capital Tegucigalpa; chief towns San Pedro Sula, Choluteca, La Ceiba, and El Progreso; pop(1985e) 4,327,487; population growth rate 3.3% (1960-78); 90% of the population is of Spanish-Indian origin; Spanish is the official language although Indian dialects are also spoken; in the Islas de la Bahía (Bay Is) English is also widely spoken; the predominant religion is Roman Catholicism; the unit of currency is the lempira of 100 centavos; national holidays 14 April (America's Day), 15 Sept (Independence Day), 3 Oct (Morazan's birthday), 12 Oct (Columbus' Day), 21 Oct

(Armed Forces Day); membership: CACM, FAO, G-77, IADB, IBRD, ICAO, ICO, IDA, IDB, IFAD, IFC, ILO, IMF, IMO, INTELSAT, INTERPOL, ISO, ITU, OAS, PAHO, SELA, UN, UNESCO, UPEB, UPU, WFTU, WHO, WMO.

Physical description. Coastal lands in the S around the Golfo de Fonseca are separated from the well-watered Caribbean coastlands by mountains that cross the country from NW to SE. In the S a plateau covered with volcanic ash and lava rises to 2,849 m at Cerro de las Minas in the Celaque range. The lowlands in the S are formed by the coastal plains of the Golfo de Fonseca on the Pacific Ocean. The Islas de la Bahía (Bay Is) in the Caribbean Sea and a group of 288 islands in the Golfo de Fonseca also belong to Honduras. Chief rivers are the Patuca, Ulúa, Guayape, and Aguán. In the extreme NE of the country is the Laguna Caratasca.

Climate. The climate is tropical in the coastal areas and temperate in the central and W parts of the country. Upland areas have 2 wet seasons, from May to July, and in Sept-Oct. Temperatures in the interior range from 15°C to 23.9°C and in the coastal plains the average is about 30°C.

History, government and constitution. Honduras was settled by Spaniards in the early 16th century and was a province of the captaincy-general of Guatemala throughout the colonial period. It gained independence from Spain in 1821 and joined the Federation of Central America. On 5 Nov 1838 Honduras declared itself an independent sovereign state free from the Federation of South America. Congress was suspended in 1972 and a military junta ruled between 1972 and 1981. Honduras is a democratic constitutional republic. The 1982 Constitution provides for an executive, 82-member unicameral legislature (National Congress), and a judiciary appointed by the National Congress. Executive authority rests with the president who is elected for 4 years.

Economy. Honduras is the least developed country in Central America, dependent largely on agriculture, livestock, forestry, and mining. Agriculture is the most important sector of the economy, constituting one-third of national income, exporting almost 70% of its output, and generating about half of total export revenues. The main export crops grown on the N lowlands are bananas, coffee, beef, cotton, tobacco, and sugar. Large areas in the E and W parts of the country are dedicated exclusively to cattle raising. The Olancho Forest Development Programme, which includes the construction of a vast pulp and paper complex, is a new development in the important forestry sector. Gold, silver, lead, and zinc are the only minerals which are mined for export. Offshore exploration of petroleum is taking place in the Caribbean, with an oil refinery at Puerto Cortés. Industry, accounting for over 17% of national income, is based on the manufacture and processing of cement, textiles, wood products, and cigars. There has been considerable growth in light manufacturing, particularly in the San Pedro Sula area. The main exports are bananas, coffee, beef, lumber, metals, and sugar, chiefly to the USA. Petroleum, chiefly from the USA and from OPEC countries, is the main import.

Communications. Honduras is connected with Guatemala, El Salvador and Nicaragua by the Pan-American Highway. The only railways are in the N coastal region and are used mainly for the transportation of bananas. There are international airports at Tegucigalpa, San Pedro Sula, and La Ceiba.

Administrative divisions. Honduras is divided into 18 departments as follows:

Department	*area (sq km)*	*pop(1983e)*
Atlántida	4,248	242,235
Choluteca	4,207	289,637
Colón	8,870	128,370
Comayagua	5,193	211,465
Copán	3,200	217,258
Cortés	3,951	624,090
El Paraíso	7,213	206,601
Francisco Morazán	7,943	736,272
Gracias a Dios	16,621	35,471
Intibucá	3,070	111,412
Islas de La Bahía	259	18,744
La Paz	2,327	86,627
Lempira	4,287	174,916
Ocotepeque	1,678	64,151
Olancho	24,339	228,122
Santa Bárbara	5,113	286,854
Valle	1,564	125,640
Yoro	7,935	304,310

Hong, river in Vietnam. See Red River.

Hong Kong, British Crown Colony, E Asia; bounded N by the Guangdong region of SE China, lying E of Zhu Jiang (Pearl River estuary) and 145 km SE of the Chinese city of Guangzhou (Canton); the South China Sea forms all other boundaries; timezone GMT +8; area 1,066.53 sq km; pop(1984) 5,394,000; pop is 98% Chinese; the colony has attracted illegal immigrants from the People's Republic of China, and refugees from Vietnam (since July 1982 Vietnamese refugees have been detained in enclosed centres, outside of which they are not allowed to seek work); capital Hong Kong (the name of the island); Victoria was the original capital of the colony but is now a district of the city of Hong Kong; English and Cantonese, spoken by 82% of the pop, are the official languages; predominant religions are Buddhism and Taoism; the official currency is the Hong Kong dollar which is divided into 100 cents; national holidays include the first 3 days of the first lunar month (the Chinese New Year), Ching Ming Festival on the 8th day of the 3rd lunar month, Tuen Ng on the 5th day of the 5th lunar month, Liberation Day on the last Monday in Aug, Mid-Autumn Festival on the 15th day of the 8th lunar month, Chung Yeung Festival on the 9th day of the 9th lunar month, 21 April (Queen's birthday); membership of ADB, IMO, INTERPOL, WMO and Multifiber Arrangement.

Physical description. The territory of Hong Kong, with its sharply indented coastline, consists principally of a rugged ridge of granite intersected by water which separates the mainland from the larger islands of Hong Kong and Lantau and from about 235 smaller islands. The hills are largely covered in dense scrub and trees planted to counteract the erosion caused by Japanese deforestation during World War II. Agriculture is only important on the flat land of narrow valleys in the New Territories, is separated from Kowloon by a ridge of mountains which are important water catchment areas.

Climate. The climate is subtropical with hot, humid summers and cool, dry winters. Average monthly temperatures vary from 16°C in Jan to 29°C in July. Such seasonal variation is unusual in the Tropics (Hong Kong is 160 km S of the Tropic of Cancer), but it is due to the effect of the monsoon winds, which blow from the N and NE during Sept-March and from the S and SW during April-Aug.

History and government. The Treaty of Nanking in 1842 ceded Hong Kong to Britain. The excellent natural harbour encouraged Hong Kong's early development from a trading post to a major port. The Convention of 1860 added Stonecutter's Island and in 1898 the New Territories were leased to Britain. Hong Kong was occupied by the Japanese during World War II. The Governor of Hong Kong, who represents the British Crown and is appointed by the British Monarch, is advised by a 16-member Executive Council and a 47-member Legislative Council. A 30-member Urban Council is responsible for the urban areas of Hong Kong Island and Kowloon, while the New Territories are

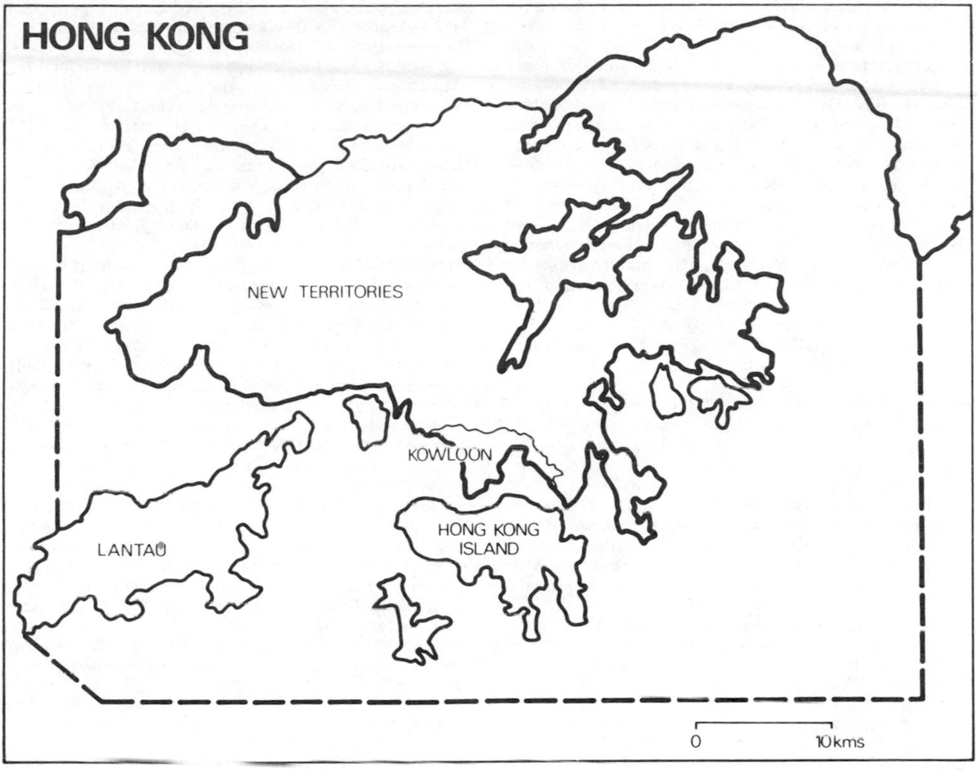

administered by their own secretary. District committees advise the governor in district affairs. The legal system is based on English common law with certain variations due to Chinese custom. Fifty-five departments carry out the administrative functions of the government. The British Government is responsible for foreign relations, but Hong Kong is largely independent in terms of commercial relations. Elections are held every 2 years for the selection of half of the elected membership of the Urban Council and the governor appoints the other members. Voting is limited to 200,000-300,000 professionals and skilled people. In 1997 Britain's 99-year lease of the New Territories will expire, whereupon, under the Sino-British Declaration initialled on 26 Sept 1984, Hong Kong will be restored to China on 1 July 1997. China has designated Hong Kong as a special administrative region as from 1997 and will allow regional independence in domestic affairs. Hong Kong will remain a freeport and a separate customs zone, foreign markets will be retained and the Hong Kong dollar will remain as the official currency. Hong Kong will be exempt from paying taxes to the central government.

Economy. The economy is based on banking, the import-export trade, shipbuilding and the manufacture of light industrial products such as textiles, electrical and electronic goods, watches, jewellery, cameras, footwear, toys and plastic goods; less than 2% of the territory's national income comes from agriculture. The main products are rice, vegetables and dairy products, but Hong Kong is required to import some 80% of its food - rice, wheat and water being the main shortages. Hong Kong's main trading partners include the USA and China. Hong Kong is an important freeport which acts as a gateway to China for the West. The airport (Kai Tak) is in Kowloon.

Administrative divisions. Hong Kong is divided into the 3 regions of Hong Kong Island, Kowloon and New Territories (includes most of the colony's 235 islands). Hong Kong Island is further subdivided into 4 dists - Central, Western, Eastern and Wan Chai, while Kowloon is divided into the 6 districts of Kowloon City, Kwun Tong, Mong Kok, Sham Shui Po, Wong Tai Po and Yau Ma Tei. The New Territories region comprises the 8 dists of the Islands, North, Sai Kung, Sha Tin, Tai Po, Tseun Wan, Tuen Mun and Yuen Long.

Hong Kong Island, island and region in the British Crown Colony of Hong Kong, SE Asia; S of New Territories, lying across the 1.5 km channel from the Kowloon peninsula and bounded on all sides by the South China Sea; ceded to Great Britain under the 1842 Treaty of Nanking; area 75 sq km; the island has a coastline of 74 km; Victoria was the original capital of the colony, but is now considered a dist of the city of Hong Kong, which lies on the island; Victoria Peak, rising to 554 m, is the highest point; the island comprises 4 city dists: Central, Western, Eastern and Wan Chai; population density of 28,500 to the sq km recorded in the 1981 census; the University of Hong Kong (1911) has some 5,700 students in 5 faculties; Hong Kong Philharmonic Orchestra was established in 1973; economy: an international financial and trading centre having 115 international banks with offices in the city; importing and exporting; light industries such as textiles, electronics and plastics.

Hongze Hu *hoong-tze hoo*, HUNGTSE HU, lake in W Jiangsu prov, E China; area 3,780 sq km; formed by the Huai He river; enters the Chang Jiang (Yangtze river) via Gaoyou Hu lake; connected with the Grand Canal; the area has now been reduced to 1,960 sq km.

Honiara *hō-nee-a'ra*, 9 28S 159 57E, pop(1979) 18,346, port and capital town of the Solomon Islands, SW Pacific, on the R Mataniko, NW coast of Guadalcanal I; the capital was transferred from Tulagi in the Florida group to Honiara on Guadalcanal after World War II; in 1568 Mendana, the European discoverer of the

Solomons, raised a cross here and claimed the island for Spain; Henderson Airport is 13 km E.

Honolulu *hon-o-loo'loo*, 21 19N 157 52W, pop(1980) 365,048, capital of state in Honolulu county, Hawaii, United States; largest city in the state and a port on Mamala Bay, Oahu I; a noted tourist resort, with the famous beach at Waikiki; ignored by Capt Cook when he explored the islands in 1778, Honolulu's harbour was entered by William Brown, an English captain, in 1794; became capital of the Kingdom of Hawaii in 1845; the Japanese attack on Pearl Harbor, the US naval base at Honolulu, on 7 Dec 1941, brought the United States into World War II; 3 universities; airport; economy: economic centre and main port of Hawaii; major industries include sugar processing and fruit canning; headquarters of the US Pacific Fleet; monuments: Bishop Museum, Pearl Harbor, Iolani Palace (the only royal palace in the United States), Aloha Tower, Diamond Head crater; events: King Kamehameha Day (June), Aloha Week (Sept).

Honshū *hon'shoo*, the largest of the 4 main islands of Japan; bounded W by the Sea of Japan, E by the Pacific Ocean; separated from Hokkaidō I to the N by the Tsugaru-kaikyō Strait, from Shikoku I to the S by the Seto Naikai Sea and from Kyūshū I to the SW by the Kammon-kaikyō Tunnels and Suō-nada Sea; c.1,290 km long and 48-240 km wide; Honshū is broadest in the centre where the land rises into the Japan Alps; Mt Fuji-san is the highest peak in Japan (3,776 m); to the W of these mountains is Biwa-ko (Lake Biwa), the largest lake in Japan; area 230,897 sq km; pop(1980) 93,246,000; the most populated areas are the coastal lowlands, including the cities of Tōkyo, Nagoya and Ōsaka; Honshū is divided into the 5 regions of Tōhoku, Kanto, Chūbu, Kinki and Chūgoku; these regions subdivide into 34 prefectures.

Hood, Mount, mountain in NW Oregon, United States; rises to 3,424 m in the Cascade range; the highest peak in Oregon state.

Hoorn, 52 38N 5 04E, pop(1984e) 50,473, city and municipality in E Noord Holland prov, W Netherlands; on an inlet of the Ijsselmeer; chief town of a wide rural area with an important market for cattle and cheese; birthplace of the navigator Willem Schouten (1580-1625), who rounded the S tip of America in 1616 and called it 'Cap Hoorn' (Cape Horn) after his home town; Jan Pieterszoon Coen (1587-1629), one of the founders of the Dutch Colonial Empire in the East Indies, was also born here; Hoorn was founded in the 14th century as a fishing and trading settlement, received its charter in 1356, expanded in the 16th and 17th centuries owing to the development of East Indies trade, then declined in importance when the harbour silted up in the 18th century; railway; economy: foodstuffs, metal and timber, tourism (2 yacht harbours); monuments: 17th-c town hall and fine gabled 17th-c houses.

Hooru, Îles de, *hoo'roo*, island group in the French overseas territory of Wallis and Futuna, central Pacific Ocean; area 115 sq km.

Hoover Dam, formerly BOULDER DAM (1936-47), 36 01N 114 45W, dam on the Colorado river between Clark county, Nevada and Mohave county, Arizona, United States; L Mead lies to the N; height 221 m; completed in 1936.

Hopeh, province in N China. See Hebei.

Hopkinsville, 36 52N 87 29W, pop(1980) 27,318, county seat of Christian county, SW Kentucky, United States; 90 km W of Bowling Green; railway; economy: leading tobacco market.

Hordaland, *hor'dahl-ahn'*, county of SW Norway, having the Hardangerfjorden (Hardanger Fjord) as its nucleus; area 15,634 sq km; pop(1983) 394,568; capital Bergen; there are many islands at the mouth of the fjord including Bømlo, Stord and Tysnesøy; the Hardangervidda range covers much of the E county with peaks including Hårteigen (1,691 m) and Hardangerjøkulen (1,862 m).

Hormozgān *hor'mōz-gan*, prov in SE Iran, bounded S by the Arabian Gulf and the Strait of Hormuz; pop(1982) 462,440; area 66,870 sq km; capital Bandar' Abbās.

Hormuz, Strait of *hor-mooz'*, passage linking the Gulf to the Arabian Sea; lies between the S coast of Iran and the Musandam Peninsula of Oman; 48-80 km wide; a strategic water route controlling ocean traffic to the oil terminals of the Gulf; Qeshm I is separated from the Coast of Iran to the NW by the Clarence Strait.

Horse Latitudes, 2 belts of ocean calm at 30° N and S of the Equator in which conditions of high atmospheric pressure exist almost permanently; it is from these belts towards the Doldrums that the Trade Winds constantly blow.

Hor'sens, 55 53N 9 53E, pop(1983) 54,779, seaport at head of Horsens Fjord, Vejle county, E Jylland (Jutland), Denmark; railway; economy: engineering; monument: early 13th-c Church of Our Saviour; the town originally developed around an early medieval stronghold.

Horsens Fjord, inlet of the Kattegat, in Århus and Vejle counties, E coast of Jylland (Jutland), Denmark; extends 21 km inland to Horsens city; at mouth of fjord are Hjarnø and Alrø Is.

Hors'forth, 53 51N 1 39W, pop(1981) 19,251, town in Leeds borough, West Yorkshire, N England; part of West Yorkshire urban area; 7 km NW of Leeds; railway.

Hor'sham, 36 45S 142 15E, pop(1983e) 12,660, town in Wimmera stat div, W Victoria, Australia; NW of Melbourne; railway; airfield; one of the largest wheat-growing areas in Victoria; home of the Victorian Wheat Institute and the Longerenong Agricultural College; monuments: Olde Horsham zoological garden; Wimmera wool factory.

Horsham, 51 04N 0 21W, pop(1981) 38,565, town in Horsham dist, West Sussex, S England; on the R Arun, 12 km SW of Crawley; railway; economy: engineering, pharmaceuticals, brewing, electronics, bricks.

Horta *or'ta*, dist of Portuguese autonomous region of the Azores comprising the Islands of Pico, Faial, Flores and Corvo; capital is Horta on Faial I; area 780 sq km; divided into 7 councils and 41 parishes; pop(1981) 19,942.

Horta, 38 32N 28 38W, pop(1981) 6,910, seaport and fortified capital of Horta dist, Portuguese autonomous region of the Azores; situated on SE coast of Faial I; possibly named after Josse van Hutere, who settled Flemish colonists here; exports wine, fruit and grain; air and naval base and radio station; monuments: churches of São Salvador and São Francisco.

Horten *hor'tun*, 59 25N 10 30E, pop(1980) 13,295, seaport on W side of Oslofjorden (Oslo Fjord), Vestfold county, SE Norway; car ferry to Moss; rail terminus; monuments: at Borrehavgene (N) is Europe's largest collection of royal burial mounds.

Hortobágy *hor'to-bad-y'*, national park in NE central Hungary; beyond the R Tisza; area 520 sq km; established in 1973; noted for its wild birds, plants and stock breeding; a nine-arched bridge, the longest stone bridge in Hungary, stands near the village of Hortobágy.

Hospitalet de Llobregat *os-pee-ta-let'* THay *lyo-vray-gat'*, 41 21N 2 06E, pop(1981) 294,033, outer industrial suburb 8 km from the centre of Barcelona city, Barcelona prov, Cataluña, E Spain; on Llobregat coastal plain; agricultural institute; economy: steel, nails, textiles, leather and petrochemicals.

Hot Springs, 34 31N 93 03W, pop(1980) 35,781, county seat of Garland county, central Arkansas, United States; 75 km WSW of Little Rock; a health and summer resort, noted for its thermal springs; economy: lumber, metal, and electrical products; event: Racing Festival (April).

Houaphan, prov (*khowèng*) of E Laos, SE Asia; capital Xam Nua.

Houghton-le-Spring *how'ton-*, 54 51N 1 28W, pop(1981) 35,361, town in Sunderland borough, Tyne and Wear, NE England; 9 km SW of Sunderland; economy: coal, engineering.

Houma *hoo'ma*, 29 36N 90 43W, pop(1980) 32,602, parish seat of Terrebonne parish, SE Louisiana, United States; a port on the Intracoastal Waterway, 74 km SW of New Orleans; railway; economy: processing of seafood, sugar cane, and oil; monument: Plantation Homes.

Houmt Souk *hoomt sook*, DJERBA, 33 55N 10 52E, pop(1975) 70,217, resort town on the Ile de Jerba, SE Tunisia, N Africa; located on N side of the island, 65 km E of Gabès; airport; monument: ruined Spanish fort.

Houndé *hoon'day*, 11 34N 3 31W, town in SW Burkina, W Africa; 105 km from Bobo Dioulasso.

Hounslow *hownz'lō*, 51 29N 0 22W, pop(1981) 200,829, borough of W Greater London, England; NW of Richmond-upon-Thames and adjacent to Heathrow airport; includes the suburbs of Feltham, Brentford and Chiswick, and Heston and Isleworth; railway; monuments: 17th-c Hogarth House and 18th-c Chiswick House.

Houston *hyoo'sten*, 29 46N 95 22W, pop(1980) 1,595,138, county seat of Harris county, SE Texas, United States; a port on the Houston Ship Channel, near Galveston Bay; the 5th largest city by pop in the USA; settled in 1836, it was capital of the republic of Texas 1837-39 and 1842-45; the city developed rapidly after the construction of the Ship Channel in 1914; 5 universities; railway; airports (Intercontinental, Hobby); economy: industrial, commercial, and financial centre, and the third-busiest port in the USA; the deep-water channel dredged between the city and the sea allows ocean-going vessels to reach the city which is a major oil centre with huge refineries and the largest petrochemical complex in the world; Houston is the corporate headquarters of numerous energy companies and a base for several space and science research firms; at nearby Clear Lake City is the NASA Johnson Space Center; industries include steel, shipbuilding, brewing, paper, rice and cotton; monuments: National Space Hall of Fame, San Jacinto battleground, Astroworld, Sam Houston Historical Park, the battleship *Texas*.

Hovd *KHovd*, KHOVD, county in W Mongolia; pop(1981e) 60,000; area 76,000 sq km; bounded W and SW by the People's Republic of China; capital Hovd; mountainous country; one-fifth of the county is steppe and desert; crossed by over 200 rivers; ibex and arkali sheep are widespread; copper, coal and iron ore are mined; industry: printing, wood processing, food processing and vehicle repair.

Hove, 50 49N 0 10W, pop(1981) 67,137, resort and residential suburb in East Sussex, SE England; part of Brighton-Worthing-Littlehampton urban area; adjoins Brighton; railway; economy: engineering.

Hövsgöl *huvs'gul*, HOEVSGOEL, county in N Mongolia; pop(1981e) 85,000; area 109,000 sq km; bounded N by the USSR; capital Mörön; at 2,600 m above sea level in the N is Hövsgöl Nuur lake (2,612 sq km); ibex, arkali sheep, bear and wild boar are common; copper, lead, phosphorite, jasper and fluorspar are mined; economy: wool laundry, open-cast mining, wood processing, cattle, animal fodder.

Howland Island, 0 48N 176 38W, uninhabited island in central Pacific Ocean, 1,150 km E of Tarawa; annexed by USA in 1856; important source of guano until 1890; US colonists landed on Howard and Baker I (58 km SE) in 1936 and an airstrip and lighthouse were built in 1937; Amelia Earhart and Fred Noonan refuelled here on their 1937 round-the-world flight before disappearing; the island is now under the jurisdiction of the US Fish and Wildlife Service.

Hoyerswerda *hoy'urs-ver-dah*, 51 28N 14 17E, pop(1981) 71,124, town in Hoyerswerda dist, Cottbus, E East Germany; founded in 14th century; railway; economy: glass.

Hoy'lake, 53 23N 3 11W, pop(1981) 24,620, coastal resort town in Wirral borough, Merseyside, NW England; at the NW end of the Wirral peninsula; railway; championship golf course.

Hradec Králové *hæra'dets krah'low-eh*, 50 13N 15 15E, pop(1984) 98,034, capital of Východočeský region, Czech Socialist Republic, NW central Czechoslovakia; at the junction of the Elbe and Orlice rivers; railway; economy: fruit and vegetable trade, textiles, tanning, musical instruments.

Hron, river in S Slovak Socialist Republic, E Czechoslovakia; rises W of Košice and flows W and S to meet the R Danube opposite Esztergom; length 270 km.

Hrvatska *her'vat-ska*, CROATIA *kro-ay'sha* (Eng), a constituent republic of Yugoslavia; bounded to the W by the Adriatic Sea, to the N by Slovenija and Romania and to the S by Bosna-Hercegovina; pop(1981) 4,601,469; area 56,538 sq km; capital Zagreb; chief towns include Rijeka, Čakovec, Split and Zadar; populated by southern Slavs, Croats (originally *Chorvats*, 'mountain people') and Serbs; from 1888 it formed a joint crownland with Slavonia; in the 1860s German peasants settled in E Croatia, creating large, regularly planned villages; here purely Slav territories have few towns.

Hsia-men, town in Fujian prov, SE China. See Xiamen.

Hsin-chu *sin-choo*, pop(1982e) 292,740, independent municipality in N Taiwan; on the railway line from Mia-oli to T'ai-pei; a science-based industrial park was opened here in Sept 1980; economy: integrated circuits and silicon wafers.

Hsin-chu, county in NW Taiwan; area 1,424.7 sq km; pop(1982e) 365,837.

Hsining, capital of Qinghai prov, W central China. See Xining.

Huainan *wī-nahn*, HUAI-NAN, 32 41N 117 06E, pop(1983e) 1,017,000, city in Anhui prov, E China; railway.

Hua-lien *hwa-lyen*, county of E Taiwan; area 4,628.6 sq km; pop(1982e) 361,017.

Huambo *wam'bō*, formerly NOVA LISBOA (1928-78), 12 42S 15 54E, pop(1970) 61,885; capital of prov of same name, W central Angola, SW Africa; 240 km E of Lobito; alt 1,695 m; founded in 1912; a hydroelectric plant is located 16 km SE; railway; airfield.

Huancavelica *wahng-ka-vay-lee'ka*, dept in W Peru; mountainous region set in the Cordillera Occidental; drained by the Río Mantaro, which separates the Cordillera Central from the Cordillera Occidental; pop(1981) 346,797; area 22,870 sq km; capital Huancavelica; the road from Huancavelica to Ayacucho (capital of Ayacucho dept) via Santa Inés averages 4,000 m in altitude for 150 km, making it the world's highest continuous road.

Huancayo *wang-kī'yō*, 12 05S 75 12W, pop(1972) 115,693, capital of Junín dept, central Peru; alt 3,271 m; commercial centre for central Peru; university (1962); railway; event: annual fiesta of the Virgin of Cocharas, commencing on 8 Sept, with feasting and dancing lasting a week.

Huang He, *wang hō*, HUANG HO, YELLOW RIVER, 2nd longest river in China; length 5,464 km; drainage area: 752,400 sq km; rises at the N foot of the Bayan Har Shan range in Qinghai prov, W central China; flows SE into Sichuan prov then NW circling the A'nyêmaqên Shan range; the Huang He then curves past the town of Lanzhou in Gansu prov, flows NE through Ningxia, through Nei Mongol (Inner Mongolia) past Baotou, then S to form the border between Shanxi and Shaanxi provs; the Huang He then turns to flow E along the Shanxi-Henan prov border before crossing Henan to the N of Zhengzhou and forming part of the prov border with Shandong; from the beginning of the Henan border with Shandong, the Huang He flows NE, past Jinan, to enter the Bohai Gulf in the NE of Shandong prov; in its upper reaches the Huang He enters a section of gorges, now used for hydroelectric power; flooding was formerly a major problem, but dykes on the river's lower reaches have been repaired and water conservancy projects on its upper and middle reaches have been extended; tributaries include the Tao He, Huang Shui, Wuding He, Fen He, Wei He, Luo He and Qin He.

Huangguoshu Falls, waterfall in W Guizhou prov, S central China; largest waterfall in China, 84 m wide and with a drop of 67 m; situated on the Bai Shui river, a headstream of the Dabang, which is a tributary of the Beipan Jiang river; the river bed consists of 9 successive drops; at the side of the falls is Waterfall Cave, a 100 m-long cavern set in the cliff face with 6 openings which look onto the falls.

Huangtu Gaoyuan *wang-too gow-yoo-an*, LOESS PLATEAU, plateau in N central China; includes Shanxi prov, N Shaanxi prov, most of Ningxia aut region, central and E Gansu and W Henan provs; bordered S by the Qin Ling range and the Wei He plain, by the Great Wall (N), the Taihang Shan range (E) and the Tao He river (W); area 400,000 sq km; alt 800-2,000 m; covered with a layer of wind-blown loess, a yellowish soil rich in nitrogen, phosphorus and potassium; the loess is generally 100 m deep, although in parts of N Shaanxi and E Gansu it is 150 m deep, and over 200 m deep in W Gansu; the looseness of the soil, sparse vegetation and frequent summer rainstorms have caused serious soil erosion, carving the land into gullies and reducing soil fertility; trees and grass are now being planted to help conserve soil and water.

Huánuco *wa'noo-kō*, dept in central Peru; slopes eastwards from the Cordillera Central; crossed by R Huallaga; pop(1981) 484,780; area 35,314 sq km; capital Huánuco.

Huánuco, 9 55S 76 11W, capital of Huánuco dept, central Peru; on the Río Huallaga; 2 universities (1964); economy: trade in sugar, cotton, coffee, cacao.

Huanuni *wa-noo'nee*, 18 15S 66 48W, pop(1976) 17,258, town in P. Dalence prov, Oruro, SW Bolivia; railway; economy: tin mining.

Huaquillas *wa-keel'yas*, 3 30S 80 15W, pop(1982) 20,117, town in El Oro prov in the Andean Sierra of SW Ecuador; on the border with Peru.

Huascarán *was-ka-ran'*, national park in Ancash dept, W Peru; consists of the Cordillera Blanca, part of the Andean Cordillera Occidental; area 3,400 sq km; established in 1975; rises to 6,768 m in Nevado de Huascarán, highest peak in Peru.

Huascarán, Nevado de, 9 07S 77 37W, height 6,768 m, extinct Andean volcano in Ancash dept, W Peru; in the Cordillera Blanca; 14 km ENE of Yungay; highest mountain in Peru and one of the highest in the Andes; set in a massif containing other snow-capped peaks.

Hubei *hoo-bay*, HUPEH, prov in E central China; bordered W by Shaanxi and Sichuan provs, S by Hunan prov, E by Jiangxi and Anhui provs and N by Henan prov; situated in the centre of the Chang Jiang (Yangtze river) valley; mountainous in the N, W and E, falling to low plains watered by numerous rivers in the central S; in the W are the Wudang Shan, Jing Shan and Wu Shan ranges, rising to 3,053 m at Dashennongjia Mt, the highest peak in central China; the Tongbai Shan range in the N forms part of the border with Henan prov, while the border with Anhui lies along the Dabie Shan and that with Jiangxi along the Mufu Shan range and the Chang Jiang river; the S and centre of Hubei is agricultural; Hubei is drained by over 1,000 rivers, the principal ones being the Chang Jiang, Han Shui and Qing Jiang; pop(1982) 47,804,150; area 187,500 sq km; capital Wuhan; principal towns Jingmen, Suizhou and Xiaogan; economy: rice, wheat, cotton, oil bearing plants, fish, timber, minerals (copper, phosphorus, iron, rock salt and gypsum), textiles.

Huber Heights, 39 48N 84 09W, pop(1980) 35,480, town in Montgomery county, W Ohio, United States; 11 km NNE of Dayton.

Hubli *hoob'lee*, HUBLI-DHERWAR, HUBLI-DHARWAR, 15 20N 75 14E, pop(1981) 526,000, city in Karnataka, S India; E of Goa; linked to Belgaum and Davangere by rail; held by the Vijayanagar kings during the 14-16th centuries; cities of Hubli and Dherwar were incorporated as one in 1961; Hubli is the trade and transportation centre for the surrounding cotton and rice-growing region, while Dherwar is the administrative centre.

Huck'nall, 53 02N 1 11W, pop(1981) 27,506, town in Newark dist, Nottinghamshire, central England; 10 km N of Nottingham; economy: electrical equipment, engineering, coal, clothing.

Ḥudaydah, Al, HODEIDA *ho-day'da*, 14 50N 43 00E, pop(1975) 32,000, industrial and commercial seaport in N Yemen; located on the Red Sea coast, it is the port for the capital city, San'ā, trading in dates, hides, and coffee; economy: oil refining.

Hud'dersfield, 53 39N 1 47W, pop(1981) 148,544, town in Kirklees borough, West Yorkshire, N England; part of West Yorkshire urban area; on the R Colne, 17 km S of Bradford; railway; economy: woollen and worsted textiles, textile machinery, clothing, dyes, carpets.

Huddinge *hu'ding-y*, 59 15N 17 57E, pop(1982) 68,524, town in Stockholm county, SE Sweden; a S suburb SW of Stockholm; economy: textiles.

Hudson, river rising in the Adirondack Mts, New York state, United States; flows 560 km S past Albany and New York City where it meets the Atlantic Ocean; navigable for large craft as far as Albany; tidal for 240 km; explored in 1609 by Henry Hudson.

Hudson Bay, large inland sea in E central Canada; area approx 1,230,250 sq km; bordered by Ontario (S), Manitoba (SW), Keewatin dist (W) and Franklin dist (N), both of Northwest Territories, and by Québec (E); length 1,368 km; breadth 1,046 km; connected with the Atlantic Ocean by the Hudson Strait in the NE and with the Arctic Ocean by the Foxe Channel in the N; in the N entrance to the bay are the islands of Southampton, Coats and Mansel; other islands and island groups include Akimsiki, Charlton, Belcher, Ottawa Sleeper and Twin islands; receives the Churchill, Nelson, Hayes, Severn, Attawapiskat, Albany, Moose, Harricana, Nottaway and Grande Rivière de la Baleine rivers; the bay is navigable from mid-July to Oct; discovered in 1610 by Henry Hudson, the bay was later explored by Sir Thomas Button in 1612 and William Baffin in 1615; the first trading post established here in 1668 at the mouth of the Rupert river was French; between 1682 and 1713 the British and French fought for control of the area; the Treaty of Utrecht in 1713 assigned all French trading posts to Britain; the Hudson's Bay Co held exclusive rights to trading in and around Hudson Bay from its charter in 1760 until the region was acquired by Canada in 1869.

Hué *hway*, 16 28N 107 35E, pop(1973e) 209,000, town in Binh Tri Thien prov, central Vietnam, Indo-China; near the mouth of the R Hué, 8 km from the South China Sea; railway; economy: rice, timber, textiles.

Huehuetenango *way-way-tay-nang'gō*, mountainous dept in W Guatemala, Central America; bounded W and N by Mexico; pop(1982e) 524,829; area 7,403 sq km; capital Huehuetenango; traversed by the Sierra los Cuchumatanes with peaks above 3,000 m; drained by the Selegua and Ixcán rivers; much of the area is devoted to subsistence agriculture.

Huehuetenango, 15 19N 91 26W, mining centre and capital town of Huehuetenango dept, W Guatemala, Central America; on the Inter-American Highway, 128 km NW of Guatemala City; chief trading centre for many outlying Indian villages; alt 1,905 m; economy: lead, copper and silver mining.

Huelva *wel'va*, prov in Andalucia region, S Spain; mineral-rich prov on the Portuguese border between the Atlantic and the Sierra Morena; to the N are tree-covered spurs of the Sierra Morena and to the S is a fertile plain (La Campina), watered by the Tinto and Odiel rivers; in the SE, along the lower R Guadalquivir, is the marshy, alluvial Las Marismas; pop(1981) 414,492; area 10,085 sq km; capital Huelva; economy: food processing and canning, non-ferrous mineral mining (Cala, Calanas, El Cerro de Andevalo), lubricants, chemicals (Palos).

Huelva, ONUBA (Lat), 37 18N 6 57W, pop(1981) 127,806, port and capital of Huelva prov, Andalucia, SW Spain; in the delta of the Odiel and Tinto rivers, 632 km SW of Madrid; bishopric; railway; economy: shipbuilding, tunny and sardine fisheries, canning, chemicals, oil refining and export of ores from Río Tinto and Tharsis; events: fiesta of the discovery of America in honour of Columbus and the discovery of the New World, in Aug with bullfights and folk events, and the patronal fair of Our Lady La Cinta in Sept.

Huesca *wes'ka*, prov in Aragón region, N Spain; the Pyrenees in the N slope down to the Ebro plain in the S; drained by the Gallego and Cinca rivers; includes the highest point of the Pyrenees (Pico Aneto, 3,404 m) and the Valle de Ordesa National Park; pop(1981) 219,813; area 15,613 sq km; capital Huesca; economy: paper (El Grado), chemical products (Monzón, Barbastro), flour, farm and construction machinery, clothes, hides, hydro-electric power.

Huesca, OSCA (anc), 42 08N 0 25W, pop(1981) 44,372, market town and capital of Huesca prov, Aragón, N Spain; 397 km NE of Madrid; bishopric; railway; monuments: cathedral (c.1400), church of San Pedro; residence of the kings of Aragon until 1118; economy: agric machinery, light engineering, aviculture, foodstuffs; events: Holy Week; fiesta of St George with pilgrimage and passion plays in April and fiesta of St Lorenzo in August with bullfights, sporting contests, folk events and parades with decorated carriages.

Hufūf, Al *al hoo-foof'*, HOFŪF, 25 25N 49 45E, pop(1974) 101,270, oasis town in Eastern prov, E Saudi Arabia; 112 km SW of Aẓ Ẓahrān (Dhahran); railway; airfield; linked by road to its Arabian Gulf port of Al 'Uqayr; monument: great mosque (19th-c).

Hugli *hoo'glee*, HOOGHLY, river channel of the R Ganga (Ganges) delta, West Bengal, NE India; length 192 km; nearly 16 km wide at its mouth; navigable to Calcutta.

Huhehot, capital of Nei Mongol aut region, N China. See Hohhot.

Huila *wee'la*, dept in S central Colombia, South America; comprises the Magdalena river valley which is flanked by the Cordillera Central and Cordillera Oriental; pop(1985) 636,642; area 19,890 sq km; capital Neiva; economy: coffee; S of Pitalito is the Cueva de los Guácharos National Park (area 90 sq km; established in 1961) with its swarms of nocturnal oilbirds (guácharos); the area is rich in archaeological and palaeontological remains; SW of Neiva, near the town of San Agustín, is the Parque Arqueológico, or Valley of the Statues, containing hundreds of large rough hewn statues of men, animals and gods, dating from 6th-c BC to just before the Spanish conquest; nothing is known of the culture which produced them, although traces of small circular bamboo straw-thatched houses have been found; some of the sculptures found here are exhibited in the national museum at Bogotá.

Huila, Nevado de, 3 00N 76 59W, Andean volcanic peak in S central Colombia, South America; on the border between Huila, Tolima and Cauca depts; rises to 5,750 m, 80 km SE of Cali; highest peak in the Cordillera Central and second highest in Colombia.

Hujirt *KHud'shirt*, KHUDSHIRT, 46 52N 102 42E, spa town in Övör-Hangay county, central Mongolia; close to a tributary of the Orhon Gol.

Hull, 45 26N 75 45W, pop(1981) 56,225, town in S Québec, SE Canada; on the Ottawa river, where it meets the Gatineau river, to the NW of Ottawa, on the Ontario border; founded in 1801 by settlers from the USA; railway; economy: lumber, paper milling, textiles, meat packing, cement.

Hull, town in Humberside, E England. See Kingston-upon-Hull.

Hulun Nur, lake in NE Nei Mongol aut region, N China; area 2,315 sq km; a semi-salt lake, fed by the Orxon Gol river; drained by the Herlen He (or Kerulen) river.

Hum'ber, river estuary in Humberside, NE England; the estuary of the Ouse and Trent rivers runs 64 km E and SE; the entrance is dominated by Spurn Head; Kingston-upon-Hull is on the N shore and the ports of Immingham and Grimsby are on the S; the Humber Bridge, completed in 1981, is the largest single-span suspension bridge in the world.

Hum'berside, county of NE England; bounded E by the North Sea, N and NW by North Yorkshire, SW by South Yorkshire, S by Nottinghamshire and Lincolnshire; drained by the R Humber which flows into the North Sea; pop(1981) 852,420; area 3,512 sq km; county town Beverley; major ports at Grimsby, Goole and Immingham on the R Humber; economy: fishing (Grimsby and Kingston-upon-Hull), sugar beet; the county is divided into 9 districts:

District	*area (sq km)*	*pop(1981)*
Beverley	404	106,628
Boothferry	647	60,595
Cleethorpes	164	68,724
East Yorkshire	1,044	75,145
Glanford	580	66,368
Great Grimsby	28	92,596
Holderness	540	46,216
Kingston-upon-Hull	71	269,539
Scunthorpe	34	66,609

Humenné *hoom'en-ya*, 48 57N 21 54E, pop(1984) 30,138, town in Východoslovenský region, Slovak Socialist Republic, Czechoslovakia; on R Laborec, SE of Prešov; railway.

Humphreys Peak, 35 21N 111 41W, mountain in Coconino county, Arizona; rises to 3,862 m in the San Francisco Mts; the highest peak in Arizona state.

Humpty Doo, 12 37S 131 14E, pop(1981) 1,265, town in Northern Territory, Australia; site of Graeme Gow's Reptile Park, containing a collection of Australia's most venomous snakes and reptiles.

Hunan *hoo-nahn*, prov in central S China; bordered S by Guangxi aut region and Guangdong prov, W by Guizhou and Sichuan provs, N by Hubei prov and E by Jiangxi prov; situated to the S of the middle Chang Jiang (Yangtze river) valley; mountainous in the W, S and E; Heng Shan peak (1,290 m) is one of China's Five Holy Mountains; Dongting Hu, China's 2nd largest freshwater lake, is one of several lakes in the N of Hunan; the province is drained by numerous rivers, the largest being the Zi Shui, Xiang Jiang, Li Shui and Yuan Jiang, all of which flow into Dongting Hu lake; pop(1982) 54,008,851; area 210,500 sq km; capital Changsha; economy: agriculture; rice, wheat, cotton, tea, timber, pig-raising, fruit; mining (coal, tungsten, antimony, lead, zinc, manganese, mercury); embroidery, porcelain.

Hunedoara *hoon-ay-dwa'ra*, county in W Romania, in the W foothills of the Transylvanian Alps; pop(1983) 548,344; area 7,016 sq km; capital Deva; iron mining (Ghelar, Teliuc).

Hunedoara, 45 45N 22 54E, pop(1983) 87,001, town in Hunedoara county, W Romania; in E foothills of the Transylvanian Alps, S of Deva; railway terminus; economy: iron and steel, metallurgy, engineering; monument: 15th-c Hunyadi Castle.

Hungary *hun'gar-i*, MAGYARORSZÁG *mod'yor-or-sag* (Hung), official name The Hungarian People's Republic, MAGYAR NÉPKÖZTÁRSASÁG, a socialist state in the Danube basin in Central Europe; bounded N by Czechoslovakia, E by the USSR and Romania, S by Yugoslavia and W by Austria; area 93,036 sq km; timezone GMT +1; capital Budapest; chief towns include Miskolc, Debrecen, Szeged, Pécs and Györ which are autonomous cities with county status; the number of cities and towns has increased from 57 in 1950 to 109 in 1984; prior to 1945 35% of the population lived in urban areas, but by 1984 the corresponding figure was 55.7%; pop(1984e) 10,679,000; 92% of the pop is Magyar, the remainder largely being German, Slovak, Romanian, gypsy and Southern Slav types; Magyar is the official language; over 67% of the pop is Roman Catholic, 20% Calvinist and 5% Lutheran; the currency is the forint of 100 fillér; national holiday 4 April (Liberation Day); membership of Warsaw Pact, CEMA, Danube Commission, FAO, GATT, IAEA, IBRD, ICAC, ICAO, ILO, IMF, IMO, IPU, ISO, ITC, ITU, UN, UNESCO, UPU, WFTU, WHO, WIPO, WMO.

Physical description. Hungary is drained by the R Danube which flows from N to S and by its tributaries the Tisza, Drava and Sava rivers. Floods are frequent, especially in the Great Plains (Alföld) region, E of the Danube. The area W of the Danube is crossed SW-NE by a low spur of the Alps (Bakony, Vertes and Philis ranges). This separates the Little Hungarian Plain (Kisalföld) from the Transdanubian downlands SE of Lake Balaton. The highest peak in Hungary is Kékestetö (1,014 m).

Climate. The landlocked position of Hungary gives it a more extreme continental type of climate compared with W Europe where there is the moderating influence of the Atlantic Ocean. There is a considerable difference between summer and winter weather with a rapid transition from one to the other. Spring and early summer are the wettest times of the year with rain often falling in heavy downpours. Winters are cold with snow lying on the ground 30 to 40 days and the R Danube occasionally frozen over for long periods. Fog is frequent during settled winter weather. There is little variation in weather and climate within Hungary.

History, government and constitution. Hungary became a kingdom under Stephen in 1000, but in the 16th century the crown passed to Ferdinand of Austria with the formation of the E part of the Hapsburg Empire. In 1867 Austria and Hungary were reconstituted as a dual monarchy, each with its own laws and parliament but under one emperor-king. After World War I Hungary became a republic under Count Karolyi but a communist revolt led by Béla Kun introduced a new régime in 1919. The monarchical constitution was restored in the following year under Admiral Horthy. After World War II a new republic was declared and a communist government was installed; the constitution of 1949, which was updated in 1972 and 1983, establishes the unicameral legislature known as the National Assembly, a body which is elected every 5 years. The National Assembly elects the executive 21-member Presidential Council and the Council of Ministers.

Economy. The major industries of Hungary include coal, bauxite and lignite mining, metallurgy, engineering, chemicals, textiles and food processing. In 1985 Hungary exported 20% of all buses sold in the world market, 8% of the alumina, 6% of the light bulbs and 4% of the pharmaceuticals. Between 1946 and 1949 most large-scale industries, mines, banks, wholesale trade and transport were nationalized as part of the centralized planning strategy of the new, post-war socialist republic. From 1968 a new system of economic management was introduced giving greater independence to individual factories and farms with a consequent decrease in central planning in favour of planning through economic regulators.

Agriculture. The main agricultural products of Hungary are grain, potatoes, sugar-beets, fruit and wine. Agricultural reform during the period 1946-65 reduced the number of small peasant holdings and private ownership by creating state farms and some 4,500 cooperative farms which by 1982 accounted for 12% and 62% respectively of the country's arable land. Co-operative farms average 41 sq km in size while privately-owned plots of half a hectare are cultivated by co-operative farm members and retired people who supply significant quantities of pigs, beef and chickens to the market. In 1983 over 50% of Hungary was under arable cultivation and over 17% under forest.

Administrative divisions. Hungary is divided into 19 counties as follows:

County	*area (sq km)*	*pop(1984e)*
Bács-Kiskun	8,363	564,000
Baranya	4,487	434,000
Békés	5,632	428,000
Borsod-Abaúj-Zemplén	7,248	801,000
Csongrád	4,263	453,000
Fejér	4,374	423,000
Györ-Sopron	4,012	430,000
Hajdú-Bihar	6,212	552,000
Heves	3,637	346,000
Komárom	2,250	323,000
Nógrád	2,544	237,000
Pest	6,394	983,000
Somogy	6,035	357,000
Szabolcs-Szátmar	5,938	586,000
Szolnok	5,608	441,000
Tolna	3,702	268,000

contd

County	*area (sq km)*	*pop(1984e)*
Vas	3,337	283,000
Veszprém	4,689	389,000
Zala	3,786	316,000

Hunsrück *hoons'rük*, mountainous region in Nordrhein-Westfalen (North Rhine-Westphalia) prov, W Germany; between the Mosel and Nahe rivers, extending SW from the R Rhine to the French border; highest peak is the Erbeskopf (818 m); geologically considered part of the Rheinisches Schiefergebirge (Rhenish Slate Mts).

Hunte, river in Niedersachsen (Lower Saxony) prov, W Germany; rises in hills E of Osnabrück, flows N into R Weser near Bremen; length 189 km; navigable length 26 km; drainage basin area 2,785 sq km.

Hunterston, 55 42N 4 51W, port facility in Cunninghame dist, Strathclyde, W Scotland; on the W coast, opposite the island of Little Cumbrae, 2.25 miles NW of West Kilbride; gas-cooled nuclear reactors came into commercial operation in 1964 and advanced gas-cooled reactors in 1976-77; economy: iron ore and coal trade.

Huntingdon, 52 20N 0 12W, pop(1981) 17,603, town linked with Godmanchester in Huntingdon dist, Cambridgeshire, E central England; 24 km NW of Cambridge; birthplace of Oliver Cromwell; railway; economy: engineering, plastics, furniture, transport equipment; monuments: 13th-c Hinchingbrooke House, 13th-c church of St Mary the Virgin, Cromwell Museum, Buckden palace (8 km SW).

Huntingdonshire, former county of E central England; part of Cambridgeshire since 1974.

Huntington, 38 25N 82 27W, pop(1980) 63,684, county seat of Cabell county, W West Virginia, United States; on the R Ohio, 80 km W of Charleston; Marshall University (1837); railway; economy: coal, glass and chemicals.

Huntington Beach, 33 40N 118 00W, pop(1980) 170,505, city in Orange county, SW California, United States; 21 km SE of Long Beach; railway; economy: petroleum, data systems, precision instruments, aerospace systems.

Huntington Park, 33 59N 118 14W, pop(1980) 46,223, city in Los Angeles county, SW California, United States; 8 km S of Los Angeles; railway; economy: clothing, oil-field equipment, metal goods.

Huntsville, 34 44N 86 35W, pop(1980) 142,513, county seat of Madison county, N Alabama, United States; 39 km NE of Decatur; university; railway; economy: major US space research centre; manufactures tyres, glass, agricultural equipment and electrical goods.

Hupeh, prov in E central China. See Hubei.

Huron *hyoo'ron*, lake in North America, in the USA and Canada; 2nd largest of the Great Lakes; bordered N, E and S by Ontario prov, Canada; bordered W by Michigan state, USA; 330 km long by 294 km wide (including Georgian Bay); max depth 229 m; area 59,570 sq km, of which 36,001 sq km belongs to Canada; receives the waters of L Superior (NW) via St Mary's river (whose rapids are bypassed by the Sault Ste Marie Canals); also receives the waters of L Michigan (W) via the Straits of Mackinac; empties into L Erie via the St Clair river, L St Clair and the Detroit river; Georgian Bay lies in the NE of the lake on the Ontario coast; Saginaw Bay is in the SW in Michigan; North Channel in the N of the lake is situated between the Manitoulin Islands and the Ontario shore; major ports in Michigan are Bay City, Alpena and Cheboygan; the major port in Ontario is Midland; the lake is generally ice-bound between mid-Dec and early April; L Huron was probably the first of the Great Lakes to be visited by Europeans; Étienne Brulé is thought to have visited Georgian Bay in approx 1612 or earlier, and Champlain crossed part of the lake in 1615.

Hurst, 32 49N 97 09W, pop(1980) 31,420, residential town in Tarrant county, NE Texas, United States; a suburb 17 km ENE of Fort Worth; economy: helicopters.

Hurstpierpoint *herst-peer'poynt*, 50 56N 0 11W, pop(1981) 11,949, town linked with Keymer in Mid Sussex dist, West Sussex, S England; 22 km N of Brighton; railway; monument: site of Roman villa.

Huşi *hoosh*, 46 40N 28 05E, pop(1983) 26,789, town in Vaslui county, E Romania; 64 km SE of Iaşi; railway terminus; economy: wine, textiles, tanning.

Hutchinson, 38 05N 97 56W, pop(1980) 40,284, county seat of Reno county, S Kansas, United States; on R Arkansas, 66 km NW of Wichita; railway; economy: commercial and industrial centre in grain, livestock and oil region; manufactures farm machinery and aircraft parts; salt mines nearby.

Hutton, oil field in the North Sea, E of the Shetland Is; linked by pipeline to Sullom Voe.

Huy *ü-ee*, dist of Liège prov, E Belgium; area 659 sq km; pop(1982) 88,645.

Huy, HOEY *hoo'ee* (Flem), 50 32N 5 14E, pop(1982) 17,451, commercial and manufacturing town in Huy dist, W Liège prov, Belgium; at the confluence of the Meuse and Hoyoux rivers, approx mid-way between Namur and Liège; it received its freedom charter in 1066 from Prince Bishop Theoduin and had reached a high degree of prosperity by the late Middle Ages because of its famous brassworks and wool industry; in a mining district (coal, iron); university (1964); railway; economy: iron foundries, sugar-refining, paper; monument: Collegiate Church of Notre-Dame (1311-1377).

Huyton-with-Roby *hī'ten-with-rō'bi*, 53 25N 2 52W, pop(1981) 61,808, town in St Helens borough, Merseyside, NW England; 10 km E of Liverpool; railway.

Hvannadalshnjúkur *hwa-nah-dals'hun-yoo'kur*, 64 02N 16 35W, highest mountain in Iceland, rising to 2,119 m in SE Iceland at S edge of Vatnajökull glacier.

Hwange *wang'kee*, WANKIE, 18 20S 26 25E, pop(1982) 39,000, town in Matabeleland North prov, Zimbabwe, S Africa; 300 km NW of Bulawayo; centre of the country's coal-mining industry; coal-fired power station; airfield; Hwange National Park (area 14,651 sq km) established in 1930.

Hwanghainam, SOUTH HWANGHAI, prov in SW North Korea; bordered W and S by Korea Bay and the Huang Hai (Yellow Sea); capital Haeju.

Hwanghaipuk *hwang-hī-puk*, NORTH HWANGHAI, prov in S central North Korea; capital Sariwŏn.

Hyde, 53 27N 2 04W, pop(1981) 30,551, town in Manchester borough, Greater Manchester, NW England; 7 km NE of Stockport; railway; economy: engineering, rubber, textiles.

Hyderabad *hī'du ru bad*, 17 22N 78 26E, pop(1981) 2,528,000, capital of Andhra Pradesh, S India; on R Musi, 611 km ESE of Bombay; founded in 1589 as capital of the kingdom of Golconda; former capital of Hyderabad state; joined with India in 1948; a Muslim stronghold in S India; 4 universities (1918, 1964, 1972, 1974); airfield; linked by rail to Warangal, Mahbunagar and Nizamabad; monuments: the ruins of Golconda fort, the tombs of the Qutb Shahi kings, a mosque built in the style of the Great Mosque of Mecca, the Char Minar (1591).

Hyderabad, HAIDARABAD, 25 23N 68 24E, pop(1981) 795,000, 2nd largest city in Sind prov, SE Pakistan; 164 km ENE of Karachi, on the E bank of the R Indus, c.190 km N of its mouth; linked by rail to Karachi and Multan; provincial capital from 1768 until captured by the British in 1843; to the W is the Kotri Barrage; university (1947); airfield; economy: gold and silver embroidery, enamelware and pottery, shoes, glass and furniture; monument: tomb of Ghulam Shah Kalhora.

Hydra, Greek island. See Ídhra.

Hyères, Iles d' *eel dyer*, LES ILES D'OR, island group in the Mediterranean Sea off the coast of Var dept, SE France, SE of Toulon; chief islands are (E-W) Levant (occupied in part by the Navy and in part by a nudist colony), Port-Cros (nature reserve) and the fortified island of Porquerolles; originally a range of the Massif des Maures; occupied by the Allies August 14-15 1944.

Hyesan *hyay-san*, 41 25N 128 12E, capital of Yanggang prov, N North Korea; close to the Chinese frontier.

Hythe *hīTH*, 50 51N 1 24W, pop(1981) 16,655, town in New Forest dist, Hampshire, S England; on the W bank of Southampton Water; ferry.

Hythe, 51 05N 1 05E, pop(1981) 13,659, town in Shepway dist, Kent, SE England; in the Romney Marsh flower-growing area, SW of Folkestone; railway; economy: horticulture, plastics.

Hyvinkaa *hoo'vin-ka*, HYVINGE (Swed), 60 37N 24 50E, pop(1982) 37,852, resort town in N Uudenmaa prov, S Finland; 48 km N of Helsinki; railway; established in 1926; winter sports resort.

I

Ialomiţa *ya'lo-mee-tsa*, county in SE Romania; traversed W-E by the R Ialomiţa; pop(1983) 298,357; area 4,565 sq km; capital Slobozia.

Ialomiţa, river in SE Romania, rising in E Transylvanian Alps; flows S and E to meet the R Danube W of Harsova; limestone caves in upper valley; receives R Prahova; length 320 km.

Iaşi *yash*, fertile agricultural county in NE Romania, bounded to the W by the R Siret and to the E by the USSR; pop(1983) 773,215; area 5,469 sq km; capital Iaşi.

Iaşi, JASSY *ya'see*, 47 09N 27 38E, pop(1983) 303,598, capital of Iaşi county, NE Romania; close to the USSR frontier; from 1565 to 1859 the city was the capital of the principality of Moldavia; temporary capital of Romania during World War I; during World War II the city's Jewish population was massacred; airfield; railway; economy: electronics, chemicals, clothing, plastics, food processing, furniture, tobacco, pharmaceuticals.

Ibadan *ee-ba-dan'*, 7 23N 3 56E, pop(1981e) 2,100,000, capital of Oyo state, Nigeria, W Africa; 113 km NNE of Lagos; founded in the 1830s; British control was established in 1896; regarded as the intellectual centre of the country; university (1948); railway; airfield; zoo; economy: metals, chemicals, brewing, motor vehicles and electronics.

Ibagué *ee-ba-gay'*, 4 35N 75 30W, pop(1985) 285,409, capital of Tolima dept, W central Colombia, South America; at the foot of the Quindío mountains; university (1954); railway; economy: hand-made leather goods and a local drink called Mistela; events: festival of St John (24 June), festival of Saints Peter and Paul (29 June), a national folklore festival is held here in the last week in June.

Ibar *ee'bar*, river in S central Yugoslavia; rises in Mokra Planina and flows E to Kosovska Mitrovica then N to meet the W Morava near Kraljevo; length 240 km; navigable for 200 km.

Ibarra *ee-ba'ra*, SAN MIGUEL DE IBARRA *san mee-gel' THay ee-ba'ra*, 0 23N 78 05W, pop(1982) 53,428, capital of Imbabura prov in the Andean Sierra of N Ecuador; 88 km NE of Quito; founded by Alvaro de Ibarra in 1597; railway; economy: drinks, tobacco, mineral and timber products; monument: Santo Domingo church; events: at weekends a unique form of paddleball is played with huge spiked paddles which are used to strike a 1 kg ball; Sept festival.

Iberian Peninsula *ī-bee'ri-an*, a name given to that area of Europe SW of the Pyrenees, including Portugal and Spain; the name is probably derived from *Iberus*, the Roman name for the R Ebro; Iberia is an ancient name for Spain.

Ibiza or **Iviza** *ee-vee'tha*, third largest island in the Mediterranean Balearic Is, Baleares autonomous region, Spain, 88 km SW of Mallorca; area 572 sq km; pop(1981) 40,000; an island of irregular relief with pine woods and groves of almond, fig and olive trees; surrounded by small islets; capital Ibiza; on the W coast is the Roman Portus Magnus, now San Antonio Abad, with its chapel-catacomb of Santa Ines which is a national monument; car ferries to Alicante, Valencia, Palma de Mallorca, Barcelona and Genoa.

Ibiza, EBUSUS (anc), 38 54N 1 26E, pop(1981) 25,489, tourist resort and capital of Ibiza I, Balearic Is, Baleares region, Spain; on the SE side of the island; the Dalta Vila district is the oldest part of the town with aristocratic houses, town hall and a cathedral; founded by the Carthaginians in 645 BC; beaches nearby at Talamanca, Figuertes and En Bosa; Ibiza is 112 km from Palma de Mallorca and 260 km from Barcelona.

Ica *ee'ka*, dept in S Peru; bordered W by the Pacific, E by the Andean Cordillera Occidental; rising gradually in the E with outliers of the Andes; pop(1981) 433,897; area 21,251 sq km; capital Ica.

Içel *i-chel'*, maritime prov in S Turkey, bounded S by the Mediterranean Sea; pop(1980) 843,931; area 15,853 sq km; capital Mersin.

Iceland *ī'sland*, ISLAND *ee'lahn* (Dan), official name Republic of Iceland, LÝÐVELDIÐ ÍSLAND (Icelandic), island state lying between the N Atlantic and Arctic Oceans, SE of Greenland and 900 km W of Norway; separated from Greenland by the Denmark Strait and from Norway by the Norwegian Sea; timezone GMT; area 103,000 sq km; pop(1983) 238,175, capital Reykjavík; the Icelandic pop is largely descended from Norwegians and Celts; the official language is Icelandic; 95% of the pop is Lutheran Protestant; the currency is the krónur of 100 aurar; national holiday 17 June (establishment of the Republic); membership of Council of Europe, EFTA, FAO, GATT, IAEA, IBRD, ICAO, ICES, IDA, IFC, IHO, ILO, IMF, INTELSAT, INTERPOL, IPU, ITU, International Whaling Commission, NATO, Nordic Council, OECD, UN, UNESCO, UPU, WHO, WMO, WSG.

Physical description. Of relatively recent geological origin, Iceland is a volcanic island of basaltic lavas and tuffs. At the N end of the mid-Atlantic Ridge, Iceland has a number of active volcanoes and is famous for its *geysers*, or hot springs. Many of the towns of Iceland are heated by subterranean hot water and a geothermal power station at Krafla is in operation. The island has a heavily indented coastline with many long fjords leading into broad valleys and high ridges that rise to 2,119 m in the SE at Hvannadalshnjúkur. Remnants of the glacial period are to be found in several large snowfields and glaciers, including Vatnajökull, Hofsjökull, Langjökull and Myrdalsjökull.

Climate. Lying in the track of warm oceanic water (Gulf Stream) and frequently crossed by depressions, Iceland experiences a changeable climate that is, in winter, remarkably mild for its latitude. Average daily temperatures range from a min of −2°C in Jan to a max of 14°C in July-Aug. Reykjavík is generally ice-free throughout the year. Summers are cool and cloudy, with brief spells of fine weather. The wettest period is from Oct to Jan, with average monthly precipitation reaching 94 mm in Oct.

History, government and constitution. Visited by the Norse as early as the 9th century, Iceland was settled by Scandinavian farming and fishing communities. In 930 the Icelanders established the world's oldest parliament, the *Althing*. Union with Norway in 1262 was followed by union with Denmark in 1380. In 1918 Iceland became an independent kingdom in personal union with Denmark, and in 1944 the island became an independent republic. The extension of the fishing limit around Iceland in 1958 and in 1975 precipitated the serious 'Cod War' disputes with the UK. The legislature of Iceland comprises a 60-member parliament (*Althing*) which includes a 20-member Upper House. The president appoints a prime minister and cabinet.

Economy. Although stock farming, dairy farming and the production of potatoes and greenhouse vegetables are important, the economy of Iceland is based on inshore and deep-water fishing which contributes three-quarters of the national income and employs one-eighth of the workforce. Aluminium (*straumsvik*) and diatomite (*mý-*

vatn) production and extensive freezing facilities are powered by geothermal and hydroelectric sources of energy. Major trade partners include EEC countries, the UK, W Germany and the USA.

Administrative divisions. Iceland is divided into 8 regions:

Region	*area (sq km)*	*pop(1983)*
Reykjavík-Revkyanes	1,920	142,564
Vesturland	9,520	15,115
Vestfirðir	9,520	10,426
Norðurland vestra	12,880	10,710
Norðurland eystra	21,680	26,190
Austurland	22,490	13,093
Suðurland	24,990	20,077

Ichihara *ee-chee'ha-ra*, 35 32N 140 04E, pop(1980) 216,394, city in Chiba prefecture, Kanto region, E Honshū island, Japan; SE of Tōkyo; railway.

Ichikawa *ee-chee'ka-wa*, 35 45N 139 55E, pop(1980) 479,439, city in Chiba prefecture, Kanto region, Japan; NE of Tōkyo; railway.

Ichinomiya *ee-chee-nō'mee-ya*, 35 18N 136 48E, pop(1980) 253,139, city in Aichi prefecture, Chūbu region, central Honshū island, Japan; 21 km NNW of Nagoya; railway.

Ichkeul, national park in Tunisia, N Africa; area 108 sq km; established in 1978.

I-ch'un, town in Heilongjiang prov, NE China. See Yichun.

Idaho *ī'da-hō*, state in NW United States; bounded W by Oregon and Washington, N by the Canadian province of British Columbia, NE by Montana, E by Wyoming, and S by Utah and Nevada; the Snake river flows generally W across S Idaho then turns N to form part of the W border before turning W again into Washington state; the R Salmon rises in central Idaho and flows N then W to empty into the Snake river on the Oregon border; the Bitterroot Range lies along much of the Montana border; rising in central and N Idaho are the Sawtooth Mts, Salmon River Mts, and Clearwater Mts; the highest point is Borah Peak (3,860 m); much of the state is rugged, mountainous country, with nearly half the state (mostly N) under national forest; along the Snake river in S Idaho is the Snake River Plain, one of the largest irrigated areas in the United States and the centre of the state's agriculture; river dams also generate hydroelectric power; where the Snake river forms the Oregon border it has cut itself a spectacular gorge, Hell's Canyon, one of the deepest gorges in the world; the state's economy is largely based on agriculture, the chief products cattle, wheat, potatoes, hay, sugar-beets, and dairy produce; industrial manufactures include wood products, processed foods, and chemicals; silver and antimony are mined; the first European exploration of the region was by Lewis and Clark in 1805; the region was held jointly by Britain and the United States until the treaty of 1846 gave the United States sole possession S of the 49th parallel; the region was part of Oregon and then Washington territories before the discovery of gold in 1860 led to an influx of settlers and the establishment of the Territory of Idaho in 1863; Idaho was admitted to the Union as the 43rd state in 1890; Idaho or Idahi was the name given to the Comanche Indians by the Kiowa-Apache tribe; also known as the 'Gem State'; pop(1980) 943,935; area 214,271 sq km; capital Boise; other chief cities include Pocatello and Idaho Falls; the state is divided into 44 counties:

County	*area (sq km)*	*pop(1980)*
Ada	2,735	173,036
Adams	3,541	3,347
Bannock	2,891	65,421
Bear Lake	2,574	6,931
Benewah	2,038	8,292
Bingham	5,450	36,489
Blaine	6,848	9,841
Boise	4,943	2,999
Bonner	4,488	24,163
Bonneville	4,784	65,980
Boundary	3,297	7,289
Butte	5,814	3,342
Camas	2,785	818
Canyon	1,518	83,756
Caribou	4,584	8,695
Cassia	6,656	19,427
Clark	4,584	798
Clearwater	5,814	10,390
Custer	12,810	3,385
Elmore	7,985	21,565
Franklin	1,726	8,895
Fremont	4,815	10,813
Gem	1,451	11,972
Gooding	1,893	11,874
Idaho	22,092	14,769
Jefferson	2,842	15,304
Jerome	1,563	14,840
Kootenai	3,224	59,770
Latah	2,800	28,749
Lemhi	11,866	7,460
Lewis	1,243	4,118
Lincoln	3,133	3,436
Madison	1,217	19,480
Minidoka	1,968	19,718
Nez Perce	2,197	33,220
Oneida	3,120	3,258
Owyhee	19,872	8,272
Payette	1,053	15,722
Power	3,648	6,844
Shoshone	6,867	19,226
Teton	1,165	2,897
Twin Falls	5,054	52,927
Valley	9,542	5,604
Washington	3,780	8,803

Idaho Falls, 43 30N 112 02W, pop(1980) 39,590, county seat of Bonneville county, SE Idaho, United States; on Snake river, 75 km NNE of Pocatello; railway; airfield; economy: commercial and processing centre for agricultural region; manufactures include concrete, steel and timber; nearby is a nuclear reactor testing station.

Idensalmi, town in Finland. See Iisalmi.

Ídhra *eedh'ru*, HYDRA *hī'dra* (Eng), island in the Aegean Sea, Greece, off the E coast of Pelopónnisos; part of Attikí nome (dept); linked by ferry to Piraiévs (Piraeus); the chief town is Ídra; a popular resort island.

Id'lib, governorate (*mohofazat*) in NW Syria; bounded N by Turkey; pop(1981) 579,581; capital Idlib; other chief town Ma'arrat an Nu'mān; the 'Āsi (Orontes) river forms part of its W boundary.

Ieper *eepr*, dist of West-Vlaanderen (West Flanders) prov, W Belgium; area 550 sq km; pop(1982) 104,042.

Ieper, YPRES (Fr), 50 51N 2 53E, pop(1982) 18,161, town in Ieper dist, West-Vlaanderen (West Flanders) prov, W Belgium; on the canalized R Ieper, close to the French border; has for long been associated with the cloth trade; devastated in World War I; the Menin Gate (great memorial), its well-kept graveyards and the beautiful Garden of Peace, make Ieper a place of pilgrimage; railway; economy: textiles, textile machinery, foodstuffs, tourism; monuments: cloth hall (13th-c), St Martin's cathedral, Menin Gate (Menenpoort); event: Festival of the Cats (2nd Sunday of May).

Ife *ee'fay*, 7 33N 4 34E, pop(1981e) 240,600, town in Oyo state, Nigeria, W Africa; 72 km E of Ibadan; university (1961); economy: metallurgy; monuments: museum, palace; events: the Olojo and Edi festivals are held in Oct and Nov.

Igualada *ee-gwal-lah'dha*, 41 37N 1 37E, pop(1981) 31,451, industrial town in Barcelona prov, Cataluña, NE Spain; 48 km NE of Barcelona; economy: textiles, leather, iron.

Iguazú *ee-gwa-soo'* (Sp), IGUAÇU (Port), national park in N Misiones prov, Argentina; borders N with Brazil; contains the Iguazú Falls; area 294 sq km; established as a park in 1934; the falls themselves lie 19 km above the junction of the Iguazú with the Paraná; their height is greater than that of Niagara by about 20 m, and they are half as wide again; the water plunges in 275 falls, many of which have separate names.

Iijoki *ee-yo'ki*, IJOÄLV (Swed), RIVER II (Eng), river in Oulu prov, N central Finland; rises in the E lake region and flows S and W past Pudasjärvi to meet the Gulf of Bothnia near the village of Ii N of Oulu; length 240 km.

Iisalmi *ee-sal'mi*, IDENSALMI (Swed), 63 33N 27 14E, pop(1982) 23,056, industrial town in the lake district of Kuopio prov, S central Finland; 80 km N of Kuopio; established in 1891; birthplace of Juhani Aho (1861-1921), founder of the realist school of Finnish literature; railway.

Ijssel *ī'sel*, a tributary of the R Rhine, in E and central Netherlands; it branches from the lower Rhine, 4 km SE of Arnhem; flows N through Gelderland prov, past Zutphen and Deventer to the Ijsselmeer, 6 km WNW of Kampen; its lower course follows the boundary between Gelderland and Overijssel provs; length 115 km; tributaries Oude (Old) Ijssel, Berkel and Vechte rivers.

Ikaría *eek-ur-ee'u*, ICARIA *ī-ka'ree-u* (Eng), Greek island in the Aegean Sea, WSW of Sámos I; part of Sámos nome (dept); area 255 sq km; named after the legendary Ikaros who flew from Kríti (Crete) with his father but plunged into the Icarian Sea; there are medicinal springs at the ancient site of Thérmai; the port of Áyios Kýrikos is a popular resort.

Ikast *ee'kahst*, 56 09N 9 10E, pop(1981) 11,716, town in Ringkøbing county, central Jylland (Jutland), Denmark; railway; economy: textiles.

Ikeja *ee-kayd'ja*, 6 28N 3 45E, capital of Lagos state, Nigeria, W Africa; 14.5 km NNW of Lagos; railway; economy: cement, textiles, brewing, chemicals, motor vehicles, food processing, electronics and glass.

Ila *ee'la*, 8 01N 4 54E, pop(1975e) 155,000, town in Oyo state, Nigeria, W Africa; 145 km NE of Ibadan.

Īlām *ee-lam'*, mountainous prov in W Iran, bounded W by Iraq; pop(1982) 246,024; area 19,042 sq km; capital Īlām.

Ilan *ee-lan*, county of NE Taiwan; area 2,137.5 sq km; pop(1982e) 447,707.

Ile-de-France *eel de frãs*, region and former prov of N central France comprising the depts of Ville de Paris, Seine-et-Marne, Yvelines, Essonne, Hauts-de-Seine, Seine-Saint-Denis, Val-de-Marne and Val-d'Oise, 22 arrond, 284 cantons and 1,281 communes; pop(1982) 10,073,059; area 12,012 sq km, it is an island in the Paris Basin between the Seine, Marne, Aisne, Oise and Ourq rivers and is surrounded by the plains of Normandy, Champagne and Beauce, and the dist of Caux; the Tertiary limestone plains covered with loess are rich farmland (wheat, sugarbeet); the region has 2 great royal palaces at Versailles and Fontainebleau, ancient abbeys at Royaumont, Chablis, châteaux at Malmaison, Dampierre, Vaux-le-Vicomte and Rambouillet, the remnants of royal hunting forests at Fontainebleau and spacious formal gardens laid out by the landscape gardener Le Nôtre at Versailles, Vaux, Sceaux, St-Cloud and Dampierre; Maisons-Laffitte, 7 km N of St-Germain, is the most important horseracing and training stables in France; the old town of Meaux annually commemorates the Battle of the Marne; there is a spa at Enghien-les-Bains, 6 km NW of St-Denis; in the 9th century the region became a dukedom, the 2nd duke, Odo, being crowned king of France in 888; Hugh Capet in 987 founded the Capetan dynasty, which ruled until 1328.

Ilesha *i-lee'sha*, 7 39N 4 38E, pop(1981e) 306,200, town in Oyo state, Nigeria, W Africa; 97 km ENE of Ibadan; economy: brewing.

Ilfracombe *il'fra-koom*, 51 13N 4 08W, pop(1981) 10,424, coastal resort town in North Devon dist, Devonshire, SW England; 15 km NNW of Barnstaple on the Bristol Channel; monument: 14th-c chapel of St Nicholas.

Ilí'a, ELIS *ee'lis*, coastal nome (dept) of Pelopónnisos region, S Greece; pop(1981) 160,305; area 2,618 sq km; capital Pírgos; drained by the R Alfiós.

Iliniza *ee-lee-nee'sa*, 0 40S 78 42W, Andean peak rising to 5,263 m in Cotopaxi prov, central Ecuador; 29 km W of Volcán Cotopaxi.

Ilkeston, 52 59N 1 18W, pop(1981) 34,840, town in Erewash dist, Derbyshire, central England; 11 km W of Nottingham; economy: clothing, plastics.

Ilk'ley, 53 55N 1 50W, pop(1981) 13,527, resort town in Bradford borough, West Yorkshire, N England; 16 km N of Bradford; in 1843 hydrotherapy was administered here for the first time in Britain; the nearby Ilkley Moor forms part of the larger Rombalds Moor; railway; economy: engineering; monuments: All Saints church, built on Roman foundations; Manor House museum and art gallery.

Ill *eel*, river in Vorarlberg, W Austria; rises in the Piz Buin glacier in the Silvretta Mt group, flowing NW to meet the R Rhine, W of Feldkirch; length 72 km; upper river dammed for hydroelectric power.

Ill, river in Haut-Rhin and Bas-Rhin depts, NE France, rising on the slopes of the Jura Mts; flows NNE to the R Rhine below La Wanzenau; length 208 km; tributaries Thur, Fecht, and Bruche rivers.

Illampu, Nevado de *eel-yam'poo*, MT SORATA, 15 51S 68 30W, highest mountain in the Andean Cordillera Oriental, in N part of range (Cordillera de la Paz); 8 km SE of Sorata; consists of two peaks, Illampu (6,485 m) and Ancohuma (6,388 m).

Ille-et-Vilaine *eel-ay-veel-en*, dept in Bretagne region of W France, on the English Channel (Golfe de St-Malo), SW of the Cotentin peninsula; comprises 4 arrond, 51 cantons and 352 communes; pop(1982) 749,764; area 6,775 sq km; watered by the R Vilaine and its tributaries; capital Rennes, the focal point of the road and rail network; there is a sea-water treatment establishment at St-Malo-Parame.

Illimani, Nevado de *eel-yee-ma'nee*, 16 37S 67 48W, Andean peak rising to 6,402 m in the Cordillera de la Paz, W Bolivia; 40 km SE of La Paz.

Illinois *il'i-noy*, state in N central United States; bounded W by Missouri and Iowa, N by Wisconsin, E by L Michigan and Indiana, and S by Kentucky; the 'Prairie State'; 21st state admitted to the Union in 1818; pop(1980) 11,426,518; area 144,677 sq km; capital Springfield; other major cities include Chicago, Rockford and Peoria; the R Mississippi forms the W border, the R Ohio follows the Kentucky border, the R Wabash forms the lower part of the Indiana border, and the R Illinois flows SW across the state to meet the R Mississippi; the highest point is Charles Mound (376 m), mostly flat prairie producing maize, soybeans and wheat and grazing pigs and cattle; explored by Jolliet and Marquette in 1673 and settled by the French who established Fort St Louis (1692); included in French Louisiana, it was ceded to the British in 1763 and by the British to the USA in 1783; the state is divided into 102 counties:

County	*area (sq km)*	*pop(1980)*
Adams	2,215	71,622
Alexander	614	12,264
Bond	980	16,224
Boone	733	28,630
Brown	796	5,411
Bureau	2,259	39,114
Calhoun	650	5,867
Carroll	1,154	18,779
Cass	972	15,084
Champaign	2,595	168,392
Christian	1,846	36,446
Clark	1,316	16,913
Clay	1,219	15,283

contd

County	*area (sq km)*	*pop(1980)*
Clinton	1,227	32,617
Coles	1,323	52,260
Cook	2,491	5,253,655
Crawford	1,160	20,818
Cumberland	900	11,062
De Kalb	1,648	74,624
De Witt	1,032	18,108
Douglas	1,084	19,774
Du Page	876	658,835
Edgar	1,620	21,725
Edwards	580	7,961
Effingham	1,243	30,944
Fayette	1,843	22,167
Ford	1,264	15,265
Franklin	1,076	43,201
Fulton	2,265	43,687
Gallatin	845	7,590
Greene	1,412	16,661
Grundy	1,100	30,582
Hamilton	1,134	9,172
Hancock	2,070	23,877
Hardin	471	5,383
Henderson	970	9,114
Henry	2,142	57,968
Iroquois	2,907	32,976
Jackson	1,534	61,522
Jasper	1,290	11,318
Jefferson	1,482	36,552
Jersey	970	20,538
Jo Davies	1,568	23,520
Johnson	900	9,624
Kane	1,362	278,405
Kankakee	1,765	102,926
Kendall	837	37,202
Knox	1,872	61,607
La Salle	2,961	112,033
Lake	1,180	440,372
Lawrence	972	17,807
Lee	1,885	36,328
Livingston	2,720	41,381
Logan	1,609	31,802
Macon	1,511	131,375
Macoupin	2,249	49,384
Madison	1,893	247,691
Marion	1,490	43,523
Marshall	1,009	14,479
Mason	1,394	19,492
Massac	627	14,990
McDonough	1,534	37,467
McHenry	1,576	147,897
McLean	3,081	119,149
Menard	819	11,700
Mercer	1,453	19,286
Monroe	1,009	20,117
Montgomery	1,833	31,686
Morgan	1,477	37,502
Moultrie	845	14,546
Ogle	1,973	46,338
Peoria	1,615	200,466
Perry	1,152	21,714
Piatt	1,142	16,581
Pike	2,158	18,896
Pope	972	4,404
Pulaski	528	8,840
Putnam	416	6,085
Randolph	1,516	35,652
Richland	936	17,587
Rock Island	1,100	165,968
Saline	1,001	28,448
Sangamon	2,252	176,089
Schuyler	1,134	8,365
Scott	653	6,142
Shelby	1,942	23,923

contd

County	*area (sq km)*	*pop(1980)*
St Clair	1,747	267,531
Stark	749	7,389
Stephenson	1,466	49,536
Tazewell	1,690	132,078
Union	1,076	17,765
Vermilion	2,340	95,222
Wabash	582	13,713
Warren	1,412	21,943
Washington	1,464	15,472
Wayne	1,859	18,059
White	1,292	17,864
Whiteside	1,773	65,970
Will	2,194	324,460
Williamson	1,110	56,538
Winnebago	1,342	250,884
Woodford	1,370	33,320

Ilmenau *il'men-ow*, river in Hamburg and Schleswig-Holstein provs, W Germany; formed below Uelzen, flows 96 km N and NW past Lüneburg to the Elbe 3 km N of Winsen; length 107 km; navigable length 29 km; drainage basin area 2,869 sq km.

Ilobasco *ee-lō-ba'skō*, pop(1980) 53,509, town in Cabañas dept, central El Salvador, Central America; NW of San Vicente; the surrounding agricultural area is devoted to cattle, coffee, sugar, and indigo; noted for its pottery; event: annual fair (29 Sept).

Iloilo *ee'lo-wee'lō*, CITY OF ILOILO, 10 41N 122 33E, pop(1980) 244,827, city in Iloilo prov, Western Visayas, Philippines; on S coast of Panay I; declared a port for foreign trade in 1855; 2 universities (1905, 1953); railway; airfield; event: summer regatta.

Ilopango, Lago de *ee-le-pang'gō*, volcanic lake in Cuscatlán, San Salvador and La Paz depts, central El Salvador, Central America; E of San Salvador.

Ilorin *ee-lo'reen*, 8 32N 4 34E, pop(1981e) 385,500, capital of Kwara state, Nigeria, W Africa; 260 km NE of Lagos; railway; airfield; economy: tobacco, wood and crafts; monuments: mosque, palace; event: Shallah festival.

Īlubabor *ee-loo'ba-bōr*, ILLUBABOR, region in W Ethiopia, NE Africa; pop(1984e) 963,327; area 47,400 sq km; high in the E, dipping W towards the Sudanese frontier; watered by the Baro Wenz, the Gīlo Wenz and the Akobo rivers; chief towns include Gorē and Gambēla.

Imathía, EMATHIA (Eng), nome (dept) of Makedhonia region, N Greece; pop(1981) 133,750; area 1,701 sq km; capital Véria; produces wheat, vegetables and wine.

Imatra *ee-mat'ra*, 61 14N 28 50E, pop(1982) 35,727, resort town in Kymi prov, SE Finland; situated by the R Vuoksi, 37 km E of Lappeenranta; established in 1948; railway; economy: steel, hydroelectric power; there is a large tourist resort on the W bank of the river.

Imbabura *eem-ba-boo'ra*, mountainous prov in the Andean Sierra of N Ecuador; situated just N of the Equator, the prov, with its crater lakes, fertile valleys and semitropical climate, is sometimes called the 'lake district of Ecuador'; pop(1982) 247,287; area 4,459 sq km; capital Ibarra; economy: fruit, vegetables, sugar, drink, tobacco, textiles, timber, minerals, wool.

Imbabura, 0 12N 78 02W, extinct Andean volcano in Imbabura prov in the Andean Sierra of N Ecuador; rises to 4,630 m, 11 km SW of Ibarra.

Im'mingham, 53 37N 0 14W, pop(1981) 11,506, port in Holderness dist, Humberside, NE England; on the S side of the R Humber estuary, NW of Grimsby; a major UK port; economy: oil refining, trade in coal, iron, petrochemical products.

Imo *ee'mō*, state in S Nigeria, W Africa; pop(1982e) 5,856,600; area 11,850 sq km; capital Owerri; chief towns Aba, Umuahia, Afikpo and Okigwe; 75% of the pop is engaged in agriculture; there are reserves of oil, lead, zinc, natural gas, limestone, clay and salt; economy: mining, brewing, ceramics, textiles, footwear, tourism and soap.

Imperatriz *eem-pay-ra-trees'*, 5 32S 47 28W, pop(1980) 220,469, town in Maranhão state, Nordeste region, NE Brazil; S of Belém, near the border with Goiás state; economy: rice, timber, cattle raising.

Imperia *eem-pay'ree-a*, prov of Liguria region, NW Italy; pop(1981) 223,738; area 1,155 sq km; capital Imperia.

Imperia, IMPERIA PORTO MAURIZIO, 43 52N 8 01E, pop(1981) 41,609, capital town of Imperia prov, Liguria region, NW Italy; on the Ligurian Sea, between Alassio and San Remo; formed in 1923 from the towns of Porto Maurizo and Oneglia; railway; economy: olive oil, tourism.

Imphal *im'pul*, 24 47N 93 55E, pop(1981) 156,622, capital of Manipur state, NE India; on R Imphal (Manipur), 60 km W of the Burmese frontier; economy: trade in sugar cane, tobacco, rice, fruit; monuments: war cemetery; ruined palaces; orchid farm (7 km).

Inagua *i-na'gwu*, southernmost islands of the Bahamas, SW of the Caicos Is; comprises Great Inagua I and Little Anagua I; pop(1980) 939; area 1,545 sq km; chief town Matthew Town; the Bahamas National Trust Park is situated on Great Inagua I.

Inarijärvi *i'na-ree-yahr'vi*, ENARE *ay'na-ru* (Swed), LAKE INARI (Eng), lake in Lappi prov, NE Finland, close to the Soviet frontier; area 1,000 sq km; length 80 km; width 41 km; 3rd largest lake in Finland; there are over 3,000 islets; the lake is drained eastwards to the Arctic Ocean by the Patsjoki which emerges 40 km NE of Ivalo; the Ivalojoki flows into the lake from the S.

Incahuasi, Cerro *se'rō eeng-ka-wa'see*, 27 03S 68 20W, Andean volcano on the Chile-Argentina border; in Atacama region, N Chile, and Catamarca prov, Argentina; 200 km ENE of Copiapó (Chile); height 6,709 m.

Inchi'ri, region in W Mauritania, NW Africa; pop(1982e) 23,000; area 46,800 sq km; capital Akjoujt; economy: gold and copper reserves.

Inch'ŏn *in-chon'*, JINSEN, CHEMULPO, 37 30N 126 38E, pop(1984) 1,295,107, special city of W Korea; W of Sŏul, on the coast of the Huang Hai (Yellow Sea); a major port for Sŏul, university (1954); subway from Sŏul; economy: fishing; the Japanese and Russian navies fought each other here in 1904; Gen MacArthur led UN forces ashore here in 1950 to regain Sŏul from North Korean forces; there is a monument to Gen MacArthur and also one to mark the landing area of the 7th US division; to the S of Inch'ŏn is Songdo leisure resort.

Independence, 39 06N 94 25W, pop(1980) 111,806, county seat of Jackson county, W Missouri, United States; residential suburb 14 km E of Kansas City; railway; site of the Civil War Battle of Westport, Oct 1864; home of Harry S. Truman, 33rd president of the United States.

India *in'dee-ah*, BHARAT *be'ret* (Sanskrit), official name Republic of India, federal republic in S Asia; bounded NW by Pakistan, N by China, Nepal and Bhutan, E by Burma and Bangladesh, SE by the Bay of Bengal and SW by the Arabian Sea; timezone GMT $+5\frac{1}{2}$; area (excluding those parts of Kashmir and Jammu which are occupied by China and Pakistan) 3,166,829 sq km; capital New Delhi; chief cities include Ahmadabad, Bangalore, Bombay, Calcutta, Hyderabad, Jaipur, Kanpur, Lucknow, Madras, Nagpur and Pune; pop(1981) 683,810,051; ethnic groups are 72% Indo-Aryan, 25% Dravidian, 3% Mongoloid and other; Hindi is the language of 30% of the people, English is important for national, political and commercial communication, Hindustani is spoken widely in N India; official languages are Hindi, English and 14 others; 83.5% of the population are Hindu, 10.7% are Muslim, 2.6% are Christian, 1.8% are Sikh, 0.7% are Buddhist; currency since 1957 is the Indian rupee of 100 paise; national holiday 26 Jan (Republic Day); membership of ADB, AIOC, ANRCP, Colombo Plan, Commonwealth, FAO, G-77, GATT, IAEA, IBRD, ICAC, ICAO, ICO, IDA, IFAD, IFC, IHO, ILO, IMF, IMO, INTELSAT, INTERPOL, IPU, IRC, ITC, ITU, IWC, NAM, UN, UNESCO, UPU, WFTU, WHO, WIPO, WMO, WSG, WTO.

Physical description. India is Asia's 2nd largest state and is divided into the 3 zones of the northern mountains, the central river plains and the southern plateau. Fifty percent of the land area of India is cultivated, 22% is forested, 20% is desert, waste and urban, 5% is pasture and 3% is occupied by inland water. The N mountain area is made up of folded mountain ridges and valleys, where the highest peaks reaching over 7,000 m are found in the Karakoram range and the Ladakh plateau, although high peaks are found all along the Himalayan borders of Arunachal Pradesh, Uttar Pradesh and Himachal Pradesh. These peaks are generally permanently ice-clad, although the lower slopes often support dense forest cover. The central river plains lying to the S of the N mountain region, cross India from Assam in the E to the Punjab in the W, extending S to end in the saline marsh and swamplands of the Rann of Kachch (Kutch), Gujarat state. It is across this region that the great rivers of India flow, such as the Ganga (Ganges), Yamuna, Ghaghari and the Brahmaputra (Jamuna). The delta of these rivers is found at the head of the Bay of Bengal, partly in the West Bengal state of India, but mostly in Bangladesh. The central and E region of the country is the heartland of India, supporting the densest cities and occupied by the best agricultural land in India. Measures of control are necessary to prevent extensive flooding in this area. Opposite to the E area of India, which is crossed by numerous rivers, the NW depends on an extensive system of canals to bring sufficient irrigation water to support any form of agriculture. The NW area of the state of Rajasthan is occupied by the Thar or Indian Desert, bordered by semi-desert areas, although the canal-irrigated regions of the state are gradually being extended so as to bring more of the state into agricultural production. The S peninsula area of India is an area of plateau, known as the Deccan Plateau, of hills and wide valleys, bounded to the W by the peaks of the Western Ghats. The coastal plains were once areas of jungle and are now important areas of rice cultivation. To the E of the Deccan Plateau are the Eastern Ghats, which are discontinuous and generally lower than the Western Ghats, with a much broader coastal plain. The Eastern and Western Ghats meet in the hilly regions of Karnataka and Tamil Nadu on the S tip of the Indian peninsula. In the centre of the Deccan Plateau are the dry, cotton and millet-growing regions of Maharashtra, Andhra Pradesh and Madhya Pradesh.

Climate. The climate of India is dominated by the Asiatic monsoon, which is a great wind system that reverses at certain times of the year to give the climate 3 distinct seasons. From June to Oct the rains come from the SW, while during Dec to Feb rainfall decreases as winds blow in from the N. The climate then becomes hotter with drought continuing until March or May when the winds turn to the SW again. India is divided climatically into 6 regions, the N mountains, the N plains, Deccan Plateau, W coast, SE coastlands and the extreme NE: (1) Rain can occur at any time over the area of the N mountains, although the main rainy season is during the SW monsoon of July to Oct. Temperatures vary greatly with altitude, with this climatic region reaching up to the high peaks of the Himalayan mountain ranges. Winters are generally cool at lower levels but temperatures increase before the monsoon storms. (2) Rainfall decreases E-W on the N plains, where desert conditions are found in the extreme W of Rajasthan state. Cool dry weather is found during the winter months of Dec to Feb, with hot dry weather continuing from March until July. The main rainy season begins in July with the start of the SW monsoon. (3) The interior region of the Deccan Plateau is affected by the seasonal changes of the SW monsoon, although rainfall is generally moderated by its position. Temperatures vary with altitude, although towards the S of the plateau region temperatures are tropical even during the cool season. (4) The west coast region, bounded E by the Arabian Sea and W by the Western Ghats, is subject to rain throughout the year, particularly in the S. Humidity is generally high and the heat becomes oppressive during the monsoon season when rainfall is most abundant. (5) The main periods of rainfall in the SE coastlands are associated with cyclones and storms developing in the Bay of Bengal during Oct-Dec. Rainfall is lighter during the period of the SW monsoon, although temperatures and humidity are high. (6) The climate of the extreme NE region, which is almost separated from the rest of India by Bangladesh, is similar to that of the N plains and the Himalayan region. The main rainy season lasts from June to Oct and is associated with the SW monsoon. Cherrapunji in Meghalaya state (alt 1,300 m), is one of the 3 wettest places in the world.

History, government and constitution. The Indus civilization, which emerged c.2500 BC, was destroyed in 1500 BC by the Aryans who developed the Brahmanic caste system. The Mauryan emperor Asoka (232 BC) unified all of India except the S tip and established Buddhism as the state religion. The collapse of the Mauryan culture in 185 BC brought the decline of Buddhism and the spread of Hinduism in India. Muslim influences were brought by the Arab invaders of Sind, Punjab and Kashmir during the 7th and 8th centuries and Muslim settlement became permanent with the establishment of a sultanate at Delhi. Gaining control over almost every independent kingdom, except that of Kashmir and those in the extreme S, this sultanate was brought to an end when Delhi was

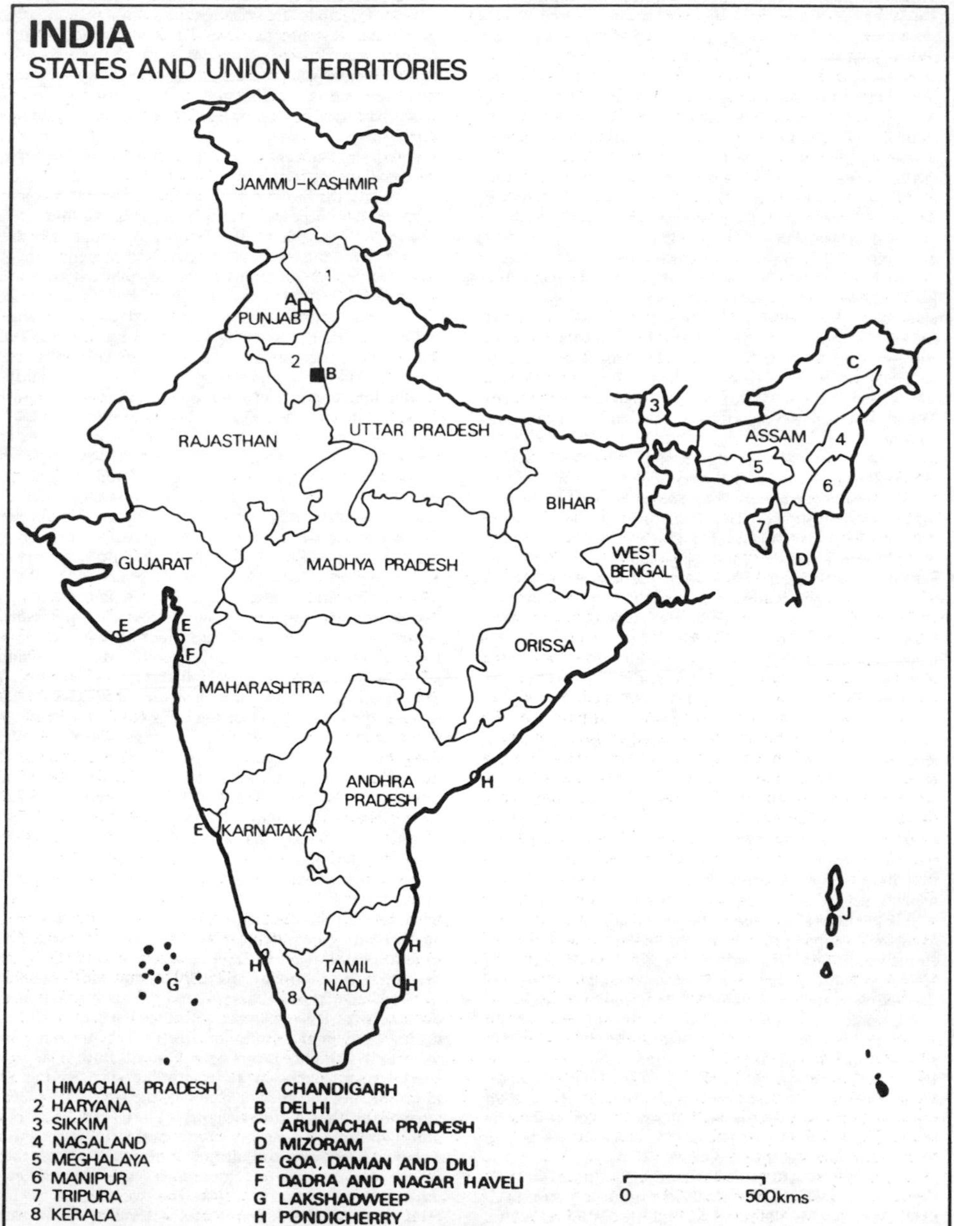

captured by Tamerlane in 1398. In 1526 the Mogul Empire was established by Babur, an invader from Afghanistan who was a descendent of Tamerlane. The empire was consolidated and extended by Akbar and Aurangzeb but began to fragment during the 18th century as the Portuguese, French, Dutch and British increased their footholds in India. As a result of an Afghan invasion in the N, a dynastic dispute and a Hindu revolt by the Mahrattas, France and Britain saw their chance to expand their hold over India. Conflict between 1746 and 1763 led to British dominance in India. The East India Company represented British interests in India, but their role was progressively regulated by the British government. After the Sepoy Rebellion, known as the Indian Mutiny (1857), all of India came under British dominance and power was transferred from the East India Company to the British Crown. Many areas continued to be ruled by native leaders who had sworn allegiance to the British Crown. By the late 19th century, Muslim and Hindu politicians pressed for independence. In 1861 the appointment of Indian councillors to advise viceroys was the first step towards Indian self-government. In the early 1900s, however, separate Muslim and Hindu constituencies of the legislative councils were a major influence in the growing split between the 2 religious communities. The cost of World War I, crop failures and an influenza epidemic which killed millions reduced British prestige in India, as did the Rowlatt Acts (1919), which dispensed with juries and trials when dealing with agitators. The Government of India Act (1919) allowed the election of Indian Ministers to share power with appointed British governors and the Government of India Act (1935) allowed for the election of entirely independent Indian provincial governments, where Great Britain would control only defence and foreign policy. After the 1937 elections and fearing Hindu domination, the Muslim nationalist movement became totally separate. At this time Mohandas K. Gandhi rose to prominence as a political figure with his passive resistance campaigns. After World War II the Congress demanded that the British leave India and in 1946 the British Government offered independence to India on condition that a settlement was reached between the Congress and the Muslim League before the withdrawal of Great Britain in June 1948. The settlement led to the creation of Pakistan, with, like India, large religious minorities. Conflict between religious groups led to over 500,000 deaths in late 1947 and in 1948 war broke out between Pakistan and India over disputed territory in Kashmir and Jammu. The constitution was passed by the Constituent Assembly in 1949 and on 26 Jan 1950 India became a sovereign democratic republic, remaining a member of the Commonwealth. In 1965 and 1971 the section of Jammu and Kashmir held by Pakistan to the W of the ceasefire line was redefined and in 1961 India incorporated the territories of Goa, Dadra and Jagar Haveli into the Union. In 1975 the princely state of Sikkim was also incorporated into the Union of India. Each of the 22 states of India is under the administration of a governor appointed by the president for a term of 5 years and each of the 9 union territories is administered by the president by way of an administrator. All executive power is vested in the president, who is head of the Union of India for a 5-year term. The president, who is advised by a Council of Ministers, appoints a prime minister. Parliament comprises the president, a Council of States or Upper House (*Rajya Sabha*) of no more than 250 members and a 544-member House of the People (*Lok Sabha*). The Legislative Assembly of each state elects members to the Council of States, while members of the House of the People are elected by adult suffrage from territorial constituencies in the states.

Economy. Despite industrial development since independence, some 70% of the Indian labour force is employed in agriculture, the majority working the land at subsistence levels. Agriculture accounts for about 40% of national income, producing 26% of Indian exports. Tea accounts for nearly 20% of these agricultural exports. Principal crops include rice, wheat, coffee, sugar cane, cotton, jute, oilseed, maize, pulses and milk. Crops are grown in the 3 farming seasons of *kharif* (monsoon), *rabi* (winter) and summer. Food production has increased at an annual rate of 3%, with a surge in productivity during the 'green revolution' of the late 1960s and early 1970s. Twenty percent of the land area of India is forested, supporting a small forest industry. Manufacturing industry employs 10% of the population and accounts for almost 20% of the national income. Major products include iron, steel and aluminium, motor vehicles, petroleum products, cement, chemicals, fertilizers, paper, jute goods, cotton textiles and sugar. Important mineral resources include coal, iron, mica, manganese, bauxite, limestone, chromite, barites, oil and gas. Major industrial exports are textiles, engineering goods and clothing, while the chief imports are machinery, transport equipment, petroleum, edible oils and fertilizers. Principal trade partners are the UK, the USA, the USSR and Japan.

Administrative divisions. India is divided into 22 states and 9 union territories as follows:

State/ Union Territory	*area (sq km)*	*pop(1981)*
Andaman and Nicobar Islands	8,293	188,254
Andhra Pradesh	276,814	53,403,619
Arunachal Pradesh	83,578	628,050
Assam	78,523	19,902,826
Bihar	173,876	69,823,154
Chandigarh	114	450,061
Dadra and Nagar Haveli	491	103,677
Delhi	1,485	6,196,414
Goa, Daman and Diu	3,813	1,082,117
Gujarat	195,984	33,960,905
Haryana	44,222	12,850,902
Himachal Pradesh	55,673	4,237,569
Jammu-Kashmir	101,283	5,981,600
Karnataka	191,773	37,043,451
Kerala	38,864	25,403,217
Lakshadweep	32	40,237
Madhya Pradesh	442,841	52,131,717
Maharashtra	307,762	62,693,898
Manipur	22,356	1,433,691
Meghalaya	22,489	1,327,824
Mizoram	21,087	487,774
Nagaland	16,527	773,281
Orissa	155,782	26,272,054
Pondicherry	480	604,136
Punjab	50,362	16,669,755
Rajasthan	342,214	34,102,912
Sikkim	7,299	315,682
Tamil Nadu	130,069	48,297,456
Tripura	10,477	2,060,189
Uttar Pradesh	294,413	110,858,019
West Bengal	87,853	54,485,560

Indian Ocean, ERYTHRÆAN SEA (anc), the 3rd largest ocean in the world, bounded W by Africa, N by Asia, E by Australia and the Malay archipelago and S by the Southern Ocean; area 73,426,500 sq km; width 6,400 km at the Equator; reaches its max depth of 7,725 m in the Java trench off S Indonesia; linked to the Mediterranean by the Suez Canal; the ocean floor is divided into E and W sections by the Mid-Oceanic Ridge, which is offset by numerous fracture zones; the rift valley, which runs along the axis of the ridge and is the centre of sea-floor spreading, is an extension of the Great Rift Valley that runs through the Gulf of Aden; other ridges, such as the Ninety East Ridge extending S from the Bay of Bengal, divide the ocean floor into a series of deep basins scattered with seamounts; the main island groups are Andaman, Nicobar, Chagos and Seychelles; Madagascar and Sri Lanka are the largest islands, while the island of La Réunion is the highest point in the Indian Ocean at

7,946 m; the ocean floor is made shallow by the cones of detrital material brought down by the Indus river into the Arabian Sea and by the R Ganga (Ganges) into the Bay of Bengal; the South Equatorial Current, Mozambique Current, South Pacific Drift and the West Australian Current flow anti-clockwise, while N currents are subject to the direction and strength of the monsoons.

Indian'a, state in E United States, S of L Michigan and W of Ohio; the 'Hoosier State'; pop(1980) 5,490,224; area 93,423 sq km; 19th state to join the Union (1816); capital Indianapolis; chief towns include Fort Wayne, South Bend, Gary, Evansville; hilly in the S, fertile plains in the centre and flat, glaciated land in the N; economy: grain, soybeans, bituminous coal, steel and iron, chemicals, motor vehicles, electrical goods; visited by La Salle in 1679 and 1681; occupied by the French who ceded the state to the British in 1763; the state is divided into 92 counties:

County	*area (sq km)*	*pop(1980)*
Adams	884	29,619
Allen	1,713	294,335
Bartholomew	1,063	65,088
Benton	1,058	10,218
Blackford	432	15,570
Boone	1,100	36,446
Brown	811	12,377
Carroll	967	19,722
Cass	1,076	40,936
Clark	978	88,838
Clay	936	24,862
Clinton	1,053	31,545
Crawford	798	9,820
Davies	1,123	27,836
De Kalb	946	33,606
Dearborn	798	34,291
Decatur	970	23,841
Delaware	1,019	128,587
Dubois	1,115	34,238
Elkhart	1,212	137,330
Fayette	559	28,272
Floyd	390	61,169
Fountain	1,035	19,033
Franklin	1,001	19,612
Fulton	959	19,335
Gibson	1,274	33,156
Grant	1,079	80,934
Greene	1,420	30,416
Hamilton	1,035	82,027
Hancock	798	43,939
Harrison	1,264	27,276
Hendricks	1,063	69,804
Henry	1,024	53,336
Howard	762	86,896
Huntington	952	35,596
Jackson	1,334	36,523
Jasper	1,459	26,138
Jay	998	23,239
Jefferson	944	30,419
Jennings	983	22,854
Johnson	835	77,240
Knox	1,352	41,838
Kosciusko	1,404	59,555
La Porte	1,560	108,632
Lagrange	988	25,550
Lake	1,303	522,965
Lawrence	1,175	42,472
Madison	1,178	139,336
Marion	1,030	765,233
Marshall	1,154	39,155
Martin	881	11,001
Miami	959	39,820
Monroe	1,001	98,785
Montgomery	1,313	35,501
Morgan	1,063	51,999
Newton	1,043	14,844

contd

County	*area (sq km)*	*pop(1980)*
Noble	1,074	35,443
Ohio	226	5,114
Orange	1,061	18,677
Owen	1,004	15,841
Parke	1,154	16,372
Perry	993	19,346
Pike	887	13,465
Porter	1,087	119,816
Posey	1,063	26,414
Pulaski	1,131	13,258
Putnam	1,253	29,163
Randolph	1,180	29,997
Ripley	1,162	24,398
Rush	1,061	19,604
Scott	497	20,422
Shelby	1,074	39,887
Spencer	1,040	19,361
St Joseph	1,193	241,617
Starke	803	21,997
Steuben	801	24,694
Sullivan	1,175	21,107
Switzerland	580	7,153
Tippecanoe	1,305	121,702
Tipton	676	16,819
Union	421	6,860
Vanderburgh	614	167,515
Vermillion	676	18,229
Vigo	1,053	112,385
Wabash	1,035	36,640
Warren	952	8,976
Warrick	1,017	41,474
Washington	1,342	21,932
Wayne	1,050	76,058
Wells	962	25,401
White	1,316	23,867
Whitley	874	26,215

Indiana'polis, 39 46N 86 09W, pop(1980) 700,807, capital of state in Marion county, central Indiana, United States; on the R White; founded in 1820 and made state capital in 1825; world-famous medical centre at Indiana-Purdue Universities campus (1969); Butler University (1855); railway; airport; economy: aircraft, motor vehicles, electronics, telephones, machinery, chemical and metal products; monuments: state museum, museum of art, City Market Internationale; event: the world-famous 'Indianapolis 500' motor-car race.

Indigirka *een-ji-geer'ku*, river in Yakutskaya ASSR, Rossiyskaya, NE Soviet Union; rises on a plateau SE of Oymyakon, between the Khrebet Tas-Kystaby (NE) and Khrebet Suntar Khayata (SW) ranges; flows generally N, cutting through the Khrebet Cherskogo range, then past Ozhogino and Chokurdakh; discharges into the E Siberian Sea where it forms a large, swampy delta; length 1,779 km; chief tributaries include the Moma, Selennyakh, and Uyandina rivers; the river is ice-free June-Sept.

Indonesia *in-do-nee'zha*, official name Republic of Indonesia, REPUBLIK INDONESIA, formerly NETHERLANDS INDIES, DUTCH EAST INDIES, NETHERLANDS EAST INDIES, UNITED STATES OF INDONESIA (1949-50), republic of SE Asia, comprising the world's largest island group, stretching from 6 08N to 11 15S and from 98 45E to 141 05E; comprises 5 main islands and 30 smaller archipelagos totalling 13,677 islands and islets of which 6,000 are inhabited; timezones GMT +7 (Jawa, Sumatera), +8 (Kalimantan, Sulawesi (Celebes), Lesser Sundas), +9 (Maluku (Moluccas), Irian Jaya); area 1,906,240 sq km; pop(1982) 146,776,473; capital Jakarta; ethnic groups, largely of Malay origin, include Javanese, Sundanese, Madurese and coastal Malays; the official language is Indonesian (a modified form of Malay) with English, Dutch and Javanese widely spoken; 90% of the pop is Muslim, 3% Hindu; the currency is the rupiah; national holiday 17 Aug (Independence Day); membership of ADB, ANRPC, ASEAN, CIPEC, ESCAP, FAO, G-77, GATT, IAEA, IBA, IBRD, ICAO, ICO, IDA, Islamic Development Bank, IFAD, IFC, IHO, ILO, IMF, IMO, INTELSAT, INTERPOL, IPU, IRC, ISO, ITC, ITU, NAM, OIC, OPEC, UN, UNESCO, UPU, WFTU, WHO, WIPO, WMO, WTO.

Physical description. Formed by intense crustal pressure, the 5 main islands of Indonesia are Sumatera, Jawa, Kalimantan (two-thirds of Borneo I), Sulawesi and Irian Jaya (W half of New Guinea I). The mountainous and densely forested islands of Sumatera, Jawa and Kalimantan stand on the Sunda shelf which extends outwards from the coast of Malaysia and Indo-China. On this shelf sea depths seldom exceed 215 m. The densely populated island of Jawa has 115 volcanic peaks of which 15 are active. The soil on Jawa is fertile and the wide coastal plains are free from swamp and marsh. Irian Jaya and the Aru Is stand on the Sahul shelf which stretches N from Australia. Between these 2 shelves are the Lesser Sunda Islands, the Maluku (Moluccas) and Sulawesi (Celebes), the summits of underwater ranges surrounded by seas that drop to depths of 4,500 m. Sulawesi is edged by a coral reef.

Climate. The equatorial climate of Indonesia is hot and humid throughout the year, and is strongly influenced by the surrounding sea. During the dry season (June-Sept) the climate is influenced by Australian continental air masses (E monsoon period). The rainy season (Dec-March) is influenced by the Asian and Pacific air masses passing over oceans. In the Moluccas, however, the rainy season occurs during June-Sept. There is an average temperature of 27°C on island coasts, falling inland and with altitude.

History, government and constitution. The islands were settled in early times by Hindus and Buddhists whose power lasted until the 14th century. Gujarati and Persian traders introduced Islam which spread throughout Indonesia during the 14th-15th centuries. Portuguese settlers established spice-trading posts early in the 16th century, but their monopoly was challenged by the Dutch who established the Dutch East India Company in 1602. This company held supreme power in the archipelago until dissolved in 1798. After a brief period of French influence Indonesia was restored to the Dutch in 1816. During the 20th century nationalist movements sprang up and Dutch influence was weakened by German occupation of Holland and Japanese occupation of the Dutch East Indies during World War II. On the defeat of the Japanese in 1945 nationalist elements under Dr Soekarno proclaimed an independent Indonesia and organized the area on a federal system which gave way to unified control in 1950 after the Netherlands government had agreed to transfer sovereignty to the republic. The 1945 constitution established a 920-member People's Consultative Assembly comprising 460 representatives from the House of People's Representatives (*Dewan Perwakilan Rakyat*), additional representatives from political parties elected by proportional representation and from functional groups such as the armed forces. The People's Consultative Assembly meets every 5 years in a general session of the Assembly. Elected for a 5-year term, the president heads a cabinet of 21 ministers. The president is advised by a 45-member Supreme National Council composed of recognized personalities at national and regional level. An Audit Board controls public financial accounts.

Economy. As the world's 4th largest country with a pop growing at an annual rate of 2.5%, Indonesia requires to import food despite moves towards self-sufficiency since 1969. Food crops produced locally, mostly by peasant farmers and smallholders, include rice, maize, cassava, sugar, sweet potatoes and bananas. Export crops include coffee, tobacco, tea, rubber, coconuts and palm oil. Fishing is important locally and extensive tropical forests provide large quantities of timber. Indonesia is a major exporter of tin and nickel ores with additional reserves of bauxite, copper and manganese. Oil, natural gas and petroleum products from Borneo and Sumatera now account for nearly 60% of national income. Manufacturing industry is small and is based on the production of textiles, paper, cement, chemicals, fertilizers, motorcycles and household goods. Major trading partners include Japan, the USA, Singapore, W Germany and Saudi Arabia.

Administrative divisions. Indonesia is divided into 27 provinces (*propinsi*), 246 districts or regencies (*kabupaten*), 54 municipalities (*kota madya*) and 3,349 sub-districts (*kecamatan*). The 3 provs of Aceh, Yogyakarta and Jakarta Raya are special territories.

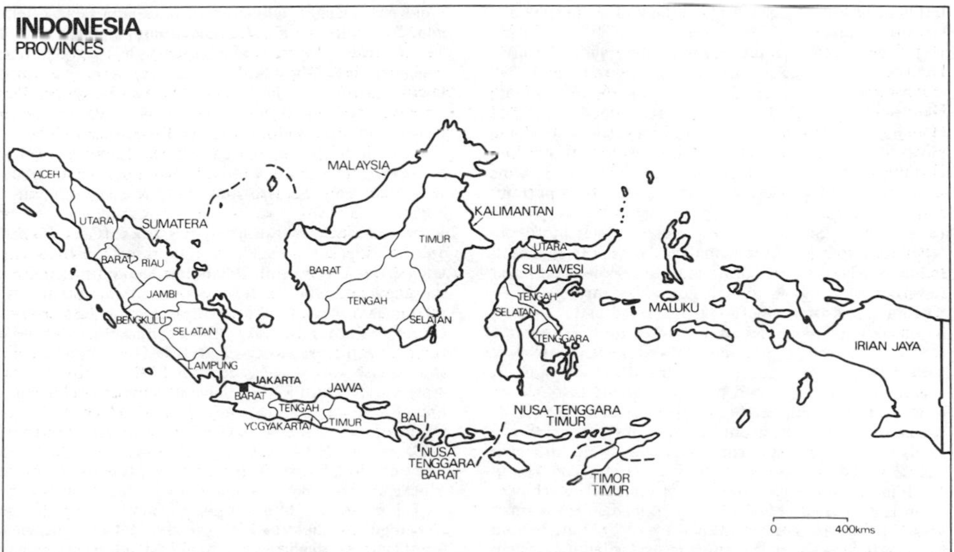

Province	area (sq km)	pop(1980)
Aceh	55,392	2,611,271
Bali	5,561	2,469,920
Bengkulu	21,168	768,004
Irian Jaya	421,981	1,173,875
Jakarta Raya	590	6,503,449
Jambi	44,924	1,445,994
Jawa Barat	46,300	27,453,525
Jawa Tengah	34,206	25,372,889
Jawa Timur	47,922	29,188,852
Kalimantan Berat	146,760	2,986,068
Kalimantan Selatan	37,660	2,064,649
Kalimantan Tengah	152,600	954,353
Kalimantan Timur	202,440	1,218,016
Lampung	33,307	4,624,785
Maluku	74,505	1,411,006
Nusa Tenggara Barat	20,177	2,724,664
Nusa Tenggara Timur	47,876	2,737,166
Riau	94,562	2,168,535
Sulawesi Selatan	27,686	442,302
Sulawesi Tengah	69,726	1,289,639
Sulawesi Tenggara	72,781	6,062,212
Sulawesi Utara	19,023	2,115,384
Sumatera Barat	49,778	3,406,816
Sumatera Selatan	103,688	4,629,801
Sumatera Utara	70,787	8,360,894
Timor Timur	14,874	555,350
Yogyakarta	3,169	2,750,813

Indore *in-dor'*, INDENE, 22 42N 75 54E, pop(1981) 829,000, town in Madhya Pradesh, central India; 335 km E of Ahmadābā; founded in the early 18th century; became capital of the princely state of Indore in 1818; university (1964); railway; economy: chemicals, cotton, hosiery, furniture; monuments: palace, temples, museums and gardens.

Indre *ī-dr*, dept in Centre region of central France, comprising 4 arrond, 26 cantons and 247 communes; it is part of the Loire basin, watered by the Indre and Creuse rivers; pop(1982) 243,191; area 6,791 sq km; capital Châteauroux, chief towns Le Blanc and La Châtre, to the N of which lies Nohant and the famous château of George Sand.

Indre, river in central France, rising in the foothills of the Massif Central, NW of Boussac; flows NW through Indre and Indre-et-Loire depts to the R Loire near Tours; length 265 km.

Indre-et-Loire *ī-dr-ay-lwar*, dept in Centre region of central France, comprising 3 arrond, 33 cantons and 277 communes; pop(1982) 506,097; area 6,127 sq km; watered by the R Loire and its S bank tributaries (Vienne, Cher, Indre); the Val de Touraine is one of the most fertile areas of France, famous for its market-gardens and for the Loire châteaux it contains; wine production and woollen manufacture are also important; capital Tours.

In'dus, (Sansk 'Sindhu', river), river of Asia, mostly in NW India; longest of the Himalayan rivers (3,059 km), it rises in the Kalias range of Xizang aut region (Tibet) near the town of Senge Khambal; flows NW through Tibet, Jammu and Kashmir, cutting through the Ladākh range; to the SE of Gilgit, the river flows S to skirt the NW section of the Punjab Himalayas and so flow into NW Frontier prov of Pakistan; within Pakistan flow is generally SSW in a broad braided channel, through the provs of Punjab and Sind to enter the Arabian Sea SE of Karachi; the river delta, cut by numerous tributaries, is a level, muddy area supporting little cultivation; the main course is fed by waters of the Karakoram and Hindu Kush mountain ranges; the area of the Indus catchment basin is estimated at 963,100 sq km; navigable for small vessels as far as Hyderabad; barrage at Sukkur, N Sind prov, provides water for an extensive irrigation system and power project; forms provincial boundaries at several places along its course; lying between the mountains of NW Frontier prov and the arid Thar desert; the Indus civilization flourished 4,000-2,000 BC, relics have been excavated at Mohenjo-Daro and Harappa.

Inglewood, 33 58N 118 21W, pop(1980) 94,245, city in Los Angeles county, SW California, United States; residential and industrial city 16 km SW of Los Angeles, just E of Los Angeles International Airport; university; railway; economy: metal goods, aircraft.

In'golstadt, 48 45N 11 26E, pop(1983) 90,500, industrial city in Oberbayern dist, Bayern (Bavaria) prov, W Germany; on the S fringe of the Fränkische Alb in a wide plain in the Danube valley, 69 km N of München (Munich); railway; economy: oil refining, motor vehicles, valves, pipelines, spinning machinery; monument: church of Maria de Victoria (1732-36).

Inhambane *ee-yam-ba'nay*, prov in SE Mozambique, SE Africa; pop(1980) 997,600; area 68,615 sq km; situated on Tropic of Capricorn; bordered N by the R Save and W by the R Changane; off the coast are the islands of Bazaruto and Benguérua; capital Inhambane; chief towns include Vilanculo, Nova Mambone and Quissico; a major part of the Zinave National Park is located in the N.

Inhambane, 23 51S 35 29E, pop(1980) 56,439, seaport capital of prov of same name, SE Mozambique, SE Africa; on Inhambane Bay, an inlet of the Mozambique Channel; NE terminus of the railway from Inharrine 370 km NE of Maputo; visited by Vasco da Gama in 1498; airfield; economy: soap, sugar milling, bricks, ceramics and trade in cotton, sugar, timber, rubber, maize, copra, peanuts.

Ink'ster, 42 18N 83 19W, pop(1980) 35,190, residential town in Wayne county, SE Michigan, United States; 21 km W of Detroit; railway.

Inland Sea, arm of the Pacific Ocean situated between Honshū island (N) and Kyūshū and Shikoku islands (S), Japan. See Seto Naikai.

Inner Mongolia, aut region in N China. See Nei Mongol.

Innsbruck *inz'brook* ('inn bridge'), 47 17N 11 25E, pop(1981) 117,287, capital of Tirol state, W Austria; situated in the wide Inn valley surrounded by mountains; there is a medieval old town, with narrow and irregular streets and tall houses in late Gothic style; a great tourist attraction, noted for its mountaineering course and tobogganing, and a popular winter skiing centre; the 1964 and 1976 Winter Olympic Games were held here; Alpine zoo; university (1914-23); bishopric; monuments: Goldenes Dachl ('golden roof'), a late Gothic oriel window roofed with 3,450 gilded copper tiles, built in 1494-96 by the Emperor Maximilian as a Royal Box from which to view theatrical performances in the square below; cathedral (1717-22); Hofburg, a 15-16th-c palace, later remodelled in Baroque and Rococo style; Hofkirche (Court Church) built in 1553-63; Altes Landhaus, a monumental Baroque palace (1725-28); events: Tirolean Summer (July-Aug), Festival of Old Music (Aug), Innsbruck Fair (Sept), Alpine Folk Music Competition (Oct).

Inowrocław *een-o-vrot'swaf*, HOHENSALZA (Ger), 52 49N 18 12E, pop(1983) 69,300, health resort in Bydgoszcz voivodship, N central Poland; saline baths; railway; economy: metallurgy, chemicals, soda, salt mining; monuments: late Gothic parish church, Romanesque church of the Virgin Mary (13th-c), museum dedicated to the poet Jan Kasprowicz.

Intibucá *een-tee-boo-kah'*, dept in S Honduras, Central America, bounded S by El Salvador; pop(1983e) 111,412; area 3,070 sq km; capital La Esperanza (Intibucá); mountainous in the N, sloping down to plains in the S.

Inuvik, 68 16N 133 40W, pop(1981) 3,421, town in the far NW of Northwest Territories, N Canada; on the Mackenzie river near its junction with the Beaufort Sea; an Eskimo centre, built on piles.

Invercar'gill, 46 26S 168 21E, pop(1981) 49,446, town in Southland, on the S coast of South Island, New Zealand; on the New River Harbour, an inlet of the Foveaux Strait; many of the town's streets are named after

Scottish rivers; famous trout-fishing rivers nearby; railway; airfield; economy: butter, cheese, wool, meat, timber, coal; monument: the Southland Centennial Museum and Art Gallery.

Inverness, 57 27N 4 15W, pop(1981) 40,010, capital of Inverness dist and of Highland region, NE Scotland; at the mouth of the R Ness, at the entrance to the Beauly Firth, 181 km NW of Edinburgh; railway; airfield; NE terminus of the Caledonian Canal; economy: electronics, textiles, tourism; monuments: Inverness museum and art gallery; Inverness castle (Victorian); 8 km E of Inverness is Culloden Moor, where Prince Charles Edward Stuart's army was defeated on 16 April 1746; event: Highland games (July).

Inverurie *in-vė-roor'ee*, 57 17N 2 23W, pop(1981) 7,680, capital of Gordon dist, Grampian region, NE Scotland; near the junction of the Don and Urie rivers, 22 km NW of Aberdeen; railway; monument: Inverurie museum.

Inyangani *in-yan-gah'ni*, 18 18S 32 54E, highest peak in Zimbabwe, S Africa; rises to 2,592 m in NE Zimbabwe near the Mozambique frontier.

Ioánnina *yō-an'yin a*, nome (dept) of Ipiros region, W Greece, bounded N by Albania; pop(1981) 147,304; area 4,990 sq km; capital Ioánnina.

Ioánnina, JANINA (Serb), 39 39N 20 57E, pop(1981) 44,829, capital town of Ioánnina nome (dept), Ipiros region, W Greece; on the W side of L Ioánnina; university (1965); airfield; economy: silver, tourism; monument: fortress (1619), now housing a folk museum; event: festival of literature and art (Aug).

Iona *ī-ō'na*, island in Argyll and Bute dist., Strathclyde region, W Scotland; off W coast of Mull, separated by the Sound of Iona; area 8.5 sq km; historic centre of Celtic Christianity, the site of the monastery established in 563 AD by St Columba, and of his burial place; restored Benedictine abbey, orig. founded in 1203, now centre of the Iona community (est. 1938); ancient burial ground of Scottish and Celtic kings.

Ionian Islands *ī-ō'nee an*, region and island group of Greece. See Ioníoi Nísoi.

Ionian Sea, part of the Mediterranean Sea, lying W of the Greek islands of Kérkira, Levkás, Kefallinía and Zákinthos and S of Italy; separated from the Adriatic Sea by the Strait of Otranto, and from the Tyrrhenian Sea by the Strait of Messina, the Malta Channel and the Sicilian Channel; connected to the Aegean Sea by the Sea of Crete.

Ioníoi Nísoi, IONIAN ISLANDS (Eng), EPTÁNISOS ('seven islands'), region and island group of W Greece, extending from the Albanian frontier to the Pelopónnisos, pop(1981) 182,651; area 2,307 sq km; comprises a chain of about 40 islands, of which the largest are Kérkira (Corfu), Kefallinía, Zákinthos and Levkás; the islands are mountainous, but with fertile plains and valleys, producing wine, olives and fruit.

Íos *ee'os*, 36 43N 25 17E, island of the Kikládhes, Greece, in the Aegean Sea, SSW of Náxos; area 108 sq km; linked by boat to Piraiévs (Piraeus), Páros and Santorin; Homer is alleged to have died here; the port of Órmos Íou lies on the W coast.

Iowa *ī'ō-wah*, state in N central United States, bounded W by Nebraska and South Dakota, N by Minnesota, E by Wisconsin and Illinois, and S by Missouri; the 'Hawkeye State'; 29th state admitted to the Union (1846); pop(1980) 2,913,808; area 145,509 sq km; capital Des Moines; other major cities are Cedar Rapids, Davenport and Sioux City; the R Mississippi follows the E border of the state and the R Des Moines flows SE across the central state before emptying into the Mississippi; the R Big Sioux forms the South Dakota state border and empties into the Missouri; the Missouri follows the Nebraska state border; the highest point is Ocheyedan Mound (511 m); Iowa is almost entirely prairie-land (95%) with rich soil; chief crops are corn and soybeans; over half the corn grown is used to feed pigs and cattle; the state leads the nation in corn and pig production, and is 2nd only to Illinois in soybean production; only California has a total farm income greater than Iowa; industry is dominated by food processing and machinery manufacture, other manufactures including chemicals and electrical equipment; Iowa became part of USA with the Louisiana Purchase in 1803, became a territory in 1838 and a state in 1846; the capital moved from Iowa City to Des Moines in 1857; the state is divided into 99 counties:

County	*area (sq km)*	*pop(1980)*
Adair	1,482	9,509
Adams	1,105	5,731
Allamakee	1,646	15,108
Appanoose	1,295	15,511
Audubon	1,154	8,559
Benton	1,867	23,649
Black Hawk	1,490	137,961
Boone	1,490	26,184
Bremer	1,141	24,820
Buchanan	1,487	22,900
Buena Vista	1,495	20,774
Butler	1,513	17,668
Calhoun	1,485	13,542
Carroll	1,482	22,951
Cass	1,469	16,932
Cedar	1,513	18,635
Cerro Gordo	1,479	48,458
Cherokee	1,500	16,238
Chickasaw	1,313	15,437
Clarke	1,121	8,612
Clay	1,479	19,576
Clayton	2,025	21,098
Clinton	1,807	57,122
Crawford	1,856	18,935
Dallas	1,537	29,513
Davis	1,310	9,104
Decatur	1,391	9,794
Delaware	1,503	18,933
Des Moines	1,076	46,203
Dickinson	991	15,629
Dubuque	1,578	93,745
Emmet	1,024	13,336
Fayette	1,901	25,488
Floyd	1,303	19,597
Franklin	1,516	13,036
Fremont	1,339	9,401
Greene	1,485	12,119
Grundy	1,303	14,366
Guthrie	1,534	11,983
Hamilton	1,498	17,862
Hancock	1,485	13,833
Hardin	1,479	21,776
Harrison	1,812	16,348
Henry	1,134	18,890
Howard	1,230	11,114
Humboldt	1,134	12,246
Ida	1,123	8,908
Iowa	1,526	15,429
Jackson	1,659	22,503
Jasper	1,901	36,425
Jefferson	1,144	16,316
Johnson	1,596	81,717
Jones	1,498	20,401
Keokuk	1,508	12,921
Kossuth	2,532	21,891
Lee	1,357	43,106
Linn	1,882	169,775
Louisa	1,045	12,055
Lucas	1,123	10,313
Lyon	1,529	12,896
Madison	1,464	12,597
Mahaska	1,485	22,867
Marion	1,456	29,669
Marshall	1,490	41,652
Mills	1,141	13,406
Mitchell	1,222	12,329

contd

County	*area (sq km)*	*pop(1980)*
Monona	1,812	11,692
Monroe	1,128	9,209
Montgomery	1,102	13,413
Muscatine	1,149	40,436
O'Brien	1,492	16,972
Osceola	1,037	8,371
Page	1,391	19,063
Palo Alto	1,461	12,721
Plymouth	2,246	24,743
Pocahontas	1,500	11,369
Polk	1,513	303,170
Pottawattamie	2,478	86,561
Poweshiek	1,521	19,306
Ringgold	1,391	6,112
Sac	1,498	14,118
Scott	1,193	160,022
Shelby	1,537	15,043
Sioux	1,999	30,813
Story	1,492	72,326
Tama	1,875	19,533
Taylor	1,396	8,353
Union	1,108	13,858
Van Buren	1,258	8,626
Wapello	1,128	40,241
Warren	1,490	34,878
Washington	1,482	20,141
Wayne	1,368	8,199
Webster	1,867	45,953
Winnebago	1,043	13,010
Winneshiek	1,794	21,876
Woodbury	2,270	100,884
Worth	1,043	9,075
Wright	1,505	16,319

Iowa City, 41 40N 91 32W, pop(1980) 50,508, county seat of Johnson county, E Iowa, United States; on the R Iowa, 40 km S of Cedar Rapids; founded in 1838; capital of Iowa territory 1839-57; university (1847); railway; major medical research and treatment centre.

Ipatinga *ee-pa-cheeng'ga*, 19 32S 42 30W, pop(1980) 105,030, town in Minas Gerais state, Sudeste region, SE Brazil; NE of Belo Horizonte; railway; economy: cattle raising.

Ipiros *ee'pi-ros*, EPIRUS *e-pī'rus* (Eng), hilly region of NW Greece, bounded N by Albania, and W by the Ionian Sea; pop(1981) 324,541; area 9,303 sq km; comprises the nomoi (depts) of Árta, Ioánnina, Préveza, and Thesprotía; the heavy rainfall favours the development of agriculture, particularly stock-farming; chief town Ioánnina; the principal ancient sites in Ipiros are Dodóna, the Nekyomanteion of Mesopótamos, and the city of Nikópolis, founded by Augustus.

Ipoh *ee-pō'*, 4 36N 101 02E, pop(1980) 293,849, capital of Perak state, W Peninsular Malaysia, SE Asia; on R Kinta, 217 km NNW of Kuala Lumpur; originally settled by Chinese miners at a point beyond which the river was not navigable; replaced Taiping as state capital in 1937; racecourse; railway; economy: tin; monuments: state mosque; rock paintings in the limestone caves nearby; Perak Tong and Sam Poh Tong Buddhist temples 6 km S.

Ip'swich, 27 38S 152 40E, pop(1981e) 73,020, city in Brisbane stat div, Queensland, Australia; on the R Bremer, 40 km W of Brisbane; railway; airfield; economy: textiles, coal mining, railway engineering, timber; the town theatre was originally designed as a rubbish incinerator by the American Burley Griffin, architect of Canberra.

Ipswich, GIPESWIC (Anglo-Saxon), 52 04N 1 10E, pop(1981) 129,908, port and county town in Suffolk, E England; at the head of the R Orwell estuary, 106 km NE of London; county town of Suffolk; a major wool port in the 16th century; birthplace of Cardinal Wolsey; home of the painter Thomas Gainsborough (1727-88); railway; economy: engineering, brewing, food processing, agricultural machinery, electrical equipment, textiles, tobacco products, fertilizers, plastics; monuments: churches of St Mary-le-Tower and St Margaret, Ipswich museum; event: music festival at Aldeburgh (32 km NE).

Iquique *ee-kee'kay* (Aymara, 'que-que', place of rest and tranquillity), 20 13S 70 09W, pop(1982) 109,033, port capital of Iquique prov, and Tarapacá region, N Chile; S of Arica; a free port; founded in 16th century on a rocky peninsula, the city was partly destroyed by an earthquake in 1877; on 21 May 1879, during the War of the Pacific, the *Esmeralda* and another wooden ship, under Captain Arturo Prat, resisted the attack of the Peruvian ironclad ship *Huáscar* here; railway; airfield; economy: trade in fishmeal, fish oil, tinned fish and salt; monuments: there are several Victorian-style painted wooden houses; at the back of the Customs House is a naval museum; the Palacio Astoreca, built in 1903, formerly the Intendencia, is now a cultural centre with exhibitions of shells and the history of the nitrate industry; events: religious festival during the ten days before 16 July (La fiesta de Tirana) at a village 70 km E of Iquique.

Iquitos *ee-kee'tōs*, 3 51S 73 13W, pop(1981) 173,629, capital of Loreto dept, NE Peru; fast-developing city on the W bank of the Amazon; facing Padre Isla island in mid-stream; completely isolated except by air and river; university (1962); chief town of Peru's jungle region and centre for oil exploration in Peruvian Amazonia.

Iráklion *eer-ah'klee-on*, HERAK'LION (Eng), CANDIA (Ital), nome (dept) of Kríti island (Crete), S Greece; pop(1981) 243,622; area 2,641 sq km; capital Iráklion.

Iráklion, 35 20N 25 08E, pop(1981) 110,958, administrative centre and capital town of Iráklion nome (dept) and Kríti (Crete) region (since 1971), S Greece, on N coast of Kríti I; airfield; ferries to Piraiévs (Piraeus) on the mainland; commercial harbour; economy: leather, soap, tourism; monuments: church of St Titos; 19th-c cathedral of Áyios Minás; the old part of Iráklion lies within the circuit of Venetian walls, begun in 1538 by the famous military engineer Sanmichele; the archaeological museum is Iráklion's most important tourist attraction, housing the largest and finest collection of Cretan antiquities; event: Navy Week (June-July).

Iran *i-ran'*, formerly PERSIA *per'zha* (-1935), official name Islamic Republic of Iran, JOMHORI-E-ISLAMI-E-IRÂN, republic in SW Asia, bounded N by USSR and the Caspian Sea, E by Afghanistan and Pakistan, S by the Gulf of Oman and the Arabian Gulf, SW by Iraq, and NW by Turkey; timezone GMT $+3\frac{1}{2}$; area 1,648,000 sq km; capital Tehrān; chief cities Mashhad, Eşfahān, Tabrīz, and Shīrāz; pop(1983) 44,444,000; ethnic groups include 63% Persian, 18% Turkic, 13% other Iranian, 3% Kurdish, 3% Arab and other Semitic; the official language is Farsi or Persian which is spoken by 45% of the population; local languages are spoken by the minorities (Kurdish, Turki); Islam is the dominant religion: 93% Shiite Muslim, 5% Sunni Muslim; the unit of currency is the rial; membership of Colombo Plan, FAO, G-77, IAEA, IBRD, ICAC, ICAO, IDA, IFAD, IFC, IHO, ILO, IMF, IMO, INTELSAT, INTERPOL, IPU, IRC, ITU, NAM, OIC, OPEC, Regional Cooperation for Development, UN, UNESCO, UPU, WFTU, WHO, WMO, WSG, WTO.

Physical description. Iran is largely composed of a vast central plateau rimmed by mountain ranges that drop down to narrow coastal lowlands. The arid central plateau, which extends E into Afghanistan, has an average elevation of 1,200 m. It comprises a number of salt and sand basins, including the Dasht-e-Kavīr (Great Salt Desert) and the Dasht-e-Lut (Great Sand Desert). There are also considerable areas of marshland. The central plateau is bounded N by the Elburz Mts which extend across N Iran and rise to 5,670 m at Qolleh-ye Damāvand (Mt Damāvand), a volcanic cone 72 km NE of Tehrān. The complex Zagros Mts, which form the W and S border of the central plateau, extend approx 1,770 km from the Turkish-Soviet frontier SE along the Persian Gulf to the E prov of Balūchestān. In the higher parts these mountains rise to between 3,000 m and 4,600 m. There are narrow coastal plains along the shores of the Arabian Gulf, Gulf of Oman, and the Caspian Sea. The Mesopotamian lowlands extend into Kuzestān prov in W central Iran.

Climate. Much of the country has a desert climate with an annual precipitation below 300 mm. Summers are warm to hot with almost continuous sunshine while winters can be extremely cold with cold airstreams blowing from the NE. Rainfall tends to be confined to the winter and spring months. Temperatures at Tehrān range from 2.2°C in Jan to 29.4°C in July and the mean annual rainfall is 246 mm. The Caspian coastal strip is much wetter than the interior. Annual precipitation here ranges from 800 to 2,000 mm and is more widely distributed throughout the year. Along the shores of the Arabian Gulf the climate is hot and humid.

History, government and constitution. A military coup on 31 Oct 1925 deposed the last Shah of the Qajar dynasty and the new leader, Reza Shah, took control of newly independent Persia. The country's name was changed to Iran on 21 March 1935. Iran's refusal to grant the USSR oil concessions at the end of World War II led eventually to revolt in the N of the country and the formation of the People's Republic of Āzarbāījān and the Kurdish People's Republic (Dec 1945). Five months later the Soviet troops withdrew under international pressure. Throughout the late 1970s protests against the Shah and his increasingly repressive regime led to the outbreak of revolution in 1978. The Shah went into exile and Ayatollah Khomeini, spiritual leader of the Shiite Muslim community, assumed control. An Islamic Republic was proclaimed on 1 April 1979. In 1980, as a result of disputed control over the Shatt al'Arab and the Gulf, Iraq invaded Iran. A president, elected for a 4-year term, is head of state. He appoints a prime minister and other ministers. The Ayatollah is the appointed religious leader with authority to protect the constitution. A 270-member national consultative assembly and a smaller senate hold administrative responsibility.

Economy. Iran is the world's 4th largest oil producer with crude oil production at 2.4 million barrels per day in 1983. The petroleum industry was severely disrupted by the 1978 revolution and Gulf War fighting between Iran and Iraq has destroyed or put out of action refineries at Ābādān and Bandar Khomeynī at the head of the Gulf and the tanker terminal on Kharg I. Other important minerals include natural gas, iron ore, copper, manganese, chromite, coal, and salt. Textiles are Iran's second most important industrial product. Other industries include sugar refining, food processing, and the production of petrochemicals, iron and steel, cement and building materials, fertilizers, and machinery. Traditional handicrafts also play an important role in the economy. The areas surrounding Tabrīz, Kermān, Arāk, Kāshān, Eşfahān, Shīrāz, and Hamadān are noted for their carpets. Eşfahān is the traditional textile manufacturing centre. In 1980 crude oil accounted for 73% and refined products for 21% of total exports. Other exports included carpets, fruit, and nuts. Japan and West Germany are the main trading partners.

Agriculture. Approx one-third of the workforce is employed in agriculture and forestry. Wheat, the most important crop, is grown mostly in the W and NW. Rice and tobacco are grown largely on the shores of the Caspian Sea. Other crops include barley, sugar-beet, cotton, dates, raisins, and tea. Sheep and goats are raised, and silkworms are bred.

Administrative divisions. Iran is divided into 24 provinces as follows:

Province	area (sq km)	pop(1982)
Āzarbāyān-e Gharbī	38,850	1,407,604
Āzarbāyān-e Sharqī	67,102	3,197,685
Bākhtarān	23,667	1,030,714
Būshehr	27,699	356,216
Chahar Mahāll va Bakhtīāri	14,820	394,357
Eşfahān	104,550	2,175,150
Fārs	133,298	2,035,582
Gīlān	14,709	1,581,872
Hamadān	20,172	1,046,628
Hormozgān	66,870	462,440
Īlām	19,042	246,024
Kermān	186,472	1,078,875
Khorāsān	313,337	3,264,398
Khuzestān	67,236	2,196,920
Kohkīluyeh va Būyer Aḩmadī	14,261	244,370
Kordestān	24,998	782,440
Lorestān	28,803	915,784
Markazī	39,895	1,230,393
Māzandarān	46,200	2,375,994
Semnān	91,214	300,640

contd

Province	area (sq km)	pop(1982)
Sīstān va Balūchestān	181,578	664,292
Tehrān	19,125	7,709,000
Yazd	63,455	369,122
Zanjān	36,398	1,117,157

Irapuato *ee-ra-pwah'tō*, 20 41N 101 21W, pop(1980) 246,308, town in Guanajuato state, S central Mexico; 107 km W of Queretaro; alt 1,725 m; railway.

Iraq *ee-rak'*, 'IRAQ (Arab), official name Republic of Iraq, AL JUMHOURIYA AL 'IRAQUIA, republic in SW Asia, bounded E by Iran, N by Turkey, NW by Syria, W by Jordan, SW and S by Saudi Arabia, and SE by Kuwait and the Arabian Gulf; timezone GMT +3; area 434,925 sq km; capital Baghdād; chief towns Al Basrah, Kirkūk, and Mosul; pop(1977) 12,029,700; the population comprises 79% Arab, 16% Kurd (concentrated largely in the NE), 3% Persian, and 2% Turkish; Islam is the dominant religion; Arabic is the official language although English is widely spoken; Kurdish is spoken in the N; the unit of

currency is the dinar; national holidays include celebrations of the 1958 and 1968 revolutions; membership of Arab League, FAO, G-77, IAEA, IBRD, ICAO, IDA, Islamic Development Bank, IFAD, IFC, ILO, IMF, IMO, INTELSAT, INTERPOL, ITU, NAM, OAPEC, OIC, OPEC, UN, UNESCO, UPU, WFTU, WHO, WIPO, WMO, WSG, WTO.

Physical description. Much of Iraq comprises the vast alluvial tract of the Tigris-Euphrates lowland, known as Mesopotamia in ancient times. Both rivers rise in Turkey and are separated in their upper courses in Iraq by the plain of Al Jazīrah, which rises to 1,547 m above sea level near the Syrian border. Below Baghdād the flood plains widen and the river channels become braided. Approx 190 km from the Arabian Gulf the 2 rivers join to form the navigable Shatt al'Arab. The lowland here contains swamp vegetation, including reed marshes and palm belts. The only mountainous terrain in Iraq is confined to the NE where heights of more than 3,000 m are attained near the Iranian border. Much of the rest of the country is desert reaching a maximum height of 100 m.

Climate. The climate is mainly arid with a wide annual range of temperature. Summers are very hot and dry while winters can be cold. Temperatures at Baghdād range from 10°C in Jan to 35°C in July, and the mean annual rainfall is 140 mm. Annual rainfall is highest in the NE with an average of 400-600 mm. Elsewhere the rainfall is low and unreliable, occurring mostly between Dec and April.

History, government and constitution. Iraq was part of the Ottoman Empire from 1638 until World War I. It was captured by British forces in 1916 and became a British-mandated territory in 1921. Independence was achieved on 3 October 1932 under the Hashemite Dynasty, which ruled as a constitutional monarchy. In 1958 the monarchy was overthrown and Iraq came under military rule. During the 1960s Kurdish nationalists in the NE of the country fought to establish a separate state with Kurds in Iran, Turkey, and the USSR. This led to limited Kurdish autonomy from 1961. In September 1980 Iraq invaded Iran in a dispute over Iranian claims to part of the Shatt al'Arab. Iraq is a democratic socialist republic currently governed under a provisional constitution. Supreme power is vested in a 9-member revolutionary command council, which elects a president. Some legislative power has now devolved to the 250-member National Assembly, elected in June 1980 for a 4-year term. The Kurdish regional assembly also has limited powers of legislation.

Economy. Oil, first discovered in 1927 and nationalized in 1972, is the mainstay of the economy. Iraq is the world's 2nd largest producer after Saudi Arabia and in 1983 crude reserves were estimated at 59 billion barrels, 3rd highest in OPEC. The main N oilfields are located at Kirkūk, Jambur, and Basi Hassau, while in the S the fields of Rumaila and Zubayr are the most important. Since the outbreak of war with Iran in 1980 oil production has been severely disrupted and major oil installations have been destroyed. Oil terminals on the Gulf were destroyed in 1980 and the trans-Syria pipeline closed in 1982. The pipeline from Kirkūk to the Mediterranean Sea via Turkey is the only means of exporting the oil. Iraq also produces natural gas and other minerals. Other industries include oil refining, and the manufacture of petrochemicals, cement, and textiles. Several new industrial plants are being developed with Soviet equipment and technical assistance. In 1980 crude oil formed 99% of all exports, of which 18% went to France, 15% to Brazil, and 14% to Japan. The chief imports of construction equipment, machinery, motor vehicles, and agricultural commodities came from Japan (18%), West Germany (15%), and France (9%).

Agriculture. Agriculture in Iraq employs 30% of the workforce and accounts for just under 10% of national income. Dates, cotton, and rice are the main products of lowland cultivation while the uplands produce winter crops of wheat, barley, and lentils. In 1980 dates, produced largely in the irrigated Shatt al'Arab, represented Iraq's largest export after oil. Sheep and cattle are raised on drier ground above the level of the floodplains. Wool is also an important export. There have been attempts to encourage private enterprise in agriculture since the government abolished its farm collectivization programme in 1981. Major irrigation schemes are also underway to extend the area under cultivation.

Administrative divisions. Iraq is divided into 18 governorates as follows:

Governorate	*area (sq km)*	*pop(1977)*
Al-Anbār	89,540	466,059
Al Basrah	19,702	1,008,626
Al-Muthanna	49,206	215,637
Al-Qādisiyah	8,569	423,006
An Najaf	26,834	389,680
Arbīl	14,428	541,456
At-Ta'mīm	9,426	495,425
Babil	5,503	592,016
Baghdād	5,023	3,189,700
Dhi-Qār	13,668	622,979
Dihōk	6,374	250,575
Diyāla	19,047	587,754
Karbalā'	52,856	269,822
Misān	16,774	372,575
Neineva	41,320	1,105,671
Salāhuddīn	21,326	363,819
Sulaymānīyah	16,482	690,557
Wāsit	17,922	415,140

The governorates of Sulaymanīyah, Dihōk, and Arbīl form the Kurdish Autonomous Region.

Ir'bid, governorate (*muhafaza*) of the East Bank, N Jordan; bounded N by Syria, E by Iraq and Saudi Arabia, and W by the R Jordan; capital Irbid; chief towns Jarash, Mafraq, and 'Ajlūn.

Irbid, 32 33N 35 51E, pop(1983e) 150,000, capital town of Irbid governorate (*muhafaza*), East Bank, N Jordan, 64 km N of Amman; university (1973).

Ireland *īr'land*, HIBERNIA (Lat), an island on the W fringe of Europe separated from Great Britain by the Irish Sea; its greatest length from Malin Head (N) to Mizen Head (S) is 486 km and its greatest E-W width is 275 km. Since 1921 the island has been divided politically into the independent 26 counties of the Irish Republic, comprising 70,282 sq km and pop(1981) of 3,440,427; and Northern Ireland which is part of the UK and contains 6 of the 9 counties of the ancient province of Ulster and has a pop(1981) 1,547,000. Known poetically as ERIN, a name derived from Strabo's name for the island which was IERNE. From 6th to 13th centuries it was often known as SCOTIA.

Irian Jaya *ir-ee-ahn jī'uh*, WEST IRIAN, formerly DUTCH NEW GUINEA, province of Indonesia, comprising the W half of the island of New Guinea and adjacent islands; incorporated into Indonesia in 1969; pop(1980) 1,173,875; area 421,981 sq km; capital Jayapura; watered by many rivers flowing from the central Pegunungan Maoke range which rises to 5,029 m at Puncak Jaya (Jaya Peak); economy: copra, maize, groundnuts, tunafish, pepper, gold, oil, coal, phosphate.

Iringa *ee-ring'ga*, 7 49S 35 39E, pop(1978) 57,182, capital of Iringa region, S central Tanzania, E Africa; 177 km S of Dodoma; economy: agricultural centre, trading in pipe tobacco, fruit, pepper and diamonds.

Irish Republic, EIRE *ayr'ē* (Gael), official name Republic of Ireland, republic occupying S, central and NW Ireland, separated from Great Britain by the Irish Sea and St George's Channel; bounded NE by Northern Ireland which is part of the UK; area 70,282 sq km; timezone GMT; pop(1981) 3,440,427; capital Dublin; chief towns include Cork, Limerick, Waterford, Galway, Drogheda, Dundalk and Sligo; the pop is largely Celtic in origin, speaking Irish Gaelic and English, which is the official language; the Gaelic-speaking areas are known as the *Gaeltacht*, mostly located on the W coast; nearly 95% of

IRISH REPUBLIC
PROVINCES AND COUNTIES

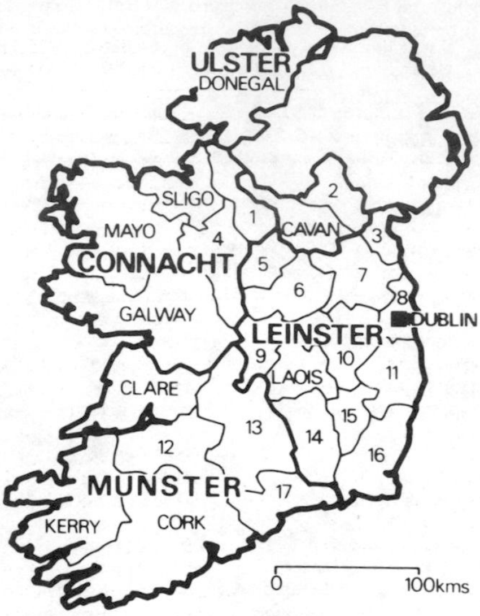

1 LEITRIM
2 MONAGHAN
3 LOUTH
4 ROSCOMMON
5 LONGFORD
6 WESTMEATH
7 MEATH
8 DUBLIN
9 OFFALY
10 KILDARE
11 WICKLOW
12 LIMERICK
13 TIPPERARY
14 KILKENNY
15 CARLOW
16 WEXFORD
17 WATERFORD

The counties of Cavan and Monaghan lie in the province of Ulster.

the pop is Roman Catholic; the currency is the Irish pound (*an punt Eirennach*); national holiday 17 March (St Patrick's Day); membership of EEC, EMS, FAO, GATT, IAEA, IBRD, ICAO, ICES, IDA, IEA, IFAD, IFC, ILO, IMF, IMO, INTELSAT, IPU, ISO, ITC, ITU, OECD, UN, UNESCO, UPU, WHO, WIPO, WMO, WSG.

Physical description. The Caledonian mountain system spreading down from Scandinavia through Scotland gives rise to the mountainous landscapes of Donegal, Mayo and Galway, where the peaks are of quartzite which has weathered to form conical mountains such as Errigal (752 m) and Croagh Patrick (765 m). In the S, the younger Armorican mountain system rises westward towards the Macgillycuddy's Reeks Mts, creating a landscape of sandstone ridges separated by limestone or shale-floored valleys. The predominantly limestone lowlands are drained S by slow-moving rivers such as the R Shannon. The Liffey drains E through Dublin and the Slaney SE to Wexford Harbour. In the S the long E-W valleys are occupied by such rivers as the Suir, Lee and Blackwater which reach the coast by making right-angled turns to pass southwards through the sandstone ridges in narrow gorge-like valleys. Most of the soils of Ireland are derived from glacial drift with thin acid peaty soils on the uplands and grey-brown podzolic soils on the fertile lowlands and acid brown earths and gleys on poorly drained lowlands.

Climate. Ireland has a mild and equable climate which is effected by the North Atlantic drift. Rainfall is heaviest in the W where it may exceed 3,000 mm in Kerry, Mayo and Donegal. The E is drier with an annual average of 785 mm at Dublin. There are few extremes of temperature but the weather can be changeable as a result of temperate depressions.

History, government and constitution. Celts, descended from earlier Neolithic and Bronze Age immigrants, occupied Ireland during the Iron Age. A high kingship was established c.200 AD with its capital at Tara (Meath). Following the conversion of the inhabitants to Christianity by St Patrick in the 5th century, Ireland became a centre of learning and missionary activity. From c.800 AD the SE ports were attacked by Norse invaders, and from the 12th century Ireland was subject to Norman influence. Henry I of England declared himself lord of Ireland in 1171 and in 1542 Henry VIII took the title 'King of Ireland' in an attempt to control Irish Catholicism. The Civil War, which began in 1641, resulted in a barbarous campaign by Cromwell (1649-50), followed by wholesale eviction and transportation. The Catholic James VII, expelled in 1689, gained support from fellow-Catholics in Ireland, but the relief of Londonderry and the victory of William III at the Battle of the Boyne (1690) marked the collapse of James's cause, and a settlement was effected by the Treaty of Limerick (1691). This treaty promised Irish Catholics some degree of religious liberty and protection, but the promises were not kept and Ireland faced over a century of suppression in order to prevent competition with England. The late 18th and the 19th centuries saw a big struggle for Irish freedom, a struggle in which the efforts of great Irish statesmen such as Henry Grattan, Daniel O'Connell and Charles Stewart Parnell were more effective than such revolutionary movements as Wolfe Tone's United Irishmen (1796-98), Young Ireland (1848) and the Fenians (1866-67). By 1801, when Ireland was united with Britain, the worst of these abuses had been removed; the Catholic Relief Act (1829) enabled Catholics to sit in parliament; the Anglican Church was disestablished in 1869; and a series of Land Acts (1870-1903) struck at the roots of Irish poverty. Prior to these Acts the population had been reduced by a half as a result of the famine of 1846. Two Home Rule Bills were introduced by Gladstone (1886-1893) and a Third Home Rule Bill was passed in 1914 but never came into effect because of the outbreak of World War I. In April 1916 armed rebellion against British rule took place and a republic was proclaimed. Renewed violence in 1919 was not prevented by the passing of an Act in 1920 by the British government dividing Ireland into North and South, with two separate parliaments. This Act was largely ignored by the National Parliament of the Irish Republic which had been elected in 1918. A treaty between the UK and the Irish Republic was signed in 1921 in which Ireland accepted dominion status subject to the right of Northern Ireland to opt out. This right was exercised and the frontier between the 26 counties of the south (*Saorstát Éireann*) and Northern Ireland was agreed in 1925. Acts of the Irish National Parliament in 1936 and 1948 subsequently severed all constitutional links between the UK and the Irish Republic. The president, elected for 7 years by direct vote, is the head of the republic. The National Parliament (*Oireachtas*) includes a representative house (*Dáil Éireann*) of 166 members elected by adult suffrage and a 60-member senate (*Seanad Éireann*), partly nominated, partly elected from vocational panels. The prime minister (*taoiseach*) is head of the government, which holds the executive power subject to the *Dáil*. Local government comprises 27 county councils, 4 county borough corporations, 7 borough corporations and 49 urban district councils.

Agriculture, forestry and fishing. Two-thirds of the country is covered by improved agricultural land and much of the remainder is used for rough grazing of sheep and cattle. Over half the farm holdings are 10-40 hectares in size, although farm size decreases westwards and northwards. The former tenancy system, predominant until the end of the 19th century, has been largely replaced by owner-occupancy. Farm products in the early 1980s contributed about 30% of the total value of exports, employing about 18% of the workforce. The mild moist climate is mostly suited to the growing of grass and consequently Irish agriculture is predominantly mixed pastoral farming with some subsidiary arable cropping. Livestock products account for more than four-fifths of output. Dairying is most important in the SW and N. Sheep are important on the dry limestone uplands of S Connacht and horses are bred in N Leinster with many stud farms around the Curragh in Kildare county. Cattle are reared in the west and fattened on the better pastures of the midlands. Tillage is mainly associated with the lighter soils and drier climate of the E coast, though oats and potatoes are commonly grown in the W. Since 1950 there has been an active state forestry programme with the planting of nearly 4,000 sq km of trees covering 4% of the land area. Ireland still remains the least afforested country in Europe apart from Iceland. There are 18 forest parks and over 400 forest sites for public recreation. The principal fishing ports of the Irish Republic are to be found at Killybegs, Howth, Rossaveel, Dunmore East and Castletownbere. The leading fish by value are herring, Dublin Bay prawns, mackerel, cod, whiting, lobster, oyster and plaice.

Manufacturing. The principal sectors of Irish manufacturing are metals, food, drink, tobacco, textiles and clothing, although in recent years there has been substantial growth in light engineering, synthetic fibres, electronics, pharmaceuticals and plastics. Manufacturing tends to be concentrated in the major urban centres. Major trade partners include other EEC countries and the USA.

Energy. Although four-fifths of the Irish Republic's energy requirements are met by imports, the country uses natural resources to the maximum to generate electricity. Since the 1920s there have been major hydroelectric schemes on the Shannon, Liffey, Lee and Erne rivers. There is a pumped storage plant in the Wicklow Mts, and by the early 1960s 11 peat-fired power stations had come into operation. Electricity is also generated from the Kinsale natural gas field in the Cork Harbour area. Larger power stations using imported coal and oil are mostly located on coastal sites.

Administrative divisions. The Irish Republic is divided into the following 26 counties which are grouped into 4 provinces:

Province/County	*area (sq km)*	*pop(1981)*
Connacht		
Galway	5,939	172,018
Leitrim	1,526	27,609
Mayo	5,398	114,766
Roscommon	2,463	54,543
Sligo	1,795	55,474
Leinster		
Carlow	896	39,820
Dublin	922	1,003,164
Kildare	1,694	104,122
Kilkenny	2,062	70,806
Laoighis	1,720	51,171
Longford	1,044	31,140
Louth	821	88,514
Meath	2,339	95,419
Offaly	1,997	58,312
Westmeath	1,764	61,523
Wexford	2,352	99,081
Wicklow	2,025	87,449
Munster		
Clare	3,188	87,567
Cork	7,459	402,465
Kerry	4,701	122,770
Limerick	2,686	161,661
Tipperary, N.R.	1,996	58,984
Tipperary, S.R.	2,258	76,277
Waterford	1,839	88,591

contd

Province/County	*area (sq km)*	*pop(1981)*
Ulster		
Cavan	1,891	53,855
Donegal	4,830	125,112
Monaghan	1,290	51,192

Irish Sea, arm of the Atlantic Ocean, between Ireland and Great Britain; area 103,600 sq km; 209 km long by 225 km at its widest point; linked by North Channel, St George's Channel and the Celtic Sea to the Atlantic.

Irkutsk *ir-kootsk'*, 52 18N 104 15E, pop(1983) 582,000, capital city of Irkutskaya oblast, S Siberian Rossiyskaya, Soviet Union; at the confluence of the Irkut and Angara rivers, 66 km W of Ozero Baykal (L Baikal); one of the largest economic centres of E Siberia; it has become a centre for fur-purchasing and gold transshipment; founded in 1661 as a fortress; university (1918); on the Trans-Siberian railway; airport; economy: foodstuffs, ship repairing, woodworking, manufacture of heavy machinery for the mining and metal industries, and machine tools.

Irlam *er'lam*, 53 28N 2 25W, pop(1981) 20,343, town in Salford borough, Greater Manchester, NW England; 13 km SW of Manchester; railway; economy: foodstuffs, engineering, soap.

Irrawaddy *ir-a-wo'dee*, division in S Burma; bounded W by Bay of Bengal, S by Preparis North Channel and E by Andaman Sea; low lying well-irrigated region, watered by the R Irrawaddy which forms part of its border with Pegu division; pop(1983) 4,991,057; capital Bassein.

Irrawaddy, major river dissecting Burma N-S; formed in Kachin state, N Burma, by the meeting of the Mali Hka and Nmai Hka 40 km N of Myitkyina; the Irrawaddy flows S through gorges, past Myitkyina to Bhamo (the head of navigation), then W into Sagaing division and S past Katha, Mandalay and Pakokku; it then flows S between the Arakan Yoma and Pegu Yoma mountain ranges, to form a delta that begins 290 km from the sea, to the N of Henzada; the R Bassein is the westernmost and principal arm of the delta; the Irrawaddy delta empties into the Andaman Sea in a broad front of tidal forests which spreads for 257 km; the easternmost arm of the delta is linked to Rangoon by canal; the chief tributary is the R Chindwin; major tributaries include the Mogaung, Mu, Chindwin, Mon, Daying Jiang (from China) and Shweli rivers; the Irrawaddy is navigable as far as Bhamo (1,287 km inland), and as far as Myitkyina for shallow-draught launches which can negotiate the rapids during the low water season of Oct-Feb; length 1,600 km; the length of the Irrawaddy plus the Nmai Hka, its longest headstream, is 2,090 km.

Irtysh *ir tish'*, chief tributary of the R Ob', mainly in Kazakhskaya SSR and W Siberian Rossiyskaya, Soviet Union; rises in N China on the W slopes of the Mongolian Altai Mts; flows W until it crosses the Soviet frontier and enters Ozero Zaysan (L Zaysan), then flows generally NW past Semipalatinsk and Omsk to join the R Ob' at Khanty Mansiysk; length 4,248 km; drainage basin area 1,643,000 sq km; chief tributaries include the Om', Tara, Ishim, Tobol, and Dem'yanka rivers; hydro-electric power stations at Ust'kamenogorsk and Bukhtarma provide power for the non-ferrous mineral industry.

Irun *ee-roon'*, 43 20N 1 52W, pop(1981) 53,445, commercial and industrial port in Guipúzcoa prov, Pais Vasco (Basque Country), N Spain; on the left bank of the R Bidassoa, near the French border, 16 km E of San Sebastian; economy: iron and lead mining, foundries, paper, porcelain, tools; agroindustrial complex; monument: 3 km E is the San Marcial Hermitage with a fine panorama; event: 30 June, festival celebrating a victory over the French in 1638.

Ir'vine, 55 37N 4 40W, pop(1981) 32,968, capital of Cunninghame dist, Strathclyde, W Scotland; at the mouth of the R Irvine on the W coast, 11 km W of Kilmarnock; railway; economy: engineering, pharmaceuticals.

Irvine, 33 41N 117 46W, pop(1980) 62,134, city in Orange county, SW California, United States; SSE of Santa Ana; university; railway.

Irving, 32 49N 96 56W, pop(1980) 109,943, town in Dallas county, NE Texas, United States; a suburb 15 km W of Dallas; university; railway; economy: building supplies, chemicals, electronic equipment and tools.

Irvington, 40 44N 74 14W, pop(1980) 61,493, town in Essex county, NE New Jersey, United States; on W edge of Newark.

Isabelia, Cordillera *ees-a-bay'lya*, mountain range in N Nicaragua, Central America; forming the boundary between the depts of Jinotega (N) and Matagalpa and Zelaya (S); the range is an E spur of the main continental divide rising to heights of over 2,000 m; forms the watershed between the Río Coco (N) and the Río Grande de Matagalpa (S); length 240 km.

Isefjord *ee'su-fyor'*, inlet of the Kattegat, on N shore of Sjælland (Zealand), Denmark; branches into Roskilde Fjord on E side; length 32 km; Orø I is 18 km S of mouth; bounded on W by Vestsjælland county, on S by Roskilde county and on E by Frederiksborg county; chief towns on shore Nykøbing, Holbæk and Hundested.

Isère *ee-zer*, mountainous dept in Rhône-Alpes region of E France, in the angle of the R Rhône as it turns S; comprises 3 arrond, 50 cantons and 532 communes; pop(1982) 936,771; area 7,431 sq km; drained also by the Isère R and its tributaries, the Drac and Romanche; the surface is mountainous and wooded in the SE, rising to 4,103 m in the Massif du Pelvoux, but levels off in the NE towards the river; notable vine-growing valley; there is abundant hydroelectric power; capital Grenoble, chief towns Vienne and Voiron; interesting caves near Balme-les-Grottes, Choranche and Sassenage; the Parc du Vercors regional nature park lies partly within the dept; there are facilities for winter sports at Alpe d'Huez (skiing in summer), Autrans, Chamrousse, Les Deux-Alpes (skiing in summer), Villard-de-Lans and St-Pierre-de-Chartreuse.

Isère, river in E France rising on the slopes of the Graian Alps near the Italian border above Val-d'Isère; flows W through winding gorges in the Savoy Alps then SW and NW to meet the R Rhône 6 km NNW of Valence; length 290 km.

Iserlohn *eez'er-lōn*, 51 22N 7 40E, pop(1983) 91,800, industrial city in Arnsberg dist, Nordrhein-Westfalen (North Rhine-Westphalia) prov, W Germany; 24 km W of Arnsberg; economy: electrical equipment, textiles.

Isernia *ee-zer'nyah*, prov of Molise region, Italy; pop(1981) 92,524; area 1,529 sq km; capital Isernia.

Isernia, 41 35N 14 14E, pop(1981) 20,145, capital town of Isernia prov, Molise region, Italy; between the Appno Abruzzese (N) and the Appno Napoletano (S); bishopric.

Iseyin *ee-say'ee*, 7 59N 3 40E, pop(1975e) 129,000, town in Oyo state, W Nigeria, W Africa; 40 km WNW of Oyo.

Ishim, river in N Kazakhskaya SSR and Tyumenskaya oblast of the Rossiyskaya, Soviet Union; largest left tributary of the R Irtysh; rises N of Karaganda in Kazakhskaya SSR, flows W past Tselinograd and Kiyma, then, on reaching Derzhavinsk, turns sharply northwards; it then flows generally N and NE until it joins the R Irtysh at Ust'ishim; length 1,797 km; chief tributary R Tersakkan.

Ishwardi or **Ishurdi** *ish-oor'dee*, 24 10N 89 04E, pop(1981) 72,123, town in Pabna dist, Pabna, NW central Bangladesh; airfield; railway.

İskenderun *is-ken-de-roon'*, formerly ALEXANDRETTA, 36 37N 36 08E, pop(1980) 94,942, seaport in Hatay prov, SW Turkey; on Gulf of İskenderun, an inlet of the Mediterranean Sea, 96 km SE of Adana; founded by Alexander the Great; an important outlet for trade from Persia and India until the opening of the Suez Canal; railway; economy: commerce, steel.

Iskur or **Iskar**, also **Isker** or **Iskr**, *ee'skar*, lake in Sofiya okrug (prov), W Bulgaria, N of Samokov and SE of Sofiya.

Iskur, river in NW Bulgaria, formed near Samokov by the meeting of three headstreams rising in the Rila Planina (Rila Mts); flows N through the Sofiya plain and W Stara Planina (Balkan Mts) and NE to meet the R Danube at Boril; length 400 km; tributaries include the Malki Iskur and Panega rivers.

Islamabad *is-lah-mah-bad'*, capital territory in Pakistan; pop(1981) 340,000; area 907 sq km.

Islamabad, ANANTNAG, 33 40N 73 08E, pop(1981) 201,000, capital city of Pakistan; on upper tributary of the R Jhelum, 16 km N of Rawalpindi; a modern planned city, with public buildings, parks, shopping centres and wide boulevards; building began in 1961; water supply from the Rawal dam which also supplies irrigation water to the surrounding agricultural region; head of navigation for larger vessels in the Vale of Kashmir; 2 universities (1965, 1974); monuments: shrine of Bari Imam; museum of folk and traditional heritage.

Islay *ī'la*, island in Argyll and Bute dist, Strathclyde region, W Scotland; the southernmost and 3rd largest of the Inner Hebrides, lying to the W of the mainland and separated from Jura to the NE by a narrow channel (Sound of Islay); mainly low-lying terrain; chief towns are Bowmore and Port Ellen; economy: distilling, farming, fishing, tourism.

Islington *iz'-*, 51 33N 0 06W, pop(1981) 160,890, borough of N Greater London, England; N of the City of London; includes the suburbs of Islington and Finsbury; railway; monuments: Sadler's Wells, Canonbury Tower, Armoury House (1735).

Isluga, Volcán *ees-loo'ga*, national park in Tarapacá region, N Chile; borders E and NE with Argentina; area 1,747 sq km; established in 1967; Isluga (5,530 m) and Cabaraya (5,869 m) volcanoes are both to the N of the park, near the frontier with Argentina; the highest point is Cerro Sillajhuay at 5,995 m on the border with Argentina in the S of the park.

Ismâ'ilîya *iz'ma-i-lee'a*, ISMAILIA, 30 36N 32 15E, pop(1976) 145,978, capital of Ismâ'ilîya governorate, NE Egypt; on the W bank of the Suez Canal by L Timsah, 72 km NNW of Suez; founded in 1863 by Ferdinand de Lesseps as a base for the construction of the Suez Canal; railway.

Isoka *ee-sō'ka*, 10 09S 32 39E, town in Northern prov, Zambia, S central Africa; 180 km E of Kasama; airfield.

Isparta *i-spar'ta*, mountainous prov in SW Turkey; pop(1980) 350,116; area 8,933 sq km; capital Isparta; economy: carpets, attar of roses.

Israel *iz'ray-el*, YISRAEL (Hebrew), official name State of Israel, MEDINAT ISRAEL, state in the Middle East, bounded W by the Mediterranean Sea, N by Lebanon, NE by Syria, E by Jordan, and SW by Egypt; timezone GMT +2; area within the boundaries defined by the 1949 armistice agreements with Egypt, Jordan, Lebanon, and Syria 20,770 sq km; capital Jerusalem; chief towns Tel Aviv-Yafo, Haifa, Beersheba, 'Akko, and Holon; pop(1984e) 3,855,345, excluding E Jerusalem and Israeli settlers in occupied territories; over 86% of all Israelis live in cities and towns; the pop comprises 83% Jewish, and 17% non-Jewish (mostly Arabs); the main religions are Judaism (85%), Islam (11%), Christianity and others (4%); Hebrew and Arabic are the official languages; the unit of currency is the shekel; membership of FAO, GATT, IAEA, IBRD, ICAC, ICAO, IDA, IDB, IFAD, IFC, ILO, IMF, IMO, INTELSAT, INTERPOL, IOOC, IPU, ITU, IWC, OAS, UN, UNESCO, UPU, WHO, WIPO, WMO, WSG, WTO.

Physical description. Israel extends 420 km from N to S, and in width varies from only 20 km to 116 km. The Mediterranean coastal plain is on average 16 km wide and is traversed by several rivers including the Qishon, Soreq, and Sarida. The Plain of Sharon is one of Israel's most fertile agricultural regions. Inland the landscape becomes mountainous, rising to 1,208 m at Mt Meron in Galilee. These mountains are composed largely of limestone or dolomite and have an average height of

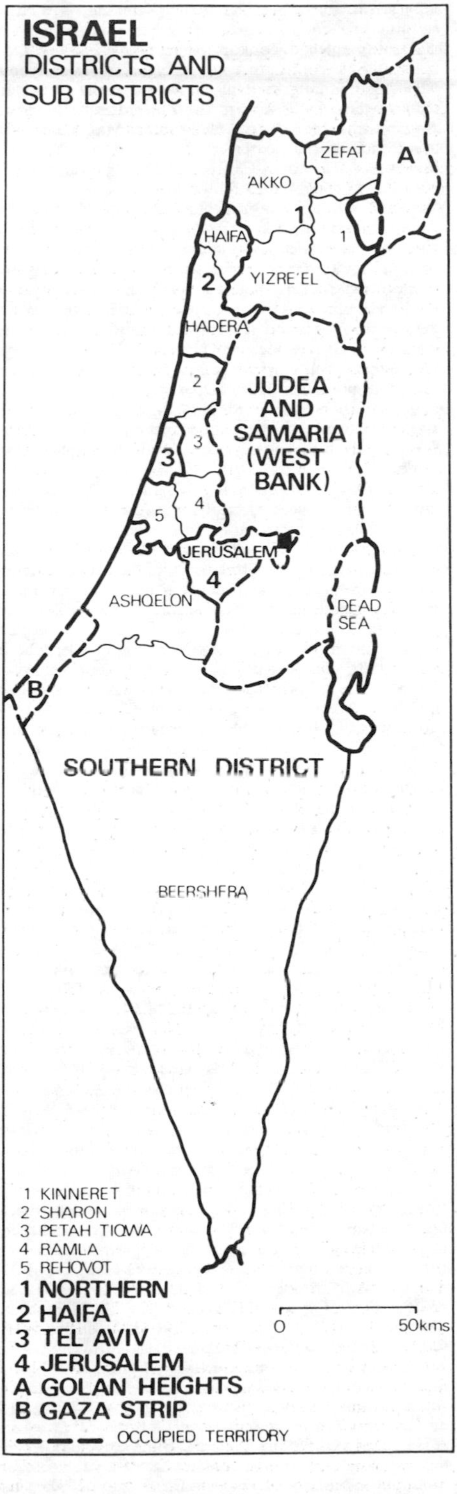

850 m. The mountains of Galilee and Samaria are dissected by faults. To the E the mountains drop down to the Jordan-Red Sea rift valley system. This rift system follows the course of the R Jordan and at L Tiberias (Sea of Galilee) is 210 m below sea-level. South of the Dead Sea it continues through the Wadi 'Araba. The occupied West Bank territory of Judea-Samaria is hilly with heights ranging from 500 m to 1,000 m. The Negev desert occupies approx 60% of the country's area stretching in a wedge from Beersheba (N) to Elat on the Gulf of 'Aqaba (S). The N section is built up of layers of chalk covered with loess soils, while further S the land becomes hilly, reaching a height of 1,935 m at Har Ramon.

Climate. N and central Israel have a typically Mediterranean climate with hot, dry summers and warm, wet winters. Temperatures at Tel Aviv-Yafo range from 14°C in Jan to 27°C in July and the mean annual rainfall is 550 mm. Further inland rainfall is heavier and snow may occasionally fall. Temperatures at Jerusalem range from 9°C in Jan to 23°C in July with a mean annual rainfall of 528 mm. In the Negev annual rainfall is low, decreasing from about 200 mm in the N to as little as 50 mm at Elat on the Gulf of 'Aqaba. Rain falls as heavy local showers any time between Sept and April.

History, government and constitution. The Zionist movement was founded by the Austrian Jewish journalist Theodor Herzl at the end of the 19th century. Inspired by Zionist ideology, thousands of Jews began to return to their ancestral homeland of Palestine, then a part of the Ottoman Empire. In 1922 the League of Nations entrusted Britain with the mandate for governing Palestine and for establishing a Jewish national home there. Nazi persecution of Jews in the 1930s greatly increased the tide of Jewish immigration. The 1947 UN Partition Plan called for the division of Palestine into a Jewish and an Arab state and for establishing Jerusalem separately as an international city under UN administration. This plan, however, was not accepted by the Arab communities. On 14 May 1948, as the British evacuated Palestine, the State of Israel proclaimed its independence in the area allocated to it by the UN. In reaction, the armies of 5 Arab nations invaded the newly-founded state. By July 1949, separate armistice agreements had been signed between Israel and its Arab neighbours, Egypt, Jordan, Lebanon, and Syria. Tension between Syria and Israel in May 1967 led to an invasion by Egyptian troops and a blockade of shipping to and from Israel in the Red Sea. Fighting broke out between Israel and Egypt, Jordan, and Syria on 5 June. After 6 days of fighting the Israelis were in control of the Gaza Strip, the Sinai Peninsula as far as the Suez Canal in Egypt, the formerly Jordanian-controlled West Bank of the R Jordan including the E sector of Jerusalem, and the Golan Heights in Syria. Further unrest in 1969 and 1973 led to renewed and intensive efforts towards peace. The Camp David conference between Egypt and Israel in Sept 1978 agreed on frameworks for peace in the Middle East. Under this peace treaty, signed in Washington on 26 March 1979, Israel withdrew from the Sinai Peninsula. Israel is a parliamentary democracy with a unicameral parliament (*Knesset*). The 120-member parliament is elected by secret ballot and universal direct suffrage for a 4-year term. The president (chief of state) is elected by parliament and may serve for a maximum of two 5-year terms. The cabinet, Israel's executive body, is appointed and headed by the prime minister and is collectively responsible to the parliament.

Economy. From a largely agricultural economy in the early 1950s, Israel has developed into a modern industrial state producing a variety of sophisticated products for domestic consumption as well as export. During the first 2 decades after independence the economic growth rate frequently exceeded 10% annually. More than 90% of all export goods are industrial products, including polished diamonds, machinery and transportation equipment, plastics, processed foods, textiles, fashion clothing, and chemicals. A growing percentage of Israel's industrial output is in high-technology fields such as electronics, medical engineering, agricultural equipment, computers and alternative energy sources. In recent years approx 5% of the country's entire industrial output has been produced from the *kibbutz*. Mineral resources in Israel include oil from the Negev, and potash, bromine, and other salt deposits in the Dead Sea. Approx 37% of Israel's imports and 34% of its exports are with the EEC, with which Israel has a free trade agreement for industrial products. Trade with the USA accounts for about 20% of both exports and imports. Tourism is a growing industry in Israel with more than one million visitors annually in the early 1980s.

Agriculture. In the early 1980s agriculture accounted for about 7% of national income. Israel's agricultural economy has traditionally been based on the export of citrus fruits, but in recent years the introduction of melons, avocados, and flowers has proved successful. Industrial crops such as cotton and sugar-beet have also been successfully introduced. Other agricultural products include vegetables, olives, tobacco, bananas, beef and dairy products. Israel has become a world leader in agrotechnology with areas of intensive cultivation. Since 1949 the total area under cultivation has increased from 1,632 to 4,268 sq km, nearly half of which is under irrigation. The 'National Water Carrier' project was introduced to transfer water from L Tiberias in the N to the Negev desert in the S. The *kibbutz* has traditionally been the backbone of Israeli agriculture, producing some 40% of the country's food output. In recent years, however, the kibbutz has turned increasingly towards industry.

Administrative divisions. Israel is divided into 6 districts:

District	*area (sq km)*	*pop(1983)*
Central	1,242	830,700
Haifa	854	576,400
Jerusalem	627	468,200
Northern	4,946	656,000
Southern	14,107	497,600
Tel Aviv	170	1,008,800

The districts of Judaea-Samaria and Gaza are Israeli-occupied territories.

Issyk-Kul', Ozero *ee-sik' kool'*, lake in Issyk-Kul'skaya oblast, NE Kirgiziya SSR, Soviet Union, in the N Tien Shan range, between the Khrebet Kungey Alatau (N) and Khrebet Terskey Alatau (S) ranges; area 6,280 sq km; length 178 km; max width 60 km; max depth 702 m; alt 1,608 m; one of the largest mountain lakes in the world; receives many streams including the R Tyup (E); intermittent link with the R Chu (W); ice-free in winter; there are health resorts along its shores.

İstanbul *is-tam'bool, is-tan-bool'* (Eng), prov in NW Turkey; pop(1980) 4,741,890; area 5,712 sq km; capital İstanbul.

İstanbul, BYZANTIUM *be-zan'tee-um* (c.660 BC-330 AD), CONSTANTINOPLE *kon-stan-ti-nō'pul* (330-1930), 41 02N 28 57E, pop(1980) 4,445,793, capital city of İstanbul prov, NW Turkey, on the Golden Horn and on both sides of the Karadeniz Boğazi (Bosporus), at its entrance on the Sea of Marmara; the only city in the world situated on 2 continents; chief city and seaport of Turkey; commercial and financial centre; the part of the city corresponding to historic Constantinople is situated entirely on the European side; founded and renamed by Constantine I in AD 330 on the site of ancient Byzantium, becoming the new capital of the Turkish Empire; ancient Constantinople was built on 7 hills and sections of its moated and turreted walls are still standing; see of the patriarch of the Greek Orthodox Church and of the patriarch of the Armenian Church; university (1453); technical university (1944); railway; once noted as the E terminus of the Orient Express and still an important rail junction linking Europe and Asia; airport; in 1973 the European and Asiatic sections of the city were linked by a suspension bridge, one of the longest in the world; economy: commerce, textiles, shipbuilding, food processing, leather, tobacco, cement, glass; monuments: Topkapi palace, palace of the Ottoman sultans from 15th to 19th century; Hagia Sophia basilica, originally built by Constantine the Great and reconstructed by Justinian; the Blue Mosque of Sultan Ahmet Camii; mosque of Süleyman the Magnificent built in the 1550s; Roman cisterns; covered bazaar; event: International İstanbul Festival (20 June-15 July).

Istiwa'iya, El, region of S Sudan. See Equatoria.

Istra *ee'stra*, ISTRIA (Eng), peninsula at the N end of the Adriatic Sea in NW Hrvatska (Croatia) and SW Slovenija republics, Yugoslavia; area 3,160 sq km; occupied by Croats, Slovenes and Italians; road signs in some towns are in Italian and Slovene; formerly part of the Italian prov of Venezia Giulia but after World War II the area around Trieste was administered as a free territory, the remainder being ceded to Yugoslavia; Pula is the chief town; tourist resorts have developed in recent years around towns such as Opatija, Poreč and Portorož.

Itabuna *ee-ta-boo'na*, 14 48S 39 18W, pop(1980) 130,163, market town in Bahia state, Nordeste region, NE Brazil; SW of Salvador; railway; economy: cocoa processing, cattle.

Itaipu *ee'tī-poo*, dam on the Río Paraná, SW Brazil; with a capacity of 12,600-megawatts, it is claimed to be the largest hydroelectric complex in the world.

Italy, ITALIA (Ital), official name The Italian Republic, REPUBBLICA ITALIANA (Ital), a republic of S Europe, comprising the boot-shaped peninsula which extends S into the Mediterranean Sea, as well as Sicilia (Sicily), Sardegna (Sardinia), and some smaller islands, bounded W by the Tyrrhenian Sea, NW by France, N by Switzerland and Austria, NE by Yugoslavia, E by the Adriatic Sea, and S by the Ionian Sea; coastline 4,996 km; area 301,225 sq km; timezone GMT +1; capital Roma (Rome); chief towns Milano (Milan), Torino (Turin), Genova (Genoa), Napoli (Naples), Bologna, Palermo, and Firenze (Florence); pop(1981) 56,556,911; the pop is largely Italian but minority ethnic groups include the German-speaking population of Bolzano prov, and the Slovenes around Trieste; the language is Italian, although parts of the Trentino-Alto Adige region are predominantly German-speaking; there is a significant French-speaking minority in Valle d'Aosta region and a Slovene-speaking minority in the Trieste-Gorizia area; the predominant faith is Roman Catholicism; the Italian currency is the lira; national holidays 25 April (Liberation Day), 1st Sunday in June (Proclamation of the Republic), 1st Sunday in Nov (National Unity Day); membership of ADB, ASSIMER, CCC, Council of Europe, DAC, ECOWAS, EIB, ELDO, EMS, ESRO, FAO, GATT, IAEA, IBRD, ICAC, ICAO, ICO, IDA, IDB, IFAD, IEA, IFC, IHO, ILO, IMO, INTELSAT, IOOC, IPU, IRC, ITC, ITU, NATO, OECD, UN, UNESCO, UPU, WEU, WHO, WIPO, WMO, WSG.

Physical description. The total area of 301,225 sq km comprises 50% cultivated land, 21% forest, 17% meadow and pasture, 9% waste or urban land. The Italian peninsula extends some 800 km SE from the Lombardo plains. Its backbone is the Apennino (Apennines), a fold of the main Alpine mountain system, rising to peaks above 2,000 m. In N Italy the Alps form an arc from Nice to Fiume, the highest peaks being along the Swiss-French frontier, Mt Blanc (4,807 m), and the Matterhorn (4,477 m). Between the Alps and the Apennino, in the basin of the R Po, spreads the broad fertile Lombardo-Venetian plain, irrigated by numerous canals and streams. Many of the Po's tributaries spread out at the foot of the Alps into considerable bodies of water, among which are L Maggiore, L di Como, and L di Garda. From Rimini to the Golfo di Trieste, the Adriatic coast is flat, marshy, and fringed by lagoons. On the Riviera, from Nice to La Spezia, the coastal mountains descend steeply to the Ligurian Sea. The island of Sicilia, separated from the mainland by the 4 km-wide Strait de Messina, includes the limestone massifs of the Monti Nebrodi and the volcanic cone of Mt Etna (3,323 m). Sardegna is a rugged island of older crystalline rocks, rising to 1,835 m in Monti del Gennargentu. Chief rivers in Italy include the Po, Tevere (Tiber), Arno, Volturno, Liri, Adige, and many shorter rivers in the E which flow into the Adriatic.

Climate. The climate varies considerably with relief and latitude. The plain of the Po river has a distinctive climate with rainfall well distributed throughout the year. Summers are hot and sunny while winters are short and cold. Hours of sunshine range from an average of 2-3 a day in winter to 9 in summer. The area around Trieste is occasionally affected by the *bora* wind, which blows cold air from central Europe. The climate of peninsular Italy and the islands varies between the mountainous interior and the coastal lowlands. The higher areas are cold, wet, and often snowy, while the coastal regions have a typical Mediterranean climate, with warm, wet winters and hot, dry summers. The length and intensity of the summer dry season increases southwards. The Adriatic coast, exposed to the NE winds, is colder than the W coast, and also receives less rainfall. In the extreme S of the mainland, and in Sicilia and Sardegna, sunshine averages 5 hours per day in winter and up to 10 or 11 hours per day in summer. In the Italian Alps, precipitation is heavier and more evenly distributed throughout the year. Summer tends to be the rainiest season and thunderstorms are frequent in spring, summer, and autumn. Around the lakes Maggiore, Como, and Garda, summers are sunnier and winters milder.

History, government and constitution. On the collapse of the West Roman Empire in 476 AD, the barbarian Odoacer ruled until overthrown by Theodoric, who founded a Gothic monarchy in Italy. Subsequent rule by the Lombards was overthrown by the Franks under Charlemagne, who was crowned emperor of the Romans

in 800 AD. In 962 Italy became part of the Holy Roman Empire under Otto, and thereafter was torn by dispute between the Guelphs and the Ghibellines and between cities and states. In the 13th century the popes became the chief power in Italy, and in the 14-15th centuries the country was divided amongst 5 powers - the kingdom of Naples, the duchy of Milan, the republics of Florence and Venice and the papacy. It was during this period that Italy made her great contribution to European culture through the Renaissance. After the French Revolution numerous republics were set up under French influence, and in 1805 Napoleon was crowned king of Italy. After the Napoleonic Wars the French left behind them democratic ideas which led to the *Risorgimento*, an upsurge of liberalism and nationalism. The unification of Italy was eventually achieved by Victor Emmanuel II of Sardinia with his prime minister Cavour. By 1870 Rome, Lombardy and Ventia had been acquired. Between 1870 and 1914 Italy struggled to establish itself as a European power. She established colonies in Eritrea (1870-89) and Somaliland (1889), and from Turkey she won Libya and the Dodecanese (1911-12). An attempt to secure a protectorate over Abyssinia was defeated at Adowa (1896). Discontent with the meagre rewards for supporting the Allies in World War I, combined with economic distress, enabled Benito Mussolini to establish a virtual dictatorship in 1922. His aggressive foreign policy resulted in the conquest of Abyssinia (1935-36) and Albania (1939). Mussolini's decision to ally himself with Hitler during World War II resulted in the downfall of his régime and the end of the Italian Empire. Italy has been a democratic republic since 2 June 1946, when the monarchy was abolished by popular referendum. The new constitution came into force on 1 Jan 1948. Parliament consists of a Chamber of Deputies and the Senate. The Chamber is elected for 5 years and consists of 630 deputies while the Senate, also elected for 5 years but on a regional basis, has 315 members. The President of the Republic is elected in a joint session of Chamber and Senate to serve for 7 years. The president appoints a prime minister, who directs a cabinet of about 20 ministers.

Industry. Industry is largely concentrated in the N around Milano, Genova and Torino, where there are good communication and transport facilities and local sources of power, such as hydroelectricity from the Alps and natural gas from the Po plain. Mineral resources are exploited elsewhere. The islands of Elba and Sardegna produce iron ore; Sardegna, Sicilia, and Lombardia are sources of non-ferrous metals, notably lead, and oil and gas fields have been exploited in the Po valley and Sicilia. However, only sulphur and mercury outputs yield a substantial surplus for export. The major industries include machinery and transportation equipment, iron and steel, chemicals, food processing, textiles, and machine tools. Italy's machine tools industry is one of the most advanced in Europe, ranking as the 5th largest producer and exporter in the world. Chief exports include machinery and transportation equipment, textiles, foodstuffs, chemicals, and footwear, while imports include machinery and transport equipment, foodstuffs, ferrous and non-ferrous metals, wool, cotton, and petroleum. Major trading partners include West Germany, France, the UK, the USA, the USSR and Saudi Arabia; Italy traditionally imports more than it exports. This trade deficit in foodstuffs and raw materials is normally offset by income derived from the tourist trade, emigrant remittances, and transportation.

Agriculture. Some 15% of the workforce are employed in agriculture, many on small peasant holdings, especially in the S. Chief crops in the fertile Po valley include wheat, maize, sugar-beet, potatoes, and rice. The Po plain is one of Italy's leading agricultural regions, producing most of the country's meat and milk (65% of the total Italian cattle stock). In the foothills of the Alps, the main products are fruit (apples, peaches, and walnuts in Alto Adige and the Adige valley) and wine. Further S, citrus fruits, vines, tomatoes, olives, and tobacco are grown. High-yielding citrus fruits are grown in terraced plantations on the volcanic soils around Vesuvius and Etna. Elsewhere, however, crop yields are low under the less intensive management of small family holdings. In 1982, S Italy generated only 35% of gross national agricultural production. Here, the average size of farm holding is 0.06 sq km compared to an average of 0.085 sq km in central and N Italy.

Administrative divisions. Italy is divided into 20 regions, which in turn are subdivided into 95 provinces as shown below:

Region/Province	*area (sq km)*	*pop(1981)*
Abruzzi		
L'Aquila	5,035	291,742
Chieti	2,587	370,534
Pescara	1,225	286,240
Teramo	1,948	269,275
Basilicata		
Matera	3,445	203,570
Potenza	6,545	406,616
Calabria		
Catanzaro	5,247	744,834
Cosenza	6,649	743,255
Reggio di Calabria	3,183	573,093
Campania		
Avellino	2,802	434,021
Benevento	2,062	289,143
Caserta	2,639	755,628
Napoli	1,171	2,970,563
Salerno	4,924	1,013,779
Emilia-Romagna		
Bologna	3,701	930,284
Ferrara	2,631	381,118
Forlì	2,911	599,420
Modena	2,691	596,025
Parma	3,450	400,192
Piacenza	2,590	278,424
Ravenna	1,860	358,654
Reggio nell'Emilia	2,292	413,396
Friuli-Venezia Giulia		
Gorizia	466	144,726
Pordenone	2,303	275,888
Trieste	210	283,641
Udine	4,864	529,729
Lazio		
Frosinone	3,240	460,395
Latina	2,251	434,086
Rieti	2,748	142,794
Roma	5,351	3,695,961
Viterbo	3,613	268,448
Liguria		
Genova	1,831	1,045,109
Imperia	1,155	223,738
Savona	1,544	297,675
La Spezia	881	241,371
Lombardia		
Bergamo	2,758	896,117
Brescia	4,758	1,017,093
Como	2,067	775,979
Cremona	1,772	332,236
Mantova	2,339	377,158
Milano	2,764	4,018,108
Pavia	2,966	512,895
Sondrio	3,212	174,009
Varese	1,199	788,057
Marche		
Ancona	1,937	433,417
Ascoli Piceno	2,088	352,567
Macerata	2,774	292,932
Pesaro e Urbino	2,893	333,488
Molise		
Campobasso	2,909	235,847
Isernia	1,529	92,524

contd

Region/Province	*area (sq km)*	*pop(1981)*
Piemonte		
Alessandria	3,561	466,102
Asti	1,510	215,382
Cuneo	6,902	548,452
Novara	3,595	507,367
Torino	6,830	2,345,771
Vercelli	3,002	395,957
Puglia		
Bari	5,128	1,464,627
Brindisi	1,836	391,064
Foggia	7,185	681,595
Lecce	2,758	762,017
Taranto	2,437	572,314
Sardegna		
Cagliari	6,895	730,473
Nuoro	7,044	274,817
Oristano	2,631	155,043
Sassari	7,520	433,842
Sicilia		
Agrigento	3,041	466,495
Caltanissetta	2,106	285,829
Catania	3,553	1,005,577
Enna	2,562	190,939
Messina	3,245	669,323
Palermo	5,017	1,198,575
Ragusa	1,614	274,583
Siracusa	2,108	394,692
Trapani	2,461	420,865
Trentino-Alto Adige		
Bolzano	7,400	430,568
Trento	6,213	442,845
Toscana		
Arezzo	3,232	313,157
Firenze	3,880	1,202,013
Grosseto	4,496	220,905
Livorno	1,220	346,657
Lucca	1,772	385,876
Massa-Carrara	1,155	203,530
Pisa	2,448	388,800
Pistoia	966	264,995
Siena	3,820	255,118
Umbria		
Perugia	6,335	580,988
Terni	2,121	226,564
Valle d'Aosta		
Aosta	3,263	112,353
Veneto		
Belluno	3,678	220,335
Padova	2,142	809,667
Rovigo	1,803	253,508
Treviso	2,476	720,580
Venezia	2,461	838,794
Verona	3,098	775,745
Vicenza	2,722	726,418

It'anagar, 27 02N 93 38E, centre of administration of Arunachal Pradesh union territory, NE India; N of the R Brahmaputra, near the frontier with Assam state; monument: ruins of ancient Mayapur.

Itapúa *ee-ta-poo'a*, dept in Oriental region, S Paraguay; bordered S and E by Argentina along the Río Paraná; pop(1982) 263,021; area 16,526 sq km; capital Encarnación; economy: timber, soya, cotton, maté, tobacco, hides; included in the dept's statistics are the islands of Yacíretá and Talavera on the Río Paraná in the SW of the dept.

Itatiaia *ee-ta-chee-ī'a*, national park in Rio de Janeiro state, Sudeste region, SE Brazil; area 119 sq km; established in 1937; situated on the Serra de Itatiaia in the Mantiqueira mountain range; contains the curious rock formations, Pedra de Taruga and Pedra de Maçã and the Véu de Noiva waterfall; just W of the Park is the Pico das Agulhas Negras (2,787 m).

Ith'aca, 42 27N 76 30W, pop(1980) 28,732, county seat of Tompkins county, central New York, United States; at the S end of L Cayuga, 75 km SSW of Syracuse; founded in 1789, achieving city status in 1888; Cornell University (1865); railway; airfield; resort; event: annual York State Crafts Fair.

Ivanovo *ee-va'nu-vu*, formerly IVANOVO-VOZNESENSK (1871-1932), 57 00N 41 00E, pop(1983) 474,000, capital city of Ivanovskaya oblast, central European Rossiyskaya, Soviet Union; on the R Uvod, 318 km NW of Moskva (Moscow); established in 1871; noted for its revolutionary activities during the strikes of 1883 and 1885 and during the 1905 revolt; historic centre of Russia's cotton-milling industry; railway; economy: manufacture of textiles, machines, chemicals, wood products, and foodstuffs.

Ivory Coast, official name Republic of the Ivory Coast, RÉPUBLIQUE DE LA CÔTE D'IVOIRE (Fr), a republic of W Africa bounded SW by Liberia, NW by Guinea, N by Mali and Burkina, E by Ghana and S by the Gulf of Guinea; timezone GMT; area 320,633 sq km; pop(1984) 9,178,000; capital Abidjan (Yamoussoukro is the capital designate); chief towns Bouaké, Daloa, Man, Korhogo and Gagnoa; there are 657 km of single track railway (Abidjan-Ouagadougou), 3,461 km of surfaced roads, 31,939 km of improved roads and 740 km of navigable rivers; ethnic groups include the Agni, Baoule, Krou, Senoufou and Mandingo tribes and about 2,000,000 foreign Africans mainly from Burkina; there are also c.40,000 French and c.25,000 Lebanese residents; 63% of the pop follows local beliefs, the remainder being either Muslim (25%) or Christian (12%); the official language is French but over 60 local dialects are also spoken, Dioula being the most widespread; the unit of currency is the franc CFA; national holiday 7 Dec; membership of AfDB, CEAO, EAMA, ECA, ECOWAS, EIB (associate), Entente, FAO, G-77, GATT, IAEA, IBRD, ICAO, ICO, IDA, IFAD, IFC, ILO, IMF, IMO, INTELSAT, INTERPOL, IPU, ITU, NAM, Niger River Commission, OAU, OCAM, UN, UNESCO, UPU, WHO, WIPO, WMO, WTO.

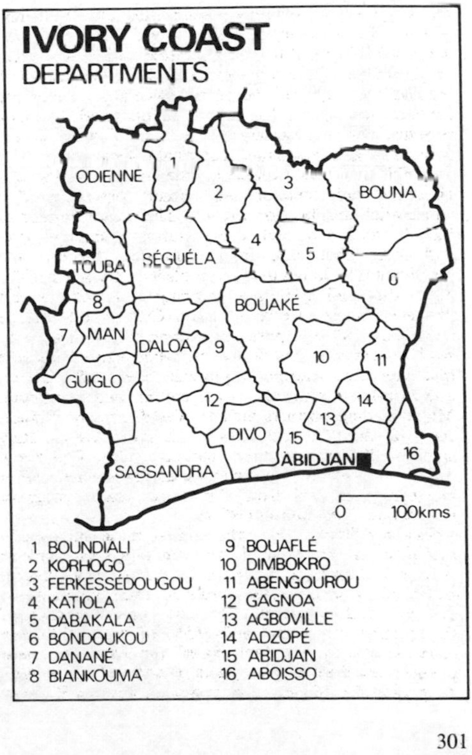

Physical description. A coast typified by sandy beaches and lagoons is backed by a broad forest-covered coastal plain. Further inland the land rises towards savannah at an alt of 300 to 350 m. The highest ground is in the W and NW with the Mt Nimba massif on the border with Liberia and Guinea rising to 1,752 m. Rivers, generally flowing N-S, include the Douobé on the Liberian border, the Sassandra, the Bandama flowing from Bandama Blanc and the Comoé. The largest lagoon is the Lagune Aby in the SE which receives the R Tano. Bandama Blanc, NE of Bouaflé, is a lake created by the damming of the R Bia at Ayamé (SE).
Climate. The Ivory Coast has a tropical climate that varies with distance from the coast. Rainfall decreases N where the two separate rainy seasons (maxima in May-June and Oct in the S) merge into a single wet season. The average annual rainfall at Abidjan is 2,100 mm and at Bouaké (central Ivory Coast) 1,200 mm. Average temperatures range between 25°C and 27°C.
History, government and constitution. French influence on the Ivory Coast dates from 1842 but it was not until 1882 that they consolidated their colonial position. In 1889 the Ivory Coast was declared a French Protectorate and subsequently a French Colony in 1893. In 1904 it became a territory within French West Africa and in 1933 was enlarged by the addition of most of what is now Burkina (Upper Volta). This territory was returned to Upper Volta in 1948. Autonomy within the French community in 1958 was followed by full independence in 1960. The constitution of 1960 was amended in 1971, 1975 and 1980. It provides for a 147-member National Assembly and an executive president (both elected for 5-year terms) plus a Council of Ministers appointed by the president. There is only one political party in the Ivory Coast.
Economy. The economy is largely based on agriculture which employs about 82% of the pop. The country is the world's largest cocoa producer and 3rd largest coffee producer. Other cash crops include bananas, rice, pineapples, cotton, coconuts, palm oil, sugar, cassava and corn. Fishing is also of importance. Since the demise of diamond mining in 1981 the country's industry has been centred around food processing, timber, textiles, clothing, vehicle assembly, small shipyards, fertilizers, battery production, oil refining and cement production. The main trading partners are France, the USA, West Germany, the Netherlands, Italy and Japan.
Administrative divisions. The Ivory Coast is divided into 26 depts:

Department	*area (sq km)*	*pop(1975)*
Abengourou	6,900	177,692
Abidjan	14,200	1,389,141
Aboisso	6,250	148,823
Adzopé	5,230	162,837
Agboville	3,850	141,970
Biankouma	4,950	75,711
Bondoukou	16,530	296,551
Bouaflé	8,500	263,609
Bouaké	23,670	808,048
Bouna	21,470	84,290
Boundiali	10,095	132,278
Dabakala	9,670	56,230
Daloa	15,200	369,610
Danané	4,600	170,249
Dimbokro	14,100	475,023
Divo	10,650	278,526
Ferkéssédougou	17,728	90,423
Gagnoa	6,900	259,504
Guiglo	14,150	137,672
Katiola	9,420	77,875
Korhogo	12,500	276,816
Man	7,050	278,659
Odiénné	20,600	124,010
Sassandra	25,800	191,994
Séguéla	21,900	157,539
Touba	8,720	77,786

Ivry-sur-Seine *eev-ree-sür-sen*, 48 49N 2 24E, pop(1982) 55,948, river port in Val-de-Marne dept, Ile-de-France region, N central France; a SE suburb of Paris on the R Seine; economy: heavy engineering, metalworking.

Iwaki *ee-wa'kee*, 36 58N 140 56E, pop(1980) 342,074, city in Fukushima prefecture, Tōhoku region, E Honshū island, Japan; railway.

Iwo *ee'wō*, 7 38N 4 11E, pop(1981e) 292,500, town in Oyo state, W Nigeria, W Africa; NE of Ibadan; economy: glass.

Iwo Jima *ee-wō jee'mah*, IŌ JIMA, the most important and the largest of the Volcano Islands; situated in the W Pacific Ocean at 24 47N 141 20E, 1,222 km S of Tōkyo; 8 km long; max width 4 km; area c.21 sq km; rises to 167 m in the S of the island at Suribachi-yama, an extinct volcano; coastguard station in the N of the island; scene of one of the severest campaigns in US military history; during World War II, the island was the heavily fortified site of a Japanese air base; it was bombed by US planes in Dec 1944 and in Jan and Feb 1945; invaded by US marines on 19 Feb 1945; Mt Suribachi-yama at the S end of the island was seized on 23 Feb 1945; Motoyama airfields were taken between 23 and 26 Feb and the island was finally taken on 15 March 1945 and occupied by the USA; it was returned to Japan in 1968.

Ixelles *eek-sel'*, pop(1982) 75,994, town in Brussel dist, Brabant prov, Belgium; a suburb of Bruxelles.

Ixtaccihuatl *ees-tah-see'wah-tul*, IZTACCIHUATL (Aztec, 'white woman'), 19 11N 98 38W, dormant volcano on the Puebla-México state border, central Mexico; rises to 5,286 m N of Popocatépetl, 56 km SE of Ciudad de México (Mexico City); irregular-shaped, snow-capped volcano with 3 summits; situated in Ixtaccihuatl-Popocatépetl National Park (area 257 sq km; established in 1935).

Izabal *ee'sa-val*, easternmost dept in Guatemala, Central America; bounded NE by Belize and the Gulf of Honduras and SE by Honduras; pop(1982e) 290,203; area 9,038 sq km; capital Puerto Barrios; chief towns Santo Tomás de Castilla and Lívingston; much of the centre of the dept is occupied by the Lago de Izabal into which the Río Polochic flows before entering the Bahía de Amatique W of Puerto Barrios.

Izabal, Lago de, lake in Izabal dept, E Guatemala, bounded S by the Sierra de las Minás; drains into the Bahía de Amatique, an inlet of the Caribbean Sea, via the Río Dulce; there is an area of swampland to the W of the lake where it receives the Río Polochic; area 1,036 sq km; length 48 km; width 24 km; largest lake in the country and an important commercial waterway; traversed by a pipeline carrying oil from the fields in NW Alta Verapaz dept to the port of Santo Tomás de Castilla.

Izalco, Volcan de *i-zal'kō*, volcano in Sonsonate dept, W El Salvador, Central America; SW of L Coatepeque; height 1,830 m; the most active volcano in Central America.

İzmir *eez-meer'*, maritime prov in W Turkey, bounded W by the Aegean Sea; pop(1980) 1,976,763; area 11,973 sq km; capital İzmir.

İzmir, formerly SMYRNA *smur'na*, 38 25N 27 10E, pop(1980) 1,226,060, seaport capital of İzmir prov, W Turkey; on an inlet of the Aegean Sea; 3rd largest city in Turkey and the 2nd most important port after İstanbul; commercial and industrial centre; the city was severely damaged by earthquake in 1928 and 1939; university (1955); railway; airfield; economy: brewing, electronics, packaging, foodstuffs, steel, trucks and engines, cement, plastics, and paper; site of the largest poultry and egg farm in the Middle East; monuments: Kadifekale (4th-c BC), fortress situated on the top of Mt Pagos; Roman remains; event: annual international fair.

İzmit', KOCAELI *ko-jah-ay'lee*, 40 47N 29 55E, pop(1980) 190,423, seaport capital of Kocaeli prov, NW Turkey; at the E end of the Sea of Marmara; centre of a rich tobacco and olive-growing region; railway.

J

Jabalpur *ju-bul'poor*, JUBBULPORE, 23 09N 79 58E, pop(1981) 757,000, town in Madhya Pradesh, central India; 240 km NNE of Nagpur, to the N of the R Narbarda; linked NE by rail to Allahabad, to the N of the Mahadeo Hills; a military post and industrial centre in an agricultural region; economy: arms, ammunition, cigarettes, limestone, clay and bauxite.

Jabiru *jab'i-roo*, 12 37S 132 54E, mining town in Northern Territory, Australia; a modern uranium-mining centre at the E end of the Arnhem highway, 251 km E of Darwin; the planned population for the town is 6,000.

Jablonec nad Nisou *yab'lon-ets nad nyis-sow*, 50 44N 15 10E, pop(1984) 44,742, town in Severočeský region, Czech Socialist Republic, Czechoslovakia; SE of Liberec; railway; economy: Bohemian glass, textiles, paper.

Jacareí *zha-ka-ray-ee'*, 23 17S 45 57W, pop(1980) 104,241, town in São Paulo state, Sudeste region, SE Brazil; E of São Paulo; railway.

Jackson, 42 15N 84 24W, pop(1980) 39,739, county seat of Jackson county, S Michigan, United States; 54 km S of Lansing; railway; economy: machinery; site of the founding of the Republican Party at a convention, 6 July 1854.

Jackson, 32 18N 90 12W, pop(1980) 202,895, capital of state in Hinds county, central Mississippi, United States; the largest city in the state, situated on the R Pearl; established as a trading post named Le Fleur's Bluff; state capital since 1821; much of the city was destroyed by General Sherman's forces during the Civil War in 1863; named after President Andrew Jackson; university; railway; airfield; economy: oil, natural gas, food processing, timber, metal and glass products; event: Dixie Livestock Show (Feb).

Jackson, 35 37N 88 49W, pop(1980) 49,131, county seat of Madison county, W Tennessee, United States; on the S fork of the Forked Deer river, 125 km ENE of Memphis; university (1834); railway; economy: processing and rail shipping point for a large farming community; monuments: Casey Jones's home and railway museum.

Jacksonville, 34 52N 92 07W, pop(1980) 27,589, town in Pulaski county, central Arkansas, United States; 24 km NE of Little Rock; railway; nearby is the Little Rock Air Force Base.

Jacksonville, 30 20N 81 39W, pop(1980) 540,920, county seat of Duval county, NE Florida, United States; a port near the mouth of the St Johns river; founded in 1816, largest city in the state, and 2nd largest city by area in the country; university (1934); railway; economy: commercial and financial centre; transport hub and a busy port, with ship-repair yards and naval installations; chief manufactures are lumber, paper, chemicals, food products and cigars; popular tourist resort; monuments: Hemming Park Confederate monument, Fort Caroline National Memorial; event: jazz festival (Oct).

Jacobabad *jay-ku-bah-bad'*, 23 16N 68 30E, pop(1981) 80,000, city in Sind prov, SE Pakistan; formerly within Upper Sind Frontier district; founded in 1847 by General John Jacob; a frontier post prior to the occupation of Quetta; railway; economy: market for millet, rice and wheat.

Jadida, El *je-dee'de*, 33 16N 8 30W, pop(1982) 81,455, town in El Jadida prefecture, Centre prov, central Morocco, N Africa; railway.

Jadotville, town in Zaire. See Likasi.

Jaén *ha-ayn'*, prov in Andalucia region, S Spain, partly wooded, mountainous country, in the upper basin of the R Guadalquivir; pop(1981) 627,598; area 13,498 sq km; capital Jaén; economy: flour, dairy produce, agric machinery (Mancha Real), olive oil, forestry and wooden products, textiles, pharmaceuticals, cement, electronics (La Carolina), confectionery (Alcaudete).

Jaén, 37 44N 3 43W, pop(1981) 96,429, capital of Jaén prov, Andalucia, S Spain; on the R Guadalbullon, at the foot of the Sierra Jabalcúz and the Sierra de la Pandera, 335 km S of Madrid; bishopric; railway; economy: pharmaceuticals, olive oil, leather, linen; monuments: Moorish walls, cathedral (16-18th-c); provincial museum with fine Roman mosaics; events: fiestas of La Patrona in April; Holy Week; Fiestas of La Virgen de la Capilla in June; Fiestas and fair of St Lucas in Oct; Lumbres de San Anton in Jan and Santa Catalina holiday in Nov.

Jaffna *jahf'na*, 9 38N 80 02E, pop(1981) 118,224, capital of Jaffna dist, Northern prov, Sri Lanka; on the N peninsula of Sri Lanka, at W entrance to the Jaffna Lagoon; financial and cultural centre of the Tamil-Hindu dominated north; 97.7% of the pop of the dist are Tamil; of great importance to the Portuguese and Dutch colonial powers; university (1974); the beaches, coralline coast and sand dunes of Manalkadu attract tourists; economy: cotton, fruit, timber and tobacco trade; monuments: Dutch fort (1680); peninsula and city have many Hindu temples and shrines.

Jaipur *jī'poor*, 26 53N 75 50E, pop(1981) 1,005,000, capital of Rajasthan state, NW India; SW of Delhi; a fine example of early town planning, with wide regularly laid out streets; planning is based on the principles of *Shilpa Shastra*, the ancient Hindu treatise on architecture; founded in 1727 by Sawai Jai Singh to replace Amber (8 km to the N) as capital; known as the 'pink city' since 1875 when Sawai Ram Singh had all the buildings of the bazaar painted pink; university (1947); linked by rail to Ajmer and Delhi; economy: textiles, metallurgy; monuments: Maharaja's palace; Sawai Man Singh Museum, housing a collection of royal robes, ancient weapons and carpets; Hawa Mahal ('hall of the winds'), built in 1799 in the shape of a giant honeycomb; Jantar Mantar, an observatory, was built in 1726 by Sawai Jai Singh.

Jajce *yī'tse*, YAITSE or YAYTSE (Eng), 44 20N 17 16E, pop(1981) 41,197, historic industrial town in Bosna-Hercegovina republic, W central Yugoslavia; situated on R Vrbas, between Split and Banja Luka; 30 m waterfall on the R Pliva nearby; anti-Fascist Congress of Liberation held here in Nov 1943; economy: steel works, chemicals, metallurgy, tourism; monuments: Museum of the National Struggle for Liberation, Esme Sultanija mosque, Mithraic shrine in Roman remains, catacombs.

Jakarta, DJAKARTA, formerly BATAVIA, 6 08S 106 45E, pop(1980) 4,576,009, seaport capital of Indonesia; on NW coast of Jawa, at mouth of R Liwung on Jakarta Bay; largest city of Indonesia; developed as a trading post in the 15th century, becoming the headquarters of the Dutch East India Company; capital of Indonesia since 1949; 11 universities (1950-1960); railway; airport; economy: timber, textiles, shipbuilding, paper, iron; exports rubber, tin, oil, coffee, palm oil, tea; monuments: Istiqlal Mosque; 90 m-high national monument; Taman Mini provincial exhibition.

Jakarta Raya *ja-kahr'tah rah-ya*, DJKARTA RAYA, special territory, NW Jawa, Indonesia, pop(1980) 6,503,449; area 590 sq km; includes the city of Jakarta, capital of Indonesia.

Jakobstad, port in Finland. See Pietarsaari.

Jalālābād *je-lal'a-bad*, JELALABAD, 34 26N 76 25E, pop(1984e) 61,900, capital of Nangarhār prov, E Afghanistan; linked by road to Kābul in the E; airfield.

Jalapa *ha-la'pa*, mountainous dept in E Guatemala,

Central America; pop(1982e) 162,907; area 2,063 sq km; capital Jalapa; drained by the Río Jalapa.

Jalapa, 14 39N 89 59W, capital town of Jalapa dept, E central Guatemala, Central America; on the Río Jalapa, 58 km E of Guatemala City; alt 1,380 m.

Jalapa Enríquez *ha-lah'pa en-ree'keth*, JALAPA, 19 32N 96 56W, pop(1980) 212,769, capital of Veracruz state, E Mexico; 80 km NW of Veracruz; university (1944); the medicinal plant from which jalap is made grows here; railway; economy: tobacco; monuments: W of the city is a museum with archaeological exhibits from the Olmec, Totonac and Huastec coastal cultures.

Jalisco *ha-lees'kō*, state in W central Mexico; bounded N by Nayarit, Zacatecas and Aguascalientes, E by Guanajuato, SW by Michoacán, S by Colima and W by the Pacific Ocean; a mountainous state with a narrow coastal plain, crossed NW-SE by the Sierra Madre Occidental and drained by the Grande de Santiago, Bolaños and Verde rivers; in the E of the state is Mexico's largest lake, Lago de Chapala; pop(1980) 4,293,549; area 80,836 sq km; capital Guadalajara; economy: agriculture (maize, chick-peas, oats, linseed), cattle and pig raising, mining (gold, silver, copper, zinc, manganese, iron), iron and steel, machinery, chemicals, textiles.

Jalon *ha-lon'*, river rising at the NE edge of the central plateau of Medinaceli, Castilla-León, Spain, flowing NE to meet the R Ebro near Alagón; length 224 km.

Jamaica *ja-may'ka* (Indian, 'xaimaca', land of springs), island in the Caribbean Sea, situated 160 km W of Haiti and 144 km S of Cuba, between 17° and 19°N and 76° and 79°W; timezone GMT −5; area 10,957 sq km; capital Kingston; chief towns Montego Bay and Spanish Town; pop(1982) 2,190,357; the pop comprises 76% African, 15% Afro-European, and 3% East Indian and Afro-East Indian; English is the official language, but most people speak a Jamaican creole dialect; Christianity is the dominant religion; the unit of currency is the Jamaican dollar of 100 cents; national holidays 1st Monday in August (Independence Day), 21 Oct (National Heroes Day); membership of CARICOM, Commonwealth, FAO, G-77, GATT, IADB, IAEA, IBA, IBRD, ICAO, ICO, IDB, IFAD, IFC, ILO, IMF, IMO, INTERPOL, ISO, ITU, NAM, OAS, PAHO, SELA, UN, UNESCO, UPU, WFTU, WHO, WIPO, WMO, WTO.

Physical description and climate. Jamaica is the third largest island in the Caribbean with a maximum length of 234 km and width varying from 35 km to 82 km. The terrain is mountainous and rugged, particularly in the E where the Blue Mts rise to heights above 1,800 m. The Blue Mountain peak (2,256 m) is the highest peak on the island. A highly dissected limestone plateau surrounds the Blue Mts and projects W over the greater part of the island. Over 100 small rivers descend from the mountains to the sea, but only the R Black in the SW is navigable. Several rivers are used to generate hydroelectric power. The climate is humid and tropical at sea-level, becoming more temperate at higher altitudes. Temperatures on the coast range from 21°C to 34°C and humidity is high. In the mountains temperatures range from 7°C to 26°C. The hottest months are June to Sept. Mean annual rainfall is 1,980 mm with the heaviest rains occurring in May and between August and November. The S and SW plains receive virtually no rainfall while some N regions receive up to 5,060 mm per annum. Jamaica lies within the hurricane belt. Extensive flood damage was caused by hurricanes in 1979 and 1980.

History, government and constitution. Originally occupied by Arawak Indians who had migrated from South America about 700-1000 AD, Jamaica was visited by Christopher Columbus in 1494. Spanish colonizers settled in 1509 and later imported West African slave labour to work on sugar plantations which were established in 1640. British occupation of Jamaica in 1655 eventually led to Britain acquiring formal possession of the island through the Treaty of Madrid in 1670. Early British settlers were harassed by runaway

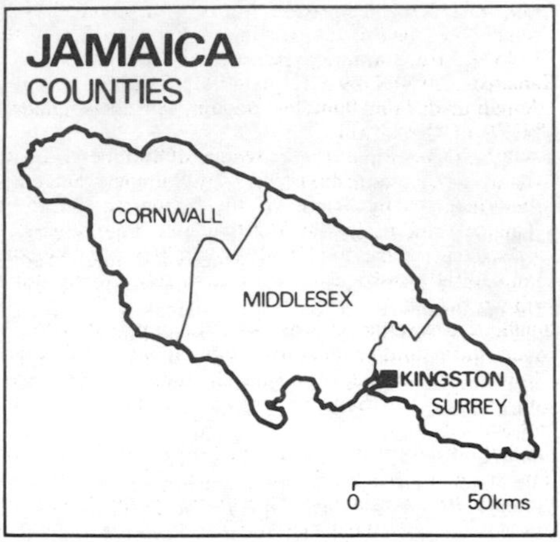

slaves called *maroons* who eventually acquired small parcels of land and some local autonomy during the first half of the 18th century. Self-government was introduced in 1944 and independence was granted on 6 August 1962. A Governor-General, appointed by the British Crown on the advice of the Jamaican prime minister, is assisted by a 6-member Privy Council. The legislature comprises a bicameral parliament consisting of an elected House of Representatives and a nominated Senate of 20 senators.

Economy. The economy has traditionally been based on plantation agriculture which still employs about one-third of the workforce producing major export crops such as sugar, bananas, citrus fruits, coffee, cocoa, ginger, coconuts and pimento. The agricultural economy has suffered from destructive weather, crop disease, fluctuating export prices and poor infrastructure. The bauxite industry developed rapidly after 1952 and has since played a dominant role in the island's economic growth. Jamaica is the 2nd largest producer of bauxite in the world (after Australia) and in 1983 bauxite and alumina represented 61% of registered export earnings. Tourism is the second most important foreign exchange earner after bauxite and alumina. Major industries in Jamaica include mining and metal refining (bauxite, alumina, gypsum), and the manufacture of textiles, foodstuffs, cement, fertilizers, rum, and chemical products. The major trade partners include the USA, the UK, Canada, Norway, Venezuela, the Netherlands Antilles and CARICOM countries.

Administrative divisions. Jamaica is divided into 3 counties which in turn are subdivided into 14 parishes as follows:

County/Parish	*area (sq km)*	*pop(1982)*
Cornwall		
Hanover	448	62,837
Westmorland	787	120,622
St Elizabeth	1,207	139,897
St James	596	135,959
Trelawny	874	69,466
Middlesex		
Manchester	827	144,029
St Ann	1,213	137,745
Clarendon	1,197	203,132
St Catherine	1,195	332,674
St Mary	608	105,969
Surrey		
St Andrew	430	482,889
Portland	812	73,656
St Thomas	742	80,441
Kingston	22	104,041

Jamalpur *jum-al'poor*, region in central Bangladesh;

pop(1981) 2,451,000; area 3,349 sq km; bounded N by Meghalaya region of Assam, India and E by the Brahmaputra (Jamuna) river; capital Jamalpur.

Jamalpur, 24 54N 89 57E, pop(1981) 91,815, capital of Jamalpur dist and Jamalpur region, central Bangladesh; NNW of Dhākā; railway.

Jambi or **Djambi** *jam'bee*, province of Indonesia, on the island of Sumatera; bounded S by Sumatera Selatan (S Sumatra), N by Riau, W by Sumatera Barat (W Sumatra) and E by the South China Sea; fringed by coastal marshland; pop(1980) 1,445,994; area 44,924 sq km; capital Jambi; economy: rattan, oil, timber, copra, rubber, pepper.

Jambi, TELANAIPURA, 1 34S 103 37E, pop(1980) 158,559, river port and commercial capital of Jambi prov, Indonesia; on Banaghari (R Hari), 96 km from the coast, on the island of Sumatera; university (1963); economy: rubber, oil.

Jambol, okrug (prov) of Bulgaria. See Yambol.

Jamestown, 15 56S 5 44W, seaport capital and only town on the British island of St Helena in the S Atlantic; pop(1976) 1,516, passenger and cargo services to the UK and S Africa.

Jamestown, 42 06N 79 14W, pop(1980) 35,775, town in Chautauqua county, SW New York, United States; at SE end of L Chautauqua, 91 km SSW of Buffalo; railway.

Jammu-Kashmir *jum'moo kash-meer'*, state in the extreme N of India; pop(1981) 5,981,600; area 101,283 sq km; bounded N by the July 1972 line of control (separating territory claimed by both India and Pakistan), W by Pakistan, E by Xizang aut region (Tibet) and by Aksai Chin (claimed by India but administered by China as part of the Xianjiang aut region); crossed by the Karakoram, Ladakh, Zaskar, Pir Panjal and Panji mountains and drained by numerous rivers including the Indus, Zaskar, Suru, Nubra and Shyok; Srinagar is the summer capital and Jammu the winter capital of the state, which is divided into the province of Kashmir, with 8 dists, and the province of Jammu, with 6 dists; the state is governed by a bicameral legislature consisting of a 36-member Legislative Council and a 76-member Legislative Assembly; 80% of the population is employed in agriculture, producing rice, wheat, maize and fruit; over one-fifth of the state is covered in forest which provides a valuable source of income; manufacturing industry is largely located in Jammu, while industries based on horticulture are widespread in Kashmir prov; traditional handicraft industries of the state include silk-spinning and carpet-weaving; Srinagar and Jammu are connected by the Jawahar Tunnel through the Banihal mountain, giving access to the Kashmir Valley during winter months; in Dec 1972 the railway line between Jammu and Pathankot was opened, linking the state to the Indian rail network; airfields are located at Jammu and Srinagar; the state of Jammu and Kashmir became part of the Mogul Empire in 1586; after Afghan rule from 1786 it was annexed to the Sikh Punjab in 1819; in 1820 Jammu came under the control of Gulab Singh, as did Kashmir in 1846; under the Indian Independence Act of 1947, which asked all states to accede either to Pakistan or to India, Kashmir requested agreements with both countries; the state came under armed attack from Pakistan and the Maharaja acceded to India on 26 Oct 1947; in 1965 there were further hostilities between India and Pakistan; a ceasefire followed in Jan 1966 and again in July 1972 when a new line of control was delineated.

Jamnagar *jahm'nu-gur*, 22 28N 70 06E, pop(1981) 317,000, city in Gujarat state, W central India; 72 km WNW of Rajkot on the Kathiawar peninsula; its port is at Bedi on the Gulf of Kachch (Kutch), an inlet of the Arabian Sea; airfield; linked to Rajkot by rail; naval and aeronautical schools; economy: pearl fishing, oilseed, chemicals, tanning, paint, soap, matches, ceramics, metalwork, sawmilling, cotton, silk and embroidery; monuments: palaces, forts and temples.

Jämsä *yam'sa*, 61 51N 25 10E, pop(1982) 12,484, industrial town in Keski-Suomi prov, S central Finland; 93 km NE of Tampere; established in 1969; railway; economy: paper.

Jamshedpur *jum-shayd'poor*, formerly SAKCHI, 22 44N 86 20E, pop(1981) 670,000, industrial city in Bihar state, E India; 225 km WNW of Calcutta, on the Sanjai river; iron and steel works were founded here in 1907 at the centre of an area of extensive coal and iron ore deposits; economy: agricultural implements, vehicles, tin plate.

Jämtland *yemt'land*, a county of W Sweden; land area 49,857 sq km; pop(1983) 134,857; capital Östersund; chief rivers include the Ljungan and the Indalsälven; L Storsjön occupies a large area in the centre of the county; other lakes include Kallsjön, Hotagen and Ströms vattudal.

Jan Mayen, *yahn mī'en*, formerly HUDSON'S TUTCHES (Eng), Norwegian volcanic island in the Arctic Ocean, 480 km E of Greenland, 576 km NNE of Iceland; area 380 sq km, length 53 km; highest point is Beerenberg (2,277 m); discovered by Henry Hudson in 1608; annexed to Norway on May 8, 1929.

Janesville, 42 41N 89 01W, pop(1980) 51,071, county seat of Rock county, S Wisconsin, United States; on the R Rock, 19 km N of Beloit; railway.

Jantra, river in Bulgaria. See Yantra.

Janūb, Al, SOUTH LEBANON, governorate (*moafazat*) of S Lebanon; bounded W by the Mediterranean Sea, S by Israel, and NE by Syria; subdivided into the 7 divisions (*cazas*) of Hâsbaīya, Jezzïne, Saïda, Nabatîyé, Soûr, Bent Jbaîl and Marjayoûn; capital Saïda (Sidon); chief towns Jezzïne, Marjayoûn, and Soûr (Tyre); drained by the R Lītāni; economy: oil refining at Az Zahrānī.

Japan', NIPPON (Jap), island state comprising a group of 4 large islands and several small ones extending between 45°N and 26°N off the E coast of Asia; bounded W by the Sea of Japan, the Korean Strait and the East China Sea, E by the Pacific Ocean, N by the Tsugaru-kaikyō Strait; timezone GMT +9; area 381,945 sq km; capital Tōkyo; chief cities include Yokohama, Ōsaka, Nagoya, Sapporo and Kyōto; pop(1982) 118,693,000; pop is 99.4% Japanese, with 0.6% other nationalities (mostly Korean); the official language is Japanese; most Japanese observe both Shinto and Buddhist religions and approx 16% belong to other faiths, including 0.8% Christian; the currency is the yen; national holidays 15 Jan (Adults' Day), 11 Feb (Commemoration of the Founding of the Nation), 21 March (Vernal Equinox Day), 29 April (Birthday of the Emperor), 3 May (Constitution Memorial Day), 6 May (Children's Day), 16 Sept (Respect for the Aged Day), 23 Sept (Autumnal Equinox Day), 10 Oct (Health Sports Day), 4 Nov (Culture Day), 23 Nov (Labour Thanksgiving Day); membership of ADB, ASPAC, Colombo Plan, DAC, ESCAP, FAO, GATT, IAEA, IBRD, ICAC, ICAO, ICO, IDA, IDB (Inter-American Development Bank), IEA, IFAD, IFC, IIIO, ILO, International Lead and Zinc Study Group, IMF, IMO, INTELSAT, INTERPOL, IPU, IRC, ISO, ITC, ITU, IWC (International Whaling Commission), IWC (International Wheat Council), OECD, UN, UNESCO, UPU, WFTU, WHO, WIPO, WMO, WSG.

Physical description. The islands of Japan consist mainly of steep mountains and hills with many volcanoes. The northernmost island, Hokkaidō, has a central range of mountains running N-S (rising to over 2,000 m), which falls in steps to coastal uplands and plains. Honshū, the largest of the Japanese islands, comprises parallel arcs of mountains bounded by narrow coastal plains. In the centre of the island, near the S coast, is Fuji-san volcano, the highest mountain in Japan at 3,776 m. In E Honshū lies the heavily populated and industrialized Kanto plain. SW Honshū, Shikoku and Kyūshū islands consist of clusters of low cones and rolling hills, mostly between 1,000 and 2,000 m high. To the S of this, Japan tails off into the Ryukyu chain of volcanic islands which curve S towards Taiwan. Okinawa is the largest in this group of islands. The main volcanic areas are S Hokkaidō, central Honshū and Kyūshū. Many of the islands' mountain streams are used for irrigation near the coast.

Climate. Japan has an oceanic climate that is influenced by the Asian monsoon. Winters are not as cold as in the same latitude on the continent and precipitation is much heavier. Winter precipitation is especially heavy on the W coasts of N Honshū and in Hokkaidō. Snowfall is heavy here since the winter monsoon blowing from Siberia and Manchuria is warmed and picks up moisture over the sea. In parts of this area winter precipitation is greater than that of the summer. Winters in N Japan are severe, with heavy falls of snow. N Japan has short but warm summers and on the E coasts the summers are wetter than the winters. Akita in N Honshū averages a daily temperature of between −5° and 2°C in Jan, rising to between 19° and 28°C in Aug, the hottest month. Rainfall is almost as heavy here during the winter as the summer, with a min of 104 mm rainfall in Feb-March and a max of 211 mm in Sept. Hakodate in S Hokkaidō records temperatures which are overall slightly lower than those for Akita, with most rainfall during July-Nov. For the rest of Japan, winter is generally a dry season. Winter weather is variable and changeable over the whole of Japan, but especially in the N and W. In summer and early autumn heavy rain is brought by typhoons, or tropical cyclones, which move N from the South China Sea. In some parts of central and S Japan rainfall is extremely heavy in early summer and again in late

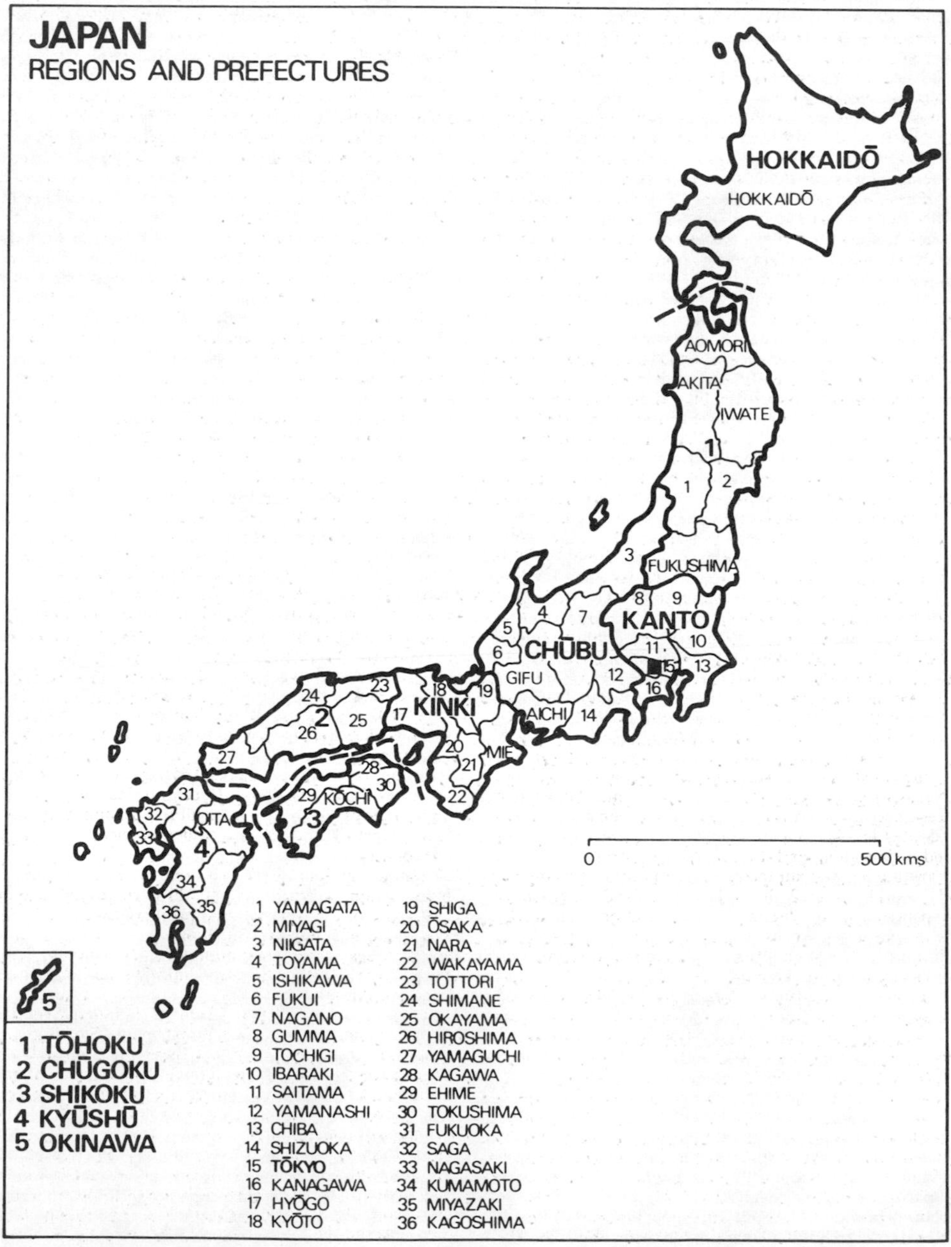

summer or early autumn. In the S of Honshū, in Shikoku and in Kyūshū the winters are mild and almost subtropical, especially on the coast of the Inland Sea. Winter rainfall is light and snow and frost very rare, while summers are warm. At Nagasaki temperatures lie between 2° and 9°C in Jan and 23° and 31°C in Aug, with rainfall heaviest in July (312 mm). Because the country is dominated in the summer by moist maritime air with frequent cloud, the summer heat is often sultry and oppressive, especially in the large cities, while temperatures in the mountains are lower.

History, government and constitution. Originally occupied by Ainu people, Japan was invaded from an early date by Manchu-Korean and Malayan settlers. In the 4th century AD Japan developed from individual communities into small states, the most powerful being Yamato which came to dominate the country by the end of the 5th century. Buddhism reached Japan in the 6th century and between the 8th and 12th centuries the country's culture was strongly influenced by China. Ruled by feudal shoguns for many centuries, there was little contact with the West. In 1853 the USA under Commander Perry used force to open Japan to trade and international commerce. After a period of political uncertainty and unrest, the power of the shoguns was finally broken in 1868, and the rule of the imperial family (the Meiji) was restored. Japan rapidly adopted Western civilization, modified its government, extended its foreign contacts and set about colonial expansion. In 1894-95 it fought a war with China over Korea, gaining territory and trade concessions. In 1904-05 Japan successfully fought Russia for rights in S Manchuria and Sakhalin. Korea was annexed in 1910, and parts of E Siberia and China were occupied temporarily after World War I, when Japan secured former German possessions in the Pacific. In 1931-32 Japan occupied Manchuria and used it as a springboard for invading the coastal cities of N China. Japan entered World War II on 7 Dec 1941 with a surprise attack on the US fleet at Pearl Harbour, Hawaii. This action was followed by the occupation of British and Dutch possessions in SE Asia. Japan attacked the Philippines on 8 Dec 1941 and occupied Manila on 2 Jan 1942, overwhelming the American and Filipino force by April of the same year. Japan seized Hong Kong on 25 Dec 1941, invaded the Malay peninsula 8-9 Dec 1941 and forced the surrender of Singapore on 15 Feb 1942. In Dec 1941 Japan also invaded Siam (Thailand), and Burma in Feb 1942. Between Jan and March 1942, Japan seized Ambon, the E coast of Borneo, Sumatra and Java. Japan received its first setback in the naval and air battles of Coral Sea (7-8 May 1942) and Midway (3-6 June 1942). From 1943 onwards, Japan gradually lost control of various areas until it was bombed by the first 2 atomic bombs used in warfare, at Hiroshima on 6 Aug 1945 and Nagasaki on 9 Aug 1945. After the war mainland Japan was occupied by Allied troops. A new constitution was adopted in 1947. Japan adopted a determined policy of industrialization and the 1960s saw strong economic growth, giving Japan the 3rd highest national income in the world. In 1972 the S Ryukyu islands reverted to Japanese control. Japan is a constitutional monarchy with the Emperor as head of state. The legislative bicameral Diet has a 491-member House of Representatives elected every 4 years and a 252-member House of Councillors elected every 6 years (one-half elected every 3 years). Executive power is vested in a cabinet composed of the prime minister and ministers of state.

Economy. With limited natural resources and less than 20% of the land under cultivation, Japan has used technical skill to increase crop production, principally of rice. Manufacturing industry has developed rapidly since 1945 and is based on metallurgical and engineering industries, electrical and electronic industries, textiles and chemicals. Major trade areas include the USA, south-east Asia, western Europe, the Middle East and communist countries; 96% of Japan's exports are manufactured consumer goods such as motor vehicles, computers, televisions, etc.

Administrative divisions. Japan is divided into 9 regions as follows:

Region	*area (sq km)*	*pop(1980)*
Chūbu	66,743	19,984,000
Chūgoku	31,847	7,586,000
Hokkaidō	83,513	5,576,000
Kanto	32,309	34,896,000
Kinki	33,038	21,208,000
Kyūshū	42,084	12,966,000
Okinawa	2,246	1,107,000
Shikoku	18,795	4,163,000
Tōhoku	66,959	9,572,000

The regions of Japan are divided into 45 prefectures. (See regional entries).

Japan, Sea of, arm of the Pacific Ocean, bounded by South and North Korea to the SW, the coasts of the USSR to the W, Sakhalin Island (USSR) to the N and the islands of Japan to the E and S; linked to the South China Sea by the Korean Strait and to Okhotskoye More (Sea of Okhotsk) by La Perouse Strait and Tatarskiy Proliv; the NE-flowing warm current keeps coastal conditions ice-free as far N as Vladivostok, USSR, the only major port in the N Pacific which is open all year.

Jarash *je'rash*, GERASA (anc), 32 10N 35 50E, village in Irbid governorate, East Bank, NW Jordan; 35 km N of Amman; built on the site of ancient Gerasa, a city of the Decapolis; monuments: paved streets and colonnades, temples, theatres, baths, and a triumphal arch.

Jarrow *ja'rō*, 54 59N 1 29W, pop(1981) 31,313, port town in South Tyneside borough, Tyne and Wear, NE England; part of Tyneside urban area; on R Tyne, 8 km E of Newcastle upon Tyne; economy: shipbuilding, iron and steel, chemicals, electronics; monument: 7th-c monastery associated with the Venerable Bede.

Järvenpää *yar'ven-pa*, TRASKANDA *tray'shen-dah* (Swed), 60 30N 25 02E, pop(1982) 24,205, town in Uudenmaa prov, S Finland; situated on L Tuusula, 32 km NNE of Helsinki; established in 1951; railway; here is 'Ainola', the former home of Sibelius.

Jasikan *ja-see-kan'*, 7 28N 0 33E, town in Volta region, E Ghana, W Africa; N of Ho, near the Togo border.

Jasper, national park in SW Alberta, SW central Canada; borders W with British Columbia; situated in the Rocky Mts; contains Mt Brazeau (3,470 m) and Mt Columbia (3,747 m); drained by the main tributary of the Athabasca river; area 10,878 sq km; established in 1907.

Jastrzębie Zdrój *yas-trown'bye-zdroo-i*, 49 52N 18 40E, pop(1983) 99,200, town in Katowice voivodship, S Poland; close to the Czechoslovak frontier; formerly a spa town; economy: coal mining.

Jászberény *ya'ber-ayn*, 47 30N 19 55E, pop(1984e) 31,000, town in Szolnok county, E central Hungary; on R Zagyva, S of Gyöngyös; agricultural school; economy: grain, livestock and tobacco trade; monument: museum of folk art.

Jaú *zha-oo'*, national park in E central Amazonas state, Norte region, N Brazil; area 22,720 sq km; established in 1980; part of the Amazon tropical rainforest.

Java, island of Indonesia. See Jawa.

Java Sea, Sea of SE Asia; bounded N by Borneo, S by Jawa (Java) and W by Sumatra; linked to the Celebes Sea by the Makassar Strait.

Jawa *jah'va*, JAVA, DJAWA, island of Indonesia; in the Greater Sunda group, SE of Sumatera and S of Borneo; comprises the provs of Jawa Barat (W Java), Jawa Tengah (central Java), Jawa Timur (E Java), the special territory of Yogyakarta and the capital territory of Jakarta; area 132,187 sq km; pop(1980) 91,269,528; one of the most densely populated islands in the world (690 persons per sq km in 1980); major cities include Jakarta, Bandung and Surabaya; this mountainous island covered with dense rainforest has 115 volcanic peaks of which 15 are active; the mountains rise to 3,371 m at Gunung Sumbung in the central Dieng plateau; in the S the mountains drop sharply into the Jawa Sea; economy: tobacco, rubber, tea, textiles, timber, rice, maize, sugar; 93% of the land is cultivated by smallholders with an average of 0.6 hectares of land; the island is noted for its batik or 'fine point' method of cloth decoration.

Jawa Barat, WEST JAVA, province of W Jawa, Indonesia, at the W end of Jawa I; pop(1980) 27,453,525; area 46,300 sq km; capital Bandung; 80% of the world's quinine comes from this region; economy: tea, rubber, coffee, rice, copra, tapioca, teakwood, gold, silver; the Ujung Kulon National Park on the W tip of the island comprises lowland forest with banteng deer and the last Javan rhinos; this 625-sq km park also includes the volcanic island of Rakata Krakatua (Krakatoa) which erupted in 1883; the 150-sq km Gunung Gede-Pangrango National Park includes the Gede crater and the Cibodas botanic garden; Mt Gede rises to 2,962 m and Mt Pangrango rises to 3,091 m.

Jawa Tengah, CENTRAL JAVA, province of central Jawa, Indonesia; pop(1980) 25,372,889; area 34,206 sq km; capital Semarang; economy: copra, rubber, tapioca, tea, sugar cane, rice, tobacco, kapok, coffee, sisal hemp, oil, iodine, teakwood; the Dieng plateau reserve includes 3 lake nature reserves, Gunung Sumbung, rising to 3,371 m, and a number of ancient Hindu temples.

Jawa Timur, EAST JAVA, province of E Jawa, Indonesia, pop(1980) 29,188,852; area 47,922 sq km; capital Sura baya; economy: sugar, rice, rubber, coffee, tapioca, copra, tobacco, kapok, maize, sisal hemp, teakwood, groundnuts, tea, oil, iodine; Meru Betiri reserve is the last refuge of the Javan tiger; 250 sq km around Gunung Baluran were declared a national park in 1980, preserving the rusa deer, banteng and feral buffalo.

Jaworzno *ya-vorzh'no*, 50 12N 19 15E, pop(1983) 93,900, town in Katowice voivodship, S Poland; SE of Katowice; railway; economy: coal mining, steel, nitrogen, three power plants.

Jayapura *jah-ya-poo'ra*, JAJAPURA, DJAJAPURA, SUKARNAPURA, 2 37S 140 39E, pop(1980) 45,786, seaport capital of Irian Jaya (West New Guinea) prov, Indonesia; on N coast W of the frontier with Papua New Guinea; headquarters of General MacArthur during World War II (1944); airfield.

Jedda, seaport in Saudi Arabia. See Jiddah.

Jefferson City, 38 34N 92 10W, pop(1980) 33,619, capital of state in Cole county, central Missouri, United States; on the R Missouri, 172 km W of St Louis; a city since 1839; Lincoln University (1866); railway; economy: government services, agricultural trade.

Jehol, town in Hebei prov, N China. See Chengde.

Jelenia Góra *yel-en'yo goor'a*, voivodship in SW Poland; bounded S by Czechoslovakia and W by E Germany; pop(1983) 504,000; area 4,278 sq km; capital Jelenia Góra; chief towns include Bolesławiec, Zgorzelec and Kamienna Góra.

Jelenia Góra, HIRSCHBERG (Ger), 50 55N 15 45E, pop(1983) 89,300, capital of Jelenia Góra voivodship, SW Poland; in a mountain valley at the confluence of Bóbr and Kamienna rivers, Polish Sudetenland; railway; economy: synthetic fibres, cellulose, pharmaceuticals, clothing, optical work; monuments: castle tower, St Anne's chapel, Baroque church of the Holy Cross, regional museum, 17-18th-c burgher houses in the Market Square.

Jena *yay'nah*, 50 56N 11 35E, pop(1982) 105,287, town in Jena dist, Gera, S East Germany; on R Saale, W of Gera; university (1588); first planetarium built here in 9th century; Napoleon defeated the Prussians here in 1806; railway; economy: chemicals, precision instruments.

Jendouba *jen-doo'ba*, governorate of N Tunisia, N Africa; pop(1984) 359,425; capital Jendouba.

Jenin *je-neen'*, sub-district of Judea-Samaria dist, Israel, in the Israeli-occupied West Bank.

Jer'ba, Ile de, ILE DE DJREBA, island off the NE coast of Tunisia, N Africa; situated in the Golfe de Gabès; chief town Houmt Souk (Jerba); the island has developed into a major international tourist resort; linked to the mainland town of Zarzis by a causeway; event: Festival of Ulysses in Aug.

Jerez or fully **Jerez de la Frontera** *he-reth' THay la fron-tay'ra*, XERES *sher'es* (Eng), 36 41N 6 07W, pop(1981) 176,238, picturesque town a few miles inland from Cádiz, Cádiz prov, Andalucia, S Spain, giving its name to sherry; airport; economy: famous for its sherry, wine and brandy; events: Fiesta of the Horse in May and wine festival in Sept with flamenco dancing.

Jericho *je'ri-kō*, ERIHA (Arab), YERIHO (Hebrew), 31 51N 35 27E, oasis town in Jerusalem governorate, Israeli-occupied West Bank, W Jordan; 36 km NE of Jerusalem; situated on the W bank of the R Jordan, 15 km NW of the Dead Sea; archaeological excavations of the mound of Tell es Sultan, the original site, were begun early in the 20th century and revealed 20 successive layers indicating different periods of settlement, the earliest dating from about 8,000 BC; NW of Old Jericho is the Mount of the Temptation where, according to Christian tradition, Jesus fasted for 40 days after being baptised by John; monuments: palace of Qirbat al-Mafyar (724 AD).

Jersey, the largest of the Channel Is; lying W of the Cotentin Peninsula of French Normandie; pop(1980) 76,100; area 116 sq km; capital St Helier; noted for its Jersey cattle and Jersey potatoes; gave its name to a woollen garment.

Jersey City, 40 44N 74 04W, pop(1980) 223,532, county seat of Hudson county, NE New Jersey, United States; port on the Hudson river and Upper New York Bay; known as Jersey City since 1838; scene of a British defeat by 'Light Horse' Harry Lee in 1779; railway; economy: chemicals, paper products; event: Harbour Festival (July).

Jerusalem *ju-roo'su-lum*, district in central Israel; pop(1983) 468,200; area 627 sq km.

Jerusalem, YERUSHALAYIM (Hebrew), 31 47N 35 15E, pop(1982) 424,400, capital city of Jerusalem dist and the State of Israel; a holy city of Christians, Jews and Muslims, situated on a dry chalk plateau on the E slope of the Judean range; the old city is surrounded by a fortified wall and divided into 4 quarters (Armenian, Muslim, Christian, Jewish) by 2 intersecting main streets; the first buildings outside the old city walls were built in 1860; capital of Palestine (1922-48); the 1949 Israel-Transjordan armistice agreement divided Jerusalem between Israel and Jordan; W Jerusalem was declared capital of Israel in 1950; E Jerusalem was annexed after the 1967 Six-Day War; Hebrew university (1925); railway; airfield; monuments: citadel (24 BC); monastery of the Armenian Patriarchate; 12th-c cathedral of St James; Temple Mount (most important Islamic shrine after Mecca and Medina) with numerous domes, temples, minarets, and mosques including El Aqsa mosque (705-15), and Dome of the Rock (685-705); Antonia Fortress (37-4 BC); church of the Holy Sepulchre, one of the holiest places in Christendom, marking the site of the crucifixion, burial, and resurrection of Jesus; Dormitio Sanctae Mariae church; Tomb of the Kings; Mount of Olives (site of Jesus' ascension).

Jerusalem, YERUSHALAYIM (Hebrew), governorate (*muhafaza*) of the Israeli-occupied West Bank, W Jordan, bounded W by Israel.

Jessore *ju-sor'*, region in SW Bangladesh; includes Jessore, Jhenaidah, Magura and Narail districts; pop(1981) 4,020,000; area 6,672 sq km; formerly a district of SE Bengal, but divided in 1947, such that six-sevenths was given to East Pakistan (now Bangladesh) and the remainder to West Bengal.

Jessore, 23 10N 89 12E, pop(1981) 148,927, capital of Jessore dist and Jessore region, SW Bangladesh; on R Ganga (Ganges), 135 km SW of Dhākā; linked to Khulna (SE) by rail; economy: trades in linseed, tobacco, tamarind, rice and sugar; manufactures celluloid, plastics.

Jette *zhet*, 50 51N 4 20E, pop(1982) 39,783, town in Brussel dist, Brabant prov, Belgium; a NW suburb of Bruxelles.

Jezerce *yez-ert'say*, 42 26N 19 46E, mountain in the N Albanian Alps on the Yugoslav border and NE of Shkodër; height 2,693 m.

Jhang Maghiana *jung mug-yah'na*, 31 19N 72 23E, pop(1981) 195,000, city in Punjab prov, Pakistan; close to the E bank of a tributary of the R Chenab, WSW of Faisalabad and 193 km WSW of Lahore; joint municipality of which Maghiana is the newer and more important; economy: trading centre of grains and cloth.

Jhansi *jahn'see*, 25 27N 78 34E, pop(1981) 281,000, agricultural market town in Uttar Pradesh state, NE India; 160 km SW of Kanpur, between the Sind and Betwa rivers; linked to Kanpur, Agra, Gwalior and Bhopal by rail; the walled, old part of the city (N) developed around a fort, which was built in 1613 by the Bundela Rajputs; came under British control in 1853, when the ruling prince died leaving no heirs; scene of a massacre of British citizens during the Indian Mutiny (1857); economy: iron and steel, brassware.

Jhelum *jay'loom*, JEHLUM, JEHLAM, HYDASPES, 32 58N 73 45E, pop(1981) 106,000, city in Punjab prov, Pakistan; 170 km NNW of Lahore, on the R Jhelum; railway; economy: trade centre and timber.

Jhelum, river of Asia; the most westerly of the five rivers of Punjab prov, Pakistan; rises in the Himalayas, in Kashmir and Jammu; flows NW through the Vale of Kashmir, past the towns of Islamabad and Srīnagar, to flow W past Baramula and the N section of the Pīr Panjāl range; close to Muzaffarābad, it receives the waters of the Kishanganga river from the NE, before flowing generally S following the border between Kashmir, NW Frontier prov and the Punjab; meets the R Chenab SW of Jhang Maghiana; length 725 km; the R Jhelum is the source of many canals and irrigation systems of the Punjab plain; famous battle between Alexander the Great and Porus fought on its banks in 326 BC.

Jiangsu *ji-ang-soo*, KIANG-SU, prov in E China; bordered E by Shanghai municipality and the Huang Hai (Yellow Sea), and by Shandong prov (N), Anhui prov (W), and Zheijiang prov (S); the flattest and most low lying prov in China; contains over 200 lakes and numerous rivers which cover 18% of the total land area; the S part of Jiangsu is divided by the Chang Jiang (Yangtze river) valley, the prov is drained by the Chang Jiang, Xinyl He, Huai He, Xinyang Gang and Dontang He rivers; the Grand Canal runs from N to S through Jiangsu; of the numerous lakes in Jiangsu, Hongze Hu and Gaoyou Hu in the E and Tai Hu in the S are the largest; pop(1982) 60,521,114; area 102,200 sq km; capital Nanjing; principal towns Lianyungang, Nantong, Suzhou, Wuxi, Yangzhou and Zhenjiang; economy: rice, wheat, freshwater fish farming, chemicals, light and heavy industry.

Jiangxi *ji-ahng-see*, KIANG-SI, prov in SE China; bordered N by Anhui prov, along the Chang Jiang (Yangtze river) in part, W by Hubei, along the Mufu Shan range and Hunan provs, E by Zhejiang prov and Fujian prov, along the Wuyi Shan and Xianxia Ling ranges, and S by Guangdong (along the Dayu Ling and Jiulian Shan ranges); mountainous in the W, S and E, with the Poyan Hu lake plain, part of the middle lower Chang Jiang (Yangtze) plain, in the N; apart from the mountain ranges which form Jiangxi's borders, the prov also rises in the W with the Jiuling Shan and Wugong Shan ranges; drained by the Gan Jiang, Xu Jiang, Yuan Shui, Xin Jiang and Le'an Jiang rivers; pop(1982) 33,184,827; area 164,800 sq km; capital Nanchang; principal town Pingxiang; economy: grain, fishing, mining, porcelain.

Jiddah *ji'du*, JEDDA, 21 29N 39 16E, pop(1974) 561,100, seaport in Makkah prov, W central Saudi Arabia; on the E shore of the Red Sea, 64 km W of Makkah (Mecca); Saudi Arabia's commercial capital and largest port; walled city; port of entry on pilgrimage route to Makkah; the W section stands on land reclaimed from the Red Sea; university (1967); airport (opened 1981); economy: shipping, steel rolling mill, cement works, oil refining.

Jihlava *yih'la-wa*, 49 24N 15 35E, pop(1984) 52,828, town in Jihomoravský region, Czech Socialist Republic, central Czechoslovakia; on R Jihlava NW of Brno; in 1436 the 'Compactata' or Magna Carta of the Hussite church was signed here; railway; economy: textiles, leather, tobacco, machinery, footwear.

Jihočeský *yi'ho-che-skee*, region in Czech Socialist Republic, W central Czechoslovakia; bisected by the R Vltava; bounded to the S and SW by Austria and W Germany respectively; area 11,345 sq km; pop(1984) 694,112; capital České Budějovice; chief towns include Písek and Tábor.

Jihomoravský *yi'ho-mo-rav-skee*, region in Czech Socialist Republic, central Czechoslovakia; bounded to the S by Austria; area 15,028 sq km; pop(1984) 2,053,497; capital Brno; chief towns include Břeclav, Gottwaldov and Hodonin.

Jijel', department in N Algeria, N Africa; area 3,704 sq km; pop(1982) 572,644; chief town Jijel.

Jilin *jee-lin*, KIRIN, prov in NE China; bordered W by Nei Mongol aut region (Inner Mongolia), SW by Liaoning prov, SE by North Korea along the Yalu and Tumen rivers, E by the USSR and N by Heilongjiang prov; mountainous in the SE (Changbai Shan range) and low lying in the NW; in the extreme E of the prov is Senlin Shan, a peak rising to 1,498 m; the prov is watered by the Dier Songhua Jiang; in the centre of the prov is Songhua Hu artificial lake; pop(1982) 22,560,053; area 187,000 sq km; capital Changchun; principal town Jilin; economy: rice, soya beans, medicinal items (deer antlers, ginseng), sable, minerals; Jilin is the ancient home of the Manchus, former nomadic hunters who became the last emperors of China.

Jilin, KIRIN, formerly YUNKI, 43 53N 126 35E, pop(1984e) 1,114,100, town in Jilin prov, NE China; E of Changchun; founded in 1673; railway; economy: chemicals, plastics.

Jīma *ji'ma*, GIMMA (Ital), 7 39N 36 47E, pop(1984e) 60,992, capital of Kefa region, SW Ethiopia, NE Africa; 240 km SW of Addis Ababa; occupied by the Italians (1936); airfield.

Jinan *jee-nahn*, TSINAN, CHI-NAN, 36 41N 117 00E, pop(1984e) 1,394,600, capital of Shandong prov, E China; situated in a valley between the lower Huang He (Yellow river) and the Taishan mts; established in Neolithic times, Jinan emerged as a commercial centre in the Tang dynasty (618-907); Shandong railway; airfield; economy: metallurgy, chemicals, textiles, paper, flour, and agricultural products such as wheat, corn, cotton, tobacco, peanuts and various types of fruit; Jinan is known as the 'City of Springs' because of its 102 bubbling natural springs found at Daming lake in the NE of the old town; the four main springs are: Wulong (Five Dragon), Zhenzhu (Pearl), Heihu (Black Tiger) and Baotu (Gushing from the Ground); just outside the town are a dam and pumping stations which prevent the Huang He river from flooding Jinan and the surrounding area; water is also used for irrigation.

Jindřichův Hradec *yin'dri-KHoof ra'dets*, 49 09N 15 01E, pop(1984) 21,367, town in Jihočeský region, Czech Socialist Republic, W central Czechoslovakia; railway; economy: textiles, glass.

Jingmen *jing-men*, 31 02N 112 06E, pop(1984e) 1,011,500, city in Hubei prov, E central China; W of Wuhan; railway.

Jinja *jin'ju*, 0 27N 33 14E, pop(1983e) 45,060, town in Busoga prov, Uganda, E Africa; on the N shore of L Victoria at the outflow of the Victoria Nile river, 33 km E of Kampala; there is a power station at Owen Falls; railway; airfield; economy: textiles, metal products, grain milling, petrol depot.

Jinotega *hee-nō-tay'ga*, dept in N Nicaragua, Central America; bounded N by Honduras and SE by the Cordillera Isabelia with peaks over 2,000 m; the Río Coco forms the entire N boundary; Lago de Apanás occupies the SW corner; pop(1981) 127,159; area 15,195 sq km; capital Jinotega; economy: sugar cane, coffee, potatoes, grain, timber.

Jinotega, 13 05N 85 59W, pop(1978) 14,088, capital town

of Jinotega dept, N Nicaragua, Central America; 5 km S of Lago de Apanás; economy: food processing, hides, straw hats.

Jinotepe *hee-nō-tay'pay*, 11 50N 86 10W, pop(1985e) 17,600, capital town of Carazo dept, W Nicaragua, Central America; on the Río Grande, 35 km SSE of Managua; alt 760 m; on the Inter-American Highway; railway; economy: salt, timber, limestone, processing of sugar cane, rice, coffee; event: fiesta (24-26 July).

Jinzhou *jin-jō*, CHIN-CHOU, 41 07N 121 06E, pop(1984e) 748,700, town in Liaoning prov, NE China; near the Laiodong Wan gulf; railway.

Jipijapa *KHee-pee-KHa'pa*, 1 23S 80 35W, pop(1982) 27,146, market town in Manabí prov, W Ecuador; famous for its Panama hats; economy: cotton, fruit and kapok.

Jiquilisco *hee-kee-lee'skō*, 13 16N 88 30W, pop(1980) 57,179, town in Usulután dept, El Salvador, Central America; 14 km W of Usulután; railway.

Jixi *chee-shee*, CHI-HSI, 45 17N 131 00E, pop(1984e) 798,900, town in SE Heilongjiang prov, NE China; E of Harbin, near the Soviet frontier; railway.

Jīzān *jee-zan'*, QIZAN *kee-zan'*, 16 57N 42 34E, pop(1974) 32,815, seaport in Jīzān prov, SW Saudi Arabia; on the E shore of the Red Sea, 168 km S of Abhā; sheltered by the Farasān Is; airfield.

João Pessoa *zhwã'ō pe-sō'a*, 7 06S 34 53W, pop(1980) 290,247, seaport and commercial and industrial capital of Paraíba state, Nordeste region, NE Brazil; on the Río Paraíba, N of Recife; port for coastal traffic; university (1955); railway.

Jodhpur *jod'pur*, MARWAR, 26 23N 73 02E, pop(1981) 494,000, city in Rajasthan state, W India; on the S edge of the Thar Desert (Indian Desert), 290 km WSW of Jaipur; the city is surrounded by a 10 km wall; founded in 1459, it replaced Rajput as the capital of Jodhpur Princely State, which joined the Union of Rajasthan in 1949; Jodhpur breeches are named after this city, where they first became popular; university (1962); airfield; linked by rail to Bikaneer, Ahmadabad and Delhi; economy: textiles, leather goods, metalwork, trade in wool, hides, cotton; monuments: a hill fort above the city contains palaces and a treasury of the maharaja.

Jod'rell Bank, 53 13N 2 21W, observatory station in Macclesfield dist, Cheshire, NW central England; 5 km NE of Holmes Chapel.

Joensuu *yo'en-soo*, 62 36N 29 45E, pop(1982) 45,584, commercial city and capital of Pohjois-Karjala prov, SE Finland, on NE fringe of the Finnish Lake Plateau; university (1969); established as a copper town in 1848; railway, airfield; economy: timber trade; event: song festival in June.

Johannesburg *jō-ha'nis-burg*, *yō-ha'nus-burKH* (Afrik), abbrev JO'BURG, 26 10S 28 02E, pop(1985) 1,609,408 (metropolitan area), largest city of Transvaal prov, South Africa; 1,290 km NE of Cape Town, 485 km NW of Durban and 50 km SSW of Pretoria; South Africa's largest city and commercial, financial and industrial centre of the Transvaal; alt 1,665 m; founded in 1886 after the discovery of gold in the Witwatersrand; originally laid out by the surveyor Josais de Villiers; now the hub of a populous conurbation of municipalities; the high cost of land has led to semi-skyscraper buildings; 2 universities (1922, 1966); railway; airport; economy: commerce, chemicals, textiles, clothing, leather products, engineering, diamond cutting, gold mining.

John o' Groats *ō grōts'*, a locality in NE Highland region, NE Scotland; on the Pentland Firth, 23 km N of Wick, near Duncansby Head; often mistakenly thought to be the northernmost point on mainland Britain; the phrase 'from Land's End to John o' Groats' is commonly used to refer to the length of Britain; there are no remains of the octagonal house which was said to have been built here by the Dutchman John de Groot, or John o' Groats, who settled in Scotland in the 16th century.

Johnson City, 36 19N 82 21W, pop(1980) 39,753, town in Washington county, NE Tennessee, United States; 145 km ENE of Knoxville; university; railway; economy: tobacco and dairy market.

Johnston Islands, 16 45N 169 32W, coral atoll enclosing 4 islets in the central Pacific Ocean, 1,150 km SW of Honolulu; comprises the islets of Johnston, Sand, North and East; 19 km in circumference; area 2.5 sq km; pop(1981e) 1,000, discovered by Captain Johnston on *HMS Cornwallis* in 1807; claimed by Hawaii in 1858; guano exported by USA during the second half of the 19th century; taken over by US Navy in 1934; now used by the US Defence Nuclear Agency under the US Air Force as a store for poisonous gas; airfield.

Johnstone, 55 50N 4 31W, pop(1981) 42,669, town in Renfrew dist, Strathclyde, W Scotland; in Clydeside urban area, 6 km W of Paisley; railway; economy: textiles; engineering.

Johnstown, 40 20N 78 55W, pop(1980) 35,496, town in Cambria county, SW Pennsylvania, United States; on R Conemaugh, 96 km E of Pittsburgh; railway; economy: traditional coal-mining centre, but diversifying more recently; suffered disastrous flood on 31 May 1889, when heavy rains caused Conemaugh Dam to burst, resulting in the deaths of over 2,200 people.

Johor or **Johore** *ju-hor'*, state in S Peninsular Malaysia, SE Asia; occupying the entire S tip of the Malay Peninsula; bounded W by the Strait of Malacca, E by the S China Sea; separated from Singapore by the Johor Strait; pop(1980) 1,580,423; area 18,985 sq km; capital Johor Baharu; chief towns include Batu Pahat, Muar and Keluang; economy: rubber, oil palm, pineapple, pepper, timber and wood products.

Johor Baharu *ju-hor' bah'roo*, 1 29N 103 44E, pop(1980) 246,395, capital of Johor state, S Peninsular Malaysia, SE Asia; at the tip of the Malay Peninsula, 365 km SE of Kuala Lumpur; connected to Singapore by a causeway; economy: tourism; monuments: the Istana Besar (Grand Palace), built in the 1860s by Sultan Abu Bakar; Abu Bakar mosque; Johor Safariworld, SE Asia's only safari park; Fiesta Village.

Joinville *zhoyn-vee'le*, 26 20S 48 49W, pop(1980) 216,986, town in Santa Catarina state, Sul region, S Brazil; near the Atlantic coast, SE of Curitaba; situated in an area with a strong German influence; railway; monuments: the museum of history in the Prince of Joinville's mansion has a collection of objects from the original German settlement; the archaeological museum has a collection of the Sambaquis period dating back to 5,000 BC; at Expoville, 4 km from the centre of town, is an exhibition on Joinville's industry and an industrial museum; event: flower festival during the first fortnight in Sept.

Joliet *jō-lee-et'*, 41 32N 88 05W, pop(1980) 77,956, county seat of Will county, NE Illinois, United States; on the Des Plaines river, 56 km SW of Chicago; state penitentiary; railway; economy: steel, petroleum products, chemicals, paper, engineering equipment.

Jonesboro, 35 50N 90 42W, pop(1980) 31,530, county seat of Craighead county, NE Arkansas, United States; 102 km NNW of Memphis, Tennessee; university (1909); railway; economy: trade, distributing, and industrial centre for a farming region; tornadoes devastated parts of the city in May 1973.

Jonglei *jong-lay'*, canal in S Sudan, NE Africa; the canal runs between Jonglei on the White Nile almost due N for approx 260 km to join the Sobat river, a tributary of the White Nile just S of Malakal.

Jönköping *yœn'kœ-ping*, a county of S Sweden, S of L Vättern; R Nissan flows S through the extreme W of the county; land area 9,943 sq km; pop(1983) 301,415; capital Jönköping; chief towns Tranås, Nässjö and Vetlanda.

Jönköping, 57 45N 14 10E, pop(1982) 107,123, industrial town and capital of Jönköping county, S Sweden; at S end of L Vättern; railway; received municipal charter in 1284; now a focus point for agriculture and forestry; economy: textiles, machinery, paper.

Jonquière *zhõ-kyayr'*, 48 25N 71 16W, pop(1981) 60,354, town in S Québec, SE Canada; on the Sable river (a tributary of the Saguenay); 14 km WSW of Chicoutimi; railway; economy: hydroelectricity, pulp and paper mills.

Joplin, 37 06N 94 31W, pop(1980) 38,893, town in Jasper county, SW Missouri, United States; 115 km W of Springfield; railway.

Jor'dan, sub-district of Judea-Samaria dist, Israel, in the Israeli-occupied West Bank of Jordan.

Jordan, official name Hashemite Kingdom of Jordan, AL MAMLAKA AL URDUNIYA AL HASHEMIYAH (Arab), kingdom in the Middle East; bounded N by Syria, NE by Iraq, E and S by Saudi Arabia, and W by Israel; timezone GMT +2; area 96,188 sq km (of which 6,644 sq km are in the West Bank); capital Amman; chief cities Irbid, Zarqa, Salt, Karak, and the port city of 'Aqaba; pop(1980) 2,152,000; slightly less than one-third of the pop lives on the West Bank; the Jordanians are mostly of Arab descent although there are small communities of Circassians, Armenians, and Kurds; approx 1 mn Palestinian Arabs live in the country; Arabic is the official language; the pop comprises 95% Sunni Muslim and 5% Christian; the unit of currency is the Jordanian dinar; national holiday 25 May (Independence Day); membership of Arab League, FAO, G-77, IAEA, IBRD, ICAO, IDA, Islamic Development Bank, IFAD, IFC, ILO, IMF, IMO, INTELSAT, INTERPOL, IPU, ITU, NAM, OIC, UN, UNESCO, UPU, WFTU, WHO, WIPO, WMO, WTO.

Physical description. The dominant topographic feature of Jordan is the Red Sea-Jordan rift valley, a branch of the great African Rift Valley system. This structural depression, which extends N-S from the foot of Jesh Sheikh (Mt Hermon) in S Syria to the Gulf of 'Aqaba in SW Jordan, divides the country into two regions: the West Bank and the East Bank. The R Jordan valley, L Tiberias (Sea of Galilee), the Dead Sea, and Wadi 'Araba all form part of this rift system. Much of the valley lies below sea level, −212 m at L Tiberias and −394 m at the lowest point of the Dead Sea. The N part of this rift valley, known as El Ghor, is the main area of irrigated cultivation. The sides of the rift rise steeply through undulating hill country to heights above 1,000 m on either side. To the E the land levels out to the Syrian desert, sandy in the S and hard and rocky further N. The highest point in Jordan is Jabal Ram (1,754 m), NE of 'Aqaba in the extreme SW of the country.

Climate. Approx 90% of Jordan is desert with an annual rainfall below 200 mm. Summers are uniformly hot and sunny, and winters can occasionally be cold with snow on higher ground. Those areas in the rift valley which are below sea level have hot summers and mild winters. The rest of the country has a typically Mediterranean climate with hot, dry summers and cool, wet winters. The wettest and most fertile part of Jordan is the hilly NW where annual rainfall may be as high as 800 mm. Temperatures at Amman, on the W edge of the desert, range from 7.5°C in Jan to 24.9°C in July, and the mean annual rainfall is 290 mm.

History, government and constitution. Following the decline of the Turkish Empire in 1918, the Arab Levant was split into British and French mandated territories. Historically, Palestine lay to the W and Transjordan to the E of the R Jordan. Transjordan became a sovereign independent state on 25 May 1946. When the British mandate over Palestine ended on 14 May 1948 the newly created state of Israel fought to control the West Bank area. Fighting broke out between the Israelis and Palestinian Arab nationalists, aided by neighbouring Arab states including Transjordan. Armistice agreements on 3 April 1949 left Jordan in control of the West Bank. The West and East Banks of Jordan were united under the Jordanian crown in 1951 and the country was renamed the Hashemite Kingdom of Jordan. The Six-day War of June 1967 between Israel and the Arab states of Syria, Egypt, Iraq, and Jordan led to Israel gaining military control of the West Bank. Attempts by the Jordanian army to expel Palestinian guerrillas from the

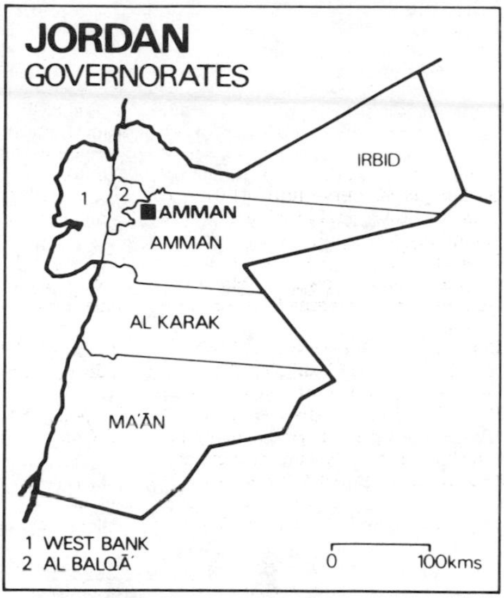

West Bank led to the outbreak of civil war in 1970-71. In 1973 King Hussein declared a general amnesty for Palestinians and the following year ceded Jordan's claims to the West Bank to the Palestine Liberation Organization (PLO). Jordan is a constitutional monarchy. Parliament consists of a 30-member senate and an elected 60-member house of representatives. On 9 Jan 1984 parliament was reconvened for the first time since it was suspended in 1974.

Economy. Manufacturing industry accounts for approx 15% of national income and is based on phosphate mining, petroleum production and refining, cement production, and light manufacturing. Phosphate, the country's main natural resource, is extracted at Al-Hassa and Wadi Al-Abyad. Jordan is the world's 3rd largest phosphate rock exporter after Morocco and the USA, and in 1984 exported 4.7 million tonnes to 29 countries. Potash is extracted from the Dead Sea and used in the manufacture of fertilizers. Oil was discovered at El Azrag, 70 km E of Amman, early in 1982. These reserves, plus oil trucked from Iraq and piped from Saudi Arabia, are refined at Zarqa. Chief exports are fruit, vegetables and phosphate rock, supplied mainly to Arab Common Market countries.

Agriculture. The agricultural sector accounts for less than 9% of national income and employs 20% of the workforce. Crops grown include cereals, vegetables, citrus fruits, and olives. The principal grain growing area is around Irbid in the N of the country. There has been considerable investment in the agricultural development of the Jordan valley which is now intensively exploited through plasticulture and drip irrigation. There is also a project in the Hamad Basin in the NW using underground water supplies.

Administrative divisions. Jordan is divided into the 8 governorates (*muhafazas*) of Amman, Irbid, Al Balqā', Al Karak, Ma'ān, Jerusalem, Hebron, and Nablus. The last 3 governorates are known collectively as the West Bank which has been occupied by Israel since 1967.

Communications. The Queen Alia International Airport at Zizya, 30 km S of Amman, was inaugurated in 1983. There are also international airports at Amman and 'Aqaba. 'Aqaba, at the head of the Gulf of 'Aqaba, is the country's only port.

Jordan, river in the Middle East, SW Asia; rises in several headstreams in the Jebel esh Sharqi (Anti-Lebanon) mountains on the Lebanon-Syria border; flows over 320 km S through L Tiberias and El Ghor to the Dead Sea;

chief tributary R Yarmūk; N half of the river forms part of the Israel-Jordan and Israel-Syria borders; the S half separates the East Bank of Jordan from the Israeli-occupied West Bank; it becomes more saline towards the Dead Sea; occupies part of the Red Sea-Jordan rift valley.

Jos *jos*, 9 54N 8 53E, pop(1981e) 143,000, capital of Plateau state, central Nigeria, W Africa; 225 km S of Kano; alt 1,222 m; university (1976); railway branchline terminus; airfield; economy: tourism, food, chemicals, textiles, tin, ceramics, bricks and brewing.

Jō-Shin-Etsu *jō-ō-shin-et'tsoo*, JOSHINETSU KOGEN, mountainous national park in Chūbu region, N central Honshū island, Japan; area 1,890 sq km; established in 1949.

Jost Van Dyke *yōst van dīk*, pop(1980) 136, mountainous island of the British Virgin Islands in the Lesser Antilles chain of the E Caribbean; W of Tortola Island; area 7.5 sq km; birthplace of William Thornton, designer of the Washington Capitol.

Jostedalsbreen *yo'stud-als-brayn'*, JOSTEDALSBRE, ice field on the Jostedalsbreen plateau, Sogn og Fjordane county, W Norway, 160 km NE of Bergen, between Nordfjord and Sognefjorden (Nord and Sogne Fjords); area 486 sq km; length 96 km; width 24 km; height 2,044 m; largest ice field in Europe, with a thickness of 300 m; the village of Jostedal lies at its E foot, 40 km N of Sogndal.

Jotunheimen, *yō'toon-hay-men*, JOTUNHEIM, ('home of the giants'), highest mountain range in Europe, N of the upper branches of Sognefjorden (Sogne Fjord), in Oppland and Sogn og Fjordane counties, S central Norway; extends c.112 km between Sognefjorden and the upper Gudbrandsval; there are more than 250 peaks over 1,900 m and over 60 glaciers; rises to 2,470 m at Glittertinden; the range lies between the R Begna to the S and the R Lågen to the N; there are many associations with folk legends and the scene of Ibsen's *Peer Gynt*.

Jōwzjān *juz-jan*, prov in N Afghanistan; bounded to the N by the USSR, with the Amudar ya river forming the boundary; pop(1984e) 683,870; area 25,553 sq km; capital Sheberghān; the Mazār-e-Sharīf to Herāt road crosses the N section of the province.

Juan Fernández *hwan fer-nan'dez*, group of 3 islands in Valparaíso prov, Chile, located in the Pacific Ocean, 640 km W of the Chile mainland; Más a Tierra, Más Afuera and Santa Clara; total area 181 sq km; Alexander Selkirk was shipwrecked on Más a Tierra island in 1704 for 4 years; Daniel Defoe based his novel *Robinson Crusoe* on his experiences.

Juan Lacaze *hwahn la-ka'say*, 34 26S 57 25W, pop(1985) 12,454, port in Colonia dept, SW Uruguay; on the Río de la Plata; 22 km SW of Rosario; railway; officially called Sauce until 1909, its port is still sometimes referred to as Puerto Sauce.

Juan-les-Pins *zhü-ĩ-lay-pĩ*, 43 39N 7 06E, fashionable resort on the Cap d'Antibes, Alpes-Maritimes dept, Provence-Alpes-Côte d'Azur, SE France; on the Mediterranean coast between Nice and Cannes, 8 km from Antibes; noted for its beaches and casinos.

Juárez, Ciudad *syoo-THATH' hwar'es*, 31 42N 106 29W, pop(1980) 567,365, town in Chihuahua state, N Mexico; on the border with the USA, opposite El Paso, Texas; on the Río Grande; alt 1,133 m; headquarters of Benito Juárez in 1865; university; railway.

Juaso *jwa'sō*, 6 41N 1 07E, town in Ashanti region, S central Ghana, W Africa; on the railway between Kumasi and Koforidua.

Juazeiro do Norte *zhwa-zay'ro dō nor'tay*, 7 10S 39 18W, pop(1980) 125,191, town in Ceará state, Nordeste region, NE Brazil; W of Recife and S of Fortaleza; railway; economy: commercial centre; manufacturing; a small pilgrimage town, it was the home of Padre Cícero, one of the unofficial saints of the NE.

Jubayl, Al *joo-bayl'*, 26 59N 49 40E, new industrial town in Eastern prov, E Saudi Arabia; on the W shore of the Arabian Gulf, approx 88 km NNW of Az̧ Z̧ahrān (Dhahran); centre of oil, petrochemical, and heavy industries; major port of Al Hasa prov in the 1920s and 1930s, until the development of the oil industry.

Júcar *hoo'kar*, river rising on W slopes of the Montes Universales, Castilla-La Mancha, Spain; flows S past Cuenca, then turning E near La Roda it flows E to enter the Mediterranean at Cullera; length 498 km; important irrigation and hydroelectric reservoirs at Embalse de Alarcón, Villa de Ves, Cofrentes and Pantano de Tous; feeds the Canal of Castile (Canal de María Cristina).

Judea *joo-dee'u*, Greco-Roman name for S Palestine, the area now occupied by SW Israel and W Jordan; it was the southernmost of the Roman divisions of Palestine; rises to 1,020 m in the S near Hebron; chief town Jerusalem; during the War of Independence of 1948-49 the W part of Judea became part of the newly-founded State of Israel while the E part, including Hebron, fell to Jordan; since 1967 the West Bank and E Jerusalem have been occupied by Israel.

Judea-Samaria *joo-dee'u su-ma'ree-u*, WEST BANK, district of Israel, in the Israeli-occupied West Bank; divided into the 7 sub-districts of Jenin, Nablus, Tulkarm, Ramallah, Jordan, Bethlehem, Hebron.

Juigalpa *hwee-gal'pa*, 12 04N 85 23W, pop(1978) 13,468, capital town and agricultural centre of Chontales dept, S central Nicaragua, Central America; on the Río Mayales, approx 18 km from the E shore of Lago de Nicaragua.

Juiz de Fora *zhoo-ees' day fo'ra*, 21 47S 43 23W, pop(1980) 299,432, town in Minas Gerais state, Sudeste region, SE Brazil; on the Río Paraibuna in a deep valley between the Mar and Mantiqueira mountain chains; university (1960); railway; economy: agriculture, cattle raising, textiles, brewing, timber, sugar refining, steel.

Jujuy *KHoo-KHooy'*, prov in Norte region, NW Argentina; founded in 1834; in Andes and Puna region; rises to 6,200 m (Nevada de Chañi); bordered by Chile (W) and Bolivia (N); drained by the Río Grande de Jujuy and the Río San Francisco; pop(1980) 410,008; area 53,219 sq km; capital Jujuy; chief towns La Quiaca and Humahuaca; economy: sugar cane, vineyards, sheep raising, fishing, timber, copper, tin, iron, lead and zinc mining.

Julian Alps, JULIJSKE ALPE (Slov), mountain range in NW Yugoslavia and NE Italy; a SE extension of the Alpine system, bounded to the N by the Karawanken Alps; rises to 2,863 m at Triglav, the highest peak in Yugoslavia.

Julianehåb *yool-yah'ne-hop*, QAQAETOQ (Esk), 60 40N 46 00W, pop(1975) 2,923, settlement in SW Greenland; economy: fishing, canning, sheep.

Jullundur *ju-lun'dur*, 31 18N 75 40E, pop(1981) 408,000, city in Punjab state, NW India; N of the R Sutlej, 120 km ESE of Lahore; capital of the Punjab from independence in 1947 until Chandigarh was built in 1954; linked by rail to Amritsar and Ludhiana.

Jundiaí *zhoon-dee-a-ee'*, 23 10S 46 54W, pop(1980) 221,888, town in São Paulo state, Sudeste region, SE Brazil; 58 km NNE of São Paulo; railway; economy: fruit trade (figs, grapes, strawberries, peaches), textiles; the town holds an annual grape festival.

Juneau *joo'nō*, 58 18N 134 25W, pop(1980) 19,528, seaport capital of state in SE Alaska, United States; on Gastineau Channel, in the Alaskan Panhandle; developed as a gold-rush town after Joseph Juneau discovered gold nearby in 1880; airport; economy: trade centre, with an ice-free harbour; chief industries are salmon and halibut fishing, lumbering, and tourism; monument: House of Wickersham; event: Salmon Derby (Aug).

Jungfrau *yoong'frow*, 46 33N 7 58E, mountain peak in the Berner Alpen (Bernese Alps), Bern canton, S central Switzerland; mountain railway near the summit; first ascended in 1811; height 4,158 m.

Junggar Pendi, DZUNGARIAN BASIN *dzen-gar-ee-an*, 2nd largest inland basin in China; in N Xinjiang aut region, NW China; bordered S by the Tien Shan range, N by the Altai Shan range; 850 km long and 380 km wide at its widest section; area 380,000 sq km; alt 500-1,000 m; in the W is the Manas He river; to the E of the Manas He lies the Gurbantunggut Shamo desert, covering an area of 47,300 sq km; moist air currents which blow in from the

NW give the Junggar Pendi more rainfall than the Tarim Pendi; the majority of the land to the W of the Manas He river is grassland and marsh; the Junggar Pendi basin is rich in minerals, provides a grazing ground for cattle and sheep, and is Xinjiang's most economically developed area.

Junín *KHoo-neen'*, 34 34S 60 55W, pop(1980) 62,080, town in Buenos Aires prov, Litoral, E Argentina; on the Río Salado; nearby lagoons supply fish sold in Buenos Aires; birthplace of Eva Peron; railway; economy: railway workshops, trade in grain and cattle.

Junín, dept in central Peru; bordered by Ene and Tambo rivers (E), Cordillera Oriental (NE) and Cordillera Occidental (W); crossed by Cordillera Central; pop(1981) 852,238; area 32,354 sq km; capital Huancayo.

Junín, Lago de, lake situated in the Andean Cordillera Central, central Peru; 13 km NNW of Junín; 10 km wide; alt 4,133 m; the Río Mantaro is its outlet.

Jura *zhü-ra, joo'ra* (Eng), dept in Franche Comté region of E France, bounded on the E by Switzerland; comprises 3 arrond, 34 cantons and 543 communes; mainly occupied by the Jura Mts, drained by the Doubs, Loué and Ain rivers; pop(1982) 242,925; area 4,999 sq km; capital Lons-le-Saunier, chief towns Dôle and St-Claude; Poligny and Arbois are known for their wines, and Morez for watches; spas at Lons-le-Saunier and Salins-les-Bains; there are interesting caves near Baume-les-Messieurs (Grotte de Baume).

Jura, limestone mountain range in E France and W Switzerland, on the Franco-Swiss border, forming a plateau 250 km long by 50 km wide; lying between the R Saône and the lakes of W Switzerland; the highest point is Crête de la Neige (1,718 m) in Ain dept, France; the highest point in Switzerland is Mt Tendre (1,682 m); the slopes, steep to the E and gentle to the W, are mostly poor pasture and forest; skiing and caving are popular; the hills are drained by the Doubs and Ain rivers and are divided from the Vosges by the Troué de Belfort; there are facilities for winter sports at Metabief-Mont-d'Or (1,000 m) and Les Rousses (1,120 m).

Jura, canton in W Switzerland; pop(1980) 64,986; area 838 sq km; capital Delémont, a French speaking and partly Catholic enclave in the German-speaking Protestant canton of Bern until 1979 when it became a separate canton.

Jurong *dyoo-rong*, 1 21N 103 42E, town and industrial estate on SW coast of Singapore I, SE Asia; W of Singapore City; area 6.3 sq km; with 1,400 factories employing 112,000 workers it is the largest industrial estate in SE Asia; railway; monuments: Bird Park, Japanese Garden and Chinese Garden.

Jutiapa *hoo-tee-ah'pa*, dept in SE Guatemala, Central America, bounded E by El Salvador and S by the Pacific Ocean; pop(1982e) 329,185; area 3,219 sq km; capital Jutiapa; chief towns Asunción Mita and Valle Nuevo; traversed by the Inter-American Highway; the dept is devoted largely to agriculture (corn, beans, vegetables, tropical fruits, and beef).

Jutiapa, 14 17N 89 50W, capital town of Jutiapa dept, SE Guatemala, Central America; 72 km ESE of Guatemala City; near the Inter-American Highway.

Juticalpa *hoot-ee-kal'pa*, 14 45N 86 12W, pop(1983e) 14,121, capital of Olancho dept, central Honduras, Central America; NE of Tegucigalpa, in a rich agricultural area; alt 820 m; airfield; economy: cattle-raising, growing of cereals and sugar cane.

Jutland, Danish peninsula. See Jylland.

Juventud, Isla de la *yoo-ven-tood'* ('isle of youth'), formerly, ISLE OF PINES, prov of Cuba, comprising an island lying 97 km off the SW coast; area 2,199 sq km; pop(1981) 57,879; capital Nueva Gerona; chief settlements Santa Bárbara and Santa Fé; La Victoria was one of Cuba's first new towns; formerly used as a penal colony; officially named Isla de la Juventud in 1958 in recognition of the contribution made by young people to development; rises to 416 m at the Sierra de Canada and 285 m at the Sierra Caballo; fine beaches on the S coast make the island an important resort area; grapefruit, mangoes and oranges are widely grown.

Jwaneng', 24 30S 24 45E, pop(1981) 5,567, independent township in Ngwaketze dist, Botswana, S Africa; located W of Gaborone; area 100 sq km; alt 1,180 m; an important diamond mining centre.

Jylland *yoo'lan*, JUTLAND (Eng), a Danish peninsula, extending N from the German mainland, and bounded by the North Sea, Skagerrak and the Kattegat; comprises the counties of Sønderjylland, Ribe, Vejle, Ringkøbing, Århus, Viborg and Nordjylland; its S border with Germany is Denmark's only land frontier; along the W coast are massive dykes, designed to protect the land from devastating storm tides; on the W coast is the major entry port of Esbjerg; formerly devoted exclusively to farming and fishing, Jylland now has well-developed industries, though agriculture still plays an important part in its economy (export of pork and bacon); chief towns include Varde, Åbenrå, Kolding, Horsens, Skanderborg and Randers.

Jyväskylä *yu'vas-ku-la*, 62 16N 25 50E, pop(1982) 64,500, commercial town and capital of Keski-Suomi prov, S central Finland; at N end of L Päijänne; established in 1837; university (1966) with a modern campus designed by Alvar Aalto; first Finnish-language secondary school established here 1858; railway; hydrofoil to Lahti; economy: paper, wood and metal products; events: arts festival in June-July; Thousand Lakes Motor Rally in Aug and the Winter Workers Festival.

K

K2, MT GODWIN-AUSTEN, second highest mountain in the world and highest in the Karakoram range, NE Pakistan; height 8,611 m; named for English topographer Henry Godwin-Austen.

Kabala *ka-ba'la*, 9 40N 11 36W, pop(1974) 8,000, capital of Koinadugu dist, Northern prov, Sierra Leone, W Africa; 97 km NNE of Makeni.

Kabalega *ka-ba-layg'a*, MURCHISON FALLS, national park in NW Uganda, E Africa; area 3,840 sq km; established in 1952; situated on the border between Northern and Western provs with L Albert forming the SW border; Victoria Nile river (including the Kabalega Falls where there is a power station) flows E-W across the park.

Kābul *ka'bool*, prov in E Afghanistan; lying to the S of the Hindu Kush; pop(1984e) 1,659,377; area 4,585 sq km; national and prov capital at Kābul.

Kābul, 34 30N 69 10E, pop(1984e) 1,179,341, capital city of Afghanistan and capital of Kābul prov, E Afghanistan; on R Kābul in a high mountain valley, it commands the approaches to the Khyber Pass and is the focus of main roads from all provinces; became Afghanistan's capital in 1773; captured in 1839 by the British during the Afghan Wars and then again in 1879 after the ambush of British troops; administrative centre of the Karmal government since the Soviet invasion in Dec 1979; university (1931); airport; economy: wool, cloth, sugar-beet, plastics, leather goods, furniture, glass, soap and heavy industry; power production was increased 25% in 1984 by the opening of a gas turbine plant.

Kabwe *kahb'way*, formerly BROKEN HILL, 14 29S 28 25E, pop(1980) 143,635, capital of Central prov, Zambia, S central Africa; 115 km N of Lusaka; mining town and centre of maize, tobacco and cattle producing area; a skull of *Homo rhodesiensis* was discovered in a mine near here in 1921; the town has been lead and zinc mining centre since 1902; nearby is the oldest operating mine in Zambia; headquarters of Zambian Railways; base of the Third Battalion, Zambia Regiment; 22 km from the town is Mulungushi Rock, the venue of several historic conferences leading to independence; railway; economy: animal feeds, pharmaceuticals, plastic products.

Kachin *ka-chin'*, state in N Burma; bordered by India (NW) and by China (N and E); mountainous in the N and E; contains Burma's highest peak (Hkakabo Razi, 5,881 m), situated on the N border with China; drained by the Mali Hka and the Nmai Hka, headwaters of the R Irrawaddy; pop(1983) 903,982; capital Myitkyina; mining of jade and amber in the NW.

Kadoma *ka-dō'ma*, GATOOMA, 18 16S 29 55E, pop(1982) 45,000, town in Mashonaland West prov, Zimbabwe, S Africa; 137 km SW of Harare; over 50% of the country's gold production is mined nearby; agricultural research station; railway; economy: textiles, mining, cattle ranching.

Kaduna *ka-doo'na*, state in N Nigeria, W Africa; pop(1982e) 6,535,400; area 70,245 sq km; capital Kaduna; chief towns Funtua, Zaria, Daura, Kafanchan and Katsina; named after the R Kaduna which flows in an arc past Kaduna on its way to meet the R Niger; main ethnic groups include the Hausa, Fulani, Kaje, Gwan and Piti; there are reserves of cassiterite, columbite, sapphire, iron ore, kyanite, graphite, gold and phosphate; economy: processing of iron ore and phosphate, petroleum, car assembly, textiles, oil milling, cigarettes, concrete, cotton (40% of Nigerian production), groundnuts and ginger.

Kaduna, 10 28N 7 25E, pop(1981e) 276,000, capital of Kaduna state, N Nigeria, W Africa; on the R Kaduna, 210 km SW of Kano; railway junction; airfield; economy: textiles, brewing, metals, cement, car assembly, animal feed and oil refining.

Kaédi *ka-ay'dee*, 16 12N 13 32W, pop(1976) 20,848, capital of Gorgol region, S Mauritania, NW Africa; on the right bank of the R Sénégal, 315 km E of Saint Louis (Senegal); airfield.

Kafr el Dauwâr *ka'fer el dow'ahr*, 31 08N 30 08E, pop(1976) 160,554, city in N Egypt; 24 km ESE of Alexandria; railway.

Kafr el Sheik *kaf'er el shayk'*, 31 07N 30 56E, capital of Kafr el Sheik governorate, N Egypt; E of the Rosetta branch of the R Nile, 35 km NNW of Tanta; railway.

Kafue *ka-foo'ay*, 15 44S 28 10E, town in Central prov, Zambia, S central Africa; on the R Kafue, 40 km S of Lusaka; railway; economy: nitrogenous fertilizer, chemicals, clothing, furniture, fibreglass.

Kafue, national park in Central prov, Zambia, S central Africa; 237 km SW of Lusaka; area 22,400 sq km; established in 1951; the park includes the Busanga plains and the upper reaches of the Kafue river; home for unusual species such as the sable and roan antelope.

Kaga Bandoro *ka-ga ban-dō'rō*, FORT CRAMPEL, 7 00N 19 10E, town in N Central African Republic; on the R Gribingui N of Sibut.

Kage'ra, national park in Rwanda, central Africa; area 2,500 sq km; established in 1934.

Kagera, region of N Tanzania, E Africa; bounded N by Uganda; includes part of L Victoria; pop(1985e) 1,298,000.

Kâğithane *kah-yi-tan'ay*, 41 05N 28 58E, pop(1980) 175,540, town in İstanbul prov, NW Turkey.

Kagoshima *ka-gō-shee'ma*, 31 37N 130 32E, pop(1980) 505,360, capital of Kagoshima prefecture, S Kyūshū island, Japan; on W shore of Kagoshima-wan Bay, opposite Sakura-jima island and volcano, to which it is joined by a bank of lava formed by the eruption of the volcano in 1914; university (1949); feudal seat of the Shimazu family (the lords of Satsuma) from the 12th to 18th centuries; St Francis Xavier landed here in 1549; centre of the Satsuma rebellion of 1877 which resulted in the destruction of the city; railway; shipping services; airport; economy: Satsuma porcelain, textiles, metal products.

Kahle Asten *kah'le ahs'tun*, 51 12N 8 30E, mountain in E Nordrhein-Westfalen (North Rhine-Westphalia) prov, W Germany; highest peak of the Rothaargebirge range, 3 km W of Winterberg; height 841 m; the Lenne river rises here.

Kahramanmaraş, mountainous prov in S central Turkey; pop(1980) 738,032; area 14,327 sq km; capital Kahramanmaraş.

Kahramanmaraş, 37 34N 36 54E, pop(1980) 178,557, capital town of Kahramanmaraş prov, S central Turkey.

Kaieteur Falls *kī'a-toor*, waterfall, central Guyana, South America; on the R Potaro in outliers of the Guiana Highlands; 161 km SW of Bartica in the heart of tropical Guyana; the falls are nearly 5 times the height of Niagara, with a sheer drop of 226 m from a sandstone tableland almost 107 m wide into a wide basin where the water drops a further 22 m; the falls were discovered in 1870 by Barrington Brown of the Geological Survey; they are set in the 116 sq km Kaieteur National Park which was established in 1929.

Kaifeng *kī-feng*, K'AIFENG, 34 47N 114 20E, pop(1984e) 619,200, town in Henan prov, N central China; Kaifeng was capital of the State of Wei from 220 to 265 and of China from 907 to 960; Jews who migrated here in the 11th century became influential in the 14th and 15th centuries, but few remain today; constant flooding of the Huang He river has always been a problem here; railway; economy: silk, electrical goods, chemicals, agricultural machinery, food processing; monuments: the pyramid-shaped Dragon Pavilion in the NW of the city marks the site of the former Song imperial stronghold; the Old Music Terrace in a park in SE Kaifeng was used for poetry recitals by Tang poets such as Du Fu and Li Bai.

Kaikoura *kī-kō'ra*, mountain ranges in NE South Island, New Zealand; two parallel ranges, the Inland Kaikoura range and the Seaward Kaikouras, extend 40 km parallel with the E coast and are separated by the lower course of the Clarence river; the highest peak is Mount Tapuaenuku (2,885 m) in the Inland Kaikoura range.

Kailahun *kī-la-hoon'*, dist in Eastern prov, Sierra Leone, pop(1974) 180,365; area 3,859 sq km; capital Kailahun.

Kailahun, 8 21N 10 21W, pop(1974) 7,000, capital of a dist of the same name, Eastern prov, Sierra Leone, W Africa; 137 km ENE of Bo.

Kailua *kī-loo'a*, 19 38N 156 00W, pop(1980) 35,812, town in Honolulu county, Hawaii, United States; on Kailua Bay, Oahu I; airfield.

Kainji *ka-in'ji*, national park in Sokoto and Niger states, W Nigeria, W Africa; situated E of the Kainji reservoir which was created by damming the R Niger; area 5,341 sq km; established in 1975.

Kairouan *kayr-wan'* ('the fortified city'), 35 42N 10 01E, pop(1984) 72,254, capital of Kairouan governorate, NE Tunisia, N Africa; 130 km S of Tunis; founded in 671 by Sidi Okba; in contrast to other Tunisian towns (excepting Mahdia) Kairouan is purely Arab in origin; capital of the Aglabite dynasty during the 9th century; now an important Muslim holy city; monuments: Great Mosque, the oldest in the Maghreb; carpet museum; 7 km S is the archaeological site of Reqqada.

Kaiserslautern *kī'zerz-low-tern*, 49 30N 7 43E, pop(1983) 98,700, industrial city in Rheinland-Pfalz (Rhineland-Palatinate) prov, W Germany; 69 km NW of Karlsruhe; situated at the intersection of important traffic routes, it is the cultural and economic centre of the Palatinate Forest; university (1975); railway; economy: motor vehicles, textiles, sewing machines, leatherworking, woodworking.

Kajaani *kah'yah-nee*, KAJANA *ki'ah-nah* (Swed), 64 17N 27 46E, pop(1982) 35,320, town in Oulu prov, central Finland; on the Kajaanjoki just SE of Oulujärvi (L Oulu); established in 1651; hydroelectric power station, railway; airport; economy: talc.

Kajang *kah jang'*, 2 59N 101 46E, pop(1980) 29,301, town in Selangor state, W Peninsular Malaysia, SE Asia; S of Kuala Lumpur; railway.

Kaka'du, national park in N Northern Territory, Australia; bordered N by the Van Diemen Gulf; in Arnhem Land, E of Darwin between the South and East Alligator rivers; includes the Jim Jim and Twin falls; the landscape is the product of continual weather erosion over the past 2 million years; Aboriginal rock paintings found here are 18,000 years old; area 6,144 sq km; established in 1979.

Kakame'ga, 0 17N 34 47E, pop(1979) 50,000, administrative centre of SE Western prov, Kenya, E Africa; 45 km N of Kisumu; centre of gold discovery in 1930; railway; economy: farming and trading centre.

Kakogawa *ka-kō-ga'wa*, 34 49N 134 52E, pop(1980) 212,233, city in Hyōgo prefecture, Kinki region, S Honshū island, Japan; 14 km ESE of Himeji; railway.

Kakopetria *ka-ko-pe'tree-a*, 34 59N 32 54E, summer resort town in Nicosia dist, Cyprus; monuments: tomb of Archbishop Makarios III; nearby are the Byzantine churches of Lagoudhera and Stavros tou Ayiasmati.

Kal'a, El, national park in Algeria; area 784 sq km; established in 1983.

Kalaha'ri, desert region of Africa; situated in SW Botswana, SE Namibia and N Cape Prov, South Africa; area c.260,000 sq km; for the most part the Kalahari has an elevation of between 850 and 1,000 m above sea-level; situated between the Orange and Zambezi rivers; though it is called a desert the Kalahari is almost entirely covered with grass and woodland, bare sand only appearing in the extreme SW where the annual rainfall falls below 200 mm; in the N rainfall peaks at over 500 mm in the Ngamiland dist of Botswana (including the Okavango delta) and gives rises to savannah woodland; annual average rainfall over the whole area is generally between 150 and 500 mm; frosts are not uncommon during the dry season.

Kalahari Gemsbok, semi-desert national park in Cape prov, South Africa, 320 km N of Upington, between the Auob and Nossob rivers, bordering Namibia; noted for its migrating game, particularly the gemsbok (oryx) antelope; area 9,591 sq km; established in 1931; facilities include 3 rest camps.

Kalámai *kal-ah'ma*, CALAMATA, KALAMÁTA (Eng), 37 02N 22 07E, pop(1981) 43,235, capital town of Messinía nome (dept), Pelopónnisos region, SW Greece; on the S coast of the island, 128 km SSE of Patrai; airfield; rail terminus; economy: cigarettes, flour milling, trade in fruit and olive oil; event: Navy Week (June-July).

Kalamazoo', 42 17N 85 35W, pop(1980) 79,722, county seat of Kalamazoo county, SW Michigan, United States; on the R Kalamazoo, 75 km S of Grand Rapids; founded in 1829, achieving city status in 1884; university (1903); railway; economy: car assembly, machinery, paper, pharmaceuticals, medical equipment.

Kalene Hill *ka-lay'nay*, 11 10S 24 12E, town in North-Western prov, Zambia, S central Africa; in the N extremity of the prov, close to the source of the Zambezi river.

Kalgoor'lie, KALGOORLIE-BOULDER, 30 49S 121 29E, pop(1981) 19,848, gold-mining town in South Eastern stat div, Western Australia, Australia; in the middle of infertile deserts and salt lakes, 550 km E of Perth; gold was discovered here in 1887-88; 60% of Australia's gold is mined in the suburb of Boulder at the Hainault gold mine; the towns of Kalgoorlie and Boulder amalgamated in 1966; the town's water supply comes from the Mundaring Weir near Perth; between Kalgoorlie and Boulder lies the 'Golden Mile', a square mile of ground, rich in gold; a flying doctor centre; railway; airfield.

Kalimantan Berat *kal-e-man'tan*, WEST KALIMANTAN, WEST BORNEO, province of Indonesia, in W Borneo; pop(1980) 2,986,068; area 146,760 sq km; capital Pontianak; mountainous in NE; watered by R Kapuas; economy: timber, pepper, copra, rubber, coffee, diamonds, gold.

Kalimantan Selatan, SOUTH KALIMANTAN, SOUTH BORNEO, province of Indonesia, in S Borneo; pop(1980) 2,064,649; area 37,660 sq km; capital Banjarmasin; rises to 1,892 m at Gunung Besar in the NE; watered by the R Barito; economy: timber, coal, rubber, iron, diamonds, gold.

Kalimantan Tengah, CENTRAL KALIMANTAN, CENTRAL BORNEO, province of Indonesia, in central Borneo; pop(1980) 954,353; area 152,600 sq km; capital Palangkaraya; mountainous to the N; watered by rivers flowing S to the Java Sea; economy: timber, coal, rubber, sugar, diamonds, gold.

Kalimantan Timur, EAST KALIMANTAN, EAST BORNEO, province of Indonesia, in E Borneo; pop(1980) 1,218,016; area 202,440 sq km; capital Samarinda; mountainous in W and NW; rivers flow SE to the Makassar Strait; economy: rattan, oil (Attaka, Tunu, Bekapai and Handil fields), coffee, copra, pepper, coal, timber.

Kálimnos *kah'leem-nos*, CALINO (Ital), CALYMNA (anc), 36 57N 26 59E, pop(1981) 10,118, port town in Sporádhes nome (dept), Aegean Islands, Greece; on the S coast of Kálimnos I; economy: sponge-fishing and processing; events: departure of the sponge divers (May); Navy Week (June-July).

Kálimnos, island of the Sporádhes, Greece, in the S Aegean Sea, N of Kós I; area 111 sq km; pop(1981) 14,295.

Kalinin *ka-lyee'nyin*, formerly TVER, 56 55N 35 55E, pop(1983) 433,000, river port capital city of Kalininskaya oblast, central European Rossiyskaya, Soviet Union; on the R Volga; established in the 12th century as a fort; Mikhail Kalinin (1875-1946), who played an important role in establishing Soviet rule in central Asia and was

Soviet president until 1946, was born in this region; centre of a flax-growing region; university (1971); railway; economy: printing, nuclear power generation, manufacture of chemicals, cotton, rolling stock, and textile machinery; monuments: White Trinity church (1563-64), Transfiguration cathedral (1689-96), 16th-c Convent of the Nativity.

Kaliningrad *ka-lyee'nyin-grat*, formerly KÖNIGSBERG (Ger), 54 40N 20 30E, pop(1983) 374,000, seaport capital of Kaliningradskaya oblast, W European Rossiyskaya, Soviet Union; on the R Pregel at the point where it flows into the Vistula Lagoon, an inlet of the Baltic Sea; founded in 1255 as a fortress; renamed in 1946 after E Prussia was ceded to Russia; university (1967); railway; airfield; a deep-water channel links it with the Baltic Sea at the port of Baltiysk; economy: machine building, metalworking, manufacture of paper and cellulose.

Kalisz *kal-eesh'*, voivodship in central Poland; traversed S-N by R Warta; pop(1983) 686,000; area 6,512 sq km; capital Kalisz; chief towns include Ostrów Wielkopolski, Krotoszyn and Jarocin.

Kalisz, KALISH (Rus), CALISIA (anc), 51 46N 18 02E, pop(1983) 102,900, industrial capital of Kalisz voivodship, central Poland; on R Prosna; described by Ptolemy in 2nd century as a trading settlement on the amber route from S Europe to the Baltic; railway; economy: transport equipment, textiles, pianos; monuments: 19th-c Franciscan monastery, collegiate church (1790), church of St Nicholas, Pulaski family mansion, regional museum, Reformation church; event: national drama festival in May.

Kalix älv *ka'liks elv*, river in Norrbotten county, N Sweden; rises near Norwegian border WNW of Kiruna; flows SE and S past Överkalix to discharge into the head of Gulf of Bothnia at Kalix; length 430 km; many rapids.

Kallavesi *kal-a-vay'si*, ISO KALLA (Swed), L KALLA (Eng), lake in the Finnish Lake Plateau of SE Finland; area 900 sq km; length 50 km; width 1-10 km; the 4th largest lake in Finland; the town of Kuopio is on the W shore.

Kal'mar, a county of SE Sweden, bounded on the E by the Kalmarsund (Kalmar Sound); includes the island of Öland; land area 11,171 sq km; pop(1983) 240,745; capital Kalmar; chief towns Nybro, Västervik and Oskarshamn.

Kalmar, CALMAR, 56 39N 16 20E, pop(1982) 53,497, capital town of Kalmar county, SE Sweden; on the Kalmarsund (Kalmar Sound) opposite Öland I; site of the Union of Kalmar which united Denmark, Sweden and Norway under a single monarchy (1397-1523); railway; economy: glass-making, foodstuffs, engineering, motor vehicles; monument: castle (early 11th-c).

Kalocsa *ko'lo-cho*, 46 32N 19 00E, pop(1984e) 20,000, town in Bács-Kiskun county, S Hungary; near the R Danube N of Baja; surrounding area noted for its embroidery; archbishopric; railway; monuments: Baroque palace (1760); library containing valuable incunabulae and facsimile editions; medieval cathedral rebuilt in 1736; museum of folk art, mobile sculpture by local sculptor Nicholas Schöffer; event: folklore festival every 3 years.

Kaluga *ku-loo'gu*, 54 31N 36 16E, pop(1983) 287,000, river port capital of Kaluga oblast, central European Rossiyskaya, Soviet Union; on the R Oka, 188 km SW of Moskva (Moscow); known since 1389 as a Muscovite outpost; railway; economy: machine building, manufacture of instruments, chemicals, and wood products.

Kalulushi *kah-loo-loo'shi*, 12 50S 28 03E, pop(1980) 59,213, mining town in Copperbelt prov, Zambia, S central Africa; NW of Ndola; part of the Kitwe conurbation.

Kalundborg *kah'loon-bor*, 55 42N 11 06E, pop(1981) 15,418, port in Vestsjælland county, W Sjælland (Zealand), Denmark; rail terminus; economy: foodstuffs; nearby is the burial-place of the Earl of Bothwell, husband of Mary Queen of Scots (died 1578 in captivity).

Kalutara *kal-u-tahr'a*, 6 35N 79 59E, pop(1981) 31,503, capital of Kalutara dist, Western prov, Sri Lanka; at the mouth of the R Kalu, on the coast of the Indian Ocean; connected NW by road to Colombo.

Kama *ka'mu*, chief left tributary of the R Volga, in E European Rossiyskaya, Soviet Union; rises in N Udmurtskaya ASSR just N of Kuligi, in the W foothills of the Ural'skiy Khrebet (Ural Mts); flows in a great loop N, E, then S before turning SW at Perm; discharges into the R Volga just S of Kazan'; length 1,805 km; drainage basin area 507,000 sq km; chief tributaries include the Zay, Syun', Tulva, Sylva, and Kolva rivers; the river is used for hydroelectric power generation.

Kamalia *ku-mahl'yu*, 30 40N 72 40E, pop(1981) 61,000, city in Punjab prov, Pakistan; N of R Ravi, NE of Multan; railway.

Kambia *kam'bi-a*, dist in Northern prov, Sierra Leone, W Africa; pop(1974) 155,341; area 3,108 sq km; capital Kambia.

Kamchatka *kum-chat'ku*, large peninsula in Kamchatskaya oblast, E Siberian Rossiyskaya, Soviet Union, separating the Sea of Okhotsk (W) from the Bering Sea (E); extends c.1,200 km S from the Koryakskiy Khrebet range to Mys Lopatka (Cape Lopatka), beyond which lie the Kuril'skiye Ostrova (Kuril Is); width 128-480 km; area 270,033 sq km; the Sredinnyy Khrebet range runs down the centre of the peninsula, bounded W by a broad, poorly drained coastal plain, and E by the valley lowland of the R Kamchatka; beyond the R Kamchatka, volcanic cones rise above lava plateaux; about a dozen of the 20-30 volcanic cones are presently active; in this volcanic zone is the highest peak on the peninsula, Klyuchevskaya Sopka (4,750 m); hot springs are abundant; the chief population centre is Petropavlovsk-Kamchatskiy on the SE coast; the peninsula was first sighted in 1697.

Kam'loops, 50 39N 120 24W, pop(1981) 64,048, town in S British Columbia, SW Canada; at the E end of Kamloops Lake, at the junction of the North and South Thompson rivers; founded in 1812 as Fort Thompson, a fur-trading post of the North West Co; later renamed Fort Kamloops; a village grew up during the Cariboo gold rush and was reached in 1885 by the Canadian Pacific Railroad; became a city in 1893; economy: fishing, hunting, tourism, lumber, cattle raising, horticulture; monument: Gold Rush museum; events: indoor rodeo in April; Indian Days festival in July.

Kamoke *kah'mō-kay*, 31 58N 74 15E, pop(1981) 71,000, city in Punjab prov, Pakistan; 18 km S of Gujranwala; railway; economy: trade in grain and rice.

Kamp, river in N Austria, rises near NW border of Niederösterreich state, flowing E and S past Zwettl Stadt to meet the R Danube E of Krems; length 153 km.

Kampala *kam-pa'la*, 0 19N 32 35E, pop(1983e) 454,974, capital of Uganda, E Africa; built on 7 hills close to the N shore of L Victoria in North Buganda prov; capital since 1963; university (1922); railway link to Nairobi; airport (Entebbe, 25 km); economy: banking, administration, fruit and vegetable trade, tea blending and packing, brewing, textiles, coffee, petrol depot.

Kampar', 4 17N 101 08E, pop(1980) 24,626, town in Perak state, W Peninsular Malaysia, SE Asia; at the foot of the Bujang Melaka, in the Kinta Valley, 39 km S of Ipoh; railway; economy: tin.

Kam'pen, 52 33N 5 53E, pop(1984e) 31,944, industrial city in W Overijssel prov, East Netherlands; on the left bank of the R Ijssel, 4 km upstream from its estuary into the Ijsselmeer; the town developed around a 12th-c fortress; noted for its theological and military colleges; tourists are attracted by a yacht harbour and by the picturesque Old Town; economy: foodstuffs, shipbuilding, timber, agricultural machinery, building materials; monuments: 14th-c town hall, restored in 1543; Gothic church (1369).

Kampot *kam-pot*, province in S Cambodia; pop(1981) 337,879; bounded S by the Gulf of Thailand, NW by Koh Kong prov, N by Kompong Speu prov and E by Takeo prov; crossed by the St Kos Sla river, upon which the port of Kampot is found; centre of Cambodia's pepper growing.

Kananga *ka-nang'ga*, LULUABOURG, 5 53S 22 26E,

pop(1976e) 704,211, capital of Kasai Occidental region, W central Zaire, central Africa; on the R Lulua, 115 km SE of Luebo; there was a mutiny here in 1895 by Congo Free State troops; railway; airfield.

Kanazawa *ka-na'za-wa*, 36 35N 136 38E, pop(1980) 417,684, capital of Ishikawa prefecture, Chūbu region, Japan; on the W coast of Honshū I, on the Sea of Japan; university (1949); became a prosperous city in the 17-19th centuries as the seat of the Maeda family; railway; economy: silk weaving, lacquer work, wood carving; monuments: 3 km from the city are the 18th-c landscape gardens of Kenroku-en, with miniature mountains, waterfalls, streams, 2 large pools and an 18th-c tea house.

Kāndāhār *kun-du-har'*, prov in S Afghanistan; bounded to the S and SE by Pakistan; pop(1984e) 625,101; area 47,676 sq km; capital Kāndāhār; crossed by the R Dori.

Kāndāhār, 31 36N 65 47E, pop(1984e) 203,177, capital of Kāndāhār prov, S Afghanistan; linked to Herāt to the NW and Kābul in the NE by main road; located on the ancient trade routes of central Asia and so was fought over by India and Persia; capital of Afghanistan between 1748 and 1773; the British occupied the city during the First Afghan War (1839-42) and from 1879 to 1881; airfield; economy: woollen cloth, silk and felt are manufactured; market for sheep, wool, grain, tobacco, fresh and dried fruits.

Kandal *kan-dal*, province in S Cambodia; pop(1981) 706,000; crossed by the Tonlé Sap river and Fleuve Bassac; chief town Ta Khmau.

Kandi *kan-dee'*, 11 05N 2 59E, pop(1979) 31,000, town in Borgou prov, NE Benin, W Africa; 520 km N of Porto Novo; railway.

Kandy *kan'dee*, CITY OF THE FIVE HILLS, 7 17N 80 40E pop(1981) 97,872, capital of Kandy dist, Central prov, Sri Lanka; looped by Sri Lanka's largest river, the Mahaweli; linked SW by road to Colombo (116 km); a royal city until 1815, when the last Kandyan king, Sri Wickrema Rajasinghe, was captured by the British; focal point of the Buddhist Sinhalese culture; monument: Dalada Maligawa (Temple of the Tooth), where the eye tooth of Buddha is enshrined; Peradeniya Botanical Gardens, 5 km SW of Kandy, were established as a pleasure garden for a Sinhala king; event: Esala Perahera, the highest religious festival in Sri Lanka, with a procession bearing the tooth casket accompanied by 80-100 elephants in July-Aug.

Ka'nem, prefecture in W Chad, N central Africa; pop(1979) 200,000; area 114,520 sq km; capital Mao; chief towns Moussoro, Rig Rig and Cheddra; economy: soda ash and trona mining, an oilfield is linked by pipeline to Laï in Tandjilé prefecture.

Kaneohe *kan-ee-ō'ee*, 21 25N 157 48W, pop(1980) 29,919, city in Honolulu county, Hawaii, United States; on Kaneohe Bay, Oahu I; a residential suburb N of Honolulu; nearby is a missile-tracking station.

Kanganda'la, national park in Angola, SW Africa; area 600 sq km; established in 1970.

Kangar *kahng'ahr*, 6 28N 100 10E, pop(1980) 12,949, capital of Perlis state, NW Peninsular Malaysia, SE Asia; on R Perlis, close to the Thailand border, 518 km NNW of Kuala Lumpur.

Kangaroo Island *kang-ge-roo'*, sparsely populated island off the coast of South Australia in the Southern Ocean; SW of Adelaide; area 4,350 sq km; chief town Kingscote; ferries to Adelaide and Port Lincoln; W is the 736 sq km Flinders Chase national park, established in 1919.

Kangchenjunga or **Kanchenjunga** *kan-chen-joong'ga*, GANGCHHENDZÖNGA (Tibetan), KUMBHKARAN LUNGUR (Nepali), 27 42N 88 09E, mountain on the border between Nepal and the Sikkim state of India, in the Himalayan range of central Asia; third highest mountain in the world; comprises 5 peaks, the highest of which is 8,586 m; considered geologically as the main axis of the Himalayan range; Zemu glacier on the E slope reaches down into Sikkim state; the Charles Evans British Expedition scaled the mountain in 1955 but turned back a few metres from the summit at the request of the Sikkim authorities.

Kanggye *kang-gyay*, 40 48N 126 38E, capital of Chagang prov, N North Korea.

KaNgwa'ne, national state or non-independent black homeland in Natal prov, South Africa; pop(1985) 392,782; achieved self-governing status in 1971; chief town Eerstehoek.

Kangwon *kang-wun*, GANGWEON-DO, mountainous prov in NE Korea; bordered N by North Korea, E by the Sea of Japan; rises to 1,577 m at Kyebang san peak; pop(1984) 1,816,365; area 16,894 sq km; capital Ch'unch'ŏn.

Kangwŏn, prov in SE North Korea; bordered S by Korea, E by the Sea of Japan and the Choson-Man bay; capital Wŏnsan.

Kanin, Poluostrov *ka'nyin*, peninsula in Arkhangel'skaya oblast, N European Rossiyskaya, Soviet Union, projecting N into the Barents Sea; separates the Beloye More (White Sea) (W) from Chëshskaya Guba (Chesha Bay) (E); the NW point is Cape Kanin Nos; tundra lowland in the S gives way to hilly terrain in the N.

Kankaanpää *kan-kahn'pah*, 63 13N 22 53E, pop(1982) 13,575, town in N Turku-Pori prov, SW Finland; established in 1967.

Kankakee' (Mohican, 'wolf land'), 41 07N 87 52W, pop(1980) 30,141, county seat of Kankakee county, E Illinois, United States; on the R Kankakee, 51 km SSE of Joliet; railway; economy: farm machinery, furniture, trade in grain and livestock.

Kankan *kan-kan'*, 10 22N 9 11W, pop(1972) 85,310, capital of Haute-Guinée region, E Guinea, W Africa; on the R Milo, 280 km SW of Bamako (Mali); railway terminus.

Kano *ka'nō*, state in N Nigeria, pop(1982e) 9,208,900; area 43,285 sq km; capital Kano; chief towns Hadejia, Kazaure, Gumel, Gwarzo and Rano; came under Fulah rule at the beginning of the 19th century, then under British control in 1903; economy: large-scale agricultural activity, based on groundnuts, tobacco and livestock.

Kano, 12 00N 8 31E, pop(1981e) 545,000, capital of Kano state, N Nigeria, W Africa; 1,130 km NE of Lagos; an ancient Hausa settlement, the modern city was founded in the 19th century; some buildings of Moorish design date from the 16th century; the city walls are 17.7 km long, 12 m thick at base and up to 12 m high; the city prospered under Fulah rule in the 19th century as a major terminus of trans-Saharan trade; university (1975); railway; airport; economy: food processing, brewing, textiles, leather, glass, metals and chemicals.

Kanpur *kahn'poor*, CAWNPORE, 26 35N 80 20E, pop(1981) 1,688,000, city in Uttar Pradesh state, N India; on the R Ganga (Ganges), 185 km NW of Allahabad; ceded to the British as a village in 1801; the entire British garrison including women and children were massacred during the Indian Mutiny of 1857; university (1966); airfield; linked by rail to Jhansi, Agra, Allahabad and Lucknow; economy: a major trade and industrial centre, producing chemicals, textiles and food products.

Kan'sas, state in central United States; bounded W by Colorado, N by Nebraska, E by Missouri, and S by Oklahoma; the R Missouri forms the upper part of the E state border; the R Republican and R Smoky Hill join in N central Kansas to form the R Kansas, which flows E to meet the R Missouri at Kansas City; R Arkansas flows E from the W border, across the S state, and then S into Oklahoma; the highest point is Mt Sunflower (1,227 m); the land rises steadily from the prairies in the E to the semi-arid high plains in the W; the state is the nation's leading wheat producer; other major crops are grain sorghum, corn and hay; cattle generate the single largest agricultural income; chief manufactures are aircraft, chemicals, processed foods, machinery, petroleum and natural gas; part of the Louisiana Purchase in 1803; in 1854-56 there was virtual civil war in the state over whether it should be a free or slave state; admitted to the Union as a free state in 1861; the 'Sunflower State'; pop(1980) 2,363,679; area 212,623 sq km; 34th state admitted to the Union, in 1861; capital Topeka; other major cities are Wichita and Kansas City; the state is divided into 105 counties:

County	area (sq km)	pop(1980)
Allen	1,313	15,654
Anderson	1,518	8,749
Atchison	1,121	18,397
Barber	2,954	6,548
Barton	2,327	31,343
Bourbon	1,659	15,969
Brown	1,487	11,955
Butler	3,752	44,782
Chase	2,020	3,309
Chautauqua	1,674	5,016
Cherokee	1,534	22,304
Cheyenne	2,655	3,678
Clark	2,535	2,599
Clay	1,643	9,802
Cloud	1,867	12,494
Coffey	1,599	9,370
Comanche	2,051	2,554
Cowley	2,933	36,824
Crawford	1,547	37,916
Decatur	2,324	4,509
Dickinson	2,215	20,175
Doniphan	1,009	9,268
Douglas	1,199	67,640
Edwards	1,612	4,271
Elk	1,690	3,918
Ellis	2,340	26,098
Ellsworth	1,864	6,640
Finney	3,385	23,825
Ford	2,857	24,315
Franklin	1,500	22,062
Geary	980	29,852
Gove	2,787	3,726
Graham	2,335	3,995
Grant	1,495	6,977
Gray	2,257	5,138
Greeley	2,023	1,845
Greenwood	2,951	8,764
Hamilton	2,595	2,514
Harper	2,085	7,778
Harvey	1,404	30,531
Haskell	1,503	3,814
Hodgeman	2,236	2,269
Jackson	1,711	11,644
Jefferson	1,391	15,207
Jewell	2,366	5,241
Johnson	1,243	270,269
Kearny	2,257	3,435
Kingman	2,249	8,960
Kiowa	1,880	4,046
Labette	1,698	25,682
Lane	1,864	2,472
Leavenworth	1,204	54,809
Lincoln	1,872	4,145
Linn	1,563	8,234
Logan	2,790	3,478
Lyon	2,194	35,108
Marion	2,454	13,522
Marshall	2,283	12,787
McPherson	2,340	26,855
Meade	2,545	4,788
Miami	1,534	21,618
Mitchell	1,864	8,117
Montgomery	1,680	42,281
Morris	1,802	6,419
Morton	1,901	3,454
Nemaha	1,869	11,211
Neosho	1,498	18,967
Ness	2,792	4,498
Norton	2,270	6,689
Osage	1,807	15,319
Osborne	2,293	5,959
Ottawa	1,875	5,971
Pawnee	1,963	8,065
Phillips	2,306	7,406
Pottawatomie	2,153	14,782
Pratt	1,911	10,275
Rawlins	2,779	4,105
Reno	3,273	64,983
Republic	1,869	7,569
Rice	1,893	11,900
Riley	1,542	63,505
Rooks	2,309	7,006
Rush	1,867	4,516
Russell	2,259	8,868
Saline	1,875	48,905
Scott	1,867	5,782
Sedgwick	2,618	366,531
Seward	1,664	17,071
Shawnee	1,427	154,916
Sheridan	2,330	3,544
Sherman	2,748	7,759
Smith	2,332	5,947
Stafford	2,049	5,694
Stanton	1,771	2,339
Stevens	1,890	4,736
Sumner	3,076	24,928
Thomas	2,795	8,451
Trego	2,314	4,165
Wabaunsee	2,072	6,867
Wallace	2,376	2,045
Washington	2,335	8,543
Wichita	1,869	3,041
Wilson	1,495	12,128
Woodson	1,295	4,600
Wyandotte	387	172,335

Kansas City, 39 07N 94 38W, pop(1980) 161,087, county seat of Wyandotte county, E Kansas, United States; port at the junction of the Kansas and Missouri rivers, adjacent to its sister city, Kansas City, Missouri; settled by Wyandotte Indians in 1843; sold to the US government in 1855 and settled by people of European origin in 1857; railway; economy: together with its sister city, a major commercial and industrial centre; market for surrounding agricultural region; stockyards, grain elevators; manufactures automobiles, metal products, processed foods, machinery and petroleum; monument: Agricultural Hall of Fame.

Kansas City, 39 06N 94 35W, pop(1980) 448,159, river port city in Jackson county, W Missouri, United States; on the S bank of the R Missouri where it follows the Kansas state border, adjacent to its sister city, Kansas City, Kansas; developed around settlements at Westport and Westport Landing in the 1830s; the Town of Kansas, which was laid out in 1838, expanded in the 1840s and was renamed the City of Kansas in 1853 and Kansas City in 1889; university (1929); railway; airport; economy: automobiles and parts, metal products, electronics, processed foods and machinery; oil refineries; railway shops; large stockyards and grain elevators; the nation's leading winter-wheat market; monuments: Nelson Art Gallery, Atkins Museum of Fine Arts.

Kansu, prov in N central China. See Gansu.

Kantchari *kan-cha'ree*, 12 37N 1 37E, town in E Burkina, W Africa; 112 km W of Niamey (Niger).

Kanto *kan-tō*, region in E Honshū island, Japan; bounded E by the Pacific Ocean, S by the Pacific and Tōkyo-wan Bay, W and NW by Chūbu region and N by Tōhoku region; low lying, densely populated region, crossed by several rivers; pop(1980) 34,896,000; area 32,309 sq km; Kanto region is divided into 7 prefectures as follows:

Prefecture	area (sq km)	pop(1980)
Chiba	5,115	4,735,000
Gumma	6,356	1,849,000
Ibaraki	6,090	2,558,000

contd

Prefecture	*area (sq km)*	*pop(1980)*
Kanagawa	2,391	6,924,000
Saitama	3,799	5,420,000
Tochigi	6,414	1,792,000
Tōkyō	2,145	11,618,000

Kanye *ka'nyay*, 24 59S 25 19E, pop(1980) 22,000, capital of Ngwaketze dist, Botswana, S Africa; 97 km NNW of Mafeking; airfield.

Kao-hsiung *'gow-shyoong*, county in SW Taiwan; area 2,792.6 sq km; pop(1982e) 1,057,725.

Kao-hsiung, TAKAO *ta-ka'ō* (Jap), 22 36N 120 17E, pop(1982e) 1,250,000, special municipality and seaport in SW Taiwan; on the SW coast, facing the Taiwan Haixia (Taiwan Strait); enjoys the status of a province; area 153 sq km; the largest seaport and industrial city in Taiwan and the world's largest shipbreaking centre; the site of the world's 2nd largest dry dock and the world's 5th largest container-handling port; the Kao-hsuing harbour at Nantze has been designated an export processing zone; the municipality is divided into 11 dists; railway; airport; economy: seaport; industry; ship-breaking; dry dock; the Cheng Ching ('clear clear') Lake resort is adjacent to the city; monument: to the S of Kao-hsiung in Kenting National Park is Fo Kuang Shan (Buddha Torch Mountain), on top of which is a 25 m tall statue of Buddha set on a 12 m high pedestal; the statue is flanked by 480 other images, each of them 1.8 m high.

Kaolack *kow'lak*, region in W Senegal, W Africa; part of Sine Saloum region until 1984; there are extensive salt marshes; capital Kaolack; monuments: megalithic stone circles near the Bao Bolong river.

Kaolack, 14 09N 16 08W, river port in W Senegal, W Africa; on the R Saloum, 153 km ESE of Dakar; capital of the Kaolack region and centre of Islam's Tidjana sect; railway; economy: cashew nuts, peanuts, canning, market gardening.

Kaolan, capital of Gansu prov, N central China. See Lanzhou.

Kapadok'ya, CAPPADOCIA *kap-e-dō'shee-a* (Eng), mountainous region of central Turkey; between Ankara and Malataya, lying between the Black Sea and the Taurus Mts; in ancient times Caesarea Mazaca (Kayseri) was its chief city at the heart of a Hittite empire; noted for its eroded landscape features and cave dwellings in the Göreme valley; Nevşehir is the largest town in the region.

Kapfenberg *kap'fan-berk*, 47 27N 15 18E, pop(1981) 25,716, town in Kärnten state, SE Austria; on the R Mur, 54 km NNW of Graz.

Kāpīsā *ku'pee-sa*, prov in NE Afghanistan; pop(1984e) 271,915; area 1,871 sq km; capital Mahmūd-e 'Eraqi.

Kaposvár *ko'posh-var'*, 46 25N 17 47E, pop(1984e) 74,000, capital of Somogy county, SW Hungary; on R Kapos, NW of Pécs; railway; economy: fruit, wine and tobacco trade, textiles.

Kapstad, city in South Africa. See Cape Town.

Ka'ra, LAMA-KARA, 9 36N 1 18E, chief town of De la Kara region, NE Togo, W Africa; 65 km N of Sokodé.

Kara Sea, KARASKOYE MORE (Rus), Arctic Sea, lying between Novaya Zemlya island and mainland USSR; separated from the Laptev Sea by Severnaya Zemlya; a shallow sea, dangerous for navigation owing to pack-ice; main arms: Baydaratskaya Guba, Obskaya Guba, Yeniseyskiy Zaliv, Gydanskaya Guba and Pyasinskiy Zaliv; major rivers: Ob', Pur, Yenisey, Pyasina and Taz.

Karachi *ka-rah'chee*, 24 51N 67 02E, pop(1981) 5,103,000; provincial capital of Sind prov, SE Pakistan; former capital of Pakistan; on the Arabian Sea coast, NW of the mouths of the Indus; 148 km SW of Hyderabad; Pakistan's principal seaport; founded in the 18th century; under British rule from 1843; beaches at Sandspit, Paradise Point and Clifton; university (1951); railway; airport; economy: exports cotton, grain, skins, wool; manufactures chemicals, textiles, plastics; shipbuilding; monuments: tomb of Quaid-i-Azam, Mohammad Ali Jinnah, founder of Pakistan; national museum.

Karadeniz Boğazi *kahr-e-de-neez' bō-gah-zee'*, BOSPORUS *bos'pu-rus* (Eng), narrow strait separating European from Asiatic Turkey and connecting the Black Sea and the Sea of Marmara; length 32 km; minimum width 640 m; at its narrowest point are two famous castles, Anadolu Hisar (1390) on the Asian side, and Rumeli Hisar (1452) on the European side; one of the world's longest suspension bridges (1,075 m) spans the strait at İstanbul; this strait plus the Çanakkale Boğazi (Dardanelles) at the W end of the Sea of Marmara have long been of great strategic importance.

Karafuto, island in the Sea of Okhotsk, E Soviet Union. See Sakhalin.

Karaganda *ku-ru-gun-da'*, 49 50N 73 10E, pop(1983) 600,000, capital city of Karagandinskaya oblast, Kazakhskaya SSR, Soviet Union; founded in 1857 as a copper-mining settlement; it is now the mining centre of the republic, with 50 coal-mining settlements scattered around the central part of the city; university (1972); airport; a canal connects Karaganda with the R Irtysh; railway junction; economy: coal, power, metallurgy, machinery.

Karaikal', district of Pondicherry union territory, E India; an enclave in Tamil Nadu state on the Coromandel coast, 240 km S of Madras; area 160 sq km; pop(1981) 120,010; held by France until 1954.

Karaj *kar-aj'*, 35 04N 51 00E, pop(1983) 526,272, town in Karaj dist, Tehrān, N Iran; 40 km WNW of Tehrān; on R Karaj, in S foothills of the Elburz Mts; agricultural market; railway.

Karak, capital town of Al Karak governorate, East Bank, W central Jordan, 80 km SSW of Amman; alt 1,006 m.

Karak, Al *el ke-rak'*, governorate (*muhafaza*) of the East Bank, central Jordan; bounded NW by the Dead Sea and E by Saudi Arabia; capital Karak.

Karaköse *ka-ra'ku-se*, AĞRI, formerly KARAKILISSE, 39 44N 43 04E, pop(1980) 40,532, capital of Ağri prov, E Turkey; on R Murat, E of Erzurum.

Karakumy, Peski, KARA-KUM *ku-ra-koom'*, extensive desert in Turkmenskaya SSR, S Soviet Union; bounded S by the Khrebet Kopet-Dag range, and N and E by the R Amudar'ya; length 960 km; width 320-400 km; traversed (SE) by the Trans-Caspian railway.

Karamoja *ka-ra-mō'ja*, prov of NE Uganda, E Africa; bounded N by Sudan; severe drought in 1980 caused widespread famine; Kidepo Valley national park is located in this area.

Karankasso *ka-ran-ka'sō*, 10 51N 3 53W, town in SW Burkina, W Africa; SE of Bobo Dioulasso.

Karawanken Alps *kar-a-vang'ken*, KARAVANKE (Yug), mountain range of the E Alps on the border between Yugoslavia and Austria, mostly in the Austrian state of Kärnten; an extension of the Carnic Alps; mostly limestone; the highest peak is Hochstuhl (2,238 m); the road from Klagenfurt to Ljubljana runs through the Loibl Tunnel.

Karbalā' *kar'ba-la*, governorate in W Iraq; bounded SW by Saudi Arabia; pop(1977) 269,822; area 52,856 sq km; capital Karbalā'; the R Euphrates lowland merges into desert in the SW.

Karcag *kor'tsog*, 47 19N 20 57E, pop(1984e) 25,000, town in Szolnok county, E central Hungary; 56 km NE of Szolnok; railway; economy: grain, fruit, vegetable and livestock trade.

Kardhítsa *kar-theet'sa*, KARDITSA (Eng), nome (dept) of Thessalía region, central Greece; pop(1981) 124,930; area 2,636 sq km; capital Kardhítsa.

Kardhítsa, 39 22N 21 55E, pop(1981) 27,291, agricultural market town and capital of Kardhítsa nome (dept), Thessalía region, central Greece; in the E foothills of the Píndhos Mts; railway; event: Karaiskakia Festival (May).

Kardzali, okrug (prov) in Bulgaria. See Kŭrdzhali.

Karelia, autonomous soviet socialist republic of the Soviet Union. See Karel'skaya.

Karel'skaya, KARELIA (Eng), an autonomous soviet socialist republic of Rossiyskaya, NW Soviet Union; bounded W by Finland and E by the Beloye More (White Sea); in medieval times an independent state with strong Finnish associations; as represented in the folk tales of the epic *Kalevala*; the area came under Swedish domination in the 17th century and in 1721 was annexed by Russia; constituted as a soviet socialist republic in 1923, the territory was extended during World War II when the Finnish-Soviet border was altered.

Karen, state in E Burma. See Kawthulei.

Kariba *ka-ree'ba*, 16 32S 28 50E, pop(1982) 124,000, town in Mashonaland West prov, Zimbabwe, S Africa; 80 km SE of Lusaka (Zambia); a rapidly growing town which was originally a construction camp for the Kariba Dam on the R Zambezi; crocodile farm; airfield.

Kariba, Lake, lake on Zimbabwe-Zambia frontier; area 5,180 sq km; 282 km long, up to 32 km wide with an average depth of 18 m; created by damming the R Zambezi in 1961; the lake's formation necessitated the removal of the Batonga people who believe that the river god Nyaminyami will destroy the dam and allow the river to flow free once again; a huge wildlife removal operation also took place with over 5,000 animals including 35 mammal species and 44 black rhinoceros being moved to the safety of the Matusaland national park; the lake provides a year-round water supply and electricity; the dam itself was 5 years in construction, is 128 m high, 528 m across at its base and 617 m across at its crest; it also serves as a bridge between Zimbabwe and Zambia; expanding town of Kariba at NE end and town of Binga near the SW end.

Karisim'bi, 1 32S 29 27E, dormant volcano in Virunga range, E central Africa; rising to 4,507 m on the Rwanda-Zaire frontier, it is the highest point of the range.

Karl Marx Stadt, county in S East Germany; pop(1981) 1,918,184; area 6,009 sq km; 2nd major industrial region of E Germany; economy: mechanical engineering (Plauen, Karl Marx Stadt), motor vehicles (Zwickau, Zschopau), textiles, electronics, carpets, toys (Seifen), musical instruments (Klingenthal), mining (Freiberg); 30% of the county is under forest; the Erzgebirge region is a major holiday and recreation area.

Karl Marx Stadt, CHEMNITZ (-1954), 50 50N 12 55E, pop(1982) 319,055, capital of Karl Marx Stadt county, S East Germany; on the R Chemnitz, at foot of the Erzgebirge Mts, SW of Dresden; college of technology; railway; economy: machine tools, machinery, chemicals, textiles, clothing.

Karleby, seaport in Finland. See Kokkola.

Karlovac *kar'lo-vats*, 45 30N 15 34E, pop(1981) 78,363, industrial town in N Hrvatska (Croatia) republic, Yugoslavia; near the junction of the Korana and Kupa rivers, 48 km SW of Zagreb; a former garrison town with the old town laid out to a rectangular plan; railway; industrial district at Banija; economy: chemicals, leather, timber, textiles, machinery, metallurgy.

Karlovy Vary *kar'lo-vi va-ri*, KARLSBAD (Ger), 50 14N 12 53E, pop(1984) 59,183, town in Západočeský region, Czech Socialist Republic, W Czechoslovakia; on R Ohre, W of Praha (Prague); famous health resort with hot alkaline springs; airport; railway; economy: kaolin, glass, footwear, mineral water.

Karlskoga *karl-skoo'ga*, 59 19N 14 33E, pop(1983) 35,952, industrial city in Örebro county, S central Sweden; 37 km W of Örebro; to the E of the town are the Bofors steelworks and rolling mills; the town received a municipal charter in 1940.

Karlskrona *karls-kroo'na*, 56 10N 15 35E, pop(1982) 59,589, seaport capital of Blekinge county, S Sweden; built on the mainland and five nearby islands in the Baltic Sea; excellent fortified harbour; principal Swedish naval base and fishing port; founded in 1680 by Charles XI; railway; economy: shipbuilding, plastics, construction of atomic reactors, manufacture of telephones and electric bulbs, fish-processing; monuments: shipping museum, Admiralty church (1685).

Karlsruhe *karls'roo-e*, dist of NW Baden-Württemberg prov, W Germany; pop(1983) 2,398,000; area 6,919 sq km; capital Karlsruhe.

Karlsruhe, 49 03N 8 23E, pop(1983) 270,300, capital of Karlsruhe dist, W Baden-Württemberg prov, W Germany; river port on the R Rhine in the NW foothills of the Schwarzwald (Black Forest), 56 km S of Mannheim; former capital of Baden; university (1825); railway; economy: oil refining, petrochemicals, machine tools, chemicals, tyres, textile and packaging machinery, precision engineering, defence equipment, rubber products, dairy produce; monument: palace (1752-85).

Karlstad', 59 24N 13 32E, pop(1982) 73,817, seaport and capital of Värmland county, SW Sweden; on N shore of L Vänern at mouth of R Klarälven; founded in 1584 by Charles IX; destroyed by fire 1865; scene of the signing of a treaty in 1905 ending the union of Sweden and Norway; see of a bishop; railway; economy: pulp, woodworking, machinery, textiles; monuments: cathedral (1723-30), bishop's house (1780).

Karmøy *kar'mu-u*, 59 15N 5 15E, pop(1980) 32,035, town on Karmøy I, off coast of N Rogaland county, SW Norway.

Karnataka, KANARA, state in SW India; pop(1981) 37,043,451; area 191,773 sq km; bounded W by the Arabian Sea; formed as Mysore under the States Reorganization Act of 1956, bringing the Kannada-speaking population of 5 states together; Kannada is the official language used in administration and is spoken by some 60% of the population; the state was renamed Karnataka in 1973; crossed by numerous rivers including the Karanja, Benithora, Bhima, Don, Krishna, Malprabha, Hagari, Gangavati, Varada, Tunga and the Kaveri; the state is divided into 4 divisions and 19 districts; a bicameral legislature comprises a 63-member Legislative Council and an elected 225-member Legislative Assembly; Bangalore is the state capital; agriculture employs more than 75% of the population, largely in the N area of the state known as *maidan* or plain country; chief crops are rice, jowar, and ragi, groundnuts, castor-seed, safflower, silk and cotton; the state grows 30% of the national ragi crop and 70% of the national coffee crop; 18% of the state is covered in forest, producing mainly sandalwood and bamboo; Karnataka is India's only source of gold and silver; there are also reserves of high-grade iron ore, manganese, limestone and chromite; the iron and steel industry is located at Bhadravati, while engineering and electronics industries are found at Bangalore; chemicals, textiles, cement, sugar and paper are also important manufactured products; sericulture is an important cottage industry; airfields are found at Bangalore, Mangalore and Belgaum; Mangalore is the state's chief deep-water port, while Karwar is a secondary intermediate port; the rail network converges on Bangalore in the S and on Hubli and Belgaum in the NW.

Karnische Alpen, mountain range on Austro-Italian frontier. See Carnic Alps.

Kärnten *kern'ten*, CARINTHIA *ka-rin'thi-a* (Eng), federal state of S Austria on the Italian and Yugoslav frontiers, comprising 10 dists and 121 communities; pop(1981) 536,727; area 9,533 sq km; capital Klagenfurt; surrounded by mountains; lakes include Wörther See, Ossiacher See, Millstätter See, Weissensee, and some 200 smaller ones; natural resources include timber and hydroelectric power; there are hydroelectric plants in the mountains (Malta, Reisseck-Kreuzeck) and on the R Drava; economy: there is mining of iron ore, lead, tungsten, zinc, and magnesite in the mountainous regions; world-famed sporting guns produced in the Ferlach area; a popular tourist attraction is the 'Carinthian Riviera', the region around the Wörther See.

Karonga *ka-rong'ga*, 9 54S 3 55E, lakeside port in Karonga dist, Northern region, N Malawi, S central Africa; situated near the N tip of L Nyasa; an Arab slave trading centre in the late 19th century; attacked by German forces in 1914; centre of the Ngonge people; N port of call for the L Nyasa steamer; airfield; economy: manufacture of honey, beeswax and propolis.

Karon'je, 2 10S 29 20E, highest mountain in Burundi, central Africa; height 2,685 m.

Karoo' ('dry'), dry steppe country in Cape prov, South Africa; descends from the Orange river down to the Cape; the Upper Karoo extends as far as the Great Escarpment at the Roggeveldberge, Nuweveldberge and Sneeuberge mts; the Great Karoo extends up to the Swartberge mts; the Little Karoo lies between the Swartberge and Langeberg ranges; the Karoo National Park, near Beaufort West, 480 km NE of Cape Town, covers 180 sq km of the arid Great Karoo and was established in 1979.

Kárpathos *kar'pa-thos*, SCARPANTO *skahr-pan'tō* (Ital), CARPATHUS (anc), mountainous, elongated island of the Sporádhes group, E Greece, in the Aegean Sea, between Ródhos (Rhodes) and the E end of Kríti (Crete); pop(1981) 4,645; area 301 sq km; length 48 km; length of coastline 160 km; rises to 1,216 m; capital Pigádhia on the SE coast; there are numerous bathing beaches, especially in the vicinity of Pigádhia.

Karpaty, Bilé *byel'eh kar-pat'i*, WHITE CARPATHIANS (Eng), steep-sided range in the Carpathian mountain group in central Czechoslovakia near the Polish frontier; rises to 970 m at Vel'ká Javorina.

Karpaty, Malé *mal'e kar-pat'i*, LITTLE CARPATHIANS (Eng), low lying range in the Carpathian mountain group, central Czechoslovakia; divides Czech Socialist Republic from the Slovak Socialist Republic; rises to 768 m at Záruby.

Karra'tha, 20 44S 116 52E, pop(1981) 8,341, town in Pilbara stat div, Western Australia, Australia; situated in Nickol Bay, E of Dampier; railway; airfield.

Kars, mountainous prov in NE Turkey, bounded E by the USSR; pop(1980) 700,238; area 18,557 sq km; capital Kars; economy: salt, textiles, carpets.

Karst, KRAS (Slov), CARSO (Ital), a barren, stony limestone plateau in the Dinaric Alps of NW Yugoslavia; extending about 80 km from the R Isonzo (NW) to the Kvarner Gulf (SE); notable caves at Postojna; geographers have come to use the term *karst* to describe limestone topography of this kind.

Karviná *kar'vin-ah*, 49 50N 18 30E, pop(1984) 77,654, town in Severomoravský region, Czech Socialist Republic, central Czechoslovakia; E of Ostrava; railway; economy: coal mining, chemicals, fertilizers.

Karwendelgebirge *kahr-ven'dul-gub-irg-u*, mountain range of Bayerische Alpen (Bavarian Alps) in Tirol, Austria, and W Germany; extending 32 km WNW from the R Inn at Schwaz to the German border at Scharnitz Pass; highest peak is the Birkkar; Isar river rises here.

Kasai Occidental *ka-sī'*, region in W central Zaire, central Africa; pop(1981e) 2,935,036; area 156,967 sq km; capital Kananga; chief towns include Luiza, Luebo, Ilebo (Port Francqui) and Tshikapa; a railway from Lusaka (Zambia) runs NW across the region past Kananga; major rivers include the Kasai, Sankuru and Lulua.

Kasai Oriental, region in S central Zaire, central Africa; pop(1981e) 2,336,951; area 168,216 sq km; capital Mbuji-Mayi; chief towns include Lomela, Lusambo and Gandajika; the R Sankuru flows across the SW corner of the region; a railway from Lusaka (Zambia) runs across the S of the region and into Kasai Occidental region.

Kasama *ka-sa'ma*, 10 10S 31 11E, pop(1980) 38,093, capital of Northern prov, Zambia, S central Africa; 645 km NE of Lusaka; alt 1,385 m; Roman Catholic cathedral; railway; airport.

Kasese *ka-say'say*, 0 10N 30 06E, town in Western prov, Uganda, E Africa; close to Uganda's W frontier with Zaire; railway; airfield; economy: petrol depot.

Kāshān *ka-shan'*, 33 59N 51 35E, pop(1983) 109,717, oasis town in Kāshān dist, Eşfahān, N central Iran; 176 km S of Tehrān; noted for its silk textiles, carpets, ceramics, copperware, and rose water; railway; monument: 13th-c minaret (45.8 m high).

Kashiwa *ka-shee-wa'*, 35 52N 139 49E, pop(1980) 239,198, city in Chiba prefecture, Kanto region, central Honshū island, Japan; NE of Tōkyo; railway.

Kashmir, region of N India. See Jammu-Kashmir.

Kásos, island of the Sporádhes, Greece, in the S Aegean Sea, SW of Kárpathos I; area 66 sq km; pop(1981) 1,184.

Kassala *ka'su-lu*, 15 24N 36 30E, pop(1973) 98,751, town in Eastern region, Sudan, NE Africa; on the intermittent R Gash, 420 km E of Khartoum; founded by the Egyptian military in 1834; held by the Madhists between 1885 and 1894 and from then till 1897 by the Italians; the town was again held by the Italians (1940-41) during World War II; railway; airfield.

Kassel *kah'sul*, N dist of Hessen (Hesse) prov, W Germany; pop(1983) 1,181,200; area 8,288 sq km; capital Kassel.

Kassel, 51 19N 9 32E, pop(1983) 190,400, cultural, economic and administrative centre of Kassel dist, Hessen (Hesse) prov, W Germany; on the R Fulda, 114 km WNW of Erfurt; an important traffic junction; university (1971); railway; economy: mineral salts, dairy products, natural gas and oil, locomotives and lorries, motor vehicles, machinery and tools, heavyweight and fine cloth, optical and geodetic instruments; Wilhelmshöhe, within the city limit, is a popular health resort noted for the Kneipp cure; monuments: Gallery of Old Masters in the Schloss Wilhelmshöhe; Bergpark Wilhelmshöhe, landscaped park; Schloss Wilhelmsthal (11 km NW), 18th-c summer palace of the Elector; events: Kurkonzerte in Wilhelmshöhe Park (May-Sept); documenta modern art exhibtion (July-Sept).

Kasserine *kahs'e-reen*, governorate in W Tunisia, N Africa; pop(1984) 297,959; capital Kasserine; there are reserves of zinc and lead.

Kastamonu *ka-sta'mo-noo*, densely forested prov in N Turkey, bounded N by the Black Sea; pop(1980) 450,946; area 13,108 sq km; capital Kastamonu; economy: fruit-growing, mohair, textiles, arsenic, hemp, coal, lignite, chromium, copper.

Kastoría *kas-to-ree'a*, nome (dept) of Makedhonia region, N Greece, on the Albanian and Yugoslav borders; pop(1981) 53,169; area 1,720 sq km; capital Kastoría.

Kastoría, 40 33N 21 15E, pop(1981) 17,133, capital town of Kastoría nome (dept), W Makedhonia region, N Greece; on a peninsula in L Kastoría; during the Turkish period it rose to prosperity as a centre of the fur trade; airfield; economy: wheat, tobacco and fur trade; monuments: there are no fewer than 72 churches and chapels, many of them with fine wall paintings; event: Fur Fair (March).

Kasugai *ka-soo-gī*, 35 15N 136 57E, pop(1980) 244,119, city in Aichi prefecture, Chūbu region, central Honshū island, Japan; N of Nagoya; railway.

Kasungu *ka-soong'goo*, national park in NW Central region, Malawi, SE Africa; an area of undulating grassland and woods; area 2,316 sq km; established in 1970; access from May to Dec.

Kasur *ku-soor'*, 31 07N 74 30E, pop(1981) 155,000, city in Punjab prov, Pakistan; 57 km SSE of Lahore; first settled by a Pathan colony; railway.

Kateríni *kaht-er-ee'nee*, KATERINE (Eng), 40 15N 22 30E, pop(1981) 39,895, agric market town and capital of Piería nome (dept), Makedhonia region, N Greece; on the main highway between Lárisa and Thessaloníki; railway; event: Olympus Festival (Aug).

Katherîna, Gebel *je-bel kath-e-ree'na*, MOUNT CATHERINE, 28 30N 33 57E, mountain in S Sinai governorate, NE Egypt; height 2,637 m; the highest point in Egypt; St Catherine's monastery (6th-c) is situated at an alt of 1,500 m on the massif.

Katherine, 14 29S 132 20E, pop(1981) 3,737, town in Northern Territory, Australia; 320 km SE of Darwin at the centre of the Never Never Land, on the Katherine river, at the meeting point of the Stuart Highway, N Australian railway and overland telegraph line; the centre of a beef cattle area; airfield; hot springs nearby; one of the town's main attractions is the Katherine Gorge; event: Katherine Show Day (July).

Katherine Gorge, national park in Northern Territory, N Australia; in the Never Never Land, 30 km NE of Katherine; spectacular gorges on the Katherine river, up to 60 m high; there are many Aboriginal rock drawings; area 1,803 sq km; the park was established in 1963.

Kathmandu or **Katmandu** *kat-man-doo'*, formerly KANTIPUR, 27 42N 85 19E, pop(1981) 195,260, capital and principal city of the Kingdom of Nepal, central Asia; 121 km from the Indian frontier in the Kathmandu Valley, at an alt of 1,373 m above sea level in the Himalayan foothills; lies on the ancient pilgrim and trade route from India to Tibet, China and Mongolia; when captured by the Gurkhas in 1768, it was made their capital and in the 18th century it became a British seat of administration; its present name is derived from Kasthamandap, which is a pagoda near Durbar Square; built in its present form by King Gunakama Deva in 723 AD, the city has many Hindu temples, Buddhist pagodas, and museums, including: the Machendra Nath Temple to the God of Rain; Hanuman Dhoka, the palace of the ancient kings of Nepal; Kasthamanadap, a wooden temple made from the timber of a single tree; Swayambhunath, one of the world's oldest Buddhist shrines (*chaitayas*); natural history museum; the Pashupatinath Temple is the centre of an annual pilgrimage.

Kati *ka-tee'*, 12 41N 8 04W, pop(1971) 13,800, town in Bamako region, SW Mali, W Africa; 10 km NW of Bamako; railway; economy: agriculture.

Katiola *kat-yō'la*, dept in N central Ivory Coast, W Africa; pop(1975) 77,875; area 9,420 sq km; capital Katiola; chief towns Niangbo, Niakaramandougou and Tafiré; the railway from Abidjan runs N through the dept.

Kat'mai, national park in SW Alaska, United States; situated on the S coast on the Shelikof Strait in the Aleutian Range; contains several lakes (including L Brooks and Naknek L) plus several volcanoes; rises to 2,331 m in Knife Peak; part of the park is known as the Valley of 10,000 Smokes, due to past volcanic activity; area 16,559 sq km; established in 1918.

Katoom'ba-Went'worth Falls, 33 42S 150 23E, pop(1981) 13,942, town in Sydney stat div, E New South Wales, Australia; W of Sydney and N of the Blue Mts National Park.

Katowice *kat-o-veet'say*, voivodship in S Poland; the Beskid Mts lie to the S; pop(1983) 3,854,000; area 6,650 sq km; capital Katowice; chief towns include Sosnowiec, Bytom, Gliwice, Zabrze, Tychy, Ruda Śląska and Chorzów; major industrial and coal mining region of Poland.

Katowice, KATTOWITZ (Ger), 50 15N 18 59E, pop(1983) 361,300, capital of Katowice voivodship, S Poland; centre of the Upper Silesian Industrial Region; university (1968); technical university (1945); airport; railway; economy: coal mining, foundries, zinc works, chemicals, optical work, mineral fertilizer; monuments: Kościuszko Park, with reconstructed old Silesian timber buildings; modern cathedral; monument to the Silesian Insurgents; event: drama festival of socialist countries in Nov.

Katrineholm *ka'treen-u-holm*, 58 59N 16 15E, pop(1983) 32,083, town in Södermanland county, SE Sweden; 112 km WSW of Stockholm; founded as a railway town in 1862; economy: light engineering.

Kattegat *kat'i-gat*, arm of the North Sea lying between Sweden and Denmark; connected to the North Sea by way of the Skagerrak and to the Baltic Sea by the Oresund; 225 km long and 64-160 km wide.

Kauai *kow'ī*, formerly KAIEIEWAHO *kah-ee-ay-ee-ay-wah-'hō*, island of the US state of Hawaii; in the Pacific Ocean, NW of Oahu I; forms Kauai county with Niihau I; area 1,692 sq km; pop(1980) 39,082; chief town Lihue; economy: tourism, sugar.

Kaufmann, mountain peak in S Soviet Union. See Lenina, Pik.

Kaunas *kow'nas*, formerly KOVNO, 54 52N 23 55E, pop(1983) 395,000, ancient town and river port in Litovskaya (Lithuania) SSR, W European Soviet Union; on the R Neman at its confluence with the R Vilnya; one of the ancient centres of artistic trades; railway; airfield; economy: chemicals, radio engineering, machine building, clothing, foodstuffs, metal and woodworking; monuments: 13-17th-c castle, early 17th-c Massalski Palace, Vytautas church (1400).

Kaválla *ku-vah'lu*, coastal nome (dept) of Makedhonia region, NE Greece, bounded S by the Aegean Sea; pop(1981) 135,218; area 2,111 sq km; capital Kaválla; includes Thásos I; produces tobacco.

Kaválla, 40 56N 24 23E, pop(1981) 56,375, major port and capital of Kaválla nome (dept), E Makedhonia region, NE Greece; N of Thásos I, on the highway between Thessaloníki and Komotiní; airfield; local ferry; economy: centre for the cotton and tobacco trades; monument: Byzantine castle; event: Navy Week (June-July).

Kavaratti *ku-vu-ru'tee*, 10 35N 72 35E, coral island and administrative centre of the Lakshadweep (Laccadive) island group, India; in the Arabian Sea.

Kavkaz *kuf-kaz'*, CAUCASUS *ko'ku-sus* (Eng), major mountain system in SW European Soviet Union; bounded S by Turkey and Iran, and comprising the Bol'shoy Kavkaz (Greater Caucasus) and the Malyy Kavkaz (Lesser Caucasus); the Bol'shoy Kavkaz is the main range and generally accepted as the physical boundary between Europe (N) and Asia (S); it extends c.1,120 km SE from the mouth of the R Kuban' on the SE shore of the Azovskoye More (Sea of Azov) to the Apsheronskiy Poluostrov (Apsheron Peninsula) on the Black Sea; it lies on the boundary between the Rossiyskaya (N) and the republics of Gruzinskaya (Georgia) and Azerbaydzhanskaya (S); constituent ranges (NW to SE) include the Bzybskiy Khrebet, Svanetskiy Khrebet, Leohkhumskiy Khrebet, Andiyskiy Khrebet, Bogosskiy Khrebet, and the Samurskiy Khrebet; in the W section is Mt El'brus (5,642 m), the highest point in the Kavkaz range; other peaks include Ushba (4,695 m), Dykh Tau (5,203 m), Shkhara (5,201 m), Tebulosmta (4,494 m), and Bazar-Dyuzi (4,480 m); in the E the range widens to over 160 km; several passes cross the Bol'shoy Kavkaz range, including the Klukhorskiy Pereval (2,786 m), Mamisonskiy Pereval (2,829 m), and the Krestovyy Pereval (2,388 m); rivers arising on the gentle N slopes include the Kuban', Kuma, Terek (one of whose tributaries, the Cherek, is fed by glaciers), and Sulak; on the steep S slopes are the sources of the Mzymta, Bzyb', Kodori, and Inguri rivers (short streams flowing into the Black Sea), the R Rioni, and the left affluents of the R Kura (Alazani, Iori); the Malyy Kavkaz lies parallel to the main range and is separated from it by the valley of the R Kura; it extends SE from the mouth of the R Rioni on the E coast of the Black Sea to the N Iranian frontier; constituent ranges are the Adzharo-Imeretinskiy Khrebet and the Trialetskiy Krebet (N), Shakhdagskiy Khrebet, and Zangezurskiy Khrebet (S); peaks include Dalidag (3,616 m), Ginaldag Gyamysh (3,724 m), and Tezhler (3,101 m); the Malyy Kavkaz consists of folded and block-faulted mountains of sedimentary and older igneous materials.

Kawagoe *ka-wag'ō-ay*, 35 55N 139 30E, pop(1980) 259,314, town in Saitama prefecture, Kanto region, E Honshū island, Japan; 37 km NW of Tōkyo; railway.

Kawaguchi *ka-wa-goo'chee*, 35 34N 138 44E, pop(1980) 379,366, town in Saitama prefecture, Kanto region, E Honshū island, Japan; N of Tōkyo; railway; economy: textiles, iron.

Kawasaki *ka-wa-sa'kee*, 35 32N 139 41E, pop(1980) 1,040,802, capital of Kanagawa prefecture, Kanto region, E Honshū island, Japan; to the S of Tōkyo, on the W shore of Tōkyo-wan Bay; in Keihin Industrial Zone; railway; economy: iron, steel, shipbuilding, machinery, chemicals, textiles.

Kawthoolay, state in E Burma. See Kawthulei.

Kawthulei *kaw-thoo-lay'*, KAWTHOOLAY, KAREN', state in E Burma; bordered E by Thailand along the R Salween; mountainous in the N and E; pop(1983) 1,057,505; capital Pa-an.

Ka'ya, 13 04N 1 09W, pop(1985e) 27,460, town in N

central Burkina, W Africa; 88 km NNE of Ouagadougou.

Kayah *kī'a*, small, mountainous state in E Burma; bordered in the W by Thailand; drained by the R Salween; pop(1983) 168,355; capital Loikaw.

Kayes *kayz*, region in W Mali, W Africa; pop(1971) 738,302; area 119,813 sq km; the R Falemé, a tributary of the R Sénégal, forms part of the western border with Senegal; the R Bafing enters the region from the S and flows through Lac de Manantali; the Bafing Dam was built after 1975 to supply water power; at Bafoulabé the Bafing joins the R Bakoye to form the R Sénégal; the Boucle de Baoulé National Park lies in the E; the Dakar-Koulikoro railway crosses the region NW-SE; capital Kayes; chief towns Nioro du Sahel, Bafoulabé, Kita, Yélimané, Kéniéba; economy: iron ore, marble and alabaster, gold and diamond mining, cement processing.

Kayes, 14 26N 11 28W, pop(1976) 44,736, river-port capital of Kayes region, W Mali, W Africa; on the Dakar-Koulikoro railway, 650 km E of Dakar; upper limit of navigation on the R Sénégal; airfield; economy: power plant.

Kayseri *kī'se-ree*, mountainous prov in central Turkey; pop(1980) 778,383; area 16,917 sq km; capital Kayseri.

Kayseri, CAESAREA MAZACA (anc), 38 42N 35 28E, pop(1980) 281,320, capital town of Kayseri prov, central Turkey; at the foot of Mt Erciyas; railway; airfield; economy: tiles, textiles, carpets.

Kazakhskaya, KAZAKHSTAN, KAZAKH, constituent republic of the Soviet Union, in the SW Asian part of the USSR, bounded E by China and W by the Caspian Sea; 2nd largest republic in the Soviet Union; a belt of steppeland in the N gives way southwards to desert (Peski Karakumy, Peski Kyzylkum); beyond the desert is a foothill zone where intensive irrigated farming is carried on; the lowest elevation in the USSR (132 m below sea-level) occurs in the Vpadina Karagiye salt marshes close to the E shore of the Caspian Sea; there are mountain ranges in the E and SE; chief rivers are the Irtysh, Syr-Dar'ya, Ural, Emba, and Ili; the Ozero Balkhash is the largest lake; pop(1983) 15,452,000; area 2,717,300 sq km; capital Alma-Ata; chief towns Karaganda, Semipalatinsk, Chimkent, and Petropavlovsk; economy: coal mining (largest coalfields are located at Karaganda and Ekibastuz), mining of iron ore, bauxite, copper, nickel, and complex ores; petroleum extraction (on the Mangyshlak Peninsula and in the vicinity of Emba) and refining; non-ferrous metallurgy; heavy engineering; chemicals; light industries (leatherwork, footwear); food processing; large hydroelectric power plants include the Ust'kamenogorsk and Bukhtarma plants on the Irtysh, the Chardar'ia on the Syr-Dar'ya, and the Kapchagai on the Ili; nomadic cattle rearing has been replaced by large-scale mechanized cultivation of grain in the N steppe region; chief crops include cotton, grapes and other fruits, grain; Kazakhskaya was made a constituent republic of the USSR in Dec 1936; the republic is divided into the 19 oblasts of Aktyubinskaya, Alma-Atinskaya, Chimkentskaya, Dzezkazgan, Dzhambulskaya, Gur'yevska, Karagandinskaya, Kokchetavskaya, Kustanayskaya, Kzyl-Ordinskaya, Mangyshlak, Pavlodarskaya, Semipalatinskaya, Severnaya Kazakhstanskaya, Taldy-Kurganskaya, Tselinograd, Turgayskaya, Uralskaya, Vostochno Kazakhstanskaya.

Kazakhstan, constituent republic of the Soviet Union. See Kazakhskaya.

Kazan' *ku-zan'yu*, 55 45N 49 10E, pop(1983) 1,031,000, river port capital of Tatarskaya ASSR, E European Rossiyskaya, Soviet Union; on the R Volga at its confluence with the R Kazanka; one of the most important industrial and cultural centres of the Volga region; founded in the 2nd half of the 13th century; Lenin spent his student days here; university (1804); railway; airport; economy: chemicals, engineering, instruments, machine building, fur, leatherwear, foodstuffs, petrochemicals; monuments: 19th-c Cathedral of the Annunciation, Governor's Palace (1845-48).

Kazan-rettō *kaz-an-re'tō*, VOLCANO ISLANDS, group of Japanese islands in the W Pacific Ocean, S of Ogasawara-shotō Is; includes the islands of Iwo Jima, Kita Iwo and Minami Iwo; administered by the USA between 1945 and 1968; returned to Japan in 1968.

Kazbek, 42 42N 44 30E, extinct volcanic peak in the central Bol'shoy Kavkaz (Greater Caucasus) range, N Gruzinskaya (Georgia) SSR, SW European Soviet Union; 112 km NNW of Tbilisi; height 5,047 m; its glaciers give rise to the R Terek; a popular tourist and sports area.

Kazincbarcika *koz'eents-bor'tsee-ko*, 48 17N 20 36E, pop(1984e) 39,000, town in Borsod-Abaúj-Zemplén county, NE Hungary; on R Sajo, NW of Miskolc; economy: iron mining, power plant.

Kéa *kay'u*, KEOS (Eng), northwesternmost island of the Kikládhes, Greece, in the S Aegean Sea; area 131 sq km.

Kearny *keer'ni*, 40 46N 74 09W, pop(1980) 35,735, town in Hudson county, NE New Jersey, United States; at the head of Newark Bay, between Passaic and Hackensack rivers.

Kebnekaise *keb'nu-kī'su*, 67 55N 18 35E, peak in the Kjölen Mts, Norrbotten county, NW Sweden, 72 km W of Kiruna, 40 km from Norwegian frontier; height 2,111 m; highest peak in Sweden; has several glaciers.

K'ech'a Mt, 7 23N 39 05E, mountain in S Ārsī region, Ethiopia, NE Africa; height 4,190 m.

Kecskemét *kech'ke-mayt*, 46 57N 19 42E, pop(1984e) 102,000, capital of Bács-Kiskun county, S Hungary; 80 km SE of Budapest; Zoltán Kodály School of Music; International Experimental Arts Studio; famous for apricot brandy; railway; economy: fruit and livestock trade, distilling, leather; monuments: many art nouveau style houses and modern houses retaining local features; museum of toys; museum of folk handicrafts; Czifra Palace.

Kedah *kay-dah'*, state in NW Peninsular Malaysia, SE Asia; bounded E by Thailand and W by the Strait of Malacca; watered by the Muda, Kedah and Baharu rivers; governed by Thailand from 1842 until 1909 when it came under British rule; pop(1980) 1,077,815; area 9,425 sq km; capital Alor Setar; chief towns Sungai Petani, Kulim and Jitra.

Kędzierzyn-Koźle *ked-yer'zhin-kozh'le*, HEYDEBRECH *hī'de-brek* (Ger), 50 20N 18 12E, pop(1983) 70,700, river port town in Opole voivodship, S Poland; at junction of R Oder (Odra) and the Gliwice Canal; one of Poland's largest inland navigation ports; two towns united, railway; economy: shipyards, papermill machinery, petrochemicals, nitrogen.

Keeling Islands, Indian Ocean. See Cocos Islands.

Keelung *kee-loong* or **Chi-lung** *jee-loong*, KIRUN' (Jap), formerly SANTISSIMA TRINIDAD (Span), 25 06N 121 34E, pop(1982e) 351,707, an independent municipality and 2nd largest seaport in Taiwan; on N coast of Taiwan I, overlooking the East China Sea; occupied by the Spanish in 1626 and the Dutch in 1641; destroyed by an earthquake in 1867.

Keetmanshoop *keet'mans-hoop*, 26 36S 18 08E, town in S Namibia, SW Africa; 450 km SSE of Windhoek and 355 km NW of Upington (South Africa); centre of the karakul (sheepskin) industry; railway.

Keewatin, district in E Northwest Territories, Canada; bounded W by Mackenzie district, S by Manitoba prov, SE and E by Hudson Bay, NE by Franklin district and N by Queen Maud Gulf and the Rae Strait; hilly in the SW and NE, with low lying land in between; Keewatin, as with Mackenzie district, is dotted with lakes and rivers; the largest lakes are Dubawn, Baker and Garry; the majority of the dist is treeless tundra, being beyond the point where trees will grow, studded with lakes and with no major drainage system; the pop is largely Indian and Eskimo; area 590,934 sq km; economy: fur trapping.

Kef, El, governorate of NW Tunisia, N Africa; pop(1984) 247,672; capital El Kef.

Kefa, mountainous region in SW Ethiopia, NE Africa; pop(1984e) 2,450,369; area 54,600 sq km; peaks include

Dulla Womba Hāyk' (3,686 m) and Mai (3,600 m); the Omo Wenz river follows the E border towards N Kenya where it flows into L Turkana as it crosses the frontier; the Gojeb Wenz flows E across the region to join the Omo Wenz; capital Jīma; chief towns include Maji, Waka and Koma.

Kefallinía *kef-al-een-ee'ah*, CEPHALONIA *sef-a-lō'ni-a* (Eng), nome (dept) of Ioníoi Nísoi region, W Greece; pop(1981) 31,297; area 904 sq km; capital Argostólion.

Kefallinía, largest of the Ioníoi Nísoi (Ionian Is), Greece, in the Ionian Sea, off the W coast of Greece; pop(1981) 27,649; area 781 sq km; length 48 km; length of coastline 254 km; it is an island of hills, rising to 1,628 m, of fertile plains and of sandy beaches and long stretches of rocky coast; with some smaller islands, including Itháki, it forms a nome (dept) of Ioníoi Nísoi region; capital Argostólion; the island was devastated by earthquakes in 1953, the highest peak being split in two.

Keflavík *kyep-lu-veek'*, 64 01N 22 35W, fishing port in Suðurland region, SW Iceland; 48 km SW of Reykjavík; pop(1983) 6,886, important trade centre since the 16th century, the 2nd largest export harbour in Iceland; first modern freezing plant started in 1929; municipal status in 1949; airport.

Kegalla *ke-gal'la*, KEGALEE, 7 14N 80 21E, pop(1981) 15,015, capital of Kegalla dist, Sabaragamuwa prov, SW Sri Lanka; linked to Colombo in the SW and Kandy in the E by road.

Keighley *keeth'li*, 53 52N 1 54W, pop(1981) 49,267, town in Bradford borough, West Yorkshire, N England; part of West Yorkshire urban area; on the R Aire, 16 km NW of Bradford; railway; economy: textiles, textile machinery, machine tools.

Kékes *kay'kesh*, mountain in N Hungary; highest peak in the Matra Mts and in Hungary, rising to 1,014 m.

Kelantan *ku-lun'tan*, state in NE Peninsular Malaysia, SE Asia; bounded N by Thailand and E by the South China sea; drained by the R Kelantan and its tributaries flowing from the mountains of the SW interior; governed by Thailand until 1909 when it came under British rule; pop(1980) 859,270; area 14,796 sq km; capital Kota Baharu; chief towns Pangkat Kalong, Peringat, Pasir Mas and Kuala Kerai.

Kells, CEANANNUS MÓR (Gael), 53 44N 6 53W, pop(1981) 2,623, urban district in Meath county, Leinster, E Irish Republic; on R Boyne NW of Dublin; noted for its monastery and the remains of 5 Celtic crosses; the *Book of Kells*, now in Trinity College, Dublin, Library, was produced here c.AD 800.

Kelowna *ki-lō'na*, 49 50N 119 29W, pop(1981) 59,196, town in S British Columbia, SW Canada; on the E shore of Okanagan L; railway; airfield; economy: fruit packing; winter ski resort; events: International Regatta in Aug; grape festival in Sept.

Kelso *kel'sō*, 55 36N 2 25W, pop(1981) 5,648, market town in Roxburgh dist, Borders, SE Scotland; at the junction of the Teviot and Tweed rivers, 29 km NE of Hawick; monuments: Kelso abbey (1128) is the largest of the Border abbeys; 3 km NW of Kelso is Floors castle, built in 1721 by William Adams and added to in the 1840s by William Playfair; a holly tree in the grounds is said to mark the spot where King James II was killed in 1460 when a cannon exploded; event: ram market (Sept).

Kemerovo *kay'mye-ru-vu*, formerly SHCHEGLOVSK, 55 25N 86 05E, pop(1983) 495,000, capital city of Kemerovskaya oblast, central Siberian Rossiyskaya, Soviet Union; on the R Tom'o; established in 1918; railway; airfield; economy: petrochemicals, coal mining, electrical machinery, foodstuffs.

Kemi *ke'mi*, 65 44N 24 34E, pop(1982) 26,679, industrial seaport on S coast of Lappi prov, N Finland; at N end of Gulf of Bothnia, just S of the mouth of the Kemijoki; established in 1869; railway; airfield (Lautiosaari); economy: commercial port, iron ore mining, steel and wood products.

Kemijärvi *ke'mi-yahr'vee*, KEMITRASK *kay'mee-tresk* (Swed), 66 40N 27 21E, pop(1982) 12,825, commercial town in Lappi prov, N Finland, on L Kemijärvi; established in 1957; railway; airfield; economy: timber.

Kemijoki *key'mi-yo-kee*, KEMIÄLV *kay'mee-elv* (Swed), L KEMI (Eng), river in Lappi prov, N Finland, rising near the Soviet border S of Inarijärvi (Lake Inari); flows S through Kemijärvi then W past Rovaniemi to meet the Gulf of Bothnia at Kemi; length 480 km; the longest river in Finland; main tributary is the Ounasjoki.

Kemo Gribingui *ke-mō gree-beeng'wee*, prefecture in S Central African Republic; the Tomi, Kémo and Kandjai rivers flow S to join the R Ubangi; pop(1968) 134,031; area 37,200 sq km; chief town Sibut; other towns include Dékoa, Griko, Yangoro and Possel.

Kempston, 52 07N 0 30W, pop(1981) 15,555, town in North Bedfordshire dist, Bedfordshire, S central England; 3 km SW of Bedford; railway.

Kempten *kemp'tun*, 47 42N 10 18E, pop(1983) 57,300, city in Schwaben dist, SW Bayern (Bavaria) prov, W Germany; on the R Iller, 104 km WSW of München (Munich); the centre of the Allgäu dairying industry and butter and cheese trade; ancient capital of the Allgäu; railway; economy: packaging systems, textile machinery; monument: Baroque church of St Mang.

Kempton Park, 26 07S 28 14E, pop(1980) 289,815, municipality in Transvaal prov, South Africa; NE of Johannesburg; railway.

Ken'dal, 54 20N 2 45W, pop(1981) 24,203, town in South Lakeland dist, Cumbria, NW England; on the R Kent, 30 km N of Lancaster; railway; economy: textiles, footwear, paper, scientific instruments; monuments: 13th-c church of the Holy Trinity, 12th-c castle, Abbott Hall (1759), Levens Hall (8 km S), Sizerburgh castle (5 km S).

Kendari *ken-da'ree*, 3 57S 122 36E, pop(1980) 41,021, capital of Sulawesi Tenggara prov, Indonesia; on the E coast of Sulawesi (Celebes) I.

Kenema *ken-e'ma*, dist in Eastern prov, Sierra Leone, W Africa; pop(1974) 266,636; area 6,053 sq km; capital Kenema.

Kenema, 7 57N 11 11W, pop(1974) 31,000, capital of a dist of the same name, Eastern prov, Sierra Leone, W Africa; 65 km ESE of Bo; economy: timber trade; airfield.

Ken'ilworth, 52 21N 1 34W, pop(1981) 18,917, town in Warwick dist, Warwickshire, central England; 8 km SW of Coventry; economy: engineering; monument: 12th-c Kenilworth castle.

Kénitra *ke-nee'tra*, MINA HASSAN TANI, 34 16N 6 40W, pop(1982) 188,194, seaport in Kénitra prefecture, Nord-Ouest prov, N Morocco, N Africa; on the R Sebou near the Atlantic coast, 35 km NE of Rabat; originally called Kénitra it was renamed Port-Lyautey in 1932 after the French Marshal Lyautey who ordered the construction of the modern city; US base located here between 1942 and 1948; railway; economy: fish processing, textiles, fertilizer, tobacco, grain, cork.

Kennedy, Cape, cape in Florida, United States. See Canaveral, Cape.

Ken'ner, 29 59N 90 15W, pop(1980) 66,382, town in Jefferson parish, SE Louisiana, United States; a suburb on the Mississippi river, 18 km W of New Orleans.

Ken'net, river rising near Marlborough in E Wiltshire, S England; flows 70 km E through Berkshire to meet the R Thames at Reading.

Kennewick, 46 12N 119 07W, pop(1980) 34,397, city in Benton county, S Washington, United States; on the Columbia river opposite the town of Pasco; the population grew rapidly during World War II in association with an atomic-energy installation near Richland to the NW; railway.

Kennoway, 56 13N 3 04W, pop(1981) 6,663, town in Kirkcaldy dist, Fife, E Scotland; 4 km NW of Leven.

Kenosha *ke-nō'sha* (Algonquian, 'pike'), 42 35N 87 49W, pop(1980) 77,685, county seat of Kenosha county, SE Wisconsin, United States; on L Michigan, 16 km S of Racine; university; railway; economy: motor vehicles, fabricated metals and tools.

Ken'sington and Chelsea *chel'si*, 51 30N 0 12W, pop(1981) 138,837, borough of central Greater London, England; N of R Thames, between the City of Westminster (E) and Hammersmith and Fulham (W); Kensington was granted the designation 'Royal Borough' by Edward VII in 1901; railway; monuments: Kensington Palace; Chelsea Royal Hospital; Victoria and Albert museum; Nottingham House, birthplace of Queen Victoria; events: Crufts dog show (Feb); Chelsea antiques fair (March and Sept); Ideal Home Exhibition (March); Chelsea Flower Show (May); Royal Tournament (July); Smithfield agricultural show (Dec).

Kent, county in SE England; bounded S by East Sussex, W by Surrey, NW by Greater London, N by the R Thames estuary and E by the English Channel; rises to 251 m in the North Downs; pop(1981) 1,467,619; area 3,731 sq km; county town Maidstone; Dover, Folkestone, Ramsgate and Sheerness are the principal cross-Channel ports; economy: tourism, cross-Channel transport, fruit, hops, horticulture, grain, vegetables, cement, paper, shipbuilding, fishing, electronics, pharmaceuticals, oil; the county is divided into 14 districts:

District	*area (sq km)*	*pop(1981)*
Ashford	581	85,968
Canterbury	311	117,169
Dartford	70	78,345
Dover	312	100,987
Gillingham	32	93,734
Gravesham	100	95,976
Maidstone	394	130,496
Rochester upon Medway	160	143,846
Sevenoaks	371	109,871
Shepway	357	86,503
Swale	369	109,647
Thanet	103	121,720
Tonbridge and Malling	240	96,848
Tunbridge Wells	331	96,509

Kent, 41 09N 81 22W, pop(1980) 26,164, town in Portage county, NE Ohio, United States; on the R Cuyahoga, 13 km ENE of Akron; university (1910); railway; economy: food processing, plastics, engineering.

Kenting, national park at the S tip of Taiwan; surrounded on 3 sides by the Taiwan Haixia (Taiwan Strait), Bashi Channel and South China Sea; area 326 sq km; divided into an ecological protection area, a special scenic area, historic sites, a recreational area (Kenting Forest) and a general management area; named after the 'ploughmen' who originally came from the Chinese mainland.

Kentucky, state in E central United States; bounded W by Missouri, NW and N by Illinois, Indiana and Ohio, E by West Virginia and Virginia, and S by Tennessee; the Mississippi river follows the Missouri state border in the SW; the R Ohio forms the entire N and NW border before emptying into the Mississippi; the Tennessee and Cumberland rivers flow NNW through the SW corner of the state to empty into the R Ohio; the R Kentucky flows NW through the centre of the state to empty into the R Ohio; the Big Sandy river and its tributary, the Tug Fork, form the West Virginia state border before emptying into the R Ohio; the Cumberland Mts lie to the SE; highest point is Mt Black (1,263 m); the central plain of the state is known as Bluegrass country, the heart and trademark of the state; to the W and E are rough uplands with vast coal reserves; in the SW corner are floodplains bounded by 3 great rivers, R Ohio, R Mississippi and R Tennessee; the state is famous for the distilling of Bourbon whisky (and still is the country's leading producer of it), and for the breeding of thoroughbred racehorses, in the Bluegrass country; chief agricultural products are tobacco, cattle, dairy produce and soybeans; major industrial manufactures are machinery, electrical equipment, processed foods, chemicals and fabricated metals; the state is the country's leading coal producer; other state minerals include petroleum and natural gas; event: the Kentucky Derby for three-year-olds, the nation's oldest continuously held classic horse race; part of the territory was ceded by the French in 1763 and explored by Daniel Boone from 1769; the first permanent British settlement was founded at Boonesborough in 1775; included in US territory by the Treaty of Paris in 1783; originally part of Virginia but admitted to the Union as a separate state (23rd) in 1792; attempted to remain neutral in the Civil War but was invaded by Confederate troops in 1862; also known as the 'Bluegrass State'; pop(1980) 3,660,777; area 103,139 sq km; capital Frankfort; major cities are Louisville and Lexington; the state is divided into 120 counties:

County	*area (sq km)*	*pop(1980)*
Adair	1,058	15,233
Allen	879	14,128
Anderson	530	12,567
Ballard	660	8,798
Barren	1,253	34,009
Bath	720	10,025
Bell	939	34,330
Boone	640	45,842
Bourbon	759	19,405
Boyd	416	55,513
Boyle	473	25,066
Bracken	528	7,738
Breathitt	1,287	17,004
Breckinridge	1,469	16,861
Bullitt	780	43,346
Butler	1,121	11,064
Caldwell	902	13,473
Calloway	1,004	30,031
Campbell	395	83,317
Carlisle	497	5,487
Carroll	338	9,270
Carter	1,058	25,060
Casey	1,157	14,818
Christian	1,877	66,878
Clark	663	28,322
Clay	1,225	22,752
Clinton	510	9,321
Crittenden	936	9,207
Cumberland	790	7,289
Davies	1,204	85,949
Edmonson	785	9,962
Elliott	608	6,908
Estill	666	14,495
Fayette	741	204,165
Fleming	913	12,323
Floyd	1,022	48,764
Franklin	551	41,830
Fulton	549	8,971
Gallatin	257	4,842
Garrard	603	10,853
Grant	673	13,308
Graves	1,448	34,049
Grayson	1,282	20,854
Green	751	11,043
Greenup	902	39,132
Hancock	491	7,742
Hardin	1,635	88,917
Harlan	1,217	41,889
Harrison	806	15,166
Hart	1,071	15,402
Henderson	1,139	40,849
Henry	757	12,740
Hickman	637	6,065
Hopkins	1,435	46,174
Jackson	900	11,996
Jefferson	1,004	685,004
Jessamine	452	26,146
Johnson	686	24,432
Kenton	424	137,058
Knott	915	17,940
Knox	1,009	30,239
Larue	684	11,922
Laurel	1,128	38,982
Lawrence	1,092	14,121
Lee	549	7,754

contd

County	*area (sq km)*	*pop(1980)*
Leslie	1,045	14,882
Letcher	881	30,687
Lewis	1,258	14,545
Lincoln	876	19,053
Livingston	811	9,219
Logan	1,446	24,138
Lyon	543	6,490
Madison	1,152	53,352
Magoffin	806	13,515
Marion	902	17,910
Marshall	790	25,637
Martin	598	13,925
Mason	627	17,765
McCracken	653	61,310
McCreary	1,110	15,634
McLean	666	10,090
Meade	796	22,854
Menifee	528	5,117
Mercer	650	19,011
Metcalfe	757	9,484
Monroe	861	12,353
Montgomery	517	20,046
Morgan	993	12,103
Muhlenberg	1,243	32,238
Nelson	1,102	27,584
Nicholas	512	7,157
Ohio	1,550	21,765
Oldham	494	27,795
Owen	920	8,924
Owsley	515	5,709
Pendleton	731	10,989
Perry	887	33,763
Pike	2,041	81,123
Powell	468	11,101
Pulaski	1,716	45,803
Robertson	260	2,265
Rockcastle	827	13,973
Rowan	733	19,049
Russell	650	13,708
Scott	744	21,813
Shelby	1,001	23,328
Simpson	614	14,673
Spencer	499	5,929
Taylor	702	21,178
Todd	980	11,874
Trigg	1,095	9,384
Trimble	385	6,253
Union	887	17,821
Warren	1,425	71,828
Washington	783	10,764
Wayne	1,160	17,022
Webster	874	14,832
Whitley	1,152	33,396
Wolfe	580	6,698
Woodford	499	17,778

Kentwood, 42 53N 85 38W, pop(1980) 30,438, town in Kent county, W Michigan, United States; 13 km SE of Grand Rapids.

Kenya *ken'ya, keen'ya,* official name Republic of Kenya; a republic of E Africa, bounded S by Tanzania, W by Uganda, NW by Sudan, N by Ethiopia, NE by Somalia and E by the Indian Ocean; area 564,162 sq km; timezone GMT +3; capital Nairobi; chief towns Mombasa, Kisumu, Nakuru, Machakos, Meru and Eldoret; pop(1979) 15,327,061; in 1985 the population growth rate was estimated at 4.1%, the world's highest rate; the principal ethnic groups include Kikuyu (21%), Luhya (14%), Luo (13%), Kalejin (11%), Kamba (11%), Kisii (6%), Meru (5%); most of the pop follow Christian beliefs (Protestant (38%) and Roman Catholic (28%)), the remainder following either local beliefs (26%) or being Muslim (6%); English and Swahili are the official languages, with numerous tribal languages also spoken; the unit of currency is the Kenya pound; national holiday 12 Dec (Independence Day); membership of AfDB, Commonwealth, FAO, G-77, GATT, IAEA, IBRD, ICAO, ICO, IDA, IFAD, IFC, ILO, IMF, IMO, INTELSAT, INTERPOL, IRC, ISO, ITU, International Wheat Council, NAM, OAU, UN, UNDP, UNESCO, UPU, WHO, WIPO, WMO and WTO.

Physical description. Crossed by the Equator, Kenya has a varied topography from coast to mountain peak. The SW plateau touching the NE corner of L Victoria rises to between 600 and 3,000 metres and includes peaks such as Mount Kenya (5,199 m), Mount Elgon (4,321 m) and the Aberdare range. The N is a dry, arid semi-desert generally under 600 m in elevation except for a few peaks such as Nyira (3,400 m) which rises out of the desert plain. L Turkana (formerly L Rudolf), a saline lake in the Rift Valley, is the largest body of water in the N. SE of L Turkana is the Chalbi desert. The coastal strip S of the R Tana is typified by coral reefs, mangrove swamps and small island groups including the Lamu archipelago. Kenya has 2 major rivers, the R Tana which rises E of Mount Kenya and flows 708 km E and then SE to enter the Indian Ocean at Formosa Bay (between Malindi and Lamu), and the R Athi which is formed at the junction of headstreams N of Nairobi and flows 547 km SE.

Climate. The coastal climate of Kenya is tropical, with an annual rainfall of about 1,000 mm which decreases from N to S. There are 2 rainy seasons during April-May and Oct-Nov. Temperatures and humidity remain high during the year but are tempered by onshore breezes and an average of 7 or 8 hours of sunshine per day. Mombasa is representative of this region with an average annual rainfall of 1,200 mm and average daily temperatures ranging from 27°C to 31°C. The N desert and lower inland plateau region is, for much of its area, characterized by annual rainfall that decreases from 500 mm in the S to 250 mm in the far N. The W and central Kenya highlands also have two rainy seasons and an annual rainfall that seldom exceeds 1,250 mm. Nairobi (alt 1,820 m) is representative of much of the region with an average annual rainfall of 960 mm, and average daily temperatures ranging from 21°C to 26°C. In the high mountains frost and snow occur. Mt Kenya has a number of glaciers and a permanent snow cap.

History, government and constitution. British control of Kenya was recognized at the Berlin Conference of 1885 and 10 years later the East African Protectorate was established and opened to white settlers. It was not until 1920 that the region became a British colony and it was not until 1944 that African participation in politics was permitted. The 'Mau Mau' rebellion between 1952 and 1960 resulted in the creation of a state of emergency and eventually Kenya gained full independence in 1963. A year later Kenya declared itself a republic within the Commonwealth. Jomo Kenyatta, a member of the Kikuyu tribe and leader of the Kenya African National Union (KANU), became the country's first leader. The 1963 constitution was amended in 1982 making Kenya a one-party state, with KANU the only legal party. The government is headed by a president elected for a five-year term. A vice-president and cabinet are appointed. There is a unicameral National Assembly of 158 members.

Economy. Agriculture accounts for one-third of national income and is dependent on export earnings from cash crops such as coffee, tea, sisal, pyrethrum, cashew nuts, rice, wheat, maize and sugar cane. Manufacturing industries accounting for 13% of national income include food processing, textiles, chemicals, cement, steel, pulp and paper, metal products, car assembly, oil refining, consumer goods, paper, tobacco and rubber. There are reserves of soda ash, fluorspar, salt, diatomite, limestone, lead, various gemstones including rubies and tsavorite, silver and gold. Soda ash is mined at L Magadi and processed on site. Fourteen national parks attract large numbers of tourists (352,300 in 1981). The main trading partners are the UK, Iran, Japan, West Germany, the USA, Tanzania, Zambia, the Netherlands and Saudi Arabia.

Administrative divisions. Kenya is divided into 8 provinces 7 of which are subdivided into 40 districts:

Province/district	*area (sq km)*	*pop(1979)*
Nairobi	684	1,161,000 (1984e)
Central Province	13,173	2,345,833
Kiambu	2,448	686,290
Kirinyaga	1,437	291,431
Murang'a	2,476	648,333
Nyandarua	3,528	233,302
Nyeri	3,284	486,477
Coast Province	83,040	1,342,794
Kilifi	12,414	430,986
Kwale	8,257	288,363
Lamu	6,506	42,299
Mombasa	210	341,148

contd

Province/district	*area (sq km)*	*pop(1979)*
Taita River	16,959	147,597
Tana River	38,694	92,410
Eastern Province	155,759	2,719,851
Embu	2,714	263,173
Isiolo	25,605	43,478
Kitui	29,388	464,283
Machakos	14,178	1,022,522
Marsabit	73,952	96,216
Meru	9,922	830,179
North-Eastern Province	126,902	373,787
Garissa	43,931	128,867
Mandera	26,470	105,601
Wajir	56,501	139,319
Nyanza Province	12,526	2,643,956
Kisii	2,196	869,512
Kisumu	2,093	482,327
Siaya	2,522	474,516

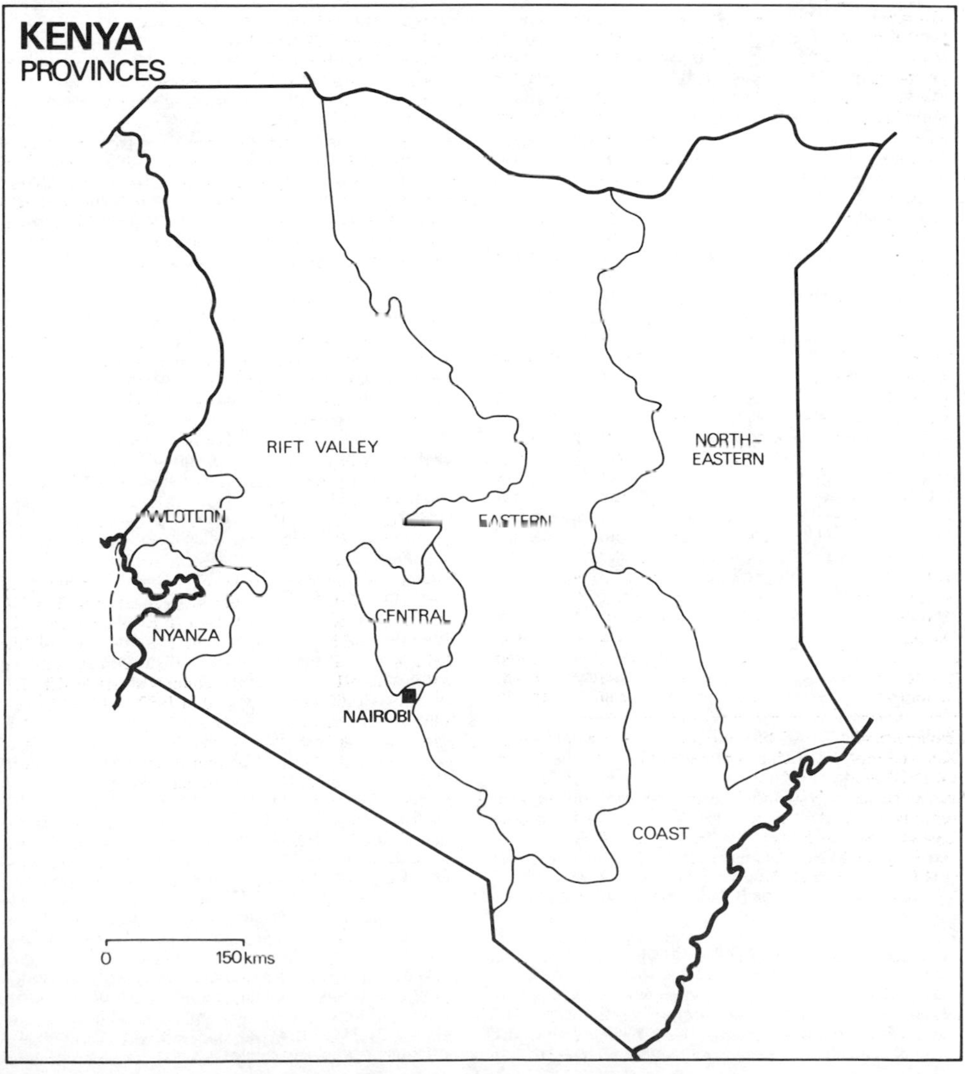

contd

Province/district	*area (sq km)*	*pop(1979)*
South Nyanza	5,714	817,601
Rift Valley Province	163,884	3,240,402
Baringo	9,885	203,792
Elgeyo Markwet	2,279	148,868
Kajiado	19,605	149,005
Kericho	3,931	633,348
Laikipia	9,718	134,534
Nakuru	5,769	522,709
Nandi	2,745	299,319
Narok	16,115	210,306
Samburu	17,521	76,908
Trans-Nzoia	2,078	259,503
Turkana	61,768	142,702
Uasin Gishu	3,378	300,766
West Pokot	9,090	158,652
Western Province	8,196	1,832,663
Bungoma	3,074	503,935
Busia	1,626	297,841
Kakamega	3,495	1,030,887

Kenya, Mount, 0 10S 37 18E, extinct volcano cone in central Kenya, E Africa; 112 km NNE of Nairobi; 2nd highest mountain on the African continent after Kilimanjaro; comprises the 3 peaks of Batian (5,199 m), Nelion (5,188 m) and Lenana (4,985 m); area includes 32 lakes and 15 glaciers (above 4,500 m); it is possible to view the summit of Kilimanjaro 323 km away, one of the longest confirmed lines of sight on Earth; thick forest extends to a high level with varied wildlife including rhinoceros, elephants and leopards; a national park of 588 sq km was established in 1949; the first European discovery was in 1849 by Krapf, a German missionary; the first ascent was by Sir Halford Mackinder, C. Ollier and J. Brocherel in 1899.

Kerala *kay'ru-lu*, state in S India; pop(1981) 25,403,217; area 38,864 sq km; bounded W along the Malabar coast by the Arabian Sea and E by the states of Karnataka and Tamil Nadu; divided into 12 administrative dists; capital Trivandrum; the state is governed by a 140-member unicameral legislature; 3 physical regions include densely forested, hilly tracts running W to E, a cultivated plain and an indented coastal region with coconut plantations and rice fields; Kerala is crossed by several rivers including the Ponnani and the Payaswani; the state of Kerala was created out of the former state of Travancore-Cochin under the 1956 States Reorganization Act; chief agricultural crops are rice, tapioca, coconut, oilseeds, sugar cane, pepper, rubber, tea, coffee and cashewnuts; Kerala produces 98% of India's black pepper and 95% of Indian rubber; 33% of the state is forested with commercial production of teak, sandalwood, ebony and blackwood; manufacturing industries include textiles, ceramics, fertilizer, chemicals, glass, electrical goods, paper; co-operative cottage industries include ivory carving, weaving, copper and brass ware, furniture; a coastal railway from Mangalore connects Kerala to the towns of Tamil Nadu; airfields are located at Cochin and Trivandrum; the seaport of Cochin is one of India's largest ports.

Kerava *ker'ah-vah*, 60 25N 25 10E, pop(1982) 24,916, town in Uudenmaa prov, S Finland; 25 km NNE of Helsinki; established in 1924; railway.

Keren *ke'ren*, 15 46N 38 30E, pop(1977e) 31,692, town in Ērtra region, NE Ethiopia, NE Africa; 72 km NW of Asmara; occupied by the Italians between 1889 and 1941; railway.

Kerewan *ke-re'wan*, local government area in The Gambia, W Africa; pop(1983) 112,047; area 2,151.5 sq km.

Kerguélen, Îles de *kur-gay'len*, DESOLATION ISLANDS (Eng), ÎLES DE DÉSOLATION (Fr), 49 30S 69 30E, French island group in S Indian Ocean comprising the island of Kerguélen and about 300 islets; about 5,300 km SE of the S tip of Africa; total area 7,215 sq km; Grande Terre, the main island (area 6,675 sq km) rises to 1,960 m at Mt Ross with snow sheet, glaciers, many lakes and a fjord-like coastline; there is some coal and the Kerguélen cabbage is peculiar to the island; discovered by the Breton navigator Yves de Kerguélen in Feb 1772; annexed by France in 1949 and incorporated in the French Southern and Antarctic Territories in 1955; scientific stations at Port-aux-Français; sheep, deer and trout have been introduced.

Kericho *ke-ree'chō*, 0 22S 35 19E, pop(1979) 30,000, town in central Rift Valley prov, Kenya, E Africa; 65 km SE of Kisumu; centre of the tea industry.

Kerinci, Gunung *goo'nung ker-in'chee*, MT KERINCI, 1 43S 101 15E, highest mountain on the island of Sumatera; rising to 3,805 m in the Bukit Barisan range, W Sumatera; source of the Banaghari (R Hari).

Kérkira *ker'kee-rah*, CORFU *kor-foo'* (Eng), nome (dept) of Ioníoi Nísoi region, W Greece; pop(1981) 99,477; area 641 sq km; includes the island of Kérkira and its neighbours; capital Kérkira.

Kérkira, CORFU (Eng), northernmost and 2nd largest of the Ioníoi Nísoi (Ionian Is), Greece, in the N Ionian Sea, off the NW coast of Greece; pop(1981) 96,533; area 592 sq km; length 64 km; length of coastline 217 km; with some lesser islands it forms a nome (dept) of Ioníoi Nísoi region; it is the 7th largest Greek island; its semi-mountainous terrain (highest point 907 m) is blanketed with dense vegetation; chief town Kérkira on the E coast; the mild climate, pleasant scenery, and numerous sandy beaches have led to the growth of tourism in recent years.

Kérkira, CORCYRA (anc), 39 38N 19 50E, pop(1981) 33,561, seaport capital of Kérkira nome (dept), Ioníoi Nísoi region, W Greece; a good harbour site on the E coast of the island; airport; local ferries to mainland Greece and to Italy, Yugoslavia, Turkey; economy: textiles, fishing, tourism, olive oil and fruit trade; monuments: church of St Spyrídon; old fortress (1386); events: Feast of St Spyrídon (April 15-21 and Nov 4); anniversary of reunion with Greece (May 21); Navy Week (June-July).

Kerkrade *kerk'rahd-u*, 50 52N 6 04E, pop(1984e) 53,231, city and municipality in SE Limburg prov, S Netherlands; on the German border 29 km E of Maastricht.

Kermadec' Islands, islands of New Zealand; 930 km NE of the Bay of Islands, North Island; includes Raoul I (Sunday I), Macaulay I, Curtis Is and L'Espérance; area 33 sq km; discovered in 1788, annexed by the UK in 1886 and declared part of New Zealand in 1887; Raoul island, with an area of 28.5 sq km, has a manned weather station.

Kermān *ker-man'*, mountainous prov in SE Iran; pop(1982) 1,078,875; area 186,472 sq km; capital Kermān.

Kermān, 30 15N 57 01E, pop(1983) 238,777, capital city of Kermān dist, Kermān, SE Iran; 800 km SE of Tehrān; its modern development has largely been due to the exploitation of mineral resources in the prov, mainly copper and precious metals; noted for making and exporting carpets; railway; airfield; monuments: ruins of 3rd-c forts; the walled city contains a citadel and 11th-c mosque.

Kerpen *ker'pun*, 50 19N 6 44E, pop(1983) 55,100, town in Köln (Cologne) dist, Nordrhein-Westfalen (North Rhine-Westphalia) prov, W Germany.

Kerry, CHIARRAIGHE (Gael), county in Munster prov, SW Irish Republic; bounded W by Atlantic Ocean; rises to Slieve Mish Mts on N side of Dingle Bay and Macgillycuddy's Reeks on the S side; watered by Feale and Blackwater rivers; the Blasket and Skellig Islands lie offshore; pop(1981) 122,770; area 4,701 sq km; capital Tralee; chief towns include Killarney and Listowel; Irish Gaelic still widely spoken; economy: tourism, fishing, textiles.

Keski-Suomi *kes-ki-soo-o'mi*, MELLERSTA FINLAND (Swed), a prov of S central Finland; the N section of L Päijänne extends into the S of the prov; area 19,356 sq km; pop(1982) 244,991; Jyväskylä, on the NW shore of L Päijänne, is the prov capital.

Keswick *kez'ik*, 54 37N 3 08W, pop(1981) 5,645, resort and market town in Allerdale dist, Cumbria, NW England; at N end of Derwent Water, on R Greta, 26 km W of Penrith; monuments: 16th-c church of St Kentigern; Greta Hall, home of Robert Southey (1803-43); Castle Rigg stone circle (3 km E); St Herbert's Island on Derwent Water, a 7th-c hermitage.

Keszthely *kest'hay*, 46 50N 17 15E, pop(1984e) 23,000, town in Veszprém county, W Hungary; on shores of L Balaton; agricultural university (1797); centre of a noted wine-producing and horse-breeding area.

Keta *ke'ta*, 5 55N 1 01E, pop(1970) 27,461, town in Volta region, SE Ghana, W Africa; on the Gulf of Guinea, ENE of Accra.

Kete-Krachi *ke'tay-kra'chee*, 7 50N 0 03W, town in Volta region, E central Ghana, W Africa; on the N shore of L Volta, NW of the junction of the White Volta and Oti rivers.

Ket'tering, 52 24N 0 44W, pop(1981) 45,389, town in Kettering dist, Northamptonshire, central England; 22 km NNE of Northampton, on the R Ise; railway; economy: soft drinks, leather, footwear, clothing, light engineering.

Kettering, 39 41N 84 10W, pop(1980) 61,186, town in Montgomery county, W Ohio, United States; 8 km S of Dayton; railway.

Keynsham *kayn'shem*, 51 26N 2 30W, pop(1981) 16,623, town in Wansdyke dist, Avon, SW England; just S of Bristol; railway.

Kgalagadi *ga-la-ga'dee*, dist in Botswana, S Africa; area 106,940 sq km; pop(1981) 24,059; capital Tsabong; chief towns Tshane and Werda; Gemsbok National Park is situated W; economy: livestock agriculture.

Kgatleng *gat-leng'*, dist in SE Botswana, S Africa; pop(1981) 44,461; area 7,960 sq km; capital Mochudi; chief town Lobatse; economy: livestock and arable agriculture.

Khabarovsk *KHu-bur-ofsk'*, HABAROVSK, 48 30N 135 05E, pop(1983) 560,000, river port capital of Khabarovskiy kray, SE Siberian Rossiyskaya, Soviet Union; close to the Chinese frontier, at the confluence of the rivers Amur and Ussuri; established in 1858 as a military outpost and prospered greatly after the coming of the railway in 1905; airfield; economy: ship repairing, engineering, oil refining, foodstuffs.

Khabur *KHa'boor*, river mainly in NE Syria; rises in the mountains of SE Turkey; flows SE past Āl Hasakah then S to the R Euphrates, 13 km N of Al Mayādīn; length 320 km; a new dam is designed to enable 10,000 sq km of land to be reclaimed for the cultivation of cotton, rice, cereals, and fruit.

Khābūrah, Al *KHa-boo'ru*, 23 57N 57 05E, seaport on the Gulf of Oman, Sultanate of Oman, SE Arabian peninsula, 56 km SE of Suḥār; linked to Maţraḩ by a modern dual carriageway.

Khálki *KHal'kee*, 36 14N 27 35E, island of the Sporádhes, Greece, in the S Aegean Sea, W of Ródhos I (Rhodes); area 28 sq km.

Khalkidhíki *KHal-kee-thee-kee'*, CHALCIDICE *kal-sid'i-se* (Eng), nome (dept) of Makedhonia region, E Greece, formed by the peninsula which stretches 3 fingers SE into the Aegean Sea; pop(1981) 79,036; area 2,918 sq km; capital Políyiros; economy: wheat, olive oil, wine; its long sandy beaches have recently led to its development as a holiday region.

Khalkidhíki, peninsula of NE Greece, projecting from Makedhonia into the Aegean Sea; it terminates in the 3 long finger-like peninsulas of Kassándra, Sithoniá, and Aktí; length 56 km; lies mostly within Khalkidhíki nome (dept); the city of Thessaloníki is at its N end.

Khalkís *KHal-kees'*, CHALCIS *kal'sis* (Eng), EVRIPOS (anc), NEGROPONT (Ital), 38 27N 23 42E, pop(1981) 44,867, capital of Évvoia nome (dept), Sterea Ellás-Évvoia region, Greece; Aristotle died here; administrative and economic centre; railway; local ferries; economy: commerce, tourism.

Khamis Mushayt *KHa-mees' moo-shayt'*, 18 00N 42 35E, pop(1974) 49,580, town in Asīr prov, SW Saudi Arabia; 32 km ENE of Abhā; on a plateau in the upper reaches of the Wadi Bisha, lying at an elevation of over 1,800 m.

Khammouan, prov (*khowèng*) of central Laos, SE Asia; capital Muang Khoummouan.

Khan Yunis *KHan yoo'nis*, sub-district of Gaza Strip dist, Israel.

Khānaqīn *KHa'nu-keen*, 34 22N 45 22E, town in Diyāla governorate, E Iraq; on R Alwand, close to the Iranian border; there is an oilfield to the S; rail terminus.

Khanewal *kahn-ay'vahl*, 30 17N 72 00E, pop(1981) 89,000, city in Punjab prov, Pakistan; NE of Multan; railway; economy: trade in grain, cotton and oilseed.

Khaniá *KHan-yah'*, CANEA *kun-ee'u* (Eng), westernmost nome (dept) of Kríti (Crete), S Greece; pop(1981) 125,856; area 2,376 sq km; capital Khaniá.

Khaniá, 35 31N 24 01E, pop(1981) 61,976, capital town of Khaniá nome (dept), Kríti (Crete), S Greece; on N shore of Kríti I; economic and administrative centre for the nome (dept); capital of Kríti until 1971; airfield; events: dance festival to commemorate the battle for Kríti (May); Chestnut Festival (Sept).

Khanpur *KHun'poor*, 28 38N 70 40E, pop(1981) 71,000, city in Punjab prov, Pakistan; SW of Bahawalpur; railway; economy: trade in oilseed, cotton and grains.

Khârga, El *kar'gu*, AL KHARIJAH, 25 27N 30 32E, capital of Al-Wadi Al-Jadid governorate, S central Egypt; in the Great Oasis, Egypt's largest oasis; railway; monuments: ruins of the temple of Hibis (around 500 BC), now a Christian necropolis, and Nadura (around 150 AD), a Christian convent.

Kharian *kahr'yan*, 32 52N 73 52E, pop(1981) 52,000, city in Punjab prov, Pakistan; 32 km NW of Gujrat; railway; economy: grain trade.

Khar'kov *KHar'kef*, KHARKIV (Ukr), 50 00N 36 15E, pop(1983) 1,519,000, capital city of Khar'kovskaya oblast, Ukrainskaya SSR, Soviet Union; on several tributaries of the R Severskiy Donets; founded 1655-56 as a fortress to protect Russia's S border; proximity to the Krivoy Rog iron mines and the Donets coal basin has provided the basis for engineering industries that produce a wide variety of heavy metal goods; university (1805); railway junction; airport; economy: machine building, metalworking, foodstuffs, building materials; monuments: Pokrovskii cathedral (1689); Uspenskii cathedral (1821-41).

Kharmanly or **Harmanli** *KHar'man-lee*, 41 55N 25 55E, pop(1981e) 20,000, agricultural centre and industrial town in Khaskovo okrug (prov), SE Bulgaria; on the lower part of the R Kharmanly; railway; economy: tobacco-processing, textiles, silk.

Khartoum *kar-toom'*, EL KHARTÛM, 15 33N 32 35E, pop(1984e) 476,218, capital of Sudan, NE Africa; also administrative centre of Khartoum region; located near the junction of the White Nile and the Blue Nile rivers, 1,600 km S of Cairo (Egypt); connected to the suburb of North Khartoum by a road and rail bridge built (1908-10) over the Blue Nile and to Omdurman by a tramway bridge built (1925-28) across the White Nile; a major communications and trade centre; with the headquarters of the Bank for African Development located here, the city is regarded as the economic link between the N Arab countries and the S African countries; founded in the 1820s the city expanded rapidly as a trade centre for slaves and goods destined for Egypt; the Gordon Memorial College was established in 1902 in memory of the British General Gordon who was killed during an unsuccessful attempt to defend the city against a siege by the Madhists in 1885; the city was regained by Lord Kitchener in 1898 and was rebuilt along more modern lines; university (1955); railway; airport; economy: commerce, banking; an oil pipeline runs NE to Port Sudan.

Khartoum North, 15 39N 32 30E, pop(1984e) 341,146, major suburb of Khartoum, Khartoum region, Sudan, NE Africa; on the R Nile; connected to the main city by a road and rail bridge; economy: textiles, food processing, tanning and trade in cotton and grain.

Khaskovo or **Haskovo** *KHas'ko-vo*, okrug (prov) of S Bulgaria in the NE foothills of the Rhodopi Planina (Rhodope Mts) on the frontier with Greece and Turkey; traversed by the R Maritsa; area 4,008 sq km; pop(1981) 296,000.

Khaskovo, 41 57N 25 32E, pop(1981) 86,204, capital of Khaskovo okrug (prov), S central Bulgaria; on a tributary of the R Maritsa; an industrial and agricultural centre on the Khaskovo plain; airfield; railway; economy: tobacco, textiles.

Khayelitsha *kī-leet'sa*, a new settlement 39 km SE of Cape Town on South Africa; False Bay, built from 1983 for Africans residing in the squatter camps of Crossroads, Langa, Guguletu, KTC and Nyanga; area 21 sq km; planned for 250,000 residents; the nature of the location and the cost of transport to work near Cape Town has resulted in opposition to settlement here.

Kherson *KHer-son'*, 46 39N 32 38E, pop(1983) 337,000, port and capital of Khersonskaya oblast, Ukrainskaya SSR, Soviet Union; on the R Dnepr, 24 km upstream from where it empties into the Black Sea; founded in 1778 as a naval station, fortress, and shipbuilding centre; in the spring the river floods nearby to a width of 25 km and forms numerous small rivers so that the area is known as Kherson's Venice; railway; airfield; economy: oil refining, shipbuilding, agricultural machinery, cotton textiles, foodstuffs; monuments: Spasskii cathedral (1806), Sviatodukhovskii cathedral (1836).

Khíos *kē'os*, CHIOS *kee'os* (Eng), SCIO *shee'ō* (Ital), nome (dept) of Aegean Is region, E Greece; pop(1981) 49,865; area 904 sq km; includes the islands of Khíos, Psará, Pasas, Andípsara and Oinousa; capital Khíos; economy: figs, olives, almonds, grapes, sheep and goats.

Khíos, Greek island in the Aegean Sea, off the W coast of Turkey; pop(1981) 48,700; area 842 sq km; length 48 km; length of coastline 213 km; 5th largest of the Greek islands; the island is traversed from N to S by a range of limestone hills rising to 1,298 m; the SE section is a fertile plain; chief town Khíos on the E coast; with some lesser islands it forms a nome (dept) of Aegean Is region; noted since classical times for its wine and figs.

Khíos, 38 23N 26 07E, pop(1981) 29,742, port and capital town of Khíos nome (dept), Aegean Islands, E Greece, on the E coast of Khíos I; home of the important Korais library, the 3rd largest in Greece; airfield; ferry to mainland and islands; economy: tanning, wine, boatbuilding, tourism; event: Navy Week (June-July).

Khon Kaen, city in Thailand. See Muang Khon Kaen.

Khorāsān *KHor-a-san'*, mountainous prov in NE Iran, bounded N and NE by the USSR and E by Afghanistan; pop(1982) 3,264,398; area 313,337 sq km; capital Mashhad.

Khorramābād *KHō-ram'a-bad*, 33 29N 48 21E, pop(1983) 199,627, capital town of Khorramābād dist, Lorestān, W central Iran; 240 km NNW of Ahvāz; trade centre for surrounding mountainous region; monuments: medieval fortress.

Khouribga *koo-reeb'ga*, 32 54N 6 57W, pop(1982) 127,181, mining capital of Khouribga prefecture, Centre prov, central Morocco, N Africa; on the Plateau des Phosphates, 104 km SE of Casablanca; economy: phosphate mining.

Khubar, Al *KHō'bar*, 26 24N 50 02E, pop(1974) 48,815, seaport in Eastern prov, E Saudi Arabia; on a peninsula which juts into the Arabian Gulf, W of Bahrain; railway.

Khulna *kool'nu*, region in SW Bangladesh; includes Bagerhat, Khulna and Satkhira districts; bounded W by West Bengal, India, and E by the R Ganges; pop(1981) 4,329,000; area 12,167 sq km; capital Khulna.

Khulna, 22 49N 89 34E, pop(1981) 646,359, capital of Khulna dist and Khulna region, SW Bangladesh; lies on a swampy forested area, close to the Ganges delta, 130 km SW of Dhākā; railway; economy: shipbuilding, textile manufacture and trade in rice, jute, salt, sugar, betel nut, coconut, oilseed.

Khushab *koo-shab'*, 32 16N 72 18E, pop(1981) 56,000, city in Punjab prov, Pakistan; on the R Jhelum, NW of Sargodha; railway; economy: trade in cotton, grain, oilseed and wool.

Khuzestān *KHoo-ses-tan'*, prov in SW Iran, bounded W by Iraq and S by the Arabian Gulf; pop(1982) 2,196,920; area 67,236 sq km; capital Ahvāz; drained by the R Kārūn, a tributary of the R Tigris; land rises towards the Zagros Mts in the E.

Khvoy *KHō'ee*, 38 32N 45 02E, pop(1983) 102,768, town in Khvoy dist, Āzarbāyān-e Gharbī, NW Iran; 120 km WNW of Tabrīz, at the N end of Daryācheh-ye Orūmīyeh (L Urmia); trade centre for a fertile agricultural region; railway.

Kiang-si, prov in SE China. See Jiangxi.

Kiang-su, prov in E China. See Jiangsu.

Kibi *kē'bē*, 6 11N 0 31W, town in Eastern region, S Ghana, W Africa; W of Koforidua.

Kibungu *kee-boon'goo*, 2 10S 30 31E, pop(1978) 360,934, city and prefecture in Rwanda, central Africa; 56 km ESE of Kigali; area 4,134 sq km; pop(1978) 360,934.

Kibuye *kee-boo'ye*, prefecture in Rwanda, central Africa; on the shore of L Kivu, W of Kigali; area 1,320 sq km; pop(1978) 337,729.

Kičevo *kee'che-vo*, 41 30N 20 59E, pop(1981) 51,422, livestock market town in W Makedonija (Macedonia) republic, Yugoslavia; on R Trska, 64 km SW of Skopje; railway.

Kid'derminster, 52 23N 2 14W, pop(1981) 50,746, town in Wyre Forest dist, Hereford and Worcester, W central England; on the R Stour, 25 km N of Worcester; railway; economy: carpets, engineering, textiles, tin-plating, chemicals, electrical equipment.

Kidepo Valley *ki-day'pō*, national park in Karamoja prov, NE Uganda, E Africa; area 1,344 sq km; established in 1958; situated on Uganda's N frontier with Sudan.

Kid'lington, 51 50N 1 17W, pop(1981) 14,012, town NE of Oxford in Cherwell dist, Oxfordshire, S central England; 8 km N of Oxford, near Oxford airport.

Kids'grove, 53 05N 2 16W, pop(1981) 28,070, town in the Potteries urban area, Staffordshire Moorlands dist, Staffordshire, central England; 10 km NW of Stoke-on-Trent; railway; economy: textiles, chemicals.

Kiel *keel*, 54 20N 10 08E, pop(1983) 248,400, port and capital of Schleswig-Holstein prov, W Germany; at S end of the Kieler Förde, an arm of the Baltic which extends some 17 km inland, 64 km NW of Lübeck; a naval base with naval command posts and training establishments; university (1665); railway; ferry service to Scandinavia; economy: merchant, fishing and naval vessels (built and serviced), engineering, electrical precision instruments, fish processing, oil, railway vehicles, foundries, telephone systems, marine electronics, defence and armaments; event: Kieler Woche (Kiel Week), sailing regattas and programme of cultural events in June.

Kielce *kyel'tsay*, voivodship in S central Poland; watered by R Nida and bounded S by R Wisła (Vistula); pop(1983) 1,094,000; area 9,211 sq km; capital Kielce; chief towns include Ostrowiec Świętokrzyski, Starachowice and Skarżysko-Kamienna.

Kielce, KELTSY (Rus), 50 51N 20 39E, pop(1983) 197,000, industrial capital of Kielce voivodship, S central Poland; main town of the Świętokrzyski tourist region; founded in the Middle Ages it was for some years the property and residence of the Bishops of Kraków; railway; economy: mining and smelting, chemicals, industrial equipment, electrical engineering, machinery, ignition plugs, ball bearings, motor vehicles; monuments: 17th-c palace; national museum; 17th-c cathedral; Zieliński mansion; geological reserve nearby.

Kielder Water *keel'der*, reservoir in Northumberland, NE England; one of the largest man-made lakes in Europe, supplying water to the industrial NE; commenced in 1974 and completed in 1982, the reservoir was created by the damming of the R N Tyne with an embankment of over 4 mn cubic m of earth; the dam was completed in 4 years; it is the first regional water grid system in the UK; planting of the nearby Kielder Forest began in 1922; with the other Border forests this area (650 sq km) constitutes the largest area of man-made forest in Europe.

Kiev, city in W Soviet Union. See Kiyev.

Kiffa *kee'fa*, 16 28N 11 38W, capital of Assaba region, Mauritania, NW Africa; 240 km N of Kayes (Mali).

Kigali *kee-ga'lee*, 1 59S 30 05E, pop(1981) 156,650, capital of Rwanda, central Africa, also capital of Kigali prefecture; 80 km E of L Kivu; airport; economy: trade in cattle and hides.

Kigoma *kee-gō'ma*, 4 52S 29 36E, pop(1978) 50,044, lake-port capital of Kigoma region, W Tanzania, E Africa; at W terminus of railway from Dar es Salaam, on the shores of L Tanganyika, 354 km W of Tabora; alt 1,189 m; important Arab trading centre till the end of the 19th century; became a free port for Belgian vessels after World War I; its importance diminished in the 1940s owing to a decrease in tin and gold shipments from Zaire; the port handles transit cargo for Rwanda, Zaire and Burundi; economy: timber, cotton and tobacco trade.

Kikinda *kee'kin-da*, 45 50N 20 30E, pop(1981) 69,854, town in autonomous province of Vojvodina, N Srbija (Serbia) republic, Yugoslavia; 80 km NE of Novi Sad; railway; economy: grain trade.

Kikládhes *kik-lah'dhis*, CYCLADES *sik'la-deez* (Eng), island group and nome (dept) of Aegean Islands region, Greece; pop(1981) 88,458; area 2,572 sq km; capital Síros; the islands are situated between Pelopónnisos to the W and the Sporádhes to the E; about 220 islands, of which the most important are Tínos, Ándros, Míkonos, Mílos, Náxos, Páros, Kíthnos, and Sérifos, lying in a circle round the island of Síros; several of these islands, in particular Míkonos, are now popular holiday resorts.

Kikwit *kee'kweet*, 5 02S 18 51E, pop(1976e) 172,450, town in Bandundu region, W Zaire, central Africa; on the R Kwilu, 400 km ESE of Kinshasa; airfield.

Kilbirnie, 55 46N 4 41W, pop(1981) 8,710, town in Kilmarnock and Loudoun dist, Strathclyde, W Scotland; on the R Garnock, at the S end of Kilbirnie Loch, 15 km NE of Ardrossan.

Kildare *kil-der'*, CHILL DARA (Gael), county in Leinster prov, E Irish Republic; SW of Dublin county and watered by Liffey and Barrow rivers and by Grand and Royal Canals; the low lying central plain is known as the Curragh; pop(1981) 104,122; area 1,694 sq km; capital Naas; chief towns include Kildare, Athy and Droichead Nua; noted for its horse breeding with a national stud at Tully and a racecourse at the Curragh.

Kilimanjaro *kil-i-man-ja'rō*, 3 02S 37 20E, mountain on the frontier between Tanzania and Kenya, E Africa; height 5,895 m; the highest point on the African continent; 280 km WNW of Mombasa (Kenya) and 200 km SSE of Nairobi (Kenya); a glaciated double peaked massif of volcanic origin capped by the dormant cone of Kibo peak (5,895 m), and the jagged extinct Mawenza peak (5,148 m), glaciers include the Great Barranco, the Heim, the Penck and the Kersten; the first European sighting was by the German missionaries Rebmann and Krapf in 1848 while working with the Chagga people; Kibo peak was first scaled by H. Meyer and L. Purtscheller in 1889 and Mawenza peak first scaled in 1912 by F. Klute and E. Oelher; from Kilimanjaro it is possible to see the summit of Mount Kenya 323 km distant, one of the longest confirmed lines of sight on the Earth's surface.

Kilimanjaro, region of NE Tanzania, E Africa; bounded N by Kenya; pop(1985e) 1,093,000; chief town Moshi, a centre of the coffee industry.

Kilinochchi *kil-ee-no'chee*, 9 23N 80 24E, pop(1981) 18,000, capital of Kilinochchi dist, Northern prov, Sri Lanka; S of the Jaffna Lagoon and N of Anuradhapura.

Kilkeel', CILL CHAOIL (Gael), 54 4N 6 00W, pop(1981) 6,036, town in Newry and Mourne dist, Down, SE Northern Ireland; on the Kilkeel river, near the coast; economy: river and sea fishing (shellfish), textiles.

Kilkenny *kil-ken'ee*, CHILL CHOINNIGH (Gael), county in Leinster prov, SE Irish Republic; fertile agricultural county watered by R Nore; Slieve Ardagh Hills rise W of Kilkenny; pop(1981) 70,806; area 2,062 sq km; capital Kilkenny.

Kilkenny, CILL CHOINNIGH (Gael), 52 39N 7 15W, pop(1981) 16,886, capital of Kilkenny county, Leinster, SE Irish Republic; on R Nore; Kilkenny College and design workshops; railway; economy: clothing, footwear, brewing; monuments: town hall (Tholsel), 18th-c Kilkenny Castle, Bishop Rothe's house; event: Kilkenny Arts Week in Aug.

Kilkís *kyeel-kyees'*, mountainous nome (dept) of Makedhonia region, N Greece, near the Yugoslav border; pop(1981) 81,562; area 2,519 sq km; capital Kilkís.

Kilkís, 41 00N 22 53E, pop(1981) 11,148, capital town of Kilkís nome (dept), Makedhonia region, N Greece; 38 km N of Thessaloníki; railway.

Killarney *kil-ar'nee*, CILL AIRNE (Gael), 52 03N 9 30W, pop(1981) 9,083, resort town in Kerry county, Munster, SW Irish Republic; centre of an area of scenic beauty which includes the Lakes of Killarney; railway; economy: engineering, container cranes, hosiery; events: pan-Celtic week with Celtavision Song Contest in May; Killarney regatta in July; Kerry boating carnival in Sept.

Killeen', 31 07N 97 44W, pop(1980) 46,296, town in Bell county, central Texas, United States; 74 km SW of Waco; railway; Fort Hood base is nearby.

Kilmarnock, 55 37N 4 30W, pop(1981) 52,083, capital of Kilmarnock and Loudoun dist, Strathclyde, W Scotland; 31 km SW of Glasgow; railway; economy: whisky blending and bottling, food processing, textiles; monuments: Dick Institute museum and art gallery; Burns Monument and museum; 14th-c Dean castle.

Kilwinning, 55 40N 4 42W, pop(1981) 16,266, town in Cunninghame dist, Strathclyde, W Scotland; on the R Garnock, 7 km E of Ardrossan; railway; economy: textiles; 13th-c Kilwinning abbey.

Kim'berley, 28 45S 24 46E, pop(1980) 144,923, city in Cape prov, South Africa; 146 km WNW of Bloemfontein and 450 km SW of Johannesburg; a major diamond mining centre since the 1870s; founded in 1871; railway from Cape Town completed in 1885; came under siege between Oct 1899 and Feb 1900 during South African War; the Big Hole, 800 m deep and 500 m across, is claimed to be the biggest hole ever created by man; airfield; economy: diamonds, metal products, furniture, clothing, cement.

Kimch'aek *keem-chak*, formerly SONGJIN *sung-jeen*, 40 40N 129 20E, pop(1972) 265,000, port in Hamgyŏngnam (North Hamyong) prov, NE North Korea; situated on the coast at mouth of R Susong; opened to foreign trade in 1889; railway; economy: fishing, steel, paper.

Kinabalu, Gunong *goon oong' kin-a-bah'loo* (Malay 'akin nabalu' home of the spirits of the departed), 6 03N 116 32E, mountain in Sabah state, E Malaysia; situated in the Crocker Range; the highest peak in SE Asia at 4,094 m; the mountain lies within the Kinabalu National Park.

Kinabatangan *kin-a-bat-ang'an*, the largest river in Sabah state, E Malaysia, SE Asia; flows 560 km E into Sandakan Bay, NE Borneo.

Kindia *kin'dyu*, 10 03N 12 49W, pop(1972) 79,861, capital of Guinée-Maritime region, W Guinea, W Africa; 115 km ENE of Conakry; railway.

Kind'ley, civil airport and United States Naval airforce base at the W end of St David's Island, Bermuda; leased to the US government for 99 years.

Kingfish, oil field in the Bass Strait, off the S coast of Victoria, Australia.

Kings Canyon, national park in E California, United States; situated in the Sierra Nevada, approx 142 km E of Fresno; contains the large, ancient sequoia trees; area 1,863 sq km; established in 1940; to the S lies Sequoia National Park.

King's Lynn, LYNN REGIS, LYNN, BISHOP'S LYNN, 52 45N 0 24E, pop(1981) 37,966, port and market town in West Norfolk dist, Norfolk, E England; S of the Wash on R Ouse, 63 km W of Norwich; railway; economy: food processing and canning, glass, agricultural equipment, refrigeration equipment; monuments: chapel of St

Nicholas (1146), Guildhall of the Holy Trinity (1421), Castle Rising, Sandringham (1867-70).

Kingsport, 36 33N 82 33W, pop(1980) 32,027, town in Sullivan county, NE Tennessee, United States; on the R Holston, 30 km NW of Johnson City and just 5 km S of Virginia border; railway; economy: printing, bookbinding, and the manufacture of film, textiles and plastics; the city stands on the old Wilderness Road, the trail followed by Daniel Boone.

Kingston, 44 14N 76 30W, pop(1981) 52,616, town in SE Ontario, SE Canada; at the mouth of the Cataraqui river, at the NE end of L Ontario, where the Rideau Canal system and L Ontario join the St Lawrence river; the site of a former fort (Fort Frontenac), the present city was founded in 1784 by United Empire Loyalists; Kingston was a Canadian naval base during the War of 1812, and the capital of United Canada from 1841 to 1844; Royal Military College (1876); Queen's University (1841); railway; economy: textiles, chemicals, mining machinery, aluminium products; monuments: the Pump House Steam Museum contains the world's largest collection of steam engines in working order; Fort Henry was used as a British garrison until 1870, then as a Canadian garrison for the next 20 years after which it was abandoned, restoration was begun in 1936 and completed in 1938.

Kingston, 17 58N 76 48W, pop(1982) 524,638, capital city and commercial centre of the Caribbean I of Jamaica, in Kingston parish, Surrey county; on the N side of a landlocked harbour, SE coast of the island; founded in 1693 after Port Royal had been destroyed by an earthquake; it has been capital of the island since 1870; Institute of Jamaica (1879); University of the West Indies (1948); Norman Manley International Airport at Palisadoes; railway; economy: oil refining; monuments: St Peter's church (1725), coin and note museum, national gallery; Hope Botanical Gardens, Tuff Gong International studio built by reggae star Bob Marley.

Kingston-upon-Hull or **Hull**, 53 45N 0 20W, pop(1981) 269,539, seaport in Humberside, NE England; at the junction of the Hull and Humber rivers, 35 km from the North Sea and 330 km N of London; named after King Edward I; city status granted in 1897 and Lord Mayor's office created in 1914; a major UK container port; university (1954); railway; car ferry service to Rotterdam, Zeebrugge; the Humber Bridge, completed in 1981, is the largest single span suspension bridge in the world; economy: chemicals, paper, pharmaceuticals, iron and steel, fishing, service industries.

Kingston-upon-Thames *-temz'*, 51 25N 0 17W, pop(1981) 132,547, borough of SW Greater London, England; on R Thames; includes the suburbs of Malden and Coombe, Surbiton, and Kingston-upon-Thames; said to have been the coronation place of Anglo-Saxon kings, the 'coronation stone' is preserved; railway; economy: chemicals, plastics, paint, light engineering.

Kingstown, 13 12N 61 14W, pop(1978) 22,782, capital and main port of St Vincent, Windward Is, E Caribbean; on Kingstown Bay, on the SW coast of the island; botanical gardens (1763); several beach resorts nearby; a breadfruit tree planted by the infamous Captain Bligh of the *Bounty* still stands; airfield; monuments: St George's cathedral, courthouse.

Kingsville, 27 31N 97 52W, pop(1980) 28,808, county seat of Kleberg county, S Texas, United States; near the head of Baffin Bay, 54 km WSW of Corpus Christi; university (1917); railway; economy: processing centre for farming, oil and gas industries.

Kingswood, 51 26N 2 30W, pop(1981) 54,956, town in Kingswood dist, Avon, SW England; part of Bristol urban area; railway.

Kingussie *king-yoo'si*, 57 05N 4 04W, pop(1981) 1,229, capital of Badenoch and Strathspey dist, Highland region, N central Scotland; on the R Spey, 45 km S of Inverness; railway; monuments: Highland Folk Museum, an open-air museum of Highland life; 1 km S are the ruins of Ruthven Barracks (1716-18) destroyed by the Jacobites in 1746.

Kinki *keen-kee*, region in S Honshū island, Japan; bounded N by the Sea of Japan, S by the Pacific Ocean, E by Ise-wan Bay and Chūbu region and W by Chūgoku region, the Harima-nada Sea, Ōsaka-wan Bay and Kii-suido Channel; pop(1980) 21,208,000; area 33,038 sq km; Kinki region is divided into 7 prefectures as follows:

Prefecture	*area (sq km)*	*pop(1980)*
Hyōgo	8,363	5,145,000
Kyōto	4,613	2,527,000
Mie	5,774	1,687,000
Nara	3,692	1,209,000
Ōsaka	1,858	8,473,000
Shiga	4,016	1,080,000
Wakayama	4,722	1,087,000

Kinneret *kee-ne'ret*, sub-district of North dist, N Israel; pop(1983) 62,620; area 521 sq km.

Kinnesswood, 56 13N 3 28W, village in Perth and Kinross dist, Tayside, central Scotland; E of Loch Leven; birthplace of the poet Michael Bruce (1746-67); until the early 20th century a centre of the Scottish parchment and vellum industry.

Kinross, 56 13N 3 27W, pop(1981) 3,496; town in Perth and Kinross dist, Tayside, central Scotland; N of Dunfermline, on the W shore of Loch Leven; economy: motor trade, cashmere spinning; monuments: 17th-c Kinross House, designed by Sir William Bruce; Loch Leven castle on an island in Loch Leven; museum; events: Sunday market; agricultural show (Aug).

Kinross-shire, former Scottish county, now part of Perth and Kinross district, Tayside region, Scotland.

Kinsha'sa, formerly LEOPOLDVILLE (-1966) (Belg), 4 18S 15 18E, pop(1981e) 2,338,246, river-port capital of Zaire, central Africa; on the Zaire river opposite Brazzaville (Congo); founded in 1887 by Henry Stanley; capital of Belgian colony transferred here from Boma in 1926; US troops stationed here during World War II; railway; airport; university (1954); economy: textiles, chemicals, brewing.

Kinston, 35 16N 77 35W, pop(1980) 25,234, county seat of Lenoir county, E North Carolina, United States; on the R Neuse, 40 km ESE of Goldsboro; railway; economy: tobacco trade, timber products, textiles and fertilizer.

Kintampo *keen-tam'pō*, 8 06N 1 40W, town in Brong-Ahafo region, central Ghana, W Africa; NE of Sunyani.

Kintyre, peninsula in Strathclyde, SW central Scotland; bounded by the North Channel and the Atlantic Ocean (W) and Kilbrennan Sound (E, an arm of the Firth of Clyde); runs S to the Mull of Kintyre from a narrow isthmus between East and West Loch Tarbert; 64 km long; average width 13 km; the chief town is Campbeltown; there is an airfield at Machrihanish.

Kintyre, Mull of, cape on the S extremity of the Kintyre peninsula, off SW Scotland; projects into the North Channel; lighthouse.

Kinyet'i, 3 56N 32 52E, mountain in Southern region, Sudan, NE Africa; height 3,187 m; located close to the Ugandan frontier, Kinyeti is the highest point in Sudan.

Kirgizskaya, KIRGIZIYA SSR, constituent republic of the Soviet Union, in NE Middle Asia; bounded SE and E by China; the Tien Shan Mts occupy much of the area, attaining a max elevation within the republic of 7,439 m at Pik Pobedy; chief river is the Naryn; the Ozero Issyk-Kul' is the largest lake; pop(1983) 3,801,000; area 198,500 sq km; capital Frunze; chief towns include Osh, Przheval'sk, and Kyzyl-Kiya; economy: non-ferrous metallurgy; machine building; coal mining and gas extraction in the SW; light industry (textiles); food processing; power generation; gold mining (started in 1986 in the upper Naryn basin); animal husbandry plays an important role in the republic's agriculture; proclaimed a constituent republic within the USSR in Dec 1936; the republic is divided into the 3 oblasts of Issyk-Kul'skaya, Naryn and Oshskaya.

Kiribati *kir-a-bas* (sic), formerly GILBERT ISLANDS, official name Republic of Kiribati, group of 33 low lying coral islands scattered over almost 3 million sq km of the central Pacific Ocean, comprising the Gilbert Group, Phoenix Is, and 8 of the 11 Line Is (the other 3 Line Is are uninhabited dependencies of the US); timezone GMT −12; total land area 717 sq km; capital Tarawa; pop(1985) 63,843; 33.2% of the population live in Tarawa (1985); the people are predominantly of Micronesian stock; Gilbertese, a Micronesian dialect, and English are the main languages; Christianity is the dominant religion, with a slightly higher number of Roman Catholics than Protestants; the unit of currency is the Australian dollar; membership of Commonwealth, ADB, GATT (de facto), ICAO.

Physical description. The islands are coral atolls, mostly flat narrow strips, seldom rising more than 4 m above sea level. In most of the atolls, a reef encloses a lagoon, on the E side of which are long narrow stretches of land, seldom more than 100 m wide. Banaba, rising to a height of 87 m, is a solid coral outcrop with a fringing reef. Kiritimati (Christmas I), in the Line group, is the largest coral atoll in the world, covering 388.4 sq km, over half the total land area of Kiribati.

Climate. The central Gilbert Is, Phoenix Is, and Banaba have a maritime equatorial climate, but the islands further N and S are tropical. The average annual temperature is 27°C, which is moderated by the E trade winds that blow for most of the year. Annual and daily ranges of temperature are small. The average annual rainfall varies from 1,020 mm near the equator to 3,050 mm in the extreme N and S. The rainy season extends from Nov to April, with rain falling in sharp irregular squalls. Some islands, particularly those in the S and central Gilbert Is, suffer from periodic drought, when as little as 200 mm of rain may fall in one year.

History, government and constitution. The Gilbert and Ellice Is were proclaimed a British protectorate in 1892 and annexed as the Gilbert and Ellice Is Colony on 10 Nov 1915. On 1 Oct 1975, the Ellice Is severed their constitutional links with the Gilbert Is to form a separate dependency called Tuvalu (now independent). Internal self-government was introduced in the Gilbert Is on 1 January 1977 and independence achieved on 12 July 1979 as the Republic of Kiribati. On independence Kiribati became the 41st member of the Commonwealth. It is a sovereign and democratic republic, with a president who is both head of state and of government, and a house of assembly composed of 36 elected members.

Economy. Agriculture is virtually non-existent due to the poor quality of the soil which is composed largely of coral sand and rock fragments. Coconut palms cover the major part of all islands, except Banaba and some of the Phoenix Is, and provide the country's only major export, copra. Copra production is a privately-owned business in the Line Is, whereas village co-operatives handle production in the Gilberts. The main food crops are babai (taro), coconuts, bananas, pandanus, breadfruit, and papaya. Sea fishing is on a small scale but has great potential. Phosphate mining, the country's major source of revenue and employment (phosphate production accounted for 86% of the country's exports by value in 1977), ceased operation in 1979 owing to the depletion of supplies. Since then, small secondary industries have been established in association with the expansion of copra production and the development of tourism.

Administrative divisions. The islands are divided into the administrative districts of Banaba, Northern Gilbert Is, Central Gilbert Is, Southern Gilbert Is, South-Eastern Gilbert Is, Line Is, and the Phoenix group.

Kirin, prov in NE China. See Jilin.

Kirin, town in Jilin prov, NE China. See Jilin.

Kiritima'ti, CHRISTMAS ISLAND, 2 00N 157 30W, largest atoll in the world, one of the Line Is, Kiribati, central Pacific Ocean, 248 km SE of Fanning I and 2,000 km S of Honolulu; area 388.4 sq km; pop(1985) 1,737; indented on the E by the Bay of Wrecks; discovered by Captain Cook in 1777, and annexed by the British in 1888; used as an air base.

Kirkby *ker'bi*, 53 29N 2 54W, pop(1981) 52,609, town in Knowsley borough, Merseyside, NW England; 10 km NE of Liverpool; Kirkby industrial estate lies to the E; railway; economy: building; engineering.

Kirkby in Ashfield, 53 06N 1 16W, pop(1981) 26,127, town in Ashfield dist, Nottinghamshire, central England; 7 km SW of Mansfield; economy: coal, hosiery, engineering.

Kirkcaldy *kir-kaw'di*, 56 07N 3 10W, pop(1981) 46,522, capital of Kirkcaldy dist, Fife, E Scotland; on the N shore of the Firth of Forth, 17 km N of Edinburgh; birthplace of the economist Adam Smith (1723) and of the architect Robert Adam (1728); railway; economy: coal, textiles, furniture, engineering, whisky; monuments: Kirkcaldy museum and art gallery; 3 km N of Kirkcaldy in Dysart is the John McDouall Stuart museum, birthplace of the explorer John McDouall Stuart (1815-66) who crossed the Australian desert in 1861.

Kirkcudbright *kir-koo'bri*, 54 50N 4 03W, pop(1981) 3,427, capital of Stewartry dist, Dumfries and Galloway, S Scotland; on the R Dee estuary, at the head of Kirkcudbright Bay; monuments: MacLellan's Castle (1582); 16th-c Tolbooth; Stewartry museum, with a display on John Paul Jones, founder of the American Navy, who was born here.

Kirkintilloch *kir-kin-til'oKH*, 55 57N 4 10W, pop(1981) 33,148, town in Strathkelvin dist, Strathclyde, W central Scotland; in Clydeside urban area, 11 km NE of Glasgow; on the Forth and Clyde Canal; economy: engineering; monument: the site of a fort on the Antonine wall.

Kırklareli *kirk-la're-lee*, prov in NW Turkey, bounded N by Bulgaria and E by the Black Sea; pop(1980) 283,408; area 6,550 sq km; capital Kırklareli; economy: canary grass, sugar-beet, cereals.

Kirkūk *kir-kook'*, 35 28N 44 26E, pop(1970) 207,852, industrial city and capital of At-Ta'mīm governorate, N Iraq; 144 km SE of Mosul, on a tributary of the R Tigris; agricultural and market centre; built on a mound containing the remains of an ancient settlement; railway; economy: gas, oil refining, and the manufacture of chemicals, cement, and textiles.

Kirkwall, 58 59N 2 58W, pop(1981) 5,995, port capital of Orkney, N Scotland; chief town and port of the Orkney mainland; at the N end of a narrow neck of land, with the Wide Firth to the N and Scapa Flow to the S; airport (4 km SE); economy: fishing, textiles, tourism, oil; monuments: Earl Patrick's palace (1607); St Magnus cathedral (1137-1200); Tankerness House, built in 1574 as a merchant-laird's mansion, is now a museum of Orkney life.

Kirkwood, 38 35N 90 24W, pop(1980) 27,987, town in St Louis county, E Missouri, United States; suburb 18 km W of St Louis; railway.

Kirov *kee'ref*, formerly VYATKA (-1934), 58 38N 49 38E, pop(1983) 404,000, river port capital of Kirovskaya oblast, central European Rossiyskaya, Soviet Union; extends 20 km along the banks of the R Vyatka; famous for its toys and wood articles; railway; airfield; economy: fertilizers, heavy engineering, tyres, clothing, footwear, timber-related industries (20% of the Soviet Union's skis are produced here); monument: Uspenskii cathedral of the Trifon Monastery (1689).

Kirovabad *kee-re-fu-bad'*, formerly GANDZHA, GANDJA, ELISAVETPOL, 40 39N 46 20E, pop(1983) 253,000, industrial town in Azerbaydzhanskaya SSR, Soviet Union; on a tributary of the R Kura; destroyed by earthquake in 1138 and rebuilt on a new site; railway; economy: textiles, carpets, cotton, foodstuffs, aluminium, instruments.

Kirovograd *kee-re-fu-grat'*, formerly KIROVO (1936-39), ZINOVIEVSK (-1924-36), ELIZAVETGRAD, YELIZAVETGRAD (-1924), 48 31N 32 15E, pop(1983) 253,000, capital city of Kirovogradskaya oblast, Ukrainskaya SSR, Soviet Union; on the R Ingul; founded in 1764; agricultural trade centre; railway; economy: machine building (one of the USSR's largest farm machinery plants), metalworking, foodstuffs, footwear, clothing.

Kırşehir *kur-she-hir'*, mountainous prov in central Turkey; SE of Ankara; pop(1980) 240,497; area 6,570 sq km; capital Kırşehir; economy: mohair, cereals, linseed oil, carpets.

Kirthar *keer'tur*, national park in Sind prov, Pakistan; established in 1974; area 819.26 sq km.

Kiruna *ki-roo'na*, 67 53N 20 15E, pop(1983) 28,638, mining town in N Norrbotten county, N Sweden; SE of L Torneträsk; on the Lappland railway between Narvik in Norway and Luleå in Sweden; originally a small Lapp settlement, the town began to develop about 1900 when the local iron ore was mined; received municipal charter in 1948; the most northerly town in Sweden.

Kisalföld *keesh'ol-fuld* LITTLE ALFÖLD (Eng), flat, lowland geographical region in NW Hungary; bounded by the R Danube, the Hungarian Alps and the Transdanubian Central Mountain Range.

Kisa'ma, national park in Angola, SW Africa; area 9,960 sq km; established in 1957.

Kisangani *kee-sen-gah'nee*, formerly STANLEYVILLE (-1966), 0 33N 25 14E, pop(1976e) 339,210, capital of Haut-Zaïre region, N central Zaire, central Africa; on the Zaire river, 1,250 km NE of Kinshasa; regarded as the beginning of the Zaire river proper; Stanley arrived here in 1877 and established Kisangani post in 1882; Stanleyville city was founded in 1898; airport.

Kishinev *ki-shi-nyof'*, CHISINAU (Rom), 47 00N 28 50E, pop(1983) 580,000, capital city of Moldavskaya SSR, SW Soviet Union; on the R Byk; founded in 1420 as a monastery town; university (1945); railway; airfield; economy: solar research and development, machine building, tobacco, textiles, foodstuffs; monument: Cathedral of the Nativity (1836).

Kishoreganj *kish-ōr'gunj*, 24 26N 90 46E, pop(1981) 52,302; town in Kishoreganj dist, Mymenshingh, E central Bangladesh; W of the R Brahmaputra (Jamuna) and NE of Dhākā; linked by rail to Mymenshingh in the NW and Dhākā in the SE.

Kisii *kee-see'*, 0 40S 34 47E, pop(1979) 31,000, town in Nyanza prov, SW Kenya, E Africa; 65 km S of Kisumu.

Kiskunfélegyháza *keesh'koon-fayl'egy'-hah'zo*, 46 42N 19 53E, pop(1984e) 36,000, town in Bács-Kiskun county, central Hungary; 24 km SE of Kecskemét; railway; established about 1743; birthplace of Hungarian novelist Ferenc Móra; economy: market centre for livestock, tobacco, fruit and wine; monuments: art nouveau town hall, prison museum.

Kiskunhalas or **Halas** *keesh'koon-ho'losh*, 46 28N 19 37E, pop(1984e) 31,000, town in Bács-Kiskun county, S Hungary; SSW of Kecskemét; famous for its lacework; a Kiskunhalas State Farm produces a prize-winning liqueur made of quails' eggs and lecithin; railway; economy: grain, cattle and wine trade, oil, lace; monuments: lace museum; museum of ethnography.

Kiskunság *keesh'koon-sog*, national park in Bács-Kiskun county, S Hungary; situated between the Danube and Tisza rivers; established in 1974; area 306.3 sq km; noted for its species of rare European birds and orchids.

Kismaayo *kees-ma'yoo*, CHISIMAIO (Ital), 0 25N 42 31E, pop(1982) 70,000, port in Jubbada Hoose prov, Somalia, NE Africa; on Indian Ocean coast near the mouth of the R Juba, 400 km SW of Muqdisho (Mogadishu); founded in 1872 by the Sultan of Zanzibar; taken by British forces in 1887 and subsequently became part of Jubaland (region ceded to the Italians in 1925); occupied again by the British during World War II; airfield.

Kissidougou *kee-see-doo'goo*, 9 05N 10 00W, town in S Guinea, W Africa; 160 km SW of Kankan.

Kistna, river of India. See Krishna.

Kisumu *kee-soo'moo*, formerly PORT FLORENCE, 0 03S 34 47E, pop(1979) 150,000, (1984e) 215,000, port, capital on L Victoria of Nyanza prov, SW Kenya, E Africa; the Mombasa railway reached here in 1901; centre of a cotton and grain growing area.

Kita *kee-ta'*, 13 04N 9 29W, pop(1971) 11,700, town in Kayes region, W Mali, W Africa; on the railway between Bamako and Kayes, 160 km WNW of Bamako; economy: power plant.

Kita-Kyūshū *kee'ta-kee-oo'shoo*, 33 52N 130 49E, pop(1980) 1,065,078, city in Fukuoka prefecture, N Kyūshū island, Japan; separated from Shimonoseki on Honshū I by the Kammon Tunnels; comprises the former towns of Tobata, Kokura, Moji, Wakamatsu and Yawata; railway; airport; Japan's leading centre for chemicals and heavy industry.

Kitale *kee-ta'lay*, 1 01N 35 01E, pop(1979) 25,000, town in Rift Valley prov, W central Kenya, E Africa; in the E foothills of Mount Elgon, 185 km NW of Nakuru; railway; airfield; economy: agricultural trading centre.

Kita'vi, national park in W Tanzania, E Africa; area 2,253 sq km; established in 1974; situated E of L Tanganyika and NW of L Rukwa.

Kitchener, 43 27N 80 30W, pop(1981) 139,734, town in SE Ontario, SE Canada; in the Grand river valley, 88 km W of Toronto; twin city with Waterloo to the NW; founded in the early 1800s by German settlers from Pennsylvania, the area is still populated by Amish and Mennonite farmers; the town was originally called Berlin, but the name was changed to Kitchener in 1916 during World War I; university (1963); railway; economy: rubber; event: 10-day Oktoberfest beer festival.

Kitgum *kit'goom*, 3 17N 32 54E, town in Northern prov, Uganda, E Africa; 80 km NE of Gulu.

Kíthira *kee'thee-rah*, Greek island in the Mediterranean Sea, SE of Pelopónnisos; area 278 sq km; produces grapes and olives.

Kíthnos *keeth'nos*, THERMIA (anc), island of the Kikládhes, Greece, in the S Aegean Sea; area 99 sq km.

Kitwe *kee'tway*, 12 48S 28 14E, pop(1980) 314,794, modern mining city in Copperbelt prov, Zambia, S central Africa; 50 km WNW of Ndola; Kitwe has grown to be Zambia's 2nd largest town; area 1,813 sq km; extended in 1970 to include the townships of Kalulushi, Chambeshi, Chibuluma and Itimpi; Mindolo Ecumenical Centre; railway; economy: copper mining, electrical equipment, batteries, paint, fibreglass, food processing, iron foundry, furniture, clothing and plastics.

Kitzbühel *kitz'bü-el*, 47 27N 12 23E, pop(1981) 7,840, winter sports resort and capital of Kitzbühel dist, Tirol, central Austria, in the Kitzbüheler Alps, on the route from St Johann to the Thurn Pass; the mining of copper and silver in the 16-17th centuries led to the town's prosperity; casino; railway; event: Kitzbühel Fair on 1st weekend of Aug.

Kivu *kee'voo*, lake in central Africa; situated on the border between Zaire and Rwanda N of L Tanganyika; area 2,655 sq km; 97 km long and up to 48 km wide, it is the highest lake of the Albertine Rift, alt 1,460 m; drains into L Tanganyika through R Ruzizi; Idjwi island occupies the middle of the lake with its town, Kashofu; the main shoreline towns include Goma, Gisenye, Kibuye, Cyangugu and Kalene; the lake is used for transporting goods; there are methane reserves under lake bed; the first European sighting of the lake was by the German Count von Gotzen.

Kivu, region in E Zaire, central Africa; pop(1981e) 4,713,761; area 256,662 sq km; capital Bukavu; chief towns include Kindu, Kibombo and Shabunda; includes a large part of L Edward (NE) and L Kivu (E), a small part of L Tanganyika (SE), and a substantial length of the Lualaba river (upper reaches of the R Zaire) which flows N past Kindu; the Lomami river forms the region's W border; mountains rising in the E include Mt Karisimbe (4,507 m), Mt Stanley (5,110 m); a railway from S Zaire runs N as far as Kindu; major reserves of columbium, tin, tantalum, tungsten and monazite (rare-earth metal) are both mined and processed.

Kiyev *kee'yef*, KIEV (Eng), KIYIV (Ukr), 50 28N 30 29E, pop(1983) 2,355,000, capital city of Kiyevskaya oblast and Ukrainskaya SSR, Soviet Union; on the R Dnepr; one of the largest industrial, cultural, and scientific centres of the USSR; earliest centre of Slavonic culture and learning; founded in the 6th or 7th century; in the 9th century Kiyev became the capital of medieval Kievan Russia, the early Russian state; university (1834); railway; airport; economy: chemicals, clothing, knitwear, leatherwork, footwear, instruments; monuments: St Sofia cathedral (1037); Zabrovsky Gate (1746); Monastery of the Caves (1051); five-domed All Saints church (17th c); Vydubetsky monastery (1070-77).

Kızıl Irmak *ku'zul ir-mak'* ('red river'), HALYS *hay'lis* (anc), longest river of Turkey; rises in the Kızıl Dağ, N central Turkey, 19 km NW of Kuruçay; flows in a wide arc SW past Sivas, then NW, N and NE to discharge into the Black Sea N of Bafra; length 1,355 km; chief tributaries Balaban, Delice, and Devrez; important source of hydroelectric power; the Hirfanli Baraji has been formed by damming the river S of Kırşehir.

Kjölen or **Kolen**, mountain range along boundary between NE Norway and NW Sweden; rises to 2,111 m at Kebnekaise, Sweden's highest peak; source of many rivers in Norrbotten county flowing SE to Gulf of Bothnia, especially Ljusnan, Ångermanälven and Lule älv.

Kjustendil, okrug (prov) in Bulgaria. See Kyustendil.

Klad'no, 50 10N 14 05E, pop(1984) 72,566, industrial town in Středočeský region, Czech Socialist Republic, W Czechoslovakia; 24 km NW of Praha (Prague); railway; economy: coal mining, metal.

Klagenfurt *klah'gen-foort*, 46 38N 14 20E, pop(1981) 87,321, capital of Kärnten state, S Austria; an industrial and commercial town on the R Glan near the Yugoslav border where the E-W routeway meets that from Wien (Vienna); founded in 1161 as a market village and granted a municipal charter in 1252; monuments: Landhaus (1574-90), Dragon Fountain (1590), 16th-c cathedral; events: Gastronomy and Tourism Trade Fair (March); Austrian Timber and Woodworking Fair (Aug), the most important of its kind in central Europe.

Klatovy *klat'o-vi*, 49 24N 13 20E, pop(1984) 22,801, town in Západočeský region, Czech Socialist Republic, W Czechoslovakia; S of Plzeň in the Bohemian Forest; railway; economy: chemicals, tanning.

Klerksdorp *klarks'dorp*, 26 52S 26 39E, pop(1980) 238,865, city in Transvaal prov, South Africa; on the Schoon Spruit river, 160 km WSW of Johannesburg, founded in 1839; mining commenced in 1933; economy: gold, uranium, lumber, beverages, machinery, grain.

Klosterneuburg *klo-ster-noy'boork*, 48 19N 16 20E, pop(1981) 22,975, town in Niederösterreich state, NE Austria; on the R Kierlingbach, separated from the Danube by a broad belt of meadowland, 12 km N of Wien (Vienna); federal college of wine-making; monument: Augustinian abbey founded in 1108, now a principal producer of wine in this rich wine-growing dist of the Wienerwald.

Klosters *klō'sterz*, 46 54N 9 54E, alpine winter skiing resort in Graubünden canton, E Switzerland; on R Landquart, NE of Davos resort town with which it shares snowfields; comprises the villages of Platz, Dörfli and Brücke; Kloster Pass (12 km E) leads to Austria; the resort is popular with young skiers and with royalty; children's ski school.

Kluane, national park in SW Yukon territory, NW Canada; borders W with Alaska and Mt Wrangell-St Elias National Park and S with British Columbia; contains part of the St Elias Mts, rising to 5,950 m at Mt Logan; area 22,015 sq km; the park was established in 1972.

Klyuchevskaya Sopka *klyoo-chif-skī'u sop'ku*, 56 03N 160 38E, highest peak in the Sredinnyy Khrebet range, Kamchatskaya oblast, E Siberian Rossiyskaya, Soviet Union; situated in the E mountain range of the Kamchatka Peninsula, on the right bank of the R Kamchatka; height 4,750 m; the highest active volcano of the Eurasian continent; the last volcanic eruption was in 1966; the volcano is a perfect cone whose crater is 200 m in diameter.

Knaresborough *nayrz'bu-ru*, 54 00N 1 27W, pop(1981) 12,994, town (just outside Harrogate) in Harrogate dist, North Yorkshire, N England; above R Nidd, 5 km N of Harrogate; railway; economy: quarrying; monuments: 14th-c castle, Mother Shipton's Cave.

Knokke-Heist *kno'ku-hīst*, 51 21N 3 19E, pop(1982) 24,082, tourist resort in Brugge dist, West-Vlaanderen (West Flanders) prov, NW Belgium; on the North Sea coast, close to the Dutch border, in an attractive landscape of dunes; after Oostende it is the most fashionable seaside resort in Belgium; its beach is 12 km long (one-fifth of the entire Belgian coastline); present tourist resort developed rapidly after 1880 when the fishing village of Knokke merged with the residential suburb of Het Zoute and the more recent settlement of Albertstrand to the W; the Zwin bird sanctuary is located nearby; railway.

Knottingley *not'ing-li*, 53 43N 1 14W, pop(1981) 15,386, town in Kirklees borough, West Yorkshire, N England; on the R Aire and the Aire and Calder Navigation, 18 km E of Wakefield; railway.

Knoxville, 35 58N 83 55W, pop(1980) 175,030, county seat of Knox county, E Tennessee, United States; a port on the Tennessee river, 160 km NE of Chattanooga; headquarters of Tennessee Valley Authority; founded in 1786; state capital 1796-1812 and 1817-18; university (1794); railway; economy: major trade and shipping centre for farm products, tobacco, coal and marble; manufactures include plastics, textiles, and marble, wood, and metal products.

Knutsford *nuts'furd*, 53 18N 2 23W, pop(1981) 13,675, town in Vale Royal dist, Cheshire, NW central England; 24 km SW of Manchester; railway; economy: chemicals, engineering, building, scientific instruments.

Kōbe *kō-ō-bay*, 34 40N 135 12E, pop(1980) 1,367,390, port capital of Hyōgo prefecture, Kinki region, central Honshū island, Japan; W of Ōsaka, on Ōsaka-wan Bay, on a narrow coastal plain 2 km wide; lies at the foot of Rokko-san mountain; Japan's leading commercial port; the harbour was built in 1868 when increased trade through nearby Ōsaka created the need for a deep-water port; the town is gradually expanding due to land reclamation on the seaward side and a tunnel under Rokko-san; university (1949); university of economics (1948); railway; economy: shipbuilding, iron and steel, saké; monuments: the harbour and naval museum; Museum of Namban Art contains an ancient map of the world and 2 painted screens of the Kano period (16-17th-c); the Minatogawa Shrine, dedicated to a popular 14th-c war hero, contains armour and other articles belonging to him; event: Nankoosai Festival of Minatogawa Shrine, with people dressed in Samurai armour (May).

København *kœ'pen-hown*, a county in E Sjælland (Zealand), Denmark; area 522 sq km; pop(1983) 619,687; capital København.

København, COPENHAGEN *kō-pen-hay'gen* (Eng), HAFNIA (anc), 55 43N 12 34E, pop(1981) 493,771, capital city of Denmark; important commercial, business and industrial city, on the E coast of Sjælland (Zealand) and N part of Amager I; developed around 12th-c fortifications, the city was chartered in 1254 and became capital of Denmark in 1443; university (1479); technical university of Denmark (1829); railway; the airport at Kastrup plays a central rôle in air traffic between Scandinavia and other European countries; København is still defended by the old citadel of Frederikshavn, and by forts on the seaward side; the older part of the city radiates from a central square; the world-famous amusement park, Tivoli (open May to mid-Sept), is on the shores of the Øresund; economy: engineering, foodstuffs; monuments: Amalienborg Palace (residence of the Danish monarch since 1794); Christiansborg Palace (rebuilt after 1907); town hall (1894-1905); national (Thorwaldsen) museum; cathedral (rebuilt after 1807); Little Mermaid; 17th-c Trinitatiskirke, with a notable round tower ascended by a spiral incline instead of steps; Rosenborg Castle (1610-24), now a historical museum.

Koblenz *kō'blents*, COBLENZ (Eng), dist of Rheinland-Pfalz

(Rhineland-Palatinate) prov, W Germany; pop(1983) 1,357,500; area 8,092 sq km; capital Koblenz.

Koblenz, CONFLUENTES (anc), 50 21N 7 36E, pop(1983) 112,200, capital of Koblenz dist, Rheinland-Pfalz (Rhineland-Palatinate) prov, W Germany; at confluence of the Mosel and Rhine rivers, 80 km SSE of Köln (Cologne); one of the leading centres of the wine trade on the Rhine; the largest garrison town in W Germany; the town is dominated by the fortress of Ehrenbreitstein on the right bank of the Rhine; railway; economy: wines, hygienic tissue products; monument: St Castor's church (836).

Kocaeli *ko-jah-ay'lee*, prov in NW Turkey; bounded NE by the Black Sea and W by the Sea of Marmara; pop(1980) 596,899; area 3,626 sq km; capital İzmit; noted for its fine beechwoods; minerals include copper, iron, manganese, lead and zinc; economy: maize, sugar-beet, flax, tobacco, cotton.

Kōchi *kō'chee*, 33 33N 133 32E, pop(1980) 300,822, port capital of Kōchi prefecture, central Shikoku island, Japan; situated on an inlet of Tosa-wan Bay, 230 km SW of Ōsaka; railway; economy: dried fish, paper, coral products.

Kodiak Island, island (160 km long) in S Alaska, United States; situated in the Gulf of Alaska; northernmost section of the Coast Range Mts; scene of the first settlement in Alaska (by the Russians in 1784); till 1804 this area was the centre for Russian interests in the USA and of the fur trade; economy: dairying, cattle and sheep raising, fur trapping, fishing and farming are all important parts of the economy; home of the Kodiak brown bear, the largest living carnivore.

Koforidua *kō-fōr-ree-doo'a*, 6 01N 0 12W, pop(1982) 62,044, capital of Eastern region, SE Ghana, W Africa; 60 km N of Accra on the railway to Kumasi; economy: civil engineering.

Køge *ku'yu*, 55 28N 12 12E, pop(1981) 25,683, town on Køge Bugt (Køge Bay), Roskilde county, E Sjælland (Zealand), Denmark; railway; economy: timber.

Koh Kong *kō kong*, province in SW Cambodia; pop (1981) 38,700; bounded S and W by the Gulf of Thailand; coastline indented by the Bay of Kompong Som; crossed by the Piphat river and the Chaines des Cardamomes; chief town Koh Kong.

Kohat *kō'hat*, 33 37N 71 30E, pop(1981) 78,000, city in North-West Frontier prov, Pakistan; 45 km S of Peshawar; former military base for the Alfridi frontier; connected to Peshawar by the 20 km-long Kohat Pass; railway; economy: textiles, baskets, trade in grain and rock salt.

Kohkīlūyeh va Būyer Aḥmadī or BOYER AHMADĪ-YE SARDSĪR VA KOHKĪLŪYEH, mountainous prov in SW Iran; pop(1982) 244,370; area 14,261 sq km; capital Yāsūj.

Koinadugu *koy-na-doo'goo*, dist in Northern prov, Sierra Leone, W Africa; pop(1974) 158,626; area 12,121 sq km; capital Kabala.

Kokkola *ko'ko-lah*, GAMLAKARLEBY *gahm'lah-kahrl'a-bu* or KARLEBY (Swed), 63 50N 23 08E, pop(1982) 34,236, seaport on NW coast of Vaasa prov, W Finland; on the Gulf of Bothnia, 112 km NNE of Vaasa; established in 1620; united with Kaarlela rural commune in 1977; one of oldest towns in Finland; the harbour at Ykspihlaja is the deepest on the W coast of Finland; railway; airfield 15 km from the town at Kruunupyy; economy: heavy industry (since the early 1960s), leather and textiles.

Koko'mo, 40 29N 86 08W, pop(1980) 47,808, county seat of Howard county, central Indiana, United States; 80 km N of Indianapolis; railway; home of Elwood Haynes, the inventor.

Kola Peninsula, peninsula in NW European Rossiyskaya, Soviet Union. See Kol'skiy Poluostrov.

Kolda *kol'dah*, region in S Senegal, W Africa; bounded S by Guinea; part of Casamance region until 1984; capital Kolda; dissected by the R Casamance.

Kol'ding, 55 29N 9 30E, pop(1983) 56,418, seaport on inlet of the Lille Bælt (Little Belt), Vejle county, SE Jylland (Jutland), Denmark; founded in the 10th century; railway; economy: engineering, foodstuffs; monument: oldest stone church in Denmark (13th-c).

Kolhapur *kōl'hah-poor*, 16 43N 74 15E, pop(1981) 351,000, market centre and city in Maharashtra state, W India; 290 km SSE of Bombay; once the capital of the former princely state of the same name, it became part of Maharashtra state in 1960; the city occupies an ancient Buddhist site and is a centre of pilgrimage; economy: matches, pottery, textiles.

Kolín *ko'leen*, 50 02N 15 10E, pop(1984) 30,937, town in Středočeský region, Czech Socialist Republic, W central Czechoslovakia; on R Elbe, 72 km E of Praha (Prague); railway; economy: oil, chemicals, food processing.

Köln *kœln*, COLOGNE *kol-ōn'* (Eng), dist of SW Nordrhein-Westfalen (North Rhine-Westphalia) prov, W Germany; pop(1983) 3,900,900; area 7,363 sq km; capital Köln.

Köln, COLOGNE (Eng), 50 56N 6 58E, pop(1983) 953,300, manufacturing and commercial river port in Köln (Cologne) dist, Nordrhein-Westfalen (North Rhine-Westphalia) prov, W Germany; on W bank of the R Rhine; one of the most important traffic junctions and commercial centres in Germany; noted for its world-famed trade fairs; archbishopric; university (1388); railway; economy: oil refining, chemicals, petrochemicals, wine, foodstuffs, heavy equipment, motor vehicles, agricultural machinery, perfumes and cosmetics, medicaments, tools; monument: Gothic cathedral (begun 1248); event: Rhineland Carnival (Feb).

Kolonjë *ko-lon'ye*, formerly ERSEKE, prov of SE Albania; area 805 sq km; pop(1980) 21,600; capital Erseke.

Kolskiy Poluostrov *kol'y'ski*, KOLA PENINSULA *ko'lu* (Eng), peninsula in Murmanskaya oblast, NW European Rossiyskaya, Soviet Union, forming the NE extension of Scandinavia; length 400 km; width 240 km; separates the Barents Sea (N) from the Beloye More (White Sea) (S); there are numerous rivers (Varzuga, Ponoy, Iokanga, Kola) and small lakes; the NE is tundra-covered while the SW is forested; road and rail transport is confined to the W; the peninsula has rich mineral deposits.

Kolwezi *kōl-we'zee*, 10 45S 25 25E, town in Shaba region, SE Zaire, central Africa; 130 km WNW of Likasi; a major copper and cobalt mining centre; railway; airfield.

Kolyma *ku-li-ma'*, river in Magadanskaya oblast and Yakutskaya ASSR, Rossiyskaya, E Soviet Union; rises in several branches on the SE Khrebet Cherskogo range, N of the Sea of Okhotsk; flows generally N and NE past Seymchan and Zyryanka to discharge into the E Siberian Sea, forming a delta W of Ambarchik; length 2,513 km; drainage basin area 647,000 sq km; chief tributaries Omolon, Berezovka and Bolshoy Anyuy rivers; swamps and small lakes are numerous in the lower floodplain of the river; its upper course crosses the rich Kolyma gold fields.

Kolymskiy, Khrebet, GYDAN, mountain range mainly in Magadanskaya oblast, but extending also into NW Kamchatskaya oblast, Rossiyskaya, NE Soviet Union; extends c.1,120 km NE from Magadan to the upper Anyuy river; forms a watershed between streams draining into the Arctic Ocean (tributaries of the R Kolyma) and those draining into the Zaliv Shelekhhova of the Sea of Okhotsk; rises to a max height of 2,222 m.

Komárno *ko'mahr-no*, KOMÁROM (Hung), 47 46N 18 07E, pop(1984) 35,396, river port on both sides of R Danube in Západoslovenský region, Slovak Socialist Republic, Czechoslovakia and Komárom county, N Hungary; divided between Hungary and Czechoslovakia in 1920 and again in 1945; railway; economy: machinery, shipbuilding, textiles, timber.

Komárom *kō'ma-rom*, industrial and mining county in N Hungary; bounded to the N by the R Danube which follows the frontier with Czechoslovakia; mountainous in the E and flat in the W; pop(1984e) 323,000; area 2,250 sq km; capital Tatabánya; chief towns include Tata and Esztergom; economy: coal and lignite mining, cement, grain, dairy produce and vegetables.

Komárom, KOMÁRNO (Slovak), 47 43N 18 07E, pop(1984e)

20,000, river port town in Komárom county, N Hungary; at junction of R Vah and R Danube NW of Budapest; divided in 1945 between Hungary and Czechoslovakia; birthplace of the Hungarian novelist M. Jokai; railway; economy: commercial and shipping centre, shipbuilding, textiles, timber.

Kombo St Mary, local government area in The Gambia, W Africa; an urban area surrounding Banjul; pop(1983) 101,431; area 75.6 sq km.

Komló *kom'lō*, 46 15N 18 16E, pop(1984e) 31,000, mining town in Baranya county, S Hungary; in Mecsek Mts, N of Pécs; economy: coal mining.

Kommunizma, Pik, COMMUNISM PEAK (Eng), formerly MT STALIN (1933-62) and MT GARMO (-1933), 39 00N 72 02E, highest peak in the Soviet Union, in the Pamir range, N Tadzhikistan SSR; height 7,495 m; first climbed in 1933.

Komodo *ke-mō'dō*, small island in Nusa Tenggara Timur prov, Indonesia; part of the Lesser Sunda Islands; situated between Sumbawa and Flores Is; a national park was established in 1980; park area 375 sq km; home of the Komodo dragon, the world's largest monitor lizard; Kampong Komodo on the E coast is the only settlement.

Komotiní *ko-mo-tee-nee'*, GÜMÜLJINA (Turk), 41 06N 25 25E, pop(1981) 34,051, ancient market town and capital of Rodhópi nome (dept), Thraki region, NE Greece; lies in a wide plain in a tobacco-growing area; on main highway between Kaválla and Alexandroúpolis; university; railway.

Kompong Cham *kom-pong cham*, province in E Cambodia; pop(1981) 820,000; bounded E by Vietnam; crossed by the Mekong and Chhlong rivers; administrative centre and river port Kompong Cham; economy: textiles; in 1973 withstood an attack by Khmer Rouge forces, the government forces being supplied via the Mekong river.

Kompong Chhnang *kom-pong shnang*, province in central Cambodia; pop(1981) 273,000; crossed by the many tributaries of the Tonlé Sap river; its chief town, Kompong Chhnang, lies on the banks of the Tonlé Sap river.

Kompong Som, 10 38N 103 30E, seaport in S Cambodia; on Gulf of Thailand; located within but politically independent of Kampot prov; city completed in 1960; chief deepwater port and commercial centre of Cambodia.

Kompong Speu *kom-pong spu*, province in SW Cambodia; pop(1981) 307,000; chief town Kompong Speu, SW of Phnom Penh; Thnot lake and dam found to the W of the town.

Kompong Thom *kom-pong tom*, province in central Cambodia; pop(1981) 322,000, bounded SW by the Tonlé Sap river; crossed by the Sen river; region noted for its gem deposits; chief town Kompong Thom.

Komsomol'sk-na-Amure *kum-su-molsk' nu u-moor'yi*, KOMSOMOLSK-ON-AMUR (Eng), 50 32N 136 59E, pop(1983) 284,000, river port city in Khabarovskiy kray, Rossiyskaya, SE Soviet Union; on the lower R Amur, 356 km NE of Khabarovsk; founded in 1932 by the Komsomol, the communist youth organization; important industrial and cultural centre of the Soviet Far East; railway; economy: logging and lumber, clothing, oil refining, heavy engineering.

Komsomolsk-on-Amur, city in SE Soviet Union. See Komsomol'sk-na-Amure.

Konar *ku-nar'*, KUNAR, KONARHA, prov in E Afghanistan; bounded to the E by Pakistan; pop(1984e) 271,470; area 10,479 sq km; capital Asadābād; the Nuristan region of the S Hindu Kush range is found in the N section of the province; crossed E-SW by the R Kunar.

Kondūz *kun'duz*, KUNDUZ, prov in N Afghanistan; bounded N by the R Pyandzh and the USSR; pop(1984e) 606,211; area 7,827 sq km; linked to Kābul by the main road to the S; crossed by the R Kundz.

Kondūz, 36 45N 68 51E, pop(1984e) 60,644; capital of Kondūz prov, N Afghanistan; S of R Kunduz; linked to Kābul by a main road running S; airfield.

Kongsberg *kongs'ber*, 59 42N 9 39E, pop(1983) 20,621, town in Buskerud county, S Norway; on the R Lågen, WSW of Oslo; the town owes its foundation and early prosperity to the nearby silver mines, which began to be worked in 1624 and remained open until 1957; the 3rd oldest town in Norway; railway.

Kongs'vinger, 60 13N 11 59E, pop(1980) 17,169, town on the R Glåma, Hedmark county, SE Norway; railway; monument: 17th-c Kongsvinger Castle.

Konin *ko-nyeen'*, agricultural voivodship in central Poland; watered by the Warta and Noteć rivers; pop(1983) 452,000; area 5,139 sq km; capital Konin; chief towns include Turek and Koło; Russian partition zone between 1815 and 1918.

Konin, 52 12N 18 12E, pop(1983) 73,000, industrial capital of Konin voivodship, central Poland; on R Warta; largely developed since 1945; railway; economy: brown coal mining, aluminium.

Köniz *ku'nits*, 46 56N 7 25E, pop(1980) 33,441, town in Bern canton, Switzerland, on the SW outskirts of Bern; railway; economy: printing; monument: 13th-c castle.

Ko'no, dist in Eastern prov, Sierra Leone, W Africa; pop(1974) 328,930; area 5,641 sq km; capital Sefadu.

Kon'stanz, CONSTANCE (Eng), CONSTANTIA (anc), 47 39N 9 10E, pop (1983) 69,100, lake port in Tübingen dist, S Baden-Württemberg prov, W Germany; on the Bodensee (L Constance), 120 km S of Stuttgart, close to the Swiss border; university (1966); once an episcopal see and later an imperial city; the town also includes the flower island of Mainau; railway; economy: tourism, commerce and wine-growing, electrical and metal-processing industries, pharmaceuticals, textiles; monuments: council hall (1388), cathedral (15th-c).

Konya *ko'nya*, prov in S central Turkey; pop(1980) 1,562,139; area 47,420 sq km; capital Konya; noted for its breeds of camel and horse.

Konya, ICONIUM (anc), 37 51N 32 30E, pop(1980) 329,139, holy city and capital of Konya prov, S central Turkey, 260 km S of Ankara; trade centre of a rich agricultural and livestock-raising region; famous for its Seljuk architecture and for its connection with the great mystical poet of Islam, Celaleddin Rumi or Mevlana; railway; airfield; economy: carpets, textiles, leather; monument: Mevlana Mausoleum, the old monastery where the Order of the Whirling Dervishes was founded by Mevlana; event: ceremony of the dance every year in Dec to commemorate the death of Mevlana.

Kópavogur, 64 06N 21 56W, 2nd largest town in Iceland, in Suðurland region, SW Iceland; pop(1983) 14,433, between Reykjavík and Hafnarfjörður; developed since 1945 to house people working in Reykjavík.

Kopparberg *ko-par-ber'yu*, formerly DALECARLIA, a county of central Sweden; land area 28,350 sq km; pop(1983) 286,166; capital Falun; chief towns Borlänge and Ludvika; drained by the Västerdalälven, Österdalälven and Fuluälven rivers; lakes include the Siljan and Trängsletsjön.

Koprivnica *kop'riv-nit-sa*, 46 09N 16 50E, pop(1981) 61,166, town in N Hrvatska (Croatia) republic, Yugoslavia; 40 km ESE of Varazdin at foot of Bilo Gora; railway; economy: petroleum, chemicals, lignite.

Kopřivnice *kop'priv-nyi-tse*, 49 36N 18 09E, pop(1984) 20,891, town in Severomoravský region, Czech Socialist Republic, central Czechoslovakia; SW of Ostrava; railway; economy: engineering, motor vehicles.

Korbu, Gunong *goon-oong' kor-boo'*, 4 43N 101 17E, mountain in Perak state, NW Peninsular Malaysia; SE Asia; rising to 2,148 m, it is the 2nd highest mountain on the Malay Peninsula.

Korçë *kor'se*, formerly KORITSA, prov in SE Albania; area 2,181 sq km; pop(1973) 175,400; capital Korçë.

Korçë, 40 37N 20 46E, pop(1980) 54,300, industrial town and capital of Korçë prov, SE Albania; near the Greek border, 112 km SE of Tiranë, at the foot of Morava ridge in a rich agric region; former Orthodox religious centre of Albania; in the Middle Ages it was an important commercial centre on the routes to the Adriatic coast; economy: textiles, leatherwork, glass, foodstuffs (especially sugar); monument: 15th-c mosque.

Kordestān *koor-dis-tan'*, KURDESTAN, prov in NW Iran, bounded W by Iraq; pop(1982) 782,440; area 24,998 sq km; capital Sanandaj; inhabited by Kurds who also occupy parts of NE Iraq, SE Turkey and NE Syria; in 1920 a Kurdish autonomous state was agreed upon at the treaty of Sèvres, but the terms were never carried out.

Kordofan', KORDUFAN, region of central Sudan, NE Africa; area 146,932 sq km; pop(1983) 3,093,294; main towns include En Nahud, El Obeid and Umm Ruwaba; the Dar Nuba mts are situated S of Umm Ruwaba.

Korea or **South Korea**, official name Republic of Korea, TAE HAN MIN'GUK *ta-han'min-gook* (Kor), Republic of E Asia occupying the southern half of the Korean peninsula; bordered W by the Huang Hai (Yellow Sea), E by the Sea of Japan, S by the Korean Strait which separates it from Japan and N by North Korea from which it is separated by a demilitarized zone at approx 38°N; timezone GMT +9; area 98,913 sq km; capital Sŏul (Seoul); pop(1984) 40,430,137; the pop is largely Korean with a small Chinese minority; the official language is Korean, but English is widely taught in secondary schools; Korea's religions include Confucianism, Shamanism, Christianity, Buddhism, Chondokyo (religion of the heavenly way) and an eclectic religion with nationalist overtones which was founded in the 19th century and has approx 1.5 million followers; the Korean currency is the won; national holidays 1 March (Independence Day), 15 April (Arbor Day), 8th day of 4th lunar month (Buddha's birthday), 5 May (Children's Day), 6 June (Memorial Day), 17 July (Constitution Day), 15 August (Liberation Day); 15th day of 8th lunar month, Ch'usŏk, or Korean Thanksgiving Day; 1 Oct (Armed Forces Day), 3 Oct (National Foundation Day), 9 Oct (Han'gŭl Day); Korea is a member of ABD (Afro-Asian League Consultative Committee), ADB (Asian Development Bank), Asian Parliamentary Union, APACL (Asian People's Anti-Communist League), ASPAC, Colombo Plan, ESCAP, FAO, G-77, GATT, Geneva Conventions of 1949 for the protection of war victims, IAEA, IBRD, ICAC, ICAO, IDA, IFAD, IFC, IHO, IMF, IMO, INTELSAT, INTERPOL, IPU, IRC, ITU, IWC (International Whaling Commission), IWC (International Wheat Council), UNCTAD, UNDP, UNESCO, UNICEF, UNIDO, UN Special Fund, UPU, WACL (World Anti-Communist League), WHO, WIPO, WMO, WTO; Korea is an official observer at the United Nations and does not hold UN membership.

Physical description. The Taebaek Sanmaek (mts), running N-S along the E coast of Korea, fall from heights in excess of 900 m through a series of ridges which extend SW to broad, undulating coastal lowlands. Most of the pop lives in the lowlands to the W of the Taebaek Sanmaek. There are few settlements on the E coast where the mts drop steeply to the sea. There are c.3,000 islands off the W and S coasts, the largest being Cheju do, which includes Korea's highest peak, rising to 1,950 m.

Climate. Korea has an extreme continental climate, with cold winters and hot summers. There is a swift transition from winter to summer conditions between April and early May, with an equally rapid reversal to winter conditions in late Oct. Affected by the Asiatic monsoon, the winter winds come from the W and N bringing cold, dry air from N China and Siberia. Summer winds come mainly from the E and S, bringing warm, moist air from the Pacific Ocean. Owing to frontal systems and depressions moving from the W, the weather can be variable from day to day in all seasons, leading to rain or snow and occasional thaws in winter and heavy rain in summer. Between June and Sept, the wettest months of the year, at least one typhoon moves up from the South China Sea with very heavy rain and strong winds. Temperatures are higher in the S than the N. Average daily temperatures in Sŏul in the N range between −9° and 0°C for the month of Jan and 22° to 31°C for Aug, with min and max monthly rainfall figures of 20 mm in Feb and 376 mm in July. The town of Pusan in the S has

average daily temperatures of −2° to 6°C in Jan and 23° to 29°C in Aug, with rainfall ranging between 31 mm in Dec and 295 mm in July.

History, government and constitution. Until the 1st century BC Korea was ruled by the ancient Chosŏn dynasty. Thereafter the country was split into 3 rival kingdoms until united again in 668 by the Silla dynasty which ruled until 935 when it was succeeded by the Koryŏ dynasty. The last dynasty, the Yi, ruled from 1392 until 1910. China, having formerly claimed suzerainty over Korea, recognized the country's independence in 1895. After the Russo-Japanese war of 1904-05 Korea became a virtual Japanese protectorate until final annexation by Japan took place in 1910. In 1945 the Russians and Americans entered Korea, from the N and S respectively, to enforce the surrender of the Japanese troops there, dividing the country by the 38th parallel of latitude. Negotiations between the 2 countries on Korea's future broke down in May 1946. On 25 June 1950 North Korean forces invaded Korea. Sixteen UN member nations assisted South Korea in holding back the North Korean forces in a war lasting from 1950 to 1953, at which time the border was re-established at 38°N. Talks since then between the 2 Koreas on unification have failed. A new constitution was approved by national referendum in 1980 under which a president with reduced executive powers is elected indirectly by a 5,000-member electoral college for a single 7-year term. A State Council is appointed and led by the President. The new constitution also made provision for a 4-year National Assembly consisting of 276 representatives, 184 directly

elected and 92 chosen by proportional representation. Suffrage is universal for those over the age of 20.
Economy. Since the early 1960s Korea has progressed towards economic, military and industrial independence. The country's manufacturing industry has concentrated on the production of light consumer goods, but more recently has shifted towards heavy industries and petrochemicals. Principal exports include textiles and clothing, electrical machinery, footwear, steel, ships and fish. Although Korea's Sangdong mine is one of the world's largest deposits of tungsten, the country suffers from shortages in base metals, petroleum, timber and certain food grains. Major trade partners include the USA and Japan.
Agriculture. Only one-fifth of Korea is suitable for cultivation, with 25% of the population living and working on the land. Major crops are rice, barley, wheat, beans, grain and tobacco. The raising of cattle, pigs and poultry has become a flourishing industry. Korea's major food shortages are in wheat, dairy products and corn. Deep-sea fishing plays an increasing role in the economy, with a total of 5 ships in 1962 rising to 849 in 1976.
Administrative divisions. Korea consists of 9 provinces and 4 special cities which have provincial status (Sŏul, Inch'ŏn, Taegu and Pusan):

Province	*area (sq km)*	*pop(1984)*
Cheju	1,824	482,031
Chŏllanam	12,189	3,824,322
Chŏllapuk	8,052	2,288,707
Ch'ungch'ŏngnam	8,807	3,056,198
Ch'ungch'ŏngpuk	7,430	1,419,921
Kangwon	16,894	1,816,365
Kyŏnggi	10,958	4,581,009
Kyŏngsangnam	11,850	3,574,035
Kyŏngsangpuk	19,425	3,083,690

Korea, North, official name Democratic People's Republic of Korea, CHOSŎN MINJUJUŬI IN'MIN KONGHWAGUK (Kor), socialist state in East Asia; situated in the N half of the Korean peninsula; bordered N by China, NE by the USSR, S by a demilitarized zone and Korea, W by Korea Bay and the Huang Hai (Yellow Sea) and E by the Sea of Japan; timezone GMT +9; area 122,098 sq km; separated from South Korea to the S by a demilitarized zone of 1,262 sq km; capital P'yŏngyang; pop(1983e) 18,490,000; the official language is Korean; although religious activities in North Korea are now almost non-existent, Buddhism and Confucianism are the traditional religions; the currency is the won (of 100 chon); national holiday 9 Sept; membership of FAO, G-77, IAEA, ICAO, IPU, ITU, NAM, UN (with observer status only), UNCTAD, UNESCO, UPU, WFTU, WHO, WIPO, WMO.
Physical description. North Korea lies on a high plateau which occupies the N portion of a mountainous peninsula which projects SE from China. The N is mountainous with many areas rising to heights between 1,800 and 2,450 m. In the NW the plateau falls to the Yalu R valley, which forms the border with China. To the S of the plateau are lower mountains and foothills which descend to narrow coastal plains in the E and wider coastal plains in the W. Good harbours are found on the E coast.
Climate. The climate of North Korea is temperate with warm summers and severely cold winters. In winter snowfall, although light, tends to lie for long periods. North Korea is exposed to the cold winds which blow from Manchuria and Siberia in the winter. The severe winter weather causes rivers to freeze for 3 to 4 months and ice forms along the coast, blocking harbours. Summer months are generally warm, but not warm enough in the far north for rice to be grown. There is little difference in temperatures and rainfall between the E and W coasts. Daily temperatures at P'yŏngyang, in W North Korea, lie between −3° and −13°C in Jan, the coldest month, while Wŏnsan on the E coast fares slightly better with −8° to 1°C in Jan. In the warmest months of July-Aug P'yŏngyang temperatures rise to between 20° and 29°C, while Wŏnsan records slightly lower temperatures of 19° to 27°C in July and 20° to 27°C in Aug. Rainfall in P'yŏngyang ranges between a min of 11 mm in Feb and a max of 237 mm in July, while Wŏnsan has a min of 31 mm in Dec and Jan and a max of 318 mm in Aug, the wettest months on either side of the country being July-Sept.
History, government and constitution. The Korean Peninsula was conquered in 1392 by the Chinese Yi dynasty who governed from Sŏul (Seoul) for over 500 years. In 1895 at the end of the Sino-Japanese War, Japan formally annexed Korea and deposed the last Yi monarch in 1910. With the downfall of the Japanese in 1945, Korea was occupied by Soviet troops from the N and US troops from the S, both meeting along latitude 38°. The 2 countries set up governments in each zone, each claiming to represent the whole of the country, but failing to agree on policies for unification. In 1950 North Korean troops invaded the S and were driven back by UN forces. Southern forces were then opposed and swept southwards by a Chinese army. The armistice line established in 1953, now a demilitarized zone, remains the official border between North and South Korea. Talks on reunification began in 1980 but were broken off by North Korea. The political structure of North Korea is based on the constitution of 1972 which replaced the earlier 1948 constitution. A Supreme People's Assembly, elected every 4 years, theoretically supervises the legislative and judicial function. In practice the country is centrally ruled by the Korean Workers' (Communist) Party, which elects a Central Committee which in turn appoints a Politburo, the first 4 members of which constitute its Standing Committee.
Economy. North Korea's population is concentrated on the low coastal zones in the E and W of the country and is

traditionally agricultural. The country suffered from extensive destruction during the Korean War, but with aid from the USSR and China economic recovery has been rapid. During the 1970s the importation of western technology and increased military spending resulted in considerable overseas debt, with North Korea being the first communist country to default on loan payments. The country's major industries are machine building, electricity production, chemicals, mining, metallurgy, textiles and food processing. North Korea has a large mineral wealth in coal, refractory clays, phosphates and iron, magnesium, tungsten, copper, lead and zinc ore. The country has little oil or natural gas, but hydroelectric power is well developed. Major trade partners include the USSR, Eastern Europe, Japan, W Germany, France.

Agriculture. Approx 48% of the North Korean workforce is employed in agriculture, generally on large-scale collective farms. The main crops produced are rice, maize and vegetables. Livestock (especially pigs) is also important. Other crops grown are wheat, barley, rape, sugar, millet, sorghum, beans and tobacco. Timber is mainly exploited for domestic use, while inshore and deep-water fishing is important.

Administrative divisions. North Korea is divided into the 9 provinces of Hamgyŏngpuk (North Hamgyong), Hamgyŏngnam (South Hamgyong), Hwanghaipuk (North Hwanghai), Hwanghainam (South Hwanghai), Kangwŏn, Chagang (Jagang), P'yŏnganpuk (North Pyongan), P'yŏngannam (South Pyongan) and Yanggang.

Korhogo *kor-hō'gō*, dept in N Ivory Coast, W Africa; pop(1975) 276,816; area 12,500 sq km; capital Korhogo; chief towns Katiali, Dikodougou and Boron; airfield; until 1981 an important diamond mining area.

Kórinthos *ko'rin-thos*, CO'RINTH (Eng), nome (dept) of Pelopónnisos region, S Greece; pop(1981) 123,042; area 2,290 sq km; capital Kórinthos.

Kórinthos, 37 56N 22 55E, pop(1981) 22,658, capital town of Kórinthos nome (dept), Pelopónnisos region, Greece; at the foot of the hill of Akrokórinthos (575 m), and on a narrow isthmus separating the Adriatic Sea from the Aegean; on the rocky Isthmus of Corinth the city had 3 harbours, one to the W and two to the E; since 1893 it has been cut by a canal; the town was transferred to a new site in 1858 after a severe earthquake and rebuilt after a further earthquake in 1928 and a great fire in 1933; the site of ancient Kórinthos, which has been excavated since 1896 by the American School, lies 7 km SW; railway; ferry to Italy; economy: wine trade, tourism; monuments: extensive remains, mostly dating from the Roman period, including the Archaic Temple of Apollo and several basilicas; event: Navy Week (June-July).

Kōriyama *kō-ree-ya'ma*, 37 23N 140 22E, pop(1980) 286,451, city in Fukushima prefecture, Tōhoku region, E central Honshū island, Japan; 40 km SSW of Fukushima; railway; economy: textiles, chemicals.

Koropí *ko-ro-pee'*, 37 54N 23 52E, pop(1981) 11,214, town in Attikí nome (dept), Sterea Ellás-Évvoia region, Greece, SE of Athínai (Athens).

Koror *kō'ror*, 7 21N 134 31E, capital town of the Republic of Belau, W Caroline Is, W Pacific Ocean, on Koror I, 1,300 km SW of Guam, and 1,200 km N of Biak (Indonesia); airport on neighbouring island of Babeldoab; economy: catching, storing and shipping of tuna, copra crushing mill, boatbuilding; monument: the Belau National Museum has exhibits depicting 2 centuries of Belauan history.

Körös *ku'rush*, river in SE Hungary; formed by the junction of the Rapid and the White Körös SE of Gyoma, rivers that rise in the Romanian Carpathian Mts; the river is also joined by the Black Körös which rises on Mt Bihor in Romania; flows 80 km W and SW to meet the R Tisza near Csongrád.

Korsør *kor'sœr*, 55 19N 11 09E, pop(1981) 15,281, seaport on the Store Bælt (Great Belt), in Vestsjælland county, SW Sjælland (Zealand), Denmark; rail terminus; ferry services across the Store Bælt; economy: engineering.

Kortrijk *kort'rik*, dist of West-Vlaanderen (West Flanders) prov, W Belgium; area 403 sq km; pop(1982) 272,038.

Kortrijk, COURTRAI *koor-tray* (Fr), 50 50N 3 17E, pop(1982) 10,944, capital town of Kortrijk dist, West-Vlaanderen (West Flanders) prov, W Belgium; on the R Leie, which is connected by canal to the R Schelde; railway; economy: synthetic fibres, clothing, linen, carpets, canvas, textiles, rubber, furniture, printing, machine building, electrical engineering, steel wire and wire products; the economy has been based on the textile industry since the beginning of the 14th century; flax, grown in the surrounding dist of Flanders, is still the most important raw material; attempts to diversify the economy, however, have led to the introduction of numerous new industries; the polishing of precious stones is also a well-known and economically important activity; monument: St Martin's church (13th-c).

Koryakskiy Khrebet, mountain range in Magadanskaya and Kamchatskaya oblasts, Rossiyskaya, NE Soviet Union, extending NNE from the neck of the Kamchatka Peninsula to the Anadyrskiy Zaliv (Anadyr Gulf) of the Bering Sea; rises to 2,562 m at Gora Ledyanaya in the central section; continued SW by the Sredinnyy Khrebet range; source of the R Velikaya and several tributaries of the R Anadyr.

Kós *kos*, COS (Eng), island of the Sporádhes, E Greece, in the Aegean Sea, off the SW coast of Turkey; area 290 sq km; length 43 km; length of coastline 112 km; width 2-11 km; the E part of the island is hilly, reaching a height of 846 m in Mt Díkaios; the island has become a popular tourist attraction, offering a mild climate, numerous bathing beaches, and an ancient sanctuary of Asklepios with extensive remains; it was famous in antiquity for its wine, amphorae, and 'Coan garments', and for the cult of Asklepius and its great school of doctors, notably represented by Hippocrates; it was severely damaged by earthquakes in 1933.

Kós, COO (Ital), 36 53N 27 19E, pop(1981) 11,851, town and port in Sporádhes nome (dept), Aegean Islands region, Greece; on NE coast of Kós I; airfield; local boat service; economy: cereals, olive oil, wine, fruit, tourism; monuments: the Asklepieion (sanctuary of Asklepios) lies 6 km SW of the town, with several temples, Roman baths, and an altar erected to Asklepios, son of Apollo, about 350 BC; 15th-c Castle of the Knights of St John; several mosques; notable is the Plane Tree of Hippocrates, where, legend has it, the great teacher of medicine in Kós (460 BC) taught; event: Navy Week (June-July).

Kosciusko, Mount *koz-ee-es'kō*, 36 28S 148 17E, highest mountain in Australia; rising to 2,228 m in SE New South Wales in the Snowy Mts of the Australian Alps, 386 km SW of Sydney; the 6,458 sq km Kosciusko National Park was established in 1944; Mount Townsend, a nearby peak, was formerly called Mount Kosciusko; a popular winter sports area.

Köseg *ku'seg*, 47 14N 16 37E, pop(1984e) 14,000, historic town in Vas county, W Hungary; at the foot of the Alps, close to the Austrian frontier; the highest town in Hungary; the advance of the Turks against Vienna was halted here in 1532; monuments: historic Jurisich Square, castle with Jurisich Miklós Museum.

Koshigaya *kō-shee-ga'ya*, 35 53N 139 47E, pop(1980) 223,241, city in Saitama prefecture, Kanto region, E central Honshū island, Japan; on the Tobu Isesaki railway line, N of Tōkyo.

Košice *ko'shi-tse*, 48 43N 21 14E, pop(1984) 214,270, industrial capital of Východoslovenský region, Slovak Socialist Republic, E Czechoslovakia; on R Hornad; 5th largest city in Czechoslovakia and 2nd largest in Slovak Socialist Republic; formerly part of Hungary; technical university (1952); airport (Barca); railway; economy: textiles, chemicals, tobacco, brewing; monument: St Elizabeth cathedral.

Kos'ovo, KOSOVO-METOHIJA, autonomous prov in the republic of Srbija (Serbia), S Yugoslavia; bounded to the S by the Yugoslav republic of Makedonija (Macedonia) and to the W by Albania; pop(1981) 1,584,440; area

10,887 sq km; capital Priština; chief towns Prizren, Peć, Uroševac and Kosovska Mitrovica; two-thirds of the pop are of Albanian stock, the remainder being Turks, Serbs and Montenegrins; both Albanian and Serbian are recognized languages with signs being written in both forms; the territory was acquired by Srbija in 1913 but during World War II it was ceded to Albania which was then under German-Italian control; Kosovo became an autonomous prov in 1948, 3 years after being returned to Yugoslavia; a poorly-developed mountainous region with reserves of lead, zinc, nickel and other non-ferrous metals; power sources at thermal and hydroelectric power stations; the Kosovo Polje (Field of Kosovo) valley, in which the capital town of Priština is located, is noted for its sweet wines.

Kosovska Mitrovica or **Mitrovica** *kos'ov-ska mee'tro-veet-sah*, 42 54N 20 52E, pop(1981) 105,323, town in autonomous province of Kosovo, S Srbija (Serbia) republic, Yugoslavia; on R Ibar, NNW of Priština; railway; economy: mining and smelting.

Kosrae, formerly KUSAIE *koo-sī'e*, island group, one of the Federated States of Micronesia, W Pacific; area 100 sq km; pop(1980) 5,522; capital Lelu, Kosrae was part of the Ponape dist of the Trust Territory of the Pacific Islands until 1977; tourism has recently developed on the volcanic island of Kosrae; there is a new harbour and an airport on Kosrae I.

Kosti *kōs'tee*, 13 11N 32 38E, pop(1973) 65,257, town in Central region, Sudan, NE Africa; on Bahr el Ablad (White Nile), 270 km S of Khartoum; railway.

Kostroma *ku-stru-ma'*, 57 50N 40 58E, pop(1983) 264,000, port capital of Kostromskaya oblast, E European Rossiyskaya, Soviet Union, on both banks of the R Volga, 372 km NE of Moskva (Moscow); founded in the 12th century; airfield; railway; economy: linen-processing, machine building, woodworking, furniture, clothing; monuments: cathedral of Bogoiavlenshii Monastery (1559-65), Troitskii Cathedral (1650-52), church of Ioann Bogoslov (1681-87);

Koszalin *kōsh-a'leen*, voivodship in NW Poland; bounded N by Baltic Sea; source of the Drama, Gwda, Rega and Parsęta rivers; pop(1983) 478,000; area 8,470 sq km; capital Koszalin; chief towns include Kołobrzeg, Szczecinek and Białograd.

Koszalin, KÖSLIN *kus'lin* (Ger), 54 10N 16 10E, pop(1983) 97,800, capital of Koszalin voivodship, NW Poland; near the Baltic coast; school of advanced engineering (1969); railway; airport; capital of voivodship since 1950 when its population was 19,000; sports centre; economy: electronics, vehicle parts, building equipment; monuments: Gothic cathedral (14th-c), castle of the Pomeranian dukes, archaeological museum; event: annual international festival of Polonia choirs.

Kota *kō'tu*, KOTAH, 25 11N 75 58E, pop(1981) 347,000, industrial city in Rajasthan state, NW India; on the R Chambal, 192 km S of Jaipur; linked by rail to Mathura and Ratlam; airfield; economy: textiles, trade in locally produced oilseed and sugar; monuments: city walls enclose many temples, the most famous of which is the Mathureshi temple.

Kota Baharu *kō'tu bah'roo*, 6 07N 102 15E, pop(1980) 167,872, capital of Kelantan state, NE Peninsular Malaysia, SE Asia; northernmost town on the E coast of the Malay Peninsula, near the mouth of the R Kelantan; economy: fishing, batik; monuments: Istana Balai Besar (palace with a large audience hall) built in 1844; Istana Jahar, now a state museum; 10 km S is the Kampung Laut mosque, the oldest mosque in Malaysia; event: bird-singing competition in June.

Kota Kinabalu *kō'tu kin-a-bah'loo*, formerly JESSELTON (-1968), 5 59N 116 04E, pop(1980) 55,997, capital of Sabah state, E Malaysia, SE Asia; situated on the W coast, between the mountains and the South China Sea; islands of the Tun Abdul Razak National Park lie offshore; frequently destroyed by pirates in the 19th century, the town was rebuilt by the Chartered Company, whose vice-chairman, Sir Charles Jessel, gave his name to the town; renamed after Mt Kinabalu, SE Asia's highest mountain.

Kotka *kot'kah*, 60 26N 26 55E, pop(1982) 60,384, seaport in Kymi prov, SE Finland; on a small island in the Gulf of Finland, E of Helsinki; established in 1878; railway; economy: shipbuilding, shipping of pulp, paper and timber.

Kotte *kō'tay*, 6 54N 79 55E, pop(1981) 101,653, town in Colombo dist, Western prov, Sri Lanka; a suburb SE of Colombo; former Sinhalese capital (14-15th century).

Koudougou *koo-doo'goo*, 11 43N 4 40W, pop(1985e) 52,431, town in Burkina, W Africa; 88 km W of Ouagadougou; railway; airfield.

Kouilou *koo-ee'loo*, province of SW Congo, W Africa; area 13,694 sq km; pop(1980) 261,370; capital Pointe-Noire.

Koulamoutou *koo-la-moo-too'*, 1 12S 12 29E, capital of Ogooué-Lolo prov, S central Gabon, W Africa; on the R Bwenguidi, 345 km ESE of Port Gentil; the centre of a number of uprisings in pre-1940 colonial times; the centre of cattle-rearing country; Roman Catholic mission; airfield.

Koulikoro *koo-lee-kō'rō*, 12 55N 7 31E, pop(1976) 16,876, river-port town in Bamako region, SW Mali, Africa; on the R Niger, 52 km ENE of Bamako; terminus of the railway from Dakar (Senegal); from July to Dec there are river connections to Gao; economy: trade, power plant.

Koulouri *koo-loo'ri* town in Attiki nome (dept), Sterea Ellás-Évroia region, Greece. See Salamís.

Koupéla *koo-pay'la*, 12 07N 0 21W, town in E central Burkina, W Africa; between Ougadougou and Fada N'Gourma.

Kourou *koo-roo'*, 5 08N 52 37W, pop(1984e) 7,000, town in Cayenne dist, French Guiana, NE South America; on the R Kourou where it meets the Atlantic, 56 km W of Cayenne; French space centre built here in 1967; known as 'white city' by the Guyanais because of the number of French people living there; tourism is important, with boats to the Iles du Salut, bathing, fishing and an aero club.

Kouroussa *koo-roo'sa*, 10 45N 9 45W, town in E Guinea, W Africa, 440 km ENE of Conakry; railway.

Koutiala *koot-ya'la*, 12 20N 5 23W, pop(1971) 14,600, town in Sikasso region, S Mali, W Africa; 27 km E of Bamako; economy: power plant.

Kouvola *ko'vo-la*, 60 54N 26 45E, pop(1982) 31,453, capital of Kymi prov, SE Finland; established in 1921; railway; economy: pulp, paper, power station.

Kowloon, peninsula and region of the British Crown Colony of Hong Kong, in SE Asia; area 10.56 sq km; in some areas of Kowloon, population density of 20,500 to the sq km was recorded in the 1981 census; railway from Hung Hom Station links Kowloon to Guangzhou (Canton) and is the only railway in Hong Kong; Hong Kong's airport is built out into the sea from the peninsula of Kowloon at Kai Tak and is one of the busiest in S Asia, handling 8.6 million passengers each year; Victoria Harbour (Hong Kong Harbour) lies between the Kowloon peninsula and Hong Kong Island and is one of the finest natural harbours in the world, ranking 7th in terms of tonnage handled.

Kozáni *koz-ah'nee*, inland nome (dept) of Makedhonia region, N Greece; E of Píndhos mts; pop(1981) 147,051; area 3,516 sq km; capital Kozáni; watered by the R Aliákmon.

Kozáni, 40 18N 21 48E, pop(1981) 30,994, capital town of Kozáni nome (dept), Makedhonia region, N Greece; 105 km WSW of Thessaloniki; events: Bourbousaria festival (6 Jan); Fanos festival with bonfires and folk dancing (March).

Kpali'mé, 6 55N 0 44E, pop(1980e) 25,500, town in Des Plateaux region, W Togo, W Africa; 104 km NW of Lomé; railway terminus; economy: cotton ginning, trade in cacao, cotton and palm products.

Kpandu *ku-pan'doo*, 7 00N 0 25E, town in Volta region, E Ghana, W Africa; N of Ho on the E shore of L Volta; economy: civil engineering.

Kpong *ku-pong'*, 6 11N 0 09E, town in Eastern region, S Ghana, W Africa; on the R Volta N of Accra.

Kra, Isthmus of, narrow section of the Malay Peninsula in S Thailand; 65 km wide at its narrowest; the Pachkan R forms a frontier with SE Burma; the port of Ranong is located to the W; there have been plans to build a canal linking the Andaman Sea with the Gulf of Thailand.

Kragerø *kra'gu-ru*, 58 54N 9 25E, pop(1980) 10,812, town on the Skagerrak, E coast of Telemark county, SE Norway; NE of Arendal; rail terminus.

Kragujevac *kra'goo-ye-vats*, KRAGUYEVATS (Slov), 44 01N 20 55E, pop(1981) 164,823, town in central Srbija (Serbia) republic, E central Yugoslavia; situated 96 km S of Beograd; university (1976); railway; economy: canning, fruit.

Kraków *krak-oof'*, voivodship in S Poland; Beskid Mts rise in the S; watered by Wisła (Vistula) and Raba rivers; pop(1983) 1,197,000; area 3,254 sq km; capital Kraków; chief towns include Skawina.

Kraków or **Cracow**, KRAKAU (Ger), CRACOVIA (anc), 50 04N 19 57E, pop(1983) 735,200, industrial capital of Kraków voivodship, S Poland; N of the Beskids, on R Wisła (Vistula); 3rd largest city in Poland; university (1364); technical university (1945); includes Nowa Huta industrial centre built after 1949; railway; airport; economy: pig iron, metallurgy, chemicals, food processing, clothing, printing; monuments: Gothic cathedral (14th-c), royal castle, city museum, churches of St Andrew, SS Peter and Paul, St Barbara and the Virgin Mary; in the central Market Square are a number of 14th-c buildings including the clothiers' hall; events: Kraków Days in June.

Kralendijk *kra-lun-dīk'*, 12 09N 68 18W, capital town of Bonaire I, S Netherlands Antilles, E Caribbean, on a W inlet of the island.

Kraljevo *kral-ye'vō*, RANKOVIĆEVO *ran'ko-vi-che-vo* (Slov), 43 44N 20 41E, pop(1981) 121,622, industrial town in Srbija (Serbia) republic, Yugoslavia; on R Ibar near its junction with R Morava; railway; economy: agricultural centre noted for its dairy produce; magnesium oxide; wagon building; wood and metal products; monuments: nearby are the monasteries of Kalenić, Žiča, Studenica, Veluće and Ljubostinja.

Kranj *krī'nya*, KRAINBURG (Ger), CARNIUM (anc), 46 15N 14 20E, pop(1981) 66,879, town in N Slovenija republic, Yugoslavia; on R Sava, 24 km NNW of Ljubljana; railway junction; economy: precision tools, textiles, leather.

Kranjska Gora *krīn'ska go'ra*, 46 29N 13 48E, winter sports complex in NW Slovenija republic, Yugoslavia; at N foot of the Julian Alps; chair-lift and ski trails on Mt Vitranc (1,631 m); there are also several mountaineering huts.

Krasnodar *krus-nu-dar'*, formerly EKATERINODAR, YEKATERINODAR (-1920), 45 02N 39 00E, pop(1983) 595,000, capital city of Krasnodarskiy kray, SE European Rossiyskaya, Soviet Union; on the R Kuban', 80 km from the Black Sea; founded as a military camp in 1793; university (1970); railway; airport; economy: solar research and development, machine building, oil refinery, chemicals, clothing, textiles.

Krasnoyarsk *krus-nu-yarsk'*, 56 08N 93 00E, pop(1983) 845,000, fast-growing river port capital of Krasnoyarskiy kray, W Siberian Rossiyskaya, Soviet Union; on the R Yenisey; founded in 1628 as a military fort; the town grew rapidly after the discovery of gold and later with the construction of the Trans-Siberian railway; university (1969); airport; economy: manufacture of heavy machinery, grain harvesters and other industrial equipment, electrical goods, steel, aluminium.

Kratie *krat-yay'*, province in E Cambodia; pop(1981) 136,000; crossed by the Mekong river; the chief town, Kratié, lies on the E bank of the Mekong river, to the S of the Sambor Dam and is the market town for the surrounding agricultural region.

Krefeld *kray'felt*, 51 20N 6 32E, pop(1983) 222,100, industrial river port in Düsseldorf dist, W Nordrhein-Westfalen (North Rhine-Westphalia) prov, W Germany; on R Rhine, 30 km WSW of Essen; railway; economy: chemicals, rail cars, textiles, hydraulic presses, special steel.

Kremenchug *krye-myen-chook'*, 49 03N 33 25E, pop(1983) 220,000, river port and administrative centre in Poltavskaya oblast, Ukrainskaya SSR, Soviet Union; on the R Dnepr; established in 1571 as a fortress; centre of an industrial complex based near a hydroelectric plant; railway; economy: machinery, metalwork, mining, oil, footwear, clothing.

Krems an der Donau *krems an der do'now*, 48 25N 15 36E, pop(1981) 23,056, industrial and commercial river port and capital of Krems dist, Niederösterreich, NE Austria; on the R Danube (Donau); the old town is built on higher ground at the mouth of the Kremstal, while the newer dists are on the banks of the Danube; railway; school of wine and fruit-growing; economy: engineering and wine trade.

Krib'i, 2 56N 9 56E, port and resort town in Sud-Ouest prov, SW Cameroon, W Africa; S of Douala, on the coast of the Gulf of Guinea; Lobe Cascades nearby; economy: timber, fishing, coffee, cocoa.

Kriens *kree-ens'*, 47 03N 8 17E, pop(1980) 21,097, industrial suburb of Luzern, in Luzern canton, Switzerland; W of Vierwaldstätter See; economy: engineering, transport equipment.

Krishna *krish'nu*, KISTNA, river in S India; rises in the Western Ghats, 65 km to the E of the Arabian sea; length 1,288 km; flows generally SE through the state of Maharashtra, entering Andhra Pradesh to the N of Raichur; flows SE, E, NE and SE through the state to its mouth in the Bay of Bengal; the mouth of the river marks the N boundary of the Coromandel Coast; the source of the R Krishna is sacred to the Hindus.

Kristiansand *krees-tyan-san'*, CHRISTIANSAND, 58 08N 8 01E, pop(1983) 61,824, seaport and capital of Vest-Agder county, SW Norway; on the Skagerrak, SW of Oslo; see of a bishop; founded in 1641 by Christian IV; railway; monuments: 17th-c neo-Gothic cathedral, 11th-c church.

Kristianstad *krist-yan'stad*, a county of S Sweden, bounded on the E by the Hanöbukten, a bay of the Baltic Sea, and on the NW by the Kattegat; land area 6,048 sq km; pop(1983) 280,220; capital Kristianstad; chief towns Hässleholm and Simrishamn.

Kristianstad, 56 02N 14 10E, pop(1982) 69,207, seaport and capital of Kristianstad county, S Sweden; railway; on R Helge; founded in 1614 by Christian IV of Denmark, ceded to Sweden in 1658, captured by the Danes in 1676 and finally recaptured by Sweden in 1678; the earliest example of Renaissance town-planning in N Europe; economy: engineering, textiles, sugar.

Kristiansund *kri-styan-soon'*, CHRISTIANSUND, 63 06N 7 58E, pop(1980) 18,013, commercial town and fishing port on W coast of Møre og Romsdal county, W Norway; built on 3 small islands enclosing a harbour, WSW of Trondheim; base of a large fishing fleet; large trade in the shipment of fish products; founded 1742.

Kristinehamn *kri'stin-u-ham*, 59 17N 14 09E, pop(1983) 26,623, lake port in Värmland county, SW Sweden; on W shore of L Vänern; founded in 1642; railway; economy: shipment of iron and timber.

Kríti, CRETE *kreet* (Eng), CAN'DIA (Ital), CRE'TA *kree'tee* (Lat) (whence the word for 'chalk', from which the geological Cretaceous system is named), island region of Greece, in the Mediterranean Sea, S of the Kikládhes island group in S Aegean Sea; pop(1981) 502,165; area 8,336 sq km; comprises the nomoi (depts) of Iráklion, Khaniá, Réthimnon, and Lasíthi; length 256 km; length of coastline 1,046 km; width 14-60 km; largest of the Greek islands and 5th largest in the Mediterranean; at the W end of the island are the Lévka Óri (White Mts), rising to 2,452 m; in the centre the Ídhi Óros rise to the highest point of the island, Psiloritis (2,456 m); the N coastline is deeply indented with fertile plains; the climate of the N coast is Mediterranean, while the S coast is sub-tropical; capital Iráklion; chief ports Khaniá, Iráklion, Áyios

Nikólaos; Knossos, Górtys and Lató are famous ancient Greek and Roman sites; economy: fruit, olive oil, wine, sheep, goats, tourism.

Krivoy Rog *kryi-voy' rok'*, KRYVYJ RIH (Ukr), 47 55N 33 24E, pop(1983) 674,000, industrial town in Dnepropetrovskaya oblast, Ukrainskaya SSR, Soviet Union; on the upper course of the R Ingulets; centre of the Krivoy Rog iron ore basin; founded in the 17th century; industrial growth dates from 1881 when several foreign interests founded a mining syndicate; railway; airfield; economy: metallurgy, machine building, power engineering, wood products.

Krka *kur'ka*, river in W Hrvatska (Croatia) republic, Yugoslavia; rises N of Knin and flows 72 km SSW to the Adriatic Sea near Šibenik; the Krka Falls between Zadar and Split are a major tourist attraction; the river is a source of hydroelectric power.

Krnov *kœr'nof*, 50 05N 17 40E, pop(1984) 26,079, town in Severomoravský region, Czech Socialist Republic, central Czechoslovakia; on R Opava, NW of Ostrava, near the Polish frontier; summer resort and winter sports centre; railway; economy: textiles, organ-building.

Kroměříž *krom'yer-ish*, 49 18N 17 24E, pop(1984) 25,904, town in Jihomoravský region, Czech Socialist Republic, W central Czechoslovakia; on R Morava, SE of Olomouc; railway; economy: agricultural trade, engineering, footwear; 18th-c summer palace of the archbishop of Olomouc where the first Austrian Constituent Parliament met in 1848.

Kronoberg *kroo-noo-ber'yu*, a county of S Sweden; numerous lakes including Åsnen, Möckeln and Bolmen; land area 8,459 sq km; pop(1983) 173,981; capital Växjö; chief towns Ljungby and Alvesta; economy: glass-making.

Kronshlot *kron'shlet*, formerly KRONSHTADT or KRONSTADT, 60 00N 29 40E, fortress and port on Kotlin I, Leningradskaya, NW European Rossiyskaya, Soviet Union; the island was taken by Peter the Great in 1703; laid out (1710) soon after St Petersburg (now Leningrad) to serve as its port; as principal Russian naval base and headquarters of the Russian admiralty the scene of four mutinies, the last (1921) suppressed by the Soviets; it played an important part in the siege of Leningrad (1941-44).

Krosno *krosh-nyo'*, voivodship in SE Poland; bounded S by Czechoslovakia and E by the Ukrainian USSR; watered by the Wisłok, San and Wisłoka rivers; pop(1983) 465,000; area 5,702 sq km; capital Krosno; chief towns include Sanok and Jasłlo.

Krosno, 49 40N 21 46E, pop(1983) 43,000, capital of Krosno voivodship, SE Poland; on R Wisłok; at centre of Carpathian oil bearing region since mid-19th century; Petroleum Institute; economy: oil, glass; monuments: statue of Ignacy Łukasiewicz (1822-82), inventor of the kerosene lamp; bishops' palace (17th-c) and regional museum.

Kruger *kroo'gur*, national park in E Transvaal, South Africa; stretches from Komatipoort N to the Mozambique frontier, 480 km from Johannesburg; area 19,485 sq km; established in 1926; facilities include 14 rest camps.

Krugersdorp *kroo'gurz-dorp*, 26 06S 27 46E, pop(1980) 102,940, city in Transvaal prov, South Africa; 32 km W of Johannesburg, on the Witwatersrand; named after P. Kruger, the last President of the Transvaal Republic; railway; economy: uranium, manganese and gold mining.

Krujë *kroo'ye*, CROIA (Ital), prov of W Albania; area 607 sq km; pop(1980) 88,200; capital Krujë.

Krujë, 41 31N 19 48E, town and capital of Krujë prov, W Albania; 19 km N of Tiranë; was a bishopric (1246-1694); bauxite deposits nearby; the population is largely Muslim in origin.

Kruševac *kroo'she-vats*, KRUSHEVATS (Slov), 43 34N 21 20E, pop(1981) 132,972, industrial town in S central Srbija (Serbia) republic, E central Yugoslavia; on R Rasina near its junction with the R Morava; in an agricultural region; railway; capital of Serbija during 14th century; economy: chemicals, hydroelectric power, mineral water; monument: Lazarica church.

Krym *krim*, CRIMEA *krī-mee'a* (Eng), peninsula in S Ukrainskaya SSR, Soviet Union; bounded S and W by the Black Sea, and E by the Azovskoye More (Sea of Azov); coterminous with Krymskaya oblast, of which Simferopol' is the capital; formerly an autonomous republic (from 1921), degraded to an oblast of the Rossiyskaya in 1946, and then transferred to the Ukrainskaya SSR in 1954; separated from the mainland (N) by the narrow Perekop Isthmus, and from the Taman Peninsula (E) by the Kerchenskiy Proliv (Kersh Strait); area 25,900 sq km; length (including the Kersh Peninsula) 320 km; along the S coast the Krymskiye Gory range rises a little over 1,500 m; dry steppeland extends southwards covering approx 80% of the total area; the Kerch Peninsula is arid but rich in minerals (iron, gypsum, limestone); chief cities include Simferopol', Sevastopol', and Kerch; the subtropical Black Sea littoral (S coast) is a major tourist attraction, with Yalta the most famous resort; Greek colonization began in the 7th century BC; thereafter came Goths (250 AD), Huns (373), Khazars (8th century), Byzantine Greeks (1016), Kipchaks (1050), and in the 13th century Tatars; in 1475 the Tatars established an independent khanate in N and central Krym; the Ottoman Empire conquered the peninsula in the late 15th century and in 1736 Russian armies first invaded the Krym; in the Crimean War (1854-55) Britain, France and Sardinia defeated the Russians; in 1918 the peninsula formed part of the short-lived republic of Taurida and in 1921 an autonomous republic was set up.

Ksar-El-Kébir *ke-sar-el-ke-beer'*, ALCAZARQUIVIR (Sp), 35 04N 5 56W, pop(1982) 73,541, commercial centre and market town in Kénitra prefecture, Nord-Ouest prov, NW Morocco, N Africa; 123 km S of Tanger (Tangiers) and SE of Larache, on the R Loukkos; the king of Portugal was killed near here in 1578 at the Battle of the Three Kings.

KTC, African squatter camp SE of central Cape Town, Cape prov, South Africa; between Guguletu and Nyanga townships; 500 Africans moved here from Crossroads camp after violence in 1983.

Kuala Belait *kwa'la bal-īt'*, 4 38N 114 58E, pop(1981) 19,281, town in Belait dist, E Brunei, SE Asia; at the mouth of Sungai Belait river; a centre of the Brunei oil industry; port serves oilfield around Seria; a main highway connects it to Tutong and Bandar Seri Begawan.

Kuala Lumpur *kwah'la loom'poor* (Malay, 'muddy estuary'), 3 08N 101 42E, pop(1980) 937,875, capital of Malaysia, in Wilayah Persekutuan federal territory, E Peninsular Malaysia, SE Asia; developed round the tin and later rubber industries since 1873; the city has a large Chinese and Indian pop, university (1962); technical university (1954); railway links with Thailand; airport to the W at Subang; monuments: national mosque, one of the largest in SE Asia; Sri Mahamariamman (1873), the largest and most ornate Hindu temple in Malaysia; national museum, national museum of art; Selangor Turf Club, founded in 1896; Istana Negara, home of the head of state; Mimaland recreational complex 1.8 km NE; event: annual Malaysian golf tournament at the Royal Selangor Golf Club; national holiday 1 Feb (founding of Kuala Lumpur).

Kuala Terengganu *kwah'la treng-gah'noo*, 5 20N 103 07E, pop(1980) 180,296, in Terengganu state, E Peninsular Malaysia, SE Asia; at the mouth of the R Terengganu where it meets the South China Sea, on the E coast of the Malay Peninsula, 491 km NE of Kuala Lumpur; economy: offshore oil, fishing, yacht-building: monuments: Istana Maziah, official residence of the Sultan of Terengganu; state museum.

Kuantan *kwan-tan'*, 3 50N 103 19E, pop(1980) 131,547, capital of Pahang state, E Peninsular Malaysia, SE Asia; at the mouth of the R Kuantan where it meets the South China Sea, on the E coast of the Malay Peninsula, 274 km ENE of Kuala Lumpur; fine beaches at Telok Chempedak, 1 km N; batik centre N at Beserah.

Kuban', river in S European Rossiyskaya, Soviet Union; rising on the W slopes of Mt El'brus, in the W section of the Bol'shoy Kavkaz (Greater Caucasus) range, close to the N frontier with Gruzinskaya SSR; flows generally N, NW, then W past Cherkessk, Armavir, and Krasnodar, to discharge into the Azovskoye More (Sea of Azov) in a swampy lagoon-filled delta just N of Temryuk; length 934 km; chief tributaries include the Adagum, Laba, Belaya, Urup, and Zelenchuk rivers.

Kuching *koo-ching'*, 1 32N 110 20E, pop(1980) 72,555, capital of Sarawak state, E Malaysia, SE Asia; on the R Sarawak where it meets the South China Sea; formerly associated with the Brooke dynasty of 'white rajahs'; airfield; economy: rubber, pepper, sago, copra; monuments: Fort Margherita, now a police museum, Sarawak museum, built in the style of a Normandy town house in 1891; event: gawai batu festival at the start of padi planting.

Küçükköy *koo-chook'oy*, 41 05N 28 47E, pop(1980) 100,406, town in İstanbul prov, NW Turkey.

Kudat *koo-daht'*, 6 54N 116 47E, pop(1980) 10,938, town in Sabah state, E Malaysia, SE Asia; on the NE coast of Sabah; airfield; event: folk festival of the Rungus tribe in October.

Kuei-yang, capital of Guizhou prov, S China. See Guiyang.

Kujū-san *koo'joo-sahn*, 33 07N 131 14E, highest peak on Kyūshū island, Japan; situated in Ōita prefecture, N Kyūshū; rises to 1,788 m within the 730 sq km Aso national park which was established in 1934.

Kukës *koo'kes*, prov of NE Albania; area 1,564 sq km; pop(1980) 81,900; capital Kukës; chrome is mined.

Kukës, 42 05N 20 24E, town and capital of Kukës prov, NE Albania; near the border with Yugoslavia, 72 km E of Shkodër, on the R Drin; iron and chrome deposits nearby.

Kulim *koo-lim'*, 5 20N 100 35E, pop(1980) 26,817, town in Kedah state, NW Peninsular Malaysia, SE Asia; ESE of Butterworth, near the Pulau Pinang frontier; economy: rubber.

Kumamoto *koo-ma-mō'tō*, 32 50N 130 42E, pop(1980) 526,662, capital of Kumamoto prefecture, W Kyūshū island, Japan; on R Shira, 80 km E of Nagasaki; university (1949); railway; economy: food processing, fishing, textiles; monument: Buddhist temple.

Kumanovo *koo'mah-no-vo*, 42 07N 21 40E, pop(1981) 126,368, town in N Makedonija (Macedonia) republic, S Yugoslavia; 25 km ENE of Skopje; railway; economy: tobacco trade.

Kumasi *koo-mah'si*, 6 45N 1 35W, pop(1982) 439,717, capital of Ashanti region, S central Ghana, W Africa; 180 km NW of Accra; known as the 'Garden City' or the 'City of the Golden Stool'; centre of the Ghanaian transport network; headquarters of wealthy Ashanti kingdom since the 17th century; university (1951); National Cultural Centre including a zoo, art gallery and open-air theatre; nearby is Bonwire, a woodcarving and cloth centre; airfield; railway; economy: large market centre for cocoa growing region.

Kumba *koom'ba*, 4 39N 9 26E, pop(1984e) 61,000, market town in Sud-Ouest prov, Cameroon, W Africa; 61 km NNE of Buéa; was called Johann-Albrechtshöhe by the Germans; daily market; railway; nearby is Barombi crater lake.

Kumi *koo'mee*, 1 29N 33 56E, town in Eastern prov, Uganda, E Africa; 44 km SE of Soroti; railway.

Kundelungu *koon-de-loong'goo*, national park in SE Zaire, central Africa; area 7,600 sq km; established in 1970; situated in the Kundelungu Mts.

Kungsbacka, 57 30N 12 05E, pop(1982) 45,176, town in N of Halland county, SW Sweden, a S suburb of Göteborg (Gothenburg), on the Kattegat; established in 1557; railway.

Kunlun Shan *koon-loon*, mountain range in W China; extends 2,500 km along the border of Xinjiang prov and Xizang aut region (Tibet); to the S lies the Xizang Gaoyuan (Tibetan Plateau), to the N the Taklimakan Shamo desert and Tarim Pendi basin; the Kunlun Shan divides E to form the Altun Shan and Hoh Xil Shan ranges; rises to 7,723 m in Muztag peak.

Kunming *koon-ming*, formerly YUNNAN, 25 04N 102 41E, pop(1984e) 1,355,300, capital of Yunnan prov, S China; situated on a flat, fertile plain in the Yunnan plateau; alt 1,894 m; circled by mountains to the N, E and W, with Dianchi lake to the SW of the city; major market and transport centre from the first settlement in 279 BC to the 19th century; Kunming is known as the 'city of eternal spring' because of its spring-like weather and scenery; university (1934); agricultural university; railway; airfield; economy: minerals, heavy and light engineering, metallurgy, food processing, chemicals, textiles; monuments: Qiongzhu Si (Bamboo Temple) 11 km W of Kunming, a 700-year-old temple with 500 life-like statues of Buddha's Chinese disciples (made between 1883 and 1890); in the temple is a 14th-c tablet bearing the edict of a Yuan dynasty emperor, unusual because it is written in both Chinese and Mongolian; 126 km SE of Kunming is the Stone Forest, with limestone peaks which rise to 30 m covering 0.8 sq km.

Kuntaur *koon-ta'oor*, local government area in The Gambia, W Africa; pop(1983) 57,608; area 1,466.5 sq km.

Kuopio *kwō'pyō*, a prov of S central Finland; area 19,956 sq km; pop(1982) 254,056; chief towns include Kuopio, Varkaus and Iisalmi; talc mining at Luikonlahti.

Kuopio, 62 51N 27 30E, pop(1982) 75,972, capital of Kuopio prov, S central Finland; on W shore of Kallavesi (L Kalla); established in 1782; university (1972); railway; airfield; boats to Savonlinna, Iisalmi and Joensuu; monuments: Museum of orthodox Church Art, revolving tower (75 m) on Puijo Hill (232 m); events: dance and music festival in June; winter games in March.

Kupa *koo'pa*, river in W Yugoslavia; rises NE of Rijeka and flows 295 km E to meet the R Sava near Sisak; navigable for 135 km; used for hydroelectric power.

Kupang *koo-pahng'*, 10 13S 123 38E, pop(1980) 52,698, capital of Nusa Tenggara Timur prov, Indonesia; on SW coast of the island of Timor; former Dutch trading post and port of call for whalers; university (1962); military base; airfield.

Kurashiki *koo-ra-shee'kee*, 34 36N 133 43E, pop(1980) 403,785, city in Okayama prefecture, Chūgoku region, SW Honshū island, Japan; 16 km WSW of Okayama, on the R Takahashi; the town's prosperity was built on the rice trade; railway; economy: textiles, wood and metal products; monuments: the Museum District contains former merchants' houses and granaries; Ohara art museum, containing Western and Japanese paintings, archaeological finds, wood engravings and printed fabrics; folkcraft museum, which houses Japanese craftwork from various regions; toy museum, with collections of toys from all over the world; archaeological museum.

Kŭrdzhali or **Kardzali**, also **Kirdzhali** *keer-ja'lee*, okrug (prov) in S Bulgaria at the E end of the Rhodopi Planina (Rhodope Mts) on the Greek frontier; area 4,020 sq km; pop(1981) 286,000.

Kŭrdzhali, 41 38N 25 21E, capital of Kurdzhali okrug (prov), S Bulgaria; 41 km from the Greek frontier and 262 km SE of Sofiya; railway; economy: tobacco, food processing, lead.

Kure *koo-ray*, 34 14N 132 32E, pop(1980) 234,549, city in Hiroshima prefecture, Chūgoku region, SW Honshū island, Japan; situated on Hiroshima-wan Bay, 19 km SSE of Hiroshima; railway; economy: shipbuilding, engineering, iron and steel.

Kurgan *koor-gahn'*, 55 30N 65 20E, pop(1983) 334,000, capital city of Kurganskaya oblast, W Siberian Rossiyskaya, Soviet Union; on the R Tobol; originated as a tax-exempt settlement in 1553; railway junction; airfield; economy: machine building, chemicals, foodstuffs, leatherwork, knitwear.

Kuria Muria Islands *koo'ree-a moo'ree-a*, JAZA'IR BIN GHALFAN *jaz-a'eer bin gal-fan'*, group of 5 granitic islands in the Arabian Sea off the S coast of Dhofar prov, Oman; ceded to the UK in 1854 by the Sultan of Oman; formerly important site for a cable station and for guano export.

Kurikka *koor'i-ka*, 62 36N 22 25E, pop(1982) 11,386, town in Vaasa prov, W central Finland; established in 1966.

Kuril Islands, archipelago in E Siberian Rossiyskaya, Soviet Union. See Kuril'skiye Ostrova.

Kuril'skiye Ostrova, KURIL ISLANDS *koo-reel'* (Eng), archipelago in Sakhalinskaya oblast, Rossiyskaya, E Soviet Union, between the N Pacific Ocean (E) and the Sea of Okhotsk (W); extends c.1,200 km from the S tip of Kamchatka Peninsula to the NE coast of Hokkaido I, Japan; area 15,600 sq km; rises to 2,339 m; comprises approx 56 islands of which the largest are (N to S) Ostrova Paramushir, Ostrova Onekotan, Ostrova Urup, Ostrova Iturup, and Ostrova Kunashir; they are actively volcanic and hot springs are abundant; the islands were discovered in 1634 by the Dutch navigator Martin de Vries and were divided between Russia and Japan in the 18th century; the entire group passed to Japan in 1875 when Russia assumed full control of Sakhalin; occupied by Soviet troops in 1945 and 2 years later became part of the Soviet Union; the islands are claimed by Japan.

Kurri Kurri-Weston, KURRI KURRI, 32 49S 151 30E, pop(1981) 12,795, coal-mining town in Hunter stat div, E New South Wales, Australia; WNW of Newcastle; railway.

Kursk *koorsk*, 51 45N 36 14E, pop(1983) 404,000, capital city of Kurskaya oblast, central European Rossiyskaya, Soviet Union; on a tributary of the R Seym and on the Moskva (Moscow)-Simferopol' highway; founded in the 10th century; the Kursk region is famous for its nightingales and its Antonovka apples; railway; airfield; economy: electrical engineering, synthetic fibres, rubber, glass, textiles, foodstuffs; monument: 18th-c St Sergius cathedral.

Kurume *koo'roo-may*, 33 20N 130 29E, pop(1980) 216,972, city in Fukuoka prefecture, NW Kyūshū island, Japan; 22 km SSE of Fukuoka; university; railway; economy: textiles.

Kurunegala *koo-roon-ay'ga-la*, 7 28N 80 23E, pop(1981) 26,198, capital of Kurunegala dist, North Western prov, Sri Lanka; 87 km NE of Colombo; economy: rice, coconuts and rubber trade.

Kuşadası *kush-ah-de-see'*, 37 51N 27 16E, pop(1980e) 8,000, seaport and resort on the Kuşadası Gulf (an inlet of the Aegean), İzmir prov, W Turkey; the largest yachting marina in Turkey lies N of the town; monument: Mehmet Pasha Caravanserai.

Kushiro *koo-shee'rō*, 42 58N 144 24E, pop(1980) 214,694, port in Saitama prefecture, E Hokkaidō island, Japan; on the Pacific Ocean; railway.

Kushtia *koosht'yu*, region in W Bangladesh; includes Chuadanga, Kushtia and Meherpur districts; pop(1981) 2,292,000; area 3,439 sq km; bounded W by India and NE by the R Ganga (Ganges); capital Kushtia.

Kushtia, 23 54N 89 07E, pop(1981) 74,892, capital of Kushtia dist and Kushtia region, W Bangladesh, on R Haringhat, 140 km W of Dhākā; linked by rail to Faridpur and Rangpur; economy: sugar, cotton, textiles and trade in rice, sugar, jute, grain and linseed.

Kuskokwim *kus'ko-kwim*, river in W Alaska, United States; rises in 4 branches on the W slope of the Alaska Range; the North Fork, East Fork and South Fork join at Medfra (63 05N 154 52W), the West Fork joins the river 18 km downstream; flows generally SW past McGrath, Kalskag and Kwethluk to the Kuskokwim Bay of the Bering Sea; length 1,287 km; receives numerous small tributaries; navigable as far as McGrath.

Kūt, Al *al koot*, KŪT AL IMĀ'RA, 32 30N 45 51E, pop(1970) 58,647, capital town of Wāsit governorate, E central Iraq, 160 km SE of Baghdād, on the R Tigris; river port; market centre for grains, dates, fruit, and vegetables.

Kütahya *ku-ta'ya*, prov in W Turkey; pop(1980) 497,089; area 11,875 sq km; capital Kütahya; minerals include iron, mercury, chromium, magnesite, lignite; economy: mohair goats, cotton, fruit, sugar-beet, carpets, ceramics, Meerschaum clay.

Kutaisi *koo-tī'si*, KUTAIS, 42 15N 42 44E, pop(1983) 207,000, town in W Gruzinskaya SSR, Soviet Union; on the R Rioni, where it leaves a ravine to flow over the Colkhidian Plateau; railway; airfield; economy: machine building, motor works, electro-mechanics, chemicals, foodstuffs, silk, leatherwork, power generation; monuments: cathedral (1003).

Kutch, Rann of, KACHCH, CUTCH, region of salt marsh lying in the Indian state of Gujarat and the Sind province of Pakistan; bounded W by the Arabian Sea and N by the Thar Desert; area 9,000 sq km; once a shallow arm of the Arabian Sea, but since the times of Alexander the Great, when it was a navigable lake, it has silted up; extensive mud flats have great accumulations of salt on their surfaces when dry, but are inundated during the season of the SW monsoon; scene of Indo-Pakistani fighting 1965.

Kutná Hora *koot'nah ho'ra*, 49 58N 15 18E, pop(1984) 21,386, town in Středočeský region, Czech Socialist Republic, NW central Czechoslovakia; on R Elbe, SE of Praha (Prague); railway; formerly noted for its silver mines and silver mint; economy: agricultural trade; monuments: St Barbara cathedral (14th-c), St James cathedral, church of St Marie.

Kuusankoski *koo'san-kos'kee*, 60 55N 26 42E, pop(1982) 22,345, town in Kymi prov, SE Finland; established in 1957; railway.

Kuwait *koo-wayt'*, official name State of Kuwait, DOWLAT AL KUWAIT, independent oil-rich state situated at the head of the Arabian Gulf between 28° and 30° N and 46° and 48° E, bounded N and W by Iraq, S by Saudi Arabia, and E by the Arabian Gulf; timezone GMT +3; area 17,818 sq km; capital Al Kuwayt (Kuwait City); chief ports Shuwaikh and Mīnā' al Aḥmadī; pop(1980) 1,400,000; virtually all settlements and 90% of the pop are within 10 km of the Arabian Gulf; the pop comprises 41.5% Kuwaiti, 40% other Arab, 5% Indian and Pakistani, and 4% Iranian; the percentage of non-Kuwaitis rose from 52.5% in 1975 to 58.5% in 1980; the dominant religion is Islam; Arabic is the official language but English is widely spoken; the unit of currency is the dinar; national holiday 25 Feb (National Day); membership of Arab League, FAO, G-77, GATT, GCC, IAEA, IBRD, ICAO, IDA, Islamic Development Bank, IFAD, IFC, ILO, IMF, IMO, INTELSAT, INTERPOL, IPU, ITU, NAM, OAPEC, OIC, OPEC, UN, UNESCO, UPU, WFTU, WHO, WMO, WTO.

Physical description. The State of Kuwait comprises the mainland and nine offshore islands, including Faylakah (inhabited) and Jazīrat Būbīyān (the largest island). The terrain is flat or gently undulating, rising towards the SW to a height of 271 m. The Wādī al Bātin, Kuwait's most prominent topographic feature, runs along the W border with Iraq. In places the wadi cuts some 45 m into the plateau. Another prominent feature is the Zor escarpment which stretches approx 60 km from Atraf NE to Al Bahrah. There are numerous wadi systems which drain

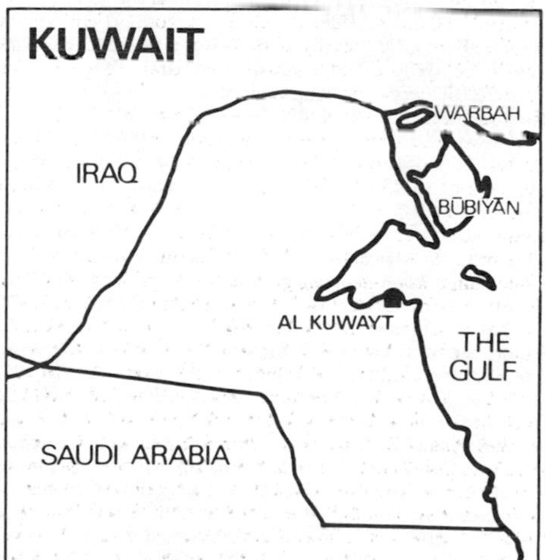

mostly into the interior. The gradual sinking of the Arabian Gulf geosyncline is thought to explain the distinctive topography of NE Kuwait. Here, gravel-topped ridges trending in a NE direction and rising in height to only about one metre alternate with narrow, sandy depressions. The NE also includes part of the Shatt al 'Arab delta. The terrain is generally stony with a sparse vegetation cover of grasses and low shrubs.

Climate. The climate is hot and dry with an annual rainfall of only 111 mm. Most of the rainfall occurs as light winter showers brought by westerly depressions. Summer temperatures are extremely high, often reaching above 45°C during July and August. Winter temperatures often rise to over 20°C during the day but then fall rapidly at night when frosts are not uncommon, especially inland. Humidity is generally high, often rising to over 90%. Dust and sandstorms are common throughout the year.

History, government and constitution. The port of Al Kuwayt was founded by Arabs at the beginning of the 18th century. In 1899 the ruler of Kuwait signed a treaty that made Britain responsible for Kuwait's foreign affairs. In 1914 Britain recognized Kuwait as an independent sovereign state and in 1961 this was reaffirmed with the additional recognition of the country's responsibility for both internal and external affairs. The state is governed by a parliament of 50 elected members and a nominated council of ministers. A prime minister is appointed by the ruler who is head of state.

Economy. Until the discovery of oil in the Burgan area in 1938 Kuwait's economy was based on pearl diving, seafaring, boatbuilding, fishing, and nomadic herding. Although Kuwait was exporting crude oil from 1946 onwards it did not become a major Middle East oil producer until the Abadan crisis in 1951 when Iranian oil production was halted for 3 years. By 1979 petroleum and its products accounted for 95% of government revenue and over 75% of national income. In 1980 Kuwait had the world's 3rd largest per capita GNP after Qatar and the UAE. Oil production peaked in 1972 with an annual total of 1,202 million barrels per day. In the aftermath of the 1973 oil crisis Kuwait began a policy of restricting oil production partly for conservation reasons and partly as a result of OPEC policy. By 1981 production had fallen to about 965,000 barrels per day. During the 1950s and 1960s approx 65% of Kuwait's oil was exported to W Europe. By 1980, 50.2% of the crude oil production was exported to Asia and only 32.3% to Europe. In 1980, 52.4% of the refined product was exported to Japan, 14.7% to Europe, and 7.4% to the Arab States. The entire gas yield is either consumed on the home market or processed for export. Exports from the two liquid petroleum gas plants in operation are exported mainly to Japan. Low grade sulphur fuel oil, produced at the Mīnā' al Aḩmadī refinery, is being used in the country's power and desalination plants. Industrial development is concentrated at Shuaiba, S of Al Kuwayt. Here there are plants for the manufacture of petrochemicals, fertilizers, construction materials, asbestos, and lead acid batteries. The government is pursuing an active programme of economic diversification and gradually creating a post-oil, high-technology state. Petroleum and petroleum products are the main exports to the EEC, Japan, and the Americas. Re-exports include chemicals, machinery, vehicles and manufactured goods, exported mainly to Saudi Arabia.

Agriculture. Agriculture plays a relatively insignificant role in the economy, accounting for only 0.2% of national income and 3.5% of the workforce. Less than 0.1% of the land is farmed and only 7.5% is pasture. Attempts have been made to lessen the dependence on imported foods by expanding the cultivation of dates, citrus fruits, and timber, and by increasing livestock and poultry farming. By the mid 1980s Kuwait was able to supply 46% of its vegetable requirements, 41.4% of milk, 20% of eggs, and 34% of poultry.

Communications. There are no railways in Kuwait. The 2,875 km of highways comprises 2,585 km bituminous road and 290 km earth, sand and light gravel track. The chief ports include Shuwaikh and Shuaiba while oil exporting operations are handled at the terminals of Mīnā' al Aḩmadī, Mīnā' Abdulla, and Az Zawr. Kuwait International Airport is located 16 km S of the capital city.

Kuwait City, capital of Kuwait. See Kuwayt, Al.

Kuwayt, Al *al koo-wayt'*, KUWAIT CITY, formerly QUREIN, 29 20N 48 00E, pop(1981) 276,356, capital city of the State of Kuwait, on the S shore of Kuwait Bay, at the head of the Arabian Gulf; the city expanded considerably in the late 1940s following oil development in the state; communications centre; university (1966); the suburban port of Shuwaikh is situated SW of the city centre; airport (16 km S); there is a ferry service to Faylakah I; Al Kuwayt has recently become important as a banking and investment centre; shipbuilding is also important.

Kuybyshev *koo'i-bi-shef*, formerly SAMARA, 53 10N 50 10E, pop(1983) 1,242,000, river port capital of Kuybyshevskaya oblast, E central European Rossiyskaya, Soviet Union; on the R Volga where it meets the R Samara; founded in 1586 as a fortress; during World War II the Soviet government was transferred here (1941-43) from Moskva (Moscow); university (1969); railway; airport; economy: machine building, metalworking, oil refining, foodstuffs.

Kuznetz Basin, basin of the Tom river in Kemerovo oblast, Rossiyskaya, central Soviet Union; stretches from Tomsk SE to Novokuznetzk; a major industrial zone based on the rich deposits of coal and iron ore.

Kvaløy, South *kval'u-u*, Norwegian island in the Norwegian sea off NW coast of Norway; separated from Tromsø, which is on an islet between S Kvaløy and the mainland, by an arm of Tromsø Sound; rises to 1,035 m in the W (Skitntind Mt); area 736 sq km; length 48 km; administered by Troms county.

Kvinn'herad, formerly SUNDE, 60 00N 6 00E, pop(1980) 12,833, town on the Hardangerfjorden (Hardanger Fjord), W coast of Hordaland county, SW Norway; economy: fishing, ship repair, canning.

Kwa Ibo *ee'bō*, town with tanker terminal facilities, Cross River state, SE Nigeria, W Africa; on the Gulf of Guinea, SW of Calabar; linked by pipeline to offshore oil fields.

Kwai Chung *kwī choong*, container port near Tsuen Wan new town, Kowloon, Hong Kong; Asia's largest container port.

KwaNdebe'le, national state or non-independent black homeland in Transvaal prov, NE South Africa; pop(1985) 235,855; area 2,860 sq km; situated NE of Johannesburg and E of Pretoria; achieved self-governing status in 1981; chief town Moutjana.

Kwangchow, capital of Guangdong prov, S China. See Guangzhou.

Kwangju *kwang-joo*, KWANGCHU, 35 07N 126 52E, pop(1984) 869,874, capital of Chŏllanam prov, SW Korea; railway; airfield.

Kwangsi Chuang, aut region in S China. See Guangxi.

Kwangtung, prov in S China. See Guangdong.

Kwa'ra, state in W Nigeria, W Africa; pop(1982e) 2,734,000; area 66,869 sq km; bounded E by the R Niger and W by Benin; capital Ilorin; chief towns Ajaokuta, Bacita, Okene, Kaiama, Lafiagi, Lokoja and Kabba; cotton, rice, sugar, cereals and tobacco are the main cash crops in the S; there are reserves of tantalite and gold; marble is mined N of Ilorin.

KwaZu'lu, national state or non-independent black homeland in Natal prov, E South Africa; pop(1985) 3,747,015; situated close to the Indian Ocean between the Transkei and Durban; achieved self-governing status in 1971.

Kweichow, prov in S China. See Guizhou.

Kweilin, town in Guangxi aut region, S China. See Guilin.

Kwe'neng, dist in S Botswana, S Africa; pop(1981) 117,127; area 35,890 sq km; capital Molepolole; the other main town is Letlhakeng; economy: livestock and arable farming.

Kwesui, former name for the capital of Nei Mongol aut region (Inner Mongolia), N China. See Hohhot.

Kwina'na, 32 15S 115 46E, pop(1981) 12,355, town in Perth stat div, Western Australia, Australia; on the W coast, S of Fremantle; railway.

Kymi *ku'mee*, KYMMENE *ku'mu-nu* (Swed), a prov of SE Finland; S section of L Saimaa crosses the N border with Mikkeli prov; area 12,828 sq km; pop(1982) 343,055; Kouvola, situated in the W of the prov, is the capital; chief towns include Lappeenranta and Imatra.

Kymijoki *ku'mee-yo'kee*, R KYMI (Eng), river in Kymi prov, SE Finland, flowing from the SE corner of L Päijänne to meet the Gulf of Finland at Kotka; length 140 km; catchment area 37,000 sq km, 19% of which is covered by lakes; hydroelectric plants supply power to the industry of S Finland.

Kyoga, Lake *kee-ō'ga*, lake in central Uganda, E Africa; N of Kampala; area 4,427 sq km; the Victoria Nile river passes through from L Victoria.

Kyŏnggi *kyong-gee*, GYEONG-GI DO, prov in NW Korea; bordered N by North Korea; drained by the Hangang, Imjingang and Puk'angang rivers; pop(1984) 4,581,009; area 10,958 sq km; capital Suwŏn.

Kyŏngju *kyong-joo*, 35 52N 129 15E, pop(1983e) 130,157; town in Kyŏngsangpuk prov, SE Korea; in a valley between Taegu and Pusan; railway; ancient capital of the Silla dynasty from 57 BC to 935 AD and of the whole of Korea which they united, from 668 to 935 AD; the town is filled with remains and artifacts from the ancient Silla kingdom; monuments: Tumuli Park, a large walled park in the centre of the town, was the burial place of Silla royalty and contains 20 ancient tombs; Ch'ŏmsŏngdae (Star Tower) is a stone observatory constructed during the reign of Queen Sŏndŏk (632-646 AD); the 12 stones of the base perimeter of the tower represent the 12 months of the year, there are 30 layers from top to bottom, one for each day of the month and the tower uses a total of 366 stones, one for each day of the year; Anjapi Pond, constructed by King Munmu in 674, was built to commemorate the unification of Silla and was built in the actual shape of the unified kingdom; when drained for repair in 1975 the pond revealed many Silla artifacts, including a perfectly preserved royal barge; in the museum grounds is the Emille Bell, one of the largest and most resonant bells in Asia, said to have been built only with the aid of a child sacrifice, which was said to give the bell its mournful undertone; Punhwangsa Pagoda, built in the 600s by Queen Sŏndŏk, is believed to be the oldest datable pagoda in Korea; when it was restored in 1915 a box containing some of the Queen's personal effects was found; the pagoda is noted for its carvings of stone lions and its guardian buddhist statues; the Onŭng Tombs contain 5 of the most ancient tombs in Kyŏngju, including the 2,000-year-old tomb of the kingdom's founder; overlooking Kyŏngju is the tomb of General Kim Yu-shin who, in the 7th century, led the armies of kings Muyŏl and Munmu in the campaigns which resulted in the unification of Korea; Pulguksa Temple to the SE of Kyŏngju is one of the 5 great temples of Korea; first built in the 8th century AD, the wooden structures have been destroyed and rebuilt numerous times; here also are the intricately designed Tabot'ap and Sŏkkat'ap pagodas, the one representing the process of ascension, the other that of the descent to the earthly world; Sŏkkuram Grotto Shrine was dedicated in the 8th century and was thought to protect the kingdom from Japanese pirates; it contains an enormous Buddha, carved out of granite, surrounded by engraved wall panels and niches holding smaller figures; UNESCO undertook a major cultural survey of Kyŏngju as part of its preservation of important world historic sites.

Kyŏngsangnam *kyong-sang-nam*, SOUTH KYONGSANG, prov in SE Korea; bounded E by the Sea of Japan, S by the Korea Strait; watered by the Namgang and Naktong rivers; rises to 1,915 m in Chiri san peak; pop(1984) 3,574,035; area 11,850 sq km; capital Masan.

Kyŏngsangpuk *kyong-sang-puk*, NORTH KYONGSANG, prov in E Korea; bordered E by the Sea of Japan; drained by the Naktong river; rises to 1,439 m in Sobaek san peak on the border with Ch'ungch'ŏngpuk prov; pop(1984) 3,083,690; area 19,425 sq km; capital Taegu.

Kyōto *kee-ō'tō*, 35 02N 135 45E, pop(1980) 1,473,065, capital of Kyōto prefecture, Kinki region, central Honshū island, Japan; SW of Biwa-ko (Lake Biwa); founded in the 8th century; capital of Japan from 794 AD until 1868, when the capital moved to Tōkyo; university (1897); university of industrial arts and textiles (1949); railway; economy: electrical goods, machinery, silk, craftwork; monuments: the city contains over 2,000 temples and shrines; Nijo Castle, begun in 1603, contains the Imperial Palace, the home of the emperors until 1868; Kinkaku ji, the Golden Pavilion, and the surrounding gardens were built in 1394 by the Shogun Ashikaga Yoshimitsu for his retirement; the Ryoan ji temple of the Zen sect was founded in 1450, rebuilt in 1499 and again in 1797 after a fire; it is famous for its garden of stones and sand; first laid out in the 16th century by the painter Soami, it consists of carefully raked sand on which are arranged 15 stones, each lying on a bed of moss; the Daitoku ji monastery is a complex of over 30 temples dating from the 14th century; the Kiyomizu dera temple on the hillside overlooking Kyōto was founded in the 8th century; 12th-c Sanjusangen do contains 1,001 gilded wooden figures of Kannon, the Goddess of Mercy; events: Mikayo Odori cherry blossom dance in April; the Kamogawa Odori in May and Oct; Aoi (hollyhock) Matsuri processions on 15 May; Mifune Matsuri boat festival on 3rd Sunday in May; Gion Matsuri parade of decorated floats in July; Jidai Matsuri parade of historical costumes of different periods in Oct.

Kyrenia *kī-ree'nyu*, dist in N Cyprus; area 639 sq km; pop(1973) 32,586; capital Kyrenia; entirely under Turkish occupation since the 1974 coup and invasion.

Kyrenia, 35 20N 33 19E, pop(1973) 3,892, port and capital town of Kyrenia dist, N Cyprus; on the Mediterranean Sea; evacuated after the 1974 Turkish invasion; monument: Byzantine castle.

Kyūshū *kee-oo'shoo*, island region in Japan; southernmost and most densely populated of the 4 main islands of Japan; the island has 4 volcanic ranges, rising to 1,788 m at Mt Kujū-san in Aso national park and to 1,935 m at Mt Miyanoura-dake on Yaku-shima island to the S of Kyūshū; Kyūshū is heavily forested apart from the NW which is an extensive rice growing area; pop(1980) 12,966,000; area 42,084 sq km; major industrial towns include Fukuoka, Kita-Kyūshū, Ōita, Kagoshima, Nagasaki; there are many spas; economy: rice, grain, sweet potatoes, fruit, silk, timber, fishing; Kyūshū is divided into 7 prefectures as follows:

Prefecture	*area (sq km)*	*pop(1980)*
Fukuoka	4,946	4,553,000
Kagoshima	9,153	1,785,000
Kumamoto	7,399	1,790,000
Miyazaki	7,734	1,152,000
Nagasaki	4,102	1,591,000
Ōita	6,331	1,229,000
Saga	2,418	866,000

Kyustendil or **Kjustendil** *kyoo-sten-deel'*, okrug (prov) of W Bulgaria in the Rila Planina (Rila Mts) bordering Yugoslavia; area 3,002 sq km; pop(1981) 199,000; fruit-growing, vineyards and tobacco are important.

Kyustendil, PAUTALIA (anc), 42 16N 22 41E, spa town and capital of Kyustendil okrug (prov), W Bulgaria; a health resort since Roman times; railway; economy: food processing, distilling and textiles; monuments: Roman temple, archaeological museum.

Kyzyl-Kum, desert in S Soviet Union. See Kyzylkum, Peski.

Kyzylkum, Peski, KYZYL-KUM, extensive desert in Uzbekskaya and Kazakhskaya republics, S Soviet Union, between the Amudar'ya (W) and Syr-Dar'ya (E) rivers; extends SE from the Aral'skoye More (Aral Sea); rises to 922 m in the centre; partially covered with sand dunes.

L

La Massa'na, parish in the Principality of Andorra. See Massana, La.

La Paz, in Bolivia, El Salvador, Honduras, Mexico, Uruguay. See Paz, La.

La Salle, town in S Québec, Canada. See Salle, La.

Labé *la-bay'*, 11 17N 12 11W, pop(1972) 79,670, capital of Moyenne-Guinée region, W central Guinea, W Africa; near the source of the R Gambia, 260 km NE of Conakry; airfield.

Labrador, part of Newfoundland prov, E Canada; bounded W and S by Québec prov and E by the Labrador Sea; separated from the island of Newfoundland by the Strait of Belle Isle; the E coast is heavily indented and the area to the W and N of Churchill Falls is studded with many lakes (Joseph, Gabbro, Lobstick, Menihek); area 110,000 sq km; economy: fishing, iron ore, hydroelectric power (Churchill and Twin falls).

Labrador City, 52 54N 66 50W, pop(1981) 11,538, city in Newfoundland, E Canada, on the W frontier of Labrador with Québec prov, near Wabush lake; largest settlement in Labrador; airfield.

Labrador Sea, arm of the Atlantic Ocean, between Newfoundland and Greenland; connected to Baffin Bay by the Davis Strait; depths fall from the continental shelves below 3,200 m towards the Mid-Oceanic Canyon, which dissects the Labrador Sea; the cold Labrador Current, flowing SE from the Davis Strait, brings icebergs into the sea, while the warm NW-flowing West Greenland Current helps modify the climate of the SW shore of Greenland.

Lac *lak*, prefecture in W Chad, N central Africa; pop(1979) 139,000; area 22,320 sq km; lies along the NW shores of L Chad; capital Bol; chief towns Kouloa, Baga Sola, Mondo and N'Gouri.

Laccadive Islands, island group of India. See Lakshadweep.

Lachine *la-sheen'*, 45 27N 73 41W, pop(1981) 37,521, town in S Québec, SE Canada; on S shore of Montréal island, at E end of L St Louis; named 'Chine' by Cartier in 1535 who thought he had reached China; founded in 1667; in 1689 the town was the scene of the worst-ever Indian raid suffered by the French; W terminus of the Lachine Canal (built 1821-25), the first canal along the St Lawrence; also W terminus of the present Montréal Water Works Canal; railway.

Lach'lan, river in New South Wales, Australia; rises in the Great Dividing Range, N of Canberra; flows 1,484 km in a curve NW then SW to join the Murrumbidgee river.

Ladakh *lah-dahk'*, dist of Jammu-Kashmir state, N India; area 118,524 sq km; pop(1981) 68,380; borders Xinjiang prov and Xizang aut region (Tibet) of China; capital Leh; crossed by the R Indus to the N of which lies the Ladakh range with peaks in excess of 6,000 m; economy: cereals, livestock.

Lādhiqīyah, Al, *la-tu-kee'u*, LATAKIA *la-tu-kee'u*, governorate (*mohofazat*) in W Syria; bounded W by the Mediterranean Sea, N by Turkey, and S by Lebanon; pop(1981) 554,384; capital Al Lādhiqīyah; other chief town Bāniyās; the R 'Āsi (Orontes) forms part of its E boundary; comprises a narrow coastal plain backed by the Jabal al Nuşayrīyah range which rises to about 1,500 m; drained by the R Kabir; economy: oil refining, production of industrial refrigeration plant.

Lādhiqīyah, Al, 35 30N 35 45E, pop(1970) 196,791, commercial seaport capital of Al Lādhiqīyah governorate W Syria; on the Mediterranean Sea; university (1971); railway; boat services to Beyrouth (Beirut), 240 km to the S, and to Cyprus; economy: famous for the tobacco (Latakia) which it exports, tourism.

Ladoga, Lake, lake in NW European Soviet Union. See Ladozhskoye, Ozero.

Ladozhskoye, Ozero *lad'esh-ke-ye*, LAKE LADOGA (Eng), LAATOKKA *laht'o-ka* (Finn), largest lake in Europe, in Rossiyskaya, NW European Soviet Union, close to the Finnish border, between the Karelian (W) and Olonets (E) isthmuses; area 17,700 sq km; length 219 km; maximum depth 230 m; average depth 51 m; alt 4 m; the S shore is low and marshy while the N shore is rocky and indented; receives the R Svir' (E) from Ozero Onezhskoye and the R Vuoksa (W) from L Saimaa in Finland; 92% of the outflow is via the R Neva into the Gulf of Finland; there are c.660 islands in the lake, mostly located along the NW coast; Ostrov Valaam island in the N has a Greek Orthodox monastery; autumn storms and ice-cover for between 2 and 4 months during the winter render navigation difficult; chief ports include Priozersk, Sortavala, Petrokrepost', and Novaya Ladoga; until 1940 the Soviet-Finnish border passed NE-SW through the centre of the lake; an extensive network of canals has developed.

Lae *lah'ay*, 6 45S 147 00E, pop(1980) 61,617, seaport and industrial city in Morobe prov, Papua New Guinea, SW Pacific, on the S coast of Huon Peninsula, E New Guinea, c.320 km N of Port Moresby; it was made capital in 1941 when Rabaul was evacuated following volcanic eruptions; in 1942 the town was taken by the Japanese and became one of their chief bases in New Guinea.

Lafayette, 40 25N 86 54W, pop(1980) 43,011, county seat of Tippecanoe county, W Indiana, United States; on the R Wabash, 93 km NW of Indianapolis; railway; agricultural market centre; site of the Battle of Tippecanoe, where General William Harrison defeated the Indians in 1812.

Lafayette, 30 14N 92 01W, pop(1980) 81,961, parish seat of Lafayette parish, S Louisiana, United States; on the R Vermilion, 84 km WSW of Baton Rouge; founded in 1824; university (1900); railway; economy: commercial and shipping centre for an agricultural and oil-producing region; manufactures include building materials, electrical appliances, auto parts, metal products, and furniture; event: Festivals Acadiens (Sept).

Lafonia *la-fo'nee-a*, the S half of East Falkland in the Falkland Is, joined to the N half by a narrow isthmus at Goose Green settlement; the terrain is flat and wet with many small lakes and streams.

Lag Bada'na, national park in Somalia, NE Africa; area 3,340 sq km; established in 1978.

Lågen *lo'gun*, NUMEDALSLÅGEN *noo'me-dals-law'gen*, LAAGEN, river in S Norway, rising in the E Hardangervidda, N of Rodberg; flows SSE through Buskerud and Vestfold counties to discharge into the Skagerrak at Larvik; length 337 km.

Laghmān *lag-man'*, prov in E Afghanistan; pop(1984e) 337,274; area 7,210 sq km; crossed by the R Alungar, flowing SW from the Nuristan region of the Hindu Kush; capital Mehtar Lām.

Laghouat, department of N Algeria, N Africa; area 112,052 sq km; pop(1982) 371,863; chief town Laghouat.

Lagos *lay'gos*, state in SW Nigeria, W Africa; pop(1982e) 2,644,800; area 3,345 sq km; bounded S by the Bight of Benin; capital Ikeja; chief towns Lagos, Mushin, Epe,

Badagri and Ikorodu; economy: cement processing, fishing, chemicals, timber, textiles.

Lagos (Port, 'lagos', lagoons), 6 27N 3 28E, pop(1975e) 1,060,848, seaport capital of Nigeria, W Africa; 120 km SW of Ibadan and 420 km ENE of Accra (Ghana); the city centre is situated on Lagos island (8 km long and 1.6 km wide) which is connected to the mainland by two bridges; port facilities are located at Apapa and Tin Can I; settled by Yoruba peoples around 1700 as a refuge from attack; the city was an infamous slave trade centre until the mid-19th century; Admiral Boscowen defeated the French off Lagos in 1759; occupied by the British in 1851 and ceded to them in 1861; the Colony of Lagos was created in 1862 and administered from Sierra Leone between 1866 and as part of the Gold Coast 1874-1886; became part of the Southern Nigeria protectorate in 1906 and capital of Nigeria in 1960; university (1962); racecourse; Murtala Muhammed airport (24 km); tanker terminal; economy: tourism, metals, chemicals, fish, gas, and brewing; monuments: national museum, palace.

Lagos *la'goosh*, LACOBRIGA (Lat), 37 05N 8 41W, pop(1981) 10,000, old fishing town in Faro dist, S Portugal; on W side of the estuary of the R Alvor, 80 km W of Faro; former capital of Algarve prov and birthplace of Gil Eanes, the first navigator to sail round Cape Bojador in W Africa (1434); monuments: church of Santa Maria where Henry the Navigator was originally buried before being transferred to the Batalha Abbey; town walls enclosing the Governor's palace; Fortaleza and town hall (1798).

Lagos, Los *lōs la'gōs*, region of S central Chile; bordered E by Argentina; comprises the provs of Valdivia, Osorno, Llanquihue, Chiloe and Palena; constitutes the main part of the Chilean lake district; pop(1984) 899,300; area 68,247 sq km; capital Puerto Montt; chief towns Valdivia and Osorno; economy: grain, vegetables, fruit, fish canning and tourism; includes the Ranco, Llanquihue and Puyehue lakes and Vicente Pérez Rosales and Puyehue national parks.

Laguna, La *la la-goo'na*, pop(1981) 112,635, second largest town and former capital of Tenerife I, Canary Is, Canarias region, at the N end of the island and W of Santa Cruz de Tenerife; bishopric; university (1701); economy: textiles, brandy, leather, tobacco; monuments: 16th-c cathedral and the church of the Conception (1502).

Laḥij, governorate of SW South Yemen; formerly the Second Governorate; chief town Al Ḥawṭah.

Lahn, river predominantly in Hessen (Hesse) prov, W Germany; rises at an alt of 600 m in the S Rothaargebirge; flows E by way of the holiday resorts of Laasphe and Beidenkopf, turns S past the university towns of Marburg and Gießen, then W through Wetzlar; flows into the R Rhine at Oberlahnstein; length 245 km; navigable length 148 km; drainage basin area 3,947 sq km.

Lahore *la-hor'*, 31 34N 74 22E, pop(1981) 2,922,000, city in Punjab prov, Pakistan; between the Ravi and the Sutlej rivers, 1,030 km from Karachi and 438 km NW of New Delhi; 2nd largest city in Pakistan; in the 15th century Lahore was the capital of the Ghaznevid dominions E of the Indus; during the 16th and 17th centuries flourished under Mogul rule; regained prominence under Sikh rule; taken in 1849 by the British who made it the capital of the prov of Punjab; trade and communications centre of Pakistan; railway; economy: textiles, carpets, footwear, electrical goods, railway engineering, metal goods; considered the cultural capital of Pakistan; 2 universities (1882, 1961); monuments: museum of Lahore, housing the statue of fasting Buddha; historical monuments of fine Muslim architecture include Badshahi mosque of Emperor Aurangzeb, Wazir Khan mosque, Shalimar Gardens of the Mogul Emperor Shahjahan and the royal fort of Akbar, with its hall of mirrors.

Lahti *lah'tee*, LAHTIS *lah'tis* (Swed), 61 00N 25 40E, pop(1982) 94,603, city in Häme prov, S Finland; S of L Päijänne and 103 km NNE of Helsinki; established in 1878; railway; winter sports centre with an Olympic size ski jump; hydrofoil to Jyväskylä; economy: metal, glass, textiles, furniture, electrical goods; event: organ festival in Aug.

Laï *lay*, DE BEHAGLE, 9 22N 16 14E, capital of Tandjilé prefecture, SW Chad, N central Africa; on the route from Bongor to Doba, 100 km NNE of Moundou; economy: a refinery is linked to oil fields in Kanem prefecture.

Laiwu *lī-woo*, 36 14N 117 40E, pop(1984e) 1,035,800, city in Shandong prov, E China; railway.

Lajes or **Lagens** *la'shish* or *la-zhensh'*, 38 45N 27 06W, pop(1981) 3,361, village in Angra do Heroísmo dist, central Azores, on NE shore of Terceira I; US airbase.

Lake Charles, 30 14N 93 13W, pop(1980) 75,226, parish seat of Calcasieu parish, SW Louisiana, United States; port on the R Calcasieu, 16 km NE of the N end of L Calcasieu; settled in 1852; university; railway; economy: major petrochemical industry; oil refining; other manufactures include rubber, tyres, plastics, and aluminium; event: Contraband Days (May).

Lake Clark, national park in S Alaska, United States; situated in the Chigmit Mts, on Cook Inlet on the S coast, contains several lakes (including L Clark) and volcanoes; rises to 3,108 m in Redoubt Volcano; area 16,374 sq km; established in 1978.

Lake District, part of Cumbria, NW England; an area of approx 1,810 sq km noted for its lake and mountain scenery; includes L Windermere, Derwent Water, Ullswater, Bassenthwaite, Thirlmere, Buttermere and Coniston Water; L Windermere is the largest lake in England; mountains include Scafell (the highest peak in England), Skiddaw and Helvellyn; chief towns include Keswick, Windermere, Ambleside and Grasmere; the area is associated with the poets Wordsworth, Coleridge and Southey and the writer John Ruskin; a national park protects 866 sq km of the Lake District.

Lake Placid, 44 18N 74 01W, resort in Essex county, N New York state, United States; in the Adirondack Mts, 65 km SW of Plattsburg on Mirror Lake; scene of Winter Olympic events.

Lake Worth, 26 37N 80 03W, pop(1980) 27,048, town in Palm Beach county, SE Florida, United States; on L Worth (a lagoon), 10 km S of West Palm Beach; railway; a winter resort.

Lakefield, national park in NW Queensland, NW Australia; bounded N by Princess Charlotte Bay; area 5,370 sq km; established in 1979.

Lakeland, 28 03N 81 57W, pop(1980) 47,406, town in Polk county, central Florida, United States; 48 km E of Tampa; railway; economy; tourism; processing and shipping centre for citrus fruit.

Lakewood, 33 49N 118 08W, pop(1980) 74,654, city in Los Angeles county, SW California, United States; SSE of Los Angeles.

Lakewood, 39 44N 105 05W, pop(1980) 112,860, town in Jefferson county, N central Colorado, United States; a residential suburb 8 km W of Denver; railway.

Lakewood, 41 29N 81 48W, pop(1980) 61,963, town in Cuyahoga county, NE Ohio, United States; residential suburb on L Erie at the mouth of the Rocky river, 8 km W of Cleveland.

Lakonía, LACONIA *la-kō'ni-a* (Eng), coastal nome (dept) of Pelopónnisos region, S Greece; pop(1981) 93,218; area 3,636 sq km; capital Spartí; economy: grain, olives, fruit.

Lakshadweep *lahk'shad-weep*, LACCADIVE ISLANDS (Sanskrit 'laksha divi', 100,000 islands), union territory of India, comprising 10 inhabited and 17 uninhabited coral islands in the Arabian Sea 300 km off the Malabar Coast of Kerala state; pop(1981) 40,237; area 32 sq km; the Amindivi Is lie to the N and the Laccadive (Cannanore) Is to the S of the group; Minicoy I lies to the S of the Laccadives from which it is separated by the Nine Degree Channel; Androth I, the largest island of the group at 4.8 sq km, is nearest to the coast of Kerala; the centre of administration is on Kavaratti I; the majority of the population is Muslim; the Malayalam language is widely spoken, although Mahl is spoken on Minicoy; economy: coconut-husk fibre (coir), coconuts and fishing; tourism is now important, with resort developments on the formerly uninhabited island of Bangarem; named the Laccadive, Minicoy and Amindivi Islands, the islands became a union territory in 1956; the territory was renamed Lakshadweep in Nov 1973.

Lambaréné *lam-ba-ray-nay'*, 0 41N 10 13E, pop(1974) 22,682, capital of Moyen-Ogooué prov, W Gabon, W Africa; on the R Ogooué, 160 km E of Port Gentil; noted for its mission hospital for lepers opened by Albert Schweitzer on an island in the river in 1913; a trading post was established on same site in 1886 by a British company which paid the local people with rum; trading activities led to vastly diminished reserves of such commodities as ebony, natural rubber and ivory; airfield.

Lambayeque *lam-bī-yay'kay*, dept in NW Peru; bordered by the Pacific (W) and Cordillera Occidental (E); includes Mórrope and Olmos deserts; situated mainly on a coastal plain, its rivers are used for irrigation purposes; pop(1981) 674,442; area 16,585 sq km; capital Chiclayo; economy: Peru's largest producer of rice and second largest sugar-producer.

Lam'beth, 51 30N 0 07W, pop(1981) 246,426, borough of S Greater London, England; S of R Thames; associated with the traditional 'coster' Cockney type; railway; monuments: Lambeth Palace, residence of the Archbishop of Canterbury; Queen Elizabeth Hall; Festival Hall; event: English Bach Festival (May).

Lamdjya *lam'ja*, MÉDÉA, 36 15N 2 48E, pop(1982) 135,364, chief town of Lamdjya dept, N Algeria, N Africa; 24 km SW of Blida; railway.

Lamía *lah-mee'a*, formerly ZITUNI *zee-too'nee*, 38 55N 22 26E, pop(1981) 41,667, agric market town and capital of Fthiótis nome (dept), Sterea Ellás-Évvoia region, Greece; near the junction of the R Sperkhiós with the Gulf of Lamía, at the foot of Mt Óthris, on the main highway between Athínai (Athens) and Thessaloníki; it was claimed in ancient times to be the home of Achilles; the site of the acropolis is now occupied by a medieval castle; railway.

Lampung *lam'poong*, province of Indonesia; at the S tip of Sumatera I; bounded N by the prov of Sumatera Selatan and separated from Jawa by the Selat Sunda; the remains of the volcano Rakata Krakatua (Krakatoa) which erupted in 1883, killing 36,000 people, lie in the strait; pop(1980) 4,624,785; area 33,307 sq km; capital Tanjungkarang; economy: pepper, coffee, cinchona bark, oil, copra, timber.

Lan Hsü *lan shoo*, HUNG-T'OU, LANYU, ORCHID ISLAND (Eng), mostly hilly island belonging to Taiwan; area 45 sq km; situated in the W Pacific, 68 km E of the southernmost tip of Taiwan; home of the Yami, the smallest and most primitive aborigine tribe in Taiwan; inhabited by approx 2,600 Yami; economy: fishing, vegetables, fruit; the tribe live in 6 coastal villages, each village having its own fishing grounds, fields and irrigated terraces; the Yami maintain their own tribal customs and traditional way of life; the men wear silver helmets, made of flattened silver coins; their boats are made out of planks joined by wooden pegs, no saws or nails are used; during the Japanese occupation of Taiwan (1895-1945) the Japanese regarded Lan Hsü as an anthropological museum and carried out an intensive study of the Yami; the island was known as Orchid Island because of the profusion of wild orchids which grow there; Lan Hsü is reached by domestic flights from T'ai-pei and T'ai-tung.

Lanai *la-nī'*, island of the US state of Hawaii; in the Pacific Ocean W of Maui and S of Molokai; part of Maui county; area 365 sq km; pop(1980) 2,119; chief town Lanai City; economy: pineapples.

Lanark, 55 41N 3 48W, pop(1981) 9,806, market town and capital of Clydesdale dist, Strathclyde, S central Scotland; on the R Clyde, 18 km SE of Motherwell; railway; monuments: 1.5 km S of Lanark is the former mill village of New Lanark, on the Falls of Clyde; founded in 1784 by David Dale and Richard Arkwright, it was the scene of early experiments in providing proper conditions for workers and their families.

Lancashire *lang'ka-shir*, county of NW England; bounded W by the Irish Sea, N by Cumbria, E by North and West Yorkshire, S by Greater Manchester and Merseyside; drained by the Lune and Ribble rivers; pop(1981) 1,376,519; area 3,063 sq km; county town Preston; chief towns include Lancaster, Blackpool, Blackburn, Burnley; economy: the traditional textile, footwear and fishing industries have given way to high-technology aerospace and electronics; the county is divided into 14 districts:

District	*area (sq km)*	*pop(1981)*
Blackburn	137	141,928
Blackpool	35	148,482
Burnley	118	94,078
Chorley	205	91,203
Fylde	165	68,904
Hyndburn	73	79,043
Lancaster	577	121,311
Pendle	168	85,744
Preston	142	126,155
Ribble Valley	579	52,121
Rossendale	138	64,690
South Ribble	111	97,464
West Lancashire	332	107,271
Wyre	283	98,125

Lancaster *lang'kas-ter*, 54 03N 2 48W, pop(1981) 44,447, town in Lancaster dist, Lancashire, NW England; 32 km N of Preston; chartered in 1193; city status in 1937; university (1964); railway; economy: paper, plastics, chemicals; monuments: 12th-c castle, priory church of St Mary.

Lancaster, 34 42N 118 03W, pop(1980) 48,027, city in Los Angeles county, SW central California, United States; in Antelope Valley (W Mojave Desert), c.72 km N of Los Angeles; railway.

Lancaster, 39 43N 82 36W, pop(1980) 34,953, county seat of Fairfield county, central Ohio, United States; on the R Hocking, 43 km SE of Columbus; railway; economy: market centre for dairying and livestock region; birthplace of William T. Sherman.

Lancaster, 40 02N 76 19W, pop(1980) 54,725, county seat of Lancaster county, SE Pennsylvania, United States; 56 km ESE of Harrisburg; was briefly capital of the USA in 1777; railway; economy: market centre in a region of diversified agriculture; monument: farm museum.

Lanchow, capital of Gansu prov, N central China. See Lanzhou.

Lancy *lãs-ee'*, pop(1980) 23,527, town in Genève canton, SW Switzerland; a suburb on the S outskirts of Genève; economy: engineering.

Landes *lãd*, dept in Aquitaine region of SW France, on the Bay of Biscay; comprises 2 arrond, 30 cantons and 331 communes; pop(1982) 297,424; area 9,243 sq km; mostly marshy tracts of Pliocene sands and pine plantations; drained by the Leyre, Douze and Adour rivers; some of the lagoons (Étang de Cazaux and Étang de Biscarrosse), cut off by dunes (showing the former coastline), have valuable fishing; capital Mont-de-Marsan; spas at Préchacq-les-Bains, Dax, Tercis-les-Bains and Eugénie-les-Bains; the Parc des Landes de Gascogne regional nature park lies partly within the dept.

Land's End, BOLERIUM (anc), 50 03N 5 44W, Cornwall, SW England; a granite headland, the westernmost extremity of England; Longships lighthouse lies offshore.

Landshut *lants'hoot*, 48 31N 12 10E, pop(1983) 56,400, town in Niederbayern dist, Bayern (Bavaria) prov, W Germany; on the R Isar, NE of München (Munich); railway; economy: electrical and mechanical engineering, car manufacturing, textiles, dyestuffs, building; monuments: St Martin's church (14-15th-c); Burg Trausnitz, founded with the town by Duke Ludwig I c.1204; event: historical pageant play, *Die Landschuter Hochzeit* (The Landshut Wedding), every three years.

Landskrona *lants-kroo'na*, 55 53N 12 50E, pop(1983) 35,983, seaport and industrial town on W coast of Malmöhus county, SW Sweden; on the Øresund (The Sound), 26 km NNE of København (Copenhagen); nearby is the island of Hven or Ven, on which Tycho Brahe built his castle and observatory of Uraniborg; ferry services to København and the Swedish island of Hven or Ven in the Øresund; railway; monument: 16th-c castle.

Lan'ga, pop(1985) 25,500, African township E of central Cape Town, Cape prov, South Africa.

Langeland *lang'e-lan*, elongated Danish island in Baltic Sea, off SE coast of Fyn I, N tip extends into the Store Bælt (Great Belt); area 285 sq km; length 53 km; width 5 km; chief town Rudkøbing; administered by Fyn county; noted for its magnificent beech trees.

Langjökull *lang'ye-kootl*, glacier in W central Iceland; NE of Reykjavík; 2nd largest glacier in Iceland; area 1,021 sq km.

Langkawi *lang-kah'wee*, island group in Perlis state, off the NW coast of Peninsular Malaysia; a group of 99 islands situated in the Strait of Malacca close to the Thailand frontier; the main island (*pulau*) is Pulau Langkawi; the 2nd largest island is Pulau Dayang Bunting; 3 of the islands are populated; pop(1980) 30,000; the chief village is Pekan Kuah; noted for its birds, butterflies and fine scenery; ferry to Kuala Perlis on the mainland.

Langøy *lang'u-u*, ('long island'), Norwegian island in the Norwegian Sea off NW Norway, westernmost island of the Vesterålen group, separated from Hinnøy to the E by a narrow strait; deeply indented in the SE by Vesterål Fjord; area 860 sq km; length 56 km; administered by Nordland county.

Langtan, national park, Nepal, central Asia; to the N of Kathmandu on the border between Nepal and the Tibet region of the People's Republic of China; founded in 1976; covers an area of 3,555 sq km.

Languedoc *lã-ge-dok*, former prov between the R Rhône, the Mediterranean and Guyenne and Gascogne, S France, now occupying the depts of Ardèche, Gard, Lozère, Hérault, Aude, Tarn and parts of Haute-Garonne, Haute-Loire, Ariège and Pyrénées Orientales; includes the dists of Vivarais, Gevaudan, Velay, Garigues, Causses and Albigeois; the Cévennes Mts are in the E; the name is derived from the langue d'oc (Provençal) as distinct from the langue d'oîl.

Languedoc-Roussillon *lã-ge-dok-roo-see-yõ*, region of S France on the Mediterranean coast, comprising the depts of Lozère, Gard, Hérault, Aude and Pyrénées-Orientales, 14 arrond, 178 cantons and 1,539 communes; pop(1982) 1,925,514; area 27,376 sq km; bounded on the S by Spain, on the SE by the Mediterranean Sea and on the E by the R Rhône; watered by the Allier, Gard, Hérault, Orb and Aude rivers; the Canal du Midi (formerly the Canal des Deux-Mers) is 200 km long and joins the Mediterranean to the R Garonne and so to the Atlantic; the plateaux of the Massif Central are extremely arid, but as one descends from the limestone Causses to the coastal plains, the climate rapidly changes to Mediterranean; sheep and goats are grazed on the plateaux, the sheep being principally kept for milk, from which Roquefort cheese is made; the valleys are fertile, planted with vines and fruit trees; from Roussillon come the early fruit and vegetables which supply the markets of France; the heart of the region is the wine-growing belt that stretches from W of Montpellier to beyond Carcassonne; the coastal plains are commonly referred to as the 'Midi'; seaside resorts include Cerbère, Port-Camargue, La Grande-Motte, Gruissan (the most recent of the new Mediterranean resorts, started in 1974), Canet-Plage, Port-Barcares; Sète is France's 2nd largest Mediterranean port; there are spas at Amélie-les-Bains-Palalda, Vernet-les-Bains and Lamalou-les-Bains; Font-Romeu, near the Franco-Spanish border, is a wintersports centre; there are several interesting caves including Grotte de Clamouse, in the Gorges of the R Hérault (its principal attraction is a series of illuminated stalactites and stalagmites) and Grotte des Demoiselles, 4 km SE of Ganges; a principal tourist attraction is the Gorges du Tarn, a fault in the earth's surface which separates the Causse de Sauveterre on one side from the Causse Méjean on the other, and is deepened by the R Tarn; the popular Perrier water (bottled) comes from Vergèze in Gard dept, while Vernières comes from Lamalou-les-Bains; the early establishment of human settlements in this region is reflected in an early flowering of art; the earliest sculptured figures in the whole of western art, dating from 1020, are to be found in the church of St-Genis-des-Fontaines, S of Perpignan.

Lanín *la-neen'*, Andean national park in SW Neuquén prov, Andina, Argentina; area 1,946 sq km; established in 1937; borders W with Chile and S with Nahuel Huapí National Park; includes Volcán Lanín (3,776 m) and L Huechulaufquen.

Lansing, 41 34N 87 33W, pop(1980) 29,039, town in Cook county, NE Illinois, United States; on Indiana border, 38 km S of Chicago.

Lansing, 42 44N 84 33W, pop(1980) 130,414, capital of state in Ingham county, S central Michigan, United States; on the R Grand, 80 km WSW of Flint; railway; economy: car and truck manufacturing centre; also manufactures machinery and fabricated metals.

Lantau *lan-dow*, island in New Territories region of Hong Kong, SE Asia; separated from Hong Kong I by the Lamma Channel and linked by an expressway to the mainland at Tsuen Wan via Tsing Yi I; the highest point is Lantau Peak which rises to 934 m.

Lanzhou *lan-jō*, LANCHOW, KAOLAN, 36 01N 103 19E, pop(1984e) 1,455,100, capital of Gansu prov, N central China; on the upper Huang He (Yellow river) in the Longxi Basin; the centre for China's atomic energy industry since 1960; university (1946); railway; airfield; economy: trade in wheat, millet, tobacco, sorghum, melons; oil refining, metallurgy, light engineering, textiles; monument: Gansu province museum contains early Chinese artifacts and the sculpture, the 'Flying Horse of Gansu'.

Laoighis *lay'ish*, LEIX *layks*, formerly QUEEN'S COUNTY, county in Leinster prov, S central Irish Republic; watered by R Nore; Slieve Bloom Mts rise in NW, pop(1981) 51,171; area 1,720 sq km; capital Portlaoighise (Maryborough); huge tracts of peat used to fuel power stations.

Laon, La *la-õ*, LAUDUNUM (anc), 49 33N 3 35E, pop(1982) 29,074, ancient town and capital of Aisne dept, Picardie region, N France, on an elongated ridge of hills rising abruptly to 100 m above the Paris Basin, 123 km NE of Paris and 45 km from Reims; alt 181 m; railway junction; the oldest part of the town, the Cité, lies at the E edge of the ridge; monuments: 12th-c Gothic cathedral with 7 towers; old episcopal palace (now used as the Palais de Justice); 12th-c church; the abbey of Premontre to the SW (1119); from the 13th-c ramparts, the Plaine de Champagne stretches towards the SE; in the 8-10th centuries, La Laon was capital of France and residence of the kings until Hugues Capet, elected King in 987, broke the tradition and moved to Paris.

Laos *lah'ōs*, official name the Lao People's Democratic Republic, a republic in SE Asia, bounded E by Vietnam, S by Cambodia, W by Thailand and N by Burma and China; timezone GMT +7; area 236,800 sq km; pop(1984e) 3,800,000; capital Vientiane; chief towns Luangphrabang, Pakse and Savannakhét; most of the E has been depopulated by war; ethnic groups include 60% Laotian, 35% hill tribes and 5% Vietnamese and Chinese; Lao is the official language; the Lao-Lum are mostly Buddhist, the Lao Theung are mostly animists and the Lao-Soung in the N are a mixture of animist, Christian and Confucian; the currency is the kip of 100 att; national holiday 2 Dec; membership of Asian Development Bank, Colombo Plan, ESCAP, FAO, G-77, IBRD, ICAO, IDA, IFAD, ILO, IMF, INTERPOL, IPU, IRC, ITU, Mekong Committee, NAM, UN, UNCTAD, UNESCO, UPU, WFTU, WHO, WMO, WTO.

Physical description and climate. Laos is a landlocked

country on the Indochinese Peninsula of SE Asia. The E frontier with Vietnam is dominated by dense jungle and rugged mountains rising to 2,751 m. These mountains form a watershed from which streams flow down to meet the R Mekong which flows NW-SE following the W frontier of Laos with Thailand for much of its course. The climate is monsoonal, with heavy rain from May to Sept. From Feb to April Laos is hot and dry. Temperatures in Vientiane range between 14°C and 34°C.
History, government and constitution. First united by the legendary King Fa Ngum, much of what is now Laos was dominated by Thailand in the 19th century. The Franco-Siamese Treaty of 1907 established the present boundaries of Laos. The Kingdom of Laos gained independence from France in 1949 but remained within the French Union until 1954. The period 1957-75 was marked by instability and internal conflict between the Royal Lao Government and the Patriotic Front (*Pathet Lao*). On 2 Dec 1975 the monarchy was abolished and the Communist Lao People's Democratic Republic was established. A People's Supreme Council was appointed to draw up a constitution. The country is headed by a president and governed by a prime minister, who is also Secretary General of the Central Committee of the Lao People's Revolutionary Party. Provinces are administered by People's Revolutionary Committees which are directly responsible to the Central Committee.
Economy. The agricultural economy of Laos suffered severely from the 20 years of civil war, with millions of hectares of paddy fields and forest being destroyed. The main crops are rice, coffee, tobacco, cotton and spices, but opium grown under state control in W Laos is of major importance to the economy. The country is now self-sufficient in rice which is the staple food. In 1979 the government abandoned its attempt to set up farming cooperatives and relaxed its restrictions on private enterprise. There are rich deposits of iron ore in Xiangkhoang prov and potash in Vientiane prov, but the

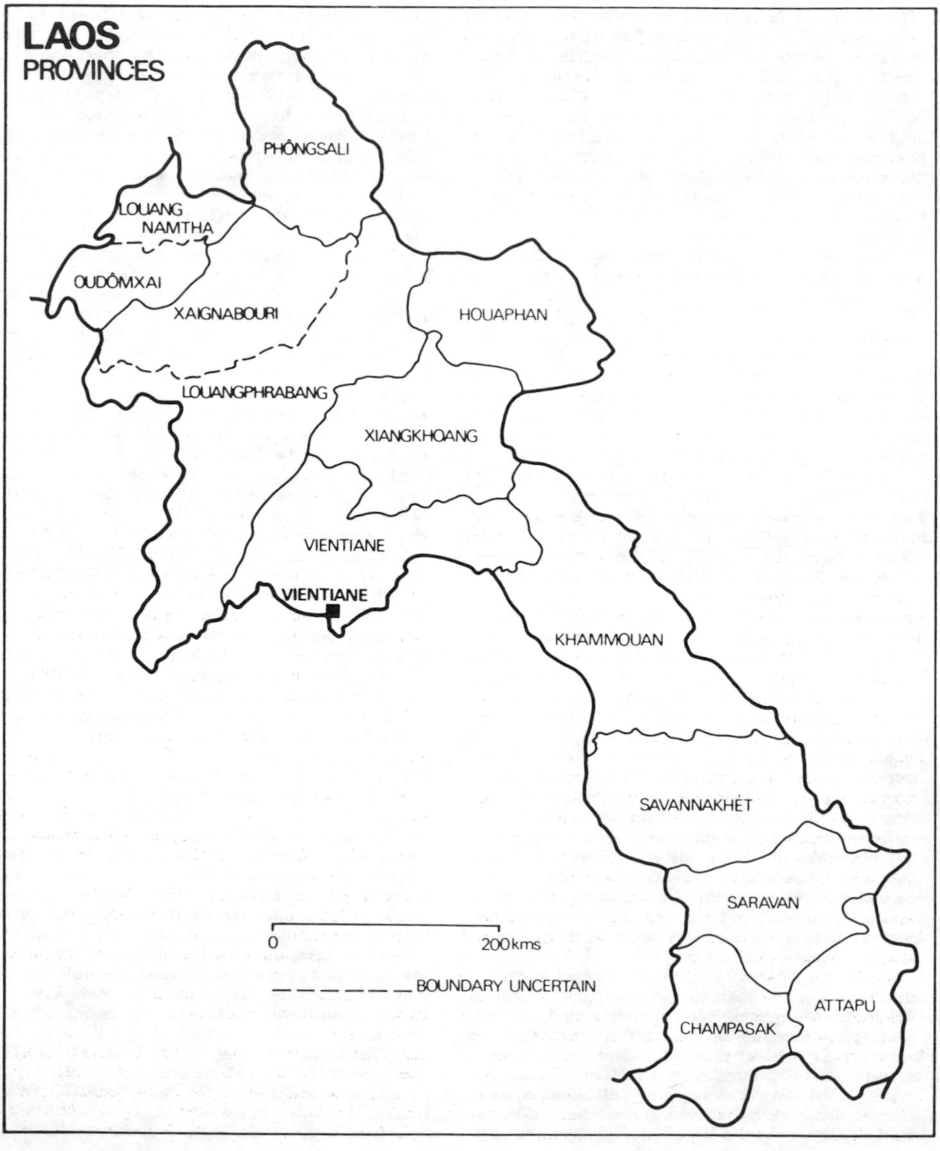

only mineral to be mined and exported in any quantity is tin. The forest industry is being developed with Russian and Swedish aid. The industrial sector is limited to the small scale manufacture of rubber, cigarettes, matches, textiles, food and drinks. The country's main exports are coffee and timber. Major trade partners include the UK, the USSR, Thailand and Japan.

Administrative divisions. Laos is divided into the 13 provs (*khowèng*) of Attapu, Champasak, Houaphan, Khammouan, Louang Namtha, Louangphrabang, Oudômxai, Phôngsali, Saravan, Savannakhét, Vientiane, Xaignabouri and Xiangkhoang.

Lappeenranta *lap'en-ran-ta*, VILLMANSTRAND *vil'man-strand* (Swed), 61 04N 28 05E, pop(1982) 53,891, town in Kymi prov, SE Finland, near border of Soviet Karelian ASSR; established in 1649 by Queen Christina; railway; airfield; boats to the Finnish lakes and through the Saimaa Canal.

Lappi *lap'i*, LAPPLAND (Swed), a prov of N Finland, bounded on the W by Sweden, the NW by Norway and on the E by USSR; drained by the rivers Kemijoki, Ounasjoki and the Kitinen; occupies nearly 30% of the total area of Finland; L Inarijärvi, the 3rd largest lake in Finland, occupies the NE corner; Mt Haltia, the highest peak in Finland (1,328 m), lies on the frontier with Norway; area 98,938 sq km; pop(1982) 198,011; Rovaniemi, on the banks of the Kemijoki (R Kemi), is the prov capital; chromium mining at Kemi and iron mining at Mustavaara and Rautuvarra; the Pallas-Ounastunturi, Lemmenjoki and Urho Kekkonen national parks are located to the W, N and E of the prov respectively.

Lappland, prov of N Finland. See Lappi.

Laptev Sea, *lahp'tev*, NORDENSKJÖLD, Arctic sea situated N of mainland USSR, between Poluostrov Taymyr and Novosibirsky Ostrova; area 649,830 sq km; linked to the East Siberian Sea by Proliv Dimitriya Lapteva and to the Kara Sea by the Proliv Vilkitskogo; the Laptev is a shallow sea situated on a long continental shelf; part of the Northern Sea Route, but only navigable during Aug-Sept due to pack-ice throughout the rest of the year; fed by the Anabar, Olenek, Yana, Omoloy and Lena rivers; main arms are Khatangskiy Zaliv, Guba Buorkhaya and Yanskiy Zaliv.

Lapua *lap'oo-a*, 62 57N 23 00E, pop(1982) 14,593, town in Vaasa prov, W central Finland; established in 1964; railway.

Lara *la'ra*, mountainous state in N Venezuela; containing NE section of the great Andean spur (S), outliers of the coastal range (E) and the arid Segovia Highlands; drained by Río Tocuyo; pop(1980) 1,047,633; area 19,793 sq km; capital Barquisimeto.

Larache *le-rash'*, LIXUS (anc), 35 12N 6 10W, pop(1982) 63,893, fortified seaport in Tétouan prefecture, Nord-Ouest prov, NW Morocco, N Africa; on the Atlantic coast, 87 km SSW of Tanger (Tangiers); part of Spanish North Africa from 1912 to 1956; 400 sq km hunting reserve stretches to the S; economy: fishing, trade in wool, cork, wax, fruit, vegetables and hides.

Laredo *le-ray'dō*, 27 30N 99 30W, pop(1980) 91,449, county seat of Webb county, S Texas, United States; a port on the Rio Grande river, opposite Nuevo Laredo, Mexico; settled in 1755, achieving city status in 1852; university; railway; airfield; economy: a major port on the USA-Mexico border, with an important import-export trade; a wholesale and retail centre for a large area on either side of the border, with ranching, farming, oil production, mining and smelting nearby; manufactures include clothing, electronic equipment, ceramics, medical supplies, leather goods.

Largo, 27 55N 82 47W, pop(1980) 58,977, resort town in Pinellas county, W Florida, United States; on Pinellas Peninsula, 6 km S of Clearwater; railway; economy: packing, canning and shipping centre for citrus fruit area.

Largs, 55 48N 4 52W, pop(1981) 9,905, resort town in Kilmarnock and Loudoun dist, Strathclyde, W Scotland; on the Firth of Clyde, opposite the island of Great Cumbrae; railway; monuments: Largs museum; Skelmorlie Aisle mausoleum (1636); Haylie chambered tomb.

Lárisa, rich agricultural nome (dept) of Thessalía region, E Greece; pop(1981) 254,295; area 5,381 sq km; capital Lárisa; drained by the R Piniós; economy: fruit, wheat, olives.

Lárisa, 39 38N 22 25E, pop(1981) 102,048, capital town of Lárisa nome (dept), Thessalía region, Greece; on a bend of the R Piníos, S of Mt Ólimbos (Olympus); centre of an agricultural region; airfield; road and rail junction; economy: textiles, agric trade.

Larkana *lahr-kah'na*, 27 32N 68 18E, pop(1981) 123,000, city in Sind prov, SE Pakistan; 322 km NE of Karachi, close to the W bank of the R Indus; economy: cotton, silk, leather and metalware; monuments: prehistoric remains of the Mohenjo-Daro civilization which thrived from 3000 to 1700 BC.

Larkhall, 55 45N 3 59W, pop(1981) 16,216, town in Hamilton dist, Strathclyde, W central Scotland; in Clydeside urban area, 6 km SE of Hamilton; economy: engineering, textiles.

Larnaca *lar'na-ka*, dist in S Cyprus; area 1,126 sq km; pop(1973) 60,714; capital Larnaca; largely in Greek Cypriot control (82%); its population has increased dramatically since 1974 with the influx of refugees; includes part of the Dhekelia British base area (E).

Larnaca, 34 55N 33 36E, pop(1973) 19,608, port and capital town of Larnaca dist, S Cyprus; on Larnaca Bay on the S coast; situated SW of the Dhekelia British base area; airport; monument: old Turkish fort (1625), used as a prison and barracks during the early period of British rule, now a museum.

Larne, LATHARNA (Gael), 54 51N 5 49W, pop(1981) 18,224, port town in Larne dist, Antrim, E Northern Ireland; on the E coast, on Lough Larne, near its mouth on the North Channel, 29 km N of Belfast; railway; ferry service to Stranraer; economy: quarries, cement works, textiles, engineering; monument: the remains of Olderfleet castle date from the 13-14th centuries.

Las Vegas, city in Nevada, United States. See Vegas, Las.

La-sa, capital of Xizang aut region (Tibet), China. See Lhasa.

Lashkar Gāh, LASH-KAR-GAR', 31 35N 64 21E, pop(1984e) 23,677, capital of Helmand prov, S Afghanistan; lies on the R Helmand; airfield.

Lasíthi, easternmost nome (dept) of Kriti region, Greece; pop(1981) 70,053; area 1,823 sq km; capital Ayios Nikólaos.

Last Chance Gulch, Montana. See Helena.

Latacunga *la-ta-koong'ga*, 0 58S 78 36W, pop(1982) 28,764, capital of Cotopaxi prov in the Andean Sierra of N central Ecuador; 29 km SE of Cotopaxi volcano; railway; economy: dairy products, flour, drinks, paper, mineral products; monuments: a botanical garden in the Parque Vicente León; the Pasaje Catedral is a colonial building recently renovated and turned into an arcade of shops, offices and a small art gallery which contains a 17th-c aerial view painting of Latacunga; event: 22-24 Sept (Fiesta de Nuestra Señora de la Merced).

Latakia, governorate and city in Syria. See Lādhiqīyah, Al.

Latina *lah-tee'nah*, prov of Lazio region, Italy; pop(1981) 434,086; area 2,251 sq km; capital Latina.

Latina, formerly LITTORIA, 41 28N 12 53E, pop(1981) 93,738, capital town of Latina prov, Lazio region, central Italy; 66 km SE of Roma (Rome), near the coast of the Tyrrhenian Sea.

Látrabjarg *low-trah-byark'*, 65 30N 24 32W, westernmost point of Iceland and one of the highest cliff faces in the world; in Vestfirdir region, W Iceland; the British trawler *Dhoon* ran aground below the cliff in 1947, the entire crew being saved by men lowered down the cliff on ropes in one of the world's greatest rescue achievements.

Latvia, constituent republic of the Soviet Union. See Latviskaya.

Latviskaya, LATVIYA SSR, LATVIA (Eng), constituent republic of the Soviet Union, in NW European USSR, bounded W and NW by the Baltic Sea; a flat, glaciated region, the NW coast is indented by the Rizhskiy Zaliv (Gulf of Riga) of the Baltic Sea; the chief river is the

Zapadnaya Dvina (Daugava); forests, primarily coniferous, cover more than 40% of the territory; pop(1983) 2,569,000; area 63,700 sq km; capital Riga; chief towns Daugav'pils and Liepāja; economy: machine building and metalworking, specializing in the manufacture of instruments, transportation and agricultural machinery, power generators, and electrical engineering and electronic equipment; chemicals; lumber industry (production of furniture and matchwood); light industry (knitwear); food processing; it is the main producer of electric railway passenger cars and long-distance telephone exchanges in the USSR; animal husbandry, notably the raising of cattle for meat and dairy products and the raising of pigs for bacon, is the chief agricultural activity; oats, barley, rye, potatoes, and flax are the main agricultural crops; incorporated into Russia in 1721, it became an independent state in 1918 after occupation by Germany; it was proclaimed a Soviet Socialist Republic on 21 July 1940; under the Czarist régime, Latvia was economically one of the most highly developed regions of Russia, possessing metalworking, shipbuilding and chemical industries; at that time, 25% of Russian exports passed through its ports; occupied alternately by Swedes, Oles and Russians, the Latts found national expression in a well-developed folklore, particularly in the 1860s when the Latvian theatre was founded in Riga (1868); the Latvian language belongs to the Baltic group of the Indo-European languages.

Lauderdale Lakes, 26 10N 80 13W, pop(1980) 25,426, town in Broward county, SE Florida, United States; residential suburb 10 km NW of Fort Lauderdale.

Lauderhill, 26 08N 80 13W, pop(1980) 37,271, town in Broward county, SE Florida, United States; a residential suburb 8 km NW of Fort Lauderdale.

Launceston *lon'ses-ten*, 41 25S 147 07E, pop(1981) 64,555 (Greater Launceston), city in Northern stat div, Tasmania, Australia; 65 km S of the Bass Strait at the confluence of the N Esk, S Esk and Tamar rivers; 2nd largest city in Tasmania; railway; airfield; economy: timber, textiles, brewing; monument: the Cataract Gorge with its suspension bridge and chair-lift.

Laurentian Plateau, area of ancient pre-Cambrian rock covering over half of Canada. See Canadian Shield.

Lausanne *lō-zan'*, 46 32N 6 39E, pop(1980) 127,349, tourist resort, convention centre, and capital of Vaud canton, W Switzerland; built on terraces on the N shore of Lac Léman (Lake of Geneva), in the S foothills of the Jura Mts where Mt Jorat descends to the lake, 51 km NE of Genève; seat of the International Olympic Committee; Ouchy, in the S outskirts, is a popular resort; the Old Town is situated higher on the slopes; nearby is Mon Repos Park where the Olympic Museum honours the memory of Baron Coubertin who founded the modern Olympic Games; university (1891); airfields at Blecherette and Montricher; railway junction; economy: clothing, confectionery, printing, leather; monuments: Gothic cathedral (1275), 17th-c town hall, ancient Bishop's Palace; events: Fête of Lausanne (late June); biennial Festival of Tapestry.

Laval *la-val'*, 45 34N 73 40W, pop(1981) 268,335, town in S Québec, SE Canada; on W bank of Rivière des Prairies on Ile Jésus, W of Montréal; railway.

Laval, 48 04N 0 48W, pop(1982) 53,766, market town and capital of Mayenne dept, Pays de la Loire region, NW France; on two heights above the R Mayenne, 70 km E of Rennes; the centre of an agric region; the town was founded before the 9th century; birthplace of Henri Rousseau (1844-1910) and Alain Gerbault, the single-handed circumnavigator who died in the South Seas in 1941; economy: dairy produce; monuments: Château Neuf (Renaissance, altered in the 19th century, houses the Palais de Justice), Vieux Château (13-16th-c), Romanesque church of La Trinité (11th-c, a cathedral since 1855), 15-16th-c church of St Venerand, Clermont Abbey (15 km NW, former Cistercian abbey founded by St Bernard in the 11th century).

Lavalleja *la-val-yay'KHa*, dept in SE Uruguay; bounded by the Cuchilla Grande range (W); drained (N) by the Río Cebollatí; pop(1985) 61,241; area 12,485 sq km; capital Minas; dept was formed in 1816.

Lavant *la'fant*, river in S Austria, rising S of Judenburg in Kärnten state, and flowing S to meet the R Drau at Lavammund; length 72 km.

Lavra, Pacific island. See Choiseul.

Lawra *lo'ra*, 10 40N 2 49W, town in Upper region, NW Ghana, W Africa; on the Ivory Coast frontier, W of Bolgatanga.

Lawrence, 39 50N 86 02W, pop(1980) 25,591, residential town in Marion county, central Indiana, United States; 14 km NE of Indianapolis; railway.

Lawrence, 38 58N 95 14W, pop(1980) 52,738, county seat of Douglas county, E Kansas, United States; on the R Kansas, 40 km E of Topeka; university (1863); railway; economy: food processing.

Lawrence, 42 43N 71 10W, pop(1980) 63,175, city in Essex county, NE Massachusetts, United States; on the R Merrimack, 14 km NE of Lowell; city status since 1853; railway; economy: textiles, paper, plastics, rubber, leather.

Lawton, 34 37N 98 25W, pop(1980) 80,054, county seat of Comanche county, SW Oklahoma, United States; 125 km SW of Oklahoma City; railway; economy: commercial and trade centre for agricultural area and for nearby Fort Sill, a US field artillery base; event: Easter Sunrise Pageant.

La'youn *la-yun'*, prov in Western Sahara, NW Africa; pop(1982) 113,411; area 39,360 sq km; claimed by Morocco.

La'youn, EL AAIUN, 27 10N 13 11W, pop(1982) 96,784, capital of La'youn prov, Western Sahara, NW Africa; airfield.

Lazarevac *la'zar-e-vats*, 44 23N 20 19E, pop(1981) 51,068, town in N Srbija (Serbia) republic, Yugoslavia; 48 km SSW of Beograd.

Lazio *lat'see-o*, LATIUM *lay'shi-um* (anc), region of W central Italy, bounded E by the Appno Abruzzese and W by the Tyrrhenian Sea; drained by the R Tevere (Tiber); comprises the provs of Frosinone, Latina, Rieti, Roma, and Viterbo; pop(1981) 5,001,684; area 17,203 sq km; chief towns Roma, Frosinone, Gaeta, Rieti, and Palestrina; varied arable and sheep farming region; the lower-lying areas produce corn, vegetables and sugar-beet, while the volcanic soils of the uplands yield citrus fruits, olives, and wine; industry has developed rapidly around Roma (Rome), in the Sacco and Liri valleys, and in the catchment area of the Autostrada del Sole (chemicals, pharmaceuticals, textiles, metal-working, building materials, etc); tourism, particularly in and around Roma, also makes a considerable contribution to the economy.

Lea or **Lee**, river rising N of Luton, Bedfordshire, SE England; flows 75 km SE and S to meet the R Thames at Blackwall; receives the R Stort E of Hoddesden.

Leamington Spa, Leamington or **Royal Leamington Spa** *lem'ing-ton*, 52 18N 1 31W, pop(1981) 57,347, health resort in Warwick dist, Warwickshire, central England; part of Warwick-Leamington Spa urban area; on the R Leam, 13 km S of Coventry; a Royal Spa since 1838; mineral springs; railway.

Leatherhead, 51 18N 0 20W, pop(1981) 42,629, town in Mole Valley dist, Surrey, SE England; part of Greater London urban area; on the R Mole, 10 km S of Kingston-upon-Thames; railway; economy: engineering, electrical goods.

Leavenworth *lev'-*, 39 19N 94 55W, pop(1980) 33,656, county seat of Leavenworth county, E Kansas, United States; on the R Missouri, 30 km NW of Kansas City; railway; economy: trade and industrial centre with flour mills and a shipyard.

Leb'anon, LIBAN *lee-bã'* (Fr), official name Republic of Lebanon, AL-JUMHOURIYA AL LUBNANIYA, republic on the E coast of the Mediterranean Sea, SW Asia; bounded N and E by Syria, and S by Israel; timezone GMT +2; area 10,452 sq km; capital Beyrouth (Beirut); chief towns Trâblous (Tripoli), Saïda (Sidon), and Zahlé; pop(1984e)

2,601,000; the urban population is concentrated mostly in Beyrouth and Trâblous; Arabs make up the majority of the pop (93%) with additional numbers of Armenian, Kurdish, Assyrian, Jewish, Turkish, and Greek minorities; Arabic is the official language although French, English, and Armenian are also spoken; 55% of the people are Christians (Maronite, Greek Orthodox and Catholic, Roman Catholic, and Protestant) and 44% Muslims (Sunni, Shi'a, Druze); the unit of currency is the Lebanese pound; membership of Arab League, FAO, G-77, IAEA, IBRD, ICAO, IDA, Islamic Development Bank, IFAD, IFC, ILO, IMF, IMO, INTELSAT, INTERPOL, IPU, ITU, IWC, NAM, OIC, UN, UNESCO, UPU, WFTU, WHO, WMO, WSG, WTO.

Physical description. Lebanon comprises 4 distinct topographic regions. The narrow Mediterranean coastal plain rises gradually E over a distance of some 30 km to the Jebel Liban (Lebanon) range. This mountain range extends almost the entire length of the country and covers more than a third of the area. Peaks include Qornet es Saouda (3,087 m) and Harf Sannine (2,628 m). Its arid E slopes fall abruptly to the fertile El Beqa'a plateau which has an average elevation of 1,000 m. Further E, the remote Jebel esh Sharqi (Anti-Lebanon) range forms the frontier between Lebanon and Syria. The R Līṭāni flows S between the 2 mountain ranges and discharges into the Mediterranean N of Soûr (Tyre).

Climate. The climate is Mediterranean with hot, dry summers and warm, moist winters. Temperature and precipitation, however, vary considerably with altitude. The average annual rainfall at Beyrouth (Beirut) is 920 mm, falling mostly during the winter months when Mediterranean depressions are frequent. Average temperatures at Beyrouth range from 13°C in Jan to 27°C in July. Winter rainfall turns to snow on the Jebel Liban. Inland, the El Beqa'a valley and the Jebel esh Sharqi range are much drier. Winters here are cooler than on the coast, with frequent snow and frost. In general, precipitation decreases from W to E, making irrigation essential in the El Beqa'a valley which has a rainfall of 380 mm per annum.

History, government and constitution. From the early 16th century Lebanon was part of the Ottoman Empire. In 1861, following the massacre of Maronites (a sect of the Roman Catholic church) by Druzes (an Islamic sect), the predominantly Maronite area around Jabal Lubnān was granted special autonomous status. Following the collapse of the Ottoman Empire after World War I the State of Greater Lebanon, based upon Maronite Christian Jabal Lubnān, was created in 1920 under French mandate. Despite considerable opposition, the predominantly Muslim coastal regions of Beyrouth, Soûr, Saïda, and Trâblous were incorporated into this new state. Although Lebanon became a constitutional republic in 1926 independence was not proclaimed until 26 Nov 1941. By the late 1960s Palestinian resistance units had established themselves in Lebanon despite opposition from the government. A series of Palestinian raids into Israel followed by Israeli reprisals led to the Cairo agreement of 1969 in an attempt to regulate the activities of the guerrillas. Several militia groups came into prominence in the mid-1970s. Shi'ite Muslims formed the Afwaj al-Muqawama al-Lubnaniyya (AMAL) militia group in 1974 and another powerful Muslim force, the Lebanese National Movement (LNM), was also established. Palestinian firepower was used to back up the political struggle of the LNM against the Maronite Christian and Sunni Muslim establishment. Muslim and Christian differences grew more intense with occasional clashes between private sectarian militias. From March 1975 Lebanon was beset by civil disorder as rival political and religious factions sought to gain control. Palestinian commandos joined the predominantly leftist-Muslim side. By November 1976 it was estimated that 40,000 people had been killed and up to 100,000 injured. The Syrian-dominated Arab Deterrent Force (ADF) was created to prevent Palestinian fighters gaining control in Lebanon. After the Oct 1976 cease fire Palestinian forces moved from Beyrouth to S Lebanon where the ADF was unable to deploy. W Beyrouth, also outside government control, was the scene of frequent conflict between opposing militia groups. Meanwhile Christian militias (backed by Israel) sought to regain control in E Beyrouth and areas to the N. In mid-1978 fighting broke out between the ADF and Christian militias. This eventually led the ADF to withdraw from the E Beyrouth area. Following a Palestinian terrorist attack in Feb 1978 Israel invaded S Lebanon and occupied the area up to the R Līṭāni. When the Israelis withdrew their forces in June they failed to hand over all their positions to the UN peace-keeping force (UNIFIL). Instead they installed Israeli-controlled Lebanese militia forces inside the Lebanese border. Following an assassination attempt against the Israeli ambassador in London on 3 June 1982, Israeli forces once again invaded Lebanon. By mid June they had reached Beyrouth and there began a two-and-a-half month siege of Palestinian and Syrian forces in the city. In September, Palestinian forces evacuated the city. The unilateral withdrawal of Israeli forces from Lebanon, beginning on 4 September 1982, led to clashes between the Druze (backed by Syria) and Christian Lebanese militia in the Shouf area, SE of Beyrouth. On 25 Sept a cease-fire for Beyrouth and the nearby mountain area was announced. Since then there have been various international efforts to achieve a lasting internal political reconciliation. Lebanon is an independent republic ruled by a 99-member parliament, a council of ministers, and a president. Executive authority is vested in the president who must be a Maronite Christian and who is elected for 6-year terms. He in turn elects the prime minister, who must be a Sunni Muslim, and the cabinet. Parliament comprises 53 Christian seats (30 Maronites, 11 Greek Orthodox, 6 Greek Catholic, 4 Armenian Orthodox, 1 Armenian Catholic, 1 Protestant), 39 Muslim seats, 6 for Druzes and one other.

Economy. Before the outbreak of civil war in 1975 Lebanon was considered the commercial and financial centre of the Middle East with a valuable and prosperous entrepôt trade. The civil war severely damaged the country's economic infrastructure and dramatically reduced industrial production. Chief industries include oil refining, the manufacture of cement, textiles, and chemicals, food processing, service industries, and some metal fabricating. A good deal of revenue is derived from transit trade and remittances from citizens abroad. Since the 1975-76 civil war the tourist industry has virtually collapsed. Exports are mainly to the Arab states of Saudi Arabia, Syria, Kuwait, Libya, and Iraq. Imports come mainly from the USA, W Germany, France, Italy, and the UK. Agriculture accounts for approx 9% of national income and employs 17% of the workforce (1981). About 1,080 sq km of land are under cultivation, the chief crops being citrus fruits, grapes, bananas, sugar-beet, olives, and wheat. Chief farming regions are the narrow coastal plain and the fertile El Beqa'a valley. Irrigation projects are under way to harness the waters of the Līṭāni river and make the area even more productive. Grapes, olives, and apple trees are grown on the less fertile lower slopes of the 2 main mountain ranges. The civil war also disrupted the country's agricultural development, particularly in the S.

Administrative divisions. Lebanon is divided into the 5 regional governments (*moafazats*) of Ash Shamāl, El Beqa'a, Beyrouth, Al Janūb, and Jabal Lubnān. These in turn are subdivided into divisions (*cazas*).

Lebanon, 40 20N 76 26W, pop(1980) 25,711, county seat of Lebanon county, SE Pennsylvania, United States; 40 km E of Harrisburg; railway.

Lebo'wa, national state or non-independent black homeland in N Transvaal prov, NE South Africa; pop(1985) 1,835,984; situated NE of Pretoria; achieved self-governing status in 1972.

Lebu *lay'boo*, 37 36S 73 39W, pop(1981) 20,197, port and capital of Arauco prov, Bío-Bío, central Chile; at the mouth of the Río Lebu, SW of Concepción; railway; economy: coal mining, tourism.

Lecce *let'chay*, prov of Puglia region, SE Italy; pop(1981) 762,017; area 2,758 sq km; capital Lecce.

Lecce, 40 21N 18 11E, pop(1981) 91,289, capital town of Lecce prov, Puglia region, SE Italy; 40 km SE of Brindisi; railway; economy: pottery, papier-mâché, trade in textiles, tobacco-growing and food products; monuments: cathedral (1658-70), church of Santa Croce (begun 1549), church of Santi Nicolo e Cataldo (1180); a Greek theatre was excavated in 1931.

Lech *leKH*, river in Austria and S Bayern (Bavaria) prov, W Germany; rises in the Vorarlberg, 16 km E of Bludenz, Austria, flows NE to German border, then N, past Füssen, Landsberg and Augsburg, to the R Danube, E of Donauwörth; length 250 km.

Lechtaler Alpen *leKH'tal-er al'pen*, LECHTAL ALPS (Eng), mountain range of the Eastern Alps in Tirol state, W Austria, bounded on the S by the Stanz valley and its continuation the Inn valley, and on the N by the Lech valley; rises to 3,036 m at Parseierspitze; there are numerous lakes including the Spullersee; in the W the Arlberg is a famous skiing area.

Ledyanaya, Gora, 61 49N 171 39E, highest peak of the Koryakskiy Khrebet range, NE Kamchatskaya oblast, E Siberian Rossiyskaya, Soviet Union; height 2,562 m; source of the R Il'pi.

Leeds, 53 50N 1 35W, pop(1981) 451,841, town in Leeds borough, West Yorkshire, N England; part of West Yorkshire urban area; on the R Aire, 315 km NNW of London; 6th largest city in England; there was a ford across the R Aire here in Roman times; in the 18th century the town became an important centre of cloth manufacture; birthplace of Lord Darnley (Temple Newsam); incorporated by Charles I in 1626; the first railway line in the world was opened here in 1758, transporting coal from Middleton to the R Aire in Leeds; university (1904); railway; economy: textiles, clothing, leather, chemicals, furniture, plastics, paper, electrical equipment; monuments: civic hall (1933), town hall (1858), churches of St John (1634) and St Peter (1841); events: Leeds Music Festival (every 3 years in April); International Pianoforte Competition (every 3 years in Sept); film festival.

Leek, 53 06N 2 01W, pop(1981) 18,535, town in Staffordshire Moorlands dist, Staffordshire, central England; 15 km NE of Stoke-on-Trent; economy: textiles.

Lee's Summit, 38 55N 94 23W, pop(1980) 28,741, town in Jackson county, W Missouri, United States; 28 km SE of Kansas City; railway; economy: tools, machinery and plastics.

Leeuwarden *lay'vahr-den*, LIOUWERT *lyœ'vert* (Fris), 53 12N 5 48E, pop(1984e) 85,435, capital city of Friesland prov, N Netherlands; on the R Ee, on fertile fenland of the former Middelzee; its cattle market is the largest in the Netherlands; the economic and cultural capital of Friesland; the town was created by the amalgamation of 3 former 'Wurt' settlements, which merged in 1435 when they received their town charters; it became a prosperous trading place but, when the Middelzee was enclosed and drained, the town lost its sea harbour and became an agricultural market and commercial capital of the Ostergos; the world-famous dancer and spy, Mata Hari, was born here in 1876; railway; canal junction; economy: foodstuffs (dairy products, flour mill products), tourism; formerly celebrated for gold and silverware; monuments: Grote Kerk (13-16th-c).

Leeward Islands, ISLAS DE SOTAVENTO (Sp), West Indian islands; all the islands of the Lesser Antilles in the Caribbean Sea S of the Puerto Rico Trench and N of the Windward Islands, from the Virgin Islands in the N to Dominica in the S; sheltered from the NE prevailing winds; the term was formerly used by the Spanish to include the Greater Antilles; sometimes referred to as the North Caribees; also formerly a division of the West Indies Federation (1958-62) comprising Anguilla, Antigua and Barbuda, British Virgin Islands, Montserrat, St Kitts, Nevis, Redonda, Sombrero.

Leeward Islands, French Polynesia. See Vent, Îles sous le.

Leganes *lay-ga-nays'*, 40 20N 3 46W, pop(1981) 163,426, town in Madrid prov, central Spain; 11 km SSW of Madrid with mineral springs; economy: electronics, perfume, mineral water.

Leghorn, prov and town in NW Italy. See Livorno.

Legnica *leg-neet'sa*, voivodship in W Poland; heavily wooded to the NW and watered by the tributaries of the R Oder (Odra); pop(1983) 478,000; area 4,037 sq km; capital Legnica; chief towns include Lubiń and Głogów.

Legnica, LIEGNITZ (Ger), 51 12N 16 02E, pop(1983) 96,500, capital of Legnica voivodship, W Poland; on R Kaczawa; railway; economy: copper foundry, electronics, pianos; monuments: around the Market Square are the churches of SS Peter and Paul (14-15th-c); 18th-c church of St John with Piast monuments and Baroque frescoes; 13th-c castle of the Piast Dukes.

Legon *lee-gōn'*, 5 36N 0 16W, town in Greater Accra region, S Ghana, W Africa; W of Accra; University of Ghana (1948).

Leicester *les'ter*, BATAE CORITANORUM (Lat), 52 38N 1 05W, pop(1981) 280,324, city and county town of Leicestershire, central England; 160 km N of London; an important royal residence in medieval times; charter granted by Elizabeth I (1589); university (1957); railway; economy: hosiery, knitwear, footwear, engineering; monuments: 14th-c cathedral of St Martin; churches of St Margaret, St Mary de Castro and St Nicholas; 17th-c Guildhall; Belgrave Hall museum.

Leicestershire *les'ter-shir*, county of central England; bounded N by Nottinghamshire, NE by Lincolnshire, NW by Derbyshire, SW by Warwickshire and S by Northamptonshire; drained by the R Soar; pop(1981) 844,525; area 2,553 sq km; county town Leicester; chief towns include Market Harborough, Loughborough; economy: arable farming, cheese, coal mining, limestone, engineering; the county is divided into 9 districts:

District	*area (sq km)*	*pop(1981)*
Blaby	130	77,348
Charnwood	279	134,542
Harborough	593	60,934

contd

District	*area (sq km)*	*pop(1981)*
Hinckley and Bosworth	297	87,617
Leicester	73	280,324
Melton	482	43,363
North-west Leicestershire	280	78,779
Oadby and Wigston	24	50,813
Rutland	394	30,805

Leiden *lī'den*, LEYDEN *lay'den*, 52 09N 4 30E, pop(1984e) 176,360, university city in Zuid Holland prov, W Netherlands; on the R Oude Rijn (which here divides into several branches linked by canals); the town developed around the castle of the Counts of Holland in the 11th century, received its charter in 1266 and in the 14th century became famous for its weaving (Leiden still manufactures cloth and blankets); besieged by the Spaniards in 1573, it held out for a year, relief coming from the sea when William the Silent ordered the dykes to be cut for the Dutch fleet to sail over the flooded polders to the city walls; as a reward for their bravery the citizens had the choice of tax remission or being given Holland's first university, they chose the university which was founded in 1575; several painters of the 16th and 17th centuries were born here, among them Rembrandt, Jan Steen and Gerard Dou; the electric cell known as the 'Leyden jar' was invented here in 1745; the university is noted for the study of law and medicine; former students include Grotius, Descartes, Linnaeus, Goldsmith and Fielding, and among its famous professors were Arminius and Scaliger; economy: hardware, machinery, printing; monuments: church of St Pancras (15th-c), church of St Peter (St Pieterskerk, Reformed, 1315), town hall (17th-c).

Leigh *lee*, 53 30N 2 33W, pop(1981) 42,929, town in Wigan borough, Greater Manchester, NW England; 19 km W of Manchester at the junction of the Bridgewater Canal with a branch of the Leeds and Liverpool Canal; economy: electrical goods, coal, textiles

Leighton Buzzard *lay'ton buz'ard*, 51 55N 0 41W, pop(1981) 29,808, town in South Bedfordshire dist, Bedfordshire, S central England; 18 km WNW of Luton; railway.

Leikanger *lay'kang-ur*, formerly HERMANNSVERK, 61 10N 6 52E, capital town of Sogn og Fjordane county, SW Norway; on the N shore of Sognefjorden (Sogne Fjord); located in a fertile, fruit-growing region; monument: 13th-c stone church.

Leine *lī'nu*, river in Niedersachsen (Lower Saxony) prov, W Germany; rises near Worbis, flows W then generally N, past Göttingen and Hannover, to the R Aller at Schwarmstedt, 18 km NW of Wietze; length 241 km; navigable length 112 km; drainage basin area 6,006 sq km.

Leinster *len'stur*, prov in E Irish Republic; comprises the counties of Louth, Meath, Westmeath, Longford, Offaly, Kildare, Dublin, Laoighis, Wicklow, Carlow, Kilkenny and Wexford; pop(1981) 1,790,521; area 19,633 sq km; capital Dublin.

Leipzig *līp'tsiKH*, county in S East Germany; pop(1981) 1,402,130; area 4,966 sq km; economy: mechanical engineering, coal mining, chemicals, machine tools, farm machinery, printing presses, iron, glass, ceramics, furs; 70% of the county is farmed and 13% is under forest; the scenic regions of Altenburg and Dübener Heide have a wide range of recreational facilities.

Leipzig, LIPSIA (anc), 51 20N 12 23E, pop(1982) 558,414, capital of Leipzig county, S East Germany; commercial centre with many trade fairs; centre of music and education; Karl Marx University (1409); college of technology; airport; railway; economy: mechanical engineering, manufacturing plant for mining and chemical industry, machine tools, furs, publishing; monuments: St Thomas' church, with the tomb of Johann Sebastian Bach; museum of fine art; Battle of the Nations monument; Renaissance town hall; Lenin Memorial and Dimitrov museum; events: Documentary and Short Film Week; annual trade fairs.

Leiria *lay-i-ree'a*, dist in W central Portugal, part of Estremadura and Beira Litoral provs; area 3,516 sq km; pop(1981) 420,229; divided into 16 councils and 131 parishes; chief towns are Leiria, Caldas da Rainha, Peniche, Alcobaça and Nazaré; airfield at Gandara dos Olivais; economy: wool, milk, cheese, rice, olives, vegetables, fruit, horticulture, cork, timber, resin; minerals: asphalt, peat, hydrocarbons.

Leiria, COLLIPO (anc), 39 46N 8 53W, pop(1981) 11,200, industrial town and capital of Leiria dist, central Portugal; on left bank of R Liz, 133 km N of Lisboa; episcopal see; industries: tanning, woodwork, glass, iron, cement and agricultural trade; railway; protected from Atlantic by Portugal's largest pine forest; monuments: Leiria Castle (1135); royal palace; cathedral; churches of Our Lady of Pena (1314) and 12th-c Romanesque São Pedro; 12 km to the S is the splendid Dominican Batalha Abbey (1388) with the tombs of Portuguese royalty including Henry the Navigator.

Leith *leeth*, port on the Firth of Forth, Lothian region, Scotland. See Edinburgh.

Leitha *lī'tah*, LAJTA *loi'to* (Hung), river rising in E Austria, NE of Erlach; flows 167 km NE and E, then SE to meet the R Danube near Mosonmagyarovar in Hungary; length 191 km.

Leitrim *lee'trim*, LIATHDROMA (Gael), county in Connacht prov, Irish Republic, stretching SE from Donegal Bay; bounded NE by N Ireland; pop(1981) 27,609; area 1,526 sq km; capital Carrick-on-Shannon; coarse angling on R Shannon and L Allen; cattle farming on the hills to the N; considerable land drainage in recent times.

Leixlip *layks'lip*, LÉIM AN BHRADÁIN (Gael), 53 22N 6 30W, pop(1981) 9,306, town in Kildare county, Leinster, E Irish Republic; on R Liffey and Grand Canal; railway; hydroelectric power.

Leixões *lay-sho'ish*, 41 11N 8 42W, pop(1981) 15,000, seaport in Leça da Palmeira parish, Porto dist, NW Portugal, near Matosinhos.

Lek, river in central Netherlands; a N arm of the Rhine delta; flows 64 km WSW past Culemborg, Vianen and Lekkerkerk; joins the R Noord, 1 km W of Krimpen aan den Lek, to form the R New Maas; entire length navigable (64 km).

Lekoui *le'kwi*, 12 37N 3 40W, town in NW Burkina, W Africa; NW of Dédougou.

Lékoumou *lay-koo'moo*, province of SW Congo, W Africa; area 20,950 sq km; pop(1980) 62,730; capital Sibiti.

Lelystad, pop(1984e) 55,100, municipality Flevoland prov, W Netherlands, NE of Amsterdam; land area 229 sq km; administrative centre of the Flevoland polders; established in 1967; natural gas power station.

Leman Bank, gas field in the North Sea, E of Norfolk, England; linked by pipeline to Bacton on the Norfolk coast, SE of Mundesley.

Léman, Lac *lay-mã'*, LAKE OF GENEVA (Eng), GENFERSEE *gen'fer-zay* (Ger), LACUS LEMAN'US (anc), crescent-shaped lake in Vaud, Genève and Valais cantons, SW Switzerland, and Haute-Savoie dept, France; area 581 sq km, 60% falling within Switzerland, 40% in France; it is the largest of the lakes in the Alps, lying between the Savoy Alps, the Swiss Jura Mts and the Vaud Alps, at a mean height of 371 m; max depth 310 m; max width 14 km; the R Rhône enters in the SE and leaves at Genève; there are vineyards on the luxuriantly fertile slopes which rise gently from the lake in the wine-growing areas of Lavaux and La Côte; chief towns on the N shore include Morges, Rolle, Lausanne and Vevey; the S shore rises abruptly to snow-capped mountains; there are numerous steamer services.

Lemberg *lem'berk*, mountain in SW Baden-Württemberg prov, W Germany; highest peak of the Schwäbische Alb (Swabian Jura range), 8 km ESE of Rottweil; height 1,015 m.

Lem'pa, river in Central America, rising near Esquipulas in

Guatemala; flows S entering El Salvador at Citalá, then winds S, E, and S past San Marcos to the Pacific Ocean 61 km ESE of La Libertad; length c.320 km; tributaries Río Quezalapa, Río Acahuapa, and the Río Mocal.

Lempira *lem-pee'ra*, formerly GRACIAS *gras'yas*, dept in SW Honduras, Central America, bounded S by El Salvador; pop(1983e) 174,916; area 4,287 sq km; capital Gracias.

Lena *lyen'a*, river in Siberian Rossiyskaya, E Soviet Union; rises in the Baykal'skiy Khrebet range, close to the W shore of Ozero Baykal (L Baikal); flows generally NE through Irkutskaya oblast and Yakutskaya ASSR, past Kirensk and Olekminsk; at Yakutsk it turns NW then N, flowing parallel to and 160-240 km W of the Khrebet Orulgan range; discharges into the Laptev Sea in a wide swampy delta, NW of Tiksi; length 4,400 km; drainage basin area 2,490,000 sq km; chief tributaries are the Muna, Linde, Vilyuy, Aldan, and Olekma rivers; coal, oil, and gold are found along the R Lena and its tributaries.

Lengwe *leng'gwe*, national park in SW Southern region, Malawi, SE Africa; area 887 sq km; established in 1970.

Lenina, Pik, formerly MT KAUFMANN, 39 21N 73 01E, highest peak in the Alayskiy Khrebet range, on the border between the republics of Tadzhikskaya and Kirgizskaya, S Soviet Union, 136 km S of Osh; height 7,134 m; it was considered to be the highest point in the USSR until 1932-33 when Pik Kommunizma (7,495 m) was found to be higher; first ascended in 1928.

Leninakan *lyay-nyi-na-KHahn'*, formerly ALEKSANDROPOL (-1924), 40 47N 43 49E, pop(1983) 218,000, industrial town in Armyanskaya (Armenia) SSR, Soviet Union; 10 km from the Turkish border; founded in 1837 on the site of a Turkish fortress; railway; economy: cotton textiles, clothing, knitwear, machine building; monuments: ruins of a 6th-c church, 17th-c domed Astvatsatsin basilica.

Leningrad *lyay'nyin-grat*, formerly ST PETERSBURG (1703-1914), later PETROGRAD (1914-24), 59 55N 30 25E, pop(1983) 4,779,000, seaport capital of Leningradskaya oblast, NW European Rossiyskaya, Soviet Union; on the R Neva, at the head of the Gulf of Finland; the largest Soviet Baltic port and 2nd largest city in the USSR; former capital of the Russian Empire (1712-1918); founded by Peter the Great in 1703 in the delta of the R Neva; the Great October Socialist Revolution, directed by Lenin, began here in 1917; university (1819); railway junction; airport; economy: manufacture of nuclear power equipment, ships, tractors, machine tools, and precision optical instruments, solar research and development; monuments: Academy of Sciences (1726); Winter Palace (1754-62); 19th-c St Isaac cathedral; Kazan cathedral (1801-11); fortress of Peter and Paul (1703); St Nicholas Navy cathedral (1753-62); there are over 60 museums including the Hermitage, one of the biggest museums in the world; event: White Nights art festival (21-29 June).

Len'vik, 69 22N 18 10E, pop(1980) 11,422, town in Troms county, N Norway; SW of Tromsø.

Léo *lay'ō*, 11 07N 2 08W, town in W central Burkina, W Africa; 145 km SSW of Ouagadougou.

Leoben *lay-ō'ben*, 47 23N 15 06E, pop(1981) 31,989, capital of Leoben dist, Steiermark, SE Austria; on a bend of the R Mur, NW of Graz; railway; mining college; economy: iron, steel (Donawitz) and lignite; event: Gösser Kirchweih, fair on the 2nd Thursday in Oct.

Leomil *lay-o-meel'*, 40 59N 7 31W, mountain in Serra de Leomil range NE of Viseu and S of R Douro, N central Portugal; height 1,010 m.

Leominster, 42 32N 71 46W, pop(1980) 34,508, city in Worcester county, central Massachusetts, United States; 29 km NNE of Worcester; city status in 1915; birthplace of Johnny Appleseed; railway; economy: furniture, paper, plastics.

León *lay-ōn'*, 21 06N 101 41W, pop(1980) 655,809, town in Guanajuato state, S central Mexico; 200 km N of Morelia; alt 1,804 m; railway; economy: shoes and leather work, including decorated saddles.

León, maritime dept in W Nicaragua, Central America; bounded SW by the Pacific Ocean; the Cordillera Horno Grande extends along the NE boundary; part of Lago de Managua occupies the SE corner; pop(1981) 248,704; area 6,097 sq km; capital León; chief towns La Paz and Nagarote.

León, 12 24N 86 52W, pop(1978) 81,647, capital city of León dept, NW Nicaragua, Central America; approx 20 km from the Pacific coast; founded in 1524 at León Viejo, 32 km from the present site; moved to present site when the original settlement was destroyed by an earthquake in 1609; capital of the country until Managua replaced it in 1858; university (1804); airfield; railway; monuments: largest cathedral in Central America (begun 1746); parish church of Subtiava (1530); numerous colonial churches.

León *lay-on'*, prov in Castilla-León region, NW Spain; with the Cordillera Cantabrica to the N and drained by the Esla and Sil rivers; pop(1981) 517,973; area 15,468 sq km; capital León; economy: anthracite mining, pharmaceuticals, cement, wood and metal products, dairy products, foodstuffs, clothes, glass.

León, 42 38N 5 34W, pop(1981) 131,132, capital of León prov, Castilla-León, NW Spain; at the junction of the R Torio and R Bernesga, 333 km NW of Madrid; bishopric; capital of medieval kingdom; railway; economy: anthracite, glass, leather, iron, timber; monuments: Gothic cathedral (13-14th-c); town walls; San Isidore, with its Royal pantheon and treasury; Monastery of St Mark; events: fiesta of Las Cabezadas on second Sunday after Easter; fiestas of St John and St Peter in June; Foro and Oferta pageant in the cathedral in Aug and pilgrimages in Sept-Oct to the chapel of the Virgin of the Way (Virgen del Camino), 5 km to the W.

Leopoldville, capital of Zaire. See Kinshasa.

Leptis Magna, LEBDA, 32 59N 14 15E, ancient Roman seaport of N Africa; the ruins of the site lie in NE Libya, E of Al Khums on the Mediterranean coast of the Gulf of Sirte; founded by Phoenicians it was one of the 3 main cities of ancient Tripolis; the birthplace of the Roman emperor, Septimus Severus.

Lérida *lay'ri-da*, prov in Cataluña, NE Spain, extending from the crest of the Pyrenees down to the Urgel plain and R Ebro; bounded to the N by France and Andorra; includes the Aigües-Tortes National Park and Alto Pallars-Aran National Game Reserve; pop(1981) 355,451; area 12,028 sq km; capital Lérida; economy: hydroelectric power, mining, livestock, animal feed, vegetable oils, pharmaceuticals, market gardening.

Lérida, 41 37N 0 39E, pop(1981) 109,573, capital of Lérida prov, Cataluña, NE Spain; on R Segre, 465 km NE of Madrid; bishopric; railway; economy: trades in wine, leather, wool, cattle, animal feed, fruit and vegetables; monuments: 18th-c new cathedral and Byzantine and Gothic old cathedral; events: Holy Week; fanalets de Sant Jaime in July and a fair in Sept.

Léros, island of the Sporádhes, Greece, in the S Aegean Sea, off the W coast of Turkey; area 53 sq km.

Lerwick, 60 09N 1 09W, pop(1981) 7,561, capital of Shetland, N Scotland; on E Mainland, by Bressay Sound, 35 km N of Sumburgh Head; airfield (Sumburgh Head); ferry terminus for boats from the Scottish mainland; economy: fishing, oil supply services; monuments: Lerwick museum; Fort Charlotte, originally built in 1665 to protect Bressay Sound; both the fort and Lerwick town were burnt by the Dutch in 1673; 1 km SW of Lerwick is Clickhimin Broch, a 5 m-high Iron Age broch; event: Up-Helly-Aa, annual festival of pagan origin (last Tuesday in Jan).

Lesbos, nome (dept) and island of Greece. See Lésvos.

Leskovac *le'sko-vahts*, LESKOVATS, 43 00N 21 57E, pop(1981) 159,001, town in SE Srbija (Serbia) republic, Yugoslavia; 37 km S of Niš; railway; economy: wine trade, soap, furniture, textiles; monument: nearby 6th-c Byzantine ruins of Caračin Grad; event: international textile fair in July.

Lesotho *le-sō'tō*, official name Kingdom of Lesotho; a S African kingdom completely bounded by South Africa; timezone GMT +3; area 30,460 sq km; pop(1984e)

1,474,000; capital Maseru; chief towns Leribe, Mokhotlong, Marakabeis, Mafeteng, Mohale's Hoek, Quthing and Roma; the majority of the pop (99.7%) are Bantus of Southern Sotho stock (Basotho), the remainder includes Zulu, Tembu and Fingo; 80% of the pop are Roman Catholic, the remainder following local beliefs; official languages are Sesotho and English, but Zulu and Xhosa are also spoken; the unit of currency is the loti (pl. maloti); national holidays 4 Oct (Independence Day), 2 May (King's birthday) and 13 June (Commonwealth Day); membership of AfDB, the Commonwealth, FAO, G-77, GATT (de facto), IBRD, ICAO, IDA, IFAD, IFC, ILO, IMF, ITU, NAM, OAU, SADCC, UN, UNESCO, UPU, WHO and WMO.

Physical description. Lesotho is approx 230 km from E to W and 200 km from N to S. The Drakensberg Mountains lie in the NE and E and include Lesotho's highest peak Thabana-Ntlenyana (3,482 m). Other high peaks within Lesotho include Makheke (3,461 m), Mafadi (3,450 m) and Mont-aux-Sources (3,299 m). The Mulati Mountains run from the NE border SW across the country forming a steep escarpment. The southernmost section is called the Thaba Putsoa. The highlands are characterized by montane grasses, gorges and deep river valleys. W of the highlands is a region between 30 and 65 km wide with an elevation of between 1,500 and 1,800 m. It is in this area that most of the pop lives and within which the majority of the agricultural land lies. Serious soil erosion occurs (particularly in the W) mainly due to heavy rainfall, overgrazing and poor agricultural methods (including the cultivation of steep slopes). The Orange and the Caledon are the two main rivers. The former rises in the Drakensberg Mountains and flows S through the centre of the highlands and then W to cross the frontier into South Africa W of Quthing. The R Caledon (a tributary of the Orange River) also rises in the NE Drakensberg and flows SW past Ficksburg (South Africa) and Meseru forming the N and W borders of Lesotho with South Africa before flowing into South Africa itself NW of Wepener.

Climate. Lesotho has mild and dry winters although temperatures frequently drop below freezing point during the night with snow falling at higher altitudes. The summer season from Oct to April is warm with temperatures rarely excessive. The lowland temperatures range from a summer max of 32.2°C to a winter min of −6.7°C. Rainfall is heaviest in Jan and averages 725 mm per year.

History, government and constitution. The area which is now Lesotho was originally inhabited by hunting and gathering bushmen. During the 16th century the first Bantu peoples arrived, settling in the upper Caledon river valley. Further migration of S Sotho groups into the area resulted in the establishment of the Basotho nation which by 1831 included an association of 23 different tribes. Visited by French and English missionaries, the area was eventually taken over by the Boers and incorporated in the Orange Free State in 1854. In 1869 the country came under British protection and was named Basutoland. By 1884 the people of Basutoland had chosen to come under direct British rule with the proviso that no white person be allowed to acquire any land within their country. Internal affairs were left largely to the inhabitants and in 1910 an advisory Basutoland council was created. The council requested internal self-government in 1955 and in 1960 the first independence constitution came into effect. The constitution was modified in 1965 and in the following year the independent state of the Kingdom of Lesotho came into being under the rule of King Moshoeshoe II. The country is a constitutional monarchy with a king as head of state, a National Assembly of 60 elected members and a Senate of 22 chiefs and 11 others appointed by the king. There is a prime minister who governs with a cabinet of about 14 ministers.

Economy. The Lesotho economy is based on intensive agriculture and male contract labour working in South Africa. Of the total land area available only 13% is suitable for cultivation. Much of this land is suffering from soil erosion. The main crops, mostly sold to South Africa, include maize, sorghum, wheat, peas, beans and barley. Lesotho remains dependent on food imports. Diamonds represent the only significant natural resource although coal, oil and uranium prospecting continues. The country has only a small industrial sector which is based on food processing and the manufacture of textiles, electrical consumer goods, carpets, pharmaceuticals, jewellery and crafts, tyre retreading and tractor assembly. Wool and mohair represent over half of Lesotho's export earnings. Lesotho has suffered both economically and politically owing to its compliance with the UN resolution which does not recognize South Africa's creation in 1976 of the 'independent' homeland of Transkei. The border between Lesotho and Transkei has remained effectively closed since 1978.

Administrative divisions. Lesotho is divided into the districts of Butha-Buthe, Leribe, Berea, Maseru, Mafeteng, Mohale's Hoek, Quthing, Qacha's Neck, Mokhotlong and Thaba-Tseka.

Lésvos, LES'BOS, nome (dept) of Greece in E Aegean Sea; comprises islands of Lésvos, Áyios Evstrátios and Límnos; pop(1981) 104,620; area 2,154 sq km; capital Mitilíni.

Lésvos, Greek island in the E Aegean Sea, off the NW coast of Turkey; 3rd largest island of Greece; with the islands of Áyios Evstrátios and Límnos it forms a nome (dept) of Sterea Ellás-Évvoia region; area 1,630 sq km; length 61 km; length of coastline 370 km; it is a hilly island rising to 969 m; chief town Mitilíni on the E coast; home of the poet Terpandros who is credited with the invention of the seven-stringed Greek lyre; joined Greece in 1913.

Leszno *lesh'nō*, voivodship in W Poland; pop(1983) 369,000; area 4,154 sq km; capital Leszno; chief towns include Kościan.

Leszno, LISSA (Ger), 51 51N 16 35E, pop(1983) 52,900, capital of Leszno voivodship, W Poland; historical town on railway between Wrocław and Poznań; centre of metallurgy and light industry since 1975; monuments: several interesting Baroque houses and churches; events: international gliding competitions.

Letch'worth, 51 58N 0 14W, pop(1981) 38,142, town linked with Baldock in North Hertfordshire dist, Hertfordshire, SE England; 9 km N of Stevenage; the first English 'garden city', founded in 1903; railway; economy: engineering, high technology, furniture, publishing.

Lethbridge, 49 43N 112 48W, pop(1984) 58,586, town in S Alberta, S Canada; on the Oldman river, in the foothills of the Rocky Mts; settled before 1867 when Fort Whoop-Up was built; coal was mined from 1872 and the traders at Whoop-Up vanished with the arrival of the Mounted Police in 1874; the last great Indian battle in Canada was fought nearby in 1870 between the Blackfoot and the Crees, who lost 40 and between 200 and 300 men respectively; university (1967); railway; airfield; economy: agricultural trade, minerals, natural gas and oil; monuments: the Nikka Yuko Japanese Gardens, created in 1967, is one of the largest authentic Japanese gardens in N America; to the S of Lethbridge is Fort Whoop-Up, a fort founded by Americans in 1867 as a trading depot exchanging whisky for furs and hides; in Galt Park a plaque commemorates the first coal-mine in Alberta opened in 1872; Indian Battle Park, site of the battle between Crees and Blackfoot.

Leticia *lay-tees'ya*, 4 09S 69 57W, pop(1985) 13,210, capital of Amazonas administrative territory, SE Colombia, South America; on the frontier with Brazil and Peru; merging with the town of Marco in Brazil; airfield; in recent years the drug trade has replaced tourism as the major industry.

Letterkenny *le-tur-ke'nee*, LEITIR CEANAINN (Gael), 54 57N 7 44W, pop(1981) 7,992, fishing port and market town in Donegal county, Ulster, N Irish Republic; at head of L Swilly; technical college; administrative centre; monument: cathedral (1901).

Leuser, Gunung *goon'ung loo'ser*, MT LEUSER, 3 46N 97 12E, mountain in Aceh territory, NW Sumatera, Indonesia; rising to 3,381 m; the 9,464 sq km Gunung Leuser National Park, created in 1980, includes the mountain and the Alas Valley.

Leuven *lœ'ven*, dist of Brabant prov, Belgium; area 1,163 sq km; pop(1982) 416,299.

Leuven, LOUVAIN *loo-vĩ*, LOWEN (Ger), 50 53N 4 42E, pop(1983e) 85,068, university town in Leuven dist, Brabant prov, Belgium; on both banks of the R Dijle at the W fringe of the Hageland, E of Bruxelles; world-famous catholic university (1425, since 1835 independent of the state); the oldest university town in Belgium; industry is concentrated in the N of the town, along a canal linking the R Dijle with the Rupel; the town is circular in shape, once surrounded by moats, all traffic junctions converge on the Grote Markt; railway; economy: beer and soft drinks, fertilizers, animal feed-stuffs; monuments: town hall (1448-63), church of St Peter (15-16th-c), church of St Michael (1650-6), Premonstratensian Abbey of the Park (SW of the city, 1129).

Levádhia *lee-vah'dhee-u*, LEBADEA, LIVADEA (Eng), 38 26N 22 53E, pop(1981) 16,864, capital town of Voiótia (Boeotia) nome (dept), Sterea Ellás-Évvoia region, Greece; in the E foothills of the Píndhos Mts, between 2 tributaries of the R Kifissós.

Levallois-Perret *le val-wa-pê-ray*, 48 54N 2 17E, pop(1982) 53,777, town in Hauts-de-Seine dept, Ile-de-France region, N central France; economy: automobiles, aeronautics, clock-making, printing inks, rubber, hand tools, laminated metal products.

Levanger *lay-vang'ur*, 63 44N 11 20E, pop(1980) 16,080, town in Nord-Trøndelag county, W Norway; at the head of Trondheimsfjord (Trondheim Fjord); railway; economy: timber, textiles.

Levant States, formerly (1920-41) part of the French Mandate of Syrie comprising the states of Syria and Lebanon.

Levant, The *le-vahnt'*, ('the place of the sun rising as seen from Italy'), general name given to describe the E shores of the Mediterranean Sea from W Greece to Egypt.

Leven *lee'vėn*, 56 12N 3 00W, pop(1981) 8,624, town in Kirkcaldy dist, Fife, E Scotland; on the N shore of the Firth of Forth, on the W side of Largo Bay.

Leven, Loch, loch in Perth and Kinross dist, Tayside, Scotland; drained by the R Leven in the SE; largest freshwater loch in lowland Scotland; area 13.7 sq km; famous for its trout fishing and its associations with Mary Queen of Scots who abdicated the throne of Scotland during her imprisonment here in 1567-68; designated a nature reserve protecting large numbers of breeding wildfowl and migrating geese.

Leven, Loch, loch in Lochaber dist, Highland region, W Scotland; linked W to Loch Linnhe; crossed by a bridge at Ballachulish.

Leverkusen *lay-ver-koo'zen*, 51 02N 6 59E, pop(1983) 157,400, industrial city in Köln (Cologne) dist, Nordrhein-Westfalen (North Rhine-Westphalia) prov, W Germany; on the R Rhine, 26 km SE of Düsseldorf; railway; economy: chemicals, iron and steel, pharmaceuticals, office equipment, photographic products.

Levice *lev'i-tse*, 48 13N 18 35E, pop(1984) 28,499, town in Západoslovenský region, S Slovak Socialist Republic, E Czechoslovakia; railway; economy: agricultural trade.

Levkás *lef'kas*, SANTA MAURA *san'ta mow'ra* (Ital), LEUCA'DIA (anc), nome (dept) of Ioníoi Nísoi region, Greece; comprises the island of Levkás and some smaller islands; pop(1981) 21,863; area 356 sq km; capital Levkás.

Levkás, one of the Ioníoi Nísoi (Ionian Is), Greece, in the Ionian Sea, off the W coast of Greece, N of Kefallinía I; pop(1981) 19,947; area 303 sq km; length 32 km; the island is mountainous, rising to 915 m; chief town Levkás; with some lesser islands it forms a nome (dept) of Greece.

Lewes *loo'is*, 50 52N 0 01E, pop(1981) 14,971, county town of East Sussex, SE England; on the R Ouse, 13 km NE of Brighton; site of the Battle of Lewes (1264) in which King Henry III was defeated by Simon de Montfort, a defeat that led to the birth of the English parliament; railway; economy: light engineering, brewing, printing; monuments: churches of St Anne (12th-c), St John the Baptist (12-18th-c) and St Michael.

Lewis with Harris, island in the Western Isles, NW Scotland; the largest and northernmost of the Hebrides, lying to the W of the mainland and separated from it by the North Minch and from Skye to the SE by the Little Minch; Lewis in the N is linked by a narrow isthmus to Harris in the S; total area 2134 sq km; chief towns are Stornoway and Tarbert; economy: fishing, crofting, tweed manufacture.

Lewisham *loo'i-shem*, 51 27N 0 01W, pop(1981) 231,324, residential borough of SE central Greater London, England; includes the suburbs of Lewisham and Deptford; includes the Ladywell dist (after a miraculous spring discovered in the 15th century); crossed by the R Ravensbourne which flows into Deptford Creek via Greenwich; railway.

Lewiston, 46 25N 117 01W, pop(1980) 27,986, county seat of Nez Perce county, NW Idaho, United States; at the confluence of Snake and Clearwater rivers, on the Washington border; the first capital of Idaho Territory (1863-64); the Nez Perce Indian reservation lies to the E; economy: commercial and industrial centre in a forestry and farming region; manufactures include processed foods, timber and paper products, ammunition primers and concrete.

Lewiston, 44 06N 70 13W, pop(1980) 40,481, town in Androscoggin county, SW Maine, United States; on the R Androscoggin, opposite Auburn and 48 km N of Portland; railway; economy: textiles, dyes, footwear, electronics.

Lexington, 38 03N 84 30W, pop(1980) 204,165 (with Fayette), county seat of Fayette county, N central Kentucky, United States; 35 km ESE of Frankfort; founded in 1779, the city was named in commemoration of the Battle of Lexington in 1775; university (1865); railway; economy: a noted centre for the raising of thoroughbred horses; major tobacco, and bluegrass seed market; industries include railway engineering, meat packing, distilling, and the manufacture of electronic equipment and paper products.

Lexington, 42 27N 71 14W, pop(1980) 29,479, town in Middlesex county, NE Massachusetts, United States; 16 km NW of Boston; the American War of Independence started here in April 1775, when minutemen resisted British soldiers marching to seize stores at Concord; monument: the Munro Tavern.

Leyland *lay'-*, 53 42N 2 42W, pop(1981) 37,151, town in Preston urban area and South Ribble dist, Lancashire, NW England; 8 km S of Preston; railway; economy: vehicles, rubber, paint, paper, printing, engineering.

Leyte *lay'tee*, island in the Visayas group, E Philippines; SW of Samar I and N of Mindanao; irregular shaped island with many bays and offshore islets; area 8,000 sq km; chief towns Tacloban and Ormoc.

Lezhë or **Lesh** *lesh*, ALESSIO (Ital), prov of NW Albania; area 479 sq km; pop(1980) 50,500; capital Lezhë.

Lezhë, LISSUS (anc), 41 47N 19 39E, town and capital of Lezhë prov, NW Albania; near the mouth of the R Drin, 32 km SSE of Shkodër; railway; linked by road with its Adriatic port, Shengjin; monument: ruins of a 15th-c Venetian citadel with tomb of Scanderbeg; founded by Dionysius of Syracuse in 385 BC.

Lhasa *lah-sa*, LA-SA ('abode of the gods'), 29 41N 91 10E, capital of Xizang aut region (Tibet), SW China; in the Gyi Qu valley in SW central Xizang; alt 3,600 m; often known as 'the forbidden city'; airfield; monuments: the Potala in the centre of Lhasa is a fortress consisting of 13 storeys and 1,000 rooms; it was built during the 17th century on the site of a similar 7th-c fortress; the upper storeys contain enormous Buddhas decorated with jewels, solid gold crypts and many chapels with human skull and thighbone wall decorations; under the Potala are jails including the Cave of Scorpions where people were allegedly eaten alive; in the centre of the Potala is the Red Palace, the former headquarters of Tibetan religious and political life and home of the Dalai Lama; 5 km outside the town is the Drepung Monastery, one of the 10 active lamaseries which remain in Xizang; the monastery dates from 1416 and was once the largest cloister in the world; approx 300 lamas still live and work here (compared to approx 10,000 in 1959); the Jokhang Temple in Lhasa was built in the 6th century AD to house a golden Buddha, and remains one of Xizang's holiest shrines; it contains the Sakyamuni Buddha, a gold Buddha encrusted with jewels brought to Tibet in 652 by a Chinese princess; as well as the gold Buddha of the Future, Jokhang contains embroidered likenesses of the princess and her husband, King Songstang Kampo, who was later designated as the first Dalai Lama.

Lianyungang *lyahn-yoong-gang*, 34 40N 119 11E, pop(1984e) 446,100, deep-water port in Jiangsu prov, E China; on the Huang Hai (Yellow Sea); a special economic zone trading with 50 countries; Haizhou Bay off the coast is one of China's richest fishing grounds; centre of a district rich in agriculture, minerals, salt and marine life; during the Tang dynasty (618-907) Lianyungang was a port for China's sea-going fleets; ocean terminal for railway from Xinjiang aut region; economy: fishing, mining, light and heavy industry, tea trade.

Liaoning *li-ow-ning*, prov in NE China; bordered W by Hebei prov, NW by Nei Mongol aut region (Inner Mongolia), NE by Jilin prov, SE by North Korea along the Yalu Jiang river and S by the Bohai gulf and Korea Bay; extends S into the sea via Liaodong Bandao peninsula; the Qian Shan range rises in the centre of the prov; drained by the Liao He river; pop(1982) 35,721,693; area 151,000 sq km; capital Shenyang; principal town Fushun; economy: agricultural trade, silk, iron, coal mining, salt, oil.

Liard *lee'ard*, river in NW Canada; rises in the Pelly Mts, S Yukon terr, E of Whitehorse; flows ESE into British Columbia to Nelson Forks where it is joined by the Fort Nelson river; it then flows N into Mackenzie dist, Northwest Territories, past Fort Liard (head of navigation) to join the Mackenzie river at Fort Simpson; length 1,115 km.

Liban, Jebel, *lee-bã'*, LEBANON, mountain range in Lebanon; extending approx 160 km NNE-SSW parallel to the Mediterranean coast; separated from the Jebel esh Sharqi (Anti-Lebanon) range to the E by the fertile El Beqa'a valley; rises to 3,087 m at Qornet es Saouda; traversed by the Beyrouth (Beirut)-Damascus railway; remains of the Cedars of Lebanon can be found at the foot of the Dahr el Qadib; grapes, olives, and apple trees are grown on the lower slopes.

Liberec *lib'er-ets*, REICHENBERG (Ger), 50 48N 15 05E, pop(1984) 99,623, city in Severočeský region, Czech Socialist Republic, W Czechoslovakia; on R Lausitzer Neisse, NE of Praha (Prague), near the E German and Polish frontiers; railway; economy: textiles, textile machinery, motor vehicles, electrical equipment, footwear, food processing.

Liberia *lī-bee'ri-a*, official name Republic of Liberia, a republic in W Africa, bounded NW by Sierra Leone, N by Guinea, E by the Ivory Coast and S by the Atlantic Ocean; pop(1985e) 2,189,000; area 1,758,610 sq km; timezone GMT; 499 km of railways, 804 km of bitumen roads; capital Monrovia; chief towns Harper, Greenville, Buchanan and Robertsport; 95% of the pop is of indigenous origin; tribes include Kpelle, Bassa, Gio, Kru, Grebo, Mano, Krahn, Gola, Gbandi, Loma, Kissi, Vai and Bella, the remaining 5% are repatriated slaves from America known as Americo-Liberians; the official language is English but over 20 Niger-Congo dialects are also spoken; 75% of the pop follow indigenous beliefs with the remainder either Muslim (15%) or Christian (10%); the unit of currency is the Liberian dollar; national holidays 12 April (National Redemption Day), 26 July (Independence Day), 15 March (J.J. Roberts' birthday); membership of AfDB, ECA, ECOWAS, FAO, G-77, IAEA, IBRD, ICAO, ICO, IDA, IFAD, IFC, ILO, IMF, IMO, IPU, IRC, ITU, Mano River Union, NAM, OAU, UN, UNESCO, UPU, WHO, WMO.

Physical description. Liberia is divided into 3 distinct geographical regions: (1) A low coastal belt c.80 km deep typified by lagoons, beaches, tidal creeks and mangrove marshes. (2) A rolling plateau between 500 and 800 m high with grasslands and forest. (3) Further inland the land rises towards a mountainous area, reaching 1,768 m at Mt Nimba, the highest point in Liberia. Other mountain groups include the Wologisi Mts (NW), the Bomi Hills (W) and the Niete Mts in the SE. There are important iron deposits in the Bomi Hills. Rivers cutting SW down through the plateau include the Mano (on the W border), St Paul, St John, Cess (on the NE border) and Douobé (on the SE border).

Climate. Liberia has an equatorial climate characterized by constantly high temperatures and abundant rainfall. There is a decline in the rainfall from S to N. The rainy season extends from April to Sept. During this period high humidity levels, especially on the coast, make the climate distinctly uncomfortable. The average annual rainfall at Monrovia is 4,150 mm.

History, government and constitution. The area was mapped by the Portuguese in the 15th century and subsequently visited by the British, Dutch and other Europeans in search of slaves, spices and gold. The country of Liberia was created as a result of the activities of several American philanthropic societies, including the American Colonization Society which aimed to establish a homeland for former American slaves. This began with the founding of what is now Monrovia in 1822. In 1847 the country was constituted as the Free and Independent Republic of Liberia, being recognized by France and Britain initially and then by others. Borders were specified in 1885 by the Anglo-Liberian Agreement and in 1882 and 1907-10 by the Franco-Liberian agreements. The Kailahun territory was exchanged by Sierra Leone for an area S of the R Mano in 1911. The US-style constitution was suspended in 1980 as the result of a military coup which established a People's Redemption Council comprising a chairman and a cabinet of ministers. In 1984 a new constitution was approved following a referendum and in 1985 elections for the 26-member Senate took place.

Economy. Liberia's economy is largely based on the extraction and export of minerals of which iron ore is the most important, representing 62% of exports (1981). Liberia is the 4th largest supplier of iron ore to the USA. Gold and diamonds are also major export earners and in addition platinum group metals, barite, titanium, zirconium, rare earth metals and clay are also mined. Approximately two-thirds of the pop rely on subsistence agriculture. Rubber is the most important cash crop followed by timber and palm oil. Other crops include rice, cassava, coffee, cocoa and coconuts. Main trading partners include West Germany, the USA, Italy, France, Belgium, Luxembourg, the Netherlands, the UK, Japan and Spain; Liberia relies heavily on foreign aid mainly from the USA. About 70% of energy requirements are met by hydroelectric power.

Administrative divisions. Liberia is divided into the counties of Grand Cape Mount, Montserrado, Grand Bassa, Sinoe, Maryland, Lofa, Bong, Nimba and Grand Gedeh; in addition there are 6 territories and the district of Monrovia.

Liberia *lee-bay'ree-a*, 10 39N 85 28W, pop(1983e) 14,770, capital town of Guanacaste prov, NW Costa Rica, Central America; on the Río Liberia; cattle market; airfield; on the Inter-American Highway.

Libertad, La *la lee-ber-tad'*, maritime dept in S El Salvador, Central America; bounded S by the Pacific Ocean; pop(1971) 293,076; area 1,650 sq km; capital Nueva San Salvador; chief towns San Juan Opico and Quezaltepeque; the Río Lempa forms its N boundary with Chalatenango dept.

Libertad, La, dept in NW Peru; bordered by the Pacific (W) and Andean Cordillera Central (E); includes E section of Cordillera Occidental, separated from Cordillera Central by the Río Marañón; pop(1981) 962,949; area 23,241 sq km; capital Trujillo; 5 km N of Trujillo are the crumbling adobe ruins of Chan-Chan, imperial city of the pre-Inca Chimú civilization; the ruins cover 28 sq km and consist of 9 great citadels housing storerooms, wells and burial mounds; Chimú kings were buried here, along with their attendant women and treasures, in a burial mound which could hold up to 1,000 sacrificial victims; the city was taken by the Incas in 1450, but not looted until the arrival of the Spaniards; a few km S of Trujillo are the enormous Moche pyramids, built out of millions of adobe bricks, said to be the largest pre-Colombian structures in South America.

Libertador General Bernardo O'Higgins *lee-bayr-ta-THōr' KHay-nay-ral' bayr-nar'THō ō-hee-geens'*, region of S Chile; bordered E by the Andes and Argentina; comprises the provs of Cachapoal, Colchagua and Cardenal Caro; pop(1984) 586,000; area 16,456 sq km; capital Rancagua; chief town San Fernando; economy: the region has the largest underground copper mine in the world at El Teniente; the manufacture of motor vehicles, phosphorus, paper, dairy products and mineral water.

Librazhd *lee-brazhd'*, prov of E Albania; area 1,013 sq km; pop(1980) 59,300; capital Librazhd.

Librazhd, 41 12N 20 21E, town and capital of Librazhd prov, central Albania; on the R Shkumbin, 22 km ENE of Elbasan; railway.

Libreville *lee-bri-veel'*, 0 30N 9 25E, pop(1974) 251,400, capital of Gabon, W Africa; also capital of Estuaire prov; at the mouth of the R Gabon, 520 km NW of Brazzaville; a Roman Catholic mission was established in 1843 and the city was founded in 1849 as a refuge for slaves freed by the French; attacked and occupied by the British and Free French in 1940; until 1946, when Pointe-Noire (Congo) was completed, it was the main port of what was then French Equatorial Africa; the discovery of oil has caused rapid development since the 1970s; Owendo Port has been built nearby (12 km) to handle iron ore extraction at Belinga (NE); the first Central African Games were held here in 1976; university (1970); engineering college; railway; airport; economy: banking, commerce, administration, timber, cement, ceramics, explosives, food processing, oil exploration, power machinery, refrigeration, paints and packaging, beer, soft drinks, polyurethane, metal alloys, fishing; monuments: Sainte-Exupéry French Cultural Centre; Cathedral of Sainte-Marie; museum of arts and traditions; art gallery.

Libya *lib'i-a*, official name The Great Socialist People's Libyan Arab Jamahiriya; a N African state, bounded NW by Tunisia, W by Algeria, SW by Niger, S by Chad, SE by Sudan, E by Egypt and N by the Mediterranean Sea; timezone GMT +1; area 1,758,610 sq km; pop(1984e) 3,684,000; capital Tarābulus al-Garbh (Tripoli); chief towns Misrātah, Banghāzī and Sabhā; 97% of the pop is of Berber and Arab origin with a small number of Tebou and Touareg nomads and semi-nomads in the S; there are also minorities from many other Arab and Asian countries; the majority belong to the Sunni Muslim sect; the official language is Arabic with Italian and English widely understood in major cities; the unit of currency is the Libyan dinar of 1,000 millemes; national holidays 1 Sept (Independence Day), 11 June (US evacuation day), 7 Oct (Italian evacuation day); membership of AfDB, Arab League, FAO, G-77, IAEA, IBRD, ICAO, IDA, Islamic Development Bank, IFAD, IFC,

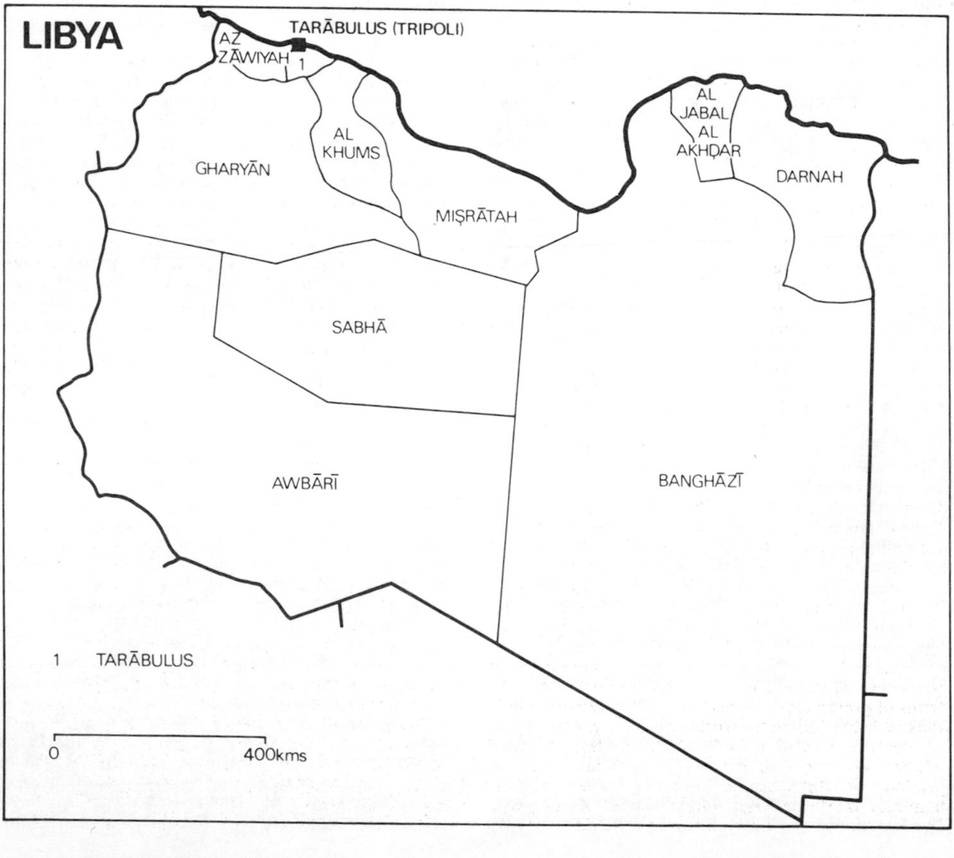

ILO, IMF, IMO, INTELSAT, INTERPOL, IOOC, ITU, NAM, OAPEC, OAU, OIC, OPEC, UN, UNESCO, UPU, WHO, WIPO, WMO and WSG.

Physical description. South of the Mediterranean coast, the greater part (93%) of Libya's land area is comprised of Saharan desert or semi-desert. Generally a low-lying country, there are 2 areas of upland in the N at Jebel al Akhdar (E of Banghāzī) and Jebel Nafūsah (S of Tripoli). In the S the land rises to over 2,000 m in the Tibesti massif on the frontier with Chad and to nearly 1,900 m in the Uweinat massif on the border with Sudan and Egypt. The highest point in Libya (2,286 m) is Pic Bette on the Chad frontier. There are no permanent rivers in Libya and surface water is limited to infrequent oases. Cultivation and settlement are therefore largely restricted to the narrow coastal strip and the slopes of the N mountains which attract winter rain.

Climate. The coastal region experiences a Mediterranean climate with variable amounts of rain falling between Oct and March. Generally, rainfall is highest (up to 600 mm per year) in the N uplands near Tarābulus (Tripoli) and Banghāzī. The coast around the Gulf of Sirte receives less rain than other parts of the coast and consequently the desert extends N to the sea. Tripoli is representative of the coastal region with an average annual rainfall of 385 mm and average max daily temperatures ranging between 16°C and 30°C. The major part of the country is desert with rainfall seldom in excess of 100 mm per year. Temperatures in the S reach an average daily max of over 40°C for 3 months of the year.

History, government and constitution. Variously under the control of the Phoenicians, Carthaginians, Greeks, Vandals and Byzantines, the Arabs gained a foothold during the 7th century. Turkish domination of the area began in the 16th century and lasted until the Italians gained control in 1911. In 1934 the Italians named their colony Libya (previously used by the Greeks to name all of N Africa bar Egypt). The colony was composed of the 3 provinces of Tripolitania (NW), Cyrenaica (E) and Fezzan (SW). After heavy fighting during World War II, Italian and German forces were defeated and the provinces of Tripolitania and Cyrenaica came under British control and Fezzan under French control. In accordance with the 1947 peace treaty the Italians waived any claims to the territory. Two years later the UN declared that Libya should become independent by 1952. Libya became the independent Kingdom of Libya, a constitutional and hereditary monarchy under the Amir of Cyrenaica, in late 1951 and was the first country to become independent under the auspices of the UN. In 1969 a military coup established a republic under Mu'ammar al-Qadhafi. The constitution was abolished and the country declared a republic under the administration of a Revolutionary Command Council. During the early 1970s foreign military installations including the US facilities near Tarābulus (Tripoli) and British bases at Tobruk and El Adem were closed down. In 1977 constitutional government was reinstated. Government policy since the revolution has been based on the promotion of Arab unity and the furtherance of Islam. Controversial activities including the alleged organization of international terrorism have strained relations with other countries. In 1984 the UK severed diplomatic relations with Libya after the murder of a policewoman in London, and in 1986 the US Air Force bombed Tarābulus and Banghāzī in response to terrorist activity.

Economy. Once a relatively poor country, with an agricultural economy based on barley, olives, fruit, dates, almonds and tobacco, Libya's economy was transformed when oil and natural gas were discovered in 1959. In terms of proven crude oil and natural gas reserves Libya ranks 9th and 16th in the world respectively. The oil and gas fields are located in the W and inland from the Gulf of Sirte. There are a number of pipelines which carry the products to the coast for shipment. There are oil terminals at Mersa Brega, Mersa Hariga, Zuetina and Ras Lanuf, and there are oil refineries at Zawia (1974) and Ras Lanuf (1980). In addition, there is a natural gas liquefaction plant at Mersa Brega. Most of the extracted oil and gas is exported and represents 99% of foreign earnings. Until 1982 the USA, Italy, West Germany and Spain bought much of the exported crude oil. At that date an oil embargo was imposed on Libyan oil by the USA. On a much smaller scale, iron ore, gypsum, sulphur and cement are also produced in Libya. Industry is centred around petroleum processing, iron, steel and aluminium production, food processing, textiles and crafts. Oil revenues ensured an annual growth rate of 5% between 1960 and 1980. In the 1980s oil prices dropped and serious attempts were made to diversify into light industry. Libya's main trading partners are Italy, West Germany, France, Spain, Turkey and the UK.

Administrative divisions. Libya is divided into the 10 provinces of Tarābulus, Az Zāwiyah, Al Khums, Gharyān, Misrātah, Sabhā, Awbārī, Banghāzī, Al Jabal al Akhdar and Darnah.

Lich'field, 52 42N 1 48W, pop(1981) 25,738, town in Lichfield dist, Staffordshire, central England; 20 km SW of Burton-on-Trent; birthplace of Samuel Johnson, the famous lexicographer (1709-84), compiler of the first major dictionary of the English language; railway; economy: engineering; monuments: cathedral of St Mary and St Chad, Johnson museum, the Staffordshire Regiment museum; event: Dr Johnson's birthday celebrations (18 Sept).

Lichin'ga, 13 13S 35 11E, pop(1980) 39,004, capital of Niassa prov, NW Mozambique, SE Africa; close to E shore of L Nyasa, N of Beira and E of Pemba; railway terminus; airfield.

Lidingö *lee'ding-u*, 59 22N 18 10E, pop(1983) 37,631, city and island in Stockholm county, SE Sweden; residential suburb NE of Stockholm; economy: electrical equipment, shipbuilding; monument: Millesgarden, the former home and studio of the Swedish sculptor Carl Milles (1875-1955).

Lidköping *leed-ku'ping*, 58 30N 13 10E, pop(1983) 21,253, port and industrial town in Skaraborg county, SW Sweden; on the S shore of L Vänern where it is joined by the R Lida; railway; received its municipal charter in 1446; economy: timber, matches, porcelain, metalwork.

Liechtenstein *liKH'ten-shtīn*, official name Principality of Liechtenstein, FÜRSTENTUM LIECHTENSTEIN (Ger), an independent Alpine principality in central Europe, situated between the Austrian prov of Vorarlberg (E) and the Swiss cantons of St Gallen and Graubünden (W); timezone GMT +1; area 160 sq km; fourth smallest country in the world; land boundary 76 km; capital Vaduz; pop(1985) 27,076; the average population density in 1985 was 169 inhabitants per sq km; the Liechtensteiners are of Alemannic origin; the official language is German but the populace speaks it in the form of an Alemannic dialect; the predominant faith is Roman Catholic (86.9%); the currency is the Swiss franc, membership Council of Europe, CEPT, EFTA, EPO, EUTELSAT, International Court of Justice, IAEA, INTELSAT, ITU, UNCTAD, UNIDO, UNICEF, UPU, WIPO.

Physical description. Liechtenstein is bounded on the W by the R Rhine, whose valley occupies about 40% of the country. This broad flood plain, where much of the agriculture is concentrated, lies at a mean alt of 450 m. Much of the rest of the country is mountainous, rising to 2,599 m in the Grauspitz. The mountains are extensively forested with meadows at higher levels. The plains, once marshy, are now drained and cultivated.

Climate. The climate is mild, in spite of the mountain situation. In winter, temperatures rarely fall below −15° C, while in summer the average high temperature varies between 20° C and 28° C. Mean annual rainfall varies between 1,050 mm and 1,200 mm, rising to 1,800 mm in the Alpine regions. The warm south wind (Föhn) greatly influences the climate and enables grapes and maize to flourish.

Government and constitution. Liechtenstein is a constitutional monarchy ruled by the hereditary princes of the House of Liechtenstein. The present constitution of 5 Oct 1921 provides for a unicameral parliament (*Diet*) of 15 members elected for 4 years. The country is governed jointly by the Prince, who is Head of State, and the parliament. On parliamentary recommendation the Prince appoints a government of 5, a prime minister and 4 councillors, for a 4-year term.

Industry. Despite its small size and limited natural resources, Liechtenstein has, since the 1950s, developed from a poor hill-farming area to a highly-industrialized nation with a per capita income higher than that of its rich neighbour, Switzerland. This transition has led to the immigration of foreign workers (Swiss, Austrians, Germans, Italians, Spaniards). In 1985, 44.1% of the labour force was employed in industry and commerce. The industrial sector is export-based and centred on specialized and high-tech production. The most important industries include metalworking, engineering and instrument making, and also more traditional industries such as chemicals, pharmaceuticals, textiles, ceramics, and foodstuffs. There has been a rapid growth in the export of high-technology goods, metals, ceramics and chemicals, mainly to Switzerland (under customs union) and re-exports to West Germany and the USA. Imports, mainly from EEC and EFTA countries, consist largely of raw materials and foodstuffs. International banking and finance (attracted by the favourable tax structure and legal system), the sale of postage stamps, and a flourishing tourist industry, bring in important revenue. Tourism has become increasingly important to the economy, the number of visitors reaching 85,851 in 1985.

Agriculture. In 1986 less than 3% of the workforce was employed in agriculture. The rearing of cattle, for which the Alpine pastures are well suited, is highly developed. Livestock, vegetables, corn, wheat, potatoes, and grapes are the main agricultural products. Nearly 35% of the total land area of the country is covered by forest, 41% of which is regularly used for timber extraction and 91% of which is public property belonging to the 11 communes and the 8 Alpine cooperatives.

Administrative divisions. The Principality is divided into two districts, Oberland (Upper Country) and Unterland (Lower Country), which are divided into 11 communes. The Oberland contains the communes of Vaduz, Balzers, Triesen, Triesenberg, Schaan, and Planken, while the communes of Eschen, Mauren, Gamprin, Ruggell, and Schellenberg lie in the Unterland.

Commune	*area (sq km)*	*pop(1985)*
Balzers	19.6	3,460
Eschen	10.3	2,785
Gamprin	6.1	927
Mauren	7.5	2,703
Planken	5.3	293
Ruggell	7.4	1,326
Schaan	26.8	4,697
Schellenberg	3.5	674
Triesen	26.4	3,043
Triesenberg	29.8	2,241
Vaduz	17.3	4,927

Liège *lee-ayzh*, prov of E Belgium; area 3,863 sq km; pop(1982) 998,007; comprises 4 dists of Huy, Liège, Verviers and Waremme; capital Liège; chief towns Huy, Eupen and Verviers; bounded on the E by W Germany; drained chiefly by the R Meuse and its tributaries; includes in the SE, part of the Ardennes, with a rich pastoral area at their base; in the NW is a fertile agricultural region, while in the centre lies one of Belgium's richest coalfields; the inhabitants are Walloons.

Liège, dist of Liège prov, E Belgium; area 798 sq km; pop(1982) 602,637.

Liège, LUIK *loyk* (Flem), LÜTTICH *lüt'eeKH* (Ger), 50 38N 5 35E, pop(1982) 211,528, river port and capital city of Liège dist, Liège prov, E Belgium; at the confluence of the Ourthe and Meuse rivers; bishopric; university (1817); 5th largest city in Belgium; associated with Europe's earliest coal mining; one of the largest river ports in Europe (accommodates vessels up to 2,000 tons); railway; economy: blast furnaces, metalworking, construction, civil engineering, cigarettes and tobacco, textiles, foodstuffs, electronics, chemicals, glassware, arms; monuments: church of St Jacques (11th-c, rebuilt 1513-38); Palace of Justice (1526-40); Gothic St Paul's cathedral (former palace of the Bishop Princes).

Lieksa *lee'ek-sa*, 63 13N 30 01E, pop(1982) 18,882, town in Pohjois-Karjala prov, E central Finland between L Pielinen and the Soviet border; established in 1936; railway.

Lier *li'er*, LIERRE *lee-er* (Fr), 51 08N 4 35E, pop(1982) 31,300, town in Mechelen dist, Antwerpen prov, N Belgium; 17 km SE of Antwerpen, at the confluence of the Grote and Kleine Nete rivers; has boat connections with Antwerpen via the Nete Canal (ships up to 1,350 tons); birthplace of the popular Flemish author Felix Timmermans (1886-1947); railway; economy: textiles (tradition of silk-spinning, lace-making and embroidery), more recently brewing, synthetic fibres, building materials; monument: Gothic church of St Gommarus (1425-1557).

Lier *lee'ur*, 59 57N 10 14E, pop(1980) 17,932, town in Buskerud county, SE Norway; railway.

Lierre, town in Belgium. See Lier.

Liestal', 47 29N 7 43E, pop(1980) 12,158, capital of Basel-Land demicanton, Basel canton, NW Switzerland, 13 km SE of Basel; monument: 16th-c town hall.

Liffey, *li'fee*, river in E Irish Republic, rising in N Wicklow county, Leinster and flowing W, NE and E through Dublin to meet the Irish Sea at Dublin Bay; length 80 km; crossed by the Grand Canal.

Liguria *lee-goo'ri-a*, region of NW Italy, extending in an arc around the Golfo di Genova (Ligurian Sea); the mountains of the Appno Ligure descend steeply to the coast; the region comprises the provs of Genova, Imperia, La Spezia, and Savona; pop(1981) 1,807,893; area 5,411 sq km; tourism along the coastal Riviera is of prime importance; industry is concentrated around the ports of Genova (Genoa), La Spezia, and Savona; the region is famed for flowers used in the manufacture of perfume.

Ligurian Sea, an arm of the Mediterranean Sea, bounded N and E by NW Italy and S by Corsica and Elba; the Golfo di Genova lies to the N; chief ports include Genova, Livorno and Bastia.

Lika'si, formerly JADOTVILLE (-1966), 10 58S 26 47E, pop(1970) 146,394, mining town in Shaba region, SE Zaire, central Africa; 105 km NW Lubumbashi; railway.

Likouala *lik-wah'la*, province of NE Congo, W Africa; area 66,044 sq km; pop(1980) 31,930; capital Impfondo.

Lille *leel*, formerly LISLE, RYSSEL (Flem), INSULA (anc), 50 38N 3 03E, pop(1982) 174,039, industrial and commercial city and capital of Nord dept, Nord-Pas-de-Calais region, N France; near the Belgian frontier, 208 km NNE of Paris; university (1560); road and rail junction; forms part of the industrial urban metropolis of Lille-Roubaix-Tourcoing, the largest economic and industrial centre of N France; economy: cotton, wool, industrial fabrics, linen, clothing, tents, sugar-processing, hygiene goods, foodstuffs, chemicals, engineering, metalworking, printing, brewing, heavy machinery; monuments: Gothic church of St-Maurice; 16th-c church of Ste-Catherine (enlarged in the 17th century); cathedral (begun in 1854, still unfinished); 16th-c citadel, Vauban's finest fortification; mid 17th-c Flemish-style old exchange; the Palais des Beaux-Arts houses one of France's finest museums, with sculptures, decorative art, ethnographical material, paintings and drawings; event: international trade fair in April.

Lille Bælt *li-lu belt'*, LITTLE BELT (Eng), strait between Fyn I and the Danish mainland, connecting the Kattegat with the Baltic Sea; length 48 km.

Lillehammer *lil'le-ham-mer*, 61 06N 10 27E, pop(1983) 21,981, capital city of Oppland county, S central Norway; 136 km N of Oslo, in a valley of the R Lågen at N the end of L Mjøsa; railway; popular tourist resort, winter sports centre; monument: Maihaugen, N Europe's largest open-air museum with manned workshops.

Lilongwe *lee-long'gway*, 13 58N 33 49E, pop(1984e) 172,000, capital of Malawi, SE Africa; in Lilongwe dist, Central region, on the R Lilongwe, 210 km NW of Zomba; alt 1,100 m; capital transferred from Zomba in 1975 with all government ministries arriving by 1979; the pop has expanded from only 19,000 in 1966; railway; Kamuzu airport opened in 1983; economy: seeds, light engineering, clothes, tourism and commerce.

Lim *leem*, river rising in N Albanian Alps and flowing 218 km N through Yugoslavia to meet the R Drina SW of Višegard; navigable for 170 km.

Lim Fjord, fjord in Denmark. See Limfjorden.

Lima *lee'ma*, dept in W central Peru; bordered W by the Pacific; crossed by the Cordillera Occidental; pop(1981) 4,745,877; area 33,894 sq km; capital Lima; economy: agriculture in the Rímac valley and mining at Cerro de Pasco.

Lima, 12 06S 77 03W, pop(1981) 4,164,597, federal capital of Peru, in Lima dept, central Peru; built on both sides of the Río Rímac, at the foot of the Cerro San Cristóbal; founded in 1535 by Pizarro who named it the 'city of the kings', Lima was the chief city of Spanish South America until the independence of the S American republics in the early 19th century; the city was devastated by the earthquake of 1746 which left only 20 houses standing and killed 4,000 inhabitants; 10 universities; railway; airport (Jorge Chávez) at 10 km; monuments: around the Plaza de Armas, just S of the Río Rímac, are the cathedral, the Palacio del Gobierno (built in 1938 on the site of Pizarro's palace), the archbishop's palace, Unity Hall and the Unión Club; the cathedral has been partly reconstructed several times; in it is the glass coffin said to contain Pizarro's remains; La Merced church, near the Plaza de Armas, has a beautiful restored façade and cloister; also of interest are the Santo Domingo church (1549) containing an urn with the remains of Santa Rosa de Lima, the first saint of the New World, and the San Francisco church (a baroque church finished in 1674); the National Museum of Art in the Palacio de la Exposición (1868) contains more than 7,000 exhibits, giving a chronological history of Peruvian cultures from the 2,000-year-old Paracas civilization up to the present day; Museum of Peruvian Culture; the Parque de las Leyendas is arranged so as to represent the country's 3 regions of: the coast, the mountainous Sierra and the jungle; events: founding of Lima (18 Jan), the Cañete during the last week of Aug, the month of Our Lord of the Miracles in Oct, the Pacific International Fair (Nov).

Lima, LIMIA (Sp), river in N Portugal and NW Spain, rising in L Antela, Orense, Spain, flows SW to Atlantic at Vila Nova de Milfontes near Viana do Castelo; navigable 40 km to Ponte da Barca, length 130 km, of which 65 km is in Portugal; area of basin 1,145 sq km; principal tributaries Laboreiro and Vez.

Lima, 40 44N 84 06W, pop(1980) 47,381, county seat of Allen county, W Ohio, United States; 109 km SSW of Toledo; railway.

Limache *lee-ma'chay*, SAN FRANCISCO DE LIMACHE, 33 00S 71 16W, pop(1982) 20,694, town in Quillota prov, Valparaíso, central Chile; in the Aconcagua valley; railway.

Limassol *lim'a-sol*, dist in S Cyprus; area 1,388 sq km; pop(1973) 124,855; capital Limassol; remains entirely within the Greek Cypriot zone; includes the Akrotiri British base area.

Limassol, 34 41N 33 02E, pop(1973) 79,641, port and capital town of Limassol dist, S Cyprus; on Akrotiri Bay, NE of the British base of Akrotiri; the influx of Greek Cypriot refugees since the 1974 Turkish invasion has swollen the town's pop dramatically; airfield; economy: wine-making, export of fruit and vegetables, distilling; monument: 14th-c castle; events: spring carnival; arts festival (July); wine festival (Sept).

Limavady, LEIM AN MHADAIDH (Gael), 55 03N 6 57W, pop(1981) 8,015, town in Limavady dist, Derry (Londonderry), NW Northern Ireland; on the R Roe, 24 km ENE of Derry; economy: textiles, engineering.

Lim'be, formerly VICTORIA, 4 01N 9 12E, pop(1976) 31,222, seaport in Sud-Ouest prov, Cameroon, W Africa; 75 km W of Douala; founded in 1858 by Alfred Saker, an English missionary; airfield (Tiko, 20 km); botanical gardens include a small cemetery for the soldiers of the Nigerian Regiment (1914-42); railway; economy: centre of an area of banana, rubber, palm tree, tea and pepper plantations; palm oil, palm kernel and natural rubber production; oil refining.

Limbe *leem'bay*, 15 50S 35 03E, town in Southern region, S Malawi, SE Africa; situated in a hilly region 8 km SE of Blantyre; Anglican and Roman Catholic cathedrals; became a township in 1909; headquarters of Malawi Railways; economy: tea and coffee trade, food processing, tobacco, textiles, handicrafts, clothing, mattresses, detergents, furniture.

Limbourg, prov of Belgium. See Limburg.

Lim'burg, LIMBOURG *lĩ-boor* (Fr), prov of NE Belgium, bounded on the N and E by the Netherlands; area 2,422 sq km; pop(1982) 720,766; comprises 3 dists of Hasselt, Maaseik and Tongeren; capital Hasselt; chief towns Genk and Tongeren; drained chiefly by the R Demer.

Limburg *lim'boork*, prov in S Netherlands, bounded on the E by W Germany and on the SW by France, drained by the R Maas and its tributaries; land area 2,171 sq km; pop(1984e) 1,083,600; capital Maastricht; chief towns Heerlen, Roermond and Weert; university (1975); economy: predominantly mixed farming on mainly sandy soils, some horticulture on the banks of the R Maas (around Maastricht and in the NE of the prov); the marl of S Limburg formerly used for building is now used for the manufacture of cement and calcareous fertilizers; clay, sand and gravel are also used for building; includes the S Limburg industrial area; the declining coal mining industry was replaced by chemical industries between 1966 and 1975; in 1973 it was designated a 'Restructuring Region' within the framework of the regional socio-economic policy, permitting the establishment of new industries and the augmentation of jobs in the service sector, by, for example, transferring central government services from W Netherlands.

Limeira *lee-may'ra*, 22 34S 47 25W, pop(1980) 137,809, town in São Paulo state, Sudeste region, SE Brazil; railway; economy: sugar cane, oranges (Limeira is the largest centre of orange cultivation in São Paulo state); the town has a large modern meat packing plant.

Limerick *lim'ur-ik*, LUIMNEACH (Gael), county in Munster prov, SW Irish Republic; pop(1981) 161,661, area 2,686 sq km; bounded to the N by R Shannon; capital Limerick; economy: dairy farming, hydroelectric power (Ardnacrusha), lace.

Limerick, 52 40N 8 38W, pop(1981) 75,520, county borough and river port capital of Limerick county, Munster, SW Irish Republic; a major industrial city at the head of the Shannon Estuary; founded in 1197 on a former Norse settlement; the scene of famous sieges by the armies of Cromwell and later of William of Orange; teacher training college; institute for higher education; Belltable arts centre; railway; economy: export of farm produce, brewing, fishing, lace; monuments: 12th-c St Mary's cathedral, St John's cathedral (19th-c), remains of city walls, King John's Castle, treaty stone, Boru House (home of the writer Kate O'Brien); events: festival of Irish dancing and Gaelic drama in March; Seisiún, traditional Irish entertainment in the summer.

Limfjorden *lim'fyord-en*, LIM FJORD (Eng), fjord in N section of Jylland (Jutland), Denmark; extends 176 km from the North Sea ENE across the peninsula to the Kattegat; opens into a 24 km wide lagoon in its middle course; shallow in parts, max depth 15 m; many islands, largest of which is Mors I; chief towns on the shore area Thisted, Ålborg and Skive with Nykøbing on Mors I.

Límnos *leem'nos*, Greek island in the N Aegean Sea, off the NW coast of Turkey; area 476 sq km; length 40 km; rises to 430 m; capital Kástron.

Limoges *lee-mōzh*, AUGUSTORITUM LEMOVICENSIUM (anc), later LEMOVICES, 45 50N 1 15E, pop(1982) 144,082, ancient town and capital of Haute-Vienne dept, Limousin region, central France; in the R Vienne valley, 176 km NE of Bordeaux; university (1808, suppressed 1840, reopened 1965); the incorporation of natural gas into porcelain firing techniques, the rapid growth of the shoe industry, the development of hydroelectric power and, above all, the discovery of uranium near Ambazac, have led to the rapid post-war expansion of Limoges; there are now large industrial zones in the suburbs to the S and NE; the old fortified city walls have been converted into promenades; meteorological observatory; formerly a Gallic tribal capital destroyed in the 5th century; 2 separate towns which had developed by the 9th century merged in 1792; sacked by the English in 1370; road and rail junction; economy: electrical fittings; famed for its manufacture of enamels and porcelain; the chief seat of the porcelain industry in France since 1736 although enamel art work flourished as early as the 12th century; monuments: Gothic cathedral of St-Étienne (begun in 1273 and continued in later periods, completed in the 19th century, noted for its 16th-c Flamboyant Gothic doorway); church of St-Pierre-du-Queyroix (13th-c belfry, 16th-c facade); church of St-Michel-des-Lions (14-16th-c).

Limón *lee-mōn'*, maritime prov in E Costa Rica, Central America; bounded E by the Caribbean Sea, NE by Nicaragua, and SE by Panama; the Cordillera de Talamanca extends along the SW border with San José and Puntarenas provs; drained largely by E flowing rivers including the Río Parismina and the Río Tortuguero; pop(1983e) 153,638; area 9,189 sq km; capital Limón.

Limón or **Puerto Limón**, 10 00N 83 01W, pop(1983e) 38,916, container port and capital of Limón prov, E Costa Rica, Central America; on the Caribbean coast; built on the site of the old Indian village of Carare, landing place of Columbus on his last American expedition (1502); an industrial free zone; airfield; railway terminus; economy: port trade and oil refining.

Limousin *li-moo-sī*, region and former prov of central France, comprising the depts of Corrèze, Creuse and Haute-Vienne, 8 arrond, 103 cantons and 747 communes; pop(1982) 737,153; area 16,942 sq km; in the sparsely peopled, granitic Central Plateau; bounded on the SW by Périgord and on the SE by Quercy; the Mts du Limousin cover much of Haute-Vienne dept, while the Plateau de Millevaches rises to 978 m in the centre of the region; watered by the Creuse, Vienne, Auvézère and Corrèze rivers; capital Limoges, chief towns Brive-la-Gaillarde, Tulle and Gueret; there are large dams on the R Dordogne at Bort-les-Orgues and Marèges, and smaller ones like the Barrage de l'Aigle and Barrage du Chastang near Argentat; Aubusson is world-famous for its tapestries.

Limpopo *lim-pō'pō*, or CROCODILE RIVER, river in South Africa, Botswana, Zimbabwe and Mozambique, SE Africa; length c.1,600 km; rises in the S Transvaal N of Johannesburg (South Africa) and flows NNW past Brits; follows the Botswana-Transvaal (South Africa) and Transvaal-Zimbabwe borders; enters Mozambique at Pafuri and flows into the Indian Ocean 130 km NE of Maputo; major tributaries include the Sashe (Botswana-Zimbabwe), the Bubye (Zimbabwe) and the Oliphants (South Africa); Vasco da Gama named it the Rio do Espiritu Santo in 1497.

Linares *lee-na'rays*, 35 51S 71 35W, pop(1982) 56,009, capital of Linares prov, Maule, central Chile; S of Santiago; railway.

Linares, 38 10N 3 40W, pop(1981) 54,549, mining town in Jaén prov, Andalucia, S Spain; at the foot of the Sierra Morena, 53 km NE of Jaén; mineral springs; railway; economy: lead mining, mining machinery, motor vehicles, tools; monument: ruins of Iberian settlement of Castulo 3 km S.

Lincoln *ling'ken*, LINDUM COLONIA (Lat), 53 14N 0 33W, pop(1981) 76,9755, county town of Lincolnshire, E central England; on the R Witham, 230 km N of London and 64 km from the North Sea; an important centre of the wool trade in the Middle Ages; railway; economy: pharmaceuticals, vehicles, engineering; monuments: parts of 3rd-c Roman wall remain; Lincoln castle; cathedral (1073), including Wren Library with one of 4 original Magna Carta manuscripts; event: cycle of mystery plays (June-July).

Lincoln, formerly LANCASTER (-1867), 40 49N 96 41W, pop(1980) 171,932, capital of state in Lancaster county, SE Nebraska, United States; 82 km SW of Omaha; state capital since 1867 when it was renamed after Abraham Lincoln; 2 universities (1867, 1887); railway; economy: trade in grain and livestock; monuments: planetarium, art gallery, sculpture garden.

Lincoln Park, 42 15N 83 11W, pop(1980) 45,105, residential town in Wayne county, SE Michigan, United States; 15 km SW of Detroit; railway.

Lincoln Sea, Arctic sea, located off NE Ellesmere Island and off Peary Land, NW Greenland; linked via Nares Strait and Baffin Bay to the Atlantic Ocean.

Lincolnshire *ling'ken-shir*, flat agricultural county in E central England; bounded E by the North Sea, N by Humberside, W by Nottinghamshire, SW by Leicestershire, S by Cambridgeshire and SE by Norfolk; drained by the Welland, Witham and Trent rivers; pop(1981) 550,758; area 5,915 sq km; county town Lincoln; chief towns include Grantham, Gainsborough, Spalding; economy: intensive farming, tourism; the county is divided into 7 districts:

District	*area (sq km)*	*pop(1981)*
Boston	360	52,908
East Lindsey	1,762	105,243
Lincoln	36	76,975
North Kesteven	923	79,242
South Holland	737	62,040
South Kesteven	943	98,245
West Lindsey	1,154	76,105

Lin'den, 5 59N 58 19W, pop(1979e) 50,000, bauxite mining town in W Demerara dist, N Guyana, South America; on the R Demerara; railway; comprises the towns of Mackenzie, Wismar and Christianburg; the latter 2 towns are separated from Mackenzie by the R Demerara, on whose banks they all lie in dense jungle; the river is navigable up to the bauxite mine.

Linden, 40 38N 74 15W, pop(1980) 37,836, town in Union county, NE New Jersey, United States; 6 km SSW of Elizabeth; railway; economy: chemicals, paints, petroleum products.

Lindenhurst, 40 41N 73 23W, pop(1980) 26,919, town in Suffolk county, SE New York, United States; on Great South Bay, Long Island, 56 km E of New York City; railway.

Lindesnes or **Lindesnaes** or **Lindesnas** *lin'dus-nays*, THE NAZE (Eng), 57 59N 7 03E, cape on the S extremity of Norway, W of Mandal in Vest-Agder county, projecting into the North Sea at the entrance to the Skagerrak; first beacon light in Norway established here.

Lindi *lin'dee*, region of SE Tanzania, E Africa; bounded E by the Indian Ocean; pop(1985e) 604,000; chief town Lindi.

Lindisfarne, island off the coast of Northumberland, NE England. See Holy Island.

Line Islands, coral island group of Kiribati, central and S Pacific Ocean, comprising the N Line Is and the S Line Is; the 3 larger N Line Is of Kiritimati (Christmas I) (388.4 sq km), Fanning I (33.7 sq km), and Washington I (9.6 sq km), are inhabited by employees who work the coconut plantations; the S Line Is have been worked for guano in the past but are now uninhabited; pop(1985) 2,508.

Línea de la Concepción, La *la lee'nya THay la con-thay-pthee-ōn'*, 36 15N 5 23W, pop(1981) 56,282, port in Cádiz prov, Andalucia, S Spain; on isthmus at Algeciras Bay, 9 km N of Gibraltar; Spanish customs post beyond which is the frontier with Gibraltar; economy: food canning.

Lingqu *ling-koo*, a canal linking the Lijiang (Li river) and the Haiyang river, Guangxi prov, S China; the oldest mountain canal in China, it was built by the Emperor Qin 2,000 ago.

Linköping *leen'kœ-ping*, 58 25N 15 35E, pop(1982) 113,997, industrial town and capital of Östergötland county, SE Sweden; near S shore of L Roxen, 176 km SW of Stockholm; see of a bishop; college (1967); railway; economy: aircraft, vehicle and railway engineering, textiles, brewing; monuments: 12-15th-c cathedral, 13th-c castle, bishop's palace (1733).

Linlithgow *lin-lith'gō*, 55 59N 3 37W, pop(1981) 9,582, town in West Lothian dist, Lothian, E central Scotland; 26 km W of Edinburgh; railway; monuments: Linlithgow Palace on the S side of Linlithgow Loch dates from the late 15th century; Mary Queen of Scots was born here (1542); the palace was burned in 1746; the Canal Museum contains a display on the Union Canal which was opened in 1822 and ran from Edinburgh to the Forth and Clyde Canal.

Linyi *lin-yee*, 35 10N 118 18E, pop(1984e) 1,351,000, city in Shandong prov, E China; NE of Xuzhou; railway.

Linz *lints*, 48 18N 14 18E, pop(1981) 199,910, industrial town and capital of Oberösterreich, N Austria; situated on both banks of the R Danube, centre of a rich agricultural region; among those who lived and worked in Linz were the novelist Adalbert Stifter, Mozart, Kepler and Anton Bruckner; extensive port installations; bishopric; University of Social and Economic Sciences (1966); 3rd largest city in Austria; economy: iron and steel, fertilizers, tobacco, chemicals, pharmaceuticals; monuments: early 16th-c castle, Martinskirche (the oldest church in Austria preserved in its original form), Landhaus (former seat of the state assembly), Minoritenkirche (1758); events: Bruckner Festival (Sept).

Lipetsk *lyee'pyetsk*, 52 37N 39 36E, pop(1983) 432,000, capital city of Lipetskaya oblast, E central European Rossiyskaya, Soviet Union; on the R Voronezh, 508 km SE of Moskva (Moscow); founded in the 13th century; one of the oldest Russian mud-bath resorts and spas; centre of an iron ore-mining area; railway; airfield; economy: ferrous metallurgy, building materials, chemicals, thermoelectric power plant, foodstuffs.

Lipica *lee'peet-sa*, village in Slovenija republic, Yugoslavia; near Sežana, close to the Italian border; has a notable stud-farm which breeds the world-famous high-stepping, white Lipizzaner horses used at the Riding School in Wien (Vienna); the stud was established in 1580 by the Archduke Charles of Austria; the area had been noted since Roman times for horse breeding.

Lipp'stadt, 51 41N 8 20E, pop(1983) 60,700, industrial city in Arnsberg dist, Nordrhein-Westfalen (North Rhine-Westphalia) prov, W Germany; on the R Lippe, 61 km SE of Münster; railway.

Liptovský Mikuláš *lip'tof-skee mi'koo-lahsh*, 49 06N 19 38E, pop(1984) 26,695, town in Středoslovenský region, Slovak Socialist Republic, E central Czechoslovakia; on R Váh; railway; economy: timber, tanning.

Lira *lee'ra*, 2 15N 32 55E, town in Northern prov, Uganda, E Africa; 80 km SE of Gulu; railway; economy: textiles.

Lisboa *leezh-bō'a*, dist in E central Portugal, in parts of Ribatejo and Estremadura provs, bounded by the Atlantic (W and S) and the R Tagus (SE); area 2,762 sq km; pop(1981) 2,069,467; divided into a municipal dist and 14 councils with 6 bairros and 191 parishes; economy: meat, wool, honey, eggs, cork, resin, timber, olives, vegetables, cereals, fruit; notable wines produced at Bucelas, Carcavelos and Colares, near Sintra, where the vines grown in sand are the oldest in Europe, having escaped the Phylloxera disease.

Lisboa, LISBON *liz'bon* (Eng), OLISIPO or FELICITAS JULIA (anc), 38 42N 9 10W, pop(1981) 812,400, seaport and capital of Portugal and of Lisboa dist, situated on hills overlooking the N bank of R Tagus where the river expands to form the Mar da Palha (Sea of Straw); largest city in Portugal; university (1911); archbishopric; the old town (Alfama) is built on the slopes of a hill crowned by the Castelo de São Jorge and on hills to the NE; the new town (Bairro Alto) lies on hills to the W and the lower town (Cidade Baixa) built after the 1755 earthquake occupies the depression between the old and the new towns; the suburb of Benfica with its elegant villas and gardens lies on the NW outskirts; since the 1930s government housing developments (bairros sociais) have been built on the outskirts and since the mid-1970s makeshift housing has been erected largely by refugees from former overseas territories; the city is administratively divided into 4 bairros and 53 parishes; botanical garden; airport; railways; monuments: Convento de los Jeronimos built by Manuel I to commemorate the voyage to India of Vasco da Gama, Tower of Belem built in 1512-21 to protect the Restelo harbour from which many of the voyages of discovery set out, Monument of the Discoveries (1960), cathedral (1344), church of São Roque, São Jorge Castle, National Museum of Art and Eiffel's elevator; event: São Antonio 13 June, a municipal holiday.

Lisbon, capital of Portugal. See Lisboa.

Lisburn *liz'burn*, LIOS NA GCEARRBHACH (Gael), 54 31N 6 03W, pop(1981) 40,391, town in Lisburn dist, Antrim, NE Northern Ireland; on the R Lagan, 13 km SW of Belfast; in 1627 Charles I granted the town to the Conways, who built a castle which was burned down in 1707; Lisburn grew after 1694 when a colony of Huguenots introduced new improved methods of manufacturing into the linen industry; railway; economy: textiles, engineering.

Lisdoonvarna, 53 02N 9 17W, pop(1981) 607, spa town 37 km NW of Ennis, Clare county, Munster, W Irish Republic; Ireland's leading sulphur spring health centre; events: Lisdoonvarna fair in Oct, with its famous mating game when shy bachelors go in search of a wife; 3-day folk festival in July.

Lismore, 28 48S 153 17E, pop(1981) 24,033, town in Richmond-Tweed stat div, NE New South Wales, Australia; on the Wilson river, S of Brisbane; railway; economy: engineering, clothing, brewing, dairy produce, fruit; monuments: historical museum and Tucki Tuckurimba koala reserve.

Lītāni *lee-ta'nee*, river in El Beqa'a and Al Janūb governorates, Lebanon, SW Asia; rises near Baalbek and flows SSW through the fertile El Beqa'a valley between the Jebel Liban (W) and Jebel esh Sharqi (E) ranges; then turns abruptly W to discharge into the Mediterranean Sea 8 km N of Soûr (Tyre); length 144 km; this was the N limit of the 1978 Israeli invasion of S Lebanon.

Lith'erland, 53 28N 2 59W, pop(1981) 21,918, town in Liverpool borough, Merseyside, NW England; on R Mersey, just N of Bootle; railway; economy: engineering, clothing, rubber.

Lithgow *lith'gō*, 33 30S 150 09E, pop(1981) 12,793, town in Central West stat div, E New South Wales, Australia; at the foot of the Blue Mts, WNW of Sydney; railway.

Lithuania, constituent republic of the Soviet Union. See Litovskaya.

Litoměřice *lit'o-myer-i-tse*, 50 33N 14 10E, pop(1984) 24,844, river port town in Severočeský region, Czech Socialist Republic, W Czechoslovakia; on R Elbe where it meets the R Ohre; railway; economy: agricultural trade.

Litovskaya, LITVA *leet'va*, LITHUANIA (Eng), constituent republic of the Soviet Union, in the W part of European USSR; bounded SW by Poland and W by the Baltic Sea; glaciated plains cover much of the area; the chief river is the Neman; pop(1983) 3,506,000; area 65,200 sq km; capital Vilnius; chief towns Kaunas, Klaipeda, and Šiauliai; economy: electronics; electrical and radio engineering; manufacture of computer hardware, instruments, and machine tools; shipbuilding; chemicals (synthetic fibres, mineral fertilizers, and plastics); light industry; food processing; petroleum refining is being developed at Mazeikiai in the NW; the principal branches of agriculture are cattle raising for meat and dairy products, pig raising for bacon, and poultry farming; from 1385 to 1795 it was united with Poland; intensive russification led to the revolts of 1905 and 1917; occupied by Germany 1915-18; proclaimed a republic in 1918; annexed by the Soviet Union in 1940 as a Socialist Republic.

Little Belt, Denmark. See Lille Bælt.

Little Cayman *kay-man'*, smallest of the Cayman Is, W Caribbean, 96 km ENE of Grand Cayman; area 26 sq km; length 16 km; width 1.6 km; administrative centre Blossom Village.

Little Rock, 34 45N 92 16W, pop(1980) 158,461, capital of state in Pulaski county, central Arkansas, United States; largest city in the state and a port on the R Arkansas; settled in 1821; in 1957 Federal troops were sent to the city to enforce a 1954 US Supreme Court ruling against segregation in schools; university; railway; economy: processing of fish, beef, poultry, bauxite and timber; monuments: Territorial Restoration, old statehouse; event: Riverfest (May).

Littlehampton, 50 48N 0 33W, pop(1981) 46,632, coastal resort town in Arun dist, West Sussex, S England; part of Brighton-Worthing-Littlehampton urban area; at the mouth of the R Arun, 12 km SW of Worthing; railway; economy: foodstuffs, light engineering.

Littleton, 39 37N 105 00W, pop(1980) 28,631, county seat of Arapahoe county, N central Colorado, United States; a suburb 14 km S of Denver; railway; economy: petroleum research and aerospace industries, tyres, precision castings, photographic equipment and trucks.

Litvínov *lit'veen-of*, 50 38N 13 30E, pop(1984) 21,769, town in Severočeský region, Czech Socialist Republic, W Czechoslovakia; in the N foothills of the Erzgebirge Mts, NW of Most, near the E German frontier; railway; economy: lignite mining, chemicals, powerplant.

Liupanshui *lyoo-pan-shway*, SUICHENG, 25 45N 104 40E, pop(1984e) 2,166,400, city in Guizhou prov, S China; W of Guiyang; railway.

Livermore, 37 41N 121 47W, pop(1980) 48,349, city in Alameda county, W California, United States; in Livermore Valley in the Coast Ranges, 48 km ESE of Oakland; railway; economy: in wine-producing region.

Liverpool, 53 25N 2 55W, pop(1981) 544,861, urban area pop(1981) 509,981, seaport in Merseyside, NW England; on the right bank of the R Mersey estuary, 5 km from the Irish Sea and 312 km NW of London; founded in the 10th century, Liverpool became a borough in 1207 and a city in 1880; port trade developed in the 16th and 17th centuries; in the 18th century the slave trade and the Lancashire cotton industry enhanced its importance; today Liverpool is a major world trading centre and the UK's most important seaport for Atlantic trade; railway; container terminal (1972); linked to Birkenhead under the R Mersey by road and rail tunnels (Queensway (1934) and Kingsway (1974)); ferries to Belfast, Dublin, Isle of Man; airport; economy: imports include petroleum, grain, ores, non-ferrous metals, sugar, wood, fruit and cotton; monuments: Catholic cathedral, designed by Sir Frederick Gibberd and consecrated in 1967; Anglican cathedral, designed by Sir Giles Gilbert Scott and completed in 1980; event: Grand National steeplechase at Aintree (Apr).

Livingston, 55 53N 3 32W, pop(1981) 38,954, town in West Lothian dist, Lothian, E central Scotland; 21 km W of Edinburgh; designated a 'new town' in 1962; railway; economy: industrial research and development centre; paper, asbestos, engineering, scientific instruments, electronics, steel.

Livingstone, town in Zambia. See Maramba.

Livo'nia, 42 23N 83 23W, pop(1980) 104,814, city in Wayne county, SE Michigan, United States; 27 km W of Detroit; economy: vehicle parts, paint, tools.

Livorno *lee-vor'nō*, prov of Toscana region, NW central Italy; pop(1981) 346,657; area 1,220 sq km; capital Livorno; bounded E by Tyrrhenian Sea.

Livorno, LEG'HORN (Eng), 43 33N 10 18E, pop(1981) 175,741, port and capital of Livorno prov, W Toscana region, Italy; on the low-lying coast of the Tyrrhenian Sea, SW of Pisa; railway; ferries to Bastia in Corsica; linked with the R Arno by a canal 15 km long; economy: shipbuilding, engineering, cement, soap, straw hats and trade in wine, olive oil and marble; monument: 17th-c cathedral.

Lizard Point, 49 56N 5 13W, Cornwall, SW England; the most southerly point on the mainland of Britain, near Lizard Town.

Ljubljana *lyoob'lyah-nah*, LUBIANA (Ital), EMONA (anc), 46 00N 14 30E, pop(1981) 305,211, capital of Slovenia republic, N Yugoslavia; on Sava and Ljubljanica rivers, 120 km WNW of Zagreb; founded by Augustus in 34 BC; capital of the former kingdom of Illyria (1816-49); ceded to Yugoslavia in 1918; university (1595); education and convention centre; airport; railway; Tivoli sports park; economy: textiles, paper, chemicals, food processing, electronics; monuments: national museum, castle, cathedral and Ursuline church; events: Alpe-Adria International Trade Fair in April; Ljubljana Festival (July-Aug); International Festival of Graphic Art in alternate years (June-Aug); International Wine Fair at the end of Aug; flower show (mid Sep); International 'Ski Expo' Fair in Nov.

Ljusnan *yus-nan'*, LJUSNA (Eng), river in central Sweden; rises on Norwegian border, W of Röros; flows SE through Jämtland and Gävleborg counties past Ljusdal and Bollnas; discharges into Gulf of Bothnia at Ljusne, S of Söderhamn; length 430 km.

Ljutomer *lyoo'to-mer*, formerly LOTMERK, 46 31N 16 11E, pop(1981) 18,770, town in NE Slovenija republic, Yugoslavia; railway; in a notable wine-growing area.

Llandrindod Wells *hlan-drin'dod*, 52 15N 3 23W, pop(1981) 4,438, county town in Radnor dist, Powys, E Wales; in the Cambrian Mts, NW of Builth Wells; spa town with magnesium, sulphur and chalybeate springs; railway; event: bowling festival (summer).

Llandudno *hlan-did'nō*, 53 19N 3 49W, pop(1981) 14,372, resort town in Aberconwy dist, Gwynedd, NW Wales; on the R Conwy, on a small peninsula terminating in Great Ormes Head; railway; economy: electrical goods, tourism.

Llanelli, LLANELLY *hla-ne'hlee*, 51 42N 4 10W, pop(1981) 45,657, town in Llanelli dist, Dyfed, SW Wales; on Carmarthen Bay, NW of Swansea; railway; economy: tinplate, chemicals, lenses, engineering, mining machinery.

Llanfairpwllgwyngyll *hlan'vir-poohl-gwin'gihl* ('St Mary's pool of the white hazel'), 53 13N 4 12W, village on the island of Yns Môn (Anglesey), Gwynedd, NW Wales; situated W of Menai Bridge; gained notoriety by the extension of its name by a poetic cobbler in the 18th century to Llanfairpwllgwyngyllgogerychwyrndrobwllantysiliogogogoch.

Llangollen *hlan-go'hlen* ('St Collen'), 52 58N 3 10W, pop(1981) 3,072, resort town in Glyndŵr dist, Clwyd, NE Wales; on the R Dee, 15 km SW of Wrexham; economy: hide and skin dressing, printing, crafts, agricultural trade; monuments: 14th-c St Collen's church; nearby is Valle Crucis abbey (c.1200) and Eliseg's Pillar, an 8-9th-c cross; Plâs Newydd, S of the town, has been the headquarters of the Welsh National Theatre since 1943; event: annual international *eisteddfods* have been held here since 1947.

Llano Estacado *lah'nō e-sta-kah'dō*, STAKED PLAIN, vast semi-arid S portion of the Great Plains; situated in E New Mexico and W Texas, United States; extends over the Texas panhandle and the portion of New Mexico situated to the E of the Pecos river; consists of flat, windswept grasslands broken by streams; the region was formerly devoted to cattle raising but now also contains natural gas and oil fields and irrigated farming.

Llanquihue, Lago *lyan-kee'way*, lake in Los Lagos region, S central Chile; 16 km N of Puerto Montt; area 780 sq km; 35 km long, 40 km wide; on E shore is Osorno Volcano (2,660 m); to SE is Calbuco Volcano (2,016 m); depths of almost 1,500 m have been measured; its outlet is the Río Maullín; around the lake are the resort towns of Puerto Octay (N), Frutillar (W), Puerto Varas (S) and Ensenada (E); fishing and water sports are popular during the summer and skiing in the winter.

Llantwit Major-St Athan *hlan'twit-*, 51 25N 3 30W, pop(1981) 13,697, urban area comprising 2 towns in Vale of Glamorgan dist, South Glamorgan, S Wales; W of Barry and S of Cowbridge.

Lleyn Peninsula, peninsula in Dwyfor county, Gwynedd, NW Wales; separates Cardigan Bay and Tremadog Bay (S) from Caernarfon Bay (N); chief towns are Pwllheli and Porthmadog.

Llullaillaco, Cerro *yoo-yī-ya'kō*, 24 43S 68 30W, a snow-capped extinct volcano on the Chile-Argentina border, in Antofagasta region, N Chile and Salta prov, Argentina; situated 300 km W of Salta (Argentina); height 6,723 m; Socampa Pass and railway are to the NE.

Lobatse *lō-ba'tsee*, 25 11S 25 40E, pop(1981) 19,034, independent township in South East dist, Botswana, S Africa; 72 km N of Mafeking; alt 1,175 m; area 30 sq km; a railhead for cattle transportation; airfield; economy: meat processing, light industry, livestock trade.

Lobaye *lō-bī'*, prefecture in SW Central African Republic; the Lobaye and Pama rivers flow SE to the R Ubangi; pop(1968) 150,510; area 24,500 sq km; chief town M'baiki; other towns include Boda, Yaka, Bogali, Ngoto, Bagandou and Mongoumba.

Lobito *loo-bee'too*, 12 20S 13 34E, pop(1970) 59,258, seaport on Lobito Bay, Benguela prov, W Angola, SW Africa; 385 km S of Luanda and 1,530 km W of Lubumbashi (formerly Elizabethville), Zaire; founded in 1843; the port is protected by a lengthy sand bar along which the town has expanded since the completion of the railway in 1929; the original harbour was constructed in 1905; airfield; economy: ship repair, metallurgy, food processing.

Lochgelly *loKH-gel'lī*, 56 08N 3 19W, pop(1981) 7,334, town in Dunfermline dist, Fife, E Scotland; 11 km SW of Glenrothes; railway; economy: open-cast mining, gas.

Lochgilphead *loKH-gilp'hed*, 56 03N 5 26W, pop(1981) 2,461, capital of Argyll and Bute dist, Strathclyde, W Scotland; at the head of Loch Gilp, at the E end of the Crinan Canal.

Locks Heath, 50 51N 1 15W, pop(1981) 25,220, E suburb of Southampton, Hampshire, S England; railway.

Lodi *law'dee*, 38 08N 121 16W, pop(1980) 35,221, city in San Joaquin county, central California, United States; on the Mokelumne river at the N tip of the San Joaquin Valley, 21 km N of Stockton; railway; at the centre of a wine-producing area.

Łódź *woodsh*, voivodship in central Poland; watered by the Bzura, Ner and Moszczenica rivers; pop(1983) 1,147,000; area 1,523 sq km; capital Łódź; chief towns of the Łódź Industrial Region include Pabianice, Zgierz and Ozorków.

Łódź, 51 49N 19 28E, pop(1983) 848,600, industrial capital of Łódź voivodship, central Poland; 2nd largest city in Poland; chartered in 500 AD, but owes its development since 1820 to the textile industry; university (1945); technical university (1945); film studios; railway; power heating plant; economy: chemicals, electrical engineering, synthetic fibres, textiles, clothing, textile machinery, transformers, radios; monuments: museum of art, archaeological and ethnographical museum, central textile industry museum, several parks and botanical gardens; event: artistic spring festival in May.

Loess Plateau, plateau in N central China. See Huangtu Gaoyuan.

Lofoten Islands, *lō-fō'ten*, island group in the Norwegian Sea, off the NW coast of Norway, SW of the Vesterålen group, separated from the mainland by Vest Fjord; off the NW coast of Norway, running spurwise SW from the Vesterålen, in a jagged mountain wall; area 1,425 sq km; principal islands include Hinnøy, Austvågøy, Vestvågøy and Moskenesøya; administered by Nordland county.

Lofty-Flinders Ranges, Mount, mountain ranges in SE South Australia, Australia; extending 800 km N from Cape Jervis to the N end of L Torrens, running roughly N-S; in the S the Mount Lofty Ranges are comparatively low, with Mount Lofty, the highest peak, rising to 727 m; in the W steep cliffs drop down to the Adelaide Plains; on the E the slopes merge with the Murray basin; the Flinders Ranges to the N commence at the E shore of St Vincent's Gulf and end approx 600 km N of Adelaide; they include an 802 sq km national park established in 1970; the highest point, St Mary Peak, rises to 1,166 m; to the N of Peterborough a divergence from the main range stretches NE via the Olary Ridges to the Barrier Range at Broken Hill; the Flinders Ranges diverge again in the far N to circle the N end of L Torrens and the N end of L Frome; the Flinders Ranges contain some unusual basins, of which Wilpena Pound is the best known; their multi-coloured rock faces and wild flowers make them a popular tourist attraction; numerous examples of Aboriginal art are scattered throughout Flinders Ranges, some of them 10,000 years old; copper, coal and gold have been mined here.

Logan, 27 38S 153 00E, pop(1981e) 87,370, city in Brisbane stat div, Queensland, E Australia.

Logan, 41 44N 111 50W, pop(1980) 26,844, county seat of Cache county, N Utah, United States; on the R Logan, 60 km N of Ogden; university (1888); economy: processing centre in a farming area; manufactures include cheese, farm machinery, pianos and plastics; monuments: Mormon Tabernacle, Living Historical Farm; event: American West Festival (July).

Logan, Mount, 60 34N 140 24W, highest mountain in Canada and 2nd highest in North America; rises to 5,950 m in the St Elias Mts in SW Yukon terr, W Canada; 289 km W of Whitehorse; lies to the N of the Seward Glacier, in Kluane National Park.

Logone *lo-gōn'*, river in SW Chad, N central Africa; formed by the confluence of the M'Béré and Pendé rivers 45 km SSE of Laï; flows 390 km NW and N past Laï and Bongor to join the R Chari at N'Djamena; its length including the R M'Béré is 800 km; forms extensive swamps along much of its course; fishing is important; follows the border between Chad and Cameroon between Ham and N'Djamena.

Logone Occidental *aw-ri-den-tal'*, prefecture in SW Chad, N central Africa; pop(1979) 295,000; area 8,965 sq km; land rises in SW; the R Logone forms the SE border; capital Moundou; chief town Boumo.

Logone-Oriental *o-ri-en-tal'*, prefecture in SW Chad, N central Africa; pop(1979) 307,000; area 28,035 sq km; land rises towards SW; the R Logone forms the NW border; capital Doba; chief towns Baïbokoum, Gore, Bebouguei, Kagopai and Bekoutou.

Logroño, prov of Spain. See Rioja.

Logroño *lō-grō'nyō*, JULIOBRIGA (Lat), VAREIA (anc), 42 28N 2 27W, pop(1981) 110,980, market town and capital of Logroño prov, Rioja, N Spain; on R Ebro, 336 km N of Madrid; centre of Rioja wine-growing region; at Clavijo, 17 km to the S, is the battlefield where Ramiro I defeated the Moors with the aid of St James in 844; railway; economy: wine, rubber, coachbuilding, metal work, tools, textiles; monuments: churches of St Bartholomew and St Mary; events: fiesta of St Barnabus in June and grape harvest festival in Sept.

Lohja *lo'ya*, LOJO *loo'yoo* (Swed), 60 12N 24 10E, pop(1982) 14,333, town in Uudenmaa prov, S Finland; W of Helsinki; established in 1926.

Loikaw *loy'ko*, 19 40N 97 17E, capital of Kayah state, E Burma; on R Nam Pilu; SE of Mandalay and NE of Rangoon; economy: timber.

Loing *lwã*, river in central France rising near St-Sauveur in Yonne dept; flows N through Loiret and Seine-et-Marne depts to meet the R Seine below Moret-sur-Loing; length 166 km; tributary R Ouanne.

Loire *lwar*, dept in Rhône-Alpes region of E France, on the upper R Loire and the E edge of the Massif Central, W of the middle Rhône; comprises 3 arrond, 39 cantons and 327 communes; pop(1982) 739,521; area 4,781 sq km; the surface rises from the river valley to the Monts du Forez (1,640 m) on the W, and the Monts du Beaujolais, du Lyonnais and du Vivarais on the E; the hills to the W of the river grow vines; capital St-Étienne, chief towns Roanne and Rive-de-Gier; spa at Montrond-les-Bains; includes the Parc du Pilat regional nature park, covering an area of 593 sq km.

Loire, LIGER (anc), river in E France rising in the Massif Central in Ardèche dept, WNW of Privas; flows N and NW past Nevers to Orléans, then turns W and flows through Blois, Tours and Nantes to empty into the Bay of Biscay by a wide estuary below St-Nazaire; the principal river of France; length 1,020 km; tributaries Allier, Cher, Indre, Vienne, Sèvre, Nièvre, Maine, Erdre and Nantaise rivers.

Loire-Atlantique, dept in Pays de la Loire region of W France, on the Bay of Biscay; comprises 4 arrond, 56 cantons and 221 communes; pop(1982) 995,498; area 6,815 sq km; cut in half by the Loire estuary, and drained by its tributaries, the Erdre and Sèvre-Nantaise rivers; includes the Lac de Grand-Lieu, SW of Nantes; capital Nantes, chief port St-Nazaire; includes the Parc de Brière regional nature park, covering 395 sq km.

Loiret *lwar-ay*, dept in Centre region of central France, includes parts of the dists of Sologne, Gâtinais and Beauce; comprises 3 arrond, 41 cantons and 334 communes; pop(1982) 535,669; area 6,775 sq km; drained by the R Loire and its tributaries; the Plaine de la Beauce extends into the W part of the dept; the river banks between Orléans and Tours are noted for their market-gardens, nurseries and vineyards; capital Orléans, chief towns Gien and Montargis, at the junction of the Orléans and Briare Canals; there is a 14-17th-c chateau at Malesherbes.

Loir-et-Cher, dept in Centre region of central France, comprising 3 arrond, 28 cantons and 291 communes; pop(1982) 296,220; area 6,343 sq km; drained by the Loir and Cher rivers in the N and S and by the Loire in the middle, lying across the fertile region of Beauce; the Sologne around Romorantin between the Loire and Cher is infertile marshland; Blois is the centre for a tour of some of the Loire châteaux; capital Blois; there are châteaux at Cellettes, Tour-en-Sologne and Cheverny.

Loja *lō'KHa*, semitropical prov in the Andean Sierra of SW Ecuador; bordered S and W by Peru; watered by Catamayo and Zamora rivers; pop(1982) 360,767; area 11,214 sq km; capital Loja; the international border with Peru was adjusted in 1942; economy: drinks, tobacco, meat packing, dairying, sugar refining, timber, chemicals.

Loja, 3 59S 79 16W, pop(1982) 71,652, capital of Loja prov, in the Andean Sierra of SW Ecuador; surrounded by hills; 2 universities (1943, 1971); noted law school; economy: drinks, tobacco, meat packing, dairy products, flour, sugar refining, wood products, chemicals; monuments: there are crude but original paintings on the patio walls of many of the old houses; the cathedral and the San Martín church have fine painted interiors.

Lokeren *lō'ke-ren*, 51 06N 3 59E, pop(1982) 33,534, manufacturing town in Sint-Niklaas dist, Oost-Vlaanderen (East Flanders) prov, NW Belgium; 19 km NE of Gent; railway.

Lolland *lo'lahn*, LAALAND, Danish island in Baltic Sea, S of Sjælland (Zealand), W of Falster I, separated from S Sjælland by the strait of Smålandsfarvandet; area 1,235 sq km; length 27 km; rises to 30 m; Sakskøbing Fjord in N and Nakskov Fjord in W break coastline; ferry services; economy: sugar-beet, tourism; chief towns Maribo and Nakskov; administered by Storstrøm county.

Lombard, 41 53N 88 01W, pop(1980) 37,295, town in Du Page county, NE Illinois, United States; 32 km W of Chicago; railway; residential.

Lombardia *lom-bar'dia*, LOMBARDY *lom'bar-di* (Eng), region of N Italy, comprising the provs of Bergamo, Brescia, Como, Cremona, Milano, Mantova, Pavia, Sondrio, and Varese; pop(1981) 8,891,652; area 23,833 sq km; capital Milano (Milan); chief towns Brescia, Pavia, and Varese; S Lombardia, in the plain of the R Po, is one of Italy's most highly developed industrial regions (chemicals, pharmaceuticals, metalworking, motor vehicles, engineering, textiles, leather goods) as well as one of its most productive agricultural regions (corn, maize, market gardening, fodder crops); tourism is important around the Alpine lakes (Maggiore, Como, and Garda) and in the mountains (winter sports, climbing).

Lombok *lahm'bak* (Jav, 'chili pepper'), volcanic island in the Lesser Sunda group, Indonesia; part of the prov of Nusa Tenggara Barat, lying between the islands of Bali (W) and Sumbawa (E); area 4,727 sq km; chief town Mataram; Gunung Rinjani (2nd highest mt in Indonesia) rises to 3,775 m in the N; of interest to biologists as it falls on Wallace's line, marking the meeting point of Asian and Australian species; economy: coffee, rice, textiles.

Lomé *lō'may*, 6 10N 1 21E, pop(1983) 366,476, seaport capital of Togo, W Africa; an important market centre, noted for its marble, gold and silver craftsmen; university (1965); airport; railway junction; economy: oil refining, steel processing and tourism.

Lomond, Loch *lō'mond*, largest lake in Scotland and the largest stretch of inland water in Britain; in W Central and NE Strathclyde regions, 32 km NW of Glasgow; area 70 sq km; 34 km long; narrow in the N, opening out to 8 km at the S end; up to 190 m deep; Loch Sloy hydroelectric power scheme in the NW has its outfall into Loch Lomond at Inveruglas; its outlet is the R Leven at the S end of the loch; the waters join the Clyde estuary at Dumbarton; pleasure cruises.

Lomphat, LUMPHAT, 13 30N 106 59E, chief town of Ratanakiri prov, NE Cambodia; lies to the E of the R Srepok; airfield.

Lom'poc, 34 38N 120 28W, pop(1980) 26,267, city in Santa Barbara county, SW California, United States; on the Santa Ynez river, c.72 km WNW of Santa Barbara.

Łomża *lom-za'*, voivodship in NE Poland; watered by the Narew, Biebrza and Pisa rivers; pop(1983) 334,000; area 6,684 sq km; capital Łomża; chief towns include Zambrów and Ciechanowiec.

London *lun'dun*, LONDINIUM (Lat), (in the 4th century AUGUSTA), 51 30N 0 10W, pop(1981) 6,713,165 (Greater London), pop(1981) 5,864 (City of London), capital city of England and the United Kingdom; on the R Thames in SE England; the area of Greater London is 1,579 sq km; from the 1st to the 5th century London was a Roman town; the Roman town which developed after 43 AD occupied 2 low gravel hills divided by a brook (Walbrook) where the R Thames narrowed to its lowest convenient crossing; sacked by Boadicea (c.AD 61), the city was later surrounded by a defensive wall, fragments of which remain; developing as the leading trade and administrative centre of England, it received charter privileges from William the Conqueror in 1067; the mayoralty was established in 1191 and in 1215 King John granted a new charter requiring the mayor to be elected annually; after the plague of 1665 and the great plague of 1666, London developed into a major trade centre and one of the largest cities in the world; the city was administered by London County Council from 1888 until 1963 and by the Greater London Council until 1986; the City Corporation is independent of the local authority administration in certain respects and retains its ancient electoral system in which a great part is played by the livery companies, successors of the former trade guilds; the City of London, occupying the approximate area of the old medieval city N of the R Thames, is the financial and business centre of the city, including within its bounds the Bank of England, the Stock Exchange and the Royal Exchange; the City of Westminster is the administrative and judicial heart of the United Kingdom with the Houses of Parliament, the Abbey of Westminster, Buckingham Palace and government departments within its bounds; additional monuments of the City of London include Sir Christopher Wren's cathedral of St Paul (begun in 1675), the Guildhall, the Mansion House (residence of the Lord Mayor), the Tower of London; the outer boroughs comprise mixed residential and industrial developments; railway and underground; airports at Luton (N), Heathrow (W) and Gatwick (S); events: Trooping of the Colour on the Queen's official birthday in June; procession to the Royal Courts of Justice (Lord Mayor's Show) in Nov; Greater London consists of 32 boroughs and the City of London:

Borough	*area (sq km)*	*pop(1981)*
Barking and Dagenham	34	149,930
Barnet	90	292,441
Bexley	61	214,078
Brent	44	253,275
Bromley	152	282,394
Camden	22	172,014
Croydon	87	300,508
Ealing	55	279,846
Enfield	81	258,770
Greenwich	47	212,987
Hackney	19	180,434
Hammersmith and Fulham	16	148,447
Haringey	30	203,553
Harrow	51	195,478
Havering	118	239,344
Hillingdon	110	230,159
Hounslow	59	200,829
Islington	15	160,890
Kensington and Chelsea	12	138,837
Kingston-upon-Thames	38	132,547
Lambeth	27	246,426
Lewisham	35	231,324
London, City of	3	5,864
Merton	38	166,100
Newham	36	209,494
Redbridge	56	228,542
Richmond-upon-Thames	55	159,693
Southwark	29	211,840
Sutton	43	167,100
Tower Hamlets	20	142,841
Waltham Forest	40	215,947
Wandsworth	35	254,898
Westminster, City of	22	191,098

Londonderry, city and county in Northern Ireland. See Derry.

Londrina *lon-dree'na*, 23 18S 51 13W, pop(1980) 257,899, town in Paraná state, Sul region, S Brazil; W of São Paulo; university (1971); railway; airfield; economy: commerce, brewing, vegetable oils.

Long Beach, 33 47N 118 11W, pop(1980) 361,334, city in Los Angeles county, SW California, United States; 32 km S of Los Angeles on San Pedro Bay; developed rapidly after the discovery of oil in 1921; there is a long bathing beach; university (1949); railway; economy: tyres, vehicle assembly, aircraft, soap, chemicals, oil refining, fish processing, fruit canning; monuments: the cruise liner *Queen Mary*, which has been converted into a museum-hotel-convention centre; Long Beach Marine Stadium where the 1932 Olympic boating events were held.

Long Beach, 40 35N 73 39W, pop(1980) 34,073, resort town in Nassau county, SE New York, United States; on Atlantic Beach, Long Island, 48 km SE of New York City; railway.

Long Branch, 40 18N 74 00W, pop(1980) 29,819, resort town in Monmouth county, E New Jersey, United States; on the Atlantic coast, 65 km ENE of Trenton.

Long Cay, FORTUNE ISLAND, island in the S Bahamas, SW of Crooked I; pop(1980) 33; area 23 sq km; length 16 km; chief settlement Albert Town.

Long Eaton, 52 54N 1 15W, pop(1981) 42,494, town in Erewash dist, Derbyshire, central England; part of Nottingham urban area; 14 km E of Derby; railway; economy: clothing, electronics, engineering.

Long Island, elongated island in the S central Bahamas, between Great Exuma I (NW) and Crooked I (SE); pop(1980) 3,358; area 595 sq km; chief towns Deadman's Cay and Clarence Town.

Long Island, island in SE New York state, United States; situated E of New York City it is bounded N by Long Island Sound, S by the Atlantic and W by the mouth of the Hudson river; separated from the Bronx and Manhattan by the East river and from Staten I by the Narrows; comprises the New York state counties of Kings (which includes the borough of Brooklyn), Nassau, Queens, Suffolk; length 190 km; land area 3,627 sq km; there are many residential towns (Lindenhurst, Garden City, Ronkonkoma, etc) and resort beaches (Coney I, Fire I, Freeport, Long Beach, etc); settled by the Dutch in 1623 and by the English c.1640, Long Island became part of the British colony of New York in 1674.

Longbenton-Killingworth, 55 01N 1 34W, pop(1981) 36,944, amalgamated towns in Newcastle upon Tyne borough, Tyne and Wear, NE England; part of Tyneside urban area; 5 km N of Newcastle upon Tyne.

Longford, LONGPHUIRT (Gael), county in NW Leinster prov, central Irish Republic; drained by R Shannon and its tributaries; crossed by Royal Canal; hilly in NW; pop(1981) 31,140; area 1,044 sq km; capital Longford.

Longford, LONGPHORT (Gael), 53 44N 7 47W, pop(1981) 6,548, capital of Longford county, NW Leinster, central Irish Republic; on R Camlin and branch of Royal Canal; former literary centre; railway; monuments: St Mel's cathedral; Tullynally Castle at Castlepollard is the home of Lord Longford.

Longmont, 40 10N 105 06W, pop(1980) 42,942, town in Boulder county, N Colorado, United States; 40 km NW of Denver; railway; economy: trading and processing centre in an irrigated farm area; manufactures include campers, trailers and batteries.

Longueuil *lõ-gu'ee*, 45 32N 73 31W, pop(1981) 124,320, town in S Québec, SE Canada; on the E bank of the St Lawrence river, opposite Montréal; railway.

Longview, 32 30N 94 44W, pop(1980) 62,762, county seat of Gregg county, NE Texas, United States; 192 km E of Dallas; railway; economy: oil and natural gas production, oil refining, livestock trade.

Longview, 46 08N 122 57W, pop(1980) 31,052, a deep-water port in Cowlitz county, SW Washington, United States; at the junction of the Cowlitz and Columbia rivers, on the border with Oregon state.

Lons-le-Saunier *lõ-le-so-nyay*, LEDO SALINARIUS (anc), 46 40N 4 50E, pop(1982) 21,886, ancient town and capital of Jura dept, Franche-Comté region, E France; in a basin of the Jura Mts surrounded by vine-clad hills, 70 km NW of Genève (Geneva), Switzerland; warm saline springs; railway; economy: wine, optical equipment; salt mines in a W suburb; monument: 12-15th-c church.

Lop Nur, salt lake in E Xinjiang aut region, NW China; E of the Tarim Pendi basin; area 2,570 sq km; alt 780 m; 2nd largest salt lake in China; watered by a tributary of the Konqi He river.

Lopatka, Mys *lu-pat'ku*, 50 50N 156 33E, the S extremity of Kamchatka Peninsula, Kamchatskaya oblast, E Siberian Rossiyskaya, Soviet Union; projects S into the Kuril Strait, opposite Ostrov Shumshu, northernmost of the Kuril'skiye Ostrova (Kuril Is).

Lorain', 41 28N 82 11W, pop(1980) 75,416, town in Lorain county, N Ohio, United States; port on L Erie, 40 km W of Cleveland; railway; economy: steel, motor vehicle assembly plants, construction equipment.

Lorca *lor'ka*, ILLURCO (Lat), LURKA (Arab), 37 41N 1 42W, pop(1981) 60,627, agric market town in Murcia prov, SE Spain; on the R Guadalentin, 62 km SW of Murcia; economy: textiles, clothes, meat processing, wine, lead mining, pottery; monuments: Moorish castle, church of St Patrick and cave dwellings 3 km to the N of the town; event: Holy Week procession.

Lord Howe Island, 31 33S 159 04E, pop(1982) 420, volcanic island in the Pacific Ocean, 702 km NE of Sydney; part of New South Wales; area 16.56 sq km; rises to 866 m at Mt Gower; discovered in 1788; a popular resort island.

Lorenskog *lo'ren-skōg*, 59 56N 10 45E, pop(1980) 22,533, town in Akershus county, SE Norway; a suburb of Oslo.

Lorestān *loor-is-tan'*, mountainous prov in W central Iran; pop(1982) 915,784; area 28,803 sq km; capital Khorramābād.

Loreto *lō-ray'tō*, dept in NE Peru; bounded E by Brazil along the Río Yavari and the Serra de Divisor mountain range, N by Colombia along the Río Putumayo; watered by the Marañón, Ucayali, Napo and Amazon rivers; the Amazon forms part of Peru's NE border with Ecuador; pop(1981) 445,368; area 478,336 sq km; capital Iquitos.

Lorient *lor-yã*, formerly L'ORIENT, 47 45N 3 21W, pop(1982) 64,675, fortified seaport in Morbihan dept, Bretagne region, W France; on the Bay of Biscay, at the junction of the Blavet and Scorff estuaries, 46 km WNW of Vannes; created by Colbert in 1666 under Louis XIV to elude the English ships patrolling the Channel; became a military fort in 1690; a naval base was designed here to support the activities of France's India Company trading in the East; used as a submarine base by the Germans in World War II; railway; economy: fishing, fish processing, shipbuilding.

Loro Sae, prov of Indonesia. See Timor Timur.

Lorraine *lo-rayn*, LOTHRINGEN (Ger), region and former prov of NE France comprising the depts of Meurthe-et-Moselle, Meuse, Moselle and Vosges, 19 arrond, 148 cantons and 2,303 communes; pop(1982) 2,319,905; area 23,547 sq km; comprises the region of the upper Meuse and the Moselle rivers, and is bordered on the W by the Plaine de Champagne and on the E by the Vosges, while in the N it extends to the Ardennes Mts and in the S to the Monts Faucilles; there are forests dotted with lakes, large areas of cornfields, orchards of cherries and plums (distilled into liqueurs such as kirsch, mirabelle and quetsche), and near Hohneck on the high ridge of the thickly-forested Vosges Mts is a stretch of pastureland; notable are the cheeses of Munster and Gerome; there are deposits of iron-ore, coal and salt, and mineral springs at Vittel and Contrexéville; after the Franco-Prussian War in 1871 the region was ceded to Germany as part of Alsace-Lorraine; chief towns Metz, Nancy, Luneville and Épinal.

Los Islands *lōs*, ÎLES DE LOS (Fr), 9 30N 13 50W, group of islands off the coast of Guinea, W Africa; there are five larger islands including Tamara, Roume and Factory; ceded to France by the British in 1904.

Lošinj *lo'shin-ya*, 45 35N 14 25E, popular resort island in the Adriatic Sea off the coast of W Hrvatska (Croatia) republic, Yugoslavia; area 75 sq km; linked with Cres I by a bridge; the main village is Mali Lošinj; many naturist beaches on the island; events: international underwater fishing contests in December.

Lossiemouth *los'ee-mowth*, 57 43N 3 18W, pop(1981) 6,847, port town in Moray dist, Grampian region, NE Scotland; on the coast, 8 km N of Elgin; the first Labour prime minister, Ramsay Macdonald, was born here in 1866; economy: fishing, tourism.

Lost World, name applied by the novelist Arthur Conan Doyle to an imaginary range of mountains where prehistoric animals survived into the 20th century; the name first appeared in the title of a serial in the *Strand Magazine* (1912) and later as a novel; the idea for the story was based on Col. Percy Fawcett's description of the Ricardo Franco Hills in the Mato Grosso state of W Brazil.

Lot, dept in Midi-Pyrénées region of S France, where the S edge of the Central Plateau descends to the Garonne corridor; comprises 3 arrond, 30 cantons and 340 communes; pop(1982) 154,533; area 5,216 sq km; drained by the R Dordogne in the N and the Lot in the S; capital Cahors; spa at Miers-Alvignac; there are interesting caves near St-Céré, Padirac, Lavace, Cabrerets and Gourdon.

Lot, OLTIS (anc), navigable river in S France rising in Lozère dept, on the slopes of the Lozère Mts; flows W through Aveyron, Lot and Lot-et-Garonne depts to meet the R Garonne at Aiguillon; length 480 km; tributaries Truyère and Célé rivers; used as a canal as far as Entraygues.

Lota *lō'ta*, 37 07S 73 10W, pop(1982) 62,662, port in Concepción prov, Bío-Bío, central Chile; railway; economy: coal-mining, ceramics; monument: nearby is the Parque Cousiño Isidora, laid out with views of the sea by an English architect about 100 years ago.

Lot-et-Garonne, dept in Aquitaine region of SW France, comprising 4 arrond, 39 cantons and 313 communes; pop(1982) 298,522; area 5,361 sq km; drained by the R Garonne and its tributaries, the Lot, Gers and Baise; mostly fertile lowland; the Garonne Canal cuts across the middle of the dept; capital Agen, chief towns Marmande (known for its stuffed prunes) and Villeneuve.

Lothian *lō'THi-an*, region in E Scotland; bounded N by the Firth of Forth, NE by the North Sea, S by Borders, SW by Strathclyde and W by Central region; in the S are the Pentland Hills and Moorfoot Hills; the Lammermuir Hills lie in the SW; pop(1981) 738,372; area 1,755 sq km; chief town Edinburgh; major towns include Livingston, Musselburgh, Haddington, Dalkeith and Penicuik; Lothian is divided into 4 districts:

District	*area (sq km)*	*pop(1981)*
East Lothian	713	80,666
Edinburgh City	261	436,936
Midlothian	358	82,411
West Lothian	423	138,359

Louang Namtha, prov (*KHowèng*) of N Laos, SE Asia; capital Louang Namtha.

Louangphrabang *loo-ang'pra-bang*, LUANG PRABANG *loo-ang pre-bang'*, 19 53N 102 10E, pop(1973) 44,244, town in Louangphrabang prov, W Laos, SE Asia; on R Mekong at its limit of navigation; linked by road to Vientiane.

Loubomo *loo-bom'ō*, formerly DOLISIE, 4 09S 12 47E, pop(1980) 30,830, town in Niari prov, SW Congo, W Africa; on the railway between Pointe-Noire and Brazzaville; airfield; economy: timber.

Louga *loo'ga*, region in NW Senegal, W Africa; pop(1976) 417,137; the area of Diourbel and Louga regions combined is 33,547 sq km; capital Louga.

Loughborough *luf'bur-u*, 52 47N 1 11W, pop(1981) 46,122, town in Charnwood dist, Leicestershire, central England; 16 km N of Leicester; formerly noted for its lace; university of technology (1966); railway; economy: clothing, electrical goods, bell founding, pharmaceuticals; monument: war memorial tower, with a chime of 47 bells.

Louisiade Archipelago *loo-i-zi-ahd'*, mountainous island group in Milne Bay prov, Papua New Guinea, SW Pacific, SE of New Guinea; comprises the islands of Tacuta, Rossel, and Misima, plus numerous other small islands and coral reefs; area 1,553 sq km; gold has been worked on Tacuta.

Louisiana *loo-zi-an'a*, state in S United States; bounded W by Texas, N by Arkansas, E by Mississippi, and S by the Gulf of Mexico; the Mississippi river flows S forming the upper part of the Mississippi state border, and then flows SE into the Gulf of Mexico; the Red river enters the state in the NW and flows SE to empty into the Mississippi; the R Sabine forms the lower part of the Texas state border and empties into the Gulf of Mexico; the R Pearl forms the lower part of the Louisiana state border, and empties into the Gulf of Mexico; the highest point is Mt Driskill (162 m); the coastal area includes vast areas of marsh, lagoon, and fertile delta lands; further inland are plains and low, rolling hills; rich alluvial soils predominate in this area; over half the land area is forested, supporting a major lumber and paper industry; the favourable climate and fertile soil makes Louisiana highly productive in agriculture; chief products include soybeans, rice, sugar cane, sweet potatoes, cotton, cattle, and dairy; fishing, particularly for shrimps and oysters, is a major industry; the state is a major source of pelts, especially muskrat furs but also mink, coypu, otter, opossum and racoon; the state is 2nd only to Texas in oil and natural gas production, much of which is obtained offshore; there are associated oil refineries and petrochemical plants in cities such as Baton Rouge; Louisiana also leads the nation in salt and sulphur production; manufactures include foods, clay, glass, and transportation equipment; the name originally applied to the entire Mississippi river basin, claimed for France by La Salle in 1682; the first successful settlement within the present state was at New Orleans (1718); the region E of the Mississippi was ceded to the USA in 1783, except for the area known as West Florida; the region W of the Mississippi was sold to the USA by France in 1803 (the Louisiana Purchase); part of this region was established as the Territory of Orleans in 1804, and was admitted to the Union as the state (18th) of Louisiana in 1812; the part of the state E of the Mississippi was acquired in 1813 when the USA occupied West Florida; the state seceded from the Union in 1861 and joined the Confederacy; readmitted to the Union in 1868; the state experienced an economic revolution in the early 1900s when large deposits of oil and natural gas were discovered; also known as the 'Pelican State'; pop(1980) 4,205,900; area 115,755 sq km; capital Baton Rouge; other major cities include New Orleans and Shreveport; the state is divided into 64 parishes:

Parish	*area (sq km)*	*pop(1980)*
Acadia	1,708	56,427
Allen	1,989	21,390
Ascension	780	50,068
Assumption	889	22,084
Avoyelles	2,200	41,393
Beauregard	3,024	29,692
Bienville	2,122	16,387
Bossier	2,197	80,721
Caddo	2,324	252,358
Calcasieu	2,813	167,223
Caldwell	1,407	10,761
Cameron	3,604	9,336
Catahoula	1,903	12,287
Claiborne	1,989	17,095
Concordia	1,864	22,981
De Soto	2,288	25,727
East Baton Rouge	1,191	366,191
East Carroll	1,108	11,772
East Feliciana	1,183	19,015
Evangeline	1,734	33,343
Franklin	1,651	24,141
Grant	1,698	16,703
Iberia	1,531	63,752
Iberville	1,659	32,159
Jackson	1,505	17,321
Jefferson	905	454,952
Jefferson Davis	1,703	32,168
La Salle	1,659	17,004
Lafayette	702	150,017
Lafourche	2,967	82,483
Lincoln	1,227	39,763
Livingston	1,719	58,806
Madison	1,641	15,975
Morehouse	2,098	34,803
Natchitoches	3,286	39,863
Orleans	517	557,515
Ouachita	1,630	139,241
Plaquemines	2,691	26,049
Pointe Coupée	1,472	24,045
Rapides	3,487	135,282
Red River	1,024	10,433
Richland	1,464	22,187
Sabine	2,223	25,280
St Bernard	1,264	64,097
St Charles	744	37,259
St Helena	1,063	9,827
St James	645	21,495
St John the Baptist	554	31,924
St Landry	2,434	84,128
St Martin	1,947	40,214
St Mary	1,594	64,253
St Tammany	2,270	110,869
Tangipahoa	2,036	80,698
Tensas	1,620	8,525
Terrebonne	3,554	94,393
Union	2,298	21,167
Vermilion	3,133	48,458
Vernon	3,463	53,475
Washington	1,758	44,207
Webster	1,565	43,631
West Baton Rouge	504	19,086
West Carroll	936	12,922
West Feliciana	1,056	12,186
Winn	2,478	17,253

Louisville *loo'i-vil*, 38 15N 85 46W, pop(1980) 298,451, county seat of Jefferson county, NW Kentucky, United States; largest city in the state and a port at the Falls of the R Ohio; University of Louisville (1798) is the oldest municipal university in the USA; railway; economy: a major centre for horse breeding; important shipping point for coal; chief products include whisky, cigarettes, machinery, electrical appliances, fabricated metals and foods; monuments: J.B. Speed Art Museum, Kentucky Railway Museum, Kentucky Derby Museum; event: Kentucky Derby (May), at Churchill Downs.

Louny *low'ni*, 50 22N 13 50E, pop(1984) 24,545, town in Severočeský region, Czech Socialist Republic, W Czechoslovakia; on R Ohre; railway; economy: agric, fruit and vegetable trade, metal.

Lourdes *loord*, 43 06N 0 00W, pop(1982) 18,000, town and important site of pilgrimage in Hautes-Pyrénées dept, Midi-Pyrénées, S France; Bernadette Soubirous was led by a vision of the Virgin Mary to the famous healing springs at the Grotte de Massabielle in 1858; monuments: Basilica of the Rosary (1885-89), church of St-Pie-X completed in 1958.

Lousa, Serra de *lo'za*, small mountain range, SE of Coimbra, central Portugal; a SW quartz and schist outlier of the Serra da Estrêla, rising to 1,204 m in the Alto do Trevim.

Louth *lowth*, LUGHBHAIDH (Gael), county in NE Leinster prov, Irish Republic; bounded N by N Ireland and E by Irish Sea; pop(1981) 88,514; area 821 sq km; capital Dundalk.

Louth, 53 22N 0 01W, pop(1981) 13,304, town in East Lindsey dist, Lincolnshire, E central England; 38 km ENE of Lincoln; economy: light engineering, plastics, agricultural machinery.

Louvain, city in Belgium. See Leuven.

Louvière, La *lah loov-yer'*, 50 29N 4 12E, pop(1982) 76,961, manufacturing town in Soignies dist, Hainaut prov, SW Belgium; economy: steel works, wire products.

Lovech or **Lovec** *lo'vech*, okrug (prov) of N central Bulgaria in the N foothills of the Stara Planina (Balkan Mts); area 4,129 sq km; pop(1981) 211,000.

Lovech, 43 08N 24 45E, capital of Lovech okrug (prov), N central Bulgaria; on the R Osam, 32 km S of Pleven; a former Roman settlement and later strategically important to the Turks (15-19th c); railway.

Loveland, 40 24N 105 05W, pop(1980) 30,244, town in Larimer county, N Colorado, United States; 75 km N of

Denver; named after the railway official, W.A.H. Loveland; railway; economy: food processing and industrial centre.

Lowell, 42 38N 71 19W, pop(1980) 92,418, town in Middlesex county, NE Massachusetts, United States; on the R Merrimack, 37 km NW of Boston; formerly a noted centre of textile production; state college (1894); technological institute (1895); the Pawtucket Falls on the R Merrimack are a major source of power; birthplace of James Whistler; railway; economy: plastics, chemicals, electronics.

Lower Austria, federal state of Austria. See Niederösterreich.

Lower Hutt, 41 12S 174 54E, pop(1981) 63,245, city in Wellington, North Island, New Zealand; 10 km NNE of Wellington; railway; economy: meat freezing, engineering, vehicle assembly, textiles, furniture; monuments: Dowse art gallery; Vogel House, the prime minister's residence.

Lower Tunguska, river in the Soviet Union. See Nizhnyaya Tunguska.

Lowestoft *lō'is-toft*, 52 29N 1 45E, pop(1981) 59,875, port town and resort in Waveney dist, Suffolk, E England; on North Sea, 62 km NE of Ipswich; Lowestoft Ness is the most easterly point in England and Lowestoft the most easterly town; railway; economy: transport equipment, fishing and fish processing, radar and electrical equipment.

Lowgar, LOGAR, prov in E Afghanistan; lying S of Kābul; pop(1984e) 234,789; area 4,652 sq km; capital Barakī Barak; crossed by the R Logar.

Loyauté, Îles *loy-ō-tay'* (Fr), LOYALTY ISLANDS *loy'al-ti* (Eng), group of coral islands in the SW Pacific Ocean, 128 km E of New Caledonia, comprising Ouvéa (130 sq km), Lifu (1,150 sq km), Mare (650 sq km), Tiga (12 sq km) and many small islets; they are a dependency of the Territory of New Caledonia; area 1,981 sq km; pop(1976) 14,518; capital We (Lifu I); noted for fine sandy beaches and a vegetation of coconut and sandalwood trees; the chief export is copra.

Lozère *lō-zer*, mountainous dept in Languedoc-Roussillon region of S France, on the S edge of the Central Plateau and the Massif Central; comprises 2 arrond, 25 cantons and 185 communes; pop(1982) 74,294; area 5,167 sq km; rises to 1,567 m at Mt Aigoual on the S border; includes the Monts d'Aubrac (NW), the Monts de la Margeride (N) and the Causse Méjean (S); the landscape is diversified by limestone *causses* deeply cut by the Lot and the Tarn rivers; capital Mende; one of the most sparsely populated areas in France.

Loznica *loz'nit-sa*, 44 31N 19 14E, pop(1981) 84,180, town in W Srbija (Serbia) republic, Yugoslavia; near R Drina; railway; economy: fruit trade, antimony mining.

Luanda *lwan'du*, formerly also LOANDA or SÃO PAULO DE LOANDA (Port), 8 50S 13 15E, pop(1982e) 700,000, seaport capital of Angola, on Bay of Bengo, SW Africa; also capital of prov of same name in NW Angola; on the R Cuanza estuary 530 km SSW of Kinshasa (formerly Leopoldville), Zaire; founded in 1575, the city was the centre of Portuguese administration from 1627; a major slave trading centre with Brazil in 17th and 18th centuries; university (1962); railway; airport; economy: oil refining, export of minerals and agricultural produce; monuments: cathedral, governor's palace, São Miguel fortress.

Luang Prabang, prov and town in Laos. See Louangphrabang.

Luangwa, South and North *loo-ang'gwa*, national parks in Zambia, S central Africa; areas 9,050 sq km and 4,636 sq km respectively; established in 1938 and 1939 respectively; 522 km E of Lusaka; large numbers of elephant plus black rhinoceros, lion, leopard, hyena, zebra, giraffe (including rare Thornicroft's giraffe in the S); diverse antelope species including puku, wildebeest and kudu; Luangwa river is the home of crocodiles and hippopotamus.

Luanshya *lwan'shya*, 13 09S 28 24E, pop(1980) 132,164, mining town in Copperbelt prov, Zambia, S central Africa; 32 km SW of Ndola; large copper mine which began operation in 1931; economy: copper wire and cable manufacture, metal fabrication, clothing, fibreglass, vehicle assembly.

Luapula *loo-e-poo'la*, prov in NW Zambia, S central Africa; pop(1980) 412,789; area 50,567 sq km; L Bangweulu lies on the SE border with Northern prov and L Mweru on the N border with Zaire; the Luapula river (headstream of the Zaire river) flows from L Bangweulu; capital Mansa; chief towns include Kawambwa, Mwendo, Chipili and Kabunda; the 880 sq km Lusenga Plain National Park located in the N was established in 1942.

Lubango *loo-bang'gō*, formerly SÁ DA BANDEIRA (-1978), 14 55S 13 30E, pop(1970) 31,674, capital of Huíla prov, SW Angola, SW Africa; 260 km S of Benguela; originally called Lubango then Sá da Bandeira (Port), reverting to its old name again after independence; railway; airfield.

Lub'bock, 33 35N 101 51W, pop(1980) 173,979, county seat of Lubbock county, NW Texas, United States; in the Llano Estacado, 230 km WNW of Abilene; the city was originally settled in 1879 by Quakers; achieved city status in 1910; university (1957); railway; airfield; economy: trade centre for cotton and grain; nearby is Reese Air Force Base.

Lü'beck, 53 52N 10 40E, pop(1983) 216,100, commercial and manufacturing seaport in E Schleswig-Holstein prov, W Germany; 56 km NE of Hamburg, on R Trave; railway; W Germany's most important Baltic port, handling timber, coal, machinery, meat, salt and other products; economy: machinery, electrical and oxygen equipment, aeronautical and space equipment, steel, structural ironwork, ceramic tiles, foodstuffs, fish canning, merchant, fishing and naval vessels (built and serviced); monuments: twin-towered Holstentor (1477), the emblem of Lübeck; town hall (13-15th-c); St Mary's church (13-14th-c); Holy Ghost hospital (13th-c); cathedral (1173); Lübeck has long been noted for its red wine trade and its marzipan.

Lubiń *woo-been'*, LÜBEN (Ger), 51 23N 16 10E, pop(1983) 70,500, town in Legnica voivodship, W Poland; N of Legnica; the development of the copper industry since 1960 has increased its pop from 5,500; sports centre; railway; economy: copper, stringed instruments (lutes); monuments: 14-16th-c House of Culture, 14th-c tower of former Głogowska Gate.

Lublin *loob-yeen'*, voivodship in E Poland; watered by the Wisła (Vistula), Wieprz and Bystrzyca rivers; pop(1983) 967,000; area 6,792 sq km; capital Lublin; chief towns include Puławy, Świdnik and Kraśnik.

Lublin, 51 18N 22 31E, pop(1983) 320,200, capital of Lublin voivodship, E Poland; on a plateau crossed by the R Bystrzyca; a castle town gaining urban status in 1317; the Act of Union between Poland and Lithuania was signed here in 1569; Poland's first Council of Workers' Delegates was formed here in 1918; Majdanek concentration camp was located near the city during World War II; catholic university (1918); railway; economy: food processing and manufacture of lorries and agricultural machinery; monuments: Kraków Gate, cathedral (16th-c), castle, St Brigittine's convent, Bernardine monastery.

Lubnān, Jabal, MOUNT LEBANON, governorate (*moafazat*) of W central Lebanon; bounded W by the Mediterranean Sea; subdivided into the 6 divisions (*cazas*) of Kesrouâne, Metn, Gaza, Ba'abdā, A'aley, Choûf; capital B'abdā; chief towns Jôunié, Bikfaiya, and Jbail; the land rises in the E towards the Jebel Liban (Mount Lebanon) range.

Lubombo *loo-bōm'bō*, dist in E Swaziland, SE Africa; bounded E by the Lubombo Mts which follow the frontier with Mozambique; chief towns include Big Bend, Siphofaneni and Nokwane; economy: sugar and citrus.

Lubumbashi *loo-boom-ba'shee*, formerly ELISABETHVILLE (-1966), 11 40S 27 28E, pop(1976e) 451,332, capital of Shaba region, SE Zaire, central Africa; on R Lualaba, close to Zambia frontier; founded in 1910; railway;

airport; economy: copper mining and smelting, food processing.

Lucan *loo'kun*, LEAMHCÁN (Gael), 53 22N 6 27W, pop(1981) 11,763, town in Dublin county, Leinster, E Irish Republic; on R Liffey, W of Dublin.

Lucca *look'kah*, prov of Toscana region, N Italy; pop(1981) 385,876; area 1,772 sq km; capital Lucca.

Lucca, 43 50N 10 30E, pop(1981) 91,246, capital town of Lucca prov, Toscana region, N Italy, NE of Pisa; centre of a fertile agricultural region; archbishopric; railway; economy: silk and woollen products, olive oil; monuments: cathedral of San Martino (6th-c), with a cedar crucifix (the Volto Santo) reputed to have been brought miraculously to Lucca in 782; church of San Frediano (said to have been founded in the 6th century by an Irish saint); remains of a Roman amphitheatre; event: Luminara di Santa Croce (13 Sept).

Lucena *loo-thay'na*, 37 27N 4 31W, pop(1981) 29,717, industrial town in Córdoba prov, Andalucia, S Spain; 60 km SE of Córdoba; railway; economy: furniture, chemical products, copper and zinc products, horse breeding.

Lučenec *loot'chen-ets*, 48 20N 19 10E, pop(1984) 27,477, town in Středoslovenský region, S Slovak Socialist Republic, E central Czechoslovakia; SE of Banská Bystrica; railway; economy: tobacco and agriculture trade, magnesite mining, textiles.

Lucerne, town and canton in Switzerland. See Luzern.

Lucerne, lake in Switzerland. See Vierwaldstätter.

Luchow, former name for the capital of Anhui prov, E China. See Hefei.

Lucknow *luk'now*, LAKHNAU, 26 50N 81 00E, pop(1981) 1,007,000, capital of Uttar Pradesh state, N central India; 410 km SE of New Delhi, on the R Gomati at the centre of the plain between the Ganga (Ganges) and the Ghaghara rivers; an important centre of the Mogul Empire during the 16th century, it became capital of the kingdom of Oudh (1775-1856) and later capital of the United Provinces when Agra and Oudh merged in 1877; the British Garrison was besieged for 5 months in Lucknow during the Indian Mutiny (June-Nov 1857) and suffered heavy casualties before relief arrived; the city was the focal point of the 1942-47 movement for an independent Pakistan; university (1921); linked to Kanpur, Shahjahanpur, Gorakhpur, Faizabad and Varanasi by rail; airfield; economy: paper, chemicals and electrical products; monuments: Imamabara Mausoleum (1784) of Asaf-ud-Daula, 4th nawab; several large palaces and 4 royal tombs.

Luda, town in Liaoning prov, NE China. See Dalian.

Lüdenscheid *lü'den-shīt*, 51 13N 7 38E, pop(1983) 73,800, industrial city in Arnsberg dist, Nordrhein-Westfalen (North Rhine-Westphalia) prov, W Germany; 59 km E of Düsseldorf; economy: domestic electric engineering.

Lüderitz *lü'du-rits*, formerly ANGRA PEQUENA, 26 38S 15 10E, seaport in SW Namibia, SW Africa; on Lüderitz Bay, an inlet of the Atlantic Ocean coast, 290 km W of Keetmanshoop; Bartholomew Diaz landed here in 1486; a German merchant named F.A.E. Lüderitz acquired the area in 1883 and was given German protection the following year; taken by South African forces during World War I; railway; economy: fishing (including pilchards, anchovies and mackerel).

Lud'low, 52 22N 2 43W, pop(1981) 8,130, historic market town in Shropshire, W central England; on R Teme, 38 km S of Shrewsbury; developed in the 12th century around a Norman fortress; economy: clothing, agricultural machinery, precision engineering; monuments: 11th-c Ludlow castle, 12-14th-c church of St Lawrence, Reader's House.

Lud'wigsburg, 48 54N 9 12E, pop(1983) 79,000, industrial city in Stuttgart dist, Baden-Württemberg prov, W Germany; W of the R Neckar and 13 km N of Stuttgart; railway; economy: machine tools; monument: palace (1704-1733).

Lud'wigshafen, LUDWIGSHAFEN AM RHEIN, 49 29N 8 27E, pop(1983) 157,400, commercial and manufacturing river port in E Rheinland-Pfalz (Rhineland-Palatinate) prov, W Germany; on W bank of the R Rhine, opposite Mannheim; railway; economy: chemicals, synthetic and industrial resins, plastics, dyestuffs, pharmaceuticals, medicaments, fertilizers, consumer goods, insulating materials, preserving equipment.

Luf'kin, 31 21N 94 44W, pop(1980) 28,562, county seat of Angelina county, E Texas, United States; 185 km NNE of Houston; railway; economy: forest industries, oil-field equipment, engines, steel castings.

Luga *loo'ga*, 35 52N 14 31E, pop(1983e) 5,567, town on the main island of Malta, S of Valletta and Grand Harbour; Malta's main international airport (Luqa) and the St Vincent de Paule hospital are located just outside the town.

Lugano *loo-gah'nō*, 46 01N 8 57E, pop(1980) 27,815, resort town in Ticino canton, S Switzerland; flanked by Monte San Salvatore and Monte Brè, on the N shore of Lago di Lugano (L Lugano); the town lies on the N-S road and rail route over the St Gotthard Pass; the third largest financial centre in Switzerland; economy: clothing, engineering; monuments: town hall (1844), cathedral of St Lawrence (originally Romanesque).

Lugano, Lago di or **Lago Ceresio** *chay-rayz'yo*, lake on the S edge of the Alps, mainly within the Swiss canton of Ticino, the remainder being in the Italian provs of Varese and Como; area 48.7 sq km; max depth 288 m; consists of 3 irregular arms, the SW and NE extremities being Italian; from the W end of the lake the R Tresa drains into Lago Maggiore; the climate is typically Mediterranean; the principal town on the lake is Lugano on the N shore.

Lugo *loo'gō*, mountainous prov in Galicia, NW Spain, with a rocky coastline on the Bay of Biscay; includes the fertile basin of the upper R Minho (Miño); pop(1981) 399,185; area 9,803 sq km; capital Lugo; economy: fishing, electrical equipment, livestock, meat products, vegetables, leather, cheese.

Lugo, LUCUS AUGUSTI (Lat), 43 02N 7 35W, pop(1981) 73,986, capital of Lugo prov, Galicia, NW Spain; on R Minho (Miño), 511 km NW of Madrid; bishopric; railway; hot springs nearby; economy: electrical equipment, leather, trades in cattle and meat, cheese; monuments: town walls and 12th-c cathedral; events: Holy Week; fiestas of St Froilan in Oct.

Lugoj *loo'gozh*, 45 41N 21 57E, pop(1983) 51,763, commercial town in Timiş county, W Romania; on R Timiş; founded in the 15th century on a former Roman site; railway; economy: grain, fruit, livestock trade, distilling, textiles; monuments: monastery, 18th-c Minorite church, Roman fortress.

Luik, city in Belgium. See Liège.

Lule *loo'lay*, river in Norrbotten county, N Sweden; rises in N Norway near Swedish border, SW of Narvik; flows SE through Stora Lulevatten L, passing over falls at Porjus and Harsprånget; discharges into Gulf of Bothnia at Luleå; length 450 km; source of hydroelectric power.

Luleå *loo'lay-o*, 65 35N 22 10E, pop(1982) 66,360, seaport and capital of Norrbotten county, N Sweden; on the Gulf of Bothnia, at the mouth of R Lule älv, 110 km from the Arctic Circle; founded in 1621 by Gustavus Adolphus and moved to present site in 1649; see of a bishop and seat of the regional governor; rail terminus; economy: ironworks; shipment of iron-ore transported from Gällivare and Kiruna; monument: cathedral (1887-93).

Luluabourg, city in W central Zaire. See Kananga.

Lumbini, town and centre of pilgrimage in the W Terai of Nepal, central Asia; 431 km SW of Kathmandu; the birthplace of Buddha; preserved here are the broken Ashokan Pillar, the remains of a monastery and images of Maya Devi (Buddha's mother); the town is being developed with the help of international aid.

Lund *loond*, 55 42N 13 10E, pop(1982) 79,791, ancient city in Malmöhus county, SW Sweden; NE of Malmö; prior to 1658 Lund was intermittently under Danish rule; see of a bishop; educational centre with university (1666) and technical institute (1961); railway; economy: paper, textiles, furniture, printing, sugar; monument: Romanesque cathedral (1080).

Lun'dy, island in the Bristol Channel, off the NW coast of Devon, SW England; 19 km NNW of Hartland Point; noted for its interesting flora and birdlife; there are 2 lighthouses; area 9.6 sq km.

Lune *loon*, river rising NE of Sedbergh in Cumbria, NW England; flows 72 km S and SW to meet Morecambe Bay SW of Lancaster.

Lün'eburg, dist of Niedersachsen (Lower Saxony) prov, W Germany; pop(1983) 1,468,700; area 15,346 sq km; capital Lüneburg.

Lüneburg, 53 15N 10 24E, pop(1983) 61,100, capital city of Lüneburg dist, NE Niedersachsen (Lower Saxony) prov, W Germany; SE of Hamburg, on the navigable R Ilmenau, on the edge of the Elbe lowlands; railway, terminal point of the Harz Heathland Highway and starting point of the Old Salt Road to Lübeck; an inland harbour on the Elbe Branch Canal; economy: chemicals, woodworking, wallpaper manufacture, paper, metalworking; monuments: St John's church (14th-c), town hall (13-18th-c); one of the principal centres of North German brick-built architecture; an old salt-working and Hanseatic town frequently visited as a health resort.

Lünen *lü'nun*, 51 37N 7 31E, pop(1983) 85,300, industrial city in Arnsberg dist, Nordrhein-Westfalen (North Rhine-Westphalia) prov, W Germany; on the R Lippe, 40 km S of Münster; railway; economy: aluminium and copper.

Lungkiang, former name for town in Heilongjiang prov, NE China. See Qiqihar.

Lunsar *loon-sar'*, MARAMPA *ma-ram'pa*, 8 41N 12 32W, pop(1974) 17,000, town in Port Loko dist, Northern prov, Sierra Leone, W Africa; near the R Rokel, 35 km ESE of Port Loko.

Luoyang *lō-yang*, HONAN, 34 47N 112 26E, pop(1984e) 1,023,900, town in Henan prov, N central China; capital of ancient China during the Eastern Zhou dynasty (770-256 BC); railway; economy: trade in wheat, sorghum, corn, sesame, peanuts, cotton; mining equipment, glass, construction equipment, light engineering; monuments: Wangcheng (Royal Town) Park contains 2 Han dynasty tombs in subterranean caves, with wall paintings and bas-relief carvings; Luoyang museum contains archaeological exhibits relating to its period as a dynastic capital; 8 km NE of the city is Baimasi (White Horse) temple, built during the Ming dynasty and restored in the 1950s; the original monastery (built in 75 AD) was one of the first Buddhist temples in China - it is still an active centre for Dhyana Buddhism; 14 km S of Luoyang are the Longmen Caves: there are over 1,300 caves containing 2,100 grottoes and niches, several pagodas and inscriptions and approx 100,000 images and statues of Buddha; carving began here in 494 and continued until the 7th century, marking the high point of Buddhist culture.

Lupeni *loo'payn*, 45 20N 23 10E, pop(1983) 30,603, town in Hunedoara county, W central Romania; on R Jiu in the Transylvanian Alps, 64 km SSE of Deva; railway terminus; economy: coal mining, cellulose.

Lur'gan, AN LORGAIN (Gael), 54 28N 6 20W, pop(1981) 20,991, town in Craigavon dist, Armagh, central Northern Ireland; situated near Lough Neagh, 30 km WSW of Belfast; railway; economy: linen manufacturing, engineering.

Lusaka *loo-sa'ka*, 15 26S 28 20E, pop(1980) 538,469, capital of Zambia; 370 km NE of Livingstone and the Victoria Falls; originally a railway town, Lusaka replaced Livingstone as capital of former Northern Rhodesia in 1935; university (1965); railway; airport (24 km NE); economy: banking, administration, cement, chemicals, insecticides, clothing, metal products, plastic products, refined sugar products; monuments: Anglican cathedral (1957); geological survey museum with exhibits from the copper industry; national archives; Livingstone museum; Munda Wanga Gardens (including over 300 flower species) and Zoo.

Lushnjë *loosh'nye*, prov of W Albania; area 712 sq km; pop(1980) 110,900; capital Lushnjë.

Lushnjë, 40 56N 19 41E, pop(1975) 21,000, agric centre and capital of Lushnjë prov, W central Albania; 34 km NW of Berat; railway.

Lu-ta, town in Liaoning prov, NE China. See Dalian.

Luton *loo'ten*, 51 53N 0 25W, pop(1981) 164,743, industrial town in Bedfordshire, S central England; 45 km NW of London; railway; airport; economy: engineering, clothing, hats, motor vehicles; 13-15th-c church of St Mary; Luton Hoo (3 km S), within a park laid out by 'Capability' Brown.

Luxembourg *lük-sã-boor'*, prov of SE Belgium; area 4,441 sq km; pop(1982) 222,437; comprises the 5 dists of Arlon, Bastogne, Marche-en-Famenne, Neufchâteau and Virton; capital Arlon; chief towns Bastogne, St Hubert and Bouillon; drained by the Ourthe and Semois rivers; bounded on the E by Luxembourg and on the S by France.

Luxembourg or **Luxemburg** *luk'sem-burg*, official name **Grand Duchy of Luxembourg**, GRAND-DUCHÉ DE LUXEMBOURG *lük-sã-boor'* (Fr), GROSS-HERZOGTUM LUXEMBURG (Ger), GROUSHERZOGDEM LËTZEBUERG (Letzeburgish), an independent, constitutional monarchy, bounded E by Germany (135 km), W by Belgium (148 km), and S by France (73 km); area 2,586 sq km; timezone GMT +1; capital Luxembourg; chief towns Esch-sur-Alzette, Dudelange and Differdange; total pop(1981) 364,606, situated as it is at the crossroads of the French and German civilizations, Luxembourg has used the languages of its two largest neighbours since the Middle Ages; education is in both French and German although the spoken tongue is the Luxembourg or Letzeburgish dialect of Moselle Frankish origin; German is the language of the press, French the language of the civil service, the law and parliament; descended from the Moselle Franks, 97% of the pop is Roman Catholic; 25% of the pop is foreign; French francs are the accepted currency; national holiday 23 June; membership of Benelux Customs Union, Belgium-Luxembourg Economic Union, EEC, EIB, EMS, FAO, GATT, IAEA, IBRD, ICAO, IDA, IEA, IFAD, IFC, ILO, IMF, INTELSAT, IOOC, IPU, ITU, NATO, OECD, UN, UNESCO, UPU, WEU, WHO, WIPO, WMO.

Physical description. Luxembourg is divided into the two natural regions of Ösling in the N, covering 32% of the territory and Gutland in the S, covering 68%; Ösling is a continuation of the Belgian Ardennes consisting of naturally infertile, wooded, hilly land with an average height of 450 m above sea level; it largely comprises Lower Devonian schistose or schisto-sandstone with no limestone or phosphorus; a continuation of the French Lorraine plateau, the more fertile Gutland is twice as large and more recent in geological terms; it consists largely of Triassic and Jurassic limestone from which are derived loam or sandy soils; in the SW there is a narrow strip of dogger iron; Gutland is less hilly than Ösling with an average height above sea level of 250 m; the country's water resources have been greatly developed since the war, by canalization of the R Moselle and by the construction of hydroelectric dams on the R Our and of water reservoirs on the upper R Sûre; part of the 72,500 ha German-Luxembourg Nature Park is located in the NE.

Climate. The S of the country is drier and sunnier than the N but winters can be severe; its inland position and the shelter of the Ardennes excludes the milder influence of the sea; in the sheltered Moselle valley of the SE, summers and autumns are warm enough for vines to be cultivated.

History, government and constitution. In 1815, after 400 years of domination by various European powers, Luxembourg was made a Grand Duchy by the Congress of Vienna; it was granted political autonomy in 1838 under King William I of the Netherlands, who was also Grand Duke of Luxembourg; by the Treaty of London in 1867, Luxembourg was recognized as a neutral indepen-

dent state; on becoming a member of NATO in 1949 neutrality was abandoned; the Constitution of 1868 established a hereditary monarchy with a Grand Duke (House of Nassau) as head of state; Parliament has a Chamber of Deputies with 59 members elected every 5 years and a State Council with 21 members appointed for life by the Grand Duke who also appoints the govern ment and its head, the Minister of State.

Industry. Twenty-five per cent of national income in 1983 was accounted for by the iron and steel industries based on the iron ore of the SW; also important are food processing, chemicals, tyres, metal products and engi neering; the principal exports are iron and steel products; the principal imports are coal and consumer goods; most of its trade is with W Germany, Belgium, France and other EEC countries.

Agriculture and forestry. Agriculture is largely based on mixed farming, dairy farming and vine-growing; farmland covers 50% of Luxembourg's total area; 44% of farmland is arable, 55% grazing; total cultivated land (1983) 1,274.22 sq km; small or medium-sized holdings predominate (average 0.32 sq km); total forest land (1983) 821 sq km.

Administrative divisions. Luxembourg is divided into 3 districts (Luxembourg, Diekirch and Grevenmacher) and 12 cantons as follows:

Canton	*area (sq km)*	*pop(1981)*
Luxembourg		
Luxembourg	238	114,228
Esch-sur-Alzette	243	114,474
Capellen	199	27,159
Mersch	224	16,546

contd

Canton	*area (sq km)*	*pop(1981)*
Diekirch		
Diekirch	239	21,873
Redange	268	10,271
Wiltz	294	8,997
Vianden	54	2,642
Clervaux	302	9,580
Grevenmacher		
Grevenmacher	211	16,393
Remich	128	11,790
Echternach	186	10,653

The country is also divided into 4 parliamentary constituencies, the number of members being proportional to population.

Luxembourg, S dist of the Grand Duchy of Luxembourg, comprising the cantons of Luxembourg, Esch-sur-Alzette, Capellen and Mersch; pop(1981) 272,407; area 904 sq km.

Luxembourg, canton in central Luxembourg dist, S Luxembourg; area 238 sq km; pop(1981) 114,228; pop excluding Luxembourg city 35,304 (Luxembourg-Camp).

Luxembourg, 49 37N 6 08E, pop(1981) 78,924, capital of the Grand Duchy of Luxembourg and of the dist and canton of Luxembourg, on the Alzette and Petrusse rivers; residence of the Grand Duke of Luxembourg and seat of government; also here are the Court of Justice of the European Communities, the General Secretariat of the European Parliament, the Consultative Committee, the European Investment Bank, the European Monetary Fund and the Coal and Steel Union; General G. Patton is buried at Hamm 5 km from the city; Luxembourg was originally built on an impregnable, defensive location as a fortress controlling the route between France and Germany; its fortifications were destroyed in 1866; the city is divided into 24 districts; airport (6 km from the city); railway; economy: steel, chemicals, textiles, food processing; monument: Musée de l'État with the 8th-c Echternach stone, the oldest altar crown ever found; events: Emais'chen traditional festival on Easter Monday; international trade fair for 9 days in late May; 23 June (National Day); Schobermesse amusement fair and market in late Aug; pilgrimages and processions to the statue of the Virgin in the cathedral after Christmas, Easter and Whitsun.

Luxor *luk'sor*, EL UQSOR, AL-UQSUR (Arab), 25 41N 32 24E, winter resort town in Qena governorate, E central Egypt; on the E bank of the R Nile, 50 km SSW of Qena and 676 km S of Cairo; Homer's 'city of a hundred gates'; known as Thebes to the Greeks and then Luxor ('the palaces') to the Arabs; monuments: numerous tombs of the pharaohs in the Valley of the Kings; temples include the Theban ruins and the temple of Luxor (built by Amenhotep III of the 18th Pharaonic dynasty); one of the obelisks was removed to the Place de la Concorde in Paris (France).

Luzern *loo-tsern'*, LUCERNE *loo-surn'* (Eng), canton in central Switzerland; pop(1980) 296,159; area 1,494 sq km; capital Luzern; joined the Swiss Confederacy in 1332.

Luzern, 47 03N 8 18E, pop(1980) 63,278, resort capital of Luzern canton, central Switzerland; on the W shore of Vierwaldstätter See (Lake of Lucerne), where it narrows to become the R Reuss, 40 km SSW of Zürich; developed as a trade centre on the St Gotthard route; railway junction; lake steamers; economy: engineering; monuments: Thorvaldsen's Lion Monument to the Swiss Guards; the wood-roofed footbridge (Kapellbrücke) decorated with 120 wooden paintings (early 16th-c) of the history of the town; 17th-c town hall; events: Luzern Music Festival (Aug), numerous folk festivals and a carnival in winter.

Luzon *loo-zahn'*, largest island of the Philippines; bounded W by the South China Sea, E by the Philippine Sea, N by the Luzon Strait; area 108,130 sq km; forms an irregular shape with many bays and offshore islets; the Cordillera Central rises to 2,929 m in the NW at Mt Puog; the Sierra Madre rises in the NE; Laguna de Bay, SE of Manila is the largest lake; chief city and capital of the Philippines, Manila, is on Luzon I.

L'vov *li-vof'*, LWOW (Pol), LEMBERG (Ger), LWIW (Ukr), 49 50N 24 00E, pop(1983) 711,000, capital city of L'vovskaya oblast, Ukrainskaya SSR, Soviet Union; close to the Polish border, near the R Poltva, a tributary of the R Bug; founded in 1256; became an important centre on the Black Sea-Baltic trade route; Ivan Franko University (1661); airfield; railway junction; economy: oil refining, machine building, heavy engineering, clothing, knitwear, pottery, footwear; monuments: Baroque St Yuri's Uniate cathedral; Church of the Assumption (1596-1629).

Lwow, city in W Soviet Union. See L'vov.

Lyallpur, Pakistan. See Faisalabad.

Lyme Bay *līm*, inlet of the English Channel off the S coast of Dorset and Devon, SW England; Sidmouth and Lyme Regis are the chief coastal towns.

Lymington *lim'-*, 50 46N 1 33W, pop(1981) 11,955, resort town in New Forest dist, Hampshire, S England; 25 km E of Bournemouth; recreational sailing centre; railway; ferries to Isle of Wight; economy: transport equipment.

Lynchburg, 37 25N 79 09W, pop(1980) 66,743, independent city, S central Virginia, United States; on the R James, 70 km E of Roanoke; railway; economy: textiles and electrical equipment.

Lynn, formerly SAUGUS (-1637), 42 28N 70 57W, pop(1980) 78,471, city in Essex county, NE Massachusetts, United States; on Massachusetts Bay, 16 km NE of Boston; established in 1629, achieving city status in 1850; formerly a major centre of footwear production; railway; economy: electrical goods.

Lynwood, 33 56N 118 13W, pop(1980) 48,548, city in Los Angeles county, SW California, United States; residential city 14 km S of Los Angeles.

Lyon *lee-õ*, LYONS *lī'onz* (Eng), LUGDUNUM (anc), 45 46N 4 50E, pop(1982) 418,476, manufacturing and commercial capital of Rhône dept, Rhône-Alpes region, S central France; at the confluence of the Rhône and Saône rivers, 93 km NW of Grenoble; 3rd largest city in France and principal centre of the French textile industry, particularly silk production; the heart of the city is on the narrow peninsula, no more than 600 m across, that lies between the 2 rivers; nearly 2 dozen bridges, most of them modern, link the peninsula with the opposite banks; the important walled city of Lugdunum occupying the strategic Fourvière hilltop site was the Roman capital of Gaul; Lyon guarded the vital river junction and was the centre of a network of military highways radiating to all parts of the country; much of its 20th century development was due to the energy of the famous Radical leader Édouard Herriot, mayor of the city from 1905 to 1955; there is an international exhibition hall, Eurexpo, with 85,000 sq m of space; archbishopric; university (1896); Catholic university (1875); Olympic swimming pool and artificial ski piste; road and rail junction; Lyon-Satolas airport (opened in 1975); economy: pharmaceuticals, electro-domestic products, tinned milk, electrical equipment for cars and aeroplanes, industrial fans and blowers, armaments, nuclear equipment, chemicals, metallurgy, heavy vehicle manufacturing; monuments: 17th-c Palais St-Pierre, a former Benedictine nunnery for noble ladies, now housing the Musée des Beaux-Arts; church of St-Nizier, a former cathedral of Lyon, rebuilt in the 15th century in Gothic style, with a beautiful Renaissance doorway and a 6th-c crypt); Hôtel de Ville, erected in 1646-72 and restored in 1674 after a fire; 12-15th-c cathedral of St-Jean, badly damaged in the Revolution but still impressive with its 4 square towers, beautiful Romanesque choir and 13th-c stained-giass; 19th-c basilica of Notre-Dame-de-Fourvière (1872-96) situated on the hill of Fourvière, 130 m above the R Saône.

Lyonnais *lee-on-ay*, former prov of S central France, lying W of Lyon; now occupies most of the depts of Rhône and Loire and parts of the dists of Beaujolais and Forez; the Monts du Lyonnais link the Cévennes and the Beaujolais ranges.

Lys *lees*, LEIE (Flem), river in N France and Belgium, rising in the Artois Hills near Fruges in Pas-de-Calais dept, France; flows NE past Aire along the Franco-Belgian border then into Belgium to meet the R Schelde at Ghent; length 214 km; tributary R Deule.

Lytham St Anne's *liTH'em*, 53 45N 3 01W, pop(1981) 40,136, resort town in Blackpool urban area and Fylde dist, Lancashire, NW England; on the R Ribble estuary, 20 km W of Preston; railway; championship golf course; economy: engineering.

M

Ma'alla *mu-a'lu*, LITTLE ADEN (Eng), 12 50N 44 08E, pop(1981e) 44,625, suburb of Aden, Aden governorate, South Yemen; on the N shore of Aden peninsula.

Ma'ān *ma-an'*, governorate (*muhafaza*) of the East Bank, S Jordan, bounded W by the Wadi 'Araba and Israel, SW by the Gulf of 'Aqaba, and S and E by Saudi Arabia; capital Ma'ān; chief port 'Aqaba; traversed N-S by the Hejaz railway.

Ma'ān, 30 11N 35 43E, capital town of Ma'ān governorate, East Bank, S central Jordan; 160 km S of Amman; economic centre of S Jordan; alt 1,066 m; airfield; on the Hejaz railway; economy: sheet glass.

Maarianhamina *mar'yan-ha-een'a*, MARIEHAMN *ma-ree'u-ha'mun* (Swed), 60 05N 19 55E, pop(1982) 9,733, resort, seaport and capital of the Ahvenanmaa (Åland) island group which is an admin dist of Finland in the Gulf of Bothnia; the town is located on the S coast of the main island of Ahvenanmaa; established in 1861.

Maaseik *mah'zīk*, dist of Limburg prov, NE Belgium; area 884 sq km; pop(1982) 189,332.

Maastricht *mahs'triKHt*, TRAIECLUM AD MOSAM or TRAIECTUM TUNGORUM (anc), 50 51N 5 42E, pop(1984e) 157,329, capital city of Limburg prov, S Netherlands, on the R Maas, near the Belgian border; the commercial hub of a wider area extending beyond the national boundary well into Belgium; noted for its vegetable and butter markets; one of Maastricht's great tourist attractions is the huge St Pietersburg underground gallery, a network of passages with wall paintings and pillars autographed in charcoal by thousands of people, including the Duke of Alva, Napoleon and Sir Walter Scott; railway junction; economy: paper, packaging, leatherwork, brewing, printing, ceramics, glass, tourism, electricity generation; monuments: 6th-c church of St Servatius, the oldest in the Netherlands; Romanesque basilica (10-11th c).

McAllen, 26 12N 98 14W, pop(1980) 66,281, city in Hidalgo county, S Texas, United States; a port on the Rio Grande river, 80 km W of Brownsville; railway; economy: packing and processing centre for citrus fruit, vegetables and other agricultural products of the area; oil refining, chemicals.

Macapá *ma-ka-pa'*, 0 04N 50 32W, pop(1980) 115,000, capital of Amapá terr, Norte region, N Brazil; on a branch of the Amazon, 320 km NW of Belém; airfield; economy: grain and livestock trade.

Macará *ma-ka-ra'*, 4 25S 79 57W, pop(1982) 10,510, town in Loja prov, SW Ecuador; on the border with Peru.

Macarena, Sierra de la *ma-ka-ray'na*, E outlier of the Cordillera Oriental in Meta dept, S central Colombia, South America; rises to 2,134 m S of Bogotá; the 5,014 sq km range was designated a national park in 1948, exclusively for the scientific study of its unique vegetation.

Macas *ma'kas*, 2 22S 78 8W, pop(1982) 5,015, capital of Morona Santiago prov, SE Ecuador; at 1,200 m on the lower E slopes of the Andes in the tropical *Oriente*; Sangay volcano rises to the NW; economy: the area is now being developed for beef production.

Macau or **Macao** *ma-ka'oo*, overseas prov of Portugal consisting of a flat, maritime tropical peninsula in SE China and the nearby islands of Taipa and Colôane; situated on the Zhujiang river (Pearl River) delta 64 km W of Hong Kong; a Chinese territory under Portuguese administration; area 16 sq km; pop(1981) 261,680; capital Nome de Deus de Macau; about 90% of the land is under urban development; 99% of the Macauese pop is Chinese; Portuguese is the official language but Cantonese is generally spoken; Buddhism and Roman Catholicism are the main religions; the currency is the pataca of

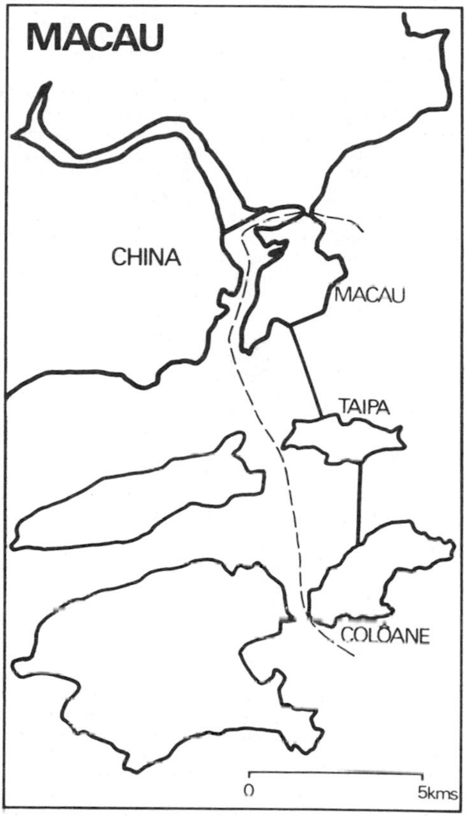

100 avos (tied to the Hong Kong dollar); ferry links with Hong Kong; Macau is governed by an 18-member legislative assembly established in 1974; a governor assisted by 5 secretaries is nominated by the president of Portugal; economy: textiles, electronics, toys, tourism, gambling and fishing; major trade partners include the USA, W Germany, France and Hong Kong; most of Macau's water and food is imported from China.

Macau, NOME DE DEUS DE MACAU, formerly AMACAO, free port capital of the Portuguese overseas prov of Macau, E Asia; on SE China peninsula; founded in 1557 and declared a city in 1586 when it was given the same status as the city of Evora in Portugal; originally developed by the Portuguese in the early 16th century as a trading post en route to China and Japan; in 1557 the Chinese agreed to Portuguese settlement of Macau but not to Portuguese sovereignty; a right of perpetual occupation was recognized by the Manchu government in 1887 (Protocol of Lisbon); grand prix racing; airport at Kai Tak; monuments: fortresses of Barra, Mong-ha and Monte; Jaialai palace.

Macclesfield *mak'elz-feeld*, 53 16N 2 07W, pop(1981) 48,071, town in Macclesfield dist, Cheshire, NW central England; on the R Bollin, 17 km S of Stockport; railway; economy: silk, textiles, textile machinery, paper, plastics, pharmaceuticals.

Macdhui, Ben *muk-doo'ee*, BEN MUICH-DHUI (Gael), 57 04N 3 40W, 2nd highest mountain in Britain; in the Cairngorm Mts, SW Grampian region, N central Scotland, 29 km WNW of Braemar; height 1,309 m.

MacDonnell Ranges *mak-don'el*, mountain ranges in S Northern Territory, central Australia; extending 320 km W from Alice Springs and rising to 1,524 m at Mount Liebig, highest point in the state.

Macedonia, region of Greece. See Makedhonia.

Macedonia, republic in Yugoslavia. See Makedonija.

Maceió *ma-say-ō'*, 9 34S 35 37W, pop(1980) 375,771, port capital of Alagoas state, Nordeste region, NE Brazil; on the Atlantic coast, S of Recife; the port is located in the Jaraguá dist; the residential area is in the Farol dist, about 1 km from the sea; 2 km S of the town is the lagoon, Lagoa do Mundau; the beaches nearby are considered to be some of the finest in Brazil; university (1961); railway; economy: commerce, metal industry, sugar and tobacco trade; monuments: recently restored cathedral, government palace and church of Bom Jesus dos Mártiresare.

Macerata *ma-chay-rah'ta*, prov of Marche region, central Italy; pop(1981) 292,932; area 2,774 sq km; capital Macerata.

Macerata, 43 18N 13 27E, pop(1981) 43,782, capital town of Macerata prov, Marche region, E central Italy; 48 km S of Ancona, between the rivers Chiento and Potenza; founded in the 12th century; university (1290); railway.

Macgillycuddy's Reeks *mak-gi-li-kud-eez reeks'*, mountain range in Kerry county, Munster, SW Irish Republic, rising to 1,041 m at Carrantuohill, the highest peak in the Irish Republic.

Machakos *mach-a'kōs*, 1 32S 27 16E, pop(1979e) 80,000, pop(1984e) 118,000, capital of Eastern prov, Kenya, E Africa; 65 km SE of Nairobi; former headquarters of British East Africa, but because it was bypassed by the railway the capital was transferred to Nairobi.

Machala *ma-cha'la*, 3 20S 79 57W, pop(1982) 105,521, capital of El Oro prov, SW Ecuador; situated near the Golfo de Guayaquil in a prosperous irrigated banana-growing area; university (1969); railway; economy: printing, drinks, tobacco, bananas, coffee, cacao, timber products, minerals; event: banana fair in Sept.

Machida *ma-chee'da*, 35 33N 139 28E, pop(1980) 295,405, city in Tōkyo prefecture, Kanto region, E Honshū island, Japan; in SW Tōkyo; university; railway.

Machinga *ma'ching-ga*, dist in Southern region, Malawi, SE Africa; area 5,968 sq km; pop(1977) 341,836.

Machu Picchu *ma'choo peek'choo*, ruined Inca city in Cuzco dept, S central Peru; situated on the saddle of a high mountain with terraced slopes falling away to the Río Urubamba below; overlooked by Huayna Picchu mountain; comparatively well preserved because it was never found by the Spaniards; discovered in 1911 by Hiram Bingham, then explored by an archaeological expedition from Yale; the ruins consist of staircases, temples, terraces, palaces, towers, fountains and a famous sundial; below the ruins is the Museo de Sitio museum; near the Río Urubamba is the Temple of the Moon; the site is approached from Cuzco by rail.

McIlwaine, Lake *mak'il-wayn*, 17 50S 30 55E, lake in Mashonaland East prov, Zimbabwe, S Africa; area 57 sq km; located 35 km SW of Harare; created by the damming of the Hunyani river in 1952 and named after Sir Robert McIlwaine, first chairman of the country's Natural Resources Board; the lake and its N shore are a major recreational area; the S shore is a game park protecting zebra, giraffe and a variety of antelope; profuse birdlife with over 200 species being recorded in a single day; lake fauna includes tiger fish, bream and barbel; at scattered locations in the granite hills around the park are ancient rock paintings; Harare's main water supply.

Macina *ma-see'na*, depression in central Mali, W Africa; a large lacustrine region stretching c.480 km SW-NE from Ségou to Tombouctou and up to 95 km wide; includes a network of R Niger channels, swamps and lakes including L Debó in the SW and L Faguibine in NE; a dam at Sansanding is linked to irrigation projects.

Mackay, 21 10S 149 10E, pop(1981) 35,361, seaport in Mackay stat div, Queensland, Australia; on the E coast, NNW of Rockhampton; railway; airfield; economy: coal, coral, sugar, cattle; the Sugar Bulk Terminal in Mackay harbour is the largest in the world; W of the town is the Eungella National Park.

Mackay, Lake, salt lake in W central Australia; on Western Australia and Northern Territory frontier, 515 km WNW of Alice Springs; 105 km long by 64 km wide.

Mckeesport, 40 21N 79 52W, pop(1980) 31,012, town in Allegheny county, W Pennsylvania, United States; at the confluence of the Monongahela and Youghiogheny rivers, 16 km SE of Pittsburgh; railway.

Mackenzie, district of W Northwest Territories, Canada; bounded W by Yukon terr, S by British Columbia, Alberta and Saskatchewan provs, E by Keewatin dist and N by the Beaufort Sea, Amundsen Gulf, Dolphin and Union straits, Coronation Gulf, Dease Strait and Queen Maud Gulf; on the Yukon frontier the Mackenzie Mts rise to 2,972 m at Mt Keele; the Mackenzie river separates the mountainous W from the low, lake-studded land to the E; the Great Bear Lake and the Great Slave Lake are the largest lakes in the Northwest Territories; the N and NE corners of Mackenzie dist comprise tundra beyond the N limit of tree growth; in the SW, situated along the South Nahanni river, is the Nahanni National Park (area 4,765 sq km, established in 1972); area 1,364,620 sq km of which 88,746 are freshwater; chief towns include Yellowknife, Coppermine, Inuvik and Fort Franklin.

Mackenzie, mountain range in E Yukon terr and W Mackenzie dist, Northwest Territories, NW Canada; N range of the Rocky Mts; extends approx 800 km SE-NW between the British Columbia border and the Peel river valley; forms S part of Yukon-Northwest Territories border; rises to 2,972 m in Keele Peak on the prov border; the range acts as the watershed for the tributaries of the Mackenzie and Yukon rivers; in the S of the Mackenzie Mts is the Nahanni nature park.

Mackenzie, river in W Mackenzie dist, Northwest Territories, NW Canada; issues from the W end of the Great Slave Lake; flows WNW to Fort Simpson where it is joined by the Liard river, then NW between the Franklin Mts (E) and the Mackenzie Mts (W) past Wrigley, Fort Norman, Norman Wells, Fort Good Hope and Arctic Red River to enter the Beaufort Sea through a 110-130 km-wide delta near the boundary with Yukon terr; the W channel of the delta flows NNW, past Aklavik; the E channel flows N, past Inuvik; length 4,241 km; the river is navigable from mid-June to mid-Oct; major tributaries include the Keele, Great Bear, Hare Indian and Arctic Red rivers; the Mackenzie river basin extends into Alberta, British Columbia and Saskatchewan; major headstreams include the Liard, Peace, Athabasca, Slave and Hay rivers.

McKinley, Mount, 63 04N 151 00W, mountain in S central Alaska, United States; situated 209 km NNW of Anchorage in Denali National Park and Preserve (area 24,413 sq km, established in 1917); highest peak in the USA and in North America; consists of two peaks, the highest being 6,194 m, the other 5,934 m; the Indian name for the mountain was Denali.

McKinley Sea, WANDEL SEA, Arctic sea, lying N of NE Greenland; Independence, Hagen and Danmark are the main coastal fjords.

Mâcon *ma-kõ*, MATISCO (anc), 46 19N 4 50E, pop(1982) 39,866, manufacturing city and capital of Saône-et-Loire dept, Bourgogne region, central France; on the W bank of the R Saône, 35 km WNW of Bourg; episcopal see from the 6th century until the Revolution; commercial centre of the Mâconnais, the wine area which stretches N and W to Tournus and Cluny and beyond; road and rail junction; economy: wine, brandy, textiles, agricultural machinery, casks; monuments: remains of a 12th-c cathedral, almost entirely destroyed at the time of the

Revolution; birthplace of the French poet and novelist Lamartine, 1790; in the municipal museum are the objects excavated at the prehistoric site of Solutre, 8 km W of Mâcon, as well as paintings, drawings and engravings by notable French artists.

Macon *māk'on*, 32 51N 83 38W, pop(1980) 116,896, county seat of Bibb county, central Georgia, United States; on the R Ocmulgee, 123 km SSE of Atlanta; university (1833); railway; economy: processing and shipping centre for large farming area; manufactures include textiles, clay products, tile brick and explosives.

Madagas'car, official name Democratic Republic of Madagascar, REPOBLIKA DEMOKRATIKA N'I MADAGASKAR, island republic in the Indian Ocean, separated from E Africa by the Mozambique Channel; the world's 4th largest island; length (N-S) 1,580 km; area 592,800 sq km; timezone GMT +3; pop(1983) 9,472,000; capital Antananarivo; chief towns Toamasina, Mahajanga, Fianarantsoa, Antseranana and Toliara; main ethnic groups include 18 Malagasy tribes, and small numbers of French, Chinese, Indians, Pakistanis and Comorans; Malagasy, of Malayo-Polynesian origin, is the official language but French is also widely spoken; about 40% of the pop are Christian, 7% Muslim, the remainder holding indigenous beliefs largely based around ancestor worship; national holiday 26 June; the currency is the Malagasy franc of 100 centimes; membership of AfDB, EAMA, FAO, G-77, GATT, IAEA, IBRD, ICAO, ICO, IDA, IFAD, IFC, ILO, IMF, IMO, INTELSAT, IRC, ISO, ITU, NAM, OAU, OCAM, UN, UNESCO, UPU, WFTU, WHO, WMO, WTO.

Physical description. Madagascar is dissected N-S by a ridge of mountains commencing at the semi-desert Isalo and Horombe plateaus in the S. The ridge climbs in a series of crests and domes to a height of 2,658 m at Boby in the Andringitra massif and then on to the Ankaratra range, where it reaches 2,643 m at Tsiajajavona before extending to the Massif du Tsarantanana which rises to 2,876 m at Maromokotra. To the E is a line of cliffs about 50 km wide, dropping down to a coastal plain through tropical forest. To the W a more gentle terraced descent leads down through savannah to a coastline which is heavily indented in the N.

Climate. In the highlands the climate is temperate with warm, rainy weather from Nov to April and cooler temperatures from May to Oct. There the annual rainfall varies between 1,000 and 1,500 mm. The coastal region is tropical with an annual rainfall at Toamasina on the wetter E coast of 3,500 mm falling on 240 days of the year. The island is occasionally exposed to rains and high wind associated with tropical storms from the E.

History, government and constitution. The French, who had established trading posts in Madagascar during the late 18th century, claimed the island as a protectorate in 1885 and eventually removed the Merina monarchy by force in 1895-96. The Malagasy Republic was set up in 1958 as an autonomous overseas French territory, and in 1959 a new constitution paved the way for full independence in 1960. In 1977 the country became known officially as Madagascar. Executive power is held by a president who is elected for 7 years. The president appoints a Council of Ministers and is guided by a 20-member Supreme Revolutionary Council. The legislature comprises a 137-member National Assembly elected every 5 years.

Economy. The main industries of Madagascar include food processing, tanning, cement, soap, glassware, paper, textiles, refined petroleum products and the mining of graphite, chrome, coal, bauxite, ilmenite and semi-precious stones. The agricultural economy is largely based around the production of rice, coffee, sugar, vanilla, cloves, cotton, peanuts, sisal and tobacco. Major trading partners include the USA, France and other EEC member countries.

Administrative divisions. Madagascar is divided into 6 provinces:

Province	*area (sq km)*	*pop(1978)*
Antananarivo	57,775	2,322,019
Antsiranana	42,725	620,228
Fianarantsoa	100,326	1,908,465
Mahajanga	152,165	857,610
Toamasina	72,212	1,254,639
Toliara	162,283	1,084,083

The provs are further divided into 18 prefectures, 92 sub-prefectures and 11,000 communes (*fokontany*).

Madang', province in Papua New Guinea; on the E coast of the mainland; includes Long Island and the islands of Karkar, Bagabag, Manam in the Solomon Sea; area 29,000 sq km; pop(1980) 209,656; capital Madang.

Madaoua *ma-da'wa*, 14 02N 5 59E, town in Tahoua dept, SW central Niger, W Africa; situated between Birni n'Konni and Maradi; economy: textiles.

Madaripur *ma-da'ree-poor*, 23 09N 90 11E, pop(1981) 63,917, town in Madaripur dist, Faridpur, S Bangladesh; W of R Tetulia, on the Ganges delta.

Madeira *ma-day'ra*, river in NW Brazil; longest tributary of the Amazon, and third longest river in South America (after the Amazonas and the Plata-Paraná); formed by the Beni and Mamoré rivers at Villa Bella, N Bolivia; flows N along the Bolivia-Brazil border for approx 95 km; then flows NE past Pôrto Velho, through Rondônia and Amazonas states, Brazil; joins the Amazon 152 km E of Manaus; a minor distributary enters the Amazon 160 km ENE, forming a large marshy island; length with the Mamoré is over 3,200 km; the river is navigable from Pôrto Velho.

Madeira or **Ilha de Madeira**, *ma-dee'ra* (Eng) ('island of timber'), 32 45N 17 00W, main island of archipelago in E Atlantic Ocean off the coast of N Africa, 535 nautical miles SW of Lisbon, Funchal dist of Portuguese autonomous region; group consists of Madeira, Ilha do Porto Santo, Ilhas Desertas and Ilhas Selvagens (5 uninhabited islets); capital Funchal; highest point is the Pico Ruivo de Santana (1,861 m), in the W is the Paul da Serra plateau, in the E the smaller plateau of Santo Antonio da Serra; economy: sugar cane, fruit, farming, fishing, wine, embroidery and tourism; occupied by Portuguese since 16th century.

Mädelegabel *may'dul-ug-ah-bul*, 47 18N 10 12E, mountain in SW Bayern (Bavaria) prov, W Germany; highest peak of the Allgäuer Alpen (Allgäu Alps), on Austro-German border 11 km S of Obersdorf; height 2,645 m.

Madero, Ciudad *syoo-THaTH' mah-THay'rō*, 22 19N 97 50W, pop(1980) 132,444, town in Tamaulipas state, E Mexico; on the Gulf of Mexico, just N of Tampico; railway.

Madhya Pradesh *mu'dyu pru-daysh'*, state in central India; pop(1981) 52,131,717; area 442,841 sq km; bounded N by Rajasthan and Uttar Pradesh states, W by Gujarat state, E by Orissa and Bihar states and S by Andhra Pradesh state; lies between the Deccan and the Ganga (Ganges) plains; crossed by numerous rivers including the Narmada, Mahanadi, Tapi, Son, Sonar and Betwa; major hill ranges within the state are the Maikala, the Satpura, the Bhanrer, the Kaimur and the Maliadeo; the state is the largest in area in India and the 6th largest in population; there are 11 administrative divisions and 45 districts; capital Bhopal; the state is governed by a bicameral legislature comprising a 90-member Upper House (*Vidhan Parishad*) and an elected 320-member Lower House (*Vidhan Sabha*); 80% of the population of Madhya Pradesh is employed in agriculture; 42% of the state is cultivable land, 13% of which is irrigated; the major irrigation schemes are those of the Chambal Valley, Tawa, Barna and Hasdeo Projects; principal agricultural crops include sugar cane, oilseed and cotton; 35% of the state is under forest, a valuable source of best-quality teak, sal, saja and bamboo; 60% of domestic fuel is derived from firewood; economy: steel, electrical engineering, aluminium, paper mills, textiles, machine tools, synthetic fibres and food processing; the state is noted for its handicrafts which include handloom weaving, calico printing, pottery, lacework, zari thread work and leather work; Madhya Pradesh has 35% of India's coal reserves, 30% of its iron ore, 50% of its manganese and 44% of its bauxite; the region was ruled during the 16th and 17th centuries by the Gonds and during the 18th century by the Mahrattas; in 1820 it was occupied by the British; from 1903 to 1950 the state was called Central Provinces and Berar; the state of Madhya Pradesh was formed under the States Reorganization Act of 1956; it comprises the 17 Hindi districts in the former state of that name, the former state of Madhya Bharat (except the Sunel enclave), the former state of Bhopal and Vindhya Pradesh and the Sironj division, an enclave of Rajasthan in Madhya Pradesh.

Madīnah, Al, *mah-dee'nu*, MEDINA, 24 35N 39 52E, pop(1974) 198,200, Islamic holy city in Madīnah prov, W Saudi Arabia; 336 km N of Makkah (Mecca) and approx 192 km from the Red Sea coast; situated in a basin of the coastal plateau, at the head of the Wadi Hamdh; second most important holy city of Islam (after Makkah), containing the tomb of Mohammed; it was the nucleus of the rapidly growing Islamic state until the caliphal residence at Damascus was established in AD 622; there is an important pilgrimage trade, served by the Red Sea port of Yanbu' al Baḩr; after his flight from Makkah, Mohammed sought refuge here; the city is closed to non-Muslims; Islamic university (1961); airfield; monuments: numerous mosques, Islamic monuments; economy: centre of a large date-growing oasis, producing also grapes and other fruit, grain, and clover.

Madison, 43 04N 89 24W, pop(1980) 170,616, capital of state in Dane county, S Wisconsin, United States; on L Mendota and L Monona; state capital since 1836 and a city since 1856; university (1836); railway; airfield; economy: trading and manufacturing centre in agricultural region; manufactures include farm machinery and medical equipment; event: World Dairy Exposition (Oct).

Madison Heights, 42 30N 83 06W, pop(1980) 35,375, town in Oakland county, SE Michigan, United States; suburb 21 km N of Detroit.

Madras *mad-ras'*, 13 08N 80 19E, pop(1981) 4,277,000, capital of Tamil Nadu state, SE India; 1,360 km SW of Calcutta, on the R Cooum where it meets the Coromandel coast of the Bay of Bengal; 4th largest city in India and chief port of the state of Tamil Nadu; Madras was founded by the British in the 17th century around Fort St George which was situated close to a Tamil village known as Madraspatnam; it became the chief English trading station on the E coast; Madras was captured in 1746 by the French, but regained by the English in 1749; the city expanded, gradually absorbing nearby villages which have since given their names to sections of the city; airport; linked to Tiruchchirāppalli, Vellore, Vijayawada and Bangalore by rail; economy: textiles, chemicals, tanning, glass, engineering, jewellery, clothing, trade in leather, wool, cotton, tobacco, mica, magnesite; monuments: Fort St George (1639) houses the offices of the Madras Government Secretariat and the State Legislative Council; the Fort museum records the history of the East India Company; St Mary's church (1680) is believed to be the oldest Anglican church in Asia; on the seafront there are 2 statues, one of Mahatma Gandhi and the other representing 'Triumph of Labour'; temples include the Kapaleeswara, which is built in the classical style of Tamil temples with an entry through a Gopuram gate; the 8th-c temple of Pathasarathy is dedicated to the god Vishnu in his incarnation as Krishna; San Thome cathedral dominates the Portuguese area, known as Mylapore; near the city is the Mount St Thomas, which is the traditional site of martyrdom of the 'doubting' apostle of Jesus Christ; Raj Bhavan is the official residence of the Governor.

Madre de Dios *ma'dray THay dyōs*, dept in SE Peru; low lying region bordered E by Brazil and Bolivia; situated almost entirely in the Amazon basin; drained by the Río Madre de Dios and the Río de las Piedras; pop(1981) 33,007; area 78,402 sq km; capital Puerto Maldonado; in NW is the Manú National Park.

Madrid *mah-THreeTH'*, region and prov in central Spain, situated on the flat central plateau (Meseta) and bounded to the NW by the Sierra Guadarrama; watered by tributaries of the R Tagus including the Henares, Jarama,

Manzanares and Tajuña; its capital, Madrid, is the capital and largest city of Spain; pop(1981) 4,726,987; area 7,995 sq km; economy: livestock and some cereals, vegetables and fruit; industry is based in Madrid, Alcalá de Henares, Alcobendas, Alcorcon, Aranjuez, Colmenar, Coslada, Getafe, Las Rozas, Leganes, Mostoles, Pinto, Pozuleo, San Sebastian de los Reyes, Torrejón, Valdemoro, Villaverde Alto.

Madrid, 40 25N 3 45W, pop(1981) 3,188,297, industrial capital and largest city of Spain and capital of Madrid prov, Castilla-La Mancha, central Spain; on R Manzanares; alt 655 m, the highest capital city in Europe; area 531 sq km; metro; railway; airport; universities (1508 and 1968); archbishopric; seat of the government; for many years a small settlement until the Moors built a fortress here; from time to time in later years it was a royal residence until Philip II made it the capital in 1561 in place of Valladolid; the city was under siege for nearly 3 years during the Civil War; monuments: Plaza Major, a square in the heart of old town was once the scene of bullfights, plays, heretic-burnings and such entertainments; 18th-c Royal Palace, built for Philip V; Prado museum with its world-famous art galleries; archaeological museum housing a collection of Iberian and Classical antiquities; Lazaro Galdiano museum with its collection of enamels and ivories; El Retiro park, once a royal hunting seat; events: Holy Week; fiesta of St Anthony in Jan and pilgrimage of St Isidore in May.

Madriz *ma-drees'*, dept in N Nicaragua, Central America; bounded W by Choluteca dept, Honduras; drained by the Río Coco and its tributaries; pop(1981) 72,408; area 1,375 sq km; capital Somoto.

Madurai *mu-doo-rī'*, 9 55N 78 10E, pop(1981) 904,000, city in Tamil Nadu state, S India; on the R Voigai, 425 km SW of Madras; capital of the Pandyan kingdom and later the Nayak dynasty; between 1743 and 1801 it was under the control of the nawabs of Arcot, thereafter it was occupied by the British; university (1966); airfield; linked to Dindigul and Rajapalaiyam by rail; economy: silk and muslin weaving, woodcarving, brassware, trade in coffee, tea and cardamon; monument: large Dravidian temple complex, built in the 14-17th centuries.

Maebashi *ma-ye-bash'ee*, 36 24N 139 04E, pop(1980) 265,169, capital of Gumma prefecture, Kanto region, central Honshū island, Japan; 96 km NW of Tōkyo; Gumma University (1949); railway; economy: silk.

Maesteg *mī-stayg'*, 51 37N 3 40W, pop(1981) 21,917, town in Ogwr dist, Mid Glamorgan, S Wales; 19 km E of Swansea; railway; economy: coal mining, engineering, car components, cosmetics, clothing.

Ma'fra, 38 55N 9 20W, pop(1981) 7,000, town in Lisboa dist, central Portugal, 50 km NW of Lisboa, famed for its palace-monastery, the largest of its kind in the Iberian peninsula.

Magallanes-La Antártica Chilena *ma-gal-ya'nays la ant ar'tee-ka chee-lay'na*, region of S Chile extending southwards from 48° 40'S; comprises the provs of Ultima Esperanza, Magallanes, Tierra del Fuego and Antártica Chilena; includes numerous channels, islands, glaciers, lakes and forests; Chile lays claim to the slice of Antarctica between 53° and 90°W, and, like Argentina, maintains a number of military bases along the Antártica Peninsula; pop(1984) 116,400; area (continental) 132,033 sq km, (Antarctic) 1,250,000 sq km; total area 1,382,033 sq km; capital Punta Arenas; economy: sheep, cattle, forestry, oil, natural gas, food canning; amongst other national parks are included those of Bernardo O'Higgins and Fernando de Magallanes; just N of the town Puerto Natales is the Cueva de Miladón, a huge cave in which remains of the *Mylodon listai*, a prehistoric giant sloth-like animal, were found; excavation began in 1895, the bones, about 14 of them, were estimated to be c.8,000 years old.

Magaria *ma-ga'ria*, 13 00N 8 59E, town in Zinder dept, SE central Niger, W Africa; 90 km S of Zinder; power plant.

Magburaka *mag-boo-ra'ka*, 8 44N 11 57W, pop(1974) 10,000, capital of Tonkolili dist, Northern prov, Sierra Leone, W Africa; on the R Rokel, 19 km SSE of Makeni.

Magdalena *mag-da-lay'na*, dept in N Colombia, South America; on the Caribbean sea; bounded W by the Río Magdalena and by marshy lowlands; pop(1985) 760,611; area 23,188 sq km; capital Santa Marta.

Magdalena, major river of Colombia, South America; rises in SW Colombia at 2 00N 76 30W in the Cordillera Central, 56 km S of Popayán; flows N 1,610 km to enter the Caribbean 14 km NW of Barranquilla; in its upper course it flows between the Cordilleras Central and Oriental then into the northern lowlands where it is joined by the Río Cauca before reaching the Caribbean in a wide delta; principal tributaries include the Cauca, San Jorge, Bogotá and Sogamoso rivers; navigable for the majority of its course; its fertile valley in the upper and mid course produces coffee, sugar cane, tobacco, cacao and cotton.

Magdeburg *mahk'du-boork*, county in W East Germany; pop(1981) 1,262,291; area 11,526 sq km; capital Magdeburg; the largest farming area in E Germany, producing cereals, sugar beet, potatoes, vegetables, milk, eggs and fatstock; 25% of the county is under forest, mainly in the Harz Mts; the Wernigerode dist is a popular holiday area; industry: heavy engineering, plant construction, potash, chemical engineering, electrical engineering, electronics.

Magdeburg, 52 8N 11 36E, pop(1982) 287,579, river port capital of Magdeburg county, W East Germany; on R Elbe WSW of Berlin, near the W German frontier; a former capital of Saxony, it was an important medieval trading town by virtue of its position at the centre of the N German plain; received a further stimulus in 1938 when the Mittelland Canal was opened, giving access to the Ruhr and Rhine rivers; college of medicine; college of technology (1953); railway; economy: iron and steel, heavy engineering, chemicals; monument: 13-16th-c cathedral.

Maggiore, Lago *ma-jō'ray*, LAKE MAGGIORE (Eng), VERBANUS LACUS (anc), 2nd largest of the N Italian lakes, in Lombardia (E) and Piemonte (W) regions, N Italy; its N end is in the Swiss canton of Ticino; area 212 sq km; length 60 km; width 3-5 km; max depth 372 m; principal tributaries Ticino and Maggia (N), Toce (W); outflow R Ticino (S end); surrounded by mountains to the N and W, mostly wooded; lake resorts include Ispra, Stresa, Arona, and the Swiss town of Locarno; on the W arm of the lake, between Pallanza and Stresa, the Borromean Is are a major tourist attraction.

Magherafelt, *mah'KHėr-felt*, MACHAIRE FIOLTA (Gael), 54 45N 6 36W, pop(1981) 5,044, town in Magherafelt dist, Derry (Londonderry), Northern Ireland; 24 km WSW of Ballymena.

Maghreb, MAGHRIB (Eng) ('far west'), an area of NW Africa, including the countries of Morocco, Algeria and Tunisia; area c.9 mn sq km, half of which is unleached fertile farmland with a pop density of 24 persons per sq km; the other half is poor land with a pop density of 8 persons per sq km; the area is largely occupied by sendentary and nomadic Berbers of the Kabyle, Shluh and Tuareg groups.

Maghull *me-gul'*, 53 28N 2 57W, pop(1981) 30,577, town linked with Lydiate in Sefton borough, Merseyside, NW England; 13 km N of Liverpool; railway.

Magnisía, coastal nome (dept) of Thessalía region, E Greece; pop(1981) 182,222; area 2,636 sq km; capital Vólos; economy: cereals, fruit, tobacco, livestock, almonds, fishing.

Magnitogorsk *mag-nyi'te-gorsk*, formerly MAGNITNAYA, 53 28N 59 06E, pop(1983) 419,000, industrial town in Chelyabinskaya oblast, SW Siberian Rossiyskaya, Soviet Union; on the R Ural; built (1929-31) under the first 5-year plan on the site of iron and magnetite deposits; one of the largest centres of the metallurgical industry in the Soviet Union; railway; airfield; economy: ferrous metallurgy, construction materials, clothing, footwear; monument: Palace of Metallurgists (1936).

Mago, national park in Ethiopia, NE Africa; area 2,200 sq km.

Magwe *mag-way'*, division in W central Burma; mountainous in the N, W and E, and dissected by the low lying valley of the R Irrawaddy running N-S through the centre of the division; Magwe's NE border with Sagaing division is formed by the Chindwin river, a tributary of the Irrawaddy, which forms part of the border with Mandalay division to the E; pop(1983) 3,241,103; capital Magwe.

Magwe, 20 08N 94 55E, river port capital of Magwe division, W central Burma; on R Irrawaddy; airfield; economy: rice, cotton, teak.

Mahajanga, MAJUNGA (Swahili 'mji angaïa', city of flowers), formerly PORT-BERGÉ, 15 40S 46 20E, pop(1978e) 57,500, port on NW coast of Madagascar overlooking the bay of Bombetoka and the Betsiboka estuary, 618 km NW of Antananarivo; chief town of a prov of the same name; former capital of the Boina kingdom; Amborovy beach nearby; airfield; economy: sugar cane, cotton, cashews, rice trade, cement, fishing.

Mahalapye *ma-ha-la'pyay*, 23 05S 26 51E, pop(1980) 19,000, town in Central dist, Botswana, S Africa; 320 km NNE of Mafeking; railway.

Mahalla El Kubra, El *el ma-hal'el koo'bra*, AL-MAHALLAT AL-KUBRA, 30 59N 31 10E, pop(1976) 292,853, town in Gharbîya governorate, N Egypt; in the R Nile delta, 105 km N of Cairo; railway.

Mahanadi *ma-ha'na-dee*, river of India, rising in the Eastern Ghats of SE Madhya Pradesh state almost 50 km ESE of Kanker, it flows generally NE and E into Orissa state where it turns S to Sonapur; flows ESE past Cuttack to its mouth in the Bay of Bengal; length 885 km; the Mahanadi marks the N extent of the Eastern Ghats mountain system; subject to flooding during the rainy season when huge volumes of water are discharged; the river is dammed to form the Hirakud Reservoir.

Maharashtra *mu-hah'rush-tra*, state in W central India; pop(1981) 62,693,898; area 307,762 sq km; bounded N and E by Madhya Pradesh state, S by Andhra Pradesh, Karnataka and Goa, W by the Arabian Sea and NW by Daman and Gujarat; crossed by several mountain ranges including the Sahyadriparvat (Ajanth), Satmala, Nirmal and Balaghat ranges; the state is drained by numerous rivers which include the Sina, Godāvari, Purna, Penganga, Tāpi, Tapti, Ghod, Wainganga and the Wardha; capital Bombay; governed by a bicameral legislature comprising a 78-member Legislative Council and an elected 287-member Legislative Assembly; 17.4% of the state is under forest; 10% of cultivated land is irrigated, the chief agricultural crops being rice, jowar, bajri, sugar cane, groundnuts and cotton; manufacturing industries include textiles, electrical equipment, machinery, chemicals and petroleum products; industry is largely concentrated in Bombay, Pune and Thana; mineral reserves include coal, chromite, iron ore and bauxite; Bombay has a major airport and is the state's largest seaport; Maharashtra was ruled by the Muslims from the 14th to the 17th centuries, by Portugal in the 16th century and by Great Britain from the early 19th century; the States Reorganization Act of 1956 created Bombay state by merging the former states of Kutch and Saurashtra with the Marathi-speaking areas of Hyderabad and Madhya Pradesh in the old state of Bombay; the state of Maharashtra was eventually formed by the Bombay Reorganization Act of 1960 when the 17 predominantly Gujarati-speaking districts of N and W Bombay State became the state of Gujarat.

Mahaweli Ganga *mu-ha've-lee gung'ga*, MAHAVELI GANGA, major river (ganga) of Sri Lanka; flows N from Central prov to meet the Bay of Bengal S of Trincomalee; an important source of hydroelectric power; length 332 km.

Mahdia, governorate of E Tunisia, N Africa; pop(1984) 270,435; capital Mahdia.

Mahé *ma-hay'*, district of Pondicherry union territory, SW India; on the Malabar coast; an enclave in Kerala state, 64 km N of Calicut; until 1954, the only French settlement on the W coast of India; area 10 sq km; pop(1981) 28,413.

Mahé, 4 41S 55 30E, pop(1985e) 65,245, main granitic island of the Seychelles, Indian Ocean; about 1,200 km E of Mombasa on the E African coast of Kenya; area 153 sq km; Victoria, the capital of the Seychelles, is situated on the NW coast; international airport (Anse Déjeuner); 68 beaches are a major tourist attraction; the island includes the mountainous Morne Seychelles National Park.

Mahmūd-e 'Eraqī, 35 1N 69 20E, pop(1984e) 1,315, capital of Kapīsā, E Afghanistan; lies N of Kābul, on the R Ghorband.

Mahon *ma-ōn'*, PORT MAHON (Eng), 39 53N 4 16E, pop(1981) 21,860, port and capital of the island of Menorca in the Balearic Is, Baleares autonomous region, Spain; on the E coast of the island on the S side of a long inlet and under the shelter of the fortified hill of La Mola; its buildings are characteristic of the period of British occupation; airport.

Mahrah, Al, governorate of E South Yemen; formerly the Sixth Governorate; chief town Al Ghayḑah.

Maidenhead, 51 32N 0 44W, pop(1981) 60,461, town in Windsor and Maidenhead dist, Berkshire, S England; on the R Thames, 8 km W of Slough; a former staging post and resort town; railway; economy: printing, plastics, engineering, computer software, pharmaceuticals; monument: railway bridge (1838), with the largest brick-built arches in the world.

Maidstone *mayd'stun*, 51 17N 0 32E, pop(1981) 87,068, county town in Maidstone dist, Kent, SE England; on the R Medway, S of Chatham; birthplace of the essayist, William Hazlitt (1778-1830); railway; economy: paper, fruit canning, brewing, cement, confectionery; monuments: 14th-c All Saints church, 14th-c Archbishop's palace, Chillington manor, Tyrwhitt Drake museum of carriages.

Maiduguri *mī-doo'gu-ree*, 11 53N 13 16E, pop(1981e) 258,000, capital of Borno state, NE Nigeria, W Africa; 515 km E of Kano; railway terminus; airfield; economy: leather, bricks and groundnut processing; monuments: museum, palace; event: Shallah festival in Nov or Dec.

Mai'ko, national park in E Zaire, central Africa; area 10,830 sq km; established in 1970; situated on the border between Kivu and Haut-Zaïre regions.

Main *mīn*, river in Bayern (Bavaria) and Hessen (Hesse) provs, W Germany; formed by the junction of the Weisser Main (White Main), which rises on the Ochsenkopf in the Fichtelgebirge, and the Roter Main (Red Main) coming from the Frankenwald (Franconian Forest), which meet below Kulmbach; flows W into the R Rhine opposite Mainz, passing through Würzburg, Aschaffenburg and Frankfurt am Main in its course; length 524 km; navigable length 396 km; drainage basin area 26,507 sq km; connected to the R Danube by the Ludwig Canal; receives the Fränkische Saale and Tauber rivers; the Mainfranken region is famous for a wide range of wines (Würzburger Stein, Escherndorfer Lump and Randersackerer Pfulben); tobacco and hops are grown in the valley.

Maine *men*, former prov in NW France, now occupying the depts of Mayenne, Sarthe and part of Orne and including the dist of Perche; the chief town is Le Mans.

Maine *mayn*, a New England state in the NE corner of the United States, bounded S by the Atlantic Ocean, SW by New Hampshire and NW, N and E by Canada; the 'Pine Tree State'; pop(1980) 1,124,660; area 80,587 sq km; 23rd state admitted to the Union in 1820; the capital is Augusta and the largest town is Portland; the Kennebec and Penobscot rivers run S through the state to the Atlantic Ocean; the state is crossed by the Appalachian Mts which rise to 1,605 m at Mt Katahdin in Baxter State Park; the N coast is characterized by rocky promontories and in the W the terrain is rugged; the state is dotted with over 1,600 lakes, the largest being L Moosehead; the northern 80% of the state is forested while the southern coastal strip is predominantly arable with potatoes the major crop; agriculture, forestry and fishing are the main industries; explored by the Cabots in the 1490s, Maine was settled first by the French in 1604 and later by the English in 1607; in 1820 Maine separated from Massachusetts; the state is divided into 16 counties as follows:

County	*area (sq km)*	*pop(1980)*
Androscoggin	1,240	99,657
Aroostook	17,475	91,331
Cumberland	2,278	215,789
Franklin	4,417	27,098
Hancock	3,996	41,781
Kennebec	2,278	109,889
Knox	962	32,941
Lincoln	1,191	25,691
Oxford	5,338	48,968
Penobscot	8,918	137,015
Piscataquis	10,364	17,634
Sagadahoc	668	28,795
Somerset	10,218	45,028
Waldo	1,898	28,414
Washington	6,724	34,963
York	2,621	139,666

Maine-et-Loire *men-ay-lwar*, dept in Pays de la Loire region of W France, comprising 4 arrond, 41 cantons and 364 communes; pop(1982) 675,321; area 7,166 sq km; flat and watered by the R Loire and its tributaries, the Mayenne, Sarthe, and Loir, which form the Maine, some 8 km N of the Loire; capital Angers, other towns include Cholet and Saumur.

Mainz *mīnts*, MAYENCE *mī-âs'* (Fr), 50 00N 8 16E, pop(1983) 186,400, old Roman city and capital of Rheinland-Pfalz (Rhineland-Palatinate) prov, W Germany; on the left bank of the R Rhine (Rhine) opposite the mouth of the R Main; university (1477); an important traffic junction and commercial and industrial centre, with the headquarters of radio and television corporations and publishing houses; centre of the Rhine wine trade; tourist river cruises along the Rhine to Köln (Cologne) are very popular; railway; economy: glass materials, electronics; monument: cathedral (begun in 975 but mostly 11-13th-c); event: Mainzer Fastnacht (Shrovetide).

Maio *mah'yoo*, 15 08N 23 13W, small island in the Sotavento or leeward group of Cape Verde, 15 minutes by air from Praia, there are air connections to 6 of the neighbouring islands; area 269 sq km; pop(1980) 4,103, rises to 429 m at Monte Penoso; occupied by the British until the end of the 18th century; salt is mined for export.

Maisons-Alfort *may zõ ahl for'*, 48 48N 2 27E, pop(1982) 51,591, town in Val-de-Marne dept, Ile-de-France region, N central France, on the Marne R; a SE suburb of Paris.

Maitland, 32 33S 151 33E, pop(1981) 38,865, town in Hunter stat div, E New South Wales, Australia; NE of Newcastle; railway; airfield.

Maíz, Islas del *eel'as del mah-ees'*, CORN ISLANDS (Eng), group of 2 small islands in Zelaya dept, Nicaragua, off the Caribbean coast, 80 km ENE of Bluefields; comprises Grande and Pequeña Is; the larger island is a popular Nicaraguan holiday resort.

Majorca, island in the Mediterranean. See Mallorca.

Makassar, seaport in Indonesia. See Ujung Padang.

Makassar, Selat *se-laht' ma-kas'ar*, MAKASSAR STRAIT, stretch of water between the islands of Borneo in the W and Sulawesi (Celebes) in the E, linking the Java Sea (S) to the Celebes Sea (N); length 720 km.

Makati *mah-kah'tee*, 14 34N 121 01E, pop(1980) 372,631, city in Capital prov, Philippines; on Luzon I, E of Manila.

Makedhonia, MACEDONIA *ma-se-dō'ni-a* (Eng), N region of Greece, extending from the Albanian frontier in the W to the R Néstos (Mesta) in the E, and from the Yugoslav frontier in the N to Mt Ólimbos (Olympus) in the S; pop(1981) 2,121,953; area 34,177 sq km; capital Thessaloníki; chief towns Kaválla, Dráma, Edhessa, and Kastoría; comprises the nomoi (depts) of Kaválla, Dráma, Kilkís, Thessaloníki, Khalkidhíki, Sérrai, Grevená, Piería, Imathía, Pélla, Flórina, Kastoría, Kozáni, and the autonomous administration Pangaíon Óros; the region is mountainous with fertile plains watered by the Struma and Vardar rivers; Thessaloníki is the chief industrial and commercial centre; there are several important ancient sites, notably Pélla (once capital of the region), and Véryina; economy: livestock, grain, tobacco, olives, grapes.

Makedonija, MACEDONIA (Eng), republic in S Yugoslavia, bounded to the W by Albania, to the S by Greece, to the E by Bulgaria and to the N by the Yugoslav republic of Srbija (Serbia); pop(1981) 1,909,112; area 25,713 sq km; capital Skopje; chief towns include Bitola, Gostivar, Tetovo and Kumanovo; populated by Slavs, Serbs, Albanians and Turks; incorporated into Srbija after the Balkan Wars; the towns are of varied origin, some are early Byzantine and some are of more recent Turkish colonial origin; to the SW are L Ohrid and L Prespa; market gardening is important.

Makeni *ma-ke'nee*, 8 57N 12 02W, pop(1974) 27,000, capital of Bombali dist, Northern prov, Sierra Leone, W Africa; 137 km ENE of Freetown.

Makeyevka *ma-kay'yef-ka*, formerly DMITRIEVSKY, (-1920), DMITRIEVSK (1920-31), 48 01N 38 00E, pop(1983) 446,000, industrial town in Donetskaya oblast, Ukrainskaya SSR, Soviet Union; 19 km NE of Donetsk; the town arose on the site of the ancient workers' settlement of Dmitrievsk; during the post-war period it became one of the largest industrial cities of the Donbas and an important centre of the metallurgical and coal industries; railway; economy: heavy metallurgy, coal, building materials, foodstuffs, footwear.

Makgadikgadi *ma-ga-di-ga'di*, salt pans in N Central dist, Botswana, S Africa; in prehistoric times it formed a large lake but now only parts of the pan flood during the wet season; individual pans within the whole area include the Sua Pan and the Ntwetwe Pan; during the wet period large flocks of flamingoes and herds of wildebeest, zebra and gemsbok arrive from the Nxai Pan (N); after the wet season the fauna migrate to the R Boteti and then begin their trek N back to the Nxai Pan; occasionally the Makgadikgadi pans are flooded from the Okavango delta.

Makhachkala *muk-hach-ku-la'*, formerly PORT PETROVSK (-1922), 42 59N 47 30E, pop(1983) 287,000, seaport capital of Dagestanskaya ASSR, Rossiyskaya, Soviet Union; on the W coast of the Caspian Sea, in the foothills of the Bol'shoy Kavkaz (Greater Caucasus) range; founded in 1844 as a fortress; university (1957); railway; airfield; economy: machine building, chemicals, foodstuffs, cotton textiles.

Makira, Pacific island. See San Cristobal.

Makkah *mak'ku*, MECCA *me'ku*, MACORABA (anc), 21 30N 39 54E, pop(1974) 366,800, Islamic holy city in Makkah prov, W central Saudi Arabia; 64 km E of its Red Sea port, Jiddah (Jedda); situated in a barren, stony valley surrounded by low hills; birthplace of Mohammed (570 AD) and site of the Kaaba, the chief shrine of Muslim pilgrimage (hadj); it is estimated that between 1.5 and 2 million pilgrims visit Makkah annually; the city is closed to non-Muslims; large bazaars; monuments: Al-Harram mosque with the Kaaba and sacred Black Stone.

Makó *mo'kō*, 46 14N 20 33E, pop(1984e) 30,000, agricultural market town in Csongrád county, S Hungary; on R Maros, E of Szeged; economy: agricultural trade, textiles, onions, machinery.

Makokou *ma-kō-koo'*, 0 38N 12 47E, capital of Ogooué-Ivindo prov, NE Gabon, W Africa; on R Ivindo.

Makurdi *ma-koor'dee*, 7 44N 8 35E, pop(1969e) 62,585, capital of Benue state, Nigeria, W Africa; on the R Benue, 185 km NNE of Port Harcourt; railway; economy: brewing.

Mala, Pacific island. See Malaita.

Mala'bo, 3 45N 8 50E, pop(1983) 15,253, seaport capital of Equatorial Guinea, W Africa; on the island of Bioko (formerly Fernando Póo), in the Gulf of Guinea, 240 km NNW of Bata on the mainland (Río Muni); founded by the British in the 1820s when it was called Clarencetown or Port Clarence; subsequently known as Santa Isabel; airfield; economy: coffee, cocoa and timber trade.

Malacca, state and town in Malaysia. See Melaka.

Malacca, Strait of, channel between the Malaysia Peninsula and the Indonesian island of Sumatra; 805 km long by 50-320 km wide; links the Andaman Sea to the South China Sea; one of the world's most important passages for shipping; Singapore is the largest port.

Má'laga, prov in Andalucia region, S Spain, bounded on the S by the Strait of Gibraltar; crossed by the Sierra de Ronda in the NW and drained by the Guadalhorce and Guadiaro rivers and by tributaries of the Guadalquivir; pop(1981) 1,036,261; area 7,276 sq km; capital Málaga; economy: the lowlands produce fruit, vegetables, almonds, cereals and wine; industries include textiles, clothes, sugar (Antequera), chemicals, pharmaceuticals, paper, beer, light engineering, food processing.

Málaga, MALACA (anc), 36 43N 4 23W, pop(1981) 503,251, port and capital of Málaga prov, Andalucia, S Spain; at the mouth of the R Guadalmedina, 544 km S of Madrid; bishopric; large boating harbour and beaches; university (1972); airport; car ferries to Casablanca, Tangier, Genoa; railway; economy: tourism, textiles, beer, Málaga wine chemicals, pharmaceuticals, food processing and export of fruit; a 265 km oil pipeline links Málaga with the Puertollano refinery; monuments: Moorish Alcazaba, cathedral (1528-1765), Roman theatre, fine arts museum, Gibralfaro lighthouse hill and gardens; events: Holy Week; fiestas of La Virgen del Carmen in July; fair in Aug; Festival of Spain in Aug-Sept and Costa del Sol Rally in Dec.

Malahide *ma'lu-hīd*, MULLACH IDE (Gael), 53 27N 6 09W, pop(1981) 9,158, resort town in Dublin county, Leinster, Irish Republic; on an inlet of the Irish Sea, NNE of Dublin.

Malaita *ma-lay'ta*, MALA, most populous of the Solomon Islands, SW Pacific, 48 km NE of Guadalcanal I; area 4,070 sq km; length 184 km; width 24 km; pop(1976) 58,721; main town Auki on the NW coast; noted for its shell money and its handicrafts.

Malanje *mu-lan'zhu*, 9 36S 16 21E, pop(1970) 31,559, capital of Malanje prov, NW central Angola, SW Africa; railway terminus and main road junction 355 km ESE of Luanda; alt 1,160 m; airfield.

Mälaren *me'la-run*, MÄLAR (Eng), lake in Västmanland, Uppsala, Stockholm and Södermanland counties, SE Sweden; extends 113 km inland from the Baltic Sea; area 1,140 sq km; the city of Stockholm is on both sides of the strait connecting the lake with the Baltic Sea.

Malatya *ma-la'tya*, mountainous prov in E central Turkey, bounded E by the R Euphrates; pop(1980) 606,996; area 12,313 sq km; capital Malatya; economy: grain, fruit and opium.

Malatya, MELITENE (anc), 38 22N 38 18E, pop(1980) 179,074, capital town of Malatya prov, E central Turkey; SW of Elâziğ; airfield.

Malawi *ma-lah'wi*, official name Republic of Malawi, a SE African republic bounded SW and SE by Mozambique, E by L Nyasa (L Malawi), N by Tanzania and W by Zambia; timezone GMT +2; area 118,484 sq km; pop(1984e) 6,839,000; capital Lilongwe; chief towns Blantyre, Limbe and Salima; the main ethnic groups include Chewa, Nyanja, Tumbuka, Yao, Lomwe, Sena, Tonga and Ngoni tribes (98%) and Asian and European (2%); the majority of the pop is Christian (Protestant (55%) and Roman Catholic (20%)), the remainder largely being Muslim (20%); the official languages are English and Chichewa with Tombuka as a second African language; the unit of currency is the kwacha of 100 tambala; national holidays 3 March (Martyrs' Day), 6 July (Republic Day) and 21 Dec (National Tree-planting Day); membership of AfDB, the Commonwealth, EEC (associate), FAO, G-77, GATT, IBRD, ICAO, IDA, IFAD, IFC, ILO, IMF, INTERPOL, IPU, ISO, ITU, NAM, OAU, SADCC, UN, UNESCO, UPU, WHO, WIPO, WMO and WTO.

Physical description. Situated in SE Africa, Malawi is traversed N-S by the Great Rift Valley which at this stage contains the African continent's third largest lake, Lake Nyasa (Lake Malawi), which covers 20% of the country. The only outlet from L Nyasa is the Shire river, a tributary of the R Zambezi, bisecting the Southern region. Part of Malawi's E border with Mozambique runs N-S down the middle of the lake. On either side of the Rift valley are high plateaux (900 to 1,200 m) with the Nyika Uplands in the N peaking at 2,600 m. To the S of L Nyasa are situated the Shire highlands (600 to 1,060 m) whose 2 main peaks are Mt Zomba (2,130 m) and Mt Mulanje (3,000 m). In the extreme S the land dips to between 30 and 90 m in elevation.

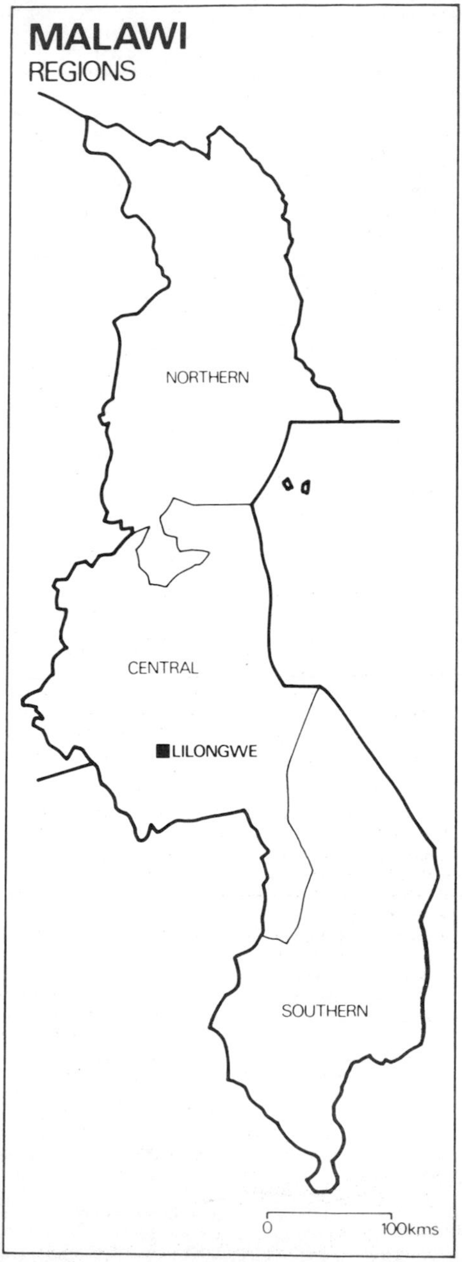

Climate. In the S, around the Shire river, conditions are tropical with high year-round temperatures ranging between 28°C and 37°C and an average yearly rainfall of 740 mm. At Lilongwe in central Malawi there are more moderate temperatures and even occasional frost during the dry season. The average annual rainfall here is 775 mm and the max daily temperature ranges between 23°C and 30°C. The mountainous areas of Malawi overlooking L Nyasa have a higher rainfall ranging between 1,500 and 2,000 mm. Rain falls in all months but the wettest period throughout the country is from Oct to Feb.

History, government and constitution. European contact was first established in this area by David Livingstone in 1859. Subsequently, a number of missions were established in the area by Scottish churches with the aim of abolishing the slave trade. In 1878 a group of traders set up the African Lakes Company to supply these missions and in 1883 the British government appointed a consul to the 'Kings and Chiefs of Central Africa'. Eight years later the area was claimed as the British Protectorate of Nyasaland, acquiring colonial status in 1907. In the 1950s the colony was joined with Northern and Southern Rhodesia to form the Federation of Rhodesia and Nyasaland. The main independence figure was Dr H.K. Banda who returned from the USA in 1958 and took over leadership of the Nyasaland African Congress which later became the Malawi Congress Party (MCP). In 1961 the MCP achieved considerable success in elections to the Legislative Assembly and also gained influence on the executive council. After a constitutional conference self-government was granted in 1963. In the same year a highly autonomous constitution came into effect and the Federation of Rhodesia and Nyasaland was abolished. In 1964 Malawi became a fully independent country and a member of the Commonwealth. In 1966 a new constitution was invoked and Malawi became a republic with Dr Banda as its first president. Malawi's president is elected every 5 years though in 1970 Dr Banda was elected for a life term. There is a Cabinet appointed by the president and a unicameral National Assembly of 112 members, 97 of whom are elected and 15 appointed.

Economy. Malawi's economy is based on agriculture which employs 90% of the pop and generates 95% of export earnings. Tobacco, sugar and tea, which in general are grown on large plantations, are the main export crops. Other export crops include cotton and groundnuts and more recently maize which is also the main subsistence crop. Malawi's industrial sector developed rapidly after independence, with an economic growth rate of over 10% in the 1970s. The industrial sector includes the manufacture of textiles, matches, cigarettes, beer, spirits and shoes. Cement production at Zomba represents the only significant mineral contribution to the economy. The main trading partners are South Africa, the UK, Japan, the USA, the Netherlands and Zimbabwe.

Administrative divisions. Malawi is divided into 3 regions and 24 districts:

Region/district	*area (sq km)*	*pop(1977)*
Central	35,592	2,143,716
Kasungu	7,878	194,436
Nkhota-Kota	4,259	94,370
Ntchisi	1,655	87,437
Dowa	3,041	247,603
Salima	2,196	132,276
Lilongwe	6,159	704,117
Mchinji	3,356	158,833
Dedza	3,624	298,190
Ntcheu	3,424	226,454
Northern	26,931	648,853
Chitipa	3,504	72,316
Karonga	2,955	106,923
Nkhata Bay	4,090	105,803
Rumphi	5,952	62,450
Mzimba	10,430	301,361

contd

Region/district	*area (sq km)*	*pop(1977)*
Southern	31,756	2,754,891
Mangochi	6,272	302,341
Machinga	5,968	341,836
Zomba	2,580	352,334
Chiradzulu	767	176,184
Blantyre	2,012	408,062
Mwanza	2,295	71,405
Thyolo	1,715	322,000
Mulanje	3,450	477,546
Chikwawa	4,755	194,425
Nsanje	1,942	108,758

Malawi, Lake, see Nyasa, Lake.

Malaysia *me-lay'zha*, official name Malaysia, independent federation of states in SE Asia, comprising Peninsular Malaysia and the E states of Sabah and Sarawak on the island of Borneo; timezone GMT +8; area 329,749 sq km; pop of Peninsular Malaysia (1980) 10,944,844; pop of Sabah and Sarawak (1980) 2,191,265; capital Kuala Lumpur; chief cities George Town, Petaling Jaya, Ipoh, Melaka, Johor Baharu, Kuching and Kota Kinabalu; ethnic groups include Malay (59%), Chinese (32%) and Indian (9%); Bahasa Malaysia (Malay) is the official language, but Chinese, English and Tamil are also spoken; religions include Muslim, Hindu, Buddhist, Confucian and Christian; the currency is the Malaysian ringgit; national holiday 31 Aug (National Day); membership of ADB, ANRPC, ASEAN, Colombo Plan, Commonwealth, FAO, G-77, GATT, IAEA, IBRD, ICAO, IDA, Islamic Development Bank, IFC, ILO, IMF, IMO, INTELSAT, INTERPOL, IPU, IRC, ITC, ITU, NAM, OIC, UN, UNESCO, UPU, WHO, WMO, WTO.

Physical description. Peninsular Malaysia consists of a mountainous chain of granite and limestone running N-S separating the narrow E plain from the much broader W coastal plain. The highest peak on the peninsula is Gunong Tahan (2,189 m) in Pahang state. The peninsula

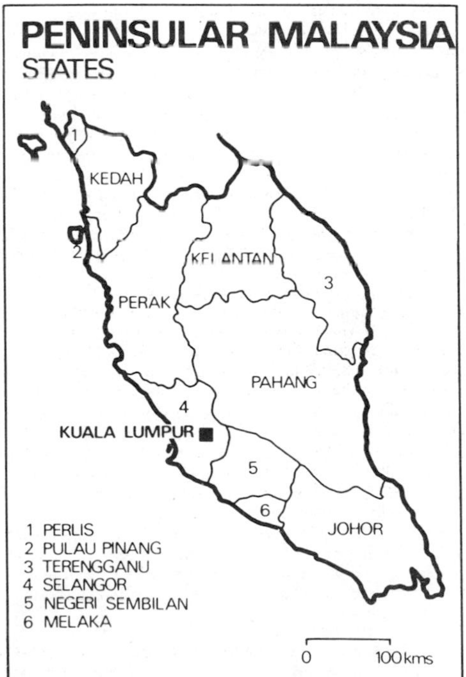

is 700 km long and up to 320 km wide and is mostly covered with tropical rain forest and mangrove swamp. The W lowlands are covered in deep, fertile alluvial soil. As a result, this side of the peninsula is the most densely populated. The E coastal plain is widest at the Penang delta where fertile alluvial soils extend inland for about 32 km. Generally the coastline consists of long, narrow beaches. The longest rivers in Peninsular Malaysia are the Pahang (456 km), which runs into the South China Sea, and the Perak (320 km), which runs into the Strait of Malacca. On the NW coast of the island of Borneo, Sarawak consists of a narrow, swampy coastal belt which is backed by foothills rising sharply towards mountain ranges on the Indonesian frontier. In the NE, near the Sabah border, the highest peak is Gunong Murud (2,423 m). The largest of many rivers that flow down through gorges to the coastal plain is the R Rajang (560 km). Sabah in the NE corner of Borneo has a deeply indented coastline, particularly in the E where there are good deep anchorages. The narrow W coastal plain rises sharply into the Crocker Range reaching 4,094 m at Gunong Kinabalu, Malaysia's highest peak. The forests and limestone caves of N Borneo provide a home for one of the largest and most varied bird populations in the world as well as a wide range of wildlife.

Climate. Malaysia has a tropical climate that is strongly influenced by monsoon winds which blow from the SW from May to Oct and from the NE from Oct to Feb. Humidity is high throughout the year. In Peninsular Malaysia average annual rainfall varies from 260 mm in the S to 800 mm in the N. In Sarawak annual rainfall varies between 470 mm and 670 mm and in Sabah from 260 mm to 670 mm. Average daily temperatures vary from 21°C to 32°C in the coastal areas and from 12°C to 25°C in the mountainous districts.

History, government and constitution. In competition with Sumatran colonists, Portugal, the Netherlands and Britain vied for control of the Malay Peninsula from the 16th century. In the 19th century Britain's hold over the area was increased as a result of a series of treaties with local sultans. In 1826 Singapore, Malacca and Penang were formally incorporated into the British Colony of the Straits Settlements. From 1874 British protection extended over Perak, Selangor, Negeri Sembilan and Pahang which were constituted into the Federated Malay States in 1895. In 1885 Johor entered into a treaty of protection with Britain and between 1910 and 1930 protection treaties were agreed with Kedah, Perlis, Kelantan and Terengganu which, along with Johor, were known as the Unfederated Malay States. After World War II Sarawak became a British colony, Singapore became a separate colony, the colony of North Borneo was formed and the Malay Union was established to unite the Malay states and Straits Settlements of Malacca and Penang. Opposition to the Malay Union resulted in the formation of the Federation of Malaya in 1948. After several years of communist insurrection the Federation of Malaya gained independence in Aug 1957. In 1963 Britain relinquished sovereignty over Sabah (North Borneo) and Sarawak and the constitutional monarchy of Malaysia came into existence. In 1965 Singapore withdrew from the Malaysian Federation. The bicameral Federal Parliament (*Majlis*) of Malaysia consists of a 58-member Senate (*Dewan Negara*) elected for 6 years and a 154-member House of Representatives (*Dewan Rakyat*) elected for 5 years. The head of state is a monarch elected for a period of 5 years by his fellow sultans. He is advised by a prime minister and cabinet.

Economy. The discovery of tin in Perak, Selangor and Negeri Sembilan in the late 19th century introduced European investment to Malaysia and laid the foundation of the modern economy. By the turn of the century the planting of rubber trees from Brazil added a new element to the plantation economy that had previously been based on coffee-growing. Today, tin and other minerals such as iron ore, ilmenite and gold provide substantial export revenues, and the discovery of oil and natural gas has helped to reduce the country's dependence on fuel imports. The diverse wealth of natural resources has enabled Malaysia to achieve one of the highest standards of living in Asia. In addition to the export of natural resources there is a rapidly growing manufacturing sector producing textiles, rubber products, petroleum products, chemicals, electronic components and electrical goods. Major trade partners include Japan, Singapore, the USA, EEC countries.

Administrative divisions. Malaysia is a federation of 11 peninsular states, 2 eastern states (Sabah and Sarawak) and a federal territory (Wilayah Persekutuan):

State	*area (sq km)*	*pop(1980)*
Johor	18,985	1,580,423
Kedah	9,425	1,077,815
Kelantan	14,796	859,270
Melaka	1,657	446,769
Negeri Sembilan	6,643	551,442
Pahang	35,965	768,801
Perak	21,005	1,743,655
Perlis	818	144,782
Pulau Pinang	1,044	900,772
Sabah	73,711	955,712
Sarawak	124,449	1,235,553
Selangor	7,997	1,426,250
Terengganu	12,928	525,255
Wilayah Persekutuan	243	919,610

Malden, 42 26N 71 04W, pop(1980) 53,386, town in Middlesex county, E Massachusetts, United States; residential suburb, 8 km N of Boston; railway.

Maldives *mol'dīvz*, formerly MALDIVE ISLANDS, official name The Republic of Maldives, DIVEHI JUMHURIYA (Divehi), an island archipelago 670 km SW of Sri Lanka, in the Indian Ocean; comprises 1,190 islands of which 202 are inhabited; the archipelago measures 823 km N-S and 130 km E-W at its greatest width; total land area 300 sq km; timezone GMT $+5\frac{1}{2}$; capital Male'; pop(1983e) 158,500, only 33 islands have more than 1,000 inhabitants; the Maldivians are mostly of Aryan origin comprising an admixture of Sinhalese, Dravidian and Arab; the official language is Divehi, a dialect of Sinhala with script derived from Arabic, but English is spoken by most government officials; Islam (Sunni) is the religion of the state; the currency is the Maldivian rupee (*rufiyah*) of 100 laaris; national holidays include most Islamic festivals, 27 July (Independence Day), 12 Nov (Republic Day) and 16 Nov (National Day); membership of Colombo Plan, Commonwealth (special member), FAO, GATT, G-77, IBRD, ICAO, IDA, IDB, IFAD, IMF, IMO, ITU, NAM, OIC, UN, UNESCO, UPU, WHO, WMO.

Physical description. The islands, which are grouped into atolls protected by coral reefs, are small and low lying, with sandy beaches fringed with coconut palms. Other trees and foods of value include breadfruit, banana, mango, cassava, sweet potato, millet and screwpine.

Climate. The Maldives are generally warm and humid and are affected by wet SW monsoons from April to Oct. The dry NE monsoons prevail between Dec and March. Annual rainfall averages 2,100 mm and the mean daily temperature at 22°C varies little throughout the year.

History, government and constitution. Apart from a brief period of Portuguese rule in the 16th century the Maldives has been an independent state. Between 1887 and 1965 the Maldives was a British protectorate. The first constitution was proclaimed in 1932 and since then the country has changed from being a constitutional monarchy to a republic which was declared in Nov 1968. The constitution of 1968 provided for the election every 5 years of a president who is head of state and chief executive. The president appoints a Ministers' *Majlis* (cabinet of ministers). A Citizens' *Majlis*, elected for a 5-year term, includes 2 members from each of the 19 atolls and Male', and 8 members appointed by the president.

Economy. The economy of the Maldives is largely based

on fishing, tourism (since 1972) and the production of coconuts and copra. Major trading partners include Japan, Sri Lanka and Thailand.

Administrative divisions. The Maldives is divided into 19 administrative atolls:

Atoll	*pop(1977)*
North Thiladhunmathi (Haa Alifu)	8,601
South Thiladhunmathi (Haa Dhaalu)	9,923
North Miladhunmadulu (Shaviyani)	6,363
South Miladhunmadulu (Noonu)	6,282
North Maalhosmadulu (Raa)	7,904
South Maalhosmadulu (Baa)	5,758
Faadhippolhu (Lhaviyani)	5,655
Male' Atoll (Kaafu)	4,153
Ari Atoll (Alifu)	6,219
Felidhu Atoll (Vaavu)	1,078
Mulakatholhu (Meemu)	3,095
North Nilandhe Atoll (Faafu)	1,986
South Nilandhe Atoll (Dhaalu)	2,999
Kolumadulu (Thaa)	6,214
Hadhdhunmathi (Laamu)	6,090
North Huvadhu Atoll (Gaafu Alifu)	4,977
South Huvadhu Atoll (Gaafu Dhaalu)	7,717
Foammulah (Gnaviyani)	4,202
Addu Atoll (Seenu)	14,094

Maldon, 51 45N 0 40E, pop(1981) 14,754, town in Maldon dist, Essex, SE England; 14 km E of Chelmsford; economy: scientific instruments.

Maldonado *mal-dō-nah'dō*, dept in S Uruguay, on the Atlantic at the mouth of the Río de la Plata; pop(1985) 92,618; area 4,111 sq km; capital Maldonado; the seaside resorts between Punta del Este in the S of Maldonado dept and the city of Montevideo make this part of Uruguay extremely popular with tourists; the largest and best known of these resorts is Punta del Este, with its beaches, yacht and fishing clubs and casinos; S of this town is the Isla de Lobos, a government reserve with a sealion colony; also on the island is South America's largest and most powerful lighthouse; in Dec 1939, the German pocket battleship *Graf Spee* encountered British warships off the coast of Punta del Este before retiring to Montevideo.

Maldonado, 34 57S 54 59W, pop(1985) 33,498, port capital of Maldonado dept, S Uruguay; near the mouth of the Río de la Plata; its port is protected by the fortified Gorriti Island; railway; airport; the town was sacked by the British in 1806; it contains many colonial remains.

Male' *ma'lee*, DAVIYA'NI (Divehi), 4 00N 73 28E, pop(1985e) 38,000, chief atoll and capital of the Maldives in the Indian Ocean; over 700 km WSW of Sri Lanka; area 2 sq km; all trade passes through Male'; land is being reclaimed from the shallow waters of the surrounding reef; airport; economy: trade in breadfruit, copra, palm mats.

Malekula *ma-le-koo'la*, MALLICOLO *ma-le-kō'lō*, 2nd largest island in the SW Pacific Vanuatu group; 40 km SW of Espiritu Santo; rises to 8,906 m at Mt Penot; area 2,024 sq km.

Mali, official name Republic of Mali, RÉPUBLIQUE DU MALI (Fr), a republic in W Africa, bounded NE by Algeria, NW by Mauritania, W by Senegal, SW by Guinea, S by Ivory Coast, SE by Burkina and E by Niger; timezone GMT; area 1,240,192 sq km; pop(1984) 7,562,000; there are 1,663 km of paved roads; capital Bamako; chief towns include Ségou, Mopti, Sikasso, Kayes, Gao, Tombouctou; the majority of the pop (50%) belong to tribes from the Mande group including Bambara, Malinké and Sarakole; other tribes include the Peul (17%), Voltaic (12%), Songhai (6%), Tuareg and Moor

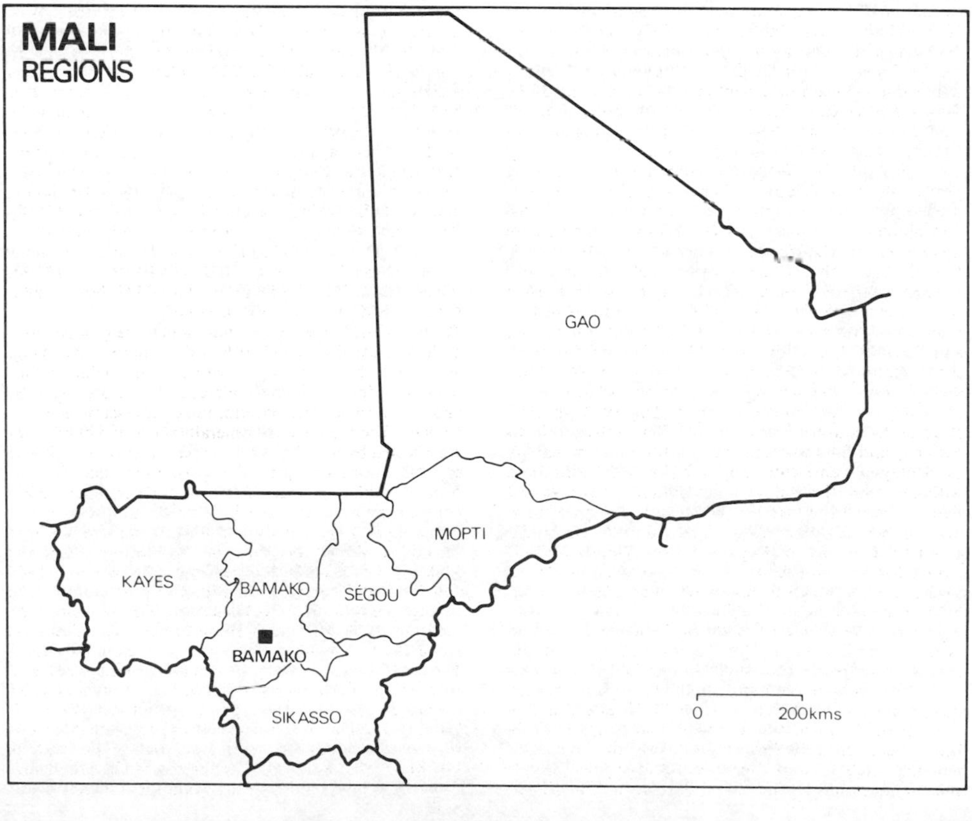

(5%); the official language is French, but the most widely spoken languages belong mainly to the Mande group including Bambara which is spoken by 60% of the pop, Soninke, Malinké and Dogon; non-Mande languages include Fulani, Songhai, Senufo and Minianka; most of the pop is Muslim (90%), the rest holding local (9%) or Christian (1%) beliefs; the unit of currency is the Mali franc; national holidays 20 Jan (Army Day), 25 Aug (African Freedom Day), 22 Sept (Independence Day), 19 Nov (Liberation Day); Muslim holidays are also observed; membership of AfDB, APC, CEAO, ECA, ECOWAS, FAO, GATT (de facto), IAEA, IBRD, ICAO, IDA, IDB (Islamic Development Bank), IFAD, IFC, ILO, IMF, INTELSAT, INTERPOL, IRC, ITU, NAM, Niger River Commission, OAU, OIC, Organization for the Development of the Niger River Valley, UN, UNESCO, UPU, WHO, WMO, WTO.

Physical description. Mali is a landlocked country of varying environments on the fringe of the Sahara desert. In the N is located the lower part of the Hoggar (Ahaggar) massif of S Algeria and in the SW there are the uplands which rise from the Ivory Coast and Guinea. Arid plains lie between 300 and 500 m above sea level and in the N there is a featureless desert with sand dunes and little surface water. The S is mainly savannah land. The R Niger flows NE from the Guinea border, watering the arid grazing lands of the Sahel. Turning E at Tombouctou, the river flows SE into Niger. In the SW the Sénégal river system drains westward; both rivers have eroded deep into the plains creating cliffs up to 1,000 m high.

Climate. Mali is divided into 4 climatic zones. (1) The desert land N of the 17th parallel receives little rainfall and suffers from extremes of temperature. (2) Between 16° and 17°N (33% of the country) there is a Sahelian transition zone with a 3-month rainy season that makes this area suitable for stock rearing. (3) Immediately to the S in the Sudanese zone the rainfall season extends to 5 months during the period June-Oct. (4) In the far SW max rainfall occurs in Aug with a dry season from Nov to May. The S of the country receives about 1,000 mm of rain per year, this level decreasing to almost zero in the Saharan N. A persistent E or NE wind (the *harmattan*) blows between Nov and May everywhere. At Bamako the average annual rainfall is 1,120 mm whilst in Tombouctou the figure is 231 mm.

History, government and constitution. Between 1881 and 1895 Mali was governed by France, after which it became the territory of French Sudan within French West Africa. Autonomy within the French community which came in 1958 was followed in 1959 by a partnership with Senegal to form the Federation of Mali. The federation gained independence in 1960 and in the same year Mali proclaimed itself an independent republic with a National Assembly. This was dissolved in 1968 with power being assumed by a military committee in 1969. A new constitution was approved by referendum in 1974 and constitutional elections were held in 1979 when an 82-member National Assembly was elected from the sole political party, the Democratic Union of Malian People (UDPM). Executive power is vested in an 18-member central executive bureau headed by the president.

Economy. Mali has limited mineral resources though marble limestone, bauxite, nickel and manganese are extracted in small amounts. Fishing from the rivers especially the Niger is important to a population largely living at a subsistence level on sorghum, millet, rice and maize crops. Both subsistence crops and cash crops, which include cotton and groundnuts, have been severely affected by drought conditions (eg 1972-76). Livestock rearing is also important to the nomadic sector of the population. The major manufacturing industries include food processing, textiles, leather and cement. Because of Mali's landlocked location and limited transport facilities the transport of imports and exports is expensive. The main trading partners are the African franc zone countries, W European countries, the USSR and China.

Administrative divisions. Mali is divided into 6 regions:

Region	*area (sq km)*	*pop(1971)*
Bamako	90,100	958,767
Gao	808,920	630,632
Kayes	119,813	738,302
Mopti	88,752	1,086,945
Ségou	56,127	779,125
Sikasso	76,480	948,513

These regions are further subdivided into 42 *cercles* or subdepartments which are themselves divided into 279 arrondissements.

Malindi *ma-leen'dee,* 3 14S 40 08E, pop(1979) 23,000, seaport in E Kenya, E Africa; on the Indian Ocean, 105 km NNE of Mombasa, near the mouth of the Athi river; Vasco da Gama visited in 1497 and built a fort, the remains of which are preserved; airfield; economy: tourism, fishing and agricultural services, port trade.

Malines, city in Belgium. See Mechelen.

Mallorca *ma-lyor'ka,* MAJORCA *ma-yor'ka* (Eng), BALEARIS MAJOR (anc), largest island in the Balearic Is, Baleares autonomous region of Spain; in the W Mediterranean, 240 km N of Algiers; pop(1981) 561,215; area, 3,640 sq km; in the NW, the tree-covered Sierra del Alfabia rises to 1,445 m at Torrellas and on the E the smaller Sierra de Levante hills rise to 500 m at San Salvador and Farruch; between these ranges there is a flat plain indented by the bays of Alcudia Pollensa to the NE and by Palma Bay to the SW; rainfall is low and the fields of the plain are watered with the aid of windmills; many Roman, Phoenician and Carthaginian remains as well as limestone caves; taken in 1229 by James I of Aragón; visited by painters and artists in the 19th-c such as George Sand and Frédéric Chopin the island has in recent years become a popular tourist resort; in the Middle Ages the island was famous for its porcelain, much of which was exported to Italy, hence the name majolica for the ware; the main town is Palma; Manacor is also an important manufacturing town; economy: tourism, pottery, brandy, jewellery, mining, sheep, timber, fishing.

Mallow *ma'lō,* MAGH EALLA (Gael), 52 08N 8 39W, pop(1981) 7,482, resort and market town in Cork county, Munster, S Irish Republic; on R Blackwater, NNW of Cork; railway; economy: agricultural trade, sugar.

Malmö *mal'mœ,* 55 35N 13 00E, pop(1982) 230,022, fortified seaport and capital of Malmöhus county, SW Sweden; on the Øresund (The Sound) opposite København (Copenhagen), Denmark; 3rd largest city in Sweden; under Danish rule until 1658, conquered and made a part of Sweden by Charles X; railway; economy: engineering, shipbuilding, textiles, cement; monuments: 16th-c town hall, 14th-c church of St Peter.

Malmöhus *mal-mœ-hoos',* a county of the extreme S tip of Sweden, bounded on the W by the Øresund (The Sound); land area 4,909 sq km; pop(1983) 744,081; capital Malmö; chief towns Lund, Landskrona, Hälsingborg and Trelleborg.

Malta *mawl'ta,* MELITA (anc), official name Republic of Malta, REPUBBLIKA TA' MALTA (Maltese), an archipelago in the central Mediterranean Sea comprising the islands of Malta (246 sq km), Gozo (67 sq km) and Comino (2.7 sq km) with some uninhabited islets including Cominotto, Filfla and St Paul's Island; situated 93 km S of Sicily and 290 km E of Tunisia; total area 316 sq km; timezone GMT +2; capital Valletta; chief towns Sliema, Birkirkara, Qormi and Rabat; chief port Grand Harbour, Valletta; international airport (Luqa) 6 km from Valletta; pop(1967) 314,216; pop(1983e) 329,189; the population is European, speaking both English and Maltese; Malta was taken from the Byzantine Empire in 870 by the Arabs who occupied the island for two centuries, injecting many Arab words into the local vocabulary; the religion, according to the constitution, is Roman Catholic Apostolic; the Maltese pound (lira matija) is the accepted currency; national holiday 31 March (National Day); membership of Commonwealth,

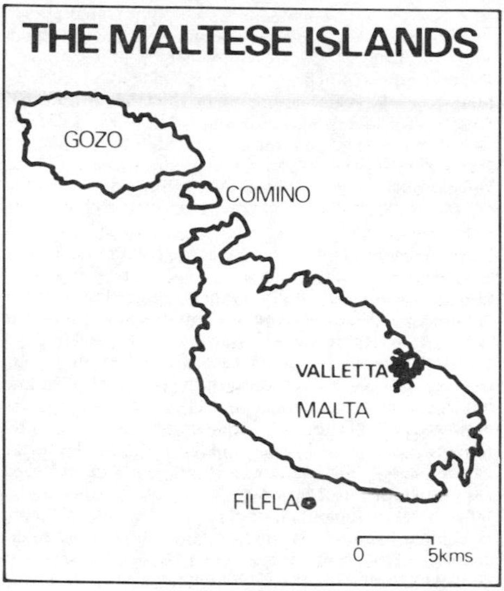

Council of Europe, FAO, G-77, GATT, ICAO, IFAD, ILO, IMF, IMO, INTERPOL, ITU, NAM, UN, UNDP, UNESCO, UNICEF, UPU, WHO, WIPO, WMO; Malta was an important strategic base in World War I and in World War II the island resisted frequent heavy air attacks; in recognition of the hardship suffered by the people of Malta the island was awarded the George Cross in 1942; the British Military Facilities agreement expired in 1979.

Physical description. The islands are generally low lying, the highest point being 244 m above sea level; there are no rivers or mountains and the coastline (136 km around Malta and 43 km around Gozo) is well indented with numerous harbours, bays and rocky coves. The soil, which contains much lime, is largely shallow except on the lowest ground.

Climate. The climate which has made Malta a major tourist resort is characterized by a dry summer season and a mild winter season (Nov-March); the average annual rainfall is about 400 mm and the average daily winter temperature is 13°C.

History, government and constitution. Malta was formally established as a British Crown Colony by the Treaty of Paris in 1814 and subsequently became a free port servicing British trade with the Near East and the Adriatic; in 1960 Malta was given internal self-government with foreign affairs and defence still the responsibility of the British Government; in 1962 the Nationalist Party was successful at the polls and a move was made to obtain independence which was eventually granted in Dec 1974 when Malta became a republic. The Constitution is largely based on the 1964 Malta Independence Constitution with subsequent amendments; the Parliament consists of the President who is elected for 5 years and the 65-member House of Representatives, also elected for 5 years from 13 districts; executive authority is vested in the President who appoints a Prime Minister and a Cabinet of Ministers. The Constitution contains a declaration of principles concerning, amongst others, social assistance and insurance, the right to work, the rights of women workers, hours of work, free education and the encouragement of private enterprise.

Economy. Tourism and ship repair are major industries but Malta's main exports include tobacco, canned foods, light engineering products and a wide range of semi-manufactured items ranging from textiles, paints and detergents to plastic and steel goods; the main imports are fuels, chemicals, machinery and a wide range of consumer goods. Major trade partners include EEC member countries and the USA.

Energy. Three thermal power stations (85, 30 and 12 MW) supply the Maltese Is, the largest also incorporating 4 seawater desalination plants with a potential production of 6 mn gallons of drinking water per day.

Agriculture. There are 132.27 sq km of arable land, the main crops being potatoes, tomatoes, onions, wheat, barley, grapes, oranges and cut flowers; there are also large numbers of cattle, sheep, goats and poultry; in 1982 agriculture employed 4,332 full-time and 11,026 part-time farmers.

Maltby, 53 26N 1 11W, pop(1981) 16,771, town in Doncaster borough, South Yorkshire, N England; 11 km S of Doncaster; economy: coal, engineering; monument: Romanesque St Bartholomew's church.

Maluku *me-loo'koo*, MOLUCCAS, SPICE IS, island group and province of Indonesia; lying between Sulawesi (Celebes) in the W and New Guinea (E); includes about 1,000 islands, the 3 largest of which are Halmahera, Seram and Buru; mostly volcanic and mountainous; pop(1980) 1,411,006; area 74,505 sq km; capital Ambon; discovered by the Portuguese in 1512 the islands came under Dutch rule in the early 17th century; economy: copra, spices, sago, coconut oil, tunafish.

Mamelo'di, black African township on the outskirts of Pretoria, Transvaal, South Africa.

Mamou *ma-moo'*, 10 24N 12 05W, town in W central Guinea, W Africa; 200 km ENE of Conakry; railway.

Mamoudzou or **Mamutzu** *mam-oo-tsoo*, 12 47S 45 14E, pop(1978) 7,798, largest commune on the island of Grande Terre, Mayotte, in W Indian Ocean; administered by France.

Mampong *mam-pong'*, 7 06N 1 20W, town in Ashanti region, S central Ghana, W Africa; 50 km NE of Kumasi.

Mamry *mam'ri*, lake in Suwałki voivodship, NE Poland; in Węyrtgorapa river basin; second largest lake in Poland; area 104.4 sq km; greatest depth 43.8 m.

Man, dept in W Ivory Coast, W Africa; pop(1975) 278,659; area 7,050 sq km; capital Man; chief town Logoualé; economy: iron ore.

Man, Isle of, British island situated in the Irish Sea, W of England and E of Northern Ireland; rises to 189 m at Snaefell in the centre of the island; pop(1981) 64,679; area 572 sq km; capital Douglas; other towns are Castletown, Peel and Ramsey; the circular artificial mound called Tynwald Hill, at St John's, near the centre of the island, where all acts of the Manx parliament must be proclaimed, is a relic of Scandinavian antiquity; seat of the Bishop of Sodor and Man, ruled by the Welsh during the 6-9th centuries, then by Scandinavians until Magnus, king of Norway, ceded it and the Hebrides to Alexander III of Scotland in 1266; granted to the Earls of Derby in 1406, it passed to the Dukes of Atholl in 1736; the island was purchased by the British Government partly in 1765 and wholly in 1828; the island has its own parliament, the Court of Tynwald, composed of the governor, the Legislative Council and the elected House of Keys, Acts of the British parliament do not generally apply to Man; event: annual Tourist Trophy motorcycle races.

Mana Pools, national park in N Zimbabwe, S Africa; area 2,196 sq km; established in 1963; situated NE of L Kariba and bordered NW by 70 km of the R Zambezi (also the frontier with Zambia); the park sits astride what is known as the Middle Valley and for several km back from the river are fertile river terraces; in this part of the valley are the remains of old river channels, some still holding water; the Middle Valley is inhabited by an extensive range of wildlife; during the dry season animals migrate toward the river in huge numbers; profuse birdlife includes Goliath herons, Egyptian and spurwing geese, cormorants, storks, eagles, vultures.

Manabí *ma-na-bee'*, tropical lowland prov of W Ecuador; bounded W by the Pacific; traversed by the Equator; consists of low Andean ridges and forested lowlands; drained by the Portoviejo and Chone rivers; pop(1982) 906,676; area 18,853 sq km; capital Portoviejo; chief towns Jipijapa and Chone; economy: fish, flour, vegetables, drink, tobacco, food processing, animal foodstuffs, mining (sand, clay), textiles, leather, paper products, minerals.

Manacor *ma-na-kor'*, 39 34N 3 13E, pop(1981) 24,153, town in the SE of Mallorca I, Balearic Is, Baleares autonomous region, Spain; nearby is the great limestone cavern of Drach, with subterranean lakes; economy: tourism, brandy, pottery, jewellery.

Managua *ma-na'gwa*, maritime dept in W Nicaragua, Central America; bounded SW by the Pacific Ocean; Lago de Managua occupies much of the centre of the dept; the Cordillera del Pacifico extends NW-SE across the dept; pop(1981) 819,679; area 3,448 sq km; capital Managua; chief towns Tipitapa and San Rafael del Sur.

Managua, 12 06N 86 18W, pop(1981) 819,679, commercial centre and capital city of the republic of Nicaragua, Central America; in Managua dept, W Nicaragua, on the S shore of Lago de Managua, 45 km inland from the Pacific Ocean; bounded W by the Cordillera del Pacifico; destroyed by earthquake in 1931 and 1972 and by civil war in the late 1970s; nearby is the archaeological site of the Huellas de Acahualinca where prehistoric animal footprints are preserved in solidified lava; university (1961); airport; railway; economy: textiles, matches, cigarettes, cement; event: Fiesta of Santo Domingo (1-10 Aug).

Managua, Lago de, lake in León and Managua depts, W Nicaragua, Central America; 2nd largest lake in Nicaragua; area 1,010 sq km; length 37 km; width 26 km; connected to Lago de Nicaragua (SE) by the short Río Tipitapa; Managua is on the SE shore; other ports include Puerto Momotombo and Mateare.

Manāmah, Al or **Manama** *me-na'me*, 26 12N 50 38E, pop(1981) 121,986, seaport capital of the State of Bahrain; on N coast of Bahrain I in the Arabian Gulf; connected by a causeway with Muharraq I to the NE; a free trade port with facilities at Mina Sulman near Sitra Wharf; economy: oil refining, entrepôt trade, commerce, banking.

Manas *ma-nas'*, NYAMYANG CHU (Chin), DANGME CHU (Bhut), river rising in the Himalayas of SE Tibet, China; flows S through Bhután and the Indian state of Assam to meet the R Brahmaputra opposite Goālpāra; length 352 km.

Manaus *ma-nã'os*, 3 06S 60 00W, pop(1980) 611,736, river-port capital of Amazonas state, Norte region, N Brazil; on the N bank of the Río Negro just above its influx into the Amazon; the city is built on a series of gentle hills divided by numerous creeks; the collecting point for produce of a vast area, including parts of Peru, Bolivia and Colombia; because of the variation in the level of the Río Negro (which has an annual rise and fall of 14 m) the harbour installations have a floating ramp about 150 m long leading from street level to the passenger-ship floating dock; founded in 1660; a free zone was established in 1967; university (1965); airfield; economy: timber, rubber, natural fibres; monument: the Teatro Amazonas opera house completed in 1896 during the great rubber boom and rebuilt in 1929 and 1974 seats over 1,000 people; event: folklore festival at the end of June.

Manche *mãsh*, dept in Basse-Normandie region of NW France, on the English Channel; comprises 4 arrond, 52 cantons and 597 communes; pop(1982) 465,948; area 5,938 sq km; bounded on the W by the Golfe de St-Malo and on the E by the Baie de la Seine; consists of the Cotentin peninsula; watered by the Sélune and Vire rivers, and many small streams; the cliffs have several harbours, of which Cherbourg is the most important; of the numerous islands, Mont-St-Michel is the most notable; rises in the E to the Collines de Normandie; capital St-Lo; chief towns Cherbourg, Avranches and Coutances.

Man'chester, MANCUNIUM (Lat), 53 30N 2 15W, pop(1981) 448,674, metropolitan dist in Greater Manchester urban area, NW England, on the R Irwell, 256 km NW of London; the Roman town was located at a major crossroads; became the centre of the local textile industry in the 17th century and the focal point of the English cotton industry during the Industrial Revolution in the 18th century; incorporated in 1838 and became a city in 1853; university (1880); railway; airport; connected to the Irish Sea by the 57 km Manchester Ship Canal (1894); economy: textiles, chemicals, engineering, paper, foodstuffs, rubber, electrical equipment, printing; monuments: 15th-c cathedral; Chetham's Hospital and Library, the oldest public library in England; Free Trade Hall (1843); Liverpool Road Station, the world's oldest surviving passenger station.

Manchester, 43 00N 71 28W, pop(1980) 90,936, town in Hillsborough county, S New Hampshire, United States; on the R Merrimack, 24 km S of Concord; airfield; railway.

Manchuria *man-choo-ree-a*, former region of NE China; now part of Liaoning, Jilin and Heilongjiang provs; most of the region is hilly and mountainous and for centuries the area was sparsely populated by nomadic tribes; the Manchus overthrew the Ming dynasty to become the last Chinese emperors (Qing dynasty, 1644-1911); the region contains vast natural resources in the form of timber and minerals (coal, iron, magnesite, oil, uranium and gold); during the 19th century these minerals were sought after by Western powers; Russia, looking for an outlet to the Pacific, leased Port Arthur (Lüshun) in 1898 and took military control of Manchuria in 1900; after the Russo-Japanese War Japan captured most of S Manchuria; in 1932 Japan captured the whole of Manchuria, installed the deposed Manchu emperor, Pu Yi, and established the puppet state of Manchukuo, consisting of Manchuria and Jehol prov; Russia re-asserted its control over Port Arthur after the defeat of Japan in 1945; in 1950 Russian troops were withdrawn and Chinese sovereignty recognized.

Manda *mã-da'*, national park in Moyen-Chari prefecture, S Chad, N central Africa; 27 km from Sarh; area 1,140 sq km; established in 1965.

Mandal, *mahn'dahl*, 58 02N 7 30E, pop(1980) 12,134, town on the S coast of Vest-Agder county, SW Norway; on the Skagerrak, W of Kristiansand; most southerly town in Norway.

Mandalay *man-da-lay'*, division in central Burma; N and NW borders with Sagaing and Magwe divisions formed by the R Irrawaddy; pop(1983) 4,580,923; capital Mandalay; in the extreme W of the division is the town of Pagan (founded in 109 AD); known as the city of four million pagodas, it contains the largest concentration of pagodas and temples in Burma, most of which were built from the 11th to the 13th century; Pagan attained national and historical greatness in 1044 under King Anawrahta when it became the seat of Buddhist learning and the centre of Burmese culture.

Mandalay, 21 57N 96 04E, pop(1983) 417,226, river port capital of Mandalay division, central Burma; on R Irrawaddy, N of Rangoon; university (1964); railway; airfield; monuments: Kuthodaw Pagoda contains 729 marble slabs on which are inscribed the entire Buddhist canons; Shwenandaw Kyaung is a traditional Burmese wooden monastery.

Mandalgovĭ *man'dal-gō'bee*, MANDALGOV, MANDAL GOBI, 45 40N 106 10E, capital of Dundgovĭ county, central Mongolia; economy: agricultural trade, camel breeding and coal mining.

Mandaluyong *mahn-dah-loo'yong*, 14 36N 121 02E, pop(1980) 205,366, city in Capital prov, Philippines; on Luzon I, near Manila.

Mandeville *man'di-vil*, 18 02N 77 31W, pop(1982) 34,502, capital town of Manchester parish, Middlesex county, W central Jamaica, 72 km W of Kingston; alt 1,950 m; the Manchester Club has the oldest golf course on the island; economy: bauxite, tourism and Pickapepper sauce factory to the NE.

Mandi Burewala, city in Pakistan. See Burewala.

Mandurah *man-doo'ra*, 32 31S 115 41E, pop(1981) 10,978, resort town in South-West stat div, Western Australia, Australia; on the Peel Inlet, S of Perth.

Mangaia *mang-ī'a*, 21 56S 157 56W, volcanic island of the Cook Is, S Pacific, 176 km SE of Rarotonga; area 52 sq km; pop(1981) 1,364; a cliff of coral limestone (*makatea*), surrounds low hills in the centre of the island; pineapples, bananas, and coconuts are grown.

Mangalia *man-ga'lya*, CALLATIS (anc), 43 48N 28 36E, pop(1983) 37,167, port and health resort town in Constanța, SE Romania; situated on the W shores of the Black Sea S of Constanța; established by the Greeks in 504 BC and later restored by the Romans and then by Constantine the Great in the 4th century; railway terminus.

Mangalore *mung'ga-lor*, 12 54N 74 51E, pop(1981) 306,000, seaport in Karnataka state, S India; on the Malabar coast of the Arabian Sea, 725 km SSE of Bombay at the mouth of the Netravati river; an important trade centre with the Persian Gulf in the 14th century; in 1763 it became a strategic shipbuilding centre for the sultans of Mysore; Mangalore was ceded to the British in 1799; linked by rail to Calicut and Coimbatore; airfield; economy: tiles, textiles, hosiery, trades in spices, coffee, rice, nuts and timber.

Mango *mang'gō*, SANSANNÉ-MANGO *san-sa'nay*, 10 23N 0 35E, town in Des Savanes region, NW Togo, W Africa; on the R Oti, 160 km NNW of Sokodé.

Mango'chi, dist in Southern region, Malawi, SE Africa; area 6,272 sq km; pop(1977) 302,341; the Shires river leaves L Nyasa through Mangochi dist.

Mangotsfield, 51 29N 2 29W, pop(1981) 28,758, town in Kingswood dist, Avon, SW England; part of Bristol urban area.

Manhat'tan, 39 11N 96 35W, pop(1980) 32,644, county seat of Riley county, NE central Kansas, United States; on the R Kansas, 76 km W of Topeka; university (1863); railway; economy: processed foods and farm machinery.

Manhattan, an island forming one of the 5 boroughs of the City of New York, New York state, E United States; at the N end of New York Bay, bounded W by the Hudson river; co-extensive with New York county; area 57 sq km; pop(1980) 1,428,285; settled by the Dutch as part of New Netherlands in 1626; taken by the British in 1664; major financial and commercial centre based around Wall Street and the World Trade Center; headquarters of the United Nations; 3 universities (1754, 1831, 1848); the island is named after a tribe of Indians who lived there when the Dutch first settled the area.

Manhattan Beach, 33 54N 118 25W, pop(1980) 31,542, resort city in Los Angeles county, SW California, United States; on the Pacific Ocean in Santa Monica Bay, 24 km SW of Los Angeles.

Manica *ma-nee'ka*, prov in W central Mozambique, SE Africa; pop(1980) 641,200; area 61,661 sq km; Mount Binga (2,436 m), the highest point in Mozambique is located on the W border with Zimbabwe; capital Chimoio, chief towns include Manica, Catandica, Tambara, Guro and Sussundenga; the railway from Beira runs E-W across prov before crossing into Zimbabwe just W of Manica.

Manicaland *ma-nee'ka-land*, region of E Zimbabwe, S Africa; bounded E by Mozambique; Mutare is the chief town.

Manihiki *ma-nee-hee'kee*, 10 24S 161 01W, coral atoll of the Cook Is, S Pacific, 1,048 km NNW of Rarotonga; area 5.4 sq km; pop(1981) 405; the administrative centre is Tauhuna; exports include copra and pearl shells; taro is grown in large man-made pits.

Manila *ma-nee'la*, *ma-ni'la*, 14 36N 120 59E, pop(1980) 1,630,485, cultural, commercial and industrial capital of the Philippines; on Manila Bay, SW Luzon I; on R Pasig; founded by Legazpi in 1571, it became an important trade centre under the Spanish; occupied by the British (1762-63); taken by the USA in Aug 1898 during the Spanish-American War; 15 universities; railway; airport; economy: shipbuilding, chemicals, textiles, timber, food processing.

Manipur *mun'i-poor*, state in NE India; pop(1981) 1,433,691; area 22,356 sq km; bounded N by Nagaland state, E by Burma and Mizoram state and W by Assam state; divided into 6 administrative districts; capital Imphal; governed by a 60-member Legislative Assembly; principal agricultural crops are rice, wheat, maize and pulses; fruits and vegetables are grown mainly in the river valleys; problems of soil erosion, produced by shifting cultivation, are gradually being lessened by the terracing of valley slopes; manufacturing industries include weaving, sugar, cement; Manipur was a state under the political control of the Government of India and was administered from the state of Assam until 1947 when it became a union territory; Manipur became a state in Jan 1972.

Manisa *ma'ni-sa*, prov in W Turkey; NE of İzmir; pop(1980) 941,941; area 13,810 sq km; capital Manisa; economy: fruit, grain, tobacco.

Manitoba *ma-ni-tō'ba*, formerly RED RIVER SETTLEMENT (-1870), province in central Canada; the westernmost of Canada's prairie provs; bounded by Saskatchewan (W), Keewatin dist of the Northwest Territories (N), Hudson Bay (NE), Ontario (E) and the United States (S); much of the prov consists of glacial lakes, the largest of which are lakes Winnipeg, Winnipegosis, Manitoba, Southern Indian, Moose and Cedar; drained by the Assiniboine, Red, Saskatchewan, Winnipeg and Dauphin rivers flowing into L Winnipeg and by the Nelson, Churchill, Hayes and Gods rivers flowing into Hudson Bay; 25% of the water of North America drains through Manitoba as it makes its way N to Hudson Bay; from a coastal plain on Hudson Bay in the NE the land gradually rises in the W and S; rises to 832 m in Baldy Mountain in the Duck Mts to the NW of L Dauphin; in the W of the prov are Duck Mountain Provincial Park and Riding Mountain National Park (area 2,975 sq km, established in 1927); pop(1981) 1,026,241; area 547,704 sq km; capital Winnipeg; major town: Brandon; economy: agriculture (grain cereals, especially wheat, livestock, vegetables), fishing, timber, hydroelectric power, food processing, mining, machinery, farm and transportation equipment, tourism; known as the 'land of 100,000 lakes', L Winnipeg and the lakes around it are the remains of the ice-age L Agassiz; first visited in 1612 by Sir Thomas Button who discovered the mouth of the Nelson river; in 1670 King Charles II granted trading rights in the area to the Hudson's Bay Co of London; the territory was named Rupert's Land; due to constant fighting between the English and the French over the fur trade, the Frenchman La Vérendrye had a series of forts built between L Superior and the Lower Saskatchewan river, including Fort Rouge in 1738 (now the site of Winnipeg); French claims were turned over to the British under the Treaty of Paris in 1763; in 1783 the North West Co was established to compete with the Hudson's Bay Co; settlement on the Red river was begun by the Earl of Selkirk in 1812 with the arrival of Scottish and Irish settlers; in 1869 Canada bought Rupert's Land (covering 3.9 million sq km) from the Hudson's Bay Co; Manitoba entered the confederation in July 1870, but was under the control of Louis Riel, leader of the Red River Insurrection, until August; at that time its area included only the settled region around Winnipeg, it was extended westward to the present Saskatchewan boundary in 1881, and N to Hudson Bay and the boundary with Northwest Territories in 1912; the Canadian Pacific Railroad reached Winnipeg in the 1880s, and led to the area's prosperity and development; Manitoba is governed by a Lieutenant-Governor assisted by an Executive Council which is responsible to the 57-member Legislative Assembly which is elected every 5 years.

Manitoba, lake in SW Manitoba prov, S Canada; W of L Winnipeg and SE of L Winnipegosis; 24 km N of Portage la Prairie; 209 km long by 45 km wide; area 4,659 sq km; the lake is drained into L Winnipeg in the NE via the Dauphin river; it receives the waters of L Winnipegosis in the NW; L Manitoba was once part of the glacial L Agassiz.

Man'itowoc, 44 05N 87 40W, pop(1980) 32,547, county seat of Manitowoc county, E Wisconsin, United States; port on L Michigan, at the mouth of the R Manitowoc; railway.

Manizales *ma-nee-sa'lays*, 5 03N 75 32W, pop(1985) 327,806, capital of Caldas dept, central Colombia, South America; straddles a narrow ridge in the Cordillera Central at 2,153 m; founded in 1848; university (1950); railway; the Teatro de los Fundadores is believed to have the largest stage in Latin America; the city is dominated by an enormous, unfinished concrete cathedral; facilities for skiing and mountain climbing at Nevado del Ruiz; experimental coffee plantation and freeze-dried coffee plant at Chinchiná; event: coffee festival in Jan.

Mankato *man-kay'tō*, 44 10N 94 00W, pop(1980) 28,651, county seat of Blue Earth county, S Minnesota, United States; on the R Minnesota, 104 km SW of Minneapolis; university; railway; economy: trade centre in a dairy farming region; site of Camp Lincoln, where 38 Sioux Indians were hanged in 1862.

Mannar', 8 58N 79 54E, pop(1981) 13,931, capital of Mannar dist, Northern prov, Sri Lanka; on Mannar I, off the NW coast of Sri Lanka; airfield at Mantota (SE); Mannar I is linked to India (Pamban I) by Adam's Bridge, a line of coral islands protected on either side by reefs; 64% of the pop of the dist is Tamil.

Mannheim *man'hīm*, 49 30N 8 28E, pop(1983) 299,700, commercial and manufacturing river port in Karlsruhe dist, NW Baden-Württemberg prov, W Germany; on right bank of R Rhine at the outflow of the canalized R Neckar, 70 km S by W of Frankfurt; university (1907); railway, one of the largest inland harbours in Europe; economy: agricultural machinery, motor vehicles (Daimler-Benz), electrical engineering, metalworking machines, oil refining, chemicals, pharmaceuticals, plastics, sugar refining, power cables, insulation materials.

Mano River Union, trade and economic alliance of the W African countries of Guinea, Liberia and Sierra Leone; established in 1981.

Manresa *man-ray'sa*, 41 48N 1 50E, pop(1981) 67,014, manufacturing and marketing town in Barcelona prov, Cataluña, NE Spain; on the R Cardoner, 45 km NW of Barcelona; economy: textiles, glass, tyres, metal products; monuments: Roman bridge, 14th-c collegiate church of St Mary and 17th-c Dominican convent over a cave once the retreat of Ignatius Loyola.

Mans, Le *le mã*, 48 00N 0 10E, pop(1982) 150,931, commercial city and capital of Sarthe dept, Pays de la Loire region, NW France; on the R Sarthe, 187 km SW of Paris; an agric trade centre; rail junction; it was the ancient capital of Maine; the old quarter, with many medieval streets and old houses, lies close to the E bank of the river; as the Gallic Oppidum Suindinum, it was fortified by the Romans in the 3rd-4th centuries; the Roman Wall is the best preserved of any in France; economy: motor vehicles (Le Mans has been associated with the motor industry for over 100 years); monuments: cathedral of St Julien (Romanesque and Gothic styles), Notre-Dame-de-la-Coutore (former abbey church dating from the 11th century); event: 'Vingt-Quatre Heures du Mans', annual 24-hour motor race in June.

Mansa *mahn'se*, formerly FORT ROSEBERY (-1967), 11 10S 28 52E, capital of Luapula region, N Zambia, S central Africa; 160 km NE of Lubumbashi (Zaire); airfield.

Mansakon'ko, local government area in The Gambia, W Africa; pop(1983) 55,266; area 1,547.5 sq km.

Mans'field, 53 09N 1 11W, pop(1981) 72,108, urban area pop(1981) 155,466, town in Mansfield dist, Nottinghamshire, central England; on the R Maun, 22 km N of Nottingham; railway; economy: coal, footwear, chemicals, textiles, engineering.

Mansfield, 40 45N 82 31W, pop(1980) 53,927, county seat of Richland county, central Ohio, United States; 86 km WSW of Akron; railway.

Mansfield, Mount, highest point in Vermont state, United States; rises to 1,339 m E of L Champlain.

Mansfield Woodhouse, 53 10N 1 11W, pop(1981) 17,609, town in Mansfield dist, Nottinghamshire, central England; N of Mansfield; economy: coal, engineering.

Mansôa *man-sō'a*, 12 08N 15 18W, pop(1979) 5,390, town in Guinea-Bissau, W Africa; NE of Bissau.

Mansûra, El *man-soo'ru*, EL MANSURA, 30 08N 31 04E, pop(1976) 257,866, capital of Daqahlîya governorate, N Egypt; in the R Nile delta, 58 km SW of Dumyât (Damietta); founded in 1221; occupied by the Crusaders; Louis IX and his forces were defeated here in 1250; university (1972); railway.

Manta *man'ta*, 0 59S 80 44W, pop(1982) 100,338, port in Manabí prov, W Ecuador; on the Pacific coast, W of Portoviejo; economy: commerce, tobacco, drinks, fish packing, flour milling, vegetable oil, textiles and clothing, leather, paper, mining (clay, sand).

Mantiqueira, Serra da *man-chee-kay'ra*, mountain range in SE Brazil; approx 320 km long; runs parallel to the coast along Minas Gerais-São Paulo and Minas Gerais-Rio de Janeiro border; forms the N limit of the Paraíba river valley; rises to 2,787 m at Pico das Agulhas Negras; traversed by railways from Rio de Janeiro to the interior of Minas Gerais; contains several health resorts; merges in the NE with the Serra do Espinhaço.

Mantova *mahn'to-vah*, prov of Lombardia region, N Italy; pop(1981) 377,158; area 2,339 sq km; capital Mantova.

Mantova, MANTUA *man'tyoo-a* (Eng), 45 10N 10 47E, pop(1981) 60,866, capital town of Mantova prov, Lombardia region, N Italy; between Lago di Garda and the Po river, on the lower course of the R Mincio, which surrounds it on 3 sides; Virgil was born near here; railway; economy: sugar-refining, brewing, tanning, printing; monuments: the town is still surrounded by a ring of ancient walls and bastions; church of Sant'Andrea (1472-94), containing the tomb of Mantegna; cathedral (10-18th-c); Palazzo Ducale, the residence of the Gonzagas, now housing a number of important museums and collections; Castello San Giorgio (1395-1406), with frescoes by Mantegna.

Manú *ma-noo'*, national park in Madre de Dios dept, SE Peru; area 15,328 sq km; established in 1973.

Manu'a *man-oo'ah*, island group and district of American Samoa, in the S Pacific Ocean; comprises the islands of Ta'u (60 sq km), Ofu, and Olosega.

Manuae *ma-noo-a'e*, 19 21S 158 58W, coral atoll of the Cook Is, S Pacific, 198 km NE of Rarotonga; comprises 2 islets (Manuae and Te Au o tu) inside a barrier reef; area 6.2 sq km; pop(1981) 12; the island is owned by the people of Aitutaki and used as their copra plantation; the government has offered the atoll as an international marine park.

Manukau *ma-nu-kow'*, 37 03S 174 32E, pop(1981) 159,363, city in Central Auckland, North Island, New Zealand; 20 km SE of Auckland; railway.

Man'us, province in N Papua New Guinea; situated on the Equator, it comprises the Admiralty, Hermit and Ninigo island groups in the Solomon Sea N of mainland Papua New Guinea; area 2,100 sq km; pop(1980) 25,859; the chief town is Lorengau on Manus I in the Admiralty group; there is a naval base at Lombrom on Manus I.

Manzini, dist in the Highveld of W Swaziland, SE Africa; chief town Manzini.

Manzini, formerly BREMERSDORP (-1960), 26 30S 31 22E, pop(1976) 10,472, town in Swaziland, SE Africa; SE of Mbabane; Swaziland's main industrial and agricultural centre and the country's first administrative capital between 1890 and 1902; university (1964); airfield.

Mao *ma'ō*, 14 06N 15 11E, capital of Kanem prefecture, W Chad, N central Africa; NE of L Chad, 140 km WNW of Moussoro.

Maotai *mow-tī*, 27 54N 106 12E, town in Guizhou prov, S central China; on R Chishui, NW of Guiyang; noted as the centre of production of Chinese maotai liqueur since 1741; maotai is made from sorghum and wheat which is fermented then distilled 7 times; with the dredging of the river in the 18th century, Maotai became an important salt port.

Mapimí, Bolsón de *bōl-sōn' day mah-pee-mee'*, arid depression in N Mexico; in E Chihuahua, W Coahuila and N Durango states; a partially-irrigated plateau region with an average alt of approx 914 m.

Maple Heights, 41 25N 81 34W, pop(1980) 29,735, town in Cuyahoga county, NE Ohio, United States; residential suburb 16 km SE of Cleveland.

Maplewood, 45 00N 93 03W, pop(1980) 26,990, town in Ramsey county, SE Minnesota, United States; residential suburb 7 km NE of St Paul; railway.

Maputo *mah-poo'tō*, prov in S Mozambique, SE Africa;

pop(1988e) 903,621; area 25,756 sq km; capital Maputo; chief towns include Moamba and Bella Vista; coastline encircles Bay de Lourenço Marques (Delagoa Bay); railways emanating from Maputo run N and SW across the prov.

Maputo, formerly LOURENÇO MARQUES (-1976), 25 58S 32 32E, pop(1980) 755,000, seaport capital of Mozambique, SE Africa; also capital of district and prov of same name; on the Maputo Bay (Bay de Lourenço Marques), 485 km E of Johannesburg (South Africa); the first European visitor was António do Campo in 1502; later explored by the trader Lourenço Marques; became capital of Portuguese East Africa in 1907; one of 3 major outlets for mineral production; university (1962); railway (linked to the Transvaal in 1895); airport; economy: steel, textiles, ship repair, footwear, cement, furniture.

Mar Chiquita, Lago *mar chee-kee'ta*, salt lake in a swampy region of NE Córdoba prov, Argentina; area 1,500 sq km; c.72 km long and 24 km wide; 145 km NE of Córdoba; receives the Río Primero (SW), Río Segundo (SE) and Río Dulce (N); has no outlet; to the N are the Porongos salt lakes; tourist resort at Miramar on S shore; contains a group of islets, the largest of which is El Médano.

Mar del Plata *mar dhel pla'ta*, 38 00S 57 30W, pop(1980) 407,024, port on the Atlantic coast in SE Buenos Aires prov, Litoral, E Argentina; founded in 1874; one of the prime holiday resorts of South America, with up to 2 million visitors in the summer months (Dec-April); university (1750); railway; airfield; economy: meat packing, fish canning, tourism.

Ma'ra, region of N Tanzania, E Africa; bounded W by L Victoria and N by Kenya; pop(1985e) 862,000; chief town Musoma.

Maracaibo *ma-ra-kī'bō*, 10 44N 71 37W, pop(1981) 890,553, capital of Zulia state, NW Venezuela; on NW shore of L Maracaibo; 2 universities (1891, 1973); airport (La Chinita) at 3.5 km; 70% of the nation's oil output comes from the nearby lake area; the town consists largely of modern buildings, but some colonial houses remain around the docks.

Maracaibo, Lago de, lake in NW Venezuela; area 12,800 sq km; approx 209 km long and 120 km wide; linked to the Gulf of Venezuela through narrows and the Tablazo Bay; situated in the humid lowlands of Maracaibo Basin, surrounded by mountains; contains one of the world's greatest oilfields, discovered in 1917; the production of oil began in 1918, the N is semi-arid, but in the S the annual rainfall is 1,270 mm; the Maracaibo Lowlands are noted for the highest annual average temperatures in Latin America.

Maracay *ma-ra-kī'*, 10 15N 67 36W, pop(1981) 387,682, administrative and agricultural capital of Aragua state, N Venezuela; railway; the Ministry of Agriculture has a school and experimental stations here; monuments: the former Hotel Jardín with its park and fountain is now a government centre; Maracay's bullring is an exact replica of the one at Seville in S Spain; there is a mausoleum with a large triumphal arch built in honour of General Gómez.

Maradi *ma-ra-dee'*, dept in S central Niger, W Africa; a low-lying region with extensive seasonal floodplains; the R Gada flows NW from its source in Nigeria across the SW corner of the region; area 38,581 sq km; pop(1977e) 842,000; comprises 4 arrond; capital Maradi; chief towns Tessaoua, Gazaoua and Kournaka.

Maradi, 13 29N 7 10E, pop(1983) 65,100; capital of Maradi dept, S central Niger, W Africa; 200 km W of Zinder; airfield; economy: chemicals and tanning.

Maralin'ga, 30 13S 131 24E, ghost town, South Australia, Australia; on the E Nullarbor Plain, N of the transcontinental railway; this area was used by the British as a nuclear testing site in the 1950s.

Maramba *ma-ram'ba*, formerly LIVINGSTONE, 17 50S 25 53E, pop(1980) 71,987, capital of Southern prov, Zambia, S central Africa; 5 km from the R Zambezi and the Victoria Falls, 370 km SW of Lusaka; capital of former Northern Rhodesia between 1911 and 1935; a major tourist centre in Zambia; railway; airport; economy: clothing, car assembly, radio manufacture; monument: Livingstone Museum with exhibits relating to David Livingstone.

Maramureş *mar-moor'esh*, county in N Romania, bounded to the N by Ukrainskaya (Ukraine SSR); pop(1983) 529,732; area 6,215 sq km; capital Baia Mare.

Maranhão *mah-rahn-yã'ō*, state in Nordeste region, NE Brazil; bounded N by the Atlantic, E by the Gurupi and Tocantins rivers, W by the Río Parnaíba; situated on a low coastal plain with tropical rainforest and savannah vegetation; pop(1980) 3,996,404; area 328,663 sq km; capital São Luís; chief town Imperatriz; economy: babaçu nuts, rice, cattle raising, oil, salt; the Boa Esperança hydroelectric plant is located on the Río Parnaíba.

Marañón *ma-ra-nyōn'*, river in Peru, one of the Amazon's major headstreams; rises in the Andes, 137 km E of the Pacific; flows NNW along high Andean ranges until it nears the Ecuadorean border, then turns NE to break through the Pongo de Manseriche gorge into the Amazon basin; flowing E past Barranca and Nauta, it joins the Río Ucayali to form the Amazon 88 km SSW of Iquitos at 4 30S 73 27W; its estimated length is 1,600 km; main tributaries include the Santiago, Morona, Pastaza, Tigre, Huallaga rivers; navigable as far as the Pongo de Manseriche gorge.

Marão, Serra do *ma-rown'*, small mountain range, N of R Douro, Vila Real dist, N Portugal, rising to 1,415 m.

Marbella *mar-bay'ya*, 36 30N 4 57W, pop(1981) 67,822, port and resort on the Costa del Sol, Málaga prov, Andalucia, S Spain; lying in the shelter of the Sierra Blanca, between Málaga and Algeciras; watersports; large bathing beaches; economy: tourism, iron and steel, furniture; events: Fiesta del Sol in Jan; Pilgrimage to La Cruz de Juana in May; fiestas of San Bernabe with bullfights, market and procession, pilgrimage to Guadalpin in June; Semana del Sol in Aug and the Costa del Sol Rally car race in Dec.

Mar'burg, 50 49N 8 36E, pop(1983) 79,100, city in Gießen dist, Hessen (Hesse) prov, W Germany; on the R Lahn, 74 km N of Frankfurt; university (1527); railway; economy: pharmaceuticals, opticals; monuments: St Elizabeth's church (1235-83), castle (15-16th-c).

March, 52 33N 0 06E, pop(1981) 14,236, town in Fenland dist, Cambridgeshire, E central England; on the R Nene, 22 km E of Peterborough; railway; economy: railway engineering, agricultural trade; monument: 15th-c church of St Wendreda.

Marche *mar'kay*, mountainous region of central Italy, comprising the provs of Ancona, Ascoli Piceno, Macerata, and Pesaro-Urbino; pop(1981) 1,412,404; area 9,692 sq km; extends between the rivers Foglia and Tronto down the E slopes of the Appno Umbro-Marchigiano to the Adriatic Sea.

Marche-en-Famenne *mahrsh-ã-fah-men'*, dist of Luxembourg prov, SE Belgium; area 955 sq km; pop(1982) 43,003.

Mar'ço, Pico 21 de *mar'sō*, mountain in N Amazonas state, Norte region, N Brazil; on the border with Venezuela; in the Serra do Imeri mountain range; 2nd highest mountain in Brazil; height 2,992 m.

Mardan *mur-dan'*, 34 14N 72 05E, pop(1981) 148,000, city in North-West Frontier prov, Pakistan; NE of Peshawar; railway.

Mardin *mar-din'*, prov in SE Turkey, bounded S by Syria and E by the R Tigris; pop(1980) 564,967; area 12,760 sq km; capital Mardin; economy: cereals, textiles.

Margarita, Isla de *mar-ga-ree'ta*, island in Nueva Esparta state, Venezuela; lying in the Caribbean, N of the Venezuelan mainland and SW of Grenada; a free port and holiday resort.

Mar'gate, formerly MERGATE, 51 24N 1 24E, pop(1981) 54,980, resort town in Thanet dist, Kent, SE England; on Isle of Thanet, N of Ramsgate; railway; economy: textiles, scientific instruments.

Margate, 26 15N 80 12W, pop(1980) 36,044, town in Broward county, SE Florida, United States; 15 km NNW of Fort Lauderdale.

Mariager Fjord *mahr-ee-yer'*, inlet of the Kattegat in E Jylland (Jutland), Denmark; forms boundary between Århus and Nordjylland counties; extends 40 km inland to Hobro; Mariager is on S shore; the inner part is often called Hobro Fjord.

Mariana Islands, Commonwealth of the Northern, group of 14 islands in the NW Pacific, c.2,400 km E of the Philippines and 5,280 km W of Hawaii; area 471 sq km; capital Saipan; the islands are mainly volcanic (3 are still active) with coral limestone and lava shores; includes the islands of Saipan, Tinian, Rota, Pagan and Guguan; after World War II the US held the islands under UN mandate as part of the US Trust Territory of the Pacific Islands; they were awarded separate status in 1975 and self-government in 1978; economy: tourism.

Mariana Trench, a deep marine trench in the Pacific Ocean, situated E of the S Honshū Ridge, S of Japan. The Challenger Depth (11,022 m) is the greatest ocean depth in the world.

Maribor *ma'ree-bor*, MARBURG *mar'boork* (Ger), 46 35N 15 40E, pop(1981) 185,699, town in Slovenija republic, N Yugoslavia; on the R Drava, between the Pohorje and Kozjak hills, 106 km NE of Ljubljana; in recent times the town has expanded on the R bank of the river; sports stadium; university (1975); airfield; railway; economy: transport, metalworking, footwear, textiles; monuments: Gothic cathedral; palace of former prince-bishop.

Marica, river in Bulgaria, Greece, Turkey. See Maritsa.

Marie-Galante *ma-ree'ga-lāt'*, island belonging to the Overseas Department of Guadeloupe, Lesser Antilles, E Caribbean; 40 km E of Basse-Terre I; area 158 sq km; pop(1982) 13,757; chief town Grand-Bourg; the island is of limestone formation and circular in shape with a diameter of 16 km.

Mariestad *ma'ree-u-stad*, 58 44N 13 50E, pop(1982) 24,236, industrial town and capital of Skaraborg county, S Sweden, on the E shore of L Vänern opposite the island of Torsö; railway; monuments: cathedral (1593-1619), Marieholm Castle (residence of the governor of Skaraborg county).

Mariet'ta, 33 57N 84 33W, pop(1980) 30,829, county seat of Cobb county, NW Georgia, United States; 26 km NW of Atlanta; railway; economy: major aircraft-manufacturing centre; summer resort; nearby Mt Kennesaw was the scene of a Union defeat during the Civil War, in 1864; many of the dead are buried in the national cemetery in the city.

Marikina *mah-ree-kee'nah*, 14 37N 121 04E, pop(1980) 211,613, city in Capital prov, Philippines; on R Marikina, Luzon I, near Manila.

Marília *ma-reel'ya*, 22 13S 49 58W, pop(1980) 103,815, town in São Paulo state, Sudeste region, SE Brazil; NW of São Paulo; railway; economy: cotton, coffee, brewing, timber.

Maringá *ma-reen-ga'*, 23 36S 52 02W, pop(1980) 158,091, town in Paraná state, Sul region, S Brazil; W of São Paulo; founded in 1947; half the pop is Japanese; university (1970); railway; economy: commerce, coffee, wheat, agricultural implements, vegetable oils.

Marion, 40 32N 85 40W, pop(1980) 35,874, county seat of Grant county, central Indiana, United States; on the R Mississinewa, 45 km NW of Muncie; railway.

Marion, 40 35N 83 08W, pop(1980) 37,040, county seat of Marion county, central Ohio, United States; 69 km N of Columbus; railway; home of Warren G. Harding, 29th president of the United States.

Marismas, Las *mah-reez'mas*, an area of swamp and marshland at the mouth of the R Guadalquivir, Andalucia, SW Spain; 16 km S of Sevilla.

Marit'sa or **Marica**, HEVROS, EVEROS or HEBROS (Gr), MERIC (Turk); river in Bulgaria, Greece and Turkey; rises on Musala Peak in the Rila Planina (Rila Mts) SE of Sofiya, Bulgaria; flows 275 km E and ESE in Bulgaria; follows the Greco-Bulgarian border for 16 km and then the Greco-Turkish line for 185 km before turning S at Edirne and then SW to the Aegean Sea where it forms a delta on the Gulf of Enos; length 480 km; tributaries include the Vacha, Asenovitsa, Arda, Topolnitsa, Strema, Tundzha and Ergene rivers.

Mar'ka, 1 42N 44 47E, pop(1982) 60,000, port in Shabeellaha Hoose prov, Somalia, NE Africa; on Indian Ocean coast, 72 km SW of Muqdisho (Mogadishu); formerly part of Zanzibar, the area was leased (1892) and then sold (1905) to the Italians.

Markazī *mar-kah'zee*, mountainous prov in W central Iran; pop(1982) 1,230,393; area 39,895 sq km; capital Arāk.

Market Harborough *har'bu-ru*, 52 29N 0 55W, pop(1981) 15,966, town in Harborough dist, Leicestershire, central England; 23 km SE of Leicester; railway; economy: foodstuffs, electrical goods, clothing.

Markham, 43 54N 79 16W, pop(1981) 77,037, town in SE Ontario, SE Canada; situated on the Rouge river; 24 km NNE of Toronto; railway; event: autumn fair.

Markoy, 14 39N 0 02E, town in NE Burkina, W Africa; N of Dori.

Marl, 51 38N 7 06E, pop(1983) 88,000, city in Münster dist, Nordrhein-Westfalen (North Rhine-Westphalia) prov, W Germany, N of Gelsenkirchen; economy: chemicals, synthetic rubber, fertilizers, coal mining, sandlime bricks.

Marlboro, MARLBOROUGH, 42 21N 71 33W, pop(1980) 30,617, town in Middlesex county, E Massachusetts, United States; 21 km ENE of Worcester.

Mar'lin, gas field in the Bass Strait, off the S coast of Victoria, Australia.

Mar'low, 51 35N 0 48W, pop(1981) 18,598, town in Wycombe dist, Buckinghamshire, S central England; 7 km S of High Wycombe; railway.

Marmara Denizi *mar'mu-ru de-ni-zee'*, SEA OF MARMARA, PROPONTIS (anc), sea in NW Turkey, between Europe (N) and Asia (S); connected on the E with the Black Sea through the Karadeniz Boğazi (Bosporus) and on the W with the Aegean Sea through the Çanakkale Boğazi (Dardanelles); area 11,474 sq km; İstanbul is on its NE shore, at the entrance to the Karadeniz Boğazi; Marmara I (from which the sea gets its modern name) is in the W part.

Marmaţiei *mar-mat'yee*, SIGHETU MARMATIEI, 47 56N 23 53E, pop(1983) 42,118, town in Maramureş county, N Romania; railway; economy: textiles, timber, fruit, animal products.

Marmolada *mar-mo-la'dah*, highest peak in the Alpi Dolomitiche (Dolomites), N Italy, 40 km ESE of Bolzano; height 3,342 m.

Marne *marn*, dept in Champagne-Ardenne region of NE France, on the middle Marne R; comprises 5 arrond, 42 cantons and 618 communes; pop(1982) 543,627; area 8,162 sq km; the Plaine de Champagne covers the entire dept; watered by the Marne, Vesle and Aisne rivers and cut by numerous canals; capital Châlons-sur-Marne, chief towns Épernay, Reims and Ay, all noted centres of the rich Champagne wine trade; includes the Parc de la Montagne de Reims regional nature park, covering 494 sq km.

Marne, MATRONA (anc), river in central France rising in the Langres Plateau in Haute-Marne dept; flows NW and W across the dry chalk of Champagne, past Châlons, Épernay and Meaux, to meet the R Seine at Charenton-le-Pont, near Paris; length 525 km; navigable to St Dizier; it is joined to the rivers Rhine, Rhône and Aisne by a canal; tributaries Blaise, Petit-Morin, Grand-Morin, Saulx and Ourcq rivers; on its banks were fought 2 of the major battles of World War I.

Marondera *mahr-on-day'ra*, MARANDELLAS, 18 10S 31 36E, pop(1982) 20,000, town in Mashonaland East prov, Zimbabwe, S Africa; 65 km SE of Harare; railway.

Maroua *ma-roo'a*, MARUA, 10 35N 14 20E, pop(1984) 97,000, capital of Extrême-Nord prov, Cameroon, W Africa; on R Kaliao, 805 km NNE of Yaoundé and 195 km SSW of Ndjamena (Chad); centre of Foulbe culture and Islam; airfield; economy: dyed cotton, crafts, and the tanning of cattle, crocodile, lizard and python hides.

Marowijne *ma-ro-vī'na*, dist in E Surinam, NE South America; bordered E by the Marowijne and Litani rivers which follow the frontier with French Guiana, S by Brazil and the Serra de Tumucumaque and N by the Atlantic; Surinam has claimed the territory to the W of the R Marowijne; area 45,980 sq km; pop(1980) 23,402; capital Albina.

Marquesas, islands of French Polynesia. See Marquises, Îles.

Marquises, Îles *mar-keez'*, MARQUESAS ISLANDS *mar-kay'suz* (Eng), mountainous, wooded volcanic island group of French Polynesia, 1,184 km NE of Tahiti, S Pacific Ocean; comprises Nuku Hiva (where Herman Melville, author of *Moby Dick*, lived), Ua Pu, Ua Huka, Hiva Oa (where Gaugin painted), Tahuata, Fatu Hiva, and 5 smaller (uninhabited) islands; area 1,189 sq km; the chief centre is Taiohae on Hiva Oa; copra is the chief export; acquired by France in 1842.

Marra, Jebel, 12 59N 24 30E, mountain in Dafur region, Sudan, NE Africa; height 3,071 m; situated in Sudan's western desert, WSW of El Fasher.

Marrakech or **Marrakesh** *ma-ra-kesh'*, 31 49N 8 00W, pop(1982) 439,728, city in Marrakech prefecture, Tensift prov, central Morocco, N Africa; in the N foothills of the Haut Atlas, 241 km S of Casablanca; the Tensift river flows N of the city; one of Morocco's 4 imperial cities, founded in 1062 by Yusuf ibn Tashfin; university; railway; airport; economy: leather, carpets; monument: Koutoubia mosque (including 67 m tower) which was constructed by the Andalucians under the Almoravid dynasty during the 12th century.

Mar'sa, 35 52N 14 31E, pop(1983e) 9,486, community on the main island of Malta, situated at the head of Marsa Creek, an inlet of Grand Harbour; sports club; power stations.

Marseille *mar-se'y'*, MARSEILLES *mar-saylz'* (Eng), MASSILIA (anc), 43 18N 5 23E, pop(1982) 878,689, principal commercial port and capital of Bouches-du-Rhône dept, Provence-Alpes-Côte d'Azur region, S France; on the NE shore of the Golfe du Lion (Gulf of Lions), 40 km E of the mouth of the R Rhône, 130 km WSW of Nice; 2nd largest city in France and leading port of the Mediterranan; founded about 600 BC by Greeks from Asia Minor, on the rocky peninsula N of the Vieux Port (Old Port); the city's main thoroughfare is La Canebière which leads W to the Vieux Port, a natural inlet reaching far into the town and used as a harbour since the time of the Greek settlers; all the restaurants around the Vieux Port serve the famous bouillabaisse (fish soup); archbishopric; university; railway; airport; economy: shipbuilding, chemicals, iron, bauxite, copper, oil refining, engineering, soap, glass, cigarettes, alcoholic and non-alcoholic beverages, dairy produce, trade in fruit, wine, olive oil, vegetables, spices, hides; monuments: church of St-Victor, built in the 5th century by St-Cassien, in its present form dates from the 11th to 14th centuries with catacombs, a martyrium and a fine series of sarcophagi; 19th-c neo-Byzantine basilica of Notre-Dame-de-la-Garde (replaced an earlier pilgrimage chapel); town hall (1663-83); Cathédrale de la Major (1852-93), the largest church built in the 19th century, 141 m long; 11-12th-c Cathédrale St-Lazare (originally founded in the 4th century); the Musée des Beaux-Arts, with imposing murals by Puvis de Chavannes (1824-98) contains works by Perugino, Brueghel, Rubens and Tiepolo, together with paintings and drawings by Marseillais artists Puget (1622-94) and Daumier (1808-79); the New Harbour (Port Moderne), begun in 1844, has 25 km of quays and covers an area of more than 2 sq km; the Basin de la Joliette is used by passenger ships; event: international trade fair (mid-April until late Sept).

Marshalltown, 42 03N 92 55W, pop(1980) 26,938, county seat of Marshall county, central Iowa, United States; on the R Iowa, 77 km NE of Des Moines; railway.

Martha's Vineyard, island in the Atlantic off the SE coast of Massachusetts, United States; part of Duke's county; area 280 sq km; the chief town is Edgartown; so called because the first English settlers found an abundance of wild grapes growing here.

Martin *mar'tyin*, 49 05N 18 55E, pop(1984) 59,933, town in Středoslovenský region, Slovak Socialist Republic, E central Czechoslovakia; railway.

Martinique *mar-teen-eek'*, island in the Windward group of the Lesser Antilles, E Caribbean, situated between Dominica and St Lucia; since 1946 an overseas department of France; timezone GMT −4; area 1,079 sq km; capital Fort-de-France; pop(1982) 328,566; 90% of the pop is of African and African-Caucasian-Indian descent; Roman Catholicism is the dominant religion; French is the official language with creole dialect widely spoken; the unit of currency is the French franc; membership of WFTU.

Physical description and climate. Martinique, 61 km long and 24 km wide, rises steeply from the sea, particularly on the N coast where high cliffs are capped by a narrow dissected plain. Here the volcanic massif of Mt Pelée rises to 1,397 m, the highest point on the island. Mt Pelée erupted in 1902 killing approximately 26,000 people and destroying the town of St Pierre. The climate is tropical with high humidity. In Fort-de-France, the likely temperature range from Jan to March is 21°C to 29°C and from June to Oct it is 23°C to 31°C. There is a wet season from July to Nov. The lower S end of the island tends to be drier.

History, government and constitution. Visited by Columbus in 1502, Martinique became a French colony in 1635. In 1946, its status was changed to that of an overseas department and, as such, it is represented in the French national assembly by 3 deputies and 2 senators. The island is administered by a commissioner appointed by and representing the French government and an elected council of 36 members.

Economy. The economy is based largely on agriculture. The chief commercial crops include sugar cane, bananas, rum, and pineapples. In 1981 there were 45.5 sq km under sugar-cane, 72 sq km under bananas, and 6.2 sq km under pineapples. The major industries include construction, rum distilling, cement manufacturing, oil refining, light industry, and tourism. The tourist industry is developing, catering mainly for visitors from W Europe and USA. Chief imports include petroleum products, foodstuffs, construction materials, vehicles, clothing, and other consumer goods. The main items of export are petroleum products (45%), bananas (21%), and rum (11%). France and Guadeloupe are the main trade partners.

Administrative divisions. Martinique is divided into 3 arrondissements which in turn are sub-divided into 34 communes.

Communications. Lamentin International Airport is located 14 km from Fort-de-France.

Maryborough, 25 32S 152 36E, pop(1981) 20,111, town in Wide Bay-Burnett stat div, Queensland, Australia; near the mouth of the Mary river, N of Brisbane; situated among sugar plantations; railway; airfield; economy: commercial and administrative centre for the Hervey Bay and Wide Bay-Burnett region; shipbuilding, iron and steel, railway engineering, timber, coal, fruit.

Maryborough, 37 05S 143 47E, pop(1983e) 8,290, town in Loddon Campaspe stat div, W central Victoria, Australia; NW of Melbourne; railway; Maryborough railway station is a classical building from the Victorian era; nearby in Bowensvale is a eucalyptus distillery.

Maryland, state in E United States; bounded W by West Virginia, N by Pennsylvania, E by Delaware and the Atlantic Ocean, and S by Virginia and West Virginia; Chesapeake Bay stretches N through the state, almost splitting it in two; the District of Columbia makes a rectangular indent into the state at the Virginia border; the R Potomac forms most of the S border; the R Susquehanna flows SE across the extreme NE corner of the state, emptying into Chesapeake Bay; the R Patuxent flows SE through the centre of the state to empty into Chesapeake Bay; the highest point is Mt Backbone (1,024 m); the Fall Line, running between Baltimore and Washington, DC, divides the state in two; to the N and W is the rolling Piedmont, rising up to the Blue Ridge and Pennsylvania Hills; to the S and E the region is dominated by Chesapeake Bay with indented shores that form a popular resort area; the farm economy is reliant on water transport; the Eastern Shore with over 12,000 sq km of forest is noted for its scenic beauty; economy: iron and steel, shipbuilding, electrical equipment, machinery and processed foods; the chief agricultural products are poultry, dairy products, corn, soybeans and tobacco; the 'Old Line' or 'Free State'; Maryland is often called 'America in miniature'; the first settlement (1634) was located at St Mary's (state capital until 1694); 7th of the original 13 states to ratify the Constitution (1788); gave up territory for the establishment of the District of Columbia; abolished slavery in 1864; pop(1980) 4,216,975; area 25,576 sq km; capital Annapolis; the other major city is Baltimore; the state is divided into 23 counties and one city:

County	*area (sq km)*	*pop(1980)*
Allegany	1,095	80,548
Anne Arundel	1,087	370,775
Baltimore	1,555	655,615
Baltimore City	208	786,775
Calvert	554	34,638
Caroline	835	23,143
Carroll	1,175	96,356
Cecil	936	60,430
Charles	1,175	72,751
Dorchester	1,542	30,623
Frederick	1,724	114,792
Garrett	1,708	26,498
Harford	1,165	145,930
Howard	653	118,572
Kent	723	16,695
Montgomery	1,287	579,053
Prince George's	1,266	665,071
Queen Anne's	967	25,508
Somerset	879	19,188
St Mary's	970	59,895
Talbot	673	25,604
Washington	1,183	113,086
Wicomico	985	64,540
Worcester	1,235	30,889

Masan *mah-sahn*, 35 10N 128 35E, pop(1984) 440,773, industrial capital of Kyŏngsangnam prov, SE Korea; situated on the S coast, facing the Korea Strait; railway.

Masaya *ma-sī'a*, dept in W Nicaragua, Central America; smallest dept in the republic; there are several lakes including Lago de Tisma on the E border and Lago de Apoyo on S border; pop(1981) 149,015; area 601 sq km; capital Masaya.

Masaya, 11 59N 86 03W, pop(1978) 47,276, capital town of Masaya dept, W Nicaragua, Central America; 30 km SE of Managua; Lago de Masaya is to the W of the town; centre of a rich agricultural area growing tobacco; railway; economy: Indian handicrafts; event: fiesta (30 Sept).

Masbate *mahs-baht'ee*, mountainous island in central Philippines; S of Luzon I and W of Samar; area 4,047 sq km; chief town Masbate.

Masca'ra, department of NW Algeria, N Africa; area 5,845 sq km; pop(1982) 502,022; chief town Mascara.

Mascerenes Islands *maz-ker-een'*, ARCHIPEL DES MASCAREIGNES *mas-ka-ren'ye* (Fr), island group in the Indian Ocean; 700-800 km E of Madagascar; includes the islands of Réunion, Mauritius and Rodrigues; named after the 16th-c Portuguese navigator Mascarenhas.

Maseru *ma'zu-roo*, 29 19S 27 29E, pop(1976) 45,000; capital of Lesotho, S Africa; on the R Caledon, 130 km E of Bloemfontein (South Africa); alt 1,506 m; university (1964); experimental crop station; railway terminus; airport; economy: administration, commerce, diamond processing and tourism.

Mashhad *mash-had'*, MESHED *me-shed'*, 36 16N 59 34E, pop(1983) 1,119,748, capital city of Mashhad dist, Khorāsān, NE Iran; 75 km from the USSR border, just S of the R Kashaf; 2nd largest city in Iran; industrial and trade centre; railway; airport; monument: golden-domed 9th-c shrine of Imam Ali Reza, one of the leading centres of Shiite pilgrimage.

Mashonaland *ma-shō'na-land*, tableland region of NE Zimbabwe, S Africa; divided into the 3 administrative regions of Mashonaland West, Mashonaland East and Mashonaland Central; bounded NE by Mozambique and NW by Zambia; Harare, the capital of Zimbabwe, is located in Mashonaland East; named after the Mashona Bantus; the territory was acquired by the British South Africa Company in 1890; in 1923 it became part of the British colony of Southern Rhodesia.

Masindi *ma-seen'dee*, 1 41N 31 45E, town in Western prov, Uganda, E Africa; 180 km NW of Kampala.

Maşīrah *me-sir'a*, island in the Arabian Sea off the E coast of Oman.

Masjed Soleymān *mas-jed' sō-lay-man*, 31 59N 49 18E, pop(1983) 116,851, industrial town in Masjed Soleymān dist, Khuzestān, W central Iran; 32 km E of Shushtar and 200 km NE of Ābādān (to which it is linked by a pipeline); situated in the S foothills of the Zagros Mts, on a tributary of the R Kārūn; site of the first discovery of petroleum in Iran (1908); airfield; rail terminus; economy: oil refining.

Mask, Lough, lake in Mayo and Galway counties, W Irish Republic; E of Connemara at N end of L Corrib to which it is linked; receives R Robe.

Mason City, 43 09N 93 12W, pop(1980) 30,144, county seat of Cerro Gordo county, N Iowa, United States; 99 km NW of Waterloo; railway.

Masqaţ *mos'kot*, MUSCAT *mus'kat*, 27 37N 58 36E, pop(1974e) 25,000, seaport capital of the Sultanate of Oman, SE Arabian peninsula; on a peninsula which juts into the Gulf of Oman and backed by mountains of the E Hajar; occupied by the Portuguese from 1508 to 1650; the town was once of great commercial importance but has now lost much of its trade to the adjacent port of Maţraḩ, the starting point for trade routes into the interior; residence of the Sultan; Seeb International Airport is situated 43 km to the W; economy: natural gas, chemicals; monuments: 2 forts built between 1527 and 1587-88.

Massa *mas'sa*, 44 02N 10 07E, pop(1981) 65,687, capital town of Massa-Carrara prov, Toscana region, NW Italy; near the Ligurian coast, between Pisa and La Spezia; airfield; railway; economy: marble quarries.

Massa-Carrara *mas'sa-ka-ra'ra*, prov of Toscana region, NW Italy; pop(1981) 203,530; area 1,155 sq km; capital Massa.

Massachusetts, *ma-sa-choo'sets*, a New England state in NE United States, bounded W by New York, N by Vermont and New Hampshire, E by the Atlantic Ocean and S by the Atlantic Ocean, Rhode Island and Connecticut; the 'Bay State' or 'Old Colony'; pop(1980) 5,737,037; area 20,342 sq km; one of the original states of the Union, 6th to ratify the Federal Constitution; capital Boston; major towns include Cambridge, Springfield and Worcester; rises from an indented coastline to a stony, upland interior and gentle, rolling hills to the W; the R Connecticut flows N-S across W part of the state, the R Housatonic flows S near W border and the R Merrimack enters the Atlantic Ocean in the NE; the Berkshire Hills rise between the Housatonic and Connecticut rivers; the highest point is Mt Greylock (1,049 m); economy: electronics, printing and publishing, timber, nursery and greenhouse produce, vegetables, cranberries; the Pilgrim Fathers who settled at Plymouth in 1620 held the first Thanksgiving Day in the following year; the first shots of the War of Independence were fired at Lexington in 1775; the state is divided into 14 counties as follows:

County	*area (sq km)*	*pop(1980)*
Barnstable	1,040	147,925
Berkshire	2,415	145,110
Bristol	1,448	474,641
Dukes	265	8,942
Essex	1,287	633,632
Franklin	1,825	64,317
Hampden	1,607	443,018
Hampshire	1,373	138,813
Middlesex	2,137	1,367,034
Nantucket	122	5,087

contd

County	*area (sq km)*	*pop(1980)*
Norfolk	1,040	606,587
Plymouth	1,703	405,437
Suffolk	148	650,142
Worcester	3,934	646,352

Massa'na, La, pop(1982) 2,705, one of the seven parishes of the Principality of Andorra with a village seat of the same name situated 5 km NW of Andorra la Vella in the Valira del Nord valley; alt 1,300 m.

Mas'sillon, 40 48N 81 32W, pop(1980) 30,557, town in Stark county, E Ohio, United States; 13 km W of Canton; railway.

Masvingo *mas-ving'gō*, formerly FORT VICTORIA or NYANDA, 20 10S 30 49E, pop(1982) 30,600, capital of Victoria prov, Zimbabwe, S Africa; 130 km SE of Gweru; the oldest town in Zimbabwe; Lake Kyle (90 sq km, SE) was created by damming the R Mtilikwe to provide irrigation water for agricultural projects; the lake also serves as a recreational park; railway; airfield; economy: construction materials; monuments: 2 towers of a fort constructed by early settlers remain; 28 km SE near L Kyle are the ruins of Great Zimbabwe; a chapel 3 km from Masvingo was built by Italian prisoners of war during World War II.

Mat, prov of N central Albania; area 1,028 sq km; pop(1973) 53,500; capital Burrel.

Matabeleland *mat-e-bee'lee-land*, region of W and S Zimbabwe, S Africa; between the Zambezi and Limpopo rivers; comprises the administrative regions of Matabeleland North and Matabeleland South; Bulawayo is the chief town of Matabeleland North; named after the Matabele Bantu, a Zulu tribe originally located in Natal and the Transvaal; the territory was acquired by the British South Africa Company in 1889; in 1923 it became part of the British colony of Southern Rhodesia.

Matadi *ma-ta'dee*, 5 50S 13 32E, pop(1976e) 162,396, river-port capital of Bas-Zaïre region, W Zaire, central Africa; on S bank of the Zaire river, 40 km E of Boma; close to the Angolan border and 130 km from the Atlantic Ocean.

Matagalpa *ma-ta-gal'pa*, dept in central Nicaragua, Central America; traversed by the Cordillera Dariense (W-E) which rises to over 1,000 m, and by the Inter-American Highway; pop(1981) 220,548, area 8,746 sq km; capital Matagalpa; the other chief town is Esquipulas.

Matagalpa, 12 52N 85 58W, pop(1978) 26,986, capital town of Matagalpa dept, central Nicaragua, Central America; in a rich coffee-growing district; railway; economy: powdered milk.

Matale *mat'el-ay*, 7 28N 80 37E, pop(1981) 29,752, capital of Matale dist, Central prov, Sri Lanka; 18 km N of Kandy; monuments: temple of Alu Vihara and a Buddhist monastery.

Matamoros *ma-ta-mōr'ōs*, 25 53N 97 31W, pop(1980) 238,840, town in Tamaulipas state, NE Mexico; 280 km E of Monterrey, on the Río Grande where it follows the border with the USA, opposite Brownsville, Texas; railway; economy: cotton, distilling, tanning, vegetable oil.

Matan'zas, prov in NW Cuba, extending from the Atlantic Ocean (N) to the Caribbean Sea (S); the Zapata Peninsula in the S is marshy; area 11,669 sq km; pop(1981) 557,628; capital Matanzas; chief towns Colón and Cárdenas; Varadero is a popular tourist centre.

Matanzas, 23 04N 81 35W, pop(1983e) 103,605, seaport and capital town of Matanzas prov, NW Cuba; on the N coast of the island, between the Yumuri and San Juan rivers, 104 km E of La Habana (Havana); on the Via Blanca which links La Habana with Varadero Beach, 34 km E of Matanzas; founded in 1690; railway; originally noted as a centre for coffee and tobacco production; between 1851 and 1861 over half of Cuba's sugar was produced here; nicknamed 'the Athens of Cuba' because of its former association with poets, scientists and artists.

Matara *maht'e-re*, 5 57N 80 32E, pop(1981) 38,843, capital of Matara dist, Southern prov, Sri Lanka; at the tip of the S coast, midway between Galle and Tangalla; centre of cinnamon trade during colonial times; famed for white zircons, locally known as Matara diamonds; monuments: 2 Dutch forts.

Mataram *ma-tah'rem*, 8 36S 116 07E, pop(1980) 68,964, capital of Nusa Tenggara Barat, Indonesia; on the W coast of Lombok I.

Mataro *ma-ta-ro'*, ILLURO (anc), 41 32N 2 29E, pop(1981) 96,467, industrial port in Barcelona prov, Cataluña, NE Spain; 25 km NE of Barcelona; divided into upper old town and lower new town; the first railway in Spain was built from Barcelona to Mataro (1848); beaches and harbour.

Mataura *ma-tow'ra*, river in S South Island, New Zealand; rises in the Garvie mountain range; flows S past the towns of Gore, Mataura and Wyndham to enter the Foveaux Strait in Toetoes Bay, ESE of Invercargill; length 240 km.

Matera *ma-tay'ra*, prov of Bascilicata region, S Italy; pop(1981) 203,570; area 3,445 sq km; capital Matera.

Matera, 40 40N 16 37E, pop(1981) 50,712, capital town of Matera prov, Bascilicata region, S Italy; 75 km NW of Taranto, above the rocky gorge of the R Gravina; archbishopric; there was severe earthquake damage in Nov 1980; economy: olive oil, cereals, pottery, pasta; monument: 13th-c cathedral.

Mátészalka *mah'tay-sol-ko*, 47 58N 22 20E, pop(1984e) 20,000, town in Szabolcs-Szátmar county, E Hungary; on R Kraszna E of Nýiregyháza; railway; economy: tobacco, grain, livestock trade, machinery.

Mat'lock, 53 08N 1 32W, pop(1981) 13,867, county town in West Derbyshire dist, Derbyshire, central England; 14 km SW of Chesterfield; formerly a spa town; railway; economy: transport equipment, engineering.

Mato Grosso *ma'tō gro'sō*, formerly MATTO GROSSO; state in Centro-Oeste region, central W Brazil; bordered SW by Bolivia; drained in the N by R Amazon tributaries, S by those of the Río Paraguay and E by those of Río Araguaia (which forms the E border with Goiás state); Chapada dos Parecis mountain range rises in the W; the Planalto Mato Grosso lies in the S; half the area is under forest; the extensive, swampy Pantanal is located in the S; SW is the 611-sq km Cará-Cará biological reserve set up in 1971; in NE is the Xingu National Park; pop(1980) 1,138,691; area 881,001 sq km; capital Cuiabá; economy: food processing; coffee, cotton, timber; rubber; metallurgy; on 1 Jan 1979, Mato Grosso was divided into the 2 states of Mato Grosso (the N section) and Mato Grosso do Sul (the S section).

Mato Grosso do Sul *dō sool*, state in Centro-Oeste region, W central Brazil; bounded W by Bolivia and Paraguay (along the Río Paraguay), S by Paraguay and E by the Río Paraná; part of Mato Grosso state until 1979; includes part of the swampy Pantanal (NW and W); pop(1980) 1,369,567; area 350,548 sq km; capital Campo Grande; economy: agriculture, cattle raising, minerals.

Matosinhos or **Matozinhos** *ma-too-zee'nyoosh*, 41 11N 8 42W, pop(1981) 25,000, port, resort and industrial town in Porto dist, N Portugal; 9 km N of Porto, at the mouth of R Leca; economy: fish canning, electrical machinery, steel tubes and frames and beer; event: Senhor de Matosinhos festival at Whitsun.

Matra *ma'tro*, mountain range in N Hungary; NE of Budapest; a S spur of the Carpathian Mts; rises to 1,014 m at Mt Kékes, the highest peak in Hungary.

Maṭraḥ, 23 37N 58 30E, pop(1980e) 15,000, commercial town and major port on the Gulf of Oman, Sultanate of Oman, SE Arabian peninsula; on a peninsula backed by the E Hajar hill country; E terminus of the dual carriageway which runs parallel to the Gulf of Oman; monuments: forts built by the Portuguese.

Matrûh *mat'roo*, MERSA MATRÛH, 31 21N 27 15E, capital of Mersa Matrûh governorate, N Egypt; on the Mediterranean coast, 250 km W of Alexandria; British planes based here stopped the Senussi invasion of Egypt in 1915; the town fell to German forces in June 1942 but was recaptured by British forces in Nov of the same year after

Rommel's defeat at El Alamein; Rommel's Cave which he used as a desert headquarters has been converted into a war museum; railway; airport.

Matsudo *ma-tsoog'-dō*, 35 48N 139 54E, pop(1980) 400,863, town in Chiba prefecture, Kanto region, E Honshū island, Japan; suburb of NE Tōkyo.

Matsuyama *ma-tsoo-ya'ma*, 33 50N 132 47E, pop(1980) 401,703, port capital of Ehime prefecture, NW Shikoku island, Japan; 2 universities; railway; airport; economy: oil refining, agricultural machinery, chemicals, textiles, fruit canning.

Matt'erhorn, MONT CERVIN (Fr), MONTE CERVINO *mon'te cher-vee'no* (Ital), 45 59N 7 39E, mountain peak in Valais canton, Switzerland, SW of Zermatt, in the Pennine Alps, on the Swiss-Italian border; height 4,478 m; first climbed by Edward Whymper in 1865.

Matu Utu, MATAUTU, 13 22S 176 12W, capital of Wallis and Futuna Is, S central Pacific Ocean, on Uvea I in the Wallis Is.

Maturín *ma-too-reen'*, 8 49N 63 10W, pop(1981) 154,976, capital of Monagas state, NE Venezuela; railway; airport; economy: important commercial centre.

Maui *mow'ee*, 2nd largest island of the US state of Hawaii; in the Pacific Ocean, NW of Hawaii I; forms Maui county with the islands of Lanai and Molokai; area 1,885 sq km; pop(1980) 62,775; chief town Wailuku; resort at Kanapali; former capital of Hawaii at Lahaina; rises to 3,055 m at Haleakela; has the only railway in the Pacific; economy: sugar, tourism.

Mauke *mow'kay*, 20 09S 157 23W, low coral island of the Cook Is, S Pacific, 240 km NE of Rarotonga; area 18.42 sq km; pop(1981) 681; airfield; citrus fruits, ginger, and arrowroot are grown; the government is experimenting with beef cattle.

Maule *mow'lay*, region of S central Chile; bordered W by Argentina; comprises the provs of Curico, Talca, Linares and Cauquenes; pop(1984) 735,400; area 30,661 sq km; capital Talca; chief towns Curicó, Cauquenes and Linares; economy: rice, wine, sugar refining, fruit, chick-peas, vegetables.

Maun *mown*, 20 00S 23 25E, pop(1980) 16,000, capital of Ngamiland dist, Botswana, S Africa; situated on the SE edge of the Okavango delta, 355 km SW of Livingstone (Zambia); airfield.

Mauna Kea *mow'na kay'a*, 19 50N 155 28W, dormant volcano in N central Hawaii, United States; rises to 4,205 m; highest island mountain in the world; has numerous cinder cones; snow-capped in winter.

Mauna Loa *lō'a*, 19 28N 155 35W, active volcano in central Hawaii, United States; situated in Hawaii Volcanoes National Park (area 990 sq km, established in 1916); rises to 4,169 m; has numerous craters, notably Kilauea, the 2nd largest active crater in the world, which also contains Halemaumau fiery pit; on its summit is Mokuaweoweo crater, one of the largest active craters in the world; last erupted in 1984.

Mauren *mow'ren*, 47 12N 9 34E, pop(1985) 2,703, commune in Unterland dist, Principality of Liechtenstein, central Europe; area 7.5 sq km.

Mauritania *mo-ri-tay'nee-a*, MAURITANIE (Fr), official name

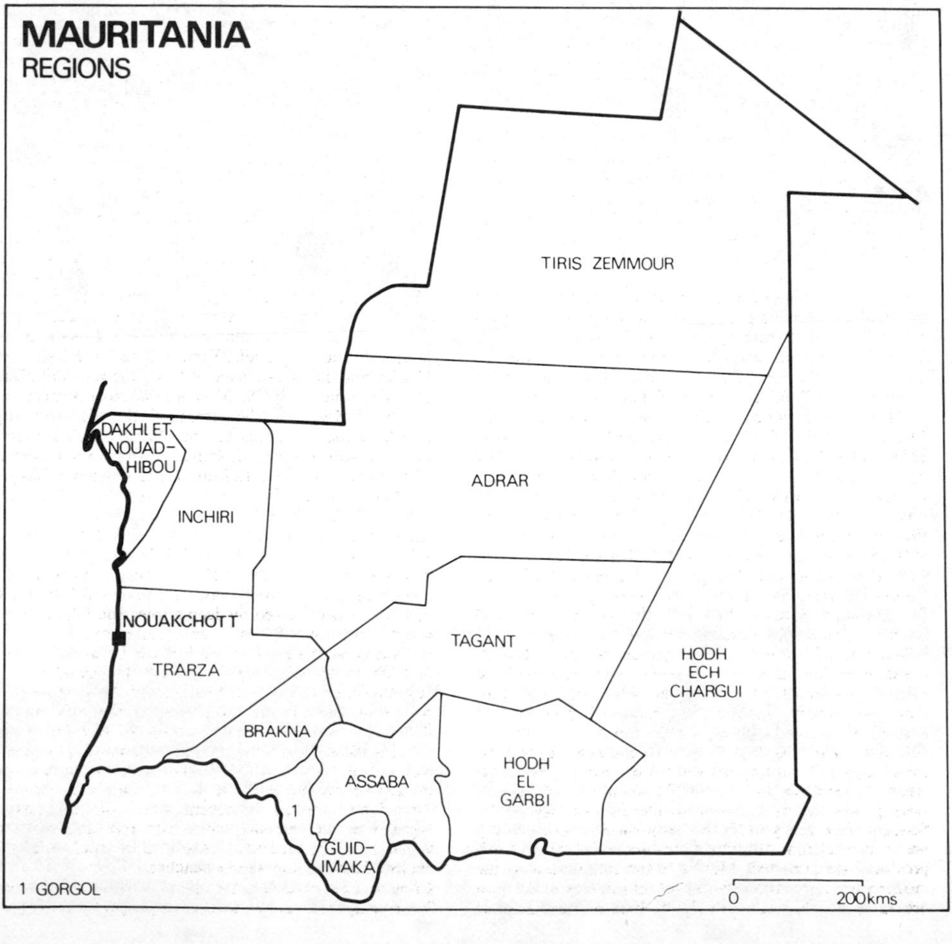

Islamic Republic of Mauritania, RÉPUBLIQUE ISLAMIQUE DE MAURITANIE (Fr), a republic in NW Africa, bounded SW by Senegal, S and E by Mali, NE by Algeria, N by Western Sahara and W by the Atlantic Ocean; timezone GMT; area 1,029,920 sq km; pop(1985e) 1,874,000; the country has 1,514 km of paved roads and 652 km of railway largely used for iron ore transportation; capital Nouakchott; chief towns Nouadhibou, Adrar, Assaba, Atar, Fderik, Kaédi, Rosso and Zouîrât; 40% of the pop is of mixed Moorish-black origin, the remainder being Moor (30%) and black (30%); virtually the entire pop is Muslim, most from the Makerite group; the official language is French, Hasanya Arabic is the national language and Toucouleur, Fula, Sarakole and Wolof are also spoken; the unit of currency is the ouguija of 5 khoum; national holiday 28 Nov (Independence Day), a number of Muslim religious holidays are also observed; membership of AfDB, AIOEC, Arab League, CEAO, CIPEC (Assoc), EAMA, EIB (Assoc), FAO, G-77, GATT, IBRD, ICAO, IDA, IDB (Islamic Development Bank), IFAD, IFC, ILO, IMF, IMO, INTELSAT, INTERPOL, IPU, ITU, NAM, OAU, OIC, OMVS, UN, UNESCO, UPU, WHO, WIPO, WMO.

Physical description. Mauritania is divided into 4 geographical zones: (1) the Saharan zone, accounting for the northern two-thirds of the country, is typified by shifting sands, sand dunes, mountainous plateaux and occasional oases; (2) the coastal zone, which is characterized by minimal rainfall and is consequently almost devoid of vegetation; (3) the Sahelian zone with its savannah grasslands and (4) the Sénégal river zone (*Chemama*), Mauritania's chief agricultural region with its rich alluvial soils; highest point Kediet Ijill (915 m) in the NW.

Climate. Mauritania has a dry tropical climate typified by sparse and sporadic rainfall. Rainfall is highest in the *Chemama* zone (S) with 300 to 600 mm per annum, the rainy season being from May to Sept during which time tornadoes are frequent. Rainfall in the Sahel zone decreases northward from about 350 mm per annum in the S. The coastal zone is humid but temperate and averages less than 25 mm of rain per annum. The Saharan zone has a rainy season extending from July to Sept with temperatures ranging from 0°C to over 49°C. The dry and often dust-laden *harmattan* wind blows from the E creating sandstorms. The average annual rainfall at Nouakchott is 158 mm.

History, government and constitution. Mauritanians are by tradition nomadic Moors. The country was proclaimed a French Protectorate within French West Africa in 1903 and became a French colony in 1920. It was not until 1934, however, that the area came fully under French control and until independence internal government largely depended on the authority of tribal chiefs. Autonomy within the French community was granted in 1958 and full independence was achieved in 1960. The adopted constitution allowed for an elected 70-member National Assembly. The country became a one-party state in 1964. In 1976 the Spanish withdrew from Western Sahara and Mauritania occupied 88,672 sq km in the S under the name of Tiris el Gharbia. However, in 1979 they renounced all rights after a conflict with the Frenta Polisario guerillas who were seeking independence for Western Sahara. In 1979 the constitution and National Assembly were suspended following a coup which placed power in the hands of the Military Committee for National Recovery (later renamed the Military Committee for National Salvation). The military government appoints an executive president, a council of ministers and a prime minister.

Economy. The majority of Mauritanians (80%) rely on subsistence agriculture, the main products being livestock, cereals, vegetables and dates. The main area of agricultural production is restricted to the alluvial soils of the Sénégal river valley in the S. Crop success is constantly under threat from drought. Gum arabic, dates and fish products are exported. Mining is the foundation of the modern economy and is based on the country's vast iron ore reserves which are principally located near Zouîrât and Guelb in the N. There is also an important gypsum mine at N'Dahamcha, N of Nouakchott. Fish processing is also of major importance, with factories near the capital. Tax is paid by foreign fishing boats in Mauritanian waters. Other industries include textiles, plaster and cement production, bricks, paints and industrial gas. The economy continues to rely heavily on foreign aid supplied mainly by France. Main trading partners for exports included France, Japan, Spain, Italy and the USSR.

Administrative divisions. Mauritania is divided into 12 regions and a capital district:

Region	*area (sq km)*	*pop(1982e)*
Hodh ech Chargui	182,700	235,000
Hodh el Gharbi	53,400	154,000
Assaba	36,500	152,000
Gorgol	13,600	169,000
Brakna	33,000	171,000
Trarza	67,800	242,000
Adrar	215,300	60,000
Dakhlet-Nouadhibou	22,300	30,000
Tagant	95,200	84,000
Guidimaka	10,300	102,000
Tiris Zemmour	252,900	28,000
Inchiri	46,800	23,000
Capital District		
Nouakchott	120	150,000

The regions are further sub-divided into 44 departments.

Mauritius *mo-rish'as*, a small island in the Indian Ocean about 800 km E of Madagascar; includes about 20 surrounding islets and the dependencies of Rodrigues I, Agalega Is and the Cargados Carajos Is (St Brandon Is); the sovereignty of the island of Tromelin is under dispute between France and Mauritius; the Chagos Archipelago was transferred to the British Indian Ocean Territory in 1965 but Mauritius maintains mineral rights there; 61 km long by 47 km wide; area 1,865 sq km; timezone GMT +4; pop(1983) 980,499 (excluding Rodrigues I); capital Port Louis; chief towns include Beau Bassin-Rose Hill, Curepipe, Vacoas-Phoenix, Quatre Bornes; more than 44% of the pop live in the urban belt from Port Louis to Curepipe; over two-thirds of the pop are Indo-Mauritians, descendants of the indentured labourers brought to Mauritius after the abolition of slavery in 1833; the pop also includes Chinese, African Creoles, descendants of former slaves and descendants of early French settlers; languages include Creole, French, English, Hindi, Urdu, Hakka and Bojpoori; over 50% of the pop are Hindu, 30% Christian and 17% Muslim; Plaisance airport in SE corner of Mauritius; the currency is the Mauritius rupee of 100 cents; Mauritius has no standing defence forces; national holidays include Hindu, Christian, Chinese and Muslim holidays, also 12 March (Independence Day) and 1 May (Labour Day); membership of FAO, G-77, GATT, IAEA, IBRD, ICAO, IDA, IFAD, IFC, ILO, IMF, IMO, ISO, ITU, IWC, NAM, OAU, OCAM, UN, UNESCO, UPU, WFTU, WHO, WIPO, WMO, WTO.

Physical description. Mauritius is volcanic in origin with a central plateau reaching between 550 m and 730 m in the S, where it is dissected by deep gorges and falls steeply to the narrow coast lands in the S and SW. The 3 main mountain ranges are the Black River-Savanne on the W and SW, rising to the highest peak on the island, Piton de la Petite Rivière Noire or Little Black River Mt (826 m); Moka or Port Louis range lies to the NW and the Bambou or Gran Port range to the E. The dry lowland coast lands fringed with coconuts, bananas and casuarinas are generally wooded savannah intermixed with mangrove swamp and in the E, bamboo. Although extensively drained in recent times the uplands are typified by wet marshy areas with fern and pandanus vegetation. The island is surrounded by coral reefs which enclose lagoons and sandy beaches.

Climate. Mauritius has a tropical-maritime climate with mean temperatures at sea-level varying from 26°C (Nov-

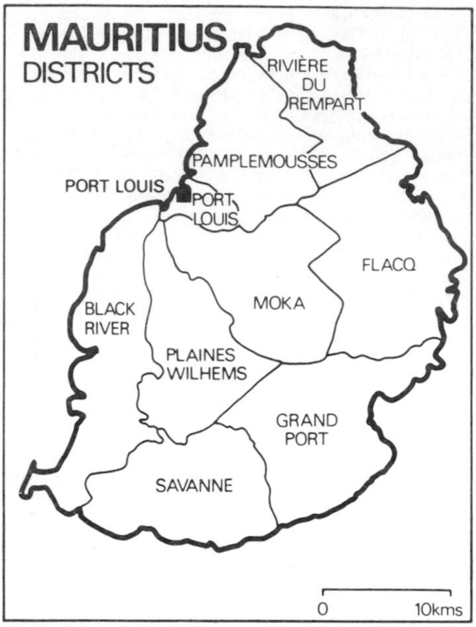

April) to 22°C (May-Oct). Temperatures decrease with altitude to about 19°C at 600 m. Humidity also increases with altitude. Trade winds from the SE tend to blow throughout the year but are stronger during Nov-April when most of the rain falls. Average rainfall varies from 850 mm in the NW to 5,000 mm on the central plateau. *History, government and constitution.* The Dutch, who visited the island in 1598, named Mauritius after their ruler, Prince Maurice of Nassau. Ships from many European countries called here for provisions, and the first settlement was established by the French in 1722. In 1814 the island was ceded to Britain which governed Mauritius jointly with the Seychelles as a single colony until 1903. In 1968 Mauritius, with a new constitution, became an independent sovereign state within the Commonwealth with the Queen as Head of State. The Queen is represented by the Governor-General who is guided by the advice of the cabinet. The Governor-General appoints a prime minister who presides over a cabinet which is composed of not more than 20 members and is responsible to the unicameral Legislative Assembly which has 62 members elected every 5 years.
Economy. The economy is largely based on knitwear, clothing, diamond-cutting, watches, rum and fertilizer, industries which are mostly located in the urban area between Port Louis and Curepipe. The island's main source of revenue is derived from agricultural crops including sugar, tea, tobacco, potatoes and vegetables. There are 21 estates on the island growing sugar cane, a major industry that employs more than 25% of the workforce and exports over 50% of its produce to the UK. *Administrative divisions.* The island of Mauritius is divided into the following 9 districts:

District	*area (sq km)*	*pop(1983)*
Port Louis	42.7	135,629
Pamplemousses	178.7	91,782
Rivière du Rempart	147.6	82,188
Flacq	297.9	109,290
Grand Port	260.3	94,490
Savanne	244.8	59,611
Plaines Wilhems	203.3	308,015
Moka	230.5	62,024
Black River	259.0	37,470

May Pen *may' pen*, 17 58N 77 15W, pop(1982) 40,962, market centre of Clarendon parish, Middlesex county, S Jamaica, on the R Minho, 48 km W of Kingston; alt 500 m; railway; economy: fruit canning.

Maya Mountains, forested mountain range in S Belize and Guatemala, Central America; rises to 1,120 m at Victoria Peak; important refuge for wildlife; the Cockscomb Basin was declared the world's first jaguar reserve in 1986.

Mayaguana *may-ug-wa'nu*, island in the SE Bahamas, between Acklins I (NW) and the Caicos Is (SE); pop(1980) 476; area 285 sq km; chief town Abraham's Bay.

Mayaguez *mī-ag-wez'*, 18 12N 67 09W, pop(1980) 96,193, trading centre on W coast of Puerto Rico, E Caribbean; on Mona Passage, S of Arecibo; founded in 1760; Las Mesas limonite deposits nearby; noted for its embroidery and needlework; airfield.

Maydān Shahr *mī-dan'*, MAIDAN, 34 23N 68 58E, pop(1984e) 2,245, capital of Vardak prov, central Afghanistan; lies to the SW of Kābul.

Mayenne *ma-yen*, MEDUANA (anc), dept in Pays de la Loire region of W France, comprising 3 arrond, 30 cantons and 259 communes; pop(1982) 271,784; area 5,175 sq km; furrowed by numerous valleys and ravines; watered by the Mayenne and Oudon rivers; the hills of Maine rise in the W and NW; capital Laval; the Parc Normandie-Maine regional nature park lies partly within the dept; there are limestone caves near Saulges.

Mayenne, river in W France rising in Orne dept on the slopes of Mont des Avalois; flows W then S through a narrow and deep valley past Mayenne and Laval (between which it is navigable) to form the R Maine with the Loir and Sarthe rivers near Angers; length 195 km; tributaries Varenne and Oudon rivers.

Mayo *may'ō*, MHUIGHEO (Gael), county in Connacht prov, W Irish Republic; bounded N and W by Atlantic Ocean; drained by R Moy which is noted for its salmon fishing; Achill I lies off the W coast; the Nephin Beg Range rises to the NW; pop(1981) 114,766; area 5,398 sq km; capital Castlebar; sheep and cattle farming in E. The parish church of Knock, which was the scene of an apparition of the Virgin Mary on 12 Aug 1879, is one of Ireland's most important places of pilgrimage and is served by a new airport; Croagh Patrick is Ireland's holy mountain, visited annually at the end of July by thousands of pilgrims.

Mayo-Kebbi *mah-yō-ke-bee'*, prefecture in SW Chad, N central Africa; pop(1979) 684,000; area 30,105 sq km; includes an extensive area of marshland; the R Logone follows the W border; capital Bongor; chief towns Pala, Lamé and Léré.

Mayotte *ma-yot'*, MAHORE (Eng), pop(1984e) 59,000, small island group of volcanic origin situated E of the Comoro Is at the N end of the Mozambique Channel, W Indian Ocean; administered by France as a *collectivité territoriale*, being of intermediate status between an overseas territory and an overseas department; area 374 sq km; the 2 main islands are Grande Terre (area 360 sq km) which rises to 660 m at Mt Benara, and La Petite Terre or Îlot de Pamandzi (area 14 sq km); capital Dzaoudzi (on La Petite Terre); main settlements include Mamoudzou; the main languages are French and Mahorian (a Swahili dialect); a French colony between 1843 and 1914, it was attached with the Comoros Islands to Madagascar; the Comoros were granted autonomy within the French Republic and became an overseas territory, but when the rest of the group voted to become independent in 1974 Mayotte voted to remain a French dependency; airport; economy: fishing, vanilla, coffee, copra and ylang-ylang. *Administrative divisions.* Mayotte is divided into 17 communes:

Commune	*area (sq km)*	*pop(1978)*
Acoua	12.62	1,910
Bandraboua	32.37	2,551
Bandrele	36.46	2,148
Boueni	14.06	2,211
Chiconi	8.29	2,880

contd

Commune	*area (sq km)*	*pop(1978)*
Chirongui	28.31	2,244
Dembeni	38.80	1,518
Dzaoudzi	6.66	4,147
Kani-Keli	20.51	1,962
Koungou	28.41	2,362
Mamoudzou	41.94	7,798
Mtsamboro	13.71	2,976
M'tsangamouji	21.84	2,349
Ouangani	19.05	1,924
Pamandzi	4.29	2,832
Sada	11.16	3,228
Tsingoni	34.76	2,206

May'wood, 41 53N 87 51W, pop(1980) 27,998, town in Cook county, NE Illinois, United States; 19 km W of Chicago; residential.

Māzandarān *ma-zan-da-ran'*, mountainous prov in N Iran, on the Caspian Sea; pop(1982) 2,375,994; area 46,200 sq km; capital Sari; occupied largely by the Elburz Mts.

Mazār-e-Sharīf *ma-za'ree she-reef'*, 36 43N 67 05E, pop(1984e) 117,723, capital of Balkh prov, N Afghanistan; linked to Kābul by main road running SE and to Herāt by main road running generally SW.

Mazaruni *ma-za-roo'nee*, river in N Guyana, South America; rises in the Guiana Highlands at 5 50N 60 08W; flows approx 560 km in a wide curve N then E and NE through tropical forests to the R Essequibo at Bartica shortly after receiving the R Cuyuni; because of its many rapids, the river is navigable near the mouth only.

Mazatenango *ma-sa-tay-nan'gō*, 14 31N 91 30W, pop(1983e) 38,318, capital town of Suchitepéquez dept, SW Guatemala, Central America; Chitalón airfield is 3 km away; railway.

Mazatlán *ma-sat-lan'*, 23 11N 106 25W, pop(1980) 249,988, seaport in Sinaloa state, W Mexico; on the Pacific coast S of the Golfo de California, on a peninsula at the foot of the Sierra Madre; 400 km NW of Guadalajara, railway; airfield at 26 km; largest Mexican port on the Pacific Ocean; main industrial and commercial centre in the W; tourist resort; economy: fishing, textiles, sugar refining, distilling, trade in tobacco and bananas.

Mbabane *um-ba-ba'nay*, 26 18S 31 06E, pop(1976) 22,262, capital of Swaziland, SE Africa; 320 km E of Johannesburg (South Africa) and 160 km WSW of Maputo (Mozambique) in the Dalgeni Hills of the Highveld; capital transferred here from Manzini in 1902; administrative and commercial centre; less stringent gaming laws bring tourists from South Africa to the town's casino.

M'baiki *um-bay'kee*, 3 53N 18 01E, chief town in Lobaye prefecture, SW Central African Republic; on the R Lobaye, 88 km SW of Bangui.

Mbala *um-ba'la*, formerly ABERCORN (-1967), 8 50S 31 24E, town in Northern prov, N Zambia, S central Africa; close to the S end of L Tanganyika and 153 km N of Kasama; established as a British trade post in 1889; airfield.

Mbale *um-ba'lay*, 1 04N 34 12E, pop(1983e) 28,039, town in Eastern prov, Uganda, E Africa; at the W foot of Mount Elgon, 130 km NE of Jinja; railway; economy: petrol depot.

Mbandaka *em-ban-dak'a*, formerly COQUILHATVILLE (-1966), 0 03N 18 28E, pop(1976e) 149,118, river-port capital of Equateur region, NW Zaire, central Africa; on the Zaire river where it meets the R Ruki, 595 km NNE of Kinshasa; founded in 1883; airfield.

Mbarara *um-ba-ra'ra*, 0 36S 30 40E, town in Southern prov, Uganda, E Africa; SW of Kampala.

M'Béré *um-bay'ray*, a W headstream of the R Logone, rising 105 km SE of N'Gaoundéré (Cameroon); flows 443 km NE, forming part of the Central African Republic's border with Cameroon and Chad, then past Baïbokoum and Moundou (both in Chad) to join the R Pendé (an E headstream of the R Logone) 45 km SSE of Laï (Chad).

Mbeya *um-bay'ya*, 8 54S 33 29E, pop(1978) 76,606, capital of Mbeya region, SW Tanzania, E Africa; 404 km SW of Dodoma; airfield; economy: soap, cement.

Mbini, Río *um-bee'ni*, formerly Río Benito (-1974), WOLEU (Gabon), river in Gabon and Río Muni, Equatorial Guinea, W Africa; flows 320 km W to meet the Gulf of Guinea near Senye.

M'bomou *um-bō'moo*, prefecture in SE Central African Republic; rivers flowing SW to join the M'bomou include the Kotto and the M'Bari; pop(1968) 127,240; area 61,150 sq km; chief town Bangassou; other towns include Kouki, Batangafo, Bouca, Marali and Kabo; economy: diamond mining.

Mbuji-Mayi *um-boo'jee-mī-ee*, BAKWANGA, 6 10S 23 39E, pop(1976e) 382,632, capital of Kasai Oriental region, S central Zaire, central Africa; on Bushimaie river; airport; economy: diamonds.

Mburo, Lake *um-boo'rō*, national park in S Uganda, E Africa; between Mbarara and Masaka.

Mchin'ji, dist in Central region, Malawi, SE Africa; area 3,356 sq km; pop(1977) 158,833.

Mdina *ma-dee'nah*, 35 53N 14 15E, pop(1983e) 926, town in central Malta; situated just N of Rabat; the former capital of Malta; also known as the 'Silent City'; the town was relatively unaffected by the Knights of St John who developed Valletta and the harbour area, leaving Mdina to Malta's old aristocracy; the town was completely walled at the time of the Arab invasions but still retains two gates, some fine family houses and a cathedral which was rebuilt in 1697 after an earthquake.

Meath *meeth*, NA MIDHE (Gael), county in Leinster prov, E Irish Republic; bounded E by Irish Sea; watered by Boyne and Blackwater rivers; crossed by Royal Canal; a former kingdom; pop(1981) 95,419; area 2,339 sq km; capital Trim; economy: sheep and cattle.

Mecca, Islamic holy city in Saudi Arabia. See Makkah.

Mechelen *meKH'eln*, dist of S Antwerpen prov, Belgium; area 510 sq km; pop(1982) 292,910.

Mechelen, MALINES *ma-leen* (Fr), 51 02N 4 29E, pop(1982) 77,067, ancient city in Mechelen dist, S Antwerpen prov, Belgium; SSE of Antwerpen, on the tidal waters of the R Dijle; former capital of the Netherlands; since the 16th century it has been the religious capital of the country; known for market-gardening (asparagus, peas); archbishopric; railway; economy: furniture, food canning, lace-making (formerly famous), carpets, wool processing, railway workshops; many factories founded here within the framework of the European Community by the member states; monuments: cathedral church of St Rombout (13-16th-c), town hall (1320-6), Alderman's House (13th-c); event: a famous Carillon concert every Monday, June to mid-Sept at 8.30 pm.

Mecsek *me'chek*, mountain range in S Hungary; W of R Danube; rises to 682 m at Mt Zengövar.

Medan *ma-dahn'* ('battleground'), 3 35N 98 39E, pop(1980) 635,562, seaport capital of Sumatera Utara prov, Indonesia; on R Deli, near the NE coast of the island of Sumatera; the economic centre of Sumatera, handling 65% of Indonesia's exports through the port of Belawan; the centre of a Dutch plantation district during the late 19th century; 2 universities (1952); railway; airfield; economy: palm oil, rubber and tobacco trade.

Medellín *me-del-yeen'*, 6 15N 75 36W, pop(1985) 2,068,892, industrial and commercial capital of Antioquia dept, NW central Colombia, South America; Colombia's leading industrial centre; 5 universities; railway; airport (Olaya Herrera) at 6 km; economy: coffee trade, textiles, chemicals, pharmaceuticals, rubber products, wood products, metal products, food processing; monuments: many of the city's colonial buildings have been demolished to make way for modern office blocks, but some 17th-c churches still remain; the new cathedral of Villanueva in the Parque Bolívar is said to be one of the largest brick buildings in the world; in the suburb of El Poblado is the Museo El Castillo, one of Medellín's most beautiful buildings; the Museo Folklórico Tejicondor has exhibitions of native handicrafts and costumes; the zoo in the S of the city contains a large collection of South American animals and birds.

Medenine *mayd-neen'*, governorate of SE Tunisia, N Africa; pop(1984) 295,889; capital Medenine.

Medford, 42 25N 71 07W, pop(1980) 58,076, town in Middlesex county, E Massachusetts, United States; residential suburb, 8 km N of Boston; Tufts University (1852); railway; economy: vehicle parts, leather goods.

Medford, 42 19N 122 52W, pop(1980) 39,603, capital of Jackson county, SW Oregon, United States; on the Bear river (a small tributary of the Rogue river); founded in 1883; railway; airfield; Crater Lake National Park is 72 km NE.

Medgidia *me-jee'dya*, 44 15N 28 16E, pop(1983) 46,668, town in Constanţa, SE Romania; W of Constanţa; on the Danube-Black Sea Canal, WNW of Constanţa; railway junction; economy: limestone, tools, ceramics.

Mediaş *med-yash'*, 46 10N 24 21E, pop(1983) 70,933, town in Sibiu county, central Romania; one of the first 7 towns established by German colonists in the 12th century; railway; airfield; economy: wine, cattle trade, textiles, hardware, leather.

Medicine Hat, 50 03N 110 41W, pop(1984) 41,493, town in SE Alberta, S Canada; near Saskatchewan border, at the foot of the Cypress Hills, on the South Saskatchewan river; chosen in 1882 as site of a North West Mounted Police post; the Canadian Pacific Railroad arrived here in 1873 in the same year that deposits of natural gas were discovered; soldiers were stationed here during the Riel rebellion of 1885; in 1898 Medicine Hat was incorporated as a town and in 1906 became a city; railway; airfield; economy: natural gas; glass blowing; chemical fertilizers; petrochemicals; clay products; monument: Dinosaur Provincial Park, 104 km W of Medicine Hat, is an actual graveyard full of partially excavated dinosaur skeletons, exhibitions of fossils and relics and weird rock formations; event: rodeo, the oldest in Alberta (July).

Medina, Islamic holy city in Saudi Arabia. See Madīnah, Al.

Mediterranean Sea *med-i-te-ray'nee-an*, MEDITERRANEUM, MARE INTERNUM (anc), the world's largest inland sea, lying between the continents of Africa, Asia and Europe; connected with the Atlantic by the 14.5 km-wide Straits of Gibraltar, with the Black Sea by the Dardanelles, Sea of Marmara and Bosporus, and with the Indian Ocean by the Suez Canal and the Red Sea; subdivided into the Ligurian, Adriatic, Aegean, Ionian and Tyrrhenian Seas; area 2,499,350 sq km; 3,860 km long, with a max width of 1,610 km; off Cape Matapan, Greece, the max depth is 4,405 m; thought to be the remains of the Tethys Sea, enclosed by the S European and NW African fold ranges; divided into 2 main basins by shallows between Cape Bon, Tunisia and W Sicily, the E basin being the larger; higher salinity than the Atlantic owing to excess of evaporation over precipitation, limited river intake and the constricted exit; incoming currents from the Atlantic and the Black Sea also prevent higher salinities developing; high temperatures at depth are due to the effect of the submarine sills at the Straits of Gibraltar and Sicily; the warmer water exercises a moderating effect on the climate; hot, dry summers, intensified by the Scirocco wind and mild winters with rainstorms typify the 'Mediterranean Climate'; the seaboard is highly favoured as a holiday and health resort; maritime highway since ancient times for the Phoenicians, Greeks, Venetians and Crusaders; a vital link connecting Europe with the E; eclipsed during the 14-16th centuries owing to the dominance of the Turks and the opening of new ocean highways, particularly around Africa; Suez Canal (1869) restored much of its importance; strategic importance demonstrated during and after World War II.

Médoc *may-dok*, dist in Gironde dept, Aquitaine region, SW France; occupying the flat alluvial plain on the W bank of the Gironde estuary, N of Bordeaux; bounded W by the Atlantic Ocean; inland lagoons include the Étang d'Hourtin et de Carcans and the Étang de Lacanau; famous for its clarets, the best wines come from the Haut-Médoc which lies between St-Estephe and Macau; the Bas-Médoc to the N stretches as far as the Pointe de Grave; Lesparre and Pauillac are the chief towns.

Med'way, river rising in headstreams in East Sussex and Surrey, SE England; flows 112 km NE through Kent, turning N at Maidstone; the R Medway estuary meets the R Thames estuary opposite Southend-on-Sea; the estuary separates the Isle of Sheppey from the Isle of Grain; navigable to Maidstone.

Medway Towns, The, pop(1981) 216,694, urban area in Kent, SE England; includes Gillingham, Rochester, Strood on the R Medway, E of London; railway.

Meerut *mee'rut*, 29 1N 77 50E, pop(1981) 538,000, city and agricultural market centre in Uttar Pradesh state, N India; 60 km NE of Delhi; in 1192 Meerut was conquered by the Muslims and in 1399 it was sacked by Tamerlane; in May 1857 the first outbreak of the Indian Mutiny began in Meerut British military cantonment; university (1966); economy: chemicals, soap, pottery, flour milling and the processing of vegetable oils.

Mégara *me'ga-ra*, 38 00N 23 20E, pop(1981) 17,719, town in Attikí nome (dept), Sterea Ellás-Évvoia region, Greece; on N coast of Saronikós Kólpos (Gulf of Saronica), W of Athínai (Athens), on the main highway between Athínai and Kórinthos; railway; economy: trade in wine and olive oil.

Meghalaya *may-gu-lay'u*, state in NE India, pop(1981) 1,327,824; area 22,489 sq km; bounded N and E by Assam state and S and W by Bangladesh; the R Brahmaputra forms part of the W boundary with Bangladesh; the state is crossed by the Krishnal, Bogai, Someswari and Kapili rivers and includes the Garo, Khāsi and Jaintia hills; the state is divided into 2 administrative districts and is governed by a 60-member Legislative Assembly; capital Shillong; 80% of the population is employed in agriculture, the chief crops being potatoes, cotton, jute and fruit; 27% of cultivated land is irrigated; mineral resources include coal, limestone, white clay, corundum; 95% of India's sillimanite is mined here, mostly in the United Khasi and Jaintia Hills district; large reserves of coal and sandstone have not yet been extracted, largely because of access problems; there is no railway within the state and no airfield; Meghalaya was formed under the Assam Reorganization Act (Meghalaya, 1969) when its status was that of a state within Assam state; in April 1972 it became a separate state comprising the former Garo Hills district and United Khasi and Jaintia Hills district of Assam.

Mehedinţi *me-he-deen'tee*, county in SW Romania, in the W foothills of the Transylvanian Alps; bounded to the W by Yugoslavia; pop(1983) 328,030; area 4,900 sq km; capital Drobeta-Turnu Severin.

Mehtar Lām, METHARLAM, METERLAM, 34 39N 70 10E, pop(1984e) 4,370, capital of Laghmān prov, E Afghanistan; lies on the Alungar river to the NE of Kābul.

Meissen *mī'sun*, 51 10N 13 28E, pop(1981) 39,276, ancient town in Meissen dist, Dresden, SE East Germany; on R Elbe; renowned for the manufacture since 1710 of the famous 'Dresden China', made from local kaolin; monuments: 15th-c castle, 13-14th-c cathedral.

Mejicanos *me-hee-kah'nos*, 13 40N 89 18W, pop(1980) 93,911, town in San Salvador dept, central El Salvador, Central America; a N suburb of San Salvador.

Mekelē, MAKALE *ma-ka'lay*, 13 32N 39 33E, pop(1984e) 61,580, capital of Tigray region, NE Ethiopia, NE Africa; 97 km SE of Aduwa; a major refugee centre during the severe drought which began in 1983.

Meknès *mek-nes'*, 33 53N 5 37W, pop(1982) 319,783, city in Meknès prefecture, Centre-Sud prov, N Morocco, N Africa; in the Moyen Atlas, 50 km WSW of Fès; one of Morocco's 4 imperial cities; founded during the 12th century; gained importance when the second Sultan of the Alaouite dynasty, Moulay Ismail (1672-1727), built a palace to rival Louis XIV's Versailles here in the 1670s; capital of Morocco until moved to Fès in 1728; divided into the imperial city and the modern city; Moulay Ismail's tomb; railway; economy: leather, wine, carpets, pottery; monuments: Musée des Arts Marocains; Bou Inania Médersa, a religious college built during the 14th century by Abu el Hassan; Grand mosque; gardens of El Haboul.

Mekong *mee'kong*, LANGCANG JIANG (Chin), river in Indo-China, SE Asia; rises on the Xizang Plateau in S Qinghai prov, China, as the Zi Qu and the Za Qu, which join to form the Langcang Jiang on the border of Xizang Autonomous Region; flows S through E Xizang Autonomous Region then through W Yunnan prov to the border with Laos and Burma; flowing generally SW it forms the boundary between Laos and Burma; flows SE forming the boundary between Thailand and Laos to the town of Pak Tha, turning E to Luang Prabang and S to the Thailand-Laos border; flows generally E forming the border between Thailand and Laos; at Pak Sane it turns SE, forming the entire E border of Thailand and Laos to Ubon Ratchahani; turns S crossing the Cambodian and Laos border to the W of Veun Kham, then meanders generally SW to its confluence with the Tonlé Sap at Phnom Penh; crosses the Cambodia-Vietnam boundary close to Chau Phu, then turns SE, splitting into 4 major tributaries at the Mekong delta where it enters the South China Sea; Mekong is linked to the Tonlé Sap lake in central Cambodia, which acts as its flood reservoir during the wet season.

Melaka *mul-a'ku*, MALACCA, state in SW Peninsular Malaysia, SE Asia; bounded W by the Strait of Malacca; one of the former Straits Settlements; pop(1980) 446,769; area 1,657 sq km; capital Melaka; economy: rubber, tin, rice.

Melaka, 2 14N 102 14E, pop(1980) 88,073, capital of Melaka state, SW Peninsular Malaysia, SE Asia; 148 km SE of Kuala Lumpur, at the mouth of the R Melaka where it meets the Strait of Malacca on the SW Malay Peninsula; the centre of a great trading empire since the 15th century; the settlement of rich Moorish merchants from Pasai in Sumatra resulted in the spread of Islam throughout the Malayan Peninsula during the 15th century; held by the Portuguese, Dutch and British in turn; large Chinese pop; monuments: state museum, St John's fort, St Peter's church (1710), Cheng Hoon Teng temple, the oldest Chinese temple in Malaysia, Kampung Kling mosque, Vinayagar Moorthi Hindu temple.

Melanesia *mel-an-ee'zha*, ethnographic area in the W Pacific Ocean; includes the islands of Fiji, New Caledonia, Vanuatu, Solomon Is and the islands of Papua New Guinea.

Melbourne *mel'bun* 37 45S 144 58E, pop(1986) 2,942,000, port and state capital in Melbourne stat div, Victoria, Australia; on the lower reaches of the Yarra river, at the head of Port Phillip Bay; Melbourne stat div is divided into 56 local government areas, the largest of which include Waverley (pop 129,400), Broadmeadows (pop 108,100), Moorabbin (pop 101,400) and Nunawading (pop 101,100); founded in 1835 and named after the British prime minister, Lord Melbourne; capital of Victoria since 1851; university (1855); Monash University (1958) in the suburb of Clayton; La Trobe University (1964) in the suburb of Bundoora; site of 1956 summer Olympic Games; capital of Australia 1901-27; Australia's first federal parliament met here in 1901; underground; railway; 2 airports; economy: major financial and communications centre; manufacturing industries, which account for almost 80% of Victoria's output, include heavy engineering, textiles, paper, electronics, chemicals, foodstuffs, metal processing and car manufacturing, shipbuilding; the port of Melbourne is Australia's biggest cargo port; monuments: Melbourne Cricket Ground, which holds over 115,000 spectators; Flemington racecourse, where the Melbourne Cup horse-race is held; events: Moomba 10-day festival of street parades, sporting events and cultural activities (March); Melbourne Royal Agricultural Show (Sept); Melbourne Cup Day (Nov).

Melbourne, 28 05N 80 37W, pop(1980) 46,536, resort town in Brevard county, E Florida, United States; on the R Indian (a lagoon), 92 km SE of Orlando; railway.

Melhus *mel'hoos*, 63 17N 10 18E, pop(1980) 11,116, town in Sør-Trøndelag county, central Norway; just to the SE of where the R Gaula joins Trondheimsfjord (Trondheim Fjord), S of Trondheim; railway.

Melilla *may-leel'ya*, RUSSADIR (anc), 35 21N 2 57W, pop(1981) 53,593 (with Ceuta), free port and modern commercial city, with Ceuta a region of Spain; on SE coast of Cap des Trois Fourches or Cape Tres Forcas in Er Rif region, on N African Coast of Morocco; a 'plaza de soberania' administered by Cádiz prov; founded as a port by the Phoenicians; a free port since 1863 it was reoccupied by Spain in 1926 after the Riffian revolt of 1921, and was the scene of a revolt of army commanders which led to the Spanish Civil War in 1936; airport (Tahuima); car ferries to Málaga; the old town is divided into three walled sections separated by deep moats which are crossed by drawbridges; naval shipyard; monument: 16th-c church of the Purisima Concepción.

Melipilla *may-lee-peel'ya*, 33 41S 71 13W, pop(1982) 38,675, capital of Melipilla prov, Santiago, central Chile; railway.

Melk, 48 14N 15 21E, pop(1981) 5,062, capital of Melk dist, Niederösterreich, NE Austria, where the R Danube enters the Wachau region; monuments: 18th-c Benedictine abbey, on a promontory above the river; fine Baroque church.

Melk'sham, 51 23N 2 09W, pop(1981) 13,300, town in West Wiltshire dist, Wiltshire, S England; 14 km E of Bath; economy: engineering, rubber products, agricultural trade.

Mellersta Finland, prov of Finland. See Keski-Suomi.

Melo *may'lō*, 32 22S 54 10W, pop(1985) 41,963, capital of Cerro Largo dept, NE Uruguay; near the Brazilian frontier; railway; airfield.

Melrose, 42 27N 71 04W, pop(1980) 30,055, town in Middlesex county, E Massachusetts, United States; residential suburb, 11 km N of Boston.

Melton Mowbray *mel'ten mō'bray*, 52 46N 0 53W, pop(1981) 23,592, town in Melton dist, Leicestershire, central England; on the R Wreake, 22 km NE of Leicester; railway; economy: foodstuffs, pet foods, footwear.

Melun *me-lœ*, MELODUNUM (anc), 48 32N 2 39E, pop(1982) 36,218, market town and capital of Seine-et-Marne dept, Ile-de-France region, N central France; on the R Seine, 46 km SSE of Paris and 6 km SW of Vaux; railway; conquered by the Romans in 53 BC; taken by the English in 1420 and retaken by Joan of Arc in 1430; monuments: 11th-c Romanesque church, on an island in the middle of the river.

Melville Island, island in W Franklin dist, Northwest Territories, Canada; N of Victoria island; area 42,149 sq km; largest of the Parry Islands, part of the Queen Elizabeth Islands; the explorer Parry wintered here in 1819.

Memphis *mem'fis*, 35 08N 90 03W, pop(1980) 646,356, county seat of Shelby county, SW Tennessee, United States; largest city in the state and a port on the R Mississippi, in the extreme SW corner of the state; a military fort was built here in 1797; the city was established by Andrew Jackson, Marcus Winchester and John Overton in 1819; captured by Union forces during the Civil War after the battle of Memphis (1862); severe yellow-fever epidemics struck the city in the 1870s, killing thousands and causing so many to flee the city that it lost its charter; 2 universities (1848, 1912); railway; airfield; economy: important market for cotton, hardwood lumber, livestock and poultry; manufactures include food and paper products, chemicals, textiles, and fabricated metals; monuments: Graceland, home of the singer Elvis Presley; Beale Street, made famous by blues composer W.C. Handy and regarded as the birthplace of the blues; Mud Island Park.

Menado *ma-nah'doo*, MANADO, 1 32N 124 55E, pop(1980) 169,684, seaport capital of N Sulawesi Utara prov, Indonesia; at the NE tip of Sulawesi I on the Minahasa peninsula, on W slopes of Mt Klabat; founded by the Dutch in 1657; university (1961); airfield.

Mende *mãd*, MIMATUM (anc), 44 31N 3 30E, pop(1982) 12,113, ancient town and capital of Lozère dept, Languedoc-Roussillon region, S France; on the R Lot, at the foot of the cliff of the Causse de Mende (1,258 m), 122 km NW of Avignon; alt 739 m; railway; formerly chief town of the region known as the Gevaudan; in the Middle Ages, Mende possessed the largest bell in Christendom, weighing 20 tons, but it was destroyed in 1579 by militant Protestants; monuments: 14th-c Gothic bridge (the Pont-Notre-Dame), cathedral (15th-c, rebuilt early 17th-c); above the town is the Ermitage of St-Privat, a resort of pilgrims on the way to Compostella; there is a zoological park at Chastel Nouvel.

Menden *men'dun*, 51 26N 7 47E, pop(1983) 52,500, city in Arnsberg dist, Nordrhein-Westfalen (North Rhine-Westphalia) prov, W Germany, ESE of Dortmund; economy: electrical and metal goods.

Men'dip Hills, hill range in Somerset and Avon, SW England; extending 37 km NW-SE from Weston-super-Mare to near Shepton Mallet; rises to 326 m at Blackdown; includes the limestone caves of the Cheddar Gorge; there are traces of former Roman lead mines.

Mendoza *men-THō'sa*, prov in Andina region, W Argentina; bordered W by the Andes and Chile, S by the Río Barrancas, N and E by the Río Desaguadero and Río Salado; rises to 6,960 m at Cerro Aconcagua which is the highest point in the Western hemisphere; pop(1980) 1,196,228; area 150,839 sq km; capital Mendoza; chief town San Rafael; the Trans-Andean railway (built 1887-1910) runs to Chile via the Uspallata Pass; until 1776 the area was part of Chile; the most notable wine-producing area of S America; economy: vineyards, fruit, sheep and some cattle raising, fishing, timber, copper, lead, salt, sand and limestone mining, oil, hydroelectricity.

Mendoza, 32 48S 68 52W, pop(1980) 596,796, capital of Mendoza prov, Andina, W Argentina; at foot of Sierra de los Paramillos Andean mt range; on the Río Tulumaya, in the Mendoza valley irrigation area; alt 756 m; colonized by Chile in 1561; named after a Chilean governor; belonged to Chile until 1776; destroyed by fire and earthquake in 1861; 4 universities (1939, 1959, 1960, 1968); railway; airport (Pulmerillo) at 8 km; economy: trading and processing centre for a large, irrigated agricultural area dealing principally in wine; local holidays 18 Jan (crossing of the Andes), 25 July (St James), 8 Sept (Virgin of Carmen de Cuyo); annual wine festival in mid-Feb.

Menlo Park, 37 24N 122 12W, pop(1980) 26,369, city in San Mateo county, W California, United States; c.40 km SSE of San Francisco, NW of Palo Alto; railway; Stanford University (1891) is to the S.

Menom'onee Falls, 43 11N 88 07W, pop(1980) 27,845, town in Waukesha county, SE Wisconsin, United States; on the R Menomonee, 23 km NW of Milwaukee.

Menorca *may-nor'kah*, MINORCA *min-or'kah* (Eng), BALEARIS MINOR (anc), 2nd largest island in the Balearic Is, Baleares autonomous region of Spain; in the W Mediterranean, NE of Mallorca; pop(1981) 58,727; area 1,296 sq km; measuring 47 km in length by 10 to 19 km in breadth; generally flat and windswept but rising to 357 m at Monte Toro in the centre of the island; noted for its ancient broch-like talayots, the table-shaped taulas and its caves; the island was occupied by the British during most of the 18th century until its loss to the French; airport at Mahon, the island capital; economy: tourism, lead, iron and copper.

Mentor, 41 40N 81 21W, pop(1980) 42,065, town in Lake county, NE Ohio, United States; residential suburb on L Erie, 35 km NE of Cleveland; railway.

Menûfîya *mi-noo-fee'yu*, governorate in N Egypt; pop(1976) 1,710,982; area 1,612 sq km; capital Shibîn el Kom.

Merapi Gunung *me-rah'pee goon'ung* (Indon, 'fire mountain'), 7 32S 110 26E, volcano in central Jawa, Indonesia; rises to 2,911 m N of Yogyakarta; erupts every 5 or 6 years; major eruption in 1006.

Merced *mur-sed'*, 37 18N 120 29W, pop(1980) 36,499, capital of Merced county, central California, United States; in the San Joaquin Valley, 88 km NW of Fresno; railway.

Mercedario, Cerro *mer-say-da'ree-ō*, 31 58S 70 10W, Andean peak rising to 6,770 m in San Juan prov, Andina, W Argentina, near the Chilean border.

Mercedes *mer-say'THays*, VILLA MERCEDES, 33 41S 65 28W, pop(1980) 50,856, town in San Luis prov, Centro, central Argentina; on the Río Cuinto; railway; economy: trade in maize, wheat, alfalfa.

Mercedes, 33 16S 58 05W, pop(1985) 37,110, capital of Soriano dept, SW Uruguay; on S bank of Río Negro, 48 km above its confluence with the Río Uruguay; railway; economy: livestock trading centre and resort; a yachting and fishing centre during the season; monuments: the Eusebio Giménez museum contains a gallery of paintings.

Meric, river in Bulgaria, Greece, Turkey. See Maritsa.

Mérida *may'ree-THa*, 20 59N 89 39W, pop(1980) 424,529, capital of Yucatán state, SE Mexico; on the NW Yucatán peninsula; founded in 1542 on the site of the Mayan city of Tihoo; port at Progresso; university (1624); railway; airport; economy: ropes, sacking, sisal and trade in sugar, indigo, hides and henequen; monuments: 16th-c cathedral; Montejo House, originally built in 1549 by the conquistador of the region and rebuilt c.1850; the Museo de Arqueología is situated in the Casa de los Gobernadores; the Museum of Peninsular Culture is a contemporary crafts museum.

Mérida, AUGUSTA EMERITA (Lat), 38 55N 6 25W, pop(1981) 41,783, city in Badajoz prov, Extremadura, W Spain; on the R Guadiana, 61 km E of Badajoz; railway; economy: textiles, leather, soap, cork, hats; monuments: Roman theatre, built by Agrippa in 24 BC; Roman arena; events: cattle market and fair in Sept; fiesta of St Eulalia in Dec.

Mérida, state in W Venezuela; mountainous region crossed SW-NE by the Cordillera de Mérida which rises to Pico Bolívar (5,007 m), the highest peak in Venezuela; a narrow neck of the state borders on L Maracaibo; in the N of the state is the Sierra Nevada National Park; pop(1980) 463,880; area 11,296 sq km; capital Mérida.

Mérida, 8 35N 71 09W, pop(1981) 143,209, capital of Mérida state, W Venezuela; situated on an alluvial terrace 15 km long and 2.5 km wide; surrounded by high cliffs and plantations; alt 1,640 m; founded in 1558; university (1785); airfield; monument: the Parque de las Cinco Repúblicas contains the first monument built to commemorate Bolívar (1842), it also contains soil from the 5 countries he liberated; events: Feria del Sol in Dec; the city is famous for its bullfights.

Mérida, Sierra Nevada de, mountain range situated in W Venezuela; a spur of the Andes; goes from Colombia's Cordillera Oriental NE between the Orinoco *llanos* plain and the Maracaibo Lowlands to Barquisimeto, at the foot of the Caribbean coastal range; 483 km long and 48-80 km wide, it includes a number of snow-capped peaks; rises to 5,007 m at Pico Bolívar, the highest peak in Venezuela; the world's highest cable railway runs to Pico Espejo (4,765 m).

Mer'iden, 41 32N 72 48W, pop(1980) 57,118, town in New Haven county, S Connecticut, United States; 27 km SSW of Hartford; railway.

Meridian, 32 22N 88 42W, pop(1980) 46,577, county seat of Lauderdale county, E Mississippi, United States; 135 km E of Jackson; railway; airfield; economy: agricultural trade.

Merignac *mer-een-yac*, 45 42N 0 06E, pop(1982) 52,785, town in Gironde dept, Aquitaine region, W France; a suburb of Bordeaux; monument: 13th-c dungeons (Tour de Veyrines).

Merksem *merk'sum*, 51 14N 4 29E, pop(1982) 41,782, town in Antwerpen dist, Antwerpen prov, Belgium.

Mer'rillville, 41 29N 87 20W, pop(1980) 27,677, town in Lake county, NW Indiana, United States; 18 km SE of Hammond; railway.

Mersa Matrûh *mur'su mu-troo'*, governorate in N Egypt; pop(1976) 112,772; area 298,735 sq km; capital Matrûh.

Mersch *mersh*, canton in N part of Luxembourg dist, central Luxembourg; area 224 sq km; pop(1981) 16,546; springs at Hunnebour; prehistoric caves at Mamer and Dreibouren; many wooded walks; traversed N-S by the R Alzette and its tributaries the Mamer and Eisch rivers.

Mersch, 49 45N 6 06E, pop(1981) 4,000, capital of Mersch canton, Luxembourg dist, central Luxembourg; 17 km N of Luxembourg; a crossroad of tourist routes at the entrance to the Valley of the Seven Castles.

Merseburg *mer'zu-boork*, 51 22N 12 0E, pop(1981) 50,932, town in Merseburg dist, Halle, SW central East Germany; on R Saale, S of Halle; former residence of the dukes of Sachsen-Merseburg; college of technology; railway; economy: paper, chemicals, beer; monuments: 15th-c episcopal palace, 13th-c cathedral.

Mersey *mer'zi*, river in NW England; formed at the junction of the Goyt and Etherow rivers; flows 112 km W past Warrington, Runcorn and Liverpool to form a wide estuary that meets Liverpool Bay, an inlet of the Irish Sea, between Wallasey and Bootle; tributaries include the Weaver and Irwell rivers and the Manchester Ship Canal.

Merseyside *mer'zi-sīd*, metropolitan county of NW England; pop(1981) 1,511,915; area 652 sq km; on both sides of the R Mersey estuary; economy: chemicals, vehicles, electrical equipment; the metropolitan council was abolished in 1986; county town Liverpool; Merseyside includes 5 boroughs:

Borough	*area (sq km)*	*pop(1981)*
Knowsley	97	172,957
Liverpool	113	509,981
Sefton	151	299,724
St Helens	133	189,759
Wirral	158	339,494

Mersin *mer-seen'*, IÇEL, 36 47N 34 37E, pop(1980) 216,308, seaport capital of Içel prov, S Turkey, on the Mediterranean Sea; rail terminus; economy: oil refining, trade in cotton, wool and chromium; event: Mersin fashion and textile show (Sept-Oct).

Merthyr Tydfil *mær'THer tid'vil*, 51 46N 3 23W, pop(1981) 39,483, town in Merthyr Tydfil dist, Mid Glamorgan, S Wales; on R Taff, 38 km N of Cardiff; railway; economy: chemicals, engineering, printing, furniture.

Mer'ton, 51 25N 0 12W, pop(1981) 166,100, residential borough of S Greater London, England; includes the suburbs of Wimbledon, Mitcham, Merton and Morden; railway; event: Wimbledon lawn tennis championships (June-July).

Meru *may'roo*, 0 03N 37 38E, pop(1979) 73,000, (1984e) 98,000, town in Eastern prov, central Kenya, E Africa; on the NE slope of Mt Kenya, 177 km NNE of Nairobi.

Meru, SOCIALIST PEAK, 3 14S 36 45E, dormant volcanic cone in NE Tanzania, E Africa; height 4,565 m; 71 km WSW of Mt Kilimanjaro; last erupted in 1910.

Mesa *may'sa*, 33 25N 111 50W, pop(1980) 152,453, town in Maricopa county, S central Arizona, United States; 25 km E of Phoenix; railway; economy: electronic components, fabricated metals, aircraft, and machine tools.

Mesa, La *may'sa*, 32 45N 117 00W, pop(1980) 50,308, city in San Diego county, SW California, United States; E of San Diego.

Mesoamerica *mee-zō-a-mer'i-ka*, an area at the heart of Middle America, including those portions of Mexico and Central America that were occupied before the Spanish conquest of the 16th century by advanced indigenous populations with centres at locations such as Teotihuacán, Monte Albán, Chichén Itzá and Tikál.

Mesolóngion *mes-o-long'gee-on*, MISSOLONGHI, MESOLONGHI (Eng), pop(1981) 10,164, capital town of Aitolía and Akarnanía nome (dept), Sterea Ellás-Évvoia region, Greece; on the highway between Návpaktos and Árta; event: Vyronia Festival of Literature and Art (Sept).

Mesopotamia *me-su-pu-tay'mee-u*, ancient region of SW Asia, extending from the Arabian Gulf N to the mountains of Armenia and now included in modern Iraq; S Mesopotamia, the region of the lower Tigris and Euphrates rivers, was long thought to be the birthplace of ancient civilization until earlier settlements (probably dating from around 5,000 BC) were discovered in N Mesopotamia; civilization was well established here by the 4th millenium BC and a sophisticated irrigation system developed which rendered the area extremely fertile; the region is the legendary locale of the Garden of Eden; the ruins of Ur, Babylon, and other ancient cities can be found here.

Mesquite *mes-keet'*, 32 46N 96 36W, pop(1980) 67,053, town in Dallas county, NE Texas, United States; a suburb 19 km E of Dallas; railway.

Messina *mes-see'na*, prov of Sicilia region, Italy; pop(1981) 669,323; area 3,245 sq km; capital Messina.

Messina, ZANCLE *zang'klee* (anc), 38 13N 15 33E, pop(1981) 260,233, port and capital town of Messina prov, Sicilia region, Italy; near the NE tip of the island of Sicilia, on the W shore of the Strait de Messina; after a severe earthquake in 1908 Messina was rebuilt in modern style, with wide streets intersecting at right angles; archbishopric; university (1548); railway; ferries to Reggio and Napoli (Naples); economy: pasta, soap, olive oil, wine, tourism; monuments: cathedral, originally built in the 12th century; 12th-c Norman church; event: Fiera di Messina (industrial, agricultural and craft fair) in Aug.

Messina, Strait de, FRETUM SICULUM (anc), channel between Sicilia (Sicily) and the Italian mainland, separating the Ionian and Tyrrhenian Seas; it tapers northward to a minimum width of 3 km; length 32 km; chief ports Messina (Sicilia) and Reggio di Calabria (mainland Italy); its whirlpools and strong currents were feared by early sailors.

Messinía *me-see'ni-a*, coastal nome (dept) of Pelopónnisos region, S Greece; pop(1981) 159,818; area 2,991 sq km; capital Kalámai.

Meta *may'ta*, dept in central Colombia, South America; extends E from the Cordillera Oriental; bounded N by the Río Meta, S by the Río Guaviare; pop(1985) 321,563; area 85,635 sq km; capital Villavicencio; in the SW is the Sierra de la Macarena, an outlier of the Cordillera Oriental, now a national park for scientific study.

Metapán *may-ta-pan'*, 14 20N 89 28W, pop(1980) 57,412, town in Santa Ana dept, NW El Salvador, Central America; 32 km N of Santa Ana and 10 km NE of Laguna de Güija, in the S foothills of the Cordillera Metapán; a mountain track leads from Metapán to the Montecristo National Nature Reserve, El Salvador's last remaining cloud forest; economy: cement works, lime kilns; monument: Baroque cathedral.

Metéora *me-te'or-a*, 39 44N 21 38E, rock formations in Tríkkala nome (dept), Thessalía, NE Greece; rising to 300 m from the Piniós plain; the rocks have been weathered into bizarre forms; perched on these rocks are the monasteries of Metéora, first settled in the 9th century AD; nearest towns are Kastráki and Kalambáka.

Metz, DIVODURUM MEDIOMATRICUM (anc), later MEDIOMATRICA, also METIS, 49 08N 6 10E, pop(1982) 118,502, fortified town and capital of Moselle dept, Lorraine region, NE France; on the R Mosel at a point where it divides into several branches and is joined by the R Seille, near the German border, 285 km ENE of Paris; Metz has been a strategic focus of crossroads for over 2,000 years, surrounded by strongly defended forts; in the 6th century it was the residence of the Merovingian kings, later it became a free imperial city and in 1552 it was incorporated into France; the German defence of Metz in 1944 held up Eisenhower's advance for over 2 months; when Alsace and Lorraine were annexed to the German Empire, Metz became the chief town of Lorraine; nearby is a military cemetery of World War I; bishopric; road and rail junction; airport; economy: brewing, tanning, food products, cement, metal goods, footwear; monuments: Gothic cathedral of St-Étienne (1250-1380), with the bell known as Dame Mutte (1605), incorporated an older church built on the same site; St-Pierre-aux-Nonnains, the oldest basilica in France, belonged to a 7th-c abbey and stands on the foundations of a 4th-c Roman basilica; Église Ste-Thérèse (consecrated in 1954); town hall (18th-c); at the E end of the town is a 13th-c chateau-fort, Porte des Allemands ('Germans' Gate'), a relic of the medieval fortifications (has two 13th-c round towers); event: Mirabelle Plum Festival (first Sunday in Sept).

Meurthe *mœrt*, river in NE France rising in the Vosges Mts above Fraize; flows NW through Vosges and Meurthe-et-Moselle depts to meet the R Mosel at Frouard above Nancy; length 170 km; tributaries Vezouze and Mortagne rivers.

Meurthe-et-Moselle *mœr-tay-mo-zel*, dept in Lorraine region of NE France, comprising 4 arrond, 40 cantons and 587 communes; pop(1982) 716,846; area 5,241; a plateau cut by the valleys of the R Mosel and its tributary, the Meurthe; capital Nancy, a road, rail and canal junction; the Parc de Lorraine regional nature park lies partly within the dept.

Meuse *mœz*, dept in Lorraine region of NE France, bounded on the NE by Belgium; comprises 3 arrond, 31 cantons and 482 communes; pop(1982) 200,101; area 6,216 sq km; watered by the upper Meuse, Aire and Aisne rivers; elevated in the S; the forested ridges of the Argonne and the Côtes de Meuse run along both banks of the Meuse; capital Bar-le-Duc, chief towns Verdun and Commercy; the countryside was ravaged by the battles of Verdun and Argonne in World War I; the Parc de Lorraine regional nature park lies partly within the dept.

Meuse, MAAS (Dut), MOSA (anc), river in NE France, Belgium and the Netherlands, rising on the Langres Plateau in Haute-Marne dept, NE France; flows N past Verdun and Mézières in France through the Ardennes, NE past Namur and Liège in Belgium, then N past Maastricht and Venlo, forming a section of the NE boundary of Belgium; enters Netherlands and as the Maas, curves W to unite at Gorinchem with the Waal branch of the R Rhine, entering the North Sea through Hollandsch Diep; length 950 km; navigable for 578 km; tributaries Sambre, Lesse and Ourthe rivers in Belgium, Niers and Ruhr rivers in Netherlands from W Germany; its valley, especially in NE France, was the scene of severe fighting in World War I.

Mexicali *may-hee-ka'lee*, 32 36N 115 30W, pop(1980) 510,554, capital of Baja California Norte state, NW Mexico; 160 km E of San Diego, adjacent to Calexico on the border with the state of California, USA; centre of irrigated agriculture; university (1957); railway; economy: cottonseed oil, soap.

Mexico *mek'si-kō*, MÉXICO *may'hee-kō* (Sp), official name United Mexican States, ESTADOS UNIDOS DE MÉXICO (Sp), federal republic in S North America; bounded by the USA (N), the Golfo de California (W), the Pacific Ocean (W and SW), Guatemala and Belize (S) and the Gulf of Mexico (E); situated between 14°N and 32°N; timezones: Baja California Norte GMT −8, Baja California Sur, Sonora, Sinaloa and Nayarit GMT −7, all the other states are GMT −6; area 1,978,800 sq km; capital Ciudad de México (Mexico City); pop(1984e) 76,791,819; pop is 60% mestizo (Indian-Spanish), 30% Amerindian, 9% white; the official language is Spanish; 97% of the pop are nominally Roman Catholic, 3% are Protestant; the Mexican currency is the peso of 100 centavos; national holiday: 16 Sep (Independence Day); membership of FAO, G-77, IADB, IAEA, IBRD, ICAC, ICAO, ICO, IDA, IDB (Inter-American Development Bank), IFAD, IFC, ILO, ILZSG, IMF, IMO, INTELSAT, INTERPOL, IRC, ISO, ITU, IWC (International Whaling Commission), LAIA, NAMUCAR, OAS, PAHO, SELA, UN, UNESCO, UPU, WHO, WIPO, WMO, WSG, WTO.

Physical description. Bisected by the Tropic of Cancer, Mexico lies at the S end of the North American Western Cordillera which extends S through Mexico as far as Panama. From narrow coastal plains bordering the Pacific Ocean and the Gulf of Mexico the land rises steeply to a central plateau which is bounded by the Sierra Madre Occidental (W) and the Sierra Madre Oriental (E). The rugged central tableland is 2,400 km in length with a max width of 800 km. From a low desert plain in the N the central plateau rises to 2,400 m above sea-level around Ciudad de México to the S of which rise volcanic peaks such as Citlaltépetl (5,699 m), Popocatépetl (5,452 m) and Ixtaccihuatl (5,286 m). South of the plateau the lower Sierra Madre del Sur extends into Guatemala. In the SE the subtropical limestone lowlands of the Yucatán peninsula stretch into the Gulf of Mexico. Mexico is subject to earthquakes, the most recent significant tremor in Sept 1985 causing extensive damage in and around Ciudad de México.

Climate. Mexico is divided into 3 climatic regions: the *tierra caliente*, comprising the coastlands and plateaux below 600 m, the *tierra templada*, lying between 600 and 1,800 m and the *tierra frío* of the mountains and plateaux above 1,800 m. Apart from altitude three important features influence the local climate of Mexico: (1) the cold Californian current which sweeps S along the Pacific coast lowers temperatures and reduces rainfall on the W coast as far S as the tip of the peninsula of Baja California. Coupled with the influence of the North Pacific anticyclone, the cold current is responsible for much of desert or semi-desert conditions of NW Mexico. Guaymas on the Golfo de California records an average daily temperature of 13° to 23°C in the coldest months of Jan-Dec and 27° to 35°C in Aug. Rainfall, mostly during July-Sept, varies monthly from an average of 91 mm in Aug to 0 mm in Feb; (2) the warm waters of the Caribbean and the NE trade winds combine to give the E coast a typically tropical climate with a single wet season in summer. At Mérida in N Yucatán a max of 173 mm of rain falls in June, with temperatures ranging from 17° to 28°C in Jan to 23° to 33°C in June-Aug. The S coasts are generally wetter, with an average annual rainfall of 1,400 mm at Acapulco; (3) N Mexico suffers extreme temperature variations as a result of winds from the N American continent. This area becomes very cold in winter and very warm in summer. In winter cold air sweeps down from the Canadian Arctic, bringing near-freezing conditions as far down the E coast as Tampico. The W coast is protected from these winds by the mountains and plateaux of central Mexico. Monterrey is representative of the interior of Mexico and at an alt of 538 m is at the upper range of the *tierra caliente*. Temperatures here range between 9° to 20°C in Jan and 22° to 33°C in Aug, with rainfall highest in the summer months, reaching a max of 132 mm in Sept and a min of 15 mm in Jan. Ciudad de México at an alt of 2,235 m is typical of the *tierra frío*, with rainfall heaviest from June to Sept reaching a max of 170 mm in July and a min of 5 mm in Feb. Temperatures range between 6° and 19°C during the coldest months of Dec-Jan, rising to 13° to 24°C in July. There can be sharp changes of temperature between day and night.

History, government and constitution. Before the arrival of the Spanish conquistadores in the 1520s Mexico had been the centre of a succession of Indian civilizations for over 2,500 years. The chronology of pre-Columbian history is generally classified into pre-Classic (1500 BC-200 AD), Classic (200-900 AD) and post-Classic (900-1520) periods. Dominant groups developing urban centres included the Gulf Coast Olmecs based at La Venta, the Zapotecs at Monte Alban near Oaxaca, the Mixtecs at Mitla, the Toltecs at Tula, the Maya of the Yucatán and the Aztecs at Tenochtitlán, the site of present-day Ciudad de México. In 1516 Hernández de Cordoba landed in the Yucatán and in 1519 Hernán Cortés came ashore near Veracruz with approx 500 men. Within 2 years Cortés had captured and destroyed the Aztec capital. For 300 years Mexico was held by the Spanish as the Viceroyalty of New Spain with Ciudad de México as its capital. Under the Spanish, the mineral wealth of Mexico was heavily exploited using Indian labour. In 1810 the struggle for independence began. Eventually, Agustín de Iturbide proclaimed the independence of Mexico in 1821 and a federal republic was created on 4 Oct 1824, with General Guadalupe Victoria as the country's first president. During the succeeding 2 decades Mexico lost territory to the USA, first with the rebellion of Texas in 1836 and later after 3 years of conflict (1845-48), the annexation of the border provinces of California, Utah and New Mexico. Civil war broke out between 1858 and 1861 as a result of the reform programme of president Benito Juárez. His victory was followed by the suspension of international debt payments, an action that forced Britain, France and Spain to land troops in Mexico. The British and Spanish forces soon left, but the French pushed inland, occupying Ciudad de México in 1863 and declaring Archduke Maximilian of Austria Emperor of Mexico. The French troops were forced to withdraw in 1867, and Maximilian was captured by Juaristas at Querétaro and shot. Benito Juárez resumed control until his death in 1872. Under the dictatorship of Porfirio Díaz (1876-1911) considerable developments took place, but the continued depressed state of the peasants led to the revolution of 1910-17. The presidency of Lázaro Cárdenas (1934-40) introduced agrarian reform, with the division of large estates into communal *ejidos*. Under the 1917 constitution Mexico is a federal republic operating under a centralized government. A president, who is elected for 6 years and cannot be re-elected, appoints a cabinet of about 20 ministers. The legislature comprises a bicameral Congress with a 64-member Senate elected every 6 years and a 400-member House of Deputies elected every 3 years. Each state has a governor and an elected Chamber of Deputies.

Economy. The economy of Mexico prior to the revolution of 1910 had largely been based on the export of minerals such as gold, silver, lead and zinc and of agricultural products such as sugar, maize, coffee, tobacco and fruit grown on plantations. In more recent times mineral exports have been extended to include fluorite, arsenic, cadmium, phosphates, sulphur, copper, antimony and iron. With a long-established oil and natural gas industry boosted by major discoveries in the 1970s, Mexico has become the 4th largest producer in the world. Nationalized oil production now supports a large petrochemical industry. Manufacturing industry is also based on iron, steel and aluminium production, motor vehicles, cement, food processing, textiles, clothing, pottery and craft work. Major exports include cotton, coffee, non-ferrous metals (including lead and zinc), shrimps, petroleum, sulphur, salt, cattle and meat, fresh fruit, tomatoes, machinery and equipment. Major trade partners include the USA, the EEC and Japan.

Administrative divisions. Mexico is divided into 31 states and the Federal District of Ciudad de México (Mexico City) as follows:

State	*area (sq km)*	*pop(1980)*
Aguascalientes	5,471	503,410
Baja California Norte	69,921	1,225,436
Baja California Sur	73,475	215,139
Campeche	50,812	372,277
Chiapas	74,211	2,096,812
Chihuahua	244,938	1,933,856
Coahuila	149,982	1,558,401
Colima	5,191	339,202
Durango	123,181	1,160,196
Guanajuato	30,491	3,044,402
Guerrero	64,281	2,174,162

contd

State	*area (sq km)*	*pop(1980)*
Hidalgo	20,813	1,516,511
Jalisco	80,836	4,293,549
México	21,355	7,545,692
México, Ciudad de	1,479	9,373,353
Michoacán	59,928	3,048,704
Morelos	4,950	931,675
Nayarit	26,979	730,024
Nuevo León	64,924	2,463,298
Oaxaca	93,952	2,518,157
Puebla	33,902	3,279,960
Querétaro	11,449	726,054
Quintana Roo	50,212	209,858
San Luis Potosí	63,068	1,670,637
Sinaloa	58,328	1,880,098
Sonora	182,052	1,498,931
Tabasco	25,267	1,149,756
Tamaulipas	79,304	1,924,934
Tlaxcala	4,016	547,261
Veracruz	71,699	5,264,611
Yucatán	38,402	1,034,648
Zacatecas	73,252	1,145,327

México *may'hee-kō*, state in central Mexico; bounded by Querétaro (NW), Hidalgo (N and NE), Tlaxcala and Puebla (E), Morelos and Guerrero (S) and Michoacán (W); surrounds most of the Ciudad de México federal district in the S; a mountainous region rising above 2,400 m; in the SE, on the border with Puebla are the volcanoes of Ixtaccihuatl (5,286 m) and Popocatépetl (5,452 m); drained by the Lerma river; pop(1980) 7,545,692; area 21,355 sq km; capital Toluca; economy: agriculture (maize, alfalfa, wheat, barley, broad beans, fruit), stock raising, mining in the W and SW (silver, zinc, copper, gold, iron, lead), motor cars, textiles, food processing, chemicals, electrical goods, iron and steel.

Mexico City, capital of Mexico. See México, Ciudad de.

México, Ciudad de *syoo-THaTH' THay*, MEXICO CITY (Eng), 19 25N 99 10W, pop(1980) 9,373,353, federal district and capital of Mexico; largest city in the world; situated in central Mexico, bounded N, E and W by México state, and S by Morelos state; mountainous in the SW; flat in the NE, at an alt of 2,200 m; area (Federal District) 1,479 sq km; situated in a small, high intermontane basin measuring 50 sq km; 7 universities; the oldest capital in continental America; built on the remains of the Aztec capital, Tenochtitlán; captured by Cortés in 1521 when it became the capital of the Viceroyalty of New Spain for 300 years until independence; held by the French 1863-67; the modern city was developed under the dictator Porfirio Díaz prior to the 1910 revolution; location of the 1968 summer Olympics; scene of an industrial accident in Nov 1984, when a liquefied gas tank belonging to the state-owned Petróleos Mexicanos exploded at the San Juan Ixhuatepec storage facility, resulting in 452 people dead and 4,248 injured; in Sept 1985 an earthquake killed an estimated 2,000 people and injured 5,000; railway; airport; economy: motor vehicles, iron and steel, chemicals, tobacco, glass, food processing, textiles; monuments: the Zócalo is Ciudad de México's largest square; on one side of it is the cathedral (commenced in 1573 and completed in the 19th-c); the national palace (built in 1692 on the ruins of the Palace of Moctezuma) is now the seat of the president of the Republic; the Castle of Chapultepec, once the residence of Emperor Maximilian and Empress Charlotte, is now the National Museum of History; the National Museum of Anthropology contains archaeological finds from all parts of Mexico; 40 km NE lie the extensive ruins of Teotihuacán.

Mexico, Gulf of, gulf on the SE coast of N America forming a basin enclosed by the US states of Florida, Louisiana, Mississippi, Alabama and Texas to the N and the E coast of Mexico as far as the Yucatán Peninsula; Cuba lies at the entrance to the gulf which is linked to the Caribbean Sea by the Yucatán Channel and to the Atlantic by the Straits of Florida; area 1,813,000 sq km; surface water enters via the Yucatán Channel, is heated as it moves in a clockwise fashion to exit by the Straits of Florida as the Gulf Stream; Campeche and Apalachee Bays are the largest arms; Sigsbee Deep (3,877.8 m) is the deepest point; the basin is significantly shallowed by the Mississippi Cone; Mississippi and the Rio Grande del Norte are the major rivers; the gulf has a low, sandy shoreline with many marshes, lagoons and deltas; offshore wells exploit oil and natural gas resources found on the continental shelves; violent *Nortes* winds blow from the NE during Sept-March.

Meymaneh, *mī-ma'na*, MAYMANA, MAIMANA, 35 54N 64 43E, pop(1984e) 41,929, capital of Fāryab prov, N Afghanistan; lies on the Qausar Andkhua river on the road between Herāt and Mazār-e Sharīf; airfield.

Mezada, 31 19N 35 21E, ancient mountaintop fortress in South dist, Israel; in the Judean desert; the final outpost of the Zealot Jews in their rebellion against Roman authority (AD 66-73); between 37 and 31 BC Herod the Great, king of Judea, added further fortifications.

Mezötúr *mez'ü-toor*, 47 00N 20 41E, pop(1984e) 22,000, town in Szolnok county, E central Hungary; on a branch of the R Berettyo SE of Szolnok; railway; economy: livestock and grain trade, textiles.

Mezzogiorno *met-zo-jee-or'no*, geographical region comprising all the regions of S Italy excluding Sardegna (Sardinia) and the provs of Latina, Frosinone and Rieti in S Latium; a largely agricultural area; development is aided by the Cassa (Fund) per il Mezzogiorno.

Miami *mī-a'mi*, 25 47N 80 11W, pop(1980) 346,865, county seat of Dade county, SE Florida, United States; a port on Biscayne Bay, at the mouth of the R Miami; settled around a military post in the 1830s; since 1945, one of the country's most famous and popular resorts; railway; airport; economy: major tourist industry with extensive recreational facilities (receives nearly 6 million visitors each year); the processing and shipping hub of a large agricultural region; industries include printing and publishing, fishing, and the manufacture of clothing, aluminium products, furniture, transportation equipment; it is the air gateway to Latin America and receives vast numbers of immigrants; nearly half of Miami's metropolitan population is Hispanic; monuments: Dade County Art Museum, Seaquarium, Villa Vizcaya, the Everglades, Biscayne Boulevard; event: Orange Bowl Festival (Dec).

Miami Beach, 25 47N 80 08W, pop(1980) 96,298, town in Dade county, SE Florida, United States; on an island across Biscayne Bay from Miami; railway; connected to Miami by 4 causeways; popular year-round resort, famous for its 'gold coast' hotel strip.

Mianwali *myang'vahl-ee*, 32 32N 71 33E, pop(1981) 59,000, town in Punjab prov, Pakistan; 170 km S of Peshawar, close to the E bank of the R Indus; railway.

Mia-oli *mya-ō-lee*, county of NW Taiwan; area 1,820.3 sq km; pop(1982e) 548,790.

Michalovce *miKH'al-ov-tse*, 48 44N 21 54E, pop(1984) 33,099, town in Východoslovenský region, Slovak Socialist Republic, E Czechoslovakia; on R Laborec, E of Košice; railway; economy: agricultural trade.

Michigan *mish'i-gun*, state in N central United States, divided in two by L Michigan and L Huron; the upper peninsula is bounded SW by Wisconsin, N by L Superior, NE by Canada, and S by L Huron and L Michigan; the lower peninsula is bounded W by L Michigan, N by L Michigan and L Huron, E by L Huron, Canada, L St Clair and L Erie, and S by Ohio and Indiana; the R Montreal forms the extreme W part of the Wisconsin border; the 'Great Lake State' or the 'Wolverine State'; 26th state admitted to the Union (1837); pop(1980) 9,262,078; area 148,080 sq km; capital Lansing; other major cities include Detroit, Grand Rapids, Warren and Flint; the R Brule and R Menominee form the E part of the Wisconsin border; the R St Clair flows between L Huron and L St Clair, forming the border with Canada;

the R Detroit flows between L St Clair and L Erie, also forming part of the border with Canada; 99,909 sq km of the Great Lakes lie within the state boundary; the highest point is Mt Curwood (604 m); the upper peninsula and N part of the lower peninsula are predominantly forested, containing several state parks; the S part of the state is highly industrialized; economy: motor vehicles and parts, machinery, cement, and iron and steel (2nd in the country for iron ore production); principal agricultural products are corn and dairy products; settled by the French in 1668 and ceded to the British in 1763; handed over to the USA in 1783 and became part of Indiana Territory; became the Territory of Michigan in 1805; its boundaries were greatly extended in 1818 and 1834; the state is divided into 83 counties:

County	*area (sq km)*	*pop(1980)*
Alcona	1,765	9,740
Alger	2,371	9,225
Allegan	2,163	81,555
Alpena	1,474	32,315
Antrim	1,248	16,194
Arenac	954	14,706
Baraga	2,343	8,484
Barry	1,456	45,781
Bay	1,162	119,881
Benzie	837	11,205
Berrien	1,498	171,276
Branch	1,321	40,188
Calhoun	1,851	141,557
Cass	1,290	49,499
Charlevoix	1,095	19,907
Cheboygan	1,872	20,649
Chippewa	4,134	29,029
Clare	1,482	23,822
Clinton	1,490	55,893
Crawford	1,453	9,465
Delta	3,050	38,947
Dickinson	2,002	25,341
Eaton	1,505	88,337
Emmet	1,217	22,992
Genesee	1,669	450,449
Gladwin	1,313	19,957
Gogebic	2,873	19,686
Grand Traverse	1,212	54,899
Gratiot	1,482	40,448
Hillsdale	1,568	42,071
Houghton	2,636	37,872
Huron	2,158	36,459
Ingham	1,456	275,520
Ionia	1,500	51,815
Iosco	1,420	28,349
Iron	3,024	13,635
Isabella	1,500	54,110
Jackson	1,833	151,495
Kalamazoo	1,461	212,378
Kalkaska	1,464	10,952
Kent	2,241	444,506
Keweenaw	1,412	1,963
Lake	1,477	7,711
Lapeer	1,711	70,038
Leelanau	887	14,007
Lenawee	1,958	89,948
Livingston	1,492	100,289
Luce	2,350	6,659
Mackinac	2,665	10,178
Macomb	1,253	694,600
Manistee	1,412	23,019
Marquette	4,735	74,101
Mason	1,284	26,365
Mecosta	1,456	36,961
Menominee	2,717	26,201
Midland	1,365	73,578
Missaukee	1,469	10,009
Monroe	1,448	134,659
Montcalm	1,854	47,555
Montmorency	1,430	7,492
Muskegon	1,318	157,589
Newaygo	2,202	34,917
Oakland	2,275	1,011,793
Oceana	1,407	22,002
Ogemaw	1,482	16,436
Ontonagon	3,409	9,861
Osceola	1,479	18,928
Oscoda	1,477	6,858
Otsego	1,342	14,993
Ottawa	1,474	157,174
Presque Isle	1,706	14,267
Roscommon	1,373	16,374
Saginaw	2,119	228,059
Sanilac	2,506	40,789
Schoolcraft	3,050	8,575
Shiawassee	1,404	71,140
St Clair	1,908	138,802
St Joseph	1,308	56,083
Tuscola	2,111	56,961
Van Buren	1,589	66,814
Washtenaw	1,846	264,748
Wayne	1,599	2,337,891
Wexford	1,472	25,102

Michigan City, 41 43N 86 54W, pop(1980) 36,850, town in La Porte county, NW Indiana, United States; port on L Michigan; yachting centre; nearby is the Indiana Dunes National Lakeshore.

Michigan, Lake, 3rd largest of the Great Lakes (area 58,016 sq km) and the only one lying entirely within the USA; bordered E and N by Michigan, W by Illinois and Wisconsin and S by Indiana; 494 km long; 190 km wide; Green Bay, a large W arm, indents the Wisconsin shore; the lake is linked in the NE with L Huron via the Strait of Mackinac; from Chicago the Chicago Ship Canal, Illinois river, and the Illinois and Mississippi Canal all link L Michigan with the Mississippi river and the Gulf of Mexico; major ports: Michigan City and Gary (Indiana); Chicago, Evanston and Waukegan (Illinois); Kenosha, Racine, Milwaukee and Manitowoc (Wisconsin); Escanaba, Muskegon and Grand Haven (Michigan).

Michoacán *mee-chō-ah-kahn'*, *meech-wah-kahn'*, MICHOACÁN DE OCAMPO, mountainous state in W central Mexico, bounded NW by Colima, N by Jalisco and Guanajuato, NE by Querétaro, E by México, S by Guerrero (along the Río Balsas) and W by the Pacific Ocean; crossed by the Sierra Madre Occidental; drained by the Balsas and Lerma rivers; in the SE is the Lago Infiernillo dam; pop(1980) 3,048,704; area 59,928 sq km; capital Morelia; major town: Uruapan; economy: agriculture (wheat, maize, sorghum, cotton, rice, sugar cane, chick-peas, fruit), cattle and pig raising, fishing, mining (silver, lead, zinc, copper, gold, iron), chemicals, fertilizers, meat, fruit and vegetable packing, textiles, tobacco, soap, tourism.

Micronesia, one of the 3 main divisions of the Pacific Is, W Pacific. See United States Trust Territory of the Pacific Islands. Guam, Kiribati, and Nauru are not part of the Trust Territory but are ethnically and geographically Micronesian.

Micronesia, Federated States of, group of 4 states in the W Pacific Ocean (Yap, Truk, Ponape, and Kosrae) belonging to the United States Trust Territory of the Pacific Islands; comprises all the Caroline Is except Belau; the constitution of the Federated States came into effect on 10 May 1979; land area 700 sq km.

Mid Glamorgan, county in S Wales; bounded S by South Glamorgan, W by West Glamorgan, SW by the Bristol Channel, E by Gwent and N by Powys; drained by R Taff; pop(1981) 538,474; area 1,018 sq km; administrative centre Cathays Park, Cardiff; economy: farming, iron and steel, engineering, textiles, electrical goods, vehicle components; created in 1974, the county is divided into 6 districts:

District	*area (sq km)*	*pop(1981)*
Cynon Valley	181	67,197
Merthyr Tydfil	112	60,708
Ogwr	285	130,349
Rhondda	97	81,955
Rhymney Valley	176	104,973
Taff-Ely	168	93,292

Mid'delburg, 51 30N 3 36E, pop(1984e) 38,854, capital city of Zeeland prov, W Netherlands, on the former island of Walcheren, on the Veere-Vlissingen Canal; seat of a bishop since 1561; built as a defensive fortress in the 9th century; received its town charter in 1217; in the 14th and 15th centuries it was a rival to Brugge in the prosperous wool trade; became famous through its cloth-making and as a depot for French goods; economy: tourism, electrics, chemicals, metalworking, electricity generation; monuments: Gothic town hall (15-16th-c); 12th-c abbey, burned down in 1940 but now completely restored).

Middelfart *mi'dul-fahrt*, 55 30N 9 44E, pop(1981) 12,064, seaport on the Lille Bælt (Little Belt), NW Fyn I, Fyn county, Denmark; railway; to the N (at Strib) is the Lille Bælt Bridge (1935) to Fredericia; economy: transport equipment.

Middle America, a geographical region encompassing Mexico, Central America and the West Indies; includes the Gulf of Mexico and Caribbean area.

Middle East, a loosely defined geographical region encompassing the largely Arab states to the E of the Mediterranean together with Cyprus, Turkey and the countries of N Africa; includes Syria, Lebanon, Israel, Jordan, Egypt, Iraq, Iran, Kuwait, Saudi Arabia, Bahrain, Qatar, Oman, United Arab Emirates, Yemen Arab Republic, Sudan, Libya, Tunisia, Algeria and Morocco.

Middle West, an area of the USA comprising the N central states of Illinois, Indiana, Iowa, Michigan, Minnesota, Ohio and Wisconsin; a major cereal growing area of the USA.

Middlesbrough *mid'lz-bru*, 54 35N 1 14W, pop(1981) 150,430, port town in Middlesbrough dist, Cleveland, NE England; on the R Tees estuary; developed around the iron industry in the 19th century; part of the Teesside conurbation; railway; economy: iron and steel, chemicals, fertilizer; monuments: town hall (1846), custom house (1840), the Captain Cook birthplace museum commemorates the great voyager Captain James Cook (1728-79).

Middlesex, county on the Caribbean I of Jamaica; located in central Jamaica between Cornwall county (W) and Surrey county (E); comprises the parishes of Manchester, Clarendon, St Ann, St Catherine and St Mary; area 5,040 sq km; pop(1982) 923,549; chief towns Spanish Town, Mandeville, Port Esquivel, May Pen.

Middleton, 53 33N 2 12W, pop(1981) 51,437, town in Rochdale borough, Greater Manchester, NW England; 6 km N of Manchester; economy: textiles, chemicals; monument: 15th-c St Leonard's church.

Middletown, 41 34N 72 39W, pop(1980) 39,040, town in Middlesex county, S Connecticut, United States; on the R Connecticut, 22 km S of Hartford; university (1831); railway; economy: textiles, footwear.

Middletown, 39 31N 84 24W, pop(1980) 43,719, town in Butler county, SW Ohio, United States; 46 km N of Cincinnati; railway.

Midi-Pyrénées, region of S France comprising the depts of Ariège, Aveyron, Haute-Garonne, Gers, Lot, Hautes-Pyrénées, Tarn and Tarn-et-Garonne, 22 arrond, 281 cantons and 3,019 communes; pop(1982) 2,325,319; area 45,348 sq km; stretches from the Pyrenees in the S to the W edge of the Massif Central in the N; drained by the Garonne, Tarn, Lot, Gers, Adour and Midour rivers; there are interesting prehistoric caves at Cabrerets, 18 km E of Cahors, Lot dept; Ax-les-Thermes is a well-known Pyrenean spa and wintersport centre; other wintersport centres include Bagnères-de-Luchon, Cauterets and Gavarnie; the Grottes de Lacave (8 km SE of Souillac), Grottes de Betharram (12 km W of Lourdes) and the Grottes du Mas-d'Azil (23 km NW of Foix, one of the most important prehistoric sites in the Pyrénées) are all interesting caves worth visiting; chief towns Toulouse, Montauban, Cahors, Rodez, Lourdes, Albi, Castres, Foix, Millau and Tarbes.

Midland, 43 37N 84 14W, pop(1980) 37,250, county seat of Midland county, E Michigan, United States; on the R Tittabawassee, 29 km W of Bay City; railway.

Midland, 32 00N 102 05W, pop(1980) 70,525, county seat of Midland county, W Texas, United States; 225 km WSW of Abilene; railway; economy: oil and cattle trade, clothing, mobile homes, aircraft, fabricated steel, plastics, and drilling tools.

Midleton, MAINISTIR NA CORAN (Gael), 51 55N 8 10W, pop(1981) 6,243, market town in Cork county, Munster, S Irish Republic; at NE end of Cork harbour; economy: distilling.

Midway Islands, 28 15N 177 25W, a circular atoll enclosing 2 small islands in the central Pacific Ocean 1,850 km NW of Oahu in the Hawaii Is; comprises Sand I and Eastern Island separated by Brooks Channel; the reef has a circumference of 24 km; area 3 sq km; pop(1981) 2,300, mostly comprising US naval personnel; discovered by US sailors in 1859 and annexed by the USA in 1867; used as a submarine cable station since 1905, a commercial aircraft stopover since 1935 and an important military airbase since 1941; the Battle of Midway (1942) was a turning point during World War II.

Midwest City, 35 27N 97 24W, pop(1980) 49,559, city in Oklahoma county, central Oklahoma, United States; a residential suburb 11 km E of Oklahoma City.

Miercurea-Ciuc *mer-koor'ya-chook*, 46 21N 5 46E, pop(1983) 43,578, capital of Harghita county, N central Romania; on R Olt, in the W foothills of the E Carpathian Mts; railway; economy: timber; monument: Simuleu pilgrimage site 3 km NE, with 13th-c statue of the Virgin.

Mikhailovgrad or **Mihajlovgrad**, also **Mikhaylovgrad** *mee-KHĪ'lov-grat*, okrug (prov) of NW Bulgaria to the N of the Stara Planina (Balkan Mts) bordering Yugoslavia to the W and Romania to the N; the R Danube follows its N frontier with Romania; area 3,628 sq km; pop(1981) 236,000; nuclear power plant at Kozloduy on the Danube.

Mikhailovgrad, MONTENENSIA (Lat), 43 25N 23 11E, capital of Mikhailovgrad okrug, NW Bulgaria, situated at the meeting point of the Barzija and Ogosta rivers; formerly known as Golyama Kutlovitsa and then Ferdinand; railway.

Mikkeli *mi'kel-i*, SANKT MICHEL (Swed), a prov of S Finland; one-third of the area is covered by lakes including L Saimaa which extends into S part of the prov; area 21,660 sq km; pop(1982) 208,523; includes the towns of Mikkeli, Savonlinna, Pieksämäki, and Heinola; economy: timber, grain, livestock, metalwork, mining.

Mikkeli, SANKT MICHEL (Swed), 61 44N 27 15E, pop(1982) 28,946, summer and winter sports resort and capital of Mikkeli prov, S central Finland; on one of the W arms of L Saimaa; established in 1838; bishopric; railway; airfield.

Míkonos *mee'ko-nos*, island of the Kikládhes, Greece, in the Aegean Sea; area 85 sq km; noted resorts on the island; near to Hora is the Agios Panteleímon monastery.

Miku'mi, national park in E central Tanzania, E Africa; area 3,230 sq km; established in 1964; situated SE of Dodoma and W of Dar es Salaam.

Milagro *mee-la'grō*, 2 11S 79 36W, pop(1982) 77,010, agricultural market town in Guayas prov, W Ecuador; in the tropical lowlands E of Guayaquil and W of the Andes; on the railway from Guayaquil to Riobamba.

Milan, prov and city in N Italy. See Milano.

Milano *mee-lah'no*, MILAN (Eng), MAILAND *mī'lant* (Ger), MEDIOLAN'UM (anc), prov in Lombardia region, N Italy; pop(1981) 4,018,108; area 2,764 sq km; capital Milano.

Milano, 45 28N 9 12E, pop(1981) 1,604,773, commercial city and capital of Milano prov, Lombardia region, N Italy; on R Olna, in a fertile plain near the S end of important passes through the Alps; its general plan is radial, with the Piazza del Duomo at the centre; a leading banking and commercial centre; a Gallic town taken by the Romans in 222 BC, later becoming the chief city of the Western Roman Empire; rebuilt after its destruction in 1162, the city was ruled by the dukes of Milan who controlled much of N Italy; the Duchy of Milan (The Milanese) was held by Spain in the 16th century, was ceded to Austria in 1713 and eventually became a kingdom in 1805; held by Austria between 1815 and 1860; linked by shipping canals with the Ticino, the Po, Lago Maggiore, and Lago di Como; university (1923); Catholic university (1920); airports at Forlanini di Linate (8 km E) and Malpensa (45 km NW); railway junction; underground railway system (opened in 1964); economy: textiles, iron and steel, non-ferrous metals, metalworking, manufacture of cars, machinery and rolling-stock, chemicals, pharmaceuticals, electrical apparatus, watches and clocks, domestic appliances, glass products, data processing equipment, foodstuffs, engineering, papermaking, publishing and printing; monuments: 14th-c Gothic cathedral, faced with white marble, and its roof adorned with many pinnacles and statues; church of San Lorenzo, dating from the Early Christian period, with a Renaissance dome (1574); church of Sant'Ambrogio, founded in 386 AD by St Ambrose; in the refectory of the 15th-c church of Santa Maria delle Grazie, is the famous 'Last Supper' of Leonardo da Vinci; Palazzo dell'Ambrosiana (1603-09), with a famous library and picture gallery; Castello Sforzesco (built in 1368), housing the Musco d'Arte Antica - its greatest treasure is the 'Pietà Rondanini', Michelangelo's last masterpiece; Teatro alla Scala (1776-78) is one of the largest and most important opera-houses in the world; event: Milan trade fair in April.

Mildura *mil-dyoo'ra*, 34 14S 142 13E, pop(1983e) 16,920, town in Northern Mallee stat div, NW Victoria, Australia; on the Murray river, 550 km NW of Melbourne; on the state boundary with New South Wales at the centre of irrigated farming; railway; airfield; economy: citrus growing, wine; monuments: Aboriginal Arts Centre; the bar in the Mildura Working Men's Club is said to be the longest bar in the world at 90.8 m with 27 beer taps.

Milford, 41 14N 73 04W, pop(1980) 49,101, town in New Haven county, SW Connecticut, United States; on Long Island Sound at the mouth of the R Housatonic, 16 km SW of New Haven; settled in 1639, achieving city status in 1959; formerly an important shipbuilding centre; railway; economy: electronics, metal goods, fisheries.

Milford Haven, formerly MILFORD, 51 44N 5 02W, pop(1981) 13,927, port town in Preseli dist, Dyfed, SW Wales; on N coast of Milford Haven estuary; railway; economy: oil refining, engineering, fishing.

Millicent, 37 36S 140 22E, pop(1981) 5,255, urban centre in South East stat div, SE South Australia, Australia; SE of Adelaide on the Princes Highway; railway; monuments: the Millicent Historical Museum and Admella Gallery has historical and maritime displays together with paintings and craft work; Shell Garden is decorated with shells, bottles and glass; the Old School Building (1873) is an historical museum; nearby is a narrow gauge steam engine.

Millstätter See *mil'shtet-ar zay*, lake in Kärnten state, SE Austria, 40 km NW of Villach; area 13.3 sq km; length 12 km; width 1.5 km; max depth 140 m; popular for water sports; Millstatt, on the N shore, is the largest locality.

Milne Bay, province at the SE tip of Papua New Guinea; includes the Louisiade, D'Entrecasteaux and Trobriand island groups which separate the Solomon Sea (N) from the Coral Sea (S); area 14,000 sq km; pop(1980) 127,725; chief town Alotau.

Mílos *mee'los*, southwesternmost island of the Kikládhes, Greece, in the S Aegean Sea; area 151 sq km; the 'Venus de Milo' sculpture, now in the Louvre museum (Paris), was discovered here; the main town is Plaka; there is a port at Adámas on the E coast.

Milpitas *mil-pee'tas*, 37 26N 121 55W, pop(1980) 37,820, city in Santa Clara county, W California, United States; at the S end of San Francisco Bay.

Milton Keynes *-keenz*, 52 03N 0 42W, pop(1981) 37,048, town in Milton Keynes dist, Buckinghamshire, S central England; planned 'new town' 80 km NW of London; Open University; railway; event: festival (Feb).

Milwaukee *mil-wo'kee*, 43 02N 87 55W, pop(1980) 636,212, county seat of Milwaukee county, SE Wisconsin, United States; on the W shore of L Michigan; largest city in the state; founded by German immigrants in the mid-19th century; 2 universities (1857, 1908); railway; airfield; economy: major lake port shipping heavy cargo via the St Lawrence Seaway; manufactures heavy machinery and electrical equipment; a leading manufacturer of diesel and petrol engines, and tractors; home of several breweries and famed for its beer-producing tradition; monuments: Pabst Museum, brewery tours, Mitchell Park Horticultural Conservatory, Milwaukee Public Museum, art museum.

Mīnā' al Aḩmadī *mee'na al a-ma-dee'*, 29 03N 48 06E, oil-exporting terminal on the Arabian Gulf, E Kuwait, 8 km ESE of Al Aḩmadī and 35 km SSE of Al Kuwayt (Kuwait City); developed after 1946 following the discovery of oil; economy: oil refining; sea water desalination plant; production of low grade sulphur fuel oil used in the country's power and desalination plants.

Mina Jebel Ali, 24 10N 55 18E, seaport on the Arabian Gulf, Dubayy (Dubai) emirate, United Arab Emirates; 35 km SW of Dubayy; there is an earth satellite tracking station nearby; economy: the industrial port complex, declared a free trade zone in 1980, was the first of its kind in the Gulf area; there is a gathering and processing plant for associated gas; aluminium smelter, desalination plant, copper and aluminium cables factory, and steel fabrication facility.

Minas *mee'nas*, 34 20S 55 15W, pop(1985) 34,611, capital of Lavalleja dept, SE Uruguay; set in wooded hills NE of Montevideo; the surrounding hills are mined for granite and marble; railway; birthplace of the independence hero, Lavalleja, leader of the 'Thirty-Three'; 8 km S, on the slopes of the Sierras de las Animas, is the Parque Salus, with a brewery, mineral springs and bottling plant.

Minas Gerais *mee'nas zhe-ra'ees*, state in Sudeste region, SE Brazil; bounded SW by the Río Grande, NE by the Río São Francisco; drained N by the Río São Francisco, E by the Jequitinhonha, Doce and Mucuri rivers, SW by the Río Grande and Río Paranaíba, headstreams of the Río Paraná; separated from the coast by numerous small mountain ranges; to N of Belo Horizonte are rich grazing lands, this wedge of land, between Goiás (N) and São Paulo (S), is known as the Triângulo Mineiro because it accounts for half of Brazil's mineral production; pop(1980) 13,378,553, area 587,172 sq km; capital Belo Horizonte; economy: coffee, iron ore, gold (the only 2 working mines in Brazil), diamonds, metal-working, timber, textiles, food processing, cattle raising, mineral waters (there are spa towns in the S); the Tres Marias Dam lies in central Minas Gerais, while in the SW is the Fumas Dam and the 715-sq km Serra da Canastra National Park established in 1972; SE of Belo Horizonte lies the colonial town of Ouro Preto, former capital of Minas Gerais, which was declared a national monument in 1933; the town was founded in 1711 as a result of a series of gold rushes to central Minas Gerais and Mato Grosso; the state is famous for its 400 caves and grottoes, the best known is the Gruta de Maquiné, which has 7 chambers.

Minás, Sierra de las *meenahs'*, mountain range between Alta Verapaz and Izabal depts (N) and Zacapa dept (S), E central Guatemala, Central America; extends 96 km W-E between the Río Polochic (N) and the Río Motagua (S); rises to over 2,500 m; the Sierra del Mico lies to the E.

Minatitlán *mee-na-teet-lahn'*, 17 58N 94 32W, pop(1980) 145,268, town in Veracruz state, SE Mexico; on the Río

Coatzacoalcos, 175 km W of Villahermosa; economy: petrochemicals, oil refining.

Mindanao *min-de-nah'ō*, island in S Philippines; bounded SW by Celebes Sea, W by Sulu Sea and N by Bohol Sea; area 99,040 sq km; irregularly shaped with many bays and offshore islets; the island is mountainous, rising to 2,954 m at Mt Apo near Davao; major rivers include the Agusan in the NE and the Mindanao in the S; Laguna Lanao is the largest lake.

Mindelo *meen-day'loo*, 16 54N 25 00W, city and chief port (Porto Grande) of Cape Verde on the NW shore of São Vicente I; pop(1970) 28,797.

Minden *min'dun*, MINTHUN (anc), 52 18N 8 54E, pop(1983) 76,400, manufacturing city in Detmold dist, Nordrhein-Westfalen (North Rhine-Westphalia) prov, W Germany; at the point of intersection between the R Weser and the Mittelland Canal, N of the Porta Westfalica; notable brine baths; railway junction; economy: porcelain, coffee, tea, fruit juice, domestic equipment, tobacco; monument: cathedral (11-13th-c).

Mindoro *min-dōr'ō*, island of the Philippines, situated SW of Luzon I and NW of Panay I; bounded S by Sulu Sea and W by South China Sea; separated from Palawan by the Mindoro Strait; area 9,732 sq km; rises to 2,585 m at Mt Halcon; wide coastal plains to the E.

Mine'head, 51 13N 3 29W, pop(1981) 11,211, resort town in West Somerset dist, Somerset, SW England; on the Bristol Channel; railway; economy: shoemaking.

Mingaora *ming-gow'ra*, MINGORA, MONGORA, 34 47N 72 22E, pop(1981) 88,000, city in North-West Frontier prov, Pakistan; close to the R Swat, 113 km NE of Peshawar; economy: grain, sugar cane and wool market.

Minho *meen'yoo*, former region and prov of NW Portugal, includes parts of present day Braga and Viana do Castelo dists, bounded by Spain (N) and the Atlantic (W), lying between the R Douro and R Minho; formerly part of Castile; area 4,782 sq km; noted for the production of young vinho verde wine; in the densely populated fertile valleys wheat, maize and animal fodder are produced while in the mountains to the north near the Spanish border the land is used primarily as sheep pasture; in 1951, 1964 and 1972 the upper reaches of the R Cávado were dammed to provide hydroelectric power, the largest of these reservoirs being the Barragem do Alto Rabagão; Portugal's first national park was established in the Peneda-Gerês ranges to protect forest and mountain scenery.

Minho, MINO (Sp), MINIUS (anc), river rising in Sierra de Meira S of Mondonedo (Lugo dist), NW Spain; flows S for 234 km to Portuguese border which it follows in a SW direction before entering the Atlantic near Caminha (Viana do Castelo dist, Port); length 310 km; 75 km in Portugal; navigable 45 km to Monção; the principal tributary is the R Coura.

Minicoy Island, island of India. See Lakshadweep.

Minna *mee-na'*, 9 39N 6 32E, pop(1969e) 69,567, capital of Niger state, W central Nigeria, W Africa; 322 km SSW of Kano; railway; economy: cattle trade, brewing, gold mining.

Minneapolis *min-i-ap'o-lis*, 44 59N 93 16W, pop(1980) 370,951, county seat of Hennepin county, SE Minnesota, United States; a port on the Mississippi river W of, and adjacent to, its twin city, St Paul; part of Fort Snelling military reservation in 1819; later developed as a centre of the timber and flour milling industries; a city since 1867; university (1851); railway; airport; largest city in the state; economy: important processing, distributing and trade centre for enormous grain and cattle area; chief manufactures are machinery, electronic equipment and computers, food processing and flour-milling; the financial capital of the upper Midwest, with a Federal Reserve Bank; monuments: Institute of Arts, Guthrie Theatre, American Swedish Institute, Grain Exchange; event: Aquatennial (July).

Minnesota *min-e-sō'ta* (Siouan, 'watery cloud'), state in N United States; bounded W by South Dakota and North Dakota, N by Canada, E by L Superior and Wisconsin, and S by Iowa; the 'North Star State' or the 'Gopher State'; 32nd state admitted to the Union (1858); pop(1980) 4,075,970; area 206,825 sq km; capital St Paul; other major cities are Minneapolis and Duluth; the R Mississippi has its source in the N central region and flows SE to form the S part of the E state border; the Minnesota river emerges from L Big Stone on S Dakota border and flows SE then NE across S region to empty into R Mississippi at St Paul; R St Croix forms the central part of Wisconsin border and empties into R Mississippi; the Red River of the North forms the upper part of the W border; over 11,000 lakes are scattered over the state, and 5,729 sq km of L Superior lies within the state boundary; the Sawtooth Mts rise in the extreme NE; the highest point is Mt Eagle (701 m); the N region has a typical glaciated terrain with boulder-strewn hills, marshland and large areas of forest; in the E are mountains from which iron ore is mined, and in the S and W are the prairies; agriculture is the leading industry and the state is the nation's 2nd biggest producer of dairy products, hay, oats, rye and turkeys; the chief manufactured products are processed foods, machinery, electrical equipment and paper products; the land E of the R Mississippi was included in the Northwest Terr in 1787 and the land to the W became part of the USA with the Louisiana Purchase (1803); permanently settled after the establishment of Fort Snelling in 1820 the area became Minnesota Territory in 1849 and a state in 1858; a Sioux Indian rebellion took place in S Minnesota in 1862; the state is divided into 87 counties:

County	*area (sq km)*	*pop(1980)*
Aitkin	4,768	13,404
Anoka	1,118	195,998
Becker	3,411	29,336
Beltrami	6,518	30,982
Benton	1,061	25,187
Big Stone	1,292	7,716
Blue Earth	1,947	52,314
Brown	1,586	28,645
Carlton	2,246	29,936
Carver	913	37,046
Cass	5,286	21,050
Chippewa	1,518	14,941
Chisago	1,084	25,717
Clay	2,727	49,327
Clearwater	2,597	8,761
Cook	3,671	4,092
Cottonwood	1,664	14,854
Crow Wing	2,621	41,722
Dakota	1,492	194,279
Dodge	1,141	14,773
Douglas	1,672	27,839
Faribault	1,856	19,714
Fillmore	2,241	21,930
Freeborn	1,833	36,329
Goodhue	1,984	38,749
Grant	1,422	7,171
Hennepin	1,407	941,411
Houston	1,466	18,382
Hubbard	2,434	14,098
Isanti	1,144	23,600
Itasca	6,919	43,069
Jackson	1,817	13,690
Kanabec	1,370	12,161
Kandiyohi	2,038	36,763
Kittson	2,870	6,672
Koochiching	8,081	17,571
La Sueur	1,160	23,434
Lac Qui Parle	2,007	10,592
Lake	2,053	13,043
Lake of the Woods	3,370	3,764
Lincoln	1,399	8,207
Lyon	1,856	25,207
Mahnomen	1,453	5,535
Marshall	4,576	13,027

contd

County	*area (sq km)*	*pop(1980)*
Martin	1,836	24,687
McLeod	1,271	29,657
Meeker	1,622	20,594
Mille Lacs	1,503	18,430
Morrison	2,922	29,311
Mower	1,847	40,390
Murray	1,825	11,507
Nicollet	1,144	26,929
Nobles	1,856	21,840
Norman	2,280	9,379
Olmsted	1,703	92,006
Otter Tail	5,130	51,937
Pennington	1,607	15,258
Pine	3,695	19,871
Pipestone	1,212	11,690
Polk	5,153	34,844
Pope	1,737	11,657
Ramsey	400	459,784
Red Lake	1,126	5,471
Redwood	2,293	19,341
Renville	2,558	20,401
Rice	1,303	46,087
Rock	1,256	10,703
Roseau	4,360	12,574
Scott	928	43,784
Sherburne	1,131	29,908
Sibley	1,542	15,448
St Louis	15,925	222,229
Stearns	3,479	108,161
Steele	1,121	30,328
Stevens	1,456	11,322
Swift	1,932	12,920
Todd	2,447	24,991
Traverse	1,495	5,542
Wabasha	1,396	19,335
Wadena	1,399	14,192
Wascca	1,097	18,448
Washington	1,014	113,571
Watonwan	1,131	12,361
Wilkin	1,953	8,454
Winona	1,638	46,256
Wright	1,747	58,681
Yellow Medicine	1,971	13,653

Minneton'ka (Siouan, 'water-big'), 44 56N 93 27W, pop(1980) 38,683, town in Hennepin county, SE Minnesota, United States; residential suburb 15 km WSW of Minneapolis; railway.

Minot *mī'not*, 48 14N 101 18W, pop(1980) 32,843, county seat of Ward county, N North Dakota, United States; on the R Souris, 160 km N of Bismarck; railway; airfield; commercial centre in an agricultural region.

Minsk *myeensk*, 53 51N 27 30E, pop(1983) 1,405,000, capital city of Minskaya oblast and Belorusskaya SSR, Soviet Union; on the R Svisloch'; one of the oldest towns in the Soviet Union; university (1921); railway junction; airport; economy: machine tools, motor vehicles, instrument-making, electronics, electrical engineering; monuments: 17th-c Bernardine convent, 17th-c cathedral of the Holy Spirit.

Min'ya, El, 28 49N 30 05E, pop(1976) 146,423, river port capital of El Minya governorate, NE central Egypt; on the R Nile, 225 km SSW of Cairo; railway; economy: food processing, cotton.

Mira *mee'ra*, river rising in the Serra do Mu, Beja dist, S Portugal; flows NW to the Atlantic at Vila Nova de Milfontes; length 130 km; navigable 30 km to Odemira; area of basin 1,781 sq km; principal tributary R Torto.

Mira'da, La, 33 51N 118 02W, pop(1980) 40,986, city in Los Angeles county, SW California, United States; SE of Los Angeles.

Mir'amar, 25 59N 80 15W, pop(1980) 32,813, town in Broward county, SE Florida, United States; 18 km SSW of Fort Lauderdale.

Miranda *mee-ran'da*, mountainous state in N Venezuela; on the Caribbean; bounded N by the federal district of Caracas; watered by the lower Río Tuy, the state also includes the Tacarigua Lagoon along the Caribbean coast; in the S of the state is part of the Guatopo National Park; pop(1980) 1,380,430; area 7,946 sq km; capital Los Teques.

Miranda de Ebro *mee-ran'da dhay e'brō*, 42 41N 2 57W, pop(1981) 36,812, town in Burgos prov, Castilla-León prov, N Spain on the R Ebro, 72 km NE of Burgos; railway; economy: cereals, wine, fruit, textiles, canning, confectionery, tools.

Mirditë *meer-dee'te*, prov of N central Albania; area 698 sq km; pop(1980) 42,400; capital Rrëshen.

Miri *mī'ree*, 4 28N 114 00E, pop(1980) 52,125, town in Sarawak state, E Malaysia, SE Asia; W of Brunei on the South China Sea coast; airfield.

Mirim, Lago *mee-reem'*, lake in E Uruguay and Río Grande do Sul prov, SE Brazil; area 2,966 sq km; 177 km long; up to 40 km wide; separated from the Atlantic by a low marshy bar; discharges (at the N end) into the Lagoa dos Patos via the São Gonçalo Canal, more than three-quarters of the lake is in Brazil; the international boundary traverses the lake's S half from the mouth of the Río Jaguarão to the southernmost tip of the lake W of Chuy.

Mirpur Khas *meer'poor KHas*, 25 33N 69 05E, pop(1981) 124,000, city in Sind prov, SE Pakistan; ruins of Buddhist stupa and monastery; noted for cloth weaving and embroidery.

Misahöhe *mee-sa-ho'hay*, 6 59N 0 40E, town in Des Plateaux region, S Togo, W Africa; NW of Plaimé, close to the Ghanaian border.

Misān', formerly MAYSAN, governorate in E Iraq; bounded E by Iran; pop(1977) 372,575; area 16,774 sq km; capital Al 'Amārah; comprises the R Tigris lowland.

Mishawak'a (Potawatomi, 'dead trees place'), 41 40N 86 11W, pop(1980) 40,201, town in St Joseph county, N Indiana, United States; 7 km SE of South Bend; railway.

Misiones *mees-yō'nays*, prov in Litoral region, NE Argentina; bordered by the Río Uruguay and Brazil (E), the Río Iguazú and Brazil (N) and the Río Paraná and Paraguay (W); subtropical, densely forested region with low mountain ranges; tourists are attracted to the Iguazú Falls on the Brazilian border; Jesuit missions founded here in 17th century were later dissolved; pop(1980) 588,977; area 29,801 sq km; capital Posadas; chief town Eldorado; economy: tea, maté, sugar cane, timber, basalt and sandstone mining.

Misiones, dept in Oriental region, S Paraguay; bounded S by Argentina along the Río Paraná and N by the Río Tebicuary; consists of forested marshy lowlands; pop(1982) 79,278; area 7,835 sq km; capital San Juan Bautista de las Misiones; the dept is so called because it was here that the Jesuits first set up their missions in the 17th and early 18th centuries before embarking upon the conversion of S Paraguay, NE Argentina, S Brazil and N Uruguay.

Miskolc *meesh'kolts*, 48 07N 20 50E, pop(1984e) 212,000, capital of Borsod-Abaúj-Zemplén county, NE Hungary; on R Sajo at the foot of the Bükk Mts; 2nd largest city in Hungary; technical university of heavy industry (1870); a city of county status; airfield; railway; economy: iron and steel, food processing, textiles, wine; monuments: castle of Diósgyör, 15th-c church on Avas Hill, Fazola furnace.

Misrātah, MISURATA *mee-zoo-ra'ta*, 32 24N 15 04E, pop(1982) 285,000, seaport in Misrātah prov, N Libya, N Africa; at the W entrance of the Gulf of Sirte (an inlet of the Mediterranean Sea), 195 km ESE of Tarābulus (Tripoli); there is a fishing port at Ra's Misrātah, 11.5 km E; economy: iron and steel.

Mississauga *mi-si-saw'ga*, 43 38N 79 36W, pop(1981) 315,056, town in SE Ontario, SE Canada; situated on L Ontario, S of Toronto; railway.

Mississip'pi, state in S United States; bordered W by

Louisiana and Arkansas, N by Tennessee, E by Alabama, and S by the Gulf of Mexico and Louisiana; the Mississippi river forms the W border; the R Pearl flows SW and S through central Mississippi and forms the S part of the Louisiana state border before emptying into the Mississippi Sound; the R Tennessee follows the state border in the extreme NE; the highest point is Mt Woodall (246 m); much of the S part of the state, to within a few miles of the fertile coastal plain, is covered in a large belt of pine woods; the land rises in the NE; between the Mississippi and Yazoo rivers is the Delta region, a flat alluvial plain which is a major cotton-producing area; other agricultural products are soybeans, cattle, dairy products and poultry; petroleum and natural gas are the state's most important mineral resources and more than one-third of the land is given over to oil and gas development; manufactured products including clothing, wood products, foods and chemicals; fisheries are prominent along the Gulf coast; Mississippi has the lowest per capita income in the USA; monuments: Old Spanish Fort, Vicksburg National Military Park, historic Natchez; the territory was held by France, Britain, and Spain in turn, until eventually accepted as belonging to the USA in 1795; Mississippi became a state (20th) in 1817 but seceded from the Union in 1861; re-admitted to the Union in 1870, but white supremacy was maintained, particularly by the constitution of 1890; also known as the 'Magnolia state'; pop(1980) 2,520,638; area 122,806 sq km; capital Jackson; other chief cities are Biloxi, Meridian, Hattiesburg, Greenville and Gulfport; the state is divided into 82 counties:

County	*area (sq km)*	*pop(1980)*
Adams	1,186	38,035
Alcorn	1,043	33,036
Amite	1,903	13,369
Attala	1,916	19,865
Benton	1,058	8,153
Bolivar	2,319	45,965
Calhoun	1,490	15,664
Carroll	1,648	9,776
Chickasaw	1,308	17,853
Choctaw	1,092	8,996
Claiborne	1,284	12,279
Clarke	1,799	16,945
Clay	1,079	21,082
Coahoma	1,453	36,918
Copiah	2,025	26,503
Covington	1,082	15,927
De Soto	1,256	53,930
Forrest	1,219	66,018
Franklin	1,472	8,208
George	1,256	15,297
Greene	1,867	9,827
Grenada	1,095	21,043
Hancock	1,243	24,537
Harrison	1,511	157,665
Hinds	2,275	250,998
Holmes	1,973	22,970
Humphreys	1,118	13,931
Issaquena	1,056	2,513
Itawamba	1,404	20,518
Jackson	1,901	118,015
Jasper	1,763	17,265
Jefferson	1,360	9,181
Jefferson Davis	1,063	13,846
Jones	1,810	61,912
Kemper	1,992	10,148
Lafayette	1,739	31,030
Lamar	1,297	23,821
Lauderdale	1,833	77,285
Lawrence	1,131	12,518
Leake	1,518	18,790
Lee	1,173	57,061
Leflore	1,573	41,525
Lincoln	1,526	30,174

contd

County	*area (sq km)*	*pop(1980)*
Lowndes	1,344	57,304
Madison	1,867	41,613
Marion	1,425	25,708
Marshall	1,843	29,296
Monroe	2,007	36,404
Montgomery	1,061	13,366
Neshoba	1,487	23,789
Newton	1,508	19,944
Noxubee	1,815	13,212
Oktibbeha	1,193	36,018
Panola	1,804	28,164
Pearl River	2,127	33,795
Perry	1,693	9,864
Pike	1,066	36,173
Pontotoc	1,297	20,918
Prentiss	1,087	24,025
Quitman	1,056	12,636
Rankin	2,033	69,427
Scott	1,586	24,556
Sharkey	1,131	7,964
Simpson	1,537	23,441
Smith	1,651	15,077
Stone	1,160	9,716
Sunflower	1,836	34,844
Tallahatchie	1,693	17,157
Tate	1,056	20,119
Tippah	1,191	18,739
Tishomingo	1,128	18,434
Tunica	1,196	9,652
Union	1,082	21,741
Walthall	1,050	13,761
Warren	1,550	51,627
Washington	1,906	72,344
Wayne	2,114	19,135
Webster	1,102	10,300
Wilkinson	1,763	10,021
Winston	1,586	19,474
Yalobusha	1,243	13,139
Yazoo	2,426	27,349

Mississippi, river in central USA; rises in N Minnesota in the small creeks draining into L Itasca and flows generally S past Grand Rapids, St Cloud and the twin towns of Minneapolis and St Paul; from the Minnesota border the Mississippi curves southwards to form the border between the states of Minnesota, Iowa, Missouri, Arkansas and Louisiana on the W and Wisconsin, Illinois, Tennessee and Mississippi on the E; it passes St Louis, Missouri, Memphis, Tennessee, and Baton Rouge and New Orleans, Louisiana before finally entering the Gulf of Mexico in SE Louisiana, near New Orleans; length 1,884 km, making the Mississippi the 2nd longest river in the USA (the longest being its tributary, the Missouri); however, the Missouri is often considered part of the main stream, and from the Missouri's longest headstream, the Red Rock-Jefferson river, the length of the Mississippi is 6,019 km; major tributaries: the Minnesota, Des Moines, Missouri, Arkansas and Red rivers (W), and the Illinois and Ohio rivers (E); the river system drains an area of approx 3,250,000 sq km between the Appalachian and the Rocky Mts and including part of Alberta and Saskatchewan, Canada; from its source the Mississippi follows a semi-circular course through the glacial lakes and swamps of the moraine of Minnesota; to the S of Minneapolis the river descends rapidly in the Falls of St Anthony; much of the river from here S as far as Cape Girardeau in S Missouri is flanked by steep limestone and sandstone bluffs; to the S of this, the hills disappear and the Mississippi continues over its own alluvial plain; artificial levees have been constructed on the banks at several points to cope with flooding; the Mississippi delta, situated S of the Red river, consists of salt marsh, wooded swampland and low lying alluvial tracts, dissected by numerous distributaries (bayous); the river enters the Gulf of Mexico in 5 main passes, approx 160 km SE of New Orleans; practically no tide ascends the Mississippi; the main river is navigable as far as Minneapolis; major river ports: New Orleans, St Louis, Memphis, St Paul and Minneapolis.

Missoula *me-zoo'le*, 46 52N 114 01W, pop(1980) 33,388, county seat of Missoula county, W Montana, United States; on the Clark Fork of the R Columbia, near its junction with the R Bitterroot; university (1893); railway; economy: commercial and medical centre in an area of farming and forestry.

Missouri *miz-oo'ri*, state in central United States; bounded W by Oklahoma, Kansas and Nebraska, N by Iowa, E by Illinois, Kentucky and Tennessee, and S by Arkansas; the 'Show Me State'; 24th state admitted to the Union (1821); pop(1980) 4,916,686; area 179,257 sq km; capital Jefferson City; major cities are St Louis, Kansas City, Springfield and Independence; the R Mississippi forms the E frontier and the R Missouri forms upper part of the W border, before turning E across the central state to empty into the Mississippi just N of St Louis; the R Des Moines forms the extreme NE border with Iowa, before emptying into the Mississippi; the Ozark Plateau lies in the SW; highest point is Mt Taum Sauk (540 m); the state is split into two parts by the R Missouri; N of the river is open prairie-land with corn and livestock, particularly hogs and cattle; S of the river are foothills and the Ozarks, much of which is forested; Missouri has more farms than any other state except Texas; manufactures include automobiles, aircraft and aerospace components, processed foods and chemicals, machinery, fabricated metals and electrical equipment; the state's mines yield over 90% of the nation's lead; the state's position at the junction of the nation's two greatest rivers has been the major factor controlling its development as a transport hub, and as the starting point for the pioneering advance westwards across the continent; the area became part of USA with the Louisiana Purchase in 1803; Missouri became a territory in 1812, but its application for admission as a state in 1817 caused tremendous controversy as it had introduced slavery; eventually it was admitted as a state in 1821 under the Missouri Compromise; the state is divided into 115 counties:

County	*area (sq km)*	*pop(1980)*
Adair	1,474	24,870
Andrew	1,131	13,980
Atchison	1,409	8,605
Audrain	1,812	26,458
Barry	2,010	24,408
Barton	1,550	11,292
Bates	2,207	15,873
Benton	1,895	12,183
Bollinger	1,615	10,301
Boone	1,786	100,376
Buchanan	1,063	87,888
Butler	1,815	37,693
Caldwell	1,118	8,660
Callaway	2,189	32,252
Camden	1,667	20,017
Cape Girardeau	1,500	58,837
Carroll	1,807	12,131
Carter	1,323	5,428
Cass	1,823	51,029
Cedar	1,222	11,894
Chariton	1,971	10,489
Christian	1,466	22,402
Clark	1,318	8,493
Clay	1,048	136,488
Clinton	1,100	15,916
Cole	1,019	56,663
Cooper	1,474	14,643
Crawford	1,934	18,300
Dade	1,277	7,383
Dallas	1,412	12,096

contd

County	*area (sq km)*	*pop(1980)*
Davies	1,477	8,905
De Kalb	1,105	8,222
Dent	1,963	14,517
Douglas	2,116	11,594
Dunklin	1,422	36,324
Franklin	2,397	71,233
Gasconade	1,355	13,181
Gentry	1,282	7,887
Greene	1,760	185,302
Grundy	1,136	11,959
Harrison	1,885	9,890
Henry	1,895	19,672
Hickory	985	6,367
Holt	1,188	6,882
Howard	1,209	10,008
Howell	2,413	28,807
Iron	1,435	11,084
Jackson	1,589	629,266
Jasper	1,667	86,958
Jefferson	1,719	146,183
Johnson	2,168	39,059
Knox	1,318	5,508
Laclede	1,997	24,323
Lafayette	1,643	29,925
Lawrence	1,594	28,973
Lewis	1,323	10,901
Lincoln	1,630	22,193
Linn	1,612	15,495
Livingston	1,396	15,739
Macon	2,072	16,313
Madison	1,292	10,725
Maries	1,373	7,551
Marion	1,139	28,638
McDonald	1,404	14,917
Mercer	1,180	4,685
Miller	1,542	18,532
Mississippi	1,066	15,726
Moniteau	1,084	12,068
Monroe	1,742	9,716
Montgomery	1,404	11,537
Morgan	1,544	13,807
New Madrid	1,711	22,945
Newton	1,630	40,555
Nodaway	2,275	21,996
Oregon	2,059	10,238
Osage	1,576	12,014
Ozark	1,901	7,961
Pemiscot	1,344	24,987
Perry	1,230	16,784
Pettis	1,784	36,378
Phelps	1,752	33,633
Pike	1,750	17,568
Platte	1,095	46,341
Polk	1,654	18,822
Pulaski	1,430	42,011
Putnam	1,352	6,092
Ralls	1,253	8,911
Randolph	1,240	25,460
Ray	1,477	21,378
Reynolds	2,103	7,230
Ripley	1,641	12,458
Saline	1,963	24,919
Schuyler	803	4,979
Scotland	1,139	5,415
Scott	1,100	39,647
Shannon	2,610	7,885
Shelby	1,303	7,826
St Charles	1,451	144,107
St Clair	1,817	8,622
St Francois	1,173	42,600
St Louis	1,316	973,896
St Louis City	159	453,085

contd

County	*area (sq km)*	*pop(1980)*
Ste Genevieve	1,310	15,180
Stoddard	2,119	29,009
Stone	1,173	15,587
Sullivan	1,693	7,434
Taney	1,581	20,467
Texas	3,068	21,070
Vernon	2,176	19,806
Warren	1,115	14,900
Washington	1,981	17,983
Wayne	1,981	11,277
Webster	1,544	20,414
Worth	692	3,008
Wright	1,773	16,188

Missouri, longest river in the USA and chief tributary of the Mississippi; the river is formed near the town of Three Forks, SW Montana by the confluence of the Jefferson, Madison and Gallatin rivers; the Madison and Gallatin rise in Yellowstone National Park, Wyoming; the Jefferson rises further W, its headstream being the Red Rock river; from Three Forks the river flows N between the Big Belt Mts and the Lewis Range; after passing through a gorge known as the Gates of the Mountains the river turns NE towards Great Falls and Fort Benton; at Great Falls the river narrows by two-thirds to 274 m and descends 107 m in 24 km by a series of cataracts (the highest being 26.5 m); after Fort Benton the Missouri flows E through Fort Peck L and is joined by the Milk river; at the Missouri-North Dakota border it is joined by the Yellowstone river and curves through W North Dakota, flowing E through L Sakakawea then S past Bismarck and into South Dakota where it flows through L Oahe and L Sharpe and is joined by the Cheyenne, Bad and White rivers; it flows generally SSE, forming the border between SE South Dakota and NW Nebraska and then forms the borders between Nebraska and Kansas (W) and Iowa and Missouri (E); to the S of Omaha the Missouri is joined by the Platte river; the Missouri continues SSE until it reaches Kansas City, where it is joined by the Kansas river and turns E to flow across Missouri and joins the Mississippi approx 16 km N of St Louis; length 3,725 km; length with longest headstream 4,125 km; major tributaries: the Musselshell, Milk, Yellowstone, Little Missouri, Grand (of South Dakota), Moreau, Cheyenne, Bad, White, Niobrara, James, Platte, Kansas, Grand (of Iowa and Missouri), Gasconade and Osage rivers; the Missouri is used for irrigation, flood-control and hydroelectricity; the major dams along its length are: the Canyon Ferry, Hauser L, Holter L and Fort Peck L dams (Montana), Garrison Dam (North Dakota, at the head of L Sakakawea), Oahe and Fort Randall dams (South Dakota); although the river is navigable as far as Fort Benton, or to the mouth of the Yellowstone river in the low-water season, navigation of the Missouri is dangerous due to its tortuous and obstructed channel.

Misti, Volcán El *mees'tee*, volcano (5,843 m) in Arequipa dept, S Peru; in the Andean Cordillera Occidental; flanked NW by Chachani (6,096 m) and SE by Pichu-Pichu (5,669 m) volcanoes; 16 km N of Arequipa; of religious significance to the Incas, the volcano is mentioned in poetry and legends; an observatory was established by Harvard University near its summit.

Mitiaro *mee-tee-a'rō*, 19 49S 157 43W, coral island of the Cook Is, S Pacific, 227 km NE of Rarotonga; area 22.3 sq km; length 6.4 km; width 1.6 km; pop(1981) 256; Mitiaro is a low island with 2 lakes and vast areas of swampland; there are large banana plantations in the interior of the island.

Mitilíni *mit-il-een'ee*, formerly KASTRO, 39 06N 26 34E, pop(1981) 24,115, capital town of Lésvos nome (dept), Aegean Islands, Greece; on the E coast of Lésvos I, opposite the Turkish mainland; airfield; ferries to mainland and islands; commercial harbour; event: Navy Week (June-July).

Mitla *meet'lah* ('place of the dead'), 16 54N 96 16W, ancient city in central Oaxaca, S Mexico; situated in the Sierra Madre del Sur, 40 km ESE of Oaxaca; became the centre of the declining Zapotec civilization after the Mixtecs began their expansion around 1000 AD; the architecture is a blend of Zapotec and Mixtec styles and features intricate geometric facades of stone mosaic work; monuments: the well-preserved ruins include temples, subterranean tombs and a building known as the 'hall of monoliths'.

Mito *mee'tō*, 36 22N 140 29E, pop(1980) 215,566, capital of Ibaraki prefecture, Kanto region, E Honshū island, Japan; 96 km NE of Tōkyo, on the R Naka; railway.

Mits'iwa, MASSAWA *me-sah'we*, 15 37N 39 28E, seaport in Ērtra region, N Ethiopia, NE Africa; on the Red Sea coast, 65 km NE of Asmara; occupied by the Italians in 1885; capital of Italian Eritrea until 1897; suffered an earthquake in 1921 after which it was largely rebuilt with much of the building stone coming from the Dahlak Is which are separated from the mainland by the Mits'iwa (Massawa) Channel; railway.

Mittelfranken *mi'tul-frahng-kun*, MIDDLE FRANCONIA *frang-kō'nee-u* (Eng), dist of Bayern (Bavaria) prov, W Germany; pop(1983) 1,520,700; area 7,245 sq km; chief towns include Nürnberg, Erlangen and Fürth.

Mitú *mee-too'*, 1 07N 70 05W, pop(1985) 3,414, capital of Vaupés administrative territory, SE Colombia, South America; situated on the Río Vaupés, near the border with Brazil; airfield.

Miyazaki *mee-yaz'a-kee*, 31 56N 131 27E, pop(1980) 264,855, capital of Miyazaki prefecture, SE Kyūshū island, Japan; on the Pacific Ocean, 160 km SE of Nagasaki; university (1949); railway; airfield; economy: chemicals, porcelain, charcoal, wood pulp; monuments: Miyazaki jingu temple is sacred to the memory of Emperor Jimmu (660 BC); Heiwadai Park contains a peace column built in 1940.

Mizoram *mi-zor'am*, union territory in NE India; pop(1981) 487,774; area 21,087 sq km; bounded N by Assam state, NW by Tripura state, W and SW by Bangladesh, S and E by Burma and NE by Manipur state; Mizoram is crossed by the Langai, Kaladan and Dhaleswari rivers; the territory includes the 3 districts of Aizawl, Chhimtuipui and Lunglei; chief town Aizawl; Mizoram is governed by a Council of Ministers which is responsible to a 30-member Legislative Assembly; 90% of the population is Christian; agriculture employs 46% of the population and 17% of the cultivated land is irrigated; forest products are the basis of local industry; there are no railways in the territory and no national highways; Mizoram became a union territory in Jan 1972, comprising the former Mizo Hills district of the state of Assam.

Mjøsa or **Mjøsen** *myœ'sen*, elongated lake in Hedmark, Oppland and Akershus counties, SE Norway; extends from Eidsvall in S to Lillehammer in N; fed by the Lågen; area 368 sq km; length 100 km; max depth 443 m; Norway's largest lake; heavily stocked with trout; chief towns on its banks are Lillehammer, Hamar and Gjøvik.

Mladá Boleslav *mœlad'ah bol'es-laf*, 50 26N 14 55E, pop(1984) 47,686, town in Středočeský region, Czech Socialist Republic, NW central Czechoslovakia; on R Jizera, 40 km SW of Liberec; railway; economy: metal, motor vehicles, textiles.

Mladenovac *mla'den-o-vats*, 44 29N 20 41E, pop(1981) 52,489, town in N central Srbija (Serbia) republic, Yugoslavia; 40 km SSE of Beograd; railway.

Moa *mō'a*, 20 42N 74 57W, town in Holguín prov, E Cuba; on the NE coast of the island; a nickel-mining centre.

Mobaye *mō-bay'*, 4 25N 21 10E, chief town in Basse-Koto prefecture, E Central African Republic; on the R Ubangi, 177 km SSE of Bambani.

Mobile *mō'beel*, 30 41N 88 03W, pop(1980) 200,452,

county seat of Mobile county, SW Alabama, United States; a major US port on Mobile Bay; settled by the French in 1711 and ceded to the British in 1763; achieved city status in 1819; scene of a Federal victory at the naval battle of Mobile Bay in 1864; university (1963); railway; economy: Alabama's only seaport; economy: shipbuilding, oil refining, paper, textiles, aluminium, and chemicals; event: Azalea Trail Festival (March-May).

Mobuto Sésé Seko, lake in E central Africa. See Albert, Lake.

Moca *mō'ka*, 19 26N 70 33W, pop(1982e) 169,164, town in S Espaillat prov, Dominican Republic, 21 km ESE of Santiago, bounded N by the Cordillera Septentrional; centre of cacao-growing area.

Moçambique *moo-sã-beek'*, 15 00S 40 44E, seaport in NE Nampula prov, Mozambique, SE Africa; on Mozambique Island about 5 km from the mainland and 845 km NE of Beira; the railway terminates on the mainland at Lumbo; 11.5 km NW of Lumbo is the residential town of Mossouril, formerly popular with European settlers; there is a sheltered port located between an island and the mainland; the city is dominated by three forts, the most notable being Fort St Sebastian which was built between 1508 and 1511; Vasco da Gama visited this part of the coast in 1498; the town was the capital of Portuguese East Africa until 1907; airfield.

Moçâmedes, port in Angola. See Namibe.

Mochis, Los *lōs mo-chees'*, 25 47N 108 59W, pop(1970) 129,375, town in Sinaloa state, NW Mexico; 156 km S of Ciudad Obregon; railway; economy: sugar cane, fishing.

Mochudi *mō-choo'dee*, 24 28S 26 05E, pop(1980) 20,000, capital of Kgatleng dist, Botswana, S Africa; on the R Limpopo, 177 km NNE of Mafeking.

Mocoa *mō-kō'a*, 1 07N 76 38W, capital of Putumayo intendency, SW Colombia, South America.

Modena *mod'ay-na*, prov of Emilia-Romagna region, N Italy; pop(1981) 596,025; area 2,691 sq km; capital Modena.

Modena, 44 39N 10 55E, pop(1981) 180,312, capital town of Modena prov, Emilia-Romagna region, N Italy; near the S edge of the N Italian plain, 39 km NW of Bologna; archbishopric; university (1175); railway; economy: glass, vehicles, pasta, sausages; monuments: Romanesque cathedral; 17th-c Palazzo Ducale, now a military academy.

Modes'to, 37 39N 121 00W, pop(1980) 106,602, capital of Stanislaus county, central California, United States; in the San Joaquin Valley, on the Tuolumne river, 40 km SE of Stockton; railway.

Moe *mō'ee*, MOE-YALLOURN, 38 11S 146 18E, pop(1983e) 18,220, town in Central Gippsland stat div, SE Victoria, Australia; SE of Melbourne; railway.

Moengo *moong'ō*, 5 45N 54 20W, pop(1980) 2,865, town in Marowijne dist, NE Surinam, NE South America; on the R Cottica, 160 km ESE of Paramaribo; economy: bauxite mining and loading centre for the Surinam Aluminium Company.

Moero, Lac, lake in central Africa. See Mweru, Lake.

Moeskroen, town in Belgium. See Mouscron.

Mogadishu, capital of Somalia, NE Africa. See Muqdisho.

Mogilev *me-gi-lyof'*, MOGILEV ON THE DNIEPER (Eng), 53 54N 30 20E, pop(1983) 325,000, industrial capital city of Mogilevskaya oblast, Belorusskaya SSR, Soviet Union; on the R Dnepr; railway junction; airfield; economy: manufacture of tractors and chemicals (mineral fertilizers); monument: church of St Nicholas (begun 1669).

Mohács *mo'hach*, 45 58N 18 41E, pop(1984e) 21,000, river port town in Baranya county, S Hungary; on R Danube, SE of Pécs, near the Yugoslav frontier; railway; economy: coal trade, timber, metallurgy.

Mohammedia *mō-ha-me-dya'*, 33 44N 7 24W, pop(1982) 105,120, seaport in Mohammedia-Zenata prefecture, Centre prov, W Morocco, N Africa; NE of Casablanca; railway; economy: oil refining, tourism.

Mohéli *mo-ay'lee*, MOHILA, MWALI, 12 15S 43 45E, pop(1980) 19,000, island of the Comoros group in the Mozambique Channel; situated W of Anjouan and SE of Grande Comore; area 290 sq km; chief town Fomboni; consists of low hills and wide fertile valleys.

Moineşti *moin-esht'*, 46 27N 26 31E, pop(1983) 22,194, industrial and health resort town in Bacău county, E Romania; 32 km SW of Bacău, in E foothills of the E Carpathian Mts; railway terminus; economy: oil, gas, wood products.

Mojave Desert *mō-hah'vee*, desert in S California, United States; part of the Great Basin; situated S of the Sierra Nevada and Death Valley, N of the San Gabriel and San Bernardino Mts and NW of the Colorado Desert; the region is one of flat basins with interior drainage separated by low, bare ranges; the area receives little rain and supports agriculture only where artesian water occurs; the Mojave river is the desert's only stream; it flows mainly underground 160 km NE until it loses itself in the desert by the Mojave sink.

Moji das Cruzes *mō-zhee' das kroo'zays*, 23 33S 46 39W, pop(1980) 122,434, town in São Paulo state, Sudeste region, SE Brazil; E of São Paulo; university (1973); railway; economy: aviculture, brewing, iron and steel.

Moka, district of central Mauritius; area 230.5 sq km; pop(1983) 62,024.

Mokp'o *mok'po*, 34 50N 126 25E, pop(1983e) 228,075, port town in Chŏllanam prov, SW Korea; situated on the SW coast, on the Huang Hai (Yellow Sea); railway; main ferry terminal for the SW coastal area; hydroelectric power and flood control are planned for the Yŏngsan-gang river.

Mold, 53 10N 3 08W, pop(1981) 8,505, county town of Clywd in Delyn dist, Clwyd, NE Wales; on the R Alyn 18 km WSW of Chester; railway; economy: agricultural trade, light industry.

Moldau, river in Czechoslovakia. See Vltava.

Moldavia *mol-day'vi-a*, MOLDAU (Ger), geographical region of NE Romania lying SW of the R Prut; divided by the R Siret into a W region of wooded uplands and a fertile E plain where livestock farming, sericulture and vine-growing are the main agricultural activities; formerly a principality founded in the 14th century and ruled by the Turks (1712-1821); united with Walachia in 1859-61 to form Romania.

Moldavia, constituent republic of the Soviet Union. See Moldavskaya.

Moldavskaya, MOLDAVIYA SSR, MOLDAVIA (Eng), constituent republic of the Soviet Union, in the extreme SW of European USSR, bounded W by Romania; the terrain consists of a hilly plain which attains a height of 429 m in the centre of the republic; chief rivers are the Dnestr and the Prut; pop(1983) 4,052,000; area 33,700 sq km; capital Kishinev; chief towns Tiraspol' and Bendery; economy: Moldavskaya takes 3rd place in the USSR in the production of wine, tobacco, and food-canning; machine building; electrical engineering; instrument-making; manufacture of farm machinery; light industry (knitwear, textiles); agriculture is dominated by fruit growing, particularly viticulture; proclaimed a Soviet socialist republic in 1940.

Molde *mol'du*, 62 44N 7 08E, pop(1983) 21,047, fishing port and capital of Møre og Romsdal county, W Norway; on N shore of Molde Fjord; economy: textiles, ship fittings; event: annual summer jazz festival.

Moldoveanu *mol-do-vya'noo*, 45 37N 24 49E, mountain in the central Transylvanian Alps, central Romania, SE of Sibiu; rises to 2,543 m.

Mole *mōl'e*, national park in Northern region, N Ghana, W Africa; area 4,921 sq km; established in 1961.

Mole *mōl*, river rising in West Sussex, S England; flows 48 km N through Surrey to meet the R Thames at East Molesey.

Molenbeek-Saint-Jean *mō'lun-bayk-sī-zhã*, SINT-JANS-MOLENBEEK *sint-yahns'-mō-lu-bayk* (Flem), 50 51N 4 20E, pop(1982) 71,181, town in Brussel dist, Brabant prov, Belgium; a W suburb of Bruxelles.

Molepolole *mō-lay-pō-lō'lay*, 24 25S 25 30E, pop(1980) 19,000, capital of Kweneng dist, Botswana, S Africa; situated on the edge of the Kalahari Desert, 160 km N of Mafeking.

Molina de Segura *mo-lee'na* THay *say-goo'ra*, 38 03N 1 11W, pop(1981) 31,322, town in Murcia prov, SE Spain; on the R Segura, 10 km NW of Murcia; economy: fruit, vegetables, cocoa and chocolate, metal boxes, clothes.

Moline *mō-leen'*, 41 30N 90 31W, pop(1980) 45,709, town in Rock Island county, NW Illinois, United States; on the R Mississippi, just upstream of Rock Island; railway; economy: agricultural machinery, furniture.

Molise *mo-lee'ze*, region of E central Italy, comprising the provs of Campobasso and Isernia; pop(1981) 328,371; area 4,437 sq km; chief towns Campobasso and Isernia; the Appno Napoletano (Neopolitan Apennines) cover much of the area; the economy is based on subsistence arable and pastoral farming.

Molndal *muln'dal*, 57 40N 12 00E, pop(1982) 48,198, industrial town in S of Göteborg och Bohus county, SW Sweden; a S suburb of Göteborg (Gothenburg); railway.

Molokai *mo-lo-kī'*, island of the US state of Hawaii; in the Pacific Ocean, NW of Maui; in Maui county; area 670 sq km; Kalaupapa leper settlement is on the N coast; economy: cattle.

Molucca Sea, SE Asian sea, lying between the Minahassa Peninsula, Sulawesi and the Halmahera Islands of the Moluccas; linked to the Seram, Celebes and Banda seas.

Moluccas, island group and prov of Indonesia. See Maluku.

Mombasa *mom-ba'su*, 4 04S 39 40E, pop(1979) 341,148, (1984e) 478,000, seaport in Coast prov, SE Kenya, E Africa; Kenya's main port and 2nd largest city; on Mombasa island; connected to the mainland by Mukapa causeway; Kilindini harbour is one of Africa's best anchorages and was used as a naval base by the British during World War II; Fort Jesus, built by the Portuguese in 1593 as protection against the Arabs and Turks, changed hands on numerous occasions before being surrendered to the Arabs in 1729; the fort became a prison after a British naval attack in 1875 and is now a museum; Mombasa was capital of the British East Africa Protectorate between 1888 and 1907; railway terminus; airport; economy: car assembly, oil refining and tourism.

Mon, coastal state in SE Burma; bounded W by the Gulf of Martaban and drained by the R Sittang (which forms the state border with Pegu in the NE) and by the Salween river; pop(1983) 1,682,041; capital Moulmein.

Monaco *mon'ak-ō*, official name Principality of Monaco, a constitutional monarchy on the Mediterranean Riviera, close to the Italian frontier with France and surrounded landward by the French department of Alpes-Maritimes; area 1.9 sq km; timezone GMT +1; pop(1984) 27,000; 19% of the pop is Monegasque, 58% French; capital Monaco; the principality is for some administrative purposes divided into the districts of Monaco-Ville, Monte Carlo, Fontvieille and La Condamine; office and residential developments are taking place on reclaimed land at Fontvieille; the nearest airport is at Nice; heliport at Fontvieille; the climate is characterized by warm, dry summers and mild winters, Monaco being less exposed to the cold blasts of the northerly mistral; French francs are the accepted currency; economy: tourism, chemicals, printing, textiles, precision instruments, electronics, metalwork, plastics; national holidays: 27 Jan (Fête of St Dévote, the patron saint of Monaco), Ascension Day, Whit Monday, Corpus Christi, May Day, 15 Aug (Assumption), 1 Nov (All Saints), 19 Nov (Prince Rainier's birthday), 8 Dec (Immaculate Conception); membership of IAEA, ICAO, IHO, INTELSAT, INTERPOL, IPU, ITU, UN, UNESCO, UPU, WHO, WIPO.

Constitution and government. From 1297 Monaco belonged to the House of Grimaldi, coming under the protection of Sardinia in 1815 and France in 1861; a constitution of 1911 was suspended in 1959 and 3 years later elections re-established the legislative National Council, comprising 18 members elected every 5 years, and the Communal Council, with 16 members elected every 4 years; in 1962 a new Constitution was promulgated; executive power is held by the Prince as Head of State, the Minister of State as Head of Government and the Council of Government as Cabinet; Monaco has close ties with France in both internal and external affairs.

Monaco-Ville *mon'ak-ō-veel'*, 43 46N 7 23E, capital and oldest part of the Principality of Monaco, situated on a rocky promontory of the Côte d'Azur on the S side of the Port de Monaco; monuments: 13th-c Palais du Prince, Musée Océanographique including many marine specimens donated by Jacques Cousteau, stalactitic caves in the Jardin Exotique.

Monagas *mō-na'gas*, state in NE Venezuela; bounded by the Río Orinoco (SE), the Caño Mánamo (E) and the Gulf of Paria (NE); apart from a coastal range in the N, it consists of *llanos* plain and low tablelands, with marshes in the area of the Orinoco delta; pop(1980) 390,083; area 28,888 sq km; capital Maturín; in the N is the Cueva del Guáchero, a series of caves inhabited by large numbers of oilbirds, first scientifically explored by Humboldt in 1799.

Monaghan *mo'nu-gun*, MHUINEACHAIN (Gael), county in Ulster prov, Irish Republic; bounded N by N Ireland and watered by R Finn; pop(1981) 51,192; area 1,290 sq km; capital Monaghan.

Monaghan, MUINEACHÁN (Gael), 54 15N 6 58W, pop(1981) 6,275, market town and capital of Monaghan county, Ulster, Irish Republic; on Ulster Canal; event: fiddler of Orie festival in July.

Monarag'ala, 6 52N 81 22E, pop(1981) 6,020, capital of Monaragala dist, Uva prov, SE Sri Lanka; 120 km E of Ratnapura and 61 km W of Arugam Bay on the E coast.

Monastir *mon-us-teer'*, RUSPINA (Lat), 35 46N 10 59E, port and capital of Monastir governorate, NE Tunisia, N Africa; 18 km ESE of Sousse; built on the site of Roman and Phoenician settlements; summer residence of the country's president; there is a modern yacht and pleasure-boat harbour; railway; airport; monument: cloister (founded in 180 AD) now the centre of the kasbah; event: Festival of Monastir in July.

Mönchengladbach *mün'KHen-glad'baKH*, MÜNCHEN-GLADBACH, 51 12N 6 23E, pop(1983) 258,200, city in Köln dist, W Nordrhein-Westfalen (North Rhine-Westphalia) prov, W Germany, 24 km WSW of Düsseldorf, on the R Niers; railway; economy: textile machinery, technical fabrics, textiles.

Monclova *mon-klō'va*, 26 53N 101 25W, pop(1980) 119,609, town in Coahuila state, NE central Mexico; 194 km NW of Monterrey; railway; economy: steel (with one of the largest steel mills in Mexico).

Moncton *munk'tun*, 46 04N 64 50W, pop(1981) 54,743, town in SE New Brunswick, SE Canada; situated on the Petitcodiac river; settled in 1763 by Dutch and German families from Pennsylvania who were joined by United Empire Loyalists in 1784; Lt-Col Robert Monckton ended French occupation of the area in 1755 with the capture of the nearby Fort Beauséjour; famous for shipbuilding, Moncton grew as an important railway and road junction; university (1864); railway; economy: textiles; food processing; wood and metal working; monuments: the Free Meeting House, built in 1827, was used by people of all denominations until they had built their own churches; at the entrance to the town's Centennial Park are a Canadian National steam locomotive and a CF 100 jet aircraft, symbolizing the importance of the town as a centre of communications.

Mondego, *mon-day'goo*, river in N central Portugal, rises in the Serra da Estrêla 16 km N of Covilhã, flows SW across Coimbra plain to the Atlantic at Figueira da Foz; largest river flowing entirely in Portugal; length 220 km; navigable 85 km to Foz do Dão; area of basin 6,772 sq km; principal tributaries Dão, Alva, Ceira and Arunca.

Mondego, Cabo, 40 11N 8 54W, rocky headland on Atlantic coast of Portugal, Coimbra dist.

Mondolkiri *mon-dol-kee-ri*, province in E Cambodia; pop(1981) 14,300; bounded E and S by Vietnam; crossed by the Srepok, Chhlong and Te rivers; chief town Sen Monorom.

Mondsee *mōnt'zay*, 47 52N 13 21E, lake in Oberösterreich state, N Austria; area 14.2 sq km; length 11 km; width 2 km; max depth 68 m; the market town of Mondsee is at the NW end; water sports centre.

Mongo *mon-gō'*, 12 14N 18 45E, capital of Guéra prefecture, S central Chad, N central Africa; 120 km SSE of Ati; airfield.

Mongolia, formerly **Outer Mongolia** *mon-gō'li-a*, official name the Mongolian People's Republic, BÜGD NAYRAMDAKH MONGOL ARD ULS, a republic of E central Asia, bounded N by the USSR and E, S and W by the People's Republic of China; timezone GMT +7 (W), +8 (central), +9 (E); area 1,564,619 sq km; capital Ulaanbaatar; chief towns Darhan, Erdenet; pop(1984) 1,860,000, (1986e) 1,962,000; ethnic groups include 90% Mongol, 4% Kazakh, 2% Chinese and 2% Russian; Khalkha Mongol is the official language and is used by over 90% of the population, with Turkic, Russian and Chinese also spoken; Tibetan Buddhism has traditionally been the main religion although the country is a communist state; the official currency is the turgik of 100 möngö; national holiday 11 July (People's Revolution Day); membership of CEMA, ESCAP, FAO, IAEA, ILO, IPU, ITU, UN, UNESCO, UPU, WFTU, WHO, WIPO and WMO.

Physical description. Mongolia is a mountainous country, with an average height above sea level of 1,580 m. The highest point is Tavan-Bogdo-Uli, in the Mongolian Altai-Nayramdal ridge, at 4,373 m. The high ground is concentrated in the W, with folded mountains lying NW-SE to form the Mongolian Altai mountain chain. The SE section of this chain is lower and runs into the arid Gobi Desert. The Khenti Mts are the only area of upland in the E. The largest lakes are found in the NW and include Uvs Nuur, Hösgol Nuur, and Hyargas Nuur. Major rivers flowing N and NE from central Mongolia include the Kereulen, Orhon Gol, Selenge Mörön, Dzavhars Gol, Haraa Gol and Tuul Gol; Lake Baikal, USSR, receives the waters of the main rivers of the E plateau. Ten per cent of the country, mostly in the W, is forested. The lowland plains are for the most part arid grasslands, but the mountain steppe provides important pasture for sheep, goats, cattle and camels.

Climate. Mongolia is a landlocked country with a continental climate. Winter is characterized by hard and long lasting frosts, although little snow falls. The mean temperature at Ulaanbaatar in Jan is −27°C, while July temperatures vary between 9° and 24°C. Precipitation is generally low, but is much greater in the mountainous NE than the S, where arid desert conditions prevail. Most rain falls during summer months (July-Aug), with frequent thunderstorms.

History, government and constitution. Mongolia was originally the homeland of nomadic tribes which united under Ghengis Khan in the 13th century to become part of the great Mongol Empire which stretched from China to the Danube in Eastern Europe. Mongolia was later assimilated into China and divided into Inner and Outer Mongolia. With the fall of the Chinese Manchu dynasty in 1911, Outer Mongolia declared itself an independent monarchy, with the support of Tsarist Russia. In 1913 and 1915 treaties with China established Mongolia as an autonomous state, but during 1919-21 China again tried to re-establish its former sovereignty. The Mongolian People's Republic (MPR) was formed in 1924, but not recognized by China until 1946. In 1936 the MPR signed a mutual assistance pact with the USSR. Mongolia is a communist state, with a mixed legal system comprising Russian, Chinese and Turkish elements. The present constitution was adopted in 1960. The 350 members of the Great People's Khural (parliament) are elected for 5 years, and an executive council of ministers and a 9-member Presidium are elected for 9 years. The head of state is the chairman of the Presidium. One deputy per 2,500 inhabitants is elected to the Great People's Khural, by universal suffrage of citizens over 18 years. Power is largely in the hands of the only political party, the communist Mongolian People's Revolutionary Party.

Economy. For centuries Mongolia had a pastoral nomadic economy, but in recent years the government, under a series of 5 year plans, has tried to develop an agricultural-industrial economy. The 1976-80 five year plan increased national income by 30.9%, industrial production by 50% and agricultural production by 6.3%. The economy of Mongolia is nevertheless still mainly based on agriculture, with 70% of agricultural production being derived from cattle raising. Industry is small-scale and local, but has a greater share of GNP per capita than agriculture. The food industry accounts for more than 20% of the total industrial production. Livestock, animal products, wool, hides, fluorspar, non-ferrous metals and minerals are the main exports, while machinery, clothing, chemicals, building materials, sugar and tea are the chief imports. Trade is mostly with other communist countries, with the USSR taking an 80% share. Mongolia is heavily dependent on financial aid from the USSR.

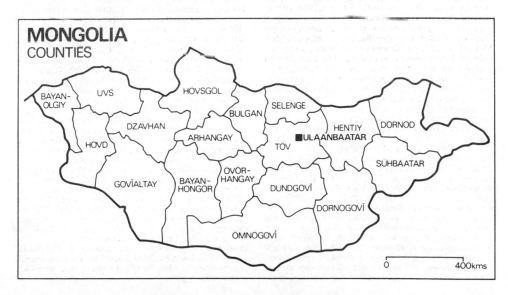

Administrative divisions. The Mongolian People's Republic is divided into 18 counties (*aimag*) as follows:

County	*area (sq km)*	*pop(1981e)*
Arhangay	55,200	80,000
Bayan-Hongar	116,000	61,000
Bayan-Ölgiy	45,800	72,000
Bulgan	50,000	40,000
Dornod	122,000	50,000
Dorngovǐ	111,000	40,000
Dundgovǐ	78,000	40,000
Dzavhan	82,000	80,000
Govǐaltay	142,000	40,000
Hentiy	85,000	50,000
Hovd	76,000	60,000
Hövsgöl	109,000	85,000
Ömnögovǐ	165,000	30,000
Övör-Hangay	63,500	80,000
Selenge	43,000	60,000
Sühbaatar	82,900	40,000
Töv	77,900	800,000
Uvs	69,200	70,000

Mongu *mong'goo*, 15 13S 23 09E, capital of Western prov, Zambia, S central Africa; 400 km NW of Maramba (Livingstone) and 676 km W of Lusaka; airfield.

Mono *mo'nō*, coastal prov in S Benin, W Africa; the W border with Ghana is formed by the R Mono; chief town Grand-Popo.

Mono, river mainly in Togo, W Africa; rises near Benin border NE of Sokodé and flows S for 560 km to enter the Gulf of Guinea W of Grand Popo; the lower course follows the border between Togo and Benin.

Monroe, 32 30N 92 07W, pop(1980) 57,597, parish seat of Ouachita parish, NE Louisiana, United States; on the R Ouachita, 152 km E of Shreveport; settled in 1785; university; railway; airfield; economy: centre of a large natural gas field; chemical and carbon-black plants; lumber and paper mills; event: Louisiana Legend (July).

Monroeville, 40 26N 79 45W, pop(1980) 30,977, residential town in Allegheny county, W Pennsylvania, United States; 18 km E of Pittsburgh.

Monrovia *mon-rō'vee-u*, 6 20N 10 46W, pop(1981) 306,460, seaport capital of Liberia, W Africa; 362 km SSE of Freetown (Sierra Leone); situated on an area divided by lagoons into islands and peninsulas; the main port and industrial sector is on Bushrod Island; the national museum is located on Providence Island; founded in 1822 by the American Colonization Society as a home for repatriated slaves from America, it was originally named Christopolis, this being changed to Monrovia after the US President James Monroe; a modern harbour and submarine base developed during 1945; the large Firestone rubber plantation and processing centre is located about 50 km from the city; university (1862); railway terminus; airport (Robertsfield, 56 km E); economy: petroleum and cement processing.

Monrovia, 34 09N 118 00W, pop(1980) 30,531, city in Los Angeles county, SW California, United States; 24 km ENE of Los Angeles, at the base of the San Gabriel Mts.

Mons *mõs*, dist of Hainaut prov, S Belgium; area 585 sq km; pop(1982) 256,025.

Mons, BERGEN *ber'KHen* (Flem), 50 28N 3 58E, pop(1982) 93,377, commercial and cultural city and capital of Mons dist, Hainaut prov, S Belgium; on the crest of low hills between the rivers Haine and Trouille; the inland harbour, which is connected to the R Schelde and to the Charleroi-Bruxelles Canal, handles mostly coal mined in the Borinage, one of the largest coal-mining and industrial dists in Belgium; built on the site of one of Caesar's camps, Mons has often been contended for by France, Spain and Austria; in 1914 the British army made first contact with the advancing Germans here (monument 1952); railway; university (1965); economy: textiles, leather, pharmaceuticals, metal processing, aluminium products; monuments: Gothic cathedral, town hall (15th-c); event: Battle of the Lumecon (annually).

Mont Blanc *mô blâ*, the highest alpine massif of SE France, SW Switzerland and NW Italy; the highest peak is Mont Blanc (4,807 m); there are 25 peaks over 4,000 m; the ridge runs mostly W to E and is bounded in the N by the valley of the Arve and in the S by Val Veni and Val Ferret; the 160 km Sentier International du Tour du Mont Blanc is an important walking route; the frontiers of France, Switzerland and Italy meet at Mt Dolent (3,823 m); Mont Blanc was first climbed in 1786 by J. Balmat and M.G. Paccard; the first ascent by a dog took place in 1837; Chamonix is an important resort.

Monta'na, state in NW United States, bounded W by Idaho, N by the Canadian provinces of British Columbia, Alberta, and Saskatchewan, E by North Dakota and South Dakota, and S by Wyoming and Idaho; the R Missouri rises in the SW and flows N, then E, across the state; the R Yellowstone flows N from Wyoming through Yellowstone National Park into Montana, and then flows NE to meet the R Missouri just over the North Dakota border; the Bitterroot Range, part of the Rocky Mts, lies along much of the W border; the highest point is Granite Peak (3,901 m); the Great Plains (E) are largely occupied by vast wheat fields and livestock farms; the W of the state is dominated by the Rocky Mts which are covered in dense pine forests; a small section of Yellowstone National Park lies in the S and the Glacier National Park is located in the W; the natural beauty and wildness of these parks and the Rocky Mts make tourism a major state industry; recreational attractions include hunting and fishing, skiing, hiking, and boating on the state's glacier lakes; the mountainous W Montana has deposits of copper, silver, gold, zinc, lead and manganese; E Montana produces petroleum and natural gas and has large coalmines; major manufactures include timber, wood products, refined petroleum and processed foods; the chief agricultural products are cattle, wheat, hay, barley, and dairy products; except for a small section of NW Montana, the state was part of the Louisiana Purchase of 1803; the region was crossed by the Lewis and Clark expedition in 1805; the Oregon Treaty of 1846 settled its border with Canada; having been successively part of the territories of Oregon, Washington, Nebraska, Dakota and Idaho, it became the Territory of Montana in 1864; ranchers moved into the area in 1866, taking over Indian land; this resulted in conflict with the Sioux who defeated General George Custer in 1876 at the Battle of the Little Bighorn, one of the greatest Indian victories; there are now 6 Indian reservations in the state, the largest being the Blackfeet, Fort Peck and Crow Indian reservations; Montana became a state (41st) in 1889; also known as the 'Treasure State'; pop(1980) 786,690; area 378,009 sq km; capital Helena; other chief cities are Billings and Great Falls; the state is divided into 56 counties and part of Yellowstone National Park:

County	*area (sq km)*	*pop(1980)*
Beaverhead	14,375	8,186
Big Horn	12,956	11,096
Blaine	11,068	6,999
Broadwater	3,091	3,267
Carbon	5,346	8,099
Carter	8,689	1,799
Cascade	7,017	80,696
Chouteau	10,366	6,092
Custer	9,818	13,109
Daniels	3,710	2,835
Dawson	6,172	11,805
Deer Lodge	1,924	12,518
Fallon	4,220	3,763
Fergus	11,284	13,076
Flathead	13,291	51,966
Gallatin	6,526	42,865
Garfield	11,677	1,656
Glacier	7,784	10,628

contd

County	*area (sq km)*	*pop(1980)*
Golden Valley	3,047	1,026
Granite	4,495	2,700
Hill	7,532	17,985
Jefferson	4,308	7,029
Judith Basin	4,865	2,646
Lake	3,757	19,056
Lewis and Clark	8,999	43,039
Liberty	3,708	2,329
Lincoln	9,402	17,752
Madison	9,334	5,448
McCone	6,828	2,702
Meagher	6,219	2,154
Mineral	3,162	3,675
Missoula	6,713	76,016
Musselshell	4,865	4,428
Park	6,929	12,660
Petroleum	4,295	655
Phillips	13,338	5,367
Pondera	4,243	6,731
Powder River	8,549	2,520
Powell	6,055	6,958
Prairie	4,503	1,836
Ravalli	6,198	22,493
Richland	5,411	12,243
Roosevelt	6,128	10,467
Rosebud	13,049	9,899
Sanders	7,147	8,675
Sheridan	4,371	5,414
Silver Bow	1,867	38,092
Stillwater	4,662	5,598
Sweet Grass	4,948	3,216
Teton	5,915	6,491
Toole	5,021	5,559
Treasure	2,535	981
Valley	12,834	10,250
Wheatland	3,689	2,359
Wibaux	2,309	1,476
Yellowstone	6,822	108,035
Yellowstone Nat Park (part)	637	275

Montauban *mõ-to-ba*, 44 00N 1 21E, pop(1982) 53,147, ancient town and capital of Tarn-et-Garonne dept, Midi-Pyrénées region, S France; situated on a plateau, on the right bank of the R Tarn, 50 km N of Toulouse; it is the marketing centre for the district's fruit and vegetable produce; built largely of pink brick; one of the earliest bastides, founded in 1144 by the Count of Toulouse, as a new settlement to encourage the productivity of the area; the centre of the town is the Place Nationale, an irregular rectangle lined by 4-storey brick terraced houses over double arcades, surrounded by narrow streets arranged in a rough grid pattern; ancient capital of Quercy; rail junction; economy: food products, furniture, textiles; monuments: fortified church of St-Jacques (formerly the town's cathedral, superseded in 1739 by a new cathedral); cathedral of Notre-Dame; episcopal palace; early 14th-c bridge.

Montclair, 40 49N 74 13W, pop(1980) 38,321, town in Essex county, NE New Jersey, United States; a residential suburb 10 km NNW of Newark.

Mont-de-Marsan *mõ-de-mar-sã*, 43 54N 0 31W, pop(1982) 30,894, capital town of Landes dept, Aquitaine region, SW France; at the confluence of the Douze and Midour rivers, where they merge to become the R Midouze, 106 km S of Bordeaux, on the S edge of the Landes pine forests; site of an important military experimental aircraft establishment; railway, airport (N of the town); well-known racecourse; economy: sawmills, resin distilling; event: local bullfighting.

Monte Albán *mon'tay ahl-bahn'*, ancient ruins in central Oaxaca, S Mexico; situated at the top of Monte Albán, 5 km SW of Oaxaca; alt 1,948 m; a sacred city of the Zapotec culture until 900 AD; after the Zapotecs abandoned the site in favour of Mitla, the Mixtecs used many of its earlier tombs for their own royal burials; the summit of the mountain, which was levelled, contains pyramids, temples, palaces and observatories; monuments date from the 1st occupation of the site (c.600 BC) and illustrate the earliest use of the calendar and of writing in Middle America; the Danzantes building depicts dancers, possibly the corpses of sacrificial victims; there are over 100 tombs in which archaeologists have discovered grave furniture, paintings and vases; in 1932 tomb No 7 in the NE of the city was excavated, revealing Mexico's largest-ever treasure-trove comprising over 500 pieces of Mixtec jewellery, including gold, silver, jade, turquoise, rock crystal and carved bone.

Monte Carlo *mon'tay kar'lõ*, 43 46N 7 23E, resort town on a rocky promontory of the Mediterranean Riviera, in the Principality of Monaco, situated on the N side of the harbour looking across to the town of Monaco; the famous Casino, providing an estimated 4% of national revenue, was built in 1878 by Charles Garnier, architect of the Paris Opéra; the luxury Monte Carlo Palais des Congrès (Les Spélugues) comprising a hotel and 100 flats was opened in 1978; famous for its annual car rally and its world championship Grand Prix motor race.

Monte, El, 34 04N 118 02W, pop(1980) 79,494, city in Los Angeles county, SW California, United States; 19 km E of Los Angeles.

Montebel'lo, 34 00N 118 07W, pop(1980) 52,929, city in Los Angeles county, SW California, United States; 13 km E of Los Angeles.

Montegiardino *mon-te-jar-dee'no*, castle (dist) in the Republic of San Marino, central Italy; area 3.31 sq km; pop(1980) 618; population density in 1980 was 187 inhabitants per sq km.

Montego Bay *mon-tay'go*, locally MOBAY, 18 27N 77 56W, pop(1982) 70,265, port and capital city of St James parish, Cornwall county on the NW coast of the Caribbean I of Jamaica; a free port and principal tourist centre of the island; derives its name from *manteca*, the Spanish for butter or lard which was derived from pigs and cattle and shipped from here; fine beaches; railway; Sangster International Airport; monuments: Rose Hall Great House (1770), old British fort, 18th-c church.

Montemuro, Serra de *mon-ti moo'roo*, mountain range, Viseu dist, N Portugal, S of R Douro, rising to 1,382 m.

Montenegro, republic of Yugoslavia. See Crna Gora.

Monterey *mon-te-ray'*, 36 37N 121 55W, pop(1980) 27,558, resort in Monterey county, W California, United States; on the Pacific Ocean, in the S of Monterey Bay, c.137 km S of San Francisco; Gaspar de Portolá established a presidio here in 1770, capital of Alta California from 1775 to 1846; US occupation commenced in 1846 and was followed by a state constitutional convention in 1849; monuments: the presidio chapel; California's first theatre (1844) and the first brick building (1847).

Monterey Park, 34 04N 118 08W, pop(1980) 54,338, city in Los Angeles county, SW California, United States; 8 km E of Los Angeles.

Montería *mon-tay-ree'a*, 8 45N 75 54W, pop(1985) 229,207, agricultural market town and capital of Córdoba dept, NW Colombia, South America; on E bank of the Río Sinú; university (1966).

Montero *mon-tay'rõ*, 17 20S 63 15W, pop(1976) 28,686, town in O. Santiesteban prov, Santa Cruz, Bolivia; set in fertile lowlands; railway; economy: sugar refining, cotton gins.

Monterrey *mon-te-ray'*, 25 40N 100 20W, pop(1980) 1,916,472, capital of Nuevo León state, NE Mexico; in Santa Catarina river valley, 157 km S of Nuevo Laredo on the US frontier; founded in 1579; a centre of the metal industry since the 1880s; 3 universities (1933, 1957, 1969); institute of technology (1943); railway; airport (Aeropuerto del Norte) at 24 km; economy: produces over 75% of Mexico's iron and steel; lead smelting, textiles, chemicals, glass, tobacco; monuments: the main square, Plaza Zaragoza, contains an 18th-c cathedral which was badly damaged in the war against the USA (1846-47) when

Mexican troops used it as a powder magazine; the institute of Technology (1943) has valuable collections of books on 16th-c Mexican history, rare books printed in Indian languages and 2,000 editions of Don Quixote in all languages.

Montes Claros *mon'tays kla'rōs*, 16 45S 43 52W, pop(1980) 151,713, town in Minas Gerais state, Sudeste region, SE Brazil; N of Belo Horizonte; university (1962); railway; airfield; economy: cotton, maize, timber, textiles.

Montevideo *mon-tay-vee-day'ō*, dept in S Uruguay; on the N bank of the Río de la Plata; pop(1985) 1,296,089; area 664 sq km; capital Montevideo; the smallest dept in the country, comprising the city of Montevideo; the dept has an indented coastline and is bounded by the Santa Lucía river mouth (W); the well-protected bay of Montevideo port has a number of good beaches.

Montevideo, 34 55S 56 10W, pop(1985) 1,296,089, federal and prov capital of Uruguay; on the Río de la Plata; founded in 1726, although most of the city is modern in style; founded by the Spanish to counteract Portuguese influences in the area; capital of Uruguay since 1830; Montevideo city is the centre for all of Uruguay's commercial, industrial, cultural and political activities; almost 90% of the country's imports and exports pass through Montevideo; university (1849); railway; airport (Carrasco) at 20 km; economy: meat packing, food processing, tanning, footwear, soap, matches, trade in meat, skins, wool; monuments: the main square, the Plaza Independencia, is set between the old town and the new city; in its centre is a statue of Artigas, above an underground mausoleum; on the S side is the Government House, on the W, the Palacio Salvo; on the Plaza Constitución, the oldest square in Montevideo, in the old part of the city, is the cathedral (1790-1804); the city has several parks; the oldest, El Prado, contains the Museums of Fine Art and History; the Parque Rodó has an open-air theatre, amusement park and boating lake, and at its E end is the National Museum of Fine Arts, housing works by living artists; in the Parque Batlle y Ordóñez there are athletics fields, a bicycle race track and a sports stadium (Estadio Centenario) with a seating capacity of 70,000; at the W end of the bay is the Cerro, the hill from which Montevideo gets its name; the fort on top of it is now a military museum; in the port the ship's bell of *HMS Ajax* has been set up to commemorate the scuttling of the *Graf Spee*; the *Graf Spee*'s anchor was set up at the entrance to the port in Dec 1964 to mark the 25th anniversary of the battle; the wreck itself lies about 3 km offshore, but is no longer visible as it was dismantled some years ago; plates from its bulkhead were used in the construction of the city stadium.

Montezinho, Serra de *mon-te-zeen'yoo*, mountain range, Bragança dist, Trás-os-Montes, NE Portugal, lying N of Bragança and rising to 1,438 m.

Montgomery *-gom'-*, 32 23N 86 19W, pop(1980) 177,857, capital of state in Montgomery county, central Alabama, United States; on the R Alabama, just downstream from its junction with the Coosa and Tallapoosa rivers; became state capital in 1847; in Feb 1861 the Confederate States of America was formed here, with Jefferson Davis inaugurated as Confederate President; the city was occupied by Federal troops in 1865; university (1874); railway; economy: important market centre for farming produce, particularly cotton, livestock, and dairy products; many manufacturing industries, including machinery, glass, textiles, furniture, foods, and paper.

Montluçon *mo-lü-sō*, 46 20N 2 36E, pop(1982) 51,765, industrial town in Allier dept, Auvergne region, central France; on the R Cher, at the foot of the Massif Central, 75 km NW of Clermont-Ferrand; a road and rail junction; on the right bank of the river is the small old quarter, where narrow streets slope up to the castle; economy: chemicals, rubber, foundries; monuments: 15th-c Bourbon castle; in the castle is a museum illustrating natural history and folklore of the region; 8 km SE is the thermal spa of Neris-les-Bains, a well-known health resort for many centuries.

Montpel'ier, 44 16N 72 35W, pop(1980) 8,241, capital of Vermont state in Washington county, N Vermont, United States; on the R Winooski; settled in 1780; state capital since 1805; Vermont College (1834); notable skiing areas nearby at Pinnacle Mt, Judgement Ridge, Glen Ellen, Bolton Valley, Sugarbush Valley and Mad River Glen; birthplace of Admiral George Dewey; railway; economy: textiles, machinery, wood products, granite quarrying, printing.

Montpellier *mô-pel-yay*, 43 37N 3 52E, pop(1982) 201,067, industrial and commercial city and capital of Hérault dept, Languedoc-Roussillon region, S France; near the Golfe du Lion (Gulf of Lions), 123 km WNW of Marseille; birthplace of the philosopher Comte; the central part of the town is the Place de la Comédie, with the Esplanade, a spacious promenade laid out in the 18th century, opening out to the N; the city was founded in the 8th century around a Benedictine abbey; bishopric; university (1289); railway; Montpellier-Frejorgues airport; economy: textiles, printing, concrete, machinery, wood products; monuments: Gothic cathedral of St Pierre (1364), restored in 1867; many 17-18th-c patrician and merchants' houses with fine decorated facades; Doric triumphal arch, constructed in 1691 in honour of Louis XIV; Château d'Eau, terminal of an aqueduct which was constructed in 1753-66 by Pitot to bring water from a source at St-Clement 14 km distant, it is a hexagonal pavilion with Corinthian columns and steps flanked by sculptured reliefs; the Jardin des Plantes was France's first botanical garden (1593); the Musée Fabre, one of the most important provincial collections in France, has paintings and sculptures by Courbet, Delacroix and Matisse; the Atger Museum, in the 16th-c former bishop's palace, has a collection of Baroque drawings.

Montréal, MONTREAL *mō-ray-al'*, *mon-tree-ol'* (Eng), 45 30N 73 36W, pop(1981) 980,354, river-port city in S Québec prov, SE Canada; situated on Montréal island, on the St Lawrence river which is ice-free from May to Nov; 2nd largest French-speaking city in the world; first visited by Cartier in 1535 when it was the Indian village of Hochelaga; Champlain visited the area in 1603 and built a fort here in 1611; the settlement slowly developed into a fur-trading centre; in 1725 stone fortifications were added; Montréal surrendered without resistance to the British in 1760; from 1775-76 it was occupied by the Continental Army under Montgomery; capital of Canada 1844-49; the British garrison was withdrawn in 1870; the 1976 Olympic Games were held here; McGill University (1821); University of Montreal (1876); Université du Québec à Montréal (1969); Concordia University (1974); metro; railway; 2 airports; economy: aircraft, railway equipment, clothing, plastics, footwear, cement, brewing (Molson Brewery, founded in 1786, is Canada's oldest operating brewery), trade in grain, timber and paper; monuments: S of the Place d'Armes, the town's original market square, is the neo-Gothic Notre Dame church (1829) with 'Le Gros Bourdon', a bell weighing 11,240 kg and a museum containing paintings, sculptures and ornaments; to the W of Notre Dame church is the Séminaire de Saint-Sulpice, established in Montréal in 1658 and noted for its woodwork clock which dates from 1710; the Maisonneuve Monument in the Place d'Armes was erected in 1895 to commemorate the founder of the city; the Château de Ramezay (now a museum), to the E of Notre Dame in the oldest part of the city, was built in 1705 by the French governor of Montréal, Claude de Ramezay and is one of the oldest buildings in N America; the business complexes in the centre of Montréal are linked by a vast system of underground passages lined with shops, restaurants, theatres and cinemas.

Montréal North, MONTRÉAL NORD, 45 36N 73 38W, pop(1981) 94,914, town in S Québec, SE Canada; a N suburb of Montréal, situated on Montréal island, on the Rivière des Prairies; railway.

Montreuil *mō-trœy'*, MONTREUIL SOUS BOIS, 48 52N 2 28E, pop(1982) 93,394, E suburb of Paris in Seine-Saint-Denis dept, Ile-de-France region, N central France; economy: engineering; monument: 12th-c church.

Montreux *mõ-trœ'*, 46 27N 6 55E, pop(1980) 19,685, winter-sports centre and resort town in Vaud canton, SW Switzerland; at E end of Lac Léman (L of Geneva), SE of Lausanne and Vevey; its mild Mediterranean climate has gained it the reputation of being the centre of the Vaud Riviera; the centre of the resort, Montreux Ville, lies on the steep slopes above the Baye de Montreux, a swiftly flowing mountain stream; figs, cypresses and palms grow by the lake and vines and walnuts are to be found in the hills; railway; casino; monument: 13th-c Château de Chillon is nearby; events: Golden Rose Television Festival (spring); International Jazz Festival (June-July); music festival (Sept).

Montrose *mon-trōz'*, 56 43N 2 29W, pop(1981) 12,325, port town in Angus dist, Tayside, E Scotland; on the E coast, 42 km NE of Dundee; railway; economy: pharmaceuticals, food processing, distilling, textiles, fishing, oil supply; to the W of the town is Montrose Basin, a large tidal lagoon; monuments: museum; the William Lamb Memorial Studio contains various works by the sculptor and etcher, including some studies of members of the royal family.

Montserrat *mont-se-rat'*, EMERALD ISLE, volcanic island lying 43 km SW of Antigua in the Leeward Is group of the Lesser Antilles, E Caribbean; a British dependent territory; timezone GMT −4; area 106 sq km; capital Plymouth; pop(1980) 12,034; over 25% of the pop lives in the capital; many inhabitants are of mixed Negro or European descent; Christianity is the dominant religion; English is the official language; the unit of currency is the East Caribbean dollar; membership of CARICOM, Economic Commission for Latin America (associate), overseas territory associated with the EEC.

Physical description and climate. The island, 18 km long and 11 km wide, is rugged and mountainous, comprising the ranges of Silver Hills, Centre Hills and Soufrière Hills, all of which are heavily forested. The highest point is Chance's Peak (914 m) in the S of the island. There are 7 active volcanoes (*soufrières*). The climate is tropical with no well-defined rainy season and low humidity. The average annual rainfall is 1,500 mm. The coolest time of the year is between Dec and March when temperatures can reach as low as 18.5°C. Hurricanes may occur between June and Nov when temperatures are higher.

History, government and constitution. In 1632 Montserrat was colonized by a group of English and Irish settlers who had moved from the overcrowded island of St Christopher. They established a plantation economy based on slave labour but the island did not become a British Crown Colony until 1871. Between 1958 and 1962 the island was a member of the Federation of the West Indies. Montserrat is administered by a governor appointed by and representing the British sovereign. There is a 6-member executive council and a legislative council consisting of 7 elected, 2 nominated, and 2 appointed members.

Economy. Just over 10% of the working population is employed in agriculture. Attempts have been made to halt the decline in the agricultural sector by revising land tenure and settlement arrangements and by extending agriculture-based industries. Emphasis has been placed on the production of sea-island cotton (supplying the raw material for the local garment and craft industry), peppers and their processing for export, tree crops, market gardening, and livestock production for both home consumption and export. Light industry is also being developed (electronic assembly, handicrafts, rum distilling). Tourism is the mainstay of the economy, accounting for 25% of national income. Chief imports include manufactured goods, foods and beverages, machinery and transport equipment, and fuel. Chief exports include hot peppers, tomatoes, manufactured goods, beef, cotton and cotton goods. Revenue is also obtained from the sale of postage stamps.

Communications. There is an international airport 13 km from Plymouth.

Moorab'bin, 37 45S 144 58E, pop(1983e) 101,400, city suburb of SE Melbourne in Melbourne stat div, Victoria, Australia; airport; monuments: Moorabbin Air Museum contains vintage and antique aircraft.

Moore, 35 20N 97 29W, pop(1980) 35,063, city in Cleveland county, central Oklahoma, United States; 17 km S of Oklahoma City; railway.

Moorhead, 46 53N 96 45W, pop(1980) 29,998, county seat of Clay county, W Minnesota, United States; on the Red River of the North, opposite Fargo, North Dakota; founded in 1871; university; railway; shipping centre for dairy and farm area.

Mopti *mop'tee*, fertile region in central Mali, W Africa; pop(1971) 1,086,945; area 88,752 sq km; encompasses the Macina depression which runs SE-NE, as does the R Niger in several courses; the R Bani joins the R Niger at Mopti; lakes in the NE include L Haogoundou and L Debó; higher ground in E and SE rises to the Mts du Hombori which run along the border with Gao region; capital Mopti; chief towns Bandiagara, Bankasa, Djenné, Douentza, Koro, Niafunké, Ténekou, Hombori.

Mopti, 14 29N 4 10W, pop(1976) 53,885, capital of Mopti region, central Mali, W Africa; situated on 3 islands joined by a dyke, Mopti or the 'Venice of Mali' lies at the confluence of the Niger and Bani rivers, 450 km ENE of Bamako in the Macina depression; airfield; economy: agricultural trade, power plant.

Moquegua *mo-kay'gwa*, dept in S Peru; bordered by the Pacific (W); the W is low lying, the E is crossed by ridges of the Cordillera Occidental; watered by the Tambo and Moquegua rivers; pop(1981) 101,610; area 16,174 sq km; capital Moquegua.

Moradabad *mō-rah'dah-bahd*, 28 50N 78 50E, pop(1981) 348,000, city in Uttar Pradesh state, N India; on the R Ramganga, 150 km ENE of Delhi; the British stronghold of Rohilla came under the control of the nawab of Oudh in the late 18th century but was ceded to the British in 1801, an important rail junction linked to Rampur, Saharanpur and Delhi; economy: cotton, carpets, brassware, agricultural trade; monuments: 17th-c mosque; ruined Rohilla fort to the N of the city.

Morar, Loch, loch in W Highland region, W Scotland; SE of Mallaig, on the W coast; 19 km long; the deepest loch in Britain (310 m); drains into the Sound of Sleat via the Morar river.

Moratuwa *me-ret'e-wu*, 6 47N 79 53E, pop(1981) 135,610, town in Colombo dist, Western prov, Sri Lanka; on L Bolgoda, 20 km S of Colombo, university (1966); railway.

Morava *mo'ra-va*, river in central Czechoslovakia; rising near the Polish frontier it flows 350 km S through the historic prov of Moravia to meet the R Danube W of Bratislava.

Morava, MARCH (Ger), river in Srbija (Serbia) republic, Yugoslavia; formed by the junction of the S and W Morava near Stalac; flows N 218 km to meet the R Danube near Smederevo.

Moravia *mur-ay'vee-a*, MORAVA *mo'ra-va* (Czech), MÄHREN *mah'ren* (Ger), historic prov of central Czechoslovakia; bounded N by Poland, S by Austria, W by historic prov of Bohemia and E by Slovakia; separated from Slovakia by the Little and White Carpathian Mts; a corridor known as the Moravian Gate provides an important communication link (N-S) between the SE Sudetes Mts and the W Carpathians; chief towns include Brno, Ostrava and Olomouc; major rivers include the Morava, Oder (Odra), Opava and Dyje; under Hapsburg rule from early 16th century until 1918 when it became a prov of Czechoslovakia; united with Silesia between 1927 and 1949, thereafter divided into modern administrative units.

Morazán *mō-re-zan'*, formerly GOTERA, dept in NE El Salvador, Central America; bounded N by Honduras; pop(1971) 170,706; area 1,364 sq km; capital San Francisco Gotera; chief towns Guatajiagua and Chilanga; the Cordillera Cacaguatique extends W-E across the centre of the dept; economy: gold and silver mining at San Cristóbal.

Morbihan *mor-bee-ã*, dept in Bretagne region of W France, bounded on the S by the Bay of Biscay; comprises 3 arrond, 42 cantons and 461 communes; pop(1982) 590,889; area 6,823 sq km; includes several islands; the coast is very irregular, carved into bays and estuaries, the largest of which are the Gulf of Morbihan (E of Quiberon peninsula) and the estuary of the Blavet; the littoral (Vannetais) is fertile, but the low hills of the interior are mostly wooded or waste; the land rises in the NW to the Montagne Noire (over 300 m); the dept is remarkable for its concentration of prehistoric megaliths, especially the tombs and alignments of Carnac and the megaliths of Locmariaguer; capital Vannes; chief towns Lorient and Pontivy; there is a Renaissance château at Josselin; a sea-water treatment establishment centre at Quiberon.

Møre og Romsdal *mu'ru o roms'dal*, a county of W Norway; area 15,104 sq km; pop(1983) 237,268; capital Molde; chief towns Kristiansund and Ålesund; drained by the Driva and Rauma rivers; its W coastline is heavily indented by fjords including the Halsa Fjord; rises to 1,999 m at Mt Pyttegga; there are many islands along the W coast including Averøa, Smøla and Otrøy.

Morecambe *mor'kam*, 54 04N 2 53W, pop(1981) 42,057, resort town in Lancaster dist, Lancashire, NW England; NW of Lancaster on the Irish Sea coast; railway; economy: clothing, plastics, engineering, shrimp fishing.

Morecambe Bay, inlet of the Irish Sea, between the Furness peninsula of Cumbria and Lancashire, NW England.

Moree', 29 29S 149 53E, pop(1981) 10,459, town in Northern stat div, N New South Wales, Australia; SW of Brisbane; railway; base for the Overseas Telecommunications station on the Queensland border; large Aboriginal settlement.

Morelia *mo-ray'lee-a*, 19 40N 101 11W, pop(1980) 353,055, capital of Michoacán state, W central Mexico; 310 km W of Ciudad de México (Mexico City); alt 1,923 m; founded in 1541; university (1917); railway; monuments: contains many old colonial houses and churches including the 17th-c cathedral, the only church in Mexico in the Plateresque style; the Colegio de San Nicolás (1540) is the oldest surviving institution of higher education in Latin America; there are plaques on the houses of Melchior Ocampo, Morelos (the revolutionary) and those of the 2 Emperors of Mexico (Agustín de Iturbide and the Archduke Maximilian of Austria).

Morelos *mo-ray'lōs*, state in S central Mexico; bounded SW by Guerrero, NW and NE by México, N by Ciudad de México federal district and E and SE by Puebla; situated mainly on the S slope of the great central plateau; slopes from N to S; drained by the Río Grande de Amacuzac and the Chinameca river; pop(1980) 931,675; area 4,950 sq km; capital Cuernavaca; economy: agriculture (sugar cane, rice, maize, cotton, soft fruit), cattle, pig, goat, sheep and horse raising, timber, motor cars, chemicals, paper, textiles, tourism.

Morena, Sierra *mo-ray'na*, a long low mountain range in Andalucia, SW Spain, rising to 1,300 m and separating the basins of the R Guadiana and the R Guadalquivir; rich in mineral deposits.

Morgantown, 39 38N 79 57W, pop(1980) 27,605, county seat of Monongalia county, N West Virginia, United States; port on the R Monongahela, 24 km NE of Fairmont; university (1867); railway; economy: shipping point for coal mining region; manufactures glass, textiles and chemicals.

Morioka *mō-ree-ō'ka*, 39 43N 141 08E, pop(1980) 229,114, capital of Iwate prefecture, Tōhoku region, N Honshū island, Japan; 170 km N of Sendai; railway; economy: metal goods, toys.

Mor'ley, 53 46N 1 36W, pop(1981) 44,671, town in Leeds borough, West Yorkshire, N England; part of West Yorkshire urban area; 7 km SW of Leeds; railway; economy: textiles, coal, engineering.

Morne Diablotin *morn dyah-blot-ī'*, 15 30N 61 25W, highest mountain peak on the island of Dominica, Windward Is, E Caribbean Sea; located in NW of the island in St Andrew parish; height 1,447 m.

Morobe, province on the Huon peninsula of Papua New Guinea; includes the Siassi Is between the islands of New Guinea and New Britain; the Rawlinson range lies to the N and the Kuper range to the S; area 34,500 sq km; pop(1980) 305,356; chief town Lae.

Morocco *me-rok'ō*, official name The Kingdom of Morocco, AL-MAMLAKAH AL-MAGHRIBĪYAH (Arab), a N African kingdom, bounded SW by the Western Sahara, SE and E by Algeria, NE by the Mediterranean Sea and W by the Atlantic Ocean; area 409,200 sq km; timezone GMT; capital Rabat; chief towns include Casablanca, Fès, Tanger (Tangiers), Meknès, Kénitra, Tétouan and Oujda; pop(1984e) 23,565,000; 99% of the pop is of Arab-Berber origin; nearly all are Muslim; the official language is Arabic with several Berber dialects; French is the language used in government, in business and in post-primary education; the unit of currency is the dirham of 100 centimes; national holiday 18 Nov (Independence Day); membership of AfDB, Arab League, EC (associate), FAO, G-77, IAEA, IBRD, ICAO, IDA, Islamic Development Bank, IFAD, IFC, ILO, ILZSG, IMF, IMO, INTELSAT, INTERPOL, IOOC, IPU, ITU, NAM, OAU, OIC, UN, UNESCO, UPU, WHO, WIPO, WMO, WTO.

Physical description. Morocco's relief is dominated by a series of folded mountain ranges, from the Er Rif in the N, through the Moyen Atlas limestone plateau to the Haut Atlas in the S which rises to 4,165 m at Jbel Toubkal, Morocco's highest peak. The Atlas Mts descend SE to the NW edge of the Sahara desert. In the N the Atlas descends steeply towards the Mediterranean between Tanger and Melilla and to a broad coastal plain bounded W by the Atlantic Ocean. The country's longest river, the Dra'ar rises in the Haut Atlas and flows 1,200 km down to the Atlantic near Tan-Tan.

Climate. Morocco can be divided into 4 main climatic regions: (1) the N coast with a Mediterranean-type climate; settled and hot from May to Sept, there is annual rainfall between 400 and 800 mm per year, falling mostly during Nov-March; (2) the Atlantic coast where annual rainfall decreases from over 400 mm N of Casablanca to over 200 mm at Agadir and even lower further S as the Sahara desert reaches W to the coast. The Atlantic coastline is relatively cool compared to the Mediterranean coastline owing to the effect of the Canaries current. Winters in this area are mild with no snow. Rabat is representative with 500 mm of rain per year and average max daily temperature ranging between 17°C and 28°C; (3) the inland High Atlas region where heavy winter snowfall lasts well into the summer on the higher ground. At lower altitudes the summer months become hot with low humidity. At intermediate altitudes the climate can be pleasant. Marrakech at 460 m receives 240 mm of rain per annum and average max daily temperatures range between 18°C and 33°C; (4) the Sahara desert region is virtually rainless, with extreme heat in the summer, but chilly and often frosty winter nights in the winter. The heat is moderated by sea breezes where the desert reaches the Atlantic Ocean.

History, government and constitution. The N coast of Morocco has been invaded and occupied by Phoenicians, Carthaginians and Romans since the 12th century BC, but it was not until the 7th century AD that Arab invaders penetrated inland, mixing with the local Berber population. In the 20th century European countries have laid claim to parts of Morocco. Spain took control of the N and Atlantic coast as well as the enclave of Ifni in 1904 and in 1912 France gained control of the rest of the country. The Treaty of Fès in 1912 established Spanish Morocco with its capital at Tétouan and French Morocco with its capital at Rabat. The international zone of Tanger was created in 1923 by France, Britain and Spain. In 1956 the treaty of Fès was terminated,

France and Spain gave full independence to their protectorates and Tanger's international status came to an end. In 1975 the former Spanish Sahara (Western Sahara) came under the joint control of Spain, Morocco and Mauritania. Spain withdrew in 1976 and Mauritania in 1979, leaving the administration of Western Sahara to Morocco. The Spanish still hold sovereignty over the 2 small enclaves of Ceuta and Melilla as well as the 3 islands of Alhucemas, Chafarinas and Peñon de Vélez. Under the 1972 constitution, Morocco is a constitutional monarchy under a king with paramount executive powers. A unicameral 267-member Chamber of Representatives is elected every 6 years and the monarch as head of state appoints about 23 ministers to a cabinet headed by an executive prime minister. Two-thirds of the Chamber are directly elected.

Economy. More than half the population are engaged in the agricultural sector which accounts for approx one-fifth of national income. Agricultural crops include cereals (wheat and barley), citrus fruits, olives, vegetables, sugar-beet, cotton and sunflowers. Fishing is important on the Atlantic and Mediterranean coasts with catches brought ashore and processed at Agadir, Safi, Essaouira and Casablanca. Mineral extraction is of vital importance to the Moroccan economy representing over 50% of the country's export earnings. Morocco is the world's 3rd largest producer, the largest exporter (over 17,000,000 tonnes per year) and has the largest known reserves of phosphate. Coal and minerals such as barite, cobalt, copper, manganese, antimony, zinc, iron ore, fluorspar, lead and silver are also extracted. Manufacturing industry is based on the production of textiles, cement, soap, tobacco, chemicals, paper, timber products and vehicle assembly. Tourism centred on the 4 imperial cities and the warm Atlantic resorts is crucial to the Moroccan economy with a total of 1,900,000 visitors arriving in 1982. Main trading partners are France, the USA, West Germany, Holland, India, the USSR, Spain, Italy, Saudi Arabia, the UK and Poland.

Administrative divisions. Morocco is divided into 7 provinces and 41 prefectures:

Prov/prefecture	*area (sq km)*	*pop(1982)*
Centre		
Azilal	10,050	387,115
Beni Mellal	7,075	668,703
Benslimane	2,760	174,464
Casablanca Anfa		2,923,630
Ben M'Sik-Sidi Othmane		639,558
Aïn-es-Sebaâ-H. Mohammadi	1,615	421,272
Aïn Chock Hay Hassani		298,376
Mohammedia-Zenata		153,828
El Jadida	6,000	763,351
Khouribga	4,250	437,002
Settat	9,750	692,359
Centre-Nord		
Al Hoceima	3,550	311,298
Boulemane	14,395	131,470
Fès	5,400	805,464
Taounate	5,585	535,972
Taza	15,020	613,485
Centre-Sud		
Errachidia	59,585	421,207
Ifrane	3,310	100,255
Kénifra	12,320	363,716
Meknès	3,995	626,868
Nord-Ouest		
Kénitra	4,745	715,967
Khémisset	8,305	405,836
Chefchaouen	4,350	309,024
Rabat-Salé	1,275	1,020,001
Tanger	1,195	436,227
Tétouan	6,025	704,205
Sidi-Kacem	4,060	514,127

contd

Prov/prefecture	*area (sq km)*	*pop(1982)*
Oriental		
Figuig	55,990	101,359
Nador	6,130	593,255
Oujda	20,700	780,762
Sud		
Agadir	5,910	579,741
Guelmim	28,750	128,676
Ouarzazate	41,550	533,892
Tan-Tan	17,295	47,040
Taroudant	16,460	558,501
Tata	25,925	99,950
Tiznit	6,960	313,140
Tensift		
El Kelaa-des Srarhna	10,070	577,595
Essaouira	6,335	393,683
Marrakech	14,755	1,266,695
Safi	7,285	706,618

The 4 provinces of former Spanish Sahara (Western Sahara) are also administered by Morocco.

Morogoro *mō-rō-gō'rō*, 4 49S 37 40E, pop(1978) 61,890, capital of Morogoro region, E Tanzania, E Africa; 185 km W of Dar es Salaam; railway; economy: tobacco, footwear, kapok, sugar, mica mining.

Mörön *mu'run*, MOEROEN, 49 36N 100 08E, county centre of Hövsgöl county, N Mongolia; economy: textiles, foodstuffs.

Morona Santiago *mo-rō'na san-tya'gō*, tropical prov in SE Ecuador; borders with Peru (E); pop(1982) 70,217; area 24,261 sq km; capital Macas; economy: drinks, tobacco.

Moroni *mo-rō'nee*, 11 40S 43 16E, capital of Comoros in the Mozambique Channel and chief town of Grande Comore I; pop(1978) 16,000; airport.

Moroto *mō-rō'tō*, 2 32N 34 41E, town in Karamoja prov, Uganda, E Africa; NE of Soroti, close to Uganda's E frontier with Kenya; airfield.

Mor'peth, 55 10N 1 41W, pop(1981) 14,496, town in Castle Morpeth dist, Northumberland, NE England; on the R Wansbeck, 23 km N of Newcastle upon Tyne; railway; economy: light engineering, market gardening, mineral water.

Morphou *mor'foo*, 35 11N 33 00E, pop(1981e) 6,650, town in Nicosia dist, N Cyprus; occupied by the Turkish army in 1974; the surrounding agricultural area produces citrus fruits, strawberries, vegetables, and cereals; monument: Byzantine monastery of Ayios Mamas (rebuilt 15th century), in which is preserved the tomb of St Mamas.

Morris Jesup, Kap, most northerly point of land in the Arctic, at the ice-free N tip of Peary Land, N Greenland.

Mörs *mœrs*, 51 27N 6 36E, pop(1983) 98,700, industrial city in Düsseldorf dist, Nordrhein-Westfalen (North Rhine-Westphalia) prov, W Germany, WNW of Duisburg.

Morton, national park in E New South Wales, Australia; situated in the Great Dividing Range, SW of Sydney; area 1,526 sq km; established in 1938.

Moscow, capital city of the Soviet Union. See Moskva.

Moselle *mō-zel*, dept in Lorraine region of NE France, bounded on the N by Luxembourg and on the NE by W Germany; comprises 9 arrond, 46 cantons and 718 communes; drained by the Moselle R and its tributaries; pop(1982) 1,007,189; area 6,216 sq km; capital Metz; chief towns Thionville, Forbach and Sarrebourg; the Parc de Lorraine and the Parc des Vosges du Nord regional nature parks lie partly within the dept.

Moselle, MOSEL *mō'zel* (Eng), MOSELLA (anc), river in W Germany, Luxembourg and NE France; rises at the Col de Bussang in the French Vosges, NE France; flows N, forming a section of the boundary between W Germany and Luxembourg, turns NE and enters the R Rhine at Koblenz; length 514 km; length in Germany 242 km; navigable length 240 km; drainage basin area 9,387 sq km; chief tributaries Orne, Sauer, Meurthe and Saare;

since 1964 the Moselle has been canalized, with a series of 10 dams (at Trier, Detzem, Wintrich, Zeltingen, Enkirch, St Aldegund, Fankel, Muden, Lehmen and Koblenz) to regulate its flow; Bernkasteler Doktor and Wehlener Sonnenuhr rank among the finest Moselle valley wines.

Moskva *musk-va'*, MOSCOW (Eng), 55 45N 37 42E, pop(1983) 8,396,000, capital city of the Soviet Union, also of Moskovskaya oblast and the Rossiyskaya; on the R Moskva; a major political, economic, scientific, and cultural centre of the Soviet Union; largest city of the Soviet Union; linked to the R Volga by a canal; the Kremlin ('citadel') is linked with the epoch of the Great October Socialist Revolution and the strengthening of Soviet power; today it is the centre of the country's political life and venue for the congresses of the Communist Party of the Soviet Union and sessions of the Supreme Soviet of the USSR; the rise of Moskva as capital of a small municipality began in the 12th century and continued until the Princes of Moskva became, with Ivan III (1462-1505), the Tsars of Russia; during this period it became the national capital; in 1703 Peter the Great transferred the seat of government to St Petersburg, where it remained until 1918; 2 universities (1960, 1975); railway; airport; economy: solar research and development, clothing, knitwear, footwear, textiles, oil refining, chemicals; monuments: the Kremlin (built in 1300) is situated on a hill and surrounded by walls and towers; the Spassky Tower, surmounted by a ruby star, has long been the symbol of Moskva and the Soviet state; of the many churches within the Kremlin the most notable are the Uspenski (Assumption) cathedral (1475-79), the cathedral of the Archangel (1333, rebuilt 1505-09), and the Blagoveshchenski (Annunciation) cathedral, where the Tsars were christened and married; other notable buildings within the Kremlin are the imperial Great Palace (1838-49), Granovitaya Palace (1487-91), Oruzheinaya Plata or Armoury (1849-51, now a museum of decorative art containing the most valuable Russian antiquities), the 17th-c Palace of the Patriarchs, the former arsenal (1701-36), and the Hall of the Senate (1775-84), now seat of the government; in the Kitaigorod, just outside the Kremlin, is the famous Red Square, the scene of annual political parades; other notable monuments include the 16th-c St Basil cathedral (now a museum), the granite mausoleum of Vladimir Ilyich Lenin, and the Tower of the Soviets surmounted by a colossal figure of Lenin (begun in 1932); there are numerous theatres, art galleries, and museums including the V.I. Lenin Museum, with more than 13,000 exhibits tracing the life and work of the founder of the Soviet state, and the USSR Museum of the Revolution (1924).

Mosonmagyaróvár *mo'shon-mog'yor-ō-var*, ALTENBURG (Ger), 47 52N 17 18E, pop(1984e) 30,000, town in Györ-Sopron county, NW Hungary; at junction of R Latja with R Danube, NW of Györ; economy: agricultural machinery, fertilizer, aluminium, chemicals.

Mosquito Coast, LA MOSQUITIA, an undeveloped coastal lowland strip in Colón and Gracias a Dios depts, E Honduras and Zelaya dept, E Nicaragua, Central America; follows the Caribbean coast in a 65 km-wide narrow strip of tropical forest, lagoons and swamp; inhabited by the Meskito Indians; economy: timber and fruit growing; the British controlled this area from 1665 until 1860, appointing a succession of Mosquito kings who ruled over the Indian population; there were several unsuccessful attempts to settle the Río Negro.

Moss *mos*, 59 26N 10 41E, pop(1983) 24,975, seaport and capital of Østfold county, SE Norway; on the E side of Oslofjorden (Oslo Fjord); railway; economy: wood-processing; the union of Norway and Sweden was concluded here in 1814.

Mossel Bay *mo'sel*, MOSSELBAI, 34 12S 22 08E, port and resort in S Cape prov, South Africa; W of Port Elizabeth; W point on the 'Garden Route'; Diaz landed here in 1488; noted for its Post Office Tree, where sailors' letters used to be placed in boots suspended from the tree; famous for its mussels after which the port is named.

Mossmorran, industrial location in Fife region, E Scotland; developed on the site of a former peat bog, N of the Firth of Forth; fractionation and ethylene plants, converting North Sea natural gas liquids into products for the chemical industry, are linked by pipeline to St Fergus in Grampian region and on to the Brent gas field in the North Sea E of the Shetland Is.

Mossoró *mo-so-ro'*, 5 10S 37 20W, pop(1980) 117,971, town in Rio Grande do Norte state, Nordeste region, NE Brazil; SE of Fortaleza; university (1968); railway; economy: cotton, maize, mining of salt and chalk, timber.

Most *most*, 50 31N 13 39E, pop(1984) 62,097, town in Severočeský region, Czech Socialist Republic, W Czechoslovakia; between the R Ohre and the Erzgebirge Mts on the E German frontier; railway; gas pipeline to Slovakia begins here; economy: metal, chemicals, coal mining.

Mos'ta or **Musta** *moo'stah*, 35 51N 14 27E, pop(1983e) 9,203, town on the main island of Malta; 8 km W of Valletta; monuments: Mosta Dome which is one of the largest domes in the world and the St Anton Church.

Mostaganem *me-stahg-e-nem'*, MESTGHANEM, 35 40N 0 05W, pop(1982) 169,526, seaport capital of Mostaganem dept, NW Algeria, N Africa; 72 km ENE of Oran; founded in the 11th century; occupied by France in 1833; expansion since the beginning of the 20th century as a result of the development of port facilities; railway.

Mos'tar, 43 20N 17 50E, pop(1981) 110,377, town in Bosna-Hercegovina republic, W Yugoslavia; on R Neretva, 80 km SW of Sarajevo; the chief town of Hercegovina; sports stadium; university (1976); airfield; railway; economy: wine, tobacco and fruit trade, aluminium production, tourism; monuments: the old town has many interesting buildings including several mosques; Turkish bridge; Karadjoz Beg Džamija mosque; event: diving competition from the Turkish bridge into R Neretva on July 27.

Mostoles *mo'sto-les*, 40 19N 3 53W, pop(1981) 149,649, town in Madrid prov, central Spain; 18 km SW of Madrid, in the centre of an agricultural region; railway; economy: electrical equipment, furniture.

Mosul *mō-sool'*, 36 21N 43 08E, pop(1970) 293,079, capital town of Neineva governorate, NW Iraq, on the W bank of the R Tigris, 352 km NNW of Baghdād; agricultural market centre; from the 8th to the 13th century Mosul was the chief town of N Mesopotamia, but it later declined under the Mongols and Turks; on the other side of the river are the ruins of ancient Nineveh; university (1967); railway; airfield; economy: power generation, oil refining, the manufacture of cement and textiles.

Motagua *mō-ta'gwa*, longest river in Guatemala, Central America; rises S of Santa Cruz del Quiché in the central highlands; flows E through Quiché dept then forms the boundary between Baja Verapaz (N) and Guatemala (S); continues E through El Progreso dept then turns NE through the depts of Zacapa and Izabal; discharges into the Bahía de Omoa on the Honduras border, 38 km E of Puerto Barrios; length 400 km; in the upper course it is known as the Río Grande; chief tributary Río Chiquimula; bananas are grown in the lower stretches of the valley.

Motala *mō-tah'la*, 58 34N 15 05E, pop(1982) 41,460, industrial town in Östergötland county, SE Sweden; on NE shore of L Vättern, 32 km WNW of Linköping; summer resort; incorporated in 1881, the town became important only after the construction of the Göta Canal; railway; economy: railway engineering, radios; monument: 14th-c church.

Motherwell *muTH'er-wel*, new African township in Port Elizabeth, SE Cape prov, South Africa; N of Bluewater Bay; built to house 120,000 African squatters; completed in 1985.

Motherwell, 55 48N 4 00W, pop(1981) 30,676, capital of Motherwell dist, Strathclyde, central Scotland; in Clydeside urban area, 20 km SE of Glasgow; united with Wishaw burgh in 1920; railway; economy: engineering; monument: 3 km N of Motherwell, in the village of Carfin, is the Grotto of Our Lady of Lourdes, to which pilgrimages are made.

Motril *mo-treel'*, 36 31N 3 37W, pop(1981) 39,784, industrial town on the Mediterranean coast, Granada prov, Andalucia, S Spain; 71 km S of Granada; economy: petroleum, bitumen, sugar, fruit, vegetables, paper.

Motru *mō'tru*, 44 33N 23 27E, pop(1983) 20,429, town in Gorj county, SW central Romania.

Mouila *mwee-la'*, 1 50S 11 02E, capital of Ngounié prov, SW Gabon, W Africa; on the R Ngounié, 305 km SSE of Libreville; economy: banking.

Moulay Idriss *moo'lay id'ris*, small town in Meknès prefecture, Centre-Sud prov, NW Morocco, N Africa; 30 km N of Meknès; a holy city containing the tomb of Moulay Idriss I, father of the founder of Fès; founded in 8th century; the site of the ancient Roman city of Volubilis lies 4 km W; event: *moussem* (fête) in May in honour of the town's founder Moulay Idriss.

Moulins *moo-lī*, 46 35N 3 19E, pop(1982) 25,548, manufacturing city and capital of Allier dept, Auvergne region, central France; on the Allier R, 93 km SE of Bourges; road and rail junction; a busy agric market; once the ancient capital of the independent duchy of Bourbon; economy: hosiery, brewing, tanning; monuments: 15th-c Gothic cathedral; 12 km W is the former Cluniac abbey of Souvigny founded in the 10th century, with 15th-c enlargement; there is an old quarter, with cobbled streets, old houses and a well-known 'Jacquemart' bell-tower (reconstructed after being burnt down in 1946).

Moulmein *mool-mayn'*, 16 30N 97 39E, pop(1973) 202,967, port and capital of Mon state, SE Burma; railway; airfield.

Moundou *moon-doo'*, 8 36N 16 02E, capital of Logone-Occidental prefecture, SW Chad, N central Africa; 420 km SSE of N'Djamena; airfield.

Mount Albert, pop(1981) 26,462, borough in N North Island, New Zealand; a residential suburb of Auckland.

Mount Aspiring *a-spīr'ing*, national park, SW South Island, New Zealand; N of Fiordland National Park; rises to 3,027 m at Mount Aspiring; in the N is Haast Pass (563 m), the most southerly route through the Southern Alps to the W coast; area 2,856 sq km; established in 1964.

Mount Athos, autonomous administration in Makedhonia region, Greece. See Pangaion Óros.

Mount Gam'bier, 37 51S 140 50E, pop(1981) 19,880, town in South East stat div, SE South Australia, Australia; W of Melbourne; built on the slopes of an extinct volcano from which it takes its name; railway; airfield; economy: agricultural trade, clothing, textiles; monuments: Black's Museum contains a collection of shells, rifles, pistols and Aboriginal artifacts; the Old Courthouse Museum charts Mount Gambier's pioneering days; the Town Hall (1876), built of pink dolomite and limestone with a clocktower; Centenary Tower on the summit of Mount Gambier (10 m high, with battlemented parapet, flat roof and balcony) was built to commemorate the centenary of the sighting and naming of Mount Gambier; nearby is the volcanic crater, the Blue Lake, whose waters change colour according to the season.

Mount Isa *ī'za*, 20 50S 139 29E, pop(1981) 23,679, town in North-West stat div, W Queensland, Australia; on the Leichhardt river, at the junction of the Flinders and Barkly highways; railway; airfield; economy: commercial, industrial and administrative centre for NW Queensland; mining (gold, opals, garnets; lead, zinc, silver, copper); the Mount Isa mine is the largest producer of lead and 2nd largest producer of silver in the western world; cattle farming; event: the Rotary Rodeo (Aug).

Mount Prospect, 42 04N 87 56W, pop(1980) 52,634, town in Cook county, NE Illinois, United States; 34 km NW of Chicago; railway.

Mount Roskill, pop(1981) 33,577, borough in N North Island, New Zealand; a residential suburb of Auckland.

Mount Vernon, 40 54N 73 49W, pop(1980) 66,713, town in Westchester county, SE New York, United States; suburb of New York City on the R Bronx; railway; laid out in 1852 by the Industrial Home Association as an alternative to high-rent locations in New York City.

Mountain Ash-Abercynon *-a-ber-ku'nun*, 51 42N 3 24W, pop(1981) 23,547, valley town in Cynon Valley dist, Mid Glamorgan, S Wales; on R Cynon, SE of Aberdare; railway; economy: coal mining, engineering.

Mountain View, 37 23N 122 05W, pop(1980) 58,655, city in Santa Clara county, W California, United States; SE of Palo Alto; railway.

Mountain Zebra, mountainous national park in central Cape prov, South Africa; near Cradock; area 65.36 sq km; established in 1937; protects the slow-breeding mountain zebra.

Mourne Mts *morn*, mountain range in SE Co Down, SE Northern Ireland; extends 24 km from Carlingford Lough NE to Dundrum Bay; a granitic hill range which supplies most of Belfast's water; rises to 852 m in Slieve Donard.

Mousalla, mountain in Bulgaria. See Musala.

Mouscron *moos-krō*, dist of Hainaut prov, Belgium; area 101 sq km; pop(1982) 72,769.

Mouscron, MOESKROEN *moos-kroon* (Flem), 50 44N 3 14E, pop(1982) 54,562, frontier town in Mouscron dist, NW Hainaut prov, Belgium; SW of Kortrijk; railway; economy: woven and tufted carpets and rugs.

Moyam'ba, dist in Southern prov, Sierra Leone, W Africa; pop(1974) 188,745; area 6,902 sq km; capital Moyamba.

Moyen-Chari *mwa-yen sha-ree'*, prefecture in S Chad, N central Africa; pop(1979) 524,000; area 45,180 sq km; drained by numerous rivers including the Chari, Man Dadji, Ouham and Bahr Béché; L Iro lies in the NE; capital Sarh; chief towns Kyabé, Moïssala and Maro; economy: petroleum.

Moyo *mō'yō*, 3 38N 31 43E, town in Nile prov, Uganda, E Africa; close to Uganda's NW frontier with Sudan, 40 km W of Nimule.

Mozambique *mō-zam-beek'*, official name People's Republic of Mozambique, REPÚBLICA POPULAR DE MOÇAMBIQUE (Port), a SE African republic bounded S by Swaziland, SW by South Africa, W by Zimbabwe, NW by Zambia and Malawi, N by Tanzania and E by the Mozambique Channel and the Indian Ocean; timezone GMT +2; area 789,800 sq km; pop(1984e) 13,413,000; capital Maputo; chief towns Lichinga, Pemba, Nampula, Quelimane, Tete, Chimoio, Beira, Inhambane and Xai-Xai; the majority of the pop belongs to local tribal groups including the Makua-Lomwe (37%, mainly in Nampula and Zambézia provs), the Shona (10%, in Manica and Sofala provs) and the Thonga (23%, in the S); there is also a small number of Europeans, Euro-Asians and Indians; most (60%) follow local beliefs with the remainder being either Christian (30%) or Muslim (10%); the official language is Portuguese but local dialects and Swahili are widely spoken; national holiday 25 June (Independence Day); since 1980 the unit of currency has been the metical of 100 centavos; membership of AfDB, FAO, G-77, GATT (de facto), ICAO, IFAD, ILO, IMO, ITU, NAM, OAU, SADCC, UN, UNESCO, UPU, WHO and WMO.

Physical description. The R Zambezi, Africa's 4th largest river, cuts the country in half. It enters Mozambique from Zimbabwe and Zambia at Zumbo, flows through the sizeable lake created by the Carona Bassa Dam and then SE past Tete to enter the Mozambique Channel between Quelimane and Beira. Mozambique's other main river is the Limpopo which enters the country at Pafuri and flows SE to meet the Mozambique Channel near Xai-Xai. S of the Zambezi the coast is low lying and typified by sandy beaches and mangroves. Inland there are low hills of volcanic origin and further N the high edge of the Zimbabwe plateau. The coast N of the Zambezi is more rugged and is backed by a narrower coastal plain. Inland there is a savannah plateau with a mean elevation of between 800 and 1,000 m. The highest ground is along the frontier with S Malawi which rises to 2,436 m at Mount Binga in Manica prov. Within Mozambique's borders is part of L Nyasa (L Malawi) (NW). The country's N border with Tanzania is, for the greater part of its length, formed by the R Rovuma.

Climate. Mozambique has a tropical climate. The coastal lowlands which are sheltered from the SE trade winds by the mountainous island of Madagascar have relatively low rainfall. The N coast is occasionally affected by Indian Ocean cyclones which bring heavy rain and high winds S through the Mozambique Channel. Most, however, pass E of Madagascar. Beira is representative of the central coast zone with an average annual rainfall of 1,520 mm and max daily temperatures ranging between 25°C and 32°C. Maputo is more representative of the drier S with an average annual rainfall of 760 mm and max daily temperatures ranging between 24°C and 31°C. Precipitation falls to between 500 and 750 mm in the drier areas of the inland lowlands, most notably the Zambezi valley. An average annual rainfall of 590 mm and average daily max temperatures ranging between 29°C and 37°C at Tete are indicative of general conditions inland. Throughout Mozambique there is one rainy season between Dec and March.

History, government and constitution. Originally inhabited by Bantu peoples who had migrated from the N during the first 4 centuries AD, the Mozambique coast was settled by Arab traders and visited by Portuguese explorers by the late 15th century. Coastal ports were developed to service ships sailing to and from the East Indies while inland exploration concentrated on the search for ivory, gold and slaves. Administered as part of Portuguese India since 1751 Mozambique acquired separate colonial status as Portuguese East Africa during the late 19th century. The colony became an Overseas Province of Portugal in 1951. In 1962 a number of political groups united to form the Frente de Libertação de Moçambique (FRELIMO) and 2 years later armed resistance to colonial rule began. In 1975 the country gained full independence from Portugal. Mozambique is a socialist one-party state. The party leader, who is president and head of state, appoints a council of about 20 ministers and presides over a 210-member legislative people's assembly. Local authority is vested in provincial and district governments.

Economy. Between 1970 and 1979 national income dropped by 42% as a result of the change from colonial status, the emigration of large numbers of Portuguese and Mozambicans, the end of a trade agreement with South Africa and international economic sanctions aimed at Southern Rhodesia. During the 1980s the economy has also been adversely affected by drought (1981-84), internal strife and a lack of foreign exchange. Eighty-five per cent of the pop is involved with agriculture either on state farms or in communally run villages. The main export crops include cashew nuts, tea, cotton, sugar cane, copra, sisal, groundnuts and fruit. For the domestic market the main crops include maize, rice, cassava and tobacco. Forestry and livestock raising are also important although cattle are severely affected by the tsetse fly in the N. Geological surveys have revealed the potential of minerals, indicating reserves of gemstones, diamonds, iron ore, copper, marble and alabaster, aluminium, fluorspar, coal, tin and gold. In 1981 industry was centred on coal mining at Moatize and tantalum metal production NW of Quelimane. On a smaller scale copper, asbestos, cement, clays, gem beryl and tourmaline, scrap mica and marine salt are also produced. There are also commercial reserves of oil and natural gas under exploration. The ports of Beira, Maputo and Nacala serve as outlets (by rail and sea) for mineral production destined for countries including Zimbabwe, South Africa, Swaziland, Malawi and Zambia. The USA, Portugal, France, Iraq, Japan and Singapore are also major trade partners.

Administrative divisions. Mozambique is divided into 10 provinces:

Province	*area (sq km)*	*pop(1980)*
Cabo Delgado	82,625	940,000
Niassa	129,055	514,000
Nampula	81,606	2,402,700
Zambézia	105,008	2,500,000
Tete	100,714	831,000
Manica	61,661	641,200
Sofala	68,018	1,065,200
Inhambane	68,615	997,600
Gaza	75,709	990,900
Maputo	25,756	491,800

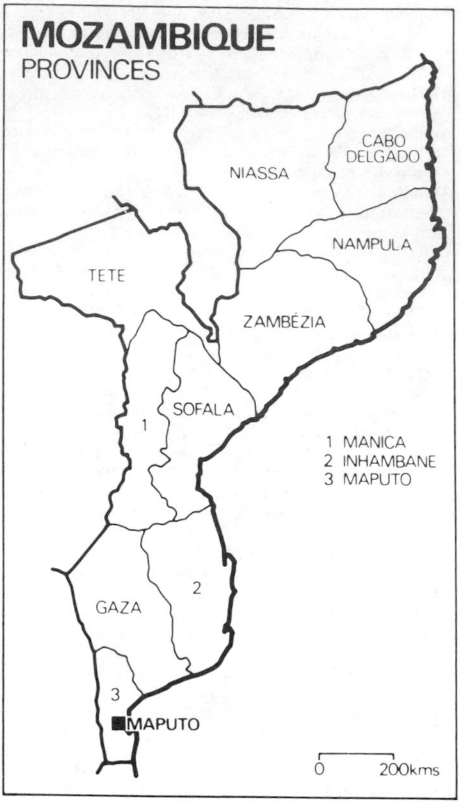

contd

Mozambique Channel, arm of the Indian Ocean, lying between India and the island of Madagascar; average depths of 55 m on the narrow continental shelf off the coast of Mozambique at the mouth of the Zambezi river; depths of 3,570 m are reached in the channel, between Madagascar and the submarine Mozambique Plateau, while depths of 4,980 m exist in the Natal Basin, between the Madagascar and Mozambique plateaus; Maputo and Sofala are the chief ports of Mozambique, both of which are developing as they are the seaward termini of important railways into interior Africa; the islands of the Comoros group and Mayotte lie to the N.

Mpika *um-pee'ka*, 11 50S 31 30E, town in Northern prov, Zambia, S central Africa; 195 km SSE of Kasama; railway; airfield.

Mpraeso *um-prī'se*, 6 36N 0 43W, town NW of Koforidua in Eastern region, S central Ghana, W Africa.

Msida *mi-see'dah*, 35 53N 14 30E, pop(1983e) 13,171, community on the main island of Malta, W of Valletta on Msida Creek, an inlet of Marsamxett Harbour.

M'Sila, department of N Algeria, N Africa; area 19,824 sq km; pop(1982) 500,364; chief town M'Sila.

Mtwara *um-twah'ra*, 10 17S 40 11E, pop(1978) 48,510, seaport capital of Mtwara region, SE Tanzania, E Africa; 56 km SE of Lindi; economy: craftwork, cashew nut trade.

Muang Khon Kaen *mwung kon ken*, KHON KAEN, 16 25N 102 50E, pop(1982) 108,444, city in E central Thailand; at the centre of the NE plateau, NE of Bangkok; university (1964); railway; airfield.

Muang Nakhon Sawan *mwung nah-kon' sa-wahn'*, NAKHON SAWAN, 15 42N 100 64E, pop(1982) 93,101, river port in central Thailand; at the confluence of the Ping and Nan rivers, NNE of Bangkok; port developed as part of the inland waterways project, providing a transport axis for the N and N central provs; airfield.

Muar *moo'ahr*, BANDAR MAHARANI *ban-dar' ma-ha-ra'nee*, 2 01N 102 35E, port town in Johor state, S Malaysia, SE Asia; on R Muar where it meets the Strait of Malacca, 145 km NW of Johor Bahru; airfield; economy: fruit, rubber, fishing.

Muara *mwah'ru*, 5 01N 115 01E, port in Brunei-Muara dist, Brunei, SE Asia; at the mouth of the R Brunei, 20 km from the capital at Bandar Seri Begawan; the main port for the capital since the opening of a deep-water port in 1972.

Mubarraz, Al, 25 30N 49 40E, pop(1974) 54,325, N oasis suburb of Al Hufūf, Eastern prov, E Saudi Arabia; railway; economy: oil.

Mubende *moo-ben'day*, 00 35N 31 24E, town in N Buganda prov, Uganda, E Africa; 140 km WNW of Kampala.

Mufulira *moo-foo-lee'ru* ('place of abundance'), 12 30S 28 12E, pop(1980) 149,778, mining city in Copperbelt prov, Zambia, S central Zambia; 65 km NW of Ndola; 4th largest city in Zambia; the 2nd largest underground copper mine in the world is located nearby; railway; economy: copper mining, clothing, explosives.

Muğla *moo-la'*, maritime prov in SW Turkey; bounded W by the Aegean Sea and S by the Mediterranean; pop(1980) 438,145; area 13,338 sq km; capital Muğla; economy: minerals, grain, tobacco, sesame, olives.

Muharraq, Al *moo-hah'rek*, 26 15N 50 39E, pop(1981) 61,853, 2nd largest city in the State of Bahrain; on Muharraq I, NE of Bahrain I; airport (1934).

Mühlhausen *mül-how'zun*, MÜLHAUSEN IN THÜRINGEN, 51 13N 10 28E, pop(1981) 43,348, town in Mühlhausen dist, Erfurt, SW East Germany; N of Eisenach, near the W German frontier; railway.

Mujeres, Isla *moo-her'es* ('island of women'), resort island in the Caribbean, off the NE coast of Quintana Roo, Mexico; 8 km long by 0.75 km wide; linked by boat to Punta Sam and Puerto Juárez.

Mukallā, Al *moo-ka'lu*, 14 33N 49 02E, pop(1981e) 50,000, seaport capital of Ḩaḑramawt governorate, South Yemen; on Mukallā Bay, an inlet of the Gulf of Aden, 480 km ENE of Aden; airfield.

Mukden, capital of Liaoning prov, NE China. See Shenyang.

Mukhā, Al, MOCHA *moKH'a*, 12 52N 43 00E, seaport in N Yemen, at the N end of the entrance to the Red Sea (Bāb al Mandab); noted for the export of coffee during the 16th and 17th centuries; it gave its name not only to its coffee but also to Mocha stones, agates with dendritic markings.

Mulan'je, dist in Southern region, Malawi, SE Asia; area 3,450 sq km; pop(1977) 477,546.

Mulanje, Mount, 16 00S 35 37E, mountain in S Malawi, SE Africa; at 3,000 m it is the highest peak in Malawi.

Mulde *mool'de*, river, East Germany; rises in the Erzgebirge range and flows N about 250 km to meet the R Elbe near Dessau.

Mülheim *mül'hīm*, 51 26N 6 35E, pop(1983) 177,200, commercial and manufacturing city in Düsseldorf dist, Nordrhein-Westfalen (North Rhine-Westphalia) prov, W Germany; on the R Ruhr near its mouth 11 km WSW of Essen; railway; economy: iron and steel, building materials, construction.

Mulhouse *mul-ooz*, MULHAUSEN *mul'how-zen* (Ger), 47 45N 7 21E, pop(1982) 113,794, industrial and commercial river port in Haut-Rhin dept, Alsace region, NE France; on the R Ill and the Rhine-Rhône Canal, 35 km S of Colmar; 2nd largest town in Alsace, after Strasbourg; Mulhouse was an imperial free city from 1308, allied with the Swiss 1515-1648, an independent republic until 1798 when it voted to become French, under German rule 1871-1918, reverted to France in 1918; a model working men's colony was founded here in 1853; university; railway; economy: linen-weaving and spinning, printed fabrics, dyes, machinery, chemicals, fertilizers, car manufacturing (Peugeot); monuments: Renaissance town hall (1552, has a council chamber); Protestant church of St-Étienne; the Musée National de l'Automobile, 2 km from the town centre, contains some 600 vintage and veteran cars; the French Railway Museum, in the suburb of Dornach, has locomotives and rolling-stock from 1844 to the present day; in the Place de l'Europe is the 31-storey Tour de l'Europe, with a revolving restaurant at the top.

Mull, island in Argyll and Bute dist, Strathclyde region, W Scotland; 2nd largest of the Inner Hebrides with an area of 925 sq km; separated from the mainland to the NE by a narrow channel (Sound of Mull) and to the E and SE by the Firth of Lorne; mountainous terrain which peaks to 3169m at Ben More; chief town is Tobermory in the NE (in Tobermory bay there is reputed to be a Spanish galleon sunk, with its treasure, 1588); ferry link to Oban on the mainland to the E; ancient castles include Aros and Duart, seat of the clan Maclean; economy: fishing, crofting, tourism.

Mullaittivu *moo-lī tee'voo*, 9 15N 80 48E, pop(1981) 7,192, capital of Mullaittivu dist, Northern prov, Sri Lanka; on the NE coast, NW of Trincomalee, on a lagoon of the Bay of Bengal; 90% of the pop in the dist are Tamil.

Mullingar *mu-lin-gahr'*, MUILEANN CEARR (Gael), 53 32N 7 20W, pop(1981) 11,703, market town and capital of Westmeath county, Leinster, E Irish Republic; on Royal Canal, WNW of Dublin; railway; economy: cattle trade.

Multan *mool-tan'*, 30 10N 71 36E, pop(1981) 730,000, city in Punjab prov, Pakistan; 314 km SW of Lahore; captured in 1006 by Mahmud of Ghazi and in 1338 by Tamerlane; ruled 1526-1779 by the emperors of Delhi and by the Afghans until 1818 when the city was seized by the Sikhs under the leadership of Ranjit Sikh; came under British sovereignty in 1849; airfield; railway; linked by natural gas pipeline to Sui and Karachi, economy: trade in grain, cotton, wool and fruits; monuments: 14th-c tombs of Muslim saints.

Mulu *moo-loo*, national park in Sarawak state, E Malaysia, SE Asia; on the island of Borneo, near the NE border with Sabah; the area around Gunong Mulu has one of the world's largest limestone cave systems; established as a park in 1975; an expedition of the Royal Geographical Society explored the caves in 1978.

Mun *moon*, river in E and central Thailand; rises in the hills NE of Bangkok and flows WSW, meeting the Khong R at Khong Chiam; length 673 km.

München *mün'KHun*, MUNICH *myoo'niKH* (Eng), 48 08N 11 35E, pop(1983) 1,284,300, capital of Bayern (Bavaria) prov, W Germany; on the R Isar, 40-60 km from the Alps; third largest city in Germany; founded in 1158 and became capital of Bavaria in the 14th century; site of summer Olympic Games (1972); university (1471); technical university (1868); railway; economy: mineral oil products, chemicals, pharmaceuticals, cosmetics and perfumes, rubber, precision engineering, optical and electrical apparatus, building materials, machine building, motor vehicles, military and civil aircraft, defence systems, paper, printing and publishing, clothing, animal feedstuffs, brewing, cigarettes, confectionery, wine, dairy produce, fruit and vegetables; monuments: church of St Peter (1181), town hall (1470).

Muncie *mun'si*, 40 12N 85 23W, pop(1980) 77,216, county seat of Delaware county, E Indiana, United States; on W fork of the R White, 27 km NE of Anderson; settled in 1824, achieving city status in 1865; university (1918);

railway; economy: electrical equipment, glassware, furniture, vehicle parts.

Munich, city in W Germany. See München.

Munku-Sardyk, Gora *moon-koo-sur-dik'*, 51 48N 100 30E, highest peak in the Vostochnyy Sayan range (E Sayan Mts), on the Soviet-Mongolian border, W of Mondy; height 3,491 m; has small glaciers.

Münster *mün'stur*, N dist of Nordrhein-Westfalen (North Rhine-Westphalia) prov, W Germany; pop(1983) 2,412,000; area 6,898 sq km; capital Münster.

Münster, MÜNSTER IN WESTFALEN, 51 58N 7 37E, pop(1983) 273,500, capital city of Münster dist, Nordrhein-Westfalen (North Rhine-Westphalia) prov, W Germany; on the R Aa and on the Dortmund-Ems Canal, 125 km NNE of Köln (Cologne); see of a Roman Catholic bishop; Treaty of Westphalia (1648), ending Thirty Years War, signed here; university (1780); railway; economy: civil engineering, construction, gases; monument: cathedral (1225-65).

Munster *mun'stur*, province in S Irish Republic; bounded S and W by Atlantic Ocean, N by Connacht and NE by Leinster; comprises the counties of Clare, Cork, Kerry, Limerick, Tipperary (N and S Ridings) and Waterford; pop(1981) 998,315; area 24,127 sq km.

Muqdisho, MOGADISHU *mo-gu-di'shoo* (Eng), MOGADISCIO (Ital), 2 02N 45 21E, pop(1982) 377,000, seaport capital of Somalia, NE Africa; on the Indian Ocean coast in Banaadir prov; taken by the Sultan of Zanzibar in 1871; the following year the Sultan leased the area along with Marka to the Italians; both areas were sold in 1905; occupied by British forces during World War II (1941); deep-water port built with World Bank assistance; university (1954); airport; economy: refining of imported oil, uranium mining, food processing; monuments: fort (including museum); 13th-c mosques; cathedral (1928).

Mur *moor*, river rising in the Hohe Tauern of Austria; flows E then S for 348 km before following the Austro-Yugoslav border for 32 km; flows SE across Yugoslavia and into Hungary where it meets the R Drau at Legrad; length 444 km; navigable below Graz.

Muramvya *moo-ra-vee'ya*, 3 14S 29 36E, capital of prov of same name, Burundi, central Africa; 80 km NW of Gitega.

Murchison Falls, Uganda. See Kabalega.

Murcia *moor'thya, mur'sha* (Eng), region and prov of SE Spain between Valencia and Andalucia; pop(1981) 957,903; area 11,313 sq km; thinly populated, except in the river valleys where oranges, lemons and dates are grown, the region is largely dry steppeland growing esparto grass and low scrub; apart from coastal tourism, the mining of lead, zinc and iron plays an important part in the economy.

Murcia, 38 20N 1 10W, pop(1981) 288,631, capital of Murcia prov, SE Spain; on R Segura, 401 km SE of Madrid; bishopric; university (1915); airport, railway; university (1915); economy: agricultural market and manufacture of silk, textiles, flour, pharmaceuticals, tinned food and leather goods; monuments: 14th-c cathedral; Salzillo museum featuring the polychrome wood sculptures of Francisco Salzillo; events: Holy Week followed by Spring Festival with fancy dress parades, battle of flowers, etc; Our Lady of La Fuensanta in Sept.

Mureş *moo'resh*, county in N central Romania, to the W of the E Carpathian Mts; pop(1983) 614,296; area 6,696 sq km; capital Tîrgu Mureş.

Mureş, river in E central Romania and E Hungary; rising in the Carpathians and flowing NW, SW and W to meet the R Tisza at Szeged in Hungary; length 880 km; navigable for 320 km.

Mur'freesboro, 35 51N 86 24W, pop(1980) 32,845, county seat of Rutherford county, central Tennessee, United States; on the W fork of the R Stone, 50 km SE of Nashville; site of the battle of Murfreesboro (or Stone River) 31 Dec 1862 to 2 Jan 1863; university (1909); railway; economy: food processing, electrical equipment, furniture and rubber tyres.

Müritz-See, LAKE MÜRITZ *moor-ets*, lake in Neubrandenburg county, East Germany; largest natural lake in East Germany; area 117 sq km.

Murmansk *moor'munsk*, ROMANOV-NA-MURMANE (-1917), 68 59N 33 08E, pop(1983) 405,000, seaport capital of Murmanskaya oblast, Rossiyskaya, Soviet Union; on the E coast of Kol'skiy Zaliv (Kola Bay) of the Barents Sea, 50 km from the open sea; founded in 1916; it is the Soviet Union's most important fishing port and the northernmost tourist centre of the USSR; an ice-free seaport, it stands 5th in the USSR for cargo turnover; railway; airfield; economy: fishing, fish processing, shipbuilding and repairing, building materials.

Murrat el Kubra, Buheiret, lake in NE Egypt. See Great Bitter Lake.

Murray, longest river in Australia; rises in the Australian Alps near Mount Kosciusko S of Canberra in New South Wales; flows 2,570 km W and WNW past Albury, Swan Hill, Mildura, then S past Murray Bridge, through L Alexandrina to enter the Southern Ocean at Encounter Bay SE of Adelaide; it forms the border between New South Wales and Victoria for 1,930 km; 640 km from its mouth it receives the Darling river (the Murray-Darling is 3,750 km long); the waters of the Murray river are used extensively for irrigation and as a source of hydroelectric power; navigation is generally confined to tourist steamers; major tributaries include the Darling, Murrumbidgee, Mitta Mitta, Goulburn, Campaspe and Loddon rivers.

Murray, 40 40N 111 53W, pop(1980) 25,750, town in Salt Lake county, N Utah, United States; a suburb 12 km S of Salt Lake City; railway.

Murray Bridge, 35 10S 139 17E, pop(1981) 8,664, river port in Murray Lands stat div, SE South Australia, Australia; on the lower Murray river, ESE of Adelaide; railway; economy: dairy products; the town has the world's smallest cathedral, and the southern hemisphere's largest milk and cheese factory.

Murree *mu'ree*, 33 55N 73 26E, hill resort in Punjab prov, N Pakistan; NE of Rawalpindi at an alt of 2,295 m.

Murrumbidgee *mu-rem-bij'ee*, river in S New South Wales, Australia; rises in the Snowy Mts near Cooma and flows 1,759 km N through Australian Capital Territory then W past the towns of Wagga Wagga, Narrandera and Hay before finally joining the Murray river on the New South Wales-Victoria border; its major tributary is the Lachlan river; at an alt below 600 m, the floodplain of the Murrumbidgee and the Molonglo rivers forms the major part of the low land of the Australian Capital Territory, irrigating a large agricultural basin.

Murska Sobota *moor'ska so-bo-ta*, 46 40N 16 11E, pop(1981) 64,299, town in NE Slovenija republic, Yugoslavia; on R Lendava, 40 km ENE of Maribor; railway; economy: grain, meat and poultry trade.

Murud, Gunong *goo-noong' moo'rood*, 3 54N 115 45E, the highest mountain in Sarawak state, E Malaysia, SE Asia; rising to 2,423 m near the border with Sabah state.

Mururo'a, remote atoll in French Polynesia, S Pacific Ocean; pop(1985) 3,000, used by France as a nuclear testing site; between 1966 and 1974 nuclear tests were carried out in the atmosphere; since then tests have been held between 700 and 1,200 m underground within the basalt remains of an extinct volcano.

Mürz *moorts*, river in N Austria, rising in the Schneealpe of Niederösterreich state, and flowing SE and SW to meet the R Mur at Bruck; length 85 km.

Muş *moosh*, mountainous prov in E Turkey; pop(1980) 302,406; area 8,196 sq km; capital Muş.

Musa'la or **Mous'alla**, also **Rila Dagh**, 42 10N 23 25E, mountain in Rila Planina (Rila Mts) of W Bulgaria rising to 2,925 m; this is the highest point in Bulgaria and was called Stalin Peak between the 1930s and 1960s.

Musandam *mu-san'dam*, point on the SE Arabian peninsula sticking out into the Strait of Hormuz; a governorate of Oman separated from the rest of the country by part of the UAE.

Musay'id *moo-sa-eed'*, UMM SAID *oom' sa-eed'*, 25 00N 51 40E, pop(1975) 6,000, industrial port town on the SE coast of Qatar Peninsula, State of Qatar; 30 km SSE of Ad Dawḥah (Doha); economy: 2 oil refineries, petrochemical plant, liquefied natural gas plant, fertilizer plant, and a huge steel complex; there is a pipeline from the Dukhān oil field.

Muscat, capital town of the Sultanate of Oman, SE Arabian peninsula. See Masqaṭ.

Musgrave Ranges *muz'grayv*, mountain ranges in NW South Australia, close to the Northern Territory border, to which they run parallel; extending 80 km, they rise to 1,440 m at Mount Woodroffe, highest point in the state.

Muskegon *mu-skee'gen* (Algonquian, 'swamp-at'), 43 14N 86 16W, pop(1980) 40,823, county seat of Muskegon county, W Michigan, United States; port on L Michigan at the mouth of the R Muskegon, 56 km WNW of Grand Rapids; railway; economy: machinery and transport equipment.

Muskogee, 35 45N 95 22W, pop(1980) 40,011, county seat of Muskogee county, E Oklahoma, United States; near the confluence of Arkansas, Verdigris, and Neosho rivers, 70 km SE of Tulsa; named after an Indian tribe; railway; economy: important transportation, trade, and industrial centre in an agricultural region; food-processing plants; monument: Five Civilized Tribes museum; event: Azalea Festival (April).

Musselburgh, 55 57N 3 04W, pop(1981) 19,081, town in East Lothian dist, Lothian, E central Scotland; on the S shore of the Firth of Forth, at the mouth of the R Esk, 9 km E of Edinburgh; racecourse; economy: engineering.

Musters, Lago *moos'ters*, lake in the Patagonian Highlands of S Chubut, Patagonia, S Argentina; area 434 sq km; length 41 km; width 5-13 km; 9 km W of L Colhué Huapí, to which it is linked by a small stream; receives the Río Senguerr.

Mutare or **Mutari** *moo-tah'ri*, formerly UMTALI, 19 00S 32 40E, pop(1982) 70,000, capital of Manicaland prov, Zimbabwe, S Africa; 220 km SE of Harare, near Mozambique frontier; 29 km SE are the Vumba botanical gardens; railway; airfield; economy: mining, farming, tobacco.

Muyinga *moo-yin'ga*, 2 50S 30 20E, capital of prov of same name, Burundi, central Africa; NE of Gitega.

Muzaffargarh *moo-zuf'fur-gur*, 30 04N 71 15E, pop(1981) 53,000, city in Punjab prov, Pakistan, close to the R Chenab, 24 km SW of Multan; railway; trading centre for the surrounding agricultural region.

Mwali, island of Comoros. See Mohéli.

Mwan'za, dist in Southern region, Malawi, SE Africa; area 2,295 sq km; pop(1977) 71,405.

Mwanza, 2 30S 32 54E, pop(1978) 110,611, lakeport capital of Mwanza region, NW Tanzania, E Africa; a railway terminus on the S shore of L Victoria, 280 km N of Tabora; economy: fishing, textiles and textile machinery parts.

Mweru, Lake *mwe'roo*, LAC MOERO, lake in central Africa; situated on the frontier between Zaire and Zambia; alt 919 m; island of Kilwa located at S end of lake; receives Lualpula river; Luvua river flows from N end; main lakeside settlement is Kilwa (Zaire).

Mwinilunga *mwee-nee-loong'ga*, 11 44S 24 24E, town in North-West prov, Zambia, S central Africa; 240 km NW of Kasempa.

Myingyan *myin'jan*, 21 25N 95 20E, pop(1973) 220,129, town in Mandalay division, central Burma; situated on the Irrawaddy river; railway.

Myitkyina *myit-chee'na*, 25 24N 97 25E, capital of Kachin state, N Burma; at the head of low water navigation on R Irrawaddy, NNE of Mandalay; railway; economy: rice, tobacco, sugar; amber and jade mining to the NW.

Mymenshingh or **Mymensingh** *mī'mun-sing*, region in N central Bangladesh; includes Kishoreganj, Mymenshingh and Netrokona districts; pop(1981) 6,568,000; area 9,668 sq km; bounded to N by Meghalaya, India and to the E by the Brahmaputra (Jamuna) river; capital Mymenshingh.

Mymenshingh, MAIMANSINGH, NASIRABAD, 24 45N 90 23E, pop(1981) 190,911, river port capital of Mymenshingh dist and region, N central Bangladesh; on a channel of the R Brahmaputra (Jamuna); agricultural university (1961); railway; economy: trading in sugar cane, rice, jute, oilseeds, tobacco and mustards; formerly noted for its manufacture of glass bangles.

Mysłowice *mis-wo-vit'ze*, 50 15N 19 09E, pop(1983) 84,800, mining and industrial town in Katowice voivodship, S Poland; E of Katowice, at confluence of Czarna and Biała Przemsza rivers; known as 'three emperors' corner' after the partitioning of Poland by Prussia, Russia and Austria in 1815; railway.

Mysore *mī-sor'*, MAISUR, 12 17N 76 41E, pop(1981) 476,000, city in Karnataka state, SW India; 850 km SSE of Bombay and 400 km WSW of Madras; prior to the formation of the state of Karnataka, Mysore was the dynastic capital of the Mysore state; the city was founded in the 16th century; linked to Bangalore by rail; university (1916); known as 'the garden city of India' because of its wide streets and numerous parks; monuments: in the city centre is the maharaja's palace, within an ancient fort which was rebuilt in the 18th century; On Chamundi Hill to the SE of the city is the statue of Nandi, the sacred bull of Shiva, a sacred place of pilgrimage.

Mystic (Algonquian, 'big-(tidal)-river'), 41 21N 71 58W, pop(1980e) 3,000, historic seaport suburb of Stonington, S Connecticut, United States; at the mouth of the Mystic river; monument: famous maritime museum.

Mývatn *mee-vah'tun*, shallow lake in Nordurland eystra region, NE Iceland; E of Akureyri and S of Húsavík; Iceland's 4th largest lake, area 37 sq km; a popular tourist location, noted for its scenery and wildlife; interesting volcanic formations; a small village has developed around a diatomite factory; geothermal power station at Krafla.

Mzim'ba, dist in Northern region, Malawi, SE Africa; area 10,430 sq km; pop(1977) 301,361.

N

Naab *nahp*, river in Bayern (Bavaria) prov, W Germany; rises as the Waldnaab 3 km S of Bärnau; flows generally S, past Weiden and Schwandorf, to the R Donau (Danube), 5 km W of Regensburg; length 160 km; navigable length 20 km; drainage basin area 5,225 sq km; chief tributaries Fichtelnaab and the Vils.

Naas *nays*, NÁS NA RIOGH (Gael), 53 13N 6 39W, pop(1981) 8,345, market town and capital of Kildare county, Leinster, Irish Republic; on branch of Grand Canal, SW of Dublin; former capital of the kings of Leinster; noted horse racing area.

Nabeul *nah-bul'*, governorate in NE Tunisia, N Africa; pop(1984) 461,405; capital Nabeul; economy: citrus.

Nablus *na-bloos'*, sub-district of Judea-Samaria dist, Israel, in the Israeli-occupied West Bank of Jordan.

Nablus, governorate (*muhafaza*) of the Israeli-occupied West Bank, NW Jordan; capital Nablus.

Nablus, 32 13N 35 16E, pop(1971e) 44,200, capital town of Nablus governorate, Israeli-occupied West Bank, NW Jordan; 48 km N of Jerusalem; market centre for the surrounding agricultural region (wheat, olives, sheep, goats); monument: Great Mosque (rebuilt 1167 as church of the Crusaders).

Naca'la, 14 30S 40 37E, seaport in Maiaia dist, Nampula prov, Mozambique, SE Africa; N of Moçambique and S of Pemba; one of 3 major outlets for mineral production.

Nacaome *na-ka-ōm'ee*, 13 30N 87 31W, capital of Valle dept, S Honduras, Central America; SW of Tegucigalpa, near the Golfo de Fonseca.

Náchod *na'KHot*, 50 26N 16 10E, pop(1984) 20,034, town in Východočeský region, Czech Socialist Republic, NW central Czechoslovakia; NE of Hradec Králové, near Polish frontier; railway; monument: 14th-c cathedral.

Na'cka, 59 17N 18 12E, pop(1982) 58,398, town in Stockholm county, SE Sweden; a suburb SE of Stockholm; a city since 1950.

Nacogdoches *nak-e-dō'chez*, 31 36N 94 39W, pop(1980) 27,149, county seat of Nacogdoches county, E Texas, United States; 215 km NNE of Houston; named after an Indian tribe; the Spanish made their first permanent settlement here in 1779; after the Louisiana Purchase, the city was twice seized in American raids, and in 1820 100 American families were issued land grants here; this settlement resulted in the Fredonian Rebellion of 1826; the city was actively involved in the Texas Revolution of 1835-36; university; railway; economy: lumbering, clay refining, meat packing and the manufacture of feeds and fertilizer, wood products, and brass valves; tourism is an important industry, the city being situated in a large recreational area.

Nador *na-dor'*, 35 12N 2 55W, pop(1982) 62,040, seaport capital of Nador prefecture, Oriental prov, NE Morocco, N Africa; on the Mediterranean coast 16 km S of Melilla; the centre of a sheep farming region; airfield.

Næstved *nest'veTH*, 55 14N 11 47E, pop(1981) 38,455, town in Storstrøm county, S Sjælland (Zealand), Denmark; on R Susa; railway; monument: St Peter's church, largest Gothic church in Denmark.

Nafūd *na-food'*, desert area in the N part of the Arabian Peninsula, connected to the Rub al Khālī (S) by the Dahnā, a corridor of gravel plains and sand dunes; approx 290 km long and 225 km wide; occasional violent windstorms have formed crescent-shaped dunes, rising to heights of 183 m; this area of white-red sand, which occupies a structural depression, is surrounded by sandstone outcrops; dates, vegetables, barley, and fruit are grown in oases, particularly near the Hejāz Mts.

Nagaland *nah'ga-land*, state in NE India; pop(1981) 773,281; area 16,527 sq km; bounded N by Assam state and Arunchal Pradesh union territory, W by Assam state, S by Manipur state and E by Burma; the Barail range lies to the SW of the state which is crossed by the Dayang, Dikhor and Tuzu rivers; Nagaland is divided into 7 districts; administrative centre Kohima; the state is governed by a 60-member State Assembly; more than 80% of the population is employed in agriculture, the principal crop being rice; terraced slopes and wet paddy cultivation are common in the Kohima district, while a traditional form of shifting cultivation (known as *jhumming*) is practised elsewhere; 17.6% of the state is under forest; there are no railways or airfields within the state; a national highway links Kohima to the states of Assam and Manipur; formerly the Naga Hills-Tuensang territory of Assam, Nagaland became a state of the Indian Union in 1961; a strong movement for independence exists amongst the Naga tribesmen; the 'Revolutionary Government of Nagaland', a breakaway government of the Naga Federal Government, was dissolved in 1973; talks with the Naga tribes underground movement produced the Shillong Peace Agreement in Nov 1975.

Nagano *na-ga'nō*, 36 39N 138 10E, pop(1980) 324,360, capital of Nagano prefecture, Chūbu region, central Honshū island, Japan; on a branch of the R Shinano, 178 km NW of Tōkyo; founded in 7th century AD; university; railway; monuments: Buddhist temple and monastery.

Nagasaki *na-ga-sa'kee*, 32 45N 129 52E, pop(1980) 447,091, capital of Nagasaki prefecture, W Kyūshū island, Japan; first Japanese port opened to foreign trade; visited by the Portuguese in 1545; opened to the Dutch in 1560, the USA in 1854 and other Western countries in 1858; became a centre for missionaries, leading to the persecution of Christians from 1597 onwards, with 3,125 Christians martyred in the 17th century; target for the 2nd atomic bomb of World War II which was dropped here on 9 Aug 1945, killing or wounding c.75,000 people and destroying over one-third of the city; university (1949); railway; airport to N; economy: fishing, shipbuilding, engineering, metal products; monuments: the R Nakajima near the Suwa jinja temple is crossed by several stone bridges, including the Megane bashi, or Spectacles Bridge, built in 1634 by a Chinese priest; the Sofuku ji pavilions contain a huge bronze cauldron used to feed poor people during famine; the houses of 3 British traders and industrialists have associations with a (mythical) Madame Butterfly; in the Peace Park is a tall peace statue which commemorates the victims of the 2nd atom bomb; event: Suwa Shrine festival in Oct.

Nagoya *na-gō'ya*, 35 08N 136 53E, pop(1980) 2,087,902, port capital of Aichi prefecture, Chūbu region, central Honshū island, Japan; on NE shore of Ise-wan Bay; the city did not develop until the 17th century, when the Emperor Tokugawa Ieyasu built a castle here; university (1939); institute of technology (1905); railway; airport; economy: engineering, metal products, bicycles, watches, sewing machines, textiles; monuments: Nagoya Castle (destroyed during World War II and rebuilt in 1959) contains a museum with a collection of weapons and painted sliding doors; the Atsuta Shrine, which was founded in the 1st or 2nd century AD, is one of the oldest and most sacred shrines in Japan, containing the royal sword, one of the 3 emblems of the emperors of Japan; Tokugawa art museum contains objects which belonged to the Tokugawa family; in a pavilion near Nittai-ji temple are 500 painted figures of the deity Rakan dating from the 18th century.

Nagpur *nahg'poor*, 21 08N 79 10E, pop(1981) 1,298,000, city in Maharashtra state, W central India; 675 km ENE of Bombay, on the R Pench; founded in the 18th century; the fortified hill of Sitabaldi in the centre of the town was the scene of the final British overthrow of the Mahrattas in 1817; former capital of Berar and Madhya Pradesh states; university (1923); airfield; linked by rail to Bhopal and Raipur; economy: cotton textiles, paper, trade in oranges.

Nagykanizsa *no'dy'-kon-i-zho*, 46 28N 17 00E, pop(1984e) 55,000, town in Zala county, W Hungary; 100 km WNW of Pécs; economy: grain and livestock trade, foodstuffs.

Nagykörös *no'dy'-kü'rüsh*, 47 5N19 48E, pop(1984e) 27,000, town in Pest county, N Hungary; NNE of Kecskemét; economy: market centre for grain, fruit and grape-growing region.

Na'ha, 26 10N 127 40E, pop(1980) 295,778, port capital of Okinawa prefecture, SW Okinawa island, Japan; on the W coast on the China Sea; university; airport; economy: pottery, textiles, sugar, fishing.

Nahariya *na-ha-ree'a*, 33 01N 35 04E, seaside resort town in North dist, NW Israel; on the Mediterranean Sea, 30 km NE of Haifa; founded by Jews in 1934 as an agricultural settlement; railway.

Nahuel Huapí, Andean national park in NW Río Negro and SW Neuquén provs, Argentina; area 3,300 sq km; established in 1934; borders W with Chile; includes L Nahuel Huapí (area 550 sq km); the resort town of San Carlos de Bariloche is at the SE end of the lake.

Nailsea, 51 26N 2 43W, pop(1981) 15,191, town in Woodspring dist, Avon, SW England; W of Bristol.

Nairn, 57 35N 3 53W, pop(1981) 7,705, capital of Nairn dist, Highland region, NE Scotland; on the S shore of the Moray Firth, on the R Nairn, 12 km E of Fort George; railway; economy: tourist resort; monuments: Nairn Fishertown Museum; 8 km SW of the town is Cawdor castle, dating from 1372.

Nairobi *ni-ro'bee*, 1 17S 36 50E, pop(1984e) 1,161,000 prov and capital of Kenya, E Africa; on the central Kenya plateau, 450 km NW of Mombasa and midway between the Indian Ocean and L Victoria; largest city in E Africa, highly developed communications and commerce centre; expanded rapidly in the 20th century; was seat of the British governor of Kenya; headquarters of the United Nations Environment Programme Secretariat; university (1956); airport (16 km); monuments: cathedral (1963), Sikh temple, national museum (including largest collection of African butterflies in the world), Snake Park with around 200 species of snake.

Najaf, An *an na'jaf*, governorate in S central Iraq, bounded SW by Saudi Arabia; pop(1977) 389,680; area 26,834 sq km; capital An Najaf; the R Euphrates (Al Furāt) lowland merges into desert in the SW.

Najaf, An, 31 59N 44 19E, pop(1970) 179,160, capital town of An Najaf governorate, S central Iraq; on R Euphrates; on the highway between Al Basrah and Baghdād.

Najafābād *na-jaf'a-bad*, 32 38N 51 23E, pop(1983) 113,835, town in Najafābād dist, Eşfahān, central Iran; 30 km W of Eşfahān; noted for its pomegranates.

Najd, tribal prov of Saudi Arabia, occupying the centre of the Arabian Peninsula; it is a vast plateau ranging in height from 762 m to 1,525 m; population is concentrated around scattered oases in the E, such as Ar Riyāḍ (Riyadh); became the centre of the Wahabi movement in the mid-18th century; the union of Najd and Hejāz in 1932 led to the formation of the Kingdom of Saudi Arabia.

Najrān *nej-ran'*, 17 31N 44 19E, pop(1974) 47,500, oasis town in Najrān prov, SW Saudi Arabia; close to the border with N Yemen; airfield; economy: agriculture (dates, alfalfa, wheat, millet, stock raising).

Nakhon Ratchasima *nah-kon' rah-chah-see'mah*, 15 00N 102 06E, pop(1982) 89,261, ancient walled city and trade centre in E central Thailand; on R Mun, on the edge of the NE plateau, 260 km NE of Bangkok; railway; monuments: many temples.

Nakhon Sawan, river port in Thailand. See Muang Nakhon Sawan.

Nakskov *nahk'skow*, 54 50N 11 10E, pop(1981) 16,218, seaport and industrial town on W coast of Lolland I, at head of Nakskov Fjord, in Storstrøm county, Denmark; rail terminus; economy: sugar refining, shipyard; monument: 15th-c St Nicholas church.

Naktong *nak-tong*, NAKDONGGANG, longest river in Korea; rises in central Korea, flows S then SE to enter the Korea Strait to the W of Pusan; length 525 km.

Nakuru *na-koo'roo*, 0 16S 36 04E, pop(1979) 93,000, (1984e) 130,000, industrial town in Rift Valley prov, W central Kenya, E Africa; 160 km NW of Nairobi; nearby is Menengai Crater (2,260 m); SSE is the 52 sq km L Nakuru, a salt lake with the world's largest colony of pink flamingoes.

Nal'chik *nal'chik*, 43 31N 43 38E, pop(1983) 218,000, capital city of Kabardino-Balkarskaya ASSR, S European Rossiyskaya, Soviet Union; on the R Nal'chik, in the N foothills of the Bol'shoy Kavkaz (Greater Caucasus) range; founded in 1817-18 as a fortification; now a health and tourist resort; university (1957); railway; on the highway between Rostov-na-Donu and Baku; economy: machine building, metallurgy, electrical engineering, chemicals.

Nam Co, salt lake in central Xizang aut region, W China; situated to the N of Lhasa; area 1,920 sq km; alt 4,718 m; the highest large salt lake in China; regarded as a holy place by Tibetans, the people of Xizang aut region.

Namangan *nu-mun-gan'*, 40 59N 71 41E, pop(1983) 256,000, capital city of Namanganskaya oblast, Uzbekskaya SSR, S Soviet Union; on the R Syr-Dar'ya; railway; economy: cotton ginning, silk, clothing, footwear, foodstuffs, chemicals.

Namaqualand *num-a'ku-land* or *na-ma'kwa-lant* (Afrik), region in S Namibia and W South Africa, SW Africa; comprises (1) Little Namaqualand extending S from the Orange river on the Namibia-South Africa frontier with Springbok as its main town; diamonds discovered at Orange river mouth (1929) and (2) Great Namaqualand extending N from Orange river into central Namibia with Keetmanshoop as its main town; a European presence was first established by Governor Van der Stel who came to the region in search of copper (1665); indigenous peoples of region known as Namaquas or Nama; rebellion in 1903 led to their decimation.

Namen, city in Belgium. See Namur.

Namhoi, town in Guangdong prov, SE China. See Foshan.

Namib *na'mib*, desert in W Namibia, SW Africa; follows almost the entire Atlantic Ocean seaboard of Namibia; c.1,300 km long and between 50 and 160 km wide; characterized by low rainfall and temperatures moderated by the cold Benguela current; midday temperatures rise higher on a few days each month especially during the winter when a hot föhn-type wind blows from the interior; the highest sand dune in the world is located in the Namib desert.

Namibe *na-mee'be*, formerly MOÇÂMEDES (Port), 15 10S 12 10E, seaport in Namibe prov, SW Angola, SW Africa; rail link E to Menongue.

Namibia *na-mib'ee-a*, SOUTH-WEST AFRICA (Eng), SUIDWES-AFRIKA (Afrik), formerly GERMAN SOUTH-WEST AFRICA, territory in SW Africa administered by the republic of South Africa; bounded N by Angola, NE by Zambia, E by Botswana, S by South Africa and W by the Atlantic Ocean; timezone GMT −2; area 823,144 sq km; pop(1981) 1,038,000; capital Windhoek; chief towns include Lüderitz, Keetmanshoop and Grootfontein; the majority of the pop is black African (85%) with over half of these belonging to the Ovambo tribe; official languages Afrikaans, German and English plus a number of indigenous languages; the unit of currency is the South African rand; membership of FAO, ILO, UNESCO, WFTU, WHO.

Physical description. Namibia is divided into 3 topographical regions: (1) the coastal desert which follows the entire Atlantic Ocean coast of the country. This region, which includes the Namib desert, is on average about 100 km wide, receives little rain and is sparsely inhabited; (2) an inland plateau with a mean elevation of about 1,500 m and isolated massifs such as the Tsaris Mts (SW), the Anas Mts (central) and the Erongo Mts (W) rising above the plateau level. The highest point in Namibia is Brandberg (2,606 m), located N of Walvis Bay; (3) to the E and S of this plateau spreads the dune- and grass-covered Kalahari desert. The Orange river forms the S frontier with South Africa and the Rio Okavango part of the N frontier with Angola. The Fish (Vis) river flows S from central Namibia to join the Orange river.

Climate. The Namib or coastal desert is an arid region with low rainfall and temperatures moderated by the cold Benguela current. Midday temperatures can rise high on a few days each month (particularly in winter) when a föhn-type wind blows from the interior. This region also experiences frequent coastal fog. Walvis Bay is representative of this region with an annual average rainfall of 24 mm and an average max daily temperature ranging between 19°C and 25°C. The interior has a slightly higher annual rainfall, most of which falls Jan-March. The Namibian capital of Windhoek (alt 1,728 m) is representative of this region with an average annual rainfall of 360 mm and an average max daily temperature ranging between 20°C and 30°C.

History, government and constitution. The Namib desert represented a significant barrier to exploration by European colonizers and it was not until the late 18th century that British and Dutch missionaries moved into the area. In 1878 Great Britain claimed the Walvis Bay enclave as part of the Cape Colony and it was subsequently incorporated in 1884. The area between the Orange river and 26°S was claimed by a German merchant, F.A.E. Lüderitz. As a result of negotiations with the British the Germans took over the whole of the coastal territory (excluding the Walvis Bay enclave) in 1892 and established their capital at Windhoek. The interior was recognized as a German sphere of influence the following year. During World War I the Germans were removed by South African forces. The South Africans administered the former German West Africa after it was mandated to them by the League of Nations in 1920. In the post-1946 period the United Nations attempted to place the territory under a trusteeship but faced stubborn resistance from the South African government. In 1966 the UN withdrew South Africa's mandate and assumed direct responsibility for the territory. Two years later its name was changed to Namibia and although attempts were made for early independence the area was, and still is, administered as South-West Africa by the Republic of South Africa. Government takes the form of an 18-member elected legislative assembly which appoints a 12-member executive ministerial council. The South African government appoints an advisory Administrator-general with overall control. The UN currently recognizes the South-West Africa People's Organization (SWAPO) as representatives of the Namibian people. SWAPO commenced guerrilla activities in 1966 and after Angolan independence (1975) bases were established in S Angola escalating the conflict in Ovamboland.

Economy. Agriculture employs approx 60% of the population in 2 distinct sectors. The first sector is usually white-owned, utilizes modern techniques and concentrates almost exclusively on livestock ranching. Where rainfall is higher (central and N areas) cattle tend to be reared whilst in the S, where less rain falls, karakul farming for sheepskins predominates. The second sector is the traditional subsistence farming of the indigenous peoples concentrated in the N. Agriculture generates about 7% of the country's export earnings. Fishing is also important and is centred at Lüderitz and Walvis Bay where catches include pilchards, anchovies, tuna and mackerel. Recent years have seen catches decreasing owing to overfishing by both local and overseas vessels. Mining is by far the most important sector of the Namibian economy accounting for about 77% of export earnings. Namibia is a major world producer of diamonds and uranium. Diamonds are mined on the SW coast at Oranjemund and uranium is extracted from a mine near Swakopmund on the Atlantic Ocean coast, just N of Walvis Bay. Tsumeb (N) is a major mining centre for copper, lead, zinc, arsenic and cadmium. Other minerals extracted include salt, silver, tin and tungsten. Manufacturing industry generates only a small part (6%) of national income, chiefly because of a small and widely dispersed local market and close proximity to the highly developed South African manufacturing economy. The main manufacturing activities include food processing, brewing, plastic products, furniture, textiles and assembly plants. Namibia's main trading partners include South Africa, West Germany, the USA and the UK.

Administrative divisions. Namibia is divided into 22 administrative districts.

Namib-Nau'kluft, national park in W Namibia, SW Africa; area 24,010 sq km; established in 1979; situated on the Atlantic coast around the South African enclave of Walvis Bay.

Nam'pa, 43 34N 116 34W, pop(1980) 25,112, town in Canyon county, SW Idaho, United States; 27 km W of Boise; named after a local Shoshone Indian chief; railway; economy: commercial, processing and shipping centre in the irrigated Treasure Valley; sugar and food processing, trailers, mobile homes, and wood products; event: Snake River Stampede (July).

Nampula *nam-poo'la*, prov in N Mozambique, SE Africa; pop(1980) 2,402,700; area 81,606 sq km; capital Nampula; chief towns include Moçambique, Nacala, Angoche, Memba and Mossuril; the railway from Lumbo and Nacala runs E-W across the prov before branching into S Malawi and NW Mozambique (Lichinga).

Nampula, 15 09S 39 14E, pop(1980) 145,722, market town and capital of prov of same name, N Mozambique, SE Africa; on the main road S to Beira and on the railway W of Moçambique.

Namsen *nahm'sen*, NAMS (Eng), river in N central Norway, issues from L Namsen 16 km NNE of Gjersvika; flows SSW and W through Nord-Trøndelag county past Namsos to discharge into the Namsen Fjord, an inlet of the Norwegian Sea; length 210 km.

Namsos *nahm'sōs*, 64 28N 11 30E, pop(1980) 11,816, port in Nord-Trøndelag county, W Norway; on N shore at head of Namsen Fjord, at mouth of Namsen R, 205 km from Trondheim; ferry; rail terminus; economy: timber.

Namur *na-mür*, prov of S Belgium; area 3,666 sq km; pop(1982) 408,134; comprises the 3 dists of Namur, Dinant and Philippeville; capital Namur; chief towns Dinant and Genbloux; drained by the Sambre, Meuse and Lesse rivers.

Namur, dist of Namur prov, Belgium; area 1,165 sq km; pop(1982) 261,292.

Namur, NA'MEN (Flem), 50 28N 4 52E, pop(1982) 102,075, capital city of Namur dist, Namur prov, Belgium; at the confluence of the rivers Sambre and Meuse; had military significance in the Roman era; with its outer forts, built in 1889-1902, Namur became one of the key strategic points of the Belgian defence line on the R Meuse; conquered by the Germans in 1914 and 1940; railway; private university (1831); economy: glass, porcelain, enamel, paper, steel; monuments: cathedral (1751-67), citadel (17th-c, on a rocky spur between the Sambre and the Meuse).

Namwŏn *nam-wun*, 35 23N 127 23E, pop(1983e) 843,465, town in Chŏllapuk prov, S Korea; railway.

Nanaimo *na-nī'mō*, 49 08N 123 58W, pop(1981) 47,069, town in SW British Columbia, SW Canada; on SE Vancouver island; on the Strait of Georgia; founded as a Hudson's Bay Co post; economy: pulp, timber; monuments: Petroglyph Park on the outskirts of the city contains prehistoric rock carvings and drawings; the Bastion Museum, part of the old Hudson's Bay fort built in 1852, contains relics of pioneering days; event: Nanaimo Bathtub Race, between Nanaimo and Vancouver across the Strait of Georgia (mid-July).

Nana-Mambéré *na-na-mam-bay'ray*, prefecture in W Central African Republic; the sources of the Pendé, Ouham and Mambéré rivers are in the N; pop(1968) 198,720; area 26,600 sq km; chief town Bouar; other towns include Baboua, Baoro, Nadjiboro and Bouala; economy: gold processing.

Nanchang *nan-chang*, NANCH'ANG-HSIEN, 28 38N 115 56E, pop(1984e) 1,088,800, industrial capital of Jiangxi prov, SE China; founded during the Eastern Han dynasty; on Aug 1 1927 30,000 peasants revolted, defeating the nationalist forces and holding the town for several days; railway; airfield; economy: distribution centre for kaolin pottery; monuments: Jiangxi provincial museum contains geographical and historical exhibitions; the Bada Shanren Exhibition Hall, former monastery and home of Zhu Da (one of the Bada Shanren, the 8 Great Hermit artists who worked in the area in the 17th century), with a display of paintings and calligraphy; headquarters of the Nanchang Uprising, it has been converted into a museum.

Nanch'ang-hsien, capital of Jiangxi prov, SE China. See Nanchang.

Nancy *nã-see*, 48 42N 6 12E, pop(1982) 99,307, manufacturing city and capital of Meurthe-et-Moselle dept, Lorraine region, NE France; on R Meurthe and Marne-Rhine Canal, 285 km E of Paris; former capital of Lorraine; episcopal see; university (founded in 1572 at Pont-á-Mousson, removed here in 1768); road and rail junction; economy: iron and steel, tubes, boilers, catering equipment, glass, footwear, tobacco, yeast, brewing; monuments: the town is noted for its 18th-c Baroque architecture; the Place Stanislas (Place Royale) is flanked by 5 handsome palaces and a 17th-c town hall; the 13th-c ducal palace, restored in the 19th century, now houses a museum of Lorraine history; 15th-c Église des Cordeliers with tombs of the dukes of Lorraine; the 14th-c Porte de la Craffe has 2 imposing round towers, the remnants of ancient fortifications; Baroque cathedral (1703-42).

Nangarhār *nan-gar-har'*, prov in E Afghanistan; pop(1984e) 812,466; area 7,616 sq km; bounded to the E by Pakistan; main road from Kābul to Pakistan crosses Nangarhār; Khyber Pass links Pakistan to Afghanistan; capital Jalālābād.

Nanjing *nan-king*, NANKING, formerly CHIANNING, 32 03N 118 47E, pop(1984e) 2,207,500, capital of Jiangsu prov, SE China; on the Chang Jiang (Yangtze river) at the foot of the Zijin mts; founded in 900 BC, Nanjing was the capital of China from 220 to 589 AD, 907 to 979 AD and from 1928 to 1949; the city grew in importance as a river port and trade centre; Nanjing was attacked by the British during the Opium War (1840-42); the Treaty of Nanjing was signed in 1842 on board a British gunboat in Nanjing harbour, forcing the city to remain open to foreign trade; university (1902); railway; airfield; economy: coal, metallurgy, petroleum refining, heavy and light engineering, shipbuilding; monuments: Nanjing is one of 24 historical and civilized cities designated by the State Council and contains 145 listed historical relics and sites; the Nanjing museum contains exhibits which cover 5,000 years of China's history; the Zhongshanling mausoleum was erected in memory of Sun Yatsen after his death in 1925; Mingxiaoling (Ming Emperor's Tomb) is the tomb of the first Ming emperor; to the E of Nanjing is the Zijin mountain observatory, China's 3rd largest observatory, which also has a museum showing ancient star charts and globes; Yuhuatai Park, said to have been founded in the 6th century AD, serves as a memorial to over 100,000 people allegedly executed during the 22 years of nationalist rule under Chiang Kaishek (1927-49).

Nanking, capital of Jiangsu prov, E China. See Nanjing.

Nanning *nan-ning*, NAN-NING, 22 50N 108 06E, pop(1984e) 902,900, capital of Guangxi aut region, S China; China's most southerly city; founded during the Yuan dynasty (1279-1368 AD) but did not develop industrially until the 20th century; it was used as a military supply town during the Vietnam War of the 1960s and in 1979 in the Sino-Vietnamese confrontation; Nanning was closed to foreigners until 1977; railway; airfield; economy: food processing, coal, bauxite, leather; event: annual Dragon Boat Regatta, a 2,000-year-old Han festival, traditionally held on the 5th day of the 5th lunar month (late May or early June).

Nanterre *nã-ter*, 48 53N 2 13E, pop(1982) 90,371, capital of Hauts-de-Seine dept, Ile-de-France region, central France; at the foot of Mont Valerien; a W suburb of Paris; economy: civil engineering and construction; birthplace of the Revolutionary hero Hanriot.

Nantes *nãt*, NAONED (Bret), CONDIVINCUM (anc), later NAMNETES, 47 12N 1 33W, pop(1982) 247,227, manufacturing and commercial seaport and capital of Loire-Atlantique dept, Pays de la Loire region, W France; at the head of the Loire estuary, 171 km W of Tours; connected by canal to St-Nazaire; 7th largest city in France; between the 16th and 18th centuries the prosperity of Nantes was based on trade in sugar and ebony; by the end of the 18th century Nantes was France's leading port; following the French Revolution and economic recession in the 19th century, it fell into a decline which was not arrested until the construction in 1856 of the outer harbour and deep-water port of St-Nazaire, at the mouth of the river; more recent dredging has enabled Nantes to regain much of its former importance; war-time destruction (World War II) by Allied bombing and postwar reconstruction affected many parts of the town but left the old medieval quarters largely untouched; birthplace of Jules Verne (1828-1905); university (1962); railway; economy: oil refining, sugar refining, boatbuilding, tobacco, soap, textiles, food products, building materials; monuments: Gothic cathedral of St-Pierre-et-St-Paul (badly damaged by fire in 1943 and 1972), containing the tomb of François II, the last Duke of Brittany; Château des Ducs, 10th-c stronghold of the Dukes of Brittany, rebuilt in 1466 and enlarged in the 16th century (the Edict of Nantes was signed here in 1598); museum of fine arts, one of the best in France outside Paris, with a rich collection of French paintings from the 19th century to the present day.

Nantong *nahn-toong*, 32 05N 120 51E, pop(1984e) 402,700, city in Jiangsu prov, E China; at the mouth of the Chang Jiang (Yangtze river); a special economic zone.

Nantou *nan-tow*, county of central Taiwan; area 4,106.4 sq km; pop(1982e) 532,750.

Nantucket (Algonquian, 'narrow-(tidal)-river-at'), island in the Atlantic off the SE coast of Massachusetts, United States; with Muskeget and Tuckernuck islands it forms Nantucket county; area 122 sq km; pop(1980) 5,087, now a summer resort, it was formerly an important whaling centre.

Nanyuki *nan-yoo'kee*, 0 01N 37 05E, pop(1979) 19,000, town in central Kenya, E Africa; at the foot of Mt Kenya, 145 km NNE of Nairobi; railway; economy: tourism and farming.

Naogaon *now'gown*, 24 49N 88 59E, pop(1981) 52,975, town in Naogaon dist, Rajshahi, W Bangladesh; on the W bank of the R Jannuna.

Náousa *now'su*, 40 38N 22 04E, pop(1981) 19,383, town in Imathía nome (dept), Makedhonia region, Greece; W of Thessaloníki; event: carnival (Feb).

Na'pa, 38 18N 122 17W, pop(1980) 50,879, capital of Napa county, W California, United States; at the head of navigation on the Napa river, 56 km N of Oakland; economy: shipping point for the wine-producing Napa Valley.

Naperville, 41 46N 88 09W, pop(1980) 42,330, city in Du Page county, NE Illinois, United States; on the W branch of the Du Page river, 45 km W of Chicago; railway.

Napier *nay'pyer*, 39 29S 176 58E, pop(1981) 48,770, seaport in Hawke Bay on the E coast of North Island, New Zealand; at the centre of a rich farming area; largely destroyed by an earthquake in 1931, Napier is now a modern seaside city built largely on reclaimed land; railway; airfield; economy: electronics, food processing, trade in wool, meat, fruit, pulp, tobacco.

Naples, prov and city in S Italy. See Napoli.

Napo *na'pō*, tropical prov in NE Ecuador; bounded N by Colombia and E by Peru; crossed by the Río Napo (1,120 km) which rises SW of Cotopaxi and flows E and SE across the *Oriente* of Ecuador into Peru where it meets the Amazon NE of Iquitos; pop(1982) 115,110; area 53,835 sq km; capital Tena; economy: crude oil, natural gas, timber.

Napoli *na'po-lee*, prov of Campania region, Italy; pop(1981) 2,970,563; area 1,171 sq km; capital Napoli.

Napoli, NEAPEL (Ger), NAPLES *nay'p'lz* (Eng), (Latin 'Neapolis', new city), 40 50N 14 15E, pop(1981) 1,212,387, seaport and capital city of Napoli prov, Campania region, SW Italy; on the Tyrrhenian Sea, 189 km SE of Roma (Rome); founded c.600 BC by refugees from the Greek colony of Cumae; capital of Napoleon's Parthenopean Republic (1799) and of the Sicilian kingdom (1806); joined Italian kingdom in 1860; in Nov 1980 there was severe damage from earthquakes; archbishopric; university (1224); airport; railway; car ferries to Cagliari (Sardinia), Messina and Palermo (Sicily); economy: aerospace industry, glass and bottles, tourism; monuments: cathedral of San Gennaro, originally built between 1294 and 1323 in French Gothic style, then restored and altered after an earthquake in 1456; church of San Lorenzo Maggiore (1266-1324); Porta Capuana, a beautiful Renaissance gateway (1485, further work 1535); 14th-c church of San Giovanni a Carbonara; the national museum is famous for its collection of Greek and Roman antiquities; events: San Gennaro (feast of St Januarius) on the 1st Saturday in May; Feast of Santa Maria del Carmine (16 July); Madonna della Piedigrotta Folk Song Festival (5-7 Sept).

Na'ra, 34 41N 135 49E, pop(1980) 297,953, capital of Nara prefecture, Kinki region, S Honshū island, Japan; 29 km E of Ōsaka; first capital of Japan founded here in 710; became a cultural and religious centre and the centre for Buddhism in Japan; the Emperor Kammu, feeling that clerical influence was becoming excessive, moved the capital to Kyōto; women's university (1908); railway; economy: textiles, dolls, fans; monuments: the Daibutsu-den (Great Buddha Hall) is the main building of the Todai-ji (East Great Temple) which was founded in 743; it houses a large bronze statue of Buddha (22 m tall) and is said to be the largest wooden structure in the world, being 57 m long and 48 m high; Nara national museum contains Buddhist art from various temples in the city; the 8th-c Shoso-in contains collections of the Emperor Shomu, works of art from India, China and Korea and the oldest example of Japanese painting of the Nara period; the Kasuga-taisha shrine is the most important Shinto shrine in the region with buildings surrounded by approx 3,000 lanterns in bronze, stone or iron; 12 km from Nara are the buildings of Horyu-ji (6th-c), the oldest temple complex in Japan, and the oldest wooden buildings in the world; events: Kasuga Shrine, Lantern Festival (3-4 Feb); Tode-ji, Emperor Shomu Festival in May; Nigatsu do, 'Omizutori' Festival on 12 May; Kasuga Shrine, 'Bon Matsuri' Festival on 15 Aug.

Naranjito *na-ran-KHee'tō*, 2 08S 79 28W, pop(1982) 10,523, town in Guayas prov, W Ecuador; E of Guayaquil and W of the Andes; on the railway from Guayaquil to Riobamba.

Narayanganj *na-ra'yung-gunj*, 23 36N 90 28E, pop(1981) 405,562, town in Narayanganj dist, Dhākā, SE Bangladesh; on R Meghna, E of Dhākā; river port for Dhākā and one of the busiest trade centres; Narayanganj and Dhākā together make up the main industrial region of Bangladesh; collection centre for jute, hides and skins; industries include jute mills, cotton textile mills, leather, glass and shoe manufacturers.

Narew *nar'ef*, river in NE Poland and W USSR, rises SE of Białystok near USSR-Polish frontier and flows 484 km to meet R Wisła (Vistula) NW of Warszawa (Warsaw); length in Poland 448 km; navigable for 300 km; tributaries include Biebrza, Pisa, Bug and Wkra rivers; the 17.6 km Żerańki Canal links the river with the Wisła; dammed at Dębe.

Nariño *na-reen'yō*, dept in SW Colombia, South America; bounded W by the Pacific and S by Ecuador; the indented coastal lowlands rise to volcanic Andean peaks in the E; pop(1985) 848,618; area 33,268 sq km; capital Pasto; economy: agriculture, cattle.

Narmada, NARBADA, river of India, rising in the Maikala range of Madhya Pradesh state; flows W and N to Jabalpur then generally WSW across Madhya Pradesh to form parts of the boundaries between Madhya Pradesh and Maharashtra states and between Maharashtra and Gujarat states; the river meanders across the state of Gujarat in a general WSW direction to meet the Gulf of Khambat (Cambay); length 1,245 km; unsuitable for navigation and irrigation owing to its confinement within steep banks and the many falls along its course; the Narmada is a sacred river to Hindus who believe that it sprang from the body of the god Shiva; along its course are found many pilgrimage centres and bathing ghats; the river is the boundary of the traditional regions of Hindustan and Deccan.

Narodnaya, Gora *na'rud-nī-u*, 65 02N 60 01E, highest peak in the Ural'skiy Khrebet (Ural Mts), on the border between Komi ASSR and Tyumenskaya oblast, Rossiyskaya, W Soviet Union; situated in the N section of the range, E of Pechora; height 1,894 m; source of the R Kos'yu.

Narrogin *nar'u-jun*, 32 58S 117 10E, pop(1981) 4,969, town in Upper Great Southern stat div, Western Australia, Australia; SE of Perth; railway.

Narshingdhi *nur'shing-dee*, 23 56N 90 40E, pop(1981) 76,841, town in Narsingdi dist, Dhākā, SE Bangladesh; ENE of Dhākā.

Narvik *nahr'vik*, 68 26N 17 25E, pop(1980) 19,339, seaport in Nordland county, N Norway; at W end of a peninsula in the Ofoten Fjord opposite the Lofoten Is; airfield; rail terminus; the town is of great economic importance as the terminus of the Lappland railway from the Kiruna iron-ore mines in Sweden and as an ice-free harbour; occupied by Germans 9 April, 1940; scene of World War II naval battles in which two British and 9 German destroyers were lost.

Nash'ua (Algonquin, 'between-water'), 42 45N 71 28W, pop(1980) 67,865, county seat of Hillsborough county, S New Hampshire, United States; on R Merrimack, 24 km S of Manchester, near Massachusetts border; railway.

Nashville, 36 10N 86 47W, pop(1980) 455,651, capital of state in Davidson county, N central Tennessee, United States; a port on the R Cumberland; settled in 1779 as Nashborough; renamed Nashville in 1784; state capital since 1843; scene of Civil War battle (1864) in which Union forces defeated Confederates; 3 universities (1867, 1872, 1909); railway; airfield; economy: chemicals, automobile glass, clothes, footwear, tyres, food products, publishing, railway engineering; famed for its music industry; monuments: the Capitol (with the tomb of James K. Polk), Country Music Hall of Fame, Opryland, USA (family entertainment complex); event: Country Music Fan Fair (June).

Nasik *nah'sik*, 20 02N 75 30E, pop(1981) 916,000, city in Maharashtra state, W central India; on a tributary of the Darna river, 145 km NE of Bombay; a holy place of Hindu pilgrimage connected with the legend of Rama; economy: cattle, poultry, brassware; monuments: many Vishnuite temples and shrines; Buddhist caves of the 2nd century AD.

Nāṣirīyah, An *a-na-sir-ee'u*, 31 04N 46 17E, pop(1970) 62,368, capital town of Dhi-Qār governorate, S central Iraq; on R Euphrates (Al Furāt), on the highway between Al Basrah and Al Kūt; railway; economy: metallurgy.

Nassau *na'so*, 25 05N 77 20W, pop(1980) 10,213, capital of the Bahamas in Montagu district, New Providence I; on NE coast of the island; its pleasant climate has made it a popular winter tourist resort; frequented by pirates during the 18th century and captured briefly by Americans in 1776; Fort Nassau (1697), Fort Charlotte (1787-94) and Fort Fincastle (1793) were built to protect the city from Spanish invasion; airport.

Nassau, 11 33S 165 25W, coral island of the Cook Is, S Pacific, 1,080 km NW of Rarotonga; area 1.2 sq km; pop(1981) 134.

Nas'ser, Lake, BUHEIRET EN NASER (Egypt), lake in S Egypt; length 500 km; area c.5,000 sq km; created as a result of the building of the Aswân High Dam which was completed in 1971; named after a former president of Egypt.

Natal *na-tal'*, 5 46S 35 15W, pop(1980) 376,446, port capital of Rio Grande do Norte state, Nordeste region, NE Brazil; on the right bank of the Río Potengi on the Atlantic coast N of Recife; Marine Research Institute at the Praia da Areia Preta; 20 km S of Natal is the rocket base of Barreira do Inferno, near the town of Eduardo Gómes; university (1958); railway; airfield (at 13 km); monuments: cathedral, 16th-c fort, folk museum.

Natal, prov in E South Africa; pop(1985) 2,145,018; area 91,355 sq km; bounded E by the Indian Ocean, N by Mozambique and Swaziland, S by Cape prov and SW by Lesotho; the Drakensberg mountains follow the NW frontier; capital Pietermaritzburg; chief towns include Durban, Pinetown, Vryheid, Ladysmith, Glencoe and Empangeni; annexed to the Cape Colony in 1844, with a separate government in 1845; became a separate colony in 1856; Zululand prov annexed in 1897 and Vryheid, Utrecht and part of Wakkerstroom dists, which formerly belonged to the Transvaal prov, were annexed in 1903; became an original prov of the Union of South Africa in 1910; economy: sugar cane, citrus, grain, vegetables, chemicals, paper, food processing, iron and steel, oil refining, explosives, fertilizers, meat canning.

National City, 32 41N 117 06W, pop(1980) 48,772, city in San Diego county, SW California, United States; S of San Diego, on San Diego Bay.

Natitingou *na-tee-ting'goo*, 10 17N 1 19E, pop(1979) 50,800, town in Atakora prov, NW Benin, W Africa; 180 km NW of Parakou.

Natron, Lake *nay'trun*, lake in N Tanzania, E Africa; situated in the Rift Valley, 112 km NW of Arusha, close to the Kenyan frontier; 56 km long and 24 km wide; the Gelai volcano (2,942 m) is located to the SE; noted for its salt and soda deposits.

Naugatuck *naw'ge-tuk* (Algonquian, 'lone tree'), 41 30N 73 03W, pop(1980) 26,456, town in New Haven county, SW Connecticut, United States; on the R Naugatuck, 8 km S of Waterbury; railway.

Nauru *na-oo'roo*, official name Republic of Nauru, 0 32S 166 56E, small isolated island in the W central Pacific Ocean, lying 42 km S of the equator and 4,000 km NE of Sydney, Australia; its nearest neighbour is Ocean Island, 306 km to the E in the Republic of Kiribati; timezone GMT +11½; area 21.3 sq km; circumference 20 km; pop(1977) 7,254; Nauru has no capital city as such; Parliament House and the government offices are in Yaren dist; the inhabitants live in small settlements scattered throughout the island, mostly in the coastal belt; indigenous Nauruans, of mixed Polynesian, Micronesian, and Melanesian descent, make up half the population (4,174 in 1977); the rest are a mixture of Australians and New Zealanders (564), Chinese (626), and other Pacific islanders (1,890); Nauruan is the national language, although English is widely understood; the Nauruans are Christians, the majority belonging either to the Nauru Protestant Church or to the Roman Catholic Church; Australian currency is used; membership of the Commonwealth (special member), ESCAP, ICAO, ITU, UPU, South Pacific Commission, South Pacific Forum.

Physical description. Nauru is one of the 3 great phosphatic-rock islands of the Pacific (the other 2 are Ocean Island, part of Kiribati, and Makatea in French Polynesia). It is oval-shaped and is bounded by a reef which is exposed at low tide. The ground rises gently from the sandy beaches to form a fertile coastal belt, 100-300 m wide, bearing the only cultivable soil on the island. Inland, coral cliffs rise to a central plateau whose highest point is 65 m. This plateau, which covers more than three-fifths of the island's total area, is composed largely of phosphate-bearing rocks.

Climate. The climate is tropical with daily temperatures ranging between 24.4°C and 33.9°C, and average humidity between 70 and 80 %. Annual rainfall averages 1,524 mm, much of it occurring during the monsoon season from Nov to Feb. However, annual rainfall is subject to marked yearly deviations from the average. In 1950 only 305 mm of rain fell, whereas in 1930 and 1940, rainfall of more than 4,572 mm occurred.

History, government and constitution. Nauru was under German administration from the 1880s until 1914. In 1919, a League of Nations mandate was granted to Australia, New Zealand, and the UK, and Nauru was thereafter administered by Australia on behalf of the 3 governments. During the time of German administration, the country's high-grade phosphates were discovered and exploited. By the 1960s, the Nauruans began to press their claim for independence and ownership of the phosphate industry. In 1966, the Nauruans were given self-government, and on 31 Jan 1968, full independence was achieved. The constitution of 29 Jan 1968 established a republic with a parliamentary system of government. The unicameral parliament consists of 18 members elected by universal adult suffrage. Parliamentary elections are held every 3 years. Parliament elects the president, who combines the functions of both head of state and prime minister, and who in turn appoints 4 or 5 members of parliament to serve concurrently as cabinet ministers in his government.

Economy. Nauru's economy is based mainly on the phosphate mining industry which has been run since 1970 by the Nauru Phosphate Corporation. Phosphate revenues bring the island one of the highest per capita incomes in the world. At present about 2 mn tons are exported annually, just over 50% to Australia, 25% to New Zealand, and the rest to Japan and other Far Eastern countries. However, in 1978, it was estimated that some 32 mn tons of phosphate remained to be worked, representing a life-span for the industry of less than 20 years at the present rate of extraction. Since independence, over 60% of revenue from phosphate exports has been invested in long-term trust funds, designed to provide the inhabitants with a future income. Agriculture is concentrated in the fertile coastal belt. Coconuts are the main crop and small quantities of vegetables are grown. All additional food has to be imported from Australia and New Zealand. Apart from foodstuffs, other imports include building construction materials and machinery for the phosphate industry.

Navan *na'vun*, AN UAIMH (Gael), 53 39N 6 41W, pop(1981) 11,136, market town in Meath county, Leinster, Irish Republic; NW of Dublin; 8 km NW in the Hill of Tailte, ancient site of the All-Irish Games; before mid-6th century the Hill of Tara was the 'capital' of Celtic Ireland and seat of the kings of Meath; railway; economy: textiles, furniture, zinc and lead, farm tools.

Navarra *na-var'a*, NAVARRE *na-var'* (Eng), former kingdom and region of N Spain, co-extensive with the prov of the same name and formerly including the French Basses-Pyrénées; pop(1981) 507,367; area 10,421 sq km; bounded in the E by Aragón its shape is determined by the rivers that flow down from the Pyrenees; from the valley of the R Ebro and the arid salt-steppe of Los Bardenas the land rises towards the W Pyrenees, with rainfall and forest cover increasing with altitude; the former kingdom had complete control over the Pyrenean passes and was an early centre of resistance against the Moors; the capital, Pamplona, lies in a treeless basin; cereals, vegetables and vines are grown close to the R Ebro; economy: food canning, cement, footwear, textiles, clothes, electrical equipment, iron and steel, furniture, metal products, agric machinery, naval construction (Tudela).

Návplion or **Nauplion** *naf'plee-on*, NAUPLIA *naw'plia* (Eng), 37 34N 22 48E, pop(1981) 10,609, seaport and capital town of Argolís nome (dept), Pelopónnisos region,

Greece, on the Argolikós Kólpos (Gulf of Argolis), under the rocky promontory of Akrónafplia (85 m) and the fortified hill of Palamídi (216 m); rail terminus; local boat service; yacht supply station; economy: fruit, vegetable and tobacco trade, tourism; event: Navy Week (June-July).

Navrongo *nav-rong'gō*, 10 51N 1 03W, town in Upper region, N Ghana, W Africa; near the Burkina frontier NW of Bolgatanga and 170 km NNW of Tamale.

Nawabshah *nu-vahb'shah*, NAWABASHAH, 26 15N 68 26E, pop(1981) 102,000, city in Sind prov, SE Pakistan; 209 km NE of Karachi; economy: trade in grain, cotton and dates.

Náxos *nak'sos*, largest island of the Kikládhes, Greece, in the S Aegean Sea, E of Páros I; area 428 sq km; length 35 km; length of coastline 148 km; width 26 km; rises to 1,002 m; chief town Náxos on NW coast; the island is famous for its wines and sandy beaches.

Naxxar or **Nashar** *nah-shahr'*, 35 55N 14 27E, pop(1983e) 5,022, town on the main island of Malta, 6 km W of Valletta; Malta International Trade Fair grounds.

Nayarit *nī-ah-reet'*, state in W Mexico; bounded by the Pacific Ocean (W), Sinaloa (NW), Durango (NE) and Jalisco (E and S); narrow coastal lowlands (marshy in the NW) in the W and outliers of the Sierra Madre Occidental in the E; drained by the Río Grande de Santiago, Huaynamota and Pedro Mezquital rivers; NE is the L de Agua Brava; the Islas Marías in the Pacific also form part of this state; pop(1980) 730,024; area 26,979 sq km; capital Tepic; economy: agriculture is the most important activity in Nayarit (major crops: tobacco, maize, sugar cane, peppers, sorghum, bananas, vegetables, coffee, fruit), cattle raising, fishing, mining (silver, copper), cigars, fertilizers, sugar refining; in the SE of the state near the town of Ixtlán are the ruins of a Toltec ceremonial centre.

Nazaré *na-zar-e'*, 39 36N 9 04W, pop(1981) 9,000, picturesque fishing town in Leiria dist, central Portugal; lying in a wide bay sheltered on the N by Monte Sitio, 33 km SW of Leiria; also a popular resort with fine beaches; since the harbour has long been silted up the brightly-coloured fishing boats are launched from the beach and on their return are pulled on shore by oxen; events: carnival in the days before Ash Wednesday and pilgrimage of the Senhora de Nazaré at the beginning of Sept, with bullfights and folk events.

Nazareth *na'zu-rith*, NAZERAT (Hebrew), 32 41N 35 16E, capital town of North dist, N Israel; above the Yizre'el (Jezreel) plain on the S edge of the hills of Galilee; its inhabitants are mostly Christian; site of the Annunciation and the place where Jesus spent most of his life; monuments: church of the Annunciation incorporating the grotto where the Angel Gabriel is said to have appeared before Mary mother of Jesus; church of St Joseph.

Naze, The, Norwegian cape. See Lindesnes.

Naz'rēt, NASSET, NAZARETH, 8 39N 39 19E, pop(1984e) 76,284, capital of Shewa region, central Ethiopia, NE Africa; SW of Addis Ababa; railway.

Nazwá *naz-wa'*, 22 56N 57 33E, pop(1983e) 10,000, commercial town in N Oman, SE Arabian peninsula; in the S foothills of the Jabal Akhdar; once capital of Oman; monument: tower built by Sultan bin Seif during the late 17th century; famous for its silversmiths.

Ndélé *un-day'lay*, 8 25N 20 38E, chief town in Bamingui-Bangoran prefecture, N Central African Republic; 500 km NE of Bangui; repeatedly destroyed by Senussite raids in the 19th and early 20th centuries.

N'Djamena *un-jam-ee'na*, formerly FORT LAMY (–1973), 12 10N 14 59E, pop(1984e) 402,000, capital of Chad, N central Africa, also capital of Chari-Baguirmi prefecture, W central Chad; at the confluence of Logone and Chari rivers, close to the Cameroon border; the junction of caravan routes; founded in 1900 by the French it became a centre for the pacification of the Negro kingdoms of central Sudan (1903-12); bombed by Italians in 1942; university (1971); airport; monument: museum with a collection relating to the Sao culture since the 9th century.

Ndola *un-dō'la*, 13 00S 28 39E, pop(1980) 282,439, capital of Copperbelt prov, central Zambia, S central Africa; 275 km N of Lusaka; major mining centre; aeroplane carrying Dag Hammarskjoeld, the Secretary-General of the United Nations, crashed here in 1961; technical college; railway; airport; economy: cement, oil refining, metal fencing products, bitumen, paint, adhesive, tyres, furniture, clothing, mining and quarrying equipment, food processing, stationery, printing, neon signs, industrial gases, vehicle assembly.

Neagh, Lough *loKH nay*, large lake in central Northern Ireland; bounded by Derry (Londonderry) (NW), Antrim (N and E), Armagh (S) and Tyrone (W); length 29 km; width 18 km; area 396 sq km; largest lake in the British Isles; well known for its eels; fed by the Main, Bann (Upper), Blackwater, Ballinderry and Moyola rivers; the lake's outlet is the lower half of the Bann river which flows out of the N end of Lough Neagh to the N coast; large deposits of lignite have recently been discovered around the lake and are being mined with the prospect of using the fuel for electricity.

Neamţ *nyamts*, county in NE Romania, in the E foothills of the E Carpathian Mts; pop(1983) 558,813; area 5,890 sq km; capital Piatra-Neamţ.

Neath *neeth*, 51 40N 3 48W, pop(1981) 49,128, town in Neath dist, West Glamorgan, S Wales; in Swansea urban area, on the R Neath; railway; economy: engineering.

Neblina, Pico da *pee'kō da neb-lee'na*, 1 45N 66 01W, mountain in Amazonas state, Norte region, N Brazil; rises to 3,014 m in the Serra Imeri mountain range on the frontier with Venezuela; recently discovered to be the highest mountain in Brazil; situated in a 22,000-sq km national park which was established in 1979.

Nebras'ka, state in central United States; bounded W by Wyoming, N by South Dakota, E by Iowa and Missouri, and S by Kansas and Colorado; the R Missouri forms the E border; the North Platte and South Platte rivers unite to form the R Platte which flows E across the state to empty into the Missouri; the highest point is Johnson Township in Kimball county (1,654 m); the E part of the state is undulating fertile farmland growing corn; further W, on the Great Plains, grass cover is helping to stabilize eroded land; in the far W, the ground rises to the foothills of the Rocky Mts; agriculture dominates the economy, the chief products being cattle (the state is the 2nd largest producer in the country), corn, hogs, wheat and grain sorghum; the main manufacturing industries are food processing, electrical machinery and chemicals; part of the Louisiana Purchase in 1803; Bellevue was established as the first permanent settlement; in 1854 Nebraska became a territory stretching as far as the Canadian border, but its area was reduced in 1863; became a state in 1867; in the same year the Union Pacific Railroad completed its transcontinental line, resulting in a land boom; the 'Cornhusker State'; pop(1980) 1,569,825; area 199,274 sq km; 37th state admitted to the Union, in 1867; capital Lincoln; other chief cities are Omaha and Grand Island; the state is divided into 93 counties:

County	*area (sq km)*	*pop(1980)*
Adams	1,466	30,656
Antelope	2,233	8,675
Arthur	1,849	513
Banner	1,942	918
Blaine	1,856	867
Boone	1,786	7,391
Box Butte	2,800	13,696
Boyd	1,383	3,331
Brown	3,156	4,377
Buffalo	2,457	34,797
Burt	1,264	8,813
Butler	1,518	9,330
Cass	1,448	20,297
Cedar	1,924	11,375

contd

County	*area (sq km)*	*pop(1980)*
Chase	2,324	4,758
Cherry	15,499	6,758
Cheyenne	3,110	10,057
Clay	1,492	8,106
Colfax	1,066	9,890
Cuming	1,495	11,664
Custer	6,685	13,877
Dakota	671	16,573
Dawes	3,632	9,609
Dawson	2,553	22,304
Deuel	1,136	2,462
Dixon	1,232	7,137
Dodge	1,388	35,847
Douglas	866	397,038
Dundy	2,392	2,861
Fillmore	1,498	7,920
Franklin	1,498	4,377
Frontier	2,538	3,647
Furnas	1,875	6,486
Gage	2,231	24,456
Garden	4,368	2,802
Garfield	1,482	2,363
Gosper	1,199	2,140
Grant	2,015	877
Greeley	1,482	3,462
Hall	1,396	47,690
Hamilton	1,412	9,301
Harlan	1,443	4,292
Hayes	1,854	1,356
Hitchcock	1,843	4,079
Holt	6,256	13,552
Hooker	1,875	990
Howard	1,466	6,773
Jefferson	1,495	9,817
Johnson	980	5,285
Kearney	1,349	7,053
Keith	2,701	9,364
Keya Paha	1,999	1,301
Kimball	2,475	4,882
Knox	2,873	11,457
Lancaster	2,181	192,884
Lincoln	6,565	36,455
Logan	1,485	983
Loup	1,492	859
Madison	1,495	31,382
McPherson	2,222	593
Merrick	1,243	8,945
Morrill	3,653	6,085
Nance	1,141	4,740
Nemaha	1,063	8,367
Nuckolls	1,498	6,726
Otoe	1,599	15,183
Pawnee	1,126	3,937
Perkins	2,301	3,637
Phelps	1,404	9,769
Pierce	1,495	8,481
Platte	1,739	28,852
Polk	1,136	6,320
Red Willow	1,867	12,615
Richardson	1,438	11,315
Rock	2,608	2,383
Saline	1,495	13,131
Sarpy	619	86,015
Saunders	1,958	18,716
Scotts Bluff	1,885	38,344
Seward	1,495	15,789
Sheridan	6,378	7,544
Sherman	1,466	4,226
Sioux	5,382	1,845
Stanton	1,121	6,549
Thayer	1,495	7,582
Thomas	1,854	973
Thurston	1,017	7,186
Valley	1,474	5,633
Washington	1,004	15,508
Wayne	1,152	9,858
Webster	1,495	4,858
Wheeler	1,495	1,060
York	1,498	14,798

Neck'ar, river in Baden-Württemberg prov, W Germany; rises at Villingen-Schwenningen on the E fringe of the Schwarzwald (Black Forest); flows NE, past Rottweil, Rottenburg and Tübingen, turns NNW at Plochingen, continues past Esslingen and Heilbronn to Eberbach, then turns W to the R Rhine at Mannheim; length 367 km; navigable length 203 km; drainage basin area 13,958 sq km; chief tributaries Jagst, Kocher, Fils and Rems rivers (right), Enz and Elsenz rivers (left); between 1921 and 1968 the Neckar was canalized on the 200 km stretch from Plochingen to Mannheim.

Necochea *nay-kō-chee'a*, 38 31S 58 46W, pop(1980) 50,939, port in Buenos Aires prov, Litoral, E Argentina; on the Atlantic at the mouth of the Río Quequén Grande; tourist resort; municipal recreation complex with modern casino and sports facilities; 24 km-long beach.

Ñeembucú *nyay-em-boo-koo'*, dept in Oriental region, SW Paraguay; bordered S and W by Argentina (S along the Río Paraná, W along the Río Paraguay); bounded NE by L Vera and L Cabral; the dept's marshy lowlands are intersected by the Río Tebicuary; pop(1982) 70,689; area 13,868 sq km; capital Pilar.

Negeri Sembilan *nug-ree' sum-bee-lahn'* (Malay, 'nine states'), state in SW Peninsular Malaysia, SE Asia; bounded W by Strait of Malacca, SE by Melaka, NW by Selangor, NE by Pahang; pop(1980) 551,442; area 6,643 sq km; capital Seremban.

Neg'ev, hilly desert region of S Israel, extending in a wedge from Beersheba in the N to Elat on the Gulf of 'Aqaba; the N section is built up of layers of chalk covered with loess soils while further S the land becomes hilly reaching a height of 1,935 m at Har Ramon; the N Negev is irrigated by a conduit leading from L Tiberias in the N.

Negoiul *neg-oy'ool*, 45 35N 24 31E, mountain in the Transylvanian Alps of S central Romania, rising to 2,548 m; the highest mountain in Romania.

Negombo *ni-gam'bo*, 7 13N 79 51E, pop(1981) 61,376, seaport and fishing town in Gampaha dist, Western prov, Sri Lanka; on the W coast 20 km N of Colombo; held by the Portuguese until taken by the British in 1796; important centre of cinnamon cultivation; the Dutch cinnamon canal ended here; now a popular coastal tourist resort.

Ne'gotin, 44 14N 22 32E, pop(1981) 63,973, town in E Srbija (Serbia) republic, Yugoslavia, near the R Danube; railway; economy: fruit, vegetables and wine trade.

Negro, Río *nayg'rō*, Patagonian river in Río Negro prov, S central Argentina; formed by junction of Neuquén and Limay rivers at Neuquén, flows 635 km S and SE (parallel to Río Colorado) past Allen General Roca and Viedma to the Atlantic 32 km SE of Viedma; navigable for 400 km upstream; used for hydroelectric power; vineyards in irrigated valleys; length of the Neuquén-Negro is 1,130 km.

Negro, Río, important N tributary of the Amazon, N Brazil; known as the Guaianí from its source in Vaupés admin terr, SE Colombia until its junction with the Río Casiquiare on the Colombia-Venezuela border; generally flows SE through Amazonas state, NW Brazil, through the Amazon tropical rainforest; joins the Amazon 18 km below Manaus; length approx 2,253 km; chief tributaries Branco, Içana and Uaupés; connected to the Orinoco river via the Casiquiare Canal; the Río Negro contains numerous islands; up to 32 km wide above Manaus, the river narrows to 2.5 km at its mouth; one of the main transport channels in NW Brazil.

Negros *nay'gros*, island in the Visayas group, central Philippines; lies between Panay I (NW) and Cebu I (E); area 13,665 sq km; chief town Bacolod.

Nei Mongol *nay mung-goo*, INNER MONGOLIA, autonomous region in N China; bordered N by Mongolia and the USSR, E by Gansu prov and W by Heilongjiang and Jilin provs; to the S, from W to E, Nei Mongol borders on Gansu, Ningxia aut reg, Shaanxi, Shanxi, Hebei and Liaoning provs; part of its S border is formed by the Great Wall of China; approx two-thirds of Nei Mongol consists of grasslands, the remainder being desert; the Da Hinggan Ling (Greater Khingan range) in the NE rises to over 1,000 m; W is Hulun Nur lake; the Hetao Plain, a fertile, grain-growing area, is situated between the Lang Shan and Yin Shan ranges and the Huang He (Yellow river); to the S of the Huang He are the Hobq Shamo and Mu Us Shamo deserts; the Ulan Buh Shamo desert lies S of the Lang Shan range and W of the Huang He river; part of the border between Nei Mongol and Ningxia is formed by the Helan Shan range; to the W of this lies the Tengger Shamo desert; further W, to the N of the Yabrai Shan range, is the Badain Jaran Shamo desert; the Bor Ul Shan range is situated in the extreme W of Nei Mongol; drained by the Hailar He, Gan He, Nuomin He and Chaor He rivers (NE), the Xar Moron He (E), the Huang He (central), the Shiyang He (W) and the Ruo Shui river (NW); pop(1982) 19,274,279; area 450,000 sq km; capital Hohhot; principal town Baotou; economy: horse breeding, cattle and sheep raising, forestry, iron and steel, coal mining.

Neineva, formerly NINEVEH, governorate in NW Iraq, bounded W by Syria; pop(1977) 1,105,671; area 41,320 sq km; capital Mosul; drained by the R Tigris; the ruins of the ancient capital of Assyria lie on the R Tigris opposite Mosul; excavations began here in 1845.

Neiva *nay'va*, 2 58N 75 15W, pop(1985) 193,101, capital of Huila dept, S central Colombia, South America; founded in 1539, destroyed by Indians and later rebuilt in 1612; railway; airfield (La Marguita) at 1.5 km; has interesting horse-driven sugar cane presses.

Nekemte, 9 04N 36 30E, pop(1984e) 28,824, capital of Welega region, W Ethiopia, NE Africa; W of Addis Ababa.

Nelson, river in N Manitoba prov, central Canada; issues from NE end of L Winnipeg; flows NE through lakes Playgreen, Cross and Split to Hudson Bay at Port Nelson, 19 km W of York Factory; length 740 km; since the Saskatchewan river enters L Winnipeg in the NW of the lake, a continous watercourse is formed (Saskatchewan-L Winnipeg-Nelson) with a total length to the head of the Bow river of 2,671 km; the first post of the Hudson's Bay Co was established at the mouth of the Nelson river at Port Nelson in 1670; the river was used for many years by fur traders as an inland routeway.

Nelson, 41 18S 173 17E, pop(1981) 33,304, port on the N coast of South Island, New Zealand; on Tasman Bay; centre of fruit, hop and tobacco growing areas; one of the world's major apple producing regions; noted as an arts and crafts centre; airfield; economy: food processing, timber products and trade in fruit, vegetables, tobacco and timber.

Nelson, 53 51N 2 13W, pop(1981) 30,494, town in Pendle dist, Lancashire, NW England; 6 km N of Burnley; railway; economy: textiles, clothing.

Nelson Lakes, national park, N South Island, New Zealand; contains Rotoiti and Rotoroa lakes (area 10 sq km and 23 sq km respectively); surrounded by rugged, forest-clad mountains rising to over 1,830 m; area 961 sq km; established in 1956.

Néma *nay'ma*, 16 32N 7 12W, capital of Hodh ech Chargui region, SE Mauritania, NW Africa; situated at the junction of desert tracks 470 km N of Bamako (Mali); airfield.

Neman *nee'mun*, MEMEL *may'mul* (Ger), river in Belorusskaya and Litovskaya (Lithuania) republics, W Soviet Union; rises 48 km SSW of Minsk, in central Belorusskaya SSR; flows generally W past Stolbtsy and Grodno, N through S Litovskaya SSR, and at Kaunas turns W and forms the border between Kaliningradskaya oblast, Rossiyskaya, and Litovskaya SSR; discharges into the Baltic Sea in the extreme SW corner of Litovskaya SSR, forming a small delta; length 955 km; chief tributaries Vilnya and Shchara rivers; the meeting between Tsar Alexander I and Napoleon I on a raft in the middle of the river resulted in the signing of the Treaty of Tilsit (1807).

Nenagh *nee'nahKH*, AONACH URMHUMHAN (Gael), 52 52N 8 12W, pop(1981) 5,871, market town in Tipperary county, North Riding, Munster, S central Irish Republic; NE of Limerick and N of the Silvermine Mts; railway; economy: textiles.

Nene *neen*, river rising SW of Daventry in Northamptonshire, central England; flows 145 km E and NE through Northampton and Peterborough to meet the Wash S of Sutton Bridge; navigable to Peterborough.

Nepal *ne-pawl'*, *nay-pal'*, official name The Kingdom of Nepal, SRI NEPALA SARKAR, an independent kingdom lying along the S slopes of the Himalayas, central Asia; bounded N by the Tibet region of the People's Republic of China, E by Sikkim and West Bengal, India and S by Bihar and Uttar Pradesh, India; timezone GMT $+5\frac{1}{2}$; area 145,391 sq km, length E-W 880 km and width 144-240 km N-S; capital Kathmandu; chief towns include Patan and Bhadgaon; pop(1983e) 16 million; ethnic groups descended from 3 major migrations from India, Tibet and central Asia include Gurungs and Magars groups (W), Rais, Limbus and Sunwars in the E mountains, Sherpas ('tigers of the snow') in the Himalayan regions up to 4,500 m, Newars in the Valley of Kathmandu, Tharus and Dhimals in the Terai region, and Brahmins, Kshetriyas and Thakuris throughout Nepal; one-third of the population live in the lowland Terai, while two-thirds live in the central hilly region; the highlands are only sparsely populated; 20 languages are spoken and English is widely used, but the official language understood by all groups is Nepali; Hinduism (90%), Buddhism and Islam are the main religions; Nepal is the only official Hindu kingdom in the world; the currency is the Nepalese rupee which has a decimal system of coinage down to one-hundredth of a rupee; tourists (other than Indians) are not allowed to bring Indian currency into Nepal; national holidays 11 Jan (birthday of the late King Prithvinarayan Shah), 18 Feb (National Democracy Day), 29 Dec (birthday of the King and National Day); membership of ADB, Colombo Plan, FAO, G-77, IBRD, ICAO, IFAD, IFC, ILO, IMF, IMO, INTERPOL, IPU, IRC, IYU, NAM, UN, UNESCO, UPU, WHO, WMO and WTO.

Physical description. Roughly rectangular in shape, Nepal rises steeply in a series of hills and mountains from that narrow part of the Ganges Basin called the Terai which occupies 17% of the total land area of the country. This is an area of swamp and forest with an extensive river network watering agricultural land growing rice. High fertile valleys, such as the Vale of Kathmandu in the 'hill country' at 1,310 m, are enclosed by ranges of fold mountains behind the escarpments and forested valleys of the Siwalik Hills. The Vale of Kathmandu is Nepal's most densely populated area, but the connecting railways with India (the Janakpur-Jayanager and the Amiek-Hgunj-Raxaul railways) do not reach this valley because of the rugged nature of the topography. Higher still are the glaciated peaks of the Himalayas, the highest of which is Mount Everest which rises to 8,848 m on the Nepal-Tibet border. A landlocked country, the nearest sea coast is 1,127 km SE in India. Only 14% of the land is cultivated, the rest being under forest, riverbed or snow.

Climate. The climate varies from subtropical lowland with hot, humid summers and mild winters to an alpine climate in the N at altitudes over 3,300 m, where mountain peaks are permanently snow-covered and temperatures remain below freezing for most of the year. At Kathmandu the temperature varies from 40°C in May to 1.6°C in Dec. The monsoon season occurs during the summer (June-Sept), with average annual rainfall decreasing from 1,778 mm in the E to 889 mm in the W.

History, government and constitution. Modern Nepal was formed from a group of independent hill states united in the 18th century by Prithvi Narayan Shah, ruler of the Gorkha kingdom (source of the term 'Gurkha' for Nepalese soldiers). After a period of internal turmoil the country was stabilized by the Rana family which established itself in power and pursued a policy of isolation and national independence. In 1950 the Shah family was restored to power and by 1959 a constitution paved the way for parliamentary democracy and the country's first election to a National Assembly. After 18 months of government by the Nepalese Congress Party, the King declared the parliamentary experiment a failure and dissolved the government. Stating that Nepal needed a democratic system nearer to Nepalese traditions, the King established the partyless system of *panchayats* (village councils) in a new constitution on 16 Dec 1962. After student unrest in 1979, a referendum in May 1980 reinforced the *panchayat* system. Nepal is a constitutional monarchy ruled by a hereditary king who is advised by a hierarchical system of councils. Village and town councils, elected by assemblies (of which every Nepalese citizen over 21 years is a member), send representatives to district assemblies, from which an 11-member district council is formed. The National Council is composed of 112 members elected by universal adult suffrage in addition to 28 members appointed by the King from professional organizations. The judges of the Supreme Court are appointed by the King.

Economy. Nepal is one of the least developed countries in Asia, receiving aid from many countries including India, China, the USA, West Germany and the UK. Agriculture is Nepal's chief economic activity, providing over one-half of the country's income and employing 90% of the people. Rice, wheat and jute are the main crops of the Terai, while millet, maize, wheat, barley and sugar-cane are grown in the hill valleys. Few areas in Nepal are irrigated sufficiently to produce maximum yields. Nepal is 33% forested, but pressure to produce local firewood and timber for export has resulted in considerable deforestation. Few minerals are exploited commercially, although there are known deposits of coal, copper, iron, mica, zinc and cobalt. Most of Nepal's foreign trade is with India owing to its landlocked situation, but trade is carried out with over 50 countries. Nepal chiefly exports agricultural and forest-based goods, but also a number of manufactured products, principally jute, handicrafts, carpets, medicinal herbs, ready-made garments, shoes and woollen goods. Cottage industries are important, accounting for 8% of Nepal's total overseas exports. Tourism has become increasingly important since 1951 and has now developed into a major source of income, with Himalayan trekking, a rich culture and religious sites attracting large numbers of tourists.

Administrative divisions. Nepal is divided into 14 zones, each of which is administered by a commissioner with one or two assistant commissioners. The country is further divided into 75 districts.

Neretva *ne'ret-va,* river in W Yugoslavia flowing from the Dinaric Alps to meet the Adriatic Sea near Ploče; length 216 km; navigable for 104 km.

Nerja *ner'KHa,* 36 45N 3 53W, pop(1981) 11,500, resort town in Málaga prov, S Spain; on a promontory of the Mediterranean coast, 50 km E of Málaga; named the Balcón de Europa by King Alfonso XII; beaches at Burriana, El Corrillo, Calahonda, El Salón and El Playazo; limestone caves were discovered nearby in 1959.

Nes *nays,* 59 56N 10 45E, pop(1980) 14,034, suburb of Oslo, in Akershus county, SE Norway.

Ness, Loch, loch in Highland region, N Scotland; extending NE from Fort Augustus along the Great Glen to 9.5 km SW of Inverness; 38 km long; average width 2 km; max depth 230 m (near Castle Urquhart); Loch Ness forms part of the course of the Caledonian Canal; fed by the Oich, Moriston, Foyers, Enrick and Farigaig rivers; drained by the R Ness, in the N end of the loch, which flows 11 km NNE to the Moray Firth; in 1933 and later there were newspaper reports of a 12-15 m-long 'monster' which was said to have been seen in the loch; since then there have been several unconfirmed sightings of the Loch Ness monster; the earliest known reference to the existence of a large aquatic animal in Loch Ness was made by St Columba; a Loch Ness Monster Exhibition Centre has been established at Drumnadrochit, on the W shore of the loch.

Neston, formerly NESTON AND PARKGATE, 53 18N 3 04W, pop(1981) 14,979, town in Ellesmere Port and Neston dist, Cheshire, NW central England; on the Wirral peninsula, 11 km W of Ellesmere Port; railway; economy: glass, printing.

Netherlands Antilles *an-til'eez,* island group in the Caribbean Sea comprising the S Netherlands Antilles (Aruba, Bonaire, Curaçao) and the N Netherlands Antilles (Saba, St Maarten, St Eustatius); an autonomous region of the Kingdom of the Netherlands; timezone GMT −4; area 993 sq km; capital Willemstad; pop(1981) 231,932; 85% of the population are of mixed African descent; Dutch is the official language, with English and a local patois called Papiamento widely spoken; the unit of currency is the Antillian guilder; membership: EEC (associate), INTERPOL, UPU, WMO.

Physical description and climate. The Leeward Is of Curaçao (444 sq km), Aruba (193 sq km), and Bonaire (288 sq km) are situated 60 to 110 km N of the Venezuelan coast between 12°N and 13°N and 68°W and 71°W. St Maarten (34 sq km), St Eustatius (21 sq km), and Saba (13 sq km) belong to the Windward group lying E of Puerto Rico. St Maarten, Aruba, Bonaire, and Curaçao are composed of coralline limestone fringing an igneous core. There are no permanent rivers on these islands. Saba and St Eustatius are part of the volcanic inner arc of the Lesser Antilles. Saba is the highest island in the group rising to 870 m at Mt Scenery. St Maarten lies on the non-volcanic outer arc with a geology similar to the islands of the S Netherlands Antilles. The climate is tropical maritime with a mean annual temperature of 27.5°C. Mean annual rainfall varies from 500 mm on the S islands to 1,000 mm on the N islands. There is a short rainy season from Oct to Jan.

History, government and constitution. Visited by Columbus, the Netherlands Antilles were initially claimed for Spain. Dutch settlers occupied the islands during the 17th century and although subsequently held by Britain or France they all eventually reverted to Dutch ownership. The Netherlands Antilles are an autonomous part of the Kingdom of the Netherlands. The sovereign of the Netherlands is the head of state and is represented by a governor. Executive power in internal affairs rests with the governor and council of ministers, who together form the government. The ministers are responsible to the unicameral legislature or *staten.* The *staten* comprises 22 members and is elected every 4 years by universal suffrage. The *staten* and governor together form the legislative authority.

Economy. The economy is largely based on the refining of crude oil imported from Venezuela to Curaçao and Aruba. The refineries and their shipping establishments account for approx 25% of the workforce on Curaçao and 30% on Aruba. More than 98% of the refined products are exported, chiefly to the USA. Reserves of salt and phosphate on Bonaire and Curaçao are mined and exported. In order to diversify the economy attempts have been made to encourage the establishment of new industries including tourism. In order to cope with increasing numbers of tourists, chiefly from the USA, large, modern hotels have been constructed in recent years on every island and airport facilities have been extended. Other industries include rum distilling, textiles, petrochemicals, beverages, and ship repairing. Agriculture plays a relatively minor role in the economy of the Netherlands Antilles.

Netherlands, The, or **Holland,** NEDERLAND (Du), official name Kingdom of the Netherlands, KONINKRIJK DER NEDERLANDEN (Du), a maritime kingdom of NW Europe, bounded on the N and W by the North Sea, on the E by West Germany, and on the S by Belgium; coastline 451 km; area 33,929 sq km; timezone GMT +1 ; capital Amsterdam; seat of government 's-Gravenhage (The Hague); largest city Rotterdam; chief towns Utrecht, Haarlem, Eindhoven, Arnhem and Groningen; pop(1984e) 14,394,600; with an average population density of 424 inhabitants per sq km (1982), the Netherlands is among the most densely populated countries in the world; nearly half the population lives in the four western provs, while the remaining eight provs, which account for 79% of the area, accommodate only a little more than half the population; the most densely populated prov is Zuid Holland, with 1,080 inhabitants per sq km of land; the Dutch are primarily of Germanic stock with some Gallo-Celtic mixture; in addition, 1% of the pop comprises Indonesian and Surinamese groups from the former colonies of the Dutch East Indies; the official language is Dutch; 40% of the pop are Roman Catholic and 31% are members of the Dutch Reformed Church and other Protestant churches; the currency is the gulden (guilder) of 100 cents; national holiday 30 April (Queen's Day); membership of EEC, Benelux Economic Union, European Space Agency, INTELSAT, ADB, DAC, ECE, EIB, ELDO, EMS, ESRO, FAO, GATT, IAEA, IBRD, ICAC, ICAO, ICES, ICO, IDA, IDB, IEA, IFAD, IFC, IHO, ILO, IMO, INRO, IPU, IRC, ITC, ITU, NATO, OECD, UN, UNESCO, UPU, WEU, WHO, WIPO, WMO, WSG.

Physical description. The total area of 33,929 sq km includes 70% cultivated land, 8.5% forest, 8% inland water and 5% urban. The country is generally low and flat except in the SE where hills rise to 321 m above sea level. Much of the coastal area between the Oosterschelde and the mouth of the R Eems lies below sea level, protected by coastal dunes and man-made dykes; without these sea defences two-fifths of the country would be submerged. The lowest point is N of Rotterdam at 6.7 m below sea level. Of the total land area, 27% is below sea level, an area inhabited by about 60% of the total population. The country is largely a delta comprising silt from the mouths of the Rhine, Waal, Maas, Ijssel and Schelde rivers. These rivers provide water routes for sea-going ships, and with connecting canals totalling 6,340 km in length, give access to the inland waterways of Belgium and Germany. The land is underlain by Tertiary sedimentary rocks which are overlain by Quaternary sand and gravel in the E. In the N and W, peat and polder clay merge into coastal dunes. Areas of infertile, sandy heathlands in the E and N are mainly planted with conifers, but river and marine clays, and in many places the peat, are fertile and support a prosperous agriculture. The reclamation of land from the sea by the creation of polder dykes has been carried out for many centuries. The reclamation of the Zuiderzee (the remnant of which now forms the Ijsselmeer) began in 1920. The 'Delta Project', scheduled to be completed in the 1980s, comprises the building of enclosure dams in the estuaries between the islands at the mouth of the R Schelde in the SW.

Climate. The climate is cool, temperate maritime with an average Jan temperature of 1.7°C and a July average of 17°C. There are no average monthly temperatures below freezing point, although cold winds from continental Europe occasionally bring severe winter conditions. The total annual precipitation exceeds 700 mm and is distributed fairly evenly throughout the year.

History, government and constitution. The name Netherlands, or Low Countries, was long applied to an area embracing not merely modern Holland, but also Belgium. In Roman times this area lay across the frontier of Gaul which rested on the R Rhine. The land S of the Rhine was then occupied by Belgic tribes and the land N by Teutonic peoples, notably the Frisii. By the 8th century the area had become part of the Frankish Empire before being incorporated into the Holy Roman Empire. Ruled by petty princes in the Middle Ages, the towns of Holland grew in wealth and power as commerce expanded. In the 15th century the Netherlands passed into the possession of the dukes of Burgundy and then by inheritance to Philip II of Spain, who succeeded to Spain and the Netherlands in 1555. His attempts to stamp out Protestantism provoked a rebellion in 1572, and with the Union of Utrecht the 7 N provinces united against Spain in 1579. The United Provinces declared their independence in 1581, and so founded the modern Dutch state. Between 1795 and 1813 the Netherlands were overrun by the French, who established the Batavian Republic. Thereafter it was united with Belgium as the Kingdom of the United Netherlands, but Belgium broke away to form a separate kingdom in 1830. The Netherlands is a parliamentary democracy under a constitutional monarchy. The kingdom also consists of the islands of the Netherlands Antilles in the Caribbean. The first Constitution of the Netherlands after its restoration as a sovereign state was promulgated in 1814. The central executive power of the State rests with the Crown, while the central legislative power is vested in the Crown and States-General (*Staten-Generahl*) which consists of two chambers, the first of 75 members, elected by the Provincial States for 6 years, and the second of 150 members, elected by universal suffrage for 4 years.

Industry and trade. Major industries of the Netherlands include engineering, chemicals, petroleum products, foodstuffs, electrical and high technology goods and natural gas. The small amount of coal mined in S Limburg was exhausted in the 1970s just as natural gas and oil from the North Sea and the Groningen came on line. Current gas production accounts for more than 14% of total government revenue, half of which is exported to EEC member countries. Wind turbines alongside the traditional windmill are making a growing contribution to the country's energy needs. Although Dutch gas accounts for nearly 50% of energy demand, this is expected to decline in the late 1980s as gas is replaced by coal. The traditional industries of shipbuilding and construction have suffered considerably in recent years, while the energy-intensive chemical and electrical engineering sectors have been the fastest growing. Amsterdam is a world centre of the diamond industry. Major exports include foodstuffs, machinery, chemicals, petroleum products, natural gas and textiles. Major trade partners are West Germany, Belgium, Luxembourg, France, the USA and East Europe. Rotterdam and the newly-constructed Europort are major European ports of transshipment, handling goods for EEC member countries.

Agriculture and forestry. The Netherlands has developed a specialized and highly intensive agriculture. Farm exports account for 25% of total exports, the Netherlands being the world's largest exporter of dairy produce. Animal husbandry dominates the agricultural scene. Grassland accounts for 60% of cultivated land, and animal husbandry for 67% of the value of all agricultural produce. The world famous horticultural industry produces flowers, bulbs, fruit and vegetables. The area under glass has doubled over the last 30 years to nearly 900 sq km. The average farm size is 0.15 sq km. Ninety per cent of all farms are family-run. The processing and marketing of many products is handled by large co-operatives. The main crops include potatoes, sugar-beet, grains and horticultural crops. Of the male working population, 6% are still directly employed in agriculture and horticulture. The Netherlands is one of the least wooded countries on the European continent, with 3,000 sq km of forest covering 8.5% of the total land area. Total state forest (including areas of natural beauty) accounts for 800 sq km.

Administrative divisions. The Netherlands is divided into 12 provinces as follows:

Province	*area (sq km)*	*pop(1984e)*
Drenthe	2,653	427,300
Flevoland	562	77,300
Friesland	3,352	597,200
Gelderland	5,008	1,735,800
Groningen	2,334	561,500
Limburg	2,171	1,083,600
Noord Brabant	4,963	2,103,000
Noord Holland	2,667	2,307,400
Overijssel	3,811	1,042,100
Utrecht	1,331	929,400
Zeeland	1,786	355,500
Zuid Holland	2,907	3,139,200

Neubrandenburg *noy-brahn'dun-boork*, county in NE East Germany; bounded on the E by R Oder; pop(1981) 620,760; area 10,948 sq km; an important agricultural and industrial region; capital Neubrandenburg; 60% of the county is farmed, producing cereals, potatoes, sugar beet and fodder crops; 20% of the pop is employed in industry, producing vehicle parts, tyres, cardboard, and food processing machinery; there are over 800 lakes in the county; trade union holiday homes are located in Klink on L Müritz, Feldberg and Lychen.

Neubrandenburg, 53 33N 13 17E, pop(1981) 79,813, capital of Neubrandenburg county, NE East Germany; at N end of the Tollense See; founded in the 13th century; railway; economy: chemicals, machinery, vehicle parts, tyres; monument: 14th-c city walls.

Neuchâtel *nœ-shah-tel'*, NEUENBURG *noi'un-boork* (Ger), canton in W Switzerland, in the Jura Mts; pop(1980) 158,368; area 797 sq km; capital Neuchâtel; includes Lac de Neuchâtel; the land rises steeply on either side of the Val de Travers; some of the best-known Swiss wines come from vineyards lying in a long, narrow strip SW of the lake, and along its N shore to the town of Neuchâtel and the Bieler See beyond; joined the Swiss Confederacy in 1815.

Neuchâtel, 44 60N 6 56E, pop(1980) 34,428, capital town of Neuchâtel canton, W Switzerland; on the steep W shore of Lac de Neuchâtel, 40 km W of Bern; a research centre for the Swiss watch industry; university (1909); railway; economy: scientific instruments, electronics, tobacco, wine trade; monuments: 13th-c university church; in the Old Town above the lake there are 16-17th-c houses; in the castle of the counts (mainly 16th-c) are the cantonal administrative departments.

Neuchâtel, Lac de, largest lake to lie wholly within Switzerland, running SW-NE at the foot of the Jura Mts, SW of Bieler See, on the S border of Neuchâtel canton, W Switzerland; area 217.9 sq km; the sunny slopes of the Jura foothills produce some of the best wine in Switzerland; regular boat services link lakeside towns; chief towns on the shore include Neuchâtel (NW) and Yverdon (S).

Neuenburg, town and canton in Switzerland. See Neuchâtel.

Neufchâteau *nü-shaht-ō'*, dist of Luxembourg prov, SE Belgium; area 1,353 sq km; pop(1982) 51,636.

Neuilly-sur-Seine *nœ-yee-sur-sen*, 48 53N 2 16E, pop(1982) 64,450, NW suburb of Paris in Hauts-de-Seine dept, Ile-de-France region, N central France, near Bois de Boulogne; economy: fertilizers, pharmaceuticals, cotton and bandages, medical equipment, engineering, foodstuffs, paper, cellulose, electrical and electronic equipment, soap and detergents; the first level bridge in France was built here over the R Seine in 1772; the Treaty of Neuilly was signed here on 27 Nov, 1919 between the Allies and Bulgaria after World War I.

Neumünster *noy'mün-ster*, 54 05N 9 59E, pop(1983) 79,600, commercial and manufacturing city in Schleswig-Holstein prov, W Germany, SSW of Kiel; railway junction; economy: textiles, paper, machinery.

Neunkirchen *noyn'kirKH-en*, 49 21N 7 12E, pop(1983) 50,800, industrial city in E Saarland prov, W Germany; 19 km NE of Saarbrücken; railway; economy: coal mining, iron.

Neuquén *nay-oo-kayn'*, prov in Andina region, W central Argentina; Andean mountainous area, bordered W by Chile; S border formed by the Río Limay, the N border by the Colorado and Barrancas rivers; intersected by the Río Neuquén; there are numerous volcanoes to the W (Copahue, Lanín) and a lake region in the SW (L Nahuel Huapí, L Traful and L Huechulaufquen); much of the prov is in a national park; the climate varies with alt but is generally temperate and dry; near the capital is the Cerros Colorados Dam, used for hydroelectricity and flood control; pop(1980) 243,850; area 94,078 sq km; capital Neuquén; chief town Zapala; economy: vineyards, fruit, sheep and some cattle raising, copper and iron mining, natural gas, oil.

Neuquén, 38 55S 68 55W, pop(1980) 90,037, capital of Neuquén prov, Andina, W Argentina; industrial city near confluence of Limay and Neuquén rivers; transport centre for Mendoza (N), Bahía Blanca and Buenos Aires (E), Zapala and Chile (W) and Bariloche (S); university (1971), railway; airfield (at 7 km); economy: equipment and construction materials for oilfields to the W and irrigated fruit-producing valley to the E.

Neusiedler See *noi'zeed-lar zay*, FERTŐ TÓ *fer'tu tō* (Hung), 47 50N 16 47E, lake in Burgenland state of E Austria and Győr-Sopron dist of NW Hungary, SE of Wien (Vienna); area 152 sq km; length 35 km; width 5-15 km; maximum depth 1.8 m; the only steppe lake in Europe; the shallow water which is slightly saline warms up quickly in summer; surrounded by reed beds up to 5 km wide; monumental sculptures in the Leitha limestone quarry between Rust and St Margarethen; stone from here was used to build St Stephen's Cathedral, Wien.

Neuss *noys*, NOVESIUM (anc), 51 12N 6 42E, pop(1983) 146,800, industrial city in Düsseldorf dist, W Nordrhein-Westfalen (North Rhine-Westphalia) prov, W Germany; 8 km W of Düsseldorf; railway; economy: diesel engines, machine building, agricultural machinery.

Neuwied *noy'veet*, 50 26N 7 28E, pop(1983) 59,200, industrial river port in Koblenz dist, Rheinland-Pfalz (Rhineland-Palatinate) prov, W Germany; on the R Rhine, 11 km NNW of Koblenz; founded in 1653; railway;

economy: tinplate and sheet, nonwoven fabrics, hospital supplies.

Neva'da, state in W United States; bounded S and W by California, N by Oregon and Idaho, and E by Utah and Arizona; the Colorado river forms the lower part of the Arizona border; the R Humboldt rises in the NE and flows W and then SW, emptying into the alkali sink of L Humboldt; L Pyramid and L Winnemucca lie to the W and L Tahoe is on the Californian border; the highest point is Boundary Peak (4,006 m); most of the state lies in the Great Basin, a huge area of arid desert interspersed with barren mountain ranges; it is an area of internal drainage, with most of the state's rivers petering out in the desert or ending in alkali sinks; in the rain shadow of the Sierra Nevada Mts of California, it is the driest of all the states and most of the land is unpopulated and uncultivated, though there are some oases of irrigation; tourism and mining are major industries; the gambling resorts of Las Vegas and Reno attract around 20 mn visitors each year, and gaming taxes are a primary source of state revenue; the shores of L Tahoe and Death Valley National Monument (part of which is in Nevada) are also major tourist attractions; Nevada is a major supplier of gold; oil was discovered in 1954; agriculture is not highly developed in the state but products include cattle, sheep, dairy products, hay and alfalfa; manufactures include clay and glass products, chemicals, electrical machinery, and lumber; the state was part of the region ceded by Mexico to the United States in the Treaty of Guadalupe Hidalgo in 1848 and was included in Mormon-ruled Utah Territory in 1850; settlement expanded after the Comstock Lode silver strike in 1859 and Nevada was made a separate territory in 1861; in order that President Lincoln could gain more votes to pass the Thirteenth Amendment, Nevada was rapidly made a state (36th) in 1864; also known as the 'Sage Brush State', 'Battle Born State' or the 'Silver State'; pop(1980) 800,493; area 285,724 sq km; capital Carson City; other major cities are Las Vegas and Reno; the state is divided into 16 counties and the independent Carson City:

County	*area (sq km)*	*pop(1980)*
Carson City	380	32,022
Churchill	12,974	13,917
Clark	20,491	463,087
Douglas	1,841	19,421
Elko	44,551	17,269
Esmeralda	9,326	777
Eureka	10,855	1,198
Humboldt	25,215	9,434
Lander	14,339	4,076
Lincoln	27,651	3,732
Lyon	5,218	13,594
Mineral	9,734	6,217
Nye	47,203	9,048
Pershing	15,694	3,408
Storey	686	1,503
Washoe	16,424	193,623
White Pine	23,145	8,167

Nevada, Sierra *ne-va'THa*, ('snowy range'), mountain range in Andalucia, S Spain, rising to 3,478 m at Mulhacén which is the highest peak in continental Spain; a core of gneiss and crystalline schists is lapped about with Triassic limestone; skiing has been developed at Solynieve on the slopes of the Pico de Veleta (access by cable-car).

Never Never Land, area of Northern Territory, N Australia; SE of Darwin; chief town Katherine; first explored by Leichardt in 1844; featured in Mrs Aeneas Gunn's book, *We of the Never Never*.

Nevers *ne-ver*, NOVIODUNUM (anc), 47 00N 3 09E, pop(1982) 44,777, capital of Nièvre dept, Bourgogne region, central France; built on high ground facing S across the R Loire, at the confluence of the Loire and Nièvre rivers, 61 km ESE of Bourges; capital of the old dukedom of Nivernais; renowned for the manufacture of fine china since the 16th century when one of the dukes introduced the craft from Italy; episcopal see (since 506); railway; economy: pharmaceuticals, metal goods, pottery, wine; monuments: 10-16th-c cathedral; Renaissance Palais Ducal (now the courthouses); 14th-c Porte du Croux (one of the remaining gateways of the old ramparts); 11th-c Romanesque church of St-Étienne (damaged in the Revolution).

Nevis, Ben, 56 48N 5 00W, highest mountain in Britain; in the Grampian Mts, Highland region, W Scotland, 7 km E of Fort William; height 1,344 m.

Nevşehir *nev-she-hir'*, mountainous prov in central Turkey; in the Kapadokya (Cappadocia) region; pop(1980) 256,933; area 5,467 sq km; capital Nevşehir; economy: grain and vegetables.

New Albany, 38 18N 85 49W, pop(1980) 37,103, county seat of Floyd county, SE Indiana, United States; on the Ohio river, opposite Louisville, Kentucky; university (1941); railway.

New Amsterdam, 6 18N 57 30W, pop(1979e) 25,000, port capital of W Berbice dist, N Guyana, South America; on the right bank of the R Berbice near its mouth; 105 km SE of Georgetown.

New Bedford, 41 38N 70 56W, pop(1980) 98,478, town in Bristol county, SE Massachusetts, United States; port on Buzzards Bay, 80 km S of Boston; railway; economy: fishing; monument: whaling museum, reflecting the town's past as a major whaling port.

New Berlin, 42 59N 88 06W, pop(1980) 30,529, city in Waukesha county, SE Wisconsin, United States; 18 km WSW of Milwaukee.

New Britain, formerly NEU-POMMERN, 5 38S 148 25E, largest island of the Bismarck archipelago, Papua New Guinea, SW Pacific, E of New Guinea; separated from New Ireland by St George's Channel; to the S is the Solomon Sea and to the N the Bismarck Sea; area 37,799 sq km; length 480 km; width 80 km; capital Rabaul; other towns include Kokopo, Talasea, Rabaul, Hoskins, and Keravat; Whiteman Range, source of numerous S flowing rivers, extends W-E across the island; highest point is Mt Sinewit (2,438 m) on the Gazelle peninsula in the extreme NE; the country's first large oil palm scheme was established S of Hoskins; economy: coconut plantations.

New Britain, 41 40N 72 47W, pop(1980) 73,840, town in Hartford county, central Connecticut, United States; 14 km SW of Hartford; railway.

New Brunswick, province in E Canada; bounded by Québec (NW and N), the United States (Maine, W), the Baie des Chaleurs (NE), the Gulf of St Lawrence and the Northumberland Strait (E), Nova Scotia (SE) and the Bay of Fundy (S); the forested, rocky land is generally low and level, rising in the NW with an extension of the Appalachian Mountain system; drained by the St John, Restigouche, Nipisiguit, Tobique, Miramichi and Petitcodiac rivers; the S part of the border with the US is formed by the Croix river; there are several lakes in New Brunswick, especially in the SW of the prov; the largest is Grand Lake (area: 174 sq km); in the E of the prov is Fundy National Park (area 205 sq km, established in 1948); pop(1981) 696,403; area 71,569 sq km; capital Fredericton; major towns include St John and Moncton; economy: paper and wood products, potatoes, seafood, mining (zinc, lead, silver, potash, bismuth), tourism, food processing, dairy products, livestock, poultry; known as Acadia, the region was first settled by French fur traders; in the 1600s it was twice conquered by the British, who were forced to return it to France each time; the French ceded it to Britain in 1713 (the Peace of Utrecht) and British ownership was confirmed by the Treaty of Paris in 1763; in 1755 the British forced the Acadians to swear allegiance to the King of England, those who refused (approx 6,000) were deported; in 1783 14,000 United Empire Loyalist settlers arrived, and New Brunswick was separated from Nova Scotia; in 1867 economic factors led the province into confederation; New Brunswick is governed by a Lieutenant-Governor and an elected 58-member Legislative Assembly.

New Brunswick, 40 30N 74 27W, pop(1980) 41,442, county seat of Middlesex county, central New Jersey, United States; on the R Raritan, 14 km W of Perth Amboy; settled in 1681, achieving city status in 1784; the starting point for George Washington's march to Yorktown in 1781; Rutgers, the State University (1766); railway; economy: chemicals, pharmaceuticals, hospital supplies, motor vehicles, clothing, food processing.

New Caledonia, NOUVELLE CALÉDONIE *noo-vel' ka-lay-do-nee'* (Fr), territory in the SW Pacific Ocean, 1,100 km E of Australia, comprising the island of New Caledonia, Îles Loyauté (Loyalty Is), Îsle des Pins, Îsle Bélep and the uninhabited Chesterfield and Huon Is; timezone GMT +11; land area 18,575 sq km; capital Nouméa; pop(1983) 145,368; the pop comprises 37.1% Europeans, 42.6% Melanesians, 8.4% Wallisians, 3.8% Polynesians, 3.7% Indonesians, 1.6% Vietnamese; more than half the inhabitants live in the capital city; French is the official language but English is widely understood; the Roman Catholic church predominates; the unit of currency is the French Pacific franc; national holidays 14 July (National Day), 24 Sept (New Caledonia Day).

Physical description and climate. The long and narrow main island of New Caledonia is 400 km in length and rises to a height of 1,639 m at Mt Panie. The central mountain chain divides the island into 2 distinct natural regions - the dry W coast, covered mostly by gum-tree savannah, and the tropical E coast. The other islands of the territory are either high and volcanic or dry limestone platforms, and all are surrounded by coral reefs. New Caledonia has a mild Mediterranean-type climate with an average July temperature of 19.9°C and an average Jan temperature of 25.8°C. December-March is warm and humid while April-Nov is cool and dry. Rainfall is heaviest from Dec to March, particularly on the E coasts of the islands.

History, government and constitution. New Caledonia was discovered in 1774 by Captain Cook, but was annexed by France as a penal settlement in 1853. It became a French Overseas Territory in 1946. The territory is administered by a high commissioner and a 7-member government council elected from the 36-member territorial assembly. New Caledonia is represented in the French national assembly by 2 deputies and in the senate by 1 senator. There were serious disturbances in the mid-1980s when the indigenous Melanesians began their struggle for independence.

Economy. The chief agricultural products are beef, pork, poultry, coffee, maize, fruit and vegetables. Coffee and copra are produced for export. Stock raising is concentrated on the W coast and has developed considerably since the introduction of Hereford and Charolais cattle. Mineral ores are the territory's chief asset, particularly nickel, chrome, and iron. New Caledonia is the world's 3rd largest producer of nickel, after Canada and the USSR, accounting for over 90% of total exports. The nickel boom of the 1960s brought thousands of settlers from France and other Pacific states. Local industries include chlorine and oxygen plants, cement, soft drinks, clothing, and foodstuffs. France is the major trade partner (32.5% of imports and 67% of exports in 1981). The main tourist resorts are on the E coast of New Caledonia, on the Ile des Pins, Ile Ouen, and the islands of Uvéa and Lifu in the Loyaute group.

Administrative divisions. The territory is divided into 4 circonscriptions and sub-divided into 32 communes which are administered by locally elected councils and mayors:

Commune	*area (sq km)*	*pop(1976)*
Bélep	69.5	686
Bouloupari	865.6	1,139
Bourail	797.6	3,410
Canala	821.7	3,842
Dumbéa	254.6	5,638
Farino	48.0	263
Hienghène	1,068.8	1,729
Houaïlou	940.6	3,995
Île des Pins	152.3	1,287
Kaala-Gomen	718.2	1,231
Koné	373.6	2,919
Koumac	550.0	1,405
La Foa	464.4	2,094
Lifou	1,207.1	8,128
Mare	641.7	4,614
Moindou	321.9	378
Mont-Dore	643.0	14,614
Nouméa	457.0	60,112
Ouégoa	656.8	1,468
Ouvéa	132.1	2,772
Païta	699.7	4,834
Poindimié	673.1	3,644
Ponérihouen	707.3	1,932
Pouébo	202.8	1,503
Pouembout	674.3	692
Poum	469.4	816
Poya	845.8	1,961
Sarraméa	106.4	483
Thio	997.6	3,019
Touho	283.0	1,901
Voh	804.9	1,586
Yaté	1,338.4	1,387

New Castle, 41 00N 80 21W, pop(1980) 33,621, county seat of Lawrence county, W Pennsylvania, United States; on the R Shenango, 70 km NNW of Pittsburgh and 15 km E of the Ohio border; railway.

New Delhi, capital of India. See Delhi.

New Forest, national park in Hampshire, S England; area 269 sq km; mostly woodland, heath and bog; ponies and pigs are reared locally; a former royal hunting ground.

New Georgia Islands, SW Pacific island group in the Solomon Islands; NW of Guadalcanal and S of Choiseul; includes the islands of New Georgia, Gizo, Kolombangara, Ganongga, Rendova, Tetepari, Vangunu and Gatukai; chief town is Hobu Hobu; economy: copra.

New Hampshire, state in NE United States, bounded W by Vermont, N by Canada, E by Maine, SE by the Atlantic Ocean and S by Massachusetts; the 'Granite State'; pop(1980) 920,610; area 23,382 sq km; 9th of the original 13 states to ratify the Federal Constitution; capital Concord; chief cities are Manchester, Nashua and Portsmouth; the R Connecticut forms W border of state and the R Merrimack flows S through the centre into Massachusetts; a low, rolling coast is backed by hills and mountains which include the White Mts in the N; the highest point is Mt Washington (1,917 m); the mountainous N is forested while the S is largely devoted to arable farming and grazing; chief agricultural products include dairy and greenhouse products, maple syrup, hay, apples and eggs; explored by Champlain and Pring (1603-05); the first settlement was established at Little Harbor in 1623; the state is divided into 10 counties as follows:

County	*area (sq km)*	*pop(1980)*
Belknap	1,050	42,884
Carroll	2,426	27,931
Cheshire	1,849	62,116
Coos	4,690	35,147
Grafton	4,469	65,806
Hillsborough	2,278	276,608
Merrimack	2,434	98,302
Rockingham	1,817	190,345
Strafford	962	85,408
Sullivan	1,404	36,063

New Haven, formerly QUINNIPIAC (-1640), 41 18N 72 55W, pop(1980) 126,109, port town in New Haven county, S

Connecticut, United States; on Long Island Sound, 58 km SSW of Hartford; founded by Puritans in 1638; joint capital of state with Hartford (1701-1873); industrial development was associated with names such as Samuel Morse and Charles Goodyear; Yale University (1701); railway; economy: firearms, aircraft parts.

New Hebrides, SW Pacific Island group. See Vanuatu.

New Iberia, 30 01N 91 49W, pop(1980) 32,766, parish seat of Iberia parish, S Louisiana, United States; 30 km SE of Lafayette; railway; economy: processing centre for sugar cane, oil, dairy products, vegetables, rock salt, and fish; salt mines; shipyards; monument: Plantation Homes.

New Ireland, formerly NEU-MECKLENBURG *noy mek'len-boorKH*, second largest island in the Bismarck archipelago, Papua New Guinea, SW Pacific, separated from New Britain to the SW by St George's Channel; with the islands of New Hanover, Lihir, Tabar, Feni, and St Matthias constitutes a prov of Papua New Guinea (New Ireland); area 8,647 sq km; length 480 km; average width 24 km; capital Kavieng; low limestone mountains form a spine down the centre of the island; Mt Gilaut (2,399 m) is the highest peak; Buluminshi Highway extends for 264 km down the E coast of the island between Kavieng and Namatanai; economy: tuna fishing, copra.

New Jersey, state in E United States; bounded W by Pennsylvania, N by New York, E by New York and the Atlantic Ocean, and S by the Atlantic Ocean, Delaware Bay and Delaware; the 'Garden State'; pop(1980) 7,364,823; area 19,417 sq km; one of the original states of the Union, 3rd to ratify the Federal Constitution; capital Trenton; other major cities include Newark, Jersey City, Paterson and Elizabeth; the Hudson river follows the NE border and the R Delaware follows the W border; the Appalachian Highlands fall down through Piedmont Plateau to low coastal plains which are broken by ridges of the Palisades; the highest point is Mt High Point (550 m); 40% of the land is forested, mostly in the SE; the NE is highly industrialized and densely populated; the rest is mainly arable and grazing, producing dairy products, hay and soybeans; economy: chemicals, electronics, metals, machinery; colonized after the explorations of Verrazano (1524) and Hudson (1609); the area between the Delaware and Hudson rivers was granted to Lord John Berkeley and Sir George Carteret after the British took control of New Netherlands in 1664; the state is divided into 21 counties as follows:

County	*area (sq km)*	*pop(1980)*
Atlantic	1,477	194,119
Bergen	616	845,385
Burlington	2,093	362,542
Camden	580	471,650
Cape May	684	82,266
Cumberland	1,295	132,866
Essex	330	851,116
Gloucester	850	199,917
Hudson	120	556,972
Hunterdon	1,108	87,361
Mercer	590	307,863
Middlesex	822	595,893
Monmouth	1,227	503,173
Morris	1,222	407,630
Ocean	1,667	346,038
Passaic	486	447,585
Salem	879	64,676
Somerset	793	203,129
Sussex	1,368	116,119
Union	268	504,094
Warren	933	84,429

New London, 41 22N 72 06W, pop(1980) 28,842, port town in New London county, SE Connecticut, United States; on Long Island Sound at the mouth of R Thames, 69 km E of New Haven; major US nuclear submarine base; railway; economy: shipbuilding.

New Mexico, state in SW United States; bounded W by Arizona, N by Colorado, E by Oklahoma and Texas, and S by Texas and Mexico; the Rio Grande flows S through the centre of the state and forms part of the S border with Texas state; the R Pecos rises in the N and flows SSE into Texas; the S end of the Sangre de Cristo Mts lies to the N; the highest point is Wheeler Peak (4,011 m); the state is characterized by broad deserts, forested mountain wildernesses, and towering barren peaks; isolated mountain ranges, part of the Rocky Mts, flank the Rio Grande; forests, such as the Gila Wilderness, lie mainly in the SW and N; most of the state, particularly in the S and E, is semi-arid plain with little rainfall; farming is centred in the valley of the Rio Grande which is extensively irrigated; chief agricultural products are cattle, dairy products, sheep, hay, wheat and cotton; chief manufactures include processed foods, chemicals and electrical equipment; the military establishments and atomic energy centres in the state are major employers; mineral resources include uranium, potash and perlite; oil and coal are also produced in large quantities; tourism is a major industry, visitors being attracted by the warm, dry climate and the state's striking scenery; among the state's major attractions are the Carlsbad Caverns National Park and the Aztec Ruins, White Sands, Chaco Canyon, Gila Cliff Dwellings and Gran Quivira national monuments; first explored by the Spanish in the early 1500s, the first white settlement in the region was at Santa Fe (1609); governed by Mexico from 1821, but ceded to the United States in the Treaty of Guadalupe Hidalgo in 1848; in 1850 New Mexico was organized as a territory including Arizona and part of Colorado and in 1912 it was admitted to the Union as the 47th state; in 1943 Los Alamos atomic research centre was built and in July 1945 the first explosion of an atomic bomb took place at White Sands proving grounds; Navajo, Zuni, Apache, Acoma, Mescalero, Canoncito, Isleta, Laguna and Ute mountain Indian reservations are located in the state; New Mexico is also known as the 'Land of Enchantment'; pop(1980) 1,302,894; area 315,471 sq km; capital Santa Fe; other main cities are Albuquerque, Las Cruces and Roswell; the state is divided into 32 counties:

County	*area (sq km)*	*pop(1980)*
Bernalillo	3,039	419,700
Catron	18,015	2,720
Chaves	15,772	51,103
Colfax	9,781	13,667
Curry	3,661	42,019
De Baca	6,040	2,454
Dona Ana	9,929	96,340
Eddy	10,878	47,855
Grant	10,319	26,204
Guadalupe	7,883	4,496
Harding	5,517	1,090
Hidalgo	8,957	6,049
Lea	11,411	55,993
Lincoln	12,563	10,997
Los Alamos	283	17,599
Luna	7,709	15,585
McKinley	14,149	56,449
Mora	5,018	4,205
Otero	17,228	44,665
Quay	7,472	10,577
Rio Arriba	15,226	29,282
Roosevelt	6,378	15,695
San Juan	14,355	81,433
San Miguel	12,243	22,751
Sandoval	9,638	34,799
Santa Fe	4,953	75,360
Sierra	10,863	8,454
Socorro	17,225	12,566
Taos	5,730	19,456
Torrance	8,671	7,491
Union	9,958	4,725
Valencia	14,602	61,115

New Milton, 50 45N 1 39W, pop(1981) 20,922, town linked with Barton-on-Sea in New Forest dist, Hampshire, S England; part of Bournemouth urban area; 8 km W of Lymington; railway.

New Orleans *or-lee'enz*, 29 58N 90 04W, pop(1980) 557,515, parish seat of Orleans parish, SE Louisiana, United States; between the Mississippi river and L Pontchartrain; founded by the French in 1718 and made capital of French Louisiana in 1722; the colony was ceded to Spain in 1763, and returned to French hands briefly in 1803 before passing to the US in the Louisiana Purchase; the French influence is still evident in the city today; in the 19th century the city prospered as a market for slaves and cotton, at the same time gaining a lasting reputation for glamour and wild living; during the Civil War, the city fell to Union troops and suffered under the occupation of General Butler's forces; during the 20th century the city has experienced industrial growth following the discovery of vast deposits of oil and natural gas in the region; jazz music originated in New Orleans in the late 1800s, among black musicians; 5 universities; railway; airport; economy: situated at the head of the Mississippi, the city is one of the nation's busiest ports, handling a wide range of goods; oil and petrochemical industries; shipbuilding yards; monuments: the French Quarter, the Cabildo, St Louis cathedral, jazz museum, Isaac Delgado Museum of Art; events: Mardi Gras (Feb-Mar), Jazz and Heritage Festival (April).

New Plymouth, 39 03S 174 04E, pop(1981) 36,048, port on the W coast of North Island, New Zealand; S of the North Taranaki Bight; to the S is Mount Egmont; railway; airfield; economy: centre of Taranaki dairying prov; nearby are the Taranaki gas fields; monuments: the Pukeiti Rhododendron Trust park and bird sanctuary covers 3.6 sq km.

New Providence, island in the N central Bahamas, between Andros I (W) and Eleuthera I (E), on the Great Bahama Bank; pop(1980) 135,437; area 207 sq km; length 32 km; capital Nassau; most important island in the Bahamas, having more than half of the total population of the group; popular tourist resort; Nassau International Airport is located W of L Kilarney; the island is divided into 20 enumeration districts as follows:

District	*pop(1980)*
Ann's Town	5,228
Bain Town	5,837
Bamboo Town	8,925
Carmichael	9,521
Centerville	5,593
Delaporte	6,528
Englerston	7,639
Fort Charlotte	5,323
Fort Fincastle	7,016
Fox Hill	8,384
Grant's Town	5,702
Montagu	10,213
Pinedale	7,368
St Agnes	5,051
St Barnabas	7,950
St Michael	5,756
Salem	4,429
Shirlea	4,144
South Beach	9,819
Yellow Elder	5,011

New Rochelle *re-shel'*, 40 55N 73 47W, pop(1980) 70,794, town in Westchester county, SE New York, United States; on Long Island Sound, 42 km NE of New York City; railway.

New Ross, BAILA NUA (Gael), 52 24N 6 56W, pop(1981) 6,141, medieval town and river port in Wexford county, Leinster, SE Irish Republic; on R Barrow, NE of Waterford; a farmhouse in Dunganstown 8 km S was the home of the Kennedy family and nearby is the J.F. Kennedy Memorial Park.

New Siberian Islands, archipelago in the Arctic Ocean, NE Soviet Union. See Novosibirskiye Ostrova.

New South Wales, state in SE Australia; bordered N by Queensland, S by Victoria, W by South Australia and E by the South Pacific Ocean and Tasman Sea; the coastal lowlands give way to tablelands, formed by the Great Dividing Range which rises to 2,228 m at Mount Kosciusko, the highest point in Australia; to the W of the tablelands are the fertile western slopes and irrigated plains; the western plains comprise two-thirds of the area of New South Wales; the main coastal rivers are the Hawkesbury, Hunter, Macleay and Clarence; the main inland rivers are the Darling, Murray, Murrumbidgee, Lachlan and Macquarie-Bogan; pop(1986) 5,605,269 (including Lord Howe Island, with 287 residents); area 801,428 sq km (including the 16.54 sq km Lord Howe I and 71 sq km of harbours and rivers); capital Sydney; principal towns include Newcastle, Wollongong and Wagga Wagga; economy: beef cattle, dairy farming, wool, cereals, fishing, forestry, textiles, electrical machinery, chemicals, food processing and the mining of lead, zinc and coal; the most populous and heavily industrialized state in Australia, it was the first colony to be established by Britain in Australia, and was named by Captain Cook who landed at Botany Bay in 1770; the first settlement was established at Port Jackson (Sydney) in 1788; New South Wales joined the other Australian states to form the Commonwealth of Australia in 1901; state holidays: Bank Holiday in Aug; Labour Day (Oct); the state of New South Wales comprises 12 statistical divisions:

Statistical division	*area (sq km)*	*pop(1982e)*
Central West	63,262	159,665
Far West	147,143	31,644
Hunter	31,011	458,686
Illawarra	8,485	293,743
Mid-North Coast	25,922	178,635
Murray	90,003	97,920
Murrumbidgee	63,522	139,709
North-Western	199,076	106,270
Northern	98,617	174,230
Richmond-Tweed	9,757	135,916
South-Eastern	52,163	140,541
Sydney	12,407	3,204,211

New Territories, region of the British Crown Colony of Hong Kong, SE Asia; N of the Kowloon Peninsula and bounded N by Guangdong prov, China; covers an area of 950 sq km over the mainland, Lantau Island and other associated islands; the coastline of the New Territories is 354 km long and the boundary between New Territories and the Chinese mainland is 31 km; leased to Britain until 1997, when under the Sino-British Agreement of 1984, Hong Kong is restored to China; population density 792 persons to the sq km (1981).

New Westminster, 49 10N 122 58W, pop(1981) 38,550, seaport in SW British Columbia, SW Canada; on the N bank of the Fraser river, 14 km ESE of Vancouver; the town was founded in 1859 and originally named Queensborough; it was the capital of British Columbia until the colonies of British Columbia and Vancouver island were united in 1886; railway; economy: timber, fishing, canning, machinery.

New York, state in NE United States; bounded W by Pennsylvania, L Erie and Canada, N by L Ontario and Canada, E by Vermont, Massachusetts and Connecticut, and S by the Atlantic Ocean, New Jersey and Pennsylvania; the 'Empire State'; pop(1980) 17,558,072; 2nd most populous state; area 123,180 sq km; one of the original states of the Union, 11th to ratify the Federal Constitution; capital Albany; other major cities include New York, Buffalo, Rochester, Yonkers and Syracuse; the R Hudson flows S through the E part of the state and near its mouth forms the border with New Jersey, the St Lawrence river forms part of N border and the R

Delaware forms part of the S border; the Adirondack Mts rise in the N and the Catskill Mts in the S; the highest point is in the Adirondack Mts at Mt Marcy (1,629 m); the state contains 11,334 sq km of the Great Lakes, as well as L Oneida and the Finger Lakes in the centre; there is extensive woodland and forest in the NE and a mixture of cropland, pasture and woodland elsewhere; economy: clothing, pharmaceuticals, publishing, electronics, automotive and aircraft components; dairy products, corn and beef; explored by Hudson and Champlain in 1609; the Dutch established posts near Albany in 1614 and settled Manhattan in 1626; the New Netherlands were taken by the British in 1664; the state is divided into 62 counties as follows:

County	*area (sq km)*	*pop(1980)*
Albany	1,362	285,909
Allegany	2,683	51,742
Bronx	109	1,168,972
Broome	1,851	213,648
Cattaraugus	3,396	85,697
Cayuga	1,807	79,894
Chautauqua	2,766	146,925
Chemung	1,069	97,656
Chenango	2,332	49,344
Clinton	2,712	80,750
Columbia	1,659	59,487
Cortland	1,300	48,820
Delaware	3,744	46,824
Dutchess	2,090	245,055
Erie	2,720	1,015,472
Essex	4,696	36,176
Franklin	4,269	44,929
Fulton	1,292	55,153
Genesee	1,287	59,400
Greene	1,685	40,861
Hamilton	4,475	5,034
Herkimer	3,682	66,714
Jefferson	3,310	88,151
Kings	182	2,230,936
Lewis	3,336	25,035
Livingston	1,646	57,006
Madison	1,706	65,150
Monroe	1,724	702,238
Montgomery	1,050	53,439
Nassau	746	1,321,582
New York	57	1,428,285
Niagara	1,368	227,354
Oneida	3,169	253,466
Onondaga	2,038	463,920
Ontario	1,674	88,909
Orange	2,148	259,603
Orleans	1,017	38,496
Oswego	2,480	113,901
Otsego	2,610	59,075
Putnam	601	77,193
Queens	283	1,891,325
Rensselaer	1,703	151,966
Richmond	153	352,121
Rockland	455	259,530
Saratoga	2,106	153,759
Schenectady	536	149,946
Schoharie	1,622	29,710
Schuyler	855	17,686
Seneca	850	33,733
St Lawrence	7,093	114,254
Steuben	3,630	99,217
Suffolk	2,369	1,284,231
Sullivan	2,538	65,155
Tioga	1,349	49,812
Tompkins	1,240	87,085
Ulster	2,941	158,158
Warren	2,293	54,854
Washington	2,174	54,795
Wayne	1,573	84,581

contd

County	*area (sq km)*	*pop(1980)*
Westchester	1,139	866,599
Wyoming	1,547	39,895
Yates	881	21,459

New York, 40 43N 74 00W, pop(1980) 7,071,639, county seat of New York county, SE New York, United States; at the mouth of the R Hudson; largest city in the United States and largest port, with 1,200 km of waterfront including that in neighbouring New Jersey; originally the site of a trading post established in 1609 by Henry Hudson, it was colonized by the Dutch and named New Amsterdam; it was captured by the British in 1664 and named New York after the King's brother, the Duke of York; scene of the reading of the Declaration of Independence on 4 July 1776, but the city was held by the British throughout the War of Independence; George Washington was inaugurated as first president of the United States in Federal Hall, on the site of the present US sub-Treasury building on Wall Street; the city experienced rapid commercial and industrial growth following the opening of the Erie canal in 1825; 8 universities; railway; airports (La Guardia and J.F. Kennedy); a major world financial centre, with Stock Exchange in Wall Street; economy: advertising, the media, printing and publishing, textiles, food processing, metal products, scientific equipment, vehicles, shipbuilding, machinery, pharmaceuticals; the country's centre for fashion, the arts and entertainment; monuments: United Nations headquarters, World Trade Centre, Statue of Liberty, Empire State Building (448 m high), Guggenheim museum, Frick museum, Metropolitan museum; the city is divided into 5 boroughs, each co-extensive with a county:

Borough	*area (sq km)*	*pop(1980)*
Bronx (Bronx co)	109	1,168,972
Brooklyn (Kings co)	182	2,230,936
Manhattan (New York co)	57	1,428,285
Queens (Queens co)	283	1,891,325
Staten Island (Richmond co)	153	352,121

New Zealand *zee'land*, independent state, comprising a group of islands in the Pacific Ocean SW of Australia lying between 34°S and 47°S in the South Pacific Ocean, midway between the Equator and the South Pole; bounded W by the Tasman Sea and E by the South Pacific Ocean; includes 2 principal islands (North and South) separated by the Cook Strait, Stewart island, and several minor inhabited and uninhabited islands; timezone GMT +12; area 268,812 sq km; pop(1981) 3,157,737; pop is 87% European, 9% Maori and 2% Pacific Islander; the official language is English, Maori is also spoken; 81% of the pop is Christian; the currency is the New Zealand dollar of 100 cents; national holiday 6 Feb (Waitangi Day); membership of ADB, ANZUS, ASPAC, Colombo Plan, Commonwealth, DAC, ESCAP, FAO, GATT, IAEA, IBRD, ICAO, ICO, IDA, IEA, IFAD, IFC, IHO, ILO, IMF, IMO, INTELSAT, INTERPOL, IPU, ISO, ITU, OECD, UN, UNESCO, UPU, WHO, WMO, WSG.

Physical description. The 2 main islands, North and South islands, are long and narrow, with 1,770 km separating the northernmost and southernmost points. North Island is mountainous in the centre with many hot springs and peaks rising to 2,797 m at Mt Ruapehu, 2,291 m at Mt Ngauruhoe, 2,518 m at Mt Egmont, and 1,727 m at Mt Makorako. North Island has New Zealand's longest river, the Waikato river (425 km) and largest lake, L Taupo (606 sq km). South Island is mountainous for the whole of its length, rising in the Southern Alps to 3,764 m at Mt Cook, New Zealand's highest peak. There are many glaciers and mountain lakes including L Te Anau (344 sq km), L Wakatipu (293 sq km) and L Wanaka (193 sq km). Over three-quarters of the land is over 200 m above sea-level, the largest area of level lowland being the Canterbury Plain on the E side of South Island.

Climate. Situated just S of the subtropical high pressure belt, the climate of New Zealand is dominated by E-moving anticyclones. Weather patterns are highly changeable throughout the year, and all months are moderately wet. Sunshine averages 4-5 hours per day in the winter and 6-7 in the summer; the N of the country and the E coast experience more sunshine than the extreme S and W coast of South Island. The high mountains in both North and South islands carry snow throughout the year. Snow can occur almost anywhere at

sea-level, but is very rare in the extreme N of North Island, where the climate is almost subtropical with mild winters and warm, humid summers. Auckland daily temperatures, representative of the warmest part of New Zealand, range from 8°C to 13°C in July and 16°C to 23°C in Jan with max and min monthly rainfalls of 145 mm in July and 79 mm in Dec and Jan. Temperatures in South Island are lower than those given for Auckland. Dunedin on the E coast has an average daily temperature of 3°C to 9°C during July and 10°C to 19°C in Jan. Christchurch, farther N, averages 2°C to 10°C in July and 12°C to 21°C in Jan. Hokitika on the W coast of S Island has an average monthly rainfall ranging from 191 mm in Feb to 292 mm in Oct. Christchurch, situated on the Canterbury Plains, the driest part of the country, receives as little as 43 mm and as much as 69 mm of rain per month. The lowlands to the E of the Southern Alps are often affected by a warm, dry wind which raises the temperature for a few hours. This occurs when strong westerly winds crossing the mountains are warmed as the air descends on the sheltered side. The wind melts snow in winter but can dessicate crops in summer.

History, government and constitution. Settled by Maoris who came from SE Asia before 1350, the first European sighting of New Zealand was by Abel Tasman in 1642, when he named it Staten Landt. It later became known as Nieuw Zeeland after the Dutch province. Captain Cook sighted the islands in 1767. The first settlement on New Zealand was established by a sealing party which landed in 1792. Whaling stations were established and a trade began with New South Wales, Australia. Increasing disorder led to the British government's acceptance of New Zealand and to their authorizing New South Wales to include the islands as part of their colony. A new immigration scheme was set up, and the Maoris ceded all rights and powers of sovereignty in the Treaty of Waitangi, on 6 Feb 1840. New Zealand remained a dependency of New South Wales until 1841, when it was made a separate colony. Partial self-government through representative institutions was granted to New Zealand in 1852. Disputes between immigrants and Maoris led to outbreaks of war between the 2 groups from 1860 to 1870; as a result, 4 Maori electorates were established in 1867. The discovery of gold in South Island gave it the lead in commercial and political development. Adult male suffrage was introduced in 1879 and in 1893 New Zealand became the first country to give women the right to vote. In 1907 the country became the Dominion of New Zealand. New Zealand troops distinguished themselves in World War I at Gallipoli and in France. Between the two World Wars New Zealand, following the economic depression of 1930, passed social legislation which turned the country into the first welfare state. In 1947 New Zealand gained complete autonomy as an independent state within the Commonwealth, recognizing Elizabeth II as head of state. The legal system is based on English law, with special land legislation and land courts for Maoris. There is a 3-level court system consisting of magistrates' courts, a Supreme Court and a Court of Appeal. The legislature consists of a unicameral 92-member House of Representatives (parliament) and a Cabinet responsible to parliament. Elections are held every 3 years, or sooner if parliament is dissolved by the prime minister.

Economy. Farming is still the basis of the New Zealand economy with pastoral production providing 75% of the country's export income. New Zealand is one of the world's major exporters of dairy produce and the 3rd largest exporter of wool. In addition to the traditional products, New Zealand farmers have been producing kiwi fruit, venison and mohair. Principal exports are meat, dairy products, fish and wool. Main trading partners include Australia, the UK, Japan and the USA. Although New Zealand has substantial coal and gas reserves, and 80% of its electricity is supplied by hydroelectric power, almost 50% of its energy requirements are met from imported oil. While producing some oil, New Zealand has developed a programme to convert natural gas found in the Taranaki gas fields near New Plymouth into compressed natural gas and liquefied petroleum gas with a view to using these as alternative fuels. Methanol is also being exported as a raw material for industrial, petrochemical and plastics industries. Income derived from tourism, a growing sector, increased by 40% between 1983 and 1984.

Statistical divisions. Since 1971 New Zealand has been divided into 13 statistical divisions:

Division	*area (sq km)*	*pop(1981)*
North Island		
Northland	12,653	114,295
Central Auckland	5,581	829,519
South Auckland -Bay of Plenty	36,902	491,304
East Coast	10,914	48,573
Hawke's Bay	11,289	147,722
Taranaki	9,729	105,153
Wellington	27,766	586,423
South Island		
Marlborough	11,080	36,027
Nelson	17,675	77,223
Westland	15,415	23,489
Canterbury	43,579	424,280
Otago	37,105	183,559
Southland	29,124	108,170

Local government regions. Since 1974 New Zealand has been divided into 22 regions for the purposes of planning and civil defence:

Region	*pop(1981)*
North Island	
Northland	113,994
Auckland	827,980
Thames Valley	54,343
Bay of Plenty	172,480
Waikato	221,850
Tongariro	40,089
East Cape	53,295
Hawke's Bay	137,840
Taranaki	103,798
Wanganui	68,702
Manawatu	113,238
Horowhenua	49,296
Wellington	323,162
Wairarapa	39,689
Remainder of North Island	3,233
South Island	
Nelson Bays	65,934
Marlborough	37,557
West Coast	34,178
Canterbury	336,846
Aorangi	84,772
Clutha-Central Otago	45,402
Coastal-North Otago	138,164
Southland	107,905
Remainder of South Island	1,990

Newark *nyoo'erk*, NEWARK-ON-TRENT, 53 05N 0 49W, pop(1981) 33,390, town in Newark dist, Nottinghamshire, central England; at junction of a branch of the Trent and Devon rivers, 25 km SW of Lincoln; railway; economy: foodstuffs, brewing, engineering, agricultural machinery, gypsum, limestone.

Newark *noo'erk*, 37 32N 122 02W, pop(1980) 32,126, city in Alameda county, W California, United States; 37 km SSE of Oakland.

Newark, 39 41N 75 46W, pop(1980) 25,247, town in New

Castle county, N Delaware, United States; 20 km WSW of Wilmington; university (1743); economy: automobiles and paper products.

Newark, 40 44N 74 10W, pop(1980) 329,248, county seat of Essex county, NE New Jersey, United States; port on the R Passaic and Newark Bay, 14 km W of New York; an important road, rail and air transportation centre; settled by Puritans from Connecticut in 1666, it achieved city status in 1836; university (1934); railway; airport; economy: chemicals, electrical equipment; insurance and financial centre; linked to New York by underground rail.

Newark, 40 03N 82 24W, pop(1980) 41,200, county seat of Licking county, central Ohio, United States; 48 km E of Columbus; railway; monument: Newark prehistoric earthworks covering over 10 sq km.

Newbridge, town in Wales. See Abercarn.

Newburn, 54 58N 1 44W, pop(1981) 43,701, town in Newcastle upon Tyne borough, Tyne and Wear, NE England; part of Tyneside urban area; on the R Tyne, 8 km W of Newcastle upon Tyne.

Newbury *nyoo'ber-i*, 51 25N 1 20W, pop(1981) 31,894, industrial town in Newbury dist, Berkshire, S England; on the R Kennet and the Kennet and Avon Canal, 25 km WSW of Reading; as a centre of the cloth industry it was England's first industrial town; racecourse; railway; economy: chemicals, coal products, plastics, engineering; monuments: Cloth Hall museum; church of St Swithin at Wickham (15 km NW).

Newcastle, 32 55S 151 46E, pop(1986) 429,300, city in Hunter stat div, New South Wales, Australia; on the E coast, 160 km N of Sydney; founded in 1804 as a penal settlement; university (1965); railway; airfield; economy: coal mining, iron and steel, dockyards, shipbuilding, railway engineering, chemicals, fertilizers, textiles, trade in coal, grain, wool and dairy produce.

Newcastle, AN CAISLEAN NUA (Gael), 54 12N 5 54W, pop(1981) 6,246, resort town in Down dist, Down, SE Northern Ireland; on the coast, on Dundrum Bay, 45 km S of Belfast; a tourist centre for the Mourne Mts

Newcastle upon Tyne, PONS AELII (Lat), MONKCHESTER (Anglo-Saxon), 54 59N 1 35W, pop(1981) 203,591, county town of Tyne and Wear, NE England; part of Tyneside urban area; on the R Tyne, 440 km N of London; cultural, commercial and administrative centre for the NE of England; founded in the 11th century, most of the streets of the inner city were laid out in the early 19th century by Richard Grainger to the plans of John Dobson; city status in 1882; university (1963); the R Tyne is crossed by 7 bridges; railway; underground; ferries to N Europe; economy: heavy engineering, shipbuilding, aircraft, chemicals, pharmaceuticals, coal trade; monuments: 12th-c castle keep, 15th-c cathedral of St Nicholas, Roman Catholic cathedral (1844).

Newcastle-under-Lyme, 53 00N 2 14W, pop(1981) 73,526, town in the Potteries of Staffordshire, central England; 3 km W of Stoke-on-Trent; railway; economy: high-technology industries including computers, industrial control equipment, defence systems.

Newfoundland *nyoo'fun-land*, province in E Canada; consists of the island of Newfoundland and the coast of Labrador, which are separated from each other by the Strait of Belle Isle; Labrador, with its heavily indented coastline, is bounded to the W and S by Québec and E by the Labrador Sea and Atlantic Ocean; Labrador is drained by many rivers which flow from the interior to the coast; the island of Newfoundland is roughly triangular in shape and has a deeply indented coastline; the Long Range Mts run the length of the Great Northern peninsula in the NW; the island rises to 814 m in the Lewis Hills in the extreme W; the majority of Newfoundland island consists of a rolling plateau with low hills; the most important of its peninsulas are the Great Northern (NW), Burin (S) and Avalon (SE); the latter contains the majority of the Newfoundland pop; there are several lakes in the W and S, the largest being Grand, Red Indian, Victoria, White Bear, Meelpaeg and Gander; the island is drained by the Humber, Victoria, Gander, Exploits and Terra Nova rivers; on the W coast of Newfoundland is Gros Morne National Park (area 1,942 sq km, established in 1970); pop(1981) 567,681; area 371,635 sq km; capital St John's; economy: food processing, pulp and paper, mining (iron ore), fishing, oil, hydroelectric power, dairy products, poultry; Vikings are thought to have visited Labrador c.1000 AD; Cabot rediscovered the island for England in 1497; Spain claimed ownership soon afterwards, but British sovereignty was declared in 1583, making Newfoundland Britain's first colony; settlement was discouraged as Britain considered the long fishing voyages good training for naval recruits; in 1855 it became a self-governing colony; in 1934, owing to financial problems, it was placed under a Commission of Government appointed by Britain; in 1946 the people of Newfoundland were asked to vote whether to remain under the commission, whether to return to self-government, or whether to unite with Canada; in 1949, after two votes, Newfoundland united with Canada; Newfoundland is governed by a Lieutenant-Governor and an elected 58-member House of Assembly.

Newham *nyoo'em*, 51 32N 0 02E, pop(1981) 209,494, borough of E central Greater London, England; N of the R Thames; includes the suburbs of West Ham and East Ham which united in 1965; includes the former Royal Docks; railway; economy: engineering, chemicals, sugar refining.

Newhaven, 50 47N 0 03E, pop(1981) 10,773, port town in Lewes dist, East Sussex, SE England; at mouth of R Ouse, 14 km E of Brighton; container and cross-Channel passenger (to Dieppe) terminals; railway.

Newman, 23 20S 119 34E, pop(1981) 5,466, town in Pilbara stat div, NW Western Australia, Australia; SE of Dampier and E of Mount Newman; built around the ore deposit at Mount Whaleback; railway; Newman's iron ore is transported to Port Hedland on the longest railway in the world (426 km) to be built exclusively for the transportation of iron ore.

Newmarket, 52 15N 0 25E, pop(1981) 16,179, town in Forest Heath dist, Suffolk, E England; 20 km E of Cambridge; famous horse-racing centre; railway; economy: electrics, engineering.

New'port, 51 35N 3 00W, pop(1981) 116,658, town in Newport dist, Gwent, SE Wales; on the R Usk, 32 km WNW of Bristol; railway; economy: steel, aluminium, electronics, chemicals, market gardening.

Newport, 50 42N 1 18W, pop(1981) 20,324, river port, market town and county town in Medina dist, Isle of Wight, S England; on the R Medina, 8 km from its mouth; Parkhurst prison is nearby; economy: construction equipment, valves, printing; monument: 12th-c Carisbrooke castle.

Newport, 41 29N 71 19W, pop(1980) 29,259, county seat of Newport county, SE Rhode Island, United States; port at the mouth of Narragansett Bay, at S end of Rhode I; settled in 1639; a haven for religious groups including Quakers and Jews; railway; large naval base; economy: shipbuilding, electrical goods, jewellery, precision instruments; monuments: the Breakers, the sloop *Providence*, Tennis Hall of Fame; event: jazz festival (July).

Newport Beach, 33 37N 117 56W, pop(1980) 62,556, city in Orange county, SW California, United States; on a peninsula between Newport Bay and the Pacific Ocean, 29 km SE of Long Beach.

Newport News, 36 59N 76 25W, pop(1980) 144,903, seaport and independent city, SE Virginia, United States; at the mouth of the R James at the entrance to Hampton Roads channel; railway; economy: shipbuilding; monuments: Mariners' Museum, War Memorial Museum of Virginia.

Newport Pag'nell, 52 05N 0 44W, pop(1981) 10,932, town just N of Milton Keynes in Milton Keynes dist, Buckinghamshire, S central England; economy: transport equipment, engineering.

Newquay *nyoo'kee*, 50 25N 5 05W, pop(1981) 15,209, town in Restormel dist, Cornwall, SW England; 17 km N of Truro; formerly a fishing port, now a resort town; railway; economy: clothing, tourism.

New'ry, AN TLUR (Gael), 54 11N 6 20W, pop(1981) 19,426, port town in Newry and Mourne dist, Down, SE Northern Ireland; on the Newry river and the Newry Canal, at the head of Carlingford Lough; the town grew up around an abbey founded in the 12th century by Maurice McLoughlin, King of Ireland; economy: engineering, food processing; monuments: St Patrick's church (1578) is one of Ireland's first Protestant churches.

Newton, 42 21N 71 12W, pop(1980) 83,622, town in Middlesex county, E Massachusetts, United States; residential suburb, 11 km W of Boston; railway.

Newton Abbot, 50 32N 3 36W, pop(1981) 20,744, market town in Teignbridge dist, Devonshire, SW England; at the head of the the R Teign estuary, NW of Torbay; railway; economy: quarrying, engineering, clay.

Newton Aycliffe, 54 36N 1 34W, pop(1981) 24,485, town in Sedgefield dist, Durham, NE England; 10 km N of Darlington; designated a 'new town' in 1947; railway.

Newton Mearns *mĕrnz*, 55 48N 4 19W, pop(1981) 15,543, town in Eastwood dist, Strathclyde, W central Scotland; in Clydeside urban area, 10 km SW of central Glasgow.

Newton-le-Willows, NEWTON-IN-MAKERFIELD, 54 17N 1 40W, pop(1981) 19,675, town in St Helens borough, Merseyside, NW England; 8 km E of St Helens; railway; economy: engineering, coal, printing.

Newtown St Boswells *-boz'-*, 55 34N 2 38W, pop(1981) 1,095, capital of Ettrick and Lauderdale dist and of Borders region, SE Scotland; 4 km SE of Melrose.

Newtownabbey, BAILE NA MAINISTREACH (Gael), 54 40N 5 55W, pop(1981) 56,149, town in Newtownabbey dist, Antrim, NE Northern Ireland; on the W shore of Belfast Lough, N of Belfast; economy: textiles, engineering, food processing.

Newtownards, BAILE NUA NA HARDA (Gael), 54 36N 5 41W, pop(1981) 20,531, town in Ards dist, Down, E Northern Ireland; at the N end of Strangford Lough, 16 km E of Belfast; Walter de Burgh founded a Dominican priory here in 1244; airfield; economy: linen, engineering; a tourist centre for the coast and the Mourne Mts; monument: nearby are the remains of a 6th-c abbey founded by St Finian.

Ngami *un-ga'mi*, lake in Ngamiland dist, Botswana, S Africa; situated on the S edge of the Okavango delta; European discovery by David Livingstone in 1849 led to the opening up of the area and the arrival of traders, hunters and missionaries; the lake dried up during the 1890s but was recharged in 1963; its size fluctuates depending on the flood levels of the Okavango delta; great numbers of birds migrate to the lake in times of high water.

Ngamiland, district in NW Botswana, S Africa; bounded S by the Kalahari Desert, N and W by Namibia; area 129,930; pop(1981) 75,997; chief town Maun; includes the Okavango swamps at the delta of the Okavanga river; chief towns are Toteng, Nokaneng, Gumare, Shakwe and Mohembo; Nxai Pan National Park is located in the E.

Ngaoundéré *un-ga-oon'day-ray*, 7 20N 13 35E, pop(1984) 57,000, capital of Adamaoua prov, Cameroon, W Africa; 295 km S of Garoua; alt 1,100 m; a Muslim town; Ardo Njobdi founded the town's Lamidat (palace of the local Muslim chief) in 1835; local markets include the covered central market and the Mboumbalal; railway terminus; economy: cereal trade, hide tanning.

Ngauruhoe *now-ru-hoy'*, 39 19S 175 40E, active volcano rising to 2,290 m on North Island, New Zealand; in Tongariro National Park.

Ngorongoro Crater *ung-gō'rong-gō'rō*, crater in N Tanzania, E Africa; in the Tanzanian section of the Rift Valley, 130 km W of Arusha; the rim of the crater is over 2,100 m in alt and the floor lies about 600 m below this level; the total area of the crater is about 260 sq km; the crater is the centre of a conservation area covering 7,770 sq km; it serves a dual purpose by allowing the Masai to live and farm their cattle within the area whilst still providing a 'free range' to wildlife which includes large numbers of wildebeeste, gazelle, zebra; L Eyasi, Olduvai Gorge and the craters of Olmoton, Embulbul and Empakai are part of this area.

Ngozi *ung-goo'zee*, 2 54S 29 49E, capital of prov of same name, Burundi, central Africa; 58 km NNW of Gitega.

Nguigmi *ung-geg'mi*, 14 19N 13 06E, town in Diffa dept, SE Niger, W Africa; 450 km E of Zinder, close to L Chad; economy: agriculture and livestock.

Ngwaketze *un-gwa-ketz'i*, BANGWAKETSE, district and tribal area in S Botswana, S Africa; bounded S by Cape prov, South Africa and N by the Kalahari Desert; area 28,470 sq km; pop(1981) 119,653; chief town Kanye.

Nhulunbuy, 12 09S 136 44E, pop(1982) 4,138, bauxite-mining centre in Arnhem Land, Northern Territory, Australia; on the Gove Peninsula; the centre of Aboriginal occupied territory.

Niagara Falls *nī-a'gra, nī-a'ga-ra*, 43 05N 79 06W, pop(1981) 70,960, town in SE Ontario, SE Canada; situated on the Niagara river, opposite Niagara Falls (New York, USA); on the border with the United States; a favourite resort for honeymooners; railway; economy: tourism, pulp, paper, fertilizer, machinery, hydroelectricity; monuments: Horseshoe Falls on the Canadian side is separated from the American Falls by Goat Island; in the S part of Queen Victoria Park which lies alongside the falls is Table Rock House, with an observation tower for viewing Horseshoe Falls; two steamers with the name *Maid of the Mist* take visitors close to the falls; Houdini Magical Hall of Fame, a tribute to the famous illusionist Houdini; Movieland Wax Museum, with wax models of film stars; Louis Tussaud's English Wax Museum.

Niagara Falls, waterfalls in W New York, USA and S Ontario, Canada; situated on the international border between the 2 countries between the cities of Niagara Falls, Ontario and Niagara Falls, New York; the American Falls are 55.5 m high and 328 m wide; the Canadian Falls, known as Horseshoe Falls, are 54 m high and 640 m wide; the two waterfalls are separated by Goat Island; behind the American Falls is the Cave of the Wind, a natural chamber created by the action of water; below the falls is Rainbow Bridge (built in 1941) between Canada and the USA, the previous bridge was destroyed in 1938; a treaty between the USA and Canada signed in 1951 agreed on the diversion of water for hydroelectric power; weirs divert part of the flow above the Canadian Falls to supplement the shallower American Falls; 6-15% of the water passes over American Falls; the mean daily flow of water over both falls before diversion is approx 5,800 cu m; all but 2,800 cu m is diverted for power during summer daylight hours; in the evenings and the winter months an additional 1,400 cu m is diverted; a world-famous tourist attraction since the early 19th century, developed after the arrival of the railway in 1836; much of the surrounding area has been parkland since 1885; tourists were once attracted by daredevil activities such as the tightrope crossings of the falls in 1859 by Blondin and Annie Edson Taylor's 'shooting' of the Horseshoe Falls in a sealed barrel in 1901.

Niagara Falls, 43 06N 79 03W, pop(1980) 71,384, town in Niagara county, W New York, United States; on the R Niagara, 27 km N of Buffalo; situated opposite Niagara Falls, Ontario to which it is connected by bridge; built on the site of a fort, it achieved city status in 1892; often visited by honeymoon couples; university (1856); railway; airfield; economy: chemicals, plastics, aerospace industries, ceramics, hydroelectricity, tourism.

Niamey *nee-a-may'*, dept in SW Niger, W Africa; a low-lying region traversed by the R Niger which flows SE; the Yatakala, Dargol and Sirba rivers join the R Niger from the SW; area 90,293 sq km; pop(1977e) 1,065,000; comprises 6 arrond; capital Niamey; chief towns Tillabéri, Karma, Kirtachi and Filingué; the Niger section of the W National Park is located in the S; there are reserves of iron ore.

Niamey, 13 32N 2 05E, pop(1983) 399,100, river-port capital of Niger, W Africa; 1,100 km E of Bamako (Mali) and 800 km NNW of Lagos (Nigeria); terminus of the railway which runs N from Gulf of Guinea through Benin to Niger; the Small Market sells mainly foods whilst the Great Market's wares include indigo tie-dye cloth and leather, iron and copper craftwork; there is a national museum which includes a zoo and botanical gardens; university (1971); airport; economy: textiles, metals, food processing, ceramics, plastics, chemicals and pharmaceuticals.

Niari *nee-ah'ree*, province in SW Congo, W Africa; area 25,942 sq km; pop(1980) 137,210; capital Loubomo.

Nias *nee'as*, island in the Indian Ocean, 125 km off the W coast of Sumatera, Indonesia; 240 km long by 80 km wide; airfield; linked by boat to Sibolga; chief town Gunungsitoli; populated by the agricultural Niah tribe; headhunting and human sacrifice recorded here as late as 1935 despite the efforts of Lutheran missionaries since 1907; notable stone sculptures date from the megalithic period.

Niassa *nī-a'sa*, prov in N Mozambique, SE Africa; pop(1980) 514,100; area 129,055 sq km; bounded W by L Nyasa and N by the R Rovuma; the Jeci mountain rises to 1,836 m N of the capital, Lichinga; chief towns include Cuamba and Marrupa.

Nicaragua *nik-ar-ag'wa*, official name Republic of Nicaragua, REPÚBLICA DE NICARAGUA (Sp), largest of the Central American republics, bounded N by Honduras and S by Costa Rica; timezone GMT −6; area 148,000 sq km; capital Managua; chief towns León, Granada, Masaya, Chinandega, and Matagalpa; Corinto is the major port; pop(1981) 2,820,000; it is the most thinly populated of the Central American republics; over 70% of the population are of mixed Indian, Spanish, and Negro blood; the dominant religion is Roman Catholicism although the inhabitants of the Atlantic coast are largely Protestant; Spanish is the official language although English is spoken on the Atlantic coast; the unit of currency is the córdoba of 100 centavos; the illiteracy rate fell from 50% in 1970 to just under 13% in 1980; national holiday 15 Sept (Independence Day); membership: CACM, CEMA, FAO, G-77, GATT, IADB, IAEA, IBRD, ICAC, ICAO, ICO, IDA, IDB, IFAD, IFC, ILO, IMF, IMO, INTELSAT, INTERPOL, IPU, IRC, ISO, ITU, NAM, NAMUCAR, OAS, ODECA, PAHO, SELA, UN, UNESCO, UPEB, UPU, WFTU, WHO, WMO, WTO.

Physical description and climate. The W half of Nicaragua is mountainous with volcanic ranges in the NW rising to over 2,000 m. A chain of volcanic peaks, some active, runs parallel to the Pacific coast. Two large lakes, Lago de Nicaragua and Lago de Managua, lie in a broad structural depression which extends NW-SE behind the coastal mountain range. E of this depression there are rolling uplands and forested plains. Numerous short rivers flow into the Pacific Ocean and the 2 large lakes. Those which flow E into the Caribbean (Río Escondido, Río Grande de Matagalpa) tend to be much longer with large drainage basins. The Río San Juan, which forms much of the S border with Costa Rica, connects Lago de Nicaragua with the Caribbean Sea. The climate is tropical with average annual temperatures ranging from 15°C to 35°C according to altitude. There is a rainy season from May to Nov when humidity is at its highest. Temperatures at Managua range from 26°C in Jan to 30°C in July, and the mean annual rainfall is 1,140 mm.

History, government and constitution. The Pacific coast was colonized by Spaniards from Panama in the early 16th century. Nicaragua gained independence from Spain in 1821 and left the Federation of Central America in 1838. Meanwhile the plains of E Nicaragua, named the Mosquito Coast, remained largely undeveloped under British protection until 1860. Nicaragua was a dictatorship from 1938 to 1979, initially under Anastasio Somoza, and then under his 2 sons. In 1979 the Sandinist National Liberation Front seized power and established a 5-member junta of national reconstruction. In 1981 the junta was reduced from 5 to 3 members. A 51-seat council of state, established in May 1980, advises the junta. The former supporters of the Somoza government (the Contras) based in Honduras have carried out guerrilla activities against the present junta since 1979.

Economy. Agriculture is the mainstay of the economy accounting for over two-thirds of total exports. The main crops are cotton, coffee, sugar cane, rice, corn, and beans. In the early 1980s a policy of export diversification led to shellfish, tobacco, and bananas becoming of major importance to the economy. Government plans for agricultural reform aim to redistribute some 25,000 sq km of land formerly held by the Somoza family and ultimately reduce the portion of agricultural land under private control to around 45%. Major industries include food processing, chemicals, metal products, textiles and clothing, petroleum, and beverages. The principal mineral resources are gold and silver, mined chiefly for export. Main imports in 1983 included food and non-food agricultural products, chemicals and pharmaceuticals, transportation equipment, machinery, construction materials, clothing, and petroleum. Chief exports were cotton, coffee, chemical products, meat, and sugar.

Administrative divisions. Nicaragua is divided into 16 departments as follows:

Department	*area (sq km)*	*pop(1981)*
Boaco	5,398	88,862
Carazo	950	109,450
Chinandega	4,598	228,573
Chontales	5,310	98,562
Estelí	1,999	110,076
Granada	1,401	113,102
Jinotega	15,195	127,159
León	6,097	248,704
Madriz	1,375	72,408
Managua	3,448	819,679
Masaya	601	149,015
Matagalpa	8,746	220,548
Nueva Segovia	4,124	97,765
Río San Juan	7,252	29,001
Rivas	2,198	108,913
Zelaya	63,005	202,462

Nicaragua, Lago de, GRAN LAGO, largest lake of Nicaragua and Central America, bounded E by the Sierra de Amerrique and separated from the Atlantic Ocean (W) by a 15 km-wide isthmus; area 8,026 sq km; length 148 km; width 55 km; connected to the Caribbean Sea by the Río San Juan and to Lago de Managua (NW) by the small Río Tipitapa; there are approx 310 small islands in the lake; the largest is Isla de Ometepe which comprises 2 volcanoes rising to 1,610 m and 1,394 m respectively; Granada is on the NW shore.

Nice *nees*, NIZZA (Ital), NICAEA (anc), 43 42N 7 14E, pop(1982) 338,486, fashionable coastal resort and capital of Alpes-Maritimes dept, Provence-Alpes-Côte d'Azur region, SE France; encircled by hills on the Baie des Anges, a bay of the Mediterranean Sea, 157 km ENE of Marseille; 5th largest city in France; tourist attractions include casinos, Palais de la Mediterranée, Palais des Expositions and a 19th-c Opera House (featuring Italian opera throughout the winter); the Promenade des Anglais is the lively seafront promenade, lined with palms; at its E end is the rocky plateau, site of a former château destroyed in 1706, but now laid out as a park with magnificent views; university (1965); railway; airport; economy: textiles, perfume, soap, olive oil, furniture; monuments: cathedral (1650), several 17-18th-c Baroque churches, 17th-c Palais Lascaris, all in the Italianate old town below the plateau; events: Carnival during the 2 weeks preceding Lent, with parades and celebrations; May book festival; international dog festival (June); ballet festival (July-Aug); there is a flower market in the old town.

Nicholas II Land, archipelago in the Arctic Ocean, N Soviet Union. See Severnaya Zemlya.

Nickerie *ni-kay'ree-a*, dist in W Surinam, NE South America; bordered W by Guyana (along the R Correntyne), N by the Atlantic and S by Brazil and the Serra de Tumucumaque; Surinam lays claim to further territory SW of the dist beyond the R Correntyne in Guyana; area 64,610 sq km; pop(1980) 34,480; capital Nieuw Nickerie.

Nicobar Islands, island group of India in the Indian Ocean. See Andaman and Nicobar Islands.

Nicosia *nik-ō-see'a*, LEVKOSIA *lef-kos-ee'a* (Gr), dist in central Cyprus; area 2,726 sq km; pop(1973) 232,702; capital Nicosia; covers the N part of the Troödos range; at present 37% of the area is under Turkish occupation.

Nicosia, 35 11N 33 23E, pop(1982) 161,100, capital city of Nicosia dist and the Republic of Cyprus; on R Pedias, in the centre of the Mesaoria plain; capital of the island since the 12th century; agricultural trade centre; old Nicosia is surrounded by Venetian-built walls dating from the late 16th century; technical institute (1968); monument: cathedral of St John; events: International State Fair and Nicosia Art Festival (end of May).

Nicoya *nee-koy'a*, peninsula in Guanacaste and Puntarenas provs, NW Costa Rica, Central America; separated from the mainland by the Golfo de Nicoya; largest peninsula in the republic; length 120 km; width 32-48 km.

Nidelv *need'elv*, NID (Eng), river in S Norway, issues from L Nisser, Telemark county; flows S through Aust-Agder county to discharge into the Skagerrak at Arendal; length 209 km; several falls provide hydroelectric power; a railway follows the river.

Nidwalden *need'val-den*, NIDWALD *need-vald'* (Fr), demi-canton in Unterwalden, central Switzerland; pop(1980) 28,617; area 274 sq km; capital Stans; joined the Swiss Confederacy in 1291.

Niederbayern *nee'dur-bī-urn*, LOWER BAVARIA, (Eng), E dist of Bayern (Bavaria) prov, W Germany; pop(1983) 1,007,500; area 10,332 sq km; chief towns include Landshut and Passau.

Niedere Tauern *nee'da-ra tow'arn*, mountain range of the Eastern Alps in Salzburg and Steiermark states of central Austria, rising to 2,863 m at Hochgolling; there are many small mountain lakes in the higher valleys and hollows; the Radstädter Tauern (W section) range is a popular skiing area.

Niederösterreich *nee'der-œs'ter-īKH*, LOWER AUSTRIA (Eng), federal state of NE Austria on the Czech frontier, comprising 25 dists and 559 communities; pop(1981) 1,439,137; area 19,171 sq km; the state government is centred in Wien (Vienna); it is the largest state in Austria and has the largest percentage of its area under cultivation, mainly agriculture (wheat, beet-sugar) and wine-growing; Austria's biggest oilfield is N of the R Danube, and there is a refinery at Schwechat near Wien; in the S Wien basin there are textiles, foodstuffs, chemicals, iron and metal plants; there are hydroelectric plants on the Danube, and a tributary river, the Kamp.

Niedersachsen *nee'-der-zahk-sen*, LOWER SAXONY (Eng), prov in northern W Germany; pop(1983) 7,248,500; area 47,447 sq km; comprises the dists of Braunschweig, Hannover, Lüneburg and Weser-Ems; drained by the Ems, Hunte, Weser, Oste and Leine rivers; in the SE the Harz Mts rise prominently from the surrounding lowlands; capital Hannover; chief towns Oldenburg, Braunschweig and Göttingen; economy: machine construction, motor vehicles, electrical engineering; Lüneburg Heath, an infertile expanse of heather, juniper bushes, deciduous and coniferous trees, extends from the R Weser to the city gates of Hamburg; home of Grimm's Fairy Tales and the Pied Piper of Hameln (Hamelin).

Nieuw Nickerie *nee'oo ni-kay'ree-a*, 6 00N 56 59W, pop(1980) 6,078, capital of Nickerie dist, NW Surinam, NE South America; port on S bank of the R Nickerie, 5 km from its mouth.

Nieuwegein, 52 05N 5 07E, pop(1984e) 53,601, city in the W Netherlands; S of Utrecht, near the junction of the Rhine-Amsterdam canal with the Gorinchem artery; part of the Dutch *Randstad* conurbation; economy: industrial chemicals, toiletries, cosmetics, detergents.

Nièvre *nee-evr*, dept in Bourgogne region of central France, comprising 4 arrond, 30 cantons and 312 communes; pop(1982) 239,635; area 6,817 sq km; drained by the Loire and Yonne rivers; it is hilly and barren in the E where the Monts du Morvan rise to 902 m; named from a minor tributary of the Loire at Nevers; capital Nevers, chief towns Cosne and Clamecy; spas at Pouques-les-Eaux and St-Honoré-les-Bains; the Parc de Morvan regional nature park lies partly within the dept.

Niğde *nee-de'*, mountainous prov in S central Turkey; pop(1980) 512,071; area 14,294 sq km; capital Niğde.

Niger *nī'jer*, river in W Africa; at 4,100 km it is the 3rd longest river in Africa after the Nile and the Congo; rises in the Loma mountains on the Sierra Leone-Guinea border only 280 km from the Atlantic coast; flows NE through Guinea, where it receives the Bale and Milo rivers, and into Mali SE of Bamako where it is joined by the R Sankarani; continues NE past Bamako and Ségou to be dammed at Markala and Sansanding; in central Mali it splits into several courses and a cluster of lakes in the Macina depression; it receives the R Bani at Mopti; reforms S of Tombouctou and curves SE past Gao and Ansongo; enters Niger passing through Niamey and as it forms part of Niger's SW border with Benin it receives the Mekrou and Alibori rivers from the SW before entering NW Nigeria; receives R Kebbi and is dammed to form the Kainji reservoir after which it flows SE (receiving the R Kaduna) and S (receiving the R Benue); the Niger spreads into a delta about 320 km across and 36,000 sq km in area before entering the Gulf of Guinea; known as Upper Niger or Djoliba between its source and Tombouctou, the Middle Niger as far as Jebba in W Nigeria and the Lower Niger or Kovarra (Kawarra, Kwara) from Jebba to its delta; with a drainage basin of 1,555,000 sq km in area there is immense irrigation potential which is beginning to be tapped; only navigable in sections and seasonally; the river is frequently interrupted by rapids; for many years geographers were unclear as to the river's course and at one stage considered it as an arm of the R Nile; first explored by Mungo Park 1795-96 and again in 1805-06; other important explorers have included Clapperton (1827) and Lander (1827-34).

Niger, official name Republic of Niger, RÉPUBLIQUE DU

NIGER (Fr), a republic in W Africa, bounded NE by Libya, NW by Algeria, W by Mali, SW by Burkina, S by Benin and Nigeria and E by Chad; area 1,186,408 sq km; timezone GMT +1; pop(1985e) 6,475,000; capital Niamey; chief towns Agadez, Diffa, Dosso, Maradi, Tahoua and Zinder; there are 18,400 km of roadway of which 1,761 km is paved; ethnic groups include the Hausa (54%), Songhai and Djerma (10%), Fulani (10%), Beriberi-Manga (9%) and Tuareg (3%) plus a small number of French; Hausa, Songhai and Djerma are agricultural groups concentrated in the S, while the Fulani are semi-nomadic and live amongst the Hausa when not travelling with their cattle; the official language is French but Hausa and Djerma are widely spoken; the majority of the pop hold Islamic beliefs; the unit of currency is the franc CFA; national holidays 3 Aug (Independence Day), 18 Dec (Republic Day); Muslim holidays are observed; membership of AfDB, APC, CEAO, EAMA, ECA, ECOWAS, Entente, FAO, G-77, GATT, IAEA, IBRD, ICAO, IDA, IDB (Islamic Development Bank), IFAD, IFC, ILO, IMF, INTELSAT, INTERPOL, IPU, ITU, Lake Chad Basin Commission, NAM, OAU, UN, UNESCO, UPU, WHO, WIPO, WMO.

Physical description. Niger is situated on the southern fringe of the Sahara desert and occupies a high plateau of old, croded rock. In the far N lies the Hamada Manguene, a high, arid plateau and in the centre is the Aïr massif. In the E is the Ténéré du Tafassasset desert which is interspersed with oases. Large areas of shifting sand occupy much of the W Talk desert, central and N Niger. Only in the SW around the R Niger and its tributaries and in the SE around L Chad is there water in any quantity. Fossil river valleys flow from the Aïr massif S towards the R Niger.

Climate. Niger is one of the hottest countries of the world and is divided into 3 climatic zones. (1) In the highly cultivated S there is a marked rainy season from June to Oct preceded by stormy weather. (2) The arid centre of Niger with lower rainfall is suitable for pasture. (3) Rainfall decreases northwards to almost negligible levels in the desert areas where the dry, dusty *harmattan* wind Niamey in the S is 554 mm and in the N is as little as 20 mm.

History, government and constitution. Niger was occupied by the French between 1883 and 1899 and became a territory within French West Africa in 1904. In 1958 it became an autonomous republic within the French community with full independence being granted in 1960. The constitution, which was suspended in 1974 after a military coup, provides for a National Assembly. The country is governed by a Supreme Military Council of 12 officers led by the president who appoints a Council of Ministers. A 150-member National Development Council has limited legislative powers.

Economy. Niger's economy is dominated by agriculture and mining. Ninety per cent of the workforce are pastoralists or farmers with important cash crops including groundnuts, cotton, cowpeas and gum arabic. In the 1970s agricultural exports dropped from 70% to 10% of total exports as a result of severe drought conditions. Oil reserves have been located near L Chad. Large uranium deposits and tin ore have been mined since 1971 in the Aïr mountains. Phosphates, coal, salt and natron are also important. Manufacturing industries cover basic needs such as building materials, textiles and food processing. The main trading partners are France, other EEC countries, Nigeria, UDEAC countries and the USA.

Administrative divisions. Niger is divided into 7 depts and 32 arrondissements with a total of 150 communes. Each dept is headed by a prefect assisted by a Regional Advisory Council:

Department	*area (sq km)*	*pop(1977e)*
Agadez	634,209	95,000
Diffa	140,216	150,000
Dosso	31,002	640,000
Maradi	38,581	842,000
Niamey	90,293	1,065,000
Tahoua	106,677	1,015,000
Zinder	145,430	1,034,000

Niger, state in W central Nigeria, W Africa; pop(1982e) 1,904,800; area 65,037 sq km; bounded S and SW by the R Niger; capital Minna; chief towns Bida, Kontagora, Mokwa and Abuja; the 2 main linguistic groups are the

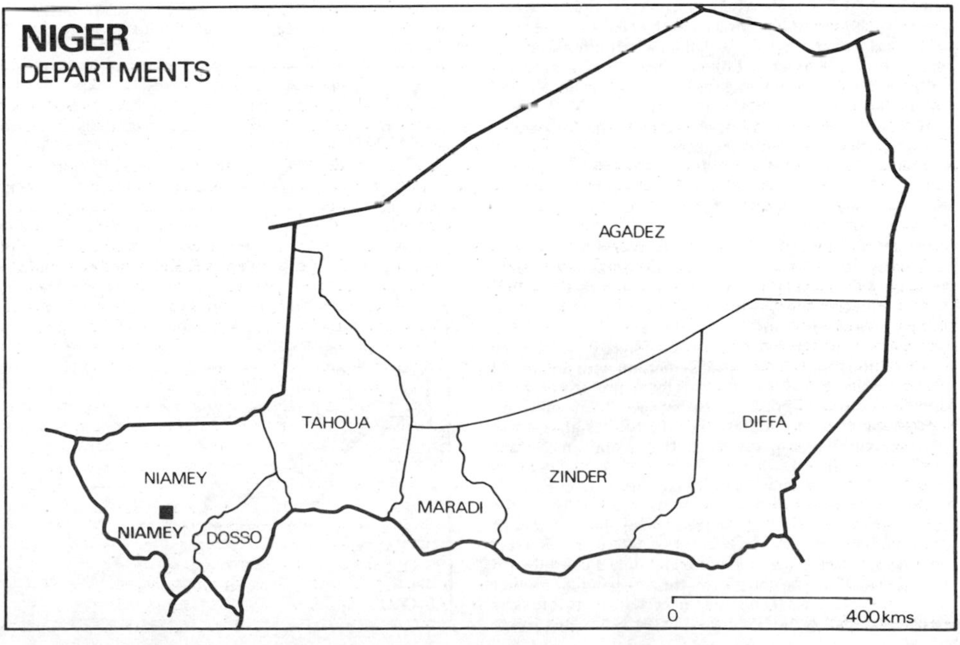

Afro-Asian (mainly Koro, Kadara and Bassa) and the Kwa-Sub (Nupe, Gwari and Kamuku); an agricultural state, the main crops are groundnuts, rice and cotton; livestock and fisheries also important; Kainji National Park is located on the W border; there are reserves of glass sands, kaolin and marble; economy: brasswork, embroidery, pottery, dyeing, marble processing, bricks, propylene sacks and sugar refining.

Nigeria, official name Federal Republic of Nigeria, a republic in W Africa, bounded W by Benin, N by Niger, NE by Chad, E by Cameroon and S by the Gulf of Guinea; timezone GMT +1; area 923,768 sq km; pop(1984e) 88,148,000, making it the most populous nation on the African continent; capital Lagos; proposed capital at Abuja; chief towns Ibadan, Ogbomosho, Kano, Oshogbo, Ilorin, Abeokuta, Port Harcourt, Zaria, Ilesha, Onitsha, Iwo and Kaduna; there are more than 250 tribal groups in Nigeria, the Hausa and Fulani in the N, the Yoruba in the S and the Ibos in the E comprise about 60% of the pop; there are about 27,000 non-Africans; about half of the pop is Muslim, 34% Christian and 18% follow local beliefs; English is the official language with Hausa, Yoruba, Edo and Ibo widely used; the unit of currency is the naira of 100 kobos; national holiday 1 Oct (Independence Day); membership of AfDB, APC, Commonwealth, ECA, ECOWAS, FAO, G-77, GATT, IAEA, IBRD, ICAO, ICO, IDA, IFAD, IFC, ILO, IMF, IMO, INTELSAT, INTERPOL, IRC, ISO, ITC, ITU, IWC, Lake Chad Basin Commission, Niger River Commission, NAM, OAU, OPEC, UN, UNESCO, UPU, WHO, WMO and WTO.

Physical description. With a max length from N to S of 1,046 km and max width from E to W of 1,127 km Nigeria is divided into four geographical regions: (1) A coastal strip between 16 and 97 km wide, bounded S by the Bight of Benin and the Gulf of Guinea and typified by a long sandy shoreline with mangrove swamp intersected by creeks and lagoons which provide navigable waterways. This area is dominated by the R Niger delta. (2) N of the coastal strip is an undulating area of tropical rain forest and oil palm bush between 80 and 160 km wide. (3) The relatively dry central plateau is characterized by open woodland and savannah. (4) The far north of the country is on the edge of the Sahara desert and is largely a gently undulating savannah with tall grasses. The country is watered by numerous rivers, the chief of which are the R Niger, which flows from the NW to its delta W of Port Harcourt, and the R Benue, which flows from the E to join the R Niger at Lokoja. The only sizeable lakes in Nigeria are the SW corner of L Chad in the far NE and the reservoir created by a dam at Kainji on the R Niger. There are a number of plateaux, notably the Jos plateau in the central area which reaches a peak at Share Hill (1,780 m). The highest ground is in the Gotel Mts, along the SE frontier with Cameroon. It is in this area that Nigeria's highest point, Mount Vogel (2,024 m), is located.

Climate. Nigeria can be divided into two climatic zones: (1) Areas on or near to the coast experience two rainy seasons with maxima in May or June and in Oct. Rain falls in all other months to a lesser extent with least rain falling between Dec and Feb and between July and Sept. The wettest part of Nigeria is in the Niger delta and the mountainous SE frontier with Cameroon with an annual rainfall rising above 2,500 mm. This figure decreases W and in central Nigeria falls to between 1,250 mm and 1,500 mm. Ibadan (alt 200 m) in the SE has an average daily maximum temperature of 31.2°C and an average annual rainfall of 1,120 mm. (2) In the N of the country there is only one rainy season. The dry season extends from Oct to April during which little rain falls. In the same period the dry and frequently dust-laden Saharan *harmattan* blows from the NE. Between Dec and Feb this wind reaches much further south and only a coastal strip escapes its effects. In contrast to the S the annual rainfall in the N is below 1,000 mm and in certain areas it falls as low as 600 mm. Kano (alt 467 m) in the N has an average daily max temperature of 33.2°C and an average annual rainfall of 870 mm.

History, government and constitution. The centre of the Nok culture between 500 BC and 200 AD, Nigeria was later influenced by Muslim immigrants in the 15-16th centuries and by eastward migrating Fulani pastoralists. European interest in gold and the Atlantic slave trade superseded the first Portuguese trading posts along the Guinea coast. British interest in Nigeria began in 1861 when Lagos was declared a colony. An international conference in Berlin in 1885 recognized Britain's claim to the Oil Rivers protectorate which had been created in 1882 in the Niger delta. It was subsequently enlarged and renamed the Niger Coast protectorate in 1893. The protectorate of Northern Nigeria was created in 1900 out of territories which had belonged to the Royal Niger Company. The protectorate of Southern Nigeria was created at the same time. Expeditions led by Lugard between 1898 and 1906 succeeded in suppressing the powerful Fulah empire which had been in control of the Hausa states. Lagos Colony was added to the Southern Nigeria protectorate in 1906 to become the Colony and Protectorate of Southern Nigeria. The Colony and Protectorate of Nigeria was created in 1914 by the amalgamation of the N and S halves of the country. In 1954 Nigeria became a federation, administered by a Governor-General and in 1960 it became an independent sovereign state within the Commonwealth. A federal republic was declared in 1963. The bicameral National Assembly consists of the 95-member Senate (5 from each of the 19 states) and the 449-member House of Representatives. Elections for the presidency, National Assembly, state governorships and state houses of assembly are held every 4 years.

Economy. Until commercial oil production began in the late 1950s Nigeria's economy was based on agriculture. About half the pop is still engaged in producing cocoa, rubber, palm oil, groundnuts, cotton, yams, cassava, rice, sugar cane and tobacco. Development schemes largely based on irrigation have been promoted in the N states of Sokoto, Kaduna, Kano and Borno. The oil and gas industries are located in the S states of Bendel, Rivers, Imo and Cross River. Between Enugu and the R Benue are the coalfields of Nigeria. There are reserves of tin, lead, zinc, lignite, iron ore, columbite and tantalite. The mining of limestone and marble is also important. Industry is dominated by light, low technology produc-

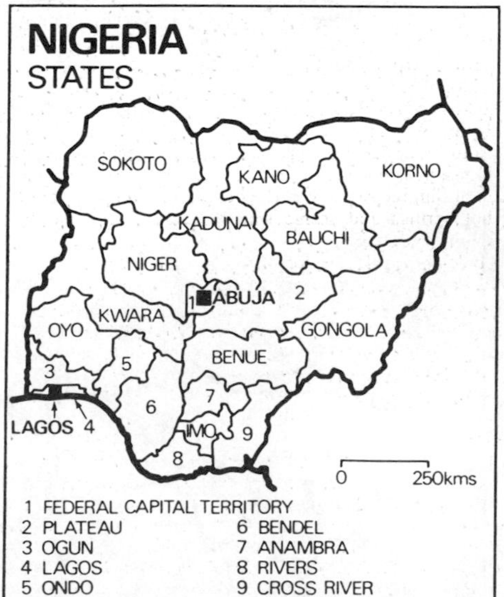

tion of food, pulp and paper, textiles, rubber, sugar, beer, vehicles and pharmaceuticals. The main trading partners are the UK, West Germany, the USA, Japan and France. *Administrative divisions*. Nigeria is divided into 19 states and a Federal Capital Territory:

State	*area (sq km)*	*pop(1982e)*
Anambra	17,675	5,735,400
Bauchi	64,605	3,877,100
Bendel	35,500	3,924,400
Benue	45,174	3,870,300
Borno	116,400	4,780,000
Cross River	27,237	5,546,400
Gongola	91,390	4,154,500
Imo	11,850	5,856,600
Kaduna	70,245	6,535,400
Kano	43,285	9,208,900
Kwara	66,869	2,734,000
Lagos	3,345	2,644,800
Niger	65,037	1,904,800
Ogun	16,762	2,473,300
Ondo	20,959	4,532,900
Oyo	37,705	8,306,400
Plateau	58,030	3,231,800
Rivers	21,850	2,742,700
Sokoto	102,535	7,237,800
Federal Capital Territory	8,094	

Nigg, village and port in Ross and Cromarty Dist, Highland, N Scotland; on the Cromarty Firth, E of Invergordon; linked by pipeline to the Beatrice oil field in the Moray Firth; economy: oil rig maintenance, petrochemicals.

Niigata *nee-ga'ta*, 37 58N 139 02E, pop(1980) 457,785, port capital of Niigata prefecture, Chūbu region, N Honshū island, Japan; on W coast opposite Sado island; on the Sea of Japan at the mouth of the R Shinano; university (1949); railway; airport; economy: oil refining, machinery, chemicals, textiles.

Nijmegen *nī'me* KHen or **Nimeguen** *nim'ay-gen*, 51 50N 5 52E, pop(1984e) 233,992, city in S Gelderland prov, E Netherlands; on the R Waal, 19 km S of Arnhem and 7 km from the German border; founded in 69 AD as a hilltop Roman fort; in 105 AD it became the Roman city of Noviomagus; former residence of the Carlovingian kings and later a member of the Hanseatic League in the Middle Ages; university (1923); railway; economy: metalworking, electrical engineering, textiles, printing, foodstuffs, chemicals; monuments: 16th-c town hall; 13th-c Groote Kerk; remains of Charlemagne's 8th-c Valkhof Palace.

Nikki *nee'kee*, 9 55N 3 18E, town in Borgou prov, NE Benin, W Africa; 95 km NE of Parakou.

Nikko *neek'ko*, national park in W Kanto region, E central Honshū island, Japan; mountainous area rising to 2,578 m at Shirane-san; the park contains cryptomeria forests, hot springs and scenic waterfalls; area 1,401 sq km; established in 1934.

Nikolainkaupunki, seaport in Finland. See Vaasa.

Nikolayev *nyi-ke-la'yef*, VERNOLENINSK, 46 57N 32 00E, pop(1983) 474,000, port and capital city of Nikolayevskaya oblast, Ukrainskaya SSR, W Soviet Union; at the confluence of the Ingul and Yuzhnyy Bug rivers, close to the N shore of the Black Sea; founded as a fortification in 1784; railway junction; airfield; economy: shipbuilding, knitwear, clothing, foodstuffs, furniture.

Nikšić *neek'shich*, OGONOSTE (Turk), 42 48N 18 56E, pop(1981) 72,299, town in W Crna Gora (Montenegro) republic, Yugoslavia; near R Zeta, NNW of Titograd; founded in 6th century; railway.

Nile *nīl*, NAHR EN NIL (Arab), river in E and NE Africa; the longest river in the world and one of only 4 over 6,000 km in length; from its most remote headstream (the Luvironza river) at 3 75S to the Mediterranean Sea at 31 30N the Nile is 6,695 km long and from L Victoria 5,600 km long; area of drainage basin estimated at 1,900,000 sq km; the Luvironza river rises in S central Burundi (SW of Bujumbura) and flows generally NE becoming the Ruvuvu river; on reaching the Tanzanian frontier the river becomes known as the Kagera river and subsequently forms the border between E Rwanda and NW Tanzania as it flows N; the Kagera then flows generally E, close to the Tanzanian-Ugandan frontier to enter L Victoria on its W shore N of Bukoba (Tanzania); the Victoria Nile flows from the N of L Victoria near Jinja (Uganda), through L Kyoga and into the NE extremity of L Albert; the Albert Nile issues from the N of L Albert (close to the Victoria Nile's delta) and flows through NW Uganda toward the Sudanese frontier which it crosses at Nimule whereupon it becomes known as the Bahr el Jebel (White Nile); it flows generally N through Sudan and upon reaching Khartoum it is joined by the Bahr el Azraq (Blue Nile) which rises in the mountains of Ethiopia; from Khartoum the R Nile flows c.3,000 km from its delta on the Mediterranean Sea; at Atbara the river is joined from the E by the R Atbara, the Nile's only significant tributary; the Nile then flows in an S-shape through N Sudan before entering Egypt where it flows into L Nasser which was created by the building of the Aswân High Dam; N of Aswân the river flows past river ports such as Idfu, Luxor, Qena, Sohâg, Asyût, El Minya, Beni Suef and finally Cairo, the Egyptian capital; the Nile opens out into a broad delta N of Cairo, stretching along the Mediterranean coast from Alexandria (W) to Port Said (Bûr Sa'id); the delta is 250 km from E to W and 160 km from N to S; historically the Nile had 7 mouths in its delta but presently there are 2, the Massab Rashîd (Rosetta Mouth) and the Massab Dumyât (Damietta Mouth), both of which are about 240 km long; James Bruce made the European discovery of the source of the Blue Nile (T'ana Hāyk or L Tana, Ethiopia) and travelled along it between 1768 and 1773; J.H. Speke was the first person to establish L Victoria as the Nile's main reservoir (1858); Speke and J.A. Grant explored L Victoria (1860-62); Samuel Baker made 2 expeditions (1861-62 and 1863-65) and made the European discovery of L Albert and the Kabalega (Murchison) Falls.

Niles, 42 02N 87 48W, pop(1980) 30,363, town in Cook county, NE Illinois, United States; 22 km N of Chicago; residential.

Nilgiri Hills *neel'gi-ree*, hills linking the Eastern Ghats with the Western Ghats, Tamil Nadu state, S India; connected to the S Deccan Plateau; the highest point is Doda Betta (2,636 m); separated from the Anaimallai Hills by the Palghat Gap; there are many coffee and tea plantations in the locality.

Nîmes *neem*, NISMES, NEMAUSUS (anc), 43 50N 4 23E, pop(1982) 129,924, ancient town and capital of Gard dept, Languedoc-Roussillon region, S France; below a semi-circle of limestone commanding the routes to Narbonne and the Carcassonne Gate, in the Cévennes foreland, 102 km NW of Marseille; thought to have been founded by Greek colonists; for 5 centuries Nîmes was one of the principal cities of Roman Gaul; a Protestant stronghold in the 16th century; the Pacification of Nîmes was signed here in 1629; scene of an uprising in 1815; birthplace of the 19th-c writer Alphonse Daudet (1840-97); centre of the wine and fruit trade and the silk industry; a type of cloth known as de Nîmes was once made here, the name contracted to 'denim', a well-known clothing material today; noted for its ancient Roman buildings and monuments, the town hosts summer courses in archaeology; bishopric; Nîmes-Garons airport (8 km S), railway; economy: textiles, clothing, footwear, carpets, agric machinery, trade in grain, wine and brandy; monuments: amphitheatre (Les Arènes), built in the 1st century AD, with a seating capacity of 21,000; Maison Carrée ('Square House'), a Corinthian temple, restored in 1824, now a museum of antiquities; remains of the ancient tower (Tour Magne) on Mont Cavalier, formerly part of the town fortifications; Temple of Diana; 11th-c cathedral of St-Castor on the site of the former temple of Apollo.

Nīmrūz *nim'rōz*, CHAKHNSUR, prov in SW Afghanistan; pop(1984e) 112,536; area 41,356 sq km; bounded W by Iran and S by Pakistan; capital Zaranj; crossed in the S by the R Helmand and NE-SW by the Khash Rud in the N; Khash Desert lies in the N section.

Ningbo *ning-pō*, NINGPO, YIN-HSIEN, 29 54N 121 33E, pop(1984e) 615,600, port city in Zhejiang prov, E China; at the confluence of the Fenghua, Tong and Yuyao rivers; for 800 years an important outlet for silk and porcelain; a special economic zone; railway; economy: fishing, shipbuilding, high-technology industries relating to oil and shipping have developed in recent years; monuments: the Tianyi Ge Library, the oldest library in China, was built in 1561; the Tianfeng Ta pagoda, highest building in Ningbo, was originally built in the 6th century; the present pagoda was built in 1330.

Ningpo, town in Zhejiang prov, E China. See Ningbo.

Ningsia Hui, autonomous region in N China. See Ningxia.

Ningxia *ning-shi-ah*, NINGXIA-HUI, NINGSIA HUI, aut region in N China; bounded by Nei Mongol (Inner Mongolia) aut region (N and W), by Gansu prov (W and S) and by Shaanxi prov (E); the S section of Ningxia is part of the Huangtu Gaoyuan (Loess Plateau), with the Quwu Shan and Liupan Shan ranges in the S and part of the Baiyu Shan range in the E; in the N is the middle Huang He (Yellow river) valley; drained by the Huang He and Qingshui He rivers; pop(1982) 3,895,578; area 170,000 sq km; capital Yinchuan; economy: grain, sheep raising, coal mining.

Ninian, oil field in the North Sea, E of the Shetland Is; linked by pipeline to Sullom Voe.

Nini-Suhien *nee-nee-sow-hyen'*, national park in Ghana, W Africa; area 104 sq km; established in 1976.

Niokolo-Ko'ba, national park and game reserve in E Senegal, W Africa; area 9,130 sq km; established in 1953; principally watered by the R Gambia; villages include Simenti and Niokolo Koba; Mt Asirik rises to 311 m.

Nioro du Sahel *nyō'rō dü sa-hel'*, 15 12N 9 35W, pop(1971) 13,200, town in Kayes region, W Mali, W Africa; 210 km NE of Kayes, close to the Mauritania border; economy: power plant.

Niort *nyor*, 46 19N 0 29W, pop(1982) 60,230, market town and capital of Deux-Sèvres dept, Poitou-Charentes region, W France; on one of the 2 arms of the R Sèvre-Niortaise, 133 km SE of Nantes; developed around a castle built by Henry II Plantagenet and Richard Coeur-de-Lion in 1155; in the 18th century the tanning of pelts imported from Canada became a major industry, the leather breeches worn by the Cavalry in the American Civil War were made in Niort; today it is best known as the headquarters of the Mutual Assurance Companies of France, and for the growing of angelica, from which a local liqueur is made; road and rail junction; economy: footwear, gloves, chipboard panels, plywood; monuments: former 16th-c town hall (now a museum of antiquities); 15-16th-c church of Notre-Dame; 12-13th-c castle; Niort is noted for its gardens.

Niquero *nee-kay'rō*, 20 3N 77 34W, port town in Granma prov, SE Cuba; 56 km SW of Manzanillo; centre of a rich agricultural region.

Niš or **Nish** *neesh*, NAISUS (anc), 43 20N 21 54E, pop(1981) 230,711, industrial town in SE central Srbija (Serbia) republic, Yugoslavia; on R Nišava near its junction with the R Morava; crossing point for N-S and E-W road routes; formerly an important stronghold on the road to Byzantium; occupied by Bulgaria until 1918; open-air theatre; university (1965); airfield; railway; economy: wine, grain, cattle trade, electronics, electrical equipment; monuments: Tower of Skulls, Turkish citadel and the nearby site of Constantine's villa at Mediana; event: film festival.

Nishinomiya *nee-shee-nō'mee-ya*, 34 44N 135 22E, pop(1980) 410,329, city in Hyōgo prefecture, Kinki region, S Honshū island, Japan; situated on Ōsaka-wan Bay, between Kōbe (W) and Amagasaki (E); university; railway; economy: chemicals, machinery, soap, saké.

Niterói *nee-tay-roy'*, 22 54S 43 06W, pop(1980) 382,736, port in Rio de Janeiro state, Sudeste region, SE Brazil; situated on SE shore of Guanabara Bay opposite Rio de Janeiro; founded in 1573; former capital of Rio de Janeiro state; connected to the capital by a 14 km-long bridge; university (1960); railway; economy: commerce, shipbuilding, canning, fishing, tourism; monuments: colonial forts include Santa Cruz, built in the 16th-c and still a military establishment, Barão do Rio Branco (1633), Gragoatá and Nossa Senhora da Boa Viagem; the church of Boa Viagem (1633) is situated on an island connected to the mainland by a short causeway; the Museu de Arqueologia de Itaipu is situated in the ruins of the 18th-c Santa Teresa Convent and also covers the archaeological site of Duna Grande on Itaipu beach.

Nitra *nyi'tra*, 48 20N 18 05E, pop(1984) 81,673, town in Západoslovenský region, Slovak Socialist Republic, SE central Czechoslovakia; on R Nitra NE of Bratislava; site of first Christian church in Czechoslovakia established in the 9th century; railway; economy: agricultural industries.

Nit'tedal, 60 05N 10 55E, pop(1980) 14,128, town in Akershus county, SE Norway, NE of Oslo; railway.

Niue *nee-oo'ay*, 19 02S 169 55W, coral island in the S Pacific Ocean, S of the American Samoa and 2,140 km NE of New Zealand, of which it is a self-governing dependency; GMT +12; area 262.65 sq km; pop(1986e) 3,000; main settlement Alofi; New Zealand currency is used; the inhabitants live in small villages scattered along the coast, with a slight concentration around Alofi, on the W coast; Christianity is the dominant religion; English is the official language with a Polynesian dialect widely used.

Physical description and climate. Niue is mainly coralline with a flat, rolling interior and porous soils. The highest point is 70 m. The climate is subtropical and damp, supporting woodland in the central uplands. Dec to March are the hottest months, and hurricanes can occur during this season. Rainfall is evenly distributed throughout the year.

History, government and constitution. James Cook discovered Niue in 1774, and was so badly received by the natives that he named it 'Savage Island'. In the mid-19th century, European missionaries arrived to convert the population to Christianity. The islanders petitioned for British sovereignty and became a protectorate in 1900. In 1901 Niue was annexed to New Zealand. Since Oct 1974 Niue has had internal self-government in free association with New Zealand, which still maintains responsibility for defence and foreign affairs. The island is governed by an elected legislative assembly of 20 members, headed by a premier.

Economy. The economy is mainly agricultural although many are employed by the government on relief work. Exports include passionfruit, copra, and a few handicrafts. New Zealand supplies the island with an annual grant-in-aid and remittances from Niueans abroad are an important supplement to the economy.

Nivelles *nee-vel*, dist of Brabant prov, Belgium; area 1,090 sq km; pop(1982) 292,939.

Nivelles, 50 36N 4 20E, pop(1982) 21,535, town in Nivelles dist, S Brabant prov, Belgium; 30 km S of Bruxelles; developed from an agricultural base into a modern industrial town; railway; economy: metalworking, railway equipment, machinery, paper; monument: former convent church of St Gertrude (consecrated 1046).

Nivernais *nee-ver-nay*, former prov in central France, now occupying the dept of Nièvre; formerly a duchy with its seat at Nevers it came to the French crown in 1669; it gives its name to a breed of beef cattle.

Nizhniy Tagil *nyeezh'nyee tu-geel'*, formerly NIZHNETAGIL'SKII ZAVOD, 58 00N 59 58E, pop(1983) 411,000, town in Sverdlovskaya oblast, E European Rossiyskaya, W Soviet Union, in the central Ural'skiy Khrebet (Ural Mts), on the R Tagil; founded in 1725 and became a city in 1917; railway; economy: ferrous metallurgy, machine building, plastics, foodstuffs.

Nizhnyaya Tunguska, LOWER TUNGUSKA, river in Irkutskaya oblast and Krasnoyarskiy kray, Rossiyskaya, Soviet Union; rises N of Ust'-Kut in N central Irkutskaya oblast, then flows N and WNW to join the R Yenisey at Turukhansk; length 3,200 km; chief tributaries Vivi and Taymura rivers; its upper course approaches within 29 km of the R Lena.

Njazidja, island of Comoros. See Grande Comore.

Nkawkaw *ung-ko'ko*, 6 32N 0 46W, town in Eastern region, S Ghana, W Africa; NW of Koforidua; economy: civil engineering.

N'Ka'yi, formerly JACOB, 4 07S 13 17E, pop(1980) 32,520, town in Niari prov, SW Congo, W Africa; on the railway between Pointe-Noire and Brazzaville.

Nkha'ta Bay, dist in Northern region, Malawi, SE Africa; area 4,090 sq km; pop(1977) 105,803.

Nkhota-Ko'ta, dist in Central region, Malawi, SE Africa; area 4,259 sq km; pop(1977) 94,370.

Nkongsamba *ung-kong-sam'ba*, 4 29N 9 53E, pop(1973) 71,298, town in Littoral prov, Cameroon, W Africa; 225 km NW of Yaoundé; developed since 1914; Martin-Paul Samba attempted a revolt against the German colonists from here but was captured and shot.

Noakhali *nō-ah-kah'lee*, region in SE Bangladesh; includes Feni, Lakshmipur and Noakhali districts; pop(1981) 3,816,000; area 5,459 sq km; bounded E by Tripuria, Assam, India and W by the Meghna river; capital Sudharam (formerly Noakhali).

Nógrád *no'grad*, county in N Hungary; bounded to the N by R Ipoly which follows the border with Czechoslovakia; Börzsöny Mts to the W and Cserhat Mts to the S; pop(1984e) 237,000; area 2,544 sq km; capital Salgótarján; economy: grain, vegetables, livestock, lignite mining.

Nogueira, Serra de, *nog-we-ee'ra*, mountain range, Bragança dist, Trás-os-Montes, NE Portugal, lying SW of Bragança and rising to 1,318 m.

Noirmoutier, Ile de *eel de nwar-moot-yer*, island in the N Bay of Biscay off the NW coast of Vendée dept, W France; separated from the mainland by the Goulet de Fromentine, an arm of the Baie de Bourgneuf; area 48 sq km; approximately 19 km long by 7 km wide; it is reached from Fromentine on the mainland by a viaduct toll-bridge; the island is flat and bare, except for the wooded Bois de la Chaise; capital town is Noirmoutier-en-L'île, in the NE part of the island; in the capital is the church of St-Philibert, with the remains of a monastery founded by St Philibert in 680 AD; economy: market-gardening, fishing.

Nokia *no'kya*, 61 29N 23 31E, pop(1982) 23,857, town in Turku-Pori prov, SW Finland; SW of Tampere; established in 1937; railway; airfield.

Nokoue, Lake *no'kway*, lagoon in S Benin, W Africa; just N of Cotonou; receives the R Ouémé and connects with adjoining Porto Novo lagoon; area 150 sq km.

Nola *nō-lah'*, 3 28N 16 08E, town in SW Central African Republic; at the head of the R Sanga, 88 km SSE of Berbérati.

Noord Brabant *nōrt'brahb-ahnt*, NORTH BRABANT (Eng), pop(1984e) 2,103,000, prov in S Netherlands, bounded on the S by Belgium and on the N and E by the R Maas, comprises the entire S part of the so-called 'Geest-Holland' and in the W it merges into the Schelde marshes in Zeeland; land area 4,963 sq km; capital 's-Hertogenbosch; chief towns Breda, Tilburg and Eindhoven; economy: predominantly mixed farming interspersed with patches of heath and moorland (agricultural land has largely replaced the original heathland of Noord Brabant), traditional cloth-making around Tilburg and Eindhoven.

Noord Holland *nōrt'hol-ahnt*, NORTH HOLLAND (Eng), pop (1984e) 2,307,400, prov in West Netherlands, bounded on the E by the Ijsselmeer, on the W by the North Sea and on the N by the Waddenzee; includes Texel I (one of the West Frisian Is); the North Sea Canal cuts across the S of the prov; land area 2,667 sq km; capital Haarlem; chief towns Amsterdam (the national capital), Zaanstad and Alkmaar; economy: important bulb growing area S of Haarlem, well-suited to the lime-rich sandy soils of the excavated old dunes; arable farming in the drained lakes on fertile, well-drained, marine clays growing cereals, potatoes, sugar beet; predominantly livestock farming elsewhere.

Nord, industrial dept in Nord-Pas-de-Calais region of N France, on the English Channel (N) and the Belgian frontier (E); comprises 6 arrond, 76 cantons and 652 communes; pop(1982) 2,520,526; area 5,743 sq km; the region saw much fighting preceding the Dunkerque (Dunkirk) evacuation in World War II; capital Lille, chief towns Dunkerque, Douai, Valenciennes and Armentières; spa at St-Amand-les-Eaux; the Parc de St-Amand-Raismes is a regional nature park, with facilities for riding and water-sports.

Norderstedt *nor-dur-shtet'*, pop(1983) 65,700, city in Schleswig-Holstein prov, W Germany.

Nordeste *nor-des'tay*, region in NE Brazil; comprises Maranhão, Piauí, Ceará, Rio Grande do Norte, Paraíba, Pernambuco, Alagoas, Sergipe and Bahia states and Fernando de Noronha territory; from Rio Grande do Norte to the S of Bahia, the land is fertile and the climate humid, with 2,000 mm of rain well-distributed throughout the year; inland is the region known as the *Sertão*, with a semi-arid climate and infrequent rain; principal rivers include the São Francisco, Parnaíba, Paraguaçu; pop(1980) 34,812,356; area 1,584,672 sq km; Brazil's major oil-producing region, the population is largely located along the coast, where most of the state capitals are situated; people flock to these cities in times of extreme drought in the Sertão.

Nordfjord *nord'fyord*, NORD FJORD (Eng), inlet of Norwegian Sea, Sogn og Fjordane county, SW coast of Norway, lies parallel with Sognefjorden (Sogne Fjord) to the S; lies almost exactly on the 62°N latitude; length 106 km; max depth 565 m; extends from Husevagøy in W to Loen.

Nordjylland *nor-yoo'lan*, a county in N Jylland (Jutland), bounded on the E by the Kattegat and on the W by the Skagerrak, the Limfjorden (Lim Fjord) runs W-E through the middle of the county; area 6,173 sq km; pop(1983) 482,409; capital Ålborg, chief towns include Brønderslev, Skagen and Frederikshavn.

Nordkapp *nör'kap*, NORTH CAPE (Eng), 71 10N 25 48E, cape on N Magerøy I, Finnmark county, N Norway; 96 km NE of Hammerfest; considered to be the most northerly point of Europe.

Nordkyn or **Nordkinn** *nōr'chun*, formerly KINNARODDEN, 70 55N 27 45E, rocky cape on N coast of Finnmark county, NE Norway; 152 km ENE of Hammerfest, 72 km E of Nordkapp or North Cape.

Nordland *nor'lahn*, a county of N central Norway, lying mostly within the Arctic Circle; area 38,327 sq km; pop(1983) 244,974; capital Bodø; chief towns Narvik and Mo; drained chiefly by the R Vefsna; mountainous terrain rising to 1,915 m at Mt Okstind; the W coastline is indented by the Vega, Salt and Ofot Fjords.

Nordliche Kalkalpen *nord'liKH-ë kal-kal'pen*, mountain range of the Eastern Alps in Oberösterreich, Niederösterreich, Salzburg and Steiermark states of central Austria, rising to 2,995 m at Hoher Dachstein.

Nord-Pas-de-Calais, region of NW France comprising the depts of Nord and Pas-de-Calais, 13 arrond, 137 cantons and 1,550 communes; pop(1982) 3,932,939; area 12,414 sq km; includes the old provinces of Flanders and Artois; in the extreme NE corner of France, bounded on the E by Belgium and on the N by the English Channel; drained by the Canche, Lys and Scarpe rivers; there are numerous canals; chief towns Calais, Boulogne-sur-Mer, Lille, Lens, Arras and Cambrai; Le Touquet is the liveliest of the many new seaside resorts that established themselves during the 19th century along the coastline; the vast urban-industrial metropolis of Lille-Roubaix-Tourcoing is the greatest economic centre of N France; economy:

coal, chemicals, metallurgy, cotton, linen, biscuits, printing, chocolate, distilling, brewing, machines, diesel engines; there are numerous World War I memorials and cemeteries, the principal sites being at Vimy, Albert, Villers-Bretonneux and Bellicourt.

Nordrhein-Westfalen *nord'rīn vest'fa-len*, NORTH RHINE-WESTPHALIA *-fay'li-a* (Eng), pop(1983) 16,836,500, prov of W Germany; comprises the five administrative dists of Düsseldorf, Köln, Münster, Detmold, Arnsberg; area 34,062 sq km; drained by the R Rhine and its tributaries, Lenne, Lippe and Ruhr; predominantly low-lying but rises to the Sauerland range in the SE and the Teutoburger Wald (Teutoburg Forest) in the NE; capital Düsseldorf; chief towns Münster, Essen, Dortmund, Köln (Cologne) and Aachen; economy: machine building, petrochemicals and chemicals, ferrous metallurgy, coal mining, electrical engineering, textiles, foodstuffs, motor vehicles, cotton and wool cloth; the most densely populated prov in W Germany; its core is the Ruhr area, Germany's most important industrial centre with Europe's largest inland port, Duisburg.

Nordstrand *nort'shtrahnt*, third largest island of the Nordfriesische Inseln (North Frisian Is), W Germany; in the North Sea, off the W coast of Schleswig-Holstein prov; area 50.1 sq km.

Nord-Trøndelag *nor træn'de-laKH*, formerly NORDRE TRONDHJEM, a county of central Norway; area 22,463 sq km; pop(1983) 126,696; capital Steinkjer; chief towns Namsos and Levanger; the upper section of Trondheimsfjord (Trondheim Fjord) penetrates the centre of the county in the SW; drained chiefly by the R Namsen; L Tunnsjøen lies near the E border with Sweden; rises to 1,390 m in the E.

Norfolk *nor'fok*, flat, arable county in E England; drained by Yare, Ouse, Waveney and Bure rivers; pop(1981) 694,566; area 5,368 sq km; county town Norwich; Great Yarmouth is a major resort and fishing port; the county is divided into 7 districts:

District	*area (sq km)*	*pop(1981)*
Breckland	1,305	96,458
Broadland	552	98,417
Great Yarmouth	173	80,819
North Norfolk	965	81,903
Norwich	39	122,890
South Norfolk	907	93,194
West Norfolk	1,426	120,885

Norfolk, 36 51N 76 17W, pop(1980) 266,979, seaport and independent city, SE Virginia, United States; on the R Elizabeth, just S of the Hampton Roads channel; settled in 1682, achieving city status in 1845; Norfolk State College (1935); railway; airfield; largest city in the state; headquarters of the US Atlantic Fleet, the largest naval base in the world; economy: shipbuilding, automobiles, chemicals machinery, trade in coal, grain, tobacco, timber and vegetables; monuments: Chrysler Museum, Douglas MacArthur Memorial, Hampton Roads Naval Museum, Botanical Gardens; event: Azalea Festival (April).

Norfolk Broads, area of shallow lakes in E England, extending from Norfolk into northern Suffolk; over 150 miles of navigable waterways created by lakes which formed from submerged Saxon and early medieval peat cuttings, linked by the rivers Waveney, Yare, Bure and tributaries; popular recreational area for boating; important nature reserves; tourist centres include Wroxham, Stalham and Yarmouth.

Norfolk Island, 29 04S 167 57E, fertile, hilly island in the W Pacific Ocean, 1,488 km NE of Sydney, Australia; pop(1982e) 16,220; area 34.55 sq km; length 8 km; a British penal settlement 1788-1806, and again 1826-55; in 1856 many people from the Pitcairn Is were transferred here; the pop comprises 'islanders' or descendants of the mutineers from *HMS Bounty* and 'mainlanders' from Australia, New Zealand and the UK; both English and Tahitian are spoken; an Australian external territory since 1913, it was formerly part of the colony of New South Wales and then Van Diemen's Land, later coming under the jurisdiction of the state of New South Wales; the island is governed by the Norfolk Island Legislative Assembly and is represented in the Australian Ministry for Territories and Local Government by an Administrator appointed by the Governor-General; economy: postage stamps, tourism.

Norge. See Norway.

Noril'sk *nu-reelsk'*, 69 21N 88 02E, pop(1983) 183,000, industrial city in W Krasnoyarskiy kray, N Siberian Rossiyskaya, E Soviet Union; 90 km E of Dudinka and the Yenisey river; established in 1935; northernmost major city in the USSR; leading Soviet nickel mining and processing centre; Noril'sk is being developed as a non-ferrous metals complex, with copper its most important product; the coldest city in the world, with a mean annual temperature of −10.9°C; railway; airfield.

Normal, 40 31N 88 59W, pop(1980) 35,672, residential town in McLean county, central Illinois, United States; 8 km N of Bloomington; at the centre of a dairy and livestock farming area; university (1857); railway.

Norman, 35 13N 97 26W, pop(1980) 68,020, county seat of Cleveland county, central Oklahoma, United States; 30 km S of Oklahoma City; founded in 1889; university (1892); railway.

Normandie *nor-mã-dee*, NORMANDY (Eng), former duchy and prov in NW France along the littoral of the English Channel between Bretagne and French Flanders; now occupying the regions of Haute-Normandie and Basse-Normandie.

Nor'manton, 53 42N 1 25W, pop(1981) 17,190, town in Wakefield borough, West Yorkshire, N England; 6 km E of Wakefield; railway; economy: electrical goods, engineering, coal, textiles.

Norra Karelen, prov in Finland. See Pohjois-Karjala.

Norrbotten *nor-bot'tun*, a county of N Sweden, largest in country, bounded on the SE by the Gulf of Bothnia, the NE by Finland and on the W by Norway; land area 98,906 sq km; pop(1983) 265,275; capital Luleå; chief towns Piteå and Gällivare; drained by the Tornio, Pite and Lule rivers; many NW to SE orientated lakes including Stora Lulevatten and Uddjaur; rises to 2,111 m at Kebnekaise, the highest peak in Sweden; important iron-ore deposits in the Kiruna-Malmberget area; Sweden's largest copper mine at Aitik.

Norristown, 40 07N 75 21W, pop(1980) 34,684, county seat of Montgomery county, SE Pennsylvania, United States; on the R Schuylkill, 27 km NW of Philadelphia; railway.

Norrköping *nawr'kyœ-ping*, 58 35N 16 10E, pop(1982) 118,242, industrial town and seaport in Östergötland county, SE Sweden; SW of Stockholm, on the R Motala where it enters the Bråviken, a fjord of the Baltic; railway; economy: metalworking, textiles; monuments: 17th-c castle, neo-Gothic St Matthew's church (1892).

Norrtälje *nor-tel'yu*, 59 46N 18 42E, pop(1982) 41,466, town in NE Stockholm county, SE Sweden.

Norte *nor'tay*, the largest and least populated region of South America, in N and NW Brazil comprising of Acre, Amazonas, Pará and Rondônia states and Amapá and Roraima territories; the majority of the region lies in a vast plain, crossed by relatively low mountain ranges; in the N are the highest points in Brazil: the Pico da Neblina (3,014 m) and the Pico 21 de Março (2,992 m); the area is covered by tropical rainforest; principal rivers include the Amazonas, Negro, Xingu, Tapajós, Tocantins, Madeira; pop(1980) 5,880,268; area 3,581,180 sq km; Manaus is the major industrial centre; the region is thought to contain large deposits of iron, gold, bauxite and manganese; poor communications have made mineral exploitation difficult; the government's main programme in this region is the Projeto Carajás, a project to explore the enormous mineral reserves in the Serra de Carajás mountain range in Pará state; this includes the building of the new Tucuruí hydroelectric dam and a railway from the mountain range to Pôrto de Itaqui, in Maranhão state; the pop is mostly located by rivers in the N; after the 1960s the S of Pará state became more populated as a result of the construction of a road between Belém and Brasília; in the 1970s Rondônia became one of the most populated areas in the country; the construction of the Transamazônica road helped to draw more people to this region; one-third of the population is still to be found in Norte's port cities of Belém and Manaus.

Norte de Santander *nor'tay day san-tan-der'*, dept in NE Colombia, South America; bordered E and N by Venezuela; located in the deeply dissected Cordillera Oriental; pop(1985) 871,966; area 21,658 sq km; capital Cúcuta; economy: coffee, tobacco, cattle.

North America, 3rd largest continent after Asia and Africa, extending 9,600 km from 70 30N to 15N; area c.24 mn sq km; roughly bisected by 100 W meridian; separated from Asia by the Bering Strait (90 km wide), bounded on the NW by the Beaufort Sea, on the N by the Arctic Ocean, on the NE by Baffin Bay and Davis Strait, on the E by the Atlantic Ocean and on the W by the Pacific Ocean; includes Canada, United States of America and Mexico; numerous islands include Queen Elizabeth Islands, Baffin Island, Newfoundland, the West Indies; mountain ranges include the Rocky Mts extending along the W coast, the Alaska Range (including Mount McKinley, highest point in N America), and the Appalachian Mts, running parallel to the Atlantic; lakes include Great Slave L, L Winnipeg and the Great Lakes; rivers include Columbia, Delaware, Hudson, Mackenzie, Mississippi, Missouri, Potomac, Rio Grande and St Lawrence.

North Bay, 46 20N 79 28W, pop(1981) 51,268, town in SE Ontario, SE Canada; situated on the E shore of L Nipissing, 160 km E of Sudbury; military base; university (1967); railway; airfield; economy: tourism, mining equipment; events: competitions involving dog sledding, log chopping and sleigh riding take place each Feb.

North Cape, Norwegian cape. See Nordkapp.

North Carolina, state in SE United States; bounded W by Tennessee, N by Virginia, E by Atlantic Ocean, and S by South Carolina and Georgia; the R Roanoke flows SE across the NE corner of the state before emptying into the Albemarle Sound; the R Yadkin rises in the NW and flows SE through central North Carolina to form the Pee Dee river; the highest point is Mt Mitchell (2,037 m); off the coast lies a chain of islands with constantly shifting sand dunes, enclosing several lagoons; the sandy beaches attract many tourists; the coastal strip on the mainland is flat, swampy, tidewater country; inland, this low land gives way to the rolling hills of the Piedmont, whose fast-flowing rivers provide hydroelectric power for the manufacturing industries of the state; in the W the land rises further to the Blue Ridge and Great Smoky Mts; the state has 4 national forests; the state grows 40% of all US tobacco, and manufactures cotton, silk goods, synthetic fibres, furniture, electrical machinery and chemicals; agricultural products include poultry, corn, soybeans, peanuts and hogs; mineral resources include feldspar, mica and lithium; the state formed part of the Carolina grant given in 1663 by Charles II to 8 court favourites, and became known as North Carolina in 1691; became a royal province in 1729; North Carolina was 12th of the original 13 states to ratify the Constitution (1789); following the Declaration of Mecklenburg the state withdrew from the Union on 20 May 1861; slavery was abolished on 7 Oct 1865 and the state was re-admitted to the Union on 11 July 1868; also known as the 'Tar Heel State' or the 'Old North State'; pop(1980) 5,881,766; area 126,992 sq km; capital Raleigh; other major cities are Charlotte, Greensboro, Winston-Salem and Durham; the state is divided into 100 counties:

County	*area (sq km)*	*pop(1980)*
Alamance	1,126	99,319
Alexander	673	24,999
Alleghany	611	9,587
Anson	1,386	25,649
Ashe	1,108	22,325

contd

County	*area (sq km)*	*pop(1980)*
Avery	642	14,409
Beaufort	2,148	40,355
Bertie	1,823	21,024
Bladen	2,285	30,491
Brunswick	2,236	35,777
Buncombe	1,713	160,934
Burke	1,310	72,504
Cabarrus	946	85,895
Caldwell	1,225	67,746
Camden	624	5,829
Carteret	1,368	41,092
Caswell	1,113	20,705
Catawba	1,030	105,208
Chatham	1,841	33,415
Cherokee	1,175	18,933
Chowan	473	12,558
Clay	556	6,619
Cleveland	1,217	83,435
Columbus	2,439	51,037
Craven	1,823	71,043
Cumberland	1,708	247,160
Currituck	666	11,089
Dare	1,017	13,377
Davidson	1,425	113,162
Davie	694	24,599
Duplin	2,129	40,952
Durham	775	152,785
Edgecombe	1,316	55,988
Forsyth	1,071	243,683
Franklin	1,284	30,055
Gaston	928	162,568
Gates	879	8,875
Graham	751	7,217
Granville	1,388	34,043
Greene	692	16,117
Guilford	1,693	317,154
Halifax	1,882	55,286
Harnett	1,563	59,570
Haywood	1,443	46,495
Henderson	972	58,580
Hertford	926	23,368
Hoke	1,017	20,383
Hyde	1,622	5,873
Iredell	1,492	82,538
Jackson	1,277	25,811
Johnston	2,067	70,599
Jones	1,222	9,705
Lee	673	36,718
Lenoir	1,045	59,819
Lincoln	775	42,372
Macon	1,344	20,178
Madison	1,173	16,827
Martin	1,199	25,948
McDowell	1,136	35,135
Mecklenburg	1,373	404,270
Mitchell	577	14,428
Montgomery	1,274	22,469
Moore	1,823	50,505
Nash	1,404	67,153
New Hanover	481	103,471
Northampton	1,399	22,584
Onslow	1,984	112,784
Orange	1,040	77,055
Pamlico	887	10,398
Pasquotank	593	28,462
Pender	2,275	22,215
Perquimans	640	9,486
Person	1,035	29,164
Pitt	1,708	90,146
Polk	619	12,984
Randolph	2,051	91,728
Richmond	1,240	45,481
Robeson	2,467	101,610
Rockingham	1,479	83,426

contd

County	*area (sq km)*	*pop(1980)*
Rowan	1,349	99,186
Rutherford	1,477	53,787
Sampson	2,462	49,687
Scotland	829	32,273
Stanly	1,030	48,517
Stokes	1,175	33,086
Surry	1,401	59,449
Swain	1,368	10,283
Transylvania	983	23,417
Tyrell	1,058	3,975
Union	1,661	70,380
Vance	647	36,748
Wake	2,220	301,327
Warren	1,110	16,232
Washington	863	14,801
Watauga	816	31,666
Wayne	1,440	97,054
Wilkes	1,955	58,657
Wilson	972	63,132
Yadkin	874	28,439
Yancey	816	14,934

North Charleston, 32 53N 80 00W, pop(1980) 62,534, town in Charleston county, SE South Carolina, United States; on the R Cooper, 10 km N of Charleston; railway.

North Chicago, 42 19N 87 51W, pop(1980) 38,774, town in Lake county, NE Illinois, United States; on L Michigan, 8 km S of Waukegan; railway.

North Dakota *dah-kō'ta*, state in N central United States; bounded W by Montana, N by Canada, E by Minnesota, and S by South Dakota; the R Missouri flows E into the state and turns SE, then S, to cross into South Dakota; the Red river follows the E state border; highest point is White Butte (1,069 m); the W part of the state receives little rainfall and semi-arid conditions prevail; cultivation is only possible in the river valleys, the rest of the land being covered in short, easily eroded prairie grasses, where cattle are grazed; the E part of the state is a flat fertile plain, covered almost entirely by crops, chiefly spring wheat, barley, sunflowers and flaxseed (North Dakota is the nation's leading producer of all these crops); cattle are the 2nd most important product of the state; major mineral products include oil (NW), and lignite coal (W); manufactures include processed foods and machinery; there are Indian reserves at Turtle Mt, Fort Berthold, Fort Totten and Standing Rock; North Dakota became part of USA as a result of the Louisiana Purchase of 1803; included in Dakota Territory which was formed in 1861; separated from South Dakota to become a state in 1889; pop(1980) 652,717; area 180,180 sq km; 39th state admitted to the Union, in 1889; capital Bismarck; other chief cities are Fargo, Grand Forks and Minot; the state is divided into 53 counties:

County	*area (sq km)*	*pop(1980)*
Adams	2,569	3,584
Barnes	3,895	13,960
Benson	3,671	7,944
Billings	2,995	1,138
Bottineau	4,337	9,239
Bowman	3,021	4,229
Burke	2,907	3,822
Burleigh	4,207	54,811
Cass	4,594	88,247
Cavalier	3,918	7,636
Dickey	2,961	7,207
Divide	3,349	3,494
Dunn	5,182	4,627
Eddy	1,648	3,554
Emmons	3,897	5,877
Foster	1,664	4,611
Golden Valley	2,608	2,391

contd

County	*area (sq km)*	*pop(1980)*
Grand Forks	3,744	66,100
Grant	4,316	4,274
Griggs	1,841	3,714
Hettinger	2,946	4,275
Kidder	3,541	3,833
La Moure	2,990	6,473
Logan	2,600	3,493
McHenry	4,906	7,858
McIntosh	2,558	4,800
McKenzie	7,160	7,132
McLean	5,369	12,383
Mercer	2,714	9,404
Morton	4,995	25,177
Mountrail	4,776	7,679
Nelson	2,577	5,233
Oliver	1,880	2,495
Pembina	2,912	10,399
Pierce	2,696	6,166
Ramsey	3,227	13,048
Ransom	2,241	6,698
Renville	2,272	3,608
Richland	3,734	19,207
Rolette	2,376	12,177
Sargent	2,228	5,512
Sheridan	2,571	2,819
Sioux	2,857	3,620
Slope	3,169	1,157
Stark	3,479	23,697
Steele	1,854	3,106
Stutsman	5,884	24,154
Towner	2,691	4,052
Traill	2,239	9,624
Walsh	3,354	15,371
Ward	5,307	58,392
Wells	3,349	6,979
Williams	5,392	22,237

North Downs Way, long-distance footpath in S England; length 227 km; follows the crest of the North Downs from Farnham to Dover.

North Island, smaller, but more densely populated of the 2 major islands of New Zealand; separated from South Island by the Cook Strait; irregularly shaped with long peninsula projecting NW; Ruahine range is the largest of several mountain ranges; the highest volcanic mountains in North Island are Ruapehu (2,797 m) and Mount Egmont (2,518 m); in the centre of the island is the largest of New Zealand's lakes, L Taupo (606 sq km); there are many hot springs in the N central area; fertile plains lie in the coastal areas; the N of the island is a narrow indented peninsula and is sparsely populated; pop(1981) 2,322,989; area 114,834 sq km; principal towns include Wellington (capital of New Zealand), Auckland, Napier, Hastings, New Plymouth and Palmerston North; economy: citrus fruit, wine, farming (N); farming, dairying, horse breeding, agriculture, coal mining, natural gas (central); mineral spas and health resorts, horse breeding, citrus and subtropical fruit, wine (E); sheep farming, industry (S); Maoris, comprising 9% of the pop, mostly live on North Island; 15,000 sq km of their land is protected and farmed as corporate enterprises or planted in forest; North Island consists of 7 statistical divisions:

Division	*area (sq km)*	*pop(1981)*
Central Auckland	5,581	829,519
East Coast	10,914	48,573
Hawke's Bay	11,289	147,722
Northland	12,653	114,295
South Auckland-Bay of Plenty	36,902	491,304
Taranaki	9,729	105,153
Wellington	27,766	586,423

North Land, archipelago in the Arctic Ocean, N Soviet Union. See Severnaya Zemlya.

North Las Vegas, 36 12N 115 07W, pop(1980) 42,739, town in Clark county, SE Nevada, United States; a suburb of Las Vegas; railway; monument: the Garden of Cities.

North Little Rock, 34 45N 92 16W, pop(1980) 64,288, town in Pulaski county, central Arkansas, United States; on the R Arkansas, opposite Little Rock; railway; economy: food products, lumber, insecticides and fertilizers, fabric, metal products, mattresses.

North Miami, 25 54N 80 11W, pop(1980) 42,566, resort town in Dade county, SE Florida, United States; residential suburb on Biscayne Bay, N of Miami; railway.

North Miami Beach, 25 56N 80 11W, pop(1980) 36,553, resort town in Dade county, SE Florida, United States; on Atlantic Ocean, N of Miami Beach; railway.

North Pole. See Poles.

North Richland Hills, 32 50N 97 14W, pop(1980) 30,592, town in Tarrant county, NE Texas, United States; a residential suburb 12 km NE of Fort Worth.

North Sea, GERMAN OCEAN, arm of the Atlantic Ocean, lying between the continent of Europe (E) and Great Britain (W); stretches from the Shetland Is in the N to the Straits of Dover in the S; bounded by the shores of Great Britain, Norway, Denmark, the Netherlands, West Germany, Belgium and the N coast of France; length 965 km; max width 645 km; approx area 574,980 sq km; deepest in the trench along Norway's coast where depths of 660 m are reached; generally shallow owing to its location on the wide continental shelf lying off the coast of NW Europe; the sea floor is irregular, being shallowed by banks running across from the Yorkshire coast, in particular the Dogger Bank; shoals of sediment are also deposited by major rivers such as the Thames, Ouse, Humber, Tyne, Tweed, Forth, Tay, Scheldt, Maas, Rhine, Weser and Elbe; important fishing grounds, but since the mid-1960s mackerel, herring, cod and haddock have declined in proportion to smaller species; territorial disputes caused by competition for existing fish stocks led to the Cod Wars of the 1960s and 1970s between Iceland and Great Britain; discovery of oil and gas in the 1960s and 1970s has led to extensive offshore oil and gas exploitation; the 1969 Bonn Agreement controls pollution from oil spillage in the North Sea and safeguards vulnerable coastlines, while member countries agree to co-operate in the clean-up of any spillages; pressure on land resources has led to reclamation of a small part of the North Sea in the Dutch polder area.

North Shields, 55 01N 1 26W, pop(1981) 41,608, residential town in North Tyneside borough, Tyne and Wear, NE England; part of Tyneside urban area; on the N bank of the R Tyne, 11 km E of Newcastle upon Tyne.

North York, 43 44N 79 26W, pop(1981) 559,521, town in SE Ontario, SE Canada; a N suburb of Toronto; railway; airfield (Downsview).

North York Moors, national park in North Yorkshire and Cleveland, England; area 1,432 sq km; established in 1952; follows the coast N of Scarborough to Hambleton Hills (W); the coast is characterized by headlands and sandy beaches; the interior consists of open moorland and wooded valleys; Mount Grace Priory and Rievaulx and Byland abbeys are located in the park; there are information centres at Danby Lodge, Pickering, Sutton Bank, Ravenscar, Helmsley and Hutton-le-Hole.

North Yorkshire, county in N England; pop(1981) 666,951; area 8,309 sq km; largest county in England; stretching from Lancashire in the W to the North Sea in the E; includes the North Yorkshire Moors and the Cleveland Hills; economy: electrical and mechanical equipment, footwear, clothing, vehicles, plastics, foodstuffs, tourism; county town Northallerton; North Yorkshire includes 8 districts:

District	*area (sq km)*	*pop(1981)*
Craven	1,176	47,537
Hambleton	1,312	74,150
Harrogate	1,334	139,799
Richmondshire	1,317	42,498
Ryedale	1,598	84,236
Scarborough	817	101,515
Selby	725	77,306
York	29	99,910

Northal'lerton, 54 20N 1 26W, pop(1981) 13,858, county town in Hambleton dist, North Yorkshire, N England; 23 km S of Darlington; railway.

North'am, 31 41S 116 40E, pop(1981) 6,791, town in Midlands stat div, Western Australia, Australia; on the R Avon, E of Perth; a major railway centre.

Northamp'ton, 52 14N 0 54W, pop(1981) 155,694, county town in Northampton dist, Northamptonshire, central England; on R Nene, SE of Coventry and 97 km NW of London; originally a Saxon town, Northampton was destroyed by fire in 1675; Thomas à Becket was tried here in 1164; railway; economy: boot and shoe manufacture; monuments: 12th-c church of the Holy Sepulchre, one of 4 round churches in England; All Saints' church and the church of St Peter.

Northampton, 42 19N 72 38W, pop(1980) 29,286, county seat of Hampshire county, W Massachusetts, United States; on the R Connecticut, 24 km N of Springfield; the home of Calvin Coolidge, 30th president of the United States; railway; economy: plastics, optical instruments, wire products; event: traditional New England country fair (Sept).

Northamptonshire, agricultural county in central England; drained by the Welland and Nene rivers; pop(1981) 528,448; area 2,367 sq km; county town Northampton; economy: wheat, iron mining; the county is divided into 7 districts:

District	*area (sq km)*	*pop(1981)*
Corby	80	52,515
Daventry	666	57,692
East Northamptonshire	510	61,194
Kettering	234	71,336
Northampton	81	157,217
South Northamptonshire	634	64,295
Wellingborough	163	64,199

Northbrook, 42 08N 87 50W, pop(1980) 30,778, town in Cook county, NE Illinois, United States; 31 km N of Chicago.

Northern, region in Ghana, W Africa; pop(1984) 1,162,645; area 70,338 sq km; predominantly low-lying with higher ground mainly in the W and E; the White Volta river flows S to join L Volta; the Black Volta flows from the W into L Volta and forms the W and SW border of the region; the R Oti, in the E, forms part of the Ghana-Togo border before entering L Volta; capital Tamale; chief towns Yendi, Salaga, Damongo and Bole; the Mole (1961) and Bui (1971) national parks are located in the region; economy: iron ore, diamond, limestone, marble and alabaster extraction.

Northern Ireland, constituent division of the United Kingdom of Great Britain and Northern Ireland; often called ULSTER; occupies the NE part of Ireland; Northern Ireland is centred on Lough Neagh, with the granite Mourne Mts in the SE, limestone and sandstone in the W, and basalt in the N along the coast of Antrim; pop(1981) 1,481,959; 28% of the pop are Roman Catholic, 22.9% are Presbyterian, 19% are Church of Ireland and 4% are Methodist; timezone GMT; area 14,120 sq km (including 663 sq km of inland water); capital Belfast; chief towns Derry, Lisburn, Ballymena, Armagh; the Government of Ireland Act 1920 established

a separate parliament for Northern Ireland, having a House of Commons of 52 members and a Senate of 26 members; following sectarian disturbances the parliament was prorogued in 1972 and abolished in 1973, the former powers of the Northern Ireland ministers being vested in the Secretary of State for Northern Ireland; a 78-member Assembly was set up in 1973; the Assembly was replaced by a Constitutional Convention in 1975; in 1982 an Assembly was re-formed but nationalist members did not take their seats; Northern Ireland is divided into 6 counties:

County	*area (sq km)*	*pop(1981)*
Antrim	2,831	642,267
Armagh	1,254	118,820
Derry	2,067	186,751
Down	2,448	339,229
Fermanagh	1,676	51,008
Tyrone	3,136	143,884

Northern Territory, one of the 3 mainland territories of Australia, covering about one-sixth of the continent; bordered W by Western Australia, S by South Australia, E by Queensland and N by the Arafura Sea and the Gulf of Carpentaria; four-fifths of the territory lies within the tropics; from Arnhem Land in the N the land rises S to the Macdonnell Ranges, reaching 1,510 m at Mt Zeil; there is good pasture land in the N and the NE on the Barkly Tableland, an elevated tract of flat grassland, but the S is largely flat and arid (Simpson Desert); there are many islands off the N coast, the largest being Groote Eylandt in the Gulf of Carpentaria and Melville and Bathurst islands off the NW coast; only 3 of the terr's sheltered bays are used by shipping: Darwin, Nhulunbuy on Gove Peninsula (NE), and Alyangula on Groote Eylandt; in the SW, in Uluru national park, is Ayers Rock; in the N major rivers include the Victoria, Daly, South Alligator, East Alligator, McArthur and Roper (the territory's longest river); rivers in the interior flow only after heavy rain and include the Finke and Todd; pop(1986) 158,402; area 1,346,200 sq km; capital Darwin; chief towns include Alice Springs, Katherine and Nhulunbuy; much of the territory is occupied by Aborigines; in 1824 the territory became part of New South Wales; by 1863 the colony of South Australia had annexed the territory; after joining the Commonwealth of Australia in 1901, the Northern Territory was transferred to Federal Government control in 1911; in 1947 the first Legislative Council took office and in 1978 self-government was achieved; economy: beef cattle, fishing, minerals (bauxite, bismuth, uranium, gold, manganese, copper), oil, gas; state holidays: May Day and Picnic Day in Aug.

Northfleet, 51 27N 0 20E, pop(1981) 21,413, town in Gravesham dist, Kent, SE England; on the R Thames, 2 km W of Gravesend; railway; economy: cement, paper, cables.

Northglenn, 39 53N 104 58W, pop(1980) 29,847, town in Adams county, N central Colorado, United States; a residential suburb 16 km N of Denver.

Northum'berland, county in NE England; bounded N by Scotland, E by the North Sea and W by Cumbria from which it is separated by the Pennines; rises to 755 m at The Cheviot; drained by the Tyne, Blyth, Wansbeck, Coquet, Aln and Till rivers; Holy Island and the Farne Is lie off the coast; pop(1981) 299,484; area 5,032 sq km; county town Morpeth; chief towns include Berwick-upon-Tweed, Ashington, Blyth, Alnwick; economy: sheep, barley, oats, fishing, forestry, coal; the county is divided into 6 districts:

District	*area (sq km)*	*pop(1981)*
Alnwick	1,080	28,626
Berwick-upon-Tweed	975	26,191
Blyth Valley	70	76,711
Castle Morpeth	619	50,505
Tynedale	2,221	54,976
Wansbeck	66	62,475

Northumberland, national park in NE England; area 1,031 sq km; established in 1956; bounded S by Hadrian's Wall and N by the Cheviot Hills (Scottish border); information centres are located at Byrness, Ingram, Rothbury, Housesteads, Hexham and Harbottle Hills.

North-West Frontier, federal province in Pakistan; pop(1981) 11,061,000; area 74,521 sq km; bounded W and S by Afghanistan and N by Northern Areas, India; crossed by the R Indus; linked to Afghanistan by the Khyber Pass; capital Peshawar.

Northwest Territories, territory in N Canada; extends over the N of Canada; consists of the Arctic islands, the islands in Hudson and Ungava bays and the land N of 60° N, between Hudson Bay and the Yukon terr; the parallel of 102° W divides the mainland into Mackenzie dist (W) and Keewatin dist (E); Franklin dist (N) includes the Arctic islands and Melville and Boothia peninsulas; the area to the N of a line from the mouth of the Mackenzie river diagonally SE to Hudson Bay in N Manitoba is treeless; pop(1981) 45,471; area 3,246,389 sq km; capital Yellowknife (since 1967); economy: mining (lead, zinc, gold), handicrafts, fur products, fishing, tourism, oil; the land held by the Hudson's Bay Co (Rupert's Land and North West Territory) changed its name to Northwest Territories in 1870 when it entered the Canadian federation; the area then included Manitoba (which became a prov in the same year), Saskatchewan and Alberta (which became provs in 1905) and parts of British Columbia and Québec; the territory was organized under the Northwest Territories Act in 1875; in 1905 the present form of administration was adopted, and the S border at 60° N was established in 1912; Northwest Territories is governed by a Commissioner and a 24-member Legislative Assembly elected every 5 years.

North'wich, 53 16N 2 32W, pop(1981) 32,832, town in Macclesfield dist, Cheshire, NW central England; at the junction of the Dane and Weaver rivers, 31 km SW of Manchester; railway; economy: salt, chemicals, steel, foodstuffs, glass, engineering.

Norton, 17 52S 30 40E, pop(1982) 12,400, town in Mashonaland West, Zimbabwe, S Africa; rapidly growing centre SE of Harare; economy: agricultural equipment, non-ferrous metals.

Norton-Radstock, 51 18N 2 28W, pop(1981) 17,769, amalgamated towns in Bath dist, Avon, SW England; 12 km SW of Bath.

Norwalk, 33 54N 118 05W, pop(1980) 85,286, city in Los

Angeles county, SW California, United States; 23 km SE of Los Angeles; railway.

Norwalk, 41 07N 73 22W, pop(1980) 77,767, town in Fairfield county, SW Connecticut, United States; on Long Island Sound, 19 km WSW of Bridgeport; railway.

Norway, NORGE (Nor), originally NORDWEG ('the northern way'), official name Kingdom of Norway, KONGERIKET NORGE (Nor), a NW European kingdom, occupying the W part of the Scandinavian peninsula, bounded N by the Arctic Ocean, E by Sweden, Finland and the Soviet Union, W by the North Sea, and S by the Skagerrak Straits; area 323,895 sq km; timezone GMT +1; capital Oslo; chief towns Bergen, Trondheim, Stavanger and Kristiansand; pop(1983) 4,122,511; Bokmål and Nynorsk are the 2 official languages in use today, the latter having its origin in the major rural dialects, while Bokmål reflects the language of the towns; 16-17% of children attend schools where Nynorsk is the official language; the majority of the population is of Nordic descent; the Sâmi people (Lapps) form an ethnic minority of some 20,000 in the far north; 95% of the population belong to the Norwegian State Church, which is Evangelical-Lutheran; the Norwegian currency is the krone of 100 øre; national holiday 17 May (Constitution Day); membership of the Council of Europe, the Nordic Council, DAC, EFTA, ESRO, FAO, GATT, IAEA, IBRD, ICAC, ICAO, ICES, ICO, IDA, IEA, IFAD, IFC, IHO, ILO, IMF, IMO, INTELSAT, IPU, ITU, NATO, OECD, UN, UNESCO, UPU, WHO, WIPO, WMO, WSG.

Physical description. A mountainous country with the Kjölen Mts forming the N part of the boundary with Sweden, the Jotunheimen group in S central Norway (Glittertind 2,470 m, Galdhøpiggen 2,469 m), and extensive plateau regions called fjells or vidde, especially in SW and central parts (Hardangervidda, Dovrefjell). Much of the interior rises above 1,500 m. There are numerous lakes, the largest of which is L Mjøsa (368 sq km). Major rivers include the Glåma, Dramselv and Lågen. The northernmost mainland point is Nordkapp or North Cape, while the most southerly point of mainland is the Lindesnes cape. The 21,347 km coastline is irregular with many long deep fjords (Sognefjorden, Hardangerfjorden, Oslofjorden) and innumerable small islands; excluding fjords and bays, the coastline is only 2,650 km in length. Lofoten and Vesterålen are the 2 largest island groups, off the NW coast. There are also many large individual islands including Senja, Søröya, Ringvassøy and Hitra.

Climate. The interior highlands have an Arctic climate in winter with snow, strong winds and severe frosts. By contrast, the coastal areas are influenced by the Gulf Stream and so have comparatively mild conditions in winter. Rainfall is heavy and frequent on the W coast (annual rainfall at Bergen is 1,958 mm). In the more extensive areas of lowland in the S the winters are colder with more frequent frost than on the Atlantic coast, but summers are warmer and drier.

History, government and constitution. In early history the Norwegians, a people of Nordic stock, were ruled by petty chieftains (*jarls*) whose followers made a precarious living by agriculture, fishing and piracy. A royal race from Sweden established itself in Vestfold, S Norway in the 7th century and a descendant, Harold Haarfager (863-930) proclaimed himself chief king of Norway. He extended his control over the Orkney Is and the Scottish Hebrides. The establishment of Norway as a united kingdom was achieved by St Olaf (1015-31) whose successor, Cnut, brought Norway under Danish rule. In 1389 Norway was united with Sweden and Denmark, a union that lasted until 1814 when Sweden was allowed to annex Norway as a reward for her assistance to the western allies against Napoleon. Growing nationalism resulted in independence in 1905, with Norway becoming a limited, hereditary monarchy under the rule of Prince Karl of Denmark who was elected as Haakon VII. The constitution, voted by the constituent assembly at Eidsvoll on 17 May, 1814 and modified at various times,

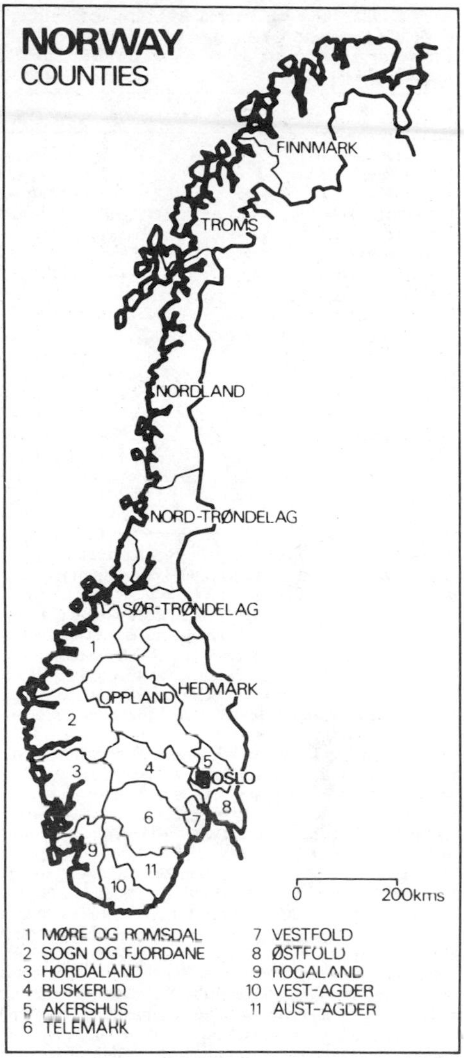

vests the legislative power of the realm in the *Storting* (Parliament). The *Storting* comprises an upper house (*Lagting*) and a lower house (*Odelsting*). Members are elected every 4 years by proportional representation. Executive power is vested in the Crown but is exercised by the Cabinet.

Industry. Industry is chiefly based on the extraction and processing of raw materials with the aid of a plentiful supply of water power. Crude petroleum and natural gas production, the manufacture of paper and paper products, industrial chemicals and basic metals are the most important export manufactures. Major trade partners include the UK, West Germany, Sweden and Denmark. In 1984 around 18.5% of national income was derived from the North Sea oil and gas sector, compared with 0.2% in 1972.

Agriculture and forestry. Norway is a largely barren and mountainous country with limited tracts of land available for cultivation. Arable soil is found mainly in deep, narrow valleys and around coastal fjords and lakes. Of the total land area of Norway less than 3% is under cultivation, the principal crops being barley, hay and oats. In 1985, the area covered with productive forests was 66,000 sq km (21%).

Administrative divisions. Norway is divided into 19 counties (*fylker*) as follows:

County	*area (sq km)*	*pop(1983)*
Akershus	4,916	376,202
Aust-Agder	9,212	92,738
Buskerud	14,933	217,348
Finnmark	48,649	77,383
Hedmark	27,388	187,779
Hordaland	15,634	394,568
Møre og Romsdal	15,104	237,268
Nordland	38,327	244,974
Nord-Trøndelag	22,463	126,696
Oppland	25,260	182,126
Oslo	450	448,775
Østfold	4,183	234,726
Rogaland	9,141	312,550
Sogn og Fjordane	18,633	106,140
Sør-Trøndelag	18,831	246,206
Telemark	15,315	161,939
Troms	25,953	147,690
Vest-Agder	7,280	138,739
Vestfold	2,216	188,664

Norwegian dependencies include Svalbard, Jan Mayen, Bouvetøya (Bouvet Island), Peter I Øy (Peter I Island) and Queen Maud Land.

Norwegian Sea *nor-wee'jan*, N Atlantic sea bounded by the NW coast of Norway and the E coast of Iceland, lying between the Greenland Sea and the North Sea; separated from the Atlantic Ocean by a submarine ridge linking Iceland and the Færøerne (Faeroe Is) and from the Greenland Sea by the Jan Mayen Ridge; depths in the Norwegian Basin to the NW of the Færøerne reach 1,240 m, while in the Jan Mayen Fracture Zone, close to the continental shelf, depths reach 2,740 m; surface circulation is such that the warm North Atlantic Drift enters the Norwegian Sea by the channel between the Færøerne and the Shetland Is, therefore the sea is generally ice-free even at these high latitudes.

Norwich *nor'ich*, 52 38N 1 18E, pop(1981) 122,890, county town in Norwich dist, Norfolk, E England; near the confluence of the Yare and Wensum rivers, 160 km NE of London; provincial centre for the largely agricultural East Anglia; University of East Anglia (1963); regional headquarters for IBA television franchise; the North Sea is reached via R Yare and Great Yarmouth (32 km E); railway; economy: commerce, engineering, printing, chemicals, electrical goods, silk, foodstuffs, trade in grain and livestock; monuments: cathedral, church of St Peter Mancroft (1430-55).

Norwich, 41 31N 72 05W, pop(1980) 38,074, town in New London county, SE Connecticut, United States; on the R Shetucket, 20 km N of New London.

Norwood, 39 09N 84 27W, pop(1980) 26,342, town in Hamilton county, SW Ohio, United States; residential suburb surrounded by Cincinnati, 8 km NE of the city centre; railway; monument: the Athenaeum of Ohio.

Noteć *no'ech*, river in W Poland; rises in lakes SW of Włocławek and flows 388 km NW and W to meet R Warta near Gorzów Wielkopolski; the 24.7 km Bydgoski Canal, built in 1914, links the Noteć to the R Brda.

Notodden *nōt-od'dun*, 59 35N 9 18E, pop(1980) 12,877, town at the head of L Hiterdal, on R Tinne, Telemark county, SE Norway; 50 km N of Skien; railway; economy: textiles, timber, chemicals, hydroelectricity.

Nottingham *not'ting-am*, 52 58N 1 10W, pop(1981) 272,141, urban area pop(1981) 598,867, county town in Nottingham dist, Nottinghamshire, central England; on the R Trent, 200 km NNW of London; university (1948); founded by the Danes; became a city in 1897; name derived from Anglo-Saxon *Snotingaham* or *Notingeham* ('village or home of the sons of Snot the Wise'); the Civil War started here in 1642; connected to both the Irish and North Seas by canal; railway; economy: cigarettes, textiles, tanning, engineering, furniture, typewriters, pharmaceuticals; monuments: 17th-c Nottingham Castle, 15th-c St Mary's church; event: Goose Fair during the first week in Oct.

Nottinghamshire, county in the R Trent basin of central England; bounded N by South Yorkshire and Humberside, E by Lincolnshire, S by Leicestershire and W by Derbyshire; pop(1981) 985,283; area 2,164 sq km; county town Nottingham; chief towns include Worksop, Newark and Mansfield; economy: arable farming, coal, gypsum, limestone, textiles and chemicals; the county is divided into 8 districts:

District	*area (sq km)*	*pop(1981)*
Ashfield	110	106,575
Bassetlaw	637	102,227
Broxtowe	81	102,891
Gedling	112	104,280
Mansfield	77	99,928
Newark	662	104,366
Nottingham	74	272,141
Rushcliffe	410	92,875

Nouadhibou *noo-ad-ee-boo'*, PORT ÉTIENNE (Fr), 20 54N 17 00W, pop(1976) 21,961, seaport capital of Dakhlet-Nouadhibou region, Mauritania, NW Africa; situated at N end of the Bay of Levrier; Mauritania's main seaport; linked by rail to the iron ore mines near Zouîrât; airport; economy: iron ore export, fish processing and refrigeration, industrial gas.

Nouakchott *nwak'shot*, 18 09N 15 58W, pop(1982e) 150,000, capital of W Mauritania, NW Africa; near the Atlantic coast, 240 km NNE of Saint Louis (Senegal); a harbour is located 7 km SSW of the city; founded in 1960 on an important caravan route; airport; economy: salt, cement, insecticides, matches, trade in gums and grains; event: camel markets.

Nouméa *noo-may'a*, formerly PORT DE FRANCE *pawr de frãs*, 22 16S 166 26E, pop(1983) 60,112, seaport capital of New Caledonia, SW Pacific, on a peninsula at the SW end of the island of New Caledonia; it was a US air base during World War II; became the capital of the territory in 1854; beaches nearby; Tontouta airport; economy: tourism, nickel smelter; monuments: cathedral.

Nouna *noo'na*, 12 44N 3 54W, town in NW Burkina, W Africa; 97 km WSW of Tougan.

Nova Gorica *no'va go'rit-sa*, 45 57N 13 39E, pop(1981) 56,758, town in W Slovenija republic, Yugoslavia; E of Gorizia in Italy; developed after World War II following settlement of Yugoslav-Italian border dispute.

Nova Gradiška *no'va gra'dish-ka*, 45 15N 17 22E, pop(1981) 61,267, town in N Hrvatska (Croatia) republic, Yugoslavia; at S foot of Psunj Mt, W of Slavonski Brod; railway; economy: fruit trade, petroleum, lignite.

Nova Lisboa, Angola. See Huambo.

Nova Scotia *nō'va skō'sha*, province in SE Canada; bounded by the Atlantic Ocean (E, S and W), the Bay of Fundy (W), New Brunswick (NW), the Northumberland Strait (N) and the Gulf of St Lawrence (NE); the prov includes Cape Breton island to the NE which is separated from the mainland by the Strait of Canso, 3 km wide; the two are connected by Canso causeway; Nova Scotia is a peninsula connected with the mainland by the isthmus of Chignecto; the coastline is deeply indented with numerous bays and inlets, the largest are Chignecto Bay, Cobequid Bay, St George's Bay, Chedabucto Bay, Minas Basin, Minas Channel, St Mary's Bay, St Ann's Bay and Mahone Bay; low hill ranges extend between the W of the prov and the Minas Basin and along the N coast along the Northumberland Strait; of the numerous lakes, Rossignol is the largest on the peninsula, while Cape Breton island is almost bisected by Bras d'Or Lake; the prov is drained by many small rivers; the Atlantic coast of the prov is generally rocky, while the slopes facing the

Bay of Fundy and the Gulf of St Lawrence in the E consist of fertile plains and river valleys because they are sheltered from the storms of the Atlantic to the W by a series of low ridges which run through the centre of the prov; in the S of Nova Scotia is Kejimkujik National Park (area 381 sq km, established in 1968); in the N of Cape Breton island is Cape Breton Highlands National Park (area 950 sq km, established in 1936); pop(1981) 847,442; area 52,841 sq km; capital Halifax; other towns are Dartmouth, Sydney, Glace Bay, Truro and New Glasgow; economy: dairy farming, fruit, fishing (especially lobster), timber, coal, gypsum, tin, tourism; probably first visited by Norsemen and European fishermen; settled by the French in 1604-05, who called the region Acadia; mainland of the prov assigned to England in the Treaty of Utrecht (1713) while Cape Breton island remained French; British domination was established by the foundation of Halifax (1749) as a military and naval base; in 1755 the Acadians, the original French settlers, were expelled; the Treaty of Paris in 1763 gave Cape Breton island to Britain; 30,000 United Empire Loyalists settled here after the American Revolution; Cape Breton island was a separate prov from 1784 and was reincorporated into Nova Scotia in 1820; Nova Scotia entered the confederation in 1867; the prov is governed by a Lieutenant-Governor and a 52-member House of Assembly which is elected every 5 years.

Nova'ra, prov of Piemonte region, NW Italy; pop(1981) 507,367; area 3,595 sq km; capital Novara.

Novara, NOVARIA (anc), 45 27N 8 37E, pop(1981) 102,086, industrial town and capital of Novara prov, Piemonte region, NW Italy; 35 km W of Milano (Milan), on a plain between the rivers Ticino and Sesia; has a large map-making institute (De Agostini); railway; economy: rice, foodstuffs, wine, tourism; monument: cathedral (1831-1865) with a 5th-c baptistry.

Nova'to, 38 06N 122 35W, pop(1980) 43,916, city in Marin county, W California, United States; 16 km N of San Rafael.

Novaya Zemlya *zim-lyu'*, archipelago in the Arctic Ocean, between the Barents Sea (W) and Karskoye More (Kara Sea) (E), in Arkhangel'skaya oblast, Rossiyskaya, NW Soviet Union; separated from the island of Ostrov Vaygach to the SE by the Proliv Karskiye Vorota strait; comprises 2 large islands separated by the narrow Proliv Matochkin Shar strait; there are also numerous offshore islands; area 81,279 sq km; length 960 km; glaciated land in the N gives way to tundra lowland in the S; the mountains, which are an extension of the Ural'skiy Khrebet range (Ural Mts), rise to heights above 1,000 m; permanent settlement is mostly concentrated along the heavily indented W coast; there are mineral deposits of copper, lead, zinc, and asphaltite; the islands have been used by the Russians for thermonuclear testing.

Nové Zámky *no'voh zahm'ki*, 49 00N 18 10E, pop(1984) 37,946, town in Západoslovenský region, Slovak Socialist Republic, SE central Czechoslovakia; on R Nitra SE of Bratislava and N of Komárno; railway; economy: tobacco, sugar, tanning.

Novgorod *nof'gu-rut*, 58 30N 31 20E, pop(1983) 210,000, capital city of Novgorodskaya oblast, NW European Rossiyskaya, Soviet Union; on the R Volkhov, 6 km from Ozero Il'men' (Lake Il'men'); one of the oldest cities in the USSR; the centre of an important agricultural area; railway; on the highway between Leningrad and Moskva (Moscow); economy: electrical and radio engineering, woodworking (particularly matches), ship repairing, foodstuffs; monuments: St Sophia's cathedral (1045-50); 12th-c Dukhov monastery.

Novi Pazar *no'vee pa-zar'*, RASCIA (anc), 43 09N 20 29E, pop(1981) 74,000, town in W Srbija (Serbia) republic, Yugoslavia; on R Raska; important 17-18th-c trading town.

Novi Sad *no'vee saht*, NEUSATZ *noy'satz* (Ger), 45 15N 19 51E, pop(1981) 257,685, commercial and industrial capital of the autonomous province of Vojvodina, N Srbija (Serbia) republic, Yugoslavia; on R Danube; formerly an important stronghold against the Turks; Niška Banja health resort is nearby; university (1960); railway; economy: wine, fruit and vegetable trade, leather, textiles, tobacco; monuments: bishop's palace, Petrovaradin castle, cathedral; events: international agricultural show in May; Danube regatta - international rowing (Aug); autumn fair in Oct.

Novo Hamburgo *nō'vō am-boor'gō*, 29 37S 51 07W, pop(1980) 133,221, town in Rio Grande do Sul state, Sul region, S Brazil; N of Pôrto Alegre; railway.

Novo Mesto *no'vo mes'to*, RUDOLFSWERTH or NEUSTÄDTL (Ger), 45 58N 15 10E, pop(1981) 55,584, market town in S Slovenija republic, Yugoslavia; on R Krka, SE of Ljubljana; founded in 1365 by Duke Rudolf of Austria; railway.

Novokuznetsk *no-vu-kooz-nyetsk'*, KUZNETSK SIBIRSKI, formerly KUZNETSK and STALINSK, 53 45N 87 10E, pop(1983) 564,000, industrial city in Kemerovskaya oblast, S central Siberian Rossiyskaya, Soviet Union, on both banks of the R Tom'o, at the confluence of the Aba and Kondoma rivers; the old town of Kuznetsk was founded by Cossacks in 1617 and declared a city in 1622; one of the major metallurgical centres of the USSR; railway; economy: aluminium and ferroalloy plants, coal mining, machine building, chemicals.

Novosibirsk *no-vu-syi-byeersk'*, formerly NOVONIKOLAEVSK, 55 00N 83 05E, pop(1983) 1,370,000, river port capital of Novosibirskaya oblast, S Siberian Rossiyskaya, Soviet Union; on the R Ob', at the NE end of the Novosibirsk reservoir; founded in 1893 when a railroad bridge was built across the river during construction of the Trans-Siberian railway; its growth is due largely to the proximity of the Kuznetsk basin coal and iron deposits; university (1959); railway; economy: machine building, metallurgy, chemicals, foodstuffs, light industry, power generation.

Novosibirskiye Ostrova *no-vu-syi-byeer'skyi-ye*, NEW SIBERIAN ISLANDS, uninhabited archipelago in the Arctic Ocean, lying between the Laptev Sea (W) and the E Siberian Sea (E), in Yakutskaya ASSR, Rossiyskaya, NE Soviet Union; area 28,230 sq km; rises to 374 m; chief islands are Ostrov Kotel'nyy, Ostrov Faddeyevskiy, and Ostrov Novaya Sibir'; separated from Ostrov Bol'shoy Lyakhovskiy to the S by the Proliv Sannikova strait; discovered in 1773 by a Russian merchant; mammoth fossils found here.

Nový Jičin *no'vee yit'cheen*, 49 36N 18 00E, pop(1984) 32,498, town in Severomoravský region, Czech Socialist Republic, central Czechoslovakia; SW of Ostrava; railway; economy: machinery, textiles, tobacco.

Nowa Huta *no'va hoo-ta*, 50 03N 19 55E, pop(1983) 200,000, industrial suburb of Kraków, Kraków voivodship, S Poland; constructed along with the Lenin steelworks after 1949; economy: coke, pig iron, metallurgy, metal products, cement; monuments: museum of aviation and astronautics, Wanda Mound prehistoric cave, 13th-c Cistercian abbey.

Nowra-Bomader'ry, 34 50S 150 36E, pop(1981) 17,887, town in Illawarra stat div, E New South Wales, Australia; the amalgamation of two towns S of Sydney; railway.

Nowshera *now'shu-ra*, 34 00N 72 00E, pop(1981) 75,000, city in North-West Frontier prov, NW Pakistan; 32 km E of Peshawar; railway; economy: leather and copper products.

Nowy Sącz *nov'i-satch*, voivodship in S Poland; bounded S by Czechoslovakia; Beskid Mts rise in the S; watered by the R Dunajec; pop(1983) 652,000; area 5,576 sq km; capital Nowy Sącz; chief towns include Zakopane, Nowy Targ and Gorlice.

Nowy Sącz, NEU SANDEC (Ger), 49 39N 20 40E, pop(1983) 68,300, capital of Nowy Sącz voivodship, S Poland; railway; monuments: 14th-c Gothic church E of the Market Square; 14th-c castle, open-air regional museum.

Nsan'je, dist in Southern region, Malawi, SE Africa; area 1,942 sq km; pop(1977) 108,758.

Nsawam *un-sa-wam'*, 5 47N 0 19W, pop(1970) 57,350,

town in Eastern region, S Ghana, W Africa; on the railway between Koforidua and Accra.

Ntcheu *un-chay'oo*, dist in Central region, Malawi, SE Africa; area 3,424 sq km; pop(1977) 226,454.

Ntchisi *un-chee'see*, dist in Central region, Malawi, SE Africa; area 1,655 sq km; pop(1977) 87,437.

Nubian Desert *nyoo'bee-an*, desert in NE Sudan, NE Africa; a sandstone plateau situated between the Red Sea and the R Nile; area c.406,630 sq km; the ancient state of Nubia occupied the area from the First Cataract of the Nile to Khartoum.

Nueva Asunción *nway'va a-soon-syōn'*, dept in Occidental region, Paraguay; bordered W by Bolivia; mostly part of the dry, flat Gran Chaco; pop(1982) 231; area 46,000 sq km; capital General Eugenio Garay.

Nueva Esparta *nway'va es-par'ta*, state consisting of Caribbean Islands, off the coast of Venezuela; the free port of Isla de Margarita, a popular weekend and holiday resort, constitutes most of the state, which also includes Coche and several smaller islands; pop(1980) 196,911; area 1,149 sq km; capital La Asunción; Isla de Margarita consists of 2 sections, linked by a spit of land which separates the sea from the Laguna Arestinga; also belonging to Venezuela are the Islas de Aves, Isla Blanquilla, the Los Hermanos islands and the Islas los Roques - the only coral atolls in the Caribbean-Atlantic.

Nueva Gerona *nway'va hay-rō'na*, 21 53N 82 49W, capital town of Isla de la Juventud prov, SW Cuba; on the N coast of the island, 144 km SSW of La Habana (Havana); economy: marble, woodwork, ceramics; Fidel Castro was imprisoned near here in the 1950s.

Nueva San Salvador *nway'va san sal'va-dor*, SANTA TECLA *tay'kla*, 13 40N 89 18W, pop(1980) 69,126, capital town of La Libertad dept, El Salvador, Central America; 13 km W of San Salvador on the Pan-American Highway; railway; alt 920 m; in a coffee-growing district; nearby is the crater of the San Salvador volcano.

Nueva Segovia *nway'va say-gō'vya*, dept in N Nicaragua, Central America; bounded N by Honduras; the Cordillera de Jalapa and the Cordillera de Dipilto run along the N boundary; drained by tributaries of the Río Coco; pop(1981) 97,765; area 4,124 sq km; capital Ocotal.

Nuevo Laredo *nway'vō la-ray'dō*, 27 29N 99 30W, pop(1980) 203,286, town in Tamaulipas state, NE Mexico; on the border with the USA, opposite Laredo, Texas; on the Río Grande; railway; economy: on a major route into E and central USA.

Nuevo León *nway'-vō lay-ōn'*, state in NE Mexico; bounded by Coahuila (W), San Luis Potosí (SW), Tamaulipas (E and NE) and by the USA along the Río Grande (N); crossed NW-SE by the Sierra Madre Oriental; drained by the Salado, San Juan and Pesquería rivers, tributaries of the Río Grande; pop(1980) 2,463,298; area 64,924 sq km; capital Monterrey; economy: agriculture (citrus fruits, maize, wheat, sorghum), goat and cattle raising, mining (barite, phosphorus, chalk, limestone, marble, dolomite, gypsum, fluorite), iron and steel, machinery, motor cars, chemicals, electrical goods, glasswork.

Nuku'alofa *noo'koo-a-lō-fah*, 21 09S 175 14W, port and capital town of Tonga, S Pacific, on Tongatapu I, 691 km SE of Suva, Fiji; university; economy: coconut processing; monument: royal palace (1867).

Nukunonu *noo-koo-nō'nō*, 9 10S 171 55W, central atoll of Tokelau, S Pacific Ocean, 56 km WNW of Fakaofo; area 5.46 sq km; pop(1981) 368.

Nul'larbor Plain, vast plateau in SW South Australia and S Western Australia; extends 480 km W from Ooldea, South Australia to Kalgoorlie, Western Australia; situated between the Great Victoria Desert and the Great Australian Bight; rises to a max height of 305 m; consists of sand dunes and sparse vegetation; the Trans-Australian Railway which crosses the plain is the world's longest straight stretch of railway, covering 478 km; on the coast of SW South Australia is Nullarbor national park (area 2,319 sq km); Nullarbor Plain was successfully crossed in 1841 by Edward John Eyre.

Numazu *noo-ma'tzoo*, 35 08N 138 50E, pop(1980) 203,695, town in Shizuoka prefecture, Chūbu region, central Honshū island, Japan; on NE shore of Suruga wan Bay, 45 km ENE of Shizuoka; railway.

Nunawading, 37 45S 144 58E, pop(1983e) 101,100, city suburb of E Melbourne; in Melbourne stat div, Victoria, Australia.

Nuneat'on, 52 32N 1 28W, pop(1981) 60,948, urban area pop(1981) 81,879, town in Nuneaton and Bedworth dist, Warwickshire, central England; on the R Anker, 13 km NNE of Coventry; railway; economy: engineering, textiles, electronics.

Nuoro *nwo'ro*, E prov of Sardegna (Sardinia), Italy; pop(1981) 274,817; area 7,044 sq km; capital Nuoro.

Nuoro, 40 20N 9 21E, pop(1981) 35,779, capital town of Nuoro prov, E central Sardegna (Sardinia), Italy; birthplace of the writer Grazia Deledda (1893-1936); railway; event: feast of the Saviour (29-31 Aug), when local costumes are worn.

Nuremberg, city in W Germany. See Nürnberg.

Nuristan *noo-ris-tan'*, region of the S Hindu Kush range, mostly in Konar prov, NE Afghanistan.

Nurmes *noor'mes*, 63 31N 29 10E, pop(1982) 11,588, town in Pohjois-Karjala prov, E central Finland; at the head of L Pielinen; established in 1876; railway; economy: timber.

Nürn'berg, NUREMBERG *nyoo'rum-burg* (Eng), 49 27N 11 05E, pop(1983) 476,400, commercial and manufacturing city in Mittelfranken dist, Bayern (Bavaria) prov, W Germany; on the R Pegnitz and the Rhine-Main-Danube Canal, 147 km NNW of München (Munich); 2nd largest city in Bayern and one of the leading industrial and commercial cities in S Germany; the first German railway opened between here and Fürth in 1835; annual meeting place of Hitler's Nazi Party after 1933; scene of trials of German war criminals (1945-46); birthplace of Albrecht Dürer and Hans Sachs; railway; economy: radio electronics, electrical equipment, pharmaceuticals, non-ferrous metal products, cars, office machinery, toys, meat products, bakery and brewing; monuments: St Lawrence's church (13-15th-c), Imperial Castle; event: Annual International Toy Fair.

Nusa Tenggara Barat *noo-se teng-gah'ra*, WEST NUSA TENGGARA, province of Indonesia, comprising the islands of Lombok and Sumbawa in the Lesser Sunda group; pop(1980) 2,724,664; area 20,177 sq km; capital Mataram on the island of Lombok; economy: maize, onions, salt, groundnuts, cattle.

Nusa Tenggara Timur, EAST NUSA TENGGARA, province of Indonesia, comprising the islands of Sumba, Flores and part of Timor in the Lesser Sunda group; pop(1980) 2,737,166; area 47,876 sq km; capital Kupang on the island of Timor; economy: maize, cattle, fish.

Nutley, 40 49N 74 09W, pop(1980) 28,998, town in Essex county, NE New Jersey, United States; residential suburb on R Passaic, 10 km N of Newark; railway.

Nuwara-Eliya *noo-wa-ra-ay'lee-ye* ('above the clouds'), 6 58N 80 46E, pop(1981) 20,471, health resort and capital of Nuwara-Eliya dist, Central prov, Sri Lanka; 138 km E of Colombo in the heart of tea-country; highest town on the island at 1,900 m; favourite summer retreat of British colonists; there is a bridle path to World's End, a precipice of 1,050 m; 60% of the pop of the dist are Tamil.

Nxai Pan *un-ksī*, national park in E Ngamiland dist, Botswana, S Africa; area 2,590 sq km; established in 1971; during the wet season (Dec-March) large herds of wildebeest, zebra and gemsbok migrate into the park; after this period they migrate S to the Makgadikgadi Pans.

Nyabisindu *nee-ya-bi-sin'oo*, 2 20S 29 43E, town in Rwanda, central Africa; situated between Kigali and Butare (SSW).

Nyainqêntanglha Shan *nyen-ching-tang-goo-la shan*, NYENCHEN TANGLHA RANGE, SE Trans-Himalayan mountain range in E Xizang aut region (Tibet), SW China; borders with Gangdisê Shan range in the W, extends SE to join the Hengduan Shan range; averages between 5,000 and 6,000 m above sea-level; rises to 7,088 m in Nyainqêntanglha Feng; watershed between the Yarlung Zangbo Jiang river to the S and the Nu Jiang river to the N.

Nyan'ga, pop(1985) 23,969, black African township E of Cape Town, Cape prov, South Africa; the squatter settlement of Crossroads lies immediately E.

Nyanza *nī-an'za*, prov of NW Kenya; divided into 4 districts; area 12,526 sq km; pop(1979) 2,643,956; capital Kisumu.

Nyanza-Lac *nī-an'za-lak'*, 4 20S 29 35E, town in Burundi, central Africa; on the E shore of L Tanganyika.

Nyasa, Lake *ni-a'sa*, NIASSA (Moz), LAKE MALAWI, lake in SE central Africa; the 3rd largest lake on the African continent; area 28,500 sq km; situated in the S section of the Great Rift valley within Malawi and Mozambique and bordering Tanzania; 580 km long and between 24 and 80 km wide; alt 437 m; main inflowing rivers include the Lilongwe, the Ruhuhu, the Lufilya, the Songwe, the Bupache, the Dwanwa and the Bua; flowing S from Mangochi at the S end of L Nyasa, the R Shire is the only outlet; navigation is possible over the whole area of the lake; the main landing points include Karonga, Salima, Mangochi, Chipoka, Nkhotakota, Lokoma Island, Nhkata Bay, Chitimba and Kambwe; first European discovery by the Portuguese in the early 17th century; rediscovered by David Livingstone in 1859; sometimes known as the 'Calendar Lake' because it is 365 miles long and 52 miles across (at its widest point).

Nyborg *nü'bor*, 55 19N 10 48E, pop(1981) 15,466, seaport and industrial town on the Store Bælt (Great Belt), E coast of Fyn I, Fyn county, Denmark; rail terminus; economy: foodstuffs, engineering; the town was a royal capital from 1200 to 1430, the royal castle was built in the 12th century to control the Store Bælt.

Nyeri *nye'ree*, 0 25S 36 56E, pop(1979) 36,000, administrative centre of Central prov, Kenya, E Africa; N of Nairobi; Lord Baden-Powell lived here from 1938 to 1941; centre of Mau Mau revolt in the 1950s; nearby is the Treetops Hotel where, in 1952, Princess Elizabeth learned of her father's death and her succession to the British throne; economy: farming and tourism.

Nyika *nyee'ka*, national park in Northern region, Malawi, SE Africa; situated on the Nyika plateau with an elevation of between 2,000 and 2,600 m; fauna includes numerous rare birds and butterflies.

Nyinahin *un-yin'a-hin*, 6 43N 2 03W, town in Ashanti region, SW central Ghana, W Africa; W of Kumasi.

Nýiregyháza *nyee're-dy'-hah'zo*, 47 58N 21 47E, pop(1984e) 114,000, capital of Szabolcs-Szátmar county, E Hungary; N of Debrecen; railway; teachers' colleges; economy: market town for tobacco and vegetables.

Nykøbing *nü'kœ-ping*, NYKØBING FALSTER, 54 47N 11 53E, pop(1981) 19,038, seaport and capital of Storstrøm county, Denmark, on W coast of Falster I, on the Gulborgsund (Gulborg Sound); a bridge connects Lolland with Falster; founded in the 12th century as a fortress against the Wends; bishopric; railway; economy: engineering, foodstuffs; monument: Franciscan church (1540).

Nyköping *nü'chœ-ping*, 58 45N 17 03E, pop(1982) 64,548, seaport and capital of Södermanland county, SE Sweden; 48 km ENE of Norrköping, on the Baltic Sea; in the Middle Ages it was one of the most important towns in Sweden, and between the 13th and 16th centuries it was the meeting-place of the *Riksdag* (Parliament) on fifteen occasions; railway; economy: electric bulbs, motor vehicles, furniture; monuments: town hall (1720), governor's residence (1803), Nyköpingshus Castle (burned down in 1665 and later partly restored).

Nyland, prov of Finland. See Uudenmaa.

Nyslott, town in Finland. See Savonlinna.

N'Zérékoré *un-zay-ray-kō'ray*, 7 49N 8 48W, pop(1972) 23,000, capital of Guinée-Forestière region, S Guinea, W Africa; 265 km NE of Monrovia (Liberia); airfield.

Nzwami, island of Comoros. See Anjouan.

O

Oad'by, 52 36N 1 04W, pop(1981) 18,372, town in Leicester urban area and Oadby and Wigston dist, Leicestershire, central England; a SE suburb of Leicester; economy: light engineering.

Oahu *ō-ah'hoo*, 3rd largest of the islands of the US state of Hawaii; in the Pacific Ocean SE of Kauai; part of Honolulu county; area 1,526 sq km; pop(1980) 797,367; chief town Honolulu; rises to 1,233 m at Kaala; economy: sugar, fruit, tourism; naval base at Pearl Harbor.

Oak Forest, 41 37N 87 44W, pop(1980) 26,096, residential town in Cook county, NE Illinois, United States; 32 km S of Chicago; railway.

Oak Lawn, 41 43N 87 44W, pop(1980) 60,590, town in Cook county, NE Illinois, United States; 19 km SW of Chicago; railway.

Oak Park, 41 53N 87 47W, pop(1980) 54,887, town in Cook county, NE Illinois, United States; 16 km W of Chicago; railway; residential.

Oak Park, 42 28N 83 11W, pop(1980) 31,537, town in Oakland county, SE Michigan, United States; 18 km NW of Detroit.

Oak Ridge, 36 01N 84 16W, pop(1980) 27,662, town in Anderson county, E Tennessee, United States; on the R Clinch, 30 km W of Knoxville; centre of atomic energy and nuclear physics research; nuclear fuel, complex nuclear instruments and electronic instrumentation are manufactured; founded by the US Government in 1942 to house the workers involved in the development of the uranium-235 and plutonium-239 isotopes for the atomic bomb; the existence and purpose of the community was kept secret until after the first atomic bombs were dropped in 1945; monument: American Museum of Atomic Energy.

Oakdale-Pontllanfraith *ōk-dayl-pont-hlahn-vrīth'*, 51 41N 3 11W, pop(1981) 12,395, town in Islwyn dist, Gwent, SE Wales; NE of Caerphilly in Islwyn urban area.

Oakengates, 52 42N 2 28W, pop(1981) 26,907, town linked with Donnington in Wrekin dist, Shropshire, W central England; part of Telford North urban area; 6 km E of Wellington; designated with Telford North and South, Telford Dawley and Wellington as a 'new town' in 1963; railway; economy: iron founding and coal mining.

Oakland, 37 49N 122 16W, pop(1980) 339,337, port capital of Alameda county, W California, United States; on the E shore of San Francisco Bay, opposite San Francisco and the Golden Gate; linked by the San Francisco-Oakland Bay Bridge; founded in 1850; railway; airports (Oakland, Hayward); economy: vehicles, chemicals, paint, food processing, metal products, office equipment; monuments: observatory; art gallery; museums.

Oakville, 43 27N 79 41W, pop(1981) 75,773, town in SE Ontario, SE Canada; on W shore of L Ontario, 32 km SW of Toronto; the Ford Motor Company built a large car factory here in 1953, making Oakville one of the wealthiest communities in Canada; railway.

Oaxaca *wah-KHah'kah*, state in S Mexico; bounded by Guerrero (W), Puebla (NW), Veracruz (NE), Chiapas (E) and the Pacific Ocean (S); mountainous in the NW and centre; in the NE and E the land drops to the low lying Istmo de Tehuantepec; drained by the Verde, Tehuantepec, Jaltepec and de la Lana rivers; pop(1980) 2,518,157; area 93,952 sq km; capital Oaxaca; economy: agriculture (pineapples, tobacco, coffee, sugar cane, maize, bananas, figs), timber, fishing, mining (gold, silver, lead, copper), fruit packing, sugar refining, tourism; the Zapotec language is used by over 300,000 people in the state as their 1st or 2nd language; the archaeological sites of Mitla and Monte Albán are located at the centre of the state to the S and SE of Oaxaca.

Oaxaca, OAXACA DE JUÁREZ, 17 05N 96 41W, pop(1980) 157,284, capital of Oaxaca state, S Mexico; in the Sierra Madre del Sur at an alt of 1,657 m; founded by the Aztecs in 1486; university (1827); home of Benito Juárez and Porfirio Díaz, both presidents of Mexico; economy: textiles, handicrafts, pottery; monuments: the monastery adjoining the church of Santo Domingo is now the regional museum; the church itself is extremely ornate, inside is a genealogical tree of the family of Santo Domingo de Guzmán (died 1221) whose lineage was indirectly related to the royal families of Castile and Portugal; the Museo Rufino contains a display of pre-Columbian artifacts; events: on the first 2 Mondays after 16 July, los Lunes del Cerro, a festival of regional Indian dances; the Day of the Dead, with a competition on the decoration of family altars and the selling of traditional wares and foods representing skulls, skeletons, coffins etc (2 Nov); 8, 12, 19 Dec (Soledad) and 23 Dec (Rábanos) with huge radishes carved in grotesque shapes being sold as fake money; a parade of floats (24 Dec).

Ob' *op*, chief river of the Zapadno Sibirskaya Ravnina (W Siberian Lowlands) and one of the largest rivers in Asiatic Rossiyskaya, central Soviet Union; formed by the union of the Biya and Katun' rivers, in the N foothills of the Altay Mts, SW of Biysk, Altayskiy kray; flows generally NW past Barnaul and Novosibirsk, through swampy forests in Tomskaya oblast, then turns W past Surgut to the mouth of the R Irtysh at Khanty-Mansiysk; the Ob' then turns N and divides into numerous channels, flowing parallel to and E of the Ural'skiy Khrebet range (Ural Mts); discharges into Obskaya Guba (Ob' Bay), an inlet of the Karskoye More (Kara Sea), 120 km ENE of Salekhard; length 3,650 km; with the R Irtysh, its chief tributary, it is 5,570 km long and the world's 4th longest river; drainage basin area 2,990,000 sq km; chief tributaries are the Kazym, Irtysh, Vakh, Tym, and Ket rivers; although frozen for 5 to 6 months of the year, the Ob' is an important transport route; there are vast oil reserves within the sedimentary basin drained by the R Ob' and its tributaries.

Oban *ō'ban*, 56 25N 5 29W, pop(1981) 8,111, port town in Argyll and Bute dist, Strathclyde, W Scotland; situated in the Sound of Kerrera, off the Firth of Lorne, 97 km NW of Glasgow; railway; ferry services to the Inner and Outer Hebrides; economy: fishing, textiles, tourism, glass making; monuments: McCaig's Tower on the hillside above Oban was built between 1897 and 1900 to provide local craftsmen with work; event: Argyllshire Highland Gathering (Sept).

Obando *ō-ban'dō*, PUERTO INÍRIDA, 3 54N 67 53W, pop(1985) 3,311, capital of Guainía administrative territory, E Colombia, South America; on the Río Inirida, near the border with Venezuela; airfield.

Obeid, El *ō-bayd'*, 13 08N 30 10E, pop(1973) 90,060, town in Kordofan region, central Sudan, NE Africa; 370 km SW of Khartoum; the Mahdi defeated Hicks Pasha's Egyptian forces here in 1883; a rail connection to Khartoum was completed in 1912; airfield.

Oberbayern *ō'bur-bī-urn*, UPPER BAVARIA (Eng), S dist of Bayern (Bavaria) prov, W Germany; pop(1983) 3,687,500; area 17,528 sq km; capital München.

Oberfranken *ō'bur-frahng-kun*, UPPER FRANCONIA *frang-kō'nee-u* (Eng), N dist of Bayern (Bavaria) prov, W Germany; pop(1983) 1,044,800; area 7,231 sq km; capital Bayreuth.

Oberhausen *ō'bur-how-zen*, 49 16N 8 29E, pop(1983) 226,200, industrial city in Düsseldorf dist, Nordrhein-Westfalen (North Rhine-Westphalia) prov, W Germany; in the Ruhr valley, 11 km WNW of Essen; railway; economy: heavy equipment, non-ferrous metals, building materials, plastics, chemicals.

Oberhof, 50 42N 10 44E, popular winter sports resort in Sühl county, S East Germany; NE of Sühl, in the Thüringer Wald (Thüringian Forest) region.

Oberland ('upper country'), one of the 2 dists of the Principality of Liechtenstein, central Europe; comprises the communes of Vaduz, Balzers, Triesen, Triesenberg, Schaan, and Planken; the division is historical, geographical and political; formerly an independent Lordship until its union with Unterland dist under the Princes of Liechtenstein; physically separated from Unterland dist by a broad plain.

Oberösterreich *ō'bur-œs'ter-īKH*, UPPER AUSTRIA (Eng), federal state of N Austria on the W German frontier, comprising 18 dists and 445 communities; pop(1981) 1,270,426; area 11,979; capital Linz; lakes include the Attersee, Traunsee and Wolfgangsee; there are reserves of oil and gas in the granite and gneiss hills to the N; there are hydroelectric power stations along the Danube and its tributary, the Enns; economy: engines, tractors, lorries, ball-bearings, iron and steel, chemicals; Austria's largest aluminium plant is situated near Ranshofen; Lenzing is a major cellulose and synthetic fabrics centre.

Oberpfalz *ō'bur-falts*, UPPER PALATINATE (Eng), E dist of Bayern (Bavaria) prov, W Germany; pop(1983) 966,200; area 9,691 sq km; chief towns include Regensburg.

Oberpfälzer Wald *ō-bur-falt'tsur vahlt*, low NW section of the Böhmerwald (Bohemian Forest) proper, in E Bayern (Bavaria) prov; extends between the Fichtelgebirge and Bayerische Wald (Bavarian Forest); highest peak is the Cerchov (Czech); highest peak in Germany is the Entenbuhl (901 m).

Óbidos *o'bee-doosh*, 39 19N 9 10W, pop(1981) 5,000, old walled town in Leiria dist, central Portugal; above the R Vargem at the W edge of the Lagoa de Óbidos, 55 km NW of Santarem; the town, which is set in a commanding position, was strongly fortified against the Moors and is now a national monument popular with tourists and artists; railway; monuments: the castle which is now a government-run hotel (Pousada) and the Gothic-Renaissance parish church of Santa Maria.

Obo *o-bō'*, 5 18N 26 28E, chief town in Haut-M'Bomou prefecture, SE Central African Republic; 420 km ENE of Bangassou.

Obock *ō'bawk*, 11 59N 43 20E, seaport in E Djibouti, on the N coast of the Gulf of Tadjoura; former capital of French Somaliland.

Obregón, Ciudad *syoo-THaTH' ō-bray-gōn'*, 27 30N 109 56W, pop(1970) 114,805, town in Sonora state, NW Mexico; 263 km SSE of Hermosillo; railway; economy: centre of an agricultural region.

Obrenovac *ob-re'no-vats*, 44 40N 20 11E, pop(1981) 62,612, town in N central Srbija (Serbia) republic, Yugoslavia; on R Kolubara, SW of Beograd; railway; thermal power plant.

Obuasi *ō-bwa'see*, 6 15N 0 56W, pop(1970) 40,001, town in Ashanti region, S Ghana, W Africa; on the railway between Kumasi and Dunkwa.

Obwalden *op'val-den*, OBWALD *op-vald'* (Fr), demicanton in Unterwalden, central Switzerland; pop(1980) 25,865; area 492 sq km; capital Sarnen; joined the Swiss Confederacy in 1291.

Ocal'a, 29 11N 82 08W, pop(1980) 37,170, county seat of Marion county, N central Florida, United States; 56 km S of Gainesville; railway; economy: trade, processing and transportation centre for citrus-growing region; area also known for its thoroughbred horses, cattle, lumber and limestone; manufactures include wood products, clothing and metalware; also a resort (hunting and fishing in Ocala National Forest).

Oceania *o-shi-an'ya*, or OCEANICA *o-shi-an'i-ka*, a general name applied to the isles of the Pacific Ocean, including Polynesia, Melanesia, Micronesia, Australasia and sometimes the Malaysian islands.

Oceanside, 33 12N 117 23W, pop(1980) 76,698, resort city in San Diego county, SW California, United States; on the Pacific Ocean, at the mouth of the San Luis Rey river, 56 km N of San Diego; railway; economy: trade centre for agricultural region.

Ocotal', 13 38N 86 31W, pop(1985e) 3,863, capital town of Nueva Segovia dept, N Nicaragua, Central America; on a sandy plain near the Honduran border, 168 km NNW of Managua; alt 600 m; railway.

Ocotepeque *o-kō-tay-pay'kay*, dept in W Honduras, Central America; bounded S by El Salvador; pop(1983e) 64,151; area 1,678 sq km; capital Nueva Ocotepeque; drained by the Río Lempa.

Oda *ō'da*, 5 55N 0 56W, pop(1970) 40,740, town in Eastern region, S Ghana, W Africa; SW of Koforidua; railway.

Odense *ō'den-se*, 55 24N 10 25E, pop(1983) 170,648, port and chief town on Fyn I, Fyn county, Denmark; 3rd largest city of Denmark; university (1964); railway; economy: engineering, foodstuffs, timber; monuments: St Knud's church (burned down in 12th century, reconstructed in 13th century); 18th-c palace; birthplace of Hans Christian Andersen.

Oder *ō'der*, ODRA (Czech, Pol), VIADUA (anc), river in central Europe rising in E Sudetes Mts of Czechoslovakia; flows N through Poland eventually following E German frontier to meet the Baltic Sea near Szczecin; total length 854 km; length in Poland 742 km; navigable for 711 km; tributaries include the Nysa Kłodzka, Barycz, Bóbr, Nysa Łużycka and Warta rivers.

Odessa *u-dye'su*, 46 30N 30 46E, pop(1983) 1,097,000, seaport capital of Odesskaya oblast, Ukrainskaya SSR, Soviet Union; on the NW shore of the Black Sea; naval base and home port for a fishing and Antarctic whaling fleet; Odessa is the leading Black Sea port, trading in grain, sugar, machinery, coal, petroleum products, cement, metals, jute, and timber; icebreakers ensure that the port is ice free throughout the year; there are large health resorts nearby; university (1865); railway, economy: fishing, solar research and development, machine building, oil refining, metalworking, chemicals, pharmaceuticals; monument: Uspensky cathedral (1855-69).

Odess'a, 31 52N 102 23W, pop(1980) 90,027, county seat of Ector county, W Texas, United States; 186 km WNW of San Angelo; railway; economy: oil refining, chemicals, plastics, synthetic rubber, and oil-field equipment.

Odiénné *ōd-yay'nay*, dept in NW Ivory Coast, W Africa; pop(1975) 124,010; area 20,600 sq km; capital Odiénné; chief towns Tiéme and Kinbirila.

Odorhei Secuiesc *od-or-hay say-choo-esk'*, 46 18N 25 19E, pop(1983) 38,410, town in Harghita county, N central Romania; 160 km NNW of Bucureşti; railway; economy: timber, livestock trade, distilling, tanning; monuments: Franciscan monastery (17th-c), Roman remains.

Ofan'to, river in S Italy, rising in the Appno Napoletano; flows E, N, and NE through Puglia region to discharge into the Adriatic Sea 6 km NW of Barletta; length 133 km; southernmost river on the E coast.

Offaly *o'ful-ee*, UA BHFAILGHE (Gael), county in Leinster prov, central Irish Republic; bounded W by R Shannon; the Slieve Bloom Mts rise in the SW; pop(1981) 58,312; area 1,997 sq km; capital Tullamore; large tracts of peat used to fuel power stations.

Offa's Dyke Path, long-distance footpath stretching the entire N-S length of Wales, from Prestatyn to Chepstow; length 270 km.

Offenbach, OFFENBACH AM MAIN, *of'-en-baKH am mīn*, 50 06N 8 46E, industrial city in Darmstadt dist, Hessen (Hesse) prov, W Germany; on the left bank of the R Main, E of Frankfurt; headquarters of the German Meteorological Service; the Kaiser-Friedrich-Quelle, drilled in 1885, is a soda water spring with the highest alkaline content in Germany; railway; economy: household electrical appliances; noted as the centre of the

German leather industry; event: Annual International Leather Goods Fair.

Offenburg *of'-en-boork*, 48 29N 7 57E, pop(1983) 50,200, manufacturing city in W Baden-Württemberg prov, W Germany; at the point where the R Kinzig emerges from the vine-clad foothills of the Schwarzwald (Black Forest) into the fertile Upper Rhine plain, 53 km N of Freiburg; an important road and rail junction; chief town of the Ortenau dist, the 'golden land' of wine and fruit; economy: publishing, printing, soft drinks, foodstuffs, milk and dairy produce, leatherwork, cigars.

Ogaden', geographical area in SE Ethiopia, NE Africa; a dry plateau which is intermittently watered by the Fafen Shet' and Jerer rivers; it became part of Abyssinia in 1890; an incident at Wal Wal in 1934 initiated the Italian-Abyssinian war; the area was part of Italian East Africa between 1936 and 1941.

Ogasawara-shotō *ō-ga-sa-wa'ra-shō'tō*, BONIN ISLANDS (Eng), group of 27 volcanic islands in the W Pacific Ocean, c.965 km S of Tōkyo, Japan; area 104 sq km; the islands form part of Tōkyo prefecture; Chichijima in the centre of the group is the largest island; other important islands are Hahajima, Nishino-shima and Mukojima; the islands were first colonized in 1830 by a small group of Europeans and Hawaiians; they were occupied by the Japanese in 1862 and annexed by them in 1876; attacked by a US task force in Sept 1944 during World War II; the islands were administered by the USA between 1945 and 1968, when they were returned to Japan.

Ogbomosho *og-bo'mō-shō*, 8 05N 4 11E, pop(1981e) 590,600, market town in Oyo state, W Nigeria, W Africa; 88 km NNE of Ibadan; economy: cloth; events: Ebo Oba Ijeru, Egungun and Ashun festivals in Feb, July and Aug respectively.

Og'den, 41 13N 111 58W, pop(1980) 64,407, county seat of Weber county, N Utah, United States; at the junction of the Ogden and Weber rivers, 50 km N of Salt Lake City; settled by Mormons in 1847; railway; economy: aerospace industries; Hill Air Force Base and Ogden Defence Depot are nearby; monument: Union Station Museum.

Ogooué *ō-gō-way'*, river in W Africa; rises in the Congo and flows N into Gabon, NW past Franceville and Lastrousville; then W and SW past Booué, Ndjolé and Lambaréné before branching into a region of lakes and splitting into a number of arms E and SE of Port Gentil; empties into the Atlantic Ocean; tributaries include the Ivindo and Ngounié rivers; length 900 km; navigable below Lambaréné all year round.

Ogun *o-goon'*, state in SW Nigeria, W Africa; pop(1982e) 2,473,300; area 16,762 sq km; capital Abeokuta; chief towns Ijebu-Ode, Ilaro and Shagamu; the main ethnic groups are the Egbas, the Aworis, the Egbados and Ijebus, all speaking Yoruba; an agricultural state, producing cocoa, cereals and the largest quantity of kolanuts in the country; economy: cement processing, food canning and rubber foam and paint manufacture; there are reserves of limestone, clay, chalk and phosphate.

O'Higgins, Lago, lake in Chile and Argentina. See Lago San Martín.

Ohio *ō-hī'ō*, state in E United States, bounded N by Michigan and Lake Erie, W by Indiana, E and S by Pennsylvania, West Virginia and Kentucky; the 'Buckeye State'; 17th state to join the Union (1803); pop(1980) 10,797,630; area 106,610 sq km; capital Columbus; chief cities are Cleveland, Cincinnati, Toledo, Akron and Dayton; the state is part of the Allegheny plateau and is drained by the Muskingum, Scioto, Great Miami rivers which flow to meet the Ohio river and L Erie; economy: grain, soybeans, vegetables, dairy cattle, livestock, coal (E and SE Appalachian coalfield), natural gas, sand and gravel; manufactures steel, metal products, vehicles, paper, chemicals, clothing, electrical goods and foodstuffs; visited by La Salle in 1669 and settled by fur traders from 1685; the state is divided into 88 counties as follows:

County	*area (sq km)*	*pop(1980)*
Adams	1,524	24,328
Allen	1,053	112,241
Ashland	1,102	46,178
Ashtabula	1,828	104,215
Athens	1,321	56,399
Auglaize	1,035	42,554
Belmont	1,396	82,569
Brown	1,282	31,920
Butler	1,222	258,787
Carroll	1,022	25,598
Champaign	1,115	33,649
Clark	1,035	150,236
Clermont	1,186	128,483
Clinton	1,066	34,603
Columbiana	1,388	113,572
Coshocton	1,472	36,024
Crawford	1,048	50,075
Cuyahoga	1,193	1,498,400
Darke	1,560	55,096
Defiance	1,076	39,987
Delaware	1,152	53,840
Erie	686	79,655
Fairfield	1,316	93,678
Fayette	1,053	27,467
Franklin	1,412	869,132
Fulton	1,058	37,751
Gallia	1,225	30,098
Geauga	1,061	74,474
Greene	1,082	129,769
Guernsey	1,357	42,024
Hamilton	1,071	873,224
Hancock	1,383	64,581
Hardin	1,225	32,719
Harrison	1,040	18,152
Henry	1,079	28,383
Highland	1,438	33,477
Hocking	1,100	24,304
Holmes	1,102	29,416
Huron	1,284	54,608
Jackson	1,092	30,592
Jefferson	1,066	91,564
Knox	1,375	46,304
Lake	601	212,801
Lawrence	1,188	63,849
Licking	1,784	120,981
Logan	1,191	39,155
Lorain	1,287	274,909
Lucas	887	471,741
Madison	1,214	33,004
Mahoning	1,084	289,487
Marion	1,048	67,974
Medina	1,097	113,150
Meigs	1,123	23,641
Mercer	1,188	38,334
Miami	1,066	90,381
Monroe	1,188	17,382
Montgomery	1,191	571,697
Morgan	1,092	14,241
Morrow	1,056	26,480
Muskingum	1,700	83,340
Noble	1,037	11,310
Ottawa	658	40,076
Paulding	1,089	21,302
Perry	1,071	31,032
Pickaway	1,308	43,662
Pike	1,152	22,802
Portage	1,282	135,856
Preble	1,108	38,223
Putnam	1,258	32,991
Richland	1,292	131,205
Ross	1,799	65,004
Sandusky	1,063	63,267
Scioto	1,594	84,545

contd

County	*area (sq km)*	*pop(1980)*
Seneca	1,438	61,901
Shelby	1,063	43,089
Stark	1,492	378,823
Summit	1,071	524,472
Trumbull	1,591	241,863
Tuscarawas	1,482	84,614
Union	1,136	29,536
Van Wert	1,066	30,458
Vinton	1,076	11,584
Warren	1,048	99,276
Washington	1,664	64,266
Wayne	1,448	97,408
Williams	1,097	36,369
Wood	1,609	107,372
Wyandot	1,056	22,651

Ohio, river in E central USA; second longest tributary of the Mississippi (after the Missouri); formed at Pittsburgh, Pennsylvania by the union of the Monongahela and Allegheny rivers; the Ohio flows generally SW for 1,578 km to join the Mississippi at Cairo, Illinois; the Ohio forms the state boundary between Ohio, Indiana and Illinois (N) and West Virginia and Kentucky (S); chief tributaries: the Kanawha, Licking, Kentucky and Tennessee rivers (left); the Scioto, Miami and Wabash rivers (right); the Ohio is navigable all the way, with the help of a canal at the rapids at Louisville; the length of the river with its longest headstream, the Allegheny, is 2,101 km.

Ohrid *oKH'rid*, OHRIDSKO JEZERO (Yug), lake situated on the frontier between Albania and Yugoslavia to the E of Elbasan; area 350 sq km; third largest lake in Yugoslavia; bounded to the E by the Galičica Mts (1,802 m); two-thirds of the lake is in Yugoslavia; boat service on the lake joining the picturesque town of Ohrid, which is now a national monument, to Sveti Naum at the S end; there is a tourist resort at Struga.

Ohrid, 41 06N 20 49E, pop(1981) 64,245, town in SW Makedonija (Macedonia) republic, Yugoslavia; on the shores of L Ohrid (Ohridsko Jezero); hydro-biological institute; airfield; monuments: cathedral of St Sophia, castle, 13th c St Clement's church; events: weekly market; old town festival in May and August; Balkan festival of folk singing and dancing in July; 'Ohrid Summer' with cultural and tourist events during July-Aug.

O'io, region in Guinea-Bissau, W Africa; pop(1979) 135,114.

Oise *wahz*, dept in Picardie region of N France, on the lower Oise R, N of Paris; comprises 4 arrond, 41 cantons and 693 communes, pop(1982) 661,781; area 5,860 sq km; capital Beauvais, chief towns Compiègne and Creil.

Oise, river in N France and Belgium, rising in the Ardennes just inside the Belgian frontier, S of Chimay; flows SW entering the Aisne dept of NE France just N of Hirson; meets the R Seine above Andresy; length 302 km; tributary R Aisne; at Noyon it is linked by the Canal du Nord with the N industrial area and the waterways of Belgium.

Ōita *ō'ee-ta*, 33 15N 131 36E, pop(1980) 360,478, capital of Ōita prefecture, NE Kyūshū island, Japan; railway.

Oiudah *wee'da*, 6 23N 2 08E, pop(1979) 30,000, town in Atlantique prov, S Benin, W Africa; 40 km west of Cotonou; railway; monuments: the original fort was built by the Portuguese and enlarged by Dutch; cathedral and 'Temple of the Sacred Python'; nearby are a Danish fort and the British Fort Williams, both now occupied by trading companies.

Ojos del Salado, Cerro *ōKH'ōs dhel sa-la'THō*, 27 05S 68 35W, Andean peak rising to 6,908 m on the Argentina-Chile border; in Catamarca prov, Andina, Argentina, and on the border with Copiapó prov, Atacama, Chile; the 2nd highest peak in the Western hemisphere (Cerro Aconcagua is higher at 6,960 m); 24 km WSW of Cerro Incahuasi.

Okara *ō-kah'ra*, 30 49N 73 31E, pop(1981) 154,000, city in Punjab prov, Pakistan; SW of Lahore; railway; economy: trade in grain, cotton and flour.

Okavango *ō-ka-vang'gō*, CUBANGO (Port), KAVENGO (Nam), river in S Africa; the 3rd largest river in S Africa, it flows through Angola, Namibia and Botswana; length 1,600 km; rises on the Bié Plateau (central Angola) and flows SE to form the Angola-Namibia frontier; turns S to cross the Caprivi Strip at Mukwe; enters Botswana at Mohembo (NW); spreads into the Okavango delta in Ngamiland dist; the delta (approx 15,000 sq km) has a diverse range of habitats ranging from forest to swamp, marsh and lagoon; over 36 species of larger mammals, over 200 species of bird and over 80 fish species have been recorded here; when the delta floods it fills a number of other rivers including the R Thamalakene which discharges into the R Chobe; in certain years it can fill Lake Ngami; tributaries include the R Cuito in SE Angola.

Okayama *ō-ka-ya'ma*, 34 40N 133 54E, pop(1980) 545,765, port capital of Okayama prefecture, Chūgoku region, SW Honshū island, Japan; 112 km W of Ōsaka; university (1949); railway; economy: cotton, porcelain; monuments: the town is dominated by its 16th c 'Castle of the Crow'; the 17th-c Koraku-en Gardens are situated on an island in the middle of the R Asahi.

Okazaki *ō-ka-za'kee*, 34 58N 137 10E, pop(1980) 262,372, city in Aichi prefecture, Chūbu region, central Honshū island, Japan; 32 km SE of Nagoya; railway; economy: metals, textiles, chemicals, machinery.

Okeechobee *ō-ke-chō'bee*, lake in S central Florida, United States; linked to the Atlantic by the St Lucie Canal and the Miami Canal; largest lake in S USA; rivers drain S through the Everglades.

Okefenokee Swamp *ō-ke-fe-nō'kee* (Muskogean, 'water-shaking'), area of swamp land in SE Georgia and NE Florida, United States; drained SW by the Suwannee river.

Okhotsk, Sea of *ō-kotsk'*, OKHOTSKOYE MORE (Rus), NW inlet of the Pacific Ocean, bounded by the E coast of Siberia to the W, Kamchatka Peninsula and Kuril'skiye Ostrova (Kuril Islands) to the E and the Japanese island of Hokkaido to the S; connected to the Sea of Japan by La Perouse Strait and Tatarskiy Proliv and to the North-west Pacific Basin by several passages through Kuril'skiye Ostrova; main arm is the Zaliv Shelikhova, extended by the Penzhinskay Guba to the NE; Magadan and Korsakov are the main ports; cold surface currents move in an anti-clockwise direction within this sea; deepest point of 3,365 m is found near Kuril'skiye Ostrova in the Okhotsk abyssal plain; ice-bound from Nov to June and subject to heavy fogs.

Oki or **Oki Retto** *ō'kee re'tō*, OKI ARCHIPELAGO (Eng), island group of Shimane prefecture, Chūgoku region, Japan; in the Sea of Japan, 56 km N of SW Honshū; area 375 sq km; includes Dōgo (the largest island) and Dōzen (group of 3 islands); the islands are generally mountainous and forested; Dōgo rises to 608 m; economy: timber, fishing; chief town and port: Saigō on Dōgo island.

Okinawa *ō-kee-na'wa*, pop(1984e) 5,600, town in Santa Cruz dept, central Bolivia; established by Japanese settlers in 1954; the pop comprises 4,000 Bolivians and 1,600 Japanese.

Okinawa, region comprising the S part of the Ryukyu islands; bounded W by the East China Sea, E by the Pacific Ocean; pop(1980) 1,107,000; area 2,246 sq km; Okinawa itself is the largest of the Ryukyu islands (area 1,176 sq km); situated 528 km SSW of Kyūshū; capital Naha; economy: rice, sugar cane, sweet potatoes.

Oklahoma *ōk-le-hō'mah* (Muskogean, 'red people'), state in SW United States; bounded W by Texas and New Mexico, N by Colorado and Kansas, E by Missouri and Arkansas, and S by Texas; the Red river follows the S border; the R Arkansas flows SE through the NE of the state; the Canadian river flows E through the centre of the state to empty into the R Arkansas near the E border;

the R Cimarron flows SE, then S through the N part of the state before emptying into the R Arkansas in NE state; the Ouachita Mts lie to the SE and the Wichita Mts to the SW; the highest point is Black Mesa (1,516 m); W Oklahoma is predominantly a high plain, sloping W-E; livestock and wheat are the major agricultural products, but cotton, dairy products, and peanuts are also important; the state's wealth is based on its large oil reserves and its associated petroleum industry; manufactured goods include machinery, fabricated metals, and aircraft; most of the state, except the panhandle, was acquired by the USA as part of the Louisiana Purchase (1803); as the Indian Territory, it was settled by Indians (the Five Civilized Tribes) in the 1830s; Allem Wright, a chief of the Choctaw tribe, coined the name Oklahoma to describe the land held by his people; as punishment for taking the Confederate side in the Civil War, the Indians lost the W part of their territory to whites; this region, which became Oklahoma Territory in 1890, included the panhandle which had been taken from Texas in the Compromise of 1850; the Indian and Oklahoma territories merged and were admitted into the Union as a state (46th) in 1907; also known as the 'Sooner State'; pop(1980) 3,025,290; area 178,503 sq km; capital Oklahoma City; other major cities include Tulsa and Lawton; the state is divided into 77 counties:

County	*area (sq km)*	*pop(1980)*
Adair	1,500	18,575
Alfalfa	2,246	7,077
Atoka	2,548	12,748
Beaver	4,701	6,806
Beckham	2,350	19,243
Blaine	2,392	13,443
Bryan	2,345	30,535
Caddo	3,344	30,905
Canadian	2,343	56,452
Carter	2,153	43,610
Cherokee	1,945	30,684
Choctaw	1,981	17,203
Cimarron	4,789	3,648
Cleveland	1,375	133,173
Coal	1,352	6,041
Comanche	2,798	112,456
Cotton	1,706	7,338
Craig	1,984	15,014
Creek	2,418	59,016
Custer	2,551	25,995
Delaware	1,872	23,946
Dewey	2,618	5,922
Ellis	3,203	5,596
Garfield	2,756	62,820
Garvin	2,114	27,856
Grady	2,876	39,490
Grant	2,610	6,518
Greer	1,659	7,028
Harmon	1,396	4,519
Harper	2,701	4,715
Haskell	1,482	11,010
Hughes	2,096	14,338
Jackson	2,124	30,356
Jefferson	1,999	8,183
Johnston	1,661	10,356
Kay	2,395	49,852
Kingfisher	2,356	14,187
Kiowa	2,649	12,711
Latimer	1,893	9,840
Le Flore	4,121	40,698
Lincoln	2,506	26,601
Logan	1,945	26,881
Love	1,349	7,469
Major	2,491	8,772
Marshall	967	10,550
Mayes	1,674	32,261
McClain	1,513	20,291
McCurtain	4,748	36,151

contd

County	*area (sq km)*	*pop(1980)*
McIntosh	1,557	15,562
Murray	1,092	12,147
Muskogee	2,119	66,939
Noble	1,914	11,573
Nowata	1,404	11,486
Okfuskee	1,633	11,125
Oklahoma	1,841	568,933
Okmulgee	1,815	39,169
Osage	5,889	39,327
Ottawa	1,209	32,870
Pawnee	1,433	15,310
Payne	1,797	62,435
Pittsburg	3,253	40,524
Pontotoc	1,864	32,598
Pottawatomie	2,036	55,239
Pushmataha	3,684	11,773
Roger Mills	2,980	4,799
Rogers	1,776	46,436
Seminole	1,661	27,473
Sequoyah	1,763	30,749
Stephens	2,298	43,419
Texas	5,304	17,727
Tillman	2,350	12,398
Tulsa	1,487	470,593
Wagoner	1,453	41,801
Washington	1,100	48,113
Washita	2,616	13,798
Woods	3,357	10,923
Woodward	3,229	21,172

Oklahoma City, 35 30N 97 30W, pop(1980) 403,213, capital of state in Oklahoma county, central Oklahoma, United States; on the North Canadian river; settled in 1889 around a railway station, becoming state capital in 1910; the city developed rapidly after the discovery of oil in 1928; university (1911); railway; airport; largest city in the state; economy: oil production; distribution and processing centre for livestock, grain, and cotton; manufactures include aircraft, machinery, and electrical equipment; Tinker Air Force Base; monuments: National Cowboy Hall of Fame, Western Heritage Centre, state historical museum; events: festival of arts (April), Quarter Horse Show (Nov).

Olan'cho, largest dept in Honduras, Central America, adjoining the Nicaragua border; pop(1983e) 228,122; area 24,339 sq km; mountainous with fertile valleys; capital Juticalpa.

Öland *œ'land*, elongated Swedish island in Baltic Sea, off SE coast of Sweden, separated from mainland by Kalmarsund (Kalmar Sound); area 1,344 sq km; length 136 km; largest island in Sweden; chief town is Borgholm on W coast; administered by Kalmar county.

Olathe *ō-lay'the*, 38 53N 94 49W, pop(1980) 37,258, county seat of Johnson county, E Kansas, United States; 32 km SSW of Kansas City; railway.

Olavarría *o-la-va-ree'a*, 36 57S 60 20W, pop(1980) 63,686, town in S central Buenos Aires prov, Litoral, E Argentina; railway.

Old'bury, 52 30N 2 00W, pop(1981) 153,461, town linked with Smethwick in Sandwell borough, West Midlands, central England; 8 km W of Birmingham; railway; economy: metal products, engineering, chemicals.

Old'enburg, 53 08N 8 13E, pop(1983) 138,800, industrial and commercial city in Niedersachsen (Lower Saxony) prov, W Germany; on the R Hunte, 128 km W of Bremen; university (1970); railway; economy: milk and dairy products, milking machines; industry has developed considerably since the improvement of the Kustenkanal (Coastal Canal) to the Ems.

Oldham *ōld'em*, 53 33N 2 07W, pop(1981) 107,830, town in Oldham borough, Greater Manchester, NW England; 12 km NE of Manchester; railway; economy: textiles and textile machinery, clothing, plastics, electronics.

Olduvai Gorge *ol'doo-vī*, gorge within the Ngorongoro conservation area of the Rift Valley, N Tanzania, E Africa; 57 km W of Ngorongoro village; named after the *oldupai*, a succulent plant found in the gorge; though not of immense physical proportions the gorge is of extreme archaeological importance as it was here that Louis and Mary Leakey dug up some of the oldest known 'human' remains; in 1959 they came across the skull of *Zinjanthropus boisei* or 'nutcracker man' which is believed to be approx 1.75 mn years old; the original skull is housed in the national museum in Dar es Salaam; other remains uncovered include *Australopithecus*, *Homo habili*, and *Homo erectus*.

Olenëk *ul-yin-yok'*, river predominantly in N Yakutskaya ASSR, E Siberian Rossiyskaya, N Soviet Union; rises on the Sredne Sibirskoye Ploskogor'ye (Central Siberian Plateau), E Krasnoyarskiy kray, then flows generally E and N in a zigzag course, to discharge into the Laptev Sea at Ust'-Olenëk; length 2,400 km; navigable length 965 km; chief tributaries are the Kelimyar, Buolkalakh, Pur, and Ukukit rivers.

Oléron, Ile d' *eel do-lay-rõ*, ULIARUS (anc), wooded fertile island in the E Bay of Biscay, off the W coast of Charente-Maritime dept, W France; largest island in the Bay of Biscay and France's 2nd largest off-shore island after Corsica; situated to the W of Rochefort opposite the mouth of the R Charente, 3 km from the mainland to which it is linked by a modern toll-bridge crossing the Pertuis de Maumusson; area 175 sq km; length 30 km; Portuguese oysters are cultivated in the salt marshes; mild climate, beaches and fishing attract tourists; the two main towns are Le Château d'Oléron, chief port at the SE end, and St-Pierre d'Oléron, the administrative and commercial centre; it gave its name to the 12th-c code of sea-laws which forms the basis of modern maritime law.

Ölgiy *ul'gi*, OELGI, 48 54N 90 00E, capital of Bayan-Ölgiy county, W Mongolia; livestock breeding is the basis of the town's economy; linked SE to Hovd by road.

Olímbia, OLYM'PIA (Eng), 37 38N 21 39E, village and national sanctuary in Ilía nome (dept), NW Pelopónnisos region, S Greece; situated in an area of gentle hills, on the N bank of the R Alfiós; railway; the Olympic Games were held here every 4 years from 776 BC in honour of Zeus; German excavations from 1875 onwards, which led to the growth of the present village, brought to light the sacred precinct with ruins of many temples and other buildings, including the Temple of Zeus (5th-c BC), Hera's Temple, and the Stadium.

Ólimbos, OLYMPUS *o-lim'pus* (Eng), range of mountains between Makedhonia and Thessalia regions, N Greece, reaching its highest point in Mítikas (2,917 m); traditionally the abode of the dynasty of gods headed by Zeus.

Olimpos-Bey Dağları, national park in W Anadolu (Anatolia), Turkey, S of Eskişehir; area 698 sq km; established in 1972.

Olinda *o-leen'da*, 8 00S 34 51W, pop(1980) 266,751, town in Pernambuco state, Nordeste region, NE Brazil; on the Atlantic coast, 6 km N of Recife; founded in 1537; original capital of Brazil from 1537 to 1549; railway; economy: tourism, fertilizers, textiles; monuments: among the colonial buildings which remain are the Prefeitura, once the palace of the viceroys, the monastery of São Bento, with fine paintings, sculpture and furniture, the monastery of São Francisco, with its wood carving and paintings, and the Bica de San Pedro, a colonial public fountain; there are also some 17th-c houses with latticed balconies, heavy doors and pink stucco walls; Museum of Sacred Art in the 17th-c bishop's palace; Museum of Art of Pernambuco in the old jail of the Inquisition.

Olivares, Cerro de *THay o-lee-va'rays*, 30 19S 69 50W, mountain rising to 6,252 m on the Argentina-Chile border; in San Juan prov, Andina, W Argentina bordering with Elquí prov, Coquimbo, Chile; 64 km WSW of Rodeo.

Olmsted, North, 41 25N 81 56W, pop(1980) 36,486, town in Cuyahoga county, NE Ohio, United States; 21 km WSW of Cleveland.

Olomouc *ol-o-mow'tse*, 49 40N 17 15E, pop(1984) 104,332, town in Severomoravský region, Czech Socialist Republic, central Czechoslovakia; on R Morava, SW of Ostrava; university (1576); airport (Holice); railway; economy: iron, steel, food processing, agricultural machinery; monuments: 12th-c St Wenceslaus cathedral; pilgrimage site of Svatý Kopeček.

Olsztyn *ol-shtin'*, voivodship in N Poland; bounded N by the USSR and watered by the R Łyna which flows S-N; a region of many lakes; pop(1983) 707,000; area 12,327 sq km; capital Olsztyn; chief towns include Ostróda, Kętrzyn, Iława and Szczytno.

Olsztyn, ALLENSTEIN (Ger), 53 48N 20 29E, pop(1983) 144,700, capital of Olsztyn voivodship, N Poland; on R Łyna at the centre of the Mazurian Lake District; between 1918 and 1939 the Union of Poles in Germany operated from here; agricultural and technical academy; Olsztyn mime theatre of deaf-mutes is internationally renowned; railway; economy: tyres; monuments: 14th-c castle of the Warmia Chapter with Masurian museum, 15-16th-c cathedral.

Olt, county in S Romania; bounded to the S by the R Danube which follows the frontier with Bulgaria; traversed N-S by the R Otul; pop(1983) 529,149; area 5,507 sq km; capital Slatina.

Olt, river in S Romania, rising on the slopes of the Romanian Carpathian Mts and crossing the Transylvanian Alps; flows S to meet the R Danube near Turnu Măgurele; length 557 km.

Olteniţa *ol-tay-nee'tsa*, 44 05N 26 40E, pop(1983) 27,837, river port in Călăraşi county, SE Romania; on R Danube, close to the Bulgarian frontier; railway; economy: port trade, fishing.

Olympia, 47 03N 122 53W, pop(1980) 27,447, seaport capital of Washington state and Thurston county, W Washington, United States; at the S end of Puget Sound, 40 km SW of Tacoma, at the mouth of the Deschutes river; founded in 1850 at the end of the Oregon Trail after homesteads were staked out in 1848; became capital of Washington Territory in 1853; railway.

Olympic, national park in NW Washington, United States; protects part of the Olympic Mts with its temperate rain forest and glaciers; established in 1938; area 3,586 sq km.

Olympus *ō-lim'pus*, mountain in the Troödos range of central Cyprus, rising to 1,951 m; the highest peak on the island.

Olympus, mountain range in Greece. See Ólimbos.

Omagh *ō-mah'*, AN OMAIGH (Gael), 54 36N 7 18W, pop(1981) 14,627, county town of Tyrone in Omagh dist, Co Tyrone, W central Northern Ireland; on the R Strule; economy: footwear, engineering, salmon fishing; a centre for touring the Sperrin Mts; monument: inside the 19th-c Catholic parish church is the Black Bell of Drumragh, which dates from the 9th century.

Omaha *ōm'a-hah*, 41 17N 96 01W, pop(1980) 314,255, county seat of Douglas county, E Nebraska, United States; a port on the R Missouri, 24 km N of its junction with the R Platte; a fur-trading post was established here in 1812; city status since 1867; 2 universities (1878, 1908); air force base; railway; airport; largest city in the state; economy: major livestock market and meat-processing centre; manufactures include processed meat, farm machinery, electrical equipment and fertilizers; centre for medical treatment and research; monuments: Joslyn Art Museum, aerospace museum, Boys Town; event: College World Series (June).

Oman, formerly MASQAṬ AND OMAN, official name Sultanate of Oman, independent state occupying the extreme SE corner of the Arabian peninsula, bounded NW by the United Arab Emirates, N and W by Saudi Arabia, SW by S Yemen, NE by the Gulf of Oman, and SE and E by the Arabian Sea; timezone GMT +4; area 300,000 sq km; second largest country in Arabia; capital Masqaṭ (Muscat); chief towns Maṭraḥ, Nazwá, and Ṣalālah;

pop(1986e) 1,074,000; the capital area of Masqaṭ, Maṭraḥ, and Ruwi has an estimated population of 80,000; the majority of the pop lives in the towns and villages of the Bāṭinah coastal plain which contains 40% of Oman's cultivated land; the people are mostly of Arab origin but significant minorities of Iranians, Baluchis, Indo-Pakistanis, and East Africans live along the NE coast; Arabic is the official language but English is widely spoken; the dominant religion is Ibadhi Muslim with a Sunni minority; the unit of currency is the rial omani which replaced the rial saidi in 1972; national holiday 18-19 Nov; membership of Arab League, FAO, G-77, GCC, IBRD, ICAO, IDA, Islamic Development Bank, IFAD, IFC, IMF, IMO, INTELSAT, INTERPOL, ITU, NAM, OIC, UN, UNESCO, UPU, WFTU, WHO, WMO.

Physical description. The tip of the Musandam peninsula which juts into the Strait of Hormuz is separated from the rest of the country by a 80 km strip belonging to the United Arab Emirates. Oman also governs 2 villages within the United Arab Emirates and holds sovereignty over Maṣīrah I and the Kuria Muria and Daymaruyat Is. A chain of eroded limestone mountains (the Hajar range) runs NW-SE parallel to the coast of the Gulf of Oman. Peaks in the Jabal Akhdar range attain heights of over 3,000 m. This upland zone is dissected by wadis which flood seasonally. E and N of the Hajar is the alluvial plain of the Bāṭinah. It extends for 270 km SE from Oman's border with the United Arab Emirates and varies in width from 50 km to 150 km. Much of the rest of the country is made up of a low, rolling plateau which merges on the Saudi Arabian frontier with the Rub al Khālī ('empty quarter'). There is a vast sand desert, the Ramlat Ahl Wahībah, in the NE.

Climate. Oman has a desert climate which varies considerably from region to region. From April to Oct the coastal areas are exceptionally hot and humid with temperatures reaching a maximum of 47°C. During this summer period the interior is hot and dry. In the mountainous regions a relatively temperate climate prevails. Light monsoon rains fall in the S from June to September.

History, government and constitution. Portuguese attempts at colonization were resisted during the 16th century. Oman soon became the dominant maritime power of the W Indian Ocean, developing trade with E Africa (notably Zanzibar), Persia, and India. From 1913 to 1920 internal strife divided Oman between supporters of the Sultanate and members of the Ibadhi sect who wanted to be ruled exclusively by their religious leader. In 1964 a separatist tribal revolt which broke out in the S province of Dhofar led to a police coup that installed the present Sultan in 1970. Oman is an independent state ruled by a Sultan who is both head of state and premier. A cabinet of about 20 appointed ministers holds executive power.

Economy. Oil was discovered in commercial quantities in the Rub al Khālī basin in 1964 and production began in 1967. In 1980 a new complex of fields around Ma'mul in Dhofar prov became operational. More than 90% of government revenue comes from the sale of oil. A pipeline network carries oil from the fields in the S and mid-W of the country to the export terminal of Mīna'al Fahl in the capital area. Gas is an important source of industrial power, particularly for copper smelting and cement plants. Attempts have been made to diversify the economy with a view to post-oil exports. The Suḥār copper smelter and refinery is one of the very few copper-producing plants in the Middle East. Manufacturing still only accounts for 3-4% of the total GDP. Light industries which have developed in recent years include date processing, banana packing, and the manufacture of electric wire and cables, spark plugs, and paper bags. Chief exports are crude oil, fish, dry limes, and wheat flour. Japan is Oman's most important export market accounting for 51.4% by volume of 1983 oil exports. The UAE, the USA and the UK also trade extensively with Oman.

Agriculture. Agriculture was the mainstay of the economy before the advent of oil. Of Oman's total land area of 300,000 sq km only 0.1% is estimated to be under cultivation. Approx 70% of the pop relies on agriculture for a livelihood, although mostly at subsistence level. Dates are grown in the valleys of the interior and on the plain of the Bāṭinah. Other crops include alfalfa, wheat, tobacco, fruit, and vegetables. Desalinated water irrigates 410 sq km of agricultural land. Fishing is also an important industry employing between 7,000 and 8,000 workers.

Administrative divisions. Oman is divided into 1 province (Dhofar), 2 governorates (Musandam and Masqaṭ) and numerous districts (*wilayats*).

Communications. The 16,900 km of highways comprise 2,200 with bituminous surface and 14,700 motorable track. The road network includes a 780 km highway linking the N with Dhofar. Seeb International Airport is situated 43 km W of Masqaṭ. Maṭraḥ is the major port.

Oman, Gulf of, NW arm of the Indian Ocean, lying between the NE coast of Oman and the S coast of Iran; linked to the Arabian Gulf by the Strait of Hormuz; vital waterway for ocean traffic to and from the oil-rich Gulf states; 480 km long; connected to the Arabian Sea in the SE.

Ombella-Mpoko *om-be'la-um-pō-kō'*, prefecture in SW Central African Republic; the land dips SE to the valley of the R Ubangi and the R Darna forms SW border; other rivers include the M'Bi, the M'Poko and the Ombella; pop(1968) 94,064; area 32,430 sq km; chief town Boyali; other towns include Bossemptélé, Bodanga, Yaloké, Bogangolo, Damara and Bombére; economy: iron ore and limestone mining.

Omdurman', 15 37N 32 29E, pop(1983) 526,287, major suburb of Khartoum, central Sudan, NE Africa; connected to the main city by a tramline bridge over the White Nile; only a village in 1884 when the Mahdi made it his military headquarters; captured by Lord Kitchener in 1898 after the final defeat of Khalifa's troops at

Kerreri, 10 km to the N; Mosque Square holds the ruins of the Mahdi's tomb which the British destroyed after capturing the city; university (1912).

Ometepe, Isla de *ō-may-tay'pay*, main island in Lago de Nicaragua, Central America; 13 km ENE of Rivas, SW Nicaragua; consists of 2 islands connected by a 3 km-wide isthmus; the larger island (N) is 19 km long and 16 km wide; there are 2 volcanoes which rise to heights of 1,610 m and 1,394 m; chief villages are Moyogalpa and Alta Gracia.

Ōmiya *ō'mee-ya*, 35 54N 139 39E, pop(1980) 354,084, town in Saitama prefecture, Kanto region, central Honshū island, Japan; 27 km NW of Tōkyo; railway; economy: trade in rice, wheat and silk; monument: Shinto shrine of Susano-wo, brother of the Sun Goddess.

Omme *om*, river in W central Jylland (Jutland), Denmark; rises in W Vejle county, flows WNW through Ribe and Ringkøbing counties, discharges into Ringkøbing Fjord, SE of Ringkøbing; length 72 km.

Ömnögovĭ *un-nu-gō'bee*, OEMNOEGOV, SOUTH GOBI (Eng), county in S Mongolia; pop(1981e) 30,000; area 165,000 sq km; capital Dalandzadgad; covered in part by the Gobi Desert; light brown steppe soil is found in the N of the county and sandy soil in the S; kulan, ibexes and arkali sheep are found; there are deposits of copper, iron ore, coal, oil, turquoise and other semi-precious stones.

Omo, national park in S Ethiopia, NE Africa; area 4,015 sq km.

Omsk, 55 00N 73 22E, pop(1983) 1,080,000, river port capital of Omskaya oblast, W Siberian Rossiyskaya, Soviet Union, at the confluence of the Irtysh and Om' rivers; founded in 1716 as a fortress; it is considered to be the greenest city in Siberia with 25 sq km of boulevards and gardens; university (1974); on the Trans-Siberian railway; airport; economy: oil refining, chemicals, engineering, clothing, footwear.

Ondo *on'dō*, state in SW Nigeria, W Africa; pop(1983e) 4,352,900; area 20,959 sq km; bounded S by Bight of Benin; capital Akure; chief towns Ondo, Owo, Ado-Ekiti, and Okitipupa; economy: reserves of clay, columbite, granite, iron ore, kaolin, limestone, oil, quartz and coal; textiles, timber, rubber and brick production and cocoa processing.

Öndörhaan *un'dur-KHan*, OENDOERHKAN, 47 20N 110 35E, centre of Hentiy county, NE Mongolia; on R Kerulen; linked by road to Ulaanbaatar in the WNW; economy: agriculture, foodstuffs and printing.

Onega *un-yay'gu*, river in Arkhangel'skaya oblast, European Rossiyskaya, NW Soviet Union; rises in Ozero Lacha (Lake Lacha), S of Kargopol', then flows generally N to discharge into Onezhskaya Guba (Onega Bay), an inlet of the Beloye More (White Sea), at Onega; length 403 km; there are rapids in the middle course.

Onega, Lake, lake in NW European Rossiyskaya, Soviet Union. See Onezhskoye, Ozero.

Oneida *ō-nī'de*, lake in central New York state, United States; SE of L Ontario to which it is linked by the Oswego river and NE of Syracuse; linked to the Mohawk river by the Erie Canal; named after an Indian tribe.

Onezhskoye, Ozero *un-yesh'ku-yu*, LAKE ONEGA *on-yeg'a* (Eng), 2nd largest lake in Europe, almost entirely in Karel'skaya ASSR, NW European Rossiyskaya, Soviet Union, close to the Finnish border; situated between Ladozhskoye Ozero (Lake Ladoga) to the SW and Beloye More (White Sea) to the NE; area 9,720 sq km; length 250 km; average depth 30 m; max depth 120 m; the S shore is low and sandy while the N shore is deeply indented and rocky with narrow bays extending up to 112 km inland (Povenets Gulf); receives the Vytegra (S), Shuya and Suna (W), and Vodla (E) rivers; drains via the Svir' river into Ladozhskoye Ozero to the SW; there are numerous islands at the N end; canals connect the lake with the R Volga and the Beloye More; chief ports on the shore include Petrozavodsk, Voznesenye, and Povenets; the lake freezes over from Nov to May.

Onitsha *o-nee-cha'*, 6 10N 6 47E, pop(1981e) 300,700, town in Anambra state, S central Nigeria, W Africa; on the R Niger, 80 km WSW of Enugu; economy: metallurgy, textiles, brewing.

Ontario *on-tay'ree-ō*, province in SE Canada; bounded W and NW by Manitoba prov, N by Hudson Bay, NE by James Bay, E by Québec prov and S by the United States; much of the S border with the United States is formed by L Superior, L Huron and Georgian Bay, L Erie and L Ontario; the N section of the prov lies in the rocky Canadian Shield, but contains an enormous clay belt suitable for farming; drained by the Severn, Winisk, Attawapiskat, Albany, Moose, and Abitibi rivers flowing into Hudson and James bays, the Ottawa river flowing into the St Lawrence, and the Rainy, Nipigon, Kaministikwia, Agwa, Montréal, Thames, Trent, Grand, Saugeen, Niagara and St Clair rivers flowing into the Great Lakes; of the numerous lakes in Ontario, other than the Great Lakes, the largest are Lake of the Woods, lakes Nipigon, Seul, des Mille Lacs, St Joseph, Nipissing, Abitibi (partly in Québec), Simcoe and Muskoka; the N part of the prov is sparsely populated, densely wooded and studded with lakes; in the centre of the prov, on the N shore of L Ontario, is Pukaskwa National Park (area 1,877 sq km, established in 1971); pop(1981) 8,625,107; area 916,734 sq km; capital Toronto; major cities include Ottawa, Thunder Bay and Hamilton; economy: tobacco, corn, livestock, poultry, dairy products, fur, motor vehicles and parts, food processing, iron and steel, machinery, mining (nickel, copper, uranium, zinc, gold, iron), hydroelectricity; widely explored by French fur traders and missionaries, Ontario was virtually unsettled when it became British territory in 1763; a large number of United Empire Loyalists came to Ontario after the American War of Independence; the constitution of 1791 divided Canada into Upper Canada (Ontario) and Lower Canada (Québec); Upper Canada was invaded by American forces in the War of 1812; a separatist rebellion took place in 1837-38; the Union Act in 1840 joined Upper and Lower Canada; the prov of Ontario came into being with the establishment of the Canadian confederation in 1867; part of Keewatin dist in Northwest Territories was added to Ontario in 1912; the prov is governed by a Lieutenant-Governor, a cabinet and a 125-member legislature.

Ontario, lake in North America; the easternmost and the smallest of the Great Lakes; bordered N, W and partly S by Ontario prov, Canada, S and E by New York state, USA; length 311 km; breadth 85 km; max depth 244 m; area 19,011 sq km, of which 10,049 sq km is in Canada; connected in the SW with L Erie via the Niagara river and the Welland Ship Canal through which it receives the drainage of the entire Great Lakes system; the outlet of the lake is the St Lawrence river in the NE; receives the Black, Oswego and Genesee rivers (New York) and the Trent river (Ontario); the Welland Ship Canal carries shipping around Niagara Falls; the lake is connected with the Hudson river via a branch of the New York State Barge Canal system which terminates at Oswego; it is connected with Georgian Bay and L Huron via the Trent Canal; the Rideau Canal connects the port of Kingston (Ontario) with Ottawa; other Canadian ports include Hamilton, Toronto, Cobourg; major New York state ports include Rochester, Oswego; the lake is never ice-bound.

Ontario, 34 04N 117 39W, pop(1980) 88,820, city in San Bernardino county, SW California, United States; 56 km E of Los Angeles; railway.

Onteniente *on-ten-yen'tay*, 38 50N 0 35W, pop(1981) 28,123, town in Valencia prov, E Spain; 24 km SSW of Játiva; economy: textiles, quilts, blankets, olive oil.

Oostende *ōs-ten-de*, dist of West-Vlaanderen (West Flanders) prov, W Belgium; area 292 sq km; pop(1982) 133,142.

Oostende, OSTEND *os'tend* (Eng), OSTENDE *os-tãd'* (Fr), 51 13N 2 55E, pop(1982) 69,331, seaport in Oostende dist, West-Vlaanderen (West Flanders) prov, W Belgium; on the North Sea coast, W of Brugge; railway; principal port for passenger and ferry services to England (Dover and Folkestone); most important seaport and largest seaside resort in Belgium; headquarters of the Belgian fishing fleet; spa resort; event: Blessing of the Sea (1st Sunday of July).

Oosterschelde *ōst'ur-sKHel-du*, EASTERN SCHELDT *-skelt* (Eng), inlet of the North Sea, in Zeeland prov, West Netherlands; a former branch of the R Schelde estuary; the town of Bergen-op-Zoom is at its E end; it is linked to the Westerschelde by a canal.

Oost-Vlaanderen *ōst-vlahn'-dur-un*, EAST FLANDERS (Eng), FLANDRE ORIENTALE *flã'dru or-ee-ã-tahl'* (Fr), prov of W Belgium; area 2,982 sq km; pop(1982) 1,332,547; comprises the 6 dists of Aalst, Dendermonde, Eeklo, Gent, Oudenaarde and Sint-Niklaas; capital Gent; chief towns Aalst, Lokeren and Wetteren; drained by the R Schelde and its tributaries.

Opatija *o'pa-tee-a*, ABBAZIA (Ital), 45 20N 14 18E, pop(1981) 29,274, resort town in NW Hrvatska (Croatia) republic, Yugoslavia; in the Bay of Rijeka on the Adriatic coast of NE Istria, at the foot of Mt Učka; a noted resort for over 100 years with a fine botanic garden and an open-air theatre; originally a winter resort but more recently sand has been imported to provide beaches for summer tourists; railway.

Opava *op'a-va*, 49 58N 17 55E, pop(1984) 60,961, town in Severomoravský region, Czech Socialist Republic, central Czechoslovakia; on R Opava, NW of Ostrava on the Polish frontier; railway; economy: textiles, food processing.

Opole *o-pol'ye*, voivodship in S Poland; bounded S by Czechoslovakia and watered by the R Oder (Odra) and its tributaries; pop(1983) 996,000; area 8,535 sq km; capital Opole; chief towns include Kędzierzyn-Koźle, Nysa, Brzeg, Kluczbork and Prudnik.

Opole, OPPELN (Ger), 50 40N 17 56E, pop(1983) 121,900, river port capital of Opole voivodship, S Poland; on R Oder (Odra), NW of Katowice; the economic centre of Opole Silesia; railway; economy: engineering, cement, furniture, food processing, machinery; monuments: 15-16th-c cathedral, Franciscan church and monastery (13th-c), Piastowska tower; event: oratorio festival in Oct.

Oporto, city in Portugal. See Porto.

Oppegård *op'pu-gor*, 59 56N 10 45E, pop(1980) 16,245, town in Akershus county, SE Norway; on the Oslofjorden (Oslo Fjord), 15 km S of Oslo; railway.

Oppland *op'lahn*, formerly KRISTIANS, a county of S central Norway; area 25,260 sq km; pop(1983) 182,126; capital Lillehammer; drained chiefly by the Lågen, Dokka and Begna rivers; includes the W section of L Mjøsa and Randsfjorden (Rands Fjord); ranges include the Jotunheimen, Rondane, Dovrefjell; mountainous terrain in the N of the county with peaks Galdhøpiggen (2,469 m) and Glittertind (2470 m).

Oradea or **Oradea-Mare** *or-a'dya*, 47 03N 21 55E, pop(1983) 206,206, capital of Bihor county, NW Romania; on R Köos, near Hungarian frontier; airfield; railway; economy: textiles, machinery, food processing, woodwork.

Orahovac *or-a'ho-vats*, 42 24N 20 40E, pop(1981) 61,178, town in autonomous province of Kosovo, SW Srbija (Serbia) republic, Yugoslavia; 24 km N of Prizren.

Oran *o-rahn'*, WAHRAN, 35 45N 0 38W, pop(1984e) 450,000, seaport in Oran dept, N Algeria, N Africa; 355 km W of Alger; founded during the 8th century; has been under the rule of Arabs, Spaniards (1509-1708), Turks (1708-32), and French (1831-1962); a French naval force was largely destroyed by the British navy nearby on 3 July 1940; point of landing for a large part of Allied forces during World War II; former French naval base 8 km away at Mers el Kabir; university (1965); railway; airport; economy: iron, textiles, food processing, footwear, cigarettes and trade in grain, wool, vegetables and esparto grass; monuments: 16th-c Santa Cruz fortress, municipal museum with Roman and Punic exhibits.

Orange, 33 19S 149 10E, pop(1981) 27,626, town in Central West stat div, E New South Wales, Australia; 200 km WNW of Sydney; railway; airfield; economy: centre of a sheep-farming and fruit-growing district; wool, domestic appliances.

Orange, 33 47N 117 51W, pop(1980) 91,788, city in Orange county, SW California, United States; N of Santa Ana.

Orange, 40 46N 74 14W, pop(1980) 31,136, town in Essex county, NE New Jersey, United States; residential suburb 6 km WNW of Newark; railway.

Orange Free State, prov in E central South Africa; pop(1985) 1,776,903; area 127,993 sq km; bounded S by the Orange river, NW by the Vaal river and SE by Lesotho; capital Bloemfontein; chief towns include Springfontein, Kroonstad, Bethlehem, Harrismith and Koffiefontein; many settlements date from the Great Trek of 1831; in 1848 Sir Harry Smith claimed the area between the Orange and Vaal rivers as a British territory called the Orange River Sovereignty; independence returned after the Conference of Bloemfontein (1854); treaty with the South African Republic (Transvaal) led to involvement in the South African War (1899-1902); annexed by Great Britain as the Orange River Colony and governed as a Crown Colony until 1907; became the Orange Free State prov within the Union of South Africa in 1910; economy: oil, agricultural equipment, fertilizers, wool, clothing, cement, pharmaceuticals, grain, pottery.

Orange River, ORANJERIVIER (Afrik), river in Lesotho, South Africa and Namibia; rises on the slopes of Mont-aux-Sources (Drakensberg Mountains) in NE Lesotho and flows S and then W into South Africa; a lake is formed by the Hendrik Verwoerd Dam NE of Colesburg; the river then flows NW forming the border between the Orange Free State and Cape provs and is dammed again at the P.K. le Roux Dam before passing Hopetown; W of Douglas it is joined by the Vaal R and changes direction abruptly to flow SE past Prieska before turning NW and W; following the border between South Africa and Namibia it enters the Atlantic Ocean at Alexander Bay; length 2,090 km; main tributaries include the Caledon, the Vaal and the Great Fish rivers.

Orange Walk, dist in N Belize, Central America; bounded W by Guatemala and N by the Rio Hondo where it follows the Mexican frontier; pop(1980) 22,870; area 4,735 sq km; capital Orange Walk; economy: light industry, sugar, timber, fruit, honey.

Orange Walk, 18 06N 88 31W, pop(1980) 8,439, capital of Orange Walk dist, N Belize, Central America; on New river and linked to Belize City by Northern Highway; airfield.

Oranjestad *o-ran'yu-stat*, 12 32N 70 02W, port and capital town of Aruba I, S Netherlands Antilles, E Caribbean; on W coast of the island, 32 km N of the Venezuelan coast.

Oranjestad, ORANGE TOWN (Eng), 17 33N 63 00W, capital town of Sint Eustatius I, N Netherlands Antilles, E Caribbean, 12.8 km NW of St Kitts; monuments: 2 old forts.

Orap'a, 21 18S 25 30E, pop(1981) 5,229, independent township in Central dist, Botswana, S Africa; area 10 sq km; alt 748 m; W of Francistown; a diamond mining centre.

Orchid island, island of Taiwan. See Lan Hsü.

Ordino *or-dee'no*, pop(1982) 780, one of the seven parishes of the Principality of Andorra with a village seat of the same name situated 8 km N of Andorra la Vella in the Valira del Nord valley; alt 1,305 m.

Ordu *or-doo'*, maritime prov in N Turkey, bounded N by the Black Sea; pop(1980) 713,535; area 6,001 sq km; capital Ordu; minerals include copper, zinc and iron.

Ordzhonikidze, formerly DZAUDZHIKAU (1944-54), VLADIKAVKAZ (-1931), 43 00N 44 43E, pop(1983) 296,000, capital city of Severo-Osetinskaya ASSR, Rossiyskaya, Soviet Union; on the R Terek, in the Bol'shoy Kavkaz (Greater Caucasus) range; founded in 1784 as a fortress; university; railway; economy: metallurgy based on zinc and silver, manufacture of tractor and car equipment, textiles, sewing machines, and food products.

Örebro *œr'e-brō*, a county of S central Sweden; contains W half of L Hjälmaren and N part of L Vättern; land area 8,514 sq km; pop(1983) 273,023; capital Örebro; chief towns Karlskoga and Nora.

Örebro, 59 17N 15 13E, pop(1982) 117,258, capital city of Örebro county, S central Sweden; at W end of L Hjälmaren, 160 km W of Stockholm, at mouth of R Svårtan; railway; monuments: 18th-c St Nicholas's church, 16th-c Renaissance castle (restored 1897-1900), neo-Gothic town hall (1856-62); the castle played an important role as the meeting place of the Riksdag (Swedish Parliament).

Or'egon, state in NW United States; bounded N by Washington (mostly along the Columbia river), E by Idaho (partly following the Snake river), S by California and Nevada and W by the Pacific Ocean; Oregon is split in two by the Cascade Range; to the W lies the fertile Willamette river valley, with the Coast Ranges beyond; to the E lies the High Desert, a semi-arid plateau used for ranching and for wheat-growing; in the NE are the Blue Mts and the Wallowa Mts and in the S are the Fremont Mts and the Steens Mts; the highest point is Mt Hood (3,424 m); Oregon contains several small lakes, including Upper Klamath lake and L Albert in the S; major rivers include the Columbia, Snake and Willamette; Crater Lake National Park is situated in the SW; Oregon produces over one-quarter of the USA's softwood and plywood; industries include electronics and food processing; chief agricultural products include livestock, wheat, dairy produce, fruit, vegetables; a fur-trading post was established in 1811 on the site of the present town of Astoria, NW Oregon; the state was occupied by both Britain and the USA from 1818 to 1846 when the international boundary was settled on the 49th parallel; Oregon became a territory in 1848 and a state (33rd) with its present boundaries in 1859; the population of the state grew after 1842 with incoming settlers following the Oregon Trail and again in the late 19th century after the completion of the transcontinental railway; also known as the 'Beaver State'; pop(1980) 2,633,105; area 250,078 sq km; capital Salem; chief cities include Portland, Albany, Eugene, Springfield; the state is divided into 36 counties:

County	*area (sq km)*	*pop(1980)*
Baker	7,987	16,134
Benton	1,765	68,211
Clackamas	4,862	241,919
Clatsop	2,093	32,489
Columbia	1,693	35,646
Coos	4,176	64,047
Crook	7,758	13,091
Curry	4,235	16,992
Deschutes	7,865	62,142
Douglas	13,114	93,748
Gilliam	3,154	2,057
Grant	11,765	8,210
Harney	26,452	8,314
Hood River	1,355	15,835
Jackson	7,246	132,456
Jefferson	4,651	11,599
Josephine	4,264	58,855
Klamath	15,480	59,117
Lake	21,453	7,532
Lane	11,861	275,226
Lincoln	2,548	35,264
Linn	5,970	89,495
Malheur	25,639	26,896
Marion	3,078	204,692
Morrow	5,314	7,519
Multnomah	1,121	562,640
Polk	1,927	45,203
Sherman	2,150	2,172
Tillamook	2,863	21,164
Umatilla	8,367	58,861
Union	5,291	23,921

contd

County	*area (sq km)*	*pop(1980)*
Wallowa	8,190	7,273
Wasco	6,198	21,732
Washington	1,885	245,808
Wheeler	4,454	1,513
Yamhill	1,859	55,332

Orel *ahr-yol'*, 52 58N 36 04E, pop(1983) 322,000, capital city of Orel oblast, central European Rossiyskaya, Soviet Union; at the confluence of the rivers Oka and Orlik; an agricultural trade centre, founded in 1566 as a fortress; in the 1860s Orel served as a place of exile for Polish insurgents, and later a central prison was built to accommodate prisoners on their way to Siberia; the author Ivan Turgenev was born here; railway junction; on the Moskva (Moscow)-Simferopol' highway; economy: machine building, foodstuffs, steel-rolling, textiles, footwear; monuments: Nikolo-Peskovskaia church (1790) and the Church of the Archangel Michael (1722-1801).

Orem *ōr'em*, 40 19N 111 42W, pop(1980) 52,399, town in Utah county, N central Utah, United States; near L Utah, 9 km N of Provo; economy: steel, electronic components and canned foods.

Orenburg, formerly CHKALOV, 51 50N 55 00E, pop(1983) 505,000, capital city of Orenburgskaya oblast, Rossiyskaya, Soviet Union; on the R Ural; founded as a fortress in 1735; railway; airfield; economy: machine tools, building materials, clothing, knitwear, textiles; monument: fortress (1743).

Orense *o-ren'say*, mountainous prov in Galicia region, NW Spain; on the Portuguese frontier crossed by the fertile valley of the R Minho (Miño) and its tributaries; pop(1981) 411,339; area 7,278 sq km; capital Orense; economy: fishing, foodstuffs, mining of non-ferrous metals, slate quarrying (Carballeda), wooden and metal products.

Orense, AURIUM (Lat), 42 19N 7 55W, pop(1981) 96,085, capital of Orense prov, Galicia, NW Spain; on R Minho (Miño), 521 km NW of Madrid; bishopric; railway; economy: furniture, fishing, clothes, food processing, metal products, ironware, flour, timber; sulphur springs; monument: 12-13th-c Gothic cathedral.

Orestiás *or-est-ee-ahs'*, 41 30N 26 33E, pop(1981) 12,685, town in Évros nome (dept), Thráki region, Greece, close to the border with Turkey; railway.

Øresund *ur'u-soon*, THE SOUND (Eng), strait between Sjælland (Zealand) I, Denmark and S Sweden, connecting the Kattegat with the Baltic Sea; width of narrowest section 6 km.

Orhon Gol *or-kon*, river in Mongolia; flows for 1,117 km from the NE edge of the Gobi Desert to the W of Altanbulag, where it joins the Selenge river.

Orihuela *o-ree-way'la*, 38 05N 0 56W, pop(1981) 49,851, town in Alicante prov, Valencia, E Spain; on the R Segura, 28 km NE of Murcia; bishopric; mineral springs; railway; economy: hemp, fruit, vegetables, cotton, almonds, cereals.

Orinoco *or-in-ō'ko*, river in Venezuela, 2560 km long, rising in the Serra Parima and flowing in a wide curve W, N and E until it empties into the Atlantic through a wide delta which begins c.240 km from the Atlantic. In S Venezuela the river forks, the S branch (Casiquiare) flowing 288 km to the Río Negro, the other forming a section of the Columbia-Venezuela boundary; it passes over the cataracts of Maipures and Atures and curves round, through the Venezuelan *llanos*, crossing the width of the country; its many tributaries include the Caroni, the Pao, the Caura and the Apure.

Orissa *ur-i'sa*, state in E India; pop(1981) 26,272,054; area 155,782 sq km; bounded N by Bihar state, NW by West Bengal state, E by the Bay of Bengal, S by Andhra Pradesh state and W by Maydhya Pradesh state; the state is divided into 13 administrative divisions; capital

Bhubaneswar; Orissa is governed by a 147-member Legislative Assembly; the Eastern Ghats are located in the S central area of the state; the R Mahanadi is dammed to form the Hirakaud Reservoir; completed in 1957, this is the largest earth dam in the world; other rivers draining the state include the Brahmani, Burhābalangar, Tel, Indravati, Nagavali, Vamsadhara and the Sabari; Chilika Lake, separated from the Bay of Bengal by a narrow spit, is a major lagoon on the E coast of Orissa; the lake, originally a bay, has been silted up by deposits from the monsoon tides; agriculture employs almost 80% of the state's population; rice is the principal crop, although wheat, oilseed, sugar cane and jute are also grown; 43% of the land area of the state is forested, producing the woods sal, teak, kendu, sandalwood, bija and bamboo; Orissa produces 95% of the Indian national output of chromite, 50% of its dolomite, 80% of its graphite, 16% of its iron ore and 20% of its limestone; manufacturing industries include cement, fertilizer, industrial explosives, sugar, glass, machinery and textiles; cottage industries include handloom weaving, basket manufacture and wooden articles; tourism is important in the region known as the Golden Triangle (Konark, Puri and Bhubaneswar); Orissa was ceded to the mahrattas by Alivardi Khan in 1751, later to be conquered by the British in 1803; it was a subdivision of Bengal until 1912 when the province of Bihar and Orissa was created; in 1936 Orissa became a separate province and in 1948-49 the area of Orissa almost doubled with the addition of 24 princely states; Orissa became a constituent state of the Indian Union in 1950.

Oristano *o-rees-tah'no*, prov of Sardegna (Sardinia), Italy; pop(1981) 155,043; area 2,631 sq km; capital Oristano.

Oristano, 39 54N 8 36E, pop(1981) 29,424, capital town of Oristano prov, W Sardegna (Sardinia), Italy; on the Golfo de Oristano, 91 km NW of Cagliari, on the main highway between Cagliari and Sassari; railway; economy: potteries; monument: 18th-c cathedral.

Orizaba *ō-ri-sah'ba*, 18 51N 97 08W, pop(1980) 114,848, town in Veracruz state, SE Mexico; 150 km E of Puebla; favourite resort of the Emperor Maximilian; railway; economy: the natural springs in the valley are used for textile and paper manufacturing; monuments: much of the town was destroyed by an earthquake in 1973; the Palacio Municipal is a cast-iron Belgian pavilion brought in pieces from France after the 19th-c Paris Exhibition.

Orkney *ork'nay*, group of islands off the coast of NE Scotland; separated from the Scottish mainland to the S by the Pentland Firth; consists of 15 main islands and numerous smaller islands; approx 20 islands are inhabited; the islands are generally low lying, but have steep, high cliffs on the W side; pop(1981) 19,056; area 976 sq km; capital: Kirkwall, on the island of Mainland; Orkney and Shetland were a Norse dependency from the 9th century onwards; in 1468 the king of Norway and Denmark pledged the islands to Scotland's king, James III, as security for the dowry of Margaret, James's queen; since the dowry was not paid, the islands were annexed to Scotland in 1472; economy: fishing; farming (Orkney has a fertile soil for agriculture); there is a North Sea oil terminal on the island of Flotta, and oil service bases at Stromness on Mainland and at Lyness on Hoy; monuments: the islands contain several prehistoric remains: the Standing Stones at Stenness (W Mainland), which date from approx 3000 BC; Skara Brae (W Mainland, 12 km N of Stromness), a Neolithic village which was lived in from approx 3000 BC to approx 2700 BC; Skara Brae has remained well-preserved because it was covered by sand for 4500 years; a storm revealed the low stone 'houses' in 1850; to the NW of the island of Hoy is an isolated stack (height 137 m) known as the Old Man of Hoy; Scapa Flow, a sea area bounded N by Mainland, E by the islands of Burray and South Ronaldsay and W by the islands of Flotta and Hoy, was used in World Wars I and II as one of Britain's major naval anchorages; the German Fleet surrendered here in 1918; now the island of Flotta has been developed as an oil terminal for North Sea oil; 3 MW wind-powered generator on Burgar Hill was switched on in 1987.

Orlan'do, 28 33N 81 23W, pop(1980) 128,291, county seat of Orange county, central Florida, United States; 125 km NE of Tampa; railway; airfield; economy: tourism, aerospace and electronic industries, trade in citrus fruit and vegetables; monument: Walt Disney World.

Orléannais *or-lay-a-nay*, former prov in N central France, now occupying the depts of Loir-et-Cher, Loiret and parts of Eure-et-Loire and Seine-et-Oise; includes the dists of Beauce, Sologne and part of the Gâtinais; its chief town is Orléans; includes the Forest of Orléans and extensive areas of reclaimed marshland in Sologne.

Orléans *or-lay-ã*, AURELIANUM (anc), 47 54N 1 52E, pop(1982) 105,589, ancient town and capital of Loiret dept, Centre region, central France; on the right bank of the R Loire, in a fertile plain of the Loire Basin, 92 km SSW of Paris; a road and rail junction in a fruit and vegetable growing region; associated with Joan of Arc, 'The Maid of Orléans', who raised the English siege here on 8 May 1429 and turned the tide of French defeat; bishopric; university (1309); economy: textiles, clothing, blankets, food processing, sparkling wines, agricultural equipment; monuments: 13-16th-c cathedral, destroyed by Protestants in 1568 and restored by Henry IV in Gothic style; 16th-c town hall; episcopal palace; museum of fine art; event: Feast of Joan of Arc (7-8 May).

Orlova *or'lov-ah*, 49 50N 18 21E, pop(1984) 33,016, town in Severomoravský region, Czech Socialist Republic, central Czechoslovakia; NE of Ostrava, near the Polish frontier; railway; economy: coal mining, metallurgy.

Orms'kirk, 53 35N 2 54W, pop(1981) 22,715, town in West Lancashire dist, Lancashire, NW England; 12 km SE of Southport; railway; economy: engineering, textiles, paper.

Orne *orn*, dept in Basse-Normandie region of W France, comprising 3 arrond, 40 cantons and 507 communes; pop(1982) 295,472; area 6,103 sq km; its elevated centre forms a watershed between N (Orne, Dives and Touques) and S (upper Sarthe, Mayenne and Huisne) flowing rivers; the dept is crossed by the Collines du Perche (E) and the Collines de Normandie (W); capital Alençon; the Parc Normandie-Maine regional nature park lies partly within this dept.

Orne, river in NW France rising E of Sees in Orne dept; flows NW and N through Calvados dept, past Caen, to meet the English Channel at Ouistreham; length 152 km; tributary R Odon.

Örnsköldsvik *urn'shults-veek*, 63 19N 18 45E, pop(1982) 60,234, town in NE of Västernorrland county, E Sweden; on the Gulf of Bothnia; the town developed near a deep-water harbour and around sawmills; the harbour is ice-free for 11 months of the year; railway terminus.

Oro, El *el ō'rō*, prov in SW Ecuador; on the Golfo de Guayaquil, an inlet of the Pacific Ocean; a narrow coastal plain (W) rises steeply into the Andean uplands (E); pop(1982) 334,872; area 5,810 sq km; capital Machala; economy: tobacco, bananas, timber, fishing, minerals.

Orodara *ō-ro-da'ra*, 11 00N 4 54W, town in SW Burkina, W Africa; between Bobo Dioulasso and Sikasso (Mali).

Orontes, river in SW Asia. See 'Āsi.

Orosháza *o'rosh-hazo*, 46 32N 20 42E, pop(1984e) 36,000, town in Békés county, S Hungary; WSW of Békéscsaba; railway; economy: grain, wine, livestock trade, glassware

Oroszlany *or'osh-lah-ny'*, 47 30N 18 25E, pop(1981) 21,000, town in Komárom county, N Hungary; SW of Tatabánya, near the border with Fejér county.

Orsk, 51 13N 58 35E, pop(1983) 259,000, city in Orenburgskaya oblast, Rossiyskaya, Soviet Union; at the confluence of the Ural and Or' rivers, in the S Ural'skiy Khrebet (Ural Mts); founded as a fortress in 1735 and became a city in 1865; it has rich iron, copper, nickel, and coal deposits; railway; airfield; economy: non-ferrous metallurgy, machine building, foodstuffs, clothing.

Ørsta *ur'sta*, 62 12N 6 09E, pop(1980) 10,157, town in Møre og Romsdal county, W Norway.

Orūmīyeh *o-room'ya*, formerly REZA'IYEH *rez-a-ee'a*,

37 32N 45 02E, pop(1983) 262,588, capital city of Orūmīyeh dist, Āzarbāyān-e Gharbī, NW Iran; 40 km from the Turkish border, on the R Bardehsūr, close to the W shore of Daryācheh-ye Orūmīyeh (L Urmia); airfield.

Orumīyeh, Daryacheh-ye, LAKE URMIA *ur'mee-ah* (Eng), MATIANUS (anc), shallow saline lake in NW Iran, W of Tabrīz; area 4,700 sq km; max depth 16 m; Sharafkhāneh is its only port, on NE shore.

Oruro *o-roo'rō*, dept in W Bolivia; includes L Poopó (E) and Salar de Coipasa (SW); separated from Chile (W) by Andean Cordillera Occidental and from Potosí dept (SE) by Cordillera de Azanaques (part of the Cordillera Oriental); the Altiplano (with altitudes over 3,500 m) between ranges is drained by the Desaguadero and Lauca rivers; severe climate and arid soil conditions prevail, but the dept is rich in minerals; pop(1982) 385,121; area 53,588 sq km; capital Oruro; chief town Huanuni; economy: tin, lead, silver mining at Bolivar and San José, and tin mining at Huanuni and Santa Fe.

Oruro, 17 59S 67 08W, pop(1982) 132,213, capital of Cercado prov, Oruro, W Bolivia; built on the slopes of a hill at an alt of 3,706 m; the population is predominantly Indian; good fishing on L Uru Uru to SW of the city; there are hot springs at Obrajes; university (1892); railway; airfield; economy: important as a railway centre and for tin, silver and tungsten mining; a 20,000 tons-a-year smelter and metallurgy complex has been built nearby at Vinto, and includes tin and antimony foundries; a pesticides plant has also been built with Argentine assistance; monument: Casa de la Cultura, the former Patiño mansion, is now a museum; events: La Diablada carnival takes place on the Saturday before Ash Wednesday; there is a daily market near the railway station.

Orust *oo'rust*, Swedish island in the Kattegat, SW of L Vänern, off SW coast of Sweden, 45 km NW of Göteborg (Gothenburg), separated from the mainland by a narrow channel 1.6-5 km wide; area 346 sq km; length 22 km; width 16 km; second largest island in Sweden; administered by Göteborg och Bohus county.

Orūzgān, prov in central Afghanistan; pop(1984e) 482,091; area 29,295 sq km; capital Tarīn Kowt; Kohi Kurd is the highest point at 3,830 m.

Ōsaka *ō-sa'ka*, formerly NANIWA, 34 40N 135 30E, pop(1980) 2,648,180, port capital of Ōsaka prefecture, Kinki region, S Honshū island, Japan; on NE shore of Ōsaka-wan Bay; Ōsaka gained importance in the 16th century under Toyotomi Hideyoshi who had a castle built here; at the end of the 19th century the port was opened to foreign trade; the city was almost completely destroyed in World War II; university (1931); university of foreign studies (1949); subway; railway; airport; economy: steel, textiles, chemicals, brewing, car manufacturing, printing; monuments: Ōsaka Castle tower is now a museum containing documents relating to the history of the castle and of the Toyotomi family; municipal museum; electric science museum; the Fujita museum contains a collection of porcelain made for use in the tea ceremony; Shintenno ji temple, founded by Prince Shotoku at the end of the 6th century; the Sumiyoshi Shrine is said to have been founded by Empress Jingu in the 3rd century after her return from Korea, but the present buildings date from 1808; the Mint, founded in 1871, is the only one in Japan; in Shinsaibashi, Ōsaka's leading shopping district, is the Dotombori river, a man-made canal completed in 1615; events: Court dances at Shintenno ji temple on 22 April; Rice Planting festival at Sumiyoshi Shrine on 14 June; Tenjin Matsuri, races on the river between decorated boats on 24-25 July; Sumiyoshi Matsuri shrine festival on 31 Aug.

Oshawa *o'sha-wa*, 43 53N 78 51W, pop(1981) 117,519, town in SE Ontario, SE Canada; on N shore of L Ontario, 48 km ENE of Toronto; the French built a trading post here in 1752; in 1795 United Empire Loyalists arrived here from the USA; in 1924 Oshawa became a city; the car industry arrived in the 1920s; Oshawa's General Motors plant is the largest car manufacturing centre in Canada; railway; monuments: the Canadian Transportation Museum contains an exhibition of antique cars, illustrating the history of the motor vehicle; Parkwood, the home of Col Sam McLaughlin who became president of General Motors of Canada.

Osh'kosh, 44 01N 88 33W, pop(1980) 49,620, county seat of Winnebago county, E Wisconsin, United States; on L Winnebago, at the mouth of the R Fox; named after a famous Menominee Indian chief; established in 1836; developed as an important timber centre; achieved city status in 1853; university (1877); railway; summer resort.

Oshogbo *ōsh-og'bō*, 7 50N 4 35E, pop(1981e) 355,500, town in Oyo state, W Nigeria, W Africa; on the R Niger, 80 km NE of Ibadan; economy: dyed cloths and brewing; monuments: museum, shrine to the goddess Oshuno; event: Oshun festival in July-Aug.

Osijek *o'si-yek*, ESSEG (Ger), ESZÉK *es'ayk* (Hung), MURSA MAJOR (anc), 45 33N 18 42E, pop(1981) 158,790, industrial river port town in NE Hrvatska (Croatia) republic, Yugoslavia; on R Drava; site of a former Roman colony; cultural and educational centre; university (1975); airfield; railway; economy: petroleum, electrical goods, chemicals, machine tools; wood products; monument: cathedral; Belje state-run model farm to the N; Kopački Rit marshland and wildlife reserve to the E.

Ösling or **Oesling** *æs'ling*, a geographical region in the Ardennes in N Luxembourg; wooded and less fertile than the Gutland or 'good land' to the S but largely agricultural; occupies 828 sq km (32%) of Luxembourg.

Oslo *os'lō*, formerly CHRISTIANIA or KRISTIANIA, 59 55N 10 45E, pop(1983) 448,775, capital city of Norway and of Oslo and Akershus counties; at the head of Oslofjorden (Oslo Fjord), SE Norway; founded in the 11th century the city came under the influence of the Hanseatic League in the 14th century; its importance dwindled in the 16th century; the city was destroyed by fire in 1624, but was rebuilt by Christian IV of Denmark and Norway and renamed Christiania; experienced a cultural revival in the 19th century with notable writers such as Ibsen and Bjørnson; Oslo became capital of independent Norway in 1905 and was renamed Oslo in 1925; see of a Lutheran and a Roman Catholic bishop; university (1811); railway; airports: economy: metalworking, foodstuffs, clothing, shipbuilding, trade in timber, paper; the ice-free port is the largest in Norway and is the base of a large merchant shipping fleet; monuments: 17th-c cathedral; national gallery; royal palace (1825-1848); late 13th-c Akershus Castle; Norwegian folk museum (Bygdøy).

Oslofjorden, OSLO FJORD (Eng), inlet of the Skagerrak, extending 100 km inland from Faerder in S to Oslo in N, in Akershus, Østfold, Vestfold and Buskerud counties, SE Norway.

Osnabrück *ōz'na-brük*, 52 17N 8 03E, pop(1983) 156,100, manufacturing city in SW Niedersachsen (Lower Saxony) prov, W Germany, in the Haase valley, 48 km NE of Münster; university (1973); bishopric; railway, linked by a branch canal with the Mittelland Canal; economy: iron and steel, machine tools, cars, metalworking, textiles, paper-making; monument: 13th-c cathedral.

Osorno *ō-sor'nō*, 40 34S 73 08W, pop(1982) 93,654, capital of Osorno prov, Los Lagos, S central Chile; founded in 1558, it was destroyed soon after and was later settled by German immigrants whose descendants still live in the area; railway; linked to the Argentinian town of San Carlos de Bariloche by a road E through the Puyehue pass.

Oss, 51 46N 5 32E, pop(1984e) 50,086, city in Noord Brabant prov, S Netherlands; S of the R Maas and 18 km ENE of 's-Hertogenbosch; railway; economy: carpets.

Ossa, Mount, mountain in NW central Tasmania; highest point on the island, rising to 1,617 m; in the 1,319 sq km Cradle Mountain-Lake St Clair national park which was established in 1922.

Os'sett, 53 41N 1 35W, pop(1981) 20,415, town in Wakefield borough, West Yorkshire, N England; part of West

Yorkshire urban area; 5 km W of Wakefield; economy: textiles, engineering.

Ossiacher See *o'see-aKH-ar zay*, lake in Kärnten state, SE Austria, NE of Villach; area 10.6 sq km; length 11 km; width 1 km; max depth 47 m; 3rd largest lake in Kärnten state, surrounded by wooded hill slopes and mountain peaks; popular for water sports.

Oste *ō'stu*, river in N Niedersachsen (Lower Saxony) prov, W Germany; formed 11 km SW of Zeven, flows N past Bremervörde, to the R Elbe estuary 5 km N of Neuhaus; length 160 km; navigable length 82 km; drainage basin area 1,714 sq km.

Ostend, seaport in Belgium. See Oostende.

Östergötland *œs-ter-yœt'land*, county of SE Sweden, E of L Vättern; land area 10,566 sq km; pop(1983) 392,195; capital Linköping; largest town Norrköping; the Göta Canal, connecting L Vättern with the Baltic Sea, bisects the county S of Norrköping; the E coastline is well indented.

Ostermyra, town in Finland. See Seinajoki.

Östersund *œs'ter-soond*, 63 10N 14 40E, pop(1982) 55,982, capital town of Jämtland county, W Sweden; on elevated land above the E shore of L Storsjön; founded by Gustav III in 1786, it has preserved its original rectangular street plan; railway; economy: furniture, machinery.

Østfold *œst'fold*, formerly SMAALENENE *smaw-le-nay'ne*, county of SE Norway, on the E of Oslofjorden (Oslo Fjord), drained chiefly by the Glåma; area 4,183 sq km; pop(1983) 234,726; capital Moss; largest town Fredrikstad.

Ostrava *os'tra-va*, 49 50N 18 13E, pop(1984) 323,732, industrial capital of Severomoravský region, Czech Socialist Republic, central Czechoslovakia; near R Odra where it meets the R Ostravice; 4th largest city in Czechoslovakia; important in medieval times as a result of its strategic position guarding the Moravian lowlands; airport; railway; economy: metal industries, bituminous coal mining, chemicals, machinery, rolling stock.

Ostrołęka *os-tro-lek'a*, voivodship in NE central Poland; watered by the R Narew and its tributaries including the Omulew; pop(1983) 379,000; area 6,498 sq km; capital Ostrołęka; chief towns include Przasnysz and Wyszków.

Ostrołęka, 53 05N 21 32E, pop(1983) 41,800, capital of Ostrołęka voivodship, NE central Poland; on R Narew, NE of Warszawa (Warsaw); economy: cellulose, paper, power and heat plant; monument: Baroque 17th-c Bernardine church and monastery.

Ostrowiec Świętokrzyski *ost-ro'vyetz shvyet-o-krish'ki*, OSTROVETS (Rus), 50 58N 21 22E, pop(1983) 69,800, town in Kielce voivodship, S central Poland; on R Kamienna, S of Warszawa (Warsaw), in the NE foothills of the Gory Świętokrzyskie; railway; economy: iron, steel, metallurgy; monument: museum with a collection of Ćmielów porcelain.

Os'westry, 52 52N 3 04W, pop(1981) 13,264, town in Oswestry dist, Shropshire, W central England; 26 km NW of Shrewsbury; the town was named after St Oswald who was killed here in 642; economy: plastics; monuments: castle and 15th-c grammar school.

Otago *ō-tay'gō*, statistical division of South Island, New Zealand; bounded S by Southland division and N by Canterbury and Westland divisions; stretches from E to W coasts across the S tip of the Southern Alps; area 37,105 sq km; pop(1981) 183,559; Dunedin is the chief town.

Otavalo *o-ta-va'lō*, 0 13N 78 15W, pop(1982) 17,469, town in Imbabura prov in the Andean Sierra of N Ecuador; railway; economy: ceramics, woollens; the town has a notable market (Tuesday and Saturday).

Oti *ō'tee*, river in W Africa; rises in S Burkina and flows SW across the N tip of Togo past Mango, it subsequently forms about 95 km of the border between Togo and Ghana before entering Ghana and finally flowing into NE L Volta; length about 500 km.

Ot'ley, 53 54N 1 41W, pop(1981) 14,250, market town in Leeds borough, West Yorkshire, N England; on the R Wharfe, 15 km NW of Leeds; the town's market regulations date back to 1222; birthplace of Thomas Chippendale (1711-79), the cabinetmaker who gave his name to a style of furniture; economy: textiles, engineering, printing; monuments: 7th-c All Saints' church.

Ot'ra, river in S Norway; flows S through Aust-Agder and Vest-Agder counties to discharge into the Skagerrak at Kristiansand; length 242 km.

Ōtsu *ōt'soo*, 35 00N 135 50E, pop(1980) 215,321, capital of Shiga prefecture, Kinki region, S Honshū island, Japan; at the S end of L Biwa-ko; railway.

Ottawa *o'ta-wa*, 45 25N 75 43W, pop(1981) 295,163, capital of Canada; in SE Ontario, SE Canada; situated on the Ottawa river at its junction with the Rideau river; on the border with Québec prov, opposite the city of Hull with which it is connected by 2 bridges; founded in 1826 by Colonel By and named Bytown, as the headquarters of the English Royal Engineers who had come to build the Rideau Canal; its name was changed in 1854 to Ottawa; chosen as Canadian capital by Queen Victoria in 1858, and became capital of the new Dominion of Canada in 1867; University of Ottawa (1848); Carleton University (1942); railway; airport; economy: pulp and paper, aluminium, steel, bronze, clothing, food processing, watches and clocks, glass; monuments: the parliament buildings (built 1859-65 on Parliament Hill) were burnt in 1916 and later rebuilt to include the 88 m-high Peace Tower, a memorial to Canada's war dead; the Eternal Flame in the centre of Parliament Hill was first lit in 1967 in Canada's centennial year to symbolize unity; also on Parliament Hill are several monuments to former Prime Ministers and to those statesmen of the various colonies of British North America who played a leading part in uniting Canada into one dominion; the National War Memorial in Confederation Square was unveiled on 21 May 1939 by King George VI in memory of Canadians killed in World War I; the War Museum contains relics from both World Wars and from the war in Korea; National Library; National Gallery of Canada; National Museum of Man; National Museum of Natural Sciences; Museum of Science and Technology; events: Changing of the Guard on Parliament Hill (every morning at 10.00 am during the summer); Tulip Festival in May.

Ottawa, RIVIÈRE DES OUTAOUAIS (Fr), river in Ontario and Québec provs, central Canada; largest tributary of the St Lawrence; rises in the Laurentian Plateau, issuing from Grand Lac Victoria, in W Québec SE of Val d'Or; flows W through Réservoir Decelles, Lac Simard and Lac des Quinze to L Timiskaming on the Ontario-Québec border; from there it flows S and SE over the Long Sault Rapids to Mattawa, and then generally ESE, past Petawawa, Pembroke and Ottawa to the St Lawrence SW of Montréal; length 1,271 km; forms the border between Ontario and Québec provs for most of its course; the lower river has numerous rapids which are used to generate hydroelectric power; major tributaries include the Noire, Coulonge, Gatineau and Lièvre rivers (N) and the Montréal, Petawawa, Madawaska, Mississippi and Rideau rivers (S); connected with L Ontario via the Rideau Canal; the Ottawa river valley was an important route for explorers, fur traders and missionaries.

Ottum'wa (Algonquian, 'swift water'), 41 01N 92 25W, pop(1980) 27,381, county seat of Wapello county, SE Iowa, United States; on the R Des Moines, 120 km SE of Des Moines; railway.

Ötztaler Alpen *œts'taler al'pen*, ÖTZTAL ALPS (Eng), mountain range in Tirol state, W Austria, rising to 3,774 m at Wildspitze, Austria's 2nd highest peak.

Ouaddaï *oo-wo-day'*, prefecture in E central Chad, N central Africa; pop(1979) 347,000; area 76,240 sq km; R Batha flows W from its source SE of Abéché; capital Abéché; chief towns Mongororo, Goz Beïda, Mourra, Tilégey and Manga.

Ouagadougou *wah-ga-doo'goo*, 12 20N 1 40W, pop(1985) 442,223, capital of Burkina, W Africa; 680 km W of Bamako (Mali) and 400 km ENE of Niamey (Niger); part of the Ivory Coast until 1947; capital of the Mossi empire from the 15th century onwards; university (1969); airfield; terminus of the railway line from Abidjan (Nigeria); economy: textiles, soap, vegetable oil and trade in groundnuts, millet and livestock; monuments: the city centre avenue (Champs Elysées) has a former governor's palace at one end and a neo-romanesque cathedral at the other; palace of Moro Naba, emperor of the Mossi.

Ouahigouya *wa-hee-goo'ya*, 13 31N 2 20W, pop(1982) 38,374, town in N Burkina, W Africa; 160 km NW of Ouagadougou.

Ouaka *oo-wa'ka*, prefecture in Central African Republic; the land rises from the R Ubangi on the S border; the prefecture is watered by the Kandjia and Ouaka rivers which flow SW to meet the R Ubangi; pop(1968) 190,972; area 49,900 sq km; chief town Bambari.

Ouargla *war'gla*, largest department of Algeria, N Africa; E Algeria, S of Atlas Saharien; area 559,234 sq km; pop(1982) 237,527; chief town Ouargla; economy: oil exploration.

Oudenaarde *ow-dun-ahr'du*, dist of Oost-Vlaanderen (East Flanders) prov, W Belgium; area 418 sq km; pop(1982) 112,402.

Oudenaarde, AUDENARDE *ōd-nahrd* (Fr), 50 50N 3 37E, pop(1982) 27,226, town in Oudenaarde dist, Oost-Vlaanderen (East Flanders) prov, W Belgium; long famous for its carpet-weaving, its tapestries are still an attraction (birthplace of the art of tapestry-making); on 11 July, 1708, Marlborough and Prince Eugene defeated the French army under Vendôme near Oudenaarde; railway; monuments: town hall (1526-37), church of Onze Lieve Vrouw Pamele (begun 1235).

Oudômxai *ow-dom say*, prov (*khowèng*) in W Laos, SE Asia; capital Ban Houayxay.

Oudtshoorn *oots'horn*, 33 35S 22 12E, town in S Cape prov, South Africa; 352 km E of Cape Town in the Little Karoo; centre of the ostrich-farming industry; Cango limestone caves nearby.

Oued Eddahab *wed ed-a'hab*, OUED ED-DAHAB, prov in Western Sahara, NW Africa; pop(1982) 21,496; area 50,880 sq km; occupied by Morocco.

Oued-Zem *wed-zem'*, 32 55N 6 33W, pop(1982) 58,744, town in W Morocco, N Africa, 128 km SE of Casablanca, on the E edge of the Plateau des Phosphates; railway; economy: phosphate and iron mining, flour milling.

Ouémé *way'may*, low lying coastal prov in S Benin, W Africa; the R Ouémé follows the NW border; economy: salt and limestone processing.

Ouémé, river in Benin, W Africa; rises in the Atakora Mts and flows S for 480 km to its delta on the Gulf of Guinea, near Cotonou, where it empties into L Nokoué; its main tributaries include the Okpara and Zou rivers.

Ouessant, Ile d' *eel dwessã*, USHANT (Eng), UXANTIS (anc), island off the coast of Finistère dept, NW France; area 15 sq km; length 7 km; chief town is Lampaul; scene of naval battles in 1778 and 1794 between the French and English.

Ouham *oo-am'*, prefecture in N Central African Republic; watered by the Bakassa and Ouham rivers which flow NE; pop(1968) 262,998; area 52,250 sq km; chief town Bossangoa; other towns include Kouki, Batangafo, Bouca, Marali and Kabo.

Ouham-Pendé *oo-am-pē-day'*, prefecture in NW Central African Republic; watered by the Pendé (a tributary of the R Logone) and Nana Barya rivers which flow N and NE; pop(1968) 232,283; area 32,100 sq km; chief town Bozoum; other towns include Bocaranga, Paoua, Batara and Beouan.

Oujda *ooj-dah'*, 34 41N 1 45W, pop(1982) 260,082, capital of Oujda prefecture, Oriental prov, NE Morocco, N Africa; close to the Algerian frontier, SE of Melilla; university; railway; airfield; economy: trade in wool, grain, fruit and wine.

Oulu *ow'loo*, ULEABORG *u'lay-o-bor'yu* (Swed), a prov in central Finland; the 5th largest lake in Finland, Oulujärvi, is situated in the S of the prov; drained by the rivers Oulujoki and Iijoki; area 61,579 sq km; pop(1982) 426,155; chief towns include Oulu, Kajaani and Vaala; copper mining at Pyhäsalmi, iron mining at Otanmaki and zinc mining at Vihanti; the Oulanka national park is partially located at the NE corner of the prov.

Oulu, ULEABORG (Swed), 65 00N 25 26E, pop(1982) 96,199, seaport and capital of Oulu prov, W Finland, on the Gulf of Bothnia and at mouth of Oulujoki (R Oulu) where water has been harnessed to produce energy; established in 1605; destroyed by fire in 1822; university (1958); railway; airfield; economy: steel; events: 75 km Tar Ski Race, the world's oldest cross-country ski race (1889); Oulu Music Summer in July-Aug.

Oulujärvi *ow'loo-yer'vi*, ULE TRASK *u'lu-tresk* (Swed), L OULU (Eng), lake in Oulu prov, N central Finland; 80 km SE of Oulu; area 900 sq km; 5th largest lake in Finland; drained to the NW by the Oulujärvi.

Oum-el-Bouaghi *oom-el-bwa'gee*, department of N Algeria, N Africa; area 8,123 sq km; pop(1982) 441,114; chief town Oum-el-Bouaghi.

Ounasjoki *o'nas-yo'kee*, OUNAS (Eng), river in Lappi prov, N Finland, rising on the Norwegian border W of Inarijärvi (L Inari); flows S to meet the Kemijoki at Rovaniemi; length 336 km.

Our *oor*, river in SE Belgium and E Luxembourg, rising NE of St Vith in Belgium; flows 80 km S to join the R Sûre E of Diekirch where it meets the NE border of Luxembourg with W Germany.

Ourthe *oort*, river in SE Belgium; rises in 2 branches, joining 8 km W of Houffalize, Luxembourg prov; flows 160 km NW and N past Esneux, Tilff and Angleur; enters the R Meuse at Liège; receives the R Amblève (N of Comblain-au-Pont) and the R Vesdre at Angleur.

Ouse *ooz*, river in East Sussex, S England; rises 10 km SSW of Crawley and flows E and S for 48 km to meet the English Channel at Newhaven.

Ouse, river in Yorkshire, NE England; formed at the junction of the Ure and Swale rivers near Boroughbridge; flows 96 km SE to meet the R Trent where it becomes the Humber estuary.

Ouse or **Great Ouse**, river rising NW of Brackley in Northamptonshire, central England; flows 256 km past Buckingham and Bedford and through the S fenland, to meet the Wash NNW of King's Lynn.

Ouse or **Little Ouse**, a tributary of the Great Ouse river, E England; flows 38 km W along part of the Norfolk-Suffolk border to meet the Great Ouse at Brandon Creek.

Outokumpu *o'to-koom'poo*, 62 43N 29 05E, pop(1982) 10,131, copper mining town in Pohjois-Karjala prov, SE central Finland; between Joensuu and Kuopio; established in 1968.

Ovalle *ō-val'yay*, 30 36S 71 12W, pop(1982) 52,369, capital of Limarí prov, Coquimbo, N central Chile; situated in the valley of the Limarí river, inland from the sea, railway; economy: the centre of a fruit, sheep-rearing and mining district.

Ovamboland *ō-vam'bō-land*, region in N Namibia, SW Africa; extends W along Namibia-Angola frontier from Okavango river; Etosha salt pans and national park are situated in the S of the region; main indigenous peoples are the Ovambos; area of conflict between SWAPO guerrilla forces based in S Angola and South African forces.

Overijssel or **Overyssel** *ō-fer-īs'el*, pop(1984e) 1,042,100, prov in East Netherlands, bounded on the E by West Germany, on the W by the Ijsselmeer and on the SW by the R Ijssel, drained also by the R Vechte; land area 3,811 sq km; capital Zwolle; chief towns Enschede, Deventer and Hengelo; economy: predominantly mixed farming on the sandier soils of the High Netherlands (SE) while the largely clay and peat soils of the Low Netherlands support livestock farming; there is a large area of arable farming on the E shore of the Ijsselmeer (NW).

Overland Park, 38 58N 94 40W, pop(1980) 81,784, town in Johnson county, E Kansas, United States; suburb 15 km S of Kansas City.

Oviedo *o-vyay'do*, ASTURIAS *as-too'ree-as*, prov in Asturias region, N Spain; includes the Montana de Covadonga o de Pena Santa National Park; pop(1981) 1,127,007; area

10,565 sq km; capital Oviedo; economy: iron and steel, shipbuilding, anthracite mining, electrical equipment, dairy products, tools, cement, mineral water, clothes, pharmaceuticals, metal products, perfume, chemicals.

Oviedo, 43 25N 5 50W, pop(1981) 184,473, capital of Oviedo prov, Asturias, NW Spain; 451 km NW of Madrid; bishopric; university (1608); airport; railway; former capital of Asturias; economy: commerce, cement, pharmaceuticals, domestic appliances, metal products; monument; 14th-c cathedral; events: fiesta of La Ascension in May and fiesta of San Mateo in Sept.

Övör-Hangay *u'vur-KHan'gī*, OEVOERKHANGAI, county in Central Mongolia; pop(1981e) 80,000; area 63,500 sq km; capital Arvayheer; N, NW and W are mountainous, while the Gobi Desert extends into the S and SE; only 2% of the county is forested; ibex, arkali sheep, wild boar, lynxes and wild camel are found; coal, iron ore, copper, fluorspar and fire slate are among the most important natural resources of the county; one of the major livestock rearing counties in Mongolia.

Owendo *o-wen'dō*, 0 21N 9 29E, port on the Atlantic coast of Gabon, W Africa; 20 km S of Libreville on the Gabon estuary; important for the shipment of minerals (chiefly iron ore and manganese).

Owensboro, 37 46N 87 07W, pop(1980) 54,450, county seat of Davies county, W Kentucky, United States; on the R Ohio, 135 km WSW of Louisville; railway; economy: whisky, chemicals, electrical equipment, steel, cigars, furniture, tobacco trade.

Owerri *ō-way'ree*, 5 29N 7 02E, capital of Imo state, S Nigeria, W Africa; 56 km NW of Aba; airfield; economy: leather and brewing.

Ox'ford, OXONIA (Latin), 51 46N 1 15W, pop(1981) 99,195, university and county town in Oxford dist, Oxfordshire, S central England; 80 km WNW of London; the 12th-c university developed from the monastery school of St Frideswide's priory and was granted its first official privileges in 1214; industry is located in the suburb of Cowley; airfield; railway; economy: vehicles, steel products, electrical goods, paper; monuments: 12th-c cathedral, Magdalen College (1458), Merton College (1264), New College (1379), University College (1249), Bodleian Library (1488), Sheldonian theatre (1664-68), Ashmolean museum, Radcliffe camera; events: sunrise service (11th May); St Giles Market (Sept); Eights Week (June-July).

Oxfordshire, county in the S Midlands of England; bounded S by R Thames and Berkshire, W by Gloucestershire and Wiltshire, E by Buckinghamshire, NW by Warwickshire and NE by Northamptonshire; the Cotswold Hills lie to the NW and the Chiltern Hills to the SW; pop(1981) 519,490; area 2,608 sq km; county town Oxford; economy: agriculture, vehicles, paper, textiles; the county is divided into 5 districts:

District	*area (sq km)*	*pop(1981)*
Cherwell	590	112,700
Oxford	36	99,195
South Oxfordshire	687	129,624
Vale of White Horse	581	101,825
West Oxfordshire	715	81,087

Ox'nard, 34 12N 119 11W, pop(1980) 108,195, city in Ventura county, SW California, United States; near the Pacific Ocean, SE of Ventura and c.88 km WNW of Los Angeles; railway; economy: oil refining, sugar processing, fruit and vegetable trade.

Ox'ted, 51 16N 0 01E, pop(1981) 11,833, town in Tandridge dist, Surrey, SE England; 6 km W of Westerham; railway.

Oyem *ō-yem'*, 1 34S 11 31E, capital of Woleu-Ntem prov, N Gabon, W Africa; 275 km NE of Libreville.

Oyo *ō-yō'*, state in SW Nigeria, W Africa; pop(1982e) 8,306,400; area 37,705 sq km; capital Ibadan; chief towns Oyo, Iseyin, Ogbomosho, Ife, Ilesha, Oshogbo, Ila, Ede, and Iwo; agriculture is based on the production of cereals, cocoa, tobacco and palm oil; there are reserves of tin, gold, marble and columbite; economy: mining, iron ore processing, food canning, soft drinks, plastics, cigarettes, tyres, shoes, brewing, wire and cable production, vehicle assembly and rubber products.

Oyo, 7 50N 3 55E, pop(1981e) 207,800, town in Oyo state, W Nigeria, W Africa; 55 km N of Ibadan; Oro and Shango festivals in June and Aug respectively.

Ozark Mountains *ō'zark*, OZARKS (Fr 'aux arks', at the arks), highlands in S central USA; situated between the Arkansas and Missouri rivers, in Missouri, N Arkansas, NE Oklahoma, Kansas and S Illinois; dissected plateau (area c.129,500 sq km, alt generally 300-360 m) of horizontal limestone and dolomite overlying Pre-Cambrian igneous rocks; the Ozarks are highest in Arkansas with the Boston Mts, which rise to 747 m; Bagnell Dam on the Lake of the Ozarks in Missouri produces hydroelectricity.

Ózd *ōzd*, 48 14N 20 15E, pop(1984e) 48,000, town in Borsod-Abaúj-Zemplén county, E Hungary; WNW of Miskolc; economy: steel, iron, lignite.

Ozero Khanka, lake in SE Heilongjiang prov, NE China and SW Sikhote-Alin prov, SE USSR. See Xingkai Hu.

P

Pa-an', 16 51N 97 37E, capital of Kawthulei state, S Burma; on R Salween N of Moulmein and E of Rangoon.

Paarl *pahrl*, 33 45S 18 58E, town in SW Cape prov, South Africa; centre of South Africa's most important wine-producing region, 50 km ENE of Cape Town on the Great Berg river.

Pabna *pab'nu*, region in W Bangladesh; includes Pabna and Sirajganj districts; pop(1981) 3,424,000; area 4,730 sq km; bounded SW by R Ganga (Ganges) and E by the Brahmaputra (Jamuna) river; capital Pabna.

Pabna, 24 00N 89 15E, pop(1981) 109,065, capital of Pabna dist and region, W Bangladesh; NE of the R Ganga (Ganges) and 120 km WNW of Dhākā; economy: engineering, hosiery, rice.

Pacaás Novos, national park in W Rondônia state, Norte region, NW Brazil; area 7,648 sq km; established in 1979; crossed by the Pacaás Novos river.

Pacaraima, Sierra *sye'ra pa-ka-rī'ma*, PAKARAIMA MOUNTAINS (Guyana), mountain range of the Guiana Highlands, South America; extending approx 800 km W-E at a latitude of 4°N; forms the border between Venezuela and Brazil and between Brazil and Guyana; rises to 2,875 m at Monte Roraima and forms the drainage divide between the Orinoco and the Amazon basins.

Pachuca *pa-choo'ka*, PACHUCA DE SOTO, 20 10N 98 44W, pop(1980) 135,248, capital of Hidalgo state, central Mexico; 88 km NE of Ciudad de México (Mexico City); alt 2,426 m; university (1869); one of the oldest silver-mining centres in Mexico; mined by the Aztecs before the arrival of the Spaniards; railway; economy: silver mining at Real del Monte (10 km), where Cornish miners settled in the 19th century; monument: La Caja, the treasury for the royal tribute in Calle Cajas (1670).

Pacific Ocean, body of water extending from the Arctic to the Antarctic, lying between North and South America on the E and Asia and Oceania on the W; with an estimated area of 181,300,000 sq km, it covers one-third of the total area of the Earth and almost one-half of the total water surface area; named by the Spanish navigator and explorer Ferdinand Magellan; the S part is sometimes known as the South Sea; lat 40°S and Antarctica are both used to define the S extent of this ocean; linked to (1) the Arctic Ocean by the Bering Strait, by way of the Bering Sea, (2) the Atlantic Ocean by the Drake Passage, Straits of Magellan and the Panama Canal, (3) the Indian Ocean by the Southern Ocean and through the numerous passages of the Malay Archipelago; chief arms of the Pacific are the Bering Sea, Gulf of California, Ross Sea, Sea of Okhotsk, Sea of Japan, Yellow Sea, East China Sea, South China Sea, Philippine Sea, Coral Sea, Tasman Sea, Arafura Sea and the Celebes Sea; narrow continental shelves exist along the shores in the E, but they are wider along the W shores; a rim of volcanoes around the ocean earns the name of the Pacific 'Ring of Fire' which, coupled with the presence of deep ocean trenches and active continental margins, is evidence of subduction and causes sea-floor contraction; such convergent plate motion occurs in the Pacific Ocean at the boundaries of the Pacific Plate with the North American Plate at a rate of 5.2-5.6 cm per year in the NW Pacific; divergent plate motion and sea-floor spreading is also associated with the SE Pacific Nazca Plate, with movement at a rate of 17.2 cm per year; greatest known depth in the ocean is the Challenger Deep in the Marianas Trench at 11,040 m; there is no mid-ocean ridge, the major ridge system being the East Pacific Ridge (Albatross Cordillera); the ocean floor is largely a deep sea-plain with an average depth of 4,300 m; numerous islands are scattered throughout the ocean and are either of volcanic origin (Hawaii) or are coral islands; the majority of islands lie in the E section; surface water circulation in the northern hemisphere is clockwise, but anti-clockwise in the southern hemisphere and separated from each other by the Equatorial Counter-currents; Spain, Portugal, UK and Holland held colonies in the Pacific from the 17th century, while France and Russia established themselves in the 18th century, with the USA, Germany and Japan extending their influence in the 19th century; commercial importance has increased since the opening of the Panama Canal in 1920; the main sources of manganese nodules are found in the central regions of each hemisphere, particularly the Clarion-Clipperton Nodule Area, W of Mexico; metal-rich sediment areas are found in the S hemisphere off the W coast of South America; fishing is important in the marine pasture areas of upwelling, particularly along the E coasts and in equatorial regions; fishing catches are susceptible to local variation, as in 1972 when the catch of anchovies in the SE Pacific declined as a result of the El Niño warm water currents moving into the cool nutrient-rich Peru current, curbing upwelling and so phytoplankton production; large areas in the central E Pacific have temperature gradients between the surface layer and deep water in excess of 22°C and are seen as potentially important areas for power generation.

Pacif'ica, 37 36N 122 30W, pop(1980) 36,866, city in San Mateo county, W California, United States; on the Pacific Ocean, SSW of San Francisco.

Padang *pa-dung'*, 1 00S 100 21E, pop(1980) 196,339, capital of Sumatera Barat prov, Indonesia; main seaport on the W coast of the island of Sumatera; 3rd largest city in Sumatera; port constructed 1880-90; university (1956); railway; airfield; outlet for exports of rubber, copra, tea at Telukbajur, 6 km S.

Pad'erborn, 51 43N 8 44E, pop(1983) 110,300, industrial and commercial city in Detmold dist, E Nordrhein-Westfalen (North Rhine-Westphalia) prov, W Germany; at the source of the R Pader, 80 km ESE of Münster; university (1972); railway; economy: iron and steel products, office equipment; monument: cathedral (11-13th-c).

Padova *pa'do-vah*, prov of Veneto region, NE Italy; pop(1981) 809,667; area 2,142 sq km; capital Padova (Padua).

Padova, PADUA *pad'yoo-a* (Eng), PATAVIUM (anc), 45 24N 11 53E, pop(1981) 234,678, capital town of Padova prov, Veneto region, NE Italy; 30 km W of Venezia (Venice), on the R Bacchiglione; 16th-c university associated with Galileo, Dante, and Petrarch; birthplace of Livy and the painter Andrea Mantegna; economy: tourism; monuments: 16th-c cathedral with a 13th-c baptistry; church of Sant'Antonio (1232-1307), containing the tomb of St Anthony of Padova, a shrine visited by countless pilgrims; Donatello's equestrian statue of Gattamelata (1447); 13th-c church of the Eremitani, restored after war damage, with famous frescoes by Mantegna; botanical garden (1545), the oldest in Europe; event: Fiera del Santo trade fair in June.

Padrela, Serra da *pad-ray'la*, mountain range, Vila Real dist, N Portugal, rising to 1,147 m.

Padua, town in Italy. See Padova.

Paducah *pa-doo'ka*, 37 05N 88 37W, pop(1980) 29,315, county seat of McCracken county, SW Kentucky, United States; a port on the R Ohio, close to the mouth of the R Tennessee; named after a local Indian chief and tribe;

railway; economy: tobacco trade, railway engineering, boatbuilding; the city suffered major floods in 1884, 1913, and 1937.

Pa'get, parish in the Bermuda Islands; pop(1980) 4,497.

Pahang *pu-hang'*, state in E Peninsular Malaysia, SE Asia; bounded E by South China Sea, N by Terengganu and Kelantan, S by Johor and W by Perak, Selangor and Negeri Sembilan; watered by the R Pahang which enters the sea S of Kuantan; pop(1980) 768,801; area 35,965 sq km; capital Kuantan; chief towns Bentong, Raub and Mentakab; formerly part of the kingdom of Malacca; economy: timber, rubber, tin, tourism.

Pahang, the longest river in Peninsular Malaysia, SE Asia; flowing 456 km E into the South China Sea.

Pahsien, town in Sichuan prov, SW central China. See Chongqing.

Paignton *payn'ten*, 50 26N 3 34W, pop(1981) 40,820, resort town in Torbay dist, Devonshire, SW England; on Tor Bay, 5 km SW of Torquay; railway.

Päijänne *pi'yan-nu*, lake in Keski-Suomi and Häme provs, S central Finland; area 1,090 sq km; the largest single lake in Finland; drained southwards to the Gulf of Finland by the Kymijoki; linked to Vesijärvi by the Vaaksy Canal; boat and hydrofoil service links Jyväskylä and Lahti.

Pais Vasco *pa-ees' vas'ko*, PROVINCIAS VASCONGADAS *pro-veenth'yas vas-kon-gah'thas*, EUSKADI (Basque), BASQUE PROVINCES *bask* (Eng), autonomous region of N Spain comprising the provs of Álava, Guipúzcoa and Vizcaya; pop(1981) 2,141,809; area 7,261 sq km; coastal hills are separated from the main ridge of the Cordillera Cantabrica to the S by valleys growing wheat; the landscape of the coastal hills is one of meadow land, fields of maize and plantations of walnuts and fruit trees; at higher altitudes there are forests of oak, beech and chestnut as well as plantations of pine and eucalyptus; rivers have been dammed to provide hydroelectric power and the main industries centred around Bilbao and San Sebastian are metal-working, papermaking and furniture-making; the Basques are a pre-Indo-European people who managed to remain largely independent until the 19th-c; the Basque language (Euskara) is spoken in a number of dialects in both Spain and the Basque region of France; there is a separatist movement (ETA).

Paisley *payz'lee*, 55 50N 4 26W, pop(1981) 84,954, capital of Renfrew dist, Strathclyde, W Scotland; in Clydeside urban area, 11 km W of Glasgow; railway; economy: food producing (sugar refining), distilling, engineering, jam, thread, chemicals; monuments: observatory; museum and art gallery; Paisley abbey (1163) was fully restored in the early 20th c.

Pakistan *pak-i-stan'*, official name The Islamic Republic of Pakistan, Asian state, bounded E by India, W by Afghanistan and Iran, N by the Soviet Union and the People's Republic of China and lying between the Hindu Kush mountain range in the N and the Arabian Sea in the S; in the N is the disputed area of Jammu and Kashmir; timezone GMT +5; area 803,943 sq km; capital Islamabad; pop(1986e) 102,689,000; pop includes nearly 5 mn refugees from Afghanistan; ethnic groups include Punjabi, Sindhi, Pushtan (Pathan) and Baluchi; Urdu and English are the official languages, while some 64% of the pop speaks Punjabi, 12% Sindhi, 8% Pushtu, 7% Urdu, 9% Baluchi and others; 97% of the pop is Muslim, 3% Christian, Hindu or other; the currency is the Pakistan rupee of 100 paisas (pre-1961 the Pakistan rupee was divided into 64 pice); national holiday 23 March (Pakistan Day); membership of ADB, Colombo Plan, FAO, G-77, GATT, IAEA, IBRD, ICAC, ICAO, IDA, Islamic Development Bank, IFAD, IFC, IHO, ILO, IMF, IMO, INTELSAT, INTERPOL, IRC, ITU, IWC, NAM, OIC, Regional Cooperation for Development, UN, UNESCO, UPU, WFTU, WHO, WIPO, WMO, WSG and the WTO.

Physical description. Pakistan is largely centred on the alluvial and densely populated flood plain of the R Indus which flows from the Himalayas in the N to the Arabian Sea at Karachi in the S. Bounded N and W by mountains which rise to 8,611 m at K2 and 8,126 m at Nanga Parbat, the country S of the Karakoram range is mostly flat plateau, low lying plains and arid desert.

Climate. Dominated by the Asiatic monsoon, the climate of Pakistan varies from N to S. In the mountains and foothills of the N and W the climate is cool with summer rain and winter snow. At Islamabad temperatures range from a max of 40°C in June to a min of 2°C in Jan, with average monthly rainfall varying from 12 mm in Nov to 258 mm in Aug. In the upland plateaux summers are hot and winters are cool, and although generally dry throughout the year some rain may fall during winter. In summer the Indus valley is extremely hot and is fanned by dry winds often carrying sand. At Jacobabad temperatures range from a max of 46°C in June to a min of 7°C in Aug, with average monthly rainfall varying from 23 mm in July and Aug to 0 mm in Oct-Nov. Throughout the country, the hottest season lasts from March to June, with the highest temperatures occuring in the S. The rainy season lasts from late June to early Oct and coincides with the the SW monsoon.

History, government and constitution. Walled cities at Mohenjo-Daro, Harappa and Kalibangan are evidence of early civilization occupying the Indus valley over 4,000 years ago. Aryans from the N and W are the ancestors of present-day Pakistanis. Under the Moghul empire (1526-1761) the whole country came under Muslim rule and in the 1840s Britain extended its influence over Sind and the Punjab. Much later in 1896 Balúchistán and the NW Frontier also came under British control. Under the Indian Independence Act of 1947, Pakistan separated from India and became a Dominion comprising the former British Indian states of Balúchistán, East Bengal, NW Frontier, West Punjab and Sind. In 1949 Pakistan occupied Jammu and Kashmir, states that are still disputed territory between Pakistan and India and have been the cause of 2 wars in 1965 and 1971. On 23 March 1956 Pakistan proclaimed itself an Islamic republic. President Mirza declared martial law in 1958 and suspended the constitution. A new constitution was declared in March 1962 and amended in 1970. Differences between East and West Pakistan, which were physically separated by 1,610 km, developed into civil war in March 1971 and resulted in E Pakistan leaving the federation to become an independent state (Bangladesh). Pakistan's 3rd constitution was adopted in 1973 and provided for an elected President and a bicameral Federal Parliament. Gen Zia-ul-Haq, who seized power in a military coup in 1977, is advised by a Military

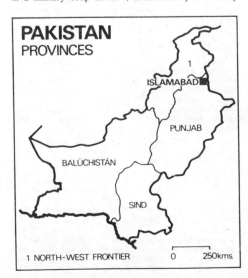

Council of 3, a larger appointed Advisory Council and a 288-member Federal Council, which was appointed in 1982 but has no controlling power and only some parliamentary functions. Organization at the provincial level is currently suspended.

Economy. Agriculture accounts for 30% of the national income and employs 55% of the labour force of Pakistan. The chief crops are wheat, cotton, maize, sugar cane and rice. Pakistan is self-sufficient in rice, wheat and sugar. Rice is a major export crop and accounts for one-fifth of the country's foreign revenue. Cotton production is important and supports the large spinning, weaving and processing industries. Agriculture is concentrated on the floodplains of the 5 major rivers of Pakistan and is supported by an extensive irrigation network. Industry employs 10% of the population and in 1982-83 contributed 17.5% of national income. Government policy since 1977 has attempted to encourage small, rural private industries and to extend transport and power supplies. Major industries include cotton textiles, food processing, tobacco, engineering, cement, fertilizers, chemicals and natural gas production. There are 4 natural gas fields in central Pakistan and gas pipelines link Sui to Karachi and Multan, and Quetta to Shikarpur, providing gas for domestic and industrial consumption. Limestone, gypsum, iron ore and rock salt are exploited, while reserves of uranium have been found at Dera Ghazi Khan. Major trade partners for exports include Japan, Saudi Arabia, the USA, the UK and W Germany.

Administrative divisions. Pakistan is divided into 4 provinces, a federal capital territory and federally administered tribal areas:

Division	*area (sq km)*	*pop(1981)*
Balúchistán	347,190	4,332,000
Federally Administered Tribal Areas	27,220	2,199,000
Islamabad	907	340,000
North-West Frontier	74,521	11,061,000
Punjab	205,334	47,292,000
Sind	140,914	19,029,000

Pakpattan *pak'pat-tun*, 30 20N 73 27E, pop(1981) 70,000, city in Punjab prov, Pakistan; 42 km SE of Sahiwal, close to the Pakpattan Canal; Muslim pilgrimage centre; railway; economy: trade in grain, cotton and hand-loom weaving.

Paks *poksh*, 46 38N 18 55E, pop(1984e) 23,000, town in Tolna county, SW central Hungary; on R Danube, NNE of Szekszárd; economy: grain and cattle trade, atomic research, textiles.

Pakse *pak-suy*, 14 09N 105 50E, pop(1973) 44,860, town in S Laos, SE Asia; on R Mekong, close to the Thailand frontier.

Paktīā *pak-tee-ay*, prov in E Afghanistan; pop(1984e) 525,389; area 9,581 sq km; bounded to the E by Pakistan; capital Gardēz; linked to Pakistan by the Batat Pass.

Paktīkā *pak-tee-kay*, KATAWAZ-URGUN, prov in E Afghanistan; pop(1984e) 266,139; area 19,336 sq km; bounded by Pakistan to the E and S; administrative centre Sheren.

Palangkaraya *pa-lahng'ka-rah'ya*, PALANGKA RAYA, 2 06S 113 55E, pop(1980) 27,132, capital of Kalimantan Tengah prov, central Borneo, Indonesia; capital of the Dayak people; airfield.

Palatinate, Upper, dist of W Germany. See Oberpfalz.

Palatine, 42 07N 88 03W, pop(1980) 32,166, town in Cook county, NE Illinois, United States; 45 km NW of Chicago; railway; residential.

Palawan *pa-lah'wan*, formerly PARAGUA (1902-05), (1902-05), island of W Philippines; a long, narrow island, with a mountain chain running almost the whole length; separated from Mindoro I (NE) by Mindoro Strait, from Sabah, Malaysia, by the Balbac Strait, and bounded E by Sulu Sea, W by South China Sea; area 11,780 sq km; chief town Puerto Princesa rises to 1,593 m in the N at Cleopatra Needle and in the S to 2,054 m at Mt Mantalingajan.

Palembang *pah-lem'bahng*, 2 59S 104 45E, pop(1980) 582,961, river-port capital of Sumatera Selatan prov, Indonesia; on R Musi, S Sumatera I; successively developed around the pepper, tin and oil trades; once the capital of the Sriwijaya Empire (7th-12th century); university (1960); airfield; economy: oil refining (Sungei Gerong) and the export of oil, rubber, fertilizers, textiles.

Palencia *pa-len'thya, pa-len'sha* (Eng), prov in Castilla-León region, NW Spain; a dry, hot, treeless plateau sloping S from the Cordillera Cantabrica and traversed by fertile valleys of subtributaries of the R Douro (Duero); pop(1981) 186,512; area 8,035 sq km; capital Palencia; economy: anthracite mining, dairy products, meat processing, paper, wood products, agric machinery, mineral water.

Palencia, PALLANTIA (anc), 41 01N 4 34W, pop(1981) 74,080, capital of Palencia prov, Castilla-León, N Spain; on R Carrión, 240 km NNW of Madrid; bishopric; railway; site of first university in Spain (1208); economy: agricultural centre, foundries, smelting and textiles; monuments: 14-15th-c Gothic cathedral, museum with 15th-c tapestries; events: Holy Week; pilgrimage of Santo Cristo del Otero in April; fair in May; Festival of Palencia in Aug.

Palenque *pah-leng'kay*, 17 30N 92 03W, remains of a Mayan city in NE Chiapas, S Mexico; situated in jungle lowland; Palenque reached the peak in its development in 692 AD and is believed to have been abandoned in the 12th century; noted for sculptures and palatial secular buildings decorated in delicate stucco and carved stonework; the ruins were discovered in 1750; the site is dominated by a great pyramid known as the Pyramid, or Temple, of the Inscriptions; in 1949 archaeologists found a stairway under its floor which led to a sealed crypt in the heart of the pyramid; inside they uncovered the remains of a Mayan chief, bedecked in jade; there is an Observatory Tower, which Mayan priests used in their astral calculations and construction of a calendar.

Paler'mo, prov of Sicilia (Sicily), Italy; pop(1981) 1,198,575; area 5,017 sq km; capital Palermo.

Palermo, 38 08N 13 23E, pop(1981) 701,782, seaport and capital of Palermo prov, Sicilia (Sicily), Italy, on the N coast of Sicilia I, bounded on the S and W by the artificially irrigated and fertile fruit-growing plain known as the Conca d'Oro (Golden Shell); founded by Phoenicians in the 8th century BC; archbishopric; university (1777); airport; railway; ferries; economy: shipbuilding, steel, glass, chemicals, furniture, tourism, trade in fruit, wine, olive oil; monuments: there is some notable Norman architecture, showing a Moorish influence, as in the 12th-c cathedral and the church of San Cataldo; ruined church of San Giovanni degli Eremiti (1132); church of La Mortorana (1143); Teatro Massimo (1875-97), one of the largest theatres in Italy; event: trade fair (May-June).

Palimé *pa-lee'may*, 6 55N 0 44E, pop(1977) 25,500, town in Des Plateaux region, S Togo, W Africa; railway terminus 105 km NW of Lomé; the centre of Togo's cocoa industry, Palimé is dominated by Mount Agou; nearby are the Kpimé and Akrowa waterfalls; economy: ceramics, pottery, trade in cocoa.

Palm Springs, 33 50N 116 33W, pop(1980) 32,271, resort city in Riverside county, S California, United States; in the N Coachella Valley, to the E of the San Jacinto Mts, 64 km ESE of Redlands; founded in 1876; developed as a luxurious desert resort in the early 1930s; airfield; near the city are Palm Canyon, with an ancient grove of native palms, and Tahquitz Bowl, a natural amphitheatre.

Palma or fully **Palma de Mallorca** *pal-ma THay ma-yor'ka*, 39 35N 2 39E, pop(1981) 304,422, seaport and capital of Baleares region, Spain and chief city of Mallorca I in the W Mediterranean; bishopric; university (1967); airport; economy: shipyard, footwear, metalwork, beer, clothes, pharmaceuticals; monuments: Bellver Castle, Church of St Francis, cathedral, Spanish Pueblo open-air museum.

Palma, La *la pal'ma*, port and capital town of Darién prov, E Panama, Central America; on the estuary of the Río Tuira, E shore of the Golfo de Panamá.

Palmas de Gran Canaria, Las, 28 07N 15 26W, pop(1981) 366,454, resort and seaport (Puerto de la Luz) and capital of Las Palmas prov, Spain; at the NE corner of Gran Canaria, Canary Islands; airport; economy: tourism, exports sugar, tomatoes, bananas; monuments: Columbus' House, where Columbus stayed in 1502, cathedral, hermitage of San Telmo and church of San Francisco; Las Cantras beach; events: Los Reyes Magos in January; Winter Festival (Feb-March); Holy Week and Festival of Spain in April-May.

Pal'mas, Las, one of 2 Spanish provs in the Atlantic Canary Is, Canarias region, comprising the islands of Gran Canaria, Lanzarote and Fuerteventura; pop(1981) 756,353; area 4,072 sq km; capital Las Palmas de Gran Canaria; economy: tourism, ship building and repair, mineral water, cement, livestock, agric produce, pharmaceuticals, drinks, textiles, fruit and vegetables, metal products (Telde), food processing and canning, furniture.

Palmerston, AVARAU, 18 04S 163 10W, coral atoll of the Cook Is, S Pacific, 432 km NW of Rarotonga; area 2 sq km; pop(1981) 51; includes some 35 tiny islands on its barrier reef; copra is exported.

Palmerston North, 40 20S 175 39E, pop(1981) 60,105, city on SW coast of North Island, New Zealand; NE of Wellington; agricultural research centre; Massey University (1926); railway; airfield; economy: dairy farming products, pharmaceuticals, textiles, electrical goods; monument: Manawatu rugby museum.

Palmyra *pal-mī'ra*, 5 52N 162 05W, uninhabited atoll enclosing 50 small islets in the Pacific Ocean 1,600 km S of Honolulu between Hawaii and Samoa; claimed by Hawaii in 1862 and annexed by the USA in 1912; an important air transport base during World War II; privately owned, but since 1962 the islands have been under the jurisdiction of the US Department of the Interior. Suggested site for nuclear waste disposal.

Palmyra, ancient city in central Syria. See Tadmur.

Palo Alto, 37 27N 122 10W, pop(1980) 55,225, city in Santa Clara county, W California, United States; near the SW end of San Francisco Bay, 48 km SSE of San Francisco; at the centre of the 'Silicon Valley' high technology area; Stanford University (1891) lies to the W; railway.

Palu *pa'loo*, 0 54S 119 52E, pop(1980) 298,584, capital of Sulawesi Tengah prov, Indonesia; at the centre of the Island of Sulawesi (Celebes).

Pampa, La *la pam'pa*, prov in Centro region, central Argentina; low grassy area (dry *pampa*) sloping gradually E from Mendoza prov border (NW); bordered S by the Río Colorado; watered by the Atuel and Salado rivers which reach the central marshes; the prov contains a number of salt marshes and salt deposits; the climate is generally dry and temperate; pop(1980) 208,260; area 143,440 sq km; capital Santa Rosa; chief towns General Pico and General Acha; economy: maize, wheat, sorghum; sheep and cattle raising, salt and gypsum mining, meat packing.

Pamplemousses *pam-ple-moos'*, district of NW Mauritius; area 178.7 sq km; pop(1983) 91,782; resorts centred around Trou aux Biches.

Pamplona *pam-plō'nah*, PAMPELUNA or POMPAELO (Lat), 42 48N 1 38W, pop(1981) 183,126, capital of Navarra prov, N Spain; on R Arga, 407 km N of Madrid; commands two important frontier roads across the Pyrenees into France - the Roncesvalles Pass and the Velate Pass; archbishopric; airport; railway; said to have been founded by Pompey who is supposed to have given the town its name; capital of the kingdom of Navarre in the 10th century; university (1952); economy: agricultural centre and manufacture of paper, rope, pottery, chemicals, kitchenware; monuments: 14-15th-c cathedral; Navarre museum with Roman mosaics; events: Holy Week; fair and fiesta of San Fermin in July with bull-running in the streets; Chiquita in Sept.

Pamporo'vo, 41 43N 24 39E, international ski resort in Smolyan okrug (prov), S Bulgaria; 15 km N of the city of Smolyan in the Rhodopi Planina (Rhodope Mts); alt 1,650 m; on Snezhanka ('snow white') Peak there are several ski runs up to 3,800 m in length.

Panaji *pan-ah'jee*, PANGIM, PANJIM *pan-zhim'*, 15 31N 73 56E, pop(1981) 76,839, largest town and seaport capital of Goa, Daman and Diu union territory, E India; at the mouth of the R Mandavi, 408 km SE of Bombay; former capital of Portuguese India; economy: trade in fish, rice, salt.

Panama *pa'na-ma*, PANAMÁ *pa-na-ma'* (Sp), official name Republic of Panama, REPÚBLICA DE PANAMÁ, republic occupying the SE end of the isthmus of Central America, bounded N by the Caribbean Sea, S by the Pacific Ocean, W by Costa Rica, and E by Colombia; timezone GMT −5; area 77,082 sq km; capital Panamá City; chief towns David, Colón, and Santiago; pop(1980) 1,831,399; the pop comprises 70% mestizo (mixed Spanish and Indian), 14% West Indian, 10% white, and 6% Indian; Spanish is the official language while English is a common second language; Roman Catholicism is the dominant religion; the unit of currency is the balboa of 100 centimes; membership: FAO, G-77, IADB, IAEA, IBRD, ICAO, ICO, IDA, IDB, IFAD, IFC, ILO, IMF, IMO, INTELSAT, INTERPOL, IRC, ITU, IWC, NAM, OAS, PAHO, SELA, UN, UNESCO, UPEB, UPU, WFTU, WHO, WMO, WTO.

Physical description and climate. Panama is mostly mountainous and hilly. The Serranía de Tabasará occupies the W part of the country and rises to peaks of over 2,000 m. From the S coast juts the mountainous Azuero peninsula. The mountain arcs are generally lower to the E of the lake-studded lowland which cuts across the isthmus from Colón to Panamá City. The E provs and the Caribbean coast are covered with dense tropical forests. The climate is tropical with a mean annual temperature of 32°C. On the Caribbean coast rainfall is much higher and there is a less clearly defined dry season. In Colón, on the Caribbean coast, annual rainfall averages 3,280 mm while in Panamá City it is approx 1,780 mm.

History, government and constitution. Panama was under Spanish colonial rule from 1538 to 1821. Thereafter it joined the Republic of Greater Colombia. A revolution, inspired by the USA, led to the separation of Panama from Colombia and ultimately to the declaration of its independence in 1903. On 10 October 1979 Panama assumed sovereignty of the 8 km-wide Canal Zone, previously administered by the USA. According to the 1972 Constitution, Panama is governed by a president, elected for 4 years, and an executive cabinet of about 13 ministers. The president is elected by and is responsible to an Assembly of 505 representatives of municipal districts.

Economy. Employing about 35% of the workforce, agriculture accounts for only just over 10% of national income. Bananas, coffee, cacao, and sugar cane are the main export crops grown chiefly on the volcanic soils of the W provs. The country's economy is centred mainly on the canal and the ports of Colón and Panamá. Revenue from the canal and registration fees from foreign ships account for approx four-fifths of the country's wealth. In recent years, however, attempts have been made to diversify the economy by introducing new sources of income. Local industries include oil refining and the manufacture of cigarettes, clothing, beverages, construction materials, and paper products. Chief exports are refined petroleum products, bananas, sugar, and shrimps. The USA supplied 33% of total imports and received 56% of exports in the early 1980s. Other trade partners include Venezuela, Japan, and West Germany. Shrimp farming is a growing industry. There are large copper deposits at Cerro Colorado in Chiriquí prov which are as yet undeveloped. The country also has gold and silver deposits. A 137 km-long pipeline transports Alaskan oil from the Atlantic port of Puerto Armuelles to the Caribbean port of Bocas del Toro. One of the most

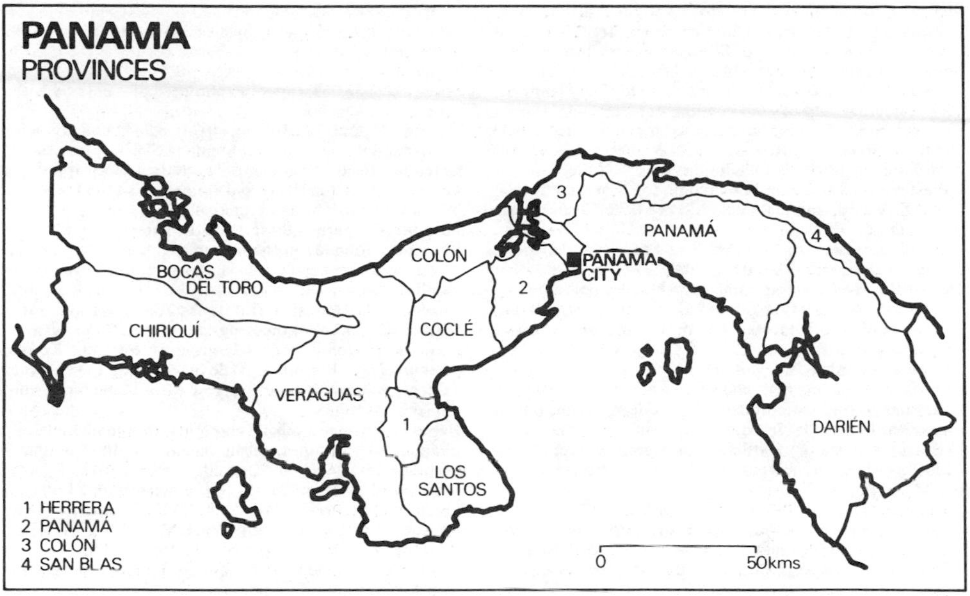

dynamic sectors of the economy is banking. Since 1970 offshore banks have increased in number from 20 to 130. *Administrative divisions.* Panama is divided into 9 provinces and 1 Indian territory as follows:

Province	*area (sq km)*	*pop(1980)*
Bocas del Toro	8,917	53,487
Chiriquí	8,758	287,350
Coclé	5,035	140,903
Colón	4,961	137,997
Darién	16,803	26,524
Herrera	2,427	81,963
Panamá	12,022	831,048
San Blas	3,206	28,621
Los Santos	3,867	70,261
Veraguas	11,086	173,245

Panamá, largest and most densely populated prov of Panama, Central America; bounded S by the Golfo de Panamá, an inlet of the Pacific Ocean; divided into W and E sections by the Panama Canal Area; drained by the Chepo and upper Chágres rivers; includes the Pearl Is in the Golfo de Panamá; pop(1980) 831,048; area 12,022 sq km; capital Panamá; chief towns La Chorrera and Chepo; traversed by the Inter-American Highway; formed originally in 1719 when it covered the entire E section of Panama.

Panamá, 8 57N 79 30W, pop(1980) 389,172, capital city of Panama, Central America, in Panamá prov; on the N shore of the Golfo de Panamá, near the Pacific end of the Panama Canal; founded on its present site in 1673; industrial and transportation centre of Panama; 2 universities (1935, 1965); airport; railway; on the Inter-American Highway; its port is Balboa in the Canal Area; monuments: church of San José, which has a famous organ and a golden altar; twin-towered cathedral; remains of the old sea wall (Las Bóvedas) built around the city to protect it from pirates; event: parades on Independence Day (3 Nov).

Panama Canal, ship canal which cuts across the isthmus of Panama, Central America, connecting the Atlantic and Pacific oceans; it is 67.5 km long from shore to shore and it has been widened in most places to 150 m; a treaty was signed on 18 Nov 1903 between the USA and Panama making it possible for the US to build and operate a canal connecting the 2 oceans; under this treaty the USA had unilateral control of canal operations and administered the Panama Canal Zone, a 1,438 sq km strip of land extending 8 km on either side of the canal and including the cities of Balboa and Cristóbal; on 1 October 1979 the Canal Zone, now known officially as the Canal Area, was formally transferred to Panamanian sovereignty, including the ports of Cristóbal and Balboa, the dry docks, the trans isthmus railway, and the naval base of Coco Solo; near the Atlantic end of the canal Gatún Dam converts the lower Chágres valley into a lake; L Gatún serves as a reservoir to hold sufficient water in the channel and for use in the locks during dry spells; 3 locks bring ships from the Atlantic level to L Gatún; they then sail up the submerged Chágres valley, through the narrow Culebra Cut, and down to Pacific level via another 3 locks.

Panama City, 30 10N 85 40W, pop(1980) 33,346, county seat of Bay county, NW Florida, United States; a port on the Gulf of Mexico, 150 km E of Pensacola; railway; economy: paper, clothing, chemicals and plastics; Tyndall Air Force Base and the US Navy Mine Defence Laboratory are nearby.

Panay *pan ī'*, island in the Visayas group, central Philippines; lies NW of Negros I; bounded W by Sulu Sea; area 12,295 sq km; chief towns are Iloilo and Roxas.

Pančevo or **Panchevo** *pahn'che-vo*, PANCSOVA (Hung), 44 52N 20 40E, pop(1981) 123,791, river port town in Vojvodina autonomous province, N Srbija (Serbia) republic, NE Yugoslavia; on R Tamiş where it meets the Danube, 16 km NE of Beograd; railway.

Pando *pan'THō*, dept in NW Bolivia; bordered by the Acre and Abuná rivers (N) and the Río Madeira (E) along the Brazil frontier, by Peru (W), by the Río Madre de Dios (SW) and by the Beni river (E); drained by the Tahuamanu, Manuripi, Orton and Madre de Dios rivers; tropical forests follow the rivers; pop(1982) 42,594; area 63,827 sq km; capital Cobija; economy: natural rubber, forestry.

Pando *pan'dō*, 34 44S 55 58W, pop(1985) 19,654, town in Canelones dept, S Uruguay; on the Río de la Plata estuary.

Pangaíon Óros, MOUNT ATHOS, autonomous administration in Makedhonia region, Greece; pop(1981) 1,472; area 336 sq km; Mt Athos, rising to 1,956 m, is the 'Holy Mountain' of the Greek Church and has been associated with the monastic order of St Basil since the 9th century; declared a theocratic republic in 1927.

Panhandle, a name used to describe any territory comprising a narrow strip of land running out from a large area in the shape of a pan handle; the term is applied in the United States to areas in (1) NW Texas (the Texas Panhandle), (2) NW Oklahoma, (3) N Idaho, (4) NE West Virginia (Eastern Panhandle), (5) N West Virginia, (6) SE Alaska, and (7) an extension of the Golden Gate Park in San Francisco.

Panna, national park in N Madhya Pradesh state, India; area 5,426 sq km; established 1981.

Pantanal', large swamp and marshland area covering 220,000 sq km in Mato Grosso and Mato Grosso do Sul states, SW Brazil; located on the E bank of the upper Paraguay river, between Cuiabá, Campo Grande and the Bolivian border; one of the world's great wildlife preserves; contains over 600 species of birds, approx 350 varieties of fish, and animals such as deer, ocelot, puma, boar, ant-eater, tapir, rhea, capybara and the jacaré (Brazilian alligator); cattle are also grazed here; 800 sq km have been designated as a biological reserve (Cará-Cará).

Paola *pow'lah*, 35 51N 14 32E, pop(1983e) 12,449, community on the main island of Malta; S of Valletta and Grand Harbour; founded in 1626 by Grand Master De Paula; monument: the underground Hypogeum discovered in 1902.

Pao-t'ou, town in Nei Mongol aut region (Inner Mongolia), N China. See Baotou.

Pápa *pa'po*, 47 22N 17 30E, pop(1984e) 34,000, town in Veszprém county, W Hungary; 40 km SSW of Györ; railway; economy: textiles, footwear, cigars; monument: 18th-c castle built by Count Esterházy.

Papakura *pa-pa-koo'ra*, 37 04S 174 59E, pop(1981) 22,482, town in NW North Island, New Zealand; SW of Auckland; railway.

Papatoetoe *pa'pa-toy-toy'*, 36 59S 174 52E, pop(1981) 21,700, town in NW North Island, New Zealand; S of Auckland; railway.

Papeete *pa-pay-ay'tay*, 17 32S 149 34W, capital and chief port of French Polynesia, S Pacific Ocean, on the NW coast of Tahiti, Archipel de la Société (Society Is); pop(1977) 62,735, economic and political centre; airport; the harbour is sheltered by a reef; exports copra, vanilla and mother-of-pearl.

Paphos *pa'fos*, dist in W Cyprus; area 1,395 sq km; pop(1973) 57,065; capital Paphos; remains entirely within the Greek Cypriot zone.

Paphos, 34 45N 32 23E, pop(1973) 8,984, holiday resort and capital town of Paphos dist, SW Cyprus; on the Mediterranean Sea; comprises Ktima, the upper and newer part of the town, and Nea Paphos, the lower area containing the harbour and main archaeological sites; capital of Cyprus during Roman times; old Paphos was probably founded in the Mycenaean period by colonists from Greece or Phoenicia; monuments: excavations within the ancient walls have revealed remains of a Roman villa (House of Dionysos); 7th-c Byzantine castle; 3rd-c BC 'Tombs of the Kings' (approx 100 tombs carved out of the solid rock underground); Saranda Kolones (remains of a Byzantine castle overlooking the harbour); Chrysopolitissa Basilica (largest early Christian basilica on the island).

Papua New Guinea, official name The Independent State of Papua New Guinea, island group in the SW Pacific Ocean, 160 km NE of Australia, comprising the E half of the island of New Guinea, the Bismarck and Louisiade archipelagos, the Trobriand and D'Entrecasteaux Is, and other off-lying groups; timezone GMT +10; area 462,840 sq km; capital Port Moresby; chief towns Lae, Madang, and Rabaul; pop(1980) 2,978,057; the average pop density in 1980 was 7 persons per sq km; the people are predominantly Melanesian except for a small number of Polynesians who inhabit some of the outlying atolls; over half of the population is nominally Christian, the remainder adhere to magico-religious beliefs and practices that are an integral part of their traditional cultures; about 750 indigenous languages exist but pidgin English is the official language and is widely used, particularly in New Guinea; Motu is the language most used in the Papuan coastal areas; English is spoken by 1-2% of the population; the unit of currency is the kina; membership of ADB, ANRPC, CIPEC (associate), FAO, G-77, GATT (de facto), IBRD, ICAO, IDA, IFAD, IFC, ILO, IMF, IMO, INTELSAT, INTERPOL, ITU, South Pacific Commission, South Pacific Forum, UN, UNESCO, UPU, WHO, WMO.

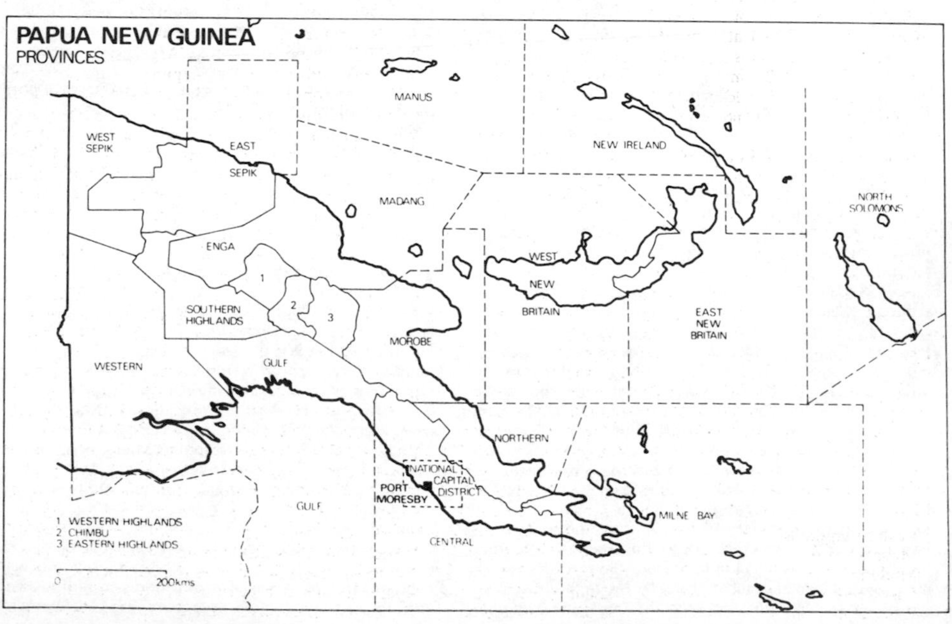

Physical description. A complex system of mountains extends from the Owen Stanley Range at the E end of New Guinea to the Victor Emanuel Range on the W boundary with Indonesian Irian Jaya. In the NE the Finisterre Range rising to 4,121 m at Mt Bangeta is separated from the Kratke Range by the R Ramu. The highest snow-covered peaks rise above 4,000 m, the highest being Mt Wilhelm (4,508 m). Large rivers, including the Fly, Sepik, and Ramu, flow to the S, N and E. Between the N and central range of mountains is the Central Depression which includes the valleys of the Sepik, Ramu, and Markham rivers. Much of the land is covered with tropical rain forest, but along the coast are vast mangrove swamps. On the SW littoral of the mainland the great delta plain of the Daru coast forms one of the most extensive swamps in the world. The archipelago islands are mountainous, mostly volcanic, and fringed with coral reefs.
Climate. The climate is typically monsoonal with temperatures and humidity constantly high throughout the year. Mean maximum temperature seldom exceeds 33°C and the mean minimum rarely falls below 22°C. The highlands, however, have a more temperate climate. Rainfall in most areas is high, averaging between 2,000 mm and 2,500 mm. The NW monsoon season, extending from December to March, is the wettest period of the year.
History, government and constitution. Britain proclaimed a protectorate over SE New Guinea in Oct 1884, and in 1899 German New Guinea was established in the NE. During World War I Australia annexed the German colony, and in the post-war years governed both the British and German areas as separate territories. The two were combined in 1949 under Australian mandate as the United Nations Trust Territory of Papua and New Guinea. Papua New Guinea achieved full independence on 16 Sept 1975. It is an independent parliamentary state within the Commonwealth. The head of state is an appointed governor-general representing the British Crown. A unicameral national parliament of 109 members is elected for a 5-year term. Executive power is vested in the cabinet led by the prime minister.
Economy. Over 66% of the workforce is engaged in farming, fishing, and forestry. Subsistence crops include yams, sago, cassava, bananas, and vegetables. The most important commercial cash crops are copra, coffee, cocoa, timber, palm oil, rubber, tea, sugar and peanuts. Copper ore is mined at Panguna on Bougainville I and the entire production is exported, mostly under long-term contracts to W Germany, Spain, Japan, and China. Large copper and gold deposits on the Ok Tedi have considerable export potential. Minerals provide over 33% of the country's export income. Hydroelectric power is generated on a large scale on the R Ramu and there is natural gas in the Sepik valley. There are few manufactures other than food processing and brewing for local consumption.
Administrative divisions. Papua New Guinea is divided into 19 provinces and a National Capital District:

Province	*area (sq km)*	*pop(1980)*
Western	99,300	78,337
Gulf	34,500	63,843
Central	29,500	116,361
National Capital District	240	112,429
Milne Bay	14,000	127,725
Northern	22,800	77,097
Southern Highlands	23,800	235,390
Enga	12,800	164,270
Western Highlands	8,500	264,129
Chimbu	6,100	178,013
Eastern Highlands	11,200	274,608
Morobe	34,500	305,356
Madang	29,000	209,656
East Sepik	42,800	220,827
West Sepik	36,300	113,849

contd

Province	*area (sq km)*	*pop(1980)*
Manus	2,100	25,859
New Ireland	9,600	65,657
East New Britain	15,500	130,730
West New Britain	21,000	88,415
North Solomons	9,300	125,506

Pará *pa-ra'*, state in Norte region, N Brazil; bordered NW by Guiana and Surinam along the Serra Acaraí and the Serra de Tumucumaque, NE by the Atlantic; lies entirely within the tropical Amazon basin; crossed by the Equator and the lower Amazon river which forms an enormous delta in the NE where the Amazon and the Pará are separated by the I de Marajó; the Amazon's main tributaries in Pará state are Tapajós, Xingu, Tocantins, Trombetas and Jari rivers; pop(1980) 3,403,391; area 1,250,722 sq km; capital Belém; economy: agriculture, cattle raising; minerals; in the NE is the Tumucumaque Indian Park; the Indian reserves of Kararão and Açurine lie in the centre of the state on the Xingu river; in the SW and S are the Mundurucania and Barotire nature reserves; in 1967 in the Serra do Carajás, to the W of the Tocantins river, an iron ore field, said to be the world's largest, was discovered; a new mining town is being built and a 940 km-long railway planned to Maranhão; New Marabá on the Tocantins river is being revitalized by power generated from the recently completed Tucuruí Dam (the old town of Marabá was flooded by the reservoir in 1974-75); the area includes 2,680 sq km which is in dispute with the state of Amazonas.

Para, district in N Surinam, NE South America; area 980 sq km; pop(1980) 14,867; capital Onverwacht.

Paraćin *pa'ra-chin*, 43 51N 21 25E, pop(1981) 64,718, town in central Srbija (Serbia) republic, Yugoslavia; near R Morava, SSE of Beograd; established in 1921; railway; economy: textiles, construction industry.

Paraguarí *pa-ra-gwa-ree'*, dept in Oriental region, S Paraguay; bounded S by the Río Tebicuary and NW by lakes Vera, Ypoá and Cabral; comprises fertile, forested lowlands with hills in NE; pop(1982) 2,021,552; area 8,255 sq km; capital Paraguarí.

Paraguay *pa-ra-gwī'*, official name Republic of Paraguay, REPÚBLICA DEL PARAGUAY, landlocked country in central South America; situated between 18° and 28°S; bordered N by Bolivia and Brazil, S by Argentina; timezone GMT −3; area 406,750 sq km; capital Asunción; pop(1982) 3,026,165; pop comprises Mestizos (95%), Amerindians, Negros and Europeans; there are over 13,000 Mennonites from Canada and Germany who settled in the Chaco between 1927 and 1947; there are about 7,000 Japanese colonists who arrived in 1937; the official language is Spanish, but Guaraní is also spoken; 97% of the pop are Roman Catholic, but small groups of Mennonites and other Protestant denominations are also present; the unit of currency is the guaraní of 100 centimos; national holidays 3 Feb (San Blas, Patron Saint of Paraguay), 1 March (Heroes' Day), 14-15 May (Independence Day), 12 June (Chaco Peace), 15 Aug (Foundation of Asunción), 25 Aug (Constitution Day), 29 Sept (Battle of Boquerón, Chaco War), 12 Oct (Día de la Raza); membership of FAO, G-77, IADB, IAEA, IBRD, ICAO, ICO, IDA, IDB, IFAD, IFC, ILO, IMF, INTELSAT, INTERPOL, IPU, IRC, ITU, LAIA, OAS, SELA, UN, UNESCO, UPU, WHO, WMO, WSG.
Physical description. Paraguay is divided into 2 distinct regions by the Río Paraguay, lying mostly at altitudes below 450 m. The country is bordered S with Argentina and E with Brazil by the Río Paraná (or the Alto Paraná, as it is called in Brazil). The Río Paraguay forms the W border with Argentina from Corrientes as far N as Asunción, then, as far N as the confluence with the Río Apa, it divides Paraguay into 2; from there on it forms the E boundary with Brazil. To the W of the Río

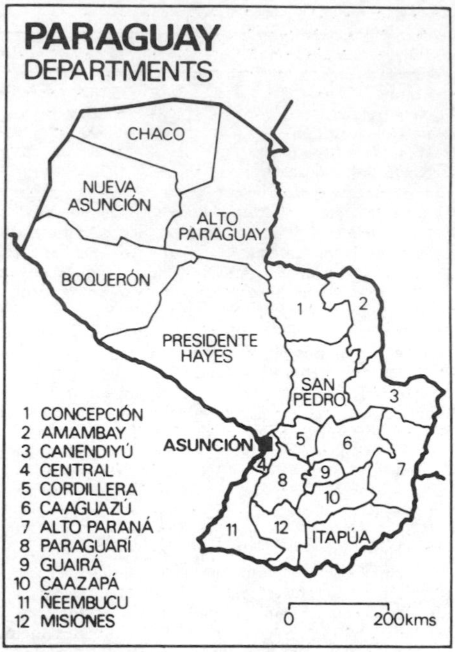

Paraguay is the dry Chaco, which is mostly cattle country or scrub forest. To the E is a more fertile and more densely populated land. The eastern half of Paraguay is further divided by a high cliffed formation which runs parallel with the Alto Paraná from a point W of Encarnación as far as the Brazilian border. The Paraná Plateau ranges in altitude from 300 to 600 m, and to the W a fertile plain stretches as far as the Río Paraguay. Much of it is wet, treeless savannah, covered in coarse grasses and is partially flooded once a year. Sugar, rice, tobacco, grains and cotton are grown here. The Chaco is drained by the Río Pilcomayo; the centre of Paraguay is watered by various tributaries of the Río Paraguay, including the Tebicuary, Jejuí-Guazú and Ypané rivers.

Climate. The NW part of Paraguay lies within the tropics and has hot summers and warm winters, with most of its rainfall in the hottest months between Oct and March. Here annual rainfall varies from 750 mm in the S to 1,250 mm in the extreme N. The SE half of the country is temperate, with temperatures lower in all months and an annual rainfall between 1,250 and 1,750 mm (averaging between 158 mm a month in the wet season and 38 mm in the dry season), increasing eastwards. Average temperatures for Asunción, at the centre of the country, indicate that the lowest temperature in the winter months will be 12°C and the hottest in the summer 35°C.

History, government and constitution. The original inhabitants of Paraguay were the Guaraní Indians. The Spanish reached Paraguay in 1537, in search of a short-cut to the gold and silver of Peru. Asunción became a major centre for Spanish settlement in South America and in 1609 Jesuits arrived in Paraguay, with the purpose of converting and civilizing the Indians. On 14 May 1811 Paraguay gained full independence from Spain and under the rule of Gaspar Rodríguez de Francia, from 1814 to 1840, a policy of complete isolation was followed, during which Paraguay achieved a high level of self-sufficiency. He was followed as president by Carlos Antonio López, who reversed Francia's policy of isolation. On his death in 1862 López was succeeded by his son, Marshal Francisco Solano López, who involved the country in the 6-year war of the Triple Alliance against Brazil, Argentina and Uruguay (1864-70), during which time Paraguay lost over 50% of its pop and was left with an imbalance of 4 women to every 1 man. Paraguay regained disputed territory in 1935 after the 3-year Chaco War with Bolivia. After 6 months of civil war in 1947 and a long period of instability, General Alfredo Stroessner seized power in 1954 and was appointed president.

Economy. Accounting for just over 15% of GNP, the major industries of Paraguay include food processing (meat, fruit, vegetables, oils, dairy produce, yerba maté), pulp, timber, textiles, fertilizers, cement, kaolin and glass. Agriculture, employing 40% of the labour force, accounts for 30% of GNP, the main agricultural crops being oilseed, cotton, wheat, manioc, sweet potato, tobacco, corn, rice and sugar cane. Although less than 5% of the country is cultivated Paraguay is self-sufficient in foodstuffs. Paraguay's major trade partners include Argentina, Brazil, the USA, the Netherlands and East Germany. Despite being a landlocked country, Paraguay has 10 ports, all of which are river ports.

Administrative divisions. Paraguay is divided into 2 regions, 19 depts and the national capital, Asunción as follows:

Department	*area (sq km)*	*pop(1982)*
Occidental region		
Alto Paraguay	37,000	4,535
Boquerón	44,000	14,685
Chaco	36,000	286
Nueva Asunción	46,000	231
Presidente Hayes	84,000	43,787
Oriental region		
Alto Paraná	13,498	188,351
Amambay	12,933	68,422
Caaguazú	14,409	299,227
Caazapá	9,496	109,510
Canendiyú	13,953	65,807
Central	2,652	494,575
Concepción	18,051	135,068
Cordillera	4,948	194,826
Guairá	3,202	143,374
Itapúa	16,526	263,021
Misiones	7,835	79,278
Ñeembucú	13,868	70,689
Paraguarí	8,255	2,021,552
San Pedro	20,002	189,751

Paraguay, Río, river in central South America; a chief tributary of the Río Paraná; rises in Brazil in central Mato Grosso prov, flows S past Corumbá, beyond which it forms the Brazil-Bolivia border (for 40 km), then the border between Brazil and Paraguay; enters Paraguay at the influx of the Apa river, flows S past Asunción and Concepción, then forms the Paraguay-Argentina border until it flows into the Paraná just above Corrientes (Argentina); length 2,300 km; in its Brazil course (between Cáceres and Paraguay border) it traverses a marshy floodplain (locally called the Pantanal) which is inundated during Nov-April; chief tributaries are the Pilcomayo and Bermejo rivers on the right and the São Lourenço (which receives the Río Cuiabá), Taquari, Miranda, Jejuí-Guazú, and Tebicuary rivers on the left.

Paraíba *pa-ra-ee'ba*, state in Nordeste region, NE Brazil; bordered E by the Atlantic; consists of a narrow coastal plain, a central plateau and semi-arid interior; drained by the Paraíba and the upper Piranhas rivers; pop(1980) 2,770,176; area 56,372 sq km; capital João Pessoa; economy: textile, metallurgy and food processing industries; whaling boats land at João Pessoa, and dried whale meat is an important part of the diet of the people in this region.

Parainen *pah'rī-nen*, PARGAS *par'gas* (Swed), 60 18N 22 20E, pop(1982) 11,267, town in Turku-Pori prov, SW Finland; on an inlet of the Gulf of Bothnia, S of Turku; established in 1948; economy: limestone quarries, cement works.

Paraíso, El *el pa-ra-ee'sō*, dept in SE Honduras, Central America; pop(1983e) 206,601; area 7,213 sq km; capital Yuscarán.

Parakou *pa-ra-koo'*, 9 23N 2 40E, pop(1979) 23,000, town in Borgou prov, NE Benin, W Africa; 150 km N of Porto Novo; airfield; railway; economy: groundnuts.

Paramaribo *pa-ra-ma'ri-bō*, urban dist in N Surinam, NE South America; part of Paramaribo federal capital; bounded N by the Atlantic; area 32 sq km; pop(1980) 67,905; capital Paramaribo.

Paramaribo, 5 54N 55 14W, pop(1980) 192,810, federal capital of Surinam, NE South America; chief port and only large town of Surinam, on the R Surinam; founded on an Indian village by the French in 1540; made capital of British Surinam in 1650; placed under Dutch rule in 1816; university (1968); airport (Zanderij) at 48 km; economy: trade in bauxite, coffee, timber, fruit; monuments: the main square in the old town is the Eenheidsplein (formerly Onafhankelijkheidsplein and before that the Oranjeplein); the People's Palace (the old Governor's Mansion) is in the square amidst many 18th and 19th-c buildings, built in traditional Dutch style; nearby is the old Fort Zeelandia, which was restored as the Surinam Museum but later repossessed by the military following their coup in 1980; the 19th-c Roman Catholic cathedral is built entirely of wood; a new harbour has been constructed about 1.5 km upstream.

Paramillo *pa-ra-meel'yō*, national park in Antioquia dept, NW central Colombia, South America; in the Cordillera Occidental, 96 km NW of Medellín; area 4,600 sq km; established in 1977; contains an Andean massif (3,959 m) of the same name.

Paramount, 33 53N 118 10W, pop(1980) 36,407, city in Los Angeles county, SW California, United States; c.18 km SSE of Los Angeles; the location of several film studios.

Par'amus, 40 55N 74 04W, pop(1980) 26,474, town in Bergen county, NE New Jersey, United States; 10 km NE of Paterson.

Paraná *pa-ra-na'*, 31 45S 60 30W, pop(1980) 159,581, capital of Entre Ríos prov, Litoral, E Argentina; founded in 1588 and capital of the republic from 1853 to 1862; railway; economy: trade in grain and cattle; monuments: cathedral; museum of fine arts; the Parque Urquiza, to the NW of town, has a statue of General Urquiza and a bas-relief showing the battle of Caseros, at which he finally defeated Rosas.

Paraná *pa-ra-na'*, state in Sul region, S Brazil; bounded W by Paraguay along the Río Paraná, SW by Argentina along the Río Peperi-Guaçu, E by the Atlantic, N by the Río Paranapanema, and S by Pelotas and Uruguay rivers; pop(1980) 7,629,392; area 199,554 sq km; capital Curitiba; chief towns Londrina, Ponta Grossa; chief port Paranaguá; economy: wheat, rye, potatoes, black beans, coffee, cattle, timber products, chemicals, food processing, non-metallic mineral products; the state was settled by Italians and Slavs; in the W is Sete Quedas National Park, on the border with Argentina is Iguaçu National Park and E of Ponta Grossa is the Vila Velha State Park, where sandstone rocks have been weathered into fantastic shapes; in the W on the Río Paraná were the great waterfalls known as the Sete Quedas in Brazil and as the Guaíra Falls in Spanish Latin America; they were drowned by the filling of the lake behind the enormous Itaipu dam in 1982.

Paraná, Río, major river of South America, forming, with its tributaries (notably the Paraguay) and with the Río Uruguay, South America's 2nd largest drainage system; rises on the plateau of SE central Brazil and flows generally S, along Paraguay's E and S border, into Argentina, where it joins the Uruguay after 3,300 km to form the Río de la Plata estuary on the Atlantic; at the junction of its two headstreams in Brazil, the Paranaíba and Río Grande, it takes the name of Alto Paraná and flows SSW along the Mato Grosso do Sul-São Paulo and Mato Grosso do Sul-Paraná prov borders; between the Guaíra Falls and the point where it meets the Río Iguazú it forms the Brazil-Paraguay border then turns SW and W, forming part of the border between Argentina and Paraguay; below Posadas (Argentina) and Encarnación (Paraguay), it is divided into several branches by large islands, and crosses 80 km of rapids (the Apipé rapids); joined by the Paraguay above Corrientes, the Paraná flows S and forms the Chaco-Corrientes, Santa Fe-Corrientes and Santa Fe-Entre Ríos prov borders; below Paraná (city) and Santa Fe it forms many small tributaries as well as the main river itself, all of which flow into the head of the Río de la Plata at points between Nueva Palmira (Uruguay) and Buenos Aires; the Paraná's chief tributaries, in addition to the Paraguay, include the Tietê, Paranapanema, Ivaí, Iguazú, Río Verde, Río Pardo, Ivinhema, Amambaí, all in Brazil, and the Salado and Carcarañá in Argentina; the river is dammed at various points for hydroelectricity, with a major scheme at Itaipu in Brazil.

Parañaque *pah-rah-nyah'kay*, 14 29N 120 59E, pop(1980) 208,552, residential city in Capital prov, Philippines; on SW shore of Manila Bay, Luzon I, S of Manila; event: Sunduan festival in Sept.

Pardubice *par'doo-bi-tse*, 50 03N 15 45E, pop(1984) 93,605, town in Východočeský region, Czech Socialist Republic, NW central Czechoslovakia; on R Elbe (Labe), E of Praha (Prague); known for horse racing and motorcycle racing; railway; economy: oil, brewing, food processing, footwear; monuments: 15th-c Kunetice castle, 13th-c cathedral.

Pargas, town in Finland. See Parainen.

Paricutín *pah-ree-koo-teen'*, 19 29N 102 17W, active volcano in W Michoacán, W central Mexico; N of Tancítaro volcano, 32 km WNW of Uruapan; erupted on 20 Feb 1943 in a cultivated field, its lava burying the Indian town of San Juan; from its base of approx 2,249 m above sea-level it had risen approx 250 m by 1950, when its activity had almost ceased; height 2,774 m; there is a festival in mid-Sept at San Juan to celebrate the saving of a Christ statue from the church; the church spires are all that can be seen of the former village.

Parima, Serra *ser'ra pa-ree'ma*, outlying mountain range in the Guiana Highlands; runs NNW-SSE along the Brazil-Venezuela border; length approx 320 km; rises to approx 1,524 m; connected with the Serra Pacaraima (NE); the Orinoco and headstreams of the Río Branco rise here.

Paris *pa-ree*, *par'is* (Eng), LUTETIA (anc), 48 50N 2 20E, pop(1982) 2,188,918, capital of France and of Ville de Paris dept, Ile-de-France, on the R Seine; named after the *Parisii*, a Celtic tribe, Paris originated as a pre-Roman settlement on an island in the R Seine; established as capital of France after the accession of Hugh Capet in 987; the city is strategically located at the convergence of several routeways including the Yonne, Marne and Oise valleys, and the railways from Dijon, Orléans and the SE; the R Seine is spanned by 30 bridges, the oldest of which is the Pont Neuf (1578-1604), and can be toured on the 'bateaux mouches'; Paris is surrounded by a ring road and is bounded W by the Bois de Boulogne and E by the Bois de Vincennes; the city is divided into 20 arrondissements but is often more simply divided between 'Left Bank' (formerly associated with the aristocracy) and 'Right Bank' (formerly associated with the middle class); since the 1950s the population has fallen from a figure of 2,725,000 to the present level; Paris is one of the most densely populated capitals of the world; headquarters of UNESCO; 12th-c Sorbonne University is named after Robert de Sorbon, confessor to St Louis, who founded a college to instruct poor students in theology; horse racing at Longchamp, Vincennes and Auteuil; there are 3 airports: Orly, to the S, and Le Bourget and Charles de Gaulle (Roissy) to the NE; métro; the main railway stations are the Gare du Nord (Lille, Calais, London, Bruxelles, Amsterdam); Gare de l'Est (Reims, Strasbourg, Switzerland); Gare d'Austerlitz (Bordeaux, Toulouse, Spain); Gare de Lyon (Lyon, Nice); Gare St-Lazare (Normandy); and Gare Montparnasse (Brittany, La Rochelle); economy: elegant hotels, night clubs, theatres, restaurants and shops make Paris an important tourist centre; the city is a world centre of high fashion and the production of luxury goods such as perfume and jewellery; heavy industry including car manufacture is located in the suburbs; monuments (Right Bank): Arc de Triomphe at the focal point of 12 avenues; Centre Pompidou, opened in 1977; Louvre museum containing a world-famous art collection; La Madeleine church; basilica of Sacré Cœur, consecrated in 1919; L'Opéra (1861-75); Tuileries gardens, named after the tiles dug out of clay here in the 15th century; monuments (Left Bank): Eiffel Tower, erected for the World Fair in 1889; Les Invalides founded by Louis XIV in 1670, with the tomb of Napoleon; Jardins des Plantes, originally a medicinal garden founded in 1626 by Louis XIII's doctors; Luxembourg Palace; Romanesque Notre-Dame cathedral (1163); events: international air show at Le Bourget in June of odd-numbered years; Festival du Quartiers du Marais in June-July; international film festival in Oct.

Paris *par'is*, 33 40N 95 33W, pop(1980) 25,498, county seat of Lamar county, NE Texas, United States; 150 km NE of Dallas; railway; economy: processing centre for a farming area.

Park Forest, 41 29N 87 40W, pop(1980) 26,222, residential town in Cook county, NE Illinois, United States; 41 km S of Chicago.

Park Ridge, 42 02N 87 51W, pop(1980) 38,704, town in Cook county, NE Illinois, United States; residential suburb 23 km N of Chicago; railway.

Parkersburg, 39 16N 81 34W, pop(1980) 39,967, county seat of Wood county, NW West Virginia, United States; port at the confluence of the Ohio and Little Kanawha rivers; railway; economy: shipping point in a coal mining region; manufactures synthetic fibres, plastics and glass.

Par'ma, prov of Emilia-Romagna region, N Italy; pop(1981) 400,192; area 3,450 sq km; capital Parma.

Parma, 44 48N 10 19E, pop(1981) 179,019, capital city of Parma prov, Emilia-Romagna region, N Italy; 126 km SE of Milano (Milan), on the R Parma, a tributary of the Po; university (1502); railway; situated on the Via Emilia; economy: oil refining, foodstuffs, pasta products; monuments: octagonal baptistry, begun in Romanesque style in 1196-1214, and completed in Gothic style in 1256-70; 12th-c cathedral; Palazzo della Pilotta (begun in 1583, left unfinished); domed church of the Madonna della Steccata (1521-39), modelled on St Peter's in Roma (Rome).

Parma, 41 23N 81 43W, pop(1980) 92,548, town in Cuyahoga county, NE Ohio, United States; a residential suburb 13 km S of Cleveland.

Parnaíba, *par-na-ee'ba*, river in NE Brazil; rises in the Serra de Tabatinga, NE Brazil, at 10 15S 45 57W; flows NNE past the town of Teresina to the Atlantic; forms the border between Maranhão and Piauí states; length approx 1,200 km; chief tributaries Balsas, Gurgueia, Canindé, Poti and Longá; the Parnaíba drainage basin is the largest between that of the Amazon (NW) and the São Francisco (SE); it covers all of Maranhão and Piauí states; the port of Parnaíba is at its mouth; SW of Teresina the river is dammed to form the Boa Esperança reservoir.

Párnon Óros *pahr'non*, mountain range in SE Pelopónnisos region, Greece, parallel to the coast of the Argolikós Kólpos (Gulf of Argolis); rises to 1,935 m, 27 km NE of Spartí.

Páros *pay'ros*, 3rd largest island of the Kikládhes, Greece, in the S Aegean Sea, W of Náxos; area 195 sq km; Páros (Paríkia) is the main port and chief town; there are beaches at Drios, Alikés and Pisso Livadi; the island was famous for its marble and its fine churches.

Parral *pa-ral'*, 36 08S 71 52W, pop(1982) 21,885, town in Linares prov, Maule, central Chile; railway.

Par'rett, river rising N of Beaminster in Dorset, S England; flows 56 km N and NW through Somerset to meet the Bridgwater Bay at Burnham-on-Sea.

Pártizánske *par'ti-zahn-ske*, formerly ŠIMONOVANÝ, 48 35N 18 23E, pop(1984) 24,766, town in Západoslovenský region, Slovak Socialist Republic, SE central Czechoslovakia; on R Nitra, NE of Nitra; economy: footwear.

Parvān *par-wan*, PARWĀN, prov in E central Afghanistan; pop(1984e) 548,001; area 9,399 sq km; capital Chāikār; crossed by the R Ghorband; part of the Hindu Kush system lies in the N section.

Pasadena *pas-e-dee'na*, 34 09N 118 09W, pop(1980) 118,550, resort city in Los Angeles county, SW California, United States; NE of Los Angeles, in the foothills of the San Gabriel Mts; railway; monuments: Pasadena Art Museum; the Civic Centre includes the City Hall, City Library and Civic Auditorium.

Pasadena, 29 43N 95 13W, pop(1980) 112,560, town in Harris county, SE Texas, United States; an industrial suburb 16 km E of Houston, on the Houston Ship Channel; airfield; economy: oil refining, chemicals, steel, paper, oil-field equipment, machinery, tools, building materials, grain trade; monuments: San Jacinto battlefield and monument.

Pasaje *pa-sa'KHay*, 3 23S 79 50W, pop(1982) 26,224, town in El Oro prov, SW Ecuador; on the Río Jubones, E of Machala and 130 km S of Guayaquil; railway; economy: timber products.

Pasay *pah'say*, 14 33N 121 00E, pop(1980) 287,770, city in Capital prov, Philippines; on Manila Bay, Luzon I, S of Manila.

Pascagoula *pas-ke-goo'la*, 30 21N 88 33W, pop(1980) 29,318, county seat of Jackson county, SE Mississippi, United States; a port on the Mississippi Sound at the mouth of the R Pascagoula; named after an Indian tribe; railway; economy: fishing, shipbuilding, paper, oil, chemicals.

Paşcani *pash-kan'*, 47 14N 26 46E, pop(1983) 33,176, town in Iaşi county, NE Romania; railway junction; economy: livestock, grain, timber trade.

Pasco *pas'kō*, dept in central Peru; in the Andes; bounded W by Cordillera Occidental, S by Cordillera Oriental, E by N outlier of the Gran Pajonal; drained by the upper Río Huallaga and headstreams of the Río Pachitea; pop(1981) 213,125; area 24,233 sq km; capital Cerro de Pasco.

Pascua, Isla de *pas'kwa*, EASTER ISLAND (Eng), 109 20W 27 05S; Chilean island just S of the Tropic of Capricorn and 3,790 km W of the Chile coast; area 166 sq km; max length 24 km; max width 12 km; pop(1985e) 2,000; the islanders are largely of Polynesian origin; capital Hanga Roa; Mataveri airport lies SE of the town; the island is triangular in shape, with an extinct volcano at each corner; rises to 652 m at Volcano Terevaka; consists of undulating grass and tree-covered hills with numerous caves and rocky outcrops; one-third of the island is covered by Rapa-Nui national park which was established in 1968, the remainder is largely used for grazing; there is a rainy season from Feb to Aug; the first European discovery was by Jacob Roggeveen on Easter Sunday 1722; in the 1850s the number of islanders was reduced by Peruvian slavers, smallpox and by emigration to Tahiti; during the last century the island was managed by sheep farmers; the island is famous for its unique *moai* stone statues depicting the human head and trunk of local ancestors and considered by their creators to have had supernatural powers; almost 1000 *moai* were carved from the slopes of Rano Raraku, where the largest one (19 m) still lies; on the SW slopes of the Rano Kau volcano crater are the remains of the ceremonial city of Orongo, consisting of 47 stone houses, an Ahu and petroglyph-covered rock outcrop honouring the birdman and the god Make Make; in the spring the chiefs appointed a representative of each tribe to swim out to the islands S of Easter Island and return with the first egg of the year; the winner became a *tangata manu*, or birdman, for the year.

Pas-de-Calais, dept in Nord-Pas-de-Calais region of N France, on the English Channel (Straits of Dover); comprises 7 arrond, 61 cantons and 898 communes; pop(1982) 1,412,413; area 6,672 sq km; drained by the Lys, Scarpe and Canche rivers; capital Arras, chief towns

Béthune, Boulogne, Calais and St-Omer; Boulogne and Calais are cross-channel terminals for car ferries and hovercraft; the dept saw bitter fighting in World War I (Vimy Ridge, Arras, etc) and in World War II preceding the Dunkerque (Dunkirk) evacuation.

Pasig *pah'seeg*, 14 32N 121 05E, pop(1980) 286,570, city in Capital prov, Philippines; on R Pasig, Luzon I, SE of Manila.

Paso de los Toros *pa'sō THay los tō'rōs*, 32 45S 56 47W, pop(1985) 12,826, town in Tacuarembó dept, N central Uruguay; at W end of the huge lake created by the Rincón del Bonete Dam on the Río Negro; railway.

Paso, El *pa'sō*, 31 45N 106 29W, pop(1980) 425,259, county seat of El Paso county, W Texas, United States; a port on the Rio Grande river opposite Ciudad Juarez, Mexico; founded in 1827; university (1913); railway; airfield; economy: trade in cattle, cotton and vegetables and the manufacture of refined petroleum, processed copper, foods, clothing and machinery; part of El Paso was transferred to Mexico in 1963, after the settlement of the Chamizal border dispute.

Passaic *pe-say'ik* (Algonquian, 'valley'), 40 51N 74 07W, pop(1980) 52,463, town in Passaic county, NE New Jersey, United States; on the R Passaic, 6 km S of Paterson; railway; economy: chemicals, pharmaceuticals.

Passaick, river rising near Morristown in NE New Jersey, United States; flows S, E and N, then S at Paterson through the Great Falls of the Passaic to meet the Newark Bay.

Passau *pas'ow*, 48 35N 13 28E, pop(1983) 51,800, city in Niederbayern dist, SE Bayern (Bavaria) prov, W Germany; at the confluence of the Danube, Inn and Ilz rivers, 149 km ENE of München (Munich), close to the Austrian border; university (1978); bishopric; railway, terminus of passenger boat services on the Donau; monuments: cathedral (15-17th-c), Oberhaus fortress; event: Spring Trade Fair.

Passo Fundo *pa'sō foon'dō*, 28 16S 52 20W, pop(1980) 103,064, town in Rio Grande do Sul state, Sul region, S Brazil; NW of Pôrto Alegre; university (1968); railway; economy: maize, soya beans, wheat, cattle.

Pastaza *pas-ta'sa*, tropical prov in E Ecuador; bounded E by Peru; pop(1982) 31,779; area 18,238 sq km; capital Puyo; economy: drinks, timber, tobacco.

Pasto *pas'tō*, 1 12N 77 17W, pop(1985) 244,559, capital of Nariño dept, SW Colombia, South America; SE of Galeras volcano; the town was a Royalist stronghold during the wars of independence; university (1964); economy: centre for Nariño's cattle and agricultural industries; famous for Pasto varnish; gold mines nearby; events: Día de los Negros (5 Jan), Día de los Blancos (6 Jan); Fiesta de las Aguas (5 Feb and 28 Dec); in the Concurso de Años Viejos, huge dolls representing the old year are burnt on 31 Dec.

Patagonia *pa-ta-gō'ni-a*, region of S Argentina comprising the provs of Chubut, Río Negro, Santa Cruz and the territory of Tierra del Fuego; a semi-arid tableland rising in terraces from the Atlantic coast to the base of the Andes which separate Chile from Argentina; watered by the Negro, Chubut, Deseado and Chico rivers; area 489,541 sq km; pop(1980) 790,803; chief towns include Rawson, Ushuaia, Comodoro Rivadavia, Rio Gallegos and the resort town of Bariloche; the name is sometimes also applied to the whole of the S part of S America including Chilean territory; in 1881 a treaty between Chile and Argentina fixed the boundary roughly along the 52nd parallel, but it was not until 1907 that demarcation was completed; in 1520 Magellan sailed along the Patagonian coast and passed through the strait that bears his name.

Pa'tan, LALITPUR ('city of beauty'), 27 40N 85 20E, pop(1971) 48,577, city in central Nepal, central Asia; 5 km SE of Kathmandu, in the Kathmandu Valley, close to the S bank of the R Bagmati; founded in the 7th century and built in a circular plan with Buddhist monuments (*stupas*) on the four points of the compass, which according to legend were built by Ashoka, the Buddhist emperor of India; capital of the Nepali kingdom in the 17th century until capture by the Gurkhas in 1768; economy: wool and leather; known as the city of artists, it is the centre of the Banra sect of goldsmiths and silversmiths; monuments: Durbar Square (the palace complex of Patan) is the focal point of the city, built in the 16th century by King Siddhi Narasingha Malla , with its palace of the Malla Kings, the temple of Lord Krishna and the Royal Bath (*Tushahity*).

Paterson, 40 55N 74 11W, pop(1980) 137,970, county seat of Passaic county, NE New Jersey, United States; on the R Passaic, 22 km N of Newark; railway; economy: clothing, chemicals; formerly a major silk-manufacturing centre.

Pátmos, island of the Sporádhes, Greece, in the Aegean Sea, off the W coast of Turkey; area 34 sq km; chief town is Hora with harbour at Skala; St John spent 2 years in Pátmos; monastery of St John built in 11th century; there are beaches at Grikos, Meloi, Netia, Diakofti and Kampos; event: church fair of Panagia in Aug.

Pat'na *pat'na*, AZIMABAD, 25 37N 85 12E, pop(1981) 916,000, winter capital of Bihar, E India; 467 km NW of Calcutta, on the S bank of the R Ganga (Ganges); the ancient city of Pataliputra, capital of the 6th-c Magadha kingdom, is buried beneath the present city; in 1732 a French trading post was established here, the rights of which were renounced in 1947; Patna lies at the centre of a major rice-growing region; the city is an industrial centre, noted for its handicrafts (brassware, furniture, carpets); university (1917); monuments: Sikh temple, mosque of Sher Shah.

Patos, Lagoa dos *pa'tōs*, tidal lagoon in SE Rio Grande do Sul state, Sul region, S Brazil; area 10,145 sq km; 240 km long; up to 48 km wide; separated from the Atlantic by a low sand bar 32 km wide in N, narrowing southward; reaches the open sea by a channel 1.5 km wide at the S end, near the port of Rio Grande; at Pelotas the lagoon receives the overflow of L Mirim via the São Gonçalo canal.

Pátrai *pa'tray*, PATRAS' (Eng), 38 14N 21 44E, pop(1981) 154,596, seaport and capital town of Akhaïa nome (dept), NW Pelopónnisos region, Greece; a thriving industrial and commercial centre; the Greek War of Independence began here in 1821; university; archbishopric; railway; ferry to Italy and the Greek islands; monument: Roman Odeon, used for concerts and theatrical performances; events: carnival (Feb); Navy Week (June-July).

Pattaya *pah-tī'ya*, 12 57N 100 53E, beach resort in E Thailand; on the NE shore of the Gulf of Thailand S of Bang Phra; the 'Riviera' of Thailand, with resort facilities.

Patuakhali *put-wah'ka-lee*, region in S Bangladesh; includes Barguna and Patuakhali districts; pop(1981) 1,843,000; area 4,095 sq km; on the Ganges delta, bounded by the R Haringhat in the W and the R Tetulia in the E; capital Patuakhali.

Patuakhali, 22 20N 90 20E, pop(1981) 267,000, capital of Patuakhali region, S Bangladesh; S of Barisal.

Patuca *pa-too'ka*, river in Olancho and Gracias a Dios depts, E Honduras, Central America; formed 37 km SE of Juticalpa by the union of the Guayape and Guayambre rivers; flows c.320 km NE to meet the Caribbean Sea at Patuca.

Pau *po*, 43 19N 0 25W, pop(1982) 85,766, economic centre and capital of Pyrénées-Atlantiques dept, Aquitaine region, SW France; on the right bank of the R Gave de Pau, 174 km S of Bordeaux; originally a hunting-lodge of the Counts of Bearn; developed into a town and became capital of Bearn (largest of the former Pyrenean provinces) in 1464; birthplace of Henry IV of France and Charles XIV (Bernadotte) of Sweden; its administrative importance has grown since the discovery in 1951 of reserves of natural gas at Lacq, 25 km to the NW; a health resort in both summer and winter, winter sports centre; during the 19th century Pau was 'discovered' by British visitors and developed rapidly thereafter; road and rail junction; economy: engineering, textiles, brewing, tanning, tourism; monuments: 12-15th-c castle (extended in later centuries, has a modern entrance); in the Musée des Beaux-Arts there are paintings by Rubens, Corot, Dégas, El Greco and many others; the Musée Bernadotte (N of the chateau) is housed in the birthplace of the famous marshal who served under Napoleon and then founded the present Swedish royal dynasty as Charles XIV; the Boulevard des Pyrénées, just under 2 km long, was laid out on the orders of Napoleon and affords magnificent views of the Pyrénées.

Paul da Serra *pa-ool' da se'ra*, plateau, W Madeira, Funchal dist, Portugal, rising to 1,419 m.

Pavia *pa-vee'a*, prov of Lombardia region, N Italy; pop(1981) 512,895; area 2,966 sq km; capital Pavia.

Pavia, TICI'NUM (anc), 45 12N 9 09E, pop(1981) 85,029, capital town of Pavia prov, Lombardia region, N Italy; on the R Ticino near its junction with the Po, in the W part of the N Italian plain; linked with Milano (Milan) to the N by a shipping canal, the Naviglio di Pavia; university (1361); railway; economy: iron and steel castings, sewing machines; monuments: cathedral (begun in 1487); coronation church of San Michele (1155); old convent church of San Pietro in Ciel d'Oro (1132), restored in 1875-99.

Pavlodar *puv-lu-dar'*, 52 21N 76 59E, pop(1983) 302,000, river port capital of Pavlodarskaya oblast, NE Kazakhskaya SSR, Soviet Union; on the R Irtysh; founded in 1720; centre of large-scale manufacturing industry; railway; airfield; road junction; economy: clothing, oil refining, ferroalloy plant, agricultural equipment, coal-fired power station, machine building.

Pawtuck'et (Algonquian, 'falls-(in)-river-at'), 41 53N 71 23W, pop(1980) 71,204, city in Providence county, NE Rhode Island, United States; on the R Blackstone at Pawtucket Falls, 7 km NE of Providence; established in 1671, achieving city status in 1885; the first US textile mill to use Arkwright machinery was established here in 1790; railway; economy: toys, textiles, machine tools, wire; monument: Slater Mill.

Payachata, Nevados de *pa-ya-cha'ta*, 18 10S 69 10W, Andean massif on Chile-Bolivia border; 129 km WNW of Arica; includes two snow-capped peaks: Cerro de Pomarepe (6,240 m) and Cerro de Parinacota (6,342 m).

Pays de la Loire, region of W France comprising the depts of Loire-Atlantique, Maine-et-Loire, Mayenne, Sarthe and Vendée, 17 arrond, 198 cantons and 1,502 communes; pop(1982) 2,930,398; area 32,082 sq km; bounded on the W by the Bay of Biscay; the land rises in E Vendée dept to 289 m in the Hauteurs de Gâtine; drained by the Loire R and its tributaries (Mayenne, Sarthe, Loir); the Pays de Retz, SE of St-Nazaire and S of the Loire estuary, is an area of marshland, on whose beaches grow the vines that produce the wine Gros-Plant; La Brière Grande, in Loire-Atlantique dept, now designated the Parc Régional de Brière, is a region of swamps where people live by fishing and marsh farming; the Forêt de Berce, in Sarthe dept, is part of the once vast forest of Le Mans; there are seaside resorts at Batz-sur-Mer, La Baule, Les-Sables-d'Olonne and St-Jean-de-Monts; there are numerous châteaux worth visiting including the Château de Craon (in Mayenne dept) and the Château de Goulaine (in Loire-Atlantique dept); chief towns Nantes, St-Nazaire (originally the deep-water port for Nantes, now an important centre of shipbuilding), Angers, Laval, Le Mans and La Roche-sur-Yon; Saumur is celebrated for its sparkling wines and cavalry school.

Paysandú *pī-san-doo'*, dept in NW Uruguay; bordered W by Argentina along the Río Uruguay, N by the Río Daymán, S by the Río Negro and E and S by the Cuchilla de Haedo range; drained by the Río Queguay; pop(1985) 103,487; area 13,252 sq km; capital Paysandú; in the NW corner of the dept is the Meseta de Artigas, home of General Artigas.

Paysandú, 32 21S 58 05W, pop(1985) 74,014, capital of Paysandú dept, NW Uruguay; on the E bank of the Río Uruguay; railway; an international toll bridge crosses here to Colón (Argentina); monuments: the 19th-c cathedral has cannonballs embedded in its walls dating from the 1865 Brazilian siege when the town was held by Paraguay; a few km N are waterfalls on the Río Queguay; 50 km N of the town are the Termas del Guaviyú thermal springs.

Paz, La *lah pahz*, dept in W Bolivia; bordered W by Peru and by Chile in extreme SW; includes E part of L Titicaca; crossed NW-SE by the Andean Cordillera Oriental, with the peaks of Illampu and Illimani; a mountain range separates the Altiplano (S) from the Yungas and tropical lowlands (N); the Río Desaguadero drains the Altiplano, the Río Beni and its affluents drain the tropical lowlands; archaeological ruins at Tiahuanaco (45 km NW from La Paz); pop(1982) 1,913,184; area 133,985 sq km; capital La Paz; economy: mining at Viloco, 264 km from La Paz; Matilde (zinc, lead, copper, silver), on NE shore of L Titicaca; Corocoro (copper), 100 km from La Paz; Caracoles (tin); and Colquiri (zinc), 235 km from La Paz.

Paz, La, 16 30S 68 10W, pop(1982) 881,404, regional capital and capital (govt) of Bolivia in Murillo prov, La Paz, W Bolivia; highest capital in the world; alt 3,665 m; set in a natural basin 370 m below the level of the Altiplano in its NE corner; founded by Spaniards in 1548; Mount Illimani (6,402 m) towers above the city to the SE; there is skiing 36 km outside the city at the world's highest ski run at Mount Chacaltaya; university (1830); railway; airport (El Alto, recently renamed Kennedy International Airport); economy: copper, wool, alpaca; the city's districts are arranged in a steppe-like formation; most of the Indians live in the higher terraces, the main business district and government offices are below, with the wealthier residential districts (Calacoto and La Florida) and their sports and social clubs further down; the traditional centre is the Plaza Murillo, to the NE of the Río Paz, with the modern cathedral, the Presidential Palace (Palacio Quemado) and the Congreso Nacional, home of Bolivia's Senate and Chamber of Deputies, grouped around it; opposite the cathedral is the National Art Museum, in the 18th-c baroque palace of the Condes de Arana; colonial buildings such as the monastery of San Francisco still remain, but much of the city is modern.

Paz, La, maritime dept in El Salvador, Central America; bounded S by the Pacific Ocean; pop(1971) 194,196; area 1,155 sq km; capital Zacatecoluca; chief towns San Juan Nonualco and Santiago Nonualco; part of Lago de Ilopango occupies its NW corner.

Paz, La, largely mountainous dept in Honduras, Central America; pop(1983e) 86,627; area 2,327 sq km; capital La Paz.

Paz, La, 24 10N 110 17W, pop(1984e) 100,000, port capital of Baja California Sur state, NW Mexico; situated in the SE of the state, in the Bahía de la Paz; a free port; ferry; airfield; economy: pearling, tourism; monuments: the Mission of Our Lady of La Paz in Plaza Constitución was founded in 1720 by the Jesuit, Jaime Bravo; the Museo Antropológico de Baja California Sur contains photographs of prehistoric paintings, the geological history of the peninsula, fossils and art exhibits.

Paz, La, 34 21S 56 18W, pop(1985) 17,680, town in Canelones dept, S Uruguay.

Pazardzhik or **Pazardzik** *pa'zar-jeek*, okrug (prov) of central Bulgaria lying between the Stara Planina (Balkan Mts) and the Rhodopi Planina (Rhodope Mts); traversed W-E by the R Maritsa; area 4,379 sq km; pop(1981) 322,000; a wine-growing area.

Pazardzhik, 42 12N 24 20E, capital of Pazardzhik okrug (prov), central Bulgaria; on the R Maritsa, 120 km SE of Sofiya; under Turkish rule during the 15-19th centuries, when the city was called Tatar-Pazari; railway; economy: textiles and food processing.

Peabody, 42 31N 70 56W, pop(1980) 45,976, town in Essex county, NE Massachusetts, United States; 23 km NE of Boston; originally part of Salem.

Peace, river in W Canada; rises in British Columbia in the

Omineca Mts (part of the Stikine Ranges) as the Finlay river; flows SE into Williston Lake and to Finlay Forks where it is joined by the Parsnip river and becomes the Peace river; it then flows E into Alberta, past the town of Peace River from where it flows generally N to Fort Vermilion then ENE through Wood Buffalo National Park to enter the Slave river near its outflow from L Athabasca near Fort Chipewyan; length 1,923 km to the head of the Finlay river.

Peacehaven, 50 47N 0 01E, pop(1981) 12,887, residential town E of Brighton in Lewes dist, East Sussex, SE England; on the English Channel, 3 km W of Newhaven.

Peak District, national park in N central England; area 1,404 sq km; established in 1951; the greater part of its area is in Derbyshire with smaller parts in Staffordshire, Cheshire, Greater Manchester, South Yorkshire and West Yorkshire; comprises limestone uplands and woodlands in the S and E, moorlands and crags in the N which is a popular walking and climbing area; there are information centres at Bakewell and Edale; there is a residential study centre at Nosehill Hall.

Pearl City, 21 24N 157 59W, pop(1980) 42,575, city in Honolulu county, Hawaii, United States; on Pearl Harbor, Oahu I; a residential suburb; severely damaged in the Japanese air attack on Pearl Harbor naval base on 7 Dec 1941.

Pearl Harbor, inlet occupied by a US naval base on the island of Oahu in the US Pacific Ocean state of Hawaii; adjacent to Honolulu; a treaty of 1887 granted the USA rights to use Pearl Harbor as a coaling and repair base; a naval base was established in 1908; the bombing of the naval base by the Japanese on 7 Dec 1941 brought the USA into World War II.

Pearl Islands, Panama. See Perlas, Archipieago de las.

Pearl River, river in S China. See Zhu Jiang.

Peary Land *pee'ri*, region of N Greenland on the Arctic Ocean, forming a mountainous peninsula; its N cape, Kap Morris Jesup, is the most northerly point of land in the Arctic; unlike most of Greenland this area is not covered by ice, explored by Peary in 1892 and 1900.

Peć or **Pech** *pech*, 42 40N 20 19E, pop(1981) 111,071, town in SW Srbija (Serbia) republic, Yugoslavia; 72 km W of Priština near the Albanian frontier in a fruit and vegetable-growing area; part of Montenegro (1913-29) and Albania (1941-44); railway; monument: Patriarchate of Peć, a Raška school monastery.

Pechora *pye-cho'ra*, river in N European Rossiyskaya, W Soviet Union, rising on the W slopes of the Ural'skiy Khrebet (Ural Mts); flows generally N through the forest and tundra regions of Komi ASSR, turns W at Trosh, then N again at Ust'tsil'ma, and finally flows through NE Arkhangel'skaya oblast to discharge into Pechorskaya Guba (Pechora Bay) of the Barents Sea, forming a delta mouth at Nar'yan Mar; length 1,790 km; drainage basin area 327,000 sq km; chief tributaries include the Izhma, Tsil'ma, Usa, and Kozhva rivers; the Pechora coal basin extends E from the middle course of the river.

Pecos *pee'kos*, river in S USA; rises in N New Mexico in the Sangre de Cristo Mts; flows S through New Mexico, past Carlsbad then SE through SW Texas, past Pecos city, to join the Rio Grande 56 km NW of Del Rio; length 1,490 km; used for irrigation.

Pécs *paytch*, FUNFKIRCHEN (Ger), SOPIANAE (Lat), 46 05N 18 15E, pop(1984e) 175,000, industrial capital of Baranya county, S Hungary; at the foot of the Mecsek Mts; capital of E Pannonia under Roman rule; surrounded by city walls during the Middle Ages; bishopric; university (1367, refounded in 1922); University of Medicine (1923); centre of a noted wine-producing area; economy: wine, leather goods; coal mining centre.

Pedro Juan Caballero *ped'rō hwahn ka-bal-yay'rō*, 22 30S 55 44W, pop(1982) 37,331, capital of Amambay dept, Oriental, E Paraguay; on the frontier, opposite Ponta Porã, Brazil; the town has become notorious as the centre of the Brazil-Paraguay drugs trade.

Peebles, 55 39N 3 12W, pop(1981) 6,692, capital of Tweeddale dist, Borders, SE central Scotland; on the R Tweed, 33 km S of Edinburgh; economy: textiles; monuments: Tweeddale museum; 1½ km W of Peebles is medieval Neidpath castle; 13 km ESE of the town is Traquair House, the oldest inhabited house in Scotland.

Pegu *pe-goo'*, division in S Burma; bordered in the SE by the Gulf of Martaban; mountainous in the N, with low lying fertile land in the S which is crossed by rivers and canals; the S part of the Pegu Yoma range extends S through the centre of Pegu division; the R Irrawaddy forms part of the W border; drained by the R Sittang (E); pop(1983) 3,800,240; capital Pegu.

Pegu, 17 18N 96 31E, pop(1983) 254,761, capital of Pegu division, SE central Burma; railway.

Pegu Yoma *yō'ma*, mountain chain in S central Burma; situated between the Irrawaddy and Sitang river valleys; the chain rises S of the Irrawaddy river bend near Myingyan and extends SSE through the centre of Pegu division; it rises to 1,518 m in Popa Mt; most peaks are below 600 m.

Pekanbaru or **Pakanbaru** *pah-kahn'bah-roo*, 0 33N 101 30E, pop(1980) 145,030, river-port capital of Riau prov, Indonesia; on R Siak at the centre of the island of Sumatera; 160 km from the coast; university (1962); airfield; economy: oil (Rumbai); monument: the Grand Mosque.

Pekin *pee'kin*, 40 35N 89 40W, pop(1980) 33,967, county seat of Tazewell county, central Illinois, United States; port on R Illinois, 16 km S of Peoria; founded in 1824; railway.

Peking, capital city and municipality in E China. See Beijing.

Pelau, Pacific island group. See Belau.

Pelée, Montagne *pel-uy'*, MOUNT PELÉE, 14 18N 61 10W, volcano on Martinique I, E Caribbean rising to 1,397 m; erupted in 1902 killing over 26,000 people in the town of St Pierre.

Peleliu *pe'le-lyoo*, flat coral island of the Republic of Belau, W Caroline Is, 50 km SW of Koror I, in the W Pacific Ocean; it was the heart of the Japanese defences during World War II; the limestone caves and tunnels where the Japanese held out to the end of the war can be visited.

Pélla, nome (dept) of Makedhonia region, N Greece; pop(1981) 132,386; area 2,506 sq km; capital Edhessa.

Pellworm *pel'vorm*, island of the Nordfriesische Inseln (North Frisian Is), W Germany; in the North Sea, off the W coast of Schleswig-Holstein prov; area 37.2 sq km; it is the remainder of a larger island which was partly flooded in 1634.

Peloponnese, region of Greece. See Pelopónnisos.

Pelopónnisos *pel-op-on'ee-sos* ('the island of Pelops'), PELEPONNESE *pel-op-on-neez'* (Eng), peninsular region of Greece; comprises the nomoi (depts) of Akhaïa, Argolís, Arkadhía, Ilia, Kórinthos, Lakonía, and Messinía; pop(1981) 1,012,528; area 21,379 sq km; it is the most southerly part of the Greek mainland, to which it is linked by the narrow Isthmus of Corinth; in the centre of the region is the thinly populated upland nome (dept) of Arkadhía, bordered on the N by a range of hills with Killíni (2,376 m) its highest peak; drained by the R Alfiós; chief towns Árgos, Kórinthos, Pátrai, Pírgos, Spartí, and Kalámai; it is a popular holiday region.

Pelotas *pe-lo'tas*, 31 45S 52 20W, pop(1980) 196,919, port in Rio Grande do Sul state, Sul region, S Brazil; at the S end of Lagoa dos Patos; on left bank of the Río São Gonçalo which connects the Lagoa dos Patos with the Lagoa Mirim; 2 universities (1883, 1960); railway; airfield; economy: rice, fruit, vegetables, soya beans, food processing.

Pelvoux, Massif du *mas-eef doo pel-voo*, largest mountain group of the Alpes Dauphiné in Isère and Hautes-Alpes depts, E France, rising to 4,103 m at Barre des Écrins.

Pem'ba, 23 43S 35 00E, pop(1980) 41,166, seaport capital of Cabo Delgado prov, N Mozambique, SE Africa; in Pemba dist; on Pemba Bay, an inlet of the Mozambique Channel, N of Moçambique; airfield.

Pemba, island region of Tanzania, E Africa; in the Indian

Ocean, N of Zanzibar and E of Tanga; area 981 sq km; pop(1985e) 256,950; capital Chake Chake; economy: cloves, copra.

Pem'broke, parish in the Bermuda Islands; pop(1980) 12,060.

Pembroke, 51 41N 4 55W, pop(1981) 15,576 (with Pembroke Dock), town in South Pembrokeshire dist, Dyfed, SW Wales; railway; ferry to Ireland; economy: engineering.

Pembroke Pines, 26 00N 80 14W, pop(1980) 35,776, town in Broward county, SE Florida, United States; a residential suburb SW of Fort Lauderdale.

Pembrokeshire Coast, national park in Wales; area 579 sq km; established in 1952; characterized by impressive stretches of coastline alternating between cliffs and sandy beaches; the area includes Milford Haven harbour, St David's cathedral and various Norman castles; information centres are located at Tenby, St David's, Pembroke, Newport, Kilgetty, Haverfordwest and Broad Haven.

Pembrokeshire Coast Path, long-distance footpath following the coast of Wales, from Amroth to Dogmaels; length 269 km.

Penafiel *pay-nya-fyel'*, 41 12N 8 17W, pop(1981) 6,000, town in Porto dist, N Portugal; on high ground between R Sousa and R Tâmega, 25 km E of Porto; until the late 18th-c the town was known as Arrifana de Sousa; monuments: 14th-c castle and Renaissance-style church of Misericordia.

Penang, state and island in Malaysia. See Pinang, Pulau.

Penarth', 51 27N 3 11W, pop(1981) 22,920, residential town in Cardiff dist, South Glamorgan, S Wales; S of Cardiff; recreational sailing and fishing centre on the Bristol Channel; railway; economy: chemicals.

Pen-ch'i, town in Liaoning prov, NE China. See Benxi.

Penco *payn'kō*, 36 45S 73 00W, pop(1982) 27,271, town in Concepción prov, Bío-Bío, central Chile; railway.

Peneda, Serra da *pen-ay'da*, border mountain range, NE Portugal, rising to 1,415 m; part of Peneda-Gerês National Park.

Peneda-Gerês, national park in a remote mountain area in Viana do Castelo, Braga and Vila Real dists, Portugal, on the Spanish border; Portugal's first national park, extending from the Castro Laboreiro plateau across the Peneda, Soajo, Amarela and Gerês mountains to the Mourela plateau; includes stands of pine, oak, cork-oak and eucalyptus forest; area 500 sq km; established in 1970.

P'eng-hu or **P'eng-hu Lieh-tao** *peng-hoo lye-dow*, PESCADORES (Span), island archipelago and county of Taiwan; situated in the Taiwan Haixia (Taiwan Strait), astride the Tropic of Cancer; consists of 64 islands, total area 126.8 sq km; pop(1982e) 104,083; 21 of the islands are uninhabitable; 85% of the pop lives on the largest island, P'eng-hu Tao; P'eng-hu Bay Bridge is the largest inter-island bridge in the Far East (5,541 m long, with 2,160 m of that over water), it links 2 of the main islands; there are no rivers on P'eng-hu Lieh-tao all water comes from wells, some of them more than 150 m deep; economy: fishing, vegetable farming, coral; monuments: the archipelago contains 147 temples, mostly built by fishermen; the oldest was built in 1593 in honour of Matsu, the Goddess of the Sea; during the Ming dynasty (1368-1644) 7 virgins allegedly drowned themselves in a well on Chimei Island (the Island of Seven Beauties) to escape possible violation by raiding pirates; the Tomb of the Seven Virgins was erected to honour them and the island named after them; P'eng-hu Lieh-tao archipelago was named the Pescadores (fishermen's islands) by Portuguese sailors in the 16th century; they were occupied by the Dutch (1622-24), then reverted to China and became a dependency of Taiwan in the late 17th century; in 1960 the archipelago was proclaimed a county of Taiwan province.

Peniche *pin-ee'shi*, 39 19N 9 22W, pop(1981) 15,600, fishing town in Leiria dist, central Portugal; situated on a rocky peninsula on the Atlantic coast, 81 km NW of Santarem; crayfish, sardine and tuna fisheries; monuments: castle and church of São Pedro; pillowlace-making school; event: festival of the Senhora da Boa Viagem, a fishermen's festival with a procession of boats at the beginning of Aug.

Penicuik *pen'i-kook*, 55 50N 3 14W, pop(1981) 17,607, town in Midlothian dist, Lothian, E central Scotland; on the North Esk river, 14 km S of Edinburgh; economy: paper, glass, scientific instruments; monuments: NE of Penicuik, in the village of Roslin, is Rosslyn Chapel, an uncompleted 15th-c chapel, famous for its stone carvings.

Pennine Chain or **The Pennines**, mountain range in N England; extends S from Northumberland to Derbyshire; consists of an anticlinal fold of carboniferous limestone and overlying millstone grit which is worn into high moorland and fell; in the N it is separated from the Cheviot Hills by the Tyne Gap and in the S the chain is dissected by the Yorkshire Dales; rises to 893 m at Cross Fell; the chain forms the main watershed for the rivers of N England; the Pennine Way footpath extends 402 km from Derbyshire to the Scottish Borders.

Pennine Way, long-distance footpath stretching from Edale in N Derbyshire, England to Kirk Yetholm in the Scottish borders; length 402 km.

Pennsylvania *pen-sil-vay'ni-a*, state in E United States; bounded W by West Virginia and Ohio, N by L Erie and New York, E by New York and New Jersey, and S by Delaware, Maryland and West Virginia (Mason-Dixon Line); the 'Keystone State'; pop(1980) 11,863,895; area 116,709 sq km; one of the original states of the Union, 2nd to ratify the Federal Constitution; capital Harrisburg; other major cities include Philadelphia, Pittsburgh and Erie; the R Delaware forms the E border; the R Susquehanna flows E, then S through the centre of the state; near the W border the R Allegheny flows S to join the R Monongahela at Pittsburgh forming the R Ohio which flows W; economy: metals, machinery, electrical equipment, grain, vegetables, apples, hay, tobacco, grapes; first settled by the Swedish in 1643; taken by the Dutch and then by the British in 1664; the region was given by King Charles II to William Penn in 1681; the state is divided into 67 counties as follows:

County	*area (sq km)*	*pop(1980)*
Adams	1,355	68,292
Allegheny	1,890	1,450,085
Armstrong	1,680	77,768
Beaver	1,134	204,441
Bedford	2,644	46,784
Berks	2,239	312,509
Blair	1,370	136,621
Bradford	2,995	62,919
Bucks	1,586	479,211
Butler	2,051	147,912
Cambria	1,797	183,263
Cameron	1,035	6,674
Carbon	998	53,285
Centre	2,876	112,760
Chester	1,971	316,660
Clarion	1,578	43,362
Clearfield	2,987	83,578
Clinton	2,317	38,971
Columbia	1,264	61,967
Crawford	2,629	88,869
Cumberland	1,422	178,541
Dauphin	1,373	232,317
Delaware	478	555,007
Elk	2,158	38,338
Erie	2,090	279,780
Fayette	2,064	159,417
Forest	1,113	5,072
Franklin	2,012	113,629
Fulton	1,139	12,842
Greene	1,500	40,476
Huntingdon	2,280	42,253
Indiana	2,155	92,281
Jefferson	1,708	48,303

contd

County	*area (sq km)*	*pop(1980)*
Juniata	1,019	19,188
Lackawanna	1,199	227,908
Lancaster	2,475	362,346
Lawrence	944	107,150
Lebanon	944	108,582
Lehigh	905	272,349
Luzerne	2,317	343,079
Lycoming	3,216	118,416
McKean	2,545	50,635
Mercer	1,747	128,299
Mifflin	1,074	46,908
Monroe	1,583	69,409
Montgomery	1,264	643,621
Montour	341	16,675
Northampton	978	225,418
Northumberland	1,199	100,381
Perry	1,448	35,718
Philadelphia	354	1,688,210
Pike	1,430	18,271
Potter	2,811	17,726
Schuylkill	2,033	160,630
Snyder	855	33,584
Somerset	2,790	81,243
Sullivan	1,173	6,349
Susquehanna	2,148	37,876
Tioga	2,941	40,973
Union	824	32,870
Venango	1,765	64,444
Warren	2,301	47,449
Washington	2,231	217,074
Wayne	1,901	35,237
Westmoreland	2,686	392,294
Wyoming	1,037	26,433
York	2,356	312,963

Penonomé *pay-nō-nō-may'*, 8 30N 80 20W, pop(1980) 7,695, capital town of Coclé prov, central Panama, Central America; 96 km SW of Panamá City, on the Inter-American Highway.

Penrhyn *pen'rin*, TONGAREVA *tong-u-re'vu*, 9 00S 158 03W, coral atoll of the Cook Is, S Pacific, 1,176 km NE of Rarotonga; area 9.84 sq km; pop(1981) 608; there is a good natural harbour on the island.

Penrith', 54 40N 2 44W, pop(1981) 12,290, town in Eden dist, Cumbria, NW England; 30 km S of Carlisle; railway; economy: engineering, timber, glass; monuments: 14-15th-c castle, St Andrew's church.

Penryn, town in Cornwall, SW England. See Falmouth.

Pensaco'la, 30 25N 87 13W, pop(1980) 57,619, county seat of Escambia county, NW Florida, United States; a port on Pensacola Bay, 16 km E of Alabama border; railway; economy: shipping and fishing; manufactures include synthetic fibres, paper products, chemicals, naval stores and nuclear-reactor parts; US naval air station nearby; monument: the ruins of Forts Barrancas, San Carlos, Pickens and McRae are on the shores of Pensacola Bay.

Penza *pyen'za*, 53 11N 45 00E, pop(1983) 515,000, capital city of Penzenskaya oblast, S central European Rossiyskaya, Soviet Union; on the R Sura, a tributary of the R Volga; founded in 1663 as an outpost on the SE border of the Russian state; centre of an extensive and fertile black-earth district; railway junction; airport; economy: clothing, leatherwork, machine tools, industrial equipment.

Penzance *pen-zans'*, 50 07N 5 33W, pop(1981) 19,579, town in Kerrier dist, Cornwall, SW England; chief resort town of 'the Cornish Riviera', 40 km SW of Truro; railway, ferry and helicopter services to Scilly Isles; economy: tourism, clothing; monument: Chysauster Iron Age village (N).

Peoria *pee-ō'ree-u*, 40 42N 89 36W, pop(1980) 124,160, county seat of Peoria county, central Illinois, United States; on the R Illinois, 107 km N of Springfield; a French fort was established in 1680 by La Salle; called Fort Clark until 1825; achieved city status in 1845; Bradley University (1896); railway.

Perak *per'ak*, (Malay, 'silver'), state in W Peninsular Malaysia, SE Asia; bounded W by the Strait of Malacca; watered by the R Perak; pop(1980) 1,743,655; area 21,005 sq km; economy: tin, timber; capital Ipoh; chief towns Taiping, Teluk Intan, Kampar, Sungai Siput, Kuala Kangsar; the sultans of Perak are descended from the sultans of Malacca; one of the wealthiest states in Malaysia since the discovery of tin in the 1840s; the Kinta Valley is the leading tin-mining area.

Perak, second longest river in Peninsular Malaysia, SE Asia; flows 320 km W to the Strait of Malacca.

Pereira *pe-ray'ra*, 4 47N 75 46W, pop(1985) 390,190, capital of Risaralda dept, W central Colombia, South America; founded in 1863; university (1961); railway; airfield (Matecaña) at 5 km; economy: a centre for the region's coffee and cattle industries.

Pergamino *per-ga-mee'nō*, 33 54S 60 40W, pop(1980) 68,989, town in Buenos Aires prov, Litoral, E Argentina; NW of Buenos Aires; railway.

Pergamon, Turkey. See Bergama.

Périgord *pay-ree-gor*, a part of the former prov of Guyenne, SW France, now mostly in the dept of Dordogne; divided into Périgord Blanc lying N of the Dordogne and Vézère valleys and Périgord Noir to the S; an extensively forested, chalky area, known for truffles; interesting caves near Montignac, Rouffignac and Le Bugue; the chief town is Périgueux.

Périgueux *per-ee-gœ*, VESUNA (anc), 45 10N 0 42E, pop(1982) 35,392, capital town of Dordogne dept, Aquitaine region, SW central France; on the right bank of the R Isle, 106 km ENE of Bordeaux; ancient settlement of the Petrocorii tribe (hence the modern name); the medieval town developed around an abbey on a hill to the NE; there was fierce rivalry between the 'old city' and the medieval city which finally ended in 1251 when they were united in one community; suffered heavily in the 16th-c Wars of Religion; bishopric; road and rail junction; economy: centre of the foie-gras and truffle industry; more recently the site of a government stamp-printing works; light metal and engineering works; monuments: 12th-c cathedral of St-Front, one of the largest churches in SW France, Romanesque in style with Byzantine influences; 12th-c church of St-Étienne which served as a cathedral until 1669, largely destroyed in 1577 leaving only 2 bays and the W tower of the original building; extensive Roman remains including the Tour de Vesone and fragments of an amphitheatre; late 15th-c Tour Mataguerre, a relic of the fortifications of Puy-St-Front.

Perito Francisco P. Moreno *pay-ree'tō fran-sees'kō puy mo ray'nō*, national park in W Santa Cruz prov, Patagonia, Argentina; area 845 sq km; established in 1937; borders W with Chile; contains several small lakes.

Per'las, Archipiélago de las, PEARL ISLANDS (Eng), Panamanian island group in the Golfo de Panamá, Central America; the largest island is San Miguel.

Perlis *per-lis'*, state in NW Peninsular Malaysia, SE Asia; the smallest state in Malaysia, bounded N by Thailand, SW by the Strait of Malacca and S by the state of Kedah; an extension of the Kedah plain; the Langkawi Is lie offshore in the Strait; pop(1980) 144,782; area 818 sq km; capital Kangar; Arau is the seat of the royal raja; economy: rice, rubber, coconut.

Perm, formerly MOLOTOV, 58 01N 56 10E, pop(1983) 1,037,000, industrial capital city of Permskaya oblast, NE European Rossiyskaya, Soviet Union; stretches for more than 80 km along the banks of the R Kama; the city dates from 1723 when a copper foundry was built here; there was rapid industrial development during the 19th century; university (1916); railway; airfield; economy: heavy engineering, chemicals, oil refining, clothing, footwear.

Përmet' or **Premet'**, prov of S Albania; area 930 sq km; pop(1980) 35,200; capital Përmet.

Përmet, 40 14N 20 20E, commercial town and capital of

Përmet prov, S Albania; on the R Vijosë, 64 km SE of Berat; a former centre of the Orthodox Church.

Pernambuco *per-nam-boo'kō*, state in Nordeste region, NE Brazil; bounded E by the Atlantic Ocean; has a narrow coastal zone with damp tropical climate, drier intermediate zone and arid interior; pop(1980) 6,141,993; area 98,281 sq km; capital Recife; chief towns: Olinda, Caruarú; economy: agriculture, chemicals, textiles, food processing.

Per'nik, okrug (prov) of W Bulgaria on the frontier with Yugoslavia; traversed by the R Struma; area 2,355 sq km; pop(1981) 175,000; coal mining in the Dimitrovo Basin.

Pernik, formerly DIMITROVO, 42 36N 23 03E, pop(1981) 93,483, capital of Pernik okrug (prov), W Bulgaria; on the R Struma, 31 km SW of Sofiya; railway; economy: electrical equipment, iron, glass; monument: Byzantine fortress.

Perpignan *per-peen-yã*, 42 42N 2 53E, pop(1982) 113,646, market town and resort capital of Pyrénées-Orientales dept, Languedoc-Roussillon region, S France; built as a strongpoint commanding the crossing of the R Tét, less than 30 km from the Spanish border, 154 km S of Toulouse; capital of the former prov of Roussillon; dates from Roman times; chartered in 1197; the church council met here in 1408; united to France in 1659; developed rapidly after the middle of the 19th century, expanding beyond its old walls; the population has increased 3-fold since 1914; 14th-c university; road and rail junction; economy: tourism and trade in olives, fruit and wine; monuments: 17-18th-c citadel; late 14th-c red-brick château (Le Castillet) now a museum for the arts and crafts of Roussillon; 13-17th-c town hall; cathedral of St-Jean (started in 1324, finished in the 17th century), became a cathedral in 1601, principally Gothic in style; 14-18th-c church of St-Jacques; 14th-c church of Notre-Dame-la-Réal; event: Midsummer Festival (June).

Persian Gulf, arm of the Arabian Sea. See Arabian Gulf.

Perth, 31 58S 115 49E, pop(1986) 1,025,300, state capital of Western Australia, Australia; near the mouth of the Swan river; an important commercial and transportation centre on the W coast of Australia; founded in 1829, it achieved city status in 1856; rapid development followed the discovery of gold and the opening of Fremantle harbour in 1897; University of Western Australia (1911), Murdoch University (1973); railway; airport; economy: textiles, clothes, cement, furniture, motor vehicles, gold mining and agricultural trade; monuments: in the Western Australian Museum are unique paintings by the Pintubi, a desert tribe; the oldest building is the Old Court House.

Perth, 56 24N 3 28W, pop(1981) 43,010, capital of Perth and Kinross dist, Tayside, E Scotland; on the R Tay, 50 km N of Edinburgh; railway; economy: whisky blending and bottling, insurance, glass making, printing, agricultural supplies; monuments: Balhousie castle contains a museum on the Black Watch; art gallery and museum; St John's Kirk dates from the 15th-c and was restored in the 1920s as a war memorial; events: festival of arts (May); agricultural show (June).

Perth Am'boy, 40 31N 74 16W, pop(1980) 38,951, city in Middlesex county, E New Jersey, United States; port at the mouth of the R Raritan, 27 km SSW of Newark; a city since 1781; economy: food processing, steel, electrical goods, plastics, oil refining, chemicals, copper smelting.

Peru *pe-roo'*, official name Republic of Peru, REPÚBLICA DE PERU (Sp), a republic situated on the W coast of South America; bordered by Ecuador (N), Colombia (NW), Brazil and Bolivia (W) and by Chile (S); timezone GMT −5; area 1,284,640 sq km; capital Lima; pop(1981) 17,762,231; ethnic groups include South American Indians (45%), mestizo (37%), white (15%), black African (3%), Japanese, Chinese and other; the official languages are Spanish and Quechua; Aymará, another Indian language, is spoken in the area around L Titicaca; the predominant religion is Roman Catholic; the currency is the sol nuevo of 100 centavos; national holiday 28 July (Independence Day); membership of the Andean Pact, AIOEC, ASSIMER, CIPEC, FAO, G-77, GATT, IADB, IAEA, IATP, IBRD, ICAO, ICO, IDA, IDB, IFAD, IFC, ILO, IMF, IMO, INTELSAT, INTERPOL, ISO, ITU, IWC, LAIA, NAM, OAS, PAHO, SELA, UN, UNESCO, UPU, WFTU, WHO, WMO, WSG, WTO.

Physical description. Peru is divided into 3 distinct geographical regions: the western coastal plains, the central mountains (the Andes) and the tropical eastern lowlands. The coastal region covers 11% of the country and contains 44% of the pop; it consists of arid plains and foothills, with areas of desert and extremely fertile river valleys. The central sierra of Peru, with an average alt of 3,000 m, covers 26% of the country and contains 50% of the pop. Rivers rising in the mountains cut through the plateau, forming deep, tropical canyons. The deep valley basins contain the best land for arable farming, while it is possible to graze animals on approx 130,000 sq km of the upland plateau. To the E is the *selva*, the forested eastern half of the Andes and the tropical forest of the Amazon basin beyond. This E region covers 62% of Peru's area, but holds only 5% of its pop which is concentrated along the river banks. The rivers are the main form of transport here. This area has immense timber reserves, and is excellent land for producing rubber, rice, jute, tropical fruits, coffee and cattle. This area is also being explored for oil. Peru's major rivers flowing down to meet the Amazon (Solimoẽs) include the Ucayali (formed by the confluence of the Urubamba and the Apurímac), the Tigre, the Pastaza, the Napo, the Marañón and the Huallaga (which flows into the Marañón).

Climate. The coastal area has mild temperatures all year. The southern part of the coastal district has a dry, arid, desert climate which is a continuation of the coastal desert of northern Chile. In N Peru, near the Equator, the coastal region has bursts of torrential rain every 10 years or so; the sea temperature also rises and the cold current retreats southwards. This phenomenon, which can cause widespread damage, is called El Niño. Unusually, the arid coastal strip experiences frequent low cloud, fog and light drizzle. Lima, representative of this area, has only 1 or 2 hours of sunshine per day during the period of low sun, and between 5 and 7 hours during the warmer months of Dec-April. The Andean region has temperatures which never rise above 23°C and a single rainy season between Nov and March. Because of the high altitude, there is a large daily range of temperature, with night frost a regular occurrence during the dry season. In the E, Peru's portion of the Amazon basin has a typically wet, tropical climate. Temperatures are warm to hot throughout the year, with a single rainy season at the time of high sun. The months of Oct to March are particularly hot and humid.

History, government and constitution. The Spanish arrived in Peru in 1531 to find a highly developed Inca civilization. Gold and silver mined in the Andes made Peru the principal source of Spanish wealth and power in South America. Peru's independence movement was led by the Argentinian, José de San Martín and by the Venezuelan, Simón Bolívar. San Martín declared Peruvian independence from Spain on 28 July 1821; emancipation was finally completed in Dec 1842. Since independence, Peru and its neighbours have engaged in various border disputes (eg the War of the Pacific, 1879-83). Following a clash between Ecuador and Peru in 1941, the Protocol of Rio de Janeiro established the boundary between the two countries. Ecuador nullified this agreement in 1960 and continuing disagreement led to severe border clashes between Ecuador and Peru in early 1981. Military coups have repeatedly interrupted civilian constitutional government in Peru; the most recent period of military rule began in 1968, led by General Juan Velasco Alvarado, who adopted a policy of nationalization and land reform. He was replaced in 1975 by the right-wing General Francisco Morales Bermúdez. A new constitution was drawn up in 1979 and elections held in 1980, in which Fernando Belaúnde was elected president. Maoist guerrillas based around the city of Ayacucho have carried out terrorist activities throughout the country. Peru is a constitutional republic, with a bicameral legislative Congress made up of a 60-member Senate and a 180-member National Chamber of Deputies elected every 5 years. Executive power is held by the president who appoints a Council of Ministers.

Economy. Peru's economy is closely related to the performance of the copper, oil and fishmeal industries. The country is one of the world's leading producers of silver, zinc, lead, copper, gold and iron ore. Peru's oil, 80% of which is extracted from the Amazon forest E of the Andes, once accounted for 20% of export earnings, but oil production has fallen steadily since 1983. Fishing, copper mining and agriculture dominate the economy of the coastal area, although a larger proportion of food production now comes from the sierra. Manufacturing industry, largely located around Lima and Callao, is largely based on the production of steel, iron, vehicles, tyres and cement.

Agriculture. Approx 38% of the pop is employed in agriculture which ranges in type from large scientific farming on the coast to small subsistence family farms in the mountains. The production of important crops such as cotton, potatoes, sugar and rice was reduced considerably in 1983 as a result of unusually severe weather. In the coastal area, cotton is grown in all regions, while sugar cane and rice are grown only in the N, and grapes, fruit and olives only in the S. In the tropical E beyond the Andes, coffee, rice, tropical fruits and cattle are the major products. Before 1982, Peru was one of the world's largest fish producers, but the severe weather conditions of 1982-83 caused schools of fish to die off or move offshore into deeper water. Most of the fishmeal or fish canning plants were forced to close at this time and output of fishmeal and fish oil fell by 40%. Continous overfishing has maintained a shortage and the depressed state of the fishing industry.

Administrative divisions. Peru is divided into the constitutional province of Callao and 24 departments as follows:

Department	*area (sq km)*	*pop(1981)*
Callao (Province)	73	443,413
Amazonas	41,297	254,560
Ancash	36,308	818,289
Apurímac	20,654	323,346
Arequipa	63,527	706,580
Ayacucho	45,503	430,289
Cajamarca	35,417	1,045,569
Cuzco	84,140	832,504
Huancavelica	22,870	346,797
Huánuco	35,314	484,780
Ica	21,251	433,897
Junín	32,354	852,238
Lambayeque	16,585	674,442
Libertad, La	23,241	962,949
Lima	33,894	4,745,877
Loreto	478,336	445,368
Madre de Dios	78,402	33,007
Moquegua	16,174	101,610
Pasco	24,233	213,125
Piura	36,403	1,045,569
Puno	72,382	890,258
San Martín	52,309	319,751
Tacna	14,766	143,085
Tumbes	4,731	103,839
Ucayali	100,831	200,669

Perugia *pay-roo'ja*, prov of Umbria region, Italy; pop(1981) 580,988; area 6,335 sq km; capital Perugia.

Perugia, 43 07N 12 23E, pop(1981) 142,348, capital town of Perugia prov, Umbria region, Italy, situated on a hill some 300 m above the Tevere (Tiber) valley, 141 km N of Roma (Rome); founded as an Etruscan city and taken by Rome in 310 BC; archbishopric; university (1276); railway; economy: woollens, furniture, chocolate, tour ism; monuments: 15th-c Gothic cathedral of San Lorenzo; Palazzo Comunale (town hall), in Italian Gothic style (1281 and 1333); Arco d'Augusto, one of the ancient Etruscan town gates; church of San Pietro dei Cassiensi, an early Christian structure; events: jazz festival (summer); music festival (Sept).

Pesaro *pay'za-rō*, 43 54N 12 54E, pop(1981) 90,412, seaside resort and capital of Pesaro e Urbino prov, Marche region, Italy; at the mouth of the R Foglia, on the NW Adriatic coast, between Rimini and Ancona; railway; economy: agricultural machinery, pottery, tourism; monuments: 15th-c fortress and 13th-c cathedral.

Pesaro e Urbino *pay'za-rō ay oor-bee'nō*, prov of Marche region, Italy; pop(1981) 333,488; area 2,893 sq km, capital Pesaro.

Pescadores, county and island group of Taiwan. See P'eng-hu.

Pesca'ra, prov in Abruzzi region, central Italy; pop(1981) 286,240; area 1,225 sq km; capital Pescara.

Pescara, 42 27N 14 13E, pop(1981) 131,330, capital town of Pescara prov, Abruzzi region, E Italy; 235 km ENE of Roma (Rome), at the mouth of the R Pescara, on the Adriatic coast; there are bathing beaches to the N and S; railway; airfield; car ferry to Yugoslavia; economy: textiles, soap, glass, furniture; tourism; monument: Palazzo della Prefettura.

Peshawar *push-ah'wur*, 34 01N 71 40E, pop(1981) 555,000, capital of North-West Frontier prov, Pakistan; 172 km W of Rawalpindi and Islamabad and 16 km E of the Khyber Pass; city of the Pathan people; major trade centre on the Afghan frontier; under Sikh rule during the early 19th century; occupied in 1849 by the British; university (1950); airfield; railway; economy: textiles, leather, food processing, copperware; monuments:

Balahisar fort, mosque of Mahabat, Qissa Khawani bazaar.

Peshkopi *pesh-ko'pee*, 41 41N 20 25E, capital of Dibrë prov, E Albania; airfield; thermal springs.

Pessac, 44 49N 0 37E, pop(1982) 50,543, town in Gironde dept, Aquitaine region, W France, 6 km SSW of Bordeaux.

Pest *pesht*, county in N Hungary; hilly in the NW but mostly flat land; bounded W by R Danube; pop(1984e) 983,000; area 6,394 sq km; capital Budapest; other chief towns include Cegléd, Nagykörös and Dunakeszi; major industries in and around Budapest.

Petah Tiqwa *pe'ta tik'va*, sub-district of Central dist, Israel; pop(1983) 297,498; area 284 sq km.

Petah Tiqwa, PETACH TIKVA, 32 05N 34 53E, pop(1982) 124,000, town in Tel Aviv dist, W Israel; E of Tel Aviv-Yafo; Jewish agricultural village founded in 1878; railway.

Petaling Jaya *pu-tah'ling jī-a*, 3 06N 101 37E, pop(1980) 207,805, industrial satellite in Selangor state, W Peninsular Malaysia, SE Asia; 6 km W of Kuala Lumpur; built in the 1950s as a squatter resettlement city.

Petaluma *pet-el-oo'ma*, 38 14N 122 39W, pop(1980) 33,834, city in Sonoma county, W California, United States; on Petaluma Creek, c.24 km above an arm of San Pablo Bay, 56 km N of San Francisco; settled in 1833.

Petange *pay-tãzh'*, 49 33N 5 53E, pop(1981) 6,416, town in Esch-sur-Alzette canton, Luxembourg dist, S Luxembourg; at the foot of the historic Tetelbierg, an ancient Roman fortification; 21 km WSW of Luxembourg; event: Remembrance Day of the Liberation, 9 Sept.

Petén *pe-ten'*, largest and northernmost dept of Guatemala, Central America; bounded W and N by Mexico and E by Belize; pop(1982e) 102,803; area 35,854 sq km; capital Flores; apart from a small area around the capital the pop density throughout the dept is less than 10 persons per sq km; most of the area is forested and agriculturally undeveloped; there is an oilfield in production in the extreme NW; the dept is drained by numerous rivers and there are large areas of swampland, particularly in the NW; contains Lago Petén Itzá; Tikal national park, with notable Mayan remains, lies NE of the lake and is served by an airfield.

Petén Itzá, Lago *eet-sa'*, lake in central Petén dept, N Guatemala, Central America; length 24 km; Flores is situated on one of its several small islands.

Peter I Øy *-u-ü*, PETER I ISLAND (Eng), 68 48S 90 35W, Norwegian island off Antarctica in the Bellingshausen Sea NE of Thurston I; area 180 sq km; length 22 km; first landing in 1929 by Norwegian expedition; on 1 May, 1931 it was placed under Norwegian sovereignty and on 24 March, 1933 incorporated in Norway as a dependency.

Peterborough, 44 19N 78 20W, pop(1981) 60,620, town in SE Ontario, SE Canada; situated on the Otonabee river, part of the Trent Waterway; the Trent Waterway negotiates the falls in the river at Peterborough by means of a hydraulic lock, which has one of the highest lifts in the world (20 m); Trent University (1963); railway; airfield; racetrack; economy: hydroelectricity, cereal milling, tourism; event: Arts and Water Festival (early Aug).

Peterborough, formerly MEDESHAMSTEDE, 52 35N 0 15W, pop(1981) 114,733, industrial city in Peterborough dist, Cambridgeshire, E central England; on the R Nene, 117 km N of London; originally developed around a Benedictine monastery; designated a 'new town' in 1967; railway; economy: diesel engines, engineering, bricks, refrigerators, agricultural machinery; monuments: 12th-c cathedral, Burghley House (24 km NW).

Peterhead, 57 30N 1 46W, pop(1981) 17,085, port town in Banff and Buchan dist, Grampian region, NE Scotland; on the NE coast, 44 km N of Aberdeen; the most easterly town on the Scottish mainland; economy: foodstuffs, textiles, machinery; principal fishing port; oilfield supply base; monuments: the Peterhead Arbuthnot Museum has displays on the development of the fishing and whaling industries.

Peterlee' 54 46N 1 19W, pop(1981) 31,570, town in Easington dist, Durham, NE England; on the North Sea, 11 km NW of Hartlepool; designated a 'new town' in 1948; economy: transport equipment, textiles, engineering.

Petersburg, 37 14N 77 24W, pop(1980) 41,055, independent city, E Virginia, United States; on the R Appomattox, 37 km S of Richmond; besieged by Union forces in the Civil War, June 1864-April 1865, until Confederate forces were forced to retreat W, abandoning Petersburg and Richmond, before surrendering at Appomattox; railway; economy: optical equipment and luggage; monuments: Centre Hill Mansion, Old Blandford Church, Siege Museum, Petersburg National Battlefield Site.

Petersfield, 51 00N 0 56W, pop(1981) 10,068, town in East Hampshire dist, Hampshire, S England; 18 km NE of Portsmouth; railway; economy: rubber, engineering.

Petra *pee'tru*, WADI MUSA (Arab), 30 20N 35 26E, ancient rock-cut city in Ma'ān governorate, East Bank, SW Jordan, 26 km NW of Ma'ān; situated in a basin in the mountains E of Wadi 'Araba; in ancient times it was the stronghold and treasure city of the Nabataeans; it was a wealthy commercial city for several centuries with an important caravan trade; the site is approached by a series of ravines, in places only 4 m wide, between red sandstone cliffs out of which are carved numerous temples, tombs, houses, shrines, altars, and a great theatre.

Petrified Forest, national park in E Arizona, United States; protects petrified wood, Indian ruins and petroglyphs; established in 1962; area 377 sq km.

Petrila *pet-ree'la*, 45 27N 23 25E, pop(1983) 25,885, town in Hunedoara county, W central Romania; NE of Petroşani, in the Transylvanian Alps; economy: coal mining, woodwork.

Petropavlovsk-Kamchatskiy *pye-tre-pav'lefsk kum-chat'skee*, PETROPAVLOVSKII PORT (1822-1924), 53 03N 158 43E, pop(1983) 237,000, seaport in Kamchatskaya oblast, E Rossiyskaya, Soviet Union; on the E shore of Kamchatka Peninsula, on Avachinskaya Guba (Avacha Bay) of the Pacific Ocean; became a city in 1822; a naval base and a base for fishing, trawling and refrigerator-ship fleets; airfield; economy: tin-plating, fish-processing, building materials.

Petrópolis *pe-tro'po-lees*, 22 30S 43 06W, pop(1980) 150,249, town in Rio de Janeiro state, Sudeste region, SE Brazil; NE of Rio de Janeiro; founded in 1843 as a summer refuge by Dom Pedro II; until 1962 it was the 'summer capital' of Brazil, with numerous picturesque private residences; university (1961); railway; economy: commerce, food processing, ceramics, textiles, tourism; monuments: the Gothic style cathedral, completed in 1925, contains the tomb of the emperor and empress; the emperor's palace, now the Museu Imperial, contains the Crown Jewels and other imperial possessions.

Petroşani *pet-ro-shan'*, 45 25N 23 22E, pop(1983) 47,289, town in Hunedoara county, W central Romania; in the Transylvanian Alps; established in the 17th century; railway; economy: important coal mining centre.

Pforzheim *pforts'hīm*, 48 53N 8 41E, pop(1983) 105,200, manufacturing and commercial city in W Baden-Württemberg prov, W Germany; on N fringe of the Schwarzwald (Black Forest) in a basin at the confluence of the rivers Enz and Nagold, 26 km SE of Karlsruhe; railway; a noted centre of the gold-smithing and jewellery industry.

Phan Thiet *pan tyet*, 10 56N 108 06E, town in Thuan Hai prov, S Vietnam, Indo-China; on South China Sea; railway.

Phenix City *fee'niks*, 32 28N 85 00W, pop(1980) 26,928, county seat of Russell county, E Alabama, United States; on the R Chattahoochee, opposite Columbus, Georgia; in 1954, the state governor placed the city under martial law for 5 months following extensive city corruption; railway; economy: timber, dairy produce.

Philadel'phia, 39 57N 75 10W, pop(1980) 1,688,210, county seat of, and co-extensive with, Philadelphia county, SE Pennsylvania, United States; major deep-water port at the confluence of the Schuylkill and Delaware rivers; noted centre for culture, education and medical research; the 5th largest city in the USA; first settled by Swedes in the 1640s; a British settlement was organized by William Penn in 1681 and the town was laid out in the following year; many Scottish and Irish immigrants settled here in the 18th century; the birth-place of the nation, where the Declaration of Independence was signed in 1776; on 17 Sept 1787, the Constitutional Convention met here and adopted the Constitution of the United States; capital of the USA 1790-1800; heavily involved in anti-slavery movement and the Civil War; site of Centennial Exposition in 1876; 4 universities (1740, 1851, 1884, 1891); railway; airport; economy: finance; manufactures machinery and electronic equipment, chemicals, printing and publishing; service economy is supplanting the dwindling manufacturing industry; naval dockyard; monuments: Pennsylvania Academy of the Fine Arts (oldest art museum in USA), museum of art, Franklin Institute Science Museum and Planetarium, Independence National Historical Park.

Philippeville, dist of Namur prov, S Belgium; area 909 sq km; pop(1982) 57,690.

Philippines *fil'e-peenz*, officially Republic of the Philippines, REPUBLICA DE FILIPINAS (Sp), a republic consisting of an archipelago of more than 7,100 islands and islets, lying NE of Borneo and S of Taiwan, between 5°N and 21°N; the name is derived from the name given to Leyte I in honour of Philip II of Spain when heir-apparent; major islands include Luzon, Mindanao, Samar, Palawan, Mindoro, Panay, Negros, Cebu, Leyte, Masbate and Bohol; separated from Borneo by the Sulu Sea; bounded E by Philippine Sea and W by South China and Luzon Seas; timezone GMT +8; area 299,679 sq km; pop(1984e) 55,528,000; capital Manila; chief cities include Quezon City, Basilan, Cebu, Bacolod, Davao, Iloilo; ethnic groups consist of descendants of Malay, Indonesian, Chinese and Spanish settlers; the official language is Pilipino (based on Tagalog) but some 87 local languages and dialects are spoken; the majority of the pop is Roman Catholic; the currency is the peso of 100 centavos; national holidays 12 June (Independence Day), 4 July (Filipino-American Friendship Day), 30 Nov (Bonifacio Day), 30 Dec (Rizal Day); membership of ADB, ASEAN, ASPAC, Colombo Plan, ESCAP, FAO, G-77, GATT, IAEA, IBRD, ICAO, IDA, IFAD, IFC, IHO, ILO, IMF, IMO, INTELSAT, INTERPOL, IPU, IRC, ISO, ITU, UN, UNESCO, UPU, WFTU, WHO, WIPO, WMO, WTO.

Physical description. The Philippine islands, being the upper portions of now inactive volcanic chains, are largely mountainous, with N-S ridges rising to heights in excess of 2,500 m. The mountains rise steeply from the sea, with narrow coastal margins and broad interior plateaux. Extensive lowland areas are only to be found on Luzon, Mindanao, Panay and Negros. Some of the islands are ringed by coral reefs. Lying within the tropics the lowlands have a warm and humid climate throughout the year, with slight variations from an average of 27°C. On Luzon rainfall averages between 890 and 5,490 mm per year with an average of 2,080 mm at Manila which has a wet season caused by the SW monsoon (June-Nov). Lying astride the typhoon belt, the Philippines are affected by about 15 cyclonic storms yearly.

History, government and constitution. When Ferdinand Magellan claimed the Philippines for Spain in 1521 he found a largely Malay population on the islands. Spanish colonization continued until 1898 when the Spanish fleet was defeated in Manila Bay during the Spanish-American War. Spain ceded the Philippines to the USA under the terms of the Treaty of Paris. A legislature and civil service were established by the Americans who handed over effective control to the Filipinos in 1935 when the country became a self-governing Commonwealth. After a period of Japanese occupation during World War II the Philippines were granted full independence on 4 July 1946. During the period 1945-53 the communist-dominated Huk rebellion was suppressed. In 1985 the 20-year rule of President Ferdinand Marcos was brought to an end by a coup that followed an election marred by irregularities. Political disturbances had led President Marcos to rule by martial law from 1972 to 1981. The constitution of 1935 was replaced in 1973 and amended in 1976 and 1981, allowing the president to formulate national policy and giving him control of the government for an unlimited number of 6-year terms. The legislature comprises a unicameral National Assembly (*Batasang Pambansa*) made up of 190 members of whom 165 are elected from the regions, the remainder including the prime minister, some members of the cabinet and sectoral representatives of youth, labour, and agriculture.

Economy. Nearly 50% of the workforce of the Philippines is engaged in farming, mostly on peasant farms and smallholdings which produce rice, maize, fruit (pineapples, mangos), vegetables and livestock for home consumption. Chief export crops include sugar, tobacco, rubber, coffee, abaca and coconuts. Forest land covering 166,300 sq km produces important exports of lumber, veneer and plywood. In addition to small amounts of oil, the mining of copper, lead, iron, nickel, chromite ore and non-metallic minerals is important. Manufacturing industry contributing 25% of national income is based on the production of textiles, petroleum products, food processing, electronics assembly, motor vehicles. Major trade partners include the USA and Japan.

Administrative divisions. The Philippines is divided into 72 provinces as follows:

Province	*area (sq km)*	*pop(1980)*
Abra	3,976	160,198
Agusan del Norte }	11,556	365,421
Agusan del Sur }		265,030
Aklan	1,818	324,563
Albay	2,553	809,177
Antique	2,522	344,879
Aurora	209	107,145
Basilan	1,372	201,407
Bataan	1,373	323,254
Batangas	3,166	1,174,201
Benguet	2,655	354,751
Bohol	4,116	806,013
Bukidnon	8,294	631,634
Bulacan	2,672	1,096,046
Cagayan	9,003	711,476
Camarines Norte	2,113	308,007
Camarines Sur	5,267	1,099,346
Camiguin	230	57,126
Capiz	2,633	492,231
Catanduanes	1,512	175,247
Cavite	1,288	771,320
Cebu	5,088	2,091,602
Davao del Norte	8,130	725,153
Davao del Sur	6,378	1,133,599
Davao Oriental	5,164	339,931
Eastern Samar	4,340	320,637
Ifugao	2,518	111,368
Ilocos Norte	3,399	390,666
Ilocos Sur	2,580	443,591
Iloilo	5,324	1,433,641
Isabela	10,665	870,604
Kalinga-Apayao	7,048	185,063
La Union	1,493	452,578
Laguna	1,760	973,104
Lanao del Norte	3,092	461,049
Lanao del Sur	3,873	404,971
Leyte	6,268	1,302,648
Maguindanao }		536,546
North Cotabato }	16,441	564,599
Sultan Kudarat }		303,785
Marinduque	959	173,715

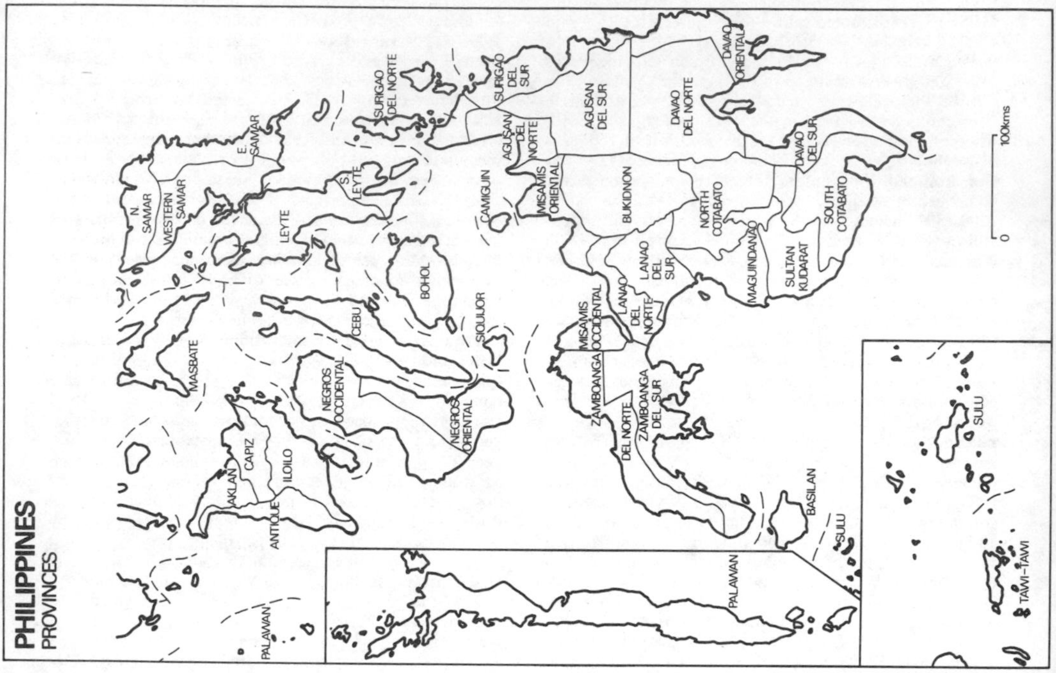
PHILIPPINES
PROVINCES
N. SAMAR
WESTERN SAMAR
E. SAMAR
LEYTE
S. LEYTE
SURIGAO DEL NORTE
SURIGAO DEL SUR
AGUSAN DEL NORTE
AGUSAN DEL SUR
DAVAO DEL NORTE
DAVAO ORIENTAL
DAVAO DEL SUR
CAMIGUIN
MISAMIS ORIENTAL
BUKIDNON
NORTH COTABATO
SOUTH COTABATO
MAGUINDANAO
SULTAN KUDARAT
LANAO DEL SUR
LANAO DEL NORTE
MISAMIS OCCIDENTAL
ZAMBOANGA DEL NORTE
ZAMBOANGA DEL SUR
BASILAN
SULU
TAWI-TAWI
PALAWAN
BOHOL
CEBU
SIQUIJOR
NEGROS OCCIDENTAL
NEGROS ORIENTAL
MASBATE
CAPIZ
AKLAN
ILOILO
ANTIQUE
0
100kms

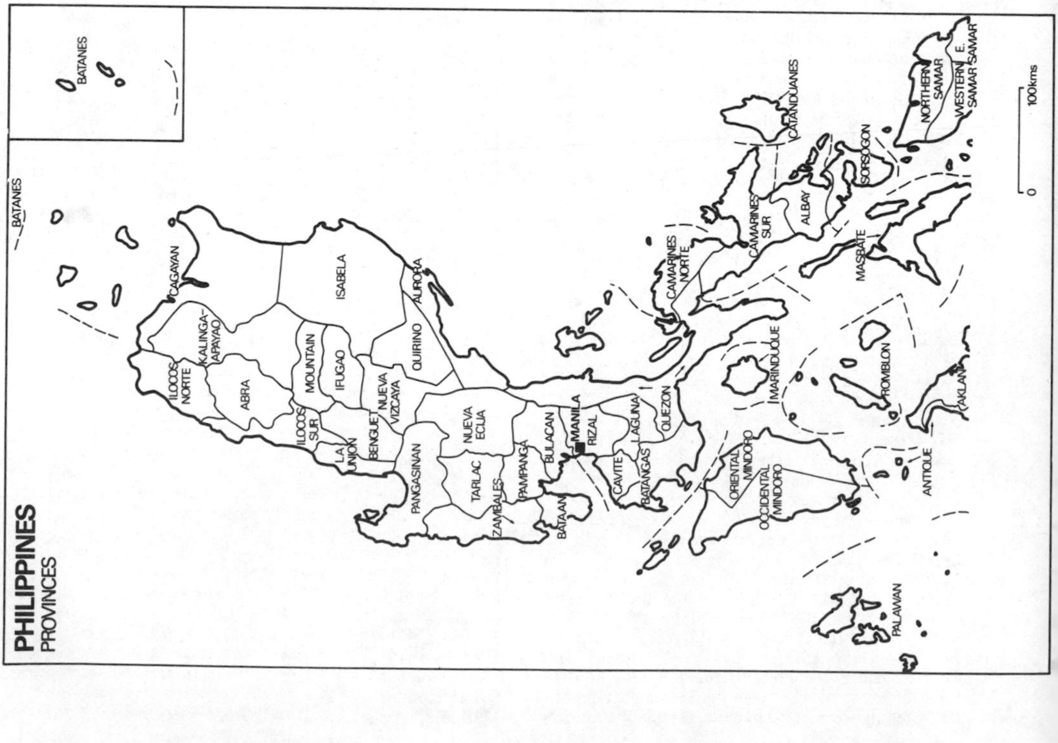
PHILIPPINES
PROVINCES
BATANES
CAGAYAN
ISABELA
AURORA
KALINGA-APAYAO
ILOCOS NORTE
ABRA
MOUNTAIN
IFUGAO
QUIRINO
NUEVA VIZCAYA
ILOCOS SUR
LA UNION
BENGUET
PANGASINAN
NUEVA ECIJA
TARLAC
ZAMBALES
PAMPANGA
BULACAN
BATAAN
MANILA
RIZAL
CAVITE
LAGUNA
BATANGAS
QUEZON
CAMARINES NORTE
CAMARINES SUR
CATANDUANES
ALBAY
SORSOGON
NORTHERN SAMAR
WESTERN SAMAR
E. SAMAR
MASBATE
MARINDUQUE
ROMBLON
ORIENTAL MINDORO
OCCIDENTAL MINDORO
AKLAN
ANTIQUE
PALAWAN
0
100kms

contd

Province	*area (sq km)*	*pop(1980)*
Masbate	4,047	584,520
Mindoro Occidental	5,880	222,431
Mindoro Oriental	4,365	446,938
Misamis Occidental	1,939	386,328
Misamis Oriental	3,570	690,032
Mountain	2,097	103,052
Negros Occidental	7,926	1,930,301
Negros Oriental	5,745	819,399
Northern Samar	3,480	378,516
Nueva Ecija	5,284	1,069,409
Nueva Vizcaya	6,961	241,690
Palawan	14,896	371,782
Pampanga	2,181	1,181,590
Pangasinan	5,368	1,636,057
Quezon }	11,946	1,129,277
Quirino }		83,230
Rizal	1,860	555,533
Romblon	1,356	193,174
Siquijor	337	70,360
Sorsogon	2,141	500,685
South Cotabato	7,356	770,473
Southern Leyte	1,735	296,294
Sulu	2,688	360,588
Surigao del Norte	2,739	363,414
Surigao del Sur	4,552	377,647
Tarlac	3,053	688,457
Tawi-Tawi	932	194,651
Western Samar	5,609	501,439
Zambales	3,714	444,037
Zamboanga del Norte	6,075	588,015
Zamboanga del Sur	9,922	1,183,845

Philipsburg, 18 03N 63 05W, capital town of St Maarten I, N Netherlands Antilles, E Caribbean; harbour facilities at Great Bay; Juliana International Airport is 7 km from Philipsburg.

Phnom Penh *nom pen*, pop(1983e) 500,000, river port capital of Cambodia; surrounded by prov of Kandal, S Cambodia; at the confluence of the rivers Mekong and Tonlé Sap; once the commercial, cultural and transportation centre of Cambodia; linked by rail to Pursat in the NW and to Bangkok; also linked by rail to Kampot in the SW; founded by the Khmers in 1371 and succeeded Angkor as the capital in 1434; abandoned as capital several times, but became the permanent capital in 1867; under Japanese occupation during World War II; after the communist victory of 1975, the population of the city was removed to work in the fields in an effort to avert widespread famine; 1970-75 population had been almost tripled by the arrival of rural refugees.

Phnum Tbêng Meanchey, 13 49N 104 58E, capital of Preah Vihear prov, N Cambodia.

Phocis, nome (dept) of Sterea Ellás-Évvoia region, Greece. See Fokís.

Phoenix *fee'niks*, 33 27N 112 04W, pop(1980) 789,704, capital of state in Maricopa county, S central Arizona, United States; largest city in the state, situated on the Salt river, 172 km NW of Tucson; settled in 1870; state capital since 1889; airport; railway; economy: hub of the rich Salt River Valley; important centre for data-processing and electronics research; manufactures include computer components, aircraft, machinery, food products and textiles; a popular winter and health resort, with its dry, sunny climate; monuments: Heard Museum of Anthropology and Primitive Arts, Pueblo Grande Museum, Desert Botanical Garden, Pioneer Arizona Museum; event: Cowboy Artists Exhibition (Nov).

Phoenix Islands, coral island group of Kiribati, S Pacific Ocean, some 1,300 km SE of the Gilbert Is; comprises the islands of Kanton, Phoenix, Hull, Enderbury, Birnie, Sydney, Gardner and McKean; pop(1985) 24 (all on Kanton I); formerly an important source of guano; in 1968, most of the inhabitants of these islands were resettled in the Solomon Is.

Phôngsali, PHONG SALY, prov (*khowèng*) of N Laos, SE Asia; capital Phôngsali.

Phthiotis, nome (dept) of Sterea Ellás-Évvoia region, Greece. See Fthiótis.

Phu Quoc *foo kwok*, island of Vietnam in the Gulf of Thailand; S of Kampot prov, SW Cambodia; chief town Duong Dong; economy: fishing, timber, pepper, rubber.

Phuket *poo-ket*, formerly SALANG or JUNKSEYLON, largest island of Thailand; situated in Phuket prov, S Thailand in the Andaman Sea, 900 km S of Bangkok; a resort area with fine beaches and hidden coves; at Phang Nga Bay the limestone is studded with dramatic caves, grottoes and columns; marine biological centre; the port of Phuket is a major Thai outlet to the Indian Ocean; event: vegetarian festival in Oct which includes fire-walking and the climbing of knife-edged ladders.

Piacenza *pya-chen'tsa*, prov of Emilia-Romagna region, N Italy; pop(1981) 278,424; area 2,590 sq km; capital Piacenza.

Piacenza, PLACENTIA (anc), 45 03N 9 41E, pop(1981) 109,039, capital town of Piacenza prov, Emilia-Romagna region, N Italy; on the R Po, N of the Appno Ligure, 61 km SW of Milano (Milan); railway; economy: agricultural machinery, pasta, leather goods; monuments: Palazzo Gotico (town hall), begun in 1281; Lombard-Romanesque cathedral, begun in 1122 and completed in the 13th century under Gothic influence; 11-12th-c church of Sant'Antonino; church of Santa Maria di Campagna (1522-28), with frescoes by Pordenone (1529-31); there is a well-preserved circuit of 16th-c walls, 6.5 km long.

Piatra or **Piatra-Neamţ** *pya'tra-nyamts*, 46 53N 26 23E, pop(1983) 102,584, industrial town and capital of Neamţ county, NE Romania; on R Bistriţa; railway; economy: chemicals, food processing, textiles, pharmaceuticals; monument: Bistriţa monastery (1402).

Piauí *pee-ow-ee'*, state in Nordeste region, NE Brazil; narrow N border on Atlantic Ocean; bounded W by the Río Parnaíba; pop(1980) 2,139,021; area 250,934 sq km; capital Teresina; economy: agriculture, fishing, food processing, textiles, chemicals; in the N is the 62-sq km Sete Cidades National Park (established in 1961).

Piave *pyah'vay*, river in NE Italy; rises on Monte Peralba in the Carnic Alps; flows S and SSW past Belluno, then SE to discharge into the Adriatic Sea 32 km ENE of Venezia (Venice); length 224 km; tributaries Boite and Cordevole rivers; for some time it formed a defence line during World War I, and was the scene of an Italian victory in June 1918.

Picardie *pee kahr-dee*, PICARDY (Eng), region and former prov of N France comprising the depts of Aisne, Oise and Somme, 13 arrond, 127 cantons and 2,293 communes; pop(1982) 1,740,321; area 19,399 sq km; bounded on the NW by the English Channel; the landscape is flat and traversed by numerous rivers (Somme, Oise) and canals; chief towns Abbeville, Amiens (with its Gothic cathedral), St-Quentin, Laon, Beauvais and Compiègne; seaside resorts include St-Valéry-sur-Somme; it was seized by Philippe-Auguste in 1185 and annexed to the crown in 1477; it was a scene of heavy fighting during World War I; Château-Thierry, in Aisne dept, is the birthplace of La Fontaine, 17th-c author of the celebrated Fables; economy: chemicals, metalworking.

Pichincha *pee-cheen'cha*, mountainous prov in the Andean Sierra of N central Ecuador; crossed by the Equator and dotted with high volcanic peaks including Pichincha, Cotopaxi, Antisana, Corazón, Rumiñahui and Cayambe; slopes W to the coastal lowlands; watered by the Río Guaillabamba; pop(1982) 1,382,125; area 12,872 sq km; capital Quito; economy: wine, cider, beer, tobacco, dairying, flour, clothes, textiles, chemicals, fruit, vegetables, animal foodstuffs, meat packing, motor vehicles.

Pichincha, 0 10S 78 35W, Andean volcano in Pichincha prov, N central Ecuador; rises to 4,794 m, 10 km NW of

Quito and approx 18 km S of the Equator; last erupted in 1881; still emits gases; on 24 May 1822 the Battle of Pichincha, which was decisive in the fight for Ecuador's independence, was fought on the volcano's lower slopes.

Pico or **Ilha do Pico** *pee'koo*, 38 28N 28 25W, most southerly island in central group of the Azores, Horta dist; 48 km long by up to 15 km wide with an area of 433 sq km; in W rises to 2,351 m at the active volcano, Pico, the highest peak in the Azores and also in Portugal; vineyards; airport; chief town is Lajes do Pico.

Pico Rivera *pee'kō ri-vay'ra*, 33 59N 118 08W, pop(1980) 53,459, city in Los Angeles county, SW California, United States; c.16 km SE of Los Angeles.

Pidurutalagala *pid-oor-oot-al-ag'a-la*, 7 01N 80 45E, the highest peak in Sri Lanka at 2,524 m; 95 km E of Colombo, to the NE of Nuwara-Eliya; sometimes called Pedrotalagala.

Piedras, Las *las pyayd'ras*, 34 42S 56 14W, pop(1985) 57,711, town in Canelones dept, Uruguay; railway; economy: wine, fruit, cattle.

Piekary Śląskie *pye-ka'i shlõ'skye*, 50 20N 18 58E, pop(1983) 66,900, mining town in Katowice voivodship, S Poland; N of Katowice; railway.

Pieksämäki *pee'ek-sah-ma'kee*, 62 18N 27 10E, pop(1982) 14,208, town in Mikkeli prov, SE central Finland; N of Mikkeli and E of Jyväskylä; established in 1930; railway; economy: timber trade.

Piemonte *pyay-mon'tay*, PIEDMONT *peed'mont* (Eng), region of N Italy, comprising the provs of Torino, Vercelli, Novara, Cuneo, Asti, and Alessandria; pop(1981) 4,479,031; area 25,400 sq km; capital Torino (Turin); chief towns Cuneo, Saluzzo, Asti, and Alessandria; drained by the upper Po and its tributaries; bounded on the S by the Appno Ligure, and on the N and W by the Alps; industrial activity (metalworking, manufacture of machinery and cars, textiles, leather goods, foodstuffs) is concentrated in the upland area round Torino, Ivrea, and Biella, with good communications and adequate energy supplies; fruit-growing, arable farming (wheat, maize, rice, fodder crops), and cattle-farming predominate on the fertile alluvial soils of the Po valley; in recent years tourism has developed rapidly in the hill regions.

Piería *pī-ee'ri-a*, coastal nome (dept) of Makedhonia region, N Greece; pop(1981) 106,859; area 1,516 sq km; capital Kateríni; one of the legendary birthplaces of Orpheus.

Pierre *pyer*, 44 22N 100 21W, pop(1980) 11,973, capital of state in Hughes county, central South Dakota, United States; on the R Missouri, just S of L Oahe; founded as a railway terminus in 1880; state capital since 1889; the centre of a grain and dairy farming region.

Pierrefonds *pyer-fõ'*, 45 28N 73 50W, pop(1981) 38,390, town in S Québec, SE Canada; situated at the SE end of Montréal island.

Pieštany *pyesh'tyan-i*, 48 35N 17 50E, pop(1984) 31,298, town in Západoslovenský region, Slovak Socialist Republic, central Czechoslovakia; on R Váh, NE of Bratislava; health resort with sulphur springs; airfield; railway.

Pietarsaari *pee'e-tar-sah'ree*, JAKOBSTAD *yah'kob-stad* (Swed), 63 41N 22 40E, pop(1982) 20,620, port in Vaasa prov, W Finland; on the Gulf of Bothnia, NE of Vaasa; established in 1652; economy: metal products.

Pietermaritzburg or **Maritzburg** *pee-ter-mar'itz-burg*, 30 33S 30 24E, pop(1980) 178,972, capital of Natal prov, E South Africa; 73 km WNW of Durban; founded in 1838 by Boers from the Cape Colony; university (1910); railway; economy: footwear, aluminium, rubber, furniture, rice; monuments: Voortrekker museum, 19th-c Macrorie House museum.

Pietrosu *pyay'tros*, 47 35N 24 39E, mountain in NE Romania in the Romanian Carpathians, rising to 2,305 m.

Pi'ing-tung *ping-toong*, county of S Taiwan; area 2,775.6 sq km; pop(1982e) 900,614.

Piła *pee'wa*, voivodship in NW Poland; watered by the Noteć and Gwda rivers; pop(1983) 455,000; area 8,205 sq km; capital Piła; chief towns include Wałcz and Wągrowiec.

Piła, SCHNEIDEMÜHL *shnī'de-mül* (Ger), 53 09N 16 44E, pop(1983) 64,600, capital of Piła voivodship, NW Poland; on R Gwda in wooded country; birthplace of Stanisław Staszic (1755-1826), writer, philosopher and political leader; 5 km NE is the resort area of L Płocie; railway junction; economy: lightbulbs, aluminium casting.

Pinang, Pulau *poo-low' pen-ang'*, PENANG (Malay, 'betel nut island'), state in NW Malaysia, SE Asia; consists of a coastal strip on the NW coast of the Malay Peninsula (Seberang Prai) around Butterworth and the island (*pulau*) of Pulau Pinang (Penang) in the Strait of Malacca; pop(1980) 900,772; area 1,044 sq km; capital George Town.

Pinar del Río *pee-nar' del ree'ō*, westernmost prov in Cuba; the N coast is fringed by numerous coral keys and there is marshland along the S coast; area 10,860 sq km; pop(1981) 640,740; capital Pinar del Río; there are modern tourist facilities at Soroa and Viñales; the Vuelta Abajo region is famous for tobacco-growing.

Pinar del Río, 22 24N 83 42W, pop(1983e) 98,825, capital town of Pinar del Río prov, W Cuba; 175 km SW of La Habana (Havana); centre of rich Vuelta Abajo tobacco-growing region; monuments: Milanes theatre (1898), Casa de Cultura, tobacco museum and museum of natural science.

Píndhos, PIN'DUS (Eng), mountain range in W central and NW Greece, on the border between Ipiros and Thessalía regions; extends from Mt Grámmos (2,503 m) and Smólikas (2,633 m) on the Albanian frontier to Gióna near the Korinthiakós Kólpos (Gulf of Corinth); forms the watershed between the rivers flowing into the Aegean Sea (Piniós, Sperkhiós rivers) and those flowing into the Ionian Sea (Árakhthos, Akhelóos rivers); it is a region of forest-covered hills, with summer grazing above the tree line.

Pindus, mountain range in Greece. See Píndhos.

Pine Bluff, 34 13N 92 01W, pop(1980) 56,636, county seat of Jefferson county, SE central Arkansas, United States; a port on the R Arkansas, 62 km SSE of Little Rock; established during World War II, Pine Bluff Arsenal is the US Army centre for chemical, biological, and toxicological research; railway; economy: agricultural trade, electrical equipment, wood and paper products, furniture.

Pinel'las Park, 27 50N 82 43W, pop(1980) 32,811, town in Pinellas county, W Florida, United States; on Pinellas Peninsula, 8 km NW of St Petersburg.

Pinetown *pīn'town*, 29 50S 30 53E, pop(1980) 336,398, municipality in Natal prov, E South Africa; a W suburb of Durban.

Ping or **Meping**, river in central Thailand; rises N of Chiang Mai and flows SSE to meet the Nan R at Muang Nakhon Sawan where it forms the Chao Phraya R; length 590 km.

Pingxiang *ping-she-ang*, 27 35N 113 46E, pop(1984e) 1,270,400, city in Jiangxi prov, SE China; SE of Changsha; railway.

Piniós *pee-nee-os'*, PENEUS *pin-ee'us*, chief river of Thessalía region, Greece; rises in the Píndhos Mts, E of Métsovon; flows SE and E past Kalabáka, Tríkkala, and Lárisa, then turns NE to discharge into the Aegean Sea at Stómion; length 205 km.

Pinkiang, former name for capital of Heilongjiang prov, NE China. See Harbin.

Pins, Île des, ISLE OF PINES, KUNIE *koo-nee'ay*, forested, mountainous island in the SW Pacific Ocean, 48 km SE of New Caledonia, of which it is a dependency; area 150 sq km; pop(1983) 1,287; the main settlement is at Vao; discovered and named by Captain Cook in 1774; formerly a penal colony; economy: fishing and tourism.

Piotrków *pyotr-koof'*, voivodship in central Poland; watered by R Pilica; pop(1983) 623,000; area 6,266 sq km; capital Piotrków Trybunalski; chief towns include Tomaszów Mazowiecki, Radomsko and Bełchatów.

Piotrków Trybunalski *pyotr-koof' tri-boon-al'skee*, PETRIKAU (Ger), 51 27N 19 40E, pop(1983) 77,000, capital of Piotrków voivodship, central Poland; SE of Łódź; from 1578, seat of royal tribunal; site of general assemblies, *Seym* (parliament) session and synods in pre-partition Poland; railway; economy: mining machinery, glass, textiles; monuments: Bernardine church and monastery (1626), 16th-c royal castle with regional museum.

Piracicaba *pee-ra-see-ka'ba*, 22 45S 47 40W, pop(1980) 179,380, town in São Paulo state, Sudeste region, SE Brazil; NW of São Paulo; railway; economy: sugar refining, iron and steel industries.

Piraiévs *pee-re-efs'*, PIRAEUS *pī-ree'us* (Eng), 37 57N 23 42E, pop(1981) 196,389, major port in Attikí nome (dept), Sterea Ellás-Évvoia region, Greece; on a hilly peninsula, 8 km SW of Athínai (Athens); it has been the port of Athínai since the 5th century BC and is now the largest in Greece; in addition to the main harbour, Kántharos, there are 2 ancient harbours still in use on the E coast; international shipping and ferries to other ports in Europe and the Middle East, and to the Greek islands; rail terminus; event: Navy Week (June-July).

Pírgos *peer'gos*, PYRGOS, 37 40N 21 27E, pop(1981) 21,958, commercial town and capital of Ilía nome (dept), Pelopónnisos region, Greece, 192 km W of Athínai (Athens); railway; Katákolo, 13 km W, is the port of Pírgos.

Pirin Planina *pee-reen' pla'nee-na*, PIRIN MTS (Eng), range of mts in SW Bulgaria forming the SW part of the Rhodopi Planina (Rhodope Mts) and rising to 2,915 m at Vikhren peak.

Pirot *pee'rot*, 43 10N 22 32E, pop(1981) 69,653, town in E Srbija (Serbia) republic, Yugoslavia; on R Nišava, ESE of Niš near Bulgarian frontier; railway; economy: rubber products, foodstuffs, carpets.

Pisa *pee'za*, prov of Toscana region, W Italy; pop(1981) 388,800; area 2,448 sq km; capital Pisa.

Pisa, 43 43N 10 24E, pop(1981) 104,509, capital town of Pisa prov, Friuli-Venezia Giulia region, W Italy, on both banks of the R Arno, 10 km from the Ligurian Sea, 67 km W of Firenze (Florence); Pisa was formerly a great port on the coast but, since Etruscan times, it has retreated 7 km inland as a result of deposition of silt by the river; birthplace of Galileo; archbishopric; university (1343); airport; railway; economy: glass, motor cycles, yachts, tourism; monuments: Romanesque cathedral (1063-1118) with fine bronze doors and notable paintings and mosaics; circular baptistry (1153-1278, with 14th-c Gothic additions) with a fine dome and famous pulpit by Pisano (1260); the campanile, the 'Leaning Tower' (1173-1350), which is 55 m high, with a series of 6 superimposed pillared galleries, deviates 2.25 m from the perpendicular (a peculiarity due to subsidence, not design); Campo Santo, the most famous cemetery of its kind, a colonnaded quadrangle (126 m long by 52 m across) in Tuscan Gothic style, built by Giovanni di Simone in 1278-83 and completed in 1462; event: carnival (Feb); Gioco del Ponte historic boat races (1st Sunday in June).

Písek *pees'sek*, 49 19N 14 10E, pop(1984) 29,094, town in Jihočeský region, Czech Socialist Republic, W central Czechoslovakia; on R Otava; school of forestry; railway; originally a gold mining town; economy: tobacco, paper, textiles, musical instruments; monuments: 12th-c cathedral, 13th-c Zvikov castle.

Pissis, Monte *pee'sees*, 27 45S 68 40W, Andean peak rising to 6,858 m on the border between Catamarca and La Rioja provs, Andina, Argentina.

Pistoia *pees-to'ya*, prov of Toscana region, Italy; pop(1981) 264,995; area 966 sq km; capital Pistoia.

Pistoia, 43 56N 10 55E, pop(1981) 92,274, capital town of Pistoia prov, Toscana region, Italy; 32 km NW of Firenze (Florence), on a spur of the Appno Tosco-Emilliano; the pistol was reputedly invented here; railway; economy: hardware; monuments: 12th-c cathedral with a magnificent altar of silver; church of the Madonna dell'Umiltà (1494-1509); 14th-c Gothic octagonal baptistry.

Pisuerga *pee-swer'ga*, river rising in the Cordillera Cantabrica near Pena Labra forming part of the boundary between Palencia and Burgos provs, N Spain, flowing S and SW past Valladolid to the R Douro (Duero); length 275 km.

Pita *pee'ta*, 11 05N 12 15W, town in W central Guinea, W Africa; in the Fouta Djallon mountains, 225 km NE of Conakry; alt 838 m.

Pitcairn Islands, island group in the SE Pacific Ocean, E of French Polynesia, comprising Pitcairn I and the uninhabited islands of Ducie, Henderson, and Oeno; timezone GMT +9; area 27 sq km; chief settlement Adamstown; most of the inhabitants are direct descendants of the mutineers from *HMS Bounty* and their Tahitian wives; the dominant faith is Seventh Day Adventism; the official language is a dialect of English; there is a primary school on Pitcairn I, but children go to New Zealand for secondary education; New Zealand decimal currency has been in use since 1967.

Physical description and climate. The islands are volcanic with high lava cliffs and rugged hills. Pitcairn (4.5 sq km), more than 2,000 km SE of Tahiti, is a high volcanic island rising to 335 m. It is surrounded by rocks and high cliffs, and even at Bounty Bay, the only landing-place, access from the sea is difficult. Oeno, an uninhabited atoll with an area of less than 1 sq km, is situated about 100 km NW of Pitcairn I. Henderson is a large raised atoll (30 sq km), and Ducie, the smallest of the 4, lies 500 km E of Pitcairn and is largely inaccessible. The climate is equable, with an average annual rainfall of 2,000 mm spread evenly throughout the year. Mean monthly temperatures range from 24°C in Jan to 19°C in July.

History, government and constitution. Pitcairn I was discovered by the British navigator Carteret in 1767 but remained uninhabited until 1790, when it was occupied by 9 mutineers from *HMS Bounty*. By 1856, the population had grown too large for the island's resources, and the 194 inhabitants were moved to Norfolk I, off the E coast of Australia. By 1864 43 Pitcairn islanders had returned and since then the island has been permanently settled. Pitcairn was brought within the jurisdiction of the High Commissioner for the Western Pacific in 1898 and transferred to the Governor of Fiji in 1952. A British Crown Colony, the islands are today governed by the High Commissioner in New Zealand (since Fiji became independent in October 1970). The Local Government Ordinance of 1964 constitutes a council of 10 members, presided over by the island magistrate who is elected triennially.

Economy. On Pitcairn I, the fertile soils of the valleys produce a wide variety of tropical and sub-tropical crops used for subsistence. However, some fruit, vegetables, and crafts are sold to passing ships running between New Zealand and Panama. Fuel oil, machinery, building materials, flour, sugar, and other foodstuffs are imported. The sale of postage stamps is the greatest source of revenue. A re-afforestation scheme was introduced in 1963 with emphasis on the planting of miro trees, which provide the wood used in making handicrafts.

Piteşti *pee-tesht'*, 44 51N 24 51E, pop(1983) 149,684, capital of Argeş county, Romania; on R Argeş; railway junction; economy: petrochemicals, motor vehicles, electric motors, textiles, wine, fruit.

Pitlochry *pit-loKH'ri*, 56 43N 3 45W, pop (1981) 2610; town in Perth and Kinross dist, Tayside region, central Scotland; on the R Tummel, 6 km S of the Pass of Killiecrankie, 18 km NW of Dunkeld; popular summer resort; Pitlochry Festival Theatre and annual Highland Games; economy: hydroelectricity, distillery, tourism.

Piton de la Petite Rivière Noire, LITTLE BLACK RIVER MT (Eng), 20 24S 57 23E, highest peak on the island of Mauritius, rising to 826 m in the Black River-Savanne range in the SW of the island.

Piton des Neiges, Le *pee-tõ day nezh'*, or LE PITON, 21 12S 55 19E, volcanic peak on the island of Réunion in the Indian Ocean, rising to 3,071 m.

Pitons, The *pee'tons*, two conical mountains of volcanic origin off the SW coast of the Windward I of St Lucia i the Caribbean; Gros Piton (798 m) and Petit Piton (750 m); Piton is the French word for a mountain peak, a term often used in the French W Indies.

Pittsburg, 38 02N 121 53W, pop(1980) 33,034, city in Contra Costa county, W California, United States; at the junction of the San Joaquin and Sacramento rivers, 40 km NE of Oakland; railway.

Pittsburgh *pits'burg*, 40 26N 80 01W, pop(1980) 423,938, county seat of Allegheny county, W Pennsylvania, United States; at the confluence of the Allegheny and Monongahela rivers where they form the R Ohio; the French built Fort Duquesne here in 1750; the fort was taken by the British and renamed Fort Pitt in 1758; achieved city status in 1816; 3 universities (1787, 1878, 1900); railway; airport; economy: the city's traditional steel industry has been largely replaced by service industries; manufactures machinery and chemicals; 3rd largest US corporate headquarters; noted for recent urban redevelopment and a dramatic reduction in air and water pollution (in 1985 judged the USA's most liveable city); monuments: Carnegie Institute, Frick Art Museum, Point State Park, Heinz Hall, Phipps Conservatory; event: arts festival (June).

Pittsfield, 42 27N 73 15W, pop(1980) 51,974, county seat of Berkshire county, W Massachusetts, United States; on the R Housatonic in the Berkshire Hills, 64 km NW of Springfield and 10 km E of the New York state border; railway; summer and winter (skiing) resort.

Piura *pyoo'ra*, dept in NW Peru; bordered W by the Pacific, N by Ecuador; the Cordillera de Guamani rises in the NE; part of the dept is occupied by the Sechura desert; pop(1981) 1,045,569; area 36,403 sq km; capital Piura; a cotton-producing area.

Piura, 5 15S 80 38W, pop(1981) 186,354, capital of Piura dept, NW Peru; founded in 1532 by the conquistadores left behind by Pizarro; 2 universities (1962, 1968); railway; economy: cotton; monuments: San Francisco church, where the city's independence from Spain was declared on 4 Jan 1821, nearly 8 months before that of Lima; Las Mercedes colonial church has ornately carved balconies, a 3-tiered archway, hand-hewn supports and massive furnishings; the Casa Museo Grau, birthplace of Admiral Miguel Grau, hero of the War of the Pacific, is now a museum containing a model of the *Huáscar*, the largest Peruvian warship in the War of the Pacific, built in Britain.

Placentia *pla-sen'ti-a*, 33 53N 117 52W, pop(1980) 35,041, city in Orange county, SW California, United States; 13 km N of Santa Ana; originally established as a health resort, with mineral springs nearby.

Plaines Wilhems, district in W central Mauritius; area 203.3 sq km; pop(1983) 308,015; chief towns are Curepipe, Beau Bassin-Rose Hill Vacoas-Phoenix and Quatre Bornes.

Plainfield, 40 37N 74 25W, pop(1980) 45,555, residential town in Union county, NE New Jersey, United States; 18 km WSW of Elizabeth; railway.

Planken *plang'ken*, 47 11N 9 33E, pop(1985) 293, commune in Oberland dist, Principality of Liechtenstein, central Europe; area 5.3 sq km.

Plano, 33 01N 96 42W, pop(1980) 72,331, town in Collin county, NE Texas, United States; 28 km NNW of Dallas; railway; economy: feed and flour mills, cotton gins, and various manufactures including metal products, boats and trailers.

Plantation, 26 08N 80 15W, pop(1980) 48,501, town in Broward county, SE Florida, United States; residential suburb 8 km W of Fort Lauderdale.

Plasencia *pla-sen'thya*, 40 30N 6 08W, pop(1981) 32,178, agric town in Cáceres prov, Extremadura, W Spain; situated N of the R Tagus, 85 km NNE of Cáceres; railway; economy: woollens, agric machinery, canning, construction equipment, mineral water; monument: 13th-c cathedral in the Plaza Mayor.

Plata, La *la pla'ta*, 34 52S 57 55W, pop(1980) 560,341, port and capital of Buenos Aires prov, Litoral, E Argentina; on Río de la Plata, SW of Buenos Aires; founded in 1882; 3 universities (1884, 1965, 1968); named Eva Perón (1946-55); railway; a motorway is being built to link La Plata with Buenos Aires; the port is accessible to ships of large tonnage and is the main outlet for produce from the pampas; economy: refrigerated meat, grain and oil trade; oil refining; a 72 km pipeline runs to the South dock at Buenos Aires; monuments: museum of natural history; zoological gardens; observatory; Garden of Peace, with each country in the world represented by one flower; local holiday: 19 Nov (foundation of the city).

Plata, Río de la *day la pla'ta*, RIVER PLATE (Eng), a wide, shallow estuary of the Paraná and Uruguay rivers, between Argentina (S and W shore) and Uruguay (N shore); area 35,000 sq km; length 320 km; width 225 km at its mouth and 45 km at Buenos Aires; its outflow is exceeded only by that of the Amazon; discovered in 1516 by Juan Diaz de Solís, explored by Magellan in 1520 and by Sebastian Cabot several years later; the first settlement on its banks was established at Buenos Aires by Pedro de Mendoza in 1536; in World War II a naval engagement (Dec 1939) between the British and Germans led to the sinking of the German pocket battleship *Graf Spee* in the river near Punta del Este; the ship was scuttled off Montevideo and her anchor set up at the port entrance in 1964; the name Río de la Plata is sometimes given to the entire river system (Paraná-Paraguay-Uruguay) draining SE central South America.

Plate, River, river estuary in South America. See Plata, Río de la.

Plateau *plat'ō*, state in central Nigeria, W Africa; pop(1982e) 3,231,800; area 58,030 sq km; bounded S by the R Benue; capital Jos; chief towns Bukuru, Nassarawa, Lafia, Akwanga, and Pankshin; there are reserves of columbite and tin; economy: rice, cattle, iron ore and cement processing, fish farming, timber, stone crushing, tailoring, soft drinks and mechanical engineering.

Platres *pla'tres*, 34 53N 32 52E, mountain resort town in Limassol dist, central Cyprus; at foot of the Troödos Mts.

Plauen *plow'un*, 50 29N 12 8E, pop(1981) 78,800, town in Plauen dist, Karl Marx Stadt, S East Germany; on R Weisse Elster SW of Zwickau; former capital of Vogtland; railway; economy: textiles, lacework, mechanical engineering.

Pleasant Hill, 37 57N 122 04W, pop(1980) 25,124, city in Contra Costa county, W California, United States; c.26 km NE of Oakland.

Pleasanton, 37 40N 121 52W, pop(1980) 35,160, city in Alameda county, W California, United States; 40 km ESE of Oakland.

Ple'ven, okrug (prov) of N Bulgaria on the frontier with Romania; traversed by the Vit and Osum rivers with the R Danube on its N boundary and the R Iskur to the W; area 4,364 sq km; pop(1981) 373,000; a nuclear power plant is located at Belene on the Danube.

Pleven, 43 25N 24 40E, pop(1981) 131,690, agricultural and industrial capital of Pleven okrug (prov), N Bulgaria; 178 km NE of Sofiya, near the R Vit; airfield; railway; economy: metal products, machinery, food processing, textiles.

Płock *pwotsk*, voivodship in central Poland; bisected by R Wisła (Vistula); pop(1983) 504,000; area 5,117 sq km; capital Płock; chief towns include Kutno and Gostynin.

Płock, PLOTSK (Rus), 52 33N 19 40E, pop(1983) 108,000, river port capital of Płock voivodship, central Poland; on R Wisła (Vistula), NW of Warszawa (Warsaw); birthplace of the poet Władysław Broniewski; railway; river service to Warszawa and Włocławek; economy: shipyard; a major oil refining and petrochemical centre since 1960, with an oil pipeline to USSR; manufacture of combine harvesters; monuments: 14-15th-c cathedral with fine collection of sacral art; castle of the Mazovian dukes; event: national festival of folk ensembles in early summer.

Ploieşti *plo-yesht'*, 44 57N 26 01E, pop(1983) 229,945, capital of Prahova county, S central Romania; railway;

major centre for the petroleum industry with pipelines to Giurgiu, Bucureşti and Constanţa; economy: petrol refining, oilfield equipment, petrochemicals, textiles, paper, furniture.

Plön, lake in W Germany. See Großer Plöner See.

Plovdiv *plov'dif*, okrug (prov) of central Bulgaria between the Stara Planina (Balkan Mts) and the Rhodopi Planina (Rhodope Mts); traversed W-E by the R Maritsa; area 5,612 sq km; pop(1981) 753,000; coal-fired Maritsa-East power plant located near Plovdiv.

Plovdiv, EVMOLPIA or TRIMONTIUM (Lat), 42 08N 24 25E, pop(1981) 358,176, capital of Plovdiv okrug (prov), central Bulgaria; on the R Maritsa, 156 km SE of Sofiya; airport; railway; 2nd largest city in Bulgaria; economy: metal products, food processing, textiles, chemicals; also a major trading centre for livestock and tobacco; monuments: Roman amphitheatre and in Old Plovdiv, many interesting buildings from the Middle Ages and the National Revival Period.

Plum, 40 29N 79 47W, pop(1980) 25,390, town in Allegheny county, W Pennsylvania, United States; suburb 20 km E of Pittsburgh.

Plymouth *pli'muth*, 16 44N 62 14W, pop(1980) 3,343, port and capital town of Montserrat, Lesser Antilles, E Caribbean; on the SW tip of the island.

Plymouth, 50 23N 4 10W, pop(1981) 242,560, seaport in Plymouth dist, Devonshire, SW England; at the confluence of the Tamar and Plym rivers, 340 km SW of London; home port of Sir Francis Drake; the Pilgrim Fathers set out from here on their voyage to the New World in the *Mayflower* (1620); a major base for the Royal Navy; ferry links to Santander (Spain), Roscoff and St Malo; railway; airfield; event: navy week (Aug).

Plymouth, 41 57N 70 40W, pop(1980) 35,913, county seat of Plymouth county, SE Massachusetts, United States; on Plymouth Bay, 29 km SE of Brockton; first permanent European settlement in New England, founded by Pilgrims in 1620; railway; economy: fishing, textiles, rope, tourism.

Plymouth, 45 02N 93 27W, pop(1980) 31,615, town in Hennepin county, SE Minnesota, United States; suburb 15 km WNW of Minneapolis.

Plynli'mon Fawr, 52 28N 3 47W, mountain rising to 752 m on the Dyfed-Powys border, central Wales; 23 km ENE of Aberystwyth.

Plzeň *pœl'zen*, PILSEN, 49 40N 13 10E, pop(1984) 174,094, modern industrial capital of Západočeský region, Czech Socialist Republic, W Czechoslovakia; at the junction of Uhlava, Uslava, Radbuza and Mze rivers, SW of Praha (Prague); railway; economy: beer, metallurgy, aircraft, armaments, motor vehicles, chemicals, clothing.

Po *po*, 11 11N 1 10W, town in central Burkina, W Africa; 130 km from Ouagadougou on the route to Bolgatanga (Ghana).

Po, national park in S central Burkina, W Africa; area 1,494 sq km; established in 1976.

Po *po, pō* (Eng), PADUS (anc), ERIDANOS (Gr), river in N Italy, rising on the Monte Viso in the Alpi Cozie (Cottian Alps) near the French frontier; flows E and NE past Torino (Turin) and Chivasso, then generally E through Piemonte region, past Piacenza and Cremona, separating Lombardia and Veneto from Emilia-Romagna; discharges into the Adriatic Sea, 56 km S of Venezia (Venice); the longest river in Italy; chief tributaries on N bank (draining the Italian lakes) Ticino, Adda, Oglio, Mincio; chief tributaries on S bank Tanaro, Trebbia, Secchia, and Panaro; the Po has an irregular flow and a tendency to silt up and alter its course; below Piacenza, much of the river has been artificially embanked since ancient times.

Pobeda, Gora, 65 10N 146 00E, highest peak in the Khrebet Cherskogo range, Yakutskaya ASSR, E Siberian Rossiyskaya, Soviet Union; height 3,147 m; several of its glaciers extend up to 70 km in length; source of several tributaries of the R Indigirka.

Pobedy, Pik, 42 25N 80 15E, highest peak in the Tien Shan range and the 2nd highest peak in the USSR, on the China-Soviet frontier, 160 km E of Ozero Issyk-Kul' (Lake Issyk-Kul'); height 7,439 m; discovered in 1943.

Pocatello, 42 52N 112 27W, pop(1980) 46,340, county seat of Bannock county, SE Idaho, United States; on the R Portneuf, near the American Falls Reservoir; named after a Bannock Indian chief; founded in 1882; Fort Hall Indian reservation lies to the N; university (1901); railway; economy: agricultural trade, food processing, mining, railway engineering.

Podol'sk *pu-dol'yusk*, 55 23N 37 32E, pop(1983) 207,000, town in Moskovskaya oblast, central European Rossiyskaya, Soviet Union; on the R Pakhra, 43 km S of Moskva (Moscow); in a fertile agricultural region; there are large limestone and marble quarries nearby; created a town in 1781; railway; economy: tin smelting, titanium and magnesium production, manufacture of sewing machines, concrete, and machinery; monument: Troitskii cathedral (1819-25).

Podujevo *po-doo'ye-vo*, 42 54N 21 10E, pop(1981) 75,427, town in autonomous province of Kosovo, S Srbija (Serbia) republic, Yugoslavia; ENE of Titova Mitrovica.

Pogradec *pog-ra'dets*, prov of E Albania; area 725 sq km; pop(1980) 59,000; capital Pogradec.

Pogradec, 40 54N 20 40E, commercial town and capital of Pogradec prov, SE Albania; on the SW shore of L Ohrid, 88 km SE of Tiranë; alt 712 m; a mountain climatic health resort and tourist centre; the population is largely of Muslim origin; economy: woodworking, foodstuffs.

P'ohang *po-hahng*, PO'HANG, 36 01N 129 23E, pop(1983e) 244,542, port town in Kyŏngsangpuk prov, E Korea; situated on the E coast on the Sea of Japan; railway; ferry terminal for Ullŭng do island off the E coast of Korea; economy: steel and commerce.

Pohjois-Karjala *po'hi-ois kar-yala*, NORRA KARELEN (Swed), a prov of E Finland, bounded on the E by USSR; contains the lakes of Pielinen and Orivesi; area 21,585 sq km; pop(1982) 177,242; Joensuu, situated on the N shore of L Orivesi, is the prov capital; copper mining at Hammaslahti, Vuonos and Keretti, talc mining at Vuonos.

Pointe-à-Pitre *pwĩt-a-pee'tre*, 16 14N 61 32W, pop(1982) 53,165 (including the suburb of Abymes), seaport and capital town of Guadeloupe, Lesser Antilles, E Caribbean; on the SW coast of the island of Grande-Terre, at the S end of the Rivière Salée; largest town in Guadeloupe; commercial centre; Le Raizet International Airport is 3 km from the centre of the town.

Pointe aux-Trembles *pwĩt'-ō-trãble*, 45 40N 73 30W, pop(1981) 36,270, town in S Québec, SE Canada; on the E shore of Montréal island, on the St Lawrence river, 18 km NNE of Montréal; railway.

Pointe-Noire *pwĩt-nwar* 4 48S 11 53E, pop(1980) 105,105, seaport in Kouilou prov, SW Congo, W Africa; on the Atlantic coast 385 km WSW of Brazzaville; W terminus of the railway from Brazzaville; development of the original harbour facilities began in 1934 and were completed after 1945; a centre of the Congo's oil industry; airfield; economy: oil refining, banking, timber, shoes.

Poitiers *pwa-tyay*, formerly POICTIERS, LIMONUM (Lat), 46 35N 0 20E, pop(1982) 82,884, market town and capital of Vienne dept, Poitou-Charentes region, W France; on a rocky plateau above the rivers Clain and Boivre which meet N of the Old Town, 160 km ESE of Nantes; bishopric; university (1431); quickly became the 3rd most important town in France after Paris and Lyon; railway and road junction; once capital of the ancient prov of Poitou, now surrounded by suburbs; has notable Romanesque churches; early Christians gathered here in the Roman city of Limonum; economy: chemicals, hosiery, trade in honey, wine and wool; monuments: 4th-c Baptistry (France's oldest Christian building), now a museum; 12-13th-c cathedral of St-Pierre (towers and upper part of the facade are 14-15th-c); 11-12th-c church of Notre-Dame-de-la-Grande (Romanesque-Byzantine, with a richly decorated W front); town hall (1869-76) containing the Musée des Beaux-Arts, 11-12th-c

Romanesque church of St-Hilaire-le-Grand (restored in the 19th-c), palace of the former counts of Poitou.

Poitou *pwa-too*, former prov in W France, now occupying the depts of Vendée, Deux-Sèvres and Vienne; the chief town is Poitiers; held by England until 1369.

Poitou-Charentes, region of W France comprising the depts of Charente, Charente-Maritime, Deux-Sèvres and Vienne, 14 arrond, 151 cantons and 1,461 communes; pop(1982) 1,568,230; area 25,809 sq km; includes the former provinces of Angoumois, Aunis and Saintonge; bounded on the W by the Bay of Biscay and on the S by the Gironde estuary; includes the islands of Oléron (France's 2nd largest off-shore island) and Ré; the land rises in the E to the Plateaux du Limousin and in the NW to the Hauteurs de Gâtine; the Plain of Poitou, E of Niort, is a land of goats, figs, fresh vegetables, salt mutton from the marshes, fat poultry, butter and fish; the Marais Poitevin is an area of marshland on either side of the Sèvre-Niortaise R (there are boat trips from Coulon, Arcais, La Garette or St-Hilaire-la-Palud); watered by the R Charente and its tributaries; of interest in the wide valley of the Charente between Angoulême and Saintes are Bassac Abbey, the Romanesque churches of Chaniers, Châteauneuf-sur-Charente and Châtre, and the town of Cognac, whose vineyards are noted for celebrated brandy, as well as for an aperitif called Pineau des Charentes; chief towns in the region include Angoulême, Niort, La Rochelle (port), Rochefort and Saintes; châteaux worth visiting include Touffou (Vienne dept), Dampierre-sur-Boutonne (Charente-Maritime dept) and Roche Courbon (Charente-Maritime dept); seaside resorts include Fouras, Meschers-sur-Gironde and Royan.

Pokhara Valley *pō'ka-ra*, Nepal, central Asia; 203 km NW of Kathmandu; the small town of Pokhara is at an alt of 913 m on a tropical plain which is dominated by the summit of Machhapuchhre, which crowns the valley, at 7,993 m; an excellent area for trekking, the valley is accessible from Kathmandu by road and daily air flights; other ice-clad peaks, which dominate the valley, are Annapurna South, Annapurna I, II, III and IV, Rock Noir, Fang, Glacier Dome, Gangapurna, Lamjung Himal, with Dhaulagiri I visible to the NW and Manaslu-Himalchuli visible to the NE; Machhapuchhre is called 'fish-tail' because it has two summit, which look like the forked tail of a fish; the R Seti drains the Pokhara Valley; several lakes including Phewa Tal (W), Begnas Tal and Rupa Tal (E) offer fishing and boating for the tourist; the Pokhara Valley floor is made up of great thicknesses of gravel cut into terraces by rivers; there is a largely Hindu population in the tropical plain and low hills, while the temperate highlands are the home of the tribal Gurungs who have villages up to 1,900 m; Pokhara is the centre of one of Nepal's 5 Development Regions.

Poland *pō'land*, POLSKA (Pol), official name The Polish People's Republic, POLSKA RZECZPOSPOLITA LUDOWA (Pol), socialist republic in central Europe; bounded N by the Baltic Sea, W by E Germany, E by the USSR and S by Czechoslovakia; its coastline extends 491 km from the E German to the USSR border; timezone GMT +1; area 312,612 sq km; the present area is some 20% less than that of 1939; 46% of Polish territory was lost to the USSR in 1945 but land was acquired from Germany on the W border; pop(1983) 36,745,000; capital Warszawa (Warsaw); chief towns include Łódź, Kraków, Wrocław, Poznań, Gdańsk, Katowice and Lublin; chief sea ports are Gdańsk, Gdynia, Szczecin and Świnoujście; chief river ports are Gliwice, Wrocław and Warszawa (Warsaw); the pop is predominantly Polish of W Slavic origin, with Ukrainian, Byelorussian and Jewish minorities comprising under 2%; 95% of the pop is Roman Catholic; the currency is the złoty of 100 groszy; national holiday 25 April; membership of Warsaw Pact, CEMA, COMECON, FAO, GATT, IAEA, ICAO, ICES, IHO, ILO, IMO, IPU, ISO, ITC, ITU, UN, UNESCO, UPU, WFTU, WHO, WIPO, WMO, WTO.

Physical description. The land is mostly part of the great European plain, with the Carpathian (Karpaty) and Sudetes Mts in the S forming a mountain wall that rises in the High Tatra to 2,499 m at Rysy on the Czechoslovak border. The Carpathians are comprised of faulted alpine formations with oil and mineral deposits while the Sudetes Mts are older denuded granites, gneisses and limestones. The glaciated and eroded granites and gneisses of the Tatra form attractive alpine scenery. To the N of these lies the Polish plateau, cut by the Bug, San and Wisła (Vistula) rivers; in the W (Silesia) Upper Carboniferous strata compose the richest coal basin in Europe. N of the plateau are the lowlands of clay and sand, formed by glaciation which left frontal moraines and fissures which glacial meltwaters have eroded and formed into many lakes; these have survived denudation in the NE, to give the hilly Mazurian lake district. The several E-W fluvioglacial valleys in which the main rivers flow, stretch from Poznań by Warszawa (Warsaw) over the USSR frontier to Polesie. The Baltic coast is flat with sandy heathland and numerous lagoons. Only on the Wisła (Vistula) delta and the almost closed Oder (Odra) estuary are there suitable places for ports. The Wisła (Vistula) and Oder (Odra) are the two greatest waterways. The rivers are often frozen in winter and are liable to flood. Forests cover one-fifth of the land with pine, beech, birch, lime and yew while patches of tundra occur in the Baltic, and steppe flora on the plateau.

Climate. The climate is continental, with severe winters and hot summers. Rain falls chiefly during the summer and seldom exceeds an annual level of 650 mm.

History, government and constitution. The kingdom of Poland dates from the year 1025 when the Poles emerged as the most powerful of a number of Slavic groups. In 1569 Poland reached its greatest extent when it united with Lithuania. Subsequently the power of the Polish state was weakened by attacks from Russia, Brandenburg, Turkey and Sweden and eventually in 1772, 1793 and 1795 Poland was divided between Prussia, Russia and Austria. In 1815 Poland reappeared as a semi-independent state following the Congress of Vienna and was incorporated into the Russian empire. The independent Polish state emerged from World War I. An authoritarian government ruled until the partition of Poland between Germany and the USSR in 1939. In 1944 a People's Democracy was established under Soviet influence and by 1947 communists controlled the government. The preliminary 'Little Charter' of 1947 was eventually succeeded in 1952 by a new and far-reaching constitution covering all phases of national life. According to this the 'workers' of town and country, who are declared the supreme authority, are represented in the *Seym* (the legislative body, elected for 4 years) in the proportion of one deputy for every 60,000 citizens, the franchise being universal from the age of 18. The single-chamber *Seym* elects a Council of State composed of the chairman, secretary and 14 members; and a Council of Ministers. Local government is carried out by People's Councils elected every 4 years. Since 1982 the united political parties formerly called the National Unity Front have been known as the Patriotic Movement of National Renaissance. The country is governed as a 'People's Republic' on the Soviet model.

Economy. In 1939 60.6% of the pop lived by agriculture. Since then industrialization has reduced that figure to about 30%, two-thirds of farm land being in private hands and one-third controlled by the state or by collectives. Nearly 50% of the land is under cultivation, the main products being rye, wheat, barley, oats, potatoes and sugar beet. Bacon, eggs, geese, turkeys and pork are exported. Poland is a major producer of coal and has deposits of lead, zinc, sulphur, potash and copper mostly located to the S in the heavy industry regions of upper Silesia around Kraków and Katowice. The production of motor vehicles, machinery, electrical equipment as well as food processing and the traditional textile industry are based around Łódź and Wrocław in lower Silesia. Nearly two-thirds of Polish trade is with E bloc countries.

Administrative divisions. Poland is divided into 49 voivodships (provinces) as follows:

Voivodship	*area (sq km)*	*pop(1983)*
Biała Podlaska	5,348	294,000
Białystok	10,055	660,000
Bielsko-Biała	3,704	857,000
Bydgoszcz	10,349	1,064,000
Chełm	3,866	237,000
Ciechanów	6,362	413,000
Częstochowa	6,182	759,000
Elbląg	6,103	458,000
Gdańsk	7,394	1,373,000
Gorzów	8,484	474,000
Jelenia Góra	4,278	504,000
Kalisz	6,512	686,000
Katowice	6,650	3,854,000
Kielce	9,211	1,094,000
Konin	5,139	452,000
Koszalin	8,470	478,000
Kraków	3,254	1,197,000
Krosno	5,702	465,000

contd

Voivodship	*area (sq km)*	*pop(1983)*
Legnica	4,037	478,000
Leszno	4,154	369,000
Łódź	1,523	1,147,000
Łomża	6,684	334,000
Lublin	6,792	967,000
Nowy Sącz	5,576	652,000
Olsztyn	12,327	707,000
Opole	8,535	996,000
Ostrołęka	6,498	379,000
Piła	8,205	455,000
Piotrków	6,266	623,000
Płock	5,117	504,000
Poznań	8,151	1,278,000
Przemyśl	4,437	389,000
Radom	7,294	719,000
Rzeszów	4,397	675,000
Siedlce	8,499	629,000
Sieradz	4,869	397,000
Skierniewice	3,960	405,000

contd

Voivodship	*area (sq km)*	*pop(1983)*
Słupsk	7,453	386,000
Suwałki	10,490	438,000
Szczecin	9,981	924,000
Tarnobrzeg	6,283	572,000
Tarnów	4,151	628,000
Toruń	5,348	627,000
Wałbrzych	4,168	728,000
Warszawa	3,788	2,382,000
Włocławek	4,402	422,000
Wrocław	6,287	1,101,000
Zamość	6,980	483,000
Zielona Góra	8,868	632,000

Polar Circle. See Arctic Circle.

Poles, the geographical poles are the 2 diametrically opposite points at which the Earth's axis cuts the Earth's surface; the N pole is covered by the Arctic Ocean, the S pole by the land mass of Antarctica; the magnetic poles are the positions towards which the needle of a magnetic compass will point; they differ from the geographical poles by an angle known as the *declination* or *magnetic variation*, which itself varies at different points of the Earth's surface and at different times; the geographical position of the magnetic poles is unstable; the S Pole was first reached by Roald Amundsen on 14 Dec 1911; the N Pole was first reached by Robert E. Peary on 6 April 1909.

Polmont, 55 59N 3 44W, pop(1981) 17,648, town in Falkirk dist, Central region, E central Scotland; 5 km E of Falkirk; railway.

Polochic *pō-lō-cheek'*, river in Alta Verapaz and Izabal depts, E Guatemala, Central America; rises near Tactic and flows 240 km E past Pancajché and Panzós to discharge into Lago de Izabal; a large swampy delta is formed SW of El Estor; chief tributary Río Cahabón.

Polonnaruwa *pō-lun-nur-oov-a*, 7 56N 81 02E, pop(1981) 11,636, capital of Polonnaruwa dist, North-Central prov, Sri Lanka; on N shore of L Parakrama Samudra, S of Trincomalee; monuments: the city has many fine buildings dating from the 11-14th centuries when it was the island's capital, including King Parakrama Bahu's palace and Kumara Pokuna (the royal baths); city once fortified by three concentric walls; an irrigation complex known as the Sea of Parakrama watered the surrounding plains.

Polska, central Europe. See Poland.

Poltava *pool-tav'a*, 49 35N 34 35E, pop(1983) 290,000, industrial capital city of Poltavskaya oblast, Ukrainskaya SSR, Soviet Union; on the R Vorskla; one of the oldest settlements in the republic, known since the 7th century; the first Marxist circles arose here in the 1890s; railway; on the Khar'kov-Kiyev highway; economy: machine building, metalworking, foodstuffs, clothing, glassworks; monument: cathedral of the Krestovozdvizhenskii monastery (1689-1709) with a campanile (1786).

Polynesia *pol-i-neez'zha*, ethnographic area in the central and SE Pacific Ocean; includes the islands of New Zealand, Hawaii, Samoa, Cook Is, Line Is, Tonga, French Polynesia, Kiribati, Tokelau and Easter I; many of the islands are small coral atolls; others are of volcanic origin.

Pomerania *pom-er-ay'nee-a*, POMMERN (Ger), POMORZR (Pol), region of N central Europe extending along the Baltic Sea from Stralsund in E Germany to the R Wisła (Vistula) in Poland; from 1919 until 1939 divided among Germany, Poland and Free City of Danzig, the Germany sector being the Prussian prov of Pomerania and the Polish sector forming the prov of Pomerelia; divided between E Germany and Poland in 1945; the region has many lakes; chief towns are Gdańsk, Szczecin and Koszalin.

Pomo'na, 34 04N 117 45W, pop(1980) 92,742, city in Los Angeles county, SW California, United States; 40 km E of Los Angeles; settled in 1875; university; railway; economy: naval ordnance, fruit, paper.

Pompa'no Beach, 26 14N 80 08W, pop(1980) 52,618, town in Broward county, SE Florida, United States; on the Atlantic Ocean, 12 km N of Fort Lauderdale; economy: pleasure boats, plastic and metal products, and electrical equipment; event: Christmas Boat Parade.

Pompei *pom-pay'*, POMPEII *pom-pay'ee* (Eng), 40 45N 14 27E, ruined ancient city in Napoli prov, Campania region, SW Italy, at the S foot of Vesuvio (Vesuvius), 20 km SE of Napoli (Naples); it was damaged by a violent earthquake in AD 63; this was followed (during the rebuilding of the city) by the great eruption of Vesuvio in AD 79, which covered the whole city, as well as Herculaneum and Stabiae, with a layer of ashes and pumice-stone 6-7 m deep; since the 18th century, systematic excavations have revealed a city roughly elliptical in shape, 3 km in circumference, with 8 gates, well-made streets with pavements, and fine examples of public buildings (forum, capitolium, amphitheatre, etc) and domestic architecture, well-preserved by the volcanic ash; two-fifths of the city still remains buried; the modern town of Pompei with the pilgrimage church of Santuario della Madonna del Rosario lies to the E of the ancient site.

Ponape *po'nu-pay*, one of the Federated States of Micronesia, W Pacific, comprising the island of Ponape (303 sq km) and 8 outlying atolls; area 345 sq km; pop(1980) 22,319, Kolonia is capital of Ponape and of the Federated States of Micronesia.

Ponca City, 36 42N 97 05W, pop(1980) 26,238, city in Kay county, N Oklahoma, United States; on the R Arkansas, 115 km WNW of Tulsa; named after an Indian tribe; railway; economy: trade, processing, and shipping centre in an agricultural and oil-producing area; oil refineries; manufactures include oil-drilling equipment.

Ponce *pon'say*, 18 01N 66 36W, pop(1980) 189,046, 2nd largest city in Puerto Rico, E Caribbean; port at Playa de Ponce on the S coast, 70 km SW of San Juan; airfield; monuments: colonial mansions, Ponce fort (1760).

Pondicherry *pon'di-che-ree*, union territory in S India; pop(1981) 604,136; area 492 sq km; the territory comprises the 4 separate enclaves of Karaikal, Pondicherry and Yanam on the Coromandel coast of Tamil Nadu and Andhra Pradesh and Mahé on the Kerala coast; capital Pondicherry; the territory is governed by a Lieutenant-Governor, appointed by the president, and a Council of Ministers responsible to a Legislative Assembly; 45% of the population is employed in agriculture, the principal food crop being rice; groundnuts, sugar cane and cotton are the main cash crops; 89% of the cultivated area is irrigated; textiles, sugar, cotton, paper and brewing are the major manufacturing industries; Pondicherry lies on a branch railway line from Madras to Madurai; founded in 1674, Pondicherry was once the chief French settlement in India; administration of the territory was transfered from France to India in Nov 1954; Pondicherry became a union territory in Aug 1962. The territory comprises 4 districts:

District	*area (sq km)*	*pop(1981)*
Pondicherry	290	444,417
Karaikal	160	120,010
Yanam	30	11,631
Mahé	10	28,413

Ponferrada *pon-fer-a'da*, 42 32N 6 35W, pop(1981) 52,499, industrial town in León prov, Castilla-León, W Spain; lying on high ground between the R Sil and R Boeza, 110 km W of León; economy: metal products; monuments: 13th-c Templars' castle; 10th-c monastery and the Mozarabic church of St Thomas; event: patronal festival in honour of the Virgin of the Oak in Sept with battle of flowers, folk music and fireworks.

Ponta Delgada *pon'ta del-ga'da*, dist in Portuguese autonomous region of the Azores comprising islands of São

Miguel and Santa Maria; divided into 7 councils and 57 parishes; capital is Ponta Delgada on São Miguel I; area 852 sq km; pop(1981) 131,295; economy: pottery, tea, tobacco, liquor, hats and fruit.

Ponta Delgada, 37 29N 25 40W, pop(1981) 21,940, capital of Ponta Delgada dist, Portuguese autonomous region of the Azores; on S coast of São Miguel I; largest town in the Azores; monuments: churches of São Sebastião and Pedro and convent of Santo Andre; events: Senhor Santo Cristo dos Milagres festival (5th Sunday after Easter), with folk events and singing competitions; Cavalhadas de São Pedro medieval equestrian games at the end of June and Divino Espirito Santo folk festival at the beginning of Aug.

Ponta Grossa *pon'ta gro'sa*, 25 07S 50 09W, pop(1980) 171,810, town in Paraná state, Sul region, S Brazil; NW of Curitiba; university (1970); railway; economy: potatoes, soya beans, wheat, fertilizers, vegetable oils, cattle raising; Ponta Grossa now calls itself the 'World Capital of Soya'.

Pon'tefract, 53 42N 1 18W, pop(1981) 29,047, town in Wakefield borough, West Yorkshire, N England; 20 km SE of Leeds; racecourse; railway; economy: coal, confectionery, distributive trades.

Pontevedra *pon-tay-vay'dra*, prov in Galicia region, NW Spain; separated from Portugal by the R Minho (Miño), its coast is cut up into *rias* or fjords which provide shelter for shipping; pop(1981) 859,897; area 4,477 sq km; capital Pontevedra; economy: fishing, shipbuilding (Vigo), metal products, tinned fish, pharmaceuticals, textiles, clothes, cement, tools, drinks, chemicals, paper, foodstuffs.

Pontevedra, PONS VETUS (Lat), 42 26N 8 40W, pop(1981) 65,137, port and capital of Pontevedra prov, Galicia, NW Spain; on Ría de Pontevedra, estuary of the rivers Lérez, Alba and Tomeza, 623 km NW of Madrid; railway; airport at Vigo; economy: textiles, pottery and trade in sardines, wine, cattle, grain and fruit; monuments: 12-arched Roman bridge (Pons Vetus), Casa de los Monteagudos, chapel of La Peregrina; events; fiesta of La Virgen de la Peregrina in Aug and pilgrimages in May and on Corpus Christi.

Pon'tiac, 42 38N 83 18W, pop(1980) 76,715, county seat of Oakland county, SE Michigan, United States; 40 km NNW of Detroit; in 1818 the settlement was named after the famous chief of the Ottawa Indians; railway; economy: car and truck manufacturing centre.

Pontianak *pon-tee-a-nahk'*, 0 05S 109 16E, pop(1980) 217,555, capital of Kalimantan Barat prov, W Borneo, Indonesia; close to the Equator, at the mouth of the R Kapuas; large Chinese pop; formerly the capital of a sultanate and major gold-exporting port; airfield; economy: shipbuilding, rubber, sugar, palm oil.

Pontoise *põ-twas*, 49 03N 3 05E, pop(1982) 29,411, historic market town and capital of Val-d'Oise dept, Ile-de-France region, central France, on the R Oise, 34 km NW of Paris.

Pontypool *pon-te-pool'*, 51 43N 3 02W, pop(1981) 36,301, town in Torfaen dist, Gwent, SE Wales; on the Afon Llwydd, 40 km NW of Bristol; railway; economy: scientific instruments.

Pontypridd *pon-te-preeth'*, 51 37N 3 22W, pop(1981) 29,796, valley town in Taff-Ely dist, Mid Glamorgan, S Wales; on the R Taff, 18 km NW of Cardiff; railway; economy: coal mining, chemicals, electronics, chains and cables.

Pool, province in S Congo, W Africa; area 34,000 sq km; pop(1980) 208,420; capital Kinkala.

Poole, 50 43N 1 59W, pop(1981) 119,316, port town in Poole dist, Dorset, S England; in Poole Harbour, 6 km W of Bournemouth; railway.

Poona, city in W India. See Pune.

Poopó, Lago *pō-ō-pō'*, lake in Oruro dept, W Bolivia; 56 km S of Oruro; 2nd largest lake in Bolivia; receives the Desaguadero (outlet from L Titicaca) and Marquez rivers; its outlet is the Río Lacahahuira; to the NE is the town of Poopó; area 2,512 sq km; length 97 km; width 32-48 km; about 2.5 m deep.

Popayán *po-pa-yan'*, 2 27N 76 22W, pop(1985) 156,530, historic city and capital of Cauca dept, SW Colombia, South America; at the foot of Puracé volcano; founded in 1536; after the conquest of the Pijao Indians the town became the regional seat of government, subject until 1717 to the Audencia of Quito and later to the Audencia of Bogotá; in March 1983 Popayán suffered a serious earthquake; university (1827); railway; economy: coffee, food processing, tanning; monuments: on the Morro de Tulcán overlooking the city is an equestrian statue of Benalcázar (founder of the city and lieutenant of Francisco Pizarro); events: Día de los Negros (5 Jan); Día de los Blancos (6 Jan).

Popocatépetl *po-pō-kah-tay'pe-tul*, POPOCATEPETL *po-pō-kah-tu-pe'tul* (Eng) (Aztec, 'smoking mountain'), 19 01N 98 38W, dormant volcano on the Puebla-México state border, central Mexico; 72 km SE of Ciudad de México (Mexico City); S of Ixtaccihuatl volcano; height 5,452 m; 2nd highest peak in Mexico, with a snow-capped symmetrical cone and a crater almost 1 km in circumference and 402 m deep; last erupted in 1702; situated in Ixtaccihuatl-Popocatépetl National Park (area 257 sq km; established in 1935).

Pop'rad, 49 03N 20 18E, pop(1984) 43,873, town in Východoslovenský region, Slovak Socialist Republic, E Czechoslovakia; on R Poprad, NW of Košice, in the High Tatra Mts; railway; economy: paper, agricultural machinery.

Pordenone *por-day-nō'nay*, prov of Friuli-Venezia Giulia region, NE Italy; pop(1981) 275,888; area 2,303 sq km; capital Pordenone.

Pordenone, 45 58N 12 39E, pop(1981) 52,094, capital town of Pordenone prov, Friuli-Venezia Giulia region, NE Italy; 28 km NW of Portogruaro; railway; monument: 15th-c cathedral.

Poreč *po'rech*, 45 14N 13 36E, resort town in W Hrvatska (Croatia) republic, Yugoslavia; on the Adriatic Sea in Istria, SE of Trieste; largely developed since the 1960s; naturist facilities nearby; monument: Byzantine Basilica of Euphrasius (6th-c).

Pori *por'ee*, BJORNEBORG *byur'na-bor'ya* (Swed), 61 28N 21 45E, pop(1982) 79,147, seaport on W coast of Turku-Pori prov, SW Finland; at the entrance to the Gulf of Bothnia, NW of Helsinki; established in 1365; the port includes the Reposaari fishing harbour, the Mäntyluoto general cargo harbour, the Tahkoluoto oil and coal harbour and a deep water harbour opened in 1985; railway; airfield; economy: commerce, shipbuilding, wood and metal products; events: jazz festival in July.

Porirua *po-ri-roo'a* (Maori, 'place of the two flowings of the tide'), 41 08S 174 52E, pop(1981) 41,104, town in SW North Island, New Zealand; on Porirua Bay, N of Wellington; railway; monuments: Gear Homestead, a colonial home, is used by spinners, weavers, potters, artists and photographers; Porirua's indigenous heritage is represented at the Takapuahia Marae, home of the Ngatitoa people.

Porsangen, PORSANGEN FJORD *pōr'sahn-gen* (Eng), inlet of Arctic Ocean, Finnmark county, on N coast of Norway, extends S inland 123 km.

Porsgrunn, *pors'groon*, 59 10N 9 40E, pop(1983) 31,251, seaport on E coast of Telemark county, SE Norway, at the head of an inlet of the Skagerrak; railway; noted for its manufacture of porcelain.

Port Arthur, 29 54N 93 56W, pop(1980) 61,251, town in Jefferson county, SE Texas, United States; a deep-water oil port on L Sabine, 26 km SE of Beaumont; the city developed after the discovery of oil at Spindletop in 1901 (the first big oil strike in the south); railway; economy: oil refining, chemicals, shipyards, oil-drilling equipment, metal, steel, and aluminium products.

Port Augusta, 32 30S 137 27E, pop(1981) 15,254, town in Northern stat div, SE South Australia, Australia; at the head of the Spencer Gulf, NNW of Adelaide; railway;

airfield; economy: wool and grain trade, engineering; starting point for the Ghan train to Alice Springs and the Indian Pacific train to Perth; base for the Royal Flying Doctor Service.

Port Dickson, 2 31N 101 48E, pop(1980) 24,389, port and resort town in Negeri Sembilan state, SW Peninsular Malaysia, SE Asia; on the Strait of Malacca, 32 km SW of Seremban; fine beaches; planned in the 19th century as an outlet for tin; also a former colonial health resort; railway.

Port Elizabeth, 33 58S 25 36E, pop(1985) 277,844, 651,993 (metropolitan area), seaport in Cape prov, South Africa; on the Algoa Bay, an inlet of the Indian Ocean, 725 km E of Cape Town and 690 km SW of Durban; Fort Frederick built here by British forces in 1799; the town was founded in 1820 by British settlers; significant development took place after completion of the railway from Kimberley in 1873; named after the wife of the acting governor of Cape prov, Sir Rufane Shaw Donkin; university (1964); railway; airfield; economy: diesel locomotives, motor vehicles, food processing, steel, wool, mohair, skins, tyres, citrus fruits.

Port Florence, Kenya. See Kisumu.

Port Gentil *por' zhã-teel'*, 0 40S 8 50E, pop(1974) 76,111, seaport capital of Ogooué-Maritime, W Gabon, W Africa; on a peninsula 160 km SSW of Libreville; the port facilities are located at Cap Lopez on Mandji I; airfield; economy: banking, agricultural services, timber processing, plywood, gun metal, oil exploration and refining.

Port Glasgow *glahz'gō*, 55 56N 4 41W, pop(1981) 22,580, town in Inverclyde dist, Strathclyde, W Scotland; on the S shore of the Firth of Clyde, 5 km E of Greenock; railway; economy: engineering, textiles, plastics; monuments: 15th-c Newark castle overlooks the Clyde.

Port Harcourt *har'kurt*, 4 43N 7 05E, pop(1981e) 330,800, seaport capital of Rivers state, S Nigeria, W Africa; on R Bonny, 65 km from the sea and 440 km ESE of Lagos; Nigeria's 2nd largest port; established during World War I (1912) and named after Sir William Harcourt; airport; linked by railway to the Enugu coalfields and to the manufacturing towns of Makurdi, Jos, Kaduna and Kano in the N; linked by oil pipeline with Makurdi; economy: metals, glass, liquid propane gas, oil refining, petrochemicals, fishing.

Port Hedland, 20 24S 118 36E, pop(1981) 12,948, port in Pilbara stat div, Western Australia, Australia; on NE coast; airfield; the largest iron-ore harbour in W Australia; salt is also shipped from here; linked by rail to iron-ore mines at Newman.

Port Huron, 42 58N 82 26W, pop(1980) 33,981, county seat of St Clair county, SE Michigan, United States; at L Huron end of R St Clair, 86 km NE of Detroit; railway; summer resort; early home of Thomas A. Edison, the inventor.

Port Lincoln, 34 43S 135 49E, pop(1981) 10,675, port in Eyre stat div, S South Australia, Australia; on Boston Bay in the S part of Eyre Peninsula; railway; airfield; economy: trade in wheat, meat and wool; a popular tourist resort; Boston Bay is the home port for the tuna fleet; the underwater filming for the motion picture *Jaws* was carried out nearby.

Port Loko *lō'kō*, dist in Northern prov, Sierra Leone, W Africa; pop(1974) 292,244; area 5,719 sq km; capital Port Loko.

Port Loko, 8 50N 12 50W, pop(1974) 11,000, capital of dist of same name, Northern prov, Sierra Leone, W Africa; 38 km NE of Freetown on Port Loko creek (a tributary of the R Sierra Leone).

Port Louis *loo'is*, 51 32S 58 08W, settlement on East Falkland, Falkland Is, in the S Atlantic, at the head of Berkeley Sound; 32 km NW of Stanley; a house incorporates the old English fort which was the original Government House used until the removal of the capital to Stanley.

Port Louis, 20 18S 57 31E, pop(1983) 135,629, seaport capital of the island of Mauritius in the Indian Ocean; established in 1735 by Mahé de la Bourdonnais; trade developed until the building of the Suez Canal; university (1965); nearly all of the trade of Mauritius passes through Port Louis; economy: sugar export, textiles, clothes, diamond cutting, watches, electrical and electronic equipment, sunglasses.

Port Macquarie *mak-wo'ri*, 31 28S 152 25E, pop(1981) 19,581, town in Mid-North Coast stat div, E New South Wales, Australia; on the E coast, N of Sydney; airfield; nearby is the open-air museum of Timbertown.

Port Moresby *maw(r)z'bi*, 9 30S 147 07E, pop(1980) 118,429, seaport and capital of Papua New Guinea, in National Capital District, on the S coast of New Guinea, SW Pacific; government, banking, educational, and commercial centre; base for overseas telecommunications and national broadcasting; gold discovered here in 1878 led to exploration of the E part of the island from the late 1880s; university (1965); Jackson's International Airport; economy: light industry; events: Hiri Moale Festival (Aug-Sept); arts festival (Sept).

Port Natal, seaport in South Africa. See Durban.

Port of Spain, 10 38N 61 31W, pop(1980) 55,800, capital city and chief port of the Republic of Trinidad and Tobago, on a gently sloping plain between the Gulf of Paria and the foothills of the Northern Range, NW Trinidad; capital of Trinidad since 1783 when it replaced St Joseph; principal commercial centre in the E Caribbean; botanical gardens (1818); Piarco International Airport is situated 26 km ESE; monuments: cathedral (1813-28), San Andres Fort (1785).

Port Pirie *pi'ri*, 33 11S 138 01E, pop(1981) 14,695, port in Northern stat div, South Australia, Australia; on the Spencer Gulf, 220 km NW of Adelaide; railway; airfield; economy: largest lead refinery in the world; smelting of metals from Broken Hill; chemicals; trade in grain.

Port Said *sa-eed'*, BÛR SA'ID, 31 17N 32 18E, pop(1976) 262,760, seaport capital of Port Said governorate, NE Egypt; on the Mediterranean coast at the N end of the Suez Canal, 169 km NE of Cairo; founded in 1859 at the beginning of the Suez Canal construction; economy: shipping services and trade in rice, cotton and salt.

Port San Carlos, 51 30S 58 59W, settlement on the W coast of East Falkland, Falkland Is, in the S Atlantic; a British Task Force landed near here in May 1982 following the invasion of the Falkland Is by the Argentine armed forces in April of that year.

Port Stanley, port in Falkland Is. See Stanley.

Port Sudan *soo-dan'*, 19 38N 37 07E, pop(1983) 206,727, seaport capital of Eastern region, Sudan, NE Africa; situated on the Red Sea coast, 400 km NE of Atbara and 480 km NNE of Kassala; Sudan's main port; founded in 1906 as a replacement for the port of Suakin which was becoming obstructed by a rapidly growing coral reef; the NE terminus of an oil pipeline from Khartoum; railway; airfield.

Port Talbot, 51 36N 3 47W, pop(1981) 40,261, town in Afan dist, West Glamorgan, S Wales; on the Bristol Channel in Swansea urban area; railway; economy: engineering, steel.

Portadown, PORT AN DUNAIN (Gael), 54 26N 6 27W, pop(1981) 21,333, town in Craigavon dist, Armagh, S central Northern Ireland; on the Bann river, to the S of Lough Neagh; railway; economy: textiles, engineering, food processing, rose growing.

Portage *por'tij*, 41 34N 87 11W, pop(1980) 27,409, town in Porter county, NW Indiana, United States; 14 km E of Gary.

Portage, 42 12N 85 35W, pop(1980) 38,157, town in Kalamazoo county, SW Michigan, United States; 13 km S of Kalamazoo; railway.

Portage la Prairie, 49 58N 98 20W, pop(1981) 13,086, town in S Manitoba, central Canada; 82 km W of Winnipeg, on the Assiniboine river; railway; economy: engineering, bricks.

Portalegre *por-tal-ay'gri*, dist in E central Portugal, part of Alto Alentejo prov, bounded by Spain (E) and R Tagus (N); area 5,882 sq km; pop(1981) 142,905; divided into 15 councils and 82 parishes; chief towns are Portalegre and

Elvas; economy: almonds, rice, grain, vegetables, fruit, wine, cork, resin, lumber, wool, skins, dairy produce, pottery; minerals: barium, lead, copper, tin, feldspar, phosphorus, quartz, titanium, wolfram.

Portalegre, AMMAIA or AMOEA (anc), 39 19N 7 25W, pop(1981) 14,800, capital of Portalegre dist, E central Portugal; on W slope of Serra da São Mamede, close to the Spanish frontier, 238 km ENE of Lisboa; economy: textiles, cork, distilling and agricultural trade; monuments: 16th-c cathedral; palaces of Amarelo, Condes de Aviles, Fonseca Acciolo, 17th-c Jesuit Convent; 13th-c Franciscan convent; castle (1290) and the Casa de Jose Regio.

Port-au-Prince *por-tō-prīs*, 18 33N 72 20W, pop(1975) 458,675, port and capital city of Haiti; on the Golfe de la Gonâve, W coast of Hispaniola I; commercial and processing centre at W end of the fertile low lying Plaine du Cul-de-Sac; an international exhibition celebrating the bi-centenary of the city was held here in 1949-50; archbishopric; university (1944); railway; airport; monument: 18th-c cathedral.

Port-de-Paix *por de-pay'*, 19 56N 72 52W, pop(1975) 21,733, port and chief town of Nord-Ouest dept, N Haiti, E Caribbean; opposite Île de la Tortue, 64 km WNW of Cap-Haïtien; Columbus landed here on 8 Dec 1492; scene of the first revolt of Negro slaves.

Porthcawl', 51 29N 3 43W, pop(1981) 15,625, seaport in Ogwr dist, Mid Glamorgan, S Wales; on the Bristol Channel SE of Port Talbot; economy: scientific instruments.

Portimão *por-tee-mown'*, 37 08N 8 32W, pop(1981) 18,000, port and industrial town in Faro dist, S Portugal; on the W side of the R Arade estuary, 18 km E of Lagos; also a resort for nearby beaches at Praia da Rocha; economy: sardine-fishing, ship-building and canning; railway.

Portishead, 51 30N 2 46W, pop(1981) 13,867, port in Bristol dist, Avon, SW England; W of Bristol, on the R Severn estuary; a major port serving Bristol.

Port'land, 38 21S 141 38E, pop(1983) 10,150, port town in South Western stat div, SW Victoria, Australia; on W Portland Bay, W of Melbourne; the only natural harbour on the coast of Victoria which can be entered by large ships; founded in 1829 by William Dutton; economy: aluminium smelting; nearby is Discovery Bay coastal park.

Portland, 43 39N 70 16W, pop(1980) 61,572, county seat of Cumberland county, SW Maine, United States; on the coast of Casco Bay, SE of Sebago Lake; business capital and chief port of Maine; established in 1632, achieving town status in 1786 and city status in 1832; state capital from 1820 to 1832; birthplace of H.W. Longfellow; Westbrook Junior College (1831); railway; economy: fisheries, ship repair, paper, chemicals, oil trade.

Portland, 45 32N 122 37W, pop(1980) 366,383, freshwater port and capital of Multnomah county, NW Oregon, United States; on the Willamette river near its junction with the Columbia river; the largest city in Oregon state; the city was laid out in 1845; it grew rapidly and served as a supply point in the 1850s during the California gold rush and later (1897-1900) during the Alaska gold rush; university (1901); railway; airport; economy: machinery, electrical equipment, food processing, wood products, metal goods, clothing, heavy vehicles, trade in timber, grain and aluminium.

Portland, Isle of, rocky peninsula on Dorset coast, S England; extends into the English Channel; connected to the mainland by a shingle ridge known as Chesil Beach; area 12 sq km; Portland Harbour is a naval base; limestone is quarried.

Portlaoighise *port lay'ish*, PORT LAOISE, formerly MARYBOROUGH, 53 02N 7 17W, pop(1981) 7,756, capital of Laoighis county, Leinster, Irish Republic; WSW of Dublin; jail; small industrial estate; railway.

Portmarnock, 53 26N 6 08W, pop(1981) 8,212, resort town in Dublin county, Leinster, Irish Republic; on Irish Sea, N of Dublin.

Porto *por'too*, dist in N Portugal, part of Douro Litoral prov, bounded by the Atlantic (W) and R Douro (S); area 2,282 sq km; pop(1981) 1,562,287; divided into 17 councils 2 bairros and 382 parishes; chief town is Porto; main ports at Douro and Leixões; economy: metal goods, cork, timber, vegetables, olives, fruit, wheat, maize, meat, dairy produce, sugar refining, metallurgy and tyres; minerals: antimony, lead, tin, feldspar, iron, manganese, gold, silver, quartz, uranium, wolfram, coal.

Porto, OPORTO (Eng) ('the port'), 41 08N 8 40W, pop(1981) 350,200, capital of Porto dist, N Portugal; 318 km N of Lisboa, on N bank of R Douro near its mouth; second largest city in Portugal; divided into 2 bairros and 15 parishes; episcopal see; university (1911); the crowded old town, with tall, painted, balconied and tiled granite houses, has its centre in the Praça da Liberdade; monuments: cathedral; stock exchange palace and Clerigos Tower; event: festival of São João at end of June; a lofty double-deck steel-arched bridge (Ponte de Dom Luis I) crosses to the suburb of Vila Nova de Gaia on the S bank of R Douro, famous for its port wine lodges; railway.

Pôrto Alegre *por'tō a-lay'gray*, 30 03S 51 10W, pop(1980) 1,114,867, port capital of Rio Grande do Sul state, Sul region, S Brazil; at NW end of Lagoa dos Patos, at the confluence of 5 rivers which flow into the Río Guaíba and then into the lagoon; stands on a series of hills and valleys, with its business area jutting out into the water on a promontory; 2 universities (1934, 1948); railway; airport; the most important commercial centre S of São Paulo; Pôrto Alegre is a freshwater port for ocean-going vessels up to 7,000 tons; vessels must come up through the town of Rio Grande and the Lagoa dos Patos, approx 275 km from the open sea; the Jockey Club holds races on Saturdays and Sundays; in the centre of town next to the Prefeitura is the Mercado Público, said to be a replica of Lisbon's Mercado da Figueira; large areas of reclaimed land have been used for housing and to extend the port facilities and quays.

Porto Novo, 6 30N 2 47E, pop(1979) 132,000, seaport capital of Benin, W Africa; on a lagoon in Ouémé prov; the seat of a native kingdom, it was settled by the Portuguese who made it their headquarters for slave and tobacco trading with Brazil; it became a French protectorate in 1863; though the official capital of Benin there is little political and economic activity, this taking place in Cotonou; railway; monuments: palace of King Toffa and museum.

Porto Santo or **Ilha do Porto Santo**, 33 04N 16 20W, island of the Madeira group, Portugal, in the Atlantic Ocean, 35 km NE of Madeira; highest point is Pico do Castelo at 507 m; chief town is Porto Santo; airport.

Pôrto Velho *vel'yō*, 8 45S 63 54W, pop(1980) 101,162, capital of Rondônia state, Norte region, N Brazil; on a high bluff overlooking the Río Madeira; an important communications centre of SW Amazonia; 20 km away is the Samuel hydroelectric scheme; railway; economy: rice, cocoa, coffee, maize, beans, rubber, timber, cattle raising; monument: cathedral (1950).

Portorož *por'to-rozh*, (Ital 'Portorose', port of roses), 45 31N 13 36E, resort town in NW Slovenija republic, Yugoslavia; on N side of Pirano Bay; naturist beaches in the Kanger campsite on S side of the bay; administered by Yugoslavia since 1947.

Portoviejo *por-tō-vye'KHō*, 1 07S 80 28W, pop(1982) 102,628, capital of Manabí prov, W Ecuador; on the Río Portoviejo, NW of Guayaquil; technical university (1952); economy: commerce, food processing, animal foodstuffs, drinks, paper.

Portree, 57 24N 6 12W, pop(1981) 1,505, port capital of Skye and Lochalsh dist, Highland region, NW Scotland; on Loch Portree, on the E coast of Skye; the largest town on the island of Skye.

Portrush, PORT ROIS (Gael), 55 12N 6 40W, pop(1981) 5,114, town in Coleraine dist, Antrim, NE Northern Ireland; on the N coast; railway; economy: engineering; a tourist centre for the Giant's Causeway, 11 km ENE.

Portsmouth *ports'muth*, 50 48N 1 05W, pop(1981) 177,905, city and seaport in Portsmouth dist, Hampshire, S

England; on Portsea Island 133 km SW of London; major naval base; birthplace of Charles Dickens; railway; ferries to the Channel Islands, France and the Isle of Wight; monuments: Lord Nelson's flagship *HMS Victory*; the Tudor warship, *Mary Rose*; Royal Navy museum; Royal Marines museum; Southsea castle including Round Tower and Point Battery; Fort Widney (Portsdown Hill); event: Navy Week (Aug).

Portsmouth, 43 05N 70 45W, pop(1980) 26,254, seaport and summer resort town in Rockingham county, SE New Hampshire, United States; on the Atlantic coast at the head of the R Piscataqua, 70 km ENE of Manchester; established in 1624, achieving city status in 1849; the treaty ending the Russo-Japanese War was signed here in 1905; there is a naval base on Seavy's I specializing in submarine construction and maintenance; railway; economy: machine tools, clothing; historic site: Strawberry Banke.

Portsmouth, 38 44N 83 00W, pop(1980) 25,943, county seat of Scioto county, S Ohio, United States; on the Ohio river where it meets the R Scioto; railway; monument: prehistoric Indian mounds and earthworks.

Portsmouth, 36 50N 76 18W, pop(1980) 104,577, port and independent city, SE Virginia, United States; on the R Elizabeth, opposite Norfolk; railway; part of a US naval complex; a base for British and then Revolutionary troops during the War of Independence; evacuated and burned by Union troops during the Civil War in 1861, and retaken in 1862; economy: railway engineering, fishing, chemicals, fertilizer, cottonseed oil, trade in tobacco and cotton.

Portstewart, PORT STIOBHAIRD (Gael), 55 11N 6 43W, pop(1981) 5,312, port and resort town in Coleraine dist, Derry (Londonderry), N Northern Ireland; on the N coast, 45 km NE of Derry; railway.

Portugal *pōrt'yoo-gal*, LUSITANIA (anc), official name Republic of Portugal, REPUBLICA PORTUGUESA (Port), a multiparty parliamentary democracy in SW Europe on the W side of the Iberian peninsula and including the semi-autonomous Azores and Madeira Is; bounded on N and E by Spain and on S and W by the Atlantic; greatest length 560 km (N-S) and greatest width 220 km; area of mainland: 88,500 sq km; area of mainland and islands 91,631 sq km; timezone GMT; pop of mainland (1981) 9,336,760; pop of mainland and islands 9,833,014; capital Lisboa (Lisbon); chief towns Porto, Setúbal, Coimbra and Évora; the currency is the escudo of 100 centavos; national holidays 25 April (Liberation Day), 5 Oct (Republic Day), 1 Nov (All Saints Day); membership of EEC (1986), EFTA, FAO, GATT, IAEA, IATP, IBRD, ICAC, ICAO, ICES, ICO, IEA, IFAD, IFC, IHO, ILO, IMF, IMO, INTELSAT, INTERPOL, IOOC, IRC, ISO, ITU, NATO, OECD, UN, UNESCO, UPU, WHO, WIPO, WMO, WSG; the colony of Macao including Taipa and Coloane in China is still administered by Portugal; the former colonies of Angola, Mozambique, Cape Verde, Timor and São Tomé and Principe gained independence in 1974-5.

Physical description. The physical geography of Portugal is linked with that of Spain. The N Portuguese provinces are invaded by spurs of the mountains of Galicia, rising to heights of 1,800 m, while the greatest mountain range of Portugal, the Serra da Estrêla (1,991 m) is a westward continuation of the Spanish system of the Sierra Guadarrama; similarly the Sierra Morena is prolonged into S Portugal. In like manner, the 4 main rivers, Douro, Minho, Tagus and Guadiana are the lower courses of rivers, the greatest part of whose lengths are in Spain.

Climate. Although the climate of Portugal, situated as it is on the Atlantic Ocean, is basically maritime, with increasing distance eastwards from the coast continental influences become stronger and the range of variation between summer and winter temperatures becomes greater. In addition, the climate is influenced from the Azores by an area of high pressure which moves north in spring and summer and south in autumn and winter. As a result, the whole of the west coast remains relatively cool in summer, fanned by winds blowing from the NW, while most of the rainfall comes in the winter particularly to the north of the country.

History, government and constitution. Portugal was a monarchy from 1143 until the revolution of 1910 when King Manuel II was driven into exile and a republic was set up by a National Assembly. After 15 years of political unrest under 18 governments and a 6-year military dictatorship that came to power in 1926 a new constitution was established in 1933, heralding a period of personalist dictatorship under the premiership of Antonio Salazar (1932-68) and his successor Marcelo Caetano (1968-74). A failure to liberalize the regime, the spiralling cost of rebellious African colonies and the continued presence of a small commercial, industrial and landholding oligarchy prompted a revolution on 25 April, 1974. After 2 years a new constitution was established with a parliamentary democracy once more under the guardianship of the military-dominated Council of the Revolution which was eventually abolished in 1982. In the 10 years following the revolution political unrest continued under 15 governments. Executive power is held by the president who is head of state and is elected for a 5-year term; the prime minister is appointed by the president; the prime minister and the council of ministers define policy; the legislature is vested in the unicameral Assembly of the

Republic whose 250 members are elected by proportional representation every 4 years; the Supreme Court of Justice is the highest court of appeal.

Trade and industry. Industry is based on intermediate technology and the productive base is narrow with a high concentration on labour-intensive sectors such as textiles, shoes, leather, woodwork, cork and ceramics. In 1983 manufacturing accounted for just under 40% of national income, employing a quarter of the labour force. Modernization is taking place as Portugal enjoys its first years as a member state of the EEC. The chief exports are textiles, cork, timber, footwear, wine, fish, chemicals and electrical machinery and the chief imports are cereals, meat, iron, steel, crude oil, motor vehicles, chemicals and industrial machinery. Exports mainly to OECD countries. There are steelworks and shipbuilding and repair yards at Lisboa and Setúbal; minerals: copper, wolfram, tin, iron ore, pyrites, zinc, lead, barium, titanium, uranium and sodium and calcium.

Transport. Main airports at Lisboa, Faro, Porto, Funchal (Madeira), Porto Santo (Madeira), Lajes, Ponta Delgada, Santa Maria and Horta. Main continental ports at Lisboa, Douro (Porto), Leixões, Faro, Portimão, Figueira da Foz, Setúbal, Viana do Castelo, Aveiro, Sines and Vila Real de Santo Antonio.

Agriculture. In 1981 agriculture accounted for 12% of national income. The main agricultural products are wheat, maize, rice, rye, beans, potatoes, fruit, olive oil, meat and dairy produce; there are large forests of pine, oak, cork-oak, eucalyptus and chestnut covering about 20% of the country.

Administrative territories. The former regions of Entre Minho e Douro, Trás-os-Montes, Beira, Estremadura, Alentejo and Algarve are still referred to, although these were partly subdivided into the following 11 mainland provinces in 1933: Minho, Douro Litoral, Trás-os-Montes, Beira Alta, Beira Litoral, Beira Baixa, Estremadura, Ribatejo, Alto Alentejo, Baixo Alentejo and Algarve. In the 1830s Portugal was divided into the following districts although the boundaries of districts and provinces do not always coincide:

District	*area (sq km)*	*pop(1981)*
Azores		
Angra do Heroísmo	703	75,010
Horta	780	19,942
Ponta Delgada	852	131,295
Central Portugal		
Castelo Branco	6,704	234,230
Coimbra	3,956	436,324
Leiria	3,516	420,229
Lisboa	2,762	2,069,467
Portalegre	5,882	142,905
Santarém	6,612	454,123
Madeira		
Funchal	796	253,891
North Portugal		
Aveiro	2,708	622,988
Braga	2,730	708,924
Bragança	6,545	184,252
Guarda	5,496	205,631
Porto	2,282	1,562,287
Vila Real	4,191	264,381
Viano do Castelo	2,084	256,814
Viseu	4,961	423,648
South Portugal		
Beja	10,240	188,420
Évora	7,393	180,277
Faro	5,072	323,534
Setúbal	5,092	658,326

Portugal is further divided for administrative purposes into 275 *concelhos* or local councils and 3,849 *freguesias* or parishes.

Portugalete *por-too-gal-ay'tay*, 43 19N 3 04W, pop(1981) 57,534, port in Vizcaya prov, Pais Vasco (Basque Country), N Spain; at the mouth of the R Nervión, NW of Bilbao; a popular resort with the people of Bilbao; iron industry nearby on the left bank of the R Nervión.

Portuguesa *por-too-gay'sa*, state in W Venezuela; contains outliers of the Andean spur in the W; consists mainly of lowland *llanos* plain; drained by secondary tributaries of the Orinoco river including the Portuguesa, Guanare and Cojedes rivers; pop(1980) 443,472; area 15,195 sq km; capital Guanare; Guanare is a national place of pilgrimage, the old colonial church contains the venerated relic of the Virgin of Coromoto, Patron of Venezuela.

Porvoo *por'vo*, BORGA *bor'go* (Swed), 60 24N 25 40E, pop(1982) 19,195, picturesque town in Uudenmaa prov, SE Finland; near the mouth of the Porvoonjoki where it flows into the Gulf of Finland; established in 1346 it is the second oldest town in Finland; bishopric; industrial development is centred around the oil port of Skoldvik; birthplace of the Finnish sculptors, W. Runeberg and V. Vallgren; home of the national poet Johan Ludvig Runeberg; boat service to Helsinki; economy: publishing; events: cycle race and Porvoo day in June; Postmaki Festival in July.

Posadas *po-sa'THas*, 27 25S 55 48W, pop(1980) 139,941, capital of Misiones prov, Litoral, E Argentina; on the Río Paraná; a 2.5 km bridge links the town to Encarnación (Paraguay); there is also a ferry link; railway; economy: tea, tobacco.

Potenza *pō-tent'sa*, POTENTIA (anc), prov of Bascilicata region, S Italy; pop(1981) 406,616; area 6,545 sq km; capital Potenza.

Potenza, 40 38N 15 48E, pop(1981) 64,358, agricultural market town and capital of Potenza prov, Bascilicata region, S Italy; 88 km E of Salerno, on a ridge above the R Basento, in the Appno Lucano; the town suffered severe damage in an earthquake in 1857; railway; monument: 18th-c cathedral.

Potomac *po-tō'mak*, river in West Virginia, Virginia and Maryland states, United States; formed at the junction of 2 branches (which rise in the Allegheny Mts) on the N boundary of Hampshire county, NW West Virginia; flows E and SE to Chesapeake Bay; navigable for large craft as far as Washington, DC; its main tributary is the Shenandoah river; the Great Falls lie 24 km above Washington.

Potosí *po-tō-see'*, department in SW Bolivia; bordered by Andean Cordillera Occidental on Chilean frontier (W) and by Argentina (S); includes the Salar de Uyuni desert (NW); the S Cordillera Oriental of the Andes crosses the dept N-S, separating the Altiplano (W) from the E valleys; the Río Grande de Lípez drains the Altiplano, the E valleys being drained by the Upper Pilcomayo river (N) and the San Juan and Cotagaita rivers (S); pop(1982) 823,485; area 118,218 sq km; capital Potosí; economy: mining at Catavi, once the largest tin producer in the world; Quechisla (tin, silver, zinc, lead, bismuth, copper, gold); Unificada (lead, copper); there is a hydroelectric dam on the Río Yura to the SW of Potosí; Pulacayo industrial plant specializes in metalwork.

Potosí, 19 34S 65 45W, pop(1982) 103,182, capital of T. Frías prov, Potosí, SW Bolivia; alt 4,060 m; the world's highest city, at the foot of the Cerro Rico from which immense amounts of silver were once extracted during the colonial period of the 17th and 18th centuries, when Potosí was one of the chief silver mining towns and the most important and populous city in South America; founded by Spaniards in 1545; the highest city of its size in the world; there are thermal baths at the Laguna de Tarapaya below the city; university (1892); railway; airfield; economy: tin, silver, copper and lead mining; monuments: around the main square, the Plaza 10 de Noviembre, are the convent of Santa Teresa (housing a collection of colonial and religious art); Las Cajas Reales (the Cabildo and the Royal Treasury) and the cathedral; nearby is the mint (Casa Real de Moneda), which was founded in 1542 and rebuilt in 1759 and is one of the chief monuments to civil building in Hispanic America, now a museum.

Pots'dam, county in central East Germany; pop(1981) 1,118,413; area 12,568 sq km; largest county in E Germany; capital Potsdam; economy: timber, livestock, cereals, fruit, iron, steel, electrical engineering, microelectronics, precision instruments, optical instruments, vehicle manufacture, chemicals (polyester and polyacryl fibres) and heavy engineering.

Potsdam, 52 23N 13 4E, pop(1982) 133,225, capital of Potsdam county, central East Germany; on the R Havel W of Berlin; Academy of Political Science and Law; colleges of cinematographic and television art; Central Meteorological Centre of the GDR; former residence of Frederick II, who encouraged the development of the city during the 18th century; at the end of World War II Potsdam was the site of a conference of British, Soviet and American leaders (July-Aug 1945); railway; economy: food processing, pharmaceuticals, electrical equipment, textiles; monuments: Sans Souci palace and park, 18th-c garrison church.

Potteries, The, pop(1981) 376,764, a NW Midlands urban area in the upper Trent valley of Staffordshire, central England; extends c.14 km (NW-SE) by 5 km (W-E); includes Stoke-on-Trent; railway; economy: since the 18th century the Potteries have been the heart of the English china and earthenware industry which is based on local clay and coal.

Potters Bar, 51 42N 0 11W, pop(1981) 22,681, residential town in Welwyn Hatfield dist, Hertfordshire, SE England; 21 km N of London; railway.

Potwar, plain in N Punjab prov, Pakistan; E of the R Indus, between Rawalpindi and Jhelum; oil fields are located at Meyal, Joya Mair, Balkassar, Tut and Dhullian.

Poughkeepsie *pa-kip'see* (Algonquian, 'rock-water-little-at'), 41 42N 73 56W, pop(1980) 29,757, county seat of Dutchess county, SE New York, United States; port on the Hudson river, 104 km N of New York City; railway; airfield; capital of state in 1778; economy: banking, electronics, precision instruments, engineering.

Poulton-le-Fylde *pool'ten-le-fīld'*, 53 51N 2 59W, pop(1981) 18,604, town in Blackpool urban area and Fylde dist, Lancashire, NW England; 5 km NE of Blackpool; railway.

Považská Bystrica *po'vahzh-skah bis'tri-tsa*, 49 08N 18 25E, pop(1984) 34,432, town in Středoslovenský region, Slovak Socialist Republic, central Czechoslovakia; on R Váh, SW of Žilina; railway.

Povoa de Varzim *po'vwa di var'zeen*, 41 25N 8 46W, pop(1981) 22,500, fishing town in Porto dist, N Portugal; on the Atlantic coast, 30 km N of Porto; a yacht harbour and beaches have made this little town a favourite resort; events: Holy Week; festival of São Pedro, a fishermen's festival with bullfights, fireworks and a parade of boats at the end of June; festival of Senhora da Assunção in mid-Aug and festival of Senhora das Dores in mid-Sept.

Powys *pow'is*, mountainous county in E Wales; bounded E by Shropshire, Hereford and Worcester, S by Gwent, Mid Glamorgan and West Glamorgan, W by Dyfed, NW by Gwynedd and N by Clwyd; drained by the Usk, Wye, Taff and Tawe rivers; source of water for the cities of Liverpool and Birmingham; pop(1981) 110,555; area 5,077 sq km; capital Llandrindod Wells; created in 1974, the county is divided into 3 districts:

District	*area (sq km)*	*pop(1981)*
Brecknock	1,794	40,879
Montgomery	2,064	48,158
Radnor	1,219	21,518

Poyang Hu, lake in N Jiangxi prov, SE China; China's largest freshwater lake; area 3,583 sq km; the lake's area was formerly 5,050 sq km, but this has been reduced by silt deposits and land reclamation; fed by the Gan Jiang, Fu Jiang, Xiu Shui, Xin Jiang and Xu Jiang rivers; merges with the Chang Jiang (Yangtze river) at the N end of the lake at Hukou.

Poza Rica *pō'sa ree'ka*, 20 33N 97 28W, pop(1980) 166,799, town in Veracruz state, SE central Mexico; railway; economy: oil; monuments: to the S are the ruins of El Tajín, capital of the Totonac culture (6-10th-c); in the centre is the Pyramid of El Tajín which has 365 squared openings; event: on Corpus Christi, Totonac rain dancers erect a 30 m mast topped by a platform; 4 *voladores* (flyers) and a musician climb to the top and while the musician dances to his own pipe and drum the roped *voladores* throw themselves into space, falling in a spiral down to the ground.

Poznań *poz'nany'*, voivodship in W Poland; watered by R Warta; pop(1983) 1,278,000; area 8,151 sq km; capital Poznań; chief towns include Gniezno, Września, Śrem and Luboń.

Poznań, POSEN (Ger), 52 25N 16 53E, pop(1983) 570,900, capital of Poznań voivodship, W Poland; on R Warta; capital of Poland until 13th century; new housing spreads over the W Grunwald district; the Wilda industrial district is to the S; university (1919); technical university (1918); noted for its choirs and the Polish Theatre of Dance; airfield; railway; economy: metallurgy, machinery, chemicals, clothing, food processing, transport; monuments: national museum with collection of medieval art; Franciscan church (1665-1728); 13th-c castle with museum of crafts; city museum; Great Poland army museum; cathedral; remains of old Prussian forts on the Citadel hill; events: Poznań Spring festival of Polish contemporary music; international violin competitions (every 5 years); international Poznań commercial fair in June.

Pra, river in S Ghana, W Africa; rises NW of Mpraeso and flows for about 250 km S past Beposo to enter the Gulf of Guinea at Shama; receives Ofin and Birnin rivers; rapids prevent navigation.

Pra'ha, PRAGUE (Eng), 50 05N 14 25E, pop(1984) 1,186,253, industrial and commercial capital of Czechoslovakia and of Středočeský region, Czech Socialist Republic, W Czechoslovakia; on R Vltava; an important trading centre since the 10th century; became capital of the newly created Czechoslovakia in 1918; historical heart of the city declared a conservation area in 1971; archbishopric; university (1348), technical university (1707); airport (Ruzyne); railway; metro; economy: chemicals, machine tools, locomotives, aircraft, glass, motorcycles, furniture, soap, perfumes; monuments: Prague Castle, cathedral of St Vitus, Royal Palace (Královsky Palác), St Nicholas cathedral, Wallenstein Palace, St George Romanesque church (10th-c), National Gallery (Šternberk Palace).

Prahova *pra'KHo-va*, county in SE central Romania, in the SE foothills of the Transylvanian Alps; crossed W-E by the R Ialomiţa; pop(1983) 853,685; area 4,694 sq km; capital Ploieşti.

Praia *prah'ya*, 14 53N 23 30W, port and capital of the Republic of Cape Verde, located on the S shore of São Tiago (Santiago) I; pop(1980) 37,500, airport connecting with Dakar and with the neighbouring islands; economy: naval shipyard, light industry, fishing, commerce.

Praslin *praz-lē*, 4 18S 55 45E, pop(1985e) 4,650, granite island in the Seychelles, Indian Ocean; NE and 2 hours by boat from the main island of Mahé; area 38 sq km; home of the coco-de-mer palm and of 3 rare bird species: the Seychelles bulbul, the fruit pigeon and the black parrot; there are tourist facilities and an airfield for light aircraft.

Preah Vihear, province of N Cambodia; bounded N by Laos, S by Kompong Thom, E by Stung Treng and W by Siem Reap-Oddar Meanchey; capital Phnum Tbêng Meanchey.

Přerov *pur-zhe'rof*, 49 27N 17 29E, pop(1984) 50,241, town in Severomoravský region, Czech Socialist Republic, Czechoslovakia; on R Becva, SE of Olomouc; railway; economy: precision instruments, textiles, food processing; monuments: 16th-c castle, botanical gardens.

Pres'cot, 53 26N 2 48W, pop(1981) 40,711, town in St Helens borough, Merseyside, NW England; 6 km SW of St Helens; railway.

Presidente Hayes *pray-see-dayn'tay ah'yes*, dept in Occidental region, W central Paraguay; bordered W by Argentina along the Río Pilcomayo and E by the Río Paraguay; comprises swamp and low, marshy grasslands intersected by numerous rivers; pop(1982) 43,787; area 84,000 sq km; capital Pozo Colorado.

Presidente Prudente *pre-see-den'tay proo-den'tay*, 22 09S 51 24W, pop(1980) 127,903, town in São Paulo state, Sudeste region, SE Brazil; WNW of São Paulo; railway; economy: cotton, coffee, maize, peanuts, food processing, cattle.

Prešov *pre'shof*, 49 00N 21 13E, pop(1984) 78,221, town in Východoslovenský region, Slovak Socialist Republic, E Czechoslovakia; on R Torysa; founded in 12th century; railway; economy: distilling, textiles, lace.

Prespa, PRESPANSKO JEZERO (Yug), lake in SW Yugoslavia, N Albania and N Greece where the three frontiers meet just to the S of Golem Grad Island; area 284 sq km; bounded on the E by the Baba Mts which reach their highest point at Pelister (2,601 m); joined to Mikry Prespa (Little Lake Prespa) by a natural channel crossing marshy land.

Prestatyn *pres-ta'tin*, 53 20N 3 24W, pop(1981) 16,414, resort town in Rhuddlan dist, Clwyd, NE Wales, United Kingdom; also in Abergele-Rhyl-Prestatyn urban area; railway.

Prestea *pres-tay'a*, 5 26N 2 07W, town in Western region, SW Ghana, W Africa; NW of Sekondi-Takoradi; railway terminus.

Pres'ton, 53 46N 2 42W, pop(1981) 126,155, county town in Preston dist, Lancashire, NW England; 45 km NW of Manchester, on the R Ribble; 18th-c centre of the cotton industry; birthplace of Richard Arkwright in 1732; railway; economy: electrical goods, engineering, plastics, chemicals; monument: Harris museum; event: Preston Guild fair every 20 years.

Prestonpans *pres-tên-panz'*, 55 57N 3 00W, pop(1981) 7,621, town in East Lothian dist, Lothian, E Scotland; on the S shore of the Firth of Forth, 5 km NE of Musselburgh; railway; economy: coal processing; monument: a cairn to the E of the town commemorates the victory of Prince Charles Edward Stuart over General Cope at the Battle of Prestonpans in 1745.

Prest'wich, 53 32N 2 17W, pop(1981) 32,035, town in Bolton borough, Greater Manchester, NW England; 6 km NW of Manchester; railway; economy: light engineering, textiles.

Prestwick, 55 30N 4 37W, pop(1981) 13,599, town in Kyle and Carrick dist, Strathclyde, SW Scotland; on the W coast, 4.8 km N of Ayr; railway; airport; economy: engineering, aerospace engineering.

Pretoria *pre-tō'ri-a*, 25 45S 28 12E, pop(1985) 443,059, 822,925 (metropolitan area), administrative capital of South Africa, also capital of Transvaal prov; 48 km NNE of Johannesburg; alt 1,369 m; founded in 1855 and named after the Boer leader, Andries Pretorius (1799-1853); became capital of Transvaal 5 years later and capital of South African Republic in 1881; Winston Churchill was imprisoned here during the South African War; the city was taken by Lord Roberts in June 1900; became administrative capital of the Union of South Africa in 1910; 2 universities (1873, 1908); railway; economy: railway engineering, motor vehicles, iron and steel, chemicals, cement, leather; monuments: Voortrekker Memorial, Paul Kruger Memorial; Transvaal museum.

Préveza *pray've-zu*, mountainous coastal nome (dept) of Ipiros region, W Greece; pop(1981) 55,915; area 1,036 sq km; capital Préveza; economy: fishing, cereals, fruit, olive oil.

Préveza, 38 58N 20 45E, pop(1981) 12,662, port and capital town of Préveza nome (dept), Ipiros region, W Greece; at the mouth of the Amvrakikós Kólpos (Ambracian Gulf), 122 km NE of Pátrai; local ferry; yacht supply station; event: Navy Week (June-July).

Prey Veng *pray veng*, province in SE Cambodia; pop(1981) 492,000; bounded S by Vietnam; lies to the E of the Mekong R; rice and corn growing area; the chief town, Prey Veng, lies 18 km ESE of Phnom Penh.

Prib'ilof Islands, a group of 4 islands in the Bering Sea, Alaska state, United States; St Paul and St George are the only inhabited islands; area 168 sq km; an important centre of the seal fur trade.

Příbram *pree'bram*, 49 41N 14 02E, pop(1984) 38,787, town in Středočeský region, Czech Socialist Republic, Czechoslovakia; SW of Praha (Prague); noted 17-18th-c gold and silver mining town; railway.

Prichard, 30 44N 88 05W, pop(1980) 39,541, town in Mobile county, SW Alabama, United States; an industrial suburb 5 km W of Mobile; railway; economy: meat and seafood packing; cotton processing; manufactures include chemicals, fertilizer, naval stores, lumber and paper products.

Prievidza *pryev'id-za*, 48 47N 18 35E, pop(1984) 44,600, town in Středoslovenský region, Slovak Socialist Republic, E central Czechoslovakia; on R Nitra 64 km NE of Nitra; railway; economy: textiles, chemicals, distilling.

Prijedor *pree'ye-dor*, 45 00N 14 41E, pop(1981) 108,868, town in Bosna-Hercegovina republic, Yugoslavia; on R Sana, 40 km NW of Banja Luka; railway; economy: iron ore and coal mining.

Prilep *pree'lep*, PERLEPE (Turk), HERACLEA PELAGONIAE (anc), 41 20N 21 32E, pop(1981) 99,770, city in Makedonija (Macedonia) republic, Yugoslavia; 72 km S of Skopje; capital of Srbija (Serbia) during 14th century; railway; economy: tobacco, wine and fruit trade, mica mining.

Prince Edward Island, province in E Canada; island prov situated in the Gulf of St Lawrence, to the NE of New Brunswick and the NW of Nova Scotia; separated from the mainland to the S by the Northumberland Strait; the irregular coastline has many large bays and deep inlets; all its inland waters are tidal except for one river and one lake; none are navigable; rises to 142 m; comprises the counties of Kings, Prince and Queens; pop(1981) 122,506; area 5,660 sq km; capital Charlottetown; other towns include Summerside, Tignish and Souris; economy: potatoes, tobacco, vegetables, grains, dairy products, fishing, food processing; discovered in 1534 by Jacques Cartier; Champlain established French claim to it as Ile St Jean; in 1798 it was renamed Prince Edward Island after Queen Victoria's father; first settled by Acadians, it was occupied by the British in 1758 and annexed to Nova Scotia in 1763; the Earl of Selkirk settled Scottish colonists here in 1803; the island became a separate prov in 1769, obtained a representative government in 1851 and joined Canada in 1873; the prov is governed by a Lieutenant-Governor and a 32-member Legislative Assembly elected every 5 years.

Prince George, 53 55N 122 49W, pop(1981) 67,559, town in central British Columbia, W Canada; on the Fraser river, at the mouth of the Nechako river; the North West Co's fur-trading post, Fort George, was established here in 1807 and taken over by the Hudson's Bay Co in 1821; the settlement expanded c.1910 when a railway to Prince Rupert was built through Fort George; the name was later changed to Prince George; railway; airfield; economy: lumber, farming, minerals, fishing and hunting.

Prince Gustaf Adolf Sea *goo'staf a'dolf*, arm of the Arctic Ocean, within the Elizabeth Is of the Northwest Territories, Canada; lies between Ringes I on the E and Borden I on the W; in 1985 the North Magnetic Pole was estimated to be located SE of Lougheed I; linked to the Beaufort Sea.

Princeton, 40 21N 74 40W, pop(1980) 12,035, borough in Mercer county, W central New Jersey, United States; 18 km NE of Trenton, on the Millstone river; founded by Quakers in 1696; a noted centre for education and research; university (1746).

Pripet, river in W Soviet Union. See Pripyat'.

Pripyat' *pree'pyut-yu*, PRIPET, river in N Ukrainskaya and S Belorusskaya republics, W Soviet Union; rises in the extreme NW of Ukrainskaya SSR, near the Polish frontier; flows generally E through Belorusskaya SSR, past Pinsk and Mozyr', to discharge into the R Dnepr 80 km N of Kiyev (Kiev); length 800 km; chief tributaries Styr', Ubort', and Zhelon' rivers; navigable below Pinsk; connected by canals with the rivers Bug and Neman; the Pripyat' Marshes are a forested, swampy area (98,420 sq km) extending along the R Pripyat' and its tributaries between Brest (W), Mogilev (NE), and Kiyev (SE); drainage of these swamps began in 1870 and the E area is now used for pasture and cultivation.

Priština *preesh'tin-a*, 42 39N 21 10E, pop(1981) 216,040, capital town of Kosovo autonomous prov, S Srbija (Serbia) republic, SE central Yugoslavia; on the edge of the Kosovo Polje valley; former capital of Srbija (Serbia); university (1976); airfield; railway; economy: motor vehicle parts; craft work; monuments: many Turkish buildings including the Sultan Murad mosque; nearby marble cave of Donje and monastery of Gračanica.

Privas *pree-vah*, 44 45N 4 37E, pop(1982) 10,638, capital town of Ardèche dept, Rhône-Alpes region, SE France; W of the R Rhône, 171 km NNW of Marseille; a Protestant stronghold in the 16th century.

Prizren *preez'ren*, 42 12N 20 43E, pop(1981) 134,526, town in Kosovo autonomous province, SW Srbija (Serbia) republic, Yugoslavia; on R Prizrenska Bistrica, not far from the Albanian frontier; built on the site of a Roman town (Theranda); important medieval trade centre; part of Albania 1941-44; railway; economy: tourism, goldsmiths and silversmiths; monuments: picturesque old town with several mosques; event: colourful weekly market.

Progreso, El *el prō-gray'sō*, mountainous dept in E central Guatemala, Central America; pop(1982e) 101,203; area 1,922 sq km; capital El Progreso; in the upper Motagua valley, bounded N by the Sierra de las Minás and the Sierra de Chuacús; the dept is predominantly agricultural producing corn, beans, vegetables, tropical fruits, and beef.

Progreso, El, 17 18N 90 56W, capital town of El Progreso dept, E central Guatemala, Central America; on a tributary of the Río Motagua, NE of Guatemala City; railway.

Progresso, El, pop(1983e) 53,835, town in Yoro dept, Honduras, Central America; on the Río Ulúa, SE of San Pedro Sula; agricultural and commercial centre; railway.

Prokop'yevsk *pru-kop'yifsk*, 54 00N 86 45E, pop(1983) 270,000, town in Kemerovskaya oblast, E Siberian Rossiyskaya, Soviet Union; on the R Aba, 269 km SE of Kemerovo; modern development dates from the 1920s; major coal producer of the Kuznetsk Basin; railway; economy: coal mining, machine building, china, clothing, foodstuffs.

Prokuplje *pro-koop'lye*, 43 14N 21 35E, pop(1981) 56,256, town in S central Srbija (Serbia) republic, Yugoslavia; on R Toplica, WSW of Niš; railway.

Prome *prōm*, PYE *pyay*, 18 50N 95 14E, pop(1973) 148,123, town in Pegu division, SW central Burma; situated on the Irrawaddy river; railway.

Prostějov *prost'ye-yof*, 49 29N 17 08E, pop(1984) 51,100, town in Jihomoravský region, Czech Socialist Republic, central Czechoslovakia; SW of Olomouc; air navigation academy; railway; economy: textiles, footwear, agricultural machinery.

Provence *pro-vās*, PROVINCIA (Lat) ('the province'), former prov in SE France on the Mediterranean coast (with the French Riviera in the W); now occupying the depts of Bouches-du-Rhône, Var, Basses-Alpes and parts of Alpes-Maritimes and Vaucluse; formerly part of the kingdom of Arles, it has a distinctive dialect; coal, bauxite, lead, zinc and salt are worked; market-gardening is important on the coast and in the upper Verdon valley.

Provence-Alpes-Côte d'Azur, region of SE France comprising the depts of Alpes-de-Haute-Provence, Hautes-Alpes, Alpes-Maritimes, Bouches-du-Rhône, Var and Vaucluse, 18 arrond, 220 cantons and 961 communes; pop(1982) 3,965,209; area 31,400 sq km; bounded on the S by the Mediterranean Sea, on the E by Italy, on the W by Languedoc-Roussillon region, and on the N by Rhône-Alpes region; watered by the Durance and Rhône rivers and their tributaries; mountainous in the E where the Alpes-Maritimes rise to over 3,000 m; the region is dry and sunny, and though much is infertile, the coast and upper Verdon valley are intensive market-garden areas, with the vine and the olive flourishing on the lower Durance and elsewhere; the Plaine de la Crau, in Bouches-du-Rhône dept, is a bare and stony plain criss-crossed by canals, some constructed for irrigation, others for industrial purposes; the Camargue is an area of 552 sq km in the Rhône delta between the Grand Rhône and the Petit Rhône rivers; the present-day Camargue, with its apex at Arles, consists of a vast, wide triangle of what was, until recently, salt marsh and lagoon; the N part of the Camargue has now been drained, desalinated, irrigated and turned into extensive rice-fields, while the S part is a natural park protecting bulls and the famous white horses; the principal town in the Camargue is Saintes-Maries-de-la-Mer, painted by Van Gogh and venue of a famous gipsy pilgrimage; the area around the Étang de Vaccares is a reserve for migratory birds (including flamingoes in summer); the Grand Canyon du Verdon, 16 km S of Castellane, is a 21 km-long canyon with cliffs varying in height from 250-700 m; the Calanques, SE of Marseille, are deep, narrow arms of the sea enclosed by rugged white limestone cliffs, some are used as natural yacht harbours; there are interesting caves at St-Cézaire and Le Thor; seaside resorts on the Côte d'Azur include Antibes, Nice, St-Raphael, St-Tropez, Monte-Carlo, Cannes and Menton; there are ski-resorts at Auron, Beuil and Valberg; there are numerous medieval hilltop villages; at Les Baux-de-Provence, in 1822, the mineral which yields aluminium was discovered and given the name bauxite; near the town of Gordes, N of Mont Ventoux, is the 'Black Village', a long-abandoned settlement of bories (primitive beehive-shaped houses in drystone construction); the Pont du Gard, a 3-tier aqueduct built towards the end of the 1st century BC, near Remoulins on the road to Uzès, is one of the most remarkable sights in the region; Gréoux-les-Bains is the oldest known health spa (pre-Roman); the Vaucluse, between the Plateau de Vaucluse and the R Coulon valley, is important for the production of ochre; Toulon is France's most important naval base; La Ciotat is the site of the most modern dockyards in France; the 'Route Napoleon', the official name given to the route followed by Napoleon on his march northwards to Grenoble after his return from Elba in 1815, runs through the region via Cannes, Grasse, Digne, Sisteron and Gap; chief towns include Marseille, Avignon, Toulon, Cannes, Nice, and Aix-en-Provence.

Providence, 41 49N 71 24W, pop(1980) 156,804, capital of Rhode I state, in Providence county, E Rhode Island, United States; port at the head of R Providence; Brown University (1764); railway; airport; economy: jewellery and silverware, fabricated metals, equipment; its excellent harbour makes it a popular sailing resort, as well as a major port for oil tankers; monuments: First Baptist church, State Capitol, museum of art.

Providence, East, 41 50N 71 28W, pop(1980) 50,980, town in Providence county, E Rhode Island, United States; on the R Seekonk close to its confluence with R Providence, 3 km E of Providence and 2 km W of the Massachusetts border; economy: jewellery, oil refining.

Providencia, island of Colombia. See San Andrés-Providencia.

Providenciales *prov-ee-den-sya'lez*, 21 48N 72 48W, island in the Caicos Is, British dependent territory of Turks and Caicos; in the W Atlantic, SE of the Bahamas; area 97 sq km; pop(1980) 977; airport; popular resort island; lobster and conch fishing.

Pro'vo, 40 14N 111 39W, pop(1980) 74,108, county seat of Utah county, N central Utah, United States; on the R Provo, near L Utah; settled by Mormons in 1849; Brigham Young University (1875); railway; economy:

distributing, processing and manufacturing centre in a mining and irrigated farming area.

Prudhoe *prood'ō*, 54 58N 1 51W, pop(1981) 11,129, town in Tynedale dist, Northumberland, NE England; 16 km W of Gateshead, S of the R Tyne; railway; economy: coal, fertilizers, foodstuffs.

Prudhoe Bay *proo'dō*, a bay on the N coast of the state of Alaska, United States; on the Beaufort Sea; a pipeline links Arctic oil fields with Valdez on the Gulf of Alaska.

Pruszków *proosh'kof*, 52 10N 20 47E, pop(1983) 52,100, town in Warszawa voivodship, central Poland; former outer suburb SW of Warszawa (Warsaw); railway.

Prut *proot*, river in SW Ukraine and E Romania; rises at the E foothills of Ukrainian Carpathians; following the E Romania frontier with the USSR it meets the R Danube above Reni in the Danube delta; length 850 km; navigable for 100 km.

Przemyśl *pshem'ish*, voivodship in SE Poland; bounded (E) by the USSR and watered by R San; pop(1983) 389,000; area 4,437 sq km; capital Przemyśl; chief towns include Jarosław and Lubaczów.

Przemyśl, 49 48N 22 48E, pop(1983) 64,100, capital of Przemyśl voivodship, SE Poland; in hilly country on R San, near USSR frontier; formerly an important trade centre on the Black Sea Kraków route; strongly fortified by the Austrians in 1873; railway; economy: lathes, high voltage equipment, light engineering, natural gas; monuments: 16-17th-c houses around the Market Square; 18th-c Franciscan church and monastery; 17th-c castle; regional museum with exhibition of icons; St Theresa's church.

Ptolemaïs *p-tol-i-mīs'*, 40 32N 21 42E, pop(1981) 22,109, town in Kozáni nome (dept), Makedhonia region, N Greece; E of Kastoría.

Ptuj *ptoo'ee*, PETTAU (Ger), POETOVIO (anc), 46 27N 15 51E, pop(1981) 67,754, town in NE Slovenija republic, Yugoslavia; on R Drava, SE of Maribor; part of Austria until 1918; railway; economy: wine trade, coal mining, footwear.

Puch'ŏn *poo-chun*, PUNWON-NI, 37 31N 126 45E, pop(1983e) 340,307, town in Kyŏnggi prov, NW Korea.

Pud'sey, 53 48N 1 40W, pop(1981) 31,946, town in Leeds borough, West Yorkshire, N England; part of West Yorkshire urban area; 10 km W of Leeds; railway; economy: textiles, tanning, engineering.

Puebla *pweb'la*, state in S central Mexico; bounded by the states of Veracruz (E and N), Hidalgo (NW), Tlaxcala, México and Morelos (W), Guerrero (SW) and Oaxaca (S); largely mountainous state; occupies part of the central Mexican plateau and is crossed by the Sierra Madre Oriental in the N; on the border with México state are Popocatépetl (5,452 m) and Ixtaccihuatl (5,286 m) volcanoes; in the E is Mexico's highest peak, the Volcán Citlaltépetl, which rises to 5,699 m; drained by the Atoyac river; pop(1980) 3,279,960; area 33,902 sq km; capital Puebla; economy: agriculture (maize, fruit, sugar cane, coffee, grains), cattle raising, aviculture, timber, machinery, motor cars, light and heavy industry, textiles, food processing.

Puebla, PUEBLA DE ZARAGOZA, 19 03N 98 10W, pop(1980) 835,759, capital of Puebla state, S central Mexico; SE of Ciudad de México (Mexico City) at an alt of 2,150 m; part of the city was damaged by an earthquake in 1973; 2 universities (1937, 1940); railway; economy: textiles, pottery, cement; monuments: the cathedral in the centre of the city has statues flanking the altar which are said to be of an English king and Scottish queen; the city is famous for its glazed tiles which cover the domes of many of its 60 churches.

Pueblo *pweb'lō*, 38 14N 104 36W, pop(1980) 101,686, county seat of Pueblo county, S central Colorado, United States; on the Arkansas river, at its junction with Fountain Creek; settled by gold miners c.1858; after the city was badly flooded in 1921, levees were constructed to contain the R Arkansas; US army ordnance depot; university; railway; economy: trade in timber, coal, livestock and arable crops; manufactures include steel, wire, concrete and lumber; monument: Thatcher Mansion.

Puelo, Lago *pway'lō*, national park in W Chubut prov, Patagonia, Argentina; N of Los Alerces National Park; area 141 sq km; L Puelo is situated in the N of the park.

Puente, La *pwen'ti*, 33 59N 117 58W, pop(1980) 30,882, city in Los Angeles county, SW California, United States; c.28 km E of Los Angeles.

Puente-Genil *pwen'tay hay-neel'*, 37 22N 4 47W, pop(1981) 25,615, industrial and agric town in Córdoba prov, Andalucia, S Spain; on the R Genil, 140 km E of Sevilla; economy: stone quarrying, conserves, olive oil, fruit, livestock.

Puerto Armuelles *ar-mway'es*, 8 19N 82 51W, pop(1980) 12,562, port in Chiriquí prov, SW Panama, Central America; on the W shore of the Golfo de Chiriquí; railway; economy: exports bananas grown in the area; an oil transit line links Puerto Armuelles with the Caribbean port of Bocas del Toro.

Puerto Ayacucho *pwer'tō ī-a-koo'chō*, 5 39N 67 32W, pop(1980) 15,000, capital of the federal territory of Amazonas, SW Venezuela; on the Orinoco river, near the Colombian frontier; close to the Atures rapids.

Puerto Ayora *pwer'tō ah-yō'rah*, 0 45S 90 19W, pop(1982) 2,404, largest town and port in the Galápagos Is, Ecuador; on the S coast of Santa Cruz island.

Puerto Barrios *pwer'to bar'ree-os*, 15 40N 88 32W, pop(1983e) 38,956, port and capital town of Izabal dept, E Guatemala, Central America; on the SE shore of the Bahía de Amatique; largely superseded as a port by Santo Tomás; railway; airfield.

Puerto Carreño *pwer'tō ka-rayn'yō*, 6 08N 69 27W, pop(1985) 3,377, capital of Vichada administrative territory, E Colombia, South America; on the Río Meta where it meets the Río Orinoco near the border with Venezuela.

Puerto Cortés *pwer'tō kor-tays'*, 15 50N 87 55W, pop(1983e) 40,249, port town in Cortés dept, NW Honduras, Central America; at the mouth of the R Ulúa, on the Caribbean Sea; principal port of Honduras; a free zone was opened in 1978; railway; economy: oil refining.

Puerto de la Cruz *pwer-to THay la krooth'*, 28 24N 16 33W, pop(1981) 39,241, largest tourist resort and agric centre on Tenerife I, in the Canary Is, Canarias autonomous region of Spain; beaches nearby; monuments: churches of St Telmo (1626) and 17th-c Our Lady of La Pena; botanical gardens; fine views nearby from the Mirador Humboldt.

Puerto de Santa Maria or **El Puerto** *pwer-to THay san-ta ma-ree'a*, 36 36N 6 13W, pop(1981) 57,437, commercial port in Cádiz prov, Andalucia, Spain; one of the oldest towns on the Bay of Cádiz; economy: sherry, brandy, wine; monuments: 13th-c Moorish castle of San Marcos and church of Our Lady of Los Milagros.

Puerto Lempira *pwer'tō lem-pee'ra*, 15 12N 83 51W, capital of Gracias a Dios dept, E Honduras, Central America; on S shore of Laguna de Caratosca; linked by road to Ahuasbila in the Montañas de Colon.

Puerto Montt *pwer'tō mont*, 41 28S 72 56W, pop(1982) 87,971, port and capital of Llanquihue prov, and Los Lagos region, S central Chile; airfield; terminus of both the railway and the Longitudinal Highway which is being extended S to Aisén; the first German colonists arrived in the prov in 1852; the port is used by fishing boats and coasting vessels; there is a handicrafts market by the port; 2 km from the centre of the town is the little fishing port of Angelmó, now a tourist centre.

Puerto Pla'ta, 19 48N 70 41W, pop(1982e) 88,079, seaport on the N coast of Puerto Plata prov, Dominican Republic, 60 km N of Santiago; founded in 1503 by Columbus; known for the native gem, amber, which is mined in a nearby mountain range; there is a cable-car to the summit of Isabel de Torres; airport; urban base for tourism on the N coast; monument: fort of San Felipe (1540).

Puerto Presidente Stroessner *pwer'tō pray-see-dayn'tay strōs-ner'*, CIUDAD PRESIDENTE STROESSNER, 25 32S

54 34W, pop(1982) 39,676, capital of Alto Paraná dept, Oriental, N Paraguay; on the Río Paraná; the fastest-growing city in the country and centre for the construction of the Itaipú dam, the largest hydroelectric project in the world; a bridge links the city with Brazil and the town of Foz do Iguaçu; named after the President of Paraguay.

Puerto Rico *pwer'to ree'ko*, formerly PORTO RICO (-1932), official name Commonwealth of Puerto Rico, easternmost island of the Greater Antilles, situated between the Dominican Republic (W) and the US Virgin Is (E), c.1,600 km SE of Miami; timezone GMT −4; area 8,897 sq km; capital San Juan; chief towns Ponce, Bayamón and Mayaguez; pop(1980) 3,196,520; 66.8% of the pop live in urban centres (1980); the people are mostly of European descent; Spanish is the official language but English is widely spoken; the dominant religion is Roman Catholicism; the unit of currency is the US dollar.

Physical description and climate. The island of Puerto Rico is almost rectangular in shape and measures 153 km in length and 58 km in width. A range of old volcanic mountains traverses the island from W to E, rising to 1,325 m at Cerro de Punta. N of these mountains is an area of *karst* or limestone country. The islands of Vieques (51.7 sq km) and Culebra also belong to Puerto Rico. Vieques is situated 16 km E of the island of Puerto Rico and in 1980 had a population of 7,662. The average annual temperature is 25°C and humidity is high. Rainfall is heaviest from June to October.

History, government and constitution. Originally occupied by Carib and Arawak Indians, Puerto Rico was visited by Columbus in 1493 and remained a Spanish colony until it was ceded to the USA in 1898. The strategic importance of its harbours in addition to gold and sugar were major attractions to both Spanish and Americans. The present constitution dates from 1952 when Puerto Rico became a semi-autonomous Commonwealth in association with the USA. There is a bicameral legislative assembly consisting of a Senate and House of Representatives, elected by universal suffrage every 4 years. A governor, elected by direct vote, appoints an executive consisting of secretaries of government departments.

Economy. Since the industrialization programme 'Operation Bootstrap' was initiated in 1948 manufacturing has become the most important sector of the economy, now accounting for just over 45% of national income. The principal manufactures are textiles, clothing, electrical and electronic equipment, and petrochemicals. Agriculture contributes approx 3% to the national income, the main activities being dairying, livestock production, and the cultivation of sugar, tobacco, coffee, pineapples, and coconuts. Tourism is of major importance to the economy. Chief exports are chemicals, petroleum products, clothing and textiles, and machinery. The USA is the main trading partner.

Puertollano *pwer-to-lya'no*, 38 43N 4 07W, pop(1981) 48,747, industrial and agric town in Ciudad Real prov, Castilla-La Mancha, S central Spain; 38 km SW of Ciudad Real; railway; economy: iron and steel, metal products, mining.

Pueyrredón, Lago *pway-re-THōn'*, LAGO COCHRANE (Chile), lake in Patagonian Andes of Argentina and Chile; in NW Santa Cruz prov, Patagonia, S Argentina and NE Capitan Prat prov, Aisen del General Carlos Ibañez del Campo, S Chile; area 271 sq km; length 32 km.

Puglia *pool'yay*, APU'LIA (Eng), region of SE Italy, comprising the provs of Foggia, Bari, Taranto, Brindisi, and Lecce; pop(1981) 3,871,617; area 19,345 sq km; chief towns Lecce, Bari, Taranto, and Brindisi; bounded E by the Adriatic Sea and W by the Appno Napoletano and Appno Lucano; main crops grown in this predominantly agricultural area include wheat, vegetables, grapes, almonds, and olives; large-scale water supply schemes have promoted considerable development of agriculture; there has recently been some industrial development, chiefly petrochemicals, in coastal areas.

Pujehun *poo-jay-hoon'*, dist in Southern prov, Sierra Leone, W Africa; pop(1974) 102,741; area 4,105 sq km; capital Pujehun.

Pujehun, 7 23N 11 44W, pop(1974) 3,000, capital of a dist of the same name, Southern prov, Sierra Leone, W Africa; on the R Waanje 64 km S of Bo.

Pukapuka *poo'ka-poo-kah*, formerly DANGER ISLAND, 10 53S 165 49W, triangular coral atoll of the Cook Is, S Pacific, 1,144 km NW of Rarotonga; area 5 sq km; pop(1981) 796; comprises 3 islets joined by reefs; copra, bananas, and papaya are grown.

Pukë *poo'ke*, prov of N Albania; area 969 sq km; pop(1980) 42,400; capital Pukë.

Pukë, 42 03N 19 53E, town and capital of Pukë prov, N Albania; 80 km N of Tiranë.

Pula *poo'lah*, POLA (Ital), PIETAS IULIA (Lat), 44 52N 13 52E, pop(1981) 77,278, seaport and resort town in W Hrvatska (Croatia) republic, Yugoslavia; on the Adriatic coast; built on the site of a former Roman colony; the town was controlled by Venice for over 400 years; airport; railway; car ferries to Italy; tourist hotels and facilities at Medulin and Premantura; economy: naval and commercial port, shipyards, tourism; monuments: Roman amphitheatre, Temple of Augustus, cathedral, 17th-c castle; events: folk displays and concerts in Roman amphitheatre during June-Aug; festival of Yugoslav feature films (July-Aug).

Pular, Cerro *se'rō poo-lar'*, 24 12S 68 05W, Andean peak in E Antofagasta region, N Chile; near the Argentinian border; height 6,225 m.

Pulau Pinang, island and state in Malaysia. See Pinang, Pulau.

Punata *poo-na'ta*, 17 32S 65 50W, pop(1976) 10,264, town in Punata prov, Cochabamba, Bolivia; railway.

Pune *poo'ne*, POONA, 18 34N 73 58E, pop(1981) 1,685,000, city in Maharashtra state, W India; 120 km SE of Bombay; once the powerful capital of the Mahrattas, it came under British rule in 1818; it then became a favourite residence of the British administrators and an important military centre; airfield; linked by rail to Bombay, Sangli and Solapur; economy: cotton, engineering, chemicals, metalwork, vehicles, soap, paper; monuments: 17-18th-c palaces and temples.

Punjab *pun'jahb*, state in NW India; pop(1981) 16,669,755; area 50,362 sq km; bounded N by Jammu and Kashmir state, NE by Himachal Pradesh territory, SE by Haryana state, S by Rajasthan state and W and NW by Pakistan; a part of the W boundary is formed by the Sutlej river; divided into 12 administrative districts; capital (jointly with Haryana) Chandigarh; major cities include Amritsar, Jalandhar, Faridkot and Ludhiana; the state is governed by a 117-member Legislative Assembly; 75% of the population is employed in agriculture, the principal crops being wheat, maize, rice, sugar cane and cotton; most of the cultivated land is irrigated; major manufacturing industries of the Punjab produce textiles, sewing machines, sugar, fertilizers, bicycles, electrical goods, machine tools and scientific instruments; the Punjab is crossed by railways linking Firozpur with Delhi and Amritsar with Ambala; there is an international airport at Amritsar and an airfield at Chandigarh; historically the Punjab region was a part of the Mogul Empire until the end of the 18th century when the Sikhs rose to power; the British annexed the Punjab and made it a province after the Sikh Wars of 1846 and 1849; in 1937 the Punjab became an autonomous province and in 1947 it was partitioned between India and Pakistan into East and West Punjab under the Indian Independence Act; the name East Punjab was changed to Punjab (India) under the constitution of India; in Nov 1966 the state was reformed as a Punjabi-speaking state, with the population of the remaining areas being shared between the states of Haryana and the union territory of Himachal Pradesh; at that time Chandigarh was made the joint capital of Punjab and Haryana; the Alkai Dai party campaigns for Sikh autonomy.

Punjab, province in Pakistan; pop(1981) 47,292,000; area

205,334 sq km; bounded E and S by India and the Thar desert and N by Baltistan; crossed by the Sutlej, Chenab, Jhelum and Indus rivers; boundary between Punjab and the North West Frontier prov is in part formed by the R Indus; capital Lahore.

Puno *poo'nō*, dept in SE Peru; bordered E and S by Bolivia; in the N it extends across the Cordillera Oriental; in the E of the dept is L Titicaca; bounded by the Cordillera Occidental (SW) and the Cordillera de Vilnacota (W); pop(1981) 890,258; area 72,382 sq km (includes part of L Titicaca); capital Puno.

Punta Arenas *poon'ta a-ray'nas*, 53 09S 70 52W, pop(1982) 80,706, port and capital of Magallanes prov, and Magallanes-La Antártica Chilena region, Chile; most southerly city in Chile; situated on the Estreitas de Magallanes (Straits of Magellan), almost equidistant from the Pacific and Atlantic oceans; airfield; economy: centre of sheep-farming, exporting wool, skins and frozen meat; crude oil is transported between the Strait oil terminals and refineries in central Chile; monuments: the museum at Colegio Salesiano features the region's Indians and its animal and bird life; on the Plaza de Armas in the Casa Menéndez, the Museo del Recuerdo contains a collection of work tools from the colonial period; the Patagonian Institute has a small zoo, a botanical garden and a collection of old local vehicles and machinery; event: Festival Folclórica de la Patagonia (26-30 July).

Punta, Cerro de *poon'ta*, highest peak on the island of Puerto Rico in the E Caribbean, rising to 1,325 m.

Punta Gorda *pun'ta gor'da*, 16 10N 88 45W, pop(1980) 2,396, capital of Toledo dist, S Belize, Central America; most southerly town of Belize; airfield; economy: fishing, small boat trading with Honduras.

Punta Negra, Salar de, salt desert in N Chile. See Atacama, Desierto de.

Puntarenas *poon-ta-ray'nas*, prov in W Costa Rica, Central America; bounded W by the Pacific Ocean and SE by Panama; largest prov in the republic; comprises the area around the Golfo de Nicoya (NW) and the basin of the Río Grande de Térraba (SE) linked by a narrow coastal strip; includes Osa peninsula and S part of Nicoya peninsula; pop(1983e) 286,082; area 11,277 sq km; economy: bananas, rice, coconuts, cattle raising; capital Puntarenas; chief port Caldera.

Puntarenas, 10 00N 84 50W, pop(1983e) 34,613, port and capital town of Puntarenas prov, W Costa Rica, Central America; on a spit of land extending out into the Golfo de Nicoya from its E shore; airfield; railway; it is being replaced as the country's main Pacific port by Caldera.

Pursat *poor-sat*, province in W Cambodia; pop(1981) 180,000; bounded W by the Gulf of Thailand and Thailand; the chief town, Pursat, lies 160 km NW of Phnom Penh on St Tamyong river, which is a tributary of the Tonlé Sap and is navigable during high water; linked by rail to Phnom Penh.

Purus *poo-roos'*, river in NW South America; an important tributary of the Amazon, NW Brazil; rises in Peru on the E slopes of the Andes at 11 00S 72 00W; flows NE across Acre and Amazonas states; joins the Amazon 160 km WSW of Manaus; its principal tributary is Río Acre; length approx 3,200 km; its winding course through the Amazon's tropical rain forest gives the Purus the title of the world's most crooked river.

Pusan or **Busan** *poo-sahn*, 35 05N 129 02E, pop(1984) 3,495,289, seaport and special city in SE Korea; situated on the SE coast on the Korea Strait in a depression surrounded by hills; 2 universities (1946-1947); international ferry; hydrofoil; railway; airport (Kimhae); economy: engineering, shipbuilding, tourism, fishing, trade in salt, fish, rice, soybeans; monuments: Pusan municipal museum contains cultural and historical exhibits dating from prehistoric times; on one of Pusan's peninsulas is the UN Memorial Cemetery containing those who died during the Korean War of 1950-53; in the centre of Pusan is Yongdu san (Dragon Head Mountain) park which contains several war memorials and a statue of Admiral Yi Sun-shin, Korea's naval hero; also in the park is Pusan Tower, a television transmission tower and observation dome; on the tip of the small peninsula to the S of Pusan is T'aejongdae park, named after King Muyŏl of the Silla Kingdom, said to have spent time here after his unification of the Three Kingdoms; approx 14 km N of Pusan is Tongnae Hot Springs, noted for its medicinal hot springs since 1691; to the N of Tongnae on the E slopes of Mt Kŭmjŏngsan is the Pŏmŏsa Buddhist temple, one of the largest Buddhist temples in Korea, originally founded in 678 AD and reconstructed in 1717; events: 27 Oct, Hansan victory festival; Kaech'on art festival on 3rd day of 10th lunar month; Arang festival on 17 May.

Puttalam *pat-el-am'*, 8 02N 79 50E, pop(1981) 21,586, seaport capital of Puttalam dist, North Western prov, Sri Lanka; 130 km N of Colombo, on the E shore of the Puttalam Lagoon.

Putumayo *poo-too-mī'yō*, intendency in SW Colombia, South America; bounded W by the Andes, S by Ecuador and Peru along the Río Putumayo and N by the Río Caquetá; pop(1973) 29,137; area 24,885 sq km; capital Mocoa; economy: sugar cane, cattle.

Puy, Le *le pwee*, ANICIUM, PODIUM ANICENSIS (anc), formerly LE PUY-EN-VELAY, 45 03N 3 52E, pop(1982) 25,968, manufacturing city and capital of Haute-Loire dept, Auvergne region, SE central France; on the E border of the Auvergne, on the right bank of the R Borne, 104 km SE of Clermont-Ferrand; alt 686 m; bishopric; the town lies on what was once the bed of a huge lake, volcanic upheavals emptied the lake, shifted the course of the R Loire and thrust up a number of pinnacles of lava rock; monuments: late 11th-c chapel of St-Michel-d'Aiguille (on the pinnacle Rocher St-Michel, 85 m high); famous pilgrimage church and cathedral of Notre-Dame du Puy (late 12th-c); the old town, famous for its handmade lace and once an important pilgrim centre, is situated on a lower hill.

Puyang *poo-yang*, 35 40N 115 00E, pop(1984e) 1,059,500, city in Henan prov, N central China; NE of Zhengzhou.

Puy-de-Dôme, dept in Auvergne region of central France, comprising 5 arrond, 61 cantons and 470 communes; pop(1982) 594,365; area 7,955 sq km; the Mts d'Auvergne rise to 1,886 m in the Puy de Sancy and to 1,463 m in the Puy de Dôme; the land rises to 1,640 m in the Monts du Forez on the E border; drained by the Allier and Dore rivers; capital Clermont-Ferrand, chief towns Thiers and Riom; there are châteaux at Orcival (15-16th-c) and Chanonat (10-18th-c) and spas at Châteauneuf-les-Bains, Chatelguyon, La Bourboule, Royat, Le Mont-Dore and St-Nectaire.

Puyehue, Lago *poo yay'way*, lake in Los Lagos region, S central Chile; 48 km E of Osorno; area 300 sq km, 32 km long; 13 km wide; on the NE shore lies Puyehue Volcano (2,240 m); on the SE shore is the resort of Puyehue.

Puyo *poo'yō*, 1 30S 77 58W, pop(1982) 9,758, capital of Pastaza prov, E Ecuador; on the Río Pastaza, E of Ambato in the E foothills of the Andes; the most important centre in the tropical *Oriente* region.

Pwa'ni, coastal region of E Tanzania, E Africa; bounded E by the Indian Ocean; pop(1985e) 578,000; chief town Kibaha.

Pyle, 51 32N 3 42W, pop(1981) 13,261, town in Ogwr dist, Mid Glamorgan, S Wales; N of Porthcawl.

P'yŏngannam, SOUTH PYONGAN, prov in central North Korea; capital P'yŏngyang.

P'yŏnganpuk *pyung-an-puk*, NORTH PYONGAN, prov in W North Korea; bordered SW by Korea Bay and NW by Liaoning prov, China, along the Yalu river; capital Sinŭiju.

P'yŏngyang *pyung-yang*, HEIJO *hay'jō* (Jap), 39 00N 125 47E, pop(1981) 1,280,000, capital of North Korea; overlooking the R Taedong; Korea's oldest city, founded allegedly in 1122 BC by remnants of the Chinese Shang dynasty; capital of Choson kingdom (300-200 BC); a colony of China in 108 BC; taken and destroyed by Japan in the 1590s; capital of North Korea since 1948; rebuilt after the Korean War; university (1946); railway; airport;

economy: iron and steel, machinery, textiles, aircraft, sugar; monuments: 1st-c tombs with fine murals.

Pyrenees *pir-en-eez'*, PYRÉNÉES *pee-ray-nay* (Fr), PIRINEOS *pee-ree-nay'os* (Sp), mountain range extending W-E from the Bay of Biscay to the Mediterranean Sea, separating the Iberian Peninsula of SW Europe from the rest of Europe; stretches 450 km along the French-Spanish frontier and includes the tiny principality of Andorra; the highest point, Pic de Aneto (3,404 m), is in Spain; other major peaks include Vignemale (3,298 m) and Montceny (2,883 m); the Gouffre de la Pierre St Martin below the Pic d'Arlas in the W Pyrenees is one of the deepest caves in the world; the Grotte Casteret is the highest ice cave in Europe; there are glaciers with a total area of 33 sq km; the Pico de la Maladetta is the largest ice field in the Pyrenees; notable scientific sites include the observatory at Pic du Midi de Bigorre (2,868 m) and the solar furnace at Font Romeau; the range is named after the legendary Pyrène who was buried there by Herakles after being killed by wild animals; Hannibal made a famous crossing in 218 BC on his way to Italy; on the Spanish side the Aragón, Gállego, Esera, Segre and Ter rivers have their source and on the French side the Adour, Garonne and Aude rivers.

Pyrénées-Atlantiques, dept in Aquitaine region of SW France, on the Spanish frontier (S) and the Bay of Biscay (W); comprises 3 arrond, 52 cantons and 539 communes; pop(1982) 555,696; area 7,633 sq km; at the NW edge of the Pyrenees Mts; drained by numerous tributaries of the R Adour; capital Pau, chief towns Bayonne and Biarritz; Maison de Louis XIV at St-Jean-de-Luz; there is a sea-water treatment establishment at Biarritz; there are interesting caves near St-Martin-d'Arberoue (Grottes d'Oxocelhaya et d'Isturits).

Pyrénées-Orientales, dept in Languedoc-Roussillon region of S France, mostly in Roussillon, on the Golfe du Lion (E) and the Spanish frontier (S); comprises 3 arrond, 21 cantons and 221 communes; pop(1982) 334,557; area 4,087 sq km; mountainous in the W, rising to 2,921 m in the E section of the Pyrénées; drained by the eastward flowing rivers of Tét, Agly and Tech; there are vineyards, olive groves and market-gardens on the upper R Tét and early vegetables are grown around Perpignan; Roussillon is noted for its wine production; capital Perpignan, chief towns Prades and Céret; there are spas at Amélie-les-Bains, Molitg-les-Bains, Vernet-les-Bains, La Preste-les-Bains and Le Boulou; there is a sea-water treatment establishment at Collioure.

Q

Qacentina, town in Algeria, N Africa. See Constantine.
Qadārif, El, town in E Sudan. See Gedaref.
Qâhira, El, capital of Egypt. See Cairo.
Qaidam Pendi, basin in NW Qinghai prov, W central China; bounded by the Kunlun Shan range (S), the Altun Shan range (NW) and the Qilian Shan range (N and NE); 800 km long and 350 km wide at its widest section; area 220,000 sq km; alt 2,700-3,000 m; there are scattered deserts in the gobi (stony) areas; in the SE are large areas of marshland and salt lakes; much of the surface of the Qaidam Pendi basin is formed by solid salt, up to 15 m thick; part of the railway to Xizang aut region (Tibet) crosses this surface; there are reserves of oil, natural gas, borax, asbestos, gypsum, metals and salt; the E and SE parts have developed into farming areas, while in other areas factories and towns have emerged.
Qā'im, Al *al kīm'*, 34 23N 41 11E, industrial town in Al-Anbār governorate, W central Iraq; on R Euphrates, on the highway between Baghdād and the Syrian border; railway; economy: manufacture of chemicals and fertilizers.
Qalāt *ka-lat'*, KALAT, KALATI GHILZAI, 34 40N 70 18E, pop(1984c) 6,518, capital of Zābol prov, Afghanistan; lies close to the W bank of the R Tarnah and on the main road between Kābul and Kandahār.
Qal'eh-ye Now *ka-la-now'*, QALAINOW, QALA NAU, 34 58N 63 04E, pop(1984c) 5,854, capital of Bādghīs prov, W Afghanistan; lies NE of Herat.
Qalyûbîya *kal-yoo-bee'yu*, governorate in NE Egypt; pop(1976) 1,674,006; area 971 sq km; capital Benha.
Qârûn, Birkat, *ka'roon*, lake in El Faiyûm governorate, N Egypt; in the Faiyûm Depression SW of Cairo and NW of the city of El Faiyûm; about 45 m below sea-level, 40 km long and up to 6.5 km wide.
Qatar *kat'ar*, official name State of Qatar, DAWLAT AL-QATAR, low lying state on the E coast of the Arabian Peninsula, comprising the Qatar Peninsula and numerous small offshore islands; bounded S by Saudi Arabia and the United Arab Emirates, and on the other 3 sides by the Arabian Gulf; timezone GMT +3; area 11,437 sq km; capital Ad Dawḥah (Doha); pop(1982e) 260,000; more than 70% of the pop lives in the capital city, most of the remainder occupying the industrial town of Musay'īd (Umm Said), the oilfield area of Dukhān, and the coastal towns of Al Wakrah and Al Khawr; only about a quarter of the pop are indigenous Qataris; the pop comprises 40% Arab, 18% Pakistani, 18% Indian, and 10% Iranian; Bedouin tribes still lead a nomadic lifestyle in the interior but their numbers are rapidly diminishing; Arabic is the official language although English is widely spoken; Islam is the dominant religion; the unit of currency is the riyal; national holiday 3 Sept (Independence Day); membership of Arab League, FAO, G-77, GATT (de facto), GCC, IBRD, ICAO, Islamic Development Bank, IFAD, ILO, IMF, IMO, INTELSAT, INTERPOL, ITU, NAM, OAPEC, OIC, OPEC, UN, UNESCO, UPU, WHO, WIPO, WMO.
Physical description and climate. The peninsula, 160 km long and 55-80 km wide, slopes gently from the W ridge of the Dukhān Heights (98 m) to the E shore. The terrain is barren, covered mainly by sand and gravel and trenched by shallow wadis. Belts of *sabkhah* or salt flats surround the much indented coastline while offshore there are numerous coral reefs and sand shoals. Qatar has a desert climate with temperatures ranging from an average of 23°C in the winter to 35°C in the summer. Because Qatar is surrounded on 3 sides by sea the humidity is exceptionally high, often reaching 90% during the summer. Total annual rainfall is sparse, not exceeding 75 mm per annum. Most of this rainfall occurs during the winter months, normally in the form of heavy thunderstorms.
History, government and constitution. After Turkish withdrawal in 1916 Qatar became a British protectorate. In 1968 attempts were made to form a federation of Gulf emirates but by 1971 the 9 shaikhdoms (Bahrain, Qatar, and the present United Arab Emirates) still had not been able to agree on terms of union. Instead, Qatar declared its independence from Britain on 3 Sept 1971. Qatar has a hereditary monarchy and has been ruled by the al-Thani dynasty since the late 19th century. There is an Emir or head of state who also acts as prime minister. There is no parliament but a council of ministers, appointed by the Emir, is assisted by a 30-member nominated consultative council.
Economy. The pearling trade brought prosperity to Qatar in the 19th and early 20th centuries but declined in the face of the production of cultured pearls from Japan. Oil was discovered at Dukhān in 1939. Subsequent exploration on land and offshore failed to yield additional findings until 1960 when the offshore fields of Idd al Sharqi and Maydan Mahzam were discovered. Since then the offshore fields of Bul Hanine and Al-Bandaq have come on stream. Oil is central to the economy, accounting for 46% of national income in 1985, almost 90% of government revenue, and 94% of export earnings. A liquefied natural gas plant uses gas derived from the Dukhān field and exports its products mainly to Japan. Gas reserves in the 1,000 sq km North Dome offshore field to the NE of the peninsula are estimated to

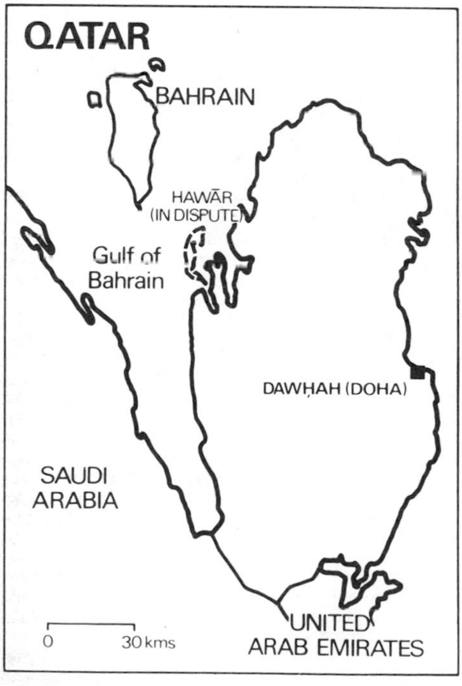

total about one-eighth of known world reserves. Using natural gas as a source of energy, industrial development is concentrated mainly at Musay'īd (Umm Said), where there are two oil refineries, a petrochemical plant, a liquefied natural gas plant, a fertilizer plant, and a huge steel complex. Steel production at Musay'īd began in 1978 with most of the output being exported to Saudi Arabia, the UAE, and Iraq. There is a cement plant at Umm Bāb near Dukhān. Ship repairing and the production of overhead cranes account for approx 5% of national income. Government incentives have encouraged private investment in light industry and there are factories in and around Ad Dawḩah involved in engineering, food processing, and the production of construction materials. Japan is Qatar's main trading partner, accounting for almost half of the country's crude oil exports in 1983. Non-oil commodities are exported mainly to neighbouring Arab countries.

Agriculture. Agriculture accounts for less than 1% of national income and employs 10% of the workforce. Only 30 sq km out of a total possible cultivable area of 300 sq km are used. The main crops are aubergine, lucerne, squash, hay and tomatoes. There are also some 200,000 date palms. Government projects include an experimental sheep farm and a poultry farm. The Qatari National Fisheries Company is one of the major exporters of Gulf shrimps. Ad Dawḩah has refrigeration and processing plants which prepare prawns for export.

Communications. The international dual carriageway which links Ad Dawḩah with the Saudi Arabian road network is part of the Trans-Arabian Highway. Musay'īd (Umm Said) and Ad Dawḩah are the main ports. There is an international airport at Ad Dawḩah.

Qazvīn *kaz-veen'*, 36 16N 50 00E, pop(1983) 244,265, town in Qazvīn dist, Zanjān, N Iran; 144 km WNW of Tehrān, in the S foothills of the Elburz Mts; repeatedly destroyed by earthquakes; railway; airfield.

Qena *kay'nu*, 26 08N 32 42E, capital of Qena governorate, E central Egypt; on the W bank of the R Nile, 50 km NNE of Luxor.

Qilian Shan *chil-yan*, mountain range in N China; situated in E Qinghai and W Gansu provs; the range averages over 4,000 m above sea level; extends NW to the Altun Shan range and SE to the Qin Ling range; Mt Qilian, the highest point, rises to 5,547 m.

Qingdao *ching-tow*, TSINGTAO, CHING-TAO, 36 04N 120 22E, pop(1984e) 1,229,500, resort seaport city in Shandong prov, E China; on S coast of the Shandong peninsula on the Huang Hai (Yellow Sea); before 1891 Qingdao was a small fishing village; in 1898 Germans took control of the town which developed into a European-type city; Japan occupied Qingdao during World War I and China did not regain control until 1922; railway; airfield; economy: cars, trains, consumer goods, brewing.

Qinghai *ching-hī*, TSINGHAI, province in W central China; bordered by Xinjiang aut region (NW), Gansu prov (N and E), by Sichuan prov (SE) and by Xizang aut region (S and SW); rises in the N with the Qilian Shan, Danghe Nanshan (Humboldt range), Tulai Shan, Datong Shan and Daban Shan ranges; the plateau in the S includes the Kunlun Shan range and its branches: the Bayan Har Shan, Ningjing Shan, Hoh Xil Shan and A'nyêmaqên Shan ranges; in the NW is the Qaidam Pendi, a large inland basin walled in by the Kunlun Shan to the S and the Qaidam Shan range to the N, consisting of numerous salt lakes and swamps; the prov takes its name from the large salt lake, the Qinghai Hu, in the NE, the largest inland lake in China; Qinghai's largest freshwater lakes, Gyaring Hu and Ngoring Hu, lie together in the centre of the prov; drained by the Huang He (Yellow river), Datong He, Huang Shui, and the Tongtian He (upper stream of the Chang Jiang (Yangtze)) rivers; pop(1982) 3,895,706; area 721,000 sq km; capital Xining; economy: sheep, yak and horse raising, medicinal materials (including caterpillar fungus, antlers, musk and rhubarb); mining.

Qinghai Hu, salt lake in NE Qinghai prov, W central China; area 4,583 sq km; alt 3,196 m; largest salt lake in China; joined by the Buh He river (NW); located in a geological fault between the Qinghai Nanshan range (S) and the Datong Shan range (N); the island in the centre of the lake, well-known for its water birds, is a nature protection zone; it contains Haixin Shan mountain which rises to 3,266 m.

Qinhuangdao *chin-whang-dow*, 39 55N 119 37E, pop(1984e) 425,300, port in Hebei prov, N China; on the NW coast of the Bohai gulf; a special economic zone since 1985; linked by 6 railway lines to the coal mining areas in the interior, the port used to be a coal depot for Shanghai's factories; it was used to land foreign troops during the Boxer Rebellion in 1900 and later to ship Chinese to the South African gold mines; linked by pipeline to the Daqing oil field; railway; economy: metallurgy, fibreglass, glass, textiles, fertilizer, chemicals, trade in fruit, chestnuts, fish, grain, coal and oil; monument: just N of the town is Shan Haiguan, the E end of the Great Wall.

Qiqihar *chi-chi-hah-er*, TSITSIHAR, formerly LUNGKIANG, 47 23N 124 00E, pop(1984e) 1,246,000, river port in Heilongjiang prov, NE China; on the R Nen; airfield; railway; economy: chemicals, matches, food processing.

Qom *koom*, 34 39N 50 57E, pop(1983) 424,048, industrial town in Qom dist, Markazī, Iran; 120 km SSW of Tehrān, on R Anarbar, in a semi-arid region; pilgrimage centre for Shiite Muslims; road and rail junction; gas pipeline; monuments: golden-domed shrine of Fatima.

Qormi *kor'mee*, 35 52N 14 30E, pop(1983e) 16,895, town on the main island of Malta, 5 km SW of Valletta.

Qornet es Saouda *koor'net es sow'da*, highest peak in the Jebel Liban (Lebanon) range, Ash Shamāl governorate, N Lebanon, 72 km NE of Beyrouth (Beirut); height 3,087 m.

Quatre Bornes *kat-re born*, 20 15S 57 28E, pop(1981e) 55,835, residential township in Plaines Wilhems dist, W Mauritius; between Port Louis and Curepipe; economy: clothes.

Que Que *kway kway*, KWEKWE, 18 55S 29 49E, pop(1981e) 62,000, town in Midlands prov, Zimbabwe, S Africa; 180 km SW of Harare; a major mineral centre with gold, chrome and iron mines; railway.

Québec, QUEBEC *kay-bek'*, *kwe-bek'* (Eng), province in SE Canada; bounded SW by Ontario, W by James Bay and Hudson Bay, NE by the Hudson Strait and Ungava Bay, E by Labrador (Newfoundland) and the Gulf of St Lawrence, SE by New Brunswick and S by the United States; the N four-fifths of the prov lie in the Canadian Shield, a partly wooded, rolling plateau dotted with lakes; the northernmost part of the prov is tundra and is beyond the limit of tree growth; pop is centred close to the St Lawrence river valley (S); rises to 1,588 m in Mont d'Iberville; in the S part of the prov are the Notre Dame Mts, an extension of the Appalachian mountain system; these mountains run along Gaspé Peninsula which extends out into the Gulf of St Lawrence; to the N of the St Lawrence and parallel with it are the Laurentian Mts: Québec prov is studded with numerous lakes, the largest being Mistassini, Sakami, Abitibi (on the Ontario border), Minto, St Jean, à l'Eau Claire and Caniapiscau; major rivers, apart from the St Lawrence, include the Mistassibi, Gatineau, Ottawa, Moisie and Péribonca flowing into the St Lawrence; the Harricana, Nottaway, Rupert, Grande Rivière and Grande Rivière de la Baleine flowing into James and Hudson bays; the aux Feuilles, aux Mélèzes, Caniapiscau, Koksoak, à la Baleine and George flowing into Ungava Bay; the Ile d'Anticosti and several smaller islands in the St Lawrence are also in Québec prov; the S of Québec prov is fertile and intensely cultivated; to the W of Québec city, bounded on the E by the St Maurice river, is La Maurice National Park (area 543 sq km, established in 1971); pop(1981) 6,438,403; area 1,357,655 sq km; capital Québec; major cities include Montréal, Laval, Sherbrooke, Verdun, Hull, Trois Rivières; economy: agriculture, timber, paper, hydroelectric power, aluminium, bauxite, iron ore, copper, gold, zinc, asbestos, textiles, high-technology industries; provincial holiday: 24 June (Jean Baptiste Day); claimed for France in 1534 by Jacques Cartier and in 1608 Champlain founded the prov of New France and the city of Québec; the prov was captured by the British in 1629 and restored to France by the Treaty of St Germain in 1632; in the Seven Years' War Wolfe took Québec city in 1759 and Montréal surrendered in 1760; the Treaty of Paris in 1763 transferred New France to Britain; the Québec Act in 1774 extended the prov's boundaries and restored French civil law; in 1775-76 the prov was invaded by the American Revolutionary Army; the constitution of 1791 divided Canada into Upper Canada (Ontario) and Lower Canada (French-speaking Québec); in 1867 Lower Canada became the prov of Québec, with English and French as official languages; during the 1960s a separatist movement emerged but in May 1980 a referendum was held in which it was decided that Québec should remain part of Canada; the prov is governed by a Lieutenant-Governor and a 122-member Legislative Assembly elected every 4 years.

Québec, QUEBEC, 46 50N 71 15W, pop(1981) 166,474, capital of Québec prov, SE Canada; in the S of the prov on the St Lawrence river where it meets the St Charles river; built on Cape Diamond, a cliff rising 100 m above the St Lawrence; 92% of the pop are French-speaking; originally the site of the Indian village of Stadacona, it was first visited in 1535 by Jacques Cartier; Champlain founded a French colony here in 1608; the first fort was built on the cape summit in 1620; originally the Lower City was occupied by tradesmen and the Upper City was reserved for the military, administration and residential life; Québec was taken by the English in 1629 and returned to France in 1632; it became the capital of the royal prov of New France in 1663; English attempts to take it in 1690 and 1711 failed; the city was finally captured in 1759 by the British under Wolfe, who defeated Montcalm on the nearby Plains of Abraham, and it was formally ceded to Britain by the Treaty of Paris in 1763; American attempts to take Québec failed (1775); it became capital of Lower Canada in 1791; for short periods after the union of Upper and Lower Canada in 1841 and before the federation in 1867 the city was the Canadian capital; Laval University (1852); Université du Québec (1968); railway; airport, economy: shipbuilding, paper, clothing, food processing, footwear, electrical goods, tobacco; monuments: the Château Frontenac on the Place d'Armes square was built as a hotel in 1892 and is still owned by the Canadian Pacific Railroad Co; it was here that Franklin D. Roosevelt, Winston Churchill and Mackenzie King met in 1943 and again in 1944 to plan strategies for World War II; S of the Château Frontenac is Dufferin Terrace and a monument to Champlain, founder of the city and first governor of New France; also on Dufferin Terrace is N America's oldest lift, which links with the Lower Town; the Musée du Fort, opposite the Château Frontenac, has a small theatre showing the 6 sieges of Québec city; the Citadel fortress is built at the highest point on Québec's promontory, approx 105 m above the St Lawrence river; the present fortress was built in 1832 by the British as part of a plan to defend Canada from possible American attack after the war of 1812-14 and was garrisoned by British troops until 1870; Battlefield Park to the W of the Citadel contains the Provincial Museum and the Plains of Abraham where, in Sept 1759, the British under Wolfe scaled the cliff to surprise the French and capture Québec; the Québec Museum contains the archives of the city, including the capitulatory document by which the city surrendered to the British in 1759; the Ursulines monastery (built in 1641 in the lower town) contains Montcalm's tomb and was the first girls' school in North America; part of the building is now a museum and contains, among other exhibits, Montcalm's skull; event: Québec Winter Carnival Canoe Race (Feb).

Queen Charlotte Islands, approx 150 islands off the W coast of British Columbia, W Canada; area 9,790 sq km; economy: timber, fishing.

Queen Elizabeth Islands, northmost islands of the Canadian Arctic Archipelago, situated N of latitude 74°N; they include Ellesmere, Devon, Prince Patrick and Cornwallis islands and the Sverdrup and Parry groups.

Queen Maud Land, Antarctica. See Dronning Maud Land.

Queenborough, 51 26N 0 45E, pop(1981) 18,695, resort town linked with Minster in Swale dist, Kent, SE England; on Isle of Sheppey, 3 km S of Sheerness; railway; economy: chemicals, transport equipment.

Queens, borough of New York City, United States; coextensive with Queens county; situated at the W end of Long Island; connected to the mainland by the Hell Gate Bridge and with Manhattan by the Queensboro Bridge; a borough since 1898; area 283 sq km; pop(1980) 1,891,325.

Queensferry, SOUTH QUEENSFERRY, 56 00N 3 25W, pop(1981) 7,540, town in Edinburgh City dist, Lothian, E central Scotland; on the S shore of the Firth of Forth, at the S end of the Forth rail and road bridges, W of Edinburgh; formerly linked by ferry to N Queensferry in Fife; railway; Port Edgar yacht harbour; monuments: South Queensferry Museum; to the W of South Queensferry is Hopetoun House: started in 1699, the house was enlarged between 1721 and 1754 by William Adam and his son Robert; further W is the 17th-c House of the Binns.

Queensland, 2nd largest state in Australia; bordered W by Northern Territory, S by New South Wales, SW by South Australia, N by the Gulf of Carpentaria, the Torres Strait and the Coral Sea and E by the South Pacific Ocean; in the N is the Cape York Peninsula; the Great Dividing Range runs N-S, separating a fertile coastal strip to the E from dry plains to the W; the climate is tropical in the N half of the state; on the border with New South Wales is the Scenic Rim mountain range; from Noosa, a point on the coast SE of Gympie, S to Bribie Island, is known as the 'sunshine coast'; this is a major resort area noted for its surfing beaches; the total coastline of Queensland is 5,200 km; pop(1986) 2,675,313; Aboriginals and Torres Strait Islanders account for 2% of the pop, most of the pop is located in the SE; area 1,727,200 sq km; capital Brisbane; principal towns: Gold Coast, Townsville, Ipswich, Toowoomba, Cairns and Rockhampton; the state accounts for 22% of Australia's agricultural production, sugar being the main export crop; wheat, sorghum, tomatoes, citrus fruit are also produced; mineral resources include bauxite (Weipa), coal (Bowen and Moreton basins), copper, zinc, lead and phosphate (Mount Isa), nickel (Greenvale), oil (Moonie), gas (Roma); industries include machinery, chemicals, textiles, food processing, furniture, plastics, rubber products, forest products, paper, motor vehicles; Queensland was established as a penal colony in 1824 and was open to free settlers in 1842 on the foundation of Brisbane; part of New South Wales until 1859; became one of the states of the Commonwealth of Australia in 1901; the state parliament consists of a Legislative Assembly; the Legislative Council was abolished in 1922; there are 134 town and country district councils elected every 3 years; the state is divided into the following 11 statistical divisions:

Statistical division	*area (sq km)*	*pop(1981)*
Brisbane	3,080	1,096,200
Central-West	370,470	14,320
Darling Downs	90,060	168,640
Far North	266,530	140,170
Fitzroy	121,880	145,520
Mackay	68,480	89,760
Moreton	19,280	312,660
North-West	311,770	40,170
Northern	101,030	156,500
South-West	332,520	28,180
Wide Bay-Burnett	52,150	153,080

Quelimane *kel-ee-ma'nay*, 17 53S 36 51E, pop(1980) 60,151, capital of Zambézia prov, N central Mozambique, SE Africa; in Quelimane dist; linked by rail to Mocuba; airfield.

Queluz *kil-oozh'*, 38 45N 9 15W, pop(1981) 46,856, market town in Lisboa dist, central Portugal, 15 km WNW of Lisboa, with a Rococo palace, once the summer residence of the Bragança kings, now used for official government receptions; event: Queluz fair in Sept.

Querétaro *ke-ray'ta-rō*, QUERÉTARO DE ARTEAGA, state in central Mexico; bounded by the states of San Luis Potosí (N and NE), Hidalgo (E, along the San Juan and Moctezuma rivers), México (S), Michoacán (SW) and Guanajuato (W); mountainous region situated mainly in the central plateau; drained by the Querétaro, Moctezuma, Santa María and San Juan rivers; pop(1980) 726,054; area 11,449 sq km; capital Querétaro; economy: barley, wheat, maize, alfalfa, lentils, oats, sorghum, chick-peas, fruit, timber, aviculture, mining (mercury, lead, silver, copper, zinc, marble, opals, bentonite), motor cars, machinery, iron and steel, chemicals, textiles, electronics, food processing, distilling.

Querétaro, 20 38N 100 23W, pop(1980) 293,586, capital of Querétaro state, central Mexico; 200 km NNW of Ciudad de México (Mexico City) at an alt of 1,865 m; university (1618); Hidalgo's rising was plotted here in 1810; Emperor Maximilian surrendered and was shot here in 1867; railway; economy: textiles, opals, mercury; monuments: the church and monastery of Santa Cruz were the headquarters of Maximilian's forces; the museum in the convent of San Francisco contains material relating to the revolution of 1810 and the reign of Emperor Maximilian; event: from the 2nd week in Dec, a *feria agricola* gloas (agricultural fair), with a special market, bullfights and cock-fights.

Quetta *kwet'ta*, 30 15N 67 01E, pop(1981) 285,000, capital of Balúchistán prov, W Pakistan; lies in the Central Brahui range, 590 km N of Karachi; for centuries a strategic location on the trade route between Kandahar, Afghanistan and the Lower Indus valley; its location controls the Bolan Pass and the Khojak Pass; occupied by the British during the First Afghan Wars of 1839-42; acquired by the British in 1876 through treaty with Khan of Kalat and developed into a strong fortress; damaged by earthquake in 1935; airfield; railway; centre of a fruit growing area; linked to Shikarpur by natural gas pipeline in 1982.

Quevedo *kay-vay'THō*, 0 59S 79 27W, pop(1982) 67,023, town in Los Ríos prov, W Ecuador; in the tropical lowlands W of the Andes; the centre of a fertile banana-growing area.

Quezaltenango *ket-sal-te-nan'go*, dept in W Guatemala, Central America; pop(1982e) 447,428; area 1,951 sq km; capital Quezaltenango; chief towns Coatepeque and Colomba; mountainous in the N, sloping down to the coastal plain towards the SW; drained by the Río Samalá; the Inter-American Highway crosses the extreme NE corner.

Quezaltenango, 14 50N 91 30W, pop(1983e) 65,733, capital town of Quezaltenango dept, SW Guatemala, Central America; W of the Río Samalá, surrounded by volcanic peaks; Guatemala's second industrial and trading centre; much of the town is modern having been rebuilt after the earthquakes of 1818 and 1902; has a branch of San Carlos University.

Quezon City *kay'son*, 14 39N 121 01E, pop(1980) 1,165,865, residential city in Capital prov, Philippines; on Luzon I, NE of Manila; laid out in 1940; formerly capital of the Philippines (1948-76); named after the first president, Manuel Luis Quezon (1878-1944); university (1908); event: night procession of La Naval de Manila in Oct, commemorating the Filipino-Spanish naval victory over the Dutch in 1646.

Quibdó *keeb-dō'*, 5 40N 76 40W, pop(1985) 47,898, river-port capital of Chocó dept, W Colombia, South America; a small jungle town on the Río Atraro, 320 km WNW of Bogotá; railway; economy: gold and platinum mining.

Quiché *kee-chay'*, mountainous dept in W central Guatemala, Central America; bounded N by Mexico; pop(1982e) 430,003; area 8,378 sq km; capital Santa Cruz del Quiché; traversed by the Sierra los Cuchumatanes and the Sierra de Chuacús mountain ranges; drained by the Río Grande and Río Chixoy.

Quillacollo *keel-ya-col'yō*, 17 26S 66 16W, pop(1976) 19,419, town in Quillacollo prov, Cochabamba, Bolivia; set in the Cochabamba basin, SW of Cochabamba; nearby is the Balneario Liriuni, thermal baths; railway; event: Sunday market.

Quillota *keel-yō'ta*, 32 53S 71 15W, pop(1982) 52,047, capital of Quillota prov, Valparaíso, central Chile; NE of Valparaíso; railway; centre of a fruit-growing region.

Quilpué *keel-pway'*, 33 05S 71 33W, pop(1982) 62,243, town in Valparaíso prov, Valparaíso, Chile; situated 1.5 km from El Retiro, a popular inland resort with medicinal springs; railway.

Quimper *kî-payr*, QUIMPER CORENTIN *kor-ã-tî*, 48 00N 4 09W, pop(1982) 60,162, manufacturing and commercial capital of Finistère dept, Bretagne region, NW France; on the long estuary of the R Odet, where it meets the R Steir, 179 km W of Rennes; capital of the old countship of Carnouailles; has a long stretch of wide quayside along the R Odet, bordering its central shopping district; has manufactured pottery, called Quimper or Brittany ware, since the 16th century; railway; monuments: 13th-c Gothic cathedral of St-Corentin; former bishop's palace (early 16th-c), now housing a history and folklore museum; event: one of the biggest folk festivals in Europe (3 days at the end of July).

Quina'ra, region in Guinea-Bissau, W Africa; pop(1979) 35,532.

Quincy, 39 56N 91 23W, pop(1980) 42,554, county seat of Adams county, W Illinois, United States; on R Mississippi, 150 km W of Springfield; railway; commercial, industrial and distributing centre in a farming area.

Quincy, 42 15N 71 00W, pop(1980) 84,743, town in Norfolk county, E Massachusetts, United States; on Quincy Bay, 13 km S of Boston; railway; birthplace of John Adams, 2nd president and John Quincy Adams, 6th president of the United States; economy: shipbuilding, foundry products.

Quindío *keen-dee'ō*, dept in W central Colombia, South America; a small dept situated in the Andean Cordillera Central; pop(1985) 375,762; area 1,845 sq km; capital Armenia; a coffee-growing area.

Quintana Roo *keen-tah'na roo*, state in SE Mexico; situated on the E section of the Yucatán peninsula; bounded E and N by the Caribbean, W by the states of Yucatán and Campeche, S by Guatemala and Belize (along the Hondo river); a flat, tree-covered state, rising gently in the W; marshy near the E coast which is indented by bays, the largest of which is the Bahía de Chetumal; the Isla de Cozumel and the resort Isla Mujeres lie in the Caribbean; pop(1980) 209,858; area 50,212 sq km; capital Chetumal; Cancún is a major resort and free port; economy: quality timber (cedar, mahogany, ebony), fishing, salt, lime, cement, tourism; there are several Mayan archaeological sites in the N, the most famous of which is Tulum.

Quito *kee'tō*, 0 14S 78 30W, pop(1982) 866,472, capital of Ecuador and of Pichincha prov in the Andean Sierra of N central Ecuador; surrounded by mountains, Quito is situated in a hollow at the E foot of Pichincha volcano; although within 25 km of the Equator, its altitude (2,850 m) gives it a temperate climate; a pre-Columbian town captured by the Spanish in 1533; Quito formerly gave its name to the Spanish presidency of Quito which became the independent republic of Ecuador in 1830; 3 universities (1769, 1869, 1946); railway; airport (Mariscal Sucre) at 8 km; economy: commerce, mining (clay, sand), drinks, tobacco, meat packing, dairying, fruit and vegetable packing, food processing, animal foodstuffs, textiles, clothing, carpet-making, pharmaceuticals, pesticides, iron and steel, motor vehicles; monuments: modern Quito extends N from the old city; in the Plaza

Independencia are the cathedral (with plaques listing the names of the founders of Quito on its outer walls and the tomb of Sucre inside), the archbishop's palace and the government palace (containing arcades filled with small curio shops in its ground floor); the Parque Alameda contains an observatory, the School of Fine Arts and a monument to Simón Bolívar with a coloured relief map of Ecuador; in the Plaza San Francisco are the church and monastery of San Francisco, the earliest religious foundation in South America, founded in 1535; nearby, the church and monastery of La Merced contains the twin clock to London's Big Ben, built in 1817 by an English firm; the numerous churches in Quito (about 86 in all) contain priceless art treasures; in the centre of the Plaza Santo Domingo is a statue of Sucre; on a hill in the centre of town is a basilica, under construction since 1926; events: Carnival in Feb; 6 Dec (public holiday).

Qunayţirah, El, *koo-nay'tru*, KUNEITRA (Fr), governorate (*mohofazat*) in SW Syria; bounded W by Israel and S by Jordan; pop(1981) 26,258; capital El Qunayţirah; chief towns Nawá and Al Khushnīyah; the land rises in the NW towards the S part of the Jebel esh Sharqi (Anti-Lebanon) range; the Yarmūk river forms its S boundary; occupied by Israel since 1967; cease-fire lines established in 1974.

QwaQwa *kwa'kwa*, national state or non-independent black homeland in South Africa; pop(1985) 181,559; achieved self-governing status in 1974.

R

Raab, RÁBA *ra'bo (Hung)*, river in E Austria and NW Hungary; rises in the Fischbach Alps of Steiermark and flows 256 km E and NE to meet the R Danube at Györ.

Raahe *rah'hay*, BRAHESTAD *brah'has-tad'* (Swed), 64 42N 24 30E, pop(1982) 18,826, town in Oulu prov, W Finland; on the Gulf of Bothnia 77 km SW of Oulu; established by Per Brahe in 1649; the town was rebuilt after a fire in 1810; economy: shipyards, steel, timber exports, light engineering.

Rab *rap*, ARBA (anc), 44 46N 14 44E, island in the Adriatic Sea off the coast of W Hrvatska (Croatia) republic, Yugoslavia; SSE of Rijeka; since the 1950s the island has become a leading resort island with hotel developments at Lopar in the N, Supetarska Daga and Kampor in the NW and Suha Punta; the main village of Rab is on the W coast; the island is also noted for its fruit and wine.

Rabat', 35 53N 14 25E, pop(1983e) 12,121, town in SW central Malta; 10 km SW of Valletta; St Paul lived in a cave here during his three-month stay on the island after his shipwreck in AD 60; monuments: Roman villa and museum of Roman antiquities; St Paul's Grotto; Verdala Castle; St Agatha and St Paul's Catacombs.

Rabat, 34 02N 6 51W, pop(1982) 518,616, capital of Morocco, N Africa; one of Morocco's 4 imperial cities in Rabat-Salé prefecture, 90 km NE of Casablanca at the mouth of the Bou Regreg; originally a 10th-c *ribat* or fortified monastery, Rabat city was founded in the 12th century by Abdu-l-Mumim and became important under the Almohads who named it Ribat el Fath (Ribat of Victory) and built defensive walls; French colonialists established a Residency-General under Marshal Lyautry in 1912; university (1957); railway; airport; economy: textiles, carpets, cement bricks, flour milling; monuments: mausoleum of Mohammed V, first king of independent Morocco; the Hassan Tower; traditional arts museum; 14th-c Chella fortress; archaeological museum.

Rabaul *ra-ba'ool*, 4 13S 152 11E, pop(1980) 14,973, seaport capital town of East New Britain prov, Papua New Guinea, SW Pacific, on the Gazelle peninsula at the NE tip of New Britain; the town was laid out by early German settlers in a regular geometric pattern with broad, tree-lined avenues running parallel to each other; Simpson Harbour is one of the deepest harbours in the world; Lakunai Airport; suffered severe damage by earthquake and eruptions of the volcano Matupi in 1937; it was bombarded many times during the Japanese occupation 1942-45; former capital of the Territory of New Guinea; economy: cocoa and copra production.

Rabnitz *rap'nits*, RÉPCE *rayp'tse* (Hung), river rising in Niederösterreich state, N Austria; flows 60 km SE across the Hungarian frontier NE of Koszeg, then N and E to meet the R Raab at Gydr; length 177 km.

Racibórz *ratch'ee-borsh*, RATIBOR, 50 05N 18 10E, pop(1983) 55,600, industrial town in Katowice voivodship, S Poland; on R Oder (Odra), SW of Katowice near the Czechoslovak frontier; ancient capital of Silesian Piast dukedom; Łężczak Forest swamp nature reserve 7 km N (396 ha); railway; economy: brewing, carbon electrodes, pressure boilers; monuments: 13th-c castle, museum of Silesian art.

Racine *ra-seen'*, 42 44N 87 48W, pop(1980) 85,725, county seat of Racine county, SE Wisconsin, United States; on L Michigan, 37 km S of Milwaukee; railway; economy: machinery and metal products.

Rădăuţi *ra-da-oots'*, 47 49N 25 58E, pop(1983) 26,989, town in Suceava county, N Romania; NW of Iaşi; railway; economy: woodwork, textiles.

Rad'cliffe, 53 34N 2 20W, pop(1981) 27,642, town in Bury borough, Greater Manchester, NW England; on the R Irwell, 4 km SW of Bury; railway; economy: textiles; light engineering.

Radom *ra-dom'*, voivodship in central Poland; bounded to the E and NE by R Wisła (Vistula) and watered by its tributaries, the Pilica and Radomka rivers; pop(1983) 719,000; area 7,294 sq km; capital Radom; chief towns include Kozienice, Zwoleń and Pionki.

Radom, 51 26N 21 10E, pop(1983) 199,000, industrial capital of Radom voivodship, central Poland; S of Warszawa (Warsaw); railway; economy: metal, chemicals, clothing, footwear, cigarettes; monuments: 15-16th-c Bernardine monastery, 19th-c Neo-classical houses in the Market Square, regional museum.

Radom, national park in Sudan, NE Africa; area 12,510 sq km; established in 1980.

Raelingen *ray'ling-un*, 59 56N 10 45E, pop(1980) 12,645, suburb of Oslo, in Akershus county, SE Norway.

Rafaela *ra-fa-e'la*, 31 16S 61 44W, pop(1980) 53,152, industrial and agricultural town in Santa Fe prov, Litoral, E Argentina; NW of Santa Fe; founded in 1881 by Italian settlers; railway.

Rafah *ra'fa*, sub-district of Gaza Strip dist, W Israel.

Ragged Islands, island group in the SW Bahamas, on the S edge of the Great Bahama Bank, SW of Long I; pop(1980) 146; area 36 sq km; consists of a chain of cays stretching approx 112 km N, including Great Ragged I and Little Ragged I.

Ragusa *ra-goo'za*, prov of Sicilia (Sicily), Italy; pop(1981) 274,583; area 1,614 sq km; capital Ragusa.

Ragusa, 36 56N 14 44E, pop(1981) 64,492, capital town of Ragusa prov, SE Sicilia (Sicily), Italy; airfield; railway; economy: tourism, potash mines, asphalt.

Rahimyar Khan *ru-heem'yur KHan*, 30 21N 71 00E, pop(1981) 119,000, city in Punjab prov, Pakistan; 170 km SW of Bahawalpur; railway; economy: soap, trade in grain, cotton.

Rahway, 40 37N 74 16W, pop(1980) 26,723, town in Union county, NE New Jersey, United States; on the R Rahway, 8 km SSW of Elizabeth; railway; economy: chemicals, pharmaceuticals.

Rainier, Mount *ray'nyer*, 46 51N 121 46W, height 4,395 m, dormant volcano in W central Washington, United States; highest point in the Cascade Range and in Washington; situated approx 64 km SE of Tacoma; has the largest single-peak glacier system in the USA; situated in Mount Rainier National Park, area 975 sq km, established in 1899; the best known of the 26 glaciers in the national park are Emmons (8 km long) and Nisqually (approx 6 km long).

Raipur *rī'poor*, 21 16N 81 42E, pop(1981) 339,000, agricultural market centre in Madhya Pradesh state, central India; 265 km E of Nagpur; linked by rail to Nagpur and Jamshedpur; economy: engineering, oilseed, rice.

Raisio *ra-ee'see-o*, 60 30N 22 10E, pop(1982) 18,507, town in Turku-Pori prov, SW Finland; W of Turku, on the 'Seven Churches Route'; established in 1966; railway.

Rajahmundry *rah'ju-mun-dree*, 17 01N 81 52E, pop(1981) 268,000, industrial city and Hindu pilgrimage centre in Andhra Pradesh state, S India; on the Godāvari river, 345 km ESE of Hyderabad; linked by rail to Vishākhapatnam; headquarters of the Godavari Irrigation Works; economy: rice, salt, tobacco, textiles, paper; event: Pushkaram Festival, held here every 12 years.

Rajang', the largest river of Sarawak state, E Malaysia, SE Asia; flows 560 km, descending through gorges to the

NW coastal plain where a delta opens out into the South China Sea beyond Sibu; navigable for 384 km.

Rajasthan *rah'ja-stahn*, state in NW India; pop(1981) 34,102,912; area 342,214 sq km; bounded N by Punjab state, NE by Haryana and Uttar Pradesh states, E by Madhya Pradesh state, S by Gujarat state and W by Pakistan; Rajasthan is divided into 27 administrative districts; capital Jaipur; the state is governed by a 200-member Legislative Assembly; Rajasthan is crossed by numerous rivers, including the Sutlej, Chambal, Kali Sindh, Porwan, Berach, Khari, Kotari, Luni, Banganga, Bandi, Mashi and the Morel; the Thar desert occupies the W of the state on the boundary between Pakistan and India; the Anavalli range of mountains is located to the S; the main agricultural crops are pulses, sugar cane, oilseed and cotton; manufacturing industry produces cotton textiles, cement, glass and sugar; the area has extensive reserves of minerals, particularly rock phosphate; other mineral resources include silver, asbestos, copper, feldspar, limestone and salt; there are airfields at Jaipur and Jodhpur; railway lines of the Indian North Western Network cross the state; the state was formed in 1948 from former principalities of Rajputana; under the States Reorganisation Act of 1956, the state of Ajmer, Abu Taluka of Bombay state and Sunel Tappa of the former state of Madhya Bharat were transferred to Rajasthan, while Sironj of Rajasthan was transferred to the state of Madhya Pradesh.

Rajkot *rahj'kōt*, 22 15N 70 56E, pop(1981) 444,000, city in Gujarat state, W India; 200 km WSW of Ahmadabad on the Kathiawar peninsula; capital of the former princely state of Rajkot; linked to Jamnagar, Ahmadabad and Junagadh by rail; airfield; university (1967); economy: textiles, machine tools, plastics, chemicals, electrical goods and vegetable oils.

Rajshahi *rahj'sha-hee*, region in W Bangladesh; includes Naogaon, Natore, Nowabganj and Rajshahi districts; pop(1981) 5,270,000; area 9,455 sq km; bounded W by West Bengal, India and S by the Ganges river; capital Rajshahi; formerly a division of N Bengal in British India, but partitioned Aug 1947, with two-thirds of the area given to East Pakistan (now Bangladesh).

Rajshahi, formerly RAMPUR BOALIA, 24 24N 88 40E, pop(1981) 253,740, capital of Rajshahi dist and region, W Bangladesh; NW of Pabna, near the Indian frontier; university (1953); railway; economy: vegetable oils, matches and lumber.

Rakahanga *ra'kah-ang-ah*, 10 03S 161 06W, coral atoll of the Cook Is, E Pacific, 1,080 km NW of Rarotonga; area 3.88 sq km; pop(1981) 272; breadfruit and taro are grown as food crops; copra is produced for export.

Rakhine, state in W Burma. See Arakan.

Raleigh *rah'lee*, 35 46N 78 38W, pop(1980) 150,255, capital of state in Wake county, E central North Carolina, United States; 105 km ESE of Greensboro; 2 universities (1865, 1887); railway; airfield; economy: foods, textiles and electrical equipment.

Ramādī, Ar *ar ra-ma'dee*, 33 27N 43 19E, pop(1970) 79,488, capital town of Al-Anbār governorate, W Iraq; on the R Euphrates (Al Furāt), 96 km W of Baghdād.

Ramallah *ra'mal-lu*, sub-district of Judea-Samaria dist, Israel, in the Israeli-occupied West Bank of Jordan.

Ramat Gan *ra-mat' gan'*, 32 04N 34 48E, pop(1982) 118,300, town in Tel Aviv dist, W Israel; 3.2 km E of Tel Aviv-Yafo; established in 1921.

Ramla *ram'le*, sub-district of Central dist, Israel, bounded E by the Israeli-occupied West Bank; pop(1983) 109,658; area 312 sq km.

Rams'gate, 51 20N 1 25E, pop(1981) 37,398, port town in Thanet dist, Kent, SE England; S of Margate on the English Channel; a resort made popular by George IV; railway; hovercraft service to France; monuments: St Augustine's abbey and church; model village; a Celtic cross marks the spot where St Augustine is supposed to have landed with 40 monks in 597 AD.

Ramu *ra'moo*, formerly OTTILIEN, river in NE Papua New Guinea rising in the Kratke range, NW of Lae and flowing about 650 km NW to meet the Bismarck Sea; an important source of hydroelectric power.

Rana, *rah'nah*, 66 11N 13 10E, pop(1980) 25,824, town in Nordland county, N Norway.

Rancagua *ran-kag'wa*, 34 10S 70 45W, pop(1982) 137,773, capital of Cachapoal prov, and Libertador General Bernardo O'Higgins region, central Chile; S of Santiago; scene of a battle fought in 1814 between O'Higgins and the Royalists; railway; economy: agricultural trade; 67 km E is El Teniente, the largest underground copper mine in the world; 37 km S are the thermal springs of Cauquenes and nearby is the hydroelectric plant of Rapel; monuments: Merced church, a national monument; historical museum; local festivals: Festival del Poroto (Bean Festival) during 1-5 Feb; the national rodeo championships are held here at the end of March.

Ranchi *rahn'chee*, 23 19N 85 27E, pop(1981) 503,000, summer capital of Bihar state, E India; 112 km NW of Jamshedpur; a health resort and spa town; university (1960); economy: machine-tools, trade in rice, maize, cotton, oilseed; monument: ruins of an 18th-c Hindu palace.

Rancho Palos Verdes *ran'chō pa'lōs ver'days*, 33 45N 118 21W, pop(1980) 36,577, city in Los Angeles county, SW California, United States; on the Pacific Ocean at Point Vicente, approx 20 km WSW of Long Beach.

Ranco, Lago *rang'kō*, lake in Los Lagos region, S central Chile; 40 km E of La Unión; area 520 sq km; 26 km long; 21 km wide; surrounded by sub-Andean peaks and forests; a noted tourist resort, its outlet is the Río Bueno.

Rand'burg, 26 07S 28 02E, pop(1980) 189,616, municipality in Transvaal prov, NE South Africa; a N suburb of Johannesburg; vintage car museum.

Randers *rah'ners*, 56 28N 10 03E, pop(1983) 61,739, seaport on the R Gudenå where it enters Randers Fjord, 24 km from the Kattegat, Århus county, E Jylland (Jutland), Denmark; railway; economy: engineering; monuments: 15th-c church; 18th-c town hall.

Randers Fjord, inlet of the Kattegat in Århus county, E Jylland (Jutland), Denmark; extends 24 km inland to Randers city, at mouth of R Gudenå.

Randsfjorden, RANDS FJORD *rans* (Eng), elongated lake in S Oppland county, SE Norway; the rivers Dokka and Eina flow into N end of lake; area 145 sq km; length 73 km; depth 108 m.

Randstad, an urban conurbation of settlements in NW Netherlands forming a horse-shoe shape situated around a central agricultural zone; administrative functions are not concentrated in one centre but are distributed over a number of cities; the majority of the population of the Netherlands is concentrated in this area; principal cities include Amsterdam, Rotterdam, Utrecht and the Hague.

Rangitikei *rang-gi-tee'kee*, river in S North Island, New Zealand; rises in central North Island in the Kaimanawa Mts; flows SW to enter the Tasman Sea 40 km SE of Wanganui; length 241 km.

Rangoon *ran-goon'*, division in S Burma; bounded S by the Gulf of Martaban; drained by the Hlaing and Rangoon rivers; in the S of the division is the Rangoon delta; pop(1983) 3,973,782; capital Rangoon.

Rangoon, YANDOON', 16 47N 96 10E, pop(1983) 2,458,712, chief port and capital of Burma; in Rangoon division, S Burma; situated on the R Rangoon which lies to the E of the great Irrawaddy delta; the city has a large Indian and Chinese pop; a town named Dagon existed here as early as the 6th century; university (1920); railway; airport (Mingaladon); economy: oil, timber, rice; monuments: in the centre of the city is the Sule Pagoda, over 2,000 years old; towering over Rangoon is the Shwedagon Pagoda, which rises to a height of 99.4 m; the Botataung Pagoda (over 2,000 years old) overlooks the waterfront; the Colossal Reclining Buddha Image of Chauk-Htat-Gyi Pagoda; the seated Buddha Image of Koe-Htat-Gyi Pagoda; the Kaba Aye (World Peace Pagoda); national museum; natural history museum.

Rangpur *rung'poor*, region in N Bangladesh; includes Gaibandha, Kurigram, Lalmonirhat, Nilphamari and

Rangpur districts; pop(1981) 6,510,000; area 9,595 sq km; bounded W by the R Brahmaputra (Jamuna); a former district of N Bengal, British India prior to the 1947 partition; capital Rangpur.

Rangpur, 25 45N 89 21E, pop(1981) 153,174, capital of Rangpur dist and region, N Bangladesh; 260 km NW of Dhākā, on a tributary of the R Brahmaputra (Jamuna); railway; economy: carpets, tobacco, oilseed, rice, jute, electrical goods, bricks, cutlery.

Rannoch, picturesque loch in Perth and Kinross dist, Tayside, Scotland; W of Loch Tummel and Pitlochry; part of the Rannoch Moor Nature Reserve with remnants of the old Caledonian pine forest S of the Loch.

Rapid City, 44 05N 103 14W, pop(1980) 46,492, county seat of Pennington county, SW South Dakota, United States; in the E part of the Black Hills, 72 km E of Wyoming border; founded in 1876; air force base; railway; airfield; economy: gold, uranium, mica and silver mines (nearby is the nation's largest underground gold mine, the Homestake); monument: nearby is Mt Rushmore, on which the faces of Washington, Lincoln, Jefferson and Theodore Roosevelt are carved.

Raqqah, Ar, *rak'ku*, RAKKA (Fr), governorate (*mohofazat*) in N Syria; bounded N by Turkey; pop(1981) 348,383; capital Ar Raqqah; bisected W-E by the R Euphrates; the Buḩayrat al Asad lake forms part of its W boundary.

Ra'ra, national park in NW Nepal, Central Asia; founded in 1976; covers an area of 106 sq km.

Rarotonga *ra-ro-tong'ah*, 21 15S 159 45W, volcanic island of the Cook Is, S Pacific; area 64.8 sq km; length 9.6 km; largest of the Cook Is; pop(1981) 9,530; rises to 652 m at Te Manga; capital Avarua; airport.

Ra's al Khaymah *ras' al KHĪ'mu*, northernmost of the seven member states of the United Arab Emirates; lying at the foot of the Hajar Mts, bounded W by the Arabian Gulf; area 1,690 sq km; pop(1980) 73,700; capital Ra's al Khaymah; economy: oil production at the Saleh offshore field began in 1984 and since then 3 more wells have been completed; industrial development is largely concentrated at Khor Khuwair where there are 2 large cement plants, a pharmaceutical factory, a limestone quarry, and a white cement plant under construction.

Ra's al Khaymah, PORT SAQR, 25 50N 56 05E, capital town of Ra's al Khaymah emirate, United Arab Emirates, SE Arabian Peninsula; on the Arabian Gulf; airport; economy: water desalination.

Ras Dashan, 13 15N 38 27E, mountain in the Simien range, NE Gonder region, NW Ethiopia, NE Africa; height 4,620 m; the highest point in Ethiopia; first ascent in 1841 by Ferret and Galinier.

Rasht, 37 18N 49 38E, pop(1983) 259,638, capital of Rasht dist, Gīlān, NW Iran; close to the S shore of the Caspian Sea, backed by the Elburz Mts; trade centre for surrounding agricultural region which produces rice, cotton, silk, peanuts; airfield; gas pipeline.

Ratanakiri *rat-tan-a-kee-ri*, province in NW Cambodia; pop(1981) 49,400; bounded E by Vietnam and N by Laos; crossed by the San and Srepok rivers; rises towards the NW of the province; 2 airfields; chief town Lomphat.

Rath'lin Island, island in N Antrim, N Northern Ireland; situated off the N coast, 5 km NW of Fair Head; the island itself is 8 km long, up to 5 km wide, rising to 137 m; area 14.4 sq km; there is a lighthouse in the NE; St Columba founded a church here in the 6th century (later destroyed by Danes); the island contains the ruins of a castle where it is reputed that Robert the Bruce took refuge in 1306 and the incident of the spider and the web took place.

Ratingen *rah'ting-un*, 51 18N 6 50E, pop(1983) 88,300, city in Düsseldorf dist, Nordrhein-Westfalen (North Rhine-Westphalia) prov, W Germany; 10 km N of Düsseldorf; economy: steam generators, boilers, bathroom fittings, textiles.

Ratnapura *rat'ne-poor-a* ('city of gems'), 6 41N 80 25E, pop(1981) 37,497, capital of Ratnapura dist, SW Sabaragamuwa prov, Sri Lanka; 90 km SE of Colombo, in the valley of the Kalu Ganga, between the Sabaragamuwa Highlands and the Central Highlands; gem pits are found throughout the paddy fields surrounding the city; gems found include sapphires, rubies, cat's-eyes, aquamarines, zircons, amethysts and topaz; cutting and polishing is carried out using traditional hand tools; the gem trade is for the most part carried on by the Muslims; nearby is the Buddhist temple of Maha Saman Dewale.

Ratzeburg, lake in W Germany. See Ratzeburger See.

Ratzeburger See *rah'tsub-oor-gur zay*, RATZEBURG LAKE (Eng), elongated lake in SE Schleswig-Holstein prov, W Germany, 10 km SSE of Lübeck; area 14.1 sq km; max depth 24 m; average depth 12 m.

Raub *rowb*, 3 54N 101 47E, pop(1980) 22,907, town in W Pahang state, central Peninsular Malaysia, SE Asia; 119 km N of Kuala Lumpur; a former gold-mining centre.

Rauma *ra-u'mah*, RAUMO *row'moo* (Swed), 61 09N 21 30E, pop(1982) 30,944, seaport on W coast of Turku-Pori prov, SW Finland; on the Gulf of Bothnia, 40 km S of Pori; established in 1442; noted for its pillowlace and its special dialect; economy: marine equipment.

Raven'na, prov of Emilia-Romagna region, N Italy; pop(1981) 358,654; area 1,860 sq km; capital Ravenna.

Ravenna, 44 25N 12 12E, pop(1981) 138,034, capital town of Ravenna prov, Emilia-Romagna region, NE Italy; 8 km from the Adriatic Sea, with which it is connected by the Naviglio Candiano; archbishopric; railway; economy: oil refining, wine-growing in the area; monuments: church of San Vitale (begun in 526) with brilliantly coloured mosaics; mausoleum of Galla Placidia; cathedral, built 1734-44 on the site of the oldest church in Ravenna; 5th-c octagonal Baptistry of the Orthodox church of Sant'Apollinare Nuovo; tomb of Theodoric, built about 520; event: Dante celebrations (mid-Sept).

Ravi *rah'vee*, HYDRAOTES (anc), river in NW India and Pakistan; one of the 5 rivers of the Punjab; source SE Pīr Pānjāl range; flows generally SW across the Pakistan Punjab, past Lahore, to join the R Chenab 53 km NNE of Multan; length 765 km; to the NE of Lahore the Ravi forms part of the border between Pakistan and India.

Rawalpindi *rahw-ul-pin'dee*, 33 40N 73 08E, pop(1981) 806,000, city in Punjab prov, Pakistan; 258 km NNW of Lahore; strategically important location controlling routes to Kashmir; occupied by the British in 1849; prior to partition in 1947 it was India's largest military station and was the Northern Army's headquarters; on 8 Aug 1919, a treaty signed here by which Britain recognized the complete independence of Afghanistan; airfield; economy: oil refining, railway engineering, iron, chemicals, furniture, trade in grain, timber, wool.

Raw'son, TRE RAWSON, 43 15S 65 53W, pop(1980) 12,891, seaport capital of Chubut prov, S central Argentina; near the mouth of the Río Chubut; named after an Argentine Minister of the Interior in the 1860s.

Rayleigh *ray'lee*, 51 36N 0 36E, pop(1981) 28,585, town in Rochford dist, Essex, SE England; 9 km N of Southend-on-Sea; railway; economy: timber, electrical goods, engineering.

Raysūt, 16 56N 54 00E, seaport on the Arabian Sea, Sultanate of Oman, S Arabian peninsula; on a coastal plain backed by mountains; economy: heavy industry.

Raytown, 39 01N 94 28W, pop(1980) 31,759, town in Jackson county, W Missouri, United States; residential suburb 15 km SE of Kansas City; railway.

Raz'grad, okrug (prov) of NE Bulgaria; area 2,646 sq km; pop(1981) 193,000; economy: grain, vegetables, sunflower and timber producing area.

Razgrad, 43 45N 26 30E, agricultural centre and capital of Razgrad okrug (prov), NE Bulgaria; on the R Beli Lom, 375 km NE of Sofiya; monument: 16th-c mosque.

Ré, Ile de *eel de ray*, island in the NE Bay of Biscay off the W coast of Charente-Maritime dept, W France; separated from La Rochelle on the mainland by the Pertuis Breton; area 85 sq km; 28 km long by 5 km wide; chief towns are St Martin, the old fortified port, and La Flotte; the terrain is flat with vineyards, beaches and market-gardens (famous for asparagus); the Phare des Baleines is a lighthouse at the NW tip of the island; there are frequent car ferries from La Pallice.

Reading *red'ing*, 51 28N 0 59W, pop(1981) 133,540, county town of Berkshire, S England; at the junction of the Kennet and Thames rivers, 63 km W of London; a centre of the textile industry in medieval times; railway; university (1926); economy: brewing, boatbuilding, food processing, metal products, engineering, printing; monuments: 12th-c Clunaic abbey, burial place of Henry I; museum of English rural life (1951); museum of Greek archaeology.

Reading, 40 20N 75 56W, pop(1980) 78,686, county seat of Berks county, SE Pennsylvania, United States; on R Schuylkill, 80 km NW of Philadelphia; railway; airfield.

Recife *re-see'fay*, 8 06S 34 53W, pop(1980) 1,183,391, port capital of Pernambuco state, Nordeste region, NE Brazil; at the mouth of the Río Capibaribe; most important commercial and industrial city in the NE; 2 universities (1951, 1954); railway; airport (Guararapes) at 12 km; the town consists of 3 portions: Recife proper, on a peninsula, Santo Antônio, on an island between the peninsula and the mainland, and Boa Vista on the mainland; the 3 districts are connected by bridges; the first Brazilian printing house was installed here in 1706; Recife claims to publish the oldest daily newspaper in South America, the *Diário de Pernambuco*, founded in 1825; monuments: São Francisco de Assisi Church, built in 1612; Conceição dos Militares, a church built in 1708, contains a large 18th-c mural of the battle of Guararapes; S of the city on Guararapes Hill is the church of Nossa Senhora das Prazeres, it was here in 1654 that the Brazilians finally ended the Dutch occupation of the NE; Fort Brum was built in 1629 by the Dutch; the fort of Conco Pontas, built by the Portuguese in 1677, houses a museum of cartographic history of the settlement of Recife; the municipal prison has been converted into the Casa da Cultura; the Museu do Açúcar contains models of colonial sugar mills, devices for torturing slaves and collections of antique sugar bowls; events: 16 July (Nossa Senhora do Carmo, patron saint of the city), 8 Dec (Nossa Senhora da Conceição).

Reck'linghausen, 51 37N 7 11E, pop(1983) 119,100, industrial and commercial city in Münster dist, Nordrhein-Westfalen (North Rhine-Westphalia) prov, W Germany; between the rivers Emscher and Lippe, 36 km SW of Münster; railway; the economy is based mainly on coal mining; event: Ruhr Festival (June-July).

Red Basin, fertile basin in Sichuan prov, S central China. See Sichuan Pendi.

Red Deer, 52 15N 113 48W, pop(1984) 51,070, town in S central Alberta, W central Canada; on the Red Deer river; 145 km S of Edmonton; Fort Normandeau was built here on the Red Deer river in 1885 during the North West rebellion; a settlement was established at Red Deer in 1884; railway; economy: agricultural trade, petroleum, petrochemicals.

Red River, river in S USA; southernmost large tributary of the Mississippi river; rises in N Texas in the Llano Estacado; flows SE and E, forming the Texas-Oklahoma and Texas-Arkansas borders; the Red river then flows SSE across Arkansas, past Shreveport and Alexandria to a point approx 72 km NNW of Baton Rouge, where it enters 2 distributaries, the Atchafalaya river which flows S to the Gulf of Mexico and the Old river, a channel which continues approx 11 km SE to join the Mississippi; length 1,966 km; major tributaries: the Pease, Wichita, Washita, Little and Black rivers; used for flood-control, irrigation and hydroelectricity.

Red River, YUAN JIANG (Chin), Hong (Viet), river rising in central Yunnan prov, China, SW of Kunming; flows SE into Vietnam near Lao Cai, past Hanoi to meet the Gulf of Tongking 32 km E of Haiphong; length approx 800 km.

Red Sea, SINUS ARABICUS (Lat), NNW arm of the Indian Ocean, lying between the Arabian Peninsula and the African countries of Egypt, Sudan and Ethiopia; connected to the Gulf of Aden by the Strait of Bāb al Mandab and to the Mediterranean Sea by the Suez Canal; divided into the Gulf of Suez and the Gulf of 'Aqaba by the Sinai Peninsula at its NW tip; a narrow sea up to 362 km wide, 2,335 km long and covering an area of approx 440,300 sq km; numerous islands are dispersed throughout the sea, while coral reefs lie parallel to the E and W shores; high salinity as a result of excessive evaporation, little freshwater input and a narrow exit into the Gulf of Aden of only 21 km; max depths of 1,200 fathoms are found near the centre, while the average depth is only 475 fathoms; the Red Sea occupies the rift valley which stretches S into the African continent; its name is probably derived from the reddish masses of the seaweed *Trichodesmium*; its importance as a trade route declined with the discovery of a sea-route around Cape of Good Hope, Africa, but the opening of the Suez Canal in 1869 made the sea once again a major trade route between Europe, the Far East and Australia; the closing of the canal after the 1967 Arab-Israeli war, the building of pipelines to the Mediterranean and the construction of massive sea-going tankers has since led to a decline in its importance as an oil trade route.

Redange *ray-dãzh'*, canton in SW part of Diekirch dist, W Luxembourg; area 268 sq km; pop(1981) 10,271; bisected in the S by the R Attert and bounded to the N by the R Sûre; on the W frontier with Belgium; the only gliding airfield in Luxembourg is at Useldange (Cercle Luxembourgeois de Vol à Voile).

Redange, 49 46N 5 53E, pop(1981) 830, capital of Redange canton, Diekirch dist, W Luxembourg; on the R Attert; a resort town in the centre of densely wooded agricultural country.

Redbridge, 51 35N 0 05E, pop(1981) 228,542, mainly residential borough of NE Greater London, England; N of the R Thames; includes the suburbs of Ilford, Chigwell, Wanstead and Woodford; also includes part of Epping Forest; railway.

Red'car, 54 37N 1 04W, pop(1981) 35,392, resort town in Langbaurgh dist, Cleveland, NE England; on North Sea, 12 km NE of Middlesbrough; racecourse; railway; economy: mining, engineering.

Redcliff, 19 00S 29 49E, pop(1982) 22,000, town in Midlands prov, Zimbabwe, S Africa; between Que Que and Gweru; railway; centre of the country's iron and steel industry.

Redcliffe, 27 12S 153 03E, pop(1981e) 44,030, city in Brisbane stat div, Queensland, Australia; 35 km N of Brisbane on the E coast; railway; economy: tourism.

Redding, 40 35N 122 24W, pop(1980) 41,995, capital of Shasta county, N California, United States; on the Sacramento river near the N end of the Central Valley, 274 km NNW of Sacramento; railway; airport, Shasta Dam and reservoir are just N of Redding, with Shasta-Trinity National Recreation Area.

Red'ditch, 52 19N 1 56W, pop(1981) 61,875, town in Redditch dist, Hereford and Worcester, W central England; 20 km SW of Birmingham; railway, economy: metal goods, batteries, aerospace components.

Redlands, 34 04N 117 11W, pop(1980) 43,619, city in San Bernardino county, S California, United States; in the San Bernardino Valley, 97 km E of Los Angeles; university (1907).

Redondela *ray-don-day'la*, 42 15N 8 38W, pop(1981) 27,202, port on the Atlantic coast of Pontevedra prov, Galicia, NW Spain; on Vigo Bay, 15 km NE of Vigo; railway; economy: linen, china, reed and cane work, tools, drinks.

Redondo Beach, 33 50N 118 23W, pop(1980) 57,102, resort city in Los Angeles county, SW California, United States; on the Pacific Ocean, 21 km S of Santa Monica.

Redruth, town in Cornwall, SW England. See Camborne.

Redwood, national park in N California, United States; at the W foot of the Klamath Mts, on the Pacific coast; protects the Coast Redwood trees (*Sequoia sempervirens*) which are amongst the tallest in the world; established in 1968; area 228 sq km.

Redwood City, 37 30N 122 15W, pop(1980) 54,951, capital

of San Mateo county, W California, United States; 40 km SSE of San Francisco; railway; connected with San Francisco Bay to the E by a deep-water channel.

Ree, Lough, lake in Roscommon, Longford and Westmeath counties, central Irish Republic; formed by a widening of R Shannon; length 25 km; Athlone is at the S end.

Regensburg *ray'genz-boorKH*, Ratisbon (Fr), CASTRA REGINA (anc), 49 01N 12 07E, pop(1983) 132,000, commercial city in Oberpfalz dist, Bayern (Bavaria) prov, W Germany; at the most northerly point in the course of the R Danube, 104 km NNE of München (Munich); a well-preserved medieval city; bishopric; university (1962); railway; river harbour with passenger services to Walhalla, Kelheim-Weltenburg and Passau; economy: electrical engineering, chemicals, clothing, sugar refining, carpet-making, river craft, construction, brewing; monuments: cathedral (13-16th-c), Old Town Hall, Benedictine monastery of St Emmeram (7th-c).

Reggio di Calabria *red'jō dee ka-la'bri-a*, prov of Calabria region, S Italy; pop(1981) 573,093; area 3,183 sq km; capital Reggio di Calabria.

Reggio di Calabria, 38 06N 15 39E, pop(1981) 173,486, seaport and capital of Reggio di Calabria prov, Calabria region, S Italy; on the E side of the Strait of Messina; archbishopric; airfield; railway; ferry to Sicilia; economy: prime producer of oil of bergamot.

Reggio nell'Emilia *red'jō nel-lay-mee'li-a*, prov of Emilia-Romagna region, Italy; pop(1981) 413,396; area 2,292 sq km; capital Reggio nell'Emilia.

Reggio nell'Emilia, 44 42N 10 37E, pop(1981) 130,376, capital town of Reggio nell'Emilia prov, Emilia-Romagna region, N Italy; on the Via Emilia, at the S edge of the N Italian plain; railway; economy: wine, cement, engineering; monuments: 13th-c cathedral, Baroque church of the Madonna della Chiaira (1597-1619).

Reghin *reg-heen'*, 46 46N 24 41E, pop(1983) 34,816, town in Mureş county, N central Romania; on R Mureş, NE of Tîrgu-Mureş; railway; economy: wine, fruit, livestock trade, fertilizer, furniture.

Regina *re-jī'na*, 50 30N 104 38W, pop(1981) 162,613, capital of Saskatchewan prov, Canada; in S Saskatchewan, S central Canada; on Moosejaw Creek; founded in 1882 as the capital of Northwest Territories and named in honour of Queen Victoria; in 1883 it became the headquarters of the North West Mounted Police; made capital of Saskatchewan when the prov was created in 1905; the town grew as the centre of a grain-growing region, and now continues to expand as the centre of a region containing reserves of potash and oil; railway; airport; economy: grain trade, oil refining, steel, engineering, meat processing, canning; monuments: the Royal Canadian Mounted Police Museum features a chronological history of the police since their foundation in 1873; the Legislative Buildings, built between 1908 and 1912, are situated in Wascana Park, a large park in the S of the city which also contains Wascana Lake, the Diefenbaker Homestead (boyhood home of John G. Diefenbaker, Canada's 13th prime minister), the Saskatchewan Centre of Arts and the Museum of Natural History; events: Buffalo Days, a pioneer celebration with horse races, bands and concerts, agricultural and industrial exhibits (July); the Canadian Western Agribition, with livestock shows and sales (autumn).

Rehovot *re-hō-vōt'*, sub-district of Central dist, W Israel; pop(1983) 233,120; area 298 sq km.

Reichenau *rī'KHen-ow*, island in the Untersee, a part of the Bodensee (L Constance), Baden-Württemberg prov, W Germany, 6 km W of Konstanz; connected with the shore by a 1.6 km long causeway; area 4.4 sq km.

Reigate *rī'gayt*, 51 14N 0 13W, pop(1981) 48,913, town linked with Redhill in Reigate and Banstead dist, Surrey, SE England; below N Downs, 15 km N of Crawley; railway; monuments: church of St Mary Magdalene, burial place of Lord Howard of Effingham (1536-1624), who led the English fleet against the Spanish Armada in 1588.

Reims *rīs*, RHEIMS *reemz* (Eng), DUROCORTORUM (anc), later REMI, 49 15N 4 02E, pop(1982) 181,985, historic town in Marne dept, Champagne-Ardenne region, NE France; on the right bank of the R Vesle, in low-lying country under the vine-clad Montagne de Reims, 133 km ENE of Paris; a bishopric since the 4th century, now an archbishopric; the textile industry, dating from Roman times, is the oldest industry in Reims; once the place where the French kings were crowned; Reims suffered extensive damage in World War I, including the partial destruction of the cathedral (restoration took place in 1927-38); scene of the signature of unconditional German surrender on 7 May, 1945; university (1967); road and rail junction; a port on the Aisne-Marne Canal; economy: textiles, champagne, chemicals, metallurgy, building, wholesale grocery (supplying supermarkets all over France), modern stained-glass workshops; monuments: 13th-c Gothic cathedral, one of the greatest Gothic structures ever built; early 11th-c church of St-Rémi, the oldest church in Reims (largely Romanesque); Roman remains including the Porte de Mars (2nd-c AD), which served as a town gate until 1544; as a major wine-producing centre (especially champagne), there is an extensive network of storage caves beneath the city and in the vicinity; the Musée St-Denis, noted for its fine art, is especially rich in French paintings from the 17th century to the present day.

Reindeer, lake in NE Saskatchewan and NW Manitoba provs, central Canada; SE of L Athabasca; 241 km long by 48 km wide; area 6,651 sq km; drained S by Reindeer river into the Churchill river.

Remich *ray'miKH*, canton in S part of Grevenmacher dist, SE Luxembourg; area 128 sq km; pop(1981) 11,790; important wine-growing area; the R Moselle forms the E frontier with W Germany here.

Remich, 49 32N 6 23E, pop(1981) 2,400, tourist town and capital of Remich canton, Grevenmacher dist, SE Luxembourg; on the R Moselle and on the European highway from Sarrbrücken to Luxembourg, 23 km SE of Luxembourg; seat of the State Viticulture Institute and National Wine Mark; boat trips on the river.

Remscheid *rem'shīt*, 51 10N 7 11E, pop(1983) 125,500, manufacturing city in Düsseldorf dist, Nordrhein-Westfalen (North Rhine-Westphalia) prov, W Germany; near the R Wuppe, 40 km ESE of Düsseldorf; economy: hardware, textile machinery, hydraulic and electronic equipment.

Renaix, town in Belgium. See Ronse.

Renfrew, 55 53N 4 24W, pop(1981) 21,458, town in Renfrew dist, Strathclyde, W central Scotland; in Clydeside urban area, on the S side of the R Clyde, 9 km W of Glasgow; economy: electronics and engineering.

Rennes *ren*, ROAZON (Bret), CONDATE (anc), 48 07N 1 41W, pop(1982) 200,390, industrial and commercial city and capital of Ille-et-Vilaine dept, Bretagne region, NW France; at the confluence of the canalised Ille and Vilaine rivers, 309 km WSW of Paris; became the capital of Brittany in the 10th century, and is now its economic and cultural centre; almost entirely a modern city, owing to rebuilding after a great fire in 1720 which damaged most of the old town, and widespread bombing during World War II; archbishopric; university (founded at Nantes in 1461, transferred to Rennes in 1735); road and rail junction; airport; economy: oil-refining, chemicals, electronics (in the highly industrialized suburbs of the SW), the Rennes-La Janais Citroën car works; monuments: Baroque town hall (1734); Palais de Justice (formerly the Parliament of Brittany, 1618-1655); former abbey church of Notre-Dame (11-13th-c); cathedral (almost completely rebuilt in the 19th century); La Porte Mordelaise, all that remains of the 15th-c ramparts; in the part of Old Rennes which survived the great fire, there are cobbled streets and some half-timbered houses with overhangs, dating from the 15th and 16th centuries; to the E of the town are the famous Thabor Gardens covering 0.1 sq km.

Reno *ray'no*, river in N central Italy; rises in the Appno Tosco-Emilliano 13 km NW of Pistoia; flows N then ESE past Argenta to discharge into the Adriatic Sea 21 km NNE of Ravenna; length 210 km; tributaries Idice, Sillaro, Santerno, and Senio rivers.

Reno *ree'nō*, 39 31N 119 48W, pop(1980) 100,756, county seat of Washoe county, W Nevada, United States; on the R Truckee, 42 km N of Carson City; settled in 1859, Reno developed with the arrival of the railway in 1868; the city is named after General J.L. Reno, killed at South Mountain in 1862; university (1874); railway; airport; noted for its casinos; couples wanting a quick divorce drive across the Californian border to Reno; events: Reno Rodeo (June), National Air Races (Sept).

Rentería *ren-tay-ree'a*, 43 19N 1 54W, pop(1981) 45,789, industrial town in Guipúzcoa prov, Pais Vasco (Basque Country), N Spain; 8 km E of San Sebastian; economy: foundries, textiles, food processing; monument: church of Christ of Lezo nearby.

Renton, 47 29N 122 12W, pop(1980) 30,612, city in King county, W central Washington, United States; on the Cedar river, just SSE of Seattle; railway.

Réo *ray'o*, 12 18N 2 37W, town in W central Burkina, W Africa; NE of Koudougou.

Resistencia *res-ees-ten'sya*, 27 28S 59 00W, pop(1980) 218,438, agricultural, commercial and industrial capital of Chaco prov, Litoral, N Argentina; on the Río Barranqueras; railway; airport (at 8 km).

Reşiţa *re'sheet-sa*, 45 16N 21 55E, pop(1983) 104,902, capital of Caraş-Severin county, W Romania; in W foothills of Transylvanian Alps; railway; iron foundries opened in 1770s; economy: metallurgy, steel, coal and iron mining, heavy equipment, marine diesel engines, food processing.

Retalhuleu *ret-a-loo-le'oo*, maritime dept in SW Guatemala, Central America; bounded S by the Pacific Ocean; pop(1982e) 206,543; area 1,858 sq km; capital Retalhuleu; chief port Champerico; the land rises inland away from the coastal plain; drained by the Río Samalá; economy: cotton is grown on the coastal plain and, further inland, there is a zone of commercial agriculture (sugar cane, corn, cotton, cocoa, bananas, coffee, and beef).

Retalhuleu, 14 31N 91 40W, capital town of Retalhuleu dept, SW Guatemala, Central America; W of the Río Samalá; on the Pacific Highway; railway; airfield; it serves a large number of coffee and sugar estates; event: fiesta (6-12 Dec).

Ret'ezat, national park in the W Transylvanian Alps (Carpatii Meridionali) of SW central Romania, extending to 130 sq km, established in 1935.

Réthimnon *reth'im-non*, RETHYMNON (Eng), RETIMO (Ital), agricultural nome (dept) of Kríti island (Crete), S Greece; pop(1981) 62,634; area 1,496 sq km; capital Réthimnon.

Réthimnon, 35 18N 24 30E, pop(1981) 17,736, capital town of Réthimnon nome (dept), Kríti region (Crete), S Greece; on the N coast of Kríti I, between Iráklion and Khaniá; the island's 3rd largest town; economy: trade in wine, cereals and olive oil; events: Cretan Wine Festival (July); commemoration of Arkádi Monastery (8 Oct).

Rethymnon, nome (dept) and town in Kríti region, Greece. See Réthimnon.

Réunion *ray-oon-yon'*, formerly BOURBON, island of the Archipel des Mascareignes (Mascerenes Is) in the Indian Ocean, 690 km E of Madagascar; pop(1982) 517,000; area 2,512 sq km; timezone GMT +4; capital St Denis; Réunion was established as a French penal colony in 1638 and became a post of the French East India Company in 1665; coffee was the main export during the 18th century but after 1815, when it could not be grown competitively, it was replaced by sugar cane; in 1946 its status was altered to that of an overseas department; in 1973 Réunion became part of an administrative region; Réunion also administers the uninhabited small islands of Juan de Nova, Europa, Bassas da India, Îles Glorieuses and Tromelin, occupying an area of about 60 sq km in various parts of the Indian Ocean; these islands remained under French control after the independence of Madagascar in 1960; Réunion is divided into the 4 *arrondissements* of St Denis, St Benoit, St Pierre and St Paul which are divided into 24 communes and 36 cantons; the island is composed of one active and several extinct volcanoes, rising to Le Piton des Neiges at 3,071 m; Le Bory was last active in 1791 and Le Dolomieu still is active; about 885 sq km of the island is under forest; most settlements and cultivation are to be found on the coastal lowlands; tourism is concentrated around the beaches of Boucan-Canot, Les Roches Noires, L'Hermitage, La Saline, St Leu, Étang-Salé and St Pierre on the the W coast; between Nov and May the average water temp is about 18°C and from May till the end of Oct about 24°C; in 1982 St Denis and St Gilles were classified as health resorts; the region is governed by a Commissioner, an elected *Conseil Général* of 36 members and an elected regional council of 45 members; airport (St Denis-Gillot); freight and passenger port at Pointe-des-Galets; economy: sugar, rum, maize, potatoes, tobacco, vanilla.

Reus *ray'oos*, 41 10N 1 05E, pop(1981) 79,245, industrial and commercial city in Tarragona prov, Cataluña, NE Spain; at the foot of the Sierra de la Musara, 10 km WNW of Tarragona; birthplace of the Catalan architect Antonio Gaudi (1852-1926); airport; railway; economy: textiles, market for flowers, dried fruit and poultry; commercial development began about 1750 after the establishment of an English colony; monument: 13th-c Gothic church of St Peter.

Reutlingen *royt'ling-en*, 48 30N 9 13E, pop(1983) 96,100, city in Baden-Württemberg prov, W Germany; on the NW slope of the Schwäbische Alb, 30 km S of Stuttgart; railway; economy: textiles, engineering, wood products, leatherwork; monument: St Mary's church (13-14th-c).

Revere *re-veer'*, 42 25N 71 01W, pop(1980) 42,423, resort town in Suffolk county, E Massachusetts, United States; on Massachusetts Bay, 8 km NE of Boston; railway; economy: tourism, chemicals, electrical goods.

Rey, el *el ray'*, national park in E Salta prov, Argentina; ENE of Salta; area 442 sq km; established in 1948.

Reykjavík *ray-kyah-veek'*, 64 09N 21 58W, pop(1983) 87,309, capital of Iceland; on the Faxaflói (Faxa Bay), SW Iceland; chief port and commercial centre of Iceland; most northerly capital of the world; founded by Ingólfur Arnarson in 874 AD; chartered in 1786; made seat of Danish administration in 1801; capital of Iceland since 1918; seat of Icelandic parliament; Lutheran bishopric; university (1911); the city's heating system uses nearby hot springs; airport (Keflavík); meeting place of US and USSR leaders in Oct 1986 to discuss arms control; economy: commerce, fishing, fish processing; monuments: national museum, Árbæjarsafn open air museum, founded in 1957.

Reynosa *ray-nō'sa*, 26 04N 98 17W, pop(1980) 211,412, town in Tamaulipas state, NE Mexico; 147 km SE of Nuevo Laredo, on the Río Grande where it follows the US frontier; railway.

Reza'iyeh, Iran. See Orūmīyeh.

Rhätikon *ray'ti-kon*, mountain range of the Eastern or Rhaetian Alps on the frontier between Austria, Switzerland and Liechtenstein, rising to 2,965 m at Schesaplana; excellent skiing terrain.

Rhein, river in Europe. See Rhine.

Rheine *rī'nu*, 52 17N 7 26E, pop(1983) 71,200, city in Münster dist, N Nordrhein-Westfalen (North Rhine-Westphalia) prov, W Germany; on the R Ems, 40 km NNW of Münster; railway; economy: textiles, machinery.

Rheinhessen-Pfalz *rīn'he-sun falts*, dist in SE Rheinland-Pfalz (Rhineland-Palatinate) prov, W Germany; pop(1983) 1,804,000; area 6,830 sq km; capital Mainz.

Rheinisches Schiefergebirge *rī'ni-shus shee'fur-gub-ir-gu*, RHENISH SLATE MTS (Eng), extensive plateau of W Germany; dissected by the Rhine and its tributaries, generally located between the Belgian border (W), the Lahn river (E), Bingen (S) and Bonn (N); includes the Eifel (NW), the Hunsrück (SW), the Taunus (SE), the Westerwald (N) and the Rothaargebirge (NE) ranges; highest peak is the Großer Feldberg (879 m) of the

Taunus; consists primarily of folded Devonian slate, and some sandstone.

Rheinland-Pfalz *rīn'lahnt-falts*, RHINELAND-PALATINATE (Eng), prov of W Germany; comprises the three administrative dists of Koblenz, Trier and Rhienhessen-Pfalz; pop(1983) 3,633,500; area 19,848 sq km; drained by the R Rhine and its left bank tributaries (Moselle, Nahe and Speyer); mountain ranges include the Westerwald (NE), Eifel (NW) and the Hunsrück (S); capital Mainz; chief towns Koblenz, Trier and Ludwigshafen; one of the most popular tourist attractions is the Rhine valley between Bingen and Koblenz, where the river has cut deeply through the Rheinisches Schiefergebirge (Rhenish Slate Mts); well-known tourist centres include Neustadt, focal point of the Palatinate wine trade and noted for its 'German Wine Harvest Festival', and Bad Durkheim, famous for its Sausage Fair and Germany's largest wine festival.

Rhenish Slate Mts, mountain range in W Germany. See Rheinisches Schiefergebirge.

Rhine *rīn*, RHEIN *rīn'u* (Ger), RIJN *rīn* (Du), RHIN *rẽ* (Fr), RHENUS (anc), river in central and W Europe, rising in SE Switzerland, in the Rheinwaldhorn glacier; flows N, adjoining Leichtenstein and Austria, to Lake Constance, continuing W and then N, forming part of the France-W Germany border, N through both scenic and highly industrialized regions of W Germany; divides into its main distributory rivers, Lek and Waal, and numerous branches, entering the North Sea through the large delta region of the Netherlands; length 1,320 km; main waterway of western Europe with Rhine-Main-Danube and Rhine-Rhone canal links; major cities on its banks are Basel, Mainz, Bonn, Köln (Cologne), Dusseldorf; main tributaries Ruhr, Main, Moselle, Neckar; flows through a flat-floored valley, 32 km wide, below Basel, and a deep and scenic gorge for 145 km between Bingen and Bonn.

Rhineland-Palatinate, prov of W Germany. See Rheinland-Pfalz.

Rhine-Westphalia, North, prov of W Germany. See Nordrhein-Westfalen.

Rhode Island, a New England state in NE United States, bounded N and E by Massachusetts, S by the Atlantic Ocean and W by Connecticut; 'Little Rhody' or the 'Ocean State'; pop(1980) 947,154; area 2,743 sq km; the smallest US state; one of the original states, 13th to ratify the Federal Constitution; capital Providence; major cities include Warwick, Cranston and Pawtucket; rises from the Narragansett Basin in the E to flat and rolling uplands in the W; the highest point is Jerimoth Hill (247 m); economy: textiles, electronics, silverware, jewellery, potatoes, apples, corn; Rhode Island gave protection to Quakers in 1657 and to Jews from the Netherlands in 1658; the state is divided into 5 counties as follows:

County	*area (sq km)*	*pop(1980)*
Bristol	68	46,942
Kent	447	154,163
Newport	278	81,383
Providence	1,082	571,349
Washington	866	93,317

Rhodes, town and island in Greece. See Ródhos.

Rhodesia, Northern. See Zambia.

Rhodesia, Southern. See Zimbabwe.

Rhodope, nome (dept) of Thráki region, Greece. See Rodhópi.

Rhodope Mts *ro-du-pee'*, RHODOPI PLANINA *ro-tho'pee pla'nee-na* or DESPOTO PLANINA *des-pa-tō'* (Bulg), RODOPI (Gr), range of mts in SW Bulgaria and NE Greece rising to 2,925 m at Musala; includes the Sredni Rodopi, Iztochni Rodopi, Rila Planina, Pirin Planina and the Zapadni Rodopi; the 290 km range of mts stretching NW-SE is a major climatic divide between the continental climate of central Bulgaria and the Mediterranean climate of the Aegean; the larger part of Bulgarian forestry is located here.

Rhön Mts *run*, upland region extending 56 km along the borders of Bayern (Bavaria) and Hessen (Hesse) provs, W Germany; main range is the Hohe Rhön (SE); highest peak is the Wasserkuppe (959 m).

Rhondda *hron'THa*, YSTRADYFODWG (Welsh), 51 40N 3 30W, pop(1981) 71,611, mining dist, Mid Glamorgan, S Wales; extends along the Rhondda Fawr and Rhondda Fach valleys; railway; economy: coal mining, engineering.

Rhône *ron*, RHONE (Eng) river in C and SW Europe, rising in the Rhône glacier in NE Valais, S Switzerland, across the Fukra pass from the sources of the Rhine, and flowing 870 km W to Lyon and S to its delta on the Mediterranean; in Switzerland it flows through Valais and SE Vaud before entering the E of L of Geneva; from the SW end, it cuts a gorge between the Jura and the Alps; at Lyon it is joined by its largest tributary, the Saône, from the N, and from Lyon it flows S past Vienne, Avignon, and Arles, where it splits into the Grand and the Petit Rhône to the E and W respectively (the Bouches-du-Rhône, 'mouths of the Rhône'), watering the Cran and the Camargue; the valley with that of the Saône forms an important routeway and is renowned for its scenery; the Ain, Ardèche, and Gard join the Rhône from the right, and the Arve, Isère, Drôme, and Durance from the left; it has extensive hydroelectric works and also provides much irrigation. Near its source the Rhône is a turbulent Alpine torrent, and still flows violently in the *cluses* or gorges of the Jura; even below Lyon the current is too strong to allow much navigation; and the spring spates of the Alpine and Cevennes tributaries can cause dangerous rises.

Rhône, dept in Rhône-Alpes region of E France, partly bounded on the E by the R Saône; comprises 2 arrond, 47 cantons and 293 communes; pop(1982) 1,445,208; area 3,215 sq km; in Lyonnais, and includes Beaujolais, whose mountains run up it S-N and form part of the steep E edge of the Central Plateau; noted for its wines which include Châteauneuf du Pape, Clairette de Die, Côtes du Rhône, Crozes-Hermitage, Gigondas and Tavel; capital Lyon, chief towns Villefranche and Tarare; spa at Charbonnières-les-Bains.

Rhône-Alpes, region of E France comprising the depts of Ain, Ardèche, Drôme, Isère, Loire, Rhône, Savoie and Haute-Savoie, 25 arrond, 312 cantons and 2,874 communes; pop(1982) 5,015,947; area 43,698 sq km; drained by the Saône, Iseŕe and Ain rivers; the Beaujolais vineyards occupy a narrow belt on the right bank of the Saône R, from just S of Mâcon to the outskirts of Lyon; the N part of this area contains the notable wine-producing villages of St-Amour, Julienos, Chenas and Fleurie; the 'Route du Beaujolais' is clearly signposted; Lyon is the 2nd largest conurbation in France after Paris; other industrial towns include Romans-sur-Isère and St-Étienne.

Rhosllanerchrugog *rōs-hla'nerKH-ree'gog*, 53 01N 3 04W, pop(1981) 11,114, town S of Wrexham in Wrexham Maelor dist, Clwyd, NE Wales.

Rhyl *ril*, 53 19N 3 29W, pop(1981) 23,318, resort town in Rhuddlan dist, Clwyd, NE Wales; in Abergele-Rhyl-Prestatyn urban area; at mouth of the Clwyd; railway; economy: furniture, tourism.

Rialto *ree-al'tō*, 34 06N 117 22W, pop(1980) 37,474, city in San Bernardino county, S California, United States; to the W of San Bernardino; railway.

Riau *ree'ow*, province on the island of Sumatera, Indonesia; bounded W by Sumatera Barat prov (W Sumatra), E by the Strait of Malacca, S by Jambi prov and N by Sumatera Utara prov (N Sumatra); the prov also includes over 1,000 islands in the Strait of Malacca and off the SE tip of the Malay Peninsula, formerly part of the Sultanate of Johore; pop(1980) 2,168,535; area 94,562 sq km; capital Pekanbaru; ethnic groups include the Sakai, Akik, Laut, Hutan, Baruk, Mantang, Talang; Mamak the modern Indonesian language originated here; economy: fishing, timber, rubber, tea, sisal, copra, pepper, rice, palm oil, tobacco, bauxite, tin, oil.

Ribatejo *ree-ba-tay'zhoo*, prov in central Portugal formed in 1936 from the former Estremadura region, includes most of Santarém dist comprising the fertile alluvial basin of the lower R Tagus valley; area 600 sq km; the dry upland region to the N is densely populated and intensively farmed by smallholders who produce wheat, olives, wine, figs and citrus fruit, while the S is more sparsely populated, like the Alentejo, with large farms producing monocultures of wheat, olives or cork-oak; for 50 km along the R Tagus seasonally flooded water meadows provide ideal land on which to grow rice and grain as well as to graze horses and the famous Ribatejo fighting bulls.

Rib'ble, river rising in the Pennine Hills of North Yorkshire, N England; flows 120 km S and SW past Preston to meet the Irish Sea in a broad estuary.

Ribe *ree'be*, RIPEN (Ger), county of SW Jylland (Jutland), Denmark; area 3,131 sq km; pop(1983) 214,700; capital Ribe, chief towns include Varde, Grindsted and Esbjerg.

Ribeirão Prêto *ree-bay-rā'ō pray'tō*, 21 09S 47 48W, pop(1980) 300,828, town in São Paulo state, Sudeste region, SE Brazil; NW of São Paulo; railway; economy: cotton, coffee, rice, grain, sugar cane, steel; distributing centre for the interior of São Paulo state and certain dists in Minas Gerais and Goiás.

Riberalta *ree-bayr-al'ta*, 10 59S 66 06W, pop(1976) 17,338, town in Vaca Diez prov, Beni, Bolivia; at the confluence of the Madre de Dios and Beni rivers; the town and region attained temporary importance during the natural-rubber boom of the late 19th century; now prospering through the cattle industry; airfield.

Ricardo Franco Hills, range of hills in Mato Grosso state, Centro-Oeste region, W Brazil; situated between the Río Verde and the Río Guaporé, near the border with Bolivia; visited by Col. Percy Fawcett whose description of the hills inspired Arthur Conan Doyle to write his novel based on a 'Lost World' where prehistoric creatures survived into the 20th century.

Richardson, 32 57N 96 44W, pop(1980) 72,496, town in Dallas county, NE Texas, United States; a suburb 20 km NNE of Dallas; railway.

Richfield, 44 53N 93 17W, pop(1980) 37,851, town in Hennepin county, SE Minnesota, United States; suburb 11 km S of Minneapolis; railway.

Richland, 46 17N 119 18W, pop(1980) 33,578, city in Benton county, Washington, United States, on the Columbia river, 16 km WNW of Pasco; developed between 1943 and 1945 as an administrative headquarters and residential community for the nearby atomic-energy research and production plant.

Richmond, 37 56N 122 21W, pop(1980) 74,676, a deep-water port and city in Contra Costa county, W California, United States; on San Francisco Bay, 16 km N of Oakland; railway.

Richmond, 39 50N 84 54W, pop(1980) 41,349, county seat of Wayne county, E Indiana, United States; on the E Fork of the R Whitewater, 114 km E of Indianapolis; railway.

Richmond, 37 33N 77 27W, pop(1980) 219,214, port and capital of state in E Virginia, United States; on the R James, 155 km S of Washington; settled as a trading post (Fort Charles) in 1645; made capital of Virginia in 1779; burned by the British under Benedict Arnold in 1781; scene of Virginia Convention in 1788 for the ratification of the Federal Constitution, and of Aaron Burr's treason trial in 1807; at the beginning of the Civil War became the Confederate capital (1861) and was captured by Union forces in 1865 after it had been abandoned and burnt; 3 universities (1804, 1832, 1865); railway; airfield; economy: corporate headquarters centre; manufactures tobacco, aluminium products, industrial fibres; monuments: Virginia Museum of Fine Arts, Museum of the Confederacy, St John's church.

Richmond Hill, 43 53N 79 26W, pop(1981) 37,778, town in SE Ontario, SE Canada; railway; 22 km N of Toronto.

Richmond-upon-Thames *-temz'*, 51 28N 0 19W, pop(1981) 159,693, borough of SW Greater London, England; on the R Thames; includes the suburbs of Twickenham, Richmond and Barnes; railway; monuments: Hampton Court Palace, Royal Botanic Gardens, Ham House; economy: engineering, plastics.

Richmond-Windsor, 33 37S 150 47E, pop(1981) 15,491, urban centre in Sydney stat div, E New South Wales, Australia; an amalgamation of 2 towns NW of Sydney; railway.

Rideau Lakes *ri-dō'*, area of lakes in E Ontario prov, E Canada; covering an area N of Kingston and SW of Ottawa.

Ridgeway Path, long-distance footpath stretching from Overton Hill near Avebury, Wiltshire, to Ivinghoe Beacon in Buckinghamshire, S England; length 137 km.

Ridgewood, 40 59N 74 07W, pop(1980) 25,208, residential town in Bergen county, NE New Jersey, United States; 8 km NNE of Paterson; railway; site of British and American encampments during the War of Independence.

Riehen *ree'un*, 47 35N 7 39E, pop(1980) 20,611, town in Basel canton, N Switzerland; between the Rhine and Wiese rivers, NE of Basel; railway.

Riesa *ree'zah*, 51 18N 13 18E, pop(1981) 51,857, town in Riesa dist, Dresden, SE East Germany; on R Elbe NW of Meissen; developed around a 12th-c monastery and later chartered in 1623; railway; economy: steel, textiles.

Rieti *ree-ay'ti*, prov of Lazio region, Italy; pop(1981) 142,794; area 2,748 sq km; capital Rieti.

Rieti, 42 24N 12 51E, pop(1981) 43,079, capital town of Rieti prov, Lazio region, Italy; on the right bank of the R Velino, 80 km NE of Roma (Rome); railway; economy: citrus fruits, olives, wine, textiles, pasta; monument: cathedral with a 13th-c campanile and a 12th-c crypt.

Rift Valley or **Great Rift Valley**, geological feature running from the Middle East S to SE Africa; extends from Syria (35°S) to Mozambique (20°S), covering one-sixth of the Earth's circumference; a depression for much of its length, it is interrupted by plateaux and mountains; parts are water-filled by seas and lakes; in the Middle East it contains the Sea of Galilee, the Dead Sea (790 m below sea-level), the Gulf of 'Aqaba and the Red Sea; in N Africa it runs between the Ethiopian highlands and the Somali plains, deepening, narrowing and containing lakes such as L Abaya; on reaching N Kenya it holds L Turkana (formerly L Rudolf); about 480 km SW of L Turkana (N of L Nyasa) it branches; the E branch is well below the E African plateau and holds lakes such as L Baringo and L Nakuru, rising to L Naivasha (1,870 m above sea-level) and L Magadi; characterized by numerous volcanic landforms it continues to the shores of L Tanganyika; the W branch (also known as the Albertine Rift) runs along the edge of the Congo basin and holds lakes such as L Albert (L Mobuto Sese Seko), L Edward (L Rutanzige), L Kivu and L Tanganyika (the bed of which is 670 m below sea-level); L Victoria is situated between the 2 branches; once rejoined the rift holds L Nyasa (L Malawi), follows the R Zambezi valley and diminishes on the Mozambique coastal lowlands.

Riga *ree'ga*, 56 53N 24 08E, pop(1983) 867,000, seaport capital of Latviskaya SSR, Soviet Union; on the R Zapadnaya Dvina (Daugava), near its mouth on the Gulf of Riga, an inlet of the Baltic Sea; founded in 1201 as a trading station on the right bank of the river; a major industrial, scientific, and cultural centre, Riga has been a famous seaside resort for many years; university (1919); military base; railway; airport; economy: hydroelectric power plant, machine tools and instruments, machine building and metalworking, woodworking, light industry, chemicals, electronics, fishing; monuments: Riga Castle (1330); 13th-c Lutheran cathedral, rebuilt in the 16th century.

Riihimäki *ree'hi-ma'kee*, 60 45N 24 48E, pop(1982) 24,046, textile and glass manufacturing town in Häme prov, S Finland; 65 km N of Helsinki; established in 1921; railway.

Rijeka *ri-ye'ka*, FIUME (Ital), 45 20N 14 27E, pop(1981) 193,044, seaport town in W Hrvatska (Croatia) republic, Yugoslavia; on R Rečina where it meets Rijeka Bay on the Adriatic coast; Yugoslavia's largest and most important port; once a Roman base (Tarsatica), it has been occupied since the 7th century by the Slavs; until 1918 Rijeka was the naval base of the Austro-Hungarian Empire; university (1973); airfield (Krk I); railway; ferries; economy: main port trade, shipyards, oil refineries; monuments: Trsat castle, Jadran palace, cathedral, national museum.

Rijn, river in Europe. See Rhine.

Rila Planina *ree'la pla'nee-na*, RILA MTS (Eng), range of mts in W Bulgaria on the border with Yugoslavia, forming the NW part of the Rhodopi Planina; this is the highest range in the Balkan peninsula, rising to 2,925 m at Musala; forestry and livestock grazing are important.

Rimavská Sobota *rim'af-skah so'bo-ta*, 48 23N 20 00E, pop(1984) 21,620, town in Středoslovenský region, Slovak Socialist Republic, E Czechoslovakia; SE of Banská Bystrica; railway; economy: fruit and grain trade.

Rìmnicu Sărat *rim'nee-koo sa-rat'*, 45 24N 27 06E, pop(1983) 34,160, town in Buzău county, SE central Romania; 120 km NE of Bucureşti; rebuilt after a fire in 1854; railway; economy: petroleum industry, textiles.

Rìmnicu Vìlcea *rim'-nee-koo vil'cha*, 45 08N 24 20E, pop(1983) 86,615, resort town and capital of Vìlcea county, S central Romania; on R Olt; summer and winter sports resort; railway; economy: chemicals, timber, animal products, wine, fruit, electric power; monument: St Demetrius church (18th-c).

Rincón del Bonete *reen-kōn' del bō-nay'tay*, LAGO DEL RÍO NEGRO, major hydroelectric plant and reservoir on the Río Negro, central Uruguay; 11 km E of Paso de los Toros; forms an artificial lake on Río Negro along Tacuarembó and Durazno dept borders; begun in 1937, it now supplies most of Uruguay's electricity.

Ringerike *ring'ur-ee-ku*, 60 09N 10 16E, pop(1983) 26,828, town in Buskerud county, SE Norway; railway; economy: timber.

Ringkøbing *ring'chœ-ping*, county of W Jylland (Jutland), Denmark, the Limfjorden (Lim Fjord) runs through the N part of the county; area 4,853 sq km; pop(1983) 264,103; capital Ringkøbing, chief towns include Holstebro and Herning.

Ringsaker *rings'a-kur*, 60 54N 10 45E, pop(1980) 30,343, town in Hedmark county, SE Norway; on E shore of L Mjøsa; economy: timber.

Ring'sted, 55 28N 11 48E, pop(1981) 16,564, town in Vestsjælland county, central Sjælland (Zealand), Denmark; railway; economy: foodstuffs; monuments: three stones (*Tingstener*) in the market square recalling the time when the town was the meeting-place of Sjælland's lawcourt; Romanesque church of St Bendt's.

Ringvassøy *ring'vas-u-ü*, Norwegian island in Norwegian Sea off NW coast of Norway, SW of Vannøy I, 16 km NNE of Tromsø; rises to 1,002 m; area 656 sq km; length 35 km; greatest width 32 km; administered by Troms county.

Ringwood, 50 51N 1 47W, pop(1981) 11,100, town in New Forest dist, Hampshire, S England; on R Avon, 16 km NE of Bournemouth.

Rio Bran'co, 9 59S 67 52W, pop(1980) 117,103, capital of Acre state and Norte region, NW Brazil; on the Río Acre, 1,100 km SW of Manaus; founded as Empreza in 1882; airfield; economy: trade in timber, nuts, rubber.

Rio Claro *ree'ō kla'rō*, 22 19S 47 35W, pop(1980) 103,119, town in São Paulo state, Sudeste region, SE Brazil; NW of São Paulo; railway; economy: sugar, oranges, textiles, ceramics.

Río Cuarto *ree'ō kwar'tō*, 33 08S 64 20W, pop(1980) 110,148, commercial, agricultural and manufacturing town in Córdoba prov, Centro, central Argentina; on the Río Cuarto; university (1962); railway.

Rio de Janeiro *ree'ō day zha-nay'rō*, state in Sudeste region, SE Brazil; bordered S and E by the Atlantic; rises to 2,787 m in SW at Pico das Agulhas Negras; pop(1980) 11,291,520; area 44,268 sq km; capital Rio de Janeiro; chief towns include Campos and Niteroi; economy: chemicals, timber, oil refining; in S on the coast Brazil's first atomic power station is located at Angra dos Reis, already noted for its fishing and shipbuilding industries; in SW is the Itatiaia national park; the state was formed on 15 March 1975, when the states of Rio de Janeiro and Guanabara were consolidated.

Rio de Janeiro, 22 53S 43 17W, pop(1980) 5,090,700, port capital of Rio de Janeiro state, Sudeste region, SE Brazil; on the Bahia de Guanabara; the city covers 20 km along a narrow strip of land between mountains and the sea; forming a background to the city is Pão de Açucar (Sugar Loaf Mountain) which rises to 396 m; 3 universities (1920, 1940, 1950); railway; metro; airport (Galeão) at 16 km; 2 airfields; discovered in 1502 by the Portuguese navigator, Gonçalo Coelho; first settled by the French in 1555 but taken by the Portuguese in 1567; in 1763 Rio de Janeiro became the seat of the Viceroy; capital of Brazil 1834-1960; the city's best known suburb is the tourist resort of Copacabana which has one of the highest pop densities in the world; beyond Copacabana are the seaside resorts of Ipanema and Leblon; SW of the city centre is the suburb of Santa Teresa, which still contains many colonial and 19th-c buildings; monuments: the monastery of São Bento (1633) contains many 17th and 18th-c paintings and examples of colonial art and architecture; the oldest religious foundation is the 17th-c convent of Carmo; on Glória hill is the famous church of Nossa Senhora da Glória do Outeiro, favourite church of the former imperial family; opposite the national museum of fine art is the municipal theatre, a replica of the Paris Opera House; the home of the emperors of Brazil up to the proclamation of the Republic in 1889 is now the national museum and contains collections of Indian tribal costumes, utensils and weapons, a mineral collection and historical documents relating to the imperial past; the museum also houses the 'Bendego' meteorite, found in 1888, probably one of the largest metallic masses to fall to earth (original weight 5,360 kg); events: São Sebastião, patron saint of Rio (20 Jan); Carnival, on Shrove Tuesday and the 3 preceding days, with parades, competitions and fancy-dress balls; festival of Iemanjá when followers of the spirit cults brought from Africa gather on beaches to sing, dance and make offerings (31 Dec).

Río Gallegos *ree'ō gah-lay'gos*, 51 35S 69 15W, pop(1980) 42,000, river-port capital of Santa Cruz prov, Patagonia, S Argentina; 15 km from the mouth of the Río Gallegos and 2,000 km SSW of Buenos Aires; railway; economy: trade in wool, skins, coal (El Turbio mines).

Rio Grande *ree'ō gran'day*, 32 03S 52 08W, pop(1980) 130,149, port in Rio Grande do Sul state, Sul region, S Brazil; at the entrance to Lagoa dos Patos, 270 km S of Pôrto Alegre; lies on a low, sandy peninsula 16 km from the Atlantic; founded in 1737; university (1969); railway; economy: oil refining, fishing, distribution centre for S part of Rio Grande do Sul state.

Rio Grande do Norte *ree'ō dō nor'tay*, state in Nordeste region, NE Brazil; bordered N and E by the Atlantic; drained by Piranhas and Apodi rivers; pop(1980) 1,898,172; area 53,015 sq km; capital Natal; economy: agriculture, textiles, food processing, offshore oil.

Rio Grande do Sul *ree'ō dō sool*, state in Sul region, S Brazil; southernmost state in Brazil; bordered W by Argentina along the Río Uruguay, S by Uruguay along the Jaguarão and Cuareim rivers, E by the Atlantic, and N by the Uruguay and Pelotas rivers; in the SE are L Mirim (area 2,966 sq km) and L Mangueira; in the E is the Lagoa dos Patos; extensive grasslands; pop(1980) 7,773,837; area 282,184 sq km; capital Pôrto Alegre; chief towns Passo Fundo, Rio Grande; economy: cattle, textiles, food processing, agriculture; in the NE is the Aparados da Serra national park and part of the São Joaquim national park; the state has numerous remains of Jesuit settlements from the colonial period.

Río Muni *ree'ō moo'ni*, mainland territory of Equatorial Guinea, W central Africa; bounded W by the Gulf of Guinea, E and S by Gabon and N by Cameroon; chief town Bata; area 26,016 sq km; the Río Mbini (Benito) flows from the mountains to the coast.

Río Negro *ree'ō nayg'rō*, prov in Patagonia region, S

central Argentina; extending from the Andes to the Atlantic; bordered by Chubut prov (S), the Río Limay (W) and the Río Colorado (N); in the W is part of the resort L Nahuel Huapí; also W, on Neuquén prov border, is the Ezequil Ramos Mexia Dam, used for irrigation, hydroelectricity, flood control and recreation; pop(1980) 383,354; area 203,013 sq km; capital Viedma; chief towns San Carlos de Bariloche and San Antonio Oeste; economy: sheep and cattle raising, timber, wine; iron, salt, lead and gypsum mining; natural gas and oil.

Río Negro, dept in W Uruguay; bordered S by the Río Negro, W by the Río Uruguay and Argentina; drained by the Arroyo Don Esteban and the Arroyo Grande; in the SE is part of the Palmar dam; pop(1985) 48,241; area 8,471 sq km; capital Fray Bentos; chief town Young; the dept was formed in 1881.

Río Pilcomayo *ree'ō peel-kō-mī'ō*, national park in E Formosa prov, Argentina; NW of Asunción; the N border with Paraguay is formed by the Río Pilcomayo; area 500 sq km; established in 1951.

Río San Juan, dept in S Nicaragua, Central America; bounded S by Costa Rica, SE by the Bahía de San Juan del Norte, and W by Lago de Nicaragua; the Río San Juan forms much of its S boundary; traversed NW-SE by the Sierra de Amerrique; pop(1981) 29,001; area 7,252 sq km; capital San Carlos.

Riobamba *ree-ō-bam'ba*, 1 44S 78 40W, pop(1982) 75,455, capital of Chimborazo prov in the Andean Sierra of central Ecuador; situated on a plateau on the Río Cebadas; 10 km N is Guano, a hemp-working and carpet-making town; university; railway; economy: drinks, tobacco, meat packing, food processing, textiles, carpet-making, timber products; monument: the restored Convento de la Concepción houses an art museum.

Riohacha *ree-ō-a'cha*, 11 34N 72 58W, pop(1985) 75,584, port capital of Guajira dept, N Colombia, South America; at the mouth of the Río César, 145 km ENE of Santa Marta; founded in 1545 by Nicolás Federmann; the town was an important centre for the pearling industry until the 18th century; economy: trade in wine, livestock and timber.

Rioja *ree-oKH'a*, region of N Spain co-extensive with the prov of Logroño; pop(1981) 253,295; area 5,034 sq km; watered by the R Ebro and its tributaries, Rioja is the best known wine producing area in Spain; capital Logroño.

Rioja, La *la ree-o'KHa*, prov in Andina region, W Argentina; bordered NW by Chile and the Andes; drained by headwaters of the Río Bermejo; the salt deserts (Salinas Grandes) lie on the E border; rises to 6,872 m (Cerro Bonete); pop(1980) 164,217; area 92,331 sq km; capital La Rioja; economy: vineyards in irrigated sub-Andean valleys, cattle raising, wolfram, copper, gold mining.

Rioja, La, 29 26S 66 50W, pop(1980) 66,826, capital of La Rioja prov, Andina, W Argentina; on the small Rioja river, at the E foot of the Sierra de Velasco; an old colonial city, founded in 1591; severely damaged by earthquake in 1894; a dam on the Rioja, completed in 1930, irrigates and supplies power to the area; folk museum; railway; economy: farming, lumbering and trading centre.

Ríos, Los *ree'ōs*, prov in W central Ecuador; bounded E by the Andes; consists almost entirely of densely forested lowlands traversed by numerous rivers (tributaries of the Guayas); pop(1982) 455,869; area 6,825 sq km; capital Babahoyo; economy: drinks, tobacco, flour, sugar, paper, animal foodstuffs.

Rip'ley, 53 03N 1 24W, pop(1981) 17,639, town in Amber Valley dist, Derbyshire, central England; part of Nottingham urban area; 15 km N of Derby; economy: quarrying, textiles.

Rip'on, 54 08N 1 31W, pop(1981) 13,232, town in Harrogate dist, North Yorkshire, N England; reckoned to be England's 2nd oldest town; economy: light engineering; monument: cathedral of St Peter and St Wilfrid; 13th-c Wakeman's House.

Risaralda *ree-sa-ral'da*, dept in W central Colombia, South America; in the Andean Cordillera Central; pop(1985) 623,756; area 4,140 sq km; capital Pereira; the Nevado de Santa Isabela National Park is popular with tourists and sportsmen.

Ris'ca, 51 37N 3 07W, pop(1981) 16,275, town in Torfaen dist, Gwent, SE Wales; in Islwyn urban area; on the Ebbw river, 42 km WNW of Bristol.

Risle or **Rille** *reel*, river in N France rising N of Courtomer in Orne dept; flows N through Eure dept to the R Seine estuary E of Honfleur; length 140 km; navigable to Pont-Audemer.

Rivas *ree'vas*, maritime dept in SW Nicaragua, Central America; bounded W by the Pacific Ocean, E by Lago de Nicaragua, and S by Costa Rica; pop(1981) 108,913; area 2,198 sq km; capital Rivas; chief towns Belén and San Juan del Sur; economy: coffee, cacao, tobacco, sesame, sugar cane, fruit, cotton, livestock.

Rivas, 11 26N 85 50W, pop(1985e) 21,000, capital town of Rivas dept, SW Nicaragua, Central America; approx 5 km from the W shore of Lago de Nicaragua; airfield; railway; on main highway leading S to Costa Rica; economy: food processing, tanning, rubber.

Rivera *ree-vay'ra*, dept in NE Uruguay; bordered by Brazil (NE and NW) and the Río Negro (SE); drained by the Tacuarembó, Cuñapirú and Yaguari rivers; pop(1985) 88,801; area 9,829 sq km; capital Rivera; the dept was created in 1884.

Rivera, 30 55S 55 33W, pop(1985) 56,335, capital of Rivera dept, NE Uruguay; railway; airfield; built on two small hills on the Brazilian frontier; divided by a street from the Brazilian town of Santa Ana do Livramento.

Rivers, state in S Nigeria, W Africa; pop(1982e) 2,742,700; area 21,850 sq km; dominated by the R Niger delta; bounded S by the Gulf of Guinea; capital Port Harcourt; chief towns Ahoada, Bonny (tanker terminal), Brass (tanker terminal), Degema (port) and Yenagoa; the economy is centred on the oil and gas industries, the state suppling about 70% of the country's crude oil output from onshore and offshore fields.

Riverside, 33 59N 117 22W, pop(1980) 170,876, city in Riverside county, S California, United States; on the Santa Ana river, 80 km E of Los Angeles; university (1907); the navel orange was introduced into California here in 1873; Citrus Experiment Station (1913); International Raceway; railway; economy: food processing, electronics, mobile homes, irrigation equipment.

Riviera Beach, 26 47N 80 03W, pop(1980) 26,489, resort town in Palm Beach county, SE Florida, United States; on L Worth (a lagoon), 6 km N of West Palm Beach; railway.

Rivière du Rempart, district in NE Mauritius; area 147.6 sq km; pop(1983) 82,188.

Riyāḍ, Ar *ri-yad'*, RIYADH, 24 41N 46 42E, pop(1974) 666,840, capital city of Saudi Arabia; in Riyāḍ prov, c.368 km SW of Ad Dammām; situated in a fertile wadi with date palms, fruit growing, and grain cultivation; political centre of Saudi Arabia and headquarters of the Wahabi movement; communications centre; formerly a walled city (demolished in the 1950s to allow for expansion of modern quarters); just N of the city is 'Solar Village', designed as a prototype project for possible use of solar power in remote regions of the country; university (1957); Islamic university (1950); King Sa'ud University (1984); over 1,000 mosques; airport; railway; monuments: royal palace, numerous mosques; economy: oil refining.

Riyadh, capital city of Saudi Arabia. See Riyāḍ, Ar.

Rize *ri-ze'*, maritime prov in NE Turkey, bounded N by the Black Sea; pop(1980) 361,258; area 3,920 sq km; capital Rize; economy: fruit, tea, maize, olives and mining of zinc, iron, manganese.

Road Town, 18 26N 64 32W, pop(1983e) 3,000, seaport and capital town of the British Virgin Is, Greater Antilles, E Caribbean, on E coast of Tortola I.

Roanoke *rōn'ōk*, 37 16N 79 56W, pop(1980) 100,220, independent city, SW Virginia, United States; on the R Roanoke, 240 km W of Richmond; railway; airfield;

economy: railway engineering, electrical equipment, furniture, textiles and metal products.

Roaring Forties, a term applied by sailors to those ocean regions in the neighbourhood of 40° S latitude, where, owing to the absence of large land masses, atmospheric depressions move W-E with great regularity, so that the W winds on their equatorial side are more constant than in the northern hemisphere and blow with great force and continuity.

Roatán *rō-a-tan'*, 16 20N 86 30W, capital of the Islas de la Bahía dept, Honduras, Central America; at the SW end of the island of Roatán in the Caribbean Sea; connected by boat with La Ceiba on the N coast of Honduras.

Robertsport, 6 45N 11 15W, pop(1962) 2,417, seaport in Liberia, on the Atlantic coast 80 km WNW of Monrovia.

Roca, Cabo da *ro'ka*, 38 46N 9 30W, westernmost point of Portugal and of continental Europe.

Rocha *ro'cha*, dept in SE Uruguay; on the Atlantic; borders NE on L Mirim and Brazil; bounded W by the Río Cebollatí; E are the fresh-water lagoons, L Rocha, L de Castillos and L Negra; pop(1985) 66,440; area 11,089 sq km; capital Rocha; the dept is known for the remains of its colonial port fortresses including San Miguel and Santa Teresa; the colonial fortress of Santa Teresa, now a national monument, was begun by the Portuguese and finished by the Spanish in the 1750s, it is set in a park of the same name (consisting of 33 sq km); the San Miguel fortress, begun by the Spanish and completed by the Portuguese, is set in a 12 sq km park, established in 1937, and has a museum attached to it.

Rocha, 34 30S 54 22W, pop(1985) 23,910, capital of Rocha dept, SE Uruguay; at N end of L Rocha; railway; airfield; the town has two casinos.

Roch'dale, 53 38N 2 09W, pop(1981) 97,942, town in Rochdale borough, Greater Manchester, NW England; on the R Roch, 16 km NE of Manchester; railway; economy: textiles, engineering.

Rochelle, La *la ro-shel*, RUPELLA (anc), 46 10N 1 09W, pop(1982) 78,231, ancient fishing and trading port and capital of Charente-Maritime dept, Poitou-Charentes region, W France; on the Bay of Biscay, 198 km SW of Tours; founded as a fishing village in the 10th century, it rapidly became a major port for salt and wine; it ranks as France's 5th largest fishing port; it was from here that the founders of Montreal and the first Canadian settlers embarked; the modern port of La Pallice, built in 1900, 6 km to the NW, operates a car ferry service to the Ile de Ré; railway; economy: shipbuilding, motor vehicles, chemicals; monuments: twin-towers (14-15th-c) guarding the entrance to the harbour, the Porte de la Grosse Horloge (13th-c medieval gateway, once separated the walled town from the port), 18th-c cathedral of St-Louis (but retains a 15th-c bell-tower).

Roch'ester, DUROBRIVAE (anc), 51 24N 0 30E, pop(1981) 24,402, town in the Medway Towns urban area and Rochester upon Medway dist, Kent, SE England; W of Chatham; an important early settlement at a ford over the R Medway; railway: monuments: 12th-c cathedral; 11th-c castle; Gad's Hill nearby was the home of Charles Dickens.

Rochester, 44 01N 92 28W, pop(1980) 57,890, county seat of Olmsted county, SE Minnesota, United States; on the R Zumbro, 112 km SSE of St Paul; railway; economy: electrical equipment and medical supplies; home of the Mayo Clinic, world-famous medical centre, established in 1889 by Dr William Mayo and Dr Charles Mayo.

Rochester, 43 10N 77 37W, pop(1980) 241,741, county seat of Monroe county, W New York, United States; port on R Genesee, 112 km ENE of Buffalo and 10 km from L Ontario; first settled in 1811, achieving city status in 1834; university (1850); railway; airfield; economy: optical and photographic instruments, machines and tools; monuments: international museum of photography, Rochester museum, Memorial art gallery; event: Lilac Festival (May).

Roche-sur-Yon, La *lah rosh-sür-yô*, formerly NAPOLEON-VENDÉE (1804-14, 1848-70), BOURBON-VENDÉE (1814-48), 46 40N 1 25W, pop(1982) 48,156, agric trade centre and capital of Vendée dept, Pays de la Loire region, W France; 59 km S of Nantes; railway junction; founded by Napoleon in 1804 to serve as capital of the dept; laid out as a copy of Washington, with a great square surrounded by neoclassical churches and public buildings.

Rock Hill, 34 56N 81 01W, pop(1980) 35,344, town in York county, N South Carolina, United States; 104 km N of Columbia; railway; economy: textiles.

Rock Island, 41 30N 90 34W, pop(1980) 47,036, county seat of Rock Island county, NW Illinois, United States; on R Mississippi, 125 km NW of Peoria; railway; US government arsenal.

Rockford, 42 16N 89 06W, pop(1980) 139,712, county seat of Winnebago county, N Illinois, United States; on the R Rock, 128 km NW of Chicago; railway; monument: Burpee Art Gallery.

Rockhampton, 23 22S 150 32E, pop(1981) 50,146, town in Fitzroy stat div, Queensland, Australia; on the Fitzroy river, NNW of Brisbane; railway; air link and hydrofoil service to Great Keppel I; economy: centre of Australia's largest beef-producing area; approx 240 km W of Rockhampton the area around the towns of Emerald, Anakie, Rubyvale, Sapphire and Willows is rich in gemstones, the 'McKiney' sapphire and the 'Black Star of Queensland' were found here; events: the Rocky Round-up (a rodeo) in April; cooeeing contest in Aug at nearby Cooee Bay (the cooee is a traditional bush yell).

Rockingham, 32 16S 115 21E, pop(1981) 24,932, resort town in Perth stat div, Western Australia, Australia; situated at S end of Cockburn Sound, S of Perth; railway.

Rockville, 39 05N 77 09W, pop(1980) 43,811, county seat of Montgomery county, W Maryland, United States; 24 km NNW of Washington; railway.

Rockville Centre, 40 40N 73 39W, pop(1980) 25,412, town in Nassau county, SE New York, United States; residential suburb on Long Island, 30 km E of New York City; railway.

Rocky Mount, 35 57N 77 48W, pop(1980) 41,283, city in Nash county, NE North Carolina, United States; on the R Tar, 78 km ENE of Raleigh; railway; economy: processing and distributing centre for agricultural area (tobacco, cotton, corn); manufactures textiles, clothing, chemicals and pharmaceuticals.

Rocky Mountains, ROCKIES, major mountain system of W North America, extending from central New Mexico generally NNW through the USA, into W Canada and N Alaska and reaching the Bering Strait N of the Arctic Circle; the mountains rise abruptly from the Great Plains on the E, while on the W they are bounded by high plateaux, basins and ranges of the intermontane region; the Rocky Mts form the easternmost belt of the North American cordillera; the Rocky Mts proper are generally considered to end in the S with the Sangre de Cristo Mts, although the link between the Rockies and a natural S extension in Mexico (the Sierra Madre Oriental) can be traced with interruptions through S New Mexico and W Texas in the Sacramento Mts, the Davis Mts and the Santiago Mts; the Rockies form the continental divide, separating the Pacific drainage from the Atlantic (via the Gulf of Mexico) and Arctic drainage; the continental divide is not a continuous chain of peaks but a vast complex of separate ranges, interrupted by wide gaps of lofty rolling plateaux; in the USA the Rocky Mts rise to 4,399 m in Mt Elbert, Colorado, while in Canada the highest peak is Mt Robson (3,954 m), situated on the British Columbia-Alberta prov border; the Rocky Mts may be subdivided into 4 sections: the Southern Rockies, the Middle Rockies, the Northern Rockies and the Arctic Mts; the Southern Rockies lie in New Mexico, Colorado and S Wyoming and constitute the highest and most homogeneous section, consisting of 2 major parallel folds, separated by a series of basins; the ranges forming this section are the Sangre de Cristo Mts, the Front Range and the Laramie Mts in the E; the Medicine Bow Mts is a NW spur of the Front Range and extends into Wyoming; the W group includes the San Juan Mts, the

Sawatch Range and the Park Range; the Río Grande, Colorado, Arkansas, North Platte, South Platte and the Pecos rivers all have their sources in this section of mountains; the Middle Rockies are separated from the Southern Rockies by the Wyoming basin and are situated in NW Wyoming, NE Utah, SE Idaho and SW Idaho; they are varied in structure, irregular in trend and do not present a solid barrier to the E; this section includes the Bighorn Mts, Owl Creek Mts, Wind River Range, Wyoming Range, Salt River Range, the lava-covered Absaroka Range, the Uinta Mts, Wasatch Range, Teton Range and Yellowstone plateau; the Snake, Bighorn, Powder and Yellowstone rivers all have their sources here; the Northern Rockies are heavily glaciated and extend through Montana, Idaho, NE Washington and almost 1,600 km into Canada where the continental divide follows the British Columbia-Alberta border; the Rocky Mountain Trench separates the ranges from those to the W, stretching from W Montana NNW to the headwaters of the Yukon; the trench is occupied one after the other by the headstreams of the Kootenai, Columbia, Fraser, Peace and Liard rivers; to the W of the British Columbia-Alberta border are the roughly parallel Purcell and Selkirk Mts, separated by grabens; the westernmost ranges of the Rocky Mts in Canada are collectively called the Columbia Mts, these include the Stikine and Cariboo Mts; the southernmost members of the Northern Rockies include the Bitterroot Range, which runs along the Idaho-Montana border, the Clearwater Mts and Salmon River Mts of central Idaho; the Arctic Rockies consist of several discontinuous parallel ranges: the Mackenzie Mts and their E outliers, the Franklin Mts, sweep 805 km across NW Northwest Territories and Yukon territory; the Richardson Mts to the N of the Mackenzie Mts stretch N to Mackenzie Bay of the Arctic Ocean; the Brooks Range continues W across the whole of N Alaska; the Rocky Mts are an important source of mineral wealth; there are several national parks along their full length including Rocky Mountain National Park (Colorado), Grand Teton National Park and Yellowstone National Park (Wyoming), Glacier National Park (Montana), Banff National Park, Jasper National Park (Alberta), Yoho National Park, Kootenay National Park, Glacier National Park (British Columbia), Northern Yukon National Park (Yukon) and Gates of the Arctic National Park (Alaska).

Rodez', SEGODUNUM (anc), 44 21N 2 33E, pop(1982) 26,346, industrial and commercial capital of Aveyron dept, Midi-Pyrénées region, S France; on a hill rising to 120 m above the R Aveyron, 125 km NE of Toulouse; a bishopric since 401 AD; former capital of the Rouergue region until 1789; a Catholic stronghold in the Wars of Religion of the 16th century; railway; economy: textiles, agric trade; monuments: 13-16th-c Gothic cathedral of Notre-Dame, standing on the highest point of the hill, the W front once formed part of the now vanished ramparts, the upper half of the belfry tower is one of the finest examples in France of Flamboyant Gothic architecture; event: the Place de la Cité has a Saturday market.

Rodhópi, RHODOPE *rod'o-pee* (Eng), coastal nome (dept) of Thráki region, NE Greece, bounded on the N by Bulgaria and the SE spurs of the Rodopi Planina (Rhodope Mts); bounded (S) by Thrakikón Pélagos; pop(1981) 107,957; area 2,543 sq km; capital Komotiní.

Ródhos ('island of roses'), largest island of the Sporádhes, Greece, in the SE Aegean Sea, off the SW coast of Turkey, NE of Kárpathos I; area 1,398 sq km; length 72 km; length of coastline 220 km; max width 35 km; 4th largest Greek island; the island is traversed by a long ridge of hills, rising to 1,215 m; capital Ródhos at northernmost tip of island; originally settled by Mycenean Greeks in 1400 BC; the 30 m statue of the sun god Chares was one of the Seven Wonders of the World (collapsed 227 BC); the ancient university was attended by Cicero and Pompey; the Knights of the Order of St John established themselves here in 1309 after the loss of the Holy Land; in 1522 the remaining 180 Knights surrendered to the Turks and moved to Malta; held by Italy (1912-1947); Ródhos has become a modern holiday and tourist centre.

Ródhos *ro'THus*, RHODES *rōdz* (Eng), RODI *rō'dee* (Ital), 36 26N 28 14E, pop(1981) 40,392, capital town of Sporádhes nome (dept), Aegean Islands, Greece; at the N tip of Ródhos I; capital of Ródhos I since 408 BC; airfield; ferries to Cyprus, Italy, Turkey; economy: wine, cereals, fruit, tobacco, tourism; monuments: temple of Aphrodite (3rd-c BC); Hospital of the Knights (1440-89), now housing the archaeological museum; the ancient acropolis lies SW of the old town; events: Kalafonon midsummer bonfires (21 June); Navy Week (June-July).

Rodrigues Island *rō-dree'gez*, 19 45S 63 20E, pop(1983) 33,572, island in the Indian Ocean; situated E of Mauritius; part of the Archipel des Mascareignes (Mascarene Is); a dependency of Mauritius; area 104 sq km; chief town Port Mathurin; rises to 396 m at Mt Limon.

Roermond *roor-mont'*, 51 12N 6 00E, pop(1984e) 38,209, manufacturing and agricultural market town in Limburg prov, S Netherlands; at the confluence of the Roer and Maas rivers, in N part of the Dutch frontier dist, between Belgium and W Germany; captured by William the Silent in 1572, Roermond was retaken by the Spaniards and remained a Spanish or Austrian possession until 1815, when it was returned to Holland; railway; economy: metalworking, electrical engineering, chemicals, textiles, paper, foodstuffs (important mushroom canning plant); monuments: 15th-c cathedral of St Christoffel; 13th-c Romanesque church.

Roeselare *roos-e-la're*, dist of West-Vlaanderen (West Flanders) prov, W Belgium; area 272 sq km; pop(1982) 137,126.

Roeselare, ROULERS *roo-ler'* (Fr), 50 57N 3 08E, pop(1982) 51,866, capital town of Roeselare dist, West-Vlaanderen (West Flanders) prov, W Belgium; 30 km S of Brugge; railway; here the French defeated the Austrians in 1794.

Rogaguado, Lago *ro-ga-gwa'THō*, lake in marshes of Beni dept, N Bolivia; 32 km WNW of Exaltación; area 1,502 sq km; length 40 km, width 13 km; empties into the Arroyo Caimanes (right-hand branch of the Río Yata).

Rogaland, *rō'gah-lahn*, formerly STAVANGER, county of SW Norway; area 9,141 sq km; pop(1983) 312,550; capital Stavanger; chief towns Eigersund and Sandnes; has the Boknafjorden (Bokna Fjord) as its nucleus; there are many small islands within and at the mouth of the fjord including Karmøy and Ombo; the land rises to 1,605 m at Snønuten in the NE.

Rogaska Slatina *ro'gash-ka sla'teen-a*, 46 15N 15 42E, resort town in NE Slovenija republic, Yugoslavia; in a wooded valley with warm mineral springs which have given it a reputation as the best-known health spa in Yugoslavia; the first spa establishment was built in 1810; railway.

Roma *ro'ma*, prov of Lazio region, Italy; pop(1981) 3,695,961; area 5,351 sq km; capital Roma (Rome).

Roma, ROME (Eng), 41 53N 12 30E, pop(1981) 2,840,259, capital city of Italy and of Roma prov, Lazio region, W central Italy; in the hilly Campagna di Roma, on the R Tevere (Tiber), 20 km from the Tyrrhenian Sea (E); on the left bank of the Tevere are the famous Seven Hills of Roma - the Capitoline (50 m), Quirinal (52 m), Viminal (56 m), Esquiline (53 m), Palatine (51 m), Aventine (46 m), and Caelian (50 m) - on which the ancient city was built during the 8th century BC; within the city's precincts, on the W bank of the Tevere, is the Vatican City, residence of the Pope and seat of the Papal Curia; Rome was the ancient capital of the Roman Republic, of the Roman Empire, and later of the States of the Church; important centre of fashion and film; headquarters of the Food and Agriculture Organisation of the United Nations and of numerous other cultural and research institutions; university (1303); airport; railway; metro; economy: oil refining, chemicals, pharmaceuticals, fertilizers, iron and steel, glass products, cement, engineering, textiles, beer and soft drinks, foodstuffs; monuments: the

Piazza Venezia is the centre of Roma, a large square from which radiate broad avenues, and which contains the huge monument to Victor Emanuel II (begun 1885); Palazzo Venezia, originally a fortress-like building erected about 1455, used from 1926-43 as Mussolini's official residence, and now a museum; Forum Romanum, on a site between the hills of Palatine and Capitoline, contains relics of ancient Roma - Arch of Titus, Via Sacra, Curia (where the Senate used to sit), and Arch of Septimius Severus (AD 203); Imperial Roma added other fora - of Julius Caesar, of Augustus, of Nerva, and of Trajan (Trajan's Column is 27 m high); the Colosseum, an amphitheatre designed for gladiatorial combats, was originally built by Vespasian (from AD 75) with 3 storeys, then heightened to 4 storeys by Titus; Baths of Caracalla (built AD 216), now used for open-air opera performances during the summer; Arch of Constantine (AD 312), Roma's best preserved triumphal arch; the best preserved monument of ancient Roma is the Pantheon, a temple built in 27 BC, which, in the 19th century, became the mausoleum of the kings of Italy; Renaissance palaces of Spada (1540), Farnese (begun in 1514, now the French embassy), Altieri, Madama (1642), and Cancelleria (1486-1511); Roma's countless churches include 5 patriarchal basilicas - St Peter's (in the Vatican), San Giovanni in Laterano (the cathedral of Roma), San Lorenzo fuori le Mura, San Paolo fuori le Mura, and Santa Maria Maggiore (founded 5th-c, rebuilt 16-17th-c); of the many Renaissance and Baroque fountains, most notable is the Fontana di Trevi (1762, by Salvi) taking up the entire facade of the Palazzo Poli; the Galleria Borghese is one of Roma's finest picture galleries, with masterpieces by Raphael, Titian, and Caravaggio; events: Festa de la Candelora (Candlemas-processions) on 2 Feb; Festa della Primavera (spring festival) in March and April; numerous religious feasts and celebrations.

Ro'man, 46 56N 26 56E, pop(1983) 67,962, town in Neamţ county, NE Romania; on R Moldava near its confluence with the R Siret; 56 km WSW of Iaşi; established in the 14th century; railway; economy: metalwork, soap, sugar, chemicals; monument: 16th-c cathedral.

Romana, La *la rō-mah'na*, 18 27N 68 57W, pop(1982e) 98,852, sugar port on the S coast of La Romana prov, Dominican Republic, on the Caribbean Sea opposite the island of Catalina, 110 km E of Santo Domingo; airfield; economy: home of the largest privately owned sugar mill in the world; cigars.

Romania or **Roumania** also **Rumania** *rō-may'nee-a*, official name Socialist Republic of Romania, REPUBLICA SOCIALISTĂ ROMÂNIA (Rom), a socialist republic of SE Europe, on the Balkan Peninsula and on the Lower Danube; bounded on the E by the Black Sea, on the S by Bulgaria, on the W by Yugoslavia and Hungary, and on the N and NE by Russia; two-thirds of the frontiers follow the course of rivers or the sea shore; area 237,500 sq km; timezone GMT +2; capital Bucureşti; chief towns include Braşov, Constanţa (Black Sea port), Iaşi, Timişoara, Cluj-Napoca; major river ports on the Danube at Drobeta-Turnu Severin, Corabia, Turnu Măgurele and Giurgiu; pop(1983) 22,553,074; 89% of the population are of Romanian nationality, of the rest 7.7% are Magyars, 1.5% Germans, 1.8% include minorities such as Ukrainians, Tartars, Jews, Croatians, Russians, Bulgarians, Serbians; the official language is Romanian, one of the Romance languages which developed from the Latin spoken in the Carpathian-Danubian-Balkan area; Hungarian and German are also spoken; about 80% of

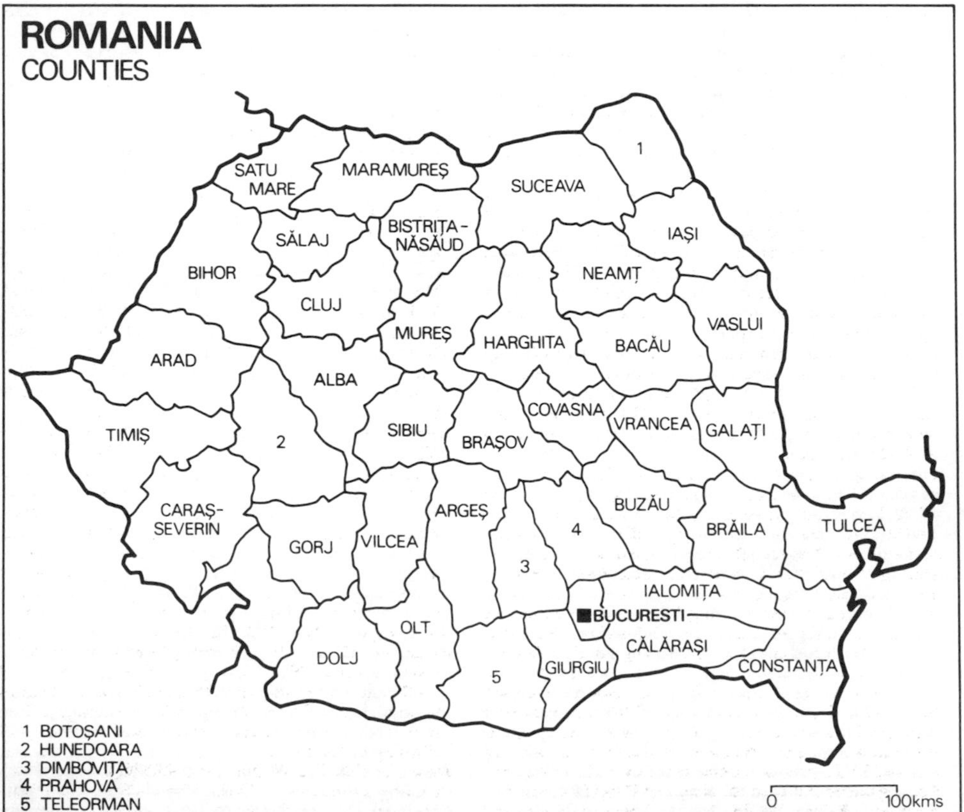

the population adhere to the Eastern Orthodox Christian Church; other denominations include the Romanian Eastern Orthdox Church (founded in 1925), Roman Catholic, Reformed Church, Evangelic of Augustan Confession, Evangelic of Synod-Presbyterian Confession, Unitarian, Mosaic, Armenian-Gregorian, Muslim, Old-Rite Christian, Baptist, Adventist, Pentecostal; the currency is the leu of 100 bani; national holiday 23 Aug (Liberation Day); membership of Warsaw Pact, CEMA, FAO, GATT, G-77, IAEA, IBRD, ICAO, IFAD, ILO, IMF, IMO, INTERPOL, IPU, ITC, ITU, UN, UNESCO, UPU, WFTU, WHO, WIPO, WMO, WTO.

Physical description. Old Romania lies to the S and E of the sickle-shaped Carpathian Mts which separate it from Transylvania and form the heart of the country. The Carpathians are divided into three ranges: the E Carpathians lying between the N frontier and the Prahova Valley, an area of extensive forest cut by many passes; the S Carpathians lying between the Prahova Valley and the Timiş-Cerna gorges, a higher range, with principal massifs in the Bucegi Mts, Făgăraş Mts, Paring Mts and Retezat Mts; and the W Carpathians lying between the R Danube and the R Someş. The Carpathian range is the watershed between the N Transylvanian rivers (such as the Mureş) which flow S to the Tisza, and those on the SE including the Prut, Siret and Olt (which breaks through the Transylvanian Alps), flowing S towards the R Danube. The highest peak in the Carpathian Mts is Negoiul (2,548 m); to the S and E the mountains are continued in the lower Sub-Carpathians which contain deposits of oil, salt and brown coal; they also form the main fruit and vine-growing area of the country. The Romanian Plain in the S includes the Bărăgan Plain (E), the richest arable area, and the Oltenian Plain (W) which is crossed by many rivers. Offshore deposits of oil have been found on the Black Sea shelf, and natural gas in the Transylvanian tableland. Coal deposits are mainly to be found in lowland depressions in Hunedoara and Bacău counties or in the uplands in Argeş, Gorj, Dolj and Sălaj counties. Iron ore is mined mostly in the W Carpathians (Banat and Poiana Ruscăi Mts) and non-ferrous ores in the Apuseni and Banat Mts. Throughout the country there are about 3,500 glacial ponds, lakes and coastal lagoons. Forest land (mostly deciduous trees) which once covered most of the country, except the SE, now accounts for only 27% of the total area. Alpine pastures spread beyond 1,800 m.

Climate. Romania has a continental type climate with cold, snowy winters and warm summers. The mildest area during the winter is along the Black Sea coast, but frosts may be as severe in the lowlands as they are in upland areas. In the Carpathians summers are cooler and wetter. During dry summers, with hot, dry winds blowing from the Russian steppes, the plains of the N and E can suffer from drought. Winds from the same direction in winter can cause severe weather. The average annual rainfall is 637 mm (1,000 mm in the mountains to 400 mm in the Danube delta).

History, government and constitution. The country has been called Romania since 1862 following the unification of Walachia and Moldavia 3 years earlier. The 1866 constitution created a monarchy and in 1918 Transylvania, Bessarabia and Bucovina united with Romania. During World War II territories were lost to Russia, Hungary and Bulgaria and in Dec 1947 the monarchy was abolished. A People's Republic was declared in that year but the later constitution of 1965 declared Romania to be a Socialist Republic. The leading political force is the Romanian Communist Party (formerly the Romanian Workers' Party) with state power expressed by the Grand National Assembly of 369 members who are elected every 5 years. Legislative power is delegated to the State Council which comprises the President as head of state, 3 Vice-presidents, one secretary and 20 members. Local government is in the hands of People's Councils.

Economy. Before World War II agriculture was the mainstay of the Romanian economy with 38% of the national income in 1938 being derived from agricultural production. By 1981 agriculture's share of national income had been reduced to just under 16% as industrial output increased, chiefly in iron and steel, non-ferrous metallurgy, engineering, chemicals, textiles, foodstuffs, electrical goods and electronics. Romania's principal trading partners are the USSR, German Democratic Republic, Federal Republic of Germany, China, France, the USA. In recent years exports of machinery, transport equipment, chemicals and rubber have risen as have the imports of fuels, raw materials and metals.

Agriculture. In 1981 there were 365 state-owned enterprises in an agricultural system where the state owns nearly 37% of farm land. Under 10% of farmland is owned by private individuals, the remainder being in the hands of agricultural production cooperatives. Animal production has risen in recent years alongside a rise in intensive structures and a fall in grain-crop farming. Vineyards and orchards occupy less than 5% of farm land.

Administrative divisions. Romania is divided into 41 counties (*judeţ*) as follows:

County	*area (sq km)*	*pop(1983)*
Alba	6,231	419,807
Arad	7,652	505,303
Argeş	6,801	660,055
Bacău	6,606	700,303
Bihor	7,535	650,707
Bistriţa-Năsăud	5,305	309,758
Botoşani	4,965	459,268
Brăila	4,724	393,291
Braşov	5,351	665,097
Bucureşti	1,521	2,227,568
Buzău	6,072	518,030
Caraş-Severin	8,503	402,939
Călăraşi	4,959	310,388
Cluj	6,650	740,580
Constanţa	7,055	693,207
Covasna	3,705	224,280
Dimboviţa	4,035	549,405
Dolj	7,413	767,624
Galaţi	4,425	623,450
Giurgiu	3,810	373,526
Gorj	5,641	370,956
Harghita	6,610	351,609
Hunedoara	7,016	548,344
Ialomiţa	4,565	298,357
Iaşi	5,469	773,215
Maramureş	6,215	529,732
Mehedinţi	4,900	328,030
Mureş	6,696	614,296
Neamţ	5,890	558,813
Olt	5,507	529,149
Prahova	4,694	853,685
Satu Mare	4,405	406,556
Sălaj	3,850	266,407
Sibiu	5,422	503,866
Suceava	8,555	664,823
Teleorman	5,760	506,647
Timiş	8,692	709,354
Tulcea	8,430	264,212
Vaslui	5,297	449,945
Vilcea	5,705	449,806
Vrancea	4,863	380,746

Rome, capital city of Italy. See Roma.

Rome, 34 15N 85 10W, pop(1980) 29,654, county seat of Floyd county, NW Georgia, United States; at the confluence of Etowah and Oostanaula rivers which join to form the R Coosa, 88 km NW of Atlanta; railway; economy: cotton market; textile and lumber mills, clothing factories.

Rome, 43 13N 75 27W, pop(1980) 43,826, town in Oneida county, central New York, United States; on the R Mohawk, 24 km WNW of Utica; railway; monument: Fort Stanwix museum.

Romsey *rum'zi*, 59 59N 1 30W, pop(1981) 15,039, town in Southampton dist, Hampshire, S England; 11 km NW of Southampton; railway; economy: electronics; monument: 10-12th-c abbey church of St Mary and St Ethelfleda.

Ron'da, 36 46N 5 12W, pop(1981) 31,383, picturesque town in Málaga prov, Andalucia, S Spain; on the R Guadalevin close to the Tajo de Ronda ravine and situated in the Sierra de Ronda; railway; famous for its school of bullfighters; economy: clothes, wine, leather, soap; events: fiesta of La Reconquista with cattle market and bullfights in May; fiesta and fair in Sept.

Rondônia *ron-don'ya*, state in Norte region, NW Brazil; bordered S by Bolivia along the Mamoré and Guaporé rivers; traversed in the W by the Río Madeira; pop(1980) 491,069; area 243,044 sq km; capital Pôrto Velho; economy: agriculture, mining of tin and gold, meat processing; Rondônia is a focus for experimental developments in agriculture and colonization; much of the state is reserved for Indians and natural forests; running SW from Pôrto Velho, parallel with the Río Madeira, then S parallel with the Río Mamoré, is the Madeira-Mamoré railway, built by Brazil in 1907-12 to compensate Bolivia for the annexation of Acre territory during the rubber boom; it cost 6,200 lives and proved of little use as it only went as far as Guajará-Mirim, instead of reaching the intended destination of Riberalta; it was replaced by a bus service in 1972; in 1956 the name was changed from Federal Territory of Guaporé to that of Rondônia; in 1981 it became a state.

Rongklang', formerly CHIN HILLS, range of mountains in Chin state, W Burma; consists of a series of parallel ranges that cover three-quarters of the state, rising to 3,053 m in Mount Victoria.

Rønne *rœn'e*, 55 07N 14 43E, pop(1981) 14,413, seaport and chief town on W coast of Bornholm I; capital of Bornholm county, Denmark; airfield; economy: foodstuffs; monument: St Nicholas's church (originally 14th-c, largely rebuilt in 1918).

Ronse *ron'se*, RENAIX *ren-ay'* (Fr), 50 45N 3 36E, pop(1982) 24,287, town in Oudenaarde dist, Oost-Vlaanderen (East Flanders) prov, W Belgium.

Roodepoort *roo'de-poort*, 26 10S 27 53E, pop(1980) 165,315, municipality in Transvaal prov, NE South Africa; a NW suburb of Johannesburg; railway; economy: gold mining, iron and steel, woodworking.

Roosendaal *rō'zen-dal*, 51 32N 4 28E, pop(1984e) 56,519, manufacturing city in W Noord Brabant prov, S Netherlands; railway.

Roraima *rō-rī'ma*, territory in Norte region, N Brazil; bordered E by Guyana (along the Río Tacutu), N along Sierra Pacaraima and NW along Serra Parima by Venezuela; drained by the Río Branco; rises to 2,772 m in NE at Monte Roraima on the border with Venezuela and Guyana; pop(1980) 79,159; area 230,104 sq km; capital Boa Vista; economy: cattle, timber; in the N is the Parima nature reserve.

Roraima, Monte *ro-rī'ma*, 5 12N 60 43W, peak at the junction of the Brazil, Guyana and Venezuela borders, South America; 442 km SE of Cuidad Bolívar (Venezuela) in the Serra de Pacaraima; highest peak (2,875 m) in the Guiana Highlands; a giant table mountain, with a total area of 67 sq km, of which 15.5 sq km are divided between Brazil and Guyana, the rest belonging to Venezuela.

Rosa Zárate *rō'sa sa'ra-tay*, 0 14N 79 28W, pop(1982) 10,658, town in Esmeraldas prov, NW Ecuador; on the Río Blanco, SE of Esmeraldas; railway.

Rosario *ro-sa'ree-ō*, 33 00S 60 40W, pop(1980) 875,623, chief city in Santa Fe prov, Litoral, Argentina; on the Río Paraná, NW of Buenos Aires; Argentina's largest inland port, founded in 1725; racecourse; golf club, boat club and aero club in the fashionable suburb of Fisherton, the headquarters of the British community; railway; airport (Fisherton) at 15 km; economy: distribution centre and export outlet for surrounding agricultural provinces; monument: memorial to General Belgrano, designer of the Argentinian flag, who first raised it here; local holiday 7 Oct (foundation of the city).

Roscommon *ros-ko'mun*, ROS COMÁIN (Gael), county in Connacht prov, W central Irish Republic; bounded E by R Shannon and watered by R Suck; pop(1981) 54,543; area 2,463 sq km; capital Roscommon.

Roscommon, 53 38N 8 11W, pop(1981) 1,673, capital of Roscommon county, Connacht, W central Irish Republic; formerly a wool town; railway; monuments: 13th-c abbey and castle.

Roseau *rō-zō'*, formerly CHARLOTTE TOWN, 15 18N 61 23W, pop(1981) 20,000, seaport and capital town of Dominica, Windward Is, E Caribbean; on the SW coast of the island, 592 km SE of San Juan, Puerto Rico; monument: cathedral (1841).

Roseires Dam *rō-say'res*, 11 52N 34 23E, dam on the Blue Nile (Bahr el Azraq), Central region, E Sudan, NE Africa; located SSE of Khartoum, the dam has created a sizeable lake and provides perennial irrigation water for over 12,000 sq km of land; over 125 megawatts of hydroelectric power is generated here.

Rosemead, 34 05N 118 04W, pop(1980) 42,604, city in Los Angeles county, SW California, United States; 16 km E of Los Angeles.

Rosenheim *rō'zen-hīm*, 47 51N 12 09E, pop(1983) 52,200, industrial town in Oberbayern dist, S Bayern (Bavaria) prov, W Germany; at foot of the Alps on the R Inn, 54 km SE of München (Munich); railway; economy: leather gloves, footwear, bags and belts.

Rosetta *rō-zet'a*, RASHID (Arab), name given to a branch of the R Nile; the town of Rashîd (Rosetta) lies E of Alexandria near the mouth of the river; the Rosetta Stone, a piece of black basalt with trilingual inscriptions, was found nearby in 1799; its discovery led to the deciphering of Egyptian hieroglyphics.

Roseville, 42 30N 82 56W, pop(1980) 54,311, town in Macomb county, SE Michigan, United States; 21 km NNE of Detroit; residential.

Roseville, 45 01N 93 10W, pop(1980) 35,820, town in Ramsey county, SE Minnesota, United States; suburb 8 km N of St Paul.

Roşiorii de Vede *rosh-yor'ya day vay'day*, 44 06N 25 00E, pop(1983) 33,223, town in Teleorman county, S Romania; NNE of Turnu Măgurele; railway; economy: textiles, foodstuffs.

Roskilde *rōs'kil-e*, a county of E Sjælland (Zealand), Denmark; area 891 sq km; pop(1983) 205,414; capital Roskilde, chief towns include Køge and Herfolge.

Roskilde, 55 39N 12 07E, pop(1981) 39,659, port and ancient town at S end of Roskilde Fjord, Roskilde county, Sjælland (Zealand), Denmark; capital of Denmark from the 10th century to 1443; by the Peace of Roskilde (1658) Denmark lost to Sweden her territory E of the Øresund; university (1970); railway; economy: engineering, foodstuffs; monuments: triple-towered cathedral (12th-c) containing Danish royal mausoleum; Viking Ships museum.

Ross Dependency, Antarctic territory administered by New Zealand, including all the islands and land between 160° E and 150° W and S of 60° S; land area 413,540 sq km; permanent shelf ice area 336,770 sq km; there are no permanent inhabitants but scientific stations near L Vanda and at Scott Base on Ross I are manned all year; came under New Zealand jurisdiction in 1923; supervised by Ross Dependency Research Committee since 1958; the territory has been explored by Sir James Ross, Captain R.F. Scott, Sir Ernest Shackleton, Roald Amundsen and Richard E. Byrd.

Ross Sea, extension of the Pacific Ocean, lying between Marie Byrd Land and Victoria Land in New Zealand's territory of Antarctica; the Ross Ice Shelf, the sea's southern arm, is located at the base of the Transantarctic Mountains; icebergs break from the 640 km seaward side of the ice shelf and are carried N by surface currents; as a result of changing ice patterns, inlets of the shelf are temporary; the Bay of Whales inlet, which was used as Roald Amundsen's base for his trek to the South Pole in

1911, existed for approx 50 years; McMurdo Sound, close to Scott Island on the W side of Ross Sea, is generally ice-free in late summer and is an important base point for exploration and scientific study; the main islands are Roosevelt Island in the E and Ross Island, with the active volcano, Mt Erebus, in the W; drilling on the continental shelf in 1972 discovered traces of methane and ethane gas; no oil yet discovered, but vast reserves are thought to be present.

Rossiyskaya, RUSSIAN SOVIET FEDERAL SOCIALIST REPUBLIC (RSFSR), largest constituent republic of the Soviet Union, occupying the E part of Europe and the N part of Asia, bounded NW by Norway and Finland, W by Poland, SE by China, Mongolia, and Korea, N by the Arctic Ocean (Barents Sea, Kara Sea, White Sea, Laptev Sea, E Siberian Sea, Chukchi Sea), E by the Pacific Ocean (Bering Sea, Sea of Okhotsk, Sea of Japan), and W and SW by the Atlantic Ocean and Caspian Sea; vast plains dominate the W half of the republic: the Ural'skiy Khrebet range (Ural Mts) separates the E European Plain (W) from the Zapadno Sibirskaya Ravnina (W Siberian Lowlands) (E); E of the R Yenisey lies the Sredne Sibirskoye Ploskogor'ye (Central Siberian Plateau), and beyond it, extending as far as the Lena basin, lies the N Siberian Plain; the Kavkaz (Caucasus), Tien Shan, and Pamir ranges lie along the S frontier; the Lena, Ob', Severnaya Dvina, Pechora, Yenisey, Indigirka, and Kolyma rivers discharge into the Arctic Ocean, while the Amur, Amgun', and rivers of the Kamchatka Peninsula discharge into the Pacific Ocean; the basin of the Caspian Sea includes the Volga and Ural rivers; there are over 20,000 lakes, the largest of which are the Caspian Sea, Ozero Taymyr, Ozero Baykal (Lake Baikal); large man-made reservoirs include the Rybinsk, Kuybyshev, Volgograd, Novosibirsk, and Bratsk; pop(1982) 141,012,000; area 17,075,400 sq km; capital Moskva (Moscow); chief cities Leningrad, Gor'kiy (Gorky), Rostov-na-Donu, Volgograd, Sverdlovsk, Novosibirsk, Chelyabinsk, Kazan', Kuybyshev, and Omsk; the fastest-growing new cities include Naberezhnyye Chelny, Angarsk, Bratsk, and Nakhodka; economy: petroleum and natural gas production (W Siberia, Volga-Ural oil-gas region, N Kavkaz, Timan-Pechora oil-gas basin); coal mining (Kuznetz and Pechora basins, E Siberia, S Yakutia and Kansk Achinsk basins); peat extraction; power generation (thermal steam-turbine plants); ferrous and non-ferrous metallurgy; machine building (transport, power industry and agricultural machinery); chemicals (mineral fertilizers, synthetic resins, plastics, chemical fibres); petrochemicals; lumber industry; light industry, particularly the manufacture of textiles; farmland occupies 2.19 mn sq km, or approx 13%, of the republic's total area; the RSFSR was formed on 25 Oct 1917; the republic is divided into the 71 administrative divisions of Altayskiy, Amurskaya, Arkhangel'skaya, Astrakhanskaya, Bashkiskaya, Belgorodskaya, Bryanskaya, Buryatskaya, Checheno Ingushskaya, Chelyabinskaya, Chitinskaya, Chuvashskaya, Dagestanskaya, Gor'kovskaya, Irkutskaya, Ivanovskaya, Kabardino-Balkarskaya, Kaliningradskaya, Kalininskaya, Kalmytskaya, Kaluga, Kamchatskaya, Karel'skaya, Kemerovskaya, Khabarovskiy, Kirovskaya, Komi, Kostromskaya, Krasnodarskiy, Krasnoyarskiy, Kurganskaya, Kurskaya, Kuybyshevskaya, Leningradskaya, Lipetskaya, Magadanskaya, Mariyskaya, Mordovskaya, Moskovskaya, Murmanskaya, Novgorodskaya, Novosibirskaya, Omskaya, Orel, Orenburgskaya, Penzenskaya, Permskaya, Primorskiy, Pskovskaya, Rostovskaya, Ryazanskaya, Sakhalinskaya, Saratovskaya, Severo-Osetinskaya, Smolenskaya, Stavropol'skiy, Sverdlovskaya, Tambovskaya, Tatarskaya, Tomskaya, Tul'skaya, Tuvinskaya, Tyumenskaya, Udmurtskaya, Ul'yanovskaya, Vladimirskaya, Volgogradskaya, Vologodskaya, Voronezhskaya, Yakutskaya, Yaroslavskaya.

Rosslare *ros-layr'*, ROS LÁIR (Gael), 52 17N 6 23W, pop(1980e) 600, port town in Wexford county, Leinster, SE Irish Republic; on St George's Channel, 8 km SE of Wexford; ferry links with Fishguard and Milford Haven.

Rosso *ros'ō*, 16 29N 15 53W, pop(1976) 16,466, river-port capital of Trarza region, SW Mauritania, NW Africa; on the R Sénégal, 88 km NE of Saint Louis (Senegal); rebuilt after floods in 1950.

Rossvat'net, lake in S Nordland county, N central Norway, N of the R Vefsna; area 210 sq km; 2nd largest lake in Norway.

Ro'stock, county in N East Germany; bounded N by the Baltic sea and includes the island of Rügen, which is linked to the mainland at Stralsund; pop(1981) 889,121; area 7,074 sq km; capital Rostock; chief towns include Wismar, Stralsund and Greifswald; economy: shipbuilding, food processing, diesel engines, fishing, electronics, industrial chalk; 70% of the county is farmed, producing grain and livestock; the Baltic coast is a popular holiday area; ferries from Rostock-Warnemünde to Gedser in Denmark, and from Sassnitz to Trelleborg in Sweden.

Rostock or **Rostock-Warnemünde** *ro-stok-var-ne-myun'du*, 54 4N 12 9E, pop(1981) 236,011, industrial port and capital of Rostock county, N East Germany; at the mouth of the R Warnow where it meets the Baltic Sea; founded in 12th century; former Hanseatic League port; rebuilt in the 1950s, Rostock is the chief cargo port of East Germany, linked to the centre of the country by rail, water and motorway; Wilhelm Pieck University (1419); railway, rail ferry to Denmark; economy: shipyard, marine engineering, fish processing, electronics; monuments: navigation museum, 15th-c town hall.

Rostov-na-Donu *re-stof'nu-du-noo'*, ROSTOV-ON-DON (Eng), 47 15N 39 45E, pop(1983) 977,000, port capital of Rostovskaya oblast, SE European Rossiyskaya, Soviet Union; on the the R Don, 46 km from the river's entrance into the Azovskoye More (Sea of Azov); became a city in 1796; it was a major grain-exporting centre throughout the 19th century; university (1917); since the completion of the Volga-Don Canal, its port has increased in economic importance; railway; airport; economy: farm machinery, machine tools, aircraft, ship building, clothing, footwear, leatherwork, foodstuffs, wine-making.

Rostov-on-Don, city in SE European Rossiyskaya, Soviet Union. See Rostov-na-Donu.

Roswell, 33 24N 104 32W, pop(1980) 39,676, county seat of Chaves county, SE New Mexico, United States; near the R Pecos, 110 km N of Carlsbad; railway; economy: rail, trade and marketing centre in an irrigated farming area; nearby is Bitter Lake National Wildlife Refuge.

Rota *rō'tu*, one of the 3 major islands in the N Mariana Is, W Pacific, 51 km NE of Guam; area 85 sq km; length 17.6 km; has a volcanic base covered with coral limestone; airport; site of ancient stone columns.

Rothaargebirge *rōt'hahr-gub-ir-gu*, mountain range in E Nordrhein-Westfalen (North Rhine-Westphalia) prov, W Germany; extends 48 km SW of Winterberg; highest peak is the Kahler Asten (841 m); geologically considered part of the Rheinisches Schiefergebirge (Rhenish Slate Mts).

Rotherham *roth'er-ėm*, 53 26N 1 20W, pop(1981) 123,312, town in Rotherham borough, South Yorkshire, N England; on the R Don, 9 km NE of Sheffield; railway; economy: coal, iron, steel, machinery, brassware, glass; monuments: late Gothic All Saints church, Chantry Chapel of Our Lady (1383).

Roth'well, 53 46N 1 27W, pop(1981) 19,172, town in Leeds borough, West Yorkshire, N England; 7 km SE of Leeds; railway; economy: coal, chemicals.

Rotorua *rō-tō-roo'a*, 38 07S 176 17E, pop(1981) 48,314, health resort, North Island, New Zealand; the town is situated in a region of thermal springs, geysers and boiling mud; monuments: Whakarewarewa is a traditional Maori village; Maori arts and crafts centre has displays of traditional carving, weaving and greenstone carving.

Rot'terdam, 51 55N 4 30E, pop(1984e) 1,025,466, industrial city and chief port of the Netherlands, in Zuid Holland prov, W Netherlands; at the junction of the R

Rotte with the Nieuwe Maas (S branch of the R Rhine), 24 km from the North Sea; the city has been a major commercial centre of NW Europe since the 14th century; since the inauguration of the Europort harbour area in 1966, Rotterdam has become one of the world's largest ports; merchant shipbuilding has declined since 1945, but the port subsequently underwent rapid development, accelerated by the westward expansion of harbour basins and industrial sites; petrochemical industries have been established along the S bank of the Nieuwe Maas (the shipping channel from Rotterdam to the sea since 1872); the approach channel was deepened in 1984, and a new container terminal was built on the Maasblakte, the westernmost harbour basin; the centre of the city, containing the chief buildings (Grote Kerk, old and new town halls, the Exchange) was almost completely destroyed by German bombing in May 1940, but it has since been reconstructed to become one of the most modern cities in Europe; birthplace of Erasmus; Erasmus university (1973); railway; economy: shipbuilding (largest shipyard in Europe), ship repairing, machinery, rolling stock, bicycles, electrical and mechanical engineering, marine and civil engineering, oil refining, petrochemicals (largest plant on the Continent), foodstuffs, mining equipment, electronic and hydraulic equipment, computer systems, clothing, paper.

Rotuma *rō-too'ma*, 12 30S 177 05E, volcanic island in the SW Pacific Ocean, 386 km N of Vanua Levu, surrounded by 8 small islands; it is now part of the Dominion of Fiji; length 12.9 km; max width 4 km; chief town Ahau; economy: copra production, manufacture of finely-plaited mats.

Roubaix *roo-bay*, 50 42N 3 10E, pop(1982) 101,886, industrial and commercial town in Nord dept, Nord-Pas-de-Calais region, NW France; on the Belgian border, 11 km NE of Lille but forming part of the same conurbation; centre of the textile industry in N France; chartered in 1469; economy: textiles, textile machinery, clothing, carpets, plastics, rubber products; monuments: 15th-c Gothic church of St-Martin.

Rouen *roo-ã*, ROTOMAGUS (anc), 49 27N 1 04E, pop(1982) 105,083, river port and capital of Seine-Maritime dept, Haute-Normandie region, NW France; lying in a hollow on the right bank of the R Seine, 86 km E of its mouth, 114 km NW of Paris; 5th largest port in France; capital of Haute-Normandie (Upper Normandy); the trial and burning of Joan of Arc took place here in 1431; the novelist Gustave Flaubert, author of *Madame Bovary*, was born here in 1821; university (1967); road and rail junction; economy: cotton, additives for lubricants; it suffered heavy damage during World War II but has been reconstructed largely as a Ville Musée (museum town); monuments: restored 13-16th-c Gothic cathedral of Notre-Dame; 14th-c abbey church of St-Ouen (where Joan of Arc was sentenced to death in 1431); late-Gothic Palais de Justice (Law Courts); Gros Horloge (Great Clock-Tower), on a Renaissance arch.

Rouerge *rwerg*, dist and former pays in S France in the E of Guyenne on the barren S edge of the Massif Central; now occupying the dept of Aveyron and part of Tarn-et-Garonne; its chief town is Rodez.

Rough *ruf*, natural gas field in the North Sea off the coast of Humberside, England.

Roulers, town in Belgium. See Roeselare.

Roumania, European socialist republic. See Romania.

Rousse, okrug (prov) in Bulgaria. See Ruse.

Roussillon *roo-see-yõ*, former prov in S France, now largely occupying the dept of Pyrénées-Orientales; chief town is Perpignan; noted for its wine production.

Rovaniemi *ro-van-yay'mee*, 66 29N 25 40E, pop(1982) 31,363, capital city of Lappi (Lapland) prov, Finland; 160 km N of Oulu, at the junction of the Kemijoki and Ounasjoki, just S of the Arctic Circle; established in 1929; railway, airfield; with river access to the Baltic Rovaniemi became an important centre for the exploitation of timber in Lapland; after a fire destroyed most of the houses in the winter of 1944-45 the town was rebuilt by Alvar Aalto who laid out the main streets in the design of a reindeer's antlers.

Rovigo *rō-vee'gō*, prov of Veneto region, N Italy; pop(1981) 253,508; area 1,803 sq km; capital Rovigo.

Rovigo, 45 04N 11 47E, pop(1981) 52,218, capital of Rovigo prov, Veneto region, N Italy; 37 km SW of Padova; railway; monument: 17th-c cathedral.

Rovno *ro'vnu*, ROWNE (Pol), ROWNO (Ger), 50 39N 26 10E, pop(1983) 205,000, capital city of Rovenskaya oblast, Ukrainskaya SSR, Soviet Union; on the R Ust'e; formerly in Poland; railway; economy: machine building, metalwork, chemicals, flax, clothing; monument: wooden Church of the Assumption (1756).

Rowne, city in W Soviet Union. See Rovno.

Rowno, city in W Soviet Union. See Rovno.

Royal Oak, 42 30N 83 09W, pop(1980) 70,893, town in Oakland county, SE Michigan, United States; residential suburb 19 km N of Detroit; railway.

Roy'ston, 52 03N 0 01W, pop(1981) 12,993, town in East Hertfordshire dist, Hertfordshire, SE England; 20 km SW of Cambridge; at the crossing of the Icknield Way and Ermine Street; railway; economy: chemicals, electronics.

Roy'ton, 53 34N 2 08W, pop(1981) 21,098, town in Oldham borough, Greater Manchester, NW England; 3 km N of Oldham; railway; economy: textiles.

Rrëshen *u-resh'en*, 41 45N 19 52E, town and capital of Mirditë prov, N central Albania; on the R Fani i Madh.

Rua'ha, national park in central Tanzania, E Africa; area 12,950 sq km; established in 1964; situated between Dodoma and Mbeya.

Ruapehu *roo-a-pay'hoo*, 39 18S 175 40E, active volcano and highest peak on North Island, New Zealand; rises to 2,797 m in Tongariro National Park.

Rub al Khālī *roob' al KHa'lee*, (Arab, 'the empty quarter'), GREAT SANDY DESERT (Eng), sand desert of the Arabian Peninsula, extending S from Najd (Saudi Arabia) to Ḩaḑramawt (S Yemen), and from the NE border of Yemen to Oman; area 582,750 sq km; approx 1,200 km long and 640 km wide; it slopes from an altitude of 1,006 m in the W to near sea-level in the E; consists of the Nafūd and Dahnā desert types in the E and very loose duneland in the extreme W; linear dunes, 90-150 m high and aligned NE-SW, cover large areas of the desert; sand dunes rise to 200 m in the SW and there are salt marshes and pans in the SE; first traversed on foot by Bertram Thomas in 1931.

Ruda Śląska *roo'da slash-ka*, 50 16N 18 50E, pop(1983) 162,800, city in Katowice voivodship, S Poland; W of Katowice; formed in 1960 from several mining and industrial settlements; has Silesia's oldest mine (1741); railway; economy: coal mining, foundries.

Rudall River, national park in central Western Australia, W Australia; includes Blanche and Dora dry salt lakes and the Rudall river; area 15,694 sq km; established in 1977.

Rudolf, Lake, lake in N Kenya. See Turkana, Lake.

Rueil-Malmaison *ru-e-y' mal-mez-õ*, 48 52N 2 11E, pop(1982) 64,545, industrial suburb on the Seine R, 13 km W of Paris in Hauts-de-Seine dept, Ile-de-France region, N central France; economy: import and distribution of motor vehicles, manufacture of automobile parts, food processing; monuments: Château de Malmaison (built in the early 17th century, enlarged in 1799), home of Napoleon and Josephine in the early 1800s, now a Napoleonic museum; burial place of the Empress Josephine and Queen Hortense.

Rug'by, 52 23N 1 15W, pop(1981) 59,720, town in Rugby dist, Warwickshire, central England; on R Avon, 17 km E of Coventry; famous boys' public school (1567) where the game of rugby football originated; railway; economy: engineering.

Rugby, 48 24N 100 00W, pop(1980) 3,335, city in Pierce county, North Dakota, United States; 120 km E of Minot; at the geographical centre of North America.

Rugeley *rooj'li*, 52 46N 1 55W, pop(1981) 23,810, town in Cannock Chase dist, Staffordshire, central England; 13 km SE of Stafford; railway; economy: coal, engineering.

Rügen *ru'gen*, Baltic Sea island off the coast of Rostock county, East Germany; area 926 sq km; connected to the mainland near Stralsund; source of industrial chalk; ferries from Sassnitz to Trelleborg in Sweden; the island of Hiddensee lies to the W.

Ruggell *roo'gel*, 47 15N 9 32E, pop(1985) 1,326, commune in Unterland dist, Principality of Liechtenstein, central Europe; area 7.4 sq km.

Ruhengeri *roo-hen-ge'ree*, 1 30S 29 39E, pop(1978) 16,025, capital of prefecture of same name, Rwanda, central Africa; 65 km NW of Kigali; alt 1,859 m.

Ruhr *roor*, river in W Germany; rises N of Winterberg, flows W past Witten, Essen and Mülheim, to the R Rhine at Duisburg; length 213 km; navigable length 41 km (head of navigation is Witten); drainage basin area 4,489 sq km; the Ruhr valley is an important mining and industrial area, including several major cities, Essen, Bochum, Duisburg, Gelsenkirchen, Dortmund.

Ruiz, Nevado del *roo-ees'*, 4 53N 75 22W, active Andean volcanic peak in W central Colombia, South America; rises to 5,399 m on Caldas-Tolima dept border in the Cordillera Central; 32 km SE of Manizales; at the NW foot are the thermal springs of Termales or Ruiz; the volcano erupted in Nov 1985, causing a flood and mudslide, resulting in the loss of many lives.

Rukwa, region of W Tanzania, E Africa; bounded W by L Tanganyika and S by Zambia; pop(1985e) 603,000; chief town Sumbawanga.

Rukwa, Lake *roo'kwa*, salt lake in SW Tanzania, E Africa; situated E of L Tanganyika and NW of Mbeya; alt 793 m; 145 km long and 16 km wide; the lake has no visible outlet; the town of Sumbawanga lies close to the NW shore.

Ruma *roo'ma*, 45 01N 19 50E, pop(1981) 55,083, town in N Srbija (Serbia) republic, Yugoslavia; S of Novi Sad; railway.

Rumania, European socialist republic. See Romania.

Rum'phi, dist in Northern region, Malawi, SE Africa; area 5,952 sq km; pop(1977) 62,450.

Runcorn *rung'korn*, 53 20N 2 44W, pop(1981) 64,216, town in Halton dist, Cheshire, NW central England, on the S bank of the R Mersey and the Manchester Ship Canal, 3 km S of Widnes; designated a 'new town' in 1964; railway; economy: chemicals, brewing, engineering, glass.

Run'nymede, a meadow on the S bank of the R Thames, Surrey, SE England; 7 km SE of Windsor, near Egham; here, or on Magna Carta Island in the river, King John in 1215 signed the Magna Carta, the basis of the English constitution; monuments: Commonwealth air forces war memorial (1953), Kennedy memorial.

Ruse *roo'say*, or **Rousse** *roo'se*, okrug (prov) of N Bulgaria on the frontier with Romania, bordered to the N by the R Danube; area 2,595 sq km; pop(1981) 297,000; a vine-growing and horticultural area.

Ruse, 43 50N 25 59E, capital of Ruse okrug (prov), N Bulgaria; on the R Danube, 327 km NE of Sofiya; a major commercial and manufacturing centre; formerly called Rustchuk by the Turks; railway; airfield; economy: metal products, food processing, textiles, petroleum refinery, tobacco.

Rush'den, 52 17N 0 36W, pop(1981) 22,434, town in East Northamptonshire dist, Northamptonshire, central England; 11 km NE of Northampton; economy: footwear.

Rush'more, Mount, MOUNT RUSHMORE NATIONAL MEMORIAL, 43 53N 103 28W, mountain in W South Dakota, United States; height 1,943 m; situated in the Black Hills near Harney Peak, 27 km SW of Rapid City; famous for the gigantic sculptures of 4 past US presidents: Washington, Jefferson, Roosevelt and Lincoln; each head is 18 m high; work was begun in 1927 under the direction of Gutzon Borglum; the details which were uncompleted at the time of his death in 1941 were finished by his son, Lincoln.

Rüsselsheim *rü'suls-hīm*, 50 00N 8 27E, pop(1983) 59,300, town in Darmstadt dist, Hessen (Hesse) prov, W Germany; on the R Main, 11 km E of Mainz; railway; economy: motor vehicles.

Russia *rush'ya*, a term used to describe (1) the whole of the Union of Soviet Socialist Republics and (2) the Russian Soviet Federated Socialist Republic (Rossiyskaya), largest of the union republics, or its historical predecessor, European Russia. The term Soviet Russia, strictly applicable to the RSFSR, is also used loosely of the USSR.

Russian Soviet Federal Socialist Republic (RSFSR), constituent republic of the Soviet Union. See Rossiyskaya.

Rutana *roo-ta'na*, 3 56S 29 59E, town in Burundi, central Africa; 55 km S of Gitega.

Rutanzige, lake in E central Africa. See Edward, Lake.

Rutland, former county of central England; part of Leicestershire since 1974.

Ruvuma or **Rovuma** *roo-voo'ma*, river in E Africa; rises E of L Nyasa and flows E for 725 km to enter the Indian Ocean SE of Mtwara and just N of Cape Delgado; receives the R Lugenda; forms nearly all of the border (E of L Nyasa) between Tanzania and Mozambique.

Ruvuma, region of S Tanzania, E Africa; pop(1985e) 691,000; bounded S by Mozambique and W by L Nyasa (Malawi).

Ruwenzori *roo-wen-zō'ri*, QUEEN ELIZABETH, national park in SW Uganda, E Africa; area 1,978 sq km; established in 1952; situated on the border between Western and Southern provs; includes L George.

Ruwenzori, mountain range in E central Africa; situated along the Zaire-Uganda frontier with L Albert to the N and L Edward to the S; approx 120 km long; mostly crystalline rocks in contrast to many other African ranges which are of volcanic origin; European discovery by Henry Stanley and Emin Pasha in 1889; first ascents by the Duke of Abruzzi's expedition (1891-1906); main peaks (N-S): Mt Emin (4,798 m), Mt Gessi (4,791 m), Mt Speke (4,896 m), Mt Stanley (5,110 m), Mt Baker (4,843 m), Mt Luigi di Savoia (4,627 m), Humphreys Peak (4,578 m); at Margherita Peak, Mt Stanley is the highest mountain in Zaire.

Ruyigi *roo-ye'ge*, 3 28S 30 14E, capital of prov of same name, Burundi, central Africa; 35 km E of Gitega.

Ružomberok *roo'zhom-ber-ok*, 49 04N 19 15E, pop(1984) 27,846, town in Středoslovenský region, Slovak Socialist Republic, E Czechoslovakia; on R Váh SE of Žilina; railway; economy: textiles, paper, cheese; monument: ethnographic museum.

Rwamagana *rwa-ma-ga'na*, 1 57S 30 26E, town in Rwanda, central Africa; 65 km E of Kigali.

Rwanda *roo-an'da*, official name Republic of Rwanda, a republic in central Africa, bounded N by Uganda, E by Tanzania, S by Burundi and W by Zaire and L Kivu; timezone GMT +2; area 26,338 sq km; pop(1984) 5,836,000, in 1984 the UNHCR recorded 49,000 refugees; capital Kigali; chief towns include Butare, Biumba, Cyangugu, Gikongoro, Gisenye, Gitarama, Kibungu, Kibuye and Ruhengeri; the majority of the pop (84%) is of Hutu origin, the remainder being Tutsi (14%), Twa (1%) and Pygmy; the official languages are French and Kinyarwanda; the Kiswahili tongue is widely used in commerce; most of pop are Christians, Roman Catholic (65%) and Protestant (9%), the rest following local beliefs (25%) or are Muslims (1%); the unit of currency is the Rwanda franc; national holiday 1 July; membership of AfDB, EAMA, FAO, G-77, GATT, IBRD, ICAO, ICO, IDA, IFAD, IFC, ILO, IMF, INTERPOL, IPU, ITU, NAM, OAU, OCAM, UN, UNESCO, UPU, WHO, WMO, WTO.

Physical description. Rwanda is bounded to the W by L Kivu and by the Virunga volcanoes along the NW border with Zaire. The country is characterized by its relatively high altitude, the highest point being Karisimbi (4,507 m) in the Virunga range. The western third of the country drains into L Kivu and then the R Congo, with the remainder draining towards the R Nile via the R Kagera and L Victoria. Lakes include L Burera and L Ruhondo (N), L Rwanye and L Ihema (E), and L Mugesera (SE). Rivers include the Luhwa and Akanyaru rivers (S border), Biruruma and Nyabarongo rivers (central), R Kagituma (NE) and R Mukungwa (N central).

Climate. Despite its equatorial situation Rwanda has, owing to its altitude, a highland tropical climate. Wet seasons run from Oct to Dec and March to May with the highest rainfall in the W, decreasing in the central uplands and to the N and E. The average annual rainfall in Kigali is 1,000 mm.

History, government and constitution. In the 16th century the Tutsi tribe moved into the country and took over from the Hutu forming a monarchy headed by a *mwami* ('king'). The Germans arrived in 1894 and in 1899 the *mwami* court accepted the country as a German Protectorate. Belgian troops from Zaire occupied Rwanda in 1916 and after World War I the League of Nations mandated Rwanda and its southern neighbour Burundi to Belgium as the Territory of Ruanda-Urundi. After World War II the territory became a United Nations Trust Territory administered by Belgium. Unrest in 1959 led to a Hutu revolt and the overthrow of Tutsi rule. Elections in 1961 led to autonomy from Belgium in 1962 and in the same year the UN granted full independence to Rwanda (and Burundi). After a military coup in 1973 all political activity was banned, and in 1978 a new constitution was created with a return to civilian rule following in 1980. The legislative body comprises the National Development Council of 70 members, a president and a council of ministers. There is only one political party.

Economy. Agriculture is important though the level of self-sufficiency in food has declined in recent years. The main cash crops are coffee, tea (both major exports) and pyrethrum. Mining is the other important sector of the economy with cassiterite (tin ore) and wolfram (tungsten ore) being the chief minerals. Columbo-tantalite, beryl and amblygonite are also mined. There are reserves of methane in L Kivu though these have not yet been developed extensively. Industry is based on agricultural processing and the production of beer and soft drinks, soap, furniture, plastic goods, textiles and cigarettes. Rwanda's main trading partners are the USA, Belgium, West Germany and Kenya.

Administrative divisions. Rwanda is divided into 10 prefectures (which are named after their capitals) as follows:

Prefectures	*area (sq km)*	*pop(1978)*
Butare	1,830	601,165
Biumba	4,987	519,968
Cyangugu	2,226	331,380
Gikongoro	2,192	369,891
Gisenye	2,395	468,786
Gitarama	2,241	602,752
Kibungu	4,134	360,934
Kibuye	1,320	337,729
Kigali	3,251	698,063
Ruhengeri	1,762	528,649

The prefectures are further sub-divided into 143 communes.

Ryazan *rya-zan'y'*, 54 37N 39 43E, pop(1983) 483,000, capital city of Ryazanskaya oblast, Rossiyskaya, Soviet Union; on the R Oka, 192 km SE of Moskva (Moscow); railway; economy: cellulosic fibres, clothing, footwear, oil refining, chemicals.

Rybinsk, port in the Soviet Union. See Andropov.

Rybnik *rib'neek*, 50 07N 18 30E, pop(1983) 133,000, industrial city in Katowice voivodship, S Poland; SW of Katowice; centre of Rybnik coal basin with large deposits of high grade coking coal; artificial lake with recreation centre; technical college; railway; economy: mining, power.

Ryde *rīd*, 50 44N 1 10W, pop(1981) 19,843, resort town in Medina dist, Isle of Wight, S England; on NE coast of the island, 11 km SW of Portsmouth; railway; ferry link with the mainland from Fishbourne to the W; economy: transport equipment, tourism; monument: Quarr abbey (1132).

Rygg *ru'gu*, 61 46N 6 07E, pop(1980) 11,311, town in Østfold county, SE Norway.

Rysy *ri'see*, mountain in the Tatry group of the Carpathian Mts, Nowy Sącz voivodship, S Poland; on Czechoslovak frontier, S of Zakopane; at 2,499 m it is the highest peak in Poland.

Rzeszów *zhe-zhoof'*, voivodship in SE Poland; watered by R Wisłok which flows from the Beskid Mts to the S; pop(1983) 675,000; area 4,397 sq km; capital Rzeszów; chief towns include Mielec and Leżajk.

Rzeszów, 50 04N 22 00E, pop(1983) 134,400, capital of Rzeszów voivodship, SE Poland; on R Wisłok; large modern housing developments to W and S; technical university (1963); sports centre; canoe jetty on the river; airfield, railway; economy: important centre of machinery and metal industries; monuments: district museum, palace of Lubomirski princes (18th-c), 17th-c castle.

S

Sá da Bandeira, Angola. See Lubango.

Saale *zah'le*, river rising in the Fichtelgebirge, E of Bayreuth, W Germany; flows 427 km N through E Germany to meet the R Elbe SE of Magdeburg.

Saar *zahr*, SARRE *sar* (Fr), river in Moselle dept, France, and Saarland and Rheinland-Pfalz (Rhineland-Palatinate) provs, W Germany; rises in two headstreams near Le Donon summit of the Vosges, flows N through Moselle and Bas-Rhin depts of NE France, and NNW across German border to the R Moselle just above Trier; length 240 km; length in Germany 120 km; navigable length 120 km; chief tributaries Blies, Suiz, Rossel, Prims and Nied rivers.

Saarbrücken *zahr'brük-en*, SARREBRUCK *sahr-u-brük'* (Fr), 49 15N 6 58E, pop(1983) 190,100, capital of Saarland prov, W Germany; on the R Saar where it follows the Franco-German frontier, 62 km SE of Trier; economic and cultural centre of Saarland; university (1948); railway; economy: ironworks, metal products, coke and coal, oil products, rubber, machine tools, electrical engineering, optical equipment, lime and cement; monument: collegiate church of St Arnual (13-14th-c); noted for its trade fairs.

Saarland, SARRE (Fr), prov in W Germany; pop(1983) 1,052,800; area 2,571 sq km; capital Saarbrücken.

Sa'ba, island of the N Netherlands Antilles, E Caribbean, 50 km S of Sint Maarten and c.900 km N of the S Netherlands Antilles; part of the inner volcanic arc of the Lesser Antilles; rises to 870 m at Mt Scenery; area 13 sq km; pop(1981) 965; capital The Bottom.

Šabac or **Shabats** *shah'bahts*, 44 45N 19 41E, pop(1981) 119,669, town in W Srbija (Serbia) republic, Yugoslavia; on R Sava, 64 km W of Beograd; railway; economy: fruit and fish trade.

Sabadell *sa-ba-dayl'*, 41 28N 2 07E, pop(1981) 194,943, industrial town in Barcelona prov, Cataluña, NE Spain; on the R Ripoll, 15 km N of Barcelona; economy: textiles, wine, agricultural trade.

Sabah *su-bah*, state in E Malaysia, SE Asia; on the N tip of Borneo, the world's 3rd largest island; bounded SW by Brunei, W by South China Sea, E by Sulu Sea and S by Kalimantan (Indonesia); pop(1980) 955,712; area 73,711 sq km; capital Kota Kinabalu; became a member of the Federation of Malaysia in 1963 when British rule in N and NW Borneo came to an end; ethnic groups include Murut, Kadazan, Bajau, Illanun and Brunei Malay; Mt Kinabalu in the Kinabalu National Park is SE Asia's highest mountain at 4,094 m; watered by the R Kinabatangan which flows into Sandakan Bay.

Sabaragamuwa *sa-ba-ru-gah'moo-va*, province in SW Sri Lanka; pop(1981) 1,478,879; area 4,901 sq km; capital Ratnapura; comprises the dists of Ratnapura and Kegalla; includes the gem-rich valley of the Kalu Ganga; Sri Pada or Adam's Peak, is the sacred mountain to which Buddhists, Hindus and Muslims make pilgrimage Dec-April; the hollow rock at the summit is believed to be the footprint of Buddha by Buddhists, of Adam by Muslims, God Siva by Hindus and St Thomas the Apostle by some Christians; there is a seasonal migration of butterflies in Sri Lanka towards Adam's Peak during March and April; intensive tea and rubber cultivation is carried out on the flanks of the highlands.

Sab'hā, 27 04N 14 25E, pop(1973) 113,000, city in Sabhā prov, W central Libya, N Africa; built round an oasis; airfield.

Sabor *sa-bor'*, river in N Portugal, rises near Bragança, flows SSW to the Douro near Torre de Moncorvo; length 104 km.

Sa'bra, Palestinian refugee camp on the outskirts of Beyrouth (Beirut), Lebanon; created following the evacuation of Palestinians from the city after the June 1982 Israeli attack on Palestinians and Syrians; scene of a massacre of Palestinians by Christian Phalangists in Sept 1983.

Sabzevār *sab-za-var'*, 36 13N 57 38E, pop(1983) 107,900, town in Sabzevār dist, Khorāsān, NE Iran; 192 km W of Mashhad; cotton-growing centre.

Sacatepéquez *sak-a-te-pay'kes*, smallest dept in Guatemala, Central America; in the mountains W of Guatemala City; pop(1982e) 137,815; area 465 sq km; capital Antigua.

Săcel or **Sacele** *sa-chel'*, 47 39N 24 23E, pop(1983) 33,811, town in Braşov county, central Romania.

Sacramen'to, 38 35N 121 29W, pop(1980) 275,741, capital of state and of Sacramento county, central California, United States; on the E bank of the Sacramento river, 121 km NE of San Francisco; founded in 1848 at the settlement of New Helvetia which was established in 1839 by John Sutter on his land grant from Mexico; expanded rapidly after gold was discovered nearby in 1848; became state capital in 1854; university (1947); railway; airport; economy: food processing, high technology; monuments: the Roman Corinthian state capitol, built in 1860 in Capitol Park; Crocker Art Gallery; Sutter's Fort (built in 1840, now restored) contains a museum of Indian and pioneer relics.

Sacramento River, longest river in California, United States; rises in the N of the state in the Klamath Mts, near Mt Shasta; longest headstream is the Pit river, which flows from Goose L in the NE of the state; the Sacramento flows 615 km S through the N part of the great central valley of California to Suisin Bay (the E arm of San Francisco Bay), which it enters just after joining the San Joaquin river in their joint delta; principal tributaries: the Pit, Feather and American rivers; navigable as far as Red Bluff (412 km) for small craft; Sacramento is the principal port and city on the river; the Sacramento and San Joaquin, along with some of their numerous tributaries, form the basis of the immense Central Valley Project undertaken for purposes of flood control, water-distribution and hydroelectricity; one of the purposes is to supply Sacramento river water to the San Joaquin valley to the S; dams and reservoirs include the Shasta and Keswick dams on the upper Sacramento, the Folsom and Nimbus dams on its tributary, the American river, and the Friant Dam which encloses Millerton L on the San Joaquin NNE of Fresno.

Sadiqabad *sa-deek-ah-bad'*, 28 16N 70 09E, pop(1981) 64,000, city in Punjab prov, Pakistan; SW of Rahimyar Khan; railway.

Sado *sah'dō*, an island forming part of Niigata prefecture, Chūbu region, Japan; in the Sea of Japan, 48 km W of Niigata, off N Honshū; 56 km long; 19 km wide; area 854 sq km; mountainous island with central plain; rises to 1,173 m in the N; economy: farming, fishing, timber; chief town and port: Ryōtsu.

Sado *sa-doo'*, river in S Portugal, rises SW of Ourique; length 176 km, flows N to Atlantic at Setúbal where it forms a wide estuary, navigable 70 km to Porto de Rei; area of basin 7,628 sq km; principal tributaries Xarrama, Alcaçovas, Marateca, Alvalade, Arcão; the 228.9 sq km Estuario do Sado nature reserve was established at the mouth of the river in 1980.

Saf'fron Wal'den, WALEDANA (Lat), 52 1N 0 15E, pop(1981) 12,058, town in Uttlesford dist, Essex, SE England; 20 km N of Bishop's Stortford; economy:

scientific instruments, engineering; monuments: 15-16th-c church of St Mary the Virgin, Audley End House.

Safi *sa-fee'*, 32 19N 9 15W, pop(1982) 197,309, seaport in Safi prefecture, Tensift prov, NW Morocco, N Africa; on the Atlantic coast, 140 km NW of Marrakech; occupied by the Portuguese 1508-41; railway; economy: fishing, chemicals, boatbuilding and trade in phosphate.

Sagaing *su-gīng'*, division in NW Burma; bordered NW and N by India along the Naga Hills; rises to 3,826 m in Mt Sarameti, which is situated on the NW border with India; drained by the Chindwin and Irrawaddy rivers; pop(1983) 3,855,991; capital Sagaing.

Sagaing, 21 55N 95 56E, capital of Sagaing division, NW Burma; 16 km SW of Mandalay on the opposite side of the R Irrawaddy; capital of Shan kingdom in 14th century and of Burma in 18th century; railway; economy: cotton, sesame and fruit trade.

Sagamihara *sa-ga'mee-ha-ra*, 35 43N 139 23E, pop(1980) 439,300, city in Kanagawa prefecture, Kanto region, central Honshū island, Japan; SW of Tōkyo, 24 km WNW of Yokohama; railway; economy: electronics, machinery.

Sag'inaw, 43 26N 83 56W, pop(1980) 77,508, county seat of Saginaw county, E Michigan, United States; port on the R Saginaw, 51 km NNW of Flint; railway; economy: fabricated metals and automobile parts.

Sagunto *sa-goon'to*, SAGUNTUM (anc), MURVIEDRO (Arab), 39 42N 0 18W, pop(1981) 54,759, town in Valencia prov, E Spain; on the right bank of the R Palancia, 25 km N of Valencia; known as Murviedro till 1877; to the N is the Costa del Azahar or 'Orange-Blossom Coast' resort region and to the E is the industrial port of Grao de Sagunto; economy: steel, fruit, linen, brandy; monuments: Roman theatre, fortress and the Gothic St Mary church.

Saha'ra (Arab, 'wilderness'), desert in N Africa; the largest desert in the world, it extends with an average width of 1,440 km across N Africa from the Atlantic to the Libyan Desert, in which it continues unbroken to the Nile, and beyond that in the Nubian desert to the Red Sea; covers parts of Morocco, Algeria, Tunisia, Libya, Egypt, Sudan, Chad, Niger, Mali, Mauritania and the Western Sahara where the desert extends W to the Atlantic Ocean; Ahaggar (Hoggar) mountain range (S Algeria) rises to 2,918 m at Mt Tahat; Tibesti mountain range (N Chad) rises to 3,265 m at Pic Toussidé and 3,415 m at Emi Koussi; Haut Atlas, Moyen Atlas and Atlas Saharien form NW border in Morocco and Algeria; receives only small amounts of rain on an unpredictable basis usually in the form of heavy but brief thunderstorms and what does fall is subject to high evaporation rates; there are scattered isolated outlets of surface water at oases, the only places where agriculture is possible; generally void of vegetation there are areas of stunted scrub; the desert includes areas of drift sand (*erg*), rock (*hamada*) or gravel and pebbles (*areg*); wind erosion is intense on these unprotected surfaces from which the wind readily picks up sharp angular fragments which are broken away by extreme changes in temperature; the climate of the Sahara has been arid since the glacial epoch when the region was relatively humid with a park savannah vegetation; parts of the Sahara are composed of marine limestone; the remainder is predominantly Archaean and Palaeozoic rocks; trade in the form of camel caravans has been carried out across and around the Sahara for many centuries following routes marked by oases but avoiding the *erg*; near the frontier between Algeria and Libya oil exploration is taking place; on the S margin, towards Sudan, there is a distinct Negro strain to the local population, and on the N margins Arabs, descended from the conquering nomads of the 11th century, are numerous.

Saharanpur *su-hah'run-poor*, 29 58N 77 33E, pop(1981) 294,000, town in Uttar Pradesh state, N India; 145 km NNE of Delhi; founded in 1340; formerly a resort town of the Mogul Empire; linked to Chandigarh and Moradabad by rail; economy: cotton cloth, wood products, railway engineering, cigarettes, paper.

Sahel' (Arab, 'sahil' coast), general term for a belt of land bordering the S edge of the Sahara desert; includes Mauritania, Chad, Mali, Senegal, Burkina and Niger; the farmland of this area often suffers from low soil moisture and from a lack of soil nutrients, such as phosphorus and nitrogen.

Sahiwal *sah'hi-val*, 30 41N 73 10E, pop(1981) 152,000, city in Punjab prov, Pakistan; on the Bari-Doab canal, SW of Lahore; railway; economy: trade in wheat, millet and cotton.

Saida *sa-ee'da*, department of NW Algeria, N Africa; area 106,777 sq km; pop(1982) 436,031; chief town Saida.

Saïda *sī'da*, SIDON ('fishing'), 33 32N 35 22E, pop(1980e) 24,740, seaport capital of Saïda division (*caza*), Al Janūb, W Lebanon, on the Mediterranean Sea, 35 km N of Soûr (Tyre); seat of the government of Al Janūb governorate; situated at the centre of a well-watered coastal plain; the ancient city was founded in the third millenium BC; once noted for the manufacture of glass and purple dyes; railway; a coastal motorway through the city is under construction; economy: oil refining; monuments: 'sea castle' built by the Crusaders (1227-28)' on an islet connected to the mainland by a short causeway; ruins of the Phoenician temple of Echmoun, situated 4 km NE of the town.

Saidpur or **Syedpur** *sī'poor*, 25 48N 89 00E, pop(1981) 126,608, town in Rangpur dist, Rangpur, N Bangladesh; SW of Rangpur; railway.

Saimaa *sī'mah*, lake system extending over the Finnish Lake Plateau in Kymi and Mikkeli provs, SE Finland; total area 4,400 sq km of which L Saimaa comprises 1,300 sq km; max depth 100 m; 5th largest lake system in Europe; rivers, channels and locks connect with about 120 lakes whose shores are mostly covered with coniferous forest; important for timber floating; boats link the towns of Lappeenranta, Savonlinna, Kuopio, Varkaus and Joensuu; L Saimaa is linked to an inlet of the Suomenlahti (Gulf of Finland) by the Saimaa Canal (60 km); the lake system is also drained by the Vuoksinjärvi which flows past Imatra to Ladozskoje Ozero (Lake Ladoga).

St Albans *awl'benz*, VERULAMIUM (Lat), 51 46N 0 21W, pop(1981) 77,187, town in St Albans dist, Hertfordshire, England; on R Ver, 40 km NW of London; named after the first Christian martyr to be executed in Britain; the Magna Carta was drafted here; Royal Charter (1553); city status (1887); agricultural research station; railway; economy: agricultural trade, micro-electronics; monuments: cathedral (1115); unique Roman theatre; museum with Iron Age and Roman exhibits.

St Albert, 53 39N 113 32W, pop(1984) 35,529, town in central Alberta, SW central Canada; on the Sturgeon river; 11 km NW of Edmonton; railway; monument: the town contains the crypt of Father Lacombe, Alberta's heroic religious figure.

St Andrews, 56 20N 2 48W, pop(1981) 11,369, town in North-east Fife dist, Fife, E Scotland; on the S side of St Andrews Bay, 17 km SE of Dundee; university (the oldest in Scotland, founded in 1412); economy: textiles; tourism; St Andrews Royal and Ancient Golf Club is the ruling authority on the game; monuments: St Andrews West Port is one of the few surviving city gates in Scotland: it was built in 1589 and restored in 1843; St Andrews Castle (founded in 1200, rebuilt several times, now in ruins); remains of St Andrews cathedral (12th-13th-c), once the largest church in the country; repertory theatre; arts centre; events: golf week in April; British Amateur Golf Championships (June).

St Anton am Arlberg, 47 08N 9 52E, winter sports resort in the Lechtal Alps (Arlberg massif), Vorarlberg, W Austria; cableway facilities on Valluga, Galzig, Brandkreuz and Kapall; Hannes Schneider and Stefan Kruckenhauser developed skiing techniques and styles here.

St Austell *o'stel*, 50 20N 4 38W, pop(1981) 20,585, town in Restormel dist, Cornwall, SW England; 20 km NE of Truro; railway; economy: quarrying, brewing.

St Barthélemy *sī bar-tayl-u-mee'*, ST BARTS, mountainous island belonging to the French Overseas Department of Guadeloupe, Leeward group of the Lesser Antilles, E Caribbean; 230 km N of Guadeloupe and 240 km E of the Virgin Is; area 21 sq km; pop(1982) 3,059; chief town Gustavia; the island was ceded to Sweden in 1784 but returned to French administration in 1877.

St-Brieuc *sî bree-œ*, 48 30N 2 46W, pop(1982) 51,399, manufacturing and commercial city and capital of Côtes-du-Nord dept, NW France; on the Golfe de St-Malo, an inlet of the English Channel, 112 km NE of Quimper, on a plateau between the 2 waterways of the Gouedic and the Gouet, their valleys crossed by large viaducts; it is a city of wide boulevards and tall skyscrapers with a centre of old streets and ancient houses; railway; monuments: 13-14th-c cathedral, built on the site chosen for the 5th-c foundation by the Welsh monk Brieuc.

St Catharines, 43 10N 79 15W, pop(1981) 124,018, town in SE Ontario, SE Canada; near L Ontario, S of Toronto, NW of Niagara Falls; originally settled by the troops of Butler's Rangers who disbanded here in 1784; Brock University (1964); railway; canal; economy: situated at the heart of Canada's fruit belt and major wine growing region; light and heavy industry; events: Royal Canadian Henley Regatta (Aug); Niagara Grape and Wine Festival (Sept).

St Catherine's, Mount, 12 10N 61 40W, volcanic peak on the island of Grenada in the Windward Is, E Caribbean; the highest peak in Grenada, rising to 843 m.

St Charles, 38 47N 90 29W, pop(1980) 37,379, county seat of St Charles county, E Missouri, United States; on the R Missouri, 32 km NW of St Louis; railway; economy: manufactures shoes and metal products; capital of state, 1821-26.

St Christopher-Nevis or **St Kitts-Nevis**, official name Federation of St Christopher and Nevis, independent state in the N Leeward Is, E Caribbean, approximately 360 km SE of Puerto Rico; comprises the islands of St Christopher (St Kitts), Nevis and Sombrero; timezone GMT −4; area 269 sq km; capital Basseterre; pop(1980) 43,309; the pop is mainly of African Negro descent; English is the official language; Christianity is the dominant religion; the unit of currency is the East Caribbean dollar; membership of CARICOM, Commonwealth, ISO, OAS, UN.

Physical description and climate. St Kitts is 37 km long and has an area of 168 sq km. A mountain range, rising

to 1,156 m at Mt Misery, extends NW-SE across the central part of the island. Mt Misery is forest-clad and dominates the crater of an extinct volcano. Nevis, 3 km to the SE, has an area of 93 sq km and is dominated by a central peak rising to 985 m. The climate is warm with an average temperature of 26°C and an average annual rainfall of 1,375 mm. Humidity is low (71.5%). The period from May to Oct is hotter with higher rainfall.

History, government and constitution. In 1623 St Kitts became the first British colony in the West Indies. Control of the islands was disputed between France and Britain during the 17th and 18th centuries until in 1783 the 2 islands were declared British under the Treaty of Versailles. St Kitts and Nevis were united by the Federal Act of 1882 along with Anguilla, a small island 104 km NW of St Kitts. In 1967 the islands became a State in Association with the UK. The Anguilla Act of 1980 formally recognized the separation of Anguilla from the state of St Kitts-Nevis. St Kitts-Nevis became an independent democratic federal state on 19 September 1983. The British monarch is head of state and is represented on the islands by a governor-general. There are 2 legislative chambers, the national assembly, whose 11 members are elected for a 5-year term, and the Nevis Island assembly with 8 members.

Economy. Sugar, grown mainly on plantations on St Kitts, supplies 60% of total exports. On Nevis, a plant to process copra and cotton seed into oil, financed by Canada, was established in mid-1983. Manufacturing industry contributed 7.6% to the GDP in 1980, the main products being electrical appliances, footware, and garments. Chief imports include machinery and transport equipment, foodstuffs, chemicals, and fuel. Sugar, molasses, cotton, and copra oil are exported, mainly to the USA and the UK.

Communications. There is a deep water port at Bird Rock, Basseterre with cargo, roll-on-roll-off and tourist facilities and an international airport on St Kitts at Golden Rock. Thirty-six miles of railway services the sugar industry.

Administrative divisions. St Kitts is divided into 9 parishes and Nevis into 5.

St Clair Shores, 42 30N 82 53W, pop(1980) 76,210, residential town in Macomb county, SE Michigan, United States; on L St Clair, 21 km NE of Detroit; sailing centre.

St Cloud, 45 34N 94 10W, pop(1980) 42,566, county seat of Stearns county, central Minnesota, United States; on the Mississippi river, 93 km NW of Minneapolis; university; railway; economy: granite quarrying, light engineering, agricultural trade.

St Croix *saynt kroy'*, largest of the 3 main US Virgin Is, Lesser Antilles, Caribbean, 120 km E of Puerto Rico and 65 km S of St Thomas; pop(1980) 49,013; area 218 sq km; main towns Christiansted (one-time Danish West Indies capital) and Frederiksted; economy: tourism, oil refining, aluminium, textiles, pharmaceuticals, rum and fragrances.

St David's, 51 54N 5 16W, pop(1981) 1,800, village in Preseli dist, Dyfed, SW Wales; 25 km NW of Milford Haven on St Bride's Bay; episcopal seat; monument: 12th-c cathedral honours the 6th-c Welsh patron saint, Dewi Ddyfrwr (David the water drinker); the saint's day (1 March) is the national day of Wales.

St David's Island, island of the Bermuda Island group joined to the Main Island of Bermuda by a bridge across the Castle Harbour; US airforce base at Kindley.

St Denis *sî de-nee'*, 20 52S 55 27E, pop(1982) 109,072, capital of the French overseas territory of Réunion in the Indian Ocean; situated on the N coast of the island; airport (St Denis-Gillot).

St-Denis *sî-dė-nee*, 48 56N 2 21E, pop(1982) 91,275, modern industrial town and railway centre in Seine-Saint-Denis dept, Ile-de-France region, N central France, a N suburb of Paris, 10 km N of its city centre; economy: paints and varnishes, automobile and aeronautical equipment; monument: 12th-c basilica of St-Denis (the first monumental Gothic structure to be built in France) with the tombs of French monarchs including Louis XII, Henry II and Francis I.

St Elias, Mount *ee-lī'as*, 60 17N 140 55W, mountain in St Elias Mts, on Yukon-Alaska border, United States; 320 km W of Whitehorse; 113 km NW of Yakutat; situated on the S edge of the Seaward Glacier; rises to 5,489 m; 2nd highest peak in the USA.

St-Étienne *sî-tay-tyen*, 45 27N 4 22E, pop(1982) 206,688, manufacturing town and capital of Loire dept, Rhône-Alpes region, SW France; in the valley of the R Furens; on the Central Plateau, 51 km SW of Lyons; railway; economy: food processing, electronics, metalworking; it has been a centre of the metallurgical industry since the 16th century and was formerly one of the leading steel-producing centres of France; its main street runs in a straight line for some 5 km from N to S.

St Fergus, gas pipeline terminal in Banff and Buchan dist, Grampian, NE Scotland; on the North Sea coast, 7 km N of Peterhead; linked to the Brent, Frigg, Bruce, Dunlin and Magnus gas fields; an overland pipeline links with fractionation and ethylene plant at Mossmorran in Fife.

Saint Floris *sĩ flo-ree'*, national park in NE Bamingui-Bangoran prefecture, Central African Republic; area 17,400 sq km; established in 1933.

St Gallen', ST GALL *sĩ-gal'* (Fr), canton in NE Switzerland, in Alps; pop(1980) 391,995; area 2,016 sq km; capital St Gallen; chief towns Grabs, Gossau; bounded on the E by the R Rhine; surrounds the cantons of Appenzell Ausser Rhoden and Appenzell Inner Rhoden; joined the Swiss Confederacy in 1803.

St Gallen, 47 25N 9 23E, pop(1980) 75,847, ancient abbey town and capital of St Gallen canton, NE Switzerland; in a narrow, high valley in the Pre-Alps, 62 km E of Zürich; the town developed around the abbey founded by St Gall in the 7th century; one of the chief commercial cities of E Switzerland; prominent as the major textile centre of Switzerland; school of economics (1899); economy: textiles, engineering; events: Olma agriculture and milk industries fair; Spring Trade Fair (end of May).

St George, 32 24N 64 42W, port in the parish of St George's on the island of St George's, Bermuda; pop(1980) 1,647, situated on the S shore; capital of Bermuda until 1815 and formerly important as a fortified military installation; modern port facilities handle cruise ships and a small amount of cargo traffic; berths at Ordnance I were improved in 1976 to accommodate vessels up to 195 m long with an 8.4 m draught; Pennos Wharf handles vessels up to 225 m long; on the N side of the island is an oil terminal; radio communication facilities are based at Fort George to the W of the town.

St George's, parish on St George's Island, Bermuda; pop(1980) 4,587.

St George's, 12 03N 61 45W, pop(1980e) 8,000, port and capital town of Grenada, Windward Is, on the SW coast of the island, E Caribbean; Pearls International Airport is located 29 km from the capital; founded as a French settlement in 1650.

St George's Channel, stretch of sea between the SE of Ireland (W) and Wales (E), connecting the Atlantic Ocean with the Irish Sea; at its narrowest between Carnsore Point (Ireland) and St David's Head (Wales), where it is 74 km across.

Saint-Gilles *sĩ-zheel'*, SINT-GILLIS *sint-KHi'lis* (Flem), 50 50N 4 20E, pop(1982) 45,184, town in Brussel dist, Brabant prov, Belgium; a SW suburb of Bruxelles.

St Gotthard, 46 34N 8 31E, mountain pass and road tunnel between Andermatt and Airolo, over the St Gotthard massif in the Lepontine Alps, S central Switzerland; height 2,108 m; it is a bare flat depression with a number of small lakes; open June to Oct; the route was made passable in the Middle Ages; monument: 14th-c St Gotthard Hospice.

St Helena, 15 58S 5 43W, volcanic island in S Atlantic; a British territory 1,920 km from the SW coast of Africa; area 122 sq km; pop(1982e) 5,499, discovered on 21 May, 1502 by the Portuguese navigator Joao da Nova Castella who named the island after the mother of Emperor Constantine the Great, whose festival falls on that day in the Eastern Church calendar; became a port of call for ships travelling to the E Indies; annexed but not occupied by the Dutch in 1633; annexed and occupied by the East India Company in 1659; brought under the direct government of the British Crown by an Act of Parliament of 1833; Napoleon Bonaparte was exiled in St Helena at Longwood House in 1815 until his death in 1821; Ascension I was made a dependency of St Helena in 1922; official language is English; an Order of Council which came into force in 1967 provided for an Executive Council and a Legislative Council consisting of the Governor, Government Secretary and Treasurer, and 12 members; districts include Hutt's Gate (E), Plantation (W) and Briars; the port and capital is Jamestown; no airfield; passenger and cargo services to the UK and S Africa; the highest point on the island is Diana's Peak (823 m); the chief agricultural crops are maize, potatoes and vegetables; there are also sheep, cattle, horses, pigs, poultry; economy: exports of fish, timber, handicrafts.

St Helens 53 28N 2 44W, pop(1981) 114,822, industrial town in St Helens borough, Merseyside, NW England; 18 km E of Liverpool; railway; economy: coal, engineering, textiles, glass.

St Helens, Mount, 46 12N 122 12W, volcano in SW Washington, USA; situated in the Cascade range, 56 km E of Kelso; rises to 2,549 m; on 18 May 1980, after earthquakes since 20 March of the same year, Mount St Helens erupted, causing damage amounting to $2.5 billion; a large area of western states was affected by volcanic ash, 100 people were killed and 276 homes were destroyed.

St Helier *hel'yer, sĩ tayl-yay* (Fr), 49 12N 2 07W, resort capital of the Channel Islands; on the S coast of the island of Jersey, at the E end of St Aubin's Bay; nearby is the Hermitage, an ancient beehive chapel, cell of Jersey's patron saint; the town was the home of Victor Hugo from 1851-55.

St Hyacinthe *hī'a-sinth, sĩ-tee-a-sĩt'* (Fr), 45 38N 72 57W, pop(1981) 38,246, town in S Québec, SE Canada; on the Yamaska river, 48 km ENE of Montréal; first settled in 1760, the town grew into an industrial centre after the arrival of the railway in 1847; economy: textiles, footwear.

St Ives, 52 20N 0 05W, pop(1981) 15,803, town linked with Hemingford Grey in Huntingdon dist, Cambridgeshire, E central England; on the R Ouse, 8 km E of Huntingdon; economy: engineering, plastics, foodstuffs.

St Ives, 50 12N 5 29W, pop(1981) 10,052, resort town in Kerrier dist, Cornwall, SW England; 12 km NNE of Penzance; railway; event: festival of music and the arts (Sept).

St Jean *sĩ zhã'*, SAINT-JEAN-SUR-RICHELIEU, 45 18N 73 16W, pop(1981) 35,640, town in S Québec, SE Canada; on the Richelieu river; railway.

St John, 45 16N 66 03W, pop(1981) 80,521, seaport in S New Brunswick, SE Canada; on the S coast, on the Bay of Fundy, at the mouth of the St John river; the St John harbour is ice-free throughout the year; a fort was established here in 1631-35; the town was involved in the Anglo-French struggle for Acadia, finally being taken by an Anglo-American force in 1758 and becoming a British possession; United Empire Loyalists landed here after the American War of Independence and established Parr Town; in 1785 it became the first incorporated city in Canada and was renamed St John; Benedict Arnold lived here 1786-91; much of the town was destroyed by a great fire in 1877; railway; airfield; economy: shipbuilding, steel, pulp; monuments: at the upper end of the harbour are the Reversing Falls, where the water falls in opposite directions over a rocky ledge according to the tide; a granite cross in King Square in the centre of the city commemorates the founding of New Brunswick in 1784; also on the square is the Old Courthouse (1830) which has an unsupported stone spiral staircase which ascends 3 storeys; Trinity Church, rebuilt in 1877 after the fire, contains a wooden coat-of-arms from the colony at Massachusetts Bay, brought here after the American War of Independence; the building known as Chubb's Corner has carved stone heads on all the cornices, and was commissioned in 1878 by Mr Chubb to portray himself, the mayor, and the members of the common council; New Brunswick Museum contains relics from the Indian, French and English periods of the province's history; Martello Tower, built on a hill in 1812 as a precaution against American attack, has walls almost 2.5 m thick; Fort Howe (1778), a reconstructed fortress built on a cliff overlooking the harbour, was built on the site of Fort LaTour, a French stronghold defended by Madame LaTour against her absent husband's fur-trading rival.

St John, smallest of the 3 main US Virgin Is, Lesser Antilles, Caribbean, 8 km E of St Thomas and 56 km N of St Croix; area 52 sq km; pop(1980) 2,360; the population is concentrated mainly in the little town of Cruz Bay and the village of Coral Bay; the Virgin Is National Park, established in 1956, covers an area of 71 sq km.

St John's, 17 06N 61 50W, pop(1975e) 24,000, port and capital city of Antigua and Barbuda, Lesser Antilles, E Caribbean, on a sheltered bay of NW Antigua I; monuments: cathedral, old fortifications.

St John's, 47 34N 52 41W, pop(1981) 83,770, capital of Newfoundland prov, E Canada; in the SE part of the island; on the NE coast of the Avalon Peninsula; John Cabot was the first to land here in 1497; Sir Humphrey Gilbert landed here in 1583 and took possession of Newfoundland for Britain; a fishing settlement was later established; held by the French, it was finally taken by the British in 1762, when the final shots of the Seven Years' War were fired here; Memorial University of Newfoundland (1925); railway; airport; economy: shipbuilding, fish processing; monuments: forts stood on Signal Hill for centuries, guarding St John's harbour; it was on Signal Hill that the first wireless message was received by Marconi in 1901; the Colonial Building (built in 1850 with stone brought from Ireland) was the site of meetings of the Newfoundland legislature from 1850 until 1960; event: Memorial Day, in memory of 1 July 1916 when, during the Battle of the Somme, the Royal Newfoundland Regiment was almost wiped out.

St Joseph, 39 46N 94 50W, pop(1980) 76,691, county seat of Buchanan county, NW Missouri, United States; a port on the R Missouri, 74 km NNW of Kansas City; railway; economy: electrical products, processed foods, wire rope and wood products; monument: Pony Express Stables.

St Julians *joo'lyan*, 35 55N 14 30E, pop(1983e) 8,715, residential and resort town on the N coast of the main island of Malta; lying between St George's Bay and St Julians Bay.

St Laurent *sĩ lō rã'*, 45 31N 73 42W, pop(1981) 65,900, town in S Québec, SE Canada; on Montréal island, W suburb of Montréal; founded in 1675; Gen Wolfe landed here in June 1759; airfield.

Saint Laurent du Maroni *sĩ lo-rã doo ma-rō-nee'*, SAINT LAURENT, 5 29N 54 03W, pop(1984e) 7,000, capital of Saint Laurent du Maroni dist, French Guiana, NE South America; 250 km W of Cayenne on the R Maroni, on the border with Surinam; near the town is the old Camp de Transportation, the original penal centre, which is now occupied by squatters.

St Lawrence, ST LAURENT (Fr), river in E Canada; one of the principal rivers of N America and the chief outlet for the Great Lakes; issues from the NE end of L Ontario and flows NE to the Gulf of St Lawrence N of the Gaspé Peninsula; from L Ontario the river forms approx 183 km of the international boundary between the USA (New York state) and Canada (Ontario); the total length from L Ontario to its mouth is 1,197 km; length of the waterway from the W end of L Superior to the Gulf of St Lawrence is 3,058 km; at the end of L Ontario, between Kingston and Brockville, Ontario, lie the Thousand Islands; the rapids which follow this section of river are used to generate hydroelectric power at the Moses-Saunders Power Dam at Cornwall, Ontario; below this the river widens into L St Francis, then passes into S Québec where it widens again into L St Louis at the mouth of the Ottawa river and descends through the Lachine rapids to Montréal; between Sorel and Trois-Rivières is L St Pierre; from Québec onwards the river is tidal, and increases gradually in width to approx 145 km; principal tributaries: the Richelieu and St François rivers (S), the Ottawa, St Maurice and Saguenay rivers (N); the Richelieu forms a navigable link with L Champlain and the Hudson river; principal cities on its banks: Kingston, Brockville and Cornwall (Ontario), Ogdensburg (New York, USA), Montréal, Sorel, Trois-Rivières and Québec city (Québec); formerly the St Lawrence was navigable for ocean-going vessels only as far as Montréal, while canals around the rapids made the entire river navigable for vessels of limited drafts; between 1955 and 1959 a waterway known as the St Lawrence Seaway was built along the upper St Lawrence river between L Ontario and Montréal to allow the passage of vessels of deep draft between the Atlantic Ocean and the Great Lakes; the Saint Lawrence Seaway includes a system of canals, locks and dams and hydroelectric power projects.

St Léonard *sĩ lay-o-nar'*, 45 35N 73 39W, pop(1981) 79,429, town in S Québec, SE Canada; on Montréal island; a N suburb of Montréal.

St-Lo *sî-lō*, BRIOVERA (anc), later LAUDUS, 49 07N 1 05W, pop(1982) 24,792, market town and capital of Manche dept, Basse-Normandie region, NW France; on a hill above the Vire valley, 54 km W of Caen; fortified by Charlemagne; almost completely destroyed in World War II, it took 20 years to rebuild; the oldest quarter, the medieval 'Enclos' in the upper part of the town, has largely been preserved; railway; monuments: 14-15th-c church of Notre-Dame (restored), old Romanesque church of Ste-Croix (restored); the St-Lo Stud breeds thoroughbred stallions of English, Norman and Percheron origin.

St Louis *saynt loo'is*, 38 37N 90 12W, pop(1980) 453,085, city independent of St Louis county, E Missouri, United States; on the R Mississippi, 16 km downstream of its junction with the R Missouri; settled by the French in 1764, it was under Spanish control from 1770 to 1800; in 1804 it was ceded to the USA and in 1822 it became a city; 3 universities (1818, 1853, 1960); railway; largest city in Missouri and busiest inland port on the Mississippi, as well as being a major land transport hub; economy: aircraft, spacecraft, machinery, metal products, food products, chemicals, and beer, trade in furs, livestock, grain and other farm produce; monuments: Gateway Arch (a giant steel arch, 192 m high, standing on the banks of the Mississippi, symbolizing St Louis as the Gateway to the West); art museum, Science Centre, Missouri Botanical Garden, Goldenrod Showboat, Sports Hall of Fame; events: Veiled Prophet Fair (July), Ragtime and Jazz Festival (June).

Saint-Louis, region in Senegal, W Africa; pop(1976) 528,473; area 44,127 sq km; called Fleuve until 1984; capital Saint-Louis.

Saint-Louis, 16 01N 16 30W, pop(1979) 96,594, seaport capital of Saint-Louis region, Senegal, W Africa; on a small island at the mouth of the R Sénégal, 177 km NE of Dakar; one of the earliest French settlements in W Africa, Saint-Louis was built in 1658 on Sor island as a trading company fort and prospered owing to the slave trade; the port was capital of French West Africa from 1895 to 1902 when Dakar became capital; railway terminal; airfield.

St Louis Park, 44 57N 93 21W, pop(1980) 42,931, town in Hennepin county, SE Minnesota, United States; suburb 7 km SW of Minneapolis; railway.

St Lucia *loo'sha* or *loo-see'a*, 2nd largest of the Windward Is, E Caribbean, situated 32 km N of the island of St Vincent and 40 km S of the French island of Martinique; area 616 sq km; timezone GMT −4; capital Castries; chief towns Vieux-Fort and Soufrière; pop(1980e) 120,300; 90.3% of the population is of African descent; the dominant religion is Roman Catholicism; English is the official language although a French patois is widely spoken; the unit of currency is the Eastern Caribbean dollar; membership of Commonwealth, CARICOM, FAO, G-77, GATT (de facto), IBRD, ICAO, IDA, IFAD, IFC, ILO, IMF, IMO, NAM, OAS, PAHO, UN, UNESCO, UPU, WFTU, WHO, WMO.

Physical description and climate. St Lucia, 43 km long and 22.5 km wide, is volcanic in origin, comprising craters and high lava ridges. It is mountainous in the centre, rising to 950 m at Mt Gimie. The twin volcanic peaks of Gros and Petit Piton rise steeply from the sea on the SW coast of the island to heights of 798 m and 750 m respectively. The climate is tropical with constant NE trade winds and an average temperature of 25°C. Temperatures range from a minimum of 18°C in the cooler months to a maximum of 34° in the hot season. The wet season extends from June to Dec and the dry season from Feb to May. Rainfall varies from 1,500 mm and 1,750 mm on the N and S coasts to 4,000 mm in the interior rain forests.

History, government and constitution. Columbus is reputed to have landed on St Lucia on 13 December 1502. Attempts to colonize the island were made by the English in 1605 and 1638. In 1650 the island was purchased, along with Grenada and Martinique, by 2 Frenchmen, and in 1659 began the great dispute between England and France over the island's ownership. In 1814 St Lucia finally became a British Crown Colony following the Treaty of Paris. It attained independence from Britain on 22 February 1979 and is now an independent constitutional monarchy within the Commonwealth. The British monarch is head of state and is represented on the island by a governor-general. There is a 17-seat house of assembly with its members elected every 5 years and an 11-seat senate whose members are nominated by the governor-general on the advice of the prime minister and leader of the opposition.

Economy. The economy is largely dependent on agriculture, tourism, and manufacturing. Agricultural output accounts for about 17% of national income, bananas (exported mainly to the UK), cocoa, copra, citrus fruits, and coconut oil being the chief agricultural products. Tourism is the fastest growing sector of the economy, accounting for 50% of the total foreign exchange. There was a 9% increase in tourist arrivals in 1983 with a 63.4% rise in the number of US tourists. The main manufacturing industries include garments, textiles, electronic components, beverages, corrugated boxes, paper products, and a vast oil complex. St Lucia exports most of its manufactured products to the CARICOM countries and to the USA. The main exports are bananas and cocoa while the main imports were foodstuffs, machinery and equipment, fertilizers, and petroleum products.

Administrative divisions. The country is divided into 16 parishes.

Communications. Hewanorra International Airport is situated at Vieux-Fort and there is an airstrip at Vigie near Castries (inter-island flights only). Castries is the country's chief port.

St-Malo *sî-mah-lō*, 48 39N 2 00W, pop(1982) 46,000, old port in Ille-et-Vilaine dept, Bretagne, W France; at the mouth of the R Rance facing Dinard; birthplace of Chateaubriand; the navigator Jacques Cartier (1491-1557) sailed to Canada from here; tidal power station nearby.

St-Marcouf, Iles *eel-sĩ mahr-coof*, 2 islands (Ile du Large and Ile de Terre) in the Baie de la Seine, S of the English Channel and off the E coast of the Cotentin Peninsula; part of Manche dept, NW France.

St Martin *sĩ mar-tĩ'*, SINT MAAR'TEN (Du), island in the Leeward group, NW extremity of the Lesser Antilles, E Caribbean, 260 km N of Guadeloupe and 310 km E of Puerto Rico; since 1648 the island's administration has been divided between (1) France and (2) the Netherlands; (1) the N two-thirds is a dependency of the French

Overseas Department of Guadeloupe; area 54 sq km; pop(1982) 8,072; chief town Marigot; (2) the remaining third belongs to the Netherlands Antilles; area 34 sq km; pop(1981) 13,156; capital Philipsburg.

St-Maur-des-Fossés *sî-mōr-day-fos-ay*, 48 48N 2 29E, pop(1982) 80,954, industrial town in Val-de-Marne dept, Ile-de-France region, N central France; a SE suburb of Paris, on the R Marne; economy: tinned foods.

St Moritz *sī mor-eets'*, SANKT MORITZ *zankt mō'rits* (Ger), SAN MUREZZAN (Roman), 46 30N 9 51E, resort town in Graubünden canton, SE Switzerland, in the Upper Engadine valley; a world-famous winter sports resort, home of the 1928 and 1948 Winter Olympics; winter sports facilities include a high ski-jump, 30 curling rinks, and the Cresta Run (tobogganing); the town comprises St Moritz Dorf, a village on a steep hill above the St Moritzer See with shops and large palatial hotels, and St Moritz Bad, a spa at the SW end of the lake, now an array of tower-block hotels; alt 1,853 m; railway; monument: Schiefer Turm in St Moritz Dorf, all that remains of the old Romanesque church of St Maurice.

St-Nazaire *sî-na-zayr*, 47 17N 2 12W, pop(1982) 68,974, seaport and industrial town in Loire-Atlantique dept, Pays de la Loire region, W France; on the right bank of the R Loire at its mouth, 53 km WNW of Nantes; believed to occupy the site of ancient Carbilo, where the Romans built a fleet in 56 BC; originally the deep-water port for Nantes, developing largely from the mid-19th century; in World War I it was a major port of debarkation for the American Expeditionary Force; a German submarine base in World War II, today the base is used for a number of industrial factories; in March 1942 the principal dock was destroyed during a British raid; much of St-Nazaire was destroyed in World War II but has now been largely rebuilt; economy: shipbuilding, marine engineering, steel, fertilizers, brewing, food canning.

St Neots *nee'ots*, 52 14N 0 17W, pop(1981) 21,290, town linked with Eaton Socon in Huntingdon dist, Cambridgeshire, E central England; on the R Ouse, 13 km SW of Huntingdon; railway; economy: paper, plastic, engineering, scientific instruments.

St Paul, 44 57N 93 06W, pop(1980) 270,230, capital of state in Ramsey county, SE Minnesota, United States; a port on the Mississippi river E of, and adjacent to, its twin city Minneapolis; founded in 1838; capital of Minnesota territory in 1849 and state capital in 1858; a city since 1854; Hamline University (1854); railway; economy: major industrial and commercial centre for a vast agricultural region; manufactures computers, electrical equipment, motor vehicles, chemicals, beer; monument: the State Capitol, modelled after St Peter's in Rome, with the largest unsupported marble dome in the world; events: Winter Carnival (Feb), Festival of Nations (April).

St Paul, Île, 38 44S 77 30E, volcanic island in S Indian Ocean, SE of Île Amsterdam; part of French Southern and Antarctic Territories; discovered in 1633 by the Dutch explorer, Van Diemen; annexed by France in 1843.

St Petersburg, 27 46N 82 39W, pop(1980) 238,647, town in Pinellas county, W Florida, United States; a port on the tip of Pinellas Peninsula, between Tampa Bay and the Gulf of Mexico; railway; airfield; economy: tourism, boatbuilding, trailers, air conditioners, electrical equipment and cement; trade in fruit and vegetables.

Saint Pierre and Miquelon, SAINT PIERRE ET MIQUELON *sã-pye-ray mee-klõ'* (Fr), French overseas territory in the N Atlantic Ocean, S of Newfoundland, Canada; comprises two islands and two communes; pop(1982) 6,041; area 240 sq km; main town St Pierre; visited and settled by Breton and Basque fishermen during the 16-17th centuries; land-based fishing and drying rights were a source of dispute between the UK and France during the 19th century; in 1946 it was classified as a French territory; economy: fishing, tourism.

St Pölten *sī pœlten*, 48 13N 15 37E, pop(1981) 50,419, industrial and commercial town and capital of Sankt Pölten dist, Niederösterreich, NE Austria; on the left bank of the R Traisen, between Linz and Wien (Vienna); bishopric; railway; monuments: noted for its Baroque architecture; 12-13th-c cathedral.

St-Quentin *sī-kã-tî*, 49 51N 3 17E, pop(1982) 65,067, industrial town in Aisne dept, Picardie region, N France; on the R Somme, 40 km NW of Laon; railway; economy: an important centre of the woollen industry during the Middle Ages; traditional textile production has now largely been overtaken by chemicals and metalworks; the St-Quentin Canal links it through the northern waterway system to the industrial capitals of Belgium and N Germany; it was surrounded by battlefields throughout World War I and occupied by the German army for 4 years; monuments: 12-15th-c basilica, late-Gothic town hall (early 16th-c facade and an 18th-c bell-tower with a 37-bell carillon); birthplace of the 18th-c pastel painter Maurice Quentin de la Tour (a collection of his works is housed in the Antoine Lecuyer Museum); the Museum of Entomology has one of the world's finest collections of butterflies and insects.

St Thomas, one of the 3 main US Virgin Is, Lesser Antilles, Caribbean, 64 km N of St Croix and 120 km E of Puerto Rico; pop(1980) 44,218; area 72.5 sq km; length 21 km; rises to 474 m at Crown Mt; capital Charlotte Amalie; at Coki Beach, on the NE coast, is the Coral World underwater observatory; airport; economy: tourism, rum distilling.

St-Tropez *sî trō-pay*, 43 16N 6 39E, fashionable resort on the Mediterranean coast of Var dept, Provence-Alpes-Côte d'Azur, SE France; SW of Cannes; a former small fishing port now frequented by yachtsmen, artists and tourists.

St Vincent, official name Saint Vincent and the Grenadines, island group of the Windward Is, E Caribbean, 160 km W of Barbados and 34 km S of St Lucia; timezone GMT −4; land area 389 sq km; capital Kingstown; chief towns Georgetown, Layou, Calliaqua, and Barrouallie; pop(1980) 123,758; the pop is mainly of African Negro descent, and there are small numbers of Asians, Europeans, and Caribs; most of the Carib pop was shipped to British Honduras (Belize) in the 1790s; English is the official language, but a local dialect is also spoken; Protestant Christianity is the dominant religion; the unit of currency is the East Caribbean dollar; membership of Commonwealth, CARICOM, FAO, G-77, GATT (de facto), IMF, IMO, OAS, UN, UPU, WFTU.

Physical description and climate. St Vincent and the Grenadines comprise the island of St Vincent and the N Grenadine Is, of which the largest are Bequia, Mustique, Canouan, Mayreau, and Union. St Vincent, some 29 km long and 16 km wide, is volcanic in origin with a ridge of mountains running the length of the island. The highest peak is Soufrière, a dormant volcano in the N rising to a height of 1,234 m. Transverse spurs divide the landscape into a series of valleys running down to the E and W coasts. The climate is tropical with an average temperature of 25°C and an average annual rainfall of 1,500 mm on the coast and 3,800 mm in the mountainous interior. During the rainy season, from June to December, temperatures may rise to 32°C.

History, government and constitution. St Vincent formed part of the West Indies Federation from 1958 to 1962. It became a self-governing Associated State of the UK in 1969 and acquired full independence on 27 Oct 1979. There is a democratically elected government. Head of state is the governor-general, appointed by and representing the British sovereign. The house of assembly consists of 13 members elected by universal adult suffrage from single-member constituencies, the attorney-general, and 6 senators appointed by the governor-general.

Economy. Agriculture forms the basis of the economy, accounting for approx 20% of national income. The main cash crops are bananas, arrowroot (the world's largest production), and coconuts. Secondary agricultural products include nutmeg, mace, cocoa, and food

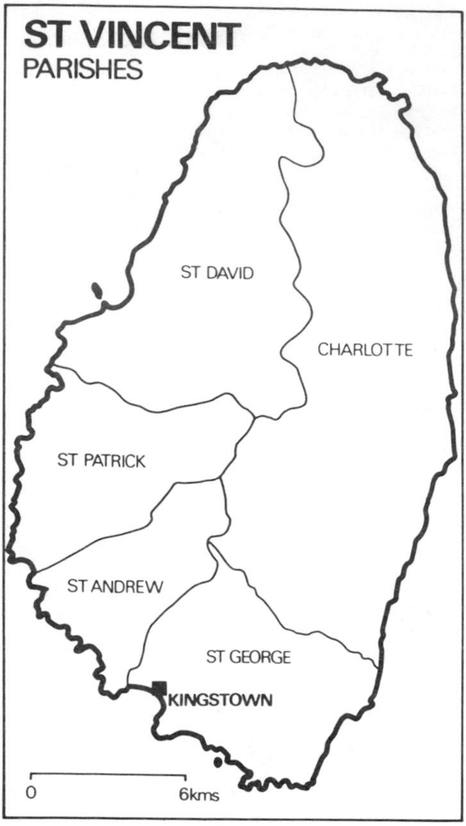

crops. The banana plantations were partly destroyed by the Soufrière eruption in 1979 and Hurricane Allen the following year. Sugar cane was reintroduced in 1980. Food processing is the major industry but small manufacturing units produce cigarettes, textiles and clothing, beverages, furniture, and concrete blocks. Chief imports included foodstuffs, machinery and equipment, chemicals and fertilizers, minerals and fuels, mainly from UK, Trinidad and Tobago, Canada and US. The main exports were bananas, arrowroot, and copra. In 1979, UK received 75% of all exports while Trinidad and Tobago accounted for 13%.

Administrative divisions. The island is divided into the 5 parishes of Charlotte, St George, St David, St Patrick, and St Andrew. For political purposes there are 13 divisions: South Leeward, North Leeward, Central Leeward, East St George, West St George, South Central Windward, North Central Windward, South Windward, North Windward, Marriaqua, East Kingstown, West Kingstown, and the Grenadines.

Sainte Foy *sĩt fwah*, 46 47N 71 18W, pop(1981) 68,883, town in S Québec, SE Canada; on the St Lawrence river; S of Québec; Québec's major residential suburb; Laval University (1852); economy: the town contains 2 of the largest shopping centres in Canada.

Saintes, Îles des *sît*, string of islands belonging to the French Overseas Department of Guadeloupe, Lesser Antilles, E Caribbean; Terre-de-Haut, Terre-de-Bas, and Îlet-à-Cabrit are the only inhabited islands; area 14 sq km; pop(1982) 2,901; chief town Terre-de-Bas.

Saintonge *sĩ-tõzh*, former prov on the Gironde estuary, W France, now occupying with Aunis the dept of Charente-Maritime.

Saipan *sī'pan*, largest of the N Mariana Is, W Pacific, 240 km NNE of Guam; area 122 sq km; length 23 km; width 8 km; a barrier reef protects a wide lagoon off the W coast; airport; in 1944 the island was taken from the Japanese by US forces after a fierce and bloody battle; economy: tourism.

Sajama, Cerro *ser'rō sa-KHa'ma*, national park in NW Oruro dept, Bolivia; area 299 sq km; established in 1945; the world's highest forest; contains the Nevado Sajama, Bolivia's highest peak at 6,542 m.

Sakai *sa'kī*, 34 35N 135 28E, pop(1980) 810,106, city in Ōsaka prefecture, Kinki region, S central Honshū island, Japan; on the E shore of Ōsaka-wan Bay, S of Ōsaka; the harbour is now silted up and of little importance; university; economy: chemicals, fertilizers, aluminium products, machinery.

Sakarya *sa-kar-ya'*, prov in NW Turkey, bounded N by the Black Sea; pop(1980) 548,747; area 4,817 sq km; capital Adapazarı.

Sakarya, river in W central Turkey; rises on the plateau of Anadolu (Anatolia), 29 km NNE of Afyon; flows generally N in a series of bends past Adapazarı to meet the Black Sea at Karasu; length 824 km; chief tributaries Aladağ, Ankara, and Porsuk; there are hydroelectric power plants on the river.

Sakhalin *sah-kah-leen'*, KARAFUTO *ka-ra'foo-too* (Jap), elongated island in the Sea of Okhotsk, Rossiyskaya, E Soviet Union, separated from the Russian mainland to the W by the Tatarskiy Proliv (Tatar Strait), and from Japan to the S by La Pérouse Strait; with the Kuril'skiye Ostrova (Kuril Is) it forms Sakhalinskaya oblast; area 74,066 sq km; length 942 km; max width 160 km; max height 1,609 m; chief towns Okha, Aleksandrovsk-Sakhalinskiy, Korsakov, Makarov, and Poronaysk; first visited by the Russian explorer Poyarkov in 1644; assumed to be a peninsula until the early 19th century; the Japanese colonized the island at the end of the 18th century while in 1853, the Russians established a military post at Korsakov; under joint Russo-Japanese control until 1875 when it was yielded completely to Russia in exchange for the Kuril'skiye Ostrova (Kuril Is); under the Portsmouth Treaty (1905) Japan gained control of the S portion of the island, named Karafuto; in 1945 the whole island was ceded to the USSR; Sakhalin was known as a place of exile for csarist prisoners; the 2 parallel mountain ranges on the island, Zapadno-Sakhalinskiy Khrebet (W) and Vostochno-Sakhalinskiy Khrebet (E), are orientated N-S and are separated by a central valley; the NW coastline is marshy; agriculture is concentrated in the central valley and the S portion of the island; the climate is severe with an annual mean temperature near freezing point and annual rainfall of 510-630 mm; forests, ruthlessly exploited at one time to supply the Japanese wood-pulp industry, still cover large areas of the island; there are oil fields in the NE.

Sakhalin Gulf, inlet of the Sea of Okhotsk. See Sakhalinskiy Zaliv.

Sakhalinskiy Zaliv, SAKHALIN GULF, inlet of the Sea of Okhotsk, between the N end of Sakhalin I and the mainland of Khabarovskiy kray, E Siberian Rossiyskaya, Soviet Union; connects with Tatarskiy Proliv (Tatar Strait) in the S.

Sal *sahl*, 16 36N 22 55N, island with fine beaches in the Barlavento or windward group of Cape Verde; area 216 sq km; pop(1980) 6,006, rises to 400 m at Monte Grande in the N; tourist facilities at Espargos and Santa Maria; international airport (Amilcar Cabral); salt is mined for export.

Šala *sha'la*, 48 09N 17 51E, pop(1984) 21,274, town in Západoslovenský region, SW Slovak Socialist Republic, central Czechoslovakia; on R Váh, SW of Nitra; railway; economy: agriculture and wine trade.

Salado del Norte, Río *del nor'tay*, river, N central Argentina; originates in the Andes in branches that rise NW and SW of Salta; flows 2,000 km SE across Salta, Santiago del Estero and Santa Fe provs to the Paraná at Santa Fe; formed by the confluence of the Toro and Guachipas rivers just E of Coronel Moldes, 56 km S of Salta, it then flows E and S for 240 km as the Pasaje or

Juramento to a swampy area in NW Santiago del Estero prov, where it takes the name Río Salado del Norte.

Salado, Río *sa-la'THō*, part of a central Argentine river system which forms a broad 960 km-long basin from the Andes of N La Rioja prov S across N Patagonia to the Río Colorado in S La Pampa prov; rises as the Bermejo in W La Rioja prov, flows 400 km S through San Juan prov, continues S along Mendoza-San Luis prov border as the Desaguadero to a point S of Salar Bebedero (a shallow salt lake); there it becomes the Río Salado and flows S into La Pampa; it turns SE and joins the Río Colorado 240 km W of Bahía Blanca; its lower course is sometimes called the Curacó; tributaries include the Atuel, Diamante and Tunuyán rivers; total length is 1,200 km.

Salaga *sa'la-ga*, 8 43N 0 28W, town in Northern region, central Ghana, W Africa; situated between Kumasi and Tamale.

Salāhuddīn *sal-a-hoo-deen'*, governorate in N central Iraq; pop(1977) 363,819; area 21,326 sq km; capital Sāmarrā'; part of the R Tigris lowland.

Sălaj *sa'lazh*, county in NW Romania, to the N of the Apuseni Mts; pop(1983) 266,407; area 3,850 sq km; capital Zálău.

Şalālah *sa-la'lu*, 16 56N 53 39E, pop(1983e) 10,000, seaport on the Arabian Sea, Sultanate of Oman, S Arabian peninsula; on a coastal plain backed by mountains; airfield; excavations are being carried out at Al Balid, an 11th-c Islamic town.

Salamá *sa-la-ma'*, 15 06N 90 15W, capital town of Baja Verapaz dept, central Guatemala, Central America; on the Río Salamá; market centre in an agricultural area.

Salamanca *sa-la-mang'ka*, 20 34N 101 12W, pop(1980) 160,040, town in Guanajuato state, S central Mexico; 100 km W of Querétaro, on the Río Lerma at an alt of 1,723 m; railway.

Salamanca, prov in Castilla-León region, N Spain; a dry steppe region on the Portuguese border; pop(1981) 368,055; area 12,336 sq km; capital Salamanca; economy: dairy products, pharmaceuticals, wool (Bejar), clothes, rubber products; uranium dioxide is mined.

Salamanca, HELMANTICA, SALMANTICA (anc), 40 58N 5 39W, pop(1981) 167,131, capital of Salamanca prov, Castilla-León, W Spain; on the R Tormes, 212 km W of Madrid; bishopric; university (1940); railway; economy: agricultural centre, rubber products, wool, pharmaceuticals, monuments: Plaza Mayor built by Philip V; 15th-c House of Shells; the Schools Square with fine examples of Salamanca Plateresque; San Stefano monastery, old and new cathedrals; events. Holy Week; patronal festival in June; fair and fiesta in Sept.

Salamat', prefecture in SE Chad, N central Africa; pop(1979) 107,000; area 63,000 sq km; extensive marshland towards the SW with rivers including the Salamay and Bahr Kelta flowing SW; the Bahr Kameur forms the SE border with Central African Republic; capital Am Timan; chief towns Abou Deïa, Kaché, Hadjera, Kouga, Cehep and Beréguile; part of Zakouma National Park found in W.

Salamís *sa'lu-mis* or *sah-lah-mees'*, also called KOULOURI *koo-loo'ri*, 37 58N 23 30E, pop(1981) 20,437, town in Attikí nome (dept), Sterea Ellás-Évvoia region, Greece, on the W coast of Salamís I, W of Piraiévs; the famous naval defeat of the Persians under Xerxes took place in 480 BC; local ferries; event: Navy Week (June-July).

Salang, tunnel and pass in the Hindu Kush, E Afghanistan; links the provs of Baghlān and Parvān; lies along the main supply route from the USSR to capital Kābul; focus of resistance activity by the Mujahideen guerrillas against the Soviet troops and the Afghan Army after the invasion of Afghanistan in 1979.

Salcantay, Nevado *nay-va'dō sal-kan-tī'*, 13 18S 72 35W, Andean peak in Cuzco dept, S central Peru; highest point in the Cordillera Vilcabamba at 6,271 m; 72 km WNW of Cuzco; to the N are the ruins of the Inca city of Machu Picchu.

Sale, 38 06S 147 06E, pop(1983e) 13,820, city in East Gippsland stat div, SE Victoria, Australia; ESE of Melbourne; railway; economy: supply centre for the Bass Strait oil fields; monuments: regional arts centre; an oil and natural gas display outlines the story of the development and production of oil in the Bass Strait oil fields; the Omega Tower (427 m) is the highest building in Australia.

Sale, 53 26N 2 19W, pop(1981) 57,933, town in Trafford borough, Greater Manchester, NW England; 8 km SW of Manchester; railway; economy: engineering.

Salé *sa-lay'*, 34 04N 6 50W, pop(1982) 289,391, city in Rabat-Salé prefecture, Nord-Ouest prov, NW Morocco, N Africa; at the mouth of the Bou Regreg opposite Rabat of which it is now essentially a suburb; there has been a settlement on this site since the 3rd century AD but the present city was founded in the 11th century and used as a base for Moorish Barbary pirates during the 17th and 18th centuries; railway; economy: fish canning, carpets, pottery.

Salem *say'lum*, 11 40N 78 11E, pop(1981) 515,000, city in Tamil Nadu state, S India; on a tributary of the R Kollidam, 270 km SW of Madras; linked by rail to Erode and Vellore; transport centre for nearby iron and manganese mines; economy: textiles and the processing of minerals.

Salem, 42 31N 70 53W, pop(1980) 38,220, county seat of Essex county, NE Massachusetts, United States; a residential suburb of Boston on Massachusetts Bay, 22 km NE of Boston; settled in 1626; developed as a port serving the east Indies trade; 20 people were executed as witches here in 1692; railway; monuments: Witch Museum, Salem Maritime National Historic Site.

Salem, 44 56N 123 02W, pop(1980) 89,233, capital of state in Marion county, NW Oregon, United States; on the Willamette river, SSW of Portland; founded in 1841 by a missionary group; became capital of Oregon Territory in 1851 and state capital in 1859 when Oregon was admitted to the Union; Willamette University (1842); railway; economy: food processing, high technology equipment, silicon wafers, metal goods.

Saler'no, prov of Campania region, S Italy; pop(1981) 1,013,779; area 4,924 sq km, capital Salerno.

Salerno, 40 40N 14 46E, pop(1981) 157,385, industrial town and capital of Salerno prov, Campania region, Italy; 50 km ESE of Napoli (Naples), on a bay of the Tyrrhenian Sea, bounded E by the Appno Napoletano; its early fame was due to its university, the earliest in Europe, a notable school of medicine, which flourished from the 11th century until it was closed down by Murat in 1812; archbishopric; university (1970); railway; monument: 11th-c cathedral.

Salford *sawl'furd*, 53 30N 2 16W, pop(1981) 98,343, city in Salford borough, Greater Manchester, NW England; on the R Irwell and Manchester Ship Canal, W of Manchester; chartered in 1230; designated a city in 1926; university (1967); railway; economy: textiles, electrical engineering, chemicals, clothing; monuments: Peel Park Museum; art gallery housing the largest collection of paintings by L.S. Lowry.

Salgótarján *shol'gō-tor-yahn*, 48 05N 19 47E, pop(1984e) 50,000, capital of Nógrád county, N Hungary; on a branch of the R Zagyvar, W of Budapest; industrial and mining centre; economy: steel, iron, coal and lignite mining, machinery.

Salima *sa-lee'ma*, 13 45S 34 29E, resort town in Salima dist, Central region, Malawi, SE Africa; situated close to L Nyasa, 80 km ESE of Lilongwe; economy: export of tropical fish, tourism.

Salina *se-lī'nah*, 38 50N 97 37W, pop(1980) 41,843, county seat of Saline county, central Kansas, United States; on the Smoky Hill river, 130 km N of Wichita; university (1886); railway; economy: trade centre in wheat-growing area; manufactures aircraft parts and dairy products.

Salinas *sa-lee'nas*, 2 15S 80 58W, pop(1982) 17,748, resort town in Guayas prov, W Ecuador; on the Punta Santa Elena, W of Guayaquil; railway; holiday resort for the residents of Guayaquil, with deep-sea fishing and water-skiing.

Salinas, 36 40N 121 39W, pop(1980) 80,479, capital of Monterey county, W California, United States; in the N of the Salinas river valley, c.72 km S of San José; railway; economy: food processing, electronics, agricultural trade.

Salisbury *sawlz'bêr-i*, NEW SARUM, 51 05N 1 48W, pop(1981) 37,831, city in Wiltshire, S England; at the junction of the Avon, Nadder, Bourne and Wylye rivers, 34 km NW of Southampton; chartered in 1270; New Sarum replaced Old Sarum in the 13th century when Bishop Richard Poore transferred his see 3 km S to the Avon valley in 1220, taking all the townsfolk with him; the Duke of Buckingham was beheaded here in 1483 when Salisbury was the headquarters of Richard III; railway; economy: engineering, tourism, agricultural trade; monuments: 13th-c cathedral, with the highest spire in Britain, contains one of 4 copies of the Magna Carta; churches of St Thomas (15th-c), St Martin (13-15th-c) and St Edmund (1407); Old Sarum (3 km N), abandoned site of a castle, cathedral and town, returned 2 members to Parliament until the passing of the Reform Bill.

Salisbury, capital of Zimbabwe. See Harare.

Salle, La, *la sahl'*, 45 26N 73 40W, pop(1981) 76,299, town in S Québec, SE Canada; in the S of Montréal island, on the St Lawrence river and the end of Lac St Louis.

Salmiya, 29 20N 48 10E, pop(1980) 145,730, E suburb of Al Kuwayt (Kuwait City), State of Kuwait, on a peninsula which juts into the Arabian Gulf.

Salo *sah-lo'*, 63 37N 23 32E, pop(1982) 19,967, town in Turku-Pori prov, SW Finland; at the head of a long inlet of the Gulf of Bothnia, 48 km E of Turku; railway.

Salonga *sa-long'ga*, national park in Zaire, central Africa; area 36,560 sq km; established in 1970; situated in NE Bandundu region, S Equateur region and NW Kasai Occidental region; main rivers include the Salonga, the Lomela and the Luilaka.

Salonica, nome (dept) and city in Greece. See Thessaloníki.

Salonta *sa'lon-ta*, 46 49N 21 40E, pop(1983) 21,113, town in Bihor county, NW Romania; SW of Oradea, near the Hungarian frontier; railway junction; economy: food processing, textiles; monument: 17th-c Turkish fortress.

Salou, Cabo *sa-lō'*, 41 03N 1 10E, cape to the S of Tarragona, Cataluña, E Spain, sheltering the resort bay near the holiday village of Salou; Jaime I sailed from here in 1229 to capture the island of Mallorca.

Saloum, Delta du *sa-loom'*, national park in SW Senegal, W Africa; area 9,130 sq km; established in 1976.

Salt, 32 03N 35 44E, pop(1978) 35,000, capital town of Al Balqā' governorate, East Bank, NW Jordan; 21 km WNW of Amman.

Salt Cay, 21 21N 71 11W, island in the Turks Is, British dependent territory of Turks and Caicos; in the W Atlantic, SE of the Bahamas; area 6.5 sq km; pop(1980) 284; airfield.

Salt Lake City, 40 45N 111 53W, pop(1980) 163,033, capital of state in Salt Lake county, N Utah, United States; on the R Jordan, near the S end of the Great Salt Lake; settled by Mormons under Brigham Young in 1849; the city expanded as a centre on the route to the California gold mines; the world centre of the Mormon Church, with 60% of the population being Mormons; university (1850); railway; economy: processing centre for an irrigated agricultural region; manufactures include aerospace components, electronic equipment, processed foods, and agricultural chemicals; silver, lead, and copper smelting plants; monuments: Temple Square, Trolley Square, Salt Lake Art Centre, Utah Museum of Fine Arts, Pioneer Memorial Museum, Hansen Planetarium, Utah Museum of Natural History; event: Utah arts festival (June).

Salta *sal'ta*, prov in Norte region, NW Argentina; in the Andes; borders Chile (W) and Bolivia (N); the Andes slope E through the dry *puna* region to the Chaco plains; rises to 6,723 m at Cerro Llullaillaco; drained by Bermejo, Juramento, Guachipas and Calchaquí rivers; there are large salt deserts in W; the climate varies from the dry cold of the highlands to the warm humidity of the fertile, inhabited valleys; the General Belgrano Dam is used for irrigation, hydroelectricity and flood control; pop(1980) 662,870; area 154,775 sq km; capital Salta; economy: wine, sorghum, sugar cane; cattle and sheep raising; timber; copper, lead and salt mining; natural gas.

Salta, 24 46S 65 28W, pop(1980) 260,323, capital of Salta prov, Norte, NW Argentina; on the Río Arias, in the Lerma valley; alt 1,190 m; founded in 1582; the cathedral contains venerated Christian images sent from Spain in 1592 - thought to have caused a miracle on 13 Sept 1692, when an earthquake ceased on their being paraded through the streets; a large parade is held each Sept in celebration of this event; Gen Belgrano defeated Spanish royalists here in 1813; a local festival on 24 Sept commemorates the battles of Tucumán and Salta; university (1967); railway; airport (General Belgrano); economy: commercial and trade centre for extensive farming, timber, stock-raising and mining area.

Saltash, 50 24N 4 12W, pop(1981) 12,460, town in Kerrier dist, Cornwall, SW England; on the R Tamar estuary, W of Plymouth; railway; economy: light engineering.

Saltcoats *sol'kōts*, 55 38N 4 47W, pop(1981) 12,834, town in Cunninghame dist, Strathclyde, W Scotland; situated on the W coast, on the Firth of Clyde, SE of Ardrossan; railway; monument: North Ayrshire museum.

Saltillo *sal-tee'yō*, 25 30N 101 00W, pop(1980) 321,758, resort capital of Coahuila state, N Mexico; 85 km SW of Monterrey; alt 1,609 m; founded in 1575; university (1867); railway; economy: clothing, textiles, ceramics, coal mining; monument: 18th-c cathedral; events: Indian dances on 30 May and 30 Aug; fiestas, with colourful ceremonies and bullfights (Oct).

Salto *sal'tō*, dept in NW Uruguay; bordered W by Argentina along the Río Uruguay and S by the R Daymán; drained by the Río Arapey; pop(1985) 105,617; area 12,603 sq km; capital Salto; the dept was formed in 1837.

Salto, 31 27S 57 50W, pop(1985) 80,787, capital of Salto dept, NW Uruguay; on Río Uruguay; railway; airfield; a ferry service crosses the river to the Argentinian town of Concordia; economy: citrus fruit processing; 20 km from Salto is the Salto Grande dam and hydroelectric plant, which was built jointly by Uruguay and Argentina; an international highway and railway run across the top of the dam, linking the two countries; 6 km N of the city lie the medicinal springs of Termas de Daymán, at Fuente Salto.

Saltpond, 5 13N 1 00W, coastal town in Central region, S Ghana, W Africa; situated NE of Cape Coast.

Salut, Îles du *sa-lü'*, island archipelago, approx 13 km off the coast of French Guiana, NE South America; 45 km NNW of Cayenne; includes the Ile Royale, Ile Saint Joseph and the Ile du Diable; housed notorious French penal colonies from 1852 to 1953; political prisoners, including Alfred Dreyfus, were incarcerated on the Ile du Diable (Devil's Island) which was almost inaccessible from the sea; the main Camp de Transportation was at Saint Laurent on the Surinam border; on Ile Royale the 20-bed hotel is the warders' former mess hall.

Salvador *sal-va-dor'*, BAHIA *ba-hee'ah*, 12 58S 38 29W, pop(1980) 1,491,642, port capital of Bahia state, Nordeste region, NE Brazil; on the Atlantic coast SE of Recife; founded in 1549, Salvador replaced Olinda as Brazil's capital; university (1946); railway; airfield at 32 km; economy: cigars, oil refining, petrochemicals, tourism; monuments: most of the city's 135 churches and the fortifications date from the 17-18th centuries; Salvador is divided into 2 zones, the Baixa or lower part, known as Comércio and the Alta or upper part, known as Centro; the commercial quarter and old port are in the lower part of the city; the older parts of the upper city are now a national monument and extensive restoration work has been undertaken; the old centre in the upper city is reached by a series of steep streets and by 4 public lifts; in the upper city around the main square (Praça Municipal) are the old government palace and the city library (built in 1811); the oldest of Salvador's forts, Santo Antônio da

Barra, was built in 1589; events: 3rd Sunday in Jan (Festa do Nosso Senhor do Bomfim); 2 July (Independence of Bahia); carnival time begins at the end of Nov and continues until the end of Jan.

Sal'vador, El, official name Republic of El Salvador, REPÚBLICA DE EL SALVADOR (Sp), smallest of the Central American republics, bounded N and E by Honduras, W by Guatemala, and S by the Pacific Ocean; timezone GMT −6; area 21,476 sq km; capital San Salvador; chief towns Santa Ana, San Miguel, Mejicanos, Delgado, Nueva San Salvador, and Sonsonate; chief ports La Unión, La Libertad and Acajutla; pop(1981) 4,672,900; 89% of the pop is of Spanish-Indian origin; Spanish is the official language but some Indians still speak Nahuatl; the predominant religion is Roman Catholicism; the unit of currency is the colón of 100 centavos; membership of CACM, FAO, G-77, IADB, IAEA, IBRD, ICAC, ICAO, ICO, IDA, IDB, IFAD, IFC, ILO, IMF, IMO, INTELSAT, INTERPOL, ITU, IWC, OAS, ODECA, PAHO, SELA, UN, UNESCO, UPU, WFTU, WHO, WIPO, WMO, WTO.

Physical description. Two virtually parallel volcanic mountain ranges running E-W divide El Salvador into three geographical regions, ranging from a narrow coastal belt in the S through upland valleys and plateaus at an average elevation of 600 m to mountains in the N. The highest volcanoes are Santa Ana (2,381 m), San Vicente (2,178 m), San Miguel (2,130 m) and San Salvador (1,885). The Río Lempa, dammed for hydroelectricity and flowing S to meet the Pacific Ocean, is the chief river and the most important volcanic lakes are Lago de Ilopango (72 sq km) and Lago de Coatepeque (26 sq km). The Laguna de Güija SW of Metapán straddles the frontier with Guatemala.

Climate. Climate varies considerably with altitude from the coastal plain and lowlands with a hot tropical climate and a single rainy season between May and Oct to the temperate uplands. At San Salvador, which lies in the lower part of the hill country at an altitude of 682 m, the average temperature is 23°C; the average temperature on the coast is 26°C. The mean annual rainfall is 1,775 mm.

History, government and constitution. El Salvador gained independence from Spain in 1821 and became a member of the Central American Federation until its dissolution in 1839. In 1841 El Salvador formally declared itself an independent republic. The 1983 constitution confirmed the executive power vested in a president elected for a term of 5 years. There is a legislative National Assembly of 52 members elected by universal suffrage. During recent times considerable guerrilla activity has been directed at the US-supported government.

Economy. The economy of El Salvador is largely based on agriculture which accounted for over 25% of national income and the employment of over 35% of the pop in 1981. Although the terrain is mountainous, a deep layer of ash and lava from successive volcanic eruptions has formed a porous soil ideal for coffee planting. Coffee and cotton are the most important crops although recent diversification has introduced sugar and maize as export crops. A few wealthy families own most of the land with the majority of agricultural workers living at subsistence level. Attempts at agrarian reform by successive governments have generally failed. El Salvador is the only producer of balsam, used for the manufacturing of medical drugs and cosmetics. Major industries include food processing and the manufacture of textiles, shoes, furniture, chemicals, fertilizers, pharmaceuticals, construction materials, cement, rubber goods, and petroleum products. The chief exports are coffee (typically 50-52% by value), cotton and clothing, and sugar. The main trading partners are the USA, countries of the CACM, the Federal Republic of Germany, Japan, Canada, France, the Netherlands, and the UK.

Administrative divisions. The republic is divided into 14 departments as follows:

Department	*area (sq km)*	*pop(1971)*
San Salvador	892	681,656
Santa Ana	1,829	375,186
San Miguel	2,532	337,325
Usulután	1,780	304,369

contd

Department	*area (sq km)*	*pop(1971)*
La Libertad	1,650	293,076
Sonsonate	1,133	239,688
La Unión	1,738	230,103
La Paz	1,155	194,196
Chalatenango	2,507	186,003
Ahuachapán	1,281	183,682
Morazán	1,364	170,706
San Vicente	1,175	160,534
Cuscatlán	766	158,458
Cabañas	1,075	139,312

Salween *sal-ween'*, NU JIANG, river in SE Asia; length 2,815 km; rises at 32° N 94° E in the Tanggula Shan range of E Xizang autonomous region, SW China; flows SE through deep gorges in parallel with the Lancang Jiang and Jinsha Jiang rivers, S through Yunnan prov, China, and into Burma; cutting a gorge through the Shan plateau, the Salween flows generally S through Shan and Kayah states, then forms part of the Burma-Thailand border (with Kawthulei state); the Salween enters the Gulf of Martaban, an inlet of the Andaman Sea, at Moulmein, forming a common mouth with the Gyaing and Ataran rivers; as the majority of the Salween is obstructed by rapids, it is navigable only as far as Kamamaung, 120 km above its mouth; major tributaries include the Nam Pang, Nam Teng, Pawn, Nam Hka, Nam Hsin and Thaungyin rivers.

Salzach *zalts'aKH*, river in W central Austria, rising in the Hohe Tauern; flows E into central Salzburg state then N to the Austro-German frontier where it meets the R Inn near Braunau; length 225 km.

Salzburg *zalts'boork*, federal state in central Austria, lying on the W German frontier and between Tirol state and the states of Kärnten, Steiermark and Oberösterreich; comprises 6 dists and 119 communities; pop(1981) 441,842; area 7,154 sq km; capital Salzburg; named after its rich salt deposits; Badgastein and Bad Hofgastein are spa resorts; the small towns of Saalbach-Hinterglemm, Zell am See and Kaprun have become well-known in recent years as winter sports centres; the state is dominated by the Dachstein massif and watered by the Traun, Enns and Mur rivers; the Salzach valley is the principal traffic route through the state; economy: salt extraction, hydroelectricity, Alpine pastoral farming, forestry, aluminium plants, tourism.

Salzburg, 47 25N 13 03E, pop(1981) 139,426, capital of Salzburg state, central Austria; on the R Salzach; since 1945 it has developed into a focal point for the international tourist trade; birthplace of Mozart, a fame reflected and maintained in the Mozarteum (musical academy) and the annual Mozart festival; the Old Town lies between the left bank of the river and the Mönchsberg ridge; railway; university (re-opened in 1962); archbishopric; economy: textiles, brewing, metallurgy; monuments: cathedral (1614-28), St Peter's church (1130-43); Franciscan church; Kollegienkirche (college church, built for the university between 1694 and 1707), town hall (1407), rebuilt in 1618 and 1772; the town is dominated by the fortress of Hohensalzburg, situated to the S of the Old Town on the SE summit of the Mönchsberg; this castle was first built in 1077, as a refuge for the archbishops in the wars between the Pope and the Holy Roman Empire; events: annual Salzburg Festival from the end of July to Aug, supplemented now by Herbert von Karajan's Easter Festival; Mozart Festival Week (end of Jan).

Salzburg Alps, division of the Eastern Alps along Austro-German border S of Salzburg; mainly in SE Bayern (Bavaria) prov, W Germany, surrounded by short, high ranges, Hagengebirge, Übergossene Alm, Steinernes Meer; highest peaks are the Hochkönig (2,938 m) in Austria, and the Watzmann (2,713 m) in Germany.

Salzgitter *zahlts'gi-tur*, formerly WATENSTEDT-SALZGITTER *vah'tun-shtet-*, 52 02N 10 22E, pop (1983) 111,100, city in Braunschweig dist, SE Niedersachsen (Lower Saxony) prov, W Germany; S of Braunschweig; railway; economy: iron and steel, shipbuilding, machine tools, tracked vehicles.

Salzkammergut *zalts'kam-ar-goot*, E Alpine region in Salzburg, Oberösterreich and Steiermark states, central Austria; a popular tourist area with many lakes (Attersee, Mondsee, Wolfgangsee; mts include Dachstein and Totes Gebirge; Gmunden, Hallstatt and Bad Aussee towns are located in this region; the name originally applied to a salt-mining area around Bad Ischl.

Samangān *sa-man-gan*, prov in N Afghanistan; pop(1984e) 284,351; area 15,465 sq km; capital Āybak (Samangān); bounded N by the R Ryandzh and the USSR; linked by road to Kābul in the SE.

Samar *sahm'ar*, island in the Visayas group, E Philippines; SE of Luzon I and NE of Leyte I; bounded E by Philippine Sea; area 13,424 sq km; chief towns Calbayog, Catarman and Catbalogan.

Samaria *su-ma'ree-u*, *su-may'ree-u*, ancient division of Palestine, now a hilly region of W Jordan in Israeli-occupied Judea-Samaria dist; bounded W by the Plain of Sharon and E by the Jordan valley.

Samarinda *sa-ma-rin'da*, 0 30S 117 09E, pop(1980) 137,521, capital of Kalimantan Timur prov, E Borneo, Indonesia; on E coast of Borneo at mouth of R Mahakam; university (1962); airfield; economy: coal, oil.

Samarkand *su-mur-kant'*, 39 40N 66 57E, pop(1983) 505,000, capital city of Samarkandskaya oblast, Uzbekskaya SSR, Soviet Union; a major industrial, scientific, and cultural centre situated in the fertile Zeravshan valley; known as the city of Timur (1333-1405), when it was named after the Tatar conqueror; university (1933); railway; airfield; economy: solar research and development, fruit growing, wine-making, manufacture of furniture, porcelain, clothing, foodstuffs, sheepskins, and silk and cotton; monuments: Gur Emir, the mausoleum of Timurids, a sepulchre capped by a tiled cupola; Ulug Begh's madrasah (1417-20).

Sāmarrā', 34 16N 43 55E, capital of Salāhuddīn governorate, N central Iraq; on R Tigris, N of Baghdād; sacred to Shiite Muslims; economy: chemicals and pesticides.

Samawah, As *sa-ma'wu*, 31 18N 45 18E, pop(1965) 33,473, capital town of Al-Muthanna governorate, S central Iraq; on R Euphrates, on the highway between Al Basrah and Baghdād; railway.

Sambre *sã-br*, river in NE France and S central Belgium, rising near le Nouvion in N Aisne dept, NE France; flows ENE through Nord dept then across the Belgian border, past Maubeuge and Charleroi, to meet the R Meuse at Namur; length 190 km.

Samokov or **Samakov** *sa'ma-kof*, 42 19N 23 34E, pop(1981e) 27,000, town in Sofiya okrug (prov), W Bulgaria, 48 km SSE of Sofiya; formerly important as an iron-mining centre; economy: textiles, agricultural trade; fruit-growing nearby.

Sámos *sah'mos*, nome (dept) of Aegean Islands region, Greece; pop(1981) 40,519; area 778 sq km; capital Vathí.

Sámos, wooded island in the E Aegean Sea, Greece, off the W coast of Turkey, from which it is separated by a strait only 2 km wide; pop(1981) 31,629; area 476 sq km; rises to 1,140 m in the centre, and 1,440 m in the W; famed for its wines; birthplace of Pythagoras; it possesses the site of one of the most important sanctuaries and cultural centres of the ancient world, the Heraion.

Samothráki *sahm-oth-rah'kee*, 40 28N 25 32E, Greek island in the NE Aegean Sea, 40 km from the mainland; area 178 sq km; rises to 1,600 m; noted particularly for its sanctuary of the Great Gods, the home of a mystery cult, and for the *Victory of Samothráki* sculpture which was found here and is now in the Louvre (Paris).

Samsun *sam'soon*, maritime prov in N Turkey, bounded N by the Black Sea; pop(1980) 1,008,113; area 9,579 sq km; capital Samsun; economy: tobacco.

Samsun, AMISUS (anc), 41 17N 36 22E, pop(1980) 198,749, seaport capital of Samsun prov, N Turkey; at the mouth of the R Murat, on the Black Sea; railway; airfield; economy: tobacco-processing; events: fair and folk-dance festival in Aug.

Samui or **Ko Samui** *kō sah-mui*, 3rd largest island (*ko*) of Thailand; one of a 60-island group in the Gulf of Thailand, 600 km S of Bangkok; includes the Angthong marine national park.

San *sã*, 13 21N 4 57W, pop(1971) 16,300, town in Ségou region, central Mali, W Africa; 345 km ENE of Bamako; airfield; economy: agricultural trade.

San, *san*, river in SE Poland; rises in Carpathian Mts near Czechoslovak frontier; flows 443 km NW, E and NW to meet the R Wisła (Vistula) NE of Stalowa Wola; tributaries include the R Wisłok; dammed at Solina and Myczkowce.

San Andrés-Providencia *san an-drays'-pro-vee-THen'sya*, intendency of Colombia, South America, comprising two small islands and 7 groups of coral reefs and cays in the Caribbean; 400 km SW of Jamaica, 180 km E of Nicaragua and 480 km N of Colombia (between 12° and 16°N and 78° and 82°W); the largest island is San Andrés; Providencia, also called Old Providence, lies 80 km NNE of San Andrés; it is 7 km long and more mountainous than San Andrés; the islands have belonged to Colombia since 1822; in the 17th century they were the headquarters of the pirate Henry Morgan; the islands are a duty free zone and San Andrés is an important international airline stopover; pop(1985) 36,515; area 44 sq km; capital San Andrés; economy: coconuts, vegetable oil, tourism.

San Angelo, 31 28N 100 26W, pop(1980) 73,240, county seat of Tom Green county, W Texas, United States; at the junction of the 2 forks of the R Concho; settled in 1867; university; railway; economy: an important wool market and a trade and shipping centre for a farming, ranching, and oil-producing area; manufactured products include processed foods, footwear, oil-drilling equipment; monument: Fort Concho Museum.

San Antonio *san an-tō'nee-ō*, 33 35S 71 36W, pop(1982) 65,174, port and capital of San Antonio prov, Valparaíso, central Chile; economy: exports copper brought by rail from the large mine at El Teniente, near Rancagua; resorts nearby include Cartagena, 8 km N; Llolleo, 4 km S; Maipo, at the mouth of the Río Maipo; and Santo Domingo.

San Antonio, 29 25N 98 30W, pop(1980) 785,880, county seat of Bexar county, S central Texas, United States; on the San Antonio river, 120 km SW of Austin; settled by the Spanish in 1718; during the Texas Revolution the city was captured by the Texans (1835), and was the scene of the Mexican attack on the Alamo (1836); during its history the city has flown 5 different flags - those of Spain, Mexico, the Republic of Texas, the Confederate States of America, and the United States; 2 universities (1852, 1869); a military aviation centre; railway; airport; economy: industrial, trade, and financial centre for a large agricultural area; manufactures include processed foods, aircraft, electronic equipment, building materials, chemicals, wood products, clothing, and machinery; monuments: the Alamo, Paseo del Rio (the Spanish Governor's palace), Museum of Art, Institute of Texan Cultures, Tower of the Americas (229 m high); events: Fiesta San Antonio (April), Folklife Festival (Aug).

San Bernardino, 34 07N 117 19W, pop(1980) 117,490, capital of San Bernardino county, California, United States; in the San Bernardino Valley, at the foot of the San Bernardino and San Gabriel Mts, near the S end of Cajon Pass, c.88 km E of Los Angeles; founded in 1851; Norton Air Force Base is nearby; university; railway; monument: San Bernardino County Museum contains exhibits of the prehistoric Indian life of California.

San Blas *san blah*, Indian territory in NE Panama, Central America; extending in a narrow strip along the Caribbean coast to the Colombia border; it forms the E part of Colón prov; pop(1980) 28,621; area 3,206 sq km; capital El Porvenir; the San Blas Is, of which there are about 365, are the home of the Cuna Indians famous for their hand-sewn *molas*.

San Bruno, 37 38N 122 25W, pop(1980) 35,417, city in San Mateo county, W California, United States; 16 km S of San Francisco; railway; just E of San Bruno is San Francisco International Airport.

San Buenaventura *bway-na-ven-too'ra*, VENTURA, 34 17N 119 18W, pop(1980) 74,393, port capital of Ventura county, SW California, United States; on the Pacific Ocean, 105 km NW of Los Angeles; railway.

San Carlos *san kar'lōs*, 36 25S 71 58W, pop(1982) 25,112, town in Linares prov, Maule, central Chile; railway.

San Carlos, river in N Costa Rica, Central America; rises in the Cordillera de Tilarán, 16 km NW of San Ramón, SW Alajuela prov; flows NNE to the Río San Juan near San Carlos; length 112 km; navigable in lower and middle course; tributaries: Río Arenal and Río Tres Amigos.

San Carlos, 11 10N 84 48W, pop(1985e) 1,500, port and capital town of Río San Juan dept, S Nicaragua, Central America; on the SE shore of Lago de Nicaragua, at the efflux of the Río San Juan.

San Carlos, 34 46S 54 58W, pop(1985) 19,854, town in Maldonado dept, SE Uruguay; railway.

San Carlos de Bariloche, BARILOCHE *ba-ri-lō'chee*, 41 11S 71 23W, pop(1980) 48,222, resort town in Río Negro prov, SW Argentina; by L Nahuel Huapí on the edge of the Cerro Otto; there are skiing facilities on Cerro Catedral; railway; airfield.

San Clemente *kli-men'tee*, 33 26N 117 37W, pop(1980) 27,325, city in Orange county, SW California, United States; on the Pacific Ocean, 42 km SSE of Santa Ana; founded in the 1920s as a real-estate development restricted to Spanish-style architecture; railway.

San Cristóbal *san krees-tō'bal*, 18 27N 70 07W, pop(1982e) 127,622, town in San Cristóbal prov, S Dominican Republic, 30 km WSW of Santo Domingo and 8 km from the Caribbean coast; on the Sanchez Highway; trading centre in a fertile agricultural area; founded in 1575 when Spanish settlers discovered gold nearby; the 1st constitution of the Dominican Republic was signed here in 1844.

San Cristóbal, MAKIRA, volcanic SW Pacific island of the Solomon Islands group; 65 km SE of Guadalcanal; economy: copra.

San Cristóbal, 7 46N 72 14W, pop(1981) 198,793, capital of Táchira state, W Venezuela; on a plateau 55 km from the Colombian border; alt 830 m; founded in 1561; the city lies on 3 terraces parallel to the Río Torbes, the top level being 200 m above the lowest; university (1962); monuments: the cathedral (1908) had its towers and frontage rebuilt in Colonial style for the city's 400th anniversary in 1961.

San Diego *dee-ay'gō*, 32 43N 117 09W, pop(1980) 875,538, seaport capital of San Diego county, SW California, United States; on the E shore of San Diego Bay, approx 24 km N of the Mexico border and 177 km SSE of Los Angeles; 4 universities; the first permanent white settlement in California; naval and marine base; railway; airport; economy: shipbuilding, food processing, aerospace industries; monuments: the Old Town district contains adobe buildings which date from the early 19th century; the San Diego de Alcalá mission (established in 1769 by Junípero Serra and now restored) was the first mission in California; Serra Museum; Cabrillo National Monument.

San Felipe *san fay-lee'pay*, SAN FELIPE DE ACONCAGUA, 32 45S 70 43W, pop(1982) 38,254, capital of San Felipe de Aconcagua prov, Valparaíso, Chile; railway; economy: agricultural and mining centre; monuments: part of the Inca highway has recently been discovered in the city (previously no traces had been found further south than La Serena).

San Felipe, 10 25N 68 40W, pop(1980) 56,000, capital of Yaracuy state, N Venezuela.

San Fernando *san fayr-nan'dō*, 34 35S 70 59W, pop(1982) 38,871, capital of Colchagua prov, Libertador General Bernardo O'Higgins region, S Chile; founded in 1742; situated in a broad fertile valley; railway; events: cowboy rodeos in Oct and Nov.

San Fernando, 36 28N 6 17W, pop(1981) 78,845, seaport and naval town in Cádiz prov, Andalucia, S Spain; on the Atlantic coast, on a rocky island in salt marshes, 17 km S of Cádiz; centre of the Isla de León with naval academy and observatory; economy: shipyard and salt production.

San Fernando, 10 16N 61 28W, pop(1980) 33,400, seaport on the Gulf of Paria, SW Trinidad, SE Caribbean; 43 km S of Port of Spain; Trinidad's 2nd largest city; originally a centre for the sugar estates; economy: petrochemicals.

San Fernando, 7 53N 67 15W, pop(1980) 54,000, capital of Apure state, W central Venezuela.

San Francisco *san fran-sees'kō*, 31 29S 62 06W, pop(1980) 58,616, town in Córdoba prov, Centro, central Argentina; E of Córdoba; railway.

San Francisco *san fran-sis'kō*, 37 47N 122 25W, pop(1980) 678,974, city co-extensive with San Francisco county, W California, United States; situated c.560 km NW of Los Angeles; on the tip of the San Francisco-San Mateo peninsula; bounded W by the Pacific Ocean, N by the Golden Gate and E by San Francisco Bay; connected to Marin county (N) by the Golden Gate bridge and to Yerba Buena island and Oakland (E) by the Transbay bridge; the Golden Gate bridge is one of the longest single-span suspension bridges in the world (1,280 m long, excluding the approaches); San Francisco is built on a series of hills; 4 universities; Don Gaspar de Portolá, the Spanish governor of Baja California, entered the Bay of San Francisco in 1769; a mission and pueblo were founded there in 1776; in 1777 Father Junípero Serra founded the pueblo of Yerba Buena; the city came under Mexican control after Mexican independence in 1821; occupied by the US Navy in 1846; the name was changed to San Francisco in 1848; the city grew rapidly after the discovery of gold nearby; those who became wealthy on the Barbary Coast waterfront built new homes higher up on Nob Hill; from the 1860s San Francisco developed as a commercial and fishing port; in 1869 it became the terminus of the first transcontinental railway; the city was badly damaged by an earthquake and fire in April 1906; tram (cable-car); railway; airport; economy: trade in fruit, cotton and mineral ores; fishing, textiles, printing, plastic and rubber products, shipbuilding, aircraft and missile parts; monuments: San Francisco's Chinatown is the largest in the USA; the Mission Dolores (1782) is now a historical monument; the Cow Palace holds livestock shows, merchandise exhibitions, political conventions, sports shows and circuses; San Francisco Museum of Art; the Civic Centre complex at City Hall includes the Opera House, War Memorial, Auditorium, Library and the State and Federal Buildings; in the centre of San Francisco Bay, E of Golden Gate, is Alcatraz island, the site of the first lighthouse on the California coast and of a Federal prison.

San Francisco de Macorís *san fran-sees'kō day ma-kō-rees'*, 19 19N 70 15W, pop(1982e) 153,447, town in Duarte prov, Dominican Republic, 55 km SE of Santiago; main highway; airfield; processing and trading centre for rich agricultural region; founded in 1777.

San Francisco Gotera *san fran-sis'kō gō-tay'ra*, 13 41N 88 06W, pop(1980) 13,015, capital of Morazán dept, E El Salvador, Central America; N of San Miguel.

San Francisco Javier *san fran-thee'skō hav-yer'*, 38 43N 1 26E, pop(1981) 749, capital of Formentera I in the Balearic Is, Baleares autonomous region, Spain; beach at Sabina Cove nearby.

San Gabriel *san gab-ree-el'*, 0 35N 77 48W, pop(1982) 11,213, town in Carchi prov in the Andean Sierra of Ecuador; SW of Tulcán, near the Colombian border; 10 km S is the grotto, Gruta de la Paz; economy: flour milling.

San Gabriel, 34 06N 118 06W, pop(1980) 30,072, city in Los Angeles county, SW California, United States; 14 km E of Los Angeles; monument: San Gabriel Mission (founded in 1771) contains rare paintings and relics.

San Ġwann *san gwahn*, 35 54N 14 30E, pop(1983e) 5,049, community on the main island of Malta, separated from Valletta by Gżira and the Marsamxett Harbour.

San Ignacio *san ig-na'see-ō*, 17 08N 89 05W, pop(1980) 5,616, town in Cayo dist, W Belize; 20 km E of the frontier with Guatemala; linked to the town of Santa Elena on the E side of the R Belize by the Hawkesworth Bridge; government agricultural station E at Central Farm; economy: citrus, livestock, light industry; monuments: Maya ruins at Xunantunich.

San Joaquin *wa-keen'*, river in central California, USA; S part of the Central Valley of California; rises in the Sierra Nevada, S of Yosemite National Park; flows SW and W past Friant and Firebaugh then NNW past Stockton to join the Sacramento river just above Suisin Bay; 510 km long; major tributaries: the Fresno, Merced and Mariposa rivers; connected with the Sacramento river in the Central Valley Project to increase irrigation, flood-control and hydroelectricity.

San Jorge, Golfo *san KHor'KHay*, GULF OF ST GEORGE (Eng), broad inlet of the Atlantic in S Chubut and N Santa Cruz provs, S Argentina; extends 135 km N-S between Cabo Dos Bahías (N), where there is a penguin rookery, and Cabo Tres Puntas (S); 160 km W-E; port of Comodoro Rivadavia on W shore.

San José *san KHō-say'*, prov in W central Costa Rica, Central America; separated from the Pacific coast by a narrow strip of Puntarenas prov; bordered E by the Cordillera de Talamanca; drained by the Naranjo and upper General rivers; the main settlements and transportation routes are concentrated on the central plateau in the N; pop(1983e) 890,443; area 4,960 sq km; capital San José; chief towns San Sebastián and Acosta.

San José, 9 59N 84 04W, pop(1983e) 271,873, capital city of Costa Rica, Central America and capital of San José prov; situated on the Inter-American Highway, in a broad fertile valley of the Meseta Central; founded in 1737 but did not become capital until 1823; alt 1,150 m; the city is laid out in a regular grid pattern; university (1940); airport (16 km from the city); railway; economy: food processing, flowers, footwear, chemicals, electronics; monuments: cathedral, national theatre; the national museum is famous for its collection of pre-Columbian art.

San José, dept in S Uruguay; on the Río de la Plata estuary; bounded E by the Río Santa Lucía and watered by the Río San José; pop(1985) 88,020; area 6,963 sq km; capital San José de Mayo; San José dept, formed in 1816, then included the depts of Florida (separated in 1856) and Flores (separated in 1885).

San José, 37 10N 121 53W, pop(1980) 629,442, capital of Santa Clara county, W California, United States; in the Santa Clara Valley, 64 km SE of San Francisco; the first city to be founded in California (1777); meeting place of the first state legislature (1849); state capital 1849-51; university; railway; economy: electronics, semiconductors, high technology, computers, guided missiles.

San José de Mayo *THay mī'yō*, 34 27S 56 27W, pop(1985) 31,732, capital of San José dept, S Uruguay; airfield; railway; founded in 1783 by Spanish settlers; proclaimed provisional capital during patriot uprising (1825).

San Juan *san hwahn*, prov in Andina region, W Argentina; bordered W by the Andes and Chile; largely mountainous with fertile irrigated valleys; crossed by Bermejo and San Juan rivers; rises to 6,770 m at Cerro Mercedario; a dry, Mediterranean-type climate in inhabited valleys; pop(1980) 465,976; area 86,137 sq km; capital San Juan; economy: vineyards in warm, sub-Andean valleys; copper, sandstone, clay, marble, aluminium sulphate, gypsum and limestone mining.

San Juan, 31 33S 68 31W, pop(1980) 117,731, industrial and commercial capital of San Juan prov, Andina, W Argentina; established in 1562; mostly destroyed by an earthquake in 1944, but the centre of the town, including the cathedral, has been rebuilt; 2 universities (1953, 1964); railway; airfield (Chacritas) at 14 km; economy: the surrounding agricultural area is known for its wine;

monument: Sarmiento Museum (birthplace of the 19th-c liberal statesman and author, Sarmiento).

San Juan, SAN JUAN DE LA MAGUA'NA, 18 49N 71 12W, pop(1982e) 120,377, agricultural centre in San Juan prov, W Dominican Republic, in a valley between the Sierra de Neiba (S) and the Cordillera Central (N); main highway; airfield; founded in 1504; became capital of the prov in 1938.

San Juan, river in Zelaya dept, SE Nicaragua, Central America; forms the E part of the frontier between Nicaragua and Costa Rica; issues from the SE end of Lago de Nicaragua; flows ESE through tropical forest past El Castillo to meet the Caribbean Sea at San Juan del Norte; chief tributaries Río San Carlos and Río Colorado; there are rapids at Toro, El Castillo, and Machuca; length 192 km.

San Juan, 18 29N 66 08W, pop(1980) 434,849, seaport capital of Puerto Rico, E Caribbean; on an island linked to the N coast of the mainland by a bridge; founded in 1510; in 1951 the city was merged with Río Piedras, seat of the University of Puerto Rico; airport; economy: cigars, tobacco, sugar, clothing; monuments: El Morro (1591, old Spanish fortress built to defend the entrance to the harbour); 16th-c cathedral; 16th-c church of San José; La Fortaleza (1533-40, official residence of the governor); Castillo de San Cristóbal (old fortress).

San Juan de los Morros *mo'rōs*, 9 53N 67 23W, pop(1980) 53,000, resort capital of Guárico state, N central Venezuela; 80 km SW of Caracas; state capital since 1934.

San Leandro *lee-an'drō*, 37 44N 122 09W, pop(1980) 63,952, city in Alameda county, W California, United States; S of Oakland; capital of Alameda county 1855-72.

San Luis *san loo-ees'*, prov in Centro region, W central Argentina; bordered W by Desaguadero and Salado rivers; drained by the Río Cuinto; a salt desert and the Sierra de San Luis lie to the N and the Sierra de Comechingones lies NE; there are extensive mineral resources; together with Mendoza and San Juan prov, it belonged to Chile until 1776; became a prov in 1832; pop(1980) 214,416; area 76,748 sq km; capital San Luis; chief town Mercedes; economy: sorghum; sheep and cattle raising; wolfram, gypsum, salt and sandstone mining.

San Luis, 33 20S 66 23W, pop(1980) 70,632, capital of San Luis prov, Centro, W central Argentina; at the S foot of the Sierra de San Luis; founded in 1596 by Martín de Loyola, governor of Chile; Potrero de Funes, an irrigation dam and hydroelectric station, is nearby; railway; airfield; economy: mining of onyx, timber, agricultural trade.

San Luis, Lago, ITONAMAS, CARMEN, lake in E Beni dept, N Bolivia; 80 km SSE of Magdalena; length 16 km; 8 km wide; receives the Río San Miguel; drained by the Río Itonamas.

San Luis Obispo *loo-is' ō-bis'pō*, 35 17N 120 40W, pop(1980) 34,252, capital of San Luis Obispo county, SW California, United States; 130 km NW of Santa Barbara; 13 km S is San Luis Obispo Bay; founded in 1772; university; railway.

San Luis Potosí *loo-ees' pō-tō-see'*, mountainous state in N central Mexico; bounded by the states of Zacatecas (W), Nuevo León and Tamaulipas (NE), Veracruz (E), Guanajuato and Querétaro (S); crossed NW-SE by the Sierra Madre Oriental; drained by the Moctezuma, Naranjos, Verde and Santa María rivers (tributaries of the Río Pánuco); pop(1980) 1,670,637; area 63,068 sq km; capital San Luis Potosí; economy: forestry, agriculture (maize, alfalfa, sugar cane, cotton, coffee, fruit, cattle, sheep) and mining (gold, silver, copper, lead, zinc, manganese, sulphur, antimony, fluorite, mercury, chalk, gypsum, salt).

San Luis Potosí, 22 10N 101 00W, pop(1980) 406,630, capital of San Luis Potosí state, N central Mexico; NNW of Ciudad de México (Mexico City) at an alt of 1,877 m; university (1826); founded as a Franciscan mission, the city became an important centre after the discovery of the San Pedro silver mine in the 16th-c; city status in 1658; seat of the government of Benito Juárez in 1863; railway; economy: refining of silver and arsenic, footwear, clothing; monuments: the Casa de la Cultura contains a collection of colonial paintings; the Palacio de Gobierno (begun in 1770) contains oil paintings of the past governors; the church of San Francisco has a blue and white tiled dome and in the transept is a suspended glass boat.

San Marcos *san mar'kōs*, westernmost dept in Guatemala, Central America; bounded W by Mexico; pop(1982) 552,094; area 3,791 sq km; capital San Marcos; chief towns Ciudad Tecún Umán and San Sebastian; the Río Suchiate forms part of the W boundary; mountainous in the N with a coastal plain in the S; a strip of land devoted to coffee growing extends W-E across the foothills of the mountains; cotton, cocoa, sugar cane, corn, bananas, and coffee are grown on the coastal plain.

San Marcos, 8 38N 75 10W, capital town of San Marcos dept, SW Guatemala, Central America; 32 km WNW of Quezaltenango; alt 2,350 m; important market centre in coffee growing zone.

San Marino *san ma-ree'nō*, official name Republic of San Marino, REPUBBLICA DI SAN MARINO, a land-locked republic in central Italy, S Europe, 20 km from the Adriatic Sea; area 61 sq km; the world's smallest republic; timezone GMT +1; land boundaries 34 km; capital San Marino; pop(1980) 20,603; population density in 1980 was 352 inhabitants per sq km; the people of San Marino are a composite of the Mediterranean, Alpine, Adriatic and Nordic ethnic types; the religion is Roman Catholic; the Sanmarinese speak Italian; the currency is the Italian lira, and, since 1972, the San Marino lira (SML); national holiday 5 Feb (Liberation of the Republic); membership of ICJ, ITU, UN, UNESCO, UPU, WHO.

Physical description. The total area of 61 sq km includes 74% cultivated, 22% meadow and pasture, and 4% urban land. The terrain is ruggedly mountainous, centred on the limestone ridges of Monte Titano (793 m) and the valley of the R Ausa.

Climate. The climate is temperate, with an average annual temperature of 16°C. Winters are cool, with alternating mild and cold spells, temperatures rarely falling below −6°C. Summers are warm, ranging from 20°C to 30°C. Rainfall is moderate throughout the year with an average annual precipitation of 880 mm.

History, government and constitution. San Marino was founded by a Christian saint in the 4th century AD as a refuge against religious persecution. In 1862, it concluded a treaty of friendship with the newly formed Kingdom of Italy, preserving the independence of the ancient republic, although completely surrounded by Italian territory. Legislative authority is vested in a unicameral parliament, the Great and General Council, consisting of 60 members elected every 5 years by popular vote. Executive power is exercised by the 11-member Congress of State (Cabinet).

Industry. The principal economic activities of San Marino are farming, livestock raising, light industry and tourism. Over the last few decades there has been considerable development of light industry and tourism. Manufacturing consists mainly of cotton textile production at Serravalle, brick and tile production at Dogane, cement production at Acquaviva, Dogane and Fiorentino, and pottery production at Borgo Maggiore. Chief exports include wood machinery, chemicals, wine, textiles, tiles, varnishes and ceramics. Manufactured consumer goods, oil, and gold are the chief imports. The largest share of government revenue is derived from the sale of postage stamps throughout the world and from payments by the Italian government in exchange for Italy's monopoly in retailing tobacco, gasoline, and a few other goods. Italy is the main trading partner. In 1980, 3.5 million tourists visited San Marino.

Agriculture. The principal crops are wheat and grapes. Other grains, fruits, vegetables, and animal feedstuffs are also grown. Livestock includes cows, oxen, and sheep.

Cheese and hinds are the most important livestock products. Approximately 4.9% of the workforce are employed in agriculture.

Administrative divisions. San Marino is divided into 9 castles (districts) as follows:

Castle	*area (sq km)*	*pop(1980)*
Acquaviva	4.9	1,087
Borgo Maggiore		3,939
Chiesanuova	5.5	702
Domagnano	6.6	1,867
Faetano	7.8	778
Fiorentino	6.6	1,392
Montegiardino	3.3	618
San Marino	16.1	4,623
Serravalle	10.5	6,531

The head of each castle is an elected committee led by an official known as the captain of the castle. Since 1980 San Marino has also been divided for statistical purposes into 15 topographical sectors as follows:

Sector	*area (sq km)*	*pop(1980)*
Falciano	2.0	624
Serravalle-Dogana	7.4	5,335
Fiorina	1.7	904
Domagnano	5.3	1,300
Cailungo	2.3	661
Ventoso	2.3	307
Gualdicciolo	2.4	670
Acquaviva	1.6	427
Borgo	5.9	2,774
San Marino	3.6	3,180
Faetano	8.8	718
Murata	3.2	1,252
Fiorentino	6.1	1,308
Chiesanuova	4.9	620
Montegiardino	3.6	523

San Marino, 43 56N 12 26E, pop(1980) 4,623, capital city of the Republic of San Marino, central Italy; on Monte Titano; accessible only by road; the electric railway, completed in 1932, was partly destroyed during World War II; monuments: surrounded by 3 enclosures of walls which include many gateways, towers and ramparts; basilica, St Francis's church with its museum and art gallery, governor's palace; event: crossbow competition on the 3rd of Sept.

San Martín *san mar-teen'*, dept in N central Peru; bounded W by the Cordillera Central it slopes eastwards to the Amazon basin; drained by the the Río Huallaga; pop(1981) 319,751; area 52,309 sq km; capital Moyobamba; in the W of the dept are the remote archaeological ruins of Gran Pajatén; unique in construction and decoration, they were only discovered in 1973.

San Martín, Lago, LAGO O'HIGGINS (Chile), lake in Patagonian Andes of Argentina and Chile; extends across the border at approx 49°S; situated in NW Santa Cruz prov, Patagonia, S Argentina and NE Capitan Prat prov, Aisen del General Carlos Ibañez del Campo, S Chile; 32 km N of Cerro Fitz Roy; bordered by the Sierra de Sangre; area 1,013 sq km; length 96 km.

San Mateo *ma-tay'ō*, 37 34N 122 19W, pop(1980) 77,561, city in San Mateo county, W California, United States; 24 km S of San Francisco; railway.

San Matías, Golfo *gol'fō san ma-tee'as*, inlet of the S Atlantic Ocean, Patagonia, Argentina, indenting Río Negro prov and bordered S by Chubut prov; c.130 km wide (W-E); c.105 km long (N-S); the port of San Antonio Oeste is on N coast.

San Miguel *san mee-gel'*, 13 28N 88 10W, pop(1980) 157,838, capital of San Miguel dept, E El Salvador, Central America; 142 km ESE of San Salvador, at the foot of the volcanoes of San Miguel and Chinameca; founded in 1530; airport; railway; economy: gold and silver mining; monument: 18th-c cathedral; event: fiesta of the Virgen de la Paz (20 Nov).

San Miguel, dept in E El Salvador, Central America; extending from Honduras (N) to the Pacific Ocean (S); pop(1971) 337,325; area 2,532 sq km; capital San Miguel; chief towns Chinameca, Ciudad Barrios, and Nueva Guadalupe; there are numerous lakes, the largest being the Laguna de Olomega in the extreme SE; crossed by several mountain ranges including the Sierra Tecapa Chinameca and the Cordillera Jucuarán-Intipuca; the volcano of San Miguel rises to 2,130 m.

San Miguel, KING, island in the Archipieago de las Perlas (Pearl Is), Golfo de Panamá, Central America; situated SW of Panamá City.

San Miguel de Tucumán *san mee-gel' THay too-koo-man'*, TUCUMÁN, pop(1980) 496,914, capital of Tucumán prov, Norte, NW Argentina; on the Río Salí (Dulce); the busiest and most populated city in N Argentina; founded in 1565 by Spaniards coming S from Peru, it moved to its present site in 1580; many colonial buildings remain; Gen Belgrano defeated Spanish royalists here on 24 Sept 1812; the congress of the United Provinces of Río de la Plata met in Tucumán on 9 July 1816 to proclaim their independence; 2 universities (1914, 1965); railway; airport (Benjamín Matienzo) at 9 km; local holiday on 24 Sept (Battle of Tucumán).

San Miguel, Volcan de, mountain in San Miguel dept, El Salvador, Central America; 11 km SW of San Miguel rising to 2,130 m.

San Miguelito *san mee-gwel-ee'tō*, 9 02N 79 03W, pop(1980) 156,611, town in Panamá prov, Panama, Central America.

San Nicolás *san nee-kō-las'*, 33 25S 60 15W, pop(1980) 96,313, river port in N Buenos Aires prov, Litoral, E Argentina; on the Río Paraná; founded in 1748; a rail junction serving an agricultural area.

San Ped'ro *san ped'rō*, 4 45N 6 37W, pop(1975) 45,000, seaport in Sassandra dept, SW Ivory Coast, W Africa; on the Atlantic coast, W of Abidjan; airfield.

San Pedro *san payd'rō*, dept in Oriental region, E central Paraguay; bounded W by the Río Paraguay and N by the Río Ypané; drained by the Río Jejuí-Guazú; largely low forested region with marshes in SW and some hills in SE and NE; pop(1982) 189,751; area 20,002 sq km; capital San Pedro.

San Pedro de Macorís *day ma-kō-rees'*, 18 30N 69 18W, pop(1982e) 115,016, port in San Pedro de Macorís prov, SE Dominican Republic, on the Caribbean Sea, at the mouth of the Rio Iguamo; main highway; airfield.

San Pedro Sula *soo'la*, 15 26N 88 01W, pop(1983e) 344,497, industrial and commercial capital of Cortés dept, NW Honduras, 58 km S of Puerto Cortés, in the fertile Ulúa valley; 2nd largest city in Honduras and one of the most rapidly growing cities in Latin America; railway; airport (Ramón Villeda Morales); economy: trade in bananas, coffee, sugar, and timber; manufacture of textiles, zinc roofing, furniture, cement and concrete blocks, and plastics; steel rolling.

San Rafael *san ra-fa-el'*, 34 35S 68 24W, pop(1980) 70,477, town in Mendoza prov, Andina, W Argentina; on the Río Diamante, at the foot of the Andes; founded in 1901; railway; economy: oil, farming, mining and manufacturing centre.

San Rafael, 37 58N 122 32W, pop(1980) 44,700, capital of Marin county, W California, United States; on the W shore of San Pablo Bay, 24 km N of San Francisco; monument: contains a replica (built in 1949) of the San Rafael Arcángel Mission which was established in 1817.

San Rafael, Laguna, national park in Aisén region, S Chile; area 17,429 sq km; established in 1967; the main feature is the San Rafael Glacier in the NW corner of the park; rises to 4,058 m at Cerro San Valentín; the Laguna San Rafael, with its icebergs, is in the N of the park.

San Salvador *san sal'va-dor*, dept in central El Salvador, Central America; pop(1971) 681,656; area 892 sq km; capital San Salvador; chief towns Aquilares and Delgado; part of the Lago de Ilopango lies on the E boundary E of San Salvador; crossed by the Sierra La Libertad in the extreme S.

San Salvador, 13 40N 89 18W, pop(1980) 425,119, capital city of El Salvador and of San Salvador dept, in an intermontane basin on the Río Acelhuate; founded in 1525 but later destroyed by earthquake in 1854; the present city has a modern layout with many parks and gardens; its buildings are specially constructed to resist seismic shocks; alt 680 m; railway; monument: cathedral; events: International Industrial Fair (held in Nov every 2 years), Fiesta of the Saviour (during Holy Week and the fortnight preceding 6 Aug), Day of the Indian processions (12 Dec).

San Salvador and Rum Cay, island group in E central Bahamas, SE of Cat I, pop(1980) 804; area 233 sq km; chief towns Port Nelson (Rum Cay) and Cockburn Town (San Salvador).

San Salvador de Jujuy *san sal-va-THor' THay KHoo-KHooy'*, JUJUY, 24 10S 65 48W, pop(1980) 124,487, resort capital of Jujuy prov, Norte, N Argentina; on the Río Grande de Jujuy; founded in 1565 and again in 1575, after being destroyed by Indians; finally established in 1593; hot springs at Termas de Reyes; railway; airport at 40 km; economy: tourism, fishing, hydroelectricity, agricultural, trade, mining and timber centre; monuments: 18th-c cathedral, government house; the Palacio de Tribunales is one of Argentina's most noted modern buildings; local holidays on 6 Aug and 23-24 Aug.

San Salvador, Volcan de, volcano in La Libertad dept, El Salvador, Central America; 11 km WNW of San Salvador; height 1,885 m; its crater and secondary cone have been made a national park; Nueva San Salvador is at its S foot.

San Sebastian *san say-vas-tyan'*, DONOSTIA (Basque), 43 17N 1 58W, pop(1981) 175,576, fortified seaport, fashionable resort and capital of Guipúzcoa prov, Pais Vasco (Basque Country), N Spain; on R Urumea, 469 km N of Madrid; bishopric; in summer the seat of the Spanish govt and the residence of the diplomatic corps; airport; railway; economy: seaport trade, fisheries, electronics, gloves, dairy produce; monuments: 18th-c Baroque church of St Mary; Mount Urgel park; events: Tamborada in Jan; Holy Week; Semana Grande in Aug and Asuncion.

San Vicente *vee-sen'tay*, dept in central El Salvador, central America; pop(1971) 160,534; area 1,175 sq km; capital San Vicente; chief towns San Sebastián and Apastepeque; the Río Lempa forms its E boundary.

San Vicente, 13 38N 88 42W, pop(1980) 62,175, capital town of San Vicente dept, central El Salvador, Central America; on the Río Alcahuapa, at the foot of the Volcan de Chinchontepec (2,178 m); monument: church of El Pilar (1762-69); event: carnival (1 Nov).

San'ā *sa-na'*, 15 27N 44 12E, pop(1975) 448,000, commercial centre and capital city of N Yemen, situated on a high plateau of the Arabian peninsula, approx 64 km inland from Al Ḩudaydah, its port on the Red Sea; it is a walled city with 8 gates and numerous mosques; alt 2,170 m; there is a museum of S Arabian antiquities; economy: textiles, cement.

Sanaba *sa-na'ba*, 12 25N 3 47W, town in NW Burkina, W Africa; W of Dédougou.

San'aga, river in Cameroon, W Africa; formed by the confluence of two rivers 145 km NNW of Batouri; flows generally WSW for approx 525 km past Bélabo, Nanga Eboko and Edéa (limit of navigation), to enter the Atlantic Ocean 50 km S of Douala; dammed upstream (NE) of Edéa.

Sanandaj *san-an-daj'*, 35 18N 47 01E, pop(1983) 172,254, capital city of Sanandaj dist, Kordestān, NW Iran; 112 km N of Kermānshāh, near the R Qeshlaq; trade centre of a grain and sheep-raising region; noted for its rugs and fine woodwork; airfield.

Sancti Spíritus *sangk'tee spee'ree-toos*, prov in central Cuba; pop(1981) 399,700; area 6,737 sq km; capital Sancti Spíritus; chief towns Trinidad and Cabaiguán.

Sancti Spíritus, 21 55N 79 28W, pop(1983e) 74,147, capital town of Sancti Spíritus prov, central Cuba; 72 km SE of Santa Clara; trading and processing centre in fertile agricultural region; founded in 1550; Cuba's largest artificial lake is at Zaza nearby; railway; monuments: parish church (1671), museum of slavery.

Sandakan *sun-du-kahn'*, 5 52N 118 04E, pop(1980) 70,420, town in Sabah state, E Malaysia, SE Asia; E of Kota Kinabalu, on the NE coast of the island of Borneo at the head of an inlet of the Sulu Sea; formerly capital of N Borneo; rebuilt after destruction during World War II; Sepilok Sanctuary is the world's largest collection of orang-utans; airfield; economy: timber.

Sandansky or **Sandanski** *san-dan'skee*, formerly SVETI VRACH (-1949), 41 35N 23 16E, pop(1981e) 22,000, spa town and agricultural centre in Blagoevgrad okrug (prov), SW Bulgaria; at the foot of the Pirin Planina (Pirin Mts), 25 km from the Greek frontier; it is believed to have been the birthplace of Spartacus.

Sandbach *san'bach*, 53 09N 2 22W, pop(1981) 14,747, town in Congleton dist, Cheshire, NW central England; 8 km NE of Crewe; railway; economy: quarrying, chemicals, salt, engineering.

Sandefjord *san'fyord*, 59 10N 10 15E, pop(1983) 35,151, seaport on E shore of Vestfold county, SE Norway; SSW of Oslo near mouth of Oslofjorden (Oslo Fjord); railway; former whaling port, now a seaside resort.

Sandnes, *sahn'nays*, 58 51N 5 45E, pop(1983) 38,085, town on W coast of Rogaland county, SW Norway; about 14 km S of Stavanger; railway.

San'down, 50 39N 1 09W, pop(1981) 16,437 (with Shanklin), town in South Wight dist, Isle of Wight, S England; on Sandown Bay, S of Ryde and N of Shanklin; home of the poet Swinburne; frequently visited by Longfellow and Keats; railway; economy: boatbuilding, electrical goods, tourism.

Sandusky, 41 27N 82 42W, pop(1980) 31,360, county seat of Erie county, N Ohio, United States; port on L Erie, 80 km W of Cleveland; railway.

Sandviken *sand-vee'kun*, 60 38N 16 50E, pop(1982) 41,956, industrial town in Gävleborg county, E Sweden; WSW of Gävle, on the N shore of L Storsjön; railway; economy:

iron and steel works (steel works established in 1862, the oldest Bessemer works in Sweden); monument: 15th-c Arsunda church.

Sandy City, 40 36N 111 53W, pop(1980) 50,546, town in Salt Lake county, N Utah, United States; 21 km S of Salt Lake City.

Sandy's, parish in the Bermuda Islands; pop(1980) 6,255.

Sanford, Mount, 62 14N 144 08W, dormant volcano in SE Alaska, United States; situated in the Wrangell Mts, 160 km NE of Valdez; in Wrangell-St Elias National Park and Preserve; height 4,949 m.

Sangay *san-gī'*, 2 00S 78 20W, active Andean volcano in Morona-Santiago prov, E central Ecuador; rises to 5,230 m, 48 km SE of Riobamba; the national park of Sangay (2,770 sq km) was established in 1975.

Sangha *sang'ga*, province in N Congo, W Africa; area 55,800 sq km; pop(1980) 41,360; capital Ouesso.

Sangli *sahng'glee*, 16 55N 74 37E, pop(1981) 269,000, city in Maharashtra state, W India; 300 km SSE of Bombay, on the Yerla river; linked by rail to Pune; economy: coffee, oilseed, cotton, peanuts, agricultural implements.

Sangolquí *san-gol-kee'*, 0 19S 78 30W, pop(1982) 15,004, town in Pichincha prov in the Andean Sierra of Ecuador; S of Quito; economy: wood products.

Sankt Michel, prov in Finland. See Mikkeli.

Sanlúcar de Barrameda *san-loo'kar THay bar-a-may'THa*, 36 46N 6 21W, pop(1981) 48,496, port in Cádiz prov, Andalucia, S Spain; at the mouth of the R Guadalquivir, 23 km NW of Jerez; economy: seaport trade and wine production.

Sanski Most *san'skee most*, 44 46N 6 40E, pop(1981) 62,467, town in NW Bosna-Hercegovina republic, Yugoslavia; on R Sana, W of Banja Luka; sulphur springs; railway; economy: coal mining.

Sant Juliá or **Sant Juliá de Loriá**, pop(1982) 4,647, one of the seven parishes of the Principality of Andorra with a village seat of the same name situated 6 km SW of Andorra la Vella on the road to Seo de Urgel in Spain; alt 939 m.

Santa An'a, dept in NW El Salvador, Central America; pop(1971) 375,186; area 1,829 sq km; capital Santa Ana; chief towns Metapán and Chalchuapa; the Río Lempa forms much of the E boundary; lakes include the Laguna de Güija (NW) and Lago de Coatepeque (S); traversed by several mountain ranges including the Sierra Apaneca y Lamatepeque, Cordillera Joya Grande, and the Cordillera Metapán Alotepeque.

Santa Ana, 14 00N 79 31W, pop(1980) 204,570, capital city of Santa Ana dept, NW El Salvador, Central America; 55 km NW of San Salvador, in an intermontane basin on the NE slopes of Santa Ana volcano; second largest city in the country; business centre of W El Salvador; coffee and sugar cane are grown in the surrounding agricultural region; railway; on the Pan-American Highway; monuments: neo-Gothic cathedral, church of El Calvario.

Santa Ana, highest volcano in El Salvador, Central America; in Santa Ana dept, SSW of Santa Ana rising to 2,381 m; Lago de Coatepeque at E foot.

Santa Ana, 33 46N 117 52W, pop(1980) 203,713, capital of Orange county, SW California, United States; on the Santa Ana river, at the base of the Santa Ana Mts, 24 km E of Long Beach; railway.

Santa Bár'bara, mountainous dept in NW Honduras, Central America; bounded W by Guatemala; pop(1983e) 286,854; area 5,113 sq km; capital Santa Bárbara.

Santa Bar'bara, 34 25N 119 42W, pop(1980) 74,414, resort capital of Santa Barbara county, SW California, United States; on the Santa Barbara Channel of the Pacific Ocean, at the foot of the Santa Ynez Mts, 137 km WNW of Los Angeles; founded in 1782; Vandenburg Air Force Base is nearby; university (1891); railway; monuments: the Santa Barbara Mission (established in 1786, present building completed in 1820) is the Western headquarters for the Franciscan order; many buildings are of Spanish architectural style; economy: tourism, space research.

Santa Catalina *san'ta ka-ta-lee'na*, one of the Santa Barbara islands in the Pacific Ocean off the coast of S California, United States; 39 km SSW of Los Angeles harbour; separated from the mainland by the San Pedro Channel; the 35 km-long island is almost split by an isthmus in the NW; it rises to 648 m; Santa Catalina is a popular tourist resort; the town of Avalon on the SE shore is the centre for resort activities.

Santa Catarina *san'ta ka-ta-ree'na*, state in Sul region, S Brazil; bordered E by the Atlantic, W by Argentina and S by the Pelotas and Uruguay rivers; pop(1980) 3,627,933; area 95,985 sq km; capital Florianópolis; economy: cattle, coal mining, food processing, textiles; carbochemicals (Imbituba); in the S is the 444-sq km São Joaquim national park established in 1961 and the 113-sq km Aparados da Serra national park established in 1959; the NE was settled mainly by Germans and Italians.

Santa Cla'ra, 22 25N 79 58W, pop(1983e) 175,525, capital of Villa Clara prov, W central Cuba; 288 km E of La Habana (Havana); centre of a rich farming and grazing region, producing sugar and tobacco; its port is Cienfuegos, 64 km distant; founded in 1689 by the Remedios family seeking refuge in the interior from pirate attacks; economy: household goods.

Santa Clara, 37 21N 121 57W, pop(1980) 87,746, city in Santa Clara county, W California, United States; university (1851); monument: the restored Santa Clara de Asís Mission (1777) is now the chapel of the university.

Santa Cruz *san'ta kroos*, prov in Patagonia region, S Argentina; southernmost area of continental Argentina; bordered by the Andes and Chile (W) and by the Atlantic (E), with Chubut prov to the N and the Straits of Magellan to the S; drained by the Deseado, Chico, Santa Cruz, Coyle and Gallegos rivers; national parks in W lakeland; L Argentino, L Viedma, L Cardiel and L Strobel all lie within Argentina; L Buenos Aires, L San Martín and L Pueyrredón are all shared with Chile; dry, cold climate, southern parts are more humid; in the N is the Cueva de las Manos, caves containing 10,000-year-old paintings of animals and human hands; pop(1980) 114,941; area 243,943 sq km; capital Río Gallegos; economy: sheep raising, salt and coal mining, natural gas, oil.

Santa Cruz, department in E Bolivia; bordered by Paraguay (S) and Brazil (E); extensive tropical areas along the Brazilian border are covered partly by marshy lakes; includes the foothills of the Cordillera de Cochabamba (W) and part of the Bolivian Chaco (S); drained by the Río Grande, Piray, San Miguel, San Martín and Paragua rivers, of which only short sections are navigable; Bolivia's largest dept and richest in natural resources; Mennonite and Japanese settlers are turning the region into an expanding produce centre; pop(1982) 942,986; area 370,621 sq km; capital Santa Cruz; chief towns Montero and Camiri; economy: cotton, rice, coffee, cattle raising, timber, oil refining, gas, iron ore and magnesium mining.

Santa Cruz, SANTA CRUZ DE LA SIERRA, 17 45S 63 14W, pop(1982) 376,917, city in A. Ibañez prov, Santa Cruz, E Bolivia; Bolivia's 2nd largest city, it lies in the plains to the E of the Cordillera Oriental; capital of Santa Cruz region; founded in 1561 by Spaniards coming from Paraguay; university (1880); railway; airport (El Trompillo) 3.5 km from the city; economy: oil refining; a gas pipeline runs from Santa Cruz to Yacuiba; monuments: the cathedral, university and the prefecture are set round the Plaza 24 de Septiembre, Santa Cruz's main square; event: carnival for the 15 days before Lent.

Santa Cruz, 36 58N 122 01W, pop(1980) 41,483, capital of Santa Cruz county, W California, United States; at the mouth of the San Lorenzo river on Monterey Bay, 96 km S of San Francisco; founded in 1791; university (1965); railway.

Santa Cruz de Tenerife *san-ta krooz THay tay-nay-ree'fay*, one of two Spanish provs in the Canary Is, Canarias autonomous region, comprising the islands of Tenerife, Palma, Gomera and Hierro; pop(1981) 688,273; area 3,170 sq km; capital Santa Cruz de Tenerife.

Santa Cruz de Tenerife, 28 28N 16 15W, pop(1981)

190,784, seaport and capital of Santa Cruz de Tenerife prov, Canary Is, Canarias autonomous region of Spain; principal city on N coast of Tenerife I in the Atlantic Ocean; airport; economy: oil refinery, wine, tobacco, pharmaceuticals, beer, pottery, tourism and export of fruit and tomatoes; events: carnival in February; Cavalcade of the 3 Wise Men (5 Jan); Holy Week; Festival of Spain in April-May; spring festival in May; commemoration of founding of Santa Cruz in first week of May; fiesta of La Virgen del Carmen in July; festivity of Santiago Apostol in July.

Santa Cruz del Quiché *san'ta kroos' del kee-chay'*, 15 02N 91 06W, capital town of Quiché dept, W central Guatemala, Central America; alt 2,000 m; mineral baths; there are remains of the former capital of Quiché, Gumarcaj, 5 km away; event: fiesta (14-20 Aug).

Santa Cruz Islands, volcanic SW Pacific island group in the Solomon Islands; E of San Cristobal; includes the islands of Ndeni, Utupua, Vanikoro and Tinakula; area 958 sq km.

Santa Elena *san'ta ay-lay'na*, 2 14S 80 38W, pop(1982) 12,859, town in Guayas prov, W Ecuador; E of the resort of Salinas on the Punta Santa Elena.

Santa Fe *san'ta fay*, prov in Litoral region, NE central Argentina; bordered E by the Río Paraná; drained by the Salado, San Javier and Carcaraña rivers; a fertile, well irrigated region which includes part of the Chaco (N) and the pampas (S); pop(1980) 2,465,546; area 133,007 sq km; its major ports on the Paraná are Santa Fe, capital of the prov, and Rosario, where ocean-going vessels load the agricultural produce of N provinces; economy: maize, wheat, sorghum, cotton, flax, sugar cane, timber, sand.

Santa Fe, 31 38S 60 43W, pop(1980) 287,240, river-port capital of Santa Fe prov, Litoral, NE central Argentina; at the mouth of the Río Salado and linked to the Río Paraná by a short canal; founded in 1573, it moved to the present site in 1651; the Constitution of 1853 was adopted in the Cabildo (town hall) here; 2 universities (1919, 1959); railway; airfield (Sauce Viejo) at 17 km; economy: rail, shipping, commercial, industrial and agricultural centre; monuments: grouped around the Plaza Mayo are the Jesuit La Merced church (1660-1754), the Casa de Gobierno, San Francisco church (1680), the Museo Histórico Provincial and a church dating from 1741; the Plaza San Martín is surrounded by modern buildings; local holidays: 30 Sept (St Jerome), 15 Nov (foundation of the city).

Santa Fe, 35 41N 105 57W, pop(1980) 48,953, capital of state in Santa Fe county, N central New Mexico, United States; at the foot of the Sangre de Cristo Mts, 90 km NNE of Albuquerque; the oldest capital city in the United States; founded by the Spanish in 1609; the centre of Spanish-Indian trade for over 200 years; after Mexico gained independence in 1821 it became the centre of trade with the United States by way of the Santa Fe Trail; occupied by US troops in 1846; became the territorial capital in 1851; railway; economy: administrative and tourist centre; noted for Indian wares; monuments: Palace of the Governors (1610), San Miguel church (1636), the Cathedral of St Francis; events: Indian Market (Aug), Santa Fe Fiesta (Sept).

Santa Isabel, Equatorial Guinea. See Malabo.

Santa Isabel, BOGHOTU (Polynesian), SW Pacific island in the Solomon Islands; N of Guadalcanal; area 4,660 sq km.

Santa Lucía *san'ta loo-see'a*, 34 26S 56 25W, pop(1985) 14,944, town in Canelones dept, S Uruguay; NW of Montevideo; railway.

Santa Luzia *san'ta loo-zee'a*, 16 45N 24 45W, small, uninhabited island in the Barlavento or windward group of Cape Verde, included in the administrative *concelho* (council) of São Vicente; mostly frequented by fishermen; access by boat from São Vicente; area 36 sq km; rises to 389 m.

Santa Maria *ma-ree'a*, 29 04S 53 47W, pop(1980) 151,156, town in Rio Grande do Sul state, Sul region, S Brazil; W of Pôrto Alegre; university (1960); railway; economy: rice, potatoes, food processing, cattle.

Santa Maria or **Ilha de Santa Maria**, 36 58N 25 07W, most southerly of the Azores Is, Ponta Delgada dist, Portuguese autonomous region of the Azores; 17 km long and 8 km wide, with an area of 97 sq km; economy: fishing, stock-rearing and crop-farming; the highest point is the double summit of Pico Alto (587 m); main town is Vila do Porto.

Santa Maria, 34 57N 120 26W, pop(1980) 39,685, city in Santa Barbara county, SW California, United States; on the Santa Maria river, 40 km SSE of San Luis Obispo.

Santa Maria, Cabo de, 36 58N 7 55 W, low lying headland on the Atlantic, the southernmost point of Portugal, SE of Faro.

Santa Marta *san'ta mar'ta*, 11 18N 74 10W, pop(1985) 215,540, Caribbean port capital of Magdalena dept, N Colombia, South America; situated at the mouth of the Río Manzanares, on a deep bay with high shelving cliffs; 96 km E of Barranquilla; the Magdalena bridge linking these two towns was opened in 1974; Santa Marta was the first town founded by the Conquistadores in Colombia (in 1525 by Rodrigo de Bastidas); Simón Bolívar died here, in Dec 1830, aged 47; Bolívar was buried in the cathedral, but 12 years later his body was taken to his birthplace at Caracas and enshrined in the Panteón Nacional; railway; airport (Simón Bolívar) at 20 km; economy: oil terminal, main export centre for the banana industry and Colombia's premier seaside resort.

Santa Marta, Sierra Nevada de, Andean massif in Magdalena dept, N Colombia, South America; E of Barranquilla; rises abruptly from the Caribbean coast to 5,800 m at Pico Cristóbal Colón, Colombia's highest peak; separated from the Cordillera Oriental (E) by the Río César depression; the mountain range was made a national park in 1964 (area 3,830 sq km); an area noted for marijuana-growing.

Santa Monica, 34 01N 118 29W, pop(1980) 88,314, residential city in Los Angeles county, SW California, United States; on the Pacific Ocean in Santa Monica Bay, 24 km W of Los Angeles; railway; monument: Santa Monica municipal pier is 512 m long.

Santa Rosa *san'ta rō'sa*, 36 37S 64 17W, pop(1980) 51,689, agricultural centre and capital of La Pampa prov, Centro, central Argentina; railway junction.

Santa Rosa, national park in Guanacaste prov, NW Costa Rica, Central America; established in 1971; area 215 sq km; thousands of Pacific turtles nest on Nancite beach within the park.

Santa Rosa, 3 29S 79 59W, pop(1982) 26,716, town in El Oro prov, SW Ecuador; S of Machala on the Golfo de Guayaquil; railway.

Santa Rosa, maritime dept in SE Guatemala, Central America; bounded S by the Pacific Ocean; pop(1982e) 249,930, area 2,955 sq km; capital Cuilapa; traversed by the Inter-American Highway; the Río Guacalate forms part of its W boundary; the N part of the dept is devoted largely to coffee growing while, further S, sugar cane, corn, cotton, cocoa, and bananas are grown.

Santa Rosa, Honduras. See Copán.

Santa Rosa, 38 26N 122 43W, pop(1980) 83,320, capital of Sonoma county, W California, United States; 80 km N of San Francisco; monuments: home and gardens of Luther Burbank, who conducted his experiments here.

Santa Venera *ven'er-ah*, 35 53N 14 30E, pop(1983e) 6,800, community on the main island of Malta, lying W of Valletta, between Hamrun and Birkirkara.

Santander *san-tan-der'*, dept in N central Colombia, South America; bounded W by the Río Magdalena; watered by Sogamoso and Suárez rivers; the Cordillera Oriental lies in the E; pop(1985) 1,427,110; area 30,537 sq km; capital Bucaramanga; economy: coffee and tobacco.

Santander, region and prov in N Spain, co-extensive with Cantabria, stretching along the Bay of Biscay and across the Cordillera Cantabrica to the headwaters of the R headwaters of the R Ebro; pop(1981) 510,816; area 5,289 sq km; capital Santander.

Santander, 43 27N 3 51W, pop(1981) 180,328, seaport, resort and capital of Santander prov, N Spain; 393 km N of Madrid; bishopric; university (1972); airport; railway; car ferries to Plymouth, Gijón; beaches; economy: pharmaceuticals, paper, glass, soap, chemicals, nuclear components, brewing, textiles, shipbuilding, fish processing; monuments: royal palace; 13th-c cathedral; prehistory museum; 7 km to the N is Cabo Mayor lighthouse; events: fiesta of Santiago in July-Aug and Semana Grande in Aug.

Santarém *san-ta-rem'*, 2 26S 54 41W, pop(1980) 102,181, river port in Pará state, Norte region, N Brazil; at the junction of the Tapajós and Amazon rivers; founded in 1661; 3rd largest town on the Brazilian Amazon; airfield; economy: commerce, jute, mining of gold and bauxite, timber, oil seed, textiles.

Santarém, district in central Portugal, part of Ribatejo prov; area, 6,612 sq km; pop(1981) 454,123; traversed by R Tagus; divided into 21 councils and 165 parishes; chief towns are Santarém, Abrantes and Tomar; economy: almonds, rice, olives, cereals, vegetables, fruit, cork, wood, resin, animal fat, meat, wool, pork sausages, honey, eggs, skins, hardware, crafts and textiles; airfield at Lago Azul.

Santarém, SCALABIS or PRAESIDIUM JULIUM (anc), 39 12N 8 42W, pop(1981) 15,300, walled capital of Santarém dist, central Portugal; 69 km NE of Lisboa; divided into 3 parishes; economy: olive oil, wine, fruit and tourism; centre of Portuguese bullfighting; railway; monuments: the Seminario (1676), churches of Santa Clara (13th-c), Senhor da Graça and São João de Alporão and Torre das Cabeças; events: festival of São Jose in March; music festival in April; festival of flowers in May; agric show at beginning of June and festival of Santa do Castelo in mid-August; food festival in October.

Santiago *san-tya'gō*, metropolitan region in central Chile; pop(1984) 4,672,700; area 15,549 sq km; capital Santiago; chief towns Talagante and Melipilla; economy: commerce, light and heavy industry, tourism, agriculture.

Santiago, GRAN SANTIAGO, 33 27S 70 38W, pop(1982) 4,039,287, capital of Santiago metropolitan zone, Santiago metropolitan region, and of Chile; the city covers approx 100 sq km and is crossed E to W by the Río Mapocho; 3 universities (1738, 1888, 1947); railway; airport (Pudahuel) at 26 km; airfield (Los Cerrillos) at 14.5 km; economy: more than half of Chile's manufacturing industry is located here; founded in 1541 by Pedro de Valdivia; became the capital of Chile at the beginning of the 19th century; has suffered on several occasions from floods, fires and earthquakes; monuments: the heart of Santiago is dominated by the Avenida O'Higgins (usually called the Alameda) which stretches for more than 3 km and is lined with ornamental gardens and with statues of Chile's national heroes; the other chief landmark is the Santa Lucía Hill, where Pedro de Valdivia built his first fort; N of the Plaza Bulnes is the principal government building, the Palacio de la Moneda; used for official receptions, it contains historic relics, paintings and sculpture; the Moneda was badly damaged by air attacks during the military coup of 11 Sept 1973; in front of the Moneda is a statue of Arturo Alessandri Palma, who was President of the Republic for 2 terms; the Parque O'Higgins contains an amusement park, a small lake, playing fields, tennis courts, a swimming pool, an open-air stage and a racecourse; the Parque Forestal contains the National Museum of Fine Arts and the Museo de Arte Contemporáneo; the National Museum contains pieces of armour worn by Valdivia's men; the Natural History Museum has an exhibition on Chilean landscapes; the Museo de la Escuela Militar features displays on General O'Higgins, the Conquest and the War of the Pacific; to the NE of Santiago lies the conical hill of San Cristóbal which is ascended by funicular railway; on one hill stands a statue of the Virgin.

Santiago, SANTIAGO DE LOS CABALLEROS *day lōs ka-ba-lyay'rōs*, 19 30N 70 42W, pop(1982e) 394,237, town in central Santiago prov, Dominican Republic, in the fertile Cibao agricultural region, 60 km S of Puerto Plata; 2nd largest city in the Dominican Republic; highway; airfield; most important trading, distributing, and processing centre in the N of the country; here was fought the decisive battle of Dominican struggle for independence (30 March 1844); economy: rum; monuments: cathedral, fort.

Santiago, 8 08N 80 59W, pop(1980) 24,205, capital town of Veraguas prov, W central Panama, Central America; on the Inter-American Highway, in a grain-growing area; one of the oldest towns in the country; its port is Puerto Mutis.

Santiago de Compostela *THay kom-pos-tay'la*, CAMPUS STELLAE (anc), COMPOSTELLA (Eng), 42 52N 8 37W, pop(1981) 93,695, city in La Coruña prov, Galicia, NW Spain; on the R Sar, SE of Monte Pedros (735 m); archbishopric; university (1501); airport; railway; former capital of the kingdom of Galicia; the shrine of St James (Iago) made it a world-famous place of pilgrimage in the Middle Ages; under a special privilege granted by Pope Calixtus II, every year in which the feast of St James falls on a Sunday ranks as a Holy Year to be marked by special celebrations; economy: linen, paper, soap, brandy, silverwork; monuments: Plaza de la Quintana and Plaza de España; Romanesque cathedral; former Benedictine monastery of San Martin Pinario; events: Ascension; Corpus Christi; fiesta of Santiago Apostol in July with a procession that features the swinging of the huge censer known as the *Botafumeiro*.

Santiago de Cuba *THay koo'ba*, prov in SE Cuba; the Sierra Maestra extends into the SW corner; drained by the upper Cauto river and its tributaries; area 6,343 sq km; pop(1981) 909,506; capital Santiago de Cuba; chief towns Palma Soriano and San Luis.

Santiago de Cuba, 20 00N 75 49W, pop(1983e) 353,373, seaport capital of Santiago de Cuba prov, SE Cuba; on a bay of the S coast; Cuba's second largest city; founded in 1514 and formerly capital of the republic; scene of events in the Spanish-American war of 1898, culminating in the town's surrender to US forces; the national hero, José Martí, is buried just W of the city; rail terminus; monuments: cathedral (1528); Moncada Barracks, the site of the first attack staged by Fidel Castro's rebels against President Batista in 1953; the residence of Diego de Velásquez, the first colonizer of Cuba, housing the Museum of Colonial Art; events: Festival de Caribe (16-19 April) with traditional African dancing; carnival in July.

Santiago del Estero *THel es-tay'rō*, prov in Norte region, N Argentina; bordered W by outliers of the mountains of Catamarca and Tucumán provs; it slopes E to the pampas and is intersected by the Dulce and Salado rivers; includes the N part of the salt deserts (Salinas Grandes) in the SW; subtropical climate; most of the prov is covered by forest; near Las Termas the Río Hondo is dammed for irrigation, hydroelectricity, flood control and recreation; pop(1980) 594,920; area 135,254 sq km; the capital, Santiago del Estero, is a major resort, along with Termas del Río Hondo (with its curative waters); economy: sheep and cattle raising, fishing, cotton, manganese, clay; gypsum and quartzite mining.

Santiago del Estero, 27 48S 64 15W, pop(1980) 148,357, capital of Santiago del Estero prov, Norte, N Argentina; on the Río Dulce; the oldest Argentinian town, founded in 1553 by settlers from Peru; university; railway; airfield; economy: agricultural trade and lumbering centre; monuments: the main square, Plaza Libertad, contains the Casa de Gobierno and the cathedral; Gothic church of San Francisco, founded in 1590 by San Francisco Solano, patron saint of Tucumán; event: festival of San Francisco (24 July).

Santo André *san'tō an-dray'*, 23 39S 46 29W, pop(1980) 549,556, town in São Paulo state, Sudeste region, SE Brazil; an outer suburb of São Paulo; railway; economy: commerce, motor vehicles, chemical products, textiles.

Santo Antão *san'too an-tã'ō*, 17 11N 25 04W, mountainous island with rocky shoreline in the Barlavento or windward group of Cape Verde, the 2nd largest island; the island is divided into 3 *concelhos* (councils): Ribeira Grande, Paul and Porto Novo; area 779 sq km; length 40 km; pop(1980) 43,198, rises to 1,948 m at the Tope da Coroa; 50 minutes by ferry from Mindelo on São Vicente; an airport for small aircraft also connects with Mindelo; sugar cane grown on the island is used in the making of rum and molasses; coffee, tobacco, oranges and beans are also grown.

Santo Domin'go, formerly CIUDAD TRUJILLO *syoo'dad troo-heel'yō*, 19 30N 70 42W, pop(1982e) 1,599,401, capital city of Distrito Nacional, S Dominican Republic, on the right bank of the Rio Ozama, 30 km E of San Cristóbal; founded in 1496 by Bartholomew Columbus; highway junction; airport; harbour; university (1538); monuments: Renaissance cathedral (1514-40) with the ornate tomb of Columbus; Alcazar castle (1514).

Santo Domingo de los Colorados *san'tō do-meeng'gō THay lōs ko-lo-ra'THōs*, 0 13S 79 09W, pop(1982) 69,235, town in Pichincha prov, W Ecuador; in the tropical lowlands to the W of the Andes; railway; economy: drinks, tobacco, roads radiate to Quito, Guayaquil, Esmeraldas and Manta; the last of the Colorados Indians are located in a reserve close to the town.

Santo Tomás or **Santo Tomás de Castilla** *san'tō tō-mahs' THay kas-teel'ya*, 15 39N 88 33W, port on the NE coast of Guatemala, Central America; SW of Puerto Barrios, on the Bahía de Amatique which is an inlet of the Gulf of Honduras; receives pipeline from Alta Verapaz dept.

Santorin', SANTORÍNI *san-tor-ee'nee* (Eng), THERA, THÍRA *thee'ra*, southernmost of the islands of the Kikládhes (Cyclades), Greece; 140 km N of Kríti (Crete); the nearby islands of Thirasía and Aspronísi are the remnants of a larger island destroyed by a volcano in the 15th century; rises to 300 m; occupied by the 2nd millenium BC.

Santos *san'tōs*, 23 56S 46 22W, pop(1980) 410,933, port in São Paulo state, Sudeste region, SE Brazil; 63 km SE of São Paulo and 5 km from the Atlantic coast, on an island; the most important Brazilian port, handling over 40% by value of all Brazilian imports and about half the total exports; outside the city is an important industrial area centred around the oil refinery and hydroelectric plant at Cubatão; the area is known locally as the Valley of Death because of the pollution from chemical factories; founded in 1534; railway; event: founding of Santos (26 Jan).

Santos, Los, prov in S central Panama, Central America; occupying the SE part of the peninsula of Azuero; bounded E and F by the Pacific Ocean; pop(1980) 70,261; area 3,867 sq km; capital Las Tablas; chief towns Los Santos and Los Asientos; a branch of the Inter-American Highway runs down the E coast.

Santurce *san-toor'say*, 43 20N 3 03W, pop(1981) 53,329, picturesque resort town and fishing port in Vizcaya prov, Pais Vasco (Basque Country), N Spain; under the Monte de Serantes, NW of Bilbao.

São Bernardo do Campo *sown ber-nar'do dō kam'pō*, 23 45S 46 34W, pop(1980) 381,097, town in São Paulo state, Sudeste region, SE Brazil; E of São Paulo; railway; economy: motor vehicles, textiles, chemical products.

São Caetano do Sul *ka-ay-ta'nō dō sool'*, 23 33S 46 39W, pop(1980) 163,082, town in São Paulo state, Sudeste region, SE Brazil; an outer suburb of São Paulo; railway; economy: motor vehicles, food processing, ceramics, chemicals.

São Carlos *kar'lōs*, 22 02S 47 53W, pop(1980) 109,167, town in São Paulo state, Sudeste region, SE Brazil; NW of São Paulo; university (1970); railway; economy: commerce, textiles, food processing, cattle.

São Cornelio *sown kor-nay'lee-o*, 40 20N 7 02W, mountain SE of Guarda near Sabugal, N Portugal; height 1,025 m.

São Filipe *fee-lee'pay*, 14 53N 24 41W, town on W coast of Fogo I, Cape Verde.

São Francisco *fran-sees'kō*, river in E Brazil; rises in the Serra de Canastra, E Brazil; flows NNE, NW then ESE to enter the Atlantic 96 km NE of Aracajú; forms the Pernambuco-Bahia state border, then the border between Alagoas and Sergipe states; length 2,900 km; with its tributaries the São Francisco forms South America's 3rd largest drainage basin; the main route of access into the interior of E Brazil; hydroelectricity is generated at several points along its length, at the Sobradinho, the Paulo Alfonso and the Tres Marias dams.

São Gonçalo *gon-sa'lō*, canal in Rio Grande do Sul state, Sul region, S Brazil; navigable natural channel (72 km long) linking L Mirim and Lagoa dos Patos, L Mirim's only outlet to the sea; the port of Pelotas is situated at the N end, 10 km from its influx into Lagoa dos Patos; receives the Río Piratini.

São Jorge or **Ilha de São Jorge** *sown zhor'zhi*, 38 40N 28 03W, in the central Azores group in Angra do Heroísmo dist, Portuguese autonomous region of the Azores, with an area of 246 sq km and measuring 45 km long; main town is Vila das Velas on SW coast; highest point is Pico da Esperanca or Morro Pelado (1,053 m) which last erupted in 1808; economy: fishing, crop-farming, stock-rearing and timber-working.

São José do Rio Prêto *sã'ō zhō-say' dō ree'ō pray'tō*, 20 50S 49 20W, pop(1980) 172,027, town in São Paulo state, Sudeste region, SE Brazil; NW of São Paulo; railway; economy: cotton, rice, coffee, oranges, maize, textiles, ceramics, timber.

São José dos Campos *dōs kam'pōs*, 23 07S 45 52W, pop(1980) 286,034, town in São Paulo state, Sudeste region, SE Brazil; ENE of São Paulo; railway; airfield; economy: motor vehicles, textiles, oil refining.

São Luís *loo-ees'*, 2 34S 44 16W, pop(1980) 182,258, port capital of Maranhão state, Nordeste region, NE Brazil; SE of Belém; situated in a region of heavy tropical rains and deep forest; the city stands on an island between the bays of São Marcos and São José; founded by the French in 1612; university (1966); airport at 15 km; economy: drinks, vegetable oils; monuments: the church of São José do Desterro (completed in 1863); the Forte do Ribeirão (1796); event: São José festival on 24 June, featuring the 'Bumba-Meu-Boi', a fantastic bull dance and masque.

São Mamede, Serra de *sown ma-may'di*, border mountain range, Portalegre dist, E central Portugal, rising to 1,025 m.

São Miguel or **Ilha de São Miguel** *sown mee-gel'*, 37 33N 25 27N, largest island in the Azores in Ponta Delgada dist, with an area of 747 sq km and measuring 65 km long by up to 16 km wide; highest points are the Pico da Vara (1,105 m) in the E and the Pico da Cruz (856 m) in the W; many extinct volcanic craters, some, occupied by lakes such as the Caldeira das Sete Cidades, the Lagoa das Furnas and the Lagoa do Fogo, are now a tourist attraction; the main town and capital of the Azores is Ponta Delgada.

São Nicolau *nee-koo-low'*, 16 37N 24 18W, small, mountainous island with two communities in the Barlavento or windward group of Cape Verde; area 388 sq km; pop(1980) 13,575, rises to 1,283 m at Monte Gordo; the chief town is Ribeira Brava; one of the first islands in the group to be settled in the 15th century; economy: horses, oranges, beans, corn.

São Paulo *pow'lō*, state in Sudeste region, SE Brazil; bordered E by the Atlantic, SW by the Río Paranapanema, NE by the Río Grande, and W by the Río Paraná; drained by the Río Tietê; in central São Paulo, on the Río Tietê is the Ibitinga Dam; pop(1980) 25,040,712; area 247,898 sq km; capital São Paulo; economy: coffee, cotton, sugar, fruit, motor vehicles, machinery; the state was transformed in the early 1900s by the coffee boom, which led to an influx of Italian, Portuguese, Spanish and Japanese immigrants.

São Paulo, 23 33S 46 39W, pop(1980) 7,032,547, capital of São Paulo state, Sudeste region, SE Brazil; on the Río Tietê, NNW of the port of Santos; founded by Jesuits in 1554; developed as a major industrial centre since the late 19th century; 3 universities (1934, 1952, 1970); railway;

airport (Congonhas) at 14 km; airfield; South America's leading commercial and industrial centre; the city accounts for approx 45% of Brazil's total industrial production and has approx 34,000 industrial establishments; economy: commerce, pharmaceuticals, machine tools, furniture, steel, chemicals, food processing; monuments: the neo-Gothic cathedral seats 8,000; the Museo de Arte de São Paulo contains a large collection of paintings by the French Impressionists, Italian Renaissance artists and other European painters; the Museum of Brazilian Art; the Iparinga Monument, commemorating the declaration of Brazilian independence, stands in the Parque da Independência in the suburb of Iparinga; São Paulo has one of the world's largest exhibition halls (the Anhembi), used by Brazil and other countries for industrial fairs and fashion and textile shows.

São Pedro do Acor *sown pay'droo doo a-kor'*, 40 12N 7 40W, mountain at SW corner of Serra da Estrêla range, central Portugal; height 1,349 m.

São Pedro Velho *sown pay'droo vel-yo*, 40 52N 8 10W, mountain SE of Porto in Serra de Arada, between R Douro and R Vouga, central Portugal; height 1,085 m.

São Tiago or **Santiago** *san-tya'goo*, 14 55N 23 31W, pop(1980) 145,923, the largest of 10 islands in Cape Verde, located in the Sotavento or leeward group; divided into the administrative *concelhos* (councils) of Praia, Santa Catarina, Tarrafal and Santa Cruz; area 991 sq km; pop(1980) 145,923, rises to 1,320 m at Antonia Peak; the chief town and capital of the Republic of Cape Verde is Praia; fine beaches at Gamboa, Prainha and Quebra-Canela; tourist developments can also be found on the N coast at Tarrafal (45 km from Praia); on the W coast Ribeira Grande, known as the 'Cidade Velha', was established in the 15th-c and was the capital of the Cape Verde Is during colonial times; an airport connects with Dakar and other islands in the group; about half of the island is cultivated, producing coffee, sugar, oranges.

São Tomé, 0 19N 6 43E, pop(1970) 25,000, seaport capital of the volcanic islands of São Tomé and Príncipe in the Gulf of Guinea; situated on Ana de Chaves Bay on the NE coast of São Tomé island; airport.

São Tomé and Príncipe *sown tō-may' and preen'si-pe*, SÃO TOMÉ E PRÍNCIPE, official name Democratic Republic of São Tomé and Príncipe, an equatorial island republic in the Gulf of Guinea off the coast of West Africa; comprising the 2 islands of São Tomé and Príncipe with a total area of 963 sq km; timezone GMT +1; pop(1983e) 100,000 (with about 80,000 on the island of São Tomé and 20,000 on Príncipe); capital São Tomé; chief towns Trinidad, Santana, Porto Alegre and Santo Antonio; ethnic groups include Mestizo, Angolares (descendants of Angolan slaves), Forros (descendants of freed slaves), Serviçaes (contract labourers from Angola, Mozambique and Cape Verde), Tongas (children of Servicais born on the islands) and Europeans (mainly Portuguese); the official language is Portuguese; the unit of currency is the dobra; national holidays: 4 Feb (Martyrs' Day), 12 July (Independence Day), 30 Sept (Farmers' Day); membership of AfDB, FAO, G-77, GATT (de facto), IBRD, ICAO, IDA, IFAD, IMF, ITU, NAM, OAU, UN, UNESCO, UPU, WHO, WMO.

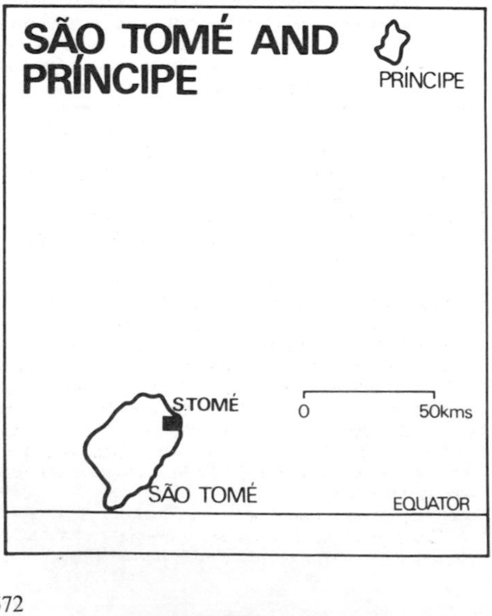

Physical description. In addition to the 2 main volcanic islands of São Tomé and Príncipe there are a number of smaller islands including Pedras Tinhosas and Rolas. São Tomé is about 440 km off the coast of N Gabon, has an area of 845 sq km and has a peak elevation of 2,024 m. Streams radiate to the sea through mountain forest. Príncipe, the smaller of the two islands, lies about 200 km off the N coast of Gabon and has similar terrain.

Climate. At sea-level the country experiences a tropical climate which is both hot and humid, though modified by the Benguela current. The average annual temperature is 27°C with little daily variation. This figure drops to around 20°C on the interior's higher altitudes where the nights are mainly cool. There is a rainy season during Oct-May with an annual average rainfall varying from 500 mm on the SW slopes to 1,000 mm on the N lowlands.

History, government and constitution. First visited between 1469 and 1472 by the Portuguese navigators, Pedro Escobar and João Gomes, the island of São Tomé was settled in 1493 by Avaro Caminha who was granted land by the Portuguese crown. The island of Príncipe to the NNE was settled 7 years later. Originally important as a source of sugar, the islands later became a port of call for ships travelling to and from the East Indies. In addition, cocoa and coffee were successfully introduced. By 1908 the territory had become the world's largest producer of cocoa, which was grown on plantations owned by Portuguese companies or absentee landlords. Resistance to Portuguese administration culminated in the 1953 riots known as the Batepa Massacre and the formation of an overseas liberation movement based in Gabon. Following the Portuguese revolution of 1974, talks were held and independence achieved a year later.

Economy. The country's economy is based on agriculture which accounts for almost 100% of exports and employs about 70% of the pop. With independence in 1975, control of the plantations, chiefly growing cocoa, passed into state hands. Other exports include copra, palm kernels and coffee. Following depressed world cocoa prices, a restructuring of the economy was announced in 1985 outlining efforts towards greater involvement in agriculture, management, commerce, banking and tourism. Aid is received from the World Bank, the UN Development Programme, the EEC and the African Development Bank and technical advice has been obtained from the USSR and other eastern bloc countries. Major trade partners include Portugal, Angola, the Netherlands, the USA, West Germany and the UK.

Administrative divisions. São Tomé and Príncipe is divided into 7 counties, 6 on the island of São Tomé and 1 on the island of Príncipe.

São Vicente *vee-sen'tay*, 23 57S 46 23W, pop(1980) 192,858, town in São Paulo state, Sudeste region, SE Brazil; on the Atlantic coast, S of São Paulo; railway; economy: commerce and tourism.

São Vicente, 16 53N 25 00W, island in the Barlavento or windward group of Cape Verde; the local government *concelho* (council) of São Vicente includes the uninhabited island of Santa Luzia; area 227 sq km; pop(1980) 41,792; rises to 762 m at Monte Verde; the chief town and port is Mindelo on the NW shore; an airport receives local flights from neighbouring islands; economy: agriculture, fishing, coal mining.

São Vicente, Cabo de, CAPE ST VINCENT (Eng), 37 01N 8 59W, rocky headland 60 m above sea level on Atlantic coast of Faro dist, SW extremity of Portugal and of continental Europe; in 12th century a ship bearing the body of St Vincent came ashore here; scene of British naval victory over Spanish fleet in 1797.

Saône *sōn*, ARAR (anc), river in E France rising SW of Épinal in the Mts Faucilles (Vosges) in Vosges dept; flows SW to Chalon-sur-Saône and then S past Bresse to meet the R Rhône at Lyon; length 480 km; canals link it with the Loire, Seine, Marne, Meuse, Moselle and Rhine rivers, and it is part of the important routeway of the Rhône-Saône valley; its seasonal maximum coincides with the minimum of the Rhône, and it has therefore a marked regularizing effect on that river; tributaries Ognon, Doubs, Seille, Tille, Ouche and Dheune rivers.

Saône-et-Loire, dept in Bourgogne region of E central France, comprising 5 arrond, 56 cantons and 573 communes; pop(1982) 571,852; area 8,565 sq km; its name is derived from the Saône R which waters its E half, and the Loire R which forms its W border; crossed by the Canal du Centre which links the 2 rivers (Chalon-Digoin); the Plaine de Bresse extends over the E part of the dept; the hilly right bank of the R Saône is an important centre of the Burgundy wine trade, especially round Mâcon; capital Mâcon, chief towns Chalon-sur-Saône, Le Creusot and Montceau-les-Mines; there are châteaux at Sully (16th-c) and Berzé-le-Chatel (18-19th-c); spa at Bourbon-Lancy; the Parc de Morvan regional nature park lies partly within the dept.

Sapporo *sap-ō'rō*, 43 05N 141 21E, pop(1980) 1,401,757, capital of Hokkaidō prefecture, W central Hokkaidō island, Japan; founded in 1871 as a centre for the development of Hohhaidō I; to the SW of the city is the Shikotsu Ioya national park; Hokkaidō University (1876); railway; subway; economy: winter sports, timber, brewing, flour, agricultural machinery; monuments: the Ainu museum in the botanical gardens contains a collection of Ainu craftwork and plants and animals native to the island; event: Snow Festival of the O dori in Jan-Feb, when c.200 sculptures made out of snow and ice are on display in the main boulevard, the O dori.

Saragossa, Spain. See Zaragoza.

Sarajevo *sa-ra-yay'vō*, 43 52N 18 26E, pop(1981) 448,500, capital of Bosna-Hercegovina republic, Yugoslavia; on R Miljacka; governed by Austria between 1878 and 1918; scene of the assassination by Gavrilo Princip of Archduke Francis Ferdinand and his wife on 28 June 1914, an event that led to the outbreak of World War I; educational and cultural centre; university (1946); airport; railway; site of 1984 Winter Olympic Games; economy: motor vehicles, brewing, engineering, chemicals, carpets, tobacco; monuments: Baščaršija quarter in the old town; Husref Bey mosque; Imperial mosque; events: Yugoslav Song Festival in April; International Festival of Military Music in June; Slivovitz and wine fair in Oct.

Saramacca *sa-ra-ma'ka*, dist in NW Surinam, NE South America; in the centre of the dist is the Voltzberg Nature Reserve, a rainforest park; area 23,420 sq km; pop(1980) 10,335; capital Groningen.

Sarandë, prov of S Albania; area 1,097 sq km; pop(1980) 74,400; capital Sarandë.

Sarandë, 39 52N 20 00E, seaport and capital of Sarandë prov, SW Albania; on the Adriatic Sea, NE of the island of Kérkira (Corfu), 80 km SE of Vlorë; became a bishopric in the 5th century; the modern port developed as an Italian naval station during World War I; monument: Byzantine church ruins nearby.

Saransk *su-ransk'*, 54 12N 45 10E, pop(1983) 293,000, capital city of Mordovskaya ASSR, central European Rossiyskaya, Soviet Union; on the R Insar; founded in 1641 as a fortress; university (1957); railway; economy: electrical engineering, machine building, chemicals, clothing; monument: church of John the Apostle (1693).

Saraso'ta, 27 20N 82 32W, pop(1980) 48,868, winter resort and county seat of Sarasota county, W Florida, United States; on Sarasota Bay, 65 km S of Tampa; university; railway; economy: yachting and fishing resort; construction industry; packing houses; monuments: John and Mabel Ringling Museum of Art, Circus Hall of Fame, Cars of Yesterday Museum.

Saratoga, 37 16N 122 02W, pop(1980) 29,261, city in Santa Clara county, W California, United States; in the foothills of the Santa Cruz Mts, 14 km SW of San José.

Saratov *sa-rat'ef*, 51 30N 45 55E, pop(1983) 887,000, river port capital of Saratovskaya oblast, E European Rossiyskaya, Soviet Union; on the R Volga; founded in 1590 as a fortress city designed to protect the Volga route from nomad raids; university (1909); railway; airport; economy: oil refining, chemicals, chemical fibres, clothing, leatherwork; monument: Troitskii cathedral (1689-95).

Saravan *sa-ra-wan*, SARAVANE, prov (*khowèng*) of S Laos, SE Asia; capital Saravan.

Sarawak *sur-ah'wak*, state in E Malaysia, SE Asia; on the NW coast of the island of Borneo; bounded S by Kalimantan (Indonesia), N by the South China Sea and NE by Brunei and Sabah; consists of a flat, narrow coastal strip, a belt of foothills and then a highly mountainous forested interior; highest peak is Gunong Murud (2,423 m); watered by the R Rajang; pop(1980) 1,235,553; area 124,449 sq km; capital Kuching; economy: oil (Miri), rice, sago, rubber, pepper, fishing; governed by the Brooke dynasty of 'white rajahs' from 1841 until 1946; became a British Protectorate in 1888 and a Crown Colony in 1946; taken by the Japanese in 1941; ethnic groups include Kayan, Kenyah, Murut, Kelabit and Punan, mostly living close to the R Rajang and its tributaries; the area around Gunong Mulu, including the spectacular limestone caves, was designated a national park in 1975.

Sarcelles *sar-sel*, 49 00N 2 24E, pop(1982) 53,732, town in Val-d'Oise dept, Ile-de-France region, N central France, 14 km N of Paris.

Sardegna *sar-day'nya*, SARDIN'IA (Eng), region and island of Italy, comprising the provs of Sassari, Nuoro, Oristano, and Cagliari; pop(1981) 1,594,175; capital and chief port Cagliari; main towns Sassari, Carbonia, Oristano and Iglesias; area 24,090 sq km; length 272 km; width 144 km; 2nd largest island in the Mediterranean, 184 km SW of the promontory of Orbetello, and separated from the neighbouring French island of Corse (Corsica) by the narrow Strait of Bonifacio; much of the island is hilly with gentler slopes in the W and more rugged country in the E, rising to 1,835 m in the Monti del Gennargentu; the centre and N are well-wooded, and the hilly mineral-bearing SW corner is cut off by the alluvial plain of Campidano, the most fertile part of the island; economy: agriculture (corn, wine, olives, citrus fruits, vegetables, and tobacco are grown in the Campidano plain, coastal areas, and the fertile valleys), pastoral farming in the uplands, fishing, mining (zinc, lead, manganese), opencast coal-mining near Carbonia, coal and hydroelectric power stations, petrochemical industries in the Cagliari area, extraction of magnesium and cooking salt from sea-water, tourism (Alghero, Santa Teresa, Costa Smeralda).

Sardinia, region and island of Italy. See Sardegna.

Sarektjåkkå, 67 29N 17 40E, peak in the Kjölen Mts, W Norrbotten county, NW Sweden, near source of Lule älv, just S of L Stora Lulevatten; height 2,089 m.

Sargasso Sea *sahr-gas'ō*, sluggish area of the Atlantic Ocean, lying between the Azores and the islands of the West Indies within the 'Horse Latitudes'; bounded to the N and NW by the NE-flowing North Atlantic Drift; a still sea, located at the centre of the clockwise-moving warm surface currents, it allows great biological activity and is particularly noted for its abundance of surface gulfweed; a breeding ground for eels which migrate to Europe; the Bermuda Islands are located on the Bermuda Rise.

Sarh *sar*, FORT-ARCHAMBAULT *ar-sham-bō* (Fr), 9 08N 18 22E, capital of Moyen-Chari prefecture, S Chad, N central Africa; 480 km SE of N'Djamena; airfield.

Sari *sa-ree'*, 36 33N 53 06E, pop(1983) 124,663, capital city of Sari dist, Māzandarān, N Iran; 32 km E of Bābol, close to the S shore of the Caspian Sea, in the N foothills of the Elburz Mts; trade centre for surrounding agricultural region which produces citrus fruits, rice, sugar cane; railway.

Sariwŏn *sa-ree-wun*, 38 30N 125 45E, capital of Hwanghai-puk prov, S central North Korea; 56 km S of P'yŏngyang; economy: textiles, coal, food processing.

Sark, SERCQ (Fr), smallest of the 4 main islands of the Channel Is, lying between Guernsey and the Cotentin Peninsula of French Normandie; consists of Great and Little Sark connected by an isthmus (La Coupée); although in the Bailiwick of Guernsey, the island has its own legislative assembly; pop(1978e) 600; area 4 sq km.

Sar'nen, 46 53N 8 13E, pop(1980) 7,600, capital town of Obwalden demicanton, and of Unterwalden canton, central Switzerland; 59 km E of Bern, at N end of the Sarner See, on the road from Luzern to Interlaken over the Brünig Pass; railway; centre for summer hiking and camping and winter cross-country skiing.

Sarnia *sar'nee-a*, 42 57N 82 24W, pop(1981) 50,892, port town in SE Ontario, S Canada; on the St Clair river, at the foot of L Huron, opposite Port Huron, Michigan (USA), with which it is linked by railway tunnel and bridge (the Blue Water International Bridge, built in 1938); founded in 1833 as a lumber port; oil was discovered nearby in 1858; railway; economy: petrochemicals, oil refining, rubber, plastics, industrial chemicals.

Sarpsborg, *sahrps'bor*, 59 17N 11 06E, pop(1980) 12,035, manufacturing town in Østfold county, SE Norway; on W bank of R Glåma with the Sarpsfoss Falls in the middle of the town, NE of Fredrikstad; founded by St Olav in the 11th century; rebuilt in 1838 on the site of a ruined medieval town; railway; economy: paper, cellulose, electrical engineering; monument: Borgarsyssel Museum.

Sarthe *sart*, dept in Pays de la Loire region of W France, comprising 3 arrond, 40 cantons and 376 communes; pop(1982) 504,768; area 6,245 sq km; watered by the Sarthe, Huisne and Loir rivers; there are several dolmens, tumuli and Roman remains; capital Le Mans, chief towns La Flèche and Mamers; there are châteaux at Le Lude (15-18th-c) and Poncé-sur-le-Loir (16th-c); the Parc Normandie-Maine regional nature park lies partly within the dept.

Sarthe, river in NW France rising in the Collines du Perche (Perche Hills) N of Mortagne in Orne dept; flows S and SW past Le Mans joining with the Mayenne and Loir rivers above Angers to form the R Maine which, only a short distance further S, meets the R Loire; length 285 km; navigable to Le Mans; tributaries include the Huisne and Loir rivers.

Sárviz *shar'viz*, river in W central Hungary; formed by the junction of the Ged and Gaja rivers W of Székesfehérvár; flows 90 km SE to meet the R Danube near Szekszárd; the Malom drainage canal runs parallel to the river.

Saskatchewan *sa-ska'choo-won*, province in W central Canada; bounded N by Mackenzie dist, Northwest Territories, W by Alberta, E by Manitoba and S by the USA; the S two-thirds of the prov consists of a fertile plain which slopes gradually to the E and N; the N third of the prov is in the Canadian Shield; rises to 1,392 m in the Cypress Hills in the SW of the prov near the border with Alberta; the lowest point is L Athabasca in the NW (alt 213 m); the prov is studded with lakes, the largest being L Athabasca (NW, on the border with Alberta), Reindeer L (NE, on the border with Manitoba) and Wollaston L in the NE; drained by the N Saskatchewan, S Saskatchewan, Saskatchewan, Beaver, Mudjatik and MacFarlane rivers; in the centre of the prov is Prince Albert National Park (area 3,874 sq km, established in 1927); pop(1981) 968,313; area 570,113 sq km; capital Regina; other major cities and towns include Saskatoon, Moose Jaw, Prince Albert and Yorkton; economy: wheat, barley, cattle, dairy farming, petroleum, potash (Saskatchewan contains the largest potash fields in the world), timber; first visited by Europeans at the end of the 17th century, Saskatchewan became an important fur-trading region; in the middle of the 18th century several French trading posts were established; these were later followed by outposts of the Hudson's Bay Co and North West Co; the Hudson's Bay Co land was acquired by Canada in 1870 and became part of Northwest Territories; the area was opened to agricultural settlement after the arrival of the Canadian Pacific Railroad in 1882-83; in 1884 the Saskatchewan Rebellion took place following land disputes between incoming settlers and Indians; Saskatchewan was made a prov of Canada in 1905; the prov is governed by a Lieutenant-Governor, an Executive Council and a 64-member Legislative Assembly elected every 5 years.

Saskatchewan, river in S Canada; formed in Saskatchewan, 48 km E of Prince Albert, by the North Saskatchewan and the South Saskatchewan rivers which rise in the Rocky Mts of W Alberta; length 1,287 km; major tributaries include the Clearwater, Brazeau, Vermilion and Battle rivers; the South Saskatchewan river is formed in S Alberta by the confluence of the Bow and Aldman rivers; it flows E past Medicine Hat, then NE into Saskatchewan and E again; after entering L Diefenbaker it turns N, passes Saskatoon and joins with the North Saskatchewan river E of Prince Albert; length 885 km; length with the Bow river: 1,392 km; from E of Prince Albert the Saskatchewan flows ENE into Manitoba, past The Pas and into Cedar L then into L Winnipeg; its length from the junction of the North and South Saskatchewan is 547 km; length to the head of the Bow river is 1,939 km; in the days of fur trading the Saskatchewan river was the main route to the western plains and to the mountain region beyond.

Saskatoon *sas-ka-toon'*, 52 10N 106 40W, pop(1981) 154,210, town in central Saskatchewan, S central Canada; on the South Saskatchewan river; first settled in 1882 by the Ontario Temperance Society as a temperance colony; the town did not grow until the early 1900s (in 1901 it had a population of only 113), when settlers arrived from the USA; University of Saskatchewan (1907); railway; airfield; economy: centre of large grain-growing area; light and heavy industry, oil-related industries, meat packing, flour milling; monuments: the Western Development Museum has re-created a Saskatchewan community of 1910; the Memorial Art Gallery is a war memorial housing paintings by Canadian artists; events: Pioneer Days and Saskachimo Exposition, a week of history pageants, antique farm equipment demonstrations, antique car displays, livestock and agriculture shows in July.

Sassandra *su-san'dru*, coastal dept in S Ivory Coast, W Africa; pop(1975) 191,994; area 25,800 sq km; the R Douobé forms the W frontier with Liberia; capital Sassandra; chief towns Tabou, San Pedro and Soubré; part of Tai National Park lies in the N; airfield; economy: cement processing.

Sassari *sas'sa-ree*, prov of Sardegna region, Italy; pop(1981) 433,842; area 7,520 sq km; capital Sassari.

Sassari, 40 43N 8 34E, pop(1981) 119,596, capital town of Sassari prov, Sardegna, Italy, on a limestone plateau in the NW of the island, 176 km NNW of Cagliari; archbishopric; university (1562); events: Cavalcata Sarda (traditional costumes) on Assumption; Processione dei Candelieri (14 Aug).

Satkhira *sat'ki-ru*, 22 43N 89 06E, pop(1981) 52,156, town in Satkhira dist, Khulna, W Bangladesh; near the border with India; railway.

Sátoraljaújhely *sha'tor-oy-o-oo-ee-hay*, 48 25N 21 41E, pop(1984e) 21,000, town in Borsod-Abaúj-Zemplén county, E Hungary; on Czechoslovak frontier NE of Miskolc; railway; economy: agricultural trade, petroleum refining, centre of a grape-growing region.

Satu Mare *sa'too ma're*, county in NW Romania; bounded

to the W by Hungary and to the N by the USSR; crossed by the R Someş; pop(1983) 406,556; area 4,405 sq km; capital Satu Mare.

Satu Mare, 47 48N 22 52E, pop(1983) 124,691, resort town and capital of Satu Mare county, NW Romania; on R Someş, near Hungarian frontier; airfield; railway junction; economy: tourism, grain, livestock, timber, wine trade, mining equipment, rolling stock, electric motors, textiles, food processing.

Saudi Arabia *sow'dee*, official name Kingdom of Saudi Arabia, AL-MAMLAKA AL-'ARABIYA AS-SA'UDIYA *al-memlek'a al-ar-e-bee'ye as-soo-dee'ya*, Arabic kingdom comprising approx four-fifths of the Arabian Peninsula, bounded W by the Red Sea, NW by Jordan, N by Iraq, NE by Kuwait, E by the Arabian Gulf, Qatar, and the United Arab Emirates, SE and S by Oman, S by S Yemen, and SW by N Yemen; timezone GMT +3; area 2,331,000 sq km (boundaries in the S and SE are undefined and disputed); capital Ar Riyāḍ (Riyadh); chief towns Jiddah (Jedda), Makkah (Mecca), Al Madīnah (Medina), Aṭ Ṭā'if, and Ad Dammām; pop(1974) 7,012,642; 1,883,987 persons were categorized as nomadic in 1974; the pop comprises 90% Arab and 10% Afro-Asian; Arabic is the official language; the dominant religion is Islam; the unit of currency is the riyal; membership of Arab League, FAO, G-77, GCC, IAEA, IBRD, ICAO, IDA, Islamic Development Bank, IFAD, IFC, ILO, IMF, IMO, INTELSAT, International Maritime Satellite Organization, INTERPOL, ITU, IWC, NAM, OAPEC, OIC, OPEC, UN, UNESCO, UPU, WHO, WMO.

Physical description. The Red Sea coastal plain, varying in width from 14 to 56 km, is bounded E by a range of mountains. The peaks in the N of this range are extremely rugged, reaching heights of about 1,200 m. The Asīr highlands in the SW contain Jebel Abhā, Saudi Arabia's highest peak (3,133 m). The Arabian Peninsula slopes gently downwards to the N and E towards the broad oil-rich Al Hasa plain on the Arabian Gulf. The interior of the country comprises two extensive areas of sand desert, the Great Nafūd in the N and the extensive Rub al Khālī ('the empty quarter') in the S. These sand deserts consist largely of linear dunes, 90-150 m high and aligned NE-SW. The rest of the country is mainly desert or semi-desert in character. The central Najd has some large oases, including Ar Riyāḍ. In the E lowlands *sabkhah* or salt flats are numerous. Saudi Arabia has no permanent rivers or bodies of water. A large network of wadis (dry river valleys) drains NE.

Climate. The climate is hot and dry, with average temperatures varying from 21°C in the N to 26°C in the S. Night frosts are common in the N and in the highlands but day temperatures may rise to 50°C in the interior sand deserts. The Red Sea coast is hot and humid. Mean

annual rainfall is sparse at approx 10 mm per annum. Rainfall is highest in the Asīr highlands, with about 370 mm a year.

History, government and constitution. Although the climate of Saudi Arabia has restricted settlement to a few major cities and oases, the country is noted as the birthplace of Islam. Modern Saudi Arabia was founded by the late King Ibn Sa'ud who, between 1902 and 1932, united the four tribal provinces of Hejāz (NW), Asīr (SW), central Najd, and Al Hasa (E). The country's S border with Yemen was settled in 1934 after a brief border war and the boundaries with Jordan, Iraq and Kuwait were established by a series of treaties negotiated in the 1920s. The border between Saudi Arabia and the United Arab Emirates was agreed upon in 1974. Saudi Arabia supported the Arab cause in the Six-day War with Israel (1967) and the Arab-Israeli conflict of 1973. Thereafter, Saudi Arabia participated in the oil boycott of the USA and the Netherlands and joined with other OPEC countries in raising oil prices. The Kingdom of Saudi Arabia is an absolute monarchy based on Islamic law and Arab Bedouin tradition. There is no formal constitution. The king, who is head of state and prime minister, is assisted by a 26-member council of ministers. In the N the former Neutral Zone between Saudi Arabia and Iraq has now been partitioned between the two countries.

Economy. Saudi Arabia's development began with the discovery of oil in the 1930s. It is now the world's leading oil exporter and its per capita income is the highest in the Arab world. Oil reserves account for approx one-quarter of the world's known supply. It has an extensive extraction, processing and shipping infrastructure capable of producing and exporting over 12 million barrels of oil per day. The main oilfields are located in the Al Hasa plain bordering the W shore of the Arabian Gulf. The construction industry employs 21% of the workforce and is the fastest-growing sector of the economy after oil. A series of 5-year development plans has sought to transform this relatively undeveloped oil-based economy into a modern industrial state. The country aims to turn its natural gas resources, previously flared as a waste product, into a wide range of chemicals and plastics, equivalent to around 5-7% of the world's demand for petrochemicals. Non-associated gas is used as fuel in local power plants and for the kingdom's liquefied petroleum gas plant at Ras Tannūrah. The new town of Al Jubayl, on the W shore of the Arabian Gulf, has been designed as a massive industrial complex. Yanbu' al Baḩr is another new industrial city which has been built around the supply of indigenous oil and gas feedstock to produce steel, petrochemicals, fertilizers, and refined oil products. The main trading partners are the USA, W Europe, and Japan.

Agriculture. The 1980-85 plan laid particular emphasis on the development of agriculture and water resources. Agricultural companies have opened up large areas for cultivation, including prairie-type wheat schemes. The country is now a net exporter of wheat and self-sufficiency has been obtained in eggs and dairy produce. Saudi Arabia has approx 45,000 sq km of cultivable land of which only 4,000 sq km are being cultivated. Chief agricultural products include dates, grains, and livestock.

Communications. There is one railway line linking Ar Riyāḑ and Ad Dammām in Eastern prov. At the end of 1981, Saudi Arabia's road network included 22,501 km of highways and 28,586 km of rural tracks. There are international airports at Aẓ Ẓahrān, Ar Riyāḑ, and Jiddah. The major ports include Jiddah, Ad Dammām, Ras Tannūrah, Al Jubayl, and Yanbu' al Baḩr.

Administrative divisions. Saudi Arabia is divided into the 14 provinces of Jawf, Qurayyat, Northern Frontier, Tabūk, Hā'il, Qassim, Madīnah (Medina), Makkah (Mecca), Baha, Asīr, Jīzan, Riyāḑ (Riyadh), Najrān and Eastern province.

Sault Ste Marie *soo saynt ma-ree'*, *sō sīt ma-ree'* (Fr), 46 32N 84 20W, pop(1981) 82,697, town in S central Ontario, S Canada; on N shore of the St Mary's river which connects L Huron and L Superior; opposite Sault Ste Marie, Michigan, to which it is connected by an international bridge; visited by French explorers and missionaries throughout the 17th century; a fort was built in 1751 which was taken by the British in 1762; the settlement was destroyed in 1814 by American naval forces after the inhabitants had helped capture an American fort; the difference in alt between L Superior (183 m) and L Huron (177 m) meant that the St Mary's river could not be used for communication and transportation until the building of the 'Soo' canals; the Soo locks on the Canadian side of the river were built in 1870 to facilitate the movement of troops W to crush Louis Riel's 2nd rebellion; the first steel plant in Ontario was opened here in 1902; railway; airport; economy: steel, lumber, paper, agricultural trade, tourism.

Sa'va, river in N Yugoslavia; a tributary of the R Danube; the longest river totally in Yugoslavia; formed by the junction of two headstreams in NW Slovenija republic, it flows SE to meet the R Danube at Beograd; length 933 km; receives Kupa, Krka, Una, Vrbas, Bosna and Drina rivers; navigable to Sisak.

Savai'i *sa-vī'ee*, 13 40S 172 16W, largest of the Western Samoan islands, in the SW Pacific Ocean, separated from Upolu I to the SE by the 17 km-wide Apolima Strait; area 1,690 sq km; pop(1981) 43,150, the volcanic island rises to 1,829 m; there are vast black lava fields in the NE of the island; the last great eruptions took place between 1905 and 1911, burying much fertile land and sending refugees to Upolu; chief town Asau, on the NW coast.

Savalou *sa-va'loo*, 7 59N 2 03E, town in Zou prov, central Benin, W Africa; 160 km NNW of Porto Novo.

Savannah, 32 05N 81 06W, pop(1980) 141,390, county seat of Chatham county, E Georgia, United States; a port near the mouth of the R Savannah; founded in 1733 by James Oglethorpe; during the War of Independence it was held by the British 1778-82; captured by Sherman during the Civil War in 1864, as he completed his march to the sea; railway; airfield; economy: trade in tobacco, cotton, sugar, clay, woodpulp; manufactures chemicals, petroleum, rubber, plastics, and paper products; fisheries; railway engineering; monuments: the city's historic district is designated a national historic landmark; event: St Patrick's Festival (March).

Savannakhét *sa-van-a-ket'*, 16 34N 104 45E, pop(1973) 50,690, town in Savannakhét prov, S Laos, SE Asia; on R Mekong, close to the Thailand frontier.

Savanne, district in S Mauritius; area 244.8 sq km; pop(1983) 59,611; the dramatic Rochester Falls are located near Souillac.

Savé *sa'vay*, 8 04N 2 37E, town in Zou prov, S Benin, W Africa; 160 km N of Porto Novo; railway; economy: sugar refinery.

Savoie, mountainous dept in Rhône-Alpes region of E France, bounded on the E by Italy; comprises 3 arrond, 34 cantons and 304 communes; pop(1982) 323,675; area 6,036 sq km; drained by the R Isère; includes the Lac du Bourget, N of Chambéry; best known of numerous spas and resorts are Chambéry, Aix-les-Bains, Challes, Salins-Moûtiers, Brides and Pralognan; capital Chambéry; there are interesting caves near Les Échelles.

Savona *sa-vō'na*, prov of Liguria region, NW Italy; pop(1981) 297,675; area 1,544 sq km; capital Savona.

Savona, 44 18N 8 28E, pop(1981) 75,353, seaport and capital of Savona prov, Liguria region, NW Italy; on the Golfo di Genova, bounded N by the Appno Ligure; as a maritime republic, Savona was long a rival to Genova, but was completely subjected by Genova in 1528; the present town is mainly modern and is surrounded by orange groves; railway; economy: tourism, steel rolling-mill; monument: 17th-c cathedral.

Savonlinna *sah'von-lee'nah*, NYSLOTT *nu-slot*, (Swed), 61 52N 28 53E, pop(1982) 28,499, resort town in Mikkeli prov, S Finland, built on a large island in the Lake Saimaa region with L Haapavesi to the N and L Pihlajavesi to the S; the town grew up around the castle of Olavinlinna or Olofsborg and received its municipal charter in 1639; spa and vacation resort; a former hunting lodge of the Russian Tsars is nearby; railway; boats to other towns on the Finnish lakes; economy: light engineering; events: opera festival and sailing regattas in July.

Sawu Sea, SAVU SEA, arm of the Indian Ocean, located between the Indonesian islands of Sumba to the W, Timor to the E and Flores to the N; linked to the Flores Sea by Selat Sape; to the Banda Sea by Selat Wetar; connected to the Timor Sea to the SE.

Saxony, Lower, prov in W Germany. See Niedersachsen.

Sayabouri, prov and town in Laos. See Xaignabouri.

Sayan *su-yan'*, mountain range predominantly in S Siberian Rossiyskaya, Soviet Union, but extending also into N Mongolia; comprises (1) the Vostochnyy Sayan (E Sayan Mts) which extend 1,090 km SE from the lower R Yenisey to within 160 km of the SW end of Ozero Baykal (Lake Baikal), forming the boundary between the Rossiyskaya and Mongolia in the E section; the highest peak, Munku-Sardyk (3,491 m), lies close to the Mongolian border and has several small glaciers; (2) the Zapadnyy Sayan (W Sayan Mts) lie entirely within the USSR and extend 640 km NE from the Altay Mts to the central section of the Vostochnyy Sayan; traversed by the R Yenisey and the Kyzyl-Minusinsk highway; the Sayan Mts yield gold, coal, graphite, silver, and lead; lumbering, hunting, and agriculture are the chief occupations.

Saynshand *sīn'shan-da*, 44 58N 110 10E, capital of Dornogovĭ county, SE Mongolia; linked by rail to Ulaanbaatar in the NW; airfield; economy: camel breeding, alabaster.

Sayreville, 40 28N 74 22W, pop(1980) 29,969, town in Middlesex county, E New Jersey, United States; on Raritan Bay Inlet, 8 km E of New Brunswick.

Scafell or **Scawfell**, *skaw-fel'*, 54 28N 3 12W, mountain in the Lake District of Cumbria, NW England; the highest peak in England, rising to 977 m in the Cumbrian Mts, W of Ambleside.

Scarborough *skahr'bru*, formerly PORT LOUIS, 11 11N 60 45W, pop(1970) 2,200, capital of Tobago I, Republic of Trinidad and Tobago, SE Caribbean; airport; originally important for the shipping of sugar.

Scarborough, 54 17N 0 24W, pop(1981) 38,048, coastal resort town in Scarborough dist, North Yorkshire, N England; on the North Sea 25 km N of Bridlington; as England's oldest spa town it has been described as 'Queen of the Yorkshire coast'; a Roman signal station in the 4th century; railway; economy: electrics, foodstuffs; monuments: 12th-c castle, museum of regional archaeology.

Schaal See *shahl'zay*, SCHAAL LAKE (Eng), 53 40N 10 57E, lake in SE Schleswig-Holstein prov, W Germany; extends 14 km N from Zarrentin; area 23.3 sq km; max depth 72 m; average depth 17 m; contains several islands; drained (S) into the R Elbe by small R Schaale.

Schaan *shahn*, 47 10N 9 31E, pop(1985) 4,697, commune in Oberland dist, Principality of Liechtenstein, central Europe; area 26.8 sq km; economy: porcelain, ceramics, dental equipment, food canning, pharmaceuticals, textiles, electrical power.

Schaerbeek *sKHahr'bayk*, SCHAARBEEK (Flem), pop(1982) 105,905, town in Brussel dist, Brabant prov, Belgium; a NE suburb of Bruxelles.

Schaffhausen *shaf-how'zen*, SCHAFFHOUSE (Fr), canton in NE Switzerland; pop(1980) 69,413; area 298 sq km; capital Schaffhausen; joined the Swiss Confederacy in 1501.

Schaffhausen, 47 42N 8 38E, pop(1980) 34,250, industrial town and capital of Schaffhausen canton, NE Switzerland; on the R Rhine, 37 km N of Zürich; one of the best preserved of Switzerland's many medieval towns; named after the 'ship houses', where cargo was stored when ships had to be unloaded for their goods to be carried past the nearby falls and rapids; railway; economy: engineering, electrics, iron and steel works, chemicals, aluminium smelting; monuments: Kastel Munot (1564-85) E of the town; Romanesque Minster (1087-1150).

Schaffhouse, town and canton in Switzerland. See Schaffhausen.

Schaumburg *shōm'berg*, 42 02N 88 05W, pop(1980) 53,305, town in Cook county, NE Illinois, United States; 40 km NW of Chicago.

Schelde *skel'de* or **Scheldt** *skelt*, ESCAUT *es-kō* (Fr), river rising in Aisne dept, N France; flows N and NE through Belgium to Antwerpen where it turns NW and flows to meet the North Sea through two estuaries (East and West Schelde) in the Netherlands.

Schellenberg *shel'en-berk*, 47 15N 9 36E, pop(1985) 674, commune in Unterland dist, Principality of Liechtenstein, central Europe; area 3.5 sq km.

Schenectady *ske-nek'ted-ee* (Iroquoian, 'beyond-pines'), 42 49N 73 57W, pop(1980) 67,972, county seat of Schenectady county, E New York, United States; on the R Mohawk, 21 km NW of Albany; settled in 1666, achieving city status in 1795; university (1795); railway; airfield; economy: major manufacturing centre for electrical equipment; an important centre of locomotive building after 1850; monument: Schenectady Stockade.

Schiedam *sKHee'dam*, 51 55N 4 25E, pop(1984e) 69,849, river port and manufacturing city in Zuid Holland prov, W Netherlands; 5 km W of Rotterdam, near the R Maas; railway; economy: aromatics, fertilizers, plasticizers, alcohols, glass products; centre of the Dutch gin industry; monuments: 17th-c town hall, 15th-c Grote Kerk.

Schifflange *shif-lãzh'*, 49 30N 6 01E, pop(1981) 6,618, town in Esch-sur-Alzette canton, Luxembourg dist, S Luxembourg; situated between the wide valley of the Alzette and a ridge of high wooded hills; omnisports centre; shooting grounds; economy: iron and steel.

Schleswig-Holstein *shles'viKH hol'shtīn*, northernmost prov of W Germany; area 15,721 sq km; pop(1983) 2,616,600; bounded on the N by Denmark and on the E by E Germany; bisected by the Nord-Ostsee Kanal; includes the Nordfriesische Inseln (North Frisian Is) off the W coast; capital Kiel; chief towns Lübeck and Flensburg; the coast between Lübeck and Flensburg is Germany's most extensive swimming and sailing resort area; economy: shipbuilding, machine construction, foodstuffs, electrical engineering.

Schneeberg *shnay'berk*, 50 03N 11 53E, mountain in Bayern (Bavaria) prov, W Germany; highest peak of the Fichtelgebirge range, 10 km WNW of Wunsiedel; height 1,051 m.

Schwaben *shvah'bun*, SWABIA *sway'bee-u* (Eng), dist in SW Bayern (Bavaria) prov, W Germany; pop(1983) 1,542,900; area 9,994 sq km; chief towns include Kempten.

Schwäbisch Gmünd *g'münt*, 48 49N 9 48E, pop(1983) 56,400, city in Baden-Württemberg prov, W Germany; in the valley of the R Rems, on the N edge of the Schwäbische Alb (Swabian Jura), 49 km E of Stuttgart; noted for its goldsmiths' and silversmiths' work and for its traditional Bohemian glassworks; railway; monument: Münster (early 14th-c).

Schwäbische Alb *shvay'bi-shu ahlp*, SWABIAN JURA (Eng), mountain range in Baden-Württemberg prov, W Germany; extends 160 km SW-NE between the Schwarzwald (Black Forest) and the R Wörnitz; highest peak is the Lemberg (1,015 m); geologically a continuation of the Jura.

Schwarzwald *shvahrts'vahlt*, BLACK FOREST (Eng), mountain range in Baden-Württemberg prov, W Germany; extends 160 km from Pforzheim in the N to Waldshut, on the Upper Rhine in the S; widens from 20 km wide at N end to 60 km in the S; highest peak is the Feldberg (1,493 m); divided by the valley of the R Kinzig into Lower (N) and Upper (S) Schwarzwald; the Danube and the Neckar rivers rise here; many medicinal baths and spas.

Schwechat *shve'KHat*, river in N Austria, rising in the Wiener Wald, E Niederösterreich state; flows E past Baden and N to meet the R Danube near Schwechat; length 64 km.

Schwedt *shvayt*, SCHWEDT AN DER ODER, 53 4N 14 17E, pop(1981) 52,291, river port in Schwedt dist, Frankfurt,

E East Germany; on a branch of the R Oder, where it follows the Polish frontier, NE of Berlin; new town; railway; economy: petro-chemicals, paper and pulp.

Schweinfurt *shvīn'foort*, 50 03N 10 16E, pop(1983) 51,800, town in Unterfranken dist, NW Bayern (Bavaria) prov, W Germany; on the R Main, 106 km E of Frankfurt am Main; railway; economy: machine construction, textile machinery, ball bearings, small motors and specialized machinery, dyeworks.

Schwerin *shvay-reen'*, county in NW East Germany; pop(1981) 590,135; area 8,672 sq km; bounded W by R Elbe and E by the lake district of the N German plain; there are over 320 lakes, including the Schweriner See (63.4 sq km); capital Schwerin; 60% of the county is farmed, producing grain, potatoes, sugar beet, oil-bearing fruit and livestock; economy: plastics, pulp, viscose staple fibres, electronics, clothing, furniture, household appliances; tourist attractions include the Renaissance palace of Güstrow and the museum in Güstrow commemorating the sculptor, Ernst Barlach.

Schwerin, 53 37N 11 22E, pop(1982) 122,700, capital of Schwerin county, NW East Germany; surrounded by 11 lakes, SW of Rostock; former capital of Mecklenburg state; railway; economy: marine engineering, power cables, sewing machines, plastics, hydraulic products, pharmaceuticals, food processing, tourism; monuments: palace, 13th-c Gothic cathedral, art museum.

Schwyz *shveets*, mountainous canton in central Switzerland; pop(1980) 97,354; area 908 sq km; capital Schwyz; economy: livestock and forestry; joined the Swiss Confederacy in 1291.

Schwyz, 47 02N 8 39E, pop(1980) 12,100, capital town of Schwyz canton, central Switzerland; on the edge of an orchard-covered plain between Vierwaldstätter See and Lauerzer See, 35 km E of Luzern; the town and canton gave their name to the whole country; the flag of Schwyz (white cross on a red ground) has become the national flag; in the Bundesbriefarchiv, the original deed of confederation between Schwyz, Uri and Unterwalden, signed on 1 Aug 1291, is displayed; railway; monument: Rathaus (1642-43).

Scilly, Isles of *si'li*, a group of c.140 islands and islets WSW of Land's End, Cornwall, SW England; includes the 5 inhabited islands of St Mary's, St Martin's, Tresco, St Agnes and Bryher; area 16 sq km; pop(1981) 1,850; economy: tourism and horticulture.

Scoresbysund *skōs'bi-sun*, 70 30N 22 00W, settlement at the head of a large inlet of the Norwegian Sea, E Greenland; founded in 1925.

Scotia Sea *skō'sha*, part of the S Atlantic Ocean, linked to the Pacific Ocean by the Drake Passage around Cabo de Hornos (Cape Horn) and connected to the Weddell Sea to the S; bounded to the N by the submarine N Scotia Ridge and the island of South Georgia; bounded to the E by the South Sandwich Islands and the South Sandwich Trench; the Antarctic Peninsula and the South Orkney Islands separate the Scotia Sea from the Weddell Sea.

Scotland, northern constituent part of the United Kingdom of Great Britain and Northern Ireland, comprising all the mainland N of the borders (from the Solway to Berwick) and the island groups of the Outer and Inner Hebrides, Orkney and Shetland; bounded W by the Atlantic and E by the North Sea; max length 441 km and max width 248 km; of 787 islands only 60 or so exceed 8 sq km in area; area 78,742 sq km (water 1,603 sq km); pop(1981) 5,130,735; 86,620 people speak, read or write the Scottish Gaelic language; the Crowns of Scotland and England united in 1603 and the parliaments united under the Treaty of Union in 1707.

Physical description. Scotland is divided into 3 physical regions: (1) the Southern Uplands rising to 843 m at Merrick; (2) the Central Lowlands, including the valleys of the Clyde, Forth and Tay rivers, is the most densely populated part of the country; (3) the Northern Highlands, which are divided in two by the fault line following the Great Glen, rise to 1,344 m at Ben Nevis, the highest peak of the British Isles. The W coast is heavily indented by sea lochs, the longest of which is Loch Fyne (68 km). Although the E coast is less indented there are several wide estuaries including the Firths of Forth, Tay and Moray. There are many freshwater lochs in the interior, the largest of which is Loch Lomond (70 sq km) and the deepest of which is Loch Ness (230 m). The longest river is the R Tay (192 km) and the highest waterfall is Eas a' Chual Aluinn (200 m).

Administrative divisions. Since 1974 Scotland has been divided into 12 regions and 53 districts:

Region	*area (sq km)*	*pop(1981)*
Borders	4,672	99,784
Central	2,631	273,391
Dumfries and Galloway	6,370	145,139
Fife	1,307	327,362
Grampian	8,704	471,942
Highland	25,391	200,150
Lothian	1,755	738,372
Orkney	976	19,056
Shetland	1,433	27,277
Strathclyde	13,537	2,404,532
Tayside	7,493	391,846
Western Isles	2,898	31,884

Scottsdale, 33 29N 111 56W, pop(1980) 88,412, resort town in Maricopa county, S central Arizona, United States; 16 km E of Phoenix; economy: electronic equipment; a popular retirement centre; event: Parade del Sol (Feb).

Scranton, 41 25N 75 40W, pop(1980) 88,117, county seat of Lackawanna county, NE Pennsylvania, United States; on the R Lackawanna, 32 km W of L Wallenpaupack; university (1888); railway.

Scun'thorpe, 53 36N 0 38W, pop(1981) 66,609, town in Scunthorpe dist, Humberside, NE England; 33 km NE of Doncaster; railway; economy: iron and steel, engineering, electronics, food processing, clothing, furniture.

Scutari, dist and town in Albania. See Shkodër.

Scutari *skoo-ta'ree*, LIGEN I SHKODRËS (Alb), SKADARSKO JEZERO (Yug), LACUS LABEATIS (anc), lake in SW Yugoslavia and NW Albania with the town of Shkodër on its SW shore; the largest lake in the Balkans; area 370 sq km (222 sq km in Yugoslavia); the lake has underwater springs.

Seaford, 50 46N 0 06E, pop(1981) 16,652, residential and resort town in Lewes dist, East Sussex, SE England; 5 km SE of Newhaven; railway.

Seaham *see'am*, 54 52N 1 21W, pop(1981) 21,884, port town in Easington dist, Durham, NE England; 8 km S of Sunderland; railway; economy: engineering, coal trade.

Seal Beach, 33 44N 118 06W, pop(1980) 25,975, city in Orange county, SW California, United States; on the Pacific Ocean, just S of Long Beach; railway.

Seaside, 36 37N 121 50W, pop(1980) 36,567, city in Monterey county, W California, United States; on the Pacific Ocean, on the S shore of Monterey Bay, 5 km E of Monterey.

Seattle *see-atl'*, 47 36N 122 20W, pop(1980) 493,846, capital of King county, W central Washington, United States; on the E shore of Puget Sound; an important commercial and financial centre of the Pacific NW; named after a local Indian chief; founded in 1851; developed rapidly as a seaport after the 1897 Alaskan gold rush and the opening of the Panama Canal; 2 universities (1861, 1892); monorail; railway; airport; economy: aircraft, shipbuilding, food canning and trade in grain, timber, fruit and fish; monuments: the Space Needle, a tower 183 m tall with a revolving restaurant and observation deck; Seattle Art Museum.

Sebba *se'ba*, 13 35N 0 32E, town in NE Burkina, W Africa; SE of Dori.

Sebeş *se'besh*, 45 58N 23 34E, pop(1983) 29,619, town in Alba county, W central Romania; S of Alba Iulia; one of 7 towns established by German colonists in the 12th century; railway; economy: wine, agricultural trade, footwear, textiles, wood products.

Sechura, Desierto de *say-choo'ra*, desert in Piura dept, NW Peru; 64 km wide, 80 km long; situated between the W outliers of the Cordillera Occidental and the Pacific; SE of the Río Piura; just SE of the city of Sechura; the desert continues in the SE as the Mórrope Desert (64 km long, 56 km wide) and the Olmos Desert (56 km long, 40 km wide).

Sefadu *se-fa'doo*, 8 41N 10 55W, pop(1974) 76,000, capital of Kono dist, Eastern prov, Sierra Leone, W Africa; 113 km NE of Bo.

Ségou *say'goo*, region in central Mali, W Africa; pop(1971) 779,125; area 56,127 sq km; the R Niger flows SW-NE across the region; the R Bani flows parallel to the S; NE of Ségou is the Macina depression; capital Ségou; chief towns San, Macina, Niono, Tominian; economy: aluminium.

Ségou, 13 28N 6 18W, pop(1976) 64,890, river-port capital of Ségou region, central Mali, W Africa; 200 km ENE of Bamako on the R Niger; centre of an irrigation scheme based on the R Niger; economy: rice, sugar and alcohol.

Segovia *say-go'vya*, prov in Castilla-León region of NW central Spain, N of Madrid in the central plateau (Meseta); bounded to the E by the Sierra de Guadarrama and drained by the Eresma and Riaza rivers; pop(1981) 149,286, area 6,949 sq km; capital Segovia; economy: tourism, forestry, pottery, meat, rubber, furniture, foodstuffs.

Segovia, 40 57N 4 10W, pop(1981) 53,237, capital of Segovia prov, Castilla-León, NW central Spain; on N slope of the Sierra Guadarrama, between R Eresma and Arroyo Clamores, 87 km NW of Madrid; alt 1,000 m; bishopric; railway; economy: wool, thread, pottery, cement, flour, fertilizers, rubber and chemicals; monuments: Roman aqueduct; 16th-c Gothic cathedral; Moor-

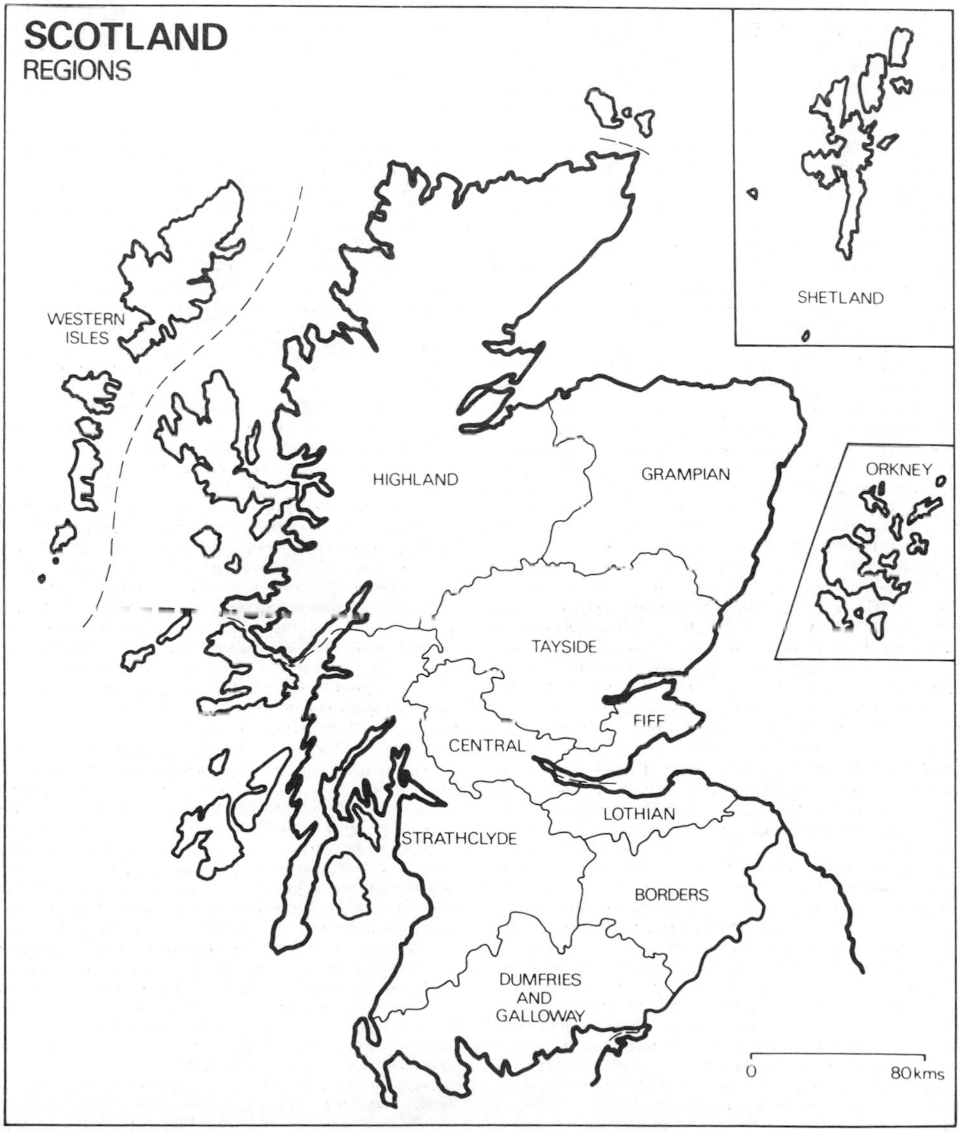

ish Alcazar; El Parral monastery; churches of St Martin and St Esteban; events: Holy Week and fiesta of St Agueda.

Segre *se'gray*, river rising above Saillagouse in E Pyrenees, S France, flowing W then SW to meet the R Ebro at Mequinenza in Spain; length 261 km; several irrigation and hydroelectric power reservoirs; feeds Urgel and other irrigation canals of Lérida; tributaries Cinca, Noguera, Pallaresa, Ribagorzana and Valira rivers.

Séguéla *say-gway'la*, dept in NW central Ivory Coast, W Africa; pop(1975) 157,539; area 21,900 sq km; capital Séguéla; chief towns Mankono, Morondo, Gouétougou and Kounioumassa.

Segura *se-goo'ra*, river rising on NE slopes of Sierra de Segura, Jaén prov, S Spain, flowing E to enter the Mediterranean SSW of Alicante; length 325 km; irrigation reservoirs at Pantano del Cenajo and Pantano de la Fuensanto; chief tributary is the R Mundo.

Sehlabathebe *say-la-ba-tay'bay*, national park in E Lesotho, S Africa; area 6.8 sq km; established in 1970.

Seiland, *say'lahn*, Norwegian island in Norwegian sea off coast of N Norway, at mouth of the Altafjord (Alta Fjord), 8 km SW of Hammerfest; glacier-covered central portion rises to 1,076 m; area 585 sq km; length 42 km; width 24 km; administered by Finnmark county.

Seinäjoki *say'na-yo'kee*, OSTERMYRA *us'ter-mu'rah* (Swed), 62 45N 22 55E, pop(1982) 25,588, town in Vaasa prov, SW central Finland; 56 km SE of Vaasa; established in 1931; railway.

Seine *sen*, SEQUANA (anc), river in N central France rising in the Langres plateau, Côte d'Or dept, 30 km NW of Dijon; flows NW past Troyes cutting through the dry pastureland of the limestone Champagne Pouilleuse, W and S across the fertile dairy country of Brie then NW to Paris from where it meanders NW past Rouen to Normandie; its estuary (Baie de la Seine) discharges into the English Channel S of Cap de la Hève; length 776 km; 3rd longest river in France; its drainage area covers 77,700 sq km of the Paris Basin; tributaries Aube, Marne, Oise, Yonne, Loing and Eure rivers; on either side of Paris it loops past the market-gardens of the Ile-de-France.

Seine-et-Marne, dept in Ile-de-France region of N France, E of Paris, including part of Gâtinais Français in the S; comprises 3 arrond, 37 cantons and 514 communes; pop(1982) 887,112; area 5,917 sq km; the Plaine de la Brie covers the NE of the dept; drained by the Seine, Marne and Yonne rivers; capital Melun; chief towns Fontainebleau, Meaux and Montereau; there are châteaux at Guermantes (17-18th-c) and Maincy (17th-c).

Seine-Maritime, formerly SEINE-INFÉRIEURE, dept in Haute-Normandie region of NW France, bounded on the N by the English Channel; comprises 3 arrond, 70 cantons and 745 communes; pop(1982) 1,193,039; area 6,254 sq km; it is crossed E-W by the Collines de Caux, whose S slopes are covered with rich pastures; the E (pays de Bray) and the banks of the Seine are wooded; the R Seine meanders across the SW section of the dept and discharges into the Baie de la Seine, S of Le Havre; watered also by the R Béthune; capital Rouen, chief towns Dieppe and Le Havre; it was renamed in 1955 because the inference of lower status was disliked; there are châteaux at Valmont (11-15th-c) and Angerville (Renaissance); the Parc de Brotonne regional nature park lies partly within the dept.

Seine-Saint-Denis, dept in Ile-de-France region of N France, N of Paris, comprising 2 arrond, 40 cantons and 40 communes; pop(1982) 1,324,301; area 236 sq km; capital Bobigny.

Seixal *say-shahl'*, 38 38N 9 06W, pop(1981) 87,581, industrial town in Setúbal dist, S central Portugal; situated on the S side of Lisboa Bay, 8 km from the centre of Lisboa; railway; ferry; economy: steel, cork, chemicals, textiles.

Sekondi-Takoradi *se-kon-dee'-ta-kor-a-di*, 4 59N 1 43W, pop(1982) 123,670, major seaport and capital of Western region, S Ghana, W Africa; on the Gulf of Guinea, 180 km WSW of Accra; founded by the Dutch in the 16th century; Sekondi expanded after construction of railway to Tarkwa (1898-1903) and merged with Takoradi; site of Fort Orange (Dutch) which is now a lighthouse; important supply base during World War II; S extremity of Ghanaian railway system; economy: railway repair, cigarette manufacture and boatbuilding.

Selangor *say-lang'gor*, state in W Peninsular Malaysia, SE Asia; pop(1980) 1,426,250; area 7,997 sq km; capital Shah Alam; economy: rubber, tin; in 1981 the federal territory of Wilayah Persekutuan was separated from Selangor.

Selby, 53 48N 1 04W, pop(1981) 12,297, town in North Yorkshire, N England; on R Ouse, 20 km S of York; linked to the R Aire by a canal; railway; economy: foodstuffs; monuments: abbey.

Selebi-Phikwe *say-lay-bee-fee'kway*, 21 58S 27 48E, pop(1981) 29,469, independent township in Central dist, Botswana, S Africa; SSE of Francistown; area 50 sq km; alt 880 m; railway; airfield; economy: copper and nickel mining centre.

Selenge *sel-eng'ga*, county in N Mongolia; pop(1981e) 60,000; area 43,000 sq km; bounded N by the USSR; lies in the river basins of the Orhon Gol and the Selenge Mörön; capital Ulaanbaatar; arable farming and hay production is important in the low, fertile valleys; 40% of Mongolia's wheat crop is grown in Selenge where cultivation is highly mechanized; one-quarter of Mongolia's beef cattle and one-half of the pure-bred sheep are bred here; copper, coal, lead, lime, silver and gold are among the county's natural resources.

Selenge, river of N central Asia; rises to the E of Uliastay, in W Mongolia, and flows E; joined by the Orhon Gol at Sühbaatar, close to the USSR border, which it crosses W of Kyakhta, Buryat ASSR; turns W at Ulan-Ude, entering Lake Baikal on the SE; length 992 km.

Selenter See, SELENTER LAKE (Eng), 54 19N 10 26E, lake in E Schleswig-Holstein prov, W Germany, E of Kiel; area 22.4 sq km; max depth 34 m; average depth 17 m.

Sélibabi or **Selibaby** *say-lee-ba-bee'*, 15 14N 12 11E, capital of Guidimaka region, SW Mauritania, NW Africa; 470 km ESE of Saint Louis (Senegal).

Selkirk, pop(1981) 10,037, town in S Manitoba, central Canada; on the Red river, 30 km NE of Winnipeg and just S of L Winnipeg; founded by the Earl of Selkirk; economy: steel, boatbuilding, dairy products, tourism.

Selkirk, 55 33N 2 50W, pop(1981) 5,437, town in Ettrick and Lauderdale dist, Borders, SE Scotland; on the Ettrick Water, 15 km N of Hawick; economy: textiles; monuments: Halliwell's House Museum; Sir Walter Scott's courtroom, where he was Sheriff of Selkirk for 30 years, is now a museum; event: Common Riding in June.

Sel'lafield, formerly WINDSCALE, 54 38N 3 30W, nuclear power plant in Cumbria, NW England; on the Irish Sea coast, W of Gosforth; processes nuclear waste; nearby are Calder Hall gas-cooled, moderated nuclear reactors which came into commercial operation 1956-59.

Selle, La *la seel'*, 18 12N 71 59W, peak in the Massif de la Selle, SE Haiti, Hispaniola I; height 2,280 m; highest mountain in Haiti.

Sel'ma, 32 25N 87 01W, pop(1980) 26,684, county seat of Dallas county, central Alabama, United States; on the R Alabama, 68 km W of Montgomery; in 1965 the city was the centre of a major rights campaign led by Dr Martin Luther King; railway; economy: farm equipment, batteries, paper, lumber, textiles and clothing.

Semarang *sa-ma-rahng'*, 6 58S 110 29E, pop(1980) 646,590, fishing port and capital of Jawa Tengah prov, central Jawa, Indonesia; a large Chinese population; the Communist Party of Indonesia was founded here in 1920; university (1960); railway, airfield; economy: shipbuilding, fishing, textiles; exports coffee, sugar, rubber; monuments: Gedung Batu cave, Mudu war memorial, Klinteng Sam Poo Kong temple; event: Hari Pembangunan (Development Day) on 2 July, with cultural performances to commemorate the development of central Jawa.

Semipalatinsk *sye-myi-pa-la'tyinsk*, formerly SEMIPALATKA, 50 26N 80 16E, pop(1983) 301,000, river port capital of

Semipalatinskaya oblast, Kazakhskaya SSR, Soviet Union; on the R Irtysh; founded in 1718 as a fortress on a site 18 km downstream; moved to the present site in 1776; railway; airport; economy: wool textiles, clothing, footwear, foodstuffs, ship repairing, meat-packing (one of the largest plants in the USSR).

Semnān *sem-nan'*, prov in N Iran; pop(1982) 300,640; area 91,214 sq km; capital Semnān.

Sen Monorom, 12 27N 107 12E, chief town of Mondolkiri prov, Cambodia; near Vietnam frontier.

Sendai *sen-dī'*, 38 16N 140 52E, pop(1980) 664,868, capital of Miyagi prefecture, Tōhoku region, NE Honshū island, Japan; on W Ishinomaki-wan Bay; Tōhoku University (1907); railway; airport; Sendai is the base for tours to the hot springs and spas in the surrounding area; economy: food processing, pottery, metal products, textiles; event: Tanabata, or Star Festival in Aug.

Senegal *sen'e-gawl*, SÉNÉGAL *say-nay-gal*, official name Republic of Senegal, RÉPUBLIQUE DU SÉNÉGAL (Fr); area 196,840 sq km; timezone GMT; pop(1984) 6,641,000; capital Dakar; chief towns Thiès, Kaolack, Saint-Louis and Ziguinchor; there are 5 railways totalling 1,186 km of track including Dakar-Kidira (continuing to Mali), Thiès-Saint-Louis (193 km), Guinguinéo-Kaolack (22 km), Louga-Linguére (129 km) and Diourbel-Touba (46 km); there are 3,461 km of paved roads and 1,505 km of inland waterways; ethnic groups include Wolof (36%), Fulani (17.5%), Serer (16.5%), Toucouleur (9%), Diola (9%), Mandingo (6.5%), other Africans (4.5%) and European and Lebanese (1%); the majority of the pop is Muslim (75%), the remainder following either local beliefs (20%) or Christian (mainly Roman Catholic) 5%; French is the official language with Wolof, Pulaar, Diola and Mandingo being widely spoken; the unit of currency is the franc CFA; national holiday 4 April (Independence Day), most Muslim holidays are observed; membership of AfDB, APC, CEAO, EAMA, ECA, ECOWAS, EIIB (associate), FAO, G-77, GATT, IAEA, IBRD, ICAO, IDA, IDB (Islamic Development Bank), IFAD, IFC, ILO, IMF, IMO, INTELSAT, INTERPOL, ITU, NAM, OAU, OCAM, OIC, Organization for the Development of the Senegal River Valley, UN, UNESCO, UPU, WFTU, WHO, WIPO, WMO, WTO.

Physical description. Senegal occupies a position on the W coast of Africa with Cape Verde, a volcanic peninsula, being the most W point of the African continent. To the N of Cape Verde the coast is characterized by dunes and to the S there are dunes, mangrove forests, estuaries and mudbanks. The N of the country is an extensive low lying basin of savannah and semi-desert vegetation with seasonal streams draining to the R Sénégal. The S, also low lying, rises toward the Guinea frontier to around 500 m. The main rivers are the R Casamance, the R Sine and the R Saloum. Senegal borders The Gambia on all sides bar its Atlantic coast.

Climate. Senegal has a tropical climate with a rainy season between June and Sept, a particularly oppressive period with high humidity levels and high night-time temperatures especially on the coast. Rainfall decreases from S (1,000-1,500 mm, rainy season extending to Oct) to N (300-350 mm). The prevailing wind during the wet season which extends to Oct in the N, is SW-W from the S Atlantic. In the dry season the dust-laden Saharan *harmattan* wind blows from the NE. The average annual rainfall at Dakar is 541 mm and the average temperature ranges from 22.2°C to 27.8°C.

History, government and constitution. The French established a fort at Saint-Louis in 1659 and later extended their territory along the coast at the expense of the Dutch. Incursions into and occupation of the interior took place between 1854 and 1865. Senegal was incorporated as a territory within French West Africa in 1902 and became an autonomous state within the French community in 1958. Senegal collaborated with French Sudan and together in 1959 they became the independent Federation of Mali but Senegal withdrew in 1960 to become a separate independent republic. In 1982 Senegal and The Gambia joined to form the Confederation of Senegambia which is designed to integrate their military, economic, communications and foreign policies whilst maintaining independence and sovereignty. There is a Legislative Assembly headed by an executive president elected for a 5-year term. The president appoints a prime minister and cabinet of about 28 ministers.

Economy. Agriculture is the most important sector of Senegal's economy, employing about 75% of the workforce. Groundnuts and cotton are the chief cash crops and sugar, millet, sorghum, manioc, maize and rice and livestock are important local food crops. Fishing and timber for railway sleepers, veneers and fuel are an adjunct to the main industries which are based on agricultural processing, salt extraction, textile manufacturing, chemicals, cement, footwear and shipbuilding and repairing. There is a phosphate fertilizer plant at Mbao and a sulphuric and phosphoric acid plant at Darou Khoudou. Mining is another significant area of the economy with phosphate rock extraction and the mining of titanium and zirconium ores. Large iron ore deposits have been located at La Falémé and gold reserves at Sabodala. Oil and natural gas have been located offshore and onshore at Dôme-Flore and Diam-Niadio Sea. The main trading partners are France, the USA, the Netherlands, West Germany, the UK, Italy, Ivory Coast, Mauritania and Nigeria.

Administrative divisions. Senegal is divided into the 10 regions of Dakar, Diourbel, Fatick, Kaolack, Kolda, Louga, Saint-Louis, Tambacounda, Thiès and Ziguinchor.

Sénégal *say-nay-gal*, river in W Africa; rises in the Fouta Djallon massif (Guinea) near the border with Sierra Leone; flows N and NW past Kayes (Mali) and after it is joined by the R Falémé (chief tributary) it forms the N frontier of Senegal with Mauritania, passing the towns of Bakel, Kaèdi and Podor; the river empties into the Atlantic Ocean at Saint-Louis; the upper course above Bafoulabé (where it is joined by the R Bakoy) is known as the R Bafing; navigable as far as Bafing at high water; length including the R Bafing 1,635 km.

Senegam'bia, Confederation of, an association between The Gambia and Senegal which came into being on 1 Feb 1982; designed to integrate military, economic, communications and foreign policies and to establish joint institutions whilst preserving independence and sovereignty; the Confederation parliament is composed of one-third Gambian and two-thirds Senegalese representation.

Senja, *sen'yah*, formerly SENJEN, Norwegian island in the Norwegian Sea off NW coast of Norway, 80 km N of Narvik; its rugged surface rises to 922 m in the N (Istind Mt); the coastline is deeply indented; area 1,590 sq km; length 72 km; administered by Troms county.

Sensuntepeque *sen-soon-tay-pay'kay*, 13 54N 88 35W, pop(1980) 50,448, capital town of Cabañas dept, El Salvador, Central America; 35 km E of Ilobasco, in the hills S of the Lempa valley; once a great source of indigo; alt 900 m; event: annual fair (4 Dec).

Seoul, capital of south Korea. See Sŏul.

Sequoia *si-kwoy'a*, national park in E California, United States; situated in the Sierra Nevada, approx 142 km E of Fresno; contains the enormous, ancient sequoia trees; area 1,631 sq km; established in 1890; to the N is Kings Canyon National Park.

Seraing *se-rĩ*, 50 37N 5 31E, pop(1982) 63,749, mining and manufacturing town in Liège dist, Liège prov, E Belgium; on the S bank of the R Meuse, 6 km SW of Liège; railway; economy: iron and steel, metallurgy, engineering, data processing; ironworks established here in 1817 by John Cockerill.

Seram or **Ceram** *say'ram*, mountainous, forested island in Maluku prov (Moluccas), Indonesia; island of the Moluccas group situated E of Buru, W of New Guinea and S of Halmahera; area 17,142 sq km; chief town Ambon; under Dutch control in 1650s.

Seram Sea, CERAM SEA, part of the Pacific Ocean, located within the Indonesian islands and bounded to the W by

Kepulian Obi and Kepulian Sula, to the S by the islands of Seram and to the E by the peninsulas of Irian Jaya of New Guinea; connected to (1) the Arafura Sea in the SE, (2) the Banda Sea by passages through the Seram Islands, particularly by the Selat Manipa and that area between Kepulian Sula and Buru, (3) the Molucca Sea by the area between Kepulian Sula and Obi and (4) the Halmahera Sea in the N; main arm: Teluk Berau, an inlet of Irian Jaya.

Serbia, republic of Yugoslavia. See Srbija.

Seremban *say-rem-bahn'*, 2 42N 101 54E, pop(1980) 132,911, capital of Negeri Sembilan state, W Peninsular Malaysia, SE Asia; 66 km SE of Kuala Lumpur; originally a Malay-Chinese tin boom town of the mid-19th century; railway.

Serena, La *la say-ray'na*, 29 45S 71 18W, pop(1982) 84,991, capital of Elquí prov, and Coquimbo region, N central Chile; N of Coquimbo, on the coast at the mouth of the Elquí river valley; nearby is La Silla observatory, the 2nd largest observatory in the world; founded in 1544 by Juan de Bohón, aide to Pedro de Valdivia; in 1546 it was destroyed by Diaguita Indians and then rebuilt by Francisco de Aguirre in 1552; in 1680 it was sacked by the English pirate, Sharpe; legends of buried treasure at Guayacán Bay, frequented by Drake, still persist; railway; airfield; monuments: the town was remodelled in the 1950s and contains many colonial-style buildings with coloured tiles; the city has a cathedral, 29 churches and several old convents; the archaeological museum has an interesting collection of Diaguita and Molle Indian artefacts.

Serengeti *se-ren-ge'ti*, national park in N Tanzania, E Africa; area 14,763 sq km; established in 1951; much of the park has a mean elevation of around 1,500 m; noted for its wildlife, a game count (1978) recorded 1.5 mn wildebeeste, 1 mn gazelle, 0.2 mn zebra, 75,000 impala, 74,000 buffalo, 65,000 topi, 18,000 eland, 9,000 each of kongoni and giraffe, 5,000 elephant, 4,000 hyena and 3,000 lion; famous for the mass migratory treks of the grass-eating animals and their predators as they follow the rains to new grazing grounds; between Dec and May they migrate to the permanent waters on the Dutwa and Ndoha plains in the W arm of the park; in Aug they move N crossing the Grumeti river, through the Ikoma Fort region to N Serengeti and the Masai Mara park in neighbouring Kenya; in Nov they trek back through the Serengeti to the Naabi Hills area.

Sergipe *ser-zhee'pay*, state in Nordeste region, NE Brazil; bounded E by the Atlantic and N by the Río São Francisco; pop(1980) 1,140,121; area 21,994 sq km; capital Aracaju; economy: agriculture, cattle, refining of offshore oil.

Seria *ser-ee'a*, 4 39N 114 40E, pop(1981) 23,511, town in Belait dist, W Brunei, SE Asia; SW of the capital Bandar Seri Begawan; Brunei's rich oil reserves are mostly located in the vicinity of Seria; in 1972 a tanker terminal for the export of crude oil was opened; cheap power for industrial and domestic use is produced from a gas turbine plant.

Sérifos or **Seriphos** *se'ri-fos*, 37 09N 24 30E, island of the Kikládhes, Greece, in the S Aegean Sea; area 73 sq km; its iron ore and copper deposits have been worked since ancient times.

Sérrai *ser'rī*, SERRES *ser'ray*, nome (dept) of Makedhonia region, NE Greece, bounded N by Bulgaria; pop(1981) 196,247; area 3,968 sq km; capital Sérrai.

Sérrai, 41 03N 23 33E, pop(1981) 45,213, commercial town and capital of Sérrai nome (dept), Makedhonia region, NE Greece; 100 km NE of Thessaloníki; rebuilt in modern style after its destruction by the Bulgarians in 1913; railway.

Serraval'le, castle (dist) in the Republic of San Marino, central Italy; area 10.53 sq km; pop(1980) 6,531; the average population density in 1980 was 620 inhabitants per sq km; economy: cotton textiles.

Serrekun'da, SERE KUNDA, 13 26N 16 41W, pop(1980) 38,800, town in The Gambia, W Africa; W of Banjul.

Serrere, Pic de *ser-er'*, mountain peak in the E central Pyrenees on the N border of the Principality of Andorra with France; height 2,911 m.

Sétif or **Stif** *say-teef'*, 36 11N 5 24E, pop(1982) 198,920, chief town of Sétif dept, NE Algeria, N Africa; WSW of Constantine; founded in the 1st century AD; French occupation began in 1838; monument: museum of Roman antiquities.

Seto Naikai *se'tō nī-kī'*, INLAND SEA, arm of the Pacific Ocean extending between Honshū I (N) and Kyūshū and Shikoku islands (S), Japan; closed at E end by Awaji-sh island; connected with the sea by 4 channels: the Akashi Strait (NE), Naruto-kaikyō Strait (SE), the Bungo-suidō Strait (SW) and the Kammon-kaikyō, or Kammon Tunnels (W); noted for its scenic beauty; contains c.300 islands and is bordered N and S by mountain chains; contains the Harima-nada, Aki-nada, Iyo-nada and Suō-nada seas; to the N of Shikoku I is the Seto Naikai National Park, established in 1934.

Settat', 33 04N 7 37W, pop(1982) 65,203, town in Settat prefecture, Centre prov, NW Morocco, N Africa; 64 km S of Casablanca; railway; airfield; economy: soap, fruit preserves, trade in wool, grain, fruit and vegetables.

Setúbal *se-too'bal*, dist in S central Portugal, part of Estremadura and Baixo Alentejo prov separated from Lisboa by R Tagus estuary, drained by R Sado which forms an enclosed inlet of the Atlantic at its mouth; divided into 13 councils and 54 parishes; area, 5,092 sq km; pop(1981) 658,326; economy: steel, fishing, sardine-canning, plums, oranges, grain, vegetables, horticulture, meat, dairy produce, Moscatel grapes, cork, resin, timber and salt; noted for production of the sweet, fortified Moscatel wine; minerals: barium, copper, iron, manganese, titanium, peat; airfield at Sines.

Setúbal, ST UBES OR ST IVES (Eng), 38 30N 8 58W, pop(1981) 76,800, industrial seaport and capital of Setúbal dist, S Portugal; at the mouth of R Sado, 32 km SE of Lisboa; divided into 4 parishes; railway; economy: cement, auto parts, domestic appliances, steel, shipyards, car assembly, fish canneries, salt pans; event: Santiago fair at end of July.

Setúbal, Baia de, inlet of the Atlantic off W coast of Portugal, bounded by Cabo de Espichel in the N and Cabo de Sines in the S; 56 km wide by 32 km long; R Sado flows into the bay past the town of Setúbal.

Sevastopol' *sye-vas-to'pul-y'*, SEBASTOPOL, 44 36N 33 31E, pop(1983) 328,000, port in Krymskaya oblast, Ukrainskaya SSR, Soviet Union; on the SW shore of a peninsula which separates the Azovskoye More (Sea of Azov) from the Black Sea; a major naval base and centre of a region noted for its health resorts; rail terminus; economy: bricks, tiles, food products, textiles, and shoes.

Sevenoaks, 51 16N 0 12E, pop(1981) 24,588, market town in Sevenoaks dist, Kent, SE England; NW of Tonbridge on the North Downs, 34 km SE of London; railway.

Se'vern, river in SE Wales and W England; rises on Plynlimon in Dyfed, central Wales and flows NE and E to Shrewsbury, then SE and S through Worcester and Gloucester; opens into a wide estuary which flows into the Bristol Channel; tributaries include the Stour, Teme, Avon, Wye and Vyrnwy rivers; navigable to Gloucester; the Severn Bridge links Aust in Somerset with Beachley on the Gwent-Gloucestershire border; linked to Gloucester from Sharpness by the Gloucester and Berkley Canal.

Severnaya Dvina, NORTHERN DVINA (Eng), river in N European Rossiyskaya, Soviet Union; formed at Kotlas by the confluence of the Sukhona and Vychegda rivers; flows NW through Arkhangel'skaya oblast to discharge into Dvinskaya Guba (Dvina Bay), an inlet of the Beloye More (White Sea), 40 km below Arkhangel'sk; length 744 km; drainage basin area 357,000 sq km; chief tributaries are the Pinega, Yemtsa, Vaga, and Uftyuga rivers.

Severnaya Zemlya *syay'vyer-na-ya zyem-lya'*, formerly ZEMLYA IMPERATORA, NORTH LAND (Eng), NICHOLAS II LAND, uninhabited archipelago in the Arctic Ocean, N of Poluostrov Taymyr (Taymyr Peninsula), Krasnoyarskiy kray, N Siberian Rossiyskaya, Soviet Union; separates the Laptev Sea (E) from the Karskoye More (Kara Sea) (W); area 37,001 sq km; chief islands are Ostrov Komsomolets, Ostrov Pioner, Ostrov Oktyabr'skoy Revolyutsii, and Ostrov Bol'shevik; the southernmost island is separated from the mainland by the Proliv Vil'kitskogo strait; there are glaciers on the larger islands; discovered in 1913 by Vilkitski.

Severočeský *se'ver-o-che-skee*, region in Czech Socialist Republic, W Czechoslovakia; bounded to N by E Germany and the Erzgebirge Mts; watered by the Elbe (Labe) and Ohre rivers; area 7,810 sq km; pop(1984) 1,177,391; capital Ústí nad Labem; chief towns include Česká Lípa, Děčín, Chomutov.

Severodvinsk, formerly SUDOSTROY (1918-38), MOLOTOVSK (1938-57), 64 35N 39 50E, pop(1983) 219,000, city in Arkhangel'skaya oblast, NW European Rossiyskaya, Soviet Union; at the mouth of the R Severnaya Dvina, on the Beloye More (White Sea), 50 km from Arkhangel'sk; became a city in 1938; railway; economy: machine building, building materials, woodworking, clothing.

Severomoravský *se'ver-o-mo-rav-skee*, region in Czech Socialist Republic, central Czechoslovakia; bounded to N by Poland; area 11,067 sq km; pop(1984) 1,948,997; capital Ostrava; chief towns include Havířov, Olomouc, Opava.

Severskiy Donets, NORTHERN DONETS or DONETS, chief tributary of the R Don, Ukrainskaya SSR and Rossiyskaya, SW Soviet Union; rises NW of Korocha, in Belgorodskaya oblast, Rossiyskaya; flows generally S then SE through E Ukrainskaya SSR, past Izyum and Kamensk-Shakhtinskiy, to join the R Don W of Konstantinovsk; length 1,010 km; chief tributaries are the Aydar, Kalitva, and Derkul rivers.

Sevilla *se-veel'ya*, SEVILLE *sev'il, sev-il'* (Eng), prov of Andalucia, S Spain, in the hot basin of the R Guadalquivir; pop(1981) 1,477,428; area 14,001 sq km; capital Seville; economy: olives, cereals, cotton, mining of non-ferrous metals, food canning, steel, electrical appliances, agric machinery, glass, plastics (Dos Hermanas), paper, leather (Pilas).

Sevilla, SEVILLE (Eng), HISPALIS (anc), 37 23N 6 00W, pop(1981) 653,833, river port and capital of Sevilla prov, Andalucia, S Spain; on R Guadalquivir, 538 km SW of Madrid; archbishopric; university (1502); airport; railway; economy: tourism, furniture, olives, pharmaceuticals, agric machinery, chemicals; monuments: 15th-c cathedral which is the largest Gothic church in the world with tomb of Columbus, Moorish Alcazar; Santa Cruz quarter formerly occupied by nobility; Maria Luisa park; fine arts museum; Pilate's House; Moorish watch tower; Palace of St Telmo; Scipio's Roman settlement of Italica, 7 km NW, has a fine amphitheatre; events: Holy Week; April fair; Festival of Spain (autumn); Corpus Christi; fiesta of La Virgen de los Reyes in Aug; St Miguel fair in Sept.

Seward Peninsula, a peninsula in Alaska, United States; separates Kotzebue Sound (N) and Norton Sound (S); the Bering Strait lies to the W; the most westerly point of the North American continent.

Seychelles *say-shelz'*, official name The Republic of Seychelles, island group in the SW Indian Ocean, N of Madagascar, comprising 115 islands scattered over 1,374,000 sq km between 4° and 5° S; Mahé (153 sq km), the main island, lies about 1,600 km E of Mombasa on the E African coast of Kenya; the other principal inhabited islands of the group are Praslin (38 sq km), La Digue (10 sq km) and Silhouette; timezone GMT +4; land area 453 sq km; pop(1985e) 65,245; the pop is largely descended from 18th-c French colonists and their freed African slaves; also small numbers of Indians, Chinese and British; the official languages are Creole, which is spoken by 95% of the pop, French and English; about 95% of the pop is Roman Catholic; capital Victoria (on Mahé); national holidays include 5 June (Liberation Day) and 29 June (Independence Day); the currency is the Seychelles rupee; membership of AfDB, FAO, G-77, GATT, IBRD, ICAO, IDA, IFAD, IFC, ILO, IMF, IMO, NAM, OAU, UN, UNESCO, UPU, WHO, WMO.

Physical description. The Seychelles islands are divided into 2 groups. The first, a compact group of 41 granitic islands which rise steeply from the sea, includes Mahé and its nearest neighbours. These islands are mountainous, rising to 906 m on Mahé, with steep forest-clad slopes dropping down to coastal lowlands with a vegetation of grass and dense scrub. The second, a group of low lying coralline islands to the SW, includes Coetivy, D'Arros, Desroches, Astove, and Assomption, as well as the atolls of St Joseph, Poivre, Alphonse, Providence, Farquhar, Aldabra and Cosmoledo Is.

Climate. The islands have a tropical climate with a rainfall that varies with altitude and is higher on the S sides of the islands, which are exposed to the SE trade winds. The wettest months are Nov to March. The Seychelles are rarely affected by tropical storms.

History, government and constitution. Colonized by French settlers in 1768, the islands were captured by Britain in 1794 and incorporated as a dependency of Mauritius in 1814. In 1903 the Seychelles became a separate colony and internal self-government was achieved in 1975. The islands became an independent republic within the Commonwealth in 1976. Aldabra, Farquhar and Desroches were transferred to the British Indian Ocean Territory in 1965 but were returned to the Seychelles in 1976. In 1979 a new constitution was introduced by the People's Progressive Front declaring itself the sole legal party for election to the 23-member unicameral People's Assembly. The president, who leads a Council of Ministers, is elected for a period of 5 years.

Economy. On the larger islands subsistence crops of fruit and vegetables with livestock are important, as are the cinnamon and copra crops from plantations. Since the opening of the international airport in 1971 tourism has become a major source of revenue for the islands, but in association with Madagascar and Mauritius the Seychelles have also been diversifying small industry which is largely based on brewing, soap, plastics, furniture, cigarettes, soft drinks and steel fabricated goods.

Seyhan *say-han'*, SARUS (anc), river in S central Turkey; rises in the Dikkulak Dağı, approx 64 km SSW of Sivas; flows SW past Adana to discharge into the Mediterranean Sea; length 560 km; cotton and grapes are grown in its valley; a dam on the river at Adana provides flood control, irrigation, municipal water and electricity.

Sfax *sfaks*, 34 45N 10 43E, pop(1984) 231,911, seaport and capital of Sfax governorate, E Tunisia, N Africa; on the Golfe de Gabès coast, 240 km SSE of Tunis; foremost port and 2nd largest city of Tunisia; the Iles de Kerkenah (Chergui and Gharbi) are situated about 32 km offshore; built on the site of Roman and Phoenician settlements; occupied by Sicilians (12th century) and Spaniards (16th century); also a base for Barbary pirates; the modern city was built after 1895; airfield; railway; economy: trade in esparto, oil, peanuts and dates, phosphate processing, fishing; monuments: museum of folk arts and traditions, archaeological museum; event: festival of music and popular arts in July.

Sfintu Gheorghe *sfin'too gyor'ge*, 45 51N 25 48E, pop(1983) 62,355, capital of Covasna county, E central Romania; on R Olt; railway junction; economy: livestock trade, wood products, textiles.

's-Gravenhage *s-KHrah'ven-hah-ge* or **Den Haag** *hahKH*, THE HAGUE (Eng), 52 05N 4 16E, pop(1984e) 672,127, capital city of Zuid Holland prov, W Netherlands; seat of the Dutch government, 3 km from the North Sea and 22 km NW of Rotterdam; 3rd largest city in the Netherlands and part of the *Randstad* conurbation; it is mainly a cultural, administrative and political city: ministries, embassies and several international organizations, including the International Court of Justice and the Permanent Court of Arbitration, have their headquarters here; industry plays a subordinate role, employing less than 30% of the population; it is often called the 'City of Arts'; many Dutch painters have lived here and the city is noted for its furniture, gold and silverware, and pottery craftwork; the chief suburbs are Scheveningen, a popular seaside resort, Rijswijk and Voorburg; a hunting lodge of the Counts of Holland from 1250, 's-Gravenhage remained unimportant until the 16th century; in 1527 it became the seat of the supreme court and meeting-place of the states-general; from the late 17th century, it was the centre of European diplomacy and many treaties were signed and conferences held here (the Triple Alliances of 1688 and 1717 and the Peace Conference of 1899); the Hague Convention (1907) formulated much of the law governing international warfare; railway; economy: textiles, electrical and electronic equipment, hardware, furniture, printing, rubber, pharmaceuticals, cigarettes, car components, tyres, food processing; monuments: 13th-c Gothic Hall of the Knights, scene of the annual opening of the states-general; Palace of Peace, erected mainly at the expense of Andrew Carnegie, inaugurated in 1913 and now the headquarters of the International Court of Justice; Nieuwe Kerk (1641), burial place of Spinoza and de Witts; the royal residence 'House in the Wood' (1647); 16th-c town hall.

Shaanxi *shen'see*, SHENSI, prov in central China; bordered N by Nei Mongol (Inner Mongolia), NW by Ningxia aut region, W by Gansu prov, S by Sichuan prov, SE by Hubei prov and E along the Huang He (Yellow river) by Shanxi prov; the N forms part of the Loess Plateau; rises in the NW with the Baiyu Shan range and in the S with the Qin Ling range and the Micang Shan and Daba Shan ranges which lie along the border with Sichuan prov; to the N of the Qin Ling range is the floodplain of the Wei He (Guanzhong), while S is the Han Shui river valley (the longest tributary of the Chang Jiang (Yangtze)); the Qin Ling range itself rises to 3,767 m in Taibai Shan, the highest peak in the prov; the Great Wall of China runs parallel with but a little inland from the prov's N boundary; Hua Shan peak (2,154 m) is one of China's Five Holy Mountains; pop(1982) 28,904,423; area 195,800 sq km; capital Xi'an; principal town Yan'an; economy: sheep, cattle and donkey raising, wheat, cotton, rice, tea, citrus fruit, textiles, mining of coal, lead, zinc, mercury, gold, silver, sulphur and limestone.

Sha'ba, region in SE Zaire, central Africa; pop(1981e) 3,823,172; area 496,965 sq km; capital Lubumbashi; chief towns include Likasi, Bukama, Kolwezi, and Kalemie (Albertville); L Mweru (Lac Moero) located on the E frontier with N Zambia; a large part of L Tanganyika is situated along the E frontier with Tanzania; lakes NE of Bukama include L Kabwe, L Kabele, L Kayeye, L Kisale, L Zimbambo and L Kabamba; other lakes include L Tshangalele (E of Likasi); L Delcommune (E of Kolwezi); the Lualuba river (major headstream of the Zaire river) flows S-N across the region; railway junction at Tenke (NW of Lubumbashi) with lines radiating SE to Zambia, W to Angola and the Atlantic coast and N to central and NE Zaire; mineral reserves include zinc, cobalt, copper, germanium, manganese, cement and cadmium.

Shabwah, governorate in central South Yemen; formerly the Fourth Governorate; chief town 'Ataq.

Shah Alam', 3 02N 101 31E, pop(1980) 24,138, state capital of Selangor, W Peninsular Malaysia, SE Asia; 32 km W of Kuala Lumpur; airport at Subang; monuments: Istana Bukit Kayangan, home of the Sultan of Selangor; the Selangor State Memorial.

Shaker Heights, 41 29N 81 32W, pop(1980) 32,487, residential town in Cuyahoga county, NE Ohio, United States; 13 km E of Cleveland.

Shakhty *shaKH'tee*, formerly ALEKSANDROVSK GRUSHEVSKII (-1921), 47 43N 40 16E, pop(1983) 216,000, mining town in Rostovskaya oblast, SW European Rossiyskaya, Soviet Union; 75 km NE of Rostov-na-Donu; a major anthracite-mining centre in the Donets basin; founded in 1829 as a coal-mining settlement; railway; economy: coal mining, cotton, footwear, flax, machine building, foodstuffs, ceramics.

Shamāl, Ash, NORTH LEBANON, governorate (*moafazat*) of NW Lebanon; bounded W by the Mediterranean Sea, and N by Syria; subdivided into the 6 divisions (*cazas*) of A'akkar, Tripoli, Koura, Zgharta, Bcharré and Batroûn; the land rises towards the SE to a height of 3,087 m at Qornet es Saouda; capital Trâblous (Tripoli); chief towns Halba and Bcharré.

Shamâlîya, Esh, NORTHERN, region of N Sudan, NE Africa; area 183,941 sq km; pop(1983) 1,083,024; chief town Wadi Halfa; crossed by the R Nile; the Nubian desert lies in the NE.

Shan, state in E Burma; bounded NE by China, E by China and Laos and SE by Thailand; a mountainous region whose area coincides largely with that of the Shan plateau, giving the state an average altitude of 915 m; drained by the R Salween; in the SW is Lake Inle; pop(1983) 3,718,706; capital Taunggyi.

Shandong *shan-tung*, SHANTUNG, prov in E China; bounded N and E by the Bohai gulf, E by the Huang Hai (Yellow Sea), S by Jiangsu prov, S and W by Henan prov and W by Hebei prov; Shandong Bandao peninsula in the E is situated to the S of the Bo Hai gulf and to the N of the Huang Hai sea; the Grand Canal flows through the W part of the prov, forming part of the border with Hebei; Shandong prov is situated in the lower Huang He (Yellow river) valley, which crosses the prov from SW to NE before flowing into the Bo Hai gulf in the N of the prov; low in the N and W, Shandong rises in the S to over 1,000 m with the Yi Shan, Lu Shan and Meng Shan ranges; in Shandong prov is Tai Shan peak (1,545 m), one of China's Five Holy Mountains; pop(1982) 74,419,054; area 153,300 sq km; capital Jinan; principal towns Linyi, Qingdao and Tai'an; economy: wheat, maize, cotton, peanuts, fruit (apples, pears, dates, watermelons), fishing, oil, textiles, iron and steel, mining of diamonds, coal, petroleum, iron, graphite, bauxite; to the S of Jinan is the town of Qufu, the birthplace of Confucius; the building of dykes along the Huang He river has greatly improved agriculture in the region.

Shanghai *shang-hī*, 31 13N 121 25E, municipality pop(1982) 115,859,748, urban centre pop(1984e) 6,881,300, port in E China; the largest city in China; on the Huangpu and Wusong rivers; bounded E by the Huang Hai (Yellow Sea); municipality area 5,800 sq km; Shanghai developed in the Yuan period (1260-1378) as a minor centre for cotton spinning and weaving; it became a trading centre in the 17th and 18th centuries after the development of silk production in the surrounding areas; by the 1800s it was a growing domestic port; after the Opium War in 1842 Shanghai was opened to foreign trade; until 1949 Shanghai grew as an enclave for Western commercial interests in China; Shanghai's industry accounts for one-eighth of national income; university (1895); 11 children's palaces (for children between 7 and 17 who show particular skills in subjects such as dance, music, mechanics and mathematics); 2 airfields; 2 airports; rail and sea links to other cities; economy: oil refining, shipbuilding, engineering, chemicals, pharmaceuticals, textiles, paper; monuments: the tree-lined avenue in the centre of Shanghai known as the Bund is the former commercial centre of foreign powers; also in the centre of the city are the People's Park and the People's Square, the square is used for celebrations, processions and political rallies; W of the park is Liberation Lane, formerly the Blood Alley red light district famous for its brothels and opium dens which were closed down in 1949-50; the Yu Yuan (Garden of Happiness) built in 1577 and consisting of a small lake, a bridge and teahouses served as the basis for 'willow pattern' chinaware; the Jade Buddha temple (1882) contains 2 rare statues of Buddha, each carved out of a single piece of white jade; Shanghai Industrial Exhibition Hall, built by the Soviet Union in the early 1950s, has a display of over 5,000 industrial and consumer products; the museum of natural history (1963) has a display of preserved corpses, dating from 1200 BC; Songjiang County Square Pagoda and Dragon Wall, an original wooden pagoda built in the 11th century; the oldest and largest temple, Longhua Temple, was built before 687 AD, the adjacent pagoda was built in 977; the site was used as the headquarters of Shanghai's Guomintang (Nationalist) garrison before World War II.

Shanklin, resort on the Isle of Wight, England. See Sandown.

Shannon RINEANNA (Gael), 52 42N 8 57W, pop(1981) 7,998, town in Clare county, Munster, W Irish Republic; W of Limerick near R Shannon; duty free airport, gateway to Ireland for transatlantic visitors; economy: electronics; event: boat show rally in July.

Shannon, river in Irish Republic, rising in Cavan county, Ulster and flowing c.385 km SW through L Allen, L Ree and L Derg to Limerick Bay; navigable for most of its length; hydroelectric power at Ardnacrusha.

Shansi, prov in NE central China. See Shanxi.

Shantou *shahn-too*, SWATOW, 23 23N 116 39E, pop(1984e) 746,400, port in Guangdong prov, SE China; on the Chaozhou-Shantou alluvial plain on the coast of the South China Sea; developed since the 16th century as a port serving southern Jiangxi and Fujian provs; designated a special economic zone in 1980; includes the districts of Longhu and Guang'ao, the Dahao zone and the Jiaoshi scenic zone; university; railway; airport (Waisha); economy: chemicals, electronics, textiles, carpets, clothing, plastic products, cellophane, handicrafts, fishing and trade in rice, sugar cane, peanuts, jute, soya beans, oranges, tangerines, lychees, bananas, tea.

Shantung, province in E China. See Shandong.

Shanxi *shan-see*, SHANSI, mountainous prov in NE central China, on the E section of the Loess Plateau; bounded N by Nei Mongol aut region (Inner Mongolia), W along the Huang He (Yellow river) by Shaanxi prov, S and SE along the Huang He by Henan prov and E along the Taihang Shan range by Hebei prov; the Great Wall of China forms the majority of Shanxi's N border with Nei Mongol; Heng Shan peak, one of China's Five Holy Mountains, rises to 2,016 m; drained by the Fen He and Qin He rivers, tributaries of the Huang He river; pop(1982) 252,891,389; area 157,100 sq km; capital Taiyuan; principal town Datong; economy: agriculture, fruit, coal mining, iron and steel.

Shar-e Kord, formerly DEH KURD, 32 20N 50 52E, pop(1983) 63,984, capital town of Chahár Mahāll va Bakhtiárí prov, W central Iran.

Shāriqah, SHARJAH *shar'ju*, 3rd largest of the seven member states of the United Arab Emirates; NE of Dubayy (Dubai); area 2,600 sq km; pop(1980) 159,000; capital Ash Shāriqah; economy: oil production began from offshore wells near the island of Abū Mūsá in 1974 but in recent years output has declined; large volumes of gas from the Sajaa field are carried via an inter-emirate gas grid to power stations in Ra's al Khaymah, Al Fujayrah, 'Ajmān, and Umm al Qaywayn; industries include ship and heavy vehicle repairing, and the manufacture of cement, paper bags, steel products, and paint.

Shāriqah, Ash, PORT KHALID, 25 20N 55 26E, capital town of Shāriqah emirate, United Arab Emirates, SE Arabian Peninsula; on the Arabian Gulf, 9 km NE of Dubayy (Dubai); airport; economy: shipping, water desalination.

Sharjah, United Arab Emirate. See Shāriqah.

Sharon, sub-district of Central dist, Israel; pop(1983) 190,405; area 348 km.

Sharpeville *sharp'vil*, 26 40S 27 52E, black African township in Transvaal prov, NE South Africa; between Vereeniging and Vanderbijlpark, S of Johannesburg; administered by Lekoa Town Council; received international attention during unrest in 1960; centre of the Sharpeville Students National Resistance Movement; L Leeukuildam is located to the E.

Sharqi, Jebel esh, ANTI-LEBANON (Eng), ANTI-LIBAN *ã-tee-lee-bã'* (Fr), barren mountain range on the E border of Lebanon with Syria; parallel to and E of the Jebel Liban (Lebanon) range from which it is separated by the fertile El Beqa'a valley; rises to 2,814 m at Jesh Sheikh (Mt Hermon); traversed by the Beyrouth (Beirut)-Damascus railway.

Sharqîya *shar-kee'yu*, governorate in NE Egypt; pop(1976) 2,621,208; area 4,180 sq km; capital Zagazig.

Shasta, Mount, 41 25N 122 12W, situated in the Cascade range in N California, United States; dormant volcano with steam vents on its slopes; has 5 glaciers on E and NE sides; rises to 4,317 m.

Shatt al'Arab *shat' al a'rab*, tidal river formed by the union of the Tigris and Euphrates rivers, SE Iraq; from Al Qurnah, 64 km NW of Al Basrah, it flows 192 km SE through marshland to discharge into the Arabian Gulf; in its lower course it forms part of the Iraq-Iran border; the delta is wide and swampy, containing the world's largest date-palm groves; navigable for ocean-going vessels as far as the port of Al Basrah; the river washes the SW shore of Jazīreh Ābādān; chief tributary Kārūn; an international commission in 1935 gave Iraq control of the Shatt al'Arab and since then navigational rights over the waterway continue to be disputed; this was one of the issues that led to the outbreak of the Gulf War in 1980.

Shaw'nee, 39 01N 94 43W, pop(1980) 29,653, town in Johnson county, E Kansas, United States; suburb 13 km SSW of Kansas City; named after an Indian tribe.

Shawnee, 35 20N 96 55W, pop(1980) 26,506, county seat of Pottawatomie county, central Oklahoma, United States; on the North Canadian river, 55 km E of Oklahoma City; named after an Indian tribe; university (1906); railway; economy: trade centre in an agricultural and oil-producing area.

Shaykh 'Uthmān, Ash, 12 52N 45 00E, pop(1981e) 30,000, town in Aden governorate, South Yemen; close to the Gulf of Aden; a N suburb of Aden.

Sheberghān *shi-ber-gan'*, SHIBERGHAN, SHIBARGHAN, 36 40N 65 42E, pop(1984e) 20,822, capital of Jōwzjān prov, N Afghanistan; lies on the R Ab-i-Safed.

Sheboy'gan, 43 46N 87 45W, pop(1980) 48,085, county seat of Sheboygan county, E Wisconsin, United States; on L Michigan, at the mouth of the R Sheboygan; railway; economy: brewing.

Sheerness, 51 27N 0 45E, pop(1981) 11,084, port and resort town in Swale dist, Kent, SE England; on Isle of Sheppey; former naval dockyard; ferry link to the Netherlands; railway; economy: steel, tourism.

Shef'field, 53 23N 1 30W, pop(1981) 477,257, urban area pop(1981) 537,557, city and county town in South Yorkshire, N England; on the R Don; separated from Manchester to the W by the High Peak of Derbyshire; developed as a cutlery-manufacturing town in the early 18th century and as a steel town in the 19th century; city status in 1893; university (1905); railway; economy: steels, engineering, tool-making, cutlery, silverware, glass, optical instruments; monuments: 12th-c cathedral church of St Peter and St Paul; Mappin Art Gallery; Crucible Theatre; Abbeydale industrial hamlet; Cutlers' Hall (1832).

Shekhupura *shay'KHoo-poor-a*, 31 42N 74 08E, pop(1981) 141,000, city in Punjab prov, Pakistan; NW of Lahore; railway;

Shelekhov Gulf, gulf of the Sea of Okhotsk, NE Soviet Union. See Shelikhova, Zaliv.

Shelikhova, Zaliv, SHELEKHOV GULF, NE extension of the Sea of Okhotsk, NE Siberian Rossiyskaya, Soviet Union; width 320 km; includes (N) the bays of Penzhinskaya Guba and Gizhiginskaya Guba, separated by the Poluostrov Taygonos peninsula; bounded NW by the Khrebet Kolymskiy range and SE by the Kamchatka Peninsula; named after an 18th-c Russian merchant.

Shelton, 41 19N 73 05W, pop(1980) 31,314, town in Fairfield county, SW Connecticut, United States; on the R Housatonic opposite Derby, 14 km W of New Haven.

Shenando'ah, river in West Virginia and Virginia states, United States; formed at the junction of the North Fork and South Fork rivers in N Virginia; flows 88 km NE to meet the Potomac river near Harper's Ferry.

Shenandoah, national park in N Virginia, United States; 775 sq km in the Blue Ridge Mts; includes the Skyline Drive which is part of the Appalachian Trail from Maine to Georgia; established in 1935.

Shensi, prov in central China. See Shaanxi.

Shenyang *shen-yang*, formerly MUKDEN, 41 50N 123 26E, pop(1984e) 4,134,800, capital of Liaoning prov, NE China; N of the Hun river; the largest industrial city in NE China; major communication and transportation centre for the NE region; although Shenyang was first settled approx 2,000 years ago it only emerged as a city in the 11th century when it became a trading centre for nomads; became capital of the Manchu state in 1625 and remained a secondary capital after Beijing (Peking) was taken in 1644; the Japanese attacked Shenyang in 1931 and set up their puppet state of Manchukuo in 1932, draining the region of its resources; the Chinese nationalists occupied the city from 1945; it fell to the communists in 1948 and was renamed in 1949; railway; airfield; economy: electrical equipment, light and heavy engineering, chemicals, textiles, food processing; the city is famous for its acrobatic troupe; monuments: the Imperial Palace, built by the Manchus between 1625 and 1636, is now a museum; Dongling (the East Tomb), situated approx 8 km E of Shenyang on the banks of the Shen river, is the tomb of Nurhachi, founder of the Manchu state; Beiling (the North Tomb) is the tomb of Nurhachi's son and heir, Abukai.

Shenzhen *shen-zen*, 22 31N 114 08E, pop(1984e) 191,400, town in Guangdong prov, SE China; on the border with Hong Kong; a special economic zone; railway; economy: garment factories, light engineering.

Shep'parton, 36 25S 145 26E, pop(1983e) 25,420, city in Goulburn stat div, N Victoria, Australia; NE of Melbourne, in the fertile Goulburn Valley; railway; economy: grain, fruit, wool, wine, food processing; headquarters of the overseas transmitter of Radio Australia; monuments: Shepparton Arts Centre contains collections of Australian paintings and Australian and Japanese ceramics; an International Village features worldwide tourist information.

Sherbro *sher'brō*, island urban dist in Southern prov, Sierra Leone, W Africa; pop(1974) 6,955; area 10 sq km; 105 km SSE of Freetown; 48 km long and up to 24 km wide; separated from mainland by R Sherbro and Shebar Strait; Turtle islands off Cape St Ann (W); port of Bonthe on E coast.

Sherbrooke, 45 24N 71 54W, pop(1981) 74,075, town in S Québec, SE Canada; on the St Francis river where it is joined by the Magog river; founded in 1794 by United Empire Loyalists; a centre of the timber and mining industries in the 19th century; during the 20th century the town grew with the coming of hydroelectric power, and with the development of textile and metalworking industries; the locality is also noted as a centre for winter sports; university (1954); railway.

Sherman, 33 38N 96 36W, pop(1980) 30,413, county seat of Grayson county, NE Texas, United States; 96 km N of Dallas; railway; economy: flour, textiles, machinery and instruments.

's-Hertogenbosch *ser'to-KHen-bos*, BOIS-LE-DUC *bwa'le dük* (Fr), (The Duke's Woods), 51 41N 5 19E, pop(1984e) 186,946, capital city of Noord Brabant prov, S Netherlands; at the confluence of the Aa and Dommel rivers; a commercial city with important cattle markets; birthplace of the famous painter Hieronymus Bosch (1450-1516) and of Theodor van Thulden (1606-69), a friend and disciple of Rubens; the name of the town recalls its origins when Henry I of Brabant built a hunting lodge (12th-c) which later developed into an important medieval fortress; railway and canal junction; economy: cement, industrial refrigeration and air-conditioning compressors, pneumatic tools, pharmaceutical products, animal feedstuffs, electricity generation, cigars, hardware, foodstuffs, brewing; monuments: 17th-c town hall; cathedral, originally Romanesque, but rebuilt 1280-1312.

Shet'land, THE SHETLANDS, ZETLAND, group of islands off the coast of NE Scotland; consists of approx 100 islands, lying 80 km NE of the Orkney islands, off the NE point of the Scottish mainland; approx 20 of the islands are inhabited; chief islands: Mainland, Unst, Yell, Fetlar and Whalsay; the Shetlands are low lying islands, the highest point is Ronas Hill in N Mainland (450 m); pop(1981) 27,277; area 1,433 sq km; capital: Lerwick, on Mainland; the Orkney and Shetland islands were annexed by Norway in the 9th c; in 1468 the king of Norway and Denmark pledged the islands to James III, king of Scotland, as security for Margaret's dowry (James's queen); since the promise was not kept, the islands were annexed to Scotland in 1472; in World War II the islands were the target of the first German air raid on Great Britain (in November 1939); economy: cattle and sheep raising; knitwear; fishing; oil service bases at Lerwick and Sandwick, on Mainland; oil terminal at Sullom Voe; the small Shetland ponies are well-known for their strength and hardiness; monuments: there are several examples of ancient civilization on the Shetlands: Staneydale Temple, on W Mainland, is a Neolithic or early Bronze Age hall; Jarlshof at Sumburgh Head, the southernmost point of Mainland, contains the remains of 3 village settlements occupied from the Bronze Age to the times of the Vikings; on the island of Mousa, to the E of S Mainland, is Mousa Broch, a 12 m-high Iron Age broch.

Shewa, SHOA *shō'a*, mountainous region in central Ethiopia, NE Africa; pop(1984e) 8,090,565; area 85,200 sq km; high peaks include Abuye Mēda (4,200 m), Jībat (3,072 m) and Dendi (3,298 m); lakes on SE border include Ziway Hāyk' and K'ok'a Hāyk'; capital Nazrēt; chief towns include Ānkober, Hosa'ina and Debra Birhan.

Shibîn el Kom *shi-been el-koom'*, SHIBIN AL-KOM, 30 33N 31 00E, pop(1976) 102,840, capital of Menûfiya governorate, N Egypt; on the Nile delta, 60 km NNW of Cairo; railway.

Shihchiachuang, capital of Hebei prov, N China. See Shijiazhuang.

Shijiazhuang *shir-jee-ah-je-wang*, SHIHCHIACHUANG, 38 04N 114 28E, pop(1984e) 1,127,800, capital of Hebei prov, N China; Shijiazhuang grew rapidly after the arrival of the railway in 1905 and is now a major railway junction; economy: mining (coal, iron ore, limestone, marble), cotton-growing, textiles, dyeing, printing; has China's largest pharmaceutical plant, specializing in antibiotics; monuments: the Longcang temple stela, built during the Sui dynasty and adorned with examples of Chinese calligraphy, is one of the oldest and most famous in China; the Zhuanlunzang pavilion (10th-c) was originally used for reciting Buddhist scriptures and contains an octagonal revolving cabinet which represents the Wheel of Life; N of Shijiazhuang, near the town of Zhengding, is the 6th-c Buddhist monastery of Longxing Si, its present buildings date back to the 10th century; the monastery contains a 10th-c bronze statue of Guanyin, the Goddess of Mercy: 22 m high and with 42 arms, the statue illustrates a period of Buddhist sculpture when the influence of the Indian artistic heritage still dominated the development of Chinese Buddhist art.

Shikarpur *shi-kar'poor*, 27 58N 68 42E, pop(1981) 88,000, city in Sind prov, SE Pakistan; 386 km NE of Karachi; railway; linked to Quetta by natural gas pipeline.

Shikoku *shi-kō'koo*, island region in Japan; smallest of the 4 main islands of Japan; situated S of Honshū and E of Kyūshū; bounded N by the Seto Naikai Sea, S by the Pacific Ocean; the island has a subtropical climate and the interior is mountainous and wooded; pop(1980) 4,163,000; area 18,795 sq km; chief towns are Matsuyama, Takamatsu; economy: rice, wheat, tobacco, soya beans, orchards; Shikoku is divided into 4 prefectures as follows:

Prefecture	*area (sq km)*	*pop(1980)*
Ehime	5,664	1,507,000
Kagawa	1,879	1,000,000
Kōchi	7,107	831,000
Tokushima	4,145	825,000

Shil'don, 54 38N 1 39W, pop(1981) 11,657, town in

Sedgefield dist, Durham, NE England; 4 km SE of Bishop Auckland; railway; economy: coal, quarrying.

Shillong', 25 34N 91 53E, pop(1981) 109,244, capital of Meghalaya state, NE India; 500 km NE of Calcutta, in the Khasi Hills, S of the R Brahmaputra; alt 1,517 m; destroyed by an earthquake in 1897; former capital of Assam; economy: trade in rice, cotton, fruit.

Shimbir'is, 10 44N 47 15E, mountain in Sanaag region, N Somalia, NE Africa; the highest point in Somalia, rising to 2,416 m.

Shimizu *shi-meed'zoo*, 35 1N 138 29E, pop(1980) 241,576, port city in Shizuoka prefecture, Chūbu region, central Honshū island, Japan; on the W shore of Suruga wan Bay; 11 km NE of Shizuoka; railway; economy: trade in rice, tea and oranges.

Shimonoseki *shi-mō-nō-se'kee*, 33 59N 130 58E, pop(1980) 268,957, port in Yamaguchi prefecture, Chūgoku region, SW Honshū island, Japan; separated from Kita-Kyūshū on Kyūshū island by the Kammon Tunnels; railway; economy: shipbuilding, engineering, metalwork, chemicals, textiles, fishing.

Shinyanga *sheen-yang'ge*, region of NW Tanzania, E Africa; S of L Victoria; pop(1985e) 1,662,000; chief town Shinyanga.

Ship'ley, 53 50N 1 47W, pop(1981) 28,856, town in Bradford borough, West Yorkshire, N England; part of West Yorkshire urban area; on the R Aire and the Leeds and Liverpool Canal, 5 km NW of Bradford; railway; economy: textiles, engineering.

Shīrāz *shee-raz'*, 29 38N 52 34E, pop(1983) 800,416, capital city of Shīrāz dist, Fārs, SW Iran; 184 km ENE of Būshehr, its port on the Arabian Gulf; situated in the Zagros Mts; 5th largest city in Iran; noted for its wines, rugs, hand-woven textiles, silverwork, and mosaics; capital of Persia from 1750-79; airfield.

Shiselwe'ni, dist in S Swaziland, SE Africa; on the border with South Africa; chief towns include Mhlosheni, Mahamba and Nhlangano.

Shizuoka *shiz-oo-wō'ka*, 34 59N 138 24E, pop(1980) 458,341, capital of Shizuoka prefecture, Chūbu region, central Honshū island, Japan; on the W shore of Suruga wan Bay; port at Shimizu; university (1949); railway; economy: tea, chemicals, machinery.

Shkodër, SCUTARI *skoo-ta'ree* (Ital), prov of NW Albania; area 2,528 sq km; pop(1980) 198,600; capital Shkodër.

Shkodër, SCUTARI (Ital), SCODRA (anc), 42 05N 19 30E, pop(1980) 66,500, market town and capital of Shkodër prov, NW Albania, between the R Drin and L Scutari; former capital of Albania; railway; economy: ferrous metallurgy, foodstuffs, tobacco, cement, leather, wood products; monuments: 14th-c citadel, cathedral.

Shkumbin *shkoom'bee*, river in central Albania; rises near L Ohrid and flows 140 km NW and W to the Adriatic Sea 32 km S of Durrës.

Shoreham-by-Sea, 50 49N 0 16W, pop(1981) 20,966, port town in Adur dist, West Sussex, S England; part of Brighton-Worthing-Littlehampton urban area; on the English Channel, at the mouth of the R Adur, 10 km W of Brighton; container terminal; railway; monument: Marlipins maritime museum.

Shortland Islands, volcanic SW Pacific island group in the NW Solomon Islands; W of Choiseul and 8 km S of Bougainville (Papua New Guinea); includes the islands of Shortland and Fauro and many small islets.

Shotton-Hawarden *hahr'den*, 53 11N 3 02W, pop(1981) 22,450, town in Alyn and Deeside dist, Clwyd, NE Wales, United Kingdom; in Connah's Quay-Shotton urban area; railway; economy: steel.

Shreveport *shreev'pōrt*, 32 31N 93 45W, pop(1980) 205,820, parish seat of Caddo parish, NW Louisiana, United States; on the Red river, 28 km E of the Texas border; the city developed rapidly after the discovery of oil in 1906; university; railway; airfield; economy: major oil and natural gas centre; manufactures include lumber and metal products, cotton, dairy goods, machinery, telephones, and chemicals; event: Red River Revel (Oct).

Shrewsbury *shrooz'ber-i* (Anglo-Saxon, 'Scrobesbyrig' town in the wood), 52 43N 2 45W, pop(1981) 59,169, county town in Shrewsbury and Atcham dist, Shropshire, W central England; on the R Severn, 63 km NW of Birmingham; headquarters of Edward I during the struggle for Wales; railway; economy: engineering, agricultural trade; monuments: church of St Mary, abbey church, Rowley's mansion (1618), 11th-c castle; events: Shropshire and W Midland agricultural show (May), National Ploughing Championships (Oct).

Shrop'shire, county in W central England; bounded W by Powys and Clwyd in Wales, S by Hereford and Worcester, E by Staffordshire and NE by Cheshire; drained by the R Severn; pop(1981) 375,715; area 3,490 sq km; county town Shrewsbury; chief towns include Telford, Oswestry, Wellington and Ludlow; economy: agriculture, engineering; the county is divided into 6 districts:

District	*area (sq km)*	*pop(1981)*
Bridgnorth	634	50,292
North Shropshire	680	50,044
Oswestry	256	30,589
Shrewsbury and Atcham	603	87,600
South Shropshire	1,028	33,790
Wrekin	291	123,835

Shuaiba *shoo-ī'ba*, 29 10N 48 10E, industrial port on the Arabian Gulf, E Kuwait; S of the port of Mīnā' al Aḩmadī; economy: oil refining, the manufacture of petrochemicals, fertilizers, construction materials, asbestos, and lead acid batteries; sea water desalination plant.

Shubra el Kheima *shoo-bra' el* KHay'*mu*, 30 03N 31 15E, pop(1976) 393,700, suburb of Cairo in Cairo governorate, N Egypt.

Shumen or **Sumen**, also **Shoumen** *shoo'men*, okrug (prov) of NE Bulgaria traversed NW-SE by the Goljama Kamcija river; area 3,374 sq km; pop(1981) 252,000.

Shumen, 43 16N 26 55E, pop(1981) 96,632, capital of Shumen okrug (prov), NE Bulgaria, 304 km NE of Sofiya; formerly known as Kolarovgrad; railway; economy: metal, leather and wood handicrafts; monuments: a 17th-c mosque which is the largest in Bulgaria; medieval fortress.

Shurugwi *shu-roog'wi*, 19 40S 30 00E, town in Midlands prov, Zimbabwe, S Africa; SE of Gweru; chrome mining centre; railway.

Shuwaikh *shoo-wī*KH*'*, 29 20N 48 00E, major commercial port of Kuwait, situated SW of central Al Kuwayt (Kuwait City), on the S shore of Kuwait Bay, an inlet of the Arabian Gulf; site of Kuwait University (1966); economy: flour mills, sea water desalination plant, container terminal.

Sialkot *syal'kōt*, 32 29N 74 35E, pop(1981) 296,000, city in Punjab prov, E Pakistan; E of the R Chenab, NE of Gujranwala; railway; economy: rubber goods, ceramics, cutlery and surgical instruments; monuments: ancient fort and mausoleum of Sikh apostle Nanak.

Sian, capital of Shaanxi prov, central China. See Xi'an.

Šibenik *shee'ben-ik*, 43 45N 15 55E, pop(1981) 80,148, seaport and resort town in E Hrvatska (Croatia) republic, Yugoslavia; NW of Split near the mouth of the R Krka which is joined to the Adriatic Sea by the Šibenik channel; held by Austria until 1919; naval harbour; Solaris resort area on the Zablaće peninsula; railway; economy: timber, bauxite, coal, wine, marble, aluminium, hydroelectric power; monuments: 15-16th-c cathedral; Municipal Loggia; Franciscan friary; the three forts of Šbićevac, St Anne and St John; events: summer festival in June-July; children's festival in early July.

Siberia *sī-bee'ri-a*, vast geographic region of Asiatic USSR, comprising the N third of Asia; stretches from the Ural'skiy Khrebet range (Ural Mts) in the W to the Pacific Ocean (Bering Sea, Sea of Okhotsk) in the E, and from the Arctic Ocean (Laptev Sea, Kara Sea, E Siberian Sea) in the N to the Kazakhskaya steppes and the Chinese and Mongolian frontiers in the S; area c.7,511,000 sq km; Arctic islands off the Siberian coast include Severnaya Zemlya, Novosibirskiye Ostrova (New Siberian Is), and Ostrov Vrangelya (Wrangel I); off its Pacific coast are Sakhalin and the Kuril'skiye Ostrova (Kuril Is); Siberia can be divided into 3 main physiographic regions: (1) the Zapadno Sibirskaya Ravnina (W Siberian Lowlands), an extensive lowland stretching more than 1,500 km from the Ural'skiy Khrebet range (W) to the R Yenisey (E), and drained by the Ob'-Irtysh river system; (2) the Sredne Sibirskoye Ploskogor'ye (Central Siberian Plateau), lying between the R Yenisey (W) and the R Lena (E); (3) the E Siberian highlands, comprising the Verkhoyanskiy Khrebet, Khrebet Cherskogo, Khrebet Kolymskiy, and Stanovoy Khrebet ranges; along Siberia's S margins lie the Amur river, Sayan Mts (Zapadnyy Sayan and Vostochnyy Sayan), and the Altay Mts, rising to 4,506 m at Gora Belukha, the highest non-volcanic summit in Siberia; the volcanic Kamchatka Peninsula rises to 4,750 m at Klyuchevskaya Sopka; there are c.155,000 rivers in Siberia, the largest of which are the Ob', Yenisey, and Lena; these northward flowing rivers freeze over for 9 months of the year, hence their use for navigation is limited; Siberia's climate is extreme continental, exposed to the cold Arctic air masses to the N; average winter temperatures are generally below −18°C and in NE Siberia, around Verkhoyansk and Oymyakon, January temperatures average −51°C; summer temperatures are relatively high, with July averages of 15°C to 18°C in the coldest winter areas; Noril'sk is the coldest city in the world with an average annual temperature of −10.9°C; precipitation is generally low, except on the E Kamchatka slopes and in the coastal areas exposed to the Pacific summer monsoon; the tundra (cold desert) extends c.320 km inland along the entire Arctic coast, merging S into taiga (boreal coniferous forest), mixed forest, and steppe; natural resources in Siberia include coal (Kuznetsk Basin), timber, gold (Vitim and Aldan plateau areas, Magadanskaya oblast, Bilibino), iron (Kuznetsk basin, E of Bratsk), copper (Noril'sk), nickel, and non-ferrous metals; industry has developed on the basis of mineral resources (particularly in the Kuznetsk basin), and the processing of agricultural products and timber; development of the huge hydroelectric power potential of Siberia's rivers began in the 1950s with construction of a power station on the Ob' river above the city of Novosibirsk; since then power stations have been built chiefly on the R Yenisey (Krasnoyarsk, Sayanogorsk) and its tributary, the Angara (Ust'Ilimsk, Bratsk, Irkutsk); principal agricultural activities in the wooded steppe and fertile black-earth areas of W Siberia are dairying and grain growing, notably spring wheat; in E Siberia a grain and cattle rearing region extends discontinuously across the S parts while further N the emphasis is on reindeer rearing and hunting; climatic conditions in the lowlands of the Amur and Ussuri rivers on the Pacific coast are ideal for the cultivation of rice, maize, sorghum, and soya beans; the chief cities of Siberia (Novosibirsk, Omsk, Krasnoyarsk, Irkutsk, Khabarovsk, and Vladivostok) lie on the Trans-Siberian railway; the Russian conquest of Siberia began in 1581-82 when the Cossacks, under the leadership of Yermak, crossed the Ural'skiy Khrebet range and conquered the Tatar khanate of Sibir; during the 17th century all of W Siberia was annexed to Russia and by 1640 the Cossacks had reached the Sea of Okhotsk; Siberia was soon used as a penal colony and place of exile for political prisoners, and the military governors who administered the region collected fur tribute from the indigenous population; with the decline of the fur trade in the early 18th century, mining became the chief economic activity; in the beginning of the 19th century there were several expeditions to Siberia, the most important being those of Litke (1821-24) and Wrangel (1820-24); by treaties of 1858 and 1860 Russia obtained possession of the Far-East territories; Russian settlement in Siberia on a large scale began with construction of the Trans-Siberian railway (1892-1905); after the Bolshevik revolution of 1917 vast areas of Siberia were occupied by the counter-revolutionary armies of Kolchak and Japanese interventionists, both of which were finally overthrown by Soviet forces in 1922; under the 5-year plans economic development in Siberia was dramatic, relying heavily on forced labour and population resettlement to establish mining, industrial, and agricultural installations; after World War II industrialization continued at a rapid pace, particularly in SW Siberia and the region around Ozero Baykal (Lake Baikal).

Siberian Lowlands, West, vast lowland area in W Siberian Rossiyskaya, Soviet Union. See Zapadno Sibirskaya Ravnina.

Siberut *see-be-root'*, island 140 km off the W coast of Sumatera, Indonesia; separated from the island of Sumatera by the Selat Mentawai, a deep submarine trench; area 500 sq km; a nature and 'traditional use' reserve area protecting the dwarf gibbon, pig-tailed langur, Mentawi leaf monkey and Mentawi macaque; air connections with Padang.

Sib'iloi, national park in NW Kenya, E Africa; on the E shore of L Turkana; area 1,570 sq km; established in 1972.

Sibiu *see-bee'oo*, county in central Romania, in the N foothills of the Transylvanian Alps; pop(1983) 503,866; area 5,422 sq km; capital Sibiu; notable wine-growing region.

Sibiu, HERMANNSTADT (Ger), 45 46N 24 09E, pop(1983) 172,117, capital of Sibiu county, central Romania; established in the 12th century; airfield; railway; economy: textiles, clothing, food processing, metallurgy, precision mechanics, brewing.

Sibu *see'boo*, 2 18N 111 49E, pop(1980) 86,000, town on the W coast of Sarawak state, E Malaysia, SE Asia; 96 km up the R Rajang, NE of Kuching; predominantly Chinese population; airfield; economy: fishing.

Sibut *see-boot'*, FORT SIBUT, 5 46N 19 06E, chief town in Kemo Gribingui region, Central African Republic; 160 km NNE of Bangui.

Sichuan *se-chwahn*, SZECHWAN, prov in SW central China; bounded N by Qinghai, Gansu and Shaanxi provs, E by Hubei and Hunan provs, S by Yunnan and Guizhou provs and W by Xizang aut region (Tibet); the E half of the prov, the Sichuan Pendi (Red Basin), is enclosed by mountains: the Longmen Shan, Micang Shan and Daba Shan ranges lie to the N, the Guanmian Shan, Wu Shan and Fangdou Shan ranges lie to the E, the Dalou Shan range to the S and the Daliang Shan and Qionglai Shan ranges to the W; the basin itself is watered by many rivers with the Min Jiang, Tuo Jiang, and Jialing Jiang all flowing into the upper Chang Jiang (Yangtze river) which also runs through this extremely fertile region; the Chengdu Plain, the major farming area in Sichuan, is watered by the ancient Dujiangyan irrigation system; in the W snow-covered mountain ranges form the Western Sichuan Plateau, these include the Qionglai Shan, Daxue Shan, Chola Shan, Shaluli Shan and Jinping Shan ranges; Sichuan rises to 7,556 m in Gongga Shan, the highest peak in Daxue Shan range; pop(1982) 99,713,310; area 569,000 sq km; capital Chengdu; principal town Chongqing; economy: largest rice-producing province in China, wheat, maize, cotton, sugar cane, silk, tea, tung oil, bamboo, citrus fruit, forestry, chemicals; pig, cattle, yak, horse and sheep raising; mining of iron ore, coal, natural gas, copper, gold, lead, zinc, mercury, asbestos, petroleum.

Sichuan Pendi, RED BASIN, basin in E Sichuan, SW central China; known as the Red Basin because of the colour of its shale and soil; bounded by the Qionglai Shan range (W), the Dalou Shan range (S), the Fangdou Shan and Wu Shan ranges (E) and the Daba Shan and Micang Shan ranges (N); alt 400-800 m; area 200,000 sq km; drained by numerous rivers which cut the basin into scattered hilly regions; the Chang Jiang (Yangtze river) flows through the S of the Sichuan Pendi basin, and is joined by the Min Jiang, Tuo Jiang and Jialing Jiang from the N and the Wu Jiang from the S; the Chengdu Plain in the W is the highest producing area in the basin, while the centre is an important farming area of flat hills, most less than 400 m in altitude; the E is made up of rows of mountains with valleys lying between them; the Chengdu Plain is well irrigated by the Dujiangyan irrigation system, in which canals and ditches are led off the most powerful river, the Min Jiang, which was first used to irrigate this area 2,000 years ago; as well as being an extremely fertile, well irrigated region producing rice, tung-oil, sugar cane, tangerines, silk, tea and rapeseed, the Sichuan Pendi basin is now a major industrial base for SW China, producing natural gas, coal, salt, phosphorus, copper and sulphur.

Sicilia *si-chee'li-a*, SICILY *sis'i-li* (Eng), largest and most populous island in the Mediterranean, separated from the mainland of Italy by the narrow Strait de Messina, 416 km SW of Roma (Rome); with some small neighbouring islands it forms a region of Italy, comprising the provs of Trapani, Palermo, Messina, Agrigento, Caltanissetta, Enna, Catania, Ragusa, and Siracusa; pop(1981) 4,906,878; area 25,706 sq km; length 288 km; width 192 km; capital Palermo; chief towns Trapani, Messina, and Catania; the terrain is mountainous with an average elevation of 442 m; a chain of mountains (Monti Nebrodi) traverses the N half of the island, rising to nearly 1,981 m and sending spurs to the S; the N and NE coasts are steep and rocky, the S and SE generally flat; there is a large earthquake zone along the E coast culminating in Mt Etna (3,323 m), the highest point on the island; drained mostly by intermittent streams and a few rivers, chiefly the Simeto, Salso and Platani; economy: intensive vegetable growing, fruit orchards and wine production (especially around Marsala) predominate in the fertile coastal areas; in the dry and hilly interior there is extensive arable cultivation (wheat alternating with beans) and some pastoral farming; coastal fisheries (tuna, anchovies, swordfish); extraction of salt in the Trapani area; petrochemicals (around Siracusa and Gela); potash mining; working of asphalt (around Ragusa) and marble; tourism.

Sicily, region and island of Italy. See Sicilia.

Sīdamo *see'da-mō*, region in S Ethiopia, NE Africa; pop(1984e) 3,790,579; area 117,300 sq km; high in N dipping S towards the Kenyan frontier; part of Ābaya Hāyk' (L Abaya) is located in the NE; the Genalē Wenz river flows along the E border; capital Awasa; chief towns include Yirga 'Alem, Sodo, Negelē and Yabēlo.

Sidi bel Abbès *bel ab-bes'*, 35 15N 0 39W, pop(1982) 165,266, chief town of Sidi bel Abbès dept, N Algeria, N Africa; 56 km S of Oran; originally a walled town, it became a military post under French occupation; one-time headquarters of the French Foreign Legion; railway.

Sidi Bouzid *see'dee boo-zeed'*, governorate in E Tunisia, N Africa; pop(1984) 288,528; capital Sidi Bouzid; economy: grain, wool, almonds, horse rearing.

Sidmouth *sid'muth*, 50 41N 3 15W, pop(1981) 11,434, resort town in East Devon dist, Devonshire, SW England; on Lyme Bay, at the mouth of the R Sid, 21 km E of Exeter; event: international folklore festival (Jul-Aug).

Sidon, seaport in Lebanon. See Saïda.

Siebengebirge *zee'ben-ge-beerge*, mountain range in Nordrhein-Westfalen (North Rhine-Westphalia) prov, W Germany; small E range of the Westerwald, extending along right bank of the R Rhine, S of Bonn; highest point is the Großer Olberg (460 m).

Siedlce *shel'tze*, voivodship in E Poland; bounded N by R Bug; pop(1983) 629,000; area 8,499 sq km; capital Siedlce; chief towns include Mińsk Mazowiecki and Łuków.

Siedlce, SESDLETS (Rus), 52 10E 22 18E, pop(1983) 61,300, capital of Siedlce voivodship, E Poland; E of Warszawa (Warsaw); teachers' college; railway; economy: metal, machinery, knitwear, food processing.

Siegen *zee'gen*, 50 52N 8 02E, pop(1983) 109,800, industrial city in Arnsberg dist, S Nordrhein-Westfalen (North Rhine-Westphalia) prov, W Germany; on the R Sieg, 78 km E of Köln (Cologne); railway; university (1972); birthplace of the painter Rubens.

Siem Reap-Oddar Meanchey, province in NW Cambodia; pop(1981) 313,000; bounded S by the Tonlé Sap; chief town, Siem Reap, lies on R Siem Reap which feeds the Tonlé Sap; ruins of the ancient capital of Angkor lie to the N of the town; province was in Thailand until 1907 and again 1941-46, with the exception of the town of Siem Reap.

Siemianowice Śląskie *shaym-yen'ov-itz shlown'ski*, 50 17N 19 02E, pop(1983) 79,600, mining and industrial town in Katowice voivodship, S Poland; N of Katowice; railway.

Siena *syay'na*, prov of Toscana region, central Italy; pop(1981) 255,118; area 3,820 sq km; capital Siena.

Siena, 43 19N 11 19E, pop(1981) 61,989, capital town of Siena prov, Toscana region, central Italy; 70 km S of Firenze (Florence); founded by the Etruscans; centre of the Ghibelline faction and a rival of Firenze; for centuries one of the great art centres of Italy; from this area comes the brown pigment known as burnt sienna; archbishopric; university (1240); monuments: 13th-c cathedral - in its library are famous frescoes of Pinturicchio and his pupils; Palazzo Pubblico (town hall), a huge Gothic building of travertine and brick (1288-1309), with a notable tower, the Torre del Mangia (1338-49); 14th-c Palazzo Buonsignori; Gothic church of San Domenico (1293-1391); house where St Catherine of Siena was born in 1347; event: Palio, a parade and horse race (2 July and 16 Aug).

Sieradz *sher-ads'*, agricultural voivodship in central Poland; bisected N-S by R Warta; pop(1983) 397,000; area 4,869 sq km; capital Sieradz; chief towns include Zduńska Wola and Łask.

Sieradz, 51 35N 18 41E, pop(1983) 34,400, capital of Sieradz voivodship, central Poland; on R Warta; sports centre; economy: knitwear, arts and crafts; monuments: open-air museum; ruins of medieval fortified town.

Sierra Leone, *li ōn'*, official name Republic of Sierra Leone; a coastal republic in W Africa, bounded N by Guinea, SE by Liberia and S by the Atlantic Ocean; timezone GMT; area 72,325 sq km; pop(1984) 3,805,000; capital Freetown; chief towns Bo, Sefadu, Makeni, Kenema and Lunsar; there are 84 km of railway; 1,225 km of surfaced roads and 600 km of perennial inland waterways; the majority of the pop are of African origin, the principal ethnic groups being the Temnes, Limbas, Lokos and Korankos in the N, the Temnes in the centre, the Mendis in the S, and the Kissis and Konos in the E; there are also some European and Asian residents; most Sierra Leoneans follow local beliefs (70%), the remainder are Muslim (25%) or Christian (5%); the unit of currency is the leone; membership of AfDB, AIOEC, Commonwealth, ECA, ECOWAS, FAO, G-77, GATT, IAEA, IBA, IBRD, ICAO, ICO, IDA, IDB (Islamic Development Bank), IFAD, IFC, ILO, IMF, IMO, INTERPOL, IPU, IRC, ITU, Mano River Union, NAM, OAU, OIC, UN, UNESCO, UPU, WHO, WMO and WTO.

Physical description. A relatively small country measuring 322 km N-S and 290 km E-W, Sierra Leone rises from a low coastal plain around 30 km wide, the only major exception being the volcanic Freetown peninsula from which the country's name originates ('lion's range'). Behind the coastal plain the W half rises to an average height of 500 m in the Loma mountains, the highest point in Sierra Leone being Loma Mansa (1,948 m) near the frontier with Guinea. South-east of the Loma mountains the Tingi mountains rise to 1,853 m. Rivers flowing SW into the Atlantic Ocean include the Great Scarcies, Rokel, Taia, Sewa, Moa and the Mano which runs along the SE frontier with Liberia.

Climate. Sierra Leone has an equatorial climate. A rainy season extends from May to Oct with most of the rain falling in July and Aug. It is the coast which experiences the highest rainfall. Either side of the dry season the country experiences monsoon type conditions with the reversal of prevailing wind direction. During this period the N districts only receive 125 mm of rain. During Dec and Jan the dry *harmattan* wind blows from the Sahara but during the rest of the year there is a cool Atlantic breeze, especially on the coast. Temperatures are uniformly high throughout the year at around 27°C. The average annual rainfall at Freetown (alt 11 m) is 3,436 mm per annum.

History, government and constitution. The area was first visited by Portuguese navigators and British slave traders. In the 1780s land was bought from local chiefs by English philanthropists who established settlements for freed slaves. In 1808 the coastal settlements became a British Crown Colony. British colonial activity increased throughout the 19th century and in 1896 the hinterland was declared a British protectorate. Full internal government in 1960 was followed by independence in 1961. In 1971 Sierra Leone became a republic. The government consists of an executive president who is head of state, a cabinet of ministers and a 104-member parliament.

Economy. Over 70% of the pop are involved in subsistence agriculture, chiefly producing rice, coffee, cocoa, ginger, palm kernels, piassava, cassava, cola nuts and citrus fruits. Coffee, cocoa and palm kernels are the main export crops. Industry is centred around food processing, soap, timber and furniture, but mining is the most important sector of the economy, with diamonds representing about 60% of exports. Bauxite, gold and titanium are other major export earners. There are reserves of iron ore at a number of locations including Marampa. Other reserves include columbium, limestone, salt, aluminium and chromite. Main trading partners are the UK, Japan, West Germany, Nigeria, China, France and the Netherlands.

Administrative divisions. Sierra Leone is divided into 4 provinces which are subdivided into districts. There are also 18 chiefdoms.

Province/district	*area (sq km)*	*pop(1974)*
Eastern Province	15,553	755,931
Kailahun District	3,859	180,365
Kenema District	6,053	266,636
Kono District	5,641	328,930
Northern Province	35,936	1,046,158
Bombali District	7,985	233,626
Kambia District	3,108	155,341
Koinadugu District	12,121	158,626
Port Loko District	5,719	292,244
Tonkolili District	7,003	206,321
Southern Province	19,694	596,758
Bo District	5,219	217,711
Bonthe District	3,458	80,606
Moyamba District	6,902	188,745
Pujehun District	4,105	102,741
Sherbro Urban District	10	6,955
Western Area	557	316,312
Freetown	13	276,247
Western Rural Area	544	40,065

Sierra Nevada *sye'ra nay-vah'da*, mountain range in W USA; situated mainly in E California; extends NW-SE for 724 km between the Cascade and Coastal ranges, from the gap S of Lassen Peak in N California to the Tehachapi Mts SE of Bakersfield; Mt Whitney (at 36 35N 118 17W) in the S portion of the range is the highest peak in the USA outside Alaska, rising to 4,418 m; the Sierra Nevada contains Yosemite, Sequoia and Kings Canyon national parks.

Sierra Nevada, national park in Mérida state, NW Venezuela; area 1,900 sq km; established in 1952; contains the Pico Bolívar, Venezuela's highest peak (5,007 m).

Sífnos, island of the Kikládhes, Greece, in the S Aegean Sea; area 73 sq km; there are many sandy bays on the E and W coasts; in ancient times it was noted for its gold, silver, and lead deposits.

Siġġiewi *si-jah'wee* or **Sijuwi** *si-joo'wee*, 35 51N 14 26E, pop(1983e) 5,316, town in S central Malta, 8 km SW of Valletta.

Sighişoara *seeg-eesh-wa'ra*, 46 12N 24 48E, pop(1983) 36,437, summer resort town in Mureş county, N central Romania; 64 km NE of Sibiu; the walled Upper Town is called the Citadel; a centre of craft guilds in medieval times; railway; economy: tourism, textiles, metalwork; monuments: within the Citadel are well preserved medieval buildings; 15th-c Tower of the Clock.

Siguatepeque *see-ga-te-pay'kay*, 14 39N 87 48W, pop(1983e) 23,235, town in Comayagua dept, W Honduras, Central America; 114 km NW of Tegucigalpa.

Siguer, Pic du *see-gwer'*, mountain peak in the E central Pyrenees on the N border of the Principality of Andorra with France; height 2,905 m.

Siguiri *see-gee'ree*, 11 31N 9 10W, town in E Guinea, W Africa; on the R Niger, 540 km from Conakry and SW of Bamako in Mali.

Siirt *seert*, mountainous prov in SE Turkey, bounded W by the rivers Tigris and Batman; pop(1980) 445,483; area 11,003 sq km; capital Siirt.

Sikasso *see-ka'sō*, region in S Mali, W Africa; pop(1971) 948,513; area 76,480 sq km; a flat region rising to 762 m at Mount Mina SSE of Sikasso; the R Baoulé, 2nd river of this name in Mali, and the R Bagoé flow NE across the region and join to form the R Bani; the R Sankarani flows through the Lac de Sélinque where it is dammed for hydroelectric power; capital Sikasso; chief towns Bougouni, Kadiolo, Kolondiéba, Koutiala, Yanfolia, Yorosso; economy: gold, lithium, lead, zinc and columbium mining, gold processing.

Sikasso, 11 18N 5 38W, pop(1976) 47,030, capital of Sikasso region, S Mali, W Africa; 290 km SE of Bamako; economy: soap, power plant.

Sikhote Alin *see'KHō-tay ah-leen'*, mountain range in Primorskiy kray, Rossiyskaya, E Soviet Union, extending c.1,280 km from Vladivostok (SW) to Nikolayevsk-na-Amure (NE), parallel to the coast of the Sea of Japan;

there are mineral resources in the S (lead, zinc, coal, tin, iron); its forests are a source of lumber; comprises 7 or 8 parallel mountain chains, the peaks of which vary in height from about 1,800 m in the centre to 1,300 m at the N and S ends; rises to 2,078 m at Tardoki Yani.

Siking, capital of Shaanxi prov, central China. See Xi'an.

Síkinos *see'keen-os*, island of the Kikládhes, Greece, in the S Aegean Sea, between Mílos and Íos; area 41 sq km.

Sikkim *sik'kim*, DENJONG ('the valley of rice'), state in NE India; pop(1981) 315,682; area 7,299 sq km; in the E Himalayas, bounded S by West Bengal state, W by Nepal, N by Xizang aut region (Tibet) of China and E by Xizang aut region and Bhutan; Sikkim is divided into 4 administrative districts; capital Gangtok; Sikkim is governed by a 32-member Assembly; the state is crossed by the Rangit and Tista rivers; Kangchenjunga mountain rises to 8,598 m on the Sikkim-Nepal border; Sikkim is inhabited mostly by Lepchas, Bhutias and Nepalis; the official language of the state was English, but now Lepcha, Bhutia, Nepali and Limboo have been declared official languages; the state religion is Mahayana Buddhism, but a large portion of the population are Hindu; the economy of the state is based on agriculture, the principal crops being rice, maize, millet, cardamon, soybean, fruit and tea; economy: cigarettes, copper, zinc and lead mining, watches, carpets, hand made paper, woodwork and silverwork; there are no railways or airfields within the state; electricity is produced within the state by 4 hydro-electric power stations; the Namgyal dynasty ruled Sikkim from the 14th century until 1975 when the last Chogyal ('king ruling in accordance with religious laws') was deposed; from 1866 until 1947 Sikkim was part of the British Empire; in Dec 1950 Sikkim became a protectorate of India, with India being responsible for Sikkim's defence and external relations; unrest and demands for political reform in 1973 led to the Chogyal requesting the Indian police to take over law and order; the Government of Sikkim Act of 1974 made the Chogyal a constitutional monarch and under the Constitutional Act of 1974 Sikkim became a state associated with the Indian Union, abolishing the office of Chogyal in 1975; Sikkim became the 22nd state of the Union of India under the Constitutional Act of 1975.

Sil *seel*, river rising in the Cordillera Cantabrica, Galicia, N Spain; flowing SW and W to the R Minho (Miño) at Los Peares, it forms part of the boundary between Lugo and Orense provs; length 225 km; irrigation and hydroelectric reservoirs; tributaries Cua, Lor, Cabe, Boeza, Cabrera, Bibley and Meo rivers.

Sil'chester, CALLEVA ATREBATUM (Lat), archaeological site in Basingstoke dist, Hampshire, S England; 12 km N of Basingstoke, near Tadley; the most completely excavated Roman town in England; there are remains of an amphitheatre, walls, basilica, etc.

Silesia *sil-ee'zha*, SLEZSKO (Czech), ŚLĄSK *slõshk* (Pol), SCHLESIEN *shlay'zhyen* (Ger), region of E central Europe on both banks of the R Oder (Odra) in SW Poland, N central Czechoslovakia and SE E Germany; bounded S by Sudetes Mts; formerly provs of Austria and Prussia; part of Silesia was held by Germany until 1919 when the region was divided into Upper and Lower Silesia; the greater part of Silesia was granted to Poland in 1945; largely an industrial region, including the coal mining and metal industries of Katowice and surrounding cities.

Siliana *seel-ya-na'*, governorate in N central Tunisia, N Africa; pop(1984) 222,038; capital Siliana.

Silicon Valley, Santa Clara county, W California, United States; an area situated SSE of San Francisco between Palo Alto and San José noted as a world centre for electronics, computing and database systems; named after the non-metallic element, silicon, which adds strength to alloys and is used in transistors, semiconductors and computer micro-chip circuitry.

Siling Co, lake in central Xizang aut region (Tibet), W China; area 1,864.8 sq km; alt 4,495 m; it joins Urru Co lake to the W.

Silistra *si-lee'stra*, okrug (prov) of NE Bulgaria on the frontier with Romania and bordered to the N by the R Danube; area 2,859 sq km; pop(1981) 174,000; an agricultural and horticultural district.

Silistra, DUROSTORUM (Lat), 44 06N 27 17E, agricultural and commercial capital of Silistra okrug (prov), NE Bulgaria; on the R Danube, 449 km NE of Sofiya; founded by the Romans in 29 BC; airfield; railway.

Siljan *sil-yan'*, SILJA (Eng), lake in central Kopparberg county, central Sweden; extends 36 km from NW to SE; area 354 sq km; width 25 km; average depth 60 m; max depth 120 m in channel from Mora to Leksand; fed by and drains into the R Dalälven; the island of Sollerön is NW; artificially regulated since 1926.

Silk Road, The, route from E China to central Asia; from the 2nd century AD, the best known route ran from Xi'an in Shaanxi prov through the Hexi Corridor; from Xi'an it went WNW to the town of Lanzhou in Gansu prov then to Wuwei, then NW as far as Dunhuang oasis; here the route split in two, with one going to the N of the Taklimakan Shamo desert via the Yumen pass and the other one going to the S of the desert through the Yangguan pass; the two roads joined up again at Kashi in W Xinjiang aut region; from there routes went to the E coast of the Mediterranean to what is now Lebanon; during the Sui dynasty (581-618) a route was opened which ran further N through Xinjiang aut region to Ürümqi then N of the Caspian and Black Seas to reach Istanbul; after the disintegration of the Tang dynasty in 907 the route was often attacked by Mongols and travel by sea to China was favoured; in exchange for silk China received grapes, cotton, chestnuts, lucerne and pomegranates from Europe and S and central Asia, while at the same time Chinese techniques for silkworm breeding, iron-smelting, paper-making and irrigation spread W; the silk road also brought Buddhism to China.

Sil'keborg, 56 10N 9 39E, pop(1981) 33,304, health resort and city in the lake region of Århus county, E Jylland (Jutland), Denmark, 43 km W of Århus; railway; economy: engineering.

Silves *seel'vish*, 37 11N 8 26W, pop(1981) 10,000, town and former Moorish capital of the Algarve, S Portugal; on R Arade, 36 km NE of Lagos; monuments: Moorish castle, 13th c cathedral and church of the Misericordia.

Silvretta *seel-vret'ta*, mountain range of the Eastern Alps in Vorarlberg state, W Austria, rising to 3,312 m at Piz Buin.

Simferopol' *syim-fye-ro'pul-y'*, 44 57N 34 05E, pop(1983) 324,000, capital city of Krymskaya oblast, Ukrainskaya SSR, Soviet Union; on a peninsula which connects the Azovskoye More (Sea of Azov) with the Black Sea; founded in 1784; university (1973); railway; airport; economy: tourism, food canning, tobacco, manufacture of agricultural machinery and equipment for the wine-making and engineering industries, machine building.

Sími *see'mee*, island of the Sporádhes, Greece, in the SE Aegean Sea, off the SW coast of Turkey; area 58 sq km.

Simi Valley *si-mee'*, 34 16N 118 47W, pop(1980) 77,500, city in Ventura county, SW California, United States; 52 km WNW of Los Angeles; railway; economy: citrus fruit.

Sim'la, 31 07N 77 09E, hill station in Himachal Pradesh state, N India; NE of Chandigarh, to which it is linked by rail; alt 2,134 m; established in 1819 as former summer capital of British India; economy: grain, timber, handicrafts.

Sim'plon Pass, PASSA DEL SEMPIONE (Ital), mountain pass between Brig, Valais canton, Switzerland and Domodossola, Italy, over the S Berner Alpen (Bernese Alps), forming a divide between the Pennine Alps (W) and the Lepontine Alps (E); height 2,006 m; the road over the pass was constructed on Napoleon's orders between 1801 and 1805; the Simplon Tunnel, opened in 1906, is one of the longest tunnels in the world.

Simpson Desert, desert in SE Northern Territory and SW Queensland, central Australia; mostly scrubland and sand dunes; first crossed in 1939 by Dr Cecil Madigan; the part of the desert in Queensland is a national park covering 5,550 sq km, established in 1967.

Simpson's Gap, national park in S Northern Territory, central Australia; 23 km W of Alice Springs; in the MacDonnell Ranges; area 309 sq km; established in 1970.

Sinai *sī'nī*, governorate in NE Egypt; pop(1976) 10,104; area 60,174 sq km; the N coastal plain rises southwards to mountains reaching 2,637 m at Gebel Katherîna, Egypt's highest point and Gebel Musa (Mount Sinai, 2,286 m); L Bardaweel (168 sq km) is situated on the Mediterranean coast; capital El 'Arîsh; in both historical and modern times the Sinai has served as a battlefield with conflicts ranging from the routing of the Hyksos armies by Ahmos I around 1500 BC to the 1967 and 1973 wars with Israel; Sinai was taken by Israel in 1967 and returned to Egypt in 1979; tourist resorts in the S include Sharm el Sheikh, Dahab, Ras Muhammad and Nuweiba.

Sinaloa *see-na-lō'a*, coastal state in NW Mexico; on the Golfo de California and the Pacific Ocean (W); bounded N by Sonora, NE by Chihuahua, E by Durango and S by Nayarit; drained by many small rivers, including the Sinaloa, del Fuerte and the San Lorenzo; pop(1980) 1,880,098; area 58,328 sq km; capital Culiacán; economy: agriculture (rice, aubergines, sugar cane, cotton, sorghum, soya, maize, wheat, cucumber, chick-peas, fruit, dairy produce), timber, fishing, mining (gold, silver, copper, lead, iron, zinc, salt), sugar refining, cotton processing, brewing.

Sincelejo *seen-say-lay'KHō*, 9 17N 75 23W, pop(1985) 133,911, capital of Sucre dept, NW Colombia, South America; 193 km S of Cartagena; economy: cattle trade; the town is well-known for its bull-chasing, similar to the San Fermín festivities in Pamplona, Spain.

Sind, province in SE Pakistan; pop(1981) 19,029,000; area 140,914 sq km; bounded E and S by India and SW by the Arabian Sea; capital and major seaport Karachi; fertile, low lying and generally flat land dissected by the R Indus supports an agricultural economy, where the chief crops are rice, cotton, barley and oilseed; Sukkur (Lloyd) Barrage, in the N of the prov, provides irrigation water; invaded by Alexander the Great in 325 BC; part of the Chandragupta Ganges Empire; made part of the Delhi Empire by Akbar; 1842-43 conquered by Charles Napier; became N part of the Bombay presidency of British India; an autonomous prov in 1937; Aug 1947 became a prov of Pakistan; 1955 provincial status of Sind was abolished but restored in 1970.

Sindelfingen *zin'dul-fing-un*, 48 43N 9 01E, pop(1983) 55,800, town in Baden-Württemberg prov, W Germany; 14 km SW of Stuttgart; economy: motor vehicles (Daimler-Benz), electronics.

Sines *see'nish*, 37 56N 8 51W, pop(1981) 10,000, new port near old fishing town in Setúbal dist, S Portugal; 17 km W of Santiago do Cacém; an industrial park with oil refinery, now one of the largest ports and industrial complexes in Portugal; the birthplace of Vasco da Gama; railway; airfield.

Sines, Cabo de, 37 58N 8 53W, headland with lighthouse on the Atlantic coast of SW Portugal, S of Setúbal.

Singapore (Sanskrit 'Singa pura', city of the lion), official name The Republic of Singapore, republic at the S tip of the Malay Peninsula, SE Asia; consisting of the island of Singapore and about 50 adjacent islets; linked to Malaysia by a causeway carrying rail, road and water pipe across the Johore Strait; timezone GMT +8; area 618 sq km; capital Singapore City; pop(1984) 2,531,000; ethnic groups include Chinese (77%), Malay (15%) and Indian (7%); the majority of the Chinese are Buddhists, the Malays are mostly Muslim, the remainder include Christians, Hindus, Sikhs, Taoists and Confucianists; English is the official language, but Malay is the national tongue; the official currency is the Singapore dollar of 100 cents; national holiday 9 Aug; membership of ADB, ANRPC, ASEAN, Colombo Plan, Commonwealth, G-77, GATT, IAEA, IBRD, ICAO, IFC, IHO, ILO, IMF, IMO, INTELSAT, IPU, ISO, ITU, NAM, UN, UNESCO, UPU, WHO, WMO, WTO.

Physical description and climate. Singapore Island, measuring about 42 km by 22 km at its widest points, is a mainly low lying island rising at its centre to 177 m at Bukit Timah. The longest river, Sungei Seletar, flows for about 15 km to meet the Johore Strait on the NE coast. Most of the jungles and swamps have been reclaimed, mainly for urban development, but part of the central plateau is maintained as a nature reserve (Bukit Timah) and water catchment area. On the SE coast the harbour at Singapore City provides deep-water anchorage in the lee of the offshore islets of Pulau Blakang Mati and Pulau Brani. Although influenced by the surrounding seas, the climate is equatorial, with high humidity, a mean annual rainfall of 2,438 mm and a daily temperature range from 21.1°C to 34.3°C.

History, government and constitution. Originally part of the Sumatran Sri Vijaya kingdom, its potential as a trading station en route to China was realized by Sir Stamford Raffles who leased the island from the Sultan of Johor in 1819. In 1826 Singapore, Malacca and Penang were incorporated as the Straits Settlements under the East India Co. and in 1867 they became a British Crown Colony. Of strategic importance, the island was taken by the Japanese (who attacked from the landward side) in Feb 1942. Restored to British rule in 1945, Singapore obtained self-government in 1959 and became part of the Federation of Malaya from 1963 until its establishment as an independent city state in 1965. The constitution is based on that of 1959 with later amendments setting up a 21-member Presidential Council (1969) to view legislation on race and religion. There is a 75-member unicameral legislature or Parliament presided over by a prime minister and elected from single-member constituencies.

Economy. Because of its unique position on the main seaway between the Indian and the Pacific Oceans and on the air-route from Europe to Australia and because of its sheltered, almost landlocked deep-water harbour, Singapore is one of the great communications entrepôts of the world. Manufacturing industry developed in the late 19th century when in 1877 the South American rubber tree was introduced and in 1887 European tin smelting processes arrived. Major industries include petroleum refining, oil-drilling equipment, rubber, food processing, chemicals, pharmaceuticals, electronics, ship repair and financial services. Less than one-sixth of the country is under cultivation and, although the country is self-sufficient in pork, poultry and eggs, and fruit and vegetables are intensively grown, most food is imported. Major trade partners include Malaysia, the USA, Japan, Hong Kong, Thailand, Australia, Indonesia and W Germany. In 1984 the per capita income was the highest in Asia after Japan and Brunei.

Administrative divisions. Singapore I is divided into the

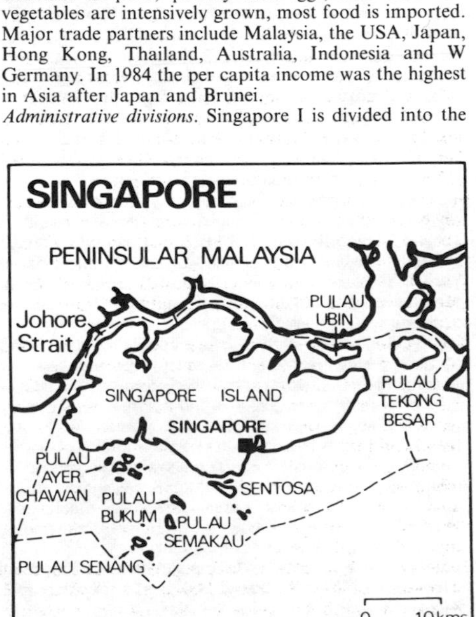

districts of Singapore City, Katong, Serangoon, Bukit Panjang and Jurong.

Singapore City, 1 20N 103 50E, seaport capital of Singapore on SE coast of Singapore I; one of the world's busiest ports, the 3rd largest oil refining centre after Houston and Rotterdam, and a production and distribution base for many international companies; in 1972 a new container port, the first in SE Asia, came into use; National University of Singapore (1964); Nanyang University (1953); Paya Lebar airport 10 km from city; railway; monuments: Tiger Balm Gardens, national museum, botanic gardens, St Andrew's Cathedral, Sultan Mosque, Monkey God temple, Poh Toh temple, Siang Lin-Si temple, House of Jade; events: Chinese New Year (Jan-Feb), birthday of Kuan Im, goddess of mercy (March), Cheng Beng (April), Buddha's birthday (June), Dragon Boat Festival (June), Festival of the Seven Sisters (Aug), Festival of the Hungry Ghosts (Aug-Sept), Market Festival (Sept), Mooncake Festival (Sept-Oct), Festival of the 9 Emperor Gods (Oct), Kusu Taoist Festival (Oct-Nov).

Singida *sin-gee'de*, region of central Tanzania, E Africa; W of Dodoma; pop(1985e) 730,000; chief town Singida.

Sining, capital of Qinghai prov, central China. See Xining.

Sinj *see'nyu*, 43 43N 16 39E, pop(1981) 59,298, town in S Hrvatska (Croatia) republic, Yugoslavia; near R Cetina, NE of Split in Dalmatia; railway; economy: bauxite and gypsum mining.

Sinkiang Uighur, autonomous region in NW China. See Xinjiang.

Sinop *si-nop'*, maritime prov in N Turkey, bounded N by the Black Sea; pop(1980) 276,242; area 5,862 sq km; capital Sinop; economy: tobacco, fruit, timber.

Sint Eustatius *sint us-tay'shus*, island of the N Netherlands Antilles, E Caribbean, c.900 km N of the S Netherlands Antilles; part of the inner volcanic arc of the Lesser Antilles; hilly in the NW; area 21 sq km; pop(1981) 1,358; capital Oranjestad (Orange Town).

Sint-Gillis-Waas *sint-KHi'lis-vahs*, SAINT-GILLES-WAAS, 50 50N 4 20E, pop(1982) 68,208, town in Sint-Niklaas dist, Oost-Vlaanderen (East Flanders) prov, Belgium.

Sint-Niklaas *sint-ni'klahs*, dist of Oost-Vlaanderen (East Flanders) prov, W Belgium; area 475 sq km; pop(1982) 210,693.

Sint-Niklaas, SAINT-NICOLAS *sĩ-neek-ō-lah'* (Fr), 51 10N 4 09E, pop(1982) 15,591, industrial town and capital of Sint-Niklaas dist, Oost-Vlaanderen (East Flanders) prov, W Belgium; between the rivers Schelde and Durme; its market square is the largest in Belgium; because of its location in relation to European trade routes, Sint-Niklaas became one of the most important industrial towns in Belgium in the 20th century; railway; economy: textiles (weaving, knitwear, carpet-making), metal, timber, tobacco processing; monuments: St Nicholas church (13th-c), town hall (neo-Gothic), 16th-c castle.

Sintra or **Cintra** *seen'tra*, 38 47N 9 25W, pop(1981) 20,000, small resort town and former summer residence of the Portuguese royal family in Lisboa dist, central Portugal; on NE slopes of Serra de Sintra (529 m), 12 km N of Estoril; railway; monuments: National Palace of Sintra; Moorish castle and Pena palace; event: São Pedro fair, an agric show at the end of June.

Sint-Truiden *sint-troy'den*, SAINT-TROND *sĩ trõ'* (Fr), 50 49N 5 11E, pop(1982) 36,591, industrial town in Hasselt dist, Limburg prov, E Belgium, 35 km NW of Liège; market town in a wide fruit-producing area; economy: sugar refining, distilleries, brewing, chemicals, metalworking, textiles, ceramics; monuments: Romanesque churches of St Peter and St Gangelof.

Sinŭiju *see-noo-ee-joo*, 40 04N 124 25E, capital of P'yŏnganpuk prov, W North Korea; on R Yalu; founded in 1910 after a bridge across the Yalu was completed; regional capital since 1923.

Siófok *shi'ō-fōk*, 16 39N 23 36E, pop(1984e) 22,000, town in Somogy county, W central Hungary; on S shore of L Balaton where R Sió leaves the lake; railway; economy: wine, grain and livestock trade.

Sioma Ngwezi *see-ō'ma ung-gway'zee*, national park in Zambia, S central Africa; area 5,276 sq km; established in 1972.

Sion *syõ*, SITT'EN (Ger), 46 14N 7 22E, pop(1980) 22,877, capital town of Valais canton, SW Switzerland; 80 km S of Bern, above the R Rhône; a bishopric since the 6th century; railway; economy: brewing and distilling; important market town for the wine, fruit and vegetables of the fertile Rhône valley; monuments: former cathedral (10-13th-c), 17th-c town hall with ancient clock; the old town is dominated by 2 castle-crowned crags, the hill of Valère, housing the battlemented church of Notre-Dame (12-13th-c), and the hill of Tourbillon, crowned by the bishop's fortress (1294); event: music festival from July to the end of Aug.

Sioux City *soo*, 42 30N 96 24W, pop(1980) 82,003, county seat of Woodbury county, W Iowa, United States; at the junction of the Big Sioux and Missouri rivers; railway; economy: shipping and trade centre in agricultural region, with grain and hog markets; manufactures fertilizer and electric tools.

Sioux Falls, 43 33N 96 44W, pop(1980) 81,343, county seat of Minnehaha county, SE South Dakota, United States; on Big Sioux river, 120 km NNW of Sioux City, Iowa; largest city in the state; railway; airfield; economy: industrial and commercial centre in a livestock farming region; meat processing; sandstone quarries.

Siracusa *seer-a-koo'zah*, prov of Sicilia region, Italy; pop(1981) 394,692; area 2,108 sq km; capital Siracusa.

Siracusa, SYRACUSE *sir'a-kyooz* (Eng), 37 04N 15 18E, pop(1981) 117,615, seaport capital of Siracusa prov, Sicilia (Sicily), Italy; 53 km SSE of Catania; it was founded in 734 BC by Corinthian settlers on the island of Ortygia, and soon spread to the adjacent mainland, becoming the chief Greek colony in Sicilia; railway; economy: petrochemicals; monuments: cathedral, built in 640 from a former temple to Minerva; Greek theatre (5th-c BC) with a semicircular auditorium hewn from the rock; Roman amphitheatre, temples, aqueducts.

Sirajganj *sir-aj'gunj*, 24 27N 89 42E, pop(1981) 106,774, river port in Sirajganj dist, Pabna, central Bangladesh; on Brahmaputra (Jamuna), NNW of Dhākā; trading centre for jute cloth; railway.

Siret *see'et*, river in E Romania and SW Ukraine; rises in the foothills of the Ukrainian Carpathians; it flows SE for 80 km into Romania and then SSE meeting the R Danube near Galaţi; length 448 km.

Síros *see'ros*, SYROS *si'ros* (Eng), island of the Kikládhes, Greece, in the S Aegean Sea; area 84 sq km.

Sirte, Gulf of *seer'tay*, KHALĪJ SURT, gulf in the Mediterranean Sea off the coast of N Libya, N Africa; situated between Misratah (W) and Banghāzī (E) on Libya's N coast; access to the Gulf waters is an area of dispute between Libya and the USA.

Sisak *see'sak*, SEGESTICA (anc), 45 30N 16 22E, pop(1981) 84,756, port town in Hrvatska (Croatia) republic, Yugoslavia; on R Sava at its junction with R Kupa, SSE of Zagreb; a major centre of communications since pre-Roman times; railway; canal from here to Podsused; economy: grain and timber trade, petroleum, gas, distilling.

Sīstān va Baluchestān *say-stan' va ba-loo-kes-tan'*, easternmost prov of Iran, bounded NE by Afghanistan, E by Pakistan, and S by the Gulf of Oman; pop(1982) 664,292; area 181,578 sq km; capital Zāhedān.

Sit'ka, national monument on W Baranof I, SE Alaska, United States; just S of the town and naval base of Sitka; preserves an Indian stockade, totem poles and a Russian blockhouse; the site was the scene of the last stand of the Tlingit Indians against the Russians in 1804; the nearby town of Sitka was founded in the same year by Baranov who named it New Archangel; the national monument was established in 1910.

Sittang *si'tang*, a major river of Burma; rises on the edge of the Shan plateau, to the NE of the town of Yamethin; flows S between the Pegu Yoma range (W) and the Shan plateau (E), then S past the town of Toungoo to enter the

Gulf of Martaban, an inlet of the Andaman Sea; length c.560 km; there is little navigation on the Sittang; in its lower course it is linked by canal with the R Pegu.

Sittingbourne *-born*, 51 21N 0 44E, pop(1981) 36,059, town in Swale dist, Kent, SE England; 13 km E of Gillingham; railway; economy: engineering, plastics.

Sittwe *sit'way*, AKYAB, 20 09N 92 55E, pop(1983) 143,215, port and capital of Arakan state, W Burma; situated on the W coast of Burma, at the mouth of the R Kaladan; airfield.

Sivas *su-vas'*, mountainous prov in N central Turkey; pop(1980) 750,144; area 28,488 sq km; capital Sivas.

Sivas, SEBASTIA (anc), 39 44N 37 01E, pop(1980) 172,864, capital town of Sivas prov, N central Turkey, on the R Kızıl Irmak; railway; airfield; economy: agricultural trade, textiles, carpets.

Siwalik Range *si-wah'lik*, CHURIA RANGE (Nepal), hill range of the S Himalayas, central Asia; stretches from SW Kashmir into Nepal; lies parallel to the main Himalayan ridge; length 1,690 km; average height 1,000-1,500 m; sometimes considered to continue into S Bhutan as far as the bend of the R Brahmaputra (Jamuna); composed of sedimentary conglomerates, clays, and sandstones of freshwater origin with many vertebrate fossil remains.

Size'well, nuclear power station in Suffolk, E England; gas-cooled, graphite-moderated reactors came into operation in 1966; site of the first UK pressurized light-water-moderated and cooled reactor.

Sjælland *she'lahn*, ZEALAND *zee'lund* (Eng), SEELAND (Ger), largest of the islands of Denmark, main island of the Sjælland group, bounded on N and NW by the Kattegat and on W by the Store Bælt (Great Belt), separated from Sweden by the Øresund (The Sound); area 7,016 sq km; length 128 km; rises to 126 m; chief towns København (Copenhagen), Roskilde, Helsingør; administered by five counties.

Sjælland, group of islands in Danish territorial waters, between Jylland (Jutland) and S Sweden; includes Sjælland, Møn, Samsø, Amager, Saltholm and other small islands; area 7,514 sq km.

Skagen *ska'yun*, 57 44N 10 37E, pop(1981) 11,743, town in Nordjylland county, NE Jylland (Jutland), Denmark, at the N extremity of Jylland, between the bays of Tannis Bugt (W) and Ålbæk Bugt (E); rail terminus; economy: foodstuffs, textiles, engineering.

Skagerrak, arm of the Atlantic Ocean, linking the North Sea with the Baltic Sea, by way of the Kattegat; bounded to the N by Norway and to the S by Denmark; main arm is the Oslo Fjord; 240 km long and 135 km wide.

Skanderborg *skah'nur-bor*, 56 02N 9 57E, pop(1981) 11,094, town in Århus county, E Jylland (Jutland), Denmark; railway; economy: engineering; the town grew up around its castle, which was frequently a royal residence during the Middle Ages.

Skaraborg *ska-ra-bor'yu*, a county of S Sweden between lakes Vättern and Vänern; land area 7,937 sq km; pop(1983) 270,537; capital Mariestad; chief towns Lidköping, Skövde and Falköping; county named from the citadel of Skara.

Skedsmo *skeds'mō*, 59 56N 10 45E, pop(1980) 32,903, town in Akershus county, SE Norway; E of Oslo; economy: motor vehicles, light engineering.

Skegness', 53 10N 0 21E, pop(1981) 16,116, resort town linked with Ingoldmells in East Lindsey dist, Lincolnshire, E central England; on the North Sea coast, 30 km NE of Boston; there is a bird reserve just S of the town; railway; economy: engineering.

Skeleton Coast, national park in NW Namibia, SW Africa; area 16,390 sq km; established in 1971; runs along Atlantic Ocean coast between Walvis Bay and the Angolan frontier.

Skellefteå *shel'ef-te-aw*, 64 45N 21 00E, pop(1982) 74,150, coastal town in Västerbotten county, N Sweden; at mouth of the R Skellefte älv; received its municipal charter in 1845; in 1912 the railway reached the town, and this, combined with the explosive expansion of the nearby Boliden mines, led to rapid development; railway; monument: 18th-c church of the Provincial Assembly.

Skel'mersdale, 53 33N 2 48W, pop(1981) 42,609, town in Wigan urban area and West Lancashire dist, Lancashire, NW England; 10 km W of Wigan; designated a 'new town' in 1961; economy: rubber, textiles, glass, engineering, electronics.

Skerries *ske'reez*, SGEIRÍ (Gael), 53 35N 6 07W, pop(1981) 5,793, resort town in Dublin county, Leinster, E Irish Republic; on Irish Sea, N of Dublin; offshore are the Skerries, a group of islands; railway; economy: fishing and tourism.

Ski, *shee*, 59 43N 10 52E, pop(1980) 19,851, town in Akershus county, SE Norway; railway.

Skíathos *skee'u-thos*, 39 10N 23 30E, island of the N Sporádhes, Greece, in the W Aegean Sea, lying only 4 km from the mainland; area 48 sq km; chief town Skíathos on the SE coast; it is now a popular holiday resort.

Skiddaw, 54 40N 3 08W, mountain in the Lake District of Cumbria, NW England; rises to 928 m E of Bassenthwaite.

Skien *shay'en*, 59 14N 9 37E, pop(1983) 46,730, ancient town and river port capital of Telemark county, SE Norway; on the R Skiensalv; in a copper and iron-mining dist; railway; economy: heavy industry.

Skierniewice *sker-nye-veet'se*, voivodship in central Poland; pop(1983) 405,000; area 3,960 sq km; capital Skierniewice; chief towns include Żyrardów, Sochaczew and Łowicz.

Skierniewice, 51 58N 20 10E, pop(1983) 35,300, capital of Skierniewice voivodship, central Poland; SW of Warszawa (Warsaw); fruit and vegetable-growing institute; railway; economy: electrical engineering; monument: 19th-c palace of Gniezno bishops.

Skikda *skeek'da*, PHILIPPEVILLE, 36 53N 6 45E, pop(1982) 134,716, seaport and chief town of Skikda dept, NE Algeria, N Africa; on Mediterranean coast, W of 'Annaba; founded by the French in 1838; railway; economy: trade in grain, wool, fruit, fish; monument: museum of Punic and Roman antiquities.

Skip'ton, 53 58N 2 01W, pop(1981) 13,185, market town in Hambleton dist, North Yorkshire, N England; 32 km NW of Bradford; railway; economy: light engineering, limestone; monument: 14th-c Holy Trinity church, burial place of the Earls of Cumberland.

Skíros *skee'ros*, 38 55N 24 34E, largest island of the N Sporádhes, Greece, in the Aegean Sea, 35 km off the E coast of Évvoia; area 209 sq km; length 36 km; max width 14 km; the coast is much indented; cultivated land is mainly restricted to the valleys in the N half of the island; it is now noted for its handicrafts, particularly hand-weaving and furniture (low chairs), with characteristic carved decoration in the Byzantine tradition.

Skive *skee'vu*, 56 34N 9 02E, pop(1981) 19,034, town in Viborg county, N central Jylland (Jutland), Denmark, on an inlet of the Limfjorden (Lim Fjord), 26 km WNW of Viborg; railway; monument: 12th-c church.

Skjeberg *shay'berk*, 59 12N 11 12E, pop(1980) 13,322, town in S of Østfold county, SE Norway, E of Fredrikstad; railway.

Skokie *skō'kee* (Algonquian, 'marsh'), 42 03N 87 45W, pop(1980) 60,278, residential town in Cook county, NE Illinois, United States; 24 km N of Chicago; railway.

Skópelos *sko'pe-los*, PEPARETHOS (anc), green and fertile island of the N Sporádhes, Greece, in the W Aegean Sea, between the islands of Skíathos and Iliodhrómia, NE of Évvoia; area 95 sq km.

Skopje or **Skoplje** *sko'pye*, ÜSKÜP (Turk), SCUPI (anc), 42 00N 21 28E, pop(1981) 506,547, industrial capital of Makedonija (Macedonia) republic, S Yugoslavia; on R Vardar, 320 km SE of Beograd (Belgrade); an earthquake in 1963 killed 1,000 people in the city; university (1949); airport; railway; economy: flour, brewing, tobacco, cement, carpets; monuments: old town and the bazaar; ethnographic museum; Daut Pasha Hammam, the largest Turkish bath-house in the Balkans (1489); Mustapha Pasha mosque; museum of contemporary art; events:

trade fair in June; international tobacco and machinery fair in Sept.

Skövde *shuv'du*, 58 24N 13 52E, pop(1982) 45,956, garrison town in Skaraborg county, S Sweden; between lakes Vänern and Vättern; associated with St Elin who is buried here, it has been a place of pilgrimage since the 12th century; railway; economy: chemicals.

Skrapar, prov of S central Albania; area 775 sq km; pop(1980) 39,800; capital Çorovodë.

Skye, island in Inverness dist, Highland region, W Scotland; 2nd largest island of the Inner Hebrides with an area of 1,665 sq km (Mull is the largest); separated from the mainland to the E by a narrow channel (Sound of Sleat); in the SW are the Cuillin Hills, a ring of peaks dominating Loch Coruisk and rising to 1,008 m at Sgurr Alasdair; in the N are Quiraing (542 m) and Storr (721 m); the coast is much indented by sea lochs (Bracadale, Dunvegan, Snizort, etc); chief towns are Portree, Broadford and Dunvegan; in the N there are ferry links from Uig to Lochmaddy (North Uist) and Tarbert (Harris); in the S there are ferry links between Armadale and Mallaig and Kyleakin and Kyle of Lochalsh; monuments: Dunvegan castle, home of the Macleods of Macleod; Kilmuir croft museum; Clan Donald centre at Ardvasar; Dunsgiath castle, a former Macdonald stronghold; Skye water mill and blackhouse, W of Dunvegan; economy: crofting, fishing, tourism.

Slagelse *slah'yul-su*, 55 24N 11 23E, pop(1981) 28,539, town in Vestsjælland county, SW Sjælland (Zealand), Denmark; an important trading town throughout the Middle Ages; it had a mint coining money as early as the 11th century; railway; economy: foodstuffs; monuments: St Michael's church (Gothic).

Slatina *sla'tee-na*, 44 26N 24 22E, pop(1983) 68,525, capital of Olt county, S Romania; near R Olt; established in the 14th century; railway; economy: grain and timber trade, aluminium.

Slavonska Požega or **Požega** *slav-on'ska po'zheg-ay*, INCERUM (anc), 45 20N 17 40E, pop(1981) 71,286, town in N Hrvatska (Croatia) republic, Yugoslavia; on R Orljava, 32 km NW of Slavonski Brod; railway; economy: wine trade, lignite.

Slavonski Brod *sla'von-skee brot*, BRÓD (Hung), MARSONIA (anc), 45 11N 18 00E, pop(1981) 106,400, river port town in N Hrvatska (Croatia) republic, Yugoslavia; on R Sava; railway; economy: wine and fruit trade, heavy equipment, fishing.

Slidell *slī-del'*, 30 17N 89 47W, pop(1980) 26,718, residential town in St Tammany parish, SE Louisiana, United States; near L Pontchartrain, 44 km NE of New Orleans; railway.

Sliema *slee'mah*, 35 55N 14 31E, pop(1983e) 20,116, residential and resort town on the N coast of the main island of Malta, across the Marsamxett Harbour from Valletta; the largest town in Malta with 3 km of sea-front, a casino, water sports facilities and a yacht repair yard; boat to the island of Comino.

Sligo *slī'gō*, SLIGEACH (Gael), county in Connacht prov, W Irish Republic; bounded N by Atlantic Ocean and watered by R Moy; Ox Mts to the W; pop(1981) 55,474; area 1,795 sq km; capital Sligo; associated with the poet Yeats.

Sligo, 54 17N 8 28W, pop(1981) 18,002, seaport capital of Sligo county, Connacht, W Irish Republic; at the head of Sligo Bay where it meets R Garrogue; technical college; Yeats international summer school and language school; railway; economy: fishing, textiles, food processing; monument: megalithic stones at nearby Carrowmore; events: Gaelic cultural activities in summer season.

Sliven *slee'ven* or **Slivno**, okrug (prov) of E central Bulgaria at the E end of the Stara Planina (Balkan Mts); area 3,618 sq km; pop(1981) 236,000.

Sliven, 42 40N 26 19E, pop(1981) 99,417, agricultural and manufacturing capital of Sliven okrug (prov), E central Bulgaria; 282 km E of Sofiya, situated on the SE slopes of the Stara Planina (Balkan Mts); railway; economy: carpets, textiles and agricultural trade.

Slivno, okrug (prov) in Bulgaria. See Sliven.

Slobozia *slo-bo'zya*, 44 34N 27 23E, pop(1983) 42,248, capital of Ialomiţa county, S Romania; on R Ialomiţa, 40 km N of Călăraşi; railway; economy: livestock trade.

Slough *slow*, 51 31N 0 36W, pop(1981) 97,389, town in Slough dist, Berkshire, S England; NE of Windsor, 30 km W of central London; railway; economy: paints, pharmaceuticals, electronics, plastics, aircraft parts, vehicle parts, foodstuffs.

Slovenija *slō-ve'nee-a*, SLOVENIA (Eng), republic in N Yugoslavia, bounded to the N by Austria, to the W by Italy, to the E by Hungary and to the S by the Yugoslav republic of Hrvatska (Croatia); pop(1981) 1,891,864; area 20,251 sq km; part of the forested Dinaric or SE Alpine foreland linked to Austria by several pass roads and dropping down towards the Adriatic karst lands; the chief rivers are the Sava and Drava; capital Ljubljana; chief towns include Maribor, Kranj and Celje; there are deposits of coal, lead and mercury; settled by Slovenians in the 6th century, but later controlled by Slavs and Franks; part of the Austro-Hungarian Empire until 1918; became a people's republic in 1946; Slovenes are the dominant ethnic group; economy: maize, wheat, sugarbeet, potatoes, livestock, timber, lignite, cotton fabrics, woollens, motor vehicles, steel.

Sloven'sko, SLOVAKIA or SLOVAK SOCIALIST REPUBLIC (Eng), republic in E Czechoslovakia; bounded N by Poland, E by the USSR, S by Hungary, SW by Austria and W by České Zemé (Czech Socialist Republic); the N half of the republic is occupied by the Tatra Mts which form the N arm of the Carpathians, rising to 2,655 m at Gerlachovsky; area 49,035 sq km; pop(1984) 5,108,817; capital Bratislava; chief towns include Košice, Banská Bystrica, Prešov; comprises the 3 administrative regions of Západoslovenský, Středoslovenský and Východoslovenský.

Słupsk *swoopsk*, voivodship in N Poland; bounded N by the Baltic Sea and watered by Słupia and Brda rivers; pop(1983) 386,000; area 7,453 sq km; capital Słupsk; chief towns include Lębork and Bytów.

Słupsk, STOLP (Ger), 54 28N 17 00E, pop(1983) 90,600, industrial capital of Słupsk voivodship, N Poland; on R Słupia; teachers' training college (1969); airfield, railway; economy: footwear, leather, furniture, ship equipment, agricultural machinery; monuments: 16th-c Renaissance castle, museum of central Pomerania; event: annual festival of Polish piano music in Sept.

Smallingerland, pop(1984e) 50,724, city in Friesland prov, N Netherlands; on a canal 19 km NE of Heerenveen.

Smederevo *sme'de-re-vo*, 44 40N 20 57E, pop(1981) 107,366, town in N Srbija (Serbia) republic, Yugoslavia; on R Danube at junction with R Morava, ESE of Beograd; railway terminus; economy: steel, petroleum refinery, machinery, wine trade, fishing; event: Danube regatta in Aug.

Smederevska Palanka or **Palanka** *sme'der-ef-ska pa'lan-ka*, 44 23N 21 00E, pop(1981) 60,945, town in central Srbija (Serbia) republic, Yugoslavia; SSE of Beograd; railway.

Smeth'wick, town in West Midlands, England. See Oldbury.

Smith's, parish in the Bermuda Islands; pop(1980) 4,463.

Smolensk *smu-lyensk'*, 54 49N 32 04E, pop(1983) 321,000, river port capital of Smolenskaya oblast, W central European Rossiyskaya, Soviet Union; on the upper Dnepr river; first mentioned in a document of 863 AD as the chief town of the large Slav tribe of Krivichi; railway; economy: linen textiles, flax-processing, clothing, nitrogenous fertilizers; monument: 12th-c cathedral of the Assumption.

Smólikas *smo'li-kus*, 40 05N 20 56E, mountain peak in the Píndhos Mts, Greece, near the Albanian frontier, 48 km NNE of Ioánnina; height 2,633 m; 2nd highest peak in Greece.

Smoljan, okrug (prov) in Bulgaria. See Smolyan.

Smolyan' or **Smoljan'**, okrug (prov) of S Bulgaria in the Sredni Rhodopi range of the Rhodopi Planina (Rhodope Mts) and on the frontier with Greece; area 3,518 sq km; pop(1981) 174,000; livestock, vegetables, tobacco and timber are important.

Smolyan, formerly PASHMAKLI (-1934), 41 34N 24 42E,

agricultural centre and capital of Smolyan okrug (prov), S Bulgaria; 258 km S of Sofiya; economy: textiles, timber and agricultural trade.

Smyrna, city in W Turkey. See İzmir.

Snake, river in NW USA; longest tributary of the Columbia river; rises in NW Wyoming; flows S then W into Idaho and crosses the S part of the state in a wide arc, passing through the Snake River Plain; turns NW and N to form part of the Oregon-Idaho and Washington-Idaho borders and flows as far as Lewiston, Idaho, where it flows into Washington and joins the Columbia river 6 km ESE of Pasco; length 1,609 km; major tributaries: the Bruneau, Boise, Owyhee, Grande Ronde, Clearwater and Palouse rivers; the Snake river contains several gorges, the largest being Snake River Canyon (or Hell's Canyon) in NW Idaho; one of the deepest gorges in the world, it is 200 km long, averages a depth of 1,676 m for approx 64 km and reaches a maximum depth of 2,408 m; it stretches N-S between the Wallowa Mts of Oregon and the Seven Devils Mts of Idaho; the Snake river is used for irrigation and hydroelectricity.

Snå'savatn, L SNASA *sno'sa* (Eng), formerly SNAASAVAND, lake in Nord-Trøndelag county, central Norway; extends 42 km SW from Snåsa village to within 11 km of Steinkjer on the Trondheimsfjord (Trondheim Fjord), into which it empties via several lesser lakes; area 118 sq km; depth 135 m.

Sneek *snayk*, 53 02N 5 40E, pop(1984e) 29,473, market town in W Friesland prov, N Netherlands; 3 km W of L Sneek, and 20 km SSW of Leeuwarden, in the middle of the Frisian lakeland; railway; a popular water sport centre, it has one of the largest yacht harbours in the country; an important market town for dairy produce; economy: tourism, foodstuffs, textiles, paper, chemicals, metalworking; monument: 17th-c town hall; event: Sneek-Week Sailing Regatta (beginning of Aug).

Śniardwy *shnyard'vi*, lake in Suwałki voivodship, NE Poland; largest lake in Poland; area 113.8 sq km; greatest depth 23.4 m.

Snoqualmie Pass *snō-kwal'mee*, winter sports area in King county, W Washington, United States; SE of Seattle.

Snowdon, 53 04N 4 05W, mountain with 5 peaks rising to 1,085 m in Gwynedd, NW Wales; the highest peak in England and Wales; at the centre of a national park.

Snowdonia, national park in Gwynedd, N Wales; area 2,188 sq km; established in 1951; an area which includes mountains, lakes, reservoirs, forests and power stations; a major walking and rock-climbing centre, with information centres at Aberdyfi, Bala, Betws-y-Coed, Blaenau Ffestiniog, Conwy, Harlech, Dolgellau, Llanberis, Llanrwst and Plas Tan-y-Bwlch (where there is also a residential study centre).

Soar *sōr*, river rising SE of Hinckley in Leicestershire, central England; flows 64 km NE and NW past Leicester to meet the R Trent S of Long Eaton.

Sochi *so'chee*, 43 35N 39 46E, pop(1983) 304,000, seaport in Krasnodarskiy kray, S European Rossiyskaya, Soviet Union; in the NW foothills of the Bol'shoy Kavkaz (Greater Caucasus) range, on the E shore of the Black Sea; established as a spa in 1910, the town stretches for more than 30 km along the shore of the Black Sea; railway; airport; monument: fortress ruins (1838).

Société, Archipel de la, SOCIETY ISLANDS (Eng), one of the 5 archipelagoes of French Polynesia, in the SE Pacific Ocean, comprising the Îles du Vent (Windward Is), which include Tahiti and Moorea, and the Îles sous le Vent (Leeward Is); area 1,535 sq km; there are 2 clusters of volcanic and coral islands in a 720 km chain stretching NW-SE; phosphates and copra are the principal exports; the islands were visited by Captain Cook in 1769 and were named by him after the Royal Society; became a French protectorate in 1844 and a French colony in 1897; capital Papeete (on Tahiti).

Södermanland *sœ'-*, county of S central Sweden, S of L Mälaren; numerous lakes include E half of L Hjälmaren; land area 6,060 sq km; pop(1983) 251,525; capital Nyköping; chief towns Eskilstuna and Katrineholm.

Södertälje *sœ'der-tel-ye*, formerly TÄLJE, 59 11N 17 39E, pop(1982) 79,794, industrial town in Stockholm county, SE Sweden; a suburb of Stockholm on the Södertälje Canal (1807-19); developed from a Viking trading station set between L Mälaren and the Baltic Sea.

Sofala *soo-fah'la*, prov in SE central Mozambique, E Africa; pop(1980) 1,065,200; area 68,018 sq km; bounded N by the R Zambezi and S by the R Save; capital Beira; chief towns include Inhaminga and Chemba; railways run W and N from Beira; Gorongosa National Park in W.

Sofiya or **Sofia** *sō-fee'a*, okrug (prov) of W Bulgaria between the Stara Planina (Balkan Mts) and the Rila Planina (Rila Mts); ski resorts at Vitosha and Borovets; the highest point is Mt Musala (2,925 m); area 7,310 sq km; pop(1981) 309,000.

Sofiya, SERDICA (Lat), 42 40N 23 18E, pop(1981) 1,070,358, capital of the People's Republic of Bulgaria; capital since 1878, situated in W Bulgaria; a modern city, well placed for communicating with the lower Danube and Struma valleys; university (1888); railway; international airport (Vrazhdebna); economy: steel, machinery and equipment, electronics, food processing, chemicals; monuments: the Mausoleum of Georgi Dimitrov; the neo-Byzantine Alexander Nevsky memorial cathedral built in the 1880s in gratitude to the Russians for liberating Bulgaria from Ottoman rule and containing the National Art Gallery branch of ancient Bulgarian art; the 4th-c St George Rotunda; the 6th-c Sofiya church and the Boyana church with its 13th-c Renaissance frescoes; events: Sofiya Musical Weeks (May-June); National Chorus Festival in May; international book fair.

Sogakofe *sō-ga-kō'fee*, 6 01N 0 35E, town in Volta region, SE Ghana, W Africa; situated between Accra and Lomé (Togo).

Sogn og Fjordane *song'en aw fyoor'a-ne*, formerly NORDRE BERGENHUS, county of SW Norway; area 18,633 sq km; pop(1983) 106,140; capital Hermansverkits; W coastline is indented by many fjords including Nordfjord (Nord Fjord) and Sognefjorden (Sogne Fjord); mountainous terrain including the Jostedalsbreen range and the peaks of Lodalskåpa (2,083 m) and Skagastølstindane (2,405 m).

Sognefjorden *song'ne-fyoor-den*, SOGNE FJORD *song'ne fyōr* (Eng), inlet of Norwegian Sea, Sogn og Fjordane county, W coast of Norway, extends E inland 204 km from Solund in W to Skjolden; largest of Norwegian fjords; average width 5 km; max depth 1,245 m.

Sohâg *sō'hag*, 26 33N 31 42E, pop(1976) 101,758, capital of Sohâg governorate, E central Egypt; on the W bank of the R Nile, 306 km NNW of Aswân.

Soignies *swa-nyee*, dist of Hainaut prov, S Belgium; area 518 sq km; pop(1982) 166,952.

Sokhondo, Gora *suk-hun'do*, 49 45N 111 10E, highest peak in the Yablonovyy Khrebet range, Chitinskaya oblast, S Siberian Rossiyskaya, Soviet Union, near the Mongolian frontier; height 2,192 m; extensive tin deposits.

Sokodé *sō-kō'day*, 8 59N 1 11E, pop(1977) 33,500, chief town of Centrale region, Togo, W Africa; 305 km N of Lomé, in the midst of Togo's forest lands; Fazao-Malfakassa National Park (area 1,920 sq km, established in 1950) lies SW of the town; railway; airfield; economy: cotton, groundnuts, livestock; events: all Muslim holidays are celebrated here including Adossa or 'Festival of Knives'.

Sokolov *sok'ol-of*, formerly FALKNOV (-1948), 50 10N 12 30E, pop(1984) 28,894, town in Západočeský region, Czech Socialist Republic, W Czechoslovakia; on R Ohre, SW of Karlovy Vary; railway; economy: chemicals.

Sokoto *sō-kō'tō*, state in NW Nigeria, W Africa; pop(1982e) 7,237,800; area 102,535 sq km; the R Niger flows across the SW corner of the state where it is joined by the R Kebbi; capital Sokoto; chief towns Gusau, Birnin Kebbi, Wurno, Kaura Namoda and Goronya; once part of the Fulah empire; inhabited by Hausa and developed between the 12th and 18th centuries under Arab and Berber influences; formerly comprising numerous small kingdoms under Muslim rulers who were suppressed in the early 19th century by Fulah tribes, the latter forming the new sultanate of Sokoto; a treaty with the British was signed in 1885 and British control was secured in 1903; the main ethnic groups are the Hausa, Fulani, Dakarkari, Dambara and Zabarima; essentially an agricultural state with over 80% of the pop involved in subsistence farming, cattle raising and the production of cotton, groundnuts, tobacco, rice; local industries are based on chemicals, leather, wood and cement.

Sokoto, 13 02N 5 15E, pop(1981e) 143,000, capital of Sokoto state, NW Nigeria, W Africa; 322 km WNW of Kano; founded in 1809; university (1975); airfield; economy: cement, wood and leather.

So'la, 58 53N 5 36E, pop(1980) 12,657, town on W coast of Rogaland county, SW Norway, just SW of Stavanger.

Solāpur *sō-lah'poor*, SHOLAPUR, 17 43N 75 56E, pop(1981) 514,000, city in Maharashtra state, W India; on the Deccan plateau, 360 km SE of Bombay; a former fortress town ruled by the Bijapur kings in the 16th century; linked by rail to Pune and Gulbarga; economy: textiles, trade in oilseed and tobacco.

Sole, West, natural gas field in the North Sea off the coast of Humberside, England.

Solent, The *sō'lent*, channel separating the Isle of Wight from mainland England.

Soleure, canton in Switzerland. See Solothurn.

Sol'ihull, 52 25N 1 45W, pop(1981) 94,613, town in West Midlands, central England; a suburb of SE Birmingham; National Exhibition Centre; airport; railway; economy: vehicles, packaging, machinery.

Solingen *zō'ling-en*, 51 10N 7 05E, pop(1983) 161,100, industrial city in Detmold dist, Nordrhein-Westfalen (North Rhine-Westphalia) prov, W Germany; in the Ruhr valley, 22 km ESE of Düsseldorf; economy: chemicals and petrochemicals, hardware.

Sollentuna *soo-lun-tu'na*, 59 26N 17 56E, pop(1982) 46,629, town in Stockholm county, SE Sweden, a NW suburb of Stockholm.

Solna *sōl-na'*, 59 22N 17 51E, pop(1982) 49,618, town in Stockholm county, SE Sweden; a N suburb of Stockholm; railway; economy: engineering, electrical equipment, film industry.

Sologne *so-lon'y'*, a pays of the Paris basin, N central France, between the Loire and Cher and the Gien and Vierzon rivers; dry and sandy in the SE, more fertile in the NW.

Sololá *sō-lō-la'*, mountainous dept in Guatemala, Central America; pop(1982e) 173,401; area 1,061 sq km; capital Sololá; chief town Santiago Atitlán; its E boundary is the Río Coyolate; much of the dept is occupied by the Lago de Atitlán.

Sololá, 14 46N 91 09W, capital town of Sololá dept, SW central Guatemala, Central America; near N shore of Lago de Atitlán; alt 2,113 m; monument: 16th-c church (rebuilt after 1902 earthquake); event: fiesta on 15 Aug.

Solomon Islands, archipelago of several hundred islands stretching some 1,400 km between Bougainville (Papua New Guinea) in the NW and Vanuatu in the SE, 1,796 km NE of Australia, SW Pacific Ocean; timezone GMT +11; land area 27,556 sq km; capital Honiara; main towns Gizu, Auki, and Kirakira; pop(1982) 244,000; the population comprises Melanesians (93.4%), Polynesians (4%), Micronesians (1.4%), Europeans (0.7%), Chinese (0.2%), and others (0.3%); the annual population growth rate is 3.4%; most people live in small, widely dispersed settlements along the coasts; overall population density is less than 9 persons per sq km; 95% of the population are Christians; English is the official language; pidgin English is widely spoken in the towns and coastal areas; the currency is the Solomon Island dollar of 100 cents; membership of Commonwealth, South Pacific Commission, South Pacific Forum, ACP/EEC, ADB, G-77, GATT, IBRD, IDA, IFAD, IFC, IMF, UN, UPU.

Physical description. The Solomon Is comprise the 6 main islands of Choiseul, Guadalcanal, Malaita, New Georgia, San Cristobal and Santa Isabel, plus a number of smaller uninhabited islands, coral reefs and lagoons. The large islands have rainforest-clad mountain ranges of mainly volcanic origin, deep narrow valleys, and coastal belts lined with coconut palms and ringed by reefs. The highest mountain is Mt Makarakomburu (2,477 m) on Guadalcanal, the largest island. Most of the smaller islands are coral atolls in various stages of development.

Climate. The climate is equatorial with few extremes around a mean temperature of 27°C. Humidity ranges from 60% to 90%. The NW trade winds from Nov to April bring more frequent rainfall and occasional squalls or cyclones on the windward side of the main islands. Minimum temperatures are recorded when the SE trades blow from April to Nov. Average rainfall is c.3,500 mm per annum.

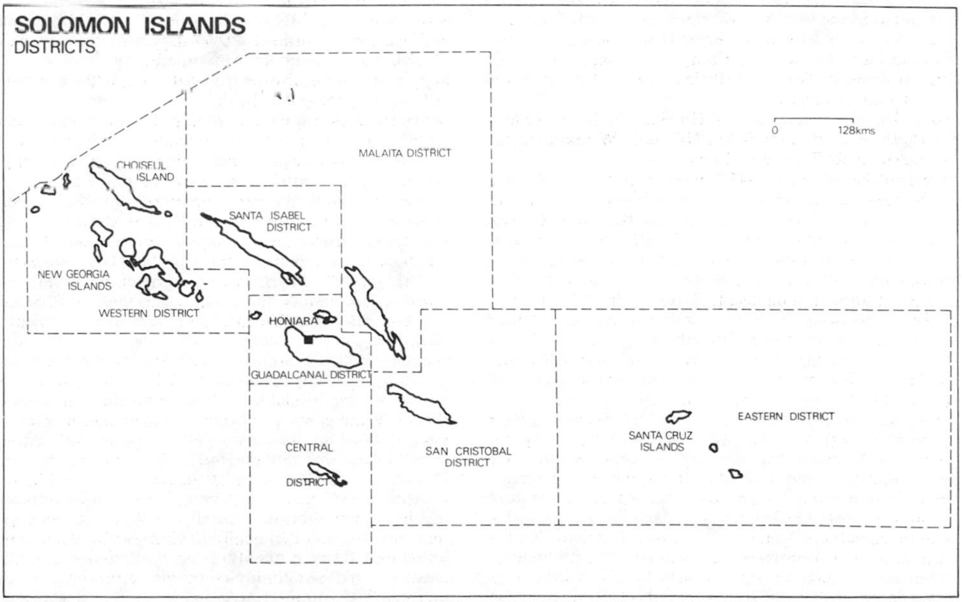

History, government and constitution. The S Solomon Is were placed under British protection in 1893, and in 1898 and 1899 the outer islands of the group were added to the protectorate. In September 1977 a constitutional conference was held in London, and on 7 July 1978 the Solomon Is became an independent state. The country's system of government is a parliamentary democracy with a unicameral legislature. The British monarch, represented locally by a governor-general, is head of state. Legislative power is vested in the national parliament, composed of 38 members elected by universal suffrage for 4 years. The prime minister is elected by members of parliament.

Economy. Agriculture, including forestry, livestock, and fisheries, is the mainstay of the economy. 90% of the population relies on subsistence agriculture, the main crops being taro, rice, bananas, and yams. Copra, the main cash crop, has for long been the traditional export from coastal areas, but this is now being supplemented by produce from large oil palm and rice plantations, particularly on the coastal plains of Guadalcanal. Export earnings from palm oil represented over 12% of export revenue in 1982. Forests cover approximately 24,000 sq km of the Solomon Is and timber is the 2nd largest export earner. The fishing industry has developed rapidly in recent years, accounting for 25% of export revenue in 1982. Japanese fishing companies have established plants at Tulagi and Noro. Manufacturing industries include palm oil milling, fish smoking, canning and freezing, saw milling, copra and cocoa drying, and handicrafts. Major exports are timber, fish, copra, and palm oil, the main markets in 1982 being Japan (59%), UK (14%), Netherlands (15%), and US (1%). Major imports are machinery and transport equipment (23%), manufactured goods (16%), and mineral fuels and lubricants (25%), supplied mainly from Australia, Singapore, and Japan.

Administrative divisions. The Solomon Is are divided into 8 administrative areas of which 7 are provinces administered locally by elected provincial assemblies (Western, Guadalcanal, Central Is, Malaita (Mala), Santa Isabel (Boghotu), Eastern Is, San Cristobal (Makira)). The 8th area is the town of Honiara administered by the Honiara town council.

Solomon Sea, SW arm of the Pacific Ocean and N part of the Coral Sea; bounded by the coast and islands of Papua New Guinea to the N, W and S and the Solomon Islands to the E; main islands: Trobriand Islands, D'Entrecasteaux and Woodlark; a depth of 9,144 m is reached in the New Britain Trench.

Solothurn *zō'lo-toorn*, SOLEURE *so-lœr'* (Fr), canton in N Switzerland; pop(1980) 218,102; area 791 sq km; capital Solothurn; joined the Swiss Confederacy in 1481.

Solothurn, 47 13N 7 32E, pop(1980) 15,778, capital town of Solothurn canton, N Switzerland; on R Aare, at the foot of the Jura Mts, 30 km N of Bern; an ancient Roman settlement which became a free Imperial city in 1218; railway junction; monument: cathedral of St Ursen (1763-73); events: Film Festival (Jan), Fasnacht (carnival, Shrovetide).

Sol'way Firth, inlet of the Irish Sea, separating Cumbria, England, from Dumfries and Galloway, Scotland; it is the estuary of the Esk and Eden rivers; length c.65 km; width at its mouth c.40 km; noted for its salmon fisheries.

Solwezi *sōl-we'zee*, 12 11S 26 23E, capital of North-West prov, Zambia, S central Africa; 160 km NNE of Kasampa.

Somalia *sō-mah'li-a*, official name Somali Democratic Republic, JAMHURIYADDA DIMUGRADIGA SOMALIYA (Arab), a NE African republic bounded NW by Djibouti, W by Ethiopia, SW by Kenya, E by the Indian Ocean and N by the Gulf of Aden; timezone GMT +3; area 686,803 sq km; pop(1984e) 6,393,000; capital Muqdisho (Mogadishu); chief towns Hargeysa, Berbera, Burco, Laascaanood, Ceerigabo, Gaalkacyo, Hobyo, Luuq, Baardhheere, Ceeldheer, Baydhabo, Jawhar and Kismaayo; there are ports at Muqdisho, Kismaayo and Berbera; 85% of the pop are of Somali origin, the rest are mainly Bantu, with Asian and European minorities; 70% of the pop are nomads; the pop is mostly Sunni Muslim; the official language is Somali, but Arabic, Italian and Swahili are also spoken; the unit of currency is the Somali shilling; national holiday 21 Oct; membership of AfDB, Arab League, EAMA, FAO, G-77, IBRD, ICAO, IDA, Islamic Development Bank, IFAD, IFC, ILO, IMF, IMO, INTELSAT, INTERPOL, ITU, NAM, OAU, OIC, UN, UNESCO, UPU, WFTU, WHO and WMO.

Physical description. Somalia occupies the E Horn of Africa where a dry coastal plain broadens to the S and rises inland to a plateau which is nearly 1,000 m in elevation. The highest peaks in the country are the forested mountains situated on the Gulf of Aden coast which rise to 2,416 m at Shimbiris, W of Ceerigabo. There are only 2 rivers of any size in Somalia, the Jubba, which enters Somalia from Ethiopia at Dolo Odo and flows S past Luuq and Baardheere before entering the Indian Ocean close to Kismaayo; and the Webi Shabeelle which also originates in Ethiopia and crosses into Somalia NW of Beledweyne, flowing S past Buulobarde and Jawhar and then SW past Qoryooley before joining the Jubba approx 80 km NNE of Kismaayo.

Climate. With a long coastline from N to S there is considerable variation in climate in Somalia. Berbera is representative of the N coast with an annual average rainfall of 61 mm and average max daily temperatures ranging betweeen 29°C and 42°C. The highest temperatures occur during April-Sept. On the E coast where rain falls during April-Sept, temperatures are moderated by a cool offshore current. Muqdisho is representative of the E coast with an annual average rainfall of 490 mm, and average daily max temperatures ranging between 28°C and 32°C. Rainfall anywhere in the country is extremely variable and the threat of drought is both serious and persistent. In 1974 drought was responsible for the death of over 1 mn animals.

History, government and constitution. Italian, French and British interest in Somalia dates from the opening of the Suez Canal in 1869. The colonial process was hampered by the resistance efforts of Sayyid Muhammad Abdille Hassan, otherwise known to the British as the 'Mad Mullah'. After World War II the Italian and British protectorates were amalgamated to form Somalia. Independence was achieved in 1960 but progress was severely hindered by territorial conflict with Ethiopia between 1964 and 1967. After a coup in 1969 the National Assembly was dissolved and the constitution suspended. Somalia is governed by a president who is nominated from the country's sole political party, an executive council of 28 ministers and a legislative People's Assembly of 121 elected members and 6 appointed deputies.

Economy. The Somalis are a largely nomadic people raising cattle, sheep and goats. Because of the dry climate it is only close to the Jubba and Webi Shabeelle rivers that significant cultivation occurs, with the main crops including bananas, sugar, spices, cotton, rice, citrus fruits, maize, sorghum, oilseeds and tobacco. The major export crop is bananas which are grown on plantations. Sugar cane is a major nationalized crop and is refined at a plant at Johar. Small industries include the manufacture of textiles and cigarettes and food processing. The main trading partners include Italy, the USSR, China, Kenya, Kuwait and Saudi Arabia.

Administrative divisions. Somalia is divided into the 16 regions of Woqooyi Galbeed, Togdheer, Sanaag, Bari, Nugaal, Mudug, Galguduud, Hiraan, Bakool, Shabeellaha Dhexe, Shabeellaha Hoose, Bay, Gedo, Jubbada Dhexe, Jubbada Hoose and Banaadir.

Som'bor, 45 46N 19 09E, pop(1981) 99,168, city in autonomous province of Vojvodina, NW Srbija (Serbia) republic, Yugoslavia; on Tisza-Danube canal, SW of Subotica; railway; economy: grain, dairy and wine trade.

Somerset *sum'er-set*, county of SW England; bounded N by Bristol Channel and Avon, E by Wiltshire, S by

Dorset and W by Devon; uplands in the W include Exmoor and the Brendon and Quantock hills; the Mendip Hills lie near the border with Avon; pop(1981) 427,114; area 3,451 sq km; county town Taunton; chief towns include Bridgewater and Yeovil; economy: agriculture, tourism, engineering, beverages, footwear; the county is divided into 5 districts:

District	*area (sq km)*	*pop(1981)*
Mendip	739	87,030
Sedgemoor	567	89,666
Taunton Deane	458	86,431
West Somerset	727	32,423
Yeovil	959	131,419

Som'erset Island, island at the W end of the Bermuda Islands group, lying between Boaz I to the N and the Main Island of Bermuda to the S.

Somerville, 42 23N 71 06W, pop(1980) 77,372, town in Middlesex county, E Massachusetts, United States; 5 km NW of Boston; railway.

Someş *so'mesh*, river in N Romania and E Hungary; formed at Dej by the meeting of the Great and Little Someş rivers, it flows NW to meet the R Tisza in Hungary; length 400 km.

Somme *som*, dept in Picardie region of N France, on the English Channel; comprises 4 arrond, 44 cantons and 783 communes; pop(1982) 544,570; area 6,175 sq km; crossed SE-NW by the Somme R; bounded on the SW by the R Bresle and on the NW by the R Authie; capital Amiens, chief town Abbeville; there is an 18th-c château at Long.

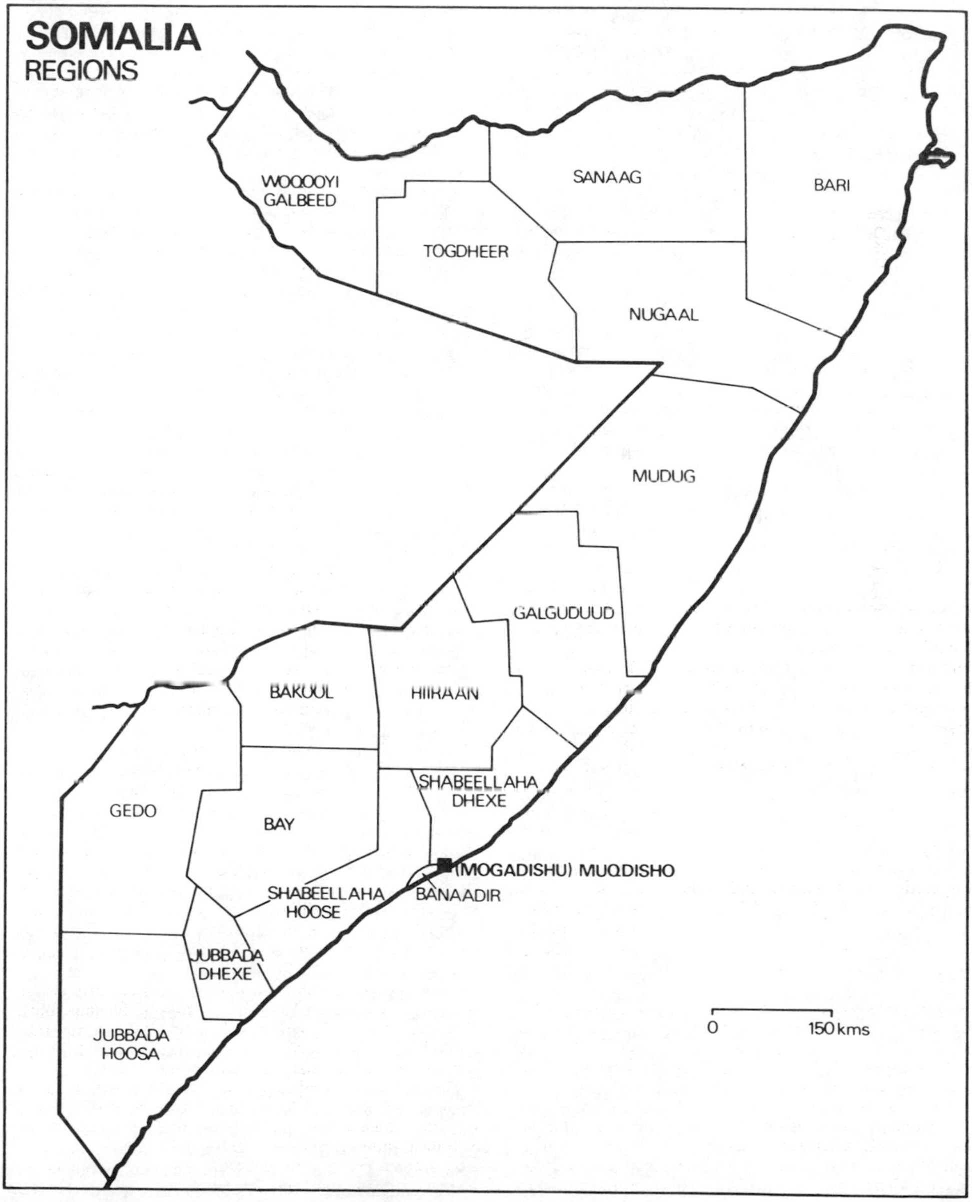

Somme, river in N France rising in Aisne dept near St-Quentin; flows SW then NW and W through Somme dept, past Amiens and Abbeville, to the English Channel near Saint-Valéry-sur-Somme; length 245 km; linked by canals to the waterways of the industrial N; on its banks took place some of the bitterest fighting of World War I; tributaries include the Ancre and Avre rivers.

Somogy *sho'mody'*, county in SW Hungary; bounded by L Balaton to the N and Yugoslavia to the S; watered by the Kapos, Fekete and Rinya rivers; pop(1984e) 357,000; area 6,035 sq km; capital Kaposvár; main industrial centres at Kaposvár and Barcs; the county is noted for its embroidery; agricultural economy: grain, vegetables, livestock, fruit.

Somoto *sō-mō'tō*, 13 29N 86 36W, capital town of Madriz dept, NW Nicaragua, Central America; on a tributary of the Río Coco; on the Inter-American Highway; airfield; economy: centre of the pitch-pine industry.

Somp'ting, 50 50N 0 21W, pop(1981) 25,870 (with Lancing), town in Adur dist, West Sussex, S England; part of Brighton-Worthing-Littlehampton urban area; 3 km E of Worthing; railway; monument: St Mary's church, associated with the Knights Templar.

Sønderborg *sœn'er-bork*, 54 55N 9 48E, pop(1981) 26,885, commercial town and holiday resort in Sønderjylland county, SW Als I, off the SE coast of Jylland (Jutland), Denmark; railway; economy: furniture, electrics; monument: 13th-c citadel, now a museum.

Sønderjylland *sœn-er-yoo'lan*, a county of S Jylland (Jutland), Denmark; area 3,930 sq km; pop(1983) 249,970; separated from Fyn I on E by the Lille Bælt (Little Belt); capital Åbenrå, chief towns include Haderslev, Sønderborg and Tønder.

Søndre Strømfjord *sœn'ru strum'fyōd*, 67 05N 50 30W, settlement on W coast of Greenland; on an inlet of the Davis Strait; airport.

Son'drio, prov of Lombardia region, N Italy; pop(1981) 174,009; area 3,212 sq km; capital Sondrio.

Sondrio, 46 11N 9 52E, pop(1981) 22,747, capital town of Sondrio prov, Lombardia region, N Italy, on the R Adda; 32 km E of Lago di Como; railway.

Songkhla *song-klah*, 7 12N 100 35E, pop(1982) 77,916, seaport and fishing port in S Thailand; on the Gulf of Thailand, E of Ban Hat Yai; university (1964); railway; airfield.

Sonora *so-no'ra*, state in NW Mexico; on the Golfo de California (W); bounded by Arizona, USA (N), Baja California Norte (NW), Sinaloa (S) and Chihuahua (E); rises from the coast to the Sierra Madre Occidental (N and E); in the NW is the Desierto de Altar; drained by the Sonora, Yaquí, Moctezuma, Mayo and Río de la Concepción rivers which are widely used for irrigation; pop(1980) 1,498,931; area 182,052 sq km; capital Hermosillo; economy: wheat, cotton, soya, maize, linseed, alfalfa, chick-peas, fruit, cattle, horses, pigs, fishing, mining (copper, gold, silver, iron, graphite, molybdenum, tungsten, manganese), vegetable oils, dairy products, meat packing, animal foods, cotton processing, fertilizers, food canning.

Sonsonate *sōn-sōn-a'tay*, maritime dept in W El Salvador, Central America; bounded S by the Pacific Ocean; pop(1971) 239,688; area 1,133 sq km; capital Sonsonate; chief towns Acajutla (port) and Nahuizalco.

Sonsonate, 13 43N 89 44W, pop(1980) 67,229, commercial town and capital of Sonsonate dept, SW El Salvador, Central America; on Río Grande de Sonsonate; founded in 1552; railway; economy: produces sugar, tobacco, rice, tropical fruits, hides, and balsam; situated in the chief cattle-raising region of the country; monument: cathedral.

Sopot *so-pot'*, ZOPPOT (Ger), 54 27N 18 01E, pop(1983) 51,500, resort town in Gdańsk voivodship, N Poland; between wooded slopes and the Bay of Gdańsk, 10 km NW of Gdańsk; with Gdańsk and Gdynia part of the *Tri-City*; hydrotherapy treatment centre; open-air opera; racecourse; railway; event: international song festival.

Sopron *shop-ron'*, ODENBURG (Ger), 47 45N 16 32E, pop(1984e) 55,000, town in Györ-Sopron county, NW Hungary; on the frontier with Austria; awarded the Europa Prize in 1975 for the conservation of its ancient monuments and buildings; university of forestry and timber industry (1808); economy: textiles, fruit, sugar; monument: Fire Tower in the Baroque main square.

Soria *so'rya*, prov in Castilla-León region of N Spain; a dry infertile area traversed by the upper course of the R Douro (Duero); pop(1981) 98,803; area 10,287 sq km; capital Soria; economy: timber and wood products, plastics, tools, meat processing, foodstuffs.

Soria, 41 43N 2 32W, pop(1981) 32,039, capital of Soria prov, Castilla-León, N central Spain; on R Douro (Duero), 231 km NE of Madrid; alt 1,063 m; railway; described by the poet Antonio Machado (1875-1939) as 'Soria pura, cabeza de Extremadura'; economy: plastics, clothes, tiles, soap, food processing, timber; monuments: former Palace of the Counts of Gomara, churches of San Juan de Duero, Santo Domingo and San Juan de Rabanera, museum of relics from nearby Numantia; event: fiesta of St John in June.

Soriano *so-rya'nō*, dept in SW Uruguay; bordered N by the Río Negro, E by the Arroyo Grande (E), S by the Cuchilla San Salvador range, W by Argentina along the Río Uruguay; drained by the Río San Salvador and the Arroyo Grande; part of the Palmar Dam is in the NE; pop(1985) 79,042; area 9,223 sq km; capital Mercedes; on the Río Uruguay (E) is La Agraciada beach, where the 'Thirty-Three' patriots landed on 19 April 1825, an act which led to Uruguay's independence; the beach has a statue of General Lavalleja, leader of the group; a festival every year celebrates this event.

Soroa *sō-rō'a*, resort area 81 km SW of La Habana (Havana), Cuba; in the Sierra del Rosario; originally noted as a coffee-growing area by the Spanish, but after 1928 the area developed as a resort around sulphur springs; noted for its orchid house.

Sorocaba *so-rō-ka'ba*, 23 30S 47 32W, pop(1980) 254,672, town in São Paulo state, Sudeste region, SE Brazil; W of São Paulo; railway; economy: sugar, cereals, coffee, alcohol, wines, minerals, cotton, textiles, railway workshops; the town has extensive orange groves and packing house installations.

Soroti *sō-rō'tee*, 1 42N 33 37E, town in Eastern prov, Uganda, E Africa; between L Kyogo and L Bisina, 100 km NW of Mbale; airfield.

Sorøy *sor'u-ü*, Norwegian island in the Norwegian Sea off NW coast of Norway, 17 km W of Hammerfest, rises to 651 m; area 816 sq km; length 64 km; width 5-29 km; administered by Finnmark county.

Sorraia *so-rah'ya*, river in central Portugal, formed by junction of the Sor and Raia E of Coruche, flows W across Santarém dist, entering the Tagus near Benavente; length 56 km.

Sør-Trøndelag *sœr-trœn'e-laKH*, formerly SONDRE TRONDHJEM, county of central Norway, including the lower section of Trondheimsfjord (Trondheim Fjord); area 18,831 sq km; pop(1983) 246,206; capital Trondheim; drained chiefly by the Orka and Gaula rivers; mountainous terrain particularly in the S and E with peaks Storvigelen (1,561 m) and Knutsho (1,690 m).

Sosnowiec *sos-nov'yetz*, SOSNOVETS (Rus), 50 16N 19 07E, pop(1983) 252,000, city in Katowice voivodship, S Poland; E of Katowice; largest town in the Dąrowa coal basin in Upper Silesia; sports centre; railway; economy: coal mining, iron, glass, machinery.

Sotavento *so-ta-ven'to*, group of leeward islands and a district, Cape Verde, comprising the islands of Maio, São Tiago, Fogo and Brava; area 1,803 sq km; pop(1980) 188,125, the district of Sotavento is divided into 7 local government *concelhos* (councils).

Soufrière or **Grande Soufrière** *grãd soo-fri-er'*, 16 03N 61 40W, volcano on Basse-Terre I, French Overseas Department of Guadeloupe, rising to 1,484 m at the S end of the island.

Soufrière, 13 21N 61 11W, volcano and highest peak on St Vincent, Windward Is, E Caribbean; height 1,234 m;

violent eruptions occurred in 1821, 1902-03, and most recently in 1979; the W slope is rugged and deeply dissected, while the E slope is gentler and undulating; the 1979 eruption destroyed large areas of banana plantation.

Sŏul *sōl*, SEOUL *se-ool*, 37 30N 127 00E, pop(1984) 9,501,413, special city and capital of Korea; situated in the Han river valley, NW Korea; area 627 sq km; founded in the late 14th century, the town of Sŏul was called Hanyang until the 20th century and was the seat of the Yi dynasty government from 1392 to 1910; 17 universities; railway; airport (Kimpo); economy: engineering, textiles, tanning, food processing; monuments: Kyŏngbok-kung palace, built in the 1390s by Sŏul's founder, King T'aejo, burned during the Japanese invasion of 1592 and rebuilt in 1867 when the regent Taewŏngun had it restored for his son Kojong who became the 26th ruler of the Yi dynasty; many of Korea's monuments and stone pagodas were moved to the grounds of Kyŏngbok-kung palace during the Japanese period of rule (1910-45): one of these is a 10-storied pagoda from the Koryŏ period; Korea's National Museum and National Folk Museum are also situated within the grounds of Kyŏngbok-kung palace; Ch'angdŏ-kung palace, built in 1405, was also burnt down in 1592 but was rebuilt in 1611 and served as royal residence until the reconstruction of Kyŏngbok-kung; the remaining members of the Yi dynasty royal family live in the Naksŏnjae section of the palace; the entrance gate to the Ch'angdŏk-kung palace, the Tonhwa-mun, is possibly the oldest original gate in Sŏul; part of the palace grounds are given over to the Piwŏn, or Secret Gardens, with numerous ponds, bridges, streams and 44 pleasure pavilions; Tŏksu-kung palace, originally a royal villa, was used as King Koyong's official residence before his abdication in 1907; several buildings in the palace grounds were built by a British architect at the turn of the century and now serve as the Museum of Modern Art; in a garden SE of Ch'angdŏk-kung palace is Chongmyo, where the ancestral tablets of Yi dynasty kings and queens are kept, the 2 courtyards and shrine buildings which contain the tablets are only open to the public on annual ceremonial days; a 16-km long wall with 8 gates was originally built around Sŏul, 5 of these gates remain and have been reconstructed; the most famous is Namdaemun (the Great South Gate) situated near Sŏul railway station; originally built in 1398, the present gate is a reconstruction of 1448; Tongdaemun (the Great East Gate) was built in 1869 as a replica of the gate already there, which had fallen beyond repair; the bell which was rung to announce the opening and closing of the city gates at sunrise and sunset is now housed in the Poshingak pavilion in the centre of Sŏul, it was cast in 1468, is approx 4 m high, and is now rung to mark the New Year; Pagoda Park, famous for its 10-storied stone pagoda, was the site of the reading of the Korean Declaration of Independence on 1 March 1919, an event which initiated a series of demonstrations against Japanese colonial rule; the zoological and botanical gardens in Sŏul Grand Park were opened in 1984-85 and with Sŏul Land (the Korean version of Disneyland), comprise the country's largest leisure park; the Chogyesa temple serves as the headquarters for over 1,500 affiliated temples throughout Korea, it is the site of the annual lantern parade held on Buddha's birthday in May; near Sŏul are 2 ancient mountain fortresses; events: first Sunday in May, annual ceremonial day; 6 June (memorial day services at the national cemetery).

Soûr *soor*, TYRE ('rampart'), 33 12N 35 11E, pop(1980e) 14,000, Mediterranean fishing port in Soûr division (*caza*), Al Janūb, SW Lebanon; the ancient city was originally built on several islands which King Hiram later joined together and which Alexander the Great connected to the mainland by a causeway; it became the most important commercial centre in the E Mediterranean for land and seaborne trade; noted for its silken garments, fine glass, and Tyrean purple, the dye from the murex sea-mussel; the introduction of the alphabet into Greece was attributed to Cadmus of Soûr; railway; monuments: excavations since 1947 have uncovered remains of Crusader, Arab, Byzantine, and Graeco-Roman cities; Roman remains include a monumental archway, aqueduct, large civic buildings, baths, a theatre, and one of the largest hippodromes of the Roman period.

Sources, Mont aux *soors*, 28 46S 28 54E, mountain in the Drakensberg Mts, Lesotho; on the N frontier with Natal prov, South Africa; rises to 3,298 m.

Sousse *soos*, 35 50N 10 38E, pop(1984) 83,509, port and capital of Sousse governorate, NE Tunisia, N Africa; 115 km SSE of Tunis; founded in the 9th century BC by the Phoenicians; came under Roman domination, but was destroyed in 434 AD by the Vandals; Port El Kantaoui marina is situated at Cape Rass Marsa, 6 km from Sousse; railway; economy: tourism, crafts (including copperwork, olive wood carving, leatherwork), clothing, ceramics, carpets; monuments: mosques include the Mosque Zakak, the Great Mosque (built in 850 AD), and the Hanafite Mosque; Ribat fortress (9th-c); events: festival of music and popular arts in April-May; Aoussou Festival in July-Aug.

South Africa, official name Republic of South Africa, REPUBLIEK VAN SUID-AFRIKA (Afrik), a South African republic bounded NW by Namibia, N by Botswana, NE by Zimbabwe, Mozambique and Swaziland, E and SE by the Indian Ocean and SW and W by the S Atlantic Ocean; Lesotho is landlocked within South Africa's borders; includes the independent homelands of Bophuthatswana, Ciskei, Transkei and Venda whose independent status is not recognized internationally; timezone GMT +2; area 1,233,404 sq km; pop(1984e) 31,698,000; administrative capital Pretoria; judicial capital Bloemfontein; legislative capital Cape Town; largest city Johannesburg; 70% of the pop is black African, 18% is white, 3% is Asian, and 9% is coloured; most whites and coloureds and about 60% of Africans are Christian; about 60% of Asians are Hindu and about 20% are Muslims; the official languages are English with Afrikaans but many African languages including Zulu, Xhosa, N and S Sotho, Swazi, Tsonga, Venda and Tswana are spoken; the unit of currency is the rand of 100 cents; national holiday 31 May (Republic Day); membership of GATT, IBRD, IDA, IFC, IHO, ILZSG, IMF, INTELSAT, ISO, International Whaling Commission, International Wheat Commission, WFTU.

Physical description. South Africa occupies the S extremity of the African plateau which is fringed by fold mountains and a lowland coastal margin to the W, E and S. The N interior of the plateau comprises the Kalahari Basin. At an altitude of 650-1,250 m above sea-level this area of scrub grassland and arid desert stretches N into

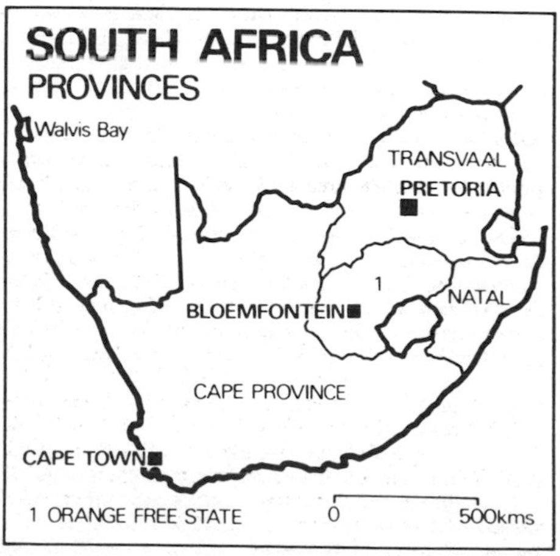

Botswana. The peripheral highlands rise to elevations over 1,200 m in the high veld of Orange Free State, NE Cape prov, and Transvaal. The Great Escarpment that fringes the interior plateau rises in the E to 3,482 m at Thabana Ntlenyana, the highest peak of the Drakensberg Mts which occupy S Transvaal, Natal, and Lesotho. In the S the Great Escarpment comprises a series of short ranges including the Roggeveldberge, Nuweveldberge and Sneeuberge which drop down to the Great Karoo NW of Port Elizabeth. The marginal coastlands vary in width from 80-240 km in the E and S to 60-80 km in the W where the land rises gently through the Namaqualand hills. South Africa's main river is the Orange river which flows W through Orange Free State to meet the Atlantic. Its chief tributaries are the Vaal and Caledon rivers. There are no lakes of any great size, although there are a number of lagoons and shallow 'pans', the largest of which is the Groot Vloers in NW Cape prov.

Climate. The climate of South Africa is influenced by 2 contrary currents, the warm Mozambique-Agulhas current originating in the equatorial region of the Indian Ocean, and the cool Benguela current from the Antarctic. In the E, along the coast of Natal, the warm Mozambique current is responsible for the subtropical climate and lush vegetation with water temperatures of about 24°C during May-Aug and 28°C during Oct-Feb. At Durban average monthly rainfall varies from 28 mm in July to 130 mm in March, with an annual average of 1,101 mm. As it moves S along the coast towards the Cape peninsula the Mozambique current becomes cooler. The Benguela current reaches the S tip of Africa from polar waters with a temperature of about 10°C. There it meets the Mozambique current and is deflected N along the W coast of Cape prov giving rise to a dry moistureless climate. At Cape Town average monthly rainfall varies from 8 mm in Feb to 89 mm in July, with an annual average of 510 mm and daily temperatures that range from an average min of 7°C in July to an average max of 26°C in Jan-Feb. The West Coast desert region further N has an annual average rainfall of less than 30 mm. On a few occasions each month (particularly in winter) the temperature can be raised by the *berg* wind which blows from the interior. The desert or scrub grassland of the W interior is characterized by low rainfall, while the E interior around Johannesburg has a more amenable climate with an annual average rainfall of 710 mm and temperatures ranging from an average min of 4°C in June-July to an average max of 26°C in Dec-Jan.

History, government and constitution. Although the first Europeans to reach the Cape of Good Hope were Portuguese navigators in the late 15th century, South Africa was not settled by Europeans until the arrival of the Dutch in 1652 and Huguenots in 1688. The arrival of the British after 1795 resulted in the annexation of the Cape to Britain in 1814, the settlement of English colonists in the 1820s and the Great Trek NE across the Orange river to Natal where the first Boer republic was founded in 1839. Natal was annexed by the British in 1846 but the Boer republics of Transvaal and Orange Free State, founded in 1852 and 1854, received recognition. The discovery of diamonds in 1866 and gold in 1886 led to rivalry between the British and the Boers and eventually to the South African Wars of 1880-81 and 1899-1902. In 1910 the states of Transvaal, Natal, Orange Free State and Cape Province were united to form the Union of South Africa, a dominion of the British Empire. In 1931 South Africa became a sovereign state within the Commonwealth and in 1961 a fully independent republic was declared. In 1966 Botswana and Lesotho gained independence and in 1968 Swaziland also gained full independence. Transkei (1976), Bophuthatswana (1977), Venda (1979) and Ciskei (1981) subsequently were granted independence from South Africa, although their independent status is not recognized internationally. Following the 1983 constitution South Africa has a tricameral legislature comprising a 166-member House of Assembly (for whites) elected for 5 years, an 85-member House of Representatives (for coloureds) and a 45-member House of Delegates (for Indians). There is a 60-member President's Council, half of which is appointed by the president, the remainder being elected by the 3 legislative houses. Since the election of the National Party in 1948 a policy of apartheid has resulted in the development of separate political institutions for the racial groups of South Africa. Africans are considered permanent citizens of the 'homelands' to which each tribal group is assigned and are not represented in the South African Parliament.

Economy. South Africa's industrial growth stems from the discovery of gold and diamonds in the 19th century, with resources exported in exchange for imported manufactured goods in the framework of an essentially colonial economy. The Pact government of 1924 diverted capital towards the build-up of local industries and a host of state-owned corporations were established, the most notable being ISCOR, the iron and steel corporation (founded in 1928). The role of foreign investment was important in the development of new products and new technologies making use of African labour. In the 1950s light industries were encouraged, but with the threat of international sanctions after the Sharpeville massacre of 1960 the emphasis changed to strategic sectors producing chemicals, vehicles, electronics and computers. Today, South Africa is largely self-sufficient in foodstuffs, with an agricultural economy based on the production of grain, wool, sugar, tobacco, citrus fruit and dairy products. Since the discovery of gold and diamonds, mineral industries have played a prominent part in South Africa's urban expansion. Manufacturing activity is focused around Pretoria-Witwatersrand-Vereeniging, Durban-Pinetown, the Western Cape and Port Elizabeth. Exports of gold account for over half of the country's export income. Manufacturing industry is diverse, accounting for 25% of national income. Products, most of which are sold domestically, include motor vehicles, machinery, chemicals, fertilizers, textiles, clothes and metal products. Sixty per cent of all power generation in Africa occurs in South Africa, with many coal-fired power stations located near open cast mines. Major exports include gold, diamonds, uranium, metallic ores, asbestos, grain, wool, sugar, fruit, hides and fish. Trade partners include the USA, W Germany, Japan, the UK and France.

Administrative divisions. South Africa is divided into 4 provinces:

Province	*area (sq km)*	*pop(1985)*
Cape	641,379	5,041,137
Natal	91,355	2,145,018
Orange Free State	127,993	7,532,179
Transvaal	262,499	1,776,903

In addition there are the 4 'independent' homelands of Transkei, Ciskei, Bophuthatswana and Venda, and the 6 non-independent national states of Gazankulu, Lebowa, QwaQwa, KwaZulu, KaNgwane, and KwaNdebele.

South America, 4th largest continent, extending c.7,500 km from 12 25N to 56S; area c.18 mn sq km; longitude 70W runs the length of the continent; linked to N America on the NW by the Isthmus of Panama, bounded on the N by the Caribbean Sea, on the E by the Atlantic Ocean and on the W by the Pacific Ocean; includes Argentina, Bolivia, Brazil, Chile, Columbia, Ecuador, Guyana, Paraguay, Peru, Surinam, Uruguay and Venezuela; outlying islands (excluding the West Indies) include the Falkland I, Galapagos I, and Tierra del Fuego at the southern tip; the Andes mountains run almost the full western length of the continent, rising to 6,960 m at Aconagua, (highest point in the western hemisphere); in the N lie the Guiana Highlands, and in the E the Brazilian Highlands rise towards the Atlantic; 3 large river basins form the lowlands: the Orinoco, Paraná, and Amazon (containing the world's largest tropical rainforest); other rivers include the Colorado, Madeira, Magdalena, Negro, Paraguay, Saõ Francisco, Tapajós, Ucayali, Uruguay and Xingu; lakes include L Titicaca, L Poopó, L Mirim and the Lago de Maracaibo; major inlets are the Rio de la Plata estuary, the Amazon delta, the Gulfs of San Matias and San Jorge.

South Australia, state in S Australia; bordered W by Western Australia, N by Northern Territory, NE by Queensland, E by New South Wales and Victoria and S by the Great Australian Bight and the Southern Ocean; much of the state is desert including the Great Victoria Desert in the NW and the Nullarbor Plain in the SW; the SE corner of the state irrigated by the Murray river is fertile agricultural land; the coastline is dissected by the Spencer and St Vincent gulfs; inland, due N of Spencer Gulf, are the dry salt lakes of Eyre, Torrens, Gairdner and Frome; the state rises in the S to the Gawler Ranges N of the Eyre peninsula and in the E and SE to the Flinders and Mount Lofty Ranges; Mount Woodroffe in the Musgrave Ranges is the highest point in the state at 1,440 m; the Murray river enters the ocean in the SE, to the E of Adelaide; covering a large area in the centre of the state is Woomera Prohibited Area, a weapons-testing range which extends across the Great Victoria Desert into Western Australia; running through much of South Australia is the 9,600 km-long Dingo Fence which protects southern grazing sheep from wild dogs; possession of a dingo is illegal in South Australia; pop(1986) 1,393,813; area 984,000 sq km; capital Adelaide; principal towns include Whyalla, Mount Gambier, Port Pirie and Port Augusta; economy: wheat and barley, fruit, wool, meat, wine, oil refining, mining of copper, silver, lead, natural gas, opals (South Australia supplies 95% of the world's opals); oranges and other citrus fruit are grown in irrigated orchards along the Murray river; almost half of Australia's wine is produced from the Barossa Valley N of Adelaide; South Australia was established as a British Crown Colony in 1836 and became a state in 1901; between 1863 and 1901 most of the Northern Territory was included as part of South Australia; state holidays: Labour Day (Oct), Proclamation Day (Dec); the state of South Australia is divided into 7 statistical divisions:

Statistical division	*area (sq km)*	*pop(1981)*
Adelaide		953,960
Eyre		34,450
Murray Lands		63,270
Northern		94,160
Outer Adelaide		69,580
South East		61,630
Yorke and Lower North		41,720

South Bend, 41 41N 86 15W, pop(1980) 109,727, county seat of St Joseph county, N Indiana, United States; on the St Joseph river, 91 km E of Gary; railway; economy: aircraft equipment, agricultural machinery, motor vehicles, clothing, engineering.

South Carolina, state in SE United States; bounded SW and W by Georgia, N by North Carolina, and E and SE by the Atlantic Ocean; the Pee Dee river flows SSE from North Carolina through the E of the state to the Atlantic; the Wateree and Congaree rivers join to form the R Santee, which flows SE to the Atlantic; the R Edisto flows SSE through the W of the state to the Atlantic; the R Savannah forms most of the Georgia state border and also empties into the Atlantic; the Blue Ridge Mts rise in the extreme NW; the highest point is Mt Sassafras (1,085 m); the coastland is flat and in the S becomes swampy where it is cut by numerous rivers and creeks to form the famous Sea Islands which attract thousands of tourists; the ground rises inland towards the rolling Piedmont, the centre of the state's agricultural and manufacturing industries; the ground rises abruptly in the NW corner of the state to the Blue Ridge Mts; reservoirs in the centre of the state include L Murray, L Marion and L Moultrie; textile and clothing manufacture relies heavily on the region's large cotton crop; other leading manufactures are lumber, chemicals, machinery and foodstuffs; tobacco and soybeans are major agricultural crops and poultry, cattle, dairy products, peaches, peanuts, sweet potatoes and corn are also important; fishing is a major industry; the area was settled by the French at Port Royal in 1562; the region was included in the Carolina grant in 1663 but returned to the Crown in 1729; brought under American control after the battle of Guilford Courthouse in 1781; 8th of the original 13 states to ratify the Constitution (1788); the first state to secede from the Union, in Dec 1860; Confederate forces attacked Fort Sumter on 12 April 1861, starting the Civil War; slavery was abolished in 1865 and the state was re-admitted to the Union on 25 June 1868; also known as the 'Palmetto State'; pop(1980) 3,121,820; area 78,528 sq km; capital Columbia; other chief cities are Charleston, Greenville and Spartanburg; the state is divided into 46 counties:

County	*area (sq km)*	*pop(1980)*
Abbeville	1,321	22,627
Aiken	2,839	105,625
Allendale	1,074	10,700
Anderson	1,867	133,235
Bamberg	1,027	18,118
Barnwell	1,451	19,868
Beaufort	1,505	65,364
Berkeley	2,881	94,727
Calhoun	988	12,206
Charleston	2,439	276,974
Cherokee	1,030	40,983
Chester	1,508	30,148
Chesterfield	2,085	38,161
Clarendon	1,565	27,464
Colleton	2,735	31,776
Darlington	1,464	62,717
Dillon	1,056	31,083
Dorchester	1,495	58,761
Edgefield	1,274	17,528
Fairfield	1,781	20,700
Florence	2,090	110,163
Georgetown	2,137	42,461
Greenville	2,067	287,913
Greenwood	1,173	57,847
Hampton	1,459	18,159
Horry	2,972	101,419
Jasper	1,703	14,504
Kershaw	1,880	39,015
Lancaster	1,435	53,361
Laurens	1,861	52,214
Lee	1,069	18,929
Lexington	1,838	140,353
Marion	1,282	34,179
Marlboro	1,256	31,634
McCormick	910	7,797
Newberry	1,648	31,242
Oconee	1,635	48,611
Orangeburg	2,889	82,276
Pickens	1,297	79,292
Richland	1,981	269,735
Saluda	1,186	16,150
Spartanburg	2,116	201,861
Sumter	1,729	88,243
Union	1,339	30,751
Williamsburg	2,428	38,226
York	1,781	106,720

South China Sea, W arm of the Pacific Ocean, bounded by the island of Taiwan to the N, the Philippines to the E, Borneo to the SE and the SE Asian coast to the NW, W and SW; covers an area of c.2,590,000 sq km and is subject to violent typhoons; linked to the East China Sea by the Formosa Strait, the Pacific Ocean by the Bashi Channel and the Luzon Strait, the Sula Sea by the Mindoro and Balabac straits and the Java Sea by that area between Singapore and Borneo; main arms are the Gulf of Tongkin and the Gulf of Kompong; the Sunda Platform in the SW, causes depths to be much shallower (61 m) than those in the deep basin to the NE (5,490 m), although depth there varies as the floor is dotted with seamounts; numerous island groups such as the Spratly Islands are scattered throughout the sea; coral reefs are found around the N tip of the Philippines, the Gulf of Tongkin and around the Malaysia Peninsula.

South Dakota *da-kō'ta*, state in N central United States; bounded W by Wyoming and Montana, N by North Dakota, E by Minnesota and Iowa, and S by Nebraska; the R Missouri flows S, then SE, bisecting the state, before forming the E part of the Nebraska state border; the Big Sioux river flows S before emptying into the R Missouri; the Bois de Sioux and Minnesota rivers form the upper part of the E border; the Black Hills rise in the SW corner of the state; the highest point is Mt Harney Peak (2,207 m); the region W of R Missouri is a semi-arid, treeless plain, one-third of which is owned by Sioux Indians; much of the area has been severely eroded to form the barren Bad Lands which feature many ancient marine and land fossils; E of the R Missouri are rich, fertile plains; the chief agricultural products are cattle, wheat, hogs, dairy products, corn, soybeans and oats; major industries include meat packing and food processing; the town of Lead in the Black Hills is the nation's leading gold-mining centre; the state is the 2nd largest gold and beryllium producer in the USA; in the Black Hills is Mt Rushmore, on which are carved the faces of George Washington, Abraham Lincoln, Thomas Jefferson and Theodore Roosevelt; the region was acquired by the USA with the Louisiana Purchase in 1803; it became part of Dakota Territory in 1861; the population swelled when gold was discovered in the Black Hills in 1874; separated from North Dakota and became a state in 1889; there are Indian reserves at Crow Creek, Rosebud, Pine Ridge and Cheyenne; pop(1980) 690,768; area 197,475 sq km; 40th state admitted to the Union, in 1889; capital Pierre; chief cities are Sioux Falls, Rapid City and Aberdeen; the state is divided into 66 counties:

County	*area (sq km)*	*pop(1980)*
Aurora	1,838	3,628
Beadle	3,273	19,195
Bennett	3,073	3,044
Bon Homme	1,435	8,059
Brookings	2,067	24,332
Brown	4,477	36,962
Brule	2,119	5,245
Buffalo	1,235	1,795
Butte	5,853	8,372
Campbell	1,903	2,243
Charles Mix	2,834	9,680
Clark	2,478	4,894
Clay	1,063	13,689
Codington	1,804	20,885
Corson	6,414	5,196
Custer	4,053	6,000
Davison	1,134	17,820
Day	2,657	8,133
Deuel	1,641	5,289
Dewey	6,006	5,366
Douglas	1,128	4,181
Edmunds	2,987	5,159
Fall River	4,524	8,439
Faulk	2,610	3,327
Grant	1,771	9,013
Gregory	2,634	6,015
Haakon	4,737	2,794
Hamlin	1,331	5,261
Hand	3,736	4,948
Hanson	1,126	3,415
Harding	6,963	1,700
Hughes	1,968	14,220
Hutchinson	2,122	9,350
Hyde	2,236	2,069
Jackson	4,867	3,437
Jerauld	1,378	2,929
Jones	2,525	1,463
Kingsbury	2,142	6,679
Lake	1,456	10,724
Lawrence	2,080	18,339
Lincoln	1,503	13,942
Lyman	4,365	3,864
Marshall	2,205	5,404
McCook	1,498	6,444
McPherson	2,985	4,027
Meade	9,051	20,717
Mellette	3,409	2,249
Miner	1,482	3,739
Minnehaha	2,106	109,435
Moody	1,352	6,692
Pennington	7,236	70,361
Perkins	7,498	4,700
Potter	2,259	3,674
Roberts	2,865	10,911
Sanborn	1,479	3,213
Shannon	5,444	11,323
Spink	3,913	9,201
Stanley	3,721	2,533
Sully	2,527	1,990
Todd	3,609	7,328
Tripp	4,207	7,268
Turner	1,604	9,255
Union	1,178	10,938
Walworth	1,838	7,011
Yankton	1,347	18,952
Ziebach	5,119	2,308

South Downs Way, long-distance footpath following the South Downs of East and West Sussex, S England; stretches from Eastbourne to Harting; length 129 km.

South Euclid, 41 31N 81 32W, pop(1980) 25,713, town in Cuyahoga county, NE Ohio, United States; suburb 16 km E of Cleveland.

South Gate, 33 57N 118 12W, pop(1980) 66,784, city in Los Angeles county, SW California, United States; 11 km S of Los Angeles.

South Georgia, 54 30S 37 00W, barren, mountainous, snow-covered island in the S Atlantic, about 500 km E of the Falkland Is; a British Dependent Territory; length 160 km and width 32 km; many glaciers descend to the sea from the mountains; probably discovered by the London merchant de la Roche in 1675; Captain James Cook landed and took formal possession of South Georgia in 1775; in 1908 and 1917 the British Government annexed South Georgia by letters patent; Grytviken is the only village; a research station is maintained here and on the neighbouring Bird Island; the island became a centre for sealing and whaling from the 19th century until 1965, by which time all shore stations had ceased operations; a magistrate, who is also the Base Commander of the British Antarctic Survey Stations, resides at King Edward Point where a research base was established in 1969 comprising 22 scientists and support personnel; there has been a British Antarctic Survey Station here since 1909; Husvik Harbour is the main anchorage; Sir Ernest Shackleton, the explorer, is buried here.

South Glamorgan, county in S Wales; bounded N and W by Mid Glamorgan, E by Gwent and S by the Bristol Channel; capital Cardiff; pop(1981) 384,042; area 416 sq km; economy: agriculture (Vale of Glamorgan), steel, plastics, engineering, vehicle components, food processing; created in 1974, the county is divided into 2 districts:

District	area (sq km)	pop(1981)
Cardiff	120	273,525
Vale of Glamorgan	296	110,517

South Island, the larger and southernmost of the 2 main islands of New Zealand; separated from North Island by the Cook Strait, and from Stewart island to the S by the Foveaux Strait; the fertile plains in the coastal areas give way further inland to mountainous areas; the Southern Alps mountain range which runs through the centre of the island contains Mount Cook (3,764 m), the highest point in New Zealand; to the W of the Alps is Westland, a narrow forested strip; to the E of the Southern Alps is the Canterbury Plain, New Zealand's largest area of flat lowland; in the SW the coast fragments into numerous bays and fiords; pop(1981) 852,748; area 153,978 sq km; chief ports include Lyttelton near Christchurch and Bluff near Invercargill; principal towns include Christchurch, Invercargill, Dunedin and Nelson; economy: tobacco, hops, apples (N); coal, cement, timber, greenstone (W); sheep, pottery (E); sheep, frozen meat, shipping, fruit (S); South Island has 6 statistical divisions:

Division	area (sq km)	pop(1981)
Canterbury	43,579	424,280
Marlborough	11,080	36,027
Nelson	17,675	77,223
Otago	37,105	183,559
Southland	29,124	108,170
Westland	15,415	23,489

South Ock'endon, 51 32N 0 18E, pop(1981) 17,582, town in Thurrock dist, Essex, SE England; 4 km NW of Grays; railway.

South Orkney Islands *ork'nee*, ORCADAS DEL SUR (Sp), group of islands in the S Atlantic, forming part of the British Antarctic Territory; situated NE of the Graham Peninsula; the main islands of the group are Coronation, Signy, Laurie and the Inaccessible Is; area 620 sq km; used by British and American whalers since 1821, the islands are now barren and uninhabited, being occasionally used as bases for scientific research; claimed by Argentina.

South Pole, S extremity of the Earth's axis from which all meridians of longitude start; surrounded by South Polar Regions in W central Antarctica. First reached by the Norwegian explorer Roald Amundsen on 14 Dec 1911, a month before the British team, led by Capt Robert Scott, which arrived at the pole on 17 Jan 1912.

South San Francisco, 37 39N 122 24W, pop(1980) 49,393, city in San Mateo county, W California, United States; S suburb of San Francisco; separated from San Francisco by the San Bruno Mts; railway.

South Sandwich Is, 56 18-59 25S 26 15W, group of small, uninhabited islands in the S Atlantic, about 720 km SE of South Georgia; a British Dependent Territory; discovered by Captain James Cook in 1775; in 1908 and 1917 the British Government formally annexed the South Sandwich Is by letters patent.

South Shetland Islands, group of uninhabited, mountainous islands in the S Atlantic, forming part of the British Antarctic Territory; situated NW of the Graham Peninsula and about 880 km SE of Cape Horn; the main islands of the group are King George, Elephant, Clarence, Gibbs, Nelson, Livingston, Greenwich, Snow, Deception and Smith, all of which are separated from the peninsula by the Bransfield Strait; area 4,622 sq km; discovered in 1819 by the British navigator William Smith. Scientific bases occasionally occupied at Admiralty Bay on King George Island and on Deception Island.

South Shields, 55 00N 1 25W, pop(1981) 87,125, town in North Tyneside borough, Tyne and Wear, England; part of Tyneside urban area; opposite North Shields, on the S bank of the R Tyne, 12 km E of Gateshead; economy: transport equipment, electrical goods, engineering; monument: Roman fort of Arbeia at the E end of Hadrian's Wall.

South West Peninsula Coast Path, long-distance footpath in Cornwall, Somerset, Devon and Dorset, SW England; stretches from Minehead to Studland near Poole.

South Yorkshire, metropolitan county in N England; bounded N by North Yorkshire and West Yorkshire, E by Humberside and S by Nottinghamshire and Derbyshire; pop(1981) 1,303,948; area 1,560 sq km; county town Sheffield; chief towns include Rotherham, Doncaster and Barnsley; the metropolitan council was abolished in 1986; economy: coal, steel, engineering; the county is divided into 4 boroughs:

Borough	area (sq km)	pop(1981)
Barnsley	329	225,084
Doncaster	582	289,532
Rotherham	283	251,775
Sheffield	368	537,557

Southamp'ton, parish in the Bermuda Islands; pop(1980) 4,613.

Southampton, CLAUSENTUM (Lat), HAMWIH (Anglo-Saxon), 50 55N 1 25W, pop(1981) 205,337, port city in Southampton dist, Hampshire, S England; at the mouth of the Test and Itchen rivers; a major UK port handling container traffic and passenger ships; high tide lasts 2 hours longer than other ports; site of both Roman and Saxon settlements; the *Mayflower* set sail from here en route to N America in 1620; the *Titanic* sailed from here on her disastrous maiden voyage on 10 April 1912; city status (1964); university (1952); railway; ferries to the Isle of Wight and continental Europe; economy: marine engineering, petrochemicals, cables, electrical goods; monuments: St Michael's church (1070); 15th-c Guildhall; 14th-c wool house now housing a maritime museum; *Mayflower* memorial.

Southampton Water, inlet of the English Channel, Hampshire, S England; formed between the estuaries of the rivers Itchen and Test, it extends 14 km from the Solent and Spithead giving access to the port of Southampton; average width about 2 km; to the S the Isle of Wight acts as a natural breakwater and creates a double tide.

Southend-on-Sea, 51 33N 0 43E, pop(1981) 155,083, resort town co-extensive with Southend-on-Sea dist, Essex, SE England; on the R Thames estuary, 57 km E of London; has a mile-long pier; railway; airfield; monument: 12th-c Prittlewell Priory museum.

Southern Alps, mountain range in W central South Island, New Zealand; extends approx 320 km NE-SW; contains New Zealand's highest peaks, Mount Cook (3,764 m), Mount Tasman (3,497 m) and Mount Dampier (3,440 m); 19 named peaks in total exceed 3,000 m; only 2 mountain passes (Haast Pass and Arthur's Pass) allow travel from E to W; national parks include Westland, Mount Cook and Arthur's Pass within which there are many glaciers; a popular area for mountain-climbing and skiing in New Zealand.

Southern Upland Way, long-distance footpath in Scotland; stretching from Portpatrick near Stranraer in the W to Cockburnspath, S of Dunbar, in the E; length 340 km; opened in 1984.

Southfield, 42 29N 83 17W, pop(1980) 75,568, town in Oakland county, SE Michigan, United States; 24 km NW of Detroit.

Southgate, 42 12N 83 12W, pop(1980) 32,058, residential town in Wayne county, SE Michigan, United States; 20 km S of Detroit.

Southport, 53 39N 3 01W, pop(1981) 90,962, coastal resort town in Sefton borough, Merseyside, NW England; on the Irish Sea, S of the R Ribble estuary, 25 km N of Liverpool; the original 'garden city'; a notable golfing area; railway; economy: chemicals, engineering.

Southwark *suTH'erk*, 51 30N 0 06W, pop(1981) 211,840, borough of central Greater London, England; S of the R

Thames; includes the suburbs of Bermondsey, Southwark and Camberwell; formerly famous for its inns and Elizabethan theatres; railway; monuments: 13th-c Southwark cathedral, Dulwich College (1621), Guy's Hospital (1721), Imperial War Museum.

South-West Africa, country in SW Africa. See Namibia.

Soviet Union, official name Union of Soviet Socialist Republics (USSR), SOYUZ SOVYETSKIKH SOTSIALISTICHESKIKH REPUBLIK (SSSR) (Rus), a federation of 15 union republics jointly forming the world's largest sovereign state, extending over 8,000 km from the Baltic Sea (W) to the Bering Strait (E), and 3,000 km from the Arctic Ocean (N) to Asia Minor (S), bounded W by Turkey, Romania, Hungary, Czechoslovakia, Poland, Finland, and Norway, and S by Iran, Afghanistan, China, Mongolia, and N Korea; timezones GMT +3 to +13; area 22,402,076 sq km; capital Moskva (Moscow); chief cities Leningrad, Kiyev (Kiev), Tashkent, Baku, Kharkov, Gork'iy (Gorky), Novosibirsk, Kuybyshev, Sverdlovsk, Tbilisi, Dnepropetrovsk, Odessa, Chelyabinsk, Donetsk, Yerevan, and Omsk; pop(1983) 271,200,000; ethnic groups include 52% Russian, 16% Ukrainian, 5% Uzbek, 4% Belorussian and over 100 other groups of Turkic, Finno-Ugric, Caucasian, and Indo-European origin; Russian is the official language but over 200 languages and dialects are spoken; Russian Orthodox is the dominant religion (18%), 9% are Muslim, 3% are Jewish and 70% are atheist; under 7% of the pop are members of the Communist Party; the unit of currency is the rouble of 100 kopeks; national holidays October Revolution Day; membership of CEMA, COMECON, Geneva Disarmament Conference, IAEA, ICAO, ILO, IMCO, ITU, UN, UNESCO, UPU, Warsaw Pact, WHO, WMO.

Physical description. The Ural'skiy Khrebet (Ural Mts) geographically divide the Soviet Union into European (W) and Asian (E) sectors. W of the Ural'skiy Khrebet lies the E European Plain, a broad plain of fertile farmland broken only by occasional low hills. Much of the land lies below 300 m and is dissected by several major rivers including the northward-flowing Pechora, Severnaya Dvina, and Mezen systems, and the southward-flowing Dnestr, Dnepr, Don, and Volga rivers. Evidence of glaciation is clearly visible here in the form of morainic hills, lakes, glacial boulder clays and sands. The Ural'skiy Khrebet extends over 2,400 km from the Arctic Ocean (N) to the sub-tropical republic of Kazakhskaya (Kazakhstan) (S). The range is narrow in the N but widens southwards until it becomes a series of parallel ridges. Narodnaya (1,894 m) is the highest peak, situated close to 65°N in a zone of sub-polar tundra. E of the Ural'skiy Khrebet lie the steppelands of the W Siberian Lowlands. This area of marshy plain extends as far E as the R Yenisey and is drained by the rivers Ob', Yenisey, and Irtysh. The land rises southwards towards Kazakhskaya SSR and the high steppes of Kirgizskaya (Kirgizkaya). E of the R Yenisey lies the Central Siberian Plateau, and beyond it, extending as far as the Lena basin, lies the N Siberian Plain. The N Siberian Plain drains northwards to the Arctic Ocean via the Lena, Olenek, Kotuy, Yenisey and other great rivers. It is bordered S and E by a complex of fold mountains extending along the Chinese-Mongolian frontier and the Pacific seaboard of E Asia. The mountain systems of the USSR occupy approx one-fifth of the total area. In central Asia the Pamir, Tien Shan, and Altay ranges rise to heights above 5,000 m. Pik Kommunizma (Commu-

nism Peak) (7,495 m) in the Pamirs is the highest mountain in the Soviet Union. The Kavkaz (Caucasus) range forms a mountainous bridge between the Black Sea (W) and the Caspian Sea (E), and Europe (N) and Asia (S). The largest lakes in the Soviet Union include Ozero Balkhash, Ozero Baykal (Lake Baikal), and Ozero Taymyr. Zemlya Frantsa-Iosifa (Franz-Josef Land), Novaya Zemlya, Severnaya Zemlya (North Land), Novosibirskiye Ostrova (New Siberian Is), Ostrov Vrangelya (Wrangel I), and Sakhalin are the chief islands of the Soviet Union.

Climate. The Soviet Union, occupying approx one-sixth of the land area of the world, comprises several different climatic regions, ranging from polar conditions in the N, through sub-arctic and humid continental, to subtropical and semi-arid conditions in the S. The country can be broadly divided into 6 climatic regions: (1) Northern and Central European Russia: this region comprises the republics of Estonskaya (Estonia), Latviskaya (Latvia), Litovskaya (Lithuania), Belorusskaya (Belorussia) and part of Rossiyskaya (RSFSR). It extends from the Barents and Kara Seas in the N to the Ukrainian border in the S. Being under the influence of weather disturbances from NW Europe, this part of the Soviet Union has variable weather both in summer and winter. Winter temperatures become increasingly severe towards the E and N, while summers become warmer eastwards and southwards. Average temperatures at Moskva range from −9.4°C in Jan to 18.3°C in July and the mean annual rainfall is 630 mm. Arkhangel'sk is much further N and has average temperatures which range from −15°C in Jan to 13.9°C in July. The mean annual rainfall here is 503 mm. Throughout the region precipitation tends to be concentrated in the summer months. (2) South European Russia: this region includes the republics of the Ukraine and Moldavia but excludes the Kavkaz (Caucasus) area. Although winters are still severe here the spring thaw comes earlier. Drier conditions prevail towards the SE, in the steppe region N of the Kavkaz and W of the Caspian Sea. Hot, dry winds often damage crops in the steppe during the summer while blizzards associated with the *buran* wind are not uncommon during the winter. Winters are particularly mild along the S coast of the Krim (Crimean) peninsula and the E shores of the Black Sea. In these areas, often known as the Russian Riviera, rain falls throughout the year. (3) The Kavkaz (Caucasus) Mts and Transcaucasia: this region comprises the republics of Gruzinskaya (Georgia), Armyanskaya (Armenia), and Azerbydzhanskaya. Winter temperatures are much higher than in the regions N of the Kavkaz range. Spells of cold weather, however, do still occur. Conditions during the summer are almost tropical. Rainfall is well distributed throughout the year in W parts of the region. The Caspian coast and some interior valleys are much drier. (4) Soviet Central Asia: this area includes the steppes and deserts of the Kazakhskaya (Kazakhstan), Uzbekskaya (Uzbekistan), and Turkmenskaya (Turkmen) republics. It is the driest part of the Soviet Union with warm to hot summers and cold but generally dry and sunny winters. Those settlements close to the Caspian Sea such as Krasnovodsk are unusually mild during the winter due to the moderating influence of the water. (5) The mountains of Soviet Central Asia: this mountainous region on the borders of Afghanistan and China includes the republics of Kirghizkaya (Kirgiztan), Tadzhikskaya (Tadzhikstan), and part of E Kazakhskaya. Winters here are cold but spring comes earlier than further N. Considering the high altitude conditions are drier than expected due largely to the sheltering effect of the Pamir and Himalayan ranges to the S and SE. (6) Siberia: this vast area extends eastwards from the Ural'skiy Khrebet (Ural Mts) to the Pacific Ocean, and southwards from the Arctic Ocean to the borders with China and Mongolia. The climate is continental with very cold and prolonged winters and short, often quite warm summers. Summer is the wettest season. The winter precipitation is quite light and falls as snow. At Vladivostok, on the Pacific coast, the E Asian summer monsoon brings warm, moist winds off the Pacific so coastal regions are comparatively wet at this time. Winters, however, are still very cold as the winds are from the W or NW. Average temperatures at Vladivostok range from −14.4°C in Jan to 18.3°C in July, and the mean annual rainfall is 599 mm.

History, government and constitution. Russia has been settled by many ethnic groups including the nomadic Slavs, Turks and Bulgars who arrived on the central steppes in the 3rd to 7th centuries. In the NW, Scandinavian merchants controlled a network of market towns and villages that were united under the Kiev Rus state in the 8th century, and by the end of the 10th century the Byzantine Christian Church had been established. During the 13th century Tatar invaders gained control over Kiyev (Kiev) and much of S Russia, while the Grand Duchy of Lithuania extended its influence eastwards over Poland into the Ukraine. Moskva (Moscow) was established as a centre of political power in the N during the 14th century, and under Ivan IV (the Terrible), Russia's first csar, the Tatars were expelled. Internal disorder amongst a feudal nobility and constant warfare with border countries such as Poland and Sweden prevented Russian development until Csar Peter I (the Great) began to introduce western ideas. Under Catherine II (the Great) Russia became a great power and extended its territories into S and E Asia. Although serfdom was abolished in 1861 the Industrial Revolution that had developed Western Europe did not take place in Russia, largely because of bureaucratic inefficiency and indifference. Defeat in the Russo-Japanese War of 1904-05 precipitated a revolution which, although unsuccessful, brought Russia's first constitution and parliament. A second revolution (1917) during the chaos of World War I ended the monarchy but initiated a 5-year political struggle between supporters of the provisional government (the Mensheviks) and those who advocated the assumption of power by the Soviets (the Bolsheviks). On 7 Nov 1917 the Bolsheviks arrested the provisional government, and their leader, Vladimir Ilyich Lenin, was named head of the first Soviet government. During the 5-year civil war that followed a constitution was adopted for the Russian Soviet Federal Socialist Republic (RSFSR), the first political successor to Csarist Russia. Other Soviet republics in the Ukraine, Belorussia and Transcaucasia joined the RSFSR in 1922. Josef Stalin succeeded Lenin after his death in 1924, adopting a totalitarian policy designed to bring Russia into the 20th century. He initiated a vigorous socialist reform that included collectivizing agriculture and enforcing a programme of rapid industrialization with emphasis on heavy industry. Russian involvement in World War II resulted in the devastation of much of W Russia, but the peace settlement of 1945 extended the country's territories in the W and created a corridor of communist-dominated countries between itself and W Europe. The 15 Union republics are governed by the bicameral Supreme Soviet which comprises the Council of the Union and the Council of Nationalities, each of 750 members elected for a term of 5 years. These chambers join to elect a Presidium of 39 members and an executive council of over 100 ministers. The Presidium of the Supreme Soviet of the USSR consists of a chairman (in effect the president of the USSR), a first vice-chairman, 15 vice-chairmen (one from each republic), 21 members, and a secretary. The Council of Ministers supervises the work of the ministries and other governmental bodies. The republics have constitutions based upon the new constitution of the USSR approved by the Supreme Soviet in Oct 1977. They have their own Supreme Soviets, Presidiums, and Council of Ministers. The republics of Estonskaya (Estonia), Latviskaya (Latvia), and Litovskaya (Lithuania) are not recognized by the USA to be part of the Soviet Union. The Communist Party exercises political authority throughout the USSR. It is the sole political party, governed by a Congress and Central Committee.

Economy. Since 1917 the Soviet government, under a system of centralized economic planning, has set itself the task of transforming a pre-eminently agrarian, backward country with a primitive system of agriculture into an industrial state supported by intensive, mechanized collective farming. Just over 10% of the land is cultivated, nearly 17% is under pasture and over 35% is wooded. About half the cultivated land is devoted to grain crops (wheat, oats, barley) and one-third to livestock fodder crops. In addition, potatoes, rice, cotton, sugar-beet, flax and sunflowers are grown extensively. The Soviet Union has considerable reserves of minerals such as coal (Don and Kuznetsk basins, Siberia, Arctic), oil, and gas (Transcaucasus, Ukrainskaya, Sakhalin, W Turkmenskaya and Siberia), iron ore, manganese, nickel, cobalt, chromium, uranium, copper, lead and zinc. Many heavy industries have been developed based on these metals, principally the manufacture of vehicles, machinery, building materials, industrial chemicals, and consumer goods. Major exports include petroleum and petroleum products, natural gas, metals, wood products, agricultural products and consumer goods. Russia trades 54% with communist countries, 32% with the industrialized West and 14% with less developed countries.

Administrative divisions. The USSR is a federation of 15 union republics, comprising 20 autonomous republics, 6 krays, 123 oblasts, 8 autonomous oblasts, and 10 autonomous okrugs:

Republic	*area (sq km)*	*pop(1983)*
Armyanskaya	29,800	3,219,000
Azerbaydzhanskaya	86,600	6,399,000
Belorusskaya	207,600	9,807,000
Estonskaya	45,100	1,507,000
Gruzinskaya	69,700	5,134,000
Kazakhskaya	2,717,300	15,452,000
Kirgizskaya	198,500	3,801,000
Latviskaya	63,700	2,569,000
Litovskaya	65,200	3,506,000
Moldavskaya	33,700	4,052,000
Rossiyskaya	17,075,400	141,012,000
Tadzhikskaya	143,100	4,239,000
Turkmenskaya	488,100	3,042,000
Ukrainskaya	603,700	50,461,000
Uzbekskaya	447,400	17,039,000

Soweto *so-way'tō*, 26 15S 27 52E, black African township in Transvaal prov, NE South Africa; the name is derived from the official title of South-West Township; linked by rail (5 km) to industrial W Johannesburg; monument: Oppenheimer Memorial.

Soyapango *soy-a-pang'gō*, 13 40N 89 18W, pop(1980) 67,312, town in San Salvador dept, central El Salvador, Central America; 4 km E of San Salvador; rail junction.

Sozo'pol, APOLLONIA (Lat), 42 23N 27 42E, fishing town and artistic centre in Burgas okrug (prov), E Bulgaria; situated on a rocky promontory on the Black Sea 34 km

S of Burgas; once a colony of the Miletian Greeks for whom it was a major trading port; 4 km to the S is the Kavatsi Resort Complex with water sports facilities.

Spain *spayn*, ESPAÑA *es-pan'ya*, IBERIA (anc), HISPANA (Lat), official name Kingdom of Spain, REINO DE ESPAÑA *ray'no THay es-pan'ya* (Sp), a parliamentary democracy in SW Europe occupying with Portugal the Iberian peninsula and including the Canary Is in the Atlantic, the Balearic Is in the W Mediterranean as well as the Presidios of Ceuta and Melilla, the 6 islands of Penon de Alhucemas, the fortified rocky islet of Penon de la Gomera (or Penon de Velez) and the 3 islands of the Chaffarinas (or Zaffarines), all on the Moroccan coast of N Africa; the Isla de Faisanes is an uninhabited Franco-Spanish condominium at the mouth of the R Bidassoa in La Higuera bay; the former provinces of Spanish Guinea, Fernando Po and Rio Muni were granted independence in 1968, the former protectorates of Spanish Morocco and Ifni were incorporated in Morocco in 1956 and 1969 respectively and in 1975 the Spanish Sahara came under joint Moroccan and Mauritanian control; mainland Spain is situated between the Atlantic (including the Bay of Biscay) and the Mediterranean and bounded by France in the N across the Pyrenees and Portugal in the W; timezone GMT +1; area of mainland 492,431 sq km; total area 504,750 sq km; total pop(1981): 37,682,355; capital Madrid; chief cities include Barcelona, Valencia, Sevilla, Zaragoza and Málaga; Castilian Spanish is the official language, but 17% speak Catalan, 7% Galician and 2% Basque; the pop is 99% Roman Catholic; the currency is the peseta of 100 centimos; national holiday 24 June; membership: ASSIMER, EEC (1986), ESRO, FAO, GATT, IAEA, IBRD, ICAC, ICAO, ICES, ICO, IDA, IEA, IFAD, IFC, IHO, ILO, IMF, IMO, INTELSAT, IOOC, IPU, ITC, ITU, NATO, OECD, UN, UNESCO, UPU, WHO, WIPO, WMO, WSG, WTO.

Physical description. The greater part of continental Spain consists of a furrowed plateau or Meseta (average height of 700 m above sea level) which is surrounded and traversed by mountains. Highest are the folded Andalucian or Baetic Mts in the SE separated from the central plateau (Meseta) by the Baetic depression along which the R Guadalquivir flows in a SW direction past Córdoba, Sevilla and out into the Gulf of Cádiz. This range of mts reaches a height of 3,478 m at Mulhacén in the Sierra Nevada, the highest point in Spain. Separated from the Meseta by a similar tectonic depression (Iberian), the Pyrenees in the N reach a height of 3,404 m at the Pico d'Aneto. The R Ebro flows in a SE direction from the Basque Country following this depression past Zaragoza and on down to the Mediterranean at the Costa Dorada. Rivers trench the Meseta from E to W, with mountain chains between. The Montes de Toledo between the R Guadiana and the R Tagus reach 1,447 m. Between the R Tagus and the R Douro (Duero) a central cordillera (Sierra de Guadarrama, 2,262 m; Sierra de Gredos, 2,592 m) runs out through Portugal to Cabo Roca, bisecting the Meseta. Further N again the Cordillera Cantabrica (Picos de Europa, 2,648 m) presents an almost unbroken rocky wall to the Bay of Biscay, while the NW coast has rias like the fjords of Norway with several good harbours. The most notable rivers are the Tagus (Tajo or Tejo), Ebro, Guadiana, Minho (Miño), Douro (Duero), Guadalquivir, Segura and Júcar. There are few natural lakes, only man-made reservoirs created in recent years by the damming of rivers in order to provide hydroelectric power and irrigation.

Climate. The varied climate of mainland Spain reflects its varied topography and the influence of both the Mediterranean and the Atlantic. The central Meseta including the R Ebro basin has a continental climate with hot summers and cold winters and lying as it does in the rain shadow of the Atlantic W winds, rainfall is low. On the surrounding mountains rainfall is high and a deep cover of winter snow encourages winter sport. The S Mediterranean coast on a narrow strip of land at the foot of high mts has the warmest winter temperatures on the mainland of Europe. The SE prov of Murcia with its palm trees has a climate of African type with low rainfall and a heat haze (*calina*) from July to Sept. On the Atlantic coast of Andalucia the summers are less hot, but further inland the temperature gradually increases as rainfall decreases. The Mediterranean coast of Cataluña and Valencia with its tourist resorts has the most equable climate with mild winters.

History, government and constitution. Prior to the departure of King Alfonso XIII and the declaration of a Republic in 1931 Spain had been a monarchy since the unification of the kingdoms of Castille, León, Aragón and Navarre, a unity that had largely been achieved by 1572. After a few months of republican rule in 1873-74 a period of relative prosperity was enjoyed under Alfonso XII (1874-1885). Less fortunate was the reign of his son, Alfonso XIII, who ruled during a period of instability in which a war with the USA in 1898 resulted in the loss of Cuba, Puerto Rico and Spain's remaining Pacific possessions. A dictatorship under General Primo de Rivera (1923-30) was followed by the exile of the king and the establishment of the second Republic (1931). The sweeping reforms undertaken by the Provisional Government which was drawn from the various Republican and Socialist parties provoked a military revolt headed by General Francisco Franco in July 1936. After a bitter civil war, in which the Republicans received assistance from Russia and a left-wing 'International Brigade', and the 'Nationalists' from Germany and Italy, Franco succeeded in establishing a dictatorship on the Fascist model. The end of World War II found Franco's Spain politically isolated, with an exiled republican government and monarchist pretender (Don Juan, son of Alfonso XIII), both challenging his authority. In July 1969 Prince Juan Carlos of Bourbon (grandson of Alfonso XIII) was nominated to succeed Franco as head of state and in Nov 1975 he acceded to the throne on General Franco's death. A new constitution was drawn up in 1977-78 replacing the uni-cameral Parliament (*Cortes de España*) of 564 members with a bi-cameral *Cortes* comprising a 350-member Congress of Deputies elected for 4 years by proportional representation, and a 208-member Senate consisting of directly elected representatives of the provinces. Since 1978 there has been a move towards local government autonomy with the creation of autonomous regions.

Trade and industry. In 1983 proposals were put forward for the restructuring of Spain's fragmented industry which was based on a narrow range of products and was suffering from low levels of technology. In 1982 manufacturing accounted for 36% of national income, the largest sector being the supply of services (58%). Overseas trade has concentrated on textiles, iron, steel, shipbuilding, electrical appliances, motor cars, cork, salt, fruit, fish, vegetables, wine and potash, the greatest volume of trade being with EEC countries. While industrial production in many sectors has declined in the 1980s energy production and consumption has risen, resulting in a fall in the country's degree of dependence on imports of fuel. The main imports are petroleum, wool, cotton, tobacco, cellulose, timber, coffee, cocoa, fertilizers, dyes, industrial machinery, motor vehicles and agricultural machinery. A variety of minerals including iron, coal, lignite, sulphur, zinc, lead, wolfram and copper are exploited.

Transport. Spain has over 145,000 km of modern roads and highways, also international airports at Alicante, Almería, Asturias, Barcelona, Bilbao, Fuerteventura, Gerona, Ibiza, Jerez de la Frontera, La Coruña, Lanzarote, Las Palmas, Madrid-Barajas, Málaga, Melilla, Menorca, Murcia, Palma de Mallorca, Reus, Santander, Santiago de Compostella, Sevilla, Tenerife Sur, Valencia, Vigo, Vitoria and Zaragoza. There are 8 foreign shipping companies that operate regularly world-wide and passenger cruisers frequently stop over in the ports of mainland Spain and of the Canary and Balearic Is.

Agriculture. In 1982 agriculture accounted for 6% of national income, the chief agricultural products being wheat, rice, maize, barley, oats, hemp and flax with a variety of fruits including olives, oranges, lemons, almonds, pomegranates, bananas, apricots and grapes. The fishing industry is important as is wine production which is largely based in Rioja, Cádiz, Málaga and Alicante provs.

Administrative divisions. Since the new constitution of 1978 there has been a policy of decentralization with the development of autonomous regional governments with limited powers. The country has been divided into the following 17 regions and 50 provinces:

Province	*area (sq km)*	*pop(1981)*
Andalucia		
Almería	8,774	405,313
Cádiz	7,385	1,001,716
Córdoba	13,718	717,213
Granada	12,531	761,734
Huelva	10,085	414,492
Jaén	13,498	627,598
Málaga	7,276	1,036,261
Sevilla	14,001	1,477,428
Aragón		
Huesca	15,613	219,813
Teruel	14,785	150,900
Zaragoza	17,252	842,386
Asturias		
Oviedo	10,565	1,127,007
Baleares		
Balearic Is	5,014	655,909
Canarias		
Las Palmas	4,072	756,353
Santa Cruz de Tenerife	3,170	688,273
Cantabria		
Santander	5,289	510,816
Castilla-La Mancha		
Albacete	14,862	334,468
Ciudad Real	19,749	468,327
Cuenca	17,061	210,280
Guadalajara	12,190	143,124
Toledo	15,368	471,806
Castilla-León		
Ávila	8,048	178,997
Burgos	14,309	363,474
León	15,468	517,973
Palencia	8,035	186,512
Salamanca	12,336	368,055
Segovia	6,949	149,286
Soria	10,287	98,803
Valladolid	8,202	751,734
Zamora	10,559	224,309
Cataluña		
Barcelona	7,733	4,618,734
Gerona	5,886	467,945
Lérida	12,028	355,451
Tarragona	6,283	516,078
Extremadura		
Badajoz	21,657	635,375
Cáceres	19,945	414,744
Galicia		
La Coruña	7,876	1,083,415
Lugo	9,803	399,185
Orense	7,278	411,339
Pontevedra	4,477	859,897
Madrid		
Madrid	7,995	4,726,987
Murcia		
Murcia	11,313	957,903
Navarra		
Navarra	10,421	507,367
Pais Vasco		
Álava	3,047	260,580
Guipúzcoa	1,997	692,986
Vizcaya	2,217	1,181,401
Presidios		
Ceuta	19	65,264
Melilla	12	53,593

contd

Province	*area (sq km)*	*pop(1981)*
Rioja		
Logroño	5,034	253,295
Valencia		
Alicante	5,863	1,148,597
Castellón	6,679	431,755
Valencia	10,763	2,066,413

Spal'ding, 52 47N 0 10W, pop(1981) 21,699, town in South Holland dist, Lincolnshire, E central England; on the R Welland, SW of the Wash, 23 km SW of Boston; railway; economy: engineering, horticulture; event: Spalding flower parade (May).

Spanish Town, 17 59N 76 58W, pop(1982) 89,097, capital city of St Catherine parish, Middlesex county, S Jamaica; on the R Cobre, 17.6 km W of Kingston; second largest city in Jamaica; capital of the island from 1535 to 1872; serves a rich agricultural area; formerly an important staging post en route to Kingston; railway; monuments: cathedral (1655), ruins of the King's House (1762), court house (1819), folk museum, statue of Admiral Rodney, White Marl Arawak museum.

Sparks, 39 32N 119 45W, pop(1980) 40,780, town in Washoe county, W Nevada, United States; 6 km E of Reno; in 1903 the settlement was named after John Sparks, state governor; economy: gold and silver mining, railway engineering.

Spar'tanburg, 34 56N 81 57W, pop(1980) 43,968, county seat of Spartanburg county, NW South Carolina, United States; 48 km ENE of Greenville; railway; airfield; economy: main manufacture is textiles; other products include machinery, ceramics, chemicals, and wood and metal products.

Spartí *spahr'tee*, SPARTE, SPARTA (Eng), 37 05N 22 25E, pop(1981) 14,388, capital town of Lakonía nome (dept), Pelopónnisos region, S Greece; on the R Evrótas, 50 km SW of Athínai (Athens); the town was refounded on an ancient site in 1834 by King Otto, with streets laid out at right angles around a large central square; economy: trade in fruit and olive oil; event: carnival (Feb).

Speightstown *spayts'town*, 13 15N 59 39W, town on the NW coast of the island of Barbados, West Indies; N of Bridgetown.

Spen'nymoor, 54 42N 1 35W, pop(1981) 18,643, town in Sedgefield dist, Durham, NE England; 6 km NE of Bishop Auckland; economy: electrical goods, textiles, coal.

Sperrin Mts, mountain range in NE Co Tyrone and W Co Derry (Londonderry), W Northern Ireland; extends 24 km SE-NW across the 2 counties; rises to 683 m in Mt Sawel, on the Tyrone-Derry border, 27 km SE of Derry.

Spey, river in Highland and Grampian regions, NE Scotland; rises near Corrieyairack Pass, SSE of Fort Augustus; flows NE past Kingussie, Aviemore, Grantown on Spey and Rothes; discharges into Spey Bay, to the E of Lossiemouth; noted for its salmon fishing; length 171 km; major tributaries include the Dulnain and Avon rivers; in the lower reaches it is the fastest flowing river in Britain.

Spezia, La *lah spet'sya*, prov of Liguria region, NW Italy; pop(1981) 241,371; area 881 sq km; capital La Spezia.

Spezia, La, 44 07N 9 48E, pop(1981) 115,392, seaport capital of La Spezia prov, Liguria region, NW Italy; near the head of the Golfo della Spezia, an inlet of the Ligurian Sea, 80 km SE of Genova (Genoa); railway; economy: tourism, shipyards, naval arsenal.

Spijkenisse *spī'kun-iss-u*, 51 52N 4 19E, pop(1984e) 54,381, city in Zuid Holland prov, SW Netherlands; on Putten I, 12 km SW of Rotterdam.

Spišská Nová Ves *spish'skah no-vah ves*, 48 58N 20 35E, pop(1984) 34,812, town in Východoslovenský region, E Slovak Socialist Republic, E Czechoslovakia; in Low Tatra, on R Hornad, NW of Košice; health resort; founded in 12th century; railway; economy: iron, timber.

Spits'bergen, island group in the Arctic Ocean, 576 km N of Norway; part of Svalbard, a Norwegian dependency; area 61,230 sq km; principal islands Spitsbergen, North East Land, Edge I, Barents I; rises to 1,713 m at Mt Newton on Spitsbergen.

Split *spleet*, SPLIT (Eng), SPALATO (Ital), 43 31N 16 28E, pop(1981) 235,922, seaport and city in W Hrvatska (Croatia), Yugoslavia; largest town on the Yugoslav Adriatic coast; university (1974); airport; railway, car ferries to Italy and Turkey; economy: shipyard, coal mining, fishing, tourism; monuments: Diocletian's palace, cathedral; events: summer festival of drama and music (June-Aug); festival of light music in July.

Spokane *spō-kayn'*, 47 40N 117 24W, pop(1980) 171,300, capital of Spokane county, E Washington, United States; on the R Spokane, near the Idaho state border; named after a Siwash Indian chief; founded in 1872, achieving city status in 1891; Gonzaga University (1887); railway; airfield; economy: commercial centre for inland farming, forestry and mining areas of E Washington; monuments: art centre; museum; Episcopal and Roman Catholic cathedrals.

Spoleto *spo-lay'to*, SPOLETIUM (Lat), 42 44N 12 44E, pop(1981) 20,000, town in Perugia prov, Umbria, central Italy; 96 km NE of Roma (Rome) on a rocky hill overlooking R Tressino; monuments: 11th-c cathedral with frescoes by Filippo Lippi; 4th-c San Salvatore basilica; Roman remains include a theatre, amphitheatre, bridge, triumphal arch of Drusus and Germanicus; events: Festival of Two Worlds, a festival of music, drama and art in June-July.

Sporádhes *spor-ah'THes*, DODECANESE *dō-dek-an-eez'* (Eng), nome (dept) of Aegean Islands region, Greece; pop(1981) 145,071; area 2,714 sq km; capital Ródhos.

Sporádhes, group of 12 islands in the SE Aegean Sea, Greece, off the SW coast of Turkey; area 2,682 sq km; chief islands include Kásos, Kárpathos, Khálki, Tílos, Sími, Astipálaia, Kós, Kálimnos, Léros, Pátmos, and Ródhos (Rhodes), the largest island; with Sámos and its neighbouring islands they form the S Sporádhes group; ancient sites in the Sporádhes include the Asklepieion on Kós and, on Ródhos, the acropolis of Ródhos and the acropolis of Líndos; some of the islands, in particular Ródhos, have developed into major tourist centres.

Spree *spray*, river in East Germany, rising near Czechoslovak frontier and flowing 382 km N through Berlin to meet the R Havel near Spandau.

Springfield, 39 48N 89 39W, pop(1980) 99,637, capital of state in Sangamon county, central Illinois, United States; 296 km SW of Chicago; home and burial place of Abraham Lincoln, 16th president of the USA; railway; economy: electrical equipment, machinery and chemicals.

Springfield, 42 06N 72 35W, pop(1980) 152,319, county seat of Hampden county, SW Massachusetts, United States; on the R Connecticut, 8 km N of the Connecticut border; railway; economy: machinery, metal and paper products; monuments: Springfield armoury (1794-1968), basketball hall of fame; event: Eastern States Expo (Sept).

Springfield, 37 13N 93 17W, pop(1980) 133,116, county seat of Greene county, SW Missouri, United States; 240 km SSE of Kansas City; established in 1829; university; railway; economy: industrial, trade and shipping centre, trading in dairy products, livestock, poultry and fruit; manufactures include clothing, furniture and typewriters; tourist centre for Ozark Mts; monument: Museum of the Ozarks.

Springfield, 39 55N 83 49W, pop(1980) 72,563, county seat of Clark county, central Ohio, United States; 35 km NE of Dayton; settled in 1799, achieving city status in 1850; university (1842); railway; economy: engineering, vehicle parts, electrical goods.

Springfield, 44 03N 123 01W, pop(1980) 41,621, city in Lane county, W Oregon, United States; on the Willamette river, E of Eugene; railway.

Springlands, port in Guyana. See Corriverton.

Springs, 26 15S 28 26E, pop(1980) 153,974, municipality in Transvaal prov, South Africa; 40 km E of Johannesburg; economy: gold, uranium, glass, machine tools, paper, bicycles.

Srbija *sur'bi-ya*, SERBIA *ser'bee-a* (Eng), republic in Yugoslavia; bounded to the E by Romania and Bulgaria, to the N by Hungary, to the S by the Yugoslav republic of Makedonija (Macedonia) and to the W by the Yugoslav republics of Hrvatska (Croatia), Bosna-Hercegovina and Crna Gora (Montenegro) and by Albania; it is mountainous, with deep river valleys such as the Morava-Vardar corridor providing access routes; the land rises from the Danube and Sava lowlands to the Dinaric Alps in the W and to the Stara Planina in the E; pop(1981) 9,313,676; area 88,361 sq km; a former kingdom of the Balkan peninsula incorporated into Yugoslavia in 1918; established as a constituent republic in 1946, including the autonomous provs of Vojvodina (N) and Kosovo (S); capital Beograd; chief towns include Niš, Priština, Prizren, Kragujevac, Leskovac; the Serbs founded a state in the 6th century but were overrun by the Turks in 1389; Srbija became a kingdom in 1882; there are many interesting monasteries of the Morava and Raška schools built between the 13th and 15th centuries.

Sredinnyy Khrebet *sre-dyee'ni KHrye byet'*, CENTRAL RANGE (Eng), mountain range in Kamchatskaya oblast, Rossiyskaya, E Soviet Union, extending the entire length of the Kamchatka Peninsula; rises to 4,850 m at Klyuchevskaya Sopka, a volcano which last erupted in 1966; other peaks include Tolbachik (3,682 m), Ichinskaya Sopka (3,621 m), and Kronotskaya Sopka (3,528 m); the average height of the range is 915 m; further N it becomes the Koryakskiy Khrebet range.

Sredne Sibirskoye Ploskogor'ye, CENTRAL SIBERIAN PLATEAU (Eng), upland region in E Siberian Rossiyskaya, Soviet Union, between the R Yenisey (W) and the R Lena (E); watered by the rivers Lena, Olenek, Kotuy, and tributaries of the Yenisey (Nizhnyaya Tunguska, Angara, Kureyka); average elevation 300-800 m; corresponds to one of Asia's stable blocks of pre-Cambrian origin.

Sremska Mitrovica *srem'ska mee'tro-veet-sa*, SIRMIUM (anc), 44 59N 19 39E, pop(1981) 85,129, town in autonomous province of Vojvodina, NW Srbija (Serbia) republic, Yugoslavia; on R Sava, SSW of Novi Sad; railway.

Sri Lanka *sree lan'kah*, formerly CEYLON *se-lon'*, official name Democratic Socialist Republic of Sri Lanka, island state lying in the Indian Ocean, separated from the Indian sub-continent by the Palk Strait, but linked by a series of coral islands known as Adam's Bridge; surrounded on all sides by the Indian Ocean and bounded by the Bay of Bengal to the E and the Gulf of Mannar to the W; timezone GMT $+5\frac{1}{2}$; area 65,610 sq km; capital (since 1983) Sri-Jayawardenapura, a suburb of former capital Colombo; chief towns Jaffna, Kandy and Galle; pop(1986e) 16,755,000; ethnic groups include Sinhalese (74%), Tamils (18%), Muslims (7%), Burghers, Malays, Veddahs (1%); Sinhala is the official language, Tamil is a national language, while English is often used in government and is spoken by 10% of the pop; religion 69% Buddhist, 15% Hindu, 8% Christian, 8% Muslim; the currency is the Sri Lankan rupee of 100 cents; national holidays 4 Feb (National Day), Sinhala and Tamil New Year (April), 22 June (National Heroes Day), Jayawardene Day (Sept); membership of ADB, ANRCP, Colombo Plan, Commonwealth, FAO, G-77, GATT, IAEA, IBRD, ICAO, IDA, IFAD, IFC, ILO, IMF, IMO, INTELSAT, INTERPOL, IPU, IRC, ITU, NAM, SAARC (South Asian Association for Regional Cooperation), UN, UNESCO, UPU, WFTU, WHO, WIPO, WMO and WTO.

Physical description. Sri Lanka is a pear-shaped island, 440 km long and 220 km wide, lying in the Indian Ocean on the continental shelf of India. It includes the island of Mannar, which is part of Adam's Bridge that links Sri Lanka to India. The N plain and S half of the island lie only just above sea level and surround a South Central upland region. The highest mountain, Pidurutalagala (2,524 m), is surrounded by lesser mountains and hills which extend SW, towards the coast. The coastal plain is fringed by fine, sandy beaches and lagoons. All rivers drain outwards from the centre, the longest (332 km) being the Mahaweli Ganga which flows NE to meet the Bay of Bengal at Trincomalee in the NE. The N region is a limestone plain and is generally arid during the dry season. Although much of the island's forest has been cleared for agriculture, 44% still remains under tropical monsoonal forest or open woodland.

Climate. Though modified near the coast, the temperatures and humidity of the N plains are high throughout the year. At Trincomalee average daily temperatures range from 24°C to 33°C. Temperatures in the interior of the country are significantly reduced by altitude, as at Nuwara-Eliya where average daily temperatures range from 7°C to 21°C. The SW coast and the mountain regions have the greatest rainfall, particularly during April-June and Oct-Nov when the SW monsoon blows onshore. The island is much drier in the NE, with hardly any rain falling during Feb-Sept. Here the main rainy period is between Oct and Jan when the NE monsoon blows onshore. Over most of the island, rain falls mainly in afternoon showers, often accompanied by thunder.

History, government and constitution. Sri Lanka was first visited in 1505 by the Portuguese who built a fort at Colombo. The Dutch ousted the Portuguese in 1658, but failed to gain control of the kingdom of Kandy in the central mountains. British occupation began in 1796 and by establishing a network of roads they were able to extend control over the whole island. The British colony of Ceylon was established in 1802. During colonial rule Tamil labourers were brought in from S India to work on coffee and tea plantations. Ceylon was made a Dominion on 4 Feb 1948, and on 22 May 1972 a constitution was adopted establishing the independent republic of Sri Lanka. The 1972 constitution was repealed and replaced in 1978. The president, elected for a 6-year term, is head of state, and may not hold office for more than 2 terms. Parliament consists of a 168-member National State Assembly, which sits for 6 years. There are acute political tensions between the Sinhalese majority and the Tamil minority, who feel at a disadvantage in government and public life and want to establish a separate independent Tamil state in the N and E.

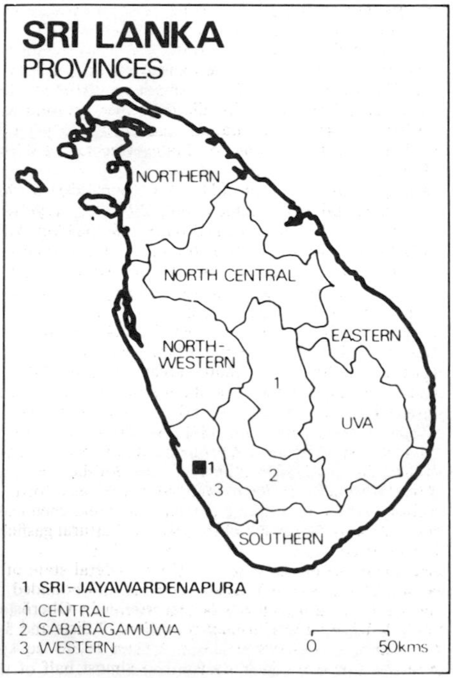

Economy. Agriculture accounts for 23% of national income and employs 46% of the labour force. The main crops are rice, rubber, tea and coconuts. In March 1976 the government took over all private tea and rubber plantations, paying compensation on condition that it was re-invested in Sri Lanka. Spices, rice, sugar-cane and other food crops are mostly grown on smaller holdings. Forests provide timber for local needs and fishing provides an important element of the local diet. Graphite, coal, precious and semi-precious stones are mined. About 85% of the country's electricity is produced by water power. Manufacturing industry is based on the production of textiles, chemicals, petroleum products, rubber, tobacco, food processing, wood products, metal products and paper. Tea, textiles, petroleum products, rubber and coconuts are the main exports, with major markets in the USA, Iraq, the UK, Egypt and Japan. Petroleum, consumer goods and wheat are the chief imports.

Administrative divisions. Sri Lanka is divided into 9 provinces and 25 districts as follows:

Province/District	*area (sq km)*	*pop(1981)*
Western province		
Colombo	652.4	1,699,241
Gampaha	1,398.8	1,390,826
Kalutara	1,606.6	829,704
Central province		
Kandy	2,157.5	1,048,317
Matale	1,988.6	357,354
Nuwara-Eliya	1,437.2	603,577
Southern province		
Galle	1,673.9	814,531
Matara	1,246.5	643,786
Hambantota	2,593.4	424,344
Northern province		
Kilinochchi } Jaffna	2,072.3	830,552
Mannar	2,002.1	106,235
Vavuniya	2,645.2	95,428
Mullaittivu	1,966.1	77,189
Eastern province		
Batticaloa	2,464.6	330,033
Amparai	4,539.2	388,970
Trincomalee	2,618.2	255,948
North Western province		
Kurunegala	4,772.8	1,211,801
Puttalam	2,976.9	492,533
North-Central province		
Anuradhapura	7,129.2	587,929
Polonnaruwa	3,403.8	261,563
Uva province		
Badulla	2,818.2	640,952
Monaragala	5,586.9	273,570
Sabaragamuwa province		
Ratnapura	3,238.0	797,087
Kegalla	1,662.0	684,944

Sri-Jayawardenapura *sree-jī-ah-war-den-a-poo'ra*, 6 55N 79 52E, official administrative capital of Sri Lanka since 1983; located in an E suburb of Colombo.

Srinagar *sree'nu-gur*, 34 08N 74 50E, pop(1981) 520,000, summer capital of Jammu-Kashmir state, N India; in the Vale of Kashmir to the NW of the Pir Panjal Range of mountains, on the Jhelum river; founded in the 6th century, it became the capital of the disputed territory of Jammu-Kashmir in 1948; airfield; river transport; economy: hand-woven woollen shawls (cashmeres), machine-made silks, woollens and carpets; monuments: Buddhist ruins and a mosque built by a Mogul empress in 1623.

Staaten River, national park in N Queensland, N Australia; area 4,600 sq km; established in 1977; crossed by the R Staaten and its tributary the Back Creek.

Staf'ford, 52 48N 2 07W, pop(1981) 62,242, county town of Staffordshire, central England; birthplace of Izaak Walton (1593-1683); railway; economy: engineering, chemicals, electrical goods, footwear, timber; monuments: churches of St Mary and St Chad; 18th-c William Salt library; Shugborough (6 km E), the ancestral home of the Earls of Lichfield.

Staffordshire, county in central England; in the basin of the R Trent; pop(1981) 1,015,620; area 2,716 sq km; county town Stafford; chief towns include Stoke-on-Trent, Newcastle-under-Lyme and Burton-upon-Trent; the county is divided into 9 districts:

District	*area (sq km)*	*pop(1981)*
Cannock Chase	79	84,763
East Staffordshire	388	95,260
Lichfield	330	88,828
Newcastle-under-Lyme	211	118,205
South Staffordshire	409	96,890
Stafford	599	118,509
Staffordshire Moorlands	576	96,110
Stoke-on-Trent	93	252,509
Tamworth	31	64,546

Staines, 51 26N 0 31W, pop(1981) 52,815, town in Spelthorne dist, Surrey, SE England; part of Greater London urban area; at the junction of the Thames and Colne rivers, 27 km W of London; railway; economy: engineering, glass, paint.

Stalowa Wola *sta-wo'va vō'a*, 50 35N 22 05E, pop(1983) 61,000, town in Tarnobrzeg voivodship, SE Poland; near R San; railway.

Stalybridge *stay'li-brij*, 53 29N 2 04W, pop(1981) 23,668, town in Tameside borough, Greater Manchester, NW England; on R Tame, 11 km E of Manchester; railway; economy: chemicals, engineering, metal products, paper.

Stam'ford, 52 39N 0 29W, pop(1981) 16,393, market town in South Holland dist, Lincolnshire, E central England; on the R Welland, 19 km W of Peterborough; railway; economy: electrical goods.

Stamford, 41 03N 73 32W, pop(1980) 102,453, town in Fairfield county, SW Connecticut, United States; on Long Island Sound, stretching NW to New York state border; railway; economy: computers and electronic components.

Standing Rock, Indian reservation in S North Dakota, United States; bounded E by the R Missouri, N by the Cedar river and S by South Dakota state; settlements include Fort Yates, Cannon Ball and Selfridge.

Stan'ford le Hope, 51 31N 0 26E, pop(1981) 32,169, town linked with Corringham in Thurrock dist, Essex, SE England; on the R Thames, 8 km NE of Tilbury; railway; economy: oil refining.

Stange *stang'u*, 60 40N 11 05E, pop(1980) 17,854, town in Hedmark county, SE Norway; on L Mjøsa, railway; church built 1250.

Stan'ley, 51 45S 57 56W, port and capital of the Falkland Is, situated on the E coast of East Falkland; pop(1980) 1,000, airport (Mt Pleasant) with links to the UK and to 31 grass and beach airstrips serving most of the settlements of the colony.

Stanley, 54 52N 1 42W, pop(1981) 20,089, town in Derwentside dist, Durham, NE England; 8 km W of Chester-le-Street; economy: textiles, chemicals, coal.

Stanley, Mount, mountain in the Ruwenzori range on the frontier between Zaire and Uganda; height of Margherita Peak 5,110 m; the highest point in Zaire and Uganda; first ascent by the Duke of Abruzzi, J Petigax, C Collier and J Brocherel in 1906.

Stanleyville, city in Zaire. See Kisangani.

Stann Creek, dist in E Belize, Central America; bounded E by the Caribbean Sea; the Cockscomb Mts rise in the W to Victoria Peak (1,120 m), watered by the Stann Creek and the Waha Leaf Creek; pop(1980) 14,181; area 2,175 sq km; chief town Dangriga (formerly Stann Creek); economy: citrus, cocoa, fishing, forestry.

Stanovoy Khrebet *stu-nu-voy' KHrye-byet'*, mountain range in SE Siberian Rossiyskaya, Soviet Union, extending c.960 km E from the R Olekma to the R Maya, a tributary of the R Uda; continued NE by the Khrebet Dzhugdzhur range; forms the watershed between the Lena and Amur river basins; rises to 2,522 m in the E; consists geologically of crystalline schists and gneiss and grey granite intrusions; traversed by the Yakutsk-Skovorodino highway.

Stans, 46 58N 8 22E, pop(1980) 5,600, capital of Nidwalden demicanton, Unterwalden canton, central Switzerland, 11 km SSE of Luzern.

Sta'ra Pa'zova, 45 00N 20 10E, pop(1981) 52,566, town in autonomous province of Vojvodina, NW Srbija (Serbia) republic, Yugoslavia; NW of Beograd; railway.

Sta'ra Zago'ra, okrug (prov) in E central Bulgaria S of the Stara Planina (Balkan Mts); area 5,013 sq km; pop(1981) 411,000; the Stara Zagora basin is an extensive agricultural, vine-growing and horticultural region, drained by the Tundzha and Maritsa rivers.

Stara Zagora, AUGUSTA TRAJANA (Lat), 42 25N 25 37E, pop(1981) 138,902, commercial and manufacturing capital of Stara Zagora okrug (prov), E central Bulgaria; 231 km E of Sofiya; airfield; railway; economy: textiles, chemicals, tobacco, food processing.

Starachowice *sta-ra-KHo'veet-sa*, 51 03N 21 00E, pop(1983) 53,400, town in Kielce voivodship, S central Poland; on R Kamienna, NE of Kielce; forest park nearby; railway; economy: lorries.

Stargard Szczeciński *star-gard shchtre-tre-cheen'ski*, 53 21N 15 01E, pop(1983) 63,300, town in Szczecin voivodship, NW Poland; SE of Szczecin, on R Ina; rebuilt after 1945; railway; monuments: 13-15th-c Gothic church of the Virgin Mary, regional museum, 13th-c town walls.

Starnberger See *shtahrn'ber-gur zay* or **Würmsee** *vürm'zay*, lake in S Bayern (Bavaria) prov, W Germany, 22 km SW of München (Munich); area 57.2 sq km; max depth 127 m; average depth 54 m; drained by the R Würm; town of Starnberg at NW tip.

State College, 40 48N 77 52W, pop(1980) 36,130, town in Centre county, central Pennsylvania, United States; 55 km NE of Altoona; university (1855).

Staten Island, borough of New York City, United States; co-extensive with Richmond county, the borough forms an island which is separated from New Jersey by Kill van Kull and Arthur Kill channels and from Long Island by the Narrows; area 153 sq km; pop(1980) 352,121; economy: oil refining, shipbuilding, paper, printing; first settled in 1641; the island was named by early Dutch settlers after the *Stahten* or States General of 17th-c Holland.

Stavanger *sta-vang'er*, 58 58N 5 45E, pop(1983) 91,964, seaport capital of Rogaland county, SW Norway; on a S branch of the Boknafjorden (Bokn Fjord), 304 km WSW of Oslo; thought to have been founded in the 8th century; important oil centre; rail terminus; airport; economy: oil refinery, fish-canning, shipyards, oil-rig construction; monument: St Swithins cathedral (12th-c).

Stave'ley, 53 16N 1 20W, pop(1981) 24,599, town in Bolsover dist, Derbyshire, central England; part of Chesterfield-Staveley urban area; 6 km NE of Chesterfield; economy: scientific instruments, chemicals.

Stavropol' *sta-vro'pul-y'*, formerly VOROSHILOVSK (1935-43), 45 03N 41 59E, pop(1983) 281,000, capital city of Stavropol'skiy kray, S European Rossiyskaya, Soviet Union; in the NW foothills of the Bol'shoy Kavkaz (Greater Caucasus) range; founded in 1777 as a fortress; railway; airfield; economy: machine building, chemicals, foodstuffs, footwear, furniture; there are natural gasfields in the area.

Steiermark *shtī'er-mark*, STYRIA (Eng), federal state of E Austria, lying on the Yugoslav frontier and bounded by the states of Burgenland, Niederösterreich, Oberösterreich, Salzburg and Kärnten; comprises 17 dists and 544 communities; pop(1981) 1,187,512; area 16,387 sq km; capital Graz; extensive forests cover almost half of the total area, grassland and vineyards account for a further quarter; often described as 'Austria's green province'; economy: mining of iron ore (from the Erzberg near the town of Eisenerz), lignite and magnesite; the iron, steel and engineering industries are based in the Mur and Mürz valleys; the Austrian vehicle industry is centred in Graz; other industries include electrics, cellulose and paper.

Steinhuder Meer *shtīn'hoo-dur mayr*, lake in Niedersachsen (Lower Saxony) prov, W Germany, 24 km WNW of Hannover; area 29.4 sq km; max depth 3 m; average depth 2 m; drains into the R Weser.

Steinkjer, *stayn'char*, 64 00N 11 30E, pop(1983) 20,692, agric market town and capital of Nord-Trøndelag county, W Norway; at the head of Trondheimsfjord (Trondheim Fjord), 125 km NE of Trondheim; railway.

Stellenbosch *stel'en-bosh*, 33 56S 18 51E, residential town in SW Cape prov, South Africa; 40 km E of Cape Town; founded in 1679; the 2nd oldest city in the country; the centre of a wine-producing region; university (1918); monuments: many fine Cape Dutch buildings including the burger house, powder magazine, coachman's cottage, St Mary's Rhenish church.

Stenhousemuir, 56 02N 3 35W, pop(1981) 19,771, town in Falkirk dist, Central, central Scotland; 3 km NW of Falkirk.

Sterea Ellás-Évvoia *ay'vi-a*, CENTRAL GREECE AND EUBOEA *yoo-bee'a* (Eng), region of Greece, bounded W by the Ionian Sea, E by the Aegean Sea, and S by Pelopónnisos region; pop(1981) 1,099,841; area 24,391 sq km; comprises the nomoi (depts) of Aitolía and Akarnanía, Attikí, Voiótia (Boeotia), Evritanía, Évvoia (Euboea), Fokís, and Fthiótis.

Sterling Heights, 42 34N 83 01W, pop(1980) 108,999, town in Macomb county, SE Michigan, United States; 30 km N of Detroit.

Sterlitamak *styir-lyee-tu-mak'*, 53 40N 55 59E, pop(1983) 233,000, town in Bashkirskaya ASSR, E European Rossiyskaya, Soviet Union; on the R Belaya, 130 km S of Ufa; founded in 1766 as a storage and transit point for salt which was shipped down the R Belaya to the Kama and Volga rivers; formerly capital of the republic (1919-22); railway; economy: chemicals, synthetic rubber, machine building, leatherwork, clothing.

Steubenville *styoo'ben-vil*, 40 22N 80 37W, pop(1980) 26,400, county seat of Jefferson county, E Ohio, United States; on Ohio river, 80 km S of Youngstown.

Stevenage *steev'nij*, 51 55N 0 14W, pop(1981) 74,523, town in Stevenage dist, Hertfordshire, SE England; 45 km N of London; designated a 'new town' in 1946; railway.

Stevenston, 55 39N 4 45W, pop(1981) 11,337, town in Cunninghame dist, Strathclyde, W Scotland; 4 km E of Ardrossan; railway; economy: iron, chemicals.

Stewart Island, island of New Zealand; lies to the S of South Island, across the Foveaux Strait; area 1,735 sq km; a refuge for animal and bird life; the small settlement of Oban on Halfmoon Bay is the main urban centre for this largely uninhabited island; the island can be reached by plane or ferry from the town of Bluff, S of Invercargill; the highest point is Mount Anglem (977 m); economy: fishing.

Steyr *shtīr*, 48 04N 14 25E, pop(1981) 38,942, capital of Steyrland dist, Oberösterreich state, N Austria, between the R Enns and its tributary, the R Steyr; economy: iron and steel, BMW bikes and trucks assembled, manufacture of the Steyr-Puch motorbike.

Stillwater, 36 07N 97 04W, pop(1980) 38,268, county seat of Payne county, N central Oklahoma, United States; 96 km W of Tulsa; settled in 1889; university (1891); railway; economy: market centre for a farming area.

Stirling, 56 07N 3 57W, pop(1981) 38,842, capital of Stirling dist and of Central region, central Scotland; on the S bank of the R Forth, 34 km NE of Glasgow; university (1967); railway; economy: brick making, coachbuilding; monuments: Stirling castle, on a 76 m-high rock, has been the scene of much of Scotland's history: it was recaptured from the English by William Wallace in 1297, taken by Edward I in 1304 until Bruce won at Bannockburn in 1314; it later became a favourite royal residence; inside part of Stirling castle is a museum on the Argyll and Sutherland Highlanders; approx 1.5 km E of Stirling are the ruins of Cambuskenneth Abbey (founded in 1147) where Bruce's parliament was held in 1326; the Church of the Holy Rude (founded in 1414) was the scene of the coronation of James VI when he was 13 months old; MacRobert Arts Centre contains a theatre, art gallery and studio; Smith Art Gallery and Museum; 2 km NNE of Stirling is the Wallace Monument (built in 1870), commemorating William Wallace, who defeated the English at the Battle of Stirling Bridge in 1297; events: Stirling Festival (May).

Stirling Range, mountain range in SW Western Australia, 64 km N of Albany; extends 64 km parallel with SW coast; rises to 1,109 m at Bluff Knoll.

Stjørdal, *styur'dahl*, 63 27N 10 57E, pop(1980) 16,173, town in Nord-Trøndelag county, W Norway; railway.

Stockholm *stok'hōlm*, county of SE Sweden; numerous small islands lie off the E coast; land area 6,494 sq km; pop(1983) 1,544,354; capital Stockholm; chief towns Södertälje and Täby.

Stockholm, 59 20N 18 03E, pop(1982) 649,587, seaport and capital of Sweden; on a group of islands and the adjacent mainland at a point where L Mälaren discharges itself by a short channel into the Saltsjö, an arm of the Baltic Sea; largest city in Sweden and its cultural, commercial and financial centre; founded in 1255, the city became an important trading centre of the Hanseatic League; the city was beautified by Queen Christina in the 17th century; see of a bishop; university (1878); underground railway system (1930); economy: metalworking, engineering, textiles, foodstuffs; monuments: 18th-c Renaissance royal palace, 17th-c German church, national museum, Drottningholm Palace (now the residence of the royal family).

Stock'port, 53 25N 2 10W, pop(1981) 136,792, town in Stockport borough, Greater Manchester, NW England; at the junction of the Tame and Goyt rivers which join to form the R Mersey, 10 km SE of Manchester; railway; airport; economy: electronics, computers, aerospace, printing, engineering, foodstuffs.

Stocksbridge, 53 27N 1 34W, pop(1981) 13,413, town in Sheffield borough, South Yorkshire, N England; on the Little Don river, 14 km NW of Sheffield; economy: steel.

Stockton, 37 58N 121 17W, pop(1980) 149,779, inland seaport and city in San Joaquin county, central California, United States; on a deep-water channel to the San Joaquin river, c.105 km E of San Francisco; university (1851); railway; economy: food processing, marine engineering, trade in agricultural products.

Stockton-on-Tees, 54 34N 1 19W, pop(1981) 87,223, town in Stockton-on-Tees dist, Cleveland, NE England; on the R Tees estuary; developed with the opening of the Stockton-Darlington railway in 1825; railway; economy: shipbuilding, engineering, chemicals.

Stoke-on-Trent, 53 00N 2 10W, pop(1981) 252,509, industrial city in Staffordshire, central England; part of the Potteries urban area; on the R Trent, 217 km NW of London; an amalgam (1910) of the former Tunstall, Burslem, Hanley, Stoke-on-Trent, Fenton and Longton municipal authorities; University of Keele (1962); railway; economy: clayware (largest producer in the world), coal, steel, chemicals, engineering, rubber, paper; monuments: Wedgwood museum at Barlaston (7 km S).

Stolberg *shtol'burk*, STOLBERG IM RHEINLAND, 50 45N 6 15E, pop (1983) 56,900, town in W Nordrhein-Westfalen (North Rhine-Westphalia) prov, W Germany; on the Belgian border, 11 km E of Aachen; railway; economy: lead, chemicals, glass, textiles.

Stone, 52 54N 2 10W, pop(1981) 12,203, town in Stafford dist, Staffordshire, central England; on R Trent, 11 km N of Stafford; railway; economy: engineering.

Stonehaven, 56 58N 2 13W, pop(1981) 7,922, port capital of Kincardine and Deeside dist, Grampian region, NE Scotland; situated on the E coast, 21 km S of Aberdeen;

railway; economy: fishing; local resort; monuments: Stonehaven Tolbooth, a 16th-c storehouse of the Earls Marischal which was later used as a prison, contains a display on local history; just S of Stonehaven are the ruins of Dunnottar Castle, a fortress built in the 14th c on cliffs above the sea; the Scottish regalia were hidden here for safety during the Commonwealth wars; when Cromwell's troops occupied the castle in 1652 the treasure was smuggled out to Kinneff church, 11 km to the S, where it remained hidden for 9 years; 5 km S of Stonehaven is Fowlsheugh Nature Reserve, a large seabird colony.

Stonehenge, prehistoric stone circle on Salisbury Plain, Wiltshire, S England; the earliest construction on the site consisted of a ring of wooden posts ('Aubrey Holes') surrounded by a bank and ditch; the 2nd phase saw the erection of a circular ring of local sarsen stones; in a 3rd phase the horseshoe of great trilithons was raised and an avenue of standing stones erected; this avenue, which was first fully revealed by aerial photography in 1923, leads first NE, then E and SSE to the R Avon at W Amesbury; in the 4th phase a smaller horseshoe and circle of 'blue stones' was erected within the larger circle; these spotted, doleritic stones are thought to have come from the Prescelly Hills of SW Wales; a 5th and final phase is represented by 2 outer rings of stone holes which have been dated to the Iron Age.

Stoney Creek, 43 13N 79 46W, pop(1981) 36,762, town in S Ontario, Canada; 6 km ESE of Hamilton; the scene of a battle between American and British forces in 1813; railway; economy: fruit growing.

Stord *stōr*, 59 47N 5 31E, pop(1980) 12,977, town on Stord I, Hordaland county, SW Norway.

Store Bælt *stor belt*, GREAT BELT (Eng), strait between Sjælland (Zealand) and Fyn I, Denmark, connecting the Kattegat with the Baltic Sea; length 64 km, average width 16 km.

Stornoway, 58 12N 6 23W, pop(1981) 8,638, port capital of Western Isles region, NW Scotland; on the E coast of the island of Lewis, 35 km S of the Butt of Lewis, the northernmost point; airfield; economy: fishing, oil supply services, tweeds and knitwear; monuments: An Lanntair art gallery; the Museum Nan Eilean Steornabhagh contains displays on the history of Lewis.

Storsjön *stoor'shun*, STOR (Eng), lake in Jämtland county, W Sweden; area 456 sq km; length 72 km; Östersund is on its E shore.

Stor'strøm, a county of Denmark including S part of Sjælland (Zealand) I and the islands of Lolland, Falster and Møn; area 3,398 sq km; pop(1983) 258,670; capital Nykøbing, chief towns include Næstved and Nakskov.

Stour *stowr*, river rising N of Gillingham in Dorset, S England; flows 88 km S and SE to meet the English Channel at Christchurch where it is joined by the R Avon.

Stour, river rising as headstreams in SE Cambridgeshire, E England; flows 75 km SE and E, following the Suffolk-Essex border, to meet the North Sea at Harwich.

Stourbridge *stowr'-*, 52 27N 2 09W, pop(1981) 55,499, town in Dudley borough, West Midlands, central England; on the R Stour, 16 km WSW of Birmingham; railway; economy: engineering, glass, metal products.

Stourport or **Stourport-on-Severn** *stowr'pōrt*, 52 21N 2 16W, pop(1981) 17,933, river and canal port in Wyre Forest dist, Hereford and Worcester, W central England; at the junction of the Severn and Stour rivers, 16 km N of Worcester; economy: electrical equipment, plastics, carpets.

Stow *stō*, 41 10N 81 27W, pop(1980) 25,303, town in Summit county, NE Ohio, United States; 11 km NE of Akron.

Stowmarket *stō-*, 52 11N 1 00E, pop(1981) 11,050, town in Mid Suffolk dist, Suffolk, E England; on R Gipping, 18 km NW of Ipswich; railway; economy: iron, tanning, engineering, foodstuffs.

Strabane *stra-ban'*, AN SRATH BAN (Gael), 54 49N 7 27W, pop(1981) 10,340, market town in Strabane dist, Tyrone, W Northern Ireland; on the Mourne and Finn rivers, where they meet to form the R Foyle; a border station on the Irish border; economy: textiles, engineering, salmon fishing.

Strakonice *stra'kon-yi-tse*, 49 17N 13 55E, pop(1984) 23,638, town in Jihočeský region, Czech Socialist Republic, W central Czechoslovakia; on R Otava NW of České Budějovice; summer resort; birthplace of the poet F.L. Celakovsky; railway; economy: industrial machinery, motorcycles, clothing; monument: castle of the Knights of St John.

Stralsund *shtrahl'zoont*, 54 18N 13 6E, pop(1981) 74,421, seaport in Stralsund dist, Rostock, N East Germany; on the Baltic coast opposite Rügen I, to which it is linked; chartered in 1234, becoming a member of the Hanseatic League in the 14th century; formerly part of Prussia; railway; economy: shipbuilding, fish processing; monument: 13th-c church of St Mary.

Strangford Lough, inlet of the North Channel, in E Co Down, E Northern Ireland; separated from the sea to the E by the Ards peninsula; its narrow entrance at the S is approx 1 km wide and 8 km long; the inlet itself is 27 km long and 6 km wide; contains several islands; the main town on the inlet is Newtownards.

Stranraer *stran-rahr'*, 54 54N 5 02W, pop(1981) 10,873, port capital of Wigtown dist, Dumfries and Galloway, SW Scotland; at the head of Loch Ryan, 37 km W of Wigtown; railway; ferries to N Ireland; economy: footwear, metal products, transport equipment; monument: Wigtown district museum.

Strasbourg *straz-boor*, STRASSBURG *stras-boorKH* (Ger), ARGENTORATUM (anc), 48 35N 7 42E, pop(1982) 252,264, industrial and commercial city and capital of Bas-Rhin dept, Alsace region, NE France; on the R Ill, 3 km W of its junction with the R Rhine, 133 km SE of Metz; 6th largest city in France; important transportation centre and major river port (largest in France); terminus of the Marne-Rhine and Rhine-Rhône Canals; part of a bishopric since 1003; university (founded in 1537, acquired university status in 1621); seat of the Council of Europe, European Parliament, European Commission of Human Rights and the European Science Foundation; the only French city on the R Rhine; the tourist centre of Alsace and the venue of numerous congresses and conferences; between 1434-1444 Gutenberg developed the art of printing here; railway junction; economy: trade in mineral ore, building materials, petroleum products and grain; industry: iron and steel, metalworking, engineering, furniture, sealing materials, foodstuffs, paper, textiles, tanning, tourism; monuments: Gothic cathedral of Notre-Dame (begun in 1015 on the foundations of an earlier Romanesque church), with a noted 14th-c astronomical clock; chamber of commerce; Château des Rohan (1728-42), until the Revolution the residence of the Cardinal-Bishops of the house of Rohan; old town hall (used as a town hall 1805-1976); Palais de l'Europe (1972-77), where the Council of Europe and the European Parliament meet; La Petite France is a charming quarter of old Strasbourg with 16th-c half-timbered buildings lining its narrow streets; to the SW are the Ponts Couverts, 4 bridges formerly roofed, crossing the R Ill, which is here divided into 4 arms; event: international music festival (16 days in June).

Stratford-upon-Avon, 52 12N 1 41W, pop(1981) 21,732, town in Stratford-upon-Avon dist, Warwickshire, central England; on the R Avon, 13 km SW of Warwick; birthplace of William Shakespeare; Royal Shakespeare Theatre; railway; economy: tourism, engineering, textiles; events: Shakespeare theatre season (April-Jan); Shakespeare's birthday and St George's Day (23 April); Mop Fair (12 Oct).

Strathclyde *strath-clīd'*, region in W and central Scotland; bounded by Highland region (N), Central region (NE), Lothian and Borders (E), Dumfries and Galloway (S) and by the Atlantic (W); the region encloses the basin of the R Clyde; to the N of the Clyde is the Highland area, made up of lochs, mountains and islands, including the islands of Mull, Jura, Islay and Arran; the lower part of the Clyde contains the city of Glasgow and the area generally known as Clydeside; this is the industrial centre of Scotland and contains almost 25% of the country's population; the land to the S of the Clyde contains part of the Southern Uplands; pop(1981) 2,404,532; area 13,537 sq km; capital Glasgow; major towns include Paisley, Motherwell, Greenock, Airdrie, Dumbarton, Hamilton, Coatbridge and Kilmarnock; Strathclyde is divided into 19 districts:

District	*area (sq km)*	*pop(1981)*
Argyll and Bute	6,497	68,834
Bearsden and Milngavie	36	39,429
Clydebank	36	52,024
Clydesdale	1,325	57,554
Cumbernauld and Kilsyth	95	62,031
Cumnock and Doon Valley	801	45,260
Cunninghame	879	138,707
Dumbarton	477	78,648
East Kilbride	285	82,949
Eastwood	116	53,572
Glasgow City	198	765,915
Hamilton	131	108,459
Inverclyde	158	100,387
Kilmarnock and Loudoun	373	82,154
Kyle and Carrick	1,322	114,565
Monklands	164	110,667
Motherwell	173	150,037
Renfrew	309	206,179
Strathkelvin	164	87,161

Středočeský *stre'do-che-skee*, region in Czech Socialist Republic, W Czechoslovakia; watered by the Elbe (Labe), Vltava, Jizera, Berounka and Sázava rivers; area 11,003 sq km; pop(1984) 1,144,360; capital Praha (Prague); chief towns include Kolín, Kladno and Mladá Boleslav.

Středoslovenský *stre'do-slo-ven-skee*, region in Slovak Socialist Republic, E Czechoslovakia; bounded S by Hungary and N by Poland, with the N arm of the Carpathian Mts culminating in the Tatra range in the N of the region; watered by the Hron and the Váh rivers; area 17,985 sq km; pop(1984) 1,559,391; capital Banská Bystrica; chief towns include Žilina, Brezno and Lučenec.

Stret'ford, 53 27N 2 19W, pop(1981) 47,771, town in Trafford borough, Greater Manchester, NW England; 6 km SW of Manchester; railway; economy: engineering, chemicals, textiles, foodstuffs.

Strimon, river in Bulgaria and Greece. See Struma.

Strongsville, 41 19N 81 50W, pop(1980) 28,577, town in Cuyahoga county, NE Ohio, United States; 22 km SSW of Cleveland.

Strood, 51 24N 0 28E, pop(1981) 32,896, town in the Medway Towns urban area and Rochester upon Medway dist, Kent, SE England; NW of Rochester; railway.

Stroud *strowd*, 51 45N 2 12W, pop(1981) 38,228, market town in Stroud dist, Gloucestershire, SW central England; on the R Frome, 13 km S of Gloucester; railway; economy: textiles, food processing, plastics, oil drilling equipment, pianos.

Struer *stroo'ur*, 56 29N 8 37E, pop(1981) 10,973, town in Ringkøbing county, W Jylland, Denmark, on S shore of Limfjorden (Lim Fjord); railway; economy: furniture, electrics.

Struga *stroo'ga*, 41 10N 20 41E, pop(1981) 56,451, town in Makedonija (Macedonia) republic, S Yugoslavia; on L Ohrid, near the Albanian frontier, SSW of Skopje; has interesting Turkish-style houses; economy: fishing.

Struma *stroo'ma*, STRIMON (Gr), river in W Bulgaria and Greece, rising in the Vitosha Mts S of Sofiya; flows SSE through agricultural land to meet the Aegean Sea WSW of Kavalla; length 346 km; tributaries include the Dzherman, Rila, Angistes and Strumica rivers.

Strumica *stroo'mit-sa*, ASTRACUM (anc), 41 26N 22 39E, pop(1981) 87,347, town in Makedonija (Macedonia) republic, S Yugoslavia; on R Strumica, SE of Skopje; economy: tobacco, livestock, cotton trade.

Stubaier Alpen *shtoo-bī'er al'pen*, STUBAI ALPS (Eng), mountain range of the Eastern Alps in Tirol state, W Austria, rising to 3,507 m at Zuckerhütl; extend immediately NE of the Ötztal Alps; numerous glaciers.

Stubbington, 50 48N 1 12W, pop(1981) 18,814 (with Lee-on-the-Solent), town in Fareham dist, Hampshire, S England; W of Portsmouth.

Studen Kladnets *stoo'dayn klad'nets*, lake in the E Rhodopi Planina (Rhodope Mts), Kŭrdzhali okrug (prov), S Bulgaria, situated E of Kŭrdzhali.

Stung Treng *stoong treng*, province in N Cambodia; pop(1981) 136,000; bounded N by Laos; crossed by the Mekong R and its tributaries the Se San and the Se Kong; administrative centre Stung Treng (13 31N 105 58E), lies to the S of the confluence of the Se San with the Mekong river.

Stura *stoo'rah*, river in NW Italy, rising on the SE slope of Maddalena Pass; flows 104 km NE past Demonte, Cuneo, and Fosano, to the R Tanaro near Cherasco.

Sturt, national park in extreme NW of New South Wales, Australia; area 3,042 sq km; established in 1972; named after the explorer, Capt Sturt.

Stuttgart *shtoot'gart*, dist of NE Baden-Württemberg prov, W Germany; pop(1983) 3,459,700; area 10,558 sq km; capital Stuttgart.

Stuttgart, 48 47N 9 12E, pop(1983) 571,100, capital of Baden-Württemberg prov, W Germany; on the R Neckar, 61 km ESE of Karlsruhe; 2 universities (1967); notable mineral springs; founded in the 10th century; former capital of the kingdom of Württemberg and seat of the Reichstag National Assembly; birthplace of the philosopher G.F.W. Hegel (1770); railway, airport; economy: car manufacturing (Daimler-Benz, Porsche), electrical equipment, office equipment, paints and varnishes, photographic products, telecommunications, engineering, precision mechanical and optical equipment, foodstuffs, metalworking machines, textiles, paper-making and publishing; it is one of Germany's largest fruit-growing and wine-producing centres; events: Spring Festival (April); Stuttgart Ballet Week (May); Lichterfest with fireworks (July); Swabian Sunday (Sept); Cannstatt Folk Festival (Sept).

Styria, federal state of Austria. See Steiermark.

Subotica *soo'bo-ti-tsah*, SZABADKA (Hung), 46 04N 19 41E, pop(1981) 154,611, largest town in autonomous province of Vojvodina, NW Srbija (Serbia) republic, Yugoslavia; Palic health resort nearby; railway; economy: fruit trade, foodstuffs, chemicals; event: Duzijanca traditional harvest festival in July.

Suceava *soo-cha'va*, county in N Romania, between the E Carpathian Mts (E) and the R Siret (N) and bounded to the N by the USSR; pop(1983) 664,823; area 8,555 sq km; capital Suceava.

Suceava, 47 37N 26 18E, pop(1983) 85,250, capital of Suceava county, N Romania; on R Suceava; famous pilgrimage centre; original capital of Moldavia (1388-1564); airport; railway; economy: food processing, wood products, mining, paper, clothing; monuments: 14th-c Mirauti church; 16th-c St George church; remains of fortress built by Stephen the Great; Dragomirna monastery 16 km N.

Suchitepéquez *soo-cheet-e-pay'kes*, maritime dept in S Guatemala, Central America; bounded S by the Pacific Ocean; pop(1982e) 304,826; area 2,510 sq km; capital Mazatenango; the land rises towards the N.

Suchow, town in Jiangsu prov, E China. See Suzhou.

Sucre *sook'ray*, formerly CHUQUISACA, 19 05S 65 15W, pop(1982) 79,941, city in Oropeza prov, Chuquisaca, S central Bolivia; official judicial and legal capital of Bolivia and capital of Chuquisaca region; founded in 1538; alt 2,705 m; university (1624); railway; airfield; economy: small oil refinery; monuments: local colonial buildings include the Legislative Palace, where the country's Declaration of Independence was signed; the modern Santo Domingo (Palace of Justice), seat of Bolivia's judiciary; 17th-c cathedral and museum; the churches of San Miguel and San Francisco contain early

17th-c wooden ceilings with intricate patterns of Moorish origin; event: Virgin of Guadalupe (8 Sept).

Sucre, dept in NW Colombia, South America; bounded W by the Caribbean; pop(1985) 523,525; area 10,917 sq km; capital Sincelejo.

Sucre, state in NE Venezuela; on the Caribbean; bordered E by Gulf of Paria; traversed by spurs of the coastal hill range; includes Araya Peninsula (W) and Paria Peninsula (E); pop(1980) 568,020; area 11,795 sq km; capital Cumaná.

Sudan *soo-dan'*, official name the Republic of Sudan, JAMHURYAT ES-SUDAN (Arab), a NE African republic bounded N by Egypt, NW by Libya, W by Chad, SW by the Central African Republic, S by Zaire, SE by Uganda and Kenya, E by Ethiopia and NE by the Red Sea; timezone GMT +2; area 2,504,530 sq km; pop(1984e) 21,103,000; capital Khartoum; chief towns Omdurman, Khartoum North, Port Sudan, Atbara, Kassala and Kosti; there are Nilotic, Negro, Nubian and Arab ethnic groups; the majority of the pop (70%) belongs to the Sunni Muslim sect (mainly in the N), the remainder either following local beliefs (20%) or Christian beliefs (5%, mainly in the S); the official language is Arabic, but Nubian, Ta Bedawie, dialects of Nilotic, Nilo-Hamitic and Sudanic languages are also spoken; the unit of currency is the Sudanese pound; national holiday 1 Jan (Independence Day); membership of AfDB, APC, Arab League, FAO, G-77, IAEA, IBRD, ICAC, ICAO, IDA, IDB (Islamic Development Bank), IFAD, IFC, ILO, IMF, IMO, INTELSAT, INTERPOL, ITU, NAM, OAU, OIC, UN, UNESCO, UPU, WFTU, WHO, WIPO, WMO, WTO.

Physical description. The largest country on the African continent, Sudan lies astride the middle reaches of the R Nile. The E edge of the country is formed by the Nubian highlands and an escarpment rising to over 2,000 m on the shores of the Red Sea. In the SE lie the foothills of the neighbouring Ethiopian highlands. In the S, along the Kenyan and Ugandan frontiers are the Imatong mountains rising to 3,187 m at Kinyeti, the highest point in Sudan. In the W the Dafur massif rises to 3,071 m at Jebel Marra. The central plain includes the fertile clays of Gezira (S of Khartoum) and the hot, sandy desert further N. Large parts of E Sudan are dominated by the R Nile and its tributaries. The White Nile crosses Sudan's S border at Nimule and flows N to meet the Blue Nile at Khartoum. The Blue Nile has its source in neighbouring Ethiopia and flows NNW past Wadi Medani, providing irrigation water and hydroelectric power.

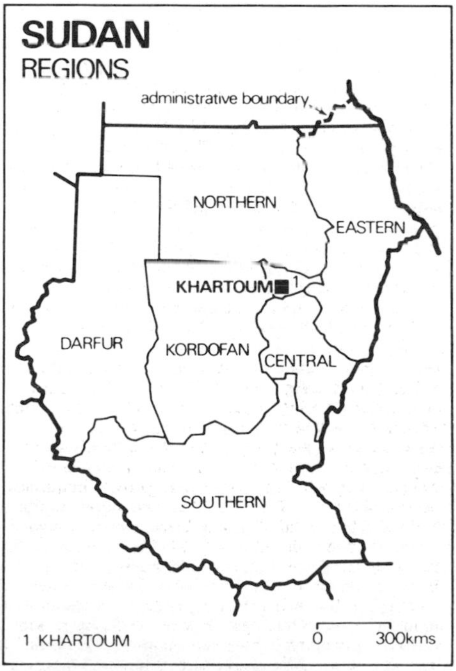

Climate. The N half of the country experiences desert conditions with a minimal rainfall of 160 mm per year at Port Sudan, but S of Khartoum the rainfall gradually increases to 1,000 mm per year. Most rain falls during April-Oct. The hottest months are July and Aug when the temperature rarely falls below 24°C in the N. Violent but brief squalls of wind (*haboobs*) can cause thick pillars of sand or dust. Juba is representative of the southern savannah region with an annual average rainfall of 970 mm and average max daily temperatures ranging between 31°C and 38°C.

History, government and constitution. In the early 19th century Egypt gained control of N Sudan but was unable to unify the fragmented tribes of the S sector. In 1881, a religious leader called Muhammed Ahmed ibn Abdalla announced himself the *Mahdi* (the 'expected one') and began to unify tribes in the western and central areas of Sudan. He initiated a revolution which ultimately led to the fall of Khartoum in 1885. Though the *Mahdi* died soon after his victory the state he had created continued until it was taken by a combined British-Egyptian offensive led by Lord Kitchener in 1898. The following year Sudan was claimed as a condominium under the joint administration of Britain and Egypt. In 1953 Sudan achieved self-government and in 1956 the country gained full independence. The military took over with a bloodless coup in 1958 but were forced to abandon power by civilian unrest at their failure to restore democratic rule. Following elections in 1965 the country was ruled by a series of coalition governments. A second military coup in 1969 resulted in the abolition of parliament and the banning of political parties. Drought and the rivalry between N and S have contributed to years of instability and a number of coups. The government is headed by a president who also acts as prime minister and appoints an executive cabinet of 28 ministers. There is a 151-member legislative National Assembly. An elected regional assembly and appointed executive council based in Juba with responsibility for the administration of the southern region were set up in 1980.

Economy. The Sudanese economy is dominated by agriculture which employs over 75% of the people. Agriculture in many areas has been made possible by large-scale irrigation schemes fed by dams such as the Sennar on the Blue Nile which provides water for 7,300 sq km. The Roseires Dam on the Blue Nile provides perennial water for over 12,000 sq km and generates more than 125 megawatts of hydroelectric power. Commercial farming is centred mainly in the N of the country in contrast to more traditional livestock farming in the S. The main cash crop is cotton which accounts for more than half the country's export earnings. The Gezira cotton scheme which is situated in the triangle formed by the White and Blue Nile rivers is one of the largest single agricultural enterprises in Africa. Such dependence on one crop has prompted efforts to encourage other cash crops such as sugar, groundnuts and castor seeds. Principal food crops grown include sorghum and wheat. Sudan produces 80% of the world supply of gum arabic. Although there are known reserves of copper, lead, iron ore, chromite, manganese, gold and salt, only small amounts of asbestos, chromium, mica and oil have been exploited. Manufacturing industry is largely based on food processing, sugar, textiles, soap, shoes, soft drinks and beer, paper products and cement. A major hindrance to general economic development within Sudan is the absence of an adequate transport system. The only main paved highway, which runs between Khartoum and Port Sudan, was completed in 1980. The main trading partners are the USSR, Iran, India, the UK, China, the USA and West Germany.

Administrative divisions. Sudan is divided into 7 regions:

Region	*area (sq km)*	*pop(1983)*
Darfur	196,555	3,093,699
Kordofan	146,932	3,093,294
Khartoum	10,883	1,802,299
Central	53,716	4,012,543
Eastern	129,086	2,208,209
Northern	183,941	1,083,024
Southern	246,389	4,871,296

Southern region includes the former regions of Equatoria, Upper Nile and Bahr al-Ghazal.

Sudbury, 46 30N 81 01W, pop(1981) 91,829, town in E central Ontario, S Canada; a settlement developed here with the arrival of the railway in 1883; construction work on the railway revealed copper ore, and the demand for nickel to use as an alloy with steel led to the development of the area; achieved city status in 1930; university (1960); railway; economy: mining (nickel, copper, cobalt, platinum, palladium), smelting, refining, pulp, paper, tourism, fishing and hunting; monuments: the Canada Centennial Numismatic Park contains the largest reproduction of a coin in the world, a Canadian 5 cents piece of 1951, minted to commemorate the 200th anniversary of the identification of nickel by the Swedish chemist Cronstedt; near the park is a model of a mine.

Sudeste *sood-es'tay*, region in SE Brazil comprising the states of Espírito Santo, Rio de Janeiro, Minas Gerais and São Paulo; in the E are mountain ranges rising to 2,890 m at the Pico da Bandeira; principal rivers include the São Francisco, Paraná, Tietê, Grande, Paraíba do Sul and the Doce; pop(1980) 51,734,125; area 924,935 sq km; the most industrially developed region in the country, with a good network of roads, railways and ports; the cities of São Paulo and Rio de Janeiro are among the most important industrial centres in South America; at São Paulo is a large proportion of Brazil's car, pharmaceutical, textile, leather and food processing industries; it also possesses a large number of chemical, metallurgical, and mechanical industries; Minas Gerais is noted for its minerals and its iron and steel industries; the region also produces meat, soya beans, maize, coffee, milk, sugar cane, poultry, eggs and wheat; the Sudeste is the most urbanized region and contains almost half of Brazil's total population.

Sudeten or **Sudetenland** *soo-day'ten-land*, mountainous territory on the border between Poland and Czechoslovakia, comprising the Sudetic Mts which rise to 1,603 m at Sněžka; during World War II the name also applied to the parts of Bohemia and Moravia occupied by German-speaking people; the Sudetenland was occupied by Germany in 1938 and restored to Czechoslovakia in 1945.

Sudharam *su-dahr'am*, formerly NOAKHALI, 22 51N 91 06E, pop(1981) 59,065; capital of Noakhali dist and region, S Bangladesh; on E side of R Ganga (Ganges); railway; airfield.

Suez *soo'ez*, EL SUWEIS (Arab), 29 59N 32 33E, pop(1976) 193,965, seaport capital of Suez governorate, E Egypt; at the S end of the Suez Canal, at the head of the Red Sea, 129 km E of Cairo; railway; economy: oil refining and storage, fertilizers, shipping services.

Suez Canal, canal connecting the Mediterranean and Red Seas; NE Egypt; built by Ferdinand de Lesseps in 10 years and opened in 1869, the canal is 184 km long including 11 km of approaches to the harbours of Suez (S end) and Port Said (N end); it has a min width of 60 m and a min draught of 16 m; the first tunnel under the canal is located 16 km N of Suez and was completed in 1980; the city of Ismâ'ilîya is located approx halfway along the canal near L Timsah through which the canal passes; between Ismâ'ilîya and Suez the canal passes through the Great and Little Bitter Lakes; according to the convention of Constantinople (1888) the canal is open (except in time of war) to vessels of any nation; the canal was blocked by Egypt during the war with Israel (1967) and re-opened in 1975; the canal is of substantial economic importance - in 1981 canal tolls totalled 621.9 mn pounds sterling and in 1980 21,603 ships totalling 285,509,207 tonnes passed through.

Suffolk *suf'uk*, county of E England; bounded E by the North Sea, N by Norfolk (along the Little Ouse and Waveney rivers), W by Cambridgeshire and S by Essex (along the R Stour); pop(1981) 598,335; area 3,797 sq km; county town Ipswich; chief towns include Lowestoft, Felixstowe and Bury St Edmunds; economy: engineering, fishing, high technology, agriculture (wheat, barley, sugar-beet), food processing; the county is divided into 7 districts:

District	*area (sq km)*	*pop(1981)*
Babergh	595	74,046
Forest Heath	374	51,978
Ipswich	40	120,908
Mid Suffolk	871	69,989
St Edmundsbury	657	86,410
Suffolk Coastal	889	95,532
Waveney	370	99,472

Suffolk, 36 44N 76 35W, pop(1980) 47,621, independent city, SE Virginia, United States; on the R Nansemond, 24 km WSW of Portsmouth; railway; economy: peanut trade.

Suḩār *sō-har'*, 24 20N 56 40E, seaport on the Gulf of Oman, Sultanate of Oman, SE Arabian peninsula; port of supply for the W Hajar hill country; linked to Masqaţ by a dual carriageway; economy: copper smelting and refining.

Sühbaatar *su'KHay-ba-tar*, SUKHE-BATOR, county in E Mongolia; pop(1981e) 40,000; area 82,900 sq km; bounded S and E by the People's Republic of China; capital Baruun Urt; ploughable land occupies 20% of the area, hay-plots 16%, pasture 57% and mountains and hills 7%; economy: sheep, cattle, furniture production, printing, foodstuffs and building material production.

Sühbaatar, 50 10N 106 14E, capital of Selenge county, N Mongolia; on R Selenge Mörön; linked to Ulaanbaatar by rail; economy: agriculture and timber.

Suhl *zool*, smallest county in SW East Germany; pop(1981) 549,075; area 3,856 sq km; dominated by the Thüringer Wald (Thuringian Forest), which covers half of the county and is a favourite tourist region with over 100 resorts; international winter sports centre at Oberhof; 38% of the land is farmed; economy: glass, potash, ceramics, tools (Suhl), timber, toys (dolls from Sonneberg), electrical engineering, electronics.

Sühl, 50 35N 10 40E, pop(1981) 49,849, capital of Sühl county, SW East Germany; SE of Eisenach; railway; economy: machinery, hunting weapons, precision tools.

Sui Xian, city in Hubei prov, E central China. See Suizhou.

Suicheng, city in Guizhou prov, S China. See Liupanshui.

Suizhou *sway-jō*, SUI XIAN, 31 46N 113 22E, pop(1984e) 1,278,900, city in Hubei prov, E China; NW of Wuhan; railway.

Sukhona *sook-ho'nu*, river in NW European Rossiyskaya, Soviet Union; issues from the SE end of Ozero Kubenskoye (Lake Kubeno), flows ENE past Velikiy Ustyug and Krasavino to join the R Vychegda at Kotlas to form the R Severnaya Dvina; navigable for entire course; chief tributaries include the Uftyuga and Bug rivers.

Sukhothai *suk-e-tī* (Thai, 'dawn of happiness'), 17 00N 99 51E, ancient ruined city of Thailand, 440 km N of Bangkok; founded in the mid-13th century when the nation of Thailand came into being; former capital of the Thai-Khmer state; now an historical park.

Sukkur *sook'koor*, SAKHAR, 27 42N 68 54E, pop(1981) 193,000, city in Sind prov, Pakistan; on E bank of R Indus, 360 km NNE of Karachi; the Sukkur (Lloyd) Barrage was built 1928-32 and comprises a 58 m-high dam and 7 canals with a total length of 26,523 km irrigating 18 mn sq km of land; economy: textiles, vegetable oils, flour milling; an important rail junction on the route between Karachi, Lahore and Quetta.

Sul *sool*, region in S Brazil, comprising the states of Paraná, Rio Grande do Sul and Santa Catarina; situated to the S of the tropic of Capricorn, it is the only region in Brazil to have a subtropical climate; a large part of the region is in the Brazilian plateau, which slopes towards the Paraná and Uruguay rivers; in the S is excellent grazing land; principal rivers are the Paraná, Uruguay, Iguaçu, Jacuí, Itajaí; pop(1980) 19,031,162; area 577,723 sq km; economy: cattle, soya beans, coffee, grapes, barley, wheat, rye, textiles (Santa Catarina), leather (Rio Grande do Sul), furniture (Paraná); all of Brazil's coal resources are located in Santa Catarina; the region has been heavily settled by Italian, German and Slav immigrants; population growth and land scarcity during the 1970s resulted in migration from this region to the states of Mato Grosso, Mato Grosso do Sul, Rondônia and Pará in the N.

Sulawesi Selatan *soo-le-way'see*, SOUTH SULAWESI, SOUTH CELEBES, province of Indonesia; between Borneo and the Moluccas; pop(1980) 442,302; area 27,686 sq km; capital Ujung Padang; economy: asphalt, rice, salt, maize, copra, kapok.

Sulawesi Tengah, CENTRAL SULAWESI, CENTRAL CELEBES, mountainous province of Indonesia; pop(1980) 1,289,639; area 69,726 sq km; capital Palu; economy: nickel, iron, coal, ebony, tunafish, mica.

Sulawesi Tenggara, SOUTH-EAST SULAWESI, SOUTH-EAST CELEBES, province of Indonesia; pop(1980) 6,062,212; area 72,781 sq km; capital Kendari; economy: rice, salt, maize, copra, kapok.

Sulawesi Utara, NORTH SULAWESI, NORTH CELEBES, province of Indonesia; includes the Sangir Is, S of the Philippines; pop(1980) 2,115,384; area 19,023 sq km; capital Menado; populated by predominantly Christian Minahasans; economy: copra, cloves, sulphur, tunafish.

Sulaymānīyah *soo-lī-ma-nee'yu*, governorate in the Kurdish Autonomous Region, NE Iraq; bounded E by Iran; pop(1977) 690,557; area 16,482 sq km; capital Sulaymānīyah; the land rises towards the Iranian border.

Sulaymānīyah, 35 32N 45 27E, pop(1970) 98,063, capital town of Sulaymānīyah governorate, Kurdish Autonomous Region, NE Iraq; trade centre and tourist resort; it is a centre of Kurdish nationalism; founded in 1789.

Sulitjelma, *soo'lit-yel-mah*, SULITELMA or SULITÄLMA (Swed), mountain range extending 48 km NW-SE along the Norwegian-Swedish border; in Nordland county, Norway and Norrbotten county, Sweden; rises to 1,913 m at Sulitjelma peak; other peaks include Olfjell and Stortoppe; permanently snow-clad, among the glaciers is Blåmannsisen (16 km long).

Sullom Voe *sul'om vō'*, 60 27N 1 20W, oil terminal in Shetland, N Scotland; at the N end of the mainland, on the W shore of Sullom Voe inlet; linked by pipeline to the Hutton, Ninian, Lyell, Dunlin, Thistle and Murchison oil fields.

Sulu Sea *soo'loo*, part of the Pacific Ocean, enclosed by the islands of the Philippines to the W, N, E and S, while the NE coast of Borneo forms the SW boundary; linked to the Pacific Ocean by the Bohol Sea, which is its main arm; several channels to the SW link it to the Celebes Sea, while the Balabac and Mindoro straits link it to the South China Sea.

Sumatera, SUMATRA *soo-mah'trah*, island in W Indonesia; S of the Malay Peninsula; comprises the provs of Aceh, Sumatera Utara, Sumatera Barat, Riau, Jambi, Bengkulu, Sumatera Selatan and Lampung; 1,760 km in length and 400 km wide; 5th largest island in the world; area 473,606 sq km; pop(1980) 28,016,100; includes the Riau archipelago off the E coast and the Mentawi Is off the W coast; major cities include Medan, Jambi, Padang, Pekanbaru and Banda Aceh; the Bukit Barisan range stretches down the W coast rising to 3,805 m at Gunung Kerinci, the highest point on the island; the Batanghari, the longest river in Sumatera, flows from Mt Kerinci across the Jambi plains; much of the SE coast, amounting to one-third of the island, is swamp and marshland; some of Indonesia's largest oilfields are located near Palembang; tin, bauxite and gold are also mined; visited by Marco Polo in the 13th century.

Sumatera Barat, WEST SUMATRA, province of Indonesia; on W coast of the island of Sumatera; separated from the Selat Mentawai Is by the Selat Mentawai; traversed by the Barisan Mts; pop(1980) 3,406,816; area 49,778 sq km; capital Padang; Bukittinggi is the cultural centre of the Minangkabau people; economy: rubber, copra, rice, coal, gold, silver.

Sumatera Selatan, SOUTH SUMATRA, province of Indonesia; in S Sumatera I; bounded N by Jambi prov, W by Bengkulu prov and S by Lampung prov; pop(1980) 4,629,801; area 103,688 sq km; capital Palembang; economy: coffee, rubber, coal, oil, tin, cinchona.

Sumatera Utara, NORTH SUMATRA, province of Indonesia; on the island of Sumatera; between Aceh territory to the N and Sumatera Barat (W Sumatra) and Riau provs to the S; pop(1980) 8,360,894; area 70,787 sq km; capital Medan; economy: tobacco, coffee, rubber, palm oil, copra.

Sumba *soom'ba*, SANDALWOOD ISLAND, flat barren island in the Lesser Sunda group of Indonesia; lying between the islands of Sumbawa and Flores and the Java Trench; bounded E by Savu Sea; area 11,148 sq km; chief town Waingapu; home of the Kupundak farmers and the isolated Bukambero people; noted for its horse breeding; economy: sandalwood, cinnamon, maize, copra and tobacco; event: tribal warfare in W Sumba during April.

Sumbawa *soom-bah'wa*, mountainous island in the Lesser Sunda group of Indonesia; lying between the islands of Lombok (W) and Flores (E); rises to 2,820 m at Gunung Tambora; area 14,739 sq km; pop(1980) 320,000; formerly divided between Bima-speaking and Sumbawa-speaking states; chief towns Sumbawa Besar, Raba and Bima.

Sumgait *soom-gī-eet'*, 40 35N 49 38E, pop(1983) 214,000, town in Azerbaydzhanskaya SSR, Soviet Union; on the W coast of the Caspian Sea, 45 km NW of Baku; developed after 1949 in connection with the republic's chemical and metallurgical industries; railway; economy: ferrous metallurgy (pipe-rolling plant); monument: Palace of Culture (1958).

Summerside, 46 24N 63 46W, pop(1981) 7,828, port and resort town on Prince Edward Island, E Canada; 55 km W of Charlottetown on Bedeque Bay; economy: trade in potatoes, dairy products, fox furs.

Šumperk *shoom'perk*, 49 58N 17 00E, pop(1984) 33,212, town in Severomoravský region, Czech Socialist Republic, central Czechoslovakia; near the R Morava, NW of Olomouc; winter sports area; railway; economy: paper, textiles.

Sumy *soo'mi*, 50 55N 34 49E, pop(1983) 248,000, capital city of Sumskaya oblast, NE Ukrainskaya SSR, Soviet Union; on the R Psel; founded in 1652; railway; airfield; economy: wool textiles, clothing, phosphate fertilizers, foodstuffs.

Sun Valley, 43 43N 114 17W, notable winter skiing resort in Blaine county, central Idaho, United States; in the Sawtooth range, NE of Ketchum; the resort developed after 1936 when the Union Pacific Railroad Company built the Sun Valley Lodge.

Sun'bury, SUNBURY-ON-THAMES, 51 24N 0 25W, pop(1981) 28,436, town in Spelthorne dist, Surrey, SE England; part of Greater London urban area; on the R Thames, 25 km WSW of London; railway.

Sunbury, town in E central Pennsylvania, USA; pop(1980e) 12,292; situated on Susquehanna R at the confluence with its W branch; industry; textiles, machinery, processed food; Fort Augusta (1756).

Sunda Islands, Greater *soon'de*, island group in Indonesia, comprising the islands of Jawa, Sumatera, Borneo and Sulawesi (Celebes), with smaller adjacent islands.

Sunda Islands, Lesser, island group in Indonesia, comprising the islands of Bali, Lombok, Sumba, Sumbawa, Flores and Timor, with small adjacent islands.

Sun'derland, WEARMOUTH *weer-*, 54 55N 1 23W, pop(1981)

195,896, port town in Sunderland borough, Tyne and Wear, NE England; part of Sunderland-Whitburn urban area; at the mouth of the R Wear, 16 km SE of Newcastle upon Tyne; railway; economy: shipbuilding, chemicals, glass, vehicles, coal trade.

Sundsvall *soons'val*, 62 22N 17 20E, pop(1982) 94,397, seaport and commercial town in SE Västernorrland county, E Sweden; on the Gulf of Bothnia, between the mouths of the Indalsälven and Ljungan rivers; received its municipal charter in 1624, having been an important trading centre as early as the 6th century; a period of prosperity began in the 19th century with the establishment of numerous sawmills; railway; economy: woodworking, papermaking, oil port.

Sungai Petani *soon-gī' pa-tah'nee*, 5 34N 100 29E, pop(1980) 45,343, town in Kedah state, NW Peninsular Malaysia, SE Asia; situated between Butterworth and Alur Setar; railway; 2nd largest city of Kedah state.

Sungai Siput *si-poot*, 4 24N 101 11E, pop(1980) 23,400, town in Perak state, W Peninsular Malaysia, SE Asia; at the N end of the Kinta Valley, 29 km N of Ipoh; railway; economy: tin.

Sunnyvale, 37 23N 122 02W, pop(1980) 106,618, city in Santa Clara county, W California, United States; between Palo Alto and San José; railway; economy: fruit canning, electronics.

Sunrise, 26 07N 80 17W, pop(1980) 39,681, town in Broward county, SE Florida, United States; suburb 10 km W of Fort Lauderdale.

Sunyani *soon-ya'nee*, 7 22N 2 18W, pop(1982) 86,903, capital of Brong-Ahafo region, SW central Ghana, W Africa; 130 km NW of Kumasi; airfield; economy: civil engineering.

Suomi. See Finland.

Superior, lake in North America, in the USA and Canada; westernmost and largest of the Great Lakes and the largest freshwater lake in the world; bordered N and E by Ontario prov, NW by Minnesota and S by Wisconsin and Michigan; length 563 km; breadth 257 km; max depth 405 m; area 82,103 sq km, of which 28,749 sq km is in Canada; connected with L Huron at its SE end via the St Mary's river (via the 'Soo' canals); receives the Nipigon and Kaministikwia rivers from Ontario, the Pigeon river (which forms part of the international border) and the St Louis river; the lake contains several islands, including Isle Royale (a US national park); to the NE of Musining, Michigan are the Pictured Rocks, red sandstone carved into fantastic shapes by the wind and water.

Superior, 46 44N 92 06W, pop(1980) 29,571, county seat of Douglas county, NW Wisconsin, United States; a major lake port at the W end of L Superior, opposite Duluth; Wisconsin State College (1896); railway; economy: trade in iron ore, coal and grain; shipbuilding, oil refining.

Sūr *soor*, 22 36N 59 32E, one of the largest ports of Oman, SE Arabian peninsula; on the Gulf of Oman at the foot of the E Hajar hill country; formerly the port of Sharqiyah for emigrants to E Africa and Zanzibar; economy: important traditional shipbuilding centre; exports dates.

Surabaya *soo-ra-bah'ya*, SURABAJA, 7 14S 112 45E, pop(1980) 1,556,255, industrial seaport capital of Jawa Timor prov, E Jawa, Indonesia; at mouth of R Kali Mas; port facilities at Tanjung Perak; allegedly founded on the site of a legendary battle between a crocodile and a shark; an important trading centre since the 14th century; university (1954); railway; airfield; naval base; economy: oil refining, textiles, glass, footwear, tobacco.

Surat *soor'ut*, 21 12N 72 55E, pop(1981) 913,000, port in Gujarat state, W India; close to the mouth of the R Tapti, on the Gulf of Khambhat (Cambay), 240 km N of Bombay; developed as a port by the Moguls; during the 17th and 18th centuries it became a rich trading centre with many European settlements; in 1612 the first English trading post in India was established here; Surat became the headquarters of the British East India Company in the late 17th century until it was transferred to Bombay in 1687; the town was sacked by the Mahrattas in 1644 when it was one of India's largest cities and busiest ports; linked to Ahmadabad, Amalner and Bombay by rail; university (1967); economy: textiles, engineering; noted for its zari thread work and diamond cutting.

Sûre *sür*, SAUER *zow'ar* (Ger), river in SE Belgium and Luxembourg, rising NW of Martelange in Belgium; flows E and SE to meet the R Moselle near Wasserbillig; length 160 km; navigable below Diekirch; reservoir at Esch-sur-Sûre; tributaries Wiltz, Alzette, Wark and Our rivers.

Surinam *soo'ri-nam*, SURINAME, official name Republic of Surinam, republic in NE South America; between 2° and 6°N; bordering W with Guyana (along the R Correntyne), E with French Guiana (along the Marowijne and Litani rivers) and S with Brazil (along the Sierra de Tumucumaque); timezone GMT $-3\frac{1}{2}$; area 163,265 sq km; capital Paramaribo; pop(1980) 352,041; the pop includes Hindustani (East Indians) 37%, Creoles 31%, Javanese 15.3%, Bush Negro 10.3%, Amerindians 2.7% and Chinese 1.7%; the official language is Dutch, although Hindustani, Javanese, Chinese, Spanish and the local language, Sranang Tongo, are also spoken; the principal religions are Hindu, Muslim, Roman Catholic, Dutch Reformed, Moravian Brethren, and other Christian groups, Jewish and Baha'i; national holidays 25 Feb (Revolution Day), 7 March (Holi Phagwa), 19 June (Ied Ul Fitre), 1 July (National Union Day), 25 Nov (Independence Day); the currency is the Surinam guilder; membership of ECLA, FAO, G-77, GATT, IBA, IBRD, ICAO, IDB, ILO, IMF, IMO, INTERPOL, ITU, NAM, OAS, PAHO, SELA, UN, UNESCO, UPU, WHO, WIPO, WMO.

Physical description. The country is divided into topographically diverse natural regions, ranging from coastal lowland through savannah to mountainous upland. Bordering the Atlantic Ocean there is a coastal strip with a width of 25 km in the E and 80 km in the W. Here the clay soil is mostly covered by swamp. Beyond this stretches 5-6 km of white, sandy soil, and a slightly undulating savannah region about 30 km wide. This region is covered with quartz sand, and overgrown with grass and shrubs. To the S is the highland interior, comprising hills and mountains overgrown with dense tropical forest and intersected by streams. Savannah reappears at the S border with Brazil. Surinam's principal

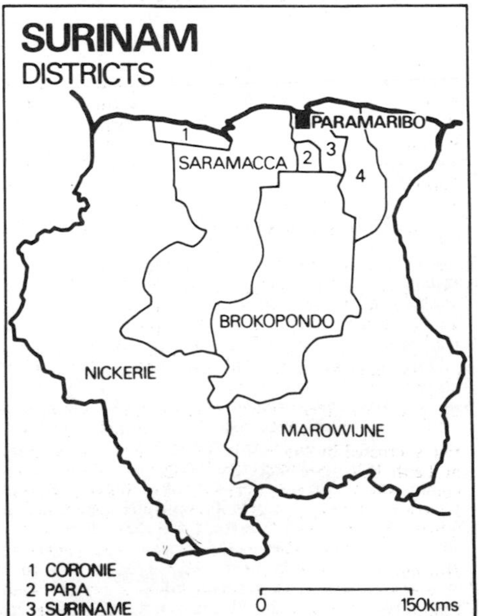

rivers, which flow from the highland interior to the Atlantic coast, include the Marowijne in the E, the Correntyne in the W, and the Suriname, Commewijne, Koppename, Saramacca and Nickerie in the centre.

Climate. Surinam's climate is tropically hot and humid with 2 rainy seasons during May-July and Nov-Jan. The coast is influenced by the trade winds and at Paramaribo temperatures range between 22° and 33°C. Average monthly rainfall varies from 310 mm in the N to 67 mm in the S.

History, government and constitution. The colony was first settled by the British on the instructions of the governor of Barbados, who sent an expedition to Surinam in 1651. In February 1667 the colony was taken by the states of Zeeland; thereafter it was decided that Surinam should remain with the Netherlands, while Nieuw Amsterdam should be given to Britain. The colony was captured by the British in 1799, but was finally restored to the Netherlands in 1818. Surinam became an independent republic on 25 Feb 1975, signing a treaty with the Netherlands for economic aid until 1985. On 25 Feb 1980 a military coup overthrew the elected government. After the execution of 15 opposition leaders on 8 Dec 1982, the Netherlands broke off relations and suspended its aid. With the suspension of the constitution and the banning of all political parties the government of Surinam is in the hands of a military-civilian executive.

Economy. Since the coup of 1980 Surinam has suffered from a lack of foreign exchange. This has hindered the development of the economy which is based on agriculture and mining. About 80% of Surinam's export income is provided through bauxite mining near the Cottica and Para rivers. Agriculture, which accounts for 10% of exports, is restricted to the alluvial coastal zone where clay soils are suitable for sugar cane, rice and citrus fruits, all of which are exported to Europe, along with small quantities of coffee and bananas. The staple food crops are rice, sugar, citrus fruits, oil palms, bananas and small amounts of coffee and cacao. Surinam has vast timber resources, mostly logged from a 10-40 km-wide strip that crosses the country 75 km inland.

Administrative divisions. Surinam is divided into 9 districts as follows:

District	*area (sq km)*	*pop(1980)*
Brokopondo	21,440	20,249
Commewijne	4,110	14,351
Coronie	1,620	2,777
Marowijne	45,980	23,402
Nickerie	64,610	34,480
Para	980	14,867
Paramaribo	32	67,905
Saramacca	23,420	10,335
Suriname	1,628	166,494

Suriname, district in N Surinam, NE South America; area 1,628 sq km; pop(1980) 166,494.

Surrey, county on the Caribbean I of Jamaica; located E of Middlesex on the E coast of the island; comprises the parishes of St Thomas, Portland, St Andrew and Kingston; area 2,006 sq km; pop(1982) 741,027; chief town Kingston (capital of Jamaica); Jamaica's highest mt, the Blue Mountain, rises to 2,256 m in Portland parish.

Surrey, county in SE England; partly in Greater London urban area; drained by the Thames, Mole and Wey rivers; crossed by the North Downs which rise to 294 m at Leith Hill; pop(1981) 1,004,332; area 1,679 sq km; county town Guildford; chief towns include Reigate, Leatherhead, Staines and Woking; the county is divided into 11 districts:

District	*area (sq km)*	*pop(1981)*
Elmbridge	97	111,616
Epsom and Ewell	34	69,568
Guildford	271	120,638
Mole Valley	259	77,048
Reigate and Banstead	129	116,773
Runnymede	78	71,155
Spelthorne	56	93,198
Surrey Heath	97	76,842
Tandridge	250	76,235
Waverley	345	109,486
Woking	64	81,773

Surtsey *sert'see*, volcanic island off S coast of Iceland; one of the Vestmannaeyjar group (Westman Is); erupted and formed in 1963; now a nature reserve; area 1.9 sq km.

Susquehanna *sus-kwi-han'a*, river rising in central New York state, USA; length 715 km; flows S across E Pennsylvania and is joined at Sunbury by its W branch which flows c.360 km NE and E from its source in the Allegheny Mountains; from Sunbury it flows c.240 km, crossing NE Maryland, to Chesapeake; main city on its banks Harrisburg; hydroelectricity; lower course passes through highly industrialized region; navigable only near its mouth by means of canals.

Sutjeska, national park in Bosna-Hercegovina republic, Yugoslavia; situated 120 km E of Dubrovnik, between the Sutjeska and Piva rivers with the foothills of Mt Volujak and Mt Bioč to the S; Maglić (2,387 m), the highest peak in Bosna-Hercegovina is located in the park; area 173 sq km; a memorial commemorates World War II partisans; bears, wild boar, chamois, red deer and roe deer live in the park.

Sut'lej, river of Asia; the longest of the 5 rivers of the Punjab; rises in La'nga Co lake in Xizang aut region (Tibet), from where it flows NW as the Xiangquan He; cuts through the Zaskar range to enter India; meanders through the Himalayas to form the boundary between Sahiwal dist, Pakistan and the Farīdot and Firozpur dists of India; flows SW to its confluence with the R Chenab just to the E of Alipur, where the combined stream flows SW for 81 km to meet the Indus; from La'nga Co to the confluence with the Chenab, the Sutlej is 1,370 km long; fed by glaciers in its upper course, water is used for irrigation, particularly at the Bhakara Dam, Himachal Pradesh, India; in the 19th century the Sutlej river was a boundary between British and Sikh spheres of influence until the Anglo-Sikh wars of the 1840s and the annexation of the Punjab in 1849.

Sut'ton, 51 22N 0 12W, pop(1981) 167,100, residential borough of S Greater London, England; includes the suburbs of Sutton and Cheam, Carshalton and Beddington and Wallington; railway; monument. 12th-c All Saints church.

Sutton Cold'field, 52 34N 1 48W, pop(1981) 103,097, town in Birmingham borough, West Midlands, central England; railway; 11 km NE of Birmingham; economy: engineering, pharmaceuticals.

Sutton in Ashfield, 53 08N 1 15W, pop(1981) 39,622, town in Ashfield dist, Nottinghamshire, central England; 5 km SW of Mansfield; economy: textiles, clothing, metal containers, engineering.

Suva *soo'vah*, 18 08S 178 25E, pop(1981) 68,178, chief port and capital of Fiji, on the SE coast of Viti Levu I, SW Pacific Ocean, overlooked by the Tholoisuva Forest Park; a city since 1953; university (1968); economy: copra processing, soap, edible oil, handicrafts, steel rolling mill (opened 1973).

Suva Reka *soo'va re'ka*, 42 21N 20 50E, pop(1981) 59,434, town in autonomous province of Kosovo, S Srbija (Serbia) republic, Yugoslavia; NNE of Prizren.

Suwałki *soo-val'ki*, voivodship in NE Poland; bounded N and E by USSR; includes Suwałki lake district and Augustowska, Poland's largest forest; L Hańcza, Poland's deepest (108.5 m) lake is 24 km NW of Suwałki; pop(1983) 438,000; area 10,490 sq km; capital Suwałki; chief towns include Ełk, Giżucko and Augustów.

Suwałki, 54 06N 22 56E, pop(1983) 46,600, capital of

Suwałki voivodship, NE Poland; NW of Augustowska Forest; railway; economy: chipboard; monuments: regional museum, birthplace of the poetess Maria Konopnicka.

Suwarrow *soo-vor'of*, SUVOROV, 13 17S 163 07W, uninhabited atoll of the Cook Is, S Pacific, 824 km NW of Rarotonga; area 0.4 sq km.

Suwaydā, As *es soo-way'da*, SOUEIDA (Fr), governorate (*mohofazat*) in SW Syria; bounded S by Jordan; pop(1981e) 193,000; capital As Suwaydā; includes the Jabal ad Durūz which rises to a height of 1,735 m.

Suwŏn *soo-wun*, SUWEON, 37 16N 126 59E, pop(1984) 402,319, industrial capital of Kyŏnggi prov, NW Korea; 48 km S of Sŏul; agricultural college; subway from Sŏul; monuments: Suwŏn's fortress walls and gates have been recently reconstructed; the Korean Folk Village nearby is a working community, with craftsmen in residence; Suwŏn *kalbi* (marinated beef ribs) is a well-known Korean delicacy.

Suzhou *soo-jō*, formerly WUHSIEN, SUCHOW, 31 21N 120 40E, pop(1984e) 695,500, town in Jiangsu prov, E China; on the banks of the Grand Canal, near Tai Hu lake; first settled in approx 1000 BC, Suzhou became capital of the Kingdom of Wu in 518 BC and developed as a market town trading in textiles, gold and silk; railway; economy: silk, light industry, chemicals, electronics; monuments: Suzhou contains over 150 ornamental gardens including Canglang (Surging Wave) pavilion, completed in about 1044, Shizilin (Lion Grove), first landscaped in 1350, Yiyuan (Garden of Harmony) and Wangshi Yuan (Garden of the Master of the Nets), which dates from the 12th century; Huqiu (Tiger Hill) is a 2,500-year-old artificial hill (height 36 m) built by the King of Wu as a tomb for his father.

Sval'bard, island group in the Arctic Ocean, about 650 km N of the Norwegian mainland; area 62,000 sq km; comprises 4 large islands and a number of smaller islands; principal islands Spitsbergen, Nordaustlandet, Edgeøya, Barentsøya and Prins; officially incorporated in Norway on 14 Aug, 1925; Longyearbyen is Svalbard's administrative centre; discovered by the Dutch seafarer Willem Barents in 1596; formerly an important whaling centre; Newtontoppen and Perriertoppen peaks rise to heights in excess of 1,700 m; there are deposits of coal (Svea Field), phosphate, asbestos, iron ore, galena, sphalerite, chalcopyrite, limestone dolerite and anhydrite.

Svartisen *svart'ee-sun*, largest ice field in N Norway, on the Arctic Circle, Nordland county, 19 km N of Mo; area 369 sq km; length 32 km; descends from alt of 1,600 m on Snetind.

Svay Rieng *swī ree-eng*, SOAIRIENG, province in SE Cambodia; pop(1981) 287,000; bounded E and S by Vietnam; chief town Svay Rieng; rice growing region.

Svendborg *sven'bor*, 55 04N 10 38E, pop(1981) 23,845, seaport on S coast of Fyn I, Fyn county, Denmark, on the narrow Svendborgsund which separates Fyn from Tasinge and other small islands; rail terminus; economy: tobacco manufacture, shipbuilding, engineering, electrics; monument: Romanesque church of St Nicholas (1220, restored 1892).

Sverdlovsk *svyerd-lofsk'*, formerly EKATERINBURG, YEKATERINBURG (-1924), 56 52N 60 35E, pop(1983) 1,269,000, industrial capital city of Sverdlovskaya oblast, E European Rossiyskaya, Soviet Union; in the E foothills of the Ural'skiy Khrebet (Ural Mts) range, on the R Iset; founded in 1821 as a Russian military stronghold and trading centre; the first ironworks were established in 1726; nearby are gold and copper mines; the Museum of Mineralogy has some 20,000 minerals, including precious stones on display (all mined in the Ural'skiy Khrebet range); university (1920); on the Trans-Siberian railway; airport; economy: heavy engineering, metallurgy, gem cutting, manufacture of clothing, wool textiles, tyres, fertilizers, and building materials.

Sveti Stefan *sve'tee ste'fan*, small Adriatic island and hotel town in Crna Gora (Montenegro) republic, Yugoslavia; linked to the mainland by a causeway; there are no permanent inhabitants; originally a fishing village, it was abandoned by its last 20 inhabitants in 1955 before its conversion to a tourist resort; on the mainland opposite is the former summer residence of King Alexander of Yugoslavia, now a hotel.

Svetozarevo *sve-to-za're-vo*, formerly YAGODINA, 44 00N 42 28N, pop(1981) 76,460, town in central Srbija (Serbia) republic, Yugoslavia; on R Morava, 112 km SSE of Beograd; railway; economy: foodstuffs, brewing.

Svir' *sveer*, river in Leningradskaya oblast, NW European Rossiyskaya, Soviet Union; issues from Ozero Onezhskoye (Lake Onega) at Voznesenye, flows W past Podporozh'ye and Lodeynoye Pole (hydroelectric stations), to Ladozhskoye Ozero (Lake Ladoga) at Sviritsa; length 224 km; navigable for entire its length as part of a canal system.

Swabian Jura, mountain range in W Germany. See Schwäbische Alb.

Swadlincote, 52 47N 1 34W, pop(1981) 33,739, town in South Derbyshire dist, Derbyshire, central England; 7 km SE of Burton-upon-Trent; economy: chemicals, coal, clay, chinaware.

Swan, major watercourse of SW Australia; in SW Western Australia; rises as the Avon river in the hills near Corrigin; flows NW and SW past the towns of York, Northam and Perth; enters the Indian Ocean at Fremantle; receives the Helena and Canning rivers; length, including the Avon river, 386 km; the Swan River Settlement established in 1829 was the first colonial settlement in Western Australia; it included the sites of Perth and Fremantle; Swanland is a fertile region producing wheat, fruit, wine, wool and timber.

Swan Hill, 35 23S 142 37E, pop(1983e) 9,110, town in Northern Mallee stat div, N Victoria, Australia; on the Murray river, 305 km NNW of Melbourne, close to the border with New South Wales; railway; airfield; economy: sheep farming, fruit growing, wine; monuments: the Pioneer Settlement is an open-air museum with old paddle steamers and reconstructions of 19th-c houses; Clockworld includes a collection of over 500 clocks and watches covering nearly 300 years in the art of clockmaking.

Swansea, ABERTAWE (Welsh), 51 38N 3 57W, pop(1981) 175,172, port city and county town in Swansea dist, West Glamorgan, S Wales; on the Bristol Channel at the mouth of the R Neath where it enters Swansea Bay; chartered in 1158-84; College of University of Wales; vehicle licensing centre; railway; airfield; economy: trade in coal, oil, ores; monuments: Norman castle, Royal Institution of South Wales (1835), Guildhall, industrial and maritime museum, marina; event: Swansea music festival (Oct).

Swatow, port in Guangdong prov, SE China. See Shantou.

Swaziland *swa'zee-land*, official name Kingdom of Swaziland, constitutional monarchy in SE Africa; the land of the Swazi, a Bantu race, bounded N, W, S and SE by South Africa and NE by Mozambique; timezone GMT +2; area 17,363 sq km; pop(1984e) 651,000; capital Mbabane; chief towns include Manzini, Big Bend, Havelock, Pigg's Peak and Mtsapa; ethnic groups include European (3%), mulatto (1%) and African (96%) - mainly Swazi with small numbers of Shangane, Zulu, Nyasa and Sutu; the majority of the pop is Christian (57%) with the remainder following local beliefs; official languages are English (government business) and Siswati; the unit of currency is the lilangeni (plural, emalangeni); national holidays 6 Sept (Independence Day), 22 June (King's birthday); membership of AfDB, FAO, G-77, GATT (de facto), IBRD, ICAO, IDA, IFAD, IFC, ILO, IMF, INTERPOL, ISO, ITU, NAM, OAU, SADCC, UN, UNESCO, UPU, WHO.

Physical description. The smallest country in S Africa, Swaziland measures 192 km from N to S and 144 km from E to W. The mountainous Highveld (*Inkangala*) in the W is a continuation of the Drakensberg Mts and has an average elevation of 1,500 m. At 1,860 m, Emblembe in the NW is Swaziland's highest point. The original forest in this area has long since been removed but in its place more than 400 sq km of Usutu pine and eucalyptus has been planted on both sides of the R Usutu. Reserves of asbestos and iron ore lie within the Highveld. To the E, the more populated Middleveld gradually descends to elevations between 600 and 700 m. Further E, at an elevation of 150-300 m, the rolling bush-covered Lowveld (*Lihlanze*) is grazed by cattle and partly cultivated with the aid of irrigation. The Lubombo plateau region to the E is similar to the Middleveld with an elevation between 400 and 825m. Its W-facing escarpment is deeply cut by rivers. One of the best-watered countries in S Africa, Swaziland is crossed from W to E by 4 major river systems, from the Komati in the N, to the Usutu and Mbuluzi in the centre and the Ngwavuma in the S. As they make their way to the Indian Ocean these rivers provide irrigation water and hydroelectric power. There are game reserves at Mlilwane and Ehlane with a varied fauna that includes antelope, zebra, rhinoceros, hippopotamus, crocodile, monkey, lion and a wide variety of birds.

Climate. The Highveld region has a humid, near temperate climate with an annual rainfall ranging between 1,000 and 2,280 mm. The Middleveld and Lubombo are sub-tropical and drier with rainfall ranging between 760 mm and 1,140 mm. The Lowveld is tropical and receives relatively little rain (500 to 890 mm per annum on average) and is susceptible to drought. Most rain falls in the summer months (Oct-March). The mean annual temperature on the Highveld is 15.6°C and on the Lowveld about 22.2°C.

History, government and constitution. Breaking away from the main Bantu group the Swazi came to this area during the first half of the 19th century. Land was later lost to Afrikaaner settlers who determined the boundaries with the Transvaal at the Pretoria Convention in 1881. Swaziland's independence was guaranteed at this time and again in 1884 in London. In 1894 the British, in contradiction to Swazi wishes, agreed to Transvaal administration of Swaziland but in 1903, after the South African War, the country became a British High Commission territory under the British Governor of Transvaal. During the 1950s the country was given its own court, national treasury and native administration under the king (*Ngwenyama*) who ruled with the advice of the *Libandia* (council consisting of all adult male Swazis). Political parties emerged in the 1960s, a constitution was invoked in 1963, and a general election held the following year. In 1967 Swaziland's first House of Assembly and Senate were formed and in 1968 the country gained independence as a constitutional monarchy. Swaziland has a bicameral parliament consisting of a 50-member National Assembly and a 20-member Senate. Forty Assembly members and 10 senators are elected, the remainder being appointed by the king. The king is advised by an 11-member cabinet headed by a prime minister and the *Libandia* advises on law, customs and traditions.

Economy. Agriculture, employing 70% of the pop, is the basis of the economy. The main subsistence crops include maize, groundnuts, beans, sorghum and sweet potatoes. Peasant cash crops include cotton, tobacco, pineapples, rice and sugar cane. Citrus and sugar grown on irrigated land around Big Bend and Mhlume are major exports. Asbestos from the Havelock mines and woodpulp from the forests of Usutu, Pigg's Peak and Nhlangano are also exported. Until 1977 high-grade iron ore was mined at Ngwenya and exported mainly to Japan. The development of coal mining operations has resulted in exports to Kenya and Mozambique. An expanding industrial sector includes timber processing, sugar refining, cotton ginning, fruit and meat canning, food and drink processing, and the manufacture of textiles, cement, paper, chemicals, clothing, agricultural machinery and televisions. The main trading partners include South Africa, the UK, Japan, Mozambique and the USA.

Administrative divisions. Swaziland is divided into the administrative dists of Shiselweni, Lubombo, Manzini and Hhohho.

Sweden *swee'den*, SVERIGE *svär'ye* (Swed), official name Kingdom of Sweden, KONUNGARIKET SVERIGE, a kingdom of N Europe, occupying the E side of the Scandinavian peninsula, bounded on the E by Finland, the Gulf of Bothnia, and the Baltic Sea, on the SW by the Skagerrak and Kattegat, and on the W and NW by Norway; timezone GMT +1; area 411,479 sq km; Europe's 4th largest country; capital Stockholm; chief towns Göteborg (Gothenburg), Malmö, Uppsala, Norrköping, Västerås and Örebro; pop(1983) 8,326,182; more than 70% of the country's area has a population density of 6 inhabitants or less per sq km; the Swedes are almost purely of Teutonic stock, with small numbers of Lapps, Finns and Germans; the predominant faith is Lutheran Protestantism (93.5%), with a small number of Roman Catholics (1%), Orthodox Catholics, and Jews; the Swedish krona of 100 öre is the currency; national holiday 30 April (King's Birthday); membership of ADB, Council of Europe, DAC, EFTA, ESRO, FAO, GATT, IAEA, IBRD, ICAC, ICAO, ICES, ICO, IDA, IDB, IEA, IFAD, IFC, IHO, ILO, IMF, IMO, INTELSAT, IPU, ISO, ITU, OECD, UN, UNESCO, UPU, WHO, WIPO, WMO, WSG.

Physical description. The total area of 411,479 sq km includes 9% inland water, the largest lakes being Vänern (5,585 sq km), Vättern (1,912 sq km) and Mälaren (1,140 sq km). The coast is distinguished by a fringe of islands, but of the larger Baltic islands, only Gotland and Öland are Swedish. The only mountainous region is in the W, where the Kjölen Mts form the boundary with Norway as far S as 64°N latitude. In these mountains are the highest peaks in Sweden, Kebnekaise (2,111 m) and Sarektjåkkå (2,089 m). The rest of the country is tableland, varying in height from 100 to 270 m. Sweden is mostly part of the ancient Pre-Cambrian Fenno-Scandian shield, with a covering of glacial deposits left when the ice-cap which covered the country melted. The run-off from the NW mountains flows SE toward the Gulf of Bothnia in some 10 rivers (Torne älv, Lule älv, Ångermanälven), which widen from time to time into long narrow lakes. There are many waterfalls of which the Harsprånget ('hare's leap'), just below the Stora Lulevatten, is the largest European cataract.

Climate. Most of Sweden has a typically continental climate with a moderate to large range of temperature between summer and winter, except in the SW of the country from Göteborg to Malmö where winter temperatures are modified by an open ocean which rarely freezes. In central and southern Sweden winters are less severe than further north and the climate permits a varied agriculture. The enclosed waters of the Baltic Sea often freeze, in whole or in part, in winter; as a result the low-lying shores of the Gulf of Bothnia tend to have much more severe winters. Further N the winters become even more severe with short, changeable summers. The average number of days with a mean temperature below freezing point increases from 71 in Malmö to 120 in Stockholm and 184 at Haparanda near the Arctic Circle. Precipitation is relatively low except on the higher mountains and is rather greater in summer than winter. N of Stockholm much of the winter precipitation is snow.
History, government and constitution. The Swedes, a people of almost pure Nordic stock, have inhabited the country since prehistoric times. In the early first millennium AD, the Svear or Suiones shared the country with the Lapps in the N and the Goths, Herules and later the Danes in the S. About the 7th century AD, the union of the kingdoms of the Goths and Svears laid the foundation of the Swedish realm, though the Danes continued to rule in the extreme S (Skåne) until 1658. In the 9th century a chieftain named Ruric founded the nucleus of the later Russia at Novgorod in the E. Finland was conquered in the 12th-13th centuries and in 1389 Sweden united with Denmark and Norway under Danish leadership. This unpopular union came to an end in 1527 following a revolt led by Gustavus Vasa, founder of modern Sweden. The present royal dynasty was founded in 1818 by the French marshal Bernadotte (Charles XIV), who had been adopted as heir to the childless Charles XIII. During the last phases of the Napoleonic War he changed allegiance and fought against Napoleon. As a consequence Sweden acquired Norway from Denmark (1814) after having surrendered Finland to Russia (1809), the union with Norway being dissolved in 1905. Since 1814 Sweden has managed to preserve her neutrality amid the many European conflicts of the last century. The present constitution came into force in 1975 and replaced the 1809 constitution. Under the present constitution, Sweden is a representative and parliamentary democracy, the central organ of government being the Parliament or *Riksdag*, which, since 1971, has consisted of one chamber of 349 members elected from 28 constituencies by proportional representation. The King is head of state, but does not participate in the government of the country.
Industry. Industry accounts for more than 75% of Sweden's exports. There has been a gradual shift from the traditional emphasis on raw materials - timber and iron ore - to more advanced products with sophisticated technology such as transportation equipment, electronics, electrical equipment and chemicals. Engineering, the largest sector of Swedish industry, accounts for 37% of Swedish industrial sales and 46% of total exports. The Swedish mining industry has ancient traditions. The iron ore industry, however, underwent a crisis in the latter part of the 1970s and Sweden's share of world iron ore production dropped to around 2% in 1982 from 4% in 1973. Steelmaking employs some 5% of the total industrial labour force. There is also a large production of non-ferrous metals (aluminium, lead, copper) and rolled semi-manufactured goods of these metals. The manufacturing sector based on Sweden's forest reserves (saw-mills, plywood factories, joinery industries) is also important to the economy, as is the rapidly expanding chemical industry, especially the petro-chemical branch. Most trade is with West Germany, Great Britain, the USA and Norway.
Agriculture and forestry. About 57% of Sweden is forest and woodland. Arable land comprises only 10% of the total area, the principal crops being wheat, barley, oats and hay. In the southern coastal areas and on Gotland I industrial crops such as sugar beets, oliferous plants and peas for processing are also cultivated. Bread grain and grain for feeding are intensively cultivated on the plains of central Sweden. Some 75% of the Swedish harvest provides fodder for livestock, of which cattle are the most important type.
Administrative divisions. Sweden is divided into 24 counties (*Län*) as follows:

County	*area (sq km)*	*pop(1983)*
Stockholm	6,494	1,544,354
Uppsala	6,987	247,101
Södermanland	6,060	251,525
Östergötland	10,566	32,195

contd

County	*area (sq km)*	*pop(1983)*
Jönköping	9,943	301,415
Kronoberg	8,459	173,981
Kalmar	11,171	240,745
Gotland	3,140	55,895
Blekinge	2,909	152,118
Kristianstad	6,048	280,220
Malmöhus	4,909	744,081
Halland	5,448	234,388
Göteborg och Bohus	5,110	709,447
Älvsborg	11,394	425,178
Skaraborg	7,937	270,537
Värmland	17,584	282,093
Örebro	8,514	273,023
Västmanland	6,302	257,782
Kopparberg	28,350	286,166
Gävleborg	18,191	292,739
Västernorrland	21,771	266,049
Jämtland	49,857	134,857
Västerbotten	55,429	245,018
Norrbotten	98,906	265,275

Świdnica *sveed-nee'tza*, SCHWEIDNITZ *shvīt'nits* (Ger), 50 51N 16 29E, pop(1983) 59,400, industrial town in Wałbrzych voivodship, SW Poland; on R Bystrzyca, in Sudetes Mts foothills, NE of Wałbrzych; railway; economy: industrial equipment, railway coachworks; monuments: 14-16th-c Gothic parish church with highest steeple in Silesia; mansions with Baroque and Renaissance facades in the Market Square; museum of old Silesian trade.

Świętochłowice *shvyẽ-toKH-wo-vee'tse*, 50 17N 18 51E, pop(1983) 60,500, town in Katowice voivodship, S Poland; NW of Katowice; railway; economy: coal mining, iron and zinc works, ship engines.

Swin'don, 51 34N 1 47W, pop(1981) 128,493, old market town in Thamesdown dist, Wiltshire, S England; 113 km W of London; Swindon developed into a modern industrial town with the arrival of the Great Western Railway in the 19th century; railway; economy: railway engineering, vehicle parts, pharmaceuticals, electronics, clothing; monuments: Great Western Railway museum (1962); 9 km E is the White Horse of Uffington.

Świnoujście *shvee-no-oo'eesh-che*, SWINEMÜNDE *sveen-e-moon'de* (Ger), 53 55N 14 18E, pop(1983) 45,000, port and coastal resort town, Szczecin voivodship, NW Poland; on Uznam and Wolin Is at mouth of R Swina on Baltic Sea coast; granted a charter in 1765; ferries to Ystad in Sweden, hovercraft service to Szczecin and ferries to several local towns; one of Europe's largest bulk cargo ports; sanatoria with mineral springs; broad sandy beaches; Wolin National Park, established in 1960, is nearby; events: student artistic festival, international sailing regatta.

Swinton, 53 32N 2 21W, pop(1981) 44,508, town linked with Pendlebury in Salford borough, Greater Manchester, NW England; 7 km NW of Manchester; railway; economy: textiles, coal, engineering.

Swit'zerland, LA SUISSE *swees* (Fr), SCHWEIZ *shvīts* (Ger), SVIZZERA *sveet'se-ra* (Ital), HELVETIA (anc), official name Swiss Confederation, CONFÉDÉRATION SUISSE (Fr), SCHWEIZERISCHE EIDGENOSSENSCHAFT (Ger), CONFEDERAZIONE SVIZZERA (Ital), a land-locked European republic, bounded on the E by Liechtenstein and Austria, on the S by Italy, on the W by France, and on the N by West Germany; land boundaries 1,884 km; timezone GMT +1; area 41,228 sq km; federal capital Bern; largest city Zürich; chief towns Luzern, St Gallen, Lausanne, Basel and Genève; pop(1980) 6,365,960; the population is concentrated mainly in the Central Plateau; more than 50% of the pop is urban; the Swiss are predominantly Alpine stock with a strong Nordic element, especially in the north and centre; languages spoken are German (65%), French (18%), Italian (12%), Romansch (1%); Romansch (Rhaeto-Roman), accepted by the electorate in 1938 as the fourth national language, is spoken by a minority in the canton of Graubünden; in Ticino canton and the S Graubünden valleys, the official language, Italian, is always spoken, except in the rural areas where local people prefer to communicate in their own Lombard dialect; the French language is spoken in 6 cantons (Fribourg, Vaud, Valais, Neuchâtel, Jura and Genève), and German is spoken by the majority of inhabitants in the remaining 19 cantons; many Swiss speak more than one language; freedom of worship is guaranteed by the 1874 constitution; religious allegiance is equally divided between Roman Catholicism and Protestantism; the Swiss franc (SFr) of 100 centimes is the currency; national holiday 1 Aug (National Day); membership of the Council of Europe, ADB, DAC, EFTA, ESRO, FAO, GATT, IAEA, ICAC, ICAO, ICO, IDB, IEA, IFAD, ILO, IMO, INTELSAT, IPU, ITU, OECD, UN, UNESCO, UPU, WFTU, WHO, WIPO, WMO, WSG, WTO, World Confederation of Labour.

Physical description. Of the total area of the country, 43% is meadow and pasture, 24% forest, 20% urban and 3% inland water. Geologically, the major regions of Switzerland are the Alps and Pre-Alps (60%), the Central Plateau (30%) and the Jura Mts (10%). The Alps chain runs roughly E and W through the S part of the country, and is divided up by the Rhône and Upper Rhine valleys lengthwise and by the Reuss and Ticino valleys crosswise. The mean altitude is around 1,700 m. While some summits average around 4,000 m, the highest peak (Dufourspitze of the Monte Rosa massif in the Valais Alps) reaches 4,634 m. On the NW slopes of the Alps, the Pre-Alps have a less complex structure, with peaks averaging around 2,000 m. The Jura Mts, an outspur of the Alps, stretch from the SW to the NW of the country. The mean altitude is 700 m, with some peaks rising to around 1,600 m. The Central Plateau has a mean altitude of 580 m, and lying as it does between the 2 main ranges, it forms a corridor which provides a natural setting for communications, commercial and cultural activity. The surface of this plain is formed of *Molasse*, a Tertiary detrital deposit derived from the denudation of earlier Alpine folds and is characterized by glacial moraines, gravels and clays. The Central Plateau is watered by the meandering R Aare and fringed with great lakes (Brienzer See, Thuner See, Bieler See, Lac de Neuchâtel). The R Rhine drains 68% of the country into the North Sea; 27.6% is drained by the Rhône, tributaries of the Po, and the Adige into the Mediterranean Sea; and 4.4% flows via the R Inn into the Danube and eventually into the Black Sea. The Swiss Alps have some 3,000 sq km of glaciers in all, the largest being the Aletsch glacier (area 117.6 sq km, length 23.6 m) in Valais and Bern cantons, S central Switzerland.

Climate. Switzerland's climate is temperate but varies considerably with relief and altitude. Summers are generally warm, with considerable rainfall; winters are characterized by clear skies and temperatures averaging 0°C. In the Central Plateau, winters are generally cold with much persistent cloud and fog. Annual rainfall here averages about 1,000 mm and average annual temperature is 7°C to 9°C. The Föhn, a warm wind bringing air of low relative humidity, is noticeable in late winter and spring in the Alps and can melt snow rapidly, often triggering dangerous avalanches at higher levels. Average annual precipitation ranges from 610 mm in Valais canton to 2,000 mm near Luzern.

History, government and constitution. The Swiss Confederation was created in 1291 when the 3 cantons of Uri, Schwyz and Unterwalden formed a defensive league. In 1315 the league won a notable victory over Leopold of Austria at Morgarten. During the 14th century, the Confederation grew, adding 5 more cantons, including Zürich and Bern. Under the Treaty of Westphalia in 1648, Swiss independence and neutrality were recognized by the other European nations. Organized as a confederation of 22 cantons in 1815 under the Federal Pact, Switzerland adopted a federal constitution in 1848, modelled in part on the US constitution. The Swiss amended their constitution extensively in 1874, establishing federal responsibility for defence, trade, and legal matters. The constitution of 1874 vests the control of federal matters in a parliament consisting of a *Ständerat* (Council of States), and a *Nationalrat* (National Council). The *Ständerat* is composed of 46 members, chosen and paid by the 23 cantons of the Confederation. The *Nationalrat* consists of 200 National Councillors, directly elected for 4 years, in proportion to the population of the cantons, with the proviso that each demicanton is represented by at least 1 member.

Industry. Industry employs c.35% of the labour force and accounts for 40% of national income. The chief manufacturing industries are based on the production of machinery, precision instruments, watches, drugs, chemicals and textiles. In recent years there has been increased specialization and development in high-technology products. Apart from watchmaking, industrial and export growth in the early 1980s has been most marked in the chemical, pharmaceutical and machinery industries. Chemicals and pharmaceuticals, concentrated principally in the Basel area, employ 2.3% of the workforce and account for 20% of exports. Major exports included power equipment and electrical appliances, instruments, watches, chemicals and dyestuffs, drugs, industrial machinery, yarn and textiles, and foodstuffs. The major markets are West Germany, France, Italy, US and UK. West Germany is Switzerland's most important trading partner; Switzerland is also a major financial centre.

Agriculture and forestry. Of the total area of the country, about 10,578 sq km (25.6%) are unproductive. Of the productive area of 30,715 sq km, 10,520 sq km are wooded. The agricultural area in 1980 consisted of 2,872 sq km of arable land (including vineyards), 1,064 sq km of artificial meadows and 5,613 sq km of permanent meadow. Dairy farming predominates, with Swiss breeds of cattle sought after in many countries of the world. Agricultural production is sufficient to satisfy around 50% of domestic food requirements. Major crops include wheat, potatoes, sugar-beet, grapes and apples. There are 121 sq km of land under vineyards, mostly in the French-speaking cantons of Vaud and Valais. However, the German-speaking N and E of the country, centred on Zürich, and the Italian Ticino in the S both have extensive areas under vine.

Administrative divisions. Switzerland is divided into 23 cantons (of which 6 are demicantons) as follows:

Canton	*area (sq km)*	*pop(1980)*
Zürich	1,729	1,122,839
Bern	6,887	912,022
Luzern	1,494	296,159
Uri	1,075	33,883
Schwyz	908	97,354
Obwalden	492	25,865
Nidwalden	274	28,617
Glarus	684	36,718
Zug	239	75,930
Fribourg	1,670	185,246
Solothurn	791	218,102
Basel-Stadt	37	203,915
Basel-Land	428	219,822
Schaffhausen	298	69,413
Appenzell Ausser Rhoden	243	47,611
Appenzell Inner Rhoden	172	12,844
St Gallen	2,016	391,995

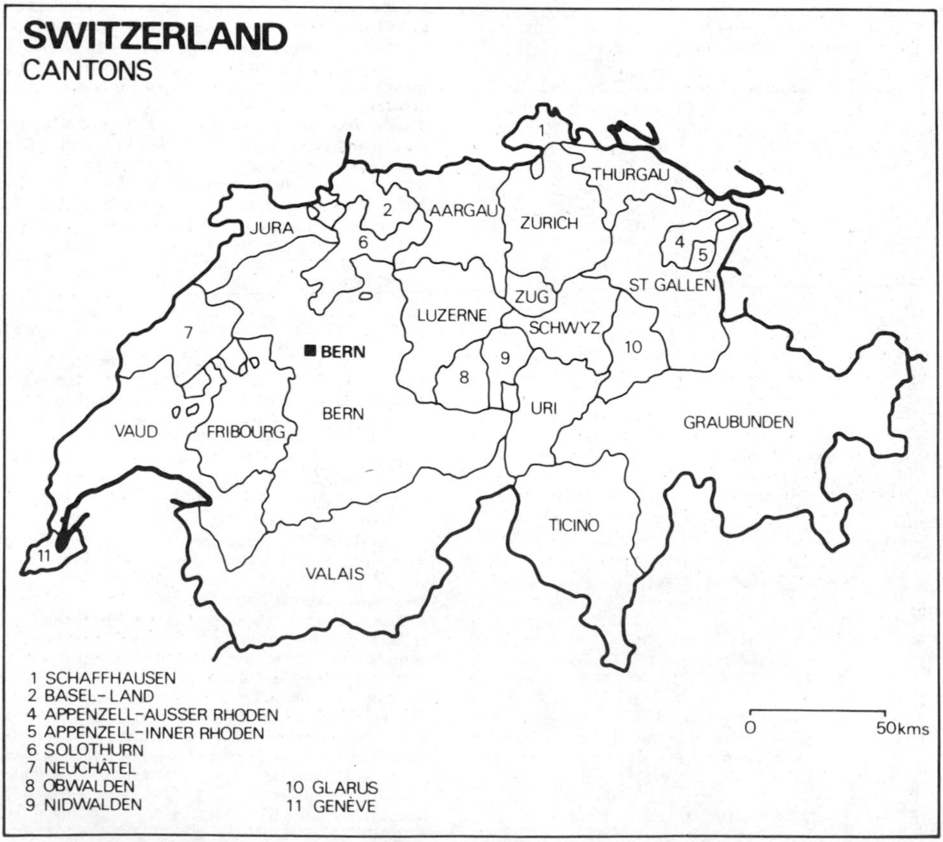

contd

Canton	*area (sq km)*	*pop(1980)*
Graubünden	7,109	164,641
Aargau	1,404	453,442
Thurgau	1,006	183,795
Ticino	2,811	265,899
Vaud	3,211	528,747
Valais	5,231	218,707
Neuchâtel	797	158,368
Genève	282	349,040
Jura	838	64,986

Swords *sordz*, SÓRD CHOLUIM CHILLE (Gael), 53 28N 6 13W, pop(1981) 11,138, town in Dublin county, Leinster, E Irish Republic; a suburban area N of Dublin; monuments: 13th-c bishop's palace and abbey church.

Sydney, 33 55S 151 10E, pop(1986) 3,430,600, port and state capital of New South Wales, on the SE coast of Australia; on the shore of Port Jackson; the largest city in Australia; Sydney stat div (1981 pop 3,204,696) comprises 44 municipalities and shires, the largest of which are Blacktown (1981 pop 181,139), Warringah (1981 pop 172,653), Sutherland (1981 pop 165,336), and Bankstown (1981 pop 152,636), founded in 1788 as the first British settlement in Australia; University of Sydney (1850); University of New South Wales (1949); Macquarie University (1964); railway; airport; economy: shipbuilding; the city's 2 major harbours are Sydney and Port Botany; economy: coal, electronics, oil refining, metal products, machinery, brewing, chemicals, paper, clothing, food processing and trade in wool, grain; monuments: Sydney Harbour Bridge (1932); Sydney Opera House on Bennelong Point peninsula; State Parliament House; national art gallery (1871); events: Festival of Sydney (Jan); Sydney Royal Easter Show; Sydney Cup Week (horse racing) in April.

Sylhet *sil'het*, region in E Bangladesh; includes Hobiganj, Moulvi Bazar, Sunamganj and Sylhet districts; pop(1981) 5,656,000; area 12,715 sq km; bounded N and E by India; crossed by the Kalni and Bibiyana rivers; rice and tea cultivation; limestone quarries.

Sylhet, 25 43N 91 51E, pop(1981) 168,371, capital of Sylhet dist and region, E Bangladesh; 200 km NE of Dhākā; centre of Islamic culture; 3 colleges; railway; airfield; economy: rice, tea, cotton, jute, oilseed, timber, electrical goods.

Sylt *zilt, zült*, northernmost German North Sea island and largest of the Nordfriesische Inseln (North Frisian Is), off the Schleswig-Holstein coast, near Danish border; area 99.1 sq km; length 37 km; connected by rail to German coast by causeway (Hindenburg Damm); popular summer resort, its particular attractions being the dunes and the 40 km of wave swept beach; preventive measures are taken to counter severe erosion.

Syracuse, ancient city of Sicilia (Sicily). See Siracuse.

Syracuse *si'ra-kyooz*, 43 03N 76 09W, pop(1980) 170,105, county seat of Onondaga county, central New York, United States; 19 km S of W end of L Oneida; developed in association with salt works during the 1780s and later at the junction of the Erie and Oswego canals; a city since 1847; university (1870); railway; airfield; economy: electrical equipment.

Syr-Dar'ya *sir-dur-ya'*, JAXARTES (anc), river predominantly in Kazakhskaya SSR, S Soviet Union; formed by the junction of the Naryn and Karadar'ya rivers, in the W section of the Tien Shan Mts, Uzbekskaya SSR; flows S and SW through a narrow gorge, turns N at Leninabad, continues through Chardara reservoir and along the E and N edges of the Peski Kyzylkum (Kyzyl-Kum Desert); discharges into the Aral'skoye More (Aral Sea) S of Aral'sk; length 2,212 km; drainage basin area 219,000 sq km; chief tributaries Arys' and Chirchik rivers; the Trans-Siberian railway parallels its lower course; its waters are used for irrigating the cotton-growing areas along its course and for hydroelectric power (Chardara and Toktogul stations).

Syria, SŪRĪYA (Arab), official name Syrian Arab Republic, AL-JUMHŪRĪYAH AL-'ARABIYAH AS-SŪRĪYAH, republic in the Middle East, bounded W by the Mediterranean Sea and Lebanon, SW by Israel and Jordan, E by Iraq, and N by Turkey; timezone GMT +2; area 185,180 sq km; capital Dimashq (Damascus); chief towns Ḥalab (Aleppo), Ḥimṣ, Ḥamāh, and Al Lādhiqīyah (Latakia); pop(1981) 9,050,204; the urban pop increased from 37% in 1960 to 50% in 1980; the pop comprises 90.3% Arab and 9.7% Kurds, Armenians, and other minority groups; Arabic is the official language; approx 90% of the population are Muslim (74% Sunni Muslim, 16% Alawite Druze and other sects) and 10% are Christian; the unit of currency is the Syrian pound; membership of Arab League, FAO, G-77, IAEA, IBRD, ICAO, IDA, Islamic Development Bank, IFAD, IFC, ILO, IMF, IMO, INTELSAT, INTERPOL, IOOC, IPU, ITU, IWC, NAM, OAPEC, OIC, UN, UNESCO, UPU, WFTU, WHO, WSG, WTO.

Physical description. Behind the narrow Mediterranean coastal plain, the Jabal al Nuṣayrīyah mountain range rises to about 1,500 m. To the E these mountains drop steeply to the 'Āsi (Orontes) river valley. In the SW of the country the Jebel esh Sharqi (Anti-Lebanon) range rises to 2,814 m at Jesh Sheikh (Mt Hermon) on the Lebanese border. The only other area of highland is the Jabal ad Durūz SE of Dimashq (Damascus) on the Jordan border. E of these mountain ranges the land slopes gently NE towards the Euphrates river valley. The vast E region consists mainly of open steppe and desert.

Climate. The coastal climate is Mediterranean with hot, dry summers and mild, wet winters. The mountainous areas have a greater rainfall and may be subject to snowfall. Approx 60% of Syria has a desert or semi-desert climate with an annual rainfall below 200 mm. At the end or beginning of the summer season the hot and dusty *khamsin* wind, blowing from the E and SE, may cause temperatures to rise as high as 43-49°C. Dimashq, situated E of the coastal mountains, has a mean annual rainfall of 225 mm and average temperatures range from 7°C in Jan to 27°C in July.

History, government and constitution. After a short period of independence in 1920 Syria was designated a French mandate. Mandatory rule came to an end on 12 April 1946 when Syria achieved complete independence. Two years later, Syria was involved in the Arab-Israeli War of 1948. In 1958 it merged with Egypt and Yemen to form

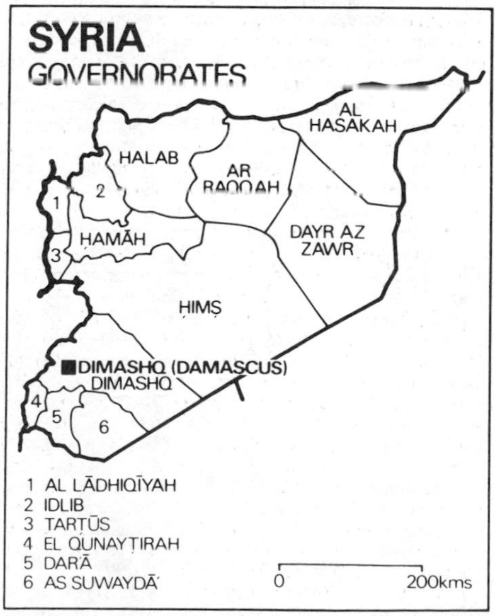

the United Arab Republic but on 28 September 1961, following a military coup, Syria re-established itself as an independent state under the title of the Syrian Arab Republic. After a coup in 1963, attempts by the Ba'ath (Renaissance) party to form a tripartite federation with Iraq and Egypt failed. Israel seized part of Syria (the Golan Heights region) in 1967. Following the outbreak of civil war in Lebanon in 1975, Syrian troops, constituting the bulk of the Arab Deterrent Force, were sent to restore order. A Treaty of Friendship and Cooperation with the USSR was signed in 1980. According to the 1973 Constitution Syria is a 'socialist popular democracy'. The president is elected for a 7-year term by universal adult suffrage. Legislative power is vested in a 195-member people's council elected for a 4-year term.

Economy. Since 1974 oil has been Syria's most important source of export revenue. Exploration first began in 1971 in the NW and in the Ḩalab area. At the outset emphasis was not so much on exports as on the development of industrial feedstock. There are refineries at Ḩimş and at Bāniyās on the Mediterranean coast. A 650 km-long pipeline links them with the oilfields and to the port of Ţarţūs. Syria's industrial sector was traditionally based on the cotton industry but in recent years phosphate mining (at Hafe, near Al Lādhiqīyah, and Tadmur) and manufacturing have become more important. Chief industries include the manufacture of textiles, beverages, tobacco, and cement, plus oil refining and food processing. Chief exports are oil, textiles, tobacco, fruits and vegetables, and cotton. Major trade partners include Saudi Arabia, W Germany, Italy, France, Romania, the USA, and the USSR. The Euphrates dam project, which presently supplies 97% of domestic demand, is planned to allow for the export of electricity to Jordan and Lebanon. The lake impounded by the dam, Buḩayrat al Asad, is designed to enable the development of a fishing industry and tourism.

Agriculture. In 1978 agriculture, forestry, and fishing accounted for 20% of national income. Agriculture has traditionally been the mainstay of the economy and now plays a major part in the country's ambitious development plans. Much of the agriculture is concentrated in the ancient 'Fertile Crescent' which extends in an arc from the inner rim of the coastal mountains, through N Syria, and down the Euphrates valley into Iraq. The main crops grown include cotton, wheat, barley, rice, olives, millet, sugar-beet, and tobacco. Cotton has traditionally been the chief export crop but in recent years exports of fruit have increased. Cattle breeding is becoming more important and there are several poultry projects under development. Arable land covers approx 48% of the total land area. The huge Euphrates dam project, inaugurated in March 1978, is planned to increase the area of arable land in Syria by 6,400 sq km. Further land reclamation schemes, notably on the Yarmūk river, are under way.

Administrative divisions. Syria is divided into 14 governorates (*mohofazats*) which in turn are subdivided into 48 *mantikas* (districts):

Governorate	*pop(1981e)*
Dar'ā	362,969
Dayr az Zawr	409,130
Dimashq	917,364
Dimashq City	1,112,214
Ḩalab	1,878,701
Ḩamāh	736,412
Āl Hasakah	669,887
Ḩimş	812,517
Idlib	579,581
Al Lādhiqīyah	554,384
El Qunayţirah	26,258
Ar Raqqah	348,383
As Suwaydā	199,194
Ţarţūs	443,290

Szabolcs-Szátmar *sa'bolch-sot'mar*, county in E Hungary; bounded to the E by the USSR and SE by Romania; mostly flat land in the Great Plains (Alföld) region; watered by the R Tisza; pop(1984e) 586,000; area 5,938 sq km; capital Nýiregyháza; chief towns include Nagyecsed and Ujfehérto.

Szarvas *sor'vosh*, 46 50N 20 38E, pop(1984e) 20,000, town in Békés county, S Hungary; on R Körös; the town has an arboretum with over 1,600 species of trees.

Szczecin *shche'tseen*, voivodship in NW Poland; bounded W by R Oder (Odra) which meets the frontier with E Germany and follows it S; also bounded N by the Baltic Sea; pop(1983) 924,000; area 9,981 sq km; capital Szczecin; chief towns include Stargard Szczeciński, Świnoujście and Police.

Szczecin, STETTIN (Ger), 53 25N 14 32E, pop(1983) 389,200, industrial river port capital of Szczecin voivodship, NW Poland; on R Oder (Odra), 60 km from Baltic Sea, near W frontier with E Germany; largest Baltic trading port; granted urban status in 1243; under Prussian rule between 1720 and 1945; the port spreads almost 5 km across between the R Oder (Odra) and the mouth of the R Regalica where it meets L Dąbie; this area, known as Międzyodrze, is crossed by natural and artificial canals with docks and transshipment facilities; maritime college; medical academy; technical university (1946); airfield; railway; economy: shipyards, yacht-building, synthetic fibres, cranes, iron, tools, deep sea fishing, fish processing; monuments: St James's cathedral, 16th-c castle of the dukes of Pomerania, 13-14th-c city walls, 15-16th-c professors' dwellings, club of 13 muses.

Szechwan, prov in SW central China. See Sichuan.

Szeged *se'ged*, 46 16N 20 10E, pop(1981) 172,000, river port capital of Csongrád county, S Hungary; on R Tisza; cultural centre of the S Alföld; university (1872, refounded 1921); university of medicine (1872, refounded 1921); biological centre of the Hungarian Academy of Sciences; medicinal baths; railway; economy: timber and salt trade, chemicals, hemp spinning and weaving, salami, red pepper; monuments: castle (1242), Votive church; event: open-air festival in July-Aug.

Székesfehérvár *say'kesh-fe-heer-var*, STUHLWEISSENBURG (Ger), ALBA REGIA (anc), 47 15N 18 25E, pop(1984e) 109,000, capital of Fejér county, W central Hungary; halfway between Budapest and L Balaton; celebrated its millennium in 1972; economy: market centre for tobacco, wine and fruit; light metal works; monument: Budenz-house, named after József Budenz, one of the founders of Finno-Ugrian comparative linguistics; Baroque cathedral; episcopal palace; Garden of Ruins with remains of 11th-c royal cathedral where 37 kings were crowned and 17 are buried.

Szekszárd *sek'sard*, 46 22N 18 42E, pop(1984e) 38,000, market town and capital of Tolna county, SW central Hungary; 128 km SW of Budapest; noted for its red wine; economy: agricultural trade.

Szentes *sen'tesh*, 46 39N 20 21E, pop(1984e) 35,000, market town in Csongrád county, S Hungary; on branch of R Tisza; economy: agricultural trade, food processing, textiles, timber, furniture, food freezers, electrical products.

Szolnok *sol'nok*, county in E central Hungary; part of the flat Great Plains (Alföld) region; watered by the Tisza and Zagyvar rivers; pop(1984e) 441,000; area 5,608 sq km; capital Szolnok; chief towns include Mezötur and Törökszentmiklós.

Szolnok, 47 10N 20 15E, pop(1984e) 78,000, industrial and commercial capital of Szolnok county, E central Hungary; at the junction of the Tisza and Zagyvar rivers, SW of Debrecen; railway; economy: footwear, paper, timber, sugar refining.

Szombathely *som'bot-hay*, STEINAMANGER (Ger), SABARIA (anc), 47 14N 16 38E, pop(1984e) 86,000, capital of Vas county, W Hungary; on R Gyöngyös; bishopric; railway; economy: chemicals, textiles, timber; monuments: cathedral, 14th-c Franciscan church, 17th-c Dominican church, Garden of Ruins with excavations of 4th-c imperial palace.

T

Ta Khmau, 11 29N 104 57E, chief town of Kandal prov, S Cambodia; lies on Fleuve Bassac, 9 km SSE of Phnom Penh.

Tabasará, Serranía de *se-ra-nee'a day ta-ba-sa-ra'*, mountain range in W Panama, Central America; forming a section of the continental divide; length approx 80 km; forms a watershed between those rivers flowing into the Caribbean (Río Chiriquí, Río Cricamola) and that flowing into the Pacific (Río Fonseca).

Tabasco *ta-bas'kō*, state in SE Mexico; bounded N by the Gulf of Mexico and Campeche, W by Veracruz, S by Chiapas and SE by Guatemala; outliers of the Sierra Madre in the S, but mostly flat subtropical jungle plain with swamps and lagoons; drained by tributaries of the Grijalva and Usumacinta rivers, which join together before entering the Gulf of Mexico at Frontera; pop(1980) 1,149,756; area 25,267 sq km; capital Villahermosa; economy: sugar cane, maize, cocoa, coconuts, bananas, coffee, pineapples and other tropical fruit, cattle, pigs, horses, fishing, sugar refining, oil and natural gas.

Table Mountain, 33 58S 18 25E, mountain in SW Cape prov, South Africa; height 1,086 m; a flat-topped central massif flanked on either side by the Lion's Head and Devil's Peak; often shrouded in cloud known as the 'Tablecloth' which is formed by moisture-laden winds from the SE; Kirstenbosch national botanical gardens situated on E slopes; Cape Town is situated at the foot of the mountain; first European sighting by Bartholomew Diaz (1488) and first European ascent in 1503 by the Portuguese explorer Antonio de Saldanha in order to ascertain whether he had rounded the Cape of Good Hope.

Tábor *tah'bor*, 49 25N 14 41E, pop(1984) 33,757, town in Jihočeský region, Czech Socialist Republic, W central Czechoslovakia; on R Lužnice, NE of České Budějovice; railway; economy: agricultural trade, tobacco, kaolin, textiles; monuments: ruins of Kozi Hradek castle nearby and pilgrimage site at Klokoty.

Tabora *ta-bō'ra*, 5 02S 32 50E, pop(1978) 67,392, capital of Tabora region, Tanzania, E Africa; 740 km WNW of Dar es Salaam; founded in 1820 by Arabs as a slave and ivory trading centre; centre of a tobacco growing area, railway; airport.

Tabrīz *tab-reez'*, TAURIS *to'ris* (anc), 38 05N 46 18E, pop(1983) 852,296, capital city of Tabrīz dist, Āzarbāyān-e Gharbī, NW Iran; 4th largest city in Iran; industrial and commercial centre, badly destroyed by 1940s earthquake; railway; monuments: ruined 15th-c Blue Mosque and citadel.

Tabūk *te-book'*, 28 30N 36 25E, pop(1974) 74,825, oasis town in Northern prov, NW Saudi Arabia; 560 km NW of Al Madīnah (Medina); airfield.

Taburiente, Caldera de la *kahl-day'rah THay la ta-boo-ree-en'tay*, LA CALDERA, 28 45N 17 45W, one of the largest volcanic craters in the world on the island of La Palma in the Canary Is, Santa Cruz de Tenerife prov, Canarias, Spain; rising to 2,433 m at the Roque de los Muchachos; a sacred place to the former native Guanches; now part of the 35 sq km Caldera de la Taburiente National Park established in 1954.

Täby *te'bu*, 59 29N 18 04E, pop(1982) 49,026, town in Stockholm county, E Sweden; a N suburb of Stockholm, 17 km from the centre of the city; monuments: runic stones.

Táchira *ta'chee-ra*, mountainous state in W Venezuela; bordered W by Colombia along the Río Táchira; traversed by the Cordillera de Mérida, its NW corner is in the Maracaibo lowlands; pop(1980) 678,660; area 11,096 sq km; capital San Cristóbal.

Tacna *tak'na*, dept in SW Peru; borders W with the Pacific, S with Chile and E with Bolivia; largely mountainous region, sloping W from the Cordillera Occidental to the ocean; watered by Sama and Locumba rivers; this department was in dispute with Chile; pop(1981) 143,085; area 14,766 sq km; capital Tacna.

Tacoma *te-kō'me*, 47 14N 122 26W, pop(1980) 158,501, port capital of Pierce county, W central Washington, United States; on Commencement Bay, an inlet of the Puget Sound, 40 km S of Seattle; settled in 1868, achieving city status in 1875; university (1888); air force base; railway; economy: a major NW Pacific container port exporting timber, fruit, tallow, agricultural machinery; industries include boatbuilding, chemicals, food processing, metalwork, wood and paper products; monuments: state historical society; Chinese museums; Fort Nisqually.

Tacora, Volcán de *ta-kō'ra*, Andean volcano rising to 5,980 m on the border between Chile and Peru; 105 km NE of Arica.

Tacuarembó *ta-kwa-rem-bō'*, dept in N central Uruguay; bordered S by the Río Negro and the Rincón del Bonete reservoir, where there is a major hydroelectric plant; pop(1985) 82,809; area 21,105 sq km; capital Tacuarembó; chief town Paso de los Toros; the dept was formed in 1837.

Tacuarembó, 31 42S 56 00W, pop(1985) 40,470, capital of Tacuarembó dept, N central Uruguay; railway; airfield; to the N of the city is the Gruta de los Cuervos.

Tadjoura or **Tajura, Gulf of** *ta-joo'ru*, an inlet of the Gulf of Aden, on the E coast of Djibouti, E Africa.

Tadley, 51 21N 1 08W, pop(1981) 13,847, town in Basingstoke and Deane dist, Hampshire, S England; SW of Reading.

Tadmur *tahd-moor*, PALMY'RA (Gr), ('city of palm trees'), 34 36N 38 15E, ancient city in Ḥimş governorate, central Syria; 208 km NE of Dimashq (Damascus); during the first two centuries AD, Tadmur was the financial capital of the E world, and many of its fine examples of Hellenistic art and architecture date from this period; on the ancient caravan route from the Arabian Gulf to the Mediterranean Sea; rail terminus; an oil pipeline passes through the city; monuments: numerous temples including the Temple of Bēl; Monumental Arch; various tombs on the slopes of the hills to the E.

Tadohae, marine national park in S Korea; area 2,039 sq km; established in 1981; includes numerous islands off the coast of Korea.

Tadzhik, constituent republic of the Soviet Union. See Tadzhikskaya.

Tadzhikskaya, TADZHIKISTAN, TADZHIK, constituent republic of the Soviet Union, in SE Middle Asia, bounded S by Afghanistan and E by China; mountains of the Tien Shan, Gissar-Alai, and Pamir ranges cover more than 90% of the territory; Pik Kommunizma (Communism Peak), the highest mountain in the USSR, reaches an elevation of 7,495 m; the R Amudar'ya flows from E to W along the S border of the republic; other rivers include the Syr-Dar'ya, Vakhsh, and Zeravshan; Ozero Kara-Kul is the largest lake; pop(1983) 4,239,000; area 143,100 sq km; capital Dushanbe; chief towns Leninabad, Kurgan-Tyube, and Kulyab; economy: coal mining, non-ferrous metallurgy (especially mining and processing of lead and zinc ores), machine building and metalworking, chemicals, light industry (the country's main producer of fine-fibre cotton), food processing, hydroelectric power generation (R Vakhsh), extraction of petroleum and natural gas; the construction of an electrochemical combine, the largest in the USSR, has begun in Yavan steppe in the S of the republic; cotton cultivation is the most important branch of agriculture; other crops grown include wheat, maize, vegetables, and fruit (including grapes); Tadzhikskaya was formed from the regions of Bokhara and Turkestan; it became a constituent republic of the Soviet Union in Dec 1929; the republic is divided into the 4 oblasts of Gorno-Badakhshanskaya, Kulyab, Kurgan-Tyube and Leninabadskaya.

Taegu *tī-goo*, 35 52N 128 36E, pop(1984) 2,012,039, special city in SE Korea; area 455 sq km; Korea's largest inland city after Sŏul; university (1946); railway; economy: market town at the centre of Korea's apple growing area; monuments: to the W of Taegu in Kayasan national park is Haeinsa temple which was established in 802 AD and contains the Tripitaka Koreana, a set of 80,000 wooden printing blocks engraved with one of the most comprehensive compilations of Buddhist scripture in Asia; the king ordered blocks to be carved during the Mongol invasion of the 13th century, they were completed in 1236; Tonghwasa Temple is situated 22 km NNE of Taegu, the wooden temple gate dates from 1634; to the right of the entrance overlooking the road is a Buddha image carved into the cliff during the 9th cent.

Taejŏn *tī-jon*, 36 20N 127 26E, pop(1984) 842,429, capital of Ch'ungch'ŏngnam prov, central Korea; Chungnam National University (1952); railway; monuments: W of the city are the Yusŏng Hot Springs, one of the finest hot springs in Korea; the mountainous Kyeryongsan national park to the W of Taejŏn is an ancient religious home for several sects, intermingling Shamanism, Buddhism, Confucianism and Christianity; distinctive pottery was produced here during the first 100 years of the Yi dynasty.

Taff, river rising SW of Brecon, Powys, Wales; flows 64 km S through Mid and South Glamorgan to meet the Bristol Channel at Cardiff; tributaries include the Rhondda and Cynon rivers.

Taganrog *ta-gen-rok'*, 47 14N 38 55E, pop(1983) 285,000, seaport in Rostovskaya oblast, S European Rossiyskaya, Soviet Union; on the NE shore of the Taganrogskiy Zaliv (Gulf of Taganrog) of the Azovskoye More (Sea of Azov); the writer Anton Chekhov was born here; founded by Peter I in 1698 as a fortress and base for the Russian Azov Naval Fleet; the port declined after Sevastopol' became a naval base; rail terminus; economy: metallurgy, machines, foodstuffs, shipyards, leatherwork.

Tag'ant, desert region in central Mauritania, NW Africa; pop(1982e) 84,000; area 95,200 sq km; capital Tidjikdja; chief towns Tichitt, Messa, El Haoussinia and Moudjéria.

Tagus *tay'gus*, TAJO *ta'ho* (Sp), TEJO *tay'zhoo*, (Port), river rising in Sierra de Albarracin (Teruel prov, Spain), flows 785 km SW through mountainous region of Guadalajara prov and W across central plateau to the Portuguese border which it follows for 44 km before turning SW for 178 km across Santarém and Lisboa dists; below Vila Franca de Xira it opens out into the Tagus estuary which consists of Lisbon Bay or Mar da Palha and of a narrow channel that links the bay to the Atlantic; 229 sq km of the estuary were given reserve status in 1976; length 1,007 km, 275 km in Portugal, navigable 212 km to Abrantes; area of basin, 24,913 sq km; principal tributaries Erges, Alviela, Almonda, Muge, Ponsul, Ocreza, Zêzere, Sever, Sorraia, Almansor.

Tahan, Gunong *goo-noong' tah-han'*, 4 34N 102 17E, mountain in Pahang state, E Peninsular Malaysia, SE Asia; rising to 2,189 m it is the highest peak in the Malay peninsula.

Tahat', Mount, mountain in Ahaggar (Hoggar) range, S Algeria, N Africa; height 2,918 m; the highest point in Algeria; first recorded ascent by Dr Wyss Dunant in 1931.

Tahiti, Archipel de *ta-ee'tee* (Fr), *ta-hee'ti* (Eng), 17 37S 149 27W, largest island of French Polynesia, S Pacific Ocean, belonging to the Îles du Vent (Windward) group of the Archipel de la Société (Society Is); area 1,042 sq km; length 48 km; pop(1977) 95,604, capital Papeete; consists of a large mountainous island (Tahiti Nui) and a small peninsula (Tahiti Iti), joined by a low isthmus; rises to 2,237 m in the volcanic peak of Mt Orohena; the NE coast is rugged and rocky; there are numerous vanilla plantations and coconut groves; became a French colony in 1880; the French artist Gauguin lived and painted here; visited in 1788 by *HMS Bounty*.

Tahoua *ta'wa*, dept in SW central Niger, W Africa; there are shifting sands in the N with some seasonal floodplains in the S and far N; area 106,677 sq km; pop(1977e) 1,015,000; comprises 7 arrond; capital Tahoua; chief towns Birni n'Konni and Madaoua; economy: phosphate and limestone mining, cement processing.

Tahoua, 14 57N 5 19E, pop(1983) 41,900, capital of Tahoua dept, SW central Niger, W Africa; 360 km ENE of Niamey; airfield; economy: power plant.

Tai, national park in Guiglo and Sassandra depts, SW Ivory Coast, W Africa; area 3,300 sq km; established in 1972.

Tai Hu, lake in S Jiangsu prov, E China; flows into the Chang Jiang (Yangtze river) via the Wusong He and Huangpu He rivers; area 2,425 sq km; alt 3.14 m; a centre for tourism and for the water network to the S of the Chang Jiang river.

Tai Mo Shan *dī-mō-shan*, 22 24N 114 07E, highest mountain peak in the British Crown Colony of Hong Kong, SE Asia; rising to 957 m in the mountain ridge that separates Kowloon from the New Territories.

Tai'an *tī-ahn*, 36 15N 117 10E, pop(1984e) 1,309,900, city in Shandong prov, E China; at the foot of Tai Shan mountain (1,545 m), one of China's Five Holy Mountains; railway.

T'ai-chung *tī-choong*, 24 09N 120 40E, pop(1982e) 636,406, an independent municipality and 3rd largest city in Taiwan; area 163.4 sq km; economic, cultural and commercial centre of central Taiwan; international seaport 16 km W opened in 1976; designated an export processing zone.

T'ai-chung, county of W Taiwan; area 2,051.4 sq km; pop(1982e) 1,094,776.

Taieri *tī'ree*, river in SE South Island, New Zealand; rises in the Rock and Pillar mountain range to the E of Roxburgh; flows N then SE to enter the Pacific Ocean 32 km SW of Dunedin; length 288 km.

Ţā'if, Aţ, *ta'if*, 21 05N 40 27E, pop(1974) 204,857, summer resort town in Makkah prov, W central Saudi Arabia; 64 km ESE of Makkah (Mecca); on a high plateau at an altitude of 1,158 m; it is the unofficial seat of government during the summer; airfield; economy: centre of fruit-growing district (grapes, apricots, pomegranates); noted for its wine.

T'ai-nan *tī-nahn*, 23 01N 120 14E, pop(1985e) 622,073, an independent municipality and oldest city in Taiwan; on SW coast of Taiwan I; capital of the island from 1684 to 1887; area 175.6 sq km; monuments: tomb of the warrior Koxinga; the oldest Confucian temple in Taiwan (1665); Yi T'sai castle (1874).

T'ai-nan, county of SW Taiwan; area 2,003.6 sq km; pop(1982e) 983,528.

Taipa *tī'pa*, 22 10N 113 33E, island of the Portuguese overseas prov of Macau, E Asia; W of Hong Kong; linked to the mainland by a bridge (Ponte Macau-Taipa) and to the island of Colôane to the S by a causeway (Istmo Taipa-Colôane); the name Taipa describes the rammed clay construction of pre-17th-c houses and churches; pop(1982) with Colôane 7,224; area 4 sq km; monuments: temple of the goddess Kun Iam, junk-building village.

T'ai-pei *tī-bay*, TAIPEI, 25 05N 121 32E, pop(1982e) 2,300,000, capital of Taiwan; special municipality enjoying the status of a province; situated at the NW end of the island; area 272 sq km; divided into 16 dists; one of the fastest-growing cities in Asia, T'ai-pei was proclaimed the provisional capital of the Republic of China on 7 Dec

1949; 52 km SW of T'ai-pei is Shinmen (Stone Gate) Dam, a man-made reservoir (area 8 sq km) which is also used as a recreational lake; railway; airport (Chiang Kaishek), 40 km SW of T'ai-pei; airfield (Sungshan); economy: textiles, plastics, electronics, machinery; monuments: the National Palace Museum contains over 600,000 priceless Chinese treasures, some over 4,000 years old; near the presidential office is the Chung Cheng (Chiang Kaishek) Memorial Hall, dedicated in April 1980; Lung Shan (Dragon Mountain) Temple was dedicated to Kuan Yin, the Buddhist Goddess of Mercy; first built in 1740, it was destroyed by an earthquake in 1817 and its replacement destroyed by a typhoon in 1867; since then it has twice been completely rebuilt, once in 1926 and again in 1959; many other deities as well as Kuan Yin, including non-Buddhist ones, are now enshrined in the temple.

T'ai-pei, county of N Taiwan; area 2,052.2 sq km; pop(1982e) 2,514,191.

Taiping *tī-ping* (Chinese, 'peace'), 4 54N 100 42E, pop(1980) 146,002, city in Perak state, W Peninsular Malaysia, SE Asia; NW of Ipoh; formerly capital of Perak state; on Gunong Hijau (Maxwell's Hill) is Malaysia's oldest hill station; railway; airfield; monuments: Allied War Cemetery, state museum.

Tairona *tī-rō'na*, national park in N Colombia, South America; on the Caribbean, 35 km E of Santa Marta; area 150 sq km; established in 1964; an unspoilt piece of coastal woodland containing numerous relics of the ancient Tairona culture.

Taisetsuzan *tī-set'soo-zahn*, national park in E central Hokkaidō island, Japan; area 2,309 sq km; established in 1934; the park contains hot springs, gorges and several volcanic peaks; it rises to 2,290 m in Asahi-dake volcano, the highest point on Hokkaidō.

Tai-tung *tī-toong*, county of SE Taiwan; area 3,515.2 sq km; pop(1982e) 279,829.

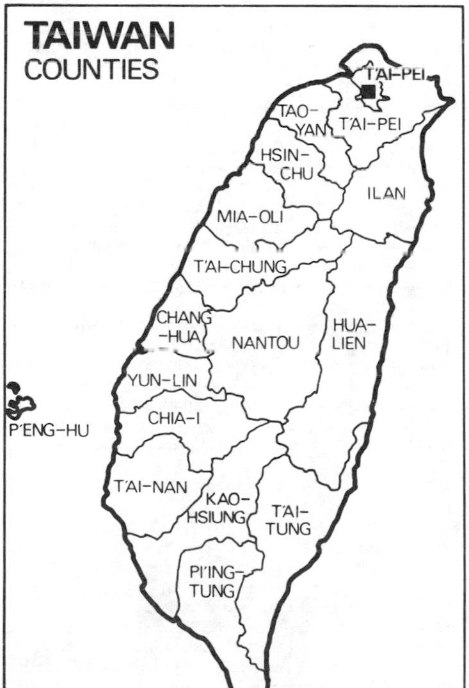

Taiwan *tī-wan*, FORMO'SA, official name Republic of China, island republic consisting of Taiwan island, the P'eng-hu Lieh-tao (or Pescadores) Islands to the W of Taiwan, Lan Hsü and Lü Tao off the E coast of Taiwan and several small offshore islands near the China mainland, including the island of Quemoy off the coast of Fujian prov and other smaller islands further N; Taiwan is situated between 22° and 25° N, lying approx 130 km off the SE coast of China; separated from China to the W by the Taiwan Haixia (Taiwan Strait); to the S is the South China Sea, to the N the East China Sea and to the E the Pacific Ocean; timezone GMT +8; area 36,000 sq km; capital T'ai-pei; pop(1982e) 18,270,749; pop comprises 98% Han Chinese and 2% Aborigines; Mandarin Chinese is the official language; principal dialects are Taiwanese, Hakka and a variation of Hokkien (the dialect of S Fujian prov, China); religions include Confucianism, Buddhism, Taoism and Christianity; the currency is the new Taiwan dollar; national holidays 1 Jan (founding of the Republic of China), 29 March (Youth Day), 5 April (death of President Chiang Kaishek, observed on April 4 in leap years), 28 Sept (the birthday of Confucius, observed as Teachers' Day), 10 Oct (Double Tenth National Day), 25 Oct (Taiwan Retrocession Day), 31 Oct (birthday of President Chiang Kaishek, observed as Veterans' Day), 12 Nov (Dr Sun Yat-sen's birthday), 25 Dec (Constitution Day).

Physical description. Taiwan island is approx 395 km long and 100-145 km wide. A mountain range running N-S covers two-thirds of the island, the highest peak is Yu Shan (3,997 m). Most of the low lying land is on the W side of the island, which is generally flat, fertile and well cultivated. The Tropic of Cancer crosses Taiwan slightly below the middle of the island.

Climate. Taiwan has the same tropical monsoon-type climate as S China. Rainfall is generally over 2,000 mm per year on low-lying land increasing with altitude, the wettest period being the summer (May-Sept). Typhoons from the South China Sea also bring heavy rains between July and Sept. Summers are hot and humid; winters are mild and short. In winter the N and E coasts are wetter and colder than the S. T'ai-pei in the N has an average daily temperature of 12° to 19°C in Jan and 24° to 33°C in the summer months of July and Aug, whilst the town of Hengch'un in the S averages 17° to 24°C in Feb and 25° to 31°C in July. Minimum and maximum monthly rainfall figures for T'ai-pei are 71 mm in Dec and 290 mm in June, while Hengch'un receives an average of 18 mm in Dec and 544 mm in Aug.

History, government and constitution. Chinese migration to Taiwan began in the 6th century. From the 17th century large numbers of Chinese migrated to Taiwan from Fujian and Guangdong provs. The Dutch held a base on Taiwan (1624-61) but were driven out by Cheng Ch'engkung who used the island as a base to defeat the Manchu invaders and restore the Ming dynasty. The Manchus conquered the island in 1683 and the Chinese ruled over it until it was ceded to Japan in 1895 after the Sino-Japanese war. It was placed back into the hands of the Chinese government in 1945 after World War II. In 1949, following the conquest of the Chinese mainland by the communists, the government leader, Chiang Kaishek, moved the nationalist government to Taiwan and established the capital at T'ai-pei in Dec of that year. Taiwan, still controlled by the remnants of the nationalist government, claims to represent the whole of China. Under the 1947 constitution the sovereignty of the people is exercised by the National Assembly which has about 1,400 members, those members elected in 1947-48 holding their seats indefinitely. The legislative parliament (*Yuan*) has about 400 members. The president appoints the premier of the executive *Yuan* which comprises the cabinet and is responsible for policy and administration. The Control *Yuan* monitors the efficiency of public services.

Economy. Since the 1950s the base of Taiwan's economy has changed from agriculture to industry. The emphasis is now changing within industry itself from light industry and consumer goods to sophisticated heavy industry and high technology, with 41% of the population employed in industry and commerce. In 1985 industry accounted for over 45% of national income, the major manufacturing industries being textiles, footwear, electronics, plastics, cement, furniture, consumer goods, iron, steel and petrochemicals. Taiwan's principal export markets are the USA, Japan and Hong Kong. Major exports include textiles, machinery, plastics, metal products, plywood and canned food. Taiwan has small deposits of coal, natural gas, limestone, marble and asbestos. Agriculture accounts for less than 8% of national income, exporting frozen pork, sugar, canned mushrooms, canned asparagus, bananas, pineapples, citrus fruits, fresh vegetables, tea and fish. There are 3 nuclear power stations, a thermal power station (Hsinta) and a hydroelectric scheme (Minghu).

Transport. Taiwan has two international airports, T'ai-pei's Chiang Kaishek International Airport, and the Kao-hsiung International Airport. Kao-hsiung is the island's largest international seaport. Other major new seaports include Keelung on the N coast, T'ai-chung on the central W coast, and Su-ao and Hua-lien on the E coast. As well as a road linking all of Taiwan's important ports, there is an electrified railway system.

Administrative divisions. Taiwan is divided into the 2 special municipalities of T'ai-pei and Kao-hsiung; the 5 municipalities of T'ai-chung, Keelung, T'ai-nan, Chia-i and Hsin-chu; and 16 counties (*hsien*) as follows:

County	*area (sq km)*	*pop(1982e)*
Chang-hua	1,061.7	1,203,970
Chia-i	1,891.4	574,712
Hsin-chu	1,424.7	365,837
Hua-lien	4,628.6	361,017
Ilan	2,137.5	447,707
Kao-hsiung	2,792.6	1,057,725
Mia-oli	1,820.3	548,790
Nantou	4,106.4	532,750
P'eng-hu	126.9	104,083
P'ing-tung	2,775.6	900,614
T'ai-chung	2,051.4	1,094,776
T'ai-nan	2,003.6	983,528
T'ai-pei	2,052.2	2,514,191
T'ai-tung	3,515.2	279,829
Taoyuan	1,220.9	1,160,709
Yün-lin	1,290.8	796,751

Taïyetos Óros *tī'ye-tos*, TAYGETUS *tay-i'ju-tus* (Eng), mountain range in S Pelopónnisos region, Greece; extends for 104 km along the border between Messinía and Lakonía nomoi (depts); rises to a height of 2,407 m; the only route through the range is the recently built road, largely following the old mule-track through the Langáda gorge, which links Spartí with Kalámai.

Taiyuan *tī-yoo-ahn*, YANGKU, 37 50N 112 30E, pop(1984e) 1,838,100, capital of Shanxi prov, NE central China; at the N end of the Taiyuan Basin; Taiyuan was founded during the Western Zhou dynasty (c.1066-771 BC); the city's development was promoted in the late 19th century by Western powers; railway; economy: coal, iron, steel, chemicals, textiles; monuments: Shanxi museum contains a display of Neolithic artifacts found in the area; c.25 km SE of Taiyuan is Jinci, a group of temples built during the Northern Wei dynasty (386-534 AD) in memory of Shu Yu, son of the King of Wu; the largest, Shengmudian (Sacred Mother Hall), contains 44 statues of Song ladies-in-waiting.

Ta'izz *ta-iz'*, 14 40N 44 40E, pop(1975) 119,570, town in the highlands of North Yemen; 51 km E of Al Mukhā; airfield to the NE; alt 1,402 m.

Takamatsu *ta-ka-mat'soo*, 34 20N 134 01E, pop(1980) 316,661, port capital of Kagawa prefecture, N Shikoku island, Japan; on the Harima-nada (Inland Sea), 136 km WSW of Ōsaka; Kagawa University (1949); railway; airport; economy: cotton, pulp, paper, fans; monuments: the 17th-c Ritsurin koen Park at the foot of Mt Shiun with its notable Japanese gardens.

Takapuna *tah-ka-poo'na*, 36 48S 174 47E, pop(1981) 65,407, city on North Island, New Zealand; on the Hauraki Gulf; N of Auckland.

Takasaki *ta-ka-sa'kee*, 36 20N 139 00E, pop(1980) 221,429, town in Gumma prefecture, Kanto region, central Honshū island, Japan; just SW of Maebashi; railway.

Takatsu *ta-kat'soo*, 35 32N 139 42E, pop(1980) 283,996, town in Kanagawa prefecture, Kanto region, Honshū island, Japan; W of Tōkyo; railway.

Takatsuki *ta-kat-soo'kee*, 34 50N 135 35E, pop(1980) 340,720, town in Ōsaka prefecture, Kinki region, S Honshū island, Japan; 24 km NNE of Ōsaka; railway; economy: textiles, machinery.

Takeo *tah'kay-ō*, province in S Cambodia; pop(1981) 467,000; bounded S and SE by Vietnam; crossed by the Takeo river; crossed by railway line, linking Phnom Penh with Kompong Som; chief town, Takeo, lies on the SW bank of the R Takeo.

Takhār *ta-kar'*, prov in NE Afghanistan; pop(1984e) 564,545; area 12,376 sq km; bounded N by the R Ryandzh and the USSR; lies N of the Hindu Kush; crossed by the R Kokcha; capital Tāloqān.

Taklimakan Shamo, desert in the centre of the Tarim Pendi basin, S Xinjiang aut region, NW China. See Tarim Pendi.

Takutea *ta-koo-tay'ah*, 19 49S 158 18W, uninhabited coral island of the Cook Is, S Pacific, 189 km NE of Rarotonga; area 1.2 sq km.

Talagante *ta-la-gan'tay*, 33 39S 70 56W, pop(1982) 26,111, capital of Talagante prov, Santiago, Chile; railway.

Talamanca, Cordillera de *THay ta-la-mang'ka*, mountain range in SE Costa Rica and NW Panama, Central America; forming a section of the main continental divide; extends 160 km SE from S Cartago prov, forming the boundary between the provs of Puntarenas (W) and Limón (E) in its middle section; rises to 3,819 m at Chirripó Grande, the highest peak in Central America; other peaks include Cerro Kamuk (3,554 m) and Cerro Durika (3,280 m).

Talamanca, Cordillera de, largest national park in Costa Rica, Central America; covering an area of 1,905 sq km in the Cordillera de Talamanca; established in 1979.

Talavera de la Reina *ta-la-vay'ra THay la ray'na*, CAESAROBRIGA, TALABRIGA (anc), 39 55N 4 46W, pop(1981) 64,136, town in Toledo prov, Castilla-León, central Spain; on the R Tagus, S of the Sierra de Gredos and 110 km SW of Madrid; economy: timber, textiles, pharmaceuticals, animal feed, soap, cement, embroidery and pottery; monuments: the Moorish Torres Albarranas, Gothic collegiate church of Santa Maria la Mayor and the Ermitá de la Virgen del Prado faced with 16-18th-c Talavera tiles.

Talca *tal'ka*, 35 25S 71 39W, pop(1982) 134,721, capital of Talca prov, and Maule region, central Chile; S of Santiago; railway; founded in 1692, destroyed by earthquake in 1742 and again in 1928; it has been completely rebuilt since 1928; Chilean independence was declared in Talca on 1 Jan 1818; Talca prov is noted as the greatest wine-producing area in Chile; monuments: Museo O'Higgins, featuring the history of the War of the Pacific.

Talcahuano *tal-ka-hwa'nō*, 36 40S 73 10W, pop(1982) 208,941, port in Concepción prov, Bío-Bío, central Chile; on a peninsula jutting out into the sea, 12 km from Concepción; has the best harbour in Chile; contains Chile's main naval base and dry docks; 1.5 km away at Huachipato is a steel plant with its own wharf to unload the iron ore shipped from the N; railway; the remains of the Peruvian warship *Huáscar*, captured during the War of the Pacific, are on display in the naval base.

Tallahas'see (Muskogean, 'town-old'), 30 27N 84 17W, pop(1980) 81,548, capital of state in Leon county, NW Florida, United States; 40 km N of Apalachee Bay; originally a settlement of Apalachee Indians; made the state capital in 1824; ordinance of secession from the Union was adopted here in 1861; 2 universities; railway; economy: the state government and the universities are the main employers in the city; lumber and wood products, and processed foods are manufactured.

Tallinn *ta'lin*, formerly REVEL or REVAL (-1917), 59 22N 24 48E, pop(1983) 454,000, seaport capital of Estonskaya (Estonia) SSR, NW European Soviet Union; on the S coast of the Gulf of Finland; the city has extensive military and naval installations and is a major transportation junction; railway; airfield; economy: manufacture of electric motors, refining and production of superphosphates; shale gas is supplied by pipeline from Kohtla-Järve; monuments: citadel (begun in the 13th century), former Governor's Palace (1767-73), Toomkirik (cathedral, 13-15th-c).

Tāloqān, TALIQ-AN, 36 48N 69 29E, pop(1984e) 21,841, capital of Takhār prov, NE Afghanistan; lies E of Kondūz and N of the Hindu Kush range; airfield.

Tamale *ta-ma'le*, 9 26N 0 49W, pop(1982) 226,715, capital of Northern region, Ghana, W Africa; 430 km N of Accra; an educational centre; airfield; economy: civil engineering.

Tamanras'set, department in E Algeria, N Africa; area 556,000 sq km; pop(1982) 63,592; chief town Tamanrasset.

Tamar *tay'mer*, river rising in N Cornwall, SW England; flows 96 km SE along the Devon-Cornwall border to meet the English Channel at Plymouth Sound.

Tam'arac, 26 11N 80 16W, pop(1980) 29,376, town in Broward county, SE Florida, United States; 15 km NW of Fort Lauderdale.

Tamarugal, Pampa del *pum'pu del tah-mah-roo-gal'*, desert plateau in N Chile. See Atacama, Desierto de.

Tamaulipas *tah-mow-lee'pas*, state in NE Mexico; bounded E by the Gulf of Mexico, N by Texas, USA along the Río Grande, W by Nuevo León and S by San Luis Potosí and Veracruz; the Sierra Madre Oriental lies in the W, dropping to a well-cultivated coastal plain; coastal lagoons include the Laguna Madre in the NE; drained by the San Fernando, Soto la Marina and Guatalejo rivers; pop(1980) 1,924,934; area 79,304 sq km; capital Ciudad Victoria; economy: wheat, cotton, sorghum, sugar cane, maize, fruit, livestock, timber, fishing, oil and natural gas, food processing, textiles, chemicals, sugar refining.

Tambacounda *tam-ba-koon'da*, region in S Senegal, W Africa; pop(1976) 286,148; area 59,602 sq km; called Sénégal-Oriental until 1984; capital Tambacounda.

Tambacounda, 13 45N 13 40W, pop(1976e) 20,000, capital of region of same name, S Senegal, W Africa; an important government, commercial and tourist centre 420 km ESE of Dakar; railway; airfield.

Tambov *tam-bof'*, 52 44N 41 28E, pop(1983) 286,000, capital city of Tambovskaya oblast, S central European Rossiyskaya, Soviet Union; on a tributary of the R Oka; founded in 1636 as a fort to defend Moskva (Moscow); railway; airfield; economy: synthetic resins and plastics, clothing.

Tâmega *ta'mi-ga, ta'may-ga* (Sp), river in NW Spain and N Portugal; rises in Orense prov E of L Antela, flows SW to the R Douro 30 km SE of Porto; length 160 km.

Tamil Nadu *tu'mil nahd'oo*, state in S India; pop(1981) 48,297,456; area 130,069 sq km; bounded N by Karnataka and Andhra Pradesh states, W by Kerala state and E and S by the Bay of Bengal, Indian Ocean; the state is divided into 18 administrative districts; capital Madras; the state is governed by a bicameral legislature comprising a 63-member Legislative Council and a 234-member Legislative Assembly; separated from Sri Lanka by the Palk Strait and the Gulf of Mannar, but linked to each other by Adam's Bridge shoal chain; Pondicherry and Karaikal, enclaves of the union territory of Pondicherry, are located on the Coromandel coast of Tamil Nadu; Cape Comorin forms the most S point; hill ranges W of the coastal plain include the Javadi, Melagiri, Sheveroy, Pachaimalai, Nilgiri and Palni hills; the state is drained by many rivers including the Rānipettai, Cheyyar, Ponnaiyar, Kaveri, Kollidam, Vaippar, Amaravati and the Bhavani; almost 90% of Tamil Nadu's population is Hindu, the remainder being mostly Christian or Muslim; 29% of the population is employed in agriculture, the principal crops being paddy rice, maize, jawar, bajra, pulses and millets, with sugar cane, cotton, oilseed, tobacco, coffee, tea, rubber and pepper being grown as cash crops; almost 50% of the land area of the state is forested, producing teak, sandalwood, softwood and cinchona bark; mineral reserves include coal, chromite, bauxite, limestone and manganese; major industries include cotton textiles, silks, tanning, textile and electrical machinery, and rubber tyres; Madras and Mandurai are the main centres of the rail network in Tamil Nadu; there is an airport at Madras and airfields at Madurai and Truchchirāppalli; Madras is the chief seaport of the state, other ports include Cuddalore and Nagappattinam; during the 10-13th centuries the Tamil Nadu region was under the control of the Chola Empire; the first British trading settlement was established at Peddapali (Nizampatnam) in 1611 and Fort St George was founded in 1639 at present-day Madras; the region was largely under British control by 1801; the boundaries of Mysore state were altered in 1956 and 1960, and in Aug 1968 the state was renamed Tamil Nadu.

Tammerfors, city in Finland. See Tampere.

Tammisaari *tam'is-ah'ree*, EKENAS *ay'ka-nes'* (Swed), 60 00N 23 30E, pop(1982) 11,179, summer resort town in Uudenmaa prov, S Finland; at the head of the Hanko Peninsula on an inlet of the Gulf of Finland, W of Helsinki; established in 1546; 80% Swedish-speaking; railway.

Tam'pa, 27 57N 82 27W, pop(1980) 271,523, county seat of Hillsborough county, W Florida, United States; a port on the NE coast of Tampa Bay; developed around a military post established in 1824 and later expanded as a cigar-making centre and then as a resort; university (1931); railway; airport; economy: tourism; processing and shipping centre for citrus fruit and phosphates; industries include brewing, printing and publishing, and the manufacture of electrical equipment, food products (mainly shrimp), fabricated metals, chemicals and cigars; monuments: David Falk and Tampa theatres, Museum of Science and Industry, Tampa Museum, Busch Gardens; event: Gasparilla Invasion (Feb).

Tampere *tam'per-e*, TAMMERFORS *tah'mar-fors* (Swed), 61 32N 23 45E, pop(1982) 167,211, city in Häme prov, SW Finland; on the Tammerkoski rapids by L Näsijärvi, about 160 km NNW of Helsinki; 2nd largest city in Finland; has many notable public buildings in contemporary styles; technological institute (1965); university (1966); established in 1779; developed as an industrial centre in 19th century; railway; boat trips to Virrat; airfield; economy: footwear, leather, textiles, metal, paper; events: Theatre Summer in Aug at the unique open-air theatre which has a revolving auditorium.

Tampico *tam-pee'kō*, 22 18N 97 52W, pop(1980) 267,957, seaport in Tamaulipas state, NE Mexico; on the Veracruz-Tamaulipas state border, on the Gulf of Mexico; railway; airport; economy: oil refining, petroleum products, boatbuilding, timber, fishing and fish processing.

Tam'worth, 31 07S 150 57E, pop(1981) 29,657, town in Northern stat div, NE New South Wales, Australia; on R Peel, at the centre of a rich agricultural area N of Sydney; railway; airfield.

Tamworth, 52 39N 1 40W, pop(1981) 64,546, town linked with Fazeley in Tamworth dist, Staffordshire, central England; on the R Tame, 21 km NE of Birmingham; in the 8th century King Offa maintained a royal palace and mint here; railway; economy: vehicles, engineering, asbestos, clothing, paper, bricks and tiles; monuments: 14th-c church of St Editha, castle museum.

Ta'na, longest river in Kenya; rises in S Central prov and flows NE, E then SE to meet the Indian Ocean at Formosa Bay, N of Malindi; length 700 km.

Tana, TENOJOKI (Finn), river in NE Norway forming a

section of the boundary between Finnmark county, Norway and Lapi county, Sweden; rises on the border near 68 45N; flows N and NE to Tana where it discharges into the Tanafjorden (Tana Fjord) of the Barents Sea; length 360 km.

T'ana Hāyk', LAKE TANA (Eng), lake in Gonder and Gojam regions, NW central Ethiopia, NE Africa; area 3,600 sq km; alt 1,829 m; situated S of Gonder and NNW of Debra Markos; source of the Ābay Wenz (Blue Nile), one of the R Nile's main tributaries, which flows from the SE corner of the lake; notable for its 40 monasteries which are located on islands in the lake; the monasteries contain important works of art and religious artifacts.

Tana, Lake, Ethiopia. See T'ana Hāyk'.

Tandil *tan-deel'*, 37 18S 59 10W, pop(1980) 78,821, health and pleasure resort in Buenos Aires prov, Litoral, E Argentina; at the N end of the Sierra del Tandil, a ridge of hills which runs W from the sea into the pampa for 250 km; founded in 1823; university; railway; economy: agricultural centre in a dairying region (Tandil cheese); monument: in the Parque de Independencia there is a statue of General Martín Rodríguez who took part in the wars against the Indians.

Tandjilé *tan-jeel-ay'*, prefecture in SW Chad, N central Africa; pop(1979) 302,000; area 18,045 sq km; the R Logone flows NW across the prefecture; capital Laï; chief towns Kélo and Beri.

Tando Adam *tun'dō ah'dum*, ADAM-JO-TANDO, 25 44N 68 41E, pop(1981) 63,000, city in Sind prov, SE Pakistan; 58 km SSE of Nawabshah; linked to Hyderabad and Sukkur by rail; local market centre.

Tanga *tang'gu*, 6 10S 35 40E, pop(1978) 103,409, seaport capital of Tanga region, NE Tanzania, E Africa; on the Indian Ocean opposite Pemba island, 193 km N of Dar es Salaam; formerly the starting point for caravans heading into the interior, it later became a point of entry for German settlers; occupied by the British in 1916; a hydroelectric power station is located on the nearby Pangani river; Tanzania's second largest port; lies at the centre of an important agricultural area; economy: tourism, sisal, cocoa, clothing, seafoods, fruit, coconut oil, tea.

Tangail *tun-gīl'*, region and district in central Bangladesh; pop(1981) 2,444,000; area 3,403 sq km; capital Tangail; separated from the Dhākā region by the Madhuper jungle in the S; separated from Mymenshingh region by the R Brahmaputra (Jamuna); capital Tangail.

Tangail, 24 15N 89 55E, pop(1981) 77,518, capital of Tangail dist and region, central Bangladesh; close to the R Brahmaputra (Jamuna), NW of Dhākā.

Tanganyika, Lake *tang'gun-yee'ku*, freshwater lake in E central Africa; situated for most of its length along the frontier between Tanzania and Zaire with smaller sections within the Zambian (S) and Burundian (NW) frontiers; extending for over 645 km NNW-SSE, it is the longest, deepest (over 1,400 m deep) and 2nd largest lake (after L Victoria) on the African continent; 2nd only to L Baikal (USSR) in depth; width ranges between 25 km and 80 km; alt 772 m; its only outlet is on the W shore via the R Lukaga which frequently silts up altering the level of the lake; the R Ruzizi (which drains L Kivu) and the R Malagarasi flow into the lake; the lake has steep shores which rise to over 2,700 m at the N end; the main ports are at Kigoma (Tanzania), Kalémié (Zaire) and Bujumbura (Burundi); the European discovery of the lake was made in 1858 by John Speke and Sir Richard Burton; the region was subsequently explored by Henry Stanley and David Livingstone in the 1870s; these two men met at Ujiji (S of Kigoma) in 1871; a small-scale naval warfare took place on the lake between British and German forces between 1915 and 1916.

Tanger *tã-zhay'*, TANGIER, TANGIERS *tan-jeer(z)'*, TINGIS (anc), 35 48N 5 45W, pop(1982) 266,346, seaport capital of Tanger prefecture, Nord-Ouest prov, N Morocco, N Africa; at the W end of the Strait of Gibraltar; strategically, an important position at the entrance to the Mediterranean; held in past centuries by the Vandals, Byzantines and Arabs; occupied by the Portuguese in 1471; came under Spanish rule between 1580 and 1660 and subsequently reverted to Portuguese control for 2 years; came under English control in 1662 when Charles II married Catherine of Braganza; Moorish occupation began in 1684; France, England and Spain signed a treaty in 1923 assuring the area's neutrality as an International Zone; became part of Morocco in 1959; free port status restored in 1962; a royal summer residence; railway; airport; monuments: kasbah fortress, with antiquities museum in the Dar Shorfa palace; the Caves of Hercules lie on the coast to the W, just S of Cap Spartel.

Tangshan *tang-shahn*, T'ANGSHAN, 39 37N 118 05E, pop(1984e) 1,366,100, town in E Hebei prov, N China; ESE of Beijing (Peking); railway.

Tanjungkarang *tahn-joong-kah-rahng'*, 5 27S 105 16E, pop(1980) 198,986, capital of Lampung prov, Indonesia, at the S tip of the island of Sumatera; N of Telukbetung; railway; airfield.

Tano *ta'nō*, river in Ghana, W Africa; rises in Ashanti region 65 km NW of Mampong; flows S for about 400 km past Tanaso (head of navigation) to enter the Gulf of Guinea at Aby lagoon; its lower course forms the border between Ghana and Ivory Coast.

Tânout *ta-noot'*, 14 55N 8 49E, town in Zinder dept, SE central Niger, W Africa; airfield; economy: stock raising, agriculture and trade.

Tanta *tan'ta*, 30 48N 31 00E, pop(1976) 284,636, capital of Gharbīya governorate, N Egypt; 84 km NNW of Cairo and 113 km ESE of Alexandria; university (1972); railway; economy: cotton, sugar; events: 3 annual festivals in honour of Ahmad al-Badwi, 13th-c Muslim saint who is buried in a Tanta mosque.

Tanzania *tan-zan-ee'a*, official name United Republic of Tanzania, an E African republic bounded S by Mozambique and Malawi, SW by Zambia, W by Zaire, NW by Burundi, Rwanda and Uganda, N by Kenya and E by the Indian Ocean; includes the islands of Zanzibar, Pemba and Matia; area 939,652 sq km; timezone GMT +3; capital Dodoma; chief towns Dar es Salaam, Zanzibar, Mwanza, Tanga and Arusha; pop(1984e) 21,202,000; 99% of the pop is of Bantu origin; on the mainland 35% are Christian; on Zanzibar the pop is almost exclusively Muslim; the official languages are English and Swahili although many local languages and dialects are spoken; the unit of currency is the Tanzanian shilling; national holidays 9 Dec (Independence Day), 26 April (Union Day); membership of AfDB, Commonwealth, FAO, G-77, GATT, IAEA, IBRD, ICAC, ICAO, ICO, IDA, IFAD, IFC, IMF, IMO, INTELSAT, INTERPOL, ITU, NAM, OAU, SADCC, UN, UNESCO, UPU, WHO, WMO, WTO.

Physical description. The largest E African country, Tanzania is situated just S of the Equator. It stretches for 1,190 km from N to S and 1,123 km from E to W. Its total area of 939,652 sq km includes c.53,000 sq km of inland water and 2,850 sq km of islands. The latter include Zanzibar which lies 40 km off the coast and Pemba which lies 40 km NE of this. SE of Dar es Salaam and E of Mohoro lies the island of Matia. The coast is fringed by long sandy beaches protected by coral reefs with mangrove swamps near the mouths of larger rivers such as the Pangani, Mandera, Rufiji and Mbemkuku. The Rovuma river, which forms the S frontier with Mozambique, flows E from just E of L Nyasa (L Malawi) to enter the Indian Ocean SE of Mtwara. Beyond the coast lies a narrow coastal plain about 15-65 km wide, rising towards a central plateau with an average elevation of 1,000 m. In the centre and S the land rises to high grasslands and to mountain ranges such as the Uruguru Mts which rise to 2,959 m at Rungwe in the S. The Rift Valley branches round L Victoria in the N where there are several high volcanic peaks including Mt Kilimanjaro (5,895 m). To the W of the mountain lies the extensive Serengeti plain. The E branch of the Rift Valley runs through central Tanzania from NE of L Victoria and contains lakes such as L Natron, L Manyara and L Eyasi before joining the W branch at L Nyasa. The Ngorongoro Crater is located on the rim of the valley in N Tanzania. The W branch runs S down the W side of L Victoria to form the W frontier of Tanzania with Zaire holding L Tanganyika, L Rukwa and other smaller lakes. Approx half of L Victoria lies within N Tanzania. This sector of the lake includes Ukerewe island and receives the Grumeti and Mbalageti rivers from the SE. Zanzibar is a coral island with ridges along the W side which rise to nearly 120 m. The island of Pemba has a peak elevation of around 95 m.

Climate. Tanzania has 3 distinct climatic zones: (1) The coast and offshore islands have a hot, humid tropical climate with average temperatures around 23°C during June-Sept and 27°C during Dec-March. Rainfall here averages over 1,000 mm per year and falls in 2 rainy seasons in March-May and Nov-Dec. (2) Further inland, the central plateau is hot and dry with an average annual rainfall of only 250 mm mostly falling between Dec and May. Dodoma at an alt of 1,120 m has average max daily temperatures ranging between 26°C and 31°C. Around L Victoria rainfall averages 1,000 mm and falls throughout the year. (3) At altitudes above 1,500 m the climate is semi-temperate, with cool nights, more evenly distributed rainfall, occasional frosts and permanent snow on high peaks.

History, government and constitution. The mainland coast and the islands of Zanzibar and Pemba had strong links with Arab, Indian and Persian traders before the arrival of the first Europeans. Between the 10th and 15th centuries the Swahili (Arab, 'coast') culture developed as a result of contact between these traders and the African Bantu. Zanzibar, with a monopoly on the clove trade, became the capital of the Omani empire under Seyyid Said during the 1840s. In the same decade German missionaries such as Krapf and Rebmann and British explorers such as Burton, Speke and Livingstone began to penetrate the interior. Much of this area came under German influence as treaties were signed with local chiefs and settlers moved in to plant cotton, sisal and rubber. In 1890 Zanzibar was declared a British protectorate and in the following year the German government took over the colonial administration of the protectorate of German East Africa. In 1919 Britain received a mandate to administer the former German territory (except Ruanda-Urundi) which was renamed Tanganyika. After 1953 an independence campaign was pursued by the Tanganyikan African National Union (TANU) under the leadership of Julius Nyerere. In 1957 a ministerial system of government was introduced and the following year TANU gained major successes in the country's first general election. Internal self-government was granted in 1961 and later the same year Tanganyika became independent as a constitutional monarchy with the Queen as head of state. It was the first E African country to gain independence and become a member of the Commonwealth. In 1962 Tanganyika became a republic with Julius Nyerere as president. Zanzibar, meanwhile, had taken a different path and had won independence as a constitutional monarchy with the Sultan as head of state. A coup in 1964 overthrew the Sultan and established a republican regime. In the same year Zanzibar signed an Act of Union which joined it with Tanganyika to form the United Republic of Tanzania. An interim constitution in 1965 was amended in 1977, establishing the principles of socialism and self-reliance. The constitution provides for a legislative National Assembly with 127 nominated and 111 elected members serving for a 5-year term. An executive president, also elected for 5 years, is assisted by a cabinet consisting of about 28 appointed members. Tanzania is a one-party state.

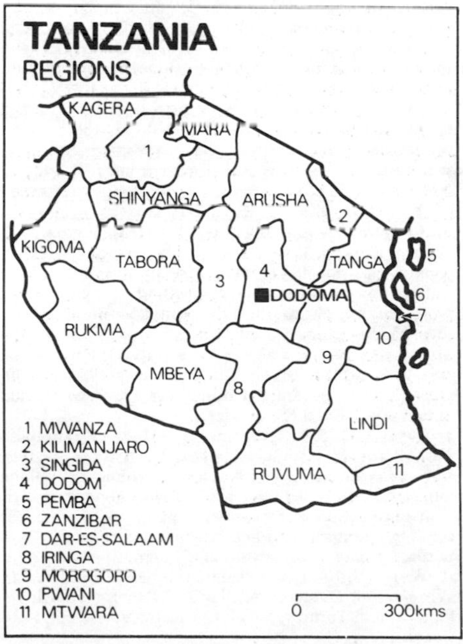

Economy. The economy of Tanzania is largely based on subsistence agriculture within village co-operatives and the cultivation of export crops such as rice, sorghum, coffee, sugar, cloves, coconuts, tobacco and cotton. The island region of Zanzibar still provides the majority of the world's clove market with c.400 sq km under cultivation. A major project, the National Agricultural Development Programme, was initiated in 1979 in order to improve agriculture and move towards self-sufficiency in food. Tanzania has reserves of iron, coal, tin, gypsum, salt, phosphate and gold, but diamonds are the only major mineral export. A small petroleum industry is centred around Dar es Salaam. Manufacturing industry is centred on food processing, cotton, cement and cigarette production. The tourism industry is based largely on the attraction of Mt Kilimanjaro, the sandy beaches, coral reefs and the country's wildlife which is preserved in 10 national parks and 5 game reserves. Main trading partners include the UK, the USA, Singapore, Hong Kong, Iran, West Germany, Italy, India, Japan and China.

Administrative divisions. Tanzania is divided into 20 mainland and 2 island regions (Pemba and Zanzibar) as follows:

Region	*pop(1985e)*
Arusha	1,183,000
Dar es Salaam	1,394,000
Dodoma	1,171,000
Iringa	1,100,000
Kagera	1,298,000
Kigoma	782,000
Kilimanjaro	1,093,000
Lindi	604,000
Mara	862,000
Mbeya	1,335,000
Morogoro	1,134,000
Mtwara	878,000
Mwanza	1,736,000
Pemba	256,950
Pwani	578,000
Rukwa	603,000
Ruvuma	691,000
Shinyanga	1,662,000
Singida	730,000
Tabora	1,089,000
Tanga	1,236,000
Zanzibar	571,000

Taoyuan *tow-yoo-ahn*, county of NW Taiwan; area 1,220.9 sq km; pop(1982e) 1,160,709.

Tapachula *ta-pa-choo'la*, 14 55N 92 16W, pop(1970) 108,056, town in Chiapas state, SE Mexico; near the SE frontier, on one of the main routes into Guatemala; railway; airport.

Tapajós *ta-pa-zhos'*, national park in W Pará state, Norte region, N Brazil; established in 1974; area 10,000 sq km; situated on the Río Tapajós.

Tapajós, river in W Pará state, Norte region, N Brazil; the river is formed at the border of Amazonas, Pará and Mato Grosso states with the junction of the Juruena and Teles Pires (or São Manuel) rivers; flows NNE to join the Amazon at Santarém; contains numerous rapids along its course; length c.800 km; length with the Arinos, its longest headstream, is 2,010 km.

Tarābulus or **Tarābulus al-Gharb** *ta-rahb'u-lus al-garb'*, TRIPOLI (Eng), OEA (anc), 32 54N 13 11E, pop(1982) 980,000, seaport capital of Libya, N Africa; on the Mediterranean coast, 345 km SSW of Malta and 645 km W of Banghāzī; established by the Phoenicians and subsequently developed by the Romans; one of the few reminders of the Roman presence is the arch of Marcus Aurelius (1st century BC); the old city is partly surrounded by Byzantine and medieval walls; an important Axis base during World War II; bombed (1941-42) and finally occupied by the British (1943); bombed by US Air Force in 1986 in response alleged to international terrorist activities; university (1973); railway; airport (35 km); economy: port trade in olive oil, fruit, fish and textiles.

Tarangire *ta-rang-gee'ri*, national park in Tanzania, E Africa; area 2,600 sq km; established in 1970; situated between Dodoma and Arusha; wildlife includes the rare black rhinoceros, biera oryx and lesser kudu.

Taranto *ta'ran-tō*, prov of Puglia region, SE Italy; pop(1981) 572,314; area 2,437 sq km; capital Taranto.

Taranto, 40 28N 17 15E, pop(1981) 244,101, capital town of Taranto prov, Puglia region, SE Italy; 78 km SSE of Bari, on the Golfo di Taranto; it ranks with La Spezia as one of Italy's 2 principal naval bases; archbishopric; airfield; railway; economy: fishing, the culture of oysters and shellfish, steelworks; monument: cathedral (originally built 1072-84, rebuilt in the 18th century).

Tarapacá *ta-ra-pa-ka'*, most northerly region of Chile; bordered by Peru (N) and by Bolivia and the Andes (W); comprises the provs of Arica, Parinacota and Iquique; contains Lauca and Volcán Isluga national parks; has many high Andean peaks in the W, including Volcán Parinacota, Volcán Guallatiri, Volcán Isluga and Cerro Sillajhuay; largely a desert, rich in minerals; pop(1984) 263,400; area 58,785 sq km; capital Iquique (a free port); chief town Arica; economy: fishing, agriculture, commerce, motor vehicles.

Tar'awa, 1 30N 173 00E, capital town of Kiribati, on Tarawa atoll in the Gilbert Is, central Pacific Ocean; pop(1985) 21,191, Bonriki airport.

Tarbes *tarb*, BIGORRA (anc), 43 15N 0 03E, pop(1982) 54,055, industrial and commercial city and capital of Hautes-Pyrénées dept, Midi-Pyrénées region, S France; on the left bank of the R Adour, 37 km ESE of Pau; a road and rail junction; an important settlement in Roman times; ancient capital of the prov of Bigorre; economy: firearms, furniture, footwear; monuments: 12-14th-c cathedral, archiepiscopal palace (now the prefecture); just S of the cathedral is the celebrated national stud-farm, Les Haras, founded in 1806; the Jardin Mussey has a 15th-c cloister rebuilt among the trees and a local museum whose tower affords panoramic views of the surrounding plain, the Adour valley and the Pyrénées.

Taree', 31 54S 152 26E, pop(1981) 14,697, town in Mid-North Coast stat div, NE New South Wales, Australia; on the E coast, 135 km NE of Newcastle; economy: dairy products; railway; airfield.

Targoviste, okrug (prov) in Bulgaria. See Tŭrgovishte.

Tarija *ta-ree'KHa*, department in SE Bolivia; bordered by the San Juan (W) and Pilaya (N) rivers, Argentina (S) and Paraguay (E); situated on the easternmost outliers of the Andean Cordillera Oriental; descends towards the Chaco plain; drained by the upper Pilcomayo, Bermejo and Tarija rivers; pop(1982) 246,691; area 37,623 sq km; capital Tarija; economy: maize, vegetables, wheat, potatoes, edible oil, wine, sugar, oil.

Tarija, 21 33S 64 45W, pop(1982) 54,001, town in Cercado prov, Tarija, SE Bolivia; founded in 1574; alt 1,958 m; situated in the rich valley of the Guadalquivir river; university (1946); airfield; economy: agricultural trade, sugar refining, edible oil, oil; event: the city is famous for its niño processions, which take place during the processions of San Roque, a 3-day festival beginning on the first Sunday in Sept.

Tarim He, river in NW China; the largest inland river in China; situated in the N Tarim Pendi basin, Xinjiang aut region, to the N of the Taklimakan Shamo desert; formed by the Yarkant He and Asku He rivers; fed by glaciers and melting snow from the Tien Shan mountains to the N; constant seepage and evaporation along the Tarim He's middle and lower course causes a decrease in flow, a build-up of mud and silt, the appearance of numerous branching streams and a constant change in river course; length 2,179 km.

Tarim Pendi, basin in S Xinjiang aut region, NW China; the largest inland basin in China; area 530,000 sq km; bounded by the Kunlun and Altun Shan ranges in the S and the Tien Shan range in the N; length 1,500 km; width 400-500 km; ringed by mountains, the land becomes dry towards the centre, passing from stony foothills to desert and salt lakes; the Taklimakan Shamo desert at the centre of the Tarim Pendi basin covers an area of 327,000 sq km and is the largest desert in China; to the N of the desert is the Tarim He river; the area is rich in salt and non-ferrous metals.

Tarīn Kowt, TERINKOT, 32 38N 65 52E, pop(1984e) 3,686, capital of Orūzgān prov, central Afghanistan; connected by road to Kandahār in the S and to Kābul in the NE.

Tarkwa *tar-kwa'*, 5 16N 1 59W, town in Western region, SW Ghana, W Africa; NW of Sekondi-Takoradi; railway.

Tarn, dept in Midi-Pyrénées region of S France, where the S edge of the Central Plateau slopes down to the plains of Toulouse; comprises 2 arrond, 42 cantons and 324 communes; pop(1982) 339,345; area 5,751 sq km; watered by the Tarn R and its tributary, the Agout; fertile in the W; capital Albi; chief towns Castres and Carmaux; the Parc du Haut-Languedoc regional nature park lies partly within the dept.

Tarn, river in S France rising on the S slopes of Monts de Lozère in the Cévennes; flowing W it cuts the limestone plateaux of Lozère and Aveyron into picturesque *causses*, separated by deep gorges, before turning SW and then NW past Albi and Montauban; it eventually meets the R Garonne E of Moissac; length 375 km.

Tarn-et-Garonne, dept in Midi-Pyrénées region of S France, comprising 2 arrond, 28 cantons and 195 communes; pop(1982) 190,485; area 3,716 sq km; watered by the Tarn, Garonne and Aveyron rivers; crossed by the Canal du Midi; capital Montauban, chief towns Moissac and Castelsarrasin.

Tarnobrzeg *tarn-o-bzheg'*, voivodship in SE Poland; watered by R Wisła (Vistula) and R San; pop(1983) 572,000; area 6,283 sq km; capital Tarnobrzeg; chief towns include Stalowa Wola and Sandomierz.

Tarnobrzeg, 50 35N 21 40E, pop(1983) 40,800, capital of Tarnobrzeg voivodship, SE Poland; on R Wisła (Vistula); since 1953 the town has developed around the sulphur industry; 7 km E there is a large sulphur mine at Jeziórko with purification and processing plants producing pure sulphur, sulphuric acid and phosphate fertilizer.

Tarnów *tar-noof'*, voivodship in S Poland; bounded N by R Wisła (Vistula) and watered by its tributaries the Wisłoka and Dunajec; pop(1983) 628,000; area 4,151 sq km; capital Tarnów; chief towns include Dębica and Bochnia.

Tarnów, 50 01N 20 59E, pop(1983) 111,000, capital of Tarnów voivodship, S Poland; E of Kraków; a former centre of culture and learning during the Renaissance; branch of Jagiellonian university; railway; economy: chemicals, electric motors; monuments: 15th-c Gothic cathedral, mausoleum to general Jósef Bem.

Tarnowskie Góry *tar-noof'skye goo'ri*, 50 28N 18 40E, pop(1983) 71,100, mining and industrial town in Katowice voivodship, S Poland; N of Katowice in upper Silesian industrial region; known in 13th century as a centre of lead and silver mining; important railway junction; economy: mining machinery; events: annual miners' week in Sept.

Ta'ro, river in N Italy, rising in the Appno Ligure, 16 km NE of Chiavari; flows 125 km NNE to the Po, 13 km W of Casalmaggiore; receives Ceno and Stirone rivers.

Taroudant *tar-oo-dã'*, 30 31N 8 55W, pop(1982) 35,848, fortified town in Taroudant prefecture, Sud prov, W Morocco, N Africa; on the Oued Sous river, E of Agadir; amidst olive groves, citrus orchards and green fields at the centre of the Sous plain; economy: leather, copperware, carved stone, wrought iron.

Tarragona *ta-ra-go'na*, prov in Cataluña, NE Spain, on the Mediterranean, with inland mountains and a coastal plain drained by the R Ebro; pop(1981) 516,078; area 6,283 sq km; capital Tarragona; economy: chemicals, electrical equipment, coffee, footwear, nuclear power stations at Asco and Vandellos; oilfields offshore.

Tarragona, TARRACO (Lat), 41 05N 1 17E, pop(1981) 111,689, port and capital of Tarragona prov, Cataluña, NE Spain; 534 km ENE of Madrid; archbishopric; airport at Reus; railway; beaches; economy: seaport and agricultural market town producing chemicals and vegetable oils; monuments: Roman aqueduct, amphitheatre, Romanesque-Gothic cathedral, Archaeological Museum with interesting mosaics; Cyclopean walls; events: fiesta of St Magin in Aug and fiesta of Santa Tecia in Sept.

Tarrasa *ta-ra'sa*, 41 34N 2 01E, pop(1981) 155,360, industrial town in Barcelona prov, Cataluña, NE Spain; on the right bank of the R Palau, in the fertile Valles district, 32 km N of Barcelona; economy: noted for silk production, textiles, glass, electrical appliances; monuments: the churches of St Peter, St Miguel and St Mary.

Tarsus *tar'sus*, 36 52N 34 52E, pop(1980) 121,074, town in Içel prov, S Turkey, on the W bank of the R Pamuk; agricultural trade centre; ancient Tarsus was one of the most important cities of Asia Minor; the Apostle Paul was born here; railway.

Tarṭūs, *tar-toos'*, governorate (*mohofazat*) in W Syria; pop(1981) 443,290; capital and major port at Tarṭūs; traces of old Crusader strongholds here.

Tarutao *tahr-e-tow'*, marine national park in Thailand; a group of 51 islands 30 km off the W coast, near the Thailand-Malaysia frontier, N of the Langkawi Is; area 1,400 sq km.

Tarxien *tahr-sheen'*, 35 52N 14 31E, pop(1983e) 7,566, community on the main island of Malta, S of Valletta and the Grand Harbour; monuments: the 3 Tarxien megalithic monuments discovered in 1915.

Tashkent *tush-kyent'*, 41 16N 69 13E, pop(1983) 1,944,000, capital city of Tashkentskaya oblast and Uzbekskaya SSR, Soviet Union; in the foothills of the Tien Shan Mts, in the R Chirchik valley; virtually rebuilt after earthquake damage in 1966; venue for many international symposia and conferences; alt 440-480 m; university (1920); railway; airport; economy: solar research and development, chemicals, heavy engineering, clothing, footwear, cotton textile; American cotton was planted here experimentally in 1878 and it has become one of Uzbekistan's principal agricultural crops; monuments: madrasah Kukeldash (c. 17th-c) and madrasah Barakkhana (c. 15-16th-c).

Tasman Sea *taz'man*, part of the Pacific Ocean separating the E coast of Australia and the island of Tasmania from New Zealand; linked to the Indian Ocean by the Bass Strait; connected to the Coral Sea in the N; shallow, narrow continental shelf off Australia, sinking to depths of 4,570 m in the Tasman abyssal plain; seamounts are scattered across the floor to the S of the Lord Howe Rise of the Coral Sea; named for the Dutch explorer Abel Tasman.

Tasmania *taz-may'nee-a*, formerly VAN DIEMEN'S LAND, island state of Australia, comprising a group of islands separated from mainland Australia by the Bass Strait; the group includes the main island of Tasmania, and smaller islands including King I (1,099 sq km), Flinders I (1,374 sq km) and Bruny I (362 sq km); the smallest of Australia's 6 states; the interior of Tasmania is mountainous with a Central Plateau rising to 1,617 m at Mt Ossa, which is situated in the 1,319 sq km Cradle Mountain-Lake St Clair National Park; Tasmania has a temperate maritime climate that is influenced by the westerly 'Roaring Forties' winds; the most fertile regions lie along the NW and E coasts and along the river valleys of the midlands and SE plateau; pop(1986) 449,135; area 67,800 sq km; capital Hobart; chief towns include Devonport, Launceston, Burnie-Somerset, Queenstown and New Norfolk; economy: sheep, cattle, pigs, cereals, wood, paper, chemicals, machinery, textiles, mining of tin, copper, zinc, lead, silver, gold and coal; abundant hydroelectric power from 25 stations has contributed to industrial development; the first Aborigines to settle here crossed the land bridge now formed by the Bass Strait 25,000 years ago; the islands contain numerous unique plants and animals, notably the Tasmanian Tiger (now feared to be extinct) and the Tasmanian Devil, both carnivorous marsupials; discovered by Abel Tasman in 1642, Europeans first settled here in 1803 when Tasmania became a British dependency of New South Wales; Port Arthur on the E coast became the largest penal colony in Australia, while Hobart was a major whaling station; after transportation stopped in 1852 large numbers of immigrants arrived; during the 2nd half of the 19th century the Tasman Aboriginal race were in conflict with the newly arrived settlers; the link with New South Wales was severed in 1825 and a Legislative Council was established in 1851; in 1869 Tasmania became the first colony of the British Empire to make education compulsory; in 1901 Tasmania joined the Commonwealth of Australia; the bicameral Tasmanian State Parliament comprises a 19-member Legislative Council and a 35-member House of Assembly; state holidays: Labour Day (March), Bank Holiday in April, 4 Nov (Recreation Day in N Tasmania only); the state of Tasmania is divided into the 4 statistical divisions of Hobart (940 sq km), Mersey-Lyell (22,700 sq km), Northern (20,610 sq km) and Southern (24,090 sq km).

Tassili N'Ajjer, national park in E Algeria, N Africa; NE of the Ahaggar (Hoggar) Mts; area 1,000 sq km; established in 1972.

Tata *to'to*, 47 37N 18 19E, pop(1984e) 25,000, town in Komárom county, N Hungary; E of Györ; economy: textiles, porcelain, foodstuffs; monument: remains of 15th-c Gothic castle.

Tatabánya *to'to-ban-yo*, 47 32N 18 25E, pop(1984e) 77,000, capital of Komárom county, N Hungary; 48 km W of Budapest; school of mining; economy: aluminium, lignite, chemicals.

Tatra, mountains in Czechoslovakia. See Tatry.

Tatry *tah'tree*, TATRA (Eng), mountain group in the central Carpathian Mts comprising the Vysoké Tatry (High Tatra) and Nízké Tatry (Low Tatra); the highest group of the Carpathians and of Czechoslovakia rising to 2,655 m at Gerlachovsky; the High Tatra National Park covering 500 sq km was established in 1948.

Ta-t'ung, town in Shanxi prov, N central China. See Datong.

Taubaté *tow-ba-tay'*, 23 00S 45 36W, pop(1980) 155,376, town in São Paulo state, Sudeste region, SE Brazil; NE of São Paulo; university; railway; economy: motor vehicles, smelting, textiles.

Taumo'tu Archipelago, island group of French Polynesia, E of the Archipel de la Société (Society Is), S Pacific Ocean; pop(1977) 8,537, consists of 2 parallel ranges of 78 atolls lying between 135° and 143° W and between 14° and 23° S; it forms the largest group of coral atolls in the world; area 826 sq km; chief islands include Rangiroa, Hao, and Fakarava; the atolls have been used for nuclear testing by the French since 1962.

Taunggyi *town-jee'*, 20 49N 97 01E, capital of Shan state, E Burma; 160 km SE of Mandalay; at an alt of 1,433 m it is a popular summer resort; at Khaungdine village by L Inle there is a vacation camp for outstanding students and workers; railway; monument: Taunggyi museum with a collection of local Shan costumes; event: Oct festival at Phaung-Daw-Oo pagoda on L Inle.

Taunton, 51 01N 3 06W, pop(1981) 48,863, county town in Taunton Deane dist, Somerset, SW England; on the R Tone, in the Vale of Taunton Deane; founded in 705 by Ine, king of the West Saxons; in 1497 the rebellion of Perkin Warbeck ended here; in 1685 the Duke of Monmouth was crowned king here; railway; economy: cider, textiles, leather, optical instruments, light engineering; monument: Somerset county museum.

Taunton, 41 54N 71 06W, pop(1980) 45,001, county seat of Bristol county, SE Massachusetts, United States; on the R Taunton, 52 km S of Boston; railway.

Taunus *tow'noos*, mountain range in SW Hessen (Hesse) prov, W Germany, between the rivers Rhine, Main, Lahn and the Wetter; extends 80 km ENE from the Rhine; highest point is the Großer Feldberg (880 m); geologically considered part of the Rheinisches Schiefergebirge (Rhenish Slate Mts); S slopes produce excellent fruit, almonds and, at Kronberg, sweet chestnuts; rich in mineral springs with famous spas at Wiesbaden, Bad Nauheim and Bad Soden.

Taupo *tow'pō*, 38 42S 176 06E, pop(1981) 13,936, borough on North Island, New Zealand; on the NE shore of L Taupo; a resort region with thermal springs; nearby are the Wairakei geothermal borefield, the Huka Falls and the Aratiatia Rapids; airfield.

Taupo, Lake, lake in central North Island, New Zealand; length 40.2 km; breadth 27.4 km; area 606 sq km; largest New Zealand lake; used as a reservoir, L Taupo fills an old volcanic crater; the lake is also used for fishing and water sports; at the NE end of the lake is the town of Taupo; an area of extensive thermal activity and location of a geothermal power scheme; at the S end of L Taupo is the settlement of Waihi; there are thermal pools at Tokaanu.

Tauranga *tow-rang'ga*, 37 42S 176 11E, pop(1981) 37,099, town on the E coast of North Island, New Zealand; on the Bay of Plenty, in a subtropical citrus fruit-growing region with mineral pools nearby; its Mission House is one of New Zealand's oldest buildings; Katikati is a garden of exotic birds; charter launches run from here to the big-game fishing waters around Mayor Island; across the harbour from Tauranga is the deep-water port of Mount Maunganui; nearby is an international motor-racing circuit; railway; airfield; economy: kiwi fruit, dairy produce, meat, timber.

Taurus, mountain range in Turkey. See Toros Dağları.

Tavastehus, prov in Finland. See Häme.

Tavira *ta-vee'ra*, 37 07N 7 39W, pop(1981) 11,614, resort and fishing town in Faro dist on S coast of Portugal, at the mouth of the Ribeira da Asseca; divided into 2 parishes; railway; numerous canals; economy: tunny fishing; caramel and salt; event: municipal holiday third week in June; monuments: Moorish castle; Roman bridge; Renaissance-style Church of the Misericordia (1541).

Tavoy *ta-voy'*, 14 02N 98 12E, pop(1983) 101,536, capital of Tenasserim division, SE Burma; situated at the mouth of the R Tavoy; airfield.

Taw, river rising in Dartmoor, Devon, SW England; flows 80 km N and NW to meet Barnstaple Bay near Appledore.

Tawau *tah-wow'*, 4 16N 117 54E, pop(1980) 45,249, town in SE Sabah state, E Malaysia, SE Asia; airfield.

Tawi-Tawi *tah-wee-tah-wee*, island group and province of SW Philippines; in Sulu archipelago, NE of Borneo; comprises the islands of Sanga Sanga, Tawi-Tawi, Simunul and about 100 small islands; area 932 sq km; pop(1980) 194,651.

Tay, longest river in Scotland (length 192 km); in Central and Tayside regions, E Scotland; its headstream, the Fillan, rises on Ben Lui in NW Central region; it flows through Loch Dochart, where it becomes the R Dochart, then NE to the town of Killin and Loch Tay; the Tay itself flows out of the NE end of the loch and flows 87 km E, past Aberfeldy, then SE past Dunkeld and Perth to the confluence with the R Earn; from here it becomes the Firth of Tay, extending 40 km ENE and E past Dundee, to the North Sea at Buddon Ness; crossed at Dundee by the Tay Bridge; major tributaries: Tummel, Isla and Earn rivers; noted for its salmon fishing.

Taygetus, mountain range in Greece. See Taïyetos Óros.

Taylor, 42 14N 83 16W, pop(1980) 77,568, town in Wayne county, SE Michigan, United States; 22 km WSW of Detroit.

Taymyr, Ozero *tī-mir'*, lake in Krasnoyarskiy kray, N Siberian Rossiyskaya, Soviet Union, on the N Poluostrov Taymyr (Taymyr Peninsula); area 4,560 sq km; length 250 km; average depth 2.8 m; max depth 26 m; the R Verkhnyaya Taymyra flows into the lake in the SW and the Nizhnyaya Taymyra flows out in the N to discharge into the Karskoye More (Kara Sea); the lake is frozen over from late September to June; there are coal deposits nearby.

Taymyr, Poluostrov, tundra-covered peninsula in Krasnoyarskiy kray, N Siberian Rossiyskaya, Soviet Union, between the mouths of the Yenisey (W) and Khatanga (E) rivers; bounded W by the Karskoye More (Kara Sea) and E by the Laptev Sea; the islands of the Severnaya Zemlya (North Land) are to the N; length (NE-SW) 1,120 km; the N extremity is Cape Chelyuskin; contains the Gory Byrranga (Byrranga Mts) and Ozero Taymyr (Lake Taymyr).

Tayside, region in E Scotland; bounded N by Grampian and Highland regions, NW by Strathclyde, W and S by Central region, SE by Fife and E by the Firth of Tay and the North Sea; the Grampian Mts lie in the NW of the region; the 'Highland Line' which separates the Highlands from the Lowlands runs NE through Tayside, through Crieff, Dunkeld, Blairgowrie, Kirriemuir and Edzell; drained by the Tay, Isla, Ericht, Earn and South Esk rivers; the region's largest lochs are Lochs Rannoch, Tummel and Tay; pop(1981) 391,846; area 7,493 sq km; capital Dundee; major towns include Forfar, Arbroath, Montrose and Perth; Tayside is divided into 3 districts:

District	*area (sq km)*	*pop(1981)*
Angus	2,023	93,038
Dundee City	235	179,674
Perth and Kinross	5,235	119,134

Taza *tah'ze*, 34 16N 4 00W, pop(1982) 77,216, capital of Taza prefecture, Centre-Nord prov, N Morocco, N Africa; 88 km E of Fès in the 'Taza gap' which separates the Er Rif mts (N) from the Moyen Atlas (S); railway; economy: carpets, footwear.

Tbilisi *ut-bil-yee'see*, TIFLIS (-1936), 41 43N 44 48E, pop(1983) 1,125,000, capital city of Gruzinskaya (Georgia) SSR, SE European Soviet Union; on the R Kura, between the Bol'shoy Kavkaz (Greater Caucasus) range (N) and the Malyy Kavkaz (Lesser Caucasus) range (S); from ancient times the site of Tbilisi has been a trading point between Europe and India; the first funicular railway, 501 m in length, was built on Mt David (on the W side of the city) in 1905; alt 400-522 m; university (1918); railway junction; airport; economy: machine building, film-making, printing and publishing, foodstuffs, silk weaving, manufacture of electrical equipment, locomotives, and plastics; monuments: ruins of the citadel of Narikala (4-17th-c); 6th-c stone Anchiskhati church; 6-7th-c Sioni cathedral.

Tchibanga *chee-bang-ga'*, 2 49S 11 00E, capital of Nyanga prov, SW Gabon, W Africa; on the R Nyanga, 340 km SSE of Libreville.

Tczew *tchef*, DIRSCHAU *dir'show* (Ger), 54 05N 18 46E, pop(1983) 56,700, port town in Gdańsk voivodship, N Poland; on R Wisła (Vistula), SE of Gdańsk; considered a seaport since 1928; railway junction; economy: timber and grain trade, shipyards.

Te Anau *tee a-now'*, lake in SW South Island, New Zealand; 2nd largest lake in New Zealand; on the E edge of Fiordland National Park; length 61.2 km; breadth 9.7 km; area 344 sq km; largest lake on South Island; on the W side of the lake are the Te Anau glow-worm caves; the lake is used for water sports.

Tébes'sa, department of N Algeria, N Africa; area 16,574 sq km; pop(1982) 423,202; chief town Tébessa.

Tecuci *te-kooch'*, 45 50N 27 27E, pop(1983) 42,449, town in Galaţi county, E Romania; on R Birlad, 64 km NW of Galaţi; established in 15th century; railway junction; airfield; economy: agricultural trade, leather, distilling.

Tees *teez*, river of NE England; rises on Cross Fell, Cumbria and flows 128 km SE through Durham, along the North Yorkshire border and into Cleveland where it develops into a broad estuary that meets the North Sea below Middlesbrough; the river passes through the heavily industrialized Teesside area; the Tees is linked to the R Tyne as part of the UK's first regional water grid system supplying water to the industrial NE of England.

Teesside, pop(1981) 382,690, urban area surrounding the R Tees estuary in Cleveland, NE England; includes Stockton-on-Tees, Redcar, Thornaby, Middlesbrough; formed in 1967 and part of Cleveland since 1974; railway; airport (Middleton St George).

Tegucigalpa *tay-goo-si-gal'pa*, ('silver hill'), 14 05N 87 14W, pop(1983e) 532,519, capital city of Honduras, in Francisco Morazán dept, S Honduras, Central America; founded as a mining camp in 1524, it comprises 2 distinct towns, the almost flat Comayagüela and the hilly Tegucigalpa, separated by the Rio Choluteca; alt 975 m; capital of Honduras since 1880; university (1847); airport (Toncontín); monuments: 18th-c cathedral, 18th-c church of Virgen de los Dolores.

Tehrān *te-ran'*, mountainous prov in N Iran; pop(1982) 7,709,000; area 19,125 sq km; capital Tehrān.

Tehrān, TEHERAN *tay-e-ran'*, 35 44N 51 30E, pop(1983) 5,734,199, capital city of Iran, in Tehrān prov, N Iran; situated in the S foothills of the Elburz Mts, SW of Mt Damāvand; largest city in Iran; administrative, commercial, and industrial centre; superseded Eşfahān as capital of Persia in 1788; largely rebuilt by Reza Shah after 1925; alt 1,200-1,700 m; university (1935); airport; road and rail junction; economy: carpet manufacture, textiles, tanning, chemicals, glass, monuments: Pahlevi palace; Shahyad Tower, symbol of modern Iran.

Teide, Pico de *tay'day*, TEYDE, PEAK OF TENERIFE (Eng), 28 17N 16 39W, dormant volcanic peak on the island of Tenerife in the Canary Is, Santa Cruz de Tenerife prov, Canarias region, Spain; rises to 3,718 m from the Canadas plateau; the highest peak in Spain; the subsidiary crater of Pico Viejo or Montana de Chaorra last erupted in the late 18th-c; now part of the 117 sq km Teide National Park which was established in 1954.

Teifi *tī'vee*, river in Dyfed, W Wales; rises in the Cambrian Mts of central Wales and flows 80 km SW and W to meet Cardigan Bay at Cardigan.

Teignmouth *tin'muth*, 50 33N 3 30W, pop(1981) 12,345, resort town in Teignbridge dist, Devonshire, SW England; at the mouth of the R Teign, N of Torquay; railway.

Tejo, river in Spain and Portugal. See Tagus.

Tekirdağ *te-kir'da*, prov in NW Turkey, bounded SE by the Sea of Marmara; pop(1980) 360,742; area 6,218 sq km; capital Tekirdağ; economy: linseed, flax, grain.

Tel Aviv *tel' a-veev'*, district in W Israel, bounded W by the Mediterranean Sea; pop(1983) 1,008,800; area 170 sq km; capital Tel Aviv-Yafo.

Tel Aviv-Yafo *ya'fa*, TEL AVIV/JAFFA, 32 05N 34 46E, pop(1982) 325,700, twin cities in Tel Aviv dist, W Israel, a commercial port on the Mediterranean Sea; Israel's largest conurbation; Tel Aviv was founded in 1909 as a garden suburb of Yafo; Yafo is the most ancient port in Israel and today is an artists' centre; former capital (pre-1950) of Israel; university (1953); railway; airport; economy: food processing, textiles, chemicals; monument: Franciscan monastery of St Peter (1654).

Tel'a, 15 46N 87 25W, pop(1983e) 27,343, town in Atlántida dept, N Honduras, Central America; on the Caribbean coast, 50 km E of Puerto Cortés; railway; economy: banana trade.

Telde *tel'day*, 28 01N 15 25N, pop(1981) 63,442, resort town in Las Palmas prov, Canarias autonomous region, Spain; in the Canary Is, on the E coast of Gran Canaria I, S of Las Palmas in a fertile fruit-growing district; economy: fruit, tourism, tobacco, chemicals, metal products and fertilizer; monuments: Basilica of Santo Cristo and the church of St John the Baptist; nearby are caves occupied by the original inabitants of the island.

Telemark *tel'u-mark*, formerly BRATSBERG, county in S Norway, bounded on the SE by the Skagerrak; area 15,315 sq km; pop(1983) 161,939; capital Skien; chief towns Porsgrunn and Notodden; drained chiefly by the Måna and Mår rivers which together flow through the lakes of Tinnsjø and Norsjø; rises to 1,883 m at Mt Gausta in the N; the Rjukanfos waterfall (104 m), formerly largest in the country, has been depleted by the hydroelectric plants for the chemical industries of Rjukan and Notodden.

Teleorman *tyel-yor-man'*, county in S Romania, bounded to the S by the R Danube which follows the Bulgarian frontier; pop(1983) 506,647; area 5,760 sq km; capital Alexandria.

Tel'ford Daw'ley, 52 42N 2 28W, pop(1981) 28,662, town in Shrewsbury and Atcham dist, Shropshire, W central England; an established settlement included as part of the 'new town' of Telford, designated in 1963.

Telford North, pop(1981) 53,165, urban area in Shropshire, W central England; on the R Severn SE of Shrewsbury, 55 km NW of Birmingham; developed as a 'new town' after 1963 with Telford South, Oakengates, Wellington and Telford Dawley; originally designated as Dawley New Town; railway; economy: electronics, plastics, vehicles, metal products.

Telford South, pop(1981) 23,354, urban area in Shropshire, W central England; part of the Telford 'new town', designated in 1963.

Tema *te'ma*, 5 41N 0 00W, pop(1982) 323,909, seaport in Greater Accra region, S Ghana, W Africa; E of Accra; railway; economy: civil engineering and metal smelting.

Temburong, BANGAR, dist of Brunei, SE Asia; bounded N by Brunei Bay and the South China Sea and on all other sides by the E Malaysian state of Sarawak; pop(1981) 6,230; chief towns Bangar and Labu.

Teme *teem*, river rising S of Newtown in Powys, E Wales; flows 96 km E through Hereford and Worcester to meet the R Severn S of Worcester.

Temirtau *tay'mir-tow*, SAMARKANDSKII (-1945), 50 05N 72 56E, pop(1983) 223,000, industrial town in Karagandinskaya oblast, Kazakhskaya SSR, Soviet Union; at the W end of the Nura reservoir, 32 km NW of Karaganda; railway; economy: iron and steel works, heat and power plant, synthetic rubber, machines.

Tempe *tem-pee'*, 33 25N 111 56W, pop(1980) 106,743, health resort in Maricopa county, S central Arizona, United States; 15 km E of Phoenix; university (1885); railway; event: Fiesta Bowl (Jan).

Temple, 31 06N 97 21W, pop(1980) 42,483, town in Bell county, central Texas, United States; 52 km SSW of Waco; railway; economy: grain trade, textiles, railway engineering.

Temple City, 34 07N 118 01W, pop(1980) 28,972, city in

Los Angeles county, SW California, United States; 18 km ENE of Los Angeles.

Temuco *tay-moo'kō*, 38 44S 72 35W, pop(1982) 162,058, capital of Cautín prov, and La Araucanía region, Chile; founded in 1881; the market town of the Mapuche Indians; railway; monument: on the Cerro Ñielol is La Patagua, the tree under which the final peace with the Mapuches was signed in 1881; this hill gives a good view of the town and contains a large array of native plants, including Chile's national flower, the Copihue Rojo.

Tena *tay'na*, 1 00S 77 48W, pop(1982) 5,457, capital of Napo prov, NE Ecuador; to S of Sumaco volcano, in the E foothills of the Andes; to the W are the famous Cuevas de Jumandi and Anaconda Island, on the Rio Napo; a large lowland Quechua Indian population lives nearby.

Tenasserim *tun-a'su-rim*, division in SE Burma; bordered E by Thailand along the Bilauktaung Range; to the W lies the Andaman Sea and numerous small islands, including the Mergui Archipelago; mountainous in the E with low coastal land in the W; pop(1983) 917,628; capital Tavoy.

Tenkodogo *ten-kō-dō'gō*, 11 54N 0 19W, chief town in E central Burkina, W Africa; 137 km from Ouagadougou on the route to Lomé (Ghana).

Tennant Creek, 19 31S 134 15E, pop(1981) 3,118, town in Northern Territory, Australia; on the Stuart Highway between Darwin and Alice Springs; airfield; an important mining centre since the 1930s; 114 km S are the Devil's Marbles, an outcrop of weathered round granite boulders situated in a scenic reserve; event: Goldrush festival in May.

Tennessee', state in SE central United States; bounded W by Arkansas and Missouri, N by Kentucky and Virginia, E by North Carolina, and S by Georgia, Alabama and Mississippi; the Mississippi river follows the W border of the state; the R Tennessee is formed by the confluence of the Holston and French Broad rivers and flows SW into Alabama; the highest point is Clingmans Dome (2,025 m); in the E lie the Great Smoky Mts, Cumberland Plateau, narrow river valleys and heavily forested foothills, which severely restrict farming; the centre of the state, which is hemmed in by the great loop of the R Tennessee, is fertile 'bluegrass' country, ideal for livestock and dairy farming; in the W, between the Tennessee and Mississippi, is a rich floodplain where most of the state's cotton is grown; the state has many lakes created by the Tennessee Valley Authority's damming of the Tennessee and Cumberland rivers; the chief agricultural crops are tobacco, soybeans, hay and cotton; cattle and dairy products are also important; the main manufactures are chemicals, processed foods, textiles and apparel, and electrical equipment; the state is the nation's largest producer of both zinc and pyrites; coal and cement are also important industries; the region was ceded by France in 1763 and explored by Daniel Boone in 1769; after the War of Independence the temporary state of Franklin was formed (1784) and in 1790 the Federal government created the Territory South of the Ohio; admitted as a state (16th) to the Union in 1796; Tennessee seceded from the Union in 1861 and was the scene of many battles during the Civil War, including Shiloh, Chattanooga and Stone River; slavery was abolished in 1865 and the state was re-admitted to the Union in 1866; in the same year the Ku Klux Klan was founded in Tennessee, at Pulaski; known as the 'Volunteer State'; pop(1980) 4,591,120; area 107,003 sq km; capital Nashville; other major cities include Memphis, Knoxville and Chattanooga; the state is divided into 95 counties:

County	*area (sq km)*	*pop(1980)*
Anderson	881	67,346
Bedford	1,235	27,916
Benton	1,019	14,901
Bledsoe	1,058	9,478
Blount	1,451	77,770
Bradley	850	67,547
Campbell	1,245	34,923

contd

County	*area (sq km)*	*pop(1980)*
Cannon	692	10,234
Carroll	1,560	28,285
Carter	887	50,205
Cheatham	790	21,616
Chester	751	12,727
Claiborne	1,123	24,595
Clay	590	7,676
Cocke	1,123	28,792
Coffee	1,113	38,311
Crockett	692	14,941
Cumberland	1,773	28,676
Davidson	1,303	477,811
De Kalb	757	13,589
Decatur	858	10,857
Dickson	1,277	30,037
Dyer	1,352	34,663
Fayette	1,833	25,305
Fentress	1,295	14,826
Franklin	1,412	31,983
Gibson	1,565	49,467
Giles	1,586	24,625
Grainger	710	16,751
Greene	1,609	54,422
Grundy	939	13,787
Hamblen	406	49,300
Hamilton	1,401	287,740
Hancock	580	6,887
Hardeman	1,742	23,873
Hardin	1,503	22,280
Hawkins	1,264	43,751
Haywood	1,388	20,318
Henderson	1,352	21,390
Henry	1,456	28,656
Hickman	1,586	15,151
Houston	520	6,871
Humphreys	1,373	15,957
Jackson	801	9,398
Jefferson	689	31,284
Johnson	772	13,745
Knox	1,316	319,694
Lake	439	7,455
Lauderdale	1,232	24,555
Lawrence	1,604	34,110
Lewis	733	9,700
Lincoln	1,485	26,483
Loudon	611	28,553
Macon	798	15,700
Madison	1,451	74,546
Marion	1,331	24,416
Marshall	978	19,698
Maury	1,602	51,095
McMinn	1,115	41,878
McNairy	1,461	22,525
Meigs	491	7,431
Monroe	1,685	28,700
Montgomery	1,401	83,342
Moore	335	4,510
Morgan	1,360	16,604
Obion	1,430	32,781
Overton	1,126	17,575
Perry	1,071	6,111
Pickett	413	4,358
Polk	1,139	13,602
Putnam	1,037	47,690
Rhea	803	24,235
Rhoane	928	48,425
Robertson	1,238	37,021
Rutherford	1,576	84,058
Scott	1,373	19,259
Sequatchie	692	8,605
Sevier	1,534	41,418
Shelby	2,007	777,113
Smith	814	14,935

contd

County	*area (sq km)*	*pop(1980)*
Stewart	1,180	8,665
Sullivan	1,079	143,968
Sumner	1,375	85,790
Tipton	1,180	32,930
Trousdale	296	6,137
Unicoi	484	16,362
Union	567	11,707
Van Buren	710	4,728
Warren	1,121	32,653
Washington	848	88,755
Wayne	1,908	13,946
Weakley	1,511	32,896
White	970	19,567
Williamson	1,518	58,108
Wilson	1,482	56,064

Tennessee, river in SE USA; formed just E of Knoxville, Tennessee, between the Cumberland and Great Smoky Mts, by the confluence of the French Broad and Holston rivers; flows generally SW past Knoxville and Chattanooga and into N Alabama, where it continues SW then curves NNW, forming part of the Alabama-Mississippi border; the river then re-enters Tennessee and flows N through the state and into Kentucky to join the Ohio river at Paducah; length, with its longest headstream, the French Broad, 1,398 km; major tributaries: the Little Tennessee, Clinch, Hiwasee, Elk and Duck rivers; used for irrigation, flood-control and hydroelectric power.

Tensift', province of W Morocco, N Africa; includes the prefectures of El Kelaa-des Srarhna, Essaouira, Marrakech and Safi; area 38,445 sq km; pop(1982) 2,944,591.

Teotihuacán *tay-ō-tee-wah-kahn'*, 19 42N 98 51W, ancient ruined city in central Mexico; 40 km NE of Ciudad de México (Mexico City); the most powerful political and cultural centre in Middle America during the early Classic Period (200-900 AD); monuments include the Pyramid of the Sun, the Pyramid of the Moon, the Citadel and the Temple of Quetzalcóatl; leading N is the 3 km-long Street of the Dead.

Tepelenë *tay-pay-lay'ne*, prov of S Albania; area 817 sq km; pop(1980) 43,300; capital Tepelenë.

Tepelenë, 40 18N 20 00E, town and capital of Tepelenë prov, S Albania; on the R Vijosë, 48 km SE of Vlorë; monument: ruins of a Turkish fortress.

Tepic *tay-peek'*, 21 30N 104 51W, pop(1980) 177,007, capital of Nayarit state, W Mexico; 127 km NW of Guadalajara, at the foot of the extinct Volcán Sanganguey (2,352 m); founded in 1531; university (1969); railway; economy: cotton spinning, sugar, rice; monuments: the Casa de Amado Nervo (Mexican poet and diplomat), regional museum.

Teplice *tep'li-tse*, 50 40N 13 50E, pop(1984) 53,508, town in Severocesky region, Czech Socialist Republic, W Czechoslovakia; SW of Ústí nad Labem in the foothills of the Erzgebirge, near the E German frontier; health resort with radioactive springs; railway; economy: clothing, paper, glass.

Teques, Los *lōs te'kays*, 10 20N 67 02W, pop(1981) 112,857, capital of Miranda state, N Venezuela; railway.

Téra *tay'ra*, 14 01N 0 45E, town in Niamey dept, SW Niger, W Africa; on the R Dargol, a tributary of the R Niger, 160 km NW of Niamey; economy: stock raising.

Teramo *tay'ra-mō*, prov of Abruzzi region, E central Italy; pop(1981) 269,275; area 1,948 sq km; capital Teramo.

Teramo, 42 40N 13 43E, pop(1981) 51,092, capital town of Teramo prov, Abruzzi region, E central Italy; 25 km W of the Adriatic, on the R Tordino; economy: textiles, food products; monuments: 12th-c cathedral, remains of a Roman amphitheatre.

Terceira or **Ilha Terceira** *ter-say'ra* ('third island'), 38 43N 27 13W, the third island to be discovered and the third largest of the Azores archipelago, Angra do Heroísmo dist, Portuguese autonomous region of the Azores; 31 km long and up to 18 km wide with an area of 397 sq km; highest point is the Caldeira de Santa Barbara (1,067 m); the 90,000 inhabitants are mostly descended from first Flemish settlers of the 15th century; economy: crop-farming, stock-rearing and seaweed gathering; the fortified main town of Angra do Heroísmo lies on the S coast.

Terengganu *treng-gah'noo*, state in NE Peninsular Malaysia, pop(1980) 525,255; area 12,928 sq km; capital Kuala Terengganu; economy: fishing, offshore oil; the sultans of Terengganu are direct descendants of the royal families of Johor and Malacca; the state was once a fief of Malacca and then Johor before coming under the rule of Thailand; in 1909 it was transferred along with Kelantan to British sovereignty.

Teresina *tay-ray-see'na*, 5 09S 42 46W, pop(1980) 339,042, river-port capital of Piauí state, Nordeste region, NE Brazil; on the Río Parnaíba, SW of Fortaleza; university (1968); railway; economy: commerce, alcohol, vegetable oils.

Terni *ter'nee*, prov of Umbria region, central Italy; pop(1981) 226,564; area 2,121 sq km; capital Terni.

Terni, 42 34N 12 39E, pop(1981) 111,564, industrial capital town of Terni prov, Umbria region, central Italy, in the fertile valley of the R Nera, bounded E by the Appno Umbro-Marchigiano, some 100 km N of Roma (Rome); railway; monument: 13-17th-c cathedral.

Terre Haute *ter hōt*, 39 28N 87 25W, pop(1980) 61,125, county seat of Vigo county, W Indiana, United States; on the R Wabash, 110 km WSW of Indianapolis; university (1865); railway.

Terschelling *ter-skel'ling*, one of the West Frisian Is, in Friesland prov, N Netherlands, between the North Sea (N) and the Waddenzee (S); area 107 sq km; length 26 km; width 5 km; Brandaris lighthouse, a landmark, is on the W shore; chief village Westterschelling; ferry to Harlingen on the mainland; the N of the island is protected by dunes, the S by heavy dykes.

Teruel *ter-oo-el'*, prov in Aragón region, E central Spain; stretching from the Sierra de Albarracín and the Montes del Maestrazgo in the S almost to the R Ebro; pop(1981) 150,900; area 14,785 sq km; capital Teruel; economy: clothes, hydroelectric power, timber, lignite mining (Escucha, Palomar de Arroyos).

Teruel, TURBA (anc), 40 22N 1 08W, pop(1981) 28,225, capital of Teruel prov, Aragón, E central Spain; on R Turia, 302 km from Madrid; bishopric; railway; economy: clothes, woollens, soap, leather, flour, wood products, foodstuffs; monuments: 16th-c cathedral; Los Arcos aqueduct; church of St Peter.

Tessin, canton in Switzerland. See Ticino.

Test, river rising W of Basingstoke, Hampshire, S England; flows 48 km W and S to meet Southampton Water at Southampton.

Tetaumatawhakatangihangakoauauotamateaturipukakapikimaungahoronukupokaiwhenuakitanatahu, location with a Maori place-name in Hawke's Bay, North Island, New Zealand; it translates as 'the hill on which Tamatea, man with the hot knees, who climbed mountains and slid down the other sides and thus travelled the land, played a flute to his loved one'; said to be the longest place-name in the world.

Tete *te'tay*, prov in W Mozambique, SE Africa; pop(1980) 831,000; area 100,714 sq km; the R Zambezi (including Canora Bassa Dam) flows E and SE; capital Tete; chief towns include Moatize, Furancungo and Zumbo.

Tete, 16 10S 33 35E, pop(1980) 45,119, capital of dist and prov of same name, NW Mozambique, SE Africa; on the R Zambezi, NNW of Beira.

Tétouan or **Tetuán** *tay-twahn'*, 35 34N 5 22W, pop(1982) 199,615, city in Tétouan prefecture, Nord-Ouest prov, NE Morocco, N Africa; 60 km SE of Tanger (Tangiers); settled by Moorish exiles expelled from Spain after the reconquest of the 15th century; captured in 1860 by the Spanish; permanent Spanish occupation commenced in 1915; airfield; economy: textiles, leather, soap, tiles.

Tetovo *tet-ō'vo*, KALKANDELEN (Turk), 42 00N 20 59E,

pop(1981) 162,414, town in NW Makedonija republic, Yugoslavia; 40 km W of Skopje; skiing on nearby Sar Mts; railway; economy: fruit and vegetable trade.

Tevere *tay've-ray*, TIBER *tī'ber* (Eng), TIBERIS (anc), 2nd longest river of Italy, rising in the Appno Tosco-Emilliano (Etruscan Apennines) on Monte Fumaiolo; flows SSE, S and SSW past Umbertide, Orte, Roma (Rome) and Ostia; discharges into the Tyrrhenian Sea, which it enters in 2 mouths; the chief mouth is the Fiumara, 27 km SE of Roma, which is silted up; the other is the Fiumicino, further N, which is kept navigable by canalization; chief tributaries include the Nera, Aniene, Paglia; receives the waters of the Lago di Albano, SE of Roma.

Texarka'na, 33 26N 94 03W, pop(1980) 31,271, town in Bowie county, NE Texas, United States; on the Arkansas state border, near the Red river; railway; economy: cotton, timber, clay products, mobile homes, furniture, and clothing.

Texas *teks'as*, state in SW United States; bounded N by Oklahoma, E by Arkansas and Louisiana, SE by the Gulf of Mexico, SW by Mexico, and W by New Mexico; the Red river forms the E part of the Oklahoma state border, and a few miles of the Arkansas border; the R Sabine flows SE and S forming the lower part of the Louisiana state border, before emptying into the Gulf of Mexico; the R Rio Grande forms the state's entire international border with Mexico, and flows into the Gulf of Mexico; the Trinity, Brazos and Colorado rivers all flow SE through the state to empty into the Gulf; the Davis and Guadalupe Mts rise in the extreme W part of the state, the highest point being Guadalupe Peak (2,667 m); much of E Texas is hilly, forested country with cypress swamps and cotton and rice cultivation; extensive oil fields underlie the land here; the Gulf coastal plains around Houston are heavily industrialized; tourism and heavy industry are based on the drier S coastal region; intensive agriculture is centred in the irrigated lower Rio Grande valley, producing citrus fruits and winter vegetables; in central and N central Texas are the blackland prairies, the richest agricultural land in the state; in the N, Dallas and Fort Worth are major industrial centres; W of the blacklands are the S central plains and Edwards Plateau with vast wheat and cotton farms and cattle ranches; the far N is dry, barren and mountainous; Texas is the nation's leading producer of oil and natural gas, providing one-third of the nation's petroleum and half of its known reserves; manufactures include chemicals, processed foods, machinery and fabricated metals; the state is a major producer of cattle, sheep, and cotton; other important agricultural products are wheat, sorghum, dairy produce, rice, and vegetables; the chief fishing catches are shrimp, oysters, and menhaden; the Spanish first settled in the area in the late 1600s; in 1821 300 American families crossed the R Sabine and founded the first American settlement in Texas; the newly independent government of Mexico was initially pleased by this colonization and encouraged further American settlers; when the Texans' request for separate statehood was turned down by Mexico and Mexican troops re-garrisoned Texas the Americans rebelled (1835); in March 1836 Texas declared its independence from Mexico; a large Mexican army under General Santa Ana entered Texas and defeated the Texans at the Alamo; subsequently a small Texan force led by Sam Houston surprised and defeated the Mexican army at San Jacinto in April 1836 capturing Santa Ana who was forced to recognize the independence of Texas; Texas remained an independent republic for nearly 10 years before it was admitted to the Union in 1845 as the 28th state; this action precipitated the US-Mexican War, but Mexican defeats at Palo Alto and Resaca de la Palma forced the Mexicans to retreat across the Rio Grande; Texas joined the Confederate states in the Civil War and was the only one not to be overrun by Union troops; it was re-admitted to the Union in 1870; the discovery of extensive oil deposits from 1901 onwards transformed the state's economy; also known as the 'Lonestar State'; pop(1980) 14,229,191; area 681,244 sq km; capital Austin; other major cities include Houston, Dallas, San Antonio, El Paso and Fort Worth; the 2nd largest state in the Union; the state is divided into 254 counties:

County	*area (sq km)*	*pop(1980)*
Anderson	2,800	38,381
Andrews	3,903	13,323
Angelina	2,098	64,172
Aransas	728	14,260
Archer	2,358	7,266
Armstrong	2,363	1,994
Atascosa	3,167	25,055
Austin	1,706	17,726
Bailey	2,148	8,168
Bandera	2,062	7,084
Bastrop	2,327	24,726
Baylor	2,241	4,919
Bee	2,288	26,030
Bell	2,743	157,889
Bexar	3,245	988,800
Blanco	1,856	4,681
Borden	2,340	859
Bosque	2,571	13,401
Bowie	2,317	75,301
Brazoria	3,658	169,587
Brazos	1,531	93,588
Brewster	16,039	7,573
Briscoe	2,306	2,579
Brooks	2,449	8,428
Brown	2,434	33,057
Burleson	1,739	12,313
Burnet	2,584	17,803
Caldwell	1,420	23,637
Calhoun	1,404	19,574
Callahan	2,337	10,992
Cameron	2,356	209,727
Camp	528	9,275
Carson	2,402	6,672
Cass	2,436	29,430
Castro	2,337	10,556
Chambers	1,602	18,538
Cherokee	2,735	38,127
Childress	1,838	6,950
Clay	2,824	9,582
Cochran	2,015	4,825
Coke	2,361	3,196
Coleman	3,320	10,439
Collin	2,213	144,576
Collingsworth	2,363	4,648
Colorado	2,509	18,823
Comal	1,443	36,446
Comanche	2,418	12,617
Concho	2,579	2,915
Cooke	2,322	27,656
Coryell	2,748	56,767
Cottle	2,327	2,947
Crane	2,033	4,600
Crockett	7,296	4,608
Crosby	2,337	8,859
Culberson	9,919	3,315
Dallam	3,913	6,531
Dallas	2,288	1,556,390
Dawson	2,348	16,184
De Witt	2,366	18,903
Deaf Smith	3,892	21,165
Delta	723	4,839
Denton	2,369	143,126
Dickens	2,358	3,539
Dimmit	3,398	11,367
Donley	2,415	4,075
Duval	4,667	12,517
Eastland	2,402	19,480
Ector	2,348	115,374
Edwards	5,515	2,033

contd

County	*area (sq km)*	*pop(1980)*
El Paso	2,636	479,899
Ellis	2,441	59,743
Erath	2,808	22,560
Falls	2,002	17,946
Fannin	2,327	24,285
Fayette	2,470	18,832
Fisher	2,332	5,891
Floyd	2,579	9,834
Foard	1,828	2,158
Fort Bend	2,278	130,846
Franklin	764	6,893
Freestone	2,309	14,830
Frio	2,946	13,785
Gaines	3,910	13,150
Galveston	1,037	195,940
Garza	2,327	5,336
Gillespie	2,759	13,532
Glasscock	2,340	1,304
Goliad	2,233	5,193
Gonzales	2,777	16,883
Gray	2,395	26,386
Grayson	2,428	89,796
Gregg	710	99,487
Grimes	2,077	13,580
Guadalupe	1,854	46,708
Hale	2,613	37,592
Hall	2,280	5,594
Hamilton	2,174	8,297
Hansford	2,395	6,209
Hardeman	1,789	6,368
Hardin	2,335	40,721
Harris	4,508	2,409,547
Harrison	2,361	52,265
Hartley	3,801	3,987
Haskell	2,343	7,725
Hays	1,763	40,594
Hemphill	2,348	5,304
Henderson	2,309	42,606
Hidalgo	4,079	283,229
Hill	2,517	25,024
Hockley	2,361	23,230
Hood	1,105	17,714
Hopkins	2,051	25,247
Houston	3,208	22,299
Howard	2,343	33,142
Hudspeth	11,874	2,728
Hunt	2,184	55,248
Hutchinson	2,267	26,304
Irion	2,735	1,386
Jack	2,392	7,408
Jackson	2,194	13,352
Jasper	2,395	30,781
Jeff Davis	5,868	1,647
Jefferson	2,436	250,938
Jim Hogg	2,954	5,168
Jim Wells	2,254	36,498
Johnson	1,898	67,649
Jones	2,421	17,268
Karnes	1,958	13,593
Kaufman	2,049	39,015
Kendall	1,724	10,635
Kenedy	3,611	543
Kent	2,283	1,145
Kerr	2,878	28,780
Kimble	3,250	4,063
King	2,376	425
Kinney	3,533	2,279
Kleberg	2,218	33,358
Knox	2,197	5,329
La Salle	3,944	5,514
Lamar	2,389	42,156
Lamb	2,634	18,669
Lampasas	1,856	12,005

contd

County	*area (sq km)*	*pop(1980)*
Lavaca	2,525	19,004
Lee	1,641	10,952
Leon	2,805	9,594
Liberty	3,052	47,088
Limestone	2,418	20,224
Lipscomb	2,426	3,766
Live Oak	2,748	9,606
Llano	2,441	10,144
Loving	1,742	91
Lubbock	2,340	211,651
Lynn	2,309	8,605
Madison	1,227	10,649
Marion	1,001	10,360
Martin	2,376	4,684
Mason	2,428	3,683
Matagorda	2,930	37,828
Maverick	3,346	31,398
McCulloch	2,785	8,735
McLennan	2,681	170,755
McMullen	3,024	789
Medina	3,461	23,164
Menard	2,345	2,346
Midland	2,345	82,636
Milam	2,649	22,732
Mills	1,945	4,477
Mitchell	2,371	9,088
Montague	2,413	17,410
Montgomery	2,722	128,487
Moore	2,353	16,575
Morris	666	14,629
Motley	2,493	1,950
Nacogdoches	2,441	46,786
Navarro	2,777	35,323
Newton	2,431	13,254
Nolan	2,379	17,359
Nueces	2,202	268,215
Ochiltree	2,389	9,588
Oldham	3,861	2,283
Orange	941	83,838
Palo Pinto	2,467	24,062
Panola	2,111	20,724
Parker	2,345	44,609
Parmer	2,301	11,038
Pecos	12,420	14,618
Polk	2,759	24,407
Potter	2,345	98,637
Presidio	10,028	5,188
Rains	632	4,839
Randall	2,384	75,062
Reagan	3,050	4,135
Real	1,812	2,469
Red River	2,740	16,101
Reeves	6,828	15,801
Refugio	2,005	9,289
Roberts	2,379	1,187
Robertson	2,246	14,653
Rockwall	333	14,528
Runnels	2,746	11,872
Rusk	2,423	41,382
Sabine	1,264	8,702
San Augustine	1,362	8,785
San Jacinto	1,487	11,434
San Patricio	1,802	58,013
San Saba	2,954	6,204
Schleicher	3,403	2,820
Scurry	2,340	18,192
Shackelford	2,379	3,915
Shelby	2,057	23,084
Sherman	23,999	3,174
Smith	2,423	128,366
Somervell	489	4,154
Starr	3,188	27,266
Stephens	2,324	9,926

contd

County	*area (sq km)*	*pop(1980)*
Sterling	2,400	1,206
Stonewall	2,405	2,406
Sutton	3,783	5,130
Swisher	2,345	9,723
Tarrant	2,257	860,880
Taylor	2,384	110,932
Terrell	6,128	1,595
Terry	2,306	14,581
Throckmorton	2,371	2,053
Titus	1,071	21,442
Tom Green	3,939	84,784
Travis	2,571	419,573
Trinity	1,799	9,450
Tyler	2,397	16,223
Upshur	1,526	28,595
Upton	3,232	4,619
Uvalde	4,066	22,441
Val Verde	8,190	35,910
Van Zandt	2,223	31,426
Victoria	2,306	68,807
Walker	2,044	41,789
Waller	1,336	19,798
Ward	2,174	13,976
Washington	1,586	21,998
Webb	8,741	99,258
Wharton	2,824	40,242
Wheeler	2,350	7,137
Wichita	1,576	121,082
Wilbarger	2,462	15,931
Willacy	1,531	17,495
Williamson	2,956	76,521
Wilson	2,098	16,756
Winkler	2,184	9,944
Wise	2,345	26,575
Wood	1,791	24,697
Yoakum	2,080	8,299
Young	2,389	19,083
Zapata	2,597	6,628
Zavala	3,375	11,666

Texas City, 29 24N 94 54W, pop(1980) 41,403, town in Galveston county, SE Texas, United States; a port on Galveston Bay, opposite Galveston; railway; economy: oil refining, petrochemicals, tin smelting, fertilizer, valves, pipes.

Tex'el, TESSEL, largest and southernmost of the West Frisian Is, in Noord Holland prov, W Netherlands, between the North Sea (N) and the Waddenzee (S); area 185 sq km, length 24 km, width 10 km; there are dunes on the W coast and dykes along the E coast; Eijerland polder (NE) was drained in 1835; a large breeding ground for sea birds; chief village Burg (or Den Burg), port Oudeschild (ferry from here to Helder on the mainland); important in Anglo-Dutch naval warfare.

Thabana-Ntlenyana *ta-ba'na-ent-len-yan'a*, THADENTSONYANE, 29 28S 29 16E, mountain in E Lesotho, S Africa; in the Drakensberg Mountains; at 3,482 m it is the highest peak in Lesotho as well as being the highest peak in Africa S of Mount Kilimanjaro; the first European ascent was in 1951 by D. Watkins, B. Anderson and R. Goodwin.

Thailand *tī'land*, MUANG THAI (Thai), formerly SIAM, official name Kingdom of Thailand, kingdom in SE Asia, situated N and W of the Gulf of Thailand and bounded W by the Andaman Sea, W and NW by Burma, NE and E by Laos, E by Cambodia and S by Malaysia; timezone GMT +7; area 513,115 sq km; capital Bangkok; chief cities include Chiang Mai, Ban Hat Yai, Nakhon Ratchasima; pop(1980) 44,824,540; ethnic groups include Thai (75%), Chinese (14%) and minority groups such as Khmer and Mon; the official language is Thai, but there are many local dialects; over 95% of the pop is Buddhist; the currency is the baht; national holidays 6 April (Chakri Memorial Day), 13 April (Thai New Year), 5 May (Coronation Day), 9 May (Ploughing Ceremony Day), 12 Aug (Queen's birthday), 5 Dec (King's Birthday), 10 Dec (Constitution Day); membership of ADB, ANRPC, ASEAN, Colombo Plan, ESCAP, FAO, G-77, GATT, IAEA, IBRD, ICAO, IDA, IFAD, IFC, IHO, ILO, IMF, IMO, INTELSAT, INTERPOL, IPU, IRC, ITC, ITU, UN, UNESCO, UPU, WHO, WMO, WTO.

Physical description. Located at the heart of SE Asia, Thailand stretches from the mountainous Burmese frontier in the N down into the Malay Peninsula. The country can be divided into 4 topographical regions: (1) A central agricultural region dominated by the floodplain of the Chao Praya R and an extensive network of canals and irrigation projects. (2) A NE plateau rising above 300 m and covering one-third of the country. Much of this land is of poor quality, with a topography that makes seasonal flood control and irrigation difficult, except near the Mekong R and its tributaries. (3) A mountainous N region rising to 2,594 m at Doi Inthanon. Fertile valleys support intensive rice cultivation while the forested hill slopes provide most of the country's timber. (4) A narrow, low lying S region separating the Andaman Sea from the Gulf of Thailand. Covered in tropical rainforest, this area supplies rubber and coconuts and is a centre of the tin-mining industry. Mangrove-forested islands off the coast have become popular resorts or are conserved as national parks protecting important marine life.

Climate. In the S the climate is equatorial, while in the N and centre a tropical monsoon climate predominates. Blowing from the Indian Ocean between May and Oct, the SW monsoons bring heavy rainfall and warm, humid air. The extreme N is virtually dry during the NE monsoon period when the wind blows overland from China. The NE winds bring cooler weather to the mountainous N during Nov-April, but elsewhere temperatures vary little from month to month.

History, government and constitution. Archaeological studies suggest that Bronze-Age communities had emerged in Thailand as early as 4,000 BC. The cultivation of wet rice was important in the socio-political development of the country. Migration from China and territorial struggles for power amongst Malay, Khmer, Tai and Mon tribes resulted in the founding of the Thai nation in the 13th century. Despite occupation by Burma during the 18th century Thailand is the only country in S and SE Asia to have escaped colonization by a European power. A revolution in 1932 transformed the Thai form of government from an absolute to a constitutional monarchy. Since then there have been 14 new constitutions, the last, in 1978, establishing the king as head of state. The king is advised by a 14-member Privy Council. The bicameral National Assembly consists of a 324-member House of Representatives and a 243-member Senate. Members of the House of Representatives are elected while members of the Senate are appointed by the king on the advice of the prime minister who heads a cabinet of 44 ministers. Provincial governors and district officers are appointed to the provinces by the Ministry of the Interior, while larger towns are administered by elected municipal assemblies and appointed district officers.

Economy. Nearly 80% of the population of Thailand is rural, with agriculture the most important economic activity in the country. Important crops for domestic consumption as well as export include rice, manioc, maize, bananas, pineapple, sugar cane and rubber. Manufacturing industry, contributing about 20% to the national income, is based on the production of textiles, electronics, chemicals and food processing. Thailand is the world's 3rd largest supplier of tin but also exports tungsten (world's 2nd largest supplier), manganese, antimony, lead, zinc and copper. Natural gas has been brought ashore since 1981. Major trade partners include Japan, the USA, the Netherlands, Hong Kong, Malaysia, Singapore, the UK, W Germany, Saudi Arabia.

Administrative divisions. Thailand is divided into provinces (*changwats*) which have the same name as their capitals:

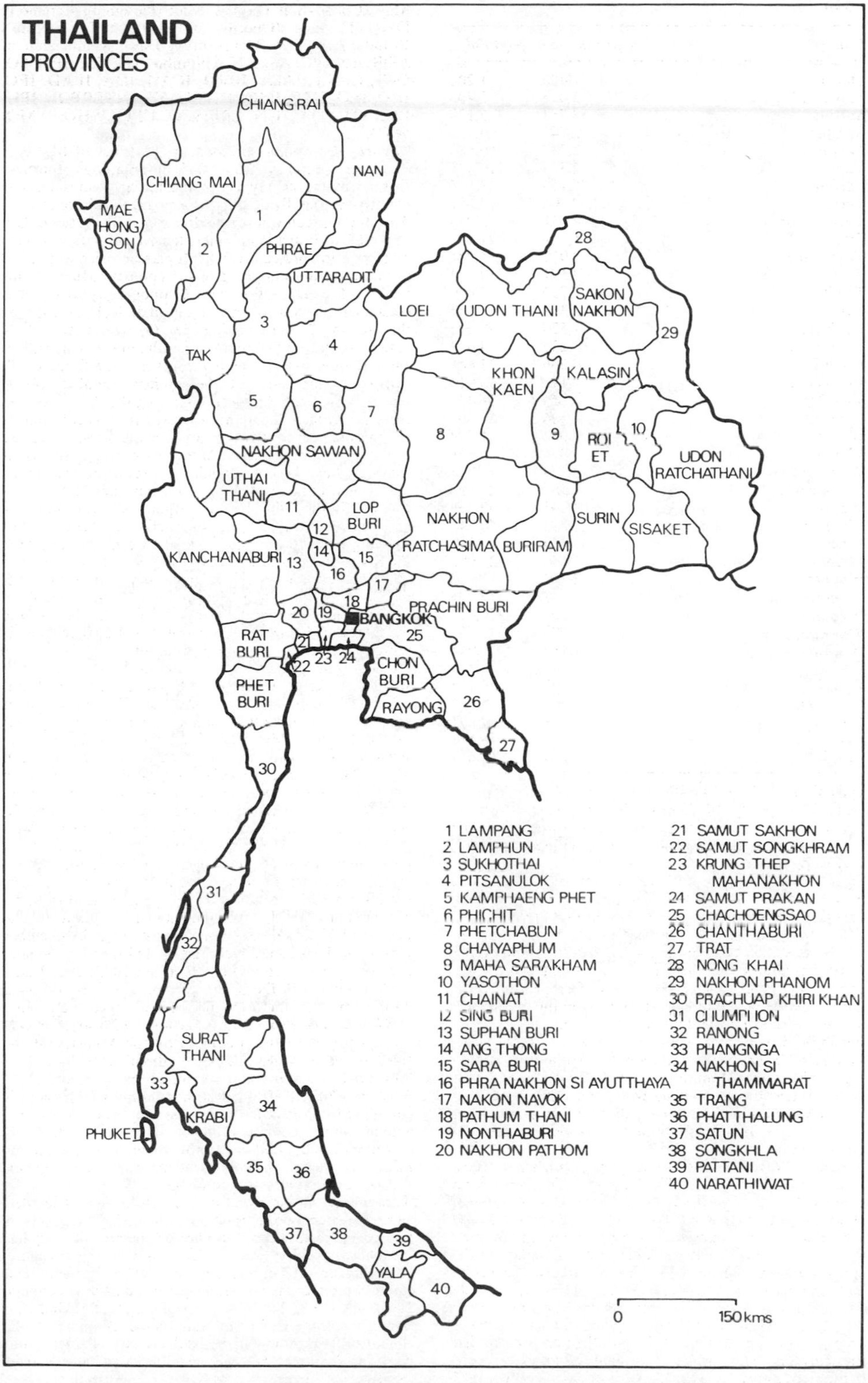
THAILAND
PROVINCES
CHIANG RAI
NAN
CHIANG MAI
MAE HONG SON
PHRAE
UTTARADIT
LOEI
UDON THANI
SAKON NAKHON
TAK
KHON KAEN
KALASIN
ROI ET
UDON RATCHATHANI
NAKHON SAWAN
UTHAI THANI
LOP BURI
NAKHON RATCHASIMA
BURIRAM
SURIN
SISAKET
KANCHANABURI
PRACHIN BURI
BANGKOK
RAT BURI
CHON BURI
PHET BURI
RAYONG
SURAT THANI
KRABI
PHUKET
YALA
1 LAMPANG
2 LAMPHUN
3 SUKHOTHAI
4 PITSANULOK
5 KAMPHAENG PHET
6 PHICHIT
7 PHETCHABUN
8 CHAIYAPHUM
9 MAHA SARAKHAM
10 YASOTHON
11 CHAINAT
12 SING BURI
13 SUPHAN BURI
14 ANG THONG
15 SARA BURI
16 PHRA NAKHON SI AYUTTHAYA
17 NAKON NAVOK
18 PATHUM THANI
19 NONTHABURI
20 NAKHON PATHOM
21 SAMUT SAKHON
22 SAMUT SONGKHRAM
23 KRUNG THEP MAHANAKHON
24 SAMUT PRAKAN
25 CHACHOENGSAO
26 CHANTHABURI
27 TRAT
28 NONG KHAI
29 NAKHON PHANOM
30 PRACHUAP KHIRI KHAN
31 CHUMPHON
32 RANONG
33 PHANGNGA
34 NAKHON SI THAMMARAT
35 TRANG
36 PHATTHALUNG
37 SATUN
38 SONGKHLA
39 PATTANI
40 NARATHIWAT
0
150 kms

Province	area (sq km)	pop (1980/83)
Ang Thong	968	255,240
Buriram	10,322	1,132,980
Chachoengsao	5,351	498,148
Chainat	2,470	330,385
Chaiyaphum	12,778	857,692
Chanthaburi	6,338	330,610
Chiang Mai	20,107	1,166,123
Chiang Rai	11,678	922,850
Chon Buri	4,363	725,407
Chumphon	6,009	330,455
Kalasin	6,947	755,274
Kamphaeng Phet	8,608	559,223
Kanchanaburi	19,483	518,927
Khon Kaen	10,886	1,354,855
Krabi	4,709	218,814
Lampang	12,534	659,433
Lamphun	4,506	353,607
Loei	11,425	449,535
Lop Buri	6,200	655,537
Mae Hong Son	12,681	132,391
Maha Sarakham	5,292	764,509
Nakhon Navok	2,122	201,230
Nakhon Pathom	2,168	561,346
Nakhon Phanom	9,853	760,319
Nakhon Ratchasima	20,494	1,916,681
Nakhon Sawan	9,598	976,971
Nakhon Si Thammarat	9,943	1,261,408
Nan	11,472	378,999
Narathiwat	4,475	441,803
Nong Khai	7,332	673,884
Nonthaburi	622	386,741
Pathum Thani	1,526	324,468
Pattani	1,940	457,760
Phangnga	4,171	174,973
Phatthalung	3,425	412,265
Phayao	6,335	461,620
Phetchabun	12,668	785,238
Phetburi	6,225	366,612
Phichit	4,531	534,481
Pitsanulok	12,668	709,073
Phra Nakhon Si Ayutthaya	11,958	623,242
Phrae	6,539	446,431
Phuket	543	133,669
Prachin Buri	11,958	631,276
Prachuap Khiri Khan	6,368	377,212
Ranong	3,298	83,707
Ratburi	5,197	644,746
Rayong	3,552	358,896
Roi Et	8,299	1,061,085
Sakon Nakhon	9,606	776,510
Samut Prakan	1,004	535,858
Samut Sakhon	872	265,464
Samut Songkhram	417	196,659
Sara Buri	3,577	4,700,655
Satun	2,479	164,740
Sisaket	8,840	1,082,121
Sing Buri	823	202,605
Songkhla	7,394	849,601
Sukhothai	6,596	531,624
Suphan Buri	5,358	709,364
Surat Thani	12,892	593,095
Surin	8,124	1,035,577
Tak	16,406	276,994
Trang	4,918	4,270,005
Trat	2,819	138,185
Udon Ratchathani	18,906	1,560,272
Udon Thani	15,589	1,448,066
Uthai Thani	6,730	259,464
Uttaradit	7,839	432,995
Yala	4,521	273,866
Yasothon	4,162	458,535

Thame *taym*, river rising in the Chiltern Hills, central England; flows 48 km SW to meet the R Thames NW of Wallingford.

Thames *temz*, TAMESIS (Lat), ('dark river'), river rising in the Cotswold Hills, SE Gloucestershire, England; flows 352 km E and SE through Oxfordshire, Berkshire, Surrey and Greater London where it approaches the North Sea in a long, wide estuary lying between Essex (N) and Kent (S); navigable as far as London by large ships; chief tributaries include the Cherwell, Thame, Lea, Colne, Roding, Kennet, Mole, Wey, and Medway rivers; the upper part of the river beyond Oxford is often called the R Isis (a quasi-classical form of *Ouse*); the Grand Union Canal, which links with Aylesbury and the R Ousel, joins the Thames near Brentford; the part of the river in the immediate vicinity of London Bridge is called the *Pool*; two embankments have been formed, one since 1864 on the N shore from Blackfriars Bridge to Westminster, and one since 1866 on the S shore from Westminster Bridge to Vauxhall; the Thames was given to the Lord Mayor of London in 1489 and in the 18th century its administration was put in the hands of commissioners; in 1857 the Thames Conservancy Board was established, but the Port of London Act (1908) put the administration of the river below Teddington in the hands of the Port of London Authority.

Thāne, 19 14N 73 02E, pop(1981) 389,000, city in Maharashtra state, W India; linked by rail to Bombay which is 32 km NNE; economy: textiles, matches, sugar cane, rice.

Tha'net, Isle of, pop(1981) 114,564, urban area in E Kent, SE England; includes the towns of Margate, Broadstairs and Ramsgate; railway.

Thanh Hoa *tah'nyu hwa*, 19 49N 105 48E, town in Thanh Hoa prov, N Vietnam, Indo-China; 248 km ESE of Hanoi; railway; economy: cement, agricultural trade, salt.

Thar *tahr*, GREAT INDIAN DESERT, INDIAN DESERT, arid region in NW India and E Pakistan, S Asia; 800 km long and 400 km wide; lies between the Indus and the Sutlej rivers on the W and the Aravalli range to the E; bounded S by the Rann of Kachch (Kutch); crossed in the N and W by irrigation canals, the largest of which is the Rajasthan Canal; the R Luni is the only major natural watercourse.

Tharparkar *tur-par'kur*, THAR DESERT, desert E of the R Indus on the India-Pakistan frontier; area 28,100 sq km; chief towns include Umarkot and Naukot.

Thásos *thah'sos*, island in the N Aegean Sea, Greece, opposite the mouth of the R Néstos (Mesta), separated from the mainland of Makedhonia by a 6.5 km wide channel; area 379 sq km; length 24 km; rises to 1,046 m in Mt Ypsári; the island was famed in ancient times for its gold-mines and marble quarries.

Thebes, town in Central Greece and Évvoia region, Greece. See Thívai.

Thesprotía *thes-pro-tee'a*, sparsely populated coastal nome (dept) of Ipiros region, NW Greece, extending S from the Albanian frontier; pop(1981) 41,278; area 1,515 sq km; capital Igoumenítsa; drained by the R Thiamis.

Thessalía *thes-al-ee'u*, THESSALY *the'sul-ee* (Eng), fertile agricultural region of E Greece, bounded W by the Píndhos Mts, and E by the Aegean Sea; comprises the nomoi (depts) of Kardhítsa, Lárisa, Magnisía, and Tríkkala; pop(1981) 695,654; area 14,037 sq km; capital Lárisa; famed in ancient times for its horses; it is Greece's principal producer of cereals.

Thessaloníki *thes-al-o-nee'ki*, SALONICA *sa-lon'ee-ka* (Eng), nome (dept) of Makedhonia region, N Greece; pop(1981) 871,580; area 3,683 sq km; capital Thessaloníki; produces cereals and grapes.

Thessaloníki, 40 38N 22 58E, pop(1981) 706,180, seaport and capital of Thessaloníki nome (dept), Makedhonia region, Greece; 2nd largest city of Greece; founded in 315 BC, it was the capital of Roman Macedonia (148 BC); held by Turkey (1430-1912); university (1926); airport; railway; car ferry to the mainland and islands; yacht supply station; economy: textiles, metal products, chemicals, cigarettes, tourism; monuments: Arch of Galerius, with carvings depicting the emperor's campaigns against the Persians (AD 297); 5th-c basilica of Ayía Paraskeví, occupying the site of an earlier Roman villa; 9th-c basilica of Áyios Dimítrios; events: carnival (Feb); Navy Week (June-July); international trade fair (Sept); song festival and film festival (Sept).

Thet'ford, 52 25N 0 45E, pop(1981) 19,593, town in Breckland dist, Norfolk, E England; SW of Norwich, at junction of Thet and Ouse rivers, 20 km N of Bury St Edmunds; 11th-c residence of the kings of East Anglia; formerly a bishopric with over 20 parish churches; railway; economy: light industry; monument: 15th-c Ancient House museum.

Thiamis *thee'um-is*, river in S Ipiros region, Greece; rises on the Albanian frontier, 24 km W of Kónitsa; flows S and W to discharge into the Ionian Sea, 11 km NW of Igoumenítsa; length 115 km; unsuccessfully proposed (1878) at Berlin as the N limit of Greece.

Thiès *tyes*, region in W Senegal, W Africa; pop(1976) 698,994; area 6,601 sq km; capital Thiès; formerly the meeting point of the kingdoms of Cayor, Baol and Djolof; the Fil festival at Touba-Toul and Ndingler is designed to 'ensure' abundant rainfall.

Thiès, 14 49N 16 52W, pop(1979) 126,886, capital of region of same name, Senegal, W Africa; 55 km E of Dakar; an African cultural and craft centre noted for its tapestries; railway junction; airfield; economy: aluminium, cotton, phosphates, cement, asbestos.

Thika *thee'ka*, 1 03S 37 05E, pop(1979) 41,000, (1984e) 57,000, town in S central Kenya, E Africa; NE of Nairobi; economy: car assembly.

Thimphu *thim'poo*, THIMBU *thim'boo*, TASHI CHHO DZONG *tash-ee chō jong*, 27 32N 89 43E, official capital of Bhután, central Asia; on R Raidak, 26 km SW of Punakha, W Bhután; dist population in 1969 of 60,027; founded in 1581, this fortified town was a major lamasery.

Thingvalla Water, lake in Iceland. See Thingvallavatn.

Þingvallavatn or **Thingvallavatn** *theeng-vaht-le-vatn*, THINGVALLA WATER (Eng), largest lake in Iceland; E of Rekyavik, SW Iceland; area 84 sq km.

Þingvellir or **Thingvellir** *theeng-gvet'lir*, 64 15N 21 06W, national shrine of Iceland, 52 km E of Reykjavík at the N end of Thingvallavatn (Thingvalla Water); the Icelandic *Althing*, oldest parliament in the world, was founded here in 930 AD, the focal point of the country until 1880; national cemetery.

Thíra or **Thera** *theer'u*, southernmost island of the Kikládhes. See Santorin.

Thirlmere *thirl'meer*, lake in the Lake District of Cumbria, NW England; 6 km SSE of Keswick; supplies water to Manchester.

Thisted *tee'steTH*, 56 58N 8 42E, pop(1981) 12,469, town in Viborg county, NW Jylland (Jutland), Denmark, on N shore of the Limfjorden (Lim Fjord); railway; economy: engineering, foodstuffs.

Thistle, oil field in the North Sea, E of the Shetland Is; linked by pipeline to Sullom Voe.

Thívai *thee'vay*, THEBES *theebz* (Eng), 38 19N 23 19E, pop(1981) 18,712, capital town of Voiótia (Boeotia) nome (dept), Sterea Ellás-Évvoia region, SE Greece; 52 km NNW of Athínai (Athens); 5 km from the Athínai-Thessaloníki highway; railway; event: traditional Kathara Dheftera (Ash Wednesday) celebrations.

Thompson, 55 45N 97 54W, pop(1981) 14,288, city in central Manitoba, central Canada; 785 km N of Winnipeg; a service centre for central Arctic Canada; economy: mining, smelting and refining of copper, cobalt, nickel.

Thornaby or **Thornaby-on-Tees**, 54 34N 1 18W, pop(1981) 26,309, town in Middlesbrough dist, Cleveland, NE England; on the right bank of the R Tees, S of Middlesbrough; part of Teesside conurbation; railway.

Thorn'bury, 51 37N 2 31W, pop(1981) 12,019, town in Northavon dist, Avon, SW England; 20 km N of Bristol; railway.

Thorne, 53 37N 0 58W, pop(1981) 16,692, town linked with Moorends in Doncaster borough, South Yorkshire, N England; 15 km NE of Doncaster; railway.

Thornton, 39 52N 104 58W, pop(1980) 40,343, city in Adams county, N central Colorado, United States; a residential suburb 14 km N of Denver.

Thornton-Cleveleys *-kleev'liz*, 53 53N 3 03W, pop(1981) 26,787, linked resort towns in Blackpool urban area and Wyre dist, Lancashire, NW England; 10 km N of Blackpool.

Thousand Oaks, 34 10N 118 50W, pop(1980) 77,072, city in Ventura county, SW California, United States; 40 km ESE of San Buenaventura.

Thrace, region of Greece. See Thráki.

Thráki *thrah'kee*, THRACE *thrays* (Eng), the most NE region of Greece, bounded N by Bulgaria, E by Turkey, and S by the Aegean Sea; pop(1981) 345,220; area 8,578 sq km; capital Komotiní; comprises the nomoi (depts) of Évros, Rodhópi, and Xánthi; a region of fertile plains, producing corn, wine, rice, and tobacco.

Thuin *twẽ*, dist of Hainaut prov, S Belgium; area 934 sq km; pop(1982) 141,378.

Thule *thoo'le*, 77 30N 69 29W, Eskimo settlement in NW Greenland; on coast of Hayes Halvø (peninsula); founded as a Danish trading post in 1910; Danish-US airforce base nearby; scientific installations; the name was also given by the ancients to the most northerly land of Europe, an island described c.310 BC by the Greek navigator, Pytheas.

Thun *toon*, THOUNE (Fr), 46 46N 7 38E, pop(1980) 36,891, town in Bern canton, Switzerland; on the R Aare just below its outflow from the Thuner See; Thun is the gateway to the Bernese Oberland; its old town is on a long, narrow island in the middle of the river, which is connected to the modern town by numerous bridges; railway junction; economy: engineering; monument: castle (1191) on a hill 30 m high dominating the town.

Thunder Bay, 48 27N 89 12W, pop(1981) 112,486, resort and port in S Ontario, S Canada; on NW shore of L Superior, in Thunder Bay; created in 1970 by the union of Fort William, a former French trading post, and Port Arthur; Lakehead University (1965); railway; airfield; economy: used as a grain storage and shipping point for the grain from the prairie provs; shipbuilding, paper, pulp; monuments: the Centennial Park contains a lumberman's camp from the early 1900s and a museum with Indian and early military artifacts.

Thuner See *too'nar zay*, LAKE OF THUN (Eng), lake in Bern canton, Switzerland, in the Aare valley between the towns of Thun (W) and Interlaken (E); area 48 sq km; length 18 km; between 2 and 2.8 km wide; max depth 217 m; the lake was originally joined to the Brienzer See to the E, but debris deposited by the R Lütschine and other mountain streams eventually divided the two at Interlaken.

Thurgau *toor'gow*, THURGOVIE *toor-go-vee'* (Fr), canton in NE Switzerland, on the S side of the Bodensee; the scenery is Pre-Alpine, its highest points barely rising to 1,000 m; pop(1980) 183,795; area 1,006 sq km; capital Frauenfeld; the main source of income is fruit-growing; joined the Swiss Confederacy in 1803.

Thurgovie, canton in Switzerland. See Thurgau.

Thüringer Wald THURINGIAN FOREST (Eng), region of forest land covering about two-thirds of the county of Suhl in SW East Germany between the Weisse Elster (E) and R Werra (W); formerly included in the German state of Thüringen (Thuringia), becoming part of E Germany in 1945; a popular tourist region; winter sports resort at Oberhof.

Thurles *thur'lus*, DÚRLA ÉILE (Gael), 52 41N 7 49W, pop(1981) 7,644, market town in Tipperary county, North Riding, Munster, S central Irish Republic; on R Suir, at the centre of fertile agricultural area; sports ground of the Gaelic athletic association; horse racing is popular; railway; economy: fishing, cattle trade, sugar-beet; monument: Holycross Abbey nearby.

Thurso, 58 35N 3 32W, pop(1981) 8,896, port town in

Caithness dist, Highland region, N Scotland; situated on the N coast, in Thurso Bay, at the head of the R Thurso, 30 km NW of Wick; railway; car ferry service to Orkney from Scrabster; monuments: St Peter's Church (17th-c); Thurso Folk Museum.

Thyolo *thi-ō'lo*, dist in Southern region, Malawi, SE Africa; area 1,715 sq km; pop(1977) 322,000.

Tianjin *tee-en-jin*, TIENTSIN, T'IEN-CHING, 39 08N 117 12E, municipality pop(1982) 7,764,141, urban centre pop(1984e) 5,312,100, port city in E China; 50 km W of the Bo Hai gulf on the Hai He river; municipality area 4,000 sq km; has China's largest artificial harbour, built during the Japanese occupation (1937-45) and completed in 1952; Tianjin dates from the Warring States period (403-221 BC); it grew in importance after 1368 AD as a port receiving grain from the southern provinces destined for Beijing (Peking); it was attacked by the British and French in 1860; the city was badly damaged by an earthquake in 1976, reconstruction was completed in 1982; university (1960); a special economic zone; railway; airport; economy: iron and steel, consumer goods, carpets; monuments: Tianjin Art Museum; Industrial Exhibition Hall; the city contains many European-style buildings and Victorian mansions.

Tia'ret, department of N Algeria, N Africa; area 23,455 sq km; pop(1982) 695,665; chief town Tiaret.

Tiber, river in Italy. See Tevere.

Tiberias *tī-bee'ree-us*, TEVARYA (Hebrew), 32 48N 35 32E, holiday resort town in North dist, N Israel; on the W shore of L Tiberias; founded in the time of Herod the Great and named after the Roman emperor Tiberius; its medicinal hot springs have been known since ancient times; one of the 4 holy cities of the Jews; the Talmud was edited here; Jewish settlement re-established in 1922; monument: monastery of St Peter.

Tiberias, Lake, SEA OF GALILEE, YAM KINNERET (Hebrew), SEA OF CHINNERETH (anc), lake in North dist, NE Israel; in the Jordan valley; the surface of the lake is 210 m below sea-level; area 165.8 sq km; length 22.5 km; width 12 km; maximum depth 46 m; fed and drained by the R Jordan; serves as Israel's largest reservoir with water being piped via the Kinneret-Negev conduit to various collection points and thence to the Negev; there are many places around the lake of historic and scriptural interest; the first Israeli *kibbutz* was founded just S of the lake in 1909.

Tibesti *tee-bes'tee*, mountain range in N central Africa; largely in NW Chad and partly in Libya and Sudan it covers 100,000 sq km, is 480 km in length and 280 km across and is the highest mountain group in the Sahara; the highest peak is Emi Koussi (3,415 m); the range is of volcanic origin and is extremely rugged with spectacular rock formations created by wind erosion; first explored by Gustav Nachtigal in 1869.

Tibet, autonomous region in SW China. See Xizang.

Ticino *tee-chee'nō*, TESSIN *tes'in* (Ger) or *te-sĩ* (Fr), canton in S Switzerland, bounded on the S by Italy; pop(1980) 265,899; area 2,811 sq km; capital Bellinzona; chief towns Lugano, Locarno; mountainous in the N; drained by the R Ticino, a left-bank tributary of the Po, which rises on the Nufenen Pass (Passo della Novena); the lakes of Maggiore and Lugano are on the S frontier with Italy; connections with the rest of Switzerland are mainly through the St Gotthard tunnels; economy: agriculture and tourism; there is wine-growing on a small scale (most distinguished wines are red, made largely from the Merlot variety); the indigenous population is almost exclusively Italian-speaking, but with a local dialect; it became an independent canton in 1803 when it joined the Swiss Confederacy.

Tidjikdja *tee-jeek-ja'*, 18 29N 11 31W, capital of Tagant region, central Mauritania, NW Africa; located E of Nouakchott; airfield.

Tielt *teelt*, dist of West-Vlaanderen (West Flanders) prov, W Belgium; area 329 sq km; pop(1982) 84,740.

Tien Shan *tyen*, TYAN SHAN, mountain range in central Asia, in the USSR and China; situated along the border of Xinjiang aut region, China and the USSR; extends as far W as the central Asian part of the USSR, and as far E as the border with Mongolia and Gansu prov; in Xinjiang the Tien Shan range separates the Tarim Pendi basin (S) from the Jungar Pendi (Dzungarian basin) in the N; contains glaciers up to 70 km in length; the length of the range is 2,500 km, of which 1,500 km are in China; contains two famous passes in its E section which link N and S Xinjiang: the Shengli Daban pass, to the SW of Ürümqi, and the pass at Qijiaojing to the NW of Hami in E Xinjiang; higher in the W than the E, the Tien Shan range rises to 7,439 m in Tomur (Pobedy) peak on the Sino-Soviet border; it divides into numerous branches in the W; contains rich deposits of coal, rock salt and metals; the N slopes have dense forests while the S ones are predominantly grasslands.

T'ien-ching, municipality and urban centre in E China. See Tianjin.

Tienen *tee'nun*, TIRLEMONT *teer-lmõ'* (Fr), 50 48N 4 56E, pop(1982) 32,537, town in Leuven dist, E Brabant prov, Belgium; mid-way between Liège and Bruxelles; situated in the middle of fertile loess-covered agricultural countryside (main crop sugar beet); since the 19th century Tienen has developed into an important location for Belgium's sugar industry; railway; economy: sugar refining; monuments: Gothic church of Our Lady, Romanesque church of St Germanus.

Tientsin, municipality and urban centre in E China. See Tianjin.

Tierra del Fuego *tye'ra THel fway'gō*, National Territory of Argentina; situated at the extreme S of South America; part of the island of the same name which is bounded by the Estreita de Magallanes (Magellan Strait) to the N, the Atlantic Ocean (E) and the Beagle Channel (S); mountains, forests and lakes in S, including L Fagnano (SW); also in the SW is a national park; local tax exemptions apply throughout Tierra del Fuego; established in 1884; pop(1980) 29,392; area 21,263 sq km; capital Ushuaia, the southernmost town in the world; economy: sheep raising, timber, fishing, oil and natural gas.

Tierra del Fuego, national park in SW Tierra del Fuego National Territory; borders W with Chile; to the N lies L Fagnano; area 630 sq km; established in 1960.

Tiflis, city in SE European Soviet Union. See Tbilisi.

Tigray, TIGRE *tee'gray*, region in NE Ethiopia, NE Africa; pop(1984e) 2,409,700; area 65,900 sq km; the W half of the region is mountainous with peaks including Mokada (2,295 m); the E half is low lying with a large section below sea-level at the centre of the Danakil Depression; capital Mekelē; chief towns include Adīgrat, Ādwa and Aksum; one of the most severely affected areas in Ethiopia during the drought which began in 1983 and centre of resistance to the government.

Tigris *tī'gris*, SHATT DIJLA (Arab), DICLE *deej'lay* (Turkish), river in SE Turkey and Iraq; rises in a mountain lake (Hazar Gölü), 24 km SE of Elâziğ, E central Turkey; flows SSE past Diyarbakiır and Cizre in Turkey and, before entering Iraq, forms a small section of the Syrian border; once in Iraq it continues SE, roughly parallel with the Euphrates, past Mosul, Sāmarrā', and Baghdād; at Al Qurnah, 64 km NW of Al Basrah, it unites with the Euphrates to form the Shatt al'Arab; the Tigris is much faster flowing and of greater volume than the Euphrates; chief tributaries include the Great Zab, Lesser Zab, and Diyala; navigable to Baghdād for shallow-draft vessels; the Wadi Ath Tharthar flood control project protects Baghdād and its vicinity from floods in addition to irrigating 3,119 sq km of land; other dams on the river divert water for irrigation purposes; below Al 'Amārah there is much swampland on either side of the river; in ancient times the Tigris served as an important transportation route and along its banks are the ruins or sites of ancient Mesopotamian cities such as Nineveh (opposite Mosul), Seleucia, Ashur, and Calah; length 1,850 km.

Tijuana *tee-hwah'na*, 32 32N 117 02W, pop(1980) 461,257, border town in NW Baja California Norte, NW Mexico; on the Pacific Ocean at the frontier with California, USA, 20 km SE of San Diego; airfield; a resort town with casinos and nightclubs; events: horse or dog racing daily and bullfights on most Sundays (April-Oct).

Tikal *tee-kal'*, archaeological site in Petén dept, N Guatemala, 62 km NE of Flores; major city of the Mayan civilization, including vast temples and public buildings; Tikal was declared a national park in 1955, covering an area of 576 sq km.

Tilarán, Cordillera de *tee-la-ran'*, mountain range in NW Costa Rica, Central America; forming a section of the main continental divide; extends 64 km SE from Laguna de Arenal; peaks include the Cerro San Antonio (1,385 m) and the Cerro Cedral (1,559 m).

Tilburg *til'bœrKH*, 51 31N 5 06E, pop(1984e) 221,684, industrial city in Noord Brabant prov, S Netherlands; on the Wilhelmina Canal, 54 km SE of Rotterdam; railway; economy: woollens, metalworking; after Eindhoven, it is the largest business and cultural city in South Netherlands; its traditional wool industry produces approximately 60% of all woollen goods in the Netherlands; acquired town status in 1809; it is the capital of Dutch Catholicism.

Til'bury, 51 28N 0 23E, pop(1981) 11,468, port town in Grays-Tilbury urban area, Thurrock dist, Essex, SE England; on the R Thames estuary, E of London; railway; major port for London and the SE.

Tillicoultry *til-i-coo'tree*, 56 09N 3 46W, pop(1981) 6,161, town in Clackmannan dist, Central region, central Scotland; 5 km NE of Alloa; economy: textiles, stone quarrying.

Tílos *tee'los*, island of the Sporádhes, Greece, in the S Aegean Sea, off the SW coast of Turkey, NW of Ródhos I; area 63 sq km.

Timanfaya, Macizo de *ma-thee'thō THay tee-man-fa'ya*, national park on the island of Lanzarote in the Canary Is, Gran Canaria prov, Canarias region, Spain; area 50 sq km; established in 1974; centre of volcanic activity; the last eruption through 25 orifices took place in 1824.

Timaru *ti-ma'roo*, 44 23S 171 14E, pop(1981) 28,412, port and resort on the E coast of South Island, New Zealand; SW of Christchurch and the Canterbury plain; railway; airfield; economy: trade in meat, wool and grain.

Timiş *tee'meesh*, county in W Romania, bounded to the W by Yugoslavia and to the N by Hungary; pop(1983) 709,354; area 8,692 sq km; capital Timişoara; iron deposits near the capital city.

Timişoara *tee-meesh-wa'ra*, 45 45N 21 15E, pop(1983) 303,499, capital of Timiş county, W Romania; on Bega Canal; university (1962); technical university (1920); fine arts academy; ceded to Romania in 1919; railway; economy: electrical engineering, textiles, chemicals, pharmaceuticals, food processing, footwear, metal; monument: 15th-c Hunyadi Castle.

Timmins, 48 30N 81 20W, pop(1981) 46,114, town in E Ontario, SE central Canada; on the Mattagami river, at the mouth of the Mountjoy river; railway; airfield; economy: mining (zinc, silver).

Timor *tee'mor*, island in SE Asia, the easternmost of the Lesser Sunda group, NW of Australia; comprises part of the Indonesian prov of Nusa Tenggara Timur (former Dutch-ruled territory) in the W and Timor Timur prov (former Portuguese overseas prov now claimed by Indonesia) in the E; area 33,912 sq km; chief towns Kupang, Dili.

Timor Sea, part of the Pacific Ocean, lying SE of the Indonesian island of Timor and NW of the coast of Northern Territory, Australia, between Van Diemen Gulf and Kings Sound; major arm is the Joseph Bonaparte Gulf; receives water from the Daly, Victoria, Ord and Fitzroy rivers; the warm surface current moves SW through the sea; to the NW of Australia, it lies over a wide continental shelf, with depths down to 110 m, but deepens due to the trench off the SE slope of Timor Island.

Timor Timur, EAST TIMOR, LORO SAE, E half of the island of Timor, Indonesia; former Portuguese overseas prov, claimed by Indonesia since 1975 when Indonesian troops entered this half of the island; this annexation was not recognized by the UN; an independence movement established by Fretilin claims to be the 'Revolutionary Government of the Democratic Republic of East Timor'; pop(1980) 555,350; area 14,874 sq km; capital Dili; economy: maize and coffee.

Timsah, Lake *tim-sah'*, BUHEIRET AL TIMSAH, lake on the Suez Canal, NE Egypt; the city of Ismâ'ilîya is situated beside it; connected to the Nile by the Ismâ'ilîya canal.

Tinian *ti'nee-un*, one of the N Mariana Is, W Pacific, 5 km SW of Saipan; area 101 sq km; length 17.6 km; width 7.2 km; there are 4 vast 2,600 m runways, built by the USA at the N end of the island; beside one of the runways a plaque commemorates the bombing of Hiroshima during World War II with the words 'From this loading pit the first atomic bomb ever used in combat was loaded aboard a B-29 aircraft and dropped on Hiroshima, Japan, August 6, 1945;' site of ancient stone columns;

Tinley Park, 41 35N 87 47W, pop(1980) 26,171, town in Cook county, NE Illinois, United States; suburb 39 km SSW of Chicago; railway.

Tínos *tee'nos*, 37 32N 25 08E, 4th largest island of the Kikládhes, Greece, in the S Aegean Sea, SE of Ándros I; area 194 sq km.

Tioman, Pulau *poo-low' tee-ō-man'*, resort island in the South China Sea, SE Asia; situated off the E coast of Pahang state, E Peninsular Malaysia; area 137 sq km.

Tipperary *ti-pu-re'ree*, THIOBRAD ÁRANN (Gael), county in Munster prov, S central Irish Republic; divided into North Riding with a pop of 58,984 and an area of 1,996 sq km, and South Riding with a pop of 76,277 and an area of 2,258 sq km; watered by R Suir; Silvermine Mts to N, Galty Mts to S and Slieve Ardagh Hills to W; capital Clonmel; rich dairy farming area; centre for horse and greyhound breeding.

Tipperary, TIOBRAID ÁRANN (Gael), 52 29N 8 10W, pop(1981) 5,169, market town in Tipperary county, South Riding, Munster, S central Irish Republic; railway; economy: computers, dairy products; event: festival of Irish and modern music and dance at the end of June.

Tiranë *tee-ra'ne*, prov of central Albania; area 1,222 sq km; pop(1980) 297,700; capital Tiranë.

Tiranë, 41 20N 19 50E, pop(1980) 194,000, capital town of Albania and of Tiranë prov; situated in an intermontane valley in the foothills of the Kruja-Dajti Mts, 40 km from the Adriatic Sea; the main political, economic and cultural centre of the country; founded by Turks in the early 17th century; created capital of Albania in 1920; residential section built by the Italians (1939-43); industrial section to the W; university (1957); railway; airport (Rinas); economy: textiles, foodstuffs, footwear, metalworking, ceramics, glass, engineering, wood products, distilling, building materials, furniture; there are coal mines nearby, at Krraba and Priska; in 1951 the V.I. Lenin Hydroelectric Power Plant, the first in the country, was built near Tiranë with Soviet assistance.

Tîrgovişte *tir-go'veesh-te*, 44 56N 25 27E, pop(1983) 82,034, capital of Dîmboviţa county, central Romania, on R Ialomiţa, NW of Bucureşti; railway; formerly capital of Walachia (1383-1698); economy: oil refining, iron, steel, oilfield equipment; monuments: 16th-c cathedral; 14th-c palace.

Tîrgu Jiu *tir'goo joo*, 45 03N 23 17E, pop(1983) 81,488, capital of Gorj county, SW Romania; on R Jiu; established in the 15th century; railway; economy: livestock and timber trade, mining equipment, furniture, clothing.

Tîrgu Mureş *tir'goo moo'resh*, OSORHEI (anc), 46 33N 24 34E, pop(1983) 154,506, capital of Mureş, N central Romania; on R Mureş; the city was rebuilt after a fire in 1876; airfield; railway junction; economy: timber, grain, oil, wine and tobacco trade, fertilizer, furniture; monuments: Cultural Palace containing art gallery, library, museum and music conservatory; Telekiana library (13th-c).

Tiris Zemmour, region in N Mauritania, NW Africa; pop(1982e) 28,000; area 252,900 sq km; capital Fderik; chief towns Zouîrât and Bir Moghrein (Fort Trinquet);

the Route du Mauritanie runs from the SE to the N tip of the region; iron ore, manganese and uranium reserves are mined.

Tìrnăveni *tir-nav-vayn'*, 46 20N 24 17E, pop(1983) 28,634, town in Mureş county, N central Romania; 32 km NE of Blaj; railway; economy: chemicals, power plant.

Tírnavos *tir'nu-vos*, TYRNAVOS (Eng), 39 45N 22 18E, pop(1981) 10,965, town in Lárisa nome (dept), Thessalía region, E Greece; 16 km NW of Lárisa, on a tributary of the R Piniós.

Tirol', federal state of W Austria, bounded by Vorarlberg state to the W, Salzburg and Kärnten states to the E, W Germany to the N and Italy to the S; comprises 9 dists and 278 communities; pop(1981) 586,139; area 12,647 sq km; capital Innsbruck; economy: tourism (earning more foreign currency than any other state), hydroelectric power (Zillertal, Kaunertal), powder metallurgy, diesel engines, vehicles, optical instruments; situated at the junction of numerous trans-continental communications links; drained by the R Inn; lakes include the Achensee, Walchsee, Tristacher See and Schwarzsee.

Tirso, river in central Sardegna (Sardinia); rises on a plateau W of Budduso; flows SW through Lago Omodeo to discharge into the Golfo de Oristano, 5 km WSW of Oristano; length 149 km; chief river of the island; receives R Flumineddu.

Tiruchchirāpalli *ti-roo-chi-ru-pah'li*, 10 45N 78 45E, pop(1981) 608,000, city in Tamil Nadu state, S India; on the Kāveri river; airfield; linked by rail to Dindigul and Neyveli; an educational, religious and commercial centre, noted for its gold, silver and brass working; monuments: fort, shrine of Sringam and a monument to the Hindu god Shiva.

Tirunelveli *ti'roo-nel-vel-ee*, TINNEVELLY, 8 45N 77 43E, pop(1981) 324,000, city in Tamil Nadu state, S India; 135 km SW of Madras; a former imperial city of the Chola kingdom (900-1200 AD); there is an important mission station (St Francis Xavier); economy: sugar refining.

Tisza *ti'sa* or *ti'so* (Hung), TISA (Czech, Rom, Serb), TISSA (Rus), longest tributary of the R Danube in E Europe; rises in the W Ukrainian Carpathian Mts and flows S to meet the Romanian frontier and then the Great Plain (Alföld) of Hungary where it is used for irrigation and hydroelectric power; known as the 'blond' river because of the yellowish loess silt in its water; during the last 100 years 120 bends have been cut off and 4,000 km of flood prevention embankments have been built, enabling 30,000 sq km of farmland to be reclaimed in Hungary; there are power stations at Tisalök and Kisköre; the chemical industry has developed on the banks of the Tisza at the new town of Leninváros; the river passes through the S prairie of Hortobágy National Park; the Tisza meets the Danube SW of Beograd; length 962 km (595 km in Hungary); navigable for 780 km.

Titicaca *tee-tee-ka'ka*, lake in SE Peru and W Bolivia; largest lake in South America (area 8,289 sq km) and highest large lake (3,812 m) in the world; a major transportation artery between Peru and Bolivia; length 177 km; width 56 km; max depth 475 m; consists of two sections connected by the Strait of Tiquina: L Chucuito (NE, 137 km long, 56 km wide) and L Uinamarca (SW, 24 km long, 56 km wide); receives the Río Suches in Bolivia and the Ayaviri, Lampa and Huenque rivers in Peru; its only outlet is the Río Desaguadero which flows into L Uru Uru and on into L Poopó; steamers run from Guaqui (Bolivia), the most important port on the lake, to the Peruvian port of Puno; the mining centre, Matilde, is on the lake's NE shore; the lake is a hunting (ducks, partridge) and fishing (trout) resort; the Bolivian Yacht Club is based here; contains 36 islands, including the islands of Titicaca and Coati with archaeological remains; on the SW shore is Copacabana which served as a place of recreation for the Royal Inca family, it is famous for its sanctuary (which contains valuable paintings and jewels gifted to the Virgin) and temple (a Franciscan monastery) constructed at the beginning of the 17th century, which contains a statue of the Virgin de Copacabana, carved in 1576 by the Indian Tito Yupanqui; many pilgrimages are made here. The ruins of Tiahuanaco, former centre of Tiahuanaco empire, lie near the lake, 60 km from La Paz.

Titograd *tee'tō-grad*, formerly PODGORICA, 42 28N 19 17E, pop(1981) 132,290, capital of Crna Gora (Montenegro) republic, Yugoslavia; on R Morava, N of L Scutari; birthplace of Diocletian; university (1973); airfield; railway; economy: aluminium, metalworking, furniture making, tobacco.

Titov Veles *tee'tov ve'les*, KOPRÜLU (Turk), 41 43N 21 49E, pop(1981) 64,799, town in Makedonija republic, Yugoslavia; on R Vardar, SSE of Skopje; railway junction; economy: fruit and vegetable trade.

Titovo Užice *tee'to-vo oo'zhit-se*, 43 52N 19 50E, pop(1981) 77,049, town in W Srbija (Serbia) republic, Yugoslavia; SSW of Beograd; railway; economy: chromium and manganese mining nearby; fruit and livestock trade; bacon, sausages and smoked meat; cheese; distilling (slivovitz and prepečenica); hydroelectric power.

Titusville, 28 37N 80 49W, pop(1980) 31,910, county seat of Brevard county, E Florida, United States; on the R Indian (a lagoon), 55 km E of Orlando; railway; the construction of the space centre at nearby Cape Canaveral in the 1950s caused a ten-fold population increase in less than a decade.

Tivaouanné *tee-va-wa'nay*, 14 57N 16 45W, town in Senegal, W Africa; 72 km ENE of Dakar; railway.

Tivat *tee'vaht*, 42 25N 18 42E, pop(1981) 9,315, town in SW Crna Gora (Montenegro) republic, Yugoslavia; on Tivat Bay, an inlet of the Gulf of Kotor on the Adriatic coast; tourist spot with bathing beaches often visited by asthma sufferers during winter; airfield; economy: naval harbour, shipyard, pottery, tourism.

Tiv'erton, 50 55N 3 29W, pop(1981) 14,982, town in Mid Devon dist, Devonshire, SW England; on the R Exe, 20 km N of Exeter; railway; economy: textiles, engineering.

Tizi-Ouzou *tee-zee' oo-zoo'*, 36 44N 4 05E, pop(1982) 181,920, chief town of Tizi-Ouzou dept, N Algeria, N Africa; 88 km E of Alger; railway.

Tjörn *churn*, Swedish island in the Skagerrak, at N entrance to the Kattegat, off SW coast of Sweden, 32 km NW of Göteborg (Gothenburg), just S of Orust I, separated from mainland by 3 km wide channel; area 147 sq km; length 16 km; width 5-13 km; administered by Göteborg och Bohus county.

Tlaxcala *tlahs-kah'lah*, state in central Mexico; bounded N by Hidalgo, NW by México and otherwise surrounded by Puebla; a mountainous region situated in Mexico's central plateau; in the S is Malinche volcano (4,461 m); drained by the Zahuapan river; pop(1980) 547,261; area 4,016 sq km; capital Tlaxcala; economy: maize, alfalfa, barley, onions, garlic, wheat, lentils, oats, cattle (raised for milk and for bullfighting), textiles, chemicals.

Tlaxcala, TLAXCALA DE XICOHTÉNCATL, 19 20N 98 12W, pop(1980e) 15,000, capital of Tlaxcala state, central Mexico; 96 km E of Ciudad de México (Mexico City); economy: food processing, alcohol (*pulque*), textiles; monuments: the church of San Francisco (1521) is the oldest in Mexico; the first Christian sermon was preached to the 'New World' here; 5 km from Tlaxcala are the ruins of the pyramid of San Esteban de Tizátlan; event: annual fair 29 Oct-15 Nov.

Tlemcen *tlem-sen'*, 34 53N 1 21W, pop(1982) 220,884, chief town of Tlemcen dept, NW Algeria, N Africa; 113 km SW of Oran; capital of major Moroccan dynasties between the 12th and 16th centuries; despite French occupation from 1842 the town has a well-preserved Muslim culture; railway; economy: agriculture, rug manufacture, tourism; monuments: Almovarid great mosque (1135), Grand mosque, Museum of Bel Hassane.

Toamasina, TAMATAVE, 18 10S 49 23E, pop(1978e) 59,100, port on the E coast of Madagascar on the Indian Ocean and chief town of a prov of the same; 367 km NE of Antananarivo; the main port of Madagascar and a popular tourist resort; Ivoloina Gardens 11 km N contain many varieties of vegetables; surrounded by sugar cane plantations; railway to Antananarivo; airfield.

Tobago *tō-bay'gō*, island in the West Indies; part of the Republic of Trinidad and Tobago; area 300 sq km; pop(1980) 39,500; chief town Scarborough; united with Trinidad in 1889; luxury hotel-conference centre at Rocky Point and tourist complex at Minster Point; airport.

Tobol, river in N Kazakhskaya SSR and SW Siberian Rossiyskaya, Soviet Union; rises SW of Dzhetygara, N Kazakhskaya SSR, then flows NNE past Kurgan and Yalutorovsk to join the R Irtysh at Tobol'sk; length 1,667 km; chief tributaries include the Tavda, Iska, Tap, Iset', Ubagan, and Toguzak rivers; navigable in its lower course.

Tobruk, town in Libya, N Africa. See Tubruq.

Tocantins *to-kan-cheens'*, river in N central Brazil; rises in Goiás state in several headstreams; flows N, dividing Goiás in two, then forms part of the border between Goiás and Maranhão states; crosses Pará state flowing past Marabá to enter the Río Pará 80 km SW of Belém; its chief tributary is the Río Araguaia; also receives the Parańa, Somno and Manuel Alves Grande rivers.

Tocopilla *tō-kō-peel'ya*, 22 05S 70 12W, pop(1982) 26,123, port and capital of Tocopilla prov, Antofagasta, N central Chile; two sports stadiums; beaches at Punta Blanca and Caleta; railway; airfield (at Barriles, 12 km away); economy: exports nitrate and iodine from María Elena (at 76 km) and Pedro de Valdivia (at 106 km); the town contains a copper concentrate plant and an electric plant which generates power for the Chuquicamata copper mine, 150 km to the E.

Tod'morden, 53 43N 2 05W, pop(1981) 11,972, town in Calderdale borough, West Yorkshire, N England; on the R Calder and the Rochdale Canal, 12 km NE of Rochdale; railway; economy: engineering, textiles.

Todos los Santos, Lago *tō'dō lōs san'tōs*, lake in Los Lagos region, S central Chile; near the frontier with Argentina; separated from L Llanquihue by Osorno Volcano; 56 km NE of Puerto Montt; drains into the Reloncaví Sound via the Río Petrohue, a popular tourist resort, it is surrounded by wooded slopes and volcanoes; situated in the Vicente Perez Rosales National Park.

Togliatti, town in W Soviet Union. See Tol'yatti.

Togo *tō'gō*, official name Republic of Togo, RÉPUBLIQUE TOGOLAISE (Fr), a republic in W Africa, bounded W by Ghana, N by Burkina and E by Benin; timezone GMT; area 56,600 sq km; pop (1984e) 2,926,000; capital Lomé; chief towns include Sokodé, Palimé, Atakpamé, Bassar, Tsévié and Anécho; the country is ethnologically divided into 2 halves with peoples mainly of Hamitic origin in the N and of Ewe origin in the S; there are 37 different tribes in total plus a small European and Syrian-Lebanese community; French is the official language, though there are many local languages in use, including Ewe and Mana in the S, and Dagomba, Tem and Kabre of the Voltaic group in the N; 70% of the pop holds local beliefs, the remainder being either Christian (20%) or Muslim (10%); the unit of currency is the franc CFA; national holiday 27 April; membership of AfDB, CEAO (observer), EAMA, ECA, ECOWAS, Entente, FAO, G-77, GATT, IBRD, ICAO, ICO, IDA, IFAD, IFC, ILO, IMF, INTERPOL, ITU, NAM, OAU, OCAM, UN, UNESCO, UPU, WHO, WIPO, WMO, WTO.

Physical description. Togo rises from the Gulf of Guinea, with a short lagoon coast, past low lying plains to the Atakora mountains which run NE to SW across the N of the country, the highest peak being Pic Baumann (986 m). The NW of the country is characterized by flat plains. There are two major rivers in Togo, the R Oti which flows SW across the N tip of the country forming part of the Ghanaian border, and the R Mono which flows S from its source NE of Sokodé eventually to form part of the Togo-Benin border before entering the Gulf of Guinea.

Climate. Togo has a tropical climate which can be divided into 3 zones: (1) In the S rain falls in all seasons, especially during the 'Guinea Monsoon' (May to Oct); (2) the central area has 2 rainy seasons with maxima in May-June and Oct and (3) in the N these merge into one season (July-Sept). The heaviest rainfall is in the mountains of the W, SW and centre. The N dry season (Oct to April) is hot, has very low humidity and is subject to the dry and often dust-laden *harmattan* wind which blows from the NE. At Lomé the average annual rainfall is 875 mm.

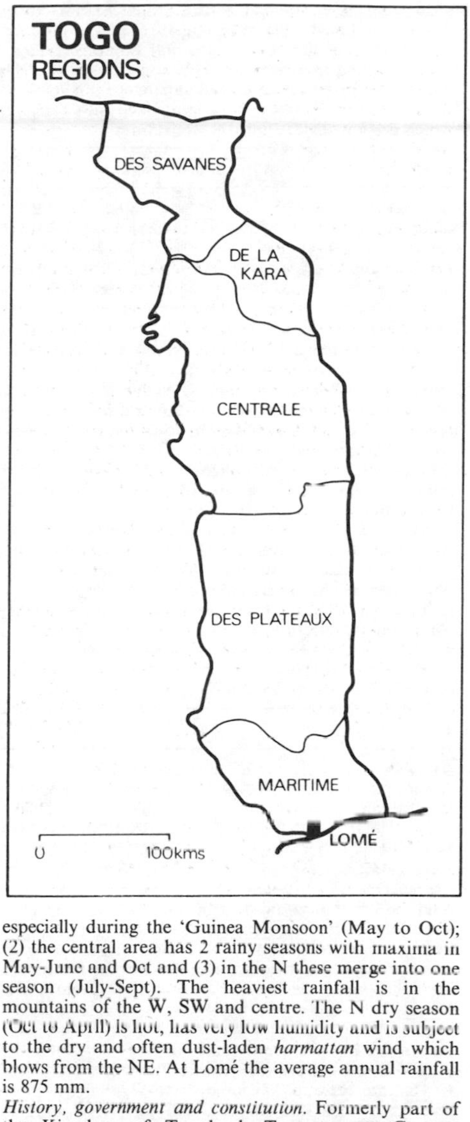

History, government and constitution. Formerly part of the Kingdom of Togoland, Togo was a German protectorate from 1894 till 1914 when French and British forces invaded. In 1922 it became a mandate of the League of Nations and was divided between France (French Togo, with its own governmental structure) and Britain (administered as part of British Gold Coast). In 1946 the mandates became trusteeships of the United Nations and in 1957 an election was held in French Togo which ultimately resulted in French Togo becoming fully independent. Meanwhile the residents of British Togoland voted (1957) to join the Gold Coast which became the new independent nation of Ghana. A bloodless military coup in 1967 installed a military government which terminated with a return to civilian rule in 1980. The constitution provides for a 67 member National Assembly, a president and cabinet elected for five year periods from a single political party.

Economy. The extraction of phosphate rock and bauxite forms a major part of the economy with limestone, iron ore and marble also important. The majority of agriculture is subsistence but cash crops include plantation-grown coffee, cocoa and cotton crops. Manufacturing industry is based on cement, steel, oil processing, food processing, handicrafts, textiles and beverages. Togo's main trading partners are France, the UK, West Germany, the Netherlands and Japan.

Administrative divisions. Togo is divided into 5 regions which are sub-divided into 21 prefectures:

Region	*area (sq km)*	*pop(1981)*
Des Savanes	8,602	326,826
De la Kara	11,630	432,626
Centrale	13,182	269,174
Des Plateaux	16,975	561,656
Maritime	6,396	1,039,700

Togo, Lake, lagoon in S Togo, W Africa; just NW of Anécho it connects with the R Mono and receives the Haho and Sio rivers.

Tōhoku *tō-hō'koo*, mountainous region in N Honshū island, Japan; bounded S by Kanto and SW by Chūbu regions, W by the Sea of Japan, E by the Pacific Ocean and N by Hokkaidō island across the Tsugaru-kaikyō Strait; the least industrialized of Honshū's regions; pop(1980) 9,572,000; area 66,959 sq km; economy: rice, fruit, timber, livestock, fishing, iron and steel, oil, winter sports; events: Osorezan Jizo festival at Mt Osore in Aomori prefecture, when people come to hear the voices of dead members of their families through the Itako, blind women who are believed to have gained supernatural powers (July); Soma-nomaoi horse-chasing festival, in Fukushima prefecture, the major event being held in Haranomachi where samurai on horseback vie with each other for a sacred banner which has been shot into the air (July); Tōhoku is divided into 6 prefectures as follows:

Prefecture	*area (sq km)*	*pop(1980)*
Akita	11,609	1,257,000
Aomori	9,614	1,524,000
Fukushima	13,782	2,035,000
Iwate	15,277	1,422,000
Miyagi	7,291	2,082,000
Yamagata	9,326	1,252,000

Tokat *to-kat'*, prov in N central Turkey; pop(1980) 624,508; area 9,958 sq km; capital Tokat.

Tokay or **Tokaj** *to'koy*, 48 08N 21 24E, town in Borsod-Abaúj-Zemplén county, NE Hungary; in the foothills of Mt Tokay where the R Bodrog meets the R Tisza, NW of Nýiregyháza; centre of a notable wine-producing area.

Tokelau *tō-kel-a'oo*, formerly UNION ISLANDS, island territory under New Zealand administration, consisting of 3 small atolls in the S Pacific Ocean, lying between 8° and 10° S and between 171° and 173° W, 480 km N of Western Samoa and about 3,500 km NNE of New Zealand; area 10.12 sq km; pop(1981) 1,572; timezone GMT −11; chief settlement Nukunonu; the population is evenly distributed between the 3 atolls; the inhabitants are Polynesian, retaining linguistic, family, and cultural links with Western Samoa; Tokelauan is usually spoken on the atolls but most people also speak English which is taught as a second language; the inhabitants are citizens of New Zealand, and there has been considerable migration from the Tokelaus to New Zealand; each atoll has a school catering for children between the ages of 5 and 15; both Western Samoa and New Zealand currencies are used.

Physical description. The 3 atolls are Atafu (2.03 sq km), Nukunonu (5.46 sq km), and Fakaofo (2.63 sq km). The central atoll, Nukunonu, lies 92 km from Atafu and 56 km from Fakaofo. Each atoll consists of a number of low lying, scrub covered, reef-bound islets encircling a lagoon. These islets, rising no higher than 5 m above sea level, vary in length from 90 m to 6 km and in width from a few metres to 200 m. The climate is hot and humid but is tempered by trade winds.

History, government and constitution. The islands became a British protectorate in 1877 and were formally annexed in 1916 when the islands, then known as the Union Is, were included with the Gilbert and Ellice Islands Colony. In 1925, the islands were separated from the Gilbert and Ellice group and administrative control was transferred to New Zealand; the 1948 Tokelau Islands Act, included Tokelau within the boundaries of New Zealand from 1 Jan 1949. The Office of Tokelau Affairs in Apia, Western Samoa, is the administrating body, although the local people generally govern themselves through their own customs and village councils (one council for each island).

Economy. Soils are thin and infertile, and apart from copra, agricultural products are of a basic subsistence nature, notably coconuts, pulaka, breadfruit, ta'amu, pawpaw, the fruit of the edible pandanus and bananas. Livestock comprises pigs and fowls. The principal revenue earners are copra, stamps, souvenir coins, and handicrafts. Money is also remitted to Tokelauan families from relatives in New Zealand.

Tokorozawa *tō-kō-rō-dza'wa*, 35 48N 139 28E, pop(1980) 236,476, city in Saitama prefecture, Kanto region, E Honshū island, Japan; NW of Tōkyo; railway.

Tokushima *to-koo-shee'ma*, 34 03N 134 34E, pop(1980) 249,343, port capital of Tokushima prefecture, NE Shikoku island, Japan; on the Kii-suido Channel; university (1949); railway; economy: cotton, saké.

Tōkyo *tō'kyō*, 35 40N 139 45E, pop(1980) 8,351,893 (metropolitan dist), seaport capital of Japan, in Tōkyo prefecture, Kanto region, E Honshū island; on N shore of Tōkyo-wan bay; founded in 12th century, rising in importance after 1603 when it became the headquarters of the founder of the Tokugawa shogunate; became the imperial capital in 1868, with the restoration of imperial power, taking over from Kyōto; Ginza is Japan's most famous shopping dist; Kanda dist contains schools, colleges, publishers and universities; residential areas include Shitamachi (on the banks of the R Sumida), Yamanote (W Tōkyo), Roppongi and Akasaka (diplomatic quarter); 32 universities; railway; airport; economy: shipbuilding, engineering, chemicals, textiles, electrical goods, vehicles; monuments: Tōkyo Tower (1958) is the tallest metal tower in the world and contains shops, restaurants and a science museum; the Idemitsu art gallery contains Japanese ceramics and prints; in Chiyoda ku dist is the 17th-c Imperial Palace; the Imperial Palace Gardens are only opened to the public twice a year, on 2 January and 19 April, the Emperor's birthdays; the Meiji Shrine, completed in 1920 in honour of the Emperor Meiji and his wife, is situated in a park in the centre of Tōkyo; the park also contains an iris garden with over 150 different varieties of iris and the Homotsu den museum, which contains objects belonging to Emperor Meiji; Asakusa Kannon temple was founded in 645; 10 km SE of central Tōkyo, on reclaimed land in the N of Tōkyo-wan Bay, is the Tōkyo Disneyland, opened in April 1983; events: Sanja Matsuri at the Asakusa Shrine in May; Sanno festival at the Hie Shrine in June.

Tolbukhin or **Tolbuhin** *tol-boo'KHin*, okrug (prov) of NE Bulgaria bounded to the E by the Black Sea and to the N by Romania; area 4,716 sq km; pop(1981) 252,000.

Tolbukhin, 43 34N 27 51E, pop(1981) 97,310, commercial and agricultural capital of Tolbukhin okrug (prov), NE Bulgaria; 512 km NE of Sofia; formerly called Dobrich but in 1949 it was named after the Russian general who captured the city in 1944; railway; economy: food processing, metal products and textiles.

Toledo *to-lee'dō*, dist in S Belize, Central America; bounded W and S by Guatemala and E by the Gulf of Honduras; the Maya mountains rise to 1,000 m at Richardson Peak; pop(1980) 11,762; area 4,647 sq km; capital Punta Gorda; Maya ruins at Lubaantun; economy: rice, timber, bananas.

Toledo *to-lay'dō*, prov in Castilla-La Mancha region, central Spain; in the middle of the R Tagus basin with mountains to N and S reaching into La Mancha;

pop(1981) 471,806; area 15,368 sq km; capital Toledo; economy: footwear, furniture, pharmaceuticals, cocoa, chocolate, clothes, linen, cement, meat processing.

Toledo, TOLETUM (Lat), 39 50N 4 02W, pop(1981) 57,769, capital of Toledo prov, Castilla-La Mancha, Spain; on R Tagus, 71 km SSW of Madrid; former capital of Visigothic kingdom of Castile and Spain; formerly famous for its sword-blades; railway; economy: tourism, engraved metalwork, silk, artwork, confectionery; monuments: Moorish Alcazar; French-Gothic cathedral; El Greco's House; churches of St Thomas and St Romanus; El Transito synagogue with Mudejar decoration; Santa Cruz museum with paintings by El Greco; convent of San Juan de los Reyes; events: Holy Week; fiesta of Olivio in April, May; fiesta and fair in Aug.

Toledo *to-lee'dō*, 41 39N 83 33W, pop(1980) 354,635, county seat of Lucas county, NW Ohio, United States; a port at the mouth of the R Maumee, at the W end of L Erie; formed by the union of 2 settlements in 1833; university (1872); railway; economy: vehicles, glass and fabricated metal products, machinery; trade in coal and grain; one of the country's largest rail centres; monuments: museum of art, zoological gardens, Crosby Gardens, Fort Meigs State Memorial, Bluebird Passenger Train. involved in the 'Toledo War', 1835-36, when there was a boundary dispute between Ohio and Michigan.

Toliara, TOLIARY, formerly TULÉAR, 23 20S 43 41E, pop(1978e) 34,000, port in SW Madagascar, at the end of Highway 7, overlooking the Mozambique Channel, 945 km SW of Antananarivo; chief town of a prov of the same name; airfield.

Tolima *to-lee'ma*, dept in W central Colombia, South America; extends along the Magdalena valley, flanked by the Cordillera Central (W) and the Cordillera Oriental (E); includes the volcanic peaks Nevado del Ruiz, Nevado del Tolima (W) and Nevado de Huila (S); pop(1985) 1,028,239; area 23,512 sq km; capital Ibagué.

Tolima, Nevado del, Andean volcano in Tolima dept, W central Colombia, South America; rises to 5,215 m in the Cordillera Central, 27 km NNW of Ibagué; at the foot are the thermal waters of El Rancho.

Tolna *tol-nah*, county in SW Hungary; bounded to the E by the R Danube; drained by Danube, Sió and Sárviz rivers; pop(1984e) 268,000; area 3,702 sq km; capital Szekszárd; chief towns include Paks, Bonyhad and Gyönk; there are over 100 villages; game reserve at Gemenc; economy: leather, food processing, wine, pig farming, agricultural machinery, precision tools, tapestries (Sarkoz); there are nuclear power plants at Paks.

Toluca *to-loo'ka*, TOLUCA DE LERDO, 19 17N 99 39W, pop(1980) 357,071, capital of México state, central Mexico; 66 km W of Ciudad de México (Mexico City) at an alt of 2,675 m; founded in 1535; university (1956); economy: textiles, pottery, food processing; monuments: the Tercer Orden and Vera Cruz churches; convent of Carmen; Museo de Bellas Artes; Palacio de Gobierno; the Museo del Arte Popular has a display of local craft work.

Toluca, Nevado de *nay-vah'dō day*, national park in S México state, S central Mexico; area 510 sq km; established in 1936; contains the extinct volcano, Nevado de Toluca, which rises to 4,577 m; the peak has deep crater lakes; the volcano was known to the Aztecs as Zinantécatl.

Tol'yatti, TOGLIATTI, STAVROPOL' (-1964), 53 32N 49 24E, pop(1983) 560,000, town in Kuybyshevskaya oblast, Rossiyskaya, Soviet Union; on the Kuybyshev reservoir; founded in 1738; the entire city was relocated in the mid-1950s when it was flooded by the reservoir of the nearby hydroelectric power plant; rail terminus; economy: synthetic rubber, fertilizers, machine building, foodstuffs.

Tomar *too-mar'*, 39 36N 8 25W, pop(1981) 13,800, town in Santarém dist, central Portugal; on the R Nabão, 45 km SE of Leiria; divided into 2 parishes; railway; economy: textiles, paper, cork and distilling; monuments: convent-castle of the Knights Templar and Church of São João Baptista; events: municipal holiday first week in March; festival of the Tabuleiros, July in even numbered years; Santa Cita in Sept and Santa Iria in late Oct.

Tomaszów Mazowiecki *tom-a'shoof mazh-ov-yet-skee*, 51 33N 20 02E, pop(1983) 65,600, industrial town in Piotrków voivodship, central Poland; on R Pilica; originally a weavers' settlement; in SE part of town is the Niebieskie Źródła (Blue Springs) nature reserve with mineral springs; railway; economy: synthetic fibres, woollens; monument: regional museum in a former manor house (1812).

Tomba'li, region in Guinea-Bissau, W Africa; pop(1979) 55,099.

Tombouctou *tō-book-too'*, TIMBUKTU *tim-buk-too'* (Eng), 16 49N 2 59W, pop(1976) 20,483, town in Gao region, N Mali, W Africa; 690 km NE of Bamako at the NE end of the Macina depression; settled in 1098 it expanded commercially and became one of the chief centres of Muslim learning; the city's wealth was destroyed by an invading Moroccan army in 1551; the abolition of slavery caused a further decline in prosperity; Tombouctou was seized by the French in 1893; airfield; a camel caravan from the Taoudeni salt mines arrives each year with salt to be sold and distributed throughout the Sahel; the adjoining town of Kabara serves as a port on the R Niger; economy: tourism, salt, power plant; monuments: 13th-c Djinguereber Mosque; Sankore and Sidi Yahya mosques, dating from the 14th and 15th centuries respectively; the tombs of Sheikh el Moktar and Sidi Ahmed Ben Amar.

Tomé *tō-may'*, 36 38S 72 57W, pop(1982) 40,032, town in Concepción prov, Bío-Bío, central Chile; railway.

Tomelloso *to-me-lyō'so*, 39 10N 3 02W, pop(1981) 26,655, town in Ciudad Real prov, Castilla-La Mancha, S central Spain; 86 km ENE of Ciudad Real; railway; economy: livestock, wine, vegetables, grain, light engineering.

Tomorrit, MT TOMOR (Eng), mountain in SE Albania rising to 2,480 m S of Elbasan.

Tomsk, 56 30N 85 05E, pop(1983) 459,000, river port capital of Tomskaya oblast, W central Siberian Rossiyskaya, Soviet Union; on the R Tom', 60 km from its confluence with the R Ob'; founded in 1604 around a fort, Tomsk was a major Siberian trade centre until bypassed by construction of the Trans-Siberian railway in the 1890s; university (1888); railway; airfield; economy: machine building, metalworking, chemicals, pharmaceuticals.

Tonawan'da, North (Iroquoian, 'swift water'), 43 02N 78 53W, pop(1980) 35,760, town in Niagara county, W New York, United States; 18 km N of Buffalo; railway; economy: timber, paper, metal goods.

Tonbridge *tun'brij*, 51 12N 0 16E, pop(1981) 34,491, town in Tonbridge and Malling dist, Kent, SE England, N of Royal Tunbridge Wells; railway.

Tong'a, FRIENDLY IS, island group in the SW Pacific Ocean, 2,250 km NE of New Zealand and 640 km E of Fiji; area 646 sq km; pop(1984) 96,592; capital Nuku'alofa, timezone GMT +13; 68% of the population lives on the main island of Tongatapu; the population comprises mainly Tongans (98%), a Polynesian group with a small mixture of Melanesian; Christianity is the dominant religion; English is the official language with Polynesian dialects widely spoken; the unit of currency is the pa'anga; membership: ADB, Commonwealth, ESCAP, ITU, UPU, South Pacific Commission, South Pacific Forum, South Pacific Bureau for Economic Cooperation, WHO.

Physical description. The 169 islands of Tonga, 36 of which are inhabited, are divided into 3 main groups: Vava'u, Ha'apai, and Tongatapu-Eua. Tongatapu, the largest island, has an area of 258.6 sq km. The Tongatapu and Ha'apai groups are low lying islands of coral formation. The islands of the Vava'u group, in the extreme N, are high and mountainous. The W islands are mainly volcanic, with low cones (some still active), between 500 and 1,000 m high. Those on the E side are mostly low coral atolls. Most of the non-volcanic low lying islands have no running streams. The extinct volcano of Kao, rising to 1,014 m, is the highest point in Tonga.

Climate. The climate is semi-tropical with a mean annual temperature of 23°C and a mean annual rainfall of 1,750 mm on Tongatapu and 2,750 mm on Vava'u. It is hot and humid between Jan and March, with temperatures of 32°C, but pleasantly cool during the rest of the year. There are occasional hurricanes during the summer months.

History, government and constitution. Tonga became a British protectorate in 1899, though still under its own monarchy. On 4 June 1970, it became a fully independent country. Its constitution, dating from 1875, provides for a government consisting of sovereign, privy council, cabinet, unicameral legislative assembly and the judiciary. The legislative assembly consists of cabinet members, 7 nobles (elected by the 33 hereditary nobles of Tonga), and 7 people's representatives elected by universal adult suffrage for 3-year terms.

Economy. The economy is largely based on agriculture. Copra, coconuts, bananas, and water-melons are the chief exports, sent mainly to New Zealand, Australia, and Holland. Yams, taro, cassava, groundnuts, rice, maize, tobacco, sugar cane, and citrus fruits are among the products grown for local consumption. The processing of coconuts into copra and dessicated coconut is the only significant industry. Tourism and cottage handicrafts are small but growing industries. The chief imports are textiles, foodstuffs, fuel oils, machinery and transport equipment, and building supplies and materials.

Tongariro *tong-ga-ree'roo*, 39 08S 175 42E, active volcano rising to 1,968 m in Tongariro national park in central SW North Island, New Zealand; the national park also contains the active volcanoes of Ruapehu and Ngauruhoe; a skiing resort in winter; the park contains many historical Maori sites; area 765 sq km; established in 1894.

Tongatapu *tong'a-ta-poo*, 21 10S 175 10W, coral island of S Tonga, S Pacific Ocean; area 258.6 sq km; pop(1984) 66,420; chief town and capital of Tonga is Nuku'alofa; the island is flat, rising to only 18.2 m, and covered by coconut plantations; site of Fua'amotu Airport; offshore there are a number of uninhabited coral islands.

Tongeren *tong'ur-un*, dist of Limburg prov, NE Belgium; area 631 sq km; pop(1982) 176,819.

Tongeren, TONGRES *tō̃gre* (Fr), 50 47N 5 28E, pop(1982) 29,765, rural market town in Tongeren dist, S Limburg prov, Belgium; on the banks of the R Jeker; founded in the 1st century AD, it is the oldest town in Belgium; monument: basilica of Our Lady.

Tongking, Gulf of *tang-king*, gulf of Indo-China, situated E of Vietnam and W of Hainan I, China; an inlet of the South China Sea.

Tongshan, town in Jiangsu prov, E China. See Xuzhou.

Tonkolili *ton-kō-lee'lee*, dist in Northern prov, Sierra Leone, pop(1974) 206,321; area 7,003 sq km; capital Magburaka.

Tonlé Sap *ton-lay sap'*, GREAT LAKE (Eng), freshwater lake in W central Cambodia; lies in a depression on the Cambodian Plain and acts as a natural flood reservoir; area 2,850 sq km during the dry season; linked to the Mekong R by the Tonlé Sap R (115 km long), the confluence of the 2 being at Phnom Penh; seasonal reversal of the Tonlé Sap R, such that during the dry season the flow of the Tonlé Sap R is toward the Mekong R, while during the wet season (June-Nov), the Tonlé Sap lake receives the floodwaters of the Mekong R; the height of the lake is raised by some 9 m, while the area of the lake is almost tripled during the wet season; some 6,475 sq km of forest surrounding the lake is inundated with floodwater during the wet season providing an excellent breeding ground for fish; Tonlé Sap fish are one of the major natural resources of Cambodia; Tonlé Sap lake and river are an important communications route, but problems of silting during the dry, low-water season restrict navigation to between Phnom Penh and Kompong Chhnang; the lake is considered to have been a gulf, which has gradually been cut off from the sea by the sediments of the Mekong river.

Tønsberg *tœns'ber*, 59 16N 10 25E, seaport and capital of Vestfold county, SE Norway, on N end of Notteroy I, at head of Tønsberg Fjord, an inlet on the W of Oslo Fjord; nautical college; railway; economy: shipbuilding; whaling ships sailed from here until whaling was stopped for conservation reasons in 1951; oldest city in Norway.

Toowoom'ba, 27 35S 151 54E, pop(1981) 63,401, city in Darling Downs stat div, Queensland, Australia; 130 km W of Brisbane; railway; airfield; economy: commercial centre for the rich agricultural Darling Downs area; trading in meat, wool, wheat, dairy produce; engineering, food processing, iron, clothing, agricultural machinery; monuments: Early Settlers Museum; St Matthew's church (1859); event: carnival of flowers in Sept.

Topeka *te-pee'ka* (Siouan, 'potato-good-place'), 39 03N 95 40W, pop(1980) 115,266, capital of state in Shawnee county, E Kansas, United States; on R Kansas, 88 km W of Kansas City; settled by anti-slavery colonists in 1854; capital since 1867; university (1865); railway; economy: marketing and processing centre for agricultural products, particularly cattle and wheat; railway engineering; an important centre for psychiatric research and therapy.

Topes de Collantes *tō'pez dhay co-lan'tez*, resort area in the Escambray Mts of central Cuba; 21 km N of Trinidad; originally noted as a health resort for tuberculosis patients; the sanatorium (1936-54) is now a teacher training college.

Topol'čany *top'pl-cha-ni*, 48 33N 18 10E, pop(1984) 34,319, town in Západoslovenský region, W Slovak Socialist Republic, Czechoslovakia; on R Nitra, N of Nitra; railway.

Torbay', pop(1981) 116,200, urban area in Devonshire, SW England; includes the resort towns of Torquay and Paignton; railway; economy: tourism, horticulture, electronics.

Torino *to-ree'no*, prov of Piemonte region, NW Italy; pop(1981) 2,345,771; area 6,830 sq km; capital Torino.

Torino, TURIN *tyoo-rin'* (Eng), AUGUSTA TAURINORUM (anc), 45 04N 7 40E, pop(1981) 1,117,154, capital city of Torino prov, Piemonte region, NW Italy; in a fertile plain on the left bank of the R Po; founded by the Taurini, the city retains its rectangular street plan from Roman times; a Roman colony under Augustus; capital of the kingdom of Sardinia (1720); centre of the 19th-c *Risorgimento*; first capital of the kingdom of Italy until 1865; archbishopric; university (1404); airport; railway; economy: iron, steel and non-ferrous metal products; manufacture of cars, agricultural equipment, engines and rolling-stock, underwater defence systems, man-made fibres, clothing, woollens, cotton, vermouths, confectionery, printing and publishing, domestic electrical equipment, plastic and rubber products; monuments: Porta Palatina (city gate), chief surviving Roman structure; 15th-c cathedral, on the site of a 4th-c basilica; palaces include the Palazzo Reale (1646-58), Palazzo Carignano (by Guarini, 1680) and Palazzo Madama (1718-20); Mole Antonelliana, begun in 1863 as a synagogue, with a tall spire added in 1879-80 (167 m high); events: carnival (Feb); Salone dell'Automobile (International Motor Show) and Salone del Veicolo Industriale (Industrial Vehicle Show) in alternate years.

Tornea, town in Finland. See Tornio.

Torness', nuclear power station, 7 km SE of Dunbar, East Lothian, Scotland; came into operation, using advanced gas-cooled reactors, 1987.

Torneträsk *tor'nu-tresk*, TORNE (Eng), elongated lake in N Norrbotten county, N Sweden; near Norwegian border; extends NW to SE parallel with road from Narvik to Kiruna; area 322 sq km; drains into the R Tornio in the SE.

Tornio *tor'nee-o*, TORNEA *tor'na-o* (Swed), 65 52N 24 10E, pop(1982), town in Lappi prov, NW Finland; at the mouth of the Tornionjoki where it meets the Gulf of Bothnia and on the Swedish frontier opposite Haparanda; established in 1621; railway; economy: steel, brewing, timber, leather and salmon fishing; events: Tornio Valley Summer, Rapids Shooting contest and White Fish Festival in July.

Tornio, TORNE ÄLV (Swed), river in N and NE Sweden; issues from L Torneträsk in NW Sweden; flows SE and S through Norrbotten county, forming in its lower course a section of the Swedish-Finnish border; discharges into head of the Gulf of Bothnia at Tornio; length 566 km.

Törökszentmiklós *tu'ruk-sent-mi'klosh*, 47 11N 20 27E, pop(1984e) 25,000, town in Szolnok county, E central Hungary; 16 km E of Szolnok; economy: grain and livestock trade, machinery.

Toronto *to-ron'tō*, 43 42N 79 25W, pop(1981) 599,217, pop(1981) 2,998,947 (metropolitan area), capital of Ontario prov, SE Canada; on the N shore of L Ontario, at the mouth of the Don river; the largest city in Canada; founded as an early fur-trading centre, the French built a fort here in 1749; it was destroyed by its garrison in 1759 and the site was occupied by the British; settled by the United Empire Loyalists in 1793, the town was named York; capital of Upper Canada in 1796; the town was twice captured by the Americans in the War of 1812; it was incorporated as a city in 1834 when its name was changed to Toronto; in 1837 it became the centre of a separatist rebellion; the Act of Union in 1840 removed the capital to Kingston; in 1849 Toronto again became the capital of Upper Canada and in 1867 it became capital of Ontario; University of Toronto (1827); the harbour is ice-free April-Nov; railway; 2 airports; economy: meat packing, metal products, machinery, clothing, food processing, petroleum products, trade in coal and grain; monuments: the O'Keefe Centre theatre seats 3,300 and is the home of the Canadian Opera Co; Osgoode Hall (1828) has been the headquarters of the Law Society of Upper Canada since 1832 and once housed Ontario's Supreme Court; the old City Hall (1891-99) is noted for its 91 m-high clocktower and its clock which is 6 m in diameter; Fort York was built in 1793 to guard Toronto harbour, it fell into ruins after 1841 but was restored in 1934; the Ontario Centennial Centre of Science and Technology features displays on space science, the earth sciences and molecular science; the Sigmund Samuel Canadiana Gallery houses historical portraits, prints and watercolours of early Canadian life; events: Canadian National Exhibition and Canadian National Horse Show and Dog Show (Aug-Sept); Royal Agricultural Winter Fair (Nov).

Tororo *tō-rō'rō*, 00 42N 34 12E, town in Eastern prov, Uganda, E Africa; close to Uganda's SE frontier with Kenya, 40 km S of Mbale; railway; airfield; economy: cement, hessian.

Toros Dağları *to-ros dag-lah-ree*, TAURUS MTS *to'rus* (Eng), mountain chain of S Turkey, extending in a curve SE, E, and NE from Eğridir Gölü (L Eğridir) roughly parallel to the Mediterranean coast as far as the R Seyhan; it forms the S border of the plateau of Anadolu (Anatolia); the Ala Dağları (3,910 m), at the E end, is the highest peak in the range; its NE extension across the R Seyhan is called the Anti-Taurus; in the SE, between the Ala Dağları (NE) and the Bolkar Dağları (SW) are the Cicilian Gates, an important pass in ancient times; mineral deposits include chromium, copper, silver, zinc, iron and arsenic.

Torquay *tor-kee'*, 50 28N 3 30W, pop(1981) 57,491, resort town in Torbay dist, Devonshire, SW England; 30 km S of Exeter; centre for recreational sailing; railway; event: regatta (Aug).

Torrance, 33 50N 118 19W, pop(1980) 129,881, city in Los Angeles county, SW California, United States; industrial and residential city 24 km S of Los Angeles; founded in 1912; economy: chemicals, computer parts, oil refining, electronic and aerospace research.

Torrejon de Ardoz *tor-ay-hōn' THay ar-doth'*, 40 27N 3 29W, pop(1981) 75,398, town in Madrid prov, central Spain; 20 km NE of Madrid; economy: electrical appliances, light engineering.

Torrelavega *to-ray-la-vay'ga*, 43 20N 4 05W, pop(1981) 55,786, industrial town in Santander prov, Cantabria, N Spain; 24 km SW of Santander; economy: timber, plastics, chemical products, iron, arms, tools.

Torrens, Lake, salt lake in S central South Australia; W of the Flinders Ranges; 145 km N of Port Pirie; 240 km long; 64 km wide; area 5,775 sq km.

Torrente *tor-en'tay*, 39 27N 0 28W, pop(1981) 51,361, town in Valencia prov, E Spain; WSW of Valencia; economy: plastics, electrical appliances, textiles.

Torreón *tor-ray-ōn'*, 25 34N 103 25W, pop(1980) 363,886, town in Coahuila state, N Mexico; on the border with Durango state, on the Río Nazas, opposite the 2 towns of Gómez Palacio and Ciudad Lerdo; railway; economy: cotton, wheat.

Torres Vedras *to'rish vay'drash*, 39 05N 9 15W, pop(1981) 10,700, ancient town in Lisboa dist, central Portugal; 60 km N of Lisboa; railway; monument: Castelo dos Mouros; event: Carnival on the four days before Ash Wednesday; the centre of a wine-producing area.

Torrington, 41 48N 73 07W, pop(1980) 30,987, town in Litchfield county, NW Connecticut, United States; on R Naugatuck, 38 km W of Hartford.

Tórshavn or **Thorshavn** *tors'hown*, 62 02N 6 47W, seaport capital of Færøerne in N Atlantic; on Nolso Fjord, SE Stromo I; pop(1981) 13,91, economy: commerce and fishing.

Tortola Island *tor-tō'la*, pop(1980) 9,322, chief island of the British Virgin Islands in the Lesser Antilles chain of the E Caribbean; situated between St John and Virgin Gorda islands; chief town Road Town; area 54 sq km; rises to 543 m at Mt Sage; first settled by Dutch pirates in 1648; economy: livestock, fruit, vegetables, sugar, charcoal.

Tortosa *tor-tō'sa*, DERTOSA (anc), 40 49N 0 31E, pop(1981) 31,445, port in Tarragona prov, Cataluña, NE Spain; at the mouth of the R Ebro, 72 km SW of Tarragona; railway; economy: timber, olive oil, pharmaceuticals; monuments: Baroque cathedral and St Luis College founded by Charles V.

Tortuguero *tor-too-gway'rō*, national park on the Caribbean coast, NE Limón prov, Costa Rica, Central America; established in 1970; it protects the egg-laying grounds of the Atlantic green turtle and an area of Caribbean rain forest; area 189.5 sq km.

Toruń *tor-oo-nye'*, voivodship in N central Poland; bounded W by R Wisła (Vistula) and watered by its tributary the R Drmęca; pop(1983) 627,000; area 5,348 sq km; capital Toruń; chief towns include Grudziądz, Brodnica and Chełmno.

Toruń, THORN *torn* (Ger), 53 01N 18 35E, pop(1983) 182,400, industrial river port and capital of Toruń voivodship, N central Poland; on R Wisła (Vistula); well preserved city with fine example of Gothic urban architecture; birthplace of the astronomer Copernicus; Nicolaus Copernicus University (1945); railway; economy: synthetic fibres, electronics, wool, phosphate fertilizer; monuments: 13th-c church of St John, palace of the bishops of Kuyawy (1693), 13th-c teutonic knights' castle, ethnographical museum, burghers' manor (15th-c); event: annual Polish theatre festival.

Toscana *tos-kah'na*, TUS'CANY (Eng), region of Italy, comprising the provs of Massa-Carrara, Lucca, Pistoia, Firenze, Livorno, Pisa, Arezzo, Siena, and Grosseto; pop(1981) 3,581,051; area 22,989 sq km; capital Firenze (Florence); chief towns Pisa, Siena, Lucca, and Livorno (Leghorn); watered chiefly by the Arno and Ombrone rivers; it is mostly mountainous, with fertile valleys and a marshy coastal plain; industrial activity is concentrated in the Arno valley, between Firenze and Livorno, and from there N along the coast to Carrara; economy: working of minerals (iron, lignite, mercury) and marble, engineering, shipbuilding, pharmaceuticals, glass and crystal, textiles, craftwork; agriculture is the predominant activity in the upland areas; there is market-gardening and flower-growing along the coast and in the Arno valley; Toscana is the home of the famous dry dark red wine, Chianti; great art centres include Firenze (Florence), Siena, and Pisa.

Tosontsengel, 48 50N 98 20E, town in Dzavhan county, NW Mongolia; economy: timber products.

Totes Gebirge *tō'tus ga-bir'ga* ('dead mountains'), mountain range of the E Alps in Oberösterreich state, N Austria, rising to 2,515 m at Grosser Priel; bounded on the W and S by the Traun valley.

Totonicapán *tō-tō-nee-ka-pan'*, dept in W Guatemala, Central America; pop(1982e) 236,033; area 1,061 sq km; capital Totonicapán; traversed by the Inter-American Highway.

Totonicapán, 14 58N 91 12W, capital town of Totonicapán dept, W Guatemala, Central America; alt 2,500 m; economy: pottery, weaving, costume making; events: fiestas on 29 Sept and 25 July.

Totton, 50 56N 1 29W, pop(1981) 20,927, town in New Forest dist, Hampshire, S England; at the head of the R Test estuary, 6 km W of Southampton; railway.

Touba *too'ba*, dept in W Ivory Coast, W Africa; pop(1975) 77,786; area 8,720 sq km; capital Touba; chief towns Koro, Borotou, Guinetéguela and Gouekan; until 1981 an important diamond mining area.

Toubkal, Jbel *toob-kal'*, 31 03 7 57W, mountain in Haut Atlas range, Morocco, N Africa; height 4,165 m; the highest point in Morocco; first ascended by Marquis de Segonzac, Berger and Dolbeau in 1923; national park of same name with an area of 360 sq km was established in 1942.

Tougan *too-gan'*, 13 06N 3 03W, town in NW Burkina, W Africa; 177 km NW of Ouagadougou.

Toulon *too-lõ*, TILIO MARTIUS (Lat), 43 10N 5 55E, pop(1982) 181,405, fortified naval port and capital of Var dept, Provence-Alpes-Côte d'Azur region, SE France; on the Mediterranean Sea, 70 km SE of Marseille, backed by limestone hills; episcopal see; railway; the most important naval port in France; the harbour basin consists of the inner 'Petite Rade' and the outer 'Grande Rade' and is protected by the peninsula St-Mandrier; in Roman times it was renowned for a purple dye obtained from the murex, a shellfish; its rise to importance dates from the 17th century when Richelieu and Louis XIV turned it into a first-class naval base; in World War I it was an important port of entry and naval station; a large part of the French Mediterranean fleet was stationed here after the French armistice of 1940; economy: shipbuilding, oil refining, armaments, chemicals, textiles; monuments: early Gothic cathedral of Ste-Marie-Majeure (11-12th-c, extended in the 17th century); naval museum, opera house, zoo.

Toulouse *too-looz*, TOLOSA (anc), 43 37N 1 27E, pop(1982) 354,289, capital city of Haute-Garonne dept, Midi-Pyrénées region, S France; on the R Garonne and the Canal du Midi, 213 km SE of Bordeaux; once the capital of the former prov of Languedoc; 4th largest city in France; archbishopric; road and rail junction; university (1229); observatory; botanical gardens; Catholic Institute of Toulouse (1877); the cultural and economic centre of S France; known as the 'red city' because of its numerous brick buildings; it is the principal centre of the electronics industry and aircraft research and construction in France; monuments: the old quarter on the right bank of the river, built largely of local faded red brick, has many churches, aristocratic old houses, open squares and museums; 11-12th-c church of St-Sernin, the largest and best preserved Romanesque church in S France, with a 65 m high 6-storey tower and a magnificent 12th-c Romanesque sculpture on the Porte Miegeville in the S aisle; church of the Jacobins (church of a monastery, founded 1216), a fine example of S French Gothic architecture, recently restored; 11-17th-c cathedral of St-Étienne.

Touraine *too-ren*, former prov in central France, now occupying the dept of Indre-et-Loire and part of Vienne; chief town is Tours.

Tourcoing *toor-kwî*, 50 44N 3 10E, pop(1982) 97,121, rapidly growing industrial satellite town in Nord dept, Nord-Pas-de-Calais region, NW France; on the Belgian frontier, 12 km NE of Lille; one of the principal textile centres of France; economy: textiles, electronics.

Tournai *toor-nay*, dist of W Hainaut prov, Belgium; area 603 sq km; pop(1982) 141,291.

Tournai, DOORNIK *dōr'neek* (Flem), TORNACUM (anc), 49 52N 5 24E, pop(1982) 67,576, administrative and cultural town in Tournai dist, W Hainaut prov, Belgium; on the R Schelde, near the Belgian-French frontier, 22 km E of Lille; bishopric; founded 275 AD, it is the 2nd oldest city in Belgium (after Tongeren); railway; economy: cement, machinery, foodstuffs, traditional textiles (especially carpet-weaving), tourism; monument: cathedral (11-12th-c, restored in the 19th century, one of the finest in Christendom).

Tours *toor*, CAESARODUNUM, TURONI (anc), 47 22N 0 40E, pop(1982) 136,483, industrial and commercial city and capital of Indre-et-Loire dept, Centre region, W central France; between the Loire and Cher rivers, 206 km SW of Paris; made an episcopal see in the 3rd century AD; the original city grew up around the tomb of St-Martin who died in 397, the church which was built over his grave in 470 became a place of pilgrimage and centre of healing; a prosperous silk industry developed in the 15th and 16th centuries; birthplace of Balzac; Tours has developed a vigorous industrial zone on the N bank of the Loire between the river and the airport; road and rail junction, airport; university; economy: metallurgy, plastics, electronics, wine; monuments: 12-16th-c cathedral of St-Gatien; the centre of the former ecclesiastical city in the W part of Tours is the Place Plumereau, with its half-timbered houses and adjoining medieval streets; there are several silk museums, a museum of the wines of Touraine (in a vaulted cellar in the remains of the abbey of St-Julien) and a fine art museum, with 2 important Mantegna paintings, 'Christ in the Garden of Olives' and 'The Resurrection'.

Töv *tuv*, TOEV, CENTRAL COUNTY (Eng), county in central Mongolia; pop(1981e) 800,000; area 77,900 sq km; capital Dzunnmod; there is a radial network of roads, converging on Ulaanbaatar; crossed by the Tuul Gol river and by the railway from N to SE via Ulaanbaatar; arable agriculture and livestock farming are the basis of the county's economy; 170 sq km are under cultivation; industry: foodstuffs, wood processing, vehicle repair, building and printing.

Tower Hamlets, 51 32N 0 02W, pop(1981) 142,841, borough of E central Greater London, England; N of the R Thames at the heart of London's 'East End'; includes the suburbs of Bethnal Green, Stepney and Poplar; also the districts of Wapping, Limehouse, Millwall and Bow; railway.

Townsville, 19 13S 146 48E, pop(1986) 103,700, industrial port and resort in Northern stat div, Queensland, Australia; on Cleveland Bay, NW of Rockhampton; founded in 1864 it is the largest city in tropical Australia; headquarters of the Great Barrier Reef Authority; James Cook University (1970); Magnetic I attracts tourists; railway; airport; army and air-force bases; economy: copper, lead, nickel, cobalt and silver mining, food processing, engineering, trade in beef, wool and sugar; event: Townsville Pacific Festival (June).

Towy, river in Wales. See Tywi.

Toyama *tō-ya'ma*, 36 42N 137 14E, pop(1980) 305,055, capital of Toyama prefecture, Chūbu region, central Honshū island, Japan; 240 km NW of Tōkyo, on the S shore of Toyama-wan Bay, on the Sea of Japan; university (1949); railway; economy: textiles, chemicals, pharmaceuticals, machinery.

Toyohashi *tō-yō-ha'shee*, 34 46N 137 22E, pop(1980) 304,273, city in Aichi prefecture, Chūbu region, central Honshū island, Japan; on E shore of Mikawa-wan Bay; railway; economy: cotton, food processing, metal goods.

Toyonaka *tō-yō-na'ka*, 34 48N 135 35E, pop(1980) 403,174, town in Ōsaka prefecture, Kinki region, S Honshū island, Japan; 16 km N of Ōsaka; railway; economy: trade in grain, rice and flowers.

Toyota *tō-yō'ta*, 35 05N 137 09E, pop(1980) 281,608, town in Aichi prefecture, Chūbu region, central Honshū island, Japan; SE of Nagoya; railway.

Trâblous *ta-ra'boo-loos*, TRI'POLI (Eng), TRIPOLIS (Gr), OEA (anc), 34 27N 35 50E, pop(1980e) 175,000, seaport capital of Trâblous division (*caza*), Ash Shamāl, NW Lebanon; 2nd largest city in Lebanon; trade centre for N Lebanon as well as for the coastal cities of NW Syria; mostly occupied by Sunni Muslims; there are 2 Palestinian refugee camps near the city; railway; El Mina is the port area; economy: port trade and oil refining; monuments: Tower of the Lion, 12th-c Crusader Castle of St Gilles, 13th-c Mamelukes' Grand Mosque.

Trabzon *trab-zon'*, maritime prov in NE Turkey, bounded N by the Black Sea; pop(1980) 731,045; area 4,685 sq km; capital Trabzon; economy: vegetables, tobacco, opium.

Trabzon, TRAPEZUS (anc), 41 00N 39 43E, pop(1980) 108,403, seaport capital of Trabzon prov, NE Turkey; at the mouth of the R Degirmen, on the Black Sea; founded in the 8th century BC by Greek colonists; technical university (1963); airfield.

Trafalgar, Cabo *tra-fal-gar'*, *tra-fal'gar* (Eng), PROMONTORIUM LUNOSIS (Lat), (Arab 'Tarif-al-ghar', cape of the cave), 36 10N 6 02W, cape on the Atlantic coast of Cádiz prov, SW Spain, off which Nelson defeated the French and Spanish fleet in 1805.

Traisen *trī'zan*, river in N Austria, rising near Sankt Aegyd am Neuwalde, Niederösterreich state; flows N past St Pölten to meet the R Danube E of Krems; length 70 km.

Tralee *tru-lee'*, TRÁIGHLÍ (Gael), 52 16N 9 42W, pop(1981) 17,035, capital of Kerry county, Munster, SW Irish Republic; NE of Slieve Mish Mts; connected to the Atlantic Ocean by a canal; technical college; railway; economy: agricultural trade, bacon-curing, tourism; events: St Patrick's Week festival in March; Rose of Tralee festival in Sept, with street dancing and singing.

Tramore *tru-mor'*, TRÁIGH MHÓR (Gael), 52 10N 7 10W, pop(1981) 5,635, resort town in Waterford county, Munster, SE Irish Republic; SW of Waterford on S coast of Ireland at the head of Tramore Bay.

Tranent, 55 57N 2 57W, pop(1981) 8,079, town in East Lothian dist, Lothian, E Scotland; 6 km E of Musselburgh.

Transcaucasia *tranz-ko-kay'zha*, region of the Soviet Union, extending S from the Bol'shoy Kavkaz (Greater Caucasus) range to the Turkish and Iranian frontiers, between the Black Sea (W) and the Caspian Sea (E); comprises the republics of Gruzinskaya (Georgia), Azerbaydzhanskaya, and Armyanskaya (Armenia), which from 1922 until 1936 formed the Transcaucasian SFSR, one of the original constituent republics of the USSR; the R Kura and its tributaries separate the Bol'shoy Kavkaz range (N) from the Malyy Kavkaz (Lesser Caucasus) range (S); chief towns include Kutaisi, Batumi, Tbilisi, Kirovabad, and Baku.

Transdanubia, region of Hungary. See Dunántúl.

Transkei *tranz-kī'*, independent black homeland in SE South Africa; pop(1984e) 2,912,408; area 42,276 sq km; between the Kei and Mtamvuna rivers on the Indian Ocean; area includes the 2 separate districts of Herschel (N) and Umzimkulu (NE); capital Umtata; chief towns include Gcuwa, Kwabhaca, Umzimvubu and Lusikisiki; traditional territory of the Xhosa nation; granted self-government in 1963 and then independence by South Africa, but independent status is not recognized internationally; rail link from Umtata to East London; agricultural activities include forestry, livestock raising and the cultivation of crops such as maize, sorghum, coffee, tea and sugar cane; over 372,000 people are commuters or migrant workers in South Africa.

Trans-Siberian Railway, major railway system in Asiatic USSR, linking European Russia with the Pacific coast; construction began in 1892 from Chelyabinsk in the E Ural'skiy Khrebet (Ural Mts) range; the original line ran E through Omsk, Novosibirsk, Krasnoyarsk, Irkutsk, Chita, and as the Chinese Eastern railway through Manchuria to Vladivostok; during World War I the Russians lost control over the Chinese Eastern line and responded by constructing a line between Chita and Vladivostok, following the Amur and Assuri rivers; its E section runs S of the recently constructed Baykal-Amur railway.

Transvaal *tranz-vahl'*, prov in South Africa; pop(1985) 7,532,179; area 262,499 sq km; bounded N by the Limpopo river following the frontier with Botswana and Zimbabwe; Transvaal Drakensberg Mts lie in the SE; capital Pretoria; chief towns include Alberton, Benoni, Boksburg, Brakpan, Germiston, Johannesburg, Kempton Park, Krugersdorp, Springs and Vereeniging; settled by the Boers who migrated from the Cape Colony in the Great Trek of 1831; independence following the Sandy River Treaty (1852) was recognized by the UK; subsequently known as the South African Republic; annexed by Great Britain in 1877; Boer rebellion in 1880-81 led to the restoration of the republic; annexed as a British colony in 1900, granted self-government in 1906 and joined the Union of South Africa in 1910 as one of the original 4 provs; discovery of diamonds in 1867 and gold in 1886; economy: gold, diamonds, iron, oil, engineering, hydroelectricity, grain, tobacco, clothing.

Transylvania *tran-sil-vay'nya*, ERDÉLY *er'day* (Magyar), SIEBENBÜRGEN *zee'ben-* (Ger), geographical region and former prov of N and central Romania, separated from Walachia and Moldavia by the Carpathian Mts; a former principality that became part of the Austro-Hungarian Empire, Transylvania was incorporated with Romania in 1918; part of the region was ceded to Hungary by Hitler during World War II; the chief towns are Cluj-Napoca and Braşov.

Transylvanian Alps, mountain range in Romania. See Carpatii Meridionali.

Trapani *tra'pa-nee*, prov of Sicilia region, Italy; pop(1981) 420,865; area 2,461 sq km; capital Trapani.

Trapani, DREP'ANUM (anc), 38 02N 12 32E, pop(1981) 71,927, port and capital town of Trapani prov, Sicilia (Sicily), Italy; on the NW coast of the island; airfield; railway; economy: its port ships salt, wine and tuna fish; monument: 17th-c cathedral.

Trar'za, region in SW Mauritania, NW Africa; pop(1982e) 242,000; area 67,800 sq km; capital Rosso; chief towns Boutilimit, Mederdra and Kroufa; the R Sénégal follows the S border.

Traskanda, town in Finland. See Jarvenpaa.

Trás-os-Montes *traz-oozh-mo'tesh* ('beyond the mountains'), mountain area and former region of NE Portugal bounded on N and E by Spain on the W and SW by the former Minho and Douro Litoral regions and on the S by the Beira Alta; geologically part of the Spanish Meseta; area, 10,784 sq km; the population is concentrated in the fertile valleys where grapes and fruit are the main produce while on the bare upland plateaux sheep and goats graze the thin pasture.

Traun *trown*, river in N Austria, rising in the Totes Gebirge near Bad Aussee, Oberösterreich state; flows N past Wels to meet the R Danube SE of Linz, length 153 km.

Traun, 48 14N 14 15E, pop(1981) 21,464, town in Steyrland dist, Oberösterreich, N Austria; S of Linz; economy: textiles.

Traunsee or **Gmundner See** *trown'zay* or *ga-moon'dan-er zay*, LAKE TRAUN (Eng), lake in Reutte dist, Tirol, central Austria; area 24.5 km; length 12 km; width 3 km; max depth 191 m; at the N end Gmunden is the chief locality; Traunkirchen, Ebensee and Rindbach are also popular summer resorts; water sports are popular.

Trave *trah'vu*, river in Schleswig-Holstein prov, W Germany; rises 8 km S of Eutin, flows SW, S and E to Lübeck, where it forms a 24 km-long estuary which reaches Lübeck Bay on the Baltic Sea at Travemünde; receives the Elbe-Trave Canal at Lübecker Bucht (Lübeck Bay); length 118 km; navigable length 53 km; drainage basin area 1,854 sq km.

Travnik *trahv'nik*, 44 13N 17 40E, pop(1981) 64,100, town in Bosna-Hercegovina republic, Yugoslavia; on R Lasva, NW of Sarajevo; winter sports centre; noted for sheep's cheese; much of the town was destroyed in a fire in 1903;

founded in 15th century; a former Turkish capital of Bosnia; Novi Travnik is an industrial suburb, 10 km from the town centre; monuments: Many-coloured Mosque; Ivo Andrić House, now a museum, but formerly the home of the Nobel prize-winning novelist.

Třebič *tre'beech*, 49 13N 15 33E, pop(1984) 35,154, town in Jihomoravský region, Czech Socialist Republic, W central Czechoslovakia; on R Jihlava, W of Brno; railway; economy: footwear; monument: 13th-c basilica.

Tredegar *tre-dee'gar*, 51 47N 3 16W, pop(1981) 16,203, town in Blaenau Gwent dist, Gwent, SE Wales; on the R Sirhowy, 53 km WNW of Bristol; economy: engineering, transport equipment, plastics.

Treinta y Tres *trayn'ta ee trays*, dept in E central Uruguay; bordered E by Brazil (and L Mirim), W by the Cuchilla Grande range, NE by the Río Tacuarí, and SE by Cebollatí river; drained by Río Olimar; pop(1985) 46,599; area 9,539 sq km; capital Treinta y Tres; named after the 'Thirty Three' patriots who landed at Soriano in April 1825.

Treinta y Tres, 33 16S 54 17W, pop(1985) 27,987, capital of Treinta y Tres dept, E Uruguay; lies near the Río Olimar; railway; airfield; nearby is the Quebrada de los Cuervos National Park.

Trelew *tre-loo'*, 43 13S 65 15W, pop(1980) 52,073, agricultural centre in Chubut prov, Patagonia, SE Argentina; on Chubut river; founded in 1888 and first settled by Welshmen; railway junction; economy: agricultural trade, trout and salmon fishing; events: founding of Chubut (28 July), Petroleum Day (28 Dec).

Trelleborg *trel'e-bor-yu*, TRALLEBORG, 55 22N 13 10E, pop(1983) 34,285, seaport on S coast of Malmöhus county, SW Sweden; on the Baltic Sea; founded in the 12th century; owed its prosperity in the Middle Ages to the abundant supply of herring in the Baltic; rail terminus; ferry link to Travemünde; monument: 13th-c church rebuilt at the end of the 19th-century.

Tremiti, Isole *tray'mee-tee*, TREMITI ISLANDS (Eng), rocky limestone archipelago in Foggia prov, Puglia, S Italy, in the Adriatic Sea, 20 km N of the Monte Gargano promontory; area 3 sq km; chief islands San Domino, San Nicola, and Caprara; the precipitous coasts with their numerous inlets and sea caves offer ideal conditions for scuba diving.

Trenčin *tren'cheen*, 48 54N 18 03E, pop(1984) 50,553, town in Západoslovenský region, Slovak Socialist Republic, central Czechoslovakia; on R Váh, NE of Bratislava; railway; economy: agricultural trade, textiles, glass.

Trent, river rising S of Biddulph in N Staffordshire, central England; flows 275 km SE, then E and NE through Derbyshire, Nottinghamshire and Humberside to meet the Humber estuary near Whitton; many Midland industrial towns are linked to the Trent by canal; tributaries include the Blythe, Dove, Derwent, Tame, Soar and Devon rivers.

Trentino-Alto Adige *tren-tee'nō al'tō ah'di-jay*, region of Italy, comprising the provs of Bolzano and Trento; pop(1981) 873,413; area 13,613 sq km; bounded N by Austria.

Tren'to, TRIENT *tree-ent'* (Ger), prov of Trentino-Alto Adige region, N Italy; pop(1981) 442,845; area 6,213 sq km; capital Trento.

Trento, 46 04N 11 08E, pop(1981) 99,179, capital town of Trento prov, Trentino-Alto Adige region, N Italy; on the left bank of the R Adige, in a fertile valley enclosed by high limestone hills; on the main highway between Bolzano and Verona; archbishopric; railway; economy: electrical goods, chemicals, cement, wine; monuments: 11-12th-c cathedral; Castello del Buon Consiglio, former residence of the prince-bishops, now a museum.

Trenton, 40 14N 74 46W, pop(1980) 92,124, state capital of New Jersey in Mercer county, W New Jersey, United States; on the E bank of the R Delaware, 45 km NE of Philadelphia; settled by English Quakers in the 1670s, it achieved city status in 1792; in the War of Independence, it was the scene of an American victory in Dec 1776; railway; economy: manufactures steel, machinery, ceramics; research and development centre; monuments: a monument marks the spot where Washington's troops opened fire on the British; State House complex; William Trent House.

Tres Cruces, Nevado *nay-va'THō trays kroo'says*, 27 05S 68 46W, mountain rising to 6,330 m on the border between Argentina and Chile; in Catamarca prov, Andina, Argentina and Copiapó prov, Atacama, Chile; 48 km WSW of Cerro Incahuasi.

Treves, town in W Germany. See Trier.

Treviso *tray-vee'zo*, TARVIS'IUM (anc), prov of Veneto region, NE Italy; pop(1981) 720,580; area 2,476 sq km; capital Treviso.

Treviso, 45 40N 12 15E, pop(1981) 87,696, capital town of Treviso prov, Veneto region, NE Italy; in a fertile plain at the junction of the Botteniga and Sile rivers, 27 km from Venezia (Venice); the town is surrounded by well-preserved 15th-c walls and a circuit of canals and moats; railway; economy: paper, machinery; monuments: 15-16th-c cathedral, with paintings by Titian and Bordone; Gothic church of San Nicolo (13-14th-c).

Trier *treer*, dist of NW Rheinland-Pfalz (Rhineland-Palatinate) prov, W Germany; pop(1983) 472,000; area 4,925 sq km; capital Trier.

Trier, TRÈVES *trev* (Fr), TREVES *treevz* (Eng), AUGUSTA TREVERORUM (anc), 49 45N 6 39E, pop (1983) 94,700, river port capital of Trier dist, Rheinland-Pfalz (Rhineland-Palatinate) prov, W Germany; on the R Moselle near the Luxembourg border, 93 km SW of Koblenz; one of Germany's oldest towns; a considerable centre of wine-production and the wine trade; a bishopric since the 4th century; university (1970); Roman Catholic Theological College; railway; monuments: Porta Nigra (late 2nd-c), cathedral (4th-c, 11th-c and 12th-c), Roman basilica.

Triesen *tree'zen*, 47 07N 9 32E, pop(1985) 3,043, commune in Oberland dist, Principality of Liechtenstein, central Europe; area 26.4 sq km; economy: manufacture of sausage skins and cotton fabrics.

Triesenberg *tree'zen-berk*, 47 08N 9 33E, pop(1985) 2,241, commune in Oberland dist, Principality of Liechtenstein, central Europe; area 29.8 sq km; economy: philatelic requisites.

Trieste *tree-est'ay*, *tree-est'* (Eng), prov in Friuli-Venezia Giulia region, NE Italy; pop(1981) 283,641; area 210 sq km; capital Trieste. After World War II it was a debatable territory with Yugoslavia; the UN constituted a Free Territory which included an Italian zone in the N and the less populous Yugoslav zone in the S with its headquarters at Capodistria; in 1954 the territory was partitioned by agreement.

Trieste, 45 39N 13 47E, pop(1981) 252,369, seaport and capital town of Trieste prov, Friuli-Venezia Giulia region, NE Italy, on the NE Adriatic coast; largest port in the Adriatic; university (1938); airport; railway; economy: shipbuilding and repairing (merchant and naval vessels), oil refining, spirits and liqueurs; monuments: town hall (1874); cathedral of San Giusto, formed in the 14th century by joining up two 6th-c churches; neo-classical church of Sant'Antonio (1849); 15-18th-c castle; event: International Trade Fair (end of June until the beginning of July).

Triglav *tree'glaf*, 46 21N 13 50E, mountain in NW Slovenija republic, Yugoslavia; highest peak in the Julian Alps and in Yugoslavia, rising to 2,863 m.

Trikhonis *tree-KHo-nees'*, lake in Aitolía and Akarnanía nome (dept), Sterea Ellás-Évvoia region, Greece, 16 km NNE of Mesolóngion; drains into the R Akhelóös; area 96,513 sq km; length 19 km; width 4.8 km; largest lake in Greece.

Tríkkala *tree'ka-la*, nome (dept) of Thessalía region, W Greece; pop(1981) 134,207; area 3,384 sq km; capital Tríkkala; produces cereals and olive oil.

Tríkkala, TRICCA (anc), 39 33N 21 46E, pop(1981) 40,857, market town and capital of Tríkkala nome (dept), Thessalía region, W Greece; in the flood plain of the R Piniós; centre for the surrounding agricultural region;

devastated by an earthquake in 1954; famed in ancient times for its horses; railway.

Trincomalee *tring-kō-me-lee'*, TRINKOMALI, 8 44N 81 13E, pop(1981) 44,313, seaport capital of Trincomalee dist, Eastern prov, Sri Lanka; 257 km NE of Colombo on Koddiyar Bay, Bay of Bengal, at the mouth of the Mahaweli river; one of the earliest Tamil settlements; held by Dutch, French and Portuguese until finally taken by the British in 1795; principal British naval base during World War II after the fall of Singapore; the port has an excellent deep-water harbour, described by Lord Nelson in 1770 as the finest harbour in the world; economy: exports dried fish and coconuts; monuments: ruins of Temple of a Thousand Columns (3rd century BC), destroyed by the Portuguese in 1662; Hindu temple; Fort Fredrick, at the foot of the Swami Rock.

Třinec *trin'ets*, 49 41N 18 39E, pop(1984) 44,976, town in Severomoravský region, Czech Socialist Republic, central Czechoslovakia; on R Olse, SE of Ostrava, near the Polish frontier; railway; economy: iron.

Tring, 51 48N 0 40W, pop(1981) 10,738, town in Dacorum dist, Hertfordshire, SE England; 8 km NW of Berkhamsted; railway; economy: chemicals, electronics.

Trinidad *tree-nee-dad'*, 14 46S 64 50W, pop(1976) 27,487, market town and capital of Cercado prov, Beni, N Bolivia; founded in 1686; linked to its port on a mud bank 8 km from the town on a tributary of the Río Mamoré; university (1967); railway; airfield.

Trinidad, 21 48N 80 00W, town in Sancti Spíritus prov, central Cuba; 72 km S of Santa Clara; trading and processing centre for rich agricultural area; its port, Casilda, is 5 km S; rail terminus.

Trinidad, 33 30S 56 51W, pop(1985) 18,271, capital of Flores dept, SW central Uruguay; NW of Montevideo; railway.

Trinidad and Tobago, official name Republic of Trinidad and Tobago, southernmost islands of the Lesser Antilles chain, SE Caribbean, just off the South American mainland; timezone GMT −4; area 5,128 sq km; capital Port of Spain; chief towns San Fernando, Arima, and Scarborough; pop(1980) 1,055,800; only 3.7% of the pop lives on Tobago I; most of the pop are of East Indian or Negro origin (81.5%); English is the official language but a small percentage also speak Hindi, French, and Spanish; the main religions are Roman Catholicism (33.6%), Hindu (25%), and Anglican (15%); the unit of currency is the Trinidad and Tobago dollar; membership: CARICOM, Commonwealth, FAO, G-77, GATT, IADB, IBRD, ICAO, ICO, IDA, IDB, IFC, ILO, IMF, IMO, INTELSAT, ISO, ITU, IWC, NAM, Non-Aligned Movement, OAS, PAHO, SELA, UN, UNESCO, UPU, WFTU, WHO, WMO, WTO.

Physical description. The island of Trinidad (4,828 sq km) is roughly rectangular in shape with promontories at the SW and NW corners. It is separated from Venezuela (S) by the 11 km-wide Gulf of Paria. Three mountain ranges, Northern, Central, and Southern, traverse the island. The heavily forested Northern Range crosses the entire width of the island and includes the 2 highest peaks of El Tucuche (936 m) and El Cerro del Aripo (940 m). Apart from these ranges, the land is fairly low lying. There are several plains including the Caroni, Nariva, and Naparima, with large areas of mangrove swamps near the coasts. Principal rivers include the Caroni, Ortoire, and Oropuche. Tobago lies 30 km NE of Trinidad and has an area of 300 sq km. A range of hills called the Main Ridge extends almost the entire length of the island. These hills are of volcanic origin and rise to 576 m. Crown Point, at the SW tip of the island, is low-lying coral limestone and off the coast is a coral lagoon bounded by the Buccoo Reef. Tropical forests cover nearly half of the land area of the 2 islands.

Climate. The climate is tropical with an annual average temperature of 29°C. Tobago is less humid and has slightly lower temperatures than Trinidad due to more constant exposure to the E trade winds. There is a cool dry season from Jan to May. Average rainfall ranges from 1,270 mm in W Trinidad to 3,048 mm in the NE; in Tobago the average is 2,184 mm.

History, government and constitution. Both islands were visited by Columbus in 1498. Trinidad was settled by Spain in the 16th century and later periodically raided by French, British, and Dutch forces. In 1802 it was ceded to Britain under the Treaty of Amiens. After being colonized by Dutch, English, and French settlers, Tobago became a British colony of the Windward Is group in 1814. It was linked administratively with the colony of Trinidad in 1889 following the collapse of the sugar industry and in 1899 Trinidad and Tobago became a joint British Crown Colony. Trinidad and Tobago became an independent member of the Commonwealth on 31 August 1962 and the country became a republic on 1 Aug 1976. Legislative power is vested in a bicameral parliament, comprising a senate with 31 members appointed by the president, and a house of representatives with 36 members elected by universal suffrage. The president is constitutional head of state elected for 5 years by both houses of parliament.

Agriculture. Agriculture's share of the economy has fallen in recent years, accounting for 2.6% of national income in 1984 compared with 5.2% in 1974. Trinidad, a net exporter of food in the 1960s, now imports 75% of requirements. Approximately 40% of the 1,821 sq km of agricultural land is held by large estates producing the main export crops of sugar, cocoa, citrus fruits, and coffee. Trinidad's sugar industry has declined in the past decade to such an extent that it is now engaged in refining raw sugar from its CARICOM partners.

Industry. For the past 2 decades the oil and gas industry has been the mainstay of the country's economic growth. In 1980 the petroleum industry accounted for over 40% of the national output, 64% of government revenues and 85% of merchandise exports. However, since the 1978 high of 229,500 barrels per day Trinidad and Tobago's crude oil production has declined considerably. In an effort to broaden the base of its oil-dependent economy, Trinidad and Tobago has developed a 6 sq km industrial complex at Point Lisas on the W coast of Trinidad. The industries in this complex, including a steel mill, 2 ammonia plants, and facilities for producing methanol and urea, are fed by gas piped 112 km across the island from off-shore platforms in the Atlantic Ocean. Pitch Lake, at La Brea in SW Trinidad, is the world's chief source of natural asphalt. Limestone, found chiefly in the

Northern and Central Ranges, provides some of the raw material for the country's cement industry. Major industries include petroleum refining (at Pointe-à-Pierre and Point Fortin), petrochemicals (Savonetta), asphalt refining, and the processing of sugar, cocoa, coffee, and fruit. Chief exports include petroleum, chemicals, foodstuffs, and asphalt. The main destinations are the USA (typically 67-71% of total value), Puerto Rico, the US Virgin Is, the Netherlands Antilles, Surinam, the UK, the Netherlands, and Canada. Tourism accounts for about 3% of national income and is the country's largest foreign exchange earner after oil. Tourist development projects on Tobago, traditionally the country's main tourist centre, include a luxury hotel-conference centre at Rocky Point and a resort complex at Minster Point. There are plans for a deep water harbour at Tobago's capital, Scarborough, with the aim of providing berthing facilities for passing cruise liners.

Administrative divisions. The republic is divided into 4 self-governing cities, 6 counties, and semiautonomous Tobago.

County	*pop(1980)*
Tobago	39,500
Trinidad	
St George	370,600
Caroni	140,400
Nariva-Mayaro	30,900
St Andrew-St David	50,200
Victoria	187,000
St Patrick	123,900

Tripoli, seaport in Lebanon. See Trâblous.

Tripoli, capital of Libya, N Africa. See Tarābulus.

Trípolis *tree'po-lis*, TRIPOLITSA (Eng), 37 31N 22 22E, pop(1981) 21,311, capital town of Arkadhía nome (dept), Pelopónnisos region, SW Greece; railway; event: Holy Week celebrations.

Tripolitania *tri-pol-i-tayn'ya*, region of N Africa, lying between Tunis and Cyrenaica; a former prov of W Libya; under Turkish control from the 16th century until 1911, under Italian control until 1943 and British control until 1952.

Tripura *trip'oo-ru*, state in E India; pop(1981) 2,060,189; area 10,477 sq km; bounded N, W and S by Bangaldesh, E by Mizoram territory and NE by Assam state; the boundary with Mizoram follows the R Langai; there are 3 administrative districts; capital Agartala; the state is governed by a 60-member Legislative Assembly; the terrain is mostly hilly, with a cover of rain forest of which an estimated 8% has not been exposed to shifting cultivation or replaced by rubber plantation trees; 23% of the state is cultivable, with traditional tribal shifting cultivation gradually being replaced by more modern farming methods; principal crops are rice, wheat, tea, cotton, jute, oilseed, mesta and sugar cane; manufacturing industry is based on food processing, jute, steel and handicrafts such as weaving and cane-work; the state was ruled by Maharajas for over 1,300 years before it became a state of the Union of India in Oct 1949; under the States Reorganization Act of 1956 Tripura became a union territory; Tripura was made a state in Jan 1972.

Tristan da Cunha *tri'stan da koon'ya*, 37 15S 12 30E, a small volcanic island in the S Atlantic lying about midway between S Africa and S America; a British dependency of St Helena; area 98 sq km; pop(1982) 324, volcanic cone rises to 2,060 m; occupied by a British garrison in 1816 during the exile of Napoleon in St Helena; when the garrison was withdrawn, 3 men, headed by Corporal William Glass, elected to stay and became the founders of the present settlement; before steam navigation the island occupied an important position on a main shipping route; became a dependency of St Helena in 1922 along with the unoccupied islands of Gough, Inaccessible and Nightingale; main settlement Edinburgh; in 1961 the islanders were evacuated after a volcanic eruption but returned in 1963; administered by an Island Council; electricity and a radio telephone service were established in 1969; economy: fishing (a fish freezing factory has been established); the sale of postage stamps.

Trivandrum *tri-vun'droom*, TRIVANDRAM, 8 31N 77 00E, pop(1981) 520,000, capital of Kerala state, SW India; 1,255 km SSE of Bombay, on the Malabar coast; university (1937); airfield; linked by rail to Quilon; economy: textiles, soap, copra, coir ropes; also noted for its wood and ivory carving; monument: early 18th-c temple to Vishnu.

Trnava *tær'na-va*, 48 22N 17 36E, pop(1984) 67,768, town in Západoslovenský region, Slovak Socialist Republic, S central Czechoslovakia; NE of Bratislava; formerly part of Hungary; railway; economy: iron, food processing.

Trogir *tro'eer*, 43 32N 16 15E, resort and historic medieval town in Hrvatska (Croatia) republic, Yugoslavia; on the Adriatic Sea, W of Split; in 3rd century BC the Greek colony of Tragourion was founded here; later held by Venice, France and Austria; monument: Romanesque cathedral.

Trois'dorf, 50 49N 7 09E, pop(1983) 59,400, town in Köln dist, Nordrhein-Westfalen (North Rhine-Westphalia) prov, W Germany; economy: explosives, chemicals, plastics.

Trois-Rivières *trwah ree-vyayr'*, 46 21N 72 34W, pop(1981) 50,466, river port in S Québec, SE Canada; built on a series of terraces where the St Maurice river enters the St Lawrence river; founded by Champlain in 1634; a major port in French times; university (1969); railway; economy: paper, iron, steel, cotton, shipbuilding, hydroelectricity.

Trollhättan *trol'het-an*, 58 17N 12 20E, pop(1982) 48,773, industrial town in Älvsborg county, SW Sweden, on the R Göta älv near L Vänern; received its municipal charter in 1916; railway; economy: electro-chemicals, engineering.

Tromelin *trom-lã'*, 15 52S 54 25E, small island in the Indian Ocean, E of Madagascar; ownership has been disputed between France and Mauritius.

Troms, a county of N Norway, lying within the Arctic Circle; numerous offshore islands including Ringvassøy, Senja and the N part of Hinnøy; area 25,953 sq km; pop(1983) 147,690; capital Tromsø.

Tromsø *trom'sæ*, 69 42N 19 00E, pop(1983) 47,316, seaport capital of Troms county, N Norway; on a small island between South Kvaløy and the mainland; the town developed around a church founded in the 13th century; received its municipal charter in 1794; largest town in N Norway; a base for expeditions to the Arctic; see of the Lutheran bishop of Halogaland; university (1972); an observatory for the study of the aurora borealis; monuments: Tromsdalen church (1975), Tromsø museum.

Trondheim *trond'hīm*, formerly NIDAROS, later TRONDHJEM, DRONTHEIM (Ger), 63 36N 10 23E, pop(1983) 134,665, seaport and capital of Sør-Trøndelag county, central Norway, at the mouth of the R Nidelv (Nea) on S shore of Trondheimsfjord (Trondheim Fjord); see of both a Lutheran and Roman Catholic bishop; former capital of Norway during the Viking period; in World War II occupied by the Germans April 1940 until May 1945; college of technology; railway; economy: trade, industry, shipping; monuments: Romanesque and Gothic cathedral (1066-93); 18th-c royal palace; 13th-c church of Our Lady, near the monument of the town's founder, Olav Trygvason.

Trondheimsfjord, TRONDHEIM FJORD (Eng), inlet of Norwegian Sea, Nord-Trøndelag and Sør-Trøndelag counties, W coast of Norway, extends inland 126 km from Agdenes to Steinkjer.

Troödos *tro'e-thos*, mountain range in central Cyprus rising to 1,951 m at Mt Olympus, the highest peak on the island.

Troon, 55 32N 4 40W, pop(1981) 14,233, town and golf resort in Kyle and Carrick dist, Strathclyde, W Scotland;

at the N end of Ayr Bay, 9 km N of Ayr; railway; economy: boatbuilding.

Tropics (Greek, 'tropē' turning), 2 parallels of latitude on the terrestrial globe, passing through the most northerly and southerly points on the Earth's surface at which the sun can be vertically overhead at noon; the tropics include between them all points on the Earth's surface at which the sun is ever vertical; the tropic N of the Equator is called the Tropic of Cancer, because the sun at the summer solstice (when it is vertically over that tropic) enters the sign of Cancer; and the southern one is, for a similar reason, called the Tropic of Capricorn; though usually said to be in $23\frac{1}{2}$°N and S latitude, the tropics are not fixed at a uniform distance from the Equator, but the limits of their variation are extremely narrow.

Tropojë *tro-po'ye*, prov of N Albania; area 1,043 sq km; pop(1980) 38,800; capital Bajram Curri.

Trowbridge *trō-*, 51 20N 2 13W, pop(1981) 27,476, county town in West Wiltshire dist, Wiltshire, S England; 12 km SE of Bath; railway; economy: foodstuffs; brewing, clothing, printing, dairy products.

Troy, ancient city in W Turkey. See Truva.

Troy, 42 37N 83 09W, pop(1980) 67,102, residential town in Oakland county, SE Michigan, United States; 12 km ESE of Pontiac; railway; economy: aerospace components.

Troy, 42 44N 73 41W, pop(1980) 56,638, county seat of Rensselaer county, E New York, United States; on the Hudson river, opposite the mouth of the R Mohawk, 13 km NE of Albany; railway; burial place of 'Uncle Sam' Wilson who supplied beef to the US army in the war of 1812; soldiers stationed near Troy interpreted the government stamp 'US Beef' to mean 'Uncle Sam's Beef'; later a caricature of Sam Wilson came to personify the United States.

Troyes *trwa*, AUGUSTOBONA TRICASSIUM (anc), 48 19N 4 03E, pop(1982) 64,769, capital city of Aube dept, Champagne-Ardenne region, NE central France; on the braided channel of the R Seine, 150 km SE of Paris; a bishopric since the 4th century; once the capital of the old prov of Champagne; has been a city of importance since Gallo-Roman days; still a traditional centre of the hosiery trade; railway; monuments: 13-16th-c cathedral of St-Peter and St-Paul, with fine 13-14th-c stained-glass; 13th-c church of St-Urbain; 16th-c church of Ste-Madeleine; the former abbey of St-Loup houses an outstanding library of some 300,000 books and manuscripts dating back to the 7th century, and the Musée des Beaux-Arts contains paintings ranging from the 15th century to the present; there is a museum illustrating the development of the local hosiery industry.

Trstenik *tar-ste'nik*, 43 56N 2 54E, pop(1981) 53,695, town in central Srbija (Serbia) republic, Yugoslavia; on R Morava, W of Krusevac; railway; economy: wine and tobacco trade.

Trujillo *troo-KHeel'yō*, 15 55N 86 00W, pop(1985e) 6,971, seaport capital of Colón dept, N Honduras, Central America; on Trulillo Bay, an inlet of the Caribbean, E of Puerto Cortés; founded in 1525 when it became the 1st capital of the Spanish prov of Honduras; destroyed by the Dutch in 1643 and resettled in 1787 by Galicians; its port is located at Puerto Castillo (20 km N); economy: trade in timber, fruit, hides.

Trujillo, 8 06S 79 00W, pop(1981) 354,557, capital of La Libertad dept, NW Peru; founded by Pizarro in 1536; La Libertad University (1824); much of the area between Trujillo and Casma (approx 170 km S) was severely damaged in the May 1970 earthquake; railway; airfield (Martínez de Pinillos) at 4 km; monuments: besides the cathedral, there are 10 colonial churches and several old convents and monasteries; 2 of the old colonial mansions on the central plaza have been taken over by the Banco Central and the Banco Hipotecario, and are partly maintained as museums; in the centre of the plaza is a sculpted group of the heroes of the Liberation; near here is the house where General Iturregui lived when he proclaimed the city's freedom from Spain in 1820; it is now the exclusive Club Central and the Chamber of Commerce.

Trujillo, mountainous state in W Venezuela; bounded NW by L Maracaibo; pop(1980) 501,178; area 7,397 sq km; capital Trujillo.

Trujillo, 9 20N 70 38W, pop(1980) 42,000, capital of Trujillo state, W Venezuela.

Truk, one of the Federated States of Micronesia, W Pacific, comprising 11 high volcanic islands in the Truk lagoon and numerous outlying atolls; area 127 sq km; pop(1980) 37,742, capital Moen; more than 60 ships of the Japanese wartime fleet lie sunk at various depths in the Truk lagoon, one of the largest in the world.

Truro *troo'rō*, 45 24N 62 18W, pop(1981) 12,552, town in Colchester county, Nova Scotia, E Canada; near the head of the Minas Basin, 100 km N of Halifax; the original Acadian settlement was destroyed in 1755; resettled in 1761 by New England colonists; agricultural college (1905); economy: timber, dairy farming, clothing.

Truro, 50 16N 5 03W, pop(1981) 18,557, county town in Carrick dist, Cornwall, SW England; on R Truro, 20 km SW of St Austell; Royal Institution of Cornwall; railway; economy: foodstuffs, engineering, seaweed fertilizer; monuments: cathedral (1880-1910), Pendennis castle (1543).

Truth or Consequences, commonly TRUTH OR C., formerly HOT SPRINGS (-1950), 33 08N 107 16W, pop(1980) 5,219, town in Sierra county, SW New Mexico; on the Rio Grande, 96 km N of Las Cruces; the new name was adopted by a vote of the citizens of the town who accepted the offer made by the master of ceremonies of a famous radio programme that if the town adopted the name of his show he would hold a yearly fiesta with the programme presented from that town.

Trutnov *troot'nof*, 50 34N 15 55E, pop(1984) 30,278, town in Východočeský region, Czech Socialist Republic, NW central Czechoslovakia; in the Sudeten area near the Polish frontier; railway; economy: textiles, glass.

Truva *troo'va*, TROY or ILIUM (anc), ancient ruined city in Çanakkale prov, W Turkey; the archaeological site lies S of the Dardanelles, near Hisarlik; in Greek legend it was beseiged by a confederation of Greek armies for 10 years (Trojan War); this story was recounted by Homer in the *Iliad*; from the Stone Age to Roman times, over a period of 4,000 years, the city was rebuilt on the same site 9 times; a well-known brand of Turkish brandy takes its name from this site.

Tryav'na, 42 50N 25 29E, pop(1981e) 13,000, resort town in Gabrovo okrug (prov), central Bulgaria, 20 km E of Gabrovo; a centre of the arts during the Bulgarian Renaissance period, specializing in icon painting, wood-carving and building construction.

Tsaratanana, Massif du, mountain range in N Madagascar rising to 2,876 m at Maromokotra; to the N is Ambre mountain nature reserve.

Tsavo *tsah'vō*, national park in SE Kenya, E Africa; area 20,821 sq km; established in 1948.

Tselinograd, formerly AKMOLINSK (-1961), 51 10N 71 30E, pop(1983) 253,000, capital town of Tselinograd oblast, Kazakhskaya SSR, Soviet Union; on the R Ishim, 222 km NW of Karaganda; founded in 1830 as a fortress; railway junction; airport; economy: agricultural machinery, ceramics, foodstuffs, clothing.

T'seng-wen *seng-wen*, reservoir in the western foothills of the central mountain range of Taiwan; 60 km NE of T'ai-nan; completed in Oct 1973; created by damming of R T'seng-wen; area 17 sq km; the largest lake in Taiwan; the reservoir provides water to Coral Lake, which distributes it for household, irrigation, and industrial use.

Tsetserleg, ZEZERLEG, 47 26N 101 22E, capital of Arhangay county, Central Mongolia; lies on the Urd Tamil Gol; economy of the town is based on stock breeding in the surrounding area.

Tsévié *tsay'vyay*, 6 26N 1 18E, pop(1977) 15,900, town in S Togo, W Africa; on the railway 32 km N of Lomé.

Tsinan, capital of Shandong prov, E China. See Jinan.

Tsinghai, province in W central China. See Qinghai.

Tsingtao, town in Shandong prov, E China. See Qingdao.

Tsitsihar, town in Heilongjiang prov, NE China. See Qiqhar.

Tsitsikama *sit-si-ka'ma*, national park on the S coast of Cape prov, South Africa; divided into (1) the 4.78 sq km De Plaat forest on the N side of the Garden Route, c.100 km E of Knysana and (2) a coastal strip of 18.4 sq km extending from the Groot river estuary W of Humansdorp to the estuary E of Nature's Valley; established in 1964; protects one of the last jungles containing the yellowwood and stinkwood trees.

Tsodilo Hills *tsō-dee'lō*, range of hills in NW Ngamiland dist, Botswana, S Africa; highest point 4,511 m; noted for its 1,700 rock paintings discovered at over 200 different sites.

Tsuen Wan *choo-an wan*, town in S New Territories dist, Hong Kong, SE Asia; NW of Kowloon; had 3,000 inhabitants when leased by Britain in 1898; during the 1930s industrial development began; an influx of Shanghai industrialists in 1949-50 further boosted development; since the 1960s Tsuen Wan has become one of Hong Kong's 3 new towns; Asia's largest container port is located here at Kwai Chung; population density of 28,500 to the sq km recorded in the 1981 census.

Tsumeb *soo'meb*, 19 13S 17 42E, town in N Namibia, SW Africa; 56 km NW of Grootfontein; alt 1,290 m; major mining centre for copper, lead, zinc, arsenic and cadmium; railway.

Tsushima *tsoo-shee'ma*, island in Nagasaki prefecture, Kyūshū, Japan; area 702 sq km (including offshore islets); situated 96 km NW of Kyūshū, off the SE tip of South Korea; 72 km long; 10 km wide; the larger N portion is separated from the S part at high tide; rocky, arid island, rising to 661 m; in 1905, during the Japanese war with Russia, the Russian fleet was destroyed near here; economy: fishing; chief town Izuhara.

Tua *too'a*, river in N Portugal, rises near Spanish border, flows SSW to the R Douro near São João da Pesqueira; length 102 km.

Tuam *too'um*, TUAIM (Gael), 53 31N 8 50W, pop(1981) 6,093, town in Galway county, Connacht, W Irish Republic; NE of Galway; area rich in prehistoric remains; railway; economy: sugar refining.

Tübingen *tü'bing-un*, dist of SE Baden-Württemberg prov, W Germany; pop(1983) 1,516,200; area 8,917 sq km; capital Tübingen.

Tübingen, 48 32N 9 04E, pop(1983) 74,700, capital of Tübingen dist, Baden-Württemberg prov, W Germany; in the Neckar valley near the point where it is joined by the R Ammer, 27 km S of Stuttgart; university (1477); railway; economy: publishing, paper, textiles, machinery.

Tubruq, TOBRUK *tu-brook'*, 32 06N 23 56E, seaport in Darnah prov, N Libya, N Africa; on the Mediterranean coastline, 144 km SE of Darna; occupied by the Italians in 1911; one of the most famous battle sites in N Africa during World War II; the Australians took it in Jan 1941 and were subsequently besieged by Rommel's forces for 8 months until Dec 1941; attacked and recaptured by Rommel in June 1942 and finally retaken by British forces in late 1942; economy: naval ship repair.

Tubuai, Îles *too-bwa'ee*, TUBUAI ISLANDS or AUSTRAL ISLANDS, *o'strul* (Eng), volcanic island group of French Polynesia, 528 km S of the Archipel de la Société (Society Is), S Pacific Ocean; comprises a 1,300 km chain of volcanic islands and reefs; chief islands include Rimatara, Rurutu, Tubuai, Raivaevae, Rapa, and the uninhabited Maria atoll; area 137 sq km; pop(1977) 5,208, the chief centre is Mataura on Tubuai.

Tucson *too'son*, 32 13N 110 58W, pop(1980) 330,537, county seat of Pima county, SE Arizona, United States; on the Santa Cruz river, 172 km SE of Phoenix; the Spanish founded the Presidio of San Augustín de Tuguison in 1776 near the site of the San Xavier del Brac Indian mission which had been established in 1700; the site was ceded to the USA in 1853 and achieved city status in 1883; it was state capital 1867-77; university (1885); airport; railway; economy: electronic, optical and research industries; processing and distributing centre for cotton, livestock and nearby mines; a major tourist and health resort owing to its warm, dry climate; nearby is Davis-Monthan Air Force Base; to the SW of the city is Kitt Peak National Observatory; event: Tucson festival (April).

Tucumán *too-koo-man'*, prov in Norte region, NW Argentina; in the E outliers of the Andes; bordered W by Catamarca prov; it slopes from high ground in the W to Santiago del Estero prov (E); drained by the Río Salí (Dulce) and the Río Santa María (Cajón) which are dammed for hydroelectric power and for irrigation; the climate is humid and warm in lower, populated parts; pop(1980) 972,655; area 22,524 sq km; capital San Miguel de Tucumán; economy: salt and gypsum mining, sugar, timber, sorghum, cattle raising.

Tucupita *too-koo-pee'ta*, pop(1980) 29,000, capital of Delta Amacuro territory, NE Venezuela; NE of Ciudad Bolívar, on an arm of the Orinoco delta.

Tula *too'lah*, ancient Toltec city in W Hidalgo, central Mexico; capital of the Toltecs from c.900 AD until northern tribesmen destroyed it at the end of the 12th century; remains include a pyramid surmounted by huge Atlantes which once supported the roof of an upper sanctuary.

Tula, 54 11N 37 38E, pop(1983) 527,000, industrial capital town of Tul'skaya oblast, N central European Rossiyskaya, Soviet Union; on the R Upa, 193 km S of Moskva (Moscow); built on a plan of concentric circles centring on the Kremlin; the town's prosperity dates from 1712 when Peter the Great founded the Imperial Small Arms Factory; railway; airfield; economy: ferrous metallurgy, machine building, chemicals, biscuits; monument: Uspenskii cathedral (1762-64).

Tulcán *tool-kan'*, 0 50N 77 48W, pop(1982) 30,985, capital of Carchi prov, N Ecuador; close to the Colombian border; the centre of a rich farming area; economy: drinks, tobacco, dairy products, food processing, textiles, wood and metal products.

Tulcea *tool'cha*, county in E Romania; bounded to the W by the R Ialomiţa, to the E by the Black Sea and to the N by the USSR; pop(1983) 264,212; area 8,430 sq km; capital Tulcea.

Tulcea, 45 10N 28 50E, pop(1983) 79,290, river port and capital town of Tulcea county, E Romania; in the Danube delta; airfield; railway; economy: port trade, shipbuilding, non-ferrous metallurgy, fishing, wine, tobacco, wood products.

Tulkarm *tool'karm*, sub-district of Judea-Samaria dist, Israel, in the Israeli-occupied West Bank of Jordan.

Tullamore *tu-lu-mor'*, TULACH MHÓR (Gael), 53 16N 7 30W, pop(1981) 8,724, capital of Offaly county, Leinster, central Irish Republic; a road junction on the Grand Canal, W of Dublin; railway; economy: agricultural trade, spinning, distilling; monument: nearby at Durrow is an abbey founded by St Columba.

Tulle *tül*, TUTELA (anc), 45 16N 1 46E, pop(1982) 20,642, capital of Corrèze dept, Limousin region, S central France; an industrial city that has given its name to the fabric known as 'tulle'.

Tul'sa, 36 10N 95 55W, pop(1980) 360,919, county seat of Tulsa county, NE Oklahoma, United States; a port on the R Arkansas, 157 km NE of Oklahoma City; settled as a Creek Indian village in the 1830s, the modern city developed in the 1880s; university (1894); railway; airport; economy: a major national centre of the petroleum industry; oil refining, petrochemicals, aerospace industry, telecommunications and the manufacture of machinery and metal goods; monument: Gilcrease Institute of Art; events: May Festival, Great Labour Day Raft Race.

Tum'ba, 59 12N 17 48E, pop(1983) 29,425, town in Stockholm county, E Sweden; SW of Stockholm; railway; economy: production of Swedish banknotes.

Tumbes *toom'bays*, dept in the extreme NW of Peru; bordered by the Pacific and the Gulf of Guayaquil (W and N) and by Ecuador (E); largely a plain, rising in the

E to the Andean foothills; pop(1981) 103,839; area 4,731 sq km; capital Tumbes.

Tumen *too-mun*, river on the border between China (Jilin prov) and North Korea; rises in the NE of the Changbai Shan range; flows NE along the border, turns E then SE at the town of Tumen then flows into the Sea of Japan, forming the border between North Korea and the Soviet Union near its mouth; length 521 km.

Tumu *too'moo*, 10 55N 1 59W, town in Upper region, NW Ghana, W Africa; W of Bolgatanga, near the Burkina frontier.

Tumucumaque, Serra de *too-moo-koo-ma'kay*, TUMUCHUMAC MOUNTAINS, mountain range of N South America; rising to 853 m on the border between Brazil, Surinam and French Guiana; extends c.290 km E-W at 2°N; N watershed of the Amazon basin.

Tunas, Las *too'nas*, prov in E central Cuba; swampy along the N coast; area 6,373 sq km; pop(1981) 436,341; capital Victoria de las Tunas; chief towns Puerto Padre and Jobabo.

Tunbridge Wells or **Royal Tunbridge Wells**, 51 08N 0 16E, pop(1981) 58,141, spa town in Tunbridge Wells dist, Kent, SE England; 50 km SE of London; in 1606 Lord North discovered iron-rich springs here, and 30 years later the town was founded; 'Royal' since 1909, a legacy of visits made by Queen Victoria; railway; economy: light industry, printing.

Tunceli *toon-je-lee'*, prov in E central Turkey; pop(1980) 157,974; area 7,774 sq km; capital Tunceli; minerals include tin and copper.

Tune *too'ne*, formerly GREAKER, 59 16N 11 02E, pop(1980) 18,438, town in Østfold county, SE Norway, on R Glåma, NE of Fredrikstad; railway; economy: timber, paper, ship repair.

Tungi, 23 55N 90 24E, pop(1981) 94,580, town in Dhākā dist, Dhākā, central Bangladesh; close to the R Daleswari in the SW and the R Brahmaputra (Jamuna) in the E; linked by road and rail to Dhākā in the S and Mymenshingh in the N.

Tungurahua *toon-goo-ra'wha*, mountainous prov in the Andean Sierra of central Ecuador; includes Tungurahua and Carihuairazo volcanoes and is watered by the Patate and Chambo rivers, headstreams of the Pastaza; the prov was severely hit by an earthquake in 1949; pop(1982) 326,777; area 3,128 sq km; capital Ambato; nearby is the spa town of Baños; economy: fruit, vegetables, drinks, tobacco, food processing, textiles, leather, timber products, motor vehicles, chemicals.

Tungurahua, 1 26S 78 26W, Andean volcano in Tungurahua prov, central Ecuador; rises to 5,016 m, 30 km SE of Ambato; the spa town of Baños is at its N foot; dormant, though emits vapours from time to time; erupted in 1886, devastating Baños.

Tunhuang, town in Gansu prov, NW China. See Dunhuang.

Tunis *tyoo'nis*, 36 50N 10 13E, pop(1984) 556,654, seaport capital of Tunisia, N Africa; on a hilly isthmus between the Lake of Tunis and the Sedjoumi salt flat, 240 km from Sicily and 645 km E of Alger; the town is of Phoenician origin, later coming under the domination of Carthage; during the Aglabite dynasty Tunis succeeded Kairouan as capital (1236) and became an important trade centre with major European links; the Turks captured Tunis in 1533 and under Turkish governors the town achieved notoriety as a pirate base; the Treaty of Le Bardo recognized the French occupation of 1881; Ain Cheffa Korbous, a hydropathic spa, is located 48 km from Tunis on the N coast of Le Cap-Bon; the city holds a strategically important position in the Mediterranean Sea; university (1960); airport; railway; monuments: Great Mosque of Zitouna built by the Aghlabid Prince, Ibrahim Ibn Ahmed between 856 and 863 with abandoned pillars from other temples and buildings of Roman Carthage; Dar Ben Abdullah, a 19th-c house exhibiting the finest skills of Tunisian craftsmen; museum of Islamic art, palace of Dar Hussein which includes the National Institute of Archaeology; Dar Beb Abdallah museum; Dar Lasram museum; Bardo National Museum (5 km N); event: film festival of Carthage in Oct.

Tunisia *tyoo-niz'i-a*, official name Republic of Tunisia, AL-DJOUMHOURIA ATTUNUSIA (Arab), a N African republic bounded W by Algeria, SE by Libya and NE and N by the Mediterranean; timezone GMT +1; area 164,150 sq km; pop(1984) 6,344,071; capital Tunis; chief towns Bizerte, Sousse, Sfax; the pop is mostly Arabic (98%) with a few Europeans; the majority of the pop is Muslim (98%), the remainder being either Christian or Jewish; the official language is Arabic but French is also widely spoken; the unit of currency is the dinar of 1,000 millines; national holiday 1 June (Independence Day); membership of AfDB, Arab League, AIOEC, FAO, G-77, GATT (de facto), IAEA, IBRD, ICAO, IDA, Islamic Development Bank, IFAD, IFC, ILO, ILZSG, IMF, IMO, INTELSAT, INTERPOL, IOOC, ITU, International Wheat Council, NAM, OAPEC, OAU, OIC, UN, UNESCO, UPU, WHO, WIPO, WMO, WTO.

Physical description. The Atlas Mts of N Africa extend into NW Tunisia, rising to 1,544 m at Chambi, W of Kasserine. From the Téboursouk and Tébessa Heights in the N the mountain ridges drop down through the Upper Steppes and the Gafsa Heights to central Tunisia where a W-E depression runs from Nefta to the Golfe de Gabès. This area contains a number of saline lakes including

Chott El Jerid and Chott El Fejai. South of this region is a dry, sandy upland. The Iles de Kerkenah (Chergui and Gharbi) lie in the Golfe de Gabès off Sfax. The Ile de Jerba, also in the Golfe de Gabès, is situated opposite the town of Gabès and is connected by causeway to the mainland town of Zarzis.

Climate. The mountainous NW and coastal region of Tunisia experiences a Mediterranean climate with hot, dry summers and wet winters. Temperatures are modified by sea breezes and range between a daily max of 14°C and 33°C. Average annual rainfall in the N ranges from 420 mm at Tunis to levels in excess of 900 mm in the Atlas Mts. Inland regions experience colder winters, hotter summers and a lower annual rainfall than the coastal region. Gafsa is representative of this region with an annual average rainfall of 150 mm and max average daily temperatures ranging between 14°C and 38°C. Further S, rainfall decreases and temperatures can be extreme. The *chili* wind (*khamsin* in Egypt) which is hot, dry and sandy, occasionally blows from the Sahara desert across this region.

History, government and constitution. Variously ruled by Phoenicians, Carthaginians, Romans, Byzantines, Arabs, Spanish and Turks, the French gained a foothold in Tunisia establishing a protectorate in 1883. Independence was achieved in 1956 and in the following year the monarchy was abolished and a republic declared. The constitution of 1959 established a 136-member National Assembly, elected every 5 years and headed by a president who appoints a prime minister and a cabinet of 22 ministers.

Economy. Agriculture, employing 50% of the pop, though significant is of declining importance within the economy. Olives are the main cash crop, Tunisia being the world's 4th largest producer of olive oil. Other important crops include wheat, barley, henna, almonds, cork, citrus fruits, dates, grapes and vegetables. Irrigation schemes supported by external aid from West Germany and Canada are being undertaken in the N. There is a sizeable fishing industry employing over 20,000 people and 6,000 boats. The industrial sector includes sugar refining, cellulose and marble processing, petroleum refining, cement production, tyre, textiles and carpet manufacture, food processing, and paper pulp and phosphoric acid production. Tunisia is the world's 5th largest producer of phosphate rock and Africa's 7th largest oil producer with oil its most valuable export. Other important minerals include iron ore, lead and zinc. There are also reserves of gold, barite and fluorspar. The main trading partners are France, West Germany, Italy, the USA and Greece.

Administrative divisions. Tunisia is divided into 18 governorates (*gouvernorats*):

Governorate	*pop(1984)*
Béja	274,706
Bizerte	394,670
Gabès	245,016
Gafsa	235,723
Jendouba	359,425
Kairouan	421,607
Kasserine	297,959
El Kef	247,672
Mahdia	270,435
Medenine	295,889
Monastir	278,478
Nabeul	461,405
Sfax	577,992
Sidi Bouzid	288,528
Siliana	222,038
Sousse	322,491
Tunis Nord	944,130
Tunis Sud	205,907

Tunja *toon'KHa*, 5 33N 73 23W, pop(1985) 93,159, capital of Boyacá dept, E central Colombia, South America; in an arid mountainous area at an alt of 2,819 m; university (1953); one of the oldest cities in Colombia (refounded as a Spanish city in 1539 by Gonzalo Suárez Rendón); before that it was the seat of the Zipa, one of the two Chibcha kings; the city formed an independent junta in 1811; in 1818 Bolívar fought the decisive battle of Boyacá 16 km to the S of Tunja; railway; monuments: the church of Santo Domingo, begun in 1594, has a richly carved wooden interior; the Santa Clara Chapel (built in 1580), now the hospital of San Rafael, also has fine wood carvings; in the Parque Bosque de la Republica is the adobe wall against which 3 martyrs of the Independence were shot in 1816; the Casa del Fundador Suárez Rendón on the main square which dates from 1540-43 is now a museum of colonial Tunja.

Tupiza *too-pee'sa*, 21 27S 65 45W, pop(1976) 10,702, town in Sud Chichas prov, Potosí, SW Bolivia; railway; economy: silver, tin, lead and bismuth mining.

Tupungato, Cerro *too-poon-ga'tō*, 33 22S 69 50W, mountain rising to 6,800 m on border between Argentina and Chile; between Mendoza prov, Andina, Argentina and Aconcagua region, Chile; c.80 km SSE of Cerro Aconcagua.

Turbat *toor'but*, 26 00N 63 06E, pop(1981) 52,000, town in Balúchistán prov, W Pakistan; 402 km WNW of Karachi on the R Dasht.

Turda *toor'da*, 46 35N 23 50E, pop(1983) 59,695, town in Cluj county, NW central Romania; on R Argeş; former Roman colony; economy: chemicals, gas, cement, food processing, salt; monuments: palace, Roman remains.

Turfan Depression, TURPAN DEPRESSION, basin in E Xinjiang aut region, NW China; situated to the N of the Qoltag Shan range and to the S of the Bogda Shan range; surrounded by mountains averaging between 1,500 and 4,500 m above sea level; the basin is 245 km W-E and 75 km N-S, with an area of 50,000 sq km; Aydingkol Hu lake at the centre of the Turfan Depression is the lowest point in China, with its surface lying 154 m below sea level; little rain falls here, and summer temperatures average 30°C, sometimes reaching 47°C; water from the surrounding mountains melts and flows into the rivers of the depression from where it seeps into the ground and irrigates the land through an underground system of channels known as the *karez*; the Turfan Depression is a major farming area for NW China, growing wheat, cotton, melons and grapes.

Tŭrgovishte or **Targoviste** *tur-go'veesh-te*, okrug (prov) of NE Bulgaria to the N of the Stara Planina (Balkan Mts); area 2,754 sq km; pop(1981) 172,000.

Tŭrgovishte, formerly ESKI DZHUMAYA (-1909), 43 14N 26 37E, capital of Tŭrgovishte okrug (prov), NE central Bulgaria; 340 km NE of Sofiya, on the R Vrana; once a cultural centre of the Bulgarian Moslems under Turkish rule; airfield; railway; economy: textiles and handicrafts.

Turia *too'rya*, river rising in the Sierra de Albarracín, Teruel prov, E central Spain, flowing SE into Valencia prov where it meets the Mediterranean at Valencia; length 280 km; irrigation reservoirs at Pantano del Generalisimo and Pantano del Loriguilla.

Turin, prov and city in NW Italy. See Torino.

Turkana, Lake *toor-ka'na*, formerly LAKE RUDOLF, lake in NW Kenya, E Africa; 400 km N of Nairobi; its N extremity extends into Ethiopia; length from N to S is 290 km; width 56 km; depth approx 70 m; area 6,405 sq km; receives the Omo, Kibish and Turkwell rivers but has no surface outlet; owing to high evaporation rates the lake is shrinking and hence becoming increasingly saline; there are a few volcanic islands; European discovery by Count Teleki in 1888, who named it L Rudolf after the crown prince of Austria.

Turkey *tur'kee*, TÜRKIYE *tyur-ki-ye'* (Turk), official name Republic of Turkey, TÜRKIYE CUMHURIYETI (Turk), republic lying partly in Europe and partly in Asia, bounded W by the Aegean Sea and Greece, N by Bulgaria and the Black Sea, E by the USSR and Iran, and S by Iraq, Syria, and the Mediterranean Sea; timezone GMT +3; area 779,452 sq km; capital Ankara; chief cities İstanbul, İzmir, Adana, Bursa and Gaziantep; pop(1980) 44,737,957; the population comprises 85% Turkish and 12% Kurd; the Kurds constitute an ethnic and linguistic minority and live mostly in the poor, remote areas of the E and SE; Turkish is the official language; the dominant religion is Islam; the unit of currency is the Turkish lira; national holiday 29 Oct (Republic Day); membership of ASSIMER, Council of Europe, EEC (associate member), ECOSOC, FAO, GATT, IAEA, IBRD, ICAC, ICAO, IDA, Islamic Development Bank, IEA, IFAD, IFC, IHO, ILO, IMF, IMO, INTELSAT, INTERPOL, IOOC, IPU, ITC, ITU, NATO, OECD, OIC, Regional Cooperation for Development, UN, UNESCO, UPU, WHO, WIPO, WMO, WSG, WTO.

Physical description. Of the total area of 779,452 sq km, 755,688 sq km lie in that part of Asia known as Asia Minor or Anadolu (Anatolia) and 23,764 sq km lie in that part of Europe known as E Thrace. The straits of Canakkale Boğazi (Dardanelles), Marmara Denizi (Sea of Marmara) and Karadeniz Boğazi (Bosporus), known collectively as the Turkish Straits, separate the 2 continents and connect the Black Sea (NE) and the Mediterranean Sea (SW). Turkey is a mountainous country with an average elevation of 1,130 m. Mountain ranges extend from W to E along the N and S coasts of Anadolu and between them is a high plateau with an average altitude between 1,000 and 2,000 m. The Toros Dağları (Taurus Mts) cover the entire S part of Anadolu and comprise an irregular succession of folded ranges roughly parallel with the Mediterranean Sea. E Anadolu is Turkey's highest region, reaching its highest peaks at Mt Ağrı Dağı (Ararat) (5,165 m) and Küçük Ağrı Dağı (Little Ararat) (3,907 m). The mountains of W Anadolu extend in spurs from the plateau towards the Aegean Sea. On the European side of Turkey is the Yıldız range. The alluvial coastal plains range in width from 20 to 30 km although some penetrate considerable distances inland (the Büyük Menderes Plain extends inland for 200 km). On the Aegean coast there are numerous peninsulas, capes, gulfs, and bays of various sizes. Steep, high cliffs extend along the full length of the Mediterranean coast. The 2 main inlets here are Antalya Körfezi (Gulf of Antalya) and İskenderun Körfezi (Gulf of Iskenderun). The largest lakes in Turkey are Van Gölü, Tuz Gölü (Salt Lake), Beyşehir Gölü, and Eğridir Gölü. Keban Baraji (675 sq km) in E Anadolu and Hirfanli Baraji (263 sq km) in central Anadolu are artificial lakes created by the damming of rivers. Chief rivers are the Kızıl Irmak (1,355 km), Sakarya (824 km), Seyhan (560 km), and Yeşilırmak (519 km). The R Tigris (Dicle) and the R Euphrates (Firat) have their origins in Turkey.

Climate. The narrow coastlands and mountain slopes facing the Black Sea on the N, the Aegean on the W, and the Mediterranean on the S have wetter and milder winters than the interior. Turkish Thrace, around İstanbul and the Black Sea coast, tends to be colder in winter than the W and S coasts and rainfall is well distributed throughout the year. Temperatures at İstanbul range from 5°C in Jan to 23°C in July, and the mean annual rainfall is 723 mm. Further E along the Black Sea coast rainfall becomes heavy in summer and autumn. The Aegean and Mediterranean coasts have a typically Mediterranean climate with hot, dry summers and warm,

TURKEY
PROVINCES

1 KIRKLARELI
2 EDIRNE
3 TEKIRDAĞ
4 İSTANBUL
5 KOCAELI
6 BURSA
7 BALIKESIR
8 ÇANAKKALE
10 KUTAHYA
11 UŞAK
12 DENIZLI
13 AYDIN
14 MUĞLA
15 İZMIR
16 ANTALYA
17 BURDUR
18 ISPARTA
19 AFYONKARAHISAR
20 ESKIŞEHIR
21 BILECIK
22 SAKARYA
24 ANKARA
25 ÇANKIRI
26 ZONGULDAK
27 KASTAMONU
28 SINOP
29 SAMSUN
30 ÇORUM
31 KIRŞEHIR
32 YOZGAT
33 TOKAT
34 AMASYA
35 ORDU
36 GIRESUN
37 TRABZON
38 RIZE
39 ARTVIN
40 KARS
41 ERZURUM
42 AĞRI
43 GÜMÜSHANE
45 ERZINCAN
46 KAYSERI
47 NIĞDE
49 IÇEL
51 KAHRAMANMARAŞ
52 GAZIANTEP
53 HATAY
55 ADIYAMAN
56 MALATYA
57 ELÂZIĞ
58 TUNCELI
59 DIYARBAKIR
62 BITLIS
63 BINGÖL
64 MUŞ
66 HAKKÂRI
67 NEVŞEHIR

0 60kms

wet winters. At İzmir on the Aegean coast, temperatures range from 8°C in Jan to 27°C in July with a mean annual rainfall of 700 mm. The interior plateau has low rainfall and cold or very cold winters. Summers are warm or even hot with occasional thunderstorms. Ankara has a mean annual rainfall of 367 mm and temperatures range from 0.3°C in Jan to 23°C in July.

History, government and constitution. In the 13th century the Turks were pressed W by the Mongols where they were rewarded for services to the Seljuk sultan of Iconium with lands in Asia Minor. When the Seljuk sultanate disintegrated in the 15th century, it was replaced by the Ottoman sultanate, so called from the first sultan, Othmân. By 1350 the little clan of nomads had gained a foothold in NW Asia Minor. Then began the Turkish invasion of Europe, first in the Balkans (1375). In 1453 Constantinople fell to the Turks, whose influence spread into the Crimea, Hungary, Syria, Egypt, Arabia and Cyprus. Under Suleyman the Magnificent (1520-66) the empire reached its peak. Despite the defeat of the Turkish fleet at Lepanto (1571) the Ottoman Empire continued to expand into Russia, Crete, Iraq and Tunisia. The empire fell into decay in the 17th century as Russian and Austrian armies pressed the Turks back towards the Bosporus. In the 19th century Britain regarded Turkey as a bulwark against Russian expansion. Thus in the Crimean War Britain and France fought to protect Turkey against the imperialist policy of Russia. Nationalist revolts in the lower Danube resulted in the Treaty of Berlin (1878) giving independence to Bulgaria, Serbia and Romania. Bosnia and Hercegovina were placed under Austrian control; Russia annexed Bessarabia and Britain Cyprus; France seized Tunis (1881) and Britain occupied Egypt (1882). Following alleged Armenian massacres, public opinion forced Britain to abandon the support of Turkey. In 1908 the Young Turks seized power and became embroiled in the Balkan War of 1912-13. Turkey allied with Germany during World War I and shared in her defeat. The Treaty of Sèvres, signed by the sultan in 1920, was repudiated by the Turks and a period of confusion followed. Order was restored when the Republic of Turkey was founded on 29 Oct 1923 following a revolt of the Young Turk movement led by Kemal Atatürk. With the collapse of the Ottoman Empire Atatürk embarked upon a policy of westernization and economic development, transforming Turkey into a modern state based on the European pattern. In 1980 Turkey came under military rule and the bicameral Grand National Assembly was dissolved. According to the new constitution introduced in 1982, Turkey has a democratic, parliamentary form of government. The constitution provides for a single-chambered grand national assembly. A president and head of state hold office for 7 years. The prime minister and council of about 25 ministers are appointed by the president.

Economy. Although largely an agricultural country, Turkey has a wide range of important mineral resources. Turkey is one of the 4 principal producers of chrome in the world and other minerals include coal, lignite, copper concentrate, and sulphur. Oil is produced in E Turkey. Manufacturing industries include food processing and the production of textiles, iron and steel, cement, and leather goods. Chief exports in 1983 were tobacco, cotton, textiles, cement, raisins, nuts, leather, glass and ceramics. Turkey's main trading partners are Iraq, West Germany, the USA, France, the UK, Italy, Libya, Iran and E Europe.

Agriculture. Agriculture accounts for almost 20% of national income and employs over 60% of the workforce. The principal products are cotton, tobacco, cereals (especially wheat), figs, silk, olives and olive oil, dried fruits, liquorice roots and nuts. The main tobacco districts are Samsun, Bafra, Çarşamba, İzmit and İzmir. The USA receives about two-thirds of the leaf tobacco exports. The area around Bursa is the principal centre for silk production. Mohair from goats, wool and hides are also important to the rural economy.

Administrative divisions. Turkey is divided into 67 provinces as follows:

Province	*area (sq km)*	*pop(1980)*
Adana	17,253	1,485,743
Adıyaman	7,614	367,595
Afyonkarahısar	14,230	597,516
Ağri	11,376	368,009
Amasya	5,520	341,387
Ankara	30,715	2,854,689
Antalya	20,591	748,706
Artvin	7,436	228,997
Aydın	8,007	652,488
Balıkesir	14,292	853,177
Bilecik	4,307	147,001
Bingöl	8,125	228,702
Bitlis	6,707	257,908
Bolu	11,051	471,751
Burdur	6,887	235,009
Bursa	11,043	1,148,492
Çanakkale	9,737	391,568
Çankırı	8,454	258,436
Çorum	12,820	571,831
Denizli	11,868	603,338
Diyarbakır	15,355	778,150
Edirne	6,276	363,286
Elâziğ	9,153	440,808
Erzincan	11,903	282,022
Erzurum	25,066	801,809
Eskişehir	13,652	543,802
Gaziantep	7,642	808,697
Giresun	6,934	480,083
Gümüşhane	10,227	275,191
Hakkâri	9,521	155,463
Hatay	5,403	856,271
Içel	15,853	843,931
Isparta	8,933	350,116
İstanbul	5,712	4,741,890
İzmir	11,973	1,976,763
Kahramanmaraş	14,327	738,032
Kars	18,557	700,238
Kastamonu	13,108	450,946
Kayseri	16,917	778,383
Kırklareli	6,550	283,408
Kırşehir	6,570	240,497
Kocaeli	3,626	596,899
Konya	47,420	1,562,139
Kütahya	11,875	497,089
Malatya	12,313	606,996
Manisa	13,810	941,941
Mardin	12,760	564,967
Muğla	13,338	438,145
Muş	8,196	302,406
Nevşehir	5,467	256,933
Niğde	14,294	512,071
Ordu	6,001	713,535
Rize	3,920	361,258
Sakarya	4,817	548,747
Samsun	9,579	1,008,113
Siirt	11,003	445,483
Sinop	5,862	276,242
Sivas	28,488	750,144
Tekirdağ	6,218	360,742
Tokat	9,958	624,508
Trabzon	4,685	731,045
Tunceli	7,774	157,974
Urfa	18,584	602,736
Uşak	5,341	247,224
Van	19,069	468,646
Yozgat	14,123	504,433
Zonguldak	8,629	954,512

Turkmenskaya, TURKMENISTAN (Eng), constituent republic of the Soviet Union, in SW Middle Asia, bounded S by Iran and Afghanistan, and W by the Caspian Sea; the Peski Karakumy (Kara-Kum Desert) occupies c.80% of the territory; the chief river is the Amudar'ya which forms part of the E boundary; pop(1983) 3,042,000; area 488,100 sq km; capital Ashkhabad; chief towns Chardzhou, Mary, Krasnovodsk, and Nebit-Dag; economy: power generation, petroleum refining, chemicals, food processing, rugs, machine building; the republic's agriculture specializes in the production of cotton, karakul, and raw silk; Turkoman horses and the famous Karakul sheep are bred; proclaimed a Soviet Socialist Republic in Oct 1924 and became a republic of the USSR in May 1925; the republic is divided into the 5 oblasts of Ashkhabadskaya, Chardzhouskaya, Krasnovodskaya, Mary, Tashauzskaya.

Turks and Caicos Islands *kay'kas*, two island groups comprising c.30 islands and cays forming the SE archipelago of the Bahamas chain, W Atlantic Ocean, situated 144 km N of the Dominican Republic and Haiti and 920 km SE of Miami; timezone GMT −5; the unit of currency is the US dollar; area 500 sq km; capital Grand Turk; pop(1980) 7,413; 41.4% of the population are under 14 years; the majority of the pop is of African descent; Christianity is the dominant religion; the official and spoken language is English.

Physical description and climate. These low lying islands stand on an E extension of the Great Bahama Bank, separated from the Bahamas by the deep Caicos Passage. The territory comprises 2 groups, the Turks Is and the Caicos Is, separated by the 35 km-wide Turks I Passage. Only 6 of the islands are inhabited: Grand Turk and Salt Cay in the Turks Is, and S Caicos, Middle Caicos, N Caicos, and Providenciales in the Caicos Is. The climate is subtropical, cooled by SE trade winds which blow throughout the year. Average annual rainfall is 525 mm on Grand Turk, but tends to be higher on the Caicos Is. Temperatures range from 24°C to 27°C in the winter months and from 29°C to 32°C in the summer. The islands have occasionally been subject to severe hurricanes.

History, government and constitution. The islands were linked formally to the Bahamas in 1765 but in 1848 responsibility was transferred to Jamaica. On 6 August 1962 Jamaica attained independence and the Turks and Caicos Is were again associated with the Bahamas until they became a British Crown Colony in 1972. The 1976 constitution provides for an executive council and a legislative council. A governor, appointed by and representing the British sovereign, presides over the 8-member executive council.

Economy. Salt production was at one time the principal occupation on these islands but difficulty in finding markets eventually led to the closure of all operations. Apart from corn and beans grown for subsistence on the Caicos Is (except S Caicos) there is practically no agriculture. The principal natural resource of the islands is fish, principally spiny lobster and conch, much of the catch being exported to the US. Fish-processing plants operate on S Caicos and Providenciales. Tourism is a rapidly expanding industry and further developments, particularly of club-type complexes, are under way. Manufacturing industries employ only 1.4% of the working population. Chief imports include foodstuffs, tobacco, clothing, beverages, and petroleum. Chief exports include conch, crawfish, and other fishmeat. The main trade partners are the USA and the UK.

Communications. The main seaports are Grand Turk, Salt Cay, Providenciales, and Cockburn Harbour on S Caicos. Grand Turk, S Caicos, and Providenciales (opened 1985) have airports and the remaining inhabited islands have airfields.

Turku *toor'koo*, ÅBO *o'boo* (Swed), 60 27N 22 15E, pop(1982) 163,484, seaport and capital of Turku-Pori prov, SW Finland; on the Aurajoki near its mouth on the Gulf of Bothnia; University of Åbo (1918); University of Turku (1920); established in the 11th century, it was the capital of Finland until 1812; a peace between Sweden and Russia was signed here in 1743; railway; airport; ferries to Sweden and Åland islands; Rantasipi Congress Centre; economy: shipbuilding, engineering, foodstuffs, textiles; events: music festival in Aug.

Turku-Pori *toor'koo-po'ree*, ÅBO-BJORNEBORG *o'boo-byur'na-bor'ya* (Swed), a prov of SW Finland, bounded on the W by the Gulf of Bothnia; area 23,166 sq km; pop(1982) 707,401; Turku, the 3rd largest town in Finland, is the prov capital; chief towns include Pori and Rauma; nickel mining at Vammala.

Tur'lock, 37 30N 120 51W, pop(1980) 26,287, city in Stanislaus county, central California, United States; in the San Joaquin Valley, 21 km SE of Modesto; railway.

Turmero *toor-may'rō*, 10 13N 67 28W, pop(1981) 110,186, town in Aragua state, N Venezuela; railway.

Turneffe Islands *tur-nef'*, island group surrounding a central lagoon in the W Caribbean Sea, separated from Belize City to the W by a barrier reef which is the 2nd longest in the world.

Turnhout *tærn-howt'*, dist of Antwerpen prov, N Belgium; area 1,365 sq km; pop(1982) 361,402.

Turnhout, 51 19N 4 57E, pop(1982) 37,567, industrial town in Turnhout dist, Antwerpen prov, N Belgium; economy: textiles; monuments: Palais de Justice (1371), church of St Peter (14th-c); here in 1597 the Netherlanders defeated the Spaniards.

Turnu Măgurele *toor'noo ma-goo-ray'le*, 43 44N 24 53E, pop(1983) 33,451, river port in Teleorman county, S Romania; on the R Danube; railway; economy: port trade, fishing, furniture; monuments: 14th-c fortress, remains of a Roman camp.

Turpan Depression, basin in E Xinjiang aut region, NW China. See Turfan Depression.

Turquino, Pico *pee'kō toor-kee'nō*, 19 59N 76 50W, peak in the Sierra Maestra, SE Cuba; on the border between Granma and Guantánamo provs, 104 km W of Santiago de Cuba; highest peak in Cuba; height 2,005 m.

Tuscaloo'sa (Choctaw, 'black warrior'), 33 12N 87 34W, pop(1980) 75,211, county seat of Tuscaloosa county, W Alabama, United States; on the Black Warrior river, 76 km WSW of Birmingham; state capital 1826-46; railway; economy: manufacturing and medical centre; industry is based on the region's coal, iron, cotton and timber; products include tyres, chemicals, paper, processed foods, petroleum products, plastics and textiles.

Tuscany, region of Italy. See Toscana.

Tus'tin, 33 44N 117 49W, pop(1980) 32,317, city in Orange county, SW California, United States; 5 km E of Santa Ana.

Tuticorin *too-ti-kor-in'*, 8 48N 78 10E, pop(1981) 251,000, seaport in Tamil Nadu state, SW India; on the Gulf of Mannar, 128 km S of Madurai; founded by the Portuguese in 1540; later held by the Dutch who established it as a centre of the pearl trade until 1825, when it passed to the British; linked by rail to Palayankottai; economy: cotton, coffee, salt.

Tutong *too-tawng*, dist of Brunei, SE Asia; bounded N by the South China Sea, W by the Belait dist of Brunei, NE by Brunei-Muara dist and on all other sides by the E Malaysian state of Sarawak; pop(1981) 21,640; chief town Tutong.

Tutong, 4 51N 114 40E, town on N coast of Tutong dist, Brunei, SE Asia; at the mouth of the Sungei Tutong river; linked to the towns of Bandar Seri Begawan and Kuala Belait by a main highway; a centre of the Brunei oil industry.

Tutuila *too-too-ee'la*, 14 17S 170 41W, largest island of American Samoa, in the S Pacific Ocean; area 109 sq km; harbour at Pago Pago; rugged in the E, fertile plain in the SW; rises to 653 m at Mt Matafao.

Tuvalu *too-va'loo* (Polynesian, 'cluster of eight'), formerly ELLICE IS, island group in the SW Pacific, between 5° and 11° S and 176° and 180° E, situated 1,050 km N of Fiji and 4,020 km NE of Sydney, Australia; includes the islands of Funafuti, Nukufetau, Nukulailai, Nanumea, Niutao, Nanumanga, Nui, Vaitupu and Niulakita; area 26 sq km; pop(1985) 8,229; capital Funafuti; the pop density in 1985 was 316 inhabitants per sq km; the people are almost entirely of Polynesian stock and have close ties

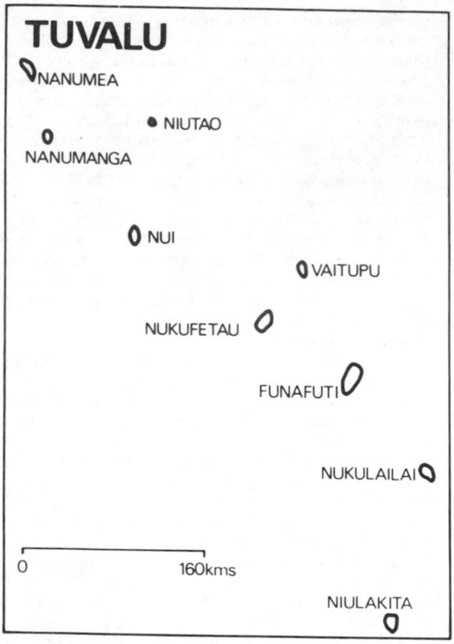

with the Samoans and Tokelauans to the S and E; Tuvaluan and English are the main languages; Christianity is the dominant faith; the unit of currency is the Australian dollar; membership of Commonwealth, ACP state of the EEC.

Physical description and climate. Tuvalu comprises 9 islands, all of them low lying coral atolls, running NW-SE in a chain 579 km long. Only 5 of the atolls have central lagoons. The climate is hot and humid throughout the year, with temperatures averaging 30°C. Trade winds from the E moderate conditions for much of the year. Rainfall averages 3,535 mm per year.

History, government and constitution. Tuvalu was invaded and occupied by Samoans in the 16th century, and between 1850 and 1875 many of the islanders were taken as forced labour for the guano mines and coffee plantations of South America. Tuvalu was declared a British protectorate in 1892 and administered as a colony jointly with the Gilbert Is (now Kiribati) from 1915. In the early 1970s the Polynesian Ellice islanders expressed a desire to separate from the Micronesian Gilbertese. On the basis of a referendum in 1974, separate constitutions for the Ellice Is, renamed Tuvalu, and the Gilbert Is came into force on 1 Oct 1975 and administrative separation was implemented on 1 Jan 1976. On 1 Oct 1978 Tuvalu became a fully independent nation. It is a constitutional monarchy with the Queen as head of state, represented in the islands by a Tuvaluan governor-general. Parliament consists of a single chamber with 12 members elected by universal adult suffrage. The cabinet comprises a prime minister and 4 ministers.

Economy. Agriculture is virtually non-existent due to the poor quality of the soil which is composed largely of coral sand and rock fragments. The main food crops are coconuts, pulaka, pandanus fruit, bananas and pawpaws. Copra is the chief cash crop and only export. The chief source of income is remittances from Tuvaluans working abroad, either employed in the phosphate industry on Nauru, or as crew on foreign ships. A small amount of income is derived from handicrafts marketed through co-operatives and the sale of postage stamps. Chief imports include foodstuffs, machinery and transport stamps. Chief trading partners are Australia, Fiji, and New Zealand.

Tuxer Alpen *took'ser al'pen*, mountain range in the E Alps in Tirol state, W Austria; the highest peak is Olperer (3,476 m).

Tuxtla Gutiérrez *toos'tla goo-tyayr'rays*, 16 45N 93 09W, pop(1980) 166,476, capital of Chiapas state, S Mexico; S of Villahermosa; university (1975); economy: coffee, cacao, sugar, tobacco, fruit; monuments: state archaeological museum; to the N of the city is the El Sumerido canyon, into which Indian warriors threw themselves during the Spanish Conquest rather than surrender to the Conquistadores; event: the fair of Guadalupe (12 Dec).

Tuz Gölü *tooz go-loo'*, shallow salt lake in central Turkey, 104 km NE of Konya; area 1,500 sq km; length 80 km; width 51 km; swampy on the W and S coasts; yields large quantities of salt.

Tuzla *tooz'la*, SALINAS (Lat), 44 33N 18 41E, pop(1981) 121,717, town in NE Bosna-Hercegovina republic, Yugoslavia; 80 km N of Sarajevo; university (1976); mineral springs; railway; economy: salt, lignite, petroleum, gas, coal; fruit trade.

Tweed, river in SE Scotland and NE England; rises in SW Borders region at Tweed's Well, 9.6 km NNW of Moffat; flows NNE to Peebles, then generally E past Innerleithen, near Galashiels and past Kelso; from just before Coldstream until near Berwick-upon-Tweed, the Tweed forms the border between England and Scotland; enters the North Sea at Berwick-upon-Tweed; major tributaries: Ettrick Water, Gala Water, Leader Water, Teviot river and Whiteadder Water; length 155 km; navigable only for a few km in its tidal section; the river has a catchment area of 4,843 sq km.

Twin Falls, 42 34N 114 28W, pop(1980) 26,209, county seat of Twin Falls county, S Idaho, United States; in the Snake river valley, 185 km ESE of Boise; airfield; economy: originally the centre of a private irrigation project, now supplemented by the Minidoka project of the US Bureau of Reclamation; food processing, trout farms; one of the falls in the nearby gorge is harnessed for hydroelectric power.

Tychy *tich'i*, TICHAU *ti'KHow* (Ger), 50 08N 18 56E, pop(1983) 178,100, city in Katowice voivodship, S Poland; amidst forest near L Paprocańskie, S of Katowice in upper Silesian industrial region; developed since 1950; railway; economy: brewing, motor vehicles, coal mining, fruit and vegetable farming.

Tyldesley *tilz'li*, 53 32N 2 29W, pop(1981) 27,903, town in Wigan borough, Greater Manchester, NW England; 8 km SW of Bolton; economy: chemicals, textiles, coal.

Tyler *tī'ler*, 32 21N 95 18W, pop(1980) 70,508, county seat of Smith county, E Texas, United States; 147 km ESE of Dallas; railway; economy: situated in the centre of the East Texas oil field, the city has oil refineries and many oil-based industries; manufactures include pipes, tyres, and electrical equipment; there is a large rose-growing industry; event: Texas Rose Festival (Oct).

Tyne *tīn*, river of NE England; formed by the confluence of the N Tyne and the S Tyne, NW of Hexham, Northumberland; flows 48 km E across the Kielder Moor and through Tyne and Wear to meet the North Sea between Tynemouth and South Shields; the S Tyne rises on the slopes of Cross Fell, E Cumbria; the N Tyne rises in the Cheviot Hills on the border with Scotland and is dammed to form the Kielder Water reservoir; the Tyne is linked to the R Tees as part of the UK's first regional water grid system supplying water to the industrial NE of England; the river is navigable 13 km above Newcastle; the Tyne serves the industrial towns of Newcastle, Jarrow, Gateshead, Wallsend and South Shields; tributaries include the Derwent and Team rivers.

Tyne and Wear *-weer*, metropolitan county of NE England; bounded E by the North Sea, N and W by Northumberland and S by Durham; drained by the Tyne and Wear rivers; pop(1981) 1,142,675; area 540 sq km; county town Newcastle upon Tyne; chief towns include Gateshead, Jarrow, Wallsend, Sunderland; economy: shipbuilding, engineering, coal mining, chemicals; the metropolitan council was abolished in 1986; the county is divided into 5 boroughs:

Borough	*area (sq km)*	*pop(1981)*
Gateshead	143	211,333
Newcastle upon Tyne	112	277,829
North Tyneside	84	198,209
South Tyneside	64	160,410
Sunderland	138	294,894

Tyneside, pop(1981) 782,410, urban area in Tyne and Wear, NE England; includes Newcastle upon Tyne, Gateshead, Jarrow, Felling, Hebburn, Newburn, Longbenton-Killingworth, Wallsend and North and South Shields; airport (Woolsington); railway.

Tyre, seaport in Lebanon. See Soûr.

Tyrifjorden *tu'ree-fyord-en*, TYRI FJORD (Eng), lake in SE Buskerud county, SE Norway, 24 km W of Oslo; fed by the Begna R in the N and waters of Rands Fjord; drains SW into the Drammen R; SE arm is called Hols Fjord; area 136 sq km; length 32 km; maximum depth 281 m.

Tyrone *tī-rōn'*, TIR EOGHAIN (Gael), county in W Northern Ireland; bounded N by Co Derry, E by Lough Neagh, SE by Armagh along the R Blackwater, SW by Fermanagh and NW and S by the Republic of Ireland along the R Foyle; a hilly county with the Sperrin Mts rising in the N to 683 m in Mt Sawel, on the border with Co Derry (Londonderry); drained by the Blackwater, Foyle and Strule rivers; pop(1981) 143,884; area 3,136 sq km; county town Omagh; major towns include Dungannon, Cookstown and Strabane; economy: agriculture (oats, potatoes, flax, turnips, sheep and cattle raising); Tyrone consists of 4 districts:

District	*area (sq km)*	*pop(1981)*
Cookstown	623	26,624
Dungannon	779	41,073
Omagh	1,129	41,159
Strabane	870	35,028

Tyrrhenian Sea *tī-ree-nee'an*, arm of the Mediterranean Sea; bounded by the Italian Peninsula, Sicily, Sardinia and Corsica; connected to the Ligurian Sea in the NW and to the Ionian Sea in the SE, by the Strait of Messina; Naples and Palermo are the major ports.

Tyumen' *tyoo-myayn'y'*, 57 11N 65 29E, pop(1983) 397,000, capital city of Tyumenskaya oblast, SW Siberian Rossiyskaya, Soviet Union; on the R Nitsa; founded in 1585 on the site of a Tatar settlement; the first settled Russian town E of the Ural'skiy Khrebet (Ural Mts) range; formerly an important centre of trade with China; university; important railway junction linking the lines that serve the Arctic regions of the country; economy: cotton textiles, clothing, machine tools and instruments, rapidly expanding oil-refining industry.

Tywi or **Towy** *tu'wee*, river in Dyfed, SW Wales; rises in the Cambrian Mts of central Wales and flows 108 km SW to meet Carmarthen Bay.

U

Ubangi *oo-ban'gee*, OUBANGUI (Fr), a major tributary of the R Zaïre (Congo) in N and W Central Africa; formed by the confluence of the Bomu and Uele rivers; follows the frontier between the Central African Republic and Zaire, flowing past Mobaye, Bangui, Libenge and Impfondo to join the R Zaire 97 km SW of Mbandaka (Coquilhatville) on the Zaire-Congo border; length 1,060 km; length including the R Uele 2,250 km; receives the Lua, Giri and Kotto rivers; explored in 1884 and a complete hydrographic survey of the entire course was carried out by the French in 1910-11.

Ubeda *oo'vay-THa*, 38 03N 3 23W, pop(1981) 28,717, town in Jaén prov, Andalucia, S Spain; 56 km NE of Jaén; economy: foundries, motor parts, timber, livestock, olives, pottery, ironwork, esparto grass; monuments: Plaza Vazquez de Molina; churches of El Salvador and St Paul.

Uberaba *oo-bay-ra'ba*, 19 47S 47 57W, pop(1980) 180,228, town in Minas Gerais state, Sudeste region, SE Brazil; on the Río da Prata, W of Belo Horizonte; an important rail and road junction; airfield; economy: rice, coffee, maize, soya beans, cattle; event: at the beginning of May the Rural Society of the Minas Triangle holds an annual cattle and agricultural exhibition.

Uberaba, Lago, lake in E Santa Cruz dept, E Bolivia; on the Bolivia-Brazil border, 153 km N of Puerto Suárez; 16 km long, 8 km wide; connected to L Gaiba (SSE) by the Canal Pedro II which forms part of the border.

Uberlândia *oo-bayr-lan'dya*, 18 57S 48 17W, pop(1980) 230,185, town in Minas Gerais state, Sudeste region, SE Brazil; WNW of Belo Horizonte; founded in 1888; university (1969); railway; economy: maize, aviculture, timber.

Ubon Ratchathani *oo-bon rah'chah-tah'nee*, MUANG UBON, 15 15N 104 50E, pop(1982) 99,567, city in E Thailand; on R Mun, 65 km W of the Laos frontier; airfield.

Ucayali *oo-kī-a'lee*, dept in N Peru; area 100,831 sq km; pop(1981) 200,669; capital Pucallpa.

Ucayali, river in E Peru; one of the Amazon's main headstreams; formed by the union of the Apurímac (or Tambo) and Urubamba rivers at 11 17S 73 47W; flows approx 1,600 km N through Loreto dept, joining the Río Marañón to form the Amazon 88 km SSW of Iquitos at 4 30S 73 27W; navigable for its entire length by small craft; main tributaries the Pachitea and Tapiche rivers.

Uccle *ü'klu*, UKKEL *u'kul* (Flem), pop(1982) 75,552, town in Brussel dist, Brabant prov, Belgium; a suburb of Bruxelles.

Uck'field, 50 58N 0 06E, pop(1981) 10,938, town in Wealden dist, East Sussex, England; 12 km NE of Lewes; railway.

Uddevalla *ood-de-val'la*, 58 20N 11 56E, pop(1982) 46,033, industrial town in Göteborg och Bohus county, SW Sweden, near coast 72 km N of Göteborg (Gothenburg), on the Byfjord; railway; economy: shipyards.

Udine *oo'dee-nay*, prov of Friuli-Venezia Giulia region, NE Italy; pop(1981) 529,729; area 4,864 sq km; capital Udine.

Udine, 46 04N 13 14E, pop(1981) 102,021, industrial town and capital of Udine prov, Friuli-Venezia Giulia region, NE Italy; at the E end of the N Italian plain, 61 km NW of Trieste; archbishopric; railway; economy: textiles, chemicals; monuments: Romanesque cathedral, Gothic town hall.

Udon Thani *oo'don tah'nee*, BAN MAK KHAENG, 17 25N 102 45E, pop(1982) 81,909, town in NE Thailand; SSE of Vientiane near the Laos border; railway; airfield.

Ufa *oo-fa'*, 54 45N 55 58E, pop(1983) 1,034,000, capital city of Baskirskaya ASSR, E European Rossiyskaya, Soviet Union; in the Ural'skiy Khrebet (Ural Mts) range, on the R Ufa, at its confluence with the Dema and Zilim rivers; founded in 1586 as a fortress; university; railway; airport; economy: clothing, cotton textiles, oil refining, chemicals.

Uganda *yoo-gan'da*, official name Republic of Uganda, an E African republic bounded S by Rwanda, L Victoria and Tanzania, E by Kenya, N by Sudan and W by Zaire; timezone GMT +3; area 238,461 sq km; pop(1984e) 14,819,000; capital Kampala; chief towns Jinja, Mbale, Tororo and Soroti; the majority of the pop (99%) is African, the remainder being European, Asian or Arab; two-thirds of the pop is Christian (Protestant (33%) and Roman Catholic (33%)), 16% is Muslim and the remainder follow local beliefs; the official language is English with Luganda and Swahili widely used; other Bantu and Nilotic languages also spoken; the unit of currency is the Uganda shilling; national holidays: 9 Oct (Independence Day), 1 May (Labour Day); the main Christian festivals also observed; membership of AfDB, the Commonwealth, FAO, G-77, GATT, IAEA, IBRD, ICAC, ICAO, ICO, IDA, Islamic Development Bank, IFAD, IFC, ILO, IMF, INTELSAT, INTERPOL, ISO, ITU, NAM, OAU, OIC, UN, UNESCO, UPU, WHO, WIPO, WMO, WTO.

Physical description. Much of Uganda is plateau with an elevation of between 900 and 1,000 m. N of L Kyoga is a dry savannah or semi-desert area similar to the Turkana region of NW Kenya. The L Victoria basin is a fertile area which stretches from Mount Elgon in the E across the N shore of L Victoria to the Tanzanian frontier in the W. This region is bounded N by L Kyoga and W by the Rift Valley and the Ruwenzori range. Most of Uganda's pop is concentrated in this region and it is here that the coffee and cotton industries were established after 1945. The W Rift Valley runs along Uganda's frontier with Zaire. The Ruwenzori range of mountains lies along the Uganda-Zaire frontier between L Albert and L Edward. The Mount Stanley massif which straddles the frontier includes Margherita Peak (5,110 m), the highest point in Uganda and Zaire. In the SW is the NE end of the Virunga volcanic range, the main section of which runs along the Zaire-Rwanda frontier. The Ugandan section includes Muhavura (4,127 m) on the frontier with Rwanda. In the E is the Mount Elgon (4,321 m) massif on the frontier with Kenya. Further N on the same frontier are the Turkana and Karasuk hills. Of Uganda's total area (238,461 sq km) 39,000 sq km is swamp and 98,823 sq km is open water. The main lakes comprising the latter area include L Victoria (SE), L George (SW), L Edward (SW), L Albert (W), L Kwania (central), L Kyoga (central) and L Bisina (formerly L Salisbury, E). The 2 main rivers in Uganda are upper reaches of the R Nile, the Victoria Nile and the Albert Nile. The former flows from the N end of L Victoria, through L Kyoga and empties into the NE extremity of L Albert. The latter flows from just N of the Victoria Nile in a NE direction crossing into Sudan at Nimule. The Semliki river which flows between L Edward and L Albert forms the frontier between Uganda and Zaire for approx one-third of its lower length.

Climate. Uganda's climate is influenced by the presence of L Victoria, Africa's largest lake. The areas which receive the highest rainfall are along the shores of L Victoria and in the mountains to the W and SW. In these areas annual rainfall exceeds 1,500 mm. Entebbe (alt

1,182 m) is representative of lakeside climate with an annual average rainfall of 1,510 mm and average max daily temperatures ranging between 24°C and 28°C. In contrast, areas in the centre and NE of the country receive under 1,000 mm of rain annually. In common with Kenya, most of Uganda has 2 rainy seasons which merge into one long rainy season and one long dry season in the N of the country.

History, government and constitution. Visited by Arab traders in the 1830s and explored by Captain John Speke in the 1860s, Uganda was granted in 1888 to the Imperial British East Africa Company. Five years later the company withdrew and the administration of the area was assumed by a commissioner. In 1893 the kingdom of Buganda became a British Protectorate and between 1900 and 1903 treaties with Uganda's 4 main kingdoms resulted in all of the territory coming under British protection. Following 2 general elections in 1961 and 1962, Uganda was granted self-government and then full independence. In 1966 a complex political situation led to Dr Milton Obote, the country's prime minister, suspending the constitution, removing the president and assuming all powers. A new constitution was invoked the same year followed by another in the following year. In 1971 a coup led by General Idi Amin Dada resulted in the suspension of the constitution again and the establishment of rule by presidential decree. In 1979 Tanzanian troops along with Ugandan exiles marched on Kampala, overthrowing the government of Idi Amin who fled into exile in Saudi Arabia. Dr Milton Obote returned to power in 1980 but was ousted by a military coup in 1985 led by General Tito Okollo. Gen Okollo suspended both the parliament and the constitution pending the holding of elections and a return to civilian government. The parliament normally consists of 156 members (136 elected directly, 10 elected indirectly and 10 appointed from the armed forces). The government is headed by a military council whose chairman is also head of state. A cabinet appointed by the council is led by an executive prime minister.

Economy. Agriculture is the main economic activity, the main export crops being coffee, cotton, tea, tobacco and sugar. Fishing and livestock production are also important for local consumption as are millet, sorghum and groundnuts. The agricultural sector suffered during the Amin era when world prices fell. Since 1979 there have been attempts to improve both farming and manufacturing industry with the help of overseas aid. The major manufacturing industries include textiles, fertilizers and other agricultural requirements, food processing (coffee, sugar, tea and dairy products), construction materials, plywood, brewing, tobacco and cotton processing. Mineral resources include tungsten, copper, tin, beryl, phosphate, limestone, with the mineral industry ranking

third after coffee and cotton during the 1960s as a foreign-exchange earner. Tungsten is extracted in the Kilembe region (Western prov). Phosphate is extracted and cement processed (from limestone reserves) near Tororo and there are reserves of copper and cobalt near Kasese. Uganda earns foreign exchange by selling electricity to Kenya under a 50-year contract. Main trading partners for imports are Kenya, Tanzania, the UK, West Germany, Italy, Hong Kong and Japan; and for exports the USA, the UK, the Netherlands, Japan, Spain and Australia.

Administrative divisions. Uganda is divided into the 10 provinces of Busoga, Central, Eastern, Karamoja, Nile, Northern, North Buganda, Southern, South Buganda and Western. These provs are further divided into 34 districts.

Uherské Hradiště *oo'er-skeh rad-yish-tye*, 49 05N 17 30E, pop(1984) 37,313, town in Jihomoravský region, Czech Socialist Republic, central Czechoslovakia; on R Morava, SE of Brno; founded 1257; railway; economy: agricultural trade; monument: 17th-c Franciscan abbey.

Ujjain *oo'jīn*, 23 11N 75 50E, pop(1981) 282,000, city in Madhya Pradesh state, central India; on the R Sipra, 51 km NNW of Indore; one of the 7 sacred cities of the Hindus; capital of Gwalior from 1750 to 1810; linked by rail to Bhopal, Indore and Ratlām; economy: textiles; event: Kumbh Mela Festival every 12 years; monument: remains of old observatory (1730).

Ujung Padang *oo-joong' pa-dang'*, formerly MAKASSAR (-1973), 5 09S 119 28E, pop(1980) 434,766, seaport capital of Sulawesi Selatan prov, Indonesia; in SW corner of Sulawesi (Celebes) I; important trade centre of E Indonesia; established by Dutch in 1607; a free port in 1848; university (1956); airfield; economy: coffee, rubber, copra, resin, spices trade.

Ukraine, constituent republic of the Soviet Union. See Ukrainskaya.

Ukrainskaya, UKRAINA SSR, UKRAINE (Eng), constituent republic of the Soviet Union, in SW European USSR, bounded W by Poland, Czechoslovakia, Hungary, and Romania, and S by the Black Sea; the terrain is predominantly a plain with high elevations in the W, S and SE; the Ukrainian Carpathians in the W rise to a max elevation of 2,061 m at Mt Goveria; chief rivers are the Dnepr, Dnestr, Severskiy Donets, and Prut; there are more than 23,000 artificial bodies of water, including the Kiyev, Kanev, Kremenchug, and Dnepropetrovsk reservoirs and lakes Lenin and Kakhovka; pop(1983) 50,461,000; area 603,700 sq km; capital Kiyev (Kiev); chief towns Kharkov, Donetsk, Odessa, Dnepropetrovsk, L'vov, Zaporozh'ye and Krivoy Rog; economy: the Donets coalfield (area 25,900 sq km), stretching from Donetsk to Rostov-na-Donu, is the chief source of hard coal in the Soviet Union; large coal deposits have recently been discovered near Novo-Moskovsk, Kharkov, Lugansk, and on the left bank of the R Dnepr; iron-ore mining (Krivoy Rog); manufacturing industries include ferrous metallurgy, machine building, chemicals (mineral fertilizers, chemical fibres, synthetic resins, plastics, dyes, and rubber products), food processing, power generation, extraction and refining of natural gas and petroleum; Ukrainskaya is the major grain exporting republic within the USSR; chief crops grown include wheat, buckwheat, sugar-beet, sunflower, cotton, flax, tobacco, soya, hops, the rubber plant kok-sagyz, fruit, and vegetables; proclaimed a Soviet Socialist Republic in Dec 1917; the republic is divided into the 25 oblasts of Cherkasskaya, Chernigovskaya, Chernovitskaya, Dnepropetrovskaya, Donetskaya, Ivano-Frankovskaya, Khar'kovskaya, Khersonskaya, Khmel'nitskiy, Kirovogradskaya, Kiyevskaya, Krymskaya, L'vovskaya, Nikolayevskaya, Odesskaya, Poltavskaya, Rovenskaya, Sumskaya, Ternopol'skaya, Vinnitskaya, Volynskaya, Voroshilovgradskaya, Zakarpatskaya, Zaporozhskaya, Zhitomirskaya.

Ulaanbaatar *oo'lan-ba'tar*, ULAN BATOR, URGA (-1924), 47 54N 106 52E, pop(1978) 40,000, capital of Mongolia, in Selenge county, central Mongolia; the Mongolian railway and road network converges on the city; surrounded by the foothills of the Khenti Mountains; centre of Mongolia's political, economic, scientific and cultural life; founded as Urga in 1639 to form the centre of the Lamaistic religion in Mongolia; in the 18th century the city was a trading centre on the caravan routes between Russia and China; centre of the first Mongolian revolt in 1911; after Soviet occupation in 1921 the city was made capital of the Mongolian secular state, changing its name to Ulaanbaatar ('red valiant warrior') in 1924 by a decision of the first Party Congress of the Mongolian People's Party; recent industrial development has brought meat processing, carpet, brewing, wood processing and veterinary medicine factories into the city; mining and foodstuffs are also important.

Ulaangom *oo'lan-gom*, 49 59N 92 00E, capital of Uvs county, N Mongolia; bounded N by USSR; stock breeding is the basis of the economy.

Ulan-Ude *oo-lan'oo-de'*, formerly VERKHNEUDINSK (-1934), 51 45N 107 40E, pop(1983) 321,000, capital city of Buryatskaya ASSR, SE Siberian Rossiyskaya, Soviet Union; on the R Selenga, 75 km E of Ozero Baykal (Lake Baikal); founded in 1666 as a Cossack winter encampment; railway junction; airfield; economy: meat processing (largest plant in the country), machine building, metalwork, building materials, woodwork, thermal electric power plant; monument: Odigitrievskii cathedral (1741-85).

Ulcinj *ool'tsin-ya*, DULCIGNO *dool-chee'nyo* (Ital), 41 56N 19 12E, fishing village and resort in Crna Gora (Montenegro) republic, Yugoslavia; near the Albanian frontier, 56 km S of Titograd; the most southerly Yugoslav holiday resort area, with chalets and hotels in and around the village and a naturist camp on Ada I.

Uleaborg, prov in Finland. See Oulu.

Ulhasnagar *ool'has-nu-gur*, 19 15N 73 10E, pop(1981) 648,000, city in Maharashtra state, W India; NW of Bombay.

Uliastay *ool'ya-sa-tī*, ULIASTAI, JIBHALANTA, 47 42N 96 52E, capital of Dzavhan county, NW Mongolia; economy: agriculture and mining.

Ullapool, 57 54N 5 10W, pop(1981) 1,146, port town in Ross and Cromarty dist, Highland region, NW Scotland; on the E shore of Loch Broom; ferry service to Stornoway, Isle of Lewis; economy: tourist resort; fishing; fish processing (mackerel); monument: Ullapool museum.

Ullensaker *ool'en-say-ker*, 60 11N 11 06E, pop(1980) 16,837, town in Akershus county, SE Norway, near Oslo; airport.

Ullswater *ulz'-*, lake in the Lake District of Cumbria, NW England; SW of Penrith; 2nd largest lake in England; length 12 km; width 1 km; depth 64 m.

Ulm *oolm*, 48 24N 10 00E, pop(1983) 99,400, industrial and commercial city in Baden-Württemberg prov, W Germany; on the R Danube near mouth of R Iller, 72 km SE of Stuttgart; Napoleon defeated the Austrians near here in 1805; birthplace of Albert Einstein; university (1967); railway; economy: car manufacturing, transport equipment, light metal products, electrical engineering, textiles, leatherwork; monument: Minster (1377-1529), with the world's highest spire (161 m).

Ulsan *ool-sahn*, 35 32N 129 21E, pop(1984) 535,186, town in Kyŏngsangnam prov, SE Korea; railway; economy: coal, agriculture.

Ulster *ul'stur*, province in the Irish Republic; comprises the counties of Cavan, Donegal and Monaghan; Donegal is separated by part of Connacht and lies W of N Ireland; Cavan and Monaghan lie to the S of N Ireland; pop(1981) 230,159; area 8,012 sq km; chief towns include Donegal, Letterkenny, Cavan and Monaghan.

Ulúa *oo-loo'ah*, river in W Honduras, Central America; rises E of Marcala then flows c.320 km N to meet the Caribbean Sea, 24 km E of Puerto Cortés.

Ul'verston, 54 12N 3 06W, pop(1981) 11,970, town in South Lakeland dist, Cumbria, NW England; 13 km NE of Barrow-in-Furness; railway; economy: electronics, engineering.

Ul'yanovsk *ool-ya'nufsk*, SIMBIRSK (-1924), 54 19N 48 22E, pop(1983) 509,000, river port capital of Ul'yanovskaya oblast, W central European Rossiyskaya, Soviet Union; on a high hill in the Volga-Sviyaga watershed; founded in 1648 as a fortress; Lenin was born here in 1870 and lived here for 17 years; after his death in 1924 the town was renamed after his family name, Ulyanov; railway; airfield; economy: machine building, metalworking, leatherwork, footwear; monument: Palace of Books (1847).

Umag *oo'mag*, 45 26N 13 31E, fishing port in W Hrvatska (Croatia) republic, Yugoslavia; on the Adriatic coast SW of Trieste; part of Yugoslavia since 1947; industrial suburb to the S and tourist complexes to the N; Kanegra naturist camp; events: daily events in the Mon Plaisir entertainment complex, the largest of its kind in Yugoslavia.

Umbria *oom'bree-a*, region of Italy, comprising the provs of Perugia and Terni; pop(1981) 807,552; area 8,456 sq km; capital Perugia; chief towns Foligno and Terni; watered chiefly by the streams of the upper Tevere (Tiber) basin; Lago Trasimeno, W of Perugia, is the largest lake on the Italian peninsula; Umbria has long been a prosperous farming region (corn, olives, wine, sugar-beet, tobacco, market gardening, sheep farming); there is considerable industrial development around the towns of Terni, Narni, and Foligno (chemicals, metalworking), where power is supplied by large hydroelectric stations; textile manufacture and the production of craft articles have also been established in the Perugia and Spoleto areas.

Ume älv *ü'mu-elv*, UME (Eng), river in Västerbotten county, N Sweden; rises on Norwegian border, SE of Mo; flows SE through L Storuman past Vännäs and Umeå to discharge into Gulf of Bothnia at Holmsund; length 460 km; receives R Vindelälven just S of Vännäs; source of hydroelectric power; salmon hatchery at Sörfors (15 km NW of Umeå) which releases 100,000 young salmon annually into the river.

Umeå *ü'may-ō*, 63 50N 20 15E, pop(1982) 82,925, seaport and capital of Västerbotten county, N Sweden; on the Gulf of Bothnia at the mouth of the R Ume älv; seat of the Provincial Appeal Court; university (1963); received municipal charter for second time in 1622; town developed with rise of woodworking industry in late 19th century; railway; economy: woodworking.

Umm al Qaywayn *oom' al kī-wīn'*, one of the seven member states of the United Arab Emirates, lying between Shāriqah and Ra's al Khaymah, at the end of a sand spit 23 km along the coast from 'Ajmān; area 750 sq km; pop(1980) 12,300; capital Umm al Qaywayn; economy: fishing, light industry; agriculture is concentrated in the fertile enclave of Falaj al Mualla.

Umm al Qaywayn, 25 32N 55 35E, capital town of Umm al Qaywayn emirate, United Arab Emirates, SE Arabian Peninsula; on a sand spit extending out into the Arabian Gulf.

Umm Qaşr *oom kahs'er*, 30 02N 47 55E, town in Al Basrah governorate, SE Iraq; close to the Kuwait border; rail terminus; economy: metallurgy, oil refining.

Umm Said, port in Qatar. See Musay'īd.

Umtali, town in Zimbabwe. See Mutare.

Una *oo'na*, river in Bosna-Hercegovina republic, W Yugoslavia; rises in the Dinaric Alps and flows 254 km N and NE to meet the R Sava SW of Sisak; navigable for 70 km.

Union City, 37 36N 122 01W, pop(1980) 39,406, city in Alameda county, W California, United States; 30 km SE of Oakland; railway.

Union City, 40 45N 74 02W, pop(1980) 55,593, city in Hudson county, NE New Jersey, United States; on the Hudson river, on the N edge of Jersey City; railway.

Unión, La *la yoon-yōn'*, 40 15S 73 02W, pop(1982) 26,600, town in Valdivia prov, Los Lagos, S central Chile; railway.

Unión, La, easternmost dept of El Salvador, Central America; bounded N and E by Honduras and S by the Golfo de Fonseca; pop(1971) 230,103; area 1,738 sq km; capital La Unión; chief towns Santa Rosa de Lima and San Alejo; there is an extensive area of marshland on the E shore of the Bahía de La Unión; the Río Goascorán forms the E boundary; the Cordillera Conchagua and the Cordillera Jucuarán-Intipuca extend across the S part of the dept; includes also the islands in the Golfo de Fonseca (Isla Conchaguita, Isla Meanguera, etc).

Union of Soviet Socialist Republics. See Soviet Union.

United Arab Emirates, formerly TRUCIAL STATES *troo'shal*, a federation comprising seven internally self-governing emirates, E central Arabian Peninsula, bounded N by the Arabian Gulf, E by Oman, S and W by Saudi Arabia, and NW by Qatar; the 7 member states of the federation are Abū Ẓabī, 'Ajmān, Dubayy, Al Fujayrah, Ra's al Khaymah, Shāriqah, and Umm al Qaywayn; timezone GMT +4; area 83,600 sq km; capital Abū Ẓabī (Abu Dhabi); chief towns 'Ajmān, Dubayy (Dubai), Al Fujayrah, and Ra's al Khaymah; pop(1980) 1,040,275; approx 1 million people live in the emirates of Abū Ẓabī, Dubayy, and Shāriqah; the pop comprises 19% Emirian, 23% other Arabs, 50% S Asian, and 8% other expatriates (including Westerners and E Asians); fewer than 20% of the pop are UAE citizens (1982); the official language is Arabic but English is widely understood; the dominant religion is Islam; the unit of currency is the dirham; national holiday 2 Dec; membership of Arab League, FAO, G-77, GATT, GCC, IAEA, IBRD, ICAO, IDA, Islamic Development Bank, IFAD, IFC, ILO, IMF, IMO, INTELSAT, INTERPOL, ITU, NAM, OAPEC, OIC, OPEC, UN, UNESCO, UPU, WHO, WIPO, WTO.

Physical description. With the exception of Al Fujayrah the emirates lie along the S shore (Trucial Coast) of the Arabian Gulf, between the base of the Qatar Peninsula in the W and the Musandam Peninsula in the E. Al Fujayrah has a coastline along the Gulf of Oman. Salt marshes predominate along the Arabian Gulf coast while further inland they give way to barren desert and stretches of gravel plain. The only mountainous area is in Al Fujayrah where the Hajar Mts rise to peaks above 1,000 m.

Climate. The climate is hot with rainfall both limited and erratic. In winter temperatures average 21°C and humidity is high (70% or over). When the NE *shimal* wind blows off the Iranian highlands temperatures may fall as low as 8°C. In summer conditions are less humid and maximum temperatures may rise to 45°C. Sandstorms are common when the *khamsin* blows from the S. Mean annual rainfall ranges from only 32 mm in Abū Ẓabī to 120 mm in the wetter areas. The period May-Nov is generally rainless, while the wettest months are Feb and March.

History, government and constitution. In 1820 the rulers of the Trucial States signed a treaty prescribing peace with the British government. The idea of federation was considered in 1968 but by the time Britain withdrew its forces in 1971 Bahrain and Qatar had already dropped out of all negotiations. The new state of the United Arab Emirates was formed on 2 Dec 1971 with 6 members. Ra's al Khaymah abstained from joining until February 1972. The UAE is a sovereign state headed by a supreme council comprising the hereditary rulers of the 7 emirates. The supreme council appoints a council of ministers.

Economy. The economy of the UAE is based, either directly or indirectly, on oil and gas. Until February 1984 the only oil-producing emirates were Abū Ẓabī, Dubayy, and Shāriqah. Since then the Saleh offshore oil and gas field in Ra's al Khaymah has commenced production. Abū Ẓabī remains the major producer, accounting for nearly 70% of the UAE's total petroleum output in 1983. Dubayy produced 29.5% and Shāriqah 0.5%. The main offshore fields are Umm Shaif, Mubarraz, Zakum, Al-Bandaq (shared with Qatar), Fath, SW Fath, Falah, and Rashid. The main onshore fields are Bū Haşā, Al' Asab, Murban-Bab, and Margham. In 1984 oil reserves in the

UAE were estimated at over 32 billion barrels, estimated to last for more than 80 years at current rates of production. Natural gas production and its export in liquefied form is becoming an increasingly important activity and revenue earner. Reserves are estimated at about 3.1 trillion cubic metres, approx 3% of the global total. The UAE thus has the second largest gas reserves among the Gulf states. Abū Ẓabī is the main exporter of liquefied natural gas in the lower Gulf area. Offshore oil and gas is collected at Dās I, now the centre of a rapidly developing petrochemical and gas liquefaction industry. A gas treatment plant at Mina Jebel Ali in Dubayy exports propane and butane products to Japan as well as supplying some of the energy requirements of local industry. The Ar Ru'ays industrial complex, 250 km W of Abū Ẓabī, was opened in 1982 to support and complement the oil-related industries already located there. Areas are set aside for the production of iron and steel, petrochemicals, and light industries. There is also considerable industrial development at the Mina Jebel Ali port complex in Dubayy. The manufacture of cement has become the second largest industry in the country and one of the most important in diversifying sources of income. The cement industry is strongly based in the N emirates. The deep-water ports of Mina Zayed in Abū Ẓabī, Mina Rashid in Dubayy, and Mina Khaled for Shāriqah have been developed to handle the country's entrepôt trade. Crude oil accounts for approx 95% of the total value of exports. The main trade partners include Japan, France, the Netherlands, the USA, Spain, the UK, Italy and the Netherlands Antilles. In 1983 Saudi Arabia took the largest share of the UAE's non-oil exports. Other industries include construction, ship repairing ('Ajmān), tourism (currently being developed in Fujayrah), and fishing. The UAE has also recently developed as an important commercial and trading centre.

Agriculture. Only 5.5% of land in the UAE is said to be cultivable. Saline water supplies have restricted agriculture to the oasis of Al Buraymī, Al Liwa, Ra's as Sa'dīyāt I off Abū Ẓabī, and the irrigated valleys of the Hajar Mts. At Ra's as Sa'dīyāt an experiment in desert cultivation under shelter has proved successful. The agricultural land comprises 24% vegetables, 30% fruits and 10% feed crops. Although dates are the major crop in terms of area cultivated they are being outstripped in importance by fruit and vegetables. Dairy farming is concentrated in Ra's al Khaymah where climatic conditions and water resources are more favourable.

Communications. There are four international airports in the UAE at Abū Ẓabī, Dubayy, Ash Shāriqah, and Ra's al Khaymah. The chief ports are Mina Zayed in Abū Ẓabī, Mina Rashid and Mina Jebel Ali in Dubayy, Mina Khalid in Shāriqah, and Mina Saqr in Ra's al Khaymah. Mina Jebel Ali is one of the busiest container ports in the UAE.

Administrative divisions. The United Arab Emirates comprises the following 7 emirates:

Emirate	*area (sq km)*	*pop (1980)*
Abū Ẓabī	67,600	449,000
'Ajmān	250	36,100
Dubayy	3,900	278,000
Al Fujayrah	1,150	32,200
Ra's al Khaymah	1,690	73,700
Shāriqah	2,600	159,000
Umm al Qaywayn	750	12,300

United Kingdom of Great Britain and Northern Ireland. See Great Britain.

United States, sometimes referred to as AMERICA, official name United States of America, a federal republic of North America; includes the detached states of Alaska, NW of Canada and Hawaii in the Pacific Ocean; timezones: mainland GMT −5 (E coast) to −8 (Pacific Coast), Alaska GMT −9, Hawaii GMT −10; the 4th largest country in the world; area 9,160,454 sq km;

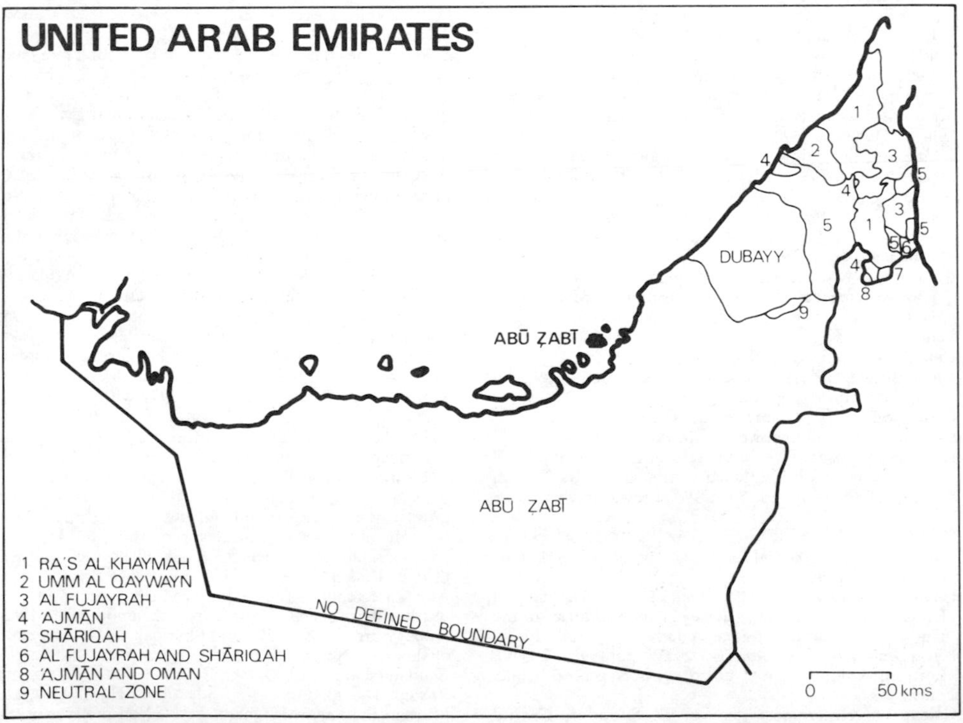

capital Washington; chief cities include New York, Chicago, Los Angeles, Philadelphia, Detroit, Houston; pop(1980) 226,545,805; ethnic groups are 86.2% of European origin (including 6.2% Hispanic), 11% black, 1.6% Asian and Pacific and 0.7% American Indian, Eskimo and Aleut; the official language is English, but there is a sizeable Spanish-speaking minority; the currency is the US dollar of 100 cents; national holiday 4 July (Independence Day); membership of ADB, ANZUS, CCC, CENTO, Colombo Plan, DAC, FAO, GATT, Group of Ten, IADB, IAEA, IBRD, ICAC, ICAO, ICEM, ICES, ICO, IDA, IDB, IEA, IFAD, IFC, IHO, ILO, IMF, IMO, INTELSAT, INTERPOL, IPU, IRC, ITC, ITU, IWC, NATO, OAS, OECD, PAHO, SPC, UN, UPU, WHO, WIPO, WMO, WSG, WTO.

Physical description. The E Atlantic coastal plain 320 km in width is backed by the Appalachian Mts from the Great Lakes in the N to the N of Alabama state in the S. This mountain system of ancient folded sedimentary rocks is divided into several parallel ranges including the Allegheny Mts, Blue Ridge Mts and Catskill Mts, and is a source of coal, iron ore and zinc. S of the Appalachians the E coastal plain broadens out towards the Gulf of Mexico, spreading down into the Florida peninsula. W of the Appalachians the Gulf Plains stretch N to meet the higher Great Plains from which they are separated by the Ozark Mts. W of the Great Plains the Rocky Mts rise to heights over 4,500 m. The NE is drained by streams such as the Genesee river which flow into the St Lawrence or the Great Lakes. On the E coast rivers such as the Susquehanna, Hudson, Delaware, Potomac, Roanoake and Savannah flow E to meet the Atlantic Ocean. The central plains are drained by the great Red River-Missouri-Mississippi river system and by the Trinity, Saline, Alabama and Flint rivers which flow into the Gulf of Mexico. In Washington state the Columbia river cuts across the Cascade Range to the Pacific and in the SW the Colorado river flows into the Gulf of California.

Climate. The climate of the USA varies from conditions characteristic of hot tropical deserts to those typical of Arctic continental regions. Most regions are affected by westerly depressions that can bring cloud, rain and changeable weather. In the Great Plains between the Rocky Mts and the Appalachian Mts wide temperature variation is the result of cold air blowing S from the Arctic as well as warm tropical air blowing N from the Gulf of Mexico. At Des Moines in Iowa average daily temperatures vary from a min of −11°C in Jan to a max of 30°C in July. On the W coast the influence of the Pacific Ocean results in a smaller range of temperatures between summer and winter. At Los Angeles average daily temperatures range from a min of 8°C (Dec-Feb) to a max of 28°C in Aug. On the E coast there is a gradual increase in winter temperatures southwards with a min

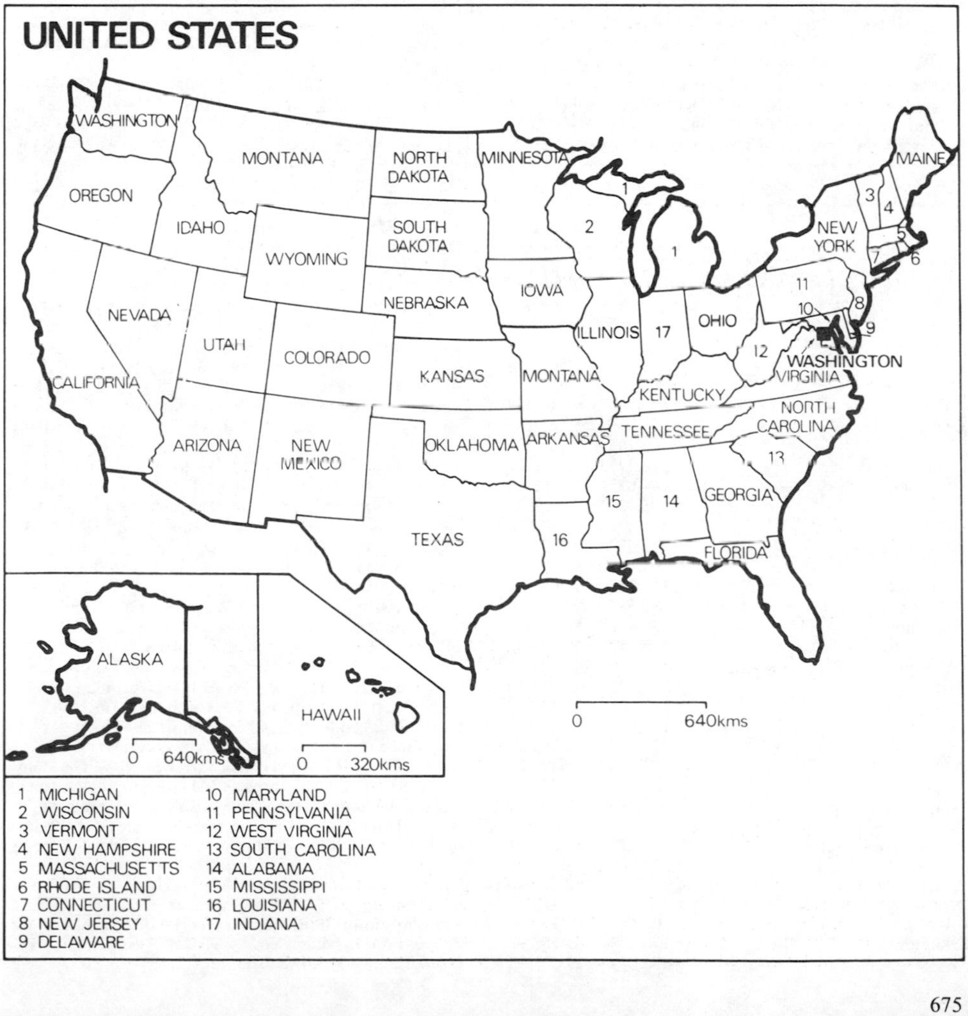

average daily temp of −7°C in Jan at Boston compared with −2°C at Miami. The states bordering the Gulf of Mexico are subject to hurricanes and tornadoes moving NE from the Caribbean.
History, government and constitution. First settled by 'Indian' groups who migrated from Asia across the Bering land-bridge over 25,000 years ago, the country was explored by the Norse in the 9th century and later by the Spanish who settled in Florida and Mexico in the 16th century. British, French (Great Lakes and Louisiana), Dutch (New Jersey) and Swedish (Delaware) from the E coast followed in the 17th century. The Swedish settlement of Delaware and Dutch New Jersey were acquired by the British who occupied the territory from New England to the Carolinas. Under the 1763 Treaty of Paris, Canada, Florida and E Louisiana passed to Great Britain. A revolt of the English-speaking colonies in the War of Independence (1775-83) resulted in the creation of the United States of America which then stretched W as far as the Mississippi and from the Great Lakes in the N to Florida in the S. Louisiana was sold to the USA by France in 1803 (the Louisiana Purchase) and the westward movement of settlers began. Florida was ceded by Spain in 1819 and further Spanish states joined the Union between 1821 and 1853. In 1867 Alaska was purchased from Russia and the Hawaiian Is were annexed in 1898. Both were admitted as states in 1959. The bicameral Congress comprises a 435-member House of Representatives elected for 2-year terms and a 100-member Senate elected for 6-year terms. The President, who is elected every 4 years by a college of state representatives, appoints an executive cabinet which is responsible to Congress.
Administrative divisions. The USA is divided into 50 federal states and the District of Columbia, each state having its own bicameral legislature and governor:

State	*area (sq km)*	*pop(1980)*
Alabama	131,994	3,893,888
Alaska	1,484,165	401,851
Arizona	295,121	2,718,215
Arkansas	135,403	2,286,435
California	406,377	23,667,902
Colorado	269,347	2,889,964
Connecticut	12,667	3,107,576
Delaware	5,023	594,338
District of Columbia	164	638,333
Florida	140,798	9,746,324
Georgia	150,946	5,463,105
Hawaii	16,705	964,691
Idaho	214,271	943,935
Illinois	144,677	11,426,518
Indiana	93,423	5,490,224
Iowa	145,509	2,913,808
Kansas	212,623	2,363,679
Kentucky	103,139	3,660,777
Louisiana	115,755	4,205,900
Maine	80,587	1,124,660
Maryland	25,576	4,216,975
Massachusetts	20,342	5,737,037
Michigan	148,080	9,262,078
Minnesota	206,825	4,075,970
Mississippi	122,806	2,520,638
Missouri	179,257	4,916,686
Montana	378,009	786,690
Nebraska	199,274	1,569,825
Nevada	285,724	800,493
New Hampshire	23,382	920,610
New Jersey	19,417	7,364,823
New Mexico	315,471	1,302,894
New York	123,180	17,558,072
North Carolina	126,992	5,881,766
North Dakota	180,180	652,717
Ohio	106,610	10,797,630
Oklahoma	178,503	3,025,290
Oregon	250,078	2,633,105
Pennsylvania	116,709	11,863,895
Rhode Island	2,743	947,154
South Carolina	78,528	3,121,820
South Dakota	197,475	690,768
Tennessee	107,003	4,591,120
Texas	681,244	14,229,191
Utah	213,390	1,461,037
Vermont	24,110	511,456
Virginia	103,230	5,346,818
Washington	172,929	4,132,156
West Virginia	62,709	1,949,644
Wisconsin	141,508	4,705,767
Wyoming	252,171	469,557

United States Trust Territory of the Pacific Islands, MICRONESIA, group of more than 2,000 islands in the W Pacific Ocean, N of Papua New Guinea, extending from 1° to 22° N and from 142° to 172° E; comprises the Commonwealth of the N Mariana Is, Federated States of Micronesia, Republic of Belau, and the Marshall Is; area 1,779 sq km; pop(1980) 116,974, excluding the N Mariana Is; the population is mostly Micronesian with a small proportion of Polynesian; English is the official language.
Physical description. The islands are mostly of volcanic origin, varying from coral-fringed mountains to almost completely submerged atolls (most of the Marshall Is). Few rise above 120 m.
History, government and constitution. The islands were administered by Japan in the inter-war years. In 1947 the USA placed the islands under the newly formed United Nations trusteeship system as a 'strategic trust' because of their military value. In 1975 the N Mariana Is concluded with the US a covenant to establish a Commonwealth of the N Mariana Is in political union with the US. In April 1976 the US government separated the administration of the N Mariana Is from that of the rest of the Trust Territory. The people of the N Mariana Is have adopted a constitution which allows them to elect their own governor and legislature. The rest of the Trust Territory is divided into 3 entities, each with its own constitution. The Marshall Is, Federated States of Micronesia, and Republic of Belau are all negotiating a status of free association with the US government. Free association grants the US the authority to control military and defence activities in return for federal government assistance and budget supports to the autonomous constitutional governments.
Economy. The economy of the US Trust Territories is based on agriculture, fisheries, and tourism. Crops include coconuts, cane sugar, cassava, and yams. Copra and locally-processed fish products are the major exports. Efforts have been made to increase copra production and develop cacao and pepper.

University City, 38 40N 90 20W, pop(1980) 42,738, town in St Louis county, E Missouri, United States; residential suburb 11 km WNW of St Louis; railway.

Unna *oon'na*, 51 32N 7 41E, pop(1983) 56,500, industrial town in Arnsberg dist, Nordrhein-Westfalen (North Rhine-Westphalia) prov, W Germany; 16 km E of Dortmund; economy: coal mining, machinery.

Unterfranken *oon'tur-frahng-kun*, LOWER FRANCONIA (Eng), dist of NW Bayern (Bavaria) prov, W Germany; pop(1983) 1,199,900; area 8,531 sq km; chief towns include Aschaffenberg, Schweinfurt and Wurzburg.

Unterland *oon'ter-lant* ('lower country'), one of the 2 dists of the Principality of Liechtenstein, central Europe; comprises the communes of Eschen, Mauren, Gamprin, Ruggell, and Schellenberg; the division is historical, geographical and political, formerly an independent Lordship until united with Oberland dist under the Princes of Liechtenstein; physically separated from Oberland dist by a broad plain.

Upem'ba, national park in Zaire, central Africa; area 11,730 sq km; established in 1939; situated in Shaba region and includes L Upemba.

Upernavik *oo-per-nah-vik*, 72 47N 56 10W, Eskimo settlement on the W coast of Greenland; on Baffin Bay.

Upland, 34 06N 117 39W, pop(1980) 47,647, city in San Bernardino county, SW California, United States; midway between Los Angeles and San Bernardino; railway.

Upolu *oo-pō'loo*, 13 58S 171 35W, 2nd largest of the Western Samoan islands, in the SW Pacific Ocean, separated from Savai'i I to the NW by the 17 km-wide Apolima Strait; area 1,121 sq km; pop(1981) 114,980, chief town Apia; rises to 1,097 m; many sandy beaches; Mulifauna is the site of the largest coconut plantation in the S hemisphere; the Scottish writer, Robert Louis Stevenson, settled on the island in 1890, died here in 1894, and was buried on Mt Vaea, overlooking Apia.

Upper, region in N Ghana, W Africa; pop(1984) 1,210,745; area 27,319 sq km; predominantly high ground over 200 m; the R Sisili flows S from its source in Burkina to join the White Volta river; capital Bolgatanga; chief towns Lawra, Tumu, Bawku, Navrongo and Wa; economy: iron ore mining.

Upper Austria, federal state of Austria. See Oberösterreich.

Upper Hutt, 41 06S 175 06E, pop(1981) 31,405, town on North Island, New Zealand; situated in the centre of the Hutt Valley, 33 km NNE of Wellington; railway.

Upper Nile, A'ALI EN NIL, area of S Sudan, NE Africa; (province prior to 1983); area 92,269 sq km; pop(1983) 1,599,605; chief town Malakal.

Upper Volta. See Burkina.

Uppsala *up'sa-la*, county of E Sweden, bounded on the NE by the Gulf of Bothnia; L Mälaren occupies the S tip of the county; land area 6,987 sq km; pop(1983) 247,101; capital Uppsala.

Uppsala, 59 55N 17 38E, pop(1982) 149,333, capital city of Uppsala county, E Sweden, 64 km NNW of Stockholm, N of L Mälaren; see of the Lutheran archbishop of Sweden; railway; educational centre with university (1477) and many other academic institutions; economy: engineering, pharmaceuticals, printing; monuments: 13-15th c cathedral with tombs of Linnaeus and Swedenborg, as well as Gustavus Vasa and other kings; 16th-c castle (now the governor's residence).

Ural *oo-ral'*, formerly YAIK, river in SE European Rossiyskaya and NW Kazakhskaya SSR, Soviet Union; rises on the SE slopes of the Ural'skiy Khrebet (Ural Mts) range; flows S past Magnitogorsk and Omsk, W though Orenburgskaya oblast, turns S at Ural'sk, and finally flows through W Kazakhskaya SSR, discharging into the Caspian Sea at Gur'yev; length 2,520 km; chief tributaries Kushum, Utva, Kumak.

Urals, mountain range in the Soviet Union. See Ural'skiy Khrebet.

Ural'skiy Khrebet *oo-ral'y'ski KHrye-byet'*, URAL MTS *yoo'rul* or THE URALS *yoo'ralz* (Eng), mountain range in the Soviet Union, forming the traditional physiographic boundary between Europe and Asia, and separating the E European Plain (W) from the Zapadno Sibirskaya Ravnina (W Siberian Lowlands) (E); the range extends 1,750 km S from Novaya Zemlya in the Arctic Ocean to the N Kazakhskaya border; relief consists of low, parallel N-S ridges, broken in many places by cross-faulting; the bulk of the region is between 200 and 1,000 m above sea-level; the Ural'skiy Khrebet is commonly divided into: (1) the N Urals, which extend as far S as 61°N and contain Mt Narodnaya (1,894 m), the highest peak in the whole system; (2) the central Urals, extending from 55°N to 61°N and forming a plateau which generally lies between 305 and 610 m above sea-level; traversed by numerous transport routes, including the Trans-Siberian railway W of Sverdlovsk; the highest peak is Konzhakovskiy Kamen (1,569 m) in the N section; (3) the S Urals, extending from 51°N to 55°N, consist of several parallel ranges and reaching a max width of 150-200 km; peaks include the Yoman Tau (1,639 m) and Yeremal (1,595 m); in the extreme S the range fans out to form a broad, dissected plateau; the Ural'skiy Khrebet forms the watershed between the Volga and Pechora river basins in the W and the Ob'-Irtysh basin in the E; the mountains are heavily forested and lumbering is an important activity; there are rich mineral deposits, including oil (along the Kama and Belaya rivers), iron ore, coal, copper, manganese, gold, aluminium, potash, bauxite, asbestos, zinc, lead, silver, nickel, and various precious metals (emerald, topaz, amethyst); the central and S Ural'skiy Khrebet, and the adjacent lowlands, are the most heavily industrialized areas.

Urawa *oo-ra'wa*, 35 52N 139 40E, pop(1980) 358,185, capital of Saitama prefecture, Kanto region, E Honshū island, Japan; 24 km NNW of Tōkyo; university (1949); railway; monument: ancient Shinto shrine.

Urbana *ur-ban'a*, 40 07N 88 12W, pop(1980) 35,978, county seat of Champaign county, E Illinois, United States; adjoins Champaign, 75 km ENE of Decatur; settled in 1824, achieving city status in 1864; university (1867).

Urewera *oo-re-we'ra*, national park, E North Island, New Zealand; the largest lake is L Waikaremoana (54 sq km); area 2,074 sq km; established in 1954.

Urfa *oor-fa'*, prov in SE Turkey, bounded S by Syria and W by the R Euphrates pop(1980) 602,736; area 18,584 sq km; capital Urfa; economy: wheat.

Urfa, EDESSA (anc), 37 08N 38 45E, pop(1980) 147,488, capital town of Urfa prov, SE Turkey; c.40 km from the Syrian border; scene of alleged Armenian massacres in 1895; agricultural market centre.

Uri *oo'ree*, canton in central Switzerland; pop(1980) 33,883; area 1,075 sq km; capital Altdorf; joined the Swiss Confederacy in 1291.

Urmia, Lake, Iran. See Orumīyeh, Daryacheh-ye.

Urmston *ermz'ten*, 53 27N 2 21W, pop(1981) 44,030, town in Salford borough, Greater Manchester, NW England; 8 km SW of Manchester; railway; economy: electrical goods, soap, textiles, steel, rubber.

Uroševac *oo'ro-she-vats*, UROSHEVATS (Slov), 42 21N 21 09E, pop(1981) 113,680, town in autonomous province of Kosovo, S Srbija (Serbia) republic, Yugoslavia; 32 km S of Priština; railway.

Uruapan *oo-roo-ah'pan*, URUAPAN DEL PROGRESO, 19 25N 102 04W, pop(1980) 146,998, town in Michoacán state, SW Mexico; located in the Barranca del Cupatitzio national park at an alt of 1,610 m; railway; economy: local woodwork, lacquerwork, pottery and embroidery; monuments: in the Jardín de los Mártires square is a 16th-c church; the ceramics museum is housed in the restored hospital built by Fray Juan de San Miguel in the 16th-c; event: at San Juan (W of Uruapan), a festival in mid-Sep to celebrating saving a Christ statue from the San Juan church during the eruption of Paricutín volcano in 1943.

Uruguay *yoor'ė-gwī, oor'oo-gwī*, official name Oriental Republic of Uruguay, REPÚBLICA ORIENTAL DEL URUGUAY, formerly known as LA BANDA ORIENTAL ('the eastern bank' of the Río Uruguay), republic in E South America; bordered E by the Atlantic Ocean, N by Brazil and W by the Río Uruguay and Argentina; area 176,215 sq km; timezone GMT −3; capital Montevideo; chief towns include Salto, Paysandú and Mercedes; the pop is 90% European in origin and 5-10% mestizo; 66% of the pop are Roman Catholic; the official language is Spanish; the currency is the nuevo peso of 100 centésimos; national holiday 25 Aug (Independence Day); membership of FAO, G-77, GATT, IADB, IAEA, IBRD, ICAO, IDB, IFAD, IFC, ILO, IMF, IMO, INTELSAT, INTERPOL, IRC, ITU, LAIA, OAS, PAHO, SELA, UN, UNESCO, UPU, WHO, WIPO, WMO, WSG.

Physical description. Merging with the rolling Argentine *pampas*, the grass-covered plains of S Uruguay gradually rise towards the N to merge with a high sandy plateau that is crossed N-S by two ridges, the Cuchilla Grande (E) and the Cuchilla de Haedo (NW). These ridges are separated by the wide basin of the Río Negro which flows SW across the lowland plain to meet the Río Uruguay on the Argentine frontier. The NE border passes through the large L Mirim and the estuarine lagoons of the SE coast afford good harbours, as at Montevideo.

Climate. The climate of Uruguay is temperate with warm summers and mild winters. The prevailing E winds impose a marine influence which moderates temperatures in all seasons. The average temperature at Montevideo is 16°C with an average of 978 mm of rain. Most rain falls during the autumn and early winter (April-June).

History, government and constitution. Originally occupied by South American Charrúas Indians, the Spanish first visited Uruguay in 1515. Rivalry with Portugal and Amerindian resistance delayed the settlement of the territory, but in 1726 Uruguay became part of the Spanish Viceroyalty of Río de la Plata. From 1814 until independence in 1825 the region was a prov of Brazil after being overrun by the Argentine federation forces, and annexed by Portugal. Independence was finally recognized in 1828 and after many years of political instability a new constitution of 1919 severed Church and State, established universal suffrage and prevented the president from assuming dictatorship. An amendment to the constitution in 1952 replaced the president as head of the executive by a 2-party National Council with 9 members. In 1966 the country returned to a presidential system, appointing a president advised by a council of 11 ministers. The bicameral legislature consists of a 30-member Senate and a 99-member Chamber of Representatives, both elected for 4 years.

Economy. The Uruguayan economy has traditionally been based on the production of livestock products such as meat, wool and hides, and the production of agricultural products such as maize, wheat, sorghum, rice, citrus fruit, potatoes, and vegetable oils. In addition to agriculture, fishing has made a growing contribution to export income in recent years. Manufacturing industry is largely centred on food processing and packing, cement, chemicals, textiles, leather, steel, light engineering and transport equipment. With little oil, coal or gas, Uruguay is largely dependent on hydroelectric power. Major trade partners include the USA, the EEC, Argentina and Brazil.

Administrative divisions. Uruguay is divided into the following 19 departments:

Department	*area (sq km)*	*pop(1985)*
Artigas	11,738	68,994
Canelones	4,752	359,349
Cerro Largo	14,929	77,985
Colonia	5,682	112,348
Durazno	14,315	53,864
Flores	4,519	24,381
Florida	12,107	65,873
Lavalleja	12,485	61,241
Maldonado	4,111	92,618
Montevideo	664	1,296,089
Paysandú	13,252	103,487
Río Negro	8,471	48,241
Rivera	9,829	88,801
Rocha	11,089	66,440
Salto	12,603	105,617
San José	6,963	88,020
Soriano	9,223	79,042
Tacuarembó	21,105	82,809
Treinta y Tres	9,539	46,599

Uruguay, Río *oo-roo-gwī'*, South American river; rises in the coastal range of S Brazil and flows in a wide arc W, SW, S along the Brazil-Argentina and Uruguay-Argentina border, joining the Paraná river above Buenos Aires to form the Río de la Plata; length c.1,600 km; its principal headstream, the Pelotas, rises 64 km from the Atlantic on the W slope of the Serra do Mar (Brazil), and forms the Santa Catarina-Río Grande do Sul border; after receiving the Canoas and Peixe rivers it takes the name Uruguay and forms the Brazil-Argentina border below the influx of the Peperi-Guacu river when it turns SW; it forms the Argentina-Uruguay border after meeting the Quarai river, just above Bella Unión (Uruguay) and continues S to join the Río de la Plata; because of rapids, the majority of the river is not navigable until its lower course; the main ports are Concepción del Uruguay (Argentina) and Paysandu (Uruguay); tributaries include the Ijui, Ibicui, Quarai (Cuareim), Arapey, Río Negro on the left and Aguapey, Miriñay on the right.

Urumchi, capital of Xinjiang aut region, NW China. See Ürümqi.

Ürümqi *oo-room-chee*, URUMCHI, WU-LU-K'O-MU-SHI, 43 43N 87 38E, pop(1984e) 1,147,300, capital of Xinjiang aut region, NW China; 8 universities; 2 medical schools; agricultural college (1952); railway; airfield; economy: steel, oil, chemicals, textiles, farm machinery; monument: Ürümqi was the headquarters of the communist forces during the 1930s and 1940s; a memorial hall to communist martyrs is situated at the Eighth Route Army Headquarters.

Uşak *oo-shak'*, prov in W Turkey; pop(1980) 247,224; area 5,341 sq km; capital Uşak; economy: carpets and sugar.

Usborne, Mount, 51 35S 58 57W, mountain on the island of East Falkland, S Atlantic, situated about 65 km W of Stanley; the highest point in the Falkland Is, rising to 705 m.

Ushuaia *oos-wī'a*, 54 57S 68 20W, pop(1980) 11,000, capital of Tierra del Fuego national territory, S Argentina; on the S coast of the island of Tierra del Fuego; chief port on the Beagle Channel; the most southerly town in the world; founded in 1884 as a penal settlement; Italian immigrants settled near here in 1948; airfield; economy: sheep, timber, livestock.

Usk, WYSG (Welsh), river rising on the Dyfed-Powys border W of Brecon, Wales; flows 96 km E, SE and S to meet the Bristol Channel at Newport.

Uspallata *oos-pa-ya'ta*, 32 50S 70 04W, pass in the Andes between Mendoza in Argentina and Santiago, Chile, on the border between the two countries; at the foot of Aconcagua; rises to 3,900 m; a statue of Christ of the

Andes was erected in 1904 to commemorate peaceful boundary settlements.

Uster *oo'stur*, 47 21N 8 49E, pop(1980) 23,702, town in Zürich canton, Switzerland, E of the Greifensee; railway; economy: textiles, engineering.

Ústí nad Labem *oos'tyee nad la-bem*, 50 41N 14 00E, pop(1984) 90,177, river port and industrial capital of Severočeský region, Czech Socialist Republic, W Czechoslovakia; on R Elbe (Labe), 72 km NW of Praha (Prague); founded in 13th century; railway; economy: chemicals, food processing, textiles.

Ustinov, formerly IZHEVSK, 56 49N 53 11E, pop(1983) 594,000, capital city of Udmurtskaya ASSR, Rossiyskaya, Soviet Union; established in 1760; university; railway; airfield; economy: metalworking, machine building, paper, foodstuffs.

Ust'-Kamenogorsk *oost-kum-yin-u-gorsk'*, 50 00N 82 36E, pop(1983) 296,000, river port capital of Vostochno Kazakhstanskaya oblast, Kazakhskaya SSR, Soviet Union; in the foothills of the W Altay Mts, on the right bank of the R Irtysh; founded in 1720 as a fortress; railway; airfield; economy: machine building, nonferrous metallurgy.

Usulután *oo-soo-loo-tan'*, maritime dept in S El Salvador, Central America; bounded S by the Pacific Ocean; pop(1971) 304,369; area 1,780 sq km; capital Usulután; chief towns Santiago de María and Puerto El Triunfo; the Río Lempa forms its W boundary with San Vicente dept; mountainous in the N with a fertile coastal plain.

Usulután, 13 20N 88 25W, pop(1980) 63,533, capital town of Usulután dept, S El Salvador, Central America; railway.

Usumacinta, Río *oo-soo-mah-seen'tah*, river in Guatemala and Mexico; formed by the meeting of the Pasión and Chixoy rivers on the border between Guatemala and Mexico (Chiapas state); forms part of the international border between Mexico and Guatemala; follows a winding course NW into Chiapas and Tabasco; enters the Bahía de Campeche and the Gulf of Mexico at the town of Frontera in Tabasco; near its mouth it is joined by the Río Grijalva; in Tabasco part of the Usumacinta branches directly N to enter the Bahia de Campeche as the Río San Pedro y San Pablo; the Río Palizada branches off from the Usumacinta and flows into the Laguna de Términos; length (with the Chixoy which rises in Guatemala) approx 965 km; navigable for 483 km.

Utah *yoo'taw*, state in W United States, bounded W by Nevada, N by Idaho, NE by Wyoming, E by Colorado, and S by Arizona; the Colorado river flows SW through SE Utah; the Green river enters NE Utah from Colorado and flows S to empty into the Colorado; in the NW lies the Great Salt Lake, the largest salt-water lake in the country (2,590 sq km); L Utah is a freshwater lake S of Great Salt Lake; the Wasatch Range, part of the Rocky Mts, runs N-S through the state; the Uinta Mts rise in the NE; the highest point is Kings Peak (4,123 m); the E is a mountainous and sparsely inhabited region dissected by deep canyons; along the W foothills of the Wasatch Range lie Utah's major cities with four-fifths of the state's population; further W is the Great Basin and in the NW is the arid Great Salt Lake Desert; agricultural income is based on cattle, sheep, poultry, hay, wheat, barley, and sugar-beets; minerals include copper, petroleum, coal; major industries include aerospace research, machinery, transportation equipment, electronic components, fabricated metals, and processed foods; the first Europeans to explore the region were Spaniards sent out by Coronado in 1540; the discovery of the Great Salt lake is credited to James Bridger (1824); the United States acquired the region from Spain in 1848 as part of the Treaty of Guadalupe Hidalgo; permanent settlement began in 1847 with the arrival of the Mormons under Brigham Young; Utah Territory, a large area including the present state, was organized in 1850; several petitions for statehood were denied because of the Mormons' practice of polygamy, and antagonism between the Mormon Church and the Federal law over this issue led to the 'Utah War' of 1857-58; Utah finally became a state (45th) in 1896; also known as the 'Beehive State'; pop(1980) 1,461,037; area 213,390 sq km; capital Salt Lake City; other chief cities include Provo and Ogden; the state is divided into 29 counties:

County	*area (sq km)*	*pop(1980)*
Beaver	6,724	4,378
Box Elder	14,596	33,222
Cache	3,045	57,176
Carbon	3,845	22,179
Daggett	1,817	769
Davis	777	146,540
Duchesne	8,406	12,565
Emery	11,567	11,451
Garfield	13,385	3,673
Grand	9,591	8,241
Iron	8,583	17,349
Juab	8,830	5,530
Kane	10,135	4,024
Millard	17,727	8,970
Morgan	1,568	4,917
Piute	1,973	1,329
Rich	2,688	2,100
Salt Lake	1,966	619,066
San Juan	20,085	12,253
Sanpete	4,126	14,620
Sevier	4,966	14,727
Summit	4,849	10,198
Tooele	17,989	26,033
Uintah	11,645	20,506
Utah	5,247	218,106
Wasatch	3,097	8,523
Washington	6,297	26,065
Wayne	6,399	1,911
Weber	1,472	144,616

Utica *yoo'ti-ka*, 43 06N 75 14W, pop(1980) 75,632, county seat of Oneida county, central New York, United States; on the R Mohawk, 75 km E of Syracuse; railway; monument: Munson-Williams-Proctor Institute (art).

Utrecht *oo'treKHt*, pop(1984e) 929,400, prov in West Netherlands, bounded on the S by the R Lek; land area 1,331 sq km; capital Utrecht; chief towns Zeist and Amersfoort; economy: predominantly livestock farming; there is a large expanse of heath and moorland to the E of Utrecht.

Utrecht, TRAJECTUMAD RHENUM (Lat), 52 06N 5 07E, pop (1984e) 501,357, capital of Utrecht prov, W Netherlands; on the R Kromme Rijn (which divides here into the Old Rhine and the Vecht) and on the Amsterdam Rhine Canal, on the geographical divide between the marshes and the sandy area of the Geest, 32 km SSE of Amsterdam; Utrecht forms the NE corner of the *Randstad* conurbation and is one of the most important political, economic and cultural cities in the country; industry has developed especially in the W of the city, where railway lines, roads and canals converge; a centre for trade fairs; seat of a Catholic and Dutch Old Catholic archbishop; university (1634); economy: steel rolling, machinery and rolling stock, building materials, heavy electrotechnical equipment, pharmaceuticals, industrial chemicals, fertilizers, construction, electrics, foodstuffs, petrochemicals, textiles, railway repair yards, furniture, tourism; monument: cathedral of St Michael (1254), a Dutch Reformed church with the highest tower in the country (112 m).

Utsunomiya *oot-soo-nō'mee-ya*, 36 33N 139 52E, pop(1980) 377,746, tourist centre and capital of Tochigi prefecture, Kanto region, E Honshū island, Japan; 96 km N of Tōkyo; railway.

Uttar Pradesh *oo-tar pru-daysh'*, state in N central India; pop(1981) 110,858,019; area 294,413 sq km; bounded W by Rajasthan state, S by Madhya Pradesh state, E by Bihar state and N by Himachal Pradesh territory, Nepal and Xizang aut region (Tibet) of the People's Republic of

China; there are 11 administrative divisions and 57 districts; capital Lucknow; the state is governed by a bicameral legislature comprising a 108-member Legislative Council and a 426-member Legislative Assembly; the official language is Hindi; the state is crossed by the rivers Yamuna, Ganga (Ganges), Chauka, Ghaghara, Saryu, Kali Nadi, Gomati, Sai, Little Gandak, Rapti, Sarju and Kosi; much of the state is criss-crossed by canals; 78% of the labour force is employed in agriculture; the state is the largest producer of foodgrains in India and one of India's chief producers of sugar; manufacturing industries produce sugar, edible oils, textiles, leather, paper and chemicals; handloom weaving is an important village industry; mineral resources include coal, copper, limestone, bauxite, silica, phosphorite and pyrophyllite; the region was known as the Bengal Presidency until 1833, when it was divided into the 2 provs of Agra and Oudh; in 1877 the 2 provs were put under the one administrator and in 1902 the name was changed to the United Provinces of Agra and Oudh; in 1935 it became simply the United Provinces; in 1947 the states of Rampur, Banaras, and Tehri-Garwal were merged with the United Provinces and the state changed its name to Uttar Pradesh in 1950.

Uttoxeter *yoo-tok'sit-ėr*, 52 54N 1 51W, pop(1981) 10,013, town in East Staffordshire dist, Staffordshire, central England; 20 km NW of Burton-upon-Trent; railway; economy: agricultural machinery, biscuits.

Uudenmaa *oo'den-ma*, NYLAND *nu'land* (Swed), a prov of S Finland, bounded on the S by the Gulf of Finland; area 10,404 sq km; pop(1982) 1,150,930; Helsinki, the capital of Finland, is also the prov capital; chief towns include Tammisaari (Ekenäs), Loviisa and Porvoo.

Uusikaupunki *oo'si-kow'poong-kee*, NYSTAD *nu'stad* (Swed), 60 48N 21 30E, pop(1982) 13,768, port and commercial town in Turku-Pori prov, SW Finland; on the Gulf of Bothnia 56 km NW of Turku; established in 1617; railway; boats to offshore islands; economy: granite, marine equipment.

Uva *oo'va*, province in SE Sri Lanka; comprises the dists of Badulla and Monaragala; pop(1981) 922,636; area 8,481 sq km; capital Badulla; mountainous in the W.

Uvea *oo-vay'a*, 13 22S 176 12W, island in the French overseas territory of Wallis and Futuna in the Wallis group, central Pacific Ocean; enclosed by a coral reef; pop(1982) 7,843; chief town and capital of Wallis and Futuna is Matu Utu.

Uvs *oovs*, county in NW Mongolia; pop(1981e) 70,000; area 69,200 sq km; capital Ulaangom; bounded N by the USSR; mountains and forest steppe cover more than half of the county, with steppe and semi-desert over the remaining area; Uvs Nuur, Mongolia's largest lake (area 3,350 sq km), is found in the N of the county close to the USSR frontier; coal, common salt, iron ore, turquoise and emerald are amongst the county's natural resources; cattle rearing is the base of the county's economy; industry: fodder, alabaster, spirits and agricultural machinery.

Uxmal *ooz-mahl'*, *oosh-mahl'*, 20 21N 89 46W, ruined Maya city in W Yucatán state, SE Mexico; contains well-preserved buildings built of white limestone in the Puuc style; the buildings include the Nunnery Quadrangle, the Palace of the Governor and the Pyramid of the Soothsayer; the friezes of the palaces are decorated with stone mosaics in geometrical design; Uxmal is believed to have been founded as an aristocratic centre in the 10th century by the Tutul Xiu family, a Maya nation; it was abandoned in 1441.

Uzbekskaya *ooz-bek-skī'a*, UZBEKISTAN (Eng), constituent republic of the Soviet Union, in central and N Middle Asia, bounded S by Afghanistan and NW by the Aral'skoye More (Aral Sea); the Peski Kyzylkum (Kyzyl-Kum Desert) occupies a large area of the republic; in the S and E are the foothills of the Tien Shan, Pamir, and Gissar-Alai ranges; chief rivers are the Amudar'ya, Syr-Dar'ya, and Chirchik; pop(1983) 17,039,000; area 447,400 sq km; capital Tashkent; chief towns Samarkand, Andizhan, and Namangan; economy: coal mining, oil extraction and refining, power generation, ferrous and non-ferrous metallurgy, chemicals (mineral fertilizers for cotton growing), machine building, cotton-ginning, cotton fabric and silk production, food processing; the land is intensively cultivated with the aid of artificial irrigation; it is the chief cotton-growing area in the USSR and 3rd largest in the world; grain is grown in the higher-lying plains; the desert and semi-desert area of W Uzbekskaya is largely pastureland; proclaimed a Soviet Socialist Republic in Oct 1924 and became a constituent republic of the USSR in May 1925; the republic is divided into oblasts and republics:

Oblast/republic	*pop(1983)*
Andizhanskaya	1,349,000
Bukharskaya	969,000
Dzhizak	511,000
Ferganskaya	1,695,000
Kara-Kalpakskaya	1,009,000
Kashkadar'inskaya	1,120,000
Khorezmskaya	840,000
Namanganskaya	1,100,000
Navoi	556,000
Samarkandskaya	1,837,000
Surkhandar'inskaya	499,000
Syr-dar'ya	499,000
Tashkentskaya	1,792,000

Navoi oblast was created in 1982 because of the significance of the gold-mining centre of Zarafshan and the uranium-mining centre of Uchkuduk. The area of the new oblast was carved mainly from the Bukharskaya and Samarkandskaya oblasts.

V

Vaal River *vahl*, river in South Africa; length 1,200 m; a major tributary of the Orange river which it joins near Douglas (NE Cape prov, SW of Kimberley); rises in SE Transvaal prov close to the Swaziland frontier; flows W and then SW along the border between Transvaal and Orange Free State provs (dammed at Bloemhof); flows into Cape prov near Warrenton.

Vaasa *vah'sah*, VASA *vah'sah* (Swed), a prov of W Finland, bounded on the W by the Gulf of Bothnia; drained by the Lapuanjoki; lakes include the Lappajärvi and the Lestijärvi; area 27,319 sq km; pop(1982) 439,082; Vaasa is the provincial capital; chief towns include Kristiinankaupunki (Kristinestad) and Pietarsaari (Jakobstad).

Vaasa, VASA (Swed), formerly NIKOLAINKAUPUNKI, 63 06N 21 38E, pop(1982) 54,249, seaport and capital of Vaasa prov, SW Finland; on the Gulf of Bothnia, about 352 km NW of Helsinki; established in 1606; destroyed by fire in 1852 but rebuilt on the present site about 1860; in Dec 1917, after the proclamation of Finnish independence, Vaasa was the temporary capital of the country when the socialists seized control of Helsinki; the shortest route between Finland and Sweden is on the Vaasa-Umeå ferry (the northernmost year-round car ferry line in the world); railway; airfield; economy: metal products; events: Vaasa Festival in June and Stundars Feast in July.

Vác *vats*, 47 49N 19 10E, pop(1984e) 36,000, river port and summer resort town in Pest county, N central Hungary; on R Danube 32 km N of Budapest; bishopric; railway; economy: textiles, footwear, cement, distilling, tools; monuments: Baroque triumphal arch; cathedral with Maulbertsch's frescoes.

Vacaville, 38 21N 121 59W, pop(1980) 43,367, city in Solano county, W central California, United States, 48 km WSW of Sacramento.

Vacoas-Phoenix *va-kō-as-fee'niks*, 20 18S 57 29E, pop(1981) 54,833, township in Plaines Wilhems dist, W Mauritius; between Port Louis and Curepipe; economy: clothes, watch parts, precision tools for cutting precious stones.

Vadsø *vahd'sœ*, 70 05N 29 47E, pop(1970e) 5,625, seaport on N shore of Varangerfjorden (Varanger Fjord), capital of Finnmark county, N Norway; ferry services to Hammerfest and Bergen; ice-free harbour; economy: fishing, fish-processing.

Vaduz, 47 08N 9 32E, pop(1983e) 4,927, capital of the Principality of Liechtenstein, Oberland dist, in the R Rhine valley; area 17.3 sq km; economy: metalworking, engineering, tourism, agricultural trade; monuments: 12th-c castle, rebuilt after being burned down during the Swabian War in 1499; the Red House, seat of the Vaistlis during the High and Late Middle Ages; the Prince's picture gallery, State art collection, and Postal museum are all housed in the 'Engländerbau'.

Váh, river in E Czechoslovakia; rises on the slopes of the Nízké Tatry (Low Tatra) as two headstreams and flows S to meet the R Danube at Komárno; length 392 km.

Vakaga *va-ka-ga'*, prefecture in NE Central African Republic; the land dips toward the W and is watered by the Bar Aouk river and its tributaries; pop(1968) 178,602; area 46,500 sq km; chief town Birao; other towns include Ngourou, Gerdil, Ouanda and Djailé; the André Félix reserve lies in the SE.

Valais *va-lay'*, WALLIS *val'is* (Ger), French-speaking canton in SW Switzerland; pop(1980) 218,707; area 5,231 sq km; capital Sion; there are vineyards on the N valley slopes; the wines produced here are predominantly white and mostly from the Chasselas grape variety; the Valais is in one of Switzerland's driest areas, requiring the vines to be watered from snowfields and glaciers by means of wooden-walled canals; joined the Swiss Confederacy in 1815.

Valasske Meziriči *val'ash-skeh mez'ir-ee-chee*, 49 29N 17 57E, pop(1984) 26,870, town in Severomoravský region, Czech Socialist Republic, Czechoslovakia; SW of Ostrava and W of the White Carpathians; railway.

Val-de-Marne *val-de-marn*, dept in Ile-de-France region of N France; E of Paris; comprises 3 arrond, 39 cantons and 47 communes; pop(1982) 1,193,655; area 244 sq km; capital Créteil; château of Gros-Bois (Louis XIII) at Boissy-St-Léger.

Valdivia *val-deev'ya*, 39 49S 73 14W, pop(1982) 113,565, capital of Valdivia prov, Los Lagos, S central Chile; situated in a rich agricultural area, 18 km from the Pacific Ocean, where 2 rivers join to form the Río Valdivia; founded by Pedro de Valdivia in 1552; university (1955); railway.

Val-d'Oise *val-dwaz*, dept in Ile-de-France region of N France, N of Paris; comprises 3 arrond, 35 cantons and 185 communes; pop(1982) 920,598; area 1,249 sq km; watered by the R Oise; capital Pontoise; monument: 13th-c Royaumont Abbey at Asnières-sur-Oise.

Valdos'ta, 30 50N 83 17W, pop(1980) 37,596, county seat of Lowndes county, S Georgia, United States; 138 km SE of Albany and only 22 km N of the Florida border; railway; economy: processing, distributing and commercial centre for tobacco, cotton and livestock area; lumber, and wood and paper products.

Valence *va-lãs*, VENTIA, VALENTIA JULIA (anc), 44 57N 4 54E, pop(1982) 68,157, market town and capital of Drôme dept, Rhône-Alpes region, SE France; on the left bank of the R Rhône, 186 km NNW of Marseille; railway; had a university from the 15th century until 1790; economy: electromechanical and electronic equipment and components for aerospace, domestic and industrial appliances; monuments: 11th-c Romanesque cathedral (considerably rebuilt in the 17th century), and many interesting old houses including the temple of St Ruf; before the construction of the present boulevards (from 1785), the town was surrounded by ramparts and fortifications and was only accessible from the harbours.

Valencia *va-len'THya*, *va-len'see-a* (Eng), VALENTIA, autonomous region of E Spain, comprising the provs of Alicante, Castellón and Valencia; the region occupies a narrow coastal area from the Ebro delta to the mouth of the R Segura and includes the popular tourist resorts on the Costa Blanca and Costa del Azahar; the central plateau (Meseta) is cut by rivers such as the Guadalaviar, Júcar and Turia which water some of the most fertile land in Spain; irrigation has been assisted by the construction of reservoirs and channels; pop(1981) 3,646,778; area 23,260 sq km; 534 municipalities; economy: the main agricultural crops are maize, wheat, lucerne and vegetables and fruit; car plant at Almusafes.

Valencia, prov in Valencia region, E Spain; bounded on the W by the edge of the central plateau of Spain which slopes down to the Mediterranean; drained by the Turia and Júcar rivers; pop(1981) 2,066,413; area 10,763 sq km; capital Valencia; economy: oil refining (Masanasa), butane (Sedavi), fruit, vegetables, olive oil, timber, iron and steel, naval construction, tiles and ceramics, textiles, electrical appliances.

Valencia, 39 27N 0 23W, pop(1981) 751,734, capital of Valencia prov, E Spain; on R Turia, 352 km E of Madrid; archbishopric; university (1500); car ferries to Balearics and Canary Is; airport; railway; nearby port at El Grao; economy: tourism, wine, fruit, chemicals, shipyards, textiles, motor vehicles, ironwork; monuments: silk exchange; ceramics museum; fine arts museum; 14th-c Serranos military towers; Gothic-Baroque cathedral; events: fallas in March; fiesta of La Virgen de los Desamparados in May; St James fair in July.

Valencia *va-len'sya*, 10 11N 67 59W, pop(1981) 616,177, capital of Carabobo state, N Venezuela; situated on the W bank of the Río Cabriales, 5 km from L Valencia; university (1852); railway; Valencia is famous for its oranges; monument: on the central Plaza Bolívar is the 18th-c cathedral; event: on the 2nd Sunday in Nov the statue of the Virgin del Socorro is paraded through the streets.

Valencia, Lago de, lake in Carabobo and Aragua states, N Venezuela; in a basin of the coastal hill range just E of Valencia; 80 km WSW of Caracas; area approx 320 sq km; 29 km long; up to 16 km wide; the 2nd largest freshwater lake in Venezuela; situated in a fertile agricultural region, one of its many affluents is the Río Aragua.

Valenzuela *vah-len-sway'lah*, 14 44N 120 57E, pop(1980) 212,363, city in Capital prov, Philippines; on Luzon I, N of Manila.

Valera *va-lay'ra*, 9 21N 70 38W, pop(1981) 102,068, town in Trujillo state, W Venezuela; SW of Trujillo.

Valjevo *va'lye-vo*, 44 16N 19 56E, pop(1981) 95,449, town in W Srbija (Serbia) republic, Yugoslavia; 72 km SW of Beograd; economy: fruit and livestock trade, agricultural machinery, magnesite mining nearby.

Valkeakoski *vahl'kay-ah-kos'kee*, 61 17N 24 05E, pop(1982) 22,638, pulp and paper-making town in Häme prov, S Finland, SE of Tampere; established in 1923.

Vall de Uxo *val* THay *oo-shō'*, 39 49N 0 15W, pop(1981) 26,145, town in Castellón de la Plana prov, Valencia, E Spain; 20 km SW of Castellón; economy: footwear.

Valladolid *val-ya-do-leed'*, prov in Castilla-León region, NW central Spain, consisting of flat, plateau country in the middle R Douro (Duero) basin; pop(1981) 751,734; area 8,202 sq km; capital Valladolid; economy: motor vehicles, metal products, cement, dairy produce, animal feed, mineral water, textiles, cocoa, chocolate, mining machinery, sugar.

Valladolid, 41 38N 4 43W, pop(1981) 330,242, capital of Valladolid prov, Castilla-León, NW central Spain; on R Pisuerga, 193 km NE of Madrid; archbishopric; Columbus died here; university (1346); airport; railway; economy: motor vehicles, cement, ironwork, flour, leather goods; monuments: 16th-c cathedral; Cervantes museum, Santa Cruz college; events: Holy Week; International Film Week in April; fair and fiesta in Sept and Festival of Spain (Oct-Nov).

Valle *val'lay*, dept in S Honduras, Central America; bounded W by El Salvador and S by the Golfo de Fonseca; pop(1983e) 125,640; area 1,564 sq km.

Valle d'Aosta *val'lay da-os'ta*, VAL D'AOSTE (Fr), autonomous region of Italy, bounded W by France and N by Switzerland; pop(1981) 112,353; area 3,263 sq km; contains the valleys of the Dora and Baltea, and the Valle d'Aosta itself, running SE from Mont Blanc; economy: tourism, wine-growing, livestock raising; the population is mostly French-speaking; the valley has been important since ancient times as the access route to the Great and Little St Bernard Passes through the Alps.

Valle de Cauca *val'yay day kow'ka*, dept in W Colombia, South America; bounded W by the Pacific and E by the Cordillera Occidental; pop(1985) 2,833,940; area 22,140 sq km; capital Cali; principal sugar-producing region of Colombia.

Valledupar *val-yay-doo-par'*, 10 31N 73 16W, pop(1985) 196,984, capital of César dept, N Colombia, South America; SE of Santa Marta and the Pico Cristóbal Colón.

Vallejo *val-ay'hō*, 38 07N 122 15W, pop(1980) 80,303, port in Solano county, W California, United States; at the mouth of the Napa river on San Pablo Bay, N of Oakland; maritime academy (1929); economy: trade in livestock, fruit and processed food.

Vallenar *val-yay-nar'*, 28 34S 70 45W, pop(1982) 42,309, capital of Huasco prov, Atacama, Chile; noted for the production of the sweet, white Pajarete wine; railway.

Valletta or **Valetta** *val-et'a*, 35 54N 14 32E, pop(1983e) 14,040, capital of Malta, situated on a peninsula between the Grand Harbour and the Marsamxett Harbour; the town was built by the French Grand Master of the Knights of St John, Jean de Valette after the siege of 1565; university (1769); airport at Luqa (6 km); economy: Grand Harbour is the main port with dockyards, and at Marsamxett Harbour there is a yachting centre; monuments: Palace of the Grand Masters, 16th-c St John's co-cathedral, the National Museum of Fine Arts.

Valley Forge, state park in Chester county, Pennsylvania, United States; 7 km SE of Phoenixville, on the R Schuylkill; winter headquarters of George Washington 1777-78.

Valley Stream, 40 40N 73 42W, pop(1980) 35,769, town in Nassau county, SE New York, United States; residential suburb on Long Island, 26 km E of New York.

Valparaíso *val-pa-ra-ee'sō*, *val-pa-rī'zo* (Eng), ACONCAGUA, region of central Chile; situated between the Pacific and the Andes; comprises the provs of Petorca, Los Andes, San Felipe, Quillota, Valparaíso, San Antonio, Isla de Pascua (Easter I); to the E on the Argentine frontier are high Andean peaks including Aconcagua, Plomo, Juncal and Leones; includes Isla de Pascua and the Archipiélago Juan Fernández, where Alexander Selkirk was marooned in 1704 for over 4 years; Daniel Defoe based his novel *Robinson Crusoe* on his experience; pop(1984) 1,316,200; area 16,396 sq km; capital Valparaíso; chief towns Los Andes, San Felipe, Quillota and San Antonio; economy: tobacco, alcohol, shoes, metal, fish, oil refining, foodstuffs, copper; to the ENE of Valparaíso (city) is Los Andes National Park.

Valparaíso, 33 03S 71 07W, pop(1982) 266,577, port and capital of Valparaíso prov, and Valparaíso region, central Chile; Chile's main port and one of the main commercial centres on the west coast of South America; the city is divided into lower and upper areas, the business and commercial centre lying around the bay, the poorer sector lying further up the hill; these lower and upper cities are connected by winding roads and funicular railways; although founded in 1536, most of its old buildings have been destroyed by earthquakes (the last serious one occurred in July 1971); most of the principal buildings date from reconstruction after the 1906 earthquake; the main financial street is the Calle Prat, which runs S from the Plaza; the main shopping area is around the Calle Esmeralda; a lift runs from the Plaza Aduana to the Paseo Veintiuno de Mayo terrace on Cerro Artillería, which gives a panoramic view of the bay and the hills beyond the city; also on Cerro Artillería is a Naval Academy and a park; 2 universities (1926, 1928); railway; event: New Year is celebrated with a firework display on the bay.

Vammala *vahm'mah-lah*, 61 20N 22 55E, pop(1982) 16,024, town in Turku-Pori prov, SW Finland; on R Kokema, 48 km WSW of Tampere; established in 1912; railway.

Van, mountainous prov in SE Turkey; bounded E by Iran; pop(1980) 468,646; area 19,069 sq km; capital Van; economy: fruit, grain, coal mining.

Van Gölü *van go-loo'*, LAKE VAN, salt lake in mountainous E Anadolu (Anatolia), Turkey; largest lake in the country; area 3,173 sq km; length 120 km; width 80 km; the rivers Deli, Zilan, Kara, and Micinger flow into the lake; there is no outlet; a ferry service operates from Tatvan to Van across the S part of the lake; the ancient Armenian civilization grew up around its shores.

Vancouver *van-koo'ver*, 49 13N 123 06W, pop(1981) 414,281, pop(1981) 1,310,600 (Greater Vancouver), seaport in SW British Columbia, SW Canada; near the Washington state frontier, opposite Vancouver island, on a peninsula between Burrard Inlet to the N and the Fraser river to the S; 3rd largest city in Canada; first settled c.1875 and named Granville; reached by the

Canadian Pacific Railroad in 1886, in the same year that the city was incorporated and renamed Vancouver; the city was named after Captain George Vancouver who entered Burrard Inlet in 1792 aboard the *Discovery*; University of British Columbia (1908); railway; airport (at 19 km); economy: shipbuilding, fishing, oil refining, distilling, brewing, timber, trucks and trailers, machinery; monuments: the older part of the city occupies the S part of the peninsula; the Lipsett Indian Museum in Hastings Park contains one of the most complete collections of British Columbian Indian life and art; Stanley Park contains a zoo, aquarium and totem poles carved by British Columbia's Coast Indians; at Prospect Point the Lions Gate Bridge, the longest bridge in the Commonwealth, crosses the narrows to residential West Vancouver; Chinatown in Vancouver is the 2nd largest Chinese community in N America; event: Pacific National Exhibition, held in Hastings Park exhibition grounds (Aug).

Vancouver, 45 38N 122 40W, pop(1980) 42,834, port capital of Clark county, SW Washington, United States; on the Columbia river, opposite Portland, Oregon; founded in 1825 by the Hudson's Bay Co; became a US possession in 1846; railway; economy: paper, aluminium, chemicals, trade in grain and timber; monuments: Fort Vancouver National Monument includes the site of the headquarters depot of Hudson's Bay Co and old Fort Vancouver, which was the early seat of military and political authority and the trading centre of the Pacific NW.

Vanda, town in Finland. See Vantaa.

Van'derbijlpark, 26 41S 27 50E, pop(1980) 294,082, town in Transvaal prov, South Africa; SW of Vereeniging; Sharpeville lies NE; railway; economy: steel.

Vänern *ve'nurn*, VANER (Eng), lake in Värmland, Skaraborg and Älvsborg counties, SW Sweden; lies NW of road from Göteborg (Gothenburg) to Örebro; area 5,585 sq km; length 146 km; max depth 98 m; largest lake in Sweden; lies in a tectonic basin, with the water level falling c.8 cm per century; in two parts: Stora Vänern to NE and Dalbosjön to SW; chief towns on its banks are Karlstad, Vänersborg, Lidköping and Mariestad.

Vänersborg *ve'nurs-bor-yu*, 58 23N 12 19E, pop(1983) 34,976, capital town of Älvsborg county, SW Sweden; at S end of L Vänern at outlet of the R Göta älv; railway; monument: 18th-c governor's residence.

Vannes *van*, DARIORIGUM (anc), 47 40N 2 47W, pop(1982) 45,397, port and capital of Morbihan dept, Bretagne region, NW France; on the Gulf of Morbihan, 107 km WNW of Nantes; railway; economy: animal feedstuffs, chicken and turkey processing, petfoods; monuments: has a picturesque Old Town, the Place Henri IV is lined with 15-16th-c half-timbered overhanging houses; also in the old quarter is the 15th-c residence of Bishop Jean de Malestroit, which was Brittany's first Parliament building (Château Gaillard), now housing a comprehensive museum of prehistoric antiquities; 13-19th-c cathedral of St-Pierre with a 13th-c Romanesque belfry and a 16th-c circular granite Renaissance chapel; 14-17th-c fortifications with 14th-c Tour du Connetable (Constable's Tower).

Vantaa *van'tah*, VANDA (Swed), 60 10N 25 02E, pop(1982) 136,607, town in Uudenmaa prov, S Finland, N of Helsinki; formerly a suburb of Helsinki established as a separate town in 1972; railway; international airport (Helsinki-Vantaa); economy: light engineering; monuments: greystone church built in 1494, formerly the parish church of Helsinki.

Vanua Levu *va-noo'ah lay'voo*, mountainous volcanic island in the SW Pacific Ocean, 2nd largest of the Fiji Is, 32 km NE of Viti Levu I; area 5,556 sq km; length 176 km; chief town Labasa; the most intensively cultivated areas are in the lower reaches of the Labasa valley which drains northwards; coconut plantations predominate on the wet E side of the island; the Great Sea Reef of Vanua Levu is the 3rd longest barrier reef in the world; Natewa Bay indents the E coast.

Vanuatu *va-noo-ah'too*, formerly NEW HEBRIDES, official name Republic of Vanuatu, an irregular Y-shaped island chain in the SW Pacific Ocean, 400 km NE of New Caledonia, between 13° S and 21° S and 166° E and 171° E; timezone GMT +11; area 14,763 sq km; capital Vila; pop(1979) 112,596; approximately 60% of the population lives on the 4 main islands of Efate, Espiritu Santo, Malekula, and Tanna; other islands include Aoba, Aurora, Pentecost, Ambrym, Epi and Erromango; 95% of the population is Melanesian, with small numbers of Europeans, Polynesians, and Micronesians making up the rest; under the independence constitution, Bislama (a form of pidgin English) has been named the national language, while English and French are the official languages; Catholicism is the dominant religion; the unit of currency is the vatu (since 1982); membership of ADB, Commonwealth, G-77, IFC, IMF, ITU, South Pacific Forum, UN.

Physical description and climate. The archipelago comprises 12 islands and 60 islets, the largest islands being Espiritu Santo (3,947 sq km), Malekula (2,024 sq km), and Efate (985 sq km). Most of the islands are volcanic and rugged, with raised coral beaches fringed by reefs. The highest peak, on Espiritu Santo, rises to 1,888 m. There are active volcanoes on Tanna, Ambrym, and Lopevi, and an underwater volcano near Tongoa. Most of the islands are covered with dense forests, but there are narrow strips of cultivated land around the coast. The climate is tropical, with a hot and rainy season between Nov and April. During this rainy season winds are variable and cyclones may occur. Trade winds from the SE moderate conditions between May and Oct. Temper-

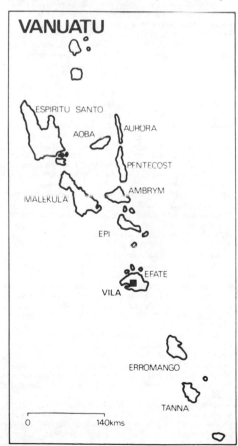

atures at Vila vary between 16°C and 33°C, and annual rainfall averages 2,310 mm.
History, government and constitution. In 1906 an Anglo-French Condominium was established providing for the joint administration of the islands. On 30 July 1980 the Condominium of the New Hebrides achieved independence and became the Republic of Vanuatu. Vanuatu is governed by a representative assembly of 42 members, replacing the former advisory council. The assembly elects the president, who as head of state appoints an executive prime minister and cabinet.
Economy. Cultivated land covers 607 sq km and is generally restricted to the coastal plains and low plateau land. The main subsistence crops include yams, breadfruit, taro, manioc, and bananas. Copra, cocoa, and coffee are major cash crops. Cattle and pigs are reared on coconut plantations. Meat (frozen, tinned, or chilled) is now the country's 3rd largest export after copra and fish. At Santo, the South Pacific Fishing Company operates a fish-freezing plant where tuna and bonito are frozen and prepared for export to the USA, Japan, and elsewhere. Manganese deposits on Efate comprise the country's only mineral wealth and provide export income. Light industries include food processing and handicrafts for a steadily increasing tourist market. The number of tourists and cruise ship visitors nearly doubled between 1974 and 1978, and totalled 69,000 in 1979. The principal imports are food and drink, metal products and hardware, oil, machinery, ships, and motor vehicles. Australia, UK, and France are the major sources of imports.

Var, dept in Provence-Alpes-Côte d'Azur region of SE France, on the Mediterranean Sea; comprises 3 arrond, 41 cantons and 153 communes; pop(1982) 708,331; area 5,993 sq km; the R Verdon forms part of the N border; watered also by the R Argens; hilly and wooded inland; hot, dry and infertile, except for the littoral where market-garden produce is grown (especially flowers, olives and vines); capital Toulon, chief towns Draguignan and La Seyne; tourist resorts on the Côte d'Azur include St-Raphael, St-Tropez and Fréjus; there are sea-water treatment establishments at Toulon and St-Raphael; includes the Parc National de Port-Cros which covers an area of 73 sq km and extends over the island of Port-Cros and the seabed around it.

Varanasi *va-ran'-e-see*, BENARES, BANARAS, KASI (anc), 25 22N 83 08E, pop(1981) 794,000, city in Uttar Pradesh state, N India; on the N bank of the R Ganga (Ganges), 120 km E of Allahabad; one of the 7 most sacred Hindu cities, it is reputed to be Siva's capital while on earth; it is also a holy city of Buddhists and Jains; a Hindu city since the 6th century, it was invaded by the Afghans in 1033; Muslims, who subsequently ruled the city until the 18th century, destroyed all early Hindu temples, replacing them with mosques; the city was ceded to Britain in 1775; universities (1916, 1958); connected by rail to Jaunpur, Allahabad and Gorakhpur; airfield; economy: textiles, brassware, jewellery; monuments: the city has over 1,400 Hindu temples and shrines including the Golden Temple (built in 1777 and dedicated to Siva) and Durga Temple, also known as Monkey Temple for the swarms of monkeys which surround it; along almost 7 km of the high bank of the R Ganga are *ghats* or stairs, which lead to numerous temples and from where pilgrims bathe in the sacred waters of the river; cremation of Hindus takes place here; Manirkarnika Ghat is the most sacred cremation *ghat*, near which is a holy well; Hindus believe that to die in Varanasi releases them from the cycle of rebirth and so allows them to enter heaven; Buddhists believe that Buddha began preaching at Sarnath, which lies only 6.5 km from Varanasi; a mosque dedicated to the Muslim emperor Aurangzeb stands on the city's highest ground.

Varaždin *var-azh'din*, 46 18N 16 21E, pop(1981) 90,729, town in N Hrvatska (Croatia) republic, Yugoslavia; on R Drava, NNE of Zagreb; radioactive sulphur springs nearby; railway junction; economy: wine trade, textiles, lignite mining nearby; monuments: market square and many interesting burghers' houses; Patačić palace, 13th-c castle.

Varberg *var-ber'yu*, 57 06N 12 15E, pop(1982) 45,034, fishing port on the coast of Halland county, SW Sweden, on the Kattegat, about 72 km S of Göteborg (Gothenburg); railway.

Vardak *war-dak*, WARDAK, prov in E central Afghanistan; pop(1984e) 312,135; area 9,023 sq km; capital Maydān Shahr; part of the Kūh e Bābā range in the NW; borders Kābul prov in the E.

Varde *vahr'du*, 55 38N 8 30E, pop(1981) 10,888, industrial town in Ribe county, SW Jylland (Jutland), Denmark, on the R Varde; railway; economy: engineering.

Varde, river in central Jylland (Jutland), Denmark; rises in W Vejle county, flows W and SW through Ribe county, discharges into North Sea NW of Esbjerg; length 72 km.

Varese *va-ray'zay*, prov of Lombardia region, NW Italy; pop(1981) 788,057; area 1,199 sq km; capital Varese.

Varese, 45 49N 8 49E, pop(1981) 90,527, capital town of Varese prov, Lombardia region, NW Italy; between Lago di Como and Lago Maggiore, in the S foothills of the Alps; railway; economy: footwear, kitchen appliances, tourism.

Varkaus *var'kows*, 62 15N 27 45E, pop(1982) 24,736, industrial town in Kuopio prov, S central Finland; on the L Saimaa canal system; established in 1929; railway; airfield; boats to Kuopio and Savonlinna; economy: paper, cellulose, timber, light engineering, shipyards.

Värmdö *verm'du*, Swedish island in the Baltic Sea, off E coast of Stockholm county, 16 km E of Stockholm; area 180 sq km; length 22.5 km; width 6.5-22 km; irregular in shape with deeply indented coastline; administered by Stockholm county.

Värmland *verm'land*, county of SW Sweden; comprises much of N section of L Vänern; chief river is the Alvdalen; land area 17,584 sq km; pop(1983) 282,093; capital Karlstad; chief towns Kristinehamn and Arvika; tourist industry now taking over from iron industry and forestry as the main activity.

Var'na, okrug (prov) of E Bulgaria bordered to the E by the Black Sea; area 3,810 sq km; pop(1981) 467,000; traversed by the R Kamchiya; agriculture and fishing are important, and there are summer resorts such as Drouzhba on the Black Sea coast.

Varna, ODESSUS (Lat), 43 13N 27 56E, pop(1981) 293,950, resort and capital of Varna okrug (prov), E Bulgaria; in a bay (Varnenski Zaliv) of the Black Sea, 469 km E of Sofiya; 3rd largest town and largest harbour in Bulgaria; for some years after 1949 the city was known as Stalin; airport; railway; economy: shipbuilding, chemical industry and power production; monument: Roman thermae and baths; in 1972 a gold hoard, dated between 3,500 and 3,000 BC, was discovered in the Varna necropolis; event: Varna Summer International Music Festival.

Várpalota *var'po-lō-to*, 47 10N 18 06E, pop(1984e) 28,000, town in Veszprém county, NW central Hungary; in SE foothills of Bakony Mts, E of Székesfehérvár; economy: fertilizer, lignite mining.

Vas *vosh*, county in W Hungary; bounded to the W by Austria and SW by Yugoslavia; mountainous in the W falling to the Kisalföld (Little Alföld) plain in the N; drained by Raab (Rába) and Gyöngyös rivers; pop(1984e) 283,000; area 3,337 sq km; capital Szombathely; chief towns include Kormend and Köseg; there are 209 villages in the county; since 1969 40% of the population has been rehoused; 97% of arable farms are state owned; spa at Bük; Europe's largest natural deposit of carbon dioxide is located near Répcelak; economy: fruit, vegetables, grain, dairy produce, machinery, dry ice and liquid carbon dioxide.

Vasa, prov in Finland. See Vaasa.

Vaslui *vas-loo'ee*, county in E Romania; bounded to the E by the R Prut which follows the USSR frontier; pop(1983) 449,945; area 5,297 sq km; capital Vaslui.

Vaslui, 46 37N 27 46E, pop(1983) 57,571, capital of Vaslui county, E Romania; on R Birlad; established in the 15th century; railway; economy: grain and livestock trade, animal products; monument: remains of Stephen the Great's palace.

Västerås *ves-ter-aws'*, 59 36N 16 32E, pop(1982) 117,797, capital city of Västmanland county, E Sweden; on the N shore of L Mälaren at the mouth of the R Svartån; major inland port; scene of parliament 1527 which formally introduced Reformation into Sweden; railway; economy: electrical appliances; monuments: Gothic cathedral, 13th-c castle.

Västerbotten *vest'er-bot'en*, county of N Sweden, bounded on the E by the Gulf of Bothnia; land area 55,429 sq km; pop(1983) 245,018; capital Umeå; chief towns Skellefteå and Lycksele; drained by the Vindelälven, Ume älv and Ångermanälven rivers; numerous NW to SE orientated lakes including the Storuman, Vojmsjön and Malgomaj; sulphide ore in Skellefteå district.

Västernorrland *vest'er-nor'land*, county of E Sweden, bounded on the E by the Gulf of Bothnia; drained by the rivers Ångermanälven and Indalsälven; land area 21,771 sq km; pop(1983) 266,049; capital Härnösand; chief towns Sundsvall, Kramfors and Örnsköldsvik.

Västervik *vest'-e-vik*, 57 45N 16 40E, pop(1982) 40,893, seaport in Kalmar county, SE Sweden, on the Baltic Sea 117 km N of Kalmar; rail terminus; ferry services to Gotland I; one of most attractive examples of the old wooden 18th-c towns of Sweden; monument: 15th-c St Gertrude's Church.

Västmanland *vest'-man-land*, county of E Sweden; comprises much of the W section of L Mälaren; land area 6,302 sq km; pop(1983) 257,782; capital Västerås; chief towns Köping and Arboga; economy: iron industry.

Vaté, Pacific island. See Efate.

Va'tican, official name The Vatican City, STATO DELLA CITTA DEL VATICANO (Ital), a papal sovereign state in Rome, Italy, on the W bank of the R Tiber; created in 1929 by the Lateran Treaty between the Pope and the Italian government of Mussolini; this treaty ended the long-standing dispute arising from the Italian occupation of the Papal States and the seizure of Rome in 1870; the state is under the protection of the 1954 La Haye Convention; area 44 hectares; timezone GMT +1; pop about 1,000; pop with citizenship about 300, the Holy See is the actual seat (ie residence) of the Pope, but is the term generally used to indicate the Pope together with those associated with him in the government of the Roman Catholic Church at its headquarters; the Vatican uses 3 different types of passport: Holy See Diplomatic passports, Holy See Service passports and Vatican City State passports, the last being reserved for citizens of the Vatican City State; the correct adjectival form depends on the context - diplomatic representation to the Holy See should be described as Apostolic (or less correctly papal) Nunciature, while it is correct to speak of the Vatican Radio or of a Vatican stamp; the Vatican City includes St Peter's, the Vatican Palace and Museum, and neighbouring buildings as well as 13 buildings in Rome and the Pope's summer villa at Castel Gandolfo all of which have the same rights as the Vatican City itself; the territory is surrounded in part by a wall extending to St Peter's Square where a line of travertine joins the two wings of the colonnade at the ground, signalling the boundaries of the State at the end of the piazza, to which anyone has free access; the city has 3 entrances, whose care is entrusted to the Pontifical Swiss Guard: 'The Bronze Doors' at the end of the right-hand colonnade, the entrance under the Arch of Charlemagne or 'The Arch of the Bells' and the Via di Porta Angelica. Within the city are some of the world's finest museums and works of art: the Belvedere, with its great collection of classical statuary, including the Laocoon, the Apollo Belvedere and the Venus of Cnidus; Raphael's Stanze and Loggie and the Sistine Chapel containing Michelangelo's magnificent frescoes. The Apostolic Vatican Library, with 800,000 volumes, 80,000 manuscripts, 10,000 incunabula and 100,000 engravings, is one of the world's great libraries, and at the Printing Press are printed books in practically all the world's languages; the city has its own stamps and coinage; national holiday 30 June; membership of FAO, IAEA, INTELSAT, ITU, IWC, OAS, UN, UNESCO, UPU, WIPO, WTO.

Government and constitution. The Vatican City State is a monarchical-sacerdotal state with the Supreme Pontiff, the Pope, as head of state; the Pope is elected for life by the Sacred College of Cardinals and has full legislative, judicial and executive powers; these powers during the period of Vacant See are held by the College of Cardinals; legislative regulations are issued by the Pope or through his delegate, by the Pontifical Commission for the Administration of the State of the Vatican City and by the Governor of the State; judicial powers reside in one Judge, a Court of First Instance, a Court of Appeal and a Court of Cassation; executive power is delegated to the Pontifical Commission and to its dependent, the Special Delegate; the Papal Military Corps, with the exception of the Swiss Guard, was disbanded in 1970.

Vatnajökull *vaht'nah-ye-kootl*, largest glacier of Iceland, in SE Iceland; area 8,456 sq km.

Vät'tern *vet'ern*, VETTER, WETTER, lake in Skaraborg, Östergötland, Jönköping and Örebro counties, S Sweden, E of L Vänern; extends 130 km from Askersund in N to Jönköping in S; area 1,912 sq km; max width 30 km; Sweden's 2nd largest lake; connected with the Baltic by the Göta Canal.

Vaucluse *vō-klooz*, dept in Provence-Alpes-Côte d'Azur region of SE France, bounded on the S by the Durance R and on the W by the R Rhône; comprises 3 arrond, 24 cantons and 151 communes; pop(1982) 427,343; area 3,566 sq km; mountainous in the E where the Alpes du Dauphiné reach 1,912 m at Mt Ventoux; watered by the Coulon, Nesque, Ouvèze and Aigues rivers; it takes its name from a spring at the village of Vaucluse, near Avignon, celebrated by Plutarch, and gives its name to a type of reappearing spring in limestone country; notable wines from Châteauneuf-du-Pape; capital Avignon, chief towns Cavaillon and Carpentras; there are caves near Cavaillon; the Parc du Luberon regional nature park lies partly within the dept.

Vaud *vō*, WAADT *vaht* (Ger), canton in W Switzerland; pop(1980) 528,747; area 3,211 sq km; capital Lausanne; Switzerland's biggest wine-producing area, lying around the fertile shores of Lac Léman; the most important areas are La Côte (producing mainly light red Gamays and Chasselas whites), Lavaux, and Chablais; joined the Swiss Confederacy in 1803.

Vaupés *vow-pes'*, administrative territory in SE Colombia; bounded E by Brazil, S by Apaporis and Ajaju rivers and N by the Río Guaviare; crossed by Vaupés and Inirida rivers, part of the Amazon system; pop(1985) 3,414; area 65,268 sq km; capital Mitú.

Vava'u *va-vow'*, coral island group of N Tonga, S Pacific, 112 km from the Ha'apai group; area 119.2 sq km; pop(1984) 15,077; main settlement Neiafu; the main island of Vava'u is surrounded by a number of smaller islands which are separated from the mainland by numerous small channels.

Vavuniya *vuv'oon-i-ya*, 8 45N 80 30E, pop(1981) 18,512, capital of Vavuniya dist, Northern prov, Sri Lanka; 52 km N of Anuradhapura; 86% of the pop of the dist are Tamil.

Växjö or **Vexiö** *vek'shœ*, 56 52N 14 50E, pop(1982) 65,424, capital town of Kronoberg county, S Sweden, 96 km WNW of Kalmar, at N end of L Växjö; traditionally founded in the 11th century by an English missionary, St Siegfrid; became a religious focal point in the 12th century; long predominany a garrison town and episcopal see; railway; monuments: 12th-c cathedral, Småland museum.

Vefsna, *vefs'nah*, 65 51N 13 10E, pop(1980) 13,236, town on R Vefsna, Nordland county, W Norway.

Vega, La *vay'ga*, 19 15N 70 33W, pop(1982e) 178,510, town in N La Vega prov, Dominican Republic, on the Rio Camú; on the Duarte highway between Santo Domingo and Santiago.

Vegas, Las *vay'gas* (Sp, 'meadows'), 36 10N 115 09W,

pop(1980) 164,674, county seat of Clark county, SE Nevada, United States; largest city in the state; named after the natural meadows which served as camping sites on early trails to the W; settled by Mormons 1855-57; purchased by a railway company in 1903 it achieved city status in 1911; university (1957); railway; airport; noted for its gaming casinos and 24-hour entertainment; also a commercial centre for a mining and ranching area; industries include printing and publishing, and the manufacture of chemicals and glass products; monuments: Mormon Fort, Liberace Museum.

Vejle *vī'lu*, a county of E Jylland (Jutland), Denmark, the E coast is indented by the fjords of Horsens and Vejle; area 2,997 sq km; pop(1983) 327,102; capital Vejle, chief towns include Horsens, Kolding and Fredericia.

Vejle, 55 43N 9 30E, pop(1981) 43,300, seaport and manufacturing town, capital of Vejle county, E Jylland (Jutland), Denmark, at head of Vejle Fjord; railway; economy: engineering, foodstuffs; monuments: 13th-c St Nicholas's church; 28 km W is Billund, with Legoland, a miniature town built of the famous Lego plastic bricks.

Vejle Fjord, inlet of the Lille Bælt (Little Belt) in Vejle county, E Jylland (Jutland), Denmark; extends 21 km inland to Vejle city.

Velasco Ibarra *vay-las'kō ee-ba'ra*, EL EMPALME, 1 00S 79 35W, pop(1982) 17,017, town in Guayas prov, W Ecuador; W of Quevedo in the tropical lowlands N of Guayaquil.

Velbert *fel'bert*, 51 22N 7 03E, pop(1983) 91,300, manufacturing city in Düsseldorf dist, Nordrhein-Westfalen (North Rhine-Westphalia) prov, W Germany; in the Ruhr valley, 22 km NE of Düsseldorf; economy: hand and electric hoists.

Velence *ve'len-tse*, lake in Fejér county, W central Hungary; SW of Budapest and W of the R Danube; area 26 sq km.

Veleta, Pico de la *vay-lay'ta*, second highest peak in the Sierra Nevada, Granada prov, Andalucia, Spain, rising to 3,392 m; skiing resort at Solynieve; access by cable-car.

Velika Gorica *ve'li-ka go'rit-sa*, 45 44N 16 05E, pop(1981) 54,474, town in N Hrvatska (Croatia) republic, Yugoslavia; SSE of Zagreb; railway; economy: timber.

Velika Plana or **Plana** *ve'li-ka pla'na*, 44 20N 21 01E, pop(1981) 52,619, town in N central Srbija (Serbia) republic, Yugoslavia; near R Morava, 72 km SE of Beograd; railway junction; economy: foodstuffs.

Ve'liko Tŭr'novo or **Veliko Tarnovo**, okrug (prov) of NE central Bulgaria traversed S-N by the R Yantra; area 4,719 sq km; pop(1981) 347,000.

Veliko Tŭrnovo, 43 04N 25 39E, pop(1981e) 65,000, capital of Veliko Tŭrnovo okrug (prov), NE central Bulgaria; on the R Yantra, 241 km NE of Sofiya; airport; railway; capital of the second Bulgarian kingdom between 1187 and 1393; monuments: Tsarevets Hill with its fortress walls, patriarch's palace, royal palace and defensive tower; the Forty Martyrs Church (1230); Renaissance museum in the former Hadji Nicoli's inn, which was built by Kolyu Ficheto, the master builder.

Vel'ingrad, 42 01N 23 59E, pop(1981e) 25,000, spa town in Pazardzhik okrug (prov), S Bulgaria; in the Rhodopi Planina (Rhodope Mts); a well known balneotherapeutic centre with 70 thermal springs; created by the amalgamation of three settlements; railway.

Velsen or **Velzen** *vel'tsen*, 52 27N 4 40E, pop(1984e) 125,016, manufacturing city in Noord Holland prov, W Netherlands, at mouth of the North Sea Canal.

Venda *ven'du*, independent black homeland in NE South Africa; pop(1985) 459,986; area 6,500 sq km; close to the Zimbabwe frontier, SE of Messina; granted self-government in 1973 and independence in 1979 by South Africa; its independent status is not recognized internationally; capital Thohoyandou; chief towns include Makhade and Sibasa; traditional territory of the Vhavenda peoples who speak Luvenda, English and Afrikaans; the economy is largely dependent on agriculture, including the cultivation of sisal, tea and coffee; over 60,000 people commute to work or are migrant workers in South Africa; there are reserves of coal, magnesite, copper, corundum, lead, graphite and phosphate.

Vendée *võ-day*, dept in Pays de la Loire region of W France, on the Bay of Biscay; comprises 3 arrond, 31 cantons and 282 communes; pop(1982) 483,027; area 6,721 sq km; rises inland to 285 m in the Hauteurs de Gâtine; marshy in the S, and moderately fertile, with considerable livestock; watered by the Lay, Vendée and Boulogne rivers; it was the scene of bitter civil fighting (1793-95) between the Revolutionaries and the royalist Vendéans; capital La-Roche-sur-Yon, chief towns Fontenay-le-Comte and Les Sables-d'Olonne; the Parc du Marais Poitevin regional nature park lies partly within the dept.

Veneto *vay'nay-to*, VENEZIA *vay-net'sya*, VENETIA (Eng), region of NE Italy, comprising the provs of Verona, Vicenza, Belluno, Treviso, Venezia, Padova, and Rovigo; pop(1981) 4,345,047; area 18,379 sq km; in the N and W, between Lago di Garda and Austria, the terrain is mountainous (Alpi Dolomitiche); chief rivers include the Po, Adige, Brenta, and Piave; the population is concentrated mainly in the larger cities of the Po plain; economy: agriculture (grains, wine, fruit, vegetables, cattle-farming) and industry (textiles, building materials, metalworking, chemicals, petrochemicals, shipbuilding) are also concentrated in the Po plain; industrial development has been promoted by an abundant supply of power (hydroelectric schemes in the Alps, natural gas resources in the Po plain); Lago di Garda, the area round Cortina d'Ampezzo in the Alpi Dolomitiche, and the old cities of Venezia (Venice), Padova (Padua), Verona, and Vicenza are popular with tourists.

Venezia *vay-net'sya*, prov of Veneto region, NE Italy; pop(1981) 838,794; area 2,461 sq km; capital Venezia.

Venezia, VENICE *ven'is* (Eng), VENETIA (Lat), 45 26N 12 20E, pop(1981) 346,146, seaport capital of Venezia prov, Veneto region, NE Italy; on the Golfo di Venezia, at the head of the Adriatic Sea; the city lies 4 km from the Italian mainland in the Laguna Veneta, a salt-water lagoon (40 km long and up to 15 km wide) which is separated from the Adriatic by a series of narrow spits of land (*lidi*); it is built on 118 small islands and is traversed by numerous canals, notably the Grand Canal, which runs NW-SE in a reversed S-curve and forms the main artery of traffic; another large canal, that of Giudecca, separates the city proper from the islands of Giudecca; the houses and palaces are built on piles and present a variety of Byzantine, Gothic, and Renaissance architecture; also in the city area are the mainland industrial suburbs of Porto di Maghera and Mestre; connection with the mainland is by a causeway for road and rail traffic and by ferries; see of a patriarch-archbishop; airport; railway; monuments: 11th-c Basilica di San Marco (St Mark's church) with its 4 great bronze horses; Campanile di San Marco, a 99 m high bell-tower rebuilt in 1905-12 after the collapse of the original campanile in 1902; the old Mint housing the library of St Mark; 14-15th-c Doge's Palace (Palazzo Ducale), said to have been the residence of the Doge since about 814; Bridge of Sighs, built about 1595 to link the palace with the prison, its name recalling the sighs of the criminals led over the bridge to the place of execution; church of Santi Giovanni e Paolo (1333-90); church of the Redentore (1577-92); there are several fine art collections including that of the Accademia di Belle Arti containing more than 800 paintings, mainly by Venetian artists; events: Festa del Redentore (3rd Saturday in July); Gondola Race (1st Sunday in Sept); Venetian Carnival (annually, end of Feb until beginning of March); Festival of Modern Art (Sept).

Venezuela *vay-nay-sway'la*, official name Republic of Venezuela, REPÚBLICA DE VENEZUELA, the most northerly country in South America; situated between 1° and 12°N; bounded N by the Caribbean, S by Brazil, E by Guyana, SW and W by Colombia; timezone GMT −4; area 912,050 sq km; capital Caracas; principal towns Maracaibo and Ciudad Guayana; pop(1971) 10,721,522;

ethnic groups include 67% mestizo, 21% European, 10% African and 2% South American Indian; the official language is Spanish, but Indian dialects are spoken by about 200,000 Amerindians in the remote interior; the main religion is Roman Catholicism (96%); the currency is the bolívar of 100 céntimos; national holidays Carnival Monday (the day before Shrove Tuesday); 19 April (Act of Independence), 24 June (Battle of Carabobo), 24 July (Bolívar's birthday); 12 Oct (Columbus Day); membership of the Andean Pact, AIOEC, FAO, G-77, IADB, IAEA, IBRD, ICAO, ICO, IDB, IFAD, IFC, IHO, ILO, IMF, IMO, INTELSAT, INTERPOL, IPU, IRC, ITU, IWC, LAIA, NAMUCAR, OAS, OPEC, PAHO, SELA, UN, UNESCO, UPU, WFTU, WHO, WMO, WTO.

Physical description. Venezuela can be divided into 4 distinct geographical regions, the Venezuelan Highlands to the W and along the coast; the Maracaibo Lowlands around the freshwater lake of Maracaibo; the vast central plain of the *llanos* of the Orinoco (the lowland area in the valley of the Orinoco river); and the Guiana Highlands, which cover over half the country. The Venezuelan Highlands are an offshoot of the Andes. They extend NE from the Colombian border S of the Maracaibo Lowlands; this section is known as the Cordillera de Mérida. To the N of Barquisimeto the mountains broaden out into the Segovia Highlands before turning E in parallel ridges along the coast to form the Central Highlands. They rise again to the E of Barcelona, forming the North-Eastern Highlands. Over three-quarters of Venezuela is drained by the Orinoco, which crosses the country in a wide arc from the S to the NE where it enters the Atlantic in a large swampy delta. The Orinoco receives other large rivers including the Guaviare, the Meta (which forms part of the Venezuelan border), the Apure, the Caura and the Caroní.

Climate. The climate of Venezuela is generally hot and humid, although the coast is fanned by cooling trade winds. Throughout the country there is one single rainy season from April to Oct. The N slopes of the Andes tend to have less rain than the S slopes. Sunshine ranges from 6 hours per day in the wetter months to as much as 8 hours per day in the dry months. Caracas in the N coastal range has annual temperatures ranging between 13° and 27°C, and monthly rainfall between 10 mm and 109 mm. On the coast the annual rainfall increases from the very low amounts around L Maracaibo to as much as 1,000 mm in the E. The lowlands around L Maracaibo are very hot in all months, Maracaibo's average daily temperatures ranging between 23° and 34°C. The *llanos* have a typical, hot tropical climate with an annual rainfall of 1,000-1,500 mm. There is little variation in temperature here. In the SE in the Guiana Highlands rainfall is heavier (1,500 mm per annum). Temperatures are moderated by the altitude and humidity is lower here than in the *llanos*. Santa Elena, representative of this plateau region, has average daily temperatures which range between 16° and 30°C and an average monthly rainfall of between 51 mm and 252 mm.

History, government and constitution. Originally inhabited by various tribes of Caribs and Arawaks, the first Spanish settlers established themselves at Cumaná in 1520. Revolt against Spanish colonial rule occurred in 1749, 1775, 1797, and again under Francisco Miranda in 1806 and 1811. The struggle for independence was carried on by Simón Bolívar who established the state of Gran Colombia (Colombia, Ecuador and Venezuela),

driving out the last of the Spanish Royalist forces who finally surrendered at Puerto Cabello in 1823. Venezuela became an independent Republic in 1830 on the dissolution of Gran Colombia. The 1958 constitution provides for elections every 5 years to a bicameral National Congress which comprises a Senate and a Chamber of Deputies. The president is advised by a council of 26 ministers.

Economy. Venezuela was predominantly an agricultural country until the 1920s when the development of oil from Maracaibo began to transform the economy. Over 90% of the country's export revenue is derived from oil, providing funds for large public-works and industrial programmes. Iron ore, gas and oil are nationalized industries. An investment fund (the Fondo de Inversiones de Venezuela) has been set up to channel oil profits into industrial and agricultural development projects. Apart from oil exploration in the Orinoco valley, emphasis is now being given to further development of the interior of Venezuela. Oil exploration is still taking place offshore but the aluminium industry has expanded rapidly to provide the country's 2nd largest export commodity. Other important minerals include gold, nickel, iron, copper and manganese. Manufacturing industry is largely based on the production of cement, steel, chemicals, food, shipbuilding and motor vehicles.

Agriculture. Although 20% of the land is under cultivation Venezuela imports half its food. The chief agricultural crops include coffee, cocoa, maize, tobacco and sugar. Dairying (Zulia state) and beef production (Zulia and the *llanos*) are the most important farming activities.

Administrative divisions. Venezuela is divided into 20 states, 2 territories and 1 federal district as follows:

State	*area (sq km)*	*pop(1980)*
Anzoátegui	43,283	689,555
Apure	76,471	196,808
Aragua	5,380	854,121
Barinas	35,187	318,401
Bolívar	237,908	666,362
Carabobo	4,647	1,019,042
Cojedes	14,793	135,579
Falcón	24,790	507,899
Guárico	64,961	371,423
Lara	19,793	1,047,633
Mérida	11,296	463,880
Miranda	7,946	1,380,430
Monagas	28,888	390,083
Nueva Esparta	1,149	196,911
Portuguesa	15,195	443,472
Sucre	11,795	568,020
Táchira	11,096	678,660
Trujillo	7,397	501,178
Yaracuy	7,096	313,073
Zulia	63,076	1,680,890
Federal territory		
Amazonas	170,503	45,600
Delta Amacuro	40,184	69,257
Federal district		
Caracas	119	2,074,203

Venice, seaport in NE Italy. See Venezia.

Vénissieux *vay-nees-yœ*, 45 42N 4 46E, pop(1982) 64,982, town in Rhône dept, Rhône-Alpes region, E France; 5 km SSE of Lyons; economy: injection equipment for diesel engines.

Venlo, *ven-lō'*, formerly VENLOO, 51 22N 6 10E, pop(1984e) 62,935, city in E Limburg prov, S Netherlands; on the R Mahs, near the W German border; an important traffic junction between Rotterdam and the Ruhr Basin, Venlo has become noted as a centre for industry and international business; railway; economy: machinery, optical apparatus, wire drawing, electrical equipment, textiles, building materials, timber; monument: 14th-c town hall.

Vennesla *ven'nayz-lah*, 58 15N 8 00E, pop(1980) 10,857, town in SE of Vest-Agder county, SW Norway; on the banks of the R Otra, N of Kristiansand; economy: timber products, hydrolectricity.

Vent, Îles du, *vē*, WINDWARD ISLANDS (Eng), island group of the Archipel de la Société (Society Is), French Polynesia, SE Pacific Ocean; comprises Tahiti (1,042 sq km), Moorea (132 sq km), and the smaller Mehetia, Tetiaroa and Tubuai Manu islands; pop(1977) 101,392; capital Papeete.

Vent, Îles sous le, LEEWARD ISLANDS (Eng), island group of the Archipel de la Société (Society Is), French Polynesia, SE Pacific Ocean; comprises the volcanic islands of Huahine, Raiatea, Tahaa, Bora-Bora, and Maupiti, together with 4 small (uninhabited) atolls; area 507 sq km; pop(1977) 16,311; chief town Uturoa on Raiatea.

Ventanas *vayn-ta'nas*, 1 28S 79 30W, pop(1982) 15,869, town in Los Ríos prov, W Ecuador; on the Río Zapotal, in the tropical lowlands W of the Andes and N of Babahoyo.

Vent'nor, 50 36N 1 11W, pop(1981) 6,980, health resort, South Wight dist, Isle of Wight, S England; on the SE coast of the island, on cliff-side terraces; the poet Swinburne is buried in the churchyard at Bonchurch nearby.

Veracruz *vay-ra-kroos'*, VERACRUZ-LLAVE *-lyah'vay*, state in E Mexico; on the Gulf of Mexico (E); bounded N by Tamaulipas, W by San Luis Potosí, Hidalgo, Puebla and Oaxaca, S by Chiapas and SE by Tabasco; a narrow state, between 48 and 160 km wide; rises from a coastal plain in the E to the Sierra Madre Oriental in the W; on the border with Puebla is Volcán Citlaltépetl (5,699 m), Mexico's highest peak; in the N along the coastline is the Laguna de Tamiahua; drained by the Pánuco, Blanco, San Juan Evangelista, Coatzacoalcos and Río Tonalá rivers; pop(1980) 5,264,611; area 71,699 sq km; capital Jalapa Enríquez; economy: maize, rice, beans, sugar cane, tropical fruit, fodder, livestock, timber, fishing, oil, sulphur, petrochemicals, food processing, sugar refining, light and heavy industry.

Veracruz, 19 11N 96 10W, pop(1980) 305,456, seaport in Veracruz state, E Mexico; situated on the Gulf of Mexico, on a low alluvial plain; Cortés landed here on 17 April 1519; railway; airport; principal port of entry for Mexico; economy: textiles, chemicals, soap, sisal and trade in coffee, vanilla and tobacco; monuments: 17th-c Palacio Municipal; the castle of San Juan de Ulúa (1565) on Gallego island was formerly used as a political prison; Chucho el Roto, the Robin Hood of Mexico, was imprisoned here; city museum; the Baluarte de Santiago fort once formed part of the city walls.

Veraguas *ve-ra'gwas*, prov in central Panama, Central America; extending across the entire isthmus from the Golfo de los Mosquitos (N) to the Pacific Ocean (S); includes the W part of the peninsula of Azuero and the Isla de Coiba in the Pacific; drained by the San Pablo and Santa Maria rivers; pop(1980) 173,245; area 11,086 sq km; capital Santiago; chief towns Soná and San Francisco; traversed by the Inter-American Highway.

Vercelli *ver-chel'lee*, prov of Piemonte region, NW Italy; pop(1981) 395,957; area 3,002 sq km; capital Vercelli.

Vercelli, VERCELLAE (anc), 45 19N 8 26E, pop(1981) 52,488, capital town of Vercelli prov, Piemonte region, NW Italy; 23 km S of Novara, between Torino (Turin) and Milano (Milan); centre of the largest rice-growing area in Europe; archbishopric; railway; economy: knitwear; monuments: Baroque cathedral, 13th-c church of Sant'Andrea.

Verde, Cape, See Cap Vert.

Verdun *ver-dun'*, 45 28N 73 35W, pop(1981) 61,287, town in S Québec, SE Canada; on the S shore of Montréal island; on the St Lawrence river, opposite Isle des Soeurs (Nuns' Island); a S suburb of Montréal.

Vereen'iging, 26 41S 27 56E, pop(1985) 60,584, 540,142 (metropolitan area), city in Transvaal prov, NE South Africa; on Vaal river, 56 km S of Johannesburg, close to the Orange Free State prov border; founded in 1892;

Treaty of Vereeniging (May 1902) terminated the South African War; economy: coal, chemicals, light industry.

Verkhoyanskiy Khrebet *vyerk-hu-yan'ski* KHrye-bet', arc-shaped mountain range in NE Yakutskaya ASSR, E Siberian Rossiyskaya, Soviet Union; entends 1,520 km along the right banks of the Lena and lower Aldan rivers; separates the Lena river basin (W) from the Yana and Indigirka basins (E); rises to a height of 2,390 m in the SE; traversed W-E by the Yakutsk-Magadan highway; the world's lowest temperatures for inhabited places have been recorded in this region.

Vermont', a New England state in NE United States, bounded W by New York, N by Canada, E by New Hampshire and S by Massachusetts; the 'Green Mountain State'; pop(1980) 511,456; area 24,110 sq km; 14th state admitted to the Union in 1791; the capital is Montpelier and the largest town is Burlington; the Green Mts run N-S through the centre of the state; rivers drain W from the mountains into L Champlain which forms much of the W border, and E into the R Connecticut which forms much of the E border; the highest point is Mt Mansfield (1,339 m); economy: forestry and timber products, arable farming, grazing, dairy products, maple syrup, marble and granite; explored by Champlain in 1609; the first settlement was established at Fort Dummer in 1724; the state is divided into 14 counties as follows.

County	*area (sq km)*	*pop(1980)*
Addison	2,010	29,406
Bennington	1,760	33,345
Caledonia	1,693	25,808
Chittenden	1,404	115,534
Essex	1,732	6,313
Franklin	1,687	34,788
Grand Isle	231	4,613
Lamoille	1,199	16,767
Orange	1,794	22,739
Orleans	1,812	23,440
Rutland	2,423	58,347
Washington	1,794	52,393
Windham	2,046	36,933
Windsor	2,527	51,030

Vernier *vern-yah'*, 46 13N 6 05E, pop(1980) 27,962, town in Genève canton, SW Switzerland; economy: engineering.

Véroia *ve'ree-u*, KARAFERIEH (Turk), BEROIA (anc), 40 32N 22 11E, pop(1981) 37,087, capital town of Imathía nome (dept), Makedhonia region, NE Greece; on the R Aliákmon, 75 km SW of Thessaloníki; base for winter sports; event: popular festival (1 Jan).

Verona *vay-rō'na*, prov of Veneto region, N Italy; pop(1981) 775,745; area 3,098 sq km; capital Verona.

Verona, 45 26N 11 00E, pop(1981) 265,932, capital town of Verona prov, Veneto region, N Italy; on the R Adige, 25 km E of the S tip of Lago di Garda; an important communications centre; railway; economy: agricultural market centre (especially fruit and vegetables); monuments: many Roman and medieval remains, including the Ponte di Pietra (Roman) and the Ponte Scaligero (1354), which were destroyed during World War II; 12th-c cathedral; 16th-c church of San Giorgio in Braida; Castel Vecchio (1354-55); 11-12th-c church of San Zeno Maggiore; tombs of the della Scala family (the Scaligers) who were lords of Verona in the 13th and 14th centuries; events: Gnocco (Festival of Bacchus) on the Friday before Shrovetide; operatic festival in the Roman amphitheatre (July-Aug).

Versailles *ver-sī'*, 48 48N 2 08E, pop(1982) 95,240, capital of Yvelines dept, Ile-de-France region, central France; 20 km SW of Paris; monuments: 18th-c cathedral (now a military hospital); Palace of Versailles, built by Louis XIV and served as a royal palace until 1793; the palace was converted into a national historical museum by Louis Philippe; nearby are the Petit Trianon and Grand Trianon châteaux; an end to the War of Independence and peace between Britain and the USA was concluded here in 1782; treaty signed here ending the Franco-Prussian War in 1871; peace treaty between the Allies and Germany signed here in 1919 ended World War I.

Vert, Cap. See Cap Vert.

Verviers *ver-vyay*, dist of E Liège prov, E Belgium; area 2,016 sq km; pop(1982) 245,859.

Verviers, 50 36N 5 52E, pop(1982) 54,800, industrial town and capital of Verviers dist, E Liège prov, Belgium; on the R Vesdre, mid-way between Aachen and Liège; developed after the 18th century into the main town of a textile region reaching as far as Eupen, its basis was the traditional wool industry (sheep rearing in the Ardennes and Eifel ranges); railway; economy: leatherware, machinery, paper, building materials, tourism (gateway to the picturesque Herve region and to the Ardennes).

Vesoul *ve-sool*, VESULUM (Lat), 47 40N 6 11E, pop(1982) 20,269, holiday resort, market town and capital of Haute-Saône dept, Franche-Comté region, W France; 93 km ENE of Dijon; built in a curve round the foot of a hill called 'La Motte' which rises steeply to 160 m above the town; from the hill there are views of the Vosges, the Jura Mts, and the Alps; railway; monuments: many attractive old houses and a classic 18th-c church; depopulated by plague in 1586.

Vest-Agder *vest-ahg'der*, formerly LISTER OG MANDAL, a county of S Norway, opposite the entrance of the Skagerrak, drained by the R Kvina; area 7,280 sq km; pop(1983) 138,739; capital Kristiansand; chief towns Mandal and Farsund.

Vesterålen *ves'ter-ol-un*, VESTERAALEN, island group in the Norwegian Sea, off the NW coast of Norway, WSW of Narvik, just N of the Lofoten group; principal islands Hinnøy, Langøya, Andøya and Hadseløy; administered by Nordland and Troms counties.

Vestfold, *vest'fol*, a county of SE Norway, lying W of Oslofjorden (Oslo Fjord), drained chiefly by the R Lågen; area 2,216 sq km; pop(1983) 188,664; capital Tønsberg; chief towns Larvik and Horten.

Vestmannaeyjar *vest'mahn-e-ay'yahr*, WESTMAN ISLANDS (Eng), a group of 15 islands and 30 reefs off the S coast of Iceland; includes the volcanic island of Heimaey which erupted in 1973; pop(1983) 4,743; the island of Surtsey was formed during eruptions in 1963-66; economy: fish processing.

Vestsjælland *vest yoo'lan*, a county of W Sjælland (Zealand), Denmark, bounded on the W by Store Bælt (Great Belt) and Samsø Bælt (Samsø Belt) and on the NE by the Isefjord; area 2,984 sq km; pop(1983) 277,914; capital Sorø; chief towns include Ringsted, Holbæk and Slagelse.

Vestvågøy *vest'vo-gu-ü*, 68 10N 13 50E, pop(1980) 11,142, town on Vestvågøy I, off W coast of Nordland county, W Norway.

Vesuvio *ve-zoo'vyo*, VESUVIUS *vus-oo'vee-us* (Eng), 40 49N 14 26E, active volcano in Campania region, S Italy, 15 km SE of Napoli (Naples); height 1,277 m; since the 17th century it has been the only volcano on the European mainland which is still intermittently active; the crater has a circumference of 1,400 m, a max diameter of 600 m, and a depth of 216 m; NE of the main crater, and separated from it by a deep steep-walled valley, is Monte Somma (1,132 m), a relic of the caldera of an older volcano; intermittent earthquakes (from AD 63) preceded the first recorded eruption, that of AD 79, which overwhelmed Pompei, Herculaneum, and Stabiae; after that, eruptions occurred only at long intervals, until 1631, since when the volcano has been in a state of fairly regular activity; the last eruption was on 20 March 1944, when the funicular up the mountain was destroyed; the ash cone and more recent lava flows are almost devoid of vegetation, but the older weathered lavas form a fertile soil on which fruit and vines (Lacrima Christi wine) are grown below 500 m.

Veszprém *ves-praym*, county in W Hungary; with forested slopes of the Bakony Mts to the N and L Balaton to the S; watered by the Tolna and Sió rivers; pop(1984e)

389,000; area 4,689 sq km; capital Veszprém; chief towns include Pápa and Ajka; there is a spa at Balatonfüred on N shore of L Balaton; economy: fruit, grain, vegetables, livestock, wine.

Veszprém, 47 08N 17 57E, pop(1984e) 60,000, capital of Veszprém county, W Hungary; on S slopes of Bakony Mts, near the N shore of L Balaton; bishopric; economy: textiles, wine; monuments: castle, Calvary Hill with 11th-c cemetery and 13th-c St Nicholas church; episcopal palace (18th-c).

Veurne *vur'nu*, FURNES *fürn* (Fr), dist of West-Vlaanderen (West Flanders) prov, W Belgium; area 275 sq km; pop(1982) 48,094.

Viamão *vee-a-mā'ō*, 30 05S 51 00W, pop(1980) 117,657, town in Rio Grande do Sul state, Sul region, S Brazil; SE of Pôrto Alegre; economy: agricultural equipment, grapes, rice, wine.

Viana do Castelo *vyah'na doo kas-tel'oo*, dist in N Portugal, part of Minho prov bounded by Spain (N) and the Atlantic (W); divided into 10 councils and 288 parishes; area, 2,084 sq km; drained by R Lima; pop(1981) 256,814; economy: textiles, olives, fruit, vegetables, grain, horticulture, wine, figs, cork, timber, resin, dairy produce, fish; minerals: kaoline, tin, feldspar, gold, quartz, wolfram.

Viana do Castelo, VELOBRIGA (anc), 41 42N 8 50W, pop(1981) 15,100, capital of Viana do Castelo dist, N Portugal; fishing port, naval shipyard and resort on N bank of R Lima, 70 km N of Porto; divided into 2 parishes; railway; monuments: Santiago da Barra castle, 16th-c town hall and churches of the Misericordia and São Domingo; events: Santa das Candeias in late Jan; municipal holiday in mid-Aug; Santa da Agonia in Aug; Santa Marta in Aug.

Vianden *vee-ahn'den*, canton in E part of Diekirch dist, NE Luxembourg; area 54 sq km; pop(1981) 2,642; the R Our forms the E frontier with W Germany; the Our Dam, 2 reservoirs and an underground power station are situated 5 km N of the town of Vianden; part of the German-Luxembourg Nature Park is in Vianden.

Vianden, 49 56N 6 12E, pop(1981) 1,600, resort town and capital of Vianden canton, Diekirch dist, E Luxembourg; on the R Our, 46 km NNE of Luxembourg; economy: manufacture of refrigerators; monument: castle (12-17th-c), the family seat of the Counts of Vianden and later of Nassau-Orange; events: nut market 2nd Sunday in Oct; 'Chasing of Judas' on Good Friday.

Viangchan, capital of Laos. See Vientiane.

Viborg *vee'bor*, a county of N central Jylland (Jutland), Denmark, the Limfjorden (Lim Fjord) runs through the N central part of the county while the Skagerrak bounds the county on the W side; area 4,122 sq km; pop(1983) 230,909; capital Viborg; chief towns include Skive and Thisted.

Viborg, 56 28N 9 25E, pop(1981) 28,659, ancient city and capital of Viborg county, N central Jylland (Jutland), Denmark; railway; economy: engineering; monument: 12th-c Gothic cathedral (restored 1864-76).

Vicente Perez Rosales *vee-sen'tay pe'res rō-sa'lays*, national park in Los Lagos region, S central Chile; borders E with the Argentinian national park of Nahuel Huapí; area 2,510 sq km; established in 1926; in the N of the park is L Todos los Santos.

Vicenza *vee-chen'tsa*, prov of Veneto region, NE Italy; pop(1981) 726,418; area 2,722 sq km; capital Vicenza.

Vicenza, VICETIA (anc), 45 33N 11 33E, pop(1981) 114,598, capital town of Vicenza prov, Veneto region, NE Italy; 35 km NW of Padova (Padua), on the edge of the Po plain; railway junction; economy: textiles, cotton, knitwear, clothing, carpets, woollens; monuments: the architect Palladio was a native, and there are fine examples of his work including the Basilica Palladiana (1549-1614), Teatro Olimpico, and Rotonda; Gothic cathedral, with a facade of white and red marble (15th-c).

Vich *veech*, AUSA, VICUS AUSONENSIS (anc), 41 58N 2 19E, pop(1981) 30,057, town in Barcelona prov, Cataluña, NE Spain; 65 km N of Barcelona; railway; economy: textiles, paper, tanning, meat processing; monuments: 18th-c cathedral and Episcopal museum.

Vichada *vee-cha'da*, administrative territory in E Colombia, South America; bounded E and N by Venezuela, S by the Río Guaviare and N by the Río Meta; crossed by the Vichada and Tomo rivers, affluents of the Orinoco; pop(1985) 3,377; area 100,242 sq km; capital Puerto Carreño.

Vichy *vee-shee*, 46 07N 3 25E, pop(1982) 35,000, famous spa town in Allier dept, Auvergne, central France; the seat of Marshall Pétain's government between 1940 and 1944; noted for its medicinal water.

Vicksburg, 32 21N 90 53W, pop(1980) 25,434, county seat of Warren county, W Mississippi, United States; a port on the Mississippi river, 64 km W of Jackson; headquarters of US Mississippi River Commission; first settled in 1791; the city was captured by Union forces during the Civil War, on 4 July 1863, after 14 months of naval shelling, 7 months of land assault, and 47 days of total siege; nearby is a national cemetery where c.13,000 unknown Union troops are buried, brought from all over the south; railway; economy: important processing and shipping centre for cotton, timber and livestock area; manufactures include lumber products, machinery, mobile homes, chemicals, fertilizers, and food products; monument: Vicksburg National Military Park.

Victor'ia, state in SE Australia; bordered W by South Australia, N by New South Wales along the Murray river, S by the Bass Strait and SW by the Southern Ocean; 2nd smallest of the 6 Australian states; E is the Great Dividing Range, known here as the Australian Alps and rising to 1,986 m at Mt Bogong; approx 36% of land is occupied by forest, mostly owned by the state; the SW region is known as Gippsland; the state contains a number of inland lakes, most with high levels of salinity; man-made irrigation storages include L Eildon on the Goulburn river and L Hume on the Murray; pop(1986) 4,207,689; Victoria contains 25% of the Australian pop concentrated into 3% of the land; area 227,600 sq km; capital Melbourne; principal towns include Geelong and Ballarat; economy: produces approx one-fifth of Australia's agricultural output of wheat, oats, barley, maize, tobacco, hops and fodder crops, citrus fruits, grapes, apples, vegetables, wool, hides, mutton, lamb and dairy products; industry: timber, coal mining (the Latrobe Valley to the E of Melbourne has one of the world's largest deposits of brown coal), motor parts; oil and natural gas fields have been developed in the Gippsland Basin, off the E coast of Victoria, and the Bass Strait to the S; discovered by Capt Cook in 1770; Melbourne was settled in 1835; separated from New South Wales in 1851 with Melbourne as its capital; gold was discovered in 1851 at Ballarat; state holiday: Labour Day (March); the state of Victoria is divided into 12 statistical divisions:

Statistical division	*area (sq km)*	*pop(1983e)*
Barwon	8,171	203,040
Central Gippsland	12,823	141,470
Central Highlands	12,700	122,050
East Central	4,109	42,700
East Gippsland	28,100	58,770
Goulburn	23,105	137,640
Loddon-Campaspe	21,738	154,770
Melbourne	6,109	2,865,700
North Eastern	18,044	81,090
Northern Mallee	35,324	74,500
South Western	24,018	101,280
Wimmera	33,359	54,590

Victoria, 48 25N 123 22W, pop(1981) 64,379, capital of British Columbia prov, W Canada; at the SE end of Vancouver island, on the Juan de Fuca Strait; founded in 1843 by the Hudson's Bay Co as a fur-trading post; a town was laid out in 1851-52 and named Victoria; became capital of Vancouver island in 1859 and the capital of British Columbia in 1866; its development was closely associated with the fur trade and later with the British Columbia gold rush; university (1963); railway; airfield; economy: shipbuilding, timber, fish canning, computer software; monuments: the Parliament Buildings (1893-97) with a provincial museum; the Empress Hotel, built by the Canadian Pacific Railroad in 1906-08, is the largest hotel in British Columbia; Thunderbird Park contains a unique collection of totem poles; Butchart Gardens, 19 km from Victoria, contains flowers from all over the world.

Victoria, 38 15S 72 27W, pop(1982) 21,497, town in Malleco prov, La Araucanía, central Chile; railway.

Victoria, 36 03N 14 14E, pop(1983e) 5,406, chief town of the Maltese island of Gozo in the Mediterranean.

Victoria, 4 37S 55 28E, pop(1985e) 23,000, seaport capital of the Seychelles, Indian Ocean; situated on the NE coast of Mahé I; area of Greater Victoria 10 sq km; economy: trade in copra, vanilla, cinnamon, tortoiseshell and guano.

Victoria, 28 48N 97 00W, pop(1980) 50,695, county seat of Victoria county, S Texas, United States; on the R Guadalupe, 190 km SW of Houston; railway; economy: food processing, aircraft parts, petrochemicals, concrete, machinery, clothing, and boats.

Victoria, Ciudad *syoo-THaTH' vik-tōr'ya*, 23 43N 99 10W, pop(1980) 153,206, capital of Tamaulipas state, NE Mexico; 208 km NW of Tampico at E end of Sierra Madre Oriental; university; railway; economy: mining, agricultural trade, textiles, tanning.

Victoria de las Tunas, LAS TUNAS, 21 38N 79 34W, pop(1983e) 88,006, capital town of Las Tunas prov, E central Cuba; on the edge of a wide plain, 123 km SE of Camagüey; centre of sugar cane-growing and cattle-breeding area; railway; founded in 1759.

Victoria Falls, waterfalls on the Zambezi river, on the Zambia-Zimbabwe frontier, S central Africa; height ranges between 61 and 108 m; width 1,688 m; comprises 5 main falls: the Eastern Cataract, Rainbow Falls, Devil's Cataract, Horseshoe Falls and Main Falls; estimated age of crevice formation is 150 million years; European discovery by David Livingstone in 1855; Livingstone named the falls after Queen Victoria; indigenous name Mosi oa Tunya which means 'the smoke that thunders' with reference to the spray generated by the falls; impressive not so much for height (the falls are only the 4th highest on the Zambezi river) but for volume (ranked 9th in world terms) of water that passes over them; in 1958 a record flow of 700,000 cubic metres per minute was recorded; the towns of Maramba (Livingstone) and Victoria Falls are situated on the Zambia and Zimbabwe sides of the falls respectively; now a major tourist attraction.

Victoria Island, island in SW Franklin dist, Northwest Territories, Canada; situated in the Arctic Ocean; separated from the Canadian mainland by the Dolphin and Union Strait, Coronation Gulf, the Dease Strait and Queen Maud Gulf; area 217,290 sq km; 515 km long; 274-595 km wide; the island is deeply indented with Prince Albert Sound in the SW and Hadley Bay in the N.

Victoria, Lake, lake in E Africa; bounded S by Tanzania, NW by Uganda and NE by Kenya; the largest lake on the African continent; lies between 0 28N and 3 00S, 31 38E and 34 53E; area 69,500 sq km; alt 1,300 m; 400 km long; 240 km wide; dam built at Owen Falls near Jinja in 1954 raised level by about a metre; receives the Kagera, Mara and Nzoia rivers; islands include the Sese archipelago the largest of which is Bugala island, Rubondo (SW), Buvuma (N) and Ukerewe (SE); the Winam Gulf lies NE and the Speke Gulf SE; the main lakeside ports are Kisumu (Kenya) on the Winam Gulf and Mwanza (Tanzania) on the S shore; European discovery by John Speke in 1858; extensively explored by Stanley in 1875; though originally called Ukewere, it was renamed in honour of Queen Victoria.

Victoria Nile, upper reach of River Nile in NW Uganda, E Africa; flowing generally in a NW direction from the N end of L Victoria close to Jinja, the river passes Namasagali before entering L Kyoga; it exits the lake at its W end and is shortly joined by the R Kafu from the S; it then flows in a NW arc past Atura, Karuma Falls and into the Kabalega national park which includes the Kabalega (Murchison) Falls (power station); terminates as a swampy delta at the NE extremity of L Albert.

Victoria Peak, mountain in the Maya mountains, Belize, Central America; highest peak in the country, rising to 1,120 m in the Cockscomb range, SW of Dangriga, Stann Creek dist.

Victoria Peak, 22 18N 114 08E, principal peak on Hong Kong Island, Victoria dist, Hong Kong, SE Asia; lies in the western area of the dist and rises to 554 m; named after Queen Victoria, who was monarch when Britain acquired Hong Kong Island in 1842; the Peak Tramway (opened in 1888) takes tourists up to Victoria Peak, where a magnificent panorama of Hong Kong city and harbour can be seen.

Vidin *vee'din*, okrug (prov) of NW Bulgaria bounded to the W by Yugoslavia and to the E by Romania; part of its border follows the R Danube; area 3,066 sq km; pop(1981) 169,000.

Vidin, BONONIA (Lat), 44 00N 22 50E, pop(1981e) 57,000, capital of Vidin okrug (prov), NW Bulgaria; on the R Danube, 199 km NW of Sofiya; the centre of a fertile agricultural region; there is a ferry to Calafat in Romania; airfield; railway; economy: wine, porcelain, agricultural trade.

Viedma *vyeTH'mah*, 40 45S 63 00W, pop(1980) 20,000, capital of Río Negro prov, Patagonia, S central Argentina; on the Río Negro, 760 km SW of Buenos Aires; an agricultural trade centre.

Viedma, Lago, lake in Patagonian Andes of W Santa Cruz prov, Patagonia, S Argentina; 40 km N of Lago Argentino, to which it is joined by a stream and which it flows into; the E part of the lake is in a national park (Los Glaciares); area 1,088 sq km; length 72 km.

Vienna, capital of Austria. See Wien.

Vienne *vyen*, dept in Poitou-Charentes region of W France, comprising 3 arrond, 38 cantons and 281 communes; pop(1982) 371,428; area 6,084 sq km; watered by the Clain and Vienne rivers; the foothills of the Plateaux du Limousin extend into the S of the dept; capital Poitiers, chief town Châtellerault; spa at La Roche-Posay.

Vienne, navigable river in central France rising in the Plateau de Millevaches (978 m) SE of Limoges, N Corrèze dept; flows W across Haute-Vienne dept then N past Châtellerault to meet the R Loire SE of Saumur; length 350 km; tributaries Clain, Taurton and Creuse rivers.

Vientiane *vyen tyan*, VIANGCHAN (Lao), 17 59N 102 38E, pop(1973) 176,637 and pop(1979e) 90,000, capital city of Laos, SE Asia; situated N of the R Mekong, close to the Thailand frontier, W Laos; airport; 72 km N is the Nam Gum Dam, inaugurated in 1971.

Viersen *feer'zen*, 51 16N 6 24E, pop(1983) 79,600, city in Düsseldorf dist, W Nordrhein-Westfalen (North Rhine-Westphalia) prov, W Germany; 29 km W of Düsseldorf; railway; economy: textiles.

Vierwaldstätter See *feer-valt'shtet-er-zay*, LAKE LUCERNE (Eng), irregular and indented lake in Uri, Schwyz, Obwalden, Nidwalden and Luzern cantons, central Switzerland; known as the 'lake of the four forest cantons'; area 113.6 sq km; 4th largest of the Swiss lakes; length from Luzern to Flüelen 38 km; max depth 214 m; the main arm of the lake runs E and SE from Luzern, then S in a narrower arm, Urner See, a fjord-like strip of water enclosed between massive rock walls; the main arms of the lake include Luzerner See, Alpnacher See, Küssnachter See and Urner See; the R Reuss feeds it from the S, and drains it from the NW to the Aare and Rhine rivers; the lake is associated with the origins of the Swiss Confederation and the legend of William Tell; resorts on its shores include Weggis, Gersau, Brunnen and Vitznau.

Vietnam *vee-et-nam'*, official name The Socialist Republic of Vietnam, CÔNG HÒA XÃ HÔI CHU NGHĨA VIÊT NAM (Viet), independent socialist state in Indo-China, bounded E by the South China Sea, W by Laos and Cambodia and N by China; timezone GMT +7; area 329,566 sq km; pop(1979e) 52,741,766; capital Hanoi; chief cities Ho Chi Minh (Saigon), Haiphong and Da Nang; 20% of the pop is urban; the majority of the pop is Vietnamese, with 3% Chinese and minority groups including Khmer, Muong, Meo, Thai, Man, Cham and other mountain tribes; religious beliefs include Confucian, Buddhist, Taoist, Roman Catholic; the official language is Vietnamese, but French, Chinese, English, Khmer and tribal languages are also spoken; the currency is the dông; national holiday 2 Sept; membership of ADB, CEMA, Colombo Plan, ESCAP, FAO, G-77, IAEA, IBRD, ICAO, IDA, IFAD, IFC, ILO, IMF, INTELSAT, IRC, ITU, Mekong Committee, NAM, PAHO, UN, UNDP, UNESCO, UNICEF, UPU, WFTU, WHO, WIPO, WMO, WTO.

Physical description. Occupying a narrow strip along the coast of the Gulf of Tongking and the South China Sea, Vietnam broadens out in the S at the delta of the Mekong R and in the N along the valley of the Red R (Hong) where it divides the steep-sided mountains of N Vietnam. The lowlands close to these 2 rivers contain the majority of the pop and the most productive rice-growing areas. Fan si Pan is the highest peak in the country, rising to 3,143 m SW of Lao Cai in N Vietnam. The narrow coastal plain of central Vietnam (formerly known as Annam) lies between the sea and the Annamite chain of mountains. Further S, where the mountains reach down to the coast, a limestone plateau stretches W into Cambodia.

Climate. Vietnam has a tropical monsoon-type climate dominated by S-SE winds during May-Sept, the period of highest rainfall, and N-NE winds during Oct-April. Annual rainfall averages from 1,000 mm in the lowlands to 2,500 mm in the uplands. In central Vietnam heaviest rainfall is between Sep and Jan when the coast is subject to tropical storms. During the rainy season humidity is high. In the S temperatures remain high throughout the year but during Oct-April it can be cooler in the N as colder air moves in from China.

History, government and constitution. The original Annamite population which was of Mongoloid nomadic stock settled in the Red R delta over 2,000 years ago. Under the influence of China for many centuries, the Vietnamese spread S to the Mekong Delta, asserting their nationhood and establishing the present-day boundaries of Vietnam. French interest in the area during the mid-19th century resulted in Cochin-China (S Vietnam) becoming a colony in 1867. In 1884 Annam (central Vietnam) and Tongking (N Vietnam) became French protectorates. The whole area became a colony, forming with Cambodia and Laos the French Indochinese Union. Nationalism sprang up after the Russo-Japanese war but was ruthlessly suppressed. After Japanese occupation (1941-45) the communist Viet-Minh League under the leadership of Ho Chi Minh forced the abdication of the Japanese-sponsored emperor and set up a republic. After 9 years of war the Viet-Minh were only able to gain control of the territory N of the 17th parallel while the French retained South Vietnam. In 1954 an armistice was signed, effectively dividing the country between the communist 'Democratic Republic' in the N and the 'State' of Vietnam in the S. Continued resistance between N and S resulted in US intervention in 1965. An intensive war continued until a ceasefire was prescribed in Jan 1973 at a conference held in Paris. The ceasefire order was not observed until the fall of Saigon in 1975. With the defeat of S Vietnam nearly 200,000 Vietnamese fled the country and in 1976, following elections to a National Assembly, Hanoi declared the reunification of the country as the Socialist Republic of Vietnam. The creation of a socialist state on the Marxist-Leninist pattern is heavily influenced by neo-Confucianism which retains a respect for the past and an implicit belief in the rulers' right to rule. The highly centralized government consists of a bicameral legislature comprising a National Assembly and a Council of State. The only political party is the Vietnam Communist Party, formerly known as the Vietnam Workers' Party.

Economy. Although over 70% of the workforce is employed in agriculture and much of the country is ideal for rice-growing, Vietnam is dependent on the import of foodstuffs. In addition to rice, maize, sorghum, beans, sugar and sweet potatoes are staple food crops. Tea, coffee, rubber, tobacco and groundnuts are grown for

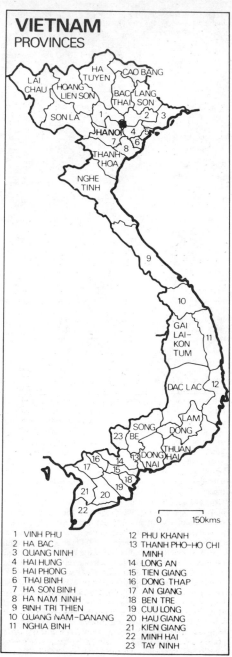

VIETNAM
PROVINCES

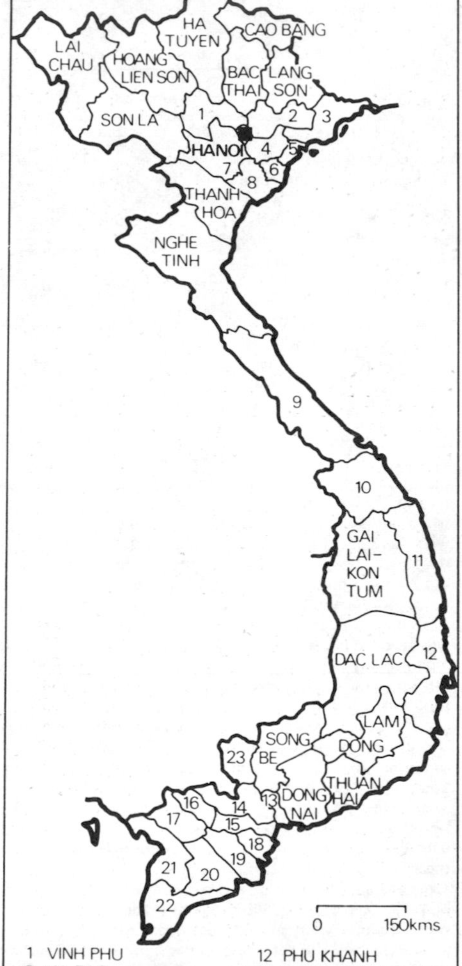

1 VINH PHU
2 HA BAC
3 QUANG NINH
4 HAI HUNG
5 HAI PHONG
6 THAI BINH
7 HA SON BINH
8 HA NAM NINH
9 BINH TRI THIEN
10 QUANG NAM-DANANG
11 NGHIA BINH
12 PHU KHANH
13 THANH PHO-HO CHI MINH
14 LONG AN
15 TIEN GIANG
16 DONG THAP
17 AN GIANG
18 BEN TRE
19 CUU LONG
20 HAU GIANG
21 KIEN GIANG
22 MINH HAI
23 TAY NINH

export. Both fishing (shrimp) and forestry make important contributions to exports and to local markets. Manufacturing industry is based on the production of wood products, rubber products, textiles, paper, fertilizers, glass, cement, food processing and light engineering. Since the end of the Vietnam War in 1975, depopulation of the countryside, destruction of forest and farmland, and towns overcrowded with refugees have contributed to the economic problems of Vietnam, as have natural hazards caused by typhoon and flood. The restoration of rail, air and road links, the development of industry, the resettlement of small farmers and the limited introduction of private enterprise are all strategies for economic recovery in the 1980s. Major trade partners include the USSR, East European countries and Japan.

Administrative divisions. Vietnam is divided into the autonomous cities of Hanoi, Haiphong and Ho Chi Minh (Saigon), the special area of Vung Tau-Con Dao and the following 38 provinces:

Province	*area (sq km)*	*pop(1979)*
An Giang	40	1,532,362
Bac Thai	8,615	815,105
Ben Tre	2,400	1,041,838
Binh Tri Thien	19,048	1,901,713
Cao Bang	13,731	479,823
Cuu Long	4,200	1,504,215
Dac Lac	18,300	490,198
Dong Nai	12,130	1,304,799
Dong Thap	3,120	1,182,787
Gai Lai-Kon Tum	18,480	595,906
Ha Bac	4,708	1,662,671
Ha Nam Ninh	3,522	2,781,409
Ha Son Binh	6,860	1,537,190
Ha Tuyen	13,519	782,453
Hai Hung	2,526	2,145,662
Hai Phong	1,515	1,279,067
Hau Giang	5,100	2,232,891
Hoang Lien Son	14,125	778,217
Kien Giang	6,000	994,673
Lai Chau	17,408	322,077
Lam Dong	10,000	396,657
Lang Son	13,731	484,657
Long An	5,100	957,264
Minh Hai	8,000	1,219,595
Nghe Tinh	22,380	3,111,989
Nghia Binh	14,700	2,095,354
Phu Khanh	9,620	1,188,637
Quang Nam-Danang	11,376	1,529,520
Quang Ninh	7,076	750,055
Son La	14,656	487,703
Song Be	9,500	659,093
Tay Ninh	4,100	684,006
Thai Binh	1,344	1,506,235
Thanh Hoa	11,138	2,532,261
Thanh Pho-Ho Chi Minh	1,845	3,419,878
Thuan Hai	11,000	938,255
Tien Giang	2,350	1,264,498
Vinh Phu	5,187	1,488,348

Vieux Fort *vye for'*, 13 46N 60 58W, port on the S coast of St Lucia, Windward Is, E Caribbean, 56 km S of Castries; Hewanorra International Airport; economy: foodstuffs, beverages, clothing, paper products, electrical and electronic machinery appliances.

Vigo *vee'go*, 42 12N 8 41W, pop(1981) 258,724, naval and commercial port in Pontevedra prov, Galicia, NW Spain; on the SE side of the long Ria de Vigo estuary; Spain's chief port for transatlantic traffic, with shipbuilding and metal industries; the granite-built old town and fishing quarter (Berbes) to the SW has narrow streets on hilly ground and to the NE lies the more spaciously planned new town with tall modern buildings, wide avenues and beautiful parks; beaches; watersports; airport; boat services to the Canary Is; monuments: castle of St Sebastian and Castro castle; events: El Carmen fiesta in July with a procession of boats; El Cristo de la Victoria fair in Aug and the Pilgrimage to Monte de Santa Tecia with folk events in Aug.

Vijayawada *vi-ju-yu-vah'du*, BEZWADA, 16 31N 80 39E, pop(1981) 545,000, city in Andhra Pradesh state, SE India; on the N bank of the R Krishna, 250 km ESE of Hyderabad; a trade and transport centre of the E Ghats; economy: engineering, rice, oilseed; a Buddhist religious centre; also the scene of a Hindu bathing festival.

Vijosë *vee-yo'se*, VIJOSA (Gr), VOIUSSA (Ital), river in N Epirus, Greece and S Albania; rises in the Pindus Mts, N of Metsovon; flows NW across Albania, discharging into the Adriatic Sea 22 km N of Vlorë; tributary R Drin; length 237 km; flows through deep gorges in its upper course.

Vikhren *vee'KHren* or **Eltepe**, 41 47N 23 22E, highest mountain peak of the Pirin Planina (Pirin Mts) of SW Bulgaria, rising to 2,915 m.

Viking, gas field in the North Sea, NE of Norfolk, England; linked by pipeline to Bacton on the Norfolk coast and to Theddlethorpe, NW of Sutton on Sea, on the Lincolnshire coast.

Vila *vee'la* or **Port-Vila**, 17 45S 168 18E, port and capital town of Vanuatu, on the SW coast of Efate I, SW Pacific; pop(1979) 14,801.

Vila do Conde *vee'la doo kon'di*, 41 21N 8 45W, pop(1981) 20,200, resort and industrial town at the mouth of the R Ave in Porto dist, N Portugal; industries: shipbuilding, textiles, clothes and pillow-lace; monument: convent of Santa Clara (1318); event: Midsummer Night, folk fair at end of July.

Vila Franca da Xira *vee'la fran'ka di shee'ra*, 38 57N 8 59W, pop(1981) 17,600, industrial town in Lisboa dist, central Portugal; on lower R Tagus, 30 km NNE of Lisboa; industries: chemicals, detergents, iron, steel, motor cars and agric processing; military airport; events: agric fair in May; Colete Encarnado festival in July, a traditional festival in honour of the campinos or herdsmen of Ribatejo; annual fair in Oct with bullfights.

Vila Real *vee'la ray-ahl'*, dist in N Portugal, part of Trás-os-Montes prov; divided into 14 councils and 264 parishes; area, 4,191 sq km; pop(1981) 264,381; chief towns are Vila Real, Chaves and Peso de Regua; mountainous to the E near Spanish border; economy: almonds, olives, vegetables, grain, wine, cork, resin, wood, wool, meat, honey, pork sausage, dairy produce, bacon fat, textiles; minerals: copper, tin, iron, molybdenum, gold, silver, quartz, wolfram, zinc, feldspar; airfields at Vila Real, Chaves and Sergio da Silva.

Vila Real, 41 17N 7 48W, pop(1981) 13,300, capital of Vila Real dist, N Portugal; on R Corgo, on the N side of the Serra de Marão, 116 km ENE of Porto; divided into 3 parishes; airfield; monuments: Gothic cathedral; church of São Pedro (16th-c); Baroque Mateus House (4 km E) and Roman sanctuary of Panoias (7 km SE); economy: port wine, pottery, tanning and textiles; the famous Mateus rosé is produced nearby; event: municipal holiday third week in June.

Vilaine *veel-en*, navigable river in NW France rising NE of Vitre in Mayenne dept; flows W to Rennes then turns SW through Ille-et-Vilaine dept to meet the Bay of Biscay near St-Nazaire; length 225 km; tributaries include the Ille, Meu, Oust and Don rivers.

Vilcea *veel'shya*, county in S central Romania, in the S foothills of the Transylvanian Alps; pop(1983) 449,806; area 5,705 sq km; capital Rimnicu Vilcea.

Villa Alemana *veel'ya a-lay-ma'na*, 33 02S 71 25W, pop(1982) 50,089, town in Valparaíso prov, Valparaíso, central Chile; railway.

Villa Clara *klah'ra*, prov in W central Cuba, bounded N by the archipelago de Sabana; land rises in the S and E; area 8,069 sq km; pop(1981) 764,743; capital Santa Clara; chief towns Sagua La Grande and Caibarien.

Villa de María *veel'ya THay ma-ree'a*, 32 25S 63 15W, pop(1980) 67,490, agricultural town in Córdoba prov, Centro, central Argentina; NE of Córdoba; railway.

Villach *fil'aKH*, 46 37N 13 51E, pop(1981) 52,692, industrial capital of Villach dist, Kärnten, S Austria; on the R Drau opposite the Karawanken Alps, W of Klagenfurt; a communications centre; the thermal springs of Warmbad Villach, S of the town, attract numerous visitors; railway; economy: tourism, timber, iron, lead; monument: 15th-c Gothic church with fine tombs and a detached tower.

Villagarcia de Arosa *veel-ya-gar-thee'a* THay *ah-rō'sa*, 42 34N 8 46W, pop(1981) 29,453, Atlantic port and resort in Pontevedra prov, Galicia, NW Spain; 23 km NW of Pontevedra; economy: port trade and fish processing, boatbuilding, canning, paper, tiles, bricks, soap, metal products.

Villahermosa *veel-ya-er-mō'sa*, 18 00N 92 53W, pop(1980) 250,903, river-port capital of Tabasco state, SE Mexico; on the Río Grijalva; university (1958); economy: agricultural trade, distilling, sugar refining; monuments: the Centro de Investigaciones de las Culturas Olmecas houses Mayan and Olmec artifacts; NW are the Mayan brick-built ruins of Comacalco.

Villarrica *veel-ya-ree'ka*, 25 45S 56 08W, pop(1982) 21,203, capital of Guairá dept, Oriental, E Paraguay; set on a hill amidst orange trees; railway; there are 3 German settlements nearby.

Villarrica, Lago *veel-ya-ree'ka*, lake in S La Araucanía region, central Chile; in N part of the Chilean lake district; 64 km SE of Temuco; area 168 sq km; 21 km long; 8 km wide; Villarrica Volcano (2,840 m) lies to the SE; the tourist resorts of Villarrica and Pucón are on the lake shore.

Villavicencio *veel-ya-vee-sen'syō*, 4 09N 73 38W, pop(1980) 116,000, capital of Meta dept, central Colombia, South America; SE of Bogotá, in the E foothills of the Andes; airfield; economy: rice-milling.

Villazón *veel-ya-sōn'*, 22 05S 65 35W, pop(1976) 12,565, town in M. Omiste prov, Potosí, SW Bolivia; on the border with Argentina; railway.

Ville de Paris, dept in Ile-de-France region of N France including the city of Paris and comprising 1 arrond, 20 cantons and 1 commune; pop(1982) 2,176,243; area 105 sq km; capital Paris.

Villejuif *veel-zhweef*, 48 47N 2 23E, pop(1982) 52,488, town in Val-de-Marne dept, Ile-de-France region, N central France; a S suburb of Paris.

Villena *veel-yay'na*, 38 39N 0 52W, pop(1981) 28,279, city in Alicante prov, Valencia, E Spain; 48 km NE of Alicante; railway; economy: flour, soap, distilling.

Villeurbanne *veel-œr-ban*, 45 46N 4 54E, pop(1982) 118,330, town in Rhône dept, Rhône-Alpes region, E France; an E suburb of Lyon; economy: chemical and petroleum production, road-making materials, floor coverings.

Villingen-Schwenningen *fi'ling-un-shve'ning-en*, 48 03N 8 28E, pop(1983) 77,300, manufacturing city in Baden-Württemberg prov, W Germany; 48 km ENE of Freiburg; railway; economy: electrical goods, data processing and print-out equipment.

Villmanstrand, town in Finland. See Lappeenranta.

Vilnius *veel'nee-oos*, formerly WILNO (1920-1939), 54 40N 25 19E, pop(1983) 525,000, capital city of Litva SSR, W European Soviet Union, on the R Vilnya; one of the largest industrial centres of the Soviet Baltic region; formerly part of Poland; university (1579); railway junction; airport; economy: machine building, metalworking, chemicals, foodstuffs, textiles; monuments: cathedral (1777-1801); Gediminas Castle.

Vilvōorde *veel-vōrd*, VILVORDE, 50 56N 4 25E, pop(1982) 33,007, manufacturing town in Halle-Vilvoorde dist, N Brabant prov, Belgium; 10 km N of Bruxelles; railway; economy: steel, coke, cement, oil refining, paint, varnishes, enamels, motor vehicles.

Vilvorde, town in Belgium. See Vilvoorde.

Viña del Mar *veen'ya* THel *mar*, 33 02S 71 35W, pop(1982) 290,014, town in Valparaíso prov, Valparaíso, central Chile; 9 km from Valparaíso city, for which it is a residential suburb and to which it is connected by electric railway; economy: one of the most popular South American social resorts; monuments and sights: at the entrance to the town is the Cerro Castillo, summer palace of the Presidents of the Republic; the municipally owned Quinta Vergara houses a collection of pictures and an art school; in part of the grounds is an outdoor auditorium where concerts and ballets are performed during the summer months; on the Plaza Vergara is the Teatro Municipal; near the Valparaíso Sporting Club, with its racecourse and playing fields, are the Granadilla Golf Club and a large sports stadium; in the hills behind the town is a large artificial lake, the Tranque Sausalito, frequented by picnickers and water-skiers; nearby is the Salinas golf course; events: an international musical festival is held in Viña del Mar each Feb; festival of El Roto, in homage to the working men and peasants of Chile (20 Jan).

Vinces *veen'says*, 1 37S 79 45W, pop(1982) 14,608, town in Los Ríos prov, W Ecuador; on the Río Vinces, in the tropical lowlands W of the Andes and NW of Babahoyo.

Vineland, 39 29N 75 02W, pop(1980) 53,753, town in Cumberland county, S New Jersey, United States; 53 km SSE of Philadelphia; railway.

Vinh *vin*, 18 42N 105 41E, town in Nghe Tinh prov, N central Vietnam, Indo-China; 256 km S of Hanoi; railway.

Vinkovci *veen'kof-tse*, 45 16N 18 49E, pop(1981) 95,245, city in NE Hrvatska (Croatia) republic, Yugoslavia; on R Bosut, S of Osijek; railway; economy: agricultural trade, wood products.

Vinnitsa *vee'nyit-su*, 49 11N 28 30E, pop(1983) 350,000, capital city of Vinnitskaya oblast, Ukrainskaya SSR, SW European Soviet Union; on the R Yuzhnyy Bug; a railway junction at the centre of a sugar-beet district; economy: foodstuffs, footwear, clothing, knitwear, chemicals, fertilizers, metalworking.

Vinson Massif, highest peak in Antarctica, rising to 5,140 m in the Ellsworth Mts.

Virgin Gorda *gor'du*, pop(1984e) 1,000, island of the British Virgin Islands in the Lesser Antilles chain of the E Caribbean; 13 km E of Tortola; chief settlement Spanish Town; rises to 418 m at Virgin Peak; formerly important for its copper; economy: livestock, vegetables, charcoal.

Virgin Islands, British, island group lying at the NW end of the Lesser Antilles chain, E Caribbean, N and E of the US Virgin Is and approx 80 km E of Puerto Rico; a British dependent territory; timezone GMT −4; area 153 sq km; capital Road Town (Tortola I); other main town is East End Long Look; pop(1980) 12,034; the majority of people are of Negro or mixed Negro and European descent; English is the official language; Protestant Christianity is the dominant religion; the unit of currency is the US dollar; membership: overseas territory associated with the EEC.

Physical description and climate. The British Virgin Is comprise 4 large islands (Tortola, Virgin Gorda, Anegada, Jost Van Dyke) and about 36 islets and cays. Only 16 islands are inhabited. Apart from Anegada they are hilly and wooded with no surface drainage. The highest point is Sage Mt (540 m) on Tortola I. Anegada, surrounded by dangerous reefs, is a flat island composed entirely of limestone. The climate is sub-tropical moderated by trade winds. Temperatures range from 17°C to 28°C in the winter and from 26°C to 31°C in the summer. Average annual rainfall is 1,270 mm.

History, government and constitution. British planters colonized Tortola in 1666, taking over from the Dutch who had settled there in 1648. Constitutional government was granted in 1774 and in 1834 slavery was abolished. The islands became part of the colony of the Leeward Is in 1872 and continued as such until 1956 when they became a separate Crown Colony. The colony is administered by a governor representing the British sovereign. There is a 5-member executive council and a legislative council of 11 members.

Economy. The main industries are tourism and related activities, notably construction, and rum distilling. Tourism is now the mainstay of the economy contributing over 50% of national income and nearly 30% of employment. Other industries include paint manufacturing, and gravel and stone extraction. Agricultural production is limited with the chief products being livestock, coconuts, sugar cane, and fruit and vegetables. Only 15% of potential agricultural land is under arable cultivation. Chief imports include building materials, foodstuffs, machinery and equipment, motor cars, and beverages. The main exports are fish, livestock, rum, and sand and gravel. Exports are almost entirely confined to the US Virgin Is.

Communications. Beef Island International Airport is situated 15 km from Road Town on Tortola I. Road Town is the main seaport.

Virgin Islands, United States, formerly DANISH WEST INDIES (-1917), official name Virgin Islands of the United States, a group of more than 50 islands in the S and W of the Virgin Is group, Lesser Antilles, Caribbean Sea, 64 km E of Puerto Rico; timezone GMT −4; area 342.5 sq km; capital Charlotte Amalie; pop(1980) 95,591; 20-25% of the population is native-born, 35-40% from other Caribbean Is, 10% from mainland USA, and 5% from Europe; Protestant Christianity is the dominant faith; unit of currency is the US dollar; English is the official language.

Physical description and climate. The 3 main inhabited islands are St Croix (218 sq km), St Thomas (72.5 sq km), and St John (52 sq km). The islands are of volcanic origin, and except for St Croix, are rugged and mountainous. St Croix lies 65 km S of the main group, separated by a deep channel. Crown Mt (474 m) on St Thomas is the highest peak in the American group. The temperature ranges from 21°C to 29°C from December to March and from 24°C to 31°C from June to September. Humidity is generally low and periods of prolonged rainfall are rare.

History, government and constitution. In 1671 Denmark chartered the Danish West Indies Company, colonizing St Thomas and St John. In 1733 Denmark bought St Croix from France and, apart from a brief period during the Napoleonic Wars, the islands remained Danish for almost 200 years. Recognizing the value of their strategic position commanding the approach to the Panama Canal the United States purchased the islands in 1917. The United States Virgin Is are an unincorporated territory of the United States with a republican form of government. Executive authority is exercised by a governor elected for a 4-year term by popular vote. There is a 15-member unicameral legislature also elected by popular vote. Since 1973, the people of the US Virgin Is have been represented in the US House of Representatives by a non-voting delegate.

Economy. Tourism is the islands' principal industry particularly on St Thomas where a deep natural harbour at Charlotte Amalie caters for a growing number of cruise ships. The Virgin Is National Park on St John (71 sq km) and the Coral World underwater observatory off the NE coast of St Thomas also attract many visitors. Manufacturing is more important on St Croix where the main industries include oil refining, alumina refining, and the manufacture of clocks and watches, woollen textiles and garments, rum and fragrances, and pharmaceuticals. Although sugar plantations were set up in the mid-17th century, sugar production has been phased out and an estimated 15 sq km of land released for the growing of other crops such as vegetables, fruit, and sorghum. Agriculture is not well-developed and much of the country's food requirements have to be imported from the USA. Chief exports include petroleum products, alumina, chemicals, clocks and watches, meat, and rum. The main trading partner is the USA.

Virginia, state in E United States; bounded W by Kentucky and West Virginia, N by West Virginia and Maryland, E by Maryland, Chesapeake Bay and the Atlantic Ocean, and S by North Carolina and Tennessee; a small part of Virginia occupies the S tip of the Delmarva peninsula across Chesapeake Bay; the R Potomac follows the Maryland state border before emptying into Chesapeake Bay; the Rappahannock, York and James rivers all flow ESE across the state to Chesapeake Bay; in the W, running SW-NE, are the Blue Ridge Mts; the highest point is Mt Rogers (1,743 m); the coastal region in E Virginia is flat and swampy, and is known as the Tidewater region; to the W the land rises into the Piedmont, rolling, fertile land, which is interrupted further W by the Blue Ridge Mts; W of these, but E of the Allegheny Mts of West Virginia, lies the Valley of Virginia, a series of beautiful valleys, the best known of which is the Shenandoah valley; the chief agricultural crop is tobacco; other important agricultural products are dairy produce, cattle (in the Valley of Virginia), hay, corn, peanuts, sweet potatoes and apples; manufactures include chemicals, tobacco products (Richmond), electrical equipment and ships (centred on the shores of Hampton Roads channel); the scenic mountains, valleys and shores of Virginia, as well as its history, makes tourism a major state industry; coal mining is important in the SW; the first permanent British settlement in America was made at Jamestown in 1607; Virginia was one of the first colonies to actively move for independence; the scene of the surrender of the British general, Lord Cornwallis, at Yorktown in 1781; 10th of the original 13 states to ratify the Constitution (1788); at the beginning of the Civil War the W counties remained loyal to the Union and split from the rest of Virginia, becoming admitted to the Union as the state of West Virginia in 1863; Virginia was the scene of several major battles in the Civil War; re-admitted to the Union in 1870; also known as 'Old Dominion'; pop(1980) 5,346,818; area 103,230 sq km; capital Richmond; other major cities include Norfolk, Virginia Beach and Newport News; the state is divided into 95 counties and 41 independent cities:

County/city	*area (sq km)*	*pop(1980)*
Accomack	1,238	31,268
Albemarle	1,885	55,783
Alexandria	39	103,217
Alleghany	1,160	14,333
Amelia	928	8,405
Amherst	1,245	29,122
Appomattox	874	11,971
Arlington	68	152,599
Augusta	2,571	53,732
Bath	1,399	5,860
Bedford	1,942	34,927
Bedford	18	5,991
Bland	933	6,349
Botetourt	1,417	23,270
Bristol	31	19,042
Brunswick	1,464	15,632
Buchanan	1,310	37,989
Buckingham	1,516	11,751
Buena Vista	8	6,717
Campbell	1,313	45,424
Caroline	1,391	17,904
Carroll	1,243	27,270
Charles City	471	6,692
Charlotte	1,240	12,266
Charlottesville	26	39,916
Chesapeake	884	114,486
Chesterfield	1,128	141,372
Clarke	463	9,965
Clifton Forge	8	5,046
Colonial Heights	21	16,509
Covington	10	9,063
Craig	858	3,948
Culpeper	993	22,620
Cumberland	780	7,881
Danville	44	45,642
Dickenson	861	19,806
Dinwiddie	1,318	22,602
Emporia	5	4,840
Essex	684	8,864

contd

County/city	*area (sq km)*	*pop(1980)*
Fairfax	1,024	596,901
Fairfax (city)	16	19,390
Falls Church	5	9,515
Fauquier	1,693	35,889
Floyd	991	11,563
Fluvanna	754	10,244
Franklin	1,776	35,740
Franklin (city)	10	7,308
Frederick	1,079	34,150
Fredericksburg	16	15,322
Galax	21	6,524
Giles	941	17,810
Gloucester	585	20,107
Goochland	731	11,761
Grayson	1,160	16,579
Greene	408	7,625
Greensville	780	10,903
Halifax	2,122	30,599
Hampton	133	122,617
Hanover	1,215	50,398
Harrisonburg	16	19,671
Henrico	619	180,735
Henry	993	57,654
Highland	1,082	2,937
Hopewell	26	23,397
Isle of Wight	829	21,603
James City	398	22,763
King and Queen	824	5,968
King George	468	10,543
King William	723	9,334
Lancaster	346	10,129
Lee	1,136	25,956
Lexington	5	7,292
Loudoun	1,355	57,427
Louisa	1,292	17,825
Lunenburg	1,123	12,124
Lynchburg	130	66,743
Madison	837	10,232
Manassas	21	15,438
Manassas Park	5	6,524
Martinsville	29	18,149
Mathews	226	7,995
Mecklenburg	1,602	29,444
Middlesex	348	7,719
Montgomery	1,014	63,516
Nelson	114	12,204
New Kent	554	8,781
Newport News	169	144,903
Norfolk	138	266,979
Northampton	588	14,625
Northumberland	481	9,828
Norton	18	4,757
Nottoway	822	14,666
Orange	889	18,063
Page	814	19,401
Patrick	1,251	17,647
Petersburg	60	41,055
Pittsylvania	2,587	66,147
Poquoson	44	8,726
Portsmouth	78	104,577
Powhatan	1,764	13,062
Prince Edward	920	16,456
Prince George	692	25,733
Prince William	881	144,703
Pulaski	827	35,229
Radford	18	13,225
Rappahannock	694	6,093
Richmond	502	6,952
Richmond (city)	156	219,214
Roanoke	653	72,945
Roanoke (city)	112	100,220
Rockbridge	1,568	17,911
Rockingham	2,249	57,038

contd

County/city	*area (sq km)*	*pop(1980)*
Russell	1,245	31,761
Salem	36	23,958
Scott	1,391	25,068
Shenandoah	1,331	27,559
Smyth	1,175	33,366
South Boston	16	7,093
Southampton	1,568	18,731
Spotsylvania	1,050	34,435
Stafford	705	40,470
Staunton	23	21,857
Suffolk	1,063	47,621
Surry	731	6,046
Sussex	1,277	10,874
Tazewell	1,352	50,511
Virginia Beach	666	262,199
Warren	564	21,200
Washington	1,461	46,487
Waynesboro	21	15,329
Westmoreland	590	14,041
Williamsburg	13	9,870
Winchester	23	20,217
Wise	1,053	43,863
Wythe	1,209	25,522
York	294	35,463

Virginia Beach, 36 51N 75 59W, pop(1980) 262,199, independent city, SE Virginia, United States; on the Atlantic Ocean, 29 km E of Norfolk; a major summer resort; naval air station; railway; monuments: Cape Henry Memorial (commemorates English landing in 1607); Marine Science Museum.

Virton *veer-tõ'*, dist of Luxembourg prov, SE Belgium; area 77 sq km; pop(1982) 44,142.

Virunga *vee-rong'ga*, MFUMBIRO *mu-foom'bee-rō*, volcanic range in E central Africa running along Rwanda's NW border with Zaire and into SW Uganda, N and NE of L Kivu; highest point is Karisimbi (4,507 m), a dormant volcano; also in E section is Mukavura (4,127 m); W section comprises 2 active volcanoes, Nyiragongo (about 3,470 m) and Nyamaragira (about 3,056 m); the uprising of the Virunga range has been put forward as a mechanism which contributed to the drying up of Egypt in Pleistocene times by blocking the N outlets of L Tanganyika and hence substantially reducing the water to the R Nile. Volcanoes National Park, established in 1929, covers a mountain area of 120 sq km.

Visalia *vi-sal'-ye*, 36 20N 119 18W, pop(1980) 49,729, city in Tulare county, S central California, United States; in the San Joaquin Valley, 64 km SE of Fresno.

Visayan Islands *ve-sī-en*, island group in central Philippines; N of Mindanao I, S of Luzon I and bounded W by Sulu Sea and E by Philippine Sea; chief islands include Cebu, Bohol, Panay, Leyte, Samar, Negros and Masbate; area 61,991 sq km; inhabited by Visayan people; economy: sugar, coconut.

Visby *vees'boo*, WISBY *viz'bee* (Ger), 57 37N 18 18E, pop(1984e) 20,000, seaport and capital of Gotland county, S Sweden; on W coast of Gotland I in the Baltic Sea; a major commercial centre of N Europe from the 10th to the 14th century; member of Hanseatic League; seat of the governor of Gotland; see of a bishop; monument: St Mary's Church.

Viseu *vee-zay'oo*, dist in N central Portugal, in parts of Beira Alta and Trás-os-Montes provs; divided into 24 councils and 366 parishes; area 4,961 sq km; pop(1981) 423,648; traversed by R Vouga; economy: wine, almonds, meat, wool, dairy produce, fruit, olives, grain, tobacco, cork, pine wood for lumber and resin; minerals: kaoline, lead, feldspar, gold, silver, quartz, uranium, wolfram, zinc; chief towns: Viseu and Lamego; airfield at Viseu.

Viseu, 40 40N 7 55W, pop(1981) 21,000, capital of Viseu dist, N central Portugal; 138 km SE of Porto on wooded hills on left bank of the R Pavia, a tributary of the R

Mondego; divided into 2 parishes; bishopric; airfield; railway; in the 16th century Viseu was the headquarters of one of the great Portuguese schools of painting represented by Gaspar Vaz and Vasco Fernandes, known as Grąo Vasco (c.1480-1543); industries: textiles and tanning; agricultural centre well known for its Dão wines; airfield; monuments: cathedral; Viriato Fortifications; Grão Vasco Museum.

Vişeul de Sus *vee-she'ool day zhos*, 47 43N 23 24E, pop(1983) 21,352, resort town in Maramureş county, N Romania; 40 km SE of Sighet; railway; economy: timber trade, tanning, stone quarrying.

Vishakhapatnam *vi-shahk-u-put'num*, 17 45N 83 20E, pop(1981) 594,000, seaport in Andhra Pradesh state, SE India; 500 km ENE of Hyderabad, on the Bay of Bengal; linked by rail to Rajahmundry; economy: shipbuilding, oil refining, trade in manganese and oilseed.

Vista, 33 12N 117 14W, pop(1980) 35,834, city in San Diego county, SW California, United States; 13 km E of Oceanside.

Vistula, river in Poland. See Wisła.

Vitebsk *vyee'tyepsk*, 55 10N 30 14E, pop(1983) 324,000, river port capital of Vitebskaya oblast, NE Belorusskaya SSR, Soviet Union; on the Zapadnaya Dvina river; established in the 11th century; railway; airfield; economy: wool textiles, clothing, knitwear, footwear, machine tools.

Viterbo *vee-ter'bo*, prov of Lazio region, central Italy; pop(1981) 268,448; area 3,613 sq km; capital Viterbo.

Viterbo, 42 24N 12 06E, pop(1981) 57,632, capital town of Viterbo prov, Lazio region, central Italy; at the foot of the Monti Cimini, some 80 km NW of Roma (Rome); the town suffered severe damage during World War II; railway; monument: 12th-c cathedral.

Viti Levu *vee'tee lay'voo*, largest and most important island of Fiji, in the SW Pacific Ocean, separated from Vanua Levu I, 32 km to the NE, by the Koro Sea; area 10,429 sq km; length 144 km; width 104 km; the interior of the island is mountainous, rising to 1,324 m in Tomaniivi (Mt Victoria); main rivers Rewa, Sigatoka, Nadi, Ba, and Navua; the lower reaches of the main rivers provide fertile alluvial flats and fan out into substantial deltas; there are experimental irrigated rice projects at Navua and in the Rewa area near Suva; capital Suva; chief towns Lautoka, Nadi, Navua, Nausori, and Sigatoka; Nadi International Airport is 6 km from Nadi on the W coast of the island, the Tholoisuva Forest Park is a mahogany forest with 3.6 km of trails, waterfalls, and natural swimming pools; tourism is important along the S coast; there is gold-mining at Vatukoula, and Lautoka is the main sugar milling centre.

Vitória *vee-to'ree-a*, 20 19S 40 21W, pop(1980) 165,090, port capital of Espírito Santo state, Sudeste region, SE Brazil; situated on an island; connected to the mainland by 2 bridges; university (1961); airfield; economy: commercial and industrial centre; mineral exports; growing centre for sea fishing; connected westwards with Minas Gerais by the Vitória-Minas railway, which transports for export millions of tons of iron ore and a large tonnage of coffee and timber; founded in 1551; S of Vitória is the small settlement of Vila Velha; on a hill above this town are the ruins of the fortified monastery of Nossa Senhora da Penha, built in 1558; it was attacked by the Dutch in 1625 and again in 1640.

Vitoria, VITTORIA (Eng), pop(1981) 192,773, capital of Álava (Vitoria) prov, Pais Vasco (Basque Country), N Spain; near the R Zadorra, 351 km N of Madrid; bishopric; airport; railway; economy: motor vehicles, steel, electronics, explosives, arms, agric machinery, furniture, sugar refining; monuments: church of St Peter; old and new cathedrals; events: fiesta of St Prudence in April, La Virgen Blanca fair in August; pilgrimage to Olarizu in Sept and autumn music festival.

Vitória da Conquista *da kon-kees'ta*, 14 53S 40 52W, pop(1980) 125,516, town in Bahia state, Nordeste region, NE Brazil; SW of Salvador; economy: coffee, beans, maize, cattle.

Vitosha or **Vitosa** *vee'to-sha*, 42 40N 23 15E, ski resort in Sofiya okrug (prov), W Bulgaria's largest ski resort 20 km E of Sofiya overlooking the Sofiya plain; alt 1,810 m; well endowed with facilities for skiing and tasting Bulgarian slivovitsa.

Vitry-sur-Seine *veet-ree-sür-sen*, 48 47N 2 24E, pop(1982) 85,820, town in Val-de-Marne dept, Ile-de-France region, N central France; a suburb to the SSE of Paris; economy: electrical and electronic equipment.

Vizcaya *veeth-ka'ya*, BISCAY *bis'kay* (Eng), one of three Pais Vasco (Basque Country) provs in N Spain; NE spurs of the Cordillera Cantabrica slope down to a rocky coastline on the Bay of Biscay; drained by the R Nervión; pop(1981) 1,181,401; area 2,217 sq km; capital Bilbao; economy: refinery at Somorrostro; nuclear power plant at Lemoniz, shipbuilding, electrical equipment, wine, food canning.

Vlaanderen *vlan'der-en*, FLANDERS (Eng), FLANDRE (Fr), historical region of N Belgium covering the territory of the former County of Flanders; it is a densely populated industrial region with an average population density of 400 inhabitants per sq km; chief towns Brugge, Gent, Antwerpen, Hasselt, Sint-Niklaas, Aalst and Ronse; the traditional textile industry plays a dominant role; the production of linen and silk still exists but has been overtaken by cotton processing, primarily around Gent; new industries have been located in the canal zone of Gent, extending N of the city, where transport conditions are favourable (petro-chemicals, motor industry); the region is also intensively farmed, the main crops being wheat, sugar-beet, oats, barley, potatoes and certain industrial plants such as flax, chicory, tobacco and hops.

Vlaar'dingen, 51 55N 4 21E, pop(1984e) 76,466, river port city in Zuid Holland prov, W Netherlands; on the R Nieuwe Maas, 10 km W of Rotterdam; railway; economy: chemical fertilizers, animal feed supplements; centre of the Dutch herring and cod fishing industry.

Vladimir *vla-dyee'myir*, 56 08N 40 25E, pop(1983) 320,000, capital city of Vladimirskaya oblast, W central European Rossiyskaya, Soviet Union; on the R Klyaz'ma, 190 km NE of Moskva (Moscow); founded in 1108 by Prince Vladimir Monomakh when it was designed to serve as a frontier fortress guarding his domain; railway, on the highway between Moskva and Gor'kiy (Gorky); economy: thermal power plant, machine building, chemicals, building materials, clothing, electrical machinery, light industry; monuments: Zolotiye Vorota (the Golden Gate) (1158-64), a unique masterpiece of ancient Russian defence architecture; Uspensky cathedral (1160) with a museum of religious art and tombs of the early princes of Vladimir.

Vladivostok *vlu-dyee-vu-stok'*, 43 10N 131 53E, pop(1983) 504,000, seaport capital of Primorskiy kray, Rossiyskaya, E Soviet Union; on the Sea of Japan; chief Soviet port on the Pacific Ocean (kept open in winter by ice-breakers); a base for fishing and whaling fleets; established in 1860 as a military post; university (1920); terminus of the Trans-Siberian railway; economy: shipbuilding and repairing, precision instruments, building materials.

Vliss'ingen, FLUSHING (Eng), FLESSINGUE *fles-ĩg* (Fr), 51 27N 3 35E, pop(1984e) 46,150, seaport on the S coast of the former island of Walcheren, Zeeland prov, W Netherlands; at the mouth of the Schelde river estuary, here more than 4 km wide; the seaport is separated by locks from 2 interior docks, connected to Middelburg by the Walcheren Canal; when the project known as the 'Delta Plan' is completed, the industrial zone of Vlissingen will be extended by c.300 sq km; site of a nuclear power station; birthplace of the famous Admiral Michiel Adriaanszoon de Ruyter (1607-76) and of the poet Jacobus Bellamy (1557-86); railway; economy: shipbuilding, machinery, vehicles, leather, fish processing, crude aluminium ingots and alloys, chemical and petrochemical works; monument: 14th-c Grote Kerk.

Vlorë *vlo're*, prov of SW Albania; area 1,609 sq km; pop(1980) 149,600; capital Vlorë.

Vlorë, VALONA (Ital), AULON (anc), 40 27N 19 30E,

pop(1980) 58,000, seaport and capital of Vlorë prov, SW Albania; on the Bay of Vlorë, 112 km SW of Tiranë; a bishopric in the 5th century; railway; has a well-protected harbour.

Vltava *vul'ta-va*, MOLDAU *mol'dow* (Ger), river in W Czechoslovakia; formed in the Bohemian Forest by the junction of two headstreams; flows SE and N to meet the R Elbe (Labe) near Melnik; length 427 km; navigable for about 80 km; tributaries Berounka, Sázava, Otava, Lužnice and Malse rivers.

Vogan *vō-gan'*, 6 20N 1 33E, town in S Togo, W Africa; 37 km NE of Lomé.

Voiótia *be-ō'sh-a*, BOEOTIA (Eng), nome (dept) of Stérea Ellás-Évvoia region, E Greece, lying NE of the Korinthiakós Kólpos (Gulf of Corinth); pop(1981) 117,175; area 2,952 sq km; capital Levádhia.

Vojvodina *voi'vo-dee-na*, autonomous province in the N of the republic of Srbija (Serbia), E Yugoslavia; bounded on the N by Hungary, on the E by Romania, and on the W by the Yugoslav republic of Hrvatska (Croatia); a flat plain intersected by the Fruška Gora and Vršački Breg mountain ranges and drained by the R Danube, R Tisza and R Sava; pop(1981) 2,034,772; area 21,506 sq km; in addition to Serbs the population includes Croats, Ukrainians and Montenegrins; Serbo-Croat and Hungarian are the main languages; capital Novi Sad; chief towns include Subotica, Pančevo, Zrenjanin; wildfowling, fishing and hunting are popular; economy: wine, fruit.

Volcano Islands, group of islands in the W Pacific Ocean. See Kazan-rettō.

Volga, RHA (anc), largest river of Europe, central European Rossiyskaya, Soviet Union; rises in the marshy Valdayskaya Vozvyshennost' (Valdai Hills), N Kalininskaya oblast, Rossiyskaya; flows in a large bend past Kalinin to the Rybinsk reservoir; on leaving the reservoir near Andropov the river flows generally SE, past Yaroslavl', Kostroma, and Gor'kiy (Gorky), to Kazan'; continues S past Ul'yanovsk, Kuybyshev, and Saratov, turns SE at Volgograd, finally discharging into the Caspian Sea, forming a broad delta below Astrakhan'; length 3,531 km; drainage basin area 1,360,000 sq km; chief tributaries Torgun, Tereshka, Sok, Sura, Oka, and Kostroma rivers; the R Volga is the principal navigable waterway in the USSR; the Volga-Baltic Waterway links the Volga with the Baltic Sea and with the Volga-White Sea Canal; the Volga-Don Canal links the Volga with the Azovskoye More (Sea of Azov) and the Black Sea; reservoirs along the course of the river (Kuybyshev, Saratov, and Volgograd) were designed primarily for power generation, industrial and urban water supply, flood-control, and added benefits for navigation; the dry steppe and semi-desert zones lying to the E of the middle and lower course of the river are now being irrigated with Volga water.

Volgograd, formerly TSARITSYN (-1925), STALINGRAD (1925-61), 48 45N 44 30E, pop(1983) 962,000, capital city of Volgogradskaya oblast, SE European Rossiyskaya, Soviet Union; extending more than 70 km along the right bank of the R Volga; E terminus of the Volga-Don Canal; administrative and economic centre; founded in the 16th century to protect the Volga trade route at the junction of the Volga and Don rivers; railway; airport; economy: hydroelectric power generation, aluminium plant, oil refining, manufacture of clothing, footwear, leatherwork, tractors; the Volgograd region now ranks 6th in the Soviet Union's oil producing areas.

Vologda *vo'lug-du*, 59 10N 39 55E, pop(1983) 260,000, capital city of Vologodskaya oblast, N central European Rossiyskaya, Soviet Union; on the R Vologda; railway junction; economy: machine building, metalworking, foodstuffs, pharmaceuticals, flax processing, lace-making; 'monuments: cathedral of St Sophia (1568-70), Voskresenskii cathedral (1772-76).

Vólos *vo'los*, 39 22N 22 57E, pop(1981) 107,407, major port and capital of Magnisía nome (dept), Thessalía region, E Greece; 160 km NNW of Athínai (Athens); important for the shipment of agricultural produce; airfield; rail terminus; ship routes; economy: weaving mills, cement works, tobacco factories; event: re-enactment of the sailing of the Argonauts (June-July).

Vol'ta, region in SW Ghana, W Africa; pop(1984) 1,201,095; area 20,651 sq km; the R Volta flows S from L Volta to the Gulf of Guinea; capital Ho; chief towns Jasikan, Kete and Sogakofe; economy: salt processing, bauxite.

Volta, river in Ghana, W Africa; formed by the junction of Black Volta and White Volta rivers near New Tamale as they enter L Volta; the river flows S to enter the Gulf of Guinea at Ada; receives Pru, Sene, Afrim, Daka and Oti rivers; river has been dammed at Akosombo to form L Volta; the Volta River Scheme was a joint enterprise of the British and former Gold Coast governments and of British and Canadian private interests, designed to supply power, improve navigation and help develop the great bauxite deposits of the region; length including L Volta about 480 km.

Volta, Lake, reservoir in SE Ghana, W Africa; area 8,500 sq km; created by the damming of the R Volta at Akosombo for hydroelectric power; the White Volta, Black Volta and Oti rivers meet in the lake area.

Volta Redonda *vol'ta ray-don'da*, 22 31S 44 05W, pop(1980) 180,126, town in Rio de Janeiro state, Sudeste region, SE Brazil; on the Río Paraíba, NW of Rio de Janeiro; railway; Brazil's chief steel centre, the town has one of the largest steel works in Latin America.

Volubilis *vol-yoobl'is*, remains of an ancient Roman town in NW Morocco, N Africa; 4 km W of Moulay Idriss and 30 km N of Meknès.

Volzhskiy, 48 48N 44 45E, pop(1983) 232,000, port in Volgogradskaya oblast, Rossiyskaya, Soviet Union; on the the R Volga, 25 km from Volgograd; established in 1951 and became a city in 1954; railway; economy: hydroelectric power generation, synthetic rubber and ball-bearings.

Vorarlberg *for'arl-berk* ('in front of the Arlberg'), federal state of W Austria, bounded by Tirol state to the E, W Germany to the N and Switzerland to the W; comprises 4 dists and 96 communities ranging from the well-cultivated shores of the Bodensee (L Constance) to the forested uplands (Bregenzer Wald) and snow-covered peaks of the Silvretta; pop(1981) 305,615; area 2,601 sq km; capital Bregenz; the painter Angelica Kauffmann (1741-1807) lived at Schwarzenberg in the Bregenzer Wald; economy: tourism, textiles (Dornbirn), embroidery (Lustenau), hydroelectricity; the Arlberg massif on the border between Vorarlberg and Tirol enjoys an international reputation as an alpine skiing centre.

Voronezh *ve-ro'nyesh*, 51 40N 39 10E, pop(1983) 831,000, river port capital of Voronezhskaya oblast, E central European Rossiyskaya, Soviet Union; on the left bank of the R Voronezh; founded as a fortress in 1586; university (1918); railway; airport; economy: production of equipment for agriculture and the food industry, construction machinery such as excavators, chemical products (especially synthetic rubber), and food products, atomic power generation.

Voroshilovgrad *ve-re-shi'lef-grat*, formerly LUGANSK (-1935, 1958-70), 48 35N 39 20E, pop(1983) 485,000, capital city of Voroshilovgradskaya oblast, E Ukrainskaya SSR, Soviet Union; on a tributary of the R Severskiy Donets; founded in 1795 when the nearby coal mines were opened; railway; airfield; economy: wool textiles, clothing, leatherwork, footwear, mining equipment.

Vosges *vozh*, dept in Lorraine region of NE France, to the W of the Vosges Mts; comprises 3 arrond, 31 cantons and 516 communes; pop(1982) 395,769; area 5,903 sq km; hilly and wooded, but fertile to the W; rises in the S to 504 m in the Monts Faucilles; watered by the Meuse and Moselle rivers; capital Épinal, chief towns Neufchâteau and St-Dié; there are spas at Contrexeuille, Vittel, Bains-les-Bains, Plombières-les-Bains and Bussang.

Vosges, VOSEGUS (anc), range of hills extending between the Haut-Rhin and Vosges depts in NE France near the

Franco-German frontier; separated from the Jura to the S by the Belfort Gap and parallel and similar to the Black Forest across the R Rhine; this is a classical rift valley (or graben) landscape; from the thickly-wooded hills rivers descend steeply to the Rhine and more gently to Lorraine and the Central Plateau of France; the highest point is Grand Ballon or Ballon de Guebwiller (1,423 m); the range is 250 km in length; skiing and rock climbing are popular; La Bresse, Le Bonhomme, Gerardmer and St-Maurice-sur-Moselle are all down-hill skiing resorts; all summits are accessible from the scenic 'Route des Crêtes' which was constructed during World War I; the 'Route du Vin' follows the full length of the E-facing vineyard slopes at the foot of the Vosges; pop(1982) 311,019; area 7,425 sq km; watered by the lower Yonne R; mostly flat, although rising to 377 m in the Collines de Puisaye in the SW; capital Auxerre, chief towns Avallon and Sens.

Voss, *vos*, 60 38N 6 25E, pop(1980) 14,166, town in Hordaland county, SW Norway; ENE of Bergen, on L Vangsvatnet; railway; alpine resort; monument: church (1270).

Vos'tock, 78 27S 106 51E, Soviet scientific station in Antarctica; the lowest temperature ever recorded on Earth (−88.3°C) was measured here; the South Geomagnetic Pole (1985) is nearby.

Vouga *vō'ga*, river in N central Portugal; rises in Serra da Lapa, flows WSW to Atlantic near Aveiro where it forms a shallow lagoon; length 136 km; navigable 50 km to Pessegueiro; area of basin 3,656 sq km; principal tributaries Sul, Caima, Ul, Agueda.

Vraca, okrug (prov) of Bulgaria. See Vratsa.

Vrancea *vran'cha*, county in E central Romania, in the SE foothills of the E Carpathian Mts; pop(1983) 380,746; area 4,863 sq km; capital Focşani.

Vrangelya, Ostrov *vran'gil*, WRANGEL *rang'gel* (Eng), tundra-covered island in the W Chukchi Sea, Khabarovskiy kray, E Siberian Rossiyskaya, Soviet Union, near the NE extremity of Asia; area 5,180 sq km; length 120 km; width 72 km; rises to 1,097 m; named after F.P. Wrangel (Vrangel'), a 19th-c Russian navigator; claimed by Russia, Canada, and the USA, it was finally left to Russia in 1924; there is a government Arctic station and trading post on the SE shore.

Vranje *vra'nye*, 42 33N 21 54E, pop(1981) 82,527, town in S Srbija (Serbia) republic, Yugoslavia; on R Morava, 80 km S of Niš; railway; economy: wine trade, textiles, metal products.

Vranov or **Vranov nad Toplou** *vra'nof nad top'low*, 48 54N 21 41E, pop(1984) 20,197, town in Východoslovenský region, Slovak Socialist Republic, E Czechoslovakia; NE of Košice; railway; economy: hydroelectric power.

Vra'tsa or **Vraca**, okrug (prov) of NW Bulgaria to the N of the Stara Planina (Balkan Mts) and bordered to the N by Romania, its N frontier follows the R Danube; area 4,006 sq km; pop(1981) 291,000; vine-growing is important.

Vratsa, 43 12N 23 32E, capital of Vratsa okrug (prov), NW Bulgaria; 116 km N of Sofiya; founded in the 15th century; railway; economy: chemicals, textiles, silk, metal products and agricultural trade.

Vrbas *vur'bas*, river in Bosna-Hercegovina republic, Yugoslavia; rises SE of Sarajevo and flows 238 km N to meet the R Sava; navigable for 80 km.

Vrsac *vur'shats*, 45 07N 21 19E, pop(1981) 61,005, town in autonomous province of Vojvodina, N Srbija (Serbia) republic, Yugoslavia; ENE of Beograd, near the Romanian frontier; Vrsac Canal, a branch of the Timiş Canal, is nearby; railway; economy: meat, wine and fruit trade, textiles, foodstuffs.

Vsetin *fset'yeen*, 49 20N 18 00E, pop(1984) 30,828, town in Severomoravský region, Czech Socialist Republic, central Czechoslovakia; on R Horní Bečva, NE of Gottwaldov, in the W Beskids; railway.

Vucitrn *voo'chee-tarn*, 42 49N 20 59E, pop(1981) 65,512, town in autonomous province of Kosovo, S Srbija (Serbia) republic, Yugoslavia; on R Sitnica, SE of Kosovska Mitrovica; railway.

Vukovar *voo-ko'var*, VALDASUS (anc), 45 19N 19 01E, pop(1981) 81,203, river port town in Hrvatska (Croatia) republic, Yugoslavia; at the junction of R Vuka with R Danube, 32 km SE of Osijek; economy: agricultural trade, horticulture, foodstuffs, fishing.

Vulcan *vool-kan'*, 45 22N 23 16E, pop(1983) 32,125, town in Hunedoara county, W central Romania; on R Jiu in Transylvanian Alps; railway; economy: coal mining.

Vung Tau *vung-tow*, formerly CAPE SAINT JACQUES (Fr), 10 19N 107 05E, point and town on the S coast of Vietnam; on the Mekong Delta, SE of Ho Chi Minh City (Saigon); with Con Dao, it is a 'Special Area' of Vietnam.

Vyatka *vyat'ku*, river in E central European Rossiyskaya, Soviet Union; rises E of Omutninsk, E Kirovskaya oblast, in the W foothills of the Ural'skiy Khrebet (Ural Mts) range; flows N, SW, then SSE, past Kirov and Malmyzh, to join the R Kama below Mamadysh; length 1,358 km; chief tributaries Kil'mez, Pizhma, Moloma, and Kobra rivers; freezes over from November to April.

Vychegda *vi'chig-du*, river in N European Rossiyskaya, Soviet Union, rising in several headstreams in the S Timanskiy Kryazh (Timan ridge); flows S then generally W past Syktyvkar, turns SW at Irta, and joins the Severnaya Dvina at Kotlas; length 1,120 km; navigable length 960 km; chief tributaries Yarenga, Vym', and Sysola rivers; in the 16th century the Vychegda was an important water route to Siberia.

Východočeský *vee'KHo-do-che-skee*, region in Czech Socialist Republic, central Czechoslovakia; area 11,240 sq km; pop(1984) 1,247,086; capital Hradec Králové; chief towns include Náchod, Pardubice.

Východoslovenský *vee'KHo-do-slo-ven-skee*, region in Slovak Socialist Republic, E Czechoslovakia; area 16,191 sq km; pop(1984) 1,440,536; capital Košice; chief towns include Prešov, Michalovce.

W

W, national park in W Africa; located at the meeting point of SW Niger, E Burkina and N Benin; the areas and dates of establishment in each country are 2,200 sq km (1954), 2,350 sq km (1953) and 5,680 sq km (1953) respectively.

Wa, 10 07N 2 28W, town in W Upper region, NW Ghana, W Africa; 185 km NW of Tamale.

Waadt, canton in Switzerland. See Vaud.

Waal *vahl*, river in S central Netherlands, an arm of the R Rhine, formed near Millingen, where it joins the lower Rhine and the Waal rivers; flows W through Gelderland prov, past Nijmegen, Tiel and Zaltbommel; joins the R Maas at Woudrichem to form the upper R Merwede; length 83 km.

Wabash *waw'bash* (Algonquian, 'white-shining'), river in Ohio, Indiana and Illinois states, United States; rises in Darke county, W Ohio; flows 764 km W and SW across Indiana to meet the Ohio river SW of Evansville.

Waco *way'kō*, 31 33N 97 09W, pop(1980) 101,261, county seat of McLennan county, central Texas, United States; on the R Brazos, 152 km NNE of Austin; named after an Indian tribe; founded in 1849; university (1845); railway; airfield; economy: trading, shipping, and industrial centre in the heart of the blacklands; manufactures include tyres, glass, and paper; monument: Texas Ranger Hall of Fame.

Wadi Meda'ni, 14 24N 33 30E, pop(1983)141,065, chief city of Central (Annil el Azraq) region, E Sudan, NE Africa; 180 km SE of Khartoum, on the Blue Nile; the centre of a cotton growing area watered by the Gezira irrigation scheme.

Wageningen *va'KHė-ning-an*, 5 44N 56 42W, pop(1980) 2,927, agricultural and manufacturing company town in Nickerie dist, Surinam, NE South America; economy: centre of the Surinam rice-growing area; one of the largest fully-mechanized rice farms in the world is located here.

Wagga Wag'ga, 35 07S 147 24E, pop(1981) 36,837, town in Murrumbidgee stat div, SE New South Wales, Australia; at the centre of a rich agricultural area W of Canberra; railway; airfield.

Waikato *wī-ka'tō*, river in North Island, New Zealand; flowing 425 km from its source, the Upper Waikato river, it is the longest river in New Zealand; rises in L Taupo then flows NW past the town of Hamilton to enter the Tasman Sea at a point 40 km S of Manukau Harbour; a source of hydroelectric power.

Waikiki Beach *wī-kee-kee'*, resort beach in SE Honolulu on the Pacific island of Oahu, Hawaii state, United States; the International Market Place is a complex of shops, vendors' carts, restaurants and nightclubs; concerts and hula shows are featured at the Kapiolani Park.

Waipahu *wī-pah'hoo*, 21 23N 158 01W, pop(1980) 29,139, city in Honolulu county, Hawaii, United States; on the NW shore of Pearl Harbor, Oahu I; damaged in the Japanese air attack on Pearl Harbor naval base, on 7 Dec 1941.

Wakatipu *wah-kah-tee'poo*, lake in S central South Island, New Zealand; 145 km WNW of Dunedin; length 77.2 km; breadth 4.8 km; area 293 sq km; the tourist resort of Queenstown is on its E shore; a steamer operates on the lake.

Wakayama *wa-ka-ya'ma*, 34 12N 135 10E, pop(1980) 400,802, capital of Wakayama prefecture, Kinki region, S Honshū island, Japan; 56 km SSW of Ōsaka, on the Tomogashima-suido Channel between Ōsaka-wan Bay and Kii-suido Channel; damaged by an earthquake and tidal wave in 1946; university (1949); railway; economy: iron, steel, chemicals, textiles.

Wake Islands, 19 18N 166 36E, horseshoe-shaped coral atoll enclosing 3 islands in central Pacific Ocean, 1,200 km N of Kwajalein in the Marshall Is; comprises the islands of Wilkes, Wake and Peale; area 10 sq km; pop(1981) 1,600, discovered by Captain William Wake and charted in 1841 by Captain Charles Wilkes accompanied by a naturalist named Peale; annexed by the USA in 1898; seaplane base opened in 1935 and the island became important for trans-Pacific air flights; under the control of the US Air Force since 1972.

Wake'field, 53 42N 1 29W, pop(1981) 75,838, county town of West Yorkshire, N England; part of West Yorkshire urban area; on the R Calder, 13 km S of Leeds; a woollen centre since the 16th century; railway; economy: textiles, chemicals, mining machinery, machine tools.

Walachia or **Wallachia** *wol-ay'ki-a*, geographical region in S Romania, lying E and W of the R Olt to the S of the Transylvanian Alps; held by Hungary and Turkey until its unification with Moldavia in 1859-61 to form Romania.

Wałbrzych *vow-brzhits'*, voivodship in SW Poland; bounded S by Czechoslovakia and watered by the Nysa Kł and Bystrzyca rivers; pop(1983) 728,000; area 4,168 sq km; capital Wałbrzych; chief towns include Świdnica, Dzierżoniów, Bielawa, Kłodzko and Nowa Ruda.

Wałbrzych, WALDENBURG (Ger), 50 48N 16 19E, pop(1983) 137,400, mining and industrial capital of Wałbrzych voivodship, S Poland; the centre of the lower Silesian coal basin; repatriated miners from France and Belgium form a large part of the pop; Piaskowa Góra modern housing development in N part of the city; polytechnic; railway; economy: coal mining, iron, steel, glass, porcelain; monuments: arcaded Baroque houses in Market Square; regional museum with geology and porcelain collections.

Walchensee *val'KHen-zay*, 47 36N 11 23E, lake in S Bayern (Bavaria) prov, W Germany, in the Bayerische Alpen (Bavarian Alps), 61 km SSW of München (Munich); area 16.4 sq km; max depth 192 m; average depth 92 m.

Wales *waylz*, CYMRU *koom'ree* (Welsh), principality on the W coast of the United Kingdom; bounded E by England, W by St George's Channel, N by the Irish Sea and S by the Bristol Channel; includes the island of Anglesey off the NW coast; timezone GMT; area 20,761 sq km; pop(1981) 2,791,851; nearly 20% of the population speak Welsh; capital Cardiff; chief towns Swansea, Newport, Merthyr Tydfil; rises to 1,085 m at Snowdon in the NW; drained by the Severn, Clwyd, Dee, Conway, Dovey, Taff, Teifi, Tawe, Towy, Usk and Wye rivers; economy: coal, slate, lead, steel, engineering, oil refining, fishing, forestry, sheep, dairy products; the Anglo-Saxon invaders of Britain drove the Brythonic Celts into Wales, calling them *Waelisc* or Welsh meaning 'foreign'; in the 8th century Welsh territory was lost to Offa, King of Mercia, who built a frontier dyke from the Dee to the Wye; in the 9th century Rhodri Mawr united Wales against the Saxons, Norse and Danes; Lewellyn ap Gruffydd, the last native prince, was killed during hostilities between English and Welsh in 1282, allowing Edward I of England to establish his authority over Wales; in Feb 1301 Edward I's son was created Prince of Wales, a title which has been borne by the eldest son of the sovereign ever since; Wales has been politically united with England since the Act of Union of 1535; national day 1 March (St David's Day); since 1974 Wales has been divided into 8 counties as follows:

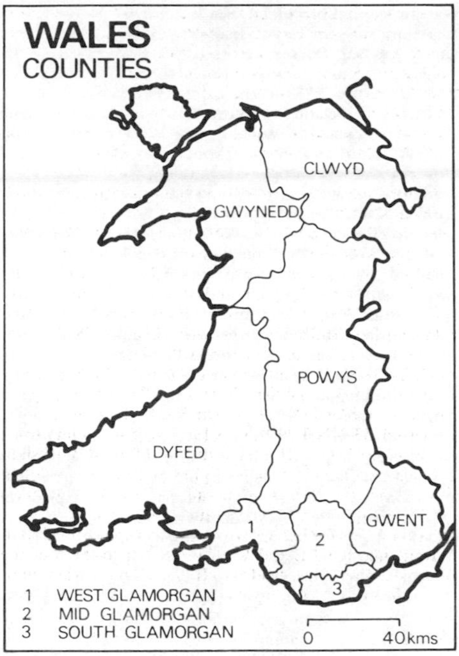

County	*area (sq km)*	*pop(1981)*
Clwyd	2,426	391,081
Dyfed	5,768	330,178
Gwent	1,376	439,875
Gwynedd	3,869	230,048
Mid Glamorgan	1,018	538,474
Powys	5,077	110,555
South Glamorgan	416	384,042
West Glamorgan	817	367,598

Walk'den, 53 32N 2 24W, pop(1981) 39,466, town in Bury borough, Greater Manchester, NW England; 7 km S of Bolton, railway.

Walla Walla, 46 04N 118 20W, pop(1980) 25,618, county seat of Walla Walla county, SE Washington, United States; on the Walla Walla river, near the Oregon state border; named after an Indian tribe; railway; airfield; monuments: 9 km W of the town is the Whitman Mission National Monument, situated on the site of a religious mission founded by Marcus Whitman and his wife who were killed in 1847 by Cayuse Indians.

Wallasey *wol'e-si*, 53 26N 3 03W, pop(1981) 62,531, town in Wirral borough, Merseyside, NW England; on the Wirral peninsula, N of Birkenhead; a dormitory town for Liverpool; railway; economy: foodstuffs, engineering.

Wallis and Futuna Islands, official name Territory of the Wallis and Futuna Islands, island group in the S central Pacific Ocean, NE of Fiji; a French overseas territory comprising the Wallis Is and the Îles de Hooru; area 274 sq km; pop(1982) 11,943; capital Matu Utu on Uvea I in the Wallis group; the inhabitants are almost entirely Polynesian; the majority of the population is Roman Catholic; Uvean and Futunan, distinct Polynesian languages, are spoken; the unit of currency is the franc.
Physical description and climate. The Territory comprises 2 groups of islands: the Wallis Is (159 sq km) and the Hooru Is (115 sq km), the latter including Futuna I. The 2 island groups lie 230 km apart. Wallis has a central island, Uvea, rising to 145 m at Mt Lulu, and ringed by low lying coral reefs. The Hooru Is, comprising Futuna and Alofi, are mountainous and volcanic. Futuna rises to 765 m at Mt Puke, and is surrounded by a fringing reef. Alofi, 2 km SE of Futuna, is uninhabited due to lack of water. The climate is warm and damp, with a cyclone season between October and March.
History, government and constitution. The islands were discovered by European seamen during the 18th century and became a French protectorate in 1842. In 1959 the inhabitants voted in favour of changing their status to an Overseas Territory of France, which took effect from 29 July 1961. The islands are governed by an appointed administrator, assisted by an elected 20-member territorial assembly, and represented in the French parliament by a deputy and senator.
Economy. Subsistence farming and fishing are the main activities. Chief agricultural products are copra, yams, taro roots, and bananas. Copra is the only significant export.

Wallonia, French-speaking region of S Belgium; approximately 3.5 million Walloons constitute 36% of the total population of Belgium; the dividing line with Flanders to the N is a belt of industry from Liège to Tournai; many Walloon towns are renowned for their art treasures (Tournai, Huy, Namur and especially Liège); economy: steel, engineering.

Wallsend, 53 00N 1 31W, pop(1981) 44,622, town in North Tyneside borough, Tyne and Wear, NE England; part of Tyneside urban area; at the E end of Hadrian's Wall, 6 km E of Newcastle upon Tyne, on the R Tyne; economy: shipbuilding, transport equipment, engineering, rope, coal.

Walnut Creek, 37 54N 122 04W, pop(1980) 53,643, city in Contra Costa county, W California, United States; in the San Ramon Valley, 21 km NE of Oakland.

Walsall *wol'sawl*, 52 35N 1 58W, pop(1981) 178,852, town in Walsall borough, West Midlands, central England; 13 km NW of Birmingham; centre of the lock and key industry in the 17th century; railway; economy: coal, engineering, machine tools, aircraft parts, plastics, electronics, chemicals, leather; monuments: England's only lock museum; museum and art gallery, containing the Garman-Ryan collection gifted by Lady Epstein in 1973.

Waltham, 42 23N 71 14W, pop(1980) 58,200, city in Middlesex county, E Massachusetts, United States; 14 km W of Boston; settled in 1636, achieving city status in 1884; the first US paper mill was founded here in 1788; Brandeis University (1947); railway; economy: electronics, precision instruments.

Waltham Cross, town in Hertfordshire, England. See Chesunt.

Waltham Forest, 51 37N 0 01W, pop(1981) 215,947, residential borough of N Greater London, England; includes the suburbs of Chingford, Walthamstow and Leyton; railway; economy: brewing, engineering.

Walton and Weybridge *-way'-*, 51 24N 0 25W, pop(1981) 50,402, residential town in Elmbridge dist, Surrey, SE England; an amalgamation of Walton-on-Thames and Weybridge in Greater London urban area; on the R Wey, 25 km SW of London; railway; economy: aircraft industry on the site of the former Brooklands racetrack.

Walvis Bay *wol'vis*, WALVISBAAI (Afrik), 22 59S 14 31E, pop(1980e) 25,000, seaport in W central Namibia, SW Africa; located on Atlantic Ocean coast 275 km WSW of Windhoek; the Walvis Bay enclave (area 1,128 sq km) is administered by South Africa as part of the Cape prov; the area was originally annexed by the Dutch in 1792 and subsequently became a British territory in 1878; incorporated into the Cape Colony in 1884; remained British territory during German annexation of the then South-West Africa in 1892; railway terminus; airfield; economy: fishing (pilchards, anchovies, tuna, mackerel, etc).

Wanaka *wan'e-ke*, lake in W of South Island, New Zealand; length 45.1 km; breadth 4.8 km; area 193 sq km; the town of Wanaka is situated on the lake's S shore; skiing in the surrounding mountains; the lake is also used as a reservoir.

Wandsworth *wondz'werth*, 51 27N 0 11W, pop(1981)

254,898, borough of SW central Greater London, England; S of R Thames; includes the suburbs of Wandsworth and Streatham; Battersea Park and Putney Heath; railway; event: Easter parade (March-April).

Wanganui *wong'a-noo-ee*, 39 56S 175 00E, pop(1981) 37,012, town on North Island, New Zealand; near the mouth of the Wanganui river; railway; airfield; an outdoor resort area specializing in jet boat trips, guided canoe treks, white-water rafting expeditions and an annual motorboat-racing event; monuments: Queen's Park in the centre of the city contains a museum, art gallery and public library.

Wanganui, river in W North Island, New Zealand; rises NW of L Taupo; flows S, past the town of Taumarunui, to enter the Tasman Sea near the town of Wanganui, 195 km N of Wellington; length 290 km; the Wanganui is the longest navigable river in New Zealand; paddle-boats visit a local winery.

Wangarat'ta, 36 22S 146 20E, pop(1983e) 16,710, town in North Eastern stat div, NE Victoria, Australia; on R Ovens, 200 km NE of Melbourne; railway; economy: tobacco, hops, wine, textiles; monument: Drage's Airworld contains the largest collection of biplane aircraft in the world.

Wankie, town in Zimbabwe. See Hwange.

Wanneroo', 31 40S 115 35E, pop(1981) 6,745, town in Perth stat div, Western Australia, Australia; N of Perth.

Wapping *wop'ing*, district in Tower Hamlets borough, Greater London, England; on the R Thames just W of the Rotherhithe Tunnel, close to the former London docks; airport (1987); economy: newspaper industry.

Warangal *vu-rung'gul*, 18 0N 79 35E, pop(1981) 336,000, city in Andhra Pradesh state, SE India; 136 km NE of Hyderabad, on the Deccan Plateau; linked to Hyderabad and Vijayawada by rail; economy: carpets, cotton, printing, trade in grain and oilseed; monuments: Hindu temple (1160); 8 km SW is Warangal Fort, which is the original site of the city.

Ware, 51 49N 0 02W, pop(1981) 15,471, town in East Hertfordshire dist, Hertfordshire, SE England; on the R Lee, 33 km N of London; railway; economy: electronics, engineering.

Waremme *vahr-em'*, BORGWORM *borKH'vorm* (Flem), dist of Liège prov, E Belgium; area 390 sq km; pop(1982) 60,866.

Warminster, 51 13N 2 12W, pop(1981) 15,222, town in West Wiltshire dist, Wiltshire, S England; railway; on the edge of Salisbury Plain, 13 km S of Trowbridge; economy: clothing, agricultural machinery, foodstuffs.

Warner Robins, 32 37N 83 36W, pop(1980) 39,893, town in Houston county, central Georgia, United States; 24 km S of Macon; railway; adjacent is Robins Air Force Base, one of the largest air force installations in the South (headquarters of Continental Air Command).

Warren, 42 31N 83 02W, pop(1980) 161,134, city in Macomb county, SE Michigan, United States; suburb 20 km N of Detroit; railway.

Warren, 41 14N 80 49W, pop(1980) 56,629, county seat of Trumbull county, NE Ohio, United States; 21 km NW of Youngstown; railway.

Warrenpoint, AN POINTE (Gael), 54 06N 6 15W, pop(1981) 4,798, seaport in Newry and Mourne dist, Down, SE Northern Ireland; situated near the head of Carlingford Lough, 10 km SE of Newry; economy: textiles; a seaport for Newry and a tourist centre for the Mourne Mts.

Warrington *wor'-*, 53 24N 2 37W, pop(1981) 82,522, town in Warrington dist, Cheshire, NW central England; on the R Mersey, 25 km SW of Manchester; designated a 'new town' in 1968; railway; economy: brewing, tanning, wire, chemicals, soap.

Warrnambool', 38 23S 142 03E, pop(1983e) 26,690, city in South Western stat div, SW Victoria, Australia; on the coast, 263 km WSW of Melbourne; railway; airfield; former whaling town; economy: woollens, clothing, dairy produce, tourism; monument: Flagstaff Hill Maritime Village restored seaport.

Warsaw, capital of Poland. See Warszawa.

Warszawa *var-shav'a*, GREATER WARSAW (Eng), voivodship in E central Poland; crossed SE-NW by R Wisła (Vistula); Kampinowska Forest in NW; pop(1983) 2,382,000; area 3,788 sq km; capital Warszawa (Warsaw); chief towns include Pruszków, Otwock, Legionowo and Wołomin; Żelazowa Wola, 54 km W of Warszawa was the birthplace of Frédéric Chopin; Łowicz is a centre of folk art and has an open-air museum.

Warszawa, WARSCHAU (Ger), VARSHAVA (Rus), WARSAW (Eng), 52 15N 21 00E, pop(1983) 1,641,400, river port capital of Poland, on R Wisła (Vistula), in Warszawa (Greater Warsaw) voivodship; on the Mazovian plain; the mid town and old town are on the left bank of the Wisła, with parks and squares sloping down to the river bank; Praaga dist lies on the left bank; established near a castle in the 13th century the town became capital of the duchy of Mazovia in 1413 and of Poland in 1596; in 1815 Warsaw became the capital of the Russian-held kingdom of central Poland and in 1915 it was occupied by German troops; after liberation in 1918 the city was again proclaimed capital of the restored Polish state; the city was largely destroyed during World War II; the postwar reconstruction of the medieval old town was carried out following the old prewar street pattern; birthplace of Marie Curie; Polish Academy of Sciences; university (1818); technical university (1945); airport; railway; economy: steel, metallurgy, machinery, electrical engineering, clothing, food processing, pharmaceuticals, printing; monuments: restored 14th-c cathedral of St John; royal castle, former home of the Mazovian dukes; Adam Mickiewicz museum of literature; Łazienkowski palace, the summer residence of the last king of Poland; events: international book fair in May; folk fair in May; modern music festival in Sept; international Chopin piano competitions every 5 years; fête of the daily Trybuna Ludu and jazz festival in October; Warsaw poetry autumn.

Warta *var'te*, WARTHE (Ger), river in W Poland; rises 56 km NW of Kraków and flows 808 km W and N to meet the R Wisła (Vistula) on the E German frontier, SW of Debno; navigable for 407 km; tributaries include the Prosna, Wełna, Obra and Noteć rivers; the 32 km Ślesiński Canal (built in 1950) links the river with L Gopło.

Warwick *wor'ik*, 28 12S 152 00E, pop(1981) 8,853, town in Darling Downs stat div, Queensland, Australia; 162 km SW of Brisbane; on the Condamine river; railway; economy: bacon and dairy products, wool, grain; noted area for horse and cattle studs.

Warwick, parish in the Bermuda Islands; pop(1980) 6,948.

Warwick, 52 17N 1 34W, pop(1981) 21,990, county town in Warwick dist, central England; on the N bank of the R Avon, 15 km SW of Coventry; founded in 914 and partly destroyed by fire in 1694; railway; economy: agriculture, engineering, carpets, tourism; monuments: 14th-c Warwick castle, Lord Leycester hospital (1383).

Warwick, 41 42N 71 28W, pop(1980) 87,123, summer resort in Kent county, E Rhode Island, United States; on Narragansett Bay at the mouth of the R Providence, 16 km S of Providence.

Warwickshire, county of central England; drained by R Avon; pop(1981) 476,315; area 1,981 sq km; county town Warwick; chief towns include Nuneaton, Royal Leamington Spa, Rugby, Stratford-upon-Avon; economy: agriculture, tourism, engineering, textiles; the county is divided into 5 districts:

District	*area (sq km)*	*pop(1981)*
North Warwickshire	286	59,929
Nuneaton and Bedworth	79	114,011
Rugby	356	86,632
Stratford-upon-Avon	977	101,148
Warwick	283	114,595

Wash, The, an inlet of the North Sea on the E coast of England; situated between Norfolk (S) and Lincolnshire (W and N); the Welland, Witham, Nene and Ouse rivers drain into the Wash which is bounded by a low marshy coast.

Washington, 54 54N 1 31W, pop(1981) 48,832, industrial town in Sunderland borough, Tyne and Wear, NE England; part of Chester-le-Street-Washington urban area; 9 km W of Sunderland; designated a 'new town' in 1964; economy: electronics, chemicals, textiles, vehicles, electrical goods, engineering.

Washington, 38 54N 77 02W, pop(1980) 638,333, capital of the United States of America, co-extensive with the District of Columbia, E United States; situated between Maryland and Virginia, on the E bank of the R Potomac at its junction with the R Anacostia; 5 universities; the legislative, administrative, and judicial centre of the United States; the Federal government provides most of the city's employment; in 1790 rivalry between northern and southern states over the location of the country's capital was ended by the agreement to build it on the R Potomac; the exact spot was chosen by President Washington, and planned by Major Pierre L'Enfant; occupied by the Federal government in 1800; Washington was sacked and burned by the British in 1814; in 1871 the city lost its charter and with the absorption of Georgetown in 1878 it became coterminous with the District of Columbia; monuments: the White House, home of the US president; the Senate and House of Representatives in the Capitol, Library of Congress, the Pentagon (US military centre), the Federal Bureau of Investigation Building, the Supreme Court Building, Washington Monument, Lincoln Memorial, Thomas Jefferson Memorial, National Gallery of Art, Smithsonian Institution buildings, John F. Kennedy Center for the Performing Arts; Arlington national cemetery; railway (Union Station); 2 airports (Washington National, Dulles).

Washington, state in NW United States; bounded N by Canada (British Columbia), NW by the Strait of Juan de Fuca, W by the Pacific Ocean, S by Oregon (mostly along the Columbia river) and E by Idaho; drained by the Columbia, Snake, Okanogan, Sanpoil and Yakima rivers; in the NW of the state, S of the Strait of Juan de Fuca, is the Olympic Peninsula with the Olympic Mts, part of the Coast Ranges, rising to 2,428 m at Mt Olympus; to the E of the Olympic Peninsula is Puget Sound, an inlet of the Pacific Ocean which extends c.160 km inland and contains numerous bays and islands; the Cascade Range runs N-S through the middle of the state; mountainous and forested country lies to the W, dry and arid land to the E; rises to 4,395 m at Mt Rainier; in the S is Mount St Helens volcano which erupted in May 1980; in the N of the state is the North Cascades National Park; economy: agricultural products include apples (Washington produces the USA's largest crop), wheat, livestock, dairy produce; industries include aluminium smelting, petroleum refining, food processing, aerospace; Washington's substantial Indian population (c.60,000) is largely employed in the fishing and farming industries; Washington was first settled in the late 18th century when it was part of Oregon Territory, a prosperous fur-trading area; Britain and the USA quarrelled over the region until the international boundary was fixed by treaty to lie along the 49th parallel (1846); Washington became a territory in 1853 and a state (42nd) in 1889; the railway arrived in 1887 and the state developed through its lumbering and fishing industries; Seattle became an important outfitting point during the Alaskan gold rush of 1897-99; Mokah, Quinault, Yakima, Spokane and Colville Indian reservations are located within the state; also known as the 'Evergreen State'; pop(1980) 4,132,156; area 172,929 sq km; capital Olympia; major cities are Seattle, Tacoma, Edmonds and Bellingham; the state is divided into 39 counties:

County	*area (sq km)*	*pop(1980)*
Adams	4,995	13,267
Asotin	1,651	16,823
Benton	4,459	109,444
Chelan	7,582	45,061
Clallam	4,558	51,648
Clark	1,630	192,227
Columbia	2,249	4,057
Cowlitz	2,964	79,548
Douglas	4,724	22,144
Ferry	5,720	5,811
Franklin	3,232	35,025
Garfield	1,836	2,468
Grant	6,916	48,522
Grays Harbour	4,987	66,314
Island	551	44,048
Jefferson	4,693	15,965
King	5,533	1,269,749
Kitsap	1,022	147,152
Kittitas	6,001	24,877
Klickitat	4,888	15,822
Lewis	6,263	56,025
Lincoln	6,006	9,604
Mason	2,499	31,184
Okanogan	13,731	30,639
Pacific	2,361	17,237
Pend Oreille	3,640	8,580
Pierce	4,355	485,643
San Juan	465	7,838
Skagit	4,511	64,138
Skamania	4,347	7,919
Snohomish	5,455	337,720
Spokane	4,581	341,835
Stevens	6,422	28,979
Thurston	1,890	124,264
Wahkiakum	679	3,832
Walla Walla	3,279	47,435
Whatcom	5,525	106,701
Whitman	5,593	40,103
Yakima	11,146	172,508

Wāsit, governorate in E central Iraq, bounded NE by Iran; pop(1977) 415,140; area 17,922 sq km; capital Al Kūt; part of the R Tigris lowland.

Wasserkuppe *vah'sur-koo-pu*, 50 30N 9 58E, mountain in E Hessen (Hesse) prov, W Germany; highest peak (950 m) of the Hohe Rhön range.

Waterbury, 41 33N 73 03W, pop(1980) 103,266, town in New Haven county, W Connecticut, United States; on the R Naugatuck, 38 km SW of Hartford; railway; economy: brass.

Waterford, PHORT LÁIRGE (Gael), county in Munster prov, S Irish Republic; bounded S by Atlantic Ocean with coastal inlets at Youghal, Dungarvan, Tramore and Waterford; Knockmealdown Mts rise in the W; watered by Suir and Barrow rivers; area 1,839 sq km; pop(1981) 88,591; apple growing region: popular resorts such as Tramore are situated on the S coast.

Waterford, 52 15N 7 06W, pop(1981) 39,636, seaport, county borough and capital of Waterford county, Munster, S Irish Republic; on R Suir at its mouth on Waterford harbour; technical college; railway; economy: shipyards, food processing, footwear, glass and crystal; monuments: remains of city walls, cathedral (1793), Blackfriars priory (1226); event: light opera festival in Sept.

Waterloo, 43 28N 80 32W, pop(1981) 49,428, town in S Ontario, S Canada; a twin city with Kitchener; settled in the early 1800s by German settlers, the area is still populated by Amish and Mennonite farmers; Wilfred Larier University (1911); University of Waterloo (1959); railway; economy: rubber, furniture, leather, textiles, foodstuffs.

Waterloo, 42 30N 92 21W, pop(1980) 75,985, county seat of Black Hawk county, E Iowa, United States; on the R Cedar, 83 km NW of Cedar Rapids; railway; economy: machinery and fabricated metals; soybean processing.

Waterlooville, 50 53N 1 02W, pop(1981) 57,493, town in Hampshire, S England; part of Portsmouth urban area; 11 km NE of Portsmouth.

Watertown, 43 59N 75 55W, pop(1980) 27,861, county seat of Jefferson county, NW New York, United States; on the Black river, 16 km E of L Ontario; railway.

Watford *wot'furd*, 51 40N 0 25W, pop(1981) 74,462, in Greater London urban area and Watford dist, Hertfordshire, SE England; 26 km NW of London; railway; economy: electronics, engineering, printing.

Watzmann *vahts'mahn*, 47 33N 12 55E, mountain in the Berchtesgadener Alpen (Berchtesgaden Alps), Oberbayern dist, SE Bayern (Bavaria) prov, W Germany; height 2,713 m.

Waukegan *wō-kee'gen* (Algonquian, 'old fort'), 42 22N 87 50W, pop(1980) 67,653, county seat of Lake county, NE Illinois, United States; port on L Michigan, 64 km N of Chicago and 16 km S of Wisconsin border; railway; nearby is the Great Lakes Naval Training Centre.

Waukesha *waw'ki-shaw* (Potawatomi, 'crooked river'), 43 01N 88 14W, pop(1980) 50,319, county seat of Waukesha county, SE Wisconsin, United States; on the R Fox, 24 km W of Milwaukee; railway.

Wausau *waw'saw* (Algonquian, 'far away'), 44 58N 89 38W, pop(1980) 32,426, county seat of Marathon county, N central Wisconsin, United States; on the R Wisconsin, 134 km WNW of Green Bay; railway.

Wauwatosa *waw-we-tō'za* (Algonquian, 'firefly'), 43 03N 88 00W, pop(1980) 51,308, town in Milwaukee county, SE Wisconsin, United States; a W suburb of Milwaukee on the R Menomonee.

Wave Rock, unique rock formation in S central Western Australia; near the town of Hyden; estimated to be 2,700 million years old; wave-shaped granite formation eroded by water and wind.

Waveney *wayv'ni*, river rising SW of Diss in Norfolk, E England; flows 80 km NE and N through the Norfolk Broads and along the border with Suffolk to meet the R Yare at the W end of Breydon Water.

Waverley, 37 45S 144 58E, pop(1983e) 129,400, suburb of Melbourne, Victoria, Australia.

Wa'za, national park in Nord prov, Cameroon, W Africa; 140 km N of Maroua by road; area 1,700 sq km; established in 1968; wildlife includes elephant, giraffe, antelope, guineafowl, ostrich and numerous other birds.

Wazirabad *vu-zee-rah-bad'*, 32 23N 74 10E, pop(1981) 63,000, town in NE Punjab prov, Pakistan; 30 km NNW of Gujranwala and 97 km N of Lahore on the R Chenab; railway.

Weald, The *weeld*, area in Kent, Surrey and Sussex, SE England; situated between the North and South Downs, this fertile agricultural area, growing fruit, vegetables and hops, was formerly noted for its extensive woodlands (part of the ancient forest of Anderida) which were used to provide charcoal for the iron industry in the Middle Ages; often refers strictly to the area in Kent SW of the greensand ridge which runs from Hythe, through Ashford to Westerham.

Weddell Sea *wed'el*, arm of the Atlantic Ocean, lying to the SE of Argentina and S of the Scotia Sea in W Antarctica; bounded by the Antarctic Peninsula to the W (British territory, but claimed by Argentina), Coats Land to the E, with the South Orkney and Sandwich Islands to the N; vast Ronne and Filchener ice-shelves cover the S extent of the sea, while calving produces icebergs; the seawater underlying the ice is much more saline; named after James Weddell, who claimed to have discovered the sea in 1823, but it was first explored in 1902-04 by William Bruce, and later during International Geophysical Year in 1957-58.

Weifang *way-fang*, WEIHSIEN, 36 44N 119 10E, pop(1984e) 1,033,200, city in Shandong prov, E China; E of Jinan; railway; economy: copper wire.

Weihsien, city in Shandong prov, E China. See Weifang.

Weimar *vī'mahr*, 50 59N 11 20E, pop(1981) 63,725, town in Weimar dist, Erfurt, SW East Germany; colleges of technology, music and architecture; residence of the poets Schiller and Goethe; former Nazi concentration camp of Buchenwald is nearby; railway; economy: farm machinery, chemicals; monuments: Goethe National Museum, Liszt museum, observatory, Weimar Castle, Belvedere Castle (18th-c).

Welega, WALAGA *we-lay'ge*, mountainous region in W Ethiopia, NE Africa; pop(1984e) 2,369,677; area 71,200 sq km; capital Nekemte; chief towns include Dembī and Dolo.

Welkom *vel'kem*, 27 59S 26 44E, pop(1980) 176,608, town in Orange Free State prov, South Africa; 135 km NE of Bloemfontein; railway; economy: gold mining.

Wel'land, 42 59N 79 14W, pop(1981) 45,448, town in SE Ontario, SE Canada; on the Welland Ship Canal, linking L Erie and L Huron; railway; economy: steel, paper.

Welland, river rising SW of Market Harborough, Leicestershire, central England; flows 112 km NE along the border with Northamptonshire and through the Lincolnshire fens to meet the Wash S of Boston.

Welland Ship Canal, canal in Ontario, E Canada; links L Erie and L Ontario; length 61 km; capable of being used by vessels up to 223 m in length.

Wellingborough *wel'ing-bur-u*, 52 19N 0 42W, pop(1981) 38,772, town in Wellingborough dist, Northamptonshire, central England; at the junction of the Ise and Nene rivers, 16 km NE of Northampton; railway; economy: footwear, light engineering.

Wellington, 41 17S 174 47E, pop(1981) 135,688, capital city and seat of government of New Zealand; on the S coast of North Island, on Port Nicholson shore, an inlet of the Cook Strait; founded in 1840; capital since 1865; the town is hemmed in by hills, but has expanded on land reclaimed from the sea; university (1897); ferry (from Wellington to Picton, South Island); railway; airport; economy: motor vehicles, footwear, chemicals, soap, metal products, trade in dairy produce, meat; monuments: the government building is the largest wooden building in the S hemisphere; its marble parliament buildings (1922) are adjacent to the modern hexagonal parliament, built in 1980 and known as 'the Beehive'; General Assembly library (1897); the national art gallery; War Memorial museum; St Paul's cathedral (1866); the recently completed Michael Fowler Centre is the venue for many cultural events; the national museum displays New Zealand's early colonial history.

Wells, 51 13N 2 39W, pop(1981) 9,560, market town in Mendip dist, Somerset, SW England; S of the Mendip Hills and 24 km S of Bristol; economy: electronics, printing, animal foodstuffs, engineering; monuments: 12th-c cathedral, 13th-c Bishop's palace, 15th-c church of St Cuthbert.

Welo, WALLO, region in E Ethiopia, NE Africa; pop(1984e) 3,609,918; area 79,400 sq km; part of the Danakil Depression lies to the NE; capital Desē.

Wels *vels*, OVILALA (anc), 48 10N 14 02E, pop(1981) 51,060, industrial and agric capital of Wels-land dist, Oberösterreich, N Austria; SW of Linz, on the R Traun; monument: the Stadtplatz including some fine baroque buildings and one of the towers of the old town wall; event: Wels International Agricultural Fair (beginning of Sept in even-numbered years).

Welwyn Garden City *we'lin*, 51 48N 0 13W, pop(1981) 41,102, town in Hatfield dist, Hertfordshire, SE England; 10 km NE of St Albans; designated a 'new town' in 1948; railway; economy: chemicals, plastics, pharmaceuticals, food processing.

Wenchi *wen'chee*, 7 45N 2 02W, town in Brong-Ahafo region, W central Ghana, W Africa; 120 km NNE of Kumasi.

Wenzhou *wen-jō*, 28 00N 120 38E, pop(1984e) 519,100, city in Zhejiang prov, E China; on the Qu Jiang river, near the East China Sea; became a trading port after the Sino-British Treaty of Yantai in 1876; a special economic zone; economy: textiles, medicine, agricultural trade.

Werra *ve'ru*, river in E and W Germany; rises in the Thüringer Wald (Thuringian Forest) in E Germany, 8 km N of Eisfeld; flows generally N to Münden, where it joins the R Fulda to form the R Weser; length 292 km; navigable length 89 km; drainage basin area 1,417 sq km.

Wesel *vay'zel*, 51 39N 6 37E, pop(1983) 55,700, industrial town in Düsseldorf dist, Nordrhein-Westfalen (North Rhine-Westphalia) prov, W Germany; on the R Rhine at the mouth of the Lippe, 78 km WSW of Münster; railway; economy: machinery, timber, cement.

Weser *vay'zer*, VISURGIS (anc), river in W Germany; one of Germany's major rivers; formed by the confluence of the Werra and Fulda rivers at Münden in S Niedersachsen (Lower Saxony) prov; flows generally N past Minden and Bremen to the North Sea forming an estuary at Wesermünde below Bremerhaven; length 440 km; navigable length 440 km; drainage basin area 41,094 sq km; chief tributaries Diemel, Hunte and Aller.

Weser-Ems *vay'zer ems*, dist of W Niedersachsen (Lower Saxony) prov, W Germany; pop(1983) 2,122,300; area 14,965 sq km.

West Allis, 43 01N 88 00W, pop(1980) 63,982, city in Milwaukee county, SE Wisconsin, United States; residential suburb 9 km WSW of Milwaukee; railway.

West Bank, region of Jordan, W of the R Jordan and the Dead Sea; comprises the Jordanian governorates of Jerusalem, Hebron, and Nablus; from 1949 to 1967 Jordan administered this part of the former mandate of Palestine; during the 1967 war the area was seized by Israel and remains today under Israeli occupation, administered as the dist of Judea-Samaria.

West Bengal *beng-gol'*, state in NE India; pop(1981) 54,485,560; area 87,853 sq km; bounded N by Bhutan and Sikkim state, NW by Nepal, W by Bihar state, E by Bangladesh, SW by Orissa state and S by the Bay of Bengal; there are 3 administrative divisions and 16 districts; capital Calcutta; governed by a 295-member Legislative Assembly; the state is crossed by numerous rivers including the Ganga (Ganges), Hugli, Matla, Guasaba, Damodar, Bhagrathi, Yasai and the Nagar; over 13% of the land area is covered by forest; the majority of the population is employed in agriculture, with some 74% of the land under cultivation, largely producing paddy rice; other important crops include foodgrains, oilseed and jute; one-third of the cultivated area is irrigated; the Raniganj coalfield is the 3rd largest in India; manufacturing industries produce aluminium, steel and fertilizer; Calcutta is the major port of the state; a second port is under construction at Haldia for shipment of bulk cargoes; there is an extensive rail network with junctions at Hāora, Asansol, Kharagpur, New Jalpaiguri and Calcutta; the state of West Bengal was created in 1947 when the Indian Independence Act divided the former prov of Bengal between the new state of West Bengal and the Muslim majority districts of East Bengal which became part of East Pakistan (now Bangladesh); in Jan 1950 Cooch-Behar state was merged with West Bengal and in Oct 1954 Chandernagore joined the state; sections of the state of Bihar were incorporated into the state of West Bengal in 1956 under the States Reorganisation Act.

West Bridgford, 52 56N 1 08W, pop(1981) 27,506, town in Rushcliffe dist, Nottinghamshire, central England; S of Nottingham and the R Trent; railway; economy: engineering.

West Bromwich *-brom'ich*, 52 31N 1 59W, pop(1981) 154,531, town in Sandwell borough, West Midlands, central England; 8 km NW of Birmingham; railway; economy: coal, metal goods; monument: 16-17th-c half-timbered Oak House.

West Covina *kō-veeñh*, 34 04N 117 56W, pop(1980) 80,291, city in Los Angeles county, SW California, United States; 29 km E of Los Angeles.

West Glamorgan, county in S Wales; bounded W by Dyfed, NE by Powys, E by Mid Glamorgan and S by the Bristol Channel; pop(1981) 367,598; area 817 sq km; capital Swansea; economy: steel, coal, tinplate, aluminium, chemicals; created in 1974, the county is divided into 4 districts:

District	*area (sq km)*	*pop(1981)*
Afan	151	54,637
Lliw Valley	214	59,800
Neath	206	66,572
Swansea	245	186,589

West Haven, 41 17N 72 57W, pop(1980) 53,184, town in New Haven county, S Connecticut, United States; suburb of New Haven, on R West; university (1920); railway.

West Highland Way, long-distance footpath in Scotland; stretching from Milngavie near Glasgow to Fort William; length 158 km; opened in 1980.

West Indies, a large archipelago (c.2,700 km in length) separating the Gulf of Mexico and the Caribbean Sea from the Atlantic Ocean, stretching between the coasts of Florida and Venezuela; about 1,200 islands, mainly volcanic or coral, which are divided into 3 main groups: the Bahamas and the Greater and Lesser Antilles; area c.177,000 km, the main part formed by Cuba, Hispaniola, Jamaica, Puerto Rico and Trinidad; on its discovery in 1492 by Columbus, the archipelago was so-named in the belief that the route west to India had been found; former colonial possessions of Britain, the Netherlands, Spain, France, USA and Venezuela, the islands are now largely autonomous dependencies, Crown colonies or independent republics; between 1958 and 1962 the British West Indies, comprising Antigua, Barbados, Dominica, Grenada, Jamaica, Montserrat, St Kitts-Nevis-Anguilla, St Lucia, St Vincent, Trinidad and Tobago, formed the Federation of the West Indies, whose parliament sat at Port-of-Spain.

West Jordan, 40 37N 111 56W, pop(1980) 27,192, town in Salt Lake county, N Utah, United States; a suburb 16 km S of Salt Lake City.

West Memphis, 35 09N 90 11W, pop(1980) 28,138, town in Crittenden county, E Arkansas, United States; 13 km W of Memphis, Tennessee; railway; economy: timber and cotton.

West Midlands, metropolitan county of central England; bounded N and W by Staffordshire, E and S by Warwickshire and SW by Hereford and Worcester; pop(1981) 2,648,939; area 899 sq km; county town Birmingham; other chief towns include Wolverhampton, West Bromwich, Coventry and Walsall; economy: vehicles, aircraft, engineering; the metropolitan council was abolished in 1986; the county is divided into 7 boroughs:

Borough	*area (sq km)*	*pop(1981)*
Birmingham	264	1,006,527
Coventry	97	313,815
Dudley	98	299,741
Sandwell	86	307,992
Solihull	180	199,261
Walsall	106	267,042
Wolverhampton	69	254,561

West Mifflin, 40 22N 79 52W, pop(1980) 26,279, town in Allegheny county, SW Pennsylvania, United States; on the R Monongahela, 10 km SE of Pittsburgh; railway.

West New York, 40 40N 74 01W, pop(1980) 39,194, town in Union county, NE New Jersey, United States; on the Hudson river, 6 km N of Jersey City.

West Orange, 40 47N 74 14W, pop(1980) 39,510, town in Essex county, NE New Jersey, United States; residential suburb 8 km NW of Newark; after 1887, the home of Thomas A. Edison, inventor of the electric light-bulb.

West Palm Beach, 26 43N 80 03W, pop(1980) 63,305,

county seat of Palm Beach county, SE Florida, United States; on L Worth (a lagoon), 100 km N of Miami; railway; connected by bridges to Palm Beach; research and production centre for aeronautics and electronics.

West Sussex, county of S England; bounded S by the English Channel, E by East Sussex, N by Surrey and W by Hampshire; drained by the Adur and Arun rivers; the South Downs run parallel to the coast; pop(1981) 661,847; area 1,989 sq km; county town Chichester; other major towns include Worthing, Crawley, Horsham; economy: agriculture, horticulture, tourism, electronics, light engineering; the county is divided into 7 districts:

District	*area (sq km)*	*pop(1981)*
Adur	42	58,316
Arun	221	119,625
Chichester	787	98,035
Crawley	36	73,376
Horsham	533	101,396
Mid Sussex	338	119,043
Worthing	33	92,056

West Virginia, state in E United States; bounded W by Kentucky and Ohio, N by Pennsylvania and Maryland, and E and S by Virginia; the R Ohio follows the Ohio state border, and receives several tributaries flowing W through the state; the R Potomac forms part of N border; the Allegheny Mts dominate the E part of the state; the highest point is Mt Spruce Knob (1,481 m); a rugged, hilly state, most of which is in the Allegheny Plateau; highest mean altitude of any state E of the Mississippi; 65% of the state is forested; agriculture is not a major industry, but products include cattle, dairy products, apples, eggs, corn and tobacco; the state is the nation's leading producer of bituminous coal, a major producer of natural gas; additional natural resources include stone, cement, salt and oil; the chief manufactures are glass, chemicals, primary and fabricated metals, and machinery; tourism is a major industry in both summer and winter (skiing); West Virginia was part of the state of Virginia until the Civil War when the area remained loyal to the Union and split from Confederate E Virginia in 1861; 35th state admitted to the Union as the state of West Virginia in 1863; known as the 'Mountain State'; pop(1980) 1,949,644; area 62,709 sq km; capital Charleston; other chief cities are Huntington, Wheeling, Parkersburg and Morgantown; the state is divided into 55 counties:

County	*area (sq km)*	*pop(1980)*
Barbour	892	16,639
Berkeley	835	46,775
Boone	1,308	30,447
Braxton	1,334	13,894
Brooke	234	31,117
Cabell	733	106,835
Calhoun	728	8,250
Clay	900	11,265
Doddridge	835	7,433
Fayette	1,734	57,863
Gilmer	884	8,334
Grant	1,248	10,210
Greenbrier	2,665	37,665
Hampshire	1,674	14,867
Hancock	218	40,418
Hardy	1,521	10,030
Harrison	1,084	77,710
Jackson	1,206	25,794
Jefferson	543	30,302
Kanawha	2,343	231,414
Lewis	1,011	18,813
Lincoln	1,141	23,675
Logan	1,186	50,679
Marion	811	65,789
Marshall	793	41,608

contd

County	*area (sq km)*	*pop(1980)*
Mason	1,126	27,045
McDowell	1,391	49,899
Mercer	1,092	73,942
Mineral	855	27,234
Mingo	1,102	37,336
Monongalia	944	75,024
Monroe	1,230	12,873
Morgan	598	10,711
Nicholas	1,690	28,126
Ohio	276	61,389
Pendleton	1,815	7,910
Pleasants	341	8,236
Pocahontas	2,449	9,919
Preston	1,693	30,460
Putnam	900	38,181
Raleigh	1,581	86,821
Randolph	2,704	28,734
Ritchie	1,180	11,442
Roane	1,258	15,952
Summers	918	15,875
Taylor	452	16,584
Tucker	1,095	8,675
Tyler	671	11,320
Upshur	923	23,427
Wayne	1,321	46,021
Webster	1,446	12,245
Wetzel	933	21,874
Wirt	611	4,922
Wood	954	93,648
Wyoming	1,305	35,993

West Yorkshire, metropolitan county of N England; bounded N and E by North Yorkshire, W by Lancashire, SW by Greater Manchester and S by Derbyshire and South Yorkshire; drained by the Aire and Calder rivers; pop(1981) 2,037,165; area 2,039 sq km; county town Wakefield; chief towns include Leeds, Bradford, Huddersfield, Halifax; economy: textiles, coal, engineering, machinery, machine tools; the county is divided into 5 boroughs:

Borough	*area (sq km)*	*pop(1981)*
Bradford	370	457,423
Calderdale	364	191,122
Kirklees	410	371,955
Leeds	562	704,885
Wakefield	333	311,780

Western, coastal region in SW Ghana, W Africa; pop(1984) 1,116,930; area 24,214 sq km; the R Tano flows S from its source in the Brong-Ahafo region to form the SW border with the Ivory Coast; the R Ankobra flows S from its source near Awaso and the R Pra flowing S cuts across the SE corner of the region; capital Sekondi-Takoradi; chief towns Awaso, Axim, Tarkwa, Enchi, Antubia and Prestea; Bia national park located in NW corner of region; economy: gold, aluminium, iron ore, diamond and limestone mining; gold, cement and manganese processing; oil.

Western Australia, state in W Australia; bounded E by Northern Territory and South Australia, S by the Great Australian Bight, W by the Indian Ocean and N by the Timor Sea; accounts for one-third of the total area of Australia; over 90% of Western Australia is occupied by the Great Plateau at a mean alt of 600 m above sea-level; in the NW it reaches 1,244 m at Mount Meharry in the Hamersley Range; in the E are the Great Sandy Desert, the Gibson Desert, the Great Victoria Desert and the Nullarbor Plain; to the N of the Great Sandy Desert, near the border with Northern Territory, is Wolf Crater, the world's 2nd largest meteorite crater; there are many dry salt lakes in the interior including Lake Lefroy near

Kalgoorlie and Lake McLeod near Port Hedland; groups of 100 or more islands off the coast include the Bonaparte and Buccaneer Archipelago (N), the Dampier Archipelago (NW) and the Recherche Archipelago (S); principal rivers include the Swan, Avon, Blackwood, Gascoyne, Drysdale, Murchison, Ashburton and Fitzroy; pop(1986) 1,496,059; area 2,525,500 sq km; capital Perth; principal towns: Port Hedland, Busselton, Albany, Kalgoorlie and Carnarvon; economy: fishing, wheat, sheep, gold (Kalgoorlie), iron ore (Newman), nickel, uranium, bauxite, mineral sands, superphosphates, oil and gas, agricultural machinery; the Dutch navigator Dirk Hartog landed here in 1616 and left a plaque commemorating the first landing on Australian soil by a European; in 1829 Capt James Stirling arrived to found Britain's first non-convict settlement on the R Swan; Western Australia has a bicameral parliament comprising a 55-member Legislative Assembly and a 32-member Legislative Council; state holidays: Labour Day (March), Foundation Day (June); there are 138 local government authorities; the state of Western Australia is divided into 9 statistical divisions:

Statistical division	*area (sq km)*	*pop(1981)*
Central	753,365	50,820
Kimberley	421,451	17,940
Lower Great Southern	40,528	44,040
Midlands	110,262	49,800
Perth	5,363	922,040
Pilbara	510,335	46,630
South-Eastern	614,388	43,260
South-West	26,661	101,880
Upper Great Southern	45,684	23,650

Western Isles, region in Scotland; group of islands off the W coast of Scotland; separated from the Scottish mainland by the Minch and Little Minch; bounded W by the Atlantic Ocean; the islands cover approx 209 km N-S, from the Butt of Lewis (N) to Barra Head (S); pop(1981) 31,884; area 2,898 sq km; capital Stornoway, on Lewis; chief islands: Lewis, North Uist, Benbecula, South Uist and Barra; economy: fishing, cattle and sheep raising, Harris tweed; the name, the Western Isles, is often used to refer to both the Inner and Outer Hebrides; the Hebrides became part of the Kingdom of Scotland in 1266, when they were ceded to Alexander III by Magnus of Norway.

Western Sahara, a former Spanish prov in NW Africa, between Morocco (N) and Mauritania (S) and bounded NE by Algeria; area 252,126 sq km; pop(1982) 163,868; since 1979 the country has been divided into the provs of La'youn, Oued Eddahab, Es-Semara and Boujdour; chief town La'youn; presently administered by Morocco, the country was partitioned by Morocco and Mauritania after its status as a Spanish prov came to an end in 1975; in 1979 Mauritania withdrew from the area it had occupied and Morocco gained control of the whole area; the partition of Western Sahara was opposed by the independence movement *Frente Polisario* which named the former prov the Democratic Saharan Republic; Saharan guerillas operate from within Algeria which also opposed partition; the area is rich in phosphate deposits.

Western Samoa *sa-mō'a*, official name The Independent State of Western Samoa, territory in the SW Pacific Ocean, between 13° and 15° S and between 171° and 173° W, 2,575 km NE of Auckland, New Zealand; comprising 2 large and several smaller islands; area 2,842 sq km; pop(1981) 158,130, timezone GMT −11; capital Apia; no other major towns; most people live in some 400 coastal villages, whose populations range from 100 to over 2,000; annual population growth rate 2.9% (1975); Samoans are the 2nd largest Polynesian group (after the Maoris of New Zealand) and speak a Polynesian dialect; there are also small groups of Euronesians (people of mixed European and Polynesian blood), other Pacific islanders, Chinese, and Europeans; the Samoans are Christians; the currency is the Western Samoan dollar (tala) of 100 cents; national holiday 1 Jan (Independence Day); membership: UN, South Pacific Forum, South Pacific Commission, Commonwealth, ADB, ESCAP, FAO, G-77, IBRD, IDA, IFAD, IFC, IMF, UN, WHO.

Physical description. Western Samoa comprises the 4 inhabited islands of Upolu, Savai'i, Apolima, and Manono, and the uninhabited islands of Fanuatapu, Nuutele, Nuula and Nuusafee. The main islands are formed from ranges of extinct volcanoes which rise to 1,829 m on Savai'i and 1,097 m on Upolu. The terrain is rugged and mountainous with many dormant volcanoes and old lava fields (the last period of volcanic activity was between 1905 and 1911). Of the numerous streams and rivers, the most important are the Sili, Faleata, Alia Senga in Savai'i and the Vaisingano in Upolu. Thick tropical vegetation covers much of the area and considerable parts of the coastline are fringed with coral reefs.

Climate. The climate is tropical with 2 seasons. The cooler and drier months are from May to Nov, when the fresh trade winds blow, while the rainy season extends from Dec to April. Temperatures normally range from 22°C to 30°C. Annual rainfall averages about 2,775 mm. Hurricanes occur from time to time, most recently in 1968 when property and crops were severely damaged.

History, government and constitution. First visited by Europeans in 1772 when the Dutch navigator Jacob Roggeveen landed here. Towards the end of the 19th century Germany, Britain and the USA gained privileges in Western Samoa. A commission of 1889 divided Samoa between Germany, which acquired Western Samoa, and the USA, which acquired the island of Tutuila and adjacent small islands now known as American Samoa. In 1919 New Zealand was granted a League of Nations mandate for Samoa and in 1946 the islands became a UN Trust Territory under New Zealand administration. On 1 Jan 1962, Western Samoa became an independent sovereign state, assisted by New Zealand in the field of foreign relations. The 1962 Constitution is based on the British pattern of parliamentary democracy, with modifications to take Samoan customs into account. It provides for a head of state to be elected by the legislative assembly for a term of 5 years. The Legislative Assembly which, with the head of state, constitutes the parliament, comprises 47 members, of whom 45 are elected by local chiefs (*matai*) on a territorial basis for a 3-year period, and 2 are elected by universal adult suffrage. The head of state appoints a prime minister, who must be an elected member of the Legislative Assembly. There are no political parties in Western Samoa.

Economy. Agriculture, mainly of subsistence type, forms the basis of Western Samoa's economy. Chief subsistence crops include taro, yams, breadfruit, and pawpaws. More than half the land is too rugged for agricultural use. Over 80% of all Samoan land is controlled by the *matai* or chiefs, and although soil and climatic conditions enable a large range of tropical and sub-tropical crops to be grown, traditional farming methods are favoured to more intensive, export-orientated agriculture. The 3 principal cash crops, and main exports, are coconuts, cocoa, and bananas, the chief markets being New Zealand and Japan. There are no mineral resources of commercial value and manufacturing industries are few in number. Tourism is making a growing contribution to the national economy and a Handicrafts Industry Development Corporation encourages local craft work. Principal imports are food, manufactured goods, machinery, and transport equipment, and Western Samoa's main trading partners are New Zealand, Australia, UK, Japan, Netherlands, and W Germany. More than 70% of the labour force are employed in agriculture, between 4-5% in manufacturing and construction, and approx 25% in the service sector.

Communications. The internal transportation system depends largely on roads and island-to-island ferries, and a charter air service is in operation between the 2 main islands. There are no railways. The principal ports are Apia on Upolu I, and the port of Asau, on the NW coast of Savai'i, which is used largely for timber exports. Faleolo Airport, 37 km W of Apia, is the principal airport and receives international flights from American Samoa, Fiji, Niue, and Tonga.

Administrative divisions. Western Samoa is divided into 24 districts for the purposes of local government.

Westerschelde, WESTERN SCHELDT *-skelt* (Eng), estuary of the R Schelde, in Zeeland prov, W Netherlands; formed where the river enters the Netherlands from Belgium, 14 km SSW of Bergen-op-Zoom; flows W past Terneuzen, Vlissingen and Breskens, to the North Sea; length 72 km.

Westerwald *ve'stur-vahlt*, mountainous range in W Hessen (Hesse), NE Rheinland-Pfalz (Rhineland-Palatinate) and SE Nordrhein-Westfalen (North Rhine-Westphalia) provs, W Germany; extending E of the R Rhine between the Sieg (N) and Lahn (S) rivers; highest peak is the Fuchskauten (656 m); geologically considered part of the Rheinisches Schiefergebirge (Rhenish Slate Mountains).

Westfield, 42 07N 72 45W, pop(1980) 36,465, town in Hampden county, SW Massachusetts, United States; on the R Westfield, 13 km W of Springfield; railway.

Westfield, 40 39N 74 21W, pop(1980) 30,447, residential town in Union county, NE New Jersey, United States; 11 km W of Elizabeth; railway.

Westland, national park, E South Island, New Zealand; joins the Mt Cook National Park along the main divide of the Southern Alps; it features glaciers, mountains, lakes and forest, and includes the Fox and Franz Josef glaciers and L Matheson; area 1,175 sq km; established in 1961.

Westland, 42 18N 83 23W, pop(1980) 84,603, town in Wayne county, SE Michigan, United States; 28 km W of Detroit.

Westman Islands, Iceland. See Vestmannaeyjar.

Westmeath *west'meeTH*, NA H-IARMHIDHE (Gael), county in Leinster prov, central Irish Republic; bounded on SW by R Shannon; crossed by Royal Canal; pop(1981) 61,523; area 1,764 sq km; capital Mullingar.

Westminster, 33 47N 118 00W, pop(1980) 71,133, city in Orange county, SW California, United States; 16 km E of Long Beach.

Westminster, 39 50N 105 02W, pop(1980) 50,211, city in Adams county, N central Colorado, United States; a residential suburb 10 km NNW of Denver.

Westminster, City of, 51 30N 0 09W, pop(1981) 191,098, borough of central Greater London, England; N of the R Thames; includes Hyde Park, St James's Park, Green Park and the suburbs of Paddington, Westminster and Marylebone; administrative centre of the United Kingdom; early Statutes of Westminster (1275, 1285, 1290) laid the foundations for the development of English law, and the Westminster Confession of Faith, produced in the Long Parliament of 1643-49, is a statement of Presbyterian theology; monuments: Houses of Parliament, Westminster Hall, Abbey of Westminster (burial place of 18 English sovereigns), Buckingham Palace, St James's Palace, Royal Albert Hall, Tate Gallery, National Gallery, the Cenotaph, Nelson's Column, Royal Academy.

West'morland, former county of NW England; part of Cumbria since 1974.

Weston-super-Mare *-soo-per-mayr'*, 51 21N 2 59W, pop(1981) 62,261, resort town in Woodspring dist, Avon, SW England; 28 km SW of Bristol on the Bristol Channel; railway; economy: plastics, engineering.

West-Vlaanderen *vest-vlahn'der-en*, WEST FLANDERS (Eng), FLANDRE OCCIDENTALE *flā'dre ōk-see-dāt-ahl'* (Fr), prov of W Belgium; area 3,134 sq km; pop(1982) 1,081,913; comprises the 8 dists of Brugge, Diksmuide, Ieper, Kortrijk, Oostende, Roeselare, Tielt, Veurne; capital Brugge; chief towns Oostende, Ieper and Kortrijk.

Wettersteingebirge *ve'tursh-tīn-gub-ir-gu*, mountain range in Bayern (Bavaria) prov, W Germany and Austria; range of the Bavarian Alps, extending W of the R Isar along the Austro-German border; highest peak is the Zugspitze (2,962 m); has the country's highest railway.

Wetzlar *vetz'lar*, 50 33N 8 30E, pop(1983) 50,600, town in Darmstadt dist, Hessen (Hesse) prov, W Germany; on the R Lahn near the inflow of the R Dill, 48 km N of Frankfurt am Main; railway; economy: special steel, ironworks, engineering, building materials, plastics, precision mechanics and optical instruments.

Wexford *weks'ford*, LOCH GARMAN (Gael), county in Leinster prov, SE Irish Republic; bounded by St George's Channel and Atlantic Ocean with bays at Wexford, Waterford and Bannow; Wicklow Mts rise in N and Blackstairs Mts in W; watered by R Barrow and R Slaney; pop(1981) 99,081; area 2,352 sq km; capital Wexford; Rosslare is the main seaport; rich farmland and resort area.

Wexford, 52 20N 6 27W, pop(1981) 15,364, capital of Wexford county, Leinster, Irish Republic; at the mouth of R Slaney where it meets Wexford harbour; railway; economy: machinery, motor vehicles, brewing, cheese, textiles; event: opera festival in Oct.

Wey *way*, river rising in E Hampshire, S England; flows 56 km NE past Guildford to meet the R Thames at Weybridge.

Weymouth *way'muth*, 50 36N 2 28W, pop(1981) 39,712, port and resort town in Weymouth and Portland dist, Dorset, S England; 42 km W of Bournemouth; railway; ferries to Channel Islands and France; economy: tourism, electronics, brewing.

Whangarei *(h)wang-ga-ray'*, 37 43S 174 20E, pop(1981) 36,550, city on North Island, New Zealand; N of Auckland; railway; airfield; economy: oil refining; monuments: Clapham clock museum; the spectacular Whangarei Falls; Northland regional museum.

Wharfe *worf*, river rising S of Hawes in North Yorkshire, N England; flows 96 km SE through Wharfedale, then E following the West Yorkshire border; meets the R Ouse near Cadwood, S of York.

Wheat Ridge, 39 46N 105 05W, pop(1980) 30,293, city in Jefferson county, N central Colorado, United States; a residential suburb 8 km WNW of Denver.

Wheaton, 41 52N 88 06W, pop(1980) 43,043, county seat of Du Page county, NE Illinois, United States; 40 km W of Chicago; railway.

Wheeler Peak, 36 34N 105 25W, mountain in Taos county, N New Mexico, United States; the highest peak in New Mexico; height 4,011 m.

Wheeling, 40 04N 80 43W, pop(1980) 43,070, county seat of Ohio county, N West Virginia, United States; on the R Ohio, in the N tip of the state, 75 km SW of Pittsburgh; railway; economy: commercial centre in an area rich in coal and natural gas; manufactures include steel, iron, chemicals, glass, tobacco, plastics and textiles; monuments: Fort Henry (scene of one of the last skirmishes of the Revolution in 1782), St Joseph's cathedral, Oglebay Park.

Whitburn, 55 52N 3 42W, pop(1981) 12,610, town in West Lothian dist, Lothian, central Scotland; 5 km SW of Bathgate.

Whit'by, 43 52N 78 56W, pop(1981) 36,698, port in SE Ontario, SE Canada; on the N shore of L Ontario, 45 km NE of Toronto; railway; economy: rubber.

Whitby, 54 29N 0 37W, pop(1981) 13,377, port and resort town in Scarborough dist, North Yorkshire, N England; on North Sea coast, 27 km NW of Scarborough; the Synod of Whitby in 664 affected the course of Christianity in England; former seaport and whaling station; Captain Cook sailed from here on his voyage to the Pacific in 1768; railway; economy: plastics, boatbuilding, fishing; monuments: 13th-c abbey, 12th-c St Mary's church.

White Nile, BAHR EL ABLAD, upper reach of the R Nile in S and E Sudan, NE Africa; a continuation of the Albert Nile which crosses into SE Sudan from NE Uganda at Nimule; at this point the river is called Bahr el Jebel and flows N past Juba and Bor; it then turns NW and sharply E past Tonga, flowing on to Malakal where it becomes the Bahr el Ablad; here it flows generally N past Melut, Renk, Rabak and Ed Dueim; on reaching Khartoum it is joined from the E by the Bahr el Azraq (Blue Nile), and forms the R Nile proper; the Jonglei Canal, which is part of a major irrigation project, flows between a point N of Bor, rejoining the river at Taufikia; its main tributary is the R Sobat.

White Plains, 41 02N 73 46W, pop(1980) 46,999, county seat of Westchester county, SE New York, United States; 40 km NNE of New York City; monuments: Miller Hill Restoration, Washington's headquarters; Provincial Congress ratified the Declaration of Independence here, 9 July 1776; scene of the Battle of White Plains, 28 Oct 1776.

White Russia, constituent republic of the Soviet Union. See Belorusskaya.

White Sands, a national monument surrounded by a missile testing range in S New Mexico, United States; the first nuclear explosion took place here in July 1945.

White Sea, BELOYE MORE (Rus), arm of the Arctic Ocean and inlet of the Barents Sea, lying in the NW section of European USSR, between Kol'skiy Poluostrov and Poluostrov Kanin; extended by Kandaakshskaya Guba (the deepest part of the sea), Dvinskaya Guba and Onezhskaya Guba; enclosed but for the 160 km strait between Terskiy Bereg and Zimniy Bereg, which separates the N section from the deeper S section; covers an area of approx 95,000 sq km; Belmorsk on the White Sea is connected to Leningrad on the Baltic by a 225 km long canal system which was completed in 1933; links have also been made to the Black Sea via the Dnieper, and to the Caspian Sea and to Moscow by way of the Volga; ice-breakers keep some channels of the sea open during winter to allow freight trade to be maintained; herring and cod fishing are important; discovered by Chancellor in 1553, it was the only outlet for 16th-c Muscovite trade.

Whitefield, 53 34N 2 18W, pop(1981) 27,650, town in Bury borough, Greater Manchester, NW England; 4 km S of Bury; railway; economy: textiles.

White'haven, 54 33N 3 35W, pop(1981) 27,925, town in Copeland dist, Cumbria, NW England; on the Irish Sea coast, 11 km S of Workington; railway; economy: chemicals.

Whitehorse, 60 41N 135 08W, pop(1981) 17,742, capital of Yukon territory, NW Canada; on the R Lewes just below Whitehorse Rapids, 145 km E of the Alaskan border; economy: mining, fur-trapping.

Whitley Bay, formerly WHITLEY AND MONKSEATON, 55 03N 1 25W, pop(1981) 36,325, coastal resort town in North Tyneside borough, Tyne and Wear, NE England; part of Tyneside urban area; on the North Sea coast, 3 km N of Tynemouth; economy: light engineering.

Whitstable *wit'stubl*, 51 22N 1 02E, pop(1981) 26,451, town in Canterbury dist, Kent, SE England; W of Herne Bay at the mouth of the R Swale; in 1830 George Stephenson established a passenger train to Canterbury; railway; economy: scientific instruments, oysters.

Whittier, 33 58N 118 03W, pop(1980) 69,717, city in Los Angeles county, SW California, United States; 19 km SE of Los Angeles.

Whyalla *whī al'e*, 33 04S 137 34E, pop(1981) 29,962, urban centre in Northern stat div, SE South Australia, Australia; W of Port Pirie, at the NW end of the Spencer Gulf; railway; airfield; economy: steel, shipbuilding.

Wiawso *wee-o'sō*, 6 15N 2 30W, town in Western region, SW Ghana, W Africa; 80 km NW of Dunkwa close to the R Tano.

Wichita *wich'e-taw*, 37 42N 97 20W, pop(1980) 279,272, county seat of Sedgwick county, S Kansas, United States; on the R Arkansas, 210 km SW of Topeka; settled in 1864; 2 universities (1892, 1898); largest city in Kansas; named after an Indian tribe; railway; airport; economy: chief commercial and industrial centre in S Kansas; industries include aircraft, chemical and petroleum products, railway engineering, food processing (grain and meat); event: Wichita River Festival (May).

Wichita Falls, 33 54N 98 30W, pop(1980) 94,201, county seat of Wichita county, N Texas, United States; on the R Wichita, 165 km NW of Fort Worth; settled in 1876; university; railway; economy: oil refining, textiles, electrical supplies, medical products, electronic products, trade in livestock and agricultural products.

Wick, 58 26N 3 06W, pop(1981) 7,900, capital of Caithness dist, Highland region, NE Scotland; on the NE coast, at the mouth of the R Wick; railway; airfield; economy: herring fishing; glass blowing; monuments: Wick Heritage Centre; on cliffs 5 km N of Wick are Castle Girnigoe (built at the end of the 15th century) and Castle Sinclair (1606-07), both were strongholds of the Sinclairs, the Earls of Caithness.

Wick'ford, 51 38N 0 31E, pop(1981) 24,522, town in Basildon dist, Essex, SE England; 5 km NE of Basildon; railway.

Wicklow *wik'lō*, county in Leinster prov, E Irish Republic; bounded E by Irish Sea; watered by Slaney, Liffey and Avoca rivers; Wicklow Mts rise to the W; pop(1981) 87,449; area 2,025 sq km; known as 'The Garden of Ireland'.

Wicklow, CILL MHANTÁIN (Gael), 52 59N 6 03W, pop(1981) 5,341, resort, market town and capital of Wicklow county, Leinster, E Irish Republic; on Irish Sea, S of Dublin; railway.

Widnes, 53 22N 2 44W, pop(1981) 55,926, town in Halton dist, Cheshire, NW central England; on the N bank of the R Mersey, 20 km E of Liverpool; railway; economy: furniture, fertilizers, chemicals, engineering.

Wien *veen*, VIENNA *vee-en'a* (Eng), 48 13N 16 22E, pop(1981) 1,531,346, capital city and a state of Austria; at the foot of the Wienerwald on the R Danube, surrounded by the state of Niederösterreich and close to the borders with Hungary and Czechoslovakia; it is the seat of the federal legislative bodies, the federal government, the central authorities and the supreme courts, also of the state government of Niederösterreich, and a number of international organizations; the central area is surrounded by the monumental buildings and gardens of the Ringstrasse, the area developed between 1859 and 1888 on the site of the old fortifications and surrounding *glacis* or wide open space which linked the heart of the medieval town with the older suburbs; beyond the Ringstrasse and the Donaukanal (Danube Canal) to the NE extends a circuit of inner suburban dists; UNO-City is a recently built conference and office complex (opened 1979), with the offices of the United Nations agencies based in Wien; archbishopric; university of technology (founded in 1815 as a technical college); university (1873-84); Spanish Riding School; refugees arriving in Austria are initially housed at the Traiskirchen camp amidst the Panonian vineyards near the city; economy: metal products, precision instruments, electrical goods, engines and gearboxes; monuments: Gothic St Stephen's cathedral, St Peter's church, Baroque Schottenkirche (12th-c, rebuilt 1638-48), former Bohemian Court Chancery, Gothic church of Maria am Gestade, Romanesque Ruprechtskirche (12-13th-c), Franciscan church (1603-11), Maria Theresa monument (1887), Palais Trautson (High Baroque architecture), neo-Gothic town hall (1872-83), Baroque palace of Schönbrunn; event: International Trade Fair, staged twice annually in spring and autumn.

Wiener Neustadt *vee'ner noy'shtat*, 47 49N 16 15E, pop(1981) 35,006, industrial town and capital of Wiener Neustadt dist, Niederösterreich, NE Austria; at the S edge of the Wien basin; economy: textiles, metal goods, shoes; monument: Gothic St George's church.

Wieprz *vyepsh*, VEPSH (Rus), river in central Poland; a tributary of the Wisła (Vistula); rises in S Zamość voivodship and flows W, NE, NW and then W to meet R Wisła NW of Puławy; length 303 km; tributaries include Tyśmienica; the Wieprz-Krzna Canal at 140 km is the longest in Poland (built in 1961).

Wieringermeer *vee'ring-er-mayer*, area of polder land near the Ijsselmeer barrier dam, NW Netherlands; area 200 sq km; reclaimed between 1927 and 1930; chief settlement Wieringerwerf.

Wiesbaden *veez'bah-den*, 50 05N 8 15E, pop(1983) 272,600, capital city of Hessen (Hesse) prov, in Darmstadt dist, W

Germany; on the R Rhine, 32 km W of Frankfurt am Main; railway; economy: wines and spirits, cement, hydraulics, hand and machine tools; a much frequented health resort; most of the large German Sekt (sparkling wine) cellars are in this area.

Wig'an, 53 33N 2 38W, pop(1981) 88,901, town in Wigan borough, Greater Manchester, NW England; 27 km NE of Liverpool, on R Douglas and Leeds-Liverpool Canal; a borough since 1246; railway; economy: engineering, cotton, foodstuffs, packaging.

Wight, Isle of, VECTIS (Lat), island county off the S coast of England; in the mouth of Southampton Water and separated from Hampshire by the Solent and Spithead; an irregular range of chalk hills running E-W ends at the imposing cliffs of the vertical sandstone Needles near Alum Bay; the island is drained by the R Medina; pop(1981) 118,594; area 381 sq km; county town Newport; chief towns include Cowes, Ryde, Sandown and Shanklin; ferry services to the island from Portsmouth, Southampton and Lymington; economy: tourism, hovercraft and boat building, electronics; the island has associations with the poets Longfellow, Keats, Tennyson and Swinburne; the county is divided into 2 districts:

District	*area (sq km)*	*pop(1981)*
Medina	117	67,919
South Wight	264	50,675

Wig'ston, 52 36N 1 05W, pop(1981) 32,441, town in Oadby and Wigston dist, Leicestershire, central England; in Leicester urban area; a SE suburb of Leicester; economy: textiles, light engineering.

Wilayah Persekutuan, federal territory in W Peninsular Malaysia, SE Asia; pop(1980) 919,610; area 243 sq km; comprises the capital city, Kuala Lumpur and environs; separated from Selangor in 1974.

Wildspitze *vilt'shpit-se*, 46 53N 10 53E, mountain in the Ötztaler Alpen, Tirol state, W Austria; height 3,774 m; the 2nd highest peak in Austria.

Wilhelm, Mount, 5 46S 144 59E, highest mountain peak in Papua New Guinea; in the Central Range (Bismarck Mts); SW of the upper course of the R Ramu; height 4,508 m.

Wilhelmshaven *vil'helmz-hah-fen*, 53 32N 8 07E, pop(1983) 99,100, seaport and resort town in Niedersachsen (Lower Saxony) prov, W Germany; on W shore of Jadebusen (Jade Bay), 30 km W of Bremerhaven; naval base; railway; economy: office machines, precision tools, textiles, oil storage.

Wilkes Land, area of Antarctica situated between Queen Mary Land (W) and Terre Adélie, lying mostly between 105° and 135° E; includes the Australian scientific station at Casey which was established in 1961.

Wilkes-Barre *-bar'*, 41 15N 75 53W, pop(1980) 51,551, county seat of Luzerne county, NE Pennsylvania, United States; on the R Susquehanna, 29 km SW of Scranton; railway; economy: coal mining.

Willemstad *vil'em-staht*, 12 12N 68 56W, pop(1983e) 50,000, capital town of the Netherlands Antilles, E Caribbean, on the SW coast of Curaçao I; established by the Dutch as a trading centre in the mid-17th century; Dr Albert Plessman International Airport is located 16 km from Willemstad; economy: oil refining (handling Venezuelan oil), ship repair, tourism.

Williamsburg, 37 17N 76 43W, pop(1980) 9,870, an independent city and capital of James City county, SE Virginia, United States; situated between the York and James rivers, SE of Richmond; settled in 1633, becoming capital of Virginia 1699-1780; Colonial Williamsburg, in Colonial National Historical Park, is a major building restoration and reconstruction scheme; College of William and Mary (1693).

Williamsport, 41 15N 77 00W, pop(1980) 33,401, county seat of Lycoming county, central Pennsylvania, United States; on W branch of the R Susquehanna, 112 km N of Harrisburg; railway; airfield.

Wilmette', 42 05N 87 42W, pop(1980) 28,229, residential town in Cook county, NE Illinois, United States; on L Michigan, 24 km N of Chicago; railway; coastguard station.

Wilmington, 39 45N 75 33W, pop(1980) 70,195, county seat of New Castle county, N Delaware, United States; a port at the confluence of Brandywine Creek, the R Christina and the R Delaware; founded by the Swedes as Fort Christina in 1638; later taken by the British and renamed Willington in 1731; renamed Wilmington in 1739; city status since 1832; largest city in the state; railway; airfield; economy: chemicals, explosives, automobiles and other transportation equipment; shipyards and railway engineering; home of several large corporations; monuments: State House complex, Winterthur Museum, Hagley Museum.

Wilmington, 34 14N 77 55W, pop(1980) 44,000, county seat of New Hanover county, SE North Carolina, United States; a port on the Cape Fear river, 125 km SE of Fayetteville; British troops under General Cornwallis held the town in 1781; during the Civil War it was the last Confederate port to close; Wilmington College (1947); railway; airfield; economy: the state's largest port, receiving petroleum products and shipping tobacco, lumber products and scrap metal; manufactures metal and wood products, textiles, clothing, boilers and fertilizers; event: Azalea Festival (April).

Wilmslow *wilmz'lō* or *wimz'lō*, 53 20N 2 15W, pop(1981) 28,933, town in Macclesfield dist, Cheshire, NW central England; on the R Bollin, 16 km S of Manchester; railway; economy: leather, textiles, clothing.

Wilrijk *vil'rīk*, 51 10N 4 23E, pop(1982) 42,349, town in Antwerpen dist, Antwerpen prov, Belgium; a S suburb of Antwerpen.

Wilson, 35 44N 77 55W, pop(1980) 34,424, county seat of Wilson county, E North Carolina, United States; 26 km SSW of Rocky Mount; railway; economy: textiles, metal products and processed foods.

Wiltshire, county of S England; bounded N by Gloucestershire, NE by Oxfordshire, E and S by Hampshire, S by Dorset and W by Somerset and Avon; the chalk downland of Salisbury Plain lies at the centre of the county; drained by the Avon and Kennet rivers; pop(1981) 518,545; area 3,481 sq km; county town Trowbridge; chief towns include Salisbury, Swindon, Chippenham; economy: agriculture, engineering, clothing, brewing; there are many ancient prehistoric remains at sites such as Stonehenge, Avebury, Silbury Hill; the county is divided into 5 districts:

District	*area (sq km)*	*pop(1981)*
Kennet	958	63,343
North Wiltshire	770	102,583
Salisbury	1,005	100,946
Thamesdown	230	152,145
West Wiltshire	517	99,528

Wiltz *vilts*, canton in W part of Diekirch dist, NW Luxembourg; area 294 sq km; pop(1981) 8,997; bisected NW-SE by the R Wiltz and bounded on the S by the R Sûre.

Wiltz, 49 58N 5 56E, pop(1981) 4,100, resort town and capital of Wiltz canton, Diekirch dist, W Luxembourg; in the Ösling region, 58 km NNW of Luxembourg; it consists of Oberwiltz on a high hill above the river of the same name and Niederwiltz; international meeting place for Boy Scouts; airfield; economy: plastics, electrolytic copper foil, vinyl floorcovering; monument: museum of the 'Battle of the Bulge'; events: Broom Folklore Festival on Whitsun Monday, International Open-air Theatre Festival (July-Aug).

Wimbledon, residential district in Merton borough, S Greater London, England.

Wimbourne Minster or **Wimborne**, 50 48N 1 59W, pop(1981) 20,049, town linked with Oakley in Wimborne dist, Dorset, S England; on R Stour, 11 km N of Bournemouth.

Win'chester, VENTA BELGARUM (Lat), WINTANCEASTER (Anglo-Saxon), 51 04N 1 19W, pop(1981) 35,664, city and county town in Winchester dist, Hampshire, S England; on the R Itchen, 105 km SW of London; the Roman settlement was the 5th largest in Britain; capital of the kingdom of Wessex in 519 AD and capital of England in 827 AD when Egbert was crowned here; William the Conqueror was crowned here as well as in London; *Domesday Book* was compiled here; from the 14th century the city declined into a small provincial town; railway; economy: engineering; monuments: the burial place of St Swithin; cathedral (1079-93), the longest Gothic cathedral in the world; Winchester College, one of England's most famous schools (1382); 12th-c St Cross Hospital; event: southern cathedrals' festival (July).

Win'dermere, lake in the Lake District of Cumbria, NW England; largest lake in England, extending 18 km S from Ambleside; linked to Morecambe Bay by the R Leven; the largest island is Belle Isle; on Ladyholme are the remains of a 13th-c chapel.

Windermere, 54 23N 2 54W, pop(1981) 7,956, lakeside resort town in South Lakeland dist, Cumbria, NW England; 11 km NW of Kendal, on L Windermere; railway; monuments: 15th-c church of St Martin; Rydal Mount (10 km NW), home of William Wordsworth from 1813 to 1850; Brantwood, the home of the writer, John Ruskin (1819-1900).

Windhoek *vint'hook*, 22 34S 17 06E, pop(1981e) 105,000, capital of Namibia, SW Africa; 1,450 km N of Cape Town, South Africa; alt 1,650 m; became capital of German South-West Africa in 1922; Roman Catholic cathedral; occupied by South African forces in 1915 and administrative headquarters of the mandate after World War I; railway; airport; economy: administration, meat canning, diamond mining and cutting, copper mining, trade in karakul (sheepskins).

Wind'scale, Cumbria, NW England. See Sellafield.

Windsor *win'zer*, 42 18N 83 00W, pop(1981) 192,083, town in S Ontario, SE Canada; on the Detroit river, opposite the US city of Detroit, founded as a Hudson Bay Co post in 1835, it grew rapidly with the arrival of industry in the form of Hiram Walker's steam flour mill in 1858, the pharmaceutical industry in 1884, paint manufacture in 1893 and the motor car industry in 1904; during the prohibition period in the 1920s Windsor was the main route for rum-running into the USA; to the S of Windsor is Point Pelee National Park (area 15.5 sq km, established in 1918); the park is a sanctuary of marshes and forests for over 300 species of birds and is situated on Canada's southernmost point; in late September thousands of orange Monarch butterflies rest here before migrating S; university (1857); railway; economy: vehicles, food processing, pharmaceuticals, paints, salt, distilling; monument: the Hiram Walker Historical Museum was the headquarters of the invading American army in 1812.

Windsor, 51 30N 0 38W, pop(1981) 31,544, town linked with Eton in Windsor and Maidenhead dist, Berkshire, S England; W of London, on R Thames; railway; monuments: Windsor Castle, Eton College (1540); events: Royal Windsor horse show (May); horse-racing at Royal Ascot (June); Eton wall game on St Andrew's Day (30 Nov).

Windward Islands, West Indian islands; all the islands of the Lesser Antilles in the Caribbean Sea S of the Leeward Islands, from Martinique in the N to Grenada in the S, excluding Trinidad and Tobago; so called because of their exposure to the prevailing NE trade winds; formerly the name of a British Colony comprising Dominica, St Lucia, St Vincent and Grenada.

Windward Islands, French Polynesia. See Îles du Vent.

Win'frith Heath, 50 39N 2 16W, Dorset, S England; nuclear research station 3 km W of Wool, with a steam-generating heavy-water reactor which came into commercial operation in 1968.

Winneba *wi'nee-ba*, 5 22N 0 38W, pop(1970) 36,104, town in Central region, S Ghana, W Africa; on the Gulf of Guinea between Accra and Cape Coast.

Winnebago *win-e-bay'gō*, lake in E Wisconsin, United States; N of Fond du Lac; named after an Indian tribe; area 557 sq km; the Fox river flows through the lake to Green Bay.

Winnipeg *wi'ni-peg, wi-ni-peg'*, 49 53N 97 10W, pop(1981) 564,473, capital of Manitoba prov, central Canada; on the Red river where it meets the Assiniboine river; established in 1738 as Fort Rouge, but later abandoned; in the early 19th century Fort Gibraltar was built by the North West Co and Fort Douglas by the Hudson's Bay Co; after 1812 the surrounding area was settled by Scottish colonists brought to Canada by the Earl of Selkirk; the 2 trading companies merged in 1821 and Fort Gibraltar was renamed Fort Garry and rebuilt in 1835; the settlement around the fort was incorporated as Winnipeg in 1873; the settlement expanded after the arrival of the Canadian Pacific Railroad in 1881; the city was severely damaged by a flood in 1950; since 1969 over 20 skyscrapers have been built in the centre of Winnipeg; university (1967); railway; airport; economy: meat packing, fur trading, textiles, machinery, aircraft parts; monuments: in front of the railway station is the *Countess of Dufferin*, the first locomotive to arrive in the W after the station opened in 1885; the Centennial Arts Centre contains a concert hall, planetarium and museum; beside the Civic Auditorium, home of the Winnipeg Symphony Orchestra, is the Art Gallery; outside Parliament Building is a monument to la Vérendrye, the first white man to arrive in the Winnipeg area; events: Festival du Voyageur (Feb); Folklorama (Aug).

Winnipeg, lake in S central Manitoba prov, S Canada; 64 km NNE of Winnipeg; to the W of L Winnipeg lie lakes Winnipegosis, Cedar and Manitoba; length 386 km; breadth 88 km; area 24,390 sq km; drained N into Hudson Bay by the Nelson river; receives the Red, Winnipeg, Dauphin, Saskatchewan (through Cedar L in the NW) and Berens rivers; L Winnipeg is a remnant of the glacial L Agassiz.

Winnipegosis *wi-ni-pe-gō'sis*, lake in W Manitoba prov, S Canada; 56 km NNE of Dauphin; situated between Cedar L to the N and L Manitoba to the SE; L Winnipeg lies to the E; length 201 km; breadth 40 km; area 5,374 sq km; receives the Red Deer and Swan rivers; drains S into L Manitoba and from there into L Winnipeg; once part of the glacial L Agassiz.

Winnipesau'kee, largest lake in New Hampshire, NE United States; a popular resort area N of Concord; area 184 sq km.

Winona *wi-no'na*, 44 03N 91 39W, pop(1980) 25,075, county seat of Winona county, SE Minnesota, United States; port on R Mississippi, 64 km E of Rochester; Winona is a Sioux Indian name often given to the first-born daughter, first settled in 1851, the city developed as a grain and timber shipping centre; achieved city status in 1857; university; railway; economy: machinery, metal products, electronics, plastics, knitwear, food processing.

Winsford *winz'-*, 53 11N 2 31W, pop(1981) 26,532, town in Macclesfield dist, Cheshire, NW central England, 37 km SW of Manchester; railway; economy: engineering, salt, chemicals.

Winston-Salem, 36 06N 80 15W, pop(1980) 131,885, county seat of Forsyth county, N central North Carolina, United States; 40 km W of Greensboro; Winston was founded in 1849 and Salem in 1766; the two towns united in 1913; Wake Forest University (1834); railway; economy: the nation's chief tobacco manufacturer; also manufactures textiles and furniture; monument: Old Salem.

Winterthur *vin'ter-toor*, 47 30N 8 45E, pop(1980) 86,758, town in Zürich canton, Switzerland; in a wide basin near the R Töss in the Pre-Alpine region, NE of Zürich; railway junction; economy: engineering, transport equipment, textiles; monument: 18-19th-c town hall.

Wisbech *wiz'beech*, 52 40N 0 10E, pop(1981) 23,191, river port town in Fenland dist, Cambridgeshire, E central England; on the R Nene, 19 km SW of King's Lynn, surrounded by orchards, bulb fields and fenland; many buildings have a Dutch character; economy: timber, printing, flowers, fruit; monuments: 12th-c church of St Peter and St Paul, Peckover House (1722-26).

Wiscon'sin, state in N United States; bounded W by Iowa and Minnesota, N by Lakes Superior and Michigan, E by Michigan and L Michigan, and S by Illinois; the 'Badger State'; 30th state admitted to the Union (1848); pop(1980) 4,705,767; area 141,508 sq km; capital Madison; other major cities include Milwaukee, Green Bay and Racine; the R Mississippi follows the lower part of the W state border; the R Wisconsin flows S through centre state, then W to meet the R Mississippi; the R Menominee follows the E part of Michigan border; L Winnebago lies to the E; 26,061 sq km of L Michigan lie within the state boundary; the highest point is Timms Hill (595 m); the N and W of the state comprise a typical glaciated terrain which is largely forested; economy: timber products, dairy products, paper, metal products, machinery, food processing, electrical equipment, transport equipment, grain, vegetables, brewing; Wisconsin produces more milk, butter and cheese than any other state, accounting for over one-third of the nation's cheese production; heavy industry is concentrated in the Milwaukee area; first settled in 1670 by French traders and surrendered to the British in 1763; handed over to the USA in 1783 when it became part of the Northwest Terr; contained successively in the Territories of Indiana, Illinois and Michigan before the Territory of Wisconsin was formed in 1836; the state is divided into 72 counties:

County	*area (sq km)*	*pop(1980)*
Adams	1,685	13,457
Ashland	2,725	16,783
Barron	2,249	38,730
Bayfield	3,801	13,822
Brown	1,362	175,280
Buffalo	1,817	14,309
Burnett	2,127	12,340
Calumet	848	30,867
Chippewa	2,644	52,127
Clark	3,167	32,910
Columbia	2,005	43,222
Crawford	1,472	16,556
Dane	3,133	323,545
Dodge	2,306	75,064
Door	1,279	25,029
Douglas	3,393	44,421
Dunn	2,218	34,314
Eau Claire	1,659	78,805
Florence	1,264	4,172
Fond du Lac	1,885	88,964
Forest	2,629	9,044
Grant	2,974	51,736
Green	1,516	30,012
Green Lake	928	18,370
Iowa	1,976	19,802
Iron	1,953	6,730
Jackson	2,595	16,831
Jefferson	1,461	66,152
Juneau	2,012	21,039
Kenosha	710	123,137
Kewaunee	892	19,539
La Crosse	1,188	91,056
Lafayette	1,648	17,412
Langlade	2,270	19,978
Lincoln	2,304	26,555
Manitowoc	1,544	82,918
Marathon	4,053	111,270
Marinette	3,627	39,314
Marquette	1,183	11,672
Menominee	933	3,373
Milwaukee	627	964,988
Monroe	2,350	35,074
Oconto	2,605	28,947
Oneida	2,938	31,216
Outagamie	1,669	128,799
Ozaukee	611	66,981
Pepin	601	7,477
Pierce	1,500	31,149
Polk	2,389	32,351
Portage	2,106	57,420
Price	3,266	15,788
Racine	871	173,132
Richland	1,521	17,476
Rock	1,880	139,420
Rusk	2,374	15,589
Sauk	2,179	43,469
Sawyer	3,263	12,843
Shawano	2,332	35,928
Sheboygan	1,339	100,935
St Croix	1,880	43,262
Taylor	2,535	18,817
Trempealeau	1,914	26,158
Vernon	2,101	25,642
Vilas	2,254	16,535
Walworth	1,446	71,507
Washburn	2,119	13,174
Washington	1,118	84,848
Waukesha	1,440	280,326
Waupaca	1,960	42,831
Waushara	1,633	18,526
Winnebago	1,167	131,703
Wood	2,083	72,799

Wishaw, 55 47N 3 56W, pop(1981) 37,783, town in Motherwell dist, Strathclyde, central Scotland; 5 km SE of Motherwell; railway; economy: engineering.

Wisła *vee'sla*, VISTULA, river in Poland; rises in Carpathian Mts in SW Poland and flows NE, N and NW for 1,047 km to meet the Baltic Sea at Gdańsk; tributaries include Dunajec, Nida, Wisłoka, San, Wieprz, Pilica, Narew, Bzura, Drwęca and Brda rivers; navigable for 941 km; Łączański Canal (17.2 km) built in 1961; Żerański Canal (17.6 km) built in 1963; the river is dammed at Goczałkowice.

Wismar *vis'mahr*, 53 54N 11 28E, pop(1981) 57,718, seaport in Wismar dist, Rostock, N East Germany; E of Lübeck; founded in 13th century; formerly held by Sweden and Denmark; railway; economy: shipyard, fishing.

Witham *wi'thum*, river rising S of Grantham in Lincolnshire, E England; flows 128 km N, E and SE to meet the Wash SE of Boston.

Witham, 51 48N 0 38E, pop(1981) 21,912, town in Braintree dist, Essex, SE England; 14 km NE of Chelmsford; in fertile wheat-growing fenland; railway; economy: foodstuffs, engineering.

Wit'ney, 51 48N 1 29W, pop(1981) 14,343, town in South Oxfordshire dist, Oxfordshire, S central England; on the R Windrush, 16 km W of Oxford; economy: clothing, engineering.

Witten *vit'en*, 51 27N 7 19E, pop(1983) 104,200, industrial city in Arnsberg dist, Nordrhein-Westfalen (North Rhine-Westphalia) prov, W Germany; on the R Ruhr, 14 km SW of Dortmund; railway; economy: steel, chemicals.

Wittenberg *vi'tun-berk*, 51 53N 12 39E, pop(1981) 53,874, town in Wittenberg dist, Halle, SW central East Germany; on R Elbe, SW of Berlin; university (1817); associated with the beginning of the Reformation in 1517; became part of Prussia in 1814; railway; economy: chemical plants manufacturing nitrogen and sulphuric acid; monuments: 16th-c Augustinian monastery where Martin Luther lived; Schlosskirche, to the doors of which Luther nailed his 95 theses.

Witwatersrand *wit-wah'terz-rand*, THE RAND ('ridge of white waters'), region centred on a ridge of gold-bearing rock in S Transvaal prov, South Africa; length 100 km; width 40 km; Johannesburg is located near its centre;

gold discovered in 1886; produces over half of the world's gold.

Włocławek *vwot-swaf'ek*, voivodship in central Poland; bisected by R Wisła (Vistula); pop(1983) 422,000; area 4,402 sq km; capital Włocławek; chief towns include Lipno and Rypin.

Włocławek, VLOTSLAVSK (Ger), 52 39N 19 01E, pop(1983) 113,500, industrial river port capital of Włocławek voivodship, central Poland; on R Wisła (Vistula); railway; river boat service to Płock; economy: china and earthenware, cellulose, paper, nitrogen, water power plant; monuments: 14-15th-c Gothic cathedral, 14th-c St Vitalis church, regional museum.

Woburn, 42 29N 71 09W, pop(1980) 36,626, town in Middlesex county, NE Massachusetts, United States; 16 km N of Boston; railway.

Wodonga, Australia. See Albury-Wodonga.

Wodzisław Śląski *vo-jee-swaf shlon'ski*, LOSLAU (Ger), 50 01N 18 26E, pop(1983) 106,800, industrial city in Katowice voivodship, S Poland; SW of Katowice near Czechoslovak frontier; part of the Rybnik coal basin; technical college; railway; economy: mining, power.

Woking *wō'king*, 51 20N 0 34W, pop(1981) 81,773, town linked with Byfleet in Woking dist, Surrey, SE England; part of Greater London urban area; on the R Wey, 40 km SW of London; railway; economy: commerce, printing.

Wokingham *wō'king-em*, 51 25N 0 51W, pop(1981) 30,773, town in Wokingham dist, Berkshire, S England, United Kingdom; 11 km ESE of Reading; railway; economy: electronics, engineering.

Wolds Way, long-distance footpath stretching from Hull to Filey, N England; links with the Cleveland Way; length 115 km.

Woleu, river in Gabon and Equatorial Guinea. See Mbini, Río.

Wolfgangsee *volf'gang-zay* or **Abersee**, SANKT WOLFGANGSEE, lake in Salzburg and Oberösterreich states, N Austria, SE of Salzburg; length 10 km; width 2 km; max depth 114 m; popular health resort at St Wolfgang.

Wolfsberg *volfs'berk*, 46 50N 14 50E, pop(1981) 28,097, industrial town, resort and capital of Wolfsberg dist, Kärnten, S Austria, in the Lavant valley NE of Klagenfurt.

Wolfsburg *volfs'boork*, 52 27N 10 49E, pop(1983) 124,000, city in Lüneburg dist, E Niedersachsen (Lower Saxony) prov, W Germany; 24 km NE of Braunschweig, on the Mittelland Canal and the Elbe Branch Canal; railway; economy: vehicles and engines, machinery, tools; known as the 'Volkswagen town'; it is an interesting piece of contemporary town-planning, a planned garden city with wide multi-lane traffic arteries, modern residential districts and ample provision for cultural and leisure activities.

Wollem'i, national park in E New South Wales, Australia; situated in the Great Dividing Range, NW of Sydney; area 4,801 sq km; established in 1979.

Wollongong *woo len gong'*, 34 25S 150 52E, pop(1986) 237,600, urban centre in Illawarra stat div, SE New South Wales, Australia; S of Sydney; railway; economy: steel, coal, dairy farming.

Woluwe-St-Lambert *vol-üv-e-sĩ-lã-bar'*, SINT-LAMBRECHTS-WOLUWE *sint-lahm'breKHs-vō'lüv-u* (Flem), 50 50N 4 25E, pop(1982) 49,331, town in Brussel dist, Brabant prov, Belgium; an E suburb of Bruxelles.

Woluwe-St-Pierre *vol-üv-e-sĩ-pyar*, SINT-PIETERS-WOLUWE *-pee'turs-* (Flem), 50 50N 4 26E, pop(1982) 40,681, town in Brussel dist, Brabant prov, Belgium; an E suburb of Bruxelles.

Wolverhampton *wool'-*, 52 36N 2 08W, pop(1981) 254,561, town in West Midlands, central England; in the industrial 'Black Country', 20 km NW of Birmingham; the town is named after Wulfruna (sister of King Edgar II) who endowed the first collegiate church here in 994; railway; economy: metal products, engineering; monument: 15th-c church of St Peter.

Wombourn, 52 33N 2 10W, pop(1981) 12,930, town in South Staffordshire dist, Staffordshire, central England; 7 km SW of Wolverhampton.

Wŏnsan *wen'sahn*, 39 07N 127 26E, capital of Kangwŏn prov, SE North Korea; on Sea of Japan; railway; economy: engineering.

Wood Buffalo, national park in N Alberta and S Northwest Territories, central Canada; includes part of Buffalo Lake and L Claire and part of the Caribou and Birch mountains; crossed by the Birch, Peace, Buffalo and Little Buffalo rivers; to the S lie the Great Canadian Oil Sands, deposits of oil-bearing sands, estimated to contain enough petroleum to supply all of N America for 60 years; area 44,807 sq km; established in 1922.

Woodhenge, prehistoric site in Wiltshire, S England; 3 km NE of Stonehenge, near Amesbury; discovered by aerial reconnaissance in 1926; there is little visible above ground; it apparently consisted of a number of concentric ovals of wooden pillars oriented for the same ritualistic forms as were in use at Stonehenge.

Woodland, 38 41N 121 46W, pop(1980) 30,235, city in Yolo county, central California, United States; in the Sacramento Valley, 29 km NW of Sacramento; railway.

Wookey Hole, limestone caves near the village of Wookey in Sedgemoor dist, Somerset, SW England; on the SW slopes of the Mendip Hills near the R Axe, 22 km SE of Weston-super-Mare; prehistoric tools have been found in the caves.

Woon'socket (Algonquian, 'steep-descent-at'), 42 00N 71 31W, pop(1980) 45,914, city in Providence county, N Rhode Island, United States; on the R Blackstone, 22 km NNW of Providence and 1 km S of the Massachusetts border; founded in 1666, achieving city status in 1888; railway; economy: textiles, electronics, paper, clothing.

Worcester *woos'ter*, WIGORNA CEASTER (Anglo-Saxon), 52 11N 2 13W, pop(1981) 74,790, county town of Hereford and Worcester, W central England; on the R Severn, 38 km SW of Birmingham; founded c.680 AD; Royal Worcester Porcelain Co established here in 1862; railway; economy: sauce, engineering, furniture, vehicle parts, porcelain, gloves; monuments: 14th-c cathedral; 11th-c Commandery founded by St Wulfstan; 18th-c Guildhall; Dyson Perins Museum; event: Three Choirs Festival in rotation with Hereford and Gloucester (Sept).

Worcester, 42 16N 71 48W, pop(1980) 161,799, county seat of Worcester county, central Massachusetts, United States; 59 km W of Boston; settled in 1713, achieving city status in 1848; industrial development followed the opening of the Blackstone Canal in 1828; Clark University (1887); airfield; railway; economy: textiles, engineering.

Workington, 54 39N 3 33W, pop(1981) 26,123, port town in Allerdale dist, Cumbria, NW England; 48 km SW of Carlisle, at the mouth of the R Derwent where it meets the Irish Sea; railway; economy: engineering, packaging; monuments: remains of the Roman fort of Gabrosentium; Workington Hall (1379).

Worksop, 53 18N 1 07W, pop(1981) 34,993, town in Bassetlaw dist, Nottinghamshire, central England; on the R Ryton, 40 km N of Nottingham, at the N end of the Dukeries; railway; economy: coal, glass, chemicals, food processing, light engineering.

World's View, 20 30S 28 30E, grave in Matabeleland South prov, Zimbabwe, S Africa; 40 km SW of Bulawayo; the location of Cecil John Rhodes's grave in the Matopo Hills in the N of the prov; Cecil Rhodes, 'founder' of Rhodesia, came to this area in the late 1890s attempting to make peace with the Matabele leaders with whom there had been two wars in 1893 and 1896.

Worms *vorms, wurmz* (Eng), BORBETOMAGUS (anc), 49 38N 8 23E, pop(1983) 73,000, river port in Rheinhessen-Pfalz dist, E Rheinland-Pfalz (Rhineland-Palatinate) prov, W Germany; on R Rhine, 16 km NNW of Mannheim; noted centre of the wine trade, the vineyards round the Liebfrauenkirche produce the famous Liebfraumilch; one of the oldest towns in Germany; scene of many imperial diets, notably the Diet of Worms (1521) at which Martin

Luther made his defence; railway; economy: sheeting and foils, chemicals; monument: cathedral (11-12th-c).

Wörther See *vurt'er zay*, lake in Kärnten state, SE Austria, W of Klagenfurt; area 18.8 sq km; length 4 km; width 1.5 km; max depth 86 km; popular for water sports; the lakeside town of Velden is the chief town and most fashionable resort in Kärnten.

Worthing *wær'thing*, 50 48N 0 23W, pop(1981) 92,056, resort town co-extensive with Worthing dist, West Sussex, S England; part of Brighton-Worthing-Littlehampton urban area; 17 km W of Brighton; once a fishing village, it developed into a fashionable coastal resort after its discovery by Princess Amelia, daughter of George III; railway; economy: electronics, engineering, plastics, furniture, horticulture; monuments: Cissbury Ring (2 km N), 3rd-c fort and Neolithic flint mines.

Wrangel Island, island in the W Chukchi Sea, E Soviet Union. See Vrangelya, Ostrov.

Wrangell-St Elias, national park and preserve in SE Alaska, United States; situated in the Wrangell and St Elias Mts, including parts of the Coast Ranges; contains several glaciers and dormant volcanoes; highest peak is Mt Blackburn (5,160 m) in the Wrangell Mts; area 53,441 sq km; established in 1978.

Wrexham *reks'em*, 53 03N 3 00W, pop(1981) 40,928, town in Wrexham Maelor dist, Clwyd, NE Wales; 20 km SW of Chester; burial place of Elihu Yale, founder of Yale University; railway; economy: coal, electronics, bricks, pharmaceuticals, food processing, metal goods; monument: 15th-c church of St Giles.

Wrocław *vrot'swaf*, voivodship in W Poland; pop(1983) 1,101,000; area 6,287 sq km; capital Wrocław; chief towns include Oleśnica and Oława.

Wrocław, BRESLAU (Ger), 51 05N 17 00E, pop(1983) 631,500, river port capital of Wrocław voivodship, W Poland; on R Oder (Odra); capital of lower Silesia; former base of the dukes of Silesia in their attempts to reunite Poland in 13th century; first Polish publications printed here in 1745; annexed by Prussia in 1741; technical university (1945); world famous pantomime theatre established by Henryk Tomaszewski; airport; railway junction; economy: shipyards, metallurgy, railway carriages, electronics, chemicals, clothes; monuments: 13th-c Gothic cathedral in Ostrów Tumski, the oldest part of the city; city museum; 13-14th-c church of St Mary Magdalene; national museum with a collection of Silesian art; events: international student theatre festivals; oratorio and cantata festival, festival of jazz.

Wu Yue, THE FIVE HOLY MOUNTAINS, the collective name for 5 mountains in China; regarded in Chinese legend as the gathering places of the gods; these were the places where the Chinese emperors normally offered sacrifices; the mountains are Tai Shan in Shandong prov (1,545 m), Hua Shan in Shaanxi prov (2,154 m), Song Shan in Henan prov (1,512 m), Heng Shan in Hunan prov (1,290 m) and Heng Shan in Shanxi prov (2,016 m).

Wuhan *woo-hahn*, HAN-KOW, HAN-KOU, 30 35N 114 19E, pop(1984e) 3,337,500, inland port and capital of Hubei prov, E central China; union of three closely linked municipalities: Wuchang, Hankou and Hanyang; situated at the confluence of the Han Shui and Chang Jiang (Yangtze) rivers; Hankou in NW Wuhan, originally a fishing village dating from the 3rd century BC, was designated a treaty port after the Opium Wars and expanded following the arrival of the railway in the early 20th century; S of Hankou, Hanyang first developed in approx 600 AD; in the late 19th century it became a prominent centre of political reform; China's first modern iron and steel complex was built here in 1891; since 1949 it has developed as a centre for light industry; Wuchang to the E is the oldest of the 3 municipalities which functioned as an administrative centre for the region; Wuhan university (1913); Central China Engineering Institute; railway; airfield; economy: iron, steel, fertilizer, limestone, machine tools, cotton, fisheries; monuments: the Guiyuan Buddhist Temple in Hanyang, built around 1600, is now a museum, the main worship hall containing 500 Buddhas carved out of wood; the Changjiang bridge, the first modern bridge to cross the Chang Jiang (Yangtze river), was completed in 1957, linking the 3 municipalities; Red Hill Park in Wuchang contains a 7-storey pagoda built during the Yuan dynasty (1307-15).

Wuhsi, town in Jiangsu prov, E China. See Wuxi.

Wuhsien, former name of town in Jiangsu prov, E China. See Suzhou.

Wu-lu-k'o-mu-shi, capital of Xinjiang aut region, NW China. See Ürümqi.

Wuppertal *voop'er-tahl*, 51 15N 7 10E, pop(1983) 386,000, industrial city in Düsseldorf dist, Nordrhein-Westfalen (North Rhine-Westphalia) prov, W Germany; on the R Wupper in the Ruhr valley, 26 km ENE of Düsseldorf; includes the former towns of Barmen, Elberfeld and Vohwinkel which are linked by an overhead railway constructed in 1898-1901; university (1972); economy: textiles, man-made fibres, brewing, plastics, steel cord, electronics, packaging, lime, automobile equipment, metalworking.

Würzburg *vürts'boorKH*, 49 48N 9 57E, pop(1983) 129,500, industrial city in Unterfranken dist, NW Bayern (Bavaria) prov, W Germany; on R Main, 96 km ESE of Frankfurt am Main; old university (1582-92), new university (1892-96); railway; economy: engineering; monuments: cathedral (11-13th-c), St Mary's chapel (1377-1479), Old Main bridge (1473-1543), Marienberg (fortress, mid-13th-c); the principal centre of wine production and marketing in Franconia; cultural centre of the Main region of Franconia and beginning of the 'Romantic Road'.

Wuxi *woo-shee*, WUHSI, 31 35N 120 19E, pop(1984e) 825,100, city in Jiangsu prov, E China; on the N bank of Tai Hu lake, on the Grand Canal; dates from the Shang and Zhou periods (1000 BC), but was developed during the Han dynasty (206-24 BC); railway; economy: silk, diesel engines, precision engineering, electronics, pig breeding, fishing, boat building; monuments: Xihui Park with Jichang Garden (Garden for Ease of Mind) and temple, both of which were built during the Ming dynasty (1368-1644).

Wyandotte *wīn'daht*, 42 12N 83 09W, pop(1980) 34,006, city in Wayne county, SE Michigan, United States; on R Detroit, 17 km S of Detroit; named after an Indian tribe; railway; the first Bessemer steel plant in USA established here in 1864.

Wye *wī*, river rising on Plynlimon, NE Dyfed, Wales; flows 208 km SE and E through Powys, Hereford and along the Gwent-Gloucestershire border to meet the R Severn estuary S of Chepstow.

Wye, river rising in Buckinghamshire, S central England; flows 15 km SE to meet the R Thames at Bourne End.

Wye, river rising near Buxton in Derbyshire, central England; flows 32 km SE to join the R Derwent at Rowsley.

Wylfa Head, headland on Ynys Môn (Anglesey), Gwynedd, NW Wales; on the N coast at the W end of Cemaes Bay; site of gas-cooled nuclear reactors which came into commercial operation in 1971-72.

Wynberg *wīn'berg*, 34 00S 18 28E, pop(1980) 744,706, magisterial dist of Cape prov, South Africa; a SW suburb of Cape Town; formerly a separate town but incorporated into Cape Town in the 1920s.

Wyoming *wī-ō'ming*, 42 54N 85 42W, pop(1980) 59,616, residential town in Kent county, W Michigan, United States; 8 km S of Grand Rapids.

Wyoming, state in W United States; bounded W by Utah, Idaho and Montana, N by Montana, E by South Dakota and Nebraska, and S by Colorado and Utah; the Snake river rises in NW Wyoming and flows S then W into Idaho; the Yellowstone river also rises in the NW and flows N into Montana; the Green river rises in the SW and flows S into Utah; the North Platte river flows N from Colorado into S central Wyoming and then turns SE to cross the border into Nebraska; W lies the Wind River Range, and N the Absaroka Range and Teton Mts;

the Bighorn Mts rise in N central Wyoming; all these ranges form part of the Rocky Mts, the highest point in the state being Gannett Peak (4,201 m); the fertile Great Plains (E) is ranching and farming country; the fertile plains give way to eroded 'badlands' in the extreme NE, and higher tablelands in the SE which are interrupted by the Laramie Mts; W of these plains lie the Rocky Mts much of which are forested; in the SW is the South Pass, a broad, grassy plain which is the natural gateway through the Rocky Mts; the state has two national parks at Grand Teton, which includes the most spectacular scenery of the Teton Range, and Yellowstone, the largest national park in the country, with its world-famous geysers and hot springs; chief agricultural products are cattle, sheep, sugar-beets, dairy produce, wool, hay and barley; minerals include oil, natural gas, sodium salts, uranium, coal, gold, silver, iron and copper; manufacturing industry is based on petroleum, timber and food processing; most of the region was acquired by the United States from France in the Louisiana Purchase of 1803, but Spain, Britain and the Republic of Texas all laid claims to other parts of the region; eventually the territory came under total American jurisdiction in 1848; Wyoming Territory was established in 1868; Wyoming was the first territory or state to adopt women's suffrage (1869), appointing the country's first female state governor, Mrs Nellie Taylor Ross, in 1924; admitted to the Union as the 44th state in 1890; Riverton and the territory to the N and W forms the Wind River Indian reservation; also known as 'Equality State'; pop(1980) 469,557; area 252,171 sq km; capital Cheyenne; the other chief city is Casper; the state is divided into 23 counties:

County	*area (sq km)*	*pop(1980)*
Albany	11,097	29,062
Big Horn	8,161	11,896
Campbell	12,470	24,367
Carbon	20,480	21,896
Converse	11,105	14,069
Crook	7,423	5,308
Fremont	23,871	38,992
Goshen	5,684	12,040
Hot Springs	5,213	5,710
Johnson	10,832	6,700
Laramie	6,978	68,649
Lincoln	10,582	12,177
Natrona	13,902	71,856
Niobrara	6,978	2,924
Park	18,034	21,639
Platte	5,260	11,975
Sheridan	6,583	25,048
Sublette	12,667	4,548
Sweetwater	26,915	41,723
Teton	10,429	9,355
Uinta	5,421	13,021
Washakie	5,832	9,496
Weston	6,245	7,106

X

Xaignabouri *say-na-boo'ri*, SAYABOURI, prov (*khowèng*) of NW Laos, SE Asia; capital Muang Xaignabouri.

Xai-Xai *shī'shī*, formerly VILA DE JOÃO BELO (-1976), 25 06S 33 31E, pop(1980) 43,794, seaport capital of dist of same name and of Gaza prov, SE Mozambique, SE Africa; at the mouth of the R Limpopo, NE of Maputo; railway.

Xanthe, nome (dept) of Thráki region, Greece. See Xánthi.

Xánthi *zan'thee*, XANTHE (Eng), nome (dept) of Thráki region, NE Greece, bounded N by Bulgaria; pop(1981) 88,777; area 1,793 sq km; capital Xánthi.

Xánthi, 41 07N 24 56E, pop(1981) 31,541, capital town of Xánthi nome (dept), Thráki region, NE Greece; near the E bank of R Néstos (Mesta), and in the S foothills of the Rodopi Planina (Rhodope Mts); tobacco growing area; railway.

Xau *ksa'oo*, LAKE DOW (Eng), lake in W Central dist, Botswana, S Africa; situated at the SW edge of the Makgadikgadi salt pans.

Xiamen *shah-men*, AMOY, HSIA-MEN, 24 26N 118 07E, pop(1984e) 532,600, subtropical port city in Fujian prov, SE China; on an island of the same name in the Taiwan Strait at the mouth of the Jiulong river; in 1949 the island was connected to the mainland by a 5 km-long causeway; first settled during the Southern Song dynasty (1127-1279); it was declared an open port after the Treaty of Nanjing (1842); a special economic zone since 1981; 4 deep-water berths and a new harbour have been created; university (1921); airfield; railway; economy: electronics, food products, textiles, building materials; centre of the growing unofficial trade between China and Taiwan; monuments: 5 km E of Xiamen is the 10th-c Nanputo temple; Overseas Chinese Museum.

Xi'an *shee-ahn*, SIAN, formerly CHANGAN, SIKING, 34 16N 108 54E, pop(1984e) 2,276,500, capital of Shaanxi prov, central China; inhabited as early as 6000 BC, Xi'an was the first capital of feudal China; university (1937); airport; railway; economy: tourism, heavy industry, cotton, food processing, chemicals, electrical equipment, fertilizers; monuments: Ming Dynasty Drum Tower; 14th-c Bell Tower at the centre of the city; Banpo Neolithic village (10 km E); 30 km E, the tumulus of Emperor Qin Shi Huangdi (259-10 BC), founder of the Qin dynasty; terracotta warriors of the Emperor Qin discovered in 1974; the Big Wild Goose pagoda (652 AD) was rebuilt between 701 and 704 as a Buddhist temple to store the manuscripts brought back from India by Jian Zhen, the monk who introduced Buddhism to China; Great Mosque (742 AD) currently under reconstruction; Hua Qing hot springs, a summer resort for Chinese emperors and scene of the Xi'an incident (1936) when Chiang Kaishek was captured in an attempt to force a union between nationalists and communists against the Japanese; a palace was built here in 644 by the Tang emperor, Tai Zong, reconstruction in the Tang style took place in 1949 and tourists and Chinese can now bathe in the curative mineral waters; Zhaoling, the tomb of the Tang emperor Tia Zong was the first burial of an emperor on a mountainside rather than in a burial hill.

Xiangkhoang *syeng-KHwang*, XIENG KHOUANG, prov of E central Laos, SE Asia; capital Xiangkhoang.

Xiaogan *shee-ow-gan*, HSIAOKAN, 30 58N 113 57E, pop(1984e) 1,191,200, city in Hubei prov, E central China; NW of Wuhan.

Xingkai Hu, OZERO KHANKA, lake in SE Heilongjiang prov, NE China and SW Sikhote-Alin prov, SE USSR; the N part belongs to China, the S to the USSR; area 4,380 sq km; to the N is the lesser Xingkai Hu lake, separated from the main lake by a narrow sand bar; the 2 lakes merge in the high-water season; drained by the Song'acha He river in the NE which flows into the Wusuli Jiang (Ussuri) river.

Xingtai *shin-tī*, HSINT'AI, 37 08N 114 29E, pop(1984e) 1,143,200, city in Shandong prov, E China; SE of Jinan; railway.

Xingu *sheeng'goo*, large S tributary of the Amazon river, N central Brazil; rises in several branches in the Serra de Roncador, Mato Grosso state; flows N into Pará state; enters the Amazon W of the I de Marajó; length c.1,980 km; interrupted by falls and rapids; navigable for the lower 160 km; its chief tributary is the Río Iriri; its numerous branches flow through the Xingu National Park in Mato Grosso state.

Xingu, national park in NE Mato Grosso state, Centro-Oeste region, W central Brazil; through it flow the various branches of the Xingu river which join to form the NW border of the park; created in 1961 by the Vilas Boas brothers to protect Indian tribes of the Xingu area, it has suffered as a result of pressure from property developers; the roads which now penetrate the park threaten the continued existence of the Indian tribes living there.

Xining *shee-ning*, HSINING, SINING, 36 35N 101 55E, pop(1984e) 576,400, capital of Qinghai prov, W central China; NW of Lanzhou; railway; airfield.

Xinjiang *shin-chyahng*, SINKIANG, autonomous region in NW China; bordered NE by Mongolia, N and W by the USSR, S by India, Xizang aut region (Tibet), SW by the disputed area of Northern Kashmir, SE by Qinghai prov and E by Gansu prov; the Tien Shan range forms the NW border with the USSR and continues on through the centre of Xinjiang prov; in the N is the Junggar Pendi (Dzungarian basin), containing the Gurbantunggut Shamo desert; to the S is the Tarim Pendi basin which occupies over half of the region's area; the Taklimakan Shamo desert lies in the centre of the Tarim Pendi basin; to the S of the Tarim Pendi basin, the Kunlun Shan range forms the border with Xizang aut region; further E is the Altun Shan (Astin Tagh) range; to the SE of Ürümqi is the Turfan Depression, an important farming area situated between mountain ranges; Aydingkol Hu lake in the Turfan Depression is the lowest point in China at an alt of 154 m below sea level; in the extreme SW of Xinjiang prov is Aksai Chin, an area disputed between India and China but under Chinese administration; the region rises to 8,611 m in Qogir Feng (K2) which is situated on the border with India and Pakistan; Xinjiang is drained by the Tarim He, Manas He, Ili He and Karakax He rivers; Lop Nur in the E of the Tarim Pendi basin in SE Xinjiang is the region's largest lake with an area of 2,570 sq km; pop(1982) 13,081,681; area 1,646,800 sq km; capital Ürümqi; economy: wheat, cotton, maize, rice, silkworm cocoons, melons, grapes, sheep and horse raising, forestry, oil, coal, chemicals, textiles.

Xizang *sit-sang*, TIBET, autonomous region in SW China; bordered N by Xinjiang aut reg, NE by Qinghai prov, E by Sichuan prov, SE by Yunnan prov and Burma, S by Bhutan, India and Nepal and W by India; situated in the Qinghai-Tibet plateau, the highest plateau in the world with an average alt of 4,000 m; described as 'the roof of the world'; the majority of Xizang consists of high-altitude plateaux and unpopulated mountains; the Himalayas lie in the S of Xizang along the border with India, Nepal and Bhutan where the mountains rise to 8,848 m at Qomolangma Feng (Mt Everest); in the N is the Kunlun Shan range and its branch the Tanggula Shan; N of the

Himalayas lie the Gangdisê Shan and the Nyainqêntanglha (Nyenchen Tanglha) Shan ranges; between the Kunlun Shan and the Gangdisê Shan lies the Northern Tibet Plateau; the major farming area of Xizang is situated in the southern valleys between the Gangdisê Shan range and the Himalayas; major rivers include the Yarlung Zangbo Jiang, Nu Jiang, Lancang Jiang and the Maquan He; the centre of Xizang contains numerous fresh- and salt-water lakes; the largest salt-water lake, Nam Co, is situated to the NW of Lhasa; pop(1982) 1,892,393; area 1,221,600 sq km; capital Lhasa; economy: wheat, peas, rapeseed; sheep, yak and goat raising, forestry, medicinal musk, caterpillar fungus, textiles, mining of chromium, iron, copper, lead, zinc, borax, salt, mica, gypsum; dominated by the Buddhist lamas since the 7th century AD until the departure of the Dalai Lama into exile in 1959; conquered by the Mongols in 1279-1368 and later controlled by the Manchus in the 18th century; Chinese authority was almost non-existent between 1912 and 1949; China's rule over Xizang was restored in 1951 but effective control was only achieved after a revolt in 1959; although most of the monasteries and temples are now closed or officially declared to be historical monuments, hundreds of people still worship daily; no new monks have been ordained since the Chinese took control of Xizang in 1959; there are thought to be fewer than 1,000 lamas in Xizang, compared to almost 110,000 monks in 2,500 monasteries prior to 1959.

Xizang Gaoyuan, TIBET OR QINGHAI-TIBET PLATEAU, plateau in W and SW China; includes the whole of Xizang and Qinghai, W Sichuan prov and SW Gansu prov; at an average alt of 4,000 m, it is the highest plateau in the world; area 2.3 mn sq km; bounded S by the Himalayas, N by Kunlun Shan and Qilian Shan ranges, W by Karakoram range and E by Hengduan Shan range; the plateau itself includes the Gangdisê Shan, Nyainqêntanglha Shan, Tanggula Shan and Bayan Har Shan ranges which divide the plateau into numerous basins, valleys and lakes; it is the source of many of the rivers of E, SE and S Asia, including the Chang Jiang (Yangtze river), Huang He (Yellow river), Langcang Jiang (Mekong river), Nu Jiang (Salween), Indus, Yarlung Zangbo Jiang (Brahmaputra) and the Tarim; the largest of the plateau lakes are Nam Co lake in Xizang aut region and Qinghai Hu lake in Qinghai prov; the climate varies greatly from N to S: the S is the major farming region of the plateau, with a warm, humid climate while the centre and N are cold and dry, with ice and snow covering the land for 6 months of the year; uplift continues at a rate of more than 10 mm per year.

Xuzhou *shoo-jō*, TONGSHAN, 34 17N 117 18E, pop(1984e) 806,400, town in Jiangsu prov, E China; NNW of Nanjing; railway.

Y

Ya Ya, La, pop(1983e) 1,200, town in Villa Clara prov, central Cuba; a self-sufficient village established by Fidel Castro in 1972; formerly noted as a sugar producing area but now noted for its dairy products.

Yablonovyy Khrebet *ya'blu-nu-vee KHrye-bet'*, mountain range in SE Siberian Rossiyskaya, Soviet Union, extending c.1,120 km NE from the Mongolian border, past Chita, to the headstreams of the Olekma river; rises to 2,192 m at Sokhondo in the S; forms a section of the watershed between Arctic and Pacific drainage basins; continued NE by the Stanovoy Khrebet range; traversed by the Trans-Siberian railway.

Yacuiba *ya-kwee'ba*, 22 00S 63 43W, pop(1976) 10,792, town in Gran Chaco prov, Tarija, S Bolivia; on the border with Argentina; railway; a gas pipeline runs from Yacuiba to the town of Santa Cruz.

Yade, Massif du *yahd*, mountainous massif in W Central African Republic; on frontier with Cameroon; the two main peaks are Mt Ngaoui (1,410 m) and Mt Pana (1,356 m).

Yafo, Israel. See Tel Aviv-Yafo.

Yakima *yak'ke-maw*, 46 36N 120 31W, pop(1980) 49,826, capital of Yakima county, S central Washington, United States; on the Yakima river, 160 km SE of Seattle; named after an Indian tribe; the Yakima Indian reservation lies to the S and the Hanford Works US Atomic Energy Commission reservation lies to the E; railway; airfield.

Yako *ya'kō*, 12 59N 2 15W, town in Burkina, W Africa; 97 km NW of Ouagadougou.

Yalu *ya-loo*, river forming the N border between North Korea and Jilin and Liaoning provs, NE China; rises in the Changbai Shan range, Jilin prov; flows S, W, then SW to form the majority of the border between North Korea and China; flows into Korea Bay; length 790 km.

Yamag'ata, 38 16N 140 19E, pop(1980) 237,041, capital of Yamagata prefecture, Tōhoku region, N Honshū island, Japan; 288 km NE of Tōkyo; university (1949); railway; economy: metal products, rice trade.

Yamal, Poluostrov *yu-mal'*, tundra-covered peninsula in Tyumenskaya oblast, Rossiyskaya, N Soviet Union, projecting N into the Karskoye More (Kara Sea), and bounded E by Obskaya Guba (Ob' Bay); length 640 km; max width 224 km; there are numerous small lakes and rivers; the land is generally low lying and poorly drained.

Yam'bol or **Jam'bol**, okrug (prov) of E Bulgaria traversed S-N by the R Tundzha; area 4,162 sq km; pop(1981) 205,000.

Yambol, 42 28N 26 30E, pop(1981) 84,528, agricultural and commercial capital of Yambol okrug (prov), E Bulgaria; on the R Tundzha, 304 km E of Sofiya; airfield; railway; economy: textiles, metal products and food processing; monuments: mosque and Turkish bazaar.

Yamoussoukro *ya-moo-soo'krō*, 6 49N 5 17W, pop(1983 70,000, country capital designate in Bouaké dept, S Ivory Coast, W Africa; a weekend resort town, NW of Abidjan; presidential residence; economy: agricultural trade.

Yamuna *yah'mu-na*, JUMNA, river of NW India; rises in the Himalayas of N Uttar Pradesh state, India; flows SW through the Siwalik Hills to Delhi, forming part of the boundary between Uttar Pradesh and Haryana states; flows generally SE past Mathura, Agra and Allahabad, where it joins the R Ganga (Ganges); Yamuna's confluence with the Ganga is one of the most sacred to the Hindus in India; the Taj Mahal at Agra is one of the many notable monuments located on the banks of the Yamuna; length 1,370 km.

Yanam', district of Pondicherry union territory, E India; an enclave in Andhra Pradesh state, at the mouth of the R Godavari, 480 km NNE of Madras; held by France until 1954; area 30 sq km; pop(1981) 11,631.

Yan'an *yen-ahn*, YENAN, 36 41N 109 20E, pop(1984e) 254,100, town in Shaanxi prov, central China; on the Yan He river; airfield; Yan'an was the headquarters of the Communist Party in 1936-47; the Yan'an Pagoda, built during the Song dynasty (960-1279), became a national symbol after the 1949 revolution; 4 caves in the locality were occupied by Mao Zedong and are now museums displaying the original furnishings and contemporary photographs of Chairman Mao.

Yanbu' al Baḩr *yen'bō*, 24 07N 38 04E, new industrial town in Western prov, W Saudi Arabia; on the E shore of the Red Sea, approx 320 km NNW of Jiddah (Jedda); Red Sea port for Al Madīnah (Medina); economy: centre of oil, petrochemical, and heavy industries; this new industrial project is to be fuelled by natural gas supplied from the 1,200 km pipeline from oil fields in the E of the country.

Yancheng *yan-cheng*, YENCH'ENG, 33 23N 120 08E, pop(1984e) 1,236,900, city in Jiangsu prov, E China; NE of Nanjing, on the Grand Canal.

Yangchow, city in Jiangsu prov, E China. See Yangzhou.

Yanggang *yang-gang*, RYANGGANG, province in N North Korea; bordered N by Jilin prov, China, along the Yalu river; capital Hyesan.

Yangku, capital of Shanxi prov, NE central China. See Taiyuan.

Yangtze, river in China. See Chang Jiang.

Yangudi Rassa Wild Ass, national park in Ethiopia, NE Africa; area 3,000 sq km.

Yangzhou *yang-jō*, YANGCHOW, 32 25N 119 26E, pop(1984e) 382,200, city in Jiangsu prov, E China; on the Chang Jiang (Yangtze) and Hua rivers; first settled during the Spring and Autumn Period (770-476 BC); in the 6th century AD it became a major communications centre after the building of the Grand Canal; the city has the largest multiple-purpose water control project in China; begun in 1961 and finished in 1975, the project consists of 4 electric pumping stations, check gates, navigation locks and trunk waterways with facilities for irrigation, drainage, navigation and power generation; economy: artistic centre for crafts, lacquerware screens, jade carving and printing; monuments: the Fajing Si (Fajing temple) was built by Jian Zhen, the monk who brought Buddhism to China during the Tang dynasty (618-907), and rebuilt in the 1930s; Yangzhou museum contains approx 100 paintings and calligraphy scrolls by the Eight Eccentricities, a school of unorthodox painters.

Yantai *yan-tī*, CHEEFOO, 37 34N 121 22E, pop(1984e) 699,400, town in Shandong prov, E China; on the N coast of the Shandong Bandao peninsula; a special economic zone; railway; economy: tourism, fishing, wine and brandy.

Yan'tra or **Jan'tra**, river in N Bulgaria, formed near Gabrovo by the meeting of three headstreams rising in the Stara Planina (Balkan Mts); flows N to meet the R Danube E of Svishtov; length 270 km; tributaries Bregovitsa and Rositsa rivers.

Yao *ya-ō*, 34 36N 135 37E, pop(1980) 272,706, city in Ōsaka prefecture, Kinki region, S Honshū island, Japan; a residential suburb, 8 km E of Ōsaka; railway.

Yaoundé *ya-oon'day*, YAUNDE, 3 51N 11 31E, pop(1984) 552,000, capital of Cameroon, W Africa; also capital of Centre prov; 210 km E of Douala; Mount Fébé nearby; Germans established a military post in 1899 and the town flourished from 1907 as an administrative centre; occupied by Belgian colonial troops in 1915; became capital of

French Cameroon in 1921, though replaced by Douala between 1940 and 1946; university (1962); football stadium (1972); statues commemorate Charles Atangana, one of the city's earliest Christians, who became the Ewondos chief and assisted Dr Jamot in his fight against sleeping sickness (trypanosomiasis); Jamot arrived in Cameroon in 1922 to study sleeping sickness which then affected 25% of the population; by 1929, this figure had been reduced to under 2%; there is a railway link with the coast (Douala); airport (7 km); economy: tourism, sugar refining, cigarettes, oil refining.

Yap, one of the Federated States of Micronesia, W Pacific, comprising the 4 large adjoining islands of Yap, Gagil-Tomil, Map, and Rumung, plus some 130 outer islands; area 119 sq km; pop(1980) 8,172; capital Colonia; Yap is famous for its stone money, dating back to the beginning of the Yapese civilization.

Yaracuy *ya-ra-koo'i*, state in N Venezuela, occupying the Yaracuy river valley which is flanked by the Sierra de Aroa (W) and outliers of the coastal range (E); pop(1980) 313,073; area 7,096 sq km; capital San Felipe.

Yare, river rising SSE of East Dereham, Norfolk, E England; flows 80 km E past Norwich and through the Norfolk Broads to meet the R Waveney at Breydon Water by Great Yarmouth.

Yarlung Zangbo Jiang, river in SW China, NE India and Bangladesh. See Brahmaputra.

Yar'mouth, 50 42N 1 29W, pop(1981) 920, port, South Wight dist, Isle of Wight, S England; ferry links with Lymington in Hampshire; a popular yachting centre.

Yaroslavl' *ya-re-slaf'ly'*, 57 34N 39 52E, pop(1983) 619,000, river port capital of Yaroslavskaya oblast, E European Rossiyskaya, Soviet Union; the oldest town on the R Volga, said to have been founded c.1024; university (1971); railway; on the highway between Moskva (Moscow) and Arkhangel'sk (Archangel); economy: cotton and linen fabric, synthetic rubber, motor tyres, lorries, diesel engines, electrical machinery, chemicals, and leather; tobacco and oil processing; monument: 12th-c Spaso-Preobrazhenski monastery.

Yāsūj, YASOOF', 30 40N 51 36E, pop(1983) 19,668, capital town of Kohkīlūyeh va Būyer Aḥmadī, W central Iran.

Yazd, prov in central Iran; pop(1982) 369,122; area 63,455 sq km; capital Yazd.

Ybbs *ips*, river in N Austria, rising in SW Niederösterreich state, near the Steiermark border; flows W, N and NE to meet the R Danube E of Ybbs; called the Ois in its upper course; length 126 km.

Yellow River, river in China. See Huang He.

Yellow Sea, HWANG HAI (Chin), inlet of the Pacific Ocean, lying to the NW of the East China Sea; bounded to the N and W by China and to the E by North Korea and South Korea; max width 643 km; max depth 152 m over the continental shelf; linked to the Sea of Japan by the Korean Strait; warm surface current moves in an anti-clockwise direction, deflected owing to the shape of the coastline; extended by Bo Hai gulf and Korean Bay; named for its colour, due to the silt brought down by the rivers which flow into it.

Yellowknife, 62 30N 114 29W, pop(1981) 10,500, capital of Northwest Territories, in Mackenzie dist, N Canada; on the NW shore of the Great Slave Lake at the mouth of the Yellowknife river; largest town in the Northwest Territories and capital since 1967; economy: gold mining.

Yellowstone, national park in NW Wyoming, United States; bordered W by Idaho and Montana, N by Montana; the park contains over 3,000 hot springs and geysers, including Old Faithful, a geyser that spurts water at regular intervals; the park also contains Yellowstone and Jackson lakes; the highest point is Electric Peak (3,350 m) in the extreme NW of the park; area 8,991 sq km; established in 1872.

Yemen, North or **Yemen**, official name Yemen Arab Republic, AL JAMHURIYA AL ARABIYA AL YAMANIYA, republic occupying the SW corner of the Arabian peninsula, bounded W by the Red Sea, N by Saudi

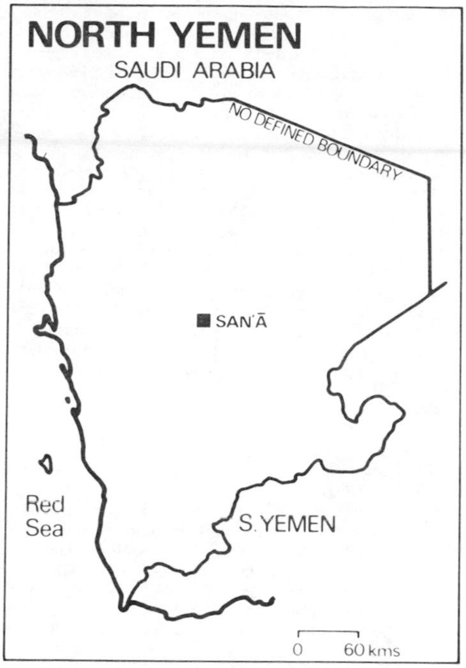

Arabia, and S by South Yemen (the NE border is undefined); timezone GMT +3; area 195,000 sq km; capital San'ā; chief towns Ta'izz and Al Ḥudaydah; pop(1980) 7,701,893; most people live in small villages and towns scattered throughout the highlands and along the Tihamat coastal plain; the dominant religion is Islam (Shi'a and Sunni sects); the official language is Arabic but English is widely understood; the unit of currency is the riyal; membership of Arab League, FAO, G-77, IBRD, ICAO, IDA, Islamic Development Bank, IFAD, IFC, ILO, IMF, IMO, INTELSAT, INTERPOL, ITU, NAM, OIC, UN, UNESCO, UPU, WFTU, WHO, WIPO, WMO.

Physical description and climate. The narrow desert plain of Tihamat bordering the Red Sea rises abruptly to a mountainous interior. These mountains, which are heavily terraced for agriculture, attain heights of between 3,000 and 3,500 m. Further E they drop in a series of precipitous steps to the fringes of the dry and arid Rub al Khālī ('empty quarter'). Rivers draining E disappear into deeply entrenched wadi beds. The W coastal strip is hot and humid with a mean annual temperature of 29°C. By contrast, the highlands are mild with summer maxima around 29°C. Winters can be cold and frosts are not uncommon. The average annual rainfall for the country is 380-500 mm, decreasing E to less than 120 mm.

History, government and constitution. Turkish occupation of North Yemen (1872-1918) was followed by the rule of the Hamid al-Din dynasty until the revolution of 1962. Territorial claims were made over Aden (formerly a British protectorate) and to British protected sultanates in S Arabia. During the revolution the republican regime was supported by Egyptian troops while the royalists sought aid from Saudi Arabia and Jordan. Fighting between the two forces continued until August 1967 when Egyptian troops were withdrawn. In 1979 there was a brief period of conflict with South Yemen. The constitution of 1970 is currently suspended. Government is the responsibility of a military command council with an appointed cabinet of about 20 ministers. A constituent people's assembly of 99 members was appointed in 1978 for a term of 2-3 years.

Economy. Agriculture is the mainstay of the economy employing approx 75% of the labour force. Most farming is at subsistence level, the staple crops being millet, wheat, barley, pulses, fruit, and vegetables. Cotton, grown largely on the Tihamat plain, has overtaken Mocha coffee as the principal cash crop. Cultivated land at present covers 13,000 sq km but irrigation schemes such as that at Wadi Mawr (watering 600 sq km) are likely to significantly increase the area under cultivation. The growing of qat, a narcotic leaf, is becoming a major agricultural enterprise. The area under qat cultivation is between 410 and 470 sq km, concentrated mainly in the mountainous interior. The industrial sector is small (6% of GDP in 1984) and is based on the manufacture of cotton textiles, cement, aluminium products, and handicrafts. Apart from oil, which was discovered in the Marib al Jawf basin, chief exports include qat, cotton, coffee, hides, and vegetables, supplied mainly to China, Italy, and Saudi Arabia. Remittances sent from Yemenis in Saudi Arabia and the Gulf states contribute significantly to the balance of payments.

Communications. There are no railways in North Yemen. Al Ḩudaydah is the major port. Airports have been built at San'ā, Ta'izz, and Al Ḩudaydah.

Administrative divisions. North Yemen is divided into 10 provs which are further subdivided into districts.

Yemen, South, official name The People's Democratic Republic of Yemen, JUMHURIJAH AL-YEMEN AL DIMUQRATIYAH AL SHA'ABIJAH, republic on the SW coast of the Arabian peninsula, bounded NW by the Yemen Arab Republic (North Yemen), N by Saudi Arabia, E by Oman, and S by the Gulf of Aden; timezone GMT +3; area 336,570 sq km (border with Saudi Arabia and N Yemen undefined); capital Aden; chief towns Al Mukallā and Ash Shaykh 'Uthmān; pop(1981e) 2,030,000; the majority of the pop are Arabs, with the addition of some Indians, Somalis, and Europeans; Arabic is the official language but English is widely understood; the dominant religion is Islam; the unit of currency is the dinar; membership of UN, FAO, G-77, GATT, IBRD, ICAO, IDA, Islamic Development Bank, IFAD, ILO IMF, IMO, ITU, NAM, OIC, UNESCO, UPU, WFTU, WHO, WMO, WTO, Arab Common Market, Arab League, Arab Fund for Economic and Social Development, Islamic Conference, World Bank.

Physical description and climate. S Yemen includes the island of Socotra in the Gulf of Aden and the islands of Perim and Kamarān in the Red Sea. The flat, narrow coastal plain is backed by a range of steep mountains rising to almost 2,500 m. N of these mountains a high plateau eventually falls to merge with the gravel plains and sand wastes of the Rub al Khālī basin. Numerous wadis descend from the mountains towards the coastal plain, the most important being the Ḩaḑramawt (240 km) and Bana valleys. The climate is hot throughout the year with max temperatures reaching over 40°C in July and Aug. Despite the aridity humidity is very high. Average temperatures at Aden vary from 24°C in Jan to 32°C in July and the average annual rainfall is 46 mm.

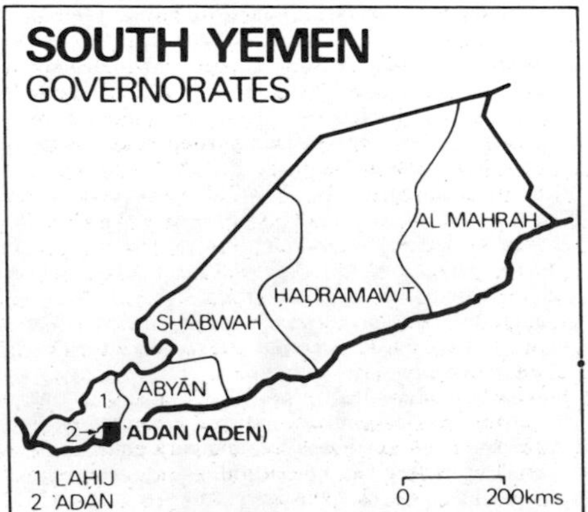

History, government and constitution. The fishing port of Aden was occupied by Britain in 1839. The town and its immediate environs became a British colony and protectorate administered from Bombay. While Aden developed as a coaling station and later as a trading city the rest of the country to the E remained pastoral. Between Aug and Oct 1967 the 17 sultanates of the Federation of South Arabia were overrun by rulers of the National Liberation Front. British troops were withdrawn from S Yemen on 29 November 1967 and on 30 November the Southern Yemen People's Republic was proclaimed. In 1969 a new constitution was adopted and the name of the country was changed to the People's Democratic Republic of Yemen. Legislative power is vested in the Supreme People's Council, a body of 101 members elected from the ruling Yemen Socialist Party.

Economy. The economy is largely based on agriculture and light industry. Millet, sorghum, dates, and cotton are grown in the fertile silted valleys and floodplains, while wheat and barley are grown at higher altitudes. Cotton is the major cash crop and principal export. Fishing is also a major industry. Oil refining and a few light industries are centred on the port of Aden. Crude oil is imported from the Arabian Gulf and the refined products are exported mainly to UK and Japan. N Yemen and E Africa are the chief trading partners but some cement and sugar is imported from communist countries.

Communications. There are no railways in S Yemen. The 5,600 km of highways include 1,700 km of surfaced road and 3,270 km of motorable track. Aden is the major port but there are also important harbours at Al Mukallā and Nashtoun. Aden International Airport is located at Khormaksar in Aden governorate.

Administrative divisions. South Yemen is divided into the 6 governorates of 'Adan, Abyān, Laḩij, Shabwah, Ḩaḑramawt and Al Mahrah.

Yenan, town in Shaanxi prov, central China. See Yan'an.

Yendi *yen'dee*, 9 30N 0 01W, town E of Tamale in Northern region, NE central Ghana, W Africa; 88 km E of Tamale.

Yengema', 8 39N 10 58W, pop(1974) 15,000, town in Kono dist, Eastern prov, Sierra Leone, W Africa; economy: diamonds.

Yenisey *yen-yi-syay'*, river in central Siberian Rossiyskaya, Soviet Union; rises in the E Sayanskiy Khrebet range, Tuvinskaya ASSR; flows generally N through Krasnoyarskiy kray, past Krasnoyarsk, Igarka, and Dudinka, until it discharges into the Karskoye More (Kara Sea) via a long estuary (Yeniseyskiy Zaliv); length 3,487 km; drainage basin area 2,580,000 sq km; chief tributaries Kureyka, Nizhnyaya Tunguska, Podkamennaya Tunguska, and Angara rivers; the navigation season is 5 months in the upper river course and 3 months in the lower reaches; forms the W boundary of the Sredne Sibirskoye Ploskogor'ye (Central Siberian Plateau); there are coal reserves in the upper valley and non-ferrous metal deposits at Noril'sk near the mouth of the river; the upper course of the river has great hydroelectric generating potential with power stations at Krasnoyarsk and Sayanogorsk.

Yeovil *yō'vil*, 50 57N 2 39W, pop(1981) 36,597, market town in Yeovil dist, Somerset, SW England; 34 km E of Taunton; airfield; railway; economy: engineering, textiles, helicopters, electronics, leather, livestock trade; monuments: 14th-c church of St John the Baptist, Cadbury castle (10 km NE), Montacute House (5 km W).

Yerevan *ye-re-van'*, ERIVAN (Eng), 40 10N 44 31E, pop(1983) 1,095,000, capital city of Armyanskaya (Armenia) SSR, SE European Soviet Union; on the R Razdan, 15 km from the Turkish frontier; the highest part of the city stands at 1,042 m above sea-level; one of the world's most ancient cities; university; railway;

airfield; economy: vodka and wine production; monument: ruins of a 16th-c Turkish fortress.

Yeu, Ile d' *eel dy'*, island in the N Bay of Biscay, 20 km off the coast of Vendée dept, W France, some 60 km S of St-Nazaire; area 23 sq km; 10 km long by 4 km wide; Port Joinville is linked by car ferry with the mainland resort of Fromentine, near Beauvoir; the S coast, called Côte Sauvage, lies exposed to rough weather; the harbour of Port-de-la-Meule, on this coast, has a lobster fishing fleet; Marshal Pétain was imprisoned here after World War II until his death in 1951.

Yiannitsá *yee-nit-sah'*, GIANNITSA (Eng), 40 46N 22 24E, pop(1981) 21,082, town in Pélla nome (dept), Makedhonia region, N Greece; on the road between Edhessa and Thessaloníki.

Yichun *ee-choon*, I-CH'UN, 47 41N 129 10E, pop(1984e) 814,300, town in central Heilongjiang prov, NE China; NE of Harbin, on the Tangwang He river; railway.

Yinchuan *yin-chwahn*, YINCH'UAN, 38 30N 106 19E, pop(1984e) 383,300, capital of Ningxia aut region, N China; NE of Lanzhou; airfield.

Yin-hsien, town in Zhejiang prov, E China. See Ningbo.

Yizre'el *yiz-re-el'*, JEZREEL *jez'reel*, sub-district of North dist, N Israel; pop(1983) 232,482; area 1,197 sq km.

Ylivieska *u'liv-ee'es-kah*, 64 05N 24 30E, pop(1982) 12,170, steel producing town in Oulu prov, W Finland, on R Kalajoki; established in 1965; railway.

Yns Môn, ANGLESEY, island district of Gwynedd, NW Wales; separated from Arfon by the Menai Strait which is spanned by a suspension road bridge (1818-26), and by a tubular railway bridge (1846-50); area 715 sq km; chief towns are Holyhead, Beaumaris, Amlwych, Llanerchymedd, Llangefni and Menai Bridge; the island is linked to Holy I by a viaduct; ferry link from Holyhead to Dun Laoghaire in Ireland; economy: agriculture, sheep rearing, tourism.

Yogyakarta *yahg-ye-kahrt'e*, JOGJAKARTA, DJOKJARKARTA, special territory, S central Jawa, Indonesia; capital Yogyakarta; formerly a sultanate; the main focus of revolutionary activity against the Dutch in the 1940s; pop(1980) 2,750,813; area 3,169 sq km; economy: cattle, cashew nuts.

Yogyakarta, or **Yogya**, 7 48S 110 24E, pop(1980) 342,267, capital of Yogyakarta special territory, S central Jawa, Indonesia; at the foot of Gunung Merapi; cultural centre of Jawa; 2 universities (1945, 1949); railway; airfield; monuments: Yogya kraton; events: Islamic and Hindu festivals such as Seketan (Mohammed's birthday), Garebeg Besar and Galungan; Siraman bathing ceremony, cleansing the royal heirlooms.

Yojoa, Lago de *yō-hō'a*, lake in W Honduras, Central America; between Tegucigalpa and San Pedro Sula; length 40 km; max width 8 km; connected with the seaport of Puerto Cortés by the Blanco and Ulúa rivers.

Yokkaichi *yō-kī'chee*, 34 58N 136 38E, pop(1980) 255,442, port city in Mie prefecture, Kinki region, central Honshū island, Japan; on NW shore of Ise-wan Bay, 32 km SW of Nagoya; railway; economy: textiles, porcelain, chemicals, oil refining.

Yokohama *yō-kō-ha'ma*, 35 28N 139 28E, pop(1980) 2,773,674, port capital of Kanagawa prefecture, Kanto region, central Honshū island, Japan; on W shore of Tōkyo-wan Bay, SW of Tōkyo; the 4th largest city in Japan, handling 30% of Japan's foreign trade; 2 universities (1949); originally a fishing village, it was chosen as the first Japanese port to be opened to foreign trade in 1858; the Japanese, on the excuse of limited space, granted foreigners access to the marshy area of Yokohama instead of Kanagawa and the settlement was abandoned in 1899; the port was absorbed into Kanagawa in 1901; Japan's first railway line linking the port with Tōkyo was opened in 1872; much of the city was destroyed by an earthquake in 1923 and by bombing in 1945; railway; economy: shipbuilding, oil refining, engineering, chemicals, glass, furniture, clothes, trade in silk, rayon and fish; monuments: Sankei en Park, laid out in the 19th century, contains a collection of monuments from all over Japan, including pagodas, pavilions and tea houses; to the S of the park is a building containing statues of the 8 saints or sages of the world; the Silk Museum has a display covering the history of Japan's silk industry; events: Port Festival in May; Black Ships' Festival in July.

Yola *yō'la*, 9 14N 12 32E, pop(1981e) 22,000, capital of Gongola state, E Nigeria, W Africa; near the frontier with Cameroon, S of the R Benue and 420 km ESE of Jos; airfield.

Yonkers, 40 56N 73 54W, pop(1980) 195,351, town in Westchester county, SE New York, United States; a residential suburb on the Hudson river, at the N edge of Greater New York about 24 km N of the city centre; named after the courtesy title ('Jonkheer') given to the early Dutch settler Adriaen van der Donck; railway; economy: retailing; monuments: St Andrews golf course (first course in the USA), Hudson River Museum, Sherwood House (restored pre-Revolution farmhouse).

Yonne *yon*, river in central France rising in Nièvre dept on N slope of Mont Beauvray in the Monts du Morvan; flows NW past Auxerre, Joigny and Sens to meet the R Seine E of Montereau; length 293 km; navigable to Auxerre; tributaries Cure, Serein and Armançon rivers.

Yopal, El *yō-pal'*, 5 20N 72 19W, pop(1985) 12,684, capital of Casanare intendency, E central Colombia, South America; in the tropical E foothills of the Andes SE of Tunja.

Yorba Linda *yor'ba lin'da*, 33 53N 117 49W, pop(1980) 28,254, city in Orange county, SW California, United States; 16 km N of Santa Ana.

York, EBORACUM (anc), 53 58N 1 05W, pop(1981) 99,910, city in North Yorkshire, N England; a Roman settlement was founded here in 71 AD as capital of the Roman province of Britannia; thereafter as a royal and religious centre it became capital of Anglo-Saxon Northumbria; captured by the Danes in 867 AD, it became known as Jorvik; the Archbishop of York bears the title Primate of England; the city expanded rapidly in the 19th century as a railway centre; university (1963); railway; economy: foodstuffs, glass, railway coaches, scientific instruments; monuments: York Minster (12-15th-c); National Railway Museum; Castle Museum; event: York Festival in June.

York, 39 58N 76 44W, pop(1980) 44,619, county seat of York county, S Pennsylvania, United States; 37 km S of Harrisburg; railway; capital of the American colonies (1777-78) while the British occupied Philadelphia.

Yorkshire Dales, national park in North Yorkshire and Cumbria, England; area 1,761 sq km; established in 1954; characterized by limestone scenery (including Kilnsey Crag, Gordale Crag and Malham Cove), popular with potholers and fell walkers; the 3 main peaks of Ingleborough, Whernside and Pen-y-Ghent; historic sites include Bolton abbey (Wharfedale) and the Roman fort at Bainbridge; there are information centres at Clapham, Grassington, Hawes, Aysgarth Falls, Malham and Sedbergh.

Yorktown, 37 14N 76 30W, county seat of York county, SE Virginia, United States; at the mouth of the R York, 32 km N of Newport News; in Colonial National Historical Park; Revolutionary troops under Washington and Rochambeau besieged British forces under Lord Cornwallis here in 1781, Cornwallis eventually surrendering; the town was also besieged during the Civil War in 1862 by Union forces under McClellan.

Yoro, dept in N Honduras, Central America, on the Caribbean coast; pop(1983e) 304,310; area 7,935 sq km; capital Yoro; largely mountainous and well-forested; drained by the Río Aguán; economy: livestock, coffee, sugar cane, bananas.

Yosemite *yō-sem'i-ti* ('grizzly bear'), national park in E California, United States; situated in the Sierra Nevada, 295 km E of San Francisco; the park consists of an 11 km-long valley full of natural granite monoliths and waterfalls; rises to 3,990 m in Mt Lyell in the SE of the park; notable features include Half Dome Mt, El Capitan and the Mariposa Grove; drained by the Merced river; area 3,083 sq km; established in 1890.

Yoshkar Ola *yush-kar-u-la'*, IOSHKAR OLA, 56 38N 47 52E, pop(1983) 223,000, capital city of Mariyskaya ASSR, E central European Rossiyskaya, Soviet Union; on the R Kokshaga, a tributary of the Volga; founded in 1578 as a Russian outpost; railway; economy: pharmaceuticals and agricultural machinery.

Youghal *yol*, EOCHAILL (Gael), 51 57N 7 50W, pop(1981) 6,145, resort and market town in Cork county, Munster, S Irish Republic; at mouth of R Blackwater, on Youghal Bay near the border with Waterford county; historically a stronghold of the Fitzgerald family; railway; economy: fishing, crafts, pottery, lace; monuments: collegiate church (1464); Myrtle Grove, the home of Sir Walter Raleigh, who is said to have planted the first potato here.

Young, 32 44S 57 36W, pop(1985) 11,939, town in Río Negro dept, W Uruguay; NE of Fray Bentos; railway.

Youngstown, 41 06N 80 39W, pop(1980) 115,436, county seat of Mahoning county, E Ohio, United States; on R Mahoning, 69 km E of Akron and 11 km W of Pennsylvania border; a city since 1859; university (1908); railway; economy: former centre of iron and steel industry in the state.

Yozgat *yoz-gat'*, mountainous prov in central Turkey; pop(1980) 504,433; area 14,123 sq km; capital Yozgat; economy: mohair, wool, lead mining, grain.

Ypres, town in Belgium. See Ieper.

Ystradgynlais-Ystalyfera *es-trad-gen'lī-es-tal-e-ve'rah*, 51 47N 3 45W, pop(1981) 10,416, valley town in Brecknock dist, Powys, E Wales.

Yu Shan *yoo shan*, MT MORRISON (Eng), highest peak on Taiwan and the highest in NE Asia; height 3,997 m; situated in the central range of the island, to the E of the town of Chia-i; Yu Shan in English means 'jade mountain'.

Yucatán *yoo-kah-tahn'*, state in SE Mexico; situated on the N Yucatán peninsula; bounded N by the Gulf of Mexico, by Campeche (W and SW) and by Quintana Roo (E and SE); subtropical limestone lowlands; approx 36% of the land is covered in forests; in the drier NW is savannah vegetation; pop(1980) 1,034,648; area 38,402 sq km; capital Mérida; economy: grain, tropical fruit, sisal and sisal products, apiculture, fishing, timber, sea salt, textiles, tobacco, brewing, tourism; there are numerous Mayan ruins including Chichén Itzá and Uxmal; the name also often applies to the whole peninsula, including the states of Quintana Roo and Campeche; the Yucatán peninsula has no river system but receives its water supply from subterranean wells (*cenotes*).

Yugoslavia or **Jugoslavia** *yoo-gō-slah'vi-a*, official name The Socialist Federal Republic of Yugoslavia, SOCIJALISTIČKA FEDERATIVNA REPUBLIKA JUGOSLAVIJA (Yug), communist state of 6 constituent federal republics in the Balkan peninsula of SE Europe; bounded W by the Adriatic Sea, E by Romania and Bulgaria, SW by Albania, N by Austria and Hungary and S by Greece; area 256,409 sq km; timezone GMT +2; capital Beograd (Belgrade); chief towns include Zagreb, Skopje, Sarajevo and Ljubljana; major seaports include Rijeka, Split, Koper, Bar, Ploce; pop(1981) 22,424,687; population comprises Serbs (36%), Croats (20%), Slovenes (8%), Albanians (8%), Macedonians (6%), Yugoslavs (5%), Montenegrins (2.5%), Hungarians (2%); 41% of the population are of the Serbian Orthodox church and 32% are Roman Catholic; in 1947 Italy ceded most of Istria including Rijeka and Zadar to Yugoslavia; the currency is the dinar of 100 paras; national holiday 29 Nov

(Proclamation of the Socialist Federal Republic of Yugoslavia); membership of ASSIMER, FAO, G-77, GATT, IAEA, IBA, IBRD, ICAC, ICAO, IDA, IDB, IFAD, IFC, IHO, ILO, IMF, IMO, INTELSAT, INTERPOL, IPU, ITC, ITU, NAM, OECD, UN, UNESCO, UPU, WHO, WIPO, WMO, WTO.

Physical description. In the N the country is dominated by the Danube, Drava, Tisza and Sava rivers, whose plains in the NE (the only low-lying part) are rich and fertile. The N is crossed by the Julian (Julijske Alpe) and Karawanken Alps, rising to 2,863 m at Triglav, which is the highest peak in Yugoslavia; the Adriatic is fringed by the Dinaric Alps; the S is a mass of ill-defined mountain ranges with summits of over 2,500 m, cut by deep river valleys, notably those of the R Morava, flowing N to the Danube, and the Vardar, flowing S to the Aegean. On the S border there are several great lakes including L Ohrid, L Prespa and L Scutari. About 34% of the country is forested with beech, oak, chestnut and pine; 32% is arable land and 25% is meadow and pasture.

Climate. A variable climate, Mediterranean on the Adriatic coast, continental in the N and NE cereal plains and almost tropically hot in Macedonia during the summer. Rain falls throughout the year with a summer maximum in the N. The upland climate is colder with considerable winter snow.

History, government and constitution. In the past the constituent republics have been governed by Rome, Turkey and Austria, their separate identities being accentuated by linguistic and religious differences. In 1918 Serbs, Croats and Slovenes united under one monarch and in 1929 the country was renamed Yugoslavia; after a period of civil war between Serbian royalists (Cetniks), Croatian nationalists and communists and the partitioning of the country during World War II, a People's Federal Republic was established in 1945 under the leadership of Josip Broz Tito. Yugoslavia is governed by a bicameral Federal Assembly which is elected every 4 years and comprises a 220-delegate Federal Chamber and smaller Chamber of Republics and Provinces; delegates are elected from republican and provincial assemblies; executive power is vested in the Federal Executive Council and the State Presidency is a collective, rotating policy-making body composed of a representative from each republic and autonomous province. The League of Communists of Yugoslavia is the only political party. Following a break with the USSR in 1948 Yugoslavia has followed an independent form of communism and a policy of non-alignment.

Economy. Since World War II Yugoslavia has extended its industrial base, particularly in the manufacture of machine tools, chemicals, textiles, the processing of food (particularly meat products), wood and metal products and the refining of oil. Agricultural output has increased with the introduction of modern farming methods, with the per hectare use of fertilizers rising 48-fold between 1948 and 1978 and a total increase in tractor power of about 60 times in the same period. The main agricultural products are wheat, maize, sugar-beet and livestock; nearly 60% of Yugoslavia's trade is with non-communist countries.

Administrative divisions. Yugoslavia is divided into 6 constituent federal republics including 2 autonomous provinces as follows:

Republic	*area (sq km)*	*pop(1981)*
Bosna-Hercegovina	51,129	4,124,256
Crna Gora	13,812	584,310
Hrvatska	56,538	4,601,469
Makedonija	25,713	1,909,112
Slovenija	20,251	1,891,864
Srbija	88,361	9,313,676
Kosovo (autonomous prov)	10,887	1,584,440
Vojvodina (autonomous prov)	21,506	2,034,772

Yukon *yoo'kon*, territory in NW Canada; bounded W by Alaska, S by British Columbia, E by Mackenzie dist, Northwest Territories and N by Mackenzie Bay and the Beaufort Sea; an area of plateaux and mountain ranges, the Yukon rises to 5,950 m at Mt Logan in the St Elias Mts, the highest point in Canada; in the E are the Selwyn Mts; S Yukon is drained by the Yukon river and its tributaries the Teslin, Pelly, Stewart, White and Klondike rivers; N Yukon is drained by the Peel and Porcupine rivers, tributaries of the Mackenzie and Yukon rivers respectively; the largest lakes are Kluane, Aishihik, Laberge and Teslin; in the N is Northern Yukon National Park; pop(1981) 22,135; area 531,844 sq km; capital Whitehorse; other towns include Watson Lake and Dawson City; economy: minerals (gold, silver, zinc, lead, copper), hydroelectric power; the Yukon-Alaska border was defined by a treaty between Britain and Russia in 1825; in 1842 a Hudson's Bay Co fur-trading post was set up in the region; the first gold prospectors entered the area in 1873 and numbers grew rapidly; in 1895 Yukon was created a district of the Northwest Territories; it was made a separate territory in 1898 when the Klondike gold rush was at its height (the gold was discovered on Bonanza Creek in Aug 1896); the W border was established in 1903 by the Alaska Boundary Tribunal; the terr is governed by a 5-member Executive Council appointed from among the 16-member Legislative Assembly which is elected every 4 years.

Yukon, major river in North America; in Yukon terr, Canada and Alaska; its headstreams rise near the border with British Columbia; from here the Yukon flows generally NW past Whitehorse, Carmacks and Minto, N past Dawson and turns NW again to flow past Forty Mile and into Alaska; the river continues through the Yukon-Charley rivers Nature Preserve and on to Fort Yukon; from here it turns W and SW to flow down through central Alaska past Tanana, Galena and Holy Cross; the Yukon then veers NW to pass Mountain Village and enters the Bering Sea in a wide delta near Alakanuk; the delta is 129-145 km wide, but only one of its mouths is navigable; length to the head of the longest headstream (the Nisutlin) near the British Columbia border is 3,185 km, 2,036 km of which lie in Alaska; the river is navigable as far as Dawson and as far as Whitehorse (approx 2,735 km upstream) for smaller vessels; the lower course of the Yukon is broad and muddy, flowing through a marshy plain; at its bend in NE Alaska the river widens into the Yukon Flats (16-32 km wide for approx 320 km); chief tributaries include the Teslin, Pelly, White, Stewart, Klondike, Porcupine, Chandalar, Tanana, Koyukuk and Innoko rivers; the river is ice-bound from Oct to June; during the 1897-98 Klondike gold rush the Yukon was a major transportation route to the Dawson gold-mining area.

Yukon, Northern, national park in N Yukon terr, NW Canada; bordered W by Alaska, N by the Beaufort Sea; most of the land lies beyond the N limit of tree growth; area 10,168 sq km; established in 1984.

Yuma *yoo'ma*, 32 43N 114 37W, pop(1980) 42,433, county seat of Yuma county, SW Arizona, United States; on the Colorado river, near its junction with the R Gila; railway; economy: cattle, citrus fruits, melons, winter vegetables, grains, and cotton; a developing resort, owing to its favourable climate; the city's economy is boosted by the nearby military installations of Yuma Proving Grounds and a US Marine Corps air station; monuments: Fort Yuma (1850), Territorial Prison museum.

Yunki, town in Jilin prov, NE China. See Jilin.

Yun-lin, county of W Taiwan; area 1,290.8 sq km; pop(1982e) 796,751.

Yunnan *yoo-nan*, prov in S China; situated on the S border of SW China; bordered W by Burma, S by Laos and Vietnam, E by Guangxi aut region and Guizhou prov, N by Sichuan prov and by Xizang aut region in the extreme NW; mountainous in the NW Hengduan Shan and Nu Shan ranges; major rivers include the Nu Jiang, Lancang Jiang, Jinsha Jiang, Yuan Jiang and the Nanpan Jiang;

Yunnan contains many fault lakes, the largest being Dian Chi to the SW of Kunming and Er Hai in the NW, both freshwater lakes; pop(1982) 32,533,817; area 436,200 sq km; capital Kunming; economy: rice, maize, wheat, tuber crops, peas, beans, rapeseed, peanuts, tobacco, tea, cotton, sugar cane, fruit, rubber, shellac, quinine, timber, mining of phosphorus, lead, zinc, tin, copper, marble; the region is subject to earthquakes.

Yunnan, former name for the capital of Yunnan prov, S China. See Kunming.

Yuscarán *yoos-ka-ran'*, 13 56N 86 45W, pop(1980e) 1,250, capital of El Paraíso dept, S Honduras, Central America; at the foot of Mount Monserrat, 48 km ESE of Tegucigalpa; economy: silver mining, trade in grain and fruit.

Yvelines *eev-leen*, dept in Ile-de-France region of N France, W of Paris; comprises 4 arrond, 38 cantons and 262 communes; pop(1982) 1,196,111; area 2,271 sq km; capital Versailles; chateaux at Thoiry (16th-c) and Dampierre (17th-c).

Yverdon *ee-ver-dõ'*, 46 47N 6 38E, pop(1980) 20,802, town in Vaud canton, Switzerland, at the SW end of Lac de Neuchâtel; railway; an important crossroads from ancient times; monument: 13th-c castle.

Z

Żabbar *zah-bahr'*, 35 53N 14 33E, pop(1983e) 10,939, town on the main island of Malta, SE of Valletta and the Grand Harbour.

Zabéré *za-bay'ray*, 11 12N 0 22W, town in E central Burkina, W Africa; E of Po.

Zābol *za'bōl*, ZABUL, prov in SE Afghanistan; pop(1984e) 194,710; area 17,293 sq km; bounded by the Toba and Kakar ranges and Pakistan to the SE; capital Qalāt; crossed by the main road from Kandahār to Kābul, and watered by the R Arghandab and the R Lora.

Zabrze *zabr'zhe*, HINDENBURG (Ger), 50 18N 18 47E, pop(1983) 196,500, mining and industrial city in Katowice voivodship, S Poland; W of Katowice; 2nd largest city in upper Silesian industrial region; granted urban status in 1922; railway; economy: coal mining, iron and steel, mining machinery.

Zacapa *za-ka'pa*, dept in E Guatemala, Central America; bounded SE by Honduras; pop(1982e) 149,267; area 2,690 sq km; capital Zacapa; chief towns Río Hondo and Gualán; bisected W-E by the Río Motagua; more mountainous in the N with peaks rising above 2,500 m.

Zacapa, 15 00N 89 30W, pop(1983e) 35,769, capital town of Zacapa dept, E Guatemala, Central America; railway; tobacco is grown in the surrounding area.

Zacatecas *zah-kah-tay'kahs*, state in N central Mexico; bounded by Coahuila (N), Durango (W), Jalisco and Aguascalientes (S) and San Luis Potosí (E); forms the N part of the large central plateau; crossed NW-SE by the Sierra Madre Occidental; semi-arid region, drained by the Juchipila and Aguanaval rivers; pop(1980) 1,145,327; area 73,252 sq km; capital Zacatecas; economy: grain, fruit, sunflowers, cattle, timber (mostly pine and oak), mining (silver, gold, lead, copper, zinc, mercury, barite, salt), food processing, tourism.

Zacatecas, 22 48N 102 33W, pop(1970) 110,000, capital of Zacatecas state, N central Mexico; NW of San Luis Potosí at an alt of 2,496 m; founded in 1548; university (1932); cablecar; railway; economy: mining (silver, gold, lead, zinc, copper, mercury); the largest silver mine in the world is at Real de Angeles; monuments: cathedral (1625); chapel of Los Remedios (1728); Francisco Goitia museum; events: bullfights on Sundays; Zacatecas Fiesta (8 Sept).

Zacatecoluca *za-ka-tay-kō-loo'ka*, 13 29N 88 51W, pop(1980) 78,751, capital town of La Paz dept, El Salvador, Central America; 56 km SE of San Salvador and 19 km S of San Vicente; railway.

Za'dar, ZARA (Ital), 44 07N 15 14E, pop(1981) 116,174, seaport and resort town in Hrvatska (Croatia) republic, W Yugoslavia; on the Zadar Channel in the Adriatic; airfield; railway; car ferries to Ancona in Italy; conquered by Venice in 1000, it passed to Austria in 1797; from 1920 to 1947 it was held by Italy as an enclave in Yugoslav territory; economy: tourism, maraschino liqueur; monuments: many Venetian buildings, Franciscan Friary, cathedral, Roman remains at nearby village of Nin; event: summer festival of music.

Zagazig *za-ga'zeeg*, ZAQAZIQ, EL ZAGAZIG, EZ ZAGAZIG, AL-ZAQAZIQ, 30 36N 31 30E, pop(1979) 202,637, capital of Sharqîya governorate, NE Egypt; in the Nile delta, 100 km NNE of Cairo; university (1974); railway; economy: cotton, grain.

Za'greb, AGRAM (Ger), ZÁGRÁB (Hung), ANDAUTONIA (anc), 45 48N 15 58E, pop(1981) 1,174,512, capital city of Hrvatska (Croatia) republic, NW Yugoslavia; on R Sava; 2nd largest city in Yugoslavia and chief Croat cultural centre; Croat has been the language of administration since 1847; before that date the educated upper classes mostly spoke German; divided between the Kaptol, the oldest part, with medieval houses and streets, and the more modern upper and lower towns; the main districts and suburbs outside the centre include Črnomerec, Dubrava, Maksimir, Medveščak, Novi Zagreb, Peščenica, Susedgrad, Trešnjevka and Trnje; university (1669); airport; railway; the city hosts important E European trade fairs; economy: electrical equipment, paper, textiles, carpets, light engineering; monuments: St Mark's church; cathedral; ethnographical museum; 40 km S at Kumrovec is the house in which Tito was born; events: spring and autumn trade fairs in April and Sept; tourism congress in April; international folk festival in July; Zagreb evenings, featuring music and drama during July-Sept.

Zagros *za'gros*, major mountain system of W Iran, extending c.1,770 km from the Turkish-Soviet frontier SE along the Arabian Gulf to the E prov of Sīstān va Balūchestān; forms the W and S border of the central Iranian plateau; tectonic movements in the NW Zagros have created large basins (Daryācheh-ye Orūmīyeh or L Urmia), *horst* blocks separated by deeply incised river valleys, and numerous volcanic cones; this section of the range is relatively well populated, particularly in the fertile valleys where wheat, barley, tobacco, cotton, and fruit are grown; the central Zagros comprises a series of parallel ridges separated by deep valleys; here salt domes and salt marsh basins are prevalent and pastoralism predominates in the uplands; the extreme SE is a desolate landscape of bare rock and sand dunes; dates and cereals are grown at oases here; Iran's major oil fields lie along the W foothills of the central Zagros; traversed by the Trans-Iranian railway and by roads to the Gulf ports of Būshehr and Bandar' Abbās.

Zāhedān *za-he-dan'*, formerly DUZDAB, 29 30N 60 52E, pop(1983) 165,038, capital city of Zāhedān dist, Balūchestān va Sīstān, SE Iran; close to the border with Afghanistan and Pakistan; renamed in the 1930s; railway; airfield.

Zahlé *zah'lu*, ZAHLAH, 33 50N 25 55E, pop(1980e) 46,800, capital town of Zahlé division (*caza*), El Beqa'a, central Lebanon; in the fertile El Beqa'a valley; railway.

Zaire, ZAÏRE *zah-eer'*, formerly CONGO FREE STATE (1885-1908), BELGIAN CONGO (1908-60), official name Republic of Zaire, RÉPUBLIQUE DU ZAÏRE (Belg), formerly DEMOCRATIC REPUBLIC OF THE CONGO, a central African republic bounded W by the Congo and the Atlantic Ocean, SW by Angola, SE by Zambia, E by Tanzania, Burundi, Rwanda and Uganda, NE by Sudan, and N and NW by the Central African Republic; timezone GMT +1 (W), +2 (E); area 2,343,950 sq km; capital Kinshasa; chief towns Lubumbashi, Kisangani, Bandundu, Mbandaka, Matadi, Mbuji-Mayi, Bukavu, Kananga, Kikwit and Likasi; pop(1984e) 32,158,000; the pop comprises over 200 ethnic groups the majority of which are of Bantu origin, the 4 largest tribes (45% of the pop) are the Mongo, the Kongo and the Luba (Bantu), and the Mangbetu-Azande (Hamitic); half of the pop is Roman Catholic, 20% are Protestant, 10% Kimbanguist, 10% Muslim; the official language is French with English, Lingala, Swahili, Kingwana, Kikongo and Tshiluba also spoken; the unit of currency is the zaïre of 100 makuta; national holidays 30 June (Independence Day), 24 Nov (Anniversary of the Regime); membership of AfDB, APC, CIPEC, EAMA, EIB (associate), FAO, G-77, GATT, IAEA, IBRD, ICAO, ICO, IDA, IFAD, IFC, IHO, ILO, IMF, INTELSAT, INTERPOL, IPU, ITC, ITU, NAM, OAU, OCAM, UDEAC, UN, UNESCO, UPU, WHO, WIPO, WMO and WTO.

Physical description. Zaire is landlocked except for a narrow strip of land that follows the R Zaire (Congo) to the Atlantic Ocean and a short 43 km coastline. The R Zaire continues inland following the country's boundary for about 650 km. From a low lying basin in the W the land rises eastwards to a densely forested plateau that is drained by many rivers flowing N to meet the R Zaire. The plateau is bounded in the E by volcanic mountains that mark the W edge of the Great Rift Valley. The Ruwenzori range in the NE on the frontier with Uganda rises to 5,110 m at Margherita Peak in the Mt Stanley massif and the Mitumbar Mts further S rise to 4,507 m at Karisimbe on the Rwanda frontier. A chain of lakes in the Rift Valley follows the E frontier of Zaire N-S and includes L Albert, L Edward, L Kivu and L Tanganyika.
Climate. Crossed by the Equator, Zaire experiences a generally hot and humid climate. The central area has an essentially equatorial climate experiencing rain all year round with max falls in March-April and Aug-Nov. Kisangani is representative of this region with an average annual rainfall of 1,700 mm and average max daily temperatures ranging between 28°C and 31°C. Elsewhere there is only one rainy season from Dec to March with a significant dry period between May and Sept. Lubumbashi is representative of this climatic region with an annual average rainfall of 1,240 mm and average max daily temperatures ranging between 26°C and 33°C. In general, humidity remains high and winds are mainly light making conditions uncomfortable. It is only near the mouth of the R Zaire and in the extreme N and S that rainfall dips much below 1,200 mm per annum and in the more mountainous areas that it rises much above 2,000 mm per annum.
History, government and constitution. The first European to visit Zaire was the Portuguese navigator Diego Cao who sailed to the mouth of the R Zaire in 1482. Following the expeditions of H.M. Stanley (1874-77) King Leopold II of Belgium laid claim to this territory, a claim that was recognized in 1895 at the Berlin Conference. The Congo Free State, which had been owned by the King of Belgium, was handed over to the state in 1907 and renamed the Belgian Congo. Inspired by the independence of former French colonies a Belgian Congo independence campaign began in the 1950s. Following riots in 1959, the colony was granted full independence in 1960. Disorder continued as the mineral-rich Katanga (Shaba) province claimed its independence and government leaders failed to establish control. A UN peace-keeping force was present in the country until 1964. Tribal conflict and resistance to central government continued in Kivu region and Belgian armed forces again became involved in helping the government to establish control. Relative stability between 1967 and 1977. During this period the country was renamed the Republic of Zaire. The constitution was renewed in 1978 and amended in 1980 to extend presidential powers. The executive president, who is elected for 7 years, appoints a National Executive Council of 27 members. Legislative power is vested in a National Legislative Council of 300 members elected every 5 years. The Mouvement Populaire de la Révolution (MPR) is the only legal political party.
Economy. Nearly 80% of the population are involved in subsistence farming which is based on livestock and the production of maize, yams, cassava, rice, beans and fruit. Cash crops include cotton, sugar, oil palm products, quinquina, coffee, tea and cocoa. Export earnings are largely based on the country's extensive mineral reserves. Zaire is the world's biggest producer of cobalt (Shaba region), industrial diamonds (Kasai region), and copper (Shaba region). Additional mineral reserves include tin, manganese, zinc, columbium, tantalum, cement, gold, silver, iron ore (Luebo area) and rare-earth metals. There are a number of small offshore oil fields (and one onshore) and in 1981 the 2,300 MW Inga hydroelectric project was completed. A sizeable manufacturing industry is largely based in Kinshasa and Lubumbashi. Industries include textiles, cotton, wood products, tobacco processing, vegetable oil, chemicals and cement production. Main trade partners are Belgium, Luxembourg, France, the USA, Canada, West Germany, the Netherlands, Italy, Japan and the UK.
Administrative divisions. Zaire is divided into 9 regions:

Region	*area (sq km)*	*pop(1981e)*
Bandundu	295,658	4,119,524
Bas-Zaïre	53,920	1,921,524
Equateur	403,293	3,418,296
Haut-Zaïre	503,239	4,541,655
Kasai Occidental	156,967	2,935,036
Kasai Oriental	168,216	2,336,951
Kinshasa City	9,965	2,338,246
Kivu	256,662	4,713,761
Shaba	496,965	3,823,172

Zaječar *zay-e'char*, 43 55N 22 16E, pop(1981) 76,681, town in E Srbija (Serbia) republic, Yugoslavia; on R Crna Reka, near Bulgarian frontier; economy: mining.

Zákinthos *zah'kin-thos*, ZANTE *zan'tee*, ZACYNTHUS *zu-sin'thus* (anc), nome (dept) and island of Ioníoi Nísoi region, W Greece, in the Ionian Sea, off the NW coast of Pelopónnisos; pop(1981) 30,014; area 406 sq km; length 40 km; capital Zákinthos on the E coast; the island was devastated by earthquakes in 1953; the W coast is steep and rugged, the E coast hilly, and there is a wide fertile plain in the central part.

Zakopane *za-ko-pa'ne*, 49 17N 19 54E, pop(1983) 29,700, chief town and winter sports resort in the Tatry (High Tatra Mts), Nowy Sącz voivodship, S Poland; close to the Czechoslovak frontier, S of Kraków; alt 800-900 m; a health resort since 1866 and popular with mountaineers since the founding of the Tatra Mountains Society in 1873; the town expanded after 1899 when the railway line reached Zakopane; well preserved local architecture and customs; monuments: home of the poet Jan Kasprowicz; home of the composer Karol Szymanowski; events: Tatra Autumn Festival and International Festival of Highland Folklore in Sept.

Zakouma *za-koo-ma'*, PARC NATIONAL DU ZAKOUMA (Fr), national park in S Chad, N central Africa; straddles the border between Guéra and Salamat prefectures; area 2,972 sq km; preserves populations of rare rhinoceros and leopards.

Zala *zo-lo*, hilly county in W Hungary; bounded to the W by Yugoslavia, with the SW tip of L Balaton in the E; the R Zala flows E and S through the county; pop(1984e) 316,000; area 3,786 sq km; capital Zalaegerszeg; chief towns include Nagykanizsa; 40% of population live in 5 towns; half of the county's 256 rural communes have a pop of less than 500; spas at Héviz and Zalakaros; there is buffalo reservation at Kápolnapuszta; economy: oil, engineering, food processing, timber, clothing, light bulbs, livestock, poultry, milk, tourism.

Zalaegerszeg *zo'lo-e'ger-seg*, 46 53N 16 47E, pop(1984e) 60,000, capital of Zala county, W Hungary; on R Zala WSW of Veszprém; railway; economy: grain, fruit and livestock trade, machines for aluminium industry, ceramics.

Zălău *za-lu'oo*, 47 10N 23 04E, pop(1983) 50,108, capital of Sălaj county, NW Romania; railway; economy: grain, fruit, livestock trade.

Zambezi or **Zambesi** *zam-bee'zee*, ZAMBEZE (PORT), river in SE Africa flowing through Angola, Zimbabwe, Zambia, Namibia and Mozambique; length approx 2,700 km, one of Africa's major rivers; rises in NW Zambia (near Kalene Hill) and flows in a large 'S' shape generally SE; from its source it crosses E Angola and then forms the border between Zambia and Namibia (Caprivi Strip); on Zimbabwe-Zambia border there are the Victoria Falls, L Kariba and Kariba Dam; the Zambezi enters Mozambique at Zumbo, flows past Tete and Sena before entering the Mozambique Channel in the form of a marshy delta 210 km NE of Beira; the river has numerous headstreams and tributaries; major tributaries are the Chobe (Botswana-Namibia), the Shangani (Zimbabwe), the Umniati, the Kafue and the Luangwa (Zambia) and the Shire (L Nyasa's outlet); the middle course of the river was explored by Livingstone in the early 1850s and by Dr J. Kirk in the late 1850s.

Zambezi, 13 33S 23 08E, town in North-West prov, Zambia, S central Africa; on the E bank of the R Zambezi; airfield.

Zambézia *zam-bay'zya*, prov in N central Mozambique, SE Africa; pop(1980) 2,500,000; area 105,008 sq km; bounded S by the R Zambezi and NE by the R Ligonha; rises W to Mount Chiperone (2,054 m) and Namuli (2,419 m); capital Quelimane; chief towns are Chinde, Mocuba and Namacurra.

Zambia *zam'bee-a*, formerly NORTHERN RHODESIA, official name Republic of Zambia, a S African republic bounded W by Angola, S by Namibia, SE by Zimbabwe and Mozambique, E by Malawi, NE by Tanzania and NW by Zaire; timezone GMT +2; area 752,613 sq km; capital Lusaka; chief towns include Ndola, Kitwe, Kabwe and Maramba (Livingstone); pop(1984e) 6,554,000; 99% of pop are African belonging to Bantu tribal groups; over 50% are Christian, the remainder following local beliefs; the official language is English but local languages such as Bemba, Tonga, Lozi, Lunda, Luvale and Nyanja are also spoken; the unit of currency is the kwacha of 100 ngwee; national holidays 24 Oct (Independence Day), 24 May (Commonwealth Day) and the main Christian festivals; membership of AfDB, the Commonwealth, FAO, G-77, GATT (de facto), IAEA, IBRD, ICAO, IDA, IEA, IFAD, IFC, ILO, ILZSG, IMF, INTELSAT, INTERPOL, IPU, ITU, NAM, OAU, SADCC, UN, UNESCO, UPU, WHO, WIPO, WMO, WTO.

Physical description. Zambia occupies a high plateau with an elevation of between 1,000 and 1,400 m. Peaks such as Chimbwingombi (1,788 m) in the Muchinga escarpment (SW of Mpika) rise from the plateau. The highest point in Zambia (2,067 m) is located SE of Mbala, close to the Tanzanian frontier and the SE tip of L Tanganyika. The Zambezi river rises in the N extremity of North-West prov near Kalene Hill and after passing briefly through Engola it flows S through W Zambia to form part of the frontier with Namibia and Zimbabwe. The N plateau country is drained by rivers flowing down to meet the Zambezi in the W and S and the R Zaire in the N. NE Zambia is drained by the R Chambeshi which flows S to the swamps around L Bangweulu.

Climate. The upland plateau of Zambia has a warm-temperate climate. Greatest rainfall occurs between Oct and March with highest humidity and temperature between Nov and Feb. The dry season extends from April to Aug. The average annual rainfall in Lusaka (alt 1,277 m) is 840 mm per annum and the max average daily temperatures range between 23°C and 35°C. The conditions in the lower river valleys are relatively uncomfortable with a typically tropical climate. The rainy season there occurs between Oct and Feb which is also the hottest period.

History, government and constitution. The various African groups which occupy Zambia today (including Bantu tribes and Ngoni peoples) had established their presence by the late 19th century. European influence followed the arrival of David Livingstone who reached the Victoria Falls in 1855. Under the leadership of Cecil Rhodes, the British South Africa Company extended its search for minerals into this area. In 1888 Northern and Southern Rhodesia were declared a British sphere of influence. Southern Rhodesia was formally annexed and granted self-government in 1923 and in the following year Northern Rhodesia became a British protectorate. In 1953 the two Rhodesias were joined with Nyasaland (now Malawi) as the Federation of Rhodesia and Nyasaland. In 1958 the United National Independence Party (UNIP), led by Kenneth Kaunda, was formed with the aim of obtaining independence. New constitutions were introduced in 1959 and 1962 and the Federation was dissolved in late 1963. At the beginning of 1964 self-government was introduced in Northern Rhodesia and Kenneth Kaunda became the first prime minister. Northern Rhodesia became the independent Republic of Zambia on 24 October 1964, the first British territory to declare itself a republic upon gaining independence. The current constitution which was invoked in 1973 provides for a National Assembly of 125 elected members and 10 appointed members serving 5-year terms, an executive president who is also head of state and a council of about 20 ministers led by a prime minister. UNIP is the only legal political party in Zambia.

Economy. Despite extensive agricultural potential the country's economy is based on the largely state-owned copper and cobalt mining industry which accounts for over half of national income. Other mineral reserves include gold, lead, silver and zinc. The agricultural, banking and construction sectors are the only sectors of the economy dominated by private enterprise. Food

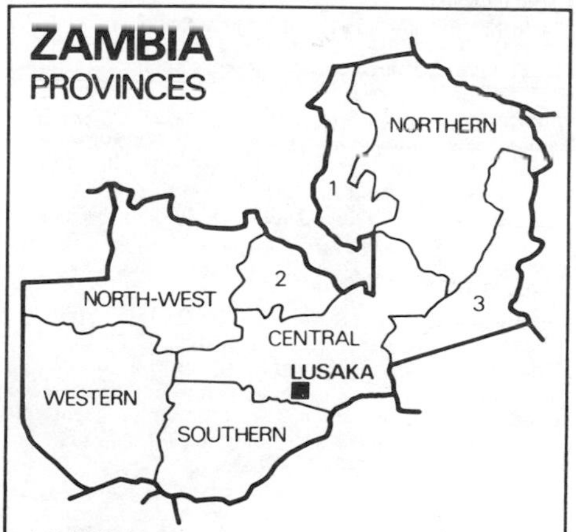

imports are high, but in normal years Zambia is self-sufficient in maize. Self-sufficiency has also been achieved in sugar which is grown on the Kafue plain. Other important food crops include cassava, millet, sorghum, pulses, groundnuts and cotton. Tobacco grown in Eastern prov supplies the local cigarette manufacturing industry. European farmers still resident in Zambia account for a large proportion of agricultural production. Cattle are kept in areas of the S and E not infested with tsetse fly. Manufacturing industry is based on the production of copper wire and cable (Luanshya), cement (Chilanga and Ndola), fertilizer (Kafue) and explosives (Kafironda). Other products include car and commercial vehicle assembly, sugar refining, food processing, textiles, clothing, glassware, tyres, bricks, brewing and oil refining. Main trading partners are the UK, West Germany, the USA, South Africa and Japan.

Administrative divisions. Zambia is divided into 8 provinces:

Province	*area (sq km)*	*pop(1980)*
Central	116,290	1,207,713
Copperbelt	31,328	1,248,888
Eastern	69,106	656,381
Luapula	50,567	412,789
Northern	147,826	677,894
North-West	125,827	301,677
Southern	85,283	686,469
Western	126,386	487,988

Zamboanga *sam-bō-ang'ga*, CITY OF ZAMBOANGA, 6 55N 122 05E, pop(1980) 343,722, seaport in Zamboanga Del Sur prov, Western Mindanao, Philippines; at W tip of Mindanao I; founded in 1635; a city since 1940s; poor anchorage during SW monsoon; airfield; economy: timber and copra trade; monument: Fort Pilar; events: Bale Zamboanga Festival in Feb, with cultural shows, fairs and regattas; feast of Our Lady of the Pillar in Oct.

Zamora *sa-mō'ra*, 4 05S 79 01W, pop(1982) 5,296, capital of Zamora Chinchipe prov, S Ecuador; on the Río Zamora, SE of Loja on the E slopes of the Andes.

Zamora *tha-mo'ra*, prov in Castilla-León region, NW Spain, lying along the Portuguese border, astride the R Douro (Duero) and its tributaries; mostly part of the central plateau (Meseta) but mountainous in the NW; pop(1981) 224,309; area 10,559 sq km; capital Zamora; wine and fruit in the river valleys, textiles, canning (Morales del Vino, Roales).

Zamora, 41 30N 5 45W, pop(1981) 59,734, capital of Zamora prov, Castilla-León, NW central Spain; near R Douro (Duero), 248 km NW of Madrid; bishopric; railway; economy: textiles, brandy, pottery, leather; monuments: Romanesque cathedral; churches of St Magdalene, St Cipriano and St Mary; events: Holy Week and St Peter fair in June.

Zamora Chinchipe *sa-mō'ra cheen-chee'pay*, prov in S Ecuador; borders Peru S and E; pop(1982) 46,691; area 23,107 sq km; capital Zamora.

Zamość *zam'osh-ke*, voivodship in E Poland; bounded E by USSR; source of R Wieprz; pop(1983) 483,000; area 6,980 sq km; capital Zamość; chief towns include Biłgoraj and Hrubieszów.

Zamość, ZAMOSTYE (Rus), 50 43N 23 15E, pop(1983) 52,900, capital of Zamość voivodship, E Poland; built between 1580 and 1600; formerly an important cultural and trade centre; university (branch of Lublin); railway; economy: meat processing, furniture; monuments: arcaded 16-17th-c houses surround the Market Square; 16-17th-c collegiate church with extensive library of rare books and manuscripts; 16th-c palace of chancellor Jan Zamoyski; 17th-c former Zamoyski Academy; zoo.

Zanesville, WESTBOURNE (-1800), 39 56N 82 01W, pop(1980) 28,655, county seat of Muskingum county, central Ohio, United States; on R Muskingum, 80 km E of Columbus; named after Ebenezer Zane who founded a settlement here which he originally name Westbourne; railway; once a major centre of the pottery industry.

Zanjān *zan-jan'*, mountainous prov in NW Iran; pop(1982) 1,117,157; area 36,398 sq km; capital Zanjān.

Zanjān, 36 40N 48 29E, pop(1983) 175,374, capital city of Zanjān dist, Zanjān, NW Iran; 288 km NW of Tehrān, in the S foothills of the Elburz Mts; trade centre for surrounding agricultural region which produces grain and fruit; airfield; railway.

Zante, Greek island. See Zákinthos.

Zanzibar *zan'zi-bar*, island region of Tanzania, E Africa; pop(1985e) 571,000; area 1,660 sq km including offshore islands such as Tumbatu (NW) and Kwale (SW); separated from the mainland by the 40 km-wide Zanzibar Channel; the island is 85 km long and 39 km wide; the capital, Zanzibar, is on the W coast; composed of coral limestone, the island has a peak elevation of 118 m; populated by Bantu peoples (from the mainland), Shiraz Persians and Arabs, the island has been predominantly Islamic since the 10th century; midway through the same century the island became part of the Zenj Empire, founded by the Persians; Swahili ruins at Kizimkazi at the S end of the island date from 1107 AD; in the 16th century it was occupied by the Portuguese as a base for raids on the mainland; in the 17th century it came under Omani Arab rule; the Sultan Seyyid Said embarked on an energetic period of building and trading which resulted in Zanzibar becoming the commercial centre of the W Indian Ocean; the Sultan introduced cloves from Indonesia to the fertile soils on the island and by the time of his death in 1856 Zanzibar had captured three-quarters of the world market; today Zanzibar is the world's 2nd largest producer of cloves; annexed by Germany in 1885, it was exchanged for the European island of Heligoland in 1890 with Britain establishing a protectorate; in 1963 Zanzibar gained internal self-government and later in the same year achieved full independence; in 1964 the ruling Sultanate was overthrown and the People's Republic of Zanzibar was created; later the same year Tanganyika, Zanzibar and Pemba united to form the United Republic of Tanganyika and Zanzibar; in Oct of 1964 the name of the union was changed to the United Republic of Tanzania.

Zanzibar, 6 10S 39 12E, pop(1978) 110,669, capital of Zanzibar island, Tanzania, E Africa; on the W coast of Zanzibar I; airfield (8 km); economy: cigarettes, cloves, clove oil, lime oil, craftwork; monuments: Beit El Ajaib or 'The House of Wonder', a palace built for Sultan Seyyid Bargash in 1833; it remained the seat of the sultanate until the British took it over in 1911 and used it for colonial offices; the residence of Dr Livingstone, where he planned his final and ill-fated expedition into the interior in 1866.

Zaozhuang *jow-zhwang*, TSAOCHUANG, 34 53N 117 38E, pop(1984e) 1,570,300, city in Shandong prov, E China; S of Jinan; railway.

Zapadnaya Dvina *zah'pud-nī-u dvee-na'*, WESTERN DVINA (Eng), river in NW European Rossiyskaya, Belorusskaya and Latviskaya (Latvia) republics, Soviet Union; rises in the W foothills of the Valdayskaya Vozvyshennost' (Valdai Hills), N of Andreapol', Kalininskaya oblast; flows SSW through N Belorusskaya SSR, turns NW at Beshenkovichi, continues past Polotsk, Daugav'pils, and Riga, to discharge into the Rizhskiy Zaliv (Gulf of Riga), an inlet of the Baltic Sea; length 1,013 km; chief tributaries Disna, Drissa, and Gobza rivers; frozen over from December to April; there is a hydroelectric power plant at Plavinas.

Zapadno Sibirskaya Ravnina *zah'pud-no sibir-skī'a rav-nee'na*, WEST SIBERIAN LOWLANDS (Eng), vast lowland area in W Siberian Rossiyskaya, Soviet Union, extending more than 1,500 km E from the Ural'skiy Khrebet (Ural Mts) range to the R Yenisey; area c.2,500,000 sq km; at least half the area lies below 100 m and nowhere does it exceed 200 m; drained mainly by the R Ob' and its tributaries the Irtysh and Tobol; most of the region is poorly drained and contains some of the world's largest swamps, notably the Vasyugan swamp; population is concentrated along the S border in the cities of Chelyabinsk, Petropavlovsk, Omsk, Novosibirsk, and Tomsk; dominant agricultural activities are dairying and grain growing; the poorly drained areas are partially used for dairy and beef cattle.

Západočeský *zah'pad-o-che-skee*, region in Czech Socialist Republic, W Czechoslovakia; area 10,876 sq km; pop(1984) 876,525; capital Plzeň; chief towns include Karlovy Vary, Cheb, Klatovy.

Západoslovenský *zah'pad-o-slo-ven-skee*, region in W Slovak Socialist Republic, central Czechoslovakia; area 14,491 sq km; pop(1984) 1,707,507; capital Bratislava; chief towns include Nitra, Komárno, Levice.

Zapaleri, Cerro *sa-pa-lay'ree*, 22 49S 67 12W, mountain rising to 5,648 m at the meeting point of Jujuy prov, Norte, Argentina, Elloa prov, Antofagasta, Chile and Potosí region, Bolivia; lies at S end of Cordillera de Lípez, 105 km E of San Pedro de Atacama (Chile).

Zapatosa, Ciénaga de *syay'na-ga day sa-pa-tō'sa*, lake on the border of Magdalena and César depts, N Colombia; in the Magdalena basin; 13 km NE of El Banco; 31 km long; 10 km wide; dotted with islands; the Río César flows through the lake to join up with the Río Magdalena.

Zaporozh'ye *za-pe-rozh'ye*, formerly ALEKSANDROVSK, 47 50N 35 10E, pop(1983) 835,000, river port capital of Zaporozhskaya oblast, Ukrainskaya SSR, S European Soviet Union; on the R Dnepr; founded in 1770 as a fortress; one of the largest industrial and energy-producing centres of the republic; railway; airfield; on the highway between Sevastopol' and Moskva (Moscow); economy: hydroelectric power generation, iron and steel, aluminium plant, car manufacturing, clothing, foodstuffs.

Zaragoza *tha-ra-go'tha*, SARAGOSSA *sa-ra-go'sa* (Eng), prov in Aragón region, NE Spain; a plain with spurs of the W Pyrenees in the N; drained by the R Ebro and its tributaries; close to the Ebro are the Imperial and Tauste irrigation canals; pop(1981) 842,386; area 17,252 sq km; capital Zaragoza; economy: textiles, food canning (Calatayud), wine, iron and steel (Zaragoza, Utebo), motor vehicles (Figueruelas), soap (Ariza), chemicals.

Zaragoza, SALDUBA (anc), 41 39N 0 53W, pop(1981) 590,750, industrial city and capital of Zaragoza prov, Aragón, NE central Spain; on R Ebro, 325 km NE of Madrid; archbishopric; university (1553); airport; railway; former residence of kings of Aragon; economy: iron and steel, agric machinery, chemicals, sugar refining, textiles, cement, soap, paper, mineral water, pharmaceuticals, foodstuffs, plastics, electrical goods, glass; monuments: El Pilar and La Seo cathedrals, 16th-c Exchange, the Aljafarería Moorish palace; events: fiesta of Our Lady of Pilar in Oct, Holy Week, and spring festival in May.

Zaranj, 31 11N 62 02E, pop(1984e) 7,100, capital of Nīmrūz prov, SW Afghanistan, situated on the border between Afghanistan and Iran, close to the banks of the R Dor, which is a tributary of the Helmand river; linked to Herāt by main road; airfield.

Zárate *sa'ra-tay*, 34 07S 59 00W, pop(1980) 65,504, town in Buenos Aires prov, Litoral, E Argentina; NW of Buenos Aires; railway; economy: paper.

Zaria *za'ree-a*, 11 01N 7 44E, pop(1981e) 306,200, town in Kaduna state, SW Nigeria, W Africa; 145 km SW of Kano; founded in the 16th century; airfield; railway junction; economy: engineering, tanning, printing, trade in sugar, groundnuts and cotton.

Zărneşti *zar-nesht'*, 45 34N 25 18E, pop(1983) 26,191, town in Braşov county, central Romania; railway; on NE slopes of the Transylvanian Alps, 24 km SW of Braşov; economy: paper, limestone.

Zarqa *zar'ka*, 32 04N 36 05E, pop(1983e) 215,000, industrial town in Amman governorate, East Bank, N Jordan; site of much of Jordan's current industrialization programme; the nearby Ruseifa area has approx one-third of the country's phosphate reserves; on the Hejaz railway; airfield; economy: oil refining, tanneries, thermal centre.

Žatec *zha'tets*, 50 20N 13 35E, pop(1984) 22,275, town in Severočeský region, Czech Socialist Republic, W Czechoslovakia; on R Ohre, NW of Praha (Prague); railway; economy: agricultural trade.

Zavidovici, *zay'vee-do-vee-chee*, 44 27N 18 09E, pop(1981) 51,861, town in central Bosna-Hercegovina republic, Yugoslavia; 64 km N of Sarajevo; economy: timber trade.

Zawiercie *zav-yer'che*, ZAVERTSE (Rus), 50 30N 19 24E, pop(1983) 55,600, industrial town in Katowice voivodship, S Poland; near the source of the R Warta, NE of Katowice; railway; economy: steel rolling, lathes, cotton.

Žd'ár or **Žd'ár nad Sázavou** *zhdyahr nad sah'za-vow*, 49 34N 16 00E, pop(1984) 25,963, industrial and resort town in Jihomoravský region, Czech Socialist Republic, central Czechoslovakia; railway.

Zealand, Denmark. See Sjælland.

Żebbuġ *ze-booj'*, 35 52N 14 27E, pop(1983e) 8,846, town in central Malta, 7 km SW of Valletta; fruit growing nearby; monuments: Roman arch, fortified tower and bishop's palace.

Zeeland *zay'lant*, pop(1984e) 355,500, prov in West Netherlands, bounded on the S by Belgium and on the W by the North Sea, in the estuary area of the Rhine, Maas and Schelde rivers, includes the islands and peninsulas of SW Netherlands (Walcheren, S and N Beveland, Schouwen-Duiveland and Tholen) and the narrow mainland strip between the Westerschelde and the Belgian frontier; land area 1,786 sq km; capital Middelburg; chief towns Vlissingen, Breskens and Terneuzen; economy: predominantly arable farming on the fertile well-drained marine clays (cereals, potatoes, sugar-beet); in the last 1,800 years the entire area has been reclaimed from the sea by man-made dykes, and is mostly below sea level; the 'Delta Plan' is intended to prevent a recurrence of the disastrous flooding of 1953, and as part of the plan, sea and river dykes throughout the country are to be strengthened and raised to the Delta level.

Zefat, sub-district of North dist, N Israel.

Zeist *zīst*, 52 05N 5 15E, pop(1984e) 60,478, city in Utrecht prov, W Netherlands, 10 km E of Utrecht.

Żejtun *zay'toon*, 35 52N 14 33E, pop(1983e) 10,633, town in E Malta, 5 km SE of Valletta.

Zelaya *zel-ī'a*, largest dept in Nicaragua, Central America; bounded E by the Caribbean Sea and N by Honduras; traversed W-E by the Cordillera de Yolaina and Montañas de Huapi; the Cordillera Isabelia, with peaks over 2,000 m, forms the NW boundary with Jinotega dept; the Río Coco forms the N boundary; all rivers drain into the Caribbean, including the Río Grande de Matagalpa and the Río Escondido, pop(1981) 202,462, area 63,005 sq km; capital Bluefields; chief ports Puerto Cabezas and Prinzapolca; the dept is virtually inaccessible from the W; the economy is based on the export of bananas, cocoa, mahogany, black walnut, rosewood, and other high-class timbers.

Zel'ler See or **Untersee** *oon'tar-zay*, lake in Salzburg state, N Austria, N of the Grossglockner; an arm of the Bodensee (L Constance) to which it is connected by the R Rhine; area 4.3 sq km; length 4 km; width 1.5 km; max depth 68 m; the Rhine leaves it from Stein in Switzerland; the resorts of Zell am See, Saalbach and Kaprun have combined to form the 'Europa Sport Region'.

Zemlya Frantsa-Iosifa *zyim'lya fran'tsa yo'syifa*, FRANZ-JOSEF LAND (Eng), archipelago in the Arctic Ocean, N of Novaya Zemlya, in Arkhangel'skaya oblast, Rossiyskaya, NW Soviet Union; area 20,720 sq km; comprises c.167 islands of volcanic origin, the largest of which are Ostrov Greem Bell (Graham Bell I), Zemlya Vil'cheka (Wilczek Land), Zemlya Georga (George Land), Zemlya Aleksandry, and Ostrov Rudol'fa; declared Soviet territory in 1926; glacier ice interspersed with poor lichen vegetation covers some 90% of the total area; most northerly land of the E hemisphere; uninhabited save for a meteorological station on Ostrov Gukera (Hooker I).

Zenica *ze'nit-sa*, ZENITSA, 44 11N 17 53E, pop(1981) 132,733, town in Bosna-Hercegovina republic, Yugoslavia; on R Bosna, 56 km N of Sarajevo; railway; economy: coal mining, steel, paper.

Zer'matt, 46 01N 7 45E, pop(1981) 3,500, fashionable skiing resort and popular mountaineering centre in the Pennine Alps, Valais canton, S Switzerland; the Matterhorn rises to the SW.

Zezere *zay'zi-ri*, river in N central Portugal; rises in Serra da Estrêla, flows SW to the R Tagus W of Abrantes; length 208 km.

Zhanjiang *zhan-jee-ang*, CHANCHIANG formerly FORT BAYARD (Fr), 21 15N 110 20E, pop(1984e) 899,500, port in Guangdong prov, SE China; on the South China Sea; a special economic zone; railway; economy: fishing, machine-building, chemicals, fertilizers, shipbuilding, paper, food processing, sugar refining, plastics, textiles, electronics, trade in rice, sweet potatoes, sugar cane, peanuts, jute.

Zhdanov, formerly MARIUPOL' (-1948), 47 05N 37 34E, pop(1983) 516,000, seaport in Donetskaya oblast, Ukrainskaya SSR, S European Soviet Union; situated where the R Kal'mius discharges into the Azovskoye More (Sea of Azov); established in the late 18th century; a noted mud-bath resort; railway; airfield; economy: iron and steel, chemicals, fertilizers, metallurgical equipment.

Zhejiang *ju-jyang*, CHEKIANG, province in E China; situated on the E coast, on the E China Sea; bounded S by Fujian prov, W by Jiangxi and Anhui provs and N by Jiangsu prov; over 70% of the prov's total area is occupied by hills and mountains; the N is low, well-watered and fertile, producing grain and silk; the W and S are hilly and mountainous with the W being an important bamboo and tea-growing region, while the intermontane valleys of the S produce grain; the Grand Canal flows S through Zhejiang as far as Hangzhou; major rivers include the Fuchun Jiang, Ling Jiang, Longquan Xi and Xiao Xi; the prov includes approx 2,000 offshore islands, the best known being the Zhoushan Dao archipelago in the S of Hangzhou Wan bay; pop(1982) 38,884,603; area 101,800 sq km; capital Hangzhou; principal towns Wenzhou and Ningbo; economy: rice, wheat, maize, sweet potatoes, jute, cotton, rapeseed, sugar cane, tea, timber, fishing (the Zhoushan Dao archipelago is the largest fishing ground in China), mining (iron, copper, lead, zinc, molybdenum, antimony, tungsten, manganese, sulphur, phosphorus, coal, fluorite, alumstone), chemicals, fish processing, crafts (stone sculpture and wood carving); produces one-third of China's raw silk brocade and satin.

Zhengzhou *jeng-jō*, CHENGCHOW, CHENGHSIEN, 34 35N 113 38E, pop(1984e) 1,551,600, capital of Henan prov, N central China; a major market and transportation centre to the S of the Huang He (Yellow river); first settled before 1000 BC, modern settlement stems from the construction of the railway in 1898; in 1937 the nationalist army attempted to harass the invading Japanese by breaching the dyke of the Huang He river to the NE of Zhengzhou; the resulting floods led to the death of thousands of people from drowning or starvation; railway junction; airfield; economy: textiles, food processing, light engineering; monuments: the cenotaph commemorates the railroad workers' general strike of Feb 1923; Henan provincial museum contains artifacts from the Neolithic era, early dynasties and the modern period.

Zhenjiang *jen-jee-ang*, CHINKIANG, 32 08N 119 30E, pop(1984e) 397,300, river port in Jiangsu prov, E China; at the confluence of the southern Chang Jiang (Yangtze river) and the Grand Canal; founded in 545 BC during the Eastern Zhou dynasty, the city gained early importance owing to its position on the Grand Canal, which opened during the Sui dynasty (581-618 AD); railway; economy: metallurgy, machinery, automobiles, shipbuilding, electronics, textiles, pharmaceuticals, chemicals; monuments: scenic spots around Zhenjiang (Jin Shan, Jiao Shan and Beigu Shan) are known as the 'Three Hills of the Capital Gateway'; NW, on Jin Shan hill, the Fahaizdong (Monk Cave) and Bailongdong (White Dragon Cave) are those featured in the Chinese fairytale 'The Story of the White Snake'; the Jinshan temple (4th-c) is one of the oldest temples in the lower Chang Jiang area; to the E of the city, on Jiao Shan, is a monastery, numerous temples and pavilions and hundreds of inscribed stone tablets; Dujinglou (Pavilion for Choosing Prospective Sons-in-Law), Shijianshi (Testing Swords Stone) and an iron pagoda dating from the Song dynasty (960-1279 AD).

Zhitomir *zhi-to'myir*, JITOMIR, 50 18N 28 40E, pop(1983) 264,000, capital city of Zhitomirskaya oblast, W central Ukrainskaya SSR, Soviet Union; on the R Teterev, 165 km W of Kiyev (Kiev); established in the 2nd half of the 9th century; railway junction; economy: machine building, metalworking, flax, clothing, footwear.

Zhongshan *zhong-shahn*, 22 30N 113 20E, pop(1984e) 1,047,200, city in Guangdong prov, SE China; S of Guangzhou, W of the mouth of the Zhu Jiang (Pearl river); hot springs nearby; birthplace of Sun Yatsen; economy: paper, electronic components, hardware, watches, household appliances, steel, shipbuilding, trade in silk, sugar cane, fish, vegetables, fruit; monument: home of Sun Yatsen.

Zhu Jiang *zhoo jyahng*, CHU-KIANG, PEARL RIVER, river in S China forming a wide estuary between Hong Kong and Macao, S of Guangzhou (Canton); formed by the confluence of the Xi Jiang, Bei Jiang and Dong Jiang rivers; the Xi Jiang rises in the mountains to the SE of Kunming, Yunnan prov; the Xi Jiang flows past Wuzhou into Guangdong, and meets the Bei Jiang at Foshan, to the W of Guangzhou; the Bei Jiang river rises in the S part of Hunnan and Jiangxi provs and flows S through Guangdong past Shaoguan to Foshan; the Dong Jiang rises in the S of Jiangxi prov then flows S and SW to Guangzhou; all 3 rivers meet in the Zhu Jiang river delta where they fan out and flow into the South China Sea in 8 outlets; the respective lengths are: Xi Jiang 2,197 km (this is taken as the length of the Zhu Jiang itself), Bei Jiang 468 km, Dong Jiang 523 km; the Zhu Jiang river valley is densely populated, fertile and covers an area of 452,616 sq km; the river is navigable as far as Wuzhou for large vessels and as far as Nanning and Liuzhou for small steamboats.

Zhuhai *zhoo-hī*, 22 17N 113 30E, pop(1984e) 144,400, city in Guangdong prov, SE China; on the W bank of the mouth of the Zhu Jiang (Pearl river), adjoining Macao and facing the South China Sea; originally a fishing village and later part of Zhongshan, it was designated a city in 1979 and became a special economic zone in 1980; the zone was extended in 1983 to cover 15.16 sq km and includes the 6 districts of Nanshan, Jida, Beiling, Lanpu, Xiangzhou and Xiawan; strong economic links with Macao and Hong Kong; an international golf course was completed in 1985; economy: quartzite, light industry, electronics, textiles, tourism, seafood, fishing.

Zibo, 36 51N 118 01E, pop(1984e) 2,280,500, city in Shandong prov, E China; E of Jinan; railway.

Zielona Góra *zhel-on-a goor'a*, voivodship in W Poland; bounded W by E Germany and watered by the R Barycz and its tributaries the Bóbr and Nysa Łużycka; pop(1983) 632,000; area 8,868 sq km; capital Zielona Góra; chief towns include Nowa Sól, Żary and Żagań; noted area for wine production.

Zielona Góra, GRÜNEBERG (Ger), 51 57N 15 30E, pop(1983) 107,800, capital of Zielona Góra voivodship, W Poland; in heavily wooded, hilly country, SW of Poznań; modern Piast housing development in SW; Piastowski Park with amphitheatre; railway; economy: wine, machinery, freight cars, electrical goods, textiles, food processing, cotton-carding machinery; monuments: regional museum with a collection of wine-making equipment, half-timbered church of Our Lady of Częstochowa (18th-c).

Ziguinchor *zee-gē-shor'*, savannah, swamp and forest region in Senegal, W Africa; part of Casamance region until 1984; capital Ziguinchor; economy: rice, peanuts, fruit, vegetables, cotton and fish.

Ziguinchor, 12 35N 16 20W, pop(1979) 79,464, capital of region of same name, Senegal, W Africa; on the R Casamance, 65 km from its mouth, 260 km SSE of Dakar; airfield; craft centre.

Žilina *zhi'li-na*, 49 14N 18 40E, pop(1984) 87,825, town in Středoslovenský region, Slovak Socialist Republic, E central Czechoslovakia; on R Váh, S of the W Beskids; railway; economy: clothing, paper.

Zillertal Alps *tsi'lar-tal*, ZILLERTALER ALPEN (Ger), ALPI AURINE (Ital), mountain range in the E Alps of N Italy and the S Tirol of Austria; extends from the Birnlücke in the E to the Brenner in the W; the highest peak is Hochfeiler (3,510 m).

Zimbabwe *zim-ba'bway*, formerly SOUTHERN RHODESIA, official name Republic of Zimbabwe, a S African republic bounded S by South Africa, SW by Botswana, NW by Zambia and NE, E and SE by Mozambique; timezone GMT +2; area 391,090 sq km; capital Harare; chief towns include Bulawayo, Kadoma, Que Que, Chinhoyi, Gweru, Hwange, Masvingo and Mutare; pop(1984e) 8,325,000; the majority of the pop (97%) is of African origin with over 77% of these people belonging to Shona tribes and 19% to Ndebele tribes; half the pop follow syncretic beliefs (part Christian, part local), with the remainder following either Christian (25%), local (24%) or Muslim beliefs; the official language is English with Shona and SiNdebele widely spoken; the unit of currency is the Zimbabwe dollar; national holiday 18 April (Independence Day); membership of AfDB, the Commonwealth, FAO, G-77, GATT, IBRD, ICAO, IDA, IFAD, IFC, ILO, IMF, INTERPOL, ITO, NAM, OAU, SADCC, UN, UNESCO, UPU, WFTU, WHO and WMO.

Physical description. Zimbabwe is a landlocked, high plateau country with a 'Middleveld' ranging in altitude from 900 to 1,200 m above sea-level. Rising above this level is the 'Highveld' which runs SW-NE with an elevation of between 1,200 and 1,500 m. To the N of the Highveld the relief dips toward the Zambezi river and to the S toward the Limpopo river. Zimbabwe's E frontier with Mozambique is marked by a mountain range rising to 2,592 m at Mount Inyangani. The R Zambezi forms Zimbabwe's NW frontier with Zambia between the NW extremity of Matabeleland North prov, NE through L Kariba to the most N point of the country. Rivers such as the Gwai, Shangani, Sanyati and Hunyani flow N from the Highveld to join the Zambezi. The Limpopo river forms a portion of Zimbabwe's S frontier with South Africa and Mozambique. The 'Lowveld' is the land below 600 m in elevation in the major river valleys.

Climate. The climate of Zimbabwe is generally subtropical and is strongly influenced by altitude. The Lowveld of Zimbabwe has a warm, dry climate with annual rainfall of between 400 and 600 mm. In contrast the mountainous terrain in the E receives between 1,500 and 2,000 mm of rain annually. The remainder of the country receives between 750 and 1,000 mm of rain annually. Most of the rain falls during Nov-March; Harare (alt 1,473 m) is representative of the Highveld with an average annual rainfall of 830 mm and average max daily temperatures ranging between 21°C and 29°C.

History, government and constitution. Visited by David Livingstone in the 1850s, Southern Rhodesia came under British influence during the 1880s as the British South Africa Company under Cecil Rhodes began its exploitation of the rich mineral reserves of the area. On the conclusion of the company's charter in 1923 Southern Rhodesia became a self-governing British colony. In 1953 Southern Rhodesia, Northern Rhodesia and Nyasaland joined together to form a multiracial federation. The federation was based on a labour supply from Nyasaland (Malawi), the mineral wealth of Northern Rhodesia (Zambia) and the technical resources of Southern Rhodesia (Zimbabwe). The federation lasted until 1963 when the protectorates of Nyasaland and Northern Rhodesia gained full independence. Opposition to the independence of Southern Rhodesia under African rule resulted in a Unilateral Declaration of Independence (UDI) by the white-dominated government on 11 Nov 1965. Although this move was deemed unconstitutional and illegal by Britain and later by the UN, economic sanctions rather than force were used in an attempt to regain control. By the mid-1970s economic pressure and internal guerrilla activity forced the government of Southern Rhodesia to negotiate with leaders of the main African groups, the Zimbabwe African People's Union (ZAPU), led by Joshua Nkomo, the Zimbabwe African National Union (ZANU), led by Robert Mugabe, the United African National Council (UANC), led by Bishop Abel Muzorewa. Agreement was eventually reached transferring power to the African majority and independence as the Republic of Zimbabwe was achieved on 18 April 1980 with Robert Mugabe as the country's first prime minister. The bicameral legislature comprises a 100-member House of Assembly and a 40-member Senate elected every 5 years. The president who is elected by parliament for 6 years appoints the prime minister and a cabinet of about 25 ministers.

Economy. Agriculture accounts for only 17% of national income but involves 70% of the population, largely in subsistence agriculture producing maize, sorghum, millet, rice, cassava and vegetables. Commercial agriculture by Africans was effectively banned by the Land Apportionment Act (1930) and the Land Tenure Act (1969) which ensured that the land most suited to cultivation was reserved for white farmers. Independence has seen the restoration of land to African farmers. Export crops include tobacco, coffee, cotton, tea, groundnuts, wheat and sugar cane. Livestock rearing is also important with over 5 million beef cattle and smaller numbers of pigs and poultry. Forestry, much of which is controlled by the Zimbabwe Forestry Commission, employs over 10,000 people and is based on the harvesting of natural forests of teak, mahogany and mukwa and the establishment of new plantations of pines, eucalyptus and wattle (mainly in the eastern mountains). Zimbabwe is rich in mineral resources which include gold, asbestos, nickel, coal, copper, chrome ore, iron ore, tin metal, silver and cobalt. Manufacturing industry is largely based on the production of iron, steel, foodstuffs, drink and tobacco, textiles, clothing and footwear, wood and furniture, and paper. The post-independence period saw an economic recovery which was moderated by depressed world demand for certain minerals and by drought. Main trading partners are South Africa, the UK, the USA and West Germany. *Administrative divisions.* Zimbabwe is divided into the 8 provinces of Matabeleland North, Matabeleland South, Midlands, Victoria, Manicaland, Mashonaland East, Mashonaland West and Mashonaland Central.

Zina've, national park in Mozambique, SE Africa; area 5,000 sq km; established in 1973; a major part of the park is in N Inhambane prov.

Zinder *zin'der*, dept in SE central Niger, W Africa; the 2nd largest region in Niger, it is predominantly low lying with extensive seasonal floodplains in the SW and NE; the Massif de Termit lies in the NE; area 145,430 sq km; pop(1977e) 1,034,000; comprises 5 arrond; capital Zinder; chief towns Tanout, Goure, Matameye.

Zinder, 13 46N 8 58E, pop(1983) 82,800, capital of Zinder dept, SE central Niger, W Africa; a typical Hausa town, 725 km E of Niamey and 1,000 km NE of Lagos (Nigeria); situated on an important trade route to Kano (Nigeria); occupied by the French in 1899 and a colonial capital until the 1920s; there is a market on Thursdays; airfield; economy: tanning, food processing, power plant; monument: Sultan's Palace (1860).

Zlatni Pyasăci *zlat'nay pya-sat'si*, GOLDEN SANDS (Eng), 43 16N 28 00E, beach resort on the Black Sea in Varna okrug (prov), E Bulgaria; 17 km NE of Varna; centre for international conferences and hydrotherapy treatment.

Zlatoust *zla-te-oost'*, 55 10N 59 38E, pop(1983) 202,000, town in W Chelyabinskaya oblast, E European Rossiyskaya, Soviet Union; in the S Ural'skiy Khrebet range (Ural Mts), W of Chelyabinsk; established when the ironworks were founded in 1754; railway; economy: machine building, toolmaking, foodstuffs.

Znojmo *znoy'mo*, 48 52N 16 04E, pop(1984) 38,321, town in Jihomoravský region, Czech Socialist Republic, central Czechoslovakia; on R Dyje, SW of Brno, near the Austrian frontier; founded in 1226; railway; economy: food processing.

Zoetermeer *zoo'tur-mayr*, 52 04N 4 30E, pop(1984e) 77,632, city in Zuid Holland prov, W Netherlands; 12 km E of 's-Gravenhage (The Hague); economy: specialized nutritional products.

Zomba *zōm'ba*, 15 22S 35 22E, pop(1984e) 49,000, town in Zomba dist, Southern region, S Malawi, SE Africa; 60 km NE of Blantyre and 480 km NNW of Beira (Mozambique); alt 880 m; capital of Malawi until 1975 when it was transferred to Lilongwe; university; railway; airfield; economy: cement, fishing tackle.

Zonguldak *zon-gool-dak'*, maritime prov in N Turkey; bounded NW by the Black Sea; pop(1980) 954,512; area 8,629 sq km; capital Zonguldak.

Zonguldak, 41 26N 31 47E, pop(1980) 109,044, seaport capital of Zonguldak prov, N Turkey; on the Black Sea; centre of a major coal-producing area; railway.

Zörs *tsurs*, 47 09N 10 12E, winter sports resort village in the Lechtal Alps, Vorarlberg, W Austria; alt 1,720 m; chairlift facilities on the Seekopf, Nördlicher Trittkopf and Krabachjoch mts.

Żory *zoo'ri*, SOHRAU *zō'row* (Ger), 50 03N 18 40E, pop(1983) 59,600, town in Katowice voivodship, S Poland; SW of Katowice in the Rybnik coal basin; railway; economy: construction industry.

Zou *zoo*, prov in S Benin, W Africa; low-lying ground in S rises towards the W and N; chief towns Abomey, Savé, Savalou; economy: marble and alabaster mining.

Zouîrât *zoo-ee-rah'*, ZOUERATE, 22 44N 12 21W, pop(1976) 17,474, town in Tiris Zemmour region, N Mauritania, NW Africa; located E of Fderik; linked by rail to the seaport of Nouadhibou on the Atlantic coast; economy: iron ore mining.

Zoutleeuw *zowt'lay-oo*, LÉAU *lay-ō'* (Fr), 50 50N 5 06E, pop(1982) 84,914, town in Leuven dist, Brabant prov, Belgium.

Zrenjanin *zren'ya-nin*, formerly VELIKI BECKEREK, PETROVGRAD, 45 22N 20 23E, pop(1981) 139,300, river port city in autonomous province of Vojvodina, N Srbija (Serbia) republic, Yugoslavia; on R Begej; railway; economy: foodstuffs, canning, machinery.

Zuarungu *zwa-roong'goo*, 10 48N 0 46W, town in Upper region, N Ghana, W Africa; close to Bolgatanga, 150 km N of Tamale, near the Burkina frontier.

Zug *tsoog*, ZOUG (Fr), canton in central Switzerland; pop(1980) 75,930; area 239 sq km; capital Zug; joined the Swiss Confederacy in 1352.

Zug, 47 10N 8 31E, pop(1980) 21,609, capital of Zug canton, central Switzerland; at the NE end of Zuger Zee, above which rises the flat-topped ridge of Zugerberg, 24 km S of Zürich; railway junction; the local kirsch is famous; monument: 15-16th-c Gothic church.

Zugspitze *tsook'shpi-tsu*, 47 25N 11 00E, mountain in S Bayern (Bavaria) prov, W Germany, rising to 2,962 m on the Wettersteingebirge of the Bavarian Alps, near Austro-German border; highest point in W Germany; near the summit is a hotel, also one of Europe's highest atmospheric sampling stations, measuring fall-out and pollution, electric charging and gradients.

Zuid Holland *zoyt'ho-lahnt*, SOUTH HOLLAND (Eng), pop(1984e) 3,139,200, prov in W Netherlands, bounded on the W by the North Sea, drained by the Oude and Lek rivers; land area 2,907 sq km; capital 's-Gravenhage; chief towns Leiden, Rotterdam and Dordrecht; economy: arable farming on fertile, well-drained marine clays, an important bulb growing area around Leiden (suited to the lime-rich sandy soils of the excavated old dunes), an important horticultural area between 's-Gravenhage, Rotterdam and Hoek van Holland (Hook of Holland), almost exclusively under glass, elsewhere livestock farming.

Zuidelijke Ijsselmeerpolders, pop(1983e) 27,500, reclaimed area in the Netherlands, NE of Amsterdam; land area 387 sq km; drained in 1957.

Zuider Zee *zī'der zee*, former shallow inlet of the North Sea in W Netherlands, divided since the 1920s into the outer Waddenzee (Wadden Sea) and the inner Ijsselmeer, which has been partially reclaimed as polder land.

Zújar *thoo'har*, river rising in the Sierra Morena, W of Fuenteovejuna, Extremadura, E Spain, flowing along the Córdoba-Badajoz border then N and W, joining the R Guadiana N of Villanueva; length 210 km; major irrigation reservoir at Pantano del Zújar.

Zulia *sool'ya*, state in NW Venezuela; on the Caribbean Gulf of Venezuela; borders W with Colombia along the Sierra de Perijá; in the N the state occupies a narrow S strip of the Guajira Peninsula; lowland around L Maracaibo rises towards outliers of the Andes; pop(1980) 1,680,890; area 63,076 sq km; capital Maracaibo; economy: a rich oil-producing region, cattle raising, dairy farming.

Zürich *tsü'reeKH*, ZURICH *zoo'rik* (Eng), canton in N Switzerland; pop(1980) 1,122,839; area 1,729 sq km; capital Zürich; rises to 1,292 m in the Schnebelhorn; joined the Swiss Confederacy in 1351.

Zürich, 47 22N 8 32E, pop(1980) 369,522, financial centre and capital of Zürich canton, N Switzerland; at the foot of the Alps on R Limmat, at the NW end of Zürichsee (Lake of Zurich), 96 km NE of Bern; largest city in Switzerland; the old town is on rising ground E of the river, between the Grossmünster and the university; the modern town is spacious and well-designed; developed as a result of its advantageous position at the crossing of E-W and N-S trade routes; railway; Kloten Airport (11 km N of the city centre); university (1833, rebuilt 1911-14); 3 of the 5 major Swiss banks have their head offices in the famous Bahnhofstrasse, one of the most notable shopping streets in Europe; economy: engineering, electrics, finance, textiles, tourism; monuments: Grossmünster (11-14th-c), Fraumünster (13th-c, restored), Rathaus (17th-c), St Peter's church (13th-c); events: International June Festival Weeks.

Zürichsee, LAKE OF ZURICH (Eng), lake in Zürich, St Gallen and Schwyz cantons, N Switzerland, stretching 39 km NW from the N foothills of the Alps to Zürich city; area

90 sq km; max width 4 km; max depth 143 m; its principal tributary, the Linth, rises in the Tödi massif, Glarus canton, flows through the Walensee and continues to the Zürichsee as a canal; the lake is drained at the NW end by the R Limmat, which flows into the R Aare below Brugg; the NE shore of the lake, with an almost continuous succession of attractive towns and villages beneath vine-clad slopes, and a whole string of beaches, is popularly known as the 'Gold Coast'; there are regular boat services linking lakeside towns; towns on the shores include Zürich, Meilen, Rapperswil, Wädenswil and Horgen.

Żurrieq *zoo-ri-ek'*, 35 50N 14 29E, pop(1983e) 7,226, town in SE Malta, 8 km SSW of Valletta.

Zvishavane *zvish-a-vah'nay*, SHABANI, 20 20S 30 05E, pop(1982) 27,000, mining town in Matabeleland North prov, Zimbabwe, S Africa; 153 km E of Bulawayo.

Zvolen *zvo'len*, 48 34N 19 08E, pop(1984) 38,445, town in Středoslovenský region, Slovak Socialist Republic, E Czechoslovakia; on R Hron, SW of Banská Bystrica; thermal springs nearby; railway; economy: timber, glass; monument: 14th-c castle.

Zwettl *tsvet'al*, 48 37N 15 11E, pop(1981) 11,479, market town and capital of Zwettl dist, Niederösterreich, NE Austria; at the junction of the Zwettlbach and Kamp rivers; centre of communications for the W Waldviertel; monuments: Cistercian abbey (1138), old town hall (1307).

Zwickau *tsvi'kow*, 50 43N 12 30E, pop(1982) 120,852, mining and industrial city in Zwickau dist, Karl Marx Stadt, S East Germany; on R Mulde, SW of Karl Marx Stadt; birthplace of Robert Schumann; a free imperial city (1290-1323); railway; economy: motor vehicles, chemicals, coal mining.

Zwolle *zvol'e*, 52 31N 6 06E, pop(1984e) 87,340, capital city of Overijssel prov, E Netherlands; on the Zwarte Water, which opens into the Ijsselmeer some 20 km NW of the town; has one of the largest cattle markets in the country; associated with Thomas à Kempis who spent most of his life nearby; railway; canal junction; economy: vehicles, machinery, foodstuffs, textiles, building materials, timber, leatherwork, chemicals, information publishing, printing, efficiency systems; monument: 15th-c St Michaelskerk.

World Atlas

Reproduced by permission of John Bartholomew & Son Ltd, Edinburgh

Printed in Scotland by
John Bartholomew & Son Ltd Duncan Street Edinburgh EH9 1TA

CONTENTS

4-5
6-7
12
13
8-9
10-11
20
14-15
16
22
21
18-19
24-25
17
26-27
23

32-33
31
35
30
34
29

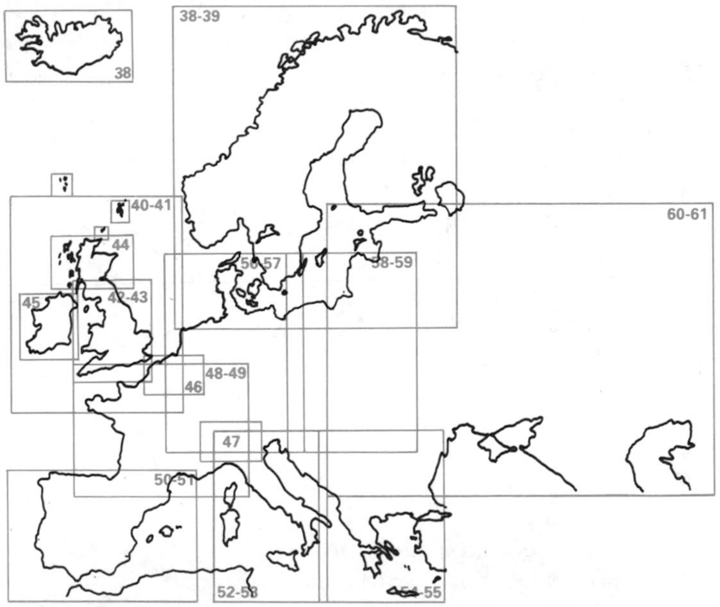
38-39
38
40-41
44
45
42-43
46
48-49
47
50-51
52-53
54-55
56-57
58-59
60-61

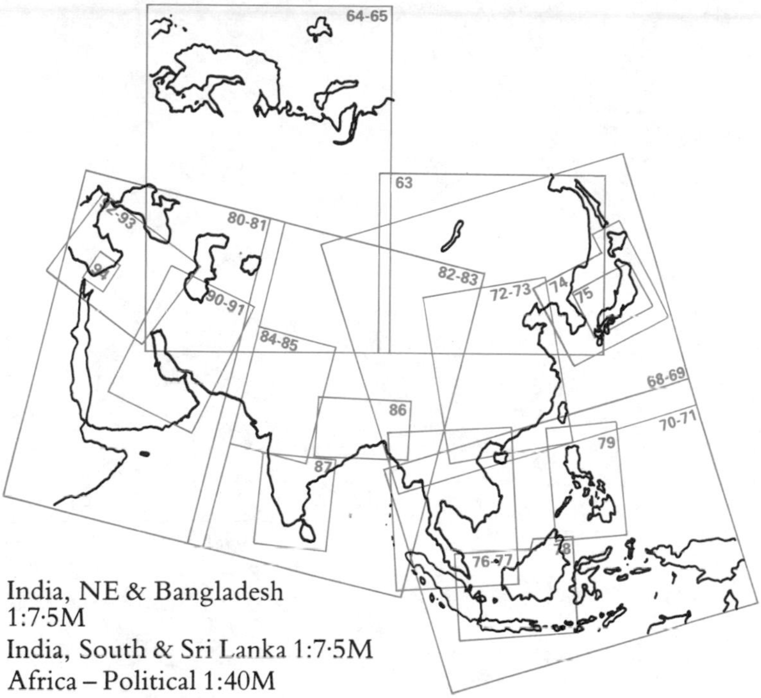

64-65
63
80-81
94
90-91
82-83
72-73
74
75
84-85
68-69
86
70-71
79
87
76-77
78

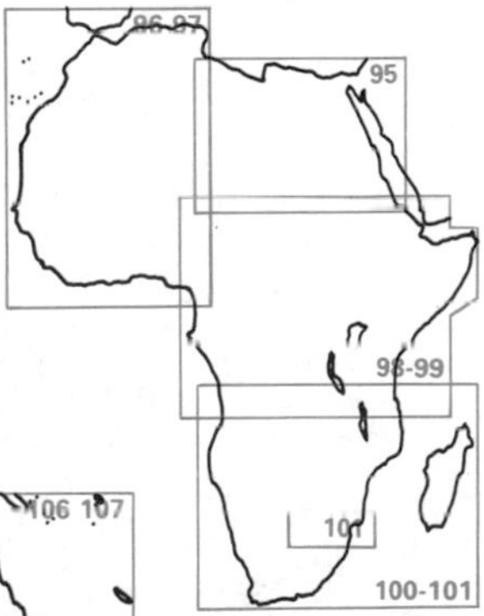

95
100-101

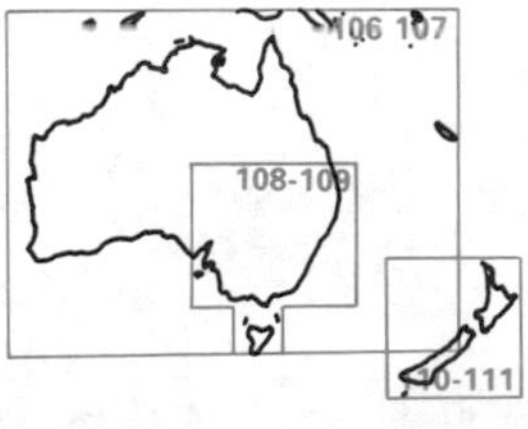

106 107

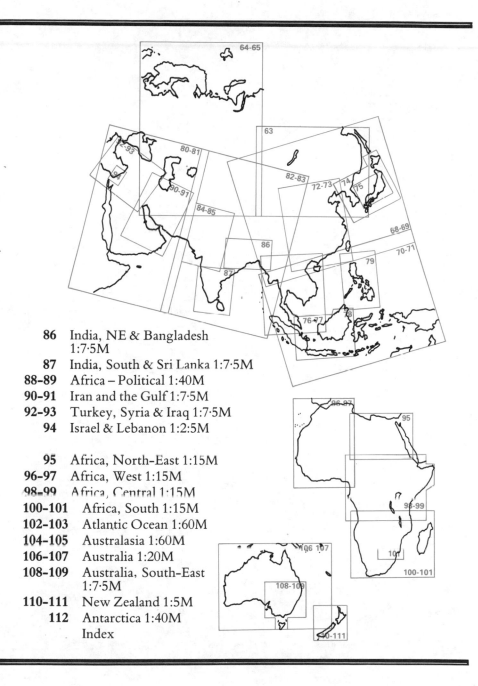

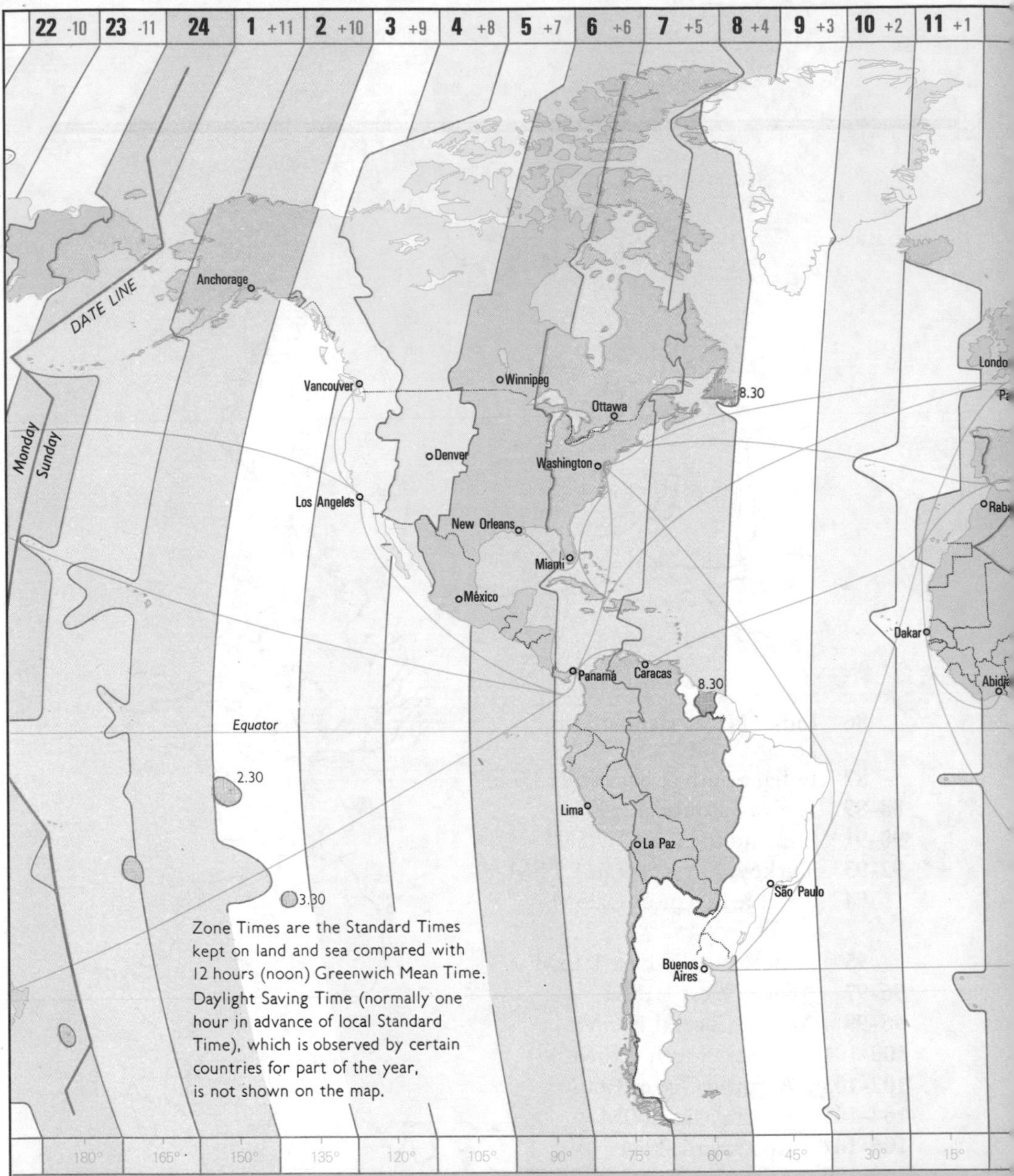

Zone Times are the Standard Times kept on land and sea compared with 12 hours (noon) Greenwich Mean Time. Daylight Saving Time (normally one hour in advance of local Standard Time), which is observed by certain countries for part of the year, is not shown on the map.

Journey Times

Sail (via Cape)
164 days

Steam (via Cape)
43 days

Steam (via Suez)
30 days

Supertanker
(via Cape)
28 days

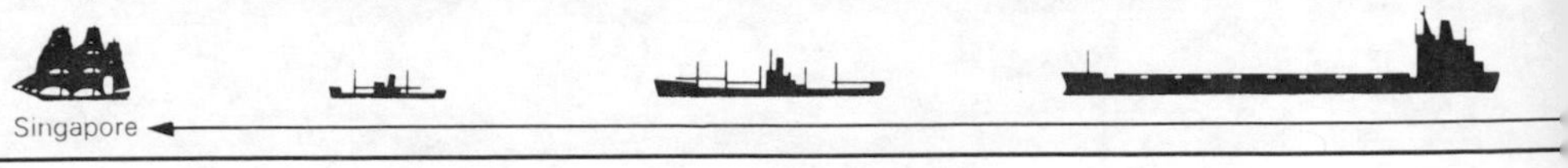

13 -1
14 -2
15 -3
16 -4
17 -5
18 -6
19 -7
20 -8
21 -9
22 -10
23 -11
24
1 +11
2 +10
Oslo
Berlin
Moskva
Sverdlovsk
Novosibirsk
Yakutsk
Magadan
Ulaanbaatar
Roma
Ankara
Beijing
Tehrān
15.30
16.30
Tōkyō
DATE LINE
Cairo
Chengdu
Shanghai
Delhi
Rīyadh
Hong Kong
17.30
18.30
Manila
Bangkok
N'Djamena
Addis Ababa
Singapore
Equator
23.30
Kinshasa
Dar es Salaam
Jakarta
18.30
Harare
21.30
Pretoria
23.30
Perth
22.30
Sydney
Cape Town
Auckland
Shipping Lanes
00.45
15°
30°
45°
60°
75°
90°
105°
120°
135°
150°
165°
180°

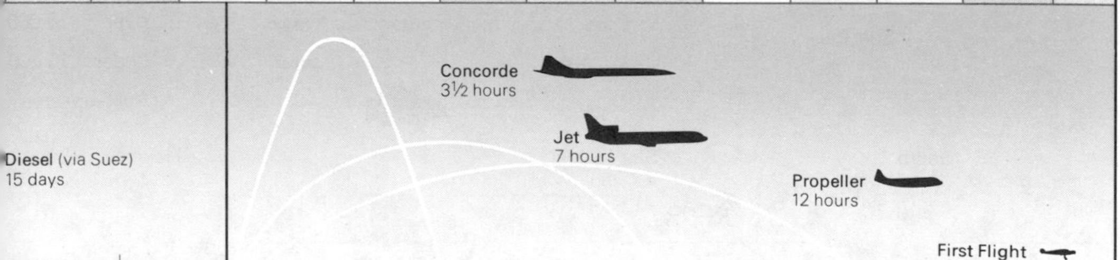
Concorde
3½ hours
Jet
7 hours
Diesel (via Suez)
15 days
Propeller
12 hours
First Flight
4½ days
London
New York

BOUNDARIES

- International
- International under Dispute
- Cease Fire Line
- Autonomous or State/ Administrative
- Maritime (National)
- International Date Line

COMMUNICATIONS

- Motorway/Under Construction
- Major/Other Road
- Under Construction
- Track
- Road Tunnel
- Car Ferry
- Main/Other Railway
- Under Construction
- Rail Ferry
- Rail Tunnel
- Canal
- International/Other Airport

LANDSCAPE FEATURES

- Glacier, Ice Cap
- Marsh, Swamp
- Sand Desert, Dunes
- Freshwater
- Saltwater
- Seasonal
- Salt Pan

OTHER FEATURES

- River/Seasonal
- Pass, Gorge
- Dam, Barrage
- Waterfall, Rapid
- Aqueduct
- Reef
- .217 ▲4231 Spot Height, Depth/ Summit, Peak
- Well
- Oil/Gas Field
- Gas / Oil — Oil/Natural Gas Pipeline
- Gemsbok Nat. Pk — National Park
- ∴UR — Historic Site

LETTERING STYLES

CANADA	Independent Nation
FLORIDA	State, Province or Autonomous Region
Gibraltar (U.K.)	Sovereignty of Dependent Territory
Lothian	Administrative Area
LANGUEDOC	Historic Region
Loire *Vosges*	Physical Feature or Physical Region

TOWNS AND CITIES

Square symbols denote capital cities		*Population*
■ ●	**New York**	over 5 000 000
■ ●	**Montréal**	over 1 000 000
□ ○	Ottawa	over 500 000
■ ●	Québec	over 100 000
□ ○	St John's	over 50 000
□ ○	Yorkton	over 10 000
□ ○	Jasper	under 10 000
		Built-up-area

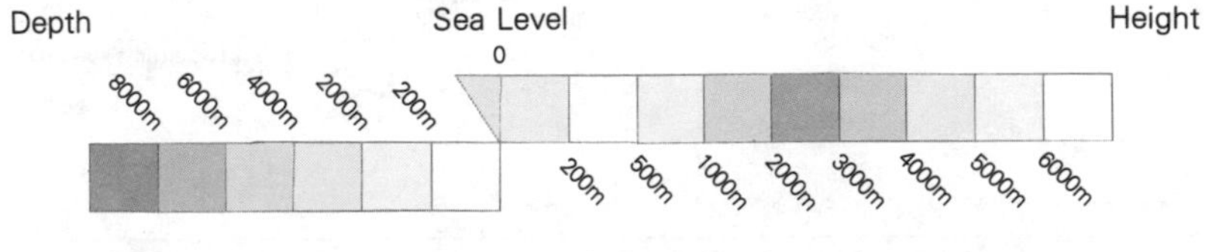

ARCTIC OCEAN
North Pole
N Magnetic Pole (1980)
Chukchi Sea
E. Siberian Sea
Laptev Sea
Kara Sea
Barents Sea
Greenland Sea
Norwegian Sea
Beaufort Sea
Lincoln Sea
Baffin Bay
Hudson Bay
Foxe Basin
Hudson Str.
Davis Str.
Denmark Strait
Nares Str.
James B.
Gulf of St Lawrence
ATLANTIC OCEAN
Arctic Circle
Tree Limit
average minimum extent of sea ice
U. S. S. R.
CHINA
FINLAND
SWEDEN
NORWAY
ICELAND
CANADA
U.S.A.
Alaska (U.S.A.)
Greenland (Den.)
ROCKY MTS
Uralskiy Khrebet
Novaya Zemlya
Severnaya Zemlya
Zemlya Frantsa Iosifa
Novosibirskiye Ostrova
O. Vrangelya
Svalbard (Spitsbergen) (Nor.)
Bjørnøya (Bear I.) (Nor.)
Jan Mayen (Nor.)
Nordkapp
Queen Elizabeth Islands
Ellesmere I.
Banks I.
Victoria I.
Baffin I.
Southampton I.
Newfoundland
Watkins Bjerge 3700
Mt McKinley 6194
K. Farvel
G. of Boothia
Gt Bear L.
Gt Slave L.
L. Athabasca
L. Winnipeg
Oz. Baykal
Amur
Lena
Yenisey
Ob'
Irtysh
Kolyma
Indigirka
Mackenzie
Yukon
Sev. Dvina
Bering
Moscow
Leningrad
Murmansk
Arkhangel'sk
Mezen'
Kotlas
Vorkuta
Salekhard
Nadym
Berezovo
Syktyvkar
Kirov
Kazan'
Gor'kiy
Yaroslavl'
Kuybyshev
Ufa
Perm'
Sverdlovsk
Magnitogorsk
Orsk
Aktyubinsk
Serov
Tobol'sk
Omsk
Novosibirsk
Krasnoyarsk
Turukhansk
Noril'sk
Dudinka
Dikson
Khatanga
Nordvik
Tiksi
Zhigansk
Yakutsk
Aldan
Verkhoyansk
Ust'Nera
Kazach'ye
Polyarnyy
Ambarchik
Pevek
Vankarem
Ust'Kut
Chita
Skovorodino
Chul'man
Blagoveshchensk
Tromsø
Narvik
Oulu
Umeå
Reykjavik
Scoresbysund
Angmagssalik
Julianehåb
Godthåb
Søndre Strømfjord
Godhavn
Upernavik
Thule
Nord
Alert
Eureka
Resolute
Pond Inlet
Inuvik
Norman Wells
Coppermine
Yellowknife
Dawson
Fairbanks
Prudhoe Bay
Barrow
Teller
Juneau
Prince Rupert
Vancouver
Seattle
Calgary
Edmonton
Saskatoon
Flin Flon
Churchill
Inukjuac
Fort George
Schefferville
Hebron
Nain
Gander

North America - Political

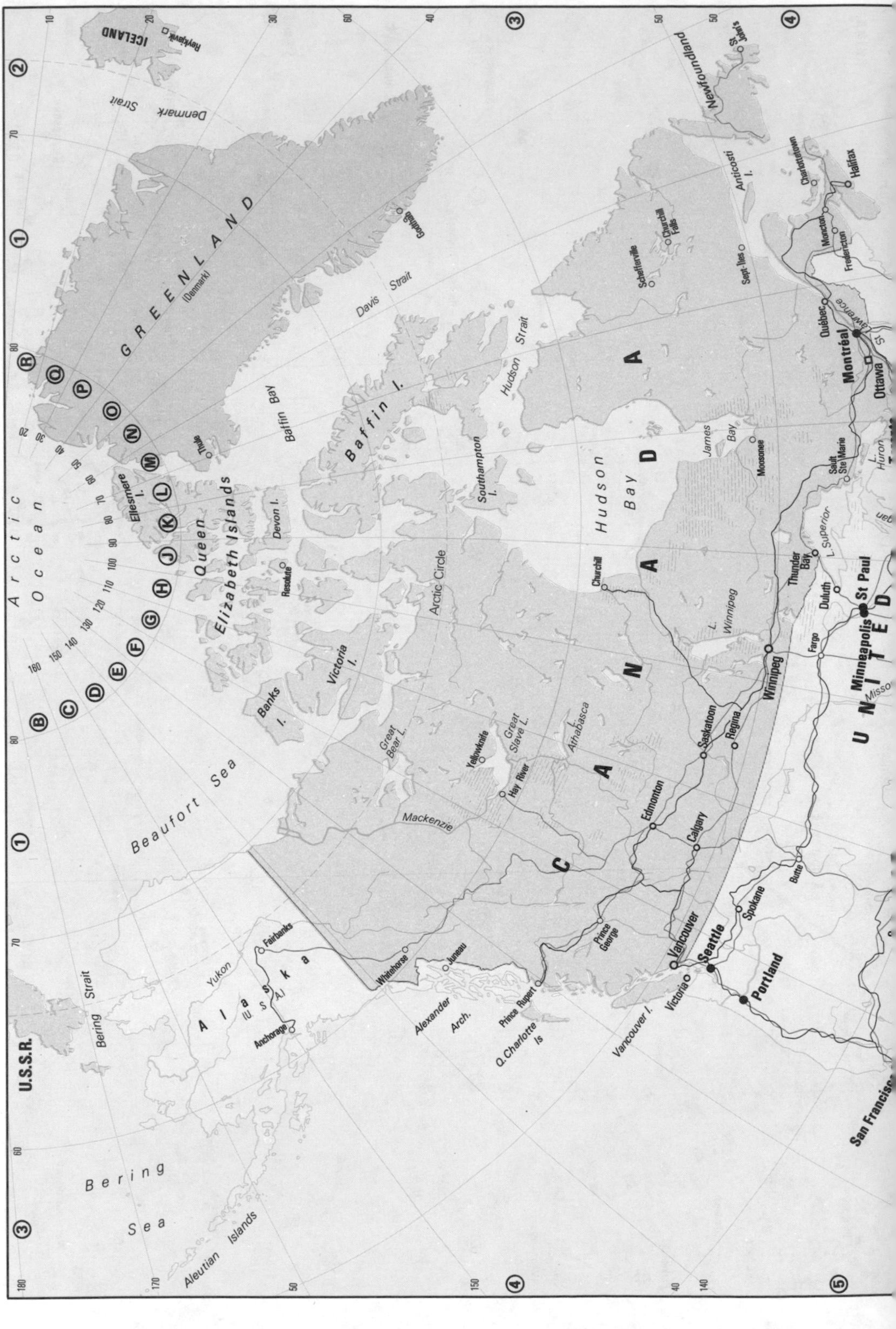

1:35M 0 250 500 750 1000 1250 km / 0 250 500 750 mls

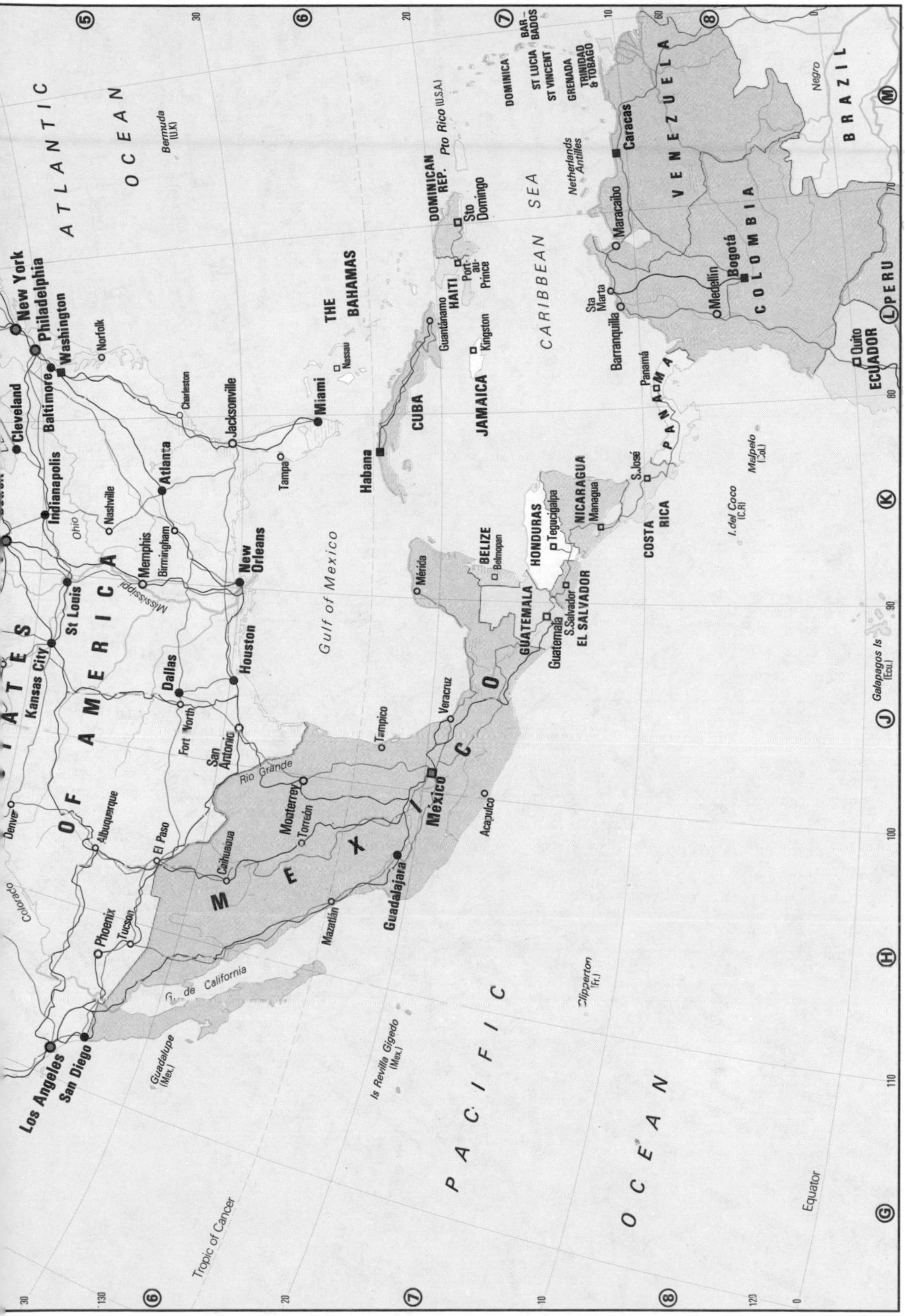

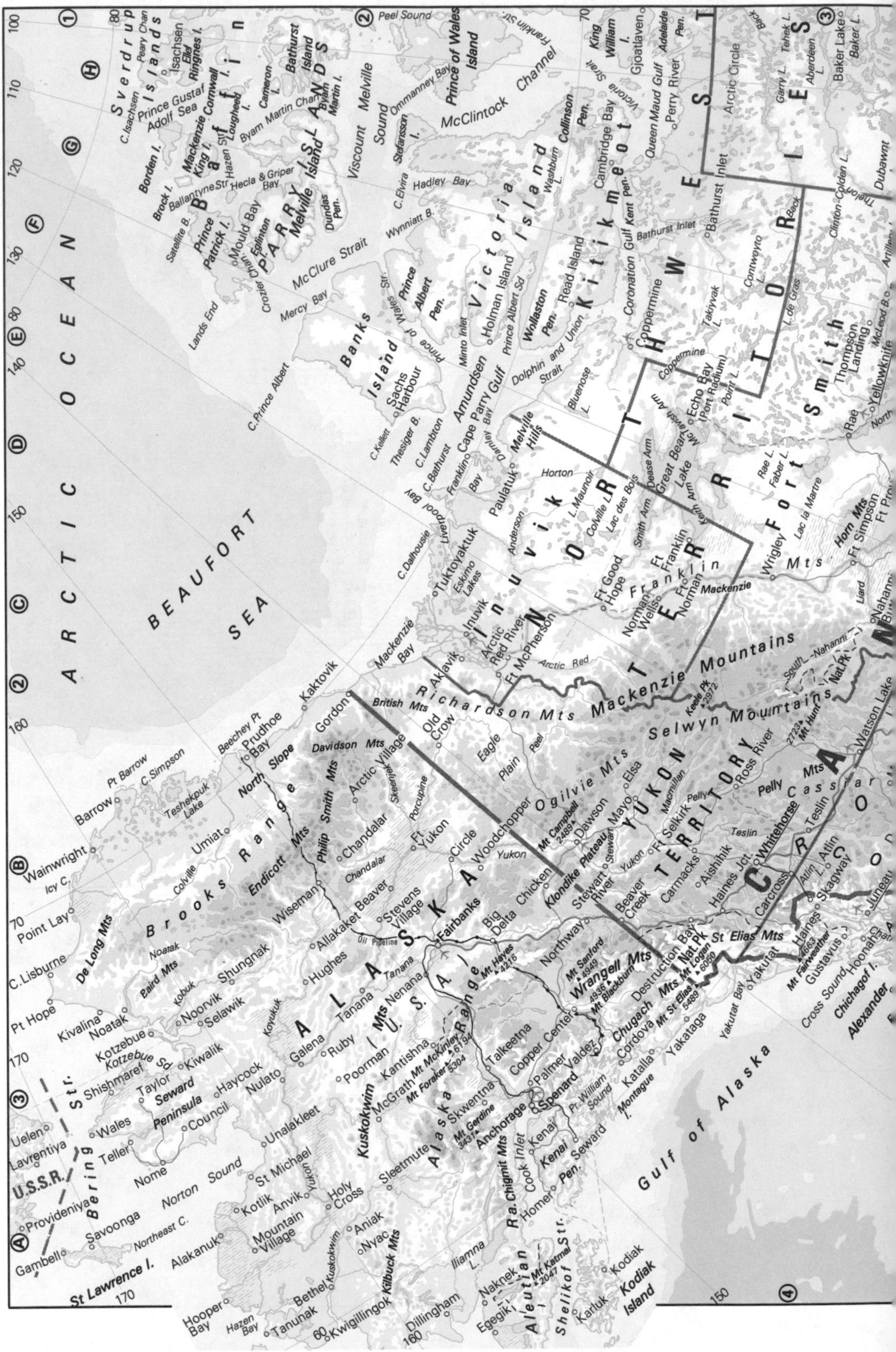
ARCTIC OCEAN
BEAUFORT SEA
Gulf of Alaska
Banks Island
Victoria Island
Prince Patrick I.
Melville Island
PARRY ISLANDS
Sverdrup Islands
Prince of Wales Island
McClintock Channel
Viscount Melville Sound
McClure Strait
Amundsen Gulf
Mackenzie Bay
Mackenzie Mountains
Richardson Mts
Selwyn Mountains
Ogilvie Mts
YUKON TERRITORY
NORTHWEST TERRITORIES
Inuvik
Kitikmeot
Fort Smith
ALASKA
U.S.A.
U.S.S.R.
Brooks Range
North Slope
Alaska Range
Wrangell Mts
St Elias Mts
Chugach Mts
Kuskokwim Mts
Seward Peninsula
Bering Str.
Norton Sound
Kotzebue Sd
Kodiak Island
Great Bear Lake
Fairbanks
Anchorage
Whitehorse
Dawson
Barrow
Prudhoe Bay
Nome
Tuktoyaktuk
Aklavik
Inuvik
Sachs Harbour
Coppermine
Yellowknife
Mt McKinley 6194
Mt Logan 6050
Mt St Elias 5489
Mt Foraker 5304
Mt Sanford 4949
Mt Hayes 4216
Keele Pk 2972
St Lawrence I.
Kenai Pen.
Cook Inlet
Shelikof Str.
Aleutian

PACIFIC
OCEAN
CANADA
U.S.A.
BRITISH COLUMBIA
ALBERTA
SASKATCHEWAN
MANITOBA
WASHINGTON
OREGON
IDAHO
MONTANA
WYOMING
NORTH DAKOTA
SOUTH DAKOTA
Rocky Mountains
Bitterroot Range
Selkirk Mts
Monashee Mts
Caribou Mountains
Omineca Mts
Skeena Mts
Cascade Range
Salmon River Mts
Big Horn Mts
Absaroka Range
Lewis Range
Queen Charlotte Islands
Vancouver Island
Queen Charlotte Sound
Hecate Str.
Dixon Entrance
Str. of Juan de Fuca
Str. of Georgia
Lake Athabasca
Wollaston L.
Reindeer Lake
Lake Winnipeg
L. Winnipegosis
Lake Manitoba
Cedar L.
Great Sandy Desert
Black Rock Desert
Harney Basin
Snake River Plain
Wood Buffalo Nat. Pk.
Vancouver
Victoria
Seattle
Tacoma
Olympia
Portland
Salem
Eugene
Spokane
Boise
Edmonton
Calgary
Red Deer
Lethbridge
Medicine Hat
Saskatoon
Regina
Moose Jaw
Prince Albert
Winnipeg
Brandon
Kamloops
Kelowna
Penticton
Prince George
Prince Rupert
Kitimat
Helena
Great Falls
Missoula
Butte
Billings
Bozeman
Bismarck
Fargo
Grand Forks
Minot
Pierre
Rapid City
Sioux Falls
Yakima
Walla Walla
Lewiston
Pocatello
Idaho Falls
Twin Falls
Klamath Falls
Medford
Redding
Eureka
Crescent City
Fort Smith
Fort McMurray
Fort Nelson
Dawson Ck
Grande Prairie
Peace River
The Pas
Flin Flon
Thompson
Mt Columbia 3747
Mt Robson
Mt Rainier
Mt Adams 3751
Mt Hood 3427
Mt Olympus 2428
Mt Baker 3285
Glacier Pk 3213
Mt Shasta
Grand Teton 4196
Gannett Pk 4202
Borah Pk 3859
Mt Waddington 4042

GREENLAND (Denmark)
ICELAND
DENMARK STRAIT
DAVIS STRAIT
HUDSON STRAIT
Labrador Sea
BAFFIN
Baffin Island
Baffin Bay
Foxe Basin
Foxe Channel
Foxe Pen.
Melville Peninsula
Keewatin
QUEEN ELIZABETH ISLANDS
PARRY ISLANDS
Ellesmere Island
Sverdrup Islands
Devon Island
Lancaster Sound
Jones Sound
Nares Strait
Kane Basin
Cumberland Sound
Cumberland Peninsula
Hall Peninsula
Meta Incognita Pen.
Frobisher Bay
Southampton Island
Boothia Peninsula
Gulf of Boothia
Somerset Island
Prince of Wales Island
Bathurst Island
Cornwallis I.
Axel Heiberg Island
Amund Ringnes I.
Graham I.
Bylot I.
Borden Peninsula
Brodeur Peninsula
Prince Regent Inlet
Admiralty Inlet
Arctic Bay
Pond Inlet
Clyde
Home Bay
Henry Kater Pen.
Penny Highlands
Pangnirtung
Cape Dyer
Kekertuk
Frobisher Bay
Lake Harbour
Amadjuak Lake
Nettilling Lake
Cape Dorset
Nuvukjuak
Igloolik
Hall Beach
Prince Charles I.
Air Force I.
Repulse Bay
Coral Harbour
Chesterfield Inlet
Baker Lake
Wager Bay
Roes Welcome Sd.
Spence Bay
Pelly Bay
Gjoa Haven
King William I.
Thom Bay
Resolute
Barrow Str.
Peel Sound
Grise Fiord
Eureka
Alexandra Fiord
Etah
Thule
Dundas
Melville Bugt
K. York
Kraulshavn
Tasiussaq
Upernavik
Søndre Upernavik
Prøven
Svartenhuk Halvø
Umanak
Disko
Disko Bugt
Godhavn
Jakobshavn
Christianshåb
Egedesminde
Holsteinsborg
Søndre Strømfjord
Sukkertoppen
Godthåb
Frederikshåb
Julianehåb
Kap Farvel
Angmagssalik
Scoresbysund
Kong Christian IX Land
Kong Frederik VI Kyst
Knud Rasmussens Land
Arctic Circle
Reykjavík
Akureyri
Keflavík
Hekla
Vatnajökull
Labrador
Resolution I.
Button Is
C. Chidley
Salisbury I.
Nottingham I.
Mansel I.
Coats I.
Evans Str.
Ivujivik
Saglouc
Kangiqsujuaq

0 200 400 600 km
0 100 200 300 mls

1:12.5M

0 100 200 300 400 500 km
0 100 200 300 mls

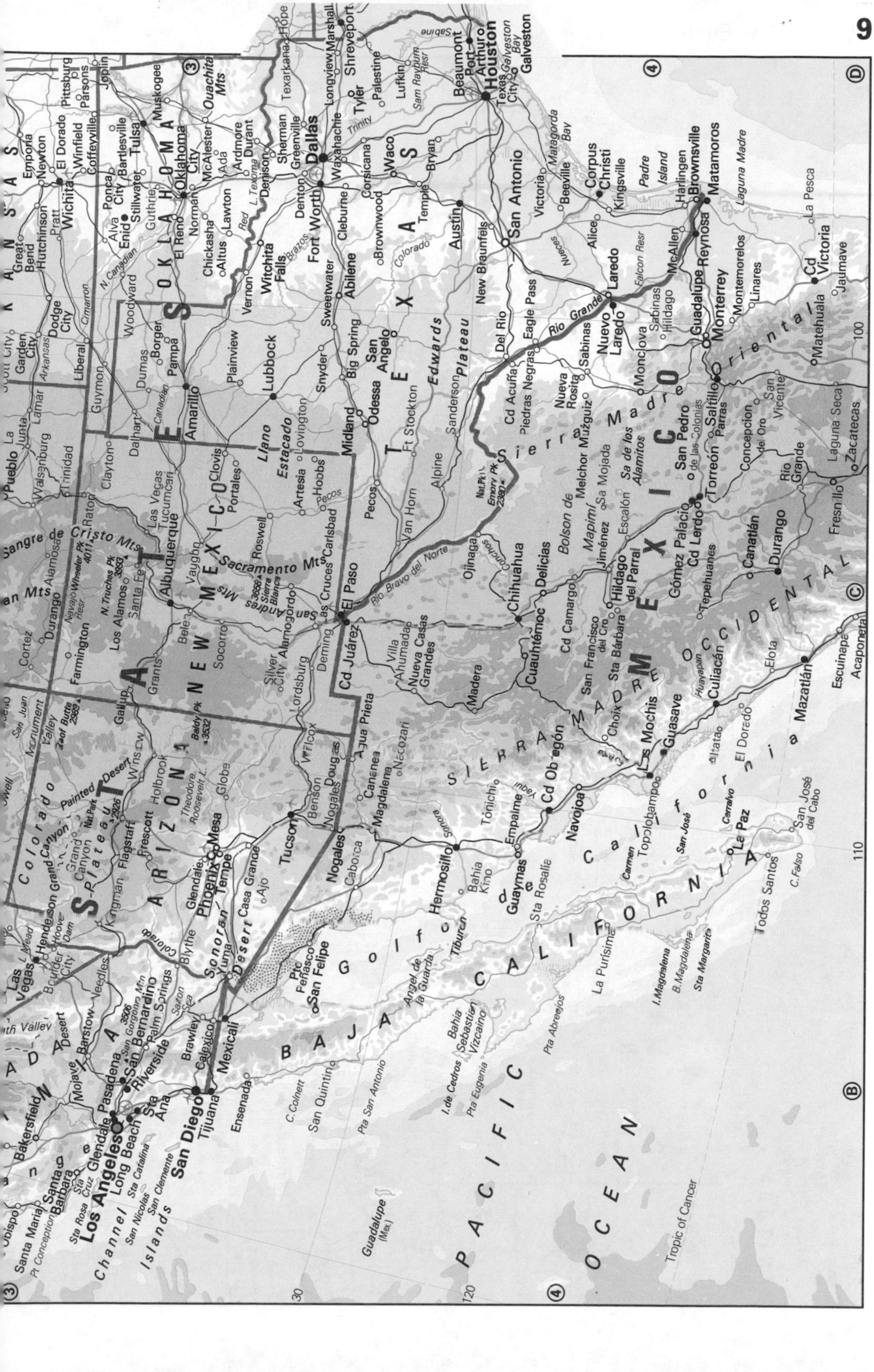
PACIFIC OCEAN
Gulf of California
BAJA CALIFORNIA
MEXICO
TEXAS
NEW MEXICO
ARIZONA
OKLAHOMA
KANSAS
NEVADA
Sierra Madre Oriental
SIERRA MADRE OCCIDENTAL
Llano Estacado
Edwards Plateau
Colorado Plateau
Sonoran Desert
Painted Desert
Sangre de Cristo Mts
Sacramento Mts
San Andres Mts
Ouachita Mts
Bolson de Mapimí
Rio Grande
Rio Bravo del Norte
Tropic of Cancer
Channel Islands
Los Angeles
San Diego
Tijuana
Mexicali
Phoenix
Tucson
Albuquerque
Santa Fe
El Paso
Cd Juárez
Chihuahua
Lubbock
Amarillo
Oklahoma City
Tulsa
Wichita
Dallas
Fort Worth
Houston
San Antonio
Austin
Corpus Christi
Laredo
Nuevo Laredo
Monterrey
Saltillo
Torreón
Durango
Culiacán
Mazatlán
Hermosillo
Guaymas
Cd Obregón
La Paz
Shreveport
Galveston
Brownsville
Matamoros
Reynosa
Zacatecas
30
100
110
120
B
C
D
3
4

MANITOBA
ONTARIO
QUEBEC
NEW BRUNSWICK
MAINE
VERMONT
NEW HAMPSHIRE
MASS.
CONN.
R.I.
NEW YORK
PENNSYLVANIA
N.J.
DEL.
MD
OHIO
INDIANA
ILLINOIS
MICHIGAN
WISCONSIN
MINNESOTA
IOWA
WEST
James Bay
LAKE SUPERIOR
L. MICHIGAN
LAKE HURON
Georgian Bay
L. ONTARIO
L. ERIE
St Lawrence
Gaspé Peninsula
Anticosti Island
Bay of Fundy
Long Island
Delaware Bay
Chesapeake
Winnipeg
Lake Winnipeg
Kenora
Thunder Bay
Sault Ste Marie
Sudbury
North Bay
Toronto
Hamilton
Ottawa
Montréal
Québec
Trois-Rivières
Sherbrooke
Chicoutimi
Baie-Comeau
Sept-Iles
Rimouski
Fredericton
Saint John
Moncton
Bangor
Augusta
Portland
Boston
Providence
Hartford
New Haven
New York
Newark
Philadelphia
Baltimore
Washington D.C.
Pittsburgh
Cleveland
Buffalo
Rochester
Syracuse
Albany
Detroit
Windsor
Toledo
Columbus
Cincinnati
Dayton
Indianapolis
Chicago
Milwaukee
Madison
Green Bay
Duluth
St Paul
Minneapolis
Fargo
Grand Forks
Des Moines
Cedar Rapids
Davenport
Peoria
Sioux Falls
Sioux City
Omaha
Lincoln
Council Bluffs
St Joseph

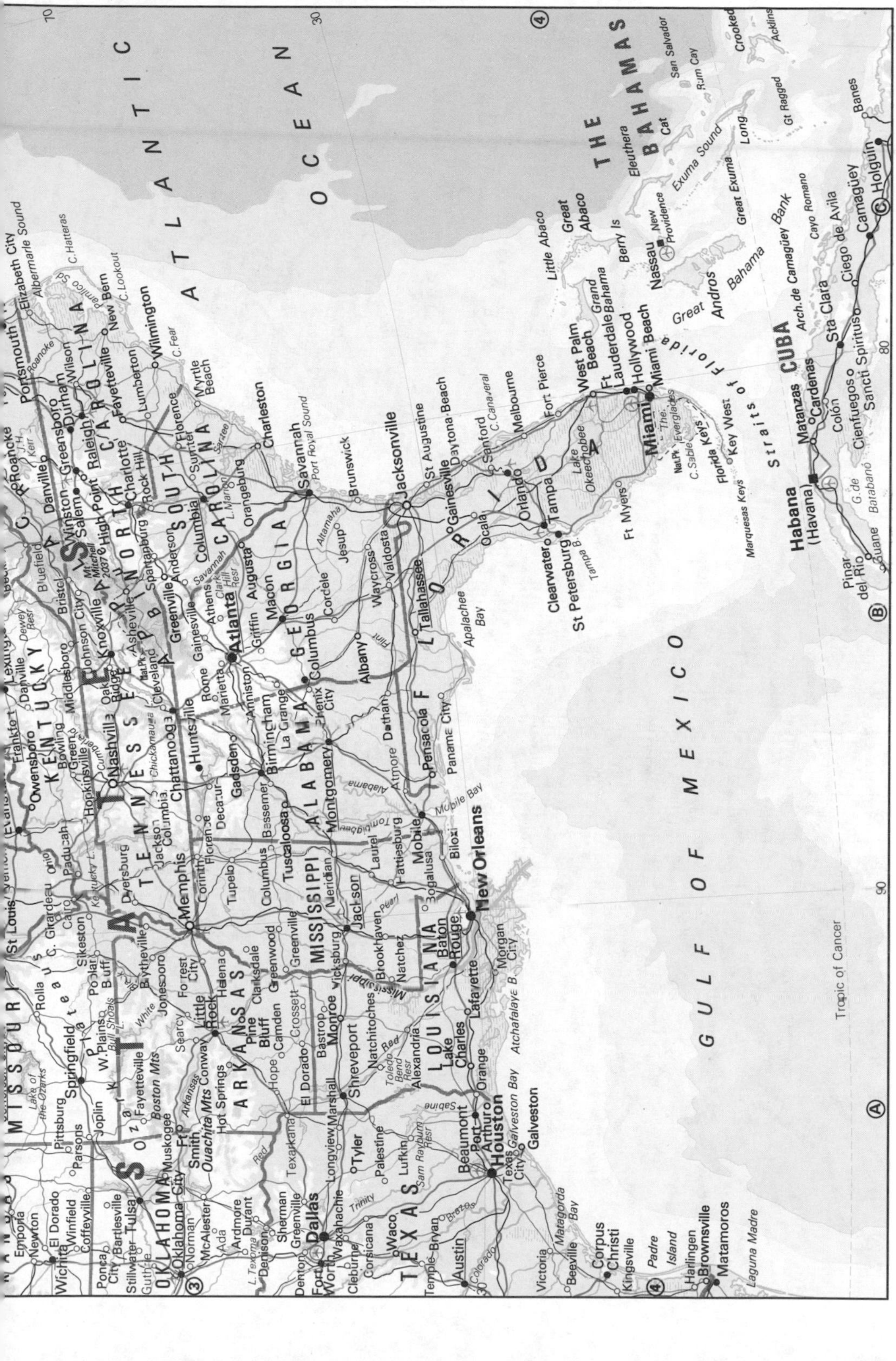
ATLANTIC OCEAN
GULF OF MEXICO
THE BAHAMAS
CUBA
MISSOURI
KENTUCKY
TENNESSEE
NORTH CAROLINA
SOUTH CAROLINA
GEORGIA
ALABAMA
MISSISSIPPI
LOUISIANA
ARKANSAS
OKLAHOMA
TEXAS
FLORIDA
Straits of Florida
Great Bahama Bank
Tropic of Cancer
Atlanta
New Orleans
Houston
Dallas
Miami
Jacksonville
Memphis
Nashville
Charlotte
Habana (Havana)
Nassau
Tampa
Orlando
Savannah
Charleston
Birmingham
Montgomery
Mobile
Tallahassee
Baton Rouge
Jackson
Little Rock
Shreveport
Oklahoma City
Tulsa
Wichita
Springfield
Knoxville
Chattanooga
Columbia
Raleigh
Greensboro
Wilmington
Augusta
Macon
Columbus
Pensacola
Gainesville
St Petersburg
Clearwater
West Palm Beach
Ft Lauderdale
Hollywood
Miami Beach
Key West
Galveston
Beaumont
Port Arthur
Austin
Corpus Christi
Brownsville
Matamoros
Camagüey
Holguín
Matanzas
Cienfuegos
Sta Clara
Ciego de Avila
Pinar del Rio
Andros
Grand Bahama
Great Abaco
Eleuthera
Cat
Great Exuma
Long
Apalachee Bay
Mobile Bay
Lake Okeechobee
A
B
C
3
4
30
70
80
90

1:10M

0 100 200 300 400 km
0 100 200 mls

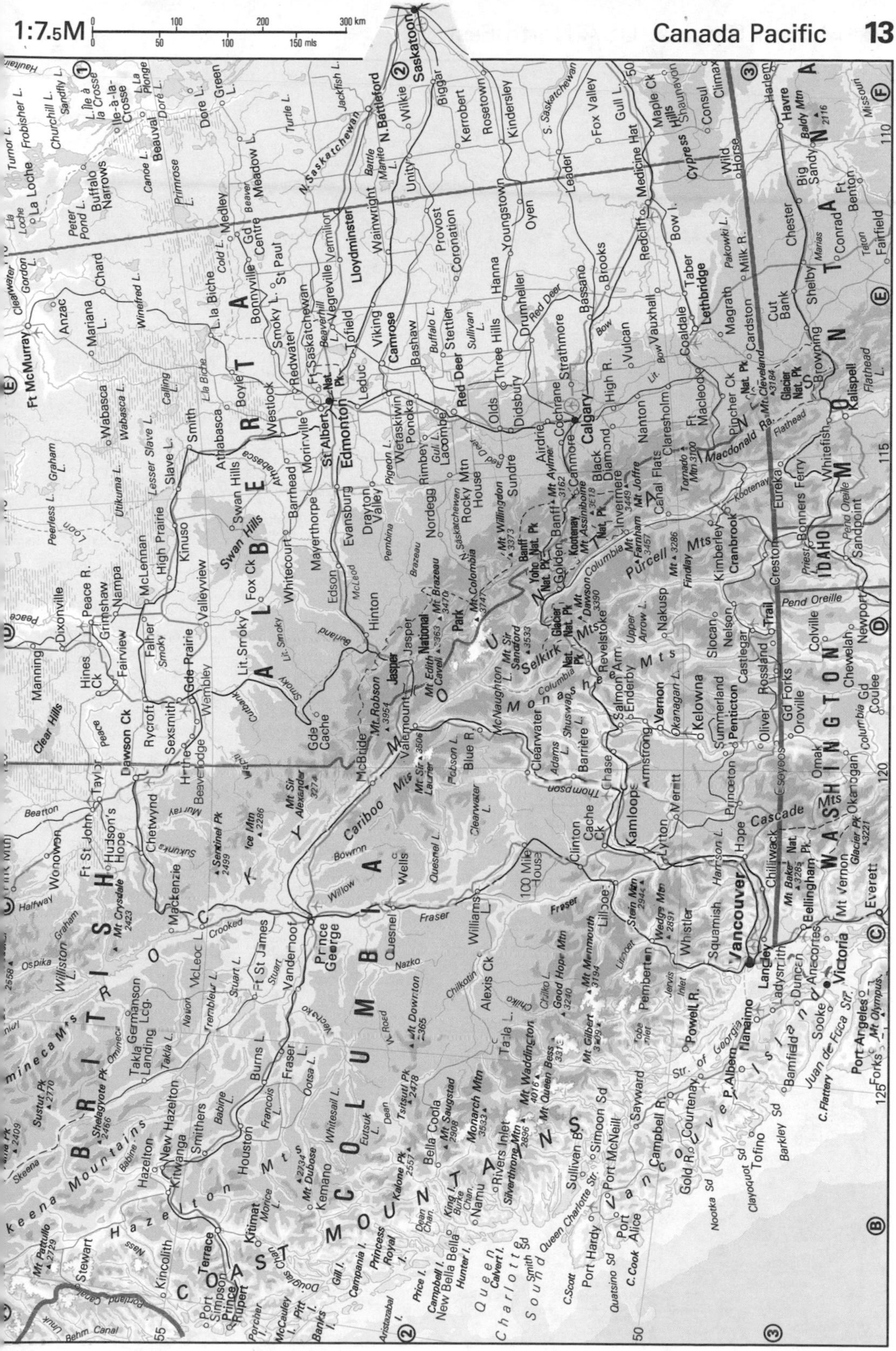
ALBERTA
BRITISH COLUMBIA
WASHINGTON
MONTANA
IDAHO
COAST MOUNTAINS
ROCKY MOUNTAINS
Monashee Mts
Selkirk Mts
Purcell Mts
Cariboo Mts
Cascade Mts
Skeena Mountains
Hazelton Mts
Swan Hills
Clear Hills
Cypress Hills
Saskatoon
N.Battleford
Lloydminster
Ft McMurray
Edmonton
St Albert
Red Deer
Calgary
Lethbridge
Medicine Hat
Camrose
Jasper
Banff
Prince George
Dawson Ck
Kamloops
Kelowna
Vernon
Penticton
Vancouver
Victoria
Nanaimo
Prince Rupert
Terrace
Kitimat
Trail
Cranbrook
Kalispell
Havre
Bella Coola
Powell R.
Campbell R.
Port Hardy
Queen Charlotte Sound
Str. of Georgia
Juan de Fuca Str.
Vancouver I.
N. Saskatchewan
Fraser
Thompson
Columbia
Peace
Mt Robson 3954
Mt Columbia 3747
Mt Waddington 4016

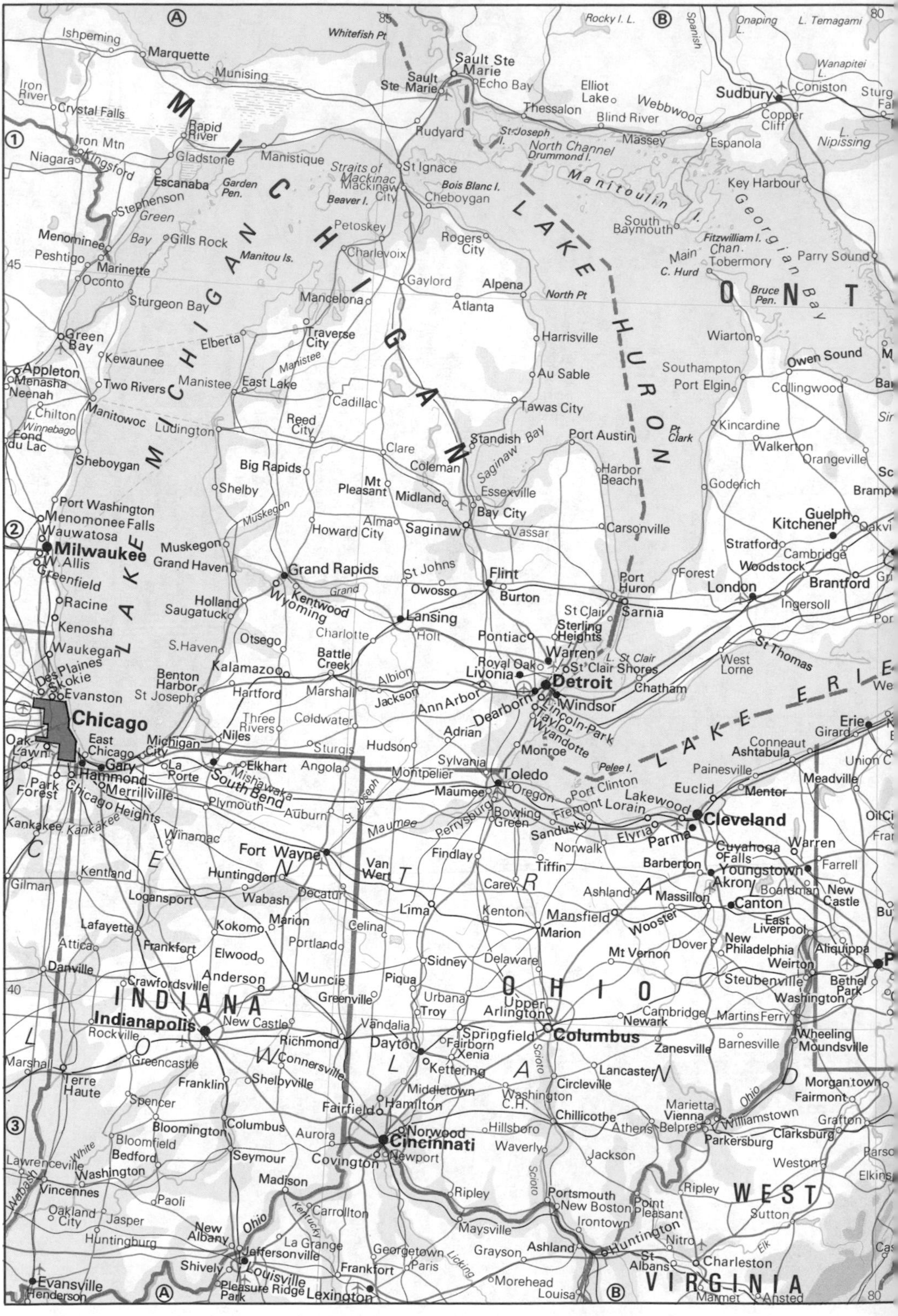

A
B
1
2
3
45
40
80
85
LAKE MICHIGAN
LAKE HURON
LAKE ERIE
MICHIGAN
INDIANA
OHIO
ONT
WEST VIRGINIA
Ishpeming
Marquette
Munising
Iron River
Crystal Falls
Rapid River
Iron Mtn
Kingsford
Niagara
Gladstone
Manistique
Escanaba
Garden Pen.
Stephenson
Green Bay
Gills Rock
Menominee
Peshtigo
Marinette
Oconto
Sturgeon Bay
Green Bay
Appleton
Menasha
Neenah
Kewaunee
Two Rivers
Manitowoc
Chilton
L. Winnebago
Fond du Lac
Sheboygan
Port Washington
Menomonee Falls
Wauwatosa
Milwaukee
W. Allis
Greenfield
Racine
Kenosha
Waukegan
Des Plaines
Skokie
Evanston
Chicago
Oak Lawn
East Chicago
Gary
Hammond
Park Forest
Chicago Heights
Merrillville
Kankakee
Gilman
Whitefish Pt
Sault Ste Marie
Sault Ste Marie
Echo Bay
Rudyard
St Ignace
Straits of Mackinac
Mackinaw City
Beaver I.
Bois Blanc I.
Cheboygan
Petoskey
Charlevoix
Manitou Is.
Rogers City
Gaylord
Alpena
North Pt
Atlanta
Mancelona
Elberta
Traverse City
Manistee
Manistee
East Lake
Cadillac
Reed City
Ludington
Clare
Big Rapids
Coleman
Mt Pleasant
Midland
Shelby
Muskegon
Muskegon
Grand Haven
Alma
Howard City
Saginaw
Saginaw Bay
Essexville
Bay City
Vassar
Standish
Harrisville
Au Sable
Tawas City
Port Austin
Pt Clark
Harbor Beach
Carsonville
Grand Rapids
Grand
Kentwood
Wyoming
St Johns
Owosso
Flint
Burton
Port Huron
Sarnia
St Clair
Sterling Heights
Holland
Saugatuck
Lansing
Holt
Charlotte
Pontiac
Warren
L. St Clair
St Clair Shores
Royal Oak
Livonia
Detroit
Windsor
Dearborn
Lincoln Park
Taylor
Wyandotte
Monroe
Otsego
S.Haven
Battle Creek
Kalamazoo
Benton Harbor
St Joseph
Hartford
Marshall
Albion
Jackson
Ann Arbor
Adrian
Three Rivers
Coldwater
Niles
Michigan City
Sturgis
Hudson
La Porte
Elkhart
Mishawaka
South Bend
Angola
Montpelier
Sylvania
Toledo
Maumee
Oregon
Plymouth
Auburn
St Joseph
Maumee
Perrysburg
Bowling Green
Fremont
Port Clinton
Pelee I.
Sandusky
Lorain
Lakewood
Elyria
Cleveland
Euclid
Mentor
Painesville
Ashtabula
Conneaut
Girard
Erie
Winamac
Fort Wayne
Findlay
Tiffin
Norwalk
Parma
Kentland
Huntingdon
Van Wert
Carey
Ashland
Barberton
Cuyahoga Falls
Youngstown
Warren
Farrell
Logansport
Wabash
Decatur
Lima
Kenton
Mansfield
Wooster
Massillon
Akron
Canton
Boardman
New Castle
Lafayette
Kokomo
Marion
Celina
Marion
East Liverpool
Attica
Frankfort
Elwood
Portland
Sidney
Delaware
Mt Vernon
Dover
New Philadelphia
Aliquippa
Weirton
Danville
Crawfordsville
Anderson
Muncie
Piqua
Steubenville
Bethel Park
Washington
Greenville
Urbana
Upper Arlington
Cambridge
Newark
Martins Ferry
Indianapolis
New Castle
Troy
Vandalia
Rockville
Richmond
Dayton
Springfield
Fairborn
Xenia
Columbus
Zanesville
Barnesville
Wheeling
Moundsville
Marshall
Greencastle
Connersville
Kettering
Scioto
Lancaster
Terre Haute
Franklin
Shelbyville
Middletown
Circleville
Morgantown
Fairmont
Spencer
Hamilton
Fairfield
Washington C.H.
Marietta
Vienna
Belpre
Williamstown
Ohio
Grafton
Bloomington
Columbus
Aurora
Norwood
Cincinnati
Hillsboro
Chillicothe
Athens
Parkersburg
Clarksburg
Bloomfield
Bedford
White
Waverly
Lawrenceville
Seymour
Covington
Newport
Jackson
Weston
Washington
Wabash
Vincennes
Madison
Ripley
Portsmouth
Point Pleasant
Ripley
Oakland City
Jasper
Paoli
Carrollton
Kentucky
New Boston
Sutton
Maysville
Irontown
New Albany
Ohio
Huntingburg
La Grange
Jeffersonville
Georgetown
Grayson
Ashland
Huntington
Nitro
Elk
Shively
Louisville
Frankfort
Paris
Licking
St Albans
Charleston
Evansville
Henderson
Pleasure Ridge Park
Lexington
Morehead
Louisa
Marmet
Ansted
Rocky I. L.
Spanish
Onaping L.
L. Temagami
Wanapitei L.
Sudbury
Coniston
Elliot Lake
Webbwood
Thessalon
Blind River
Copper Cliff
St Joseph I.
North Channel
Drummond I.
Massey
Espanola
L. Nipissing
Manitoulin I.
Key Harbour
Georgian Bay
South Baymouth
Fitzwilliam I.
Main Chan.
C. Hurd
Tobermory
Parry Sound
Bruce Pen.
Wiarton
Owen Sound
Southampton
Port Elgin
Collingwood
Kincardine
Walkerton
Orangeville
Goderich
Guelph
Kitchener
Stratford
Cambridge
Woodstock
Forest
London
Brantford
Ingersoll
St Thomas
West Lorne
Chatham
Meadville
Union C
Oil Ci
Sault
Ste Marie

1:5M 0 50 100 150 200 km 0 50 100 mls

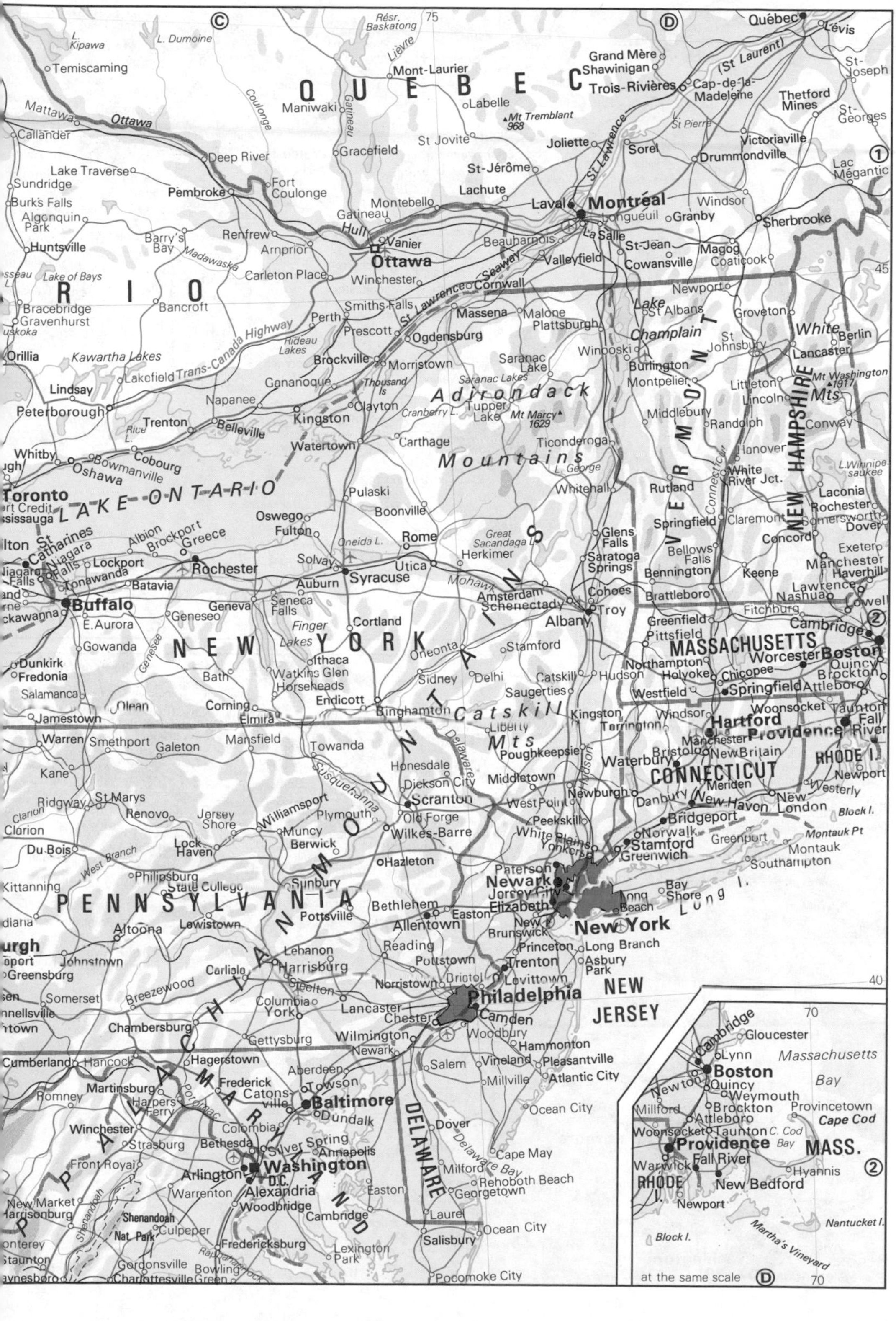

1:2.5M

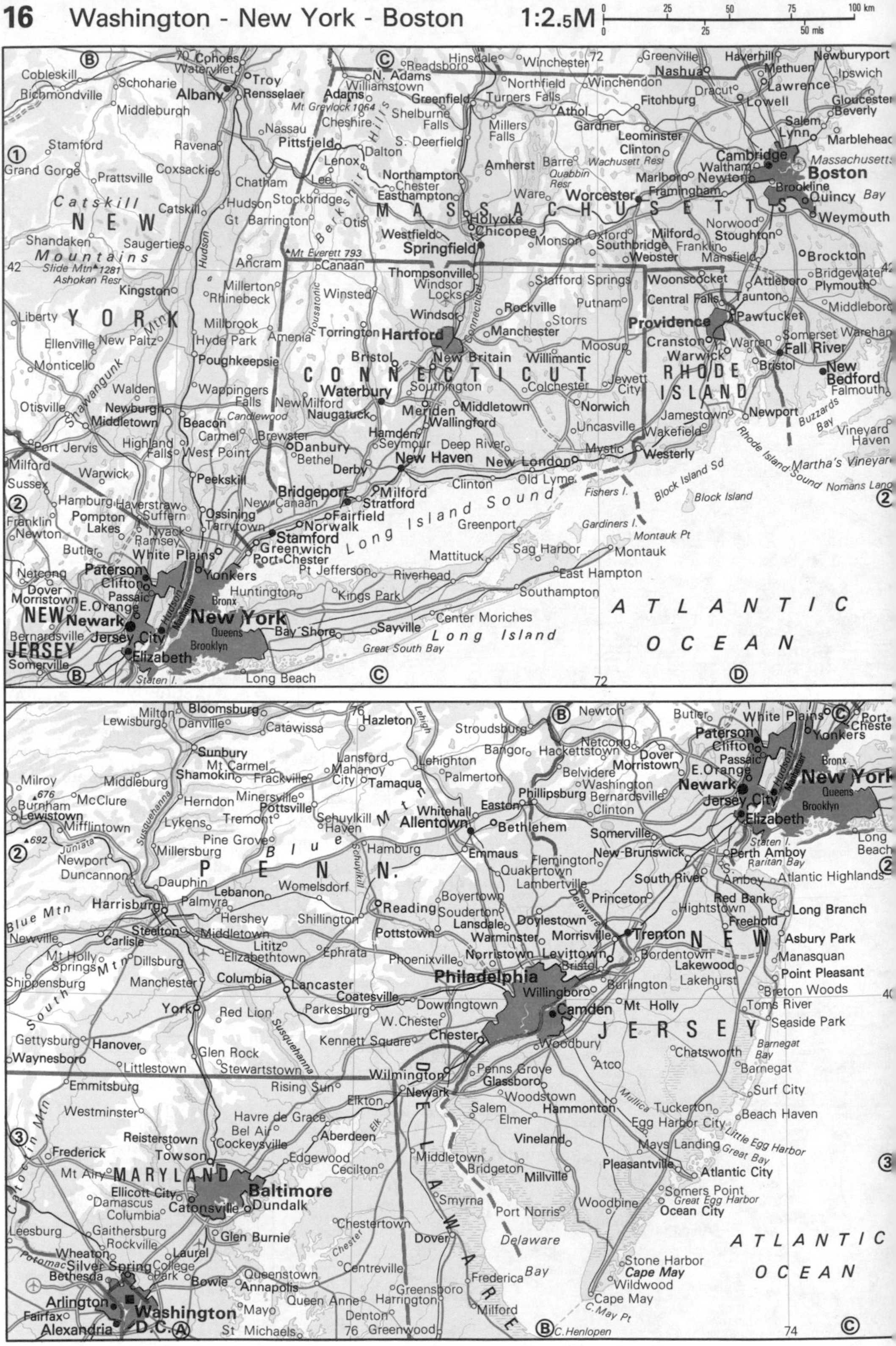
0 25 50 75 100 km
0 25 50 mls
NEW YORK
MASSACHUSETTS
CONNECTICUT
RHODE ISLAND
NEW JERSEY
PENN.
MARYLAND
DELAWARE
ATLANTIC OCEAN
Long Island Sound
Long Island
Catskill Mountains
Berkshire Hills
Shawangunk Mtn
Blue Mtn
South Mtn
Catoctin Mtn
Albany
Troy
Cohoes
Watervliet
Rensselaer
Schenectady
Cobleskill
Richmondville
Schoharie
Middleburgh
Stamford
Grand Gorge
Prattsville
Ravena
Coxsackie
Catskill
Hudson
Chatham
Nassau
Shandaken
Saugerties
Slide Mtn 1281
Ashokan Resr
Kingston
Rhinebeck
Millerton
Ancram
Liberty
Ellenville
New Paltz
Monticello
Millbrook
Hyde Park
Poughkeepsie
Amenia
Walden
Wappingers Falls
Otisville
Newburgh
Middletown
Beacon
Port Jervis
Highland Falls
West Point
Carmel
Brewster
Milford
Sussex
Warwick
Peekskill
Hamburg
Haverstraw
Suffern
Ossining
Tarrytown
Nyack
Ramsey
Franklin
Newton
Pompton Lakes
Butler
White Plains
Yonkers
Paterson
Clifton
Passaic
Netcong
Dover
Morristown
E. Orange
Newark
Jersey City
Elizabeth
Bernardsville
Somerville
Bronx
Manhattan
New York
Queens
Brooklyn
Staten I.
Long Beach
Bay Shore
Sayville
Great South Bay
Center Moriches
Huntington
Kings Park
Pt Jefferson
Riverhead
Southampton
East Hampton
Mattituck
Sag Harbor
Greenport
Montauk
Montauk Pt
Gardiners I.
Fishers I.
Block Island
Block Island Sd
Port Chester
Greenwich
Stamford
Norwalk
New Canaan
Fairfield
Bridgeport
Stratford
Milford
Derby
New Haven
Clinton
Old Lyme
New London
Mystic
Westerly
Danbury
Bethel
Seymour
Hamden
Wallingford
Meriden
Middletown
Deep River
Naugatuck
Waterbury
Southington
New Milford
L. Candlewood
Bristol
Torrington
Winsted
Hartford
New Britain
Windsor
Windsor Locks
Thompsonville
Manchester
Rockville
Storrs
Willimantic
Colchester
Norwich
Uncasville
Jewett City
Moosup
Putnam
Stafford Springs
Canaan
Mt Everett 793
Gt Barrington
Stockbridge
Lee
Lenox
Pittsfield
Dalton
Cheshire
Adams
Mt Greylock 1064
N. Adams
Williamstown
Readsboro
Hinsdale
Winchester
Northfield
Winchendon
Greenville
Nashua
Haverhill
Newburyport
Methuen
Ipswich
Lawrence
Dracut
Lowell
Gloucester
Beverly
Salem
Lynn
Marblehead
Fitchburg
Leominster
Gardner
Athol
Clinton
Wachusett Resr
Quabbin Resr
Turners Falls
Greenfield
Shelburne Falls
Millers Falls
S. Deerfield
Amherst
Barre
Northampton
Chester
Easthampton
Otis
Westfield
Holyoke
Chicopee
Springfield
Ware
Monson
Worcester
Oxford
Southbridge
Webster
Marlboro
Framingham
Waltham
Newton
Cambridge
Boston
Brookline
Quincy
Weymouth
Massachusetts Bay
Norwood
Stoughton
Milford
Franklin
Mansfield
Brockton
Bridgewater
Plymouth
Attleboro
Taunton
Middleboro
Woonsocket
Central Falls
Pawtucket
Providence
Cranston
Warwick
Warren
Somerset
Wareham
Fall River
Bristol
New Bedford
Falmouth
Jamestown
Newport
Wakefield
Buzzards Bay
Rhode Island Sound
Vineyard Haven
Martha's Vineyard
Nomans Land
Bloomsburg
Milton
Lewisburg
Danville
Catawissa
Hazleton
Lehigh
Newton
Stroudsburg
Butler
Sunbury
Mt Carmel
Shamokin
Frackville
Lansford
Mahanoy City
Tamaqua
Lehighton
Palmerton
Bangor
Hackettstown
Netcong
Dover
Morristown
Belvidere
Washington
Phillipsburg
Easton
Bernardsville
Milroy
676
Burnham
Lewistown
Mifflintown
692
Middleburg
McClure
Herndon
Minersville
Pottsville
Schuylkill Haven
Tremont
Lykens
Pine Grove
Millersburg
Juniata
Newport
Duncannon
Dauphin
Susquehanna
Hamburg
Whitehall
Allentown
Bethlehem
Emmaus
Clinton
Somerville
Flemington
New Brunswick
Quakertown
Lambertville
Perth Amboy
Raritan Bay
South Amboy
South River
Atlantic Highlands
Long Branch
Red Bank
Hightstown
Freehold
Princeton
Harrisburg
Palmyra
Lebanon
Womelsdorf
Hershey
Shillington
Reading
Boyertown
Souderton
Lansdale
Doylestown
Steelton
Carlisle
Newville
Middletown
Lititz
Ephrata
Pottstown
Warminster
Morrisville
Trenton
Asbury Park
Mt Holly Springs
Dillsburg
Elizabethtown
Phoenixville
Norristown
Levittown
Bristol
Bordentown
Manasquan
Shippensburg
Manchester
Columbia
Lancaster
Coatesville
Philadelphia
Willingboro
Burlington
Lakewood
Lakehurst
Point Pleasant
Breton Woods
York
Red Lion
Parkesburg
Downingtown
W. Chester
Camden
Mt Holly
Toms River
Seaside Park
Gettysburg
Hanover
Waynesboro
Littlestown
Glen Rock
Stewartstown
Kennett Square
Chester
Woodbury
Barnegat Bay
Chatsworth
Atco
Barnegat
Penns Grove
Glassboro
Wilmington
Newark
Emmitsburg
Rising Sun
Elkton
Elk
Woodstown
Salem
Elmer
Hammonton
Mullica
Tuckerton
Surf City
Beach Haven
Westminster
Havre de Grace
Bel Air
Aberdeen
Egg Harbor City
Little Egg Harbor
Great Bay
Reisterstown
Cockeysville
Vineland
Mays Landing
Frederick
Towson
Edgewood
Cecilton
Middletown
Bridgeton
Millville
Pleasantville
Atlantic City
Mt Airy
Ellicott City
Damascus
Columbia
Catonsville
Baltimore
Dundalk
Smyrna
Port Norris
Woodbine
Somers Point
Great Egg Harbor
Ocean City
Leesburg
Gaithersburg
Rockville
Glen Burnie
Chestertown
Chester
Dover
Delaware Bay
Wheaton
Silver Spring
Laurel
College Park
Potomac
Bethesda
Bowie
Queenstown
Annapolis
Centreville
Greensboro
Frederica
Stone Harbor
Cape May
Wildwood
Arlington
Washington
Fairfax
Alexandria
D.C.
Mayo
Queen Anne
Harrington
Denton
Milford
C. May Pt
St Michaels
Greenwood
C. Henlopen
42
40
72
74
76
70

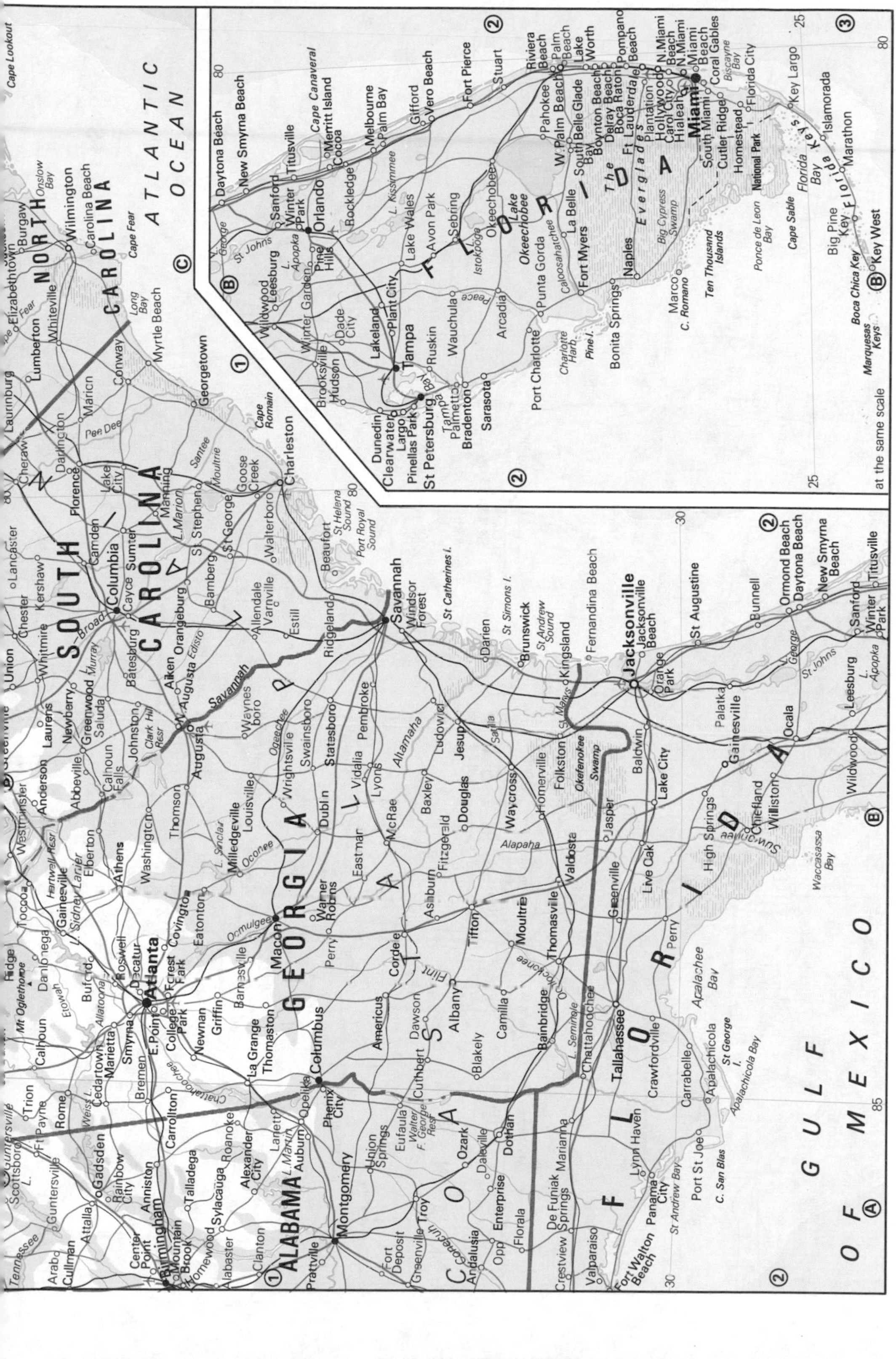
ATLANTIC OCEAN
GULF OF MEXICO
NORTH CAROLINA
SOUTH CAROLINA
GEORGIA
FLORIDA
ALABAMA
Atlanta
Savannah
Jacksonville
Tallahassee
Columbia
Charleston
Augusta
Macon
Columbus
Montgomery
Birmingham
Wilmington
Myrtle Beach
Georgetown
Florence
Brunswick
Valdosta
Albany
Gainesville
Ocala
St Augustine
Daytona Beach
Pensacola
Panama City
Orlando
Tampa
St Petersburg
Miami
Fort Lauderdale
West Palm Beach
Fort Myers
Key West
Lake Okeechobee
The Everglades
Florida Keys
Cape Canaveral
Cape Fear
Cape Lookout
Apalachee Bay
at the same scale

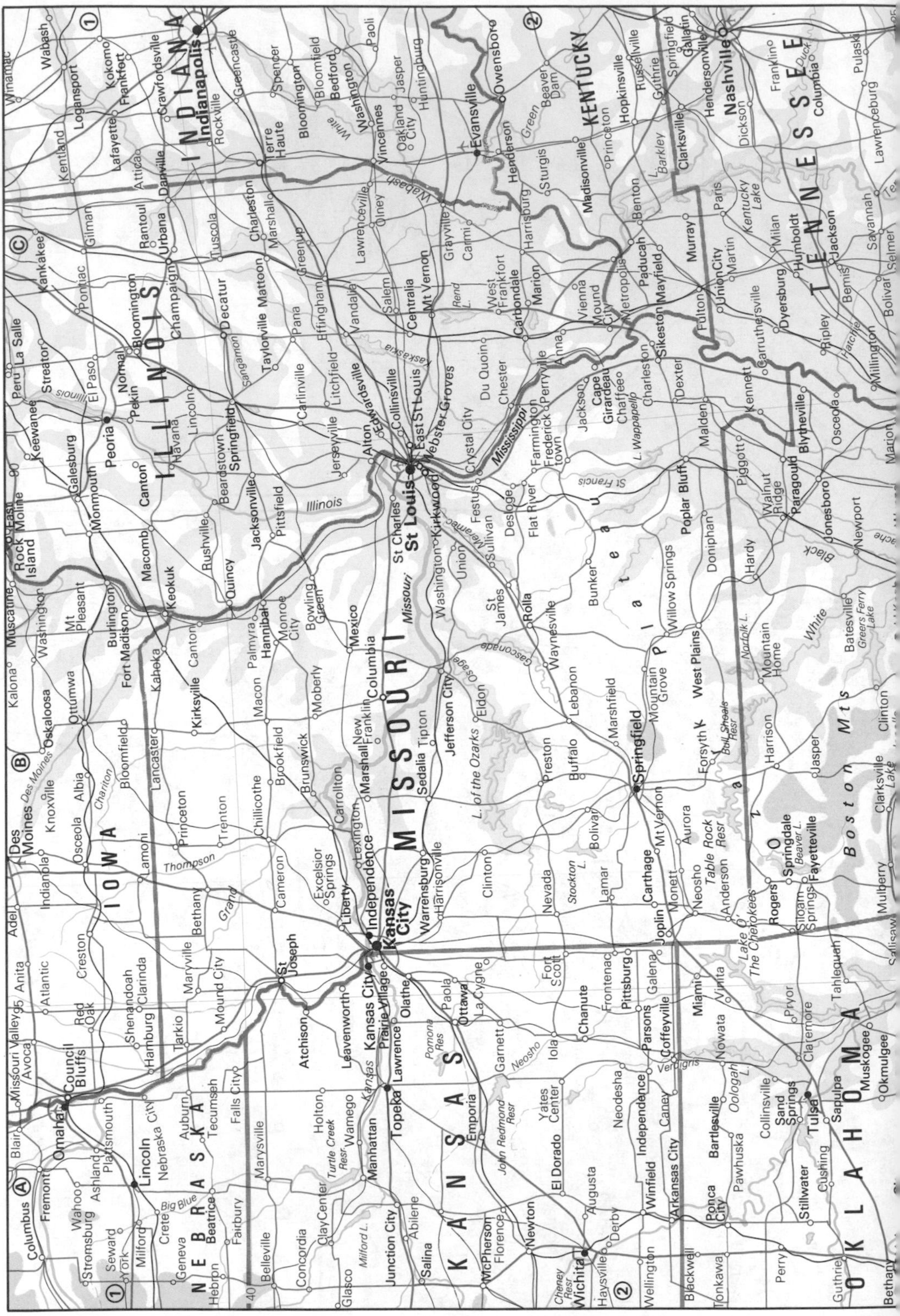
IOWA
ILLINOIS
INDIANA
KENTUCKY
TENNESSEE
MISSOURI
KANSAS
NEBRASKA
OKLAHOMA
Ozark Plateau
Boston Mts
St Louis
Kansas City
Indianapolis
Nashville
Springfield
Peoria
Evansville
Omaha
Lincoln
Topeka
Wichita
Tulsa
Des Moines
Jefferson City
Columbia
Joplin
Paducah
Mississippi
Missouri
Illinois
Wabash
Kansas
Osage
Neosho
L. of the Ozarks
Table Rock Resr
Bull Shoals Resr
Lake O' The Cherokees
Kentucky Lake
L. Barkley

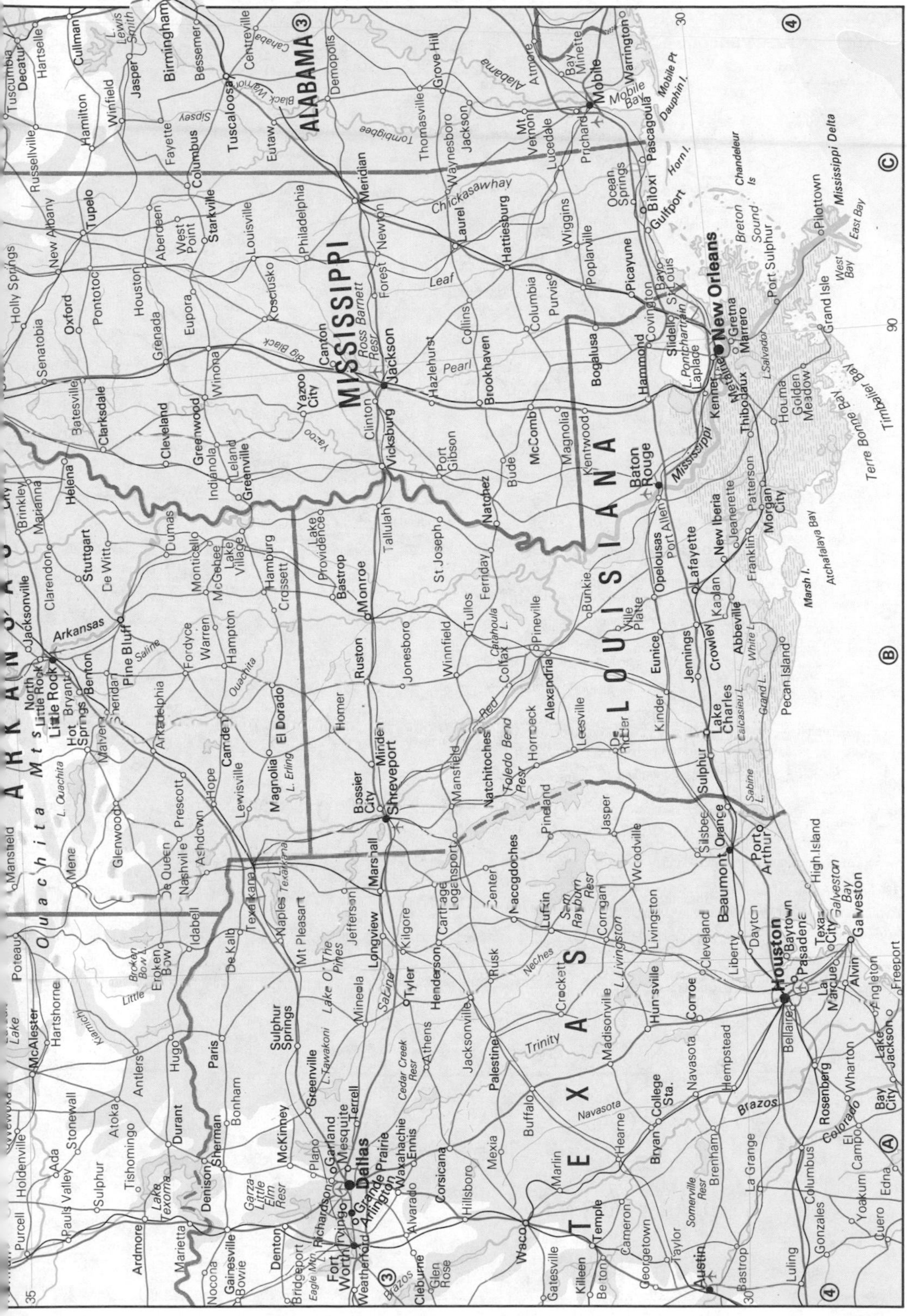
ALABAMA
MISSISSIPPI
LOUISIANA
ARKANSAS
TEXAS
Ouachita Mts
Birmingham
Tuscaloosa
Mobile
Mobile Bay
Dauphin I.
Meridian
Jackson
Vicksburg
Hattiesburg
Gulfport
Biloxi
Pascagoula
New Orleans
Baton Rouge
Lafayette
Lake Charles
Shreveport
Monroe
Alexandria
Natchez
Little Rock
Pine Bluff
Hot Springs
Texarkana
El Dorado
Dallas
Fort Worth
Arlington
Waco
Austin
Houston
Galveston
Beaumont
Port Arthur
Tyler
Longview
Sherman
Denison
Lake Texoma
Tupelo
Columbus
Greenville
Greenwood
Cleveland
Clarksdale
Yazoo City
Mississippi Delta
Breton Sound
Chandeleur Is
Terre Bonne Bay
Timbalier Bay
Atchafalaya Bay
Sam Rayburn Resr
Toledo Bend Resr
Galveston Bay
Brazos
Trinity
Colorado
Red
Pearl
Tombigbee
Arkansas
Mississippi
35
30
90
3
4
A
B
C

1:5M 0 50 100 150 200 km; 0 50 100 mls

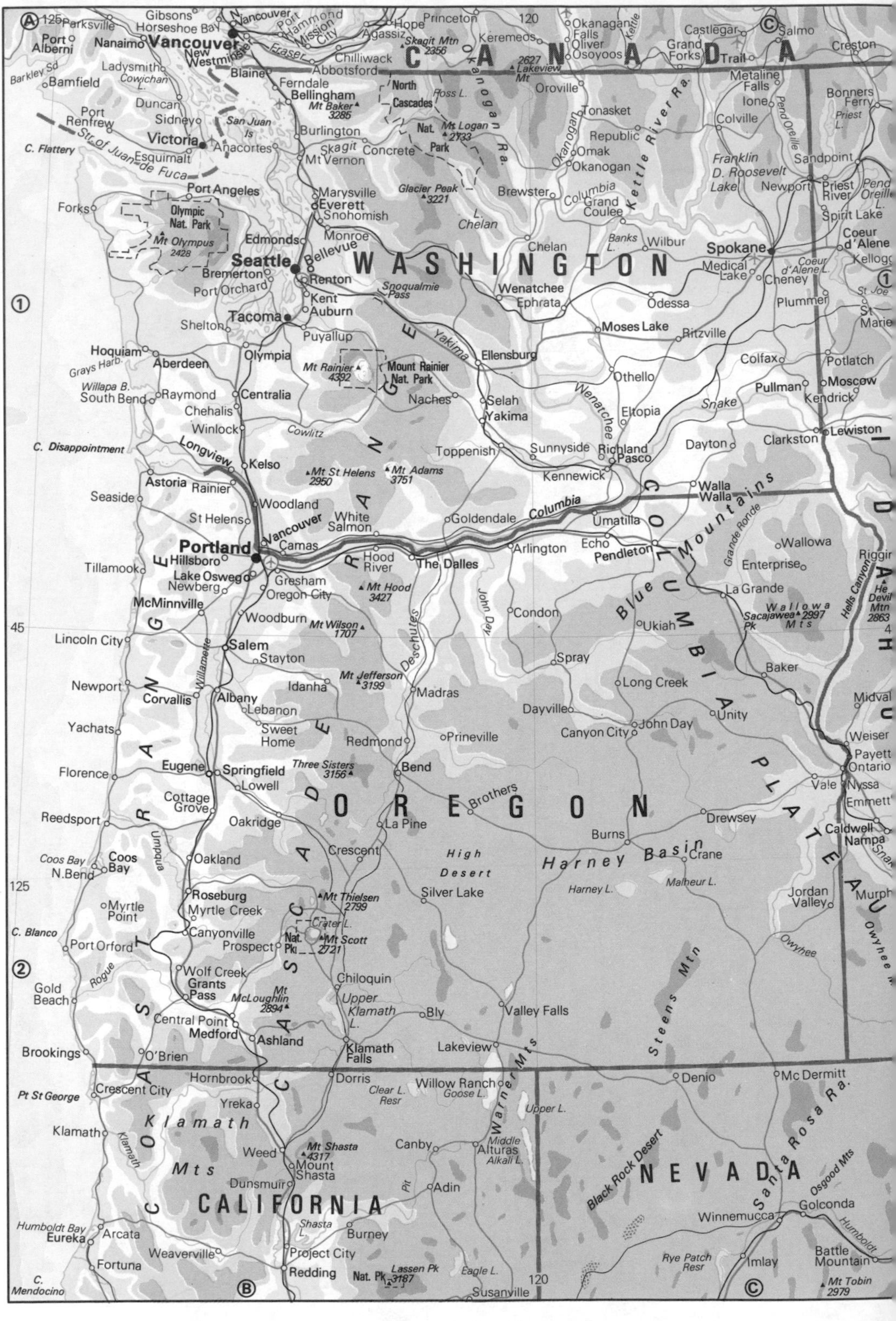

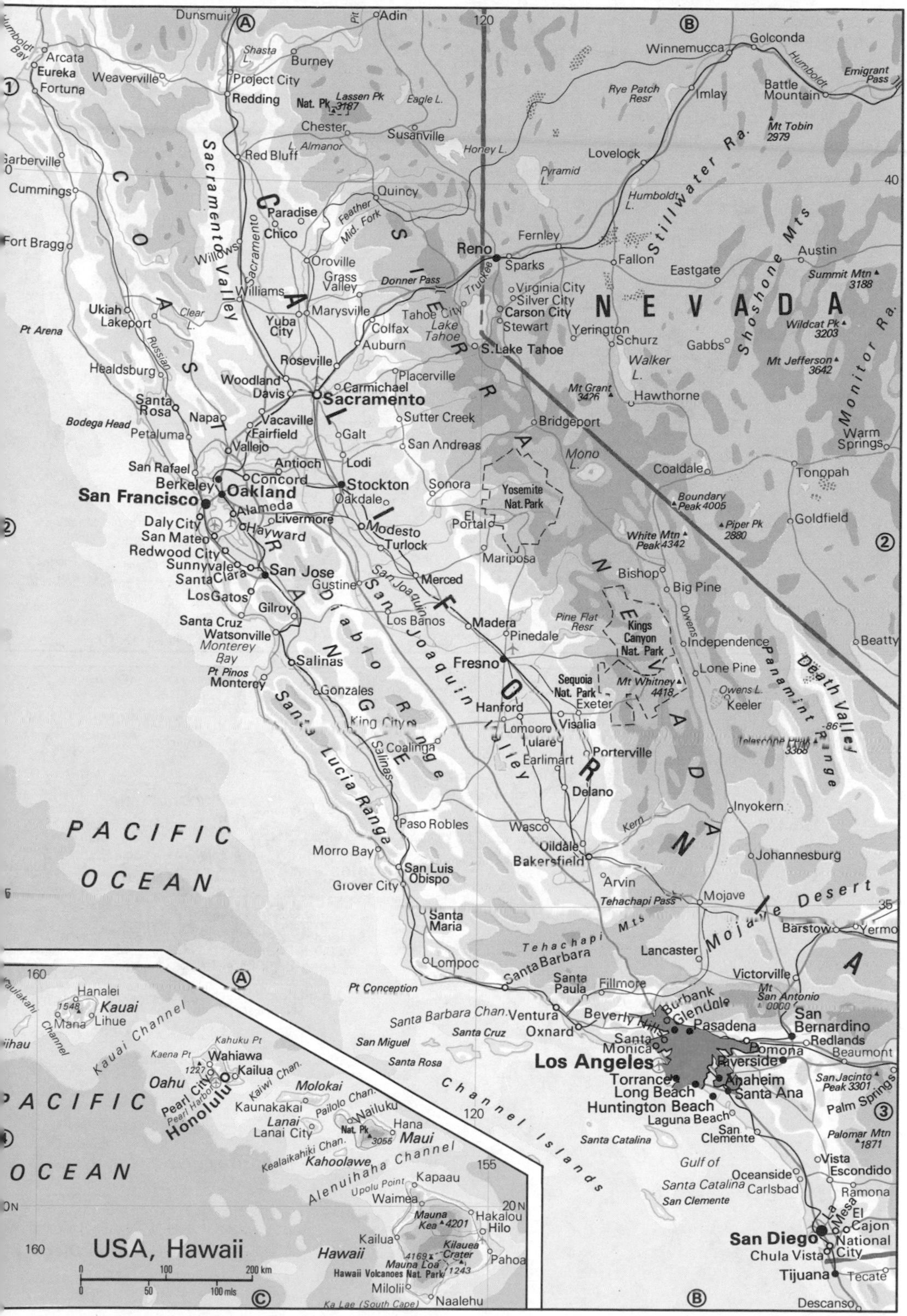
NEVADA
CALIFORNIA
SIERRA NEVADA
COAST RANGES
PACIFIC OCEAN
Dunsmuir
Adin
Arcata
Eureka
Fortuna
Weaverville
Shasta L.
Burney
Project City
Redding
Lassen Pk 3187
Nat. Pk
Eagle L.
Chester
Susanville
L. Almanor
Red Bluff
Honey L.
Garberville
Cummings
Sacramento Valley
Quincy
Paradise
Chico
Feather Mid. Fork
Fort Bragg
Willows
Oroville
Grass Valley
Donner Pass
Reno
Sparks
Williams
Marysville
Yuba City
Ukiah
Lakeport
Clear L.
Pt Arena
Russian
Tahoe City
Lake Tahoe
Colfax
Auburn
S. Lake Tahoe
Roseville
Healdsburg
Woodland
Davis
Placerville
Carmichael
Sacramento
Santa Rosa
Napa
Bodega Head
Vacaville
Fairfield
Petaluma
Vallejo
Sutter Creek
Galt
San Andreas
Antioch
Lodi
San Rafael
Concord
Berkeley
Oakland
Stockton
San Francisco
Alameda
Oakdale
Sonora
Daly City
Livermore
Modesto
San Mateo
Hayward
Turlock
Redwood City
Sunnyvale
Santa Clara
San Jose
Los Gatos
Gustine
Merced
Gilroy
Santa Cruz
Watsonville
Monterey Bay
Pt Pinos
Monterey
Salinas
Los Banos
Madera
Pinedale
Fresno
Gonzales
King City
Diablo Range
San Joaquin
San Joaquin Valley
Santa Lucia Range
Coalinga
Hanford
Lemoore
Visalia
Tulare
Earlimart
Porterville
Delano
Exeter
Paso Robles
Wasco
Oildale
Bakersfield
Morro Bay
San Luis Obispo
Grover City
Arvin
Santa Maria
Lompoc
Pt Conception
Santa Barbara
Tehachapi Pass
Tehachapi Mts
Santa Paula
Fillmore
Ventura
Oxnard
Santa Barbara Chan.
Santa Cruz
San Miguel
Santa Rosa
Channel Islands
Winnemucca
Golconda
Humboldt
Emigrant Pass
Rye Patch Resr
Imlay
Battle Mountain
Mt Tobin 2979
Stillwater Ra.
Lovelock
Pyramid L.
Humboldt L.
Fernley
Fallon
Eastgate
Austin
Shoshone Mts
Summit Mtn 3188
Truckee
Virginia City
Silver City
Carson City
Stewart
Yerington
Schurz
Gabbs
Wildcat Pk 3203
Walker L.
Mt Jefferson 3642
Monitor Ra.
Mt Grant 3426
Hawthorne
Bridgeport
Mono L.
Yosemite Nat. Park
Warm Springs
Coaldale
Tonopah
Boundary Peak 4005
Piper Pk 2880
Goldfield
El Portal
Mariposa
White Mtn Peak 4342
Bishop
Big Pine
Pine Flat Resr
Kings Canyon Nat. Park
Owens
Independence
Beatty
Lone Pine
Owens L.
Keeler
Panamint Range
Death Valley
Sequoia Nat. Park
Mt Whitney 4418
Inyokern
Kern
Johannesburg
Mojave
Mojave Desert
Barstow
Yermo
Lancaster
Victorville
Mt San Antonio
San Bernardino
Redlands
Beaumont
Burbank
Glendale
Pasadena
Beverly Hills
Santa Monica
Los Angeles
Pomona
Riverside
Torrance
Anaheim
Long Beach
Santa Ana
Huntington Beach
Laguna Beach
San Jacinto Peak 3301
Palm Springs
Santa Catalina
San Clemente
Palomar Mtn 1871
Gulf of Santa Catalina
Oceanside
Carlsbad
Vista
Escondido
Ramona
La Mesa
El Cajon
San Diego
National City
Chula Vista
Tijuana
Tecate
Descanso
USA, Hawaii
Hanalei
Kauai
Lihue
Kauai Channel
Kahuku Pt
Kaena Pt
Wahiawa
Kailua
Oahu
Pearl City
Pearl Harbor
Honolulu
Kaiwi Chan.
Molokai
Kaunakakai
Pailolo Chan.
Wailuku
Lanai
Lanai City
Hana
Maui
Kealaikahiki Chan.
Kahoolawe
Alenuihaha Channel
Upolu Point
Kapaau
Waimea
Mauna Kea 4201
Hakalau
Hilo
Kailua
Hawaii
Mauna Loa 4169
Kilauea Crater 1243
Pahoa
Hawaii Volcanoes Nat. Park
Milolii
Ka Lae (South Cape)
Naalehu
0 100 200 km
0 50 100 mls

1:2.5M 0 25 50 75 100 km / 0 25 50 mls

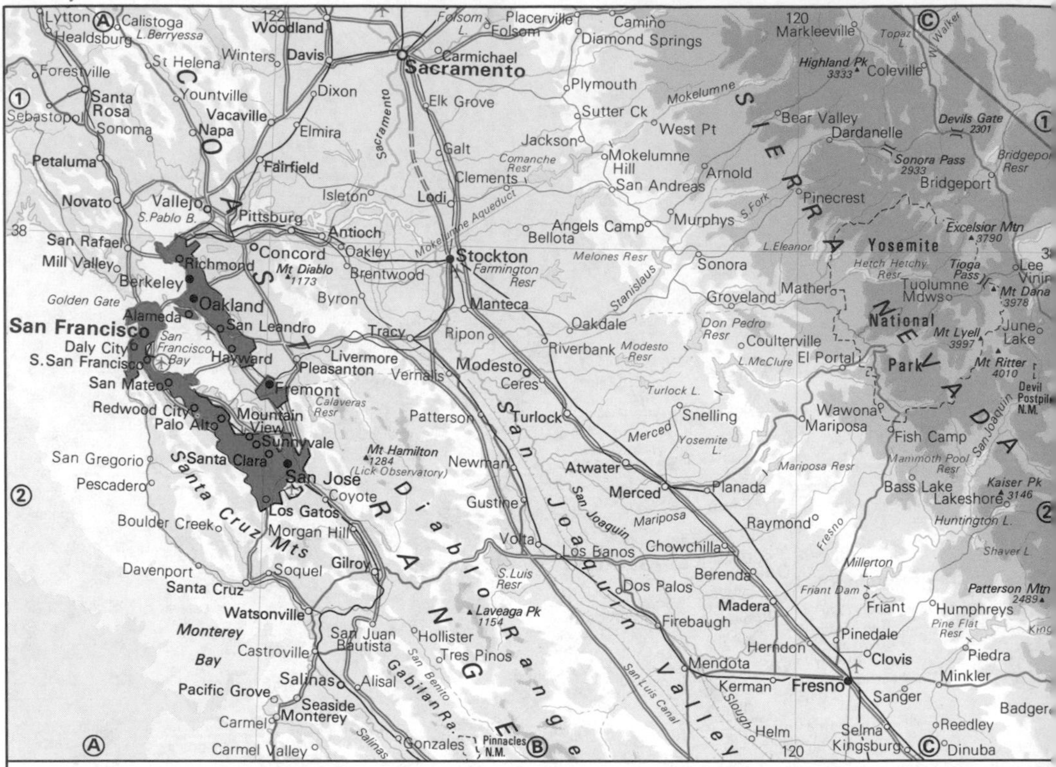

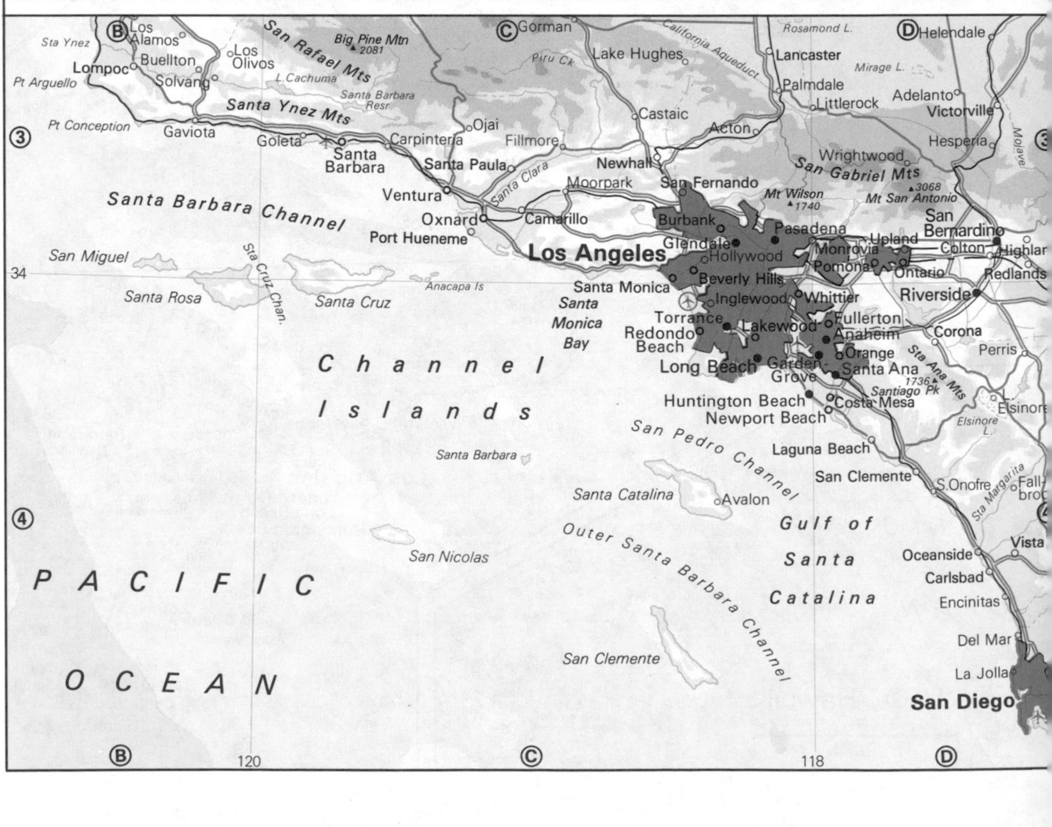

GULF OF MEXICO
Veracruz
Jalapa
Poza Rica
Tuxpan
Tampico
Cd Madero
San Luis Potosí
Querétaro
Guanajuato
León
Aguascalientes
Guadalajara
Colima
Manzanillo
Morelia
Uruapan
Toluca
México
Xochimilco
Cuernavaca
Puebla
Tlaxcala
Pachuca
Orizaba
Córdoba
Tehuacán
Oaxaca
Acapulco
Chilpancingo
Iguala
Taxco
Tehuantepec
Salina Cruz
Celaya
Salamanca
Irapuato
Zamora
Tepic
Lázaro Cárdenas
HIDALGO
QUERÉTARO
GUANAJUATO
JALISCO
COLIMA
MICHOACÁN
MORELOS
TLAXCALA
GUERRERO
OAXACA
NAYARIT
AGS.
Nev. de Toluca 4558
Popocatepetl 5450
Vol. Citlaltepetl 5700
L. de Chapala
Sierra Madre del Sur
Sierra Madre Oriental

San Diego
Brawley
Salton Sea
Tijuana
Mexicali
Ensenada
Yuma
Phoenix
Mesa
Wickenburg
Theodore Roosevelt L.
Baldy Peak 3532
ARIZONA
Casa Grande
Tucson
NEW MEXICO
Vaughn
Sacramento Mts
Sa Blanca 3658
Silver City
Alamogordo
Artesia
Roswell
Lordsburg
Las Cruces
El Paso
Cd Juárez
Tucumcari
Amarillo
Clovis
Plainview
Llano Estacado
Lubbock
Carlsbad
Big Spring
Midland
Snyder
Odessa
San Angelo
Pecos
Van Horn
Alpine
Emory Pk 2389
UNITED
TEXAS
Edwards Plateau
Oklahoma City
OKLAHOMA
El Reno
Chickasha
Lawton
Ardmore
Wichita Falls
L. Texoma
Denison
Greenville
Fort Worth
Abilene
Sweetwater
Brownwood
Colorado
Corsicana
Waco
Austin
New Braunfels
Del Rio
San Antonio
Cd Acuña
Piedras Negras
Eagle Pass
Victoria
Nueces
Beeville
Corpus Christi
Kingsville
Padre I.
Laredo
Nuevo Laredo
Falcon Resr
McAllen
Reynosa
Brownsville
Matamoros
Lag. Madre
San Quintín
Pta Baja
Baja California
Golfo de California
Caborca
Pto Peñasco
Nogales
Douglas
Agua Prieta
Cananea
Magdalena
Nacozari
Nuevo Casas Grandes
Rio Bravo del Norte
Angel de la Guarda
Cedros
Ba Sebastian Vizcaino
Pta Eugenia
Hermosillo
Sonora
Tiburón
Madera
Ojinaga
Chihuahua
Guaymas
Empalme
Yaqui
Sta Rosalía
Pta Abreojos
Ciudad Obregón
Navojoa
Cuauhtémoc
Delicias
Cd Camargo
Sierra Madre Occidental
Sierra Madre Oriental
San Francisco del Oro
Hidalgo del Parral
Sta Barbara
Choix
Fuerte
Los Mochis
Topolobampo
Guasave
I. Magdalena
Ba Magdalena
I. Sta Margarita
Bolson de Mapimí
Monclova
Sa de los Alamitos
Nueva Rosita
Sabinas
Sabinas Hidalgo
Rio Grande
Gómez Palacio
Torreón
Monterrey
Guadalupe
Saltillo
Montemorelos
Huayapan
Tepehuanes
Tropic of Cancer
Altata
Culiacán
El Dorado
La Paz
Concepción del Oro
Canatlán
Durango
MEXICO
C. Falso
San José del Cabo
Mazatlán
Matehuala
Cd Victoria
Escuinapa
Fresnillo
Acaponeta
Zacatecas
Tuxpan
Las Tres Marías
Tepic
R. Gd de Santiago
Aguascalientes
San Luis Potosí
Cd Madero
Tampico
Cd Valles
Lag. de Tamiahua
C. Rojo
Ba de Banderas
C. Corrientes
Guadalajara
Pto Vallarta
Ameca
L. de Chapala
Lagos de Moreno
León
Irapuato
Celaya
Querétaro
Ocotlán
Sahuayo
Zamora
Tuxpan
Poza Rica
Papantla
San Benedicto
Roca Partida
Revillagigedo (Mex.)
Clarión
Socorro
Autlán
Cd Guzman
Morelia
Acámbaro
Pachuca
Colima
Manzanillo
Tecomán
Apatzingan
Uruapan
México
Toluca
Popocatepetl 5452
Cuernavaca
Taxco
Puebla
Citlaltepetl 5699
Orizaba
Córdoba
Jalapa
Tehuacán
Acatlán
Iguala
Balsas
P. del Infiernillo
Ba de Petacalco
Sierra Madre del Sur
Chilpancingo
Tecpan
Acapulco
Oaxaca
Tehuantepec
PACIFIC OCEAN
Clipperton I. (France)
30
20
10
110
100
A
B
2
3
4

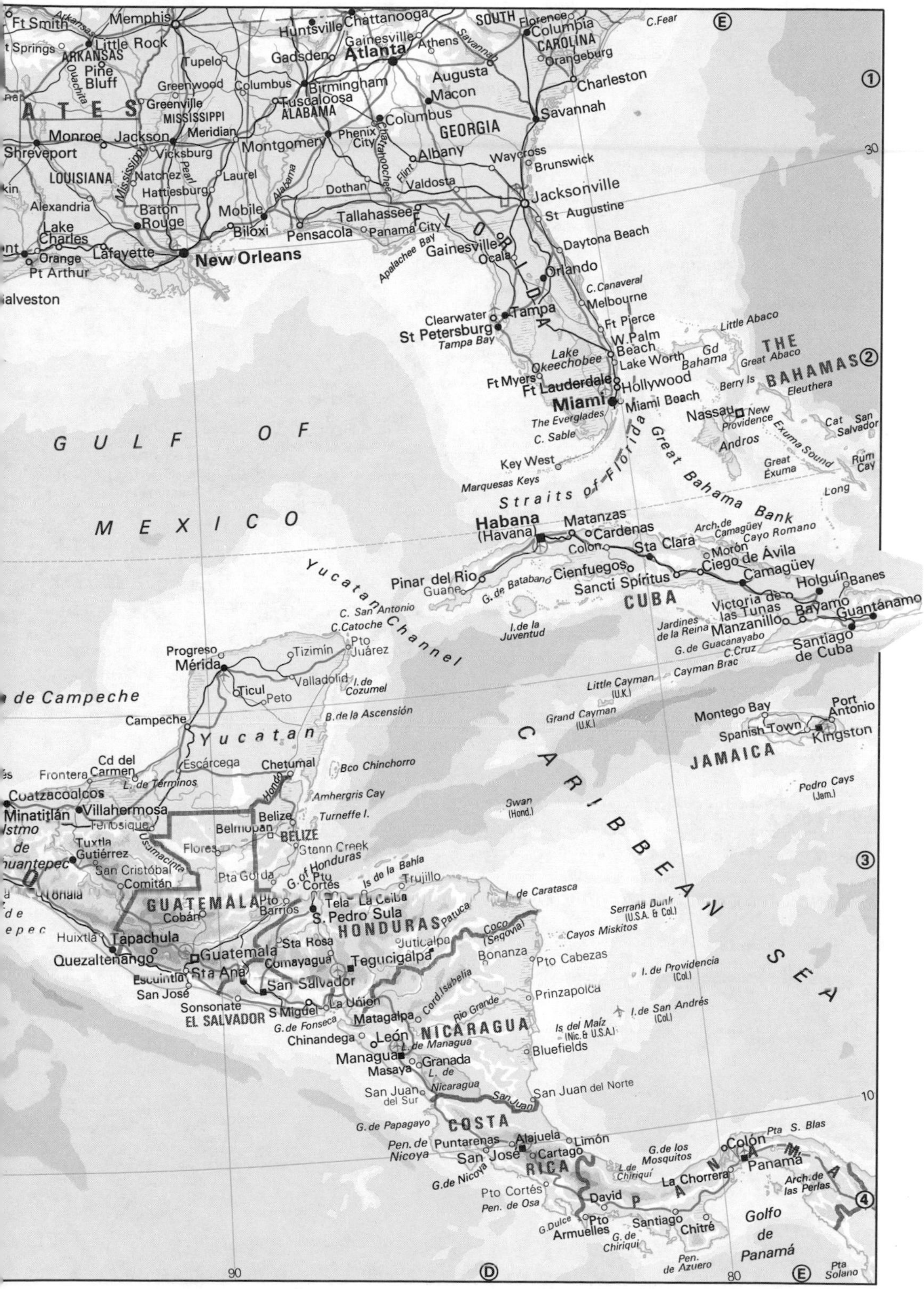
Ft Smith
Memphis
Little Rock
ARKANSAS
Pine Bluff
Tupelo
Greenwood
Columbus
Greenville
MISSISSIPPI
Meridian
Monroe
Jackson
Shreveport
Vicksburg
LOUISIANA
Natchez
Hattiesburg
Laurel
Alexandria
Baton Rouge
Lake Charles
Lafayette
Orange
Pt Arthur
New Orleans
Mobile
Biloxi
Huntsville
Chattanooga
Gainesville
Athens
Gadsden
Atlanta
Birmingham
Tuscaloosa
ALABAMA
Augusta
Macon
Columbus
GEORGIA
Montgomery
Phenix City
Albany
Dothan
Valdosta
Tallahassee
Pensacola
Panama City
Apalachee Bay
SOUTH CAROLINA
Florence
Columbia
C.Fear
Orangeburg
Charleston
Savannah
Waycross
Brunswick
Jacksonville
St Augustine
Daytona Beach
Gainesville
Ocala
FLORIDA
Orlando
C. Canaveral
Melbourne
Clearwater
Tampa
St Petersburg
Tampa Bay
Ft Pierce
W.Palm Beach
Lake Worth
Lake Okeechobee
Ft Myers
Ft Lauderdale
Hollywood
Miami
Miami Beach
The Everglades
C. Sable
Key West
Marquesas Keys
Straits of Florida
Little Abaco
Gd Bahama
Great Abaco
THE BAHAMAS
Berry Is
Eleuthera
Nassau
New Providence
Andros
Exuma Sound
Cat
San Salvador
Great Exuma
Rum Cay
Long
Great Bahama Bank
GULF OF MEXICO
Habana (Havana)
Matanzas
Cardenas
Colon
Sta Clara
Arch. de Camagüey
Cayo Romano
Morón
Ciego de Ávila
Camagüey
Pinar del Rio
Guane
G. de Batabanó
Cienfuegos
Sancti Spíritus
CUBA
Holguín
Banes
Victoria de las Tunas
Bayamo
Guantánamo
Manzanillo
Santiago de Cuba
Jardines de la Reina
G. de Guacanayabo
C.Cruz
I. de la Juventud
C. San Antonio
C.Catoche
Yucatan Channel
Progreso
Mérida
Tizimín
Pto Juárez
Valladolid
I. de Cozumel
Ticul
Peto
de Campeche
Campeche
Yucatan
B. de la Ascensión
Little Cayman (U.K.)
Cayman Brac
Grand Cayman (U.K.)
Montego Bay
Port Antonio
Spanish Town
Kingston
JAMAICA
Pedro Cays (Jam.)
Cd del Carmen
Frontera
L. de Términos
Escárcega
Chetumal
Bco Chinchorro
Coatzacoalcos
Minatitlán
Villahermosa
Ambergris Cay
Turneffe I.
Belize
Belmopan
BELIZE
Stann Creek
Flores
Usumacinta
Tuxtla Gutiérrez
San Cristóbal
Comitán
Pta Gorda
G. of Honduras
Pto Cortés
Is de la Bahía
Trujillo
Tonala
GUATEMALA
Pto Barrios
Cobán
Tela
La Ceiba
S. Pedro Sula
HONDURAS
Patuca
L. de Caratasca
Huixtla
Tapachula
Quezaltenango
Guatemala
Sta Rosa
Juticalpa
Coco (Segovia)
Cayos Miskitos
Serrana Bank (U.S.A. & Col.)
Swan (Hond.)
CARIBBEAN SEA
Escuintla
Sta Ana
Comayagua
Tegucigalpa
Bonanza
Pto Cabezas
I. de Providencia (Col.)
San José
Sonsonate
San Salvador
EL SALVADOR
S Miguel
La Unión
Cord. Isabelia
Prinzapolca
Rio Grande
Matagalpa
I. de San Andrés (Col.)
G. de Fonseca
Chinandega
León
NICARAGUA
Is del Maíz (Nic. & U.S.A.)
L. de Managua
Bluefields
Managua
Masaya
Granada
L. de Nicaragua
San Juan del Sur
San Juan
San Juan del Norte
G. de Papagayo
COSTA RICA
Pen. de Nicoya
Puntarenas
Alajuela
Limón
San José
Cartago
G. de Nicoya
Pto Cortés
Pen. de Osa
G.Dulce
Pto Armuelles
David
G. de los Mosquitos
L. de Chiriquí
G. de Chiriquí
Colón
Pta S. Blas
Panamá
La Chorrera
Arch. de las Perlas
PANAMA
Santiago
Chitré
Pen. de Azuero
Golfo de Panamá
Pta Solano
30
10
90
80
D
E
1
2
3
4

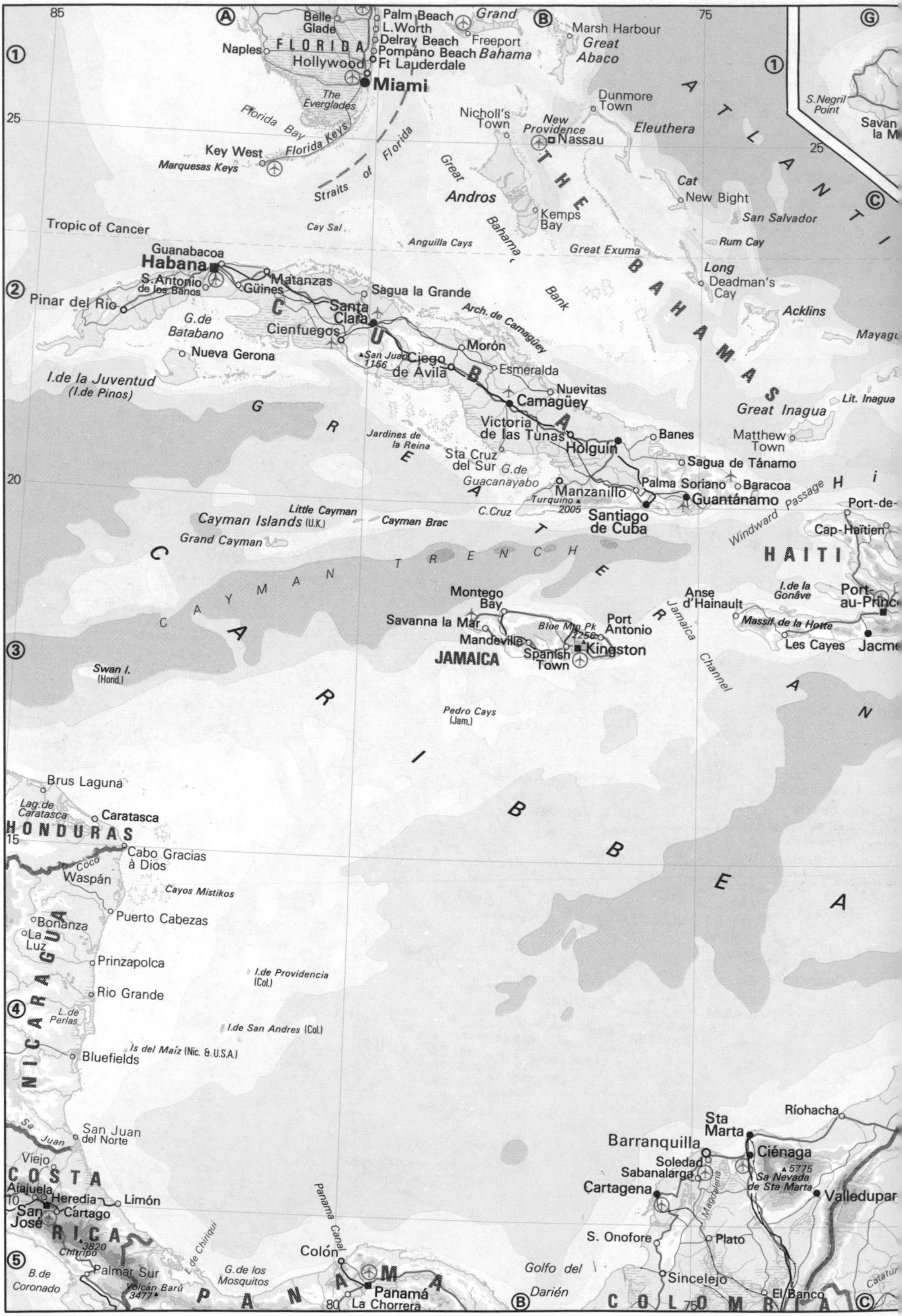

FLORIDA
Belle Glade
Palm Beach
L.Worth
Delray Beach
Pompano Beach
Ft Lauderdale
Naples
Hollywood
Miami
The Everglades
Florida Bay
Florida Keys
Key West
Marquesas Keys
Straits of Florida
Grand Bahama
Freeport
Marsh Harbour
Great Abaco
Dunmore Town
Nicholl's Town
New Providence
Nassau
Eleuthera
Great Bahama Bank
Andros
Kemps Bay
Cat
New Bight
San Salvador
Rum Cay
Great Exuma
Long
Deadman's Cay
Acklins
Mayagu
THE BAHAMAS
ATLANTIC
Cay Sal
Anguilla Cays
Tropic of Cancer
Guanabacoa
Habana
S.Antonio de los Banos
Güines
Matanzas
Sagua la Grande
Pinar del Rio
Santa Clara
G.de Batabano
Cienfuegos
CUBA
Arch. de Camagüey
Nueva Gerona
San Juan 1156
Ciego de Avila
Morón
Esmeralda
I.de la Juventud
(I.de Pinos)
Nuevitas
Camagüey
Victoria de las Tunas
Holguin
Banes
Great Inagua
Lit. Inagua
Matthew Town
Jardines de la Reina
Sta Cruz del Sur
G.de Guacanayabo
Sagua de Tánamo
Palma Soriano
Baracoa
Manzanillo
Guantánamo
Turquino 2005
Santiago de Cuba
Windward Passage
C.Cruz
Little Cayman
Cayman Brac
Cayman Islands (U.K.)
Grand Cayman
CAYMAN TRENCH
Port-de-
Cap-Haïtien
HAITI
I.de la Gonâve
Port-au-Prince
Anse d'Hainault
Massif de la Hotte
Les Cayes
Jacmel
Montego Bay
Savanna la Mar
Mandeville
Blue Mtn Pk 2256
Port Antonio
Spanish Town
Kingston
JAMAICA
Jamaica Channel
Swan I. (Hond.)
Pedro Cays (Jam.)
S.Negril Point
Savan la M
CARIBBEAN SEA
Brus Laguna
Lag.de Caratasca
Caratasca
HONDURAS
Coco
Cabo Gracias à Dios
Waspán
Cayos Mistikos
Puerto Cabezas
Bonanza
La Luz
Prinzapolca
I.de Providencia (Col.)
Rio Grande
L.de Perlas
I.de San Andres (Col.)
Is del Maíz (Nic. & U.S.A.)
Bluefields
NICARAGUA
Sa Juan
San Juan del Norte
Viejo
COSTA RICA
Alajuela
Heredia
Limón
San José
Cartago
Chirripó 3820
B.de Coronado
Palmar Sur
Volcán Barú 3477
L.de Chiriquí
G.de los Mosquitos
Panama Canal
Colón
PANAMA
Panamá
La Chorrera
Golfo del Darién
Ríohacha
Sta Marta
Barranquilla
Ciénaga
Soledad
Sabanalarga
Sa Nevada de Sta Marta 5775
Cartagena
Valledupar
Magdalena
S. Onofore
Plato
Sincelejo
El Banco
Catatur
COLOMBIA
85
80
75
25
20
15
10

1:10M 0 100 200 300 400 km / 0 100 200 mls

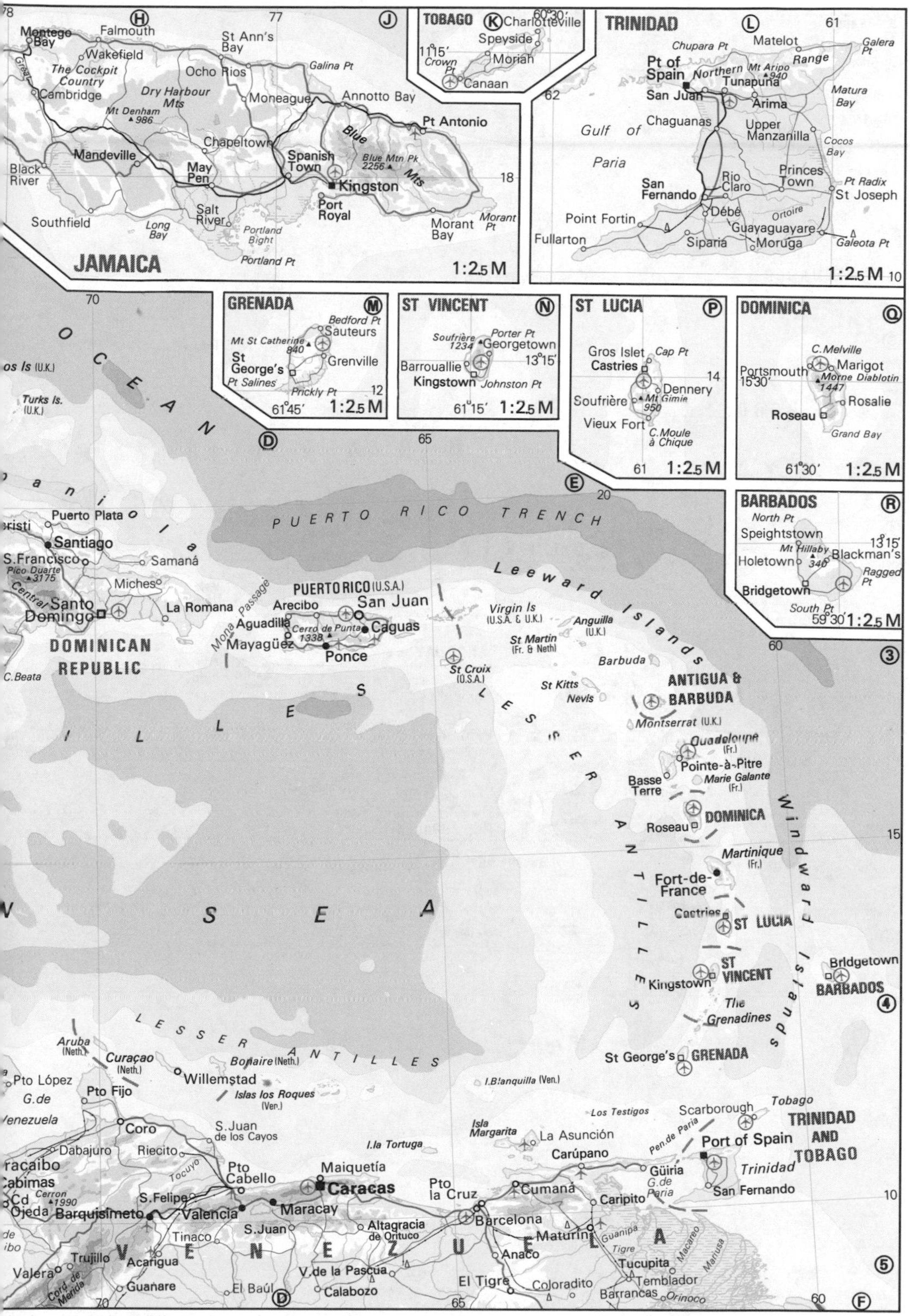

1:40M
0 400 800 1200 1600 km
0 400 800 mls
CARIBBEAN SEA
NICARAGUA
COSTA RICA
S.José
Panamá
PANAMA
Sta Marta
Barranquilla
Maracaibo
Caracas
Barcelona
ST LUCIA
BARBADOS
TRINIDAD & TOBAGO
S.Cristóbal
Orinoco
Cd Bolívar
VENEZUELA
Medellín
Bogotá
Georgetown
Paramaribo
GUYANA
Cayenne
SURINAM
FR. GUIANA
Malpelo (Col.)
Buenaventura
Cali
COLOMBIA
Popayán
Boa Vista
S.Lorenzo
Quito
ECUADOR
Guayaquil
I.de Marajó
Equator
Negro
Santarem
Belém
São Luís
Manaus
Amazonas
Iquitos
I.Fernando de Noronha (Braz.)
Xingu
Tapajós
Madeira
Purus
Ucayali
Teresina
Fortaleza
Natal
Trujillo
PERU
Pto Velho
Recife
BRAZIL
Maceió
Callao
Lima
Huancayo
Pto Maldonado
Cuzco
Salvador
Cuiabá
Goiânia
Brasília
São Francisco
Arequipa
La Paz
BOLIVIA
Cochabamba
Sucre
Sta Cruz
Corumbá
Arica
Belo Horizonte
Campo Grande
Ribeirão Prêto
SOUTH PACIFIC OCEAN
PARAGUAY
Paraná
Campos
Rio de Janeiro
São Paulo
Santos
Antofagasta
Salta
Asunción
Tropic of Capricorn
Curitiba
S.Félix (Chi.)
S.Miguel de Tucumán
Resistencia
Posadas
CHILE
ARGENTINA
Córdoba
Sante Fe
Paraná
Pto Alegre
Pelotas
Mendoza
Rosario
URUGUAY
Valparaíso
Santiago
Buenos Aires
Montevideo
R.de la Plata
Is Juan Fernández (Chi.)
SOUTH ATLANTIC OCEAN
Concepción
Mar del Plata
Bahía Blanca
Valdivia
Pto Montt
Cmd. Rivadavia
G.San Jorge
Falkland Is (U.K.)
Stanley
Río Gallegos
Punta Arenas
Tierra del Fuego
S.Georgia (U.K.)
S.Shetland Is (U.K.)
S.Orkney Is (U.K.)

0 200 400 600 km
0 100 200 300 mls

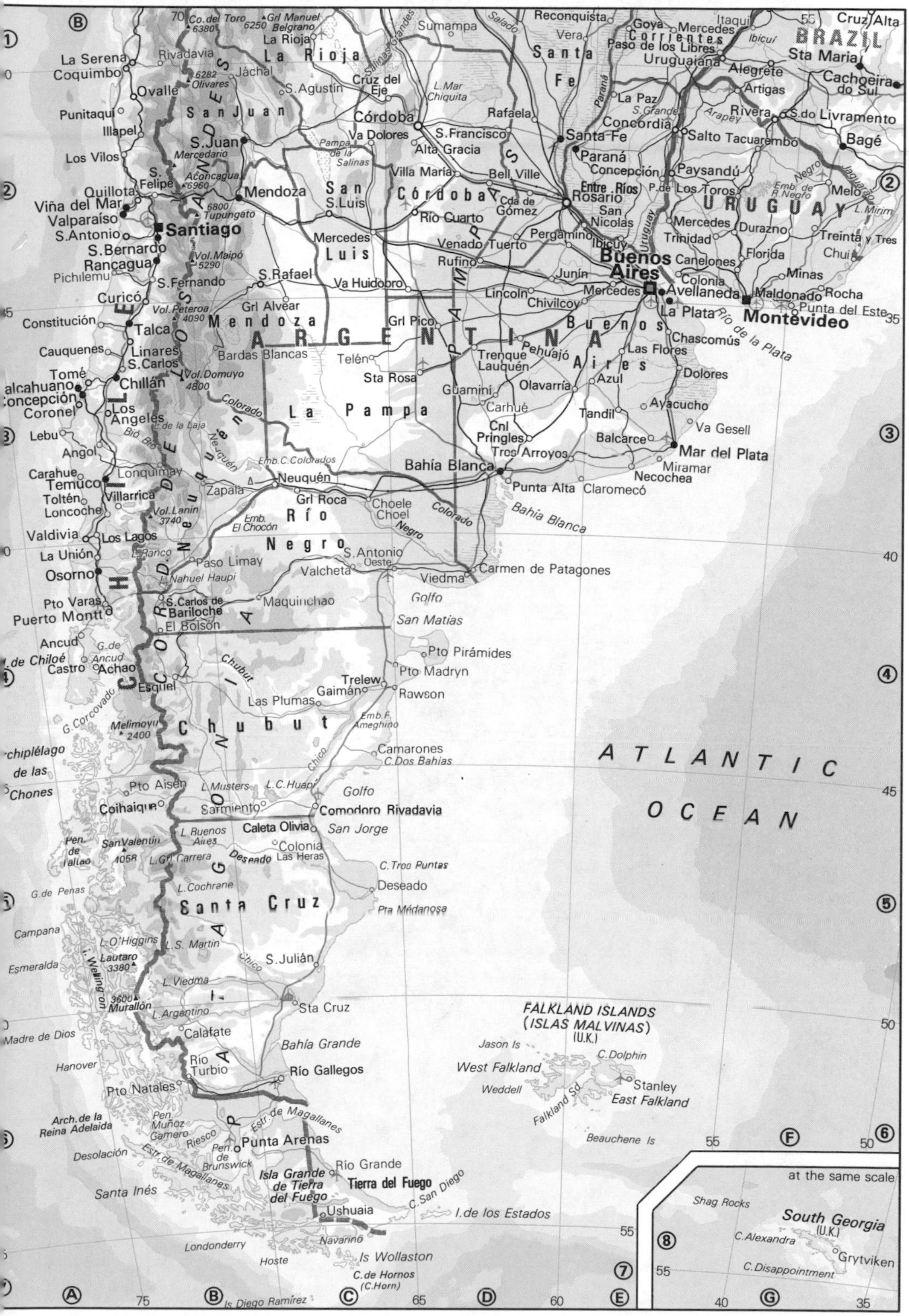

1:15M

0 200 400 km
0 100 200

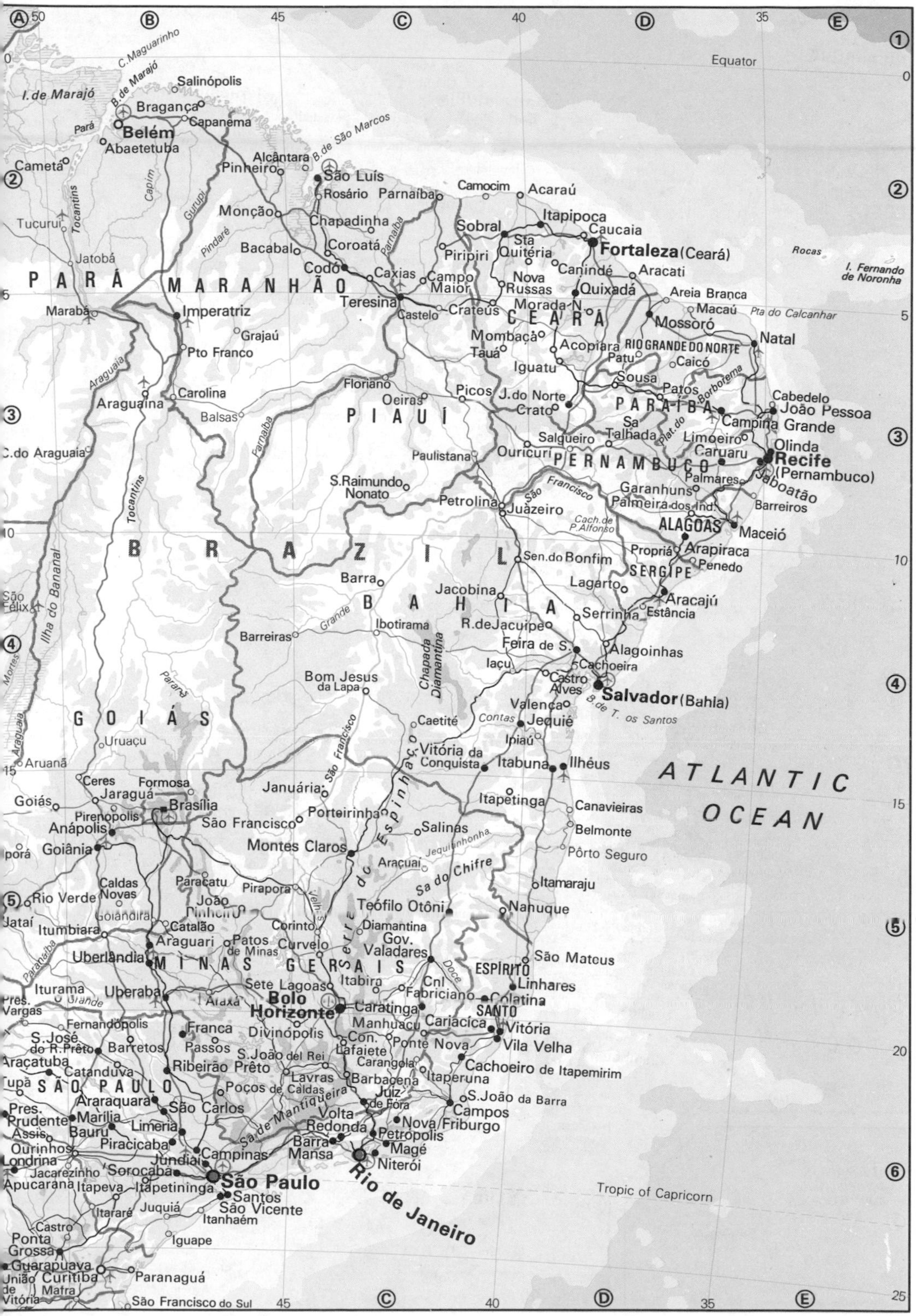
A
B
C
D
E
50
45
40
35
1
2
3
4
5
6
0
5
10
15
20
25
Equator
C.Maguarinho
B. de Marajó
I. de Marajó
Salinópolis
Bragança
Capanema
Pará
Belém
Abaetetuba
Cametá
B. de São Marcos
Alcântara
Pinheiro
São Luís
Rosário
Parnaíba
Camocim
Acaraú
Tocantins
Capim
Gurupi
Tucuruí
Monção
Chapadinha
Itapipoca
Sobral
Caucaia
Pindaré
Bacabal
Coroatá
Piripiri
Sta Quitéria
Fortaleza (Ceará)
Rocas
I. Fernando de Noronha
Jatobá
Codó
Caxias
Campo Maior
Nova Russas
Canindé
Aracati
P A R Á
M A R A N H Ã O
Quixadá
Areia Branca
Teresina
Morada N.
Macaú
Pta do Calcanhar
Marabá
Imperatriz
Castelo
Crateús
C E A R Á
Mossoró
Natal
Grajaú
Mombaça
Acopiara
RIO GRANDE DO NORTE
Pto Franco
Tauá
Patu
Caicó
Iguatu
Araguaia
Floriano
Sousa
Borborema
Carolina
Picos
J. do Norte
Patos
Cabedelo
Oeiras
Crato
P A R A Í B A
João Pessoa
Araguaina
P I A U Í
Campina Grande
Balsas
Parnaíba
Sa Talhada
Plat. do
C. do Araguaia
Salgueiro
Limoeiro
Olinda
Paulistana
Ouricuri
P E R N A M B U C O
Caruaru
Recife (Pernambuco)
Tocantins
Palmares
Jaboatão
S. Raimundo Nonato
São Francisco
Garanhuns
Petrolina
Juàzeiro
Palmeira dos Ind.
Barreiros
Cach. de P. Alfonso
ALAGOAS
Maceió
B R A Z I L
Propriá
Arapiraca
Ilha do Bananal
Sen. do Bonfim
Penedo
SERGIPE
Barra
Lagarto
Jacobina
São Félix
B A H I A
Aracajú
Estância
Serrinha
Grande
Ibotirama
R. de Jacuípe
Barreiras
Chapada Diamantina
Feira de S.
Alagoinhas
Mortes
Iaçu
Cachoeira
Paraná
Bom Jesus da Lapa
Castro Alves
Salvador (Bahia)
Valença
B. de T. os Santos
G O I Á S
Caetité
Contas
Jequié
Araguaia
São Francisco
Uruaçu
Ipiaú
Espinhaço
Vitória da Conquista
Itabuna
Ilhéus
Aruanã
A T L A N T I C
O C E A N
Ceres
Formosa
Januária
Jaraguá
Goiás
Itapetinga
Brasília
Canavieiras
Pirenópolis
Porteirinha
São Francisco
Anápolis
Salinas
Belmonte
Jequitinhonha
Goiânia
Montes Claros
Porá
Pôrto Seguro
Araçuaí
Sa do Chifre
Caldas Novas
Paracatu
Itamaraju
Rio Verde
Pirapora
Velhas
Serra do
João Pinheiro
Teófilo Otôni
Nanuque
Jataí
Goiandira
Catalão
Corinto
Diamantina
Itumbiara
Paranaíba
Araguari
Patos de Minas
Curvelo
Gov. Valadares
Uberlândia
M I N A S   G E R A I S
São Mateus
ESPÍRITO SANTO
Doce
Sete Lagoas
Itabira
Linhares
Iturama
Cnl Fabriciano
Uberaba
Grande
Pres. Vargas
Araxá
Belo Horizonte
Caratinga
Colatina
Manhuaçu
Cariacica
Fernandópolis
Franca
Divinópolis
Vitória
S. José do R. Prêto
Barretos
Passos
Con. Lafaiete
Ponte Nova
Vila Velha
S. João del Rei
Araçatuba
Ribeirão Prêto
Carangola
Cachoeiro de Itapemirim
Catanduva
Lavras
Barbacena
Itaperuna
Tupã
S Ã O   P A U L O
Poços de Caldas
Mantiqueira
Juiz de Fora
S. João da Barra
Araraquara
Campos
Pres. Prudente
São Carlos
Marília
Volta Redonda
Nova Friburgo
Assis
Bauru
Limeira
Sa de
Petrópolis
Ourinhos
Piracicaba
Barra Mansa
Magé
Londrina
Campinas
Jundiaí
Niterói
Jacarezinho
Sorocaba
Rio de Janeiro
São Paulo
Apucarana
Itapeva
Itapetininga
Santos
São Vicente
Tropic of Capricorn
Itararé
Juquiá
Itanhaém
Castro
Ponta Grossa
Iguape
Guarapuava
União
Curitiba
Paranaguá
de Vitória
Mafra
São Francisco do Sul

NICARAGUA
Bluefields
S.Carlos
I.de Perlas
I.de San Andrés (Col.)
Alajuela
Heredia
Limón
San José
Cartago
Chirripó Grande 3815
COSTA RICA
Chiriquí 3486
David
G. Dulce
Pto Armuelles
G. de Chiriquí
I. Coiba
Pta Mariato
PANAMA
Colón
Panamá
La Chorrera
Santiago
Chitré
Pen.de Azuero
Arch.de las Perlas
G.de Panamá
L.de Chiriquí
G. de los Mosquitos
G.de Urabá
La Palma
Guapá
Atrato
Pta Gallinas
Pen.de Guajira
Ríohacha
Sta Marta
Ciénaga
Barranquilla
Cartagena
Maicao
Sa Nevada de Sta Marta 5800
Valledupar
S.Jacinto
Sincelejo
El Banco
Magangué
Montería
Turbo
Sinú
Caucasia
Cauca
Magdalena
Barrancabermeja
Yarumal
Bello
Pto Berrío
Itagui
Medellín
Barbosa
Quibdó
C.Corrientes
Occidental
Oriental
Manizales
5218 Tolima
Pereira
Cartago
Armenia
Bogotá
Tuluá
Ibagué
Girardot
Buenaventura
G.de Tortugas
Buga
Palmira
Cali
Huila 5750
Cord. Central
Santander
Popayán
Neiva
Vol.Puracé 4700
Pto Rico
Pitalito
Florencia
Belén
Malpelo (Col.)
Tumaco
El Diviso
Pasto
S.Lorenzo
Ipiales
Mocoa
Tulcán
Pto Asis
Esmeraldas
Ibarra
Otavalo
Cojimíes
Equator
Quito
Jama
5896 Cotopaxi
Coca
Lago Agrio
Napo
Tena
Chone
Manta
Ambato
C. San Lorenzo
Jipijapa
ECUADOR
Guaranda
Chimborazo 6310
Babahoyo
Riobamba
Guayaquil
Milagro
Macas
La Libertad
Playas
I.Puná
Cuenca
Azogues
Gualaceo
G.de Guayaquil
Tumbes
Machala
Zaruma
Loja
Zamora
Talara
Negritos
Chira
Sullana
Paita
Piura
Chulucanas
Huancabamba
Catacaos
Pta Aguja
Jaén
Moyobamba
Lambayeque
Ferreñafe
Chachapoyas
Chiclayo
Chepén
Cajamarca
Cajabamba
Pacasmayo
Huamachuco
Otusco
Trujillo
PACIFIC OCEAN
Pomabamba
Huallanca
Huascarán 6768
Chimbote
Huaráz
Casma
Huarmey
Pativilca
Barranca
Huacho
Ancón
Callao
Lima
La Oroya
Mantaro
Jauja
Huancayo
Huancavelica
Chincha Alta
Pen.de Paracas
Pisco
Ica
Nazca
Andahuaylas
CORD. DE LOS ANDES
Pto Fijo
Aruba
Curaçao (Neth.)
Bonaire
Willemstad
G.de Venezuela
Maracaibo
Cabimas
Machiques
L.de Maracaibo
Cd Ojeda
Trujillo
Valera
Mérida
Cord. de Mérida
Bolívar 5007
Ocaña
Cúcuta
San Cristóbal
Pamplona
Bucaramanga
Málaga
Sogamoso
Tunja
Chocontá
Villavicencio
Granada
COLOMBIA
Coro
Riecito
Tocuyo
Pto Cabello
Maiquetía
Cara
Valencia
Maracay
Barquisimeto
S.Juan
Acarigua
Guanare
V.de la Pascua
Barinas
Apure
S.Fernando
LLANOS
VE
Arauca
Meta
Pto Carreño
Orinoco
Pto Ayacucho
Vichada
Ventuari
Orocué
Guaviare
Salto Angostura
Inírida
Guanía
Casiquiare
Negro
Calamar
Vaupés
Mitú
Cucuí
Içana
Yarí
Apaporis
Leguízamo
Putumayo
Salto Grande
Caquetá
Japurá
Napo
Içá
Tigre
Pastaza
Santiago
Marañón
Iquitos
Solimões (Amazonas)
Letícia
Tabatinga
Caxias
Yavarí (Javari)
Jutaí
Juruá
Elvira
SELVAS
AM
Yurimaguas
Tarapoto
Ucayali
Huallaga
Tapau
Juruá
Cruzeiro do Sul
Feijó
Purus
Bôca do Acre
ACRE
Sena Madureira
Pucallpa
Tingo María
Ucayali
La Unión
Huánuco
Oxapampa
Cerro de Pasco
La Merced
Tarma
PERU
Acobamba
Rio Branco
Abunã
Brasiléia
Riberalta
Cobija
Porvenir
Madre de Dios
Pto Maldonado
Pto Heath
L.Rogaguado
Beni
Quillabamba
Machu-Picchu
Ayacucho
Apurímac
Cuzco
Abancay
Sicuani
Ayaviri
BOL
Rurrenabaque
ISLAS GALÁPAGOS (ARCHIPIÉLAGO DO COLÓN) (Equ.)
Culpepper
Wenman
Pinta
Marchena
Genovesa
Fernandina
San Salvador
Santa Cruz
Isabela
Baquerizo Moreno
San Cristóbal
Santa María
Española
at the same scale

GRENADA
St George's
I. de Margarita
La Asunción
Carúpano
Pen. de Paria
Güiria
Port of Spain
Tobago
Trinidad
San Fernando
TRINIDAD AND TOBAGO
G. de Paria
Cumana
Caripito
Maturín
Tigre
Tucupita
Barrancas
El Tigre
Orinoco
Cd Bolívar
Cd Guayana
Upata
Cd Piar
Emb. de Guri
ZUELA
La Paragua
El Dorado
Salto del Angel
Paragua
La Gran Sabana
Roraima 2180
Sta Elena
Sa Pacaraima
Mabaruma
Charity
Suddie
Leguan I.
Georgetown
V. en Hoop
Bartica
New Amsterdam
Linden
Kaieteur Fall
Paramaribo
Nieuw Amsterdam
Marienburg
Nieuw Nickerie
Totness
Albina
Sinnamary
I. du Diable (Devil's I.)
Kourou
Cayenne
Apoera
Witagron
Blommesteinmeer
Corantijn
Maroni
GUYANA
SURINAM
Julianatop 1280
FRENCH GUIANA
Cabo Orange
Oiapoque
Ireng
Bonfim
Lethem
Boa Vista
Essequibo
Litani
Oiapoque
Sa Parima
Orinoco
RORAIMA
Caracaraí
Serra Tumucumaque
Amapá
Ilha de Maracá
AMAPÁ
Sa do Navio
Jari
Macapá
Pto Santana
Branco
purucuara
Paru
C. Maguarinho
I. de Marajó
B. de Marajó
Salinópolis
Bragança
Capanema
Pará
Belém
Abaetetuba
Cametá
Negro
Oriximiná
Obidos
Amazonas
Monte Alegre
Santarém
Xingu
Manaus
Manacapuru
Careiro
Itacoatiara
Altamira
Tefé
Aveiro
Tucuruí
Tocantins
Capim
Gurupi
AZONAS
PARÁ
Itaituba
Tapajós
Purus
Madeira
Coari
Pimenta
Jatobá
Aripuanã
Iriri
Marabá
Imperatriz
Jacareacanga
S. Félix
Pto Franco
Araguaia
Lábrea
Humaitá
Prainha
Serra do Cachimbo
Araguaína
Carolina
Xingu
Madeira
Pôrto Velho
Teles Pires
C. do Araguaia
Aripuanã
Jiparaná
Cachimbo
Tocantins
abunã
T. Roosevelt
Juruena
Guajará-Mirim
Rondônia
Arinos
Sa dos Caiabis
Sa Formosa
Ilha do Bananal
RONDÔNIA
Serra dos Parecis
São Félix
Guaporé
Itonomas
Vilhena
Pto Artur
MATO GROSSO
Paranã
Iténez
Paraguá
Mortes
Araguaia
GOIÁS
Trinidad
Mato Grosso
Uruaçu
Aruanã
ATLANTIC OCEAN
65
60
55
50
10
5
0
15

Buenos Aires
Avellaneda
La Plata
Rosario
Córdoba
Santa Fe
Paraná
Mendoza
Santiago
Valparaíso
Viña del Mar
Concepción
Talcahuano
Temuco
Bahía Blanca
Mar del Plata
Neuquén
San Luis
San Juan
Río Cuarto
Santa Rosa
San Rafael
Rancagua
Talca
Chillán
La Serena
Coquimbo
Entre Ríos
Santa Fe
Córdoba
Buenos Aires
La Pampa
San Luis
Mendoza
San Juan
Neuquén
La Rioja
Uruguay
OCEANO PACIFICO

1:7.5M 0 100 200 300 km; 0 50 100 150 mls

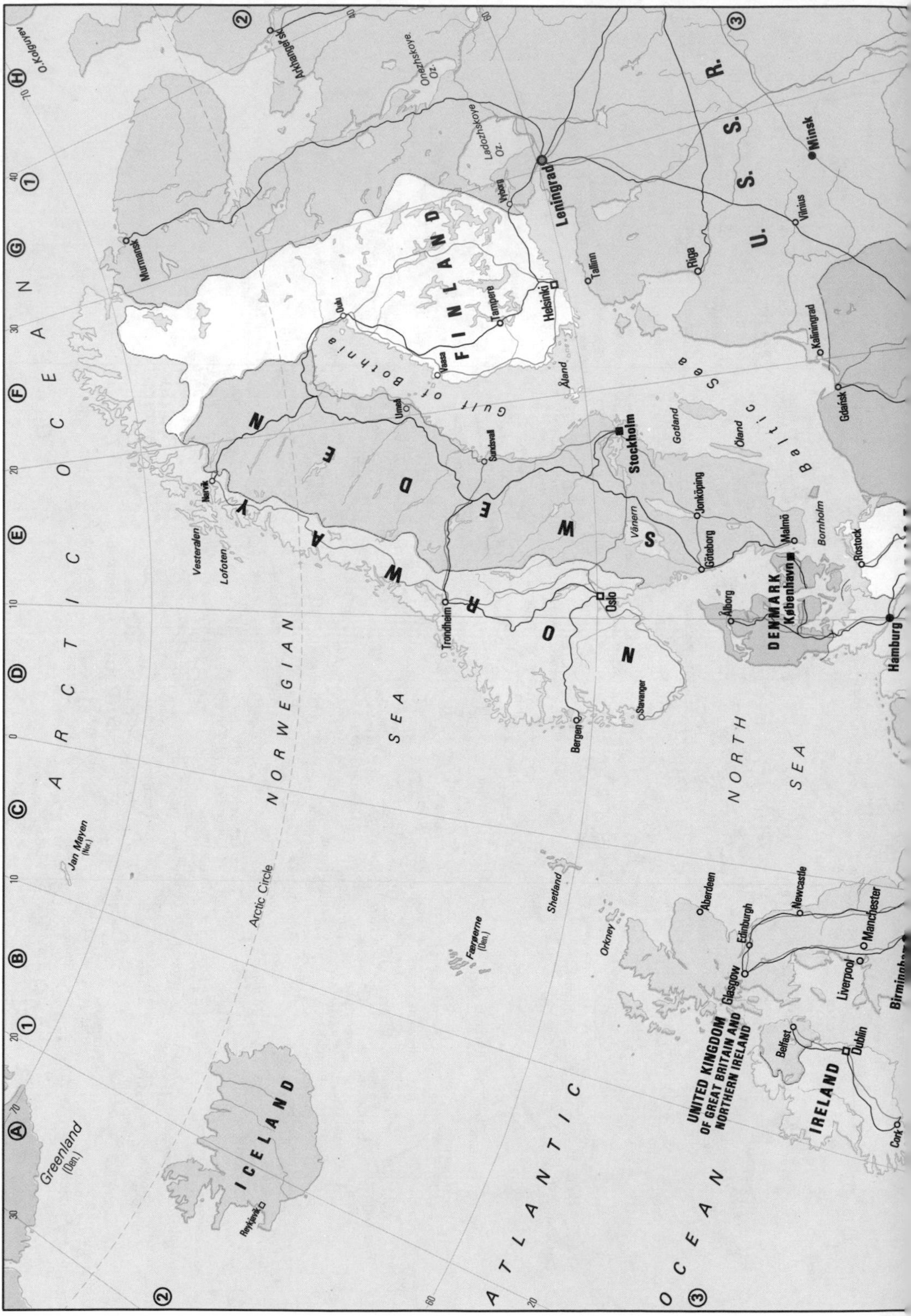
ARCTIC OCEAN
NORWEGIAN SEA
NORTH SEA
ATLANTIC OCEAN
Baltic Sea
Gulf of Bothnia
Arctic Circle
ICELAND
Reykjavik
Greenland (Den.)
Jan Mayen (Nor.)
Færøerne (Den.)
Shetland
Orkney
NORWAY
SWEDEN
FINLAND
DENMARK
U. S. S. R.
UNITED KINGDOM OF GREAT BRITAIN AND NORTHERN IRELAND
IRELAND
Murmansk
Arkhangel'sk
O. Kolguyev
Onezhskoye Oz.
Ladozhskoye Oz.
Leningrad
Vyborg
Helsinki
Tampere
Vaasa
Oulu
Åland
Tallinn
Riga
Vilnius
Minsk
Kaliningrad
Gdańsk
Umeå
Sundsvall
Narvik
Vesterålen
Lofoten
Trondheim
Stockholm
Gotland
Öland
Jönköping
Vänern
Göteborg
Malmö
Bornholm
København
Ålborg
Rostock
Hamburg
Oslo
Bergen
Stavanger
Aberdeen
Edinburgh
Glasgow
Newcastle
Manchester
Liverpool
Birmingham
Belfast
Dublin
Cork
A
B
C
D
E
F
G
H
1
2
3

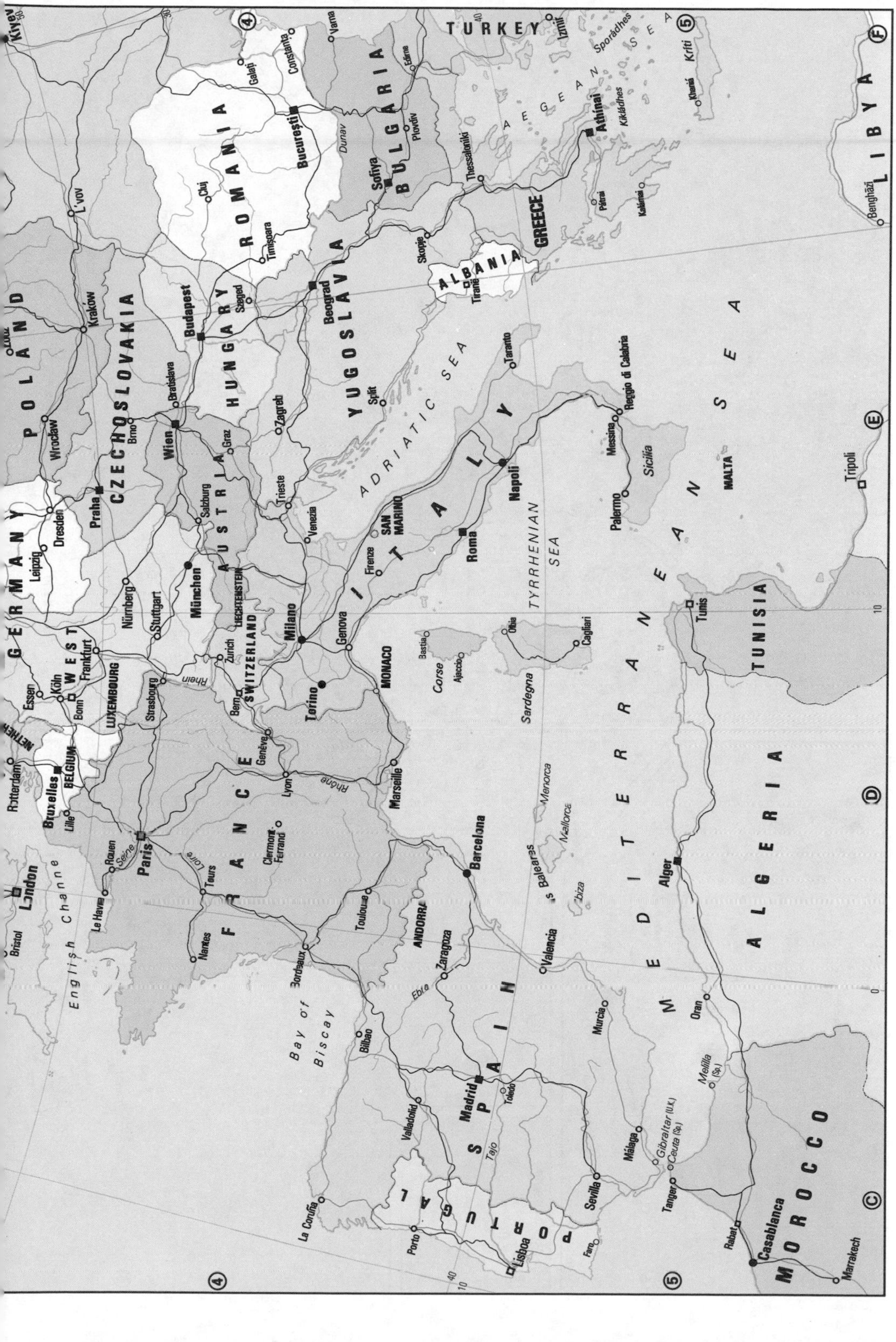
POLAND
WEST GERMANY
CZECHOSLOVAKIA
ROMANIA
BULGARIA
TURKEY
HUNGARY
YUGOSLAVIA
ALBANIA
GREECE
AUSTRIA
SWITZERLAND
LIECHTENSTEIN
ITALY
SAN MARINO
MONACO
FRANCE
LUXEMBOURG
BELGIUM
NETHERLANDS
ANDORRA
SPAIN
PORTUGAL
MOROCCO
ALGERIA
TUNISIA
LIBYA
MALTA
MEDITERRANEAN SEA
ADRIATIC SEA
TYRRHENIAN SEA
AEGEAN SEA
Bay of Biscay
English Channel
Kiyev
L'vov
Kraków
Wrocław
Praha
Dresden
Leipzig
Essen
Köln
Bonn
Frankfurt
Nürnberg
Stuttgart
München
Strasbourg
Rhein
Bern
Zurich
Genève
Salzburg
Wien
Brno
Bratislava
Budapest
Szeged
Graz
Zagreb
Trieste
Venezia
Milano
Torino
Genova
Firenze
Roma
Napoli
Taranto
Reggio di Calabria
Messina
Palermo
Sicilia
Split
Beograd
Timişoara
Cluj
Galaţi
Constanţa
Varna
Bucureşti
Dunav
Sofiya
Plovdiv
Edirne
İzmir
Sporádhes
Kikládhes
Kriti
Khaniá
Athinai
Thessaloniki
Pátrai
Kalámai
Skopje
Tiranë
Corse
Bastia
Ajaccio
Sardegna
Olbia
Cagliari
Tunis
Tripoli
Benghāzī
Rotterdam
Bruxelles
Lille
London
Bristol
Paris
Seine
Rouen
Le Havre
Tours
Loire
Nantes
Clermont-Ferrand
Lyon
Rhône
Marseille
Bordeaux
Toulouse
Barcelona
Menorca
Mallorca
Baleares
Ibiza
Valencia
Zaragoza
Ebro
Bilbao
Madrid
Toledo
Tajo
Valladolid
La Coruña
Porto
Lisboa
Faro
Sevilla
Málaga
Murcia
Gibraltar (U.K.)
Ceuta (Sp.)
Melilla (Sp.)
Tanger
Rabat
Casablanca
Marrakech
Oran
Alger
C
D
E
F
4
5

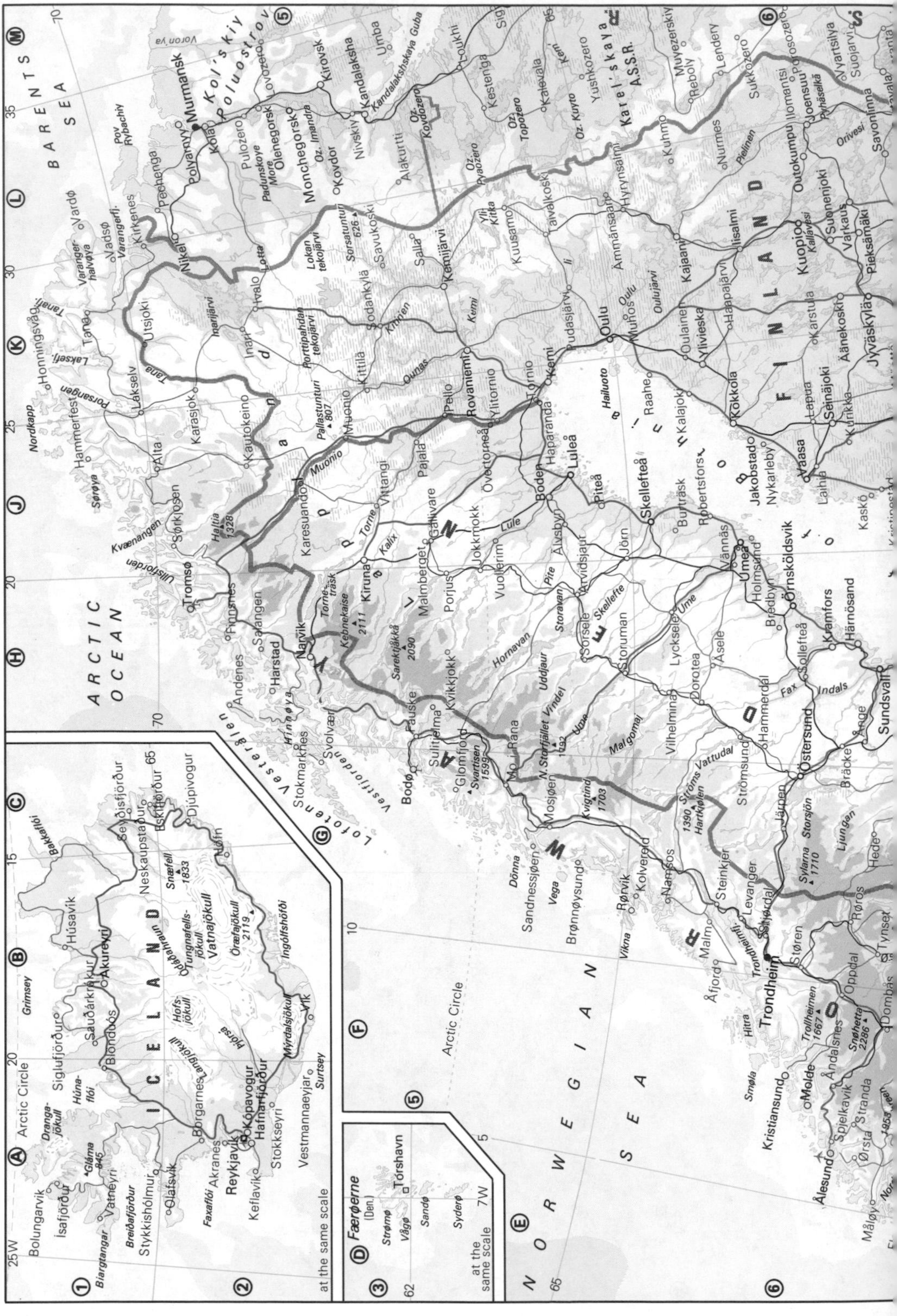
BARENTS SEA
ARCTIC OCEAN
NORWEGIAN SEA
ICELAND
FINLAND
Lapland
SWEDEN
NORWAY
Karel'skaya A.S.S.R.
Kol'skiy Poluostrov
Murmansk
Tromsø
Narvik
Kiruna
Luleå
Oulu
Trondheim
Reykjavík
Akureyri
Færøerne (Den.)
Tórshavn
Lofoten
Vesterålen
Vestfjorden
Arctic Circle
at the same scale

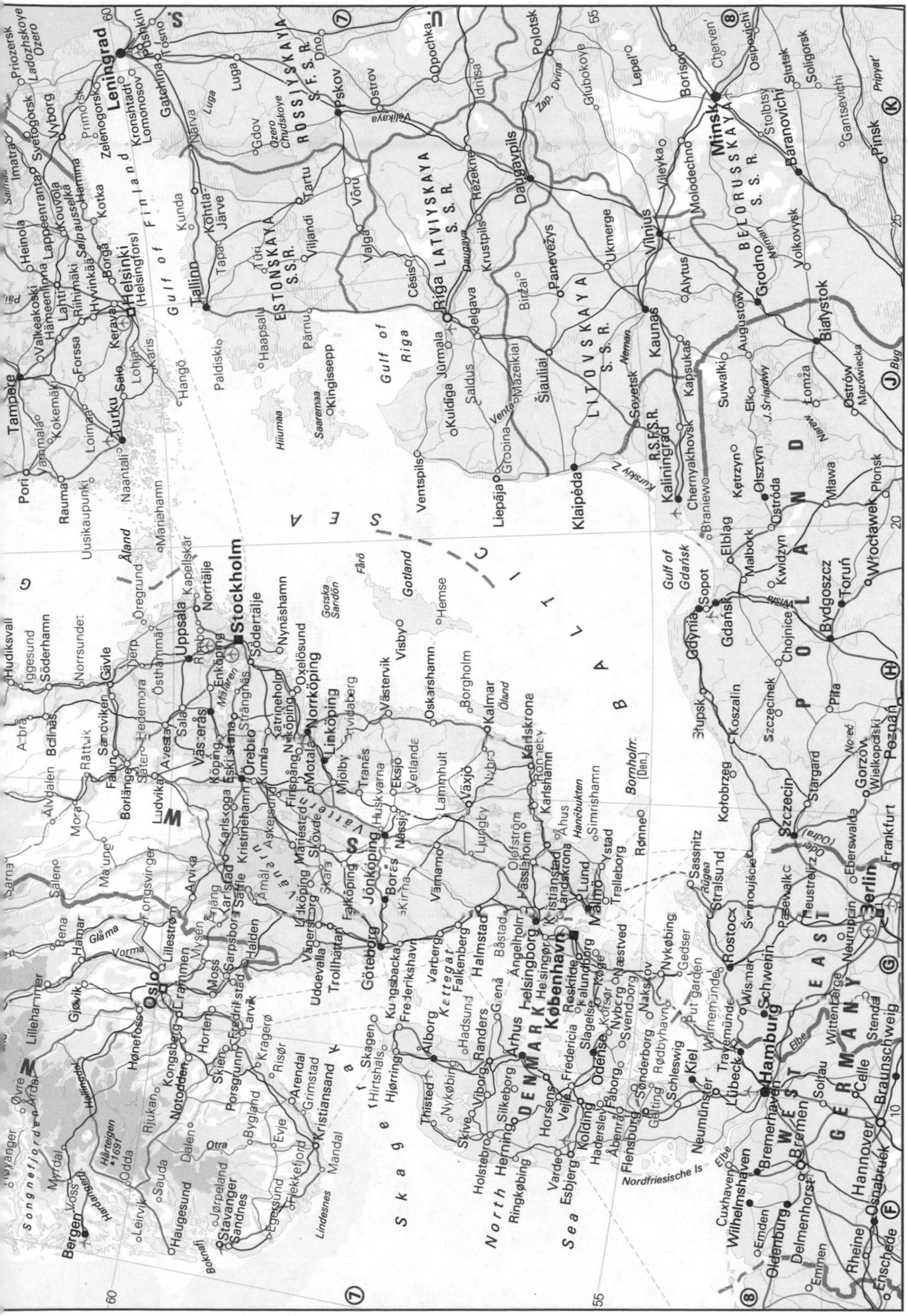
Leningrad
Helsinki (Helsingfors)
Tallinn
Riga
Vilnius
Kaunas
Minsk
Pskov
Tartu
Daugavpils
Stockholm
Oslo
Göteborg
København
Malmö
Gdańsk
Gdynia
Szczecin
Berlin
Hamburg
Bremen
Hannover
Kiel
Lübeck
Rostock
Kaliningrad
Klaipėda
Liepāja
Šiauliai
Grodno
Białystok
Toruń
Bydgoszcz
Poznań
Uppsala
Västerås
Örebro
Norrköping
Linköping
Jönköping
Kalmar
Karlskrona
Visby
Gotland
Åland
Turku
Tampere
Pori
Lahti
Kotka
Vyborg
Narva
Pärnu
Ventspils
Jelgava
Bergen
Stavanger
Kristiansand
Drammen
Lillehammer
Ålborg
Århus
Odense
Esbjerg
Helsingør
Bornholm (Den.)
Rønne
Gulf of Finland
Gulf of Riga
Gulf of Gdańsk
Kattegat
Skagerrak
North Sea
BALTIC SEA
ESTONSKAYA S.S.R.
LATVIYSKAYA S.S.R.
LITOVSKAYA S.S.R.
BELORUSSKAYA S.S.R.
ROSSIYSKAYA S.F.S.R.
R.S.F.S.R.
POLAND
DENMARK
WEST GERMANY
EAST GERMANY

1:5M

0 50 100 150 200 km
0 50 100 mls

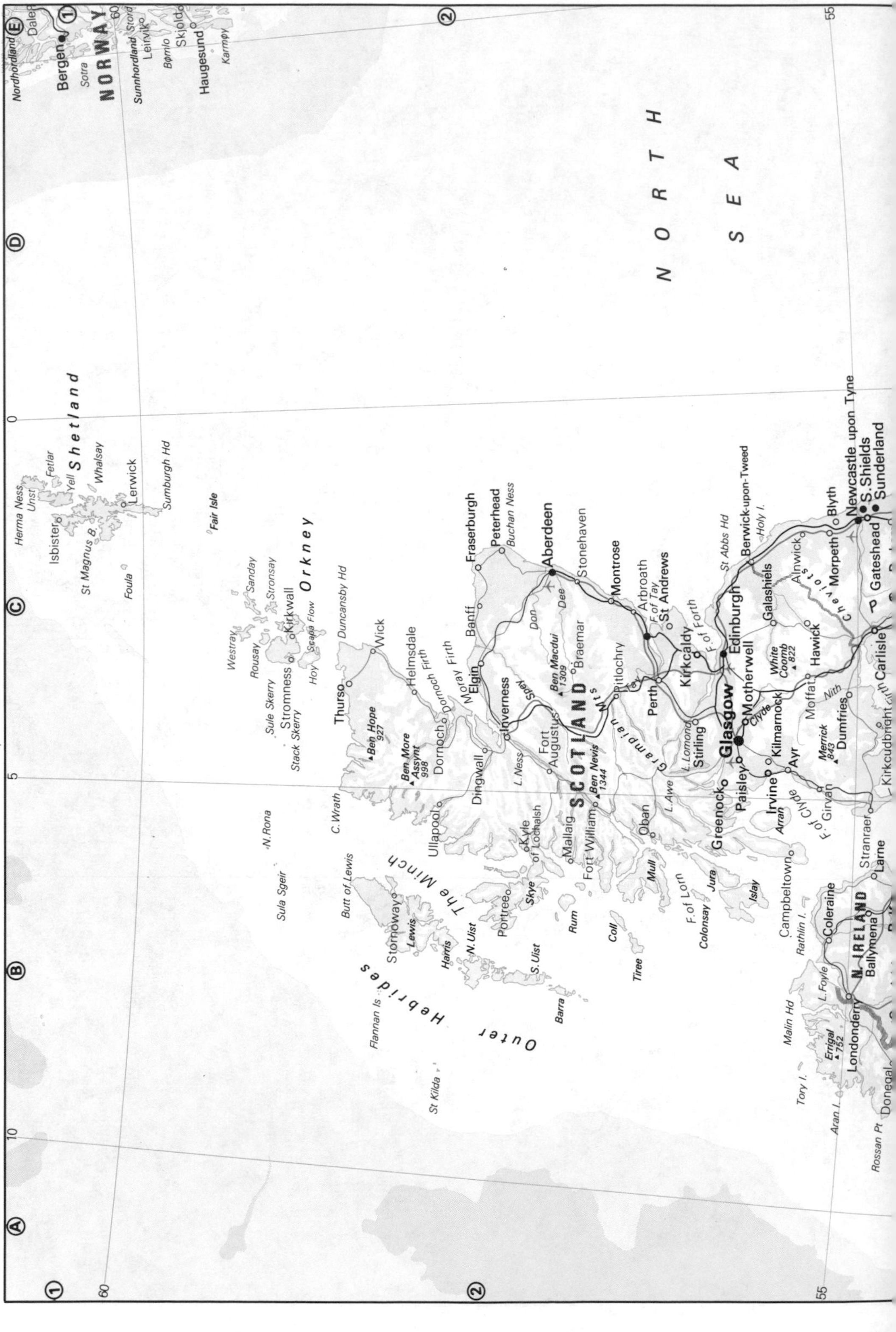

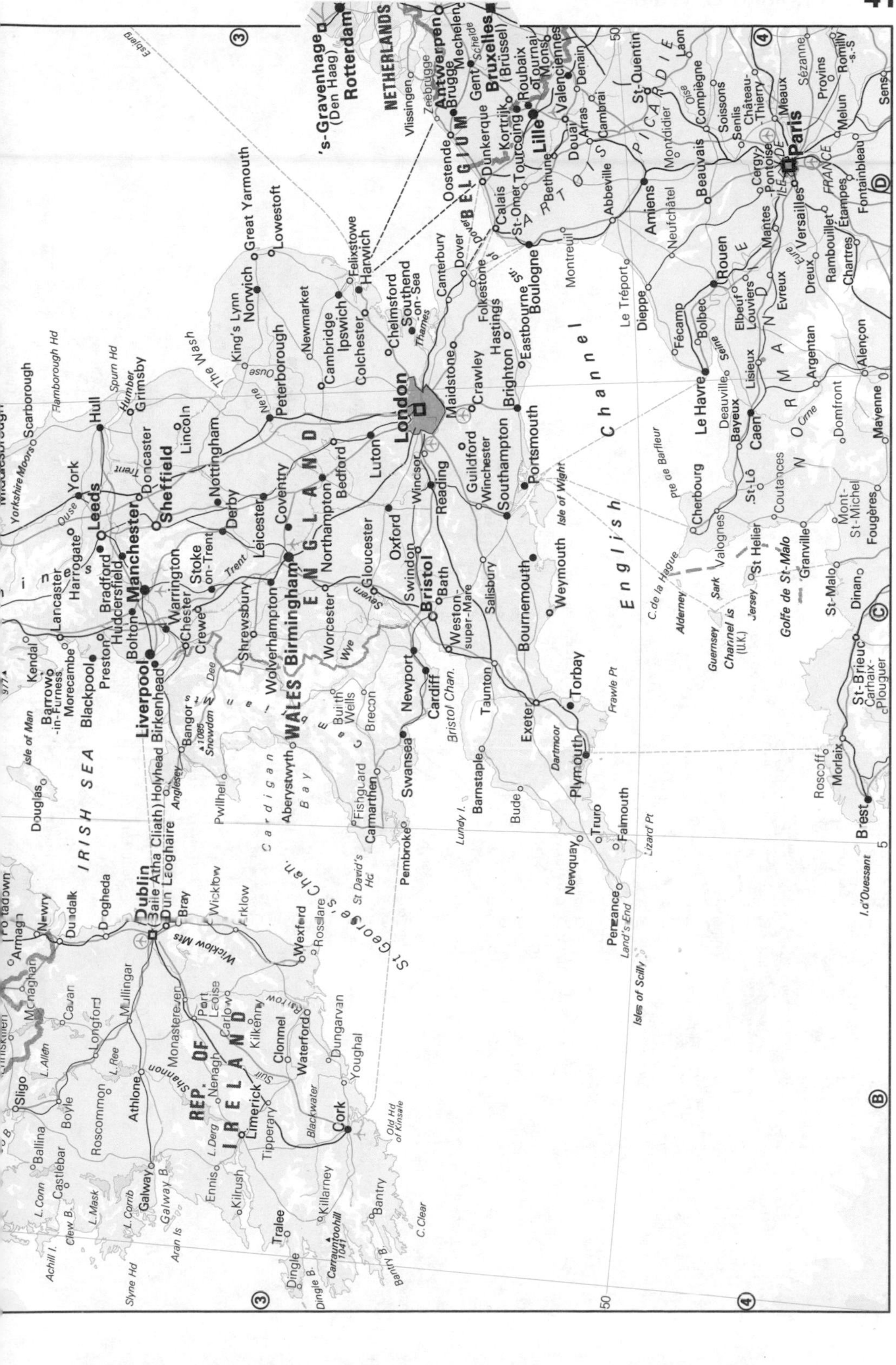
IRISH SEA
REP. OF IRELAND
ENGLAND
WALES
NETHERLANDS
BELGIUM
FRANCE
English Channel
Cardigan Bay
St George's Chan.
Bristol Chan.
PICARDIE
ARTOIS
NORMANDIE
ÎLE DE FRANCE
Dublin (Baile Átha Cliath)
Dun Laoghaire
Bray
Wicklow
Arklow
Wexford
Rosslare
Waterford
Dungarvan
Youghal
Cork
Old Hd of Kinsale
Bantry
Bantry B.
Killarney
Tralee
Dingle
Dingle B.
Carrauntoohill 1041
Kilrush
Ennis
Limerick
Tipperary
Clonmel
Kilkenny
Carlow
Port Laoise
Monasterevan
Nenagh
Athlone
Galway
Galway B.
Aran Is
Slyne Hd
Achill I.
Clew B.
L.Mask
L.Corrib
L.Conn
Castlebar
Ballina
Sligo
Boyle
Roscommon
Longford
L.Ree
L.Derg
Mullingar
Cavan
Monaghan
Armagh
Newry
Dundalk
Drogheda
L.Allen
Shannon
Suir
Barrow
Blackwater
Wicklow Mts
C.Clear
St David's Hd
Pembroke
Fishguard
Carmarthen
Swansea
Aberystwyth
Pwllheli
Anglesey
Holyhead
Bangor
Snowdon 1085
Dee
Builth Wells
Brecon
Newport
Cardiff
Lundy I.
Douglas
Isle of Man
Barrow-in-Furness
Kendal
Morecambe
Lancaster
Blackpool
Preston
Bolton
Liverpool
Birkenhead
Chester
Crewe
Warrington
Manchester
Huddersfield
Bradford
Harrogate
Leeds
York
Yorkshire Moors
Scarborough
Flamborough Hd
Hull
Humber
Spurn Hd
Grimsby
Doncaster
Sheffield
Lincoln
Nottingham
Derby
Stoke-on-Trent
Trent
Ouse
Shrewsbury
Wolverhampton
Birmingham
Coventry
Leicester
Northampton
Worcester
Wye
Severn
Gloucester
Bedford
Luton
Peterborough
Nene
The Wash
King's Lynn
Norwich
Great Yarmouth
Lowestoft
Newmarket
Cambridge
Ipswich
Felixstowe
Harwich
Colchester
Chelmsford
Southend-on-Sea
Thames
London
Oxford
Swindon
Bath
Bristol
Weston-super-Mare
Windsor
Reading
Guildford
Winchester
Southampton
Salisbury
Bournemouth
Weymouth
Portsmouth
Isle of Wight
Brighton
Crawley
Maidstone
Canterbury
Dover
Folkestone
Hastings
Eastbourne
Taunton
Exeter
Dartmoor
Torbay
Barnstaple
Bude
Plymouth
Newquay
Truro
Falmouth
Lizard Pt
Penzance
Land's End
Isles of Scilly
Frawle Pt
Alderney
Guernsey
Sark
Jersey
Channel Is (U.K.)
St Helier
C.de la Hague
Pte de Barfleur
Cherbourg
Valognes
St-Lô
Coutances
Granville
Golfe de St-Malo
St-Malo
Dinan
Mont-St-Michel
Fougères
St-Brieuc
Carhaix-Plouguer
Morlaix
Roscoff
Brest
I.d'Ouessant
Bayeux
Caen
Orne
Deauville
Le Havre
Lisieux
Argentan
Domfront
Mayenne
Alençon
Fécamp
Bolbec
Seine
Dieppe
Le Tréport
Rouen
Elbeuf
Louviers
Evreux
Eure
Dreux
Rambouillet
Chartres
Étampes
Fontainebleau
Melun
Versailles
Paris
Mantes
Cergy-Pontoise
Beauvais
Neufchâtel
Abbeville
Amiens
Montreuil
Boulogne
Calais
St-Omer
Béthune
Arras
Douai
Cambrai
Lille
Roubaix
Tourcoing
Kortrijk
Tournai
Mons
Valenciennes
Denain
St-Quentin
Laon
Montdidier
Compiègne
Oise
Soissons
Senlis
Château-Thierry
Meaux
Sézanne
Provins
Romilly-s.-S
Sens
Dunkerque
Oostende
Brugge
Zeebrugge
Vlissingen
Gent
Schelde
Antwerpen
Mechelen
Bruxelles (Brüssel)
's-Gravenhage (Den Haag)
Rotterdam
Esbjerg
50
5
0
B
C
D
3
4

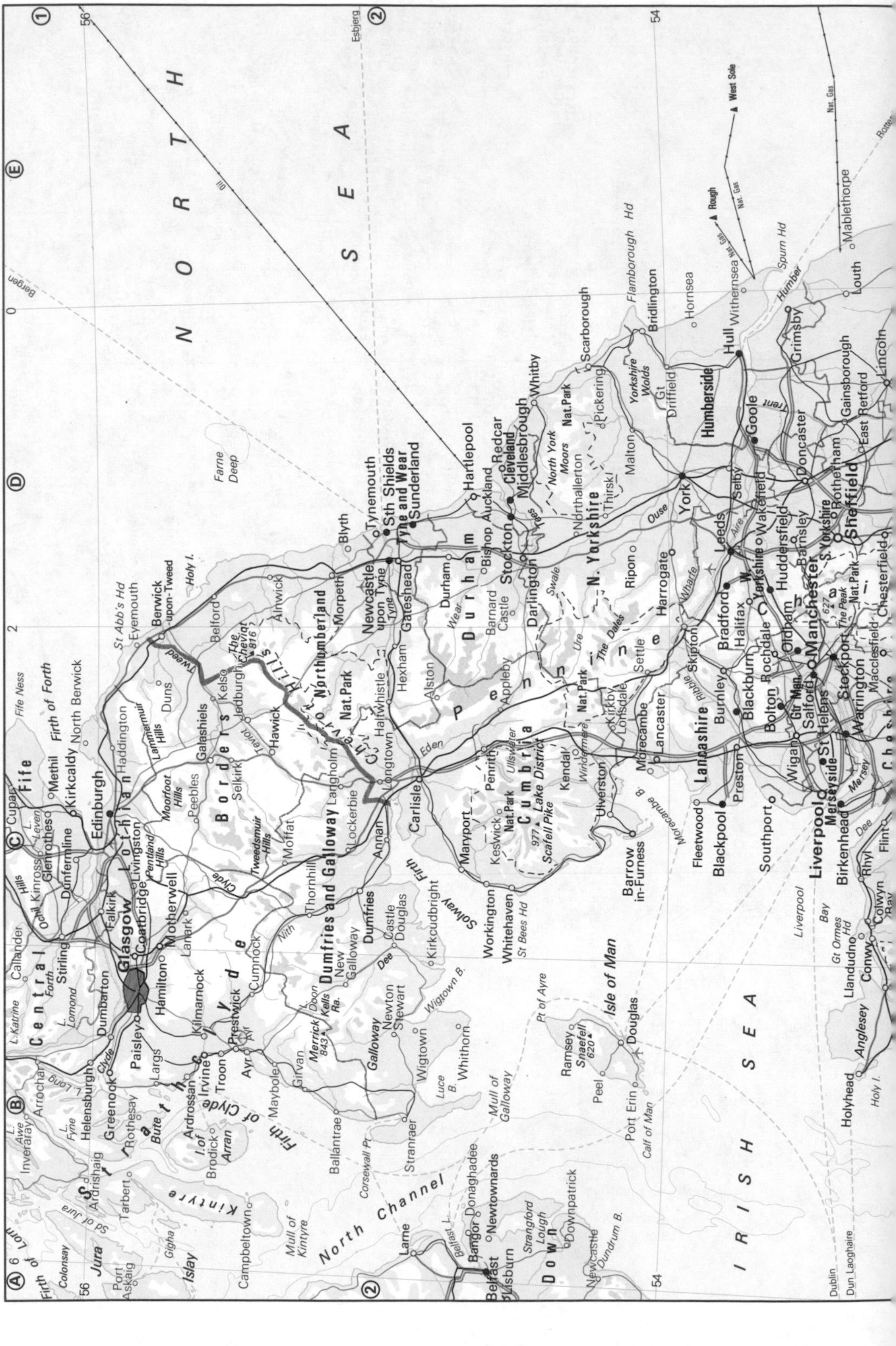
NORTH SEA
IRISH SEA
North Channel
Firth of Forth
Firth of Clyde
Solway Firth
Morecambe B.
Liverpool Bay
Isle of Man
Cumbria
Durham
N. Yorkshire
Northumberland
Tyne and Wear
Cleveland
Humberside
Lancashire
Merseyside
Gtr Man
S. Yorkshire
Borders
Dumfries and Galloway
Lothian
Central
Fife
Strathclyde
Down
Pennine
Cheviot Hills
Lake District
The Dales
The Peak
Nat. Park
Edinburgh
Glasgow
Newcastle upon Tyne
Carlisle
York
Leeds
Bradford
Manchester
Liverpool
Sheffield
Hull
Blackpool
Preston
Lancaster
Middlesbrough
Sunderland
Durham
Darlington
Stockton
Hartlepool
Scarborough
Whitby
Berwick-upon-Tweed
Dumfries
Stranraer
Belfast
Douglas
Birkenhead
Southport
Wigan
Bolton
Blackburn
Burnley
Oldham
Stockport
Warrington
St Helens
Huddersfield
Wakefield
Barnsley
Doncaster
Rotherham
Grimsby
Goole
Lincoln
Holyhead
Anglesey
Rhyl
Llandudno
Conwy
Flint
Dublin
Dun Laoghaire
Esbjerg
Bergen
West Sole
Rough
Nat. Gas
Oil
56
54
2
0
6
A
B
C
D
E
1
2

1:2.5M 0 25 50 75 100 km / 0 25 50 mls

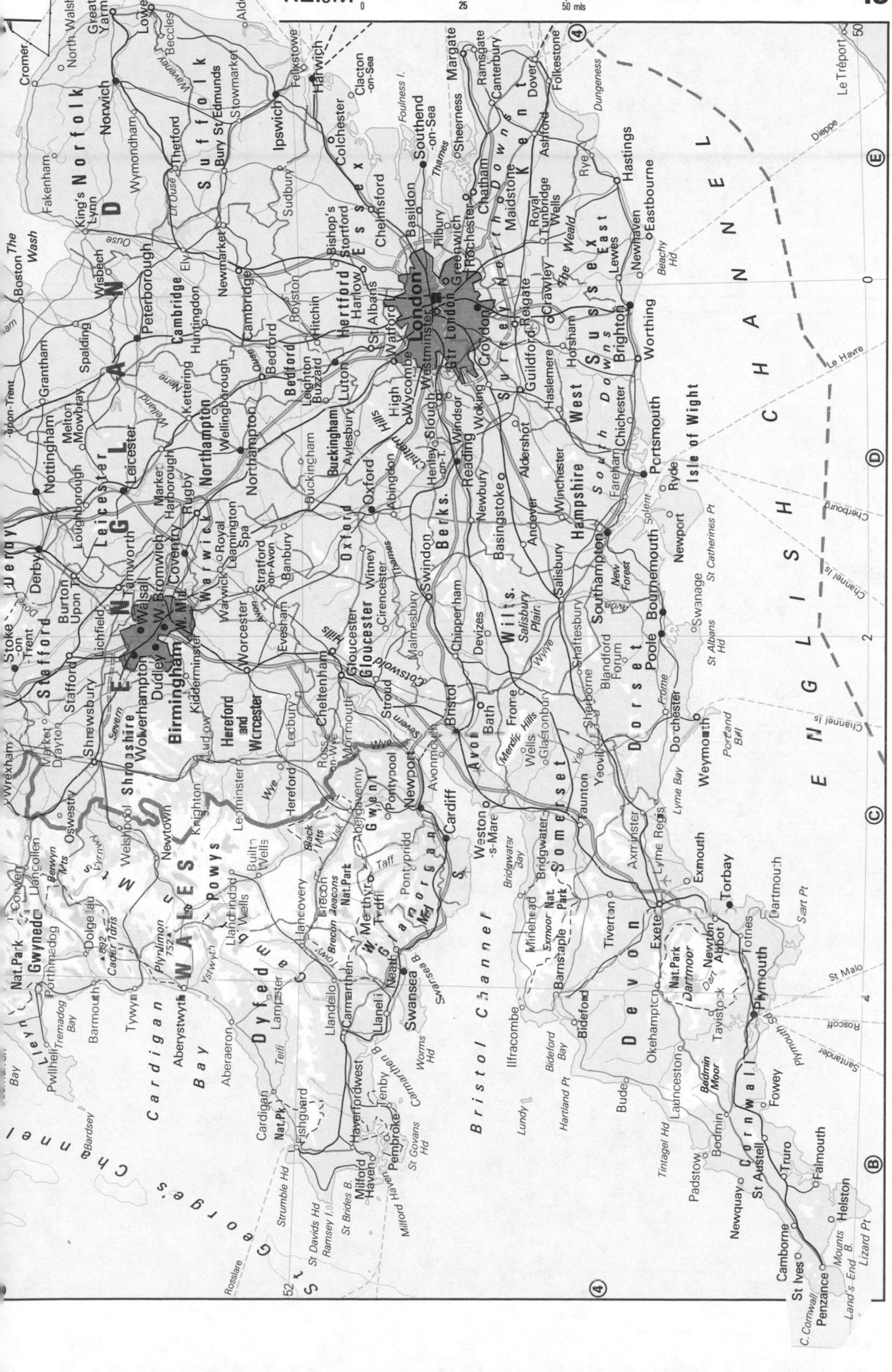

1:2.5M 0 25 50 75 100 km 0 25 50 mls

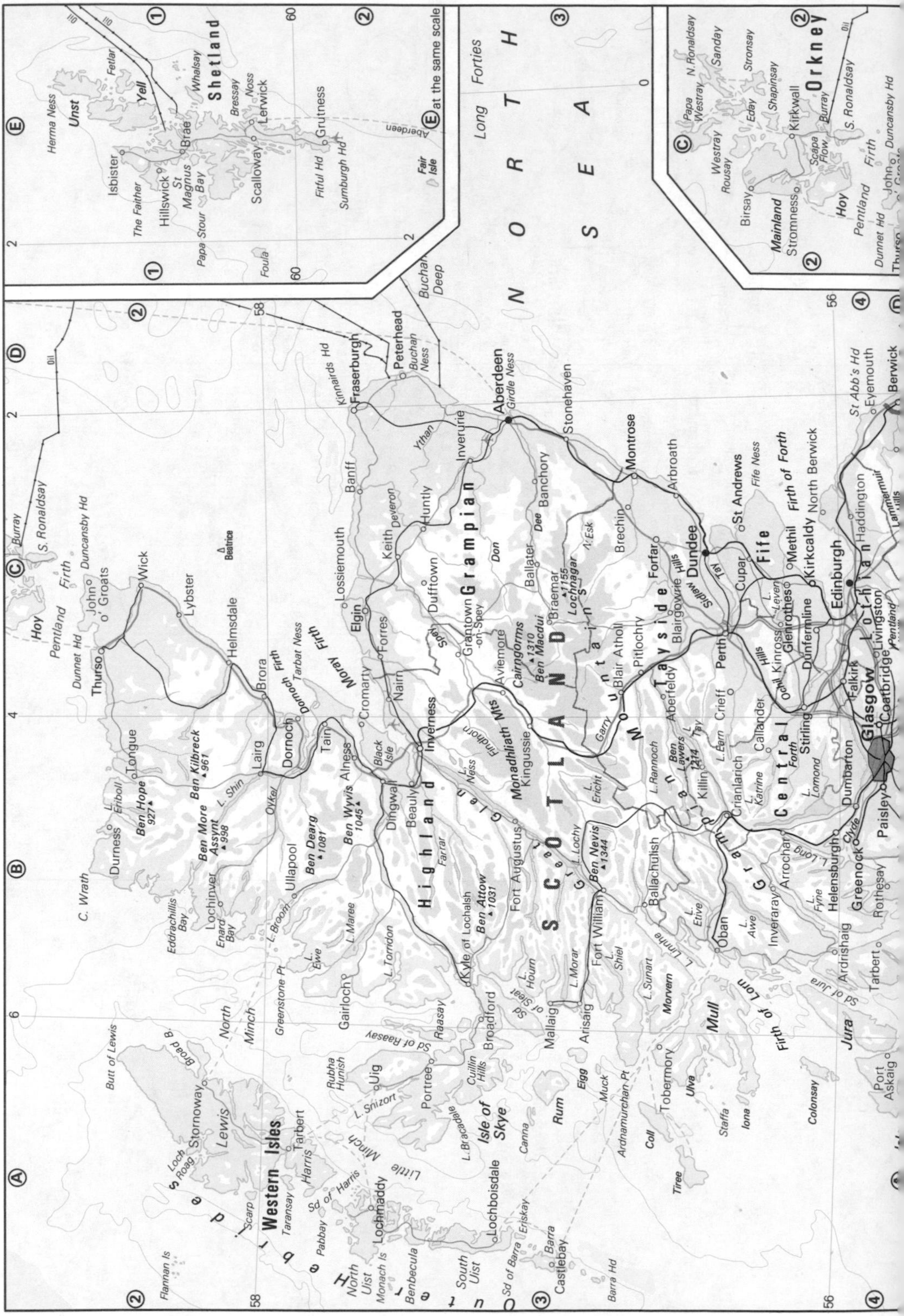

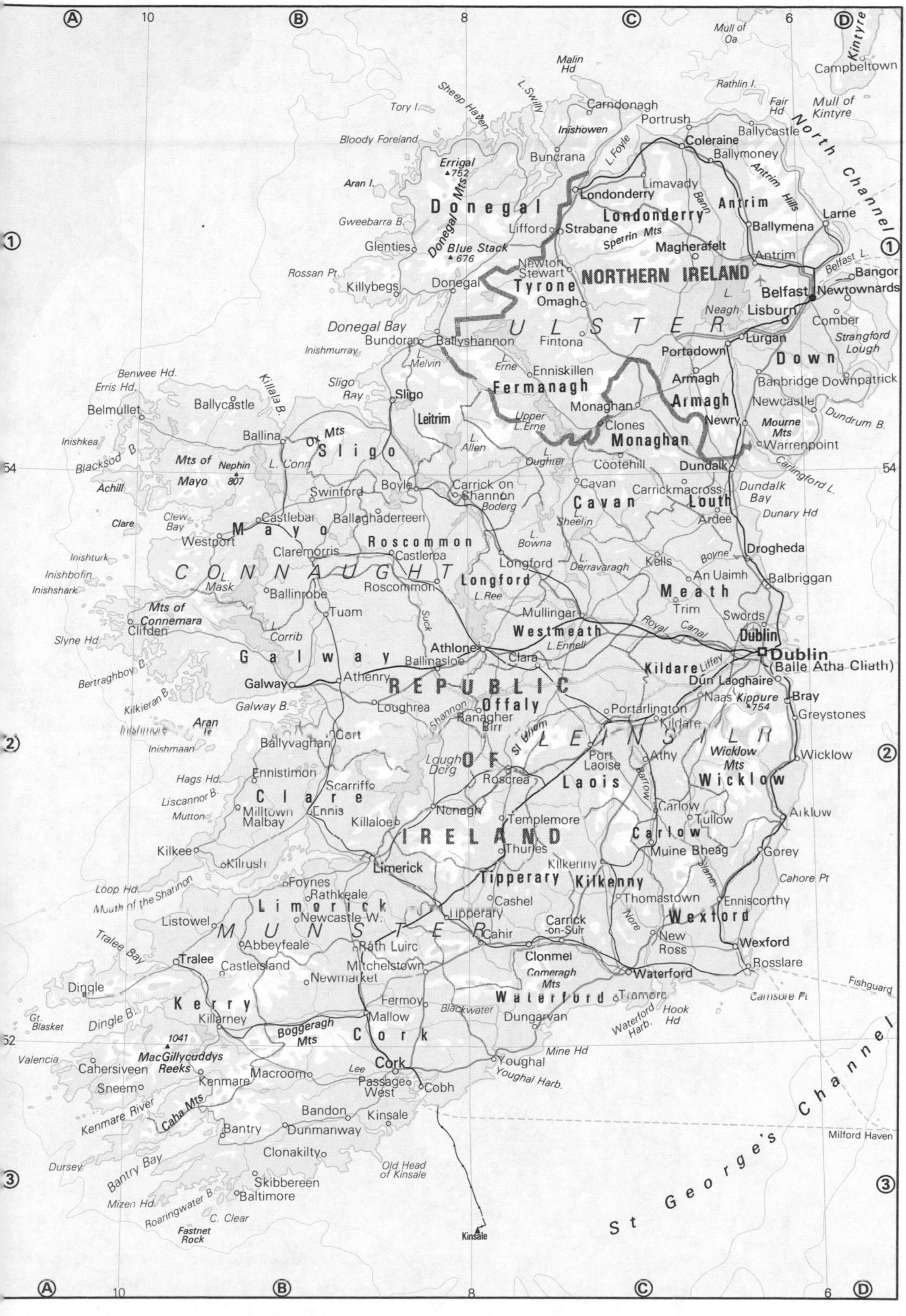
A
B
C
D
10
8
6
54
52
1
2
3
Mull of Oa
Kintyre
Campbeltown
Malin Hd
Rathlin I.
Sheep Haven
L. Swilly
Fair Hd
Mull of Kintyre
Tory I.
Carndonagh
Portrush
North Channel
Inishowen
Ballycastle
Bloody Foreland
L. Foyle
Coleraine
Buncrana
Ballymoney
Errigal 752
Antrim Hills
Aran I.
Limavady
Donegal
Londonderry
Bann
Antrim
Londonderry
Larne
Gweebarra B.
Lifford
Strabane
Sperrin Mts
Ballymena
Glenties
Donegal Mts
Blue Stack 676
Magherafelt
Antrim
Rossan Pt.
Newton Stewart
NORTHERN IRELAND
Belfast L.
Bangor
Killybegs
Donegal
Tyrone
L. Neagh
Belfast
Newtownards
Omagh
Lisburn
Donegal Bay
Comber
Bundoran
Ballyshannon
ULSTER
Strangford Lough
Fintona
Lurgan
Inishmurray
Portadown
Down
L. Melvin
L. Erne
Enniskillen
Benwee Hd.
Killala B.
Sligo Bay
Armagh
Banbridge
Downpatrick
Erris Hd.
Sligo
Fermanagh
Armagh
Belmullet
Ballycastle
Leitrim
Monaghan
Newcastle
Upper L. Erne
Newry
Mourne Mts
Dundrum B.
Ballina
Ox Mts
Clones
Inishkea
L. Allen
Monaghan
Warrenpoint
Sligo
Blacksod B.
Mts of Mayo
Nephin 807
L. Conn
L. Oughter
Cootehill
Dundalk
Carlingford L.
Achill
Boyle
Carrick on Shannon
Cavan
Dundalk Bay
Swinford
Carrickmacross
Boderg
Cavan
Louth
Clew Bay
Castlebar
Ballaghaderreen
L. Sheelin
Ardee
Dunany Hd
Clare
Mayo
Westport
Claremorris
Roscommon
L. Bowna
Drogheda
Castlerea
Inishturk
Longford
L. Derravaragh
Kells
Boyne
CONNAUGHT
Inishbofin
L. Mask
An Uaimh
Balbriggan
Longford
Inishshark
Ballinrobe
Roscommon
L. Ree
Meath
Tuam
Trim
Mts of Connemara
Mullingar
Swords
Clifden
Suck
Royal Canal
L. Corrib
Westmeath
Slyne Hd.
Dublin
L. Ennell
Athlone
Dublin
Galway
Ballinasloe
Clara
(Baile Atha Cliath)
Kildare
Liffey
Bertraghboy B.
Athenry
Galway
REPUBLIC
Dún Laoghaire
Kilkieran B.
Naas
Kippure 754
Bray
Offaly
Galway B.
Loughrea
Portarlington
Shannon
Banagher
Kildare
Greystones
Aran Is.
Birr
Inishmore
Gort
LEINSTER
Slieve Bloom
Inishmaan
Ballyvaghan
Port Laoise
Wicklow Mts
Wicklow
Lough Derg
OF
Athy
Hags Hd.
Ennistimon
Roscrea
Laois
Wicklow
Barrow
Scarriff
Clare
Liscannor B.
Milltown Malbay
Ennis
Carlow
Nenagh
Tullow
Mutton
Killaloe
Templemore
Arklow
IRELAND
Carlow
Kilkee
Thurles
Muine Bheag
Gorey
Kilrush
Limerick
Kilkenny
Slaney
Foynes
Tipperary
Kilkenny
Cahore Pt
Loop Hd.
Rathkeale
Thomastown
Mouth of the Shannon
Cashel
Enniscorthy
Limerick
Newcastle W.
Tipperary
Nore
Listowel
Wexford
MUNSTER
Carrick -on-Suir
Cahir
New Ross
Abbeyfeale
Tralee Bay
Ráth Luirc
Wexford
Tralee
Clonmel
Castleisland
Mitchelstown
Rosslare
Waterford
Comeragh Mts
Newmarket
Fishguard
Dingle
Fermoy
Waterford
Tramore
Carnsore Pt
Kerry
Mallow
Blackwater
Hook Hd
Gt. Blasket
Dingle B.
Killarney
Boggeragh Mts
Waterford Harb.
Dungarvan
Cork
1041
Mine Hd
Valencia
MacGillycuddys Reeks
Cahersiveen
Youghal
Lee
Cork
Macroom
Youghal Harb.
Kenmare
Sneem
Passage West
Cobh
Kenmare River
Caha Mts
Bandon
Kinsale
Bantry
Dunmanway
Milford Haven
Clonakilty
Dursey
Bantry Bay
Old Head of Kinsale
Skibbereen
Mizen Hd.
Roaringwater B.
Baltimore
C. Clear
Fastnet Rock
Kinsale
St George's Channel
A
B
8
C
6
D

1:2.5M 0 25 50 75 100 km / 0 25 50 mls

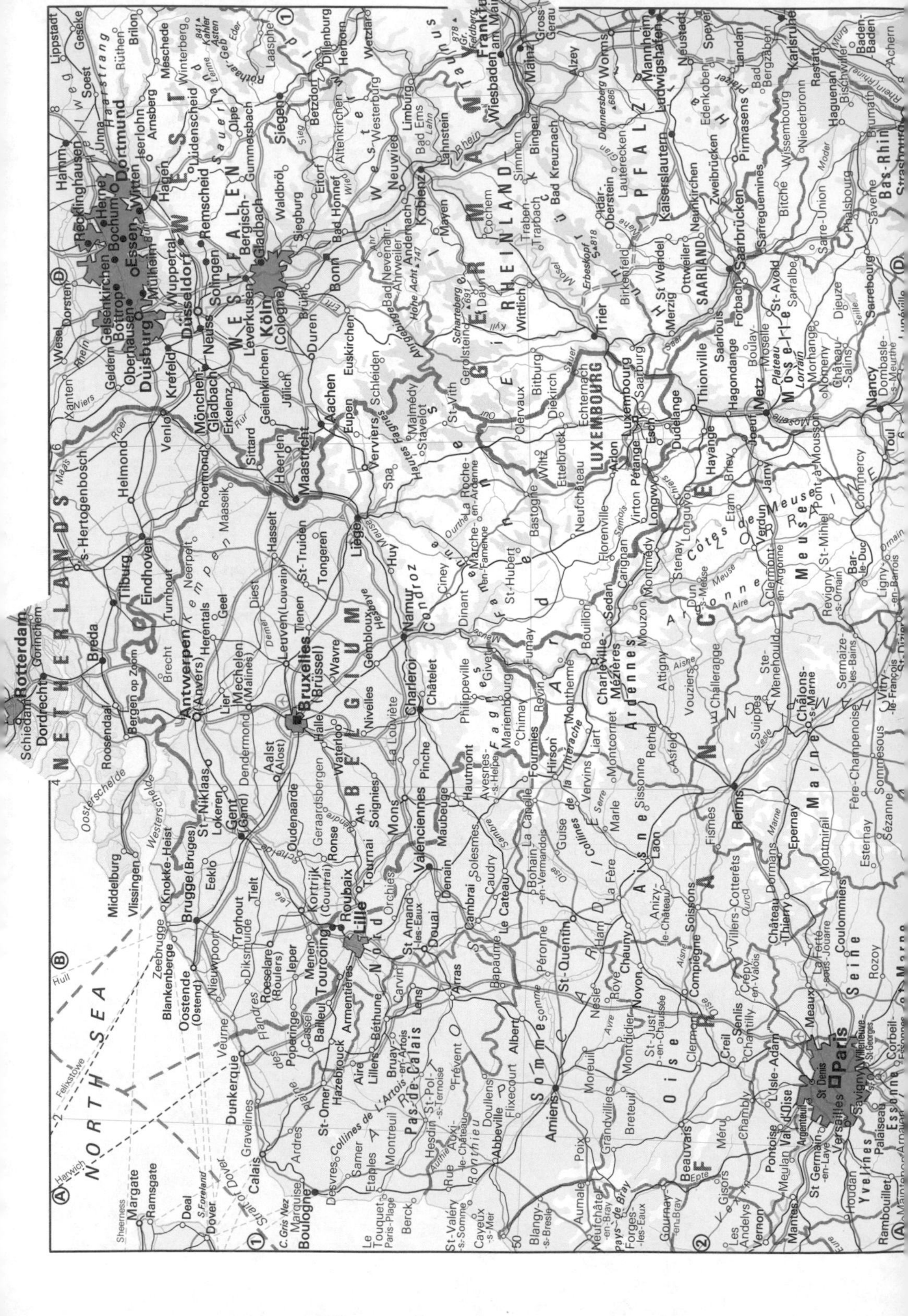

GERMANY
SWITZERLAND
AUSTRIA
FRANCE
ITALY
LIECHTENSTEIN
LOMBARDIA
PIEMONTE
TRENTINO
VENETO
VALLE D'AOSTA
VORALBERG
Innsbruck
Bolzano (Bozen)
Merano
Bressanone
Trento
Verona
Vicenza
Padova (Padua)
Venezia (Venice)
Treviso
Mestre
Bologna
Ferrara
Modena
Parma
Piacenza
Cremona
Brescia
Bergamo
Milano (Milan)
Monza
Como
Lecco
Lugano
Bellinzona
Locarno
Novara
Vercelli
Alessandria
Torino (Turin)
Aosta
Zürich
Luzern (Lucerne)
Bern (Berne)
Basel (Basle)
Lausanne
Genève (Geneva)
Annecy
Chambéry
Grenoble
Besançon
Chur
Davos
St Moritz
Sondrio
Mantova (Mantua)
Reggio nell'Emilia
Bodensee
Lago Maggiore
Lago di Garda
L. Léman (L. of Geneva)
Mt Blanc 4810
Matterhorn 4478
Jungfrau
Alpi Pennine
Alpes Cottiennes
Chablais
Vanoise
Engadin
Ortles
Dolomiti

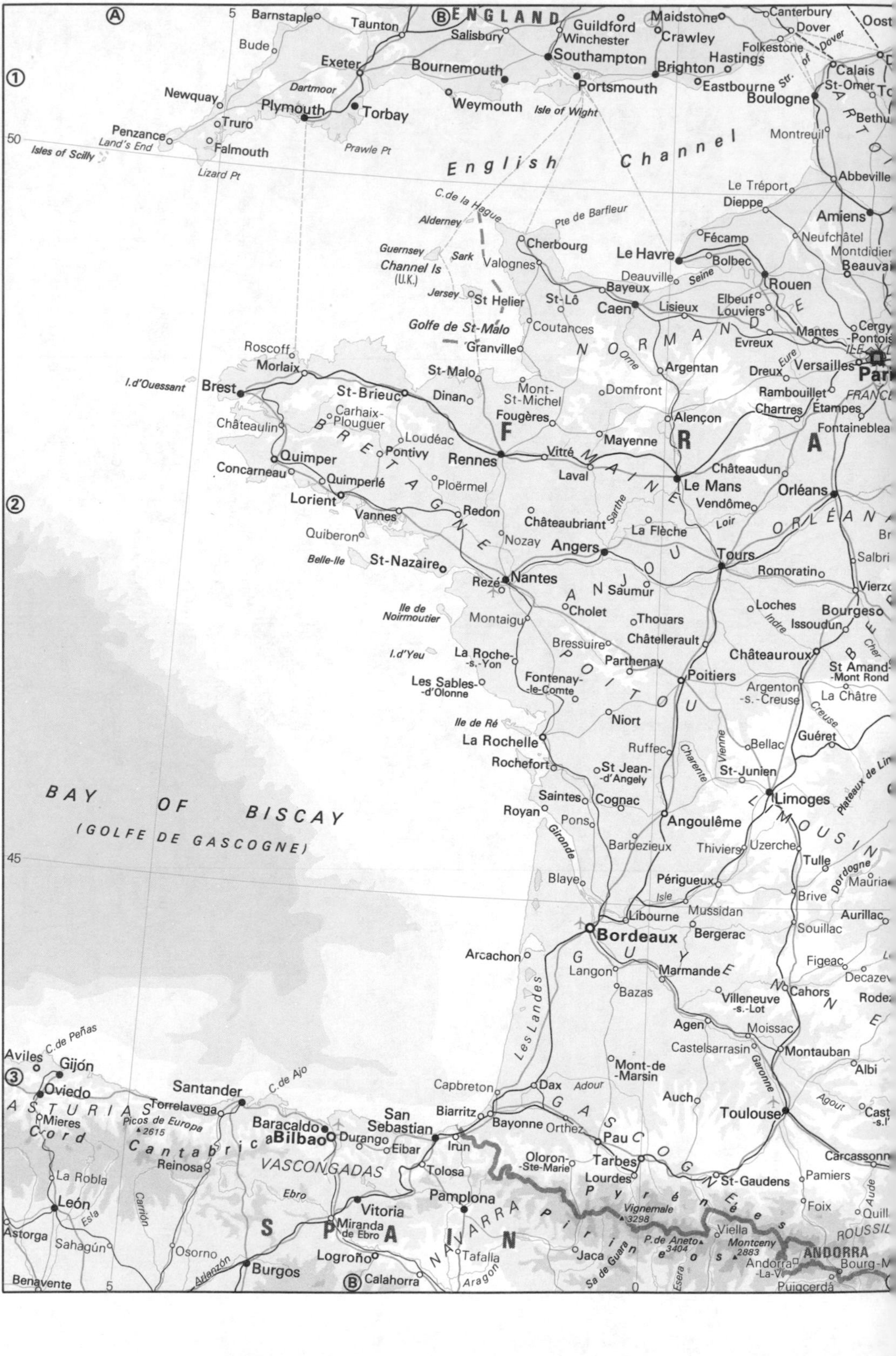
ENGLAND
Barnstaple
Taunton
Bude
Exeter
Salisbury
Guildford
Winchester
Maidstone
Canterbury
Dover
Crawley
Folkestone
Hastings
Southampton
Bournemouth
Brighton
Eastbourne
Portsmouth
Isle of Wight
Weymouth
Dartmoor
Newquay
Plymouth
Torbay
Truro
Penzance
Land's End
Falmouth
Isles of Scilly
Lizard Pt
Prawle Pt
English Channel
Str. of Dover
Calais
St-Omer
Boulogne
Montreuil
Abbeville
Le Tréport
Dieppe
Amiens
Neufchâtel
Montdidier
Beauvai
Fécamp
Le Havre
Bolbec
Seine
Rouen
C.de la Hague
Alderney
Pte de Barfleur
Cherbourg
Guernsey
Sark
Channel Is
(U.K.)
Valognes
Jersey
St Helier
St-Lô
Bayeux
Deauville
Caen
Lisieux
Elbeuf
Louviers
Golfe de St-Malo
Coutances
Granville
NORMANDIE
Evreux
Mantes
Cergy-Pontois
Versailles
Pari
Roscoff
Morlaix
I.d'Ouessant
Brest
St-Malo
Dinan
Mont-St-Michel
Argentan
Orne
Domfront
Dreux
Eure
Rambouillet
Chartres
Étampes
St-Brieuc
Carhaix-Plouguer
Châteaulin
Loudéac
Fougères
Alençon
Fontainebleau
Quimper
Pontivy
Rennes
Vitré
Mayenne
F
R
A
Concarneau
Quimperlé
Lorient
Ploërmel
Laval
MAINE
Le Mans
Châteaudun
Orléans
Vendôme
Vannes
Redon
Quiberon
BRETAGNE
Châteaubriant
Sarthe
La Flèche
Loir
ORLÉANAIS
Belle-Ile
St-Nazaire
Nozay
Angers
Tours
Salbri
Rezé
Nantes
ANJOU
Saumur
Romorantin
Vierzo
Ile de Noirmoutier
Montaigu
Cholet
Thouars
Loches
Indre
Bourges
Issoudun
I.d'Yeu
La Roche-s.-Yon
Bressuire
Châtellerault
Châteauroux
Cher
Parthenay
St Amand-Mont Rond
Les Sables-d'Olonne
Fontenay-le-Comte
POITOU
Poitiers
Argenton-s.-Creuse
La Châtre
Niort
Creuse
Ile de Ré
La Rochelle
Ruffec
Bellac
Guéret
Charente
Vienne
Rochefort
St Jean-d'Angely
St-Junien
Plateaux de Lin
Saintes
Cognac
Limoges
BAY OF BISCAY
(GOLFE DE GASCOGNE)
Royan
Pons
Gironde
Angoulême
LIMOUSIN
Barbezieux
Thiviers
Uzerche
Tulle
Dordogne
Blaye
Périgueux
Mauria
Isle
Brive
Libourne
Mussidan
Aurillac
Bordeaux
Bergerac
Souillac
Arcachon
GUYENNE
Langon
Figeac
Marmande
Decazev
Bazas
Cahors
Rode
Villeneuve-s.-Lot
Les Landes
Agen
Moissac
Castelsarrasin
Montauban
Garonne
Albi
Mont-de-Marsin
Aviles
C.de Peñas
Gijón
Oviedo
Santander
C.de Ajo
Capbreton
Dax
Adour
ASTURIAS
Torrelavega
Auch
Toulouse
Agout
Cast
Mieres
Picos de Europa
2615
Cord
Baracaldo
Bilbao
San Sebastian
Biarritz
Bayonne
Orthez
GASCOGNE
Cantabric
Durango
Eibar
Irun
Pau
Reinosa
VASCONGADAS
Oloron-Ste-Marie
Tarbes
Carcassonn
La Robla
Tolosa
Lourdes
St-Gaudens
Pamiers
Ebro
Carrión
Pamplona
Pyrénées
Pirineos
Vignemale
3298
Foix
Aude
Quill
León
Esla
Vitoria
NAVARRA
Viella
ROUSSIL
Astorga
Sahagún
S
Miranda de Ebro
A
I
N
P.de Aneto
3404
Montceny
2883
ANDORRA
Osorno
Logroño
Tafalla
Jaca
Andorra-La-V
Bourg-M
Arlanzón
Burgos
Sa de Guara
Esera
Benavente
Calahorra
Aragon
Puigcerdá

1:5M
0 50 100 150 200 km
0 50 100 mls
Vlissingen
Eindhoven
Zeebrugge
Antwerpen (Anvers)
Brugge
Mechelen
Gent
Hasselt
Maastricht
Bruxelles (Brüssel)
Leuven
St-Truiden
BELGIUM
Roubaix
Tournai
Soignies
Namur
Liège
Mons
Valenciennes
Charleroi
Denain
Maubeuge
Marche
Ardennes
Fourmies
Bastogne
St-Quentin
Charleville-Mézières
Sedan
Arlon
LUXEMBOURG
Luxembourg
Laon
Compiègne
Reims
Verdun
Longwy
Thionville
Metz
Châlons-s.-M.
Epernay
Meaux
Sézanne
Provins
Vitry-l.-F.
St-Dizier
Toul
Nancy
Romilly-s.-S
Troyes
Bar-s-A.
Chaumont
Sens
Joigny
Châtillon
Langres
Auxerre
Avallon
Dijon
Beaune
Dôle
Autun
Chalon-s.-S.
Le Creusot
Lons-l.-S.
Montceau-l.-M.
Digoin
Mâcon
Roanne
Vichy
Thiers
Tarare
Lyon
Villeurbanne
St-Chamond
St-Étienne
Annonay
Vienne
Le Puy
Mt Mézenc 1754
Pradelles
Aubenas
Mende
Montélimar
Nyons
Orange
Alès
Bagnols-s.-Cèze
Avignon
Carpentras
Cavaillon
Nîmes
Arles
Salon-d.-P.
Montpellier
Sète
Martigues
Marseille
Aubagne
Toulon
Hyères
Iles d'Hyères
Narbonne
Golfe du Lion
Perpignan
C. de Creus
Massif Central
LANGUEDOC
BOURGOGNE
NIVERNAIS
CHAMPAGNE
LORRAINE
FRANCE
FRANCHE-COMTÉ
Jura
Vosges
ALSACE
SAVOIE
DAUPHINÉ
PROVENCE
Besançon
Vesoul
Belfort
Montbéliard
Épinal
St Dié
Colmar
Mulhouse
Strasbourg
Sarrebourg
Sarreguemines
Saarlouis
Saarbrücken
SAARLAND
Kaiserslautern
Pirmasens
Trier
Bitburg
Bad-Kreuznach
Bingen
RHEINLAND PFALZ
Ludwigshafen
Mannheim
Worms
Mainz
Wiesbaden
Koblenz
Andernach
Limburg
Bonn
Bad Godesberg
Euskirchen
Aachen
Köln
Düsseldorf
Mönchengladbach
WESTFALEN
Siegen
Marburg
Giessen
Bad Hersfeld
Alsfeld
Fulda
HESSEN
Frankfurt
Offenbach
Aschaffenburg
Darmstadt
Heidelberg
Speyer
Karlsruhe
Pforzheim
Rastatt
Baden-Baden
Stuttgart
Esslingen
Ludwigsburg
Heilbronn
Crailsheim
Ansbach
BADEN-WÜRTTEMBERG
Tübingen
Reutlingen
Offenburg
Freiburg
Schwarzwald
Schwäbische Alb
Heidenheim
Ulm
Biberach
Tuttlingen
Ravensburg
Konstanz
Friedrichshafen
Lindau
Lörrach
Schaffhausen
Erfurt
Eisenach
Jena
Gera
Zwickau
E.GER.
Thüringer Wald
Plauen
Hof
Coburg
Cheb
Schweinfurt
Bamberg
Bayreuth
Würzburg
Kitzingen
Erlangen
Weiden
Amberg
Fürth
Nürnberg
Parsberg
Regensburg
Fränkische Alb
Donauwörth
Ingolstadt
Landshut
Dachau
Augsburg
München
Starnberg
Landsberg
Memmingen
Kempten
Rosenheim
Bad Tölz
Füssen
Kufstein
Garmisch-P.
BAYERN
WEST GERMANY
Donau
AUSTRIA
Innsbruck
Brenner 1370
Dornbirn
Feldkirch
Bludenz
Landeck
Wildspitze 3774
LIECHTENSTEIN
Vaduz
Basel
Olten
Zürich
Winterthur
St Gallen
Zug
Schwyz
Luzern
Biel
Bern
Neuchâtel
Pontarlier
Fribourg
Thun
Interlaken
SWITZERLAND
Lausanne
Vevey
Montreux
Jungfrau 4158
L. Léman
Genève
Brig
Rhône
Simplon 2009
Martigny
2469 Col du Gd St Bernard
Matterhorn 4477
Mt Blanc 4807
Aosta
St Gotthard 2112
Chur
Arosa
Rhein
St Moritz
Ortles 3899
Bellinzona
Domodossola
L. Maggiore
Lugano
L. di Como
Sondrio
Edolo
Merano
Bolzano
Brunico
Marmolada 3342
Trento
Rovereto
Bassano
Lôvere
Lecco
Bergamo
L. di Garda
Como
Varese
Busto Arsizio
Monza
Milano (Milan)
Biella
Novara
Ivrea
Vercelli
Lodi
Pavia
Brescia
Verona
Vicenza
Cremona
Mantova
Adige
Rovigo
Piacenza
Casale Monf.
Torino (Turin)
Asti
Alessandria
Parma
Carpi
Modena
Ferrara
Reggio n.-E.
Bologna
Novi Ligure
Ovada
Alba
Appennino Ligure
Genova (Genoa)
Rapallo
Mondovi
Cuneo
Mte Viso 3841
Stura
Gran Paradiso 4061
Col du Mt Cenis 2803
Susa
Albertville
Annecy
Aix-l.-B.
Chambéry
Bourg
Bellegarde
St Claude
Villefranche
Voiron
Grenoble
Massif du Pelvoux
Romans-s.-I.
Valence
Bourg-d.-P.
Briançon
Corps
Gap
Durance
Mt Pelat 3053
Sisteron
Digne
Var
C. de Tende 1870
Castellane
Verdon
Nice
Monte Carlo
MONACO
Grasse
Draguignan
Cannes
St Raphaël
Aix-en-Provence
St Tropez
Côte d'Azur
Savona
Alassio
Imperia
San Remo
G. di Genova
La Spezia
Ligurian Sea
Carrara
Mte Cimone 2165
Massa
Viareggio
Pistoia
Prato
Lucca
Firenze (Florence)
Pisa
Pontedera
Livorno
Cecina
Siena
Follonica
Piombino
Portoferraio
Elba
Grosseto
Pianosa
Orbetello
Giglio
Montecristo
Cap Corse
G. de St Florent
Bastia
Calvi
Mt Cinto 2710
Ponte Lecca
CORSE (CORSICA)
Corte
Ajaccio
C. Rosso
Cateraggio
ITALY
ALPS
Po
Taro
Doubs
Saône
Seine
Yonne
Aisne
Oise
Meuse
Mosel
Loire
Allier
Werra
Fulda
Main

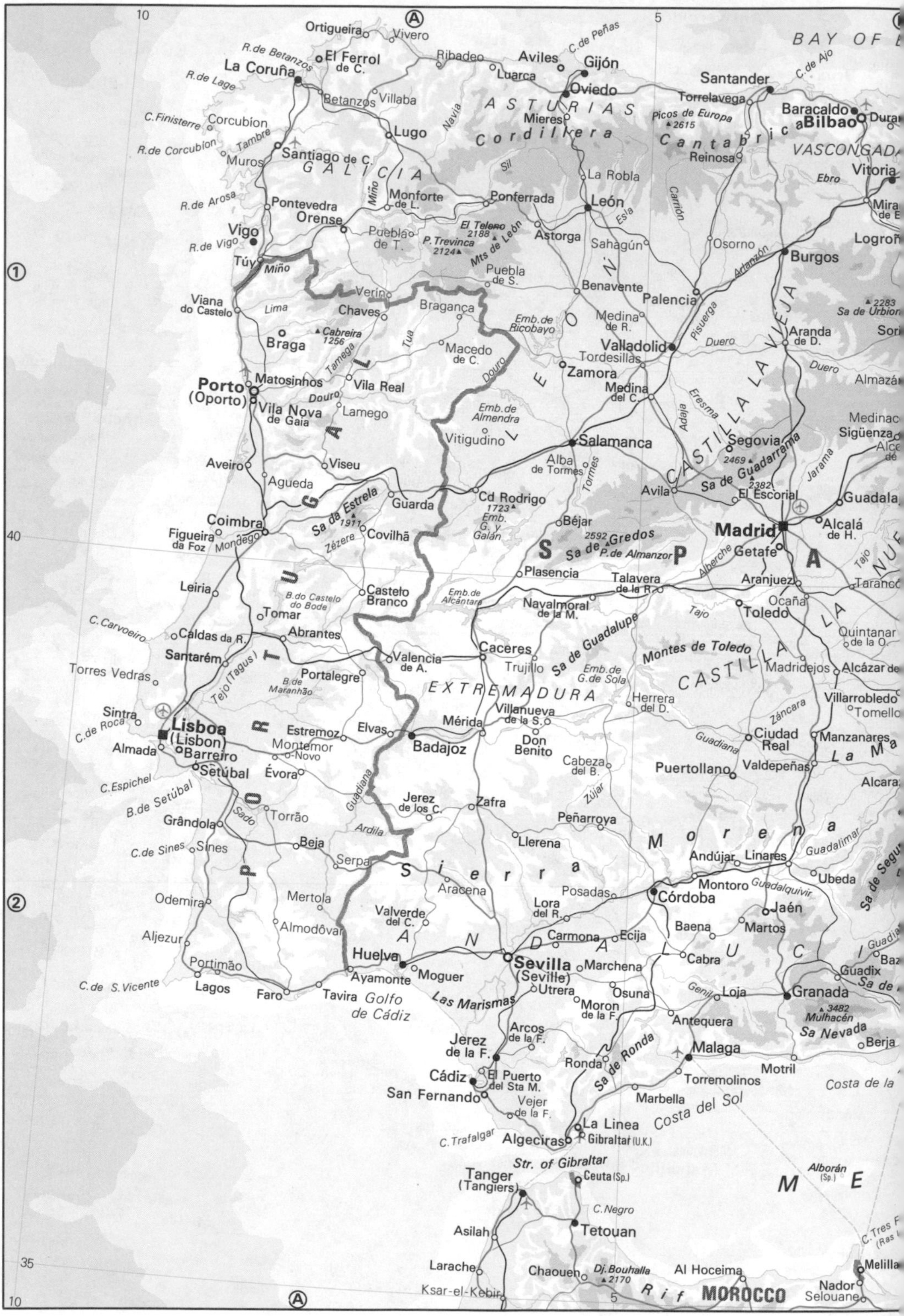

BAY OF
Ortigueira
Vivero
R.de Betanzos
El Ferrol de C.
La Coruña
R.de Lage
Betanzos
Villaba
Ribadeo
Luarca
Aviles
C. de Peñas
Gijón
Oviedo
Mieres
ASTURIAS
Cordillera Cantabrica
Santander
Torrelavega
C. de Ajo
Baracaldo
Bilbao
Picos de Europa 2615
Reinosa
VASCONGADAS
Vitoria
Ebro
C.Finisterre
Corcubíon
R.de Corcubíon
Tambre
Muros
Santiago de C.
Lugo
Navia
GALICIA
Sil
La Robla
R.de Arosa
Pontevedra
Miño
Monforte de L.
Ponferrada
León
Esla
Carrión
Orense
Vigo
R.de Vigo
Puebla de T.
El Teleno 2188
P. Trevinca 2124
Mts de León
Astorga
Sahagún
Osorno
Logroño
Túy
Miño
Puebla de S.
Burgos
Arlanzón
Viana do Castelo
Lima
Verín
Chaves
Bragança
Benavente
Palencia
Pisuerga
Sa de Urbion 2283
Braga
Cabreira 1256
Tamega
Tua
Macedo de C.
Emb.de Ricobayo
Medina de R.
Valladolid
Aranda de D.
Soria
Duero
Tordesillas
Zamora
LEON
Porto (Oporto)
Matosinhos
Vila Real
Douro
Vila Nova de Gaia
Lamego
Emb.de Almendra
Medina del C.
Eresma
Adaja
CASTILLA LA VIEJA
Almazán
Medinaceli
Sigüenza
Vitigudino
Salamanca
Segovia
Aveiro
Viseu
Alba de Tormes
Tormes
2469
Sa de Guadarrama
Jarama
Agueda
2382
El Escorial
Avila
Guadalajara
Cd Rodrigo
Guarda
1723
Emb. G. y Galán
Coimbra
Sa da Estrela
1911
Covilhã
Figueira da Foz
Mondego
Zézere
Béjar
2592 Sa de Gredos
P. de Almanzor
Madrid
Alcalá de H.
Getafe
Alberche
Tajo
SPAIN
PORTUGAL
Leiria
Castelo Branco
B.do Castelo do Bode
Plasencia
Talavera de la R.
Aranjuez
Tarancón
Emb.de Alcántara
Navalmoral de la M.
Ocaña
Toledo
Tomar
C. Carvoeiro
Caldas da R.
Abrantes
Tajo
Quintanar de la O.
Santarém
Tejo (Tagus)
Valencia de A.
Caceres
Sa de Guadalupe
Montes de Toledo
Torres Vedras
Portalegre
Trujillo
Emb.de G.de Sola
CASTILLA
Madridejos
Alcázar de
B.de Maranhão
EXTREMADURA
Herrera del D.
Villarrobledo
Tomelloso
Sintra
C.de Roca
Lisboa (Lisbon)
Estremoz
Elvas
Mérida
Villanueva de la S.
Zancara
Almada
Barreiro
Montemor-o-Novo
Badajoz
Don Benito
Guadiana
Ciudad Real
Manzanares
La Mancha
Setúbal
Évora
Cabeza del B.
Puertollano
Valdepeñas
C.Espichel
B.de Setúbal
Sado
Guadiana
Jerez de los C.
Zafra
Zújar
Alcaraz
Torrão
Grândola
Ardila
Peñarroya
C.de Sines
Sines
Beja
Llerena
Sierra Morena
Guadalimar
Serpa
Andújar
Linares
Aracena
Posadas
Montoro
Guadalquivir
Ubeda
Sa de Segura
Odemira
Mertola
Lora del R.
Córdoba
Jaén
Valverde del C.
Aljezur
Almodôvar
Baena
Martos
Carmona
Ecija
ANDALUCIA
Huelva
Sevilla (Seville)
Marchena
Cabra
Guadix
Baza
Portimão
Ayamonte
Moguer
Sa de
C. de S. Vicente
Lagos
Faro
Tavira
Golfo de Cádiz
Las Marismas
Utrera
Osuna
Genil
Loja
Granada
Moron de la F.
3482 Mulhacén
Sa Nevada
Antequera
Arcos de la F.
Jerez de la F.
Sa de Ronda
Malaga
Berja
Ronda
Motril
Cádiz
El Puerto del Sta M.
Torremolinos
Costa de la
San Fernando
Vejer de la F.
Marbella
Costa del Sol
C. Trafalgar
La Linea
Algeciras
Gibraltar (U.K.)
Str. of Gibraltar
Tanger (Tangiers)
Ceuta (Sp.)
Alborán (Sp.)
ME
C.Negro
Tetouan
Asilah
C. Tres F
Larache
Chaouen
Dj.Bouhalla 2170
Al Hoceima
Melilla
Nador
Ksar-el-Kebir
Rif
MOROCCO
Selouane
10
5
40
35
①
②
Ⓐ

FRANCE
Toulouse
Albi
Montpellier
Nîmes
Arles
Salon-d.-P.
Aix-en-Provence
Marseille
Martigues
Aubagne
Toulon
Hyères
Béziers
Sète
Golfe du Lion
Carcassonne
Narbonne
Perpignan
ROUSSILLON
Castres-s.l'A
Auch
Mont-de-Marsin
Dax
Capbreton
Biarritz
Bayonne
Orthez
Pau
Tarbes
Lourdes
Oloron-Ste-Marie
St-Gaudens
Pamiers
Foix
Quillan
GASCOGNE
Pyrénées
Vignemale 3298
P. de Aneto 3404
Montceny 2883
Viella
ANDORRA
Andorra-La-V.
Bourg-Madame
Puigcerdá
Irun
Tolosa
Pamplona
NAVARRA
Tafalla
Jaca
Calahorra
Alfaro
Tudela
Tarazona
Alagón
Zaragoza
Huesca
Barbastro
Sa de Guara
Sa del Codi
Figueras
C. de Creus
Gerona
Costa Brava
San Felíu de G.
Vich
Lérida
CATALUÑA
Sabadell
Tarrasa
Granollérs
Mataró
Badalona
Barcelona
Villanuova y G.
Valls
Reus
Tarragona
Golfo de San Jorge
Tortosa
Amposta
C. de Tortosa
Vinaroz
Benicarló
Torreblanca
ARAGÓN
Emb. de Mequinenza
Caspe
Calatayud
Daroca
Alcaniz
Monreal del C.
Sa de Albarracín
Sa de Gudar
2019 Penarroya
Teruel
Sarrion
Cuenca
Castellon de la P.
Villarreal
Segorbe
Sagunto
Is Columbretes
Golfo de Valencia
Valencia
VALENCIA
Utiel
Motilla del P.
La Roda
Albacete
Alcira
Játiva
Gandia
Onteniente
Denia
C. de la Nao
Almansa
Villena
Alcoy
Benidorm
Hellín
MURCIA
Elda
Alicante
Elche
Orihuela
Cieza
Caravaca
Murcia
Costa Blanca
Totana
Lorca
Cartagena
C. de Palos
G. de Mazarrón
Aguilas
Vera
C. de Gata
C. Formentor
C. de Caballeria
Menorca
Ciudadela
Mahón
C. Binibeca
Mallorca
Alcudia
Mayor 1445
Capdepora
Palma de Mallorca
Manacor
Santañy
C. de Salinas
Cabrera
Ibiza
S. Antonio Abad
Formentera
ISLAS BALEARES
(BALEARIC ISLANDS)
(Sp.)
MEDITERRANEAN SEA
Alger (Algiers)
Dellys
Bojaïa (Bougie)
Tizi Ouzou
Djurdjura
Kherrata
Sétif
Cherchell
Boufarik
Blida
Ténès
Dahra
Miliana
Médéa
Bouïra
Beni Mansour
Bir Rabalou
Bj bou Arréridj
Mts du Hodna
Khemis
El Asnam
Bosquet
C. Ferrat
Massif de l'Ouarsenis
Ksar El Boukhari
M'Sila
Mostaganem
Arzew
Relizane
Mers el Kebir
Oran
Sig
O. Tlelat
Mohammadia
Aïn Oussera
Aïn el Hadjel
Chott el Hodna
Barika
ALGERIA
Beni-Saf
Aïn Témouchent
Mascara
Tiaret
Plat. du Sersou
Z. Chergui
Bou Saâda
Monts des Ouled Nail
Sidi-bel-Abbès
Frenda
40
35
5
0

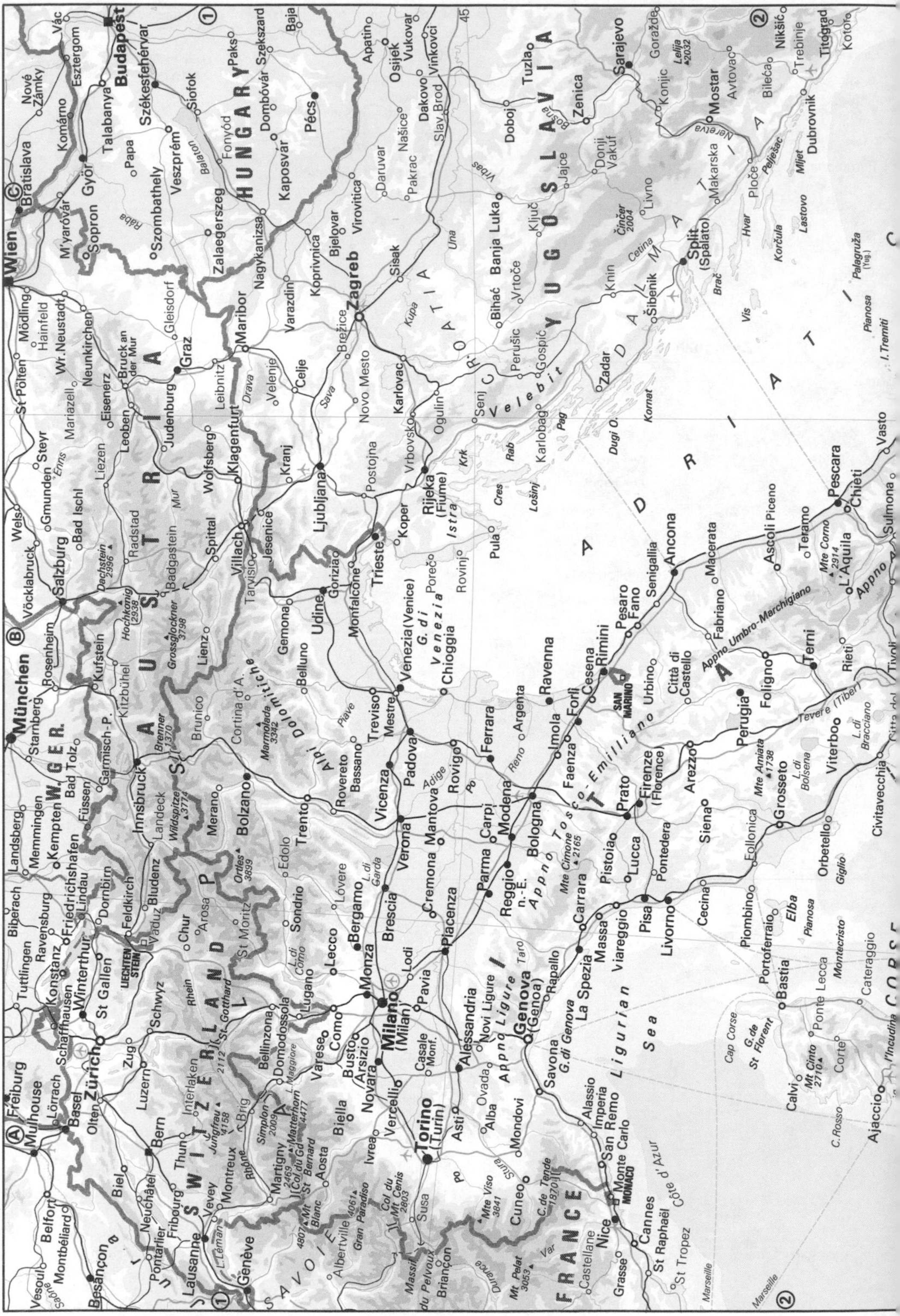
ITALY
SWITZERLAND
AUSTRIA
W. GER.
HUNGARY
YUGOSLAVIA
FRANCE
CROATIA
DALMATIA
SAVOIE
LIECHTENSTEIN
SAN MARINO
MONACO
ADRIATIC
Ligurian Sea
G. di Venezia
G. di Genova
Alpi Dolomitiche
Appno Tosco-Emilliano
Appno Umbro-Marchigiano
Appno Ligure
Velebit
Istra
Wien
Bratislava
Budapest
Győr
Sopron
Szombathely
Veszprém
Székesfehérvár
Pécs
Kaposvár
Nagykanizsa
Zalaegerszeg
Balaton
Graz
Maribor
Klagenfurt
Villach
Salzburg
Innsbruck
Linz
München
Kempten
Zürich
Basel
Bern
Luzern
Genève
Lausanne
Zagreb
Ljubljana
Rijeka (Fiume)
Trieste
Sarajevo
Split (Spalato)
Mostar
Dubrovnik
Zadar
Banja Luka
Osijek
Bolzano
Trento
Verona
Vicenza
Padova
Venezia (Venice)
Treviso
Udine
Milano (Milan)
Torino (Turin)
Genova (Genoa)
Bergamo
Brescia
Como
Novara
Piacenza
Parma
Reggio n.-E.
Modena
Bologna
Ferrara
Ravenna
Rimini
Pesaro
Ancona
Firenze (Florence)
Prato
Pisa
Livorno
Lucca
Siena
Arezzo
Perugia
Terni
Pescara
L'Aquila
La Spezia
Alessandria
Cuneo
Aosta
Nice
Cannes
Monte Carlo
San Remo
Bastia
Ajaccio
Elba
Mte Viso 3841
Gran Paradiso 4061
Mt Blanc 4807
Matterhorn 4477
Jungfrau 4158
Grossglockner 3798
Marmolada 3342
Brenner 1370
Simplon 2009
St Gotthard 2112
Mte Corno 2914
Mte Cimone 2165
Mte Amiata 1738

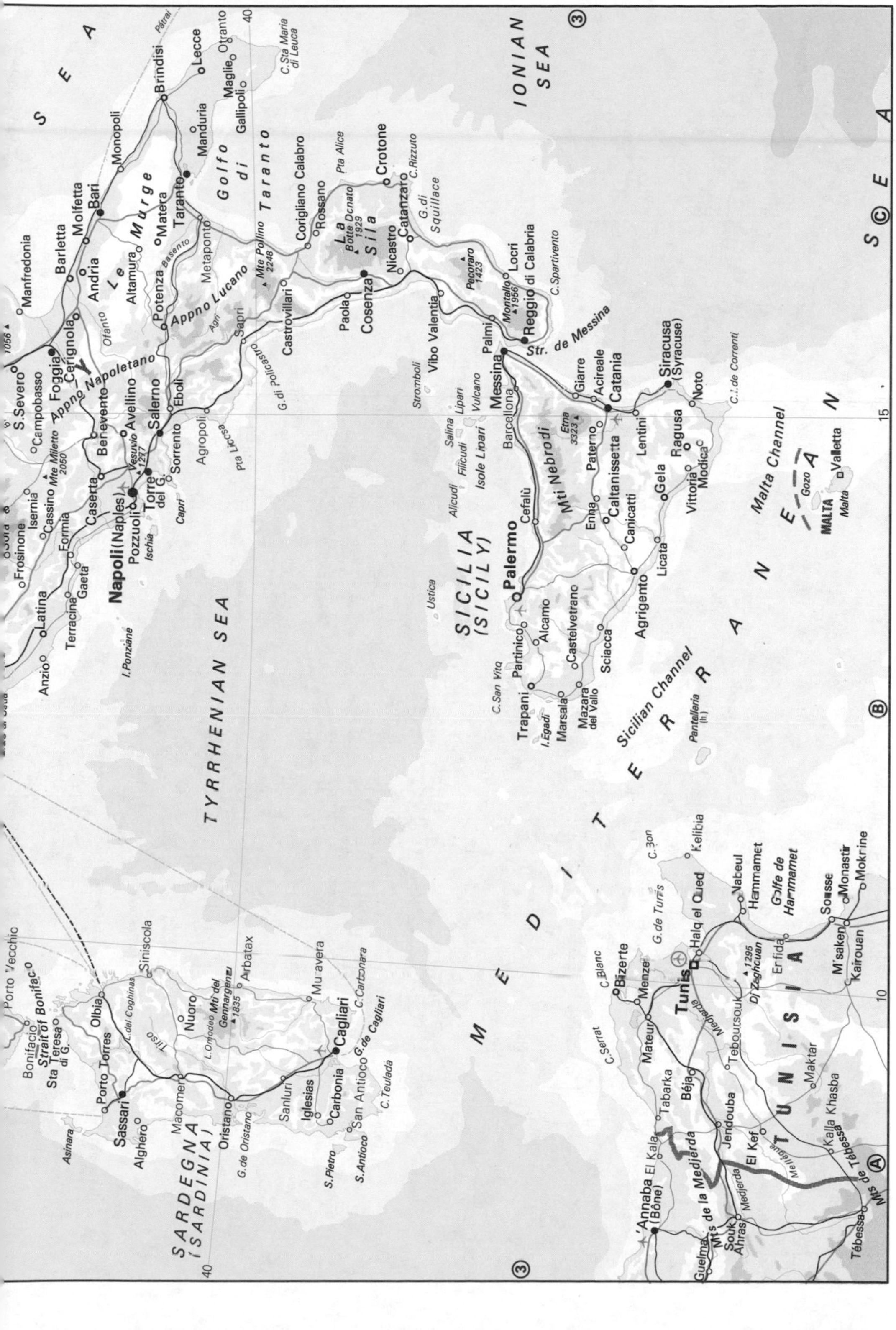
TYRRHENIAN SEA
IONIAN SEA
M E D I T E R R A N E A N S E A
SICILIA (SICILY)
SARDEGNA (SARDINIA)
TUNISIA
MALTA
Golfo di Taranto
Le Murge
Appno Lucano
Appno Napoletano
La Sila
Str. de Messina
Strait of Bonifacio
Sicilian Channel
Malta Channel
Isole Lipari
Mti Nebrodi
Etna 3323
Vesuvio 1277
Mte Pollino 2248
Mte Miletto 2050
Montalto 1956
Botte Donato 1929
Pecoraro 1423
Mti del Gennargentu 1835
Dj Zeghouan 1295
Napoli (Naples)
Pozzuoli
Torre del G.
Salerno
Sorrento
Capri
Ischia
Caserta
Benevento
Avellino
Foggia
Cerignola
Manfredonia
Barletta
Andria
Molfetta
Bari
Monopoli
Brindisi
Lecce
Otranto
Maglie
Gallipoli
Manduria
Taranto
Matera
Altamura
Potenza
Metaponto
Eboli
Agropoli
Sapri
Castrovillari
Corigliano Calabro
Rossano
Crotone
Catanzaro
Nicastro
Cosenza
Paola
Vibo Valentia
Palmi
Locri
Reggio di Calabria
Messina
Barcellona
Cefalù
Palermo
Partinico
Alcamo
Trapani
Marsala
Mazara del Vallo
Castelvetrano
Sciacca
Agrigento
Licata
Canicattì
Caltanissetta
Enna
Paternò
Catania
Acireale
Giarre
Lentini
Siracusa (Syracuse)
Noto
Ragusa
Modica
Vittoria
Gela
Ustica
Stromboli
Salina
Lipari
Vulcano
Filicudi
Alicudi
I. Egadi
Pantelleria
Gozo
Valletta
Latina
Anzio
Terracina
Gaeta
Formia
Frosinone
Cassino
Isernia
Campobasso
S. Severo
I. Ponziane
Porto Vecchio
Bonifacio
Sta Teresa di G.
Olbia
Siniscola
Nuoro
Arbatax
Muravera
Cagliari
Carbonia
Iglesias
Sanluri
Oristano
Macomer
Sassari
Porto Torres
Alghero
Asinara
S. Pietro
S. Antioco
Tunis
Bizerte
Menzel
Mateur
Béja
Tabarka
Jendouba
El Kef
Maktar
Kairouan
M'saken
Sousse
Monastir
Mokrine
Hammamet
Nabeul
Kelibia
Tebourso uk
Enfida
'Annaba (Bône)
El Kala
Souk Ahras
Guelma
Tébessa
Mts de la Medjerda
Mts de Tébessa
C. Bon
C. Blanc
C. Serrat
C. Spartivento
C. Rizzuto
C. Sta Maria di Leuca
C. de Correnti
C. San Vito
C. Teulada
C. Carbonara
G. di Squillace
G. di Policastro
G. de Oristano
G. de Cagliari
Golfe de Hammamet
G. de Tunis
15
10
40

BLACK SEA
U.S.S.R.
HUNGARY
ROMANIA
YUGOSLAVIA
BULGARIA
Odessa
Tiraspol
Kishinev
Iasi
Galati
Brăila
Tulcea
Constanța
Mangalia
Bucureşti (Bucharest)
Ploieşti
Braşov
Sibiu
Cluj-Napoca
Tîrgu Mureş
Oradea
Arad
Timişoara
Craiova
Piteşti
Budapest
Debrecen
Szeged
Kecskemét
Pécs
Novi Sad
Beograd (Belgrade)
Niš
Sarajevo
Mostar
Dubrovnik
Titograd
Skopje
Priština
Sofiya
Plovdiv
Stara Zagora
Burgas
Varna
Ruse
Pleven
Shumen
Tolbukhin
Edirne
Istanbul
Üsküdar
Carpaţii Meridionali (Transylvanian Alps)
Stara Planina
Rodopi
Ludogorie
Istranca Dağları
Dunav (Donau)
Prut (Prutul)
Dnestr
Siret
Mureş
Olt
Morava
Sava
Drina

AEGEAN SEA
IONIAN SEA
IÓNIOI NÍSOI (Ionian Islands)
Strait of Otranto
Sea of Kríti
Sea of Crete
Mirtoan Sea
Sea of Marmara
T U R K E Y
G R E E C E
A L B A N I A
SPORÁDHES
DODECANESE
Kikládhes (Cyclades)
Thermaïkós Kólpos
Lakonikós Kólpos
Messiniakós Kólpos
Kiparissiakós Kólpos
Argolikós K.
Saronikós K.
Korinthiakós K.
Saros Körfezi
Edremit K.
Çandarlı K.
Kuşadası K.
Kerme K.
Athínai (Athens)
Piraiévs
Thessaloníki (Salonica)
Izmir
Bursa
Balıkesir
Manisa
Denizli
Aydın
Muğla
Tiranë
Durrës
Brindisi
Lecce
Otranto
Gallipoli
Kérkira (Corfu)
Pátrai
Kórinthos
Iráklion
Khaniá
Réthimnon
Ródhos
Sámos
Khíos
Lésvos
Límnos
Thásos
Samothráki
Évvoia
Kríti
Kárpathos
Kásos
Kós
Náxos
Thíra
Mílos
Zákinthos
Kefallinía
Levkás
Khalkidhikí
Olimbos (Olympus) 2917
Áthos 2033
Smólikas 2637
Grámmos 2503
Tomorr 2480
Ídhi Óros 2456
Lévka Óri 2452
Dhíkti Óri 2148
Ak Dağ 2089
Boz Dağları
Larisa
Vólos
Lamía
Ioánnina
Kavála
Kalámai
Trípolis
Navplion
Bitola
Ohrid
Korçë
Vlorë
Elbasan
Kavajë
Fier
Berat
Gjirokastër
Sarandë
Çanakkale
Gelibolu (Gallipoli)
Bandırma
Karacabey
Edremit
Ayvalık
Bergama
Söke
Milas
Bodrum
Marmaris
Selçuk
Kastélli
Sitía
Ierápetra
Timbákion
Kíthira
Síros
Ándros
Tínos
Míkonos
Páros
Íos
Ikaría
Pátmos
Léros
Kálimnos
Astipálaia
Tílos
Sími
Líndos

NORTH SEA
BALTIC SEA
SWEDEN
DENMARK
POLAND
EAST GERMANY
NIEDERSACHSEN
SCHLESWIG-HOLSTEIN
NORDRHEIN-
Kattegat
Göteborg
Borås
Jönköping
Malmö
Helsingborg
Helsingør
København (Copenhagen)
Roskilde
Odense
Århus
Ålborg
Esbjerg
Kolding
Sjælland
Fyn
Jylland (Jutland)
Lolland
Bornholm
Rønne
Kiel
Lübeck
Hamburg
Bremen
Bremerhaven
Hannover
Braunschweig
Rostock
Schwerin
Berlin
Potsdam
Magdeburg
Szczecin
Poznań
Frankfurt an-der-O.
Cottbus
Dessau
Osnabrück
Bielefeld
Münster
Dortmund
Essen
Duisburg
Krefeld
Oldenburg
Wilhelmshaven
Emden
Groningen
Leeuwarden
Zwolle
Arnhem
Nijmegen
Amsterdam
Haarlem
Utrecht
Rotterdam
's-Gravenhage (Den Haag)
Antwerpen (Anvers)
Brugge
Gent
Oostende
Harwich
IJsselmeer
Elbe
Oder (Odra)

1:5M 0 50 100 150 200 km
0 50 100 mls

Gulf of Riga
(Rizhskiy Z.)
Gulf of Gdańsk
(Z.Gdańska)
Kurskiy Zaliv
Hanöbukten
Bornholm
Gotland
Öland
Rügen
B A L T I C S E A
S W E D E N
LATVIYSKAYA S.S.R.
LITOVSKAYA S.S.R.
BELORUSSKAYA S.S.R.
R.S.F.S.R.
U.S.S.R.
P O L A N D
Riga
Jūrmala
Jelgava
Tukums
Ventspils
Liepāja
Klaipėda
Kaunas
(Kovno)
Vilnius
Daugavpils
Šiauliai
Panevėžys
Minsk
Grodno
Brest
Kaliningrad
(Königsberg)
Gdynia
Gdańsk
(Danzig)
Sopot
Elbląg
Olsztyn
Białystok
Warszawa
Łódź
Toruń
Bydgoszcz
Poznań
Szczecin
Kołobrzeg
Koszalin
Słupsk
Lębork
Malbork
Grudziadz
Włocławek
Płock
Kalisz
Pabianice
Jönköping
Nässjö
Växjö
Kalmar
Karlskrona
Kristianstad
Ystad
Rønne
Visby
Polotsk
Novopolotsk
Molodechno
Borisov
Baranovichi
Pinsk
Sassnitz
Frankfurt
an-der-O
Cottbus
Słubice
Eberswalde
Prenzlau
Anklam
Świnoujście
Z.Szczeciński
Oder
(Odra)
Wisła (Vistula)
Neman
Narew
Bug
Noteć
Pripyat'
Z.Dvina (Daugava)
Venta
Lielupe
Gauja
Berezina
Nevis
Sluch
Ubort
Tsna
Pregolyu
Spree
15
20
55
B
C
D
1
2

Kostopol'
Sluch
Novograd V.
Polonnye
Korec
Slavuta
Rovno
Shepetovka
Starokonstantinov
Letichev
Khmel'nitskiy
Dubno
Kremenets
Bazaliya
Kivercy
Lutsk
Brody
Zolochev
Ternopol
Terebovlya
Gorodok
Podol'skaya Vozv.
Dunayevtsy
Kamenets Podolskiy
Dnestr
Khotin
Chortkov
Ivano-Frankovsk
Kolomya
Chernovtsy
Storozhinets
Yedintsy
Ryshkany
Prut (Prutul)
Dorohoi
Botoşani
Iaşi
Roman
Vladimir Volynskiy
Novovolynsk
Chervonograd
Rava Russkaya
L'vov
Berezhany
Khodorov
Kalush
Stryy
Drogobych
Borislav
Gorodok
Sambor
Nadvornaya
Yasinya
Goverla 2058
Rakhov
Khust
Svalyava
Mukachevo
Uzhgorod
U K R A I N S K A Y A S. S. R.
Krasnystaw
Zamość
Tomaszów Lubelski
Jarosław
Przemyśl
Kraśnik
Stalowa Wola
San
Tarnobrzeg
Rzeszów
Dębica
Sanok
Jasło
Nowy Sącz
Tarnów
Bochnia
Kraków
Beskidy Zachodnie
Bardejov
Prešov
Michalovce
Košice
Skarżysko-Kamienna
Starachowice
Ostrowiec
Kielce
Sandomierz
Mielec
Końskie
G. Świętokrzyskie
Jędrzejów
Buskozdrój
Radomsko
Częstochowa
Zawiercie
Dąbrowa-Gorn.
Sosnowiec
Katowice
Oświęcim
Myślenice
Żywiec
Bytom
Gliwice
Zabrze
Chorzów
Wieluń
Kluczbork
Opole
Odra
Nysa
Wrocław (Breslau)
Brzeg
Dzierżoniów
Bielawa
Kłodzko
Świdnica
Wałbrzych
Legnica
Jelenia Góra
Śnieżka 1603
Labe
Görlitz
Zittau
Bautzen
Ústí n.L.
Liberec
Jablonec n.N.
Mladá Boleslav
Brandys n.L.
Kladno
Praha (Prague)
Kolín
Kutná Hora
Hradec Králové
Pardubice
Ostrava
Karviná
Cieszyn
Opava
Praděd 1490
Jeseníky
Hranice
Přerov
Olomouc
Prostějov
Zábřeh
Vyškov
Brno
Svitavy
Českomoravská Vysočina
Jihlava
Třebíč
Havlíčkův Brod
Sázava
Benešov
Tábor
Písek
Vltava
České Budějovice
Kaplice
Třeboň
Gmünd
Znojmo
Mikulov
Hodonín
Břeclav
Morava
Gottwaldov
Čadca
Žilina
Martin
Ružomberok
Zakopane
Gerlachovský 2655
Tatry
Banská Bystrica
Zvolen
Rožňava
Lučenec
Trenčín
Piešťany
Nitra
Levice
Trnava
Bratislava
Malé Karpaty
Bílé Karpaty
Váh
ČESKOSLOVENSKO
Wien (Vienna)
Hollabrunn
Stockerau
Klosterneuburg
Mödling
Hainfeld
Wr. Neustadt
Neunkirchen
St Pölten
Horn
Freistadt
Linz
Donau
Steyr
Enns
Mariazell
Eisenerz
Leoben
Bruck an der Mur
Gleisdorf
Graz
Judenburg
Liezen
Wolfsberg
Leibnitz
Klagenfurt
AUSTRIA
Győr
Sopron
Mosonmagyaróvár
Komárno
Nové Zámky
Esztergom
Tatabánya
Pápa
Veszprém
Székesfehérvár
Siófok
Balaton
Fonyód
Szombathely
Zalaegerszeg
Nagykanizsa
Kaposvár
Dombóvár
Pécs
Paks
Szekszárd
Baja
Kiskunhalas
Kecskemét
Cegléd
Nagykőrös
Szolnok
Budapest
Vác
Hatvan
Gyöngyös
Salgótarján
Eger
Ózd
Kazincbarcika
Miskolc
Hajdúböszörmény
Debrecen
Nyíregyháza
Mátészalka
Kisvárda
Újfehértó
Berettyóújfalu
Karcag
Tisza
Hódmezővásárhely
Szeged
Makó
Békéscsaba
Orosháza
Szentes
Kiskunfélegyháza
Szarvas
Gyula
HUNGARY
Satu Mare
Carei
Baia Mare
Sighet
Zalău
Marghita
Oradea
Salonta
Arad
Sîntana
Lipova
Timişoara
Deta
Vršac
Caransebeş
Reşiţa
Lugoj
Hunedoara
Deva
Orăştie
Alba Iulia
Sebeş
Sibiu
Mediaş
Tîrnăveni
Turda
Cluj-Napoca
Dej
Reghin
Tîrgu Mureş
Sighişoara
Gheorgheni
Miercurea-Ciuc
Sfîntu Gheorghe
Braşov
Făgăraş
Rupea
Moldoveanu 1543
Cindrelu 2245
Peleaga 2511
Vlădeasa 1836
Bihor 1849
Mţii Apuseni
Mţii Zarandului
Mţii Rodnei
Mţii Călimanilor
Borşa
Vatra Dornei
Bistriţa
Rădăuţi
Suceava
Fălticeni
Paşcani
Piatra-Neamţ
Bicaz
Bacău
Siret
Adjud
Tecuci
Focşani
Rîmnicu Sărat
Buzău
Mizil
Ploieşti
Cîmpina
Tîrgovişte
Rîmnicu Vîlcea
Tîrgu Jiu
Carpaţii Meridionali (Transylvanian Alps)
ROMANIA
Subotica
Senta
Kikinda
Bečej
Zrenjanin
Novi Sad
Sombor
Vrbas
Vukovar
Vinkovci
Apatin
Osijek
Dakovo
Našice
Slav. Brod
Daruvar
Pakrac
Virovitica
Bjelovar
Koprivnica
Varaždin
Sisak
Zagreb
Kupa
Una
Sava
Brežice
Karlovac
Ogulin
Novo Mesto
Celje
Maribor
Velenje
Drava
Kranj
Ljubljana
Vrbovsko
Rijeka (Fiume)
YUGOSLAVIA

Stockholm
Södertälje
Nynäshamn
Nyköping
Norrköping
Linköping
Katrineholm
Tranås
Nässjö
Vättern
Oskarshamn
Västervik
Visby
Fårö
Gotland
Hemse
Borgholm
Öland
Kalmar
Karlskrona
B A L T I C S E A
Hangö
Karis
Helsinki
Borgå
Kotka
Vyborg
Gulf of Finland
Tallinn
Hiiumaa
Saaremaa
Haapsalu
Tapa
Kohtla-Järve
Lomonosovo
Gatchina
Leningrad
Pushkin
Volkhov
Tosno
Kirishi
Tikhin
Narva
Luga
ESTONSKAYA S.S.R.
Pärnu
Viljandi
Kingissepp
Ozero Chudskoye
Tartu
Gulf of Riga
Ventspils
Valga
Võru
Pskov
Ostrov
Ladozhskoye Ozero
Olonets
Podporozh'ye
Lodeynoye Pole
Vepsovskaya Vosv.
Vytegra
Kovzha
Beloye
Belozersk
Babayevo
Cherepovets
Chudovo
Novgorod
Il'men
Meta
Borovichi
Pestovo
Rybinsko Vdkhr.
Andropov
Staraya Russa
Dno
Valday
Bologoye
Valdayskaya
Vozvyshennost
Vyshniy-Volochek
Bezhetsk
Uglich
Kalyazin
Kimry
Torzhok
Ostashkov
Lovat
R O S S I
Kuldīga
Liepāja
Jūrmala
Riga
Cēsis
Jelgava
LATVIYSKAYA S.S.R.
Mazeikiai
Jekabpils
Dvina
Rēzekne
Opochka
Klaipeda
Šiauliai
LITOVSKAYA S.S.R.
Panevežys
Daugavpils
Nevel
Velikiye-Luki
Toropets
Volga
Kalinin
Dubna
Rzhev
Klin
Dmitrov
Nelidovo
Moskva (Moscow)
Noginsk
Lyublino
Gagarin
Vyaz'ma
Naro Fominsk
Podol'sk
Słupsk
Gdańsk (Danzig)
Gdynia
Kaliningrad R.S.F.S.R.
Sovetsk
Neman
Kaunas
Chernyakhovsk
Elbląg
Kapsukas
Ukmergė
Polotsk
Vilnius
Alytus
Glubokoye
Lepel
Vitebsk
Yartsevo
Smolensk
Chojnice
Wisła
Olsztyn
Suwałki
Bydgoszcz
Grudziądz
Ostróda
Ełk
Toruń
Włocławek
Smorgon'
Molodechno
Borisov
Orsha
Grodno
Lida
Białystok
Łomża
Novogrudok
Minsk
Mogilev
Dnepr
BELORUSSKAYA S.S.R.
Cherven'
Osipovichi
Krichev
Roslavl'
Kirov
Sukhinichi
Kaluga
Ugra
Aleksin
Serpukhov
Tula
Shchekino
Plavsk
Uzlovaya
Kutno
Płock
Płońsk
Ostrów Mazowiecka
Łowicz
Volkovysk
Baranovichi
Slonim
Slutsk
Bobruysk
Sozh
Warszawa (Warsaw)
P O L A N D
Łódź
Siedlce
Brest
Kobrin
Soligorsk
Dneprovskaya
Zhlobin
Unecha
Bryansk
Sredne-Russkaya Vozvyshennost
Mtsensk
Yefremov
Piotrków Trybunalski
Radom
Dęblin
Lublin
Bug
Pinsk
Pripyat'
Nizmennost
Kalinkovichi
Gomel'
Klintsy
Novozybkov
Desna
Navlya
Orel
Yelets
Częstochowa
Kielce
Ostrowiec
Chełm
Kovel'
Mozyr'
Dobrush
Khoyniki
Livny
Sosnowiec
Wisła
Vladimir Volynskiy
Sarny
Ovruch
Shchors
Shostka
Kursk
Shchigry
Kraków
Rzeszów
Lutsk
Sluch
Korosten
Chernobyl
Chernigov
Glukhov
Ryl'sk
Seym
Przemyśl
Jarosław
Dubno
Rovno
Novograd Volynskiy
Nezhin
Konotop
Bakhmach
Oboyan
Staryy Oskol
Gerlachovsky 2663
Brody
Shepetovka
Kiyev (Kiev)
Romny
Sumy
Sula
Georgiu-Dezh
Prešov
L'vov
Stryy
Ternopol'
Berdichev
Zhitomir
Fastov
Vasil'kov
Priluki
Borisovka
Belgorod
CZECH.
Košice
Dnestr
U K R A I N S K A Y A S.S.R.
Khmel'nitskiy
Lubny
Akhtyrka
Dergachi
Valuyki
Miskolc
Tisza
Uzhgorod
Ivano Frankovsk
Vinnitsa
Khar'kov
HUNGARY
Debrecen
Mukachevo
Kolomyya
Nyíregyháza
2058 Goverla
Khotin
Zhmerinka
Cherkassy
Smela
Kremenchugskoye Vdkhr.
Poltava
Sev. Donets
Kupyansk
Satu Mare
Baia Mare
Chernovtsy
Prut
Mogilev Podol'skiy
Gaysin
Tal'noye
Uman'
Kremenchug
Oradea
2305 Pietrosul
Suceava
Botoşani
Soroki
MOLDAVSKAYA S.S.R.
Kirovograd
Slavyansk
Kramatorsk
Lisichansk
Dneprodzerzhinsk
Dnepropetrovsk
Gorlovka
Békéscsaba
Dej
Cluj
Piatra Neamţ
Beltsy
Balta
Pervomaysk
Krivoy Rog
Kotovsk
Donetsk
Makeyevka
1849 Bihor
Iaşi
Voznesensk
Prichernomorskaya
Arad
R O M A N I A
Tîrgu Mureş
Roman
Kishinev
Berezovka
Zaporozh'ye
Nikopol
Timişoara
Mureşul
Bacău
Bendery
Tiraspol
Nizmennost
Nikolayev
Kakhovskoye Vdkhr.
Novocherkassk
Taganrog
Reşiţa
Sibiu
Negoiu 2544
Braşov
Bîrlad
Odessa
Kherson
Dnepr
Novaya Kakhovka
Melitopol'
Zhdanov
Yeysk
Berdyansk
Mtii Carpaţii Meridionali
Rîmnicu Vîlcea
Belgorod Dnestrovskiy
Danube
Tîrgu Jiu
Turnu Severin
Piteşti
Galaţi
Brăila
Buzău
Izmail
Bolgrad
Azovskoye More
Primorsko-Akhtarsk
YUGOS
Zaječar
Craiova
Olt
Ploieşti
Tulcea
Sulina
Karkinitskiy Z.
Dzhankoy
Bucureşti (Bucharest)
Roşiorii de Vede
Dunărea
Dunav
Cernavodă
Yevpatoriya
Krym
Kerch'
Timashevsk
Lom
Niš
Silistra
Ruse
Constanţa
Sevastopol'
Simferopol'
Feodosiya
Krasnodar
Novorossiysk
Krymsk
Stara Planina
Pleven
Tolbukhin
Veliko Turnovo
Shumen
M. Sarych
Yalta
Pernik
Sofiya (Sofia)
Kazanluk
Sliven
Varna
Tuapse
BULGARIA
Pazardzhik
Plovdiv
Stara Zagora
Yambol
Burgas
Blagoevgrad
Khaskovo
Maritsa
B L A C K S E A
55
50
45
30
35

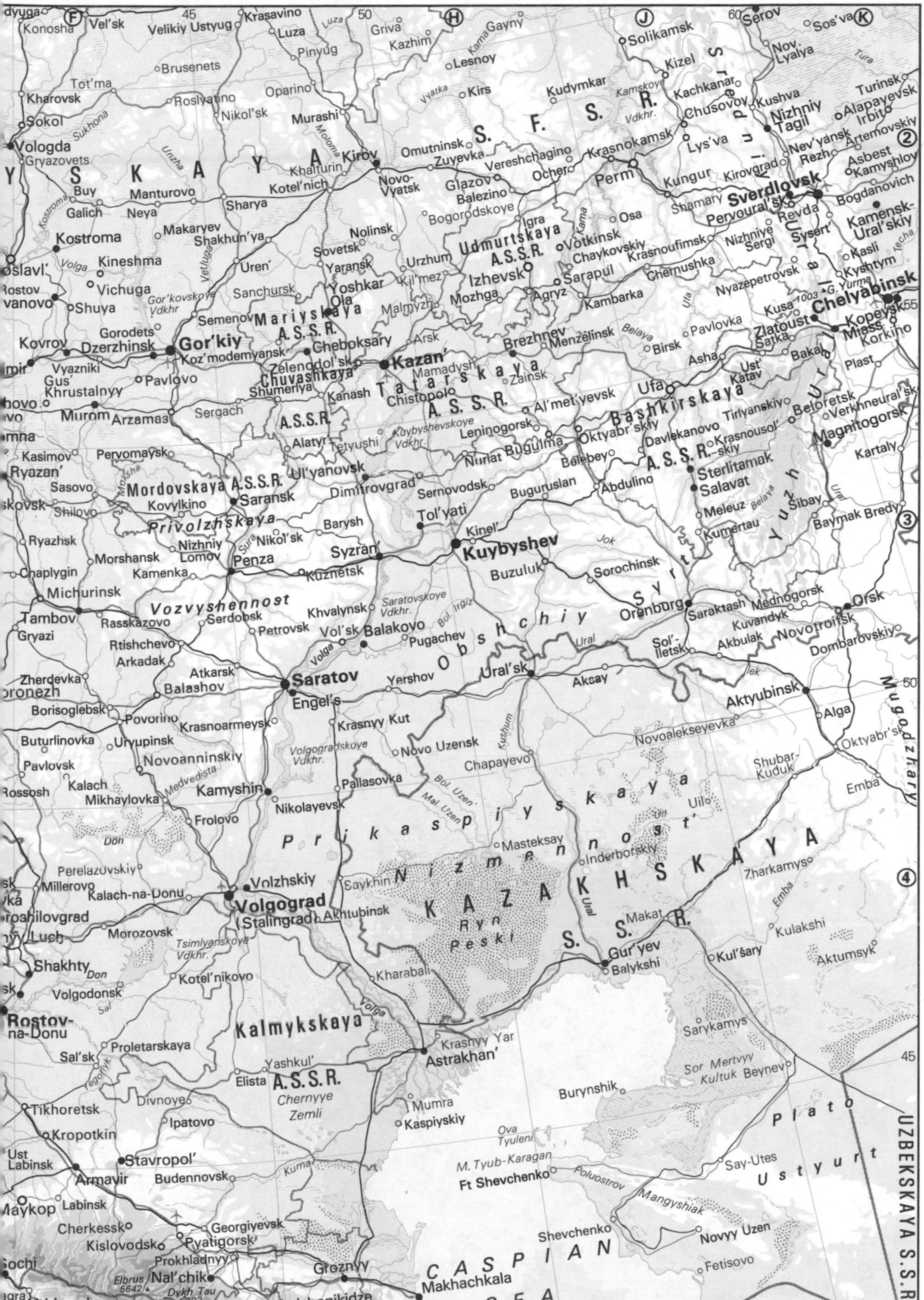
Konosha
Vel'sk
Velikiy Ustyug
Krasavino
Luza
Griva
Kazhim
Gayny
Solikamsk
Serov
Sos'va
Pinyug
Brusenets
Lesnoy
Kizel
Nov. Lyalya
Tot'ma
Kharovsk
Roslyatino
Oparino
Kirs
Kudymkar
Kachkanar
Turinsk
Sokol
Nikol'sk
Murashi
Chusovoy
Kushva
Alapayevsk
Irbit
Nizhniy Tagil
Vologda
Gryazovets
Omutninsk
Zuyevka
Vereshchagino
Krasnokamsk
Lys'va
Nev'yansk
Artemovskiy
Rezh
Asbest
Kamyshlov
S K A Y A
S. F. S. R.
Khalturin
Kirov
Novo-Vyatsk
Glazov
Ocher
Perm'
Kungur
Kirovgrad
Sverdlovsk
Bogdanovich
Buy
Manturovo
Kotel'nich
Balezino
Shamary
Pervoural'sk
Revda
Kamensk-Ural'skiy
Galich
Neya
Sharya
Bogorodskoye
Igra
Osa
Sysert'
Kostroma
Makaryev
Shakhun'ya
Nolinsk
Udmurtskaya A.S.S.R.
Votkinsk
Chaykovskiy
Krasnoufimsk
Nizhniye Sergi
Kasli
Kineshma
Sovetsk
Urzhum
Uren'
Yaransk
Izhevsk
Sarapul
Chernushka
Kyshtym
Vichuga
Sanchursk
Yoshkar Ola
Kil'mez
Mozhga
Agryz
Kambarka
Nyazepetrovsk
Chelyabinsk
Rostov
Shuya
Gor'kovskoye Vdkhr.
Mariyskaya A.S.S.R.
Malmyzh
Kusa
Zlatoust
Kopeysk
Miass
Korkino
Gorodets
Semenov
Brezhnev
Menzelinsk
Pavlovka
Satka
Kovrov
Dzerzhinsk
Gor'kiy
Cheboksary
Arsk
Birsk
Asha
Bakal
Plast
Koz'modemyansk
Zelenodol'sk
Kazan'
Mamadysh
Vyazniki
Gus' Khrustalnyy
Pavlovo
Chuvashskaya
Zainsk
Ust' Katav
Shumerlya
Tatarskaya A.S.S.R.
Chistopol
Ufa
Beloretsk
Verkhneural'sk
Murom
Arzamas
Sergach
Kanash
Al'met'yevsk
Bashkirskaya
Tirlyanskiy
Magnitogorsk
Kuybyshevskoye Vdkhr.
Leninogorsk
Oktyabr'skiy
Davlekanovo
Krasnousol'skiy
Kasimov
Pervomaysk
Alatyr
Tetyushi
Bugul'ma
Nurlat
Belebey
Kartaly
Ryazan'
Ul'yanovsk
A.S.S.R.
Sterlitamak
Sasovo
Mordovskaya A.S.S.R.
Dimitrovgrad
Sernovodsk
Buguruslan
Abdulino
Salavat
Kovylkino
Saransk
Shilovo
Tol'yati
Meleuz
Sibay
Privolzhskaya
Kinel'
Kumertau
Baymak
Bredy
Ryazhsk
Barysh
Nikol'sk
Syzran'
Kuybyshev
Jok
Morshansk
Nizhniy Lomov
Penza
Kuznetsk
Buzuluk
Sorochinsk
Chaplygin
Kamenka
Michurinsk
Vozvyshennost
Khvalynsk
Saratovskoye Vdkhr.
Orenburg
Saraktash
Mednogorsk
Orsk
Tambov
Rasskazovo
Serdobsk
Obshchiy Syrt
Kuvandyk
Novotroitsk
Gryazi
Petrovsk
Vol'sk
Balakovo
Pugachev
Akbulak
Dombarovskiy
Rtishchevo
Arkadak
Ural
Sol'-Iletsk
Atkarsk
Saratov
Yershov
Ural'sk
Aksay
Zherdevka
Voronezh
Balashov
Engel's
Aktyubinsk
Mugodzhary
Borisoglebsk
Povorino
Krasnyy Kut
Alga
Krasnoarmeysk
Ilek
Buturlinovka
Uryupinsk
Novo Uzensk
Novoalekseyevka
Oktyabr'sk
Volgogradskoye Vdkhr.
Novoanninskiy
Chapayevo
Pavlovsk
Shubar-Kuduk
Rossosh
Kalach
Medvedista
Pallasovka
Bol. Uzen
Emba
Mikhaylovka
Kamyshin
Mal. Uzen
Kushum
Prikaspiyskaya
Frolovo
Nikolayevsk
Uil
Nizmennost'
Don
Masteksay
Inderborskiy
Perelazovskiy
Zharkamys
Millerovo
Volzhskiy
Saykhin
KAZAKHSKAYA S.S.R.
Kalach-na-Donu
Volgograd (Stalingrad)
Akhtubinsk
Ryn Peski
Makat
Voroshilovgrad
Luch
Morozovsk
Tsimlyanskoye Vdkhr.
Kulakshi
Shakhty
Gur'yev
Balykshi
Kul'sary
Aktumsyk
Kotel'nikovo
Kharabali
Volgodonsk
Sal
Rostov-na-Donu
Kalmykskaya A.S.S.R.
Sarykamys
Sal'sk
Proletarskaya
Krasnyy Yar
Astrakhan'
Yashkul'
Sor Mertvyy Kultuk
Beyneu
Elista
Chernyye Zemli
Burynshik
Divnoye
Tikhoretsk
Mumra
Plato Ustyurt
Ipatovo
Kaspiyskiy
Kropotkin
Ova Tyuleni
M. Tyub-Karagan
Ust Labinsk
Stavropol'
Armavir
Say-Utes
Budennovsk
Kuma
Ft Shevchenko
Poluostrov Mangyshlak
Maykop
Labinsk
Cherkessk
Georgiyevsk
Kislovodsk
Pyatigorsk
Shevchenko
Novyy Uzen
Prokhladnyy
Sochi
Elbrus 5642
Nal'chik
Dykh Tau 5203
Groznyy
Makhachkala
Fetisovo
CASPIAN SEA
Abkhazskaya
Alagir
Ordzhonikidze
Buynaksk
UZBEKSKAYA S.S.R.

1:45M

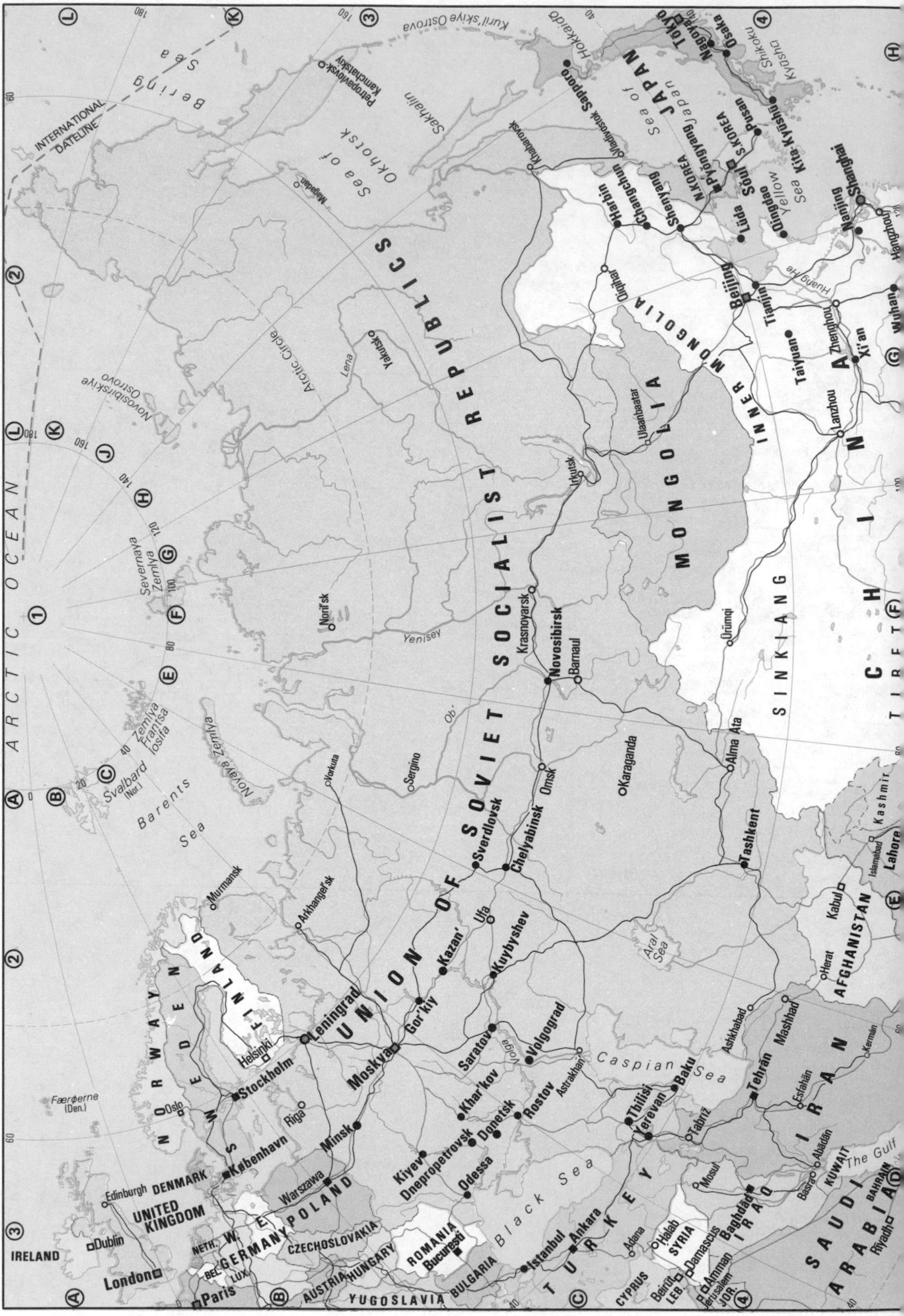
0
600
1200
1800 km
300
600
900 mls
ARCTIC OCEAN
INTERNATIONAL DATELINE
Bering Sea
Sea of Okhotsk
Sakhalin
Kuril'skiye Ostrova
Hokkaido
Sea of Japan
JAPAN
Sapporo
Tokyo
Nagoya
Osaka
Shikoku
Kyushu
Kita-Kyushu
Petropavlovsk-Kamchatskiy
Magadan
Khabarovsk
Vladivostok
N.KOREA
Pyongyang
S.KOREA
Soul
Pusan
Yellow Sea
Harbin
Changchun
Shenyang
Lüda
Qingdao
Nanjing
Shanghai
Hangzhou
Beijing
Tianjin
Huang He
Wuhan
Zhengzhou
Xi'an
Taiyuan
Lanzhou
Qiqihar
INNER MONGOLIA
MONGOLIA
Ulaanbaatar
Irkutsk
Yakutsk
Lena
Arctic Circle
Novosibirskiye Ostrova
Severnaya Zemlya
Noril'sk
Yenisey
Krasnoyarsk
Novosibirsk
Barnaul
Ürümqi
SINKIANG
CHINA
TIBET
Alma Ata
Karaganda
Omsk
Ob'
Sergino
Vorkuta
Zemlya Frantsa Iosifa
Svalbard (Nor.)
Novaya Zemlya
Barents Sea
UNION OF SOVIET SOCIALIST REPUBLICS
Sverdlovsk
Chelyabinsk
Tashkent
Kashmir
Lahore
Islamabad
Kabul
AFGHANISTAN
Herat
Aral Sea
Ashkhabad
Mashhad
IRAN
Tehran
Esfahan
Kerman
Abadan
The Gulf
KUWAIT
BAHRAIN
SAUDI ARABIA
Riyadh
Basra
IRAQ
Baghdad
Mosul
Tabriz
Baku
Caspian Sea
Tbilisi
Yerevan
Astrakhan
Volgograd
Volga
Saratov
Kuybyshev
Ufa
Kazan'
Gor'kiy
Moskva
Leningrad
Arkhangel'sk
Murmansk
FINLAND
Helsinki
SWEDEN
Stockholm
NORWAY
Oslo
Færøerne (Den.)
Riga
Minsk
Kiyev
Khar'kov
Dnepropetrovsk
Donetsk
Rostov
Odessa
Black Sea
TURKEY
Ankara
Istanbul
Adana
Halab
SYRIA
Damascus
Beirut
LEB.
Amman
Jerusalem
JOR.
CYPRUS
BULGARIA
ROMANIA
Bucuresti
YUGOSLAVIA
HUNGARY
AUSTRIA
CZECHOSLOVAKIA
POLAND
Warszawa
W. GERMANY
NETH.
BEL.
LUX.
Paris
London
UNITED KINGDOM
IRELAND
Dublin
Edinburgh
DENMARK
København

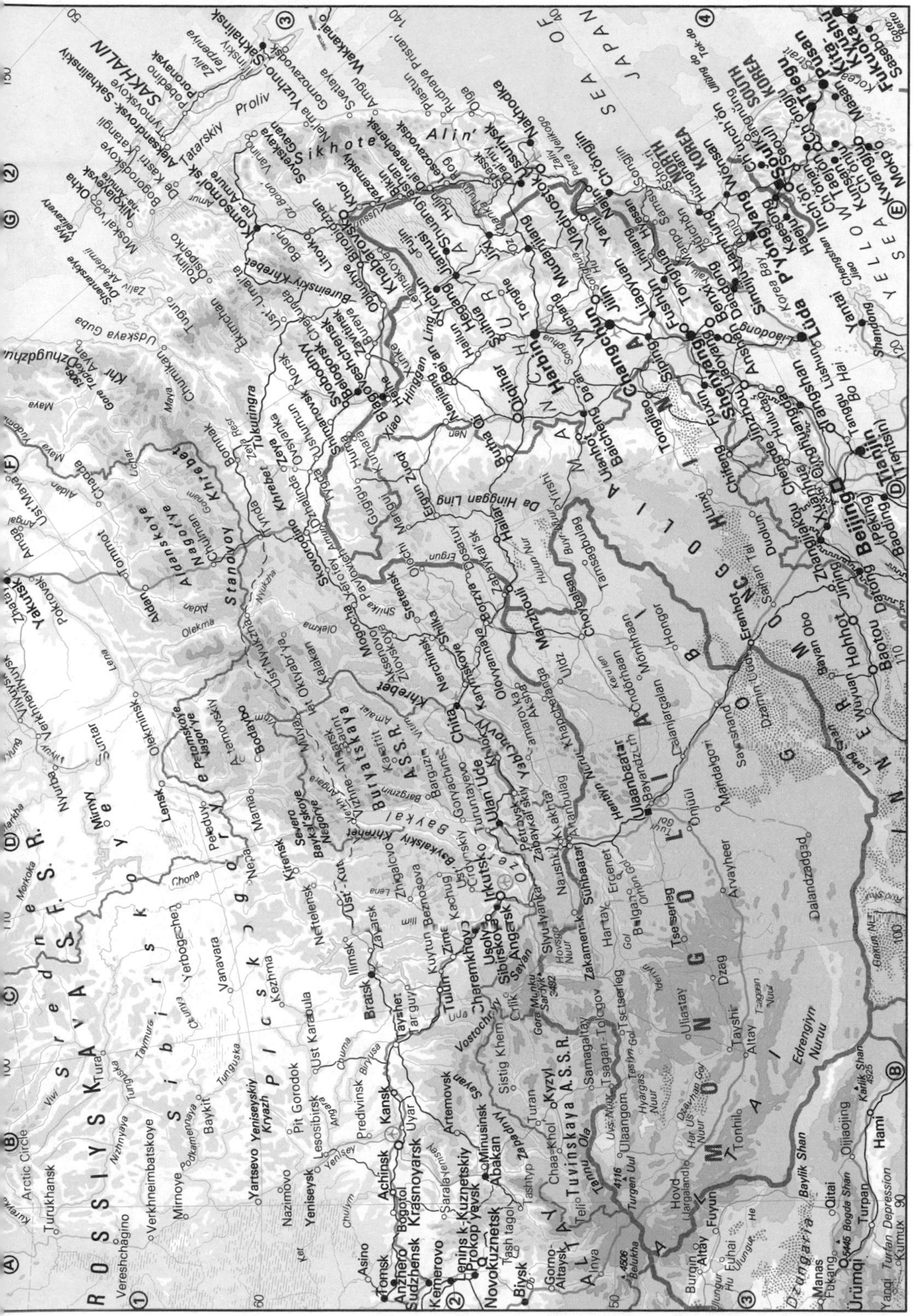
ROSSIYSKAYA S.F.S.R.
SREDNE SIBIRSKOYE PLOSKOGOR'YE
Arctic Circle
Turukhansk
Tura
Baykit
Vanavara
Yeniseysk
Lesosibirsk
Krasnoyarsk
Achinsk
Kansk
Bratsk
Ust'-Kut
Kirensk
Lensk
Mirnyy
Olekminsk
Yakutsk
Aldan
Tomsk
Kemerovo
Novokuznetsk
Biysk
Gorno-Altaysk
Abakan
Minusinsk
Kyzyl
Tuvinskaya A.S.S.R.
Irkutsk
Angarsk
Ulan-Ude
Buryatskaya A.S.S.R.
Ozero Baykal
Chita
Skovorodino
Tynda
Zeya
Svobodnyy
Blagoveshchensk
Khabarovsk
Komsomol'sk-na-Amure
Sovetskaya Gavan'
Vladivostok
Nakhodka
Ussuriysk
Sakhalin
Yuzhno-Sakhalinsk
Aleksandrovsk-Sakhalinskiy
Okha
Nikolayevsk-na-Amure
Tatarskiy Proliv
Sikhote Alin'
SEA OF JAPAN
MONGOLIA
Ulaanbaatar
Erdenet
Darhan
Choybalsan
Sühbaatar
Hovd
Uliastay
Altay
CHINA
Harbin
Qiqihar
Changchun
Jilin
Shenyang
Anshan
Fushun
Dalian
Beijing (Peking)
Tianjin (Tientsin)
Baotou
Hohhot
Datong
Ürümqi
Hami
Turpan
Dzungaria
NORTH KOREA
P'yongyang
SOUTH KOREA
Seoul
Pusan
Taegu
Inch'on
Kitakyushu
Fukuoka
YELLOW SEA
Stanovoy Khrebet
Aldanskoye Nagor'ye
Da Hinggan Ling
Xiao Hinggan Ling
Yablonovyy Khrebet
Baykal'skiy Khrebet
Vostochnyy Sayan
Zapadnyy Sayan
Yeniseyskiy Kryazh
Tannu Ola
Altay
Bogda Shan
Baylik Shan
Turfan Depression

ARCTIC OCEAN
KARA SEA
BARENTS SEA
NORWEGIAN SEA
NORTH SEA
BALTIC SEA
Arctic Circle
SVALBARD (SPITSBERGEN) (Nor.)
Spitsbergen
Nordaustlandet
Kong Karls Land
Barentsøya
Edgeøya
Hopen
Sørkapp
Prins Karls Forland
Bjørnøya
ZEMLYA FRANTSA IOSIFA (FRANZ-JOSEF-LAND)
Zemlya Aleksandry
Zemlya Georga
Ostrov Rudol'fa
Ostrov Greem Bell
Zemlya Vil'cheka
NOVAYA ZEMLYA
M.Zhelaniya
O.Mezhdusharskiy
Krasino
Proliv Karskiye Vorota
O.Vaygach
Amderma
Pechorskoye More
Ostrov Belyy
Dikson
Yeniseyskiy Zal
Gydanskiy Poluostrov
Pov Yamal
Obskaya Guba
Baydaratskaya G.
Khrebet Pay-Khoy
Vorkuta
Novyy Port
Nyda
Tazovskiy
Pur
Tarko-Sale
Labytnangi
Muzhi
Berezovo
Sev.Sos'va
G.Narodnaya 1894
G.Tel'pos-iz 1617
Nar'yan Mar
Usa
Ust'Tsil'ma
Izhma
Pechora
Ukhta
Kryazh Timanskiy
Vym
Syktyvkar
Ostrov Kolguyev
Cheshskaya Guba
Belush'ye
Kanin Nos
Pov Kanin
Mezen'
Ponoy
Gremikha
Usogorsk
Pinega
Arkhangel'sk
Kotlas
Sev Dvina
KOMI A.S.S.R.
ROSSIYSKAYA
Vardø
Pov Rybachiy
Nikel'
Murmansk
Kol'skiy Poluostrov
Kirovsk
Kandalaksha
Beloye More (White Sea)
Nordkapp
Hammerfest
Kirkenes
Inari
Lappland
Muonio
Kelloselka
Tromsø
Vesterålen
Lofoten
Narvik
Kiruna
Vestfjorden
Bodø
Mo
Haparanda
Luleå
Kemi
Oulu
Kajaani
Belomorsk
Kem
Severodvinsk
Onega
Karel'skaya A.S.S.R.
Medvezh'yegorsk
Onezhskoye Ozero
Shenkursk
Nyandoma
Vel'sk
Konosha
Sokol
Vologda
Sukhona
Sharya
Buy
Kostroma
Petrozavodsk
Vytegra
Lodeynoye Pole
Ladozhskoye Ozero
Leningrad
Cherepovets
Rybinskoye Vdkhr
Andropov
Yaroslavl
Ivanovo
Vladimir
Kalinin
Bologoye
Chudovo
Novgorod
Ozero Il'men
Vyborg
Helsinki
Lahti
Tampere
Kuopio
FINLAND
Vaasa
Gulf of Bothnia
Pori
Turku
Umeå
SWEDEN
NORWAY
Östersund
Sundsvall
Namsos
Trondheim
Kristiansund
Ålesund
Jotunheimen 2481
Gävle
Uppsala
Stockholm
Örebro
Norrköping
Oslo
Drammen
Bergen
Vänern
Vättern
Jönköping
Göteborg
Gotland
Öland
Stavanger
Kristiansand
Skagerrak
Frederikshavn
Ålborg
Helsingborg
Malmö
København
Bornholm
Odense
DENMARK
Esbjerg
Kiel
Hamburg
Bremen
Sassnitz
Gulf of Finland
Tallinn
ESTONSKAYA S.S.R.
Pärnu
Chudskoye Oz
Tartu
Pskov
Ostrov
Velikiye Luki
Rzhev
Moskva (Moscow)
Vyaz'ma
Smolensk
Serpukhov
Tula
Roslavl
Bryansk
Gulf of Riga
Riga
LATVIYSKAYA S.S.R.
Ventspils
Liepaja
Daugavpils
Vitebsk
Polotsk
Orsha
LITOVSKAYA S.S.R.
Kaunas
Vilnius
Minsk
Mogilev
Bobruysk
Gomel'
BELORUSSKAYA S.S.R.
Klaipeda
Sovetsk
Kaliningrad
RSFSR
Grodno
Bialystok
Pinsk
Pripyat'
Mozyr
Korosten'
Zhitomir
Brest
Kovel
Gdańsk
Bydgoszcz
Szczecin
Wisła
Warszawa
POLAND
Lublin
Łódź
Radom
Poznań
Warta
Oder
Berlin
Wrocław
Kraków
Przemyśl
L'vov
Rovno
Vinnitsa
Ivano-Frankovsk
Chernovtsy
Carpathian Mts
GERMANY
Dnepr
Desna
Faerøerne (Den.)
Shetland Is
Orkney Is
Wick
Hebrides
Inverness
Aberdeen
U.K.
SCOTLAND
Edinburgh
Glasgow

R.S.F.S.R.
1 Chuvashskaya A.S.S.R.
2 Checheno-Ingushskaya A.S.S.R.
3 Severo-Osetinskaya A.S.S.R.
4 Kabardino-Balkarskaya A.S.S.R.
GRUZINSKAYA S.S.R.
5 Abkhazskaya A.S.S.R.
6 Adzharskaya A.S.S.R.
AZERBAYDZHANSKAYA S.S.R.
7 Nakhichevanskaya A.S.S.R.
KAZAKHSKAYA S.S.R.
UZBEKSKAYA S.S.R.
TURKMENSKAYA S.S.R.
KIRGIZSKAYA S.S.R.
TADZHIKSKAYA S.S.R.
SINKIANG
AFGHANISTAN
IRAN
IRAQ
TURKEY
BLACK SEA
Aral'skoye More
Kara kumy
Kyzylkum
Tien Shan
Omsk
Novosibirsk
Barnaul
Tomsk
Sverdlovsk
Chelyabinsk
Kuybyshev
Kazan'
Saratov
Volgograd
Astrakhan'
Rostov-na-Donu
Donetsk
Khar'kov
Dnepropetrovsk
Odessa
Tbilisi
Yerevan
Baku
Tehrān
Tashkent
Alma Ata
Frunze
Karaganda
Semipalatinsk
Ust'-Kamenogorsk
Pavlodar
Tselinograd
Kustanay
Aktyubinsk
Gur'yev
Orenburg
Ufa
Perm'
Krasnovodsk
Ashkhabad
Mashhad
Herat
Samarkand
Dushanbe

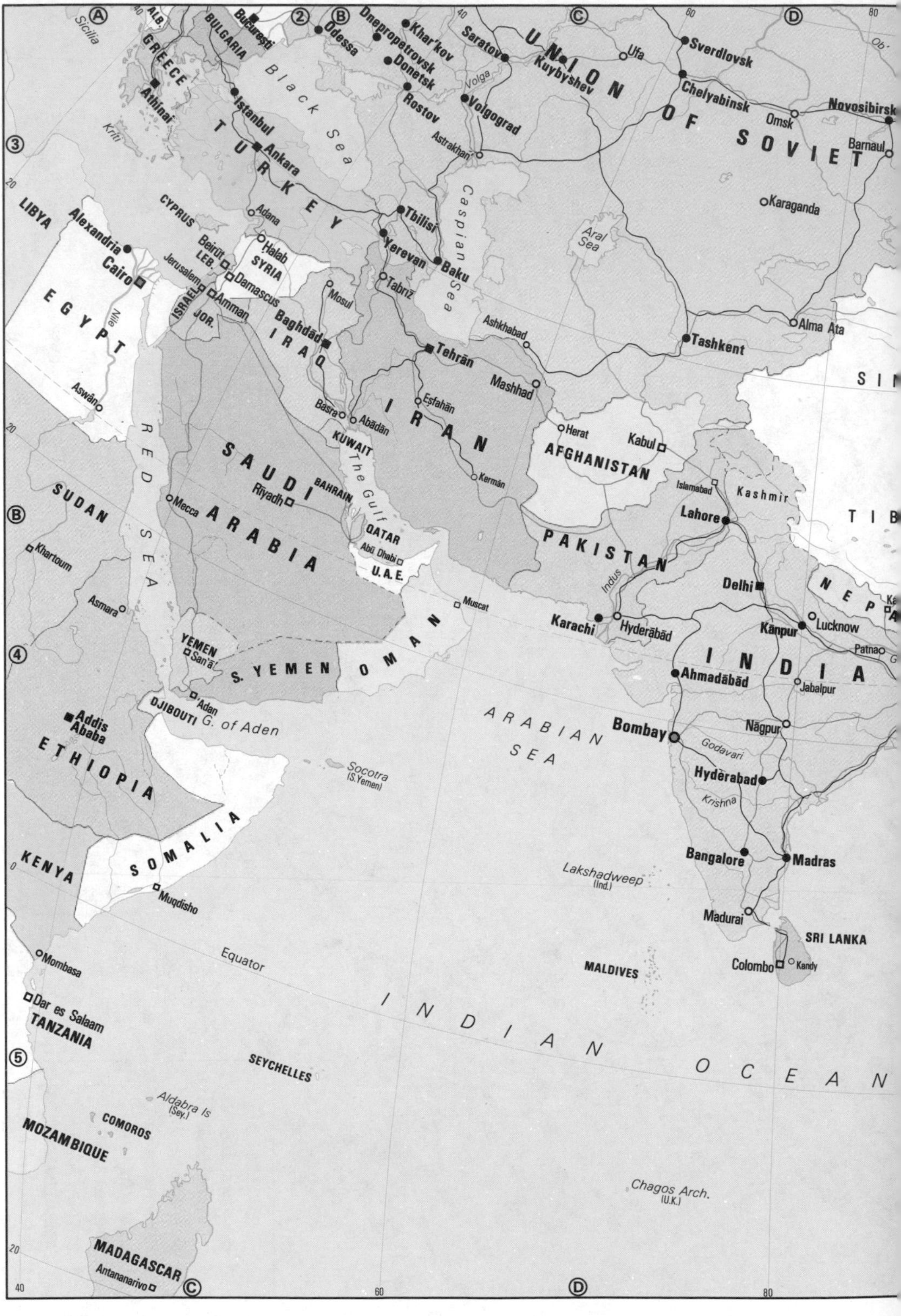

UNION OF SOVIET
TURKEY
GREECE
BULGARIA
ALB.
Bucureşti
Athínai
Sicilia
Kriti
Odessa
Dnepropetrovsk
Khar'kov
Donetsk
Rostov
Saratov
Volgograd
Volga
Kuybyshev
Ufa
Sverdlovsk
Chelyabinsk
Omsk
Novosibirsk
Barnaul
Karaganda
Astrakhan'
Black Sea
Caspian Sea
Aral Sea
İstanbul
Ankara
Adana
Tbilisi
Yerevan
Baku
Tabrīz
Ashkhabad
Tashkent
Alma Ata
LIBYA
CYPRUS
Alexandria
Cairo
Beirūt
LEB.
Jerusalem
ISRAEL
Halab
SYRIA
Damascus
Amman
JOR.
Mosul
Baghdād
IRAQ
Tehrān
Mashhad
Eşfahān
IRAN
Kermān
EGYPT
Nile
Aswân
Basra
Abādān
KUWAIT
The Gulf
BAHRAIN
QATAR
Abū Dhabi
U.A.E.
SAUDI ARABIA
Riyadh
Mecca
RED SEA
Herat
Kabul
AFGHANISTAN
Islamabad
Kashmir
Lahore
PAKISTAN
Indus
Delhi
NEPA
TIB
SI
Muscat
OMAN
Karachi
Hyderābād
Kānpur
Lucknow
Patna
INDIA
Ahmadābād
Jabalpur
SUDAN
Khartoum
Asmara
YEMEN
San'ā'
S. YEMEN
Adan
DJIBOUTI
G. of Aden
Addis Ababa
ETHIOPIA
ARABIAN SEA
Bombay
Nāgpur
Godavari
Hyderabad
Krishna
Socotra (S.Yemen)
SOMALIA
KENYA
Muqdisho
Bangalore
Madras
Lakshadweep (Ind.)
Madurai
SRI LANKA
Colombo
Kandy
MALDIVES
Equator
Mombasa
Dar es Salaam
TANZANIA
INDIAN OCEAN
SEYCHELLES
Aldabra Is (Sey.)
COMOROS
MOZAMBIQUE
Chagos Arch. (U.K.)
MADAGASCAR
Antananarivo
Ob'

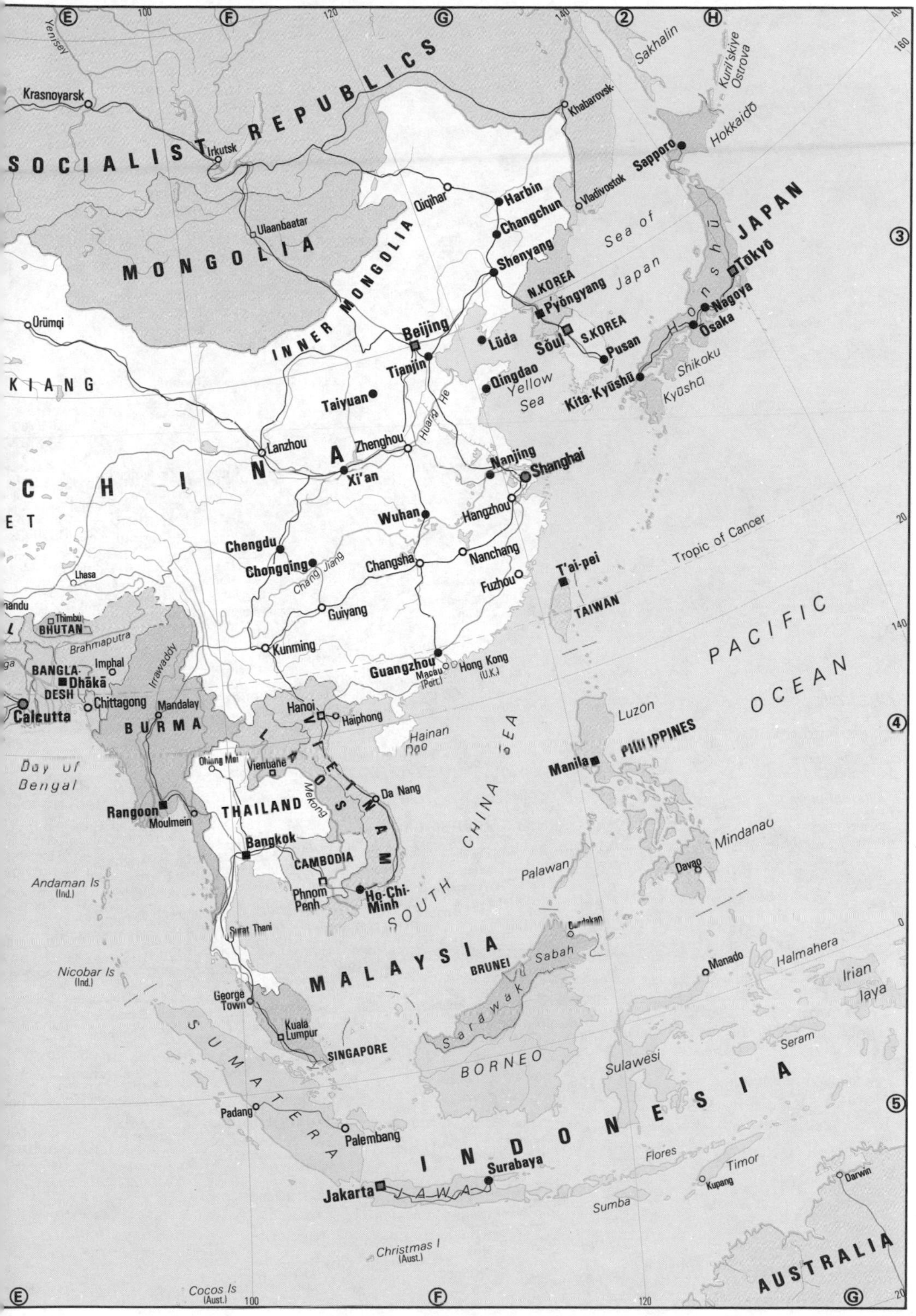
SOCIALIST REPUBLICS
Yenisey
Krasnoyarsk
Irkutsk
Khabarovsk
Sakhalin
Kuril'skiye Ostrova
Hokkaidō
Sapporo
Vladivostok
Ulaanbaatar
MONGOLIA
Qiqihar
Harbin
Changchun
Shenyang
Sea of Japan
JAPAN
Honshū
Tokyō
Nagoya
Ōsaka
N.KOREA
P'yŏngyang
S.KOREA
Sŏul
Pusan
Kita-Kyūshū
Shikoku
Kyūshū
INNER MONGOLIA
Beijing
Tianjin
Lüda
Qingdao
Yellow Sea
Ürümqi
KIANG
Taiyuan
Huang He
Lanzhou
Zhenghou
CHINA
Xi'an
Nanjing
Shanghai
Hangzhou
Wuhan
ET
Chengdu
Chongqing
Chang Jiang
Changsha
Nanchang
Fuzhou
T'ai-pei
TAIWAN
Tropic of Cancer
Lhasa
Thimbu
BHUTAN
Guiyang
Kunming
Brahmaputra
Irrawaddy
Imphal
BANGLA-DESH
Dhākā
Chittagong
Calcutta
Mandalay
BURMA
Guangzhou
Macau (Port.)
Hong Kong (U.K.)
PACIFIC OCEAN
Hanoi
Haiphong
VIETNAM
LAOS
Hainan Dao
Luzon
PHILIPPINES
Manila
Bay of Bengal
Chiang Mai
Vientiane
Mekong
Da Nang
Rangoon
Moulmein
THAILAND
Bangkok
CAMBODIA
Phnom Penh
Ho-Chi-Minh
SOUTH CHINA SEA
Palawan
Mindanao
Davao
Andaman Is (Ind.)
Surat Thani
Sandakan
MALAYSIA
BRUNEI
Sabah
Manado
Halmahera
Irian Jaya
Nicobar Is (Ind.)
George Town
Kuala Lumpur
Sarawak
SINGAPORE
SUMATERA
BORNEO
Sulawesi
Seram
INDONESIA
Padang
Palembang
Flores
Timor
Surabaya
Kupang
Darwin
Jakarta
JAWA
Sumba
Christmas I (Aust.)
AUSTRALIA
Cocos Is (Aust.)

Mikhaylovskiy
Biysk
Tashtagol
Rubtsovsk
Gorno-Altaysk
Tashtyp
Sistig Khem
Turan
Voshnyy Saytocan
100
Cheremkhovo
Zima
Kachung
Ust'-Ordynskiy
110
Karaftit
Barguzin
Yerofey Pa
Aksenovo
Zilovskoye
Mogo
Usolye Sibirskoye
Irkutsk
Angarsk
Goryachinsk
Khrebet
Vitim
Shilka
Sretensk
Nerchinsk
A L T A Y
Kyzyl
Orlik
Chaa-Khol'
Leninogorsk
Inya
Teli
Ust'-Kamenogorsk
Akzhal
Belukha 4506
Tannu Ola
G.Munku-Sardyk 3492
Slyudyanka
Ozero Baykal
Turuntayevo
Ulan Ude
Domna
Chita
Khilok
Petrovsk-Zabaykal'skiy
Karymskoye
Shilka
Zyryanovsk
Kokpekty
Turgen Uul 4116
Uvs Nuur
Samagaltay
Tsagan-Tologoy
Hövsgöl Nuur
Zakamensk
Naushki
Sühbaatar
Kyakhta
Yablonovyy
Olovyannaya
Yamarovka
Borzya
Ergun
U. S. S. R.
Ulaangom
Oz. Zaysan
Burqin
Zaysan
Ulungur Hu
Altay
Fuyun
Hyargas Nuur
Tesiyn Gol
Tsetserleg
Hantay
Ideriyn Gol
Erdenet
Altanbulag
Khapcheranga
Aksha
Dosat
Zabaykal'sk
Manzho
Uldz
Hovd (Jargalant)
Har Us Nuur
Dzavhan Gol
Uliastay
Bulgan
Orhon Gol
Hentiyn Nuruu
Hail
Hulun Nur
Fuhai
Karamay
Ulungur He
Manas Hu
Tsetserleg
M O N G O L I A
Ulaanbaatar
Tuul Gol
Bayandzürh
Kerulen
Choybalsan
Tonhil
Tayshir
Dzag
Öndörhaan
Buyr Nuur
Altay
Mönhhaan
Tamsagbulag
Dzungaria
Usa
Manas
Fukang
Qitai
Baytik Shan
Tsagaan Nuur
Arvayheer
Onjüül
Dalanjargalan
Ürümqi
Bogda Shan 5445
Turpan
Edrengiyn Nuruu
Mandalgovi
Hongor
Oijiaojing
Karlik Shan 4925
Saynshand
G O B I
Yanqi
Turfan Depression
Hami
Dalandzadgad
Dzamin Üüd
Erenhot
Bosten Hu
SINKIANG
Xingxingxia
Kuruktag
Gaxun Nur
I N N E R   M O N G O L I A
Linxi
Bei Shan
Saihan Tal
Duolun
Chifeng
40
Lop Nur
Shule He
Lang Shan
Bayan Obo
Dunhuang
Anxi
Ruo Shui
Wuyuan
Hohhot
Zhangjiakou
Chengde
Jinz
Hulu
Ruoqiang
Altun Shan
Yumen
Jiayuguan
Baotou
Jining
Xuanhua
Qinhuangda
Ala Shan
Datong
Beijing (Peking)
Tangshan
Ayakkum Hu
Mangnai
Sukai Hu
Qilian Shan
Zhangye
Ordos
Tianjin (Tientsin)
Tanggu
Harhu
Da Qaidam
Qaidam Pendi
Yinchuan
Ningwu
Baoding
Bo H
Wuwei
Huang He
Yulin
Xin Xian
Cangzhou
Hah Xil Hu
Hoh Sai Hu
Qinghai Hu
Datong
Taiyuan
Fenyang
Shijiazhuang
Golmud
Haiyang
Suide
Yangquan
Dezhou
Hoh Xil Shan
Dulan
Xining
Yanchang
Xingtai
Jinan
Ulan Ul Hu
Lanzhou
Yan'an
Handan
Zibo
90
Ngoring Hu
Donggi Cona
Qingyang
Linfen
Wei He
Qingd
Gyaring Hu
Changzhi
Anyang
Joma 6800
Huang He
Pingliang
Tongchuan
Xinxiang
Jining
Yanzhou
Bayan Har Shan
Zhengzhou
Kaifeng
Linyi
Tanggula Shan
Tianshui
Baoji
Sanmenxia
Luoyang
Tongtian He
Xi'an
Shangqiu
Xuzhou
Yushu
Wei He
Hua Shan
Xuchang
Sog Xian
Ningjing Shan
Pingwu
Hanzhong
Luohe
Zhoukouzhen
Hongze Hu
TIBET
Nagqu
Dêqê
Guangyuan
Nanyang
Bengbu
Qamdo
Dadu He
Ankang
Fuyang
Huainan
Nyainqentanglha Shan
Mianyang
Lanzhong
Daba Shan
Xiangfan
Xinyang
Nanjing
30
C H I N A
Lhasa
Batang
Yalong
Dawu
Chengdu
Sui Xian
Lu'an
Hefei
Wuhu
Namcha Barwa 7756
Red Basin
Nanchong
Wanzian
Yichang
Tai Hu
Nyingchi
Kangding
Ya'an
Tongling
Lhunze
Mekong
Gongga Shan 7556
Leshan
Hechuan
Enshi
Shashi
Wuhan
Anqing
Chang Jiang
Hangzhou
Kangto 7090
Zayü
Hengduan Shan
Chongqing
Fuling
Dongting Hu
Huangshi
Tawang
Sadiya
Yibin
Luzhou
Youyang
Changde
Yueyang
Jiujiang
Jingdezhen
Shaox
Tunxi
Dibrugarh
Putao
Zhougdian
Xichang
Yuanling
Yiyang
Nanchang
Brahmaputra
Dalou Shan
Qu X
Jorhat
Naga Hills
Kumon Ra.
Lijiang
Zhaotong
Zunyi
Lengshuijiang
Changsha
Qingjiang
Yingtan
Shangrao
Zhuzhou
Xiangtan
INDIA
Lushui
Dukou
Jinsha Jiang
Chang Jiang
Wu Jiang
Xuanwei
Guiyang
Zhijiang
Pingxiang
Fuzhou
Chong'an
Jianyang
Shaoyang
Dali
Dongchuan
Ji'an
Myitkyina
Xiaguan
Anshun
Duyun
Hengyang
Nanping
Ningde
Imphal
Baoshan
Qujing
Lingling
Wuyi Shan
Sanming
Katha
Luixi
Chuxiong
Kunming
Chen Xian
Changting
Fuzhou
Chindwin
Bhamo
Dian Chi
Guilin
Nanling
Ganzhou
Putian
Irrawaddy
Lincang
Nanpan Jiang
Hongshui
Lian Xian
Nanxiong
Quanzhou
Shwebo
Lashio
Yishan
Shaoguan
Zhangzhou
Monywa
Sagaing
Maymyo
Pu'er
Gejiu
Bose
Liuzhou
Mei Xian
Xiamen
Pakokku
Mandalay
Babian
Wenshan
Wuzhou
Xun Jiang
Qingyuan
Chao'an
Formosa Str.
Myingyan
Kengtung
Ha Giang
Nanning
Guangzhou (Canton)
Heyuan
Shantou
Meiktila
BURMA
Lao Cai
Huizhou
T'ai-nan
Arakan
Minbu
Magwe
Taung-gyi
Lai Chau
Lang Son
Pingxiang
Yulin
Foshan
Kowloon
Kao-hsiung
Muong Sing
Da
Hong
Jiangmen
Tung-Chiar
20
Salween
M. Chiang Rai
Luang Namtha
Sam Neua
Beihai
Xiangjiang
Macau (Port.)
Victoria
HONG KONG (U.K.)
B. Houei Sai
Hanoi
Bac Ninh
Leizhou
Zhanjiang
Prome
Pegu
Yoma
Toungoo
Luang Prabang
Haiphong
Nam Dinh
Gulf of Tongkin
Bandao
Xuwen
Dongsha Qundao
Myanaung
Chiang Mai
Muang Nan
Thanh Hoa
Lingao
Haikou
M. Lampang
Pak Sane
Dongfang
Wuzhi Shan 1879
Hainan Dao
Henzada
Pegu
Vinh
Bassein
Uttaradit
Vientiane
Rangoon
Tak
Sawankhalok
Nong Khai
Thakhek
Dong Hoi
Yulin
110
C. Bojea
Lao

1:20M 0 200 400 600 800 km 0 200 400 mls

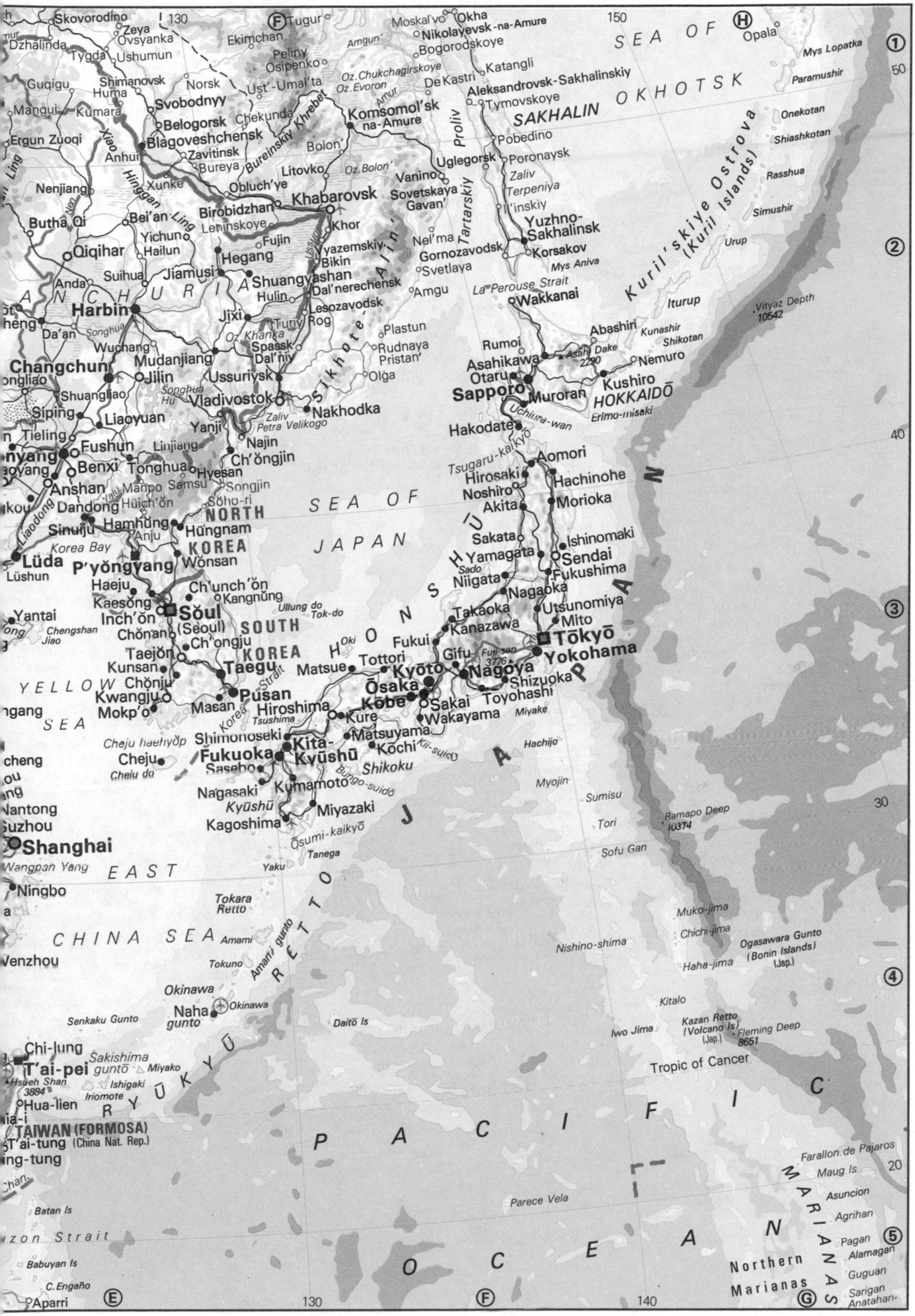

BURMA
Mandalay
Myingyan
Sagaing
Pakokku
Meiktila
Minbu
Magwe
Prome
Toungoo
Myanaung
Henzada
Bassein
Rangoon
Pegu
Moulmein
Mouths of the Irrawaddy
Ye
Tavoy
Mergui
Mergui Archipelago
Kengtung
Taunggyi
Chiang Mai
M.Chiang Rai
M.Lampang
Tak
Uttaradit
Sawankhalok
M. Phitsanulok
THAILAND
M.Nakhon Sawan
Nakhon Ratchasima
U.Ratchathani
Ayutthaya
Bangkok (Krung Thep)
Phet Buri
Prachuap Khiri Khan
Chumphon
Isthmus of Kra
Gulf of Thailand
Surat Thani
Phangnga
Ko Phuket
Phuket
Nakhon Si Thammarat
Thung Song
Trang
Songkhla
Thale Luang
B.Hat Yai
Ko Phangan
Ko Samui
Ko Chang
ANDAMAN SEA
Lampi
Vientiane
Nong Khai
Thakhek
M.Nakhon Phanom
M.Khon Kaen
Savannakhet
Saravane
Pakse
Attopeu
Luang Prabang
Muang Sing
Luang Namtha
B.Houei Sai
Sam Neua
Muang Nan
Pak Sane
LAOS
VIETNAM
CAMBODIA
ANGKOR
Sisophon
Battambang
Pursat
Kompong Chhnang
Kratie
K.Cham
Phnom Penh
Kompong Som
Trat
Phanom Dang Raek
Mekong
Srepok
Hanoi
Haiphong
Bac Ninh
Nam Dinh
Thanh Hoa
Vinh
Dong Hoi
Quang Tri
Hue
Da Nang
Quang Ngai
Pleiku
Qui Nhon
An Nhon
Ban Me Thuot
Tuy Hoa
Nha Trang
Da Lat
Phan Rang
Phan Thiet
Loc Ninh
Saigon (Ho Chi Minh)
My Tho
Can Tho
Long Xuyen
Vinh Long
Vinh Loi
Quan Long
Mouths of the Mekong
Mui Bai Bung
Con Son
Q.Phu Quoc
Lao Cai
Ha Giang
Lai Chau
Lang Son
Gulf of Tongkin
Nanning
Pingxiang
Beihai
Wuzhou
Guangzhou (Canton)
Foshan
Jiangmen
Yulin
Xiangjiang
Macau (Port.)
Heyuan
Chao'an
Shantou
Huizhou
Kowloon
Victoria
HONG KONG (U.K.)
Leizhou
Bandao
Zhanjiang
Xuwen
Lingao
Haikou
Dongfang
Wuzhi Shan 1879
Hainan Dao
Yulin
Dongsha Qundao
T'ai-nan
Kao-hsiung
Tung-Chiang
C.Bojeador
Laoag
Vigan
San Fernando
Lingayen
Tarlac
Bataan Pen.
Corregidor
San P
Batan
Mindoro
Calamian Group
Taytay
Palawan
Puerto Princesa
Brooke's Pt
Paracel Is
SOUTH CHINA SEA
INDO-CHINA
Thitu
Nanshan
Discovery Reef
Spratly Islands
Ladd Reef
Spratly
Amboyna Cay
Swallow Reef
Louisa Reef
Balabac
Balabac Str.
Banggi
Cagayan Sulu
Kudat
Kinabalu 4094
Kota Kinabalu
Sandakan
Labuk B.
Ranau
Weston
SABAH
Lahad Datu
Tenom
Tk Darvel
Bandar Seri Begawan
BRUNEI
Miri
Seria
Tawau
Niah
Malinau
Bintulu
Tarakan
Igan
Mukah
Tanjungselor
SARAWAK
Tanjungredeb
Sibu
Rajang
Hose Mts
Tamabo Ra.
G.Bulu 1252
Kayan
Kuching
Tg Datu
Paloh
Sambas
Singkawang
Serian
Niut 1701
Simanggang
Putussibau
Niapa 1380
Menyapa 2000
Sangkulirang
BORNEO
Sanggau
Kapuas
Sintang
Peg. Muller
Pontianak
Tayan
KALIMANTAN
Nangapinoh
Raya 2278
Peg. Schwaner
Samarinda
Donggala
Palu
G. Lokilalaki 3311
Balikpapan
Buntok
Meratus
Tanahgrogot
Maya
Sukadana
Karimata
Ketapang
Kendawangan
Palangkaraya
Mendawai
Sampit
Barito
Amuntai
Kandangan
Kumai
Banjarmasin
Kintap
Batakan
Tg Puting
Tg Selatan
Laut
Makassar Strait
Mamuju
Makale
Majene
Pinrang
Parepare
Ujung Pandang (Makassar)
Sala
SUL
MALAYSIA
PENINSULAR MALAYSIA
Langkawi
Kota Bharu
George Town
Pinang
Butterworth
Kuala Kerai
Kuala Trengganu
Taiping
Ipoh
Telok Anson
Kuala Lipis
Chukai
Kuantan
Pekan
Kelang
Kuala Lumpur
Gemas
Melaka
Mersing
Johor Bharu
SINGAPORE
Bintan
Kep. Riau
Kep. Anambas
Bunguran
Kep. Bunguran Selatan
Strait of Malacca
Sabang
Banda Aceh
Lhokseumawe
Calang
Takingeun
Meulaboh
Leuser 3381
Langsa
Belangpidie
Belawan
Kuala
Medan
Tanjungbalai
Kalakepen
Simeulue
Danau Toba
Tarutung
Kep. Banyak
Sibolga
Rantauparapat
Nias
Dumai
Natal
Pini
Pekanbaru
P.P. Batu
Bukittinggi
Pariaman
Padang
Muara
Solok
Rengat
Lingga
Singkep
Siberut
Kep. Mentawai
Sipora
Pagai Utara
Pagai Selatan
Tapan
Kerinci 3805
Hari
Jambi
Mentok
Pangkalpinang
Bangka
Palembang
Lubuklinggau
Toboali
Tanjungpandan
Belitung
Bengkulu
Peg. Barisan
SUMATERA
Enggano
Telukbetung
Selat Sunda
Jakarta
Tanjung Priok
Bogor
Cirebon
Bandung
Semarang
Muryo 1602
Rembang
Bawean
Madura
Pamekasan
P.P. Kangean
Genteng
Purwokerto
Slamet 3428
Surakarta
Surabaya
Kediri
Cilacap
Yogyakarta
Malang
Probolinggo
Jember
Banyuwangi
Singaraja
Denpasar
Bali
Selat Lombok
Mataram
Lombok
Rinjani 3726
Sumbawa Besar
Raba
Taliwang
Sumbawa
Waingapu
Sumba
Komodo
JAVA SEA
INDONESIA
FLORES
JAWA
INDIAN OCEAN
Christmas I. (Aust.)
Cocos Is (Aust.)
Keeling Is
A
B
C
1
2
3
4
5
20
10
0
10
100
110
120

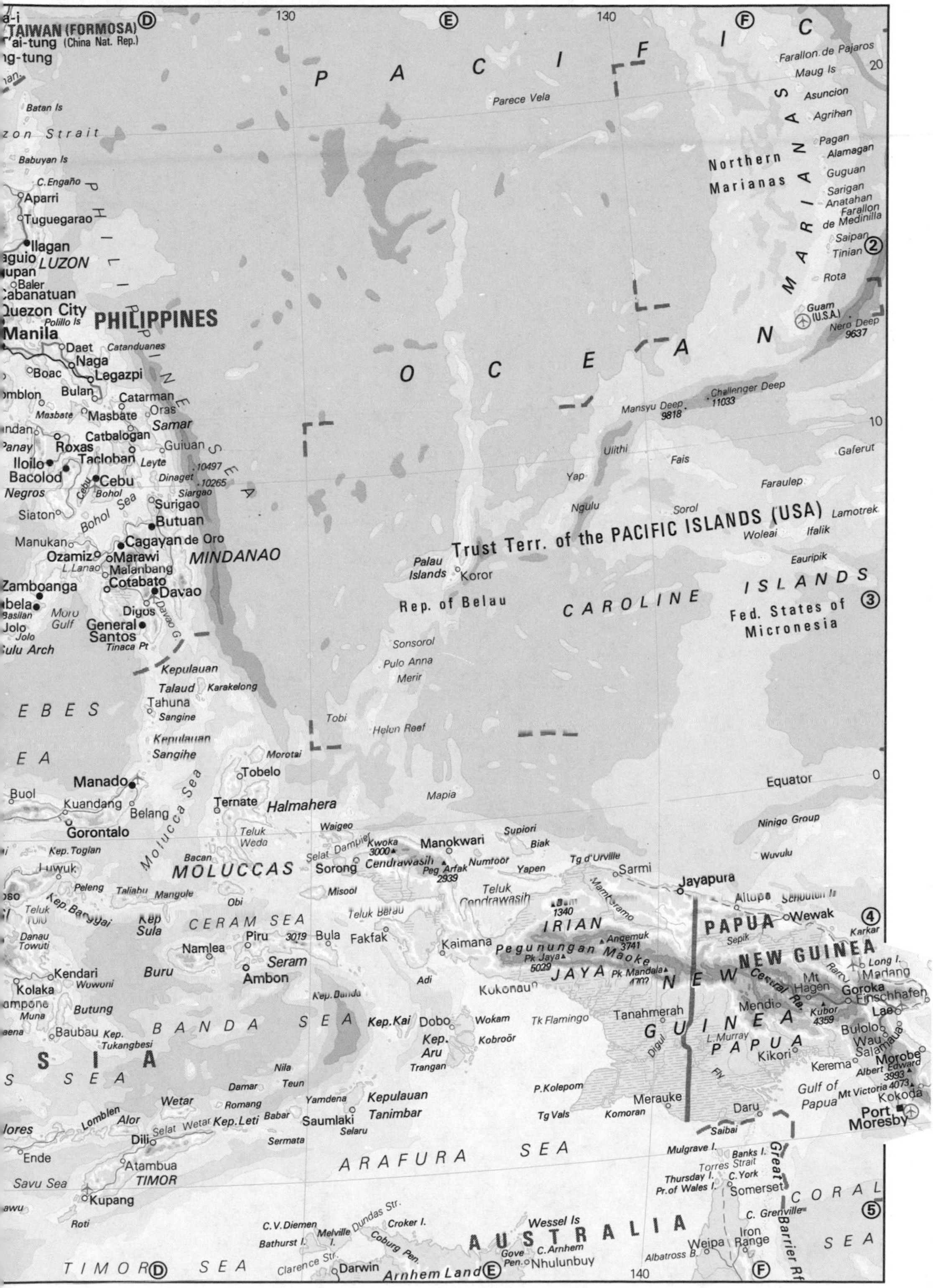
TAIWAN (FORMOSA)
T'ai-tung (China Nat. Rep.)
Batan Is
Babuyan Is
C. Engaño
Aparri
Tuguegarao
Ilagan
LUZON
Baler
Cabanatuan
Quezon City
Polillo Is
PHILIPPINES
Manila
Daet
Catanduanes
Naga
Legazpi
Boac
Bulan
Catarman
Masbate
Masbate
Oras
Samar
Catbalogan
Roxas
Guiuan
Iloilo
Tacloban
Leyte
Bacolod
Cebu
Dinaget
Negros
Bohol
Siargao
Surigao
Siaton
Bohol Sea
Butuan
Manukan
Cagayan de Oro
Ozamiz
Marawi
MINDANAO
L. Lanao
Malanbang
Zamboanga
Cotabato
Davao
Basilan
Moro Gulf
Digos
Davao G.
Jolo
General Santos
Tinaca Pt
Sulu Arch
Kepulauan Talaud
Karakelong
Tahuna
Sangine
Kepulauan Sangihe
Morotai
Tobelo
Manado
Buol
Kuandang
Belang
Gorontalo
Molucca Sea
Ternate
Halmahera
Teluk Weda
Kep. Toglan
Bacan
MOLUCCAS
Peleng
Taliabu
Mangole
Kep. Banggai
Kep Sula
Obi
CERAM SEA
Piru
3019
Bula
Namlea
Seram
Ambon
Buru
Kendari
Wowoni
Kolaka
Butung
Muna
Baubau
Kep. Tukangbesi
BANDA SEA
Kep. Banda
Nila
Teun
Damar
Romang
Wetar
Alor
Lomblen
Selat Wetar
Kep. Leti
Babar
Dili
Ende
Atambua
TIMOR
Savu Sea
Kupang
Roti
TIMOR SEA
PHILIPPINE SEA
PACIFIC OCEAN
Parece Vela
Farallon de Pajaros
Maug Is
Asuncion
Agrihan
Pagan
Alamagan
Guguan
Sarigan
Anatahan
Farallon de Medinilla
Saipan
Tinian
Rota
Northern Marianas
MARIANAS
Guam (U.S.A.)
Nero Deep 9637
Mansyu Deep 9818
Challenger Deep 11033
Ulithi
Fais
Gaferut
Yap
Faraulep
Ngulu
Sorol
Lamotrek
Trust Terr. of the PACIFIC ISLANDS (USA)
Woleai
Ifalik
Eauripik
Palau Islands
Koror
Rep. of Belau
CAROLINE ISLANDS
Fed. States of Micronesia
Sonsorol
Pulo Anna
Merir
Tobi
Helen Reef
Mapia
Equator
Ninigo Group
Wuvulu
Waigeo
Selat Dampier
Kwoka 3000
Manokwari
Supiori
Biak
Sorong
Cendrawasih
Peg Arfak 2939
Numfoor
Yapen
Tg d'Urville
Sarmi
Misool
Teluk Cendrawasih
Mamberamo
Jayapura
Schouten Is
Teluk Berau
Fakfak
1340
IRIAN JAYA
Kaimana
Pegunungan Maoke
Angemuk 3741
Pk Jaya 5029
Pk Mandala 4702
PAPUA NEW GUINEA
Wewak
Sepik
Karkar
Long I.
Madang
Mt Hagen
Goroka
Finschhafen
Central Ra.
Mendi
Kubor 4359
Lae
Adi
Kokonau
NEW GUINEA
Kep. Kai
Dobo
Wokam
Tk Flamingo
Tanahmerah
Kep. Aru
Kobroör
Trangan
Digul
L. Murray
Fly
PAPUA
Kikori
Bulolo
Wau
Salamaua
Kerema
Morobe
Albert Edward 3993
Mt Victoria 4073
Kokoda
Gulf of Papua
Port Moresby
P. Kolepom
Merauke
Komoran
Tg Vals
Daru
Saibai
Yamdena
Kepulauan Tanimbar
Saumlaki
Selaru
Sermata
ARAFURA SEA
Mulgrave I.
Banks I.
Torres Strait
Thursday I.
C. York
Pr. of Wales I.
Somerset
Great Barrier Rf
CORAL SEA
C. Grenville
C. V. Diemen
Melville I.
Dundas Str.
Croker I.
Wessel Is
Bathurst I.
Coburg Pen.
AUSTRALIA
Gove Pen.
C. Arnhem
Nhulunbuy
Weipa
Iron Range
Albatross B.
Clarence Str.
Darwin
Arnhem Land
130
140
20
10
0

MONGOLIA
NEI MONGOL
LIAONING
JILIN
HEBEI
SHANXI
SHANDONG
HENAN
SHAANXI
NINGXIA
GANSU
QINGHAI
JIANGSU
ANHUI
BO HAI
KOREA BAY
YELLOW SEA
(HUANG HAI)
Bohai Wan
Laizhou Wan
Liaodong Wan
Haizhou Wan
Jiaozhou Wan
Beijing
(Peking)
Tianjin
(Tientsin)
Shenyang
Changchun
Lüda
(Dairen)
Jinan
(Tsinan)
Qingdao(Tsingtao)
Taiyuan
Shijiazhuang
Zhengzhou
Luoyang
Kaifeng
Xi'an
(Sian)
Lanzhou
Yinchuan
Xining
Hohhot
Baotou
Datong
Zhangjiakou
Tangshan
Qinhuangdao
Anshan
Fushun
Benxi
Dandong
Jinzhou
Fuxin
Chifeng
Chengde
Baoding
Handan
Xingtai
Anyang
Xinxiang
Jiaozuo
Pingdingshan
Xuchang
Nanyang
Xuzhou
Lianyungang
Yantai
Weifang
Zibo
Jining
Bengbu
Huainan
Baoji
Tianshui
Erenhot
Mu Us Shamo
Tengger Shamo
Badain Jaran Shamo
Qin Ling
Lüliang Shan
Taihang Shan
Yin Shan
Liupan Shan
Huang He
Wei He
Fen He
Luo He
Han Shui
Da Yunhe
Dalai Nur
Ulansuhai Nur
Gaxun Nur
Helan Shan 3556
Wutai Shan 3058
Taibai Shan 3767
Maomao Shan 4070
Nemagt Uul 2768
Hörh Uul 1763
Gurvan Sayhan Uul 2825

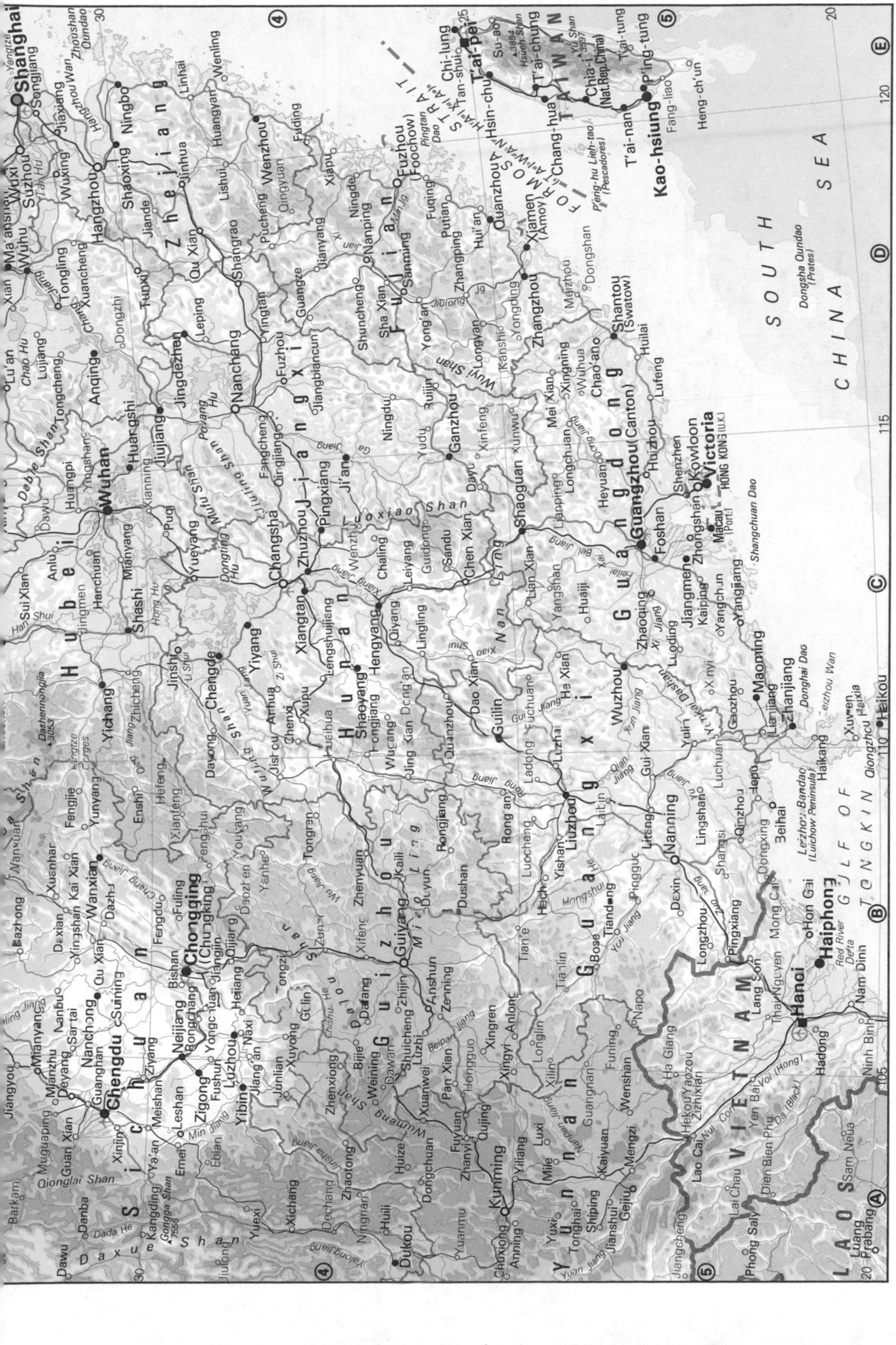
Sichuan
Hubei
Hunan
Jiangxi
Zhejiang
Fujian
Guangdong
Guangxi
Guizhou
Yunnan
TAIWAN
VIETNAM
LAOS
SOUTH CHINA SEA
GULF OF TONGKIN
FORMOSA STRAIT
TAIWAN HAIXIA
Shanghai
Wuhan
Chengdu
Chongqing (Chungking)
Changsha
Nanchang
Hangzhou
Fuzhou (Foochow)
Guangzhou (Canton)
Victoria
HONG KONG (U.K.)
Kowloon
Macau (Port.)
Guiyang
Kunming
Nanning
Guilin
Hanoi
Haiphong
T'ai-pei
Kao-hsiung
T'ai-chung
Chi-lung
Xiamen (Amoy)
Shantou (Swatow)
Wenzhou
Ningbo
Nanjing
Suzhou
Wuxi
Yichang
Shashi
Xiangtan
Zhuzhou
Hengyang
Shaoyang
Ganzhou
Shaoguan
Liuzhou
Wuzhou
Zhanjiang
Maoming
Haikou
Beihai
Zhangzhou
Quanzhou
Jingdezhen
Jiujiang
Anqing
Yibin
Luzhou
Zigong
Neijiang
Nanchong
Wanxian
Dukou
Lao Cai
Luang Prabang
Nam Dinh
Dongsha Qundao (Prates)
Leizhou Bandao (Luichow Peninsula)
Red River Delta
Dongting Hu
Poyang Hu
Nan Ling
Wuyi Shan
Wuling Shan
Daxue Shan
Qionglai Shan
Dabie Shan
Miao Ling
Dalou Shan
Luoxiao Shan
Yangtze
Han Shui
Xiang Jiang
Gan Jiang
Xi Jiang
Min Jiang
Jinsha Jiang
Yuan Jiang
4
5
A
B
C
D
E
20
25
30
105
110
115
120

0 100 200 300 km
0 100 200 mls

SEA OF JAPAN
HONSHU
JAPAN
PACIFIC OCEAN
SHIKOKU
KYUSHU
Sado-shima
Noto-hantō
Oki-shotō
Dōgo
Dōzen
Awa-shima
Hegura-jima
Ullung-do
Todong
Tok-do (Take-shima) (Liancourt Rocks)
Niigata
Sendai
Fukushima
Kōriyama
Iwaki
Mito
Tōkyō
Chiba
Kawasaki
Yokohama
Kōfu
Nagano
Matsumoto
Toyama
Kanazawa
Fukui
Gifu
Nagoya
Shizuoka
Hamamatsu
Toyohashi
Tsu
Kyōto
Ōsaka
Kōbe
Sakai
Nara
Wakayama
Himeji
Okayama
Hiroshima
Tottori
Matsue
Shimonoseki
Kita-Kyūshū
Fukuoka
Kumamoto
Ōita
Matsuyama
Kōchi
Tokushima
Takamatsu
Biwa-ko
Wakasa-wan
Ise-wan
Suruga-wan
Sagami-nada
Kii-suidō
Bungo-suidō
Tosa-wan
Harima-nada
Hiuchi-nada
Iyo-nada
Suō-nada
Fuji-san 3776
Ontake-san 3063
Yariga-take 3180
Haku-san 2702
Shirane-san 2368
Iide san 2105
Shirami-san 3192
Kuju-san 1791
Bōsō-hantō
Kii-sanchi
Shikoku-sanchi
Chūgoku-sanchi
Ō-shima
Miyake-jima
Hachijō-jima
Shiono-misaki
Muroto-zaki
Ashizuri-misaki
Inubo-saki
Nojima-zaki
Omae-zaki
35
135
140
A
B
C
1
2

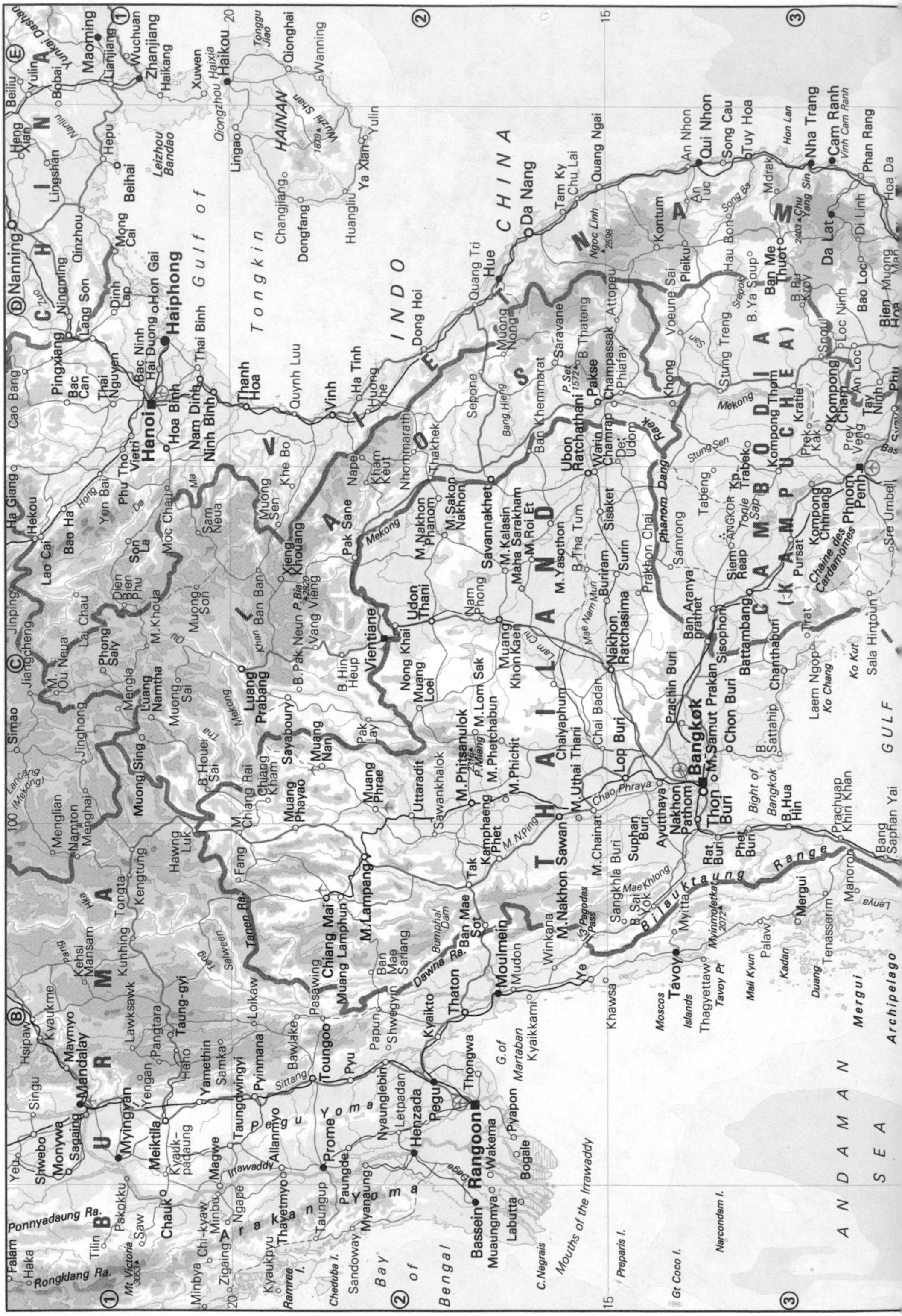
CHINA
BURMA
THAILAND
LAOS
VIETNAM
CAMPUCHEA (KAMPUCHEA)
INDO CHINA
HAINAN
Gulf of Tongkin
ANDAMAN SEA
Bay of Bengal
G. of Martaban
GULF
Mergui Archipelago
Mouths of the Irrawaddy
Rangoon
Mandalay
Bangkok
Hanoi
Haiphong
Vientiane
Phnom Penh
Da Nang
Hue
Luang Prabang
Chiang Mai
Moulmein
Haikou
Nanning
Mekong

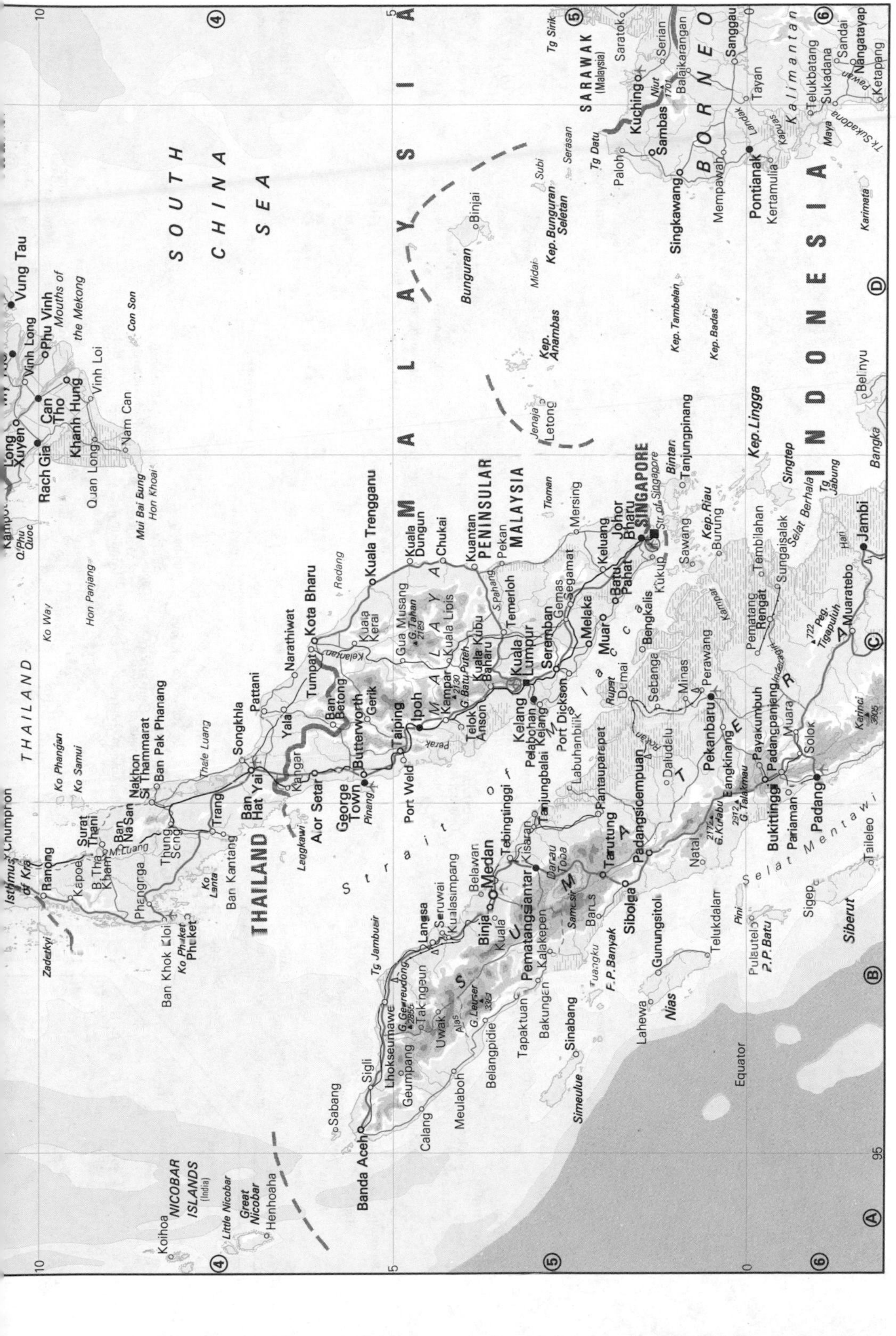
SOUTH CHINA SEA
THAILAND
MALAYSIA
INDONESIA
BORNEO
SUMATERA
PENINSULAR MALAYSIA
SARAWAK
(Malaysia)
Kalimantan
NICOBAR ISLANDS
(India)
Little Nicobar
Great Nicobar
Henhoaha
Koihoa
Banda Aceh
Sabang
Sigli
Lhokseumawe
Geumpang
Calang
Meulaboh
Belangpidie
Tapaktuan
Sinabang
Simeulue
G. Geureudong
G. Leuser
Takengeun
Uwak
Langsa
Seruwai
Kualasimpang
Binjai
Medan
Belawan
Tebingtinggi
Kisaran
Tanjungbalai
Pematangsiantar
Kabanjahe
Danau Toba
Samosir
Tarutung
Sibolga
Barus
Padangsidempuan
Gunungsitoli
Nias
Lahewa
Telukdalam
P. P. Batu
Pini
Natal
Bukittinggi
Pariaman
Padang
Padangpanjang
Payakumbuh
Solok
Muara
Pekanbaru
Bangkinang
Perawang
Dumai
Rupat
Bengkalis
Selatpanjang
Rengat
Pematang
Tembilahan
Muaratebo
Jambi
Siberut
Sigep
Taileleo
Selat Mentawai
Kerinci
Equator
Strait of Malacca
George Town
Pinang
Butterworth
Taiping
Ipoh
Kampar
G. Batu Puteh
Telok Anson
Kuala Kubu Baharu
Kuala Lumpur
Kelang
Pelabohan Kelang
Port Dickson
Seremban
Melaka
Muar
Batu Pahat
Keluang
Johor Bharu
SINGAPORE
Str. of Singapore
Kukup
Segamat
Gemas
Temerloh
Kuala Lipis
Kuala Kerai
Gua Musang
G. Tahan
Kota Bharu
Tumpat
Kuala Trengganu
Kuala Dungun
Chukai
Kuantan
Pekan
Mersing
Tioman
Alor Setar
Kangar
Langkawi
Port Weld
Gerik
Ban Betong
Yala
Pattani
Narathiwat
Songkhla
Ban Hat Yai
Trang
Nakhon Si Thammarat
Ban Pak Phanang
Thale Luang
Surat Thani
Ban Na San
Thung Song
Ranong
Kapoe
Phangnga
Phuket
Ko Phuket
Ban Khok Kloi
Ko Lanta
Ban Kantang
Ko Samui
Ko Phangan
Chumphon
Isthmus of Kra
Zadetkyi
Tg Jambueir
Rach Gia
Long Xuyen
Can Tho
Khanh Hung
Vinh Long
Phu Vinh
Vung Tau
Mouths of the Mekong
Con Son
Quan Long
Nam Can
Vinh Loi
Mui Bai Bung
Hon Khoai
Hon Panjang
Ko Wai
Redang
Bunguran
Binjai
Kep. Bunguran Seletan
Kep. Anambas
Jenaja
Letong
Midai
Subi
Serasan
Tg Datu
Tg Sirik
Kuching
Serian
Saratok
Balaikarangan
Sambas
Paloh
Singkawang
Mempawah
Pontianak
Kertamulia
Sanggau
Tayan
Telukbatang
Sukadana
Sandai
Nangatayap
Ketapang
Karimata
Kep. Tambelan
Kep. Badas
Kep. Riau
Bintan
Tanjungpinang
Sawang
Burung
Kep. Lingga
Singkep
Selat Berhala
Tg Jabung
Bangka
Belinyu
Sungaisalak
A
B
C
D
4
5
6
95
0
5
10

1:10M 0 100 200 300 400 km 0 100 200 mls

1:10M 0 100 200 300 400 km / 0 100 200 mls

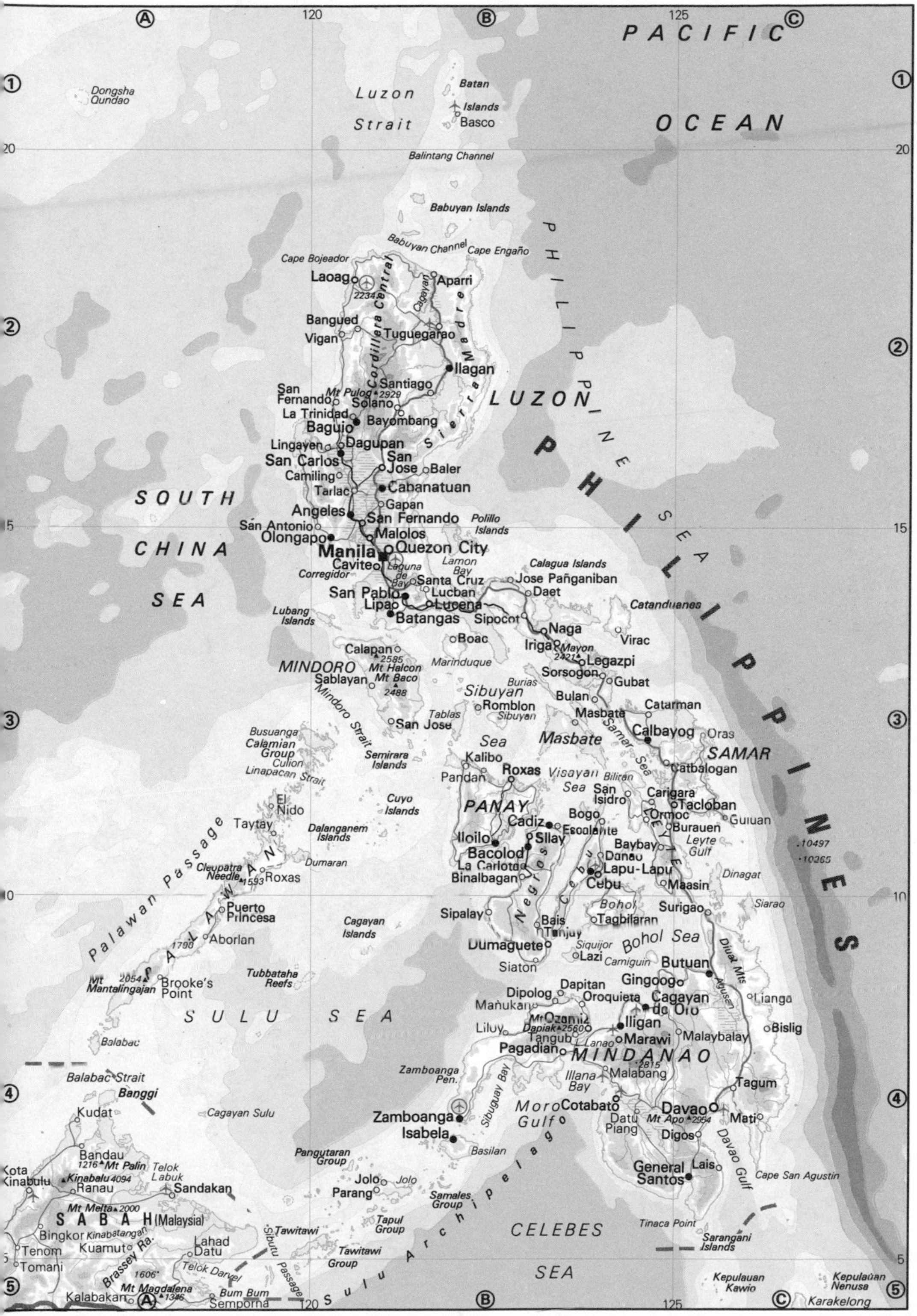

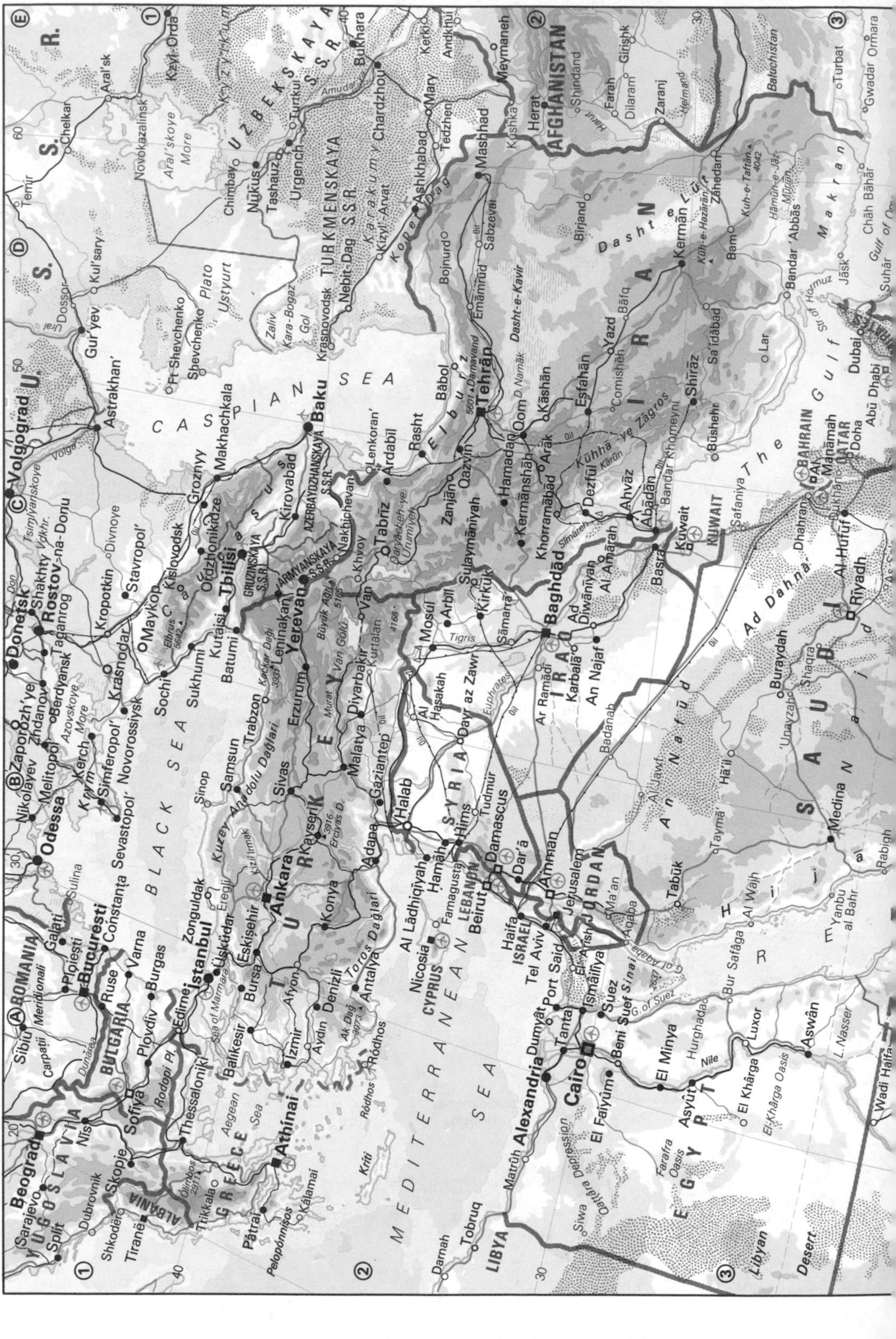
CASPIAN SEA
BLACK SEA
MEDITERRANEAN SEA
The Gulf
TURKEY
IRAN
IRAQ
SYRIA
SAUDI ARABIA
EGYPT
AFGHANISTAN
JORDAN
ISRAEL
LEBANON
CYPRUS
KUWAIT
BAHRAIN
QATAR
LIBYA
GREECE
BULGARIA
ROMANIA
YUGOSLAVIA
ALBANIA
U.S.S.R.
TURKMENSKAYA S.S.R.
UZBEKSKAYA S.S.R.
AZERBAYDZHANSKAYA S.S.R.
ARMYANSKAYA S.S.R.
GRUZINSKAYA S.S.R.
Tehrān
Baghdād
Ankara
Istanbul
Damascus
Beirut
Amman
Jerusalem
Cairo
Alexandria
Riyadh
Kuwait
Baku
Tbilisi
Yerevan
Volgograd
Odessa
Bucuresti
Beograd
Athínai
Sofiya
Nicosia
Herat
Mashhad
Esfahān
Shīrāz
Kermān
Tabrīz
Halab
Mosul
Basra
Medina
Dubai
Aswân
Nile
Tigris
Euphrates
Libyan Desert
An Nafūd
Ad Dahnā
Dasht-e Lūt
Dasht-e-Kavir
Kara-kumy
Kyzyl-kum
Aral'skoye More
Plato Ustyurt
Kavkaz
Elburz
Kūhhā-ye Zāgros
Toros Dağlari
Anadolu Dağlari
Makran
Sinai
Gulf of Suez
Str. of Hormuz
Gulf of Oman

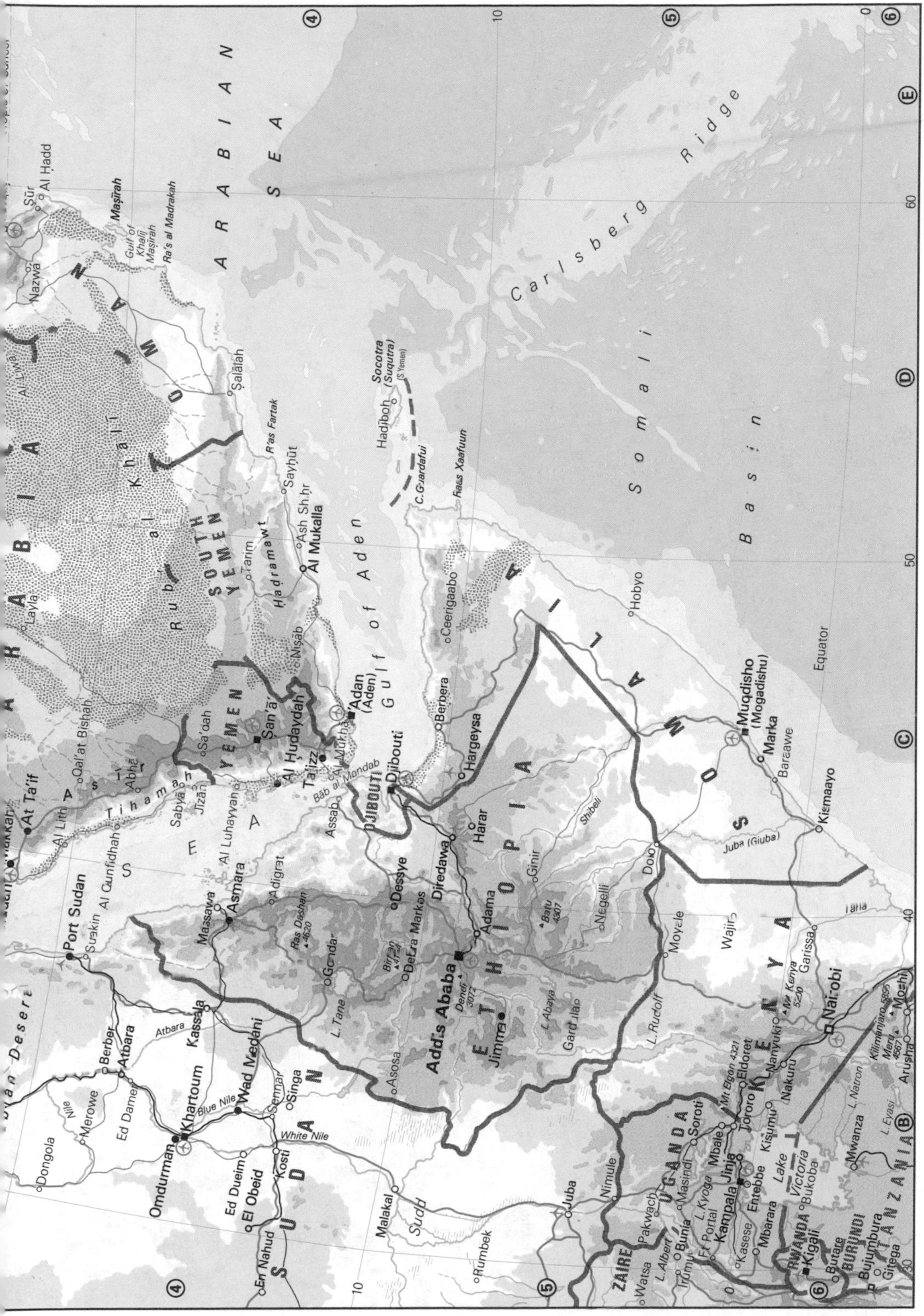
ARABIAN SEA
Carlsberg Ridge
Somali Basin
Gulf of Aden
Rub' al Khali
SAUDI ARABIA
OMAN
SOUTH YEMEN
YEMEN
Red Sea
SUDAN
ETHIOPIA
SOMALIA
DJIBOUTI
KENYA
UGANDA
TANZANIA
RWANDA
BURUNDI
ZAIRE
Nubian Desert
Al Hadd
Sur
Masirah
Gulf of Masirah
Ra's al Madrakah
Nazwa
Al Liwa
Salalah
Ras Fartak
Sayhut
Ash Sh.hr
Al Mukalla
Tarim
Hadramawt
Layla
Nisab
Adan (Aden)
San'a'
Sa'dah
Al Hudaydah
Ta'izz
Al Mukha
Bab al Mandab
Qal'at Bishah
Abha
Jizan
Sabya
Tihamah
At Ta'if
Al Lith
Al Qunfidhah
Al Luhayyah
Socotra (Suqutra)
Hadiboh
C. Guardafui
Raas Xaafuun
Ceerigaabo
Berbera
Hargeysa
Djibouti
Assab
Hobyo
Muqdisho (Mogadishu)
Marka
Baraawe
Kismaayo
Juba (Giuba)
Shibeli
Equator
Harar
Diredawa
Dessye
Adigrat
Asmara
Massawa
Ras Dashan 4620
Gondar
Debra Markos
Birhan 4154
Addis Ababa
Dendi 3072
Adama
Jimma
Ginir
Batu 4307
Negelli
Dolo
L. Abaya
Gardula
L. Tana
Asosa
Port Sudan
Suakin
Atbara
Berber
Kassala
Khartoum
Omdurman
Wad Medani
Blue Nile
White Nile
Sennar
Singa
Kosti
Ed Dueim
El Obeid
En Nahud
Dongola
Merowe
Ed Damer
Nile
Malakal
Sudd
Juba
Rumbek
Nimule
Moyale
Wajir
Garissa
Tana
L. Rudolf
Nairobi
Mt Kenya 5200
Kilimanjaro 5895
Meru 4567
Moshi
Arusha
L. Natron
L. Eyasi
Nanyuki
Nakuru
Eldoret
Mt Elgon 4321
Kisumu
Tororo
Soroti
Mbale
Jinja
Kampala
Entebbe
L. Kyoga
Masindi
Gulu
Pakwach
L. Albert
Bunia
Irumu
Ft Portal
Kasese
Mbarara
Lake Victoria
Bukoba
Mwanza
Kigali
Butare
Bujumbura
Gitega
Watsa
10
20
30
40
50
60
0

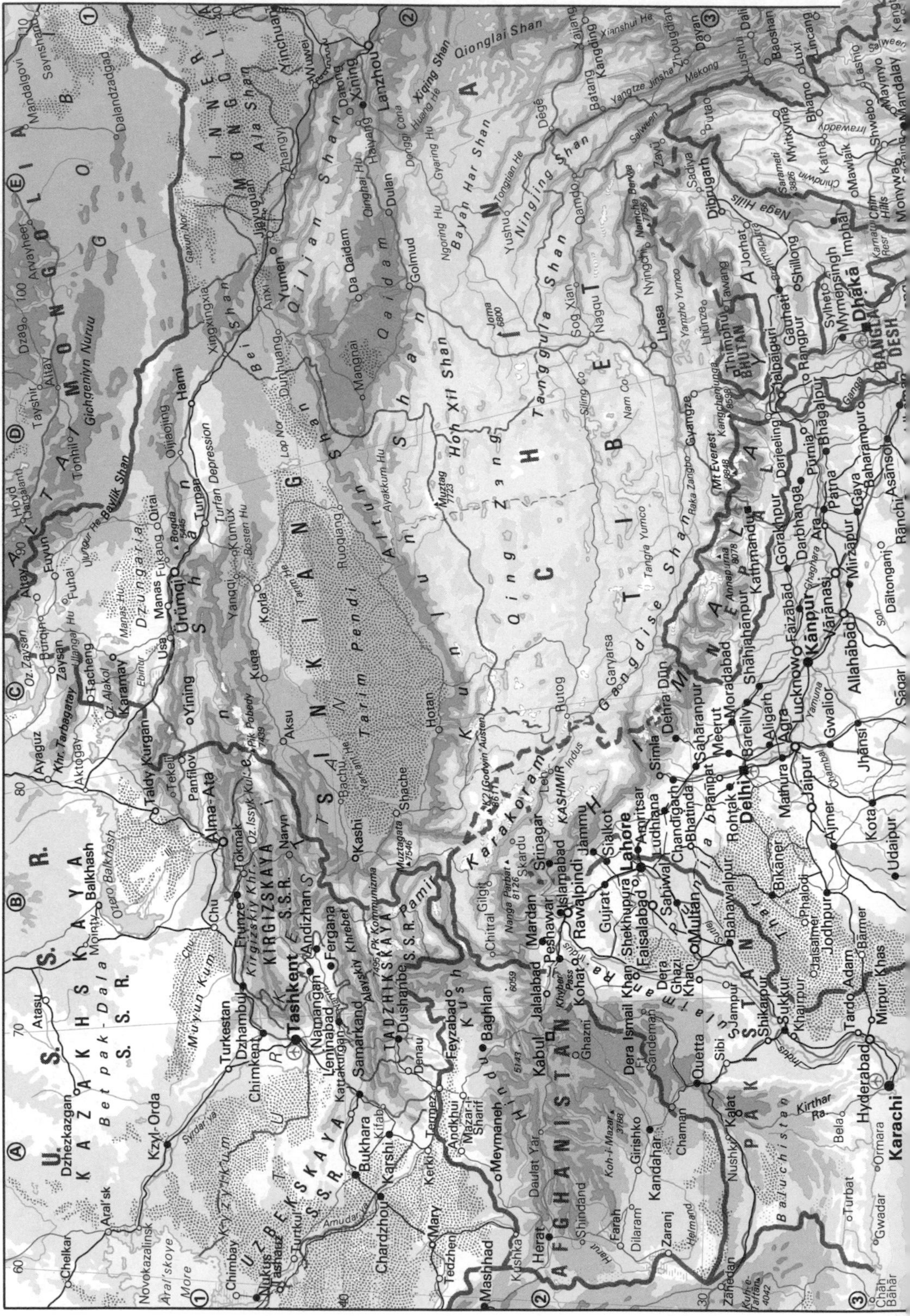
MONGOLIA
INNER MONGOLIA
Mandalgovi
Dalandzadgad
Lanzhou
Xining
Qionglai Shan
Dzungaria
Ürümqi
Turpan
Turfan Depression
Hami
Altay
Taklimakan
Tarim Pendi
Kunlun Shan
Altun Shan
Qilian Shan
Qaidam
Golmud
Bayan Har Shan
Tanggula Shan
Qing Zang
TIBET
Lhasa
Gangdise Shan
Karakoram
KASHMIR
Srinagar
Mt Everest
NEPAL
Kathmandu
BHUTAN
Thimphu
Dhaka
BANGLADESH
Delhi
Lahore
Islamabad
Rawalpindi
Peshawar
Kabul
AFGHANISTAN
Kandahar
Herat
Hindu Kush
PAKISTAN
Quetta
Karachi
Hyderabad
Multan
Kanpur
Allahabad
Varanasi
Patna
Jaipur
Agra
Lucknow
Tashkent
Samarkand
Bukhara
Dushanbe
Frunze
Alma-Ata
Balkhash
KAZAKHSKAYA S.S.R.
KIRGIZSKAYA S.S.R.
TADZHIKSKAYA S.S.R.
UZBEKSKAYA S.S.R.
Kzyl-Orda
Aral'sk
Mashhad

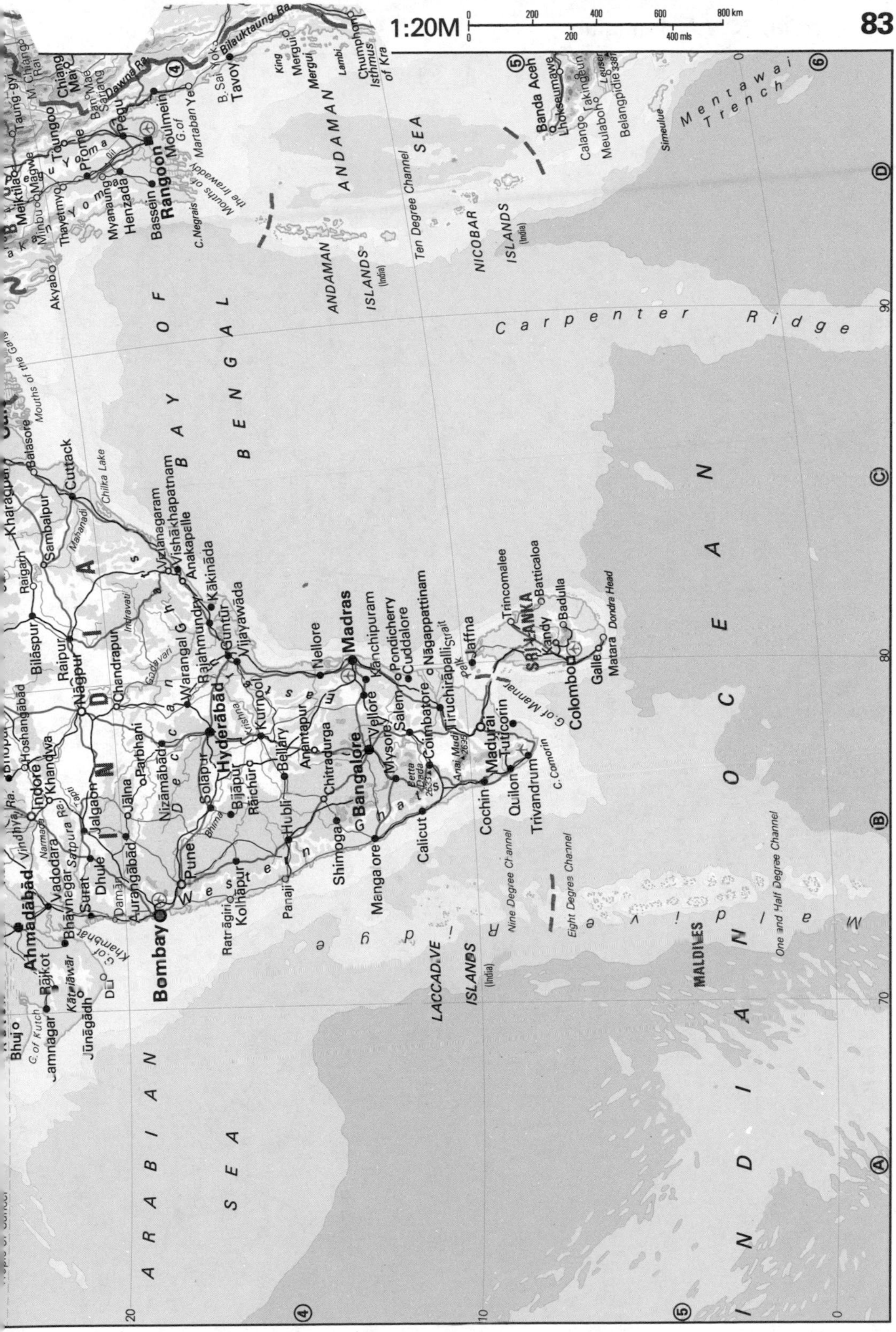
1:20M
0 200 400 600 800 km
0 200 400 mls
ARABIAN SEA
BAY OF BENGAL
ANDAMAN SEA
INDIAN OCEAN
INDIA
SRI LANKA
MALDIVES
LACCADIVE ISLANDS (India)
ANDAMAN ISLANDS (India)
NICOBAR ISLANDS (India)
Carpenter Ridge
Mentawai Trench
Ten Degree Channel
Nine Degree Channel
Eight Degree Channel
One and Half Degree Channel
Bombay
Madras
Hyderābād
Bangalore
Ahmadābād
Rangoon
Colombo
Moulmein
Tavoy
Mergui
Banda Aceh
Cuttack
Nāgpur
Pune
Madurai
Trivandrum
Cochin
Calicut
Mangalore
Jaffna
Kandy
Galle
Trincomalee
Batticaloa
Vishākhapatnam
Vijayawāda
Nellore
Pondicherry
Cuddalore
Coimbatore
Tiruchirāpalli
Salem
Mysore
Vellore
Kurnool
Bellary
Hubli
Kolhāpur
Sholāpur
Aurangābād
Jalgaon
Indore
Vadodara
Surat
Rājkot
Bhuj
G. of Kutch
G. of Khambhat
G. of Mannar
C. Comorin
Chilka Lake
Mouths of the Irrawaddy
G. of Martaban
Isthmus of Kra
A B C D
4 5 6
0 10 20
70 80 90

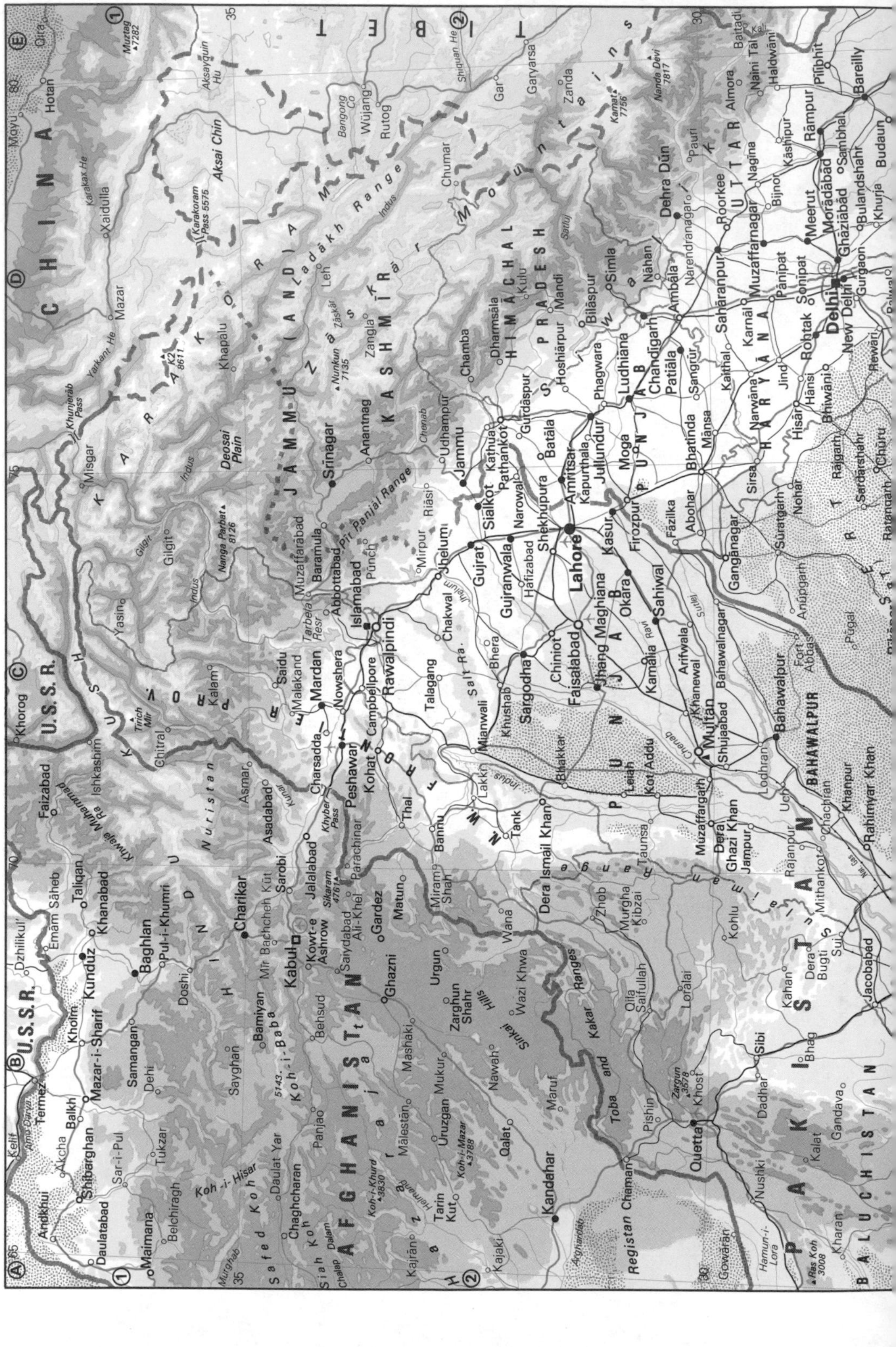
CHINA
U.S.S.R.
AFGHANISTAN
PAKISTAN
JAMMU AND KASHMIR
HIMACHAL PRADESH
PUNJAB
HARYANA
UTTAR PRADESH
BALUCHISTAN
BAHAWALPUR
N.W. FRONTIER
HINDU KUSH
KARAKORAM
Ladakh Range
Pir Panjal Range
Salt Ra.
Toba and Kakar Ranges
Sulaiman Range
Aksai Chin
Deosai Plain
Nuristan
Hotan
Xaidulla
Mazar
Khorog
Faizabad
Ishkashim
Chitral
Gilgit
Yasin
Misgar
Khapalu
Leh
Srinagar
Anantnag
Baramula
Muzaffarabad
Abbottabad
Islamabad
Rawalpindi
Mardan
Peshawar
Kohat
Bannu
Jalalabad
Kabul
Charikar
Baghlan
Kunduz
Mazar-i-Sharif
Termez
Balkh
Shibarghan
Maimana
Daulatabad
Andkhui
Bamiyan
Ghazni
Gardez
Kandahar
Qalat
Chaman
Quetta
Sibi
Jacobabad
Kalat
Zhob
Dera Ismail Khan
Dera Ghazi Khan
Multan
Bahawalpur
Sahiwal
Okara
Faisalabad
Sargodha
Jhang Maghiana
Gujranwala
Gujrat
Jhelum
Sialkot
Lahore
Kasur
Amritsar
Jullundur
Ludhiana
Chandigarh
Patiala
Firozpur
Bhatinda
Jammu
Pathankot
Simla
Dehra Dun
Saharanpur
Meerut
Moradabad
Rampur
Bareilly
Delhi
New Delhi
Rohtak
Hisar
Ganganagar
Rahimyar Khan
Khanpur
K2 8611
Nanga Parbat 8126
Nanda Devi 7817
Tirich Mir
Khyber Pass
Karakoram Pass 5575
Khunjerab Pass
Indus
Chenab
Jhelum
Sutlej
Ravi
Tarbela Resr

ARABIAN SEA
Tropic of Cancer
Karachi
Hyderabad
Sukkur
Jaisalmer
Jodhpur
Bikaner
Jaipur
Ajmer
Udaipur
Kota
Agra
Gwalior
Kanpur
Jhansi
Bhopal
Sagar
Jabalpur
Indore
Ujjain
Ahmadabad
Vadodara
Surat
Rajkot
Jamnagar
Bhavnagar
Bombay
Pune (Poona)
Nasik
Aurangabad
Nagpur
Amravati
Akola
Dhule
Jalgaon
Ahmadnagar
Nanded
Gulf of Khambhat
Rann of Kachchh
Mouths of the Indus
Thane
Alibag

1:7.5M

0 100 200 300 km
0 50 100 150 mls

1:7.5M 0 100 200 300 km 0 50 100 150 mls

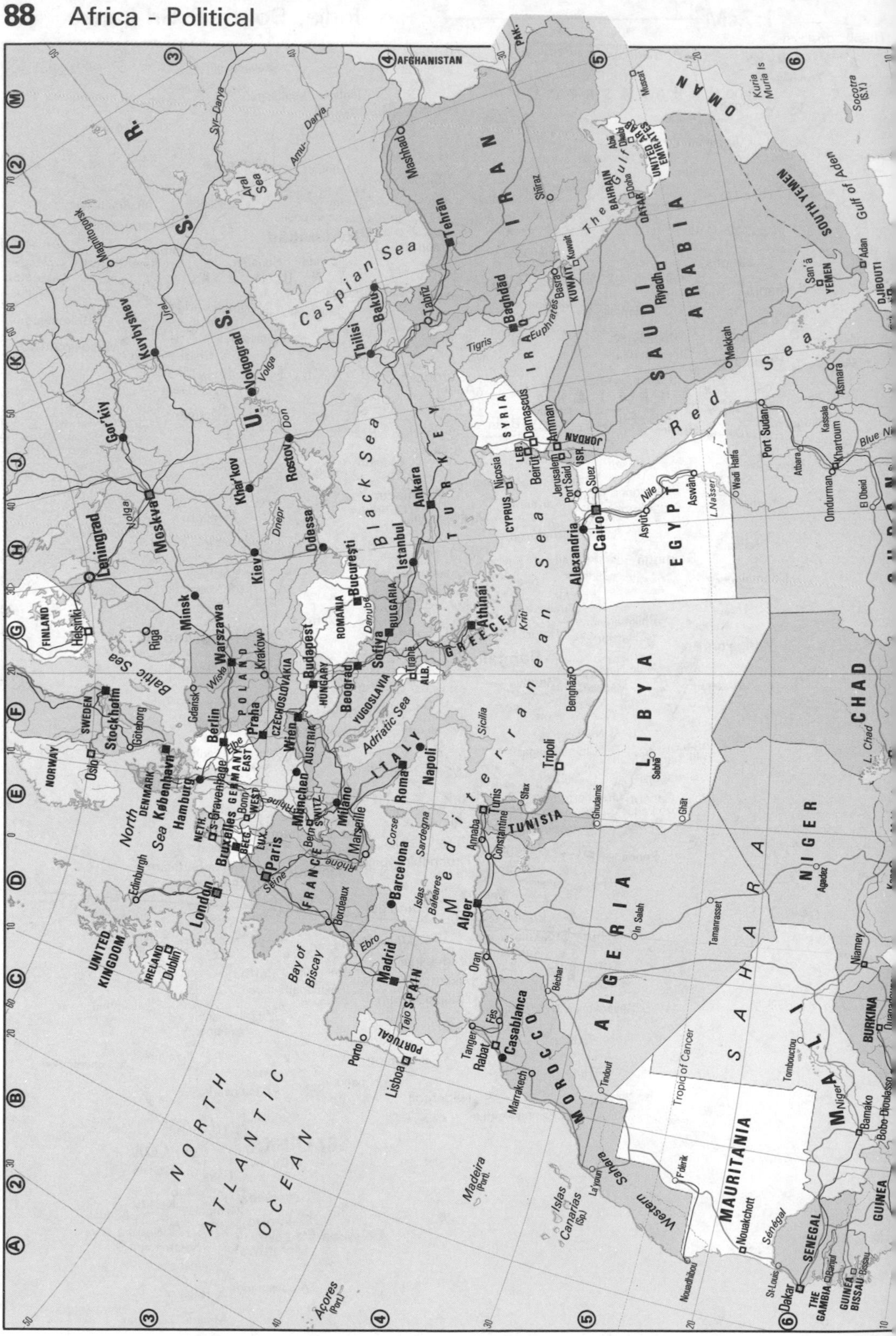
AFGHANISTAN
PAK.
IRAN
OMAN
Kuria Muria Is
Socotra (S.Y.)
SOUTH YEMEN
Gulf of Aden
YEMEN
DJIBOUTI
SAUDI ARABIA
UNITED ARAB EMIRATES
QATAR
BAHRAIN
KUWAIT
The Gulf
Caspian Sea
Aral Sea
U. S. S. R.
Black Sea
TURKEY
SYRIA
IRAQ
JORDAN
LEB.
ISR.
CYPRUS
Red Sea
EGYPT
SUDAN
LIBYA
CHAD
NIGER
ALGERIA
TUNISIA
MOROCCO
SAHARA
MAURITANIA
MALI
BURKINA
SENEGAL
THE GAMBIA
GUINEA BISSAU
GUINEA
Western Sahara
Mediterranean Sea
GREECE
ALB.
YUGOSLAVIA
BULGARIA
ROMANIA
HUNGARY
CZECHOSLOVAKIA
AUSTRIA
POLAND
GERMANY EAST
GERMANY WEST
SWITZ.
ITALY
FRANCE
SPAIN
PORTUGAL
LUX.
BELG.
NETH.
DENMARK
NORWAY
SWEDEN
FINLAND
UNITED KINGDOM
IRELAND
North Sea
Baltic Sea
Adriatic Sea
Bay of Biscay
NORTH ATLANTIC OCEAN
Açores (Port.)
Madeira (Port.)
Islas Canarias (Sp.)
Tropic of Cancer
Moskva
Leningrad
Gor'kiy
Kuybyshev
Volgograd
Rostov
Khar'kov
Kiev
Odessa
Minsk
Riga
Helsinki
Stockholm
Oslo
Göteborg
København
Warszawa
Kraków
Berlin
Praha
Wien
Budapest
Beograd
Sofiya
Bucureşti
Istanbul
Ankara
Athínai
Tiranë
Roma
Napoli
Milano
München
Bern
Marseille
Paris
Bruxelles
's-Gravenhage
Bonn
Hamburg
London
Edinburgh
Dublin
Bordeaux
Barcelona
Madrid
Lisboa
Porto
Alger
Oran
Tunis
Constantine
Annaba
Sfax
Tripoli
Benghāzi
Alexandria
Cairo
Port Said
Suez
Asyût
Aswân
L. Nasser
Wadi Halfa
Port Sudan
Khartoum
Omdurman
Atbara
Kassala
Asmara
Mekkah
Riyadh
San'a
Adan
Baghdād
Basra
Kuwait
Tehrān
Mashhad
Shīrāz
Tabrīz
Baku
Tbilisi
Damascus
Beirūt
Amman
Jerusalem
Nicosia
Doha
Abū Dhabi
Muscat
Casablanca
Rabat
Fès
Tanger
Marrakech
Bechar
Tindouf
In Salah
Tamanrasset
Ghadamis
Ghāt
Sabhā
Agadez
Niamey
Tombouctou
Bamako
Nouakchott
Nouadhibou
F'dérik
La'youn
Dakar
St-Louis
Banjul
Bissau
Bobo Dioulasso
Ouagadougou
L. Chad
El Obeid
Blue Nile
Nile
Niger
Sénégal
Danube
Dnepr
Don
Volga
Ural
Amu-Darya
Syr-Darya
Tigris
Euphrates
Elbe
Wisła
Rhine
Rhône
Seine
Ebro
Tajo
Corse
Sardegna
Sicilia
Kriti
Islas Baleares
Magnitogorsk

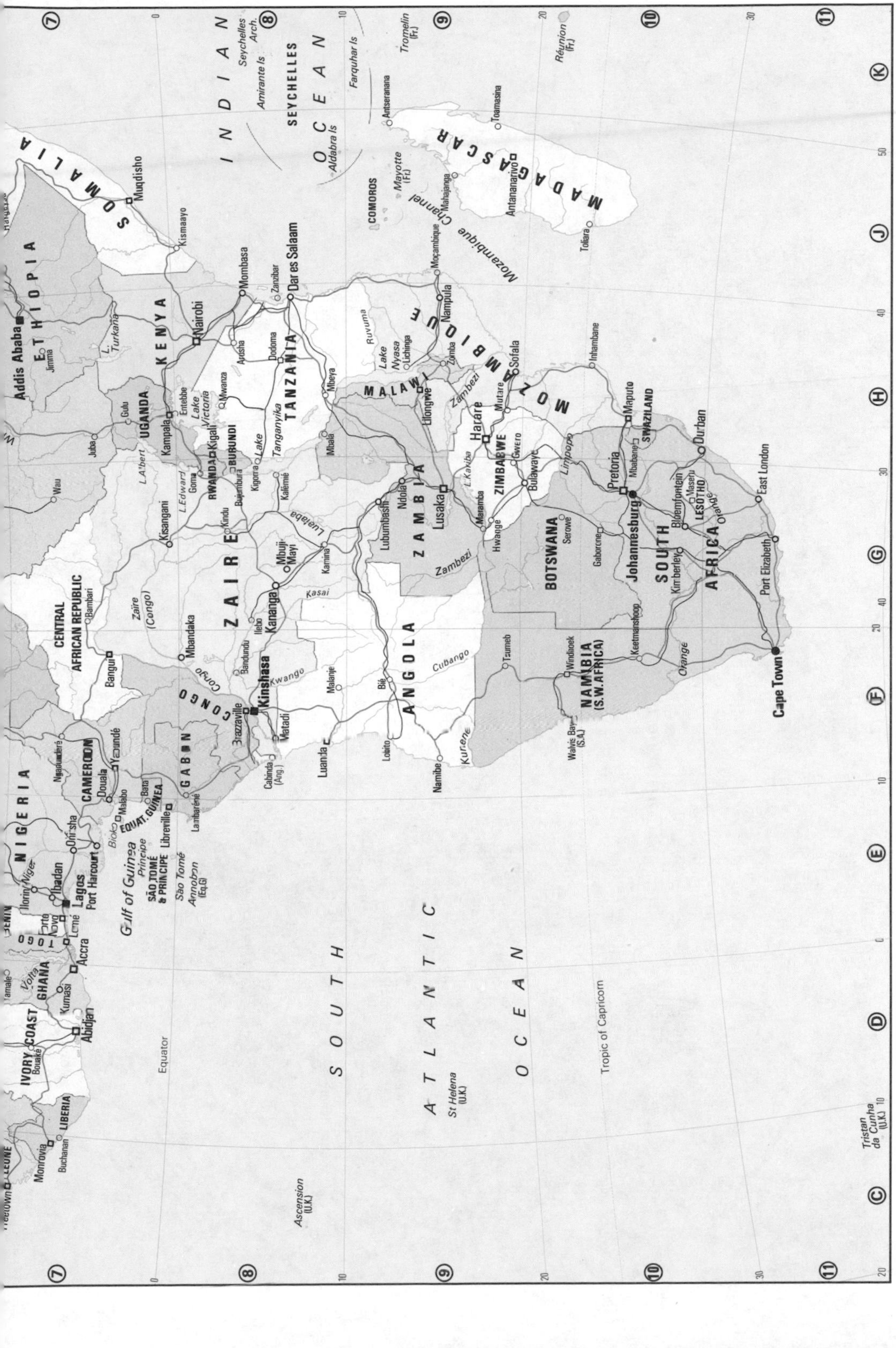
INDIAN OCEAN
SOUTH ATLANTIC OCEAN
SOMALIA
ETHIOPIA
Addis Ababa
Jimma
Muqdisho
Kismaayo
KENYA
Nairobi
Mombasa
L. Turkana
UGANDA
Kampala
Entebbe
Gulu
Juba
Wau
Lake Victoria
TANZANIA
Dar es Salaam
Dodoma
Arusha
Mwanza
Zanzibar
Mbeya
Lake Tanganyika
Kigoma
RWANDA
Kigali
BURUNDI
Bujumbura
SEYCHELLES
Seychelles Arch.
Amirante Is
Aldabra Is
Farquhar Is
COMOROS
Mayotte (Fr.)
Mozambique Channel
MADAGASCAR
Antananarivo
Mahajanga
Toamasina
Toliara
Antseranana
Tromelin (Fr.)
Réunion (Fr.)
MOZAMBIQUE
Moçambique
Nampula
Lichinga
Lake Nyasa
Ruvuma
Zomba
Sofala
Inhambane
Maputo
MALAWI
Lilongwe
ZAMBIA
Lusaka
Ndola
Lubumbashi
Zambezi
L. Kariba
ZIMBABWE
Harare
Mutare
Gweru
Bulawayo
Hwange
Maramba
Limpopo
SWAZILAND
Mbabane
BOTSWANA
Gaborone
Serowe
SOUTH AFRICA
Pretoria
Johannesburg
Durban
Bloemfontein
Kimberley
East London
Port Elizabeth
Cape Town
LESOTHO
Maseru
Orange
NAMIBIA (S.W. AFRICA)
Windhoek
Keetmanshoop
Tsumeb
Walvis Bay (S.A.)
ANGOLA
Luanda
Lobito
Namibe
Malanje
Bié
Cubango
Kunene
Cabinda (Ang.)
ZAIRE
Kinshasa
Kisangani
Mbandaka
Kananga
Mbuji-Mayi
Kindu
Kalemie
Kamina
Ilebo
Bandundu
Matadi
Lualaba
Kasai
Kwango
Zaire (Congo)
L. Albert
L. Edward
Goma
CONGO
Brazzaville
Congo
GABON
Libreville
Lambaréné
CENTRAL AFRICAN REPUBLIC
Bangui
Bambari
CAMEROON
Yaoundé
Douala
Ngaoundéré
EQUAT. GUINEA
Malabo
Bata
Bioko
NIGERIA
Lagos
Ibadan
Ilorin
Port Harcourt
Onitsha
Niger
Gulf of Guinea
Principe
SÃO TOMÉ & PRINCIPE
São Tomé
Annobon (Eq.G)
BENIN
Porto Novo
TOGO
Lomé
GHANA
Accra
Kumasi
Tamale
Volta
IVORY COAST
Abidjan
Bouaké
LIBERIA
Monrovia
Buchanan
Equator
Tropic of Capricorn
Ascension (U.K.)
St Helena (U.K.)
Tristan da Cunha (U.K.)
C D E F G H J K
7 8 9 10 11

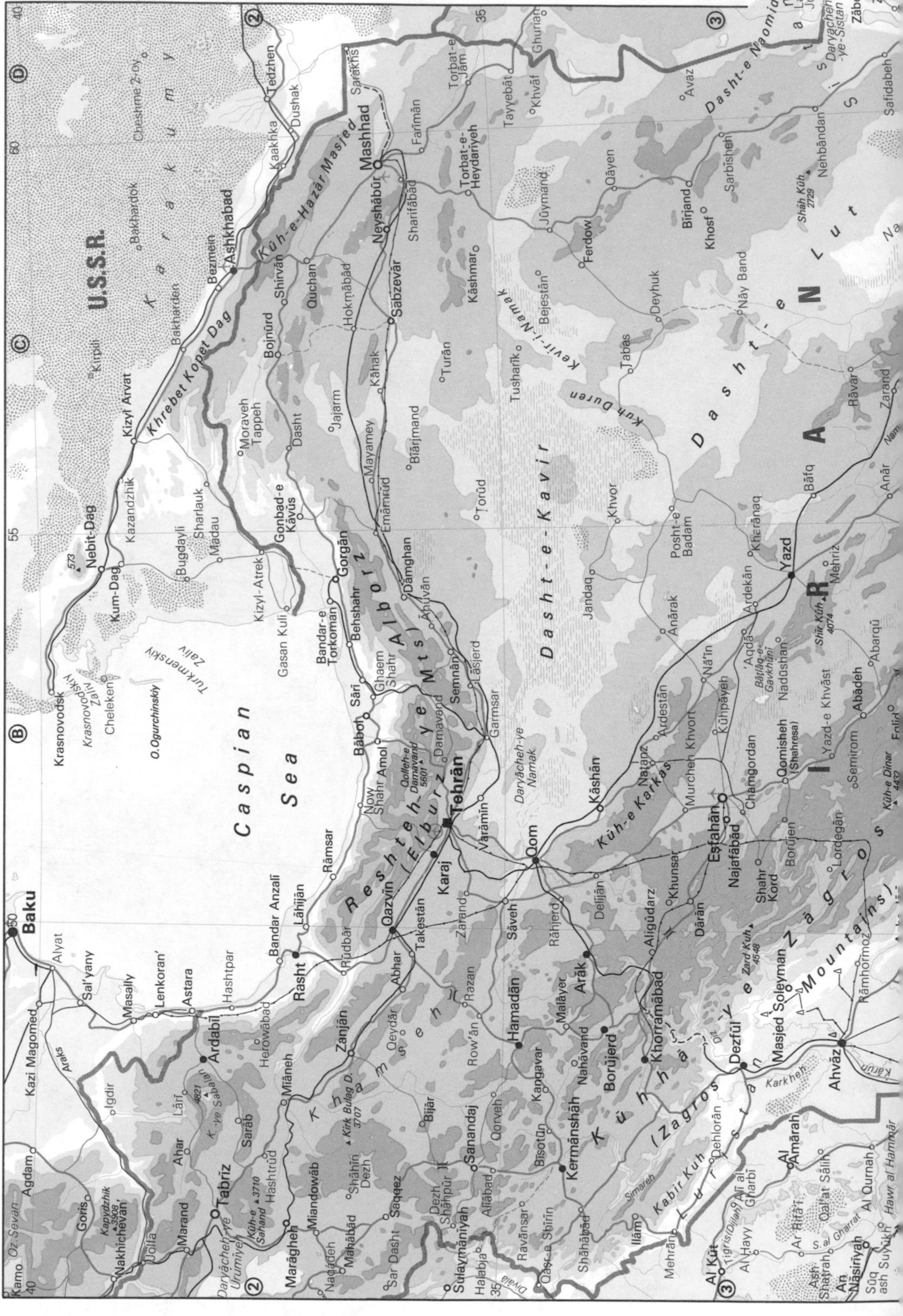
U.S.S.R.
Karakumy
Caspian Sea
Kara-Bogaz-Gol
Dasht-e Kavir
Dasht-e Lut
Dasht-e Naomid
IRAN
Reshteh-ye Alborz (Elburz Mts)
Kūh-e Kalkas
Kūhhā-ye Zāgros (Zagros Mountains)
Khrebet Kopet Dag
Kūh-e-Hazār Masjed
Kevir-i-Namak
Kuh Duren
Baku
Tehrān
Mashhad
Tabrīz
Esfahān
Yazd
Qom
Kāshān
Hamadān
Kermānshāh
Ahvāz
Dezfūl
Rasht
Qazvīn
Karaj
Gorgān
Sārī
Bābol
Semnān
Dāmghān
Sabzevār
Neyshābūr
Ashkhabad
Krasnovodsk
Nebit-Dag
Kum-Dag
Kizyl-Arvat
Tedzhen
Sarakhs
Bojnūrd
Quchan
Shirvān
Zanjān
Ardabīl
Arāk
Borūjerd
Khorramābād
Sanandaj
Marāgheh
Mahābād
Saqqez
Miāneh
Bandar Anzalī
Astara
Lenkoran'
Sal'yany
Nakhichevan'
Jolfa
Marand
Ahar
Sarāb
Bandar-e Torkoman
Gonbad-e Kāvūs
Birjand
Ferdow
Tabas
Kāshmar
Torbat-e Heydarīyeh
Torbat-e Jām
Zābol
Zarand
Rāvar
Bāfq
Nā'īn
Ardakān
Najafābād
Shahr Kord
Masjed Soleymān
Āmārah
Al Kūt
An Nāsirīyah
Qolleh-ye Damāvand 5601
Shīr Kūh 4074
Zard Kūh 4548
Kūh-e Sahand 3710
Kūh-e Sabalan 4821
Shāh Kūh 2729
Kūh-e Dīnār 4432

1:7.5M 0 100 200 300 km 0 50 100 150 mls

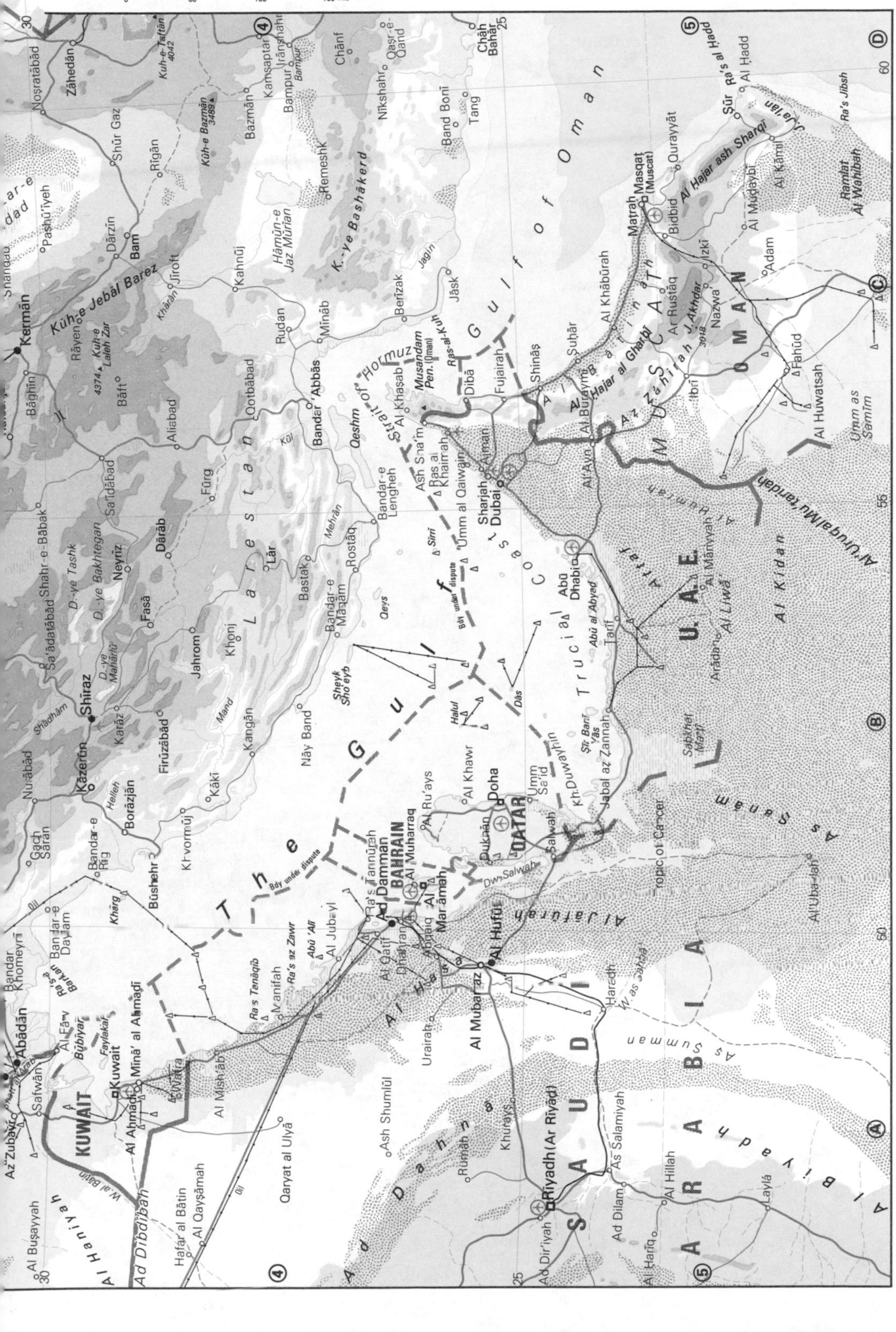

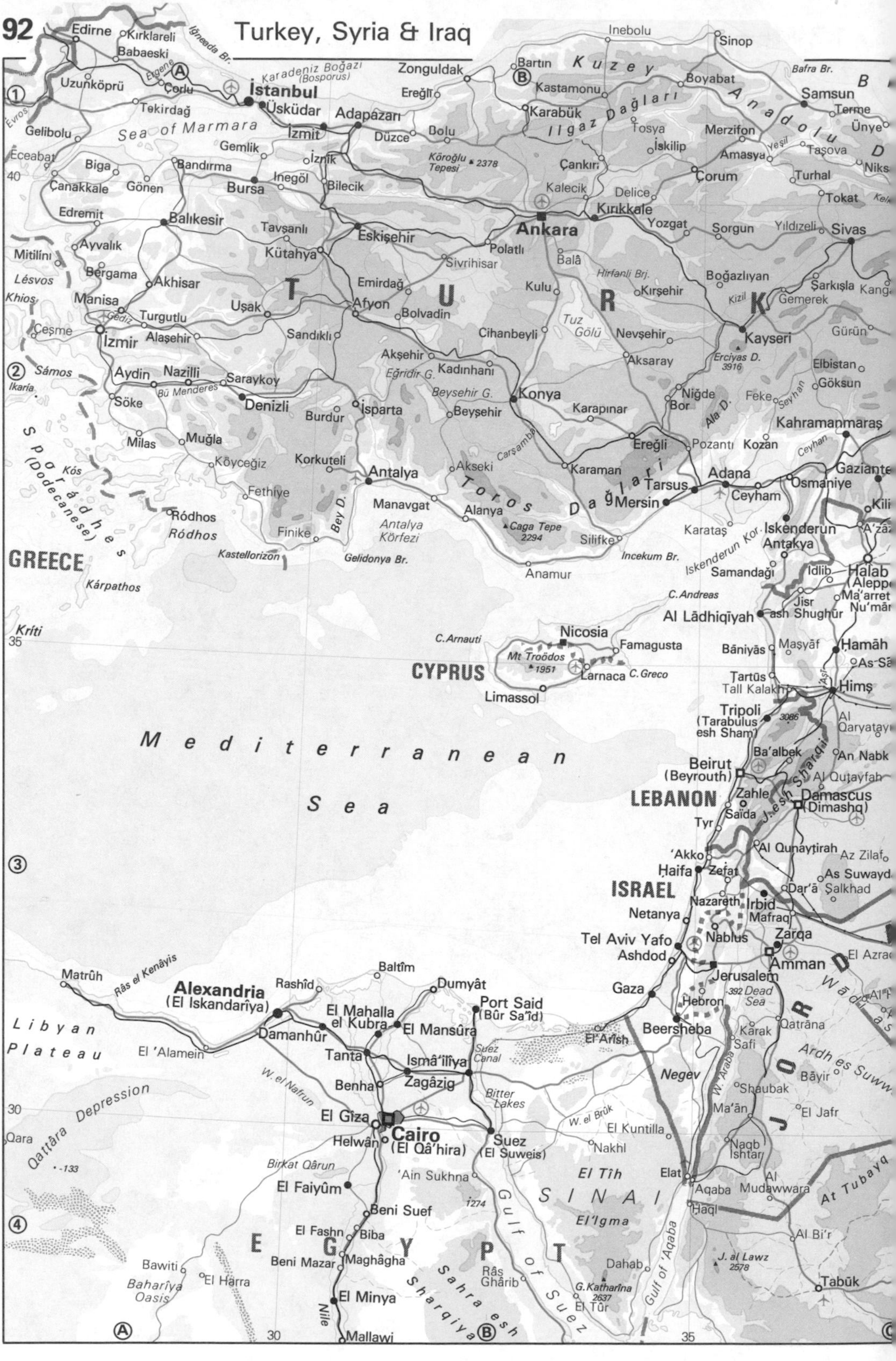
Edirne
Kırklareli
Babaeski
İğneada Br.
Karadeniz Boğazı (Bosporus)
Zonguldak
Bartın
Inebolu
Sinop
Kuzey Anadolu Dağları
Bafra Br.
Uzunköprü
Ergene
Çorlu
İstanbul
Üsküdar
Ereğli
Kastamonu
Boyabat
Samsun
Terme
Ünye
Tekirdağ
Adapazarı
Karabük
Ilgaz Dağları
Tosya
Merzifon
Yeşil
Taşova
Gelibolu
Sea of Marmara
İzmit
Düzce
Bolu
İskilip
Amasya
Niksar
Eceabat
Gemlik
İznik
Köroğlu Tepesi 2378
Çankırı
Çorum
Turhal
Biga
Bandırma
Çanakkale
Gönen
Bursa
İnegöl
Bilecik
Kalecik
Delice
Tokat
Edremit
Balıkesir
Tavşanlı
Eskişehir
Ankara
Kırıkkale
Yozgat
Sorgun
Yıldızeli
Sivas
Mitilíni
Ayvalık
Kütahya
Polatlı
Sivrihisar
Balâ
Lésvos
Bergama
Akhisar
Emirdağ
Hirfanli Brj.
Kırşehir
Boğazlıyan
Şarkışla
Kangal
Khíos
Manisa
Uşak
Afyon
T U R K
Kulu
Kizil
Gemerek
Gediz
Turgutlu
Bolvadin
Çeşme
İzmir
Alaşehir
Sandıklı
Cihanbeyli
Tuz Gölü
Nevşehir
Kayseri
Gürün
Akşehir
Kadınhanı
Aksaray
Erciyas D. 3916
Elbistan
Sámos
Ikaría
Aydin
Nazilli
Sarayköy
Eğridir G.
Beyşehir G.
Konya
Niğde
Bor
Feke
Göksun
Bü Menderes
Söke
Denizli
Burdur
İsparta
Beyşehir
Karapınar
Ala D.
Seyhan
Kahramanmaraş
Milas
Muğla
Çarşamba
Ereğli
Pozantı
Kozan
Ceyhan
Kós
Köyceğiz
Korkuteli
Antalya
Akseki
Karaman
Adana
Gaziantep
S p o r á d h e s (Dodecanese)
Fethiye
Toros Dağları
Tarsus
Ceyham
Osmaniye
Manavgat
Alanya
Mersin
Kilis
Ródhos
Ródhos
Bey D.
Finike
Antalya Körfezi
Caga Tepe 2294
Silifke
Karataş
Iskenderun
A'zāz
GREECE
Kastellorizon
Gelidonya Br.
Incekum Br.
Iskenderun Kor.
Antakya
Samandağı
Idlib
Halab (Aleppo)
Anamur
Kárpathos
C. Andreas
Jisr esh Shughūr
Ma'arret Nu'mān
Al Lādhiqīyah
Kríti
Nicosia
C. Arnauti
Famagusta
Bāniyās
Maşyāf
Ḩamāh
Mt Troödos 1951
CYPRUS
Larnaca
C. Greco
Ṭarṭūs
Tall Kalakh
As-Sa
Limassol
Ḩimş
Tripoli (Tarabulus esh Sham)
3086
Al Qaryatayn
Mediterranean Sea
Ba'albek
An Nabk
Beirut (Beyrouth)
Al Quṭayfah
J. esh Sharqi
Zahle
Damascus (Dimashq)
LEBANON
Saïda
Tyr
'Akko
Al Qunayṭirah
Az Zilaf
Ḩaifa
Zefat
As Suwayda
Ṣalkhad
ISRAEL
Dar'ā
Irbid
Nazareth
Netanya
Mafraq
Tel Aviv Yafo
Nablus
Zarqa
Ashdod
Amman
El Azraq
Matrûh
Râs el Kenâyis
Baltîm
Jerusalem
Wādī as
Alexandria (El Iskandarîya)
Rashîd
Dumyât
Port Said (Bûr Sa'îd)
Gaza
-392 Dead Sea
Hebron
Libyan Plateau
El Mahalla el Kubra
El Mansûra
Beersheba
Karak
Qatrāna
Damanhûr
El 'Alamein
El 'Arîsh
Safi
Tanta
Ismâ'ilîya
Suez Canal
Ardh es Suwwān
W. el Nafrun
Zagâzig
Negev
W. Araba
Bāyir
Benha
Bitter Lakes
Shaubak
Qattâra Depression
El Gîza
Cairo (El Qâ'hira)
W. el Brûk
Ma'ān
El Jafr
Qara
Helwân
Suez (El Suweis)
El Kuntilla
Nakhl
Naqb Ishtar
-133
Birkat Qârun
El Tîh
Elat
El Faiyûm
'Ain Sukhna
Aqaba
Al Mudawwara
At Tubayq
SINAI
Beni Suef
Gulf of Suez
El'Igma
Ḩaql
EGYPT
El Fashn
Biba
Al Bi'r
Bawiti
Beni Mazar
Maghâgha
Dahab
J. al Lawz 2578
Baharîya Oasis
El Ḩarra
Sahra esh Sharqiya
Râs Ghârib
G. Katharîna 2637
Gulf of 'Aqaba
Tabūk
El Minya
El Tûr
Nile
Mallawi
30
35
40

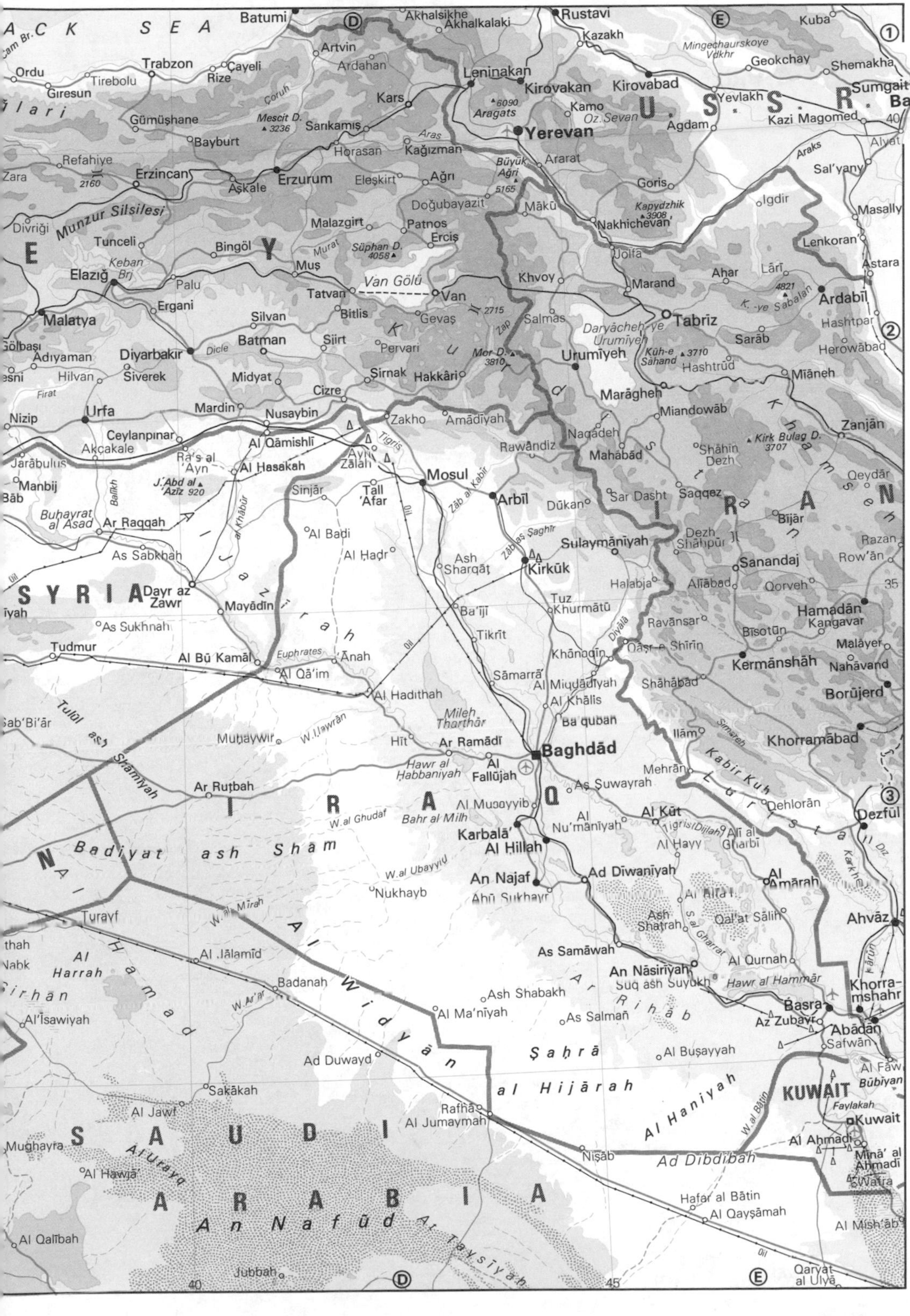
Batumi
Akhalsikhe
Akhalkalaki
Rustavi
Kazakh
Kuba
Mingechaurskoye Vdkhr
Geokchay
Shemakha
Sumgait
Baku
Trabzon
Çayeli
Rize
Ordu
Tirebolu
Giresun
Artvin
Ardahan
Leninakan
Kirovakan
Kirovabad
Yevlakh
Kazi Magomed
Kars
Aragats
Kamo
Oz. Sevan
Yerevan
Agdam
Gümüşhane
Mescit D.
Sarıkamış
Bayburt
Aras
Horasan
Kağızman
Ararat
Alyat
Refahiye
Erzincan
Aşkale
Erzurum
Eleşkirt
Ağrı
Büyük Ağrı
Goris
Araks
Sal'yany
Zara
Doğubayazit
Mākū
Kapydzhik
Nakhichevan'
Igdir
Masally
Divriği
Munzur Silsilesi
Malazgirt
Patnos
Erciş
Süphan D.
Lenkoran'
Tunceli
Bingöl
Murat
Julfa
Astara
Keban Brj
Elazığ
Muş
Van Gölü
Van
Khvoy
Marand
Ahar
Ardabīl
Palu
Tatvan
Ergani
Bitlis
Gevaş
Salmas
Tabrīz
Hashtpar
Malatya
Silvan
Daryācheh-ye Urumīyeh
Sarāb
Gölbaşı
Batman
Siirt
Pervari
Herowābad
Adıyaman
Diyarbakır
Dicle
Mor D.
Urumīyeh
Kūh-e Sahand
Hashtrūd
Hilvan
Siverek
Midyat
Şirnak
Hakkâri
Mīāneh
Fırat
Cizre
Marāgheh
Nizip
Urfa
Mardin
Nusaybin
Zakho
Amādīyah
Miandowāb
Zanjān
Ceylanpınar
Al Qāmishlī
Tigris
Naqadeh
Kirk Bulag D.
Akçakale
Ra's al 'Ayn
Rawāndiz
Mahābād
Shāhin Dezh
Jarābulus
Al Ḥasakah
Zālah
Qeydār
Manbij
J. 'Abd al 'Azīz
Sinjār
Tall 'Afar
Mosul
Arbīl
Dūkān
Sar Dasht
Saqqez
Bāb
Balīkh
Zāb al Kabīr
Bījār
Buḥayrat al Asad
Ar Raqqah
Al Badi
Dezh Shāhpūr
Razan
Al Jazīrah
Zāb aş Şaghīr
Sulaymānīyah
As Sabkhah
Al Ḥaḍr
Ash Sharqāṭ
Kirkūk
Sanandaj
Row'ān
Halabja
Alīābād
Qorveh
SYRIA
Dayr az Zawr
Mayādīn
Tuz Khurmātū
Ba'ījī
Hamadān
Kangavar
As Sukhnah
Ravānsar
Tikrīt
Bīsotūn
Tudmur
Diyālā
Malāyer
Al Bū Kamāl
Euphrates
'Ānah
Khānaqīn
Qaşr-e Shīrīn
Kermānshāh
Nahāvand
Al Qā'im
Sāmarrā'
Al Miqdādiyah
Shāhābād
Borūjerd
Al Ḥadīthah
Al Khāliş
Tulūl ash Shāmiyah
Mileh Tharthār
Ba'qūbah
Sab'Bi'ār
W. Ḥawrān
Īlām
Simareh
Khorramābad
Muḥaywir
Hīt
Ar Ramādī
Baghdād
Hawr al Ḥabbānīyah
Al Fallūjah
Mehrān
Kabīr Kūh
Ar Ruṭbah
Aş Şuwayrah
IRAQ
Dehlorān
Al Musayyib
Al Nu'mānīyah
Al Kūt
Dezfūl
W. al Ghudaf
Bahr al Milh
Tigris (Dijlah)
'Alī al Gharbī
Karbalā'
Al Ḥillah
Al Ḥayy
Bādiyat ash Shām
W. al Ubayyiḍ
Ad Dīwānīyah
Al 'Amārah
An Najaf
Abū Şukhayr
Karkheh
Nukhayb
Ash Shaṭrah
Qal'at Şāliḥ
Ahvāz
Turayf
W. al Mirah
Shaṭṭ al Gharrāf
As Samāwah
Al Qurnah
Al Ḥarrah
Al Jalāmīd
An Nāṣirīyah
Hawr al Hammār
Khorramshahr
Sirḥān
Badanah
Sūq ash Shuyūkh
Kārūn
W. Ar'ar
Ash Shabakh
Ar Riḥāb
Basra
Al Ma'nīyah
As Salmān
Az Zubayr
Abādān
Al 'Isawiyah
Al Widyān
Safwān
Şaḥrā al Ḥijārah
Al Buşayyah
Ad Duwayd
Al Fāw
Būbiyān
KUWAIT
Sakākah
Al Hanīyah
W. al Bāṭin
Faylakah
Kuwait
Rafḥā
Al Jawf
Al Jumaymah
SAUDI ARABIA
Al Aḥmadī
Mughayra
Al 'Urayq
Nişāb
Ad Dibdibah
Mīnā' al Aḥmadī
Al Hawjā'
Wafra
Ḥafar al Bāṭin
Al Qayşūmah
An Nafūd
Aṭ Ṭaysīyah
Al Qalībah
Al Mish'āb
Jubbah
Qaryat al Ulyā
Oil
40
45
35

1:2.5M 0 25 50 75 100 km 0 25 50 mls

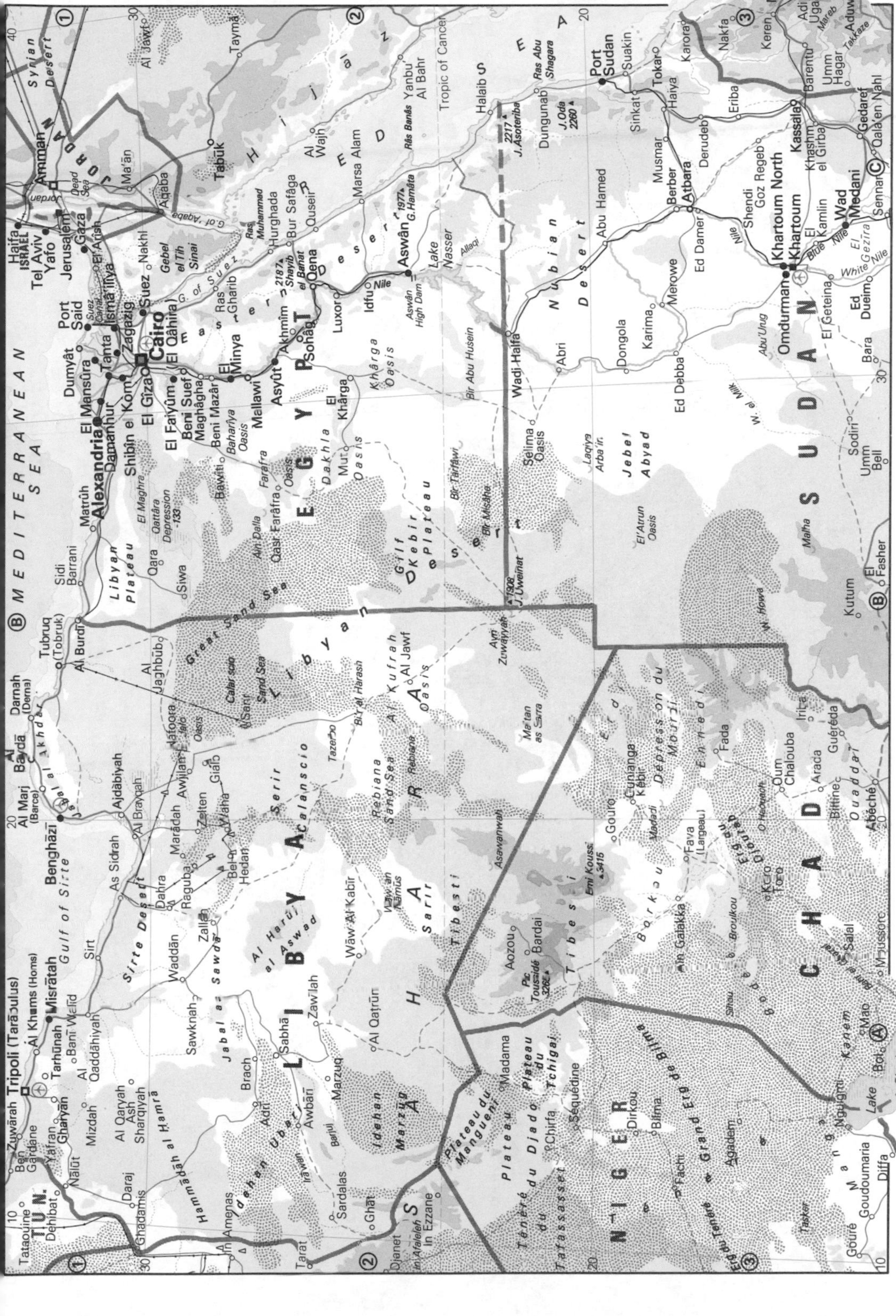
MEDITERRANEAN SEA
Tripoli (Tarābulus)
Al Khums (Homs)
Misrātah
Benghāzī
Gulf of Sirte
Sirte Desert
Al Marj (Barce)
Al Baydā
Darnah (Derna)
Tubruq (Tobruk)
Sidi Barrani
Matrûh
Alexandria
Damanhur
El Mansûra
Dumyât
Port Said
Tanta
Cairo
El Giza
El Faiyûm
Beni Suef
El Minya
Asyût
Sohâg
Qena
Luxor
Aswân
Lake Nasser
Wadi Halfa
Suez
Ismâ'ilîya
Zagazig
Sinai
Gaza
Jerusalem
Tel Aviv Yafo
Haifa
ISRAEL
Amman
JORDAN
Dead Sea
Aqaba
Tabūk
Taymā'
Syrian Desert
Yanbu' Al Bahr
Tropic of Cancer
Hurghada
Bur Safâga
Quseir
Marsa Alam
Halaib
Port Sudan
Suakin
Tokar
Massawa
Asmara
Keren
Nakfa
Kassala
Atbara
Berber
Abu Hamed
Dongola
Karima
Merowe
Omdurman
Khartoum
Khartoum North
Wad Medani
Sennar
Gedaref
Ed Dueim
El Fasher
Kutum
Abéché
Nubian Desert
Libyan Desert
Great Sand Sea
Libyan Plateau
Siwa
Qattâra Depression -133
Farafra
Dakhla Oasis
Kharga Oasis
Gilf Kebir Plateau
J. Uweinat 1908
Al Kufrah Oasis
Al Jawf
Sabhā
Marzuq
Ghāt
Ghadāmis
Tibesti
Emi Koussi 3415
Aozou
Bardai
Ennedi
Fada
Faya (Largeau)
Bilma
Dirkou
Lake Chad
Massakory
Mao
Bol
Diffa
LIBYA
EGYPT
SUDAN
CHAD
NIGER
TUN.

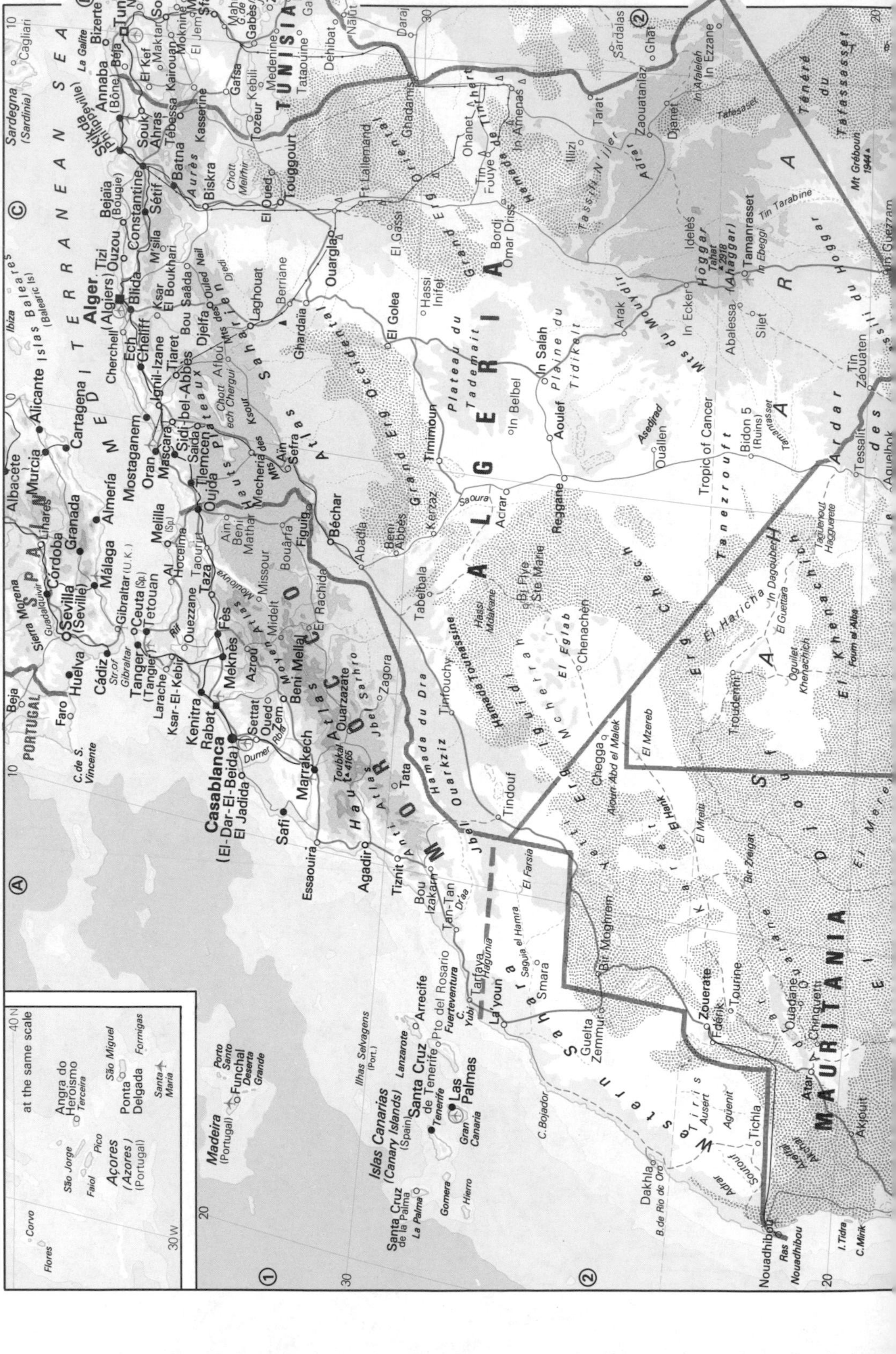
MEDITERRANEAN SEA
SPAIN
PORTUGAL
MOROCCO
ALGERIA
TUNISIA
MAURITANIA
Western Sahara
Sardegna (Sardinia)
Islas Baleares (Balearic Is)
Ibiza
Alger (Algiers)
Oran
Constantine
Annaba (Bône)
Tunis
Bizerte
Sousse
Sfax
Gabès
Casablanca (El-Dar-El-Beida)
Rabat
Kenitra
Tanger (Tangier)
Ceuta (Sp.)
Tetouan
Fès
Meknès
Marrakech
Agadir
Safi
Essaouira
Oujda
Melilla (Sp.)
Béchar
Tindouf
Ouargla
Ghardaïa
Laghouat
Biskra
Touggourt
El Oued
El Golea
In Salah
Timimoun
Reggane
Adrar
Tamanrasset
Djanet
Ghat
Ghadamis
Sevilla (Seville)
Córdoba
Granada
Málaga
Murcia
Alicante
Cartagena
Almería
Albacete
Cádiz
Huelva
Gibraltar (U.K.)
Faro
Beja
Islas Canarias (Canary Islands) (Spain)
Santa Cruz de Tenerife
Las Palmas
Arrecife
Lanzarote
Fuerteventura
Gran Canaria
Tenerife
La Palma
Gomera
Hierro
Madeira (Portugal)
Funchal
Porto Santo
Açores (Azores) (Portugal)
at the same scale
Ponta Delgada
Angra do Heroísmo
La'youn
Smara
Tarfaya
Dakhla
Nouadhibou
Zouerate
Atar
Akjoujt
Chinguetti
Ouadane
Tropic of Cancer
Hoggar (Ahaggar)
Tassili-n-Ajjer
Grand Erg Occidental
Grand Erg Oriental
Erg Chech
Tanezrouft
Haut Atlas
Anti Atlas
Moyen Atlas
Plateau du Tademait
Hamada du Dra
Tahat 2918
Toubkal 4165
Mt Gréboun 1944
Ténéré du Tafassasset

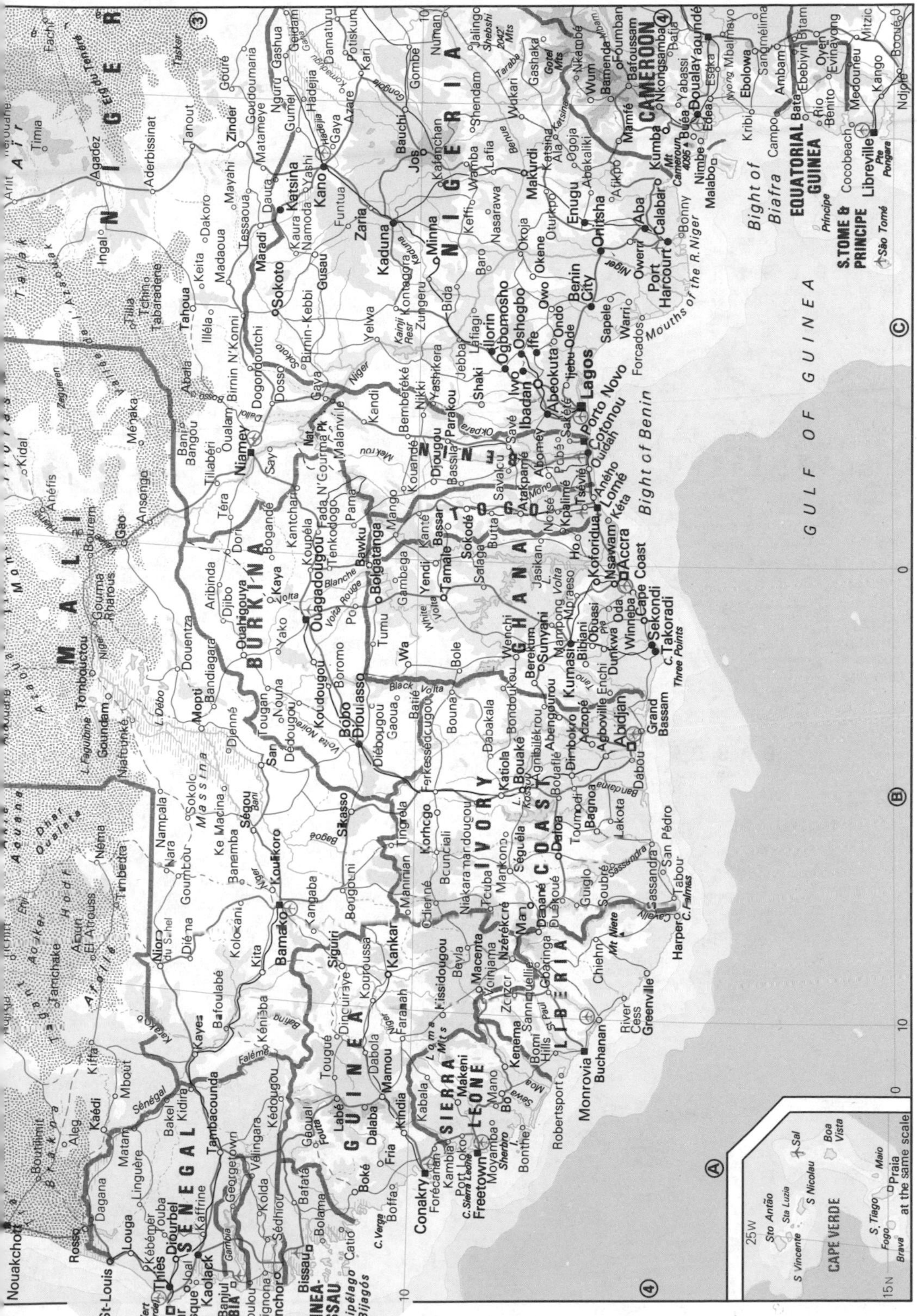
MALI
NIGER
NIGERIA
BURKINA
GHANA
TOGO
BENIN
IVORY COAST
LIBERIA
SIERRA LEONE
GUINEA
GUINEA-BISSAU
SENEGAL
THE GAMBIA
CAMEROON
EQUATORIAL GUINEA
S.TOME & PRINCIPE
CAPE VERDE
GULF OF GUINEA
Bight of Benin
Bight of Biafra
Nouakchott
Dakar
Banjul
Bissau
Conakry
Freetown
Monrovia
Bamako
Ouagadougou
Niamey
Accra
Lomé
Porto Novo
Cotonou
Lagos
Abidjan
Malabo
Libreville
São Tomé
Praia
Kano
Kaduna
Ibadan
Kumasi
Tombouctou
Gao
Mopti
Ségou
St-Louis
Kaolack
Tambacounda
Bobo Dioulasso
Tamale
Bouaké
Port Harcourt
Douala
Yaoundé
at the same scale

CHAD
NIGERIA
CAMEROON
CENTRAL AFRICAN REPUBLIC
EQUAT. GUINEA
GABON
CONGO
ZAIRE
ANGOLA
Lake Chad
Bight of Biafra
Ndjamena (Ft Lamy)
Maiduguri
Kano
Jos
Yaoundé
Douala
Bangui
Libreville
Brazzaville
Kinshasa (Léopoldville)
Luanda
Kisangani (Stanleyville)
Mbandaka (Coquilhatville)
Kananga (Luluabourg)
Mbuji-Mayi
Lubumbashi
Kolwezi
Likasi (Jadotville)
Huambo (Nova Lisboa)
Lobito
Benguela
Matadi
Boma
Pte Noire
Cabinda
Malabo
Abéché
Sarh
Moundou
Ngaoundéré
Bandundu
Kikwit
Kindu
Kamina
Massif de l'Adamaoua
Massif des Bongo
Haute Kotto
Dar Rounga
Ouaddai
Baguirmi
Bornu
Kanem
Jebel Marra
Mt Cameroun 4095
Nyala
Geneina
El Fasher

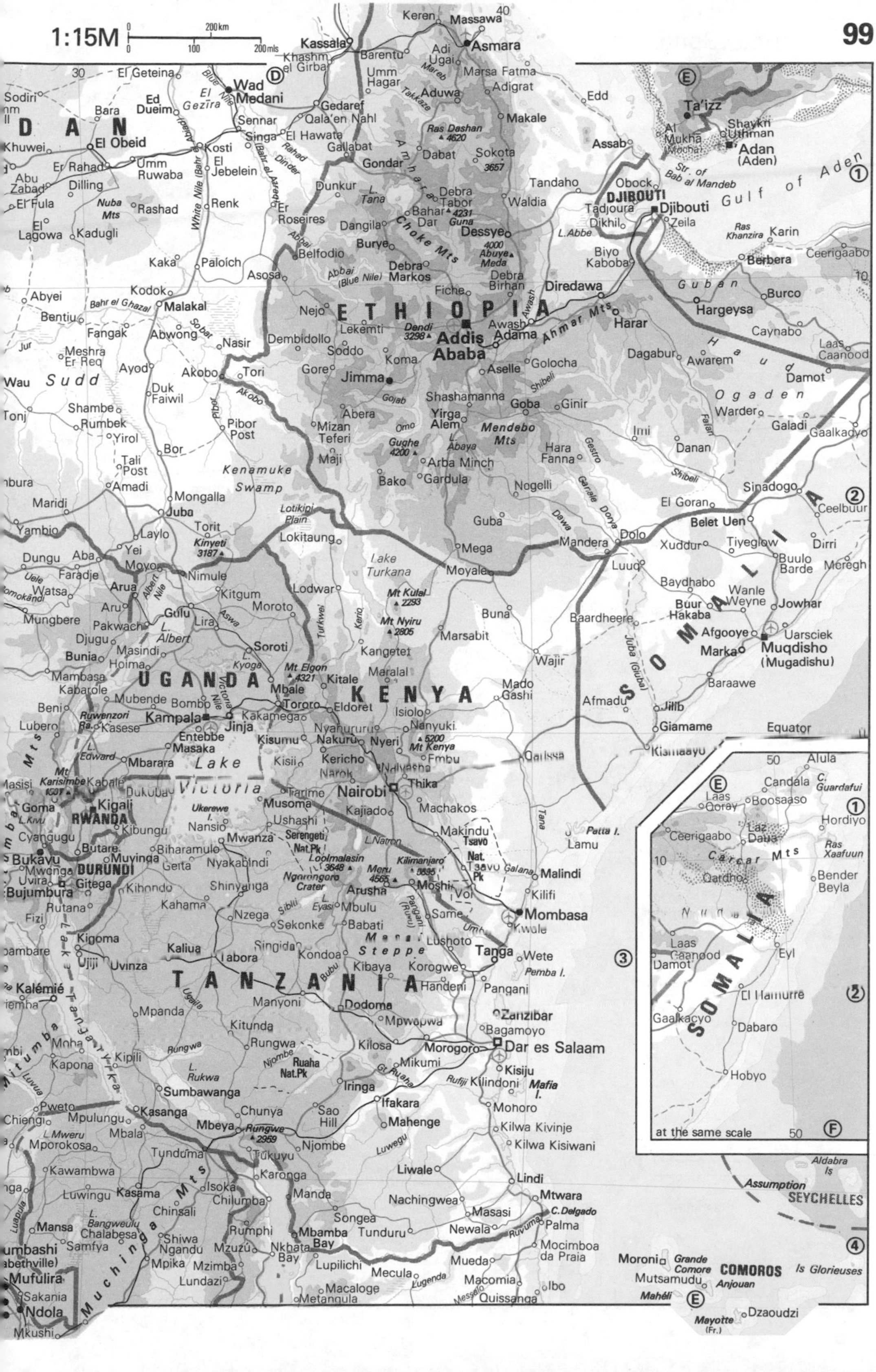
Keren
Massawa
Asmara
Kassala
Khashm el Girba
Barentu
Adi Ugai
Umm Hagar
Marsa Fatma
Adigrat
Aduwa
Edd
El Geteina
Wad Medani
Gedaref
Makale
Sodiri
Bara
Ed Dueim
El Gezira
Sennar
Qala'en Nahl
Singa
El Hawata
Ras Dashan 4620
DAN
El Obeid
Kosti
Gallabat
Dabat
Sokota 3657
Assab
Ta'izz
Al Mukha (Mocha)
Shaykh Uthman
Adan (Aden)
Khuwei
Er Rahad
Umm Ruwaba
El Jebelein
Gondar
Str. of Bab al Mandeb
Gulf of Aden
Abu Zabad
Dilling
Dunkur
L. Tana
Debra Tabor
Tandaho
Obock
El Fula
Nuba Mts
Rashad
Renk
Er Roseires
Bahar Dar
Guna 4231
Waldia
DJIBOUTI
Djibouti
Tadjoura
Dikhil
Zeila
El Lagowa
Kadugli
White Nile (Bahr el Abiad)
Blue Nile
Dinder
Rahad
Bahr el Azraq
Dangila
Choke Mts
Dessye
L. Abbe
Ras Khanzira
Karin
Burye
Belfodio
4000 Abuye Meda
Biyo Kaboba
Berbera
Ceerigaabo
Kaka
Paloich
Asosa
Debra Markos
Abbai (Blue Nile)
Debra Birhan
Guban
Kodok
Fiche
Diredawa
Burco
Abyei
Malakal
Bahr el Ghazal
Nejo
ETHIOPIA
Hargeysa
Bentiu
Sobat
Lekemti
Dendi 3298
Addis Ababa
Awash
Adama
Ahmar Mts
Harar
Fangak
Abwong
Nasir
Dembidollo
Soddo
Caynabo
Laas Caanood
Jur
Meshra Er Req
Koma
Dagabur
Awarem
Haud
Ayod
Gore
Akobo
Tori
Jimma
Aselle
Golocha
Damot
Wau
Sudd
Duk Faiwil
Shibeli
Shashamanna
Goba
Ginir
Ogaden
Gojab
Tonj
Shambe
Rumbek
Abera
Yirga Alem
Warder
Pibor
Pibor Post
Mizan Teferi
Omo
Mendebo Mts
Galadi
Yirol
L. Abaya
Imi
Gaalkacyo
Gughe 4200
Hara Fanna
Danan
Tali Post
Bor
Maji
Arba Minch
Kenamuke Swamp
Bako
Gardula
Amadi
Nogelli
Sinadogo
Maridi
Mongalla
Lotikipi Plain
El Goran
Ceelbuur
Juba
Guba
Belet Uen
Yambio
Torit
Kinyeti 3187
Lokitaung
Dolo
Mandera
Xuddur
Tiyeglow
Dirri
Laylo
Mega
Dungu
Aba
Yei
Lake Turkana
Moyale
Luuq
Buulo Barde
Meregh
Uele
Faradje
Moyo
Nimule
Watsa
Arua
Albert Nile
Kitgum
Lodwar
Mt Kulal 2293
Baydhabo
Wanle Weyne
Aru
Moroto
Buur Hakaba
Jowhar
Mungbere
Pakwach
Gulu
Lira
Aswa
Buna
Baardheere
Djugu
L. Albert
Turkwel
Kerio
Mt Nyiru 2805
Marsabit
Afgooye
Uarsciek
Bunia
Masindi
Soroti
Kangetet
Marka
Muqdisho (Mugadisho)
Hoima
L. Kyoga
Mt Elgon 4321
Maralal
Wajir
Juba (Giuba)
SOMALIA
Mambasa
UGANDA
Kitale
KENYA
Baraawe
Kabarole
Mbale
Mado Gashi
Beni
Mubende
Bombo
Victoria Nile
Tororo
Eldoret
Isiolo
Afmadu
Jilib
Ruwenzori Ra.
Kampala
Jinja
Kakamega
Lubero
Kasese
Nyahururu
Nanyuki
Giamame
Equator
Entebbe
Kisumu
Nakuru
Nyeri
5200 Mt Kenya
Masaka
Kisii
Kericho
Embu
Garissa
Kismaayo
Edward
Mbarara
Lake Victoria
Naivasha
Narok
Mt Karisimbe 4507
Kabale
Dukuba
Tarime
Nairobi
Thika
Goma
Kigali
Musoma
Kajiado
Machakos
L. Kivu
RWANDA
Ukerewe I.
Ushashi
Nansio
Kibungu
Mwanza
Serengeti Nat.Pk
L. Natron
Makindu
Tsavo Nat. Pk
Patta I.
Lamu
Tana
Cyangugu
Butare
Biharamulo
Bukavu
Muyinga
Geita
Nyakabindi
Loolmalasin 3648
Kilimanjaro 5895
Tsavo
BURUNDI
Mwonga
Uvira
Gitega
Ngorongoro Crater
Meru 4565
Galana
Malindi
Bujumbura
Kibondo
Shinyanga
Arusha
Moshi
Kilifi
Rutana
Kahama
L. Eyasi
Mbulu
Voi
Sibiti
Pangani (Ruvu)
Same
Mombasa
Fizi
Nzega
Sekonke
Babati
Kwale
Masai Steppe
Lushoto
Kigoma
Singida
Kondoa
Tanga
Wete
Ujiji
Uvinza
Kaliua
Tabora
Bubu
Kibaya
Korogwe
Pemba I.
Kalémié
Lake Tanganyika
TANZANIA
Handeni
Pangani
Ugalla
Manyoni
Dodoma
Mpanda
Mpwapwa
Zanzibar
Kitunda
Bagamoyo
Mitumba
Moba
Rungwa
Kilosa
Morogoro
Dar es Salaam
Kipili
Njombe
Ruaha Nat.Pk
Mikumi
Kapona
L. Rukwa
Gt Ruaha
Kisiju
Luvua
Iringa
Rufiji
Kilindoni
Mafia I.
Sumbawanga
Pweto
Kasanga
Chunya
Ifakara
Mohoro
Chiengi
Mpulungu
Sao Hill
Mahenge
Kilwa Kivinje
L. Mweru
Mbala
Mbeya
Rungwe 2959
Njombe
Kilwa Kisiwani
Mporokosa
Tunduma
Tukuyu
Luwegu
Kawambwa
Karonga
Liwale
Lindi
Luwingu
Kasama
Isoka
Muchinga Mts
Chilumba
Manda
Nachingwea
Mtwara
C. Delgado
Chinsali
Masasi
Luapula
L. Bangweulu
Songea
Mansa
Chalabesa
Shiwa Ngandu
Rumphi
Mbamba Bay
Tunduru
Newala
Ruvuma
Palma
Samfya
Mzuzu
Nkhata Bay
Mueda
Mocimboa da Praia
Mpika
Mzimba
Lupilichi
Mecula
Lugenda
Macomia
Mufulira
Lundazi
Ibo
Sakania
Macaloge
Metangula
Messalo
Quissanga
Ndola
Mkushi
Moroni
Grande Comore
COMOROS
Is Glorieuses
Mutsamudu
Anjouan
Mohéli
Mayotte (Fr.)
Dzaoudzi
Aldabra Is
Assumption
SEYCHELLES
Alula
C. Guardafui
Candala
Laas Qoray
Boosaaso
Hordiyo
Ceerigaabo
Laz Daua
Ras Xaafuun
Carcar Mts
Qardho
Bender Beyla
Laas Caanood
Damot
Eyl
El Hamurre
Gaalkacyo
Dabaro
Hobyo
at the same scale
50
30
40
10
D
E
F
1
2
3
4

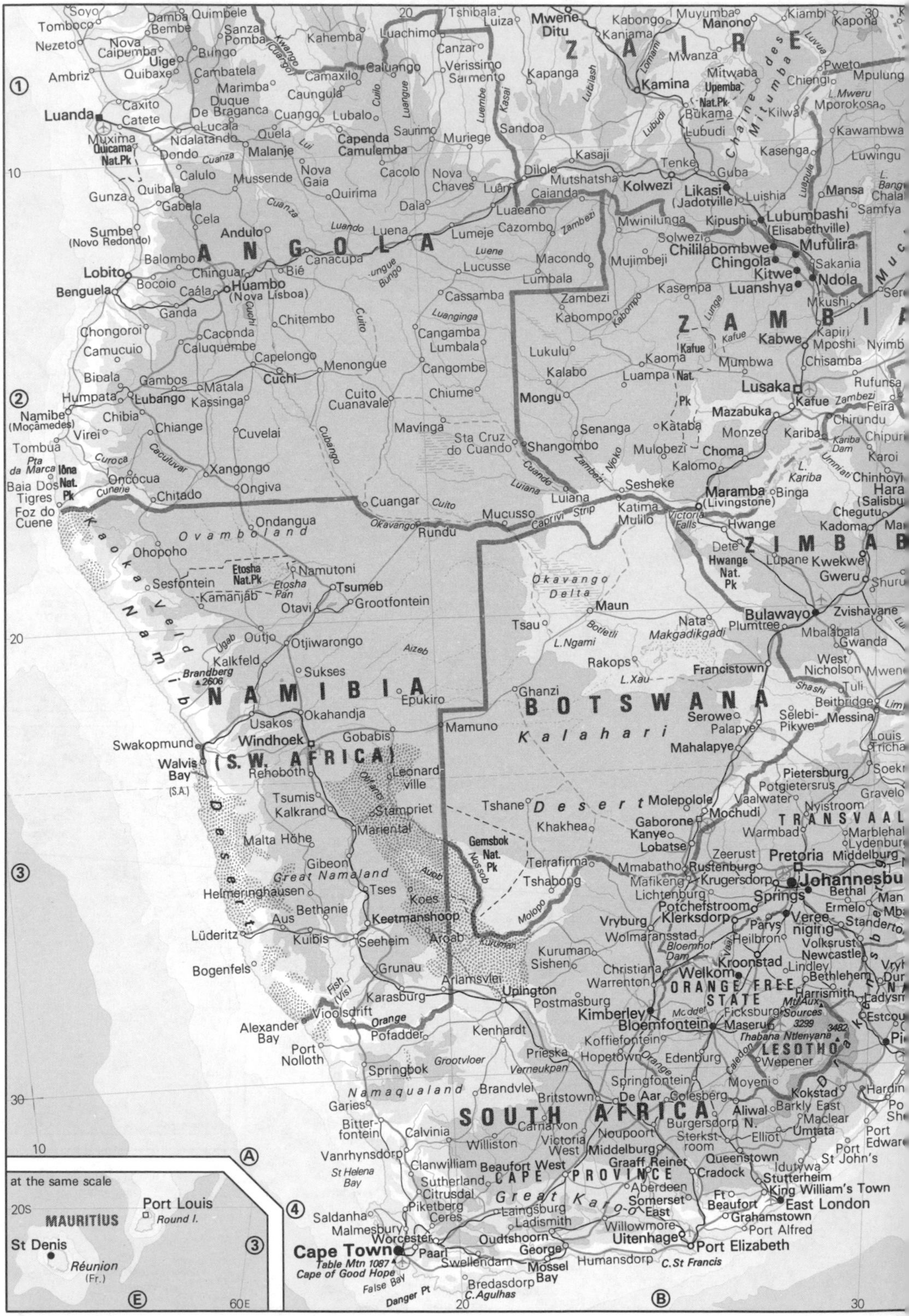
ANGOLA
ZAIRE
ZAMBIA
NAMIBIA
(S.W. AFRICA)
BOTSWANA
ZIMBABWE
SOUTH AFRICA
LESOTHO
TRANSVAAL
ORANGE FREE STATE
CAPE PROVINCE
Kalahari Desert
Namib Desert
Kaokaveld
Ovamboland
Great Namaland
Namaqualand
Great Karoo
Okavango Delta
Makgadikgadi
Chaîne des Mitumba
Luanda
Lobito
Benguela
Huambo
(Nova Lisboa)
Lubango
Namibe
(Moçâmedes)
Tombua
Menongue
Cuito Cuanavale
Luena
Malanje
Sumbe
(Novo Redondo)
Kolwezi
Likasi
(Jadotville)
Lubumbashi
(Elisabethville)
Kamina
Mwene Ditu
Chililabombwe
Chingola
Kitwe
Ndola
Mufulira
Luanshya
Kabwe
Lusaka
Livingstone
Maramba
Mongu
Hwange
Bulawayo
Gweru
Kwekwe
Francistown
Maun
Ghanzi
Gaborone
Mochudi
Serowe
Mahalapye
Lobatse
Kanye
Rundu
Tsumeb
Grootfontein
Otjiwarongo
Windhoek
Swakopmund
Walvis Bay
(S.A.)
Rehoboth
Mariental
Keetmanshoop
Lüderitz
Karasburg
Oranjemund
Alexander Bay
Port Nolloth
Springbok
Upington
Kimberley
Bloemfontein
Welkom
Kroonstad
Pretoria
Johannesburg
Springs
Vereeniging
Potchefstroom
Klerksdorp
Mafikeng
Mmabatho
Rustenburg
Pietersburg
Messina
Maseru
De Aar
Beaufort West
Calvinia
Cape Town
Table Mtn 1087
Cape of Good Hope
False Bay
Danger Pt
C.Agulhas
Worcester
Paarl
Stellenbosch
Oudtshoorn
George
Mossel Bay
Port Elizabeth
Uitenhage
Grahamstown
Port Alfred
East London
King William's Town
Queenstown
Umtata
Kokstad
Port St John's
Port Edward
Etosha Nat.Pk
Etosha Pan
Brandberg 2606
Gemsbok Nat. Pk
Hwange Nat. Pk
Kafue Nat. Pk
Quicama Nat.Pk
Iôna Nat. Pk
Upemba Nat.Pk
Victoria Falls
Caprivi Strip
L.Ngami
L.Xau
L. Kariba
L. Mweru
L. Bangweulu
Zambezi
Cuanza
Cubango
Okavango
Cunene
Orange
Fish
Molopo
Nossob
Auob
Vaal
Caledon
Mont aux Sources 3299
Thabana Ntlenyana 3482
Drakensberg
Kasai
Kwango (Cuango)
Lualaba
Luapula
Kafue
Luangwa
1
2
3
4
A
B
E
10
20
30
at the same scale
MAURITIUS
Port Louis
Round I.
St Denis
Réunion
(Fr.)
20S
60E

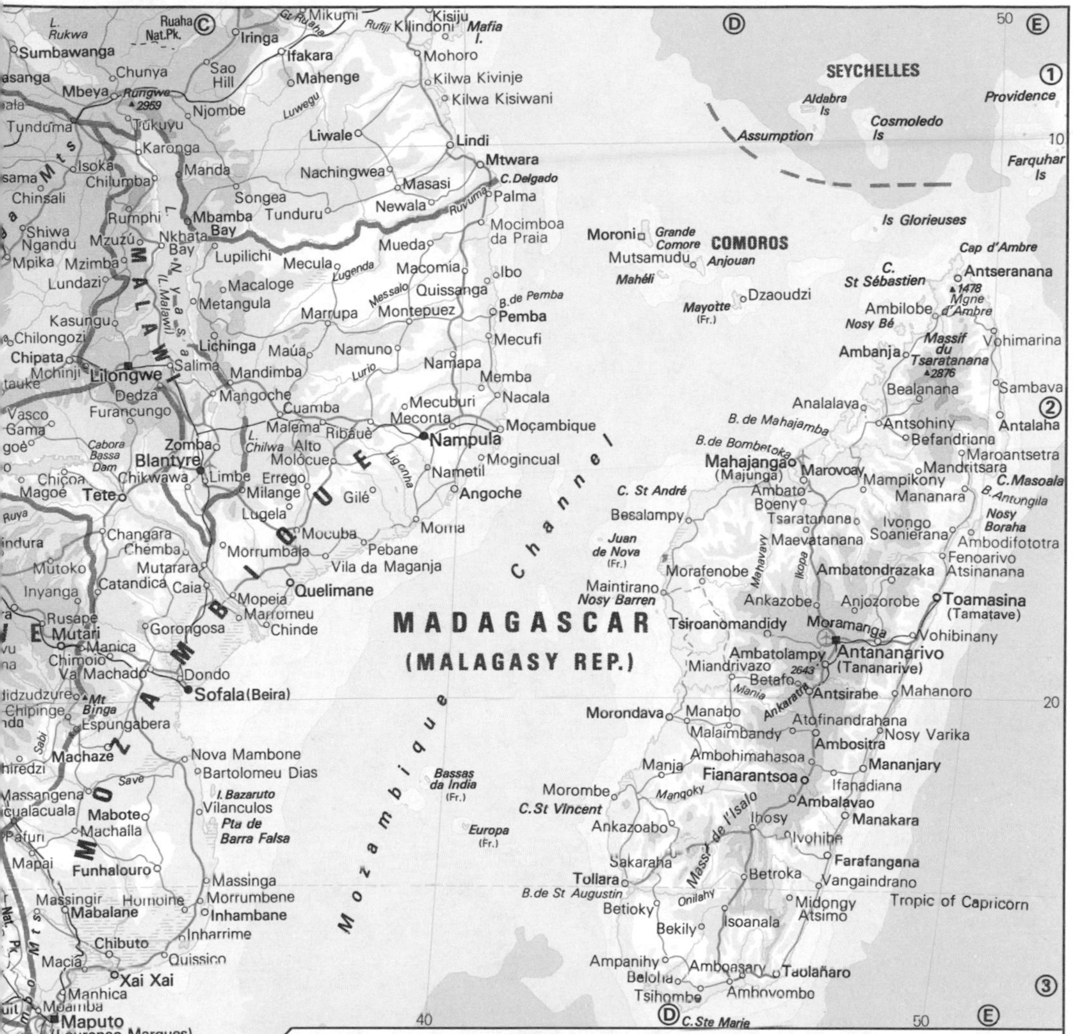
SEYCHELLES
Aldabra Is
Cosmoledo Is
Assumption
Providence
Farquhar Is
Is Glorieuses
COMOROS
Moroni
Grande Comore
Mutsamudu
Anjouan
Mahéli
Mayotte (Fr.)
Dzaoudzi
MADAGASCAR
(MALAGASY REP.)
Mozambique Channel
MOZAMBIQUE
MALAWI
Juan de Nova (Fr.)
Bassas da India (Fr.)
Europa (Fr.)
Cap d'Ambre
Antseranana
C. St Sébastien
Ambilobe
Nosy Bé
Massif du Tsaratanana
Vohimarina
Ambanja
Sambava
Bealanana
Analalava
Antalaha
Antsohiny
Befandriana
Maroantsetra
Mandritsara
Mahajanga (Majunga)
Marovoay
Mampikony
C. Masoala
Mananara
Antongila
Nosy Boraha
C. St André
Besalampy
Tsaratanana
Maevatanana
Ivongo Soanierana
Ambodifototra
Fenoarivo Atsinanana
Morafenobe
Ambatondrazaka
Maintirano
Nosy Barren
Ankazobe
Anjozorobe
Toamasina (Tamatave)
Tsiroanomandidy
Moramanga
Vohibinany
Antananarivo (Tananarive)
Ambatolampy
Miandrivazo
Betafo
Antsirabe
Mahanoro
Morondava
Manabo
Malaimbandy
Atofinandrahana
Nosy Varika
Ambositra
Ambohimahasoa
Manja
Fianarantsoa
Mananjary
Ifanadiana
Morombe
C. St Vincent
Ambalavao
Manakara
Ankazoabo
Ihosy
Massif de l'Isalo
Ivohibe
Sakaraha
Farafangana
Tollara
B. de St Augustin
Betroka
Vangaindrano
Betioky
Midongy Atsimo
Tropic of Capricorn
Bekily
Isoanala
Ampanihy
Beloha
Amboasary
Taolañaro
Tsihombe
Ambovombo
C. Ste Marie
Mikumi
Kisiju
Mafia I.
Kilindoni
Mohoro
Iringa
Ifakara
Mahenge
Kilwa Kivinje
Kilwa Kisiwani
Sumbawanga
Chunya
Sao Hill
Mbeya
Njombe
Tukuyu
Liwale
Lindi
Mtwara
C. Delgado
Karonga
Nachingwea
Masasi
Palma
Newala
Songea
Tunduru
Mocimboa da Praia
Mbamba Bay
Nkhata Bay
Mzuzu
Mueda
Macomia
Ibo
Mecula
Lupilichi
Macaloge
Metangula
Quissanga
Montepuez
Pemba
Marrupa
Mecufi
Lichinga
Maúa
Namuno
Namapa
Lilongwe
Salima
Mandimba
Memba
Dedza
Mangoche
Mecuburi
Nacala
Cuamba
Meconta
Moçambique
Nampula
Zomba
Blantyre
Mogincual
Nametil
Angoche
Tete
Milange
Gilé
Moma
Quelimane
Pebane
Vila da Maganja
Chinde
Mutare
Manica
Chimoio
Dondo
Sofala (Beira)
Machaze
Nova Mambone
Bartolomeu Dias
I. Bazaruto
Vilanculos
Pta de Barra Falsa
Mabote
Funhalouro
Massinga
Morrumbene
Inhambane
Mabalane
Inharrime
Chibuto
Quissico
Xai Xai
Manhica
Maputo (Lourenço Marques)
Bela Vista
SWAZILAND
Nongoma
St Lucia
Mtubatuba
C. St Lucia
Empangeni

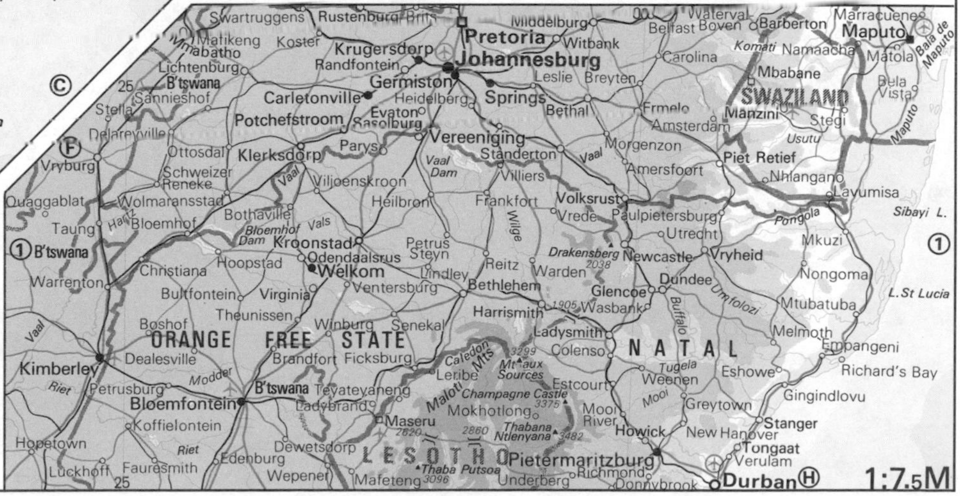
Swartruggens
Rustenburg
Pretoria
Middelburg
Witbank
Belfast
Waterval Boven
Barberton
Maputo
Marracuene
Mmabatho
Krugersdorp
Johannesburg
Randfontein
Germiston
Carolina
Namaacha
Matola
Lichtenburg
Mbabane
Springs
Carletonville
Heidelberg
SWAZILAND
Potchefstroom
Bethal
Ermelo
Manzini
Evaton
Sasolburg
Amsterdam
Vereeniging
Standerton
Morgenzon
Piet Retief
Klerksdorp
Vryburg
Amersfoort
Viljoenskroon
Villiers
Volksrust
Paulpietersburg
Bloemhof
Frankfort
Vrede
Utrecht
Kroonstad
Newcastle
Vryheid
Hoopstad
Welkom
Reitz
Bethlehem
Dundee
Glencoe
Harrismith
Wasbank
Ladysmith
ORANGE FREE STATE
NATAL
Kimberley
Colenso
Eshowe
Richard's Bay
Bloemfontein
Estcourt
Greytown
Maseru
Mooi River
Stanger
LESOTHO
Howick
Tongaat
Pietermaritzburg
Verulam
Durban
1:7.5M

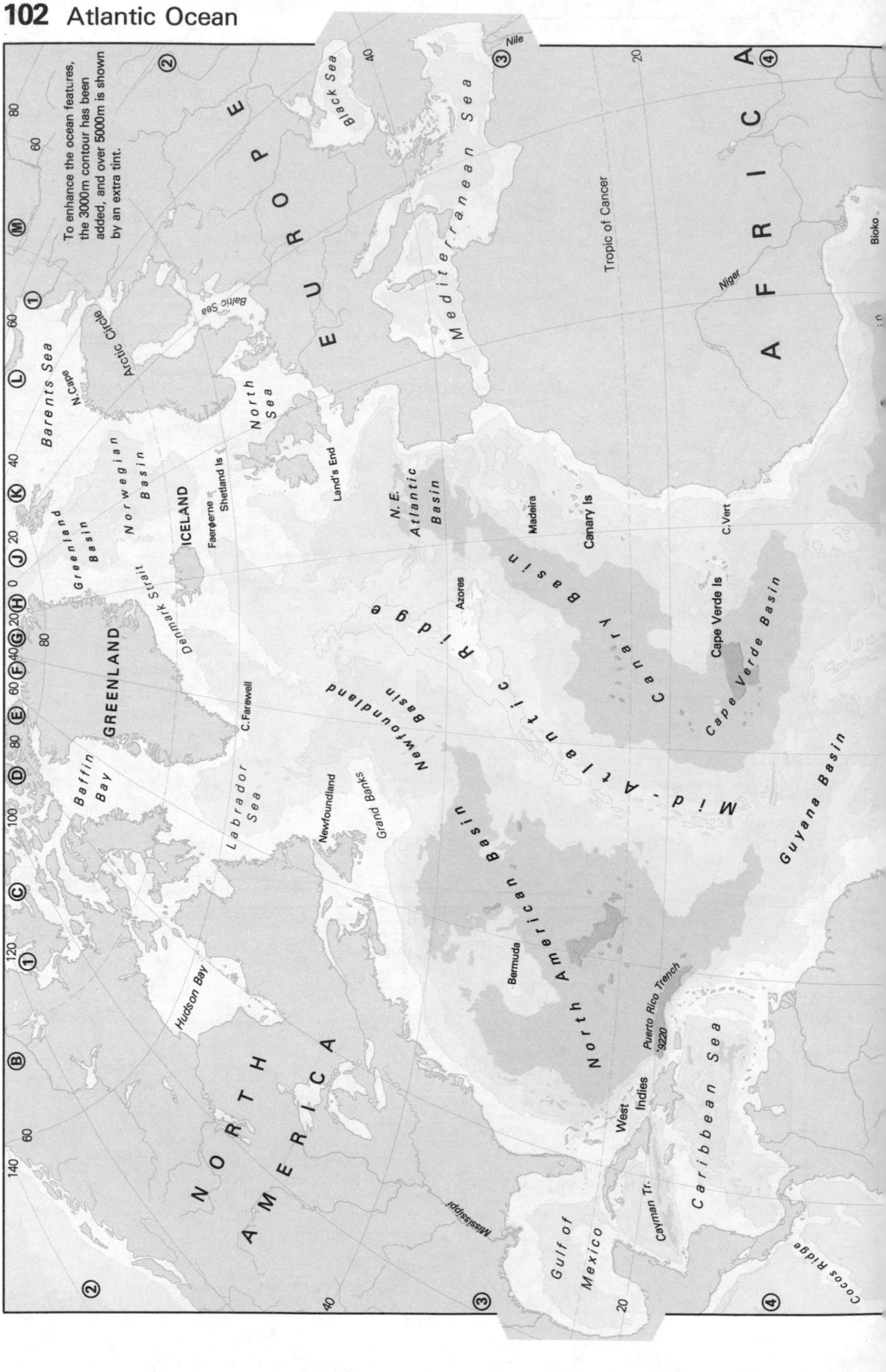
To enhance the ocean features, the 3000m contour has been added, and over 5000m is shown by an extra tint.
EUROPE
AFRICA
NORTH AMERICA
GREENLAND
ICELAND
Barents Sea
N.Cape
Arctic Circle
Baltic Sea
North Sea
Norwegian Basin
Greenland Basin
Shetland Is
Faerøerne
Denmark Strait
Land's End
N.E. Atlantic Basin
Madeira
Canary Is
Canary Basin
Azores
Mid-Atlantic Ridge
Mediterranean Sea
Black Sea
Nile
Tropic of Cancer
Niger
Bioko
C.Vert
Cape Verde Is
Cape Verde Basin
Guyana Basin
Baffin Bay
C.Farewell
Labrador Sea
Newfoundland Basin
Newfoundland
Grand Banks
Hudson Bay
North American Basin
Bermuda
Puerto Rico Trench
9220
West Indies
Caribbean Sea
Cayman Tr.
Gulf of Mexico
Mississippi
Cocos Ridge
Tropic of Cancer

1:60M 0 600 1200 1800 2400 km
0 600 1200 mls

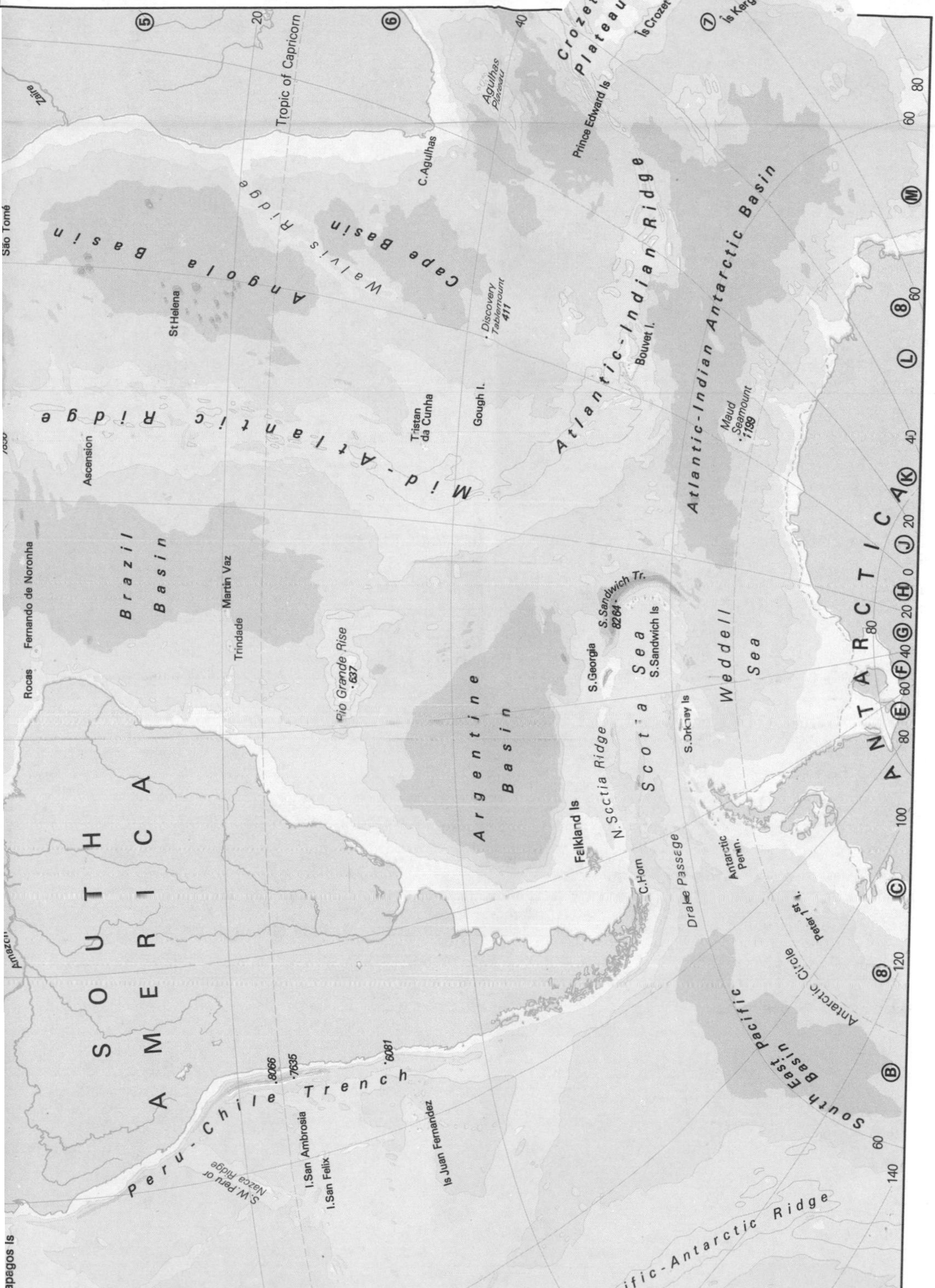

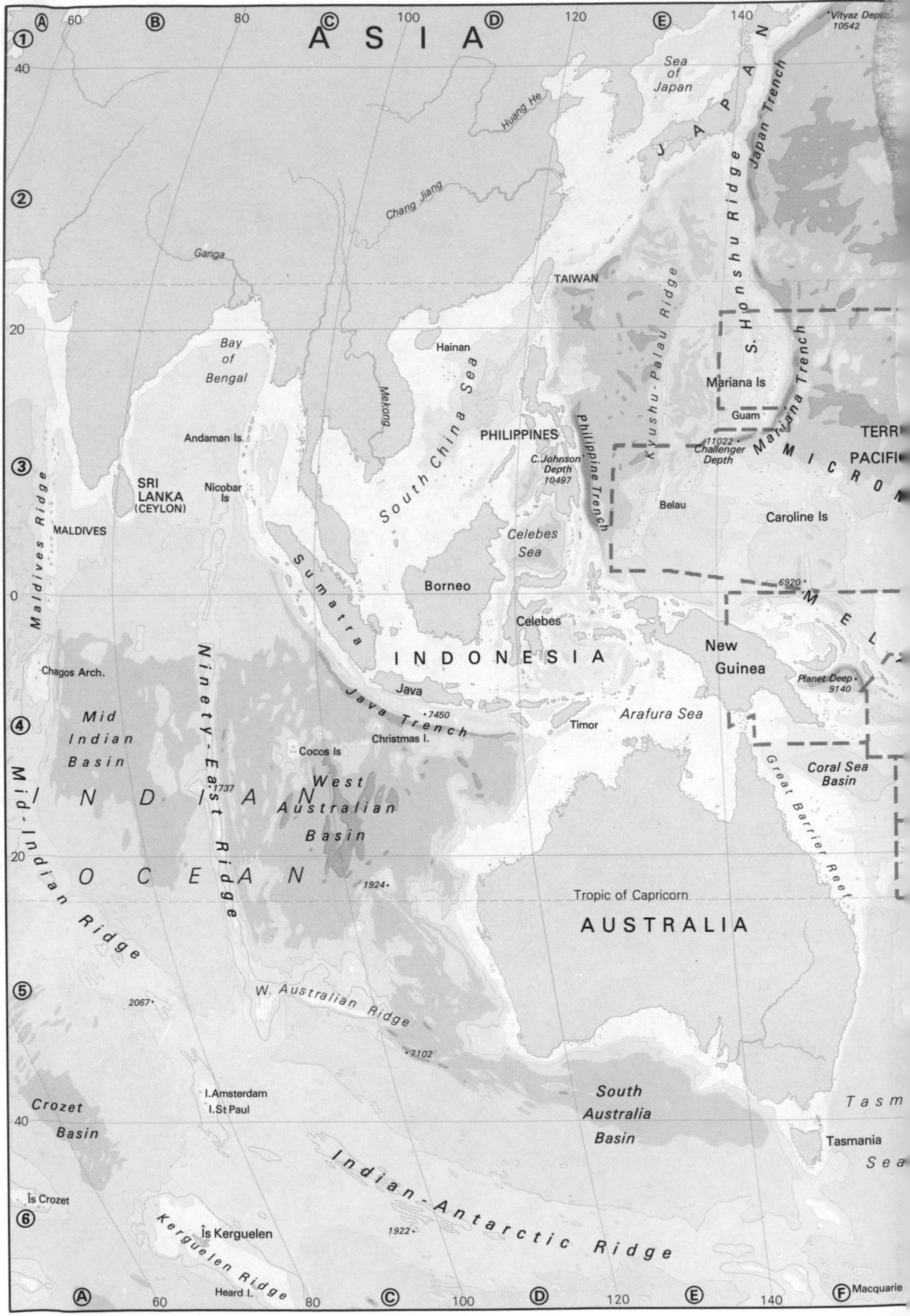
ASIA
Sea of Japan
JAPAN
Japan Trench
Vityaz Depth 10542
Huang He
Chang Jiang
Ganga
TAIWAN
Kyushu-Palau Ridge
S. Honshu Ridge
Bay of Bengal
Hainan
Mekong
South China Sea
PHILIPPINES
Philippine Trench
C.Johnson Depth 10497
Mariana Is
Guam
Mariana Trench
11022 Challenger Depth
MICRON
TERR
PACIFI
Andaman Is
SRI LANKA (CEYLON)
Nicobar Is
Maldives Ridge
MALDIVES
Belau
Caroline Is
Celebes Sea
Borneo
Sumatra
6920
MEL
Celebes
INDONESIA
New Guinea
Chagos Arch.
Planet Deep 9140
Java
Java Trench
7450
Christmas I.
Timor
Arafura Sea
Mid Indian Basin
Ninety-East Ridge
Cocos Is
1737
INDIAN OCEAN
West Australian Basin
Coral Sea Basin
Great Barrier Reef
Mid-Indian Ridge
1924
Tropic of Capricorn
AUSTRALIA
W. Australian Ridge
2067
7102
I.Amsterdam
I.St Paul
Crozet Basin
South Australia Basin
Tasm
Tasmania
Sea
Indian-Antarctic Ridge
Îs Crozet
Îs Kerguelen
1922
Kerguelen Ridge
Heard I.
Macquarie

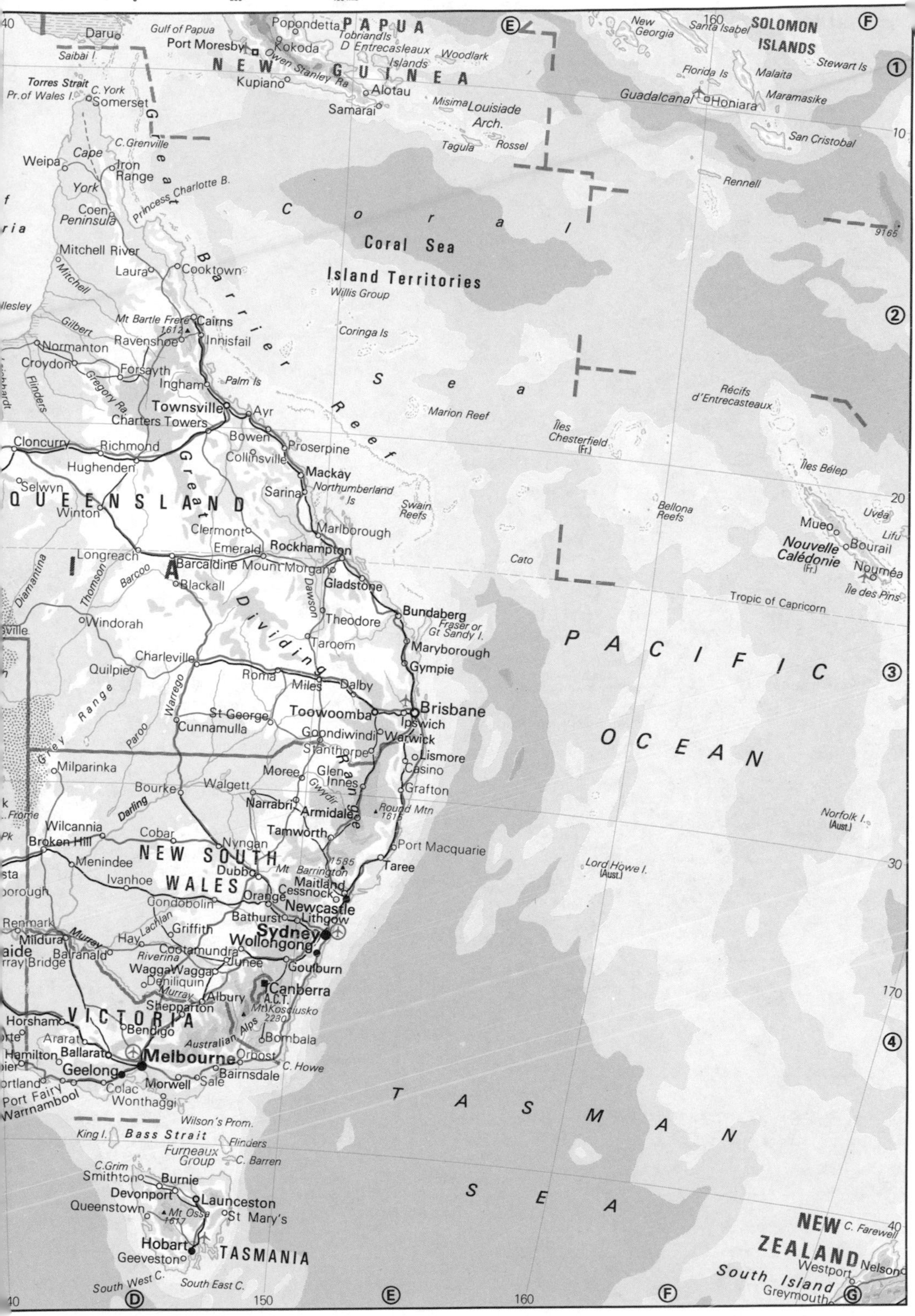
PAPUA NEW GUINEA
Gulf of Papua
Daru
Saibai I.
Port Moresby
Popondetta
Kokoda
Owen Stanley Ra
Kupiano
Tobriand Is
D'Entrecasteaux Islands
Woodlark
Alotau
Samarai
Misima
Louisiade Arch.
Tagula
Rossel
New Georgia
Santa Isabel
SOLOMON ISLANDS
Florida Is
Malaita
Stewart Is
Guadalcanal
Honiara
Maramasike
San Cristobal
Rennell
9165
Torres Strait
Pr. of Wales I.
C. York
Somerset
C. Grenville
Weipa
Cape York Peninsula
Iron Range
Coen
Princess Charlotte B.
Great Barrier Reef
Coral Sea
Coral Sea Island Territories
Willis Group
Coringa Is
Mitchell River
Mitchell
Laura
Cooktown
Gilbert
Mt Bartle Frere 1612
Cairns
Innisfail
Normanton
Ravenshoe
Croydon
Forsayth
Gregory Ra
Flinders
Ingham
Palm Is
Townsville
Ayr
Charters Towers
Bowen
Proserpine
Cloncurry
Richmond
Hughenden
Collinsville
Mackay
Marion Reef
Îles Chesterfield (Fr.)
Récifs d'Entrecasteaux
Îles Bélep
Selwyn
QUEENSLAND
Winton
Sarina
Northumberland Is
Swain Reefs
Bellona Reefs
Clermont
Marlborough
Longreach
Emerald
Rockhampton
Barcaldine
Mount Morgan
Cato
Mueo
Uvéa
Lifu
Nouvelle Calédonie (Fr.)
Bourail
Nouméa
Île des Pins
Tropic of Capricorn
Diamantina
Thomson
Barcoo
Blackall
Dawson
Gladstone
Bundaberg
Fraser or Gt Sandy I.
Windorah
Theodore
Great Dividing Range
Taroom
Maryborough
Gympie
Charleville
Quilpie
Roma
Miles
Dalby
PACIFIC OCEAN
Warrego
Grey Range
Paroo
St George
Toowoomba
Brisbane
Ipswich
Cunnamulla
Goondiwindi
Warwick
Stanthorpe
Lismore
Casino
Milparinka
Moree
Glen Innes
Gwydir
Bourke
Walgett
Grafton
Narrabri
Armidale
Round Mtn 1615
Norfolk I. (Aust.)
Darling
Wilcannia
Tamworth
Cobar
Port Macquarie
Broken Hill
Nyngan
1585
Taree
NEW SOUTH WALES
Menindee
Dubbo
Mt Barrington
Lord Howe I. (Aust.)
Ivanhoe
Maitland
Cessnock
Orange
Condobolin
Newcastle
Bathurst
Lithgow
Renmark
Lachlan
Griffith
Sydney
Mildura
Murray
Hay
Wollongong
Balranald
Riverina
Cootamundra
Junee
Goulburn
Wagga Wagga
Deniliquin
Canberra
A.C.T.
Albury
Shepparton
Mt Kosciusko 2230
Horsham
VICTORIA
Bendigo
Australian Alps
Bombala
Ararat
Hamilton
Ballarat
Melbourne
Orbost
Geelong
Bairnsdale
C. Howe
Morwell
Sale
Colac
Portland
Port Fairy
Warrnambool
Wonthaggi
TASMAN SEA
Wilson's Prom.
King I.
Bass Strait
Flinders
Furneaux Group
C. Barren
C. Grim
Smithton
Burnie
Devonport
Launceston
Queenstown
Mt Ossa 1617
St Mary's
Hobart
Geeveston
TASMANIA
South West C.
South East C.
NEW ZEALAND
C. Farewell
Nelson
Westport
South Island
Greymouth
10
20
30
40
150
160
170

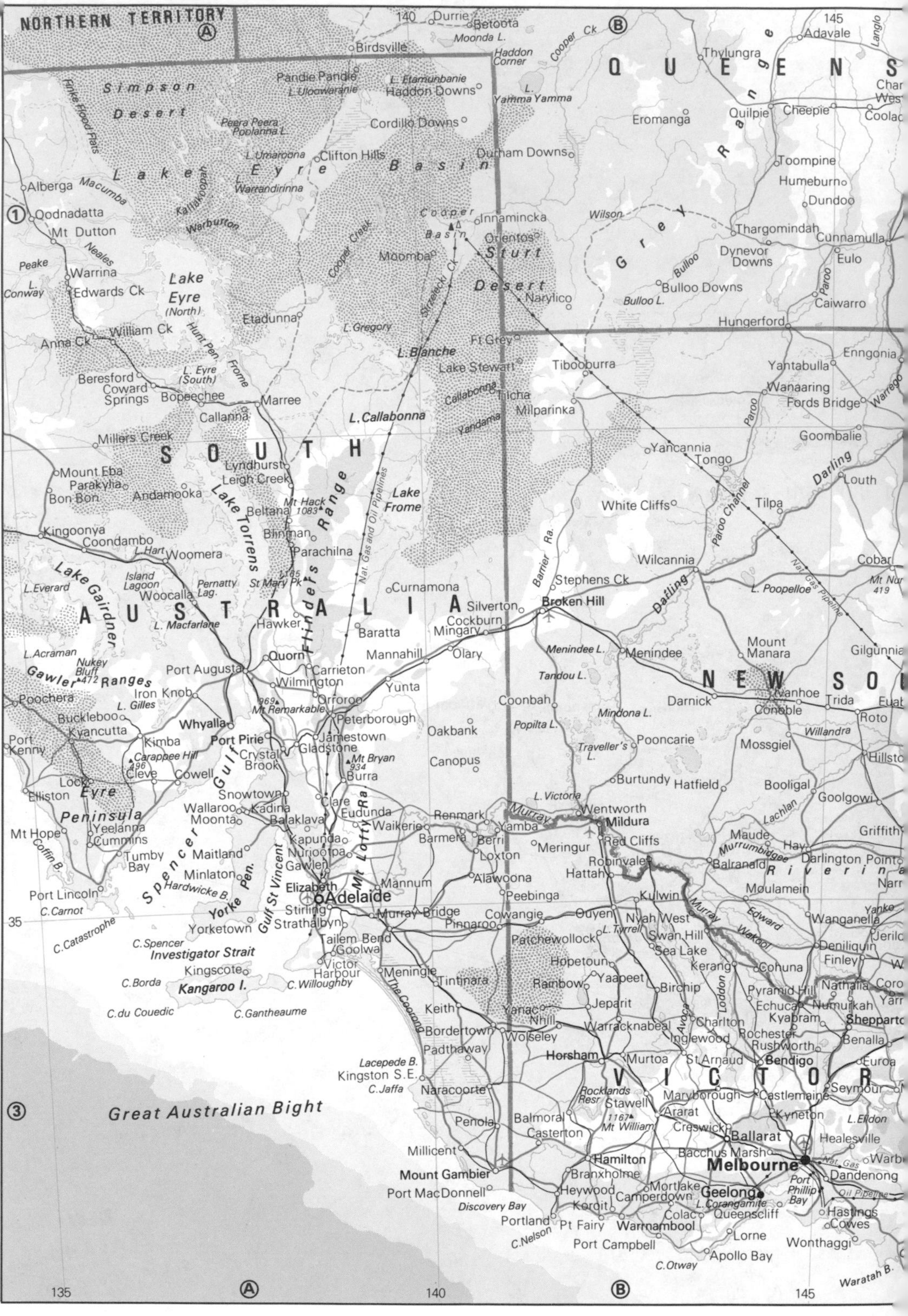
NORTHERN TERRITORY
A
B
140
145
135
35
1
3
Durrie
Betoota
Moonda L.
Birdsville
Haddon Corner
Cooper Ck
Adavale
Thylungra
Langlo
QUEENSLAND
Simpson Desert
Finke Flood Flats
Pandie Pandie
L. Uloowaranie
L. Etamunbanie
Haddon Downs
L. Yamma Yamma
Eromanga
Quilpie
Cheepie
Cooladdi
Grey Range
Peera Peera Poolanna L.
Cordillo Downs
L. Umaroona
Clifton Hills
Durham Downs
Lake Eyre Basin
L. Warrandirinna
Toompine
Humeburn
Alberga
Macumba
Kallakoopah
Dundoo
Oodnadatta
Warburton
Cooper Basin
Innamincka
Wilson
Mt Dutton
Orientos
Thargomindah
Cunnamulla
Neales
Cooper Creek
Moomba
Sturt Desert
Dynevor Downs
Eulo
Peake
Warrina
Lake Eyre (North)
Bulloo
L. Conway
Edwards Ck
Strzelecki Ck
Bulloo Downs
Paroo
Narylico
Bulloo L.
Caiwarro
Etadunna
Hunt Pen.
L. Gregory
Hungerford
William Ck
Anna Ck
Frome
Ft Grey
L. Blanche
Enngonia
Beresford
L. Eyre (South)
Lake Stewart
Tibooburra
Yantabulla
Coward Springs
Bopeechee
Callabonna
Tilcha
Wanaaring
Warrego
Marree
Milparinka
Fords Bridge
Callanna
L. Callabonna
Yandama
Millers Creek
Goombalie
SOUTH AUSTRALIA
Yancannia
Tongo
Lyndhurst
Mount Eba
Leigh Creek
Darling
Louth
Parakylia
Bon Bon
Andamooka
Lake Torrens
Mt Hack 1083
Lake Frome
Tilpa
Beltana
White Cliffs
Nat. Gas and Oil Pipelines
Paroo Channel
Kingoonya
Blinman
Coondambo
Barrier Ra.
L. Hart
Parachilna
Woomera
Flinders Range
Wilcannia
Cobar
Lake Gairdner
Island Lagoon
Pernatty Lag.
1165 St Mary Pk
Stephens Ck
Mt Nurri 419
L. Everard
Woocalla
Curnamona
Nat. Gas Pipeline
L. Poopelloe
L. Macfarlane
Silverton
Broken Hill
Hawker
Cockburn
Baratta
Mingary
L. Acraman
Mount Manara
Nukey Bluff 472
Menindee L.
Quorn
Mannahill
Olary
Menindee
Gilgunnia
Port Augusta
Carrieton
Gawler Ranges
Wilmington
Tandou L.
NEW SOUTH WALES
Yunta
Iron Knob
969 Mt Remarkable
Orroroo
Coonbah
Ivanhoe
Trida
Euabalong
Poochera
L. Gilles
Darnick
Conoble
Mindona L.
Roto
Peterborough
Buckleboo
Whyalla
Kyancutta
Popilta L.
Jamestown
Oakbank
Willandra
Port Pirie
Kimba
Port Kenny
Gladstone
Crystal Brook
Pooncarie
Traveller's L.
Mossgiel
Hillston
Carappee Hill 496
Mt Bryan 934
Canopus
Cleve
Cowell
Burra
Burtundy
Hatfield
Booligal
Lock
Spencer Gulf
Snowtown
Elliston
Eyre Peninsula
L. Victoria
Goolgowi
Clare
Wallaroo
Kadina
Eudunda
Renmark
Wentworth
Lachlan
Griffith
Moonta
Balaklava
Mildura
Mt Lofty Ra.
Murray
Yamba
Waikerie
Mt Hope
Yeelanna
Barmera
Berri
Red Cliffs
Maude
Hay
Cummins
Kapunda
Meringur
Murrumbidgee
Darlington Point
Coffin B.
Maitland
Nuriootpa
Loxton
Robinvale
Balranald
Riverina
Tumby Bay
Gawler
Hattah
Narrandera
Minlaton
Mannum
Alawoona
Moulamein
Gulf St Vincent
Port Lincoln
Hardwicke B.
Yorke Pen.
Elizabeth
Adelaide
Peebinga
Kulwin
C. Carnot
Stirling
Murray Bridge
Cowangie
Ouyen
Edward
Yanko
Strathalbyn
Pinnaroo
Nyah West
Wanganella
C. Catastrophe
Yorketown
L. Tyrrell
Wakool
Jerilderie
Tailem Bend
Patchewollock
Swan Hill
Deniliquin
C. Spencer
Investigator Strait
Goolwa
Sea Lake
Hopetoun
Finley
Kingscote
Victor Harbour
Kerang
Cohuna
Meningie
Yaapeet
Tintinara
C. Borda
Kangaroo I.
C. Willoughby
Rainbow
Birchip
Pyramid Hill
Nathalia
Corowa
The Coorong
Loddon
Echuca
Numurkah
Jeparit
Yarrawonga
C. du Couedic
C. Gantheaume
Keith
Yanac
Kyabram
Nhill
Shepparton
Warracknabeal
Avoca
Charlton
Bordertown
Rochester
Wolseley
Benalla
Inglewood
Rushworth
Padthaway
Horsham
Murtoa
St Arnaud
Bendigo
Euroa
Lacepede B.
Kingston S.E.
VICTORIA
Rocklands Resr
C. Jaffa
Naracoorte
Stawell
Maryborough
Castlemaine
Seymour
Great Australian Bight
Ararat
1167 Mt William
Kyneton
L. Eildon
Penola
Balmoral
Creswick
Casterton
Ballarat
Healesville
Millicent
Bacchus Marsh
Warburton
Hamilton
Melbourne
Nat. Gas
Mount Gambier
Branxholme
Dandenong
Port Phillip Bay
Heywood
Mortlake
Geelong
Port MacDonnell
Oil Pipeline
Camperdown
Discovery Bay
Koroit
L. Corangamite
Queenscliff
Colac
Hastings
Portland
Pt Fairy
Warrnambool
Cowes
C. Nelson
Lorne
Wonthaggi
Port Campbell
Apollo Bay
C. Otway
Waratah B.

1:7.5M 0 100 200 300 km 0 50 100 150 mls

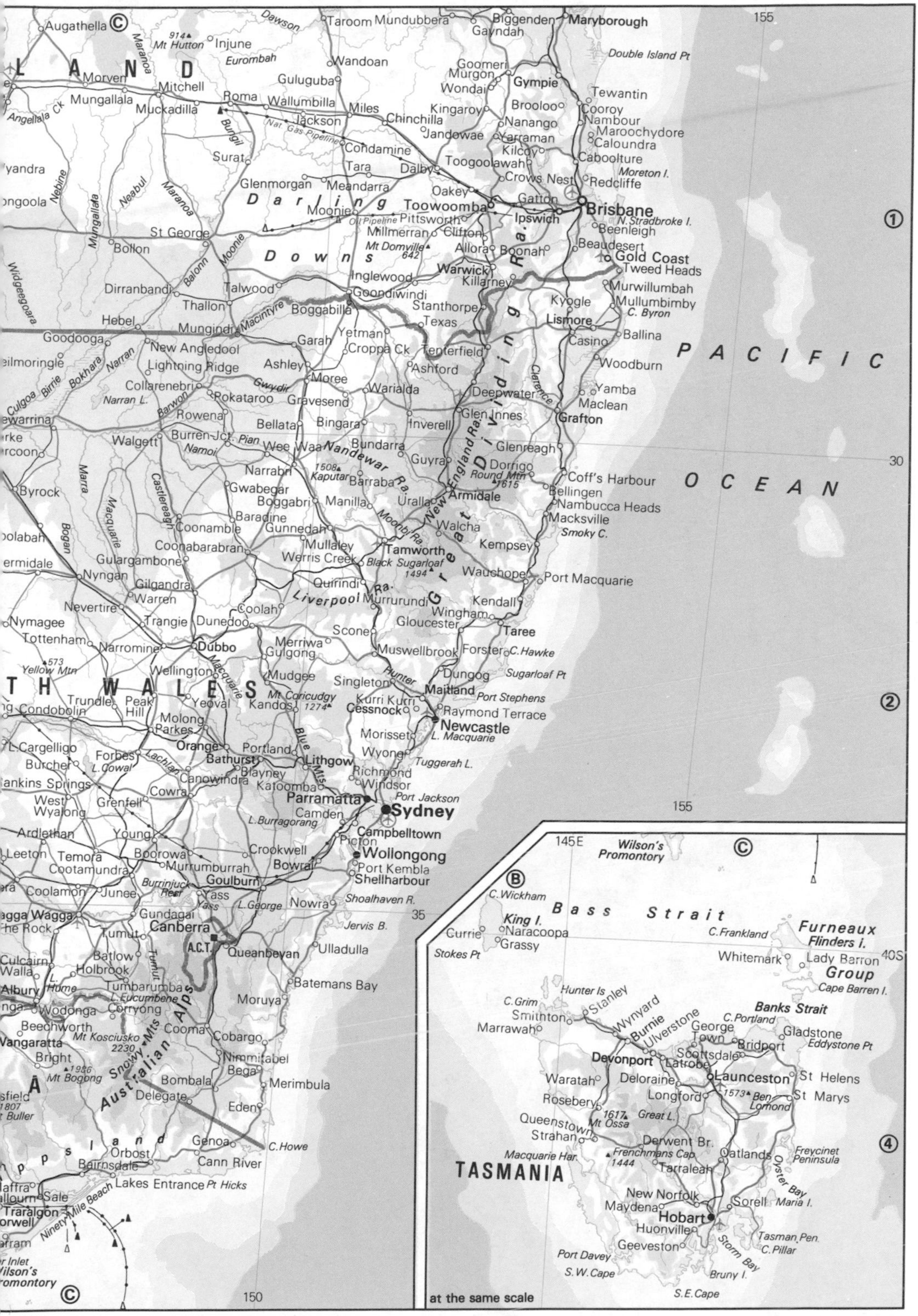

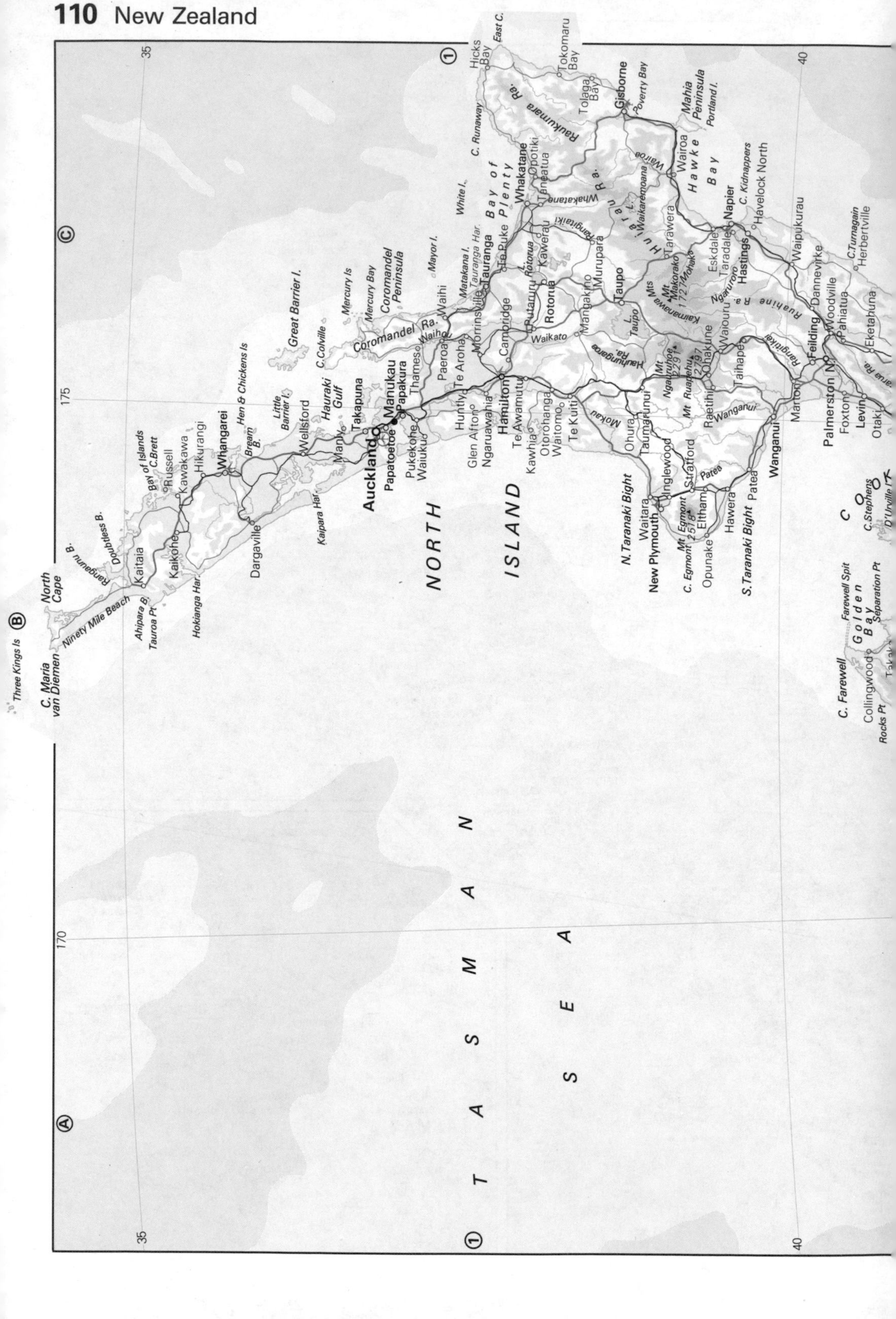
T A S M A N
S E A
NORTH
ISLAND
Three Kings Is
C. Maria van Diemen
North Cape
Ninety Mile Beach
Rangaunu B.
Doubtless B.
Kaitaia
Ahipara B.
Tauroa Pt
Kaikohe
Hokianga Har.
Bay of Islands
C.Brett
Russell
Kawakawa
Hikurangi
Whangarei
Dargaville
Kaipara Har.
Bream B.
Hen & Chickens Is
Little Barrier I.
Wellsford
Hauraki Gulf
Great Barrier I.
C.Colville
Takapuna
Manly
Auckland
Manukau
Papatoetoe
Papakura
Pukekohe
Waiuku
Thames
Coromandel Ra.
Coromandel Peninsula
Mercury Bay
Mercury Is
Waihi
Paeroa
Te Aroha
Huntly
Glen Afton
Ngaruawahia
Hamilton
Te Awamutu
Kawhia
Otorohanga
Waitomo
Te Kuiti
Cambridge
Morrinsville
Mayor I.
Matakana I.
Tauranga Har.
Tauranga
Te Puke
Bay of Plenty
White I.
Whakatane
Opotiki
Taneatua
C. Runaway
Hicks Bay
East C.
Tokomaru Bay
Raukumara Ra.
Tolaga Bay
Gisborne
Poverty Bay
Mahia Peninsula
Portland I.
Wairoa
Hawke Bay
Napier
C. Kidnappers
Havelock North
Hastings
Taradale
Eskdale
Waipukurau
Dannevirke
Woodville
Pahiatua
Eketahuna
Herbertville
C.Turnagain
Putaruru
Rotorua
Kawerau
Murupara
Mangakino
Taupo
L. Taupo
Waikato
Mt Makorako 1727
Kaimanawa Mts
Tarawera
Waikaremoana
Huiarau Ra.
Ruahine Ra.
Ngaruroro
Hauhungaroa Ra.
Mt Ngauruhoe 2291
Mt Ruapehu 2797
Ohakune
Waiouru
Taihape
Raetihi
Wanganui
Taumarunui
Ohura
Mokau
Inglewood
Stratford
Waitara
New Plymouth
N. Taranaki Bight
Mt Egmont 2518
C. Egmont
Eltham
Opunake
Hawera
Patea
S.Taranaki Bight
Marton
Feilding
Palmerston N.
Foxton
Levin
Otaki
Rangitikei
C. Farewell
Farewell Spit
Golden Bay
Separation Pt
Collingwood
Rocks Pt
C.Stephens
D'Urville I.
35
40
170
175
A
B
C
1

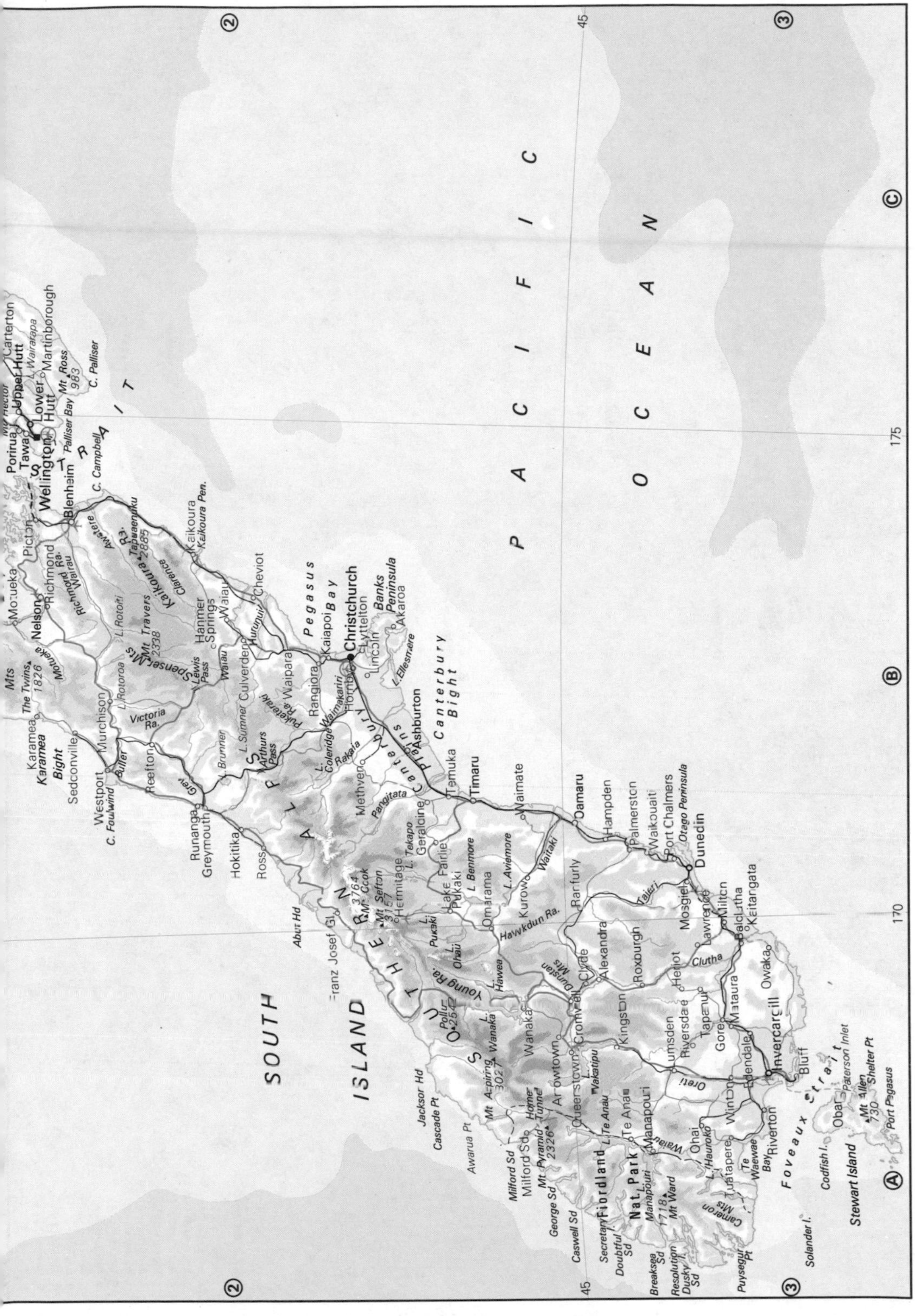
SOUTH ISLAND
PACIFIC OCEAN
Canterbury Bight
Pegasus Bay
Karamea Bight
Foveaux Strait
Westport
C. Foulwind
Sedconville
Karamea
The Twins 1826
Mts
Motueka
Nelson
Richmond
Richmond Ra.
Picton
Blenheim
Wellington
Porirua
Tawa
Lower Hutt
Upper Hutt
Carterton
Martinborough
L. Wairarapa
Mt Ross 983
C. Palliser
Palliser Bay
C. Campbell
Wairau
Awatere
Tapuaenuku 2885
Kaikoura Ra.
Clarence
Kaikoura
Kaikoura Pen.
Cheviot
Waiau
Hanmer Springs
Mt Travers 2338
L. Rotoiti
Spenser Mts
Lewis Pass
Culverden
Hurunui
Waipara
Kaiapoi
Christchurch
Lyttelton
Lincoln
Banks Peninsula
Akaroa
L. Ellesmere
Rangiora
Hornby
Waimakariri
Ashburton
Murchison
L. Rotoroa
Victoria Ra.
Buller
Reefton
Grey
Runanga
Greymouth
Hokitika
Ross
L. Brunner
L. Sumner
Arthurs Pass
L. Coleridge
Rakaia
Methven
Canterbury Plains
Rangitata
Geraldine
Temuka
Timaru
Waimate
Oamaru
Hampden
Palmerston
Waikouaiti
Port Chalmers
Otago Peninsula
Dunedin
Mosgiel
Taieri
Ranfurly
Kurow
Waitaki
L. Aviemore
L. Benmore
Omarama
Fairlie
L. Tekapo
Lake Pukaki
L. Pukaki
Hermitage
Mt Cook 3764
Mt Sefton 3157
Hawkdun Ra.
Alexandra
Clyde
Dunstan Mts
Roxburgh
Lawrence
Milton
Balclutha
Kaitangata
Clutha
Owaka
Heriot
Tapanui
Gore
Mataura
Riversdale
Lumsden
Kingston
Invercargill
Edendale
Bluff
Winton
Oreti
Riverton
Te Waewae Bay
Tuatapere
Ohai
L. Hauroko
Waiau
Manapouri
L. Manapouri
Mt Ward 1718
Te Anau
L. Te Anau
Queenstown
Arrowtown
Cromwell
L. Wakatipu
Wanaka
L. Wanaka
L. Hawea
Young Ra.
Pollux 2542
Mt Aspiring 3027
Homer Tunnel
Mt Pyramid 2326
Milford Sd
Milford Sd
George Sd
Caswell Sd
Secretary I.
Doubtful Sd
Breaksea Sd
Resolution I.
Dusky Sd
Puysegur Pt
Cameron Mts
Fiordland Nat. Park
Awarua Pt
Cascade Pt
Jackson Hd
Abut Hd
Franz Josef Gl.
SOUTHERN ALPS
Solander I.
Codfish I.
Stewart Island
Oban
Paterson Inlet
Mt Allen 730
Shelter Pt
Port Pegasus
45
170
175

1:40M
0 400 800 1200 1600 km
0 400 800 mls

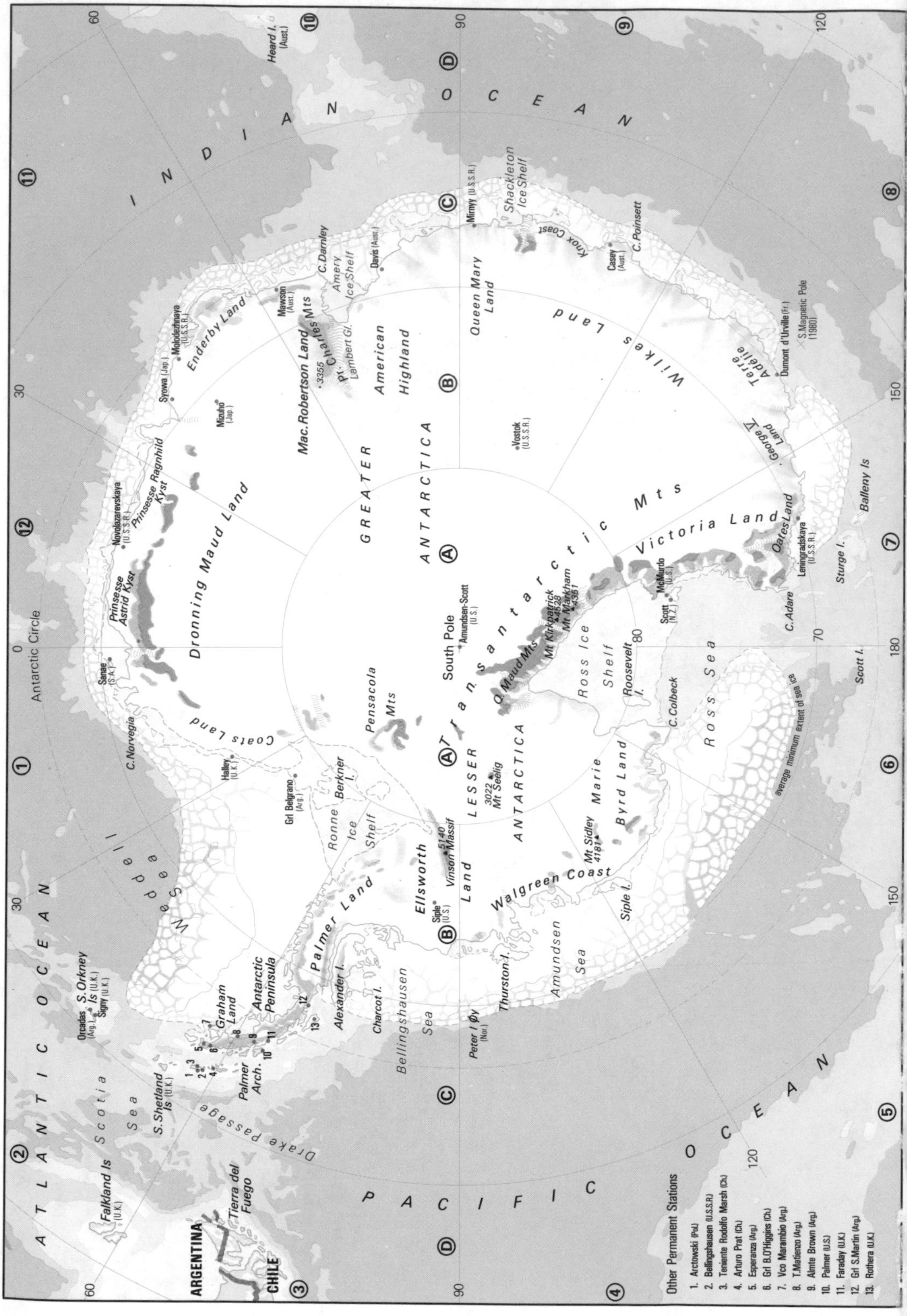
ATLANTIC OCEAN
INDIAN OCEAN
PACIFIC OCEAN
Antarctic Circle
South Pole
Amundsen-Scott (U.S.)
GREATER ANTARCTICA
LESSER ANTARCTICA
Transantarctic Mts
Dronning Maud Land
Coats Land
Prinsesse Astrid Kyst
Prinsesse Ragnhild Kyst
Enderby Land
Mac.Robertson Land
Charles Mts
American Highland
Queen Mary Land
Wilkes Land
Terre Adélie
George V Land
Oates Land
Victoria Land
Ross Ice Shelf
Ross Sea
Roosevelt I.
Marie Byrd Land
Walgreen Coast
Ellsworth Land
Vinson Massif 5140
Mt Seelig 3022
Mt Sidley 4181
Mt Kirkpatrick 4528
Mt Markham 4351
Q. Maud Mts
Pensacola Mts
Ronne Ice Shelf
Berkner I.
Palmer Land
Graham Land
Antarctic Peninsula
Alexander I.
Charcot I.
Bellingshausen Sea
Amundsen Sea
Thurston I.
Peter I Øy (Nor.)
Siple I.
Siple (U.S.)
Weddell Sea
Scotia Sea
Drake Passage
S. Shetland Is. (U.K.)
S. Orkney Is (U.K.)
Orcadas (Arg.)
Signy (U.K.)
Palmer Arch.
Falkland Is (U.K.)
Tierra del Fuego
ARGENTINA
CHILE
Halley (U.K.)
Grl Belgrano (Arg.)
Sanae (S.Af.)
C.Norvegia
Novolazarevskaya (U.S.S.R.)
Syowa (Jap.)
Mizuho (Jap.)
Molodezhnaya (U.S.S.R.)
Mawson (Aust.)
C.Darnley
Amery Ice Shelf
Lambert Gl.
3355
Davis (Aust.)
Mirnyy (U.S.S.R.)
Shackleton Ice Shelf
Knox Coast
Casey (Aust.)
C.Poinsett
Vostok (U.S.S.R.)
Dumont d'Urville (Fr.)
S.Magnetic Pole (1980)
Balleny Is
Leningradskaya (U.S.S.R.)
C.Adare
McMurdo (U.S.)
Scott (N.Z.)
Sturge I.
Scott I.
C.Colbeck
average minimum extent of sea ice
Heard I. (Aust.)
Other Permanent Stations
1. Arctowski (Pol.)
2. Bellingshausen (U.S.S.R.)
3. Teniente Rodolfo Marsh (Ch.)
4. Arturo Prat (Ch.)
5. Esperanza (Arg.)
6. Grl B.O'Higgins (Ch.)
7. Vco Marambio (Arg.)
8. T.Matienzo (Arg.)
9. Almte Brown (Arg.)
10. Palmer (U.S.)
11. Faraday (U.K.)
12. Grl S.Martin (Arg.)
13. Rothera (U.K.)